# MOON HANDBOOKS®

# HAWAII

Kalalau Valley

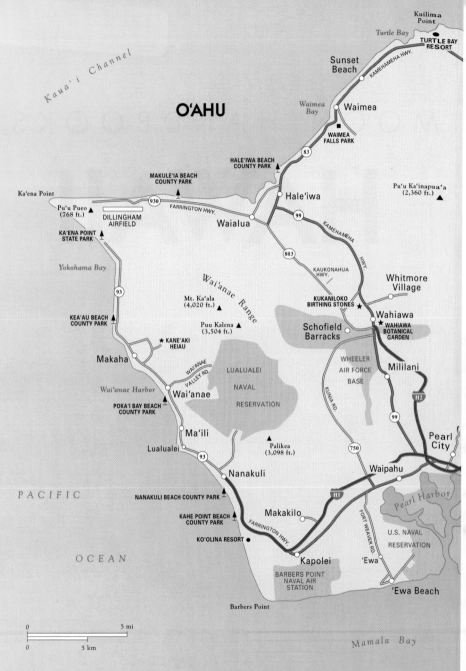

O'AHU

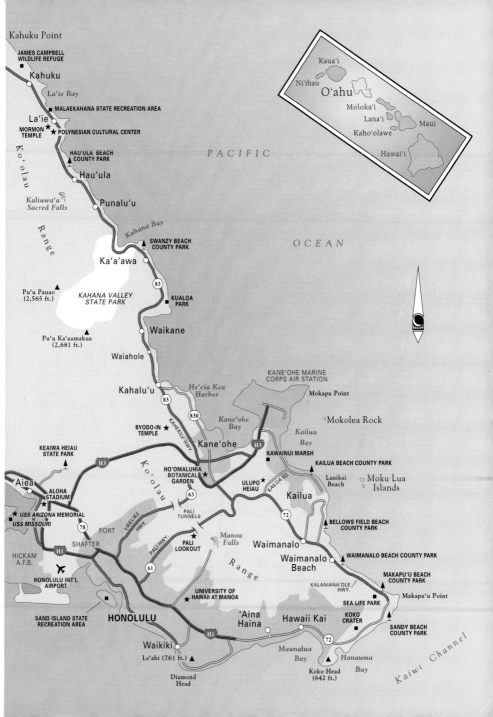

# BIG ISLAND OF HAWAI'I

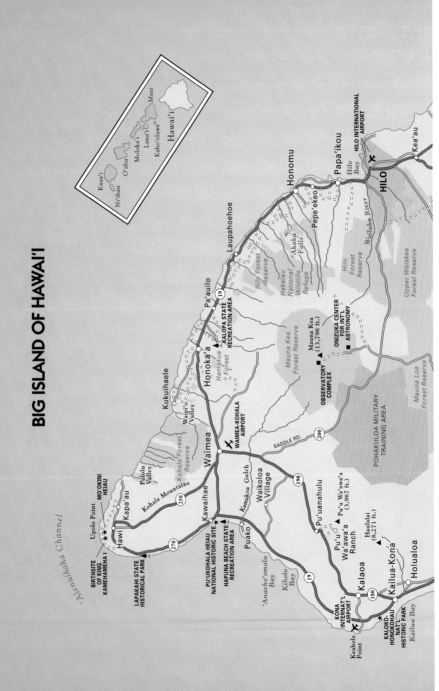

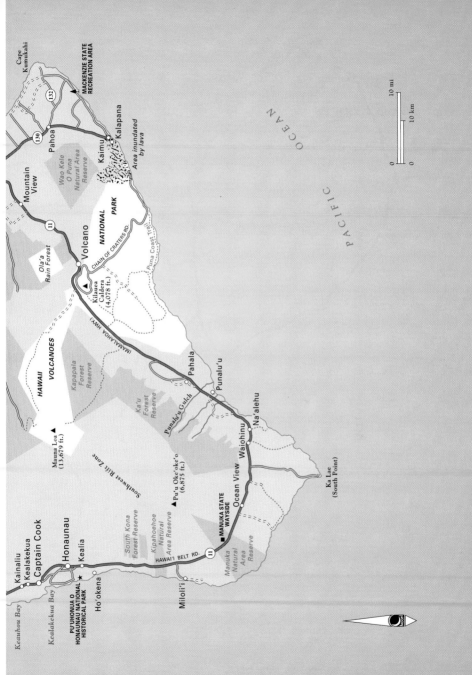

Cape
Kumukahi

MACKENZIE STATE
RECREATION AREA

132

130

Pahoa

Mountain
View

Wao Kele
O Puna
Natural Area
Reserve

Kaimu

Kalapana

Area inundated
by lava

11

Ola'a
Rain Forest

Volcano

HAWAII VOLCANOES NATIONAL PARK

CHAIN OF CRATERS RD.

Kilauea
Caldera
(4,078 ft.)

Puna Coast Trail

(MAMALAHOA HWY.)

Kapapala
Forest
Reserve

Mauna Loa
(13,679 ft.)

Ka'u
Forest
Reserve

Pahala

Punalu'u

Punalu'u Gulch

Southwest Rift Zone

Pu'u Oke'oke'o
(6,875 ft.)

Ocean View

Waiohinu

Na'alehu

Ka Lae
(South Point)

Kainaliu

Kealakekua

Captain Cook

Honaunau

Kealia

PUUHONUA O
HONAUNAU NATIONAL
HISTORICAL PARK

Ho'okena

Keauhou Bay

Kealakekua Bay

South Kona
Forest Reserve

Kipahoehoe
Natural
Area Reserve

Miloli'i

MANUKA STATE
WAYSIDE

HAWAI'I BELT RD.

11

Manuka
Natural
Area
Reserve

PACIFIC OCEAN

0                    10 mi
0                    10 km

© SANDRA E. BISIGNANI TRUST AND AVALON TRAVEL PUBLISHING, INC.

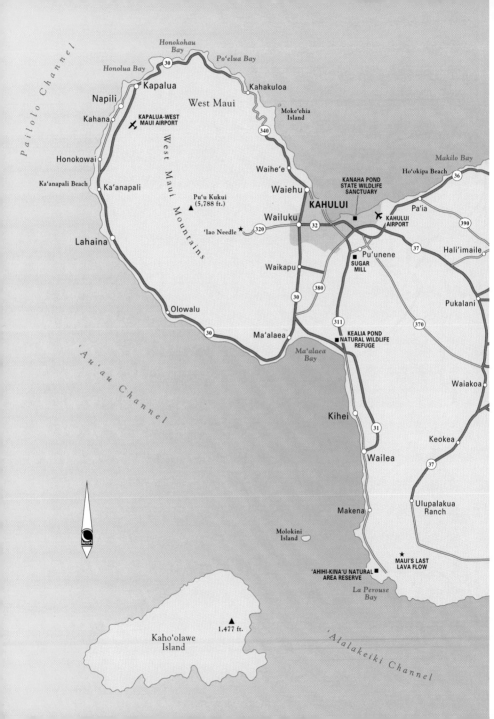

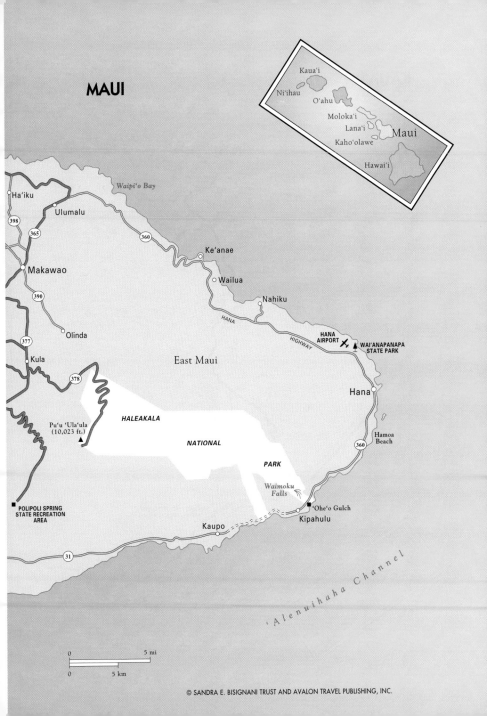

# MAUI

Kaua'i

Ni'ihau
O'ahu

Moloka'i
Lana'i
Maui
Kaho'olawe

Hawai'i

Waipi'o Bay

Ha'iku

(398)

Ulumalu

(365)

(360)

Ke'anae

Makawao

Wailua

(390)

Nahiku

Olinda

HANA

(377)

East Maui

HANA
AIRPORT

WAI'ANAPANAPA
STATE PARK

Kula

HIGHWAY

(378)

Hana

Pu'u 'Ula'ula
(10,023 ft.)

HALEAKALA

(360)

Hamoa
Beach

NATIONAL

PARK

Waimoku
Falls

POLIPOLI SPRING
STATE RECREATION
AREA

'Ohe'o Gulch

Kipahulu

Kaupo

(31)

'Alenuihaha Channel

0        5 mi

0     5 km

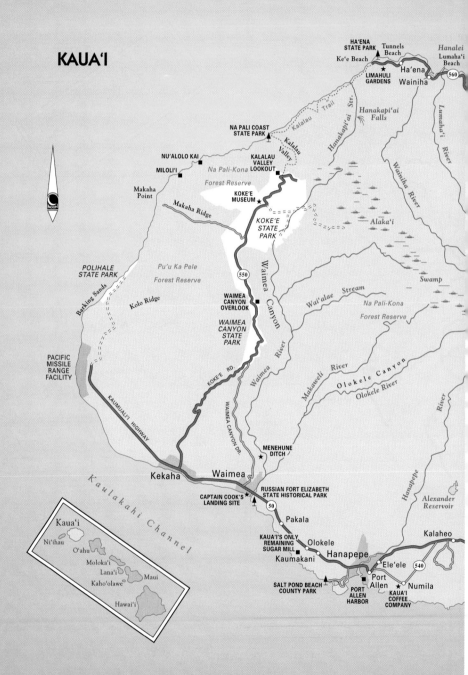

Princeville

'ANINI BEACH
COUNTY PARK

Kilauea Point    ★ KILAUEA LIGHTHOUSE
                ■ KILAUEA POINT NATIONAL WILDLIFE REFUGE

Bay             Mokolea Point

Kalihiwai       Kilauea

KUHIO
HANALEI         ✈
TARO FIELDS     PRINCEVILLE
                AIRPORT     HIGHWAY

Hanalei                                     Moloa'a
                                            Bay

                ★ GUAVA KAI
                  PLANTATION

Wai'oli Stream                              56

Halelea                 Kealia
Forest      Powerline   Forest      Anahola Mountains        Anahola
Reserve     Trail       Reserve                              Bay

                                            Anahola

            ▲ Mt. Kualapa
              (2,129 ft.)
                                                             Kealia

▲ Mt. Wai'ale'ale                                   KAPA'A
  (5,148 ft.)                                                ▲ KAPA'A BEACH
★ WORLD'S       ■ KEAHUA         580                           COUNTY PARK
  WETTEST SPOT    ARBORETUM              Wailua
                                         Homesteads          Waipouli
▲ Mt. Kawaikini                                     Wailua
  (5,243 ft.)                    581
                                 WAILUA RIVER     ★ POLI'AHU    Wailua Bay
                                 STATE PARK         HEIAU
                                         Wailua             ▲ LYDGATE
                    Wailua       River    Falls    ★ FERN        STATE PARK
                                                     GROTTO
Lihu'e Koloa                              583               56

Forest Reserve          Kilohana ☀       Hanama'ulu
                                                   ★ HANAMA'ULU BEACH
                                         Kapaia      COUNTY PARK
▲ Mt. Kahili            KAUA'I
  (3,089 ft.)           COMMUNITY                  ✈ LIHU'E AIRPORT
Papua'a                 COLLEGE
Reservoir                        Puhi    LIHU'E
            KAUMUALI'I  Highway                    Kalapaki Beach
50                                       Nawiliwili
                                         Bay
Lawa'i  'Oma'o  Waita    Ha'upu Ridge    NAWILIWILI
                Reservoir        QUEEN    HARBOR
                                 VICTORIA'S
530    520               HAWAI'I'S FIRST  PROFILE
                         SUGAR MILL       Kipu Kai
NATIONAL TROPICAL       Koloa
BOTANICAL GARDEN
       Kukui'ula  Po'ipu  Last Eruption   Maha'ulepu
★ SPOUTING                on Kaua'i ☀     Beach
  HORN          PO'IPU BEACH
                COUNTY PARK

Kaua'i Channel

0                    2.5 mi

0        2.5 km

P A C I F I C

Princeville

Kaua'i        Kapa'a

Lihu'e

Waimea    Po'ipu

Ni'ihau

Hale'iwa

O'ahu

Kane'ohe

Honolulu

Waikiki

## MAP SYMBOLS

Divided Highway
Main Road
Other Road
Railroad
Trail
US Interstate
State Highway
State Capital
City/Town
Primary Airport
Secondary Airport

★    Point of Interest
•    Accommodation
▼    Restaurant/Bar
■    Other Location
⚑    Golf Course
△    Campground
🤿    Snorkeling
▲    Mountain
🛆    State/County Park
🌴    Waterfall
〰    Swamp/Marsh

0            25 mi

0        25 km

# MAPS

O C E A N

Moloka'i

Kaunakaka'i

Kapalua

Lana'i City

Lahaina

Kahului

Lana'i

Maui

Hana

HALEAKALA N.P.

Wailea

Kaho'olawe

Waimea

Hawai'i

Hilo

Kailua-Kona

HAWAII
VOLCANOES
NATIONAL
PARK

sunset over Napili Bay

# MOON HANDBOOKS®

# HAWAII

## SEVENTH EDITION

### ROBERT NILSEN

AVALON
TRAVEL

# Contents

ROBERT NILSEN

# O'AHU

*Known as "The Gathering Place," O'ahu lives up to its name—it's home to almost 75 percent of Hawaii's diverse population and the point of entry for most visitors. Honolulu's hot spots and Waikiki's beaches are legendary for good reason—but you'll also find more remote beauty well worth exploring.*

# BIG ISLAND OF HAWAIʻI ........................... 387

*The island of Hawaiʻi is big in many ways. Its known for its beautiful orchids, black-sand beaches, and the world's largest and most active volcano—not to mention a fine cup of coffee. Big isn't necessarily better, but combined with beautiful, uncrowded, traditional, and inexpensive, it's hard to beat.*

# MAUI

*The only Hawaiian island named after a god, Maui preserves its divine legacy with a string of superlatives—including the most miles of swimmable beach—and sacred pools that have become legendary. Nearby, Lana'i caters to well-to-do travelers seeking peace and quiet, while on Moloka'i a primeval world of emerald-green awaits.*

*Kaua'i is quieter than the other islands—relaxation is unavoidable. See dolphin spin off the Na Pali Coast and watch rainbows dance along the waterfalls of Waimea Canyon. On the Garden Island, poetry is in the land itself.*

# ABOUT THE AUTHOR
## Robert Nilsen

© ROBERT NILSEN

Robert Nilsen was born and raised in Minnesota. His first major excursion from the Midwest was a two-year stint in South Korea with the Peace Corps. Following that eye-opening service, he stayed on in Korea independently, teaching and traveling, and soaking up as much of its history and culture as he could. Setting his sights on other lands and cultures, he made a two-year trek through Asia before returning home to the United States, and since then has had the good fortune to return to Asia and the Pacific on numerous occasions. Robert has written *Moon Handbooks South Korea* for Avalon Travel Publishing, and has contributed to *Moon Handbooks Indonesia*.

Since the passing of his good friend J.D. Bisignani, he has shouldered full responsibility for the revision of Moon Handbooks' Hawaii series, including *Moon Handbooks Hawaii, Moon Handbooks Kaua'i, Moon Handbooks O'ahu, Moon Handbooks Maui,* and *Moon Handbooks Big Island of Hawai'i.*

It is the many wonderful aspects of the Hawaiian Islands—slack-key guitar, palm-fringed beaches, tropical mountain hikes, the re-emergent culture of the Hawaiian people and their friendly *aloha* spirit—that keep Robert heading back each year.

*To Sandy B., who from first glance*
*filled her dad with* aloha.

# Introduction

No alien land in all the world
has any deep, strong charm for me,
            but that one;
    no other land could
so longingly and beseechingly
haunt my sleeping and waking,
    through half a lifetime,
        as that one has done.
    Other things leave me,
            but it abides.

—Mark Twain, circa 1889

# Introduction

The modern geological theory concerning the formation of the Hawaiian Islands is no less fanciful than the Polynesian legends sung about their origins. Science maintains that about 30 million years ago, while the great continents were being geologically tortured into their rudimentary shapes, the Hawaiian Islands were a mere ooze of bubbling magma 20,000 feet below the surface of the primordial sea. For millions of years this molten rock flowed up through fissures in the sea floor. Slowly, layer upon layer of lava was deposited until an island rose above the surface of the sea. The great weight then sealed the fissures, whose own colossal forces progressively crept in a southwesterly direction, to burst out again and again building the chain of what we now call the Hawaiian Islands. At the same time, the entire Pacific plate, afloat on the giant sea of molten magma, was slowly gliding to the northwest, carrying the newly formed islands with it.

In the beginning the spewing crack formed Kure and Midway islands in the extreme northwestern sector of the Hawaiian chain. This process continued for eons, and today 132 islands, islets, and shoals make up the Hawaiian Islands, stretching nearly 1,600 miles across an expanse of the North Pacific. Some geologists maintain that the "hot spot" now primarily under the Big Island

Walpi'o Valley

ROBERT NILSEN

remains relatively stationary, and that the 1,600-mile spread of the Hawaiian archipelago is due to a northwest drifting effect of about three to five inches per year. Still, with the center of activity under the Big Island, which itself is a relative youngster at about one million years old, Mauna Loa and Kilauea volcanoes regularly add more land to the only state in the country that is literally still growing. About 20 miles southeast of the Big Island is Lo'ihi Seamount, waiting 3,000 feet below the waves. Frequent eruptions bring it closer and closer to the surface; one day it will emerge as the newest Hawaiian Island and later, perhaps, merge with the Big Island itself.

# The Land

The Hawaiian Islands sit right in the middle of the North Pacific straddling the tropic of Cancer. They take up about as much room as a flower petal floating in a swimming pool. The sea makes life possible on the islands, and the Hawaiian sea is a mostly benign benefactor providing all the basics. It is also responsible for an endless assortment of pleasure, romance, and excitement, and it forms a cultural link between Hawaii and its Polynesian counterparts. The slopes of the Hawaiian Islands rise dramatically from the sea floor, not gradually, but abruptly, like temple pillars rising straight up from Neptune's kingdom.

## Physical Features

Hawaii is the southernmost state in the Union and the most westerly except for a few far-flung islands in the Alaskan Aleutians. The main islands lie just south of the tropic of Cancer at about the same latitude as Mexico City, Havana, Calcutta, and Hong Kong. Hawaii is the fourth smallest state, larger only than Connecticut, Rhode Island, and Delaware. Together, its 132 shoals, reefs, islets, and islands constitute 6,423 square miles of land. The eight *major* islands of Hawaii account for more than 99.9 percent of the total land area and are home to 100 percent of the population. They stretch over 400 miles across the Pacific from southeast to northwest: Hawai'i (the Big Island), Maui, Kaho'olawe (uninhabited), Lana'i, Moloka'i, O'ahu, Kaua'i, and Ni'ihau. The little-known Northwestern Islands, less than one-tenth of 1 percent of the state's total landmass, dot the North Pacific for more than 1,100 miles running from Nihoa, about 150 miles off Kaua'i's west shore, to Kure in the far northwest. The state has 822 miles of coastline and just over 1,000 miles of tidal shoreline. It ranges in elevation from Mauna Kea's 13,796-foot summit to Maro Reef, which is often awash by the sea.

## Volcanoes

The Hawaiians worshipped Madame Pele, the fire goddess whose name translates equally well as "Volcano," "Fire Pit," or "Eruption of Lava." When she was angry, Madame Pele complained by spitting fire and spewing lava that cooled and formed land. The Hawaiian Islands are perfect examples of **shield volcanoes.** These are formed by a succession of gentle submarine eruptions, which build an elongated dome much like a turtle shell. As the dome nears the surface of the sea, the eruptions combine with air and become extremely explosive due to the rapid temperature change and increased oxygen. Once above the surface they mellow again and steadily build upon themselves. As the island-mountain mushrooms, its weight seals off the spewing fissure below. Instead of forcing itself upward, the lava now finds less resistance to moving laterally. Eventually, the giant tube that carried lava to the top of the volcano sinks in upon itself and becomes a caldera. More eruptions occur periodically, but the lava is less dense and could be thought of as icing on a titanic cake. Then the relentless forces of wind and water take over to sculpt the raw lava into deep crevasses and cuts that eventually become valleys. The smooth, once-single mountain is transformed into a miniature mountain range, while generations of coral polyps build reefs around the islands, and the rising and falling of the surrounding seas during episodic ice ages combine with eroded soil to add or destroy coastal plains.

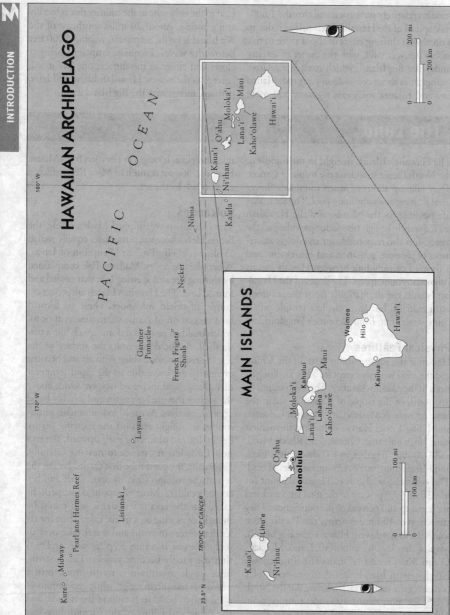

# HAWAIIAN ARCHIPELAGO

PACIFIC OCEAN

160° W

170° W

23.5° N

TROPIC OF CANCER

Kure
Midway
Pearl and Hermes Reef
Lisianski
Laysan
Gardner Pinnacles
French Frigate Shoals
Necker
Nihoa

Ka'ula
Ni'ihau
Kaua'i
O'ahu
Moloka'i
Lana'i
Maui
Kaho'olawe
Hawai'i

0       200 mi
0       200 km

## MAIN ISLANDS

Kaua'i
Lihu'e
Ni'ihau
O'ahu
**Honolulu**
Moloka'i
Lana'i
Kahului
Lahaina
Kaho'olawe
Maui
Waimea
Hilo
Hawai'i
Kailua

0       100 mi
0       100 km

© SANDRA E. BISIGNANI TRUST AND AVALON TRAVEL PUBLISHING, INC.

## Lava

The Hawaiian Islands are huge mounds of cooled **basaltic lava.** The main components of Hawaiian lava are silica, iron oxide, magnesium, and lime. Lava flows in two distinct types, for which the Hawaiian names have become universal geological terms: **'a'a** and **pahoehoe.** They are easily distinguished by appearance, but chemically they're the same. Their appearance differs due to the amount of gases contained in the flow when the lava hardens. 'A'a is extremely rough and spiny, and will quickly tear up your shoes if you do much hiking over it. Also, if you have the misfortune to fall down on it, you'll immediately know why it's called 'a'a. Pahoehoe is billowy, ropy lava that looks like burned pancake batter. Not nearly as dense as 'a'a, it can form fantastic shapes and designs.

Lava actually forms molten rivers as it barrels down the steep slopes of the volcanoes. Sometimes a lava river crusts over while the molten material on the inside continues to drain, until a **lava tube** is formed. Such a tube characteristically has a domed roof and a flat floor and would make a very passable subway tunnel. Some tubes measure more than 20 feet in diameter. One of the best examples is the Thurston

ROBERT NILSEN

pahoehoe lava: motion frozen in stone

Lava Tube at Volcanoes National Park on Hawai'i. Other lava oddities are **peridots** (green, gemlike stones called Pele's diamonds) and clear **feldspar.** Gray lichens that cover older volcanic flows are known as **Hawaiian snow,** and volcanic glass that has been spun into hairlike strands is known as **Pele's hair,** while congealed lava droplets are known as **Pele's tears.**

## LAND STATISTICS

| Island | Area | Percent of state total | Coastline | Highest Point |
|---|---|---|---|---|
| Big Island | 4,028 | 62.9 | 266 | 13,796 |
| Maui | 727 | 11.3 | 120 | 10,023 |
| Kaho'olawe | 45 | 0.7 | 29 | 1,477 |
| Lana'i | 140 | 2.2 | 47 | 3,370 |
| Moloka'i | 260 | 4 | 88 | 4,961 |
| O'ahu | 597 | 9.3 | 112 | 4,020 |
| Kaua'i | 552 | 8.6 | 90 | 5,243 |
| Ni'ihau | 70 | 1 | 45 | 1,281 |
| Northwestern Islands | 3 | - | 25 | 903 |
| Total | 6,423 | | 822 | |

## Lakes and Rivers

Hawaii has very few natural lakes because of the porousness of the lava: water tends to seep into the ground rather than form ponds or lakes. However, *underground* deposits where water has been trapped between porous lava on top and dense subterranean layers below account for many freshwater springs throughout the islands; these are tapped as a primary source for irrigation and drinking water. Hawaii's only large natural lakes happen to be on the private island of Ni'ihau and are therefore seldom seen by the outside world. Diminutive **Lake Waiau,** at 13,020 feet on the Big Island's Mauna Kea, ranks among the highest lakes in the United States. Honolulu's Salt Lake, once O'ahu's only natural inland body of water, was bulldozed for land reclamation. No extensive rivers are found in Hawaii except the **Waimea River** on Kaua'i; none are navigable except for a few miles of the **Wailua River,** also on Kaua'i. The countless "streams" and "rivulets" on the main islands turn from trickles to torrents depending upon rainfall. This is of greatest concern to hikers, who can find themselves threatened by a flash flood in a valley that was the height of hospitality only a few minutes before.

## Tsunamis

Tsunami, a word of Japanese origin, is the more correct term for what is often popularly referred to as a "tidal wave." Tsunamis rank up there with the worst of them in sparking horror in human beings. But if you were to count up all the people in Hawaii who have been swept away by tsunamis in the last 50 years, the toll wouldn't come close to those killed on bicycles in only a few Mainland cities in just five years. A Hawaiian tsunami is actually a seismic sea wave generated by an earthquake that could easily have originated thousands of miles away in South America or Alaska. Some waves have been clocked at speeds up to 500 mph. The U.S. Geological Survey has uncovered data that indicates a 1,000-foot-high wall of water crashed into the Hawaiian Islands about 100,000 years ago. They believe a giant undersea landslide about 25 miles south of Lana'i was the cause.

The wave was about 15 miles wide, and when it hit Lana'i it stripped land more than 1,200 feet above sea level. It struck the other islands less severely, stripping land up to 800 feet above sea level. The worst tsunamis in modern times have both struck Hilo on the Big Island: the one in May 1960 claimed 61 lives. Maui also experienced a catastrophic wave that inundated the Hana Coast on April 1, 1946, taking lives and destroying much property. Other waves have inexplicably claimed no lives. The Big Island's Waipi'o Valley, for example, was a place of royalty that, according to ancient Hawaiian beliefs, was protected by the gods. A giant tsunami inundated Waipi'o in the 1940s, catching hundreds of people in its watery grasp. Unbelievably, not one person was hurt. After the wave departed, many people rushed to the valley floor to gather thousands of fish that were washed ashore. Without warning, a second towering wave struck and grabbed the people again. Although giant trees and boulders were washed out to sea, not one person was harmed even the second time around. The safest place, besides high ground well away from beach areas, is out on the open ocean where an enormous wave is perceived only as a large swell. A tsunami is only dangerous when it is opposed by land.

## Earthquakes

Earthquakes are also a concern in Hawaii and offer a double threat because they can generate tsunamis. If you ever feel a tremor and are close to a beach, evacuate as soon as possible. The Big Island, because of its active volcanoes, experiences hundreds of technical earthquakes every year, although 99 percent can only be felt on very delicate equipment. The last major quake occurred on the Big Island in late June 1989, reaching 6.2 on the Richter scale and causing about a million dollars' worth of damage. Fortunately, since 1868 (when an earthquake and tsunami killed 81 people) only two lives have been lost.

Hawaii has an elaborate warning system against natural disasters. Loudspeakers high atop poles along many beaches and coastal areas warn of tsunamis, hurricanes, and earthquakes.

They are tested at 11 A.M. on the first working day of each month. All island telephone books contain a civil defense warning and procedures section with which you should acquaint yourself. Note the maps showing which areas traditionally have been inundated by tsunamis and what procedures to follow in case an emergency occurs.

## CLIMATE

Of the wide variety of reasons for visiting Hawaii, most people have at least one in common: the weather! Nowhere on the face of the earth do human beings feel more physically comfortable than in Hawaii, and a happy body almost always means a happy mind and spirit too. Cooling trade winds, low humidity, high pressure, clear sunny days, negative ionization from the sea, and an almost total lack of industrial pollution combine to make Hawaii *the* most healthful spot in America.

### "So Good" Weather

The ancient Hawaiians had words to describe climatic specifics such as rain, wind, fog, and even snow, but they didn't have a general word for "weather." The reason is that the weather is just about the same throughout the year and depends more on where you are on any given island than on what season it is. The Hawaiians did distinguish between *kau* (summer, May–October) and *ho'oilo* (winter, November–April), but this distinction included social, religious, and even navigational factors, far beyond a mere distinction of weather variations. The average daytime temperature throughout Hawaii is about 80° F (26° C), with the average winter day registering 78° and the average summer day raising the thermometer only seven degrees to 85°. Nighttime temperatures drop less than 10°. Elevation, however, does drop temperatures about three degrees for every 1,000 feet; if you intend to visit the mountain peaks of Haleakala, Mauna Loa, or Mauna Kea (all more than 10,000 feet), expect the temperature to be at least 30° cooler than at sea level. The lowest recorded temperature in Hawaii was 1° F inside the Mauna Kea summit crater on the Big Island in January 1970; the hottest day occurred in 1931 in the Puna District of the Big Island with a scorching (for Hawaii) 100°.

## GREEN FLASH

Nearly everyone who has visited a tropical island has heard of the "green flash"—but few have seen it. Some consider the green flash a fable, a made-up story by those more intent on fantasy than reality, but the green flash is real. This phenomenon doesn't just happen on tropical islands; it can happen anywhere around the midriff of the earth where an unobstructed view of the horizon is present, but the clear atmosphere of a tropical island environment does seem to add to its frequency. The green flash is a momentary burst of luminescent green color that happens on the horizon the instant the sun sets into the sea. If you've seen the green flash you definitely know; there is no mistaking it. If you think you saw something that might have been green but just weren't sure, you probably didn't see it. Try again another day.

The green flash requires a day where the atmosphere is very clear and unobstructed by clouds, haze, or air pollutants. Follow the sun as it sinks into the sea. Be careful not to look directly at the sun until it's just about out of sight. If the conditions are right, a green color will linger at the spot where the sun sets for a fraction of a second before it too is gone. This "flash" is not like the flash of a camera, but more a change of color from yellow to green—an intense green—that is instantaneous and momentary.

However romantic and magical, this phenomenon does have a scientific explanation. It seems that the green color is produced as a refraction of the sun's rays by the thick atmosphere at the extreme low angle of the horizon. This bending of the sun's light results in the green spectrum of light being the last seen before the light disappears.

Seeing the green flash is an experience. Keep looking, for no matter how many times you've seen it, each time is still full of wonder and joy.

## Precipitation

Hardly a day goes by when it isn't raining somewhere on *all* the main islands. If this amazes you, just consider each island to be a mini-continent: it would be the same as expecting no rain anywhere in North America on any given day. All islands have a windward (northeast, wet) and leeward (southwest, dry) side. It rains much more on the windward side, and much more often during winter than summer. (However, kona storms, because they come from the south, hit the islands' leeward sides most often.) Another important rain factor is the mountains, which act like water magnets. Moist winds gather around them and eventually build rain clouds. The ancient Hawaiians used these clouds—and the reflected green light on their underbellies—to spot land from great distances. Precipitation mostly occurs at or below the 3,000-foot level; thus, the upper slopes of taller mountains such as Haleakala are quite dry. The average annual rainfall on the seas surrounding Hawaii is only 25 inches, while a few miles inland around the windward slopes of mountains it can be 250 inches! Compare Lahaina and Mt. Pu'u Kukui, only seven miles distant from each other on West Maui, for a dramatic example of this phenomenon. Hot, arid Lahaina has an annual rainfall of only 15 inches; Pu'u Kukui can receive close to 35 *feet* of rainfall a year, rivaling Mt. Wai'ale'ale on Kaua'i as the "wettest spot on earth." Another point to remember: where there's rain there's also an incredible explosion of colorful flowers like an overgrown natural hothouse. You'll find this effect mostly on the windward sides of the islands. Conversely, the best beach weather is on the leeward sides: Ka'anapali, Waikiki, Kailua-Kona, Po'ipu. They all sit in the "rain shadows" of interior mountains, and if it happens to be raining at one leeward beach, just move down the road to the next. One more thing about Hawaiian rains—they aren't very nasty. Much of the time just a light drizzle, they hardly ever last all day. Because they are mostly localized, you can often spot them by looking for rainbows. Rain should never spoil your outings in Hawaii. Just "hang loose, brah," and go to the sunshine.

## The Trade Winds

One reason Hawaiian temperatures are both constant and moderate is the trade winds, moderate breezes from the northeast blowing at about 5–15 miles per hour. These breezes are so prevailing that the northeast sides of the islands are always referred to as windward, regardless of where the wind happens to be blowing on any given day. You can count on the "trades" to be blowing an average of 300 days per year, hardly missing a day during summer and occurring half the time in winter. Usually calm in the morning, they pick up during the heat of the afternoon, then weaken at night. Just when you need a cooling breeze, there they are, and when the temperature drops at night, it's as if someone turned down a giant fan.

The trade winds are also a factor in keeping down the humidity. They will suddenly disappear, however, usually in winter, and might not resume for a few weeks. The tropic of Cancer runs through the center of Hawaii, yet the latitude's famed oppressively hot and muggy weather is joyfully absent in the islands. Honolulu, on the same latitude as sweaty Hong Kong and Havana, has only a 50–60 percent daily humidity factor.

## Kona Winds

"Kona" means "leeward" in Hawaiian, and when the trades stop blowing these southerly winds often take over. To anyone from Hawaii, "kona wind" is a euphemism for bad weather because it brings in hot, sticky air. Luckily, kona winds are most common October–April when they appear roughly half the time. The temperatures drop slightly during the winter, so these hot winds are tolerable, even useful for moderating the thermometer. In the summer they are awful, but luckily—again—they hardly ever blow during this season.

A "kona storm" is another matter. These subtropical low-pressure storms develop west of the Hawaiian Islands, and as they move easterly they draw winds up from the south. Usual only in winter, they can cause considerable damage to crops and real estate. There is no real pattern to kona storms—some years they come every few weeks, while other years they don't appear at all.

# HURRICANE FACTS

A tropical depression is a low-pressure system or cyclone with winds below 39 mph. A **tropical storm** is a cyclone with winds 39–73 mph. A **hurricane** is a cyclone with winds over 74 mph. These winds are often accompanied by torrential rains, destructive waves, high water, and storm surges.

The National Weather Service issues a **Hurricane Watch** if hurricane conditions are expected in the area within 36 hours. A **Hurricane Warning** is issued when a hurricane is expected to strike within 24 hours. The state of Hawaii has an elaborate warning system against natural disasters. You will notice loudspeakers high atop poles along many beaches and coastal areas; these warn of tsunami, hurricanes, and earthquakes. These sirens are tested briefly at the beginning of each month. As the figures below attest, property damage has been great but the loss of life has, thankfully, been minimal.

## Major Hurricanes since 1950

| Name | Date | Islands Affected | Damages |
|------|------|------------------|---------|
| Hiki | Aug. 1950 | Kaua'i | 1 death |
| Nina | Dec. 1957 | Kaua'i | — |
| Dot | Aug. 1959 | Kaua'i | $5.5 million |
| Fico | July 1978 | Big Island | — |
| 'Iwa | Nov. 1982 | Kaua'i, O'ahu | 1 death; $234 million |
| Estelle | July 1986 | Maui, Big Island | $2 million |
| 'Iniki | Sept. 1992 | Kaua'i, O'ahu | 8 deaths; $1.9 billion |

## Severe Weather

With all this talk of ideal weather it might seem like there isn't any bad. Read on. When a storm does hit an island, conditions can be bleak and miserable. The worst storms occur in the fall and winter and often have the warped sense of humor to drop their heaviest rainfalls on areas that are normally quite dry. It's not infrequent for a storm to dump more than three inches of rain an hour; this can go as high as 10, making Hawaiian rainfalls some of the heaviest on earth.

Hawaii has also been hit with some walloping **hurricanes** in the last few decades. There haven't been many but they've been destructive. The vast majority of hurricanes originate far to the southeast off the Pacific coasts of Mexico and Latin America; some, particularly later in the season, start in the midst of the Pacific Ocean near the equator south of Hawaii. Hurricane season is generally considered June–November. Most hurricanes pass harmlessly south of Hawaii, but some, swept along by kona winds, strike the islands. The most recent and destructive was Hurricane 'Iniki, which battered the islands in 1992, killing eight people and causing an estimated $2 billion in damage. It had its greatest effect on Ni'ihau, the Po'ipu Beach area of Kaua'i, and on the leeward coast of O'ahu.

## Flora and Fauna

### THE MYSTERY OF MIGRATION

Anyone who loves a mystery will be intrigued by the speculation about how plants and animals first came to Hawaii. Most people's idea of an island paradise includes swaying palms, dense mysterious jungles ablaze with wildflowers, and luscious fruits just waiting to be plucked. In fact, for millions of years the Hawaiian chain consisted of raw and barren islands where no plants grew and no birds sang. Why? Because they are geological orphans that spontaneously popped up in the middle of the Pacific Ocean. The islands, more than 2,000 miles from any continental landfall, were therefore isolated from the normal ecological spread of plants and animals. Even the most tenacious travelers of the flora and fauna kingdoms would be sorely tried in crossing the mighty Pacific. Those that made it by pure chance found a totally foreign ecosystem. They had to adapt or perish. The survivors evolved quickly, and many plants and birds became so specialized that they were limited not only to specific islands in the chain but to habitats that frequently encompassed a single isolated valley. It was as if after traveling so far and finding a niche, they never budged again. Luckily, the soil of Hawaii was virgin and rich, the competition from other plants or animals nonexistent, and the climate sufficiently varied and nearly perfect for most growing things.

The evolution of plants and animals on the isolated islands was astonishingly rapid. A tremendous change in environment, coupled with a limited gene pool, accelerated natural selection. For example, many plants lost their protective thorns and spines because there were no grazing animals or birds to destroy them. Before settlement, Hawaii had no fruits, vegetables, coconut palms, edible land animals, conifers, mangroves, or banyans. The early Polynesians brought 27 varieties of plants that they needed for food and other purposes. About 90 percent of plants on the Hawaiian Islands today were introduced after Captain Cook first set foot here. Tropical flowers, wild and vibrant as we know them today, were relatively few. In a land where thousands of orchids now brighten every corner, there were only four native varieties, the least in any of the 50 states. Today, the indigenous plants and animals have the highest rate of extinction anywhere on earth. By the beginning of the 20th century, native plants growing below 1,500 feet in elevation were almost completely extinct or totally replaced by introduced species. The land and its living things have been greatly transformed by humans and their agriculture. This inexorable process began when Hawaii was the domain of its original Polynesian settlers, then greatly accelerated when the land was inundated by Western peoples.

### The Greening of Hawaii

The first *deliberate* migrants to Hawaii were Polynesians from the Marquesas Islands. Many of their voyages were undertaken when life on their native islands became intolerable. They were prompted mostly by defeat in war, or by growing island populations that overtaxed the available food supply. Whatever the reasons, the migrations were deliberate and permanent. The first colonizers were known as "the land seekers" in the old Marquesan language—probably advance scouting parties who proved true the ancient chants, which sang of a land to the north. Once they discovered Hawaii, their return voyage to the southern homeland was relatively easy. They had the favorable trade winds at their backs, plus the certainty of sailing into familiar waters. Later, both men and women would set out for the new land in canoes laden with seeds and plant cuttings necessary for survival, as well as animals for both consumption and sacrifice.

Not all the domesticated plants and animals came at once, but the colonizers brought enough to get started. The basic food plants included taro, banana, coconut, sugarcane, breadfruit, and yams. The Polynesians also brought the paper mulberry from which tapa was made and the *ti* plant necessary for cooking and making offerings at *heiau*. Various gourds were grown to be used as bowls, containers, and even helmets for Hawaiian-style defensive armor. Arrowroot and turmeric were used in cooking and by the healing *kahuna* as medicines. *'Awa* (kava) was brought by the high priests to be used in rituals; after chewing, the resulting juice was spat into a bowl where it fermented and became a mild intoxicant. Bamboo, the natural wonder material, was planted and used for countless purposes. The only domesticated animals taken to the new land were pigs, dogs, and chickens. Rats also made the journey as stowaways.

In the new land the Polynesians soon found native plants that they incorporated and put to good use. Some included: *olona,* which made the best-known fiber cord anywhere in the world and later was eagerly accepted by sailing ships as new rigging and as a trade item; koa, an excellent hardwood used for the manufacture of highly prized calabashes and the hulls of magnificent seagoing canoes; *kukui* (candlenut), eaten as a tasty nut, strung to make lei, or burned as a source of light like a natural candle. For a thousand years a distinct Hawaiian culture formed in relative isolation. When the first whites came they found a people who had become intimately entwined with their environment. The relationship between Hawaiians and the *'aina* (land) was spiritual, physical, and emotional: they were one.

## PLANTS, FLOWERS, AND TREES

Much like the Polynesian settlers who followed, it was the drifters, castaways, and shanghaied of the plant and animal kingdom that were the first to reach Hawaii. Botanists say spores and seeds were carried aloft into the upper atmosphere by powerful winds, then made lucky landings on the islands. Some hardy seeds came with the tides and managed to sprout and grow once they hit land. Others were carried on the feathers and feet of migratory birds, while some made the trip in birds' digestive tracts and were ignominiously deposited with their droppings. This chance seeding of Hawaii obviously took a very long time: scientists estimate one plant arrival and establishment every 30,000–50,000 years. By latest count more than 1,700 distinct species of endemic (only Hawaiian) and indigenous (other islands of Polynesia) plants have been cataloged throughout the island chain. It is reasonably certain all of these plants were introduced by only 250 original immigrants; the 168 different Hawaiian ferns, for example, are the result of approximately 13 colonists. Most of the seeds and spores are believed to have come from Asia and Indonesia, and evidence of this spread can be seen in related plant species common to many Polynesian islands. Other endemic species such as the koa tree, which the Hawaiians put to great use in canoe building, have close relatives only in Australia. No other group of islands between Hawaii and Australia has such trees; the reason remains a mystery. Many plants and grasses came from North and South America and can be identified with common ancestors still there. Some species have become so totally Hawaiian that relatives are found nowhere else on earth. This last category has either evolved so dramatically they can no longer be recognized, or their common ancestors have long been extinct from the original environment. An outstanding example in this category is the silversword *('ahinahina),* found in numbers only atop Haleakala on Maui, with a few specimens extant on the volcanoes of the Big Island.

### Hawaii's Flora

Hawaii's indigenous and endemic plants, flowers, and trees are both fascinating and beautiful, but unfortunately, like everything else that was native, they are quickly disappearing. The majority of flora considered exotic by visitors were introduced either by the original Polynesians or by later white settlers. The Polynesians who colonized Hawaii brought foodstuffs, including coconuts, bananas, taro, breadfruit, sweet potatoes, yams, and sugarcane. They also carried along gourds to use as containers, *'awa* to make a basic intoxicant, and the *ti* plant to use for offerings or to string into hula skirts. Non-Hawaiian settlers over the years have brought mangos, papayas, passion fruit, pineapples, and many other tropical fruits and vegetables associated with the islands. Also, most of the flowers, including protea, plumeria, anthuriums, orchids, heliconia, ginger, and most hibiscus, have come from every continent on earth. Tropical America, Asia, Java, India, and China have contributed their most beautiful and delicate blooms. Hawaii is blessed with national and state parks, gardens, undisturbed rainforests, private reserves, and commercial nurseries that offer an exhaustive botanical survey of the island. The following is a sampling of the common native and introduced flora that add dazzling color and exotic tastes to the landscape.

## Native Trees

Koa and ʻohiʻa are two indigenous trees still seen on the main islands. Both have been greatly reduced by the foraging of introduced cattle and goats, and through logging and forest fires.

The **koa,** a form of acacia, is Hawaii's finest native tree. It can grow to more than 70 feet high and has a strong, straight trunk that can measure more than 10 feet in circumference. Koa is a quickly growing legume that fixes nitrogen in the soil. It is believed that the tree originated in Africa, where it was damp. It then migrated to Australia, where dry conditions caused the elimination of leaves, leaving only bare stems that could survive in the desert climate. When koa came to the Pacific Islands, instead of reverting to the true leaf, it just broadened its leaf stem into sickle-shaped, leaflike foliage that produces an inconspicuous, pale yellow flower. When the tree is young or damaged it will revert to the original feathery, fernlike leaf that evolved in Africa millions of years ago. Koa does best in well-drained soil in deep forest areas, but scruffy specimens will grow in poorer soil. The Hawaiians used koa as the main log for their dugout canoes; elaborate ceremonies were performed when a log was cut and dragged to a canoe shed. Koa wood was also preferred for paddles, spears, even surfboards. Today it is still, unfortunately, considered an excellent furniture wood, and although fine specimens can be found in the reserve of Hawaii Volcanoes National Park on the Big Island, loggers elsewhere are harvesting the last of the big trees.

The **ʻohiʻa** is a survivor and therefore the most abundant of all the native Hawaiian trees. Com-

## ALL-PURPOSE KUKUI

Reaching heights of 80 feet, the *kukui* (candlenut) was a veritable department store to the Hawaiians, who made use of almost every part of this utilitarian giant. Used as cure-alls, its nuts, bark, or flowers were ground into potions and salves and taken as a general tonic, applied to ulcers and cuts as an effective antibiotic, or administered internally as a cure for constipation or asthma attacks. The bark was mixed with water, and the resulting juice was used as a dye in tattooing, tapa-cloth making, and canoe painting, and as a preservative for fishnets. The oily nuts were burned as a light source in stone holders, and ground and eaten as a condiment (mixed with salt) called *ʻinamona.* Polished nuts took on a beautiful sheen and were strung as lei. Lastly, the wood itself was hollowed into canoes and seeds as fishnet floats.

LOUISE FOOTE

ing in a variety of shapes and sizes, it grows as miniature trees in wet bogs or as 100-foot giants on cool, dark slopes at higher elevations. This tree is often the first life in new lava flows. The ʻohiʻa produces a tuftlike flower—usually red, but occasionally orange, yellow, or white, the latter being very rare and elusive—that resembles a natural pompon. The flower was considered sacred to Pele; it was said she would cause a rainstorm if you picked ʻohiʻa blossoms without the proper prayers. The flowers were fashioned into lei that resembled feather boas. The strong, hard wood was used to make canoes, poi bowls, and especially temple images. 'Ohi'a logs were also used as railroad ties and shipped to the Mainland from Pahoa. It's believed that the "golden spike" linking rail lines between the U.S. East and West Coasts was driven into a Puna 'ohi'a log when the two railroads came together in Ogden, Utah.

## Lobelia

More species of lobelia grow in Hawaii than anywhere else in the world. A common garden flower elsewhere, in Hawaii it grows to tree height. You'll see some unique species covered with hair or spikes. The lobelia flower is tiny and resembles a miniature orchid with curved and pointed ends, like the beak of the native *'i'iwi*. This bird feeds on the flower's nectar; it's obvious that both evolved in Hawaii together and exhibit the strange phenomenon of nature mimicking nature.

## Tropical Rainforests

When it comes to pure and diverse natural beauty, the United States is one of the finest pieces of real estate on earth. As if purple mountains' majesty and fruited plains weren't enough, the country even contains tiny, living emeralds of tropical rainforest. A tropical rainforest is where the earth takes a breath and exhales pure sweet oxygen through its vibrant green canopy. Located in the territories of Puerto Rico and the Virgin Islands, and in the state of Hawaii, these forests comprise only one-half of one percent of the world's total, and they must be preserved. The U.S. Congress passed two bills in 1986 designed to protect the unique biological diversity of its tropical areas, but their destruction has continued unabated. The lowland rainforests of Hawaii, populated mostly by native 'ohi'a, are being razed. Landowners slash, burn, and bulldoze them to create more land for cattle and agriculture and, most distressingly, for wood chips to generate electricity! Introduced wild boar gouge the forest floor, exposing sensitive roots and leaving tiny fetid ponds where mosquito larvae thrive. Feral goats roam the forests like hoofed locusts and strip all vegetation within reach. Rainforests on the higher and steeper slopes of mountains have a better chance because they are harder for humans to reach. One unusual feature of Hawaii's rainforests is that they are "upside down." Most plant and animal species live on the forest floor, rather than in the canopy as in other forests.

Almost half the birds classified in the United States as endangered live in Hawaii, and almost all of these make their homes in the rainforests. For example, Maui's rainforests have yielded the *po'ouli,* a new species of bird discovered only in 1974. Another forest survey in 1981 rediscovered the Bishop's *'o'o,* a bird thought to be extinct in the early 1900s. We can only lament the passing of the rainforests that have already fallen to ignorance, but if this ill-fated destruction continues on a global level, we will be lamenting our own passing. We must nurture the rainforests that remain and, with simple enlightenment, let them be.

## BIRD LIFE

One of the great tragedies of natural history is the continuing demise of Hawaiian bird life. Perhaps only 15 original species of birds remain of the more than 100 native families that thrived before the coming of humans, these from only 20 or so original ancestors. Experts believe that the ancient Hawaiians annihilated about 40 species, including seven species of geese, a rare one-legged owl, ibis, lovebirds, sea eagles, and honeycreepers. Since the arrival of Captain Cook in 1778, 23 species have become extinct, with 31 more in danger. Hawaii's endangered birds account for more than 40 percent of the birds officially listed by the U.S. Fish and Wildlife Service as endangered or threatened. In the last 200 years, more than four times as many birds have become extinct in Hawaii as in all of North America. These figures unfortunately suggest that a full 40 percent of Hawaii's endemic birds no longer exist. Almost all of O'ahu's native birds are gone, and few indigenous Hawaiian birds can be found on any island below the 3,000-foot level.

Native birds have been reduced in number because of multiple factors. The original Polynesians helped wipe out many species. They altered large areas for farming and used fire to destroy patches of pristine forests. Also, bird feathers were highly prized for the making of lei, for featherwork in capes and helmets, and for the large *kahili* fans that indicated rank among the *ali'i*. Introduced exotic birds and the new diseases they carried are another major reason for reduction of native bird numbers, along with predation by the mongoose and rat—especially upon ground-nesting birds. Bird malaria and bird pox were also devastating to the native species. Mosquitoes, unknown in Hawaii until they were accidentally introduced at Lahaina in 1826, infected most native birds, causing a rapid reduction in bird life. However, the most damaging factor by far is the assault upon native forests by agriculture and land developers. The vast majority of Hawaiian birds evolved into specialists. They lived in only one small area and ate a very limited number of plants or insects, which, when removed or altered, resulted in the birds demise.

## Preservation

Theodore Roosevelt established the Northwest Islands as a National Wildlife Reserve in the early 20th century, and efforts have continued since then to preserve Hawaii's unique avifauna. Many fine organizations are fighting the battle to preserve Hawaii's natural heritage, including: Hawaii Audubon Society, University of Hawai'i, U.S. Fish and Wildlife Service, World Wildlife Fund, and Hawaii Department of Natural Resources. While visiting Hawaii make sure to obey all rules regarding the natural environment. Never disturb nesting birds or their habitat while hiking. Be careful with fire and never cut living trees. If you spot an injured or dead bird do not pick it up; but report it to the local office of the U.S. Fish and Wildlife Service. Only through the conscientious effort of all concerned does Hawaii's wildlife stand a chance of surviving.

## Hawaiian Honeycreepers

One of the most amazing families of all the birds on the face of earth is known as Drepanidinae, or Hawaiian honeycreepers. More than 40 distinct types of honeycreepers currently exist, although many more are suspected to have become extinct even before the arrival of Captain Cook, when a record was started. All are believed to have evolved from *a single* ancestral species. The honeycreepers have differing body types. Some look like finches, while others resemble warblers, thrushes, blackbirds, parrots, and even woodpeckers. Their bills range from long, pointed honeysuckers to tough, hooked nutcrackers. They are the most divergently evolved birds in the world. If Darwin, who studied the birds of the Galapagos Islands, had come to Hawaii, he would have found bird evolution that would make the Galapagos seem like child's play.

## More Endangered Endemic Birds

Maui is the last home of the **crested honeycreeper** *('akohekohe)*, which lives only on the windward slope of Haleakala from 4,500 to 6,500 feet. It once lived on Moloka'i but no longer. A rather large bird, it averages seven inches long and is predominantly black. Its throat and breast are tipped with gray feathers; bright orange decks its neck and underbelly. A distinctive fluff of feathers forms a crown. It primarily eats 'ohi'a flowers, and it's believed the crown feathers gather pollen and help propagate the 'ohi'a. The **Maui parrotbill** is another endangered bird found only on the slopes of Haleakala above 5,000 feet. It has an olive-green back and yellow body. Its most distinctive feature is the parrot-like bill, which it uses to crack branches and pry out larvae.

The **po'ouli** is a dark brown, five-inch bird with a black mask and dark brown feet. It has a short tail and sports a conical bill. It was saved from extinction through efforts of the Sierra Club and Audubon Society, who successfully had it listed on the Federal List of Endangered Species. The bird has one remaining stronghold deep in the forests of Maui.

Two endangered waterbirds are the **Hawaiian stilt** *(ae'o)* and the **Hawaiian coot** *('alae ke'oke'o)*. The stilt is a 16-inch, very thin wading bird. It is primarily black with a white belly and long, pink sticklike legs. The adults will pretend to be hurt, putting on an excellent "broken-wing" performance to lure predators away from their nests. The Hawaiian coot is a web-footed waterbird that resembles a duck. Found on all the main islands but mostly on Maui and Kaua'i, it has dull gray feathers, a white bill, and white tail feathers. It builds a large floating nest and vigorously defends its young. The **dark-rumped petrel** is slightly different from other petrels that are primarily marine birds. This petrel can usually be seen around the visitors center at Haleakala Crater about an hour after dusk from May through October.

## Survivors

The *'amakihi* and the *'i'iwi* are endemic birds not endangered at the moment. The *'amakihi* is one of the most common native birds. Yellowish-green, it frequents the high branches of 'ohi'a, koa, and sandalwood looking for insects, nectar, or fruit. It's less specialized than most other Hawaiian birds, the main reason for its continued existence. The *'i'iwi* is a bright red bird with a salmon-colored hooked bill. It's found mainly on Maui, Hawai'i, and Kaua'i in forests above 2,000 feet. It, too, feeds on insects and flowers. The *'i'iwi* is known for its harsh voice, which sounds like a squeaking hinge but is also capable of a melodious song. The feathers of the *'i'iwi* were highly prized by the *ali'i* for clothing decoration.

The *'elepaio* is found on several of the islands and is fairly common in the rainforest. This longtailed, five-inch brown bird can be coaxed to come within touching distance of the observer. This bird was the special *'aumakua* (personal spirit) of canoe builders in ancient lore. The *'apapane,* the most common native bird, is the easiest to see. It's a chubby, red-bodied bird about five inches long with a black bill, legs, wing tips, and tail feathers. It's quick and flitty and has a wide variety of calls and songs, from beautiful warbles to mechanical buzzes. Its feathers, like those of the *'i'iwi,* were sought by Hawaiians to produce distinctive capes and helmets for the *ali'i.*

## Pueo

This Hawaiian owl is found on all of the main islands, but mostly on Maui, especially in Haleakala Crater. The *pueo* is one of the oldest examples of an *'aumakua* in Hawaiian mythology. It was an especially benign and helpful guardian. Old Hawaiian stories abound in which a *pueo* came to the aid of a warrior in distress or a defeated army. Arriving at a tree in which a *pueo* had alighted, the soldiers are safe from their pursuers and are under the protection of "the wings of an owl." The many introduced barn owls in Hawaii are easily distinguished from a *pueo* by their heart-shaped faces. The *pueo* is about 15 inches tall with a mixture of brown and white feathers. The eyes are large, round, and yellow, and the legs are heavily feathered, unlike those of a barn owl. *Pueo* chicks are a distinct yellow color.

## The Nene

The *nene,* or Hawaiian goose, deserves special mention because it is Hawaii's state bird and is making a comeback from the edge of extinction. The *nene* is found only on the slopes of Mauna Loa, Hualalai, and Mauna Kea on the Big Island, and in Haleakala Crater on Maui. It was extinct on Maui until a few birds were returned there in 1957, but some experts maintain the *nene* lived naturally only on the Big Island. *Nene* are raised at the Wildfowl Trust in Slimbridge, England, which placed the first birds at

ROBERT NILSEN

The *nene,* the state bird, lives mainly on the slopes of Haleakala, Mauna Loa, Mauna Kea, and Mt. Hualalai.

Haleakala, and at the Hawaiian Fish and Game Station at Pohakuloa, along the Saddle Road on Hawai'i. By the 1940s, fewer than 50 birds lived in the wild. Now approximately 125 birds live on Haleakala and 500 on the Big Island. Although the birds can be raised successfully in captivity, their life in the wild is still in question.

The *nene* is believed to be a descendant of the Canada goose, which it resembles. Geese are migratory birds that form strong kinship ties, mating for life. It's speculated that a migrating goose became disabled and remained in Hawaii along with its loyal mate. The *nene* is smaller than its Canadian cousin, has lost a great deal of webbing in its feet, and is perfectly at home away from water, foraging and nesting on rugged and bleak lava flows. The *nene* is a perfect symbol of Hawaii: let it be, and it will live.

# OTHER HAWAIIAN ANIMALS

## Insects

No one knows for sure, but it's highly probable the first animal arrivals in Hawaii were insects. Again, the theory is that most were blown here by ancient hurricanes or drifted here imbedded in floating logs and other pieces of wood. Like the plants that preceded them, their success and rapid evolution were phenomenal. A gravid female had to make the impossible journey, then happen upon a suitable medium in which to deposit her eggs. Here, at least, they would be free from predators and parasites with a good chance of developing to maturity. Again, the gene pool was highly restricted and the environment so foreign that an amazing variety of evolutionary changes occurred. Biologists believe only 350–400 original insect species are responsible for the more than 10,000 species that occur in Hawaii today. Of these 10,000, nearly 98 percent are found nowhere else on earth. Many are restricted to only one island, and most are dependent on a single species of plant or fruit. For this reason, when Hawaiian plants become extinct, many insects disappear as well.

It's very probable there were no pests before humans arrived. The first Polynesians introduced flies, lice, and fleas. Westerners brought the indestructible cockroach, mosquito larvae in their ships' stores of water, termites, ants, and all the plant pests that could hitch a ride in the cuttings and fruits intended for planting. Today visitors will note the stringent agricultural controls at airports. Some complain about the inconvenience, but they should know that in the past 50 years more than 700 new insect species have become established in Hawaii. Many are innocent enough, while others cause great problems for Hawaii's agriculture.

## Land Snails

People have the tendency to ignore snails until they step on one, and then they find them repulsive. But Hawaiian snails are some of the most remarkable and beautiful in the world. It's one thing to accept the possibility that a few insects or plant spores could have been driven to Hawaii by high winds or on birds' feet, given the fact of their uncountable billions. But how did the snails get here? Snails, after all, aren't known for their nimbleness or speed. Most Hawaiian snails never make it beyond the tree on which they're hatched. Yet more than 1,000 snail varieties, from an original 22, are found in Hawaii, and most are inexplicably found nowhere else. The Polynesians didn't bring them, seawater kills them, and it would have to be a mighty big bird that didn't notice one clinging to its foot. Biologists have puzzled over Hawaiian snails for years. One, J. T. Gulick, wrote in 1858, "These Achatinellinae [tree snails] never came from Noah's ark." Tree snails are found on O'ahu, Maui, Moloka'i, and Lana'i, but not on Kaua'i. Kaua'i has its own land dwellers, and the Big Island has land snails that have moved into the trees. Like all the other endemic species, Hawaiian land snails now face extinction. Of the estimated 1,000 species existing when the Europeans came, 600 are now gone forever, and many others are threatened. Agriculture, the demise of native flora, and the introduction of new species add up to a bleak future for the snails.

## Drosophila: The Hawaiian Fly

Most people hardly pay attention to flies, unless one lands on their plate lunch. But geneticists from throughout the world, and especially from the University of Hawai'i, make special pilgrimages to the volcano area of the Big Island and to Maui just to study the native Hawaiian drosophila. This critter is related to the fruit fly and housefly, but there are hundreds of native species that are singularly unique—more than one-third of the world's estimated total. The Hawaiian ecosystem is very simple and straightforward, so geneticists can trace the evolutionary changes from species to subspecies through mating behavior. The scientists compare the drosophila species between the two islands and chart the differences. Major discoveries in evolutionary genetics have been made through these studies.

## Indigenous Land Animals

Before humans arrived, Hawaii had a paucity of higher forms of land animals. There were no amphibians and no reptiles, and except for a profusion of bird life, insects, and snails, only two other animals were present: the **monk seal** and the **hoary bat,** both highly specialized mammals.

The monk seal has close relatives in the Caribbean and Mediterranean, although the Caribbean relatives are now believed to be extinct, making the monk seal one of the two tropical seals left on earth. It's believed that the monk seal's ancestors entered the Pacific about 200,000 years ago when the Isthmus of Panama was submerged. When the land rose, no more seals arrived, and the monk seal became indigenous to Hawaii. The main habitat for the Hawaiian monk seal is the outer islands, from the French Frigate Atolls north to Kure Island, but infrequently a seal is spotted on the shores of one of the main islands. Though the seals' existence was known to the native Hawaiians, who called them *'ilio-holo-i-ka-uaua* (dog running in the toughness), they didn't seem to play much of a role in their folklore or ecosystem. Whalers and traders certainly knew of their existence, hunting them for food and sometimes for skins. This kind of pressure almost wiped out the small seal population in the 19th century. Scientists were largely unaware of the monk seal until early in the 1900s. Finally, the seals were recognized as an endangered species and put under the protection of the Hawaiian Islands National Wildlife Refuge, where they remain in a touch-and-go battle against extinction. Today it's estimated that only 1,000 individuals are left.

The Hawaiian hoary bat *(pe'ape'a)* is a remarkable migratory animal that reached Hawaii from North and South America under its own power. The hoary bat no longer migrates, but its continental relatives still range far and wide. The Hawaiian bat has become somewhat smaller and reddish in color over the years, distinguishing it from its larger, darker brown cousins. Its tail has a whitish coloration, hence the name. The hoary bat has a 13-inch wingspan, gives birth to twins in early summer, and unlike other bats, is a solitary creature, roosting in trees. It doesn't live in caves like others of its species. The bats normally live at altitudes below 4,000 feet, but some have been observed on Mauna Loa and Mauna Kea above 6,000 feet. The main population is on the Big Island, with smaller breeding grounds on Maui and Kaua'i. Sometimes bats are spotted on the other main islands, but it remains uncertain whether they inhabit the islands or simply fly there from their established colonies. Recently, a second species of bat (now extinct) has been identified from bone fragments taken from caves on four of the Hawaiian Islands.

## Coral

Whether you're an avid scuba diver or novice snorkeler, you'll become aware of underwater coral gardens and grottoes whenever you peer at the fantastic seascapes below the waves. Although there is plenty of it, the coral in Hawaii doesn't do as well as in other more equatorial areas because the water is too wild and it's not quite as warm. Coral looks like a plant fashioned from colorful stone, but it's really the skeleton of tiny animals, zoophytes, that eat algae to live. Coral grows best on the west side of the islands where the water is quite still, the days are more sunny, and the algae can thrive. Many of Hawaii's reefs have been dying in the last 20 years, and no one seems to know why. Pesticides, used in agriculture, have been pointed to as a possible cause.

## HAWAII'S NATIONAL WILDLIFE REFUGES

### Big Island of Hawai'i

**Hakalau Forest NWR**
32 Kinoole St., Suite 101
Hilo, HI 96720
808/933-6915

Located between the 3,900–7,200 foot elevation on the windward slope of Mauna Kea, the Hakalau Forest refuge is instrumental in sustaining the naturally evolving middle elevation rainforest. It protects *'akiapola'au,* Hawaiian *'akepa,* 'io, Hawaiian creeper, *'o'u,* Hawaiian hoary bat, *nene, pueo, 'amakihi,* Hawaiian thrush, and the more common *'elepaio, 'i'iwi, 'oma'o,* and *'apapane* in a 33,000-acre habitat of koa, 'ohi'a, *opeka, pilo,* and other native species. Entry is authorized for hiking every weekend of the month, by special use permit. Contact the refuge manager.

### Moloka'i

**Kakahai'a NWR**
U.S. Fish and Wildlife Service
300 Ala Moana Blvd.
P.O. Box 50167
Honolulu, HI 96850
808/541-1201

Five miles east of Kaunakakai along Highway 450, Kakahai'a NWR protects Hawaiian coot and Hawaiian stilt in 40 acres of freshwater ponds and marsh with dense thickets of bulrush. Established 1976. A beach park on refuge land is open to the public.

### O'ahu

**James C. Campbell NWR**
O'ahu National Wildlife Refuge Complex
66-590 Kamehameha Hwy., Room 2C
Hale'iwa, HI 96712
808/637-6330

Near Kahuku on the northeastern shore of the island of O'ahu, this NWR protects Hawaiian gallinule *('alae'ula),* Hawaiian coot *('alae ke'oke'o),* Hawaiian stilt *(ae'o),* Hawaiian duck *(koloa),* black-crowned night herons, introduced birds, migratory shorebirds, and waterfowl. It covers 142 acres in two units: Punamano Pond is a natural spring-fed marsh, while the Ki'i Unit is a series of man-made ponds once used as sugarcane waste settling basins. Established in 1977. Open on specified weekends; contact manager for tours.

**Pearl Harbor NWR**
O'ahu National Wildlife Refuge Complex
66-590 Kamehameha Hwy., Room 2C
Hale'iwa, HI 96712
808/637-6330

Within Pearl Harbor Naval Base, this refuge protects Hawaiian gallinule, Hawaiian coot, Hawaiian stilt, Hawaiian duck, and black-crowned night herons on 40 acres of man-made wetlands. Established in 1977.

**O'ahu Forest NWR**
O'ahu National Wildlife Refuge Complex
66-590 Kamehameha Hwy., Room 2C
Hale'iwa, HI 96712
808/637-6330

Located in the Ko'olau Range above the Leilehua Plateau, this new refuge has been established to protect upland native birds like the *'apapapne, O'ahu 'elepaio,* and *pueo* (Hawaiian owl), and several varieties of rare trees snails.

### Kaua'i

**Kilauea Point NWR**
P.O. Box 87
Kilauea, HI 96754
808/828-1413

Kilauea Point NWR lies one mile north of Kilauea on a paved road; the headquarters and parking area are on Kilauea Point. Kilauea protects red-footed boobies, shearwaters, great frigate birds, brown boobies, red-tailed and white-tailed tropic birds, and Laysan albatross, as well as green sea turtles, humpback whales, and dolphins. It covers 31 acres of cliffs and headlands with native coastal plants. Open Mon.–Fri. 10 A.M.–4 P.M. The entrance fee is $2 adults, free for children under 16.

### Hule'ia NWR
P.O. Box 87
Kilauea, HI 96754
808/828-1413

At Hule'ia, viewing is best from the Alakoko Fish Pond overlook along Halemalu Road west of Puhi Road. This refuge protects *koloa* (Hawaiian duck), Hawaiian coot, Hawaiian gallinule, and Hawaiian stilt. It covers 238 acres of seasonally flooded river bottomland and wooded slopes of the Hule'ia River Valley. Established in 1973. No general admittance.

### Hanalei NWR
P.O. Box 87
Kilauea, HI 96754
808/828-1413

Hanalei NWR is on the north coast of Kaua'i, 1.5 miles east of Hanalei on Highway 56. Observe wildlife from Ohiki Road, which begins at the west end of Hanalei River bridge, or from the highway overlook in Princeville. This refuge protects *koloa* (Hawaiian duck), Hawaiian coot, Hawaiian gallinule, and Hawaiian stilt. It covers 917 acres of river bottomland, taro farms, and wooded slopes in the Hanalei River Valley. Established in 1972.

## Atolls

### Hawaiian Islands NWR
Hawaiian and Pacific Islands NWRs
300 Ala Moana Blvd.
P.O. Box 50167
Honolulu, HI 96850
808/541-1202

Hawaiian Islands NWR comprises far-flung islands and atolls strung 1,000 miles from Nihoa Island to Pearl and Hermes Reef—rugged volcanic remnants and sparsely vegetated low sandy islands. The refuge protects Laysan and black-footed albatross, sooty terns, white terns, brown and black noddies, shearwaters, petrels, red-tailed tropic birds, frigate birds, and boobies. Also protected are several land birds and ducks, the Hawaiian monk seal, and the green sea turtle. The refuge covers 1,800 acres of land and a quarter million acres of submerged reef and lagoons. Established in 1909. No general access.

### Remote Pacific Refuges
Hawaiian and Pacific Islands NWRs
300 Ala Moana Blvd.
P.O. Box 50167
Honolulu, HI 96850
808/541-1202

**Johnston Atoll NWR** is about 825 miles southwest of Honolulu. It protects seabird nesting rookeries, sooty terns, gray-backed terns, shearwaters, red-footed boobies, brown boobies, masked boobies, lesser and great frigate birds, red-tailed tropic birds, and brown noddies. It's been a refuge since 1926. Managed with the Defense Nuclear Agency.

**Baker Island NWR,** 340 acres, and **Howland Island NWR,** 400 acres, are about 1,600 miles southwest of Hawaii, just north of the equator. Each encompasses emerged and submerged land. Low islands covered in grasses, vines, and bush sustain various seabirds and migratory birds.

**Jarvis Island NWR** is about 1,300 miles south of Honolulu and includes 1,100 acres of nesting area for at least eight species of migratory birds.

**Rose Atoll NWR** is the easternmost point of the Samoan archipelago and the southernmost U.S. national wildlife refuge. It covers 20 acres of islets, lagoon, and reef that support a dozen species of migratory birds. Administered jointly with the American Samoa government. Baker, Howland, Jarvis, and Rose NWRs were established in 1974.

# WHALES

Perhaps it's their tremendous size and graceful power, coupled with a dancer's delicacy of movement, that render whales so esthetically and emotionally captivating. In fact, many people claim that they feel a spirit-bond to these obviously intelligent mammals, which at one time shared dry land with us and then re-evolved into creatures of the great seas. Experts often remark that whales exhibit behavior akin to the highest social virtues. For example, whales rely much more on learned behavior than on instinct, the sign of a highly evolved intelligence. Gentle mothers and protective "escort" males join to teach the young to survive. They display loyalty and bravery in times of distress, and innate gentleness and curiosity. Their "songs," especially those of the humpbacks, fascinate scientists and are considered a unique form of communication in the animal kingdom. Humpback whales migrate to Hawaii every year November–May. Here, they winter, mate, give birth, and nurture their young until returning to food-rich northern waters in the spring. It's hoped that humankind can peacefully share the oceans with these magnificent giants forever. Then, perhaps, we will have taken the first steps toward saving ourselves.

## Evolution and Socialization

Many millions of years ago, for an unknown reason, animals similar to cows—their closest land relative is the hippo—were genetically triggered to leave the land and readapt to the sea. Known as cetaceans, this order contains about 80 species of whales, porpoises, and dolphins. Being mammals, cetaceans are warm-blooded and maintain a body temperature of 96°, only 2.6 degrees less than humans. After a gestation period of about one year, whales give birth to fully formed young, which usually enter the world tail first. The mother whale spins quickly to snap the umbilical cord, then places herself under the newborn and lifts it to the surface to take its first breath. A whale must be taught to swim or it will drown like any other air-breathing mammal. The baby whale, nourished by its mother's rich milk, becomes a member of an extended family, or pod, through which it's cared for, socialized, and protected by many "nannies."

## Physiology

The best way to spot a whale is to look for its "spout," a misty spray forced from a blowhole—really the whale's nostrils, which have moved from its snout to just behind its head. The spray from the spout is not water, but highly compressed air heated by the whale's body and expelled with such force that it condenses into a fine mist. A whale's tail is called a fluke; unlike the vertical tail of fish, a whale's tail is horizontal. The fluke, a marvelous appendage for propelling the whale through the water, is a vestige of the pelvis. It's so powerful that a 40-ton humpback can lift itself completely out of the water with only three strokes of its fluke. A whale's flippers guide it through the water. The bones in the flippers closely resemble those of the human arm and hand; small, delicate bones at the ends of the flippers look like fingers. On a humpback the flippers can be one-third as long as the body and supple enough to bend over its back, like a human reaching over the shoulder to scratch an itch.

A whale's eyes are functional but very small and not the primary sensors. Instead, the whale has developed keen hearing; the ears are small holes about as big around as the lead of a pencil. They have protective wax plugs that build up over the years. Like the growth rings in a tree, the ear plugs can be counted to determine the age of a whale; its life span is about the same as that of a human being. Because of strong ocean currents and the myriad dangers inherent in being at sea, whales enjoy a very light sleep, more like a rest similar to humans just awakening, a state that is not fully conscious but aware.

## Types of Whales

Although all whales, dolphins, and porpoises are cetaceans, they are arbitrarily divided according to length. Whales are all those animals longer than 30 feet; dolphins range six to 30 feet; and porpoises are less than six feet long. There are basically two types of whales: toothed, which includes the sperm, killer, and pilot whales, as well as porpoises and dolphins; and baleen, including the blue, minke, right, fin, and humpback.

Toothed whales feed by capturing and tearing their prey with their teeth. The killer whale or orca is the best known of the toothed whales. With its distinctive black-and-white markings and propensity for aquabatics, it's a favorite at marine parks around the world. The orca hunts other cetaceans, oftentimes attacking in packs to overcome larger whales. A killer whale in the wild lives about four times as long as one in captivity, even if it is well cared for.

A baleen whale eats by gliding through the water with its mouth open, sucking in marine plankton and tiny shrimplike creatures called krill. The whale then expels the water and captures the food in row after row of a prickly, fingernail-like substance called baleen.

## Hawaiian Whales and Dolphins

The role of whales and dolphins in Hawaiian culture seems quite limited. Unlike fish, which were intimately known and individually named, only two generic names described whales: *kohola* (whale) and *palaoa* (sperm whale). Dolphins were lumped together under one name, *nai'a;* Hawaiians were known to harvest dolphins on occasion by herding them onto a beach. Whale jewelry was worn by the *ali'i.* The most coveted ornament came from a sperm whale's tooth, called a *lei niho palaoa,* which was carved into one large curved pendant. Sperm whales have upward of 50 teeth, ranging in size four to 12 inches and weighing up to two pounds. One whale could provide numerous pendants. The most famous whale in Hawaiian waters is the humpback, but others often sighted include the sperm, killer, false killer, pilot, Curvier, Blainsville, and pygmy killer. There are technically no porpoises, but dolphins include the common, bottlenose, spinner, white-sided, broad- and slender-beaked, and rough-toothed. The mahimahi, a favorite eating fish found on many

BOB RACE

humpback whale

menus, is commonly referred to as a dolphin but is unrelated and is a true fish, not a cetacean.

## The Humpbacks

The humpback gets its name from its style of exposing its dorsal fin when diving, which gives it a humped appearance. This dorsal fin also puts it into the rorqual family. There are about 10,000 humpback whales alive today, down from an estimated 100,000 at the beginning of the 20th century. The remaining whales are divided into three separate global populations: North Atlantic, North Pacific, and South Pacific groups. About 3,000 North Pacific humpbacks migrate from coastal Alaska beginning in November. Migration peaks in February, when humpbacks congregate mostly in the waters off Maui, with smaller groups heading for the waters off the other islands. In 1992, the **Hawaiian Islands Humpback Whale National Marine Sanctuary** was designated, encompassing waters off all six major islands. One hopes this will ensure a perpetual safe haven for the whales.

Adult humpbacks average 45 feet long and weigh in at a svelte 40 tons (80,000 pounds) or more. They come to Hawaii mainly to give birth to 2,000-pound, relatively blubberless calves (one per female), most of which are born by the end of January. The mother nurses her calf for about one year and becomes impregnated again the next year. While in Hawaiian waters the humpbacks generally don't eat. They wait until returning to Alaska, where they gorge themselves on krill. It's estimated they can live off their blubber without peril for six months. They have enormous mouths stretching one-third the length of their bodies and filled with more than 600 rows of baleen. Humpbacks have been known to blow air underwater to create giant bubble-nets that help corral krill. They rush in with mouths agape and dine on their catch.

Like other baleen whales, humpbacks feed in

relatively shallow waters and sound (dive) for periods lasting a maximum of about 25 minutes. In comparison, the sperm whale, a toothed bottom-feeder, can stay down for more than an hour. On the surface a humpback will breathe about once every two minutes. They also sleep on the surface or just below it.

A distinctive feature of the humpback is the 15-foot flipper that it can bend over its back. The flippers and tail flukes have white markings that differ between individuals, much as do human fingerprints. These markings are used to identify individual migrating humpbacks. Scientists photograph the distinctive tails and send prints to Seattle, Washington, a center of whale research. There a computer analysis identifies the individual or records it as a new specimen. Thereafter, any sightings become part of its life history. The humpback is the most aquabatic of all whales, and it is a thrilling sight to see one of these agile giants leap from the water and create a monumental splash.

## The Humpback's Song

Unlike other whales, humpbacks have the special ability to sing. They create their melodies by grunting, shrieking, and moaning. No one knows exactly what the songs represent, but it's clear they're a definite form of communication. The singers appear to be "escort males" who tag along with and seem to guard a mother and her calf. Some scientists believe these are lone males and perhaps the song is territorial, or a mating call. The songs are exact renditions that last 20 minutes or longer and are repeated for hours. Amazingly, all the whales know and sing the same song, and the song changes from year to year. The notes are so forceful they can be heard above and below the water for miles. Some of the deep bass notes carry underwater for 100 miles.

## Whaling History

Humans have known about whales for many thousands of years. A Minoan palace on the island of Crete depicts whales on a 5,000-year-old mural. The first whalers were probably Scandinavians who used stone harpoon heads to capture their prey more than 4,000 years ago. Inuit have long engaged in whaling as a means of survival, and for centuries many peoples living along coastal waters have harpooned migrating whales that ventured close to shore. The Basques had a thriving medieval whaling industry in the 12th century centered in the Bay of Biscay, until they wiped out all the Biscayan right whales. The height of the classic whaling industry that in-

## ENVIRONMENTAL RESOURCE GROUPS

Anyone interested in Hawaii's environmental issues can contact the following for more information:

**Earthjustice Legal Defense Fund,** 223 S. King St., 4th Fl., Honolulu, HI 96813, 808/599-2436, www.earthjustice.org

**Greenpeace,** 702 H Street NW, Ste. 300, Washington, DC 20001, 202/462-1177 or 808/263-4388 in Hawaii, www.greenpeace.org

**The Nature Conservancy,** 923 Nu'uanu Ave., Honolulu, HI 96817, 808/537-4508, www.tnc.org/hawaii

**Rainforest Action Network,** 221 Pine St., Ste. 500, San Francisco, CA 94104, 415/398-4404, www.ran.org

**Sierra Club Hawaii Chapter,** P.O. Box 2577, Honolulu, HI 96803, 808/538-6616, www.hi.sierraclub.org

**Earth Trust,** 25 Kaneohe Bay Dr., Ste. 205, Kailua, HI 96734, 808/254-2866, www.earthtrust.org

A savvy monthly newsletter that focuses on environmental and political issues facing Hawaii today is *Environment Hawai'i*, 282 Ululani St, 1st Fl., Hilo, HI 96720, 808/934-0115, www.environment-hawaii.org; individual subscription rate $35 per year. The well-researched and concisely written newsletter attempts to be fair to all parties concerned. Short on preaching and long on common sense, *Environment Hawai'i* is an excellent resource for anyone interested in the sociopolitical and environmental issues of the 50th state.

spired Melville's *Moby Dick* occurred 1820–1860. The international whaling capital perfectly situated in the center of the winter whaling grounds was Lahaina, Maui. At that time 900 sailing ships roamed the globe in search of whales. Of these, 700 were American, and they started the trend away from coastal to pelagic whaling by bringing their try-pots (blubber pots) aboard ship.

Although the killing was great during these years, every part of the whale was needed and used: blubber, meat, bone, teeth. Whale oil, the main product, was a superior lighting fuel and lubricant unmatched until petroleum came into general use in the mid-19th century. Today, every single whale by-product can be manufactured synthetically and there's absolutely no primary need to justify slaughtering whales.

During the great whaling days, the whales actually had a fighting chance. After all, they were hunted by men in wooden sailing ships that depended upon favorable winds. Once a whale was sighted by a sailor perched high in the rigging using a low-powered telescope, a small boat heaved off; after desperate rowing and dangerous maneuvering, the master harpooner threw his shaft by hand. When the whale was dead, it took every able-bodied man to haul it in.

Today, however, modern methods have wiped out every trace of daring and turned the hunt into technologically assisted slaughter. Low-flying aircraft radio the whales' locations to huge factory-ships that track them with radar and sonar. Once the pod is spotted, super-swift launches tear into them, firing cannon-propelled harpoons with lethal exploding tips. The killer launches keep firing until every whale in the pod is dead, and the huge factory-ship follows behind, merely scooping up the lifeless carcasses and hauling them aboard with diesel winches.

Many pirate whalers still roam the seas. The worst example perpetrated by these racketeers occurred in the Bahamas in 1971. A ship ironically carrying the name of *the* classic conservation group, *Sierra*, succeeded in wiping out every single humpback whale that wintered in Bahamian waters. Since 1971 not one whale has been sighted in the Bahamas, and whale-watchers lament that they will never return.

## The Last Whalers

Thanks to world opinion and the efforts of benign but aggressive organizations such as Greenpeace and Earth Trust, the International Whaling Commission (IWC), a voluntary group of 49 nations, now sets standards and passes quotas on the number and species of whales that can be killed. Over the last several decades, the blue, right, gray, bowhead, and humpback have become totally protected. However, many great whales such as the sperm, minke, sei, and fin are still hunted. Also, the IWC has no power of enforcement except public opinion and possible voluntary economic sanction.

The Japanese and Norwegians still hunt for whales, their operations often thinly disguised as "research." Native American Inuit and a few other indigenous peoples of the world, like the villagers of Lamalera on Lembata in Indonesia, hunt whales, but the number of whales taken by these groups is minuscule. The Japanese technically stay within their quotas, but they hire and outfit these and other nationals to hunt whales for them. Their main argument is that whaling is a traditional industry upon which they rely for food and jobs. This is patently false. Hardly more than 100 years old, pelagic whaling is a new industry to the Japanese. Much of the Japanese whale meat becomes pet food anyway, which is mainly exported.

Amazingly, a poll taken in Japan by the Whale and Dolphin Society of London found that 69 percent of the people opposed whaling. Finally, through the efforts of *ICEARCH* (International Cetacean Education And Research Conference), the first pillars of a bridge were laid between Japanese and Western scientists who are dedicated to finding a way for mankind and the great whales to live in harmony. In April 1993 these scientists came together on Maui for the first time to discuss the issue.

## Whale-Watching

If you're in Hawaii from late November to early May, you have an excellent chance of spotting a humpback. March is perhaps the best month. You can often see a whale from a vantage point on land, but this is nowhere near as thrilling as seeing them close up from a boat. Either way, binoculars are a must. Telephoto and zoom lenses are also useful, and you might even get a nifty photo in the bargain. But don't waste your film unless you have a fairly high-powered zoom: fixed-lens cameras give pictures with a lot of ocean and a tiny black speck. If you're lucky enough to see a whale breach (jump clear of the water), keep watching—they often repeat this a number of times. If a whale dives and lifts its fluke high in the air, expect it to be down for at least 15 minutes and not come up in the same spot. Other times they'll dive shallowly, then bob up and down quite often. If you time your arrival near sunset, even if you don't see a whale you'll enjoy a mind-boggling light show.

To learn more about whales and the Hawaiian Islands Humpback Whale National Marine Sanctuary, www.hihwnms.nos.noaa.gov, stop by its office at 726 S. Kihei Rd., Kihei, HI 96753, 800/879-2818. Another good source of information is the **Pacific Whale Foundation,** at the Ma'alaea Harbor Village in Ma'alaea, 808/249-8811, www.pacificwhale.org. Both these organizations have plenty of printed information about whales and other marine animals, and the Pacific Whale Foundation prints the free *Outdoor Adventures* tabloid, which details other information about these mammals and doings of the foundation. Additional research on whales and dolphins is being undertaken by the **Island Marine Institute,** 658 Front St., #101, Lahaina, HI 96761, 808/661-8397; www.whalewatchmaui.com.

# History

## THE ROAD FROM TAHITI

Until the 1820s, when New England missionaries began a phonetic rendering of the Hawaiian language, the past was kept vividly alive only by the sonorous voices of special *kahuna* who chanted the sacred *mele*. The chants were beautiful, flowing word pictures that captured the essence of every aspect of life. These *mele* praised the land *(mele 'aina)*, royalty *(mele ali'i)*, and life's tender aspects *(mele aloha)*. Chants were dedicated to friendship, hardship, and favorite children. Entire villages sometimes joined together to compose a *mele*—every word was chosen carefully, and the wise old *kapuna* would decide if the words were lucky or unlucky. Some *mele* were bawdy or funny on the surface but contained secret meanings, often with biting sarcasm, that ridiculed an inept or cruel leader. The most important chants took listeners back into the dim past, even before people lived in Hawaii. From these genealogies *(ko'ihonua)*, the *ali'i* derived the right to rule, since these chants went back to the gods Wakea and Papa from whom the *ali'i* were directly descended.

## The Kumulipo

The great genealogies, finally compiled in the late 1800s by order of King Kalakaua, were collectively known as the *Kumulipo, A Hawaiian Creation Chant,* basically a Polynesian account of Genesis. Other chants related to the beginning of this world, but the *Kumulipo* sums it all up and is generally considered the best. The chant relates that after the beginning of time, there is a period of darkness. The darkness, however, mysteriously brims with spontaneous life; during this period plants and animals are born, as well as Kumulipo, the man, and Po'ele, the woman. In the eighth chant darkness gives way to light and the gods descend to earth. Wakea is "the sky father" and Papa is "the earth mother," whose union gives birth to the islands of Hawaii. First born is Hawai'i, followed by Maui, then Kaho'olawe. Apparently, Papa becomes bushed after three consecutive births and decides to vacation in Tahiti. While Papa is away recovering from postpartum depression and working on her tan, Wakea gets lonely and takes Ka'ula as his second wife; she bears him the island-child of Lana'i. Not fully cheered up, but getting the hang of it, Wakea takes a third wife, Hina, who promptly bears the island of Moloka'i. Meanwhile, Papa gets wind of these shenanigans, returns from Polynesia, and retaliates by taking up with Lua, a young and virile god. She soon gives birth to the island of O'ahu. Papa and Wakea finally decide that they really are meant for each other and reconcile to conceive Kaua'i, Ni'ihau, Ka'ula, and Nihoa. These two progenitors are the source from which the *ali'i* ultimately traced their lineage, and from which they derived their god-ordained power to rule.

Basically, there are two major genealogical families: the **Nanaulu,** who became the royal *ali'i* of O'ahu and Kaua'i, and the **Ulu,** who provided the royalty of Maui and Hawai'i. The best sources of information on Hawaiian myth and

legend are Martha Beckwith's *Hawaiian Mythology* and the monumental three-volume opus *An Account of the Polynesian Race,* compiled by Abraham Fornander 1878–85. Fornander, after settling in Hawaii, married an *ali'i* from Moloka'i and had an illustrious career as a journalist, Maui circuit judge, and finally Supreme Court justice. For years Fornander sent scribes to every corner of the kingdom to listen to the elder *kupuna*. They returned with firsthand accounts, which he dutifully recorded.

## Polynesians

Since prehistory, Polynesians have been seafaring people whose origins cannot be completely traced. They seem to have come from Southeast

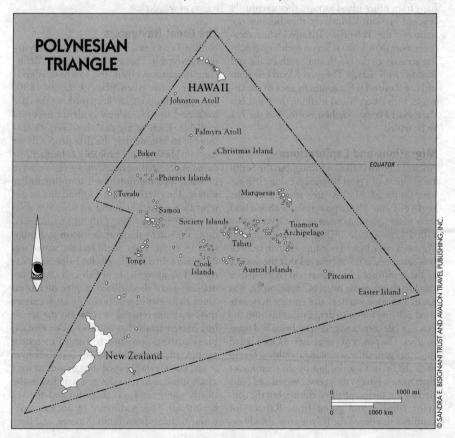

POLYNESIAN TRIANGLE

Asia mostly through the gateway of Indonesia, and their racial strain pulls features from all three dominant races: Caucasian, Negro, and Asian. They learned to navigate on tame narrow waterways along Indonesia and New Guinea, then fanned out eastward into the great Pacific. They sailed northeast to the low islands of Micronesia and southwest to Fiji, Vanuatu, and New Caledonia. Fiji is regarded as the "cradle of Polynesian culture"; carbon dating places humans there as early as 3,500 B.C. Many races blended on Fiji, until finally the Negroid became dominant and the Polynesians moved on. Wandering, they discovered and settled Samoa and Tonga, then ranged far east to populate Tahiti, Easter Island, and the Marquesas. From the Marquesas, or perhaps from other island groups, they eventually reached Hawaii. Ultimately, they became the masters of the "Polynesian Triangle," which measures more than 5,000 miles on each leg, stretching across both the North and South Pacific and studded with islands. The great Maori kingdom of New Zealand is the southern apex of the triangle, with Easter Island marking the point farthest east; Hawaii, farthest north, was the last to be settled.

## Migrations and Explorations

Ancient legends common throughout the South Pacific speak of a great Polynesian culture that existed on the island of Raiatea, about 150 miles north of Tahiti. Here a powerful priesthood held sway in an enormous *heiau* in the Opoa district called Toputapuatea. Kings from throughout Polynesia came here to worship. Human sacrifice was common, as it was believed that the essence of the spirit could be utilized and controlled in this life; therefore the mana of Toputapuatea was great. Defeated warriors and commoners were used as living rollers to drag canoes up onto the beach, while corpses were dismembered and hung in trees. The power of the priests of Opoa lasted for many generations, evoking trembling fear in even the bravest warrior just by the mention of their names. Finally, their power waned and Polynesians lost their centralized culture, but the constant coming and going from Raiatea for centuries sharpened the Polynesians' already ex-

cellent sailing skills and convinced them that the world was vast and that unlimited opportunities existed to better their lot.

Many explorers left to look for the "heavenly homeland to the north." Samoans called it Savai'i, Tongans Hawai, Rarotongans Avaiki, and Society Islanders Havai'i. Others abandoned the small islands throughout Polynesia where population pressures exceeded the limits of natural resources, prompting famine. Furthermore, Polynesians were very warlike among themselves; power struggles between members of a ruling family were common, as were marauders from other islands. So, driven by hunger or warfare, countless refugee Polynesians headed north. Joining them were a few who undoubtedly went for the purely human reason of wanderlust.

## The Great Navigators

No one knows exactly when the first Polynesians arrived in Hawaii, but the great "deliberate migrations" from the southern islands seem to have taken place A.D. 500–800, though anthropologists keep pushing the date backward in time as new evidence becomes available. Even before that, however, it's reasonable to assume that the first people to set foot on Hawaii were probably fishermen, or perhaps defeated warriors whose canoes were blown hopelessly northward into unfamiliar waters. They arrived by a combination of extraordinary good luck and an uncanny ability to sail and navigate without instruments, using the sun by day and the moon and rising stars by night. They could feel the water and determine direction by swells, tides, and currents. The movements of fish and cloud formations were also utilized to give direction. Since their arrival was probably an accident, they were unprepared to settle on the fertile but barren lands, having no stock animals, plant cuttings, or women. Forced to return southward, many undoubtedly lost their lives at sea, but a few wild-eyed stragglers must have made it home to tell tales of a paradise to the north where land was plentiful and the sea bounteous. This is affirmed by ancient navigational chants from Tahiti, Moorea, and Bora

Bora, which were passed from father to son and revealed how to follow the stars to the "heavenly homeland in the north." Possibly a few migrations followed, but it's known that for centuries there was no real reason for a mass exodus, so the chants alone remained and eventually became shadowy legend.

## From Where They Came

While some new evidence and assumptions may dispute this claim, it's generally agreed that the first planned migrations were from the violent cannibal islands that Spanish explorers called the Marquesas, 11 islands in extreme eastern Polynesia. The islands themselves are harsh and inhospitable, breeding a toughness into these people that enabled them to withstand the hardships of long, unsure ocean voyages and years of resettlement. Marquesans were a fiercely independent people whose chiefs could rise from the ranks because of bravery or intelligence. They must have also been a fierce-looking lot. Both men and women tattooed themselves in complex blue patterns from head to foot. The warriors carried massive, intricately designed ironwood war clubs and wore carved whale teeth in slits in their earlobes that eventually stretched to the shoulders. They shaved the sides of their heads with sharks' teeth, tied their hair in two topknots that looked like horns, and rubbed their heavily muscled and tattooed bodies with scented coconut oils. Their cults worshipped mummified ancestors; the bodies of warriors of defeated neighboring tribes were consumed. They were masters at building great double-hulled canoes launched from huge canoe sheds. Two hulls were fastened together to form a catamaran, and a hut in the center provided shelter in bad weather. The average voyaging canoe was 60–80 feet long and could comfortably hold an extended family of about 30 people. These small family bands carried all the staples they would need in the new lands.

## The New Lands

For five centuries the Marquesans settled and lived peacefully on the new land, as if Hawaii's

*aloha* spirit overcame most of their fierceness. The tribes coexisted in relative harmony, especially since there was no competition for land. Cannibalism died out. There was much coming and going between Hawaii and Polynesia as new people came to settle for hundreds of years. Then, it appears that in the 12th century a deliberate exodus of warlike Tahitians arrived and subjugated the settled islanders. They came to conquer. This incursion had a terrific significance on the Hawaiian religious and social system. Oral tradition relates that a Tahitian priest, Pa'ao, found the mana of the Hawaiian chiefs to be low, signifying that their gods were weak. Pa'ao built a *heiau* at Waha'ula on the Big Island, then introduced the warlike god Ku and the rigid *kapu* system through which the new rulers became dominant. Voyages between Tahiti and Hawaii continued for about 100 years, and Tahitian customs, legends, and language became the Hawaiian way of life. Then suddenly, for no recorded or apparent reason, the voyages discontinued and Hawaii returned to total isolation.

The islands remained forgotten for almost 500 years until the indomitable English sailor, Captain James Cook, sighted O'ahu on January 18, 1778, and stepped ashore at Waimea on Kaua'i two days later. At that time Hawaii's isolation was so complete that even the Polynesians had forgotten about it. On an earlier voyage, Tupaia, a high priest from Raiatea, had accompanied Captain Cook as he sailed throughout Polynesia. Tupaia demonstrated his vast knowledge of existing archipelagos throughout the South Pacific by naming more than 130 islands and drawing a map that included the Tonga group, the Cook Islands, the Marquesas, even tiny Pitcairn, a rock in far eastern Polynesia where the mutinous crew of the *Bounty* found solace. In mentioning the Marquesas, Tupaia said, *"He ma'a te ka'ata,"* which means "Food is man" or simply "Cannibals." But remarkably absent from Tupaia's vast knowledge was the existence of Easter Island, New Zealand, and Hawaii.

The next waves of people to Hawaii would be white, and the Hawaiian world would be changed quickly and forever.

# THE WORLD DISCOVERS HAWAII

The late 18th century was an extraordinary time in Hawaiian history. Monumental changes seemed to happen all at once. First, Captain James Cook, a Yorkshire farm boy fulfilling his destiny as the all-time greatest Pacific explorer, found Hawaii for the rest of the world. For better or worse, it could no longer be an isolated Polynesian homeland. For the first time in Hawaiian history, a charismatic leader—Kamehameha—emerged, and after a long civil war he united all the islands into one centralized kingdom. The death of Captain Cook in Hawaii marked the beginning of a long series of tragic misunderstandings between whites and natives. When Kamehameha died, the old religious system of *kapu* came to an end, leaving the Hawaiians in a spiritual vortex. Many takers arrived to fill the void: missionaries after souls, whalers after their prey and a good time, traders and planters after profits and a home. The islands were opened and devoured like ripe fruit. Powerful nations, including Russia, Great Britain, France, and the United States, yearned to bring this strategic Pacific jewel under their own influence. The 19th century brought the demise of the Hawaiian people as a dominant political force in their own land and with it the end of Hawaii as a sovereign monarchy. An almost bloodless yet bitter military coup followed by a brief Hawaiian Republic ended in annexation by the United States. As the United States became completely entrenched politically and militarily, a new social and economic order was founded on the plantation system. Amazingly rapid population growth occurred with the importation of plantation workers from Asia and Europe, which yielded a unique cosmopolitan blend of races like nowhere else on earth. By the dawning of the 20th century, the face of old Hawaii had been altered forever; the "sacred homeland in the north" was hurled into the modern age. The attack on Pearl Harbor saw a tremendous loss of life and brought Hawaii closer to the United States by a baptism of blood. Finally, on August 2, 1959, after 59 years as a "territory," Hawaii officially became the 50th state of the Union.

## Captain Cook Sights Hawaii

In 1776 Captain James Cook set sail for the Pacific from Plymouth, England, on his third and final expedition into this still vastly unexplored region of the world. On a fruitless quest for the fabled Northwest Passage across the North American continent, he sailed down the coast of Africa, rounded the Cape of Good Hope, crossed the Indian Ocean, and traveled past New Zealand, Tasmania, and the Friendly Islands (where an unsuccessful plot was hatched by the "friendly" natives to murder him). On January 18, 1778, Captain Cook's 100-foot flagship HMS *Resolution* and its 90-foot companion HMS *Discovery* sighted O'ahu. Two days later, they sighted Kaua'i and went ashore at the village of Waimea. Though anxious to get on with his mission, Cook decided to make a quick sortie to investigate this new land and reprovision his ships. He did, however, take time to remark in his diary about the close resemblance of these newfound people to others he had encountered as far south as New Zealand, and he marveled at their widespread habitation across the Pacific.

The first trade was some brass medals for a mackerel. Cook also stated that he had never before met natives so astonished by a ship, and that they had an amazing fascination for iron, which they called *ko'i,* Hawaiian for "adze." There is even some conjecture that a Spanish ship under one Captain Gaetano had landed in Hawaii as early as the 16th century, trading a few scraps of iron that the Hawaiians valued even more than the Europeans valued gold. It was also noted that the Hawaiian women gave themselves freely to the sailors with the apparent good wishes of the island men. This was actually a ploy by the *kahuna* to test if the newcomers were gods or men—gods didn't need women. These sailors proved immediately mortal. Cook, who was also a physician, tried valiantly to keep the 66 men (out of 112) who had measurable cases of venereal disease away from the women. The task proved impossible as women literally swarmed the ships; when Cook returned less than a year later, it was logged that signs of VD were already apparent on some natives' faces.

Cook was impressed with the Hawaiians'

**Captain James Cook**

swimming ability and with their well-bred manners. They had happy dispositions and sticky fingers, stealing any object made of metal, especially nails. The first item stolen was a butcher's cleaver. An unidentified native grabbed it, plunged overboard, swam to shore, and waved his booty in triumph. The Hawaiians didn't seem to care for beads and were not at all impressed with a mirror. Cook provisioned his ships by trading chisels for hogs, while common sailors gleefully traded nails for sex. Landing parties were sent inland to fill casks with fresh water. On one such excursion a Mr. Williamson, who was eventually drummed out of the Royal Navy for cowardice, unnecessarily shot and killed a native. After a brief stop on Ni'ihau, the ships sailed away, but both groups were indelibly impressed with the memory of each other.

## Cook Returns

Almost a year later, when winter weather forced Cook to return from the coast of Alaska, his discovery began to take on far-reaching significance. Cook had named Hawaii the Sandwich Islands, in honor of one of his patrons, John Montague, the Earl of Sandwich. On this return voyage, he spotted Maui on November 26, 1778. After eight weeks of seeking a suitable harbor, the ships by-

passed it, but not before the coastline was duly drawn by Lieutenant William Bligh, one of Cook's finest and most trusted officers. (Bligh would find his own drama almost 10 years later as commander of the infamous HMS *Bounty.*) The *Discovery* and *Resolution* finally found safe anchorage at Kealakekua Bay on the Kona Coast of the Big Island. It is very lucky for history that on board was Mr. Anderson, ship's chronicler, who left a handwritten record of the strange and tragic events that followed. Even more important were the drawings of John Webber, ship's artist, who rendered invaluable impressions in superb drawings and etchings. Other noteworthy men aboard were George Vancouver, who would lead the first British return to Hawaii after Cook's death and introduce many fruits, vegetables, cattle, sheep, and goats; and James Burney, who would become a long-standing leading authority on the Pacific.

By all accounts Cook was a humane and just captain, greatly admired by his men. Unlike many other supremacists of that time, he was known to have a respectful attitude toward any people he encountered, treating them as equals and recognizing the significance of their cultures. Not known as a violent man, he would use his superior weapons against natives only in an absolute case of self-defense. His hardened crew had been at sea facing untold hardship for almost three years; returning to Hawaii was truly like reentering paradise.

A strange series of coincidences sailed with Cook into Kealakekua Bay on January 16, 1779. It was *makahiki* time, a period of rejoicing and festivity dedicated to the fertility god of the earth, Lono. Normal *kapu* days were suspended and willing partners freely enjoyed each other sexually. Dancing, feasting, and the islands' version of the Olympic games also took place. It was long held in Hawaiian legend that the great god Lono would return to earth. Lono's image was a small wooden figure perched on a tall, mastlike crossbeam; hanging from the crossbeam were long, white sheets of tapa. Who else could Cook be but Lono, and what else could his ships with their masts and white sails be but his sacred floating *heiau?* This explained the Hawaiians' previous fascination with his ships, but to add to the remarkable coincidence, Kealakekua Harbor happened to be considered Lono's private sacred harbor. Natives from throughout the land prostrated themselves and paid homage to the returning god. Cook was taken ashore and brought to Lono's sacred temple, where he was afforded the highest respect. The ships badly needed fresh supplies so the Hawaiians readily gave all they had, stretching their own provisions to the limit. To the sailors' delight, this included full measures of the *aloha* spirit.

## The Fatal Misunderstandings

After an uproarious welcome and generous hospitality for over a month, it became obvious that the newcomers were beginning to overstay their welcome. During the interim a seaman named William Watman died, convincing the Hawaiians that the *haole* were indeed mortals, not gods. Watman was buried at Hikiau Heiau, where a plaque commemorates the event to this day. Incidents of petty theft began to increase dramatically. The lesser chiefs indicated it was time to leave by "rubbing the Englishmen's bellies." Inadvertently, many *kapu* were broken by the English, and once-friendly relations became strained. Finally, the ships sailed away on February 4, 1779.

After plying terrible seas for only a week, *Resolution*'s foremast was badly damaged. Cook sailed back into Kealakekua Bay, dragging the mast ashore on February 13. The natives, now totally hostile, hurled rocks at the sailors. Orders were given to load muskets with ball; firearms had previously only been loaded with shot and a light charge. Confrontations increased when some Hawaiians stole a small boat and Cook's men set after them, capturing the fleeing canoe that held an *ali'i* named Palea. The Englishmen treated him roughly; to the Hawaiians' horror, they even smacked him on the head with a paddle. The Hawaiians then furiously attacked the marines, who abandoned the small boat.

## Cook Goes Down

Next the Hawaiians stole a small cutter from the *Discovery* that had been moored to a buoy and partially sunk to protect it from the sun. For the first time, Captain Cook became furious. He or-

dered Captain Clerk of the *Discovery* to sail to the southeast end of the bay and stop any canoe trying to leave Kealakekua. Cook then made a fatal error in judgment. He decided to take nine armed marines ashore in an attempt to convince the venerable King Kalani'opu'u to accompany him back aboard ship, where he would hold him for ransom in exchange for the cutter. The old king agreed, but his wife prevailed upon him not to trust the *haole*. Kalani'opu'u sat down on the beach to think while the tension steadily grew.

Meanwhile, a group of marines fired upon a canoe trying to leave the bay; a lesser chief, No'okemai, was killed. The crowd around Cook and his men reached an estimated 20,000, and warriors outraged by the killing of the chief armed themselves with clubs and protective straw-mat armor. One bold warrior advanced on Cook and struck him with his *pahoa* (dagger). In retaliation, Cook drew a tiny pistol lightly loaded with shot and fired at the warrior. His bullets spent themselves on the straw armor and fell harmlessly to the ground. The Hawaiians went wild. Lieutenant Molesworth Phillips, in charge of the nine marines, began a withering fire; Cook himself slew two natives.

Overpowered by sheer numbers, the marines headed for boats standing offshore, while Lieutenant Phillips lay wounded. It is believed that Captain Cook, the greatest Western sailor ever to enter the Pacific, stood helplessly in knee-deep water instead of making for the boats because he could not swim! Hopelessly surrounded, he was knocked on the head; then countless warriors passed a knife around and hacked and mutilated his lifeless body. A sad Lieutenant King lamented in his diary, "Thus fell our great and excellent commander."

## The Final Chapter

Captain Clerk, now in charge, settled his men and prevailed upon the Hawaiians to return Cook's body. On the morning of February 16 a grisly piece of charred meat was brought aboard: the Hawaiians, according to their custom, had afforded Cook the highest honor by baking his body in an underground oven to remove the flesh from the bones. On February 17, a group of

Hawaiians in a canoe taunted the marines by brandishing Cook's hat. The English, strained to the limit and thinking that Cook was being desecrated, finally broke. Foaming with bloodlust, they leveled their cannons and muskets on shore and shot anything that moved. It is believed that Kamehameha the Great was wounded in this flurry, along with four *ali'i*; 25 *maka'ainana* (commoners) were killed. Finally, on February 21, 1779, the bones of Captain James Cook's hands, skull, arms, and legs were returned and tearfully buried at sea. A common seaman, one Mr. Zimmerman, summed up the feelings of all who sailed under Cook when he wrote, "He was our leading star." The English sailed next morning after dropping off their Hawaiian girlfriends who were still aboard.

Captain Clerk, in bad health, carried on with the fruitless search for the Northwest Passage. He died and was buried at the Siberian village of Petropavlovsk. England was at war with upstart colonists in America, so the return of the expedition warranted little fanfare. The *Resolution* was converted into an army transport to fight the pesky Americans; the once-proud *Discovery* was reduced to a convict ship ferrying inmates to Botany Bay, Australia. Mrs. Cook, the great captain's steadfast and chaste wife, lived to the age of 93, surviving all her children. She was given a stipend of 200 pounds per year and finished her days surrounded by Cook's mementos, observing the anniversary of his death to the very end by fasting and reading from the Bible.

## THE UNIFICATION OF OLD HAWAII

Hawaii was already in a state of political turmoil and civil war when Cook arrived. In the 1780s the islands were roughly divided into three kingdoms: venerable Kalani'opu'u ruled Hawai'i and the Hana district of Maui; wily and ruthless warrior-king Kahekili ruled the remainder of Maui, Kaho'olawe, Lana'i, and later O'ahu; and Kaeo, Kahekili's brother, ruled Kaua'i. War ravaged the land until a remarkable chief, Kamehameha, rose and subjugated all the islands under one rule. Kamehameha initiated a dynasty that would last

for about 100 years, until the independent monarchy of Hawaii forever ceased to be. To add a zing to this brewing political stew, Westerners and their technology were beginning to come in ever-increasing numbers. In 1786, Captain Jean de François La Pérouse and his French exploration party landed in what's now La Pérouse Bay near Makena on Maui, foreshadowing European attention to the islands. In 1786 two American captains, Portlock and Dixon, made landfall in Hawaii. Also, it was known that a fortune could be made on the fur trade between the Pacific Northwest and Canton, China; stopping in Hawaii could make it feasible. After this was reported, the fate of Hawaii was sealed.

Hawaii under Kamehameha was ready to enter its "golden age." The social order was medieval, with the *ali'i* as knights, owing their military allegiance to the king, and the serf-like *maka'ainana* paying tribute and working the lands. The priesthood of *kahuna* filled the posts of advisors, sorcerers, navigators, doctors, and historians. This was Polynesian Hawaii at its apex. But like the uniquely Hawaiian silversword, the old culture blossomed, and as soon as it did, began to wither. Ever since, all that was purely Hawaiian has been supplanted by the relentless foreign influences that began bearing down upon it.

### Young Kamehameha

The greatest native son of Hawaii, Kamehameha, was born under mysterious circumstances in the Kohala District of the Big Island, probably in 1753. He was royal born to Keoua Kupuapaikalaninui, the chief of Kohala, and Keku'iapoiwa, a chieftess from Kona. Accounts vary, but one claims that before his birth, a *kahuna* prophesied that this child would grow to be a "killer of chiefs." Because of this, the local chiefs conspired to murder the infant. When Kekuiapoiwa's time came, she secretly went to the royal birthing stones near Mo'okini Heiau and delivered Kamehameha. She entrusted her baby to a manservant and instructed him to hide the child. He headed for the rugged and remote coast around Kapa'au. Here Kamehameha was raised in the mountains, mostly by men. Always alone, he earned the nickname "The Lonely One."

Kamehameha was a man noticed by everyone; there was no doubt he was a force to be reckoned with. He had met Captain Cook when the *Discovery* unsuccessfully tried to land at Hana on Maui. While aboard, he made a lasting impression, distinguishing himself from the multitude of natives swarming the ships by his royal bearing. Lieutenant James King, in a diary entry, remarked that Kamehameha was a fierce-looking man, almost ugly, but that he was obviously intelligent, observant, and very good-natured. Kamehameha received his early military training from his uncle Kalani'opu'u, the great king of Hawai'i and Hana who fought fierce battles against Alapa'i, the usurper who stole his hereditary lands. After regaining Hawai'i, Kalani'opu'u returned to his Hana district and turned his attention to conquering all of Maui. During this period young Kamehameha distinguished himself as a ferocious warrior and earned the nickname of "The Hard-shelled Crab," even though old Kahekili, Maui's king, almost annihilated Kalani'opu'u's army at the sand hills of Wailuku.

When the old king neared death, he passed on the kingdom to his son Kiwala'o. He also, however, empowered Kamehameha as the keeper of the family war god Kuka'ilimoku: Ku of the Bloody Red Mouth, Ku the Destroyer. Oddly enough, Kamehameha had been born not 500 yards from Ku's great *heiau* at Kohala, and had heard the chanting and observed the ceremonies dedicated to this fierce god from his first breath. Soon after Kalani'opu'u died, Kamehameha found himself in a bitter war that he did not seek against his two cousins, Kiwala'o and his brother Keoua, with the island of Hawai'i at stake. The skirmishes lasted nine years, until Kamehameha's armies met the two brothers at Moku'ohai in an indecisive battle in which Kiwala'o was killed. The result was a shaky truce with Keoua, a much-embittered enemy. During this fighting, Kahekili of Maui conquered O'ahu, where he built a house of the skulls and bones of his adversaries as a reminder of his omnipotence. He also extended his will to Kaua'i by marrying his half-brother to a high-ranking chieftess of that island. A new factor would resolve this stalemate of power—the coming of the *haole.*

## The Olowalu Massacre

In 1790 the American merchant ship *Eleanora,* commanded by Yankee captain Simon Metcalfe, was looking for a harbor after its long voyage from the Pacific Northwest. Following a day behind was the *Fair American,* a tiny ship sailed by Metcalfe's son Thomas and a crew of five. Simon Metcalfe, perhaps by necessity, was a stern and humorless man who would tolerate no interference. While his ship was anchored at Olowalu, a beach area about five miles east of Lahaina, some natives slipped close in their canoes and stole a small boat, killing a sailor in the process. Metcalfe decided to trick the Hawaiians by first negotiating a truce and then unleashing full fury upon them. Signaling he was willing to trade, he invited canoes of innocent natives to visit his ship. In the meantime, he ordered that all cannons and muskets be readied with scatter shot. When the canoes were within hailing distance, he ordered his crew to fire at will. Over 100 people were slain; the Hawaiians remembered this killing as "the day of spilled brains." Metcalfe then sailed away to Kealakekua Bay and in an unrelated incident succeeded in in-

**King Kamehameha**

sulting Kameiamoku, a ruling chief, who vowed to annihilate the next *haole* ship he saw.

Fate sent him the *Fair American* and young Thomas Metcalfe. The little ship was entirely overrun by superior forces. In the ensuing battle, the mate, Isaac Davis, so distinguished himself by open acts of bravery that his life alone was spared. Kameiamoku later turned over both Davis and the ship to Kamehameha. Meanwhile, while harbored at Kealakekua, the senior Metcalfe sent John Young to reconnoiter. Kamehameha, having learned of the capture of the *Fair American,* detained Young so he could not report, and Metcalfe, losing patience, marooned his own man and sailed off to Canton. (Metcalfe never learned of the fate of his son Thomas, and was later killed with another son while trading in the South Pacific.) Kamehameha quickly realized the significance of his two captives and the *Fair American* with its brace of small cannons. He appropriated the ship and made Davis and Young trusted advisors, eventually raising them to the rank of chief. They would all play a significant role in the unification of Hawaii.

## Kamehameha the Great

Later in 1790, supported by the savvy of Davis and Young and the cannons from the *Fair American* (which he mounted on carts), Kamehameha invaded Maui, using Hana as his power base. The island's defenders under Kalanikupule, son of Kahekili who was lingering on O'ahu, were totally demoralized, then driven back into the death trap of 'Iao Valley. There, Kamehameha's forces annihilated them. No mercy was expected and none given, although mostly commoners were slain with no significant *ali'i* falling to the victors. So many were killed in this sheer-walled, inescapable valley that the battle was called *ka pani wai,* which means "the damming of the waters"—literally with dead bodies.

While Kamehameha was fighting on Maui, his old nemesis Keoua was busy running amok back on Hawai'i, again pillaging Kamehameha's lands. The great warrior returned home flushed with victory, but in two battles could not subdue Keoua. Finally, Kamehameha had a prophetic dream in which he was told that Ku would lead

him to victory over all the lands of Hawaii if he would build a *heiau* to the war god at Kawaihae. Even before the temple was finished, old Kahekili attempted to invade Waipi'o, Kamehameha's stronghold. But Kamehameha summoned Davis and Young, and with the *Fair American* and an enormous fleet of war canoes defeated Kahekili at Waimanu. Kahekili had no choice but to accept the indomitable Kamehameha as the king of Maui, although he himself remained the administrative head until his death in 1794.

Now only Keoua remained in the way, and he would be defeated not by war, but by the great mana of Ku. While Keoua's armies were crossing the desert on the southern slopes of Kilauea, the fire goddess Pele trumpeted her disapproval and sent a huge cloud of poisonous gas and mud-ash into the air. It descended upon and instantly killed the middle legions of Keoua's armies and their families. The footprints of this ill-fated army remain to this day outlined in the mud-ash as clearly as if they were deliberately encased in wet cement. Keoua's intuition told him that the victorious mana of the gods had swung to Kamehameha and that his own fate was sealed. Kamehameha sent word that he wanted Keoua to meet with him at Ku's newly dedicated temple in Kawaihae. Both knew that Keoua must die. Riding proudly in his canoe, the old nemesis came gloriously outfitted in the red-and-gold feathered cape and helmet signifying his exalted rank, accompanied by a small band of warriors. When he stepped ashore he was killed by Ke'eaumoku, a friend and ally of Kamehameha, and his warriors were slain by Kamehameha's men. His body was ceremoniously laid upon the altar along with the others who were slaughtered and dedicated to Ku, "of the Maggot-dripping Mouth."

## Increasing Contact

By the time Kamehameha had won the Big Island, Hawaii was becoming a regular stopover for numerous ships seeking the lucrative sandalwood trade with China. In February 1791, Captain George Vancouver, still seeking the Northwest Passage, returned to Kealakekua, where he was greeted by a throng of 30,000.

The captain at once recognized Kamehameha, who was wearing a Chinese dressing gown that he had received in tribute from another chief who in turn had received it directly from the hands of Cook himself. The diary of a crew member, Thomas Manby, relates that Kamehameha, missing his front teeth, was more fierce-looking than ever as he approached the ship in an elegant double-hulled canoe propelled by 46 rowers. The king invited all to a great feast prepared for them on the beach. Kamehameha's appetite matched his tremendous size. It was noted that he ate two sizable fish, a king-size bowl of poi, a small pig, and an entire baked dog. Kamehameha personally entertained the English by putting on a mock battle in which he deftly avoided spears by rolling, tumbling, and catching them in midair, all the while hurling his own spear a great distance. The English reciprocated by firing cannon bursts into the air, creating an impromptu fireworks display. Kamehameha requested from Vancouver a full table setting, with which he was provided, but his request for firearms was prudently denied. Captain Vancouver became a trusted advisor of Kamehameha and told him about the white people's form of worship. He even interceded for Kamehameha with his headstrong queen, Ka'ahumanu, and coaxed her from her hiding place under a rock when she sought refuge at Pu'uhonua O Honaunau. The captain gave gifts of beef cattle, fowl, and breeding stock of sheep and goats. The ship's naturalist, Archibald Menzies, was the first *haole* to climb Mauna Kea; he also introduced a large assortment of fruits and vegetables. The Hawaiians were cheerful and outgoing, and showed remorse when they indicated that the remainder of Cook's bones had been buried at a temple close to Kealakekua. John Young, by this time firmly entrenched into Hawaiian society, made no request to sail away with Vancouver. During the next two decades of Kamehameha's rule, the French, Russians, English, and Americans discovered the great whaling waters off Hawaii. Their increasing visits shook and finally tumbled the ancient religion and social order of *kapu*.

## Finishing Touches

After Keoua was laid to rest, it was only a matter of time until Kamehameha consolidated his power over all of Hawaii. In 1794 the old warrior Kahekili of Maui died and gave O'ahu to his son, Kalanikupule, while Kaua'i and Ni'ihau went to his brother Ka'eo. In wars between the two, Kalanikupule was victorious, though he did not possess the grit of his father nor the great mana of Kamehameha. He had previously murdered a Captain Brown, who had anchored at Honolulu, and seized his ship, the *Jackall*. With the aid of this ship, Kalanikupule now determined to attack Kamehameha. However, while en route, the sailors regained control of their ship and cruised to the Big Island to inform and join with Kamehameha. An army of 16,000 was raised and sailed for Maui, where they met only token resistance, destroyed Lahaina, pillaged the countryside, and subjugated Moloka'i in one bloody battle.

The war canoes sailed next for O'ahu and the final showdown. The great army landed at Waikiki, and though defenders fought bravely, giving up O'ahu by the inch, they were steadily driven into the surrounding mountains. The beleaguered army made its last stand at Nu'uanu Pali, a great precipice in the mountains behind present-day Honolulu. Kamehameha's warriors mercilessly drove the enemy into the great abyss. Kalanikupule, who hid in the mountains, was captured after a few months and sacrificed to Ku, the Snatcher of Lands, thereby ending the struggle for power.

Kamehameha put down a revolt on Hawai'i in 1796. The king of Kaua'i, Kaumuali'i, accepting the inevitable, recognized Kamehameha as supreme ruler without suffering the ravages of a needless war. Kamehameha, for the first time in Hawaiian history, was the undisputed ruler of all the islands of "the heavenly homeland in the north."

## Kamehameha's Rule

Kamehameha was as gentle in victory as he was ferocious in battle. Under his rule, which lasted until his death on May 8, 1819, Hawaii enjoyed a peace unlike any the warring islands had ever known. The king moved his royal court to Lahaina, where in 1803 he built the "Brick Palace," Hawaii's first permanent building. The benevolent tyrant also enacted the "Law of the Splintered Paddle." This law, which protected the weak from the exploitation of the strong, had its origins in an incident of many years before. A brave defender of a small overwhelmed village had broken a paddle over Kamehameha's head and taught the chief—literally in one stroke—about the nobility of the commoner.

However, just as Old Hawaii reached its golden age, its demise was at hand. The relentless waves of *haole* both innocently and determinedly battered the old ways into the ground. With the foreign ships came prosperity and fanciful new goods after which the *ali'i* lusted. The *maka'ainana* were worked mercilessly to provide sandalwood for the China trade. This was the first "boom" economy to hit the islands, but it set the standard of exploitation that would follow. Kamehameha built an observation tower in Lahaina to watch for ships, many of which were his own returning laden with riches from the world at large. In the last years of his life Kamehameha returned to his beloved Kona Coast, where he enjoyed the excellent fishing renowned to this day. He had taken Hawaii from the darkness of warfare into the light of peace. He died true to the religious and moral *kapu* of his youth, the only ones he had ever known, and with him died a unique way of life. Two loyal retainers buried his bones after the baked flesh had been ceremoniously stripped away. A secret burial cave was chosen so that no one could desecrate the remains of the great chief, thereby absorbing his mana. The tomb's location remains unknown, and disturbing the dead is still one of the strictest *kapu* to this day. The Lonely One's kingdom would pass to his son, Liholiho, but true power would be in the hands of his beloved and feisty wife Ka'ahumanu. As Kamehameha's spirit drifted from this earth, two forces sailing around Cape Horn would forever change Hawaii: the missionaries and the whalers.

# MISSIONARIES AND WHALERS

The year 1819 was of the utmost significance in Hawaiian history. It marked the death of Kamehameha, the overthrow of the ancient *kapu* system, the arrival of the first "whaler" in Lahaina, and the departure from New England of Calvinist missionaries determined to convert the heathen islands. Great changes began to rattle the old order to its foundations. With the *kapu* system and all of the ancient gods abandoned (except for the fire goddess Pele of Kilauea), a great void permeated the souls of the Hawaiians. In the coming decades Hawaii, also coveted by Russia, France, and England, was finally consumed by America. The islands had the first American school, printing press, and newspaper (the *Polynesian*) west of the Mississippi. Lahaina, in its heyday, became the world's greatest whaling port, accommodating more than 500 ships during its peak years.

## The Royal Family

Maui's Hana District provided Hawaii with one of its greatest queens, Ka'ahumanu, born in 1768 in a cave within walking distance of Hana Harbor. At the age of 17 she became the third of Kamehameha's 21 wives and eventually the love of his life. At first she proved to be totally independent and unmanageable and was known to openly defy her king by taking numerous lovers. Kamehameha placed a *kapu* on her body and even had her attended by horribly deformed hunchbacks in an effort to curb her carnal appetites, but she continued to flaunt his authority. Young Ka'ahumanu had no love for her great, lumbering, unattractive husband, but in time (even Captain Vancouver was pressed into service as a marriage counselor) she learned to love him dearly. She in turn became his favorite wife, although she remained childless throughout her life. Kamehameha's first wife was the supremely royal Keopuolani, who so outranked even him that the king himself had to approach her naked and crawling on his belly. Keopuolani produced the royal children Liholiho and Kauikeaouli, who became King Kamehameha II and III, respectively. Just before Kamehameha I died in 1819 he appointed Liholiho his successor, but

COURTESY OF HAWAII STATE ARCHIVES

the great Queen Kaʻahumanu, by ship's artist Louis Choris from the Otto Von Kotzebue expedition, circa 1816

he also had the wisdom to make Kaʻahumanu the *kuhina nui* or queen regent. Initially, Liholiho was weak and became a drunkard. Later he became a good ruler, but he was always supported by his royal mother, Keopuolani, and by the ever-formidable Kaʻahumanu.

### Kapu is Pau

Kaʻahumanu was greatly loved and respected by the people. On public occasions, she donned Kamehameha's royal cloak and spear: so attired and infused with the king's mana, she demonstrated that she was the real leader of Hawaii. For six months after Kamehameha's death, Kaʻahumanu counseled Liholiho on what he must do. The wise *kuhina nui* knew that the old ways were *pau* (finished) and that Hawaii could not hope to function in a rapidly changing world under the *kapu* system. In November 1819, Kaʻahumanu and Keopuolani prevailed upon Liholiho to break two of the oldest and most sacred *kapu* by eating with women and by allowing women to eat previously forbidden foods such as bananas and certain fish. Heavily fortified with strong drink and attended by other high-ranking chiefs and a hand-

ful of foreigners, Kaʻahumanu and Liholiho ate together in public. This feast became known as *ʻAi Noa* (Free Eating). As the first morsels passed Kaʻahumanu's lips, the ancient gods of Hawaii tumbled. Throughout the land, revered *heiau* were burned and abandoned and the idols knocked to the ground. Now the people had nothing to rely on but their weakened inner selves. Nothing and no one could answer their prayers; their spiritual lives were empty and in shambles.

### Missionaries

Into this spiritual vortex sailed the brig *Thaddeus* on April 4, 1820. It had set sail from Boston on October 23, 1819, lured to the Big Island by Henry ʻOpukahaʻia, a local boy born at Napoʻopoʻo in 1792, who had earlier been taken to New England. Coming ashore at Kailua-Kona, where Liholiho had moved the royal court, the Reverends Bingham and Thurston were granted a one-year trial missionary period by King Liholiho. They established themselves on the Big Island and Oʻahu and from there began the transformation of Hawaii. The missionaries were people of God, but also practical-minded Yankees. They brought education, enterprise, and most important a commitment to stay and build (unlike the transient seafarers). By 1824 the new faith had such a foothold that Chieftess Keopuolani climbed to the fire pit atop Kilauea and defied Pele. This was even more striking than the previous breaking of the food *kapu* because the strength of Pele could actually be seen. Keopuolani ate forbidden *'ohelo* berries and cried out, "Jehovah is my God." Over the next decades the governing of Hawaii slipped away from the Big Island and moved to the new port cities of Lahaina on Maui and, later, Honolulu.

## Rapid Conversions

The year 1824 also marked the death of Keopuolani, who was given a Christian burial. She had set the standard by accepting Christianity, and a number of the *ali'i* had followed the queen's lead. Liholiho had sailed off to England, where he and his wife contracted measles and died. Their bodies were returned by the British in 1825, on the HMS *Blonde* captained by Lord Byron, cousin of *the* Lord Byron. During these years, Ka'ahumanu allied herself with Reverend Richards, pastor of the first mission in the islands, and together they wrote Hawaii's first code of laws based upon the Ten Commandments. Foremost was the condemnation of murder, theft, brawling, and the desecration of the Sabbath by work or play. The early missionaries had the best of intentions, but like all zealots they were blinded by the single-mindedness that was also their greatest ally. They weren't surgically selective in their destruction of native beliefs. *Anything* native was felt to be inferior, and they set about wiping out all traces of the old ways. In their rampage they reduced the Hawaiian culture to ashes, plucking self-will and determination from the hearts of a once-proud people. More so than the whalers, they terminated the Hawaiian way of life.

## The Early Seamen

A good portion of the common seamen of the early 19th century came from the dregs of the Western world. Many a whoremongering drunkard had awoken from a stupor and found himself on the pitching deck of a ship, discovering to his dismay that he had been "pressed into naval service." For the most part these sailors were a filthy, uneducated, lawless rabble. Their present situation was dim, their future hopeless, and they would live to be 30 if they were lucky and didn't die from scurvy or a thousand other miserable fates. They snatched brief pleasure in every port and jumped ship at every opportunity, especially in an easy berth like Lahaina. They displayed the worst elements of Western culture—which the Hawaiians naively mimicked. In exchange for *aloha* they gave drunkenness, sloth, and insidious death by disease. By the 1850s the population of native Hawaiians tumbled from the estimated 300,000 reported by Captain Cook in 1778 to barely 60,000. Common conditions such as colds, flu, venereal disease, and sometimes smallpox and cholera decimated the Hawaiians, who had no natural immunities to these foreign ailments. By the time the missionaries arrived, *hapa haole* children were common in Lahaina streets.

The earliest merchant ships to the islands were owned or skippered by lawless opportunists who had come seeking sandalwood after first filling their holds with furs from the Pacific Northwest. Aided by *ali'i* hungry for manufactured goods and Western finery, they raped Hawaiian forests of this fragrant wood so coveted in China. Next, droves of sailors came in search of whales. The whalers, decent men at home, left their morals back in the Atlantic and lived by the slogan "no conscience east of the Cape." The delights of Hawaii were just too tempting for most.

## Two Worlds Tragically Collide

The 1820s were a time of confusion and soul-searching for the Hawaiians. When Kamehameha II died the kingdom passed to Kauikeaouli (Kamehameha III), who made his lifelong residence in Lahaina. The young king was only nine years old when the title passed to him, but his power was secure because Ka'ahumanu was still a vibrant *kuhina nui*. The young prince, more so than any other, was raised in the cultural confusion of the times. His childhood was spent during the very cusp of the change from old ways to new, and he was often pulled in two directions by vastly differing beliefs. Since he was royal born, he was bound by age-old Hawaiian tradition to mate and produce an heir with the highest-ranking *ali'i* in the kingdom. This mate happened to be his younger sister, the Princess Nahi'ena'ena. To the old Hawaiian advisors, this arrangement was perfectly acceptable and encouraged. To the increasingly influential missionaries, incest was an unimaginable abomination in the eyes of God. The problem was compounded by the fact that Kamehameha III and Nahi'ena'ena were drawn to each other and were deeply in love. The young king could not stand the mental pressure imposed by conflicting worlds. He became a teenage alcoholic too royal to be restrained by anyone in the kingdom, and his bouts of drunkenness and womanizing were both legendary and scandalous.

Meanwhile, Nahi'ena'ena was even more pressured because she was a favorite of the missionaries, baptized into the church at age 12. She too vacillated between the old and the new. At times a pious Christian, at others she drank all night and took numerous lovers. As the prince and princess grew into their late teens, they became even more attached to each other and hardly made an attempt to keep their relationship from the missionaries. Whenever possible, they lived together in a grass house built for the princess by her father.

In 1832, the great Ka'ahumanu died, leaving the king on his own. In 1833, at the age of 18, Kamehameha III announced that the "regency" was over and that all the lands in Hawaii were his personally, and that he alone was the ultimate law. Almost immediately, however, he decreed that his half-sister Kina'u would be "premier," signifying that he would leave the actual running of the kingdom in her hands. Kamehameha III fell into total drunken confusion, until one night he attempted suicide. After this episode he seemed to straighten up a bit and mostly kept a low profile. In 1836, Princess Nahi'ena'ena was convinced by the missionaries to take a husband. She married Leleiohoku, a chief from the Big Island, but continued to sleep with her brother. It is uncertain who fathered the child, but Nahi'ena'ena gave birth to a baby boy in September 1836. The young

prince survived for only a few hours, and Nahi'ena'ena never recovered from her convalescence. She died in December 1836 and was laid to rest in the mausoleum next to her mother, Keopuolani, on the royal island in Mokuhina Pond in Lahaina. After the death of his sister, Kamehameha III became a sober and righteous ruler. Often seen paying his respects at the royal mausoleum, he ruled longer than any other king until his death in 1854.

## The Missionaries Prevail

In 1823, the first mission was established in Lahaina, Maui, under the pastorate of Reverend Richards and his wife. Within a few years, many of the notable *ali'i* had been, at least in appearance, converted to Christianity. By 1828 the cornerstones for Waine'e Church, the first stone church on the island, were laid just behind the palace of Kamehameha III. The struggle between missionaries and whalers centered around public drunkenness and the servicing of sailors by native women. The normally God-fearing whalers had signed on for perilous duty that lasted up to three years, and when they anchored in Lahaina they demanded their pleasure. The missionaries were instrumental in placing a curfew on sailors and prohibiting native women from boarding ships, which had become customary. These measures certainly did not stop the liaisons between sailor and *wahine,* but they did impose a modicum of social sanction and tolled the end of the wide-open days. The sailors were outraged; in 1825 the crew from the *Daniel* attacked the home of the meddler, Reverend Richards. A year later a similar incident occurred. In 1827, confined and lonely sailors from the whaler *John Palmer* fired their cannons at Reverend Richards' newly built home.

Slowly the tensions eased, and by 1836 many sailors were regulars at the Seamen's Chapel adjacent to the Baldwin home. Unfortunately, even the missionaries couldn't stop the pesky mosquito from entering the islands through the port of Lahaina. The mosquitoes arrived from Mexico in 1826 aboard the merchant ship *Wellington.* They were inadvertently carried as larvae in the water barrels and democratically pestered everyone in the islands from that day forward, regardless of race, religion, or creed.

## Lahaina Becomes a Cultural Center

By 1831, Lahaina was firmly established as a seat of Western influence in Hawaii. That year marked the founding of Lahainaluna School, the first *real* American school west of the Rockies. Virtually a copy of a New England normal school, it attracted the best students, both native and white, from throughout the kingdom. By 1834, Lahainaluna had an operating printing press publishing the islands' first newspaper, *The Torch of Hawaii,* starting a lucrative printing industry centered in Lahaina that dominated not only the islands but also California for many years.

An early native student was David Malo. He was brilliant and well educated, but more importantly, he remembered the "old ways." One of the first Hawaiians to realize his native land was being swallowed up by the newcomers, Malo compiled the first history of precontact Hawaii, and the resulting book, *Mo'olelo Hawai'i* (Hawaiian Antiquities), became a reference masterpiece that has yet to be eclipsed. David Malo insisted that the printing be done in Hawaiian, not English. Malo is buried in the mountains above Lahainaluna where, by his own request, he is "high above the tide of foreign invasion." By the 1840s, Lahaina was firmly established as the "whaling capital of the world"; the peak year 1846 saw 395 whaling ships anchored here. A census in 1846 reported that Lahaina was home to 3,445 natives, 112 permanent *haole,* 600 sailors, and more than 500 dogs. The populace was housed in 882 grass houses, 155 adobe houses, and 59 relatively permanent stone and wood-framed structures. Lahaina would probably have remained the islands' capital, had Kamehameha III not moved the royal capital to the burgeoning port of Honolulu on the island of O'ahu.

## Foreign Influence

By the 1840s, Honolulu was becoming the center of commerce in the islands; when Kamehameha III moved the royal court there from Lahaina, the ascendant fate of the new capital was guaranteed. In 1843, Lord Paulet, com-

mander of the warship *Carysfort,* forced Kamehameha III to sign a treaty ceding Hawaii to the British. London, however, repudiated this act, and Hawaii's independence was restored within a few months when Queen Victoria sent Admiral Thomas as her personal agent of good intentions. The king memorialized the turn of events by a speech in which he uttered the phrase, *Ua mau ke e'a o ka 'aina i ka pono* ("The life of the land is preserved in righteousness"), now Hawaii's motto. The French used similar bullying tactics to force an unfavorable treaty on the Hawaiians in 1839; as part of these heavy-handed negotiations they exacted a payment of $20,000 and the right of Catholics to enjoy religious freedom in the islands. In 1842 the United States recognized and guaranteed Hawaii's independence without a formal treaty, and by 1860 more than 80 percent of the islands' trade was with the United States.

## The Great Mahele

In 1840 Kamehameha III ended his autocratic rule and instituted a constitutional monarchy. This brought about the Hawaiian Bill of Rights, but the most far-reaching change was the transition to private ownership of land. Formerly, all land belonged to the ruling chief, who gave wedge-shaped parcels called *ahupua'a* to lesser chiefs to be worked for him. The commoners did all the real labor, their produce heavily taxed by the *ali'i.* The fortunes of war, the death of a chief, or the mere whim of a superior could force a commoner off the land. The Hawaiians, however, could not think in terms of "owning" land. No one could *possess* land; one could only *use* land, and its *ownership* was a strange and foreign concept. As a result, naive Hawaiians gave up their lands for a song to unscrupulous traders, which remains an integral, unrectified problem to this day.

In 1847 Kamehameha III and his advisors separated the lands of Hawaii into three groupings: crown land (belonging to the king), government land (belonging to the chiefs), and the people's land (the largest parcels). In 1848, 245 *ali'i* entered their land claims in the *Mahele Book,* assuring them ownership. In 1850 the commoners were given title in fee simple to the lands they cultivated and lived on as tenants, not including house lots in towns. Commoners without land could buy small *kuleana* (farms) from the government at 50 cents per acre. In 1850, foreigners were also allowed to purchase land in fee simple, and the ownership of Hawaii from that day forward slipped steadily from the hands of its indigenous people.

# KING SUGAR

It's hard to say just where the sugar industry began in Hawaii. One story holds that a lone entrepreneur from China refined sugar on Lana'i just after 1800, but there seems to be no factual recording of his endeavor. The Koloa Sugar Plantation on the southern coast of Kaua'i successfully refined sugar in 1835. Following this, sugar refining was tried at numerous locations throughout the islands with varying degrees of success, but the industry burgeoned at Hana, Maui, in 1849. A whaler named George Wilfong hauled four blubber pots ashore and set them up on a rocky hill in the middle of 60 acres he had planted in sugar. A team of oxen turned "crushing rollers" and the cane juice flowed down an open trough into the pots, under which an attending native kept a roaring fire burning. Wilfong's methods of refining were crude, but the resulting high-quality sugar turned a neat profit in Lahaina. The main problem was labor. The Hawaiians, who made excellent whalers, were basically indentured workers. They became extremely disillusioned with their contracts, which could last up to 10 years. Most of their wages were eaten up by manufactured commodities sold at the company store, and it didn't take long for them to realize that they were little more than slaves. At every opportunity they either left the area or just refused to work.

## Imported Labor
The **Masters and Servants Act of 1850,** which allowed importation of laborers under the contract system, ostensibly guaranteed an endless supply of cheap labor for the plantations. Chinese laborers were imported, but were too enterprising to remain in the fields for a meager $3 per month. They left as soon as opportunity permitted and went into business as small merchants and retailers. In the meantime, Wilfong had sold out, releasing most of the Hawaiians previously held under contract, and his plantation fell into disuse. In 1860 two Danish brothers, August and Oscar Unna, bought land at Hana to raise sugar. They solved the labor problem by importing Japanese laborers who were extremely hard-working and easily managed. The workday lasted 10 hours, six days a week, for a salary of $20 per month with housing and medical care thrown in. Plantation life was very structured, with stringent rules governing even bedtimes and lights out. A worker could be fined for being late or for smoking on the job. Even the Japanese couldn't function under these circumstances, and improvements in benefits and housing were slowly gained.

## Sugar Grows
The demand for "Sandwich Island Sugar" grew as California was populated during the gold rush and increased dramatically when the American Civil War demanded a constant supply. The only sugar plantations on the Mainland were small plots confined to the Confederate states, whose products would hardly be bought by the Union and whose fields, later in the war, were destroyed. By the 1870s it was clear to the planters, still mainly New Englanders, that the United States was their market; they tried often to gain closer ties and favorable tariffs. The Americans also planted rumors that the British were interested in annexing Hawaii; this put pressure on the U.S. Congress to pass the long-desired **Reciprocity Act,** which would exempt sugar from import duty. It finally passed in 1875, in exchange for U.S. long-term rights to use the strategic naval port of Pearl Harbor, among other concessions. These agreements gave increased political power to a small group of American planters, whose outlooks were similar to those of the post-Civil War South, where a few powerful whites were the virtual masters of a multitude of dark-skinned laborers. Sugar was now big business and the Hana District alone exported almost 3,000 tons per year. All of Hawaii would have to reckon with the "sugar barons."

## Changing Society

The sugar plantation system changed life in Hawaii physically, spiritually, politically, and economically. Now boatloads of workers came not only from Japan but from Portugal, Germany, and even Russia. The white-skinned workers were most often the field foremen *(luna)*. With the immigrants came new religions, new animals and plants, unique cuisines, and a plantation language known as pidgin, or *da' kine*. Many Asians, and to a lesser extent the other groups, including the white plantation owners, intermarried with Hawaiians. A new class of people properly termed "cosmopolitan" but more familiarly and aptly known as "locals" was emerging. These were the people of multiple racial backgrounds who couldn't exactly say *what* they were, but it was clear to all just *who* they were. The plantation owners became the new "chiefs" of Hawaii who could carve up the land and dispense favors. The Hawaiian monarchy was soon eliminated.

# A KINGDOM PASSES

## The Beginning of the End

Like the Hawaiian people themselves, the Kamehameha dynasty in the mid-1800s was dying from within. King Kamehameha IV (Alexander Liholiho) ruled 1854–63; his only child died in 1862. He was succeeded by his older brother Kamehameha V (Lot Kamehameha), who ruled until 1872 and remained unmarried and childless. With his passing the Kamehameha line ended. William Lunalilo, elected king in 1873 by popular vote, was of royal, but not Kamehameha, lineage. He died after only a year in office, and being a bachelor left no heirs. He was succeeded by David Kalakaua, known far and wide as the "Merrie Monarch," who made a world tour and was well received wherever he went. He built 'Iolani Palace in Honolulu and was personally in favor of closer ties with the United States, helping push through the Reciprocity Act. Kalakaua died in 1891 and was replaced by his sister, Lydia Lili'uokalani, last of the Hawaiian monarchs.

Queen Lili'uokalani

COURTESY OF HAWAII STATE ARCHIVES

## The Revolution

When Lili'uokalani took office in 1891, the native population was at a low of 40,000, and she felt that the United States had too much influence over her homeland. She was known to personally favor the English over the Americans. She attempted to replace the liberal constitution of 1887 (adopted by her pro-American brother) with an autocratic mandate in which she would have had much more political and economic control of the islands. When the McKinley Tariff of 1890 brought a decline in sugar profits, she made no attempt to improve the situation. Thus, the planters saw her as a political obstacle to their economic growth; most of Hawaii's American planters and merchants were in favor of a rebellion. She would have to go! A central spokesperson and firebrand was Lorrin Thurston, a Honolulu publisher who, with a central core of about 30 men, challenged the Hawaiian monarchy. Although Lili'uokalani rallied some support and had a small military potential in her personal guard, the coup was ridiculously easy—it took only one casualty. Captain John Good shot a Hawaiian policeman in the arm and that did it.

Naturally, the conspirators could not have succeeded without some solid assurances from a secret contingent in the U.S. Congress as well as outgoing president Benjamin Harrison, who favored Hawaii's annexation. Marines from the *Boston* went ashore to "protect American lives," and on January 17, 1893, the Hawaiian monarchy came to an end.

The provisional government was headed by Sanford B. Dole, who became president of the Hawaiian Republic. Lili'uokalani surrendered not to the conspirators but to U.S. Ambassador John Stevens. She believed that the U.S. government, which had assured her of Hawaiian independence, would be outraged by the overthrow and would come to her aid. Incoming president Grover Cleveland *was* outraged, and Hawaii wasn't immediately annexed as expected. When queried about what she would do with the conspirators if she were reinstated, Lili'uokalani said that they would be hung as traitors. The racist press of the times, which portrayed the Hawaiians as half-civilized, bloodthirsty heathens, publicized this widely. Since the conspirators were the leading citizens of the land, the queen's words proved untimely. In January 1895 a small, ill-fated counterrevolution headed by Lili'uokalani failed, and she was placed under house arrest in 'Iolani Palace. Officials of the republic insisted that she use her married name (Mrs. John Dominis) to sign the documents forcing her to abdicate her throne. She was also forced to swear allegiance to the new republic. Lili'uokalani went on to write *Hawaii's Story* and the lyric ballad "Aloha O'e." She never forgave the conspirators and remained "queen" to the Hawaiians until her death in 1917.

## Annexation

The overwhelming majority of Hawaiians opposed annexation and desired to restore the monarchy. But they were prevented from voting by the new republic because they couldn't meet the imposed property and income qualifications—a transparent ruse by the planters to control the majority. Most *haole* were racist and believed that the "common people" could not be entrusted with the vote because they were childish and incapable of ruling themselves. The fact that the Hawaiians had existed quite well for a thousand years before white people even reached Hawaii was never considered. The Philippine theater of the Spanish-American War also prompted annexation. One of the strongest proponents was Alfred Mahon, a brilliant naval strategist who, with support from Theodore Roosevelt, argued that the U.S. military must have Hawaii in order to be a viable force in the Pacific. In addition, Japan, victorious in its recent war with China, protested the American intention to annex, and in so doing prompted even moderates to support annexation for fear that the Japanese themselves coveted the prize. On July 7, 1898, President McKinley signed the annexation agreement, and this "tropical fruit" was finally put into America's basket.

## MODERN TIMES

Hawaii entered the 20th century totally transformed. The old Hawaiian language, religion, culture, and leadership were all gone; Western dress, values, education, and recreation were the norm. Native Hawaiians were now unseen citizens who lived in dwindling numbers in remote areas. The plantations, new centers of social order, had a strong Asian flavor; more than 75 percent of the workforce was Asian. There was a small white middle class, an all-powerful white elite, and a single political party ruled by that elite. Education, however, was always highly prized, and by the late 19th century all racial groups were encouraged to attend school. By 1900, almost 90 percent of Hawaiians were literate (far above the national norm), and schooling was mandatory for all children ages 6–15. Intermarriage was accepted, and there was a mixing of the races like nowhere else on earth. The military became increasingly important to Hawaii. It brought in money and jobs, dominating the island economy. The Japanese attack on Pearl Harbor, which began U.S. involvement in World War II, bound Hawaii to America forever. Once the islands had been baptized by blood, the average Mainlander felt that Hawaii was American soil. A movement among Hawaiians to become part of the United States began to grow. They wanted a real voice in Washington, not merely a voteless delegate as provided under their territory status. Hawaii became the 50th state in 1959, and the jumbo-jet revolution of the 1960s made it easily accessible to growing numbers of tourists from all over the world.

## Military History

A few military strategists realized the importance of Hawaii early in the 19th century, but most didn't recognize the advantages until the Spanish-American War. It was clearly an unsinkable ship in the middle of the Pacific from which the United States could launch military operations. Troops were stationed at Camp McKinley, at the foot of Diamond Head, the main military compound until it became obsolete in 1907. Pearl Harbor was first surveyed in 1872 by General Schofield. Later, a military base named in his honor, Schofield Barracks, was a main military post in central O'ahu. It first housed the U.S. 5th Cavalry in 1909 and was heavily bombed by the Japanese at the outset of World War II. Pearl Harbor, first dredged in 1908, was officially opened on December 11, 1911. The first warship to enter was the cruiser *California*. Ever since, the military has been a mainstay of the Hawaiian economy. Unfortunately, there has been long-standing bad blood between locals and military personnel. Each group has tended to look down upon the other.

## Pearl Harbor Attack

On the morning of December 7, 1941, the Japanese carrier *Akagi*, flying the battle flag of the famed Admiral Togo of the Russo-Japanese War, received and broadcast over its public address system island music from Honolulu station KGMB. Deep in the bowels of the ship a radio man listened for a much different message, coming thousands of miles from the Japanese mainland. When the ironically poetic message "east wind rain" was received, the attack was launched. At the end of the day, 2,325 U.S. servicemen and 57 civilians were dead; 188 planes were destroyed; 18 major warships were sunk or heavily damaged; and the United States was in

the war. Japanese casualties were extremely light. The ignited conflict would rage for four years until Japan, through the atomic bombing of Nagasaki and Hiroshima, was vaporized into submission. At the end of hostilities, Hawaii would never again be considered separate from America.

## Statehood

A number of economic and political reasons explain why the ruling elite of Hawaii desired statehood, but put simply, the vast majority of people who lived there, especially after World War II, considered themselves Americans. The first serious mention of making "The Sandwich Islands" a state was in the 1850s under President Franklin Pierce, but it wasn't taken seriously until the monarchy was overthrown in the 1890s. For the next 50 years statehood proposals were made repeatedly to Congress, but there was stiff opposition, especially from the southern states. With Hawaii a territory, an import quota system beneficial to Mainland producers could be enacted on produce, especially sugar. Also, there was prejudice against creating a state in a place where the majority of the populace was not white.

During World War II, Hawaii was placed under martial law, but no serious attempt was made to intern the Japanese population as it was in California. There were simply too many Japanese, who went on to gain the respect of the American people by their outstanding fighting record during the war. Hawaii's own 100th Battalion became the famous 442nd Regimental Combat Team, which gained notoriety for saving the Lost Texas Battalion during the Battle of the Bulge and went on to be *the* most decorated battalion of the war. When these GIs returned home, *no one* was going to tell them that they were not loyal Americans. Many of these AJAs (Americans of Japanese Ancestry) took advantage of the GI Bill and received higher education. They were from the common people, not the elite, and they rallied grassroots support for statehood. When the vote finally occurred, approximately 132,900 voted in favor of statehood with only 7,800 votes against. Congress passed the Hawaii State Bill on March 12, 1959, and on August 21, 1959, President Eisenhower announced that Hawaii was officially the 50th state.

# Government

Being the newest state in the nation, Hawaii has had the chance to scrutinize the others, pick their best attributes, and learn from their past mistakes. The government of the state of Hawaii is in essence no different from that of any other state except that it is streamlined and, in theory, more efficient. With only two levels—state and county—the added bureaucracy of town or city governments is theoretically eliminated. Unfortunately, some of the state-run agencies, such as the centralized Board of Education, have become "red-tape" monsters. Hawaii, in anticipation of becoming a state, drafted a constitution in 1950 and was ready to go when statehood was ratified. Politics and government are taken seriously in the Aloha State. For example, in the election to ratify statehood, hardly a ballot went uncast, with 95 percent of the voters opting for statehood. The bill carried every island of Hawaii except for Ni'ihau, where, coincidentally, the majority of people (total population 250 or so) are of relatively pure Hawaiian blood. In the first state elections that followed, 173,000 of 180,000 registered voters voted. In recent years, the number of votes cast in primary and general elections has slipped to unprecedented lows, as in the rest of the country. These days, Hawaiians give greater importance to and show greater turnout for state elections. Because of Hawaii's location in the far west, when presidential elections are held, the result are often known before many in the state have time to cast their ballots.

## State Government

Honolulu is the state capital of Hawaii and its seat of government. All major state-level executive, legislative, and judicial offices are located there. Hawaii's State Legislature has 76 members, with 51 elected seats in the House of Representatives and 25 in the State Senate. Members serve two- and four-year terms respectively. All officials come from 76 separate electorates based on population, which sometimes makes for strange political bedfellows.

O'ahu, which has the largest number of voters, elects 19 of 25 senators and 35 of 51 representatives, giving this island a majority in both houses. Kaua'i County, in comparison, elects one state senators and three representatives.

The state of Hawaii has an overwhelming Democratic Party orientation. Of the 76 members of the legislature, 56 are Democrats. Although not exclusive, Republican strongholds are portions of the metropolitan areas of Honolulu, Kane'ohe and Kailua, on O'ahu, and the major resort areas of Maui and the Big Island.

The state is divided into four administrative counties: the **County of Kaua'i,** covering Kaua'i and Ni'ihau, with Lihu'e as the county seat; the **City and County of Honolulu,** which encompasses O'ahu and includes all of the Northwestern Hawaiian Islands, with Honolulu as its county seat; the **County of Hawai'i,** covering the Big Island, with Hilo as its county seat; and the **County of Maui,** administering the islands of Maui, Lana'i, Moloka'i, and uninhabited Kaho'olawe, with the county seat at Wailuku on Maui. Each county has an elected mayor. County councils are also elected to help administer each county. Honolulu, Hawai'i, and Maui Counties each have nine council members, while Kaua'i has seven.

## Branches of Government

The **State Legislature** is the collective body of the House of Representatives and the Senate. They meet during a once-yearly legislative session that begins on the third Wednesday of January and lasts for 60 working days. (These sessions are oftentimes extended, and special sessions of up to 30 days are frequently called.) The Legislature primarily focuses on taxes, new laws, and appropriations. The **Executive Branch** is headed by the governor and lieutenant governor, both elected on a statewide basis for four years with a two-term maximum. The governor has the right to appoint the heads of 18 state departments outlined in the constitution. The department appointees must be approved by the Senate, and they usually hold office as long as the appointing administration. The present governor is Republican Linda

Lingle, former mayor of Maui County, elected to office in 2002. The **Judiciary** is headed by a state Supreme Court of five justices, an appeals court, and four circuit courts. All jurists are appointed by the governor and serve for 10 years with Senate approval. Twenty-seven district courts have local jurisdiction; the judges are appointed for six-year terms by the chief justice of the Supreme Court.

## Special Departments

The Department of Education is headed by a board of 13 nonpartisan representatives elected for four-year terms, 10 from Oʻahu and three from the other islands. The board has the right to appoint the Superintendent of Schools. Many praise the centralized board as a democratic body offering equal educational opportunity to all districts of Hawaii regardless of sociofinancial status. Detractors say that the centralized board provides "equal educational mediocrity" to all. The University of Hawaiʻi is governed by a Board of Regents appointed by the governor. They choose the president of the university.

## Federal Government Representatives

The state of Hawaii elects two senators and two representatives to the U.S. Congress. Currently, all four are Democrats. The senators are Daniel Inouye and Daniel Akaka. Neil Abercrombie and Ed Case are the representatives.

## Political History

Before World War II Hawaii was run by a self-serving yet mostly benevolent oligarchy. The one real political party was Republican, controlled by the Hawaiian Sugar Planters Association. The planters felt that, having made Hawaii a paradise, they should rule because they had "right on their side." The Baldwin family of Maui *was* the government, with such supporters as the Rice family, which controlled Kauaʻi, and William (Doc) Hill of Hawaiʻi. These were the preeminent families of the islands; all were represented on the boards of the Big Five corporations that ruled Hawaii economically by controlling sugar, transportation, and utilities. An early native politician was Prince Jonah Kuhio Kalanianaʻole,

Queen Kapiʻolani's adopted son and heir to the throne following Liliʻuokalani, who joined with the Republicans to gain perks for himself and for his own people. Nepotism and political hoopla were the order of those days. The Republicans, in coalition with the native Hawaiians, maintained a majority over the large racial groups such as the Japanese and Filipinos who, left to their own devices, would have been Democrats. The Republicans also used unfair literacy laws, land ownership qualifications, and proof of birth in Hawaii to control the large numbers of immigrant workers who could threaten their ruling position. It was even alleged that during elections a pencil was hung on a string over the Republican ballot: if Hawaiians wanted to vote Democratic, they would have to pull the string to the other side of the voting booth. The telltale angle would be a giveaway. They would be unemployed the next day.

## The Democrats Rise to Power

The Democrats were plagued with poor leadership and internal factionalism in the early years. Their first real rise to power began in 1935 when the International Longshoremen's and Warehousemen's Union (ILWU) formed a branch in Hilo on the Big Island. In 1937, an incident known as the "Hilo Massacre" occurred when policemen fired on and wounded 25 striking stevedores, which was the catalyst needed to bind labor together. Thereafter, the ILWU, under the leadership of Jack Hall, became a major factor in the Democratic party. Their relationship was strained in later years when the ILWU was linked to Communism, but during the early days, whomever the ILWU supported in the Democratic Party won.

The Democrats began to take over after World War II when returning Japanese servicemen became active in politics. The Japanese by this time were the largest ethnic group in Hawaii. A central character during the late 1940s and '50s was Jack Burns. Although a *haole*, this simple man was known to be for "the people" regardless of their ethnic background. During the war, as a police captain he made clear his view that he considered the Japanese exemplary Americans. The

Japanese community never forgot this and were instrumental in Burns' election as governor, both in 1962 and 1966. The majority of people in the Asian ethnic groups in Hawaii tended to remain Democrat even after they climbed the socioeconomic ladder. The first special election after statehood saw the governorship go to the previously appointed Republican territorial governor William Quinn, and the lieutenant governorship to another Republican, James Kealoha, of Hawaiian-Chinese ancestry. The first congressperson elected was Japanese-American—Democrat Daniel Inouye. Since then, every governor except the present governor has been a Democrat and one out of every two political offices is held by a person of Japanese extraction. Former governor George Ariyoshi was the first governor of Japanese ancestry in the United States, and former governor Benjamin Cayetano was the first of Filipino ancestry to govern Hawaii.

# OFFICE OF HAWAIIAN AFFAIRS

In 1979, a constitutional mandate created the Office of Hawaiian Affairs (OHA). This remarkable piece of legislature recognized, for the first time since the fall of the monarchy in 1893, the special plight of native Hawaiians. For 75 years, no one in government was eager to face the "native question," but since 1979, OHA has opened a Pandora's box of litigation and accusation. For example, in 1983, a presidential commission investigated U.S. involvement in the overthrow of Hawaii's last queen, Lili'uokalani, to decide if the federal government owed reparations to her Hawaiian people. After listening to testimony from thousands attesting to personal family loss of land and freedom, complete with old deeds documenting their claims, the commission concluded the United States was guiltless and native Hawaiians had nothing coming from Uncle Sam. Jaws dropped, and even those opposed to native Hawaiian rights couldn't believe this *white* wash. Then-governor George Ariyoshi said in a newspaper interview, "A recent congressional study did not accurately portray what went on here at the turn of the

century. . . . To say that the monarchy was not overthrown . . . is something that I cannot accept. It is not historically true."

## Trouble in Paradise

Since then, OHA, as the vanguard of native political activism, has focused on gaining moneys guaranteed in the state constitution as recently as 1959 for "ceded lands." It has also been instrumental in regaining disputed Hawaiian lands and has helped in the fight to save the sacred and uninhabited island of Kaho'olawe, which was used as a bombing target from World War II until 1990. To simply state a complex issue, native Hawaiians have been eligible for benefits from revenues accrued from ceded lands and haven't been receiving them. These lands (1.8 million acres) were crown and government lands belonging to the Hawaiian monarchy and, therefore, to its subjects. When the kingdom was overthrown, the lands passed on to the short-lived Republic, followed by the U.S. Protectorate, and then finally to the state in 1959. No one disputed these lands belonged to *the people*, who were entitled to money collected from rents and leases. Since statehood, however, these tens of millions of dollars have gone into a "general fund" used by various state agencies, such as the Department of Transportation and the Department of Land and Natural Resources; the state is extremely reluctant to turn these funds over to what they derisively call an "unconstitutional special interest group." A Constitutional Convention in 1988 supposedly addressed this issue, but many problems still exist.

## Native Hawaiian Rights

The question has always been, "Just what is a native Hawaiian?" The answer has always been ambiguous. The government has used the "blood quantum" as a measuring stick. This is simply the percentage of Hawaiian blood in a person's ancestry—customarily 50 percent qualifies a person as Hawaiian. The issue is compounded by the fact that no other group of people has been so racially intermarried for so many years. Even though many people have direct ancestry to pre-Republic Hawaiians, they don't have enough

"Hawaiian-ness" to qualify. An overwhelming number of these people fall into the category of "locals": they "feel" Hawaiian, but blood-wise they're not. They suffer all of the negativity of second-class citizens and reap none of the benefits accorded Hawaiians. Those who do qualify according to blood quantum don't have the numbers or the political clout necessary to get results. In fact, many people involved with OHA would not qualify themselves, at least not according to the blood quantum! Strong factionalism within the native Hawaiian movement itself threatens its credibility. Many people who do qualify by the blood quantum view the others as impinging on their rightful claims. The most vocal activists point out that only a coalition of people who have Hawaiian blood, combined with those who "identify" with the movement, will get results. Political firebrands maintain "anti-Hawaiian rights" lobbyists such as the tourist industry, airlines, and large corporations are now stronger than the Hawaiians. They advise that the only way the Hawaiian rights movement can win is to become active "political warriors" and vote for legislators who will support their cause. The rhetoric of OHA is reminiscent of that of the equal rights movement of the 1960s.

Obviously compromise is necessary. Perhaps certain social entitlements (such as tuition grants) could be equal for all, whereas money and land entitlements could be granted by percentages equal to the claiming person's "blood quantum." OHA members appeal directly to the Hawaiian people and can build political constituencies at a grassroots level. Since they are elected by the people and not appointed by the government (the case with the Hawaiian Home Lands Department and the trustees of the Bishop Estate, two other *supposedly* Hawaiian institutions), the status quo political parties of Hawaii are wary of them. (Recently, a court finding has called into question the legitimacy of the voting system for OHA trustees, resulting in the appointment of several members by the governor.) What makes the issue even more ludicrous is that some of the state's most powerful corporate families opposed to Hawaiian rights have direct lineage not only to pre-Republic Hawaiian ancestors but to Hawaiian royalty. They themselves would receive "entitlements" from the ceded land according to blood quantum, but socioeconomically they are the natural enemies of OHA. The problem is difficult, and it is improbable that all concerned will get satisfaction. OHA maintains offices at 711 Kapi'olani Blvd., Honolulu, HI 96813, 808/594-1980; www.oha.org. It publishes a newspaper entitled *Ka Wai Ola o OHA* (The Living Water of OHA), which is available upon request.

# Economy

Hawaii's mid-Pacific location makes it perfect for two primary sources of income: tourism and the military. Tourists come in anticipation of endless golden days on soothing beaches, while the military is provided with the strategic position of an unsinkable battleship. The tourism sector nets Hawaii about $11 billion annually, about one-third the state's revenue of $33.5 billion, while military spending comes in at just over $3 billion, money that should keep flowing smoothly and even increase in the foreseeable future. These revenues mostly remain aloof from the normal ups and downs of the Mainland economy, and both attract either gung-ho enthusiasts or rabidly negative detractors. The remaining 60 percent comes in descending proportions from construction, manufacturing, and agriculture (mainly sugar and pineapples). As long as the sun shines and the balance of global power requires a military presence, the economic stability of Hawaii is guaranteed.

## TOURISM

"The earthly paradise! Don't you want to go to it? Why, of course!" This was the opening line of *The Hawaiian Guide Book* by Henry Whitney, which appeared in 1875. In print for 25 years, it sold for 60 cents during a time when a round-trip sea voyage between San Francisco and Honolulu cost $125. The technique is a bit dated, but the human desires remain the same: some of us seek paradise, all seek escape, some are drawn to play out a drama in a beautiful setting. Tourists have been coming to Hawaii ever since steamship service began in the 1860s. Until World War II, luxury liners carried the financial elite on exclusive voyages to the islands. By the 1920s 10,000 visitors a year were spending almost $5 million—cementing the bond between Hawaii and tourism.

A $25,000 prize offered by James Dole of pineapple fame sparked a transpacific air race in 1927. The success of the aerial daredevils who answered the challenge proved that commercial air travel to Hawaii was feasible. Two years later, Hawaiian Air was offering regularly scheduled flights between the major islands. By 1950 airplanes had captured more than 50 percent of the transportation market, and ocean voyages were relegated to "specialty travel," catering to the elite. By 1960 the large airbuses made their debut; 300,000 tourists arrived on eight designated airlines. The Boeing 747 began operating in 1969. These enormous planes could carry hundreds of passengers at reasonable rates, so travel to Hawaii became possible for the average-income person. In 1970, two million arrived, and by 1990 close to six million passengers arrived on 22 international air carriers. In 2000, nearly seven million visitors chose Hawaii as their destination. The first hotel in Honolulu was the Hawaiian, built in 1872. It was pre-dated by the humble Volcano House, which overlooks Kilauea Crater on the Big Island and was built in 1866. The coral-pink Royal Hawaiian, built in 1927, is Waikiki's graciously aging grande dame, a symbol of days gone by. As late as the 1950s it had Waikiki Beach almost to itself. Only 10,000 hotel units were available in 1960; today there are more than 50,000 statewide and about 20,000 condo units as well.

## Tourists: Who, When, and Where

Tourism-based income outstripped pineapples and sugar by the mid-1960s and the boom was on. Longtime residents could even feel a physical change in air temperature: many trees were removed from Honolulu to build parking lots, and reflected sunlight made Honolulu much hotter and at times unbearable. Even the trade winds,

known to moderate temperatures, were not up to that task. So many people from the outlying farming communities were attracted to work in the hotels that there was a poi famine in 1967. But for the most part, islanders knew their economic future was tied to the "nonpolluting" industry of tourism. Most visitors are Americans, and by far the largest numbers come from the West Coast. Sun-seeking refugees from frigid Alaska, however, make up the greatest proportional number, according to population figures. The remaining arrivals are, in descending numbers, from Japan, Canada, England, Australia, Korea, Germany, China, and Taiwan. The fewest come from South America, the Middle East, and Africa.

The Japanese market grew constantly until 1995, when it reached more than two million visitors per year. Due largely to the continued Asian economic crisis in the late 1990s, numbers fell somewhat but are back nearly to the high levels of the early 1990s. Japanese tourists still make up roughly 26 percent of the Hawaiian market. This is particularly beneficial to the tourist market because the average Western tourist spends about $154 per day, while a Japanese counterpart spends $241 per day. The average Japanese tourist, however, stays only about six days as opposed to 10 days for westbound travelers. Up until very recently the Japanese traveled only in groups and primarily stayed on Oʻahu. Now the trend is shifting to independent travel, or to coming with a group and then peeling off, with a hefty percentage heading for the "Neighbor Islands" (all islands other than Oʻahu).

The typical visitor is slightly affluent, and female visitors outnumber males three to two. The average age, at 35, is a touch higher than in most vacation areas because it reflects an inflated proportion of retirees heading for Hawaii, especially Honolulu, to fulfill lifelong "dream" vacations. A typical stay lasts about 10 days, down from a month in the 1950s; a full 56 percent are repeat visitors. On any given day there are about 80,000 travelers on Oʻahu, 40,000 on Maui, 21,000 on Hawaiʻi, and about 15,000 on Kauaʻi. Molokaʻi and Lanaʻi get so few visitors, 1,000 and 850, respectively, that the figures are hardly counted. In 1964 only 10 percent of the islands' hotel rooms were on the Neighbor Islands, but by 1966 the figure jumped to 25 percent, with more than 70 percent of tourists opting to visit the Neighbor Islands. Today four out of 10 hotel rooms are on the Neighbor Islands, with the figure steadily rising. The overwhelming number of tourists are on package tours, and the largest number of people congregate on O'ahu in Waikiki, which has roughly 73 percent average hotel occupancy and attracts twice as many visitors as do the Neighbor Islands together. Obviously, Waikiki is still most people's idea of paradise. Those seeking a more intimate experience can have it with a 20-minute flight from O'ahu to a Neighbor Island.

Joaquin Miller, the 19th-century poet of the Sierras, said, "I tell you my boy, the man who has not seen the Sandwich Islands, in this one great ocean's warm heart, has not seen the world." The times have certainly changed, but the sentiments of most visitors to Hawaii remain consistently the same.

## Tourism-Related Problems

Tourism is both boon and blight to Hawaii. It is the root cause of two problems: one environmental, the other socioeconomic. The environmental impact is obvious, and is best described in the lament of singer Joni Mitchell's "Big Yellow Taxi": "They paved paradise and put up a parking lot." Put simply, tourism can draw too many people to an area and overburden it. In the process, it stresses the very land and destroys the natural beauty that attracted people in the first place. Tourists come to Hawaii for what has been called its "ambient resource": a balanced collage of indulgent climate, invigorating waters, intoxicating scenery, and exotic people all wrapped up neatly in one area that can both soothe and excite. It is in Hawaii's best interest to preserve this resource.

Most point to Waikiki as a prime example of development gone mad. It is super-saturated, and amazingly enough, hotel owners themselves are trying to keep development in check. Two prime examples of the best and the worst development can be found on Maui's south shore at Kihei and Wailea, less than five miles apart. Kihei is shoulder to shoulder high-rise condo, with hardly room

## ECOTOURISM IN HAWAII

Ecotourism is economically, culturally, socially, and environmentally sensitive and sustainable tourism that helps promote local communities and organizations and works in harmony with nature. Although small potatoes yet in the Hawaiian (and worldwide) tourism economy, ecotourism and its goals are growing in importance and will become a major factor in the economic vitality of tourism in the state. For more information on ecotourism in Hawaii, contact the Hawaii Ecotourism Association, P.O. Box 61435, Honolulu, HI 96822, 808/956-2866, hea@aloha.net, www.planet-hawaii.com/hea.

The following organization can also provide related information and contacts: The International Ecotourism Society, P.O. Box 668, Burlington, VT 05420, 802/651-9818, www.ecotourism.org.

for a peek at the ocean. You can bet those who made a killing building there don't live there. Just down the road, Wailea is a model of what development could and should be. The architecture is tasteful, low-rise, unobtrusive, and done with people and the preservation of the scenery in mind. It's obviously more exclusive, but access points to the beaches are open to everyone and the view is still there for all to enjoy. It points the way for development standards of the future.

## Changing Lifestyle

Like the land, humans are stressed by tourism. Local people, who once took the "Hawaiian lifestyle" for granted, became displaced and estranged in their own land. Some areas, predominantly along gorgeous beaches that were once average- to low-income communities, are now overdeveloped, with prices going through the roof. The locals are not only forced to move out, but often must come back as service personnel in the tourist industry and cater to the very people who displaced them. At one time the psychological blow was softened because, after all, the newcomers were merely benign tourists who would stay a short time, spend a wad of money, and leave.

Today, condos are being built and a different sort of visitor is arriving. Many condo owners are well-educated businesspeople and professionals in the above-average income brackets. The average condo owner is a Mainlander who purchases one as a second or retirement home. These people are not islanders and have a tough time relating to the locals, who naturally feel resentment. Moreover, since they don't *leave* like normal tourists, they use community facilities, find those special nooks and crannies for shopping or sunbathing that were once exclusively the domain of locals, and have a say as voters in community governments. The islanders become more and more disenfranchised. Many believe that the new order instigated by tourism is similar to what has always existed in Hawaii: a few from the privileged class being catered to by many from the working class. In a way it's an extension of the plantation system, but instead of carrying pineapples, most islanders find themselves carrying luggage, cocktails, or broiled fish. One argument, however, remains undeniable: whether it's people or pineapples, one has to make a living. The days of a little grass shack on a sunny beach aren't gone, but you need a steady job or a wallet full of credit cards to afford one.

## THE MILITARY

Hawaii is the most militarized state in the United States: all five services are represented. Camp H.M. Smith, overlooking Pearl Harbor, is the headquarters of CINCPAC (Commander in Chief Pacific), which is responsible for 70 percent of the earth's surface, from California to the east coast of Africa and to both poles. The U.S. military presence dates back to 1887, when Pearl Harbor was given to the Navy as part of the Sugar Reciprocity Treaty. The sugar planters were given favorable duty-free treatment on their sugar, while the U.S. Navy was allowed exclusive rights to one of the best harbors in the Pacific. In 1894, when the monarchy was being overthrown by the sugar planters, the USS *Boston* sent a contingency of marines ashore to "keep order," which

really amounted to a show of force, backing the revolution. The Spanish-American War saw U.S. troops billeted at Camp McKinley at the foot of Diamond Head, and Schofield Barracks opened to receive the 5th Cavalry in 1909. Pearl Harbor's flames ignited World War II, and there has been no looking back since then.

About 35,000 military personnel are stationed in Hawaii (99 percent on O'ahu), with more than 53,000 dependents. This number has slowly but steadily been decreasing since 1988, when the military was at its greatest strength in the state, and is now lower than at any time since the mid-1950s. The Army has the largest contingent with some 16,000, followed by the Navy at 8,300, Marine Corps at 7,000, Air Force at 3,300, and 1,200 or so with the Coast Guard. Besides this, more than 34,000 Department of Defense personnel and 16,500 civilian support personnel account for 65 percent of all federal jobs in Hawaii. The combined services are one of the largest landholders, with almost 240,000 acres, accounting for five percent of Hawaiian land. The two major holdings are the 101,000-acre Pohakuloa Training Area on Hawai'i and 81,500 acres on O'ahu, which is a full 21 percent of the entire island. The Army controls 63 percent of the military lands, followed by the Navy at 22 percent, and the remainder goes to the Air Force, Marines, and a few small installations to the Coast Guard.

### The Military Has No Aloha

Not everyone is thrilled by the strong military presence in Hawaii. Two factions, native Hawaiians and antinuclear groups, are downright angry. Radical contingencies of native Hawaiian-rights groups consider Hawaii an independent country, besieged and "occupied" by the U.S. government. They date their loss of independence to Lili'uokalani's overthrow in 1894. The vast majority of ethnic Hawaiians, though they consider themselves Americans, are concerned with loss of their rightful homelands—with no financial reparation—and about continuing destruction and disregard for their traditional religious and historical sites. A long list of grievances is cited by native Hawaiian action groups, but the best and clearest example was the controversy over the sacred island Kahoʻolawe, which until 1990 was used as a bombing target by the U.S. Navy.

A major controversy raised by the military presence focuses on Hawaii as a nuclear target. The ultimate goal of the antinuclear protesters is to see the Pacific, and the entire world, free from nuclear arms. They see Hawaii as a big target used by the international power merchants on the Mainland as both pawn and watchdog—if war breaks out, they say, the Hawaiian Islands will be reduced to cinders. The military naturally counters that a strong Hawaii is a deterrent to nuclear war and that Hawaii is not only a powerful offensive weapon, but one of the best-defended regions of the world. Unfortunately, when you are on an island there is no place to go: like a boxer in a ring, you can run, but you can't hide.

Also, the military has been cited for disposing of stockpiles of chemical weapons by incineration on Johnston Island, a military installation southwest of the Big Island. Because there was no environmental impact study, scientists fear that wind and currents could carry the pollutants to the main Hawaiian Islands, destroying delicate coral reefs along the way.

## SUGAR

Sugarcane *(ko)* was brought to Hawaii by its original settlers and was known throughout Polynesia. Its cultivation was well established and duly noted by Captain Cook when he first sighted the islands. The native Hawaiians used various strains of sugarcane for food, rituals, and medicine. It was never refined, but the stalk was chewed and juice was pressed from it. It was used as food during famine, as an ingredient in many otherwise unpalatable medicines, and especially as a love potion. Commercial growing started with a failure on Oʻahu in 1825, followed by a successful venture a decade later on Kauaʻi. Until the mid-1990s, this original plantation was still productive. The industry received a technological boost in 1850 when a centrifuge, engineered by David Weston of the Honolulu Iron Works, was installed at a plantation on East Maui. It was used to spin the molasses out of the cooked syrup, leaving a crude crystal.

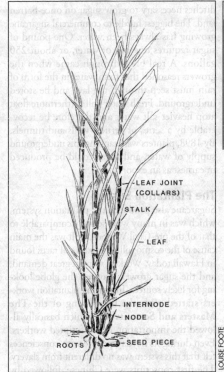

Labels: LEAF JOINT (COLLARS), STALK, LEAF, INTERNODE, NODE, ROOTS, SEED PIECE

LOUISE FOOTE

**young sugarcane**

Hawaii's biggest market has always been the Mainland. Demand rose dramatically during the California gold rush of 1849–50 and again a decade later for the Union Army during the American Civil War. At first Hawaiian sugar had a poor reputation that almost killed its export market, but with technological advances it became the best-quality sugar available.

### Irrigation and Profit Politics

In 1876 the **Reciprocity Treaty** freed Hawaiian sugar from import duty. Now a real fortune could be made. One entrepreneur, Claus Spreckels, a sugar-beet magnate from California, became the reigning Sugar King in Hawaii. His state-of-the-art refineries on Maui employed every modern convenience, including electric lighting; he was also instrumental in building marvelous irrigation ditches necessary to grow sugar on once-barren land. The biggest hurdle to commercial sugarcane growing has always been water. One pound of sugar requires one ton of water, or about 250 gallons. A real breakthrough came when the growers reasoned that fresh water in the form of rain must seep through the lava and be stored underground. Fresh water will furthermore float atop heavier salt water and therefore be recoverable by a series of vertical wells and tunnels. By 1898, planters were tapping this underground supply of water, and sugar could be produced in earnest as an export crop.

### The Plantation System

Sugarcane also produced the plantation system, which was in many ways socially comparable to that of the pre-Civil War South. It was the main cause of the cosmopolitan mixture of races found in Hawaii today. Workers were in great demand, and the sugar growers scoured the globe looking for likely sources. Importing plantation workers started with the liberalizing of the **The Masters and Servants Act,** which basically allowed the importation of conscripted workers. Even during its heyday, people with consciences felt that this system was no different from slavery. The first conscripts were Chinese, followed by Japanese, and then myriad people including other Polynesians, Germans, Norwegians, Spanish, Portuguese, Puerto Ricans, Koreans, Filipinos, and even a few freed slaves from the southern United States.

Today, with production down on Kaua'i and Maui (commercial production has ceased on O'ahu and the Big Island), yearly sugar sales have fallen from those of a few decades ago, when they were a hefty $500 million, to less than $60 million currently, 46,000 acres. Nonetheless, the state's sugarcane-producing farms and their attendant refineries still employ a large number of workers. Newcomers, startled by what appear to be brush fires, are actually witnessing the burning of sugarcane prior to harvesting. While much reduced from its heyday, Hawaii's sugarcane industry is still solvent, producing more than two million tons of raw sugar annually.

## PINEAPPLES

Next to cane, the majority of Hawaii's cultivated lands yield pineapples. The main farms are on O'ahu, on the northwest tip of Maui, and on the lower slopes of Haleakala on Maui, with Lana'i, once the world's largest pineapple plantation, now out of business. Pineapples were brought to the islands by Don Francisco Marin, an early Spanish agronomist, in the 1820s. Fresh pineapples were exported as early as 1850 to San Francisco, and a few cases of canned fruit appeared in 1876 at Hawaii's pavilion at the U.S. Centennial Exposition in Philadelphia. Old varieties of pineapples were pithier and pricklier than the modern variety. Today's large, luscious, golden fruits are the "smooth cayenne" variety from Jamaica, introduced by Captain Kidwell in 1886.

### Dole

But Hawaiian pineapple, as we know it, is synonymous with one man, James Dole, who actually *made* the industry at the turn of the 20th century. Jim Dole started growing pineapples on a 60-acre homestead in Wahiawa, O'ahu. He felt that America was ready to add this fruit to its diet and that "canning" would be the conveyance. By 1903, he was shipping canned fruit from his Iwilei plant, and by 1920 pineapples were a familiar item in most American homes. Hawaii was at that time the largest producer in the world. In 1922, Jim Dole bought the entire island of Lana'i, whose permanent residents numbered only about 100, and started the world's largest pineapple plantation. By all accounts, Jim Dole was an exemplary human being, but he could never learn to "play ball" with the economic powers that ruled Hawaii, namely the Big Five. They ruined him by 1932 and took control of his **Hawaiian Pineapple Company.** Today, the Hawaiian pineapple industry is beleaguered by competition from Asia, Central America, and the Philippines, resulting in the abandonment of many corporate farms. Hit especially hard was Moloka'i, where Del Monte shut down its operations in the mid-1980s, and Lana'i, which stopped farming the prickly fruits in 1993. The other plantations are still reasonably strong, bringing in about $100 million dollars annually from some 20,000 acres, twice as much on O'ahu as on Maui, but employment in the pineapple industry has dropped drastically in the last decade, and these jobs will not return.

## OTHER AGRICULTURE

Every major food crop known can be grown in Hawaii because of its amazingly varied climates and rich soil. Farming ventures through the years have produced cotton, sisal, rice, and even rubber trees. Until the year 2000 (now surpassed by Australia), Hawaii was the world's largest producer of the macadamia nut, considered by some the world's most useful and delicious nut. The islands' fresh exotic fruits are unsurpassed; juices and nectars made from papaya, passion fruit, and guava are becoming well known worldwide. Dazzling flowers such as protea, carnations, orchids, and anthuriums are also commercially grown. Hawaii has a very healthy livestock industry, headed by the Big Island's quarter-million-acre Parker Ranch, the largest singly owned cattle ranch in the United States. Poultry, dairy, and pork are also produced on many farms. The only coffee grown in the United States is grown in Hawaii on four islands. "Kona coffee" is of gourmet quality, well regarded for its aroma and rich flavor. Recently, chocolate manufacture was introduced to the Big Island, and production of this fine sweet is in full operation. *Pakalolo* (marijuana) is still a lucrative cash crop, but no official economic records exist. It's grown by enterprising gardeners on all the islands.

Hawaiian waters are alive with fish, but its commercial fleet is woefully small and obsolete. Fishing revenues amount to only $44 million per year, which is ludicrous in a land where fish is the obvious natural bounty. Two-third of the 21 million pounds come from tuna, and 80 percent is fished by the commercial ventures on O'ahu. Native Hawaiians were masters of aquaculture, routinely building fishponds and living from their harvest. Where once there were hundreds of fishponds, only a handful are in use today. The main aquaculture is growing freshwater prawns, which produces some $7.5 million annually. With all of these foodstuffs, unbelievable as it may sound, Hawaii must import much of its food. Hawaii can feed *itself,* but it cannot support the six million hungry tourists who come to sample its superb and diverse cuisine every year.

## ECONOMIC POWER
### The Big Five Corporations

Until statehood, Hawaii was ruled economically by a consortium of corporations known as the Big Five: **C. Brewer and Co.,** sugar, ranching, and chemicals, founded in 1826; **Theo. H. Davies & Co.,** sugar, investments, insurance, and transportation, founded in 1845; **Amfac Inc.** (originally H. Hackfield Inc.—a German firm that changed its name and ownership during the anti-German sentiment of World War I to American Factors), sugar, insurance, and land development, founded in 1849; **Castle and Cooke Inc.** (Dole), pineapple, food packing, and land development, founded in 1851; and **Alexander and Baldwin Inc.,** shipping, sugar, and pineapple, founded in 1895. This economic oligarchy ruled Hawaii with a steel grip in a velvet glove.

With members on every important corporate board, they controlled all major commerce, including banking, shipping, insurance, hotel development, agriculture, utilities, and wholesale and retail merchandising. Anyone trying to buck the system was ground to dust, finding it suddenly impossible to do business in the islands. The Big Five were made up of the islands' oldest and most well-established *haole* families; all included bloodlines from Hawaii's own nobility. They looked among themselves for suitable husbands and wives, so that breaking in from the outside even through marriage was hardly possible. The only time they were successfully challenged prior to statehood was when Sears, Roebuck and Co. opened a store on O'ahu. Closing ranks, the Big Five decreed that their steamships would not carry Sears's freight. When Sears threatened to buy its own steamship line, the Big Five relented.

Actually, statehood, and more to the point, tourism, broke their oligarchy. After 1960 too much money was at stake for Mainland-based corporations to ignore. Eventually the grip of the

Big Five was loosened, but they are still enormously powerful and richer than ever. These days, however, they don't control everything; now their power is land. With only five other major landholders, they control 50 percent of the privately held land in Hawaii.

## Land Ownership

Hawaii, landwise, is a small pie, and its slices are not at all well divided. Of the state's 6,423 square miles of land, the six main inhabited islands make up 98 percent. This figure does

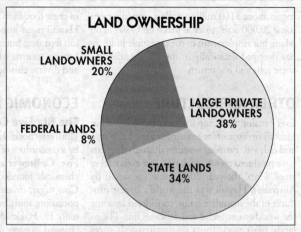

**LAND OWNERSHIP**

- SMALL LANDOWNERS 20%
- LARGE PRIVATE LANDOWNERS 38%
- FEDERAL LANDS 8%
- STATE LANDS 34%

not include Niʻihau, which is privately owned by the Robinson family and inhabited by some of the last remaining pure-blooded Hawaiians; nor does it include uninhabited Kahoʻolawe. Of the 4,110,976 acres that make up the inhabited islands, 34 percent is owned by the state and 8 percent by the federal government; the remaining 68 percent is in private hands. While only 40 owners, with 5,000 or more acres each, own 65 percent of all private lands, the top 10 control 75 percent of that. To be more specific, Castle and Cooke Inc. owns 99 percent of Lanaʻi, while 40–60 percent of Maui, Oʻahu, Molokaʻi, Kauaʻi, and Hawaiʻi is owned by fewer than a dozen private parties.

The largest private landowner, with more than 366,000 acres (nearly 9 percent of the total

land area of the state), is the Kamehameha Schools/Bishop Estate, which some years ago lost a Supreme Court battle allowing the state of Hawaii to acquire privately owned land for "the public good." More than in any other state, Hawaiian landowners tend to lease land rather than sell it, and many private homes are on rented ground. This was the case with many homes rented from the Bishop Estate. The state acquired the land and resold it to long-term lease holders. These lands had previously earned a slow but steady profit for native Hawaiians. As land prices continue to rise, only the very rich land developers are able to purchase long-term leases, and the people of Hawaii continue to become even more land poor.

# The People

Nowhere else on earth can you find such a kaleidoscopic mixture of people as in Hawaii. Every major race is accounted for, with more than 50 ethnic groups adding not only their genes, but their customs, traditions, and outlooks. The modern Hawaiian is the future's "everyman": a blending of all races. Interracial marriage has been long accepted in Hawaii, and people are so mixed it's already difficult to place them in a specific racial category. Besides the original Hawaiians, themselves a mixed race of Polyne-

sians, people in the islands have multiple ancestor combinations. Hawaii is the most racially integrated state in the United States, and although the newest, it epitomizes the time-honored American ideal of the melting-pot society.

## THE ISSUE OF RACE

This polyracial society should be a model of understanding and tolerance, and in most ways it is, but there are still racial tensions. People tend to identify with one group, and though not openly hostile, they do look disparagingly on others. Some racial barbs maintain the Chinese are grasping, the Japanese too cold and calculating, the *haole* materialistic, Hawaiians lackadaisical, and Filipinos emotional. In Hawaii this labeling tendency is a bit modified because *people,* as individuals, are not usually discriminated against, but their *group* may be. Another factor is that individuals identify with a group not along strict blood lines, but more by a "feeling of identity." If a white/Japanese man married a Hawaiian/Chinese woman, they would be accepted by all groups concerned. Their children, moreover, would be what they chose to be and, more to the point, what they "felt" like.

There are no ghettos as such, but there are traditional areas where people of similar racial strains live, and where outsiders are made to feel unwelcome. For example, the Wai'anae District of O'ahu is considered a strong "Hawaiian" area where other people may meet with hostility, and the Kahala area of O'ahu mostly attracts upwardly mobile whites. Some clubs make it difficult for nonwhites to become members; certain Japanese, Chinese, and Filipino organizations attract only members from these ethnic groups; and Hawaiian *'ohana* would question any person seeking to join unless he or she had some Hawaiian blood. Generally, however, the vast majority of people get along with each other and mix with no discernible problems.

The real catalyst responsible for most racial acceptance is the Hawaiian public school system. Education has always been highly regarded in Hawaii; the classroom has long been integrated. Thanks to a standing tradition of progressive education, democracy and individualism have always been basic maxims taught in the classroom. The racial situation in Hawaii is far from perfect, but it does point the way to the future in which all people can live side by side with respect and dignity.

## Who and Where

Hawaii has an approximate population of 1.2 million, which includes about 90,000 permanently stationed military personnel and their dependents. It has the highest ratio of population to immigration in the United States and until the year 2000, when California's white population fell below 50 percent, it was the only state where whites were not the majority. White people are, however, the fastest growing group, due primarily to immigration from the U.S. West Coast. About 56 percent of Hawaiian residents were born in Hawaii; 26 percent were born on the Mainland U.S.; and 18 percent are foreign-born. The average age is 29, and men slightly outnumber women. This is due to the large concentration of predominantly male military personnel and to the substantial number of older bachelor plantation workers who came during the first part of the 20th century and never found wives. The population has grown steadily in recent times but has fluctuated wildly in the past. Most European sources gave estimates of between 300,000 and 400,000 for the population of the Hawaiian Islands before the arrival of

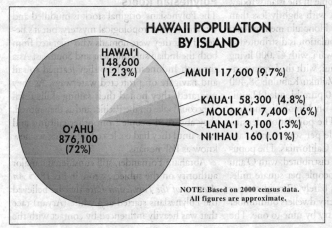

**HAWAII POPULATION BY ISLAND**

HAWAI'I 148,600 (12.3%)

MAUI 117,600 (9.7%)

KAUA'I 58,300 (4.8%)
MOLOKA'I 7,400 (.6%)
LANA'I 3,100 (.3%)
NI'IHAU 160 (.01%)

O'AHU 876,100 (72%)

NOTE: Based on 2000 census data.
All figures are approximate.

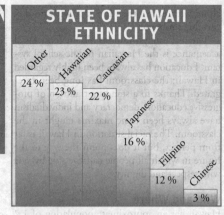

## STATE OF HAWAII ETHNICITY

Other 24%
Hawaiian 23%
Caucasian 22%
Japanese 16%
Filipino 12%
Chinese 3%

average household size in Hawaii is 3.1 persons, down from 4.5 in 1940.

## THE HAWAIIANS

The study of the native Hawaiians is ultimately a study in tragedy because it nearly ends in their demise as a viable people. When Captain Cook first sighted Hawaii in 1778, an estimated 300,000 natives were living in harmony with their ecological surroundings; within a little more than 100 years a scant 48,000 demoralized and dejected Hawaiians existed almost as wards of the state. Today, although more than 240,000 people claim varying degrees of Hawaiian blood (some official surveys record 140,000), experts say fewer than 1,000 are pure Hawaiian, and this is stretching it. A resurgence of Hawaiian ethnic pride is sweeping the islands as many people trace their roots and attempt to absorb the finer aspects of their ancestral lifestyle. It's easy to see why they could be bitter over what they've lost, since they're now strangers in their own land, much like Native Americans. The overwhelming majority of "Hawaiians" are of mixed heritage, and the wisest take the best from all worlds. From the Hawaiian side comes simplicity, love of the land, and acceptance of people. It is the Hawaiian legacy of *aloha* that remains immortal and adds the special elusive quality that *is* Hawaii.

### Polynesian Roots

The Polynesians' original stock is muddled and remains an anthropological mystery, but it's believed that they were nomads who migrated from both the Indian subcontinent and Southeast Asia through Indonesia, where they learned to sail and navigate on protected waterways. As they migrated, they honed their sailing skills until they could take on the Pacific, and as they moved, they absorbed people from other cultures and races until they had coalesced into what we now know as Polynesians.

Abraham Fornander, still considered a major authority on the subject, wrote in his 1885 *An Account of the Polynesian Race* that he believed the Polynesians started as a white (Aryan) race that was heavily influenced by contact with the

Captain Cook. Some now estimate that number as low as 200,000 or as high as 800,000. In any case, following the arrival of Europeans, the native Hawaiian population declined steadily for a century. In 1876, it reached its lowest ebb, with only 55,000 permanent residents in the islands. This was the era of large sugar plantations; their constant demand for labor was the primary cause of importing various peoples from around the world, leading to Hawaii's racially integrated society. During World War II, Hawaii's population swelled from 400,000 just prior to the war to 900,000. These 500,000 were military personnel who left at war's end, but many returned to settle after getting a taste of island living.

Of the 1.2 million people in the islands today, 881,300 live on O'ahu, with slightly less than half of these living in the Honolulu metropolitan area. The rest of the population is distributed as follows: 149,000 on Hawai'i, with 47,000 living in Hilo; 128,000 on Maui, with the largest concentration, 53,000, in Wailuku/Kahului; 58,400 on Kaua'i, including 160 pure-blooded Hawaiians on Ni'ihau; 7,200 on Moloka'i; and just over 3,200 on Lana'i. The population density, statewide, is 188 people per square mile, approximately the same as California's. The population is not at all evenly distributed, with O'ahu claiming about 1,470 people per square mile, while the Big Island has barely 37 residents per square mile. Statewide, city dwellers outnumber those living in the country by nine to one. The

## THE LITTLE PEOPLE OF HAWAII

The Mu, Wa, and 'E'epa are all "little people" of Hawaii, but the most famous are the Menehune. As a group they resemble the trolls and leprechauns of Europe, but so many stories concern them that they appear to have actually existed in Hawaii at one time. Even in the late 18th century, an official census noted King Kaumuali'i of Kaua'i had 65 Menehune, who were said to live in Wainiha Valley. It's held that the Menehune drove out the Mu and the Wa. They also differed slightly in appearance. The Menehune are about two to three feet tall with hairy, well-muscled bodies. Their red faces have thick noses, protruding foreheads, and long eyebrows, and their hair is stringy. They love to frolic, especially by rolling down hills into the sea, and their favorite foods are shrimp and poi. They seldom speak, but their chatter sounds like the low growling of a dog. Nocturnal creatures, Menehune are frightened of owls and dogs.

The Mu are mute, while the Wa are noted for their loud blustering shouts. The Mu were thought to be black-skinned and to live deep in the forest on a diet of bananas. All had their specialties, but the Menehune were stonemasons par excellence. Many feats involving stonework are attributed to the Menehune. The most famous is the "Menehune Ditch" on Kaua'i. They finished their monumental tasks in one night, disappearing by daybreak. Even in the 1950s, masons building with stone near Diamond Head insisted their work was disturbed at night, and a *kahuna* had to be called in to appease the Menehune. After that, all went well.

In a more scientific vein, the Tahitian word for Menehune means "commoner." Many feel they were non-Polynesian aboriginals who somehow made it to the islands and co-mingled with Hawaiians until their chiefs became alarmed that their little race would vanish. (Mohikia and Analike are the respective names of a Menehune prince and princess who married Hawaiians and whose names have been preserved in legend.) The Menehune assembled en masse and supposedly floated away on an island descended from the heavens called "Kuaihelani." Some say they headed for the far-flung outer islands of Necker and Nihoa, where, oddly enough, stone gods found there are unlike any on the other Hawaiian Islands. But there the trail grows cold. Today, island mothers warn their misbehaving toddlers that the Menehune will come and take them away, but in most stories they are actually pixie-like and benign.

Cushite, Chaldeo-Arabian civilization. He estimated their arrival in Hawaii at A.D. 600 based on Hawaiian genealogical chants. Modern science seems to bear this date out, although it remains skeptical of his other surmises.

Thousands of years before Europeans even imagined the existence of a Pacific Ocean, Polynesians had populated the far-flung islands of the "Polynesian Triangle," which stretches from New Zealand in the south, east thousands of miles to Easter Island, and finally to Hawaii, the northern apex. Similar language, gods, foods, and crafts add credibility to this theory. Other more fanciful versions are all long on conjecture and short on evidence. For example, Atlantis, the most "found" lost continent in history, pops up again, with the Hawaiians the supposed remnants of this advanced civilization. The slim proof is the Hawaiian *kahuna*, so well versed in the curative arts they had to be Atlanteans. In fact, they not only made it to Hawaii, but also to the Philippines, where their secret powers have been passed on to the faith healers of today. That the Hawaiians are the "lost tribe of Israel" is another theory, but this too is wild conjecture.

### The "Land Seekers"

The intrepid Polynesians who actually settled Hawaii are believed to have come from the Marquesas Islands, 1,000 miles southeast of Hawaii. The Marquesans were cannibals known for their tenacity and strength, attributes that would serve them well. They left their own islands because of war and famine; these migrations went on for centuries. Ships' logs mention Marquesan seagoing canoes setting sail in search of new land as late as the mid-19th century. The first navigator-explorers, advance scouting parties, were referred to as "land seekers." They were led northward by a few terse words sung in a chant that gave a general direction and promised some guiding stars (probably recounting the wild adventures of canoes blown far off course that somehow managed to return to the southern islands of Polynesia). The land seekers were familiar with the stars, currents, habits of land birds, and countless other subtle clues that are overlooked by "civilized" people.

After finding Hawaii, they were aided in their voyage home by favorable trade winds and familiar waters. They set sail again in canoes laden with hopeful families and all the foodstuffs necessary to colonize a new land, anticipating a one-way ride with no return. Over the centuries, the fierce Marquesans mellowed into Hawaiians and formed a new benevolent culture based on the fertility god Lono. Then, in the 12th century, a ferocious army of Tahitians invaded Hawaii and supplanted not only the ruling chiefs but also the gentler gods with their war god Ku, who demanded human sacrifice. Abruptly, contact with Polynesia stopped. Some say the voyages, always fraught with danger, were no longer necessary. Hawaii was forgotten by the Polynesians, and the Hawaiians became the most rarefied race in the world. It was to these people that Captain Cook in 1778 brought the outside world. Finding Polynesians stretched so far and wide across the Pacific, he declared them "the most extensive nation upon earth."

## Causes of Decline

When Captain Cook stepped ashore on Waimea, Kaua'i, on the morning of January 20, 1778, he discovered a population of natives living in perfect harmony with their surroundings. Their agrarian society had flourished in the last thousand years. However, the ecological system of Hawaii has always been exceptionally fragile, its people included. White arrivals found a great people who were large, strong, and virile, but when it came to fighting even minor diseases they proved as delicate as hothouse flowers. To exacerbate the situation, the Hawaiians were totally uninhibited about sex between willing partners. Unfortunately, white sailors were laden

with syphilis, gonorrhea, and all manner of other germs and common European diseases. Captain Cook tried desperately to keep sexually diseased members of his crew away from Hawaiian women, but it was impossible. The *hospitality* of Hawaiian women was legendary, and promises of "paradise" were actually used as a lure to get sailors for perilous cruises into the Pacific that could last for years. When Cook returned from the north in less than one year, there were already natives with telltale signs of venereal disease.

Hawaiian women brought venereal disease home, and it spread like wildfire. By the time the missionaries came in 1820 and halted the widespread fornication, the native population was only 140,000, less than half of what it had been only 40 years before. In 1804 alone, perhaps 100,000 died from 'oku'u (either typhoid or cholera). In the next 50 years measles, mumps, influenza, and tuberculosis ravaged the people. In 1853 a smallpox epidemic ate further into the doomed and weakened Hawaiian race, and leprosy ranged far and wide in the land. In addition, during the whaling years, at least 25 percent of all able-bodied Hawaiian men sailed away, never to return. By 1880 King Kalakaua had only 48,000 Hawaiian subjects, a cataclysmic decrease of the original population. Wherever the king went, he would beseech his people, "Ho'oulu lahui" ("Increase the race"), but it was already too late. Nature itself had turned its back on these once-proud people. Many of their marriages were barren, and in 1874 when only 1,400 children were born, a full 75 percent died in infancy. The final coup de grâce was intermarriage. With so many interracial marriages, the Hawaiians nearly bred themselves out of existence.

## Painful Adjustments

In the 19th century, the old paternalism inherent in the Hawaiian caste system was carried on by the ruling *haole* families. The remaining Hawaiians looked to the ruling class of whites as they had to their own *ali'i*, and for many years this attitude discouraged self help. Many Hawaiians fervently accepted the Christianity that had supplanted their own religion because it was a haven against a rapidly changing world in which they felt more and more alienated. Though Hawaiians were not favored as good plantation workers and were branded as lazy, they were actually hard and dedicated workers. Like all people attuned to their environment, they chose to work in the cool of the mornings and late afternoons, and could make no sense of laboring in the intense heat of the day. As fishermen they were unparalleled, and they also made excellent cowboys on the ranches, preferring the open ranges to the constricting plantation fields.

Hawaiians readily engaged in politics and were impressed with all the hoopla and fanfare. They attended rallies, performed hula and songs, and in most instances sided with the whites against the Asians. They were known to accept money for their votes and almost considered it the obligation of the leader, whom they regarded as a sort of chief, to grease their palms. Educated Hawaiians tended to become lawyers, judges, policeman, and teachers, and there is still a disproportionate number of Hawaiians, population-wise, in these fields. Hawaiians were somewhat racist toward the Japanese and Chinese. However, they would readily intermarry because, true to *aloha,* they accepted individual "people" even though they might be prejudiced against their group. In 1910, although the native population was greatly reduced, there are still twice as many full-blooded Hawaiians as mixed bloods. By 1940 mixed-blood Hawaiians were the fastest-growing group, and full bloods the fastest declining.

## Hawaiians Today

Many of the Hawaiians who moved to the cities became more and more disenfranchised. Their folk society stressed openness and a giving nature but downplayed the individual and the ownership of private property. These cultural traits made them easy targets for users and schemers until they finally became either apathetic or angry. Most surveys reveal that although they number only 13 percent of the population, they account for almost 50 percent of the financially destitute families, arrests, and illegitimate births. Ni'ihau, a privately owned island, is home to about 160 pure-blooded Hawaiians, the largest concentra-

tion per capita in the islands. The Robinson family, which owns the island, restricts visitors to invited guests only. The second largest concentration of people with Hawaiian blood is on Moloka'i, where 2,700 Hawaiians, living mostly on Hawaiian Homes lands, make up 40 percent of the population. The majority of mixed-blooded Hawaiians, 240,000 or so, live on O'ahu, where they are particularly strong in the hotel and entertainment fields. People of Hawaiian extraction are a delight to meet, and visitors so lucky as to be befriended by one long regard this friendship as the highlight of their travels. The Hawaiians have always given their *aloha* freely, and it is we who must accept it as a precious gift.

## THE CHINESE

Next to Yankees from New England, the Chinese are the oldest migrant group in Hawaii, and their influence has far outshone their meager numbers. They have long been the backbone of the small, privately owned retail trade. They brought to Hawaii, along with their individuality, Confucianism, Taoism, and Buddhism, although many have long since become Christians. The Chinese population of about 56,000 makes up only five percent of the state's total, and the vast majority reside on O'ahu. Their key to success has been indefatigable hard work, the shrewdness to seize a good opportunity, and above all, an almost fanatical desire to educate their children. As an ethnic group they account for the least amount of crime, the highest per capita income, and a disproportionate number of professionals. They are some of Hawaii's most prominent citizens.

### The First Chinese

No one knows his name, but an unknown Chinese immigrant is credited with being the first person in Hawaii to refine sugar. This Asian wanderer tried his hand at crude refining on Lana'i in 1802. He failed, but other Chinese were operating sugar mills by 1830. Within 20 years, the plantations desperately needed workers, and the first Chinese laborers brought to Hawaii were 195 coolies from Amoy who arrived in 1852 under the newly passed Masters and Servants Act. These conscripts were contracted for 3–5 years and given $3 per month plus room and board. This was for 12 hours a day, six days a week, and even in 1852 these wages were absolutely miserable. The Chinese almost always left the plantations the minute their contracts expired. They went into business for themselves and promptly monopolized the restaurant and small shop trades.

## Bad Feelings

When they left the plantations, the Chinese were universally resented, due to prejudice, xenophobia, and their success in business. The first Chinese peddler in Honolulu was mentioned as early as 1823. The Chinese Consul in Hawaii was very conservative and sided with the plantation owners, giving his own people no support. When leprosy became epidemic in the islands, it was blamed on the Chinese. The Hawaiians called it *pake* disease, their derisive name for Chinese men, which, oddly enough, was an endearment in China meaning "uncle." Although leprosy cannot be blamed solely on the Chinese, a boatload of Chinese immigrants did bring smallpox in 1880. At the turn of the 20th century, a smallpox epidemic broke out again in Honolulu's Chinatown (where half the residents were really Japanese), and the area was promptly burnt to the ground by the authorities.

Amidst all this negativity, some intrepid souls prospered. The most successful entrepreneur was Chun Afong, who, with little more than determination, became a millionaire by 1857, raised 16 children, and almost single-handedly created the Chinese bourgeoisie in Hawaii. The Chinese were also responsible for making rice Hawaii's second most important crop (1867–1872). It was another Chinese person, Ah In, who brought the first water buffalo used to cultivate rice during this period.

## The Chinese Exclusion Act

Although reforms on the plantations were forthcoming, the Chinese preferred the retail trade. In 1880 half of all plantation workers were Chinese, by 1900 10 percent were, and by 1959, only 300 Chinese worked on plantations. When the "powers that were" decided Hawaii needed compliant laborers, not competitive businesspeople, the monarchy passed the Chinese Exclusion Act in 1886, forbidding any more Chinese contract laborers from entering Hawaii. Still, 15,000 more Chinese were contracted in the next few years. In 1900 there were about 25,000 Chinese in Hawaii, but because of the Exclusion Act and other prejudices, many sold out and moved away. By 1910 their numbers were reduced to 21,000.

## The Chinese Niche

Although many people in Hawaii considered all Chinese ethnically the same, they were actually quite different. The majority came from Guangdong Province in southern China. They were two distinct ethnic groups: the Punti made up 75 percent of the immigrants, and the Hakka made up the remainder. The Hakka had invaded Punti lands over a thousand years ago and lived in the hills overlooking Punti villages. In China, they remained separate from each other, never mixing; in Hawaii, they mixed out of necessity. Few Chinese women came at first, and the ones who followed were at a premium and gladly accepted as wives, regardless of ethnic background. The Chinese were also one of the first groups to willingly intermarry with the Hawaiians, from whom they gained a reputation for being exceptionally caring spouses.

By the 1930s, there was still resentment, but the Chinese were firmly entrenched in the merchant class. Their thriftiness, hard work, and family solidarity had paid off. The Chinese accepted the social order and kept a low profile. During Hawaii's turbulent labor movements of the 1930s and '40s, the Chinese community produced not one labor leader, radical intellectual, or left-wing politician. When Hawaii became a state, one of the two first senators was Hiram Fong, a racially mixed Chinese. Since statehood, the Chinese community has carried on business as usual as they continue to rise both economically and socially.

# THE JAPANESE

Most scholars believe that (inevitably) a few Japanese castaways floated to Hawaii long before Captain Cook arrived and might have introduced the iron with which the islanders seemed to be familiar before the white explorers arrived. Other scholars refute this claim and say Portuguese or Spanish ships lost in the Pacific introduced iron. Nevertheless, shipwrecked Japanese did make it to the islands. The most famous episode involved a man named Jirokichi, who, lost at sea for 10 months, was rescued by Captain Cathcart of Nantucket in 1839. Cathcart brought him to Hawaii, where Jirokichi boarded with prominent families. This adventure-filled episode is recounted in the Japanese classic *Ban Tan (Stories of the Outside World)*, written by the scribe Yuten-sei. The first official arrivals from Japan were ambassadors sent by the Japanese shogun to negotiate with the United States in Washington. They stopped en route at Honolulu in March 1860, only seven years after Commodore Perry and his famous "Black Ships" had roused Japan from its self-imposed 200-year slumber.

A small group of Japanese plantation workers arrived in 1868, but mass migration was blocked for almost 20 years. King Kalakaua, among others, proposed that Japanese be brought in as contract laborers in 1881; it was thought that Japanese subsistence farmers held promise as an inexhaustible supply of hardworking, uncomplaining, inexpensive, resolute workers. In 1886, because of famine, the Japanese government allowed farmers (mainly from southern Honshu, Kyushu, and Okinawa) to emigrate. Among these were members of Japan's little-talked-about untouchable caste, called *eta* or *burakumin* in Japan and *chorinbo* in Hawaii. They gratefully seized this opportunity to better their lot, an impossibility in their homeland.

## The Japanese Arrive

The first Japanese migrants were almost all men. Under Robert Irwin, the American agent for recruiting the Japanese, almost 27,000 Japanese came, for which he received a fee of $5 per head.

The contract workers received $9 plus room and board, and an additional $6 for a working wife. This pay was for a 26-workday month at 10 hours per day in the fields or 12 hours in a factory. Between 1897 and 1908, migration was steady, with about 70 percent men and 30 percent women. Afterwards, immigration was nearly halted because of a "gentlemen's agreement," a euphemism for racism against the "yellow peril." By 1900, more than 60,000 Japanese had arrived in the islands, constituting the largest ethnic group.

Until 1907 most Japanese longed to return home and faithfully sent back part of their pay to help support their families. Eventually, a full 50 percent did return to Japan, but the others began to consider Hawaii their home and resolved to settle . . . if they could get wives! Between 1908 and 1924, "picture brides" arrived whose marriages had been arranged *(omiai)* by family members back home. These women clung to the old ways and reinforced the Japanese ethnic identity. Excellent plantation workers, they set about making their rude camps into model villages. They felt an obligation that extended from individual to family, village, and their new country. As peasants, they were imbued with a feeling of a natural social order that they readily accepted . . . if treated fairly.

## Changing Attitudes

Unfortunately, some plantation *luna* were brutal, and Japanese laborers were mistreated, exploited, and made to live in indecent conditions on the plantations. In unusual protest, they formed their first trade union under Yasutaro Soga in 1908 and gained better treatment and higher wages. In 1919 an unsuccessful statewide plantation strike headed by the Federation of Japanese Labor lasted seven bitter months, earning the lasting mistrust of the establishment. By the 1930s, the Japanese, frustrated at being passed over for advancement because they were nonwhite, began to move from the plantations, opening retail stores and small businesses. By World War II they owned 50 percent of retail stores and accounted for 56 percent of household domestics. Many became small farmers, especially in Kona, where they began to grow coffee. They also accounted for Hawaii's fledgling fishing fleet and would brave the deep waters in their small, seaworthy sampans. Like the Chinese, they were committed to bettering themselves and placed education above all else. Unlike the Chinese, they did not marry outside their ethnic group and remained relatively racially intact.

## Americans of Japanese Ancestry (AJAs)

Parents of most Japanese children born in Hawaii before World War II were *issei* (first generation), who considered themselves apart from other Americans and clung to the notion of "we Japanese." They held traditional beliefs of unwavering family loyalty, and to propagate their values and customs they supported Japanese-language schools, which 80 percent of their children attended before the war. This group, who were never "disloyal," were, however, proud of being Japanese. Some diehards even refused to believe Japan lost World War II and were shamed by their former homeland's unconditional surrender.

Their children, the *nissei* or second generation, were a different breed altogether. In one generation they had become Americans, and they put into practice the high Japanese virtues of obligation, duty, and loyalty to the homeland; that homeland was now unquestionably America. After Pearl Harbor was bombed, many people were terrified that the Hawaiian Japanese would be disloyal to America and would serve as spies and even as advance combatants for imperial Japan. The FBI kept close tabs on the Japanese community, and the menace of the "enemy within" prompted the decision to place Hawaii under martial law for the duration of the war. Because of their sheer numbers it was impossible to place the Hawaiian Japanese into concentration camps as was done in California, but prejudice and suspicion toward them, especially from Mainland military personnel, was fierce. It has since been noted that not a single charge of espionage or sabotage was ever reported against the Japanese community in Hawaii during the war.

## AJAs as GIs

Although Japanese had formed a battalion during World War I, they were insulted by being con-

sidered unacceptable as American soldiers in World War II. Those already in the armed services were relieved of any duty involving weapons. People who knew better supported the AJAs. One was Jack Burns, a Honolulu policeman, who stated unequivocally that the AJAs were trustworthy. They never forgot his support, and thanks to a huge Japanese vote he was later elected governor. Some Japanese-Americans volunteered to serve in labor battalions, and because of their flawless work and loyalty, it was decided to put out a call for a few hundred volunteers to form a combat unit. More than 10,000 signed up!

AJAs formed two distinguished units in World War II: the 100th Infantry Battalion and, later, the 442nd Regimental Combat Team. They landed in Italy at Salerno and even fought from Guadalcanal to Okinawa. The 442nd distinguished themselves as *the* most decorated unit in American military history. They made excellent newspaper copy; their exploits hit front pages around the nation. They were immortalized as the rescuers of a Texas company pinned down during the Battle of the Bulge. These Texans became known as "The Lost Battalion" and have periodic reunions with the AJA GIs who risked and lost so much to bring them to safety.

## The AJAs Return

The AJAs returned home to a grateful country. In Hawaii, at first, they were accused of being cocky. Actually, they were refusing to revert to the prewar status of second-class citizens and began to assert their rights as citizens who had defended their country. Many took advantage of the GI Bill and received college educations. The Big Five corporations for the first time accepted former AJA officers as executives, and the old order began to wobble. Many Japanese became involved in Hawaiian politics, and the first elected member to Congress was Daniel Inouye, who had lost an arm fighting in the war. Hawaii's former governor, George Ariyoshi, elected in 1974, was the country's first Japanese-American to reach such high office. Most Japanese, even as they climb the economic ladder, tend to remain Democrats.

Today, one out of every two political offices in Hawaii is held by a Japanese-American. In one of those weird quirks of fate, it is now the Hawaiian Japanese who are accused by other ethnic groups of engaging in unfair political practices—nepotism and discrimination. It's often heard that "if you're not Japanese, forget about getting a government job." Many of these accusations against AJAs are undoubtedly motivated by jealousy, but their record of social fairness is not without blemish, and true to their custom of family loyalty, they do stick together. Heavily into the "professions," they're committed to climbing the social ladder. The AJAs of Hawaii, now indistinguishable from "the establishment," enjoy a higher standard of living than most and are motivated to get the best education possible for their children. They are the least likely of any ethnic group to marry outside of their group—especially the men. There are now 290,000 people of Japanese ancestry in Hawaii, nearly one-quarter of the state's population.

# CAUCASIANS

White people have a distinction separating them from all other ethnic groups in Hawaii: they are all lumped together as one. You can be anything from a Protestant Norwegian dockworker to a Greek Orthodox shipping tycoon, but if your skin is white, in Hawaii, you're a *haole*. What's more, you could have arrived at Waikiki from Missoula, Montana, in the last 24 hours, or your *kama'aina* family can go back five generations, but again, if you're white, you're a *haole*.

The word *haole* has a floating connotation that depends upon the spirit in which it's used. It can mean anything from a derisive "honky" or "cracker" to nothing more than "white person." The exact Hawaiian meaning is clouded, but some say it meant "a man of no background," because white people couldn't chant a genealogical *ha'i kupuna* telling the Hawaiians who they were. The word eventually evolved to mean "foreign white man" and today simply "white person."

## White History

Next to Hawaiians themselves, white people have the oldest stake in Hawaii. They've been there as settlers in earnest since the missionaries

of the 1820s, and were established long before any other migrant group. From the 1800s until statehood, old *haole* families owned and controlled almost everything, and although they were generally benevolent, philanthropic, and paternalistic, they were also racist. They felt (not without certain justification) they had "made" Hawaii, and, consequently, that they had the right to rule. These established *kama'aina* families, many of whom made up the boards of the Big Five corporations or owned huge plantations, formed an inner social circle closed to the outside except through marriage.

Their paternalism, which they accepted with grave responsibility, at first only extended to the Hawaiians, who saw them as replacing their own *ali'i*. Asians were primarily considered instruments of production. These supremacist attitudes tended to drag on in Hawaii until quite recent times. Today, they're responsible for the sometimes sour relations between white and nonwhite people in the islands. Since the *haole* had the power over other ethnic groups for so long, they have offended each group at one time or another. Today, all individual white people are resented to a certain degree because of these past acts, even though they personally were in no way involved.

## White Plantation Workers

In the 1880s, the white landowners looked around and felt surrounded and outnumbered by Asians. Many figured these people would one day be a political force to be reckoned with, so they tried to import white people for plantation work. Some of the imported workers included: 600 Scandinavians in 1881; 1,400 Germans 1881–85; 400 Poles 1897–98; and 2,400 Russians 1909–12. None worked out. Europeans were accustomed to much higher wages and better living conditions than provided on the plantations. Although they were workers, not considered the equals of the ruling elite, they were expected to act like a special class and were treated preferentially, receiving higher wages for the same jobs performed by Asians. Even so, many proved troublesome to the landowners, unwilling to work under the prevailing conditions; they were especially resentful of Hawaiian *luna*. Most moved quickly to the Mainland, and the Poles and Russians even staged strikes after only months on the job. A contingency of Scots, who first came as mule skinners and gained a reputation for hard work and frugality, became successful plantation managers and supervisors. There were so many on the Hamakua Coast of the Big Island that it was dubbed the "Scotch Coast." The Germans and Scandinavians were well received and climbed the social ladder rapidly, becoming professionals and skilled workers.

The Depression years, not as economically disastrous in Hawaii as in the continental United States, brought many Mainland whites seeking opportunity, mostly from the South and the West. These new people tended to be even more racist toward brown-skinned people and Asians than the *kama'aina haole*. They made matters worse and competed intensely for jobs. The racial tension generated during this period came to a head in 1932 with the infamous "Massie Rape Case."

## The Massie Rape Case

Thomas Massie, a naval officer, and his young wife Thalia attended a party at the Officers Club. After drinking and dancing all evening, they got into a row and Thalia rushed out in a huff. A few hours later, Thalia was at home, confused and hysterical, claiming to have been raped by some local men. On the most circumstantial evidence, Joseph Kahahawai and four friends of mixed ethnic background were accused. In a highly controversial trial rife with racial tensions, the verdict ended in a hung jury.

While a new trial was being set, Kahahawai and his friends were out on bail. Seeking revenge, Thomas Massie and Grace Fortescue, Thalia's mother, kidnapped Joseph Kahahawai with a plan of extracting a confession from him. They were aided by two enlisted men assigned to guard Thalia. While questioning Kahahawai, they killed him and attempted to dump his body in the sea but were apprehended. Another controversial trial—this time for Mrs. Fortescue, Massie, and the accomplices—followed. Clarence Darrow, the famous lawyer, sailed to Hawaii to defend

them. For killing Kahahawai, these people served *one hour* of imprisonment in the judge's private chambers. The other four, acquitted with Joseph Kahahawai, maintain innocence of the rape to this day. Later, the Massies divorced, and Thalia went on to become a depressed alcoholic who took her own life.

## The Portuguese

The last time anyone looked, Portugal was still attached to the European continent, but for some anomalous reason the Portuguese weren't considered *haole* in Hawaii for the longest time. This was because they weren't part of the ruling elite, but merely workers, showing that at one time the word *haole* implied social standing and not just skin color. About 12,000 arrived 1878 and 1887 and another 6,000 came between 1906 and 1913. They were accompanied during the latter period by 8,000 Spanish, who were considered one and the same. Most of the Portuguese were illiterate peasants from Madeira and the Azores, while the Spanish hailed from Andalusia. The majority of Spanish and some Portuguese tended to leave for California as soon as they made passage money. Those who remained were well received because they were white, but not *haole,* making a perfect "buffer" ethnic group. Unlike other Europeans, they would take any job, worked hard, and accepted authority. Committed to staying in Hawaii, they rose to be skilled workers and the *luna* class on the plantations. However, the Portuguese did not invest as much in education and became very racist toward the upwardly mobile Asians, regarding them as a threat to their job security.

By 1920, the 27,000 Portuguese made up 11 percent of the population. After that they tended to blend with the other ethnic groups and weren't counted separately. Portuguese men tended to marry within their ethnic group, but a good portion of Portuguese women married other white men and became closer to the *haole* group, while another large portion chose Hawaiian mates and grew further away.

Although they didn't originate pidgin English, the unique melodious quality of their native tongue did give pidgin a certain lilt it has today.

Also, the ukulele (which translates as "jumping flea") was closely patterned after the *cavaquinho,* a Portuguese stringed folk instrument.

## The White Population

Today Caucasians make up the largest racial group in the islands at 25 percent of the population. With mixed white blood, that number jumps to nearly 40 percent. They are spread evenly throughout Kaua'i, O'ahu, Maui, and the Big Island, with much smaller percentages on Moloka'i and Lana'i. Numerically, the vast majority live on O'ahu, in the more fashionable central valley and southeastern sections. Heavy white concentrations are also found on the Kihei and Ka'anapali coasts of Maui and the north Kona Coast of Hawaii. The white population is also the fastest growing in the islands because most people resettling in Hawaii are white Americans predominantly from the West Coast.

# FILIPINOS AND OTHERS

The Filipinos who came to Hawaii brought high hopes of making personal fortunes and returning home as rich heroes; for most it was a dream that never came true. Filipinos had been American nationals ever since the Spanish-American War of 1898, and as such weren't subject to immigration laws that curtailed the importation of other Asian workers at the turn of the twentieth century. The first to arrive were 15 families in 1906, but a large number came in 1924 as strikebreakers. The majority were illiterate Ilocano peasants from the northern Philippines with about 10 percent Visayans from the central cities. The Visayans were not as hardworking or thrifty, but were much more sophisticated. From the first, Filipinos were looked down upon by all the other immigrant groups and were considered particularly uncouth by the Japanese. The value they placed on education was the least of any group, and even by 1930 only half could speak rudimentary English, while the majority remained illiterate. They were billeted in the worst housing, performed the most menial jobs, and were the last hired and first fired.

One big difference between Filipinos and other groups was that the men brought no Filipino women to marry, so they clung to the idea of returning home. In 1930 there were 30,000 men and only 360 women. Many of these terribly lonely bachelors would feast and drink on weekends and engage in the gruesome but exciting pastime of cockfighting on Sunday. When some did manage to find wives, their mates were inevitably part Hawaiian. Today, there are still plenty of old Filipino bachelors who never managed to get home.

Filipinos constitute 14 percent of Hawaii's population, with nearly three-quarters living on O'ahu. The largest concentration, however, is on Lana'i, where they make up 60 percent of that island's population. Some of these men are new arrivals with the same dream held by their countrymen for more than 70 years. Many visitors to Hawaii mistake Filipinos for Hawaiians because of their dark skin, and this is a minor irritant to both groups. Some streetwise Filipinos even claim to be Hawaiians, because being Hawaiian is "in" and goes over well with tourists, especially young women. For the most part, these people are hardworking, dependable laborers who do tough work for little recognition. They remain low on the social totem pole and have not yet organized politically to stand up for their rights.

## Other Groups

About 10 percent of Hawaii's population is a conglomerate of other ethnic groups. Of these, one of the largest and fastest growing is Korean, with 25,000 people. About 8,000 Koreans came to Hawaii from 1903 to 1905, when their government halted emigration. During the same period about 6,000 Puerto Ricans arrived, and today about 30,000 consider themselves a Puerto Rican mix. There were also two attempts made in the 19th century to import other Polynesians to strengthen the dying Hawaiian race, but they were failures. In 1869 only 126 central Polynesian natives could be lured to Hawaii, and from 1878 to 1885, 2,500 Gilbert Islanders arrived. Both groups were immediately disenchanted with Hawaii. They pined for their own islands and departed for home as soon as possible.

Today, however, 16,000 Samoans have settled

in Hawaii, and with more on the way they are the fastest growing minority in the state. For inexplicable reasons, Samoans and native Hawaiians get along extremely poorly and have the worst racial tensions and animosity of any groups. The Samoans ostensibly should represent the archetypal Polynesians that the Hawaiians are seeking, but it doesn't work that way. Samoans are criticized by Hawaiians for their hot tempers,

lingering feuds, and petty jealousies. They're clannish and are often the butt of "dumb" jokes. This racism seems especially ridiculous, but that's the way it is.

Just to add a bit more exotic spice to the stew, there are about 22,000 blacks, 3,500 Native American Indians, 4,000 Tongans, 7,000 other Pacific Islanders, and 8,000 Vietnamese living on the islands.

# Language

Hawaii is part of the United States, and people speak English there, but that's not the whole story. If you turn on the TV to catch the evening news, you'll hear "Walter Cronkite" English, unless of course you happen to tune in to a Japanese-language broadcast designed for tourists from that country. You can easily pick up a Chinese-language newspaper or groove to the music on a Filipino radio station, but let's not confuse the issue. All your needs and requests at airports, car rental agencies, restaurants, hotels, or wherever you happen to travel will be completely understood, as well as answered, in English. However, when you happen to overhear islanders speaking, what they're saying will sound somewhat familiar but you won't be able to pick up all the words, and the beat and melody of the language will be noticeably different.

Hawaii—like New England, the Deep South, and the Midwest—has its own unmistakable linguistic regionalism. All the ethnic peoples who make up Hawaii have enriched the English spoken there with words, expressions, and subtle shades of meaning that are commonly used and understood throughout the islands. The greatest influence on English has come from the Hawaiian language itself, and words such as "aloha," "hula," and "lu'au" are familiarly used and understood by most Americans.

Other migrant peoples, especially the Chinese, Japanese, and Portuguese, influenced the local dialect to such an extent that the simplified plantation lingo they spoke has become known as "pidgin." A fun and enriching part of the "island experience" is picking up a few words of Hawaiian and pidgin. English is the official language of the state, business, education, and perhaps even the mind; but pidgin is the language of the people, the emotions, and life, while Hawaiian remains the language of the heart and the soul.

**Note:** Many Hawaiian words are commonly used in English, appear in English dictionaries, and therefore would ordinarily be subject to the rules of English grammar. The Hawaiian language, however, does not pluralize nouns by adding an "s"; the singular and plural are differentiated in context. For purposes of this book, and to highlight the Hawaiian culture, the Hawaiian style of pluralization will be followed for common Hawaiian words. The following are some examples of plural Hawaiian nouns treated this way in this book: *haole* (not haoles), hula, *kahuna,* lei, lu'au, and *nene.*

## PIDGIN

The dictionary definition of pidgin is: a simplified language with a rudimentary grammar used as a means of communication between people speaking different languages. Hawaiian pidgin is a little more complicated than that. It had its roots during the plantation days of the 1800s when white owners and *luna* (foremen) had to communicate with recently arrived Chinese, Japanese, and Portuguese laborers. It was designed as a simple language of the here and now, and was primarily concerned with the necessary functions of working, eating, and sleeping. It has an economical noun-verb-object structure (although not necessarily in that order).

# CAPSULE PIDGIN

The following are a few commonly used words and expressions that should give you an idea of pidgin. It really can't be written properly, merely approximated, but for now, "*Study da' kine an' bimbye it be mo' bettah, brah! OK? Lesgo.*"

**an' den**—and then? big deal; so what's next?

**auntie**—respected elderly woman

**bad ass**—very good

**bimbye**—after a while; bye and bye. "Bimbye, you learn pidgin."

**blalah**—brother, but actually only refers to a large, heavy-set, good-natured Hawaiian man

**brah**—all the bros in Hawaii are brahs; brother; pal. Used to call someone's attention. One of the most common words even among people who are not acquainted. After a fill-up at a gas station, a person would say "Tanks, brah."

**chicken skin**—goose bumps

**cockaroach**—steal; rip off. If you really want to find out what *cockaroach* means, just leave your camera on your beach blanket when you take a little dip.

**da' kine**—a catchall word of many meanings that epitomizes the essence of pidgin. *Da' kine* is a euphemism for pidgin and is substituted whenever the speaker is at a loss for a word or just wants to generalize. It can mean you know? watchamacallit; of that type.

**geev um**—give it to them; give them hell; go for it. Can be used as an encouragement. If a surfer is riding a great wave, the people on the beach might yell, "Geev um, brah!"

**grinds**—food

**hana ho**—again. Especially after a concert the audience shouts "hana ho" (one more!).

**hele on**—let's get going

**howzit?**—as in "howzit, brah?" what's happening? how's it going? The most common greeting, used in place of the more formal "How do you do?"

**huhu**—angry! "You put the make on the wrong da' kine wahine, brah, and you in da' kine trouble if you get one big Hawaiian blalah plenty huhu."

**lesgo**—let's go! do it!

**li'dis an' li'dat**—like this or that; a catch-all grouping especially if you want to avoid details; like, ya' know?

**lolo buggah**—stupid or crazy guy (person). Words to a tropical island song go, "I want to find the lolo who stole my pakalolo."

**mo' bettah**—better, real good! great idea. An island sentiment used to be, "mo' bettah you *come* Hawaii." Now it has subtly changed to "mo' bettah you *visit* Hawaii."

**ono**—number one! delicious; great; groovy. "Hawaii is ono, brah!"

**pakalolo**—literally "crazy smoke"; marijuana; grass; reefer

**pakiki head**—stubborn; bull-headed

**pau**—a Hawaiian word meaning finished; done; over and done with. *Pau hana* means end of work or quitting time. Once used by plantation workers, now used by everyone.

**seestah**—sister, female

**shaka**—hand wave where only the thumb and baby finger stick out, meaning thank you, all right!

**sleepah**—slippers, flip-flops, zori

**stink face**—(or stink eye) basically frowning at someone; using facial expression to show displeasure. Hard looks. What you'll get if you give local people a hard time.

**swell head**—burned up; angry

**talk story**—spinning yarns; shooting the breeze; throwing the bull; a rap session. If you're lucky enough to be around to hear *kupuna* (elders) "talk story," you can hear some fantastic tales in the tradition of old Hawaii.

**tanks, brah**—thanks, thank you

**to da max**—all the way

**waddascoops**—what's the scoop? what's up? what's happening?

Hawaiian words make up most of pidgin's non-English vocabulary. It includes a good smattering of Chinese, Japanese, and Samoan; the distinctive rising inflection is provided by the melodious Mediterranean lilt of the Portuguese. Pidgin is not a stagnant language. It's kept alive by hip new words introduced by people who are "so radical," or especially by slang words introduced by teenagers. It's a colorful English, like "jive" or "ghettoese" spoken by American blacks, and it's as regionally unique as the speech of Cajuns from Louisiana's bayous. *Maka'ainana* of all socioethnic backgrounds can at least understand pidgin. Most islanders are proud of it, while some consider it low-class jargon. The Hawaiian House of Representatives has given pidgin an official sanction, and most people feel that it adds a real local style and should be preserved.

## Pidgin Lives

Pidgin is first learned at school, where all students, regardless of background, are exposed to it. The pidgin spoken by young people today is "fo' real" different from that of their parents. It's no longer only plantation talk but has moved to the streets and picked up some sophistication. At one time there was an academic movement to exterminate it, but that idea died away with the same thinking that insisted on making left-handed people write with their right hand. It is strange, however, that pidgin has become the unofficial language of Hawaii's grassroots movement, when it actually began as a white owners' language that was used to supplant Hawaiian and all other languages brought to the islands.

Although hip young *haole* use pidgin all the time, it has gained the connotation of being the language of the nonwhite locals, and is part of the "us against them" way of thinking. All local people, *haole* or not, consider pidgin their own island language, and don't really like it when it's used by *malihini* (newcomers). If you're in the islands long enough, you don't have to bother learning pidgin; it'll learn you. There's a book sold all over the islands called *Pidgin to da Max,* written by (you guessed it) a *haole* from Nebraska named Doug Simonson.

You might not be able to understand what's being said by locals speaking pidgin (that's usually the idea), but you should be able to *feel* what's meant.

## HAWAIIAN

The Hawaiian language sways like a palm tree in a gentle wind. Its words are as melodious as a love song. Linguists say that you can learn a lot about people through their language; when you hear Hawaiian you think of gentleness and love, and it's hard to imagine the ferocious side so evident in Hawaii's past. With its many Polynesian root words easily traced to Indonesian and Malay, Hawaiian is obviously from this same stock. The Hawaiian spoken today is very different from old Hawaiian. Its greatest metamorphosis occurred when the missionaries began to write it down in the 1820s, but in the last couple of decades there has been a movement to reestablish the Hawaiian language. Not only are courses in it are offered at the University of Hawai'i, there is a successful elementary immersion school program in the state, some books are being printed in it, and more and more musicians are performing it. Many scholars have put forth translations of Hawaiian, but there are endless, volatile disagreements in the academic sector about the real meanings of Hawaiian words. Hawaiian is, by and large, no longer spoken as a language except on Ni'ihau and in Hawaiian-language immersion classes, and the closest tourists will come to it is in place-names, street names, and words that have become part of common usage, such as "aloha" and "mahalo." A few old Hawaiians still speak it at home and there are sermons in Hawaiian at some local churches. Kawaiaha'o Church in downtown Honolulu is the most famous of these, but each island has theirs.

## Wiki Wiki Hawaiian

Thanks to the missionaries, the Hawaiian language is rendered phonetically using only 12 letters. They are the five vowels, a-e-i-o-u, sounded as they are in Italian, and seven consonants, h-k-l-m-n-p-w, sounded exactly as they are in English. Sometimes "w" is pronounced as "v," but this only occurs in the middle of a word and always follows a vowel. A consonant is always followed by a vowel, forming two-letter syllables, but vowels are often found in pairs or even triplets. A slight oddity about Hawaiian is the glottal stop, called *'okina* in Hawaiian. This is an abrupt break in sound in the middle of a word, such as "oh-oh" in English, and is denoted in this book by a reverse apostrophe ('). A good example is *ali'i* or, even better, the O'ahu and Maui towns of Ha'iku, which actually means "Abrupt Break."

## Note on Diacritics

In addition to the *'okina,* or glottal stop, there is the macron *kahako,* a short line written over a vowel indicating that the vowel is stressed. The *kahako* is not used in this book. The *'okina* is used in Hawaiian place names, names of historical persons, and ordinary Hawaiian words, where appropriate. It is not used in business names if the business itself does not use this symbol. The name Hawai'i, written with an *'okina* refers to the island of Hawai'i, the Big Island; without the 'okina, it refers to the state. The word Hawaiian, written without the glottal stop, refers to both the Polynesian inhabitants of the islands before Western contact and to those people of all races who currently reside in the state.

## Pronunciation Key

For those unfamiliar with the sounds of Italian or other Romance languages, the vowels are sounded as follows:

**A**—in stressed syllables, pronounced as in "ah" (that feels good!). For example, Haleakala is pronounced "hah-lay-AH-kah-lah." Unstressed syllables are pronounced "uh" as in "again" or "above." For example, Kamehameha would be "kuh-MAY-huh-MAY-huh."

**E**—short "e" is "eh," as in "pen" or "dent" (thus *hale* is "HAH-leh"). Long "e" sounds like "ay" as in "sway" or "day." For example, the Hawaiian goose *(nene)* is a "nay-nay," not a "nee-nee."

**I**—pronounced "ee" as in "see" or "we" (thus *pali* is pronounced "PAH-lee").

**O**—pronounced as in "no" or "oh," such as "KOH-uh" (koa) or "OH-noh" (ono).

**U**—pronounced "oo" as in "do" or "stew"; for example, "KAH-poo" *(kapu)* or "POO-nuh" (Puna).

## Diphthongs

Eight vowel pairs are known as "diphthongs" (ae-ai-ao-au-ei-eu-oi-ou). These are the sounds made by gliding from one vowel to another within a syllable. The stress is placed on the first vowel. In English, examples would be soil and bail. Common examples in Hawaiian are lei (lay) and *heiau* (hayee-aoo).

## Stress

The best way to learn which syllables are stressed in Hawaiian is by listening closely. It becomes obvious after a while. Also, some vowel sounds are held longer than others; these can occur at the beginning of a word, such as the first "a" in *'aina* (land), or in the middle of a word, like the first "a" in *lanai* (veranda). Again, it's a matter of tuning your ear and paying attention. When written, these stressed vowels, called *kahako* occur with a macron, or short line, over them. Stressed vowels with marks are not written as such in this book. No one is going to give you a hard time if you mispronounce a word. It's good, however, to pay close attention to the pronunciation of street and place-names, because many Hawaiian words sound alike and a misplaced vowel here or there could be the difference between getting where you want to go and getting lost.

# Religion

The Lord saw fit to keep His island paradise secret from humans for a few million years, but once we finally arrived we were awfully thankful. Hawaii sometimes seems like a floating tabernacle; everywhere you look there's a church, temple, shrine, or *heiau*. The islands are either a very holy place, or there's a powerful lot of sinning going on that would require so many houses of prayer. Actually, it's just America's "right to worship" concept fully employed in microcosm. All the peoples who came to Hawaii brought their own forms of devotion. The Polynesian Hawaiians praised the primordial creators, Wakea and Papa, from whom their pantheon of animistically inspired gods sprang. Obviously, to a modern world these old gods would never do. There were simply too many, and belief in them was looked down upon as mere superstition, the folly of semi-civilized pagans. So, the famous missionaries of the 1820s brought Congregational Christianity and the "true path" to heaven.

Inconveniently, the Catholics, Mormons, Reformed Mormons, Adventists, Episcopalians, Unitarians, Christian Scientists, Lutherans, Baptists, Jehovah's Witnesses, Salvation Army, and every other major and minor denomination of Christianity that followed in their wake brought their own brands of enlightenment and never quite agreed with each other. The Chinese and Japanese immigrants established all the major sects of Buddhism, Confucianism, Taoism, and Shintoism. Allah is praised, the Torah is chanted in Jewish synagogues, and nirvana is available at a variety of Hindu temples. If the spirit moves you, a Hare Krishna devotee will be glad to point you in the right direction and give you a free flower for only a dollar or two. If the world is still too much with you, you might find peace at a Church of Scientology, or meditate at a Kundalini yoga institute, or perhaps find relief at a local assembly of Baha'i. Anyway, rejoice, because in Hawaii you'll find not only paradise but perhaps salvation.

## HAWAIIAN BELIEFS

The Polynesian Hawaiians worshipped nature. They saw its forces manifested in a multiplicity of forms to which they ascribed godlike powers. Daily life was based on this animistic philosophy. Hand-picked and specially trained storytellers chanted the exploits of the gods. These ancient tales, kept alive in a special oral tradition called *mo'olelo,* were recited only by day. Entranced listeners encircled the chanter and, in respect for the gods and in fear of their wrath, were forbidden to move once the tale was begun. This was serious business during which a person's life could be at stake. It was not like the telling of *ka'ao,* which were simple fictions, tall tales, and yarns of ancient heroes, related for amusement and to pass the long nights. Any object, animate or inanimate, could be a god. All could be infused with mana, especially a dead body or a respected ancestor.

*'Ohana* had personal family gods called *'aumakua* on whom they called in times of danger or strife. There were children of gods, called *kupua,* who were thought to live among humans and were distinguished either for their beauty and strength or for their ugliness and terror. It was told that processions of dead *ali'i* called "Marchers of the Night" wandered through the land of the living, and unless you were properly protected it could mean death if they looked upon you. Simple ghosts known as *akua lapu* merely frightened people. Forests, waterfalls, trees, springs, and a thousand forms of nature were the manifestations of *akua li'i,* "little spirits" who could be invoked at any time for help or protection. It made no difference who or what you were in old Hawaii; the gods were ever-present and they took a direct and active role in your life.

Behind all of these beliefs was an innate sense of natural balance and order, and the idea that everything had its opposite—similar to the Asian idea of yin-yang. The time of darkness when only the gods lived was *po.* When the great gods descended to earth and created light, this was *ao*, and humanity was born. All of these *mo'olelo* are part of the *Kumulipo*, the great chant that records the Hawaiian version of creation. From the time the gods descended and touched earth at Ku Moku on Lana'i, the genealogies were kept. Unlike in the Bible, these included the noble families of female as well as male *ali'i*.

## Heiau

A *heiau* is a Hawaiian temple. The basic *heiau* was a masterfully built and fitted rectangular stone wall that varied in size from about as big as a basketball court to as broad as a football field. Once the restraining outer walls were built, the interior was backfilled with smaller stones, and the top dressing was expertly laid and then rolled, perhaps with a log, to form a pavement-like surface. All that remains of Hawaii's many *heiau* are the stone platforms. The buildings upon them, made from perishable wood, leaves, and grass, have long since disappeared.

Some *heiau* were dreaded temples where human sacrifices were made. Tradition says that this barbaric custom began at Waha'ula Heiau on the Big Island in the 12th century and was introduced by a ferocious Tahitian priest named Pa'ao. Other *heiau*, such as Pu'uhonua O Honaunau, also on the Big Island, were temples of refuge where the weak, widowed, orphaned, and vanquished could find safety and sanctuary.

Within *heiau*, ceremonies were conducted by the priestly *kahuna*. Offerings of chickens, dogs, fish, fruit, and tapa were laid on the *lele*, a huge stone altar, in hopes the gods would act favorably toward the people. Some buildings held the bones of dead *ali'i*, infused with their mana. Other structures were god houses in which idols resided, while still others were oracle towers from which prophecies were made. The gods were honored by *ali'i* and *maka'ainana* alike, but the *kahuna* prayed for the *ali'i*, while the commoners represented themselves. There was a patron god for every aspect of life, especially farming and fishing, but gods could be invoked for everything from weaving to help for thieves! Men and women had their own gods, with rituals governing birth, cutting the umbilical cord, sickness, and death.

Ceremonies, often lasting for many days, were conducted by *kahuna*, many of whom had highly specialized functions. Two of the most interesting were: *kahuna kilikilo*, who could see a person die in a dream and save his or her life through offerings of white dogs, chickens, tapa, and '*awa*; and *kahuna kaula*, semi-hermits who could foretell the future.

## Idols

The Hawaiian people worshipped gods who took the form of idols fashioned from wood, feathers, or stone. Some figures were more than six feet tall and crowned with elaborate head pieces. Figures were often pointed at the end so they could be stuck into the ground. The eyes were made from shells, and until these were inlaid, the idol was dormant. The hair used was often human hair, and the arms and legs were usually flexed. The mouth was either gaping or formed a wide figure-eight lying on its side, and more likely than not was lined with glistening dog teeth. Small figures were made of woven basketry, expertly covered with feathers. Red and yellow feathers were favorites taken from specific birds by men whose only work was to roam the forests in search of them.

# GREAT GODS

## Ku

The progenitors of the gods were Wakea, the "sky father," and Papa, the "earth mother," but the actual gods worshipped in Hawaii were Ku, Kane and Kanaloa, and Lono. Ku was a universal god who represented the male aspect of nature, and Hina, the moon goddess, was his female counterpart. Ku was prayed to at sunrise and Hina at sunset. Ku's maleness was represented with pointed stones, while flat ones symbolized Hina's womanhood. Ku ruled the forest, land, mountains, farming, and fishing—his benevolent side. But Ku was better known as the god of war. It was Ku who demanded human sacrifice, especially in times of calamity or in preparation for battle. At times, Ku was represented by an 'ohi'a log, and a human sacrifice was made in the forest where it was cut and also at the post

representation of the god Ku, based on a woven fiber image

hole that held it upright at the *heiau*. When Ku was invoked, the strict and serious ceremonies could go on for more than a week. The entire *'aha* (assembly) kept complete silence and sat ramrod straight with the left leg and hand crossed over the right leg and hand in an attitude called *ne'epu*. At a precise command everyone simultaneously pointed their right hands heavenward. Anyone caught dozing or daydreaming, or who for some reason missed the command, instantly became the main course for Ku's lunch.

Kamehameha the Great carried a portable Ku into battle with him at all times, and this statue was known as Kuka'ilimoku (the Snatcher of Lands). It was held that during battle this effigy, whose gaping mouth gleamed with canine incisors, would cry out in a loud voice and stir Kamehameha's warriors on to victory. After a battle, the slain enemies were taken to the *heiau* and placed upon Ku's altar with their arms encircling two pigs. Now Ku became Kuwahailo (of the Dripping Maggot Mouth). With Ku's killing nature appeased, the people would pray for

good crops, good fishing, and fertile wives. The scales were balanced and life went on.

## Kane and Kanaloa

*Kane* is the Hawaiian word for "man" or "husband," and he was the leading god worshipped when the missionaries arrived. God of life, ancestor of all Hawaiians, Kane is the center of the Hawaiian creation myth, whose events are amazingly similar to those of Genesis. Kane comes forward from *po* (darkness) into *ao* (light) and, with the help of Ku and Lono, fashions a man from clay gathered from the four cardinal points of the compass. Once the body is formed, the gods breathe (some say spit) into the mouth and nostrils and give it life. The man is placed upon a paradise island, *Kalani i hauola,* and a wife is fashioned for him out of his right side. Like Adam and Eve, these two break the law by eating from the forbidden tree and are driven from paradise by the sacred white albatross of Kane.

Kane is a forgiving god who demands no human sacrifice, because all life is sacred to him. He is a god of a higher order, not usually rendered as an idol. Instead he was symbolized by a single upright male stone splashed with oil and wrapped in white tapa. Kanaloa, the antithesis of Kane, was represented as a great squid, and often likened to the Christian devil. He warred with Kane and was driven out of heaven along with his minions. Kanaloa became the ruler of the dead and was responsible for "black" sorcery and for poisonous things. However, these two gods were often linked together. For example, prayers would be offered to Kane when a canoe was built and to Kanaloa to provide favorable winds. Farmers and diviners often prayed simultaneously to Kane and Kanaloa. Both gods were intimately connected to water and the intoxicating beverage *'awa.*

## Pele

The Hawaiian gods were toppled literally and figuratively in 1819 and began to fade from the minds of people. Two that remained prominent were Madame Pele, the fire goddess, who resides at Kilauea Volcano on Hawaii, and the demigod Maui, who is like Paul Bunyan and Ulysses rolled into one. Many versions account for how Pele wound up living in the Kilauea fire pit, but they all follow a general outline. It seems the beautiful young goddess, from a large family of gods, was struck by wanderlust. Tucking her young sister, in the convenient form of an egg, under her armpit, she set out to see the world. Fortune had its ups and downs in store for young Pele. For one, she was ravished by a real swine, Kamapua'a the pig god. Moreover, she fought desperately with her sister, Namaka o Kahai, over the love of a handsome young chief; Pele's sister stalked her and smashed her bones on the Hana Coast of Maui at a spot called Kaiwi o Pele (the Bones of Pele).

Pulling herself back together, Pele set out to make a love nest for her lover and herself. She chose the fire pit at Kilauea Volcano and has long been held responsible for its lava flows, along with anything else that deals with heat or fire. Pele can change her form from a withered old woman to a ravishing beauty; her moods can change from gentle to fiery hot. She is traditionally appeased with 'ohelo berries cast into her fire pit, but lately she prefers juniper berries in the form of gin. Pele's myth was shattered by the Hawaiian queen Keopuolani, one of the earliest and most fervent converts to Christianity. In the 1820s this brave queen made her way to Kilauea fire pit and defiantly ate the 'ohelo berries sacred to Pele. She then cast stones into the pit and cried in a loud voice, "Jehovah is my god . . . it is my God, not Pele, that kindled these fires."

Still, stories abound of Pele's continuing powers. Modern-day *kahuna* are always consulted and prayers offered over construction of an *imu,* which falls under Pele's fire domain. It's said by traditional Hawaiians and educated *haole* alike that when Kilauea erupts, the lava miraculously stops before or circles around a homestead over which proper prayers were made to the fire goddess. In addition, the rangers at Volcanoes National Park receive hundreds of stones every year that were taken as souvenirs and then returned by shaken tourists, who claim bad luck stalked them from the day they removed Pele's sacred stones from her volcano. And, no one who has lived in the islands for any length of time will carry pork over the volcano at night, lest they offend the goddess. She's perhaps still angry with that swine, Kamapua'a.

## The Strifes of Maui

Of all the heroes and mythological figures of Polynesia, Maui is the best known. His "strifes" are like the great Greek epics, and they make excellent tales of daring that elders loved to relate to youngsters around the evening fire. Maui was abandoned by his mother, Hina of Fire, when he was an infant. She wrapped him in her hair and cast him upon the sea, where she expected him to die, but he lived and returned home to become her favorite. She knew then that he was a born hero and had strength far beyond that of ordinary mortals. His first exploit was to lift the sky. In those days the sky hung so low that humans had to crawl around on all fours. A seductive young woman approached Maui and asked him to use his great strength to lift the sky. In fine heroic fashion, this big boy agreed, if the beautiful woman would, euphemistically, "give him a drink from her gourd." He then obliged her by lifting the sky.

The territory of humankind was small at the time. Maui decided that more land was needed, so he conspired to "fish up islands." He descended into the land of the dead and petitioned an ancestress to fashion him a hook out of her jawbone. She obliged, creating the mythical hook *Manai ikalani.* Maui then secured a sacred *'alae* bird that he intended to use for bait and bid his brothers to paddle him far out to sea. When he arrived at the deepest spot, he lowered *Manai ikalani* baited with the sacred bird, and his sister, Hina of the Sea, placed it into the mouth of "Old One Tooth," who held land fast to the bottom of the waters. Maui then exhorted his brothers to row but warned them not to look back. They strained at the oars with all their might and slowly a great landmass rose. One brother, overcome by curiosity, looked back, and when he did so, the land shattered into all of the islands of Polynesia.

Maui desired to serve humankind further. People were without fire, the secret of which was held by the sacred *'alae* birds, who had learned it from Maui's beneficent mother. Hina of Fire gave Maui her burning fingernails, but he oafishly kept dropping them into streams until all had fizzled out and he had totally irritated his generous progenitor. She pursued Maui, trying to burn him to a cinder, and Maui desperately chanted for rain to put out her scorching fires. When she saw her fires being quenched, Hina hid her fire in the barks of special trees and informed common mud hens where they could be found, but first made them promise never to tell humans. Maui learned of this and captured a mud hen, threatening to wring its scrawny, traitorous neck unless it gave up the secret. The bird tried trickery and told Maui first to rub together the stems of sugarcane, then of banana and even of taro. None worked, and Maui's determined rubbing is why these plants have hollow roots today. Finally, with Maui's hands tightening around the mud hen's neck, the bird confessed fire could be found in the *hau* tree and also the sandalwood, which Maui named *'ili ahi* (fire bark) in its honor. Maui then rubbed all the feathers of the mud hen's head for being so deceitful, which is why their crowns are featherless today.

Maui's greatest deed, however, was in snaring the sun and exacting a promise that it would go slower across the heavens. The people complained that there were not enough daylight hours to fish or farm. Maui's mother could not dry her tapa cloth because the sun rose and set so quickly. When she asked her son to help, Maui went to his blind grandmother for assistance. She lived on the slopes of Haleakala and was responsible for cooking the sun's bananas, which he ate every day in passing. Maui kept stealing his granny's bananas until she agreed to help. She told him to personally weave 16 strong ropes with nooses from his sister's hair. Some say these came from her head, but other versions insist that it was no doubt Hina's pubic hair that had the power to hold the sun god. Maui positioned himself, and as each of the 16 rays of the sun came across Haleakala, he snared them until the sun was defenseless and had to bargain for his life. Maui agreed to free him if he promised to go more slowly. The sun agreed, and from that time forward Haleakala (The House of the Sun) became Maui's home.

## Lono and the Makahiki Festival

Lono was a benevolent god of clouds, harvest, and rain. In a fit of temper he killed his wife, whom he thought unfaithful. When he discovered his grave error, he roamed the countryside challenging everyone he met to a boxing match. Boxing later became an event of the Makahiki, the Harvest Festival, which was held in his honor. Lono decided to leave his island home, but he promised one day to return on a floating island. Every year at the beginning of *ho'oilo* (winter), starting in October, the Makahiki was held. It was a jubilant time of harvest when taxes were collected and most *kapu* were lifted. It ended sometime in February, and then the new year began. During this time great sporting events included surfing, boxing, sledding, and a form of bowling. At night, people feasted at lu'au to the rhythm of drums and hula. Fertility was honored, and willing partners from throughout the land coupled and husbands and wives shared their mates in the tradition of *punalua*.

Lono's idol was an *akua loa,* a slender 15-foot pole with his small image perched atop. Another pole fastened at the top formed a cross. Hanging from the cross pole were long banners of white tapa cloth, and the pole was festooned with the feathers and skins of seabirds. To this image the *kahuna* offered red and white fish, black coconut, and immature *'awa.* This image, called "Long God," traveled in a procession clockwise around the island. It was met at every *ahupua'a* (land division) by the chief of that region, and new tapa was offered by the chieftess, along with roasted taro. The *maka'ainana* came and offered their produce from sea and land, and so the taxes were collected. At the end of the festival a naked man representing the god Kohoali'i ate the eyeball of a fish and one of a human victim and proclaimed the new year.

It was during the Makahiki that Captain Cook sailed into Kealakekua Bay. *Kahuna* saw his great "floating islands" and proclaimed the return of Lono. Uncannily, the masts of the sailing ships draped in canvas looked remarkably like Lono's idol. Cook himself was particularly tall and white-skinned, and at the sight of him, many natives fell to their knees and worshipped him as "Lono returned."

## THE CASTE AND KAPU SYSTEM

All was not heavenly in paradise due to horrible wars, but the people mainly lived quiet, ordered lives based on a strict caste society and the *kapu* system. Famine was contained to a regional level. The population was kept in check by herbal birth-control potions, crude abortions, and infanticide, especially of baby girls. The strict caste system was determined by birth, and there was no chance of changing one's status. The highest rank was the ***ali'i***, the chiefs and royalty. The impeccable genealogies of the *ali'i* were traced back to the gods themselves and recorded in chants *(mo'o ali'i)* memorized and sung by professionals called *ku'auhau*, who were themselves *ali'i*. Ranking passed from both father and mother, and custom dictated that the first mating of an *ali'i* be with a person of equal status. After a child was produced, the *ali'i* was free to mate with lesser *ali'i* or even with a commoner. The custom of *punalua*, the sharing of mates, was practiced throughout Hawaiian society. Moreover, incest was not only condoned but sanctioned among *ali'i*. To conceive an offspring of the highest rank, *ni'au pi'o* (coconut leaf looped back on itself), the parents were required to be full brothers and sisters. These offspring were so sacred they were considered *akua* (living gods), and people of all ranks had to literally crawl on their stomachs in their presence. *Ali'i* who ran society's affairs were of lesser rank, and they were the real functionaries. The two most important were the land supervisors *(konohiki)* and caste priests *(kahuna)*. The *konohiki* were in charge of the *ahupua'a*, pie-shaped land divisions running from mountain to sea. The common people came in contact with these *ali'i* because they also collected taxes and ruled as judges among the people.

*Kahuna* were highly skilled people whose advice was sought before any major undertaking, such as building a house, hollowing a canoe log, or even offering a prayer. The *mo'o kahuna* were the priests of Ku and Lono, in charge of praying and following rituals. These powerful *ali'i* kept strict secrets

and laws concerning their various functions. The *kahuna* dedicated to Ku were severe: it was they who sought human sacrifice. The *kahuna* of Lono were more comforting to the people but were of lesser rank than the Ku *kahuna*. Other *kahuna* were not *ali'i* but commoners. The two most important were the healers *(kahuna lapa'au)* and the black magicians *(kahuna 'ana'ana)*, who could pray a person to death. The *kahuna lapa'au* had a pharmacopoeia of herbs and spices that could cure more than 230 diseases. They employed baths and massage and used various colored stones to outline the human body and accurately pinpoint not only the organs but the internal origins of illness. The *kahuna 'ana'ana* were given a wide berth by the people, who did everything possible to stay on their good side! The *kahuna 'ana'ana* could be hired to cast a love spell over a person or cause untimely death; they seldom had to send a reminder of payment.

The common people were called the ***maka'ainana***, "people of the land." They were the farmers, craftspeople, and fishermen. Their land was owned by the *ali'i*, but they were not bound to it. If the local *ali'i* was cruel or unfair, the *maka'ainana* had the right to leave. Very unjust *ali'i* were even put to death by their own people, with no retribution if their accusations proved true. The *maka'ainana* mostly loved their local *ali'i*, and vice versa. *Maka'ainana* who lived close to the *ali'i* and could be counted on as warriors in times of trouble were called *kanaka no lua kaua*, "a man for the heat of battle." They were treated with greater favor than those who lived in the backcountry, *kanaka no hi'i kua*, whose lesser standing opened them up to discrimination and cruelty. All *maka'ainana* formed extended families *('ohana)* and usually lived on the same section of land *(ahupua'a)*. Inland farmers would barter their produce with fishermen; thus all shared equally in the bounty of the land and sea.

A special group called ***kauwa*** were a landless, untouchable caste confined to living on reservations. Their origins were obviously Polynesian, but they appeared to be descendants of castaways who had survived and become perhaps the aboriginals of Hawaii before the main migrations. It was *kapu* for anyone to go onto *kauwa* lands;

doing so meant instant death. A *kauwa* driven by necessity to leave his lands was required to cover his head with tapa cloth, his eyes focused on the ground in a humble manner. If a human sacrifice was needed, the *kahuna* simply summoned a *kauwa*, who had no recourse but to mutely comply. Through the years after discovery by Cook, the *kauwa* became obscured as a class and mingled with the remainder of the population. But even to this day, calling someone *kauwa*, which now supposedly only means servant, is still considered a fight-provoking insult.

## Kapu and Daily Life

Occasionally there were horrible wars, but mostly the people lived quiet and ordered lives based on a strict caste society and the *kapu* system. Famine was known but only on a regional level, and the population was kept in check by birth control, crude abortions, and the distasteful practice of infanticide, especially of baby girls. The Hawaiians were absolutely loving and nurturing parents under most circumstances, and would even take in *hanai* (adopted child or oldster), a lovely practice that lingers to this day.

A strict division of labor existed between men and women. Only men were permitted to have anything to do with taro, a foodstuff so sacred it had a greater *kapu* than humans themselves. Men pounded poi and served it to women. Men were also the fishermen and builders of houses, canoes, irrigation ditches, and walls. Women tended gardens and were responsible for making tapa and tending to shoreline fishing. The entire family lived in the common house *(hale noa)*. But certain things were *kapu* between the sexes. The primary *kapu* were entrance by a woman into the *mua* (men's house), nor could they eat with men. Certain foods such as pork, coconut, red fish, and bananas were forbidden to women. It was *kapu* for a man to have intercourse before going fishing, engaging in battle, or attending a religious ceremony. Young boys lived with the women until they underwent circumcision *(pule ipu)*, after which they were required to keep the *kapu* of men. A true Hawaiian settlement required a minimum of five huts: the men's eating hut, women's menstruation hut, women's eating hut, communal sleeping hut, and prayer hut. Without these five separate structures, Hawaiian "society" could not happen, since the *ia kapu* (forbidden eating between men and women) could not be observed.

*Ali'i* could also declare a *kapu*, and often did so. Certain lands or fishing areas were temporarily made *kapu* so they could revitalize. Even today, it is *kapu* for anyone to remove all the *'opihi* (a type of limpet) from a rock. The great King Kamehameha I even placed a *kapu* on the body of his notoriously unfaithful child bride, Ka'ahumanu. It didn't work! The greatest *kapu* *(kapu moe)* was afforded to the highest ranking *ali'i*: anyone coming into their presence had to prostrate themselves. Lesser ranking *ali'i* were afforded the *kapu noho*: lessers had to sit or kneel in their presence. Commoners could not let their shadows fall upon an *ali'i* or enter their houses except through a special door. Breaking a *kapu* meant immediate death.

## Fun and Games

The native Hawaiians loved sports. A type of "Olympiad" was held each year during the Makahiki Festival. Events included boxing, swimming, diving, surfing, and running. A form of bowling used polished, wheel-shaped stones that tested for distance and accuracy. Hawaiians also enjoyed a more cerebral, chesslike game called *konane*. Intricately carved *konane* boards survive to this day. Hawaiians built special downhill courses for a runnered bobsled called *holua*. Strangely enough, the Hawaiians developed a bow and arrow but never employed it in warfare. It was merely a toy for shooting at targets or rats.

The greatest sport of all was surfing. **Surfing** originated with the Hawaiians, and many old records recount this singularly exhilarating activity. The boards, made of various woods, were greatly cared for, measuring up to 15 feet long and six inches thick. James King, a lieutenant with Cook, was "altogether astonished" by surfing, and Reverend Ellis wrote in 1826, "to see fifty or a hundred persons riding on an immense billow . . . for a distance of several hundred yards together is one of the most novel and interesting sports a foreigner can witness in the islands."

## Ghosts

The Hawaiians had countless superstitions and ghost legends, but two of the more interesting involve astral travel of the soul and the "Marchers of the Night." The soul, 'uhane, was considered by Hawaiians to be totally free and independent of its body, kino. The soul could separate, leaving the body asleep or very drowsy. This disincorporated soul (hihi'o) could visit people and was considered quite different from a lapu, an ordinary spirit of a dead person. A kahuna could immediately recognize if a person's 'uhane had left the body, and a special wreath was placed upon the head for protection and to facilitate reentry. A person confronted by an apparition could test to see if it was indeed dead or still alive by placing leaves of an 'ape plant upon the ground. If the leaves tore when they were walked upon, the spirit was human, but if they remained intact it was a ghost. Also, you could sneak up and startle the vision, and if it disappeared it was a ghost. Also, if no reflection of the face appeared when it drank water from an offered calabash, it was a ghost. Unfortunately, there were no instructions to follow once you had determined you indeed had a ghost on your hands. Maybe it was better not to know! Some people would sprinkle salt and water around their houses, but this kept away evil spirits, not ghosts.

There are also many stories of kahuna restoring souls to dead bodies. First they had to catch one and keep it in a gourd. He then placed beautiful tapa and fragrant flowers and herbs about the body to make it more enticing. Slowly, the kahuna would coax the soul out of the gourd and get it to reenter the body through the big toe.

## Death Marchers

One inexplicable phenomenon that many people attest to is Ka Huaka'i o Ka Po, "Marchers of the Night." This march of the dead is fatal if you gaze upon it, unless one of the marchers happens to be a friendly ancestor who will protect you. The peak time for "the march" is 7:30 P.M.–2 A.M. The marchers can be dead ali'i and warriors, the gods themselves, or the lesser 'aumakua. When the 'aumakua march there is usually chanting and music. Ali'i marches are more somber. The entire procession, lit by torches, often stops at the house of a relative and might even carry him or her away. When the gods themselves march, there is often thunder, lightning, and heavy seas. The sky is lit with torches, and they walk six abreast, three gods and three goddesses. If you get in the way of a march, remove your clothing and prostrate yourself. If the marching gods or 'aumakua happen to be ones to which you pray, you might be spared. If it's a march of the ali'i, you might make it if you lie face upward and feign death. If you do see a death march, the last thing you'll worry about is lying naked on the ground and looking ridiculous.

# MISSIONARIES ONE AND ALL

In Hawaii, when you say "missionaries," it's taken for granted you're referring to the small and determined band of Congregationalists who arrived aboard the brig *Thaddeus* in 1820, and the "companies" or "packets" that reinforced them over the next 40 years. They were sent from Boston by the American Board of Commissioners for Foreign Missions (ABCFM), which learned of the supposed sad and godless plight of the Hawaiian people from returning sailors and especially through the few Hawaiians who had come to America to study.

The person most instrumental in bringing the missionaries to Hawaii was a young man named Henry 'Opukaha'ia. An orphan befriended by a captain and taken to New England, he studied theology and was obsessed with the desire to return home to save his people from sure damnation. His widely read accounts of life in Hawaii were the direct cause of the formation of the Pioneer Company to the Sandwich Islands Missions. Unfortunately, 'Opukaha'ia died in New England from typhus in 1819, the year before the missionaries sailed.

## "Civilizing" Hawaii

The first missionaries had the straightforward task of bringing the Hawaiians out of paganism and into Christianity and civilization. They met with extreme hostility—not from the natives, but from sea captains, sailors, and traders who were content with the open debauchery and wanton whoremongering that was the status quo in the Hawaii of 1820. The many direct confrontations between these two factions even included the cannonading of a missionary home by American sea captains who were denied the customary visits of island women, thanks to the meddlesome "do-gooders." The most memorable of these incidents involved "Mad Jack" Percival, the captain of the USS *Dolphin,* who bombed a church in Lahaina to show his rancor. In actuality, the truth of the situation was much closer to the sentiments of James Jarves, who wrote, "The missionary was a far more useful and agreeable man than his Catholicism would indicate; and the trader was not so bad a man as the missionary would make him out to be." The missionaries' primary aim might have been conversion, but the most fortuitous byproduct was education, which raised the consciousness of every Hawaiian regardless of religious affiliation. In 40 short years Hawaii was considered a civilized nation well on its way into the modern world, and the American Board of Missions officially ended its support in 1863.

Some of Hawaii's finest museums and grandest architecture are part of the missionary legacy. Some of the most notable are: Moku'aikaua Church in Kona, Hawai'i, the first Christian church, founded in 1820; the Lyman House Museum of Hilo; Kawaiaha'o Church in Honolulu, founded 1821, and next door the superb Mission Houses Museum; Waine'e Church, the first stone church in Hawaii, founded in Lahaina in 1828, and the Baldwin Home just down Front Street; and Lahainaluna High School and Printing House, the first American school and publishing house west of the Rockies. The churches, but especially the homes and museums, not only offer a glimpse of religious life, but are some of the finest "windows" into 19th-century America. Their collections of artifacts, utensils, and general memorabilia put the life and times of 19th-century Yankees in a setting that could hardly be more different from New England.

## Bonanza for Missionaries

Although the missionaries were the first, they by no means had the field to themselves. Hot on the same religious trail came the Catholics—French Sacred Hearts led by Father Bachelot, who arrived in Honolulu in July 1827 aboard *La Comete.* Immediately, Queen Ka'ahumanu, who had been converted by the Congregationalists, ordered them to leave. They refused. For the next 10 years the Catholic priests and their converts met with open hostility and persecution, which, in true missionary fashion, only strengthened their resolve. The humiliation of a young convert, Juliana Keawahine, who was tied to a tree and scourged, became a religious rallying point. After this incident the persecutions stopped. Honolulu's Our Lady of Peace Cathedral was completed in 1843, and 'Ahuimanu Catholic School, O'ahu's counterpart to Lahainaluna, opened for instruction in 1846. Today, Roman Catholicism, with 230,000 adherents, is the single largest religious group in Hawaii.

## The Saints Come Marching In

A strange episode in Hawaii's history involved the Mormons. In 1850, the Latter-day Saints arrived direct from missionary work in California gold fields. By 1852, George Cannon had already translated the *Book of Mormon* into Hawaiian. The five original Mormon missionaries spent every moment traveling and converting the Hawaiians. They had a grand plan of constructing a "City of Joseph" on Lana'i, where they managed to gain a large tract of land. In 1858 the Mormon Wars broke out in Utah, and the missionaries were called home. One of their band, Walter Murray Gibson, who stayed to manage the fledgling Mormon church, became one of the most controversial and singularly strange fixtures in Hawaiian politics. When the Mormons returned in 1864, they found Gibson had indeed carried on the "City of Joseph," but he had manipulated all of the deeds and land grants into his personal possession. Furthermore, he had set himself up as an omnipotent grand patriarch and openly denounced the polygamous beliefs of the Mormons of the day. Immediately excommunicated, Gibson was abandoned to his fate, and the Mormons moved to O'ahu, where they founded a sugar plantation and temple in La'ie.

The Church of Jesus Christ of the Latter-day Saints now has approximately 40,000 members, the largest Protestant denomination in Hawaii. Their settlement on Oʻahu at Laʻie is now home to an impressive Mormon Temple and an island branch of Brigham Young University. Close by, the Mormons also operate the Polynesian Cultural Center, which is one of the top tourist attractions in all of Hawaii.

As for Gibson, he was elected to the legislature in 1876 and became a private counselor to King Kalakaua. In 1882, he worked himself into the office of "Premier," which he ran like a petty dictator. One of his more visionary suggestions was to import Japanese labor. Two of his most ridiculous were to drive non-Hawaiians from the islands (excluding himself) and to gather Oceania into one Pacific nation with Hawaii at the forefront. By 1887 he and Kalakaua had so infuriated the sugar planters that Gibson was railroaded out of the islands and Kalakaua was forced to sign a constitution that greatly limited his power. Gibson died in 1888, and his daughter Talulah and her husband sold the lands on Lanaʻi for a song after they tried but failed to grow sugarcane.

## Non-Christian

By the turn of the 20th century, Shintoism and Buddhism, brought by the Japanese and Chinese, were firmly established in Hawaii. The first official Buddhist temple was Hongpa Hongwanji, established on Oʻahu in 1889. All denominations of Buddhism account for 17 percent of the island's religious total, and there are about 50,000 Shintoists. The Hindu religion has perhaps 2,000 adherents, and roughly 10,000 Jewish people live throughout Hawaii. About 10,000 island residents are in new religious movements and lesser-known faiths such as Bahaʻi and Unitarianism. A large number of people in Hawaii remain unaffiliated.

# Arts and Music

Referring to Hawaii as "paradise" is about as hackneyed as you can get, but when you combine it into "artists' paradise" it's the absolute truth. Something about the place evokes art (or at least personal expression) from most people. The islands are like a magnet: they not only draw artists to them, but they draw art *from* the artists. The list of literary figures who visited Hawaii and had something inspirational to say reads like a freshman survey in literature: William Henry Dana, Herman Melville, Mark Twain, Robert Louis Stevenson, Jack London, Somerset Maugham, Joaquin Miller, and of course James Michener.

The inspiration comes from the astounding natural surroundings. The land is so beautiful yet so raw; the ocean's power and rhythm are primal and ever-present; the riotous colors of flowers and fruit leap from the deep-green jungle background. Crystal water beads and pale mists turn the mountains into mystic temples, while rainbows ride the crests of waves. The stunning variety of faces begging to be rendered suggests that all the world sent delegations to the islands.

And in most cases it did! Inspiration is everywhere, as is art, good or bad.

Sometimes the artwork is overpowering in itself and in its sheer volume. Though geared to the tourist's market of cheap souvenirs, there is hardly a shop in Hawaii that doesn't sell some item that falls into the general category of "art." You can find everything from carved monkey-face coconut shells to true masterpieces. The Polynesian Hawaiians were master craftspeople, and their legacy still lives in a wide variety of wood carvings, basketry, and weavings. The hula is art in swaying motion, and the true form is rigorously studied and taken very seriously. There is hardly a resort area that doesn't offer the "bump and grind" tourist's hula, but even these revues are accompanied by proficient local musicians. Nightclubs offer "slack key" balladeers; island music performed on ukuleles and on Hawaii's own steel guitars spills from many lounges.

Vibrant fabrics that catch the spirit of the islands are rendered into muʻumuʻu and aloha shirts at countless local factories. They're almost a mandatory purchase! Pottery, heavily influenced by the Japanese, is a well-developed craft at numerous kilns. Local artisans fashion delicate jewelry from coral and olivine, while some ply the whaler's craft of etching on ivory, called scrimshaw. There are fine traditions of quilting, flower art in lei, and street artists working in everything from airbrush to glass.

## ARTS OF OLD HAWAII

Since everything in old Hawaii had to be fashioned by hand, almost every object was either a genuine work of art or the product of a highly refined craft. With the "civilizing" of the natives, most of the "old ways" disappeared, including the old arts and crafts. Most authentic Hawaiian art exists only in museums, but with the resurgence of Hawaiian roots, many old arts are being revitalized, and a few artists are becoming proficient in them.

### Magnificent Canoes

The most respected artisans in old Hawaii were the canoe makers. With little more than a stone adze and a pump drill, they built canoes that could carry 200 people and last for generations—sleek, well proportioned, and infinitely seaworthy. The main hull was usually a gigantic koa log, and the gunwale planks were minutely drilled and sewn to the sides with sennit rope. Apprenticeships lasted for years, and a young man knew that he had graduated when one day he was nonchalantly asked to sit down and eat with the master builders. Small family-size canoes with outriggers were used for fishing and perhaps carried a spear rack; large oceangoing double-hulled canoes were used for migration and warfare. On these, the giant logs had been adzed to about two inches thick. A mainsail woven from pandanus was mounted on a central platform, and the boat was steered by two long paddles. The hull was dyed with plant juices and charcoal, and the entire village helped launch the canoe in a ceremony called "drinking the sea."

### Carving and Weaving

Wood was a primary material used by Hawaiian craftsmen. They almost exclusively used koa because of its density, strength, and natural luster. It was turned into canoes, woodware, calabashes, and furniture used by the *ali'i*. Temple idols were another major product of wood carving. A variety of stone artifacts were turned out, including poi pounders, mirrors, fish sinkers, and small idols.

Hawaiians became the best basket makers and mat weavers in all of Polynesia. *Ulana* (mats) were made from *lau hala* (pandanus) leaves. Once split, the spine was removed and the leaves stored in large rolls. When needed they were soaked, pounded, and then fashioned into various floor coverings and sleeping mats. Intricate geometrical patterns were woven in, and the edges were rolled and well fashioned. Coconut palms were not used to make mats in old Hawaii, but a wide variety of basketry was made from the aerial root *'ie'ie*. The shapes varied according to use. Some baskets were tall and narrow, some were cones, others were flat like trays, while many were woven around gourds and calabashes.

A strong tradition of weaving and carving has survived in Hawaii, and the time-tested material of *lau hala* is still the best, although much is now made from coconut fronds. You can purchase anything from beach mats to a woven hat, and all share the desirable qualities of strength, lightness, and ventilation.

### Featherwork

This highly refined art was found only on the islands of Tahiti, New Zealand, and Hawaii, while the fashioning of feather helmets and idols was unique to Hawaii. Favorite colors were red and yellow, which came only in a very limited supply from a small number of birds such as the *'o'o, 'i'iwi, mamo,* and *'apapane*. Professional bird hunters in old Hawaii paid their taxes to *ali'i* in prized feathers. The feathers were fastened to a woven net of *olona* cord and made into helmets, idols, and beautiful flowing capes and cloaks. These resplendent garments were made and worn only by men, especially during battle when a fine cloak became a great trophy of war. Featherwork was also employed in the making of *kahili* and lei, which were highly prized by the noble *ali'i* women.

## Tapa Cloth

Tapa, cloth made from tree bark, was common throughout Polynesia and was a woman's art. A few trees such as the *wauke* and *mamaki* produced the best cloth, but other types could be utilized. First the raw bark was pounded into a feltlike pulp and beaten together to form strips (the beaters had distinctive patterns that also helped make the cloth supple). They were then decorated by stamping (using a form of block printing) and then were dyed with natural colors from plants and sea animals in shades of gray, purple, pink, and red. They were even painted with natural brushes made from pandanus fruit, with an overall gray color made from charcoal. The tapa cloth was sewn together to make bed coverings, and fragrant flowers and herbs were either sewn or pounded in to produce a permanent fragrance. Tapa cloth is still available today, but the Hawaiian methods have been lost, and most comes from other areas of Polynesia.

## First Western Artists

When Captain Cook made first contact in 1778, the ship's artists immediately began recording things Hawaiian. John Webber and James Clevely made etchings and pen-and-ink drawings of Hawaiian people, structures, *heiau*, and everyday occurrences that struck them as noteworthy or peculiar. William Ellis, ship's surgeon, also a fair hand at etching, was attracted to portraying native architecture. These three left a priceless and faithful record of what Hawaii was like at the moment of contact. Louis Choris, ship's artist with Otto Von Kotzebue in 1816, painted early portraits of King Kamehameha and Queen Ka'ahumanu, the two grandest figures in Hawaii's history. Jacques Arago, aboard the *Uranie* with the French Captain de Freycinet in 1819, recorded some gruesome customs of punishment of *kapu* breakers and made many drawings of island people. Robert Dampier, who sailed on the *Blonde,* the ship that returned King Liholiho's body from England, recorded one of the earliest landscapes of Honolulu, a site that has continued to be depicted more on film by tourists than almost any other city on earth. These early artists set a trend that continues unabated to this day; artists endeavor to "capture" Hawaii, and they do so with every medium available.

## Modern Masters

Countless artists working at all levels of accomplishment try to match their skills to the vigor and beauty of the islands. Some have set the standards, and their names have become synonymous with Hawaiian art. Heading this list of luminaries are Huc Luquiens, Madge Tennent, Tadashi Sato, Jean Charlot, and John Kelly.

Madge Tennent (1889–1972) was an Englishwoman who came to Hawaii via Samoa after spending years in South Africa and New Zealand. She worked in oils that she applied liberally and in bold strokes. Enamored with the people of Hawaii, her portraits are of a race striking in appearance and noble in character. Her works, along with those of other island artists, are displayed at the Tennent Art Foundation, on the slopes of Punchbowl on O'ahu.

Huc Luquiens, former chair of the art department at the University of Hawai'i, was a master at etching, especially in drypoint. His works, mainly island landscapes, are displayed in the Hawaiiana Collection of the Honolulu Academy of Arts.

Maui-born Tadashi Sato, a superbly accomplished muralist, has produced such famous mosaics as the 30-foot *Aquarius* (at the state capitol in Honolulu) and the 60-foot *Portals of Immortality* (at the Maui Memorial Gymnasium in Lahaina).

Frenchman Jean Charlot perfected his mural art in Mexico before coming to Hawaii in 1949. He is renowned for his frescoes and became a well-known art critic and the grand old man of Hawaiian art. He died in 1979 at 90.

John M. Kelly was in love with Hawaiian women; his etchings of them are both inspired and technically flawless. Kelly was infinitely patient, rendering his subjects in the minutest detail.

These artists are the "Big Five of Hawaiian Art"; their accomplishments are a gauge of what Hawaii can inspire in an artist. By observing their works you can get an instant art course and a comparative view of the state of the arts in Hawaii.

## Contemporary Artists

The crop of new artists making their marks always seems bounteous, and their works, heavily influenced by the "feeling of Hawaii," continue to be superb. Every island has art galleries, co-ops, or unofficial art centers. One of the finest groups of island artists can be found along the "fence" of the Honolulu Zoo fronting Kapi'olani Park. The following list of artists, with a short description of their work, is by no means exhaustive. It merely shows the wide range of artwork available.

Roy Tabora specializes in dramatic sea-scapes of windwhipped palm trees and crashing surf illuminated by glorious sunsets. His work is a dramatic crescendo of sea, surf, and spirit, entwined to capture the awesome power that is Hawaii.

James Hoyle, a longtime Kaua'i resident, captures the spirit of Hawaii through color and movement. His media are oil, pastel, and polymer that he applies on canvas in a distinctive style of macro-pointillism. The sense that permeates all of Hoyle's work is that humankind cannot conquer nature but must learn to live in harmony with the 'aina, which is very much alive.

Robert Nelson is a Maui artist who superbly transmits the integrated mystical life of land and sea. His watercolors are often diffused with the strange filtered light found beneath the waves. A conservationist, he has often depicted the gentle frolicking life of the whales that visit Hawaiian waters.

Bill Christian is a master of scrimshaw, which he renders on slate. He also produces fine oil paintings of the sea and old salts. A world-class artist, he

has had his works displayed at art galleries on Maui as well as at the Smithsonian and at the New Bedford Massachusetts Whaling Museum.

Pegge Hopper is often compared to Madge Tennent. She works in bold colors and strokes. Her subject matter is islanders, especially the delicacy and inner strength of women. Her works are displayed at various galleries and are often available in limited-edition serigraphs.

Alapai Hanapi is a traditionalist sculptor who re-creates the motifs of his Hawaiian ancestors. He works in wood and stone with tools that he fashions himself. His driving force is cultural awareness, and through his art he tells of the old ways. His work is known for its simplicity.

Al Furtado is a freelance artist working in Honolulu. He specializes in capturing the movement of Hawaiian dance. His depictions are often larger than life, with a strong sense of vitality and motion.

Daniel Wang was born in Shanghai, where he learned the art of Chinese watercolors. Although born deaf and mute, he speaks loudly, clearly, and beautifully through his art. Daniel has a special technique in which the palm of his hand becomes his artistic tool. He can transmit intense inner emotions directly from his body to the canvas.

The following is a potpourri of distinguished artists displayed at various galleries around the islands. Any work bearing one of their names is authentic island art considered superior by fellow artists: William Waterfall, photographer; Satoru Abe, sculptor; Ruthadell Anderson, weaver; Betty Tseng Yu-ho Ecke, *dsui* painter; Claude Horan, sculptor, ceramics; Erica Karawina, stained glass; Ron Kowalke, painter; Ben Norris, painter; Louis Pohl, printmaker; Mamoru Sato, sculptor; Reuben Tam, painter; Jean Williams, weaver; John Wisnosky, painter; and John Young, painter.

## ARTS TO BUY

Wild Hawaiian shirts or bright mu'umu'u, especially when worn on the Mainland, have the magical effect of making wearers "feel" like they're in Hawaii, while at the same time eliciting spontaneous smiles from passersby. Maybe it's the colors, or perhaps it's just the "vibe" that signifies

---

### GICLÉE

**M**any galleries now offer unbelievable prints produced by a rather expensive computer-based method called *giclée*. A picture of the original is made into a transparency that is scanned to match subtle strokes and color variations perfectly, and then airbrushed at four million droplets per second (each one-fourth the diameter of a human hair) onto paper or canvas, creating a cyberspace copy of near-perfect similarity to the original.

"party time" or "hang loose," but nothing says Hawaii like alohawear does. More than a dozen fabric houses in Hawaii turn out distinctive patterns, and many dozens of factories create their own personalized designs. These factories often have attached retail outlets, but in any case you can find hundreds of shops selling alohawear. Aloha shirts were the brilliant idea of a Chinese merchant in Honolulu, who used to hand-tailor them and then sell them to the tourists who arrived by ship in the glory days before World War II. They were an instant success. Mu'umu'u or "Mother Hubbards" were the idea of missionaries, who were appalled by Hawaiian women running about au naturel and insisted on covering their new Christian converts from head to foot. Now the roles are reversed, and it's Mainlanders who come to Hawaii and immediately strip down to as little clothing as possible.

### Alohawear

At one time alohawear was exclusively made of cotton or from man-made, natural fiber-based rayon, and these materials are still best for any tropical clothing. Beware, however: polyester has slowly crept into the market. No material could possibly be worse for the island climate, so when buying your alohawear make sure to check the label for material content. Mu'umu'u now come in various styles and can be worn for the entire spectrum of social occasions in Hawaii. Aloha shirts are basically cut the same as always, but the patterns have undergone changes, and besides the original flowers and ferns, modern shirts might depict an island scene in the manner of a silk-screen painting. A basic good-quality mu'umu'u or aloha shirt is guaranteed to be worth its price in good times and happy smiles. The connoisseur might want to purchase *The Hawaiian Shirt, Its Art and History,* by R. Thomas Steele. It's illustrated with more than 150 shirts that are now considered works of art by collectors the world over.

BOB RACE

scrimshaw of whaling scene

### Scrimshaw

This art of etching and carving on bone and ivory has become an island tradition handed down from the times of the old whaling ships. Although scrimshaw can be found throughout Hawaii, the center remains in the old whaling capital of Lahaina. There along Front Street a few shops specialize in scrimshaw. Today, pieces are carved on fossilized walrus ivory that is gathered by Inuit and shipped to Hawaii. It comes in a variety of shades from pure white to mocha, depending upon the mineral content of the earth in which it was buried. Elephant ivory or whale bone is no longer used because of ecological considerations, but there is a "gray market" in Pacific walrus tusks. Inuit can legally hunt the walrus. They then make a few minimal scratches on the tusks, which technically qualifies them to be "Native American art" and free of most governmental restrictions. The tusks are then sent to Hawaii as art objects, but the superficial scratches are immediately removed and the ivory is reworked by artisans. Scrimshaw is made into everything from belt buckles to delicate earrings and even into coffee-table centerpieces. The prices can go from a few dollars up into the thousands.

### Wood Carvings

One surviving Hawaiian art is wood carving. Old Hawaiians used koa almost exclusively because of its density, strength, and natural luster, but koa is becoming increasingly scarce. Many items are still available, but they are costly. Milo and monkeypod are also excellent woods for carving and have largely replaced koa. You can buy tikis, bowls, and furniture at numerous shops. Countless inexpensive carved items, such as hula dancers or salad servers, are sold at variety stores, but most of these are imported from Asia or the Philippines and can be bought at any variety store.

## Weaving

The minute you arrive in Hawaii you should shell out a few dollars for a woven beach mat. This is a necessity, not a frivolous purchase, but it definitely won't have been made in Hawaii. What is made in Hawaii is *lau hala*. This is traditional Hawaiian weaving from the leaves *(lau)* of the pandanus *(hala)* tree. These leaves vary greatly in length, with the largest more than six feet, and they have a thorny spine that must be removed before they can be worked. The color ranges from light tan to dark brown. The leaves are cut into strips from one-eighth to one inch wide and are then employed in weaving. Any variety of items can be made or at least covered in *lau hala*. It makes great purses, mats, baskets, and table mats.

Woven into a hat, it's absolutely superb but should not be confused with a palm-frond hat. A *lau hala* hat is amazingly supple and even when squashed will pop back into shape. A good one is expensive and with proper care will last for years. All *lau hala* should be given a light application of mineral oil on a monthly basis, especially if it's exposed to the sun. For flat items, iron over a damp cloth and keep purses and baskets stuffed with paper when not in use. Palm fronds also are widely used in weaving. They, too, are a great natural raw material, but not as good as *lau hala*. Almost any woven item, such as a beach bag, makes a good authentic yet inexpensive gift or souvenir.

## Gift Items

Jewelry is always an appreciated gift, especially if it's distinctive, and Hawaii has some of the most original. The sea provides the basic raw materials of pink, gold, and black corals, which are as beautiful and fascinating as gemstones. Harvesting coral is very dangerous work. The Lahaina beds off Maui have one of the best black coral lodes in the islands, but unlike reef coral these trees grow at depths bordering the outer limits of a scuba diver's capabilities. Only the best can dive 180 feet after the black coral, and about one diver per year dies in pursuit of it. Conservationists have placed great pressure on the harvesters of these deep corals, and the state of Hawaii has created strict limits and guidelines on the firms and divers involved.

Pink coral has long been treasured by humans. The Greeks considered it a talisman for good health, and there's even evidence that it has been coveted since the Stone Age. Coral jewelry is on sale at many shops throughout Hawaii, its value determined by the color of the coral and the workmanship.

*Puka* shells (with small, naturally occurring holes) and *'opihi* shells are also made into jewelry. Many times these items are very inexpensive, yet they are authentic and great purchases for the price. Hanging macramé planters festooned with seashells are usually quite affordable and sold at roadside stands along with shells.

Hawaii produces some unique food items that are appreciated by many people. Various-size jars of macadamia nuts and butters are great gifts, as are tins of rich, gourmet-quality Kona coffee. Guava, pineapple, passion fruit, and mango are often gift-boxed into assortments of jams, jellies, and spicy chutneys. And for that special person in your life, you can bring home island fragrances in bottles of perfumes and colognes in the exotic smells of gardenia, plumeria, and even ginger. All of the above items are reasonably priced, lightweight, and easy to carry.

# LANGUAGE OF THE LEI

The goddess Hi'iaka is Pele's youngest sister, and although many gods are depicted wearing flower garlands, the lei is most associated with her. Perhaps this is because Hi'iaka is the goddess of mercy and protection, qualities that the lei is deemed to symbolize. Hi'iaka traveled throughout the islands destroying evil spirits wherever she found them. In the traditional translation of "The Song of the Islands" by Reverend Samuel Kapu, the last verses read, "We all call to you, answer us o Hi'iaka, the woman who travels the seas. This is the conclusion of our song, o wreaths of Hawaii, respond to our call." A special day, May 1, is Lei Day in Hawaii. It started in 1928 as a project of Don Blanding, an island poet.

Hardly a more beautiful tradition exists anywhere in the world than placing a flower garland around the neck of someone special. The traditional time to give a lei is when someone is arriving or departing the islands, so every airport has lei sellers, mostly older women who have a little booth at the entrance to the airport. But lei are worn on every occasion, from marriages to funerals, and are equally apt to appear around the lovely neck of a hula dancer or as a floral hatband on the grizzled head of an old *paniolo*, or even draped around his horse's neck. In old Hawaii lei were given to the local *ali'i* as a sign of affection. When two warring chiefs sat together and wove a lei, it meant the end of hostilities and symbolized the circle of peace.

## Lei Making

Any flower or blossom can be strung into a lei, but the most common are carnations or the lovely smelling plumeria. Lei, like babies, are all beautiful, but special lei are highly prized by those who know what to look for. Of the different stringing styles, the most common is *kui*—stringing the flower through the middle or side. Most "airport-quality" lei are of this type. The *humuhumu* style, reserved for making flat lei, is made by sewing flowers and ferns to a *ti*, banana, or sometimes *hala* leaf. A *humuhumu* lei makes an excellent hatband. *Wili* is the winding together of greenery, ferns, and flowers into short, bouquet-type lengths. The most traditional form is *hili*, which requires no stringing at all but involves braiding fragrant ferns and leaves such as *maile*. If flowers are interwoven, the *hili* becomes the *haku* style, the most difficult and most beautiful type of lei.

## The Lei of the Land

Every major island is symbolized by its own lei made from a distinctive flower, shell, or fern. Each island has its own official color as well, though it doesn't necessarily correspond to the color of the island's lei.

The island of Hawai'i's lei is made from the red (or rare creamy white or orange) *lehua* blossom. The *lehua* tree grows from sea level to 9,000 feet and produces an abundance of tufted flowers. The official color of Hawai'i Island, like the lava from its active volcanoes, is red.

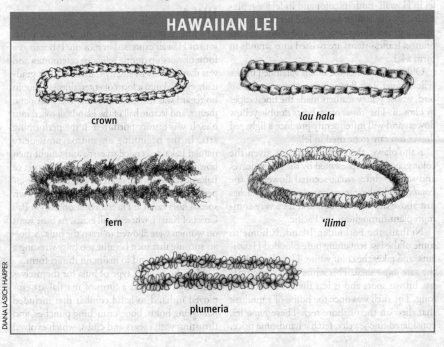

## HAWAIIAN LEI

crown

lau hala

fern

'ilima

plumeria

DIANA LASICH HARPER

Kaua'i, oldest of the main islands, is represented by the *mokihana* lei and the regal color purple. The *mokihana* tree produces a small, cubelike fruit that smells like anise. Green when strung into Kaua'i's lei, the fruit turn a dark brown and keep their scent for months.

Maui is the pink island, and its lei is the corresponding small pink rose called the *lokelani*. These flowers are not native but were imported and widely cultivated at one time. In recent years they've fallen prey to a rose beetle, and sometimes when they're scarce *roselani* is substituted for Maui's lei.

Moloka'i is the silvery green island, and its lei is fashioned from the green leaves and small white flowers of the *kukui* tree. After it's shaped and polished, the *kukui* nut makes some of the most permanent and beautiful lei for sale in Hawaii. *Kukui* nut lei are quite common and make excellent gifts. Although not the official lei of any island, they could easily be the official lei representing all the islands.

Lana'i has one of the most traditional forms of lei in Hawaii. Both its color and its lei are represented by the orange *kaunaoa*. This plant commonly grows along beaches and roadsides. Its orange, leafless stems are twisted into strands to form a lei.

O'ahu, the color of the sun, is garlanded by the yellow *'ilima*. This flower is reminiscent of the *'o'o* bird, whose yellow feathers made the finest capes in Hawaii. The *'ilima* often bears double yellow flowers and will infrequently produce a light red flower too rare to be used in lei.

Kaho'olawe, the sacred island, is given the color gray and is represented by the silvery leaves and small, white, sweet-scented flowers of the *hinahina*. This heliotrope grows on sandy beaches just above the high-water mark; it's a very common plant throughout the Pacific.

Ni'ihau, the Forbidden Island, is home to some of the last remaining pure-blooded Hawaiians, and takes the color white. The island's lei is the rare *pupu* shell. This white shell sometimes has brown spots and is less than one-half inch long. The shell was once the home of a mollusk that died on the offshore reef. These *pupu* lei, considered fine jewelry, fetch a handsome price.

Very cheap facsimiles made of *pikake* shells are sold everywhere; most have been imported from the Cook and Society Islands of the South Pacific.

The last island is the semi-submerged volcano of Molokini, just off Maui's south shore. Molokini is represented by the very traditional lei made from *limu kala*, a brown, coarse seaweed with feathery spiny leaves that makes a boa-type lei.

Besides these island lei, two others must be mentioned. A lei made from *maile* is perhaps the most traditional of all. *Maile* is a green, leafy vine. Its stiff, bonelike inner stem is removed, leaving the leaves and pliable bark intact, which are then twisted into lei. They might be ordinary to look at, but they have a delicious smell that is Hawaii. *Maile* is often used in conjunction with flowers to make top-notch lei. *Laua'e* is a common fern with large, coarse, shiny leaves. It is used to fluff out many lei; when bruised, the leaves have a mild scent of *maile*. Lei have one quality that is unsurpassed: they feel just as good to give as they do to receive.

# HULA

The hula is more than an ethnic dance; it is the soul of Hawaii expressed in motion. It began as a form of worship during religious ceremonies and was danced only by highly trained men. It gradually evolved into a form of entertainment, but in no regard was it sexual. The hula was the opera, theater, and lecture hall of the islands all rolled into one. It was history portrayed in the performing arts. In the beginning an androgynous deity named Laka descended to earth and taught men how to dance the hula. In time the male aspect of Laka departed for the heavens, but the female aspect remained. The female Laka set up her own special hula *heiau* at Ha'ena Point on the Na Pali Coast of Kaua'i, where it still exists. As time went on women were allowed to learn the hula. Scholars surmise that men became too busy wresting a living from the land to maintain the art form.

Men did retain a type of hula for themselves called *lua*. This was a form of martial art employed in hand-to-hand combat that included paralyzing holds, bone-crunching punches, and thrusting with spears and clubs, which evolved into a ritualized warfare dance called *hula kui*. During the 19th century, the hula almost vanished because the missionaries considered it vile and heathen. King Kalakaua is generally regarded as saving it during the 1800s, when he formed his own troupe and encouraged the dancers to learn the old hula. Many of the original dances were forgotten, but some were retained and are performed to this day. Although professional dancers were highly trained, everyone took part in the hula. *Ali'i*, commoners, young, and old all danced. Early drawings by ships' artists like Arago, Choris, and Webber recorded hula scenes. Old folks even did it sitting down if their legs were too weak to perform some of the gyrations.

## Hula Training

Only the most beautiful, graceful, and elegant girls were chosen to enter the hula *halau* (school). At one time, the *halau* was a temple in its own right, and the girls who entered at the ages of four or five would emerge as accomplished dancers in their early teens to begin lifelong careers of the highest honor. In the *halau*, the *haumana* (pupils) were under the strict and total guidance of the *kumu* (teacher), and many *kapu* were placed upon them. The hula was a subordination of gross strength into a sublime coupling of grace and elegance. Once a woman became a proficient and accomplished dancer, her hula showed a personal, semi-spontaneous interpretation based upon past experiences. Today, *hula halau* are active on every island, teaching hula and keeping the old ways and culture alive. (Ancient hula is called *hula kahiko* and modern renditions are known as *hula auana*.) Performers still spend years perfecting their techniques. They show off their accomplishments during the fierce competition of the Merrie Monarch Festival in Hilo every April. The winning *halau* is praised and recognized throughout the islands.

## The Special World of Hula

Hawaiian hula was never performed in grass skirts; tapa or *ti*-leaf skirts were worn. Grass skirts came to Hawaii from the Gilbert Islands, so if you see grass or cellophane skirts in a "hula revue," it's not traditional. Almost every major resort offering entertainment or a lu'au also offers a revue. Most times, young island beauties accompanied by local musicians put on a floor show for the tourists. It'll be fun, but it won't be traditional. A hula dancer has to learn how to control every part of her or his body, including facial expressions, which help set the mood. The hands are extremely important and provide instant background scenery. For example, if the hands are thrust outward in an aggressive manner, this can mean a battle; if they sway gently overhead, they refer to the gods or to creation; they can easily become rain, clouds, sun, sea, or moon. Watch the hands to get the gist of the story, though in the words of one wise guy, "You watch the parts you like, and I'll watch the parts I like!" The motion of swaying hips can denote a long walk, a canoe ride, or sexual intercourse. Foot motion can portray a battle, a walk, or any kind of conveyance. The overall effect is multidirectional synchronized movement. The correct chanting of the *mele* is an integral part of the performance. These story chants, accompanied by musical instruments, make the hula very much like opera; it is especially similar in the way the tale unfolds.

## Hula Music

Accompaniment is provided by chants called *mele* or *oli* and by a wide variety of instruments. The *ipu* is a primary hula instrument made of two gourds fastened together. It's thumped on a mat and slapped with the hand. In the background is the steady rhythm of the *pahu*, a large bass drum made from a hollowed coconut or breadfruit tree log and covered with a sharkskin membrane. Hawaii's largest drum, it was sometimes placed on a pedestal and used in ceremonies at the *heiau*. The *'uli 'uli* is a gourd or coconut filled with shells or pebbles and used like rattles, while *'ili 'ili* are stones clicked together like castanets. The *punui* is a small drum made from a coconut shell half and beaten in counterpoint to the *ipu*. Oftentimes it was played by the hula dancer, who had it fastened to her body as a knee drum. The *pu'ili* is a length of bamboo split at one end to look like a whisk, and when struck against the body it makes a rattling noise, while the *ka'eke'eke* and *kalau* are bamboo cut to various lengths and struck to make a rudimentary xylophonic sound. Two unique instruments are the *kupe'e niho 'ilio,* a dog's tooth rattle worn as an ankle bracelet by men only, now replaced by sea shells; and an *'ohe hano ihu,* a nose flute of bamboo that accompanied chants. None of these instruments are actually necessary to perform a hula. All that's needed are a dancer and a chant.

# THAT GOOD OLD ISLAND MUSIC

The missionaries usually take a beating when it's recounted how much Hawaiian culture they destroyed while "civilizing" the natives. However, they seem to have done one thing right. They introduced the Hawaiians to the diatonic musical scale and immediately opened a door to latent and superbly harmonious talent. Before the missionaries, the Hawaiians knew little about melody. Though sonorous, their *mele* were repetitive chants in which the emphasis was placed on historical accuracy and not on "making music." The Hawaiians, in short, didn't *sing.* But within a few years of the missionaries' arrival, they were belting out good old Christian hymns, and one of their favorite pastimes became group and individual singing.

Early in the 1800s, Spanish *vaqueros* from California were imported to teach the Hawaiians how to be cowboys. With them came guitars and moody ballads. The Hawaiian *paniolo* (cowboys) quickly learned how to punch cows and croon away the long lonely nights on the range. Immigrants who came along a little later in the 19th century, especially from Portugal, helped create a Hawaiian-style music. Their biggest influence was a small, four-stringed instrument called a *braga* or *cavaquinho.* One owned by Augusto Dias was the prototype of a homegrown Hawaiian instrument that became known as the ukulele. "Jumping flea," the translation of ukulele, is an appropriate name devised by the Hawaiians when they saw how nimble the fingers were as they "jumped" over the strings.

King Kalakaua (the Merrie Monarch) and Queen Lili'uokalani were both patrons of the arts who furthered the Hawaiian musical identity at the turn of the 20th century. Kalakaua revived the hula and was also a gifted lyricist and balladeer. He wrote the words to "Hawaii Pono," which became the national anthem of Hawaii and later the state anthem. Lili'uokalani wrote the hauntingly beautiful "Aloha O'e," which is often pointed to as the "spirit of Hawaii" in music. Detractors say that its melody is extremely close to the old Christian hymn, "Rock Beside the Sea," but the lyrics are so beautiful and perfectly fitted that this doesn't matter.

Just prior to Kalakaua's reign a Prussian bandmaster, Captain Henry Berger, was invited to head the fledgling Royal Hawaiian Band, which he turned into a very respectable orchestra lauded by many visitors to the islands. Berger was openminded and learned to love Hawaiian music. He collaborated with Kalakaua and other island musicians to incorporate their music into a Western format. He headed the band for 43 years until 1915, and was instrumental in making music a serious pursuit of talented Hawaiians.

## Popular Hawaiian Music

Hawaiian music has a unique twang, a special feeling that says the same thing to everyone who hears it: "Relax, sit back in the moonlight, watch the swaying palms as the surf sings a lullaby." This special sound is epitomized by the bouncy ukulele, the falsettos of Hawaiian crooners, and by the smooth ring of the "steel" or "Hawaiian" guitar. The steel guitar is a variation originated by Joseph Kekuku in the 1890s. Stories abound of how Joseph Kekuku devised this instrument; the most popular versions say that Joe dropped his comb or pocketknife on his guitar strings and liked what he heard. Driven by the faint rhythm of an inner sound, he went to the machine shop at the Kamehameha Schools and turned out a steel bar for sliding over the strings. To complete the sound he changed the cat-gut strings to steel and raised them so they wouldn't hit the frets. Voila!— Hawaiian music as the world knows it today.

The first melodious strains of **slack-key guitar** *(ki ho'alu)* can be traced back to the time of Kamehameha III and the *vaqueros* from California. The Spanish had their way of tuning the guitar, and played difficult and aggressive music that did not sit well with Hawaiians, who were much more gentle and casual in their manners.

Hawaiians soon became adept at making their own music. At first, one person played the melody, but it lacked fullness. There was no body to the sound. So, as one *paniolo* fooled with the melody, another soon learned to play bass, which added depth. But, a player was often alone, and by experimenting he or she learned to get the right hand going with the melody and play the bass note with the thumb to improve the sound. Singers also learned that they could "open tune" the guitar to match their rich voices.

Hawaiians believed knowledge was sacred, and what is sacred should be treated with utmost respect—which meant keeping it secret, except from sincere apprentices. Guitar playing became a personal art form whose secrets were closely guarded, handed down only to family members, and only to those who showed ability and determination. When old-time slack-key guitar players were done strumming, they loosened all the strings so no one could figure out how they had them tuned. If they were playing, and some folks came by who were interested and weren't part of the family, the Hawaiians stopped what they were doing, put their guitars down, and put their feet across the strings to wait for the folks to go away. As time went on, more and more Hawaiians began to play slack key, and a common repertoire emerged.

An accomplished musician could easily figure out the simple songs, once they had figured out how the family had tuned the guitar. One of the most popular tunings was the "open G." Old Hawaiian folks called it the "taro patch tune." Different songs came out, and if you were in their family and were interested in the guitar, they took the time to sit down and teach you. The way they taught was straightforward—and a test of your sincerity at the same time. The old master would start to play. He just wanted you to listen and get a feel for the music—nothing more than that. You brought your guitar and *listened*. When you felt it, you played it, and the knowledge was transferred. Today, only a handful of slack-key guitar players know how

to play the classic tunes classically. The best-known and perhaps greatest slack-key player was Gabby Pahinui, with The Sons of Hawaii. When he passed away he left many recordings behind. A slack-key master still singing and playing is Raymond Kane. Kane now teaches a handful of students his wonderful and haunting music. Not one of his students is from his own family, and most are *haole* musicians trying to preserve the classical method of playing.

Hawaiian music received its biggest boost from a remarkable radio program known as *Hawaii Calls*. This program sent out its music from the Banyan Court of the Moana Hotel from 1935 until 1975. At its peak in the mid-1950s, it was syndicated on more than 700 radio stations throughout the world. Ironically, Japanese pilots heading for Pearl Harbor tuned in island music as a signal beam. Some internationally famous classic tunes came out of the 1940s and '50s. Jack Pitman composed "Beyond the Reef" in 1948; more than 300 artists have recorded it and it has sold well over 12 million records. Other million-sellers include: "Sweet Leilani," "Lovely Hula Hands," "The Crosseyed Mayor of Kaunakakai," and "The Hawaiian Wedding Song."

By the 1960s, Hawaiian music began to die. Just too corny and light for those turbulent years, it belonged to the older generation and the good times that followed World War II. One man was instrumental in keeping Hawaiian music alive during this period. Don Ho, with his "Tiny Bubbles," became the token Hawaiian musician of the 1960s and early '70s. He's persevered long enough to become a legend in his own time, and his Polynesian Extravaganza at the Hilton Hawaiian Village packed visitors in until the early 1990s. He now plays at the Waikiki Beachcomber Hotel and still doing a marvelous although smaller show. Al Harrington, "The South Pacific Man," until his recent retirement had another Honolulu "big revue" that drew large crowds. Of this type of entertainment, perhaps the most Hawaiian was Danny Kaleikini, who entertained his audience with dances, Hawaiian anecdotes, and tunes on the traditional Hawaiian nose flute.

## The Beat Goes On

Beginning in the mid-1970s islanders began to assert their cultural identity. One of the unifying factors was the coming of age of "Hawaiian" music. It graduated from the "little grass shack" novelty tune and began to include sophisticated jazz, rock, and contemporary rhythms. Accomplished musicians whose roots were in traditional island music began to highlight their tunes with this distinctive sound. The best embellish their arrangements with ukuleles, steel guitars, and traditional percussion and melodic instruments. Some excellent modern recording artists have become island institutions. The local people say that you know if the Hawaiian harmonies are good if they give you "chicken skin."

Each year special music awards, **Na Hoku Hanohano,** or Hoku for short, are given to distinguished island musicians. The following are some Hoku winners considered by their contemporaries to be among the best in Hawaii. If they're playing on one of the islands while you're in Hawaii, don't miss them (some, unfortunately, are no longer among the living, but their recorded music can still be appreciated). Barney Isaacs and George Kuo, Na Leo Pilimihana, Robi Kahakalau, Keali'i Reichel, Darren Benitez, Sonny Kamahele, Ledward Kaapana, Hapa, Israel Kamakawiwio'ole, and Pure Heart.

Past Hoku winners who have become renowned performers include the Brothers Cazimero, who are blessed with beautiful harmonic voices; Krush, who are highly regarded for their contemporary sounds; The Peter Moon Band, fantastic performers with a strong traditional sound; Henry Kapono, formerly of Cecilio and Kapono; and The Beamer Brothers. Others include Loyal Garner, Del Beazley, Bryan Kessler & Me No Hoa Aloha, George Kahumoku, Amy Hanaiali'i Gilliom, Olomana, Genoa Keawe, and Irmagard Aluli.

Those with Internet access can check out the Hawaiian music scene at one of the following websites: Hawaiian Music Island, www.mele.com; Nahenahenet, www.nahenahe.net; and Hawaiian Music Guide, www.hawaii-music.com. While not the only sites, they are a good place to start. For listening to Hawaiian music on the Web, try: http://kkcr.org or www.hotspots.hawaii.com/IRH.

## Festivals and Events

In addition to all the American national holidays, Hawaii celebrates its own festivals, pageants, ethnic fairs, and a multitude of specialized exhibits. They occur throughout the year, some particular to only one island or locality, while others such as Aloha Week and Lei Day are celebrated on all the islands. Some of the smaller local happenings are semi-spontaneous, so there's no *exact* date when they're held. These are some of the most rewarding, because they provide the best times to have fun with the local people. At festival time, everyone is welcome. Check local newspapers and the free island magazines for exact dates of events. For additional events of all sorts throughout the state, visit the calendar of events listing on the HVB website at http://calendar.gohawaii.com, the Hawaii vacation planner website at www.hshawaii.com/vacplanner/calendar, or visit the State Foundation of Culture and the Arts calendar, which features arts and cultural events, activities, and programs at www.state.hi.us/sfca/culturecalendar.html.

**Note:** Island-specific festivals and events are listed in the individual island chapters below.

### Statewide Events

**Wesak or Buddha Day** is on the closest Sunday to April 8, and celebrates the birthday of Gautama Buddha. Ornate offerings of tropical flowers are placed at temple altars throughout Hawaii. Enjoy the sunrise ceremonies at Kapi'olani Park, Honolulu, with Japanese in their best *kimonos* along with flower festivals, pageants, and dance programs in many island temples.

May 1 is May Day to the communist world, but in Hawaii red is only one of the colors when everyone dons a lei for **Lei Day.** Festivities abound throughout Hawaii, but there are special goings-on at Kapi'olani Park, Honolulu.

Agricultural exhibits, down-home cooking, entertainment, and fresh produce are presented for four weekends starting in late May at the **50th State Fair,** at Aloha Stadium, Honolulu.

**King Kamehameha Day,** June 11, is a state holiday honoring Kamehameha the Great, with festivities on all islands. Check local papers for times and particulars. The following are the main events: O'ahu holds a lei-draping ceremony at the King Kamehameha statue in downtown Honolulu, along with parades complete with floats and pageantry featuring a *ho'olaule'a* (street party) in Waikiki; Kailua-Kona on the Big Island is hospitable with a *ho'olaule'a,* parades, art demonstrations, entertainment, and contests; on Kaua'i enjoy parades, *ho'olaule'a,* arts, and crafts centered around the Kaua'i County Building; Maui's Lahaina and Kahului are decked out for parades and pageants.

August 15 is **Admission Day,** a state holiday recognizing the day that Hawaii became a state. The date may change by a few days every year.

The **Aloha Festival** is a two-month-long celebration (Sept.–October) with more than 300 events on all of the islands, where everyone celebrates Hawaii's own "intangible quality," *aloha.* This is the state's largest multi-ethnic event. There are parades, lu'au, historical pageants, balls, and various entertainment. The spirit of *aloha* is infectious and all are welcomed to join in. Check local papers and tourist literature for happenings near you. For information, call 800/852-7690 or check online at www.alohafestivals.com.

To promote cultural understanding and awareness among people of the different ethnic groups in the state, the **Hawaii International Film Festival** showcases new and engaging films, mainly from Asian and Pacific Rim countries at various theaters around the island during November. Seminars and workshops are also held. For information, call 800/876-0567 or 800/752-8193 or visit the website at www.hiff.org.

On **New Year's Eve** hold onto your hat, because they do it up big in Hawaii. Merriment and alcohol flow all over the islands. Firecrackers are illegal, but they go off everywhere. Beware of hangovers and drunken drivers.

# Exploring the Islands

## Sports and Recreation

Hawaii is a playground for young and old with sports, games, and activities galore. Everyone can find something they enjoy, and most activities are free, relatively cheap, or once-in-a-lifetime thrills that are worth the money. The sea is the ideal playground. You can swim, snorkel, scuba, surf, bodysurf, windsurf, fish, sail, canoe, kayak, parasail, cruise, or stroll along the shore picking up shells or exploring tidepools. Every island offers tennis and golf, along with plenty of horseback riding, hiking, biking, and hunting,

with more limited freshwater fishing. Spectator sports such as baseball, basketball, polo, and especially football are popular, and the Kona Coast of the Big Island is a mecca for world-class triathletes. Whatever your desire or physical abilities may be, there'll be some activity that strikes your fancy in Hawaii.

One of the best tonics for relaxation is to play hard at something you thoroughly enjoy, so you're deliciously tired and fulfilled at day's end. For you this might be hooking onto an 800-pound marlin that'll test you to the limit, or perhaps just giving yourself to the sea and floating on

Napili Bay

gentle waves. Hawaii is guaranteed to thrill the young, invigorate the once young, put a twinkle in your eye, and add a bounce to your step.

The following sports and recreation overview is designed to give you an idea of what's available. More in-depth information can be found in the travel chapters below. There you'll also find specific entries for localized sports like jet skiing, water-skiing, snow skiing, parasailing, and much more. Whatever else you may do in Hawaii, you owe it to yourself to do one thing: enjoy it!

## BEACHES

Each island has beaches that offer wonderful space for visitors to appreciate Hawaiian waters and near-shore sea life within surrounding reefs. The largest number and greatest cumulative mileage of beaches is on Kaua'i, which has had the longest time to form these strands of sand. O'ahu and Maui also have plenty of fine beaches, several of the best known in the state. While the smaller islands of Lana'i and Moloka'i also have beaches, there are far fewer winners on each of these islands. The Big Island of Hawai'i gets the short end of the stick when it comes to the number of great beaches. While not numerous, it too has a few that will please anyone. Aside from the mostly predominant golden sand beaches, Hawaii has a handful of beaches that are salt and pepper, gray, black, green, and red in color. See the travel chapters below for specific beach entries on each island.

Generally speaking, beaches and shorelines on the north and west have high surf conditions and strong ocean currents during winter months—use extreme caution—and those on the south and east experience some high surf during the summer months. All beaches are open to the public. Most are accessed through beach parks, but some access is over private property. All hotels and condominiums must by law offer pathway access to beaches they front, and each has some parking set aside for public use. At some beaches, flags warn of ocean conditions. A yellow flag means use caution. A half-yellow, half-red sign signifies caution because of strong winds. A red flag indicates hazardous water conditions—beach closed, no swimming. In addition, yellow and black signs are sometimes posted to indicate other warnings: dangerous shore break, high surf spot, strong currents, presence of jellyfish, or beach closed.

Before you head to the beach, take a drive to the local shop for a cheap woven beach mat. Whalers General Store, ABC markets, other sundries shops, Longs Drug, Wal-Mart, Kmart, and the like have them for $1–1.50. Hotel sundries shops sometimes also carry the exact same thing for about a dollar more. On occasion, condos have them to borrow, and often B&Bs and vacation rental homes have them available for guests—but don't count on it.

## SCUBA AND SNORKELING

If you think Hawaii is beautiful above the sea, wait until you explore below. The warm tropical waters and coral growth make it a fascinating haven for reef fish and aquatic plant life. Snorkel and dive sites, varying in difficulty and challenge, are accessible from all islands. Sites can be totally hospitable ones where families snorkeling for the first time can have an exciting but safe frolic, or they can be accessible only to the experienced diver. Every island has dive shops where you can rent or buy equipment, and where dive boats and instruction on all levels can be arranged. You'll soon discover that Hawaiian waters are remarkably clear, with excellent visibility. Below, fish in every fathomable color parade by. Lavender clusters of coral, red and gold coral trees, and more than 1,500 different types of shells carpet the ocean floor. In some spots (like O'ahu's Hanauma Bay) the fish are so accustomed to humans that they'll come looking for you. In other spots, lurking moray eels add the zest of danger. Sharks and barracuda pose less danger than scraping your knee on the coral or being driven against the rocks by a heavy swell. There are enormous but harmless sea bass and a profusion of sea turtles. All this awaits below Hawaii's waters.

### Scuba

Scuba divers must show certification cards to rent gear from local shops, fill tanks, or take a charter dive. Plenty of outstanding scuba instructors will

# REEF FISH

Achilles tang

red-lipped parrotfish

moorish idol

lagoon *humu*

Hawaiian lionfish

*manini*

blue-spotted cowfish

bluestripe butterflyfish

Potter's angelfish

threadfin butterflyfish

trumpetfish

saddleback wrasse

mottled moray

manta ray

*uhu*

LOUISE FOOTE/DIANA LASICH HARPER

give you lessons toward certification, and they're especially reasonable because of the stiff competition. Prices vary, but you can take a three- to five-day semiprivate certification course, including all equipment, for $300–600. Divers unaccustomed to Hawaiian waters should not dive alone regardless of their experience. Most opt for dive tours to special dive grounds guaranteed to please. These vary also, but an introductory dive will run about $90, an *accompanied* single-tank dive where no boat is involved goes for about $85, and expect to spend $100 for a double-tank boat dive. There are charter dives, night dives, and photography dives. Most companies pick you up at your hotel, take you to the site, and return you home. Basic equipment rental costs $30–50 for the day, and most times the water is so mild you'll need only the top of a wet suit.

## Snorkeling

Scuba diving takes expensive special equipment, skills, and athletic ability. Snorkeling in comparison is much simpler and enjoyable to anyone who can swim. In about 15 minutes you can be taught the fundamentals of snorkeling—you really don't need formal instructions. Other snorkelers or dive shop attendants can tell you enough to get you started. Because you can breathe without lifting your head, you get great propulsion from the fins and hardly ever need to use your arms. You can go for much greater distances and spend longer in the water than if you were swimming. Experienced snorkelers make an art of this sport and you too can see and do amazing things with a mask, snorkel, and flippers. Don't, however, get a false sense of invincibility and exceed your limitations.

You can buy or rent snorkel equipment in dive shops and in department stores. Sometimes condos and hotels offer free snorkeling equipment for their guests, but if you have to rent it, don't do it at a hotel or condo; go to a dive shop where it's much cheaper. Expect to spend $3–9 a day for mask, fins, and snorkel. A special option is an underwater camera. These single-use cameras run about $15–20. Many boats will take you out snorkeling. Prices range from about $40 (half day, four hours) to $70 (full day, eight

hours). Activities centers can also arrange these excursions for no extra charge.

## Snuba

No, that's not a typo. Snuba offers a hybrid sport that is half snorkeling and half scuba diving. You have a regulator, a weight belt, mask, and flippers, and you're tethered to scuba tanks that float 20 feet above you on a sea-sled. The unofficial motto of snuba is "secure but free." The idea is that many people become anxious diving under the waves encumbered by tanks and all the scuba apparatus. Snuba frees you. You would think that being tethered to the sled would slow you down, but actually you're sleeker and can make better time than a normal scuba diver. The sled is made from industrial-strength polyethylene and is 2.5 feet wide by 7.5 feet long, consisting of a view window and a belly in the sled for the scuba tank. If you get tired, just surface and use it as a raft.

# KAYAKING

Kayaking has become one of the great water sports in Hawaii over the past several decades. While O'ahu seems to have little interest in the activity, it's quite popular on the Neighbor Islands. Sea kayaking is the norm but Kaua'i does have several small rivers that also offer smooth and controlled conditions. While Kealakekua Bay on the Big Island, Makena on Maui, Shipwreck Beach on Lana'i, and the south coast on Moloka'i are well visited, perhaps the most spectacular area in the state to kayak is the Na Pali Coast of Kaua'i. Because of water conditions, the south shore of any of the islands is best in the winter. North shore water conditions are better in the summer; water is generally flattest then so you'll be fighting the wind and waves less.

Before launching, check with a kayak shop to get current information on wind and water conditions. Open cockpit kayaks generally rent for about $25 single or $50 tandem and come with all necessary gear and sometimes a carriers for the car. Most shops want day-rental kayaks back by 5 P.M. Occasionally, companies will rent by the hour or week. While you can go where you want, numerous companies and individuals offer guided tours on each of the islands. Tours vary, but run about $65–80 for a half day; full-day tours may be twice that. Be sure to wear proper clothing: a swimsuit or shorts and T-shirt and some type of water shoes. Be sure to take a brimmed hat and sunglasses, put on sunscreen, take a towel and a dry change of clothes, and don't forget drinking water and snacks. A windbreaker is recommended for the open ocean.

See the individual travel chapters below for specifics of rentals and tours on each island.

# CATCHING WAVES

## Surfing

Surfing is a sport indigenous to Hawaii. When the white man first arrived, he was astonished to see natives paddling out to meet the ships on long carved boards, then gracefully riding them in to shore on crests of waves. The Hawaiians called surfing he'enalu (to "slide on a wave"). The newcomers were fascinated by this sport, recording it on engravings and woodcuts marveled at around the world. Meanwhile, the Polynesians left records of surfing in petroglyphs and in mele of past exploits. A Waikiki beach boy named Duke Kahanamoku won a treasure box full of gold medals for swimming at the 1912 Olympic Games. Thereafter, he became a celebrity, introducing surfing to California, Australia, and the rest of the world. Surfing later became a lifestyle, popularized far and wide by surf movies and the songs of the Beach Boys in the 1960s. Now surfing is a sport enjoyed around the world, complete with championships, movies, magazines, and advanced board technology.

It takes years of practice to become good, but with determination, good swimming ability, and a sense of balance you can learn the fundamentals in a short time. At surf shops on all islands you can rent a board for very reasonable prices. The boards of the ancient ali'i were up to 20 feet long and weighed more than 150 pounds, but today's board is made from ultralight foam plastic covered in fiberglass. While they come is various lengths and shapes, the smallest are about six feet long and weigh 12 pounds or so. Innova-

tions occur every day in surfing, but one is the changeable "skeg" or rudder allowing you to surf in variable conditions.

The sport of surfing is still male-dominated, but women champions have been around for years. The most famous surfing beach in the world is Sunset Beach and the Banzai Pipeline on North Shore O'ahu. Every year the nationally televised pro-tour Triple Crown of Surfing is held there, usually from late October to December. It's only a matter of time before surfing becomes an Olympic sport. One of the most brilliant books ever written on surfing is Surfing, the Ultimate Pleasure, by Leonard Lueras.

## Sailboarding

Technically called sailboarding, this sport is called windsurfing by most people, after the name of one of the most famous manufacturers of sailboards. A combination of surfing and sailing, the equipment is a rather large and stable surfboard mounted with a highly maneuverable sail. It may sound difficult, but most people find it slightly easier than surfing because you're mobilized by the wind and not at the mercy of the waves. You don't have to "read" the waves as well as a surfer, and like riding a bicycle, as long as you keep moving you can hold your balance. Boards and lessons are available on all the major islands. Sailboards are slightly more expensive than surfboards to rent, but you should be in business for about $35–50 a day.

## Kiteboarding

A cross between wakeboarding and flying a kite, kiteboarding (also known as kitesurfing) is one of the newest water sports to hit the island. With kiteboarding, a large foil-sail kite is attached by long ropes to a grab bar that is clipped to a harness that's worn around the waist. Steering is done by pulling one end of the bar or the other to raise or lower the kite, catching more or less wind. A wide ski is used, similar to a wakeboard ski, except that this one has a short rudder. Booties, a neoprene version of snowboard boots, keep you attached to the board. The proficient skim the water as fast and as freely as sailboarders. Those who really know how to use the wind to their advantage can get 20–30 feet of loft. Those who know the sport say that it's not for the timid, nor as easy as it might appear. Take lessons first. Both Maui and Oʻahu have shops that give lessons and rent gear.

## Boogie Boards

If surfing or sailboarding is a bit too much for you, try a boogie board—a foam or hard-shell board about three feet long that you lie on from the waist up. With the help of flippers for maneuverability, you can get tremendous rides on boogie boards. You can learn to ride in minutes and it's much faster, easier, and more thrilling than bodysurfing. Boogie boards are for sale all over the islands and are relatively cheap. You can rent one from a dive or surf shop for $5–7, or buy your own for $80–350.

# FISHING

Hawaii has some of the most exciting and productive "blue waters" in all the world. A statewide "sport fishing fleet" comprises skippers and crews who are experienced professional anglers. You can also fish from jetties, piers, rocks, and the shore. If rod and reel don't strike your fancy, try the old-fashioned throw net, or take along a spear when you go snorkeling or scuba diving. There's nighttime torch fishing that requires special skills and equipment, and freshwater fishing in public areas. Streams and irrigation ditches yield introduced trout, bass, and catfish. While you're at it, you might want to try crabbing for Kona and Samoan crabs, or working low-tide areas after sundown hunting octopus, a tantalizing island delicacy.

## Deep-Sea Fishing

Most game-fishing boats work the waters on the calmer leeward sides of the islands. Some skippers, carrying anglers who are accustomed to the sea, will also work the much rougher windward coasts and island channels where the fish bite just as well. Trolling is the preferred method of deep-sea fishing; this is usually done in depths of 1,000–2,000 fathoms (a fathom is six feet). The skipper will either "area fish," which means running in a crisscross pattern over a known productive area, or "ledge fish," which involves trolling over submerged ledges where game fish are known to feed. The most advanced marine

J.D. BISIGNANI

**Hawaiʻi's Kona Coast offers fishing enthusiasts a great opportunity to catch one of the "big blues."**

technology, available on many boats, sends sonar bleeps searching for fish. On deck, the crew and anglers scan the horizon in the age-old Hawaiian tradition—searching for clusters of seabirds feeding on bait fish pursued to the surface by the huge and aggressive game fish. "Still fishing," or "bottom fishing" with hand lines, can yield some tremendous fish.

## The Game Fish

The most thrilling game fish in Hawaiian waters is marlin, generically known as "billfish" or *a'u* to the locals. The king of them is the blue marlin, with record catches well over 1,000 pounds. There are also striped marlin and sailfish, which often go more than 200 pounds. The best times for marlin are during spring, summer, and fall. The fishing tapers off in January and picks up again by late February. "Blues" can be caught year-round, but, oddly enough, when they stop biting it seems as though the striped marlin pick up. Second to the marlin is tuna. *'Ahi* (yellowfin tuna) is caught in Hawaiian waters at depths of 100–1,000 fathoms. It can weigh 300 pounds, but 25–100 pounds is common. There's also *aku* (skipjack) and the delicious *ono,* which average 20–40 pounds. Mahimahi is another strong-fighting, deepwater game fish abundant in Hawaii. These delicious fish can weigh up to 70 pounds.

Shore fishing and bait-casting yield *papio,* a jack tuna. *Akule,* a scad (locally called *halalu*), is a smallish schooling fish that comes close to shore and is great to catch on light tackle. *Ulua* is a shore fish that can be found in tidepools. They're excellent eating, averaging 2–3 pounds, and are taken at night or with spears. *'O'io* are bonefish that come close to shore to spawn. They're caught by bait-casting and bottom fishing with cut bait. Although bony, they're a favorite for fish cakes and *poki. Awa* is a schooling fish that loves brackish water. It can get up to three feet long and is a good fighter. A favorite for throw netters, it's even raised commercially in fishponds. Besides these there are plenty of goatfish, mullet, mackerel, snapper, sharks, and even salmon.

## "Blue Water" Areas

One of the most famous fishing spots in Hawaii is **Penguin Banks** off the west coast of Moloka'i and the south coast of O'ahu. The "Chicken Farm" at the southern tip of Penguin Banks has great trolling waters for marlin and mahimahi. The calm waters off the Wai'anae Coast of O'ahu yield marlin and *'ahi.* The Kona Coast of the Big Island, with its crystal waters, shelters the most famous marlin grounds in Hawaii. Every year the **Hawaiian International Billfish Tournament** draws anglers from around the world to Kona. The marlin are found in 1,000 fathoms of water, but close in on the Kona Coast you can hook *ono* and hand line for *onaga* and *kahala.* Maui fishers usually head for the waters formed by the triangle of Maui, Lana'i, and Kaho'olawe, where they troll for marlin, *mahi,* and *ono,* or bottom fish for snapper. Kaua'i has excellent fishing waters year-round, with *ono, 'ahi,* and marlin along the ledges. Large schools of *'ahi* come to Kaua'i in the spring, and the fishing is fabulous with possible 200-pound catches.

## Charter Boats

The charter boats of Hawaii come in all shapes and sizes, but all are staffed by professional, competent crews and captains with intimate knowledge of Hawaiian waters. You can hire a boat for a private or share charter, staying out for four, six, or eight hours. Some captains like to go for longer runs as there is a better chance of a catch and they can get farther into the water; some now do only private charters. Boat size varies, but four anglers per midsize boat is about average. No matter the size, most boats will take no more than six anglers. Although some provide it, be sure to bring food and drink for the day; no bananas, please—they're bad luck. Deep-sea fishing on a share basis costs approximately $120 per half day (four hours) or $160 full day, per person. On a private basis, expect $500 per half day or up to $800 for a full day. No fishing licenses are required. Tackle is carried on the boats and is part of the service. It is customary for the crew to be given any fish that are caught, but naturally this doesn't apply to trophy fish; the crew is also glad to cut off steaks and fillets for your personal use. Honolulu's Kewalo Basin, only a few minutes from Waikiki, has the largest fleet of charter

## SEASICKNESS

Many people are affected by motion sickness, particularly on sailing vessels. If you tend to get queasy, try one of the following to prevent symptoms.

Oral medications widely available through pharmacies are **Dramamine, Bonine,** and **Triptone.** Running about $4 a pop, Dramamine and Bonine may cause drowsiness in some people, but Triptone seems not to. Although these medications are usually taken just before boarding a ship, they might work better if one half-dose is taken the night before and the second half-dose is taken the morning of your ride. In all cases, however, take medication as prescribed by the manufacturer.

For those who don't want to take medication, try **Seabands,** an elastic band worn around the wrist that puts gentle pressure on the inside of the wrist by way of a small plastic button. Seabands are also available at pharmacies and at most scuba shops for about $8.50 and can be reused until the elastic wears out. Follow directions for best results.

Without medication or pressure bands, you can still work to counter the effects of motion sickness. The night before, try not to eat too much, particularly greasy food, and don't drink an excess of alcohol. If your stomach begins to feel upset, try eating a few soda crackers. If you begin to feel dizzy, focus on the horizon or a mountain top—something stationary—and try to direct your thoughts to something other than your dizziness or queasiness. With children (and perhaps adults as well), talking about what animal figures they can see in the clouds or how many houses they can spot along the shoreline may be enough to distract them for a time to begin feeling better.

boats. On the Big Island, Honokohau Small Boat Harbor just north of Kailua-Kona has the largest concentration of charter boats, with some boats out of Kawaihae. Maui boats run out of Lahaina or Ma'alaea Bay. Moloka'i has a few boats berthed at Kaunakakai, Lana'i has one, and on Kaua'i most boats sail out of Nawiliwili Harbor.

### Freshwater Fishing

Due to Hawaii's unique geology, only a handful of natural lakes and rivers and a few reservoirs are good for fishing. The state maintains four "Public Fishing Areas" spread over Kaua'i, O'ahu, and Hawai'i. None are found on Maui, Lana'i, or Moloka'i. The two public fishing areas on O'ahu are **Wahiawa Public Fishing Area,** a 300-acre irrigation reservoir primarily for sugarcane near Wahiawa in central O'ahu, and **Nu'uanu Freshwater Fish Refuge: Reservoir no. 4,** in the Ko'olau Mountains above Honolulu. On Kaua'i, **Koke'e Public Fishing Area** is north of Kekaha, with 13 miles of stream, two miles of irrigation ditches, and a 15-acre reservoir offering only rainbow trout. On Hawai'i, the **Waiakea Public Fishing Area** encompasses a 26-acre estuarine pond within the city of Hilo.

### Freshwater Fish

Hawaii has only one native freshwater game fish, the 'o'opu. This goby is an oddball with fused ventral fins. It grows to 12 inches and is found on all islands, especially Kaua'i. Introduced species include largemouth and smallmouth bass, bluegill, catfish, tucunare, oscar, carp, *pongee* (snakehead), and tilapia. The only trout to survive is the rainbow, found only in the streams of Kaua'i and the Big Island. The tucunare is a tough-fighting, good-tasting game fish introduced from South America, similar to the oscar from the same region. Both have been compared to bass, but are of a different family. The tilapia is from Africa and has become common in Hawaii's irrigation ditches. It's a "mouth breeder," and the young will take refuge in their parents' protective jaws even a few weeks after hatching. The snakehead is an eel-like fish that inhabits reservoirs and is a great fighter. The channel catfish can grow to more than 20 pounds and bites best after sundown. There's also the carp, and with its broad tail and tremendous strength, it's the poor person's game fish. All of these species are best caught with light spinning tackle or with a bamboo pole and a trusty old worm. The catch limit of eight species of freshwater fish is regulated.

## Fishing Licenses

A license is needed for freshwater fishing only. A **Freshwater Game Fishing License** is good for one year, from July 1 to June 30. Licenses cost $25 for non-island nonresidents, $10 for 7-day tourist use, $20 for 30-day tourist use; $5 for residents over age 15 and active duty military personnel, their spouses, and dependents over age 15, $3 for children ages 9–15; they are free to senior citizens and children under age nine when accompanied by an adult with a license. You can pick up a license at sporting goods stores or at the Division of Aquatic Resources on each of the main islands. Be sure to ask for its *Hawaii Fishing Regulations* and *Freshwater Fishing in Hawaii* booklets. All game fish except trout may be taken year-round. Trout, on Kaua'i only, may be taken for 16 days commencing on the first Saturday of August. Thereafter, for the remainder of August and September, trout can be taken only on Saturday, Sunday, and state holidays. Fishing is usually allowed in most State Forest Reserve Areas. Owners' permission must be obtained to fish on private property.

## CAMPING AND HIKING

A major aspect of the "Hawaii experience" is the simple beauty of nature and the outdoors. Some visitors come to Hawaii to luxuriate at resorts and dine in fine restaurants, but everyone heads for the sand and surf, and most are captivated by the lush mountainous interior. What better way to savor this natural beauty than by hiking slowly through it or pitching a tent in the middle of it? Hawaii offers a full range of hiking and camping, and what's more, most of it is easily accessible. Camping facilities are located near many choice beaches and amid some of the most scenic mountain areas in the islands. They range in amenities from full housekeeping cabins to primitive hike-in sites. Camping permits can be obtained by walk-in application to the appropriate office, or by writing or phoning. Although there is usually no problem obtaining sites, when writing, request reservations well in advance, allowing a minimum of one month for letters to go back and forth.

Some restrictions to hiking apply because much of the land is privately owned, so advance permission to hike may be required. But plenty of public access trails along the coast and deep into the interior would fill the itineraries of even the most intrepid hikers. If you enjoy the great outdoors on the Mainland, you'll be thrilled by these "mini-continents," where in one day you can go from the frosty summits of alpine wonderlands down into baking cactus-covered deserts and emerge through jungle foliage onto a sun-soaked subtropical shore.

## Equipment

Like everything else you take to Hawaii, your camping and hiking equipment should be lightweight and durable. Camping equipment size and weight should not cause a problem with baggage requirements on airlines: if it does, it's a tip-off that you're hauling too much. One odd luggage consideration you might make is to bring along a small Styrofoam cooler packed with equipment. Exchange the equipment for food items when you get to Hawaii. If you intend to car camp successfully and keep food prices down, you'll definitely need a cooler. You can also buy one on arrival for only a few dollars.

Consider an internal-frame **backpack** or a convertible pack that turns into a soft-side suitcase, and a day pack. You'll need a lightweight **tent,** preferably with a rainfly and a sewn-in waterproof floor. This will save you from getting wet and miserable, and will keep out mosquitoes, cockroaches, ants, and the islands' few stinging insects. **Sleeping bags** are a good idea, although you can get along at sea level with only a blanket. Down-filled bags are necessary for Haleakala, Mauna Kea, Mauna Loa, or any high-elevation camping—you'll freeze without one.

**Campstoves** are needed because there's very little available wood, it's often wet in the deep forest, and open fires are often prohibited. If you'll be car-camping, take along a multi-burner stove; for hiking, a backpacker's stove will be necessary. Buy stove gas in Hawaii as these containers are not to be taken on a plane. The grills found at some campgrounds are popular with many families who often go to the beach parks for open-air dinners. You can buy a very inexpensive charcoal grill at many variety stores throughout Hawaii. It's a great idea to take along a **lantern.** This will add safety for car-campers. Definitely take a **flashlight,** replacement batteries, and a few small **candles.** A complete **first-aid kit** can be the difference between life and death, and it's worth the extra bulk. Hikers, especially those leaving the coastal areas, should take rain gear, a plastic ground cloth, a utility knife, a compass, a safety whistle, a mess kit, water purification tablets, biodegradable "Camp Suds" or similar soap, a canteen, nylon twine, a sewing kit (dental floss works as thread), and waterproof matches. In a film container pack a few nails, safety pins, fishhooks, line, and bendable wire. Nothing else does what these do and they're all handy for a million and one uses. If you find a staff or hiking stick at the beginning of a trail, consider using it—others obviously found it useful—but leave it at the trailhead for others to use when you return. Only a limited number of stores sell or rent camping and hiking equipment.

## Hiking Tips

Keep your eye on two things to remain safe while hiking in Hawaii: humans and nature. The general rule is: the farther you get away from towns, the safer you'll be from human-induced hassles. Hike with someone—share the experience. If possible, don't hike or camp alone, especially if you're a woman. Don't leave your valuables in your tent, and always carry your money, papers, and camera with you. At the least, let someone know where you are going and when you plan to be back; supply an itinerary and your expected route, then stick to it. Stay on designated trails—this not only preserves the fragile environment, it also keeps you out of dangerous areas. While hiking, remember that many trails are well maintained, but trailhead markers are often missing. The trails themselves can be muddy, which can make them treacherously slippery and often knee-deep. Occasionally, trails will be closed for maintenance, so stay off these routes. Buy and use a trail map.

Wear comfortable clothing. Shorts and a T-shirt will suffice on many trails, but long pants and long-sleeve shirts are better where it's rainy and overgrown, and at higher elevations. Bring a windbreaker or raingear—it can rain and blow at any time. Wear sturdy walking or hiking shoes that you don't mind getting wet and muddy—it's almost guaranteed on some trails. Some very wet spots and stream crossings may be better done in tabi or other water shoes. Your clothes may become permanently stained with mud—a wonderful memento of your trip. Officials and others often ask hikers to pick clinging seeds off their clothes when coming out at the trailhead and to wash off boots so as not to unintentionally transport seeds to nonnative areas.

Always bring food because you cannot, in most cases, forage from the land. Carry plenty of drinking water, at least two quarts per day. Heat can cause your body to lose water and salt. If you become woozy or weak, rest, take salt, and drink water as you need it. Remember, it takes much more water to restore a dehydrated person than to stay hydrated as you go; take small, frequent sips. No matter how clean it looks, water in most streams is biologically polluted and will give you bad stomach problems if you drink it without purifying it first by boiling, filtering, or adding purification tablets. For your part, please don't use streams as a toilet.

Use sunscreen. The sun can be intense and UV rays go through clouds. Bring and use mosquito lotion—even in paradise pesky bugs abound. Do not litter. Carry a dedicated trash bag and take out all that you bring in.

Some trails are used by hunters of wild boar, deer, or game birds. It's best not to use these trails during hunting season, but if you do hike in hunting areas during hunting season, wear brightly colored or reflective clothing. Often, forest reserve trails have check-in stations at trailheads. Hikers and hunters must sign a logbook, especially if they intend to camp. The comments by previous hikers are worth reading for up-to-the-minute information on trail conditions.

Twilight is short in the islands, and night sets in rapidly. In June, sunrise is around 6 A.M. and sunset 7 P.M.; in December, these occur at 7 A.M. and 6 P.M. If you become lost, find an open spot and stay put; at night, stay as dry as you can. If you must continue, walk on ridges and avoid the gulches, which have more obstacles and make it harder for rescuers to spot you. Do not light a fire. Hawaii is made of brittle and crumbly volcanic rock. Never attempt to climb steep *pali* (cliffs). Every year people are stranded, and fatalities have occurred. Be careful of elevation sickness, especially on Haleakala, Mauna Loa, and Mauna Kea. The best cure is to head down as soon as possible. Be mindful of flash floods. Small creeks can turn into raging torrents with upland rains. Never camp in a dry creekbed. Fog is encountered only at elevations of 1,500–5,000 feet, but be careful of disorientation.

Generally, stay within your limits, be careful, and enjoy yourself.

## Hiking Groups and Information

The **Department of Land and Natural Resources,** Division of Forestry and Wildlife, 1151 Punchbowl St., Room 325, Honolulu, HI 96813, 808/587-0058, is helpful in providing trail maps, accessibility information, hunting and fishing regulations, and general forest rules. This office offers an excellent, free *Recreation Map* for each of the four main islands. This state department has branch offices in Hilo on the Big Island, in Wailuku on Maui, and in Lihu'e on Kaua'i.

See the travel chapters below for organizations that offer guided hiking trips on the individual islands.

## Hiking and Camping Books

For well-written and detailed hiking guides, complete with maps, check out *Maui Trails, Kauai Trails, Oahu Trails* and *Hawaii Trails* by Kathy Morey. See also Robert Smith's *Hawaii's Best Hiking Trails,* and his *Hiking Maui, Hiking Oahu, Hiking Hawaii* and *Hiking Kauai,* as well as *Hawaiian Hiking Trails* by Craig Chisholm,

Two helpful camping books are *Hawaii: A Camping Guide,* by George Cagala, and Richard McMahon's *Camping Hawai'i.*

## Topographical Maps and Nautical Charts

For detailed topographical maps, contact **U.S. Geological Survey, Information Services,** P.O. Box 25286, Denver, CO 80225, 888/ASK-USGS, www.usgs.gov. Many types of maps are available at Borders Books throughout the islands. A wide range of topographical maps, nautical charts, and local maps can be purchased at independent shops like **Pacific Map Center,** 560 N. Nimitz Hwy., Suite 206A, Honolulu, HI 96817, 808/545-3600, and **Basically Books,** 160 Kamehameha Ave., 808/961-0144, in downtown Hilo on the Big Island. Also useful, but not for hiking, are the University of Hawai'i Press reference maps of each island.

For nautical charts, write **National Ocean Service,** Greenbelt, MD 20770-1479, 301/436-8301 or 800/638-8972.

## NATIONAL PARKS

Hawaii's two national parks sit atop volcanoes: **Haleakala National Park** on Maui and **Hawaii Volcanoes National Park** centered around Kilauea Crater on the Big Island. Camping is free at both, and permits are not required except for the cabins and campgrounds inside Haleakala crater and the back-country locations of Hawaii Volcanoes National Park. See the travel chapters for detailed information. Get free information by contacting the individual park headquarters: Hawaii Volcanoes National Park, P.O. Box 52, Hawaii National Park, HI 96718, 808/985-6000, www.nps.gov/havo; Haleakala National Park, P.O. Box 369, Makawao, HI 96768, 808/572-4400, www.nps.gov/hale. Or try the Hawaii office of the **National Park Service,** 300 Ala Moana Blvd., Honolulu, HI 96850, 808/541-2693.

## STATE PARKS

Hawaii's 54 state parks, which include historical parks, recreation areas, recreation piers, waysides, monuments, and underwater parks, are managed by the Department of Land and Natural Resources, through its Division of State Parks branch offices on each island. Some are for looking at, some are restricted to day use, and at 14 (which may change periodically without notice) there is overnight camping. At seven of these parks, A-frames, self-contained cabins, or group accommodations are available on a fee basis with reservations necessary. At the others, camping is $5 per campsite for every night of use, $10 per person per night at the Na Pali Coast State Park campsites, and permits are required. RVs are technically not allowed.

## Permits and Rules

Camping permits are good for a maximum stay of five consecutive nights at any one park, except for the Na Pali Coast State Park, which has one- and three-night limits at certain campsites. A permit to the same person for the same park is again available only after 30 days from the last day of previous use. Campgrounds are open every day on the Neighbor Islands but closed Wednesday and Thursday on O'ahu. Arrive after 2 P.M. and check out by 11 A.M., except again on O'ahu, where Wednesday checkout is 8 A.M. You must be 18 for park permits; anyone under that age must be accompanied by an adult. Alcoholic beverages are prohibited, along with nude sunbathing and swimming. Plants and wildlife are protected, but reasonable amounts of fruits and seeds may be gathered for personal consumption. Fires are allowed on cookstoves or in designated pits only. Dogs and other pets must be under control at all times (if allowed) and are not permitted to run around unleashed. Hunting and freshwater fishing are allowed in season with a license, and ocean fishing is permitted except when disallowed by posting. Permits are required for certain trails, pavilions, and remote camps, so check.

## Cabins and Shelters

With one exception, housekeeping cabins, A-frames, and group lodges are available daily at seven state parks throughout the state; at Polipoli Spring on Maui, cabins are not available on Tuesday. See specific travel chapters for details. As with camping, permits are required and have the same five-day maximum-stay limitations. Reservations are necessary because of popularity, and a 50 percent deposit within two weeks of reservation is required. There is a 15-day cancellation requirement for refunds, with payment made in cash, money order, cashier's check, or certified check. If you pay by personal or business check, it must be received 30 days before arrival. The exact balance is due on arrival in cash; check-in is 2 P.M., checkout 11 A.M.

## State Park Permit-Issuing Offices

Permit applications can be made by mail, by phone, or in person at one of the issuing offices, not more than one year in advance (30 days in advance for O'ahu). Reservations by letter must include your name, address, phone number, names and identification numbers of those over 18 years old in your party, type of permit requested, and duration of stay. Permits can be picked up from the issuing office on arrival with proof of identification. Office hours are Mon.–Fri. 8 A.M.–3:30 P.M. Usually, camping permits are no problem (O'ahu excepted) to secure on the day you arrive, but reserving ensures you a space and alleviates anxiety. The permits are available from the following offices: **O'ahu,** Division of State Parks, 1151 Punchbowl St., Honolulu, HI 96813, 808/587-0300; **Hawai'i,** Division of State Parks, 75 Aupuni St., Hilo, HI 96720, 808/974-6200; **Maui and Moloka'i,** Division of State Parks, 54 S. High St., Wailuku, HI 96793, 808/984-8109; **Kaua'i,** Division of State Parks, 3060 Eiwa St., Lihu'e, HI 96766, 808/274-3444. For lodging at **Koke'e State Park,** Kaua'i, write Koke'e Lodge, P.O. Box 819, Waimea, HI 96796, 808/335-6061 (9 A.M.–3:45 P.M.); and for **Malaekahana SRA,** O'ahu, write Friends of Malaekahana, P.O. Box 305, La'ie, HI 96762, 808/293-1736 (10 A.M.–4 P.M.).

# COUNTY PARKS

The state of Hawaii is broken up into counties, and the counties control their own parks. Of the more than 600 county parks, more than 100 are scattered primarily along the coastlines and are generally referred to as **beach parks.** Most are for day use only, where visitors fish, swim, snorkel, surf, picnic, and sunbathe, but more than 35 have overnight camping. The rules governing their use vary slightly from county to county, so check the individual travel chapters below, but most have about the same requirements as state parks. Again, the differences between individual parks are too numerous to mention, but the majority have a central pavilion for cooking, restrooms, and cold-water showers (solar heated at a few). Some have individual fire pits, picnic tables, and electricity (usually only at the central pavilion). RVs are allowed to park in appropriate spaces.

## Fees and Permits

The fees are quite reasonable at $3–5 per night, per adult, with children about $.50–1 each. One safety point to consider is that beach parks are open to the general public, and most are used with regularity. Quite a few people pass through, and your chances of encountering a hassle or rip-off are slightly higher than average. To get a permit and pay your fees for use of a county park, either write in advance or visit one of the following issuing offices. Most will accept reservations months in advance, with offices generally open during normal working hours, 8 A.M.–4 P.M. Write or visit the Department of Parks and Recreation, County Parks: **O'ahu,** 650 S. King St., Honolulu, HI 96813, 808/523-4525; **Maui,** War Memorial Gym, 1580-C Ka'ahumanu Ave., Wailuku, HI 96793, 808/270-7389; **Hawai'i,** 101 Pauahi St., Suite 6, Hilo, HI 96720, 808/961-8311; **Kaua'i,** 4444 Rice St., Mo'ikeha Bldg., Suite 150, Lihu'e, HI 96766, 808/241-6660, or during off hours Lihu'e Police Station, 3060 Umi St., 808/245-6711; **Moloka'i,** Mitchell Pauole Center, Kaunakakai, HI 96748, 808/553-3204.

## HORSEBACK RIDING

Horseback riding tours are available on each island, ranging from an easy walk along a shoreline bridle path to hard rides into mountainous interiors. But remember, all these tours are guided. On most you can canter, some let you gallop, but none will just let you take off on your own. Some stop at waterfalls, a few include a picnic lunch, and all offer fine island scenery. Important points to consider when thinking about a horseback ride are your level of expertise (or lack thereof) on a horse, the length of ride, and the terrain that the ride traverses—near the ocean, through thick valley forests, with broad vistas,

or onto a working cattle ranch. Most operations have age and weight restrictions, often taking those only above age eight or 10 and below 225 pounds, so ask. While most rides run about 60–90 minutes for $60–100, you can find easy $50, 45-minute rides as well as $345, eight-hour adventures. The options are truly many.

## BICYCLING

Bicycling in Hawaii can be both fascinating and frustrating. The countryside is great, and the weather is perfect, but for the most part, Hawaii is not as bicycle-conscious as many places in the country. Few bicycle trails and bicycle lanes exist. Most roads are well paved, and some have adequately wide shoulders. Others have no shoulders at all. While coastal roads are generally flat and offer suburb views, they are often heavily trafficked. Because of steep climbs, many mountain roads can challenge the most dedicated riders, but these offer grand vistas to those who persevere. Many roads are full of twists and turns and, while fun to bike, do not offer much sight distance for a vehicle coming up behind. Traffic in and around the Honolulu metropolitan area is heavy, and riding a bicycle can be dicey. Traffic in small towns and out in the country is much less severe. Fortunately, there are many roads with little traffic, particularly on the Big Island, so bicycling can be a very enjoyable and rewarding experience. Off-road riders have some choice of trails, but the number is still small, with more found on the Big Island than anywhere else.

If you're planning on spending any length of time on a bicycle in Hawaii, you're probably better off bringing your own bike than renting. If you do rent a bicycle, consider getting a **mountain bike** instead of a delicate road bike, which will allow for the sometimes-poor road conditions and open up the possibilities of off-road biking. Even experienced mountain bikers should be careful on off-road trails, which are often extremely muddy and rutted. While the roads are sometimes congested, pedaling around is usually safe—a fun way of seeing the sights. Always use a helmet, always lock your bike, and always take your bike bag.

You can take your bike with you interisland by plane, but it will cost about $20 one-way—just check it in as baggage. Bikes must be packed in a box or hard case, supplied by the owner. Handlebars must be turned sideways and the pedals removed or turned in. Bikes go space available only—usually not a problem, except, perhaps, during bicycle competitions. In addition, a release of liability for damage must be signed before the airline will accept the bike. If you plan ahead, you can send your bike the previous day by air freight. You can also take your bike on the interisland ferries between Maui and both Lana'i and Moloka'i. It will cost you $20 and $15, respectively, each way, but you don't need to pack it.

Getting your bike to Hawaii from the Mainland or another country will depend upon which airline you take. Some will accept bicycles as baggage traveling with you (approximate additional charge of $50 from the Mainland U.S.) if the bikes are properly broken down and boxed in a bicycle box, while others will only take them as air freight, in which case the rates are exorbitant. Check with the airlines well before you plan to go or explore the possibility of shipping it by sea through a freight company.

For general information on biking in Hawaii, contact **Hawaii Bicycling League,** P.O. Box 4403, Honolulu, HI 96812-4403. This nonprofit organization promotes biking as recreation, sport, and transportation, encourages safe biking practices, conducts biking education, and advocates for biking issues. It publishes a monthly newsletter, *Spoke-n-Words,* filled with news of the organization's business, its bicycle safety program for kids, and rides that are open to the public, as well as current bicycle issues and sponsored bicycle competitions throughout the state. Group rides for all levels of abilities are sponsored almost every weekend, and nonmembers are welcome. If you are a bicycle rider living in the islands or simply want a subscription to the newsletter, write for membership information. For mountain biking and trail information on all the major islands, pick up a copy of *Mountain Biking the Hawaiian Islands,* by John Alford.

For additional information, have a look at the *Bicycle Regulations and Illustrated Safety Tips* booklet, put out by the Department of Transportation Services, City and County of Honolulu. Although written for the island of O'ahu, the information is applicable to all the islands, except for a few minor details. On O'ahu, pick up a copy at city hall or any satellite city hall or most bike shops. From the Neighbor Islands or if coming from outside the state, write or call for a copy: Bicycle Coordinator, City and County of Honolulu, 711 Kapi'olani Blvd., Suite 1200, Honolulu, HI 96813, 808/527-5044. Also very informative for rules of the road and common sense biking tips is the *Rights and Responsibilities for Hawai'i's Bicyclists* booklet. This booklet and the *Bike Oahu* bicycle route map are available free from the State Bicycle/Pedestrian Coordinator, State Department of Transportation, 869 Punchbowl St., Honolulu, HI 96813, 808/587-2321, and may be available at city halls and tourist offices.

## GOLF AND TENNIS
### Golf

People addicted to chasing that little white ball around the links are going to be delighted with Hawaii. You can golf every day of the year on more than 80 golf courses scattered around the state. Many are open to the public and are built along some of the most spectacular scenery in the world, where pounding surf or flower-dappled mountains form the backdrop. You'll find everything from Lana'i's nine-hole Cavendish Golf Course, where you put your donation in an envelope on the honor system, to some of the most highly praised, exclusive, and exciting golf courses in the world. Master builders such as Robert Trent Jones and Jack Nicklaus have laid out links in the islands where major tournaments are yearly events. Fees range from as little as $7 for some little nine-holers up to $220 at the most exclusive resorts.

Some tipping is the norm. A $1 tip to the bag drop attendant is customary, $2 if a bag boy takes your bags from the car, and a couple bucks extra if he cleans your clubs for you.

Municipal and public courses are open to everyone. Resort courses cater to the public as

The Big Island has some of the best golf courses in the state—many situated right along the ocean.

well as to resort guests, who usually get a substantial discount. Private courses are for members only and their guests, although some set aside a day or two a week for nonmembers. Military personnel and dependents, Department of Defense personnel, and those who have access to military bases are welcome to golf at the military courses (only on O'ahu). If you wish to golf at other than municipal or public courses, be sure to call ahead to verify accessibility. Most courses have pros and pro shops; most offer lessons. Many have driving ranges, some lighted. Virtually all have clubhouses with restaurants and lounges. Greens fees listed in the charts in the following island chapters are for non-Hawaii residents and for civilians at military courses. Many courses offer reduced *kama'aina* rates, special time rates, twilight hour rates, and summer specials. Be sure to ask about these rates as they often afford substantial savings. Some courses charge higher fees for non-U.S. residents. Military courses charge different greens fees for civilians than for military personnel, and the military fees differ depending upon rank.

For printed information on golf in Hawaii, pick up a copy of *Guide to Golf: Hawaiian Is-*lands. Additionally, look for the *Maui Golf Review* magazine or the newspaper-format *Hawai'i Golf News and Travel.*

## Tennis

Tennis courts are found on every island of Hawaii and enjoyed by locals and visitors on a year-round basis. County courts, under the control and maintenance of the Department of Parks and Recreation, are open to the public for free. Play is on a first-come, first-served basis and is limited to 45 minutes if there are people waiting. Weekends are often fairly busy, but it's relatively easy to get a court on weekdays. Court rules apply and only soft-sole shoes are allowed. Some hotel and private courts are also open to the public, where fees range from complimentary to about $20 for nonguests. Most courts are of Laykold or plexi-pave asphalt. Many courts are lighted. Charts in the accompanying travel chapters list many courts open to visitors.

## HUNTING

Most people don't think of Hawaii as a place to hunt, but actually it's quite good. Seven species of introduced game animals and 15 species of game birds are regularly hunted. Not all species of game animals are open on all islands, but every island offers hunting. Please refer to the travel chapters for full details on hunting on particular islands.

## General Hunting Rules

Hunting licenses are mandatory to hunt on public, private, or military land anywhere in Hawaii. They're good for one year beginning July 1 and cost $20 residents and military, $105 nonresidents; free to senior citizens. Licenses are available from sporting goods stores and from the various offices of the Division of Forestry and Wildlife. This government organization also sets and enforces the rules, so contact it with any questions. Generally, hunting hours are from a half hour before sunrise to a half hour after sunset. Checking stations are maintained, where the hunter must check in before and after hunting.

Rifles must have a muzzle velocity greater than 1,200 foot-pounds. Shotguns larger than .20 gauge are allowed, and muzzle loaders must have a .45-caliber bore or larger. Bows must have a minimum draw of 40 pounds for straight bows, 35 pounds for a recurve bow, and 30 pounds for compounds. Arrows must be broadheads. The use of hunting dogs is permitted only for certain species of birds and game, and when dogs are permitted, only smaller caliber rifles and shotguns, along with spears and knives, may be used—no big bore guns/shotguns. Hunters must wear orange safety cloth on front and back no smaller than a 12-inch square. Certain big game species are hunted only by lottery selection; contact the Division of Forestry and Wildlife two months in advance. Guide service is not mandatory, but is advised if you're unfamiliar with hunting in Hawaii. You can hunt on private land only with permission, and you must possess a valid hunting license. Guns and ammunition brought into Hawaii must be registered with the chief of police of the corresponding county within 48 hours of arrival. Also, firearms must be unloaded and in an appropriately locked case as checked luggage to be transported by plane to the state.

## Information

Hunting rules and regulations are always subject to change. Also, environmental considerations often change bag limits and seasons. Make sure to check with the State Division of Forestry and Wildlife for the most current information. Request *Rules Regulating Game Bird Hunting, Rules Regulating Game Mammal Hunting,* and *Hunting in Hawaii.* Direct inquiries to: Department of Land and Natural Resources, Division of Forestry and Wildlife, 1151 Punchbowl St., Honolulu, HI 96813, 808/587-0166; on Maui, 54 S. High St., Wailuku, HI 96793, 808/984-8100; on Hawai'i, 19 East Kawili, Hilo, HI 96720, 808/974-4221; on Lana'i, P.O. Box 732, 911 Fraser Ave., Lana'i City, HI 96763, 808/565-7916; on Kaua'i, 3060 Eiwa St., P.O. Box 1671, Lihu'e, HI 96766, 808/274-3433; on Moloka'i, P.O. Box 347, Kaunakakai, HI 96748, 808/533-1745.

## Game Animals

All game animals on Hawaii have been introduced. Some have adapted admirably and are becoming well entrenched, while the existence of others is still precarious. **Axis deer** originated in India and were brought to Lana'i and Moloka'i, where they're doing well. The small herd on Maui is holding its own. Their unique flavor makes them one of the best wild meats. They're hunted on Lana'i from mid-February to mid-May, by public lottery. **Feral pigs** are escaped domestic pigs that have gone wild and are found on all islands except Lana'i. The stock is a mixture of original Polynesian pigs and subsequently introduced species. The pigs are hunted with dogs and usually killed with a spear or long knife—not recommended for the timid or tender-hearted. These beasts' four-inch tusks and fighting spirit make them tough and dangerous. **Feral goats** come in a variety of colors. Found on all islands except Lana'i, they have been known to cause erosion and are considered a pest in some areas, especially on Haleakala. They're openly hunted on all islands, and when properly cooked, their meat is considered delicious. **Black-tailed deer** come from Oregon. Forty were released on Kaua'i in 1961; the herd is now stabilized at around 400 and they're hunted in October by public

INTRODUCTION

lottery. **Mouflon sheep** are native to Corsica and Sardinia. They do well on Lana'i and on the windswept slopes of Mauna Loa and Mauna Kea, where they're hunted at various times, also by public lottery. **Feral sheep** haunt the slopes of Mauna Kea and Mauna Loa at 7,000–12,000 feet. They travel in flocks and destroy vegetation. It takes determination and a good set of lungs to bag one, especially with a bow and arrow. **Feral cattle** on the Big Island and **rock wallabies** from Australia, which now make their home on O'ahu, are not hunted.

## Game Birds

A number of game birds are found on most of the islands. Bag limits and hunting seasons vary, so check with the Division of Forestry and Wildlife for details. The **ring-necked pheasant** is one of the best game birds, found on all the islands. The **kalij pheasant** from Nepal lives only on the Big Island, where the **green pheasant** is also prevalent, with some found on O'ahu, Maui, and Lana'i. **Francolins,** gray and black birds from India and the Sudan, are similar to partridges. They are hunted with dogs on all islands and are great roasted. There are also **chukar** from Tibet, on the slopes of all islands; a number of **quail,** including the Japanese and California varieties; **doves;** and the wild **Rio Grande turkey** found on all islands except Kaua'i and O'ahu.

## Sporting Clays

An outgrowth of hunting, sporting clays is a sport that helps develop and maintain your hand-eye coordination. Shooting is done from different stations around a course, and the object is to hit

a small round clay disk. Different from trap or skeet shooting, sporting clays relies upon moving targets that mimic different animals and birds, hopping along the ground as if a rabbit, springing off the ground like a teal, or flying high like a pheasant. Hawaii has two sporting clays courses, one in Makena on Maui and the other on Lana'i. Although a variety of options are available for the beginner to the advanced shooter, a typical round of 100 shots with a 20-gauge shotgun would take about an hour and cost around $125.

## SIGHTSEEING TOURS

Tours offered on all the major islands will literally let you cover an individual island from top to bottom; you can walk it, drive it, sail around it, fly over it, or see it from below the water. Water tours include half-day or full-day snorkel trips, kayak expeditions up rugged lava coastlines, submarine rides, and comfortable sunset cocktail/dinner cruises. Land tours are generally very gentle bus or van trips that show you the highlights of the islands, but some now offer adventure 4WD outings to the tops of mountains or into deep forest areas. Hiking tours are also a great option to get to places that you can't get to otherwise and to open up the natural beauty of the interior and natural life of the islands. Helicopter rides and fixed-wing air tours are the most usual and ubiquitous available, but several enterprising companies offer glider rides, hang gliding, paragliding, and even parachuting for the more adventurous traveler into the experience of excitement. See the individual island chapters below for specific information.

# Accommodations

Hawaii's accommodations won't disappoint anyone. The state has an exceptionally wide range of places to stay with varieties both in style and in price. You can camp on a totally secluded beach two days down a hiking trail, have a dream vacation at one of the undisputed top resorts in the world, or get a package deal including a week's lodging in one of many island hotels for less than you would spend for a hotel at home. If you want to experience the islands as if you lived here, bed-and-breakfasts have become popular and easy to arrange. Condominiums are plentiful, and great for extended stays for families who want to set up home away from home or for a group of friends who want to save money by sharing costs. There is a smattering of youth hostels, YM/WCAs, and home exchanges. If you're a student, a summer session at the University of Hawai'i can mix education and fun.

Hawaii makes the greater part of its living from visitors, and all concerned desire to keep Hawaiian standards up and vacationers coming back. This means accommodations in Hawaii are operated by professionals who know the business of pleasing people. This adds up to benefits for you. Rooms in even the more moderate hotels are clean; the standard of services ranges from adequate to luxurious pampering. With the tips and advice given below, you should be able to find a place to stay that will match your taste and your pocketbook. For specifics, please refer to **Accommodations** in each of the travel chapters.

## HOTELS

Even with the wide variety of other accommodations available, most visitors, at least first-timers, tend to stay in hotels. At one time, hotels were the only places to stay. Characters like Mark Twain were berthed at Kilauea's rude Volcano House, while millionaires and nobility sailed for Waikiki, where they stayed in luxury at the Moana Hotel or Royal Hawaiian, which both still stand as vintage reminders of days past. Maui's Pioneer Inn dates from the turn of the

20th century, and if you were Hawaii-bound, these and a handful that haven't survived were about all that was offered. Today, there are approximately 54,000 hotel rooms statewide, and every year more hotels are built and older ones renovated. They come in all shapes and sizes, from 10-room family-run affairs to high-rise giants. A trend turned some into condominiums, while the Neighbor Islands have learned an aesthetic lesson from Waikiki and built low-rise resorts that don't obstruct the view and that blend more readily with the surroundings. Whatever accommodation you want, you'll find it in Hawaii.

## Types of Hotel Rooms

Most readily available and least expensive is a bedroom with bath. Some hotels can also offer you a studio (a large sitting room that converts to a bedroom), a suite (a bedroom with sitting room), or an apartment with full kitchen plus at least one bedroom. Kitchenettes are often available, and each contains a refrigerator, sink, and stove usually in a small corner nook or fitted together as one space-saving unit. Kitchenettes cost a bit more but save you a bundle by allowing you to prepare some of your own meals. To get that vacation feeling while keeping costs down, eat breakfast in, pack a lunch for the day, and go out to dinner. If you rent a kitchenette, make sure all the appliances work as soon as you arrive. If they don't, notify the front desk immediately, and if the hotel will not rectify the situation ask to be moved or given a reduced rate. Hawaii has cockroaches, so put all food away.

Check-in is usually 3 P.M. or 4 P.M., although if your room is ready, they can get you in early. Call. Checkout is most often 11 A.M. or noon. Some of the more expensive hotels and resorts have express checkout, and a TV video checkout system is offered by others.

## Amenities

All hotels have some of them, and some hotels have all of them. Air-conditioning is available in most, but under normal circumstances you won't need it. Balmy trade winds provide plenty of breezes, which flow through louvered windows and doors in many hotels. Ceiling fans are better. TVs are often included, but not always, as are entertainment centers with stereos and CD players; pay-per-view movies are almost always an option. In-room phones are usually provided, but a service charge of up to one dollar per call is often tacked on, even for local calls. Dataports for internet connection are also becoming common in rooms at better hotels and most provide internet access for guests in a common area. A few hotels have purposefully created an environment without phone, TV, or entertainment centers so that you can get plugged into your surroundings and stay disconnected form other distractions. Swimming pools are very common, even though the hotel may sit right on the beach. There is always a restaurant of some sort, a coffee shop or two, a bar, a cocktail lounge, and sometimes a sundries shop, clothing store, or art gallery. Most rooms have mini-refrigerators and coffee machines. While most stock complimentary coffee and tea, goodies from the honor bar (if there is one) will be charged to your bill.

Some hotels also offer tennis courts or golf courses either as part of the premises or affiliated with the hotel; usually an "activities desk" can book you into a variety of daily outings. Plenty of hotels offer laundromats on the premises, and the better places also have pickup and delivery laundry services. Hotel towels can be used at the beach and pool. Many hotels have installed lines that pull out over the bathtub and are to be used for drying wet clothes. Dry your swimsuits there because hotels don't want you to drape your wet suit over the balcony outside. Bellhops generally get about $1 tip per bag or $5 a load on a rolling cart, and maid service is free, though maids are customarily tipped $1–2 per time—a bit more if kitchenettes are involved, or if you've been a piggy. Self-parking is usually free unless you opt for valet service, which is provided at a nominal fee or by tip. Most have in-room safes for securing your valuable, but many charge $1.50–3.75 for the privilege. Most hotels offer a children's program with supervised activities, excursions, and food during weekday daytime hours—sometimes seasonally—for children 5–12. Cost ranges from free to $50 a kid. Hotels can often arrange special services like baby-sitters (in house or with a local licensed caregiver), all kinds of lessons, and special entertainment activities. A few even have bicycles and snorkeling equipment to lend. They'll receive and send mail for you, cash your traveler's checks, and take messages. For your convenience, each room should be equipped with a directory of hotel services and information, and some hotels also include information about area sights, restaurants, and activities.

## Hotel Rates: Add 11.4 Percent Tax

Every year Hawaiian hotels welcome in the New Year by hiking their rates by about 10 percent. Hawaii, because of its gigantic tourist flow and tough competition, offers hotel rooms at universally lower rates than those at most developed resort areas around the world; so, even with the 11.4 percent tax (7.25 percent transient accommodations tax, plus 4.16 percent state excise tax), there are still many reasonable rates to be had. Package deals, especially to Waikiki, almost throw in a week's lodging for the price of an air ticket. The basic **daily rate** is geared toward double occupancy; singles are hit in the pocketbook. Single rates, when available, are cheaper than doubles, but not usually by much. Many hotels will charge for a double and then add an additional charge ($10–100) for each extra person up to a certain number. Plenty of hotels offer the **family plan,** which allows children, usually 17 or 18 and under, to stay in their parents' room free if they use the existing bedding. If another bed or crib is required, there is an additional charge. Some hotels—not always the budget ones—let you cram in as many as can sleep on the floor for no additional charge. Only a limited number of hotels offer the **American plan,** in which breakfast and dinner are included with the night's lodging. **Discounts** of various sorts are offered, but these vary by hotel. Some of the typical discounts are AAA, AARP, car and room, room and breakfast, fifth-night free, and *kama'aina* (state resident) rates, but many now offer special lower internet rates when booking online as it's cheaper for hotels to sell rooms that way. **Business/corporate rates** are usually offered to anyone who can at least produce a business card. **Weekly and monthly** rates will save you approximately 10 percent off the daily rate. In all cases, make sure to ask about other-than-published rates because this information won't usually be volunteered. In addition to regular hotel charges and taxes, some luxury hotels and resorts now charge a "resort fee," generally $10–15, that is used to offset a variety of activities, services, and parking costs that would otherwise be charged for individually.

While some hotels have a single basic rate throughout the year, most have a tiered pricing policy based on times of the year. This often translates as regular- and value-season rates (which may be referred to differently at different hotels), while some also include holiday rates. Some hotels have a policy of **minimum stay,** usually three to seven days, during Christmas and New Year. While the difference between "high season" and "low season" is less distinct than it used to be, Hawaii's **peak season** still runs from just before Christmas until after Easter, and then again throughout the summer, when rooms are at a premium. Value-season rates, when rooms are easier to come by, are often about 10 percent below the regular rate.

In Hawaiian hotels you always pay more for a good view. Terms vary slightly, but usually "oceanfront" means your room faces the ocean and mostly your view is unimpeded. "Ocean view" is slightly more vague. It could be a decent view, or it could require standing on the dresser and craning your neck to catch a tiny slice of the sea sandwiched between two skyscrapers. "Garden view" means just that, and "mountain view" may mean that you have a view of a mountain or simply that you have a view away from the ocean. Rooms are designated and priced upward with garden view or mountain view being the least expensive, then ocean view and ocean front rooms. Suites are invariably larger and more expensive, and these usually get the best locations and views.

**Note:** Prices listed are based on a standard published rate, double occupancy, without taxes or other charges added, unless otherwise noted.

## Paying, Deposits, and Reservations

The vast majority of Hawaiian hotels accept foreign and domestic traveler's checks, personal checks preapproved by the management, foreign cash, and most major credit cards. Reservations are always the best policy, and they're easily made through travel agents or by contacting the hotel directly. In all cases, bring documentation of your confirmed reservations with you in case of a mix-up.

**Deposits** are not always required to make reservations, but they do secure them. Some hotels require the first (or several) night's payment in advance. Reservations without a deposit can be legally released if the room is not claimed by 6 P.M. Whether by phone call, email, fax, or letter, include your dates of stay and type of room in your request for a reservation, and make sure that the hotel sends you a copy of the confirmation. All hotels and resorts have **cancellation requirements** for refunding deposits. The time limit on these can be as little as 24 hours before arrival, or as much as a full 30 days. Some hotels require full **advance payment** for your length of stay, especially during peak season or during times of crowded special events. Be aware of the time required for a cancellation notice *before* making your reservation deposit, especially when dealing with advance payment. If you have confirmed reservations, especially with a deposit, and there is no room for you, or one that doesn't meet prearranged requirements, you should be given the option of accepting alternate accommodations. You are owed the difference in room rates if there is any. If there is no room whatsoever, the hotel is required to find you one at a comparable hotel and to refund your deposit in full.

# CONDOMINIUMS

Hawaii was one of the first states struck by the condominium phenomenon; it began in the 1950s and has increased ever since. Now condos are almost as common as hotels, and renting one is just about as easy. Condos, unlike hotel rooms, are privately owned apartments normally part of a complex or high-rise. The condo is usually an absentee owner's second or vacation home.

ROBERT NILSEN

Kanaloa at Kona is one of the premier condominiums in the Kailua–Keauhou area.

An on-premises condo manager (or rental agency) rents out vacant units and is responsible for maintenance and security.

## Things to Know

Staying in a condo has advantages and disadvantages over staying in a hotel. The main qualitative difference between a condo and a hotel is amenities. At a condo, you're more on your own. You're temporarily renting an apartment, so there won't be any bellhops, and rarely a bar, restaurant, or lounge on the premises, though many times you'll find a sundries store. The main lobby, instead of having that grand entrance feel of many hotels, is more like an apartment house entrance, although there might be a front desk. Condos can be studios (one big room), but mostly they are one- or multiple-bedroom affairs with a complete kitchen. Reasonable housekeeping items should be provided: linens, furniture, and a fully equipped kitchen. Most have TVs and phones, but remember that the furnishings are provided by the owner. You can find brand-new furnishings that are top of the line, right down to "garage sale" bargains. Inquire about the furnishings when you make your reservations. Maid service might be included on a limited basis (for example, once weekly), or you might have to pay extra for it.

Condos usually require a minimum stay, although some will rent on a daily basis, like hotels. Minimum stays when applicable are often three days, but seven is also commonplace, and during peak season two weeks isn't unheard of. Swimming pools are common, and depending on the "theme" of the condo, you can find saunas, weight rooms, hot tubs, or tennis courts. A nominal extra fee, often $10–15, is usually charged for more than two people. Generally speaking, studios can sleep two, a one-bedroom will sleep four, two-bedrooms will sleep six, and three-bedrooms will sleep eight. Most have a sleeper couch in the sitting room that folds out into a bed. You can find clean, decent condos for as little as $450 per week, all the way up to exclusive apartments for well over $2,000. Most fall into the $700–1,000 range per week. The method of paying for and reserving a condo is just about the same as for a hotel. However, requirements for deposits, final payments, and cancellation charges are much stiffer than in hotels. Make absolutely sure you fully understand all of these requirements when you make your reservations.

Their real advantage of condos is for families, friends who want to share accommodations, and especially travelers on long-term stays, for which you will always get a special rate. The kitchen facilities save a great deal on dining costs, and it's common to find units with their own washers and dryers. To sweeten the deal, many condo companies offer coupons that can save you money on food, gifts, and activities at local establishments. Parking space is ample for guests, and like hotels, plenty of stay/drive deals are offered. Like hotels, condos usually charge for local calls, credit card calls, and collect calls. Some have in-room safes, but there will be a daily charge of $1.50–1.75 for their use. Pay-per-view, in-room movie service is usually available for $8.95–16.95 per movie. Many now also have a lost key fee, which may be as steep as $75, so don't lose it! If you can't produce it, you pay for it.

## Hotel and Condominium Information

One of the best sources of hotel/condo information for the vacationer is the Hawaii Visitors Bureau. While planning your trip, either visit one nearby or write to the bureau in Hawaii. (Addresses are listed in the **Information and Services** section later in this chapter.) Request a free copy of the current Accommodation/Dining/Entertainment Guide. This handy booklet lists all the hotel/condo members of the HVB, with addresses, phone numbers, facilities, and rates. Understand that these are not all of the hotels/condos in Hawaii, just members of HVB. Entertainment, dining, transportation, and general tips are also given.

For condo booking agencies on the different islands, see the individual travel chapter introductions below.

## VACATION RENTALS

Vacation rentals are homes or cottages that are rented to visitors, usually on a basis of a week or longer. Some shorter rentals can be arranged. These rentals come with all the amenities of condo units, but they are usually free-standing

homes. Meals are not part of the option, so that is your responsibility. There are numerous vacation rentals throughout the islands, and many of these advertise by word of mouth, ads in magazines, and websites. Perhaps the best way to locate a vacation rental, at least for the first time that you visit the island, is through a rental/real estate agent—a number are listed in the travel chapters of this book. This can be handled in Hawaii or by phone, fax, email, or mail. Everything from simple beach homes to luxurious hideaways is put into the hands of rental agents. The agents have descriptions of the properties and terms of the rental contracts, and many will furnish photographs. Be aware that some places, although not all, have out-cleaning fees in addition to the rental rate. When contacting an agency, be as specific as possible about your needs, length of stay, desired location, and how much you're willing to spend. If handled through the mail, the process may take some time; write several months in advance. Be aware that during high season, rentals are at a premium; if you're slow to inquire there may be slim pickin's.

## BED-AND-BREAKFASTS

Bed-and-breakfast (B&B) inns are hardly a new idea. The Bible talks of the hospitable hosts who opened the gates of their homes and invited the wayfarer in to spend the night. B&Bs have a long tradition in Europe and were commonplace in Revolutionary America. Nowadays, lodging in private homes called bed-and-breakfasts is becoming increasingly fashionable throughout America, and Hawaii is no exception, with about 100,000 B&B guests yearly.

### Points to Consider

The primary feature of bed-and-breakfasts is that every one is privately owned and therefore uniquely different from every other. The range of B&Bs is as wide as the living standards in America. You'll find everything from a semi-mansion in the most fashionable residential area to a little grass shack offered by a down-home fisherman and his family. This means that it's particularly important for the guest to choose a host family with whom his or her lifestyle is compatible.

Unlike at a hotel or a condo, you'll be staying *with* a host (usually a family), although your room will be private, with private baths and separate entrances quite common. You can make arrangements directly or you might want to go through agencies (listed below), which act as go-betweens, matching host and guest. It is best to call these agencies, but you can also write. Agencies have a description of each B&B they rent for, its general location, the fees charged, and a good idea of the lifestyle of your host family. What the agency will want to know from you is where you want to stay, what type of place you're looking for, the price range you're willing to pay, arrival and departure dates, and other items that will help them match you with a place. (Are you single? Do you have children? Smoker? etc.) You, of course, can do all the legwork yourself, but these people know their territory and guarantee their work. If you find that a situation is incompatible, they will find another that works. They also inspect each B&B, and make sure that each has a license and insurance to operate. Most can also arrange discount rental car and interisland air fares for you.

Since B&Bs are run by individual families, the times that they will accept guests can vary according to what's happening in their lives. This makes it imperative to write well in advance: three months is good; earlier is too long and too many things can change. Four weeks is about the minimum time required to make all necessary arrangements. Expect a minimum stay (three days is common). B&Bs are not long-term housing, although it's hoped that guest and host will develop a friendship and that future stays can be as long as both desire.

As with condos, B&Bs have different requirements for making and holding reservations and for payment. Most will hold a room with a credit card deposit or check covering a certain percentage of the total bill. Be aware, however, that some B&Bs do not accept credit cards or personal checks, so you must pay in cash, traveler's checks, or money orders. Always inquire about the method of payment when making your initial inquiries.

## B&B Agencies

A top-notch B&B agency with over 200 homes is **Bed and Breakfast Hawaii,** operated by Evelyn Warner and Al Davis. They've been running this service since 1978, and their reputation is excellent. Write Bed and Breakfast Hawaii, P.O. Box 449, Kapa'a, HI 96746, 808/822-7771 or 800/733-1632, www.bandb-hawaii.com, reservations@bandb-hawaii.com.

One of the most experienced agencies, **Bed and Breakfast Honolulu** (statewide), at 3242 Kaohinanai Dr., Honolulu, HI 96817, 808/595-7533 or 800/288-4666, fax 808/595-2030, owned and operated by Marylee and Gene Bridges, began in 1982. Since then, they've become masters at finding visitors the perfect accommodations to match their desires, needs, and pocketbooks. Their repertoire of guest homes offers more than 400 rooms, with half on O'ahu and the other half scattered around the state. The agency's website is at www.hawaiibnb.com; it's email address is rainbow@hawaiibnb.com.

**All Island Bed and Breakfast,** 823 Kainui Dr., Kailua, HI 96734, 808/263-2342 or 800/542-0344, fax 808/263-0308, cac@aloha.net, can match your needs up with about 700 homes throughout the state.

**Hawaii's Best Bed and Breakfast,** P.O. Box 520, Kamuela, HI 96743, 808/885-4550 or 800/262-9912, fax 808/885-0559, www.bestbnb.com, bestbnb@aloha.net, has listings all over the state and is known for excellent service.

Since 1982, **Go Native Hawaii** has helped people find the right place to stay on the five major islands. Contact Go Native at 808/935-4178 or 800/662-8483, www.gonativehi.com, reservations@gonativehi.com.

Two of the islands have their own bed and breakfast associations, although not all of the B&Bs on those islands are members. More than just a marketing ploy, these associations try to insure the quality and high standards of their individual bed and breakfast members. For B&B on Maui, see the **Maui Bed and Breakfast Association,** www.bedbreakfastmaui.com. On the Big Island, try **Hawaii Island B&B Association,** P.O. Box 1890, Honoka'a, HI 96727; www.stayhawaii.com, hibba@stayhawaii.com.

## HOSTELS, YMCA AND YWCA

While there are very few hostels in Hawaii, each of the four major islands has at least one, although only three are official American Youth Hostel members. All are located in major towns, and several are just a few blocks from the beach in Waikiki. These are basic accommodations that offer a common room, several bathrooms, bunk rooms, and a limited number of private rooms. Kitchens are usually available, as is long-term storage. Each offers other amenities, which may include transportation to and/or from the airport, local excursions, low car rental rates, and free use of water equipment. European travelers, surfers, and backpackers make up the bulk of visitors. Generally, a bunk bed runs about $17.50–20 and private rooms are $35–50.

YM/WCAs are also quite limited in Hawaii. All those with rooms are in Honolulu. They vary as far as private rooms and baths are concerned, so each should be contacted individually. Prices vary too, but expect to pay $25 single.

Men or women are accepted at respective Ys unless otherwise stated.

## HOME EXCHANGES

One other method of staying in Hawaii, open to homeowners, is to offer the use of your home in exchange for use of a home in Hawaii. This is done by listing your home with an agency that facilitates the exchange and publishes a descriptive directory. To list your home and to find out what is available, contact one of the following agencies:

**Homelink USA,** P.O. Box 47747, Tampa, Fl 33647, 813/975-9825 or 800/638-3841, fax 813/910-8144, www.homelink.org, usa@homelink.org.

**Intervac U.S.,** 30 Corte San Fernando, Tiburon, CA 94920, 808/756-4663, fax 415/435-7440, www.intervacus.com, info@intervacus.com.

**Vacation Homes Unlimited,** 16654 Soledad Canyon Road, Suite 214, Santa Clarita, CA 91387, 808/298-0376, fax 808/298-0576 or 800/848-7927; www.exchangehomes.com.

## Food and Drink

Hawaii is a gastronome's Shangri-La, a sumptuous smorgasbord in every sense of the word. The varied ethnic groups that have come to Hawaii in the last 200 years have each brought their own special enthusiasms and cultures—and lucky for all, they didn't forget their cookpots, hearty appetites, and taste buds.

The Polynesians who first arrived found a fertile but barren land. Immediately they set about growing taro, coconuts, and bananas, and raising chickens, pigs, fish, and dogs, though the latter were reserved for nobility. Harvests were bountiful and the islanders thanked the gods with the traditional feast called the lu'au. Most food was baked in the underground oven, the *imu*. Participants were encouraged to feast while relaxing on straw mats and enjoying the hula and various entertainment. The lu'au is as popular as ever, a treat that's guaranteed to delight anyone with a sense of eating adventure.

The missionaries and sailors came next and their ships' holds carried barrels of ingredients for puddings, pies, dumplings, gravies, and roasts—the sustaining "American foods" of New England farms. The mid-1800s saw the arrival of boatloads of Chinese and Japanese peasants, who wasted no time making rice instead of bread the staple of the islands. The Chinese added their exotic spices, creating complex Sichuan dishes as well as workers' basics like chop suey. The Japanese introduced shoyu (soy sauce), sashimi, boxed lunches (bento), delicate tempura, and rich, filling noodle soups. The Portuguese brought their luscious Mediterranean dishes of tomatoes and peppers and plump spicy sausages, nutritious bean soups, and mouthwatering sweet treats like malasadas (holeless donuts) and pao dolce (sweet bread). Koreans carried crocks of zesty kimchi and quickly fired up grills for pulgogi, a marinated beef cooked over a fire. Filipinos served up their delicious adobo stews—fish, meat, or chicken in a rich sauce of vinegar and garlic.

Recently, Thai and Vietnamese restaurants have been offering their irresistible dishes next door to restaurants offering fiery burritos from Mexico and elegant marsala cream sauces from France. The ocean breezes of Hawaii not only cool the skin but waft with them some of the most delectable aromas on earth, to make the taste buds thrill and the spirit soar.

Nothing is sweeter to the appetite than reclining on a beach and deciding just what dish will make your taste buds laugh that night. Kick back, close your eyes, and let the smells and tastes of past meals drift into your consciousness.

## HAWAIIAN FOODS

Hawaiian cuisine, the oldest of the islands, consists of wholesome, well prepared, and delicious foods. All you have to do on arrival is notice the size of some of the local boys (and women) to know immediately that food to them is indeed a happy and serious business. An oft-heard island joke is that "local men don't eat until they're full; they eat until they're tired." Many Hawaiian dishes have become standard fare at a variety of restaurants, eaten at one time or another by anyone who spends time in the islands. Hawaiian food in general is called *kaukau,* cooked food is *kapahaki,* and something broiled is called *ka'ola.* Any of these prefixes on a menu indicates that Hawaiian food is served. Usually inexpensive, these dishes will definitely fill you and keep you going.

### Traditional Favorites

In old Hawaii, although the sea meant life, many more people were involved in cultivating beautifully tended garden plots of taro, sugarcane, breadfruit, and various sweet potatoes *('uala)* than with fishing. They husbanded pigs and barkless dogs *('ilio),* and prized *moa* (chicken) for their feathers and meat, but found eating the eggs repulsive. Their only farming implement was the *'o'o,* a sharpened hardwood digging stick. The Hawaiians were the best farmers of Polynesia, and the first thing they planted was taro, a tuberous root created by the gods at the same

time as humans. This main staple of the old Hawaiians was pounded into poi. Every lu'au will have poi, a glutinous purple paste. It comes in liquid consistencies referred to as one-, two-, or three-finger poi. The fewer fingers you need to eat it, the thicker it is. Poi is one of the most nutritious carbohydrates known, but people unaccustomed to it find it bland and tasteless. Some of the best, fermented for a day or so, has an acidic bite. Poi is made to be eaten *with* something, but locals who love it pop it in their mouths and smack their lips. Those unaccustomed to it will suffer constipation if they eat too much.

While poi fell out of favor during the middle of the 20th century, it is once again becoming more popular, and several sizable factories now produce poi for sale. You can find plastic containers of this food refrigerated in many supermarkets and local food stores. In addition, deep-fried slices of taro root, plain or spiced, are now packaged and sold like potato chips.

A favorite popular dessert is *haupia,* a custard made from coconut. *Limu* is a generic term for edible seaweed, which many people still gather from the shoreline and eat as a salad, or mix with ground *kukui* nuts and salt as a relish. A favorite Hawaiian snack is *'opihi,* small shellfish (limpets) that cling to rocks. Those who gather them always leave some on the rocks for the future. Cut from the shell and eaten raw by all peoples of Hawaii, *'opihi* sell for $150 per gallon in Honolulu—a testament to their popularity. A general term that has come to mean hors d'oeuvres in Hawaii is *pu pu.* Originally the name of a small shellfish, it is now used for any finger food. A traditional liquor made from *ti* root is *'okolehao.* It literally means "iron bottom," reminiscent of the iron blubber pots used to ferment it.

### Pacific Rim (a.k.a. Hawaiian Regional) Cuisine

At one time the "tourist food" in Hawaii was woeful. Of course, there has always been a handful of fine restaurants, but for the most part the food lacked soul, with even the fine hotels opting to offer second-rate renditions of food more appropriate to large Mainland cities. Surrounded by some of the most fertile and pristine waters in the

Pacific, you could hardly find a restaurant offering fresh fish, and it was an ill-conceived boast that even the fruits and vegetables lying limply on your table were "imported." Beginning with a handful of extremely creative and visionary chefs in the early 1980s, who took the chance of perhaps offending the perceived simple palates of visitors, a delightfully delicious new cuisine was born. Based upon the finest traditions of Continental cuisine—including, to a high degree, its sauces, pastas, and presentations—the culinary magic of Pacific Rim boldly adds the pungent spices of Asia, the fantastic fresh vegetables, fruits, and fish of Hawaii, and, at times, the earthy cooking methods of the American Southwest. The result is a cuisine of fantastic tastes, subtle yet robust, and satiating but health-conscious—the perfect marriage of fresh foods prepared in a fresh way. Now restaurants on every island proudly display menus labeled "Hawaiian Regional" or some version of this. As always, some are better than others, but the general result is that the "tourist food" has been vastly improved and everyone benefits. Many of these exemplary chefs left lucrative and prestigious positions at Hawaii's five-diamond hotels and opened signature restaurants of their own, making this fine food much more available and affordable.

In 1998, a new and younger group called Hawaiian Island Chefs came together to further enhance the variety and offering of innovative foods made with island-grown produce and the bounty of the sea. In addition, this group strives to influence culinary programs in the state to help carry on this fine tradition of fusion food. With the incredible mix of peoples and cultures in Hawaii, the possibilities are endless, and this new group of chefs intends to shepherd the experience along.

## Lu'au

Thick cookbooks are filled with common Hawaiian dishes, but you can get a good sampling at a well-done lu'au. The central feature is the *imu*, an underground oven. Basically, a shallow hole is dug and lined with stones upon which a roaring fire is kindled. Once the fire dies down and the stones are super-heated, the ashes are swept away

and the *imu* is ready for cooking. At one time only men could cook in this fashion; it was *kapu* for women. These restrictions have long been lifted, but men still seem to do most of the pit cooking, while women primarily serve. The main dish at a lu'au is *kalua* pork. *Kalua* refers to any dish baked underground. A whole pig *(pua'a)* is wrapped in *ti* and banana leaves and placed in the pit's hot center. The pig's stomach cavity is filled with more hot stones; surrounding it are bundles of food wrapped in *ti* leaves. These savory bundles, *lau lau*, contain the side dishes: fish, chicken, poi, sweet potatoes, breadfruit, and bananas. The entire contents are then covered with multiple layers of banana, *ti*, or sometimes ginger leaves, and a final coating of earth. A long tube of bamboo may stick up from the *imu* so that water (for steam) can be added. In about four hours the coverings are removed and the lu'au begins. You are encouraged to recline on *lau hala* mats placed around the central dining area, although tables and chairs are usually provided. There are forks and plates, but traditionally it is proper to use your fingers as utensils and a sturdy banana leaf as a plate. Professional lu'au cooks pride themselves on their cooking methods and their food, and for a fixed price you can gorge yourself like an ancient *ali'i*. All lu'au supply entertainment, and exotic drinks flow like the tides. Your biggest problem after one of these extravaganzas will be finding the strength to rise from your *lau hala* mat.

Lu'au generally range in price from $60 to $80 per adult and half that for children. This price includes entertainment. Most commercial lu'au are still put on by hotels, but many others are also very successful and well-regarded. Generally, lu'au run from about 5:30 to 8:30 P.M. On your lu'au day, eat a light breakfast, skip lunch, and do belly-stretching exercises! Lu'au food is usually served buffet-style, although some do it family-style. All lu'au have pretty much the same format, although the types of food and entertainment differ. The least expensive, most authentic, and best lu'au are often put on by local churches or community groups. They are not held on a regular basis, so peruse the free tourist literature where they advertise.

# INTERNATIONAL DISHES

Chinese and Japanese cuisines have a strong influence on island cooking, and their well-known spices and ingredients are creatively used in many recipes. Other cuisines, such as Filipino, Korean, and Portuguese, are not as well known but are now becoming standard island fare.

## Chinese

Tens of thousands of fortune cookies yield their little sprigs of wisdom every day to hungry diners throughout Hawaii. The Chinese, who came to Hawaii as plantation workers, soon discovered a brighter economic future by striking out on their own. Almost from the beginning, these immigrants opened restaurants. The tradition is still strong, and if the smallest town in Hawaii has a restaurant at all, it's probably Chinese. These restaurants are some of the least expensive, especially at lunchtime when prices are lower. In them, you'll find the familiar chop suey, chow mein, Peking duck, and fried rice. Take-out is common and makes a good, inexpensive picnic lunch.

## Japanese

For the uninitiated, Japanese food is simple, aesthetically pleasing, and delicious. Sushi bars are plentiful, especially in Honolulu, using the freshest fish from local waters. Some common dishes include: teriyaki chicken, fish, or steak, which is grilled in a marinated shoyu (soy sauce) base; tempura, or mouth-size bites of fish and vegetables dipped in a flour and egg batter and deep fried; sukiyaki, or vegetables, meat, mushrooms, tofu, and vermicelli you cook at your table (in a prepared stock kept boiling with a little burner) then dip into a mixture of egg and shoyu; shabu shabu, similar to sukiyaki though without noodles and with the emphasis on beef; donburi, various ingredients on rice in a bowl; and various tofu dishes and miso soup, which provide some of the highest sources of non-meat protein. Japanese restaurants span the entire economic range, from elegant and expensive to hole-in-the-wall eateries where the surroundings are basic but the food is fit for a samurai. Above all, cleanliness is guaranteed.

## Filipino

Most people have never sampled Filipino food. This cuisine is spicy with plenty of exotic sauces. The following is a sampling found in most Filipino restaurants: singang, a sour soup made from fish, shrimp, or vegetables, which has an acidic base from fruits like tamarind; adobo, a generic term for anything (chicken and pork are standards) stewed in vinegar and garlic; lumpia, a Filipino spring roll; pancit, many variations of noodles made into ravioli-like bundles stuffed with pork or other meats; lechon, a whole suckling pig stuffed and roasted; siopao, a steam-heated dough ball filled with chicken or other tasty ingredients; and halo halo, a confection of shaved ice smothered in preserved fruits and canned milk.

## Korean

Those who have never dined on Korean dishes are in for a sumptuous treat. Specialties include: kalbitang, a beef rib soup in a thin but tasty broth; pulgogi, marinated beef and vegetables grilled over an open flame; pulkalbi, beef ribs grilled over an open flame; pibimbap, a large bowl of rice smothered with beef, chicken, and vegetables that you mix together before eating; kimchi, fermented cabbage and hot spices made into a zesty "slaw"; kimchi chigyae, a stew of kimchi, pork, vegetables, and spices in a thick soup base.

# MONEY-SAVERS

Only one thing is better than a great meal: a great meal at a reasonable price. The following are island institutions and favorites that will help you eat well and keep prices down.

## Kaukau Wagons

These are lunch wagons, but instead of slick, stainless-steel jobs, most are old delivery trucks converted into portable kitchens. Some say they're a remnant of World War II, when workers had to be fed on the job; others say that the meals they serve were inspired by the Japanese bento, a boxed lunch. You'll see these wagons parked along beaches, in city parking lots, or on busy streets. Usually a line of local people will be placing their orders, especially at lunchtime—a tip-off that the wagon serves delicious, nutritious island dishes for reasonable prices. They might have a few tables, but basically they serve food to go. Most of their filling meals are about $3.50, and "plate lunches" are the specialty.

## Plate Lunch

One of the best island standards, these lunches give you a sampling of authentic island food that can include teriyaki chicken, mahimahi, *lau lau,* and *lomi* salmon among others. They're served on paper or Styrofoam plates, are packed to go, and usually cost less than $3.50. Standard with a plate lunch is "two-scoop rice," a generous dollop of macaroni or other salad. Full meals, they're great for keeping down food costs and for instant picnics. Available everywhere from *kaukau* wagons to restaurants.

An innovation on the regular plate lunch is starting to pop up here and there in finer restaurants and even at a few *kaukau* wagons. This is a better quality plate lunch with the freshest ingredients, more health-conscious preparation, and a greater inventiveness in the foods chosen, and they're often served in a classier manner. As would be expected, these meals are not available everywhere yet and cost up to twice as much as the ordinary plate lunch, but they're still a good deal for this variation on a standard Hawaiian tradition.

## Bento

Bento are the Japanese rendition of the box lunch. Aesthetically arranged, they are full meals. They are often sold in supermarkets and in some local eateries with take-out counters.

## Saimin

Special "saimin shops," as well as restaurants, serve this hearty, Japanese-inspired noodle soup. Saimin is a word unique to Hawaii, although some speculate that is originates from the Chinese *sai mihn,* meaning something like "fine noodles," of the Guangdong Province. In Japan, these soups would be called *ramen* or *soba,* and it's as if the two were combined in saimin. A large bowl of noodles in broth, stirred with meat, chicken, fish, shrimp, or vegetables, costs only a few dollars and is big enough for an evening meal. The best place to eat saimin is in a local hole-in-the-wall shop run by a family.

## Okazu-ya

A Hawaiian adaptation of the Japanese restaurant that sells side dishes and inexpensive food, okazu-ya usually have a full menu of savory entrées as well as side dishes that take their inspiration, like much in the islands, from all the peoples who have made Hawaii their home. Sometimes, they specialize in one type of dish or another. Usually small family-run shops that cater to the local community, they have loyal clients who demand top quality and cheap prices. While not usually on the list of dieters' delights, the food you find at these fine places is filling and will sustain you through the day, yet some places are adapting to a "leaner" menu selection. Some but not all have the word "okazu-ya" as part of the restaurant name.

## Early-Bird Specials

Even some of the island's best restaurants in the fanciest hotels offer "early-bird specials"—a sampling of the regular-menu dinners offered to diners who come in before the usual dinner hour, which is approximately 6 P.M. You pay as little as half the normal price, and can dine in luxury on some of the best foods. The specials are often advertised in the "free" tourist books, which might also include coupons for two-for-one meals or limited dinners at much lower prices. Just clip them out.

## Buffets

Buffets are also quite common in Hawaii, and like lu'au are all-you-can-eat affairs. Offered at a variety of restaurants and hotels, they usually cost $12 and up, but will run $25–35 in the better hotels. The food, however, ranges considerably from passable to quite good. At lunchtime, they're lower priced than dinner, and breakfast buffets are cheaper yet. Buffets are often advertised in free tourist literature, which often includes discount coupons.

## Tip

Many lounges and bars have a "happy hour," usually around sundown, when the price of drinks is reduced. Some also offer free *pu pu* during happy hour, and at the best, these *pu pu* could make a meal.

# FISH AND SEAFOOD

Anyone who loves fresh fish and seafood has come to the right place. Island restaurants specialize in seafood, and it's available everywhere. Pound for pound, seafood is one of the best dining bargains in Hawaii. You'll find it served in every kind of restaurant, and often the fresh catch of the day is proudly displayed on ice in a glass case. The following is a sampling of the best.

## Mahimahi

This excellent eating fish is one of the most common, most popular, and least expensive in Hawaii. It's referred to as a "dolphin" but is definitely a fish, not a mammal. Mahimahi can weigh 10–65 pounds; the flesh is light and moist. This fish is broadest at the head. When caught it's a dark olive color, but after a while the skin turns iridescent shades of blue, green, and yellow. It can be served as a main course or as a patty in a fish sandwich.

## A'u

This true island delicacy is a broad-bill swordfish or marlin. It's expensive even in Hawaii because the damn thing's so hard to catch. The meat is moist and white and truly superb. If it's offered on the menu, order it. It'll cost a bit more, but you won't be disappointed.

## Ono

*Ono* means "delicious" in Hawaiian, so that should tip you off to the taste of this wahoo, or king mackerel. *Ono* is regarded as one of the finest eating fishes in the ocean, and its white, flaky meat lives up to its name.

## Manini

These five-inch fish are some of the most abundant in Hawaii; they live in about 10 feet of water. They school and won't bite a hook but are easily taken with spear or net. Not often on a menu, but they're favorites with local people who know best.

## Ulua

This member of the crevalle jack family ranges 15–100 pounds. Its flesh is white and has a steak-like texture. Delicious and often found on the menu.

## Uku

This gray snapper is a favorite with local people. The meat is light and firm and grills well.

## 'Ahi

A yellowfin tuna with distinctive pinkish meat. 'Ahi is a great favorite cooked or served raw in sushi bars.

## Moi

This is the Hawaiian word for "king." This fish has large eyes and a sharklike head. Considered one of the finest eating fishes in Hawaii, it's best during the autumn months.

## Seafood Potpourri

Other island seafood includes *'opihi,* a small shellfish (limpet) that clings to rocks and is considered one of the best island delicacies, eaten raw; *'alo'alo,* similar to tiny lobsters; crawfish, plentiful in taro fields and irrigation ditches; *'ahipalaka,* albacore tuna; various octopuses and squid (calamari); and shark of various types.

*'A'ama* are the ubiquitous little black crabs that you'll spot on rocks and around pier areas. They're everywhere. For fun, local fishermen try to catch them with poles, but the more efficient way is to throw a fish head into a plastic bucket and wait for the crabs to crawl in and trap themselves. The *'a'ama* are about as big as two fingers and make delicious eating.

*Limu* is edible seaweed that has been gathered as a garnish since precontact times and is frequently found on traditional island menus. There's no other seaweed except *limu* in Hawaii. Because of this, the heavy, fishy-ocean smell that people associate with the sea but which is actually that of seaweed is absent in Hawaii.

*Poke* is raw, cubed fish, usually made into a seafood salad with salt, vinegar, seaweed, onions, or other such ingredients, that is often found in deli sections of supermarkets.

## Sushi

A finger-size block of sticky rice, topped with a pickled vegetable and a slice of raw fish. A delicacy in Japan and appreciated in Hawaii as a fine food. In addition to the traditional offerings, cutting-edge chefs now create a mind-boggling variety of innovative sushi morsels.

## MUNCHIES AND ISLAND TREATS

Certain finger foods, fast foods, and island treats are unique to Hawaii. Some are meals in themselves, others are snacks. Here are some of the best and most popular.

## Pu Pu

Pronounced as in "Winnie the Pooh Pooh," these are finger foods and hors d'oeuvres. They can be anything from crackers to cracked crab. Often, they're given free at lounges and bars and can even include chicken drumettes, fish kabobs, and tempura. At a good display you can have a free meal.

## Crackseed

A sweet of Chinese origin, crackseed is preserved and seasoned fruits and seeds. Favorites include coconut, watermelon, pumpkin seeds, mango, plum, and papaya. Distinctive in taste, they take some getting used to but make great trail snacks. They are available in all island markets. Also look for dried fish (cuttlefish) on racks, usually near the crackseed. Nutritious and delicious, it makes a great snack.

## Shave Ice

This real island institution makes the Mainland "snow cone" melt into insignificance. Special machines literally shave ice to a fluffy consistency. It's mounded into a paper cone and then your choice of exotic island syrups is generously poured over it. Given a straw and a spoon, you just slurp away.

## Taro Chips

Like potato ships, but made from the taro root. If you can find them fresh, buy a bunch as they are mostly available packaged.

## Malasadas and Pao Dolce

Two sweets from the Portuguese, malasadas are holeless donuts and pao dolce is sweet bread. Sold in island bakeries, they're great for breakfast or as treats.

## Lomi Lomi Salmon

This salad of salmon, tomatoes, and onions with garnish and seasonings often accompanies "plate lunches" and is featured at buffets and lu'au.

## TROPICAL FRUITS AND VEGETABLES

Some of the most memorable taste treats from the islands require no cooking at all: the luscious tropical and exotic fruits and vegetables sold in markets and roadside stands or just found hanging on trees, waiting to be picked. Experience as many as possible. The general rule in Hawaii is that you are allowed to pick fruit on public lands, but the amount should be limited to personal consumption. The following is a sampling of some of Hawaii's best produce.

## Bananas

No tropical island is complete without them. There are more than 70 species in Hawaii, with hundreds of variations. Some are for peeling and eating while others are cooked. A "hand" of bananas is great for munching, backpacking, or picnicking. Available everywhere—and cheap.

## Avocados

Brought from South America, avocados were originally cultivated by the Aztecs. They have a buttery consistency and nutty flavor. Hundreds of varieties in all shapes and colors are available fresh year-round. They have the highest fat content of any fruit except the olive.

## Coconuts

What tropical paradise would be complete

INTRODUCTION

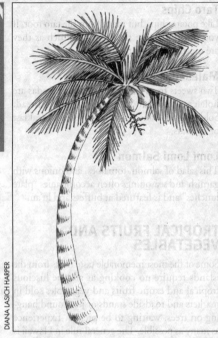

DIANA LASICH HARPER

**coconut palm**

without coconuts? Indeed, these were some of the first plants brought by the Polynesians. When a child was born, a coconut tree was planted to provide fruit for the child throughout his or her lifetime. Truly tropical fruits, coconuts know no season. Drinking nuts are large and green, and when shaken you can hear the milk inside. You get about a quart of fluid from each. It takes skill to open one, but a machete can handle anything. Cut the stem end flat so that it will stand, then bore a hole into the pointed end and put in a straw or hollow bamboo. Coconut water is slightly acidic and helps balance alkaline foods. Spoon meat is a custard-like gel on the inside of drinking nuts. Sprouted coconut meat is also an excellent food. Split open a sprouted nut, and inside is the yellow fruit, like a moist sponge cake. "Millionaire's salad" is made from the heart of a coconut palm. At one time an entire tree was cut down to get to the heart, which is just inside

the trunk below the fronds and is like an artichoke heart except that it's about the size of a watermelon. In a downed tree, the heart stays good for about two weeks.

## Breadfruit

This island staple provides a great deal of carbohydrate, but many people find the baked, boiled, or fried fruit bland. It grows all over the islands and is really thousands of little fruits growing together to form a ball that can be as big as a watermelon.

## Mangos

These are some of the most delicious fruits known to humans. They grow wild all over the islands; the ones on the leeward sides of the islands ripen April–June, while the ones on the windward sides can last until October. They're found in the wild on trees up to 60 feet tall. The problem is to stop eating them once you start!

## Papayas

This truly tropical fruit has no real season but is mostly available in the summer. Papayas grow on branchless trees and are ready to pick as soon as any yellow appears. Of the many varieties, the "solo papaya," meant to be eaten by one person, is the best. Split one in half, scrape out the seeds, and have at it with a spoon.

## Passion Fruit

Known by their island name of *liliko'i,* passion fruit make excellent juice and pies. The small yellow fruit (similar to lemons but smooth-skinned) is mostly available in summer and fall. Many grow wild on vines, waiting to be picked. Slice off the stem end, scoop the seedy pulp out with your tongue, and you'll know why they're called "passion fruit."

## Guavas

These small, round, yellow fruits are abundant in the wild, where they ripen from early summer to late fall. They're often considered a pest—so pick all you want. A good source of vitamin C, they're great for juice, jellies, and desserts.

## Macadamia Nuts

The king of nuts was brought from Australia in 1882. Now it's the state's fourth largest agricultural product. These nuts are creamy in color, crispy in texture, round in shape and about the size if a marble, slightly sweet, and available plain, roasted, candied, or buttered. Until the year 2000, Hawaii produced more of these nuts than anywhere else in the world. Now it follows Australia in total production.

## Litchis

Called nuts but really small fruits with thin red shells, litchis have a sweet, juicy white flesh that tastes somewhat like a green grape that surrounds a hard inner seed. **Rambutan** are similar in flesh but have a soft spikey and somewhat thicker red covering.

## Other Fruit

Along with the above, you'll find pineapples (including the white, sweet, and less acidic Sugarloaf variety), oranges, limes, kumquats, thimbleberries, and blackberries in Hawaii, as well as carambolas (star fruit), wild cherry tomatoes, and tamarinds.

# ISLAND DRINKS

To complement the fine dining in the islands, bartenders have been busy creating their own tasty concoctions. The full range of beers, wines, and standard drinks is served in Hawaii, but for a real treat you should try mixed drinks inspired by the islands. Most look very innocent because they come in pineapples, coconut shells, or tall frosted glasses. They're often garnished with little umbrellas or sparklers, and most have enough fruit in them to give you your vitamins for the day. Rum is the basis of many of them; it's been an island favorite since it was introduced by the whalers of the 19th

century. At fancy hotels expect to pay $6–7 for a drink; at other locations, about $5–6. Here are a few of the most famous: mai tai, a mixture of light and dark rum, orange curaçao, orange and almond flavoring, and lemon juice; chi-chi, a simple concoction of vodka, pineapple juice, and coconut syrup—a real sleeper because it tastes like a milk shake; Blue Hawaii, made with vodka and blue curaçao; Planter's Punch, composed of light rum, grenadine, bitters, and lemon juice—a great thirst quencher; and Singapore Sling, a sparkling mixture of gin and cherry brandy with lemon juice and/or pineapple, lime, and orange juices.

## Drinking Laws

There are no state-run liquor stores; all kinds of spirits, wines, and beers are available in markets and shops, generally open during normal business hours, seven days a week. The drinking age is 21, and no towns are "dry." Legal hours for serving drinks depend on the type of establishment. Hours generally are: hotels, 6 A.M.–4 A.M.; discos, and nightclubs where there is dancing, 10 A.M.–4 A.M.; bars and lounges where there is no dancing, 6 A.M.–2 A.M. Most restaurants serve alcohol, and in many that don't, you can bring your own.

## Coffee

Kona coffee at one time held the distinction of being the only coffee grown in the United States. It's been grown for about 150 years in the upland district of Kona on the Big Island and is a rich, aromatic, truly fine coffee. If it's offered on the menu, have a cup. More recently, coffee from Maui, Moloka'i, O'ahu, and Kaua'i has entered the market. About 4,000 acres of former cane land has been turned into one huge coffee production on Kaua'i, making it by far the largest in the state. The other islands have much fewer acres in production.

M

## Getting There

With the number of visitors each year approaching seven million, the state of Hawaii is one of the easiest places in the world to get to . . . by plane. Over half a dozen large North American airlines (plus additional charter airlines) fly to and from the islands. About the same number of foreign carriers, mostly from Asia and Oceania, also touch down on a daily basis. Hawaii is a hotly contested air market. The competition between carriers is fierce, and this makes for "sweet deals" and a wide choice of fares for the money-wise traveler. It also makes for pricing chaos. It's impossible to quote airline prices that will hold true for more than a month—if that long. But it's comforting to know that flights to Hawaii remain relatively cheap, and mile for mile they are one of the best travel bargains in the industry. Familiarize yourself with the alternatives at your disposal so you can make an informed travel selection. Now more than ever, you should work with a sharp travel agent who's on your side or do some research on the Web.

Airlines routinely adjust their flight schedules about every three months to account for seasonal differences in travel and route changes. Before planning a trip to and around the islands, be sure to contact the airlines directly or go through your travel agent for the most current information on routes and flying times.

### When to Go

The prime tourist season starts two weeks before Christmas and lasts until Easter. It picks up again with summer vacation in early June and ends once more in late August. Everything is usually much more heavily booked and prices are inflated. Hotel, airline, and car reservations are a must at this time of year. You can generally save considerably and deal with a lot of hassle if you go in the "off-season," September to early December and mid-April (after Easter) through the end of May. Recently, the drop in numbers of tourists during the off-season has not been nearly as substantial as in years past, indicating the increasing popularity of the islands at this time of year, but you'll still find the prices better and the beaches, trails, campgrounds, and even restaurants less crowded. The people will be happier to see you, too.

### Airflight: The Early Years

On May 20–21, 1927, the people of the world were mesmerized by the heroic act of Charles Lindbergh, The Lone Eagle, as he safely piloted his sturdy craft, *The Spirit of St. Louis,* across the Atlantic. With the Atlantic barrier broken, it took only four days for Jim Dole, of pineapple fame, to announce an air race from the West Coast to Hawaii. He offered the same first prize of $25,000 that Lindbergh had claimed, and to sweeten the pot he offered $10,500 for second place. The **Dole Air Derby** applied only to civilian flights, though the military had already been at work attempting the Pacific crossing.

In August 1925, a Navy flying boat took off from near San Francisco, piloted by Commander John Rodgers. The seaplane flew without difficulty across the wide Pacific's expanse but ran out of gas just north of the Hawaiian Islands and had to put down in a stormy sea. Communication devices went dead, and the mission was given up as lost. Heroically, Rodgers and his crew made crude sails from the wings' fabric and sailed the plane to within 12 miles of Kaua'i, where they were spotted by an incredulous submarine crew. On June 28, 1927, Army lieutenants Lester Maitland and Alfred Hegenberger successfully flew a Fokker tri-motor land plane, *The Bird of Paradise,* from Oakland to O'ahu in just under 26 hours.

On July 14, 1927, independent of the air derby, two indomitable pilots, Ernest Smith and Emory Bronte, flew their *City of Oakland* from its namesake to a forced landing on the shoreline of Moloka'i. On August 16, 1927, eight planes lined up in Oakland to start the derby. The first to take off was the *Woolaroc,* piloted by Art Goebel and Bill Davis. It went on to win the race and claim the prize in just over 26 hours. Second place went to the appropriately named *Aloha,* crewed by

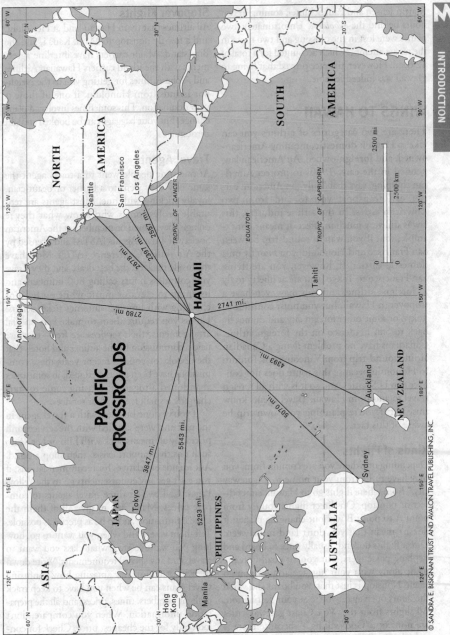

PACIFIC
CROSSROADS

NORTH AMERICA

SOUTH AMERICA

ASIA

AUSTRALIA

NEW ZEALAND

HAWAII

Seattle
San Francisco
Los Angeles
Anchorage
Tokyo
Hong Kong
Manila
Auckland
Sydney
Tahiti

JAPAN
PHILIPPINES

2557 mi.
2397 mi.
2678 mi.
2780 mi.
2741 mi.
4333 mi.
5070 mi.
5543 mi.
5293 mi.
3847 mi.

TROPIC OF CANCER
EQUATOR
TROPIC OF CAPRICORN

2500 mi
2500 km

60° N    60° N
30° N
30° S
60° W    60° W
90° W
120° W
150° W
180°
150° E
120° E
0°

Martin Jensen and Paul Schluter, coming in two hours behind the *Woolaroc*. Unfortunately, two planes were lost in the crossing and two more in the rescue attempt, which accounted for a total of 12 dead. However, the race proved that flying to Hawaii was indeed feasible.

# WINGS TO HAWAII

There are two categories of airlines you can take to Hawaii: **domestic,** meaning American-owned, and **foreign**-owned. An American law, penned in the early 1900s to protect American shipping, says that "only" an American carrier can transport you to and from two American cities. In the airline industry, this law is still very much in effect. It means, for example, that if you want a round-trip between San Francisco and Honolulu, you *must* fly on a domestic carrier. If, however, you are flying San Francisco to Tokyo, you are at liberty to fly a "foreign" airline, and you may even have a stopover in Hawaii, but you must continue to Tokyo or some other foreign city and cannot fly back to San Francisco on the foreign airline. Canadians have no problem flying a Canadian airline round-trip from Vancouver or Toronto to Honolulu because this route does not connect two U.S. cities, and so it is with all foreign travel to and from Hawaii. Travel agents know this, but if you're planning your own trip be aware of this fact.

## Kinds of Flights

Depending on where you are coming from, you may have to fly from your home to a "gateway city," from where flights go to Hawaii, either direct or nonstop. On direct flights you fly from point A to point B without changing planes; it doesn't mean that you don't land in between. Direct flights do land, usually once to board and deplane passengers, but you sit cozily on the plane along with your luggage and off you go again. Nonstop is just that; you board and when the doors open again you're at your destination. All flights from the West Coast gateway cities are nonstop, "God willing"—because there is only the Pacific in between!

## Stopover Flights

All airlines that fly to Hawaii land at Honolulu, and a few fly nonstop to Maui, Kaua'i, and the Big Island. Major carriers have interline agreements with the island carriers Hawaiian Airlines and Aloha Airlines for getting you to the Neighbor Islands from Honolulu, if one of those is your destination. This sometimes involves a plane change, but your baggage can be booked straight through.

## Travel Agents

At one time people went to a travel agent the same way they went to a barber or beautician, loyally sticking with one. Most agents are reputable professionals who know what they're doing. They should be members of the American Society of Travel Agents (ASTA) and licensed by the Air Traffic Conference (ATC). Most have the inside track on the best deals, and they'll save you countless hours calling 800 numbers and listening to elevator music while on hold or checking with umpteen internet ticket sellers. Unless you require them to make very special arrangements, their services are free—they are paid a commission by the airlines and hotels that they book for you. In recent years these commissions have been greatly reduced, in some cases abandoned altogether, causing some to start charging a small fee for their services.

If you've done business with a travel agent in the past and were satisfied with the services and prices, by all means stick with him or her. If no such positive rapport exists, then shop around. Ask friends or relatives for recommendations; if you can't get any endorsements go to the Yellow Pages. Call two or three travel agents to compare prices. Make sure to give all of them the same information and to be as precise as possible. Tell them where and when you want to go, how long you want to stay, what class you want to travel, and any special requirements. Write down their information. It's amazing how confusing travel plans can be when you have to keep track of flight numbers, times, prices, and all the preparation information. When you compare, don't look only for the cheapest price. Check for convenience in flights, amenities of hotels, and any other fringe benefits that might be included. Then make your choice of agents and, if he or she is willing to give you individualized service, stick with that agent from then on.

Agents become accustomed to offering the same deals to many clients because they're familiar with the arrangements and because the deals have worked well in the past. Sometimes these are indeed the best, but if they don't suit you, don't be railroaded into accepting them. Any good agent will work with you. After all, it's your trip and your money.

Consolidators are companies that buy blocks of seats on certain flights and then turn around and sell them. Their buying price must be very cheap because their prices are some of the best that you can find. They often list their toll-free phone numbers in local phone directories and just as often run ads in large city newspapers—often in a Sunday Travel section. With the proliferation of the Internet, the number of online travel companies has also mushroomed, and these companies offer great deals. As with consolidators, online travel companies come and go, so use a company that has previously worked with you or someone you know. Again, the range in prices is substantial, so check around with many before you send your money.

## Package Tours

For the independent traveler, practical package deals that include only flight, car, and lodging are okay. Agents put these together all the time and they just might be the best, but if they don't suit you, make arrangements separately. A package *tour* is totally different. On these you get your hand held by an escort, eat where they want you to eat, go where they want you to go, and watch Hawaii slide by your bus window. For some people, especially groups, this might be the way to do it, but everyone else should avoid the package tour. You'll see Hawaii best on your own, and if you want a tour you can arrange one there, often cheaper. Once arrangements have been made with your travel agent, make sure to take all receipts and letters of confirmation (hotel, car) with you to Hawaii. They probably won't be needed, but if they are, nothing will work better in getting results.

## Mainland and International Fares

There are many categories of airline fares, but only three apply to the average traveler: first class, coach, and excursion. Traveling **first class** seats you in the front of the plane, gives you free drinks, a wider choice of meals, more leg room, and access to VIP lounges, if they exist. There are no restrictions, no penalties for cancellations or rebooking of return flights, and no advance-booking or minimum-stay requirements.

**Coach,** the way that most people fly, is totally adequate. You sit in the plane's main compartment behind first class. Your seats are comfortable, but they're narrower and you don't have as much leg room or as wide a choice of meals. Movie headsets and drinks cost you a few dollars, but that's about it. Coach offers many of the same benefits of first class and costs about 30 percent less. You can buy tickets up until takeoff; you have no restrictions on minimum or maximum stays; you receive liberal stopover privileges; and you can cash in your return ticket or change your return date with no penalties.

**Excursion** or advance-payment excursion (APEX) fares are the cheapest. You are accommodated on the plane exactly the same as if you were flying coach. There are, however, some restrictions. You must book and pay for your ticket in advance (usually 7–14 days; sometimes up to 30 days). At the same time, you must book your return flight, and under most circumstances you can't change either without paying a stiff penalty. Also, your stopovers are severely limited and you will have a minimum/maximum stay period. Only a limited number of seats on any one plane are set aside for APEX fares, so book as early as you can. Also, if you must change travel plans, you can go to the airport and get on as a standby passenger using a discounted ticket, even if the airline doesn't have an official standby policy. There's always the risk that you won't get on, but you do have a chance, as well as priority over an actual standby customer.

**Standby** is exactly what its name implies: you go to the airport and wait around to see if any flights going to Hawaii have an empty seat. You can save some money, but you cannot have a firm itinerary or limited time. Since Hawaii is such a popular destination, standbys can wait days before catching a plane.

## Charters

Charter flights were at one time only for groups or organizations that had memberships in travel clubs. Now they're open to the general public. A charter flight is an entire plane or a block of seats purchased at a quantity discount by a charter company and then sold to customers. Because they are bought at wholesale prices, charter fares can be the cheapest available. As in package deals, only take a charter flight if it is a "fly only," or perhaps includes a car and/or a room. You don't need one that includes a guide and a bus. Most important, make sure that the charter company is reputable. It should belong to the same organizations (ASTA and ATC) as most travel agents. If not, check into the company at the local chamber of commerce.

More restrictions apply to charters than to any other flights. You must pay in advance. If you cancel after a designated time, you can be penalized severely or lose your money entirely. You cannot change departure or return dates and times. However, up to 10 days before departure the charter company is legally able to cancel, raise the price by 10 percent, or change time and dates. It must return your money if cancellation occurs, or if changed arrangements are unacceptable to you. Most charter companies are on the up-and-up and flights go smoothly, but there are horror stories. Be careful. Be wise. Investigate!

## Tips

Flights from California take about five hours, a bit longer from the Northwest or Pacific Canada; you gain two hours over Pacific Standard Time when you land in Hawaii (three hours during daylight savings time). From the East Coast it takes about 11 hours and you gain five hours over Eastern Standard Time. Flights from Japan take about seven hours and there is a five-hour difference between the time zones. Travel time between Sydney, Australia, or Auckland, New Zealand, and Hawaii is about nine hours. They are ahead of Hawaii time by 20 and 22 hours, respectively. Try to fly Mon.–Thurs., when flights

are cheaper and easier to book. Pay for your ticket as soon as your plans are firm. If prices go up no charge is added, but merely booking doesn't guarantee the lowest price. Make sure the airlines, hotels, and car agencies get your phone number too—not only your travel agent's—in case any problems with availability arise (travel agents are often closed on weekends). It's not necessary, but it's a good idea to call and reconfirm flights 24–72 hours in advance.

First-row (bulkhead) seats are good for people who need more leg room, but bad for watching the movie. Airlines will give you special meals (vegetarian, kosher, low cal, low salt) often at no extra charge, but you must notify them in advance. If you're "bumped" from an overbooked flight, you're entitled to a comparable flight to your destination within one hour. If more than an hour elapses, you get denied-boarding compensation, which goes up proportionally with the amount of time you're held up. Sometimes this is cash or a voucher for another flight to be used in the future. You don't have to accept what an airline offers on the spot, if you feel it isn't being fair.

## Traveling with Children

Fares for children ages 2–12 are often 30–50 percent of the adult fare, although the exact amount will depend on the season and flight; children under two not occupying a seat travel free. If you're traveling with an infant or active toddler, book your flight well in advance and request the bulkhead seat or first row in any section and a bassinet if available. Many carriers have fold-down cribs with restraints for baby's safety and comfort. Toddlers appreciate the extra space provided by the front-row seats. Be sure to reconfirm, and arrive early to ensure this special seating. On long flights you'll be glad you took these extra pains.

Although most airlines have coloring books, puppets, etc., to keep your child busy, it's always a good idea to bring your own. These can make the difference between a pleasant flight and a harried ordeal. Also, remember to bring baby food, diapers, and other necessities, as many airlines may not be equipped with exactly what you need. Make all inquiries ahead of time so you're not caught unprepared.

## Baggage

You are allowed two free pieces of checked luggage—one large, the other small—and a carry-on bag. The two checked pieces can weigh up to 70 pounds each; an extra charge is levied for extra weight. The larger bag can have an overall added dimension (height plus width plus length) of 62 inches; the smaller, 55 inches. Your carry-on must fit under your seat or in the overhead storage compartment. Purses and camera bags are not counted as carry-ons and may be taken aboard. Surfboards and bicycles may run about $50 extra from the Mainland but this may vary by airline; enclosed golf bags can be sent as checked luggage at no extra charge. Although they make great mementos, remove all previous baggage tags from your luggage; they can confuse handlers. Attach a sturdy holder with your name and address on the handle, or use a stick-on label on the bag itself. Put your name and address inside the bag, and the address where you'll be staying in Hawaii if possible. Carry your cosmetics, identification, money, prescriptions, tickets, reservations, change of underwear, camera equipment, and perhaps a change of shirt or blouse in your carry-on.

## Visas

Entering Hawaii is like entering anywhere else in the United States. Foreign nationals must have a current passport and most must have a proper visa, an ongoing or return air ticket, and sufficient funds for the proposed stay in Hawaii. A visa application can be made at any U.S. embassy or consular office outside the United States and must include a properly filled out application form, two photos 1.5 inches square, and a nonrefundable fee of $65. Canadians do not need a visa or passport but must have proper identification such as passport, driver's license, or birth certificate. Visitors from 28 countries do not need a visa to enter the United States for 90 days or less. As this list is amended periodically, be sure to check in your country of origin to determine if you need a visa for U.S. entry.

## Agricultural Inspection

Everyone visiting Hawaii must fill out a "Plant and Animals Declaration Form" and present it to the appropriate official upon arrival in the state (or to the airline personnel). Anyone carrying any of the listed items must have these items inspected by an agricultural inspection agent at the airport. For information on just what is prohibited, contact any U.S. Customs Office or check with an embassy or consulate in foreign countries.

Remember that before you leave Hawaii for the Mainland, all of your bags are again subject to an agricultural inspection, a usually painless procedure taking only a minute or two. To facilitate your departure, leave all bags unlocked until after inspection. There are no restrictions on beach sand from below the high-water line, coconuts, pre-packaged sugarcane, dried flower arrangements, fresh flower lei, pineapples, certified pest-free plants, seashells, seed lei, and wood roses. However, avocado, litchi, and papaya must be treated before departure. Some other restricted items are berries, fresh gardenias, roses, jade plants, live insects, snails, cotton, plants in soil, soil itself, and raw sugarcane. Raw sugarcane is okay, however, if it is cut between the nodes, has the outer covering peeled off, and is split into fourths. For any questions pertaining to plants that you want to take to the Mainland, call the Agricultural Quarantine Inspection office on any island before your planned departure.

Foreign countries may have different agricultural inspection requirements for flights from Hawaii (or other points in the United States) to those countries. Be sure to check with the proper foreign authorities for specifics.

## Pets and Quarantine

Hawaii has a very rigid pet quarantine policy designed to keep rabies and other Mainland diseases from reaching the state. All domestic pets are subject to a **120 day quarantine** (a 30-day quarantine is allowed by meeting certain pre-arrival and post-arrival requirements—inquire). Unless you are contemplating a move to Hawaii, it is not feasible to take pets. For complete information, contact the Department of Agriculture, Animal Quarantine Division, 99-951 Halawa Valley St., 'Aiea, HI 96701, 808/483-7151.

## DOMESTIC CARRIERS

The following are the major domestic carriers to and from Hawaii. The planes used are primarily wide-body D10s, L10s, and 747s, with a smaller 737, 767, or the like flown now and again. A list of the "gateway cities" from which they fly direct and nonstop flights is given, but "connecting cities" are not. The majority of flights, by all carriers, land at Honolulu International Airport, with the remainder going directly to Maui, Hawai'i, and Kaua'i. Only the established companies are listed. Entrepreneurial small airlines such as the defunct Mahalo Air pop up now and again and specialize in dirt-cheap fares. There is a hectic frenzy to buy their tickets, and business is great for a while, but then the established companies lower their fares and the gamblers fold.

### Hawaiian Airlines

Hawaiian Airlines operates daily flights from Los Angeles, San Francisco, San Diego, Ontario (California), Las Vegas (via Los Angeles), Phoenix, Seattle, and Portland to Honolulu, with flights several times a week from Los Angeles, San Francisco, and Portland nonstop to Kahului, Maui.

Scheduled flights to the South Pacific run twice a week between Honolulu and Pago Pago, Samoa, and once weekly to Papeete, Tahiti. Since about 2000, Hawaiian Airlines has expanded its service to the West Coast so there may very well be additional destinations and service in the future. Hawaiian Airlines offers special discount deals with Dollar rental cars and select major-island hotels, and has a partnership agreement with American, Continental, Alaska, and Northwest airlines. Contact Hawaiian Airlines at 800/367-5320 Mainland and Canada, 800/882-8811 in Hawaii, www.hawaiianair.com.

### Aloha Airlines

Aloha Airlines flies between Honolulu and Kahului, Maui in the islands and Vancouver, Canada, Oakland, Las Vegas (via Oakland), Burbank, Sacramento (via Burbank), Orange County, California, and Phoenix (via Orange County) on the Mainland. It also has a direct connection between Kaua'i and Oakland, and Kona on the Big Island with Vancouver and Oakland. In addition, Aloha Airlines now operates a weekly flight on Saturday to Midway Island, and twice-weekly flights to Johnston Atoll in the South Pacific, that carry on to Majuro Atoll and Kwajalein. Periodi-

Aloha Airlines and Hawaiian Airlines connect all major islands to the hub city of Honolulu.

ROBERT NILSEN

cally, charter flights also go to Christmas Island and Rorotanga in the South Pacific and flights to Midway Island have been discontinued because of its closure to the public. If you are interested in visiting these very remote islands, check with the airlines to see if those flight are currently in operation. Like Hawaiian, Aloha Airlines has been expanding its West Coast operation, so greater variety will undoubtedly be in store in the future. For information, contact the airline at 800/367-5250 Mainland and Canada or 808/244-9071 on Maui, www.alohaairlines.org.

## United Airlines

Since its first island flight in 1947, United has become top dog in flights to Hawaii. United's Mainland routes connect more than 100 cities to Honolulu. The main gateway cities of San Francisco and Los Angeles have direct flights to Honolulu; flights from all other cities connect through these. United also offers direct flights to Maui, Kona, and Kaua'i from San Francisco and Los Angeles. Continuing through Honolulu, United flights go to Tokyo (Narita), where connections can be made for other Asian cities. United offers a number of packages, including flight and hotel on O'ahu, and flight, hotel, and car on the Neighbor Islands. United interlines with Aloha Airlines and deal with Hertz Rent A Car. United is the "big guy" and intends to stay that way. Its packages are hard to beat. Contact the airline at 800/241-6522, www.ual.com.

## American Airlines

American offers direct flights to Honolulu from Los Angeles, San Francisco, Dallas/Fort Worth, and Chicago. It also flies daily from Los Angeles and Chicago direct to Maui, and from Los Angeles to Lihue. American does not fly to points in Asia or other Pacific destinations from Hawaii. American interlines with Hawaiian Airlines. Contact American at 800/433-7300, www.aa.com.

## Continental Airlines

Flights from all Mainland cities to Honolulu connect via Los Angeles, Newark, and Houston. Also available are direct flights from Honolulu to Guam, from where flights run to numerous other Asian and Pacific cities and islands. Continental interlines with Hawaiian Airlines. For information call 800/523-3273, or visit the airline's website at www.continental.com.

## Northwest Airlines

Northwest flies into Honolulu from Los Angeles and Seattle. There are onward non-stop flights to Narita and Osaka in Japan, from where all other Asian destinations are connected. Call 800/225-2525, or visit the airline's website at www.nwa.com.

## Delta Air Lines

In 1985, Delta entered the Hawaiian market; when it bought out Western Airlines its share became even bigger. It has nonstop flights to Honolulu from Dallas/Fort Worth, Los Angeles, San Francisco, Salt Lake City, and Atlanta, and a direct flight from Maui to Los Angeles. Contact Delta at 800/221-1212 or www.delta.com.

# FOREIGN CARRIERS

## Canada

Nonstop flights from Canada to Honolulu originate in Vancouver and Toronto, and to Maui from Vancouver. Call 888/247-2262 or visit www.aircanada.ca.

## Air New Zealand

Flights link New Zealand, Australia, and numerous South Pacific islands to Honolulu, with continuing flights to Mainland cities. All flights run via Auckland, New Zealand. Call 800/262-1234 in the United States and 800/663-5494 in Canada for current information, or visit the airline's website at www.airnz.com.

## Japan Air Lines

The Japanese are the second-largest group, next to Americans, to visit Hawaii. JAL flights to Honolulu originate in Tokyo (Narita), Nagoya, and Osaka (Kansai). In addition, there are flights between Tokyo (Narita) and Kona on the Big Island. JAL flights continue beyond Hawaii to San Francisco and Los Angeles. Call JAL at 800/525-3663, or go online to www.jal.co.jp/en.

## Qantas

Daily flights connect Sydney and Melbourne, Australia with Honolulu; all other flights feed through these hub. Call 800/227-4500, or visit the Qantas website at www.qantas.com.au.

## China Airlines

Routes to Honolulu with China Airlines are only from Taipei, and all go through Tokyo. Connections are available in Taipei to most Asian capitals. Call 800/227-5118, or visit the airline's website at www.china-airlines.com.

## Korean Air

Korean Air offers some of the least expensive flights to Asia. All flights are direct between Honolulu and Seoul, with connections there to many Asian cities. Call 800/438-5000 or try the website www.koreanair.com.

## Air Pacific

Air Pacific offers once weekly non-stop flights between Nadi, Fiji and Honolulu. Contact 808/227-4446 or see www.airpacific.com.

## Polynesian Airlines

If flying to Samoa, use Polynesian Airlines for weekly flights directly from Honolulu to Apia. Call 808/842-7659 or see www.polynesianairlines.co.nz.

## Philippine Airlines

Three times weekly, direct non-stop flights between Honolulu and Manila are handled through Philippine Airlines, 808/435-7725 or www.philippineair.com.

## Other Airlines

Aside from the above airlines, large volume charter operators book flights to the various island with such carriers as **Canada 3000, American Trans Air, Ryan International** and **Skyservice USA.**

# TOUR AND TRAVEL COMPANIES

Many tour companies advertise packages to Hawaii in large city newspapers every week. They offer very reasonable airfares, car rentals, and accommodations. The following companies offer great deals and most have excellent reputations. This list is by no means exhaustive.

## Pleasant Hawaiian Holidays

A California-based company specializing in Hawaii, Pleasant Hawaiian Holidays makes arrangements for flights, accommodations, and transportation only. For flights, it primarily uses American Trans Air, but also uses select commercial airlines and regularly scheduled flights. Aside from the air connection, Pleasant Hawaiian offers a choice of accommodation levels from budget ro luxury, a fly/drive option if you have your own accommodation, and numerous perks, like a flower greeting lei, first morning orientation, service desks at hotels, and coupons and gift certificates. Pleasant Hawaiian is easy to work with and stands behind its services. A deposit is required after booking and there is a time frame for full payment that depends upon when you make your reservation. Fees are accessed for changing particulars after booking, so be sure to apprise yourself of all financial particulars. Most major travel agents work with Pleasant Hawaiian but you can also contact them directly at 2404 Townsgate Rd., Westlake Village, CA 91361, 800/742-9244, www.pleasantholidays.com.

## SunTrips

This California-based tour company that runs flights to Hawaii from Los Angeles and San Francisco. It offers flight, accommodation, and/or car rental packages that match any for affordability. Your price will depend upon your choice of accommodations and type of car. Using both charter and commercial air carriers, SunTrips does not offer assigned seating until you get to the airport. They recommend you get there two hours in advance, and they ain't kidding! This is the price you pay for getting such inexpensive air travel. Remember that everyone on your incoming flight makes a beeline for the rental car's shuttle van after landing and securing their baggage. If you have a traveling companion, work together to beat the rush by leaving your companion to fetch the baggage while you head directly for the van as soon as you arrive. Pick your car up, then return for your partner and the bags. Even if you're alone, you could zip over to the car-rental center and then return for your bags without having them sit very long on the carousel. SunTrips financial regulations are similar to those at Pleasant Hawaiian; be sure to inquire. Contact SunTrips, 2350 Paragon Dr., San Jose, CA 95131, 800/786-8747, or at www.suntrips.com.

## Similar Companies

Several other companies offer similar package options from the Mainland to Hawaii. Try the following. **Happy Vacations,** 4604 Scotts Valley Drive, Scotts Valley, CA 95066, 831/461-0113 or 800/877-4277, fax 831/461-1604; www.happy-vacations.com; an older and reputable company that gives good service and stands by its policies. **Creative Leisure International,** 951 Transport Way, Petaluma, CA 94954, 707/778-1800 or 800/413/1000, fax 707/778-1223. www.creativeleisure.com. Utilizes United Airlines. **United Vacations,** 8907 Port Washington Road, Milwaukee, WI 53217, 414/228-7472 or 800/328-6877, 414/351-5826. A United Airlines affiliate.

## Council Travel Services

These full-service, budget-travel specialists are a subsidiary of the nonprofit Council on International Educational Exchange, and the official U.S. representative to the International Student Travel Conference. They'll custom-design trips and programs for everyone from senior citizens to college students. Bona fide students have extra advantages, however, including eligibility for the International Student Identification Card (ISIC), which often gets you discount fares and waived entrance fees to tourist attractions. Groups and business travelers are also welcome. For full information, call 800/226-8624, or write to Council Travel Services at one of these offices: 530 Bush St., San Francisco, CA 94108, 415/421-3473; or 205 E. 42nd St., New York, NY 10017, 212/822-2700. For additional retail locations and information, see www.counciltravel.com.

## STA Travel

STA Travel is a full-service travel agency specializing in student travel, regardless of age. Those under 26 do not have to be full-time students to get special fares. Older independent travelers can avail themselves of services, although they are ineligible for student fares. STA works hard to get you discounted or budget rates. Many tickets issued by STA are flexible, allowing changes with no penalty, and are open-ended for travel up to one year. STA has some 300 offices around the world. For information, call 800/781-4040 or visit www.statravel.com. STA also maintains Travel Help, a service available at all offices designed to solve all types of problems that may arise while traveling. STA is a well-established travel agency with an excellent and well-deserved reputation.

## Ocean Voyages

This unique company offers multi-day itineraries aboard two yachts in the Hawaiian Islands. The ships, one a six-passenger catamaran, the other a six-passenger sloop, ensure individualized sail training and service. These vessels sail throughout the islands, exploring hidden bays and coves, and berth at different ports as they go. This opportunity is for anyone who wishes to see the islands in a timeless fashion, thrilling to sights experienced by the first Polynesian settlers and Western explorers. For rates and information contact Ocean Voyages, 1709 Bridgeway, Sausalito, CA 94965, 415/332-4681 or 800/299-4444 Mainland, fax 415/332-7460.

## Ecotours to Hawaii

**Sierra Club Trips** offers Hawaii trips for nature lovers who are interested in an outdoor experience. Various trips include birding on the Big Island, and kayak and camping trips on Kaua'i. All trips are led by experienced guides and are open to Sierra Club members only ($35 per year to join). For information contact the Sierra Club Outing Department, 85 2nd St., 2nd Fl., San Francisco, CA 94105, 415/977-5522, www.sierraclub.org/outings.

**Backroads,** 801 Cedar St., Berkeley, CA 94710, 510/527-1555, fax 510/1444, or 800/462-2848, arranges an easy-on-the-environment six-day bicycle, hiking, and kayak trip on the Big Island for $2,398. This price include hotel/inn accommodations, most meals, and professional guide service. Airfare is not included, and bicycles and sleeping bags can be rented (BYO okay) for reasonable rates. The company's website is at www.backroads.com, backtalk@backroads.com.

## Educational Trips

Not a tour per se, but an educational opportunity, **Elderhostel Hawaii** offers short-term programs on five of the Hawaiian islands. Different programs focus on history, culture, cuisine, and the environment in association with one of the colleges or universities in the islands. Most programs use hotels for accommodations. For information, write Elderhostel, 11 Avenue de Lafayette, Boston, MA 02111-1746, or call 877/426-8056; www.enderhostel.org.

# BY SHIP

## Cruise Ships

Cruise lines offering ships that touch in Hawaii for day trips only on their varied routes include the following. Most travel agents can provide information on these cruise lines:

**Norwegian Cruise Lines,** 800/327-7030, www.ncl.com

**Holland America Lines,** 800/426-0327, www.hollandamerica.com

**Cunard,** 800/528-6273, www.cunardline.com

**Carnival Cruise Line,** 800/327-9501, www.carnival.com

**Princess Cruises,** 800/421-0522, www.princesscruises.com

**Royal Caribbean International,** 800/327-6700, www.royalcaribbean.com

**Crystal Cruises,** 800/446-6620, www.cruise-crystal.com

## Freighter Travel

Travel by freighter is on a working cargo ship. While the routes are usually longer than cruise ship itineraries and the ships themselves do not contain all the luxuries and amenities of the cruise liners, fares are often 30–40 percent less per day than travel on a cruise ship. If you're especially interested in traveling by freighter, contact: **Freighter World Cruises,** 180 S. Lake Ave., Suite 335, Pasadena, CA 91101-2655, 626/449-3106 or 800/531-7774, www.freighterworld.com, freighter@freighterworld.com. This company is an agent that arranges passage for travelers on over 100 ships around the world. It publishes the *Freighter Space Advisory* newsletter. Also arranging travel is **Maris Freighter Cruises, USA,** 215 Main St., Westport, CT 06880, 203/222-1500 or 800/996-2747, fax 203/222-9191, www.cruise-maris.com/frieghters.html, maris@freighter-cruises.com. Maris publishes the monthly *Freighter Travel Newsletter.* For additional information, check *Ford's Freighter Travel Guide & Waterways of the World* quarterly, which can be contacted at 19448 Londelius St., Northridge, CA 91324, 818/701-7414.

# Getting Around

## BY AIR

Interisland air travel is highly developed, economical, and completely convenient. You can go almost anywhere at any time on everything from wide-bodied jets to single-engine air taxis. Hawaiians take flying for granted, using planes the way most people use buses. A shopping excursion to Honolulu from a Neighbor Island is commonplace, as is a trip from the city for a picnic at a quiet beach. Most interisland flights are 20–40 minutes long, with some shorter and a few longer. The moody sea can be uncooperative to mass transit, but the skies above Hawaii are generally clear and perfect for flying. Their infrequent gloomier moments can delay flights, but the major airlines of Hawaii have been flying nonstop ever since Hawaiian Air's maiden flight in 1929. The fares are competitive, the schedules convenient, and the service friendly.

### Brief History

Little more than a motorized kite, the *Hawaiian Skylark* was the first plane to fly in Hawaii. On New Year's Day, 1911, it circled a Honolulu polo field, where 3,000 spectators, including Queen Lili'uokalani, witnessed history. Hawaiians have been soaring above their lovely islands ever since. The first paying customer, Mrs. Newmann, took off on a $15 joyride in 1913 with a Chinese aviator named Tom Gunn. In February 1920, Charles Fern piloted the first interisland customer round-trip from Honolulu to Maui for $150. He worked for Charles Stoffer, who started the first commercial airline the year before with one Curtiss biplane, affectionately known as "Charlie's Crate." For about 10 years sporadic attempts at interisland service amounted to little more than extended joyrides to deliver the day's newspaper from Honolulu. The James Dole Air Race in 1927 proved transpacific flight was possible, but interisland passenger service didn't really begin until Stanley C. Kennedy, a World War I flier and heir to Inter-Island Steam Navigation Co., began Inter-Island Airways in

January 1929. For a dozen years he ran Sikorsky Amphibians, considered the epitome of safety. By 1941 he converted to the venerable workhorse, the DC-3, and changed the company name to **Hawaiian Air.**

By 1948, Hawaiian Air was unopposed in the interisland travel market, because regularly scheduled boats had already become obsolete. However, in 1946 a fledgling airline named Trans-Pacific opened for business. A nonscheduled airline with only one war surplus DC-3, it carried a hunting party of businessmen to Moloka'i on its maiden flight. By June 1952, it was a regularly scheduled airline in stiff competition with Hawaiian Air and had changed its name to **Aloha Airlines.** Both airlines had their financial glory days and woes over the next decade; by the end of the 1960s both were flying interisland jets.

A healthy crop of small scheduled and unscheduled airlines always darted about the wings of the large airlines, flying to minor airfields and performing flying services uneconomical for the bigger airlines. Most of these tiny, often one-plane companies are swatted from the air like gnats whenever the economy goes sour or tourism becomes sluggish. In the past, they had names like Peacock and Rainbow, and after a brief flash of wings they were gone.

## INTERISLAND CARRIERS

The only effective way for most visitors to travel between the Hawaiian Islands is by air. Luckily, Hawaii has excellent air transportation that boasts one of the industry's safest flight records. All interisland flights have a "no smoking" regulation. There are no assigned seats on interisland flights so if you have a seating preference, get to the boarding gate early and grab your place in line. Items restricted on flights from the Mainland and from overseas are also restricted on flights within the state. Baggage allowances are the same as anywhere, except that due to space constraints, carry-on luggage on the smaller prop planes may be limited in number and size.

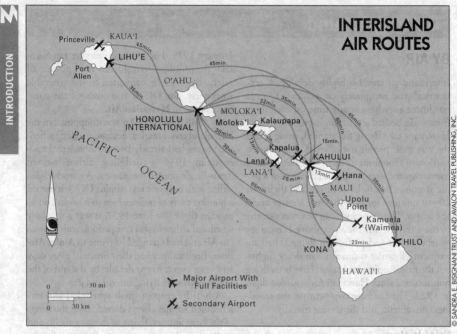

Hawaiian and Aloha have competitive prices, with interisland flights about $80 each way, with substantial savings for state residents. With both airlines, you can save per ticket by purchasing a booklet of six **flight coupons** that run $408. These are only available in state at any ticket office or airport counter, and they are *transferable*. Just book a flight as normal and present the filled-in voucher to board the plane. Perfect for families or groups of friends. Hawaiian Airlines coupons are good for six months, Aloha Airlines coupons for one year. Hawaiian also offers a 10-coupon booklet that can be mailed to Mainland visitors that is $732—allow two weeks.

Additionally, each airline offers passes good for unlimited travel anywhere that the airlines flies, but they are nontransferable and may only be used on consecutive days. You may purchase these passes in state or before you arrive in Hawaii. Hawaiian Airlines has the Hawaiian Island Pass: five days at $310, seven days at $320, 10 days at $419, and 14 days at $479. Fares for children ages 2–11 and seniors are about 10 per-

cent less. Aloha Airlines offers one 7-day Island Pass for $336 with the same conditions.

**Note:** Although every effort has been made for up-to-date accuracy, remember that schedules are constantly changing. The following should be used only as a point of reference. Please call the airlines listed below for their latest schedules.

**Hawaiian Air,** 800/367-5320 Mainland and Canada, 800/882-8811 statewide, www.hawaiianair.com, is not only the oldest airline in Hawaii, it is also the biggest. It flies more aircraft, to more airports, more times per day than any other airline in Hawaii. It services all islands, including Moloka'i and Lana'i, and flies all jets.

**Aloha Airlines,** 800/367-5250 Mainland and Canada, www.alohaairlines.com, with its all-jet fleet of 737s, is also an old and venerable Hawaiian company with plenty of flights connecting O'ahu to Kaua'i, Maui, and both Kona and Hilo on Hawai'i. It offers more flights to Maui than any other island carrier.

**Island Air** (a subsidiary of Aloha Airlines and

formerly called Aloha Island Air), 800/323-3345 Mainland, 800/652-6541 statewide, www.alohaairlines.com, offers scheduled flights to and from Honolulu, Moloka'i, Lana'i; Kahului, Kapalua-West Maui, and Hana airports on Maui; and Kona on the Big Island. About half the flights are on jet aircraft and half on Dash-8 turboprop airplanes.

A local company operating eight-seat, twin-engine Cessna 402C planes, **Pacific Wings** does the pickup routes. It connects Honolulu to Kahului, Hana, Lana'i, Moloka'i, Kalaupapa, and Kamuela on the Big Island, and connects these airports together, but on a limited schedule of less than half a dozen flights a day at most. Pacific Wings can be reached at 888/575-4546, www.pacificwings.com.

### Charter Airlines and Air Tours

Hawaii has a good but dwindling selection of charter airlines offering some regularly scheduled flights, air tours, and special flights the big carriers don't service. They're so handy and personalized they might be considered "air taxis." All use smaller aircraft that seat 6–12 people and fly low enough that their normal interisland flights are like air tours. Stories abound of passengers being invited to ride copilot, or of a pilot going out of his way to show off a glimmering coastline or a beautiful waterfall. Many times you get the sense that it's "your" flight and the airline is doing everything possible to make it memorable. The commuter airlines are limited in plane size and routes serviced. Among themselves, prices are very competitive, but, except on their specialty runs, they tend to be more expensive than the four major interisland carriers. They're also not as generous on baggage allowance. You'll be charged more for the extra bulk, or some of it may not be allowed to accompany you on the plane.

Companies include **Big Island Air,** 808/329-4868 or 800/303-8868, operating out of Kailua-Kona, with charter service and flight-seeing tours around the Big Island on eight-passenger Cessna 402s. **Paragon Air,** 808/244-3356 or 800/428-1231, www.paragon-air.com, has charter flights to all of Hawaii's airports and flight-seeing tours

to Moloka'i and the Big Island. **Maui Air,** 808/877-5500, www.volcanoairtours.com, runs its operation from Kahului and does tours and private charters in nine-passenger air-conditioned, twin-engine planes.

## BY SHIP

### Cruise Ships

In 2001, American Hawaii Cruises stopped all service within the Hawaiian Islands. For years, this company had operated seven-day cruises to four of the islands, and hopefully will resume operation at some time in the future.

From December 2001, Norwegian Cruise Lines (a subsidiary of Star Cruises PLC of Malaysia) has run a weekly seven day roundtrip cruise with their luxury liner *Norwegian Star.* This ship leaves Honolulu harbor Sunday evening and cruises to Hilo for its first stop. Leaving there, it spends a day at sea before arriving at Fanning Island in the Republic of Kiribati. One day of sailing back returns the ship to Kahului, from where it goes to Nawiliwili Harbor on

Cruise ships offer a unique way to see the islands.

Kaua'i and then back to port in Honolulu. This trip can also be started on Maui. For information and pricing, contact Norwegian Cruise Lines, 7665 Corporate Center Dr., Miami FL, 33126, 800/327-7030, www.ncl.com.

# RENTAL CARS

Does Hawaii really have more rental cars than pineapples? O'ahu's Yellow Pages have numerous pages of listings for car rental agencies. There are more than 25 firms on Maui and a dozen or so on the Big Island and Kaua'i. Moloka'i has four, and Lana'i has two. Still, it's best to reserve your car well before your arrival in Hawaii. If you visit the islands during the peak tourist frenzy without reserving your wheels in advance, you may be marooned at the airport.

There is a tremendous field of cars and agencies from which to choose. Special deals come and go like tropical rain showers; swashbuckling price-slashings and come-ons are common all over the rental car market. A little knowledge combined with some shrewd shopping around can save you a bundle. And renting a car is the best way to see the islands if you're going to be here for a limited time. Outside of O'ahu, it simply isn't worthwhile to hassle with the poor public transportation system or rely on your thumb.

You can rent anything from a subcompact to a full-size luxury land yacht, but the most common rentals seem to be compact and mid-size sedans. Gaining in popularity, however, especially for the more adventurous travelers on the Neighbor Islands, are SUVs, Jeeps, and other 4WD vehicles, and some vans are also available. Automatics far outnumber standard shift cars, and some companies don't even carry vehicles with manual transmissions anymore. What's best for you must meet your needs—and your pocketbook. If your vacation will mostly be spent at the hotel, seeing a few sights, and going out to dinner, get yourself a comfortable mid-size or luxury car. If you get a big fatso luxury car, it'll be great for puttin' on the ritz at the resort areas, but you'll feel like a hippopotamus in the back-country. Are you young and/or adventurous; on a honeymoon perhaps? Try a sporty model.

There's nothing like cruising along the coast with the top down. Got kids? Be sure to rent a car with four doors or get a van. Want to get off the main highway? A compact with standard shift or a jeep might be best for you. Main roads on Maui are broad and well paved, but the back roads, where much of the fun is, can be narrow, twisty affairs. You'll appreciate the downshifting ability of standard transmissions on curves and steep inclines, if you can get it. Most cars now come with cloth seats. If yours doesn't, sitting on your towel will help. Air-conditioning is standard on all but the cheapest, but hardly seems necessary in this environment. Automatic window and door locks are common, but will not come on all rentals. While you'll want to be paying attention to the scenes around you, a radio is great for getting in touch with local Hawaiian tunes and for weather and surf reports. Most companies have child seats available for rent on a daily basis, $6 a day or $40–50 maximum, and can install right- or left-hand controls for handicapped drivers; most agencies require 48–72 hours advance notice to install hand controls.

## Requirements

Car agencies impose various requirements on the renter, but the most important clauses are common. Before renting, check that you fulfill the requirements. Generally, you must be 21 years old, although some agencies rent to 18-year-olds, while others still require you to be 25 for certain types of vehicles. You must possess a valid driver's license—licenses from most countries are accepted, but if you are not American, get an International Driver's License to be safe. You should also have a major credit card in your name. This is the easiest way to rent a car. Some companies will take a deposit, but it will be very stiff. It could easily be $50 per day on top of your rental fees and sometimes much more. In addition, they may require a credit check on the spot, complete with phone calls to your employer and bank. If you damage the car, charges will be deducted from your deposit, and the car company itself determines the extent of the damages. Some companies *will not* rent you a car without a major credit card in your name, no matter how much of a deposit you are willing to leave, and this is often true for Hawaiian residents who want to rent a car on an island that they are not a resident of.

## When to Rent

On this one, you'll have to make up your own mind, because it's a bet that you can either win or lose. But it's always good to know the odds before you plop down your money. You can reserve your car in advance when you book your air ticket, or play the field when you get there. If you book in advance, you'll obviously have a car waiting for you, but the deal that you made is the deal that you'll get—it may or may not be the best around, but it may be quite good. On the other hand, if you wait, you can often take advantage of on-the-spot deals. However, you're betting that cars are available. You might be totally disappointed and not be able to rent a car at all, or you might make a honey of a deal.

If you're arriving during the peak seasons of Christmas, Easter, or late summer vacation, absolutely *book your car in advance*. Rental companies have their numbers down pretty well and seem to have plenty of cars, but all may be accounted for during this period. Even if you can find a junker from a fly-by-night, it'll price-gouge you mercilessly. If you're going off-peak, you stand a good chance of getting the car you want at the price you want. It's generally best to book ahead; most car companies have toll-free numbers. At least call them for an opinion of your chances of getting a car upon your intended arrival.

## Rates

The super-cheap rates on eye-catcher brochures refer to subcompacts. The price goes up with the size of the car. As with options on a new car, the more luxury you get, the more you pay. All major car rental companies in Hawaii use a flat rate option. The flat rate is best, providing a fixed daily rate and unlimited mileage. Some of the smaller local companies may have a mileage rate option. Mileage rate costs less per day, but you are charged for every mile driven. Mileage rates are best if you drive less than 30

miles per day—but even on an island that isn't much! With either rate, you buy the gas.

Rental rates vary by company, as do the names they use to refer to their types of vehicles. The following rates are fairly representative for most categories: subcompact, $45 a day, $225 a week; compact, $55/260; midsize, $65/300; full size, $75/350; luxury, $110/575; convertible and jeep, $100/500; van, $110/$575. Substantial discounts are offered for weekday, weekly, and monthly rentals. It's sometimes cheaper to rent a car for the week even if you're only going to use it for five days. If you'll be on more than one island, check to see if weekly and monthly rates can be split between Neighbor Islands. Most of the car companies, local and national, offer special rates and deals, like AAA rates. These deals fluctuate too rapidly to give any hard-and-fast information. They are common, however, so make sure to inquire. Don't expect that rental companies will let you know about any deal that they have. Also, peak periods have "blackouts," during which normally good deals no longer apply.

These rates aren't your only charges, however. On top of the actual rental fee, you must pay an airport access fee, airport concession fee, state tax, and a road tax surcharge—in total, an additional 25–30 percent. For cars not rented at the airports, you'll realize a savings of about 7.5 percent because some of the taxes can not be charged.

You may be asked about refueling options. Ordinarily, you fill the tank when you return the car or the company will fill the tank itself at an inflated rate. Some now offer you the option of prepaying for a half or full tank of gas at a reduced rate and they fill the car when it comes back. To get your money's worth this way, bring the car back exactly half empty or all the way empty, otherwise you may lose a little bit over pumping the gas yourself. Gas prices are generally higher in Hawaii than anywhere on the Mainland, and may be higher yet in "distant" locations like Hana, Moloka'i, and Lana'i.

**Warning:** If you keep your car beyond your contract, you'll be charged the highest daily rate unless you notify the rental agency beforehand. *Don't keep your car longer than the contract without notifying the company.* Companies are *quick* to send out their repossession specialists. You might find yourself in a situation with your car gone, a warrant out for your arrest, and an extra charge on your bill. A simple courtesy call notifying them of your intentions saves a lot of headaches and hassle.

## Insurance

Before signing your car rental agreement, you'll be offered various "insurance" coverages. Although these too vary somewhat by company, they fall into general categories: loss/damage option runs about $15 a day; uninsured motorist protection, $7 a day; and liability protection, $13 a day. In addition, some also offer a personal effects protection for $5 a day in case your property gets stolen. Since insurance is already built into the contract (don't expect the rental agency to point this out), what you're really buying is a waiver on the deductible ($500–1,000), in case you crack up the car. If you have insurance at home, you will almost always have coverage on a rental car—including your normal deductible—although not all policies are the same, so check with your agent. Also, if you haven't bought the waiver and you have a mishap, the rental agency will put a claim against your credit card on the spot for the amount of deductible, even if you can prove that your insurance will cover. The company will tell *you* to collect from your insurance company because it doesn't want to be left holding the bag on an across-the-waters claim. If you have a good policy with a small deductible, it's hardly worth paying the extra money for the waiver, but if your own policy is inadequate, buy the insurance. Also, most major credit cards offer complimentary car-rental insurance as an incentive for using their cards to rent the car. Simply call your credit card company to see if this service is included.

## Driving Tips

Wear your seat belt—it's the law! Police keep an eye out for miscreants and often ticket those who do not use their restraints. Protect your small children as you would at home with car seats. Either bring one from home or rent one from a car rental company. Rental prices and availability

vary, but all the agencies can make arrangements if you give them enough notice.

Mile markers on roads are great for pinpointing sites and beaches. The lower number on these signs is the highway number, so you can always make sure that you're on the right road.

In most cases, you'll get only one key for your rental car. Don't lose it or lock it inside. If you do lock it inside the vehicle, call AAA (or other auto emergency service that you have) and ask for assistance. Failing that, a local locksmith can open your car for a fee or the rental car agency can send out a second key by taxi, but both of these options can get quite pricey.

There are few differences between driving in Hawaii and on the Mainland. Just remember that many people on the roads are tourists and can be confused about where they're going. Since many drivers are from somewhere else, there's hardly a "regular style" of driving in the islands. A farmer from Iowa accustomed to poking along on back roads can be sandwiched between a frenetic New Yorker who's trying to drive over his roof and a super-polite but horribly confused Japanese tourist who normally drives on the left.

In Hawaii, drivers don't generally honk their horns except to say hello, or in an emergency. It's considered rude, and honking to hurry someone might earn you a knuckle sandwich. Hawaiian drivers reflect the climate: they're relaxed and polite. Often, they'll brake to let you turn left when they're coming at you. They may assume you'll do the same, so be ready, after a perfunctory turn signal from another driver, for him or her to turn across your lane. The more rural the area, the more apt this is to happen.

It may seem like common sense, but remember to slow down when you enter the little towns strung along the circle-island route. It's easy to bomb along on the highway and flash through these towns, missing some of Hawaii's best scenery. Also, rural children expect *you* to be watchful and will assume that you are going to stop for them when they dart onto the crosswalks.

O'ahu's **H-1, H-2, and H-3 freeways** throw many Mainlanders a Polynesian "screwball." Accustomed to driving on superhighways, Mainlanders assume these are the same. They're not.

O'ahu's superhighways are generally much more convoluted than most Mainland counterparts. Subliminally they look like normal freeways, except they've been tied into Hawaiian knots. There are split-offs, crossroads, and exits in the middle of exits. Stay alert and don't be lulled into complacency.

Respect Do Not Enter and Private Property signs—*Kapu* means the same thing.

Most insurance companies warn you that their cars are not supposed to be driven off paved roads—read your policy. This seems absolutely ridiculous for 4WD vehicles, but true nonetheless. When a road is signed for 4WD only, assume that that's the case for a good reason.

Speed limits change periodically along the highways of Hawai'i, particularly when they pass through small towns. Police routinely check the speed of traffic by use of radar equipment. Be aware of this so you don't go home with more than a suntan.

The State Department of Transportation has installed emergency call boxes on highways that are linked directly to an emergency response network. These boxes are located along major highways and to be used in emergencies only. Look for a yellow box on a tall pole topped by a small solar panel and blue light.

## BYO Car

If you want to bring your own car, write for information: Director of Finance, Division of Licenses, 1455 S. Beretania St., Honolulu, HI 96814. However, unless you'll be in Hawaii for a bare minimum of six months and will spend all your time on one island, don't even think about it. It's an expensive proposition and takes time and plenty of arrangements. To ship a vehicle from the U.S. West Coast to Hawaii, the cost is at least $825 to Honolulu, and an additional $50 to any other island. To save on rental costs, it would be better to buy and sell a car there, or to lease for an extended period.

## Four-Wheel Drives

For normal touring, it is unnecessary to rent 4WDs in Hawaii except on Lana'i, where they're a must, or if you really want to get off the beaten track on the other islands. They are expensive ($70–120 per day), and you simply don't need them. If you still want one, most car rental agencies have them, and some specialize in them. Because their numbers are limited, reservations are highly recommended.

## RENTAL AGENCIES

When you arrive at any of Hawaii's airports, you'll walk the gauntlet of car rental booths and courtesy phones shoulder to shoulder along the main hallways. Of the two categories of car rental agencies in Hawaii, each has its advantage. In the first category are the big national firms. These big guys are familiar and easy to work with, sometimes offer special fly/drive deals with airlines, and live up to their promises. If you want your rental experience to be hassle-free, they're the ones. Also, don't be prejudiced against them just because they're so well known; sometimes they offer the best deals. Although these companies carry mostly sedans, some now also rent Jeeps, sport-utility vehicles, other 4WD vehicles, trucks, and vans.

Hawaii has spawned a good crop of local entrepreneurial rental agencies. Their deals and cars can range, like rummage-sale treasures, from great finds to pure junk. Local companies have the advantage of being able to cut deals on the spot. If nothing is moving from their lot on the day you arrive, you might get a real bargain. Unfortunately, mixed in this category is a hodgepodge of fly-by-nights. Some of these are small but adequate, while others are a rip-off.

The four major islands also have rental companies that deal in vanity vehicles like the Dodge Viper, Corvette, Ferrari, Porsche, Jaguar, and Lamborghine Diablo. These cars are purely for show, but if you don't mind dropping a couple of hundred dollars for a few hours in a sports car, give it a try.

### National Agencies

All of the following national companies are represented in Hawaii. Only the 800 numbers are given below. For local numbers and for other agencies, see the individual travel chapters.

One of the best firms with an excellent reputation for service and prices is **Dollar Rent A Car,** 800/800-4000 worldwide, www.dollarcar.com. Dollar rents mostly Chrysler vehicles. All major credit cards accepted.

**Alamo,** 800/327-9633, www.goalamo.com, has good weekly rates. Mostly GM cars.

**National Car Rental,** 800/227-7368 worldwide, www.nationalcar.com, features GM and Nissan cars and accepts all major credit cards.

**Avis,** 800/321-3712 nationwide, www.avis.com, features late-model GM cars as well as most imports and convertibles.

**Budget,** 800/527-7000 worldwide, www.budget.com, offers competitive rates on late-model Ford and Lincoln-Mercury cars and specialty vehicles. Budget manages the Sears auto rental network.

**Hertz,** 800/654-3011 worldwide, www.hertz.com, is competitively priced with many fly/drive deals. Hertz features Ford vehicles.

**Thrifty,** 800/367-2277 worldwide, www.thrifty.com, uses mostly Chrysler vehicles.

**Enterprise,** 800/736-8222, www.enterprise.com, rents all types of vehicles at decent rates.

## Car Pickup

The majority of agencies listed above have booths at all of the airport terminal buildings throughout Hawaii. If they don't, they have clearly marked courtesy phones in the lobbies. Just pick one up to get directions on where to wait for the agency's shuttle. Some of the larger local agencies also have courtesy phones and booths at airport terminals, but many only work out of their lots.

## Travelers with Disabilities

**Accessible Vans of Hawaii** 296 Alamaha St., Suite C, Kahului, HI 96732, 808/871-7785 or 800/303-3750, fax 808/871-7536, is a private company owned and operated by Dave McKown, who has traveled the world with his paraplegic brother. Dave knows firsthand the obstacles faced by people with disabilities, and his disabled associate does as well. Accessible Vans of Hawaii provides a full-service travel agency, book-

ing rooms, flights, and activities for the physically disabled. Wheelchair-lift-equipped vans are rented on O'ahu and Maui for $115 a day, $599 a week, or $2,250 a month, plus tax and pickup and delivery charges. This company also does sales of new and used vans set up for disabled owners, and sells mobility equipment and travel accessories. Dave and his associate are good sources of information for any traveler with disabilities. The company's website is at www.accessiblevanshawaii.com; its email address is info@accessalohatravel.com.

# MOTORCYCLES AND MOPEDS

Driving a motorcycle can be liberating and exhilarating, yet motorcycle drivers are more vulnerable than drivers of cars and trucks. Enjoy your ride, but be very aware of traffic conditions. Drive safely and defensively, and always wear a helmet. Mopeds fall into the same vehicle category as bicycles, so become aware of all appropriate rules and regulations before you rent and ride.

Most motorcycles for rent in Hawaii are the big Harley-Davidsons, while some Japanese models are also available. Rates vary but run around $100 for half a day and $140–190 for 24 hours; longer rentals can be arranged. All drivers must be at least 21 years old, have a valid motorcycle license, and be in possession of a major credit card. Insurance is available. Companies want you to stay on good paved roads. Although wearing helmets is not required by state law, they are available, but you must wear eye protection.

# BY BOAT

Ironically, in the country's only island state, which boasts a long sailing history, modern shipping, and port towns, ferry service between the islands, except for that between Maui and Lana'i and Maui and Moloka'i, is nonexistent. Periodically, there is a cry to reinstate some sort of coastal and interisland boat or ferry service. Some say visitors and islanders alike would enjoy the experience and be able to travel more economically. Others argue that Hawaiian waters are as dangerous and unpredictable as ever, and no evidence of need or enough passengers exists. For now, interisland travelers have to be content with seeing the islands from the air.

# PUBLIC TRANSPORTATION

Public transportation is very limited in Hawaii, except for O'ahu's exemplary **TheBus.** TheBus, 808/848-4444, can take you just about anywhere you want to go on O'ahu for only $1.50 adult or 75 cents for students. Carrying more than a quarter million passengers per day, it's a model of what a bus system should be.

The MTS Line, popularly called the **Hele-On Bus,** 808/961-8744, is a very local bus system that services the Big Island. It's cheap and okay for short hops, but infrequent and slow for long distances. Travelers say they consistently make better time hitchhiking between Hilo and Kona than waiting for Hele-On to waddle by.

The **Kaua'i Bus,** 808/241-6410, runs limited routes with no service on Sundays or holidays. Still, for making shopping runs to Lihu'e or Kapa'a, it's an option if you have plenty of time on your hands.

Public bus service is new to Maui, but none exists on Moloka'i or Lana'i. Operated by MEO (Maui Economic Opportunity, Inc.) in association with a local private bus company, service is offered between Wailuku and Kahului, between the resort communities of West Maui and South Maui, and also between Wailuku/Kahului and the resort communites.

Check the travel chapter introductions below for details on what is available on each island.

# HITCHHIKING

Hitchhiking varies from island to island, both in legality and method of thumbing a ride. On O'ahu, hitchhiking is legal, and you use the tried-and-true style of facing traffic and waving your thumb—but you can only hitchhike from bus stops. Not many people hitchhike and the pickings are reasonably easy, but TheBus is only $1.50 for anywhere you want to go, and the paltry sum you save by hitchhiking is lost in "seeing time." It's legal to hitch on Kaua'i and the police don't bother you on Hawai'i. Remember that Hawai'i is indeed a "big" island; be prepared to take some time getting from one end to the other. In Maui County (Maui, Moloka'i, Lana'i), thumbing a ride is now legal again. As one of her last duties, former mayor Linda Lingle signed a bill in early 1999 to give the right to hitch a ride back to the people. Where once you had to play the game with no thumb, now you can solicit rides with that old reliable method. You can get around quite well by thumb on Maui if you're not on a schedule, but traffic is very light on both Moloka'i and Lana'i, so you should expect to wait.

In general, you will get a ride, eventually, but in comparison to the amount of traffic going by, it isn't easy. Two things work against you: many of the drivers are tourists who don't want to bother with hitchhikers, and many locals don't want to bother with nonlocal hitchhikers. When you do get a ride, most of the time it will be from a *haole* who is either a tourist on his or her own or a new island resident. If you are hitchhiking along a well-known beach area, perhaps in your bathing suit and obviously not going far, you can get a ride more easily. Women should exercise caution and avoid hitchhiking alone.

**INTRODUCTION**

# Health and Safety

In a survey published some years ago by *Science Digest*, Hawaii was cited as the healthiest state in the United States in which to live. Indeed, Hawaiian citizens live longer than anywhere else in America: men to 76 years and women to 82. Lifestyle, heredity, and diet help with these figures, but Hawaii is still an oasis in the middle of the ocean, and germs just have a tougher time getting here. There are no cases of malaria, cholera, or yellow fever. Because of a strict quarantine law, rabies is also nonexistent. On the other hand, tooth decay, perhaps because of a wide use of sugar and the enzymes present in certain tropical fruits, is 30 percent above the national average. With the perfect weather, a multitude of fresh-air activities, soothing negative ionization from the sea, and a generally relaxed and carefree lifestyle, everyone seems to feel better in the islands. Hawaii is just what the doctor ordered: a beautiful, natural health spa. That's one of its main drawing cards. The food and water are perfectly safe, and the air quality is the best in the country.

## Handling the Sun

Don't become a victim of your own exuberance. People can't wait to strip down and lie on the sand like beached whales, but the tropical sun will burn you to a cinder if you're silly. The burning rays come through more easily in Hawaii because of the sun's angle, and you don't feel them as much because there's always a cool breeze. The worst part of the day is 11 A.M.–3 P.M. Hawaii lies roughly between 19 and 22 degrees north latitude, not even close to the equator, but it's still more than 1,000 miles south of sunny southern California beaches. You'll just have to force yourself to go slowly. Don't worry; you'll be able to flaunt your best souvenir, your golden Hawaiian tan, to your green-with-envy friends when you get home. It's better than showing them a boiled lobster body with peeling skin! If your skin is snowflake white, 15 minutes per side on the first day is plenty. Increase by 15-minute intervals every day, which will allow you a full hour per side by the fourth day. Have faith;

this is enough to give you a deep golden, uniform tan. If you lie out on the beach or are simply out in the sun during the day, use sunblock lotion that has greater strength than you use at home—most people recommend SPF 25 or higher—and reapply every couple of hours. If you do burn, try taking aspirin as quickly as you can. No one knows exactly what it does, but it seems to provide some relief. Alternately, apply a cold compress or aloe juice, but be careful with aloe because it may stain clothing.

Whether out on the beach, hiking in the mountains, or just strolling around town, be very aware of dehydration. The sun (and wind) tend to sap your energy and your store of liquid. Bottled water in various sizes is readily available in all parts of Hawaii. Be sure to carry some with you or stop at a store or restaurant for a filler-up.

Don't forget about your head and eyes. Use your sunglasses and wear a brimmed hat. Some people lay a towel over their neck and shoulders when hiking; others will stick a scarf under their hat and let it drape down over their shoulders to provide some protection.

## Haole Rot

A peculiar condition caused by the sun is referred to locally as *haole* rot. It's called this because it supposedly affects only white people, but you'll notice some dark-skinned people with the same condition. Basically, the skin becomes mottled with white spots that refuse to tan. You get a blotchy effect, mostly on the shoulders and back. Dermatologists have a fancy name for it, and they'll give you a fancy prescription with a not-so-fancy price tag to cure it. It's common knowledge throughout the islands that Selsun Blue shampoo has some ingredient that stops the white mottling effect. Wash your hair with it and then make sure to rub the lather over the affected areas, and it should clear up.

## Bugs

Everyone, in varying degrees, has an aversion to vermin and creepy crawlers. Hawaii isn't infested with a wide variety, but it does have its share. Mosquitoes were unknown in the islands until their larvae stowed away in the water barrels of the *Wellington* in 1826 and were introduced at Lahaina. They bred in the tropical climate and rapidly spread to all the islands. They are a particular nuisance in the rainforests. Be prepared, and bring a natural repellent like citronella oil, available in most health stores on the islands, or a commercial product available in all groceries or drugstores. Campers will be happy to have mosquito coils to burn at night as well.

Cockroaches are very democratic insects. They hassle all strata of society equally. They breed well in Hawaii, and most hotels are at war with them, trying desperately to keep them from being spotted by guests. One comforting thought is that in Hawaii they aren't a sign of filth or dirty housekeeping. They love the climate like everyone else, and it's a real problem keeping them under control. Of a number of different roaches in Hawaii, the ones that give most people the jitters are big bombers over two inches long. Roaches are after food crumbs and the like, and very infrequently bother with a human. Be aware of this if you rent a room with a kitchenette or condo. If you are in a modest hotel and see a roach, it might make you feel better to know that the millionaire in the $1000-a-night suite probably has them too. Bring your own spray if you wish, call the desk if you see them, or just let them be.

## Poisonous Plants

A number of plants in Hawaii, mostly imported, contain toxins. In almost every case you have to eat a lot of them before they'll do you any real harm. The following is a partial list of the most common poisonous plants you'll encounter and the parts to avoid: poinsettia—leaves, stems, and sap; oleander—all parts; azalea—all parts; crown flower—juice; lantana—berries; castor bean—all parts; bird of paradise—seeds; coral plant—seeds.

## Pollution in Paradise

Calling Hawaii the healthiest state in America doesn't mean that it has totally escaped pollution. It is the only state, however, in which all of the natural beauty is protected by state law, with a statewide zoning and a general development plan. For example, the absence of billboard advertising is due to the pioneering work of a women's club, The Outdoor Circle, which was responsible for an anti-billboard law passed in 1927. It's strictly enforced, but unfortunately high-rises and other ill-advised developments have obscured some of the lovely views that these far-sighted women were trying to preserve. Numerous environmental controversies, including nuclear proliferation and the ill effects of rampant development, rage on the islands.

The most obvious infringements occur on O'ahu, with 73 percent of the state's population, which places the greatest stress on the environment. An EPA study found that almost 20 percent of O'ahu's wells have unacceptably high concentrations of DBCP and TCP. Because of Hawaii's unique water lenses (fresh water trapped by layers of lava), this fact is particularly onerous. The "Great O'ahu Milk Crisis" of 1982 saw dairies shut down when their milk was found to have abnormally high concentrations of heptachlor, a chemical used in the pineapple industry. This was traced to the tops of pineapple plants sold as fodder, which tainted the milk.

O'ahu's H-3 Freeway cuts through an ecologically sensitive valley, and an alternative biomass energy plant is denuding the islands of its remaining indigenous *'ohi'a* trees. On the Big Island, plans are always lurking for resort development near South Point and even in the magnificent Waipi'o Valley. Also on the Big Island, a thermal energy plant was bitterly challenged because its builders insisted on locating it in the middle of sensitive rainforest when other, more ecologically acceptable sites were readily available. And just to be pesky, the Mediterranean fruit fly made its appearance and Malathion had to be sprayed. Compared to those in many states, these conditions are small potatoes, but they lucidly point out the holistic global concept that no place on earth is immune to the ravages of pollution.

**M**

# WATER SAFETY

Hawaii has one very sad claim to fame: more people drown here than anywhere else in the world. Moreover, there are dozens of yearly swimming victims with broken necks and backs or with injuries from scuba and snorkeling accidents. These statistics shouldn't keep you out of the sea, because it is indeed beautiful—benevolent in most cases—and a major reason to go to Hawaii. But if you're foolish, the sea will bounce you like a basketball and suck you away for good. The best remedy is to avoid situations you can't handle. Don't let anyone dare you into a situation that makes you uncomfortable. "Macho men" who know nothing about the power of the sea will be tumbled into Cabbage Patch dolls in short order. Ask lifeguards or beach attendants about conditions, and follow their advice. If local people refuse to go in, there's a good reason. Even experts get in trouble in Hawaiian waters. Some beaches are as gentle as lambs; others, especially on the north coasts during the winter months, are frothing giants.

While beachcombing, or especially when walking out on rocks, never turn your back on the sea. Be aware of undertows (the waves drawing back into the sea). They can knock you off your feet. Before entering the water, study it for rocks, breakers, reefs, and riptides. Riptides are powerful currents, like rivers in the sea, that can drag you out. Mostly they peter out not too far from shore, and you can often see their choppy waters on the surface. If caught in a "rip," don't fight to swim directly against it; you'll lose and only exhaust yourself. Swim diagonally across it, while going along with it, and try to stay parallel to the shore. Don't waste all your lung power yelling, and rest by floating.

When bodysurfing, never ride straight in; come to shore at a 45-degree angle. Remember, waves come in sets. Little ones can be followed by giants, so watch the action awhile instead of plunging right in. Standard procedure is to duck under a breaking wave. You can survive even thunderous oceans using this technique. Don't try to swim through a heavy froth and never turn your back and let it smash you. Don't swim alone if possible, and obey all warning signs. Hawaiians want to entertain you and they don't put up signs just to waste money. The last rule is, "If in doubt, stay out."

## Yikes!

Sharks live in all the oceans of the world. Most mind their own business and stay away from shore. Hawaiian sharks are well fed—on fish—and don't usually bother with unsavory humans. If you encounter a shark, don't panic. Never thrash around because this will trigger their attack instinct. If they come close, scream loudly.

Portuguese man-of-wars put out long, floating tentacles that sting if they touch you. It seems that many floating jellyfish are blown into shore by winds on the eighth, ninth, and tenth days after the full moon. Don't wash the sting off with fresh water, as this will only aggravate it. Hot salt water will take away the sting, as will alcohol (the drinking or rubbing kind), after-shave lotion, or meat tenderizer (MSG), which can be found in any supermarket and some Chinese restaurants.

## WATER SAFETY TIPS

**O**bserve the water before you enter. Note where others are swimming or snorkeling and go there. Don't turn your back on the water. Dive under incoming waves before they reach you. Come in *before* you get tired.

When the wind comes up, get out. Stay out of the water during periods of high surf. High surf often creates riptides that can pull you out to sea. If you get caught in a riptide, don't panic. Swim parallel to the shore until you are out of the strong pull. Be aware of ocean currents, especially those within reefs that can cause riptides when the water washes out a channel.

If you are using water equipment, make sure it all works properly. Wear a T-shirt when snorkeling; it could save you from a major sunburn.

Stay off coral. Standing on coral damages it, as does breaking it with your hands.

Leave the fish and turtles alone. Green sea turtles are an endangered species, and a fine of up to $10,000 can be levied on those who knowingly disturb them. Have a great time looking, but give them space.

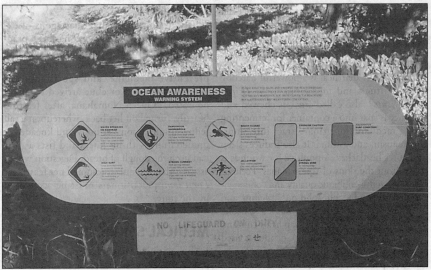

ROBERT NILSEN

**Most popular Hawaiian beaches have ocean awareness signs posted. Pay heed.**

Coral can give you a nasty cut, and it's known for causing infections because it's a living organism. Wash the cut immediately and apply an antiseptic. Keep the cut clean and covered, and watch for infection.

Poisonous sea urchins, such as the lacquer-black *wana,* can be beautiful creatures. They are found in shallow tidepools and will hurt you if you step on them. Their spines will break off, enter your foot, and burn like blazes. There are cures. Vinegar and wine poured on the wound will stop the burning. If those aren't available, the Hawaiian solution is urine. It might seem ignominious to have someone pee on your foot, but it'll put the fire out. The spines will disintegrate in a few days, and there are generally no long-term effects.

Hawaiian reefs also have their share of moray eels. These creatures are ferocious in appearance but will never initiate an attack. You'll have to poke around in their holes while snorkeling or scuba diving to get them to attack. Sometimes this is inadvertent on the diver's part, so be careful where you stick your hand while underwater.

Freshwater-borne bacteria deposited by the urine of infected animals into streams, ponds, and muddy soil cause **leptospirosis.** Two to 20 days after the bacteria enter the body, there is a *sudden* onset of fever accompanied by chills, sweats, headache, and sometimes vomiting and diarrhea. Preventive measures include: staying out of freshwater sources where cattle and other animals wade and drink; not swimming in freshwater if you have an open cut; and not drinking stream water. Although it may not always be the case, *leptospirosis* left untreated may be fatal.

## HAWAIIAN FOLK MEDICINE AND CURES

Hawaiian folk medicine is well developed, and its cures for common ailments have been used effectively for centuries. Hawaiian *kahuna* were highly regarded for their medicinal skills, and Hawaiians were by far some of the healthiest people in the world until the coming of the Europeans. Many folk remedies and cures are used to this day and, what's more, they work. Many of the common plants and fruits that you'll encounter provide some of the best remedies. When roots and seeds and special exotic plants are used, the preparation of the medicine is as painstaking as in a modern pharmacy. These prescriptions are exact and take an expert to prepare. They should never be prepared or administered by an amateur.

## Common Curative Plants

Arrowroot, for diarrhea, is a powerful narcotic used in rituals and medicines. Kava *(Piper methysticum),* also called *'awa,* is chewed and the juice is spat into a container for fermenting into a medicine for urinary tract infections, rheumatism, and asthma. It also induces sleep and cures headaches. A poultice for wounds is made from the skins of ripe bananas. Peelings have a powerful antibiotic quality and contain vitamins A, B, and C, phosphorous, calcium, and iron. The nectar from the plant was fed to babies as a vitamin juice. Breadfruit sap heals cuts and makes a moisturizing lotion. Coconut is used to make moisturizing oil, and the juice can be chewed, spat into the hand, and used as a shampoo. Guava is a source of vitamins A, B, and C. Hibiscus has been used as a laxative. *Kukui* nut oil makes a gargle for sore throats and a laxative, plus the flowers cure diarrhea. *Noni,* an unappetizing hand-grenade-shaped fruit that you wouldn't want to eat unless you had to, reduces tumors, diabetes, and high blood pressure, and the juice is good for diarrhea. Sugarcane sweetens many concoctions, and the juice of toasted cane was a tonic for sick babies. Sweet potato is used as a tonic during pregnancy and juiced as a gargle for phlegm. Tamarind is a natural laxative and contains the most acid and sugar of any fruit on earth. Taro has been used for lung infections and thrush, and as a suppository. Yams are good for coughs, vomiting, constipation, and appendicitis.

A bad-breath gargle is made from the *hapu'u* fern. The latex from inside the leaves of aloe is great for soothing burns and sunburn, as well as for innumerable skin problems. If you get chapped lips or windburned skin, use oil from the *hinu honu.* A headache is lessened with *'awa* or *'ape.* Calm nervousness with *'awa* and *lomi lomi,* Hawaiian-style massage. To get rid of a raspy sore throat, chew the bark of the root of the *'uhaloa.* A toothache is eased by the sticky narcotic juice from the *pua kala* seed, a prickly poppy.

## Lomi Lomi

This traditional Hawaiian massage is of exceptional therapeutic value. It has been practiced since very early times and is especially useful in cases of fatigue, general body aches, preventive medicine, and sports injuries. When Otto Von Kotzebue arrived in 1824, he noted, "Queen Nomahana, after feasting heartily, turned on her back, whereupon a tall fellow sprang upon her body and kneaded it unmercifully with his knees and fists as if it had been the dough of bread. Digestion was so assisted that the queen resumed her feasting." *Lomi lomi* practitioners must be accredited by the state.

# MEDICAL SERVICES

Each major island has at least one hospital that provides emergency room, long-term, and acute care facilities; clinics, for immediate care and first-aid treatment; and pharmacies, for drug prescriptions and other medical necessities. Island by island lists of these facilities are in the specific travel chapters below.

## Alternative Medicine

Most ethnic groups who migrated to Hawaii brought along their own cures. The Chinese and Japanese are especially known for their unique and effective treatments, such as herbal medicine, acupuncture, and shiatsu. The time-honored Chinese therapy of acupuncture is available throughout the islands. On O'ahu, contact the Hawaii Acupuncture Association, P.O. Box 11202, Honolulu, HI 96828, 808/538-6692, for referrals to state-licensed acupuncturists throughout the islands. Hawaii also has a huge selection of chiropractors. Referrals can be had through the Hawaii State Chiropractic Association, P.O. Box 845, Pearl City, HI 96782, 808/926-8883. All types of massage are available throughout the islands, everything from shiatsu to Hawaii's own *lomi lomi* massage. The Yellow Pages on all islands list acupuncturists, chiropractors, holistic practitioners, herbalists, naturopaths, as well as massage therapists.

## SERVICES FOR TRAVELERS WITH DISABILITIES

A person with disabilities can have a wonderful time in Hawaii; all that's needed is a little pre-planning. The following general advice should help.

### Commission on Persons with Disabilities

This state commission was designed with the express purpose of aiding handicapped people. It is a source of invaluable information and distributes self-help booklets, which are published jointly by the Disability and Communication Access Board and the Hawaii Centers for Independent Living. Any person with disabilities heading to Hawaii should write first or visit their offices on arrival. For the *Aloha Guide to Accessibility* (Part I is free; $3–5 charge for Parts II and III), write or visit the head office at: Commission on Persons with Disabilities, 919 Ala Moana Blvd., Room 101, Honolulu, HI 96814, 808/586-8121; on Maui, 54 High St., Wailuku, HI 96793, 808/984-8219; on Kaua'i, try the Hawaii Centers for Independent Living, 4340 Nawiliwili Road, Lihu'e, HI 96766, 808/345-4034. On Hawai'i, contact the Centers for Independent Living at 400 Haulani St., #16D, Hilo, HI 96820, 808/935-3777, or 81-6627 Mamalahoa Hwy., Suite B-5, Kealakekua, HI 96750, 808/323-2221.

### General Information

The key for a smooth trip is to make as many arrangements ahead of time as possible. Tell the transportation companies and hotels that you'll be dealing with the nature of your handicap in advance so that they can make arrangements to accommodate you. Bring your medical records and notify medical establishments of your arrival if you'll be needing their services. Travel with a friend or make arrangements for an aide on arrival. Bring your own wheelchair if possible and let airlines know if it is battery-powered; boarding interisland carriers requires steps. They'll board you early on special lifts, but they must know that you're coming. Many hotels and restaurants accommodate people with disabilities,

but always call ahead just to make sure. For specific services, see the individual island chapters.

## PROSTITUTION

Ever since the first ship arrived in 1778, Hawaii has known prostitution. Rampant until the missionaries arrived in 1819, was a major cause of the tragic population decline of the Hawaiian race. The tradition has carried on into more recent times. Iwilei was a notorious red-light district in Honolulu in the early 1900s, even considered by some to be an attraction—when Somerset Maugham passed through the islands in 1916 on his way to Russia as a spy for England, he was taken there as if on a sightseeing tour. The long-established military presence in Hawaii has also helped keep prostitution a flourishing business. During World War II, the consensus of the military commanders was that prostitution was a necessary evil, needed to keep up the morale of the troops.

Prostitution is still a reality in Honolulu, centered mainly around Waikiki and Chinatown (particularly along Hotel Street, where you should be careful at night). Waikiki prostitution is generally geared toward tourists, while in Chinamen it's directed toward servicemen. Honolulu also has its share of massage parlors, escort services, and exotic dance joints.

## ILLEGAL DRUGS

The use and availability of illegal, controlled, and recreational drugs are about the same in Hawaii as throughout the rest of America. Cocaine is available on the streets of the main cities, especially Honolulu. Although most dealers are small-time, the drug is brought in by organized crime. Cocaine trafficking fans out from Honolulu.

Another drug menace on the streets is "ice," smokable methamphetamine that will wire a user for up to 24 hours. Many of the violent deaths in Honolulu have been linked to the use of ice.

### Pakalolo

However, the main drug available and commonly used in Hawaii is marijuana, which is locally called *pakalolo*. In the 1960s, mostly *haole* hippies from the Mainland began growing pot in the more remote sections of the islands, such as Puna on Hawaii and around Hana on Maui. They discovered what legitimate planters had known for 200 years: plant a broomstick in Hawaii, treat it right, and it'll grow. *Pakalolo*, after all, is a weed, and it grows in Hawaii like wildfire. The locals quickly got into the act when they realized that they, too, could grow a "money tree." As a matter of fact, they began resenting the *haole* usurpers, and a quiet and sometimes dangerous feud has been going on ever since. Much is made of the viciousness of the backcountry "growers" of Hawaii. There are tales of booby traps and armed patrols guarding their plants in the hills, but mostly it's a cat-and-mouse game between the authorities and the growers. If you, as a tourist, are tramping about in the forest and happen upon someone's "patch," don't touch anything. Just back off and you'll be okay. Pot has the largest monetary turnover of any crop in the islands and, as such, is now considered a major source of agricultural revenue, albeit illicit and underground. There are all kinds of local names and varieties of pot in Hawaii. All passengers leaving Hawaii are subject to a thorough "agricultural inspection," and you can bet they're not looking only for illegal papayas.

## THEFT AND HASSLES

Theft and minor assaults can be a problem, but they're usually not violent or vicious as in some Mainland cities. Mostly, it's a local with a chip on his shoulder and few prospects, who will ransack your car or make off with your camera. A big Hawaiian or local guy will be obliged to flatten your nose if you look for trouble, but mostly it will be sneak thieves out to make a fast buck.

From the minute you sit behind the wheel of your rental car you'll be warned not to leave valuables unattended and to lock your car up tighter than a drum. Signs warning about theft at most major tourist attractions help fuel your paranoia. Many hotel rooms offer safes so you can lock your valuables away and relax while getting sun-

burned. Stories abound about purse snatchings and surly locals just itching to give you a hard time. Well, they're all true to a degree, but Hawaii's reputation is much worse than the reality. In Hawaii you'll have to observe two golden laws: if you look for trouble, you'll find it, and a fool and his camera are soon parted.

### Theft

The majority of theft in Hawaii is of the "sneak thief" variety. If you leave your hotel door unlocked, a camera sitting on the seat of your rental car, or valuables on your beach towel, you'll be inviting a very obliging thief to pad away with your stuff. You have to learn to take precautions, but they won't be anything like those employed in rougher areas of the world—just normal American precautions.

If you must walk alone at night, stay on the main streets in well-lit areas. Always lock your hotel door and windows and place valuable jewelry in the hotel safe. When you leave your hotel for the beach, there is absolutely no reason to carry all your traveler's checks and credit cards or a big wad of money. Just take what you'll need for drinks and lunch. If you're uptight about leaving money in your beach bag, stick it in your bathing suit or bikini. American money is just as negotiable if it is damp. Don't leave your camera or any electronic goods on the beach unattended. Ask a person nearby to watch it for you while you go for a dip. Most people won't mind at all, and you can repay the favor.

While sightseeing in your shiny new rental car, which immediately brands you as a tourist, again, don't take more than what you'll need for the day. Why people leave a camera sitting on the seat of their car is a mystery! Many people lock valuables in the trunk, but remember that most good car thieves can jimmy it open as quickly as you can open it with your key. If you must, for some reason, leave your camera or valuables in your car, lock them in the trunk, stash them under a seat back that's been reclined, or consider putting them under the hood. Thieves usually don't look there, and on most modern cars you can only pop the hood with a lever inside the car. It's not fail-safe, but it's worth a try.

Campers face special problems because their entire camp is open to thievery. Most campgrounds don't have any real security, but who, after all, wants to fence an old tent or a used sleeping bag? Many tents have zippers that can be secured with a small padlock. If you want to go hiking and are afraid to leave your gear in the campgrounds, take a large green garbage bag with you. Transport your gear down the trail and then walk off through some thick brush. Put your gear in the garbage bag and bury it under leaves and other light camouflage. That's about as safe as you can be. You can also use a variation on this technique instead of leaving your valuables in your rental car.

## Hassles

Another self-perpetuating myth about Hawaii is that "the natives are restless." An undeniable animosity exists between locals (especially those with some Hawaiian blood) and *haole*. Fortunately, this prejudice is directed mostly at the group and not at the individual. The locals are resentful of those *haole* who came, took their land, and relegated them to second-class citizenship. They realize that this is not the average tourist and they can tell what you are at a glance. Tourists usually are treated with understanding and are given a type of immunity. Besides, Hawaiians are still among the most friendly, giving, and understanding people on earth.

*Haole* who live in Hawaii might tell you stories of their children having trouble at school. They could even mention an unhappy situation at some schools called "beat-up-a-*haole*" day, and you might hear that if you're a *haole* it's not a matter of "if" you'll be beaten up, but "when." Truthfully, most of this depends upon your attitude and your sensitivity. The locals feel infringed upon, so don't fuel these feelings. If you're at a beach park and there is a group of local people in one area, don't crowd them. If you go into a local bar and you're the only one of your ethnic group in sight, you shouldn't have to be told to leave. Much of the hassle involves drinking. Booze brings out the worst prejudice on all sides. If you're invited to a beach party, and the local guys start getting drunk, make this your exit call. Don't wait until it's too late.

Most trouble seems to be directed toward white men. White women are mostly immune from being beaten up, but they have to beware of the violence of sexual abuse and rape. Although plenty of local women marry white men, it's not a good idea to try to pick up a local woman. If you're known in the area and have been properly introduced, that's another story. Also, women out for the night in bars or discos can be approached if they're not in the company of local guys. Maintain your own dignity and self-respect by treating others with dignity and respect. Most times you'll reap what you sow.

# What to Take

It's a snap to pack for a visit to Hawaii. Everything is on your side. The weather is moderate and uniform on the whole, and the style of dress is delightfully casual. The rule of thumb is to pack lightly: few items, and light clothing both in color and weight. What you'll need will depend largely on your itinerary and your desires. Are you drawn to the nightlife, the outdoors, or both? If you forget something at home, it won't be a disaster. You can buy everything you'll need in Hawaii. As a matter of fact, Hawaiian clothing, such as mu'umu'u and aloha shirts, is one of the best purchases you can make, both in comfort

and style. It's quite feasible to bring only one or two changes of clothing with the express purpose of outfitting yourself while there. Prices on bathing suits, bikinis, and summer wear in general are quite reasonable.

## Matters of Taste

A grand conspiracy in Hawaii adhered to by everyone—tourist, traveler, and resident—is to "hang loose" and dress casually. Best of all, alohawear is just about all you'll need for comfort and virtually every occasion. The classic mu'umu'u is large and billowy, and aloha shirts are made to be worn outside the pants. The best of both are made of cool cotton. Rayon and silk are natural fibers that isn't too bad, but polyester is hot, sticky, and not authentic. Not all mu'umu'u are of the "tent persuasion." Some are very fashionable and form-fitted with peek-a-boo slits up the side, down the front, or around the back. A *holomu* is a mu'umu'u fitted at the waist with a flowing skirt to the ankles. They are not only elegant, but perfect for "stepping out."

## Basic Necessities

As previously mentioned, you really have to consider only two "modes" of dressing in Hawaii: beachwear and casual clothing. The following list is designed for the midrange traveler carrying one suitcase or a backpack. Remember that there are laundromats and that you'll be spending a considerable amount of time in your bathing suit. Consider the following: one or two pairs of light cotton slacks for going out and about, and one pair of jeans for hiking and riding horses; two or three casual sundresses; three or four pairs of shorts for beachwear and for sightseeing; four to five short-sleeved shirts or blouses and one long-sleeved; three or four colored and printed T-shirts that can be worn anytime from hiking to strolling; a beach coverup; a brimmed hat for rain and sun—the crushable floppy type is great for purse or day pack, or pick up a straw or woven hat in the islands for about $10; two or three pairs of socks are sufficient, nylons you won't generally need; two bathing suits (nylon ones dry quickest); plastic bags to hold wet bathing suits and laundry; five to six pairs of underwear; towels (optional, because hotels provide them, even for the beach); a first-aid kit, pocket-size is sufficient; suntan lotion and insect repellent; a day pack or large beach bag. And don't forget your windbreaker, perhaps a shawl for the evening, and an all-purpose jogging suit. A few classy restaurants in the finest hotels require men to wear a sport coat for dinner. If you don't have one, most hotels can supply you with one for the evening.

## In the Cold and Rain

Two occasions for which you'll have to consider dressing warmly are visits to mountaintops and boat rides when wind and ocean sprays are a factor. You can conquer both with a jogging suit or sweat suit and a featherweight, water-resistant windbreaker. If you intend to visit Mauna Kea, Mauna Loa, or Haleakala it'll be downright chilly. Your jogging suit with a hooded windbreaker/raincoat will do the trick for all occasions. If you're going to camp or hike, you should add another layer, a woolen sweater being one of the best. Wool is the only natural fiber that retains most of its warmth-giving properties even if it gets wet. Several varieties of "fleece" synthetics currently on the market also have this ability. If your hands get cold, put a pair of socks over them. Tropical rain showers can happen at any time so you might consider a fold-up umbrella, but the sun quickly breaks through and the warming winds blow. Nighttime winter temps may drop into the lower 60s or upper 50s, so be sure to have a sweater and long pants along.

## Shoes

Dressing your feet is hardly a problem. You'll most often wear zori (rubber thongs) for going to and from the beach, leather sandals for strolling and dining, and jogging shoes for hiking and sightseeing. Teva and other types of outdoor strap sandals are good for general sightseeing and beach and water wear. A few discos require dress shoes, but it's hardly worth bringing them just for that. If you plan on heavy-duty hiking, you'll definitely want your hiking boots. Lava, especially 'a'a, is murderous on shoes. Most backcountry trails are rugged and muddy, and you'll need those good old lug soles for traction. If you plan moderate hikes, jogging shoes should do.

## Specialty Items

Following is a list of specialty items that you might consider bringing along. They're not necessities but most will definitely come in handy. A pair of binoculars really enhances sightseeing—great for viewing birds and sweeping panoramas, and almost a necessity if you're going whale-watching. A folding, Teflon-bottomed travel iron makes up for cotton's one major shortcoming, wrinkles. Most accommodations have them, but you can't always count on it. Nylon twine and miniature clothespins are handy for drying garments, especially bathing suits. Commercial and hotel laundromats abound, but many times you'll get by with hand-washing a few items in the sink. A radio/tape recorder provides news, weather, and entertainment, and can be used to record impressions, island music, and a run-

ning commentary for your slide show. Hair dryer: although the wind can be relied upon to dry wet hair, it leaves a bit to be desired in the styling department. As with the iron, most accommodations have these, but not all. Flippers, mask, and snorkel can easily be bought in Hawaii but don't weigh much or take up much space in your luggage.

# Information and Services

## HAWAII VISITORS BUREAU

In 1903 the Hawaiian Promotion Committee thought tourism could be the economic wave of the future. They began the Hawaii Tourist Bureau, which became the Hawaii Visitors Bureau. The HVB is now a top-notch organization providing help and information to Hawaii's visitors. Anyone contemplating a trip to Hawaii should visit or write the HVB and inquire about any specific information that may be required, or visit its website at www.gohawaii.com. Their advice and excellent brochures on virtually every facet of living, visiting, or simply enjoying Hawaii are free. The materials offered are too voluminous to list, but for basics, request individual island brochures, maps, and vacation planners (also on the Web at www.hshawaii.com), and an all-island members' directory of accommodations, restaurants, entertainment, and transportation. Allow two to three weeks for requests to be answered.

### HVB Offices Statewide

Statewide offices include: **HVB Administrative Office,** Waikiki Business Plaza, 2270 Kalakaua Ave., Suite 801, Honolulu, HI 96815, 808/923-1811; **Visitor Information Office,** 808/924-0266, Waikiki Shopping Plaza, 2250 Kalakaua Ave., Suite 502, Honolulu, HI 96815; **O'ahu Visitors Bureau,** 733 Bishop St., Suite 1872, Honolulu, HI 96813, 808/524-0722 or 877/525-3530, www.visit-oahu.com; **Big Island HVB, Hilo Branch,** 250 Keawe St., Hilo, HI 96720, 808/961-5797 or 800/648-2441, www.bigisland.org; **Big Island HVB, Kona Branch,** 250 Waikoloa Beach Drive, Suite B15, Waikoloa, HI

96738, 808/886-1655; **Kaua'i HVB,** 4334 Rice St., Suite 101, Lihu'e, HI 96766, 808/245-3971 or 800/262-1400, www.kauaivisitorsbureau.org; and **Maui HVB,** 1727 Wili Pa Loop, Wailuku, HI 96793, 808/244-3530 or 800/525-6284, www.visitmaui.com.

Two other helpful organizations are the **Moloka'i Visitors Association,** P.O. Box 960, Kaunakakai, HI 96748, 808/553-3876 or 800/800-6367 Mainland and Canada, or 800/553-0404 interisland, www.molokai-hawaii.com; and **Destination Lana'i,** P.O. Box 700 Lana'i City, HI 96763, 808/565-7600 or 800/947-4774, fax 808/565-9316, www.visitlanai.net.

### North American Offices
**West Coast:** 4150 Mission Blvd., Suite 200A, San Diego, CA 92109, 858/270-2390.

Salinas: 1172 South Main St., #369, Salinas, CA 93901, 831/455-1839.

**Midwest:** 625 N. Michigan Ave., Suite 1737, Chicago, IL 60611, 312/654-4542.

**East Coast:** 1100 N. Glebe Road #760, Arlington, VA 22201, 703/525-7770.

**Canada:** c/o Comprehensive Travel, 1260 Hornby St., #104, Vancouver, B.C., Canada V6Z 1W2, Canada, 604/669-6691.

### European Offices
**United Kingdom:** P.O. Box 208, Sunbury on Thames, Middlesex, England, TW16 5RJ, 208/941-4009.

**Germany:** Noble Kommunikation GmbH, Luisenstrasse 7, 63262 Neu-Isenburg, Germany, 180/223-040.

## South American Office

**Uruguay:** c/o Yamandu Rodriguez 1390, 11500 Montevideo, Uruguay, 2/606-0277.

## Asian/Pacific Offices

**Tokyo:** Kokusai Bldg., 2F, 3-1-1, Marunouchi, Chiyoda-ku, Tokyo 100, Japan, 3/3201-0430.

**Osaka:** Sumitomo Nakanoshima Bldg., 2F, 3-2-18, Nakanoshima, Kita-gu, Osaka 530, Japan, 6/6443-8015.

**Korea:** c/o Travel Press, Seoul Center Bldg., 12th Fl., 91-1, Sokong-dong, Chung-gu, Seoul 100-070, Korea, 2/777-0033.

**Beijing:** A606, COFCO Bldg., 8 Jianguomen Nei Dajie, Beijing, China 100005, 10/6527-7530.

**Shanghai:** Shanghai Centre, 1376 Nanjing Road West, Room 527, Shanghai, China 200040, 21/6279-8099.

**Taiwan:** Wish (Wei Yuan) Company, 9F-1, #21, Lane 22, Hsein Yen Road, Wen Shan Area, Taipei 117, Taiwan, 2/2934-8323.

**Hong Kong:** Pacific Leisure Group, c/o Pacam Limited, 10F, Tung Ming Bldg., Room 1003, 40 Des Voeux Road Central, Hong Kong SAR, China, 2524-1361.

**New Zealand:** c/o Walshes World, 14 Shortland Street, Level 6, Auckland, New Zealand, 9/379-3708.

**Australia:** c/o The Sales Team, Suite 602A, Level 6, 97-103 Pacific Highway, North Sydney, NSW 2060, Australia, 2/9955-2619.

## Other Information Services

The state operates **visitor information booths** at Honolulu International Airport, 808/836-6413, that offer plenty of practical brochures and helpful information. Similar visitor information booths and/or brochure stands are located at all airports in the state.

# LOCAL RESOURCES

**Police, fire, ambulance:** Dial **911** on all islands.

**Coast Guard Search and Rescue:** Dial 800/552-6458 on all islands.

For other numbers, such as non-emergency police numbers, crisis lines, consumer protec-

tion, weather and marine reports, see the individual travel chapters below.

## Foreign Consulates

All foreign consulates and diplomatic offices are in Honolulu. Most major European, Asian, and Oceanic nations, along with many South American countries, have delegates in Honolulu. They are listed under "Consulates and Other Foreign Government Representatives" in the O'ahu Yellow Pages.

## Post Offices

Post offices are located in all major towns and cities. Most larger hotels also offer limited postal services. Normal business hours are Mon.–Fri. 8 or 8:30 A.M. to 4 or 4:30 P.M.; some offices are open Saturday 8 A.M.–noon or 1 P.M. The first three zip code digits, 967, are the same for all of Hawaii, except Honolulu, where it's 968. The last two digits designate the particular post office.

The simplest way to receive mail is to have it sent to your lodgings if you'll be there long enough to receive it. Have it addressed to you in care of your hotel or condo, and include the room number if you know it. It'll be in your box at the front desk. If you plan frequent moves or a multiple-island itinerary with short stays on each island, have mail sent General Delivery to a post office in a town you plan to visit. The post office will hold your mail in general delivery for 30 days. It takes about five days for a first-class letter to arrive in Hawaii from the Mainland. It's a good idea to notify the postmaster of the post office where you will be receiving mail of the dates you expect to pick it up.

# OTHER INFORMATION

## Telephone

The telephone system in Hawaii is modern and comparable to any system on the Mainland. You can "direct dial" from Hawaii to the Mainland and more than 160 foreign countries. Undersea cables and satellite communications ensure top-quality phone service. Any phone call to a number on that island is a local call; it's long distance when dialing to another island or beyond the state. As they do everywhere else in the United States, long-distance rates go down at 5 P.M. and again at 11 P.M. until 8 A.M. the next morning. Rates are cheapest from Friday at 5 P.M. until Monday at 8 A.M. Local calls from public telephones cost 50 cents. Emergency calls are always free. Public telephones are found at hotels, street booths, restaurants, most public buildings, and some beach parks. It is common to have a phone in most hotel rooms and condominiums, though a service charge is usually collected, even on local calls. Toll-free calls are preceded by 800, 888, 877, or 866; there is no charge to the calling party. Many are listed in the text. For directory assistance call: local, 1-411; interisland, 1-555-1212; Mainland, 1-area code-555-1212; toll-free 1-800-555-1212. The **area code** for the entire state of Hawaii is 808.

## Time Zones

There is no daylight savings time in Hawaii. When daylight savings time is not in effect on the Mainland, Hawaii is two hours behind the West Coast, four hours behind the Midwest, five hours behind the East Coast, and 11 hours behind Germany. Hawaii, being just east of the international date line, is almost a full day behind most Asian and Oceanic cities. Hours behind these countries and cities are: Japan, 19 hours; Singapore, 18 hours; Sydney, 20 hours; New Zealand, 22 hours; Fiji, 22 hours.

## Electricity

The same electrical current is in use in Hawaii as on the U.S. Mainland and is uniform throughout the islands. The system functions on 110 volts, 60 cycles of alternating current (AC). Appliances from Japan will work, but there is some danger of burnout, while those requiring the normal European current of 220 will not work.

## Distance, Weights, and Measures

Hawaii, like all of the United States, employs the "English method" of measuring weights and distances. Basically, dry weights are in ounces and pounds; liquid measures are in ounces, quarts, and gallons; and distances are measured in inches, feet, yards, and miles. The metric system is known but is not in general use.

# MONEY AND FINANCES

## Currency

U.S. currency is among the drabbest in the world. It's all the same size and color; those unfamiliar with it should spend some time getting acquainted so that they don't make costly mistakes. U.S. coins include one cent (penny), five cents (nickel), 10 cents (dime), 25 cents (quarter), 50 cents (half dollar), and $1 (uncommon); paper currency is $1, $2 (uncommon), $5, $10, $20, $50, $100. Bills larger than $100 are not in common usage. Since 1996, new designs have been issued for the $100, $50, $20, $10, and $5 bills. Some color has been added since 2003. Both the old and new bills are accepted as valid currency.

## Banking

Full-service bank hours are generally 8:30 A.M.–4 P.M. Mon.–Thurs. and Friday until 6 P.M. There are no weekend hours, and weekday hours will be a bit longer at counters in grocery stores and other outlets. All main towns have one or more banks. Virtually all branch banks have ATM machines for 24-hour service, and these can be found at some shopping centers and other venues around the island. ATMs work only when the Hawaiian bank you choose to use is on an affiliate network with your home bank. Of most value to travelers, banks sell and cash traveler's checks, give cash advances on credit cards, and exchange and sell foreign currency (sometimes with a fee). Major banks are American Savings Bank, Bank of Hawaii, Central Pacific Bank, and First Hawaiian bank.

## Traveler's Checks

Traveler's checks are accepted throughout Hawaii at hotels, restaurants, and car rental agencies, and in most stores and shops. However, to be readily acceptable they should be in U.S. currency. Some larger hotels that frequently have Japanese and Canadian guests will accept their currency. Banks accept foreign-currency traveler's checks, but it'll mean an extra trip and inconvenience. It's best to get most of your traveler's checks in $20–50 denominations; anything larger will be hard to cash in smaller shops and boutiques, though not in hotels.

## Credit Cards

More and more business is transacted in Hawaii using credit cards. Almost every form of accommodation, shop, restaurant, and amusement accepts them. For renting a car they're almost a must. With "credit card insurance" readily available, they're as safe as traveler's checks and sometimes even more convenient. Be sure to write down your credit card numbers in case they're lost or stolen and keep them separate from the checks. Don't rely on them completely because some establishments won't accept them, or perhaps won't accept the kind you carry.

# NEWSPAPERS AND TOURIST PUBLICATIONS

Hawaii's two main English-language dailies are the *Honolulu Star Bulletin* and the *Honolulu Advertiser.* The Japanese-English *Hawaii Hochi* and the Chinese *United Chinese Press* are also published on O'ahu and are available on the other islands. Two foreign-language newspapers flown in are the *Ashai Shinbun* from Japan and the *Korea Times.*

There's a stampede of weeklies in Hawaii; all major islands have at least one and O'ahu has at least six. On Kaua'i look for the *Garden Island.* Maui has the *Maui News.* The Big Island offers the *Hawaii Tribune Herald* out of Hilo and *West Hawaii Today,* published in Kailua. All of these papers are great for what's happening and for money-saving coupons for restaurants, rentals, and amusements.

## Free Tourist Publications

On every island, at airports, in hotel lobbies, at shopping malls, and on main streets are racks filled with free magazines, pamphlets, and brochures. Sometimes the sheer volume is overwhelming, but most have up-to-the-minute information on what's happening and many money-saving coupons. They're also loaded with maps and directions to points of interest. The best, published in a convenient narrow format,

are *This Week . . . Oahu, Maui, Kauai, Big Island,* published weekly, the *Beach Activity Guide* for each island, and *Spotlight's Gold* series for each island. Regional magazines such as *Maui Visitor* and *Hawai'i Island Journal* are also well worth checking out, as is the *Drive Guide* available from major car rental agencies.

# TIDBITS: OFFICIAL AND UNOFFICIAL

## Official Hawaii

The state flower is the yellow hibiscus. More than 5,000 species grow in Hawaii. The state tree is the *kukui.* The candlenut was one of the most useful trees of old Hawaii, providing food, medicine, and light. The state bird is the *nene,* a goose that came to Hawaii eons ago and adapted to the rugged terrain, becoming a permanent resident and losing its instinct for migration. The state fish, with a name bigger than itself, is the *humuhumunukunukuapua'a* (*humu,* for short). Found in a few scattered beds at depths of up to 100 meters is black coral, the state gem. The humpback whale that visits Hawaii every year was made the official mammal in 1979.

Hawaii's nickname is "The Aloha State." The motto, *Ua mau ke e'a o ka 'aina i ka pono* ("The life of the land is perpetuated in righteousness"), came from King Kamehameha III, when in 1843 Hawaii was restored to self-sovereignty after briefly being seized by the British. The anthem, "Hawai'i Pono," was written by the "Merrie Monarch," King Kalakaua, and put to music by the royal bandmaster, Henry Berger, in 1876. "Hawai'i Pono" at one time was the anthem of the Kingdom of Hawai'i and later of the territory before becoming the official state anthem.

## Little-Known Facts

The Hawaiian Islands, from Kure Atoll in the north to the Big Island in the south, stretch 1,600 miles. South Point (Ka Lae) on the Big Island is the southernmost point of the United States. The oldest of the islands are some 30 million years old and were entirely created by volcanic activity. Haleakala on Maui is the world's largest inactive volcano, while Hawaii's Mauna Loa is the

## HAWAII'S LARGEST CITIES AND TOWNS

| Island | City/Town | Pop. |
|---|---|---|
| Big Island | Hilo | 47,000 |
| | Kailua-Kona | 12,500 |
| | Kealakakua/Captain Cook | 7,000 |
| Maui | Kahului/Wailuku | 41,000 |
| | Kihei | 16,000 |
| | Lahaina | 8,200 |
| Lana'i | Lana'i City | 3,200 |
| Moloka'i | Kaunakakai | 2,500 |
| O'ahu | Honolulu | 400,000 |
| | Kailua/Kaneohe | 95,000 |
| | Pearl City/'Aiea | 70,000 |
| | Waipahu | 25,000 |
| | Wahiawa | 16,000 |
| Kaua'i | Kapa'a | 7,600 |
| | Lihu'e | 5,200 |

Note: All population figures are approximate.

world's largest active volcano, and Kilauea is *the* most active volcano in the world. Kaua'i's Mt. Wai'ale'ale is the wettest spot on earth, receiving about 450 inches of rain per year on average. Honolulu's 'Iolani Palace is the only royal palace in the United States. Hawaii had the first company (C. Brewer), American school (Lahainaluna), newspaper *(Sandwich Island Gazette)*, bank (First Hawaiian), and church (Moku'aikaua, Kailua-Kona) west of the Rocky Mountains.

American captains Shaler and Cleveland brought the first horses aboard the *Lydia Byrd* and introduced them at Lahaina in 1803. Two were given to Kamehameha the Great, who was not impressed. Tattooing was common in old Hawaii; many people had the date of the death of a loved one tattooed on their body, and gouged their eyes and knocked out their own teeth as signs of mourning. The greatest insult was to inlay a spittoon with the teeth of a defeated enemy. The name of the channel between Lana'i and Kaho'olawe, Kealaikahiki, means "The Way to Tahiti." Voyagers got their bearings here for the long voyage south. "It will happen when Boki comes back" means something is impossible. Boki was a chief who sailed away in 1829 looking for sandalwood. He never returned. Only 20 of the 500 who sailed with him made it back to Hawaii.

# Introduction

# O'ahu

*It is the meeting place of East and West. The very
new rubs shoulders with the immeasurably old. And
if you have not found the romance you expected you
have come upon something singularly intriguing.*
—W. Somerset Maugham

# Introduction

It is the destiny of certain places on earth to be imbued with an inexplicable magnetism, a power that draws people whose visions and desires combine at just the right moment to create a dynamism so strong that it becomes history. The result for these "certain places" is greatness . . . and O'ahu is one of these.

It is difficult to separate O'ahu from its vibrant metropolis, Honolulu, whose massive political, economic, and social muscle dominates both the entire state and its home island. But to look at Honolulu *as* O'ahu is to look upon only the face of a great sculpture, ignoring the beauty and subtleties of the whole.

The words "Honolulu," "Waikiki," and "Pearl Harbor" conjure up visions common to people the world over. Immediately, imaginations flush with palm trees swaying, a healthy tan, bombs dropping, and a golden moon rising romantically over coiled lovers on a white-sand beach.

O'ahu is called the "Gathering Place," and to itself it has indeed gathered the noble memories of old Hawaii, the vibrancy of a bright-eyed fledgling state, and the brawny power so necessary for the future. On this amazing piece of land adrift in the great ocean, 876,100 people live; nearly seven times that number visit yearly,

ROBERT NILSEN

Lanikai Beach is one of the best family beaches on O'ahu.

and as time passes O'ahu remains strong as one of those "certain places."

O'ahu is partly a tropical garden, bathed by soft showers and sunshine, and swaying with a gentle but firm rhythm. You can experience this feeling all over the island, even in pockets of downtown Honolulu and Waikiki. However, its other side is brash—dominated by the confidence of a major American city perched upon the Pacific Basin whose music is a pounding staccato jackhammer, droning bulldozer, and mechanical screech of the ever-present building crane. The vast majority of first-time and return visitors land at Honolulu International and spend at least a few days on O'ahu, usually in Waikiki.

People are amazed at the diversity of experiences the island has to offer. Besides the obvious (and endless) beach activities, it offers museums, botanical gardens, a fantastic zoo and aquarium, nightclubs, extravagant shows, free entertainment, cultural classes, theaters, sporting events, a major university, historical sights galore, an exotic cosmopolitan atmosphere, backcountry hiking, and an abundance of camping—all easily accessible via terrific public transportation. Finally, to sweeten the pot, O'ahu can be the least expensive of the Hawaiian Islands to visit.

## Honolulu

Head for downtown and give yourself a full day to catch all the sights. It's as if a huge grappling hook attached to the heart of a Mainland city and hauled it across the sea. But don't get the idea that Honolulu is not unique, because it is! You'll find a delightful mixture of quaintly historic and future-shock new, exotic and ordinary. The center is 'Iolani Palace, the only real royal palace in America, heralded by the gilded statue of Kamehameha I. In an easy walking radius are the State Capitol and attendant government buildings. Chrome and glass skyscrapers holding the offices of Hawaii's economically mighty shade small stone and wooden structures from the late 1800s: Mission Houses Museum, Kawaiaha'o Church, and St. Andrew's Cathedral.

Down at the harbor Aloha Tower greets the few passenger ships that still make port; nearby at the Maritime Center is the floating museum ship Falls of Clyde, a nostalgic reminder of simpler times. Hotel Street takes you to old but not always venerable Chinatown, filled with alleyways housing tiny temples, herbalists, aromatic markets, inexpensive eateries, rough nightspots, dives, and the strong, distinctive flavor of transplanted Asia. If the hustle and bustle gets to be too much, head for Foster Botanical Garden or Lyon Arboretum. Or hop a bus for the serenity of the Bishop Museum, undoubtedly the best Polynesian cultural and anthropological museum in the world.

Behind the city is the Ko'olau Range. As you head for these beckoning hills, you can take a sidetrip over to the University of Hawai'i and the East-West Center while passing through Manoa Valley, epitome of the "good life" in Hawaii. Route 61 takes you up and over Nu'uanu Pali to O'ahu's windward side. En route you'll pass Punchbowl, an old crater holding some of the dead from World War II and the Korean and Vietnam Wars in the National Cemetery of the Pacific. As you climb, the road passes the Royal Mausoleum, final resting place for some of Hawaii's last kings, queens, and nobility. Then comes Queen Emma Summer Palace, a Victorian home of gentility and lace. Next is Nu'uanu Pali, where Kamehameha drove 16,000 O'ahu warriors over the cliff, sealing his dominance of the island kingdom with their blood. The view is hauntingly beautiful, as the mountains drop suddenly to the coast of windward O'ahu.

## Waikiki

Loosely, this world-famous beach is a hunk of land bordered by the Ala Wai Canal and running eastward to Diamond Head. Early in the 20th century these two golden miles were little more than a string of dirty beaches backed by a mosquito-infested swamp. Until 1901, when the Moana Hotel was built, only Hawaii's few remaining ali'i and a handful of wealthy kama'aina families had homes here. Now, more than 100 hotels, condos, and other lodgings provide more than 30,000 rooms, and if you placed a $20 bill on the ground, it would barely cover the cost of the land beneath it.

This hyperactive area will delight and disgust you, excite and overwhelm you, but never bore you. Waikiki gives you the feeling that you've arrived *someplace*. Besides lolling on the beach and walking the gauntlet of restaurants, hotels, malls, and street merchants, you can visit the **Waikiki Aquarium** or **Honolulu Zoo.** Then, ever-present Diamond Head, that monolith of frozen lava so symbolic of Hawaii, is easily reached by a few minutes' drive and a leisurely stroll to its summit.

## Central O'ahu

Hawaii's major interstate, H-1, runs west of the city center to **Pearl Harbor.** You can't help noticing the huge military presence throughout the area, and it becomes clear why Hawaii is considered the most militarized state in the country. The attraction here, which shouldn't be missed, is the **USS *Arizona* Memorial.** The museum, visitors center, and tours, operated jointly by the U.S. Navy and the National Park Service, are both excellent and free. Nearby are the **USS *Bowfin* Submarine Museum and Park** and the **USS *Missouri,*** both worthy stops.

Pearl Harbor is ringed by rather ordinary communities, suburbs of Honolulu. Because of its topography and climate it was a mainstay of the sugar industry until quite recently. In Waipahu, the museum village **Hawaii's Plantation Village** gives you a glimpse of what life was like for those living and working the ever-present sugar plantation. Farther up the plateau the land has been put to other uses. Early in the 19th century, huge pineapple plantations were started on the rich soil, and today vast tracts are still planted in this fruit. The demonstration gardens of Del Monte and Dole are good places to stop for an introduction to the history of pineapple production on the island. Also dominating huge areas of this central plain are the broad and beautiful **Schofield Barracks** Army base and **Wheeler Air Force Base,** two of the island's important military installations and significant players in America's armed conflicts

in the Pacific and Asia. The area west of Pearl Harbor also was, until not long ago, large sugar cane tracts and military bases. Now, the military is largely gone and suburban communities are taking over. While the 'Ewa coast is still rather undeveloped, the west coast does sport the **Ko 'Olina Resort,** a fashionable tourist area of hotels, condominiums, a golf course, marina, and fine beaches.

## Leeward Coast

The western edge of the island is the **Wai'anae Coast.** The towns of **Ma'ili, Wai'anae,** and **Makaha** are considered one of the last domains of the locals of O'ahu. This coastal area has escaped mass development so far, and it's one of the few places on the island where ordinary people can afford to live near the beach. Sometimes an attitude of resentment spills over against tourists; mostly, though, lovely people with good hearts live here, who will treat you as nicely as you're willing to treat them.

World-class surfing beaches along this coast are preferred by many of the best-known surfers from Hawaii. Many work as lifeguards in the beach parks, and they all congregate for the annual surfing championships held in Makaha. Here is a perfect chance to mingle with the people and soak up some of the last real *aloha* left on O'ahu.

## Southeast O'ahu

Head eastward around the bulge of Diamond Head, passing exclusive residential areas; you quickly find a string of secluded beaches that are better for surfing than swimming. The next bulge in the shoreline is **Koko Head,** below which lies **Hanauma Bay,** a nature preserve renowned for magnificent family-class snorkeling. **Koko Crater** is a short distance away, and within its circling arms lies the little-visited **Koko Crater Botanical Garden,** which specializes in dry land plants. Below **Makapu'u Point,** the easternmost tip of the island, is **Sea Life Park,** an extravaganza of the deep, and just up the coast is the sleepy village of **Waimanalo.** The beach at Waimanalo is considered one of the best on the island, and it's hard to believe the city's just 10 miles back.

Windward O'ahu is best known for its steep and deeply carved *pali*, like this section near Kualoa Beach Park.

## Windward O'ahu

On the windward side, **Kailua** and **Kane'ohe** have become suburban bedroom communities for Honolulu; this entire coast has few tourist accommodations, so it remains relatively uncrowded. The beaches are excellent, with beach parks and camping spots one after another, and the winds make this side of the island perfect for sailboarding. Inland of downtown Kane'ohe is **Valley of the Temples,** where a Christian cross sits high on a hill, and Buddha rests calmly in **Byodo-In Temple.**

Just up Route 83, the coastal highway, comes **Waiahole,** O'ahu's outback, where tiny farms and taro patches dot the valleys and local folks move with the slow beat of bygone days. Then a quick succession of beaches follows, many rarely visited by more than a passing fisherman. **Punalu'u** comes next, offering some of the only accommodations along this coast. In **La'ie** is the **Polynesian Cultural Center,** operated by the Mormon Church. **Brigham Young University** is here too, along with a solid **Mormon temple** that's open to visitors.

## North Shore

The North Shore is famous for magnificent surf. From **Hale'iwa** to **Sunset Beach,** world-class surfers come to be challenged by the liquid thunder of the **Banzai Pipeline, Waimea Bay,** and other well-known surf breaks. Art shops, boutiques, and restaurants are concentrated in Hale'iwa, the main North Shore town, but secluded hideaways line these sun-drenched miles. Beyond the former sugar town of **Waialua** lies the long and nearly unvisited **Mokule'ia Beach** and **Dillingham Airfield,** where you can take a glider ride or air tour of the island. The road ends with a very rugged jeep trail leading to **Ka'ena Point,** renowned for the most monstrous surf on the North Shore.

# The Land

When Papa, the Hawaiian earth mother, returned from vacationing in Tahiti, she was less than pleased. She had learned through a gossiping messenger that her husband, Wakea, had been playing around. Besides simply philandering, he'd been foolish enough to impregnate Hina, a lovely young goddess who bore him island children. Papa, scorned and furious, showed Wakea that two could play the same game by taking a handsome young lover, Lua. Their brief interlude yielded the manchild O'ahu, sixth of the great island children. Geologically, O'ahu is the second oldest main island after Kaua'i. It emerged from beneath the waves as hissing lava a few million years after Kaua'i and cooled a little quicker than Papa's temper to form Hawaii's third largest island.

## Land Facts

O'ahu has a total land area of 597 square miles, and measured from its farthest points it is 44 miles long by 30 miles wide. The 112-mile coastline holds the two largest harbors in the state, **Honolulu** and **Pearl.** The **Ko'olau Range** runs north-south for almost the entire length of the island, dramatically creating windward and leeward O'ahu. The **Wai'anae Range** is smaller, confined to the western section of the island. It too runs north-south, dividing the **Wai'anae Coast** from the massive **Leilehua Plateau** of the interior. **Mount Ka'ala**, at 4,020 feet, in the northern portion of the Wai'anae Range, is O'ahu's highest peak. Even with these two mountain ranges, 45 percent of O'ahu is less than 500 feet in elevation, the lowest of the six major islands. Much of the huge Leilehua Plateau is covered in pineapple. Lying between the two mountain ranges, it runs all the way from Waialua on the North Shore to 'Ewa, just west of Pearl Harbor. At its widest point, around Schofield Barracks, it's more than six miles across.

O'ahu's most impressive natural features were formed after the heavy volcanic activity ceased and erosion began to sculpt the island. The most obvious are the wall-like *pali* cliffs—mountains eroded by winds from the east, valleys cut by streams from the west. Perfect examples of these *pali* are seen from Waimanalo to the north end of Kane'ohe Bay, and examples of eroded valleys are **Nu'uanu** and **Kalihi.** Other impressive features are **Diamond Head, Koko Head,** and **Punchbowl,** three "tuff-cone" volcanoes created after the heavy volcanic activity of early O'ahu. A tuff cone is volcanic ash cemented together to form solid rock. Diamond Head is the most dramatic, formed after a minor eruption about 100,000 years ago and rising 761 feet from its base.

O'ahu has the state's longest stream, **Kaukonahua,** which begins atop Pu'u Ka'aumakua at 2,681 feet in the central Ko'olau Range and runs westward 33 miles through the Leilehua Plateau, emptying at the North Shore. En route, it runs through the **Wahiawa Reservoir,** which, at 302 acres, forms the second largest body of fresh water in Hawaii. O'ahu's tallest waterfalls are 80-foot **Kaliuwa'a** (Sacred Falls), just west of Punalu'u; and **Waihe'e Falls,** in the famous Waimea Park on the North Shore, which has a sheer drop of more than 40 feet. O'ahu's main water concern is that future usage may outstrip supply.

## THE CLIMATE

O'ahu, like all the Hawaiian Islands, has equitable weather year-round. The average daily temperature is 80° F. The mountainous interior of O'ahu experiences about the same temperatures as the coastal areas because of the small difference in elevation. However, the *pali* are known for strong, cooling winds that rise up the mountainside from the coast. The coldest temperature recorded on the island was 43° in Kane'ohe on the windward coast, while the hottest was 96° at Wai'anae on the leeward coast.

Precipitation is the biggest differentiating factor in the climate of O'ahu. Generally, the entire leeward coast, the "rain shadow," from Ka'ena to Koko Head, is dry. Wai'anae, Ho-

## O'AHU TEMPERATURE AND RAINFALL

| TOWN | | JAN. | MARCH | MAY | JUNE | SEPT. | NOV. |
|---|---|---|---|---|---|---|---|
| **Honolulu** | High | 80 | 82 | 84 | 85 | 82 | 81 |
| | Low | 60 | 52 | 68 | 70 | 71 | 68 |
| | Rain | 4 | 2 | 0 | 0 | 0 | 4 |
| **Kane'ohe** | High | 80 | 80 | 80 | 80 | 82 | 80 |
| | Low | 67 | 62 | 68 | 70 | 70 | 68 |
| | Rain | 5 | 5 | 2 | 0 | 2 | 5 |
| **Waialua** | High | 79 | 79 | 81 | 82 | 82 | 80 |
| | Low | 60 | 60 | 61 | 63 | 62 | 61 |
| | Rain | 2 | 1 | 0 | 0 | 1 | 3 |

temperature in degrees F, rainfall in inches

nolulu International Airport, and Waikiki average only 20–25 inches of rain a year. The Leilehua Plateau in the center of the island does a little better at about 40 inches a year. Rain falls much more frequently and heavily in the Ko'olau Mountains and along the windward coast. The bay town of Kane'ohe sees 75–90 inches a year, while the Nu'uanu Reservoir in the mountains above Honolulu gets a whopping 120–130 inches yearly, with some

years substantially greater than that. The maxim throughout the islands is "don't let rain spoil your day." If it's raining, simply move on to the next beach, or around to the other side of the island where it'll probably be dry. You can most often depend on the beaches of Waikiki and Wai'anae to be sunny and bright. No matter where you go for that day on the beach, however, the temperature of the ocean water will run 75–80° year-round.

## Flora and Fauna

The indigenous flora and fauna of O'ahu have suffered the same fate as those of the other Hawaiian Islands, and perhaps more so. These species are among the most endangered on earth and are disappearing at an alarming rate. Several sanctuaries on O'ahu still harbor native species, but they must be vigorously protected. Native plants and trees hang on in a few remote shoreline areas, in deep mountain valleys, and in the uplands of both the Wai'anae and Ko'olau mountain ranges. The great majority of indigenous plants have been replaced by introduced species, and while generally pleasing to the eye, these species are not native.

You would think that with O'ahu's dense human population, little room would be left for animals. In fact, they are environmentally stressed, but they do survive. The interior mountain slopes are home to **wild pigs,** and a small

population of **feral goats** survives in the Wai'anae Range. Migrating **whales** pass by, especially along the leeward coast where they can be observed from lookouts ranging from Waikiki to Koko Head. Half a dozen introduced game birds are found around the island, but O'ahu's real animal wealth is its indigenous bird life.

### Birds

The shores around O'ahu, including those off Koko Head and Sand Island, but especially on the tiny islets of Moku Manu and Manana on the windward side, are home to thriving colonies of marine birds. On these diminutive islands it's quite easy to spot a number of birds from the **tern** family, including the white, gray, and sooty tern. All have a distinctive screeching voice and approximate wingspan of 30 inches. Part of their problem is that they have little fear

# O'AHU'S PUBLIC AND PRIVATE BOTANICAL GARDENS

**Honolulu Botanical Gardens** comprises five separate gardens supported and maintained by the county. Three are open daily 9 A.M.–4 P.M., two are open sunrise to sunset. No admission fee, except for Foster Botanical Garden.

**Foster Botanical Garden,** 50 N. Vineyard Blvd., Honolulu, 808/522-7066. Thirteen-acre oasis of exotic trees and rare plants. Guided tours Mon.–Fri. at 1 P.M. Admission is $5 nonresidents, $3 children 6–12, and free children under 6.

**Ho'omaluhia Botanical Garden,** 45-680 Luluku Rd., Kane'ohe, 808/233-7323. Guided hiking tours are offered Saturday at 10 A.M. and Sunday at 1 P.M.

**Koko Crater Botanical Garden,** inside Koko Crater, 808/522-7060. Specializes in succulents, cacti, and other dry land plants. Open sunrise to sunset.

**Lili'uokalani Botanical Garden,** North Kuakini Street, Honolulu, 808/522-7060. Features mostly native Hawaiian plants, Nu'uanu Stream, and Waikahalulu Waterfall. Open sunrise to sunset.

**Wahiawa Botanical Garden,** 1396 California Ave., Wahiawa, 808/621-7321. Twenty-seven acres of cultivated trees, flowers, and ferns from around the world.

**Ha'iku Gardens,** 46-336 Ha'iku Rd., Kane'ohe. Many acres of flowers, ornamental trees, and a pond. Restaurant on site.

**Lyon Arboretum,** 3860 Manoa Rd., Honolulu, 808/988-0464. Dr. Lyon planted 194 acres of trees, flowers, and bushes in the late 1800s. Research facility of the University of Hawai'i. Open Mon.–Sat. 9 A.M.–3 P.M. Some guided tours offered. Entrance by donation.

**Senator Fong's Plantation and Gardens,** 47-285 Pulama Rd., Kane'ohe, 808/239-6775. Open daily 10 A.M.–4 P.M., except Christmas and New Year's Day. Includes 725 acres of natural and cultivated flower, tree, palm, and fern gardens. Admission is $10 adults, $6 children 5–12. Guided and narrated tram rides run several times per day.

**Waimea Arboretum and Botanical Garden,** at Waimea Falls Park, 808/638-8511. Collects, grows, and preserves rare Hawaiian flora. Some flowers and plants labeled.

---

of humans. Along with the terns are **shearwaters.** These birds have a normal wingspan of about 36 inches and make a series of moans and wails, oftentimes while in flight. For some reason shearwaters are drawn to the bright lights of the city, where they fall prey to house cats and automobiles. Sometimes Moku Manu even attracts the enormous **Laysan albatross** with its seven-foot wingspan. **Tropic birds** with lovely, streamer-like tails are quite often seen along the windward coast.

To catch a glimpse of exotic birds on O'ahu you don't have to head for the sea or the hills. The city streets and beach parks are constantly aflutter with wings. Black **mynah birds** with their sassy yellow eyes are common mimics around town. **Sparrows,** introduced to Hawaii through O'ahu in the 1870s, are everywhere, while **munia,** first introduced as cage birds from Southeast Asia, have escaped and can be found almost anywhere around the island. Another escaped cage bird from Asia is the **bulbul,** a natural clown that perches on any likely city roost and draws attention to itself with loud calls and generally ridiculous behavior.

If you're lucky, you can also catch a glimpse of the *pueo* (Hawaiian owl) in the mountainous areas of Wai'anae and the Ko'olau Range. Also, along trails and deep in the forest from Tantalus to the Wai'anae Range you can sometimes see elusive native birds like the *'elepaio, 'amakihi,* and fiery red *'i'iwi.*

# Government and Economy

O'ahu has been the center of government for about 160 years, since King Kamehameha III permanently established the royal court here in the 1840s. In 1879–82, King David Kalakaua built 'Iolani Palace as the central showpiece of the island kingdom. Lili'uokalani, the last Hawaiian monarch, lived after her dethronement in the nearby residence Washington Place. While Hawaii was a territory, and for a few years after it became a state, the palace was used as the capitol building, the governor residing in Washington Place. Modern O'ahu, besides being the center of state government, governs itself as the **City and County of Honolulu.** The county covers the entire island of O'ahu as well as the far-flung Northwestern Islands, except for Midway, which is under federal jurisdiction.

The island of O'ahu has three times as many people as the other islands combined. Nowhere is this more evident than in the representation of O'ahu in the state House and Senate. O'ahu claims 19 of the 25 state senators and 35 of the 51 state representatives. These lopsided figures make it obvious that O'ahu has plenty of clout, especially Honolulu urban districts, which elect more than 50 percent of O'ahu's representatives. Frequent political battles ensue, since what's good for the city and county of Honolulu isn't always good for the rest of the state. More often than not, the political moguls of O'ahu, backed by huge business interests, prevail.

Like the rest of the state, the voters on the island of O'ahu are principally Democratic in orientation, but not in as great a percentage as on the other islands. The current mayor is Jeremy Harris, Democrat. He is assisted by an elected county council consisting of nine members, one from each council district around the island. The O'ahu state senators are overwhelmingly Democratic, with only four Republicans. Democratic state representatives also outnumber Republicans, but not by quite as huge a margin. Most of the 12 Republican districts are in urban Honolulu and the suburban communities of Kailua and Kane'ohe. For internet information about the city and county of Honolulu, see www.co.honolulu.hi.us.

Economically, O'ahu dwarfs the rest of the islands combined. A huge military presence, an international airport that receives the lion's share of visitors, and a sizable agricultural sector keep O'ahu in the economic catbird seat. The famous "Big Five" and other major businesses all maintain their corporate offices in downtown Honolulu, from where they oversee vast holdings throughout Hawaii and the Mainland.

## Tourism

The flow of visitors to O'ahu has remained unabated ever since tourism outstripped sugar and pineapples in the early 1960s, becoming Hawaii's top moneymaker. Of the more than six million people who visit the state yearly, more than one-half stay on O'ahu. This means that on any given day, O'ahu plays host to about 80,000 visitors. Waikiki is still many people's idea of paradise. Most all the rest, en route to the Neighbor Islands, at least pass through. Hotels directly employ more than 16,000 workers, half the state's total, not including all the shop assistants, waiters and waitresses, taxi drivers, and everyone else needed to ensure a carefree vacation. Of the state's 70,000 accommodation units, O'ahu claims 36,000; of those, more than 31,000 are in Waikiki. The O'ahu hotels consistently have the highest occupancy rates in the state, hovering around 73 percent. In contrast, the average daily room rate is the lowest in the state, making accommodations on O'ahu slightly more of a bargain than on the other islands. The tourism industry generates about $11 billion of yearly revenue from direct visitor spending. With the flow of visitors seemingly endless, O'ahu has a bright economic future.

## Military

Hawaii is the most militarized state in the United States, and O'ahu is the most militarized island in the state. The U.S. military has been on O'ahu since 1887, when Pearl Harbor was opened to the U.S. Navy as part of the "Sugar Reciprocity

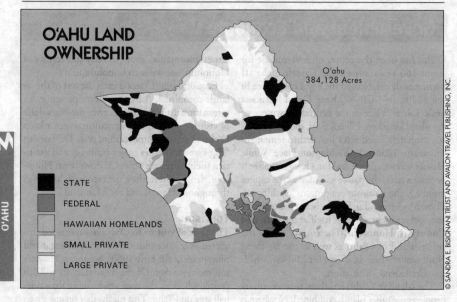

O'AHU LAND OWNERSHIP

O'ahu
384,128 Acres

■ STATE
▨ FEDERAL
□ HAWAIIAN HOMELANDS
▦ SMALL PRIVATE
□ LARGE PRIVATE

© SANDRA E. BISIGNANI TRUST AND AVALON TRAVEL PUBLISHING, INC.

Treaty." The Spanish-American War saw U.S. troops billeted at Camp McKinley at the foot of Diamond Head, and Schofield Barracks opened to receive the 5th Cavalry in 1909. Pearl Harbor's flames ignited World War II, and there has been no looking back since then. All five services are represented on O'ahu, and Camp H.M. Smith, overlooking Pearl Harbor, is the headquarters of CINCPAC (Commander in Chief Pacific), responsible for U.S. military bases and personnel from the U.S. west coast to Africa's east coast. On O'ahu today, the combined military services hold about 81,000 acres, a full 21 percent of the island. Much of this land, used for maneuvers, is off-limits to the public. Besides Pearl Harbor, so obviously dominated by battleship gray, the largest military lands are around Schofield Barracks and the Kahuku-Kawailoa Training Area. About 35,000 military personnel are stationed on O'ahu (99 percent of those in the state), with a slightly higher number of dependents.

## Agriculture

You'd think that with all the people living on O'ahu, coupled with the constant land development, there'd be hardly any room left for things to grow. But that's not the case. The land is productive, though definitely stressed.

Changing times and attitudes led to a "poi famine" that hit O'ahu in 1967 because very few people were interested in the hard work of farming taro, the source of this staple. While O'ahu has the smallest average size of farm in the state, it still manages to produce a considerable amount of pineapples and the many products of diversified agriculture. Pineapples cover 9,100 acres, with the biggest holdings on the Leilehua Plateau belonging to Dole, a subsidiary of Castle and Cooke. Due to demand and diversification, O'ahu now also raises a whole variety of organic greens, freshwater shrimp, coffee, and flowers. Only about 100 acres have been put into coffee, the smallest acreage of any of the islands—on land between Wahiawa and Haleiwa—but this land produces a respectable 50,000 pounds a year. In the hills, entrepreneurs raise *pakalolo*, which has become the state's most productive cash crop. O'ahu is also a huge agricultural consumer, demanding more than four times as much vegetables, fruits, meats, and poultry to feed its citizens and visitors than the remainder of the state combined.

### Land Ownership

The island of O'ahu is about 600 square miles in size. Although Honolulu County also includes the string of Northwest Islands, only O'ahu is inhabited. This island, smaller than the Big Island and Maui, and only slight larger than Kaua'i, has nearly three-quarters of the state's population. The federal government owns vast tracts on O'ahu, mostly military bases and military-use areas. While smaller in area, the state also owns many acres,

particularly rugged mountain sections of both the Ko'olau and Wai'anae ranges. There are two Hawaiian Home Lands sections on O'ahu, one in Waimanalo and the other in Nanakuli on the Wai'anae Coast. These are just where you might expect them, as many native Hawaiians live in these areas. Of the large landowners, the Bishop Estate, Castle and Cooke, and the James Campbell Estate control the vast majority of land, but larger in size are the plots of land held by small landowners.

## The People

For most visitors, regardless of where they've come from, O'ahu (especially Honolulu) will be the first place they've ever encountered such an integrated multiracial society. Various countries may be cosmopolitan, but nowhere will you meet so many individuals from such a diversity of ethnic groups, and mixes of these groups. You could be driven to your hotel by a Chinese-Portuguese cab driver, checked in by a Japanese-Hawaiian clerk, served lunch by a Korean waiter, and serenaded by a Hawaiian-Italian-German musician, while an Irish-English-Filipino-French chambermaid tidies your room. This racial symphony is evident throughout Hawaii, but it's more apparent on O'ahu, where the large population creates more opportunity for a racial hodgepodge. The warm feeling you get almost immediately upon arrival is that everyone belongs.

### O'ahu Population Figures

O'ahu's 881,300 or so residents account for 72 percent of the state's population. All these people are on an island comprising only 9 percent of the state's land total. About 400,000 people live in greater Honolulu, the built-up area from 'Aiea to Koko Head. The next most populous urban centers after Honolulu are the Kailua/Kane'ohe area on the windward side with about 100,000 residents, Mililani and Wahiawa on the Leilehua Plateau with about the same number, followed by Pearl City and Waipahu with a combined total of about 70,000 or so. The strip of towns on the leeward coast, including Wai'anae, totals about 40,000 inhabitants. In the last decade, the areas that have had the greatest increase in population are Mililani and 'Ewa. On O'ahu, 96 percent of the population are urban dwellers while only 4 percent live rurally.

## Festivals and Events

O'ahu has more festivities and events than all the other islands, and these times provide great social opportunities for meeting people. Everyone is welcome to join in the fun, and most times the events are either free or nominally priced. There's no better way to enjoy yourself while vacationing than by joining in with a local party or happening. Island specific information is also available on the web; check the calendar listing at www.visit-oahu.com/cal-endar.htm.

### January

January 2: **Queen Emma Museum Open House.** This is Queen Emma's birthday, and the public is invited to visit her summer home and view a well-preserved collection of her personal belongings; 808/595-3167.

**The Narcissus Festival** in Honolulu's Chinatown starts with the parade and festivities of Chinese New Year, with lion dances in the street, fireworks, a beauty pageant, and a coronation ball; call 808/533-3181 for locations.

The **Cherry Blossom Festival** in Honolulu can begin in late January and last through March. Events include a Japanese cultural and trade show, tea ceremony, flower arranging, queen pageant, and coronation ball. Check newspapers and free tourist magazines for dates and times of various Japanese cultural events.

## February

**NFL Pro Bowl.** Aloha Stadium, Honolulu. Annual all-star football game offering the best from both conferences. Call 808/486-9300 for more information.

**Punahou School Carnival.** Honolulu. Arts, crafts, and a huge rummage sale at one of Hawaii's oldest and most prestigious high schools. Great ethnic foods. You'd be surprised at what Hawaii's oldest and most established families donate to the rummage sale. Call 808/944-5711 for details.

## March

Enjoy the kites at the annual **O'ahu Kite Festival** at Kapi'olani Park or the **Honolulu Kite Festival** at Sandy Beach. For fun and competition.

**Hawaiian Song Festival and Song Composing Contest.** Kapi'olani Park Bandstand in Waikiki. Determines the year's best Hawaiian song. Presented by top-name entertainers.

**Kamehameha School Annual Song Contest.** Blaisdell Center Arena, Honolulu. Competition among secondary-grade students of Hawaiian ancestry.

## April

**Easter Sunday.** Sunrise Service at the National Memorial Cemetery of the Pacific, Punchbowl Crater, Honolulu.

**Annual Hawaiian Festival of Music.** Waikiki Shell, Honolulu. A grand and lively music competition of groups from all over the islands and

# O'AHU ARTS AND CULTURE INFORMATION

**Arts With Aloha,** www.artswithaloha.com. An association of major arts and cultural organizations in Honolulu that provides quick and easy information about its member organizations through a printed brochure and website.

**Bishop Museum,** 1525 Bernice St., Honolulu, HI 96817, 808/847-3511, www.bishop.hawaii.org. The world's *best* museum covering Hawaii and Polynesia. Exhibits, galleries, archives, demonstrations of Hawaiian crafts, and a planetarium. On the premises, Shop Pacifica has a complete selection of books and publications on all aspects of Hawaiian art and culture.

**Hawai'i Craftsmen,** P.O. Box 22145, Honolulu, HI 96823, 808/596-8128, www.hawaiicraftsmen.org. Increases awareness of Hawaiian crafts through programs, exhibitions, workshops, lectures, and demonstrations.

**Honolulu Academy of Arts,** 900 S. Beretania St., Honolulu, HI 96814, 808/532-8701, www.honoluluacademy.org. Collects, preserves, and exhibits works of fine art. Offers public art

education programs related to its collections. Also offers tours, classes, lectures, films, and publications.

**Mayor's Office of Culture and the Arts,** 530 S. King St., Rm. 404, Honolulu, HI 96813, 808/523-4674, www.co.honolulu.hi.us/moca. The City and County of Honolulu's official organ for visual and performing arts information islandwide.

**Pacific Handcrafters Guild,** P.O. Box 29389, Honolulu, HI 96820-1789, 808/254-6788, www.alternative-hawaii.com/profiles/crafters/phg.htm. Focuses on developing and preserving handicrafts and fine arts of all mediums. The guild sponsors four major crafts fairs annually.

**State Foundation on Culture and the Arts,** 250 S. King St., 2nd Floor, Honolulu, HI 96813, 808/586-0300, www.state.hi.us/sfca. Begun by state legislature in 1965 to preserve and promote Hawaii's diverse cultural, artistic, and historical heritage. Manages grants, maintains programs in folk arts and art in public places, and runs the Hawaii State Art Museum.

# O'AHU'S ARCHIVES AND LIBRARIES

**Bishop Museum Library and Archives,** 1525 Bernice St., Honolulu, HI 96817, 808/848-4148 or 808/848-4182. Open Tues.–Fri. noon–3 P.M. and Sat. 9 A.M.–noon. Extensive historical and cultural collection. Best for those doing academic research.

**Episcopal Church in Hawaii,** 229 Queen Emma Square, Honolulu, HI 96813, 808/536-7776. Records and photos of church history in Hawaii from 1862.

**Hamilton Library** at the University of Hawai'i Library at Manoa, 2550 McCarthy Mall, Honolulu, HI 96822, 808/956-7204. The 4th floor holds the Hawaiian/Pacific Collection.

**Hawaiian Historical Society,** 560 Kawaiaha'o St., Honolulu, HI 96813, 808/537-6271. Open Mon.–Fri. 10 A.M.–4 P.M. Extensive collection of 19th-century materials on Hawaiian Islands, including 10,000 photos, 12,000 books, maps, and microfilm. At the Mission Houses Museum, George R. Carter Reading Room, along with the Hawaiian Mission Children's Society Library.

**Hawaiian Mission Children's Society Library,** 808/531-0481, at the Mission Houses Museum, George R. Carter Reading Room. Open Mon.–Fri. 10 A.M.–4 P.M. Records, personal journals, letters, microfilm, and photos of early 19th-century Congregational missionaries to the Mainland. A music lover's smorgasbord offering everything from symphony to swing and all in between.

Hawaiian Islands; archive of the Congregational Church in the Pacific.

**Hawaiian State Archives,** 'Iolani Palace Grounds, Honolulu, HI 96813, 808/586-0329. Open Mon.–Fri. 9 A.M.–4 P.M. except state holidays. Archives of the government of Hawaii. Private papers of Hawaiian royalty and government officials, photos, illustrations, and etchings recording Hawaiian history. For anyone seriously interested in Hawaii.

**Hawaii Chinese History Center,** 111 N. King St., Rm. 410, Honolulu, HI 96813, 808/521-5948. Call for hours. Rare books, oral histories, and photos concerning the history of Chinese in Hawaii.

**Hawaii State Library,** 'Iolani Palace Grounds, Honolulu, HI 96813, 808/586-3500. Main branch of the statewide library system. Open Mon., Fri., and Sat. 9 A.M.–5 P.M., Wed. 10 A.M.–5 P.M., and Tues. and Thurs. 9 A.M.–8 P.M.

**Robert Allerton Library,** 900 S. Beretania St., Honolulu, HI 96814, 808/532-8700. This library at the Honolulu Academy of Arts is an indispensable site for information about the arts, containing 35,000 books on art and Hawaiiana. Started in 1927, it's been recently remodeled and is now more user-friendly. Books can only be used on site. Open Wed.–Sat. 1–4 p.m.

The **Honolulu International Bed Race Festival** holds forth in Waikiki with the race, live entertainment, a parade, games, and fireworks.

## May

**Brothers Cazimero Annual May Day Concert** is one of the most anticipated musical events of the year. These musicians perform at the Waikiki Shell in the evening, as they have done for a quarter of a century.

**Memorial Day.** Special military services held at Honolulu, National Memorial Cemetery of the Pacific, on the last Monday in May.

**50th State Fair,** at Aloha Stadium, Honolulu. Agricultural exhibits, down-home cooking, entertainment, and produce. Lasts four weekends.

## June

**Mission Houses Museum Fancy Fair** and **Festival of Hawaiian Quilts,** Honolulu. A top-notch collection of Hawaii's best artists and craftsmen for the fair, and Hawaii's best stitchery for the quilt show. A great chance to browse and buy. Also, food and entertainment; 808/531-0481.

## O'AHU'S MUSEUMS AND GALLERIES

**Bishop Museum,** 1525 Bernice St., Honolulu, 808/847-3511. Open daily 9 A.M.–5 P.M. The best collection in the world on Polynesia in general and Hawaii specifically. A true cultural treat that should not be missed.

**The Contemporary Museum,** 2411 Makiki Heights Dr., Honolulu, 808/526-0232, open Tues.–Sat. 10 A.M.–4 P.M., Sun. noon–4 P.M. The focus is on exhibitions, not collections, although there are permanent displays. Changing exhibits reflect different themes in contemporary art.

**Damien Museum,** at Saint Augustine Catholic Church, 130 Ohua Ave., Waikiki, 808/923-2690. Displays photographs, papers, artifacts, and mementos of the legendary Father Damien who helped leprosy patients on Moloka'i. Open weekdays only 9 A.M.–3 P.M. Donations gratefully accepted.

**Hawaii Maritime Center,** at Pier 7, Honolulu Harbor, 808/536-6373. Open daily except Christmas 8:30 A.M.–8 P.M. A museum chronicling the exploration and exploitation of Hawaii by the seafarers who have come to its shores. Visit the famous double-hulled canoe *Hokule'a* and the tall-masted *Falls of Clyde.*

**Hawaii's Plantation Village,** 94-695 Waipahu St., Waipahu, 808/677-0110. An open-air museum portraying sugar plantation life and the ethnic mix of plantation workers. Restored buildings and memorabilia. Open for guided tours only Mon.–Fri. 9 A.M.–3 P.M. and Sat. 10 A.M.–3 P.M.

**Honolulu Academy of Arts,** 900 S. Beretania St., Honolulu, 808/532-8701. Open Tues.–Sat. 10 A.M.–4:30 P.M., Sun. 1–5 P.M. Collects, preserves, and exhibits works of art, classic and modern, with a strong emphasis on Asian art. Permanent and special exhibitions, with tours, classes, lectures, and films. Across from the Academy of Arts, the affiliated **Academy Art Center at Linekona** displays student artwork, mostly of a contemporary Hawaiian nature.

**'Iolani Palace,** 'Iolani Palace Grounds, Honolulu, 808/538-1471. The only royal palace in the United States. Vintage artwork and antiques. Guided tours Tues.–Sat. 9 A.M.–2:15 P.M.

**Mission Houses Museum,** 553 S. King St., Honolulu, 808/531-0481. Open Tues.–Sat. 9 A.M.–4 P.M. Two homes, a printing house, and a library; an early mission compound. Guided tours only. Excellent.

**Queen Emma Summer Palace,** 2913 Pali Hwy., Honolulu, 808/595-3167. Open daily 9 A.M.–4 P.M., except major holidays. Restored historic home, built about 1848. Furniture and me-

---

**Annual King Kamehameha Hula Competition.** Blaisdell Center.

The **Taste of Honolulu** brings together food from some 30 restaurant and wine vendors plus big-name local entertainment for this weekend-long festivity at the Civic Center.

**Annual Pan-Pacific Festival—Matsuri.** Dances and festivities, parades and performances, music, arts and crafts in Honolulu at Kapi'olani Park and other locations. It's a show of Japanese culture in Hawaii. Also, *Bon Odori,* the Japanese festival of departed souls, features dances and candle-lighting ceremonies at numerous Buddhist temples throughout the islands. These festivities

change yearly and can be held anytime from late June to early August.

## July

July 4:**Hawaiian Islands Tall Ships Parade.** Tall-masted ships from throughout the islands parade from Koko Head to Sand Island and back to Diamond Head. A rare treat and taste of days gone by. Other celebrations along Waikiki Beach.

The **Prince Lot Hula Festival** is a great chance for visitors to see authentic and noncompetitive hula from some of the finest hula *halau* in the islands. A free annual event held at the beautiful Moanalua Gardens in Honolulu; 808/839-5334.

mentos of Queen Emma and her family. Some items belong to other members of the royal family.

**Queen's Medical Center Historical Room,** 1301 Punchbowl St., Honolulu, 808/547-4397. Exhibits display the history of the Queen's Medical Center (founded 1859) and the history of medicine in Hawaii. Open weekdays 8:30 A.M.–3:30 P.M., no charge.

**Tennent Art Foundation Gallery,** 201-203 Prospect St., Honolulu, 808/531-1987. Shows work of Madge Tennent. Open Tues.–Sat. 10 A.M.–noon, Sun. 2–4 P.M.

**Tropic Lightning Museum,** directly up from Macomb Gate on Schofield Barracks, 808/655-0438. Military museum on the history of Schofield Barracks Army Base and the 25th Infantry Division. Open Tues.–Sat. 10 A.M.–4 P.M.

**University of Hawai'i Art Gallery,** University of Hawai'i, Manoa, Department of Art, 808/956-6888. Showcases faculty, student, and traveling exhibitions. Open during the academic year, Mon.–Fri. 10:30 A.M.–4 P.M. and Sun. noon–4 P.M. during school sessions only. Also open on the university campus are an adjunct gallery on the third floor of the student center, the East-West Center Gallery, the John Young Museum of Art at Krauss Hall, and the School of Architecture Gallery.

**U.S. Army Museum of Hawaii,** Fort DeRussy, Waikiki, 808/438-2821. Open Tues.–Sun. 10 A.M.–4:45 P.M. Covers military history of Hawaii from the time of Kamehameha I to the activities of the U.S. Army in east Asia and the Pacific islands.

**USS Arizona Memorial,** Pearl Harbor, 808/422-2771. Free Navy launches take you on the tour of "Battleship Row," including the sleek 184-foot white concrete structure that spans the sunken USS *Arizona.* Open daily except Thanksgiving, Christmas, and New Year's Day 7:30 A.M.–5 P.M. No reservations: first-come, first-served. Launches run every 15 minutes 8 A.M.–3 P.M. Visitors center offers graphic materials and film, reflecting events of the Pearl Harbor attack.

**USS Bowfin Submarine Museum,** Pearl Harbor, 808/423-1341. Open daily except Thanksgiving, Christmas, and New Year's Day 8 A.M.–5 P.M. Guided tours of this fully restored World War II submarine offer insight into the underwater war. Fascinating. Next door to Arizona Memorial.

**USS *Missouri,*** Pearl Harbor, 808/423-2263. It was on this refurbished World War II ship that the documents ending war hostilities were signed. A fitting counterpoint to the USS *Arizona,* the destruction of which pushed the United States into the war. Open 9 A.M.–5 P.M. daily.

O'AHU

Also includes gift and craft sales, quilts, demonstrations, and food vendors.

**Queen Lili'uokalani Keiki Hula Competition,** Blaisdell Arena, Honolulu. Children ages 6–12 compete in a hula contest. Caution: Terminal Cuteness.

**Annual Ukulele Festival,** held on the last Sunday of the month at Kapi'olani Park Bandstand, Waikiki. Hundreds of ukulele players from throughout the islands put on a very entertaining show.

The annual **Dragon Boat Festival** provides fun entertainment for all at the Ala Moana Beach Park.

For the music aficionado, the **Hawaii Inter**national Jazz Festival offers great music from island and international musicians at the Hawaii Theatre and/or other venues around town; www.hawaiijazz.com.

## August

The **Pacific Taro Festival** at Windward College celebrates this important staple crop with food, music, and cultural performances.

## September

**Moloka'i to O'ahu Canoe Race.** Women in Hawaiian-style canoes race from a remote beach on Moloka'i to Fort DeRussy Beach in Honolulu. In transit they must navigate the rough Kaiwi Channel. (The men's race is in October.)

## October

**Moloka'i to O'ahu Canoe Race.** Men navigate Hawaiian-style canoes across the rough Kaiwi Channel from a remote beach on Moloka'i to Fort DeRussy Beach, Honolulu. (The women's race is in September.)

**Annual Orchid Plant and Flower Show.** Hawaii's copious and glorious flowers are displayed. Blaisdell Center Exhibition Hall, Honolulu. Blaisdell Center.

## November

November 11: **Veterans Day Parade.** National holiday. A parade from Fort DeRussy to Queen Kapi'olani Park, Waikiki. American Legion, 808/949-1140.

**Mission Houses Museum Holiday Craft Fair.** Quality items offered by Hawaii's top craftsmen in an open-air bazaar; 808/531-0481.

**Triple Crown of Surfing.** Hawaiian Pro, World Cup of Surfing, Pipeline Masters. The best surfers in the world come to the best surfing beaches on O'ahu. Wave action determines sites except for the Masters, which is always held at Banzai Pipeline, North Shore, O'ahu. Big money and national TV coverage.

The annual **World International Hula Festival** is held at the Waikiki Shell for participants from several countries. Individual, female, male, and combined events are held.

## December

**Pacific Handcrafters Guild, Winter Fair,** Thomas Square, Honolulu. A chance to see the "state of the arts" all in one locality. Perfect for early-bird and unique Christmas shopping. The best by the best, just in time for Christmas. Browse, buy, and eat ethnic foods at various stalls. This guild also holds spring, summer, and fall fairs at Thomas Square and other shows periodically around town. Call 808/254-6788 for information.

**Annual Honolulu Marathon.** An institution in marathon races. One of the best-attended and very prestigious races in the country, where top athletes from around the world turn out to compete. Call 808/734-7200.

The annual **Honolulu City Lights** festival starts off the Christmas season with the lighting of a Christmas tree at City Hall, followed by an electric light parade and other entertainment.

**Annual Rainbow Classic.** Invitational tournament of NCAA collegiate basketball teams. University of Hawai'i, Manoa.

**Aloha Bowl** and **O'ahu Bowl** are two postseason collegiate football games played at Aloha Stadium on Christmas Day.

To counter the alcohol-inspired activities, the alcohol-free **First Night Honolulu,** a festival of music and other events, is sponsored at the Honolulu City Hall the last night of the year until midnight.

# Sports and Recreation

## BEACHES

As O'ahu is the second oldest of the major Hawaiian Islands, it's had plenty of time to create wonderful beaches. Great beaches are found of all sides of the island: some are best-known as family-friendly spots or snorkel sites, others are especially known for boogie boarding or sailboarding, while others still are renown as world-class surfing locations. Generally speaking, beaches and shorelines on the north and west have high surf conditions and strong ocean currents during winter months—use extreme caution—and those on the south and east experience some high surf during the summer months. All beaches are open to the public. Most are accessed through beach parks, but some access is over private property. There are 18 beaches on O'ahu that have lifeguards on duty during summer months and during weekends the rest of the year. At some beaches, flags will warn you of ocean conditions. A yellow flag means use caution. A half-yellow, half-red sign signifies caution because of strong winds. A red flag indicates hazardous water conditions—beach closed, no swimming. In addition, yellow and black signs are sometimes posted at certain beaches to indicate other warnings: dangerous shore break, high surf spot, strong currents, presence of jellyfish, or beach closed.

Before you head to the beach, take a drive to the local shop for a cheap woven beach mat. Whalers General Store, ABC markets, other sundries shops, Longs Drug, Wal-Mart, Kmart, and the like have them for $1–1.50. Hotel sundries shops sometimes also carry the exact same thing for about a dollar more. Sometimes condos, B&Bs, and vacation rental homes will have them for guests to use, but don't necessarily count on it.

## South Shore Beaches
While there are a few beaches in the 'Ewa area west of Pearl Harbor, most of the best-known beaches on the south shore at along its eastern extent. Generally these are great family beaches with lots of sand and relatively gentle water that are best during fall, winter, and spring. Summer brings higher waves. The two closest to the city are *Ala Moana Beach* and **Waikiki Beach.** While both can become crowded, there is generally enough room for everyone. While Waikiki Beach is the haunt of tourists, Ala Moana Beach is where the citizens of Honolulu head for a fun day at the beach with family. A bit farther out is **Hanauma Bay Beach,** set inside the protective arms of a seaside crater. As part of a nature preserve, it is perhaps the best snorkeling spot in the state. Beyond that is **Sandy Beach,** a popular spot with surfers and boogie boarders. The water at this beach has plenty of power so check with the lifeguard here about conditions before entering.

## West Shore Beaches
The Wai'anae Coast beaches are much less frequented than those closer to Honolulu and Waikiki. While they too can be great for swimming when the waves are not rolling in, the beaches on this coast are perhaps best known for the surf. At the south end, **Kahe Point** and **Tracks Beach,** and **Makaha Beach** at the north

end, are surfers havens during winter. The best for swimming are **Nanakuki, Ma'ili,** and **Poka'i.** With its adjacent beach park, Poka'i is the most protected and the sand there slides gently into the calm water. The most remote beach is on Yokohama Bay at the entrance to Ka'ena Point State Park. This is the place to come for seclusion, sun, and quiet beach walking time, but much of the year the water is too rough to enter safely.

## East Shore Beaches
Many believe that the best overall beaches in the state are on O'ahu's Windward Coast. Each has a broad expanse of sand backed by trees, gentle drop-off, and is good for swimming, sailboarding, kite boarding, and kayaking for most of the year. Good beach facilities accompany these beaches and they have easy access. They are **Waimanalo Bay Beach** and **Bellows Beach** in Waimanalo and **Kailua Beach** in Kailua. As it has favorable tradewinds for much of the year and a reasonably large calm area inside the reed, Kailua Beach has become know as the major sailboarding location on O'ahu and one of the two best known in the state. A bit more secluded and with no lifeguards is **Lanikai Beach** just south of Kailua Beach. Not only gentle and safe, the golden sand and aquamarine water of Lanikai Beach is offset by the green mounds of the two small offshore islands, the deep blue of the sea beyond, and the lighter blue of the sky above. It is the most picture perfect and typically tropical of Hawaiian beaches. Farther up the coast, beaches are overall less spectacular for swimming and more conducive to snorkeling, reef fishing, and other such activities.

## North Shore Beaches
North Shore O'ahu beaches are known for their surf—and rightly so—as some of the best surfing conditions in the world manifest themselves along this shoreline during winter months. Every year, a number of surfing competitions are held at these beaches for amateurs and professionals, locals and international surfers. **Sunset, Bonzai Pipeline, Ehukai,** and **Waimea Bay,** are perhaps the best known, but many others, like **Hale'iwa Ali'i Beach** and **Mokule'ia Beach,** are also known

locally for great surf. The waves along this shore are wonderful for surfers, but for those who don't ride the board, this coastline still provides great thrills in just watching the power of the ocean. Winter is the time for surf, but during summer the water calms down and the North Shore beaches become fine for swimming.

## SCUBA AND SNORKELING

O'ahu has particularly generous underwater vistas open to anyone donning a mask and fins. Snorkel and dive sites, varying in difficulty and challenge, are accessible from the island. Sites can be totally hospitable, good for families and first-time snorkelers who want an exciting but safe frolic; or they can be accessible only to the experienced diver. There are a number of dive shops on the island from which you can rent or buy all equipment, and where dive boats and instruction on all levels can be arranged. There are dozens of well-known dive sites around the island, with many of these clustered along the Wai'anae Coast, the eastern half of the North Shore, and the southeastern corner of the island. Some features of note include drop-offs, walls, sea caves, arches, and sunken ships and planes.

### Dive Shops and Rentals

In the Honolulu area, try the following. **Waikiki Diving,** 424 Nahua St., 808/922-2121, www.waikikidiving.com, does PADI certification, beach and boat dives. Boat dive go mostly to the Koko Head area. **South Seas Aquatics,** 2155 Kalakaua Ave., Suite 112, 808/922-0852, www.ssahawaii.com, is a full-service dive shop with competitive pricing for certification, tours, and rentals. **Reef Trekkers,** 808/943-0588, www.reeftrekkers.com, has established a good reputation for scuba tours. At the Outrigger Waikiki Hotel **Aqua Zone,** 808/923-3483, www.aquazone.net, offer tours and instruction for both beginners and advanced divers.

For dives along the west and southwest coasts, try **Ocean Concepts,** 808/766-7975, www.oceanconcepts.com. Ocean concepts has several shops around the island and leaves out of Ke'ehi Lagoon and Wai'anae Boat Harbor.

**Surf and Sea,** 62-595 Kamehameha Hwy., 808/637-9887, www.surfnsea.com, is a complete dive shop on the North Shore in Hale'iwa offering certification, rentals, charters, and tours. Also offering educational dive options in Hale'iwa is **Deep Ecology,** 808/637-3992, www.deepecology.com.

**Aloha Dive Shop** at the Hawaii Kai Shopping Center (on the way to Hanauma Bay), 808/395-5922, www.alohadiveshop.com, does it all from snorkeling to boat dives at various spots near Koko Head. Excellent rates, good service. This shop is owned and run by Jackie James, the "First Lady of Diving" in Hawaii, with over 30 years of experience.

In Kailua, try the full service dive shops: **Aaron's Dive Shop,** 307 Hahani St., Kailua, 808/262-2333, www.hawaii-scuba.com; or **Oahu Dive Center,** 866/933-3483, www.oahudivecenter.com, at the Daiei Shopping Center in Kailua.

### Snorkeling

While there are countless places to snorkel around the island, several spots are easily accessible to visitors. Perhaps the best spot right at Waikiki is Sans Souci Beach or the area right in front of the Natatorium. Magic Island at Ala Moana park is also good and appropriate for kids. Going a little farther around the coast brings you to Hanauma Bay, perhaps the best, and certainly the most popular spot on the island. Along the windward shore, Makai Pier, Lanikai Beach with its offshore island, and Goat Island at Malaekahana Park offer good options. Shark's Cove and Three Tables at Waimea and Big Rock at Waimea Bay are good but only when there's no surf. More protected is Turtle Bay and the adjacent Kuilima Cove. On the leeward side, try Electric Beach at Kaha Point, which is just at the start of the road up the Wai'anae Coast.

### Snorkel Rentals

**Snorkel Bob's,** 808/735-7944, at the corner of Kapahulu Ave. and Date St., has very inexpensive deals on snorkeling. Prices start at $3.50 a day or only $9 per week for full snorkel gear, which you can take to Maui, Kaua'i, and Big Island locations and return to his shops there for free. The better

# O'AHU SNORKELING

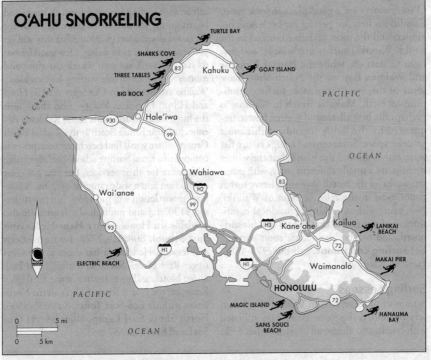

© SANDRA E. BISIGNANI TRUST AND AVALON TRAVEL PUBLISHING, INC.

equipment (still a deal) runs to $29 a week. Snorkel Bob's also has underwater cameras for about $10, boogie boards for $6.50 a day or $26 a week, and wet suits at $15 a week. It's best to stop in and peruse the selection for just what you need. **Hanauma Bay Snorkeling,** 808/373-5060, rents full equipment for $6.25 a day and underwater cameras for $12. The company offers tours to Hanauma Bay from Waikiki for $15, including transportation, equipment, instruction, a fish I.D. chart, and a map of the reef. Also running shuttle tours to Hanauma Bay from Waikiki is **Tommy's Tours,** 808/373-5060. They offer snorkel rental plus transportation for $15.00 adults, $12.50 children 5–11. At the Koko Marina Shopping Center, **Hanauma Bay Snorkel Adventure,** 808/396 9199, offers snorkel gear rental for $5, transportation to the bay for $10 per person, and even transportation from your hotel in Waikiki for $15. The $3 entrance fee into Hanauma Bay is your responsibility. If you are heading to Hanauma Bay on your own, you can rent full snorkel gear from the kiosk on the beach there for $6 a day.

## Snuba

**Snuba Adventures of Oahu,** 808/923-5700, offers snuba tours at the Ko 'Olina Resort that include instruction and some free swim time in a placid lagoon. Basic instruction is given at the JW Marriott Hotel about 11:30 A.M. and the boat leaves later for the reef off Paradise Cove. Tours run Monday, Wednesday, and Friday and cost $99 adult and $89 for kids. Call for reservations a day or so in advance.

## CATCHING WAVES
### Surfing

All the Hawaiian Islands have incredibly good surfing conditions, but O'ahu has the best. If there is such a thing as "the perfect wave,"

O'ahu's waters are a good place to look for it. Conditions here are perfect for both rank beginners and the most acclaimed surfers in the world. Waikiki's surf is predictable, and just right to start on, while the **Banzai Pipeline** and **Waimea Bay** on the North Shore have some of the most formidable surfing conditions on earth. **Makaha Beach** in Wai'anae is perhaps the best all-around surfing beach, frequented by the living legends of this most graceful sport. Summertime brings rather flat wave action around the island, but the winter months are a totally different story, with monster waves on the North Shore and heavy surf at times even in the relative calm of Waikiki. *Never* surf without asking about local conditions, and remember that "a fool and his surfboard, and maybe his life, are soon parted." For **surfing conditions,** call 808/973-4383. Heed all warnings!

## Surfing Lessons

A number of enterprises in Waikiki offer beach services. Often these concessions are affiliated with hotels, and almost all hotel activities desks can arrange surfing lessons for you. A lesson and board go for about $40 an hour, half that for the board alone. Most guarantee that they will get you standing, but as in skiing, a few good lessons to start you off are well worth the time and money. Some reputable surfing lessons along Waikiki are provided by Outrigger Waikiki Hotel and Hilton Hawaiian Village. Also check near the huge rack of surfboards along Kalakaua Avenue, just near Kuhio Beach at the Waikiki Beach Center, where you'll find beach boy enterprises at competitive rates. Surfing schools usually charge a bit more for their services, but you get great instruction and a wide range of options. A one-hour group lesson will run $65–75, a private lesson $130; day and multiple-day lessons are also available. In Honolulu, try **Hans Hedemann Surf School,** 808/924-7778, for instructions and lessons. Hedemann has shops at the Outrigger Reef Hotel, Sheraton Waikiki, and Park Shore Hotel, and gives lessons at the Turtle Bay Resort on the North Shore. Others on the North Shore include **Eco-Surf Tours,** 808/638-9503, **North Shore Surf Camp,** 808/638-5914, or **Surf and Sea,** 808/637-9887.

surfing at Ehukai Beach on O'ahu's North Shore

ROBERT NILSEN

## Boogie Boarding

The most highly acclaimed boogie-boarding beach on O'ahu is Sandy Beach (with Makapu'u Beach not far behind). It also has the dubious distinction of being the most dangerous beach in Hawaii, with more drownings, broken backs, and broken necks than anywhere in the state. Waikiki is tame and excellent for boogie boarding. Bellow Beach serves the beginner well, Waimanalo Beach is more for the intermediate boarder, and Kailua Beach has a good break at its northern end.

## Sailboarding and Kiteboarding

Far and away the most famous sailboarding and kiteboarding beach on O'ahu is Kailua Beach on the windward coast. Daily, a flotilla of wind riders glide over the smooth waters of the bay, propelled by the always-blowing breezes. In town enterprises build, rent, and sell sailboards and kiteboards. Commercial ventures are allowed to operate along Kailua Beach only on weekdays and weekend mornings, but weekend afternoons and holidays are *kapu!* The North Shore also offers decent sailboarding and kiteboarding areas.

For lessons and rentals, see the following. **Kailua Sailboard Company,** with a perfect location only a minute from the beach in Kailua at 130 Kailua Rd., 808/262-2555, open 9 A.M.–5 P.M. daily, is a full-service sailboard and kayak store. Sailboard rentals are $39 per day, half day $29; weekly rates are also available. Beginning group lessons are $49 for a three-hour session. In addition, kite boards, boogie boards, kayaks, snorkel gear, and bicycles are rented.

**Naish Hawaii,** 155 A Hamakua Dr., 808/262-6068 or 800/767-6068, open 9 A.M.–5:30 P.M. daily, is a very famous maker of custom boards, production boards, sails, hardware, accessories, and repairs. T-shirts, bathing suits, beach accessories, hats, and slippers are also for sale. Naish is the largest and oldest sailboarding company in Hawaii. The famous Naish Windsurfing School gives 90 minutes of personal instruction at Kailua Beach and an additional half-hour of board use for $55 including all equipment; $75 for two people, or $35 per person for a group. Naish rents boards and rigs for beginners, intermediate, and advanced riders from two hours to two weeks.

On the North Shore at Hale'iwa, see **Surf and Sea,** 808/637-9887 or **Eco-Surf Tours,** 808/638-9503, for lessons and rentals.

Kiteboarding lessons generally run around $100 for about three hours, but it all depends on the weather; 24-hour reservations is required. Gear rents for about $20 a day for those who don't need lessons. For kitesurfing lessons and rentals, see **Naish Hawaii,** 808/262-6068, in Kailua; **Kailua Sailboards and Kayaks,** 808/262-2555, in Kailua; and **Aloha Kiteboarding Academy,** 808/924-5483, in Haleiwa.

# THRILL CRAFT

## Parasailing

For a once-in-a-lifetime treat try **Aloha Parasail,** 808/521-2446, and **Hawaiian Parasail,** 808/591-1280, in Honolulu. With offices in the Koko Marina Shopping Center in Hawaii Kai, **Sea Breeze Watersports,** 808/396-0100, **Hawaii Sports,** 808/395-3773, and **H.O.T. Hawaii Ocean Tours and Adventures,** 808/395-6133, also offer this adventure.

## Jet Skiing

Jet skiing is not allowed in Waikiki, but you can speed across the water in Maunalua Bay near Koko Head or up in Hale'iwa on the North Shore. Jet skis usually run about $35 for a half hour or $60 an hour. Jet ski use is not allowed on Maunalua Bay on weekends and holidays, so make you plans for weekdays. Head to the Koko Marina Shopping Center and check with **Hawaii Sports,** 808/395-3773, **Sea Breeze Watersports,** 808/396-0100, and **H.O.T. Hawaii Ocean Tours and Adventures,** 808/395-6133. On the North Shore, where you can ride any day of the week—weather and water conditions permitting—check with **Watercraft Connection,** 808/637-8006, at the Hale'iwa marina.

# OCEAN TOURS

## Sail and Dinner Cruises

If you're taking a tour at all, your best bet is a sail or dinner cruise. They're touristy, but a lot of fun, and actually good value. Many times money-saving coupons for them are found in the free tourist magazines. Most of these cruises depart around 5:30 P.M. from the Kewalo Basin Marina, or from one of the piers near the Aloha Tower and cruise Waikiki toward Diamond Head before returning about two hours later. On board is a buffet, an open bar, live entertainment, and dancing.

High-tech hits the high seas on the *Navatek I,* 808/973-1311 or 800/548-6262, www.atlantisadventures.com, a unique bi-hulled ship that guarantees the "most stable ride in the islands." Sailing from Pier 6, you have a choice of various cruises, including a whale watch cruise in season for $49; a sunset buffet cruise, $59 adult and $39 children; and a sunset dinner cruise, $120 and $72, featuring gourmet food and some of the best island entertainers. Operated by Atlantis Adventures.

**Dream Cruises,** 808/592-5200 or 800/400-7300, www.dream-cruises.com, offers a morning dolphin-watching tour along the leeward coast. These 2.5-hour sails leave from Wai'anae's small boat harbor and include transportation from Honolulu and a small breakfast; $65.95 adults, $39.95 for children 12 and under. December–April, several daily whale-watching tours leave from Honolulu's Kewalo Basin and cruise off Waikiki and Diamond Head; $27.95 adults and $18.95 for children. Another offering is a dinner/dance cruise from 5:30–7:30 P.M. also off Waikiki ($49.95/$29.95). The midday Pacific Splash fun cruise ($65.95/$34.95) and the Morning Splash brunch cruise ($49.95/$29.95) take you to a mooring spot where you can play with water toys, swim, and use the two-story water slide and trampoline.

**Paradise Cruises,** 808/983-7827 or 800/334-6191, www.paradisecruises.com, also does dinner cruise and show combinations on the *Star of Honolulu, Starlet I,* and *Starlet II* ships. The *Starlet I* and *Starlet II* leave out of the Kewalo Basin 5:15 P.M. for two- to four-hour cruises. Prices range $31–71 adult for the Sunset Grill and Dinner Cruise. The larger *Star of Honolulu* offers three options from $66 to the $199 five-star, seven-course French dinner cruise with all the extras. It departs from Pier 8 near Aloha Tower at 5:30 P.M. and returns at 7:30 P.M. During the

day, these ships do whalewatch (in season) and Hawaiian cultural cruises for $42 adult and a water adventure day with barbecue off Waikiki and Diamond Head for $49.95 adult.

The *Ali'i Kai* catamaran packs them in (1,000-passenger capacity) for a sunset dinner cruise and live band dance nightly at 5:30 P.M. from Kewalo Basin. The buffet dinner runs $52 adult and $31 children. For the various full sit-down dinner options, rates are $67–124 adult and $40–74 children. The ride includes dinner, a Polynesian show, various numbers of free cocktails, and dancing. For $73 adult, $51 child, you can have a regular dinner sail plus a seat at the Magic of Polynesia illusion show in town. Call 808/539-9400 for reservations.

For the pure thrill of running under the wind in the waters off Waikiki, have a sail with *Maitai Catamaran,* 808/922-5665. Ninety-minute trips leave several times a day for $20 per person, while the sunset cocktail cruise goes for $30. These cruises leave from the beach between the Sheraton Waikiki and Halekulani hotels and cruise the waters off Waikiki. The Outrigger Waikiki also offers similar catamaran rides throughout the day.

Leaving from the Kewalo Basin Harbor, just in toward town from Waikiki, is the sleek 56-foot sailboat *Learjet* sailing yacht. A luxurious craft that's participated in numerous sailing competitions, it now offers snorkel trips, sunset sails, and go-for-broke sailing experiences daily. For information and reservations, contact Hawaii Sailing Adventures, 808/596-9696.

On the North Shore, try the catamaran *Ho'o Nanea* out of Hale'iwa Harbor, 808/638-8279, which does sailing and picnic snorkels throughout the year and whale-watching tours from January to May.

Tours from **Wild Side Specialty Tours,** 808/306-7273, wildsidehawaii.com, include reef snorkeling, whale-, turtle-, and dolphin-watching, and evening starlight cruises on its sailing catamaran *Island Spirit.* The size of the craft limits guests to 15, and the cost is $95 per person for any of the sails, which run three to four hours. As the crew are biologists, your time on the water can be as much an educational experience as simply a day on the water. Wild Side tours leave from the Wai'anae boat harbor on the Leeward Coast.

Others companies also run dolphin-watch tours on the Wai'anae coast. Touring in a high-powered mono-hull speed boat, **Dolfun,** 808/591-9599, www.dolfun-hawaii.com, offers dolphin-watch tours year round for $74 with transportation from Waikiki included. **Ko Olina Ocean Adventures,** 808/396-2068, www.ocean-adventures.com, runs boats out of the Ko 'Olina marina on dolphin and whale-watch cruises that also include some snorkel time. Rates are $75 for adults and $65 for kids. As dolphins like to play in the early morning hours, the dolphin tours leave at 7 A.M.; whale-watch tours in season go later in the morning. If that's not enough water fun for the day, this company also offers snuba/snorkel trips to the reef off Paradise Cove in the afternoon. Also leaving out of the Ko 'Olina marina is *Leid Back.* A sleek catamaran, *Leid Back* runs various snorkel, whale-watch, dolphin watch, and sunset dinner cruises throughout the day for $58–135, and can arrange full-day, week-long, wedding sails, and other specialty trips. Contact **Hawaii Nautical** at 808/255-5170.

**Captain Bob's,** 808/942-5077, tours Kane'ohe Bay aboard the *Barefoot I* catamaran daily (except Sun.) and features a picnic lunch and all the water activities that you can handle on its four-hour sail 10:30 A.M.–2:30 P.M. Prices run $69 adults, $59 for ages 13–17, and $49 for kids 4–12. You can work off lunch snorkeling or playing volleyball on the beach. The food is passable, but the setting offshore with the *pali* in the background is world-class. Transportation from Waikiki is included. Boats depart from He'eia Kea Harbor north of Kane'ohe.

For a sleeker ride with many of the same options and activities, **Serenity Sailing** runs the *Dreamer* from He'eia Kea Harbor on Monday, Wednesday, and Friday from 9 A.M.–12:30 P.M. Tours include light refreshments and snorkel gear. Call 808/306-2584 for more information.

Also operating on Kane'ohe Bay and out of He'eia Kea Harbor is the **Coral Queen,** 808/235-2192, which runs its glass-bottom boat from He'eia Kea Harbor. Daily one-hour excursions to Kane'ohe Bay run $10 adults or $5 for children 3–11. Call for reservations.

## Underwater Cruises

As beautiful as O'ahu is topside, it can be more exquisite below the waves. **Atlantis Submarines,** 808/973-9811 or 800/548-6262, www.atlantisadventures.com, costs $59 adult, $39 children 12 and under, and departs daily every hour on the hour 9 A.M.–3 P.M. from the Hilton Hawaiian Village pier, where you board the Hilton Rainbow Catamaran, which ferries you to the waiting sub. Once aboard, you're given a few instructions and then it's "run silent, run deep, run excited" for about 45 minutes. The sub is amazingly comfortable. Seats are arranged so that everyone gets a prime view through the large windows, and the air is amazingly fresh. The larger futuristic sub measures 96 feet and carries 64 passengers; the smaller is 65 feet long and carries 48 passengers. Outfitted with videocams, it allows the passengers to view the undersea world in every direction, while listening to explanations of the varied sea life through a multilanguage audio system. A thrill of a lifetime.

## Kayaking

**Go Banana Kayaks,** 799 Kapahulu, 808/737-9514, is into kayaks. Single-person kayaks run $30 per day, $42 for two-person kayaks; lessons and guided tours are available. Aside from renting kayaks, the store sells kayak and canoe gear and equipment.

Near the beach in Kailua, **Kailua Sailboard Company,** 808/262-2555, www.kailuasail-boards.com, also rents kayaks. A guided tour of the coast and islands off Kailua Beach runs $79. Good service, good prices, free pickup in Waikiki. Its prices are about the same as **Twogood Kayaks Hawaii,** 808/262-5656 or 345 Hahani St. in Kailua, www.aloha.com/~twogood, which also offers kayak rentals, sales, lessons, and group tours. Full-day rental $32, tandem $42, and the kayak will be dropped off for free at the Kailua Beach Park ($10 delivery fee for other locations in Kailua). Half-day and multi-day rates are also an option, as are various lessons, and a tour to Kailua Bay for $89 per person. Open Mon.–Fri. 9 A.M.–5 P.M., Sat.–Sun. 8 A.M.–5 P.M.

O'AHU

# FISHING

## Deep-Sea Fishing

O'ahu's offshore waters are alive with game fish. Among these underwater fighters are marlin, 'ahi, ono, mahimahi, and an occasional deepwater snapper. The deep-sea boats generally troll the Penguin Banks and the generally calm waters along the Wai'anae Coast, from Barbers Point to Ka'ena Point.

The vast majority of O'ahu's fleet moors in **Kewalo Basin,** in Honolulu Harbor along Ala Moana Boulevard next to Fishermen's Wharf. The boat harbor is a sight in itself, and if you're contemplating a fishing trip, it's best to head down there the day before and yarn with the captains and returning fishermen. This way you can get a feel for a charter to suit you best.

For a charter organization try **Hawaii Charter Skippers Association,** 808/591-9100. Many private boats operating out of Kewalo Basin include: *Sea Verse,* 808/591-8840; **Kamome Sport Fishing,** 808/593-8931; *Maggie Joe,* 808/591-8888; **Magic Sportfishing,** 808/596-2998; **Kuu Huapala Fishing Co.,** 808/596-0918, and **The Wild Bunch.**

A few boats operate out of the Wai'anae small boat harbor on the leeward coast, like **Kaimalolo Sportfishing,** 808/695-3474, and a few berth in Hale'iwa on the North Shore, like **Chupu Charters,** 808/637-3474 and *Kuuloa Kai Sportfishing,* 808/637-5783.

## Freshwater Fishing

The state maintains two public freshwater fishing areas on O'ahu. The **Wahiawa Public Fishing Area** is 300 acres of fishable waters in and around the town of Wahiawa. It's basically an irrigation reservoir used to hold water. Species regularly caught here are large and smallmouth bass, sunfish, channel catfish, *tucunare,* oscar, carp, snakehead, and Chinese catfish. The other area is the **Nu'uanu Reservoir no. 4,** a 25-acre restricted watershed above Honolulu in the Ko'olau Mountains. It's open for fishing only three times per year in May, August, and November. Fish caught there are tilapia and Chinese catfish.

# CAMPING AND HIKING

Few people equate visiting O'ahu with camping. The two seem mutually exclusive, especially when you focus on the mystique of Waikiki and the dominance of a major city like Honolulu. But among state, county, and private campgrounds, you have about 20 spots to choose from all over the island.

## State Parks

O'ahu boasts 21 state parks, recreation areas, waysides, and monuments. Less than half offer a beach for day use or shoreline access, but the majority have some combination of walking paths, picnic areas, cultural sites, picnic areas, toilets, showers, and/or pavilions. Included in these state properties are three *heiau,* **'Iolani Palace,** the **Royal Mausoleum,** and **Diamond Head.** The state parks on O'ahu close their gates and parking lots at night. Those *not* offering camping are open 7 A.M.–7:45 P.M. from April 1 to Labor Day, closing during the remainder of the year at 6:45 P.M.

Four state parks currently offer tent camping: **Sand Island State Recreation Area,** just a few minutes from downtown Honolulu; **Keaiwa Heiau State Recreation Area,** in the interior on the heights above 'Aiea; **Malaekahana Bay State Recreation Area,** a mile north of La'ie on the windward coast; and **Kahana Valley State Park** between Punalu'u and Ka'a'awa on the windward coast.

To camp at Sand Island, Keaiwa Heiau, or Kahana Valley State Park, you must acquire a permit from the Department of Land and Natural Resources, Division of State Parks, P.O. Box 621 (1151 Punchbowl St.), Honolulu, HI 96809, 808/587-0300, open weekdays 8 A.M.–3:30 P.M. Camping fees are $5 per campsite for every night of use. O'ahu campsite **permit reservations** can be made only 30 days prior to the first day of camping, but *must* be made at least one week in advance. Write for a permit application form. Information needed includes your name, address, phone number, names and identification numbers of all persons over 18 years of age in your party, type of permit requested, duration

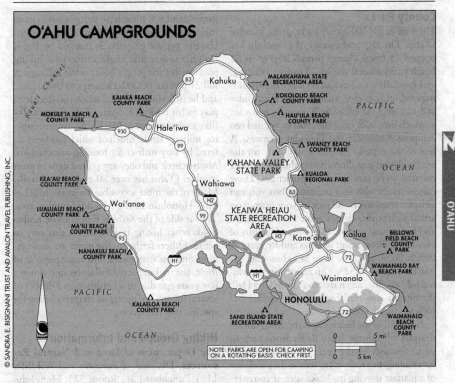

# O'AHU CAMPGROUNDS

KAUAI CHANNEL

83 Kahuku

MALAEKAHANA STATE RECREATION AREA

KAIAKA BEACH COUNTY PARK

KOKOLOLIO BEACH COUNTY PARK

PACIFIC

MOKULE'IA BEACH COUNTY PARK

930 Hale'iwa

HAU'ULA BEACH COUNTY PARK

99

SWANZY BEACH COUNTY PARK

OCEAN

KEA'AU BEACH COUNTY PARK

Wahiawa

KAHANA VALLEY STATE PARK

KUALOA REGIONAL PARK

83

LUALUALEI BEACH COUNTY PARK

Wai'anae

H2

KEAIWA HEIAU STATE RECREATION AREA

MA'ILI BEACH COUNTY PARK

99

H3

BELLOWS FIELD BEACH COUNTY PARK

93

Kane'ohe Kailua

NANAKULI BEACH COUNTY PARK

H1

72

WAIMANALO BAY BEACH PARK

H1

Waimanalo

PACIFIC

KALAELOA BEACH COUNTY PARK

HONOLULU

72

WAIMANALO BEACH COUNTY PARK

SAND ISLAND STATE RECREATION AREA

OCEAN

0     5 mi
0     5 km

NOTE: PARKS ARE OPEN FOR CAMPING ON A ROTATING BASIS. CHECK FIRST.

© SANDRA E. BISIGNANI TRUST AND AVALON TRAVEL PUBLISHING, INC.

of your stay, and specific dates requested. The permits can be picked up on arrival with proof of identification.

Camping is allowed *only* from Friday 8 A.M. to Wednesday 8 A.M. (closed all day Wednesday and Thursday for camping—other activities okay), with the shutdown, supposedly, for regrowth and maintenance. Camping on Sand Island State Recreation Area only is Friday through Monday. Camping is allowed for only five consecutive days in any one month, and don't forget a parking permit for your vehicle, which must remain within the locked park gates at night.

Camping at Malaekahana State Recreation Area is handled by the Friends of Malaekahana, 808/293-1736, fax 808/293-2066, P.O. Box 305, La'ie, HI 96762. Reservations are taken up to 12 months in advance and at least 14 days before planned arrival, although walk-in camping reservations are accepted if there is

space available. Check-in is handled 3–5 P.M.; checkout time is until noon. The office is open Mon.–Fri. 10 A.M.–4 P.M. Write or call for information and reservation applications. Firearms, fireworks, pets, and drinking of alcoholic beverages are prohibited in the park, and a quiet time is enforced 10:00 P.M.–8 A.M. Half a dozen beach houses, which sleep up to 10, run $66 a night during the week and $80 on weekends. Tent campers pay $5 per person per night. A few other cabins, pop-up trailers, and thatched huts on the property can also be rented. Outside hot showers and bathroom facilities are shared. Bring mosquito repellent. The pavilion can be rented for day events or for the day and night ($250)—it sleeps 15. Parking is limited. Make sure to call and make arrangements with the staff if you will be arriving later than office hours. The park gate is locked—for your security—7 A.M.–7 P.M.

## County Parks

There are nearly 300 county parks on the island of O'ahu. The city and county of Honolulu has opened 15 (these change periodically) of its 62 beach parks around the island to tent camping, and most allow trailers and RVs. A free permit is required, and camping is allowed only from Friday at 8 A.M. until the following Wednesday at 8 A.M., at which time your campsite must be vacated (no camping Wednesday and Thursday evenings). A few of these parks have camping only on the weekends and one allows it only during summer months, so be sure to ask for particulars. These campsites are also at a premium, but you can write for reservations and pick up your permits on arrival with proper identification. For information and reservations write or visit City and County of Honolulu, Department of Parks and Recreation, Permit Section, 650 S. King St., Honolulu, HI 96813, 808/523-4525. This office is in the Municipal Building, down the street from City Hall. Permits are also available from the satellite city halls around the island.

**Note:** All of the beach parks are closed during designated months (they differ from park to park) throughout the year. This is supposedly for cleaning, but really it's to reduce the possibility of squatters moving in. Make sure, if you're reserving far in advance, that the park will be open when you arrive. Don't count on the Parks and Recreation Department to inform you!

## Hiking

The best way to leave the crowds of tourists behind and become intimate with the beauty of O'ahu is to hike it. Although the Neighbor Islands receive fewer visitors, a higher percentage of people hike them than O'ahu. Don't get the impression that you'll have the island to yourself, but you will be amazed at how open and lovely this crowded island can be. Some cultural and social hikes can be taken without leaving the city, like a stroll through Waikiki and a historical walking tour of downtown Honolulu and Chinatown. But others—some mere jaunts, others quite strenuous—are well worth the time and effort.

Remember that much of O'ahu is privately owned, and you must have permission to cross this land, or you may be open to prosecution. Usually private property is marked by signs. Another source that might stomp your hiking plans with their jungle boots is the military. A full 21 percent of O'ahu belongs to Uncle Sam, and he isn't always thrilled when you decide to play in his backyard. Some of the finest walks (like to the summit of Mt. Ka'ala) require crossing military lands, much of which has been altered by very unfriendly looking installations. Always check and obey any posted signs to avert trouble. O'ahu has over 80 maintained trails. Many of the most accessible are in the hills behind Honolulu in the Makiki/Tantalus area. The far side of the Ko'olau Range above Kailua holds other hiking trails that are also easy to get to. Others farther to the north are more remote and less frequented. The most popular of these, the trail to Sacred Falls, was shut down a few years ago due to a landslide and deaths of several hikers. See the travel chapters below for specific trail references.

## Hiking Groups and Information

The **Department of Land and Natural Resources,** Division of Forestry and Wildlife, 1151 Punchbowl St., Room 325, Honolulu, HI 96813, 808/587-0058, is helpful in providing trail maps, accessibility information, hunting and fishing regulations, and general forest rules. This office is in the Kalanimoku Hale state office building across from the State Capitol. The following organizations can provide information on organized hiking trips. For information on the trails in the state's Na Ala Hele trail access system see www.hawaii-trails.org for the list and descriptions. **The Hawaiian Trail and Mountain Club,** P.O. Box 2238, Honolulu, HI 96804, 808/674-1459 or 808/377-5442, meets behind 'Iolani Palace on Saturday at 9 A.M. and Sunday at 8 A.M.; free for members and $2 for nonmembers. The hikes are announced on their internet site and in the *Honolulu Star Bulletin's* "Pulse of Paradise" column. For the group's *Hiker's Guide,* send $1.50 and an SASE to the above address or check its website at www.geocities.com/htm-club. **Sierra Club, Hawaii Chapter** P.O. Box 2577, Honolulu, HI 96803, organizes weekly hikes, $1 for members and $3 for nonmembers. Information about the organization and its hikes is listed in its newsletter and on its website at www.hi.sierraclub.org. Sierra Club also sells the useful booklet *Hiking Softly in Hawai'i* ($5), which gives general information about hiking in Hawaii; preparation, etiquette, and precautions; a brief chart of major trails on each island, along with their physical characteristics; and other sources of information. **Hawaii Audubon Society** can be reached at 850 Richards Street, Honolulu, HI 96813, 808/528-1432, for information about birdwatching hikes, or call the **Hawaii Nature Center**, 808/955-0100, 2131 Makiki Heights Drive, for information about hikes.

Since 1995, the ecotour operator **Oahu Nature Tours**, 808/924-2473 or 800/861-6018, www.oahunaturetours.com, natureguide@oahunaturetours.com, has offered daily hiking tours that focus on native birds and plants and the island's natural wonders. Seven tour options are available, and these can be combined for multiday touring. The Diamond Head Crater Sunrise Adventure is offered twice each morning for $20. Two different daily waterfall tours run $37 apiece, and a southeast coastal natural highlights tour is $32. Rainforest, valley, and another coastal tour go on various days of the week for $37–42. Conducted by owner Michael Walther or one of his knowledgeable guides, each tour is an environmental education experience as well as a fun outing. This is a first-class operation and all tours are well worth the time and money. You will not be disappointed. Transportation and all equipment is provided. Call for departure times.

Other hikes are offered by **Hawiian Islands Eco-Adventures**, 808/236-7766 or 866/445-3624; www.hikeoahu.com. Full-day botanical garden and coastal hikes, and half-day waterfall hikes are options. Hikes run daily and cost $40–59 for adults or $29–39 children.

**Hawaiian Isle Adventure**, 808/261-2786, is a low-key company that does a hike to a waterfall, visits a *heiau*, stops at the *pali* lookout, and gives snorkeling lessons at one of the less-visited Windward Coast beaches. Guided tours are conducted by van transportation. Hotel pickup is at 7:15 A.M. and tours run until 3:30 P.M.

**Mauka Makai Excursions**, 808/593-3525 or 877/326-6248, offers several eco-friendly drive and hiking tours around the island that focus on cultural history and places of archaeological importance. Full- and half-day trips take you to North Shore or windward O'ahu sites. Trips run $35–60 for adults, $10 less for kids 6–17 years old.

## Camping Gear and Rentals

If you've come without camping gear and wish to rent some try **The Bike Shop**, 1149 S. King St., Honolulu, 808/596-0588, renting two-person tents and backpacks at $35 each for a weekend or $70 for the week. A $200 deposit, returned when you return the equipment, is required. **Omar the Tentman**, 94-158 Leoole St., Waipahu, 808/677-8785, rents a wider variety of equipment and offers prices for one- to three-day or four- to seven-day periods. A six-person dome tent runs $52–57, sleeping bags $15–20, stoves $14–18, and lanterns (you supply the fuel) $14–18. No backpacking tents.

For sales, try The Bike Shop. Also, **The Sports Authority** has a great variety of outdoor sports and camping equipment at decent prices. Much of the camping gear is more useful for car and beach camping than backpacking but it does offer a selection. Most convenient is their store in the Ward Gateway Center. **Powder Edge** has two shops, at the Aloha Tower Marketplace and the Ward Village Shops for some outdoor equipment.

## Topographical Maps

On O'ahu, a wide range of USGS topographical maps and ocean navigational charts can be purchased at the **Pacific Map Center**, 560 N. Nimitz Hwy., 206A, Honolulu, HI 96817, 808/545-3600. This shop is in the Gentry Pacific Design Center. USGS, Defense Mapping Agency, University of Hawai'i, and Hawaii Geographical Society maps, as well as a limited selection of geographical-related books can be purchased at

**Hawaii Geographic Maps and Books,** 49 S. Hotel St., Rm. 217, Honolulu, 808/538-3952 or 800/538-3950, open Mon., Wed., and Fri. 10 A.M.–2 P.M.

## HORSEBACK RIDING

A different and delightful way to see O'ahu is from the back of a horse. The following outfits operate trail rides on different parts of the island. **Kualoa Ranch,** 808/237-7321, at the north end of Kane'ohe Bay, offers 60-minute rides along the base of the *pali* for $45 and two-hour rides into Ka'a'awa Valley for $79. Rides also are given as part of the ranch's all-day adventure packages. Hotel pickup available.

Above the town of Waimea on the North Shore, **Happy Trails Hawaii,** 808/638-7433, gets you on horseback for easy rides along the edge of the canyon looking into Waimea Valley. The one-hour and 90-minute rides run $38 and $48, respectively. The age requirement is six years old and you cannot weigh more than 235 pounds to ride. In Waimea Valley, **Waimea Falls Park,** 808/638-8511, offers horseback rides as one of their activities for $45 an hour.

At the northern tip of the island, the stable at **Turtle Bay Resort,** 808/293-8811, welcomes both resort guests and nonguests. Gentle guided trail rides through the ironwood forest and along the beach are run several times daily. Regular rides run $35 adults and $22 children age nine and above for the 40-minute saunter; advanced adult rides are $50, while evening rides run $65 per person.

## BICYCLING

Pedaling around O'ahu can be both fascinating and frustrating. The roads are well paved, but the shoulders are often torn up. Traffic in and around Honolulu is horrifying, and the only way to avoid it is to leave very early in the morning. Many, but not all, of the city buses have been equipped with bike racks, so it's easier than before to get your bike from one part of the city to another or out of town. Once you leave the city, traffic, especially on the secondary interior roads, isn't too bad. Un-

fortunately, all of the coastal roads are heavily trafficked. Pedaling around Waikiki, although congested, is usually safe, and a fun way of seeing the sights. Always use a helmet, always lock your bike, and always take your bike bag.

### Bike Rental and Bike Shops

For bicycle rentals try: **The Bike Shop,** 808/596-0588, 1149 S. King St.; **Big Mountain Rentals,** 2426 Kuhio Ave., 808/926-1644; **Blue Sky Rentals,** 808/947-0101, at 1920 Ala Moana Ave.; **Paradise Isle Rentals,** 1879 Kalakaua Ave., 808/946-7777; or **Coconut Cruisers,** 808/924-1644 at the Royal Hawaiian Shopping Center. Many rental bikes are mountain bikes or hybrids but city bikes and road bikes are also rented. Not all shops carry all types, so inquire, but many of the dealers in the Waikiki area have mountain or hybrid bikes. Expect to pay about $15–25 a day or $70–110 a week, depending upon the type.

For sales and repairs try: **The Bike Shop,** 1149 S. King St., 808/596-0588; **The Bike Factory,** 740 Ala Moana Blvd., 808/596-8844; **Island Triathlon and Bike,** 569 Kapahulu Ave., 808/732-7227; **McCully Bicycle,** 2124 S. King St., 808/955-6329; and **Raging Isle Surf and Cycle,** 66-250 Kamehameha Hwy. in Hale'iwa, 808/637-7707.

### Bike Tours

Organized bike tour companies are not numerous on O'ahu, but for a downhill ride above Honolulu or off-road adventure in Ka'a'awa Valley on the Windward side, try **Bike Hawaii,** 808/734-4214, www.bikehawaii.com. Bikes, helmets, water, and snacks are provided.

## GOLF

With 38 public, private, municipal, and military golf courses scattered around such a relatively small island, it's a wonder that it doesn't rain golf balls. These courses range from modest nine-holers to world-class courses whose tournaments attract the biggest names in golf today. Prices range from $10 a round up to $160. An added attraction of playing O'ahu's

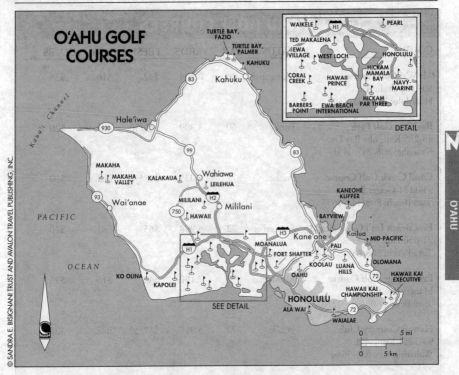

O'AHU GOLF COURSES

courses is that you get to walk around on some of the most spectacular and manicured pieces of real estate on the island. Some afford sweeping views of the coast, such as the **Ko 'Olina Golf Club,** while others, like the **Pali Golf Course,** have a lovely mountain backdrop, or, like Waikiki's **Ala Wai Golf Course,** are surrounded by city spread. The Ala Wai Golf Course also must be one of the busiest courses in the country as some 500 rounds of golf are played there daily! In 1994, the PGA rated the **Ko'olau Golf Course** the toughest course in the United States. Tough or easy, flat or full of definition, O'ahu provides ample opportunity and variety for any golfer.

For ease of use for municipal golf courses, the City and County of Honolulu has an automated tee time reservation and information system. Call 808/296-2000 to make or check your reservation or to have your inquiry answered.

## TENNIS

Grease up the old elbow, because O'ahu boasts 181 county-maintained tennis courts, 124 of which are lighted. Most courts also have backboards. To get information on where they are located, write a letter of inquiry and enclosing an SASE to the Department of Parks and Recreation, Tennis Division, 3908 Paki Ave., Honolulu, HI 96815, or call 808/971-7150. Alternately, you can stop by the Diamond Head Tennis Center at the above address and pick up a copy of a complete list. The accompanying chart is a partial listing of what's available.

## HUNTING

Game on O'ahu includes wild pig and goat, plus a variety of pheasant, francolin, quail, partridge, and dove. For information on hunting on O'ahu, contact the Department of Land and Natural

M

O'AHU

# O'AHU GOLF COURSES

| COURSE | STATUS | PAR | YARDS | FEES† | CART | CLUBS |
|--------|--------|-----|-------|-------|------|-------|
| **Ala Wai Golf Course** 404 Kapahulu Ave. Honolulu; 808/733-7387 | Municipal | 70 | 6,208 | $42 | $16 | $25 |
| **BayView Golf Park** 45-285 Kane'ohe Bay Dr. Kaneohe; 808/247-0451 | Public | 60 | 3,399 | $42/50 | incl. | $20 |
| **Coral Creek Golf Course** 91-1111 Geiger Rd. 'Ewa Beach; 808/441-4653 | Public | 72 | 6,025 | $125 | incl. | $30 |
| **Ewa Beach Int'l Golf Course** 91-050 Fort Weaver Rd. 'Ewa Beach; 808/689-8351 | Semiprivate | 72 | 5,998 | $65 | incl. | $40 |
| **Ewa Village Golf Course** Mango Tree Rd. 'Ewa Beach; 808/681-0220 | Municipal | 72 | 7,100 | $42 | $16 | $25 |
| **Hawaii Country Club** 94-1211 Kunia Rd. Wahiawa; 808/621-5654 | Public | 72 | 5,916 | $49/59 | incl. | $20 |
| **Hawaii Kai Golf Course** Championship Course Executive Course 8902 Kalaniana'ole Hwy. Honolulu; 808/395-2358 | Public Public | 72 55 | 6,222 2,386 | $90 $37 | incl. $8.50 | $30 $30 |
| **Hawaii Prince Golf Club** 91-1200 Fort Weaver Rd. 'Ewa Beach; 808/944-4567 | Resort | 36** | 3,350 | $135 | incl. | $40 |
| **Kahuku Golf Course** P.O. Box 417 Kahuku; 808/293-5842 | Municipal | 35* | 2,699 | $10 | $4 | $12 |
| **Kalakaua Golf Course** USAG-HI Bldg. 2104 Schofield Barracks 808/655-9833 | Military | 72 | 6,186 | $26 | $9 | $8 |

O'AHU

| COURSE | STATUS | PAR | YARDS | FEES† | CART | CLUBS |
|---|---|---|---|---|---|---|
| **Kapolei Golf Course**<br>91-701 Farrington Hwy.<br>Kapolei; 808/674-2227 | Semiprivate | 72 | 6,136 | $90/100 | incl. | $45 |
| **Ko 'Olina Golf Club**<br>92-1220 Ali'inui Dr.<br>Kapolei; 808/676-5300 | Resort | 72 | 6,867 | $145 | incl. | $50 |
| **Ko'olau Golf Course**<br>45-550 Kionaole Rd.<br>Kane'ohe; 808/236-4653 | Public | 72 | 6,797 | $95 | incl. | $35 |
| **Leilehua Golf Course**<br>USAG-HI Bldg. 2104<br>Schofield Barracks<br>808/655-4653 | Military | 72 | 6,521 | $32 | $9 | $6 |
| **Luana Hills Country Club**<br>770 Auloa Rd.<br>Kailua; 808/262-2139 | Semiprivate | 72 | 6,164 | $109 | incl. | $45 |
| **Makaha Resort Golf Club**<br>84-626 Makaha Valley Rd.<br>Waianae; 808/695-9544 | Public | 72 | 6,414 | $90 | incl. | $30 |
| **Makaha Valley Country Club**<br>84-627 Makaha Valley Rd.<br>Waianae; 808/695-7111 | Public | 71 | 6,369 | $100 | incl. | $30 |
| **Mid-Pacific Country Club**<br>266 Kaelepulu Dr.<br>Kailua, 808/261-9765 | Semiprivate | 72 | 6,509 | $52 | incl. | $50 |
| **Mililani Golf Club**<br>95-176 Kuahelani Ave.<br>Mililani; 808/623-2222 | Semiprivate | 72 | 6,455 | $89/95 | incl. | $25 |
| **Moanalua Golf Club**<br>1250 Ala Aolani St.<br>Honolulu; 808/839-2411 | Semiprivate | 36* | 2,972 | $25/30 | $16 | No |
| **Olomana Golf Links**<br>41-1801 Kalaniana'ole Hwy.<br>Waimanalo; 808/259-7926 | Public | 72 | 6,304 | $67 | incl. | $35 |

*continued on next page*

## O'AHU GOLF COURSES (cont'd)

| COURSE | STATUS | PAR | YARDS | FEES† | CART | CLUBS |
|---|---|---|---|---|---|---|
| **Pali Golf Course**<br>45-050 Kamehameha Hwy.<br>Kane'ohe; 08/266-7612 | Municipal | 72 | 6,524 | $42 | $16 | $20 |
| **Pearl Country Club**<br>98-535 Kaonohi St.<br>'Aiea; 808/487-3802 | Semiprivate | 72 | 6,232 | $65/70 | incl. | $30 |
| **Ted Makalena Golf Course**<br>93-059 Waipio Point Access Rd.<br>Waipahu; 808/675-6052 | Municipal | 71 | 5,976 | $42 | $16<br>$4 pull cart | $15 |
| **Turtle Bay Resort**<br>Arnold Palmer Course<br>George Fazio Course<br>57-049 Kamehameha Hwy.<br>Kahuku; 808/293-8574 | Resort<br>Resort | 72<br>72 | 6,795<br>6,535 | $160<br>$155 | incl.<br>incl. | $40<br>$40 |
| **Waikele Golf Course**<br>94-200 Paioa Place<br>Waipahu; 808/676-9000 | Semiprivate | 72 | 6,261 | $125 | incl. | $30 |
| **West Lock Golf Course**<br>91-1126 Okupe St.<br>'Ewa Beach; 808/675-6076 | Municipal | 72 | 5,849 | $42 | $16 | $15 |

*= 9 holes, ** = 27 holes (par 36 per 9), † = weekday/weekend rates*

Resources, Division of Forestry and Wildlife, 1151 Punchbowl St., Honolulu, HI 96813, 808/587-0166.

## LAND TOURS

Guided land tours are much more of a luxury than a necessity on O'ahu. Because of the excellent bus system and relatively cheap rental cars, you spend a lot of money for a narration and to be spared the hassle of driving. If you've come in a group and don't intend to rent a car, they may be worth it. Sea cruises and air tours are equally luxurious, but provide glimpses of this beautiful island you'd normally miss. The following partial list of tour companies should get you started.

### Bus and Shuttle Tours

If you're going to take a land tour, you must have the right attitude, or it'll be a disaster. Your tour leader, usually driving the van or bus, is part instructor, comedian, and cheerleader. There's enough "corn" in his or her jokes to impress an Iowa hog. On the tour, you're expected to become part of one big happy family, and most importantly, to be a good sport. Most guides are quite knowledgeable about O'ahu and its history, and they honestly try to do a good job. But they've done it a million times before, and their performance can be as stale as week-old bread. The larger the tour vehicle and the shorter the miles covered, the worse it is likely to be. If you still want a tour, take a full-day jaunt in a small

# O'AHU TENNIS COURTS

## County Courts

Under the jurisdiction of the Department of Parks and Recreation Tennis Division, 3908 Paki Ave., Honolulu, HI 96815, 808/971-7150. Courts listed are in Honolulu, Waikiki, and main towns only.

| TOWN | LOCATION | NO. OF COURTS | LIGHTED |
|------|----------|---------------|---------|
| 'Aiea | 'Aiea District Park | 2 | Yes |
| 'Ewa | 'Ewa Beach Community Park | 4 | Yes |
| Kahala | Kahala Community Park | 2 | No |
| Kailua | Kailua District Park | 8 | Yes |
| Kaimuki | Kaimuki Community Park | 2 | Yes |
| Kane'ohe | Kane'ohe District Park | 6 | Yes |
| Ke'ehi | Ke'ehi Lagoon Courts | 12 | Yes |
| Koko Head | Koko Head District Park | 6 | Yes |
| Manoa | Manoa Valley District Park | 4 | Yes |
| Maunawili | Maunawili Valley Park | 2 | Yes |
| Mililani | Mililani District Park | 4 | No |
| Pearl City | Pearl City | 2 | Yes |
| Sunset Beach | Sunset Beach Neighborhood Park | 2 | Yes |
| Wahiawa | Wahiawa District Park | 4 | Yes |
| Waialua | Waialua District Park | 4 | Yes |
| Wai'anae | Wai'anae District Park | 8 | Yes |
| Waikiki | Ala Moana Park | 10 | Yes |
| Waikiki | Diamond Head Tennis Center | 10 | No |
| Waikiki | Kapi'olani Tennis Courts | 4 | Yes |
| Waimanalo | Waimanalo District Park | 4 | No |
| Waipahu | Waipahu District Park | 4 | Yes |

## Hotel and Private Courts Open to the Public

| TOWN | LOCATION | FEE | NO. OF COURTS | LIGHTED |
|------|----------|-----|---------------|---------|
| 'Aina Haina 808/373-1282 | Honolulu Tennis Academy | $20/hr. | 2 | Yes |
| 'Ewa Beach 808/944-4567 | Hawaii Prince Golf Club | $5/hr. | 2 | Yes |
| Kahuku 808/293-8811 | Turtle Bay Resort | $20/hr. | 10 | Yes |
| Kapolei 808/679-0079 | JW Marriott Ihilani Resort | $24/hr. | 6 | Yes |

O'AHU

van: you get to know the other people and the guide, who'll tend to give you a more in-depth presentation. Tips are cheerfully accepted. Also, be aware that some tours get kickbacks from stores and restaurants they take you to, where you don't always get the best bargains. Most companies offer free hotel pickup and delivery. Lunch or dinner is not included unless specified, but if the tour includes a major tourist spot like Waimea Falls Park or the Polynesian Cultural Center, admission is usually included.

About half a dozen different tours offered by most companies are variations on the same theme, and the cost is fairly uniform. One of the more popular is a **circle-island tour,** including numerous stops around Waikiki, the windward coast, North Shore, and the center of the island. These usually run about $50, half that for children. An afternoon and evening Polynesian Cultural Center tour, including admission and dinner show, costs close to $70. Tours to the sights of Pearl Harbor run about $40, and those to Diamond Head and downtown sights run around $25.

Some reputable companies include: **Polynesian Adventure Tours,** 808/833-3000, www.polyad.com; **Roberts Hawaii,** 808/539-9400, www.robertshawaii.com; **E Noa Tours,** 808/591-2561, www.enoa.com.

With tours mostly focused on the Pearl Harbor area is **Discovering Hidden Hawaii Tours,** 808/737-3700, www.discoverhawaiitours.com. **Home of the Brave Tours,** 808/396-8112, offers tours Mon.–Fri. from 6 A.M.–2 P.M. for $69 per person, excluding lunch costs, which takes in the *USS Arizona Memorial,* several of the military installations, Punchbowl National Cemetery, and sites in downtown Honolulu.

## Special Walking Tours

The following are special tours that you should seriously consider.

**Walking Tour of Chinatown,** 808/533-3181, by the Chinese Chamber of Commerce, leaves every Tuesday at 9:30 A.M. from in front of its offices at 42 N. King Street. The cost is $5 for the 2.5-hour tour. The **Hawaiian Heritage Center** offers a similar historical and cultural two-hour

tour of Chinatown, leaving from the Ramsey Galleries at 1128 Smith St. every Friday at 9:30 A.M. The cost is $10 per person. Call 808/521-2749 for reservations.

The American Institute of Architects (AIA) offers a walking tour of downtown Honolulu and Chinatown, exploring the old edifices of the city. This walking tour starts from the institute's office at 119 Merchant St. at 9:30 A.M. on Tuesday and Saturday and returns about noon. The price is $15 per person or $25 per couple. Call 808/545-4242 for reservations.

**Walking Tour of Honolulu** is a three-hour tour led by a very knowledgeable volunteer from the **Mission Houses Museum.** Starting with a walk through the houses of the museum, you're led on a wonderfully anecdoted walk through the historical buildings of central Honolulu for only $15. Tours are given on Thursday only and start at 9:45 A.M. from the Mission Houses Museum. Reservations are required; call 808/531-0481.

Free guided **walking tours of historical sites of Waikiki** are given by the Native Hawaiian Hospitality Association. These tours follow a number of surfboard-shaped historical markers that have been set up at various points around Waikiki and are part of the Waikiki Historical Trail. Each marker give a brief description of important places, person, or happenings that relate to the history of Waikiki. Tours run about 1.5 hours and are offered Mon.–Sat. at 9 A.M., or you can follow the signs on your own with up a copy of the *Waikiki Historic Trail* brochure. For tour reservations, call 808/841-6442.

When they're happening, **Honolulu Time Walks,** 2634 S. King St., Suite 3, Honolulu, HI 96826, 808/943-0371, offers fascinating interpretive walking tours focusing on the city's colorful past. The tours, ranging in price $5–40 (most about $10), sometimes including dinner, are thematic and change regularly. Expect topics like A Journey to Old Waikiki, Mysteries of Mo'ili'ili, Scandalous Days of Old Honolulu, and the very popular Ghosts of Honolulu. Master storyteller Glen Grant, in costume, hosts many of the tours. Thematic bus and trolley tours are also offered, and several historical shows are performed at the Waikiki Heritage Theater in the International Marketplace. Extremely authentic and painstakingly researched, these tours and shows are immensely educational and entertaining. You can't find better. Reserve!

The **Hawaii Nature Center,** 2131 Makiki Heights Dr., Honolulu, HI, 808/955-0100, is a nonprofit organization dedicated to environmental education through a hands-on approach. Primarily geared toward school-age children, but welcoming the young at heart, the Hawaii Nature Center offers weekend community programs for families and the public to share in the wealth of Hawaii's magnificent natural environment through interpretive hikes, earth care projects, and nature crafts. This is a wonderful opportunity for visitors to explore Hawaii through direct interaction with the environment.

The volunteer organization **Clean Air Team,** 808/948-3299, hosts a hike up Diamond Head every Saturday 9 A.M.–noon, regardless of weather, leaving from the front entrance of the Honolulu Zoo. There is no cost for this hike, but a donation of $5 is accepted to further programs of this nonsmoker's rights advocacy group. Additionally, this group runs a hike to Jackass Ginger waterfall and natural swimming pool on Sunday, leaving at 9 A.M. from near the Mahatma Gandhi statue in front of the Honolulu Zoo. A $10 contribution is requested, and transportation is by public bus.

## AIR TOURS

When you soar above O'ahu, you realize just how beautiful this island actually is, and considering that the better part of a million people live in this relatively small space, it's amazing just how much undeveloped land still exists in the interior and even along the coast. The following are some air tours worth considering. Remember that small one- or two-plane operations come and go as quickly as cloudbursts. They're all licensed and regulated for safety, but if business is bad, the propellers stop spinning.

### Fixed-Wing Tours

Novel air tours are offered from Dillingham Airfield, located along the northwest coast, a few miles down the Farrington Highway west of Hale'iwa. Once in the air, you can soar silently above the coast with **Glider Rides,** 808/677-3404, an outfit offering one- or two-passenger piloted rides infinitely more exciting than the company's name; www.honolulusoaring.com. A plane tows you aloft and you circle in a five-mile radius with a view that can encompass 40 miles on a clear day. The rides are available daily 10 A.M.–5:30 P.M. on a first-come, first-served basis. The published rate is $100 for a single person and $120 if there are two passengers for a 20 minutes, but these flights are often greatly reduced in price. Add $25 for additional 10-minute segments if you want a longer ride. Lessons and aerobatic flights can also be arranged. Check in with "Mr. Bill."

Also at the Dillingham Airfield is **Soar Hawaii Sailplanes,** 808/637-3147; www.soarhawaii.com. This company offers 10-, 20-, 30-, 40-, 50-, and 60-minute rides for $49–99 for one person, with the option of tandem rides available. Aerobatic rides for one passenger (with parachute!) are the same length as the standard rides but $49 more per ride. A reduction in rates is usually offered during the summer season. Open 10 A.M.–6 P.M.; reservations are recommended.

Mr. Bill also operates **Stearman Biplane Rides** out of the Dillingham Airfield. A ride in one of these old-style birds brings back the days of barnstormers and pioneer aviation. Stearman runs 20-minute flights for $125 and 40-minute flights for $195 in its open-cockpit biplane. One passenger only—aside from the pilot. If your really a daredevil, you can ask for the aerobatic option, but it'll run you an extra $50. Meant for extreme aerobatic flights, a Pitts S-2B biplane is a step up in adventure. Ten-minute single-passenger roller-coaster rider go for $100 while the 15-minute flights run $150.

A throwback to the days when tourists arrived in the islands by clipper planes is a seaplane tour by **Island Seaplane Service,** 808/836-6273, located on a floating dock at 85 Lagoon Dr., on the back side of the Honolulu International Airport. These planes take off and land in Ke'ehi Lagoon, just like the Pan Am China Clippers did in the 1930s. Two runs are offered: a half-hour circle of southeastern O'ahu to get a look at Honolulu, Waikiki, Diamond Head, and the lower windward *pali*, and a one-hour ride that gives you all of that plus takes you all the way up the windward coast, circling back over the Leilehua Plateau and Pearl Harbor before landing. Six flights a day fly from 9:15 A.M.–4:45 P.M. and run $89 per person for the shorter flight, $139 for the longer. Reservations required, and you can be shuttled from Waikiki if you need.

**Eco Air Tours Hawaii,** 808/839-1499, flies out of Honolulu in a nine-passenger twin-engine Piper Chieftain. A six-island 3.5-hour scheduled excursion is offered at $249 per person leaving Honolulu at 9 A.M. or Maui at 9:30 P.M. A minimum of six passengers is needed to fly, so flights may not go every day. All flights include a narration on ecology, culture, and history of the islands. Private charters can be scheduled at $500 an hour for the plane. Reservations are necessary at least 24 hours in advance.

Using the runway for take-off and landing of the small twin-engine, glass front Observer Partenavias airplane, **Tora Flights,** 808/836-1234, leaves from its office location at 14 Lagoon Drive for daytime circle flights over the southeastern corner of the island as well as a nighttime city lights flight. Leaving up to four times during the day and twice at night, these flights run about 40–45 minutes in length. Daytime flights run $99 per person, while the night flights are $139; minimum two passengers.

**Islands in the Sky** is a one-day flying extravaganza offered by **Hawaiian Airlines.** Using regularly scheduled flights, this daily tour goes from Honolulu to Maui, on to Kona on the Big Island, and then back to O'ahu for $340 adults or $320 for kids ages 2–11. Stops in Kona and on Maui include lunch and dinner and all sightseeing ground transportation; transportation to and from your hotel in Honolulu is also included. Call 808/838-1555 for reservations or arrange this trip at any Hawaiian Airlines ticket office.

## Helicopters

Helicopter companies rev up their choppers to flightsee you around the island, starting at about $75 per person for a short 20-minute trip over Honolulu/Waikiki. Prices rise up from there to about $185 for a one-hour full-island narrated tour. Several companies even offer a night flight over Waikiki for a spectacular light show for about $100. Usually, transport to and from the heliport is included in the cost. Sometimes discounts are offered, so ask.

Chopper companies are all located at the backside of the Honolulu International Airport, except Cherry Helicopters, 808/293-2570, which operates out of the Turtle Bay Resort on the North Shore. **Makani Kai Helicopters,** 808/834-5813, www.makanikai.com, offers standard options at a fair price using Astar six-passenger aircraft. This is a respected company with a great track record. **Sandstone Helicopters,** 808/833-5678, does a one-hour circle-island flight in a Bell 407 for $145 per person. It also can operate like a "limo in the sky" if the entire aircraft is rented without sharing space. **Offshore Helicopters,** 808/838-0007, has several options daily from 20- to 50-minute flights, staying mostly in the Honolulu, Pearl Harbor, and lower Windward Coast areas.

## Parachuting

Three companies offer parachuting at the Dillingham Airfield. These drops are tandem with an instructor, unless you have certification for solo flights. After gaining about 10,000 feet, you'll free fall for a minute and parachute for several more, landing lightly on the grass (God willing) next to the airstrip. Rates vary somewhat, as do drop elevations, but expect a fee of about $150–200. For this thrill ride, contact **Drop Zone,** 808/637-7007; **Pacific International Skydiving,** 808/637-7472; or **Skydiving Hawaii,** 808/637-9700.

## Hang Gliding

**North Shore Hang Gliding,** 808/637-3178, sells hang gliders and can hook you up with a tandem instructor for lessons toward certification. The staff can also give you tips on where to fly on O'ahu if you're already certified.

# Accommodations and Food

## ACCOMMODATIONS

The innkeepers of O'ahu would be personally embarrassed if you couldn't find adequate lodging on the island. So long as O'ahu has to suffer the "slings and arrows" of development gone wild, at least you can find all kinds, qualities, and prices of places in which to spend your vacation. Of the more than 70,000 rooms available in Hawaii, 37,000 are on O'ahu, with 33,000 of them in Waikiki alone! Some accommodations are living landmarks, historical mementos of the days when only millionaires came by ship to O'ahu, dallying as if it were their own private hideaway. When the jumbo jets began arriving in the early 1960s, O'ahu, especially Waikiki, began to build frantically. The result was hotel skyscrapers that grew faster than bamboo in a rainforest. These monoliths, which offered the "average family" a place to stay, marked a tremendous change in social status of visitors to O'ahu. The runaway building continued unabated for two decades, until the city politicians, supported by the hotel keepers themselves, cried "Enough!" and the activity finally slowed down.

Now a great deal of money is put into refurbishing and remodeling what is already built. Visitors can find breathtakingly beautiful hotels that are the best in the land next door to more humble inns that can satisfy most anyone's taste and pocketbook. On O'ahu, you may not get your own private beach with swaying palms and hula girls, but it's easy and affordable to visit one of the world's most exotic and premier vacation resorts.

Rooms on O'ahu may be found in all sorts of hotels, condos, and private homes. Some venerable old inns along Waikiki Beach were the jewels of the city when only a few palms obscured the views of Diamond Head. However, most of Waikiki's hotels are now relatively new high-rises. In Waikiki's five-star hotels, prices for deluxe accommodations, with all the trimmings, can run $250 per night or (way) more. But a huge inventory of rooms go for half that amount and less. If you don't mind being one or two blocks from the beach, you can easily find nice hotels for $75–125. Waikiki's side streets also hold many apartment-hotels that are, in effect, condos. In these you get the benefit of a full kitchen for under $150. Stays of a week or more bring further discounts.

Central Honolulu has one fine business hotel and a no-frills hotel in Chinatown. Some upscale hotels around Ala Moana put you near the beach but away from the heavy activity of Waikiki. For those passing through, a few overnight-style hotels are near the airport. For those looking for less expensive accommodations, the city has a handful of YM/WCAs, youth hostels, and hostel hotels.

The remainder of the island, outside Waikiki, was mostly ignored as far as resort development was concerned, except for the venerable Turtle Bay Hilton on the North Shore and the new and luxurious JW Marriott Ihilani Resort in 'Ewa, and the remodeled Makaha Resort and Golf Club on the Wai'anae coast. In the interior towns, and along the remainder of the coasts, you'll be hard pressed to find a hotel room. Even today, only a handful of hotels, inns, and condos are found on the windward coast, at Kane'ohe, Punalu'u, and La'ie. This windward coast has more vacation rentals, bed-and-breakfasts, and a hostel or two, as does the north coast.

## FOOD

### Lu'au

The following is a listing of the lu'au available on O'ahu. The **Royal Hawaiian Lu'au** on the Ocean Lawn of the Royal Hawaiian Hotel, every Monday and Thursday 6–8:30 P.M., 808/931-7194, *is* the classic Hawaiian feast, complete with authentic foods, entertainment, and richly spiced with *aloha*. Authenticity is added by lawn seating on traditional *lau hala* mats (table seating too) while the sun sets on Waikiki Beach and the stars dance over Diamond Head. Entertainment is an hour-long Polynesian extravaganza featuring Tahitian and traditional hula, a Samoan fire dance, and bold rhythmic drumming, and the buffet is a lavish feast of traditional favorites. You are presented with a fresh flower lei and welcomed at the open bar for mai tais and other tropical drinks. Cost is $81 adults, $48 for children 5–12.

**Germaine's Lu'au,** 808/949-6626 or 800/367-5655, often claimed by local people to be *the* best, is held at a private beach at Barber's Point, Tues.–Sun. 6–8:45 P.M. Of all the lu'au on the island, Germaine's is the most down-home Hawaii of the bunch. The cost for dinner, cocktails, and the Polynesian show runs $46 for adults and $37 for kids 14–20. A free shuttle (reservations required) from Waikiki area hotels can be booked when calling for tickets.

**Paradise Cove Lu'au** at the Ko 'Olina Resort boasts a wonderful dinner with arts and crafts displays, games, and other activities on a private beach along the leeward coast. Held daily 5–8:30 P.M., tickets run $52.50 for adults, $42,50

youth 13–18, and $32.50 for kids 6–12, with enhanced packages at greater cost and a non-dinner cocktail show only for less. Paradise Cove is in a well-run, well-landscaped 12-acre park-like setting, and the production is definitely tourist oriented. Transportation by shuttle bus from Waikiki is included in the price. The shuttle bus departs from various hotels starting at 3:45 P.M. and returns by about 9:30 P.M. Call 808/842-5911 or 800/775-2683 for reservations.

In La'ie on the windward coast, try the **Ali'i Lu'au** at the Polynesian Cultural Center. The dinner and show run daily except Sunday 5:30–9 P.M. The cost is $69 adult and $48 children and this includes entrance to the Polynesian Cultural Center. The Ali'i Lu'au introduces you to a well-rounded Hawaiian feast, the *imu* ceremony, and a reenactment of a royal court procession before the show begins. For reservations, call 808/293-3333 or 800/367-7060.

# Getting There

The old adage of "all roads leading to Rome" applies almost perfectly to O'ahu, though instead of being cobblestones, they're sea lanes and air routes. Except for a handful of passenger ships still docking at Honolulu Harbor, and some limited nonstop flights to the Neighbor Islands, all other passengers to and from Hawaii are routed through Honolulu International Airport.

## Honolulu International Airport

This international airport is one of the busiest in the country, with hundreds of flights to and from cities around the world arriving and departing daily. In a routine year, over 20 million passengers utilize this facility. The three terminals (directions given as you face the main entranceway) are: the main terminal, accommodating all international and Mainland flights; the interisland terminal, a separate building at the far right end of the main terminal, handling flights between the islands by Hawaiian and Aloha airlines; and the commuter terminal, farther to the right side, taking care of the commuter and smaller interisland air carriers.

The ground floor of the **main terminal** is mostly for arriving passengers and contains the baggage claim area, car rental agencies, the USO lounge, and international and domestic arrival doors, which are kept separate. The second floor is for departing passengers, with most activity centered here, including ticket counters, shops, lounges, currency exchange, baggage handlers, the Pacific Aerospace Museum, a business center, and the entrance to most of the gates. From both levels you can board taxis and TheBus to downtown Honolulu and Waikiki.

The **interisland terminal** services flights aboard Hawaii's two major interisland carriers. It has its own snack bars, car rental information, lounges, information booths, and restrooms. It's only a leisurely 10-minute stroll between the two terminals, which is fine if you don't have much baggage; if you do, there are plenty of shuttles every few minutes.

Shuttles also service the **commuter terminal,** which lies beyond the interisland terminal. This terminal is used by Island Air and Pacific Wings, each of which has a ticket counter in the terminal

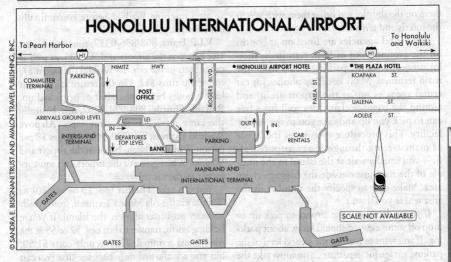

# HONOLULU INTERNATIONAL AIRPORT

To Pearl Harbor

To Honolulu and Waikiki

H1

NIMITZ  HWY.

COMMUTER TERMINAL

PARKING

POST OFFICE

ROGERS BLVD.

PAIEA ST.

● HONOLULU AIRPORT HOTEL

● THE PLAZA HOTEL

KOAPAKA  ST.

ARRIVALS GROUND LEVEL

LEI

UALENA  ST.

INTERISLAND TERMINAL

IN

DEPARTURES TOP LEVEL

BANK

PARKING

OUT

IN

AOLELE  ST.

CAR RENTALS

MAINLAND AND INTERNATIONAL TERMINAL

GATES

Noa

SCALE NOT AVAILABLE

GATES

GATES

GATES

© SANDRA E. BISIGNANI TRUST AND AVALON TRAVEL PUBLISHING, INC.

O'AHU

lobby. Here too you'll find a baggage claim area, telephones, restrooms, a small gift shop, and pick up stops for the inter-terminal shuttle and car rental shuttles. Departures are at the far end, arrivals are closest to the Interisland Terminal.

## Services, Information, Tips

For general airport information and arrival and departure information, call 808/836-6413.

The main **information booth** is on the ground level just near the central escalators. Besides general information, it has good maps of the airport, O'ahu, Honolulu, and Waikiki. Also, information booths lined up along the ground level, at the international area and interisland terminals, are friendly and helpful when there is a person in attendance, but not always stocked with as many maps as the main information booth.

**Lost and found** booths are on the ground level of the main terminal and at the interisland terminal; call 808/836-6547. The **post office** is across the street from the main entranceway toward the interisland terminal.

There are several **foreign currency exchange** booths at the airport as well as ATM machines, however, getting change can be a hassle or a downright rip-off, and very bad public relations for visitors. Unless the situation has recently changed for the better, no one will give you change, putting

you at the mercy of $1 bill-change machines located throughout the airport. These machines happily dispense 85 cents for every $1 you put in, so if you want to make a phone call, or the like, you're out of luck. Snack bars will only change money for you with a purchase. For a state that prides itself on the *aloha* spirit and depends on good relations with its visitors, this is a ridiculously poor way of greeting people or giving them a last impression before they return home.

## Airport Transportation

The free **Wiki Wiki Shuttle** takes you between the terminals and arrival/departure gates. There are three color-coded lines that service the terminals. From arrival gates, all shuttles make stops at the baggage claim areas but not all run to every section of the airport. Check with the signs outside the arrival/departure gates for this specific information. Staffed by courteous drivers, the wiki-wiki shuttle is efficient—most of the time. When it's not, a nickname could be the "Tricky Tricky Shuttle." Transfer time between the two main and interisland terminals is only about 10 minutes, which does not include baggage transfer. If you'll be going on to a Neighbor Island make sure the carrier you are using has an interline agreement with the Hawaiian domestic carrier. If not, you must fetch your own bags, place them on the shuttle, and bring them with you to the interisland terminal.

**Car rental agencies** are lined up at booths on the ground floor of both terminals; their lot offices are in the parking area outside the main terminal. Many courtesy phones for car rental agencies not at the airport are in and around the baggage claim area; call for a free van to pick you up and take you to the nearby facility. This procedure even saves the hassle of maneuvering through heavy airport traffic—you usually wait at the island in the middle of the road just outside the baggage claim area. Make sure to specify the number of the area where you'll wait.

If you're driving to the airport to pick up or drop off someone, you should know about **parking.** If you want to park on the second level of the parking garage for departures, you must take the elevator either up to the fourth floor or down to ground level, and from there cross the pedestrian bridge. There's no way to get across on levels two and three. Parking is $1 for the first half hour, $1 for each additional hour, or $10 maximum for a 24-hour period.

**Public transportation** to downtown Honolulu, especially Waikiki, is abundant. Moreover, some hotels have courtesy phones near the baggage claim area; if you're staying there, they'll send a van to fetch you. Current charges for taxis, vans, TheBus, and limousine service are posted just outside the baggage claim area, so you won't have to worry about being overcharged.

Only **taxis** that contract with the airport can pick up at the terminal. All others can drop off there but are allowed to pick up only outside the terminal, at a car rental office, for example. From the terminal to Waikiki costs about $21–26, not counting bags. Splitting the fare with other passengers can save money. Some companies charge a flat fee of $15 from outside the terminal to Waikiki. Vans and motorcoaches leave from the central island in the roadway just outside the baggage claim. They charge about $8, but a wait of up to 45 minutes for one is not out of the ordinary. Moreover, they drop passengers at hotels all over Waikiki, so if you're not one of the first stops by chance, it could be an hour or so after reaching Waikiki before you're finally deposited at your hotel.

**V.I.P Trans,** 808/836-0317, runs shuttle service between the airport and Waikiki, as well as other parts of the city. To Waikiki the rate is $7; roundtrip runs $12. On the return trip, call at least 5 hours before you want to be picked up. **Reliable Shuttle,** 808/924-9292, runs basically the same service at the same rates. **Airport Waikiki Express,** 808/539-9400, charges $8 per person ($4 for children) between the airport and Waikiki. When going to the airport, you must reserve two days in advance.

You can take **TheBus** (no. 19 or no. 20) to Waikiki via the Ala Moana Terminal, from which you can get buses all over the island. If you're heading north, transfer to bus nos. 52 or 55 at the Ala Moana terminal. TheBus only costs $1.50, but you are allowed only baggage that you can hold on your lap without infringing on other riders. Drivers are sticklers on this point.

## Interisland Carriers

**Hawaiian Airlines,** 800/367-5320 nationwide and Canada, 800/882-8811 statewide, 808/838-1555 on Oʻahu, www.hawaiianair.com, offers the most flights. From Honolulu to Kauaʻi, nearly two dozen nonstop flights go 5:30 A.M.–7:30 P.M.; flights to Maui begin at 5:15 A.M. with one every 20–30 minutes until 7:30 P.M.; flights to Hilo and Kona on the Big Island leave about every hour or so 5:20 A.M.–6 P.M. Also, daily flights are offered once a day to Lanaʻi and Molokaʻi, and between all the major island airports.

**Aloha Airlines,** 800/367-5250 Mainland and Canada, 808/484-1111 on Oʻahu, www.alohaairlines.com, connects Honolulu to Kauaʻi, Maui, and both Kona and Hilo on the Big Island of Hawaiʻi, and Maui to Kauaʻi and Kona. Routes from Honolulu to Kauaʻi run more than once an hour from 6 A.M.–7:45 P.M. A bit more often are flights to Maui. Nineteen flights a day go to Hilo and a dozen and a half run to Kona. There are 15 flights a day between Maui and Kauaʻi, but only two a day from Maui to Kona. Aloha Airlines partners with United Airlines.

**Island Air,** 800/323-3345 nationwide, 800/652-6541 statewide, and 808/484-2222 on

O'ahu, www.alohaairlines.com, connects Honolulu with Kahului, Kapalua-West Maui, Lana'i, and Ho'olehua on Moloka'i. About half the flights are on jet aircraft and half on Dash-8 turboprop airplanes. Eight flights each connect Honolulu with Lana'i and Moloka'i; six go to West Maui Airport; while one or two run to Kahului. Between the islands, flights connect Kahului to Moloka'i and Lana'i.

**Pacific Wings** is a local and reputable commercial airline that fills the gap that the bigger airlines often miss. It connects Honolulu to Kahului, Hana, Ho'olehua and Kalaupapa on Moloka'i, Lana'i City, and Kamuela on the Big Island, and connects these airports together, but on a limited schedule of three or less flights a day, except for the dozen flights a day between Honolulu and Kahului. Pacific Wings also does flightseeing tours from its base on Maui and is available for charter flights. Pacific Wings can be reached at 808/873-0877 or 888/575-4546; www.pacificwings.com.

## Charter Airlines

If you've got the bucks or just need to go when there's no regularly scheduled flight, try one of the following for islandwide service: **Paragon Air,** 866/946-4744, www.paragon-air.com; and **Maui Air,** 808/877-5500, www.maui.net/~mauisle.

# Getting Around

Touring O'ahu is especially easy, since almost every normal (and not so normal) mode of conveyance is readily available. You can rent anything from a moped to a limo, and the competition is very stiff, which helps keep prices down. A few differences separate O'ahu from the other islands. To begin with, O'ahu has a model public transportation system called The-Bus—not only efficient, but very inexpensive. Also, O'ahu is the only island that has a true expressway system, though along with it came rush hour and traffic jams. A large part of O'ahu's business is processing people, even if it's only to send them on to another island. The agencies operating these businesses on the island are masters at moving people down the road. With the huge volume of tourists who visit every year, it's amazing how smoothly it works.

## RENTAL CARS

Every reputable national and state car rental agency is here, along with some car rental hucksters that'll hook you and land you like mahimahi if you're not careful. The rule of thumb is, if the deal sounds too good to be true, it is. The competition is fierce among the reputable agencies, however, and their deals are all equally good. Always check with your travel agency for big savings on fly/drive or stay/drive packages.

Reserving a car on O'ahu is doubly important because of the huge turnover that can occur at any time. Be aware of **drop-off charges;** for example, if you rent in Waikiki and leave the car at the airport, you'll be charged. It's convenient to rent a car at the airport. But it's also convenient to take an inexpensive shuttle to and from Waikiki and rent there. Many firms have offices in Waikiki, and you can even rent a car from your hotel desk and have it delivered to you. This saves you the hassle of dealing with traffic and unfamiliar roads during arrival and departure, and avoids drop-off fees—but you don't always get the cheapest rates.

## National Agencies

All of the following national companies have locations in Waikiki. The local phone numbers given are for the main location at Honolulu International Airport and locations in Waikiki. Call for more details.

**Dollar Rent A Car,** 808/831-2330 or 808/944-1544.

**Alamo,** 808/833-4585 or 808/947-6112.

**National Car Rental,** 808/831-3800 or 808/973-7200.

**Avis,** 808/834-5536 or 808/971-3700.

**Budget,** 808/838-1111.

**Enterprise,** 808/836-2213, 808/922-0090, or 808/922-0090.

**Hertz,** 808/831-3500 or 808/971-3535.
**Thrifty,** 808/831-2277 or 808/971-2660.

## Local Agencies

These firms are established rental companies. Some may rent without a major credit card, but they will undoubtedly require a stiff deposit. Sometimes they even rent to those under 21. You usually make out all right with **Paradise Rent A Car,** 808/946-7777, 808/926-7777, or 808/924-7777, 1879 Kalakaua Ave., at 151 Uluniu Ave., and 355 Royal Hawaiian Ave. in Waikiki, which carries Jeeps, SUVs, convertibles, motorcycles, and mopeds. **VIP (Very Inexpensive Prices) Car Rentals,** 808/922-4605 or 808/924-6500, with two locations in Waikiki, handles sedans, jeeps, and stationwagons. **JN Car and Truck Rental,** 808/831-2724, has all sorts of sedans, convertibles, trucks, and vans.

## Vanity Rentals

The most distinctive and fun-filled cars on O'ahu are the sports cars and luxury imports available from **Ferrari Rentals,** 808/942-8725, in Waikiki at 2002 Kalakaua Ave. This company has a fleet of American and European classic cars, like Viper, Corvette, Ferrari, Porsche, Jaguar, Mercedes, and BMW. The magnificent Lamborghine Diablo goes for the equally magnificent price of $1,300 per day, while they let the lowly Corvette out for the mere pittance of only $260 per day.

**Paradise Rent A Car,** 808/946-7777 or 808/926-7777, or 808/923-8000 at 1879 Kalakaua Ave., 151 Uluniu Ave., and 355 Royal Hawaiian Ave., in Waikiki, also rents luxury cars like the Prowler, Viper, Mercedes, Porsche, Cabrio, Lamborghini Diablo Roadster, and Corvette convertible. Most of these run $249–599 a day with the Lanborghini triple that. Offices are open daily 8 A.M.–5 P.M.

## Motorcycles and Mopeds

For rentals, try **Paradise Isle Rentals,** 808/922-2224, at 151 Uluniu in Waikiki, where you can ride away with the wind in your face on a Nighthawk, Ninja, or Harley-Davidson for $100 a day, or scoot away on a 50cc moped for a daily rate of $35. Other options include **Adventure on 2 Wheels,** 1946 Ala Moana Ave., 808/944-3131; and **Big Kahuna Motorcycle Tours and Rentals,** 808/924-2736, at 407 Seaside Avenue. **Coconut Cruisers,** 2301 Kalakaua Ave., 808/924-1644, rents motorcycles that run $90–170 for three hours or $100–215 for up to 12 hours. **Cruzin Hawaii Motorcycles,** 808/945-9595, rents only Harleys. Open 8:30 A.M.–5:30 P.M. at 1980 Kalakaua Ave., near the Ambassador Hotel, it rents the Big Twins, Road Kings, and Heritage Softtails at $149 all day, and Sportsters for $99 all day.

# ALTERNATE TRANSPORTATION

## TheBus

If Dorothy and her mates had TheBus to get them down the Yellow Brick Road, she might have chosen to stay in Oz and forget about Kansas. TheBus, TheBus, ThewonderfulBus is the always-coming, slow-moving, go-everywhere friend of the budget traveler. Operated by O'ahu Transit Services, Inc. (OTS), it could serve as a model of efficiency and economy in any city of the world. What makes it more amazing is that it all came together by chance, beginning as an emergency service in 1971. It now services more than a quarter million passenger rides a day. Aside from crisscrossing the city, these coaches go up and down both the windward and leeward coasts, through the interior, while passing through all of the major and most of the minor towns in between, and most often stopping near the best sights.

Route signs and numbers are located on the front of the bus and near the bus doors. The **fare** is only $1.50 adult, 75 cents for students between ages 6–19, while kids under six who can sit on a parent's lap aren't charged at all. The fare is paid in *exact change* upon entering. Drivers cannot make change. A four-day unlimited-use **visitors pass** is also available for $15 from ABC Stores. Adult **monthly bus passes,** good at any time and on all routes, are $27, but be aware that they are good only from the first to the last day of every month. If you buy a pass in mid-month, or even later, it's still full price. A student monthly pass is $13.50. Passes for senior citizens and disabled passengers are good for two years and cost $25. Seniors (65 or older) must furnish proof of age and will be given the pass within a few minutes of having an ID photo taken. Monthly passes are available at **TheBus Pass Office,** open Mon.–Fri. 7:30 A.M.–4 P.M., at 811 Middle St., 808/848-4444, www.thebus.org. Bus no. 1 Kalihi stops within a few feet of The-Bus Pass Office.

**Transfers** are free and are issued upon request when entering TheBus, but you can only use them for ongoing travel in the same direction, on a different line. They are also timed and dated, good for approximately two hours.

Only baggage that can be placed under the seat or on one's lap is permitted; baby strollers that fold up are allowed. Seeing-eye dogs and other similar service animals can accompany a passenger, but all other animals must be in a carrier that fits under the seat or on the lap. No smoking is allowed, and eating or drinking is not permitted. Please use radios or similar devices with headphones only.

Some buses are now equipped with bike racks, which makes it easier to get around town or out of town without having to jostle with all the traffic. Bike racks carry two bikes only. First, let the bus driver know that you wish to load your bike. Then pull down to unfold the rack, if it isn't down already, and securely set the bike wheels into the slots. Pull up on the securing arm to lock your bike in, then board. When leaving the bus, be sure to let the driver know that you want to unload your bike, or it may go to the next stop without you. For additional instructions, consult the *How to Use the New Bike Rack for Buses* booklet, available from TheBus office.

There are about 80 routes in the system. Get full **route and schedule information** by calling TheBus at 808/848-5555, 5:30 A.M.–10 P.M., or by visiting the information booth at the Ala Moana Terminal and satellite city halls, where you can pick up fliers and maps. For other general information and attractions along the routes call 808/296-1818 and follow the directions. TheBus lost and found office can be contacted at 808/848-4444. The Customer Service number is 808/848-4500. One inexpensive guide to major bus routes and attractions is the *TheBus Map*

*and Guide Book.* Another excellent little guide is *Hawaii Bus and Travel Guide,* by Milly Singletary. Both are available in most bookstores for around $5.

The following are some popular destinations and their bus numbers. Note that buses with letter designations are express buses. **Academy of Arts,** no. 2, 13, B; **Aloha Tower,** no. 19, 20, 42; **Honolulu International Airport,** no. 19, 20; **USS *Arizona* Memorial, Pearl Harbor,** no. 20, 42; **Bishop Museum,** no. 2 "School Street;" **Chinatown,** no. 2, 13, 19, 20, 42, B; **Diamond Head entrance,** no. 22, 58; Hanauma Bay, no. 22; **Honolulu (downtown),** no. 2, 13, 19, 20, 42, B; **Kailua (and Waimanalo),** no. 57; **Punchbowl,** no. 42 to Alapai Street near City Hall, then transfer to no. 15; **Polynesian Cultural Center,** 52 Wahiawa-Circle Isle, 55 Kane'ohe-Circle Isle from the Ala Moana Terminal; **Queen Emma Summer Palace,** no. 4; **Sea Life Park,** no. 22, 58; **University,** no. 4; **Wai'anae Coast,** no. 40, 93, C; **Waikiki Beach,** no. 2, 4, 13, 19, 20, 58; **Ward Centers,** no. 19, 20. The **Beach Bus,** no. 22, starts on Kuhio Ave. near Kalakaua Ave. and services all of the beach areas, including Hanauma Bay and Sandy Point; Sea Life Park is its terminus. Once a seasonal service, the Beach Bus now operates year-round.

Circling the island by bus is a terrific way to see the sights and meet people along the way. The circle route takes about four hours if you ride the entire loop, but you can use the transfer system to give yourself a reasonable tour of only the sights that strike your fancy. The **circle-island** bus no. 52 Wahiawa-Circle Isle goes inland to Wahiawa, north to Hale'iwa, along the North Shore, down the windward coast to Kane'ohe and back over the *pali* to Honolulu. Bus no. 55 Kane'ohe-Circle Isle follows the same route but in the opposite direction.

## Trolley and Shuttles

The **Waikiki Trolley,** 808/593-2822, an open-air trolley-like bus, will take you on a tour of Waikiki and surrounding areas for $20 adults, $10 child. This all-day pass lets you board, exit, and reboard at any stop along four specific routes. Multiday passes for four consecutive days on these same four routes are available for $45 and $15, respectively. Starting from the Royal Hawaiian Shopping Center in Waikiki, the trolley runs four main routes, with several overlapping stops, mostly at 20- to 30-minute intervals. The red line (Honolulu City route) operates 8:30 A.M.–6:30 P.M., leaving its last starting point at 4:30 P.M. This line basically connects Waikiki with historical and cultural sights in downtown Honolulu. The yellow line (Shopping and Dining route) runs from 9 A.M. to about 11 P.M. and brings visitors to the Ala Moana and Ward shopping centers, downtown, Hilo Hattie, and Dole Cannery mall. The green line (Local Shopping and Gourmet route) goes every 40 minutes 10:25 A.M.–9:45 P.M. and makes its major stops by restaurants in Waikiki and out along S. King Street. The blue line (Ocean Coast route) starts at 8:30 A.M. and runs every 45 minutes until 7 P.M. It heads east to the coastal sights of southeast O'ahu and as far as Sea Life Park. In addition, there are other lines. A free DFS Galleria Waikiki line trolley operates only in the evening 5–11:50 P.M. connecting the Galleria to several major hotels in Waikiki. The purple and orange lines operate differently, and tickets run $22 adult and $8 children 4–11. The purple line (First Adventures route) runs to Diamond Head, Punchbowl, the Pali Lookout, and the State Capitol, while the orange line (Hidden Treasures route) takes you to the University of Hawai'i at Manoa, Wai'oli Tea Room, the Pali Lookout, and Moanalua Gardens. Trolleys on the orange and purple lines make two runs per day. Last is the Out Neighborhood Trolley line which runs from Waikiki, up Kapahulu Avenue, and on up Wai'alae Avenue. Going every 30 minutes 10 A.M.–11 P.M., this trolley brings you out to the shops and restaurants of Kaimuki. Fares are $1 one way, $2 for an all-day pass, or $25 for a moth pass. Pick up a map/brochure from any activity desk or call the number above. Tickets can be purchased from booths at the Royal Hawaiian Shopping Center and at Ward Warehouse.

In addition to this trolley, several shuttles run only to specified sites. All leave from various hotels in Waikiki. The **Arizona Memorial Shuttle Bus** runs about every 90 minutes 6:50 A.M.–1 P.M. to the memorial, and until about 5:15 P.M. back

from the memorial. Call 808/839-0911 for reservations (a must); $7 per person round-trip. The **Hilo Hattie/Dole Cannery Bus** runs daily to those two shopping sites, leaving every 20 minutes 7 A.M.–6 P.M. No charge. For exact schedule, call 808/537-2926. The **Waikele Trolley** heads from Waikiki hotels to the outlet shops in Waikele twice a day in the early morning and returns at three set times in the afternoon and evening for $22 adult roundtrip or $8 children. Call 808/591-2561 for reservations.

## Taxis

The law says that taxis are not allowed to cruise around looking for fares, so you can't hail them. But they do and you can, and most police officers have more important things to do than monitor cabs. Best is to summon one from your hotel or a restaurant. All are radio-dispatched, and they're usually there in a flash. The fares, posted on the taxi doors, are set by law and are fair, but still expensive for the budget traveler. The rates do change, but expect about $2 for the flag fall, and then 25 cents for each additional one-eighth mile. From the airport to Waikiki is about $25, though luggage costs extra. Most cab drivers are quite good, but you may pause to consider if your cab sports the bumper sticker "Caution! I drive like you do!"

Of the many taxi companies, some with good reputations are: **Sida,** a cooperative of owner-drivers, at 808/836-0011; **Aloha State Cab,** 808/847-3566; **Charley's,** 808/955-2211; and **City Taxi,** 808/524-2121. If you need some special attention like a Rolls-Royce limo, try: **Cloud 9 Limousines,** 808/524-7999. It is one of at least three dozen limo services on the island.

## Hitchhiking

Hitchhiking varies from island to island, both in legality and method. On O'ahu, hitchhiking is legal, and you use the tried-and-true style of facing traffic and waving your thumb. But city ordinance specifies that you can only hitchhike from a bus stop! Not many people try so the pickings are reasonably easy. TheBus, however, is only $1.50 for anywhere you want to go, and the paltry sum that you save in money is lost in "seeing time."

Two things against you: Many of the people are tourists and don't want to bother with hitchhikers, and many locals don't want to bother with nonlocal hitchhikers. When you do get a ride, most of the time it will be from a *haole* who is either a tourist on his own or a recent island resident. If you are just hitchhiking along a well-known beach area, perhaps in your bathing suit and obviously not going far, you can get a ride more easily. Women should exercise caution and avoid hitchhiking alone.

# Information and Services

## Emergencies

For **police, fire, or ambulance** anywhere on O'ahu, dial **911**. For **nonemergency police** assistance and information, call 808/529-3111.

**Civil Defense:** In case of natural disaster such as hurricanes or tsunamis on O'ahu, call 808/523-4121 or 733-4300. The **Coast Guard Search and Rescue** can be reached at 800/541-2450.

**Sex Abuse Treatment Center Hotline:** Call 808/524-7273 for cases involving sexual assault or rape crisis.

## Medical Services

Full-service hospitals include: **The Queen's Medical Center,** 1301 Punchbowl St., Honolulu, 808/538-9011; **Castle Medical Center,** 640 Ulukahiki St., Kailua, 808/263-5500; **St. Francis Medical Center,** 2230 Liliha, Honolulu, 808/547-6011; **Straub Clinic and Hospital,** 888 S. King St., Honolulu, 808/522-4000; **Kuakini Medical Center,** 347 N. Kuakini St., Honolulu, 808/536-2236; and **Wahiawa General Hospital,** 808/621-8411, 128 Lehua St. in Wahiawa.

Medical services and clinics include: **Kaiser Permanente,** 3288 Moanalua Road, Honolulu, 808/432-0000; **Doctors on Call,** 808/971-6000 (for Japanese-speaking doctors call 808/923-9966), for emergencies and "house calls" to your hotel, 24 hours a day; **Hawaii Medical Uneo Clinic,** 808/926-9911, on the lobby level of the Ilikai Hotel near the Ala Wai Marina is open 24 hours a day; **Kuhio Walk-in Medical Clinic,** 2310 Kuhio Ave., Suite 223, in Waikiki, 808/924-6688, open 9 A.M.–4:30 P.M. Mon.–Fri. and Saturday until 1 P.M. at the corner of Nahua in Waikiki; **Urgent Care clinic,** 808/597-2860, 2155 Kalakaua Ave. in the ANA Kalakaua Building, Suite 308, with lab and x-ray capability is open daily 7 A.M.–11 P.M.; and **Waikiki Health**

**Center,** 277 'Ohua Ave., 808/922-4787, for low-cost care including pregnancy and confidential VD testing, open Mon.–Thurs. 9 A.M.–8 P.M., Friday until 4:30 P.M., Saturday until 2 P.M.

Dozens of **pharmacies** dot the island, including: **Kuhio Pharmacy,** at the corner of Kuhio and Nahua, 808/923-4466; **Center Pharmacy,** 302 California Ave. in Wahiawa, 808/622-2773; **Longs Drugs,** in Honolulu at the Ala Moana Shopping Center, 808/941-4433, at the Kane'ohe Bay Shopping Center, 808/235-4511, and at over 20 other locations around the island; **Waianae Drugs,** 85-910 Farrington Hwy., Waianae, 808/696-6348; and **Waipahu Drug,** 94-748A Hikimoe, 808/677-0794. In addition, Safeway and Times Super Markets also have pharmacies in their stores.

For **alternative health care** try: **Acupuncture Clinic,** 111 N. King St., 808/545-8080; **East-West Acupuncture and Herbs,** 1481 S. King St., 808/942-0244; **Honolulu School of Massage,** 1136 12th Ave., 808/733-0000. **Chiropractic Referral Service,** 808/478-4022, offers free information and referral to qualified chiropractors. For other chiropractors, acupuncturists, and alternative health care providers, please refer to the Yellow Pages.

## Weather, Marine Report, and Time of Day

For recorded information on local island weather, call 808/973-4380; for marine conditions, phone 808/973-4382; and for the surf report, call 808/973-4383. For time of day, call 808/983-3211.

## Consumer Protection and Tourist Complaints

If you encounter problems with accommodations, bad service, or downright rip-offs, try the following: **The Chamber of Commerce of Hawaii,** 808/545-4300; **Office of Consumer Protection,** 808/587-3222; or the **Better Business Bureau,** 808/536-6956. For general information, or if you have a hassle, try the City Hall's **Office of Information,** 808/523-4385, or the **Office of Complaint,** 808/523-4381.

## Tourism Information

Perhaps the most convenient spot to garner tourist information is the **Visitor Information Office,** Waikiki Shopping Plaza, 2250 Kalakaua Ave., Suite 502, Honolulu, HI 96815, 808/924-0266. For online information, see www.visit-oahu.com.

## Post Offices

There are over a dozen post offices in Honolulu, and one in each of the major towns on the island. The main post office in downtown Honolulu is at 3600 Aolele St.; it has window hours weekdays 7:30 A.M.–8:30 P.M. In Waikiki, the post office is at 330 Saratoga Road; in Kailua, at 335 Hahani St.; in Wai'anae, at 86-014 Farrington Hwy.; in Hale'iwa, at 66-437 Kamehameha Hwy.; and in Wahiawa, at 115 Lehua St.

## Reading Material

Besides special-interest Chinese, Japanese, Korean, Filipino, and military newspapers, two major dailies are published on O'ahu. The *Honolulu Advertiser* is the morning paper, and the *Honolulu Star Bulletin* is the evening paper. They combine to make a Sunday paper. On Friday, the Advertiser runs a TGIF entertainment and arts section that's great for finding out what's happening around town. The alternative free press *Honolulu Weekly* adds a different perspective to the mix. Aside from feature articles on pertinent local issues, it does a calendar of local arts and events. Free tabloids like the *Waikiki Beach Press* and *Waikiki News* offer entertainment calendars and feature stories of general interest to visitors. Other weekly or monthly free papers that you might see around the island include the *Downtown Planet, Oahu Island News,* the *Midweek Islander* with emphasis on the Windward Coast, the *North Shore News,* and the *Ka Leo O Hawai'i,* the University of Hawai'i at Manoa campus newspaper.

Don't miss out on the **free tourist literature** available at all major hotels, shopping malls, the airport, and stands along Waikiki's streets. They all contain up-to-the-minute information on what's happening, and a treasure trove of free or reduced-price coupons for various attractions and services. Always featured are events, shopping tips, dining and entertainment, and sightseeing. The main ones are: *This Week Oahu,* the best and most complete; *Spotlights Oahu Gold,* with good sections on dining and sightseeing. Heavy on sightseeing spots, **101 Things To Do: Oahu** also has maps, advertising, and some coupons. *Oahu Drive Guide,* handed out by all the major car rental agencies, has some excellent tips and orientation maps. Especially useful to get you started from the airport.

There are 23 public libraries on O'ahu, and these include: Hawaii State Library, next to 'Iolani Palace in Honolulu at 478 S. King St., 808/586-3500; Kailua Library, 239 Ku'ulei Road, 808/266-9911; Waikiki-Kapahulu Library, at 400 Kapahulu, 808/733-8488. Business hours for each library differ, so check with the one you want to visit. Brochures listing hours and other general information are available at all libraries.

## Island Facts

O'ahu's nickname is "The Gathering Place." Its color is yellow, the island flower is the *'ilima,* and the island lei is strung from its bold blossoms. At 597 square miles, O'ahu follows Hawai'i and Maui in size and has nearly the same area as Kaua'i.

# Honolulu

Honolulu is the most exotic city in the United States. It's not any one attribute that makes this so; it's a combination of things. Honolulu's like an ancient Hawaiian goddess who can change her form at will. At one moment you see a black-eyed beauty, swaying provocatively to a deep and basic rhythm, and in the next a high-tech scion of the computer age sitting straight-backed behind a polished desk. The city is the terminus of "manifest destiny," the end of America's relentless westward drive, until no more horizons were left. Other Mainland cities are undoubtedly more historic, cultural, and perhaps, to some, more beautiful than Honolulu, but none come close to having all of these features in the same overwhelming combination. The city's face, although blemished by high-rises and pocked by heavy industry, is eternally lovely. The Koʻolau Moun-

tains form the background tapestry from which the city emerges; the surf gently foams along Waikiki; the sun hisses fire-red as it drops into the sea, and Diamond Head beckons with a promise of tropical romance.

In the center of the city, skyscrapers rise as silent, unshakable witnesses to Honolulu's economic strength. In glass and steel offices, businesspeople wearing conservative three-piece uniforms are clones of any found on Wall Street. Below, a fantasia of people live and work. In nooks and crannies is an amazing array of arts, shops, and cuisines. In a flash of festival the streets become China, Japan, Portugal, New England, old Hawaii, or the Philippines.

New England churches, a royal Hawaiian palace, bandstands, tall-masted ships, and the narrow streets of Chinatown illustrate Hono-

ROBERT NILSEN

ʻIolani Palace

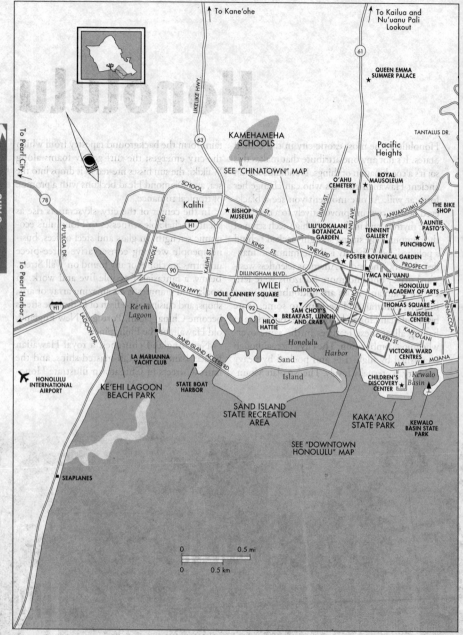

To Kane'ohe

To Kailua and
Nu'uanu Pali
Lookout

61

QUEEN EMMA
SUMMER PALACE ★

TANTALUS DR.

LIKELIKE HWY.

KAMEHAMEHA
SCHOOLS

SEE "CHINATOWN" MAP

Pacific
Heights

O'AHU
CEMETERY ★

ROYAL
MAUSOLEUM ★

SCHOOL ST.

ANUAIOUMU ST.

To Pearl City

THE BIKE
SHOP ★

78

Kalihi

★ BISHOP
MUSEUM

BISHOP ST.

LILI'UOKALANI
BOTANICAL
GARDEN

NU'UANU AVE.

TENNENT
GALLERY ★

AUNTIE
PASTO'S ★

H1

KING ST.

VINEYARD

FOSTER BOTANICAL GARDEN

PUNCHBOWL ★

PROSPECT

PU'ULOA DR.

MIDDLE RD.

KALIHI ST.

90

DILLINGHAM BLVD.

YMCA NU'UANU ★

To Pearl Harbor

NIMITZ HWY.

IWILEI

Chinatown

HONOLULU
ACADEMY OF ARTS ★

H1

LAGOON DR.

Ke'ehi
Lagoon

DOLE CANNERY SQUARE

BISHOP ST.

THOMAS SQUARE ★

PENSACOLA

92

SAM CHOY'S
BREAKFAST, LUNCH,
AND CRAB ★

BLAISDELL
CENTER ★

SAND ISLAND ACCESS RD.

HILO
HATTIE ★

Honolulu
Harbor

QUEEN ST.

KAPI'OLANI

LA MARIANNA
YACHT CLUB ●

Sand
Island

VICTORIA WARD
CENTRES

MOANA

HONOLULU
INTERNATIONAL
AIRPORT ✈

STATE BOAT
HARBOR ●

CHILDREN'S
DISCOVERY
CENTER ★

ALA

Kewalo
Basin

KE'EHI LAGOON
BEACH PARK

SAND ISLAND
STATE RECREATION
AREA

KAKA'AKO
STATE PARK

KEWALO
BASIN STATE
PARK

SEE "DOWNTOWN
HONOLULU" MAP

■ SEAPLANES

0        0.5 mi

0        0.5 km

O'AHU

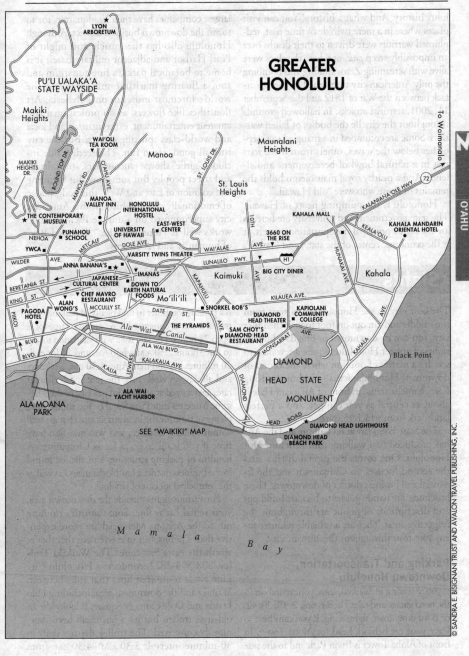

# GREATER HONOLULU

LYON ARBORETUM

PU'U UALAKA'A STATE WAYSIDE

Makiki Heights

MAKIKI HEIGHTS DR.

ROUND TOP DR.

WAI'OLI TEA ROOM

Manoa

O'AHU AVE.

MANOA RD.

ST. LOUIS DR.

Maunalani Heights

To Waimanalo

72

THE CONTEMPORARY MUSEUM

NEHOA

PUNAHOU SCHOOL

MANOA VALLEY INN

HONOLULU INTERNATIONAL HOSTEL

UNIVERSITY OF HAWAII

EAST-WEST CENTER

METCALF

DOLE AVE.

St. Louis Heights

KALANIANA'OLE HWY

KAHALA MALL

KEALA'OLU

KAHALA MANDARIN ORIENTAL HOTEL

YWCA

WILDER AVE.

BERETANIA ST.

KING ST.

ANNA BANANA'S

JAPANESE CULTURAL CENTER

CHEF MAVRO RESTAURANT

ALAN WONG'S

IMANAS

DOWN TO EARTH NATURAL FOODS

MCCULLY ST.

VARSITY TWINS THEATER

WAI'ALAE

LUNALILO FWY.

H1

Kaimuki

10TH AVE.

AVE.

KAPAHULU

KILAUEA AVE.

3660 ON THE RISE

BIG CITY DINER

HUNAKAI AVE.

KAHALA AVE.

Kahala

Black Point

PAGODA HOTEL

PIIKOI

BLVD.

BLVD.

Ala Wai Canal

DATE ST.

THE PYRAMIDS

SNORKEL BOB'S

SAM CHOY'S DIAMOND HEAD RESTAURANT

DIAMOND HEAD THEATER

KAPIOLANI COMMUNITY COLLEGE

ALA WAI BLVD.

KALAKAUA AVE.

KALIA

LEWERS

ALA WAI YACHT HARBOR

ALA MOANA PARK

MONSARRAT AVE.

DIAMOND HEAD ROAD

DIAMOND HEAD STATE MONUMENT

SEE "WAIKIKI" MAP

DIAMOND HEAD LIGHTHOUSE

DIAMOND HEAD BEACH PARK

M a m a l a    B a y

Mo'ili'ili

O'AHU

lulu's history. And what a history! You can visit places where in a mere twinkle of time past, red-plumed warriors were driven to their deaths over an impossibly steep *pali,* or where the skies were alive with screaming Zeros strafing and bombing the only American city threatened by foreign attack between the War of 1812 and the September 11, 2001, terrorist attacks. In hallowed grounds throughout the city lie the bodies of fallen warriors. Some are entombed in a mangled steel sepulcher below the waves, others from three wars rest in a natural bowl of bereavement and silence. And a nearby royal mausoleum holds the remains of those who were "old Hawaii."

Honolulu is the pumping heart of Hawaii. The state government and university are here, as are the state's principal transportation centers. It is the economic center of the state, and Hawaii's largest companies have their headquarters toe to toe in the downtown business district. Although Honolulu also has the muscle and might of Pearl Harbor and adjacent military bases, it is home to botanical parks, a fine aquarium and zoo, a floating maritime museum, and the world's foremost museum on Polynesia. Art flourishes like flowers, as do professional and amateur entertainment, extravaganzas, and local and world-class sporting events. But the city isn't all good, clean fun. The seedier side includes "girlie" shows, raucous bars, street drugs, and street people. But somehow this blending and collision of East and West, this hodgepodge of emotionally charged history, this American city superimposed on a unique Pacific setting works well as Honolulu, the "Sheltered Bay" of humanity and its dreams.

## Sights

The best way to see Honolulu is to start from the middle and fan out on foot to visit the inner city. You can *do* downtown in one day, but the sights of greater Honolulu require a few days to see. It's a matter of opinion where the center of downtown Honolulu actually is, but the King Kamehameha statue in front of Ali'iolani Hale is about as central as you can get, and a perfect landmark from which to start.

The State Foundation on Culture and the Arts has produced two walking-tour brochures for Honolulu. One covers the capital district, and the second focuses on Chinatown and the financial and business district of downtown. These brochures are handy guides to historic buildings and descriptions of public art throughout the respective areas. They are a valuable resource for any foot tour throughout this historic city.

### Parking and Transportation, Downtown Honolulu

If you're staying in Waikiki, leave your rental car in the hotel garage and take TheBus nos. 2, 19, 20, 42, or B for downtown sightseeing. If you can't bear to leave your car behind, head for Aloha Tower. In front of Aloha Tower is Irwin Park and to the side is a parking lot. Enter to find plenty of parking. The traffic is not as congested here, and the large lot is open 24 hours. The rate is $2 with validation for up to three hours 7:30 A.M.–4:30 P.M. and $1 for each 20 minutes beyond that. After 4:30 P.M. weekdays and all day on weekends, the rate is $2. Similar rates are charged at another lot just east of the Maritime Museum near Piers 5 and 6. You should have plenty of time for the local attractions that are well within walking distance, and you may also have time if you want to go as far as Chinatown. A handful of parking structures can also be found in the business district a few blocks inland as well as the municipal lot east of city hall.

For various sights outside the downtown area, your rental car is fine. Some shuttles running out to the Arizona Memorial are more expensive than TheBus, but so convenient that they're worth the extra few coins. The **Waikiki Trolley,** 808/593-2822, conducts a Honolulu City Line circle route (red line) that runs between Waikiki and the downtown area, including Hilo Hattie and Dole Cannery Square. It looks like an old-style trolley, but it's a bus that's been ingeniously converted. The trolley departs daily at 30-minute intervals 8:30 A.M.–4:30 P.M. from

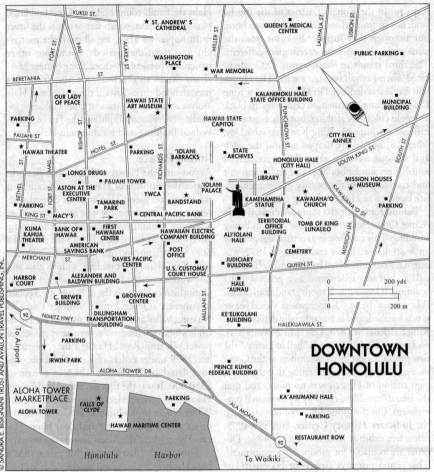

the Royal Hawaiian Shopping Center. You can get off and on at any of the 25 stops along the way or ride along for the entire two-hour trip at $20 adults or $10 children for the entire day.

## THE CAPITOL DISTRICT

The **Statue of King Kamehameha** is at the junction of King and Mililani Streets. Running off at an angle is Merchant Street, the oldest thoroughfare in Honolulu, and you might say it's "the beginning of the road to modernity." The

statue is much more symbolic of Kamehameha's strength as a ruler and unifier of the Hawaiian Islands than as a replica of the man himself. Of the few drawings of Kamehameha that have been preserved, none is necessarily a good likeness. Kamehameha was a magnificent leader and statesman, but by all accounts not very good-looking. This statue is one of three. The original, lost at sea near the Falkland Islands en route from Paris where it was bronzed, was later recovered, but not before insurance money was used to cast this second one. The original is in the town of

Kapaʻau, in the Kohala District of the Big Island, not far from where Kamehameha was born, but although they supposedly came from the same mold, they somehow seem quite different. The third stands in Washington, D.C., dedicated when Hawaii became a state. The Honolulu statue was dedicated in 1883, as part of King David Kalakaua's coronation ceremony. Its black and gold colors are striking, but it is most magnificent on June 11, King Kamehameha Day, when 18-foot lei are draped around the neck and the outstretched arms. More recently, a fourth, very similar but not exact replica was cast and erected below the county government office building in Hilo on the Big Island.

Behind Kamehameha stands **Aliʻiolani Hale** (Chief Onto Heaven), now the State Judiciary Building. This handsome structure, designed by an Australian architect and begun in 1872, was originally commissioned by Kamehameha V as a palace, but was redesigned as a general court building. It looks much more grand than ʻIolani Palace across the way. Kamehameha V died before it was finished, and it was officially dedicated by King Kalakaua in 1874. Less than 20 years later, on January 17, 1893, at this "hall of justice," the first proclamation by the Members of the Committee of Safety was read, stating that the sovereign nation of Hawaii was no more, and that the islands would be ruled by a provisional government. On the ground floor of this building, the **Judiciary History Center,** 808/539-4999, offers free exhibits weekdays 9 A.M.–4 P.M. Docents are available for groups by appointment. This center portrays aspects of Hawaiian law from the traditional *kapu* system through the introduction of Western legal codes to the present legal system. In addition, the center theater shows a 10-minute video on land law in Hawaii, there's a refurbished courtroom from the territorial period, and a special exhibition presents aspects of martial law instituted following the bombing of Pearl Harbor during World War II.

Next door to the east is the **Territorial Office Building,** which is home to several state department offices, and on the west side is the downtown **post office.** To their rear are the old **U.S. Customs and Court House** and **Kapuaiwa**

**Hale,** the family courts building. These buildings, plus **Hale ʻAuhau,** which stands across the street from Kapuaiwa Hale, are all from the monarchy and territorial periods. Numerous other structures, particularly those along or near Merchant Street to the west, are also from this prestatehood time. Toward the water from Hale ʻAuhau are newer government office buildings, including Keʻelikolani Building, the Prince Kuhio Federal Building, and Kaʻahumanu Hale.

## ʻIolani Palace

As you enter the 11-acre parklike palace grounds, notice the emblem of Hawaii in the center of the large iron gates. They're often draped with simple lei of fragrant *maile.* The quiet grounds are a favorite strolling and relaxing place for many government workers, especially in the shade of a huge banyan, purportedly planted by Kalakaua's wife, Kapiʻolani. The building, with its glass and ironwork imported from San Francisco and its Corinthian columns, is the only true royal palace in America. (Queen Emma Summer Palace in Nuʻuanu Valley and Huliheʻe Palace on the Big Island, while royal residences, were never the seat of power.) ʻIolani (Royal Hawk) Palace, begun in late 1879 under orders of King Kalakaua, was completed in December 1882 at a cost of $350,000. It was the first electrified building in Honolulu, having electricity even before the White House in Washington D.C., and it had a direct phone line to the Royal Boat House, located near where the Aloha Tower stands today.

Through the first floor of this palace runs a broad hallway with a grand stairway that leads to the second story. On the east side of the building is the large and opulent Throne Room, the scene of formal meetings and major royal functions. On the west side are the smaller Blue Room, an informal reception area, and the dining room. The upstairs level was the private residence of the king and his family. It also has a wide hallway and on each side are bedrooms, sitting rooms, a music room, and office. The basement held servants' quarters, the kitchen, and offices of certain government officials.

Non-Hawaiian Island residents of the day thought it a frivolous waste of money, but here poignant scenes and profound changes rocked the Hawaiian Islands. After nine years as king, Kalakaua built a Coronation Stand that originally stood directly in front of the palace but was later moved to the left where you see it today. In a belated ceremony, Kalakaua raised a crown to his head and placed one on his queen, Kapi'olani. During the ceremony, 8,000 Hawaiians cheered, while Honolulu's foreign, tax-paying businessmen boycotted. On August 12, 1898, after only two Hawaiian monarchs, Kalakaua and Lili'uokalani (his sister), had resided in the palace, the American flag was raised up the flagpole following a successful coup that marked Hawaii's official recognition by the United States as a territory. During this ceremony, loyal Hawaiian subjects wept bitter tears, while the businessmen of Honolulu cheered wildly. On the far side of the approach path is a raised earthen platform, the original site of the royal mausoleum, which was later moved out along the Pali Highway.

Kalakaua, later in his rule, was forced to sign a new constitution that greatly reduced his own power to little more than figurehead status. He traveled to San Francisco in 1891, where he died. His body was returned to Honolulu and lay in state in the palace. His sister, Lili'uokalani, succeeded him; she attempted to change this constitution and gain the old power of Hawaii's sovereigns, but the businessmen revolted and the monarchy fell. 'Iolani Palace then became the main executive building for the provisional government, with the House of Representatives meeting in the throne room and the Senate in the dining room. It served in this capacity until 1968. It has since been elevated to a state monument and National Historical Landmark.

'Iolani Palace is open to 45-minute guided tours only, starting every 30 minutes Tues.–Sat. 9 A.M.–2 P.M.; $20 adults, $15 *kama'aina*, $5 children 5–12, with no children under five admitted. The palace is open the same hours on the first Sunday of every month for free admission to *kama'aina*; other visitors are charged the regular fees. These tours are popular, so make reservations at least a day in advance. The **'Iolani Palace Gallery,** in the basement of the palace, is also open to visitors, but on a self-guided basis.

This gallery contains the Hawaiian crown jewels and other royal accouterments. No reservations are needed to view this site, which is open 9 A.M.–4 P.M. on days that the palace is open. The cost of viewing the galleries is $10 adults, $5 children 5–17. Tickets are sold at a window at the 'Iolani Barracks, behind the Royal Bandstand, open Tues.–Sat. 8 A.M.–3:30 P.M. Also in the barracks, the palace gift and book shop is open Tues.–Sat. 8:30 A.M.–3:30 P.M. For information and reservations, call 808/522-0832 or go online to http://openstudio.hawaii.edu/iolani.

## Palace Grounds

Kalakaua, known as the "Merrie Monarch," was credited with saving the hula. He also hired Henry Berger, first Royal Hawaiian Bandmaster, and together they wrote "Hawaii Pono," the state anthem. Many concerts were given from the Coronation Stand, which became known as the **Royal Bandstand.** Behind it is **'Iolani Barracks** (Hale Koa), built in 1870 to house the Royal Household Guards. When the monarchy of Hawaii fell to provisional government forces in 1893, only one of these soldiers was wounded in the nearly bloodless confrontation. The barracks were moved to the present site in 1965 from nearby land on which the State Capitol was erected.

To the right behind the palace are the **State Archives,** 808/586-0329. This modern building, dating from 1953, holds records, documents, and vintage photos. A treasure trove to scholars and those tracing their genealogy, it is worth a visit by the general public to view the old photos on display. Open Mon.–Fri. 9 A.M.–4 P.M.; free. Next door is the **Hawaii State Library,** housing the main branch of this statewide system. The central courtyard is a favorite lunch spot for government workers. Some of the original money to build the library was put up by Andrew Carnegie. This main library branch is open Mon., Fri., and Sat. 9 A.M.–5 P.M., Wed. 10 A.M.–5 P.M., and Tues. and Thurs. 9 A.M.–8 P.M.; for information, call 808/586-3500.

## Government Buildings

Lili'uokalani was deposed and placed under house

arrest in one room of the second floor of the palace for nine months. Later, after much intrigue that included a visit to Washington, D.C., to plead her case and an aborted counterrevolution, she sadly accepted her fate and moved to nearby **Washington Place.** This solid-looking structure fronts Beretania Street and was originally the home of sea captain John Dominis. It was inherited by his son John Owen Dominis, who married a lovely young Hawaiian aristocrat, Lydia Kapaʻakea, who became Queen Liliʻuokalani. She lived in her husband's home, proud but powerless, until her death in 1917. Washington Place was the official residence of governors of Hawaii until 2003, when a new governor's mansion was built behind it. Following renovation, Washington Place is slated to be opened to the public for tours.

To the right of Washington Place is the eternal flame **War Memorial.** Erected in 1974, this memorial replaced an older one and is dedicated to the people who perished in World War II. An approach walk and benches are provided for quiet meditation.

Directly behind ʻIolani Palace is the magnificent **Hawaii State Capitol,** built in 1969 for $25 million. The building is a metaphor for Hawaii: the pillars surrounding it are palms, the reflecting pool is the sea, and the cone-shaped rooms of the Legislature represent the volcanoes of Hawaii. It's lined with rich koa wood from the Big Island and is further graced with woven hangings and murals, with two gigantic, four-ton replicas of the State Seal hanging at both entrances. The inner courtyard has a 600,000-tile mosaic, *Aquarius,* rendered by island artist Tadashi Sato. Standing at the *mauka* entrance to the building is a poignant sculpture of *Father Damien,* while the statue *The Spirit of Liliʻuokalani* fronts the building on the ocean side. The State Legislature is in session Jan.–Mar., and opens with dancing, music, and festivities at 10 A.M. on the third Wednesday in January, public invited. Peek inside, then take the elevator to the fifth floor for outstanding views of the city.

Across Punchbowl Street to the east is the Kalanimoku Hale state office building and to its front at the corner of S. King Street stands **Honolulu**

**Hale,** Honolulu City Hall. Built in 1928, with annex additions in 1951, this office building is open 7:45 A.M.–4:30 P.M. weekdays and houses the office of the mayor, the city council, and a few city departments. It too has a courtyard where music, art, and other public events are held. Beyond is the newer Honolulu Municipal Building.

## Cathedrals

To the left of Washington Place is **St. Andrew's Cathedral.** Construction started in 1867 as an Anglican church but wasn't really finished until the late 1950s. Many of its stones and ornaments were shipped from England, and its stained-glass windows and bell tower are of particular interest. Hawaii's monarchs worshiped here, and the church is still very much in use. Open Mon.–Fri. 6 A.M.–6 P.M.; a free guided tour is offered following the 10 A.M. Sunday service.

A few steps away at Bishop Street and N. Beretania is the **Cathedral of Our Lady of Peace.** Constructed in 1843 of plastered coral blocks, this structure was Hawaii's first Roman Catholic church. Although the building has gone through numerous renovations, it has remained in continuous use.

## Kawaiahaʻo Church

This church, so instrumental in Hawaii's history, is the most enduring symbol of the original missionary work in the islands. A sign welcomes you and bids the blessing, "Grace and peace to you from God our Father." Hawaiian-language services are given here every Sunday, along with English-language services. The church was constructed 1837–1842 according to plans drawn up by Hiram Bingham, its minister, and is the oldest permanent church structure in Honolulu. Before this, at least four grass shacks of increasing size stood here. One was destroyed by a sailor who was reprimanded by Reverend Bingham for attending services while drunk; the old sea dog returned the next day and burned the church to the ground. Kawaiahaʻo (Water of Hao) Church is constructed from more than 14,000 coral blocks quarried from offshore reefs. In 1843, following Restoration Day, when the British returned the Hawaiian Islands to sovereignty after a brief pe-

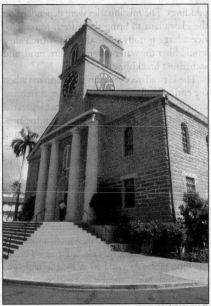

ROBERT NILSEN

**Kawaiahaʻo Church**

riod of imperialism by a renegade captain, King Kamehameha III uttered here the profound words in a thanksgiving ceremony that were destined to become Hawaii's motto, *"Ua mau ke ea o ka ʻaina i ka pono"* ("The life of the land is preserved in righteousness").

Other noteworthy ceremonies held at the church were the marriage of King Liholiho and his wife Queen Emma, who bore the last child born to a Hawaiian monarch. Unfortunately, little Prince Albert died at the age of four. On June 19, 1856, Lunalilo, the first king elected to the throne, took his oath of office in the church. A bachelor who died childless, he always felt scorned by living members of the Kamehameha clan and refused to be buried with them at the Royal Mausoleum in Nuʻuanu Valley; he is buried in a tomb at the front of the church. Buried along with him is his father, Charles Kanaʻina, and nearby lies the grave of his mother, Miriam Kekauluohi. In the graveyard at the rear of the church lies Henry Berger and many members of the Parker, Green, Brown, and Cooke families,

early missionaries to the islands. In fact, the names on the headstones here read like a veritable who's who of early missionaries, and most are recognizable as important and influential people in 19th-century Hawaiian history. Queen Liliʻuokalani's body lay in state in the church before it was taken to the Royal Mausoleum. A jubilation service was held in the church when Hawaii became a state in 1959. Kawaiahaʻo holds beautiful Christmas services with a strong Polynesian and Hawaiian flavor. Hidden away in a corner of the grounds is an unobtrusive adobe building, remains of a schoolhouse built in 1835 to educate Hawaiian children.

## MISSION HOUSES MUSEUM

The days when tall ships with tattered sails crewed by rough seamen bore God-fearing missionary families dedicated to Christianizing the savage islands are alive in the halls and buildings of the Mission Houses Museum, 553 S. King St., Honolulu, HI 96813, 808/531-0481, www.lava.net/~mhm, now a registered National Historical Landmark. Set behind Kawaiahaʻo Church, the complex includes two main houses, a printing house annex, a research library, and a fine gift shop. It's operated by the nonprofit Hawaiian Mission Children's Society, whose members serve as guides and hosts. Many are direct descendants, or spouses of descendants, of the Congregationalist missionaries who built these structures. One-hour guided tours are offered Tues.–Sat. at 10 A.M., 11:15 A.M., 1 P.M., and 2:45 P.M.; admission is $10 adults, $8 *kamaʻaina,* military, and seniors, $6 students six and older.

### Construction

If you think that precut modular housing is a new concept, think again. The first structure that you enter is the **Frame House,** the oldest wooden structure in Hawaii. Precut in Boston, it came along with the first missionary packet in 1819. Since the interior frame was left behind and didn't arrive until Christmas Day, 1820, the missionary families lived in thatched huts until it was erected. Finally the Chamberlain family occupied it in 1821. Many missionary families used it over the years, with as many as four households occupying this small structure at the same time. This is where the Christianizing of Hawaii truly began. This structure was renovated in 1996, and most artifacts and furniture are from the 1820–1860 period, with some reproductions.

The missionaries, being New Englanders, first dug a cellar. The Hawaiians were suspicious of the strange hole, convinced that the missionaries planned to store guns and arms in this "fort." Although assured to the contrary, King Liholiho, anxious to save face and prove his omnipotence, had a cellar dug near his home twice as deep and large. This satisfied everyone.

Notice the different styles, sizes, and colors of bricks used in the structures. Most of the ships of the day carried bricks as ballast. After unloading cargo, the captains either donated or sold the bricks to the missionaries, who incorporated them into the buildings. A common local material was coral stone: pulverized coral was burned with lime to make a rudimentary cement, which was then used to bind cut-coral blocks. The pit that was used for this purpose is still discernible on the grounds.

## Kitchen

The natives were intrigued with the missionaries, whom they called "long necks" because of their high collars. The missionaries, on the other hand, were a little more wary of their "charges." The low fence around the complex was symbolic as well as utilitarian. The missionaries were obsessed with keeping their children away from Hawaiian children, who at first ran around naked and played many games with overt sexual overtones. Almost every evening a small cadre of Hawaiians would assemble to peer into the kitchen to watch the women cook, which they found exceedingly strange because their *kapu* said that *men* did the cooking. In the kitchen, actually an attached cookhouse, the wood-burning stove kept breaking down. More often than not, the women used the fireplace with its built-in oven. About once a week, they fired up the oven to make traditional New England staples like bread, pies, cakes, and puddings. The missionaries were dependent on the Hawaiians to bring them fresh water. Notice a large porous stone through which they would filter the water to remove dirt, mud, and sometimes brackishness.

The Hawaiians were even more amazed when the entire family sat down to dinner, a tremendous deviation from their beliefs that separated men and women when eating. When the missionaries assembled to dine or meet at the "long table," the Hawaiians silently stood at the open door to watch the evening soap opera. The unnerved missionaries eventually closed the door and cut two windows into the wall, which they could leave opened but draped. The long table took on further significance. The one you see is a replica. When different missionaries left the islands, they, like people today, wanted a souvenir. For some odd reason, they elected to saw a bit off the long table. As years went by, the table got shorter and shorter until it was useless.

## Residents

Originally housing four families, the house was made a duplex in 1824 and into a home for one family in 1851. Although many families lived in it, two of the best known were the Binghams and the Judds. Much of the furniture here was theirs. Judd, a member of the third missionary company, assumed the duties of physician to all the missionaries and islanders. He often prescribed alcohol of different sorts to the missionary families for a wide variety of ailments; many records remain of these prescriptions, but not one record of complaints from his patients. The Binghams and Judds got along very well and entertained each other and visitors, most often in the Judds' parlor because they were a little better off. The women would often congregate here to do their sewing, which was in great demand, especially by members of the royal household. Until the missionary women taught island girls to sew, providing clothing for Hawaii's royalty was a tiresome and time-consuming obligation.

The missionaries were self-sufficient and had the unbounded energy of youth, as the average age was only 25. The husbands often built furniture for their families. Reverend Bingham, a good craftsman, was pressed by Queen Ka'ahumanu to build her a rocking chair after she became enamored of one made for Mrs. Bingham. The queen weighed almost 400 pounds, so building her a suitable chair was no small feat! Still, the queen could only use it in her later years when she'd lost a considerable amount of weight. After she died, the Binghams asked for it to be returned, and it sits in their section of the house. Compare Bingham's chair to another in the Judds' bedroom, jury-rigged by a young missionary husband from a captain's chair. An understatement, found later in his diary, confirmed that the young man was not a carpenter.

When you enter the Judds' bedroom, note how small it is, and consider that two adults and five children slept here. As soon as the children were old enough, they were sent back to the Mainland for schooling, no doubt to relieve some of the congestion. Also notice that the windows were fixed, in the New England style, and imagine how close it must have been in these rooms. The Binghams' bedroom is also small, and not as well furnished. Bingham's shaving kit remains and is inscribed with "The Sandwich Isles." In the bedroom of Mary Ward, a missionary woman who never married, the roof was raised to accommodate her canopy bed.

Another famous family that lived in the complex was the Cookes. When the missionary board withdrew its support, the Cookes petitioned them to buy the duplex, which was granted. Shortly thereafter, Mr. Cooke, who had been a teacher, formed a partnership with one Mr. Castle, and from that time forward Castle and Cooke grew to become one of Hawaii's oldest and most powerful corporations.

## Chamberlain House

The largest building in the compound is the coral-block Chamberlain House. This barnlike structure was completed in 1831 and used as a warehouse and living quarters for Levi Chamberlain's family. Chamberlain was the accountant and business agent for the mission, so goods for all mission stations in the islands were stored in most of the structure, while the family occupied three modest rooms.

Exhibits are shown on the second floor. This building went through extensive renovation inside and out in 2002.

## Printing House

The missionaries decided almost immediately that the best way to convert the natives was to speak to them in their own language and to create a written Hawaiian language that they would teach in school. To this end, they created the **Hawaiian alphabet,** consisting of 12 letters, with five vowels and seven consonants. In addition, to disseminate the doctrines of Christianity, they needed books, and therefore a printing press. On the grounds still stands the Printing House, built in 1841 but first used as annex bedrooms of the Frame House by the Hall family. The original printing house, built in 1823, was located across the street and no longer exists. In the Printing House is a replica of the Ramage press brought from New England, first operated by Elisha Loomis. He returned to the Mainland when he was 28 and soon died of tuberculosis, but not before he had earned the distinction of being the first printer west of the Rockies. Here were printed biblical tracts, textbooks, and anything that the king or passing captains were willing to pay to have printed. Although it took eight hours of hard work to set up one page to be printed, it is estimated that in the 20 years the press operated under the missionaries, more than seven million pages were produced.

## Gift Shop

While you're on the grounds, be sure to visit the bookstore and gift shop; open 9 A.M.–4:15 P.M. It's small but has an excellent collection of Hawaiiana, some inexpensive but quality items, and an outstanding collection of Ni'ihau shellwork, considered the finest in Hawaii. The shelves hold tasteful items like wood carvings, bread boards, tapa bookmarks, hats, weavings, chimes, flags of old Hawaii, and stuffed pillows with classic Hawaiian quilt motifs, as well as a good collection of Hawaiian dolls, for kids and adults. Between the bookstore and the research library are restrooms.

## Special Programs

Along with other programs, the museum hosts a Kama'aina Day program, with volunteers dressed in fashions of the period, who assume the roles of missionaries in 1830s Honolulu. Feel free to interact and ask questions, but remember that they stay in character, so the answers may surprise you. This program is usually offered on the last Saturday of the month, 9 A.M.–4 P.M., regular admission except for *kama'aina,* who get in for half price. Other special programs are also offered, like a candlelight Christmas affair, crafts and quilt fairs, and quilt classes; call 808/924-1911 for details. Also, consider the historic walking tour offered by the museum, which guides you through downtown Honolulu, hitting all the historic sights with an extremely knowledgeable narration by one of the museum's guides. The walking tour is conducted on Thursday only 9:45 A.M.–12:45 P.M.; reserve one day in advance. The cost is $15, or $10 plus the entrance to the mission houses if you want the tour there as well. For anyone wanting to delve into the history of the mission, the reference library is open Tues.–Fri. 10 A.M.–4 P.M.

# HONOLULU HARBOR AREA

## Hawaii Maritime Center

The development of this center was a wonderful concept whose time finally came. It's amazing that a state and former nation, whose discovery and birth are so intimately tied to the exploration, navigation, and exploitation of the sea, had never had a center dedicated exclusively to these profoundly important aspects of its heritage. Now the Hawaii Maritime Center, at Pier 7 across from the Aloha Tower Marketplace in Honolulu Harbor, 808/536-6373, is exactly that. Open since 1989, the center consists of three attractions: the Maritime Center building with displays of Hawaii's past; the classic, and last remaining, fully rigged, four-masted *Falls of Clyde* floating museum; and the reproduction of a Hawaiian sailing canoe, the *Hokule'a,* which has sailed back in time using ancient navigational methods to retrace the steps of Hawaii's Polynesian explorers. Take TheBus no. 19 or 20 or the Waikiki Trolley from Waikiki. Admission for all attractions is $7.50 adults, $4.50 children 4–12, and free for younger kids; open 8:30 A.M.–8 P.M. every day except Christmas. Admission includes a 48-minute taped tour that guides you through the museum. Don't just walk past or save this for last because it explains the exhibits and gives insight into what you're seeing. Also, stop in at the gift shop for a collectible of Hawaii's vintage past.

The main building of the center is the two-story museum. Upon entering you find a glass case filled with trophies and memorabilia from the days of King Kalakaua. His words have a sadly prophetic ring. "Remember who you are. Be gracious, but never forget from whence you came for this is where your heart is. This is the cradle of your life." Notice the phones installed throughout the capital in 1887, a few years before California had electricity. Kalakaua had previously installed telephones between his boathouse and the palace in 1878, just two years after Bell's invention. The bottom floor of the center recalls ancient fishing methods and the traditional division of land and sea resources among the people. Another fascinating display traces the development of surfing through the ages, from original boards—more like seagoing canoes at 18 feet long—until the modern debut of the fiberglass board. You can spot a vintage album of *Surfin' Safari* by the Beach Boys.

Here, too, is a land-surfing sled used for games during the Makahiki Festival. Trails to accommodate it were up to one mile long. Built on steep hills, they were paved in stone, layered with earth, and topped with slippery grass. Once launched there was no stopping until the bottom. Yippee! One corner of the museum is dedicated to tattooing, Polynesian and Western. It shows traditional tattoos worn by both men and women, and then how the Western style became more popular because Hawaii was a main berth for sailors, who sported these living souvenirs from around the world. Mail buoys sound uninteresting, but these tidbits of old Hawaiiana are fascinating, and the tradition is still alive today. Passing ships, mainly from Peru and Ecuador, still radio Honolulu Harbor that they are dropping one of these gaily painted metal cans. Someone, anyone, who hears the message fetches it. Inside are little gifts for the finder, who takes the enclosed mail and sends it on its way.

The second floor is dedicated to the discovery of Hawaii, both by the Polynesians and Westerners. Through ledgers, histories, and artifacts, it traces original discovery, Western discovery, the death of Captain Cook, and the role of the sea otter pelt, which brought the first whalers and traders after sandalwood. The whaling section is dripping with blood and human drama. Look at the old harpoons and vintage film footage. Yes, film footage, and photos. A remarkable display is of scrimshaw from the whaling days. Sailors would be at sea 5–7 years and would have untold hours to create beauty in what were dismal conditions. Suspended from the ceiling are replicas of double-hulled sailing canoes and one of only two fully restored skeletons of the humpback whale (this one is in diving position). One corner is a replica of H. Hackfeld and Co., a whaling supply store of the era. The rear of the second floor shows steamships that cruised between Hawaii, Japan, and the East Coast; a nature exhibit of weather, marine life, and volcanoes; and an auditorium with a video on the *Hokule'a*.

Behind the museum is the seafood Pier Seven Restaurant and an area called Kalakaua Park, a garden and observation area perfect for lunch. Eighty-one steps lead to the "crow's nest" and "widow's walk," with great views of the harbor and city.

## Falls of Clyde

This is the last fully rigged, four-masted ship afloat on any of the world's oceans; it has been designated as a National Historic Landmark. She was saved from being scrapped in 1963 by a Seattle bank that was attempting to recoup some money on a bad debt. The people of Hawaii learned of her fate and spontaneously raised money to have the ship towed back to Honolulu Harbor. The *Falls of Clyde* was always a worker, never a pleasure craft. It served the Matson Navigation Company as a cargo and passenger liner from 1898 to 1920. Built in Glasgow, Scotland, in 1878, she was converted in 1906 to a sail-driven tanker; a motor aboard was used

*The Falls of Clyde riding at anchor at the Hawaii Maritime Center*

mainly to move the rigging around. After 1920, she was dismantled and towed to Alaska, becoming little more than a floating oil depot for fishing boats. Since 1968, the *Falls of Clyde* has been a floating museum, sailing the imaginations of children and grownups to times past, and in this capacity has performed perhaps her greatest duty.

## Hokule'a

The newest and perhaps most dynamic feature of the center is the *Hokule'a*. This authentic re-creation of a traditional double-hulled sailing canoe captured the attention of the world when in 1976 it made a 6,000-mile round-trip voyage to Tahiti. It was piloted by Mau Piailug, a Caroline Islander, who used only ancient navigational techniques to guide it successfully on its voyage. This attempt to relive these ancient voyages as closely as possible included eating traditional provisions only—poi, coconuts, dried fish, and bananas. Toward the end of the voyage, some canned food had to be broken out!

ROBERT NILSEN

O'AHU

Modern materials such as plywood and fiberglass were used, but by consulting many petroglyphs and old drawings of these original craft, the design and lines were kept as authentic as possible. The sails, made from a heavy cotton, were the distinctive crab-claw type. In trial runs to work out the kinks and choose the crew, she almost sank in the treacherous channel between O'ahu and Kaua'i and had to be towed in by the Coast Guard. But the *Hokule'a* performed admirably during the actual voyage. The experiment was a resounding technical success, but it was marred by bad feelings between crew members. Both landlubber and sea dog found it impossible to work as a team on the first voyage, thereby mocking the canoe's name, "Star of Gladness." The tension was compounded by the close quarters of more than a dozen men living on an open deck only nine feet wide by 40 feet long. The remarkable navigator Piailug refused to return to Hawaii with the craft and instead sailed back to his native island. Since then, the *Hokule'a* has made six more voyages, including one to distant Rapa Nui, logging more than 90,000 miles, with many ethnically mixed crews who have gotten along admirably.

The *Hokule'a*, owned by the Hawaii Maritime Center but sailed by the Polynesian Voyaging Society, makes Pier 7 its home berth when not at sea. This double-hulled canoe, a replica and much older brother of the significantly larger ones that Captain Cook found so remarkable, will fascinate you, too. This canoe has been joined by another, the *Hawai'iloa*, which also has made a long trip to Polynesia and back. When not at sea, it too is docked at the Hawaii Maritime Center. For more information about the Polynesian Voyaging Society, check its website at http://pvs-hawaii.org.

## Aloha Tower

Next door to the Hawaiian Maritime Center, at Pier 9, is the Aloha Tower, a beacon of hospitality welcoming people to Hawaii for eight decades. When this endearing and enduring tourist cliché was built in 1926 for $160,000, the 184-foot, 10-story tower was the tallest structure on O'ahu. As such, this landmark emblazoned with the greeting and departing word, "Aloha," and with clocks embedded in all four walls, became the symbol of Hawaii. Before the days of air transport, ocean liners would pull up to the pier to disembark passengers, and on these "Boat Days," festive well-wishers from throughout the city would gather to greet and lei the arriving passengers. The Royal Hawaiian Band would even turn out to welcome the guests ashore. Almost as a re-creation of days past, similar "Boat Days" activities are held at the pier when cruise ships arrive for a stop in the islands.

Aloha Tower was originally connected to surrounding buildings. Visitors to the islands entered the huge ground-floor U.S. Customs rooms, which at one time processed droves of passengers coming to find a new life. Today, crowds come to find bargains at the adjacent Aloha Tower Marketplace. When refurbished in 1994, the tower's attached buildings were removed, making the tower stand out with more prominence. Only a few harbormasters on the top floor oversee the comings and goings of cargo ships. The observation area is reached by elevator, which has the dubious distinction of being one of the first elevators in Hawaii. The elevator is a bit like a wheezy old man, huffing and puffing, but it still gets you to the top. Once atop the tower, you get the most remarkable view of the harbor and the city. A high-rise project planned for next door would surely have ruined the view, and due to good sense and citizens with clout, this ill-considered idea thankfully met a timely end. A remarkable feature of the vista is the reflections of the city and the harbor in many of the steel and reflective glass high-rises inland. It's as if a huge mural were painted on them. The tower is open free of charge daily 9 A.M.–5 P.M.

## CHINATOWN

Chinatown has seen ups and downs in the last 150 years, ever since Chinese laborers were lured from Guangdong Province to work as contract laborers on the pineapple and sugar plantations. They didn't need a fortune cookie to tell them there was no future in plantation work, so within a decade of their arrival they had established themselves as merchants, mostly in small retail businesses and restaurants. Chinatown is roughly an area contained by Vinyard Boulevard and Nimitz Highway on the north and south and Bethel Avenue and River Street on the east and west. Twice this area has been flattened by fire, once in 1886 and again in 1900. The 1900 fire was deliberately set to burn out rats that had brought bubonic plague to the city. The fire got out of control and burned down virtually the whole district. Some contended that the fire was allowed to engulf the district in order to decimate the growing economic strength of the Chinese. Chinatown reached its heyday in the 1930s, when it thrived with tourists coming and going from the main port, which was then at the foot of Nuʻuanu Avenue.

Today, Chinatown is a mixed bag of upbeat modernization and run-down sleazy storefronts. Although still strongly Chinese, there are Japanese, Laotians, Vietnamese, Filipinos, and Koreans doing business here as well. The entire district takes only minutes to walk and is a world apart from "tourist" Oʻahu. This is Asia come to life: meat markets with hanging ducks and a host of ethnic Asian foods with their strange aromatic spices all in a few blocks. Crates, live chickens, incredible shops, down-and-outers, tattoo parlors, lei and flower shops, and Buddhist temples, shopkeepers, businesspeople, and hookers all can be found in this quarter. When Hotel Street meets River Street, it all abruptly ends. This is a different Honolulu, a Pacific port and immigrant enclave, crusty and exciting.

Chinatown is relatively safe, especially during the daytime, but at night, particularly along infamous Hotel Street (a cruising ground for prostitutes), you have to be careful. When the sun sinks, the neon lights and the area fires up.

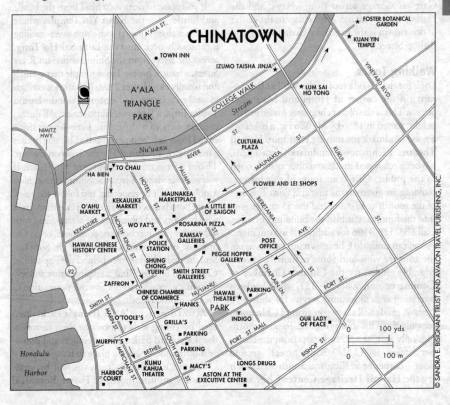

Not many tourists come this way, but walking down Hotel Street is really an adventure in and of itself. If you stay on the main drag, right down the middle, you'll be okay. At Hotel and Mauna Kea Streets you'll find the Honolulu Police Department downtown substation. A lot of nondescript places open to the street like a wound, oozing the odor of stale beer and urine; the section between Nu'uanu and Smith streets seems to be the epicenter. But it's not all down and dirty here. On the periphery of Chinatown there are upscale bars and restaurants and even a few art galleries.

Limited-time street parking is available, but finding a spot is not always easy. You'll have a better chance finding space in a parking structure. Several parking lots and structures are conveniently located along or near Bethel Street: Marks Center Garage, across Pauahi Street from the Hawaii Theatre, Macy's Garage, Chinatown Gateway Garage across from Macy's, and the Harbor Court Garage. A bit closer to the center of downtown is the Executive Center Garage on Bishop Street.

## Walking Tours

Look for the pagoda roof of the **Wo Fat Restaurant** on the corner of Hotel and Maunakea Streets. This is the oldest chop suey house in Honolulu, started in 1886 by Mr. Wo Fat, a baker. It's a good landmark for starting your tour. **Hawaii Theatre,** a Chinatown landmark (circa 1922), has been renovated inside and once again is open to the public. One-hour tours of this historic building are given on the first and third Tuesdays of the month at 11 A.M., and the $5 charge goes into the fund to refurbish the building's exterior. Call 808/528-0506 for additional information.

You can easily do Chinatown on your own, but for another view and some extremely knowledgeable guides, try the **Chinese Chamber of Commerce** tour, 808/533-3181, which has been operating as a community service for almost 30 years. A guide will show you around Chinatown for only $5. This tour is offered Tuesday mornings only at 9:30 A.M. and starts from the chamber office at 42 N. King Street, second floor—corner of S. King and Smith Streets. Or try the **Hawaii Heritage Center** Chinatown Historical and Cultural Walking Tour, which starts from the Ramsay Galleries at 1128 Smith St., every Friday at 9:30 A.M. The two-hour tours are $10 per person, minimum of three for tours to go; call 808/521-2749 for reservations, or write to P.O. Box 37520, Honolulu, HI 96837. An excellent source of general information on Chinatown is the **Hawaii Chinese History Center** at 111 N. King St., 4th Floor.

Another walking tour, but one that goes beyond the confines of Chinatown to take in historical structures in the rest of downtown Honolulu, is that given by the **American Institute of Architects (AIA),** 808/545-4242. This walking tour starts from their office at 119 Merchant Street at 9 A.M. on Tuesdays and Saturdays and returns about noon. The price is $15 per person or $25 per couple, and reservations and prepayment by credit card are necessary.

If you want to clear your head from the hustle and bustle, visit the **Kuan Yin Temple,** where Buddha is always praised with some sweet-smelling incense. Or peek into the **Lum Sai Ho Tong,** across the street from the Shinto shrine on River Street, a basic Chinese Taoist temple that is small and usually closed after 2 P.M. If that's not enough to awaken your spiritual inner self, visit the **Izumo Taisha Jinja,** a Japanese Shinto shrine. All the accouterments of a shrine are here—roof, thick coiled rope, bell, and prayer box. This one houses a male deity. You can tell by the cross on the top. There's a ferroconcrete example of a torii gate. If you've never visited a Japanese Shinto shrine, have a look here, but be respectful and follow the rules. Along both banks of the river are pedestrian malls with benches and tables that are always filled with old-timers playing checkers, dominoes, or *go.* On one side of the river is a statue of Dr. Sun Yat-Sen, the main driving force behind the Republic of China, and Dr. Jose Rizal, a Filipino writer and revolutionary opposed to the Spanish occupation of the Philippine Islands.

Across the river is **'A'ala Triangle Park,** often used by young kids to practice their moves at the skateboard park and by derelicts and down-and-outers looking for a place to hang out.

For peace and quiet, treat yourself by walking a few minutes north to **Foster Botanical**

Garden at 180 N. Vineyard for a glimpse of rare and exotic flora from around the world.

# PALI HIGHWAY

Cutting across O'ahu from Honolulu to Kailua on the windward coast is Route 61, better known as the Pali Highway. Before getting to the famous Nu'uanu Pali Lookout at the very crest of the Ko'olau Mountains, you can spend a full and enjoyable day sightseeing. Stop en route at Punchbowl's National Memorial Cemetery, followed by an optional side trip to the summit of Tantalus for a breathtaking view of the city. Open 7 A.M.–7:45 P.M., Pu'u 'Ualaka'a State Wayside, also known as Round Top, is where Honolulu lies at your feet. Numerous hiking trails cross Tantalus Drive as it circles its way up and then down these mountain ridges. You can also visit the **O'ahu Cemetery** and **Royal Mausoleum State Monument** in the vicinity. Take the H-1 freeway to Vineyard Boulevard (exit 22), cross the Pali Highway to Nu'uanu Avenue, and follow it to the mausoleum. In a minute or two, if you continue up Nu'uanu Avenue, it intersects the Pali Highway. This small chapel, built in 1865 by Kamehameha IV, holds the bodies of most of the royal family who died after 1825. Their bodies were originally interred elsewhere but were later moved here. The mausoleum at one time held 18 royal bodies but became overcrowded, so they were moved again to little crypts scattered around the three-acre grounds. Of the eight Hawaiian monarchs, only King Kamehameha I and King William Lunalilo are buried elsewhere—King Kamehameha I somewhere on the Big Island and Lunalilo at Kawaiaha'o Church. Few tourists visit this serene place, which is open weekdays 8 A.M.–4 P.M. Across Nu'uanu Avenue and down just a bit is the O'ahu Cemetery. Founded in 1844, it hold the graves of some of the oldest and best-known island families.

A short distance up the road is Temple Emmanuel and the Philippine and South Korean consulates. Next comes the Queen Emma Summer Palace and the Dai Jingu Temple, a Baptist college, a Catholic church, and several other churches and temples. It almost seems as though these sects were vying to get farther up the hill to be just a little closer to heaven. A sign, past Queen Emma Summer Palace, points you off to **Nu'uanu Pali Drive.** Take it! This few-minutes' jog off the Pali Highway (which it rejoins) takes you through some wonderful scenery. Immediately the road is canopied with trees, and in less than half a mile there's a bubbling little waterfall and a pool. The homes in here are grand, and the entire area has a parklike effect. One of the nicest little roads that you can take while looking around, this side trip wastes no time at all.

## Queen Emma Summer Palace

Called Hanaiakamalama, this summer home is more the simple hideaway of a well-to-do family than a grand palace. The 3,000-square-foot interior has only two bedrooms and no facilities for guests. John George Lewis put the house on the property in 1848. He purchased the land for $800 from a previous owner by the name of Henry Pierce and then resold it to John Young II. The exterior has a strong New England flavor, and indeed the house was prefabricated in Boston, but it definitely has a neoclassical flourish with its tall, round Doric columns. The simple square home, with a front lanai, was purchased by John Young II, Queen Emma's uncle, in 1850. When he died, she inherited the property and spent many relaxing days here, away from the heat of Honolulu, with her husband King Kamehameha IV. The huge rear room was added in 1869 for a visit by the Duke of Edinburgh. Emma used the home little after 1872, and following her death in 1885 it fell into disrepair.

Rescued from demolition by the Daughters of Hawaii in 1913, it was refurbished and has operated as a museum since 1915. In the 1970s, the Summer Palace was added to the National Register of Historic Sites. The palace, at 2913 Pali Hwy., 808/595-3167, is open daily 9 A.M.–4 P.M., except for major holidays; admission $5 adults, $4 seniors, $1 children 16 and under. Although it's just off the Pali Highway, the one and only sign comes up quickly, and many visitors pass it by. If you pass the entranceway to the O'ahu Country Club just across the road, you've gone too far.

As you enter, notice the tall *kahili,* symbols of noble rank in the entranceway, along with *lau hala* mats on the floor, which at one time were an unsurpassed specialty of Hawaii. Today they must be imported from Fiji or Samoa. The walls are hung with paintings of many of Hawaii's kings and queens, and in every room are distinctive Hawaiian artifacts, such as magnificent feather capes, fans, and tapa hangings. Many of the furnishings belonged to Queen Emma, but others were from other royal family members.

The furnishings have a very strong British influence. The Hawaiian nobility of the time were enamored with the British. King Kamehameha IV traveled to England when he was 15 years old; he met Queen Victoria, and the two became good friends. Emma and Kamehameha IV had the last child born to a Hawaiian king and queen on May 20, 1858. Named Prince Albert after Queen Victoria's consort, he was much loved but died when he was only four years old on August 27, 1862. His father followed him to the grave in little more than a year. The king's brother, Lot Kamehameha, a bachelor, took the throne but died very shortly thereafter, marking the end of the Kamehameha line; after that, Hawaii elected her kings. Prince Albert's canoe-shaped cradle is here, made in Germany by Wilhelm Fisher from four different kinds of Hawaiian wood. His tiny shirts, pants, and boots are still laid out, and there's a lock of his hair, as well as one from Queen Emma. In every room there is royal memorabilia. The royal bedroom (originally the dining room) displays a queen-size bed, covered with an exquisite bedspread or quilt that is changed periodically. In the Cloak Room, originally built as the bedroom but later used as the dining room, is a fine example of a royal feather cloak.

Throughout the house, there's vintage Victorian furniture, a piano built in London by Collard and Collard, and even a stereopticon given as a gift from Napoleon III. A royal cabinet made in Berlin holds porcelains, plates, and cups. After Queen Emma died, it stood in Charles R. Bishop's drawing room but was later returned. In the cellar of the house were the servants' quarters, and the original cookhouse once stood to the side where the paved patio is today. Queen Emma once owned 65 acres of the surrounding land. The two acres that remain are beautifully manicured, and the house is surrounded by shrubbery and trees, many of which date from when the royal couple lived here. Restrooms are around back, as is the gift shop, which is open the same hours as the palace. Managed by the Daughters of Hawaii, it's small but packed with excellent items like greeting cards, lei, books, beverage trays (reproductions of the early Matson Line menus), little Hawaiian quilt pillows, needlepoint, wraparounds from Tahiti, T-shirts with Queen Emma Summer Palace logo, and Ni'ihau shellwork, the finest in Hawaii.

Walk around back past the neighborhood park basketball court and keep to the right. Soon you'll see a modest little white building. Look for a rather thick and distinctive rope hanging across the entranceway. This is the Shinto temple **Dai Jingu**. It's not nearly as spectacular as the giant trees in this area, but it is authentic and worth a quick look. Shake the bell rope and clap your hands three times as you walk up to the entranceway. For fun, place $.25 into the *oni kuji* wooden box, and out comes a good luck fortune on the back of a small piece of paper. So, for a quarter, find out about love, marriage, business, health, and that sort of thing, and help out the temple at the same time.

## Nu'uanu Pali Lookout

This is one of those extra-benefit places where you get a magnificent view without any effort at all. Merely drive up the Pali Highway to the well-marked turnout and park. The lookout closes at 8 P.M. Rip-offs happen, so take all valuables with you when getting out of the car. Before you, if the weather is accommodating, an unimpeded view of windward O'ahu lies at your feet. Nu'uanu Pali (Cool Heights) lives up to its name; the winds here are chilly and extremely strong, and they funnel right through this notch in the mountain ridge. You may need a jacket or windbreaker. On a particularly windy day just after a good rainfall, various waterfalls tumbling off the *pali* will actually be blown uphill! Several roads, punched over and through the *pali* over the years, are engineering marvels. Originally a foot path, later expanded to a horse trail, the famous "carriage road" built in 1898 was truly amazing. It was built by John Wilson, a Honolulu boy, for only $37,500, using 200 laborers and plenty of dynamite. Droves of people come here, many in huge buses, and they all go to the railing to have a peek. By walking down the old road built in 1932 that goes off to the right, you actually get private and better views, and the wind is quieter.

Nu'uanu Pali figures prominently in Hawaii's legend history. It's said—but not without academic skepticism—that Kamehameha the Great pursued the last remaining defenders of O'ahu to these cliffs in one of the final battles fought to consolidate his power over all of the islands in 1795. If you use your imagination, you can easily feel the utter despair and courage of these vanquished warriors as they were driven ever closer to the edge. Mercy was neither shown nor expected. Some jumped to their deaths rather than surrender, while others fought until they were pushed over. The estimated number of casualties varies considerably, from a few hundred to a few thousand, and some believe that the battle never happened at all. Compounding the controversy are stories of the warriors' families, who searched the cliffs below for years and supposedly found bones of their kinsmen, which they buried. The Pali Lookout is romantic at night, with the lights of Kailua and Kane'ohe in the distance, but the best nighttime view is from Tantalus Drive, where all of Honolulu lies at your feet.

## PUNCHBOWL, NATIONAL CEMETERY OF THE PACIFIC

One sure sign that you have entered a place of honor is the hushed and quiet nature that everyone adopts without having to be told. It's like this the moment you enter this shrine. The Hawaiian name, Puowaina (Hill of Sacrifice), couldn't have been more prophetic. Punchbowl is the almost perfectly round crater of an extinct volcano. It holds the bodies of more than 33,000 men and women who fell fighting for the United States, from World War II to Vietnam, and a few notable individuals who have served the country in other ways. At one time, Punchbowl was a bastion of heavy cannon and artillery trained on Honolulu Harbor to defend it from hostile naval forces. In 1943 Hawaii bequeathed

ROBERT NILSEN

**monument at Punchbowl National Cemetery**

it to the federal government as a memorial; it was dedicated in 1949, when the remains of an unknown serviceman killed during the attack on Pearl Harbor were the first interred. One of the more recent to be buried here was astronaut Ellison Onizuka, who died in 1986 aboard the *Challenger* space shuttle. To attest to its sacredness and the importance of those who lie buried here, more than two million visitors stop here yearly to pay their respects, making this the most visited site in the state. In addition, the annual Easter sunrise service held here draws thousands.

As you enter the main gate, a flagpole with the Stars and Stripes unfurled is framed in the center of a long sweeping lawn. A roadway lined with monkeypod trees adds three-dimensional depth to the impressionistic scene, as it leads to the steps of a marble, altarlike monument in the distance. You get a visual continuous sweep of the field because there are no elevated tombstones, just simple marble slabs lying flat on the ground. The field is dotted with trees, including eight banyans, a special tree and symbolic number for the many Buddhists buried here. Brightening the scene are plumeria and rainbow shower trees, often planted in Hawaiian graveyards because they produce flowers year-round as perennial offerings from the living to the dead when they can't personally attend the grave. All are equal here: the famous, like Ernie Pyle, the stalwart who earned the Congressional Medal of Honor, and the unknown who died alone and unheralded on muddy battlefields in godforsaken jungles. To the right just after you enter is the office, 808/532-3720, with brochures and restrooms. The cemetery is open free of charge 8 A.M.–5:30 P.M. Sept. 30–March 1 and until 6:30 P.M. March 2–Sept. 29, except for Memorial Day when the grounds are open 7 A.M.–7 P.M. You are free to enter and look around as you wish. Guided walking tours for groups are conducted by the American Legion on an appointment basis. These two-hour tours cost $15 per person, and reservations must be made by calling 808/946-6383. Alternately, Roberts Hawaii, 808/539-9400, offers the Starts and Strips tour, which includes the National Cemetery as part of an all-day tour, for $47. Tour buses, taxis, and limousines line up at the front. Don't leave valuables in your car.

To get to Punchbowl take the H-1 freeway to Route 61, the Pali Highway, and exit at 21B. Immediately get to the right, where a sign points you to Punchbowl. You'll make some fancy zigzags through a residential area, but it's well marked and you'll come to Puowaina Drive, which leads you to the main gate. Take note of landmarks going in, because as odd as it sounds, no signs lead you back out, and it's easy to get lost.

## The Monument

Like a pilgrim, you climb the steps to the monument, where on both sides marble slabs seem to whisper the names of 28,778 servicemen, all MIAs whose bodies were never found or those who were buried at sea, but whose spirits are honored here. The first slabs on the right are for the victims of Vietnam, on the left are those from World War II, and you can see that time is already weathering the marble. Their names stand together, as they fought and died—men, boys, lieutenants, captains, private soldiers, infantrymen, sailors—from everywhere in America. "In proud memory . . . this memorial has been erected by the United States of America."

At the monument, built in 1966, is a chapel, and in the middle is a statue of a woman, a woman of peace, a heroic woman of liberty. Around her on the walls are etched maps and battles of the Pacific War whose names still evoke passion: Pearl Harbor, Wake, Coral Sea, Midway, Iwo Jima, the Gilbert Islands, Okinawa. Many of the visitors are Japanese. Many of Hawaii's war dead are also Japanese. Four decades ago we battled each other with hatred and malice. Today, on bright afternoons we come together with saddened hearts to pay reverence to the dead.

## UNIVERSITY OF HAWAI'I

Established in 1907, the University of Hawai'i at Manoa, www.hawaii.edu, is the main campus of a 10-branch university system. The Manoa campus teaches about 15,000 students in undergraduate and graduate programs and, like the rest of the state, is a multicultural and multiracial establishment. You don't have to be a student to head for the University of Hawai'i, Manoa Campus. For one, it houses the **East-West Center,** which was incorporated in 1975 and officially separated from the university; here nations from Asia and the Pacific present fascinating displays of their homelands. Also, Manoa Valley is one of the loveliest residential areas on O'ahu. To get to the main campus, follow the H-1 freeway to exit 24B (University Avenue). Follow University Avenue to Dole Avenue, and make a right onto campus. Stop immediately at one of the parking lots and get a parking map! Parking restrictions are strictly enforced, and this map not only helps to get you around, but also saves you from fines or having your car towed. Parking is a flat $3 for visitors each time you use the lot, so think about taking TheBus no. 4, which services this area quite well from Waikiki.

Two six-week summer sessions beginning late May and in early July are offered to bona fide students of accredited universities at the University of Hawai'i at Manoa, including courses in Hawaiian language and history and Pacific Island studies. For information, catalog, and enrollment, write Summer Session Office, Outreach College, University of Hawai'i, 2440 Campus Rd., Box 447, Honolulu, HI 96822, 808/956-5666 or 800/862-6628, www.summer.hawaii.edu.

## Campus Center

Make this your first stop. As you mount the steps, notice the idealized mural of old Hawaii: smiling faces of contented natives all doing interesting things. Inside is the **Information Center,** which dispenses information not only about the campus, but also about what's happening socially and culturally around town. Stop here for a campus map and self-guided tour brochure, and, if you're into it, pick up brochures on public artwork and significant plants on campus. The food in the cafeteria is institutional but cheap and has a Hawaiian twist. The best places to eat are either the Manoa Garden Restaurant on the ground floor of the Hemenway Center next door to the Campus Center or at the Paradise Palms Cafe next to Hamilton Library, although there are other smaller cafés and food kiosks around campus.

The **University Bookstore** on the lower level is excellent, open Mon.–Fri. 8:15 A.M.–4:45 P.M., Sat. 8:15–11:45 A.M. The bookstore is worth coming to for its excellent range of specialty items, like language tapes and a whole range of Hawaiiana. The Commons Gallery, an adjunct of the University Art Gallery in the Art Department building, www.hawaii.edu/artgallery, is on the third floor and is worth a look. Free! The exhibits change regularly and the galleries are only open during regular school sessions (Aug.–May) Mon.–Fri. 10 A.M.–4 P.M. and Sun. noon–4 P.M. Next to the gallery in the Campus Center is a lounge filled with overstuffed chairs and big pillows, where you can kick back and even take a quick snooze. This is not a very social campus. By 4:30 or 5 P.M. the place is shut up and no one is around. Don't expect students gathered in a common reading room or the activity of social and cultural events. When school lets out at the end of the day, people simply go home.

## East-West Center

Follow Dole Avenue to East-West Road and make a left. The center's 21 acres were dedicated in 1960 by the U.S. Congress to promote better relations between the countries of Asia and the Pacific with the United States. Many nations, as well as private companies and individuals, fund this institution of cooperative study and research. The center's staff, with help from University of Hawai'i students and scholars and professionals from throughout the region, focus on four broad but interconnected issues: regional security, social and cultural changes, the changing domestic political scene in nations of the region, and regional economic growth and its resultant consequences. John Burns Hall's main lobby dispenses information on what's happening, along with self-guiding maps. Imin Center–Jefferson Hall, fronted by Chinese lions, has a serene and relaxing Japanese garden behind it, complete with a little rivulet and a teahouse named Jakuan, "Cottage of Tranquillity." The murals inside are excellent, and it also contains a large reading room with relaxing couches. While you're here, check out the bookstore, which carries an impressive selection of Hawaiiana and books on

M

O'AHU

Asia, or have a peek at the East-West Center Gallery, open Mon.–Fri. 8 A.M.–5 P.M. and Sun. noon–4 P.M.

The impressive 23-ton, solid teak Thai Pavilion was a gift from the king of Thailand, where it was built and sent to Hawaii to be reconstructed. These *salas* are common sights in Thailand. The Center for Korean Studies (not part of the East-West Center, but just up the road) is also outstanding. A joint venture of Korean and Hawaiian architects, its inspiration was taken from the classic lines of Kyongbok Palace in Seoul. Most of the buildings are adorned with fine artworks: tapa hangings, murals, calligraphy, paintings, and sculpture. The entire center is tranquil, and along with the John F. Kennedy Theater of Performing Arts just across the road, is indeed fulfilling its dedication as a place of sharing and learning, culture and art.

## MANOA VALLEY

Manoa Valley, a tropical palette of green ablaze with daubs of iridescent color, has a unique designation most aptly described as urban rainforest. Although not technically true, the valley, receiving more than 100 inches of rainfall per year, is exceptionally verdant even by Hawaiian stan-

dards, but it wasn't always so. In the late 1800s, the overpopulated valley was almost denuded of trees, only to be reforested by Dr. Lyon, the founder of Lyon Arboretum, who planted trees gathered from around the world. A literal backwater, the runoff from Manoa would flood the relatively dry Waikiki until the Ala Wai Canal was built in the 1920s as a catchment for its torrential flash floods. Only a short drive from arid Waikiki, Manoa was the first place in Hawaii where coffee was grown and where pineapple was cultivated.

The great **Queen Ka'ahumanu,** who died here in 1832, favored the cool hills of the valley as a vacation spot to escape the summer heat. Manoa, favored by royalty ever since, has maintained itself as one of the most fashionable residential areas in Hawaii, even boasting its own country club at the turn of the 20th century, which is yet memorialized by the Manoa Cup held yearly at the O'ahu Country Club. In 1893, just before annexation, a bewildered and beaten group of royalists came to Manoa to hide out. They were subsequently captured by a contingency of pursuing U.S. Marines and imprisoned in an area called The Pen, on the grounds of the now-defunct Paradise Park.

Taking Manoa Road you pass **Punahou**

## THE LEGENDS OF MANOA VALLEY

Kahala-o-puna, known for her exceptional beauty, was betrothed to Kauhi, a young chief who was driven mad by unfounded jealousy. He falsely accused his lovely wife of faithlessness and killed her five times, only to have her resurrected each time by her sympathetic guardian *amakua*. Finally, left for dead, Kahala-o-puna was found by a young prince who fell in love with her. Beseeching his animal spirits, he brought her to life one last time, and through them turned the jealous Kauhi into a shark. Kahala-o-puna, warned never to go into the ocean, disobeyed, and was seized in the massive jaws of Kauhi, who fatally crushed the life from her, never to be rekindled. The warm misty rains of Manoa are the tears of the mother of Kahala-o-puna, and the gentle winds are the soft sobs

of her bereaved father, who together lament the loss of their beloved daughter.

Another legend sings of the spring, Wai-a-ke-akua, created spontaneously by the great gods Kane and Kaneloa, who came to visit this valley. While overindulging in 'awa they became intoxicated, and decided that they would dawdle in the lovely valley. Lying down, the gods could hear water running underground, so Kane took his great staff and struck the earth, causing Wai-a-ke-akua to appear. Because of the spring's divine origin, it became known as "water of the gods," making it *kapu* to all but the highest *ali'i*. When Kamehameha conquered Oahu, only he could drink from the spring, which flows with cool sweet water to this day.

**School,** one of the oldest and most prestigious high schools in Hawaii. Built in 1841 from lava rock, children of the missionary families of wealthy San Franciscans attended, getting the best possible education west of the Rockies. Manoa Road eventually crosses O'ahu Avenue—an extension of University Avenue. Follow it to **Wai'oli Tea Room,** 3016 O'ahu Ave., which is owned and operated by the Salvation Army. Set within a small parklike property, the restaurant features fresh-baked pastries and serves breakfast, sandwich and salad lunches, and a formal high tea (24-hour reservation requested) daily. The Wai'oli Tea Room is open daily 8 A.M.–4 P.M. with a fondue and à la carte dinner served on weekends only 5:30–9 P.M. Also featured here is the **Little Grass Shack** supposedly lived in by Robert Louis Stevenson when he was a resident of Waikiki. Visit the chapel with its distinctive stained-glass windows.

**Paradise Park,** 3737 Manoa Rd. (at the very end), closed in late 1993, is 13 acres of lush tropical plants founded by James Wong about 30 years ago. Magnificent blooms compete with the wild plumage of 50 species of exotic birds. However, the **Treetop Restaurant,** literally at treetop level and offering very good food and superlative views, is still operating. It serves lunch buffet only and is a bargain at $9.95 weekdays and $12.95 on weekends.

The **Lyon Arboretum,** 3860 Manoa Rd., 808/988-0464, www.hawaii.edu/lyonarboretum, is situated on 194 acres at the upper end of Manoa Road. Open to the public, it's principally a research facility and academic institution of the University of Hawai'i, a quiet shaded retreat from the noise of the city. While well cared for and orderly, this is not a highly manicured garden, just a natural beauty and profusion of greens. It not only has sections set aside for research and horticultural plants, but there is also an herb garden, ethnobotanical garden, and hundreds of tropical plants that include ginger, *ti,* heliconia, hibiscus, palms, and bromeliads. You can visit on your own Mon.–Sat. 9 A.M.–3 P.M., but guided tours are also offered Tues. 10–11:30 A.M. and Sat. 1–2:30 P.M. Call ahead and reserve. Walking-tour maps are available; sign in and leave your donation.

The arboretum book and gift shop is a great place to pick up a memento or to select one of numerous books on the flora of Hawaii and other Hawaiian subjects. In addition, various horticultural and related classes are held at the arboretum, usually on Thursday and Saturday mornings. Guided hikes, both inside the arboretum and to other locations around the island, are also offered. Both the classes and the hikes are open to anyone interested but require a fee and reservation.

Free parking for arboretum visitors is near the visitor center gift shop. Do not park in the arboretum parking lot if you're planning to walk up the Manoa Valley Trail to Manoa Falls. Park inside the trailhead gates or down the road in the residential neighborhood.

## BISHOP MUSEUM

Otherwise known as the Museum of Natural and Cultural History, this group of stalwart stone buildings holds the greatest collection of historical relics and scholarly works on Hawaii and the Pacific in the world. It refers to itself as a "museum to instruct and delight," and in one afternoon walking through its halls you can educate yourself about Hawaii's history and people and enrich your trip to the islands tenfold.

Officially named Bernice Pauahi Bishop Museum, its founding was directly connected to the last three royal women of the Kamehameha dynasty. Princess Bernice married Charles Reed Bishop, a New Englander who became a citizen of the then-independent monarchy in the 1840s. The princess was a wealthy woman in her own right, with lands and an extensive collection of things Hawaiian. Her cousin, Princess Ruth Ke'elikolani, died in 1883 and bequeathed Princess Bernice all of her lands and Hawaiian artifacts. Together, this meant that Princess Bernice owned about 12 percent of all Hawaii! Princess Bernice died less than two years later and left all of her landholdings to the **Bernice Pauahi Bishop Estate,** which founded and supported the Kamehameha School, dedicated to the education of Hawaiian children. (Although this organization is often confused with the

Bishop Museum, they are totally separate. The school once shared the same grounds with the museum, but none of the funds from this organization were, or are, used for the museum.) Bernice left her personal property, with all of its priceless Hawaiian artifacts, to her husband, Charles. Then, when Queen Emma, her other cousin, died the following year, she too desired Charles Bishop to combine her Hawaiian artifacts with the already formidable collection and establish a Hawaiian museum.

True to the wishes of these women, he began construction of the museum's main building on December 18, 1889, and within a few years the museum was opened. In 1894, after 50 years in Hawaii, Bishop moved to San Francisco, where he died in 1915. He is still regarded as one of Hawaii's most generous philanthropists. In 1961, a science wing and planetarium were added, and two dormitory buildings are still used from when the Kamehameha School for Boys occupied the same site.

To get there, take exit 20A off the H-1 freeway, which puts you on Route 63, the Likelike Highway. Immediately get into the far right lane. In only a few hundred yards, turn onto Bernice Street, where you'll find the entrance to the museum. Or, exit H-1 onto Houghtailing Street, exit 20B. Keep your eyes peeled for a clearly marked but small sign directing you to the museum. TheBus no. 2 (School-Middle Street) or route C run from Waikiki to Kapalama Street, from which you walk two blocks.

## Admission and Information

The museum is at 1525 Bernice Street, Honolulu, HI 96817, 808/847-3511, www.bishop.hawaii .org, and is open daily 9 A.M.–5 P.M., except Christmas Day. Admission is $14.95 adults, $11.95 for ages 4–12 and seniors; kids under four and museum members are free, but some exhibits and the planetarium are closed to children under six. Kama'aina, military, and other discounts are available, but you must ask. It's sometimes best to visit on weekends because many weekdays bring teachers and young students who have more enthusiasm for running around than for checking out the exhibits. Food, beverages,

and smoking are all strictly prohibited in the museum. The natural light in the museum is dim, so if you're into photography you'll need super-fast film (400 ASA performs only marginally) or a flash. Before leaving the grounds make sure to visit **Hawaiian Halau,** where a hula is performed Mon.–Fri. at 11 A.M. and 2 P.M. The **planetarium** opens up its skies daily at 11:30 A.M., 1:30 P.M., and 3:30 P.M., and the first Friday evening of each month at 7 P.M. by reservation; call 808/848-4168. Both the library and archives are open to the public Tues.–Fri. noon–3 P.M. and Sat. 9 A.M.–noon. Special exhibits are shown in the Castle Memorial Building—Sue, the most complete *Tyrannosaurus rex* fossil, had her Hawaiian debut here in 2000. For library reference services, call 808/848-4148; for the archives, 808/848-4182. The snack shop has reasonable prices, and **Shop Pacifica,** the museum bookstore and boutique, has a fine selection of materials on Hawaii and the Pacific, plus some authentic and inexpensive souvenirs.

## Exhibits

It's easy to become overwhelmed at the museum, so just take it slowly. The number of exhibits is staggering: more than 180,000 artifacts; about 20 million(!) specimens of insects, shells, fish, birds, and mammals; an extensive research library; a photograph collection; and a fine series of maps. The main gallery is highlighted by the rich tones of koa, the showpiece being a magnificent staircase. Get a map at the front desk that lists all of the halls, along with descriptions, and a suggested route to follow. Throughout the week, the hall offers demonstrations in various Hawaiian crafts like lei-making, featherwork, and quilting 9 A.M.–2:30 P.M. The following is just a small potpourri of the highlights.

To the right of the main entranceway is a fascinating exhibit of the old Hawaiian gods. Most are just called "wooden image" and date from the early 19th century. Among them are Kamehameha's war-god, Ku; the tallest Hawaiian sculpture ever found, from Kaua'i; an image of a god from a temple of human sacrifice; and lesser gods, personal 'aumakua that controlled the lives of Hawaiians from birth until death. You wouldn't want to meet any of them in a dark alley! Outside, in what's called the **Hawaiian Courtyard,** are implements used by the Hawaiians in everyday life, as well as a collection of plants that are all identified. The first floor of the main hall is perhaps the most interesting because it deals with old Hawaii. Here are magnificent examples of *kahili,* feathered capes, plumed helmets—all the insignia and regalia of the *ali'i.* A commoner sits in a grass shack, a replica of what Captain Cook might have seen.

Don't look up! Over your head a 55-foot sperm whale hangs from the ceiling. It weighed more than 44,000 pounds alive. You'll learn about the ukulele, and how vaudevillians spread its music around the world. Hula-skirted damsels from the 1870s peer provocatively from old photos, bare-breasted and with plenty of "cheesecake." Tourists bought these photos even then, although the grass skirts they're wearing were never a part of old Hawaii but were brought by Gilbert Islanders. See authentic hula instruments like a "lover's whistle," a flute played through the nose, and a musical bow, the only stringed pre-European Hawaiian instrument.

Don't miss the koa wood collection. This accomplished artform produced medicine bowls, handsome calabashes, some simple home bowls, and others reputed to be the earthly home of the wind goddess, which had to be refitted for display in Christianized 'Iolani Palace. A model *heiau* tells of the old religion and the many strange *kapu* that governed every aspect of life. Clubs used to bash in the brains of *kapu*-breakers sit next to benevolent little stone gods, the size and shape of footballs, that protected humble fishermen from the sea. As you ascend to the upper floors, the time period represented becomes increasingly closer to the present. The missionaries, whalers, merchants, laborers, and Westernized monarchs have arrived. Yankee whalers from New Bedford, New London, Nantucket, and Sag Harbor appear determined and grim-faced as they scour the seas, harpoons at the ready. Great blubber pots, harpoons, and figureheads are preserved from this perilous and unglamorous life. Bibles, thrones, and the regalia of power and of the new god are all here.

# OTHER MUSEUMS AND GALLERIES

## Hawaii State Art Museum

In 2002, the State Foundation of Culture and Arts finally got its wish—a location to house and display part of its large collection of Hawaiian art by Hawaiians. This collection is open to the public on the second floor of the No. 1 Capital District Building, a Spanish Mission–style stucco building kitty-corner from 'Iolani Palace, which sits on the site of the original Royal Hawaiian Hotel, the finest of Honolulu's early hotels. The museum's two galleries and lobby house several hundred works of art, mostly paintings, ceramics, and sculpture. These pieces are part of the foundation's Art in Public Places collection and together offer a glimpse of the diverse cultural mix of people who make Hawaii their home and their expression of the islands. The museum is open Tues.–Sat. 10 A.M.–4 P.M.; 808/586-0900. Guide tours of the galleries are offered at 11 A.M. and again at 2 P.M. for those interested. There is no entrance fee but donations are appreciated. See www.state.hi.us/sfca/hawaiistateartmuseum.htm.

## Honolulu Academy of Arts

Enjoy the magnificent grounds of this perfectly designed building, a combination of East and West with a Hawaiian roof and thick white stucco walls reminiscent of the American Southwest, created by architect Bertram Goodhue and benefactor Anna Rice Cooke expressly as a museum. The museum, at 900 S. Beretania St. opposite Thomas Square, 808/532-8700 or 808/532-8701 for recorded exhibition information, www.honoluluacademy.org, is open Tues.–Sat. 10 A.M.–4:30 P.M., Sun. 1–5 P.M. Admission fees are $7 adults, $4 seniors, students, and military personnel. Members and children under 12 get in free, as does everyone on the first Wednesday of the month. Guided docent tours are conducted daily at 11 A.M., Sun. at 1:15 P.M. The academy houses a brilliant collection of classic and modern art, strongly emphasizing Asian artwork. It is Hawaii's premier general fine arts museum.

James Michener's outstanding collection of

Japanese *ukiyo-e* is here. The story goes that an unfriendly New York cop hassled him on his way to donate it to a New York City museum, whereas a Honolulu officer was the epitome of *aloha* when Michener was passing through, so he decided that his collection should reside here. This collection is rotated frequently and displayed in a specially designed gallery to highlight and protect the prints. Magnificent Korean ceramics, Chinese furniture, and Japanese prints, along with Western masterworks from the Greeks to Picasso, make the academy one of the most well-rounded art museums in America. Some collections are permanent but others change, so the museum remains dynamic no matter how many times you visit. Discover delights like Paul Gauguin's *Two Nudes on a Tahitian Beach,* James Whistler's *Arrangement in Black No. 5,* and John Singer Sargent's *Portrait of Mrs. Thomas Lincoln Hansen Jr.* An entire wing is dedicated to religious art, while another holds furniture from medieval Europe. A small gallery has been given over to Islamic art from the collection of Doris Duke, and other galleries hold works of Hawai'i and the Philippines. The courtyards are resplendent with statuary from the 6th century A.D. and a standing figure from Egypt, circa 2500 B.C. The Hawaiian climate is perfect for preserving artwork. In 2001, the new Luce Pavilion Complex was opened with a downstairs gallery focused on traveling exhibitions and the upstairs gallery that displays engaging works on the history of art in Hawaii.

In addition to the art exhibitions, educational programs, films, and concerts are supported by the museum and held in the Academy Theater, and the Robert Allerton Library is a fine reference library open to the public for research. Stop at the Academy Shop, specializing in art books, museum reproductions, Hawaii out-of-prints, jewelry, notebooks, and postcards. The Pavilion Café is open Tues.–Sat. 11:30 A.M.–2 P.M. It has a light but terrific menu, and besides, a trip to the Academy demands a luncheon in the café.

The Academy now offers tours of Shangri La, the former home of Doris Duke, a wealthy patron of the arts in Hawaii and elsewhere. Shangri La sits on the ocean below Diamond Head and tours include transportation to and from the house. Over the years of her life, Doris Duke collected a vast quantity of Islamic Art, much of which is displayed at Shangri La, and much of the house was renovated in Middle Eastern styles. Six tours a day are given Wed.–Sat. and only by advanced reservation. Because these tours are so popular, they may be filled several months ahead. Call to reserve well in advance (808/385-3849). Tickets run $25 per person; no children under age 12.

The Waikiki Trolley and TheBus nos. 2 and 13 stop out front, but if you are driving, parking is in a lot to the rear of the Academy Art Center; $1 with validation, $2 per hour during the day, or $4 flat rate in the evening. A second lot one block to the east of the main building is open to the public only in the evening at the same rate.

## Academy Art Center at Linekona

Kitty-corner from the Academy of Arts, and affiliated with it, is the Academy Art Center. Built in 1908 as McKinley High School, and later used as Lincoln (Linekona) Elementary School, it is now on both the national and state registers of historic places. The building was renovated and reopened in 1990 as a place where art students can do and display their artwork, and where annual and special exhibitions are held. The displays change periodically, so what you'll get is potluck. It's a functioning art center, so it's a good place to see what kinds of artwork young, contemporary Hawaiian artists are doing. Works are displayed in a large, wooden-floored room with a vaulted ceiling, perhaps the old school gymnasium, where banks of windows provide plenty of natural light.

## The Contemporary Museum

Under the direction of Georgiana Lagoria, at 2411 Makiki Heights Dr., 808/526-0232, www.tcmhi.org, the museum welcomes you with two copper-green gates that are sculptures themselves. This open and elegant structure, the former Spalding House, yields seven galleries, a gift shop, an art library, and an excellent ritzy gourmet restaurant, the Contemporary Cafe. Acquired through the generosity of the *Honolulu Adver-*

*tiser*'s stockholders, the building was donated to the museum as a permanent home in 1988. The focus is on exhibitions, not collections, although works by David Hockney are on permanent display, and there are others by such well-known artists as Andy Warhol and Jasper Johns. Always-changing exhibits reflect different themes in contemporary art—from 1940 onward. Open Tues.–Sat. 10 A.M.–4 P.M., Sun. noon–4 P.M., closed Mon. and major holidays; admission $5 general, $3 students and seniors. Parking is free.

Surrounding the building are three magnificent acres sculpted into gardens perfect for strolling and gazing at the sprawl of Honolulu far below. Led by museum volunteers, a 45-minute tour of the gardens is offered by appointment only. Guided tours of the exhibitions are also given Tues.–Sat.; call 808/536-1322 for details at least a week in advance.

Aside from the main galleries, works are displayed at the museum galleries at the First Hawaiian Center, 999 Bishop St., which is open Mon.–Thurs. 8:30 A.M.–4 P.M. and Fri. until 6 P.M. Admission is free.

### Tennent Art Foundation Gallery

At 201-203 Prospect St., on the *ewa* slope of Punchbowl, this gallery is open Tues.–Sat. 10 A.M.–noon, Sun. 2–4 P.M., 808/531-1987. Free. The walls hold the paintings of Madge Tennent, one of Hawaii's foremost artists. According to her wishes, her remaining works are housed and displayed here, in what was her studio, rather than being sold or given for display elsewhere. Designed by one of Hawaii's well-known architects, the two-level gallery with its undulating roof has been placed on the State Historical Record. The gallery is a quiet sanctuary in a residential neighborhood and worth a visit. Head up Ward Avenue until it meets Prospect Street. Turn left and proceed until Prospect Street veers off to the right. From there it's not far. Look for the salmon-colored wall and gate.

### University of Hawai'i Art Gallery

Housed in the Department of Art along The Mall on the university campus, the art gallery exhibits various art shows, both national and international, as well as student art works. Its yearly International Shoebox Sculpture Exhibition is well known. The Commons Gallery, a smaller gallery in the student center, also displays pieces by students and visiting artists. Both galleries are open to the public for free during the school year, Mon.–Fri. 10:30 A.M.–4 P.M. and Sun. noon–4 P.M. Call 808/956-6888 for exhibition information or see www.hawaii.edu/artgallery for a peek at what's showing.

While on the university campus, you may want to have a look at the East-West Center Gallery, the John Young Museum of Art at Krauss Hall, and the School of Architecture Gallery.

## GARDENS
### Foster Botanical Garden

Many of these exotic trees have been growing in this 13.5-acre manicured garden for more than 100 years. In the mid-1800s it was the private estate of Dr. Hillebrand, physician to the royal court; he brought many of the seedlings from Asia. Now that the garden is on the National Register of Historic Places, two dozen of these trees enjoy lifetime protection by the state, and others are examples of rare and endangered species. A few of the huge and exceptional trees are kapok, bo, banyan, and Mindanao gum, several from the 1850s, and other sections of the garden show orchids, palms, poisonous plants, herbs, and "primitive" plants. At 180 N. Vineyard Blvd., 808/522-7065, the gardens are open daily 9 A.M.–4 P.M. except Christmas and New Year's Day. Admission is $5 nonresidents, $3 residents, $1 children 6–12, and free for those younger. Guided tours are given Mon.–Fri. at 1 P.M.; call 808/522-7066 for reservations. Free self-guided brochures are available. Give yourself at least an hour for a leisurely stroll; bring insect repellent. Along with four others on the island, these gardens are administered by the Honolulu Botanical Gardens. Before leaving, stop in for a look at the Foster Garden Gallery and Bookstore for books, postcards, tapa cloth, T-shirts, and other such gift items. The closest stop on TheBus is no. 4 from Waikiki.

O'AHU

### Lili'uokalani Botanical Garden

A stone's throw to the north over the freeway and set along the Nu'uanu Stream are the 7.5 acres of this garden. Once the secluded private garden of the last Hawaiian monarch but now hemmed in by private homes and apartment buildings, it's now part of the Honolulu Botanical Garden system. Unlike the imported magnificence of the Foster Botanical Garden, this garden features mostly native Hawaiian plants. The bottom end near the freeway is more pleasant than the upper end near the parking lot, and it seems to be used mostly for picnics.

### Moanalua Gardens

The private gardens of the Damon Estate, at 1352 Pineapple Pl., 808/833-1944, were given to the original owner by Princess Bernice Bishop in 1884. On the mountain side of the Moanalua Freeway, these gardens are open to the public but not heavily visited. More like a park with open grassy lawns and spaced monkeypod trees than a typical botanical garden, it is a welcome respite from the hustle and bustle of the city. Some magnificent old trees include a Buddha tree from Ceylon and a monkeypod called "the most beautifully shaped tree" in the world by *Ripley's Believe It or Not*. Open weekdays 7 A.M.–6 P.M. and from 7:30 A.M. on weekends; no charge.

The nonprofit cultural and educational Moanalua Garden Foundation, not affiliated with the Damon Estate, presents the noncompetitive Prince Lot Hula Festival in the Moanalua Gardens yearly on the third Saturday of July. In addition, this foundation sponsors guided hikes into Halawa Valley (the valley that the H-3 freeway runs through) four times a year on Sundays. These hikes introduce people to the historical and cultural artifacts and the botanical diversity of the valley. This three-mile, four-hour round-trip hike is $5 per person. For information and arrangements, call the foundation at 808/839-5334.

## HONOLULU BEACHES AND PARKS

The beaches and parks listed here are found in and around Honolulu's city limits. World-famous Waikiki has its own section (see the Waikiki chapter). The good thing about having Waikiki so close is that it lures most bathers away from other city beaches, which makes them less congested.

Huge monkeypod trees at Moanalua Garden create large areas of shade–a perfect spot to picnic.

The following list contains most of Honolulu's beaches, ending at Ala Moana Beach Park, just a few hundred yards from where the string of Waikiki's beaches begins.

## Ke'ehi Lagoon Beach Park

At the eastern end of Honolulu International Airport, this park is at the inner curve of Ke'ehi Lagoon, just off Route 92 (the Nimitz Highway). The water at this park is somewhat polluted, but people do swim here, and a canoe club uses it. Mostly, local people use the area for pole fishing and crabbing, picnicking, and ball games. There are restrooms, pavilions, picnic facilities, a pay phone, and lots of parking. One entrance to the Disabled American Veterans Memorial is through the park.

## Sand Island State Recreation Area

You enter this park by way of the Sand Island Access Road, clearly marked off the Nimitz Highway. On the way, you pass through some ugly real estate—scrapyards, petrochemical tanks, warehouses, and other such beauties. It's not bad once you get past this commercial/industrial strip. Don't get discouraged, keep going! Once you cross the bridge, hurry past a wastewater treatment center (hold your nose!), and pass the entrance to the U.S. Coast Guard base, you enter the actual park, 14 acres landscaped with picnic and playground facilities. Follow the road into the park. From here, you get a view of downtown Honolulu, with Diamond Head making a remarkable counterpoint. The park is well maintained, with pavilions, cold-water showers, walkways, and restrooms, and closes at 6:45 P.M. However, the camping area is usually empty (state permit required). The sites are out in the open, but a few trees provide some shade. Unfortunately, you're under one of the main glide paths for Honolulu International Airport. Many local people come to fish, and the surfing is good, but the beaches for snorkeling and swimming are fair at best. The currents and wave action aren't dangerous, but remember that this part of the harbor receives more than its share of pollutants. From the campground end of the park, you have a view of part of the inner Honolulu harbor.

## La Mariana Yacht Sailing Club

This small marina at 50 Sand Island Access Road is a love song in the middle of an industrialized area. The marina is Annette La Mariana Nahinua's labor of love that has remained true since 1955. You can read her fantastic story on the menu of the marina's Hideaway Restaurant, the only real restaurant on Sand Island. In 1955 this area was forgotten, forsaken, and unkempt. Ms. Nahinua, against the forces of nature and the even more unpredictable and devastating forces of bureaucracy, took this land and turned it into a yacht harbor. The main tools were indefatigable determination, God listening to her prayers, and a shovel and rake. It's one of the last enclaves of old Hawaii, a place to come for dinner, a drink, or just to look at the boats. The nighttime bartender is friendly but stoic after decades of seeing and hearing it all. Annette, the founder, is now a little gray-haired woman, a motherly type in Birkenstocks, who lives right here above the Hideaway. In the daytime she wanders around spreading her magic while talking to old salts or new arrivals.

The marina is adjacent to an open waterway, which means that you don't have to pay for anchorage. It comes under the old "rights of sailors" to find a free port in which to berth. This unique setup has created an atmosphere in which a subculture of people have built subsistence shacks on the little islands that dot the bay. Some also live on old scows, shipshape yachts, or on imaginative homemade crafts, afloat and semi-afloat on this tranquil bay. Many are disillusioned and disenfranchised Vietnam vets who have become misanthropes. You'll see the Stars and Stripes flying from their island hooches. Others are yachties who disdain being landlubbers, whereas others are poor souls who have fallen through the social net. La Mariana is a unique statement of personal freedom in a city where unique statements are generally not tolerated.

## Kaka'ako (Point Panic) Waterfront Park

This small state facility was carved out of a piece of land donated by the University of Hawai'i's Biomedical Research Center, and at one time was used as a dump. Next to Kewalo Basin Harbor, follow 'Ohe or Ko'ula streets off Ala Moana Boulevard to the park. From the huge parking lot, walking paths lead over the rise (which blocks out the noise of the city) to a grand promenade and picnic tables set under stout trellises. This area is poor for swimming, but it's great for fishing and surfing. Others come to enter the water for scuba dives. If you're lucky, you may even spot a manta ray, which are known to frequent these waters. Unfortunately, novices will quickly find out why it's called Point Panic. As at the Kewalo Basin Park across the opening to the adjacent harbor, a long seawall with a sharp drop-off runs the entire length of the area. The wave action is perfect for riding, but all wash against the wall. Beginners stay out! The best reason to come here is for the magnificent and unobstructed view of the Ala Moana Beach, the Waikiki skyline, and Diamond Head beyond. Although it's rather underused at present, there are plans to add more facilities in the future and hold musical concerts and cultural events here.

To the side of the park is the **Hawaii Children's Discovery Center,** 808/524-5437, an interactive educational institution where kids can learn about themselves, the community in which they live, the special things about Hawaii, and the different peoples of the world. The center is open Tues.–Fri. 9 A.M.–1 P.M. and on the weekends 10 A.M.–3 P.M. Admission is $8 adults, $5 seniors, $6.75 ages 2–17.

## Kewalo Basin State Park

Kewalo Basin Marina, developed in the 1920s to hold Honolulu's tuna fleet, is home to many charter boats for water activities, including fishing, parasailing, sunset tours, and underwater excursions. Pay parking is to the side. On the ocean side of the marina, stretching along the breakwater, is this state park (free parking) with its promenade and covered picnic tables. Surfers congregate here for the good waves that develop because of the offshore reef, which continues all the way along the front of Ala Moana Beach Park.

If you're here in the very early morning hours, check out the Honolulu Fish Auction. Your dinner might be coming off one of these boats. This auction is held about 6 A.M. on 'Ahui Street on the west side of the marina next to the John Dominus Restaurant.

## Ala Moana Beach Park

Ala Moana (Path to the Sea) Beach County Park is by far Honolulu's best. Most visitors congregate just around the bend at Waikiki, but residents head for Ala Moana, the place to soak up the local color. During the week, this beautifully curving white-sand beach has plenty of elbow room. Weekends bring families that come for every water sport O'ahu offers. The swimming is great, with manageable wave action, plenty of lifeguards, and even good snorkeling along the reef. Board riders have their favorite spots, and bodysurfing is excellent. The huge area has several restrooms, food concessions, tennis courts, softball fields, a bowling green, and parking for 500 cars. Many O'ahu outrigger canoe clubs practice in this area, especially in the evening; it's great to come and watch them glide along. A huge banyan grove provides shade and strolling if you don't fancy the beach, or you can bring a kite to fly aloft with the trade winds. Ala Moana Park stretches along Ala Moana Boulevard between the Ala Wai and Kewalo Basin boat harbors. It's across from the Ala Moana Shopping Center on the east end and Ward Centre on the west end, so you can rush right over if your credit cards start melting from the sun.

'Aina Moana (Land from the Sea) Recreation Area used to be called Magic Island because it was reclaimed land. It is actually the point of land stretching out from the eastern edge of Ala Moana Beach Park, contiguous with it. The beach here is a fine crescent strand that's protected by a breakwater and also backed by broad lawns, trees, and picnic tables.

# HONOLULU HIKING
## Manoa Valley Trail

Less than one mile long and reasonably level, the Manoa Valley Trail is one of the easiest in town to negotiate and easy to get to. Follow O'ahu Avenue past the university, then turn onto Manoa Road. Follow this until it turns sharply to the left and up the hill to Lyon Arboretum. If the gate at the trailhead is open, park inside the gate in the small parking lot. Otherwise, go back down the road to the Treetop Restaurant parking lot (pay) or farther into the neighborhood. The trail roughly follows the Manoa Stream down this tight valley. It's an easy trail that goes through mostly introduced trees and bamboo, but it may be muddy if it's rained recently. The hike takes a bit more than 30 minutes up and ends at a small pool into which the falls drop.

## Judd Trail

This is an excellent trail to take to experience O'ahu's "jungle" while visiting the historic and picturesque Nu'uanu Pali nearby. From the Pali Highway, Route 61, turn right onto the Old Pali Highway, then right again onto Nu'uanu Pali Drive. Follow it for just under a mile to Reservoir No. 2 spillway. The trail begins on the ocean side of the spillway and leads through fragrant eucalyptus and a dense stand of picture-perfect Norfolk pines. It continues through the forest reserve and makes a loop back to the starting point. En route you pass Jackass Ginger Pool. In the immediate area are "mud slides," where you can take a ride on a makeshift toboggan of *pili* grass, *ti* leaves, or a piece of plastic, if you've brought one. This activity is rough on your clothes and even rougher on your body. The wet conditions after a rain are perfect. Afterward, a dip in Jackass Pool cleans the mud and refreshes at the same time. Continue down the trail to observe wild ginger, guava, and *kukui,* but don't take any confusing side trails. If you get lost, head back to the stream and follow it until it intersects the main trail.

## Tantalus and Makiki Valley Trails

Great sightseeing and hiking can be combined when you climb the road atop Tantalus. Trails in this area offer magnificent views, and, in fact, it has the greatest concentration of easy-access hiking trails on the island. To get there, head past Punchbowl along Puowaina Drive; just keep going until it turns into Tantalus Drive. The road switchbacks past some incredible homes and views until it reaches the 2,000-foot level,

where it changes its name to Round Top Drive, then heads down the other side. To approach from the other side, take Ke'eaumoku Street across H-1. Turn right on Nehoa, then left in one block to Makiki Street. Follow this a short distance to Round Top Drive and you're on your way. Trailhead signs are along the road.

One place to start is at the half-mile-long **Moleka Trail,** which offers some excellent views and an opportunity to experience the trails in this area without an all-day commitment. The trails are excellently maintained by the State Division of Forestry and Wildlife. Your greatest hazard here is mud, but in a moment you're in a handsome stand of bamboo, and in 10 minutes the foliage parts onto a lovely panorama of Makiki Valley and Honolulu in the background. These views are captivating, but remember to have "small eyes"—check out the variety of colored mosses and fungi, and don't forget the flowers and fruit growing around you. A branch trail to the left leads to Round Top Drive, and if you continue the trail splits into three: the right one is the **Makiki Valley Trail,** which cuts across the valley for about one mile, ending up at Tantalus Drive; 'Ualaka'a Trail branches left and goes for another half mile, connecting the Makiki Valley Trail with Pu'u 'Ualaka'a State Park; straight ahead is the **Maunalaha Trail,** which descends for just over one-half mile to the bottom of the valley at the Hawaii Nature Center and Forestry Baseyard.

On the mountain side of the road across from the Moleka Trailhead, the **Manoa Cliff Trail** heads inland and swings in a 3.5-mile arch back around to meet Tantalus Drive. Intersecting this trail at approximately the halfway point is the **Pu'u Ohia Trail,** which leads to the highest point on Tantalus and the expected magnificent view. It continues inland via the **Pauoa Flats Trail,** which ends at a lookout over Nu'uanu Valley and its reservoir. Partway along this trail, the **Nu'uanu Trail** heads west down to connect with the Judd Trail. A short way farther, the **'Aihualama Trail** heads to the east to Manoa Falls and down the **Manoa Valley Trail** to the end of Manoa Valley Road, exiting near Lyon Arboretum.

## Accommodations

The vast majority of O'ahu's hotels are strung along the boulevards of Waikiki. Most are neatly clustered, bound by the Ala Wai Canal, and run eastward toward Diamond Head. These hotels will be discussed in the Waikiki section. The remainder of greater Honolulu has few accommodations, but those that do exist are some of O'ahu's cheapest. Most are clean, no-frills establishments, a handful just beyond the edge of Waikiki, one or two downtown, some near the university, with a few others at the airport.

### DOWNTOWN

**YMCA Nu'uanu** (men only), 1441 Pali Hwy., Honolulu, HI 96813, at the intersection of S. Vineyard Blvd., 808/536-3556, is a few minutes' walk from downtown Honolulu. You'll find a modern, sterile facility with a swimming pool, exercise room, a public telephone, and private rooms with a communal bathroom. Rooms do not have televisions, but there is free parking. This is a first-come, first-served facility; call in the morning for a room, which run $30 per night for a single, $160 per week, with a $5 key deposit.

The **Town Inn,** 250 N. Beretania St., Honolulu, HI 96817, 808/536-2377, is on the western edge of Chinatown. It's an inexpensive old standby hotel that's used primarily by seamen and long-term guests. Somewhat worse for the wear (particularly the carpets) and spartan, the rooms have one queen bed or two singles and rent for $44.60–57.80; weekly rates are also available. A $5 key deposit is required and there's a charge for all phone calls. There are no TVs in the rooms, but there is one in the lobby. No cooking is allowed in the rooms. Just off the lobby, a restaurant serves authentic Japanese food at moderate prices and doubles as a karaoke bar in the evening.

The only upscale hotel right in downtown Honolulu is the **Aston at the Executive Center,** 1088 Bishop St., Honolulu, HI 96813, 808/539-3000 or 800/949-3932, fax 808/523-1088, www.astonhotels.com. This triangular glass and steel building puts both businesspeople and travelers in the heart of Honolulu's financial and capital districts. Rooms look out over city streets and provide fine views of the city night lights. Each spacious air-conditioned suite is fitted with an entertainment center, telephones, data ports, and in-room safe. A continental breakfast and local newspaper are available complimentary for all guests, and an on-site restaurant, daily maid service, 24-hour business center, coin laundry, 24-hour swimming pool, fitness center, and sauna are all amenities. Business suites with a refrigerator run $190–200, while the one-bedroom suites with kitchen are $240–270. Substantial discounts of 40–50 percent are offered for corporate and government guests. If you need to be in the city for business or other reasons, the Aston at the Executive Center is a perfect location.

### NEAR WAIKIKI

The **YMCA Central Branch,** 401 Atkinson Dr., Honolulu, HI 96814, 808/941-3344, fax 808/941-8821, www.centralymcahonolulu.org, is the most centrally located and closest to Waikiki. Call ahead and make reservations at least two weeks in advance. A definite checkout date is a must. There is no curfew, no visitors allowed in the rooms, no loud noise permitted after 10 P.M., no smoking or drinking, no cooking in rooms, and a $10 key deposit, but the Y does have an outside swimming pool, sauna, weight room, gym, and racquetball court that are open to all guests. Parking is limited to two stalls and the fee for each is $5 per day. There are single and double rooms, shared and private baths. Rooms are spartan but clean with a bed, desk, and telephone. Rates for rooms with shared baths (men only) are $30 per night single or $41 double; weekly and monthly rates available. For rooms with a private bath (open to men and women), rates are $38 per day single and $53 double; rates go down after eight consecutive days. This Y is just up from the eastern end of Ala Moana Park across from the tall Ala Moana Hotel, only a 10-minute walk to Waikiki.

The **Pagoda Hotel,** 1525 Rycroft St., Honolulu, HI 96814, 808/941-6611 or 800/367-6060, www.pagodahotel.com, is behind Ala Moana Shopping Center between Kapi'olani Boulevard and S. King Street. Because this hotel is away from the action, you get good value for your money. Rooms are located in one low-rise building and one high-rise tower. All rooms in the Terrace Tower come with kitchenettes and run $130–200 for studio, one-, and two-bedroom suites. The Hotel Tower has mostly standard rooms at $130, but a few deluxe rooms cost $140 and a couple of suites go for $230; numerous packages are available. Substantial discounts are given to residents. Rooms come in a mixture of twin, double, and/or queen beds, so inquire. All rooms have a TV, a/c, an in-room safe, and a small refrigerator. There's free parking, laundry facilities, a sundries shop, two swimming pools, and access to the well-known Pagoda Restaurant, a favorite of locals for its Asian ambiance, theme buffets, koi pond, and manicured garden. The Pagoda Hotel is locally owned and operated.

The 36-story, 1,200-room **Ala Moana Hotel,** 410 Atkinson Dr., Honolulu, HI 96814, 808/955-4811 or 800/367-6025, fax 800/944-6839, www.alamoanahotel.com, is just off the Waikiki strip. It's between Ala Moana and Kapi'olani Boulevards, with a walking ramp connecting it directly with the Ala Moana Shopping Center for easy access. City-view rooms in the back Kona Tower are $125, while those in the main Waikiki Tower run $155–215, and $250–2,300 for suites; corporate and government rates are available. Each room has a/c, a TV, a mini-fridge, direct-dial telephones, data ports, and all the comforts that you would expect from a quality hotel. The hotel contains a third-level swimming pool, sundries shop, laundry facilities, the Rumours nightclub, a cocktail lounge, Japanese and Chinese restaurants, a Polynesian Revue with buffet dinner, and Aaron's restaurant on the top floor for elegant dining.

## NEAR THE UNIVERSITY

The **Honolulu International Hostel,** 2323-A Seaview Ave., Honolulu, HI 96822, 808/946-0591, fax 808/946-5904, www.hiavh.org, is near the main entrance to the university. It's an official Hostelling International hostel, so members with identity cards are given priority, but nonmembers are accepted on a space-available day-by-day basis. This hostel has 43 beds and two private rooms. A bed in a dormitory runs $14 per night for members and $17 for nonmembers. The office is open 8 A.M.–noon and 4 P.M.–midnight. It has travel and sightseeing information, can offer suggestions for what to see and do, and hosts periodic barbecues. This hostel is always busy, but it takes reservations by phone with a credit card. For information and non–credit card reservations, write to the manager and include an SASE. There is no curfew but the expectation is that everyone keeps appropriate quiet hours. A full kitchen is open for use, and there is a grill on the back patio for daytime barbecuing. A washer and dryer are available for guest use and there's limited off-street parking. Kick back in the communal room for TV, free movies, or to meet other travelers. From the hostel to the airport, take TheBus no. 6 to Ala Moana Shopping Center and transfer there to bus no. 19 or 20; to Waikiki, take bus no. 4 direct. For information about Hostelling International—American Youth Hostels and membership cards, write HI-AYH National Office, P.O. Box 37613, Washington, DC 20013-7613.

**YWCA Fernhurst** (women only), 1566 Wilder Ave., Honolulu, HI 96822, just off Manoa Rd., across from the historical Punahou School, 808/941-2231, fax 808/949-0266, offers single and double rooms with shared baths and 24-hour security. Women from around the world have found this a safe and convenient home while on the island. At the end of 2002, the Fernhurst YWCA was closed for major renovation. For rooms available in 2004 and beyond, please contact the YWCA for rates and information at the above telephone numbers, send an email to fernhurst@ywcaoahu.org, or check www.ywcaoahu.org.

ROBERT NILSEN

**Manoa Valley Inn**

The **Manoa Valley Inn,** 2001 Vancouver Dr., Honolulu, HI 96822, 808/947-6019, fax 808/946-6168, manoavalleyinn@aloha.net, www.manoavalleyinn.com, offers a magnificent opportunity to lodge in early-1900s elegance. Formerly the John Guild Inn, this country inn is listed on the national and state registers of historic places. Built in 1915 by Milton Moore, an Iowa lumberman, the original structure was a modest, two-story, boxlike home. It was situated on seven acres, but the demand for land by growing Honolulu has whittled it down to the present half acre or so. Moore sold the house to John Guild in 1919. A secretary to Alexander and Baldwin, Guild added the third floor and back porch, basically creating the structure you see today. The home went through several owners and even survived a stint as a fraternity house. It ended up as low-priced apartment units until it was rescued and renovated in 1982 by the former owner of Crazy Shirts and one of Hawaii's patrons of arts and antiques. He outfitted the house from his warehouse of antiques with furnishings not original to the house but true to the period. Since then it has been sold several times and undergone additional refurbishing and landscaping.

The current owner is Therese Wery. Rooms with double or queen-size beds and a shared bath run a reasonable $99, while the larger rooms with private baths and queen- or king-size beds are $140. One suite with a king bed goes for $190, and the detached cottage with its double bed runs $150. A continental breakfast and local phone calls are all included in the room charge. The exemplary continental breakfasts are prepared on the premises. In the morning, the aroma of fresh-brewed coffee wafts up the stairs. The daily and Sunday newspapers are available. Pick one and sink into the billowy cushions of a wicker chair on the lava-rock-colonnaded back porch. Free off-street parking is provided. Check-in is at 3 P.M., checkout at 11 A.M.

## NEAR THE AIRPORT

**Nimitz Shower Tree,** 3085 N. Nimitz Hwy., 808/833-1411, is a converted warehouse-type building, a bit like a hostel, with double-bed rooms for $22–30 for single and $36 for a couple, with one queen room for $45. If all you need is a shower and a rest during a layover, it's $7.50. Weekly rates are available. Cash only is accepted. Rooms are given on a first-come, first-served basis. The bathroom, TV lounge, pay phone, and laundry are down the hall. Only five minutes from the airport, the Shower Tree provides transportation to and from and luggage storage.

One of the closest hotels to the airport is Best Western's **The Plaza Hotel,** 3253 N. Nimitz Hwy., 808/836-3636 or 800/800-4683, fax 808/834-7406, www.bestwestern-honolulu.com. This 12-story tower has 274 small but a/c rooms, each with king or queen bed, a full bath, entertainment center, and a small refrigerator. Amenities include a restaurant and bar, coin laundry, sundries shop, small swimming pool, and courtesy van service to and from the airport. Rates run $123 for a standard, $133 for a superior, $142 for a deluxe room, and $309 for a suite, with discounts for AAA members, seniors, government employees, and military personnel. Although not in the center of the city or along the sands

of Waikiki, it is convenient for air travel, close to the military facilities that surround Pearl Harbor, and near the USS *Arizona,* USS *Missouri,* and USS *Bowfin* attractions.

With nearly the same amenities as the Best Western, the **Honolulu Airport Hotel,** 3401 N. Nimitz Hwy., 808/836-0661 or 800/800-3477 Mainland or Canada, fax 808/833-1738, www.honoluluairporthotel.com, is even a bit closer to the airport terminal. Here you have more than 300 rooms on four floors, your choice of a standard room at $125, superior at $135, executive at $146, or a suite for $350. Seniors and AAA members get 25 percent off, and other discounts are offered for airline, military, and government personnel. Day-use rates for 8 A.M.–6 P.M. are greatly reduced. There is free hotel parking and complimentary shuttle service to and from the airport.

# Food

The restaurants mentioned as follows are outside of the Waikiki area, although many are close, even within walking distance. Others are near Ala Moana, Chinatown, downtown, Kaimuki, and the less touristed areas of greater Honolulu. Some are first-class restaurants; others, among the best, are just roadside stands where you can get a satisfying plate lunch. The restaurants are listed according to price range and location, with differing cuisines mixed in each range. Besides the sun and surf, the amazing array of food found on O'ahu makes the island extraordinary.

## SHOPPING CENTER DINING

### Ala Moana Shopping Center

The following are all at the Ala Moana Shopping Center along Ala Moana Boulevard. Most are in the **Makai Food Court,** a huge central area where you can inexpensively dine on dishes from San Francisco to Tokyo—most for under $10. Counter-style restaurants serve island favorites, reflecting the multiethnic culinary traditions from around the Pacific. You take your

dish to a nearby communal dining area, which is great for people-watching.

**Patti's Chinese Kitchen,** on the first floor facing the sea, has all the ambiance you'd expect from a cafeteria-style Chinese fast-food joint, plus lines about a block long. But don't let either discourage you. The lines move incredibly quickly, and you won't get gourmet food, but it's tasty, plentiful, and cheap. Plate lunches, noodle soups, pizza, and munchies can be ordered from the **Ala Moana Poi Bowl.** The **Island Burger** has, well, burgers, while **Lahaina Chicken** does chicken in a variety of ways. For noodles, stop at **Naniwa-ya Ramen** or **Tsuruya Noodle Shop,** or if you want the Italian variety, try **Mama'a Spaghetti.** Head for **Yummy Korean BBQ** for hot and spicy Korean plates.

On the top level near the Sears end, the **China House,** is open daily for lunch and dinner. This enormous dining hall offers the usual selection of Chinese dishes but is famous for its dim sum (served 11 A.M.–2 P.M.); you pick and choose bite-sized morsels from carts. For more class and a finer environment, head for **Assaggio,** 808/942-3446, on the ground level next to Macy's. This award-winning Italian restaurant serves tasty dishes that your mama would be proud to put on the table. You might not expect to find a fine restaurant in a department store, but Alan Wong has opened the **Pineapple Room** restaurant and Patisserie Bar on the third floor of Macy's department store. These two establishments plus his Regional Cuisine Marketplace on the fourth floor are swiftly establishing a great reputation.

## Ward Warehouse

This shopping center, at 1050 Ala Moana Blvd., has a range of restaurants, from practical to semi-chic, all reasonably priced. **Benkei,** 808/591-8713, is a Japanese restaurant beautifully appointed with a rock garden at the entranceway that continues to the inside. It's bright and airy, neo-Japanese traditional. Prices are reasonable, with set menu dishes like unagi kabayaki, miso-fried fish, and plate lunches, as well as a wide selection of don buri, yakitori, and tempura. Open Mon.–Sat. 11 A.M.–2 P.M. for lunch, for dinner from 5 P.M. Nearby you'll find **Korean Barbecue Express** and **L&L Drive-In** for a cheaper bite to eat.

The **Old Spaghetti Factory,** 808/591-2513, is a huge place that feels a bit like you might imagine a San Francisco eatery at the turn of the 20th century—almost Victorian. It serves a wide variety of pasta not quite like Mama makes, but passable, and at a reasonable price. Try chicken parmigiana, spinach and cheese ravioli, or meatballs, Italian sausage, and spaghetti with meat sauce, all for under $8. Following your meal, linger over an Italian soda, coffee, tea, draft beer, or house wine. Open Mon.–Fri. for lunch 11:30 A.M.–2 P.M., daily for dinner 5–9 P.M., Sun. from 4 P.M., and Sat. right through.

More modern and expensive is **Kincaid's Fish, Chop & Steak House,** 808/591-2005, on the second floor with views out over Kewalo Basin Marina. Kincaid's dinner menu includes sirloin steak for $20.95, pasta and roasted chicken Dijon for $16.50, and grilled mixed seafood at $20. The lunch menu includes many sandwiches in the under-$12 range, garlic-roasted tiger prawns, and fettuccine with Cajun-style chicken. Soups and salads are à la carte, and a few desserts round

out the list. Kincaid's serves generous portions of honest food at decent prices.

The **Chowder House,** 808/596-7944, on the ground floor, has fresh-grilled ahi, snow crab salad, Manhattan clam chowder, bay shrimp cocktail, deep-fried shrimp, daily specials, and an all-you-can-eat crab night on Thursday.

## Ward Centre

This upscale shopping center is directly across the street from Ala Moana Park and next door to the Ward Warehouse. The following are some of its restaurants and eateries, where you can enjoy not only class, but quality as well.

Chocoholics would rather visit the **Honolulu Chocolate Company** than go to heaven. Mousse truffles, Grand Marnier truffles, and chocolate eggs with pistachio or English walnut will all send you into eye-rolling rapture. If you enter, forget any resolve about watching your weight. You're a goner!

For a quick lunch, try **Mocha Java Cafe,** a yuppie, upscale, counter-service-type place with a few tables. It has a selection of sandwiches with an emphasis on vegetarian. If you want a designer lunch, that's the place to go.

The **Yum Yum Tree,** 808/592-3580, is an affordable American standard family restaurant that features pies and cakes from its bakery, along with homestyle fresh pasta. It has an extensive dining area, quite cheerful with dark wood floors, ferns, hanging greenery, and an open-beam ceiling. Breakfast, lunch, and dinner 6:30 A.M.–10 P.M.; cocktails until closing.

Overlooking Ala Moana Park, **Compadres Mexican Bar and Grill,** 808/591-8307, open Mon.–Fri. 11 A.M.–1 A.M., Sat.–Sun. noon–1 A.M., serves from a smaller, late-night menu 10 P.M.–1 A.M. Although part of a small chain, Compadres offers made-to-order health-conscious Mexican cuisine that was voted the Best on O'ahu by the small but discerning local Mexican population. The decor is a mixture of South Seas and south of the border. The menu is huge, and no lard is used in any of the dishes except carnitas, which are pork anyway. Try the big, double-handed burritos or the Quesadillas Internacionales, which join flavors from many countries. Besides these, the menu comprises standard burritos, tacos, and plenty of vegetarian selections, and no dish is more than $19. The bar complements the meal with a full selection of domestic and imported beer, a selection of microbrewery beers, 10 different kinds of tequila, margaritas by the glass or pitcher, and island exotic drinks. Compadres is an excellent choice for a budget gourmet meal in a hospitable atmosphere where the prices are right and the service excellent. You can't go wrong!

**Ryan's Grill,** 808/591-9132, open 11:15 A.M.–2 A.M., is an ultramodern yet comfortable establishment appointed with black leather chairs, chrome railings, marble-topped tables, and a hardwood floor, which are all dominated by a huge bar and open kitchen. The menu offers standards along with nouveau cuisine and includes onion soup, sesame chicken salad, and tossed fettuccine with sliced breast of chicken and Cajun sauce. Sandwiches are everything from hot Dungeness crab to a grilled chicken club, all for about $10. More substantial meals from the grill include coffee-crusted chicken with lychee relish and pasta dishes. The bar prepares all of the usual exotic drinks and has plenty of draft beer selections from which to choose. Most menu items, along with plenty of munchies and *pu pu,* are served until 1 A.M., so Ryan's Grill makes a perfect late-night stop.

Offering pizza, pasta, and (as they say) pizzazz, **Scoozees a Go Go Bakery and Deli,** 808/597-1777, is a modern and tasteful restaurant and deli. Imported pastas, prosciutto, cheese, stromboli, and fresh baked goods are available from the counter. Menu items include Italian sausage and pepper sandwich, eggplant parmesan, rotisserie chicken, and a multitude of pastas and pizzas for around $8–12. Italian desserts, soft drinks, coffees, and smoothies round out what's available. Open for lunch and dinner and from 10 P.M.–2 A.M. for *pu pu* and drinks.

**Sushi Masa,** 808/593-2007, serves reasonable Japanese food such as tempura, shrimp, and vegetables, chicken teriyaki, and tanuki udon for under $9. You can get a sashimi combination plate for $22 or a sushi special for $16.50–18.50.

Created by the owner of the upscale Alan Wong's Restaurant, **Kaka'ako Kitchen,** 808/596-7488, puts out more inexpensive plate lunches and sandwiches for shoppers on the go. Although most items such as roast turkey sandwich, yaki tofu stir-fry, and chicken katsu curry are familiar, others like shichimi-dusted ahi steak with avocado poke and crispy fired sweet chili chicken are a bit more exotic. Always tasty and easy on the pocketbook, meals here run mostly in the $7–8.50 range. A bargain.

Upstairs is **Brew Moon Restaurant and Micro Brewery,** 808/593-0088. Food is casual American with a blend of the islands and a hint of Asian, but the real reason for stopping by should be the beer. Usually on tap are a half dozen beers brewed on site, with others offered seasonally. Several of these fine concoctions have won awards at various beer festivals around the country. The standards include Moonlight, a light body lager, Pacific Pale Ale, and Hawaii 5 Ale, an amber heartier ale. Open 11 A.M.–10:30 P.M., until midnight on the weekends, the bar stays open until 2 A.M., and there's music most nights from about 8 P.M.

On the ground level below the multiplex theater, kitty-corner in the Ward Entertainment Center, is **Wolfgang Puck Express,** 808/593-8528, which offers quick and nutritious salads, sandwiches, pizza, and a few hot entrées for reasonable prices, mostly $7–9. Some of the meat is done in a rotisserie so it imparts that special flavor, and the pizza is baked in a wood-fired oven. Order at the counter and grab one of the few tables inside or head outside for bistro seating.

Across the street in the Ward Village Shops, the **Kua 'Aina** sandwich shop, 808/591-9133, offers a hearty variety of sandwiches, burgers, and sides for an easygoing price from 10:30 A.M.–9 P.M. Some say the burgers are the best on the island.

## Aloha Tower Marketplace

Some years ago, a law was passed in Hawaii allowing beer to be sold at the place at which it was made. This allowed breweries to open pubs on premises. **Gordon-Biersch Brewery & Restaurant,** 808/599-4877, has taken advantage of this opportunity and opened a fine establishment at the Aloha Tower Marketplace. Four beers are brewed here, all lagers, with the addition of seasonal favorites: Export, a smooth, medium hop, full-bodied beer similar to a pilsner but less bitter; Marzen, an Oktoberfest beer with a little extra oomph from a combination of malts; Dunkles, a dark beer served unfiltered in the old Bavarian tradition; and Blonde Bock, a sweet light golden drink. Aside from these beers, there is a selection of wines, coffees, soft drinks, milk, and juices, but no tropical mixed drinks. The lunch and dinner menus are similar, aside from the sandwiches offered at lunch and more hearty main dishes in the evening. Appetizers include fried calamari and crispy artichoke hearts, and there are small pizzas, pasta, and stir-fry. These and the various salads are just preparation for the main courses, like a barbecue salmon with cashew rice or double-cut pork chops with mashed potatoes. Dine inside or out. Inside, with its leather booths, is more elegant and quieter for conversation. In the more casual alfresco portico, sit at stout wooden tables under canvas umbrellas and watch the tugboats shuttle ships through the harbor as the city lights sparkle across the water. The inside bar is good for a quiet drink, while you can boogie at the outside bar, where different bands come to play Wed.–Sat.

Across the walkway, **Don Ho's Island Grill,** 808/528-0807, serves lunch and dinner daily and stays open for late evening music. Cashing in on one of the best-known names in island music, this is a casual, easygoing place with good food to match. Try surfboard-shaped pizzas, fresh fish, pasta, and Hawaiian desserts. Entrés run mostly $13–17.

At the entrance to the Marketplace is **Chai's Island Bistro,** 808/585-0011, a great stop for Hawaiian regional cuisine but also the most happening place in town for the sweet sounds of island music, provided by famous island artists 7–9 P.M. For lunch, try such delicacies as fresh spinach gnocchi, Thai vegetarian green curry, grilled Atlantic salmon with truffle Madeira sauce, or a simpler marinated and grilled chicken breast pita bread sandwich. The dinner menu is partially the same with additional intriguing items like seafood rissotto cake appetizers, Long Island duck bistro style, and Asian-style osso bucco

with kabocha pumpkin. Chai's has established a great reputation and works hard at keeping the accolades coming. Lunch entrée prices run $12–20, dinner prices $26–45.

On the ground level near the water is the **Kupono's Bar and Grill,** 808/532-2161. A casual outdoor affair that capitalizes on its music and waterfront location, Kupono's generally has eats of the *pu pu* and bar food variety, but there are better entrées in the evening. Always good entertainment in the evening.

Upstairs, the **Big Island Steakhouse,** 808/537-4446, has a well-rounded menu with both meat and seafood and strolling musicians to accompany your evening meal.

## Restaurant Row

This new-age complex at 500 Ala Moana Boulevard (across from the Federal Building) points the way to people-friendly development in Honolulu's future. It houses shops and businesses, adequate public parking, and a nine-theater cineplex, but mostly restaurants, all set along its central courtyard and strolling area. Some restaurants are elegant and excellent, whereas others are passable and plain. But they are all in a congenial setting, and you can pick your palate and style preference as easily as you'd pick offerings at a buffet. Start at the central fountain area with its multicolored modernistic Lego-inspired tower.

A premier restaurant here is **Sansei Seafood Restaurant and Sushi Bar,** 808/536-6286. Following the great success of the original Sansei in Kapalua, Maui, owner D. K. Kodama opened this fine restaurant in Honolulu. Employing the same concept, but in a much larger space, the Sansei offers a full range of traditional favorites and experimental sushi, main course entrées, and a large selection of domestic and imported wines and sake. Not only is the food eminently tasty, but it's also a joy to eat and is presented in a stylish manner. The sushi is adaptive, and many of the sauces, innovations in themselves, go way beyond soy sauce and wasabi. Sushi is the focus here, and this is a great place to try several varieties. The meal menu includes mostly fish and seafood, but some meat and poultry are also available. Sample items off the menu are an award-winning Asian rock shrimp cake appetizer, spider roll sushi that's crispy, tempura soft shell crab with a sweet and hot Thai sauce and unagi glaze, and roast Peking duck breast over mushroom and potato risotto with a foie gras demi glace. When possible, locally grown greens picked daily are used, and, oddly enough but perhaps not surprising for this avant garde establishment, the desserts are as all-American as apple pie. Sushi is priced from $3.25, entrées run $16–24. But the Sansei is more than a restaurant. Open until 10 P.M. nightly and until 2 A.M. Thur.–Sat. for karaoke and food, with reduced prices on sushi and the bar menu after 10 P.M., it's become a favorite late-night spot. The Sansei is a winner and sure to please the discriminating palate.

The **Sunset Grill,** 808/521-4409, is on the corner. With wraparound windows, a long and open bar, and comfortable maple chairs, it lives up to its name. This is the place to come for a quiet evening drink in the downtown area. The food is prepared in full view on a *kiawe*-fired grill, wood-roasting oven, and Italian rotisserie. Choices include pasta, gourmet salads, calamari, fresh fish, chicken, and lamb. Lunch is a wide variety of plump, juicy sandwiches. The chefs at the Sunset aren't afraid to blend East with West in a wide variety of creations. Open weekdays 11 A.M.–10 P.M., Sat. and Sun. 5:30–11 P.M.

Others in the Row include **Ruth's Chris Steakhouse,** for the big meat, **Josie's** for Mexican, **Phillip Paolo's Italian Restaurant** for Mediterranean cuisine, and **Payao Thai Restaurant** for tastes of Asia. In the middle of the complex is **The Row,** an outdoor bar with finger food, and nearby is the **Ocean** nightclub, one of the happening nightspots in town.

# INEXPENSIVE DINING AROUND TOWN

The following restaurants are in and around the greater Honolulu area.

At the corner of Pali Highway and Vineyard is **People's Cafe,** 808/536-5789. It's run by Newton and Adelle Oshiro, and two going on three generations of the same Japanese family have been serving the full range of excellent and inexpensive

Hawaiian food at this down-home restaurant. Plate lunches and other lunches run about $6. Combination lunches like the Laulau plate, which is lomi salmon, pipikaula, chicken lu'au or chicken long rice, and poi or rice, are about $10 and served on sectioned trays. Although there's no decor to speak of, the place is clean and the people are friendly. If you want a real Hawaiian meal at a reasonable price, this is the place to come. People's Cafe is open Mon.–Fri. 10 A.M.–7:30 P.M., Sat. until 2:30 P.M.

**Down to Earth Natural Foods and Deli,** 2525 S. King St., 808/947-7678, open daily 7:30 A.M.–10 P.M., is a kind of museum of health food stores serving filling, nutritious health food dishes for reasonable prices. Get sandwiches (like a whopping avocado, tofu, and cheese) and other items such as veggie stroganoff, eggplant parmigiana, and lasagna at the deli counter, or try the salad and hot entrée bars for other prepared foods. Many items at the hot entrée bar go for $5.95 per pound. Healthwise, you can't go wrong!

**Kokua Market Natural Foods Co-op,** 2643 S. King St., 808/941-1922, is open to the public daily 8:30 A.M.–8:30 P.M. It's a full-service store with organic and fresh produce, cheese, milk, juices, bulk foods, breads, a small deli case full of sandwiches, and prepared entrées and hot soups.

Directly across from the University on O'ahu Avenue are **Volcano Joe's** for espresso and pastries and **Mamo's** for pizza, just perfect for students on a budget looking for inexpensive eats. Inside the YMCA next door is an alternative snack shop/breakfast place that can put something healthy and filling into your belly.

**Sekiya's Restaurant and Deli,** 2746 Kaimuki Ave., 808/732-1656, looks like a set from a 1940s tough-guy movie. The food is well prepared and the strictly local clientele will be amazed that you even know about the place. Open 8:30 A.M.–10 P.M., Fri. and Sat. until 11 P.M.

**Hale Vietnam,** 1140 12th Ave. in Kaimuki, 808/735-7581, has built an excellent and award-winning reputation for authentic and savory dishes at moderate prices. It gets the highest praise from local people, who choose it again and again for an inexpensive evening of delicious dining. Hours are daily 11 A.M.–10 P.M. Try such items as deep-fried Imperial roll appetizers, catfish soup, chicken curry, braised shrimp in black pepper sauce, one of the numerous vegetarian dishes, or the Vietnamese fondue.

Another winner in Kaimuki is the **Big City Diner,** 3565 Wai'alae Ave., 808/738-8855. Open for breakfast, lunch, and dinner, it serves huge portions and is so much a local favorite that you'll have to wait in line to get a seat on Saturday morning. Your breakfast might be Our Famous Big Breakfast of three eggs and choice of meat, Loco Moco, or Murphy's Famous Fresh Apple Pancakes. The lunch and dinner menu are pretty much the same, and from them you can order, among others, chow mein noodles, hamburger steak with grilled onions and mushrooms, baby back ribs with guava barbecue sauce, kimchi fried rice, burgers, or sandwiches. Most come for the food, but there's also satellite TV, live Monday night sports, and karaoke every evening starting at 10 P.M. Park in the city parking lot behind.

Literally within a few steps of the Big City Diner you can find Italian, Japanese, Chinese, Korean, Mexican, Vietnamese, and Thai restaurants, as well as a coffee shop and bakery or two. This stretch of Wai'alae Avenue is full of activity, with plenty of food options.

There are also a few opportunities in Honolulu to feed your mind and soul along with satiating your appetite.

The **Pavilion Cafe,** at the Honolulu Academy of Arts, 900 S. Beretania, 808/532-8734, is a classy place for lunch. Open Tues.–Sat. 11:30 A.M.–2 P.M.; dine inside or out. Menu items include soups, salads, and sandwiches, perhaps a goat cheese salad and tenderloin steak sandwich, and other entrées like pasta, mostly for under $10. An assortment of desserts and beverages can also be ordered. The food is delicious, but be aware that the portions are not for the hungry, being designed primarily for patrons of the arts, who seem to be wealthy matrons from the fashionable sections of Honolulu who are all watching their waistlines.

Don't let the Porsches, Mercedeses, and BMWs parked vanity plate to vanity plate in the parking lot discourage you from enjoying the **Contemporary Cafe,** at the Contemporary Museum, 2411 Makiki Heights Dr., 808/523-3362 (reservations recommended). The small but superb menu is as inspired as the art in the museum, and the prices are astonishingly inexpensive. Dine inside or out. Appetizers are house-cured gravlax, shrimp cocktail, or crostini for under $8. Salads include garden salad, soba noodle salad, or chicken taco salad for under $10. Sandwiches include smoked breast of turkey, grilled vegetable wrap, or tuna for $9.25 or less. Desserts run from cheesecake to flourless chocolate roulade, and beverages include homemade lemonade and cappuccino. For a wonderful cultural outing combined with a memorable lunch, come to the Contemporary Cafe. Open Tues.–Sat 11:30 A.M.–2:30 P.M., Sun, noon–2:30 P.M. It's just so . . . contemporary!

## MODERATE DINING AROUND TOWN

**Fisherman's Wharf,** 1009 Ala Moana Blvd. on the Kewalo Basin, 808/538-3808, is a Honolulu institution. This restaurant has been here since 1952, when it took over from Felix's Italian Garden Restaurant, which had been on this spot since the 1940s. The restaurant's design gives you the feel of being aboard ship. Its theme is nautical, displaying a collection of ship's accessories, riggings, figurines, and trophy catches from the sea. The place exudes the feel of a Honolulu of days past, and you can sit and watch through the windows as fishing boats and cruise ships arrive and depart as they have done for decades, or look out past Waikiki to Diamond Head. For lunch, start with oysters on the half shell or fresh steamed clams. Follow this with Boston-style clam chowder and a Caesar salad. Lunch sandwiches range $7.95–11.95, or choose fresh fish done in a variety of ways at market price, broiled oysters and shiitake mushrooms for $15, fish entrées $11–14, or steak, lobster, and crab $16–30. The dinner menu is similar, except a few dollars more in price, but without the sandwiches and with the addition of pastas and other special entrées. Happy hour runs 4–6 P.M., and on Friday there's live contemporary Hawaiian music. Upstairs, the Captain's Bridge is like a cabaret club that serves light meals, soups, and salads, with a full range of drinks. Friday night 8 P.M.–midnight upstairs there's karaoke, so come up and sing.

**The Hideaway Restaurant,** at La Mariana Sailing Club, 50 Sand Island Access Rd., 808/848-2800, is the only real restaurant in this neck of the woods. The Hideaway serves appetizers like sashimi, lumpia, and sautéed mushroom buttons. From the broiler come steaks, pork chops, and burgers with all the fixings. From the sea, seafood brochette, shrimp scampi served over linguini, or Cajun-style ahi will fill your plate. Chicken, lobster, and nightly specials round out the menu. The lunch menu is simpler, with soups, salads, hot and cold sandwiches, and a handful of fish and stir-fry selections. The chef is also known for his onion rings. They're not on the menu; you have to know about them. Now you know. The decor has been upgraded, but it's still very Polynesian and nautical in essence. Inside hang Japanese glass floats that are diffused with different colors at night, providing mood lighting for the cozy black booths and wooden tables with wicker chairs, carved tiki posts, lights with blowfish skins or seashell covers, and decorations scavenged from defunct former restaurants in town. The Hideaway is an out-of-the-way place, local, and real Hawaiiana. Located at a working marina, this is where all the yachties come. Half hidden behind a stand of trees and a fence, only one small sign at the entrance points the way. The restaurant serves food Mon.–Fri. 11 A.M.–2 P.M. and 5–9 P.M., Sat.–Sun. noon–5 P.M. An early-bird menu is served 3–5 P.M., and *pu pu* are served at the bar, where happy hour runs 4–7 P.M. Most evenings there's piano music from about 6 P.M., so stop by for a drink at the bar and enjoy.

**Auntie Pasto's,** 1099 S. Beretania and the corner of Pensacola, 808/523-8855, is open Mon.–Thurs. 11 A.M.–4 P.M. for lunch and until 10:30 P.M. for dinner, and weekends 4–11 P.M. only for dinner. The quiet, comfortable vibe is upbeat pizza parlor; you can even bring your own wine. Most of the Italian menu entrées are $8.50–12, and these include eggplant parmesan, calamari steak, and veal marsala. Soups come by the cup or bowl, and salads range from a garden green salad to a chicken Caesar. Antipasto

plates, sides, and desserts run $3–9. No reservations necessary.

The minute you walk into **Imanas Tei** you know you're in for a special treat. The ambiance is traditional and the smells authentic. It's like being in a small neighborhood restaurant in small-city Japan. Selections off the long menu include deep-fried and grilled tofu, meat, and fish. Sushi rolls and plates, sashimi, and various stews and noodle dishes round out the list. It's just what you'd expect from a traditional Japanese restaurant. Most items runs $3–9—you'll want more than one—but the stews and other full meals are $18.50 and more. Some claim that Imanas Tei has the best Japanese food in town. Because it always seems to be busy, regulars would probably agree. Imanas Tei is up a short alley around the corner from Puck's Alley, near the intersection of King and University streets. Limited parking. Open Mon.–Sat. 5–11:30 P.M.; call 808/941-2626 for reservations.

Across the street at 2632 S. King Street, **India House,** 808/955-7552, is open daily for lunch and dinner. Extraordinary Indian dishes include a wide selection of curries, tandoori specials, vegetarian dishes, special naan bread, kabobs, and fish tikka. Specialty desserts include halawas, gulab jamun, and kheer.

This corner of King Street and University Avenue, and its adjacent blocks, has not only India House and Imanas Tei, as well as Down To Earth and Kokua natural food stores, but also several other reasonably priced restaurants that include the following: **Taste of Saigon** serves a whole assortment of Vietnamese foods. The **Greek Corner** weighs in with the hearty dishes of the Mediterranean, like hommos, gyros sandwiches, falafel plate, and souvlaki chicken kebab. Next door, **Magoos** is a lively local hangout for beer and pizza that's boisterous and busy on the weekends. And **Maharani** serves the wonderful spiced dishes of the subcontinent.

# CHINATOWN

You can eat delicious ethnic food throughout Chinatown. If not Honolulu's best, the entire district, food-wise, is definitely one of Honolulu's cheapest. On almost every corner you've got places like **Mini Garden Noodle House, Yat Tug Chow,** and **Ting Yin Chop Suey** for breakfast, lunch, and dinner. They're basic and cheap eateries whose ambiance is a mixture of Formica-topped tables and linoleum floors. In almost all, the food is authentic, with most featuring Asian food. You can easily get meals here for around $7. Some eateries appear greasier than the Alaska Pipeline, so you'll have to feel them out. The local people eat in them regularly, and most are clean enough. One place that you shouldn't miss is **Shung Chong Yuein,** a Chinese cake shop at 1027 Maunakea. Look in to see yellow sugar cakes, black sugar cakes, shredded coconut with eggs, salted mincemeat, Chinese ham with egg, lotus seeds, and steamed buns.

As with the shops at the Chinatown Cultural Plaza, the restaurants there also come and go. One to check is **Buddhist Vegetarian Restaurant,** 808/532-8218, which is basic and about as antiseptic as a monk's cell, but the food is healthy. The varied menu includes inexpensive dim sum dishes, stir-fry vegetables, spicy hot and sour soup, and many braised or fried vegetable or tofu dishes. Most are in the under-$10 category, but the Buddhist supreme vegetarian plate goes for $23.95. Lunch is served 10:30 A.M.–2 P.M., dinner 5:30–9 P.M.

**Doong Kong Lau Seafood Restaurant** is on the river side of the Cultural Plaza, 808/531-8833. Inside it's utilitarian with leatherette seats and Formica tables. You come here for the food. Savories include stir-fried squid with broccoli, stir-fried scallops with garlic sauce, stir-fried oysters with black beans, sizzle plates like seafood combo, or shark fin with shredded chicken, all for reasonable prices. Open 7 A.M.–9 P.M.

At another stall in this complex is the **Royal Kitchen,** 808/524-4461, a popular place with local families and businesspeople. It's especially known for its takeout baked manapua, soft dough buns stuffed with pork, charsiu, or vegetables, and for its Chinese sausage, lupcheung, charsiu, roast pork, and roast duck. Open very early in the morning.

**Won Kee Sea Food Restaurant** 808/524-6877, is an eatery where you get delicious seafood in tasteful surroundings. A place for Honolulu's in-the-know crowd.

Right next door to the Won Kee is the **Forum Cafe,** 808/599-5022. Open daily 11 A.M.–2:30 P.M. and 5–11 P.M., this too is a classy joint with everything from the usual rice dishes to braised imperial shark fin soup for $38 per person.

The **Legend Seafood Restaurant,** 808/532-1868, two doors down from the Won Kee, emphasizes fish and seafood but also serves inexpensive Hong Kong–style dim sum in small, medium, large, and super-size plate sizes.

A recent phenomenon is several excellent Vietnamese restaurants that have sprung up like bamboo sprouts along Chinatown's streets. Most are meticulously clean, and the moderately priced food is "family-pride gourmet." The decor ranges from oilcloth tablecloths topped by a bouquet of plastic flowers and a lazy Susan filled with exotic spices and condiments, to down-to-earth chic with some mood lighting, candles, and even linen place settings. As a group, they represent the best culinary deals on O'ahu today. Many selections, like the grilled seasoned meatballs or marinated pork, come with noodles, fresh lettuce, mint, cucumber, bean sprouts, and ground peanut sauce that you wrap in layers of rice paper to make your own version of what can best be described as an Asian taco. Simply moisten a few sheets of the rice paper in the bowl of water provided and wrap away. Great fun, and they'll show you how! There are plenty of savory vegetarian menu choices as well.

**A Little Bit of Saigon,** 1160 Maunakea, 808/528-3663, open daily 10 A.M.–10 P.M., is the fanciest of the lot, although it is still quite basic. Specialties are rollups that include savory beef, pork, or chicken, served with lettuce, fresh herbs, vegetables, sweet and sour fish sauce, and peanut or pineapple and anchovy sauce, along with thin rice paper that you use to roll your own for $5.50–11.95. Good yet inexpensive selections are stir-fried vegetables that you can have either by themselves or with fresh fish, prawns, chicken, beef, tofu, or scallops. For the hearty appetite, try the five-course dinner for two at

$29.95 that gives a good sample of the menu. Finish with banana and tapioca dessert, $2.50.

**To Chau Vietnamese Restaurant,** 1007 River St., 808/533-4549, and **Ha Bien,** around the corner at 198 N. King St., serve basic Vietnamese fare for under $8 for most dishes.

**Rosarina Pizza,** 1111 Maunakea St., 808/533-6634, is an alternative to the Asian cuisine. They will sell you a slice of pizza for only $1.50 or a whole pie ranging from a small cheese for $8 to a large combo at $16. You can also order a 12-inch sublike pastrami and provolone for $5 or an à la carte dinner like spaghetti with meat sauce or sausage, cannelloni, or manicotti, all for under $8.

Also for an alternative, try **Zaffron** at 69 N. King St., open Tues.–Sat. 6–9:30 P.M. for Indian tandoori, curry, and other usual selections.

**Grilla's,** 808/545-7444, open for breakfast and lunch at 12 S. King Street, caters to the downtown business crowd looking for a quick, inexpensive meal. Although everything comes out on styrofoam and the food is not necessarily for the health-conscious, it's hearty and flavorful. Breakfast is eggs in many permutations and griddlecakes. Lunch might be a sub sandwich, quiche, or pasta with meatballs. Expect to eat for less than $8.

A local bar with an easygoing atmosphere and a *pu pu* and pita-deli sandwich menu is **Hanks Cafe Honolulu,** 1038 Nu'uanu Ave., 808/526-1410. Open noon–2 A.M. weekdays, 5 P.M.–midnight on Sat., and 4–10 P.M. on Sun.; there's a weekday happy hour 4–6 P.M. Monday is open-mike comedy night, while musicians hold forth the rest of the week. While you're there, have a look at the paintings on the walls—all Hank's.

At the bottom end of Nu'uanu Street are **O'-Toole's Pub,** open for beer, hard drinks, and music Wed.–Sat. evenings, and **Murphy's** bar, which is open until 2 A.M. except Sunday, when it closes at midnight. At Murphy's, you can not only order such items as fish and chips and Gaelic steak that you might expect from an Irish bar, but you can also get fresh grilled island fish, a chicken breast sandwich, or a Cajun burger, all at a reasonable $7.50–13.

The nearby and more upscale Indigo and Palomino restaurants are included in the Hawaiian Regional Cuisine section.

## ALONG KAPAHULU AVENUE

Once Kapahulu Avenue crosses Ala Wai Boulevard going away from Waikiki, it passes excellent inexpensive to moderately priced restaurants, strung one after the other. Kapahulu was the area in which the displaced Chinese community resettled after the great Chinatown fire at the turn of the 20th century. Kapahulu basically means "poor soil," and unlike most areas of Hawaii it could barely support vegetables and plants. Undaunted, the Chinese brought in soil with wagons and wheelbarrows, turning the area productive and verdant. The restaurants along Kapahulu Avenue are only a short drive away for those staying in Waikiki.

**Sam Choy's Diamond Head Restaurant,** 449 Kapahulu Ave., 808/732-8645, is open for dinner Mon.–Thurs. 5:30–9 P.M. and Fri.–Sun. 5–9:30 P.M. Reservations are accepted. Island chef Sam Choy and his staff prepare food using mostly local produce, meat, and fish, mixing and embellishing the varied ethnic cuisine traditions of the islands. There are set and daily special menus. One of the nice things here is that you always have many *pu pu* appetizers to choose from, making it easier to sample small portions of food that you wouldn't otherwise have tried. Some signature entrées include Sam's seafood *lau lau,* Asian veal osso bucco with Oriental noodles, honey macadamia nut–crusted pork chops, and oven-roasted duck. Expect most entrées in the $20–28 range. The restaurant also has a full bar and wine selection, and the decor is as soothing as the food is delicious. In addition to the dinner meals, Sam serves more island-style favorites during the Big Aloha Sunday Brunch Buffet at 9:30 A.M.–1:30 P.M. for $25.

On the ground floor below Sam Choy's is **Hee Hing** Chinese restaurant, 808/735-5544. A large establishment with decor that shouts China, Hee Hing has a menu so big that you might take longer deciding what you want than actually eating your meal. Along with the usual soups, noodle, and rice dishes, you'll find other specialties like earthen pot casseroles, sizzling plates, traditional Szechuan and Northern Chinese dishes, and plenty of selections from the sea. All this comes at a reasonable price, with most dishes in the $7.50–13 range, except for a few of the lobster, shrimp, and abalone entrées.

The **Rainbow Drive-In** at the corner of Kana'aina Avenue is strictly local, with a kids' hangout feel, but the plate lunches are hearty and well-done for under $6. Another of the same, **K C Drive Inn,** just up the road a few blocks at 1029 Kapahulu, specializes in waffle dogs and shakes and even has carhops. Both are excellent stops for picking up plate lunches on your way out of Waikiki heading for the H-1 freeway.

The sit-down **Irifune Japanese Restaurant,** 563 Kapahulu, 808/737-1141, is open Tues.–Sat. for lunch 11:30 A.M.–1:30 P.M. and for dinner 5:30–9:30 P.M., directly across from Zippy's, a fast-food joint. Irifune serves authentic, well-prepared Japanese standards in its small dining room. Most dinner meals begin at around $10, while lunch dishes are somewhat less. One item that Irifune has become especially known for is its garlic ahi, which goes for $11. Irifune is a great deal for Japanese food, much cheaper and easily as good as most other Japanese restaurants on the Waikiki strip. Known more for its food than its decor, it's a winner! Get there early because it's a popular place.

The next restaurant in line is **Ono Hawaiian Foods,** 726 Kapahulu, 808/737-2275, open Mon.–Sat. 11 A.M.–7:45 P.M., an institution in down-home Hawaiian cooking. This is the kind of place that a taxi driver takes you when you ask for "the real thing." It's clean and basic, with the decor being photos of local performers—all satisfied customers—hung on the wall. If you want to try *lomi lomi* salmon, poi, or *kalua* pig, this is *da' kine place, brah!* Prices are cheap, with plate lunches for $8.45.

If you have a sweet tooth, try **Leonard's Bakery** at 933 Kapahulu. Specializing in hot malasadas and pao dolce, Leonard's has garnered an islandwide reputation since 1952. Open 6 A.M.–9 P.M. Sun.–Thurs. and until 10 P.M. on Fri. and Sat. nights.

**The Pyramids,** 758-B Kapahulu Ave., 808/737-2900, is the place to head for Greek and Mediterranean cuisine. Open Mon.–Sat. for lunch buffet 11 A.M.–2 P.M. and daily for dinner 5:30–10 P.M., it's a small place, so reservations are recommended. Being here, you might imagine yourself to be inside King Tut's tomb with hieroglyphics and painted stone blocks on the walls. Live music and belly dancing accompany the meal every evening. All the usual favorites are on the menu: tabouleh and shawerma salads; hommos, baba ghanouj, falafel, and stuffed grape leaves appetizers; and entrées like shish kabob, moussaka, and kebbeh. Dinner prices, $13.95–18.95 for entrées, are a few dollars more than those at lunch, although the lunch buffet runs $8.95. The lunch menu also has a few sandwiches, while the dinner menu has some vegetarian options. This is about the only Middle Eastern/Egyptian restaurant on the island.

## HAWAIIAN REGIONAL CUISINE

As large a city as Honolulu is, it's able to support many innovative restaurants where locally grown foods are combined with preparation techniques from around the world to produce new and intriguing flavors. The following are restaurants where something new is always on the menu and the combination of ingredients, textures, and tastes is sure to please. Reservations are recommended.

In the semi-industrial area of Iwilei at 580 N. Nimitz Hwy., **Sam Choy's Breakfast, Lunch, and Crab,** 808/545-7979, is as popular as every other Sam Choy restaurant in the islands. The Kona poke and beef stew omelets are much-requested breakfast items, while various crab and other seafood entrées appear for lunch and dinner depending on the season. Many other island favorites are on the menu and there's always generous portions. Sam brews beer at this site, and the brewpub is open nightly until 10 P.M. Here you get *pu pu* specials and there's live music periodically. Valet parking only. Hours of operation are breakfast Mon.–Fri. 6:30–10:30 A.M. and until 11 A.M. on Sat. and Sun., lunch until 4 P.M., and dinner weeknights 5–9:30 P.M., weekends until 10 P.M.

**Indigo,** 1121 Nu'uanu Ave. in Chinatown across from the Hawaii Theatre, 808/521-2900, serves what some classify as Eurasian cuisine.

Chef Glenn Chu offers such savory items as Chinese steamed buns filled with eggplant and sun-dried tomatoes, crispy goat cheese wonton filled with fruit sauce, roasted tomato garlic crab soup, Balinese curried calamari, or grilled Mongolian rib-eye beef with black bean sauce. Some vegetarian items are available, and they offer many desserts to ponder over. Open for lunch Tues.–Fri. 11:30 A.M.–2 P.M. and dinner Tues.–Sat. 6–9:30 P.M. There's live music, dancing, and drinks at the adjacent Green Room Bar and Lounge until midnight. Valet parking is provided.

On the third floor of the Harbor Court building at 66 Queen Street, set on the edge of Chinatown and overlooking Honolulu harbor, is **Palomino,** 808/528-2811, an innovative restaurant that combines fresh island ingredients with an old-world Italian twist. A specialty here are the wood-fired oven and rotisserie, which produce some exquisite flavors. Open for lunch and dinner, the menu changes periodically but retains such favorites as chop chop salad, huli-huli lemon sage chicken, paella, honey-crusted beef tenderloin, and lamb shank. Always great are the pizza and pasta dishes and an assortment of intriguing appetizers, yet some come for the desserts, which include tiramisu, mocha crème brûlée, and the molten chocolate tower. Expect lunch entrées, which also include sandwiches, in the $8–15 range, while dinner entrées run up to $30. Only two blocks from the Hawaii Theatre, Palomino caters to the late-night theater crowd with late hours and a reasonably priced prix fixe dinner for $25. Hours are Sun.–Thurs. until 11 P.M. and Fri. and Sat. until 1 A.M.

**Alan Wong's,** just north of Waikiki at 1857 S. King St., third floor, 808/949-2526, is a Best Restaurant of the Year award winner. Try 'opihi shooters or kalbi-style beef wonton tacos as appetizers. Although the menu changes periodically, entrées might be pan-steamed opakapaka, kiawe-grilled beef tenderloin, grilled lamb chops with coconut macadamia nut crust, or a vegetarian entrée consisting of mashed potatoes, black bean salsa, grilled asparagus, and roasted shiitake mushrooms. Yum! The contemporary style of the restaurant matches the contemporary style of the food and its presentation. Valet parking is offered. Alan Wong also has the Pineapple Room restaurant for upscale dinning and Patisserie Bar for coffee, drinks, and pastries on the third floor of Macy's department store at Ala Moana Center and the Regional Cuisine Marketplace for fine island foodstuffs on the fourth floor.

At 3660 Wai'alae Avenue near where the road crests the hill in Kaimuki is **3660 On the Rise,** 808/737-1177, a casually elegant place where you can watch the cooks create behind the glass wall of the kitchen. The menu changes somewhat every night, but Chef Russell Siu's "first flavors" include pan-seared shiitake-crusted hamachi or potato-crusted crab cakes, while "second flavors" are soups and salads. "Feature presentations" might be grilled ginger breast of chicken, Burgundy braised short ribs of beef, or Chinese steamed fillet of snapper lightly seared and simmered in a Chinese black bean broth. Round out your meal with one of the "sweet endings": harlequin crème brûlée or mile-high Wai'alae pie, perhaps, or indulge in a cup of coffee or glass of cognac or port. Delightful presentation and attentive service. Open Tues.–Sun. 5:30–9 P.M.; reservations necessary.

**On Jin's Cafe,** 401 Kamake'e behind Pier 1 Imports at the Victoria Ward Centers, 808/589-1666, is a pleasant surprise. Chef On Jin Kim, who used to run the kitchen at the Hanatei Bistro before it closed, has opened a much smaller and more intimate restaurant here to everyone's delight. Open for lunch Mon.–Fri. 11 A.M.–2 P.M. and dinner Wed.–Sat. 5–9 P.M., Fri. and Sat. until 10 P.M. The food is eclectic with definite Pacific and European overtones. The clean, modern style, marble tables decorated with orchids, tile floor, and semi-open kitchen set the mood. Lunch is inexpensive, with plate lunches and sandwiches that run $5.75–7.50, but even these show class. Dinners are the best—more sophisticated and more expensive but not outrageous. Appetizers like charred ahi and Korean-style shrimp with sweet potato pancakes run about $6–8, a French onion soup $4.95, while the entrées like steamed salmon, bouillabaisse, five-spice duck, and rack of lamb are mostly $18.50–24.50. Savor the sauces.

One of the fine restaurants that has made a superb name for itself is **Chef Mavro Restau-**

rant, 1969 S. King St., 808/944-4714, at the corner of McCully, open for dinner only, daily except Monday. Formerly the executive chef of the Four Seasons Resort on Maui and before that the executive chef at the Halekulani in Waikiki, Chef Mavro is now king of his own domain, and he reigns with distinction. The restaurant is not large but comfortable and personal, tastefully elegant yet not extravagant. Booths line the perimeter of the room, tables are set in the middle, paintings of tropical flowers and raku pottery with flowers line the walls, and low lighting, linen, and crystal set the mood. Chef Mavro offers a mix of à la carte and prix fixe menus with three, four, or six options, with or without wine. The food is exceptional in its own right, but an important factor of dining here is the pairing of wine and food, a complementary union where neither overpowers the other. Each item is introduced and explained as it's set on the table, and wines are chosen for each individual dish. Nearly the entire menu changes by season, but no matter what the choices, the freshest of Hawaiian produce and seafood are always infused with subtle yet intense flavors and prepared with a French flare, resulting in tropical cuisine with French soul. This is an exceptional restaurant with masterful food. For a special night out, this is a great choice. Dining here can be expensive, but it's worth every penny. Appetizers generally run $15–20, entrées $32–39.

On the top floor of the Ala Moana Hotel, a short hop west of Waikiki, is **Aaron's.** This location affords an unsurpassed view out over the Waikiki strip as well as over downtown Honolulu. It is as much for its fabulous location that people come to dine, yet the food is first-class as well. Start your dinner with tiger eye sushi tempura, Manila clams, or kiawe beef stick appetizer, and follow this with a daily selection of soup or a nutritious nalo greens salad. Entrées include steamed island onaga with bok choy, soy-nori vinaigrette, and hot peanut oil, blackened double pork chop with pineapple marmalade, curry sauce, and toasted macadamia nuts, and clams spaghettini with pomodoro sauce and arugula. Appetizers run $8–14—with caviar at $85— and entrées fall mostly in the $25–49 range. Couple the food and location with a select wine and you have the makings for a romantic evening. Open for dinner only 5–10:45 P.M.—call 808/955-4466 for reservations—with live R&B Wed.–Sat. evenings.

## Entertainment

### Music and Dancing

**Anna Banana's,** 2440 S. Beretania, 808/946-5190, is the "top banana" for letting your hair down and boogying the night away. It's just west of the S. King Street and University Avenue intersection, just across from Star Market. Banana's has a laid-back atmosphere, reasonable beer prices, usually a small cover of about $5 that goes to the band, no dress code, and a friendly student crowd. The bar downstairs is dark and its walls covered with plenty of memorabilia. An additional bar is upstairs, and four or five nights a week there is live music. The music is potluck, so you get the whole spectrum coming through here. There is light dining downstairs and a backyard to cool off in between sets. Great place, great fun! Open 11:30 A.M.–2 A.M.

Located at Restaurant Row, 500 Ala Moana Blvd., the **Ocean Club,** 808/526-9888, is one of Honolulu's consistent hot spots. Open Tues.–Thurs. 4:30 P.M.–2 A.M., Fri. 4:30 P.M.–3 A.M., and Sat. 6 P.M.–3 A.M., Sun. and Mon. closed, it has a DJ and a large dance floor. The cocktail hour, with reduced-price *pu pu* and light meals, runs 4:30–8 P.M., while happy hour on Friday starts at 8 P.M. The age limit for entrance is 23. Apparently the owners want a more sophisticated crowd, not just a bunch of rowdy first-timers.

**Rumours Nightclub,** in the Ala Moana Hotel, 410 Atkinson St., 808/955-4811, is an established DJ disco that cranks up around 9 P.M. on Friday and Saturday and features the newest in dance and rock videos. A dress code is enforced, and a $5–10 cover is charged.

Also at the Ala Moana Hotel at the South Seas Village is **Kalo's South Seas Revue,** a Polynesian revue and buffet dinner show. Dinner starts at 5:30 P.M. and the show gets going about 6:30 P.M. Dinner includes prime rib and dozens of other treats, and the show is a mixture of music, hula, and a fire dance. Tickets run $53 adults, $28 children. Call 808/941-5205 for information and reservations.

The open-air **Kupono's Bar and Grill** at the Aloha Tower Marketplace has an elevated stage with live acts throughout the week except Sunday, ranging from Hawaiian to contemporary rock to jazz, including Henry Kupono and other big-name Hawaiian performers on occasion. The music is potluck, but you're right on the water next to Aloha Tower, so you can watch the sunset and always have a great time. Just a few steps away are **Don Ho's Island Grill, Big Island Steakhouse,** and **Gordon-Biersch Brewery and Restaurant,** all of which offer evening entertainment on weekends or extended weekends to accompany their fine menus.

**Chai's Island Bistro,** also at Aloha Tower Marketplace, has some of the best island musicians performing weekly. The Brothers Cazimero take the stage on Wednesday, Thursday is Jake Shimabukuro purforms on ukulele, Robert Camimero plays piano solo on Tuesday, Friday, and Saturday, and Olomana holds court on Sunday and Monday. Each is a class act, and together they make the best lineup of local musicians on the island. Music runs 7–9 P.M. Reservations are suggested. Free valet parking is provided.

For a complete listing of what's happening in town on the music and dance scene for the weekend and coming week, have a look at the Calendar of Events section of the Friday edition of the newspaper.

**Note:** Also see the Waikiki chapter.

## Free Entertainment

At **Centerstage,** Ala Moana Shopping Center, various shows are presented—mostly music (rock, gospel, jazz, Hawaiian) and hula. Performances usually start at noon. The **Keiki Hula Show,** every Sunday at 10 A.M., is fast becoming an institution. Here, hula is being kept alive, with many first-time performers interpreting the ancient movements that they study in their *halau.*

The **Royal Hawaiian Band,** founded more than 150 years ago, performs Friday at noon on the 'Iolani Palace Bandstand, and on Sunday at 2 P.M. at the Kapi'olani Bandstand. Call 808/527-5666 for other band performance locations, or visit the band website at www.royalhawaiianband.com.

Everyone is invited to enjoy the free **Mayor's Aloha Music Break** every Friday from noon–1 P.M. at Tamarind Park, on the corner of King and Bishop Streets, where anything from rock-and-roll to jazz to traditional music may be performed.

Honolulu Hale (City Hall) presents periodic free musical concerts in the central courtyard and art exhibitions in the central courtyard, Lane Gallery, or Third Floor Gallery. All are welcome Mon.–Fri. 8 A.M.–5 P.M.

Sometimes the university has free noontime shows by local bands at the student center and Friday evening jam sessions at the Manoa Gardens restaurant. Call the information center, 808/956-7235, for current happenings.

## Performance Arts

Like any big city, Honolulu has a whole host of musical and performance art venues and high-quality productions. Some of the best-known are as follows:

The **Honolulu Symphony,** www.honolulusymphony.com, performs indoors at the Neil S. Blaisdell Center Concert Hall and outdoors at the Waikiki Shell. Various programs take place throughout the year, with most tickets ranging $15–50, with students and seniors half price. For information and tickets at the Blaisdell Center, contact 808/538-8863; for information about shows at the Waikiki Shell, call 808/591-2211.

**Hawaii Opera Theater** also puts on shows at the Neil S. Blaisdell Center Concert Hall. The six-week season for this professional company runs late January through early March. For tickets, call 808/596-7858, or check online at www.hawaiiopera.org.

**Ballet Hawaii** also uses the Neil S. Blaisdell Center Concert Hall for performances but re-

O'AHU

hearses at its studio at Dole Cannery Square. For information about schedules and ticketing, call 808/988-7578, or check online at www.ballethawaii.com.

**Diamond Head Theater** performs at its own location, 520 Makapu'u Ave., just below Diamond Head. This company has been presenting theatrical shows since 1915 and never fails to impress. Performances are Thurs.–Sat. at 8 P.M. and Sunday at 4 P.M., and tickets range $10–40. Call the box office at 808/734-0274 for information and tickets or check online at www.diamondheadtheatre.com.

Built in 1922 and renovated inside in 1996, the **Hawaii Theatre** has thrilled crowds with its variety of shows over the years. This theater hosts local and off-island music and theater shows and is a venue of the annual Hawaii International Film Festival. The Hawaii Theatre is at 1130 Bethel Street at the edge of Chinatown, and there is ample nearby pay parking. For what's happening, stop by the box office Tues.–Sat. 9 A.M.–5 P.M. and one-half hour before shows, call 808/528-0506, or surf to www.hawaiitheatre.com.

**Kumu Kahua Theater** is a small theater that produces half a dozen plays annually about life in Hawaii by Hawaiian playwrights. Set on the corner of Bethel and Merchant streets, this 100-seat theater opens its doors Thurs.–Sat. at 8 P.M. and Sun. at 2 P.M. Admission is a reasonable $16 general, $13 seniors, $10 students, with discounts on Thursday. Call 808/536-4441 for tickets and information.

The **Academy Theater** at the Honolulu Academy of Arts hosts a full schedule of film, music, and theatrical performances throughout the year, along with lectures and other educational functions. Tickets for film showings runs $5, and

those for other events vary in price. Call 808/532-8768 for information.

On the University of Hawai'i, Manoa campus, the **Kennedy Theatre** hosts university stage productions. The building, designed by the noted architect I. M. Pei, is of interest in itself but is of greater interest for theater buffs because it is made to easily stage both Western- and Asian-style productions. For information, call 808/956-7655.

The smaller and more intimate **Manoa Valley Theatre,** Hawaii's own "off-Broadway" theater, produces more experimental stage shows throughout the years. For tickets and information, call 808/988-6131.

For first-run commercial Hollywood movies, try **Restaurant Row 9 Theater,** at Restaurant Row, 808/526-4171; the **Kahala 8 Theater,** at the Kahala Mall, 808/733-6243; or the **Ward 16 Theaters,** at the Ward Entertainment Center, 808/594-7000. About the only place in town to see art films at a commercial theater is the **Varsity Twins,** at 1106 University Ave. near the university, 808/973-5833. International films are screened during the summer at **Krauss Hall,** Yukiyoshi Room, on the University of Hawai'i campus. Films usually play on Wednesday evenings at 7:30 P.M. No admission, but donations are accepted.

## Girlie Bars and Strip Joints

Many of these "lounges" or "clubs," as they're called, are strung along the 1600 and 1700 blocks of Kapi'olani Boulevard and in the little alleys running off it. They open and shut frequently. Chinatown's Hotel Street is a cruising ground for both male and female prostitutes. A few clubs in this area offer strippers. Always be prepared for fights and bad vibes in any of these joints, and be careful along Hotel Street at night.

# Shopping

If you don't watch the time, you'll spend half your vacation moving from one fascinating store to the next. Luckily, in greater Honolulu most shopping is clustered in malls, with specialty shops scattered around the city, especially in the nooks and crannies of Chinatown.

## Ala Moana Shopping Center

This is the largest shopping center in the state, and if you want to get all of your souvenir hunting and special shopping done in one shot, this is the place. It's on Ala Moana Boulevard just across from the Ala Moana Beach Park, open Mon.–Sat. 9:30 A.M.–9 P.M., Sun. 10 A.M.–7 P.M. The center has large free parking lots for those who care to drive in, but the mall can also be reached by the Waikiki Trolley red, yellow, and green lines; TheBus nos. 8, 20, 42, and 58; and the Ala Moana Shuttle, which runs every 15 minutes daily throughout business hours from half a dozen locations in Waikiki for $1.50 each way. Recently, the Ala Moana Shopping Center has taken off its comfortable Hawaiian shirt and shorts and donned designer fashions by Christian Dior and Gianni Versace. Local people are irritated, and they have a point, to a point. The center has plenty of down-home shopping left, but it now caters as much to the penthouse as it does to the one-room efficiency. It used to be where the *people* shopped, but now portions are being aimed at the affluent tourist, especially the affluent Japanese tourists who flaunt designer labels like politicians flaunt pretty secretaries. If anything, the shopping has gotten better, but you'll have to look around a bit more for bargains.

Plenty of competition keeps prices down, with more than enough of an array to suit any taste and budget. There are about 200 stores, including all of Hawaii's major department stores like **Sears, JCPenney,** and **Macy's,** with the inclusion of a **Neiman Marcus.** Utilitarian shops and boutiques feature everything from wedding rings to swim fins, while the food court and other restaurants feed hungry shoppers. It's also a great place to see a cross-section of Hawaiian society. Another

pleasantry is the free Keiki Hula Show every Sunday at 10 A.M. on the Centerstage, but there are literally hundreds of other performances throughout the year. The center maintains an information kiosk near Centerstage to answer any questions and point you in the right direction.

The following is a mere sampling of what you'll find. For books, try **Waldenbooks,** which has a large selection of books and an inclusive Hawaiiana section. Books make inexpensive, easy-to-transport, and long-lasting mementos of your trip to Hawaii. **Longs Drugs** has good prices for film, but for cheap and fast developing, try **Fromex One Hour Photo. The Crack Seed Center** offers the best array of crackseed (spiced nuts, seeds, and fruits), which has been a treat for island children for years. Prices are inflated here, but the selection can't be beat, and you can educate yourself about these same products in smaller stores around the island. Crackseed is not to everyone's liking, but it does make a unique souvenir. Spirolina hunters can get their organic fix at **Vim and Vigor,** featuring vitamins, supplements, and minerals, and those needing a chocolate fix should head for **Godiva.**

**Shirokiya** is a Japanese-owned department store between JCPenney and Macy's on the mountain side of the complex. It has a fascinating assortment of gadgetry, knickknacks, handy items, and nifty stuff that Nippon is so famous for. It's fun just to look around, and the prices are reasonable. Japanese products are also available at **S.M. Iida Limited,** a local store dating back to the early 1900s, featuring garden ornaments and flower-arrangement sets. Specialty shops in the center include **Products of Hawai'i, Too, Hawaiian Quilt Collection,** and **The Island's Best,** selling a wide assortment of island-made goods and souvenirs, from cheap to exquisite. Aside from all these shops, Honolulu maintains a satellite city hall here, there is a post office, and both United and Continental have airline offices at the mall.

The restaurants in the **Makai Food Court** are exceptional, if not for taste, at least for price, and

O'AHU

are unbelievable for the variety of cuisines represented. In a huge open area you'll find dishes from Bangkok to Acapulco, from Tokyo to San Francisco. Most of these restaurants have only counters for ordering, with tables in a common dining area. Great for people-watching. In addition, free-standing restaurants and others in the department stores prepare a variety of excellent foods.

## Victoria Ward Centers

This cluster of more than 120 shops and nearly two dozen eateries occupying seven buildings is just a few blocks west of Ala Moana Shopping Center, across from Kewalo Basin and the west end of Ala Moana Beach Park. Shopping hours run Mon.–Sat. 10 A.M.–9 P.M. and Sun. 10 A.M.–5 P.M. The centers can be reached by Waikiki Trolley and TheBus nos. 8, 19, and 20. The modern two-story **Ward Warehouse** complex lives up to its name as a warehouse, with a motif from bygone days when stout wooden beams were used instead of steel. The wide array of shops includes inexpensive restaurants and clothing stores, but the emphasis is on arts and crafts. Give the tots their first lesson in impulse buying at **Child's Play,** an educational toy store, or show them how a pro does it by wandering into **Blue Ginger** for men's and women's fashionable alohawear. Repent past gluttony at **Aloha Health Foods,** primarily a vitamin and mineral store. Perhaps you can dress your feet at **Thongs 'n Things,** with everything in thongs from spiked golfing thongs to Teva sandals, the best all-around footwear for the island. Other shops include **Runners Route,** selling jogging shoes, shorts, and some backpacks; **Le Lotus Bleu** and **Villa Roma** for ladies' fashions; and **Beyond the Beach,** which stocks men's and women's alohawear, casual clothing, and sunglasses. Be sure to stop at **Native Books and Beautiful Things** for unique and authentic high-quality gifts, crafts, artwork, clothing, food items, and books made in Hawaii. This store is an excellent place to start looking for an authentic gift to take home from the islands. Aside from the items it sells, this cooperative offers demonstrations, classes, and other activities on an ongoing basis. Perhaps the premier shop in the Warehouse is **Nohea Gallery**

(*nohea* means "beautiful" or "handsome" in Hawaiian), which displays works by more than 500 local artists and craftspeople. Some of the finest works are created by more than 100 island woodworkers, who make everything from rocking chairs ad rolltop desks to traditional canoe paddles using rich grained woods like koa, mango, and rosewood. Nohea Gallery is where you can see the "heart of Hawaii" through the eyes of its artists. Have a look!

The **Ward Farmers Market** is just across Auahi Street, a great place to pick up fresh produce, fruits, nuts, fish, poultry, and flowers. To the side is **Ward Gateway Center,** where **Sports Authority** is the biggest shop, and behind is an **Office Depot** and **Nordstrom Rack.** Across Kamake'e Street, **Ward Village Shops** include a **Pier 1 Imports,** several clothing outlets, a **Starbucks Coffee,** and a **Kua 'Aina Sandwich** shop. At the intersection of Auahi and Kamake'e streets is the newest addition, the **Ward Entertainment Center,** where you not only have a 16-plex movie theater, but also several restaurants and the three-story **Dave and Buster's** interactive entertainment arcade for adults.

Down Ala Moana Boulevard from Ward Warehouse and across the street from the Ward Village Shops is **Ward Centre,** a sting of stores that's gaining a reputation for some exclusive shops and upscale eateries. It also has one of the few microbreweries on the island. The Ward Centre is appointed in light wood and accentuated by brick floors that give the feeling of an intimate inside mall, although much is outside. Here you can find that just-right piece of jewelry at **Black Pearl Gallery;** fashions at **Allure, Kamehameha Garment Co.,** and **Rain Bow Tique;** and artworks at the **Gallery at Ward Centre.** Next to the gallery is the **Honolulu Chocolate Co.** Like a smug little devil, it tempts with chocolate truffles, mocha clusters, and fancy nut rolls. So sin! You're on vacation.

Vibrating from a remote corner of the mall, where mystics feel more at home, is **Sedona,** a metaphysical new-age store. Inside, its shelves and cases are stocked with aromatherapy and massage oils, natural crystals, agates, books, jewelry, figurines, carvings, posters, postcards, and consciousness-lifting tapes. Recharge your spiritual batteries with a personal psychic reading done by various practitioners in a private upstairs area. **Borders Books and Music** anchors the end of this center and is a full-selection outlet with books, music, newspapers, and magazines from around the world, a very good Hawaiiana section, ongoing events, and a gallery and coffee shop upstairs. Open Mon.–Thurs. 9 A.M.–11 P.M., Fri.–Sat. to midnight, and Sun. 9 A.M.–10 P.M. Call 808/591-8995 for book information, 808/591-8996 for music.

## Aloha Tower Marketplace

Constructed in 1994, the Aloha Tower Marketplace is one of the most unique mall/shopping plazas in Honolulu, one frequented by tourists and locals alike. Set to the side of the Aloha Tower and fronting the working harbor of Honolulu, where ships from all over the world load and unload their goods, this marketplace is an old warehouse that's been tastefully converted into an upscale group of more than 100 shops offering food and beverages, apparel, art, gifts, jewelry, and specialty items. Shops are open Mon.–Sat. 9 A.M.–9 P.M. and Sun. until 6 P.M. An indoor-outdoor affair, where the sea breezes blow right through, the center atrium area lies in the shadow of the tower. This central courtyard atrium is also the spot for musical entertainment performed free throughout the day. The outside area in front of the tower is called the Boat Days Bazaar, and it's filled with cabana-type booths selling mostly apparel, gifts, and souvenirs. Inside, find fashions at **Daniella** and **Beyond the Beach,** among others. **Magnet Five-O** has all sorts of magnets from floor to ceiling. If you can't find one here, you haven't looked hard enough. The **World of Hats** carries everything from baseball caps to woven Panama hats, **Black Pearl Gallery** has designer jewelry, you can find musical instruments and hula instruments at **Hawaiian Ukulele Company** and **Island Hula Studio,** and **Island Art Gallery** carries artwork to hang on your wall. Then there is **Perfumania,** and its name says it all. Browse through **Hula Prints** or peruse **Martin & MacArthur** for mostly koa wood furniture and furnishings. Also check out

the **Endangered Species Store,** which stocks nature-inspired gift items. Part of the profits go to protect endangered species of the world. Most of the shops in this complex are locally owned, non-chain outfits. Have a walk through and support the local economy.

After having a look at the shops, sit down for a snack or a meal at one of the many food vendors or have a drink at the watering holes. At several of these fine establishments you'll find evening entertainment virtually every night of the week.

The vintage-looking, open-air yellow line Waikiki Trolley makes the connection from Waikiki to Aloha Tower, running throughout the day for $1.50 each way. Alternately, take TheBus no. 19 or 20 from Waikiki and no. 55, 56, or 57 on the return to Waikiki; or park in the pay parking lots in front of Aloha Tower or near Piers 5 and 6.

## Chinatown

For shopping in Chinatown, head to the **Chinatown Cultural Plaza Shopping Center,** on the corner of Maunakea and Beretania Streets, but note that it has been struggling lately and shops come and go with regularity. It's more fun to look at than to shop in. You'll find such stores as Dragon Gate Book Store, Phuc Hing Gift and Bookstore, Tak Wah Tong Chinese Herbalist, Bin Ching Jade Center, Excellent Gem and Diamonds, Peninsula Jewelry, and a slew of restaurants. The Cultural Plaza Moongate Stage is the centerpiece. Here they perform Chinese dances and plays, and herald in the Chinese New Year. If there is a presentation happening, attend.

At the corner of Hotel and Maunakea is the **Maunakea Marketplace,** a tight little jumble of shops with souvenirs, gifts, and an indoor food court, with mostly Asian vendors that seems more vibrant and with a steadier business than the Cultural Plaza. A half block away along Kekaulike Street is the **Kekaulike Market** with more of the same diversity, and here **Paradise Produce Co.** handles an incredible variety of fresh edibles. Many other shops sell ethnic foods and ingredients.

Nearby and close to the river is an open market, a cooperative of open-air stalls selling just about everything that Chinatown has to offer at competitive prices. Follow your nose to the pungent odors of fresh fish at **Oʻahu Market** on King Street, where ocean delectables can be had for reasonable prices. Numerous other fish markets line the streets nearby.

Several antique and collectible shops line the lower end of Nuʻuanu Avenue, many of which carry estate sale items.

**Cindy's Lei & Flower Shoppe,** on the corner of Hotel and Maunakea, has fresh lei at cheap prices. At Beretania and Smith Street is **Lita's Lei,** famous for good products and prices. Several others in the nearby streets are **Maunakea Street Florist, Lin's Lei Shop, Violet Lei Stand,** and **Lina's Leis and Flowers,** which form a garland of flower shops.

**Pegge Hopper Gallery,** 1164 Nuʻuanu St., 808/524-1160, is open Tues.–Fri. 11 A.M.–4 P.M. and Sat. 11 A.M.–3 P.M. Ms. Hopper is one of the three most famous working artists in all of Hawaii. Her original works grace the walls of the most elegant hotels and homes in the islands. If you would like to purchase one of her bold and amazing serigraphs, this shop has the best and widest selection. While you're here, check out the **Sisu Gallery** and **The Studio of Roy Venter,** both of which are only a few steps down the street. One block away on Smith Street and nearly across from one another are the **Ramsay Galleries** and **Smith Street Galleries.**

## Dole Cannery Square

Look for the giant pineapple rising 200 feet into the air. A landmark of Honolulu, it was built in Chicago and erected here in 1928. It is still used as a reservoir and holds 100,000 gallons of water, which is piped throughout the Dole Cannery, whose outer buildings were transformed in 1988 to a minimall located at 650 Iwilei Road. Upon entering the atrium area, look high on the walls to see reproductions of Dole pineapple can labels. They're pop art, conveying a feeling of simpler times past. Downstairs are photographs and explanations of the pineapple operation, including the planting, raising, harvesting, and production process. On the two levels you'll find a cluster of shops laid out as traditional store-fronts, but many seem to be empty—perhaps victims of the slow Hawaiian economy. Check **Joon's Pineapple to Go** for this golden fruit in all its forms, or to satisfy your sweet tooth, head for that mountain of sin at the **Rocky Mountain Chocolate Factory.** Across the street at the entrance to the Signature 18-plex movie theaters is **Famous Footwear** for shoes.

In the factory, workers stay busy processing the fruit with the newest generation of the marvelous Ginaca machine, first built in 1913 by Henry Ginaca, a draftsman hired by James Dole to modernize the industry. This whirring wonder can peel, core, cut, slice, and dice 100 fruits per minute. Within 20 minutes of reaching the machine, the canned fruit is ready for the grocer's shelf. Millions of Hawaii's fruits are canned, juiced, and sliced here for shipment around the world. In the summertime, at the height of the harvest, this factory can process more than three million cans of fruit per day!

Only a short distance away at 700 Nimitz Highway is the well-known **Hilo Hattie** shop. At this store you can find an incredible variety of island fashions, gifts, crafts, and food items at reasonable prices. This is a good introduction to what the islands have to offer, and to make it a sweeter deal, the store offers free transportation to its store from Waikiki on its own shuttle buses. Hilo Hattie, the largest manufacturer of alohawear in the state, also conducts free tours of its factory, which is also at this location. It's hard to resist spending: Prices and craftsmanship are good, and designs are contemporary. The store is open daily 7 A.M.–6 P.M., 808/535-6500.

## Kahala Mall

The Kahala Mall is the major shopping mall on the eastern side of Honolulu at the edge of the upscale Kahala area. **Macy's, Longs Drug, Star Market,** and the eight-plex **Kahala Theaters** anchor this mall, surrounded by dozens of apparel outlets, gift shops, and novelty stores, as well as electronics chains, jewelry stores, and specialty shops. As with most malls, there are about a dozen fast-food outlets, from pizza to plate lunch and sushi, to refresh yourself for more shopping. Both **Barnes & Noble** and **Waldenbooks** have shops here. On the east end of the city, this is the shopping center of choice. Open Mon.–Sat. 10 A.M.–9 P.M., Sun. until 5 P.M. Serviced by the Waikiki Trolley and TheBus nos. 22 and 58.

## Bargains and Discounts

**The Muumuu Factory,** 1423 Kapi'olani Blvd., offers great sales, but get there early and bring your helmet and shoulder pads to fight off the crowds. **Goodwill Thrift Shop,** 1075 S. Beretania St., displays the same bargains as on the Mainland, but with a wide assortment of alohawear. Ladies looking for appropriate islandwear that won't break the budget should head for the **Pzazz** consignment boutique, 3057 Wai'alae Ave., which sells used designer clothing. Pzazz has won accolades for being the best designer resale shop in town for moderately priced quality women's clothing. Also try the **Manufacturers Outlet,** a bevy of outlet shops under one roof at Dillingham and Kokau Streets in Iwilei.

## Miscellaneous

**Hawaiian Islands Stamp and Coin,** 1111 Bishop St., street level in the International Savings Building, displays rare coins, stamps, and paper money of Hawaii, the United States, and worldwide.

**R. Field Wine Co.,** in the Foodland supermarket at 1460 S. Beretania, is a purveyor of exquisite food, fine wines, crackers, cookies, cheeses, imported pastas, and caviar. Most of the wines are top-shelf Californian, with a nice variety of their reserve wines going back to 1968. Older French wines, as well as German wines, are also available, and while you're there peruse the humidor for a fine cigar. Most recent has been the addition of local organic produce and other Hawaiian food products. Look here for something special for that special evening. Wine tasting takes place at 2:30 P.M. on Saturdays.

Everyone, sooner or later, needs a good hardware store. You can't beat the selection at **Kilgo's,** 180 Sand Island Rd. Open 7:30 A.M.–4 A.M. daily except some holidays.

**O'AHU**

# Waikiki

Waikiki (Spouting Water) is like a fresh young starlet from the sticks who went to Hollywood to make it big, and did, although maybe too fast for her own good. Everyone always knew that she had a double-dip of talent and heart, but the fast lane has its heartaches, and she's been banged around a little by life. Even though her figure's fuller, her makeup's a little smeared, and her high heels are worn down, she has plenty of chutzpah left, and when the curtain parts and the lights come up, she'll play her heart out for her audience.

Waikiki is a classic study of contradictions. Above all, it is an example of basic American entrepreneurialism taken to the nth degree. Along the main strip, high-powered businesspeople cut multimillion-dollar deals, but on the sidewalks it's a carnival midway with hucksters, handbillers, and street people selling everything decent and indecent under the tropical sun. To get a true feeling for

Waikiki, you must put this amazing strip of land into perspective. The area covers only seven-tenths of a square mile, which at a good pace, you can walk the length of in half an hour. On any given day, about 110,000 people crowd its beaches and boulevards, making it one of the most densely populated areas on earth. Sixty thousand of these people are tourists; 30,000 are workers who commute from various towns of O'ahu and cater to the tourists, and the remaining 20,000 actually call Waikiki home. The turnover is about 80,000 new tourists per week, and the pace rarely slackens. To the head shakers, these facts condemn Waikiki as a mega-growth area gone wild. To others, these same figures make Waikiki an energized, fun-filled place to be, where "if you don't have a good time, it's your own fault."

For the naive or the out-of-touch looking for grass-shack paradise, the closest they'll come to it

view of Waikiki from Diamond Head

in Waikiki is painted on a souvenir ashtray. Those drawn to a smorgasbord of activities, who are adept at choosing the best and ignoring the rest, can't go wrong! People and the action are as constant in Waikiki as the ever-rolling surf.

## History

The written record of this former swampy area began in the late 1790s. The white man, along with his historians, cartographers, artists, and gunpowder, was already an undeniable presence in the islands. Kalanikupule, ranking chief of O'ahu, hijacked the *Jackall*, a small ship commanded by Captain Brown, with which he intended to spearhead an attack against Kamehameha I. The chief held the *Jackall* for a while, but the sailors regained control just off Diamond Head and sent the Hawaiians swimming for land. The ship then hastened to Kamehameha to report the treachery and returned with his armada of double-hulled canoes, which beached along Waikiki. The great king then defeated Kalanikupule at the famous battle of Nu'uanu Pali and secured control of the island. Thereafter Waikiki, pinpointed by Diamond Head, became a well-known landmark.

Waikiki's interior was low-lying swampland, long known to be good for fishponds, taro, rice, and bananas, but hardly for living. The beach, however, was always blessed with sunshine and perfect waves, especially for surfing, a sport heartily loved by the Hawaiians. The royalty of Hawaii, following Kamehameha, made Honolulu their capital and kept beach houses at Waikiki. They invited many visiting luminaries to visit them at their private beach. All were impressed. In the 1880s, King Kalakaua was famous for his beach house hospitality. One of his favorite guests was Robert Louis Stevenson, who spent many months here writing one of his novels. By the turn of the 20th century, Waikiki, which had been little more than a handful of grass-shack cottages, had become a highly exclusive vacation spot and home to some of the island's wealthiest families.

In 1901 the Moana Hotel was built, but immediately a protest was heard because it interfered with the view of Diamond Head. In 1906, Lucius Pinkham, then director of Hawaii's Board of Health, called the mosquito-infested area "dangerous and unsanitary," and proposed to drain the swamp with a canal so that "the whole place can be transformed into a place of unique beauty." By the early 1920s, the Ala Wai Canal was built, its dredgings used to reclaim land, and Waikiki was demarcated. By the end of the 1920s, the Royal Hawaiian Hotel, built on the site previously occupied by the royal beach house, was receiving very wealthy guests who arrived by ocean liner, loaded down with steamer trunks. They ensconced themselves at Waikiki, often staying for the duration of the season.

For about 40 years, Waikiki remained the enchanted domain of Hollywood stars, dignitaries, and millionaires. But for the brief and extraordinary days of World War II, which saw Waikiki barricaded and barbed-wired, GIs—regular guys from the Mainland—were given a taste of this reserved paradise while on R&R. They brought home tantalizing tales of wonderful Waikiki, whetting the appetite of middle America.

Beginning just before statehood and continuing through the 1960s to the mid-'70s, hotels and condos popped up like fertilized weeds, and tourism exploded with the advent of the jumbo jet. Discounted package tours began to haul in droves of economy-class tourists. Businesses catering to the tastes of penny-pinchers and first-timers elbowed their way into every nook and cranny. For the first time Waikiki began to be described as tacky and vulgar. For the old-timers, Waikiki was in decline. The upscale and repeat visitors started to snub Waikiki, heading for hidden resorts on the Neighbor Islands. But Waikiki had spirit and soul and never gave in. Its declining hotels started a campaign to regain their illustrious images. Millions upon millions of dollars have been poured into renovations and remodeling. Luxury hotels renting exclusive and expensive rooms have reappeared and are doing a booming business. To give you some perspective of just what's here, Waikiki has roughly 120 hotels with 33,000 guest rooms, 100 condominiums, 300 bars and lounges, and 250 restaurants, not to mention the hundreds of shops, sundry stores, and entertainment spots.

## Waikiki Today

The Neighbor Islands are pulling more and more

tourists away, and depending on your point of view, this is either a boon or a bust for Waikiki. Direct flights to Maui, the Big Island, and Kaua'i allow more tourists than ever to bypass O'ahu, but still a whopping 80 percent of the people visiting the islands spend at least one night in Waikiki hotels, which offer, on average, the lowest room rates in Hawaii. The sublime and the gaudy are neighbors in Waikiki. Exclusive shops are often flanked by buskers selling plastic hula dolls. Burgers and beer mingle their pedestrian odors with those of Parisian cuisine. Although

Waikiki is unique in many ways, it can also come off as "Anytown, U.S.A." But most important, it somehow works, and works well. You may not find paradise on Waikiki's streets, but you will find a willing dancing partner, and if you pay the fiddler, she'll keep the beat.

Non-Americans, especially Japanese, still flock for dream vacations, mostly staying at Waikiki hotels, many of which are owned by Japanese firms. Mainlanders and locals alike are disgruntled when they see the extent to which Waikiki has become a Japanese town. The visiting Japanese

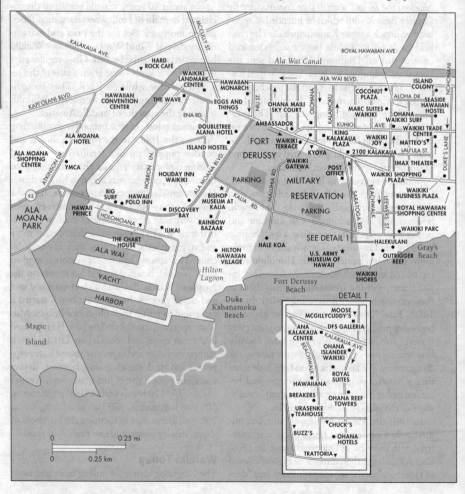

have been soundly warned by the tour operators before they arrive to never talk to strangers, especially someone on the street. Unfortunately for them, this means a vacation in which they never really leave their Japanese cocoon. They're herded into Japanese-owned shops and restaurants where prices are inflated and from which the tour operators get kickbacks. Local shopkeepers who are not on the list are aggravated. They say that the once-timid Japanese visitors will now show irritation if the shopkeeper doesn't speak Japanese and will indignantly head for the door if there is no one provided to deal with them in their native tongue. Also, these visitors have been taught to bargain with American shopkeepers, who they are told inflate prices. This makes for some rugged interaction when the price is already fair but the Japanese visitors won't believe it. While on average the Japanese tourist spends $245 per day, as opposed to a Mainlander who spends $160 per day, the Japanese really don't spread their money around as much as you would think. The money spent in Japanese shops primarily goes back to Japan. It's an incestuous system that operates in Waikiki.

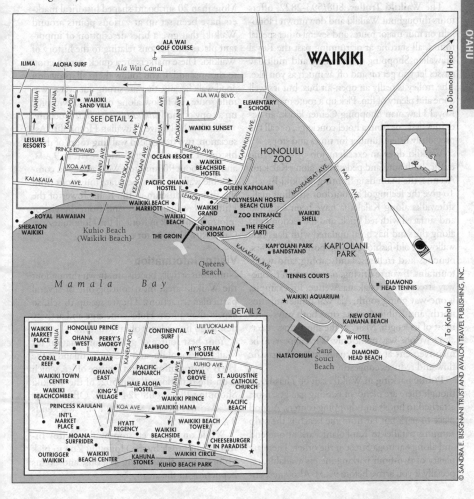

## Getting Around

Far and away the best way to get around Waikiki is on foot. For one, it's easily walked from one end to the other, and walking saves you hassling with parking and traffic jams. Also, TheBus and taxis are abundant. Those who have opted for a rental car should note that many of the agencies operate Waikiki lots, which for some can be more convenient than dropping your car at the airport on the day of departure. Check to see if this suits you. The following information is specific to Waikiki and offers some limited alternatives.

The **Waikiki Trolley,** 808/593-2822, offers tours throughout Waikiki and downtown Honolulu on four major routes and several other special routes, all starting at or running past the Royal Hawaiian Shopping Center. Day and multiday passes let you get on and off as much as you like. The trolley is really an open-air bus, but it's well done and plenty of fun. Pick up a route map at the Royal Hawaiian Shopping Center kiosk, an activities desk, or from a hotel concierge, or call the previously listed number for times and stops.

Waikiki does an excellent job of conveying traffic, both auto and pedestrian, along Kalakaua Avenue, the main drag fronting Waikiki Beach. To give the feeling of an outdoor strolling mall, sidewalks along Kalakaua have been widened and surfaced with red brick, and the section right along the sand has been updated with flagstone walkways, old-fashioned lamp posts, tiki torches, benches and trellises, landscaping, and water fountains. If you're driving, pay attention to one-way street signs. Kalakaua Avenue, for example, is one-way going south, Ala Wai Boulevard runs north, and Kuhio Avenue runs both ways—for most of its length. Many of the short cross streets also have one-way traffic only. What appears to be inconvenient at first actually helps the traffic flow and reduces congestion.

**Public parking** in Waikiki can be a hassle, although there are plenty of parking garages, most attached to hotels and shopping centers. A good place to park not far from the beach is the strip running parallel to Kapiʻolani Park at one end and along Saratoga Street at the other. There are plenty of two-hour parking meters available, especially if you arrive before 9 A.M. Also, inexpensive (for Waikiki) parking is available at the ramp adjacent to the Waikiki Theaters along Seaside Road, but only after 5:30 P.M. Parking at the Fort DeRussy parking lot runs $2.50 for the first hour, $1.50 for additional hours, and $24 for a maximum of 24 hours. Parking at hotel or private parking lots can also be expensive. Hotels usually charge $10–12 for their daily rate; some have valet parking, whereas at others you self-park. Parking lot fees often run $10–15 overnight.

## Waikiki Historical Trail Markers

More than 20 surfboard-shaped historical markers have been set up at various points around Waikiki that give a brief description of important places and persons relating to the history of Waikiki. These markers are a quick introduction to the area and, if you follow them all, provide a good walk because they are strung out over a two-mile route. To follow along on your own, pick up a copy of the *Waikiki Historic Trail* brochure.

Run by the Native Hawaiian Hospitality Association, two free guided **walking tours** of these historical sites are offered Mon.–Sat. at 9 A.M. and last about 90 minutes. Wear a hat and comfortable walking shoes. Separate tours start from the Bishop Museum at the Kalia Tower of the Hilton Hawaiian Village and from the visitor information kiosk in front of the Honolulu Zoo. Call 808/841-6442 for exact details.

## Visitor Information

Numerous activity booths are strewn throughout the Waikiki area, most touting one or several particular attractions. They're set up to sell, so expect their pitch. Hotel concierge and activity desks also have plenty of information.

Your best source of general information for Waikiki, Honolulu, and the entire inland is the **HVB Visitor Information Service** office, which is on the fifth floor, Room 502, of the Waikiki Shopping Plaza, 808/924-0266. Office hours are Mon.–Fri. 8 A.M.–4:30 P.M., weekends 8 A.M.–noon.

While on the street, stop by the **visitor information kiosk** by the Honolulu Zoo to pick up brochures about town, TheBus, and events happening in the area.

# Sights

To see Waikiki's attractions, you can simply perch on a bench or loll on a beach towel. Its boulevards and beaches are world-class for people-watching. Some of its strollers and sunbathers are visions, whereas others are real sights. And if you keep your ears open, it's not hard to hear every American accent and a dozen foreign languages being spoken. Some actual sights are intermingled with the hotels, boutiques, bars, and restaurants. Sometimes, too, these buildings are the sights. Unbelievably, you can even find plenty of quiet spots—in Kapi'olani Park, Fort DeRussy, and at churches, temples, tearooms, and ancient Hawaiian special places—sitting unnoticed amid the grandiose structures of the 20th century. Also, both the Honolulu Zoo and Waikiki Aquarium are well worth a visit.

## DIAMOND HEAD

If you're not sandwiched in a man-made canyon of skyscrapers, you can look eastward from anywhere in Waikiki and see Diamond Head, which *says* Waikiki. Western sailors have used it as a landmark since the earliest days of contact, and the Hawaiians undoubtedly before that. Ships' artists etched and sketched its motif long before the names of the newfound lands of Hawaii, Waikiki, and O'ahu were standardized and appeared on charts as Owyhee, Whytete, and Woohoo. The Hawaiian name was Le'ahi (Brow of the Ahi); legend says it was named by Hi'iaka, Madame Pele's younger sister, because she saw a resemblance in its silhouette to the yellowfin tuna. The name "Diamond Head" comes from a band of wild-eyed English sailors who found calcite crystals on its slopes and thought they'd discovered diamonds. Hawaii had fulfilled so many other dreams, why not a mountain of diamonds? Kamehameha I immediately made the mountain *kapu* until his advisor, John Young, informed him that what the seamen had found, later known as "Pele's tears," were worthless, except as souvenirs. No fortune was made, but the name stuck. Diamond Head was considered a power spot by the Hawaiians. Previously, Kamehameha had worshipped

At water's edge, Diamond Head is surrounded by Honolulu neighborhoods.

ROBERT NILSEN

O'AHU

at a *heiau* on the western slopes, offering human sacrifice to his bloodthirsty war-god, Ku.

Geologically, the 761-foot monolith is about 350,000 years old, formed in one enormous explosion when seawater came into contact with lava bubbling out of a fissure. The huge rock, actually a tuff cone, is now Hawaii's state monument and a national natural landmark since its designation in 1968. Its 350-acre crater serves as a Hawaii National Guard depot; a hiking trail to the summit leads through an installation left over from World War II. The southeast *(makai)* face has some of the most exclusive and expensive real estate in the islands. The Kahala Mandarin Oriental Hotel is regarded by many to be one of the premier hotels in the world, and nearby is the super-snobbish Waialae Country Club. Many private estates—homes of multi-millionaires, Hollywood stars, Hawaii's well-known, and high-powered multinational executives—cling to the cliffside, fronting ribbons of beach open to the public by narrow rights-of-way that are often hemmed in by the walls of the estates.

## The Hike

The most recognized symbol of Hawaii, Diamond Head is the first place you should head to for a strikingly beautiful panorama of Waikiki and greater Honolulu.

Getting there takes only 15 minutes from Waikiki, either by TheBus no. 58 or by car following Kalakaua Avenue south from Waikiki and turning onto Monsarrat Avenue just beyond the Honolulu Zoo. Monsarrat turns into Diamond Head Road, then quickly a sign points you to Diamond Head Crater. Pass through a tunnel and into the militarized section in the center of the crater; the trail starts at the end of the parking lot. Although the hike is moderate, you should bring along water, a flashlight (a must), and binoculars if you have them. Run by the Division of State Parks, the park is open daily 6 A.M.–6 P.M., and the entrance fee is $1 per person. The trail is seven-tenths of a mile long and was built to the 761-foot summit of Le'ahi Point in 1908 to serve as a U.S. Coast Artillery Observation Station. It was heavily fortified during World War II, and

part of the fun is exploring the old gun emplacements and tunnels built to link and service them.

Wildflowers and chirping birds create a peaceful setting, although the inside of the crater is mostly an arid environment. When you come to a series of cement and stone steps, walk to a flat area to the left to find an old winch that hauled the heavy building materials to the top. Here's a wide panorama of the sea and Koko. Notice too that atop several little hillocks along the rim is an old gun emplacement. Next comes a short but dark tunnel (flashlight!) and immediately a series of 99 steps. Following the steps is a spiral staircase that leads up into the four-level command post/gun emplacement and out to the ridge. If you haven't brought a flashlight, give your eyes a few minutes to adjust and follow someone who has brought one. Once on top, another stairway and ladder take you to the very summit, where Waikiki lies below.

## HONOLULU ZOO

The trumpeting of elephants and chatter of monkeys emanates from the jungle at the 42-acre Honolulu Zoo, 151 Kapahulu Ave., 808/971-7171, www.honoluluzoo.org, open daily except Christmas and New Year's Day, 9 A.M.–4:30 P.M. General admission is $6 adults, $4 locals, $1 children 6–12 with an adult, and children under five free; the Honolulu Zoo family pass is $25. Other special programs at an additional cost include a tour with a zookeeper, a campout with breakfast and tour, and a moonlight stroll through the zoo. Special evening concerts featuring local artists happen June–Aug. every Wednesday 6–7 P.M. For the free evening show, the gates reopen at 4:35 P.M. and there is no admission. For the Sunday Music Series, there is free admission after 3:30 P.M. and the concert starts at 4:30 P.M.

The zoo holds the expected animals from around the world: monkeys, giraffes, lions, big cats, a hippo, elephants, even a sun bear (what else in Hawaii?). The Honolulu Zoo has the only large snake in Hawaii—a male Burmese python named Monty—housed in the Reptile House. (Only the zoo can legally import snakes, geckos, iguanas, and similar reptiles.) Many islanders love this exhibit because snakes in Hawaii are so exotic! Just as exotic is the Komodo Dragon exhibit. From Indonesia, Komodo dragons are the world's largest lizards, often measuring three meters long. But the zoo is much more than just a collection of animals. It is an up-close escapade through the jungle of Hawaii, with plants, trees, flowers, and some vines named and described. Moreover, the zoo houses Hawaii's indigenous birdlife, which is fast disappearing from the wild: Hawaiian gallinules, coots, hawks, owls, and the *nene,* the state bird, which is doing well in captivity, with breeding pairs being sent to other zoos around the world. The zoo is also famous for its Manchurian cranes, extremely rare birds from East Asia, and for successfully mating the Galapagos turtle. A **petting zoo** of barnyard animals, small reptiles, and amphibians is great for kids, and the tropical bird and African savanna sections are also sure to please. Before leaving, have a look at the Zootique shop where you can pick up T-shirts, postcards, posters, stuffed animals, books, and other gift items. The parking lot on the Kapahulu Avenue side costs $.25 per hour.

## WAIKIKI AQUARIUM

The first Waikiki Aquarium (then called the Honolulu Aquarium) was built in 1904, its entranceway framed by a torii gate. Rebuilt and restocked in 1954, it took on its current focus as an outreach and educational facility in the 1970s. The aquarium has recently undergone a face-lift with a new entranceway, touch tanks, and an opening directly to the sea. At 2777 Kalakaua Avenue in Kapi'olani Park, the aquarium, 808/923-9741, www.waquarium.org, is open daily except Christmas Day, 9 A.M.–5 P.M., with entrance until 4:30 P.M. Admission is $7 adults, $5 seniors, students, *kama'aina,* and military, $3.50 youths 13–17, and free to children under 12. An audio wand tour in English and Japanese, included in the price of admission, explains the exhibits. Walk from points in Waikiki, take TheBus no. 2, or use the Waikiki Trolley red or blue line.

Although more than 400 species of Hawaiian and South Pacific fish, flora, and mammals live in its sparkling waters, the aquarium is much more than just a big fish tank. The floor plan contains four galleries of differing themes, all related to marine communities of the Pacific. One exhibit shows fish found in waters from Polynesia to Australia. Tanks hold sharks, turtles, eels, rays, clams, a seahorse, and colorful coral displays. Another exhibit, perhaps the most amazing of all, contains live coral that seem more like extraterrestrial flowers than specimens from our own seas. Some are long strands of spaghetti with bulbous ends like lima beans, others are mutated roses, or tortured camellias, all moving, floating, and waving their iridescent purples, golds, and greens in a watery bouquet. An Edge of the Reef exhibit shows how the low coastal waters and immediate shoreline relate to sustain the very busy reef environment.

Watch the antics of the monk seals, shameless hams, from the side of their 85,000-gallon tank, which now has a "variegated coastline" of natural nooks and crannies patterned after sections of O'ahu's coast. Hawaiian monk seals are one of only two species of tropical seals on earth. Endangered, only about 1,500 individuals still survive, and the performances are more of a detailed description of the seals' day-to-day life in their dwindling environment. The three seals inhabiting the tank are all males because placing a breeding couple would almost certainly result in the birth of a pup. Marine biologists anguished over the decision. It was felt that seals raised in captivity and then released back into the natural environment might introduce a devastating disease to the native population. This was considered too great a danger to risk.

The aquarium contains a bookshop with a tremendous assortment of titles on sealife and the flora and fauna of Hawaii, plus great gifts and mementos. The University of Hawai'i, which has run the aquarium since 1919, offers seminars and field trips through the aquarium, everything from guided reef walks to mini-courses in marine biology; information is available at the aquarium. The Waikiki Aquarium is a special opportunity for fun and education that will be enjoyed by the entire family. Don't miss it!

M

O'AHU

# U.S. ARMY MUSEUM OF HAWAII

This museum, with the hulks of tanks standing guard, is one long corridor where you feel the strength of the super-thick reinforced walls of this once-active gun emplacement. At Battery Randolph in Fort DeRussy, on the corner of Kalia and Saratoga Roads, the U.S. Army Museum of Hawaii, 808/438-2821, is open Tues.–Sun. 10 A.M.–4:45 P.M., except Christmas and New Year's Day, for self-guiding tours. Entrance is free. Guided tours can be arranged for large groups by calling several weeks in advance. Battery Randolph once housed two 14-inch coast artillery rifles meant to defend Honolulu and Pearl harbors. The architecture is typical of the Taft Period forts constructed between 1907–1920. The battery is listed in the National Register of Historic Places. As you enter there is a shop dedicated to things military, from flying jackets to wall posters. Walk the halls to learn the military history of Hawaii traced as far back as Kamehameha I. Here are rifles, swords, and vintage photos of Camp McKinley, an early-1900s (1898–1907) military station in the shadow of Diamond Head.

A side room holds models of artillery used to defend Waikiki from times when Battery Randolph was an active installation. One room shows how the guns worked in a method called "disappearing guns." The gun would raise up and fire. The recoil of the gun would swing it back down and lock it in position. After it was reloaded, a 50-ton counterweight would pop it up ready to fire. The explosive sound would rattle the entire neighborhood, so they were seldom test-fired.

Exhibits show the fledgling days of Army aviation in Hawaii, when on July 13, 1913, 14 officers began a military flying school. There are beautiful models of military equipment, especially one of an old truck unit. Then comes the ominous exhibit of "Rising Japan" with its headlong thrust into World War II. Hawaii, grossly overconfident, felt immune to attack because of the strong military presence. Photos from the 1930s and '40s depict the carefree lifestyle of visiting celebrities like Babe Ruth and Shirley Temple, which ended abruptly on December 7, 1941, in the bombing of Pearl Harbor.

An entire room is dedicated to the Pearl Harbor attack and is filled with models of Japanese planes, aircraft carriers, and real helmets and goggles worn by the Zero pilots. Most interesting are the slice-of-life photos of Hawaii mobilized for war: defense workers, both men and women, sailors, soldiers, entertainers, and street scenes. Pamphlets from the time read, "Know Your Enemies," and there's a macabre photo of people gathered at a stadium to see a demonstration of the devastating effect of flame throwers that would be employed upon the Japanese enemy. Bob Hope is here entertaining the troops, while a 442nd Regimental Battle Flag bears testament to the most decorated unit in American history, comprised mostly of *nisei* Japanese from Hawaii. Then come photos and exhibits from the soul-wrenching conflicts in Korea and Vietnam.

A gallery on the upper level tells of the heroics of Hawaiian soldiers who have been awarded the Congressional Medal of Honor and Distinguished Service Cross for combat valor, almost all posthumously. Go outside to the upper-level exhibit to see one of the old guns still pointing out to sea, which seems incongruous with sunbathers just below on the quiet and beautiful stretch of beach. On the upper deck are depth charges, torpedoes, and shells, along with a multimedia slide show. Your eyes will take a few minutes to refocus to the glorious sunshine of Waikiki after the cold gloom of the bunker. Perhaps our hearts and souls could refocus as well.

# BISHOP MUSEUM AT KALIA

An offshoot of the main Bishop Museum in Honolulu, the Waikiki branch of the museum is housed in the Kalia Tower of the Hilton Hawaiian Village Resort. Much smaller in size and more focused in concept, this museum still offers galleries dedicated to the music, craftsmanship, and beliefs of Hawaiians, navigation, the monarchy period, and historical Waikiki. As at the main museum, the items shown here are excellent examples and the displays are well done. In addition, various activities, such as *lauhala* weaving, *kapa* making, navigation techniques, games, and music and musical instruments, are scheduled throughout the day for the enjoyment of guests, and a stars and skies mini-planetarium program relates to the wisdom and beliefs of the ancient Hawaiians. In this location, the Bishop Museum is able to bring to the traveling public a glimpse of ancient Hawaii for those who do not have the time or the desire to have a look at the extensive collection of the main museum. The Bishop Museum at Kalia is open daily 9 A.M.–5 P.M.; entrance $9.95 adults, $7.95 children 4–12, and free for kids under four.

# FREE SIGHTS AND CURIOSITIES

On the beach near the Sheraton Moana Surfrider Hotel are the **kahuna stones,** a lasting remnant of old Hawaii. The Hawaiians believed these stones were imbued with mana by four hermaphroditic priests from Tahiti: Kinohimahu, Kahaloamahu, Kapunimahu, and Kapaemahu (*mahu* in Hawaiian signifies homosexuality). They came to visit this Polynesian outpost in ancient times and left these stones for the people, who have held them in reverence for more than 600 years. About 40 years ago, a group of local historians went looking for the stones but couldn't find them. Around that time, there was a bowling alley along the beach, and when it was finally torn down, it was discovered that the stones had been incorporated into the foundation. Most visitors and islanders alike no longer revered the stones and often used them as a handy spot to scrape sand off their feet. That was the case until the recent renovation of Kalakaua Avenue, when the stones were fenced off and once again given prominence as a tangible element of ancient Hawaiian belief. *Kupuna* versed in the old ways say that the mana, once put in and strengthened by reverence, is dissipating.

Even if you're not a guest at the following hotels, you should at least drop by their lobbies for a quick look. Dramatically different, they serve almost as a visual record of Waikiki's changing history. Those who have a fondness for the elegance of days gone by should take a tour of the **Shera-** **ton Moana Surfrider** and steep in the history of the hotel, admiring its early-1900s artifacts and memorabilia. The Moana, Waikiki's oldest hotel, dating from 1901, is a permanent reminder of simpler times when its illustrious clientele would dance the night away at an open-air nightclub suspended over the sea. The Moana houses the Banyan Court, named for the enormous banyan tree just outside. From here, *Hawaii Calls* beamed Hawaiian music to the Mainland by shortwave for 40 years beginning in 1935. In its heyday, the show was carried by more than 700 stations. The hotel's architecture is a classic example of the now quaint "colonial style." Free one-hour tours are offered weekdays at 11 A.M. and 5 P.M. starting at the second-floor historical room.

The **Royal Hawaiian Hotel,** built in 1927 on the site of the old royal beach house, once had fresh pineapple juice running in its fountains. Now surrounded by towering hotels, it's like a guppy in a sea of whales. However, it does stand out with its Spanish-Moorish style, painted in distinctive pink, and is surrounded by huge old tropical trees and huge coconut palms. In the old days, only celebrities and luminaries came to stay—who else could afford $3 per day? Although it's younger than the Moana, many consider it the grande dame of Hawaiian hotels. The entranceway is elegantly old-fashioned, with rounded archways, overstuffed couches, and lowboys. At the end of the main hallway, Diamond Head is framed in the arches. Historical guided tours of the building and grounds are offered for free every Monday, Wednesday, and Friday at 2 P.M. Meet in the registration lobby.

Across the street from the Sheraton Moana are the giant, modernistic, twin towers of the **Hyatt Regency Waikiki.** The lobby, like those of most Hyatts, is wonderful, with a huge waterfall and a jungle of plants, all stepped down the series of floors, making an effect like the Hanging Gardens of Babylon.

The **Pacific Beach Hotel,** farther down the street at 2490 Kalakaua Ave., is a first-rate hotel and a great place to stay in its own right. But if you don't, definitely visit the Oceanarium Restaurant just off the lobby, which has an immense three-floor-high aquarium dedicated to holding 280,000 gallons of sea water and scores of colorful tropical fish. The old mafia dons used to send their rivals to "sleep with the fishes"; here, you have an opportunity to dine with the fishes. Usually you go snorkeling to watch the fish eat, but in this particular instance the fish watch you eat.

At the corner of the DFS Galleria Waikiki building is a two-story aquarium called The Tube. Running up through it from the first to the second floor is a spiral staircase, so as you walk up or down you can see the tropical fish, small sharks, and rays from all angles. A nice touch.

As you walk along Kalakaua Avenue, directly across from the Kuhio Beach section is **St. Augustine Catholic Church.** This modernistic building squashed between high-rises is worth a quick look. The interior, serene with the diffused light of stained glass, looks like a series of A-frames. The **Damien Museum** is housed in a separate building to the rear, displaying photos and other artifacts of Father Damien, the Belgian priest who humanely cared for the lepers of Kalaupapa, Moloka'i, until his own death from complications of leprosy. The museum is open Mon.–Fri. 9 A.M.–3 P.M. and is free, although donations are gratefully accepted because they are the museum's only source of revenue.

A few blocks away at 2414 Kuhio Avenue is the **Lucoral Museum,** a showcase, giftshop, and factory of gemstones, minerals, pearls, and coral. Open weekdays 9 A.M.–5:30 P.M., this compact, almost claustrophobic, collection has an amazing display of large and small items. Some jewelry is for sale in the gift shop.

The **Urasenke Teahouse,** 808/923-3059, is an authentic teahouse donated to Hawaii by the Urasenke Foundation of Kyoto. It is at 245 Saratoga Road, which lies along the Waikiki side of Fort DeRussy. Every Wednesday and Friday at 10 A.M., volunteer students and teachers performs the ancient aesthetic art of *chanoyu* (tea ceremony). A minimum donation of $3 is asked of those who want to watch the ceremony and partake of the frothy *matcha,* a grass-green tea made from the delicate tips of 400-year-old bushes, and the accompanying sweets. Comfortable long pants and socks are requested. To find delight and sanctuary in this centuries-old

ritual among the clatter and noise of Waikiki offers a tiny glimpse into the often puzzling duality of the Japanese soul.

Delineating Waikiki from the rest of the city is the nearly two-mile-long **Ala Wai Canal.** Created in the '20s to drain the swamps that filled this flat oceanfront land, it now channels runoff from the mountains to the sea. The banks of the canal are used extensively by walkers, joggers, and runners, particularly shortly after sunrise and again before sunset; many come here to sit, relax, and watch the parade of paddlers practice for outrigger canoe races. It's cheap entertainment for one of Hawaii's favorite sports. Fishermen also use the canal, trying their luck near its mouth near the Ala Moana bridge.

Just across the canal from Waikiki proper is the new and impressive **Hawaii Convention Center.** Built to attract more convention business to the state, it's a combination of large and small meeting halls, exhibition rooms, and banquet facilities, with high-tech sound and light capabilities and instantaneous translation services. Appealing to the aesthetic side of anyone who takes the time to look inside are several waterfalls and pools, tall palm trees, numerous artworks, and a glass ceiling that brings the outside in.

## WAIKIKI BEACHES AND PARKS

In the six miles of shoreline from Kahanamoku Beach fronting the Hilton Hawaiian Village at the west end of Waikiki to the section of Kahala Beach fronting the Kahala Mandarin Oriental Hotel, there are at least a dozen choice spots for enjoying swimming or surf activities. The central Waikiki beaches are so close to each other that you can hardly tell where one ends and another begins. They are basically just names for different sections of one long strand of sand. All are generally gentle, but as you head around Diamond the beaches get farther apart and have their own personalities. Sometimes they're rough customers, particularly during winter. As always, never take *moana* for granted, especially during periods of high surf. There are at least six lifeguard stations in Waikiki, staffed daily year-round 9 A.M.–5:30 P.M. Now that you've finally arrived at a Waikiki beach, the one thing left to do is kick back and R-E-L-A-X.

Waikiki Beach stretches for two miles, broken into separate areas. A multitude of concession stands offer everything from shave ice to canoe rides. It's not news that this beach is crowded. Sometimes when looking at the rows of glistening bodies, it appears that if one person wants to tan her other side, everybody else has to roll over with her. Anyone looking for seclusion here is just being silly. Take heart—a big part of the fun is the other people.

Stands set up along Waikiki Beach fronting Kalakaua rent boogie boards, surfboards, paddle boats, and snorkel gear. They're convenient, but their prices are much more than many shops offering the same. However, all offer decent prices for surfing lessons and rides in outrigger canoes, which get you three waves and about 20 minutes of fun. Find other outrigger canoe rides—you help paddle—in front of the big hotels. Try the Outrigger Waikiki. They're great fun and a bargain at $7 per person.

## Kahanamoku Beach

This stretch of sand fronting the lagoon at the Hilton Hawaiian Village is named after Hawaii's most famous waterman, Duke Kahanamoku. Duke's extended family lived here, and the Kahanamoku boys learned to play in the water. The man-made beach and lagoon were completed in 1956, and the beach here is the widest of any section in Waikiki. The swimming is great inside the reef, and a concession stand offers surfboards, beach equipment, and catamaran cruises.

## Fort DeRussy Beach

You pass through the right-of-way of Fort DeRussy military area, where you'll find restrooms, picnic facilities, volleyball courts, and food and beverage concessions. Lifeguard service is provided by military personnel—no duty is too rough for our fighting men and women! A controversy raged for years between the military and developers who coveted this valuable piece of land. The government has owned it since the early 20th century and has developed what once was wasteland into the last stretch of noncement,

non-high-rise piece of real estate left along Waikiki. And it's a beauty. Because the public has access to the beach and its landscaped lawns, and because Congress has voted that the lands cannot be sold, it'll remain under military jurisdiction.

## Gray's Beach

This section's name comes from Gray's-by-the-Sea, a small inn once located here. The narrow white-sand beach lies in front of the House Without a Key restaurant at the Halekulani Hotel, which replaced Gray's. Rights-of-way run on either side of the hotel, or get to the beach from behind the military museum. The sea is generally mild here and the swimming is always good, with shallow waters and a sandy bottom. Offshore is a good break called Threes, a favorite with surfers.

The next section is referred to as **Royal Moana Beach** because it lies between Waikiki's oldest man-made landmarks, the Royal Hawaiian and Moana Surfrider hotels. Access is unlimited off Kalakaua Avenue. The inshore waters here are also gentle, and the bottom is sandy and generally free from coral. Offshore are three popular surfing areas: Paradise, Populars, and Canoes. Many novices have learned to surf here because of the predictability of the waves, but with so many rookies in the water and beach activities going on all around, you have to remain alert for runaway boards and speeding outrigger canoes.

## Prince Kuhio Beach and Beach Park

When people say "Waikiki Beach," this is the section to which they're usually referring. Named for Prince Kuhio—a tireless worker for Hawaiian rights and the Hawaiian representative to the U.S. Congress in the years following the demise of the Hawaiian Kingdom—this county-maintained park fronts Kalakaua Avenue as far as Kapahulu Avenue and "the groin," a cement pierlike protuberance running out into the water. Here, you'll find surfing, canoeing, and generally safe year-round swimming along the gently sloping, sandy-bottomed shoreline. The Waikiki Beach Center is at the in-town end of this beach, where you'll find comfort stations, concession stands,

ROBERT NILSEN

O'AHU

**Kuhio Beach at Waikiki**

lifeguards, and a police substation. Be careful of the rough coral bottom at the Diamond Head end of Kuhio Beach. A long retaining wall called Slippery Wall fronts the beach and runs parallel to it, creating a semienclosed saltwater pool. Covered with a coating of slick seaweed, Slippery Wall definitely lives up to its name. Although local youngsters play on the wall, the footing is poor and many knees have been scraped and heads cracked after spills from this ill-advised play. The surf on the seaward side of the wall churns up the bottom and creates deep holes that come up un-expectedly, along with an occasional rip current. A statue of Duke Kahanamoku, Hawaii's most fa-mous native son, stands prominently in this park. At the beach stage near here, a free presentation of torchlighting, hula, and music is presented Fri.–Sun. evenings.

## Kapi'olani Regional Park

In the shadow of Diamond Head is Kapi'olani Park, a quiet 140-acre oasis of greenery, just a co-conut's roll away from the gray cement and flash-ing lights of central Waikiki. It has proved to be one of the best gifts ever received by the people of

Honolulu. King Kalakaua donated this section of crown lands to them in 1877, requesting that it be named after his wife, Queen Kapi'olani. A statue of her now stands near the bandstand in the park. In times past, it was the site of horse and car races, polo matches, and Hawaii's unique *pa'u* riders, fashionable ladies in long, flowing skirts rid-ing horses decked out with lei. The park was even the site of Camp McKinley, the U.S. Army head-quarters in the islands 1898–1907.

The park remains a wonderful place for peo-ple to relax and exercise away from the hustle of Waikiki. The park is a mecca for jogging and aerobics, with many groups and classes meet-ing here throughout the day. It also serves as the starting point for the yearly Honolulu Marathon, one of the most prestigious races in the world. Its **Waikiki Shell,** an open-air amphitheater, hosts many visiting musical groups, especially during Aloha Week. The Honolulu Symphony is a reg-ular here, providing free concerts, especially on summer evenings. Nearby, the rebuilt **Kapi'olani Bandstand** hosts the Royal Hawaiian Band on Sunday afternoons at 2 P.M. and other concerts on Friday evenings at 5:30 P.M. The area around the bandstand has been landscaped, and a small lagoon once again graces its side, harkening back to the early days of the park when it had several such lagoons.

Also, under the shade of the trees toward Waikiki Beach, plenty of street entertainers, in-cluding clowns, acrobats, and jugglers, congregate daily to work out their routines to the beat of conga drums and other improvised music sup-plied by wandering musicians. Families and large groups come here to picnic, barbecue, and play softball. The park grounds are also home to the free **Kodak Hula Show,** Waikiki Aquarium, Natatorium War Memorial, and Honolulu Zoo. Just in front of the zoo, by the big banyan, are hundreds and hundreds of pigeons, the "white phantoms of Waikiki." In the morning they are especially beautiful darting through the sunshine like white spirits. Also in front of the zoo is a statue of Mohandas Gandhi and a raised octag-onal monument surrounded by a wrought iron fence that's dedicated to Hawaiian royalty once buried in the sands of Waikiki.

Although Kapi'olani Beach Park is only a short stroll down the beach from Waikiki central, it gets much less use. This is where local families and those in the know come to get away from the crowds, just a few beach-blanket lengths away. In the park and along the beach are restrooms, volleyball courts, picnic tables, lifeguard towers, and a concession stand. At water's edge near the aquarium is the **Waikiki Natatorium,** a saltwater swimming pool built in 1927 as a World War I memorial. This pool was allowed to decay over the years until it was closed in 1980. The main gate and outer walls have recently been refurbished, and plans are in the works to do the same to the pool enclosure. Be careful of the rocky areas to the front of its stone enclosure. The section of the beach between Kuhio Beach Park and the Natatorium is called **Queens Beach.** The swimming is generally good here, with the best part at the Waikiki end, where it's at its widest and the bottom is gently sloping sand. Within this section, an area called The Wall has been designated as a special bodysurfing and boogie boarding area. Supposedly, board riders are restricted from this area, but if the surf is good they're guaranteed to break the rules. Experts can handle it, but novices, especially with runaway boards, are a hazard. Beyond the Natatorium is **Sans Souci Beach,** the quiet southern end. Many families with small children come to Sans Souci because it is so gentle, yet for another crowd it's called "dig me beach" by locals because of the bronzed bodies who come to strut.

The **Waikiki Marine Life Conservation District** occupies an area that stretches from the "groin" (a seawall at the end of Kapahulu Ave.) to the Natatorium, basically the Queens Beach area, and out 500 yards into the water. It's a fish management area, so fishing is not allowed, but other water sports can be enjoyed.

The Kapi'olani Park **Visitor Information Kiosk** is on the corner of Kapahulu and Kalakaua Avenues. The kiosk uses vintage photos to give a concise history of Kapi'olani Park. An overview map shows all the features of the park. Information is available here concerning events at the aquarium, zoo, Waikiki Shell, Art at the Zoo Fence (a collection of island artists selling their creations along the fence at the Zoo), and the Kapi'olani Bandstand, where you're treated to free concerts by top-name bands and orchestras every Friday evening. Across the street and on the beach, free movies and music happen Friday and Saturday nights.

## Around Diamond Head

**Kaluahole Beach** is on the Waikiki side of Diamond Head. The water conditions are safe year-round, but the beach is small and lies along a seawall. Once a large beach, it was paved over for building purposes. It has one public right-of-way, poorly marked and sandwiched between private homes. It's almost at the end of Kalakaua Avenue. Park at Kapi'olani Park and walk. The surfing in this area is generally good, and the breaks are known as Tongg's, named after a local family that lived along this shore.

A short way farther are **Makalei Beach County Park,** with some picnic tables and shade trees, and **Le'ahi Beach County Park,** with less shade but lots of grass. Bus or walk—there is no parking.

**Diamond Head Beach Park** is an unlimited access area that covers almost two acres of undeveloped shoreline off Beach Road. Unfortunately, the beach is narrow and surrounded by unfriendly rock and coral. The waters, however, are protected and generally safe, except in periods of high surf. This area is good for fishing and finding quiet moments. Adjoining this park and running for a good way to the east is **Kuilei Cliffs Beach Park.** Diamond Head Lighthouse sits prominently along the shore here and a Coast Guard reservation is set just beyond. Like Diamond Head Beach Park, Kuilei Cliffs Beach Park lies below Diamond Head Road and has access from three lookout areas along the road. You must walk down the cliff trails to the beaches below. Here are plenty of secluded pockets of sand for sunbathing but poor swimming. The surf is generally rough, and the area is always frequented by surfers. Surfing breaks offshore are known as Diamond Head and Lighthouse. When the winds are right, sailboarders also come. Offshore is hazardous with submerged rocks, but this makes it excellent for diving and snorkeling—for experts only! Currents can be fierce, and you can be dashed against the rocks.

O'AHU

Whales can sometimes be spotted passing this point, and to add to the mystique, the area is considered a breeding ground for sharks. Most visitors just peer down at the surfers from Diamond Head Road or choose a spot of beach for peace and quiet. There are three parking areas along the road. At one of these is a memorial plaque dedicated to the famous American aviator Amelia Earhart. Lining these parking areas are unofficial gardens of grass and flowers, envisioned, planted, and maintained by a couple of surfing oldsters who wanted to replace the hardpan dirt that flanked the top of the cliff with something more visually pleasing that would also cut down on the dust.

Farther east is a protrusion of land known as Black Point, the western end of ritzy residential Kahala. This section is the Beverly Hills of Honolulu, where many celebrities have homes. The least expensive home in this section easily pushes a $1 million asking price. On the Diamond Head side of Black Point is **Ka'alawai Beach.** The swimming is good here and generally safe because of a protecting reef. Many locals come to this area to fish, and it is good for bodysurfing and snorkeling. The waters outside the reef are excellent for surfing and produce some of the biggest waves on this side of the island. Surf breaks offshore here are called Browns and Blacks. Access is by public right-of-way marked off Kulumanu Place, by small side roads that run off Kahala Avenue, or by walking along the shoreline from Kuilei Beach.

**Kahala Beach** parallels Kahala Avenue from Black Point to the Kahala Mandarin Oriental Hotel and can be reached by marked rights-of-way between the high fences of estates in the area. The swimming is not particularly good, but there are plenty of pockets of sand and protected areas where you can swim and snorkel. Local people come to fish, and the surfing is good beyond the reef. The Kahala Mandarin Oriental is at the eastern end of this beach. The swimming there is always safe and good because the hotel has dredged the area to make it deeper.

Where Kapakahi Stream enters the sea along Kahala Beach, the county has constructed **Waialae Beach County Park.** Waialae is a popular sailboarding and fishing spot, and it may be crowded on weekends. Split by the stream that's crossed by a footbridge, it's a small beach park with basic amenities in a beautiful location. Looking to the east, Koko Head gives the impression that there is an island off in the distance, but it's just the way O'ahu bends at this point.

## Accommodations

Waikiki is loaded with places to stay. These come in all categories from deluxe to dingy, and there are many cross-over accommodations that have amenities and services typical to both hotels and condos. Your problem won't be finding a place to stay, but choosing from the enormous selection. During peak season (Christmas to Easter and again in summer) you'd better have reservations, or you could easily be left out in the *warm*. The good news is that, room for room, Waikiki is the cheapest place to stay in the state. Hotels along the beach tend to be slightly more expensive than their counterparts on a side street or back lane. The beachfront hotels have the surf at the doorstep, but those a block away have a little more peace and quiet. The following listings are not exhaustive—they couldn't be! Here are just some from all categories, which you can use as a barometer to measure what's available.

### UNDER $50

If you are in the military, you can check out **Hale Koa,** 808/955-0555 or 800/367-6027, fax 808/955-9670, reservations@halekoa.com, www.halekoa.com, the Fort DeRussy Armed Forces Recreational Center. On the beach at Fort DeRussy, this hotel is solely operated for active-duty U.S. military personnel, Department of Defense civilians, and a few other categories of former military and defense-related personnel. But anyone can walk in and have a look around. This well-run and well-maintained hotel has all the dining facilities, entertainment options, activity programs, and amenities of other large hotels in Waikiki. Depending on military rank or government status, there is a bewildering array of prices for the seven categories of rooms, all at rates well below the going rate for similar hotels in Waikiki—especially as it's right on the beach, and a wonderful section at that. Call for specifics.

**Hale Aloha Hostel,** the only member of Hostelling International—American Youth Hostel Association in Waikiki, is at 2417 Prince Edward St., Honolulu, HI 96815, 808/926-8313, fax 808/922-3798, ayhaloha@lava.net, two streets behind the Hyatt Regency. A dorm room bunk is $17 for members and $20 for nonmembers. Dorm rooms are sexually integrated, and you must be at least age 18 to stay unaccompanied by an adult. Couples can rent a studio for $42 members and $48 nonmembers. It's recommended that reservations be made at least two weeks in advance, particularly during peak season. There is a seven-day maximum stay. Credit cards can be used for reservations. The business office is open 7 A.M.–3 A.M., but there is no curfew. The hostel is open 24 hours. Baggage may be stored for $5 for the day after checkout if you have a late flight. Key deposits will not be refunded if keys are not returned by 11 A.M., checkout time. Visitors are not allowed at any time, and neither alcohol nor smoking is permitted. Lockers—small, gym locker-types not big enough for a backpack but adequate for valuables—are available, but you must provide your own lock. The hostel gets visitors from around the world. It's clean and safe. The common area/TV lounge, kitchen, and bathrooms are shared by all.

The **Waikiki Beachside Hostel and Hotel** is at 2556 Lemon Rd., Honolulu, HI 96815, 808/923-9566, fax 808/923-7525, reservations@HoKondo.com, www.HoKondo.com. Rates start at $18 per person for a bunk bed in the dorm and increase to $49 for a semiprivate room. One-bedroom apartments with kitchens that sleep four go for $89 per night. All rooms have full baths and kitchens with refrigerator, a/c, and TV, and daily maid service. Guests can stay up to 30 days; only out-of-state guests are allowed in the shared rooms. On property there's a large outdoor lounge, pool table, laundry facilities, large storage lockers for $3 per day, and some parking. On the first floor is an Internet café. A clean, well-furnished, well-kept place—this is a good choice.

Just down the road is the **Polynesian Hostel Beach Club,** 2584 Lemon Rd., Honolulu, HI 96815, 808/922-1340 or 877/504-2924, fax 808/262-2817, polynesian@hawaiihostels.com, www.hawaiihostels.com. Only one block from the beach, the Polynesian is in a converted condoapartment building. A space in a shared room with shared bath runs $19, single/double rooms with in-room baths are $38-49, and a private studio with kitchen goes for $60. The hostel has a common room for reading and watching TV, free movies, a communal kitchen, laundry facilities, free use of some water equipment, and some hostel-sponsored activities. Internet connection is available. There are no storage lockers, but packs can be kept safely in the office. When arriving, there is an airport shuttle; for adventure, inexpensive van excursions depart throughout the week to points around the island. Somewhat rough around the edges, this conveniently located hostel is a good place to meet people from other countries.

The **Pacific Ohana Hostel,** 2552 Lemon Rd., 808/921-8111, was once a small apartment building, much like the other hostels along this road. Dorm rooms for up to four people, either coed or women-only, run $18 per person, shared private rooms for one or two are $30-40, and private studios with kitchenettes run $50 per night. All rooms have air-conditioning. Other amenities include a community kitchen, coin laundry, vending machines, Internet access, and a big-screen TV in the lounge, and there is staff on duty 24 hours a day. The Pacific Ohana Hostel is associated with the Island Hostel (see following entry).

On the other end of Waikiki is **Island Hostel,** 1946 Ala Moana Blvd., inside the Hawaiian Colony Building across from Fort DeRussy, tel./fax 808/942-8748. Each hostel room has a bathroom, small refrigerator, a/c, and linens. Bunks run $18 per person, and private rooms cost $50 per night. Weekly and monthly rates can be arranged, so you'll find other than travelers here. A small communal kitchen is in the office, and the lounge is open for community activities. Laundry facilities, lockers, and telephones are available, and there is some water equipment to borrow. Overpowered by the surrounding buildings, the island hostel is somewhat dark and less open and breezy than hostels at the east end of the strip.

**Seaside Hawaiian Hostel,** 419 Seaside Ave., Honolulu, HI 96815, is the most centrally located of the hostels in Waikiki, yet because it's just inland of Kuhio Avenue it's still relatively quiet. Nestled under a banyan tree, this low-rise hostel is a home away from home for short-term foreign and domestic guests. The maximum stay is seven days; identification and departure information are required. Women-only and coed bunk rooms run $15 per person, two-person shared bunk rooms are $17 per person, and semi-private rooms with a TV, mini-fridge, and shared bath go for $40 per room. Clean and safe, some of the amenities include Internet access, free shuttle from the airport if staying for at least three nights, in-room storage lockers, clean linens, a communal kitchen, lounge, outdoor courtyard, coin laundry, low-cost outings and activities, and 24-hour staff. Like most of the hostels in Waikiki, a simple continental breakfast of toast and coffee is available each morning. For information and reservations, contact the hostel at 808/924-3303 or 866/924-3303, fax 808/923-2111, info@seasidehawaiianhostel.com, www.seasidehawaiianhostel.com.

For additional listings of inexpensive YMCAs, YWCAs, and hostels in other areas of the city, see the Accommodations section in the Honolulu chapter.

## $50–100

When the hostels are full, try the **Waikiki Prince Hotel** just next door to Hale Aloha YH, 2431 Prince Edward St., Honolulu, HI 96815, 808/922-1544, fax 808/924-3712. This little hotel is about the cheapest in Waikiki at $45–60 per night during low season—Apr.–Nov. Weekly rates get you a seventh night free. While the rooms are quite small, everything is as neat as a pin. All rooms have air-conditioning and cable television, and there's a coin laundry and limited parking on premises. One of the best bargains for the price in town, this is a good quiet alternative to the noisier and busier hostels in the area.

The **Royal Grove Hotel,** 151 Uluniu Ave., Honolulu, HI 96815, 808/923-7691, fax 808/922-7508, rghawaii@gte.net, www.royalgrovehotel.com, built in 1951 and run by the Fong family since 1970, gives you a lot for your money. You can't miss its "paint-sale pink" exterior, but inside it's much more tasteful. Rooms in the older wing run $44.50–75 for two; the newer upgraded wing with a/c is $60–75; $10 for an extra person. All are studios and one-bedroom apartments with kitchenettes and air-conditioning. A tiny pool in the central courtyard offers some peace and quiet away from the street. The Royal Grove passes the basic tests of friendliness and cleanliness. It's used but not abused. During low season, Apr. 1–Nov. 30, the Royal Grove offers reduced rates; weekly and monthly rates are possible except for January and February.

A few steps away is the **Continental Surf Hotel,** 2426 Kuhio Ave., 808/922-2232, fax 808/922-1718, which offers small but clean rooms for $49–89. Spartan and rather uninspired, the rooms here are a good value for the money.

The **Waikiki Hana Hotel,** 2424 Koa Ave., Honolulu, HI 96815, 808/926-8841 or 800/367-5004, sits just behind the massive Hyatt Regency on a quiet side street. The hotel has just 73 rooms, so you won't get lost in the shuffle, and the friendly staff go out of their way to make you feel welcome. The Waikiki Hana is surrounded by high-rise hotels, so there's no view, but the peace and quiet just one block from the heavy action more than makes up for it. Rooms start at a reasonable $89 and go to $129 for a deluxe with kitchenette; low-season rates are $15–25 cheaper. All rooms have telephones, a/c, color TV, and in-room safes, and are gaily appointed with bright bedspreads and drapes. Under separate ownership, the Super Chef Restaurant, on the ground floor of the hotel, has reasonable prices. On-site parking is another good feature in crowded Waikiki, but the charge is $12 per day. For a quiet, decent but basic hotel in the heart of Waikiki, the Waikiki Hana, a Castle Resorts property, can't be beat.

At the far west end of Waikiki is **Hawaii Polo Inn,** an Aston Hotel property, 1696 Ala Moana

Blvd., across from the Ala Wai Yacht Harbor, 808/949-0061 or 800/669-7719, www.hawaiipolo.com. A small accommodation with 72 units, each is decorated in lively tropical style. All are air-conditioned, have daily maid service, and some have kitchenettes. Standard rooms run $69–71, deluxe rooms are $79–81, and junior suites go for $98–125. An inexpensive place with all the necessities, the Hawaii Polo Inn gets you close to the action yet keeps you out of the bustle.

Almost next door is the **Big Surf Hotel,** 1690 Ala Moana Blvd., Honolulu, HI 96815, 808/946-6525, fax 808/949-1142. An older high-rise that's seen plenty of use, this hotel maintains small but reasonably clean rooms at an affordable price. Simple and basic, but don't expect too much. Rooms with twin or double beds, some with their own small lanai, are studios at $39–49 and one- or two-bedroom suites with kitchens that range $65–80. Each unit has a/c, ceiling fans, and maid service.

## $100–150

**Ohana Hotels,** 303/369-7777 or 800/462-6262, fax 800/622-4852, www.ohanahotels.com, is a branch of the Outrigger Hotels and Resorts family of accommodations. Ohana has 13 properties in Waikiki offering more than 4,500 rooms. Half are clustered near the beach close to their most luxurious sister property, the Outrigger Reef Hotel, while the others lie along Kuhio Avenue. All fall into the economy to moderate categories. Although not luxurious, they do offer good accommodations, and all have full baths, air-conditioning, TV, and entertainment centers. Rooms are basic, simple, and clean, and some properties have recently been renovated. Several of the Ohana Hotels have restaurants, lounges with entertainment, shops, and swimming pools on property, and similar services. Rates vary from hotel to hotel, but seven start with rooms at $129, an additional three from $149, and three have rooms from $189. Most rooms are no more expensive than $169, but a handful of suites and studios, many with kitchenettes, run $179–229. Additional adults in a room are $20 per night. The two best of the bunch and a step above the others

are the **Ohana East,** where rooms run $189–399, and the **Ohana Islander Waikiki,** where rooms are $189–450. To help save money on these reasonably priced rooms, Ohana offers a $69–109 SimpleSaver rate, plus room and car, room and breakfast, and multiday package reductions.

**The Breakers,** 250 Beachwalk, Honolulu, HI 96815, 808/923-3181 or 800/426-0494, fax 808/923-7174, breakers@aloha.net, www.breakers-hawaii.com, is a friendly, family-style two-story hotel, where if you're a repeat visitor, the staff remembers your name, and with only 65 units, they get plenty of repeat guests. Only minutes from the beach, this little gem of a hotel somehow keeps the hustle and bustle far away. Certainly, this is what staying at Waikiki was like before the high-rises blocked the sight of the beach from street level. Having done a superb job since 1954, The Breakers is tastefully decorated and well kept. Every room has a complete kitchenette and overlooks the shaded courtyard of coconut and banana trees. In the garden is an ample swimming pool, and off to the side you can relax with a snack or light meal and tropical drink at the Cafe Terrace pool bar and lounge. Complimentary coffee is offered near the front desk all day. The rates for studios are $91–98 single and $94–100 double; garden suites run $125–151. For additional persons in any room, there is an additional $8 per-person fee. Studios hold up to three, suites five. All units have a/c, color TV, telephone, and a safe. There's limited parking at the back. The Breakers claims to be "Waikiki's most distinctive resort hotel" and it's right. It's a winner.

Next door at 260 Beachwalk is the **Hawaiiana Hotel,** 808/923-3811 or 800/367-5122, fax 808/926-5728, another low-rise cinderblock hotel with a distinctly local flavor. The Hawaiiana is a bit more boxy than the Breakers but is painted in pleasing whites and light blues. Two pools set off the nicely landscaped garden, onto which each of the fewer than 100 rooms in the six buildings has a view. All rooms have air-conditioning, a kitchenette, and electronic safe; most have showers, but a few have baths. Complimentary morning coffee and juice are served at poolside, barbecue grills are set up for guest use, and a free hula show is put on for guests every

Sunday at 6:30 P.M. In addition, the hotel offers limited parking and laundry facilities. Rates for rooms, single or double, run $85–95, the one-bedrooms are $135, and suites go for $165–190. There's no glitz here, just good honest value and close proximity to the beach.

Another property in the same category is **Leisure Resorts,** 431 Nohonani St., Honolulu, HI 96815, 808/923-7336 or 800/634-6981, fax 808/923-1622, a low-rise local place with 80 units, where each looks out over the garden courtyard with its swimming pool, spa, and coconut trees. Comfortably decorated with tropical decor, these rooms contain all the amenities to make your stay relaxing. Studio rooms are $110 and one-bedroom suites with kitchenettes run $150. Shuttle service is provided to sites around the island and to the airport for pickup and drop-off for a nominal fee. On-site parking is limited. Dwarfed by the surrounding hotels and condos, Leisure Resorts is like an old-time oasis amid new-fangled Waikiki.

Moving a few blocks back from the main drag takes you away from the congestion of town and puts you in a perfect spot to view the mountains that back this lovely city. The **Aston Aloha Surf Hotel,** 444 Kanakapolei, 808/923-0222 or 800/922-7866, fax 808/924-7160, is in such a location. Open, airy, bright, and modern, this hotel overlooks the Ala Wai Canal yet is near to what's happening in Waikiki. Room rates are $135–145 for a hotel room, $160–175 for a studio, and $200–220 for a suite. With most of the amenities of the big hotels, plus a continental breakfast daily, the Aloha Surf is a good value.

Across the street but newer and more contemporary in design is the **Waikiki Sand Villa Hotel,** 2375 Ala Wai Blvd., Honolulu, HI 96815, 808/922-4744 or 800/247-1903, fax 808/923-2541, www.waikikisandvillahotel.com. Reasonably small, with more than 200 rooms, it still has all the amenities of a big hotel, including a large pool, sundries shop, and on-site restaurant and bar. A complimentary breakfast is served daily. Housed in one tower and a three-story Mediterranean-style building to the rear, rooms run $110–139, while the larger and more spacious studios that overlook the pool are $169. Prices run about $10 less from about Easter to Christmas.

A sister hotel, the **Waikiki Gateway Hotel,** 2070 Kalakaua Ave., Honolulu, HI 96815, 808/955-3741 or 800/247-1903, fax 808/923-2541, www.waikiki-gateway-hotel.com, is across from the King Kalakaua statue near where Kalakaua and Kuhio avenues meet. Trapezoidal in shape, this hotel is the home of Nick's Fishmarket (one of the town's best dinner choices), a sundries shop, and small pool, and it serves a daily complimentary breakfast with a view up on one of the top floors. Generally, the bed arrangement is one double and one single in a room, but two doubles and three singles are also available. Room rates run $99–132, and $162 for one of the few rooms with a kitchenette; add about 10 percent from Christmas to Easter. Business accounts are welcome.

The minute you walk into the **Aston Coconut Plaza Hotel,** 450 Lewers St., 808/923-8828 or 800/922-7866, fax 808/923-3473, with plantation decor in its lobby, you feel at home and comfortable. With the Ala Wai Canal to its side, the hotel is not in the midst of the action, but it's only a few blocks to dining and entertainment. Rates are $100–145 for hotel rooms and studios and up to $195 for suites; off-season is cheaper, with special day rates for bona fide business travelers on a space-available basis. Bright and cheery, all rooms are fully air-conditioned and the studios and suites have kitchenettes. There is a small pool off the lobby, where a complimentary continental breakfast is offered daily.

Of newer design is the **Holiday Inn Waikiki,** 1830 Ala Moana Blvd., 808/955-1111 or 888/992-4545, fax 808/947-1799. Rooms here are clean, decent, away from the action, and reasonably priced at $120–130, suites at $310, with reduced rates at various times of the year according to availability. Although it's not chic, the Holiday Inn is comfortable and affordable, has its own swimming pool and small fitness center, and you always get good service. A fine choice.

## $150–200

The 21-floor **Miramar at Waikiki,** 2345 Kuhio Ave., Honolulu, HI 96815, 808/922-2077 or 800/367-2303, fax 808/926-3217, www.miramarwaikiki.com, is in the heart of Waikiki but not on the beach. This hotel offers generous rooms, with lanai, a/c, TV, a swimming pool, restaurants and lounges, and free guest parking. Rates range $125–200 for rooms and $225–400 for suites, $20 extra per person, with numerous corporate, military, and special rates available.

With its off-the-strip location and magnificent views of Diamond Head, the **Queen Kapiolani Hotel,** 150 Kapahulu Ave., Honolulu, HI 96815, 808/922-1941 or 800/367-2317, fax 808/922-2694, www.queenkapiolani.com, is one of the best and quietest hotels for the money in Waikiki. You're only seconds from the beach, and the hotel provides a spacious lobby, ample parking, air-conditioning, shops, and a swimming pool. Featured in the Peacock Dining Room is one of the best buffets in Waikiki, and the Akala Room hosts the Laugh Factory comedy show nightly. An excellent choice for the money. Rates begin at $140 standard to $220 for an ocean view and run $235–250 for studios with kitchenettes. Suites with kitchenettes run $325–425 per night and must be the best deal in town. Several packages are also available. Although it's not luxurious, the Queen Kapiolani has all you need for a comfortable and convenient vacation and is a good value for the money. During its last major renovation, the stately columns in the lobby have been redone, new wallpaper applied, and the shopping area upgraded. The overall effect is now open and airy with the living mural of Diamond Head in the background.

One block behind the Queen Kapiolani is her sister property, the **Ocean Resort Hotel Waikiki,** 175 Paoakalani Ave., Honolulu, HI 96815, 808/922-3861 or 800/367-2317, fax 808/924-1982, www.oceanresort.com. The Ocean Resort is as good a deal as the Queen, but it does not have as nice a location. Remodeled in 2000, the Ocean Resort is perhaps a bit more refined than the Queen. Two towers of rooms offer everything from standard rooms at $140–220 to suites for $225–500, and there is an on-site restaurant and lounge.

The **'Ilima Hotel,** 445 Nohonani St., Honolulu, HI 96815, 808/923-1877 or 800/367-5172, fax 808/924-8371, mail@ilima.com, www.ilima.com, overlooks the Ala Wai Canal and golf course. This high-rise condo-style hotel has the friendly *aloha* spirit and maintains a quiet and safe environment. As soon as you enter you are greeted by paintings that depict scenes from Hawaiian mythology in bold strokes. Studio units begin at a reasonable $129, one-bedroom suites at $179, two-bedroom suites at $250, with $10 each for extra persons. For families of up to eight, the three-bedroom, two-bath penthouse suite at $375 per night is an option. These rates are $10–20 less during low season, Apr.–mid-Dec., and discounts are given for corporate, military, and government travelers, AARP seniors, and AAA members. All units are spacious, have full kitchens, a/c, TV, and maid service, and each has been remodeled with new floor and wall coverings, linens, and decorations. For amenities, you'll find a small pool, exercise room, sauna, laundry facilities, a travel desk, and limited free parking. At the 'Ilima you get all the necessities at a reasonable rate. A great choice.

Directly across from the beach, the **Aston Waikiki Circle Hotel,** 2464 Kalakaua Ave., 808/923-1571 or 800/922-7866, fax 808/926-8024, has one of the best locations in Waikiki at a reasonable rate. An older landmark hotel that has been totally refurbished in a clean and cheery, whimsically modern mode, the building is built in the round so that only some of the rooms have a view of the ocean. With 14 guest floors, this hotel is dwarfed by its neighbors, but it makes it all the more intimate for its guests. Guest rooms run $155 for a city view, $170 for a partial ocean view, and $180–190 for a view facing or fronting the ocean. Rooms and amenities include a/c, private lanai, cable TV, laundry facilities, on-premise restaurant, parking, and a tour desk. For its location, this is a bargain.

Upon arrival, step onto a path of white tile leading through a tiny but robust garden to a translucent dome sheltering the outdoor reception area of the **Aston Waikiki Joy Hotel,** 320 Lewers St., Honolulu, HI 96815, 808/923-2300 or 800/922-7866, fax 808/924-4010, a lotus flower that blooms in the heart of Waikiki. Immediately, marble steps rise to a veranda, where every morning a complimentary continental breakfast is served accompanied by the soft background chanting of a tiny fountain. The hotel, with only 94 rooms, is divided into two towers: the Hibiscus and the Gardenia. It's intimate enough to make everyone feel like an honored guest. Typical hotel rooms, $129–185, and suites, $205–245, are amazingly spacious, and bigger yet are the executive one-bedroom suites with kitchen, $300. The hotel rooms each feature a refrigerator and writing desk. A king-size bed with a slanted headboard perfectly designed for propping pillows is the nerve center of the room, with controls for everything within easy reach. The suites in the Gardenia Tower feature a bedroom and attendant sitting area complete with couch and a large private lanai. Here, too, bathrooms feature a wonderful hot tub. The hotel also has a 15-room karaoke studio (reservations recommended). The hotel restaurant is Cappuccino's, a European-style bistro featuring live entertainment on the weekends. The Waikiki Joy, aptly named, is the epitome of the adage that "wonderful things come in small packages," but in this case, the wonderful thing *is* the package!

Snuggled into a corner of Fort DeRussy is Castle Resorts boutique hotel **Waikiki Terrace**, 2045 Kalakaua Ave., Honolulu, HI 96816, 808/955-6000 or 800/367-5004, fax 808/943-8555. This hotel looks out over the green space, with a nearly unobstructed view to the beach. While not on the water, it's just a short stroll away. There is a swimming pool at the hotel, a fitness center, and asundries shop, but no restaurant, although the much-appreciated Kyoya Japanese restaurant is next door. Each room is air-conditioned and all have small refrigerators, lanai, color TV, and daily maid service. Rooms run $160 for a mountain view, $170 for a city view, $180 for a partial ocean view, and $190 for an oceanview room, while the top-floor one-bedroom suite runs $330.

Renovated in 2001, the **Bamboo**, 2425 Kuhio Ave., Honolulu, HI 96815, 808/922-7777, fax 808/922-9473, www.bamboo.com, a Castle Resorts property, is a smart boutique hotel near the action. Thai-inspired, with decorative touches of bamboo, this older 12-story building has been transformed into a pleasing and intimate accommodation—and one easy on the budget. All rooms are air-conditioned, come with daily maid service, and have a lanai, color TV, and all comforts of a fine establishment; studios and suites have kitchens or kitchenettes. One thing you don't have, however, is a beach view, yet the pool area with its spa and surrounding tropical greenery make for a secluded spot to lounge. A continental breakfast is served daily, coffee is going all day in the lobby, you can enjoy a weekly hosted cocktail get-together, laundry facilities are on property, and daily newspapers are also available for those who like to keep up with the news. Parking is available but limited. Room rates run $135 for a hotel room, $145–155 for a studio, $175–255 for one of the suites, and $500 for the penthouse if you're so inclined. Children under 18 stay free with parents using existing bedding. For a small, charming, comfortable hotel, the Bamboo is hard to beat.

## $200–250

**Outrigger Hotels and Resorts** manages the most hotel and condo rooms in the state for any single owner-operator. Outrigger is an island-owned chain that has three high-end properties in Waikiki, 13 economy Ohana Hotels properties also in Waikiki (see the $100–150 section), hotels and condos on the other three major islands, and additional properties throughout the South Pacific. Its flagship property and fanciest Waikiki hotel is the **Outrigger Waikiki,** which sits right on the beach next to the Royal Hawaiian Shopping Center, between the classic Royal Hawaiian Hotel and Sheraton Moana Surfrider. A few properties to the west and also on the beach is the **Outrigger Reef,** the company's number-two property in Waikiki. Next door to that stands the **Waikiki Shores,** its premier resort condominium on Oʻahu. All of the Outrigger hotels have multiple restaurants on property, and most have lounges and in-house entertainment on a daily basis. In addition, the Outrigger Waikiki presents the popular entertainment show, Society of Seven, in its Main Showroom, and the local and perennial favorite comic Frank De Lima performs at the Palace Showroom at the Ohana

Reef Towers, a sister hotel. Each property has a pool, laundry facilities, shops, a travel desk, a/c, in-room refrigerators and safes, a kid's program, and all amenities that you'd expect from a quality establishment, plus Outrigger operates its own catamaran from the beach for snorkel tours and sunset sails. Room rates for the Outrigger Waikiki and Outrigger Reef run $220–450 per room and suites are $460 and up; studios and suites at the Waikiki Shores run $245–650. Outrigger can help you reduce your expenses by taking advantage of one of their many discount programs, like a free night with a minimum stay; room and car package; bed-and-breakfast package; and over 50, AAA, AARP, military, and corporate rates. Having been around for decades, the Outrigger gives good value and plenty of service, and knows how to treat its guests right. For additional information or reservations, contact Outrigger Hotels at 303/369-7777 or 800/688-7444, fax 800/622-4852, www.outrigger.com.

At the far eastern end of the bay next to Kapi'olani Park and just below Diamond Head is a small group of hotels and condos, amid a handful of apartments and single-family homes. One landmark of this area is the refurbished, small and intimate **The New Otani Kaimana Beach Hotel,** 2863 Kalakaua Ave., Honolulu, HI 96815, 808/923-1555 or 800/356-8264, fax 808/922-1555, www.kaimana.com. Built in 1964, it has the look of that era but has been totally brought up to date. The New Otani has all the amenities and niceties that you'd expect from such a hotel, but a big plus is that it sits on the quiet Sans Souci Beach with no building between it and the view of central Waikiki down the shore. On property are two fine restaurants, Hau Tree Lanai and Miyako, the Sunset Lanai bar, a travel desk, sundries shop, laundry facilities, fitness center, and off-street parking. Depending on direction of view, rooms run $140–325 and suites are $210–1,009, slightly more from Christmas through mid-March; $25 per additional person. If you're looking for a quiet hotel on a superb spot, yet want to be near the heart of Waikiki for easy access, the New Otani Kaimana Hotel is a great choice.

A few steps away is the **Diamond Head Beach Hotel,** 2947 Kalakaua Ave., 808/922-1928 or 800/535-0085, fax 808/924-8980. Small and slender in stature, this Marc Resort property rises up at a slight angle, making the top floors narrower than the bottom floors. Tucked between tall apartments, most rooms offer little horizon view, except for those at the ocean end of the building. Rooms have full and modern conveniences and amenities, and the hotel provides daily complimentary breakfast and staffs an activities desk. Studios have kitchenettes and suites have full kitchens. Rates run $185–205 for rooms and $245–611 for suites.

Sometimes you just hit it lucky and find yourself in a situation where you get more for your money than you expected, and delightfully so. The **Waikiki Beachcomber Hotel,** 2300 Kalakaua Ave., Honolulu, HI 96815, 808/922-4646 or 800/622-4646, fax 808/923-4889, www.waikikibeachcomber.com, is definitely one of those *sometimes* things. The Beachcomber is right in the heart of town—you couldn't be more central. The Beachcomber, living up to its name, is just a minute from the beach, and the professional and amiable staff knows exactly what you want and how to deliver it. The 500 guest rooms, outfitted in new furniture and carpet, and painted in soothing tropical tones, all feature a private lanai, a/c, TV, phone, room safe, and convenient refrigerator. The Hibiscus Cafe, a casual restaurant on the second floor, serves meals all day, from a light breakfast starter to an international evening entrée. On the property are a swimming pool, boutique shops, covered parking, and laundry facilities. Offered throughout summer, the Beachcomber Kids program can entertain and feed children while their parents are off doing other activities. Enjoy the voice and humor of one of Hawaii's consummate entertainers, Don Ho, as he presents his musical extravaganza Sun.–Thurs. evenings as he has done in Waikiki for years. To add to its image as an entertainment center, the Beachcomber also presents both the "Magic of Polynesia Show," a nightly illusionist spectacular, in its 700-seat showroom, and "Blue Hawaii: The Show," an Elvis impersonation and musical review. The rates for guest rooms range $220–270, while the sumptuous

M

O'AHU

suites run $380 and $600. There is a $25 charge for an additional adult, and children 17 and under stay free in their parents' room. A bargain special at only $129 puts you in a city view room with a rental car included or a breakfast buffet for two, while other special rates are also available. To stay within budget while having a quality experience, the Beachcomber is a sure bet!

Just off Lewers Street is the modern but casual **Waikiki Parc Hotel**, 2233 Helumoa Rd., 808/921-7272 or 800/422-0450, fax 808/923-1336, www.waikikiparc.com, where the beach is just a stroll away. The entranceway is done in marble, carpet, and subdued lighting, and coolness seems to permeate the entire property. Subdued elegance is the mode here—the building and surroundings speak for themselves. Rooms are not spacious, but efficient, yet eminently comfortable and pleasing, some with lanai and others with balconies. On the oceanview side, you look down on the distinctive orchid pool at its sister property, the Halekulani, across the street. Depending on location in the building, rooms run $225–320 per night, which includes a complimentary breakfast at the Parc Cafe, the hotel's main dining room, or the Japanese restaurant Kacho, both of which are also open for lunch and dinner. The Parc Cafe features reasonably priced buffets at all meals (à la carte available as well), but the specialty is the weekend evening prime rib and seafood buffet. The hotel pool is on the eighth floor, and there too you can get light meals and refreshments. Several special room packages are available to reduce your charges. A business center, fitness room, and hospitality room for early check-ins or late checkouts are additional amenities. Validated valet parking is standard.

Across the road from her sister hotel, the Sheraton Moana Surfrider, is the **Sheraton Princess Ka'iulani Hotel**, 120 Ka'iulani Ave, Honolulu, HI 96815, 808/922-5811 or 800/782-9488, fax 808/931-4577, www.princess-kaiulani.com. With grace and grandeur, the Princess takes her place as one of the royalty of this strip, and this is immediately apparent as you enter the hotel lobby. Princess Ka'iulani was the last generation of Hawaiian royalty, but unfortunately she died in 1899 at the young age of 23, six years after the end of the monarchy. Portraits of her hang in the lobby of the hotel, and a statue has been placed in 'Ainahau Park, the small traingular park around the side and one block back from the hotel. This hotel is built on what was her estate, 'Ainahau, and it's a big place with 1,150 rooms in three towers. Rooms run from $165 for a cityside room and $205 for a standard to $360 for a deluxe ocean view, with suites running upward from $595. Guest service helps with arranging activities and dining, kids can be taken care of through the hotel's *keiki* program, and you can safely deposit your car in the hotel parking lot. When looking for food, you need not look far. The Princess Ka'iulani has the Momoyama Japanese restaurant, the open-air Pikake Terrace, known for its evening buffets and nightly Hawaiian entertainment—music wafts across the torch-light pool for the enjoyment of all—and the Princess Food Court along Kalakaua Avenue. In addition, the Princess presents the theatrical performance "Creation: A Polynesian Odyssey," nightly in its 'Ainahau showroom.

The small but sumptuous **Aston Waikiki Beachside Hotel**, 2452 Kalakaua Ave., 808/931-2100 or 800/922-7866, fax 808/931-2129, is a boutique hotel with style and class, from the Italian Travertine marble floor covered with pink floral carpet to the hand-painted silk artwork hanging on the walls. Every little touch says classical elegance. Outside, a tiny courtyard is serenaded by a bubbling Italian fountain, perfect for complimentary breakfast of coffee and croissants. In the 12 floors above, only 79 luxurious rooms await, ranging in price $215–405. Each tastefully decorated room comes with twice-daily maid service, a mini-fridge, entertainment center, room safe, and free morning newspaper. To make your visit even more carefree, the concierge service will help with all your activities and travel plans. While not cheap, this is a gem.

Near the eastern end of the strip is the **Aston Waikiki Beach Hotel**, 2570 Kalakaua Ave., 808/922-2511 or 800/922-7866, fax 808/923-3656, www.astonwaikiki.com. Remodeled in 2001 to the tune of $30 million, this 719-room, 25-floor property has been totally reconditioned and brought up to date with retro architectural features and hip Hawaiian decor. Each room has a contemporary island feel with bold, bright colors and furnishings, and while they're small, the bathrooms are finely done. Check-in is on the second floor, and across the pool deck is Tiki's Grill and Bar, a lively, casual place with indoor and outdoor seating that looks out over Kalakaua Avenue to the beach. More than just a casual eatery, as its name and decor seem to imply, Tiki's also serves contemporary island favorites, including many fresh fish entrées, offers a bar menu until midnight, and is the venue of soothing music every evening 4–6 P.M. and again 9–11 P.M. Rising over the bar is a tapered hood with a flood of red light shining up the wall mimicking a volcano. One of the special features of this hotel is its breakfast on the beach concept, where a continental breakfast is served each morning on the pool deck. This breakfast is a wide assortment of pastries, cereal, yogurt, fruit, and drinks, which you can have on one of the poolside chaise lounges, in your room, or load into the soft-sided cooler from your room and carry across the street to enjoy while you sit under a palm tree with your feet in the sand. This hotel has valet parking only and a string of street-level shops. Room rates are standard $150–212, partial ocean view $262, ocean view $332, oceanfront $387, and suites $400. An older establishment brought back to life as a fashionable, chic spot, the Aston Waikiki Beach Hotel is a great choice for comfort and convenience.

Standing as one of the pillars of the eastern end of the strip is **Pacific Beach Hotel**, 2490 Kalakaua Ave., 808/922-1233 or 800/367-6060, fax 808/922-0129, reservation@hth.com, www.pacificbeachhotel.com. This two-tower, 830-room hotel has a perfect spot along the shore and is only on the edge of most of the busy shopping bustle. Rooms have full baths, lanai, a/c, complete entertainment centers, refrigerators, and coffee makers. On property are a swimming pool, two tennis courts, a fitness center, a bevy of shops, laundry services, and valet or self parking. The concierge or tour desk will arrange activities for the family, and the kids' program is set up to take care of the younger set. For the con-

venience of guests, the Pacific Beach has three restaurants: the unique Oceanarium, which has a three-story aquarium wall; Neptune's Garden, where the focus is on seafood; and Shogun, for Japanese dining fine enough to win local appeal. Room rates run $195–225 for standard and partial oceanview rooms, $235–250 for oceanview rooms, and $280–295 for oceanfront rooms; slightly higher from just before Christmas to the end of February. In addition, a handful of suites on the top floors of each tower run $510–2,200 per night and provide you the best of the best. For location, amenities, and ease of use, this fine hotel is hard to beat.

The intimate boutique hotel **Doubletree Alana Hotel Waikiki**, 1956 Ala Moana Blvd., 808/941-7275 or 800/222-8733, fax 808/949-0996, www.alana-doubletree.com, provides all needed amenities in a casual and relaxed atmosphere. All rooms are comfortably outfitted with king beds or two queen-size beds and have a/c, TV, computer hookups, lanai, and Italian marble entryways and baths. Rooms run $205–225, suites $260–700, and the Royal Amethyst Suite (a combined three-suite unit with boardroom) goes for $2,000. Artworks adorn the walls and works by local artists hang in the hotel's gallery. A full-service business center is available for those on working assignments, and everyone can enjoy the fitness center and swimming pool. Convenient for guests, one of Waikiki's best restaurants, Padovani's Bistro and Wine Bar, makes the Doubletree Alana its home.

## $250 AND UP
### Hilton Hawaiian Village
This mammoth first-rate resort, a 22-acre oasis of tranquillity, sits in its own quiet corner of Waikiki. You are greeted at the entrance by a larger-than-lifesize sculpture of three Hawaiian hula dancers and a reflecting pond. The Hilton, 2005 Kalia Rd., Honolulu, HI 96815, 808/949-4321 or 800/445-8667, fax 808/947-7898, www.hawaiianvillage.hilton.com, is at the far western end of Waikiki, lying between Fort DeRussy and Ala Wai Yacht Harbor. Enter along 200 yards of the private hotel driveway, passing the Rainbow

Bazaar mall with its exclusive shopping and dining. Facing you are the Hilton's six towers: the Tapa, Diamond Head, Lagoon, and Rainbow, the prestigious Ali'i Tower, and the newest, the Kalia. With more than 3,400 rooms, this resort complex is by far the largest in the state, having nearly twice as many rooms as its nearest rival. The huge multistoried rainbows on both sides of the Rainbow Tower are, according to the *Guinness Book of World Records,* the tallest ceramic-tile mosaics in the world. All rooms are deluxe and most have magnificent views. Amenities include color TV, a/c, self-service bar, refrigerator, 24-hour room service, voice mail, and a safe for personal belongings. The beachside Ali'i Tower pampers you even more with a private pool, turndown service, and concierge service. The Lagoon Tower overlooks the huge hotel lagoon, while the others lie back from the water. The Kalia, newest of the bunch, has been set up with the business traveler in mind. It has several dedicated executive floors, a bridge connection to the Mid-Pacific Conference Center, its own set of shops, the Niumalu Café, a branch of the Bishop Museum, and houses the Mandara Spa and fitness center, the Ola Pono Spa Café, and the Holistica Hawaii Health Center, a preventive health clinic, which has, among other things, an electron-beam tomography scanning machine. Room rates are $189–510 throughout the village, with suites up to $4,260. One- and two-bedroom condo units are available in the Lagoon Tower for $260–700.

The towers form a semicircle fronting the beach, not a private beach because none can be private, but about as private a public beach as you can get. Few come here unless they're staying at the Hilton. It's dotted with palms—tall royal palms for elegance, shorter palms for shade. The property has five pools. The main pool, surrounded by luxuriant tropical growth, is the largest in Waikiki. The lagoon area creates the music of water in bubbling rivulets, tiny waterfalls, and reflecting pools. Torches of fire, and ginger, banana trees, palms, ferns, and rock gardens are the grounds. The concierge can arrange a free guided tour of the grounds by a groundskeeper, who will explain the habitat, life cycle, and characteristics of each plant. Within the grounds, several dozen birds, including half a dozen penguins, make their home.

The action of Waikiki is out there, of course, just down the shore, but you don't feel it unless you want to. Relax and enjoy the sunset accompanied by contemporary Hawaiian music at any of the eight bars and lounges. Exotic and gourmet dining from throughout the Pacific rim is available at the village's 12 restaurants, especially the hotel's signature Bali by the Sea and Golden Dragon restaurants. Additional restaurants, like Benihana of Tokyo and Sergio's, are just across the driveway at the Rainbow Bazaar shopping mall, while more boutique shops can be found in each of the towers. Exclusively for kids, the Rainbow Express Keiki Club offers fun things to do each day of the week year-round. Reflecting the large-scale nature of this resort, a long list of free activities and entertainment is scheduled throughout the week. Of special note are the evening torchlighting ceremony and the Friday sunset King's Jubilee entertainment of Polynesian music and dance that's accompanied by fireworks over the water. The hotel has everything to keep its villagers contented and happy. As a complete destination resort where you can play, relax, shop, dine, dance, and retreat, the Hilton Hawaiian Village knows what it's about and has found its center.

## Hyatt Regency Waikiki

The Hyatt, 2424 Kalakaua Ave., 808/923-1234 or 800/233-1234, fax 808/923-7839, www.waikiki.hyatt.com, is a hotel resort of grand proportions. Standing directly across from the beach, two geometrical towers rise up in symmetry to the warm tropical sun. Anchoring these modernistic pillars are three floors of shops and restaurants, a day spa, and meeting and convention space. As if in imitation of a jungle forest, the entrance atrium sports copious tropical greenery and a broad waterfall that spills into a refreshing pool. Up the stairs on the second level is the front desk. More than 1,200 rooms occupy this mini-city, and each is large and plush with the latest in adornments and amenities. Nothing is skimped on when it comes to guest comforts, but this luxury comes at a price. Hotel room rates run $265–485 per night, while suites are

$800–4,000. Special deals and packages are always available, but these may change throughout the year. As with many other Hyatt hotels, this one provides professional spa service. At Na Ho'ola, you can maintain your workout regimen at the fitness center or be pampered with massage, sauna, body work, or Hawaiian healing treatments of herbal preparations. Don't want to walk across the street to the beach? Then have a dip in the hotel pool or the hot tub. Five restaurants, serving everything from award-winning Chinese cuisine to standard American steaks, grace this hotel, and there is the customary lounge and bar for relaxation. Soft sounds of Hawaiian music waft through the hotel every evening from the lobby bar. With practiced efficiency, the Hyatt will provide a memorable stay.

## Hawaii Prince Hotel Waikiki

The dynamic seascape of the tall masted ships anchored in the Ala Wai Yacht Harbor reflects in the shimmering pink-tinted glass towers of the Hawaii Prince Hotel Waikiki, 100 Holomoana St., Honolulu, HI 96815, 808/956-1111 or 800/321-6248, fax 808/946-0811. The twin towers, Diamond Head and Ala Moana, are scaled by a glass elevator affording wide-angled vistas of the Honolulu skyline. Decorated in green and tan with light burnished maple, the rooms, all oceanview, feature a marble-topped desk with full mirror, a/c, functional windows, and a full entertainment center. Each room has its own refrigerator, walk-in closet with complimentary safe, and a king-size bed. The marble bathrooms have separate shower stalls, tubs, and commodes with a full set of toiletries. Room rates are from $310 for an Oceanfront Marina to $450 for an Oceanfront Top (floors 30–33), while suites range $550–2,500; $40 per extra person. Special business rates are offered (ask when booking), and golf and other packages are available. Ride the elevator to the fifth floor, where you will find a keyhole-shaped pool and canvas shade umbrellas overlooking the harbor below. Here as well is the Promenade Deck Snack Shop, serving coffee, jumbo hamburgers, and other munchies beginning at 11 A.M. The business center gives you access to a secretary, computers, fax machines, modems for email, and a conference room. Fees vary according to services rendered. Other amenities include two excellent restaurants—the Prince Court and Hakone—a lobby lounge with evening music, a full fitness center, spa and massage service, the Prince Keiki Club children's program, valet parking, and a courtesy shuttle. The Hawaii Prince boasts its own golf course, an Arnold Palmer–designed 27-hole championship course, and two tennis courts, at the Hawaii Prince Golf Club, at 'Ewa Beach, 40 minutes away, the only one of its kind belonging to a Waikiki hotel. The Hawaii Prince, at the gateway to Waikiki, is away from the action of the frenetic Waikiki strip, but close enough to make it easily accessible.

## Sheraton Waikiki

Dominating the center of Waikiki are the 30 floors and 1,852 rooms of the Sheraton Waikiki Hotel, 2255 Kalakaua Ave., Honolulu, HI 96815, 808/922-4422 or 800/782-9488, fax 808/923-8785, www.sheraton-waikiki.com. Built in 1971 as one of the area's first convention centers, it has a perfect location on the beach—and a long stretch of the beach. Recent refurbishment brings the spirit of the sea into the hotel. In conjunction, the *honu* (green sea turtle), which has come back from the brink of extinction and feeds in the evening in the waters of Waikiki, has been incorporated into the hotel logo. Rooms are basically either ocean view or city view, and all have full amenities, including air-conditioning, TV and movies, mini-refrigerators, and in-room safes. Rooms with views away from the water run $290–350. For an oceanview or oceanfront room, rates are $440–570. Suites start at $885. The hotel has a clutch of two dozen shops for apparel, jewelry, gifts, camera needs, and sundries; two freshwater swimming pools; a fitness center; business center; and plenty of parking. On the dining and entertainment side, the Sheraton has the only nightclub in Waikiki on the beach, two cocktail lounges, nightly poolside Hawaiian music entertainment, and three fine restaurants, including the Hanohano Room (its signature restaurant on the 30th floor), the Restaurant Gion for a taste of Japan, and the more casual Ocean Terrace Restaurant, which is known for its buffets. Guests have signing privileges at the other Sheraton properties in Waikiki, all three of which are only minutes away. Free to guests are fun runs Mon.–Sat. at 7 A.M., aerobic fitness training, tai chi, and a leisurely guided historical tour along the beach various days of the week. Water activities like sailing, surfing, snorkeling, and outrigger canoe and catamaran rides can all be arranged at the hotel beach center. Outside activities can be arranged through the activities desk, and guests who have early arrivals or late-night departures can use the lockers, showers, restrooms, and lounge in the Hospitality Center 6:30 A.M.–9:30 P.M. The Keiki Aloha Club can keep your kids busy with age-appropriate, supervised activities, and baby-sitting services are also available. As the second largest resort complex in Hawaii, the Sheraton Waikiki offers something for everyone.

## Sheraton Moana Surfrider

The Moana Surfrider, 2365 Kalakaua Ave., Honolulu, HI 96815, 808/922-3111 or 800/782-9488, fax 808/923-0308, www.moana-surfrider .com, is the oldest and most venerable hotel in Waikiki. More than just recapturing early-1900s grandeur, the Moana has surpassed itself by integrating all of the modern conveniences. The original Italian Renaissance style is the main architectural theme, but like a fine opera, it joins a variety of themes that blend into a soul-satisfying finale. Later construction and restoration has connected the three main buildings—the Banyan, Tower, and Diamond wings—to form an elegant complex of luxury accommodations, gourmet dining, and distinctive shopping. The renovated Moana, filled with memories of times past, is magical. It's as if you stood spellbound before the portrait of a beautiful princess of long ago, when suddenly her radiant granddaughter, an exact image, dazzling in jewels and grace, walked into the room.

You arrive under the grand columns of a porte cochere, where you are greeted by doormen in crisp white uniforms and hostesses bearing lei and chilled pineapple juice. The lobby is a series of genteel parlor arrangements conducive to civilized relaxation. Art, urns, chandeliers, sofas, koa tables, flowers, vases, and pedestaled glass-topped tables wait in attendance. An elevator takes you to the second floor, where a room filled with 100 years of memorabilia whispers names and dates of the Moana's grand past.

Upstairs, the rooms are simple elegance. Queen-size beds, rattan chairs, and fluffy pillows and bedspreads extend their waiting arms. All rooms have a/c, and the Banyan Wing features a remote-control master keyboard for TV, lights, and music. But this is the Moana! Bathrooms are tile and marble appointed with huge towels and stocked with fine soaps, shampoos, creams, makeup mirrors, and a bathroom scale, which you can hide under the bed.

Being the first hotel built in Waikiki, it sits right on the beach with one of the best views of Diamond Head along the strip. A swimming pool with sundeck is staffed with attentive personnel, and the activities center can book you on a host of activities, including a classic outrigger canoe ride or a sunset sail on a catamaran. Three restaurants, a grand ballroom, a snack bar, and two lounges take care of all your dining needs, and in addition, traditional afternoon tea is served. Of the restaurants, the dinner-only Ship's Tavern is the hotel's fine-dining restaurant, and The Banyan Veranda is known for its sumptuous Sunday Brunch. Many rooms overlook the central Banyan Court, scene of nightly entertainment that can be chamber music or soft Hawaiian tunes. Open the windows, allowing the breezes to billow the curtains while the waves of Waikiki join with the music below in a heavenly serenade. Rooms are $270–575, with suites priced from $1,025–3,000. The Sheraton Moana Surfrider is a superb hotel offering exemplary old-fashioned service. Whether you're a guest here or not, join one of the free guided tours of the hotel's restored and refurbished original section, offered twice weekdays at 11 A.M. and 5 P.M.

## Royal Hawaiian Hotel

The Royal Hawaiian, the second oldest hotel built along Waikiki, 2259 Kalakaua Ave., Honolulu, HI 96815, 808/923-7311 or 800/782-9488, fax 808/931-7098, www.royal-hawaiian

.com, provides an ongoing contemporary experience in early-1900s charm. Affectionately know as the Pink Palace, this Spanish-Moorish–style hotel has also recently completed a $25 million restoration, which has recaptured the grand elegance of the historic boat days. Its doors first opened in 1927, at a cost of $4 million, an unprecedented amount of money in those days for a hotel. The Depression brought a crushing reduction to Hawaiian tourism, bringing the yearly total down from a whopping 22,000 to less than 10,000 (today more visitors arrive in one day), and the Royal Hawaiian became a financial loss. During World War II, with Waikiki barbedwired, the hotel was leased to the Navy as an R&R hotel for sailors from the Pacific Fleet. After the war, the hotel reverted to Matson Lines, the original owner, and reopened in 1947 after a $2 million renovation. Sheraton Hotels purchased the Royal in 1959, built the Royal Tower Wing in 1969, sold the hotel in 1975, but continued to remain as operating manager.

When you visit the Royal Hawaiian, the most elegant lobby is not where you check in. Rather, follow the long hallway toward the sea. This becomes an open breezeway, with arches and columns in grand style. Here is the heart of the hotel, with Diamond Head framed in the distance. Although hemmed in by taller and larger buildings and its property shrunk in size to a mere 12 acres, the Royal Hawaiian still maintains a fabulous garden. Feel free to walk around and see what the grounds offer, but to make the best of it, pick up a copy of the hotel's *Self-guided Garden Walking Tour* brochure.

Original double doors featured one solid door backed by a louvered door so you could catch the ocean breezes and still have privacy. Today, the hotel is fully air-conditioned, so the old doors have been removed and new solid rosewood doors carved in the Philippines have replaced them. Rooms might have four-poster beds, canopies, twins, or kings, depending on your preference. All rooms have remote-control TV, refrigerators, electronic safes, and computer hookups on telephones for laptop computers. Furniture is French provincial, with bathrooms fully tiled. Completely renovated rooms in the original section have kept the famous pink motif but are slightly more pastel. They have a marble tile bathroom, a brass butler, and louvered drawers. The tall ceilings are even more elegant with molded plaster cornices. Guests are treated to banana bread on arrival, a daily newspaper on request, and turndown service. A Hospitality Suite is provided for early morning check-ins or late checkouts and offers complimentary shower facilities. The Royal Tower is preferred by many guests because every room has an ocean view and the bathrooms are generally larger. From the balcony of most, you look down onto the swimming pool, the beach, palm trees, and Diamond Head in the distance. Not as large as its neighbors, the Royal Hawaiian has 527 rooms, 34 of which are suites. A basic guest room is $380–655, with suites ranging upward from $850.

The main dining room at the Royal is the beachfront Surf Room, open all day every day, and perhaps best known for its Friday evening seafood buffet. Lighter food is also available at the Beach Club next to the pool. If you stay at the Royal Hawaiian, you can dine and sign at the Moana Surfrider, Sheraton Waikiki, or Princess Ka'iulani, all operated by Sheraton Hotels. One of the best features of the Royal, open to guests and nonguests, is the remarkable lu'au every Monday night. Drinks and entertainment are provided daily at the hotel's famous Mai Tai bar. To the delight of many who remember, The Royal Tea is once again served on the Coconut Grove lanai 1–4:30 P.M. daily for $21.95. A blend of the East and West, tea, pastries, and sandwiches are served by kimono-clad ladies to contemporary classical music. Call 808/921-7194 to reserve a seat and experience the tradition.

## Halekulani

The Halekulani, 2199 Kalia Rd., Honolulu, HI 96815, 808/923-2311 or 800/367-2343, fax 808/926-8004, www.halekulani.com, was an experiment of impeccable taste that paid off. Some years ago the hotel was completely rebuilt and refurnished with the belief that Waikiki could attract the luxury-class visitor, and that belief has proven accurate. Since opening, the hotel has gained international recognition and has been named as a member of the prestigious Leading Hotels of the World and Preferred Hotels and Resorts Worldwide. It is one of few AAA five-diamond award hotels in Hawaii and the only one on O'ahu. In addition, its signature restaurant, La Mer, has also been given a five-diamond award rating, and the Orchids Dining Room has received a four-diamond award, making the Halekulani one of the best.

The soothing serenade of the Halekulani begins from the moment you enter the porte cochere, where an impressive floral display welcomes you. The property was first developed in 1907 by Robert Lewers as a residential grouping of bungalows, none of which survive. However, still preserved is the Main Building, dating from the 1930s when the hotel became a fashionable resort owned by Juliet and Clifford Kimball. The Main Building, a plantation-style mansion, houses the hotel's second-floor La Mer restaurant, along with the ground-floor Orchids Dining Room, serving breakfast, lunch, and dinner; Lewer's Lounge for an intimate cocktail and nightly entertainment; the genteel Living Room, where you can enjoy refreshments; and the Veranda where afternoon tea is held. Notice the Main Building's distinctive "Dickey Roof," patterned after a Polynesian longhouse, perfectly sloped to catch island breezes while repelling a sudden rain squall. Wander the grounds to be pleasantly surprised that so much is given to open space, accented with trimmed lawn, reflecting pools, and bubbling fountains. The heated Orchid Pool, with its signature mosaic orchid, is always inviting and within earshot of the surf. Close by is House Without a Key, an indoor/outdoor buffet restaurant also serving light snacks and perhaps one of the best locales in all of Waikiki for a sunset cocktail.

Enter the guest room through a solid teak door into an antechamber that opens into the room, done in shades of white. Awaiting is a platter of fine china bearing a display of fresh fruit and complimentary "Bakeshop" chocolates. King-size beds require only a small portion of the rich Berber carpet-covered floors. For ultimate relaxation and added convenience, all rooms feature a writing desk, small couch,

ROBERT NILSEN

**The upper floors of the Halekulani Hotel offer one of the best views of the waters of Waikiki and Diamond Head beyond.**

reclining chair, and Oriental-style lamps, while bathrooms have separate soaking tubs and showers. Additional amenities include a remote-controlled entertainment center with DVD player, mini-fridge, three wireless telephones, and in-room safe. Sliding louvered doors lead to a private tiled lanai. Prices are $325–520 for guest rooms, $750–1,725 for suites, with the Presidential and Royal suites at prices available on request. A third-person charge is $125 for anyone over 18 years of age or $40 for a child if a roll-away bed is needed. Additional amenities include the heated swimming pool, daily newspapers, free local telephone calls, a full-service fitness center, and free admission to numerous historical and cultural attractions around town through the "For You, Everything" program. The Halekulani awaits to show you its version of classic island charm. You won't be disappointed.

## Waikiki Beach Marriott Resort

The Waikiki Beach Marriott Resort (formerly the Hawaiian Regent Hotel), 2552 Kalakaua Ave., Honolulu, HI 96815, 808/922-6611 or 800/367-5370, fax 808/921-5255, www.marriottwaikiki.com, has a long history of treating guests like royalty. The hotel now stands on what was the original site of Queen Lili'uokalani's summer cottage. The grand tradition of the hotel is reflected in the open sweeping style, and after more than two decades, it appears extremely modern because its design was so visionary when it was built. With more than 1,300 units, the hotel ranks as the third largest hotel in Waikiki after the Hilton Hawaiian Village and the Sheraton Waikiki. There are many categories of rooms, but most fall into the $194–360 range, with suites from $1,500–2,300. All rooms are oversize and include cable TV, a/c, nightly turndown service, and in-room safes. You can step across the street to mingle with the fun-seekers on Waikiki Beach or relax at one of the hotel's two pools. A championship Laykold tennis court is open from sunrise to sunset, with lessons and rackets available. The hotel offers exclusive shops in an off-lobby mall, and an on-site beauty shop and Japanese acupressure/massage service can revitalize you after a hard day of having fun in the sun. For food and entertainment, try the family-style Kuhio Beach grill, the Moana Terrace, or the newer Japanese noodle shop Restaurant Run or the Italian restaurant Arancino. If you're after peace and quiet, head for the Garden Courtyard in the center of the hotel, where you can sit among flowers and full-grown coconut and bamboo trees. Periodically throughout the week, you can attend activities here to learn leimaking, hula, or even Hawaiian checkers from *kupua* who come just to share their *aloha*. The Marriott is a first-class hotel that really knows how to make you feel like a visiting monarch. Rule with joy!

## Kahala Mandarin Oriental

Long considered a standard-setter for Hawaiian deluxe hotels, the Kahala Mandarin Oriental, 5000 Kahala Ave., Honolulu, HI 96816, 808/739-8888 or 800/367-2525, fax 808/739-8800, www.mandarinoriental.com, is not actually in Waikiki, but in Kahala, an exclusive residential area just east of Diamond Head. The hotel, built more than 30 years ago and refurbished in 1996–1997 to the tune of $80 million, is proud that many of its key employees have been there from the first days and that they have formed lasting friendships with guests who happily return year after year. Surrounded by the exclusive Wai'alae Country Club (not even hotel guests are welcome unless they are members), the hotel gives a true sense of peace and seclusion and rightly boasts a "Neighbor Island Experience" only minutes from bustling Waikiki.

Adjacent to the lobby is the Verandah lounge. An indoor-outdoor affair, tea and light foods are served here in the afternoon 2–5 P.M., and entertainment is scheduled every afternoon and evening. Beyond the lounge and overlooking the garden and bay is the hotel's signature restaurant, Hoku's. One of many imaginative restaurants in town, Hoku's serves a grand combination of ethnic dishes encompassing the Pacific, East, and West from its open kitchen, and is open for lunch weekdays, dinner daily, and Sunday brunch. Down a grand staircase and directly below Hoku's is the more informal and open-air Plumeria Beach Cafe, which offers à la carte and buffet choices every day from morning until evening. If that's not enough, Tokyo-Tokyo offers superb Japanese food, and the poolside Honu Bar is a perfect spot for a quiet afternoon or evening drink, serving *pu pu* 4–8 P.M.

The Kahala Mandarin has 364 rooms in two towers and low-rise bungalows set around a lagoon. Average rooms are extra large and have full entertainment centers with 27-inch televisions, bathrooms with his and her sections, a wet bar, small refrigerators, and in-room safes. Rates are $295–345 for a courtyard-view room, $345 for a garden-view room, $375–425 for a mountain-view room, up to $590 for a lagoon or oceanview room, and $690 for a room on the water; add $140 for a third adult in any room. Suites run $950–3,700. Numerous promotions and packages are available.

The hotel, fronting the sheltered Maunalua

Bay, features a perfect crescent beach, the most secluded of hotel beaches in the city. Also on property are a swimming pool and beach cabana with all water-sports gear available, including kayaks, rafts, boogie boards, and snorkel gear. Behind, a waterfall cascading from a free-form stone wall forms a rivulet that leads to a dolphin lagoon and a series of saltwater ponds teeming with reef fish. A daily 30-minute in-water dolphin experience is offered by an independent company, Dolphin Quest, and runs $175 adults, $150 kids 5–12 years old. A Hawaiian cultural program offers classes free to guests, including lei-making, hula dance, or ukulele instruction. Other offerings are its arcade shops, scheduled shuttle service to Waikiki and major shopping malls, fitness and executive business centers, and the Keiki Club for kids 5–12 years old. The Kahala Mandarin is a AAA five-diamond award winner and pays excellent attention to detail and service. While not for everyone, there's no doubt you get all that you pay for.

## W Honolulu Hotel

The W Honolulu Hotel is at 2885 Kalakaua Ave., Honolulu, HI 96815, 808/922-1700 or 877/946-8357, fax 808/923-2249, www.whotels.com. Small and intimate, at the quiet end of Waikiki on Sans Souci Beach, this is a chic modern affair at the forefront of contemporary design and features, with a touch of Asia, yet the elegance is understated. Each spacious room has a superb view of Diamond Head or the ocean, and only the best of amenities and finest of service are allowed. Although not aimed exclusively to this group, the W Honolulu Hotel does cater to business travelers. To satisfy your most discriminating tastes, the Diamond Head Grill, one of the city's most chic food purveyors, is in the building. This hotel comprises only four dozen rooms, so each guest is treated with a familiarity that is not possible at a larger resort. Rooms are $375–475, suites run $600–800, with the two-bedroom penthouse at $3,000; $55 extra guest charge, no charge for kids under 18 using existing bedding. Business discounts are offered.

## CONDOMINIUMS

### $100–150

One company in Hawaii that manages many condominiums around the state is **Aston Hotels and Resorts**, 800/922-7866. Several of their Waikiki properties are listed in the following sections. For a complete listing of all hotels and condominiums, rates, and amenities, see www.aston-hotels.com.

You can capitalize on the off-beach location of the **Aston Honolulu Prince**, 415 Nahua St., Honolulu, HI 96815, 808/922-1616 or 800/922-7866, where you'll find a hotel/condo offering remarkably good value for your money. This 10-floor property invites you into its fully furnished hotel rooms and one- and two-bedroom suites. All offer a/c, color cable TV, and daily maid service, while the suites have fully equipped kitchens. Prices begin at $80–100 for a standard room, $140 one bedroom, and $165 two bedroom, with rates somewhat higher during peak season. The apartments are oversize, with a huge sitting area that includes a sofa bed for extra guests. The Honolulu Prince is not fancy, but it is clean, decent, and family-oriented. A fine choice for a memorable vacation at affordable prices.

### $150–200

Another island company that also has numerous properties around the state, and four in Waikiki, is **Marc Resorts**, 808/922-9700 or 800/535-0085, fax 808/922-2421, www.marcresorts.com. Marc Resorts basically has condominium units in various configurations, with the addition of hotel rooms in some buildings. The studios and suites come with kitchenettes or full kitchens, and the hotel rooms have small refrigerators. Some amenities differ according to property, but all are air-conditioned. Most have swimming pools, lanai, laundry facilities, sundries shops, and a restaurant. A few have daily complimentary continental breakfast, and others have weekly managers' mai tai parties. In Waikiki, the best of the Marc condominium properties is **Waikiki Royal Suites**, 255 Beachwalk, where rates run $199–329. Prices at **Island Colony** and **Marc Suites Waikiki** start a bit lower at

$155 and $149, respectively. Marc's fourth property is the Diamond Head Beach Hotel (seethe $200–250 section).

You can't beat the value at the **Aston Pacific Monarch** condo resort directly behind the Hyatt Regency, 2427 Kuhio Ave., Honolulu, HI 96815, 808/923-9805 or 800/922-7886, fax 808/924-3220. It offers some great features for a moderately priced property. Fully furnished studios are $130–150; one-bedroom condo apartments cost $155–185, all a/c, with on-site pay parking. The rooms are bright and cheery with full baths, living/dining areas, kitchens or kitchenettes, and cable TV. End units of each floor are larger, so request one for a large or shared party. The swimming pool, with a relaxing hot tub, perches high over Waikiki on the 34th floor of the hotel, offering one of the best cityscapes in Honolulu. The lobby is sufficient but small. Save money and have a great family experience by setting up temporary housekeeping at the Pacific Monarch.

## $200–250

Twinkling lights descending the residential valleys of the Ko'olau Range with Diamond Head framed in perfect symmetry are an integral part of the natural room decor of the **Aston Waikiki Sunset,** 229 Paoakalani St., Honolulu, HI 96815, 808/922-0511, or 800/922-7866, fax 808/8785, one of Waikiki's newest condominium properties. Although a condominium, the Waikiki Sunset offers all of the comfort and convenience of a hotel, including 24-hour front desk service, daily maid service, and amenities like a swimming pool, sauna, tennis court, travel desk, minimart, and even a restaurant. The entrance, cooled by Casablanca fans whirring over marble floors, sets the mood for this charming accommodation tucked away only one block from the Kalakaua strip. One-bedroom units range $190–235, and

two-bedroom units run $355–375, making this an appropriate size for families. All feature full kitchens for in-room cooking and dining. All suites feature a private lanai, an entertainment center with remote-control color TV, and a tiled bath with a Japanese-style *ofuro*, a soaking tub perfect for the start of a cozy evening.

## $250 and Up

A tunnel of white thunbergia tumbling from a welcoming arbor leads to the entrance of the **Aston Waikiki Beach Tower**, 2470 Kalakaua Ave., Honolulu, HI 96815, 808/926-6400 or 800/922-7866, fax 808/926-7380, one of Waikiki's newest mini-luxury condo hotels. A lustrous patina shines from brown on tan marble floors while glass-topped tables of black and gold lacquer hold magnificent displays of exotic blooms, and fancy French mirrors and cut-glass chandeliers brighten the small but intimate reception area. Enter your suite through a vestibule onto a white carpet leading to a combination dining/living room, accented with contemporary paintings and koa trim. The ultramodern kitchen is complete with standard-size refrigerator, a rice cooker, four-burner stove and oven, and dishwasher. The master bedroom has its own entertainment center and huge private lanai from which you can overlook Waikiki. The full bathroom has a huge walk-in closet holding a safe, steam iron and board, and a washer and dryer. Rates range $540–585 for one-bedroom suites, $640–775 for two-bedroom suites, with the addition of more opulent units up to $1,300. Special amenities include twice-daily maid service, concierge desk, valet parking, a swimming pool, spa, and sauna. For a condo, this one is right at the top, and you get all the extra amenities that make your stay a pleasure, plus you have the beach at your doorstep.

# Food

The streets of Waikiki are an international banquet, with more than a dozen cuisines spreading their tables for your enjoyment. Because of the culinary competition, you can choose restaurants in the same way that you peruse a smorgasbord, for both quantity and quality. Within a few hundred yards are all-you-can-gorge buffets, lu'au, dinner shows, fast food, ice cream, and jacket-and-tie restaurants. The free tourist literature runs coupons, and placards advertise specials for breakfast, lunch, and dinner. Bars and lounges often give free *pu pu* and finger foods that can easily make a light supper. As with everything in Waikiki, its restaurants are a close-quartered combination of the best and the worst, but with only a little effort it's easy to find great food, great atmosphere, and mouthwatering satisfaction.

**Note:** At many of the moderately priced restaurants listed and at all of the expensive restaurants *reservations are highly recommended.* It's much easier to make a two-minute phone call than it is to have your evening spoiled, so please call ahead. Also, many of the restaurants along the congested Waikiki strip provide valet parking (usually at no charge) or will offer validated parking at a nearby lot. So check when you call to reserve. Attire at most Hawaiian restaurants is casual, but at the better restaurants it is dressy casual, which means closed-toe shoes, trousers, and a collared shirt for men, and a simple but stylish dress for women. At some of the very best restaurants you won't feel out of place with a jacket, but ties are not usually worn.

## INEXPENSIVE

**Eggs and Things,** 1911 Kalakaua Ave., just where it meets McCully, 808/949-0820, is a late-night institution open 11 P.M.–2 P.M. the following afternoon. The clientele in the wee hours is a mix of revelers, hotel workers, boat captains, and even a hooker or two. The decor is tile floors and Formica tables, but the waitresses are top-notch and friendly. The food is absolutely excellent, and it's hard to spend more than $10. Daily specials are offered 1–2 A.M., while the morning special runs 5–9 A.M. Waffles and pancakes are scrumptious with fresh fruit or homemade coconut syrup. Besides the eggs and omelets, the most popular item is fresh fish, which is usually caught by the owner, Mr. Jerry Fukunaga, who goes out almost every day on his own boat. Casual attire is acceptable, and BYO wine or beer is okay.

The **Dynasty Restaurant,** 1778 Ala Moana Blvd., in Discovery Bay, 808/947-3771, has an enormous menu of various Hong Kong Chinese dishes that is acceptable but not memorable. The servers are friendly and courteous, and it's open daily 11 A.M.–1 A.M. For a very late-night repast after doing the town, the food definitely hits the spot!

**Da Smokehouse,** 444 Hobron Ln., on the ground level of the Eaton Square plaza, 808/946-0233, open daily 11 A.M.–midnight, is one of those places where the food is good and you can even get take-out and delivery. Your choices are baby back ribs, smoked beef, pork spareribs, and ham, or rotisserie chicken all served picnic style, with two choices of sides, including homemade potato salad, baked beans, rice, coleslaw, or French fries. Prices are reasonable, and desserts are only a couple of bucks. A small delivery charge makes Da Smokehouse a perfect alternative to inflated room service prices at surrounding hotels or for a home-cooked dinner in your condo. This is a pub as well, so you'll love that friendly, neighborhood bar atmosphere. As an active bar with no smoking restrictions, the smoke inside isn't all from the kitchen.

**Ruffage Natural Foods,** 2443 Kuhio, 808/922-2042, is one of a very few natural food restaurants in Waikiki. It serves a wide assortment of tofu sandwiches, burritos, natural salads, tofu burgers, fresh island fruits, and smoothies for lunch and dinner, 9 A.M.–7 P.M. Everything is homemade, and the restaurant tries to avoid processed foods as much as possible. Just about everything on the menu is less than $7. Aside from the menu items, food supplements, minerals, vitamins, and things of that nature are also available. It's a small hole-in-the-wall–type eatery around the corner from the Royal Grove Hotel that's easy to miss. A few wooden tables are available for eating outside under a portico.

**Maria's Health Food Organic Café,** 808/926-3900, is an eat-in/take-out place along Beachwalk in the ANA Kalakaua Center. Open 11 A.M.–8 P.M. Mon.–Sat., salads, wraps, sandwiches, and smoothies are on the simple menu, while supplements and other health products are also for sale.

**Ezogiku** is a small chain of Japanese restaurants; it has three locations in Waikiki at 2146 Kalakaua Ave., 2420 Koa Ave., and 2546 Lemon Road. Open until the wee hours, these no-atmosphere restaurants serve inexpensive hearty bowls of Sapporo ramen (renowned as the best), curry rice, and gyoza. Ezogiku is a no-frills kind of place: small, smoky, counter seating, and totally authentic. It's so authentic that on the dishes they spell ramen as larmen. You not only eat inexpensively, but you also get an authentic example of what it's like to eat in Japan . . . cheaply. Eat heartily for around $7.

**Perry's Smorgy,** with locations at 2380 Kuhio Ave. and at 250 Lewers St., is the epitome of the budget traveler's "line 'em up, fill 'em up, and head 'em out" kind of restaurant. What you'll find is good ol' American food. There is no question that you'll waddle away stuffed, but forget about any kind of memorable dining experience. When you arrive, don't be put off by the long lines. They move! First, you run a gauntlet of salads, breads, and potatoes, in the hopes that you'll fill your plate. Try to restrain yourself. Next comes the meat, fish, and chicken. The guys serving up the roast beef are masters of a whole lot of movement and very little action. A paper-thin slice is finally cut off and put on your plate with aplomb. Pressure comes from the long line of tourists behind, who act as if they have just escaped from a Nazi labor camp. The breakfast buffet, 7–11 A.M., is actually very good at $5.95, with all the standard eggs, meats, juices, and rolls, and the food in general, considering the price, is more than acceptable. You can't complain. The lunch buffet, 11:30 A.M.–2:30 P.M., is priced equally well at $6.95, and the all-you-can-eat dinner, 5–9 P.M., is a bargain at $9.95, as is Sunday brunch.

Building on its success in Lahaina, Maui, as a fun-loving place with good eats and affordable prices, all in a location that gives great sunsets, with the added benefit of lively music in the evening, **Cheeseburger in Paradise** opened shop in Waikiki right across from the beach at 2500 Kalakaua Ave. Try an omelet, pancakes, or French toast to get you going in the morning. For the rest of the day, burgers (meat or meatless), sandwiches, salads, and fries will do. Lots of options, and lots of logo items too, are offered. You won't have to try too hard to get out the door for under $15.

There are enough Formica-tabled, orange-colored, golden-arched, belly-up-to-the-window places selling perfected, injected, and inspected ground cow, chicken, and fish to feed an army . . . and a navy, and Marine Corps, too. Those needing a prefab meal can choose from the royal Burger King and Dairy Queen, Jack-in-his-Box, Ronnie McDonald, and Pizza Hut-2-3-4. Fast-food addicts easily find pushers throughout Waikiki!

## MODERATE

At the Ohana Edgewater Hotel you'll find **Chuck's Original Steak House,** 808/923-6111, open 4:30–10 P.M. daily. While there are others, this one is *the* original. Opened in 1959 and still going strong, they're doing something right! Chuck's has a simple menu—steak, with the addition of a few pork, chicken, and seafood items. All meals come with rice or fries, salad bar, and bread. The early-bird special is $10.95, while most entrées run $16–21. There is nothing extraordinary here, just plain good food prepared in a straightforward manner. The sister restaurants, **Chuck's Steak House** at the Outrigger Waikiki and **Chuck's Cellar** at the Ohana East, have the same basic menu and reputation. You can't go wrong here for a decent meal.

Almost next door at the Ohana Reef Lanai is **Buzz's Steak and Lobster** restaurant and lounge, 808/923-6762. Open for all three meals every day, some of what's on the evening menu are Hawaiian ono steak at $16.95, steak and crab for $24.95, and steak and lobster at a daily quote. For those who would rather have something less robust, chicken and pasta are also available. Buzz's is an old standby that serves tasty and consistent, if not memorable, food.

The **Shore Bird Beach Broiler,** open for breakfast buffet, a lunch lanai menu, and dinner, is on the beach at the Outrigger Reef Hotel, 2169 Kalia Rd., 808/922-2887, giving this restaurant one of the best gourmet locations in all of Waikiki. A walk through the lobby to the beach for a remarkable sunset takes you right past the restaurant, where you'll find a limited but adequate menu of cook-your-own selections for under $20. Included is a fresh salad bar of vegetables and fruits. Beverages are included, the setting is wonderful, and the value is excellent. Across the lobby, the Shore Bird Beach Bar serves a grill menu 11 A.M.–1 A.M. plus offers evening entertainment nightly 4 P.M.–midnight.

The **House of Hong,** 260 Lewers St., 808/923-0202, open daily 11 A.M.–10:30 P.M., Sun. from 4 P.M., is a standard, no-surprises Chinese restaurant with a flair. The decor borders on tasteful, with some tables outfitted in starchy white tablecloths accented by inlaid wall murals and painted ceilings of China scenes. Daily lunch specials run $6.25, but nothing except seafood items is over $10. Early-bird dinner specials are as much a bargain at $9.95. Not great, but no complaints either.

The **Oceanarium** at the Pacific Beach Hotel offers a full breakfast, lunch, and dinner menu. While limited à la carte menus are always available, buffets, like the nightly prime rib and seafood buffet for $29.50, are what it does best. The Oceanarium is done in elegant muted colors as if you were under water. A real treat.

**Trattoria,** in the Edgewater Hotel, 2168 Kalia Rd., 808/923-8415, serves savory dishes from northern Italy. Particularly good are the veal plates, with an appropriate bottle of Italian wine. The interior is upscale with bent-wood chairs and white linen tablecloths set with crystal. Antipasti selections include escargot and calamari salad. Combine these with pasta dishes like spaghetti puttanesca, a savory dish of fillet of anchovy and melted butter cooked in a hot sauce

with tomatoes and black olives. Complete dinners range $18–28; early-bird specials of pasta served before 6:30 P.M. run $10.95. Trattoria is a good choice for a moderate restaurant with a pleasant atmosphere and better-than-average cooking. Dinner only.

**Duke's Canoe Club, Waikiki,** at the Outrigger Waikiki Hotel, 808/922-2268, has an unbeatable location fronting Waikiki Beach. Basically a steak and seafood restaurant, it's a happening place, with plenty of Duke Kahanamoku and surfing memorabilia on the wall, with cocktails and lively local music every evening. The day starts with a filling breakfast buffet for $10.50. Lunch runs 11 A.M.–5 P.M., with its own $10.50 buffet running from 11:30 A.M.–2:30 P.M. and dinner until 10 P.M. Aside from the steak and fish items there are such selections as huli huli chicken, Big Island pork ribs, and shrimp scampi, all $14.95–24.95. The food is tasty, but you generally come here as much for the atmosphere, music, and chance to see the sun sink into the sea. Just another part of the restaurant, the Barefoot Bar has a lighter and cheaper menu of sandwiches, burgers, pizza, and plate lunches until midnight.

Whether you've tried Thai food or not, **Keo's in Waikiki,** 808/951-9355, at the Ambassador Hotel near where Kalakaua and Kuhio avenues merge, is a very good choice. Keo's has the full range of Thai entrées, from meat selections through noodles, seafood, and vegetarian dishes, and all can be adjusted from mild to fiery hot to suit your taste. Try a spicy lemongrass soup or green papaya salad to start your meal. These and appetizers are priced mostly under $10, while entrées, like Thai garlic beef with mushrooms, Thai crispy fish with red chili, pad thai noodles with vegetables, or yellow curry with chicken, generally run $9–13. Dinner is served daily from 5 P.M. and, with basically the same menu, Keo's is also open for lunch 11 A.M.–2 P.M. Reservations would be a good idea because this is a popular place.

At the Ohana East Hotel, **Keoni's,** a sister restaurant of Keo's, also serves Thai cuisine alongside many Western dishes at prices that are similar. On the Thai side, you find Thai crispy calamari appetizers, hot basil chicken, panang curry, and spicy scallops with lemongrass. From the Western side come onion soup au gratin, spaghetti Bolognese, and roasted chicken. Call for a reservation, 808/922-9888; also open for breakfast.

If you've ever eaten at or even peered into a Planet Hollywood restaurant, the **Planet Hollywood Honolulu,** 2155 Kalakaua Ave., in the ANA Kalakaua Center, 808/924-7877, will be no surprise. The place is filled with movie memorabilia and celebrity costumes, a monument to television and film. It's a happy place with enjoyable background music. Have a look around while you wait for your food. Mostly salads, sandwiches, and burgers, a fair selection of pasta, and more hearty meat dishes are on the menu. And then, of course, there are the tropical drinks and rich desserts. While the food won't win any Oscars, it'll fill you up, get you on your way, and not set you back too much. Expect most items in the $14 and under range, with entrées from the grill up to $21. Open from 11 A.M. for lunch and until 10 P.M. for dinner, with live entertainment each night of the week and salsa dancing on Saturday night until 2 A.M.

Along the same lines, but with a focus on music, is the **Hard Rock Cafe,** 808/955-7383, at the corner of Kalakaua Ave. and Kapi'olani Blvd. across from the Hawaii Convention Center. This is a large, modern eatery with vaulted ceiling, a huge bar, and an open kitchen. All-American burgers, sandwiches, and grill items fill the menu, most at $8.50–14, with lots of drink options. An easygoing, convivial eatery with heady music; a real rock 'n' roll experience. Valet parking only. Open 11 A.M.–11 P.M. daily, Fri. and Sat. until 11:30 P.M.

## UPPER END

**Benihana of Tokyo,** at the Hilton Rainbow Bazaar, 808/955-5955, is open daily for lunch and for dinner. Meals are designed to fit *gaijin* taste, and cooks flash their knives and spatulas at your table—as much a floor show as a dining experience. Good, basic Japanese food, *teppan*-style, but not cheap with many dinner meals in the $22–34 range.

**The Chart House,** 1765 Ala Moana Blvd., in the Ilikai Marina Building across from Ala Wai Yacht Harbor, 808/941-6669, is open daily 4 P.M. until 2 A.M. (from 5 P.M. on the weekends), with food served 5:30–9:30 P.M. (10 P.M. Fri., Sat., and Sun.). Seafood and beef are its specialties, with most entrées in the $25–35 range. It offers a happy hour until 7 P.M., *pu pu* off the lounge menu until midnight, and nightly entertainment. The Chart House has a great reputation with locals and visitors alike, and because it's one of the oldest restaurants in Waikiki, it definitely is doing something right. You can't go wrong here.

The word "genius" is often overused and misapplied, causing it to lose its oomph, but when it comes to creativity with food, Roy Yamaguchi is a genius par excellence! **Roy's Restaurant,** 6600 Kalaniana'ole Hwy., in Hawaii Kai Corporate Plaza, 808/396-7697, open Sun.–Thurs. 5:30–9:30 P.M., until 10:30 P.M. Friday and Saturday, from 5 P.M. Saturday and Sunday, presents Pacific Rim cuisine at its very best. Although not in Waikiki but in Hawaii Kai about 20 minutes away, it is definitely worth the trip. Through experimentation and an unfailing sense of taste, Roy's has created dishes using the diverse and distinctive flavors of French, Italian, Chinese, Japanese, Thai, and Hawaiian cuisine and blended them into a heady array of culinary delights that destroy the adage that "East is East and West is West." The twain have definitely met, and with a resounding success. Roy's dining rooms—one up and one down—are elegant casual, much like the food, featuring an open kitchen, and although pleasant enough, it is not designed for a lengthy romantic evening. Roy's dining philosophy seems to be the serving of truly superb dishes posthaste with the focus on the food as the dining experience, not the surroundings. The menu changes somewhat every evening, but you might find charred ahi and opakapaka pot stickers and wild mushroom and escargot cassoulet for appetizers, various salads, or an individual *imu*-oven pizza, most under $8. Entrées like grilled loin of lamb with rosemary, crabmeat, and risotto sauce, a teriyaki grilled chicken, or rosemary-seared yellowtail hamachi tuna are mostly in the $20–27 range. Desserts are also superb and include individually prepared (order at beginning of dinner) fresh fruit cobbler in sauce anglaise, or a richer-than-rich chocolate soufflé. Roy's is a dining experience that is universally appreciated. This was Roy's first restaurant and is still his flagship. From here the empire spread—now nearly three dozen strong.

**House Without a Key,** open for breakfast, lunch, and dinner, is a casual outdoor-indoor restaurant in a magnificent oceanside setting at the Halekulani Hotel. Named after the first novel written about Charlie Chan, Honolulu's famous fictional detective, the restaurant offers unsurpassed views in every direction and is one of the best spots on the island to enjoy a sunset cocktail. Although casual, the seating is comfortable with padded chairs at simple wood-trimmed tables. Like the environment, the menu too is casual, with prices much easier on the budget. Breakfast is buffet only at $21. Lunch and dinner are à la carte, with such entrées as Ka'u orange and poha berry-glazed chicken breast at $17.50, crab-crusted mahimahi for $18, and New York steak is $22. Entertainment is offered nightly 5–8 P.M., where you'll be entranced by the graceful beauty of hula dances done by former Miss Hawaii, Kanoe Miller, and Debbie Nakanelua. Remember, the door is never locked at House Without a Key.

The **Golden Dragon,** 808/946-5336, open nightly except Monday for dinner 6–9:30 P.M., would tempt any knight errant to drop his sword and pick up chopsticks. One of the two fine restaurants at Hilton Hawaiian Village, the Golden Dragon's walls are decorated with portraits of emperors, and the plates carry the Golden Dragon motif. The interior color scheme is a striking vermilion and black, with the chairs and tables shining with a lacquerware patina. The Golden Dragon isn't your average chop suey house, but the menu has all of the standard Cantonese fare (with some Szechuan dishes) from crispy lemon chicken to . . . well, chop suey noodles, but it doesn't end there. The food is expertly prepared, and two fine choices are the exotic Imperial Beggar's Chicken, feeding two for $44, which is a chicken wrapped in lotus leaves, encased in clay, and baked (requires 24 hours' notice to prepare); and Chef Chiang's Signature Selection (for two), which includes chicken egg rolls, crispy

wontons, island pork char siu, hot and sour soup, stir-fry chicken, scallops with lychee and asparagus, beef with snow peas, lobster and shrimp, and duck fried rice, with green tea ice cream for $36 per person. For a first-class restaurant with impeccable food and service, the prices at the Golden Dragon are reasonable.

**Hakone,** the Hawaii Prince Hotel's fine Japanese restaurant, is appointed with shoji screens and wooden tables with high-backed chairs in front of a glass wall that frames the still life of the Ala Wai Yacht Harbor. Dishes are typical, with set menus *(teishoku)* like chicken teriyaki and wafu sirloin steak at $36, nabemono $31–34, and sushi. On Friday and Saturday, the sushi buffet runs $42. Open for dinner only Wednesday through Sunday.

**Michel's,** at the Colony Surf, 2895 Kalakaua Ave., 808/923-6552, open daily at 5:30 P.M. for dinner only, is literally on the beach, so your appetite is piqued not only by sumptuous morsels, but also by magnificent views of the Waikiki skyline boldly facing the Pacific. The interior is neo-French elegant, with the dining rooms appointed in soft pastels, white tablecloths, crystal chandeliers, heavy silver service, and tasteful paintings. The bar is serpentine and made of polished koa. Food is traditional French continental, and dinner is *magnifique* with such entrées as fresh Maine lobster, potato-crusted onaga, duckling a l'Orange, filet Wellington of beef tenderloin, and chateaubriand for two; $28–42. The dining experience at Michel's is completely satisfying with outstanding food and outstanding service, all in an outstanding setting.

Almost next door is the **Diamond Head Grill,** 808/922-3734, at the W Honolulu Hotel. This chic eatery serves three meals a day, and the menu items are as light and modern as the decor. The breakfast menu has everything from a vegetable frittata to Belgian waffles. Lunch could be a cool Cobb salad or seafood linguine. While not overly complex, dinner entrées are well seasoned and freshly creative. Herb-crusted opakapaka with Kahuku corn ragout and red potato, and rosemary chicken with sundried tomatoes and asparagus risotto are two options. Expect most entrées in the $21–32 range. After dinner, the lounge comes alive with live guitar or DJ dancing music.

**Matteo's,** 364 Seaside, in the Marine Surf Hotel, 808/922-5551, open 6 P.M.–2 A.M., is a wonderfully dark and romantic Italian restaurant that sets the mood even outside by welcoming you with a red canopy and brass rail that leads to a carved door of koa and crystal. Inside is stylish, with high-backed booths, white tablecloths, and marble-top tables. On each is a rose, Matteo's signature. Dinners begin with hot or cold antipasti priced $7–13, such as portobello crustini, artichokes alla Matteo's, or seafood medley vinaigrette. Light fare of *insalada e zuppe* (salad and soup) matched with garlic bread or bruschetta make an inexpensive but tasty meal. Entrée suggestions are chicken Florentino, veal osso bucco Milanese, Grenadine of beef tenderloin, or cioppino alla Livornese, all under $32. Complete dinners come with Matteo's special salad, soup, and coffee or tea and include seafood lasagne and veal parmigiana and are priced under $36. Pastas are reasonable and besides the usual linguine dishes include gnocchi and manicotti. An extensive wine list complements the food, and for after dinner, coffee, a cordial, or cognac might suit the mood. This restaurant gets the thumbs up from local critics and has garnered awards of excellence. If you are out for a special evening of fine dining and romance, Matteo's will set the mood, and the rest is up to you.

**Hy's Steak House,** 2440 Kuhio Ave., 808/922-5555, is one of those rare restaurants that not only is absolutely beautiful (decorated in dark wood and low light like a Victorian sitting room) but serves great food as well. Its award-winning menu offers entrées other than steak and chops, but these are the specialties and worth the stiff-upper-lip price. Great care is taken in the preparation and presentation of all dishes. Expect most entrée prices in the $25–37 range. Open for dinner only from 6 P.M.; reservations necessary.

**Restaurant Suntory,** Royal Hawaiian Shopping Center, 808/922-5511, is a handsome restaurant with different rooms specializing in particular styles like shabu shabu, teppanyaki, and sushi. The prices used to be worse, but they're still expensive. However, the food preparation

and presentation are excellent, and the staff is attentive. Open for lunch and dinner.

The **Shogun Restaurant,** also at the Pacific Beach Hotel, 808/921-6113, is an award winner and a favorite spot for residents to take their visiting guests. Shogun offers breakfast and lunch buffets, à la carte menus, dinner specials, and a teppan and sushi bar. Definitely make reservations. **Neptune's Garden Restaurant,** 808/921-6112, is the hotel's fine-dining restaurant; reservations recommended. Open for dinner only 6–9:30 P.M., its focus is fish and seafood, as its name implies. Entrées run $19.75–32 and include such delicacies as Neptune's paella, seafood bouillabaisse, and grilled ono with Kona lobster.

**Furusato Sushi,** 2424 Kalakaua Ave., at the Hyatt Regency, 808/922-4991, is expensive but a top-notch Japanese restaurant. The food and service are authentic, but they are geared toward the Japanese tourist who expects, and almost demands, to pay high prices. Free valet parking is great for this congested part of Waikiki. Three other exceptional restaurants worth visiting for authentic Japanese food are **Miyako,** at The New Otani Kaimana Beach Hotel, 808/923-4739; **Kacho,** at the Waikiki Parc Hotel, 808/924-3535; and the contemporary **Kyoya,** 2057 Kalakaua Ave., 808/947-3911. All have excellent reputations and outstanding food.

**Sarento's, Top of the "I"** occupies the top floor of the Ilikai Hotel and, like its sister restaurant, Aaron's, on the top floor of the Ala Moana Hotel, it has a fabulous location that looks out over the Ala Wai Yacht Club, down along the Waikiki strip, and over downtown Honolulu. The quality of the food at Sarento's matches its setting. Start with appetizers like black and blue ahi, bruschetta rustica, or steamed clams and mussels in wine sauce, all for $6.50–13. Soups and salads follow but are only a preview to the many fine entrées that include opakapaka sautéed with rock shrimp, asparagus tips and mushrooms, veal saltimboca, charbroiled petit filet, pollo paesano sautéed chicken, and penne pasta with diced eggplant, tomato, and Italian sausage. Most entrées run $23–33, with the pastas a bit less. Sarento's is open 5–9 P.M. nightly; call 808/955-5559 for reservations.

One of the most unusual of restaurants in Waikiki is the **Top of Waikiki** at the Waikiki Business Plaza. The food and drink are good here, but many come for the great view over the town as the round restaurant makes a slow revolution. Seating is tiered so that everyone has a good view. Come before sunset and watch the lights of the city come on and (hopefully) the sun sink into the sea. Start with an appetizer like sautéed escargot in parsley butter for $8.95 before moving on to shrimp scampi at $21.95. Other entrées include a New York strip steak at $24.50, salmon supreme at $19.95, and baked chicken breast for $17.95. Sunset special entrées are offered 5–7 P.M. for $12–18.

## FINE DINING

Softly the soprano sea sings, while the baritone breeze whispers in melodious melancholy, as you float ephemerally above the waves at **La Mer,** the open-air signature dinner restaurant at the Halekulani. Splendid in their appointment, the walls, filigreed panels of teak covered in Chinese silk-screen, are predominantly browns and whites, the traditional colors of Hawaiian tapa. The superb French continental menu, with its numerous selections of seafood, is bolstered by a huge wine list and a platter of select cheeses to end the meal. Entrées like roasted Scottish salmon, bouillabaisse in a puff pastry, breast of Barbary duck, and rack of lamb are generally in the $36–45 range, with two set dinner menus at $85 and $125. La Mer sets the standard, and if you were to choose one restaurant for a night of culinary bliss, this is a perfect choice.

White, purple, and yellow orchids tumble from trellises, cascade from clay planters, and always grace your table at **Orchids Dining Room,** open for three meals a day, another seaside, indoor-outdoor restaurant at the Halekulani. Specializing in contemporary American cuisine, Orchids is also famous for its fabulous Sunday brunch. Beautifully appointed with teak wood and Hawaiian eucalyptus flooring, the setting is casual-elegant with white starched linen tablecloths, captain-style chairs with blue and white pillows, and of course heavy silver and crystal.

Arranged with a trilevel central dining area that spreads out to a covered veranda, all tables enjoy a panoramic view of the sea with Diamond Head in the distance. Start the day with a continental or American breakfast, or try it Japanese style with grilled fish, steamed rice, pickles, miso soup, seaweed, and green tea. Lunch is also casual, with the Sunday brunch drawing visitors and residents alike. The dinner specialty is seafood, although meat and poultry are available. Entrées are luscious Oriental-style onaga, Madras seafood curry, pan-seared ahi steak, and roasted lamb chops. Most entrées run $24–36.

The Hilton Hawaiian Village is one of the finest destination resorts in Hawaii. Its signature restaurant complements the resort perfectly. **Bali by the Sea,** 808/941-2254, on the first floor of the Rainbow Tower and open Mon.–Sat. for dinner 6–9:30 P.M., may sound like Indonesian cuisine, but it's more continental than anything else, and it's a consistent AAA four-diamond award winner. The setting couldn't be more brilliant. Sit by the open windows so that the sea breezes fan you as you overlook the gorgeous beach with Diamond Head off in the distance. Choose appetizers like escargot mushroom purse or sweet potato–crusted prawns with mango salsa. Ranging mostly $30–36, entrées include a magnificent selection of fish from Hawaiian waters, each prepared to bring out its essential flavor and many covered with a special sauce. Meat entrées are seared breast of chicken, sake-steamed Kona lobster, or paniolo-style rack of lamb. Bali by the Sea is a superb choice for an elegant evening of fine dining. Reservations recommended.

The signature restaurant at the Sheraton Waikiki is the **Hanohano Room,** atop the building on its 30th floor. From here, the vista before you sweeps from Pearl Harbor to Diamond Head, and behind you, the city of Honolulu runs up into the hills. Although noteworthy during the day, the view at night is stunning with the twinkle of city lights below. Aside from the usual breakfast fare, the Hanohano Room serves a breakfast buffet that, while not cheap, seems to have endless options. Along with breakfast Saturday morning, the room hosts the ever-popular Parry and Price live radio show on KSSK. The

8 A.M.–1 P.M. Sunday champagne brunch buffet is an outstanding feed, but pricey at $30.95. In the evening, the restaurant features Pacific Island cuisine. Choose your selection of entrées from such items as lemongrass-crusted onaga and duet of duck to filet mignon and lobster tail, ranging $28–49. If all the choices are too difficult, try one of the select menu combinations, $53–76. A wonderful meal may be even more romantic here to the sounds of light piano music or later in the evening when a local trio called Stardust plays contemporary jazz and top 40 tunes. The dance floor is always open. Dress code is required.

One of the most laudable achievements in the restaurant business is to create an excellent reputation and then to keep it. **Nick's Fishmarket,** 2070 Kalakaua, at the Waikiki Gateway Hotel, 808/955-6333, open nightly for dinner 5–10 P.M., until 11 P.M. on Fri. and Sat., has done just that—and keeps doing it. Many gourmets consider Nick's *the* best dining in Waikiki, and it's great fun to find out if they know what they're talking about. Adventurous and highly skilled, the chefs here, like the master of an old sailing ship, will take you to culinary ports of call that are rarely, if ever, visited. Highly professional waiters, knowledgeable about every dish, are friendly and efficient and always at hand to suggest just the right wine from the extensive list to perfectly complement your choice of dish. Start with fresh-baked oysters Rockefeller, blackened sashimi, or, if you're in the mood, how about Russian beluga caviar (don't ask how much!). The New England clam chowder is unbeatable, while the Caesar salad prepared at your table has long won honors as the best available west of California! Although Nick's is primarily renowned for its fish and lobster, don't overlook the veal, steaks, and chicken with sides of pasta. An excellent choice is one of Nick's complete dinners or lobster combinations. Most entrées run $29–37, while the lobster dishes run upward of $43. The sinless—along with those expecting salvation "tomorrow"—will enjoy the dessert menu. A Cafe Menu has been added, from which you can order while listening to live entertainment in the lounge area 5:30–10 P.M. and until midnight on Friday and Saturday. Items on the Cafe Menu are all reasonably priced under $12. Dancing to live music is featured nightly 7 P.M.–11 A.M. and 9 P.M.–1 A.M. Friday and Saturday, along with special events, such as wine-tasting evenings, scheduled throughout the year. If you had only one evening in Waikiki and you wanted to make it memorable, you'd have a hard time doing better than Nick's Fishmarket.

Another fine establishment is **Padovani's Bistro & Wine Bar,** 1956 Ala Moana Blvd., at the Doubletree Alana Hotel, 808/946-3456. With rich dark wood, a low ceiling, and semi–art deco styling, the casually elegant restaurant is downstairs and its wine bar is upstairs. In the restaurant, dinner is served nightly 6–9:30 P.M. Mostly meat and seafood in the $28–44 range, entrées include fricassee of rabbit, roasted quail, venison loin, pan-fried onaga, poached mahimahi, and salmon confit. Three prix fixe options are also available for $48–120. A more casual and less expensive menu is offered upstairs for breakfast and lunch and again for dinner from 5:30–10 P.M., when entrées like grilled shrimp fettuccini, pan-sautéed fish, and ragout of lamb tenderloin run $19–29. The wine bar has about 50 wines by the glass, appetizers, gourmet cheeses, and rich desserts. Formerly head chef of the Manele Bay Hotel on Lana'i, Padovani combines haute cuisine with the ingredients and flavors of Hawaii and Asia. Valet parking is provided.

For other fine-dining options around town, several of which are close to Waikiki, refer to the Honolulu chapter dining section.

## Entertainment

Waikiki swings, beats, bumps, grinds, sways, laughs, and gets down. If Waikiki has to bear being called a carnival town, it might as well strut its stuff. Dancing, happy hours, cocktail shows, cruises, lounge acts, Polynesian extravaganzas, and the street scene provide an endless choice of entertainment. Small-name Hawaiian trios, soloists, pianists, and sultry singers featured in innumerable bars and restaurants woo you in and keep you coming back. Big-name island entertainers and visiting international stars play the big rooms. Free entertainment includes hula shows, ukulele music, street musicians, jugglers, and artists. For a good time, nowhere in Hawaii matches Waikiki. The Friday edition of the newspaper contains a Calendar of Events section that lists events and activities throughout the area for the weekend and coming week. The free Honolulu Weekly also sports such a listing. Also see the Honolulu chapter for other happenings around town.

### Bars and Lounges

In the International Market Place, **Coconut Willy's Bar and Grill** offers free entertainment, with no minimum or cover.

In business for nearly 30 years, the gay-friendly alternative nightclub **Hula's Bar and Lei Stand** operates at 134 Kapahulu Avenue, on the second floor of the Waikiki Grand Hotel. There's music and dance that everyone can get down to. Open until 2 A.M.

The kitchen at **Kelly O'Neil's** Irish pub and grill, 311 Lewers St., 808/926-1777, produces such dishes as fish and chips, corned beef and cabbage plate, cottage pies, as well as sandwiches and burgers. It's open until 10 P.M. and the bar stays open until 4 A.M. Happy hour runs until 8 P.M., and music of the unplugged variety starts at 9 P.M., so if the noise of the Moose McGillycuddy's across the street is too overwhelming, head to the shamrock for something more mellow.

Many hotel cocktail bars and restaurants will offer evening entertainment. One is the Shore Bird Beach Bar at the Outrigger Reef Hotel, where you can catch live local music 4 P.M.–midnight.

**Duke's Canoe Club** in the Outrigger Waikiki Hotel has a great lineup of well-known local talent playing every night of the week 4–6 P.M. and then later from 10 P.M. to midnight.

For contemporary guitar or modern DJ music in a hip and happening place, visit the lounge of the **Diamond Head Grill** at the exclusive W Honolulu Hotel, at the far end of Kapi'olani Park below Diamond Head. This has become one of the city's hot spots. Open Wednesday and Thursday until midnight, Friday and Saturday until 2 A.M.

The **Paradise Lounge** at the Hilton Hawaiian Village presents the harmonies of Olomana, a well-appreciated old-time trio, Friday and Saturday evenings 8 P.M.–midnight. Also at the Hilton, the **Tapa Bar, Shell Bar,** and **Tropics Bar** offer nightly entertainment, sometimes with hula accompaniment; no cover.

The **Banyan Court** at the Sheraton Moana Surfrider Hotel was the home of the famous Hawaii Calls radio show of years gone by. Now you don't have to dial in. Just walk down and sit under the banyan tree for the sweet sounds of contemporary Hawaiian music and hula every evening 5:30–8:30 P.M.

The Halekulani offers superb nightly entertainment. There is no lovelier location for a sunset cocktail than **House Without a Key,** where The Islanders, Aloha Serenaders, Pookela, or Paahana perform contemporary tunes nightly 5–8:30 P.M. Gracing the stage are two former Miss Hawaii beauty queens, Kanoe Miller and Debbie Nakanelua, who perform their inspired hula. Sunday brunch at the hotel's **Orchids Dining Room** is made even more genteel with the musical strains of harpist Carol Miyamoto, accompanied by flutist Aileen Kawakami, who perform the hit songs of Broadway musicals. Nightly 8:30–midnight (or after) from the wood-paneled **Lewers Lounge** flows contemporary jazz selections with Noly Paa on piano, the duo of Jim Howard on keyboard and Bruce Hamada on bass and vocals, Lenny Keyes on piano accompanied by vocalist Sonya Mendez, or Lenny Keyes with Rocky Holmes on woodwinds.

**Poolside at the Sheraton Waikiki** you can find several Hawaiian music and dance groups performing on a rotating schedule. Visit the **Hanohano Room** on the 30th floor of the Sheraton for jazz and contemporary music.

Across the road at the **Sheraton Princess Kaiulani Hotel,** there is poolside musical entertainment nightly form 6:15–9:30 P.M. The stage location is such that music wafts across the pool and into the hotel lobby.

Every evening at the outdoor Moana Terrace bar and grill on the third floor of the Waikiki Beach Marriott there are great Hawaiian entertainers like Aunty Genoa Keawe, George Kua, and Martin Pahinui. Music usually starts at 6–7 P.M. and runs to about 9 P.M.

For jazz, head for the gentle ambiance of the veranda lounge at the **Kahala Mandarin Oriental Hotel,** where vocalist Loretta Ables holds court Tues.–Sat. 7:30–11 P.M. Other evenings it's the sound of classical guitar, while every afternoon 2:30–4:30 P.M. there is the heavenly sound of a harpist.

## Dancing and Nightclubs

**Nick's Fishmarket** restaurant at the Gateway Hotel, 2070 Kalakaua Ave., swings with contemporary dance music every Friday and Saturday 9 P.M.–1:30 A.M. Expect a mixed but mostly mature crowd who have stayed on to dance after a magnificent meal, which Nick's is known for.

The following are disco and/or live music nightclubs in and around Waikiki. Most have videos, a theme, a dress code of alohawear and shoes (no sandals), and start hopping around 9 P.M. with the energy cutoff around 4 A.M.

**The Wave,** 1877 Kalakaua Ave., is a rock-and-roll and new wave hotspot with live music on the weekends; $5 cover. The Wave has become an institution of late-night fun and dancing. The crowd is mixed, and you can choose to dance, perch upstairs in the balcony behind glass where you can check out the dancers below, or have a few drinks and some conversation. The Wave is a sure bet for a night of fun.

**The Red Lion,** 240 Lewers St., in the basement of the Ohana Waikiki Village Hotel, 808/922-1027, offers live rock-and-roll Wed.–Sat. and high-tech video and disco the remaining nights. They have a nice dance floor, and beachwear is okay. Bar and bar food during the day. Open 11 A.M., with dancing 9 P.M.–4 A.M.

**The Cellar,** 205 Lewers St., features mostly rock-and-roll spun by the DJ. The place jumps until 4 A.M. and has plenty of special nights like Thirsty Tuesdays and Ladies' Night. Put on your dancin' shoes and casual attire.

The **Irish Rose Saloon,** 227 Lewers St., at the Ohana Reef Towers Hotel, presents live entertainment nightly with dancing until 4 A.M. and features sporting events on its big-screen TV. Happy hour is 3–8 P.M.

Everyone trumpets the mating call at **Moose McGillycuddy's Pub and Cafe,** 310 Lewers St., 808/923-0751, especially every Wednesday, which is Ladies' Night, and Sunday, when there's a bikini contest, but really every night there's a party. Moose serves breakfast, lunch, and dinner (until 10 P.M.) in the downstairs restaurant; head upstairs for the music and dancing. The nightclub rocks 8 P.M.–4 A.M. every night, with live music until about 1 A.M. To help get the evening started, happy hour runs 4–8 P.M., and various specials on *pu pu* in the pub are always posted. This is a wild and zany place: good food, good fun, cheap drinks, and a young, energetic crowd. Try here to answer the call of the wild.

**The Esprit,** at the Sheraton Waikiki, presents dance music from the 1950s to the present Wed. and Thurs. 8:30 P.M.–12:30 A.M. and Fri. and Sat. 9 P.M.–1:30 A.M. by local bands. Come casual or dressed to the hilt. Good dance floor, $5 cover. It's the only nightclub in Waikiki that's right on the beach.

**Scruples Beach Club,** 2310 Kuhio Ave., in the Waikiki Market Place across from the end of Duke's Lane, is a disco that's attracting dancers who once filled other discos in the area that have since closed their doors. The cover entry is $5 and there's a variety of music on different nights.

Near the corner of Kuhio and Valima, in the basement of the Ohana West Hotel, is **Nashville,** 808/228-0826, a country bar with inexpensive drinks, pool tables, and occasional line dancing. Open 4 P.M.–4 A.M. No cover.

The **Zanzabar** nightclub, 2255 Kuhio Ave., in the Waikiki Trade Center, is supposedly the largest nightclub in Waikiki. It may also be one of the fanciest. Dance to live music or DJ tunes of all types of music from 8 P.M.–4 A.M.; $10 cover, 18 and older only.

If you don't want to go out alone or just desire some company, try the **Endless Days of Summer Pub Crawl,** an organized, nonstop, chauffeured tour of at least five nightspots around town for $50. Traveling by small bus with others in your group, you get cover paid, several complimentary drinks, dinner, and a chance for prizes. The party starts at 6:30 P.M. Call 808/947-2779 for information and reservations. Must be 21 years old and observe a minimal dress code.

Most of the flashy, fleshy exotic dance spots of Waikiki used to be a few blocks away along Kapi'olani Boulevard, but they have been moving ever closer to the heart of Waikiki. Now a few are set along or near Kuhio Avenue, where they're easily recognizable by garish neon lights advertising their wares.

## Dinner Shows and Polynesian Extravaganzas

Although hotel concierge staff and various ticket agents around town can sell or arrange tickets to the following shows, each show has its own dedicated ticket booth at the establishment where it performs. It's best to check in the morning for ticket availability or several days in advance during summer and winter peak seasons.

The Don Ho Show, an institution that played at the Hilton Hawaiian Village for years, is no longer. Now **Don Ho** performs at the Waikiki Beachcomber Hotel, 2300 Kalakaua Ave., where he plays one show nightly, Sun.–Thurs. at 8:15 P.M. For dinner (7 P.M.) and the show, tickets run $52; for cocktails (7:45 P.M.) and the show, it will be $32; reduced *kama'aina* rates. Gone is the glitz and glamour, leaving just Ho, his organ, his backup band, and guest performers, much in the same way as he performed at Duke Kahanamoku's Club in the 1960s. Don Ho is still a great performer and "the godfather of mod-ern Hawaiian music." For information, call 808/923-3981.

The multimillion-dollar, 700-seat showroom at the Waikiki Beachcomber Hotel fills with magical vibrations when headliner John Hirokawa suddenly appears out of nowhere. The **Magic of Polynesia** is a journey into the realm of enchantment and beauty that the entire family can enjoy. Sleight of hand, disappearing maidens, swaying hula dancers, fantastic costumes, and audience participation are all part of the magical extravaganza. Two shows nightly at 5 P.M. and 8 P.M. Dinner seating at the first show runs $69 adults, $49 kids 4–12; cocktail seating for either show runs $41 adults, $31 children. Call 808/971-4321 for information and reservations.

Also playing at the Waikiki Beachcomber is **Blue Hawaii: The Show,** a tribute to Elvis. This show of music and dance is held nightly except Tuesday 6:15–7:30 P.M. Dinner and show runs $59 and starts at 5 P.M. If you want to come just for a cocktail and the show, it will set you back $29. For information and reservations, call 808/923-1245.

**Society of Seven,** a well-established local ensemble, appears nightly except Monday at the Outrigger Main Showroom, performing musical tunes from the last 50 years, with plenty of humor and antics thrown in for good measure. In various permutations, this band has been performing locally since the late 1960s. Show time is 8:30 P.M. and tickets run $39 if you only want cocktails with your show or $57 for buffet dinner with the show. Dinner starts at 7 P.M. Call 808/922-6408 for reservations or information.

Professional funster **Frank De Lima** holds court at the Ohana Reef Towers Palace Showroom, Friday and Saturday 8:30–9:30 P.M. De Lima is guaranteed to tickle your funny bone, "island style." Tickets for this cocktail show are $19.50 and include a drink. Reserve by calling 808/923-7469.

The 'Ainahau Showroom at the Sheraton Princess Ka'iulani Hotel presents **Creation: A Polynesian Odyssey,** a story of the origins of man and the movement of the Polynesian peoples across the Pacific islands to Hawaii, ending with scenes of luxury liners, statehood, and the hope for a prosperous future. Overall, this is a quick glimpse of the people who have made Hawaii home. Dramatically produced, with plenty of flash and flair, this show is an eyeful. One show nightly except Monday and Wednesday at 6 P.M. with dinner or cocktails. Cocktail show prices are $32 and the dinner show fare runs $62–105, depending on your choice of food. Contact 808/931-4660 for information and tickets.

Now open for a barrel of laughs is the **Laugh Factory,** showing nightly at the Queen Kapiolani Hotel Akala Room. Shows play nightly in this 225-seat ballroom, where two nationally known comedians headline the performance, hosted by a local celebrity. Tickets run $25 general, $20 for military and *kama'aina;* two-drink minimum is required. Call 808/924-6616 for information and reservations.

## Free or Small-Fee Entertainment

Every evening at King's Village behind the Hyatt Regency, a changing-of-the-guard show is performed at 6:15 P.M. by the King's Guards in uniforms from the period of the monarchy to give you a peek into one of the rituals of royal ceremony.

The **Royal Hawaiian Band** plays free concerts on Sunday afternoons at 2 P.M. at the bandstand in Kapi'olani Park, often with singers and hula dancers, and again on Friday at 12 P.M. at the 'Iolani Palace in downtown Honolulu. Formed in 1836, the band plays mostly classical music and Hawaiian traditional tunes. Also in the park, free concerts are periodically given by local and visiting musicians at the Waikiki Shell.

The **Kodak Hula Show** is very popular. The show is held Tues.–Thurs. at 10 A.M. at the Waikiki Shell in Kapi'olani Park, but people start lining up at 8 A.M.; be there by 9 if you want a seat. You sit on bleachers with 3,000 people, while Hawaiian *tutu* bedecked in mu'umu'u, lei, and smiles play ukuleles and sing for the *ti*-leaf-skirted dancers. The performance dates back to 1937, and some of the original dancers, now in their eighties, still participate. At the finale, the dancers line up on stage with red-lettered placards that spell out H-A-W-A-I-I, so you can take your own photo of the most famous Hawaiian post-

card. Then the audience is invited down for a free hula lesson. People who are too hip hate it, and *kama'aina* shy away from it, but if you're a good sport, you'll walk away with a big smile on your face like everyone else.

A potpourri of contemporary entertainment is also found in Kapi'olani Park on weekends. Just across from the zoo, musicians, jugglers, clowns, unicyclists, and acrobats put on a free, impromptu circus. Likewise, street musicians perform along both Kalalaua and Kuhio avenues at appropriate spots where large groups of people can stop, listen, drop bills into an open instrument case, or buy a CD.

The **Royal Hawaiian Shopping Center** provides free craft demonstrations and lessons at various times throughout the week, including quilting, hula, lei-making, and ukulele instruction. The Polynesian Cultural Center performs a short show of song and dance Monday, Wednesday, and Friday at 6 P.M. and Tuesday, Thursday, and Saturday at 10 A.M., at the fountain courtyard, where a mini-torchlighting ceremony is also presented daily at 6 P.M. Free musical entertainment is scheduled daily at the same courtyard. For specific times for the crafts, call 808/922-2299.

A free hula show and fireworks are performed every Friday around sundown at the super pool next to the main lobby at the Hilton Hawaiian Village. Other music and dance performances, most accompanied by a torchlighting ceremony, also take place around the super pool on other days of the week. On Friday, performers from the Polynesian Cultural Center perform 6–6:45 P.M. Anyone can come and stand for the show, but if you occupy one of the seats you must purchase at least one drink.

Also staging a free hula show, albeit in a more mundane setting, is the Waikiki Town Center. Come to the second floor of the shopping mall Monday, Wednesday, Friday, and Saturday at 7 P.M. for the fun.

A slice of old Hawaii comes to life Fri.–Sun. evenings at 6:30 P.M. at Kuhio Beach Park. **Kuhio Beach Torchlighting and Hula Show,** complete with Hawaiian music and authentic hula performed by various *halau,* is offered free to the public. Head for the beach stage near the Duke

Kahanamóku statue and you'll be in the right spot. You might want to bring your beach mats for this casual show.

**Sunset on the Beach** is an event of sunset, music, and movies at the Queen's Surf Beach section of Waikiki near the Groin on Saturday and Sunday. Starting around 4 P.M. music is performed free by some of the island's known bands while food stalls dispense quick, easy, and inexpensive eats for dinner. Once the sun goes down, a free family-oriented movie is shown on a 30-foot screen. Bring your appetite and something to sit on.

"Free" tickets to some of Waikiki's most popular Polynesian extravaganzas are sometimes handed out by condo time-share outfits stationed in booths along the main drags. For attending their sales presentations, usually 90 minutes, you can get tickets, but they might be the toughest freebies you've ever earned. The presentation is a pressure cooker, where hardened sales pros try every imaginable technique to get you to sign "right now, because this is the only time that this deal can be offered." If you're really interested in time-sharing, the deals aren't too bad, but if you're there only for the tickets, what a waste of time!

The **IMAX Waikiki** theater, half a block up Seaside Ave. from Kalakaua Ave., screens several shows every day from 11 A.M.–9:45 P.M. The exciting documentary films on Hawaiian and other subjects run about 40 minutes long and are scheduled on a rotating basis. On occasion, regular feature films are also shown; $9 adults, $7 children 2–12, $8 seniors and military. Call 808/971-5033 for current showings and ticket prices, or see www.imaxwaikiki.com.

Just for the thrill of it, ride the outside glass elevators of either the Sheraton Waikiki, Ilikai, or Hawaii Prince hotel to see great sights.

# Shopping

The biggest problem concerning shopping in Waikiki is to keep yourself from burning out over the endless array of shops and boutiques. Everywhere you look someone has something for sale, and with the preponderance of street stalls lining the boulevards, much of the merchandise comes out to greet you. The same rule applies to shopping as it does to everything in Waikiki—class next door to junk. Those traveling to the Neighbor Islands should seriously consider a shopping spree in Waikiki, which has the largest selection and most competitive prices in the islands. A great feature about shopping in Waikiki is that most shops are only a minute or two from the beach. This enables your sale-hound companion to hunt while you relax. There's no telling how much money your partner can save you! "Ingrate! This bathing suit could have cost $50, but I got it for $25. See, you saved $25 while you were lying here like a beached whale." Everyone concerned should easily be mollified. Charge!

## The Fence

The best place to find an authentic island-made souvenir at a reasonable price is at The Fence, along the fence of the Honolulu Zoo fronting Kapi'olani Park. Also referred to as Art at the Zoo Fence, the Fence gathers some of the island's best artists to display and sell their works on weekends 9 A.M.–4 P.M., as they have for decades. Individual artists are allowed to display only one day a week. Established in 1953, the Fence was the good idea of Honolulu's former mayor, Frank Fasi, who decided that O'ahu's rich resource of artists shouldn't go untapped. There are plenty of excellent artists whose works are sure to catch your fancy.

## Gifts, Souvenirs, and Sundries

**ABC Stores** scattered throughout Waikiki were founded by a local man, Sid Kosasa, who learned the retail business from his father. Euphemistically referred to as the "**A**ll **B**locks **C**overed" store, this "everything store" sells groceries, sundries, and souvenirs. Prices are good, especially on specials like lotions and beach mats. Very conveniently located just about everywhere.

Those who just can't return home without a deep Hawaiian tan should visit **Waikiki Aloe,**

2168 Kalakaua Ave. It specializes in skin-care products, lotions, and tanning supplies.

The **Waikiki Business Plaza,** 2270 Kalakaua Ave., houses jewelry stores. In one stop you can get a pretty good idea of prices and availability. Look for jewelry boxes laden with jade, gold, turquoise, pearls, coral, and *puka* shells, and eel, snake, and leather goods.

Most people just can't leave the island without buying an aloha shirt or a mu'umu'u. Any why not? They *say* Hawaii. Dozens of shops in Waikiki handle these trademark items, but to get an idea of what's out there at a decent price, try **Touch of Aloha** at 205 Lewers Street. Alternately, search the numerous shops at the International Market Place. For something more classy (and more expensive), look to the upscale shops in the larger shopping malls or the boutiques at the luxury hotels along this strip.

For classic Hawaiian shirts, head for **Bailey's Antique and Aloha Shirts,** 517 Kapahulu, 808/734-7628, where you will find thousands of the vintage "collectible garments" on display. The best are made from rayon that was manufactured before 1950. Prices can range from $100–2,000. Reproductions of these old wearable artworks are also available, as are clothing, jewelry, lamps, figurines, and the like. Nearby at 732 Kapahulu is **Peggy's Picks,** with new and used gifts, treasures, and collectibles from around the world.

For **photo finishing and photo supplies** at bargain prices, try **Wolf Camera** in the Royal Hawaiian Shopping Center and at the Sheraton Moana Surfrider; **Island Camera and Gift Shops** at Princess Ka'iulani, Sheraton Waikiki, Royal Hawaiian, and Sheraton Moana Surfrider hotels; and **Outrigger Photo** at 2335 Kalakaua Avenue.

**Duty-free goods** are always of interest to international visitors. You can find a duty-free store at the Hilton Hawaiian Village. Also, if you want to see a swarm of Japanese jostling for position in a tiny little store trying to feed a buying frenzy, that's the spot. For a larger selection, try **DFS Galleria Waikiki,** 330 Royal Hawaiian Ave., opposite the Bank of Hawaii—how convenient!

## Waikiki Shopping Centers

The largest credit card oasis is the **Royal Hawai-ian Shopping Center.** This massive complex is three stories of nonstop shopping, running for three blocks in front of the Sheraton and Royal Hawaiian hotels. It's open daily 10 A.M.–11 P.M., 808/922-0588. This complex provides an excellent mixture of intimate shops, larger national chain stores, and international boutiques, with an overabundance of clothing shops and jewelry stores. If jewelry is an interest of yours, have a look at the Hawaiian Heirloom Jewelry shop on the ground floor. Also on the third floor is the Little Hawaiian Craft Shop, which carries an amazing array of high-quality, handmade gift items; most are made by local craftspeople. There's a post office on the third floor. The second and third floors of this shopping center are pretty quiet; the third floor has many of the restaurants. It's off the street, so not as many tourists find their way here. It's a good place to do some comparative browsing before making your purchases. If you get hungry while looking from store to store, stop at one of the 11 restaurants or additional snack shops to ease your pangs. The tastes of Asia predominate, but Italian, meat, and seafood are also in the mix. There is an information desk on the first level, about in the middle of the complex. The Waikiki Trolley has a stop and a ticket booth here, and a parking structure is attached.

Where the Royal Hawaiian Shopping Plaza ends, the multilevel **Waikiki Shopping Plaza** begins, but on the other side of the street. The mall's centerpiece is a five-story waterfall, an impressive sculpture of water and Plexiglas, while other fountains grace the lower level. Another feature of this mall is Waikiki Calls, a free hula show. The Hawaii Visitors Bureau (HVB) maintains its Waikiki office on the 5th floor, room 502, offering free brochures, maps, and plenty of advice for all your questions. Many inexpensive eateries are located on the bottom floor, while fancier Chinese and Japanese restaurants are on the fourth and fifth floors. Clothing and accessory shops seem to predominate. The plaza is open daily 9 A.M.–11 P.M., 808/923-1191. While here, take a ride to the top floor of the Waikiki Business Plaza next door, where you'll get a fine overview of the Honolulu-Waikiki area.

Across Royal Hawaiian Avenue is the three-story **DFS Galleria Waikiki** center. This chic shopping plaza has little but fashions and the third-floor duty-free shops. The ground floor is designed to give the impression of early-1900s plantation storefronts, all gathered around a banyan tree. On Wednesday and Friday evenings at 7 P.M. a free hula show is presented at the stage. A two-story aquarium sits at the corner of this building, and a staircase spirals up to the second floor through it.

Directly behind the International Market Place at 2301 Kuhio Avenue is the **Waikiki Town Center,** a little older, funkier three-level mall for gifts, fashions, and food. While here, enjoy the free Polynesian Show Monday, Wednesday, Friday, and Saturday 7–7:45 P.M. on the second floor.

The **Hyatt Regency Shopping Center,** also called the **Atrium Shops,** is on the first three floors of the Hyatt Regency Hotel, 2424 Kalakaua Ave., open daily 9 A.M.–11 P.M. The 60 or so shops are mighty classy: If you're after exclusive fashions or a quality memento, this is the place. There's a continental-style sidewalk café, backed by a cascading indoor waterfall. Often free entertainment and fashion shows are put on by the various shops.

**King's Village,** directly behind the Hyatt Regency, takes its theme from the late 1800s, with boardwalks passing 19th-century lookalike shops on two levels, complete with a changing-of-the-guard ceremony nightly at 6:15 P.M. Apparel and jewelry shops make up the bulk of the stores here, but there are gift shops and restaurants too. Around the walkways historical plaques briefly relate the reign of the Hawaiian kings and queens. Enter at Ka'iulani and Koa Streets.

The **Rainbow Bazaar** is a unique mall at the Hilton Hawaiian Village on the far western end of Waikiki. Fun just to walk around, shops feature three main themes: Imperial Japan, Hong Kong Alley, and South Pacific Court. The shops here sell fashions, gifts, fine arts, jewelry, and sundries.

One of the newest shopping complexes to grace the streets of this already shop-filled town is the **King Kalakaua Plaza.** Nike Town fills a good portion of this building, as does a Banana Republic store. Along Kalakaua Avenue, heading back into the center of the strip, is **2100 Kalakaua,** a series of exclusive high-fashion stores that include Tiffany & Co., Yves Saint Laurent, Chanel, Gucci, and Tod and Boucheron. If you've got plenty of dough to drop, you can feel comfortable heading this way; otherwise you may have trouble getting past the front door security guards.

## Outdoor Shops

The **International Market Place** is an open-air shopping bazaar that feels like Asia. Its natural canopy is a huge banyan, and the entire complex is tucked between the Beachcomber and Princess Ka'iulani hotels. This warren of shops opens daily about 9 A.M. and closes when the vendors get tired at night. Among some fine merchandise and a treasure or two is great junk! If you're after souvenirs like bamboo products, shellwork, hats, mats, lotions, alohawear, jewelry, and carvings, you can't do better than the International Market Place. A food court sits on the Duke's Lane side. The worst thing is that everything starts to look the same; the best is that the vendors will bargain. Make offers and try hard to work your way through the gauntlet of shops without getting scalped.

In **Duke's Lane,** a shortcut between Kuhio and Kalakaua Avenues, you'll find a row of stalls selling mostly jewelry and knickknacks.

Across Kuhio Avenue is the smaller **Waikiki Market Place,** with additional clothing shops, sundry stores, and food vendors.

## Street Artists and Vendors

You don't have to try to find something to buy in Waikiki—in fact, if you're not careful, the merchandise will come after you! This takes place in the form of street vendors, who have been gaining a lot of attention lately. Some view them as a colorful addition to the beach scene, others as a nuisance. These carnival-type salespeople set up their mobile booths mainly along Kalakaua Avenue, with some on Kuhio Avenue and the side streets in between. In dealing with them you can have a positive experience if you remember two things: They have some pretty nifty junk, and you get what you pay for.

Street artists also set up their easels along busy

thoroughfares, and especially at the entrances to small shopping malls. Most draw caricatures of patrons in a few minutes for a few dollars—fun souvenirs. Others take a spot along the sidewalk and make coconut-frond hats and baskets, basically a dying art. They're cheap, a real souvenir of Hawaii, and a fun gift to bring home.

## Activities and Rentals

Not all activities and sports rentals in Waikiki are done at the umbrella stands set up along Waikiki Beach. For a reputable shop, try **Blue Sky Rentals,** 1920 Ala Moana Blvd., 808/947-0101. Owner Luis Merino can arrange activities and rent equipment for most of your ground, air, and sea needs. Mountain bikes rent for $10 for four hours, $15 for eight hours, or $20 for a full day. Mopeds run $18, $23, and $33 for the same time increments. Snorkeling gear or boogie boards are $10 per day. Introductory scuba dives start from about $85. You'll find these and many more options for rental gear and activities.

As you might expect, **Snorkel Bob's** operates on O'ahu, as he does on all the outer islands. Always a good deal, Bob may be a bit higher priced here than on the Neighbor Islands, but he still has the same great gear. Depending on the quality, snorkel sets run from $3.50 per day to $29 per week. And if you're traveling to one of the other islands, you can drop your gear off at one of his shops there for free. Find Snorkel Bob's, 808/735-7944, at the corner of Kapahulu and Date Streets, across from the corner of the Ala Wai Golf Course.

Of the beachside sport rental shops, **Prime Time Sports (PTS),** 808/949-8952, is a good bet. At Fort DeRussy Beach in front of the Hale Koa Hotel, it rents all sorts of water equipment, beach chairs, and umbrellas, and gives scuba, surf, and sailboarding lessons, all at reasonable prices. Sample fees are surfboard, $10 per hour; surf lesson, $40 per hour; outrigger canoe rides, $10 per person; snorkel gear, $15 per day; and aqua cycles, $20 per hour.

**Kool Karz,** 808/926-5279, rents open-sided, electric cars that are street legal. Like a souped-up version of a golf cart, these babies move but can't be taken onto the highways. Seating up to four, they rent for $25 per hour, $59 for four hours, or $119 for 24 hours. Optional insurance is offered. Stop by the shop at 2301 Kuhio Avenue on the street level of the Waikiki Town Center.

O'AHU

# Central O'ahu and 'Ewa

For most uninformed visitors, central O'ahu is a colorful blur as they speed past in their rental cars en route to the North Shore. Slow down, there are things to see! For island residents, the suburban towns of 'Aiea, Pearl City, Waipahu, Mililani, and Wahiawa are home. The three routes heading north from the coast meet in Wahiawa, the island's most central town. The roads cross just near the entrance to Schofield Barracks, which served as a warm-up target for Japanese Zeros as they flew on their devastating bombing run over Pearl Harbor.

'Ewa holds few attractions for the average visitor and, as with central O'ahu, most tourists simply buzz right through. Once a broad expanse of sugar cane fields and a huge naval air station, this land now provides room for the fastest-growing suburban areas on the island, expansive golf courses, and a huge industrial estate, while much is either left fallow or as undeveloped as it has been for decades.

lagoon at Ko'Olina Resort

ROBERT NILSEN

# 'Aiea, Pearl City, and Waipahu

The twin cities of 'Aiea and Pearl City, except for the World War II military memorials and perhaps a football game at Aloha Stadium, have little to attract the average tourist. They are mainly residential areas for greater Honolulu and the large numbers of military families throughout this area. Likewise, Waipahu doesn't hold much attraction to the tourist because of its largely agricultural base, but Hawaii's Plantation Village is an attempt to interpret the importance of plantation culture for visitors.

## PEARL HARBOR HISTORICAL SITES

### Getting There

There are a few options for how to visit Pearl Harbor and its three historical military sites. If you're driving, the entrance is along Route 99, Kamehameha Highway, about one-half mile south of Aloha Stadium; well-marked signs direct you to the ample parking area. If you're on H-1 west, take exit 15A and follow the signs. You can also take TheBus, no. 20 or 42 from Kuhio Avenue in Waikiki, no. 20, 42, or 52 from Ala Moana Center or downtown, and be dropped off within a minute's walk of the entrance. Depending on stops and traffic, this trip could take over an hour.

The **Arizona Memorial Shuttle Bus,** 808/839-0911, a private operation from Waikiki run by VIP Tours, takes about half an hour and will pick you up at any Waikiki hotel. It charges $7 round-trip; reservations are necessary, so call a day in advance. It runs every 45 minutes to the memorial 6:50 A.M.–1 P.M. For your return trip, just find the bus in the parking lot and board. Return trips run 9:50 A.M.–5:15 P.M.

To see all three of these memorials—a definite recommendation—plan to be at Pearl Harbor by midmorning and make a half day of your visit. Start with the USS *Arizona* and then proceed to the other two.

Tour boat operators out of Kewalo Basin used to run extensive tours into Pearl Harbor, including a run by the USS Arizona Memorial and the USS *Missouri* battleship, but they have not been allowed to continue following the terrorist attacks of September 11, 2001. Even when operating, these tours were strictly ride-by tours and boats were not able to drop off passengers. When and if these tours will resume is uncertain, so for the foreseeable future, boat tours of the area are not an option.

## USS Arizona Memorial

Even as you approach the pier from which you board a launch to take you to the USS *Arizona,* you know that you're at a shrine. Very few spots in America carry such undeniable emotion so easily passed from one generation to another: here, Valley Forge, Gettysburg, not many more. On that beautiful, cloudless morning of December 7, 1941, at one minute before 8 o'clock, the United States not only entered the war but lost its innocence forever.

The first battle of World War II for the United States actually took place about 90 minutes before Pearl Harbor's bombing, when the USS *Ward* sank an unidentified submarine sliding into Honolulu. In Pearl Harbor, dredged about 40 years earlier to allow superships to enter, the heavyweight champions of America's Pacific Fleet were lined up, flanking the near side of Ford's Island. The naive deployment of this "Battleship Row" prompted a Japanese admiral to remark that never, even in times of maximum world peace, could he dream that the military might of a nation would have its unprotected chin stuck so far out, just begging for a right cross to the jaw. When it came, it was a roundhouse right, whistling through the air, and what a doozy!

Well before the smoke could clear and the last explosion stopped rumbling through the mountains, 3,566 Americans were dead or wounded, six mighty ships had sunk into the ooze, 12 others stumbled around battered and punch-drunk, and 323 warplanes were useless heaps of scrap. The Japanese fighters had hardly broken a sweat, and when their fleet, located 200 miles north of

O'ahu, steamed away, the "east wind" had indeed "rained." But this downpour was only the first squall; the American hurricane followed.

## Visitor Center

The Arizona Memorial Visitor Center, www.nps.gov/usar/index.htm, is a joint venture of the U.S. Park Service and the navy. It's free, but donations are accepted. The Park Service runs the visitor center, and the navy operates the shuttle boats that take you out to the memorial shrine. The displays, museum, and gift shop at the complex are open daily 7:30 A.M.–5 P.M., with daily programs at the theater and the actual shuttle

ride to the memorial operating only 8 A.M.–3 P.M. (closed Thanksgiving, Christmas, New Year's Day). If the weather is stormy, or waves rough, they won't sail. For recorded information, call 808/422-0561 or 422-2771. As many as 5,000 people visit per day, and your best time to avoid delays is before 9:30 A.M. With 1.5 million visitors yearly, this is one of the most heavily visited sites in the state.

Security measures in place following the September 11, 2001, terrorist attacks on the Mainland include not allowing any backpacks, strollers, purses, bags, and other such items larger than about 12 inches square to be brought into this

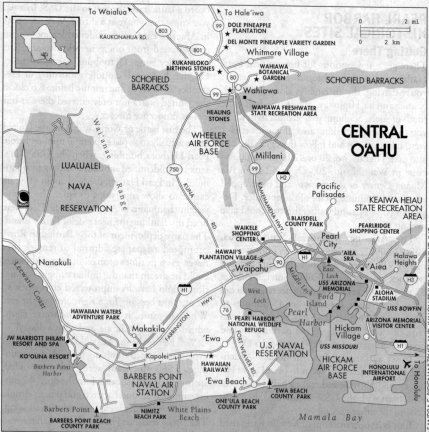

memorial, the Bowfin Museum, or to the USS *Missouri*. A storage place that charges $2 per bag has been set up in the parking lot so you can safely leave larger items that you've brought.

As you enter, you're handed a numbered ticket. Until it's called, you can visit the bookstore/gift shop and museum or, if the wait is long, the USS *Bowfin*, moored within walking distance (see USS Bowfin Submarine Museum and Park). The bookstore specializes in volumes on World War II and Hawaiiana. The museum is primarily a pictorial history, with a strong emphasis on the involvement of Hawaii's Japanese citizens during the war. There are instructions of behavior to "all persons of Japanese ancestry," from the time when bigotry and fear prevailed early in the war, as well as documentation of the 442nd Battalion, made up of Japanese American soldiers, and their heroic exploits in Europe, especially their rescue of Texas's "lost battalion." Preserved newspapers of the day proclaim the "Day of Infamy" in bold headlines.

When your number is called, you proceed to the comfortable theater where a 20-minute film includes actual footage of the attack. The film is historically factual, devoid of an overabundance of flag waving and Mom's apple pie. After the film, you board the launch: no bare feet, no bikinis or bathing suits, but shorts and shirts are fine. Thirty years ago visitors wore suits and dresses as if going to church!

## The Memorial

The launch, a large, mostly open-air vessel handled and piloted with professional deft by naval personnel, heads for the 184-foot-long alabaster memorial straddling the remains of the ship that still lies on the bottom. Some view the memorial as a tombstone; others see it as a symbolic ship, bent by struggle in the middle, but raised at the ends pointing to glory. The USS *Arizona* became the focus of the memorial because her casualties were so severe. When she exploded, the blast was so violent that it lifted entire ships moored nearby clear out of the water. Less than nine minutes later, with infernos raging and huge hunks of steel whizzing through the air, the *Arizona* was gone. Her crew went with her; more than 1,100 men were sucked down to the bottom, and only

289 somehow managed to struggle to the surface. To the left and right are a series of black-and-white moorings bearing the names of the ships that were tied to them on the day of the attack.

The deck of the memorial can hold about 200 people; a small museum holds the ship's bell, and a chapel-like area displays a marble tablet with the names of the dead. Into a hole in the center of the memorial, flowers and wreaths are dropped on special occasions. Part of the superstructure of the ship still rises above the waves, but it is slowly being corroded away by wind and saltwater. The flag, waving overhead, is attached to a pole anchored to the deck of the sunken ship. Sometimes, on weekends, survivors from the attack are aboard to give firsthand descriptions of what happened that day. Many visitors are Japanese nationals, who often stop and offer their apologies to these Pearl Harbor survivors, distinguished by special military-style hats. The navy ordered that any survivor wishing to be buried with his crew members had that right. Several veterans have been laid to rest with their buddies.

## USS Bowfin Submarine Museum and Park

The USS *Bowfin*, a World War II submarine, is moored a few short steps from the Arizona Memorial Visitor Center. In the museum building, a short pictorial history depicts progress in undersea warfare from Revolutionary times to the present. Battle flags, recruiting posters, photographs, uniforms, military medals, and weapons and hardware are displayed, while a cutaway model of the *Bowfin* depicts life aboard ship. Unique to the museum, and the only one displayed for public viewing, is a daunting Poseidon C-3 submarine missile. An ongoing film in the mini-theater describes life below the surface for the modern submarine force. For the real aficionado, the museum archives and library of submarine-related literature is open by appointment only. Here and there across the four-acre grounds lie artillery pieces, torpedoes, missiles, and the conning tower and periscope of the USS *Parche*. Next to the museum is a gift shop and snack bar. This park is open daily 8 A.M.–5 P.M., except Thanksgiving, Christmas, and New Year's Day.

Guided tours lead into the sub; the last tour starts at 4:30 P.M. Admission to the sub and museum is $8 adults or $4 for the museum only, $3 children ages 4–12 or $2 for the museum only. Children three and under are free for the museum tour but not admitted into the submarine. The rate for *kama'aina,* senior citizens, and active military personnel is $6. (See USS *Missouri* for rates combining a visit to both the USS *Bowfin* and USS *Missouri.*) The private, nonprofit organization Pacific Fleet Submarine Memorial Association, 808/423-1341, www.bowfin.org, maintains the park and museum as a memorial and educational exhibit.

Launched one year to the day after the Pearl Harbor attack, the USS *Bowfin* (SS-287) completed nine patrol tours during World War II. Nicknamed the "Pearl Harbor Avenger," it was responsible for sinking an incredible 44 enemy ships before the end of the war. Retired in 1979, restored and opened to the public in 1981, it was put on the National Historical Landmark list in 1986. It's a 312-foot-long sausage of steel with a living area only 16 feet in diameter. As you enter the sub, you're handed a telephone-like receiver; a transmitted message explains about different areas on the sub. The deck is made from teak wood, and the deck guns could be moved fore or aft, depending on the skipper's preference. You'll also notice two anchors. As you descend, you feel as if you are integrated with a machine, a part of its gears and workings. In these cramped quarters of brass and stainless steel lived 90 to 100 men, all volunteers. Fresh water was in short supply, and the only man allowed to shower was the cook. Officers were given a dipper of water to shave with, but all the other men grew beards. With absolutely no place to be alone, the men slept on tiny stacked shelves, and only the officers could control the light switches. The only man to have a minuscule private room was the captain.

Topside, twin 16-cylinder diesels created unbelievable noise and heat. A vent in the passageway to the engine room sucked air with such strength that if you passed under it, you'd be flattened to your knees. When the sub ran on batteries under water, the quiet became maddening. The main bunk room, not much bigger than an average bedroom, slept 36 men. Another 30 or so ran the ship, while another 30 lounged. There was no night or day aboard ship, just shifts. Coffee was constantly available, as well as fresh fruit, and the best mess in all the services. Subs of the day had the best radar and electronics available. Aboard were 24 high-powered torpedoes and ammo for the topside gun. Submariners, chosen for their intelligence and psychological ability to take it, knew that a hit from the enemy meant certain death. The USS *Bowfin* is fascinating and definitely worth a visit.

## USS Missouri

On June 22, 1998, the USS *Missouri* came home. Whereas the destruction of the USS *Arizona* and other ships in the harbor and the incredible loss of life and innocence brought the United States into war with Japan, it was on the deck of the USS *Missouri* that Japan, bruised and bloodied, surrendered to the United States, ending this most costly of world conflicts. Docked on Ford Island just a rifle shot from the USS *Arizona,* it proudly takes its place on "Battleship Row." At 887 feet long and 108 feet wide, this battleship is a behemoth, one of the largest ever built and the last taken off active service. Like a floating city, she had a crew of around 2,500. Commissioned in 1944, this ship participated in many battles during World War II and later during the Korean War and the Persian Gulf War. Money collected by the private, nonprofit USS Missouri Memorial Association is used to refurbish and maintain the "Mighty Mo." Since January 1999, visitors have been allowed onto the deck, where the signing of the surrender took place, and to view the bridge, climb the stairs from level to level, peer into officers' and enlisted men's quarters, enter the galley and dining rooms, and see the armaments that the ship was well known and feared for. Although later retrofitted with more sophisticated weapons, the original huge 16-inch guns could fire a 2,700-pound shell more than 23 miles, and even the smaller five-inch guns could send their projectiles a respectable nine miles. This was no light-duty ship. For protection, some of its armor plating was 17 inches thick! Several videos and other displays along the way explain the

ROBERT NILSEN

**Still an imposing ship, the USS *Missouri* is open to visitors.**

ship's history and function. A plaque on the surrender deck indicates the spot where the table used by representatives of the Japanese, U.S., and Allied governments and armed forces signed the surrender document. In future years, other areas of the ship may also be opened to tourists.

Entrance runs $16 adults, $12 *kama'aina*, $7 military, and $9 children for an unguided tour, or $6 more for the basic guided tours. Other special guided tours that take you to various parts of the ship that are not open to the general public are also offered. These tours run $22–49; ask about what's currently available. Shuttle trolleys depart every 10 minutes starting at 9 A.M. from a stand in front of the USS Bowfin Museum and run over the new Ford Bridge to the ship. Tickets are sold at the USS *Bowfin* ticket office until 4 P.M., and everyone must leave the ship by 5 P.M. For nonmilitary personnel, this is the only way to get to the ship. It's worth a couple of hours, and the emotional impact will remain much longer. If you want to combine a tour of the USS *Missouri* with the USS *Bowfin,* tickets run $18 self-guided and $24 guided for adults, and $9 unguided and $15 guided for children. For more information, contact the USS Missouri Memor-

ial Association, P.O. Box 6339, Honolulu, HI 96818, 808/423-2263, or 888/877-6477, www.ussmissouri.com.

## Visit Ships Program

The navy used to hold an **open house** on one of its ships berthed at Pearl Harbor on the first Saturday of each month. Unfortunately it no longer does so. However, on occasion—usually around public holidays—home-port ships are open to the public for tours at Aloha Tower Market Place and at piers on the Neighbor Islands where ships make port calls. For information on when ships will be open for tours, call 808/473-2888.

## BEACHES AND SIGHTS

### Keaiwa Heiau State Recreation Area

As you travel up 'Aiea Heights Road, you get a world-class view of Pearl Harbor below. It's not glorious because it is industrialized, but you do ride through suburban sprawl Hawaiian style until you come to the end of the road at Keaiwa Heiau State Recreation Area. In the cool heights above 'Aiea, these ancient grounds have a soothing effect the minute you enter. Overnight tent camping, at exceptionally large sites, is allowed here with a permit; for the few other visitors, the gates open at 7 A.M. and close at 6:45 P.M. As you enter the well-maintained park (a care-taker lives on the premises), tall pines to the left give a feeling of alpine coolness—great for a pic-nic. Below, Pearl Harbor lies open, like the shell of a great oyster.

Keaiwa Heiau was a healing temple, sur-rounded by gardens of medicinal herbs tended by Hawaii's excellent healers, the *kahuna lapaʻau*. Roots, twigs, leaves, and bark from the garden were ground into potions and mixed liberally with prayers and love. These potions were amaz-ingly successful at healing Hawaiians before the white explorers brought diseases. Walking into the *heiau* compound, it's somehow warmer and the winds seem quieter. Toward the center are nu-merous offerings, simple stones wrapped with ti leaves. Some are old, while others are quite fresh. Follow the park road to the top and the entrance to the **ʻAiea Loop Trail,** which heads back 4.8 miles round-trip onto one of the ridges de-scending from the Koʻolau Mountains. You'll pass through a forest of tall eucalyptus trees and view canyons to the left and right. Partway up is a bench in a small clearing with a grand view over the mountains and valleys. Notice, too, the softness of the "spongy bark" trees growing where the path begins. Allow three hours for the loop.

## Blaisdell County Park

The park's waters, part of Pearl Harbor's East Lock, are too polluted for swimming. It's sad to think that in the late 19th century it was clear and clean enough to support oysters. Pearl Harbor took its name from Waimomi, "Water of Pearls," which were indeed harvested from the oysters and a certain species of clam growing here. Today, however, we see firsthand the devastation caused by sewage and uncountable oil spills. Oysters from the Mainland's East Coast have been in-troduced, but signs still warn of polluted fish and shellfish. Open until 10 P.M., the park has broad grass lawns and young monkeypod and other trees. Facilities include a pay phone, ta-bles, and restrooms. From here you can see the back side of Ford Island and a few naval ships

parked on its periphery. From this point, the water looks like a lake. Local people gather here on weekends and in the cool of the evening. It's a quiet spot to watch the evening turn to night. Ac-cess is off Route 99 at the junction of Kaʻahu-manu Avenue, about 1.5 miles past Aloha Stadium and just before you enter Pearl City.

The **Pearl Harbor Bike Path,** a biking/jogging right-of-way, skirts the water through this park. It runs for several miles from near the Arizona Memorial, around the top of the bay, and out to Waipahu Depot Road in Waipahu. This path is part of the Pearl Harbor Historic Trail system, an effort by the city and community action groups to expand the recreational opportunities of city residents, and consists of this trail, future biking/jogging trails through golf courses, wildlife refuges, the ʻEwa Plain, additional parkland, the Hawaiian Railway line in ʻEwa, and a future ex-tension of that line into Waipahu.

A short way to the east of Blaisdell County Park is the much smaller **ʻAiea State Recreation Area.** Also set on the water, this diminutive green area does have grass lawns, picnic benches, rest-rooms, and a parking lot, but it seems much less used. As with its neighbor up the road, the Pearl Harbor Bike Path runs along the edge of this park.

# PRACTICALITIES
## Accommodations

Except for a handful of long-term apartment ho-tels, accommodations are virtually nonexistent in this area. One of the available places is the **Harbor Shores Apartment Hotel,** 98-145 Lipoa Place, ʻAiea, HI 96701, 808/488-5742 or 800/227-8796, fax 808/486-8537, hshores@aloha.net, www.har-bor-shores.com. This modern three-story affair has 42 two-bedroom apartments that go for $95 per night or $599 per week per couple, with re-duced TLA rates for military families. Each fur-nished unit has linoleum floors and air-condition-ing, a complete kitchen, a living room with color cable television, free local phone calls, and a full bath. As a family-oriented hotel, the Harbor Shores has a small swimming pool, fenced children's play area, barbecue grills for outdoor cooking, a laundry facility, parking, and complimentary transportation to nearby military bases and the airport. Only the Pearl Harbor Bike Path lies between it and the water. Located just off Kamehameha Highway and close to H-1, the Harbor Shores is not bothered by traffic noise yet is close to transportation routes and the nearby military bases.

Just down the road, the **Harbor Arms Apartment Hotel,** 98-130 Lipoa Pl., 808/488-5556 or 800/360-5556, fax 808/488-8385, harborarms@cvcmail.com, www.harborarms.com, offers fully furnished air-conditioned studios and apartments, all with kitchens and baths, TV, and phone. One-bedroom units start around $70 per day and two-bedroom apartments at about $80, but rates vary according to occupancy and season, so be sure to contact the hotel for a current quote; cash only, no credit cards. A laundromat and swimming pool are also available on property, and there's plenty of parking. The Harbor Arms is a three-story cement block affair, not fancy by any means but clean and well maintained and with all the necessary comforts. Because it's TLA-approved, many military personnel use this facility as temporary housing. Airport transportation provided.

## Food

**Buzz's Steak House,** 98-751 Kuahao Pl. (at the corner of Ka'ahumanu Ave., just below H-1), 808/487-6465, is open for lunch 11 A.M.–2 P.M. and again for dinner 5–10 P.M. It's futuristic, like something a kid would build with an erector set. It'd be perfect if it were down by the sea, where you could see something, but from where it's located you can peer at Pearl Harbor in the distance or have a world-class view of the freeway. The steakhouse is owned and operated by an old island family whose business grew into a small chain of restaurants from the original location in Kailua. This is one of the remaining two. Buzz's is an institution where islanders go when they want a sure-fire good meal. There's a salad bar, and you prepare your own charbroiled steaks and fish. Generally, you can get lunch sandwiches and salads for under $10, while the dinner menu has finer meat and fish dishes mostly under $28. No credit cards, please.

Just down Ka'ahumanu Avenue, try **Stuart**

**Anderson's Cattle Co. Restaurant,** 808/487-0054, open weekdays for lunch and daily for dinner with the lounge open until 2 A.M. Stuart Anderson's focus is red meat, and they cut their own daily so it's fresh and tasty, but chicken and seafood are also available. Whatever the meal, it'll "come with all the fixin's."

For something Asian, the Japanese **Gyotaku Restaurant,** 808/487-0091, is almost next door and open from 11 A.M.–9 P.M. (10 P.M. on Fri. and Sat.). Stop here for sushi, salad, miso soup, various full meal plates, a *bento* meal, udon or soba noodle dishes, or combination plates. Luncheon and dinner specials and senior and *keiki* meals all help keep the price down.

Across the road in the Waimalu Shopping Plaza is the **Elephant and Castle Restaurant & Pub,** 808/487-5591, open daily for lunch and dinner, breakfast on weekends only. This restaurant has done an excellent job of creating an English-style pub atmosphere. The interior is cool and rich with red velvet, heavy chairs, tapestries, and open beams, with a pool table and dartboards in the pub area. At night, it's one of the best places in the area for a beer and a chat. The food is good too. Try English fish and chips, a burger platter, hot sandwiches, or soup and sandwich during the day, or for dinner try seafood scampi, English-style roast prime-rib dinner, New York strip steak, or chicken Cordon bleu. Enjoy merry old England Hawaiian style.

## Shopping

The main shopping center in 'Aiea is the **Pearl-ridge Shopping Center,** open Mon.–Sat. 10 A.M.–9 P.M., Sun. until 6 P.M., with prices geared toward island residents, not tourists, so you have a good chance of coming away with a bargain. Some of the larger stores include Macy's, JCPenney, Sears, Longs, and Waldenbooks. There are also a 16-screen movie theater, two food courts with more than 25 restaurants, a satellite city hall, plus more than 150 smaller boutiques and specialty shops. Consisting of two main buildings—the "Uptown" and "Downtown" centers—and several smaller annexes, the entire complex is air-conditioned, and the two major sections are serviced by a monorail for your shopping

O'AHU

convenience. The Skycab monorail costs $.50 each way and runs 9 A.M.–9 P.M. daily. Plenty of parking is available. Aside from the shopping opportunities, you will be entertained in the Uptown section on Friday evenings at 7 P.M. by a cute *keiki* hula show and on Saturday 6–8 P.M. by musicians at the Downtown center court.

Across the street to the west is the smaller **Westridge Shopping Center,** and across the highway to the south, the **Pearl Kai Shopping Center,** both clusters of shops and eateries. Next to the Westridge complex is the **Kam Swap Meet** site. A second, similar outdoor market, the **Aloha Stadium Swap Meet,** operates at the Aloha Stadium parking lot. Both run Wednesday, Saturday, and Sunday from early morning until midafternoon. About one-half mile down Kamehameha Highway to the west past the Pearl Kai Shopping Center is the **Waimalu Shopping Center,** which is little more than a strip mall of ethnic restaurants. Here you can find Japanese, Chinese, Korean, Hawaiian, and Filipino foods, as well as the Marujyu Market, which is open 24 hours for groceries, a deli, and a pharmacy. At intervals along Route 99 to the west are additional shopping malls for everything from groceries to fashions.

# WAIPAHU
## Hawaii's Plantation Village

Hawaii's Plantation Village, an open-air museum, in Waipahu Cultural Park, 94-695 Waipahu St., Waipahu, HI 96797, 808/677-0110, offers a stroll down memory lane. Below the now-abandoned Oʻahu Sugar Mill and smokestack, these plantation buildings have been moved from other locations to create this museumlike village. The 30 original structures and the photos, artifacts, and memorabilia they contain testify to the hard work performed by Hawaii's sugar plantation communities and provide insight into the eight ethnic groups represented. From 1852 to 1946, nearly 400,000 immigrants were brought to the islands to work in the field industries. Although the Chinese were first and their numbers amounted to 46,000, the Japanese were the largest group at 180,000. These were followed by Portuguese, Puerto Ricans, Okinawans, Koreans, and a smaller number of north-

ern Europeans. The last major influx was by the Filipinos, whose numbers swelled to about 125,000. Each group contributed greatly to the economic health of the islands and over the following decades became part of the cultural mix that the state is known for today. In the museum building are homey displays illuminating everyday plantation life of the workers and the industry as a whole. The main museum building functions as an education center and is the start of all tours. It houses several displays portraying various aspects of plantation life and is a fine but brief introduction to the reality of the sugar economy in the islands. Out in the yard stands a train engine, once used to pull cane from the fields to the mill. Open for guided tours only Mon.–Fri. 9 A.M.–3 P.M. and Sat. 10 A.M.–3 P.M.; tours run about 90 minutes and start every hour. Admission is $7 adults, $5 military and *kamaʻaina,* $4 seniors, and $3 students 5–12. This is a worthy stop. From Farrington Highway, turn onto Waipahu Depot Street and then follow Waipahu Street around to the left to the entrance.

## Waipahu Bargains

Directly north, along H-1, is the large **Waikele Shopping Center,** with a typical mall selection of shops. Across the road at **Waikele Premium Outlets** you can save money on fashions, furnishings, and specialty items. You'll only find big-name stores at the outlets, with hardly as island shop in sight. If you need to travel thousands of miles to spend money at logo wear shops, this is the place. A favorite of locals, it's also well used by visiting Japanese tourists. For the convenience of shoppers, the Waikele Trolley connects the outlet mall with the shopping center. It also connects the mall with hotels in Waikiki, leaving various locations in Waikiki twice in the morning and returning three times every afternoon and evening; $22 round-trip adults, $8 kids. Reservations preferred. Call 808/591-2561, or have your hotel concierge make the arrangements.

If you haven't had enough of strip malls and shopping plazas, several others line Highway 90 west of the Waipahu Cultural Park going toward ʻEwa.

# Wahiawa and Vicinity

Wahiawa is like a military jeep: basic, ugly, but indispensable. This is a real military town, with personnel from Schofield Barracks or nearby Wheeler Air Force Base shuffling along the streets. Most are young, short-haired, short-tempered, and dressed in fatigues. Everywhere you look are cheap bars, exotic dance halls, liquor stores, burger joints, run-down discos perfumed with sweat and spilled beer, pawn shops, tattoo parlors, antique shops, and used-furniture stores. Just south of town, Route 99 turns into Route 80, which goes through Wahiawa, crossing California Avenue, the main drag, then rejoins Route 99 near the Del Monte Pineapple Variety Garden. Wahiawa has seemingly little to recommend it, and maybe because of its ugliness, when you do find beauty it shines even brighter.

Wahiawa was of extreme cultural and spiritual importance to the early Hawaiians. In town are healing stones, whose mystic vibrations were said to cure the maladies of sufferers. In a field just north of town are the Kukaniloko, the royal birthing stones, where the ruling *ali'i* labored to give birth to the future nobles of the islands. While in town you can familiarize yourself with O'ahu's flora by visiting the Wahiawa Botanical Garden, test your luck at the Wahiawa reservoir fishing area, or take a quick look at a serene Japanese temple.

As you gain the heights of the Leilehua Plateau, spread between the Waianae and Ko'olau mountain ranges, a wide expanse of green is planted in pineapple. Just like on supermarket shelves, Del Monte's Pineapple Variety Garden competes with Dole's Pineapple Plantation, a minute up the road. As a traveler's way station, central O'ahu blends services and just enough historical sites to warrant stretching your legs, but not enough to bog you down for the day.

## SIGHTS
### The Healing Stones
Belief in the healing powers of these stones has been attracting visitors since ancient times. When traveling through town on Kamehameha Highway (Route 80), take a left on California Avenue and follow it to Ka'alalo Place. To glimpse the religion of Hawaii in microcosm, in a few blocks you pass the Ryusenji Soto Buddhist Mission, followed by the healing stones, next door to Olive United Methodist Church. If you've never experienced a Buddhist temple, make sure to visit the grounds of **Ryusenji Soto Mission.** Usually no one is around, and even if the front doors are locked you can peer in at an extremely ornate altar graced by Buddha, highlighted in black lacquer and gold. On the grounds look for a stone *jizo,* patron of travelers and children. In Japan he often wears a red woven hat and bib, but here he has on a straw hat and mu'umu'u.

An HVB Warrior sign may mark the healing stones, just past the Ka'ala Elementary School, across the street from a beautiful eucalyptus grove. A small, white, humble cinder-block building built in 1947 houses the stones right at the edge of the street. Although normally locked, when the iron gate is swung open it strikes a deep mournful note, as if it were an instrument designed to announce your presence and departure. Inside the building, three stones sit atop rudimentary pedestals. Little scratches mark the stones, and an offertory box is filled with items like oranges, bread, a gin bottle, coins, and candy kisses. A few votive candles flicker before a statue of the Blessed Virgin.

### Kukaniloko Birthing Stones
Follow Route 80 through town for about a mile. At the corner of Whitmore Avenue is a stoplight: Right takes you to Whitmore Village and left puts you on a dirt track that leads to another eucalyptus grove in the midst of pineapple fields marking the birthing stones. About 40 large boulders are in the middle of a field with a mountain backdrop. One stone looks like the next, but on closer inspection you see that each has a personality. It is said they have been used for at least 800 years; the royal wives would come here, assisted by both men and women of the ruling

*ali'i*, to give birth to their exalted offspring. The baby's umbilical cord, a sacred talisman, would be hidden in the cracks and crevices of the stones. On the edge of this group of stones is a special stone that appears to be fluted all the way around, with a dip in the middle. It, along with other stones nearby, seems perfectly fitted to accept the torso of a woman in a reclining position. Notice that small fires have been lit in the hollows of these stones, and that they are discolored with soot and ashes. Nearby was a *heiau* where the newborns were consecrated.

## Wahiawa Botanical Garden

In the midst of town is an oasis of beauty, 27 acres of developed woodlands and ravine featuring exotic trees, ferns, and flowers gathered from around the world. At 1396 California Avenue, 808/621-7321, just beyond the district park and recreational center, it's open daily except Christmas and New Year's, 9 A.M.–4 P.M., admission free. The parking lot is marked by an HVB Warrior; walk through the main entranceway and take a pamphlet from the box (when available) for a self-guiding tour. When it rains, the cement walkways are treacherously slippery, especially if you're wearing thongs. The nicer paths have been left natural, but they can be muddy. Inside the grounds are trees from the Philippines, Australia, and Africa, and a magnificent multihued Mindanao gum from New Guinea. Fragrant camphor trees from China and Japan and the rich aroma of cinnamon bombard your senses. Everywhere are natural bouquets of flowering trees, entangled by vines and highlighted by rich green ferns. Most specimens have been growing for a minimum of 40 years, so they're well established, and some have been around since the 1920s when this area was an experimental tree farm. This well-kept garden is a delightful little surprise in the midst of this heavily agricultural and military area.

## Schofield Barracks

Stay on Route 99 (here called Wilikina Drive), skirt Wahiawa to the west, and go past the main entrance to Schofield Barracks. Notice the Kemoo Farms building about 50 yards past the entrance. This former outlet for farm produce is now a café/bakery and bar that caters largely to off-duty military personnel who live and work across the road. Stop here and look behind the shops at a wonderful still life created by the Wahiawa Reservoir. Schofield Barracks dates from the early 1900s, named after General John Schofield, an early proponent of the strategic importance of Pearl Harbor. A sign tells you that it is still the "Home of the Infantry, Tropic Lightning." Open to the public, the base remains one of the prettiest military installations in the world, and one of the largest, as home to more than 20,000 military personnel and dependents.

You can visit the small **Tropic Lightning Museum,** 808/655-0438, with its memorabilia going back to the War of 1812. There are tanks from World War II, Chinese rifles from the Korean War, and deadly *pungi* traps from Vietnam. The museum lost many of its exhibits some years ago to the U.S. Army Museum at Fort DeRussy in Waikiki, so it remains mostly a portrayal of the history of Schofield Barracks and the 25th Infantry "Tropic Lightning" Division. There is no charge for the museum, which is open Tues.–Sat. 10 A.M.–4 P.M., except federal holidays. The museum is on Waianae Avenue, straight up from Macomb Gate, but entrance is via the Foote Gate on Kunia Avenue. Follow the signs for parking. Since the September 2001 terrorist attacks on the mainland, nonmilitary visitors need to enter and sign in at Lyman Gate on Kunia Avenue and may not be allowed to travel anywhere accept to the museum.

## Pineapples

A few minutes past the entrance to Schofield Barracks, Route 803 goes straight ahead to Waialua, while Route 99 bears right and begins passing row upon row of pineapples. At the intersection of Route 80 is the **Del Monte Pineapple Variety Garden.** Park along the roadway, but please be careful of traffic if you cross the road to the garden. You're free to wander about this small showcase garden and read the descriptions of the history of pineapple production in Hawaii and of the genetic progress of the fruit made famous by the islands. Hawaiian pineapple production started in this area at the turn of the 20th century, and it has maintained a strong force in the economy of

# PINEAPPLE

Ananas comosus of the family Bromeliaceae is a tropical fruit that originated in southern South America. During the 1500s and 1600s, ships' captains took this unusual and intriguingly sweet fruit around the world on their journeys. Pineapples seem to have been brought to Hawaii from somewhere in the Caribbean in the early 1800s, but it wasn't until the mid-1880s that any experimentation was done with them, using the "smooth Cayenne," which is still the dominant commercial fruit variety. The first commercial plots of pineapple production were planted on the Leilehua Plateau at Wahiawa by James Dole just after the turn of the 20th century. To preserve the fruit, he built a cannery there in 1903 and later a second in Iwilei in Honolulu. Expanding his operation, Dole bought the island of Lana'i in 1922 and proceeded to turn the Palawai Basin into one huge pineapple plantation—some 18,000 acres at its greatest extent, producing a million pineapples a day during peak harvest. Relying heavily on canning, Dole made the "king of fruits" a well-known and ordinary food to the American public.

Production of pineapples is a lengthy process. First the ground must be tilled and harrowed to ready the soil for planting. The crowns of the pineapple fruit (which themselves look like miniature pineapple plants) or slips from the stem are planted by hand into long rows—some 30,000 plants per acre. A drip-irrigation system is then installed and the soil covered with ground cloth to help control pests and weeds. Fertilizers and pesticides are then sprayed as needed, and the plants grow in the warm tropical sun. After 11–13 months these plants fruit, and some seven months later the first crop is harvested. Generally each plant yields one fruit, which grows on a center stalk surrounded by sharp and spiky curved leaves. The fruit sprouts again and, about 13 months later, a second crop is taken. Sometimes a third crop is also harvested from these same plants, before the remainders are tilled into the soil and the process begins again. Pineapples are picked by hand—a hot, dusty, and prickly job—and then placed on a boom conveyor that dumps them into trucks, which then take them to the cannery. There, all are pressure-washed and sorted by size and quality before being canned or fresh-packed into boxes and shipped to market. Generally about two-thirds are used as fresh fruit; the remainder is canned. All aspects of production are rotated to keep pineapples available for market throughout the year.

O'ahu since then. This exhibit is much more scientific than the **Dole Pineapple Plantation** just up the road, the one with all the tour buses lined up outside, but it too has a small demonstration garden of pineapple varieties and a botanical garden in the back. The Dole stop is a monument to retailing with its huge gift shop, open 9 A.M.–6 P.M., where packaged and ready-to-eat pineapples (they sell more than 3,500 a week) and other food items, logo wear, and many other souvenirs made in Hawaii are yours to purchase. While at the Dole Plantation, visit the "World's Largest Maze." Certified by the *Guinness Book*

*of World Records*, the maze is nearly two acres in area and formed by more than 11,000 native Hawaiian bushes and flowering plants. The maze is open 9 A.M.–5 P.M., admission $5 adults and $3 children. Plan on 20–30 minutes to find your way through—it's a chore and a blast. The newest addition to this commercial establishment is the Pineapple Express Train, a miniature train that runs over a two-mile narrow-gauge rail line that loops for a 20-minute tour through plantation fields. Each narrated tour runs Mon.–Fri. every half hour from 9 A.M.–5 P.M. Tickets are $7.50 adults, $5.50 kids 4–12.

ROBERT NILSEN

O'AHU

## PRACTICALITIES

**Dot's Restaurant,** off California Ave. at 130 Mango St., 808/622-4115, is a homey restaurant specializing in American-Japanese food. It gives a good square meal for your money. The interior is a mixture of Hawaiian/Asian in dark-brown tones. Lunch specials include butterfish, teriyaki chicken, pork, or beef plates all for around $6. Miso soup and simple Japanese dishes are also available. The most expensive item on the menu is steak and lobster. Dot's is nothing to write home about, but you definitely won't go hungry. Open 6 A.M.–9 P.M. For something more institutional, try **Zippy's** or **L&L Drive-In,** both on the main drag.

The streets of Wahiawa are lined with stores that cater to residents, not tourists. This means that the prices are right, and if you need supplies or necessities, this would be a good place to stock up. Up California Avenue toward the botanical garden is **Wahiawa Town Center,** with eateries, Longs Drugs for sundries, a bank, video, and laundry, and the smaller **Wahiawa Shopping Center** directly adjacent with a Foodland for groceries.

# 'Ewa

As far as the average tourist is concerned, the road to 'Ewa is not a road to anywhere of interest. Located just west of Pearl Harbor and not long ago a great expanse of sugar cane fields, 'Ewa now sprouts little more than residential subdivisions and golf courses but has been a military stronghold for decades. Military bases edge the western shore of Pearl Harbor, and a huge expanse was taken by the former Naval Air Station Barbers Point, now slowly being turned to other uses. A few isolated and little-used beaches line the 'Ewa south shore, and while not the best for swimming, they are great for seclusion. West of 'Ewa is Kapolei, a new high-tech town with much development that does attract tourists to its luxury hotel, marina, man-made swimming lagoons, water park, and lu'au garden.

## Hawaiian Railway Line

No commercial passenger train lines operate in the islands today, but two trains do run for tourists: the Sugar Cane Train on Maui and the Hawaiian Railway train on O'ahu. In 'Ewa, the Hawaiian Railway Society, 91-1001 Renton Rd., 808/681-5461, gives rides, restores and shows engines and train cars, and maintains an open-air train exhibit and gift shop. This organization does more than give tourist rides; it provides an educational adventure. The 90-minute round-trip, fully narrated rides start at 1 P.M. and 3 P.M. on Sunday only; $8 adults and $5 for seniors and children under 12. No reservations; first-come, first-served. On the second Sunday of every month, the Dillingham parlor car with its luxury appointments is added to the train on both runs. Fares for the parlor car seats are $15. Group charter rides can be arranged Mon.–Fri. mornings. The train runs about seven miles along narrow-gauge track from the 'Ewa station at the end of Renton Road west to the leeward coast at Kahe Point, just past the Ko 'Olina Resort. Don't expect a rail burner—this baby moves at a mild 15 miles an hour. All aboard!

At one time, the O'ahu Railway and Land Company (OR&L) railroad totaled 72 miles of track that ran from Honolulu around Pearl Harbor, up the leeward coast, and across the north coast all the way to Kahuku, with another line up from Honolulu to the inland town of Wahiawa. It was a workhorse of a system, hauling people and goods (mostly sugar and molasses), servicing farms and commercial establishments, and, later, transferring troops and bulk items during World War II. After the war, the railroad couldn't compete with the burgeoning bus and trucking firms and the growing importance of the automobile, so the line was shut down at the end of 1947 after 58 years of service, and most of the track taken up. After much labor was expended restoring a section of the remaining track and some rolling stock, the Hawaiian Railway Society began to offer rides to the public in 1989. For additional information, see www.hawaiianrailway.com.

## 'Ewa Beaches

Unlike the small plantation-era town of 'Ewa with its renovated structures, skeleton mill, and orientation to the farm, 'Ewa Beach is a beach community and working-class town. Near the end of Fort Weaver Road is the small **'Ewa Beach County Park.** A broad, grassy area with a few coconut trees and restrooms fronts its narrow sand beach, from where you can see Honolulu and Diamond Head way off in the distance to the east. Although better swimming beaches are found elsewhere on the island, this is a good place to come if you want to have the beach to yourself—but it's a long way to come.

At the west end of Papipi Road is **One'ula Beach Park,** larger than 'Ewa Beach Park but farther off the main drag. There are some athletic fields and picnic tables here, and many young guys come to surf the mostly gentle waves along this shore. Farther to the west and reached by driving down Coral Sea Road through the old Barbers Point air base is the small and well-maintained **Nimitz Beach Park.**

# KAPOLEI
## Hawaiian Waters Adventure Park

Whether it's barreling down the four-story slide, bodysurfing at the wave pool, floating leisurely down the curvaceous and continuous "river" in an inner tube, or playing with the kids in the *keiki* pool, a day at Hawaiian Waters is good, clean fun in a safe environment, with appropriate activities for all ages. Opened in 1999 in Kapolei, this 25-acre water-theme park is the only one of its kind in Hawaii. Other amenities include a picnic area, bathrooms and changing rooms, lockers, a first-aid station, food concessions, gift shops, a musical performance stage, and plenty of free parking. Don't forget your hat and sunscreen. This is the sunniest side of the island! Hawaiian Waters, 400 Farrington Hwy., 808/674-9283, www.hawaiianwaters.com, is open 10:30 A.M.–5 P.M. through the summer and until 3:30 P.M. on weekdays and

4 P.M. on weekends the rest of the year, with periodic days off for maintenance. All-day admission runs $32.99 adults, $21.99 kids 4–11, with *kama'aina,* senior, and group rates for savings.

## Ko 'Olina Resort

Although it's still in the early stages of development, the 640-acre Ko 'Olina Resort is set up like other high-class resorts around the islands. Away from the hustle and bustle of the big city, it's a huge, manicured property of well-tended and landscaped lawns, tree-lined boulevards, the well-respected championship golf course, one luxury hotel (for now), several townhouse properties, and a timeshare accommodation. Here as well are the Paradise Cove Lu'au park, a marina and public boat launch with its store and deli, four perfectly shaped man-made lagoons for sunbathing and swimming, a seaside pathway, and public access parks—all with plenty of space for growth. Set between the Barbers Point Harbor and the bottom end of the Wai'anae Mountain Range, this resort has a very agreeable location—

This man-made lagoon at Ko 'Olina Resort is a great place for a tranquil swim.

it gets the most sun and the least rain of any section of the island. The only drawback, and this perhaps will be less obvious as the resort becomes more built up, is the specter of Campbell Industrial Park down the coast toward Barbers Point.

## JW Marriott Ihilani Resort and Spa

The courtiers anxiously waited for the grand night when the torches would be lighted and the drums beaten to announce the lovely princess as she was presented to the assembled *aliʻi*. Those closest to the young beauty were confident that their years of training had refined the grace and nobility that matched her dignified heritage. She had proven to be an enthusiastic and willing student, endearing herself to all because of her gaiety, sweetness, and loving heart. But to assume her rightful place with the most powerful in the land, she would have to gain the self-possessed assuredness that only comes from the wisdom of experience. It is much the same with the **JW Marriott Ihilani Resort and Spa,** 92-1001 Olani St., Kapolei, HI 96707, 808/679-0079 or 800/626-4446, fax 808/679-0080, www.ihilani.com.

The hotel, an alabaster specter floating amid the emerald-green acres of the Ko ʻOlina Resort, rises above a white-sand beach at the southern end of the Waiʻanae coast. It's about one-half hour west of the Honolulu airport—simply follow the H-1 expressway to the clearly marked Ko ʻOlina exit. You approach the resort by way of a cobblestone drive that winds its way up to a porte cochere, where valets and lei-bearing hostesses wait to greet you. The open breezeway leads to a towering glass-domed atrium brightened by cascading trellised flowers and ringed by living green ferns. Below, rivulets trickle through a series of free-form ponds, some like glass-reflecting sculptures, others alive and tinkling a natural refrain. The guest rooms, huge at almost 700 square feet, are pleasantly appointed in pastels and white, and all feature air-conditioning, ceiling fans, louvered doors, remote-control entertainment centers, in-room safes, mini-bars, and private lanai. Bathrooms, an intricate play of marble and tile, feature double sinks, separate commode and shower stalls, and deep oversize tubs. Evening brings turndown service. Golf-view rooms run $354, while oceanview and oceanfront rooms go for $434–595 per night; suites run $800–4,500. Many spa, golf, tennis, and honeymoon packages are also available, and these save a good deal on room rates.

Other amenities are 24-hour room service, concierge service, a small clutch of shop boutiques, a *keiki* beachcomber club, tennis courts, and a full-service spa. Free cultural activities are scheduled throughout the week, and there's evening entertainment at poolside. For the more adventurous, interactive explorations of the saltwater pools and the sharks, rays, fish, and other sea creatures that inhabit them are offered daily for $22.95 adults or $15.95 children, and a daily outrigger canoe ride gives guests a feel for the waves. For those who desire, a free shuttle offers rides to points within the resort, while another runs three times a day from the resort to Waikele Shopping Center for $10 and to Ala Moana Shopping Center for $20. The terrace is a perfect place to relax after a dip in the circular freshwater pool, but for a more athletic swim, try the gentle lagoon down below. With time and maturity, the Ihilani Resort and Spa, tucked away from the madding crowd, gives every indication of becoming one of Oʻahu's premier destinations. In fact, it has received the prestigious AAA five-diamond award for excellence in service and accommodations.

Dining at the Ihilani is a fantastic blending of East and West, relying heavily on locally grown herbs, vegetables, meats, and most important, island seafood. It is a blissful marriage built on Mediterranean, Oriental, and Hawaiian cuisine that can easily be influenced by ingredients from around the world. The Ihilani's signature restaurant, a AAA four-diamond award winner, is the dinner-only **Azul,** complemented by a magnificent wine cellar. Here the flavors of fish and seafood, mixed with the cuisines of the Mediterranean, are cooked to their finest over the wood-fired oven and grill. Select entrées might include roasted lobster for $41, seared tenderloin of beef for $32, or osso bucco alla Milanese for $31. Breakfast, lunch, and dinner of more contemporary Hawaiian cuisine and a Saturday night seafood buffet are served at the open-air **Nau-**

paka Terrace, with views of the pool and lagoon; and traditional Japanese fare, which includes Monday and Friday night buffets, is offered for dinner only at the Ushio Tei. Golfers and others who are into the casual setting overlooking the golf course's 18th hole and perimeter pond will enjoy clubhouse dining for lunch or afternoon cocktails at the Ko 'Olina Golf Club's Niblick Restaurant. (Niblick is a Scottish term for a nine iron.) For snacks during the day, try the Poolside Grill or Hokule'a Lounge. In additional to all these options, health-conscious breakfasts and lunch spa cuisine are also offered at the Ihilani Spa.

In a separate facility just a short walk across from the main entrance is the Ihilani Spa, a magnificently soothing, revitalizing, and uniquely Hawaiian spa experience. This facility is centered around Thalasso water therapy, a computer-controlled water-jet massage utilizing fresh seawater and seaweed. After being immersed in this state-of-the-art tub, you move on to the Vichy Shower, Grand Jet, or Needle Pavilion, where 12 shower heads poke stimulating sprays into every nook and cranny. Next, the superbly trained staff offers hands-on experiences in the form of therapeutic massage, including Swedish, *lomi lomi,* or shiatsu. You can also opt for a manicure, pedicure, or skin-rejuvenating facial. To keep trim and supple, head for the fitness facility on the third level, where you will find a lap pool, hot tub, aerobics room, and strengthening equipment.

The green velvet of the Ko 'Olina Championship Golf Course, designed by Ted Robinson and named as one of the finest courses in America by *Golf Digest,* fronts the hotel. Open since 1990, the course is fully matured and has already hosted prestigious tournaments. If you'd rather play tennis, day or evening, the resort's three hard and three artificial grass Kramer surface tennis courts await your pleasure on top of the hotel's parking structure. Court time can be arranged for $24 per hour, and instruction, round robins, and clinics are offered for extra fees.

## Barbers Point Beach County Park

This county park is at the end of Olai Road off Kalaeloa Boulevard. The point was named after Captain Henry Barber, who was shipwrecked here in 1795. Few people, even island residents, visit this beach park because the shoreline is rocky, it still hasn't fleshed out to become very pretty, and you have to get to it by driving through the Campbell Industrial Park. One pocket of white-sand beach is open to the public, although it fronts an adjacent residence. The swimming is safe only in summer but snorkeling is better, and you'll find picnic tables and rest-rooms.

## Practicalities

Aside from sundries, clothing racks, and a travel desk, the Ko Olina Marina Store and Deli offers a deli menu from 8 P.M.–4:30 P.M. Made for those with a light appetite and those on the go, some menu items are pastries, soups and salads, plate lunches, and sandwiches, with most items $6.50 or less.

Offering water activities along the leeward shore is Ko Olina Ocean Adventures, 808-396-2068, www.ocean-adventures.com. Running boats from the Ko 'Olina Marina, this company offers various scuba, snuba, and dolphin- or whale-watching excursions daily.

The new community of Kapolei and the older residential area of Makakilo lie just east of the Ko 'Olina Resort. Although only sparse services are available in Makakilo, in Kapolei you will find the Kapolei Shopping Center, the Marketplace at Kapolei, and other nearby shopping areas, perfect for those staying on this coast. Among the numerous shops are a Longs Drug store, a Temps Music, GNC Nutrition Center, Postal Plus for package service, plenty of boutiques, Safeway for food shopping, three banks all with ATM machines, three gas stations, and Loco Moco, Panda Express, Tasty Korean BBQ, and other fast-food eateries for inexpensive dining. A movie theater and post office are a short distance to the west on Kamokila Boulevard.

O'AHU

# The Leeward Coast

The Wai'anae (Mullet Waters) coast, the leeward face of O'ahu, is separated physically from the rest of the island by the Wai'anae Range. Spiritually, culturally, and economically, the separation is even more profound. This area is O'ahu's last stand for ethnic Hawaiians, and for that phenomenal cultural blending of people called *locals*. The idea of "us against them" permeates the consciousness of the area, but even so, native voices of moderation are raised. Guidebooks, government pamphlets, and word of mouth warn tourists against going to Wai'anae because "the natives are restless." If you follow this poor advice, you miss not only the last of undeveloped coastal O'ahu, but also the absolute pleasure of meeting people who will treat you with genuine *aloha*. Along the coast are magnificent beaches long known for their surf, condos and developments nestled in secure valleys, prime golfing, and one small community after another. Wai'anae is the home of small farms, run-down shacks, and families that hold *lu'au* on festive occasions, where the food and entertainment are the real article. Anyone lucky enough to be invited into this quickly disappearing world will be blessed with one of the last remaining authentic cultural experiences in Hawaii.

The possibility of hassles shouldn't be minimized because they do happen, but every aggressor needs a victim. The biggest problem is

coastal dunes at Ka'ena Point

Ka'ena Point

Pu'u Pueo
(768 ft.)

**KAENA POINT
STATE PARK**

Yokohama
Bay

MOKULE'IA
BEACH PARK

DILLINGHAM
AIRFIELD

Po'ohuna Point

Makua
Valley

**KANEANA
CAVE**

**THE
LEEWARD
COAST**

Ohikilolo
Beach

Kepuhi Beach
Kepuhi
Point

**KEA'AU BEACH
COUNTY PARK**

Makaha Valley

Makaha Stream

**MAKAHA BEACH
COUNTY PARK**

KILI DR.

★ **KANE'AKI HEIAU**

Makaha

● **MAKAHA RESORT AND GOLF CLUB**

MAKAHA VALLEY RD.
**WAI'ANAE REGIONAL PARK**

**MAUNA LAHILAHI
BEACH PARK**

WAI'ANAE

Wai'anae Harbor

**POKA'I BAY BEACH
COUNTY PARK**

Wai'anae

GATE

VALLEY RD.

**LUALUALEI BEACH
COUNTY PARK**

**MA'ILI BEACH
COUNTY PARK**

Ma'ili

**LUALUALEI
NAVAL
RESERVATION**

Lualualei

Maili Point

GATE

**ULEHAWA BEACH
COUNTY PARK**

Nanakuli

**NANAKULI BEACH
COUNTY PARK**

**TRACKS BEACH PARK**

**KAHE POINT BEACH
COUNTY PARK**

**HAWAIIAN WATERS
ADVENTURE PARK**

**KO'OLINA RESORT**

Makakilo

Barbers Point Harbor

Kapolei

KALAELOA
BLVD.

**BARBERS POINT BEACH
COUNTY PARK**

**BARBERS POINT
NAVAL AIR
STATION**

PACIFIC OCEAN

FARRINGTON HWY

930

To Hale'iwa

Wai'anae Range

To Honolulu

H1

90

93

0        2 mi
0        2 km

thievery, of the sneak-thief variety. You're marked as a tourist because of your new rental car. If you leave valuables in it, or lying unattended on the beach, they have a good chance of disappearing. But who does silly things like this *anywhere* in the United States? You won't be accosted, or held up at gunpoint, but if you bother a bunch of local guys drinking beer, you're asking for trouble. Moreover, the toughness of Wai'anae is self-perpetuating, and frankly some of the locals *like* the hard reputation. Some years back a feature writer reported that when he visited Wai'anae some toughs threw rocks at him. No one had ever reported this before, but after a big stink was made about it, more and more people had rocks thrown at them when they visited here.

In recent years *pakalolo* has had a tremendous effect on the area. Local guys began growing and smoking it. This brought some money back into the depressed region, and it changed the outlook of some of the residents. They felt a camaraderie with other counterculture people, many of whom happened to be *haole*. They could relax and not feel so threatened with pursuing an often elusive materialistic path. Many became more content with their laid-back lifestyle and genuinely less interested with the materialistic trip all the way around. Today, the most insidious problem is methamphetamine, which, along with other hard drugs, has compounded the social and economic burden of the community.

In truth, *we* shouldn't be warned about *them,* but vice versa. The people of Wai'anae are the ones being infringed upon, and it is they who, in the final analysis, will be hassled, ripped off, and ultimately dispossessed. A few rocks are poor weapons against developmental progress, which is defined by the big boys with the big dreams and the big bucks to back them up. Years ago, it was thought that this northeast coast would be the next large region of development, and indeed some was done. However, with the downturn in the Hawaiian economy throughout the 1990s and into the 2000s, less was accomplished than some had envisioned.

## Beaches and Sights

The Wai'anae coast is very accessible. One road takes you there. Simply follow the H-1 freeway from Honolulu until it joins the Farrington Highway (Route 93), which runs north, opening up the entire coast. A handful of side roads lead into residential areas, and that's about it! A strange recommendation, but sensible on this heavily trafficked road, is to drive north to the end of the line and then stop at the scenic sights on your way back south. This puts you on the ocean side of the highway, where you won't have to worry about cutting across traffic, which can be a steady stream, making it tough to navigate. TheBus no. 40 and express bus C run from Ala Moana Shopping Center up the Wai'anae coast to the north end of Makaha and stop at all the beaches on the way.

**Note:** Four of the beach parks along this coast offer **camping,** but their status periodically changes to no camping without notice. Many of the other campers are local people in semipermanent structures; the status changes quickly to prevent these people from squatting. Also, remember that this is the leeward coast, which gets plenty of sunshine. Many of the beach parks do not have shade trees, so be prepared. June is the prettiest month because all the flowers are in bloom, but it's one of the worst times for sunburn. The entire coast is great for snorkeling, with plenty of reef fish. However, keep your eyes on the swells, and always stay out of the water during rough seas, when waves can batter you against the rocks. The parks listed in this section run from south to north.

### Kahe Point Beach County Park and Tracks Beach Park

These parks are just where the Farrington Highway curves north along the coast. They're the first two *real* Wai'anae beaches, and they're symbolic. You come around the bend to be treated to an absolutely pristine view of the coast with the rolling sea, a white-sand beach, a cove, and the most hideous power plant you've ever seen. Facilities at Kahe Point Beach County Park are restrooms, a phone, a pavilion, and picnic tables.

The beach is poor except for a section just north of the improved park, and this is known as Electric Beach because it sits just opposite the power plant. Swimming is dangerous except on calm summer days. More often, you'll find people surfing and bodysurfing here, and some scuba companies bring guests here to enter the water.

A short way along is a mostly undeveloped area known as Tracks to island surfers because of the railroad tracks that run along the shore here. The white-sand beach is wide, and the swimming is generally safe. The mild waves are perfect for learning how to surf. If you keep your eyes trained out to sea, the area is beautiful. Don't look inland!

### Nanakuli Beach County Park

This park is on the southern outskirts of Nanakuli (Pretend to be Deaf) town, which is the first real town of the Wai'anae coast. The beach park is community-oriented, with recreational buildings, basketball courts, a baseball diamond, and children's play area. Camping is permitted with a county permit. Lifeguards work on a daily basis, and the swimming is generally safe except during periods of high winter surf. The southern section, called Piliokahe, is fronted by a cliff with a small cove below, and you'll often see fishermen casting off the cliff edge here. This cliff is lithified sandstone overlaying lava. During periods of calm surf, the waters are crystal clear and perfect for snorkeling. The northern end, called Kalaniana'ole, is generally calmer than the southern end. A pathway runs between these sections.

### Ulehawa Beach County Park

Just north of Nanakuli and running for a good long way along the coast, this park offers restrooms, picnic facilities, lifeguards, and sometimes camping. The best swimming is in a sandy pocket near the lifeguard tower at the south end. Surf conditions make for good bodysurfing. Most of the park, along a rocky cliff, is undeveloped, although the parking areas have been improved. Here you'll find unlimited fishing spots. A shallow lagoon is generally safe for swimming year-round. As always, it's best to check with the local people on the beach.

## Ma'ili Beach County Park

This park stretches along the length of Ma'ili (Pebbly) town. It lies between two streams coming down from the mountains. Amenities include restrooms, picnic facilities, and lifeguard towers, and the site is one of the best beaches along the coast. Camping is permitted with a county permit. The best swimming is in front of the lifeguard towers at the northern end. In wintertime the beach disappears, but it returns wide and sandy for the summer. Plenty of coral pockets offer good snorkeling. Don't just jump in. Ask the locals or swing by the lifeguard tower to make sure that it's safe.

## Lualualei Beach County Park

This beach lies in town and is generally decent for swimming in summer. Directly south of there and along the highway is a narrow strip of sand between the road and the water lying directly below Pu'u Ma'ili'ili, a fist of a hill that pushes nearly to the water. This park has restrooms, picnic facilities, and camping during summer. The entire park is largely undeveloped and lies along low cliffs and raised coral reef. Swimming is almost impossible. It's primarily good for fishing and looking.

## Poka'i Bay Beach County Park

This park is one of the nicest along the Wai'anae coast, just off the main drag in Wai'anae town. It provides restrooms, picnic facilities, lifeguards, and a boat ramp, which brings plenty of small craft into the area. Set on Kane'ilio Point is Kuiluiloa Heiau. Don't be surprised to see a replica of a double-hulled canoe. It's been used for publicity purposes and has appeared in a beer commercial. The park is clean, well maintained, reasonably secure, and family-oriented. There's surfing, sailboarding, snorkeling, and safe swimming year-round. If you're heading for one beach along Wai'anae, this is a top choice.

## Wai'anae Harbor

To get a look at a small working harbor or to hire a fishing boat, visit Wai'anae Boat Harbor, just across Poka'i Bay from Poka'i Park. Huge installed stones form an impressive man-made harbor, with everything from luxury yachts to aluminum fishing boats. Mahi Divers runs scuba

ROBERT NILSEN

One of the best places for a swim along the Wai'anae Coast is at Poka'i Bay Beach.

tours from here, and Dolphin Watch does (what else?) dolphin-watching tours along this coast.

## Makaha

Although Makaha can translate as "Water Breaking Out to Sea" because of the area's propensity for damming runoff waters from the mountains behind the beach until enough pressure forces it to "break out," there is another meaning for Makaha that doesn't help its image. The second translation, meaning "fierce," aptly describes a gang of bandits who long ago lived in the surrounding hills and terrorized the region. They would wait for small bands of people walking the road, then swoop down and relieve them of their earthly goods.

If you follow Kili Drive inland, you pass condos and high-rises clinging to the arid walls of this leeward valley. Turning right onto Huipu Drive, or alternately, driving up Makaha Valley Road from the highway, you reach an artificial oasis of green that is the Makaha Resort and Golf Club and Makaha Valley Country Club.

Continue up Mauanolu Street to visit the **Kaneʻaki Heiau**, a 17th-century temple restored under the direction of the Bishop Museum in 1970. This temple was dedicated to Lono, the benevolent god of harvest and fertility. The thatched huts used as prayer and meditation chambers, along with a spirit tower and carved images, have all been replicated. Because the *heiau* is within a private gated community, access is limited to Tues.–Sun. 10 A.M.–2 P.M. Stop at the guard house and let them know where you're heading. They will ask to see your identification and car registration or car rental agreement before they sign you in.

Once past Makaha, there are plenty of private places to pull off. This crab claw of land, which ends at Kaʻena Point, forms a lightly indented bay. The seascape demands attention, but look into the interior. The mountains seem naturally terraced as they form dry, deep valleys. All are micro-habitats, each different from the other.

## Makaha Beach County Park

This beach is famous for surfing, and as you approach, you can't help spotting a dominant headland called Lahilahi, which was a one-time island. Called "Black Rock" by the local fishermen, and used as a landmark, it still marks Makaha. Surfing competitions have been held here since the Makaha International Surfing Competition began in 1952. Years later, a local lifeguard named Richard "Buffalo" Keaulana, known to all who've come here, began the Annual Buffalo Big Board Riding Championship. Paul Strauch Jr., inventor of the "hang five," comes to Makaha whenever he has a chance, along with Buffalo's sons and other pro surfers, many of whom live in the area. In 1995, Buffalo retired after 36 years as a lifeguard. He has passed the torch on to his son Brian, who became captain of the whole east side. Along with protecting the beach and riding the waves, Brian has a budding acting career as a stunt man for Hollywood.

The swimming can be dangerous during high surf but excellent on calm days of summer. Winter brings some of the biggest surf in Hawaii. Always pay heed to the warnings of the lifeguards.

## Keaʻau Beach County Park

This park has restrooms, picnic facilities, and camping. The improved part of the park has a sandy beach, but mostly the park is fronted by coral and lava, and is frequented mostly by fishermen and campers. The unimproved section is not good for swimming, but it does attract a few surfers; it's good for snorkeling and scuba only during calm periods. The improved section is a flat, grassy area with picnic tables, a few shade trees, and pavilions. Farther on is Ohikilolo Ranch, a couple of homeless camps along the water, a few private homes, and more strands of solitary beach.

## Kaneana Cave

A few minutes south of Yokohama Bay on your right as you head up the coast is Kaneana Cave. You probably won't notice it on your way north because of the land formation that conceals the mouth in that direction, but it is obvious as you drive south. Legend has it that this cave was the home of Nanue the shark man. Unfortunately, people have come here with spray cans and beer bottles and trashed the cave. If you can overlook that, it's a phenomenon—a big one. Look for three yellow cement blocks, like road dividers, right in front of the entrance. It's at the foot of a 200-foot outcropping of stone. When you see local people defacing the natural beauty like this, it's hard to believe that the Hawaiians had such a spirit bond with the 'aina.

## Ka'ena Point State Park

Yokohama Bay is the end of the line; the pavement ends here at a long stretch of sandy beach. If you're headed for Ka'ena Point or beyond to the north coast, you'll have to walk through this windswept coastal park. The park is mostly unimproved except for a lava-rock bathhouse on the right just after the entrance. The area was named because of the multitude of Japanese fishermen who came to this lonely site to fish. It's still great for fishing! The swimming can be hazardous because of the strong wave action and rough bottom, but the snorkeling is superb and the sunbathing is tops. Lifeguards are on duty during summer. Mostly the area is used by surfers and local people, including youngsters who dive off the large lava rocks. This is inadvisable for people who are unfamiliar with the area. Yokohama is a great place to come if you're after a secluded beach. Weekdays, you'll have it to yourself, with a slightly greater number of people on the weekends. Definitely bring cold drinks, and remember that there are no shade trees whatsoever, so a hat or beach umbrella is a necessity. Many people camp here unofficially. You can still see cement railroad track abutments and embedded railroad ties, remnants of the sugar cane rail line that once ran around the point to the North Shore. A gigantic golf ball, really a U.S. satellite tracking station, caps the ridge above this park.

The hike out to the point or around to the end of the road on the north shore is hot and dry. There is no shade and no amenities. Bring plenty of water and a hat. The trail is level and easy to follow because it was the old railbed, but parts are rocky and may be muddy. In at least one spot the trail has been washed away, so you will have to scramble down into and out of a low gully. When the trade winds are blowing, this south side is protected from the wind, but once at the point you feel the trades. The point has been set aside as a nature preserve and is home to various shore nesting and breeding seabirds. Leave them alone and give them plenty of space.

# Practicalities

## ACCOMMODATIONS

### Makaha Resort and Golf Club

After several years of closure, then a major renovation and refurbishment, the old Sheraton Makaha Resort has reopened as the **Makaha Resort and Golf Club,** 84-626 Makaha Valley Rd., Waianae, HI 96792, 808/695-9544 or 866/576-6447, fax 808/695-7558, www.makaharesortgolfclub.com. This property has a wonderful location set back in the Makaha Valley, surrounded by the *pali,* and is accompanied by a great golf course. Its western orientation allows for perfect sunsets, which are common because this is the sunniest and driest part of the island. The location gives this resort seclusion, yet is close enough to reach the water by a short drive. From the reception building, which houses the registration desk, restaurant, lounge, and golf pro shop, detached buildings step down the gentle slope of the property. Somewhat dated by their design and style and sweeping Polynesian-style wood-shingle roofs—it was built in the 1960s—each of these buildings contains several rooms, and all of the buildings are connected by walkways. Because of the layout, you and your bags will be driven to your room by golf cart, but it's only a short walk to any point of property. The entire property has gone through a thorough renovation, and all rooms and public areas have been brought up to date. Rooms, with their pleasing island colors and decor, contain king or double beds, a full bath and private lanai, writing desk and chairs, coffee maker, television, and small refrigerator, and all are air-conditioned. To the oceanside of the large, inviting swimming pool, you have sweeping views of the mountains and coast.

Snacks are available throughout the day from the snack bar near the pro shop, and the Kaiona Restaurant offers sit-down service for three meals a day. Its short but adequate menu features a combination of reasonably priced appetizers and entrées. Breakfast items include omelettes, hot cakes, and loco moco; the lunch menu is easy-on-the-pocketbook salads, sandwiches, saimin, and hamburger steak; and dinner offers heartier meals like fried chicken, pot roast pork, spinach pasta, or kiawe-broiled baby back ribs, all for less than $20. Although not gourmet, these meals are filling and nutritious. Whether dining inside or out on the balcony, try to time your dinner meal for sunset. After dinner or a round of golf, stop for a cool drink at the Puamana Lounge, where there's live music on the weekends. Occasionally, concerts by well-known island musicians are scheduled at the restaurant or ballroom—a great opportunity to hear local talent.

Standard rooms run $109 per night, junior suites $170, and the handful of one-bedroom and two-bedroom suites are $225 and $450, respectively. Special golf/room packages are also offered. For its location and amenities, the Makaha Resort and Golf Club offers a great deal for a reasonable price.

## Condominiums

Except for camping, most inexpensive places to stay along the Wai'anae coast are in condos. Depending on the season, number of rooms, and property, rates generally fall into the $300–475 per week range for studios, $400–600 for one-bedroom units, and up to $850 for two bedrooms. Monthly rates are also available, and you usually get substantial savings for longer rentals. Most require a minimum stay of four or seven days. Some local people let rooms for a good rate, but there is no way to find this out in advance. Your best bet is to check out the bulletin boards at various stores along the coast.

The **Maili Cove,** 87-561 Farrington Hwy.

in Ma'ili, has one-bedroom apartments, a swimming pool, parking, and TV, along with a few hotel units. The least expensive accommodations are at the **Makaha Surfside,** 85-175 Farrington Hwy., just beyond the high school. The beach is rocky near the condo, but it makes up for this with two pools and a sauna. All units are individually owned and fully furnished.

Next up the way, at Lahilahi Point, are the **Makaha Beach Cabanas,** 84-965 Farrington Hwy. All units have a lanai overlooking the water. They're not fancy, but they are spotlessly clean and serviceable. All units are fully furnished with complete kitchens. Next door and a step up in quality and price is the **Hawaiian Princess,** 84-1021 Farrington Hwy. Farthest up the coast, the **Makaha Shores,** 84-265 Farrington Hwy., are privately owned units that overlook a beautiful white-sand beach and provide great viewing of the surfers challenging the waves below. All units are fully furnished.

**Makaha Valley Towers** rise dramatically from Makaha Valley, but they don't fit in. They're either a testament to man's achievement or ignorance, depending on your point of view. The condo provides fully furnished studio, one-, and two-bedroom units, a/c, TV, and pool. If you're staying in this high-rise, at least try to get a top floor, where you can take advantage of the remarkable view. Just below the Towers is the **Makaha Valley Plantation,** an aesthetic low-rise community with generally larger units that better fits the land.

For rental information on property along this coast, contact Inga's Realty, 808/695-9055, fax 808/695-8060; Sugar Kane Realty, 808/696-5833, fax 808/696-7573; Waianae Coast Realty, 808/696-6366, fax 808/696-6368; or Sun Estates, 808/696-6500, fax 808/696-5817. In addition, Don and Pat Maxwell have several units in three condos along the coast that rent for $55–75 for studios and one-bedrooms and $90–105 per night for a two-bedroom unit; weekly and monthly rates are also available and longer stays are preferred. Contact Don and Pat at 808/395-5960, maxwell@hawaiibeachcondos.com, www.hawaiibeachcondos.com.

# SHOPPING, FOOD, AND SERVICES

For your shopping and dining needs in Nanakuli, try the **Pacific Shopping Mall,** where you'll find Sack 'n Save Foods, the largest supermarket in the area for groceries, bakery, and a deli. In the complex is **Nanakuli Chop Suey Restaurant,** open 10 a.m.–8:30 P.M., serving standard Chinese fare at local down-home prices. Just behind McDonald's is the **Nanakuli Korean Bar-B-Que,** 808/668-2722, with sit-down and takeout Korean food at moderate prices; open 10 A.M.–9 P.M. daily.

The **Wai'anae Mall** is a complete shopping facility, the largest on the coast. Don't worry about bringing supplies or food if you're on a day excursion. The mall holds all you need, including Waianae Chop Suey, a few clothing and gift shops, Blockbuster Video, Longs Drugs, and Wai'anae Laundromat. Have no fear if you're addicted to fast food. Some major franchises have decided that your trip to leeward O'ahu wouldn't be complete without something processed in a Styrofoam box. Banking needs can be taken care of at the Bank of America or American Savings Bank branch offices.

For ethnic flavor, try the **Tamura Super Market,** which stocks plenty of ingredients used in ethnic foods. An **L&L Drive-In** and **Masago's Drive Inn** are here as well for plate lunch lovers. The post office sits just up the road from Tamura's, and you'll spot several gas stations in the middle of Wai'anae, along with a 7-Eleven convenience store.

Finding a two-scoop plate lunch is no problem. Little drive-in lunch counters are found in almost every Wai'anae town. Each serves hearty island food such as teriyaki chicken, pork, or mahimahi for under $6. A favorite is the **Makaha Drive-In** on Farrington Highway near the Makaha Valley Road intersection; open (at least) until 8 P.M. Near the drive-in is a 7-Eleven convenience store with an attached gas station, your last chance to fill your tank as you head up the coast.

## Arts and Crafts

The **Wai'anae Coast Culture and Arts Society** offers workshops in lei-making, *lau hala* weaving, hula, ceramics, and the Hawaiian language. The center welcomes people either to observe or participate in the programs, residents and visitors alike. The fee to participate is $3 per month plus the cost of supplies. For times and schedules, contact the Society at 808/668-1549.

# Southeast O'ahu

## Maunalua Bay to Makapu'u

It's amazing how quickly you can leave the frenzy of Waikiki behind. Once you round the bend past Diamond Head and continue traveling east toward Koko Head, the pace slackens measurably . . . almost by the yard. A minute ago you were in traffic, now you're cruising. It's not that this area is undeveloped; other parts of the island are much more laid-back, but none so close to the action of the city. In the 12 miles you travel from Honolulu to Waimanalo, you pass

the natural phenomenon of Koko Crater, a reliable blowhole, the most aquatically active marine preserve in the islands, and a string of beaches, each with a different personality.

Humanity has made its presence felt here, too. The area has some of the most exclusive homes on the island, as well as Hawaii Kai, a less exclusive project developed by the visionary businessman Henry Kaiser, who years ago created this harbinger of things to come. There's Sea Life

Local residents often rate Waimanalo Beach one of the best on the island.

ROBERT NILSEN

Park, offering a day's outing of fun for the family, plus shopping centers, the mostly Hawaiian town of Waimanalo, and the inactive Bellows Air Force Base, which now has one of the finest camping beaches on the island. This lack of development preserves the area as scenic and recreational, prized attributes that should be taken advantage of before this sunny sandbox gets paved over.

## SIGHTS, BEACHES, AND PARKS

The drive out this way accounts for half of the 360 degrees of what is called **The Circle Route.** Start by heading over the Pali Highway down to Kailua, hitting the sights on the way, or come this way first along Route 72 as you make the loop back to the city. The only consideration is what part of the day you'd rather stop at the southeast beaches for a dip. For the most part, the beaches of this area *are* the sights. The road abounds with scenic points and overlooks. This is the part of O'ahu that's absolutely beautiful in its undevelopment. It's hard to find a road on any of the Hawaiian Islands that's more scenic than this one. At first the countryside is dry because this is the leeward side, but as you approach Waimanalo it gets more tropical. The road is a serpentine ribbon with one coastal vista after another, a great choice for a joyride just to soak in the sights. The following listings assume that you follow Route 72 east from Waikiki to Waimanalo.

## Maunalua Bay

Maunalua (Two Mountain) Bay is a four-mile stretch of sun and surf between Diamond Head and Koko Head, with a beach park about every half mile. **Wailupe Beach County Park** lies on the Waikiki side of the residential Wailupe Peninsula, once a shoreline pond. This pocket-size beach park, clearly marked off the Kalaniana'ole Highway, provides restrooms and picnic facilities. Swimming is officially not recommended. Be careful of the

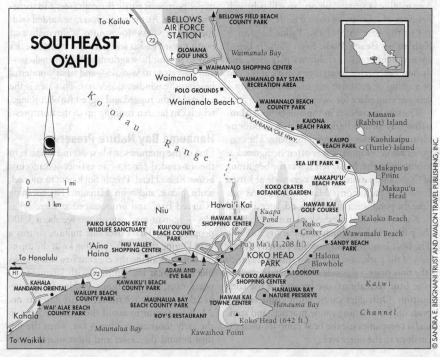

boat channel surrounding the area because the deep drop-off is abrupt.

After another fancy neighborhood is **Kawaikuʻi Beach County Park.** No lifeguard is present, but the conditions are safe year-round, and the bottom is shallow and overgrown with seaweed. In times past, islanders came to the confluence of a nearby spring to harvest special *limu* that grow only where fresh water meets the ocean. You'll find unlimited access, parking stalls, picnic facilities, and restrooms. Few people use the park, and it's ideal for sunning, but for frolicking in the water, give it a miss.

In quick succession come **Niu and Paiko Beaches,** lying along residential areas. Although there is public access, few people take advantage of them because the swimming, with a coral and sand bottom, is less than ideal. It's shallow and best at high tide when a kayak works well to scoot across the water. Some residents have built a pier at Niu Beach past the mudflats, but it's restricted to their private use. **Paiko Lagoon** is a state wildlife sanctuary; binoculars will help with sightings of a variety of coastal birds.

On the east side of the Paiko Lagoon is **Kuliʻouʻou Beach Park.** Even with its broad lawns, picnic tables, children's play area, and shallow beach, this "everyman's" park at the end of a string of exclusive neighborhoods is not a very enticing place for swimming.

The residential area in the hills behind **Maunalua Bay Beach Park** is Hawaii Kai, built by Henry Kaiser, the aluminum magnate. The controversial development was often denigrated as suburban blight. Many felt it was the beginning of Oʻahu's ruination. On the oceanside of Kuapa Pond, the park fronts Maunalua Bay. At one time the pond was a huge fishpond, later dredged by Kaiser, who used the dredged material to build the park, which he donated to the city in 1960. The boat launch constitutes the primary attraction of the park, and except for this boat launch (the only one on this side of the island), the area is of little recreational use because of the coral bottom. Outrigger canoe clubs come here to push off for morning canoe practice, and some scuba companies use the boat ramp for their excursions to the outer reef.

**Kokeʻe and Koko Kai Beach Parks,** two undeveloped parks, are along Poʻipu Drive in the wealthy Portlock area below Koko Head. The currents and beach conditions make both largely unsuitable for swimming, even though sand has recently been deposited there from dredging the channel to Kuapa Pond at Hawaii Kai marina, but they're popular with surfers. Few others come here, but the views of the bay are lovely.

## Mariner's Ridge Trail

Up above Hawaii Kai is a ridgetop subdivision called Mariner's Ridge. Turn onto Kaluanui Road just past the post office on the north side of Hawaii Kai Marina to get there. Follow the road all the way as it snakes up to the top. At the end of the road, park your car and head up the ridge trail. A steady uphill climb most of the way, this trail should take about 45 minutes and is the shortest route to the Koʻolau ridge. The bottom half is fairly open, with views over the entire residential area surrounding Maunalua Bay, but the upper portion is partly through trees and somewhat cooler. At the ridge, you're rewarded with spectacular views down onto Waimanalo and north toward Kailua and Kaneohe. From here, it's easy to see just how agricultural Waimanalo is—and how close to Waikiki—and what wonderful beaches the windward side has. This area is the tail end of the rugged and jagged Koʻolau Range, which can be seen running up to the northwest.

## Hanauma Bay Nature Preserve

One of the premier seaside spots in Hawaii is in the sea-eroded crater of an extinct volcano just below Koko Head. People flock here to snorkel, scuba, picnic, and swim. Hanauma Bay, meaning "Curved Bay" and pronounced as three syllables—"ha-nau-ma," gets on average about 3,300 people a day. That's over one million visitors a year! During the day, the parking lot at the top of the hill overlooking the crescent bay below looks like a used-car lot, jammed with Japanese imports, vans, and tour buses. Parking ($1 per vehicle) is severely restricted, so use TheBus no. 22. If you want to avoid the crowds, come in the early morning or after 4 P.M. when the sun dips behind the crater and most tourists leave

ROBERT NILSEN

**Hanauma Bay offers the premier snorkel site on O'ahu—not to mention a great day at the beach.**

O'AHU

on cue. There's still plenty of daylight, so plan your trip accordingly.

After years of overuse, this recreation area has gone through several improvements, including new facilities and an educational program. Hanauma Bay is open 6 A.M.–6 P.M. except for Tuesday when the bay is closed, and a $3 entrance fee is charged for nonresidents older than age 12 going down to the water. Before you actually head down the road to the beach, you are obliged to view a seven-minute-long video about the bay, its marine life, and how to best protect this fragile environment. A look at the Marine Education Center environmental display next door adds to your understanding of how the whole ecosystem works. A small food concession, gift shop, and restrooms are located near the ticket windows up top, and snorkel rentals, an information booth, showers, and additional restrooms are down at the beach. Lifeguards are on duty all day. Neither smoking nor alcohol consumption are allowed beyond the entrance center. From the top, you can walk down or take the trolley, $.50 down, $1 up, or $2 for all-day use; scuba tanks and other large items require an extra fee.

The reef protects the bay and sends a maze of coral fingers right up to the shoreline. A large sandy break in the reef, **Keyhole,** is a choice spot for entering the water and for swimming. The entire bay is alive with tropical fish. Many fish have become so accustomed to snorkelers that they've lost their fear entirely and come nibbling at your fingers for food. Before you enter the water, do yourself a favor and visit the information booth that describes conditions. It divides the bay into three areas, ranging from beginner to expert, and warns of sections to avoid. Be especially careful of **Witches Brew,** a turbulent area on the right at the mouth of the bay that can wash you into the Moloka'i Express, a notoriously dangerous rip current. Follow a path along the left-hand seacliff to **Toilet Bowl,** a natural pool that rises and falls with the tides. If the conditions are right, you can sit in it to float up and down in a phenomenon very similar to a flushing toilet.

**Note: Environmental Alert.** Because severe overuse has threatened the fragile ecosystem of the bay, tour companies are now banned from dropping people at the entrance expressly for snorkeling unless they have a commercial permit issued for that purpose. People wishing to explore the bay may come by rental car, moped, bicycle, or city bus, which has a stop just above the parking lot. Once the parking lot is filled, it is closed and drivers must wait until someone leaves! The bay is closed to all visitors on Tuesday when maintenance is performed. Also, please do not feed the fish. It's illegal to do so and carries a stiff fine. Let the fish feed naturally to maintain a better balance and prevent them from becoming food beggars. Most important, the reef is being destroyed by people walking on it. Please do everything you can to avoid this harm. Also, leave the sea turtles alone, and all rocks, shells, and coral as you find them. With care, Hanauma Bay will remain beautiful for all future generations.

**M**

**O'AHU**

## Koko Head

For a sweeping view, you used to be able to hike to the summit of **Koko Head,** not to be confused with Koko Crater farther east, but it's now off limits. The 642-foot summit of Koko (Blood) Head was the last place that young, wandering Madame Pele attempted to dig herself a fiery nest on O'ahu; as usual, she was flooded out by her jealous sister. The bowl of Hanauma Bay lies at the feet of Koko Head; below are two small extinct craters, Nono'ula and 'Ihi'ihilauakea.

## Halona Cove

As you round a bend on Route 72 past Hanauma Bay, you come to two scenic lookouts and the natural lookout of Halona Cove, which means "The Peering Place," an excellent vantage point from which to see whales in season. Just before Halona stands a monument and stone wall erected by the **Honolulu Japanese Casting Club.** Below on the rocks, men come to cast into the surf. The monument at one time was of O Jisan, the Japanese god of protection, but it was destroyed by overzealous patriots during World War II. The current monument was erected after the war, and O Jisan was carved into it. Below is a secluded little beach perfect for sunbathing. The only way to reach it is to scramble down the cliff. Swim only on calm days, or the waves can pull you out to sea and then suck you into the chamber of the famous **Halona Blowhole** just around the bend. There's a turnout at the blowhole for parking. The blowhole is a lava tube at the perfect height for the waves to be driven into it. The water compresses, and the pressure sends a spume into the air through a hole in its ceiling. Be extremely cautious around the blowhole. Those unfortunate enough to fall in face almost certain death.

## Sandy Beach Park

The fine white sand of Sandy Beach forms one of the best bodysurfing beaches on O'ahu, and the most rugged of them all. It's also a great surfing beach—for experts. More necks and backs are broken on this beach than on all the other O'ahu beaches combined. But because of the east-breaking waves, and bottom, the swells are absolutely perfect for bodysurfing. The lifeguards at the two towers use a flag system to inform you about conditions. The red flag means "stay out." When checking out Sandy Beach, don't be fooled by bodysurfers who make it appear easy. These are experts who are intimately familiar with the area, and even they are injured at times.

Local people refer to the beach as "Scene Beach" because this is where young people come to strut their stuff. This is where the boys are because this is where the girls are. There are restrooms, a large parking area, and two lifeguard towers. Rip-offs have happened, so don't leave valuables in your car. *Kaukau* wagons park in the area, selling refreshments. When wind conditions are right, you may see a whole parade of colorful exotic-shaped kites flying across the sky here. Some even come to practice flying kites to work on skills for kitesurfing.

As the road skirts the coastline, it passes a string of beaches that look inviting but are extremely dangerous because there is no protecting reef. The best known is **Wawamalu,** where people come to sunbathe only. Across the road is **Hawaii Kai Golf Course,** an excellent public course.

## Koko Crater

Koko Crater's Hawaiian name is Kohelepelepe (Vagina Labia Minora). Legend says that Pele's sister, Kapo, had a magical vagina that could fly and that she could send anywhere. Kamapua'a, the pig god, was intent on raping Pele when Kapo came to her aid. She dispatched her vagina to entice Kamapua'a, and he followed it to Koko Crater, where it made the crater and then flew away. Kamapua'a was unsuccessful when taking a flying leap at this elusive vagina.

The rim of Koko Crater rises to 1,208 feet. On the floor is the 60-acre **Koko Crater Botanical Garden,** 808/522-7060, which, because of the unique conditions, specializes in succulents, cacti, and other dry land plants from Hawaii, the Americas, Africa, and Madagascar. Opened in 1958, this garden is little developed and has but one trail and no other amenities. Admission is free. Open daily 9 A.M.–4 P.M., except Christmas and New Year's Day. Expect to spend 90 minutes on the two-mile circle path. To reach the gardens, follow Route 72 east to Wawamalu Beach just past Sandy Beach Park and then take a left on Kealahou Street. Turn left again at a sign that points to a riding stable and botanical garden, and follow the road to its end, where a walking path leads into the crater.

## Makapuʻu Point

The southeasternmost point of land on Oʻahu is Makapuʻu (Bulging Eye) Point. This headland overlooks Makapuʻu Beach Park and supports an important lighthouse. This lighthouse uses prism glass in its lamp and has been functioning for more than 100 years. Bunkers near the top were constructed during World War II and referred to by James Jones in his novel *From Here to Eternity.* They were manned during the war to protect the deep-water Makapuʻu Bay from possible Japanese attack. A moderate one-mile hike over an asphalt road leads to the top. Park along the highway and give yourself at least 90 minutes for the round-trip. It's dry and windy, so bring plenty of water and a hat to shade your eyes. During winter this is an excellent spot to watch for whales. Some energetic people bring a picnic lunch and hike down the sheer outer face of this promontory to a rocky tidepool area along the water to sunbathe and fish.

## Makapuʻu Beach Park

This beach park below Makapuʻu Point is a favorite launching pad for hang gliding. Makapuʻu is *the* most famous bodysurfing beach in the entire state and also used for surfing. It can be extremely rugged, however, and more people are rescued here than at any other beach on Oʻahu—except Sandy Beach. In winter the conditions are hazardous, with much of the beach eroded away, leaving exposed rocks. With no interfering reef, the surf can reach 12 feet—perfect for bodysurfing, if you're an expert. In summer, the sandy beach reappears, and the wave action is much gentler, allowing recreational swimming. There are restrooms, lifeguard towers with a flag warning system, and picnic facilities.

Offshore is **Manana (Rabbit) Island.** Curiously, it does resemble a rabbit, but it's so named because rabbits actually live on it. They were re-

leased there in the 1880s by a local rancher who wanted to raise them but who was aware that if they ever got loose on Oʻahu they could ruin much of the crop lands. During the impotent counterrevolution of 1894, designed to reinstate the Hawaiian monarchy, Manana Island was a cache for arms and ammunition buried on its windward side. Nearby, and closer into shore, is tiny Kaohikaipu Island, which, along with Manana and several other islands along this coast, is reserved as a seabird sanctuary. Efforts are being made by the National Audubon Society to attract albatross to this island from nearby Kaneohe Marine Corps Air Base. Establishing a colony here would keep these ground-nesting animals away from natural predators like mongooses, cats, and dogs.

## Sea Life Park Hawaii

Nestled below the lush Koʻolau Mountains inland of Makapuʻu Point is Sea Life Park Hawaii, 808/259-7933, www.sealifeparkhawaii.com. Within the park, a cluster of tanks hold an amazing display of marine animals that live freely in the ocean just a few hundred yards away. Admission is $24 adults, $12 children 4–12, under four free; open daily 9:30 A.M.–5 P.M. E Noa Tour's Ocean Coast Line shuttle bus runs roundtrip from major Waikiki hotels for $5 per person, or take TheBus no. 58 from Ala Moana Center or no. 22 from Waikiki past Hanauma Bay. For self-drivers, parking is $3 in the parking lot.

The park hosts a variety of shows throughout the day by trained sea lions, dolphins, and penguins and other activities with turtles and monk seals in the various pools and at the informative Hawaii Ocean Theater. The park's most impressive feature is the **Hawaiian Reef Tank,** a massive 300,000-gallon fish bowl where guests come face to face through walls of glass with more than 2,000 specimens of the island's rich marine life as they descend three fathoms down an exterior ramp. For a more in-depth and intense exposure to the training and care of dolphins, attend **Splash U,** a one-hour interactive dolphin training session where you're behind the scenes and right there with the trainers, or the more intensive **Dolphin Adventure.** Splash U costs $79 adults, $67 kids up to age 12; the Dolphin Adventure is $129 for adults only. The **Sea Trek** program lets guests actually enter the big tank in wet suits and a diver's helmet to meet the fish mask to mouth; $89 for age 12 and up. The newest interactive feature is the **Hawaiian Ray Encounter,** where you enter the stingray tank to float among those graceful creatures; $39 adults or $27 children. All of these prices include regular admission to the park. The popular sessions are held several times a day, and reservations must be made well in advance.

A full menu of island food is available at the Sea Lion Cafe for when you've worked up an appetite. Before you leave, pick up a souvenir at one of the gift shops and have a look at the collections of whaling artifacts in the front building. Sea Life Park Hawaii is a great learning and entertaining experience for the entire family or for anyone interested in exploring Hawaii's fascinating marine life.

## ACCOMMODATIONS

You're limited when it comes to accommodations in this area. Only a few B&Bs and rental homes are available. One is **Adam and Eve Bed and Breakfast,** which offers spacious rooms in a waterfront Paiko home, a few steps from the Paiko Lagoon Wildlife Sanctuary. Of mission-style, with stucco and red tile roof, this beach home is open and breezy with a great view out the back over the shallow water inside the reef of Maunalua Bay. The spacious downstairs common room or back patio and yard provide a perfect spot for sunsets. Renting for $160 per night, the master suite and its private deck occupy one side of the upstairs. An open-beam, wood-floor affair, the bedroom has a four-poster bamboo bed under a ceiling fan with a rattan couch and cushy pillows. The gigantic tile bathroom around the corner comes with a large walk-in closet, double-sink vanity, a separate commode room, shower stall, and huge spa tub. Sharing a bathroom, two smaller guest rooms are housed on the far side of the central stairway and together can accommodate up to four people if both rooms are used. They run $120 for one room or $200 for both. A continental

breakfast of fruits, yogurt, coffee, and tea is served each morning. A small swimming pool and spa occupy the front courtyard. This B&B makes a fine home away from home in a comfortable setting. For information, contact Jubal Jones or Rika at 226 Paiko Drive, Honolulu, HI 96821, 808/395-6068, fax 808/395-6069, jonesj004@hawaii.rr.com, www.adamandeveplanet.com. In addition, this couple can work with you if you are looking for property to buy on O'ahu, particularly in East Honolulu.

## FOOD AND SHOPPING

One of the first places to pick up supplies as you head east on Route 72 is the Times Super Market in the **Niu Valley Shopping Center,** about halfway between Diamond Head and Koko Head. Aside from foodstuffs, you can also get your prescription filled here, pick out flowers for your sweetie, or grab a sandwich for your trip down the highway. In the shopping center is **The Swiss Inn,** 808/377-5447, an authentic Swiss restaurant where the owner/chef pours love and attention into every dish. The food, like veal medallion Florentino, wienerschnitzel, and baked chicken, is superb, well prepared, and reasonably priced for the quality at mostly $18–22. Dinner is served from 6 P.M. and Sunday brunch 10:30 A.M.–1 P.M. If heavy Germanic food isn't what you're after, perhaps you can try Lung Fung Chinese or Castagnola's Italian. Castagnola's uses only fresh ingredients from the islands and pasta and tomatoes from the Abruzzi region of Italy for natural, flavorful, and wholesome foods cooked to order. Newest is **Le Bistro,** 808/373-7990, a small neighborhood restaurant owned by a local boy that's getting rave reviews from patrons. A mixture of Continental cuisine with a dash of the East, Le Bistro serves such items as coq au vin, pasta, and steak. Small and intimate with midrange pricing. Open 5:30–9 nightly except Tuesday.

A little less ideal for location and a bit closer to Diamond Head, the **Aina Haina Shopping Center** still has many restaurants, a Foodland Supermarket, two banks, a branch post office, and a gas station. Enter from West Hind Drive.

## Hawaii Kai Shopping

On the west side of Kuapa Pond are two shopping malls. Try **Hawaii Kai Towne Center** for Payless Shoes, General Nutrition Center, Costco, or more than a dozen other shops. Safeway, Longs Drugs, Aloha Dive Shop, and numerous other stores and restaurants are in the neighboring **Hawaii Kai Shopping Center** just up the road.

The **Aloha Dive Shop,** 808/395-5922, is a full-service dive shop. You can rent or buy snorkeling and scuba gear. So, if you haven't picked up rentals from Waikiki and you're heading out to Hanauma Bay, come here. Two-tank, two-location dives run $95 for beginners and feature all-boat diving at Maunalua Bay, Koko Head, and/or Diamond Head. Pickup in Waikiki is about 8:30 A.M. and return is 1:30–2 P.M. Three-day, open-water certification courses are given for $398; advanced and search-and-rescue courses are also taught. This is the shop of Jackie James, first lady of Hawaiian diving. She's been diving here for more than 30 years.

**Note:** For Hawaii Kai's outstanding gourmet option, Roy's Restaurant, see the Waikiki chapter.

## Koko Marina Shopping Center

Along the highway in Hawaii Kai, this center is the largest and easiest-access shopping center that you'll find on the way to Hanauma Bay. There are three banks, several gift shops, Local Motion and other shops for beachwear, and Koko Marina 8 Theaters. Foodland provides most supplies for picnics and camping, and you can dine at Bua Khao Thai, Kozo Sushi, Zippy's for plate lunches and burgers, Bubbies Ice Cream, or Assaggio's Ristorante Italiano, the best of the bunch.

The Japanese own the Koko Marina Center. In the center are water sport and thrill-ride booking agencies that will take non-Japanese tourists, but they are more for the Japanese tourists who come here by the busload and immediately head out on one of these thrill rides. They've already booked from Japan, so it's all set up and off they go.

**Hawaii Sports,** 808/395-3773, offers nearly a dozen water sports to choose from, like a 20-minute banana boat ride for $25 per person, 30-minute personal watercraft use for $39, parasail ride for $49 (10 minutes in the air), wakeboarding or water-skiing for $39 for a 15-minute pull, two-person glass-bottom boat ride for $49, and an introductory scuba dive for $49.

Several other water sports companies offer the same activities at roughly the same prices, while a few also have speed and sailboat rides or transportation to Hanauma Bay for a day of snorkeling. Other companies that also have shops at this center are **Sea Breeze Watersports,** 808/396-0100; **H.O.T. Hawaii Ocean Tours and Adventures,** 808/395-6133; and **South Pacific Hawaii,** 808/395-7474. Keep in mind that personal watercraft rentals are not allowed on weekends and holidays, so make your plans for some other day. Generally, self-powered watercraft, parasail, and scuba happens from a floating dock out in Maunalua Bay, while activities pulled by a boat take place inside the marina.

For those intending to head to Hanauma Bay to snorkel but don't care to deal with the traffic or parking, **Hanauma Bay Snorkel Adventure,** 808/396-9199, offers snorkel gear rental for $5, other beach gear rental at various rates, transportation to the bay from their office in the Koko Marina Shopping Center for $10 per person, and even transportation from your hotel in Waikiki for $15. The $3 entrance fee into Hanauma Bay is your responsibility.

O'AHU

# Waimanalo

This small rural town was at one time the center of a thriving sugar plantation owned by the *hapa* Hawaiian nobleman, John Cummins, who was responsible for introducing rabbits to Manana Island. It has fallen on hard times ever since the plantation closed in the late 1940s, and now it produces much of Honolulu's bananas, papayas, and anthuriums from small plots and farms, and a great deal of organic greens that end up on the plates of many fine restaurants on the island. The town sits in the center of Waimanalo Bay, which has the longest (three miles) stretch of sand beach on O'ahu, and to many people, especially those from O'ahu, it is also the best. The backdrop for this rather ordinary town is a finely sculpted *pali* that rises precipitously into a variegated curtain of green—and it's close. Few but adequate travelers' services are in town.

The Olomana Golf Links, a relatively easy public course, is close to town. It's also a good

ROBERT NILSEN

**Waimanalo as seen from the ridge of the Ko'olau Range.**

place to go for breakfast. You think you're in Waimanalo when you pass the first built-up area, but that isn't it. You keep going about a mile or two and then you'll come to the older section of town, which is Waimanalo proper.

For those who enjoy the sport of kings, polo matches are held at about 2:30 P.M. on Sundays from April (or May) to October at the polo field in Waimanalo across from Waimanalo Bay State Recreation Area. Matches usually last 90 minutes; $3 adults, kids are free.

## BEACHES AND PARKS

### Kaupo Beach Park

Between Sea Life Park and Waimanalo, this is the first park along the coast that's safe for swimming. The park is undeveloped and has no lifeguards, so you are advised to exercise caution. The shore is lined with a protective reef and rocks, and the swimming is best beyond the reef. Close to shore, the jutting rocks discourage most swimmers. Surfers frequent Kaupo, especially beginners, lured by the ideal yet gentle waves. At the southern end of this park is Makai Research Pier. Part of this pier is open to the public, but the rest is closed for use by government ocean research organizations. Many locals come to fish off the pier or spearfish along the coast. Some companies run scuba tours to the reef offshore.

### Kaiona Beach Park

Just before you enter the ethnically Hawaiian town of Waimanalo, you pass Kaiona Beach Park. Local people are fond of the area and use it extensively. Look inland to view some remarkable cliffs and mountains that tumble to the sea. The area was once called Pahonu, "Turtle Enclosure," because a local chief who loved turtle meat erected a large enclosure in the sea into which any turtle that was caught by local fishermen had to be deposited. Parts of the pond perimeter wall can still be seen at low tide. Facilities include restrooms, showers, and a picnic area. Swimming is safe year-round.

## Waimanalo Beach County Park

The fine powder sand of Waimanalo beaches stretches virtually uninterrupted from Sea Life Park, past the town of Waimanalo, and through Bellows Air Force Base to Wailea Point. At the south end of town, Waimanalo Beach County Park provides camping with a county permit. The beach is well protected, and the swimming is safe year-round. Snorkeling is good, and there are picnic tables, restrooms, and recreational facilities, including a ball park, basketball courts, and children's play equipment. The park is right in the built-up beach area and not secluded from the road. Although the facilities are good, the setting could be better.

## Waimanalo Bay State Recreation Area

Just up the road is Waimanalo Bay State Recreation Area. This park is good for picnicking and swimming, which can sometimes be rough. The area, surrounded by a dense ironwood grove, is called "Sherwood Forest" or "Sherwoods," because of many rip-offs by thieves who fancy themselves as Robin Hood, plundering the rich and keeping the loot for themselves. Guess who the rich guys are? Fortunately, this problem of breaking into cars is diminishing, but take necessary precautions. This is the best beach on this section of the island.

## Bellows Field Beach County Park

Part of this one-time active air force base, now used only as a rest and recreational facility, is now one of O'ahu's finest beach parks, and there's camping too! The water is safe for swimming year-round, and lifeguards are on duty on the weekends. Bodysurfing and board surfing are also excellent in the park, but snorkeling is mediocre. After entering the main gates, follow the road for about two miles to the beach area. You'll find picnic tables, restrooms, and cold-water showers. The combination of shade trees and adjacent beach make a perfect camping area that's often full. The park is marked by two freshwater streams, Waimanalo and Puha, at either end. Because of military exercises and security issues, this park may only be open on the weekends.

## FOOD AND SHOPPING

As you enter Waimanalo, look on the right for **Keneke's** plate lunch place, next to the post office. A local eatery, Keneke's offers plate lunches with a huge list of options for $3.50–6, burgers, sandwiches, shave ice, and smoothies. It's a great place to fill up for an afternoon on the beach, and the crowd at the window tells you what a good reputation it has. Nearby in what looks like an old gas station building is a small "no-name" market for sundries and snacks. A short "mile" past Keneke's is **Mel's Market,** where you can pick up almost all supplies, and you definitely have a better selection. A gift gallery is next door. Keep going along the Kalaniana'ole Highway for a mile or so to find **Waimanalo Shopping Center** in the middle of town. Here you can do all your business, pick up lunch and supplies, and head on down the road or go to the beach. In the shopping center are **Hawaii's Hidden Treasures** for jewelry, gifts, and souvenirs; **Sumo Connection Hawaii,** where wrestler Akebono's mother presides over sumo memorabilia and aloha shirts; and the well-managed **Waimanalo Laundry.** For food, try **Maria Bonita's Restaurant** for quick Mexican eats at $6.50 or less; **KimoZ Restaurant and Karaoke,** which has some of the best food and drink around in a clean family setting but which turns into a sports bar after 3 P.M.; or **Dave's Hawaiian Ice Cream,** open seven days a week 9 A.M.–9:30 P.M. Across the road and down a bit is **Shima's Market,** a small but full-service food and sundries outlet.

# Windward O'ahu

O'ahu's windward coast never has to turn a shoulder into a harsh and biting wind. The trades do blow, mightily at times, but always tropical warm, perfumed with flowers, balmy and bright. Honolulu is just 12 miles over the hump of the *pali,* but a world apart. When *kama'aina* families talk of going to "the cottage in the country," they're most likely referring to the windward coast. In the southern parts, the suburban towns of **Kailua** and **Kane'ohe** are modern in every way, with the lion's share of the services on this side. With populations of more than 35,000 each, these two towns together make the second most densely populated area on the island. Kailua has O'ahu's best sailboarding beach and a nearby *heiau,* preserved and unvisited, while Kane'ohe sits on a huge bay dotted with islands and fringed by a reef. The Kahekili Highway runs inland to the base of the *pali,* passing the **Valley of the Temples,** resplendent with universal houses of worship. At **Kahalu'u** starts a string of beaches running north, offering the full range of O'ahu's coastal outdoor experience. You can meander side roads into the mountains near the Hawaiian villages of **Waiahole** and **Waikane,** where the normal way

Ho'omaluhia Botanical Garden

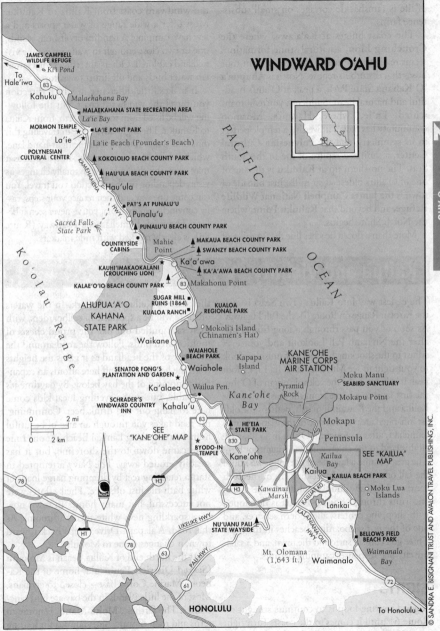

# WINDWARD O'AHU

JAMES CAMPBELL
WILDLIFE REFUGE
Kiʻi Pond

To
Haleʻiwa

83

Kahuku

Malaekahana Bay

MALAEKAHANA STATE RECREATION AREA
Laʻie Bay

MORMON TEMPLE
LAʻIE POINT PARK

Laʻie

Laʻie Beach (Pounder's Beach)

POLYNESIAN
CULTURAL CENTER

KOKOLOLIO BEACH COUNTY PARK

HAUʻULA BEACH COUNTY PARK

Hauʻula

PAT'S AT PUNALUʻU

Punaluʻu

Sacred Falls
State Park

PUNALUʻU BEACH COUNTY PARK

COUNTRYSIDE
CABINS

Mahie
Point

MAKAUA BEACH COUNTY PARK

SWANZY BEACH COUNTY PARK

Kaʻaʻawa

KAUHIʻIMAKAOKALANI
(CROUCHING LION)

KAʻAʻAWA BEACH COUNTY PARK

KALAEʻOʻIO BEACH COUNTY PARK

83  Makahonu Point

SUGAR MILL
RUINS (1864)

KUALOA
REGIONAL PARK

KUALOA RANCH

AHUPUAʻAʻO
KAHANA
STATE PARK

Mokoliʻi Island
(Chinamen's Hat)

Waikane

WAIAHOLE
BEACH PARK

Kapapa
Island

KANEʻOHE
MARINE CORPS
AIR STATION

SENATOR FONG'S
PLANTATION AND GARDEN

Waiahole

Moku Manu
SEABIRD SANCTUARY

Kaʻalaea  Wailua Pen.

SCHRADER'S
WINDWARD COUNTRY
INN

Kahaluʻu

Kaneʻohe
Bay

Pyramid
Rock

Mokapu Point

Mokapu
Peninsula

0        2 mi

0      2 km

SEE
"KANEʻOHE"
MAP

83

HEʻEIA
STATE PARK

830

BYODO-IN
TEMPLE

Kaneʻohe

Mokapu

Kailua
Bay

SEE "KAILUA"
MAP

H3

H3

Kawainui
Marsh

Kailua

KAILUA BEACH PARK

Moku Lua
Islands

78

MOON

Lanikai

78

H1

LIKELIKE HWY

NUʻUANU PALI
STATE WAYSIDE

63

PALI HWY

Mt. Olomana
(1,643 ft.)

Waimanalo

BELLOWS FIELD
BEACH PARK

Waimanalo
Bay

61

HONOLULU

To Honolulu

72

PACIFIC

OCEAN

Koʻolau Range

KAMEHAMEHA HWY

KALANIANAʻOLE HWY

KAILUA RD

OʻAHU

of life is ramshackle cottages on small subsistence farms.

The coast bulges at **Kaʻaʻawa**, where the **Crouching Lion**, a natural stone formation, seems ready to pounce on the ever-present tour buses that disturb its repose. North is **Ahupuaʻa ʻO Kahana State Park**, a peak at Oʻahu's beautiful and natural heart. Suddenly, you're in manicured **Laʻie**, where Hawaii's Mormon community has built a university, a temple perfect in its symmetry, and the **Polynesian Cultural Center**, a sanitized replica of life in the South Seas. The northern tip at **Kahuku** is the site of one of Oʻahu's oldest sugar mills. Just outside of town is the **James Campbell National Wildlife Refuge**, and beyond that **Kahuku Point**, where the North Shore begins.

More than a dozen beaches line the 24 miles of the windward coast from Kailua to Kahuku. Most offer a wide range of water sports and a few have camping. A handful of offshore islands, one or two close enough to wade to, can be visited and explored. Others are refuges for Hawaiian water birds and off limits to visitors.

It makes little difference in which direction you travel the windward coast, but the following will be listed from south to north, from Kailua to Kahuku. The slight advantage in traveling this direction is that your car is in the right-hand lane, which is better for coastal views. But, as odd as it may seem, this dynamic stretch totally changes its vistas depending on the direction you travel. You can come one way and then retrace your steps, easily convincing yourself that you've never seen it before. The road, Kamehameha Highway (Route 83), is clearly marked with mile markers.

## Kailua and Vicinity

The easiest way into Kailua (Two Seas) is over the Koʻolau Range on Route 61, the Pali Highway. As soon as you pass through a long tunnel just after the Nuʻuanu Pali Lookout and your eyes adjust to the shocking brilliance of sunshine, look to your right to see Mt. Olomana. Its 1,643-foot peak is believed to be the volcanic origin of Oʻahu, the first land to emerge from the seas. Below lies Kailua and the Kawainui marsh, perhaps the oldest inhabited area on this side of the island. Kamehameha I, after conquering Oʻahu in 1795, gave all this land to the chiefs who had fought for him. The area became a favorite of the ruling *aliʻi* until the fall of the monarchy at the turn of the 20th century. The Kawainui Canal drains the marsh and runs through Kailua. Kailua is developed with shopping centers, all modern services, and one of the *best* sailboarding beaches in the state. Three golf courses surround the town, and a satellite city hall dispenses camping permits.

## SIGHTS

A good touring loop is to continue straight on Route 61 until it comes to the coast. Turn right onto Kalaheo Avenue, which takes you along the coast to Kailua Beach Park. In the waters offshore will be a spectacle of sailboarders, with their sails puffed out like the proud chests of multicolored birds. Follow the road around the shoulder of the headland as it gains the heights from the beach; a pull-off here affords an expansive panorama of the bay below. By daytime it's enjoyable, but in the evening local kids come here to hang out and drink beer. Continuing, the road takes you through an area of beautiful homes strung along Lanikai Beach. At one time trees came down to the shoreline, but it has steadily eroded away. The Navy attempted to start a retaining reef by dumping barge loads of white bath tile just offshore. Their efforts were not successful, but many homes in town now have sparkling new, white-tiled bathrooms! As this road, Aʻalapapa Drive, loops back toward town, it changes name to Mokulua.

At the north end of Kailua Beach is **Mokapu (Sacred District) Peninsula**, home of the Kaneohe Marine Corps Base—closed to civilians. Most of the little islands in the bay are bird sanctuaries. The farthest, **Moku Manu**, is home to terns and man-oʻ-wars, birds famous for leading fishermen to schools of fish.

## Ulupo Heiau State Monument

Ulupo (Night Inspiration) is dedicated to the Ulu line of *ali'i*, who were responsible for setting up *heiau* involving the sacred births of chiefs. The umbilical cord was often cut just as a drum was sounded, and then the cord *(piko)* was placed in a shallow rock depression at a *heiau*. This temple, supposedly built by the legendary *menehune*, who usually accomplished their task within the span of one night, shows remarkable stone craftsmanship, measuring 140 feet wide and 30 feet high, although the stepped front wall has partially collapsed by rock fall. Atop the temple is

a pathway that you can follow. Notice small stones wrapped in *ti* leaves placed as offerings. The *heiau* overlooks Kawainui marsh, once a huge inland lagoon that provided great quantities of fish for the population. It is estimated that about 6,000 years ago, this marsh was a bay of the ocean. Because of the forces of nature, by 1,000 years ago it had turned into a lagoon. Its size continued to shrink, and by 200 years ago it was a much smaller fishpond, perhaps 400 acres in size. Only in the 20th century did it become a marsh, as a result of natural changes and human intervention, and today it's home to many en-

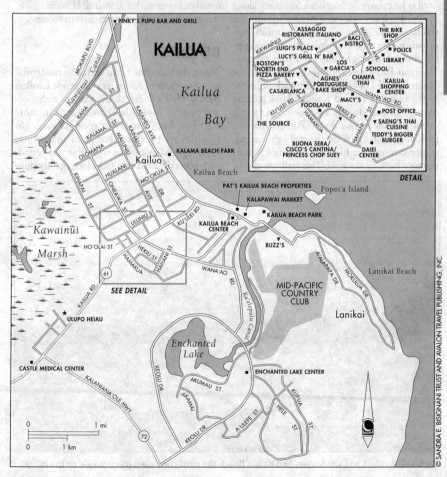

dangered water birds. A second former fishpond to the southeast called Kaʻelepulu Pond, similar but smaller, is now better known as Enchanted Lake. To get to Ulupo Heiau as you approach Kailua on Route 61, look for a red light and a 7-Eleven store. Turn left onto Uluoa Street, following it one block to Manu Aloha Street, where you turn right. Turn right again onto Manu Oʻo and park in the Windward YMCA parking lot. The *heiau* is directly behind the YMCA building.

### Maunawili Demonstration Trail

This is one of Oʻahu's newest trails. The trailhead is just above St. Stephen's Seminary along the Pali Highway, but you can't turn left into the trailhead parking lot when going uphill. Approach it from the Honolulu side or head uphill through the *pali* tunnel and turn off onto Nuʻuanu Pali Drive. Follow this up past the Nuʻuanu Pali Lookout and get back onto the highway going toward Kailua. After passing through the tunnel again, a sign points to a scenic overlook a short ways down. Pull off into the parking area and look for the trail sign and entrance through the highway guardrail a short distance back up the road. This trail can also be accessed by walking down the Old Pali Road from the Nuʻuanu Lookout. The beauty of this trail is that it is reasonably flat with little elevation gain or loss as it winds its way along the windward side of the Koʻolau Range. The whine of the Pali Highway abates almost immediately and you are suddenly in a brilliant highland tropical forest. You can continue to the end (upper Waimanalo, about three hours one-way) for a full day's hike, or just find a secluded spot after a mile or so for a picnic. The views are spectacular, and vantage points display the coast all the way from Rabbit Island to Chinaman's Hat. Remember, however, that as with all Hawaiian trails, recent rainfall makes for treacherous footing.

## BEACHES

Along the shoreline of an exclusive residential area, just south of Kailua, sits the gentle **Lanikai Beach.** Half a dozen clearly marked rights-of-way run off Mokulua Drive, the main thoroughfare, but there is not good parking. No facilities are provided, but good snorkeling, kayaking, and swimming is possible year-round, with generally mild surf and a long, gently slop-

Both sailboarders and kite surfers find Kailua Beach the most consistent place to ride on the island.

ing, sandy beach. The beach runs south for almost a mile, broken by seawalls designed to hold back erosion. Many outrigger canoes use the sandy-bottomed shore to launch and land. Popular with local people, but not visited much by tourists, this beach is consistently rated as one of the best in the state.

**Kailua Beach** is the main beach in the area and is often regarded as the best overall beach on the island. Of wide, soft, powdery sand, it runs for nearly two miles along the front of town, with the Kailua Beach Park at its southern end. Great for family outings, with safe conditions and fine facilities, this beach has become a hot sailboarding spot, and more recently kiteboarders have found it a great place for this new sport. The wind conditions attract a daily flotilla of sailboarders and kiteboarders, but they must stay beyond marked buoys that delineate the swimming area at the center of the park. Windsurfers and kiteboarders must launch their gear only from the left side of the swimming area. The park boasts a pavilion, picnic facilities, restrooms, showers, lifeguards, a boat ramp at its south end, and sometimes a food concession (they come and go). The surf is gentle year-round, and the swimming safe. Children should be careful of the sudden drop-offs in the channels formed by the Ka'elepulu Canal as it enters the sea in the middle of the beach park. Good surfing and diving are found around Popoi'a Island just offshore.

**Kalama Beach Park** is reached by making a left at the T-intersection onto North Kalaheo. Wedged between large beachfront lots and stylish houses, this small park has only parking and restroom facilities but allows access to the central stretch of Kailua Beach and is less frequented than Kailua Beach Park. At the far north end of Kailua Beach, a reef break makes better wave action for body boarders than any other place in the bay.

## ACCOMMODATIONS

Most options here are cottages, rental homes, and bed-and-breakfasts.

If looking for a rental house in Kailua, start by contacting **Pat's Kailua Beach Properties,** 204 South Kalaheo Ave., Kailua, HI 96734, 808/261-

1653, fax 808/261-0893, pats.kailua@verizon.net, www.patskailua.com. Pat's has more than 30 separate units in Kailua (and three in Waimanalo), ranging in price from $70–500 per night; monthly rates are also available, and some properties can only be rented by the month. Stays of a week or longer are appreciated, although shorter stays are accepted when they fit between other reservations. All units are fully furnished, and most are within two blocks of the water. The options are many, and Pat's has something for everyone from a young couple out for a week of water activities looking for an inexpensive vacation, all the way to a large family needing a five-bedroom luxury beachside home for a family reunion. This company can find the right place to meet your needs.

One of the finest guest homes in Kailua is **Sharon's Kailua Serenity,** 808/262-5621 or 800/914-2271, sharon@sharonsserenity.com, www.sharonsserenity.com. This beautiful property sits on a quiet side street. Sharon goes out of her way to make you feel comfortable and welcome. The coffee is always fresh-perked. Sharon also takes the time to sit with you, giving advice on where to dine, what to see, and a candid description of activities that are worthwhile. The meticulously clean, beautifully appointed home features guest rooms with color TV and refrigerator, Mexican tile throughout, a spacious family room, swimming pool, lanai, and views of the Ka'elepulu Canal, golf course, and hills beyond. The Blue Room has a queen bed and its own attached private bath. Opening onto the pool, the Poolside Room has both a king bed and a twin. The suite could easily accommodate a small family, with a queen-size bed and a twin bed set up like a daybed. It features in-room sliding doors for privacy and its own bath just across the hall. Rates are $70–85 per night, and the price includes a continental breakfast, which Sharon will have waiting in the morning. Sharon's Serenity is an excellent choice for the windward coast, perfect for getting away from it all.

Located one block from the beach, **Savannah's Cabana** is a one-bedroom detached cottage that's great for a vacationing couple. Cool and comfortable, this newly built hideaway has all modern amenities and comes with cable color TV, an efficiency cooking area, a washer and dryer, and some beach gear to borrow. Rent is $100 per night with a $75 cleaning fee upon checkout, and three nights' minimum stay is required; no credit cards please. For more information and reservations, contact the owners at 808/261-6848.

**Pacific Hawaii Reservations** and **Affordable Paradise Bed and Breakfast,** both reputable agencies with offices in Kailua, list bed-and-breakfasts and private rental homes in and around town and throughout the island. Rates and homes differ dramatically, but all are guaranteed to be comfortable and accommodating. Contacts: Ingrid Carvalho, Pacific Hawaii Reservations, 571 Pauku St., Kailua, HI 96734, 808/262-8133, fax 808/262-5030, pir@aloha.net, www.oahu-hawaii-vacation.com; Barbara Wilson, Affordable Paradise Bed and Breakfast, 332 Ku'ukama St., Kailua, HI 96734, 808/261-1693, fax 808/261-7315, barbara@affordable-paradise.com, www.affordable-paradise.com.

## FOOD

Kailua is rich in foods of the world, and the following list gives you a sampling. Most of these restaurants are in the moderate range, but several are classier fine-dining places. Enjoy!

### Uluniu Street Eateries

One block north of the main intersection is Uluniu Street. This and adjacent streets have several moderate to expensive places to eat. Try **Luigi's Place,** 808/263-5678, for Mediterranean cuisine, open Tues.–Sat. 5:30–9:30 P.M., serving pasta for $12–14 and other entrées for up to $16. Luigi's is a small eatery with an old-world atmosphere. BYOB if you desire.

A few steps up the street is the **New Chinese Garden,** 808/262-9090, a basic Chinese restaurant with decent prices that's open daily 10:30 A.M.–9 P.M.

Let the pungent aroma of garlic frying in olive oil lead you to **Assaggio Ristorante Italiano,** 354 Uluniu St., 808/261-2772, open for lunch Mon.–Fri. 11:30 A.M.–2:30 P.M., dinner

Sun.–Thurs. 5–9:30 P.M. and until 10 P.M. on Fri. and Sat. nights. You are welcomed into a bright and open contemporary dining room done in the striking colors of black, red, teal, and magenta, where tables covered in white linen and black upholstered chairs line the long window area. The typical Italian menu, served with crusty Italian bread, begins with antipasti priced $6–11. Soups like pasta fagioli, minestrone, tortellini in brodo, or vichyssoise run less. Pastas range in price $10–14, including linguine, fettuccine, and ziti, and are covered in marinara, clam, carbonara, or pesto sauce. Entrées are chicken cacciatore or chicken rolatini, baked ziti with eggplant and mozzarella, lasagna, and meat dishes such as New York strip steaks, pork chops, and osso bucco. All are priced below $19. From the sea comes fresh fish sautéed in garlic; scallops and shrimp in wine, garlic butter, and snow peas; or calamari alla parmigiana. Desserts are homemade and the full bar serves imported and domestic beers, liquors, coffees, espressos, and plenty of wine varietals.

A few steps down Aulike Street, the smaller and more intimate **Baci Bistro,** 808/262-7555, open for lunch weekdays and dinner daily, has both indoor and outdoor café seating. Soup, salad, and hot or cold appetizers prepare you for the tasty entrées to come. Try one of the traditional pastas, like rigatoni with sausage and basil or spinach tagliatelle and porcini mushrooms in cream sauce, or choose a meat or fish dish, like veal scallopine, fresh fish of the day, or grilled pork chops, all for $13–19. Baci Bistro serves a memorable meal with class.

Nearly across the street is **Lucy's Grill N' Bar,** 808/230-8188, open 5–10 P.M. daily. A fine-dining place with an eclectic menu and full bar, Lucy's has such items as blackened ahi sashimi and kalua pig tacos for appetizers, Italian sausage and shiitake mushroom pizza, and oven-baked salmon, braised lamb shanks, and Mongolian-style pork ribs for entrées. When locals want a special night out on the town, Lucy's is often the choice, but it's not cheap, as most main dishes run $16–25.

Around the corner from Uluniu Street and near the main intersection of town is **Los Garcia's,** 14 Oneawa St., 808/261-0306, open daily for lunch and dinner, a better than average Mexican restaurant. Simple yet tasteful, the south-of-the-border decor is achieved with adobelike arches, wooden tables, Mexican ceramics placed here and there, and plenty of cacti and hanging plants. The menu features combination dinners of burritos, chiles rellenos, enchiladas, tacos, or tamales all priced under $14. Shrimp and seafood dishes run $14.95, and the special meat plates cost about the same. Less expensive dishes, all $9–11, are chimichangas, asada burritos, tacos rancheros, and pizza Mexicana, while appetizers are half that. There are even a half dozen dishes for the vegetarian. Los Garcia's is definitely worth the money!

A few steps away along Kuulei Road is **Champa Thai,** 808/263-8281, serving lunch Mon.–Fri. 11 A.M.–2:30 P.M. and dinner nightly 5–9:30 P.M. A comfortable place with linens and white table cloths and a mixture of Thai and beach decoration, Champa Thai gets praise from locals for its extensive menu of well-prepared dishes that can be made to your desired spiciness level. All of the usual offerings from spring roll appetizers to green papaya salad, hot and sour lemongrass soup, curries, vegetarian dishes, rice, noodles, meat, and seafood dishes are available. Most entrées run $6.75–8.45.

## Ho'ola'i Street Eateries

Open nightly except Sunday 6–9:30 P.M., the **Casablanca,** 808/262-8196, serves Moroccan cuisine, one of the unusual tasty treats of town. Appetizers include young calamari that's pan seared in olive oil and onions, and baked phyllo dough with saffron chicken, almonds, and egg. Couscous is a mainstay and comes with vegetables, chicken, or lamb. Other herbed delicacies are fish charmoula, a spiced fish baked with sweet peppers and onions, Cornish hen with prunes and honey, or lamb brochettes. Entrées here run $13–18. If you desire wine with dinner, you must bring our own.

For a lot of something more common, try **Boston's North End Pizza Bakery,** 263-7757, which serves one size—a huge three-pound, 19-inch pizza. Prices vary from $13–19 depending on the number of toppings, while smaller calzones run $4 each. A few tables inside and out accommodate guests, but most people stop here for take-out.

For a little pick-me-up, try **Agnes' Portuguese Bake Shop** at Ho'ola'i and Uluniu Streets for Portuguese-based malasadas, pao dolce, breads, pies, and cakes, or soup, salad, cappuccino, or espresso. Open 6 A.M.–6 P.M. except Monday, this cool, clean, and inviting place is a popular stop in town.

One block over at 32 Kainehe Street is the well-established health food store **The Source,** 808/262-5604. Open weekdays 9 A.M.–9 P.M., Sat. 9 A.M.–6 P.M., and Sun. 10 A.M.–5 P.M., this place has vitamins and minerals, bulk foods, some organic fresh produce, cosmetics and hygiene products, as well as lots of essences, oils, and natural healing products to help with whatever ails you and to keep you on the straight and narrow.

## Hahani Street Eateries

Near the post office along Hahani Street is a clutch of small, moderately priced restaurants that include Teddy's Bigger Burger, Maui Taco, Jamba Juice, and Saeng's Thai Cuisine. **Teddy's Bigger Burger** is a retro place with a 1950s look: bright lights, formica, and stools. Stop here for large burgers, crispy fries, shakes, and fountain drinks. **Maui Taco** serves Mexican food with an attitude and Hawaiian twist—always good. Next door is **Jamba Juice** and its variety of cool, refreshing, and mostly healthy juice concoctions. Across the street, **Saeng's Thai Cuisine,** 808/263-9727, has been around the longest. Open weekdays for lunch, daily for dinner, it offers spicy Thai food with an emphasis on vegetarian meals, all at an agreeably reasonable price. Appetizers and starters are Thai crisp noodles, fish patties, salads like green papaya salad, yum koong shrimp salad, and chicken coconut soup. Specialties include spicy stuffed calamari, Thai red curry, and à la carte beef, pork, and chicken dishes.

If Japanese food is what you're after, try **Otaru,** 808/263-4482, across Kailua Rd. in the Kailua Shopping Center. Otaru can fill your every wish for sushi, sashimi, noodles, and full sukiyaki, tempura, and lobster meals for both lunch and dinner. Sushi runs $3.50–8 and you won't run out of choices, while most dinners are $13–19; lobster combinations are around $30.

## Hekili Street Eateries

Running into Hahani Street is Hekili Street, along which are several more restaurants. **Princess Chop Suey,** 808/262-7166, is your basic chop suey joint, open Mon.–Sat. 10 A.M.–9 P.M., Sun. 1–9 P.M. Its theme is naugahyde and formica, and everything on the menu is under $8.

Next door is **Cisco's Cantina,** 808/262-7337, featuring complete Mexican cuisine, open Sun.–Thurs. 11:30 A.M.–10 P.M., Fri. and Sat. 11:30 A.M.–11 P.M. Tostadas, tacos, burritos, enchiladas, and chiles rellenos are all under $15. More expensive dishes are those like fajitas ($19.95, or $24.95 for two). All come with Mexican corn, sautéed Tex-Mex mushrooms, and salad. Inside, the south-of-the-border atmosphere is created with hanging piñatas, stucco walls, and blue-tile tables.

An easygoing place with linens, **Buona Sera,** 808/263-7696, does reasonably priced Italian food with appetizers in the $6–8 range and main entrées $6–12. Open Sun.–Thurs. 5:30–9 P.M. and Fri. and Sat. until 10 P.M.

For more down-home cooking, step next door to **Boots and Kimo's Homestyle Kitchen.**

If that's not enough, across the street in the new shopping plaza are **Big City Diner,** a sister restaurant to the original in the Kaimuki area of Honolulu, and a **Quizno's Classic Subs.**

## Near the Water

**Buzz's Original Steakhouse,** 413 Kawailoa Rd., 808/261-4661, is really *the* original steakhouse of this small island chain owned by the Schneider family. Buzz's is just across the road from Kailua Beach Park, situated along the canal. This restaurant is an institution with local families. It's the kind of place that "if you can't think of where to go, you head for Buzz's." The food is always good, if not extraordinary. Lunch is served until 3 P.M. and consists of salads and burgers, mostly $7–10. For dinner, 5–9 P.M. daily, some menu items are top sirloin for $17.95, chicken teriyaki at $13.95, rack of lamb for $24.95, and fresh fish that usually runs about $20. Salad bar is included with all entrées, and separately costs $8.95. Everything is charbroiled. Remember, no credit cards.

At the Kailua Beach Center near the beach park is **Kailua Beach Restaurant,** 808/263-2620. Open 9 A.M.–9 P.M., this casual eatery serves egg and griddle items for breakfast and Chinese food the rest of the day. Not gourmet by any means, it gives you plenty of food at cheap prices and is a convenient stop for those spending the day on the beach. Nothing on the menu is over $7.50.

At the north end of town overlooking Kawainui Channel is **Pinky's Pupu Bar and Grill,** 808/254-6255. Pinky's is a good-time, cheery place, open and breezy, with lots of stuff hanging from the ceiling and a set of shelves that shouts vintage Hawaii. This is the place to come for familiar, feel-good food and large portions. The menu has soup and salads, plenty of sandwiches, baby back ribs, fish tacos, beer can chicken, steak, and all those meals you know and love. Full bar is available. Open until 10 P.M.

# SHOPPING

The two towns of Kailua and Kaneʻohe have the lion's share of shopping on the windward coast. You can pick up basics in the small towns as you head up the coast, but for any unique or hard-to-find items, Kailua/Kaneʻohe is your only bet. There are some shops near the main intersection of Kailua Road (Highway 61) and Oneawa, but you'll find more in the small shopping centers around town. The **Kailua Shopping Center,** with its new facelift at 540 Kailua Rd., has limited shopping that includes a Times Supermarket, open until 10 P.M.; **Under a Hula Moon** for gifts and souvenirs; an **Alpha Video** store; the well-stocked **Bookends,** 808/261-1996, open Mon.–Fri. 9:30 A.M.–9 P.M., Sat. 9:30 A.M.–5:30 P.M., Sun. until 5 P.M., for a full range of reading material; and the **Kailua Information Center** staffed by the Chamber of Commerce.

Across the street in the **Kailua Center** are **Macy's** and **Longs Drugs.** A few steps down Hahani Street is the large **Daiei** store, where you can find just about anything. Also at the Daiei center are a crackseed store, Vim 'N Vigor for vitamins and supplements, and in detached buildings to the front and side, Twogood Kayaks Hawaii shop, Oahu Dive Center, the Kailua Cinemas, and a Safeway supermarket. On the corner of Hamakua and Hekili streets sits a new **Foodland.** Incorporated into this supermarket is **R. Field,** a wine company that is much more because it carries a gourmet selection of cheeses, crackers, jams, jellies, pâté, and all sorts of other prepared foods, both local and international. In this same small shopping plaza are Big City Diner and Quizno's. Nearly across the street from Foodland is Naish Hawaii for sailboarding and kiteboarding sales, rentals, and advice.

You might pick up an heirloom at **Heritage Antiques,** at the corner of Kailua Rd. and Hamakua St., 808/261-8700, open daily 10 A.M.–5:30 P.M., which is overflowing with Asian, Hawaiian, and Americana antiques. Across the street are **The Hunter,** 808/262-4868, and **Windward Antiques,** 808/262-5526, for collectibles of all sorts. If you're really into old finds and haven't had enough yet, head to **Old Pali Road Antiques,** 808/261-7946, only a few blocks away at 320 Ku'ulei Road across from the elementary school, or around the corner to **Ali'i Antiques of Kailua,** 808/261-1705, at 21 Maluniu Ave., both old fixtures in town.

**Island Treasures,** 629 Kailua Rd., 808/261-8131, is an art gallery in Kailua. Owned and operated by Debbie Costello, who comes from a family of artists, the shop is open daily 10 A.M.–6 P.M., Sun. until 4 P.M. Debbie, an artist in her own right, does the beautiful stained-glass pieces in the shop. This shop represents Hawaiian artists only and then only if the work has an island flavor.

Across the road from the library is **The Bike Shop,** 808/261-1553, which does bike sales and

repair and also rents mountain bikes at $15 per day or $85 per week.

**Kalapawai Market,** the closest shop to the beach at the corner of Kailua Rd. and Kalaheo Ave., is open 6 A.M.–9 P.M. daily for basic food and drink supplies, wine and beer, and a deli counter that carries tasty sandwiches and pasta for under $6.

Kitty-corner is the small **Kailua Beach Center.** Aside from Kailua Beach Restaurant, there is a First Stop convenience store, two clothing stores, Ocean Art Gallery, and Kailua Sailboards for water gear and water craft sales and rental as well as bike rental.

Other smaller malls with additional retail stores are the **Enchanted Lake Shopping Center,** in the Enchanted Lake district around Ka'elepulu Pond, which has plenty of Asian restaurants to choose from; the **Keolu Mall** next door with a satellite city hall, post office, the Keolu Cinema, and a few more Asian eateries; and **Aikahi Park Shopping Center,** near the Kaneohe Marine Corps Base, with another supermarket and a handful of additional shops.

## INFORMATION AND SERVICES

Campers can get information and permits at the satellite city hall, 1090 Keolu Dr., in the Keolu Mall near Enchanted Lake. A post office is at the corner of Kailua and Hahani, just across from a First Hawaiian National Bank. Medical aid is available from Castle Medical Center, 808/263-5500, at the intersection of the Pali Highway (Route 61) and Kalaniana'ole Highway (Route 72).

# Kaneʻohe and Vicinity

The bedroom community of Kaneʻohe (Kane's Bamboo) lies along Kaneʻohe Bay, protected by Hawaii's only large barrier reef, easily seen from the Nuʻuanu Pali Lookout high above to the west. Around the edge of the bay lie six of the original 30 fishponds that once graced this fine shore. A lush, fertile land of bountiful farms, historically one of the most productive areas of Oʻahu, Kaneʻohe was the second most populous area on the island. Through the years, the major crops of this coastal town have shifted from taro to rice, sugarcane, pineapples, and bananas, and today a variety is still grown.

Where Route 83 intersects the Likelike Highway on the southern outskirts of Kaneʻohe, it branches north and changes its name from the Kamehameha Highway to the Kahekili Highway until it hits the coast at Kahaluʻu. This four-mile traverse passes two exceptionally beautiful valleys: Haʻiku Valley and the Valley of the Temples. Neither should be missed. Three golf courses grace these green hills, one near the water and two tucked into the folds of the encircling *pali*.

Offshore is Moku O Loʻe, commonly called **Coconut Island.** It became famous as the opening shot in the TV show *Gilligan's Island,* although the series was shot in California. Now home to the University of Hawaiʻi Marine Lab, in ancient times, it was *kapu* and during World War II served as an R&R camp for B-29 crews. Many of the crews felt the island had bad vibes and reported having a streak of bad luck. In recent times, Frank Fasi, Honolulu's former mayor, suggested that Hawaii's gate-crashing guests, Ferdinand and Imelda Marcos, should lease Coconut Island. It never happened.

A **sandbar,** approximately one mile wide and three miles long, occupies the center of Kaneʻohe Bay, making a perfect anchorage for yachts and powerboats. These boat people drop anchor, jump off, and wade to the bar through knee-deep, clear waters. It has become an unofficial playground where you can fling a Frisbee, drink beer, fly a kite, or just float around. Part of the sandbar rises above the water, and some barbecue chefs even bring their hibachis and have a bite to eat. Surrounding you is Kaneʻohe Bay, with Chinaman's Hat floating off to the north and a perfect view of the *pali* straight ahead. This place is the epitome of la dolce vita, Hawaiian style. Fortunately, in recent years, the once crystal-clear bay, which was becoming murky with silt because of development, is clearing again as a result of conservation efforts.

## SIGHTS

### Hoʻomaluhia Botanical Garden

Lying below the encircling H-3 freeway at the edge of town is this 400-acre tract, one component of the Honolulu Botanical Gardens system that previously was agricultural land given over to sugar cane, pineapples, and bananas. Although it includes a 32-acre lake, no swimming is permitted. This dammed reservoir, part of the flood control for Kaneʻohe, was created following several devastating floods in the 1960s. The focus of this garden is on trees and plants from various areas of the world, including Hawaii, the Philippines, India, Africa, and tropical America. Day-use and weekend overnight camping are permitted, walking is encouraged along its many trails, and jogging and bicycling can be done on its paved road. Do yourself a favor and walk down to the lake to see the ducks, geese, and moorhens, but don't forget to turn around and look up at the *pali* that rises up precipitously right behind you. Free guided nature walks are given 10 A.M. on Saturday and 1 P.M. on Sunday. Bring mosquito repellent and an umbrella. The garden, 808/233-7323, is open daily except Christmas and New Year's Day, 9 A.M.–4 P.M. The entrance is at the end of Luluku Road.

### Haʻiku Gardens

Haʻiku (Abrupt Break) Gardens, 46-336 Haʻiku Rd., is a lovely section of a residential area that includes a restaurant and some quiet condominiums. After you pass Kaneʻohe District Park and Windward Community College, turn left onto

Ha'iku Road and proceed for about one-half mile uphill. The gardens date from the mid-1800s, when Hawaiian *ali'i* deeded 16 acres to an English engineer named Baskerville. He developed the area, creating spring-fed lily ponds, building estate homes, and planting flowers, fruits, and ornamental trees. Later a restaurant was built, and the grounds became famous for their beauty, often used for outdoor weddings and special gatherings. You're welcome to walk through the gardens, but they are closed at sunset. Proceed from the restaurant down a walkway to the grassy lawn and pond, where perhaps you'll attract an impromptu entourage of ducks, chick-

ens, and guinea fowl that squawk along looking for handouts. Amid the lush foliage is a gazebo used for weddings. A path leads around the pond, whose benches and small pavilions are perfect for contemplation, and continues under a huge banyan, while a nearby bamboo grove serenades with sonorous music if the wind is blowing.

## Valley of the Temples

The concept of this universal faith cemetery is as beautiful as the sculpted *pali* that serves as its backdrop. A rainy day makes it better. The *pali* explodes with rainbowed waterfalls, and the greens turn a richer emerald, sparkling with dew-

drops. Don't miss the Valley of the Temples Memorial Park at 47-200 Kahekili Highway. Open daily 8 A.M.–4:30 P.M.; admission is $2 adults, $1 seniors and children 2–12, or *kama'aina* rates of $5 per carload, but you have to prove you're from Hawaii. Admission is charged only until 4:30 P.M. After that, you can walk in to see the grounds, but the buildings will not be open. High on a hill sits a Christian chapel, an A-frame topped by a cross. The views can be lovely from up there, but unfortunately the large windows of the chapel perfectly frame some nondescript tract housing and a shopping center below. Great planning! Different areas are set aside for Catholics, Chinese, and other groups.

The crown jewel of the valley is **Byodo-In Temple** (Temple of Equality), a superbly appointed replica of the 900-year-old Byodo-In of Uji, Japan (depicted on the 10-yen coin). This temple dates from June 7, 1968, 100 years to the day after Japanese immigrants first arrived in Hawaii. It was erected through the combined efforts of an American engineering firm headed by Ronald Kawahara in accordance with a plan designed by Kiichi Sano, a famed Kyoto landscape artist.

Across the low arched bridge and to the left as you approach the temple hall is a three-ton brass bell. This bell, which you're invited to strike after making an offering, creates the right vibrations for meditation and symbolically spreads the word of Amida Buddha. Follow the path behind the bell to a small gazebo. Here a rock, perfectly and artistically placed, separates a stream in two, sending the water to the left and right. The pagoda at the top of the path is called the Meditation House. Go to this superbly manicured area to get a sweeping view of the grounds. In front of the Meditation House is a curious tree; pick up one of the fallen leaves and feel the natural velvet on the backside. Remove your shoes before entering the temple hall proper. The walls hold distinctive emblems of different Buddhist sects. Upstairs wings are roped off, with no entry permitted. Stand on the gravel path opposite the main temple. You'll see a grating with a circle cut in the middle. Stick your face in to see the perfectly framed contemplative visage of Buddha. A small gift shop selling souvenirs, cards,

film, and some refreshments is to the right of the temple. If you wish to photograph the complex, it's best to come before noon, when the sun is at your back as you frame the red and white temple against the deep green of the *pali*.

## Along the Shore

The shoreline from Mokapu Peninsula past the downtown area is chock-a-block with homes and condos and a handful of private yacht clubs and marinas. Beyond, it's much more open and rural, more like it was in decades past. The tiny **Kane'ohe Beach Park** is accessible off Route 830 as it heads northward through town; turn onto Waikalua Road at the corner that has both the police and fire stations. This park is better for the views of Kane'ohe Bay than for any beach activities, although there are restrooms and a few picnic tables. The water is safe year-round, but it's murky and lined with mudflats and coral heads.

**He'eia State Park** is designated as an interpretive park. It sits low on Kealohi Point overlooking He'eia Fishpond and Kane'ohe Bay below. Kealohi translates as "The Brightness," because it was a visible landmark to passing voyagers, but there is a much deeper interpretation. To the Hawaiians this area was a jumping-off point into the spirit world. It was believed that the souls of the recently departed came to this point and leapt into eternity. The right side, He'eia-kei, was the side of light, while the left side, He'eia-uli, was the domain of darkness. The wise *kahuna* taught that you could actually see the face of God in the brilliant sun as it rises over the point. This point is also the site of an ancient *heiau* called Kalae'ulu'ula, but it was removed when sugar was planted in the 19th century. On the grounds are a pavilion and rest-rooms. The park contains some indigenous plants and mature trees. Because it's an interpretive park, periodic programs are offered for the community and visitors alike by the Friends of He'eia State Park.

Below is He'eia Fishpond, the finest remaining example of the many fishponds that once lined this bay. Now privately owned, it is still used to raise mullet *('ama)*, the traditional fish raised by the ancient Hawaiians and *kapu* to all except the *ali'i*. Just to the north of this park is the state-operated **Heʻeia Kea Harbor.** Generally, small fishing boats and pleasure craft use the boat launch and other facilities, and several water activity companies start their tours here. A gift shop/snack bar at the end of the pier is a good place to pick up last-minute supplies, get a bite to eat, and ask about what's operating from the harbor. Club Kona Ocean Sports, the *Dreamer* sailboat, and the *Ocean Queen* glass-bottom boat run their operations from here, catering mostly to Japanese visitors. Captain Bob's caters generally to Western tourists and spends much of the day at the sandbar for swimming, snorkeling, other water activities, and a barbecue picnic.

For a fun-filled day on the water, far from the crowds of Waikiki, try **North Bay Aquatics,** on the grounds of Schrader's Windward Country Resort, 47-039 Lihikai Dr., 808/239-5711. A small boat runs from the resort property to the sandbar on Wednesday and Saturday, where you can swim, snorkel, kayak, or hydrobike to your heart's content. Departure time is usually around 10:30 A.M. but may depend on the tides, so call a day in advance. Free for those staying at the resort, only $10 for others.

## ACCOMMODATIONS

**Camp Kokokahi,** 45-035 Kaneʻohe Bay Dr., 808/247-2124, has private and semiprivate cabins that are only open to visitors when they're not booked for groups. Call for information and reservations no more than 30 days in advance. Cabins are for sleeping only; restrooms, a kitchen, and a laundry facility are separate. Rates in a shared cabin are $15 per person, while private cabins run $90–175. Tent camping is also an option for $10 per night per person. Located at the water's edge under tall monkeypod trees, this is a restful and attractive place.

Right over the water opposite the private Makani Kai Marina is **Kaneʻohe Bay B&B,** 45-302 Puʻuloko Pl., Kaneohe, HI 96744, 808/235-4214, kaneohebaybnb@aol.com. The main rental room in this contemporary-style house not only faces east toward the bay and morning sun but is also set next to the courtyard saltwater swimming pool and hot tub. The tile floor and tradewind breezes help keep the room cool during the day, and while not overly large, this room has an attached full kitchen that's stocked with a few complimentary drinks and a bottle of wine. Although you may choose to make your evening meal, a full prepared breakfast is served each morning at the poolside lounge or on the back patio. The room runs $125 per night with a two-night minimum. For couples traveling together or for a small family, an upstairs room is also available but is not usually rented to a separate party. Located in a quiet residential neighborhood, Kaneʻohe Bay B&B is a convenient home-away-from-home, and the gracious hosts will welcome you like old friends, offer advice for sightseeing and meals, but give you space if you desire.

## FOOD

Fortunately, or unfortunately, Kaneʻohe is a bit of a wasteland as far as tourist services, nightlife, and eating out are concerned. Most people who live here head for the action in Honolulu. Kaneohe has mostly ordinary midrange restaurants, many with respectable menus, while more upscale eateries are located in Kailua. The one exception is the well-liked Haleiwa Joe's Seafood Grill.

The best cheap deal in town is at **Kim Chee One,** 46-010 Kamehameha Hwy., 808/235-5560, which has a few sister restaurants scattered around Oʻahu. The setting is plain, but you'll have no trouble finding an excellent Korean mixed barbecue plate for $7.25 or a selection of other Korean and Hawaiianized Korean dishes.

Just down the road is the **Kaneohe Bakery,** open 24 hours a day every day, with all sorts of fresh and tempting delights to satisfy your sweet tooth. Also offering quick, easy food are the Eastern Garden Chinese Restaurant, L&L Drive-In, and Tasty Korean BBQ. All are at the Kaneʻohe Bay Shopping Center, just up the road. In the Windward City Shopping Center is the inexpensive Chao Phya Thai Restaurant.

Highly recommended are **Kin Wah Chop Suey,** 808/247-4812, for the best Chinese food in the area, and **Cafe Satino,** 808/236-0062, for Italian food that's like homemade. Find Kin Wah Chop Suey in a small strip mall at the corner of Luluku Place across from the Windward City Shopping Center. Open daily 10 A.M.–9 P.M., the menu contains the full litany of meat and vegetarian dishes, plus rice, noodles, and daily specials. Most items are under $8, except for the multiple-person meals. In a no-nonsense, no-atmosphere, cinderblock building, set between an upholstery shop and an auto parts store, Satino creates wonderfully tasty food every day for dinner only from 5 P.M. Ordinary lasagna and ravioli are on the menu, but others selections of greater interest are chicken Sorrentino, veal Venezia, calamari Capri, and the like, most at a reasonable $10–12.

**Haleiwa Joe's Seafood Grill at Ha'iku Gardens,** 808/247-6671, true to its name, sits surrounded by a fragrant garden in its lovely, secluded valley. It's considered one of the most beautiful places on O'ahu, and people come here to be married. This restaurant specializes in fresh fish, steak, and prime rib, although the menu is much longer than that, and food is prepared with the flavors and spices of the Pacific and Asia. Appetizers can be Thai fried calamari at $6.25 or crunchy coconut shrimp for $9.95, and entrées include more than half a dozen kinds of fish in various preparations for around $18, herb-roasted chicken at $12.95, sticky ribs for $15.95, and prime rib for $19.95. Dinner only is served from 5:30 P.M. The bar opens at 4:30 P.M., and there are bar specials and *pu pu* until 6:30 P.M. It's first-come, first-served; no reservations are accepted.

## SHOPPING

With a series of shopping malls, independent stores, restaurants, banks, government offices, the police and fire stations, a post office, and library, the major business route through town is Kamehameha Highway (Rte. 830). Toward the north end of this strip is the **Windward Mall,** 46-056 Kamehameha Hwy., open weekdays 9:30 A.M.–9 P.M., Sat. to 5:30 P.M., Sun. 10 A.M.–5 P.M. It's the premier full-service mall on the windward coast. Besides department stores like Macy's and Sears, typical mall shops sell everything from shoes to jewelry, plus there are small, unique shops like Seeds and Things, which sells crackseed and other snacks, a requisite food court, and a multiplex movie theater.

The **Kane'ohe Bay Shopping Center** across from the Windward Mall is a little more downhome, featuring a Longs Drugs (especially good for photo supplies), a Blockbuster Video, Kinko's copy center, and several restaurants. For those staying in the area, the Safeway and Star Market here are convenient.

At the corner of Kamehameha Highway and Kane'ohe Bay Drive is the smaller **Windward City Shopping Center.** Here you'll find a Foodland Supermarket, Starbucks Coffee, Longs Drugs, several Japanese, Chinese, and Korean eateries, fast-food outlets, and two banks.

Across from the Valley of the Temples Memorial Park is the **Ko'olau Center,** which provides a gas station, a Times Supermarket, several local eateries, and the Koolau 10 Cinema.

# North Kane'ohe Bay

## KAHALU'U

This community is near the convergence of Kahekili Highway, Route 83, and Route 830, an extension of the Kamehameha Highway that cuts through Kane'ohe and hugs the coastline heading north from town. The shoreline drive out of Kane'ohe offers some of the most spectacular views of a decidedly spectacular coast, with few tourists venturing along this side road. Kahalu'u is not much more than a gas station and the Hygienic Store, which sells liquor, groceries, soda, ice, and all you'll need for an afternoon lunch, plus a few gift shop/galleries and a convenience store farther up the road. Although they may not always be around, look for little trucks parked along the road near the Hygienic Store selling hot *ono laulau,* which are snacks that come out of the *imu* oven. Across from the Hygenic Store is the large and fancy retail gift shop and jewelry store set up to cater to Japanese tour buses making a round-island trip and for those heading to the Polynesian Cultural Center.

The Waihe'e Stream, meandering from the *pali,* empties into the bay and deposits fresh water near the ancient **Kahalu'u Fishpond,** a picture-perfect tropical setting. So picture-perfect is the place that it has provided the background scenery to TV and Hollywood productions such as an episode from *Jake and the Fat Man,* a setting for *Parent Trap II,* and the famous airport and village scene from *The Karate Kid II.* To the west of the fishpond a spit of land holds a wedding chapel, and beyond that, at the mouth of the stream, is **Kahalu'u Park,** little more than a dirt parking lot, a public boat launch well-used by fishers, a canoe club, and undeveloped land that's recently been cleared of its trees so you can once again see the water.

## Senator Fong's Plantation and Gardens

Just north of Kahalu'u, Senator Fong's Plantation and Gardens, 47-285 Pulama Rd., 808/239-6775, www.fonggarden.com, is open daily 10 A.M.–4 P.M., except Christmas and New Year's Day. Follow Pulama Road inland about one-half mile to the garden entrance. Admission is $10 adults, $6 children 5–12. Guided and narrated one-hour tram tours run at 10:30 A.M., 11:30 A.M., 1 P.M., 2 P.M., and 3 P.M., taking visitors through about 200 acres of the garden. The plantation is a labor of love created by former senator Hiram Fong, who served as state senator 1959–1977. Upon retirement he returned to his home and ever since has been beautifying the gardens he started in the 1950s. The result is 725 acres of natural beauty that rise to 2,600 feet at the ridge of the Ko'olau Range above. The five major valleys and ridges of this garden—each named for a president that Senator Fong served under—preserve the native flora and fauna of the land, along with planted flower and fruit gardens and groves of trees, palms, bushes, and ferns. The large open-air entrance pavilion houses a snack window and a small but well-appointed souvenir shop, where you can get everything from aloha shirts to postcards. The tables set with baskets of

flowers inside the pavilion are where you can make your own keepsake lei for $6.50.

## Accommodations

**Schrader's Windward Country Inn,** 47-039 Lihikai Dr., Kane'ohe, HI 96744, 808/239-5711 or 800/735-5711, fax 808/239-6658, www.hawaiiscene.com/schrader, has been operating for years. It overlooks Kahalu'u Fishpond at the end of Wailau Peninsula. At first it may look like a hodgepodge of a place, but it's really a nice little community of about four dozen units in several separate buildings. Some of these units sit along the water while others step up the steep embankment. One-, two-, three-, and four-bedroom units are available, some fully furnished and others with kitchenettes. Surprisingly large, all are neat and clean, with a/c, telephone, television, and daily maid service. A complimentary breakfast is available each morning on the veranda outside the office on the top level of the main building, a free, simple dinner is served on Wednesday evening, and karaoke night is Friday. On property are a swimming pool, laundry, and barbecue pit. Also, a complimentary two-hour pontoon boat cruise into the bay for snorkeling, kayaking, and swimming at the sandbar is open for all guests; $10 for others. The boat leaves every Wednesday and Saturday (days may change) at about 10:30 A.M. Room rates run $60–125 for one-bedroom rooms, $110–190 for two-bedroom units, $200–320 for three-bedroom suites, and $400–450 for the four-bedroom deluxe suite, but room and car packages are also an option. Ask about off-season and multiple-night discounts. This rural cottage motel on the water is a fine alternative for those looking for peace and quiet.

## WAIAHOLE AND WAIKANE

If you want to fall in love with rural, old-time O'ahu, go to the northern reaches of Kane'ohe Bay around Waiahole and Waikane, a Hawaiian grassroots area that has so far eluded development. Alongside the road sit some of the best fruit stands on O'ahu. Do yourself a favor and have one of the coconuts. Sip the juice, and when it's gone, eat the custardlike contents. A real island treat, nutritious and delicious. For a glimpse of what's happening, look for the Waiahole Elementary School, and turn left up Waiahole Valley Road. The road twists its way into the valley, becoming narrower. Left and right in homey, ramshackle houses lives down-home Hawaii, complete with taro patches in the backyards and fruit and nut trees to the sides. At the turn, stop for a bite to eat at the **Ono Loa Hawaiian Foods** restaurant, a local place at the Waiahole Poi Factory. Time your trip right because this restaurant is only open 10 A.M.–2 P.M. daily, except for Thursday when it's closed. This is the real thing. Plate lunches go for about $7 and individual items for $2. Another road of the same type is about one-half mile up Route 83 just before you enter Waikane. If you're staying in Waikiki, compare this area with Kuhio Avenue only 45 minutes away!

Up the road, Waiahole Beach Park is rather undeveloped, but it gets you down to the water. This is followed by the old-style Waikane General Store a short distance before the much newer Coral Kingdom gift shop. Around the bend and on a ways is Tropical Farm at Kualoa Nursery and Garden, a macadamia nut outlet with plenty of other goodies that's just before Kualoa Re-

gional Park. Continuing on, the road passes through what was once sugarcane country. Most of the businesses failed in the 1800s, but you will see the ruins of the Kualoa Sugar Mill along the road a mile or so before reaching Kaʻaʻawa. Although it closed more than a century ago, the dilapidated mill still stands, its chimney the most obvious remnant.

Offshore stands a recognizable island. Mokoliʻi (Small Lizard) Island is commonly called **Chinaman's Hat** for its obvious resemblance to an Asian chapeau. Legend says that Mokoliʻi Island is the tail of a lizard that was killed by the goddess Hiʻiaka. Where's the body? The flat land near the old overgrown mill ruins.

## Kualoa Regional Park

With the *pali* in the background, Chinaman's Hat offshore, and a glistening white strand shaded by swaying palms, Kualoa is one of the finest beach parks on windward Oʻahu, and it has one of its longest beaches. Kualoa is one of the most sacred areas on Oʻahu, and the *aliʻi* brought their children here to be reared and educated. The area is designated in the National Register of Historic Places. It has a full range of facilities

Chinaman's Hat

ROBERT NILSEN

and services, including lifeguards, restrooms, picnic tables, and an expansive parking area. Because of its exposure to winds, Kualoa is sometimes chilly. The park is popular and often used by athletic groups for games and competitions. The park is open daily 7 A.M.–7 P.M., with overnight camping allowed with a county permit. The swimming is safe year-round along a shoreline dotted with pockets of sand and coral. The snorkeling and fishing are good, but the real treat is walking the 500 yards to Chinaman's Hat at low tide. You need appropriate footgear (old sneakers are fine) because of the sharp coral heads. The island is one of the few around offshore O'ahu that are not official bird sanctuaries, although many shorebirds do use the island and should not be disturbed.

## Kualoa Ranch

The 4,000-acre Kualoa Ranch, 49-560 Kamehameha Hwy., 808/237-8515 or 800/231-7321, www.kualoa.com, just past Kualoa Regional Park, offers four organized, prepackaged outdoor activity tours on its working cattle ranch. Activities run 9 A.M.–3 P.M. Your choice of activities includes horseback riding, personal watercraft rides, ATV dune cycle rides, gun range firing, snorkeling, scuba, beach activities, a movie set ride,

and more. Other games and activities, a petting zoo, and Hawaiian exhibits are also available for free. The Activity Adventure Tour runs $94 adults, $60 children 3–11 and includes a full-day pass for up to seven activities, discounted rates on others, transportation to and from Waikiki, as well as a barbecue lunch. The Deluxe Adventure Tour at $148 and $95, respectively, is much the same except that you have as many activity choices as you can handle in one day, plus an introductory scuba dive. With the Secret Island and Activity Tour, you get one activity at the ranch with a half day of water sports, plus transportation and lunch. Rates run $69 adults, $35 children. The fourth tour is the Horseback or ATV Tour, which gives you either of these activities plus discounts on others. For some activities, there are stipulations for the age of participant and adult accompaniment. Individual activities may also be purchased for their set fees for those who do not desire packages. Most ranch activities take place weekdays only, with adult horseback rides and ATV dune cycle ride also offered on Sunday; closed on national holidays. The Kualoa Ranch is not a cultural experience. It's an outing for activities, sun, and fun. Periodically the list of activities and tours changes, so call for current information.

# Ka'a'awa Town and Vicinity

## SIGHTS AND BEACHES

When you first zip along the highway through town you get the impression that there isn't much here, but there's more than you think. The town stretches back toward the *pali* for a couple of streets. On the ocean side is Swanzy Beach Park, primarily a local hangout. Across the road is the tiny post office and **Moani's Country Kitchen,** which serves breakfast and plate lunches, most less than $6. It has a few tables, but the best bet is to get your plate lunch and take it across the street to the beach park. Behind the post office is **Pyramid Rock,** obviously named because of its shape.

O'ahu's windward *pali* are unsurpassed anywhere in the islands, and they're particularly

beautiful here. Take a walk around. Stroll the dirt roads through the residential areas and keep your eyes peeled for a small white cross on the *pali* just near Pyramid Rock. It marks the spot where a serviceman was killed during the Pearl Harbor invasion. His spirit is still honored by the perpetually maintained bright white cross. While walking you'll be treated to Ka'a'awa's natural choir—wild roosters crowing any time they feel like it and the din of cheeky parrots high in the trees. A pair of parrots escaped from a nearby home years ago, and their progeny continue to relish life in the balmy tropics.

As you approach the bend of Mahie Point, staring down at you is a popular stone formation, the **Crouching Lion.** Undoubtedly a tour bus or two will be sitting in the lot of the Crouching Lion Inn. As with all anthropomorphic rock formations, it helps to have an imagination. Anyway, the inn is much more interesting than the lion. George Larsen built the inn in 1928 from rough-hewn lumber from the Pacific Northwest; the huge stones were excavated from the site. The inn went public as a restaurant in 1957 and has been serving tourists ever since.

Four beach parks in as many miles lie between Ka'a'awa Point and Kahana Bay. **Kalae'o'io Beach County Park,** the first, is a shaded short strip that has roadside parking only. There are a few picnic tables but no restrooms, and the beach is good but the bottom is a bit rocky. The second park, a short distance beyond, is **Ka'a'awa Beach County Park,** a popular beach with restrooms, lifeguards, picnic facilities, and limited parking at its northern end. An offshore reef running the entire length of the park makes swimming safe year-round, but perhaps the snorkeling is better. There's a dangerous rip at the south end of the park at the reef break. Lots of people come to shorefish this coastal strip.

**Swanzy Beach County Park,** two minutes north, offers a broad, grassy expanse and basketball courts and has camping with a county permit on weekends only. The sand and rubble beach lies below a long retaining wall, often underwater during high tide. The swimming is safe year-round but is not favorable because of the poor quality of the beach. Swanzy is one of the best squidding and snorkeling beaches on the windward coast. A break in the offshore reef creates a dangerous rip that should be avoided.

**Ahupua'a 'O Kahana State Park** (formerly called Kahana Valley State Park) is a full-service park with picnic facilities, restrooms, camping, a boat launch on the beach, and hiking trails inland. Camping is allowed with state permit at the beach; restrooms and information are on the mountain side of the road. It's perfectly situated for a quiet picnic under the coconut trees. Swimming is good year-round, although the waters can be cloudy at times. A gentle shorebreak makes the area ideal for bodysurfing and beginner board riders. This entire beach area is traditionally excellent for *akule* fishing, with large schools visiting the

offshore waters at certain times of year. The bay and valley once supported a large Hawaiian community, and many cultural remains dot the area, including *heiau,* housing sites, terraced fields, and irrigation ditches. Remnants of **Huilua Fishpond** lie just outside the park boundary on the south shore of the bay. Running up the valley, past a small in-park residential neighborhood, is the rest of the park. Few people visit there. The park encompasses this valley, historically an *ahupua'a,* and runs from water's edge to over 2,600 feet.

You can follow two trails within the park, one that loops about three miles back into the valley and the other a one-mile round-trip along the bayfront mountainside past a fish deity shrine to a lookout that was once used to watch for fish in the bay. For the **Kapa'ele'ele Ko'a and Keaniani Kilo Trail** to the shrine and lookout, the hike starts to the side of the park information center. This trail begins on what was a train track bed but shortly begins to climb up the hillside to a height of about 150 feet to the lookout, passing the small fishing shrine on the way. Return the same way or head down the hill and follow the roadside trail back. To reach the **Nakoa Trail,** which runs into the valley, head up the road through the residential neighborhood—park your car at the entrance to the village. From the check-in station beyond the far end of the village you can follow the loop trail either right or left. Much of this trail winds around the hillsides through stands of *hala* trees. It's wet back in the valley and easily may rain, so be prepared to get wet. It's also a great environment for mosquitoes. Once at the back end of the loop and again a couple hundred yards from the trailhead at a swimming hole, this trail crosses the Kahana Stream. Because there are no bridges, you must wade through.

## PRACTICALITIES

There was a time when *everyone* passing through Ka'a'awa stopped at the **Crouching Lion Inn.** Built in 1928, it was the only place *to* stop for many, many years. The inn has seen its ups and downs, and now, fortunately, is on the upswing again. The inn, along Route 83 in Ka'a'awa,

808/237-8511, is open daily for lunch 11 A.M.–3 P.M., cocktails from 3 P.M. onward, *pu pu* 4–5 P.M., and dinner 5–9 P.M. The inn is beautiful enough to stop at just to have a look, but if you want a reasonably quiet meal, avoid lunchtime and come in the evening when all of the tour buses have long since departed. Sitting high on a verdant green hill, the inn's architectural style is a mixture of English Tudor and country Hawaiian. Inside it is cozy with a fireplace as well as open-beamed ceilings, while the view from the veranda is especially grand.

Lunch can be a simple order of Portuguese bean soup, or appetizer, salad, and sandwich. Appetizers like royal shrimp cocktail, sautéed mushrooms, or honey garlic shrimp run $7.25–9.25. Salads include Oriental chicken, shrimp Parmesan, and fruit of kings salad. Regular lunch entrées are mahimahi melt, turkey sandwich, or *kalua* pork plate, all priced under $9. Dinner entrées, accompanied by fresh-baked rolls, soup or salad, vegetables, and choice of rice

or potatoes, include Slavonic steak, sautéed seafood, Hawaiian chopped steak, or shrimp kebabs for $14.95–24.95. Some vegetarian selections complete the menu, which is an expansion of the lunch menu. The inn's famous mile-high coconut pie, macadamia nut cream pie, and double-crusted banana cream pie, for under $5, are absolutely delicious. The limited-menu early-bird special at $10.95 is a real bargain. To complement your menu selection, a full bar serves cocktails, beer, wine, and liquors.

In an adjacent building is **Livingston Galleries,** 808/237-7165, open weekdays from 11:30 A.M. and weekends 10:30 A.M.–7:30 P.M. This gallery displays an excellent representation of original prints, sculptures, some jewelry and gifts, and edition prints of both internationally acclaimed and local island artists; some of the well-known artists shown here are Nisla, Walfrido, David Lee, and Burrows. Predominantly paintings and prints, other media are represented in smaller numbers.

## Punalu'u and Hau'ula

### PUNALU'U

Punalu'u (Coral Diving) is a long, narrow ribbon of land between the sea and the *pali,* a favorite place to come for a drive in the country. Its built-up area is about a mile or so long but only a hundred yards wide. It has gas, supplies, and camping, along with the several art galleries. In town is **St. Joachim Church.** There's nothing outstanding about it, merely a one-room church sitting meekly on a plot of ground overlooking the sea. But it's real home-grown, where the people of this district come to worship. Just look and you might understand the simple and basic lifestyle that still persists in this area.

On the northern outskirts of town is **Sacred Falls State Park** (closed indefinitely because of a landslide that killed seven hikers in 1999). There is a barricade across the entrance: no admittance. The area's Hawaiian name was Kaliuwa'a (Canoe Leak), and although the original name isn't as romantic as the anglicized version,

the entire area was considered sacred. It's a narrow valley where the gods would show disfavor by dropping rocks onto your head. Hawaiians used to wrap stones with *ti* leaves and leave them along the trail as an appeasement to the gods, so they weren't tempted to brain them. The walls of this deep valley are 1,600 feet high, but the falls drop only 90 feet or so. The pool below was ample for a swim, but the water is chilly and often murky. Although you can't hike there now, you can get a glimpse of the falls way back in the valley from over the roof of the Church of Latter-Day Saints along the highway or from the end of the road to the side of the church.

### HAU'ULA

This speck of a town is just past Punalu'u between mile markers 21 and 22. The old town center is two soda machines, the pink Ching Jong Leong store, and Wu's Sundries. At the estuary of a stream is **'Aukai Beach Park,** a flat little beach right in the middle of town. A small restaurant, a 7-Eleven, and a little church up on the hill with the *pali* as a backdrop add the finishing touches.

## Hau'ula Trails

Outdoor enthusiasts will love the little-used Hau'ula Trails. These ridge and valley trails offer just about everything you can expect from a Hawaiian trail: the mountains, the valleys, and vistas of the sea. Built by the Civilian Conservation Corps during the Depression, these manicured trails are wide, and the footing is great most of the way even in rainy periods. They run up and down several ridges and deep into interior valleys through the extraordinary jungle canopy. The hard-packed loop trail, covered in a soft carpet of ironwood needles, offers magnificent coastal views once you reach the heights and sights of inland verdant gulches and valleys. The area flora is made up of ironwoods, passion fruit, thimbleberries, *ohia*, and wild orchids, among other native and introduced species. The ridge trail has a completely different character as it passes through sections of hau trees and some hardwoods. It starts by a steep zigzag up the hillside to a covered picnic table and overlook and from there heads up the ridge only to circle back around. All three trails start beyond the end of Makakua Road, which is off Hau'ula Homestead Road. Pass a hunter's check-in station and continue on the paved trail. On your right is the start of the **Hau'ula Loop Trail.** A short way farther, the **Ma'akua Ridge Trail** heads off to the left, while the **Ma'akua Gulch Trail** goes straight ahead up the valley. Each trail round-trip should take less than two hours. The Gulch Trail may be closed periodically because of hazardous conditions.

# BEACHES

Right along the highway is **Punalu'u Beach County Park,** with restrooms, picnic tables, lots of shade, and decent snorkeling, but no lifeguards. The swimming is safe year-round inside the protected reef. Local fishermen, usually older Filipino men who are surfcasting, use this area frequently.

They're friendly and a great source of information for anyone trying to land a fish or two. They know the best baits and spots to dunk a line.

**Hau'ula Beach County Park** is an improved beach park with picnic facilities, restrooms, pavilion, volleyball court, and camping. There's safe swimming year-round inside the coral reef, with good snorkeling; surfing is usually best in winter. Rip currents are present at both ends of the beach at reef breaks, and deep holes in the floor of a brackish pond are formed where Ma'akua Stream enters the sea. Across the road are the ruins of the historic **Lanakila Church** (1853), partially dismantled at the turn of the 20th century to build a smaller church near Punalu'u.

**Kokololio Beach County Park** is next—a fine spot with lots of parking. A little dune protects the beach from road noise. There is good swimming, but many locals come to boogie board, mostly at the northern end where the beach makes a slight curve. With lots of shade trees and picnic tables, it's good for a day trip or to camp with a county permit.

# PRACTICALITIES

## Accommodations

**Pat's at Punalu'u** is one of the few condos along this coast, and one of the few buildings that approaches the height of coconut trees. Even though it's rather out of place along this coast, the building is painted light green to blend into the background color. Pat's is right on the water, and every unit has a lanai that overlooks the sea. On property are a swimming pool, sauna, patio next to the beach, and parking. Units are fully furnished with kitchens, televisions, and washers and dryers, and run $80–90 for a studio, $100–105 for one bedroom, and $180 for a three-bedroom penthouse, with the addition of a cleaning charge. Weekly and monthly rates can be arranged. A $150 damage deposit is required within 10 days of booking, and full payment is to be made one month before arrival. Punalu'u and vicinity is an easygoing area, a throwback to Hawaii as it used to be years ago, yet it's so close to the big city and all it offers. If you're looking for quiet and relaxation at a decent price, this could be the spot. Room arrangements are made through Paul Comeau Condo Rentals, P.O. Box 589, Kaʻaʻawa, HI 96730, 808/293-2624 or 800/467-6215, fax 808/293-0618, comeau001@hawaii.rr.com, www.patsinpunaluu.com.

The **Punaluʻu Guesthouse,** 808/293-8539, provides two rooms with single beds and one room with a queen-size bed. It's like a bed-and-breakfast, but no breakfast is provided. However, guests may use the kitchen to do their own cooking. Rates run $22 adults, $12 kids ages 5–12. Reservations are also done through the Honolulu International Hostel, 808/946-0591, fax 808/946-5904.

A few steps down the road from Punaluʻu Beach Park, the **Countryside Cabins,** 53-224 Kamehameha Hwy., 808/237-1203, reservations@hawaiicabins.com, www.hawaiicabins.com, is an inexpensive, somewhat funky, but enduringly charming place for the young and young at heart. It's an easygoing compound of cabins, tent space, and gardens that's half overgrown by fruit trees and tall hardwoods. Tenting here costs $7.50 per night, a bunk in the hostel is $15, and cabins furnished with full kitchens and baths run $40–65; weekly rates are an option. In addition, there is space to park cars and a laundry facility to wash clothes. Used predominantly by backpackers and others traveling on a budget, guests often congregate in the "luau hut" in the evening to eat, drink, "talk story," and play cards. Look for the small sign that says "Cabins."

## Food

Keep a sharp eye out for a truck and a sign featuring shrimp just along the road. Turn in to **Restaurant Punaluʻu,** 53-146 Kamehameha Hwy., 808/237-8474, open daily 11 A.M.–9 P.M., 8 P.M. on Sunday. This is the first place of note after passing the Ahupuaʻa ʻO Kahana State Park. The shrimp couldn't be fresher—it comes from local fishermen. In this no-frills but super-friendly restaurant, you can have 30 shrimp cooked to order as scampi, tempura, spicy, or in a cocktail for $12.95! Shrimp is the pièce de résistance, but basic sandwiches and burgers for under $6.95 are also on the menu, as well as entrées like spaghetti for $9.50, breaded chicken cutlet with

gravy at $7.25, and steak and mahimahi combo for $16.95. Complete meals come with cooked vegetables, bread, and rice or potatoes. There are plenty of appetizers and side dishes on the menu and a good selection of beer and wine. Formerly Ahi's Restaurant, the new management still serves all of its great food with authentic *aloha*. Stop in! You'll be glad you did.

## Shopping

The **Punaluʻu Art Gallery,** in Punaluʻu around mile marker 24, 808/237-8221, is the oldest art gallery on windward Oʻahu. Open daily 10:30 A.M.–6:30 P.M. Owner and candle artist Scott Bechtol is dedicated to showcasing the works of an assortment of the finest artists that the island has to offer. Scott is well known for his wonderful sculpted candles, all made from the finest beeswax. Some are lanterns shaped like a huge pita bread with the top third cut off. The remainder is sculpted with a scene that glows when the candle is lit. Others are huge tikis, dolphins, or flowers, all inspired by the islands. Some of the larger candles are $70, the man-size tiki is about $800, and Scott's unique "crying tiki" sells for only $25; small tapers go for $5–9. Scott creates all of this beautiful, glowing art with just one precision carving tool—a buck knife! Another artist shown is Bill Cupid, who creates "bananascapes." Bill removes the outer bark from the banana tree, then he tears and cuts it to make a scene of boats or mountains. The result is a three-dimensional piece. Bill's wife is an artist who specializes in seascapes made with seaweed, while Janet Stewart does watercolors and prints. Other beauty is added by Janet Holiday's silk-screen prints and Peter Hayward's landscapes and seascapes in oil. The Punaluʻu Art Gallery is a jewel case of man-made beauty surrounded by natural beauty. They harmonize perfectly.

A few steps up the way are **Wu Sundries,** a minimart in an old building for basic food supplies, and the gift shop **Ching Punaluʻu Store.**

Three other galleries here make this a mini-center for viewing artwork. The **Lance Fairly Gallery,** 53-839 Kamehameha Hwy., 808/293-9009, www.lancefairly.com, displays colorful landscapes and seascapes by fine artist Lance Fairly. His

M

OʻAHU

paintings seem to have a luminescence, an inner light, and there's an enhancement of color for a pleasing yet somewhat magical or mystical tone. Lithographs and giclée (prints created by a computer-based method that reproduces the original almost perfectly) are available for purchase. The gallery is open pretty much every day, but because this is Fairly's studio, you may have to ring the front bell to have the door opened.

Just up the road is the **Kim Taylor Reece Gallery,** 53-866 Kamehameha Hwy., www.alohadirect.com/ktr. Reece is a photographer, and many of his large-size prints are of nudes. The bulk of the work is done in black and white, but some prints are hand tinted. This gallery is open noon–5 P.M. Thurs.–Sat. only. Between these two is **Kahaunani Woods & Krafts,** displaying wooden bowls, boxes, and other such objects made of native woods by the owner in his shop in the back.

In Hau'ula look for the **Hau'ula Kai Center,** a small shopping center with a post office, Zoe's Cafe for quick eats, and a KFC. Also in Hau'ula is the Rainbow Plaza, an unabashed tourist trap, classic in its obvious tastelessness. Here you'll find beads, baubles, and jewelry. This shop has been taken over by Korean merchants who cater largely to Korean tourist groups.

# La'ie and Kahuku

## LA'IE

The "Saints" came marching into La'ie (Leaf of the 'Ie Vine) and set about making a perfect Mormon village in paradise. What's more, they succeeded! The town is squeaky clean, with well-kept homes and manicured lawns that hint of suburban Midwest America. Dedicated to education, they built a branch of **Brigham Young University** (BYU), which attracts students from all over Polynesia, many of whom work in the nearby Polynesian Cultural Center. The students vow to live a clean life, free of drugs and alcohol, and to not grow beards. In the foyer of the main entrance, look for a huge mural depicting La'ie's flag-raising ceremony in 1921, which symbolically established the colony. To reach the university from the highway, turn onto Hale La'a Boulevard and at the traffic circle follow Kulaniu Street directly to the campus. Alternately, take Naniloa Loop off the highway.

The first view of the **Mormon Temple,** built in 1919, is impressive. Square, with simple architectural lines, this house of worship sits pure white against the *pali* and is further dramatized by a reflecting pool and fountains spewing fine mists. The visitors center of this tranquil, shrinelike church is open daily 9 A.M.–8 P.M., when a slide show telling the history of the La'ie colony is presented, along with a guided tour of the grounds.

The tour guides, while not pushy, definitely want to engage you in a discussion about your beliefs. They are missionaries after all, so it's not surprising, and they'll leave you alone if you desire. "Smoking is prohibited, and shirts (no halter tops) must be worn to enter." The temple attracts more visitors than any other Mormon site outside of the main temple in Salt Lake City.

## Polynesian Cultural Center

The real showcase in La'ie is the Polynesian Cultural Center. The PCC, as it's called by islanders, began as an experiment in 1963. Smart businessmen said it would never thrive way out in La'ie, and tourists didn't come to Hawaii for *culture* anyway. Well, they were wrong, and the PCC now rates as one of O'ahu's top tourist attractions, luring about one million visitors annually. Miracles do happen! The PCC is a nonprofit organization, with proceeds going to the La'ie BYU students' educational funds and to maintaining the center.

Covering 42 acres, the primary attractions are seven model villages including examples from Hawaii, Samoa, the Marquesas, Fiji, Aotearoa (New Zealand), Tonga, and Tahiti. The villages are primarily staffed with people from the representative island homelands. Remember that most are Mormons, whose dogma colors the attitudes and selected presentations of the staffers. Still, all

O'AHU

ROBERT NILSEN

The Pageant of Canoes highlights a visit to the Polynesian Cultural Center.

are genuinely interested in dispensing cultural knowledge about their traditional island ways and beliefs, and almost all are characters who engage in lighthearted bantering with their willing audience. Walk through the villages on your own or take a canoe ride over the artesian-fed waterways. Other attractions include a Migrations Museum, art and handicraft shops, and an IMAX theater that presents two shows about Polynesia and the sea. A shuttle tram runs outside the center and will take you on a guided tour to the BYU campus, the temple, and the community.

The undeniable family spirit and pride at the PCC makes you feel welcome, while providing a clean and wholesome experience, with plenty of attention to detail. It's this quality approach and good value that has sustained the "miracle."

Throughout the day, there are various cultural presentations at each village. The Pageant of Canoes sails at 2:30 P.M. and is a waterborne show of music and dance. All day, the Keiki Activities program offers children the opportunity to tune into these cultures with kid-oriented experiences. **Horizons,** the center's largest extravaganza, runs 7:30–9 P.M. at the indoor/outdoor amphitheater. This theater hosts about 3,000 spectators

for this show of music, dance, and historical drama, which is put on by nearly 100 performers. The costumes and lighting are dramatic and inspired and the performance is spirited and genuine; it's hard to believe that the performers are not professionals.

Food is available from snack bars, or you can dine at the Gateway restaurant; at the Ambassador restaurant, your dinner is part of a package, including the Polynesian extravaganza. Another option is the Ali'i Lu'au, which introduces you to the Hawaiian feast, the ceremony of removing the roasted pig from the *imu* pit, and a reenactment of a royal court procession.

The PCC is open daily except Sunday 12:30–6 P.M. for general admission and the show, $39 adults, $24 children, under five free, but dinner is on your own. Packages are also available; they include general admission to the villages and daytime activities, dinner, and preferred seating at the evening show. The Gateway Buffet Package, $54 adults and $37 children, includes a buffet dinner at the Gateway restaurant; Ali'i Lu'au Package, $69 adults and $48 children, lets you partake in the *lu'au* dinner show; and the Ambassador Package, $104 adults and $71 children, serves you a sit-down dinner at the Ambassador restaurant, gives a guided tour, and offers special souvenirs, gifts, and other perks. For more information, contact the PCC at 808/293-3333 or 800/367-7060, www.polynesia.com. TheBus no. 52 runs to the PCC from Ala Moana Shopping Center but takes about 2.5 hours. The PCC runs its own bus transportation to the center from certain hotels in Waikiki for $13 per person round-trip and offers door-to-door mini-coach transportation for $21 round-trip from any point in Waikiki. Most island hotels and tour companies can arrange a package tour to PCC.

## Laʻie Point

Laniloa Peninsula is a spit of land that pushes out to Laʻie Point. It's a residential area that ends in an undeveloped country park, from where you can get scenic views up and down the coast and to the small islands offshore. While the peninsula is a low, rocky promontory, beaches line the coast in both directions. Of the offshore islands, there are several legends. One states that Laniloa was a legendary *moʻo* (lizard) that terrorized the inhabitants of this area and anyone who happened to pass this way. The lizard was finally dispatched by the heroic warrior and demi-god named Kana, who had it out for all lizards after one had terrorized his mother. Kana cut this lizard's head into five pieces and threw them into the ocean, and these pieces are now seen as the five small islands off the end of the Laniloa Peninsula.

## Malaekahana State Recreation Area

This state recreation area is the premier camping beach and park along the north section of the windward coast. Separated from the highway by a large stand of ironwood shade trees, this 37-acre park offers showers, restrooms, picnic facilities, local-style beach cabins, and camping. Camp sites run $5 per person for those eight and older, while the various cabins from one bedroom to four bedrooms range $66–250 per night. (See the Camping section in the On The Road chapter for more details.) For information and reservations, contact Friends of Malaekahana at P.O. Box 305, Laʻie, HI 96762, 808/293-1736, fax 808/293-2066, fom@hawaii.rr.com, www.alter-native-hawaii.com/fom; office hours are Mon.–Fri. 10 A.M.–4 P.M.

Malaekahana was Puʻuhonua of Laʻie, a place of refuge and, according to legend, the only spot on Oʻahu not conquered by King Kamehameha. The recent restructuring of the recreation area and administration by native Hawaiians was intended to bring back its traditional role as a healing and gathering place. An alternative learning center erected here is connected to Kahuku High School, where students come to reconnect culturally and spiritually.

Offshore is Mokuʻauia, better known as **Goat Island.** The island is only a stone's throw from shore. Reef walkers or tennis shoes are advised, but go only when the water is calm. You can reach this seabird sanctuary by wading across the reef during low tide. You'll find a beautiful crescent white-sand beach and absolute peace and quiet. Relax and look for seabirds, or try to spot hawksbill or green sea turtles. The swimming inside the reef is good, and it's amazing how little this area is used for such a beautiful spot. Farther offshore, about 200–300 yards, are two other small islands, which *you cannot wade to.* It is too far, and the currents are strong. Some kiteboarders now come to use this beach. Be aware that there are two entrances to the park. The south entrance, closest to Laʻie, puts you in the day-use area of the park, where there are restrooms and showers. The entrance to the camping section is north a minute or two (around mile marker 17) and is marked by a steel gate and a sign welcoming you to Malaekahana State Recreation Area. Be aware that the gate opens at 7 A.M. and is locked at 6:45 P.M.

## Beaches

At the southern end of Laʻie is **Laʻie Beach County Park,** an unimproved beach park with no facilities. The beach here is called **Pounder's Beach,** so named by students of BYU because of the pounding surf. This beach experiences heavy surf and dangerous conditions in the winter, but its excellent shoreline break is perfect for body-surfing for those with some skill. The remains of an old pier at which interisland steamers once stopped is still in evidence. The shoreline waters farther into town are safe for swimming inside the reef, but winter produces heavy and potentially dangerous surf. Good snorkeling, fishing, and net-throwing are possible here.

At the north end of town, just south of Makalawena, is the tiny **Hukilau Beach.** This is the site of real neighborhood *hukilau* of decades past and the inspiration of the *hapa-haole* song "Hukilau." Penned in 1948 by Jack Owens, it refers to fishing with *hukilau* nets at La'ie Bay and is now part of the repertoire of most Hawaiian entertainers. A fine beach in summer, winter winds bring kiteboarders.

## Accommodations

The **Laie Inn,** 55-109 Lanilau St., La'ie, HI 96762, 808/293-9282 or 800/526-4562, fax 808/293-8115, laieinn@hawaii.rr.com, www.laie inn.com, is just outside the PCC on the mountain side of the highway. It's a humble motel-like cinderblock affair—basic, as neat as a pin, and secure. Although you won't find luxury, you won't go wrong here. Five two-story buildings with four dozen units surround a quiet and relaxing central courtyard and swimming pool. All rooms have a/c, TV, mini-fridge and microwaves, and island-inspired decorations and amenities; bathrooms have been renovated with new fixtures and accessories. Rooms are $89 queen, $94 two doubles, $99 king, with a $5 reduction during off-season (Apr.–May, Sept.–Oct.); good value. The fee includes continental breakfast, free local telephone calls, and parking. Not only is this inn close to BYU, the PCC, and the Mormon temple, but it's also near windward and North Shore beaches. Hotel guests have access to a private beach area across the road near a barbecue grill. This is a good choice at reasonable rates.

**Pounder's Vacation Rentals,** 55-161 Kamehameha Hwy., La'ie, HI 96762, 808/293-1000, is between mile markers 19 and 20, ocean side, just south of Pounder's Beach. Drop-ins are certainly welcome when there is room, but reservations are encouraged. Chances of turning up and finding a vacancy are poor, so at least call from the airport to check availability. Three studios with kitchenette for two people each run $65 per day, while the downstairs self-contained, two-bedroom, full-kitchen unit, which can accommodate up to six people, starts at $85 per day for two with $10 for each additional person. There is a two-day minimum, a deposit of $100 is required to hold a reservation, a 30-day cancellation period is in effect, and most credit cards are accepted. All guests have use of the washer and dryer, and there is good off-street parking. From the house, there's a short path to Pounder's Beach, and an outdoor shower can be used to wash off beach sand when returning. This is good value in a quiet, if not spectacular, setting.

A stone's throw from the La'ie Village Shopping Center is the one-unit vacation rental **Ala Mahina,** 808/293-2275. A tropical hideaway set among thick vegetation and right on the narrow but sandy beach, it has a good-size sitting room, small but fully furnished kitchen, and one bedroom with air-conditioning. All of the art hanging on the walls has been done by Michael, the owner. The rate is $150 per night plus a cleaning fee, and weekly rates can be negotiated.

## Food and Shopping

When you enter La'ie you will be greeted by the Stars and Stripes flying over the entrance of the PCC. Next door is a whopper of a McDonald's, and in keeping with the spirit of Polynesian culture, it looks like a Polynesian longhouse. Just up the road at the **La'ie Village Shopping Center** you'll find a large and modern Foodland, along with a Bank of Hawaii, a small convenience store, a handful of other shops, La'ie Washerette, L&L Drive-In, La'ie Chop Suey, La'ie Cinemas, a post office, a hardware store—all that you'll need and more for a successful vacation.

## KAHUKU

This village—and it is a village—is where the *workers* of the North Shore live. Kahuku is "fo' real," and a lingering slice of what *was* not so long ago. Do yourself a favor, and turn off the highway for a two-minute tour of the dirt roads lined by proudly maintained homes that somehow exude the feeling of Asia. The older part of town is to the sea side of the mill; newer homes line well-paved streets up by the school and hospital. When the sugar mill closed, this community, like many throughout the state, took a nose dive and lost its economic balance. Still looking for equilibrium, some locals have turned to raising freshwater shrimp in several shrimp farms just north of town, and others grow sweet corn. Along the beach is the local, nine-hole Kahuku Golf Course. It was built for plantation workers early in the 1900s, an unusual move by owners for their workers. It is now a municipal course.

On the northern outskirts of town are the two sections of the 164-acre **James Campbell National Wildlife Refuge.** Established in 1976, this refuge consists of marshland and man-made ponds, and harbors many varieties of waterfowl and shorebirds, including the endemic and endangered Hawaiian stilt, coot, duck, and moorhen. Free and educational guided tours are offered Aug.–Jan. on Saturday mornings and afternoons and Thursday afternoons for up to 25 people. Call the refuge management office at 808/637-6330 to make arrangements.

## Practicalities

You can pick up supplies at the **Kahuku Superette,** clearly marked along Route 83, from 6:15 A.M.–10 P.M. and shorter hours on the weekends. For short-order food, stop across the road at **Amy's By the Green,** a small plate lunch place that also serves grilled items and breakfast generally for under $6. For another uniquely local experience, try **Giovanni's** white *kaukau* wagon, which sits across the roadway from the school. Open 10:30 A.M.–6:30 P.M. daily, it sells shrimp scampi, a demonly spicy shrimp, and shrimp in lemon juice that run $11 for a dozen in-the-shell pieces, which comes with rice. Picnic tables sit under an awning attached to the wagon, and to the side is another *kaukau* wagon selling smoothies. You're guaranteed to get messy eating this meal, and you'll use a pile of napkins, but your sticky fingers and sated stomach are your reward. Other similar *kaukau* trucks selling shrimp can also be seen along the highway in the vicinity.

On the north end of town is the **Mill Shop-**

**ping Center,** which is really the town's old sugar mill recycled. The interior of the old mill, which operated 1893–1971 and may be open daily except Sunday 9 A.M.–5 P.M., is dominated by huge gears and machinery, power panels, crushers, and sign boards that give you a little sugar history lesson. The 10-foot gears and conveyor belts have all been painted with bright colors and seem like a display of modern art pieces. Outside the main mill building is a little bazaar of shops and a restaurant, but it's been difficult to keep the shops filled. Here as well are two condo offices for Turtle Bay Resort condos, a post office, and a gas station out front. The **Kahuku Sugar Mill Restaurant** serves mostly Korean and American plate lunches, but, because of the area, has several shrimp dishes as well. An indoor-outdoor restaurant with a walk-up window, it is open daily 8 A.M.–5 P.M. for breakfast and lunch. Most dishes are in the under-$8 range.

On the second and fourth Saturdays of the month from 8 A.M.–noon, the Kahuku Community Hospital sponsors a **farmer's market** for produce, flowers, and crafts, as well as a health screening.

Just a mile past Kahuku, beyond the shrimp farms, is the **Tanaka Plantation Store,** 56-901 Kamehameha Hwy., a refurbished early-1900s company store that now houses **The Only Show In Town** antique shop, 808/293-1295, open daily 10:30 A.M.–5:30 P.M. Blown to Oʻahu's North Shore from Kauaʻi by Hurricane ʻIniki, Paul Wroblewski has reopened his antiques and collectibles shop and once again jammed it with Hawaiian artifacts, old bottles, costume jewelry, license plates, Japanese glass fishing floats, netsuke, scrimshaw, a collection of Marilyn Monroe memorabilia, and a full line of antique jewelry. Paul's an amiable fellow and is open to any reasonable offer. Remember, he may price according to your attitude. Also, if you have a collectible that you want to sell or get an estimate on, ask Paul to take a look.

# The North Shore

This shallow bowl of coastline stretches from Ka'ena Point in the west to Turtle Bay in the east. **Mount Ka'ala,** verdant backdrop to the area, rises 4,020 feet from the Wai'anae Range, making it the highest peak on O'ahu. The entire stretch is a day-tripper's paradise, with plenty of sights to keep you entertained. But the North Shore is synonymous with one word: surfing.

Thunderous winter waves, often measuring 25 feet but sometimes up to 40 feet (from the rear!), rumble along the North Shore's world-fa-mous surfing beaches lined up one after the other—**Waimea Bay, Pipeline, 'Ehukai, Sunset.** They attract highly accomplished athletes who come to compete in prestigious international surfing competitions. Other beaches, often less well-known, like Mokule'ia Beach, also provide excellent waves without the crowds. Be aware that *all* North Shore beaches experience heavy surf conditions with dangerous currents from Oct.–Apr. The waters, at this time of year, are not for the average swimmer. Please heed all

ROBERT NILSEN

Spectacular sunsets are a daily occurrence along the North Shore.

warnings. In summer *moana* loses her ferocity and lies down, becoming gentle and safe for anyone—leap in!

The main attractions of the North Shore are its beaches, but interspersed among them are a few sights definitely worth your time and effort. The listings below run from west to east. Although the North Shore can easily be approached from Windward O'ahu, the most-traveled route to the North Shore is from Honolulu along the H-2 freeway to Wahiawa, and then directly to the coast from there along Route 99 or Route 803. At Weed Circle or Thompson Corner, where these routes reach the coastal highway, turn left along the Farrington Highway (Route 930), following it to road's end just before Ka'ena Point, or turn right along the Kamehameha Highway (Route 83), which heads around the coast all the way to Kane'ohe.

**Hale'iwa** has become the central town along the North Shore. Its main street is lined with restaurants, boutiques, art galleries, small shopping malls, and sports equipment stores. **Waialua,** just west, is a former sugar town with an old mill and a few quiet condos on the beach

for relaxation. Farther west is **Dillingham Airfield,** where you can arrange to fly above it all in a small biplane, soar silently in a glider, or give your heart a real jolt by jumping out of a plane for a free-fall parachute ride. The road ends for vehicles not far from there, and then your feet have to take you to Ka'ena Point, where large waves pound the coast and coastal sand dunes have been set aside as a nature reserve for native plants and birds. Heading east, you'll pass a famous *heiau* where human flesh once mollified the gods, a monument to a real local hero, and **Waimea Falls Park,** the premier tourist attraction of the North Shore. Then come the great surfing beaches and their incredible waves. Here and there are tidepools rich with discovery.

Places to stay are limited along the North Shore. The best deals are beach homes or rooms rented directly from the owners, but this is a hit-and-miss proposition. You have to check the local papers or the bulletin boards outside stores and shops in Hale'iwa and Waimea. Many better homes are now handled by rental agents. The homes vary greatly in amenities. Some are palaces, whereas others are basic rooms perfect for surfers or those who consider lodging secondary.

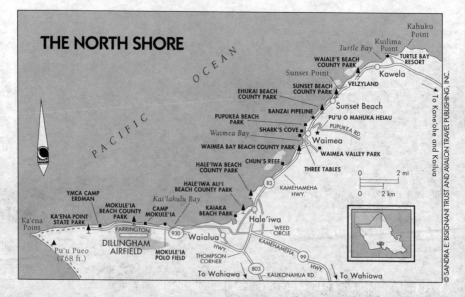

# Along the Farrington Highway

## Waialua

In the early 1900s, Waialua, a stop along the sugar-train railway, was a fashionable beach community complete with hotels and vacation homes. Today, it's hardly ever visited, and once in a while you can see horses tied up along the main street along with the parked cars in this real one-horse town. Sundays also attract a rumble of bikers, who kick up the dust on their two-wheeled steeds.

The old sugar mill, an outrageously ugly mechanical monster, dominates the town. There is no sugar now, but the area does produce some coffee, corn, bananas, and other diversified crops on mostly small plots. Quiet Waialua, with its main street divided by trees running down the middle, *is* rural O'ahu. There's a general store for supplies, a post office, a feed shop, and the **Sugar Bar,** a bar/cocktail lounge in the old Bank of Hawaii building that features a simple bar menu of *pu pu,* sandwiches, and pizza, and live music on Wednesday, Friday, Saturday, and Sunday evenings. The Sugar Bar is still a biker stop for motorcyclists who pull in for Sunday lunch on their way around the island.

If polo is your game or if you're just curious, head west of town to the Mokule'ia Polo Field and catch a Hawaii Polo Club match, Sunday at 2 P.M. from March to August.

## Coastal Points of Interest

**Mokule'ia Beach County Park** is the main public access park along the highway. It provides rudimentary picnic facilities, restrooms, a playground area, and camping, but almost no shade. In summer, swimming is possible along a few sandy stretches protected by an offshore reef. Some come to kiteboard because of the steady trade winds.

Farther down, **Mokule'ia Army Beach** is a wider strand of sand that also has little shade. It's private, and the only noise interrupting your afternoon slumber might be planes taking off from the airfield. Local people have erected semi-permanent tents in this area and guard it as if it were their own. A minute farther toward Ka'ena is an unofficial area with a wide sand beach.

During the week you can expect no more than a half dozen people on this 300-yard beach. Remember that this is the North Shore and the water can be treacherous.

Across from the YMCA camp and up the road a short ways is a trail (30 minutes) that leads uphill to a rock wall that can be seen from the road. Many consider this spot to be the best rock-climbing area on the island, and it is indeed unusual in this usually crumbly volcanic landscape.

Five minutes past the airfield, the road ends and the state park begins. This is a good place to check out giant waves in winter or have a good walk any time of year.

## Dillingham Airfield

Across the road from Mokule'ia Beach Park is Dillingham Airfield, small but modern, with restrooms near the hangars and a new parking area. Most days, especially weekends, a few local people sell refreshments from their cars or trucks. The main reason for stopping is to take a small biplane flight or glider ride or to try parachuting. **The Original Glider Rides,** 808/677-3404, takes you on a 20- or 30-minute flight. Talk to owner Bill Star, who has been flying from here since

Daredevils go skydiving at Dillingham Airfield.

1970. **Soar Hawaii Sailplanes,** 808/637-3147, also offers rides of differing lengths. Expect fees in the range of $40–70 for a 20-minute ride. This is the only place in the state where glider riders are offered. Mr. Bill also offers Stearman open-cockpit biplane rides for one person plus the pilot at $125 for a 20-minute flight or $195 for a 40-minute flight. Use the west end gate across from the control tower for these attractions.

The first entrance, at the eastern end of the field, will bring you to the three skydive operations: **Pacific International, Drop Zone,** and **Skydive Hawaii.** This is the only place in the state where skydiving is offered commercially. The thrill of a one-minute free fall followed by a five- to 10-minute parachute drop will set you back $150–200. Tandem drops only.

## Ka'ena Point State Park

Ka'ena Point lies about 2.5 miles down the dirt track after the pavement gives out. Count on three hours for a return hike and remember to bring water. The point can also be reached from road's end above Makaha on the Waianae (leeward) side of the island. The sand dunes on the point is a nature reserve for nesting sea birds, so give them wide berth. Ka'ena often has *the* largest waves in Hawaii on any given day. In winter, these giants can reach above 40 feet, and their power, even when viewed safely from the high ground, is truly amazing. Surfers have actually plotted ways of riding these waves, which include being dropped by helicopter with scuba tanks. Reportedly, one surfer named Ace Cool has already done it. For the rest of us mortals . . . "who wants to have that much fun anyway!" Ka'ena Point is the site of numerous *heiau.* Because of its exposed position, it, like similar sites around the islands, was a jumping-off point for the "souls of the dead." The spirits were believed to wander here after death, and once all worldly commitments were fulfilled, they made their leap from earth to the land beyond. Hopefully, the daredevil surfers will not revive this tradition! During winter, chances are good for seeing whales carousing off this point.

## Accommodations

**Mokuleia Beach Colony,** 68-615 Farrington Hwy., is a private gated community of 26 duplexes along a wonderfully uncrowded beach just past the polo grounds. Some owners rent their condos themselves, and others are handled by local real estate agents. For information and reservations, contact Paradise Realty, 808/637-1997, or Marianne Abrigo Properties, 808/637-3511.

Just beyond the Colony is **Mokule'ia Sunset Vacation Rentals,** 808/637-2312 or 808/637-4111. Set directly on the beach, this is a quiet place, clean, but a little funky. Other units on the property have long-term residents, but the rentals run about $685 per week for the cottage, $685 weekly for the studio, and $785 per week for the two-bedroom suite that looks right over the water.

**Camp Mokule'ia,** 68-729 Farrington Hwy., Waialua, HI 96791, 808/637-6241, fax 808/637-5505, www.campmokuleia.com, is owned and operated by the Episcopalian Church in Hawaii. This camp runs organized summer programs for kids ages 7–17, and offers space for other group meetings and retreats throughout the year. In addition, rooms in their lodge building are open to individuals and families on a space-available basis. Reserve no more than 30 days in advance. Plain and simple, rooms run $60–70 per day. Tent camping is also an option at $6 per person per night. Meals can be purchased separately when the kitchen is open for groups or you can barbecue your own. As an added attraction, Camp Mokule'ia has protected swimming on an adjacent sand beach.

**YMCA Camp H. R. Erdman,** 69-385 Farrington Hwy., Waialua, HI 96791, 808/637-4615, fax 808/637-8874, www.camperdman.net, is next, one of the best-known camps on O'ahu. This YMCA facility is named after a famous Hawaiian polo player killed in the 1930s. The full-service facility is used as a summer camp for children, throughout the year for special functions, and as a general retreat area by various organizations. Although cabins are usually rented to groups of eight or more, tenting is available Sept.–May on the weekends and daily through the summer for $50 per site (for up to 10 people), which includes use of the shower and bathrooms. At least a 48-hour advance reservation is requested.

# Hale'iwa and Vicinity

Hale'iwa (Home of the Frigate Birds) has become the premier town of the region, mainly because it straddles the main North Shore road where the highways over the Leilehua Plateau meet the coast, and it has most of the shopping, dining, and services along the North Shore. The coastal highway runs through town, but to ease traffic, Hale'iwa now has a bypass, the Joseph P. Leong Highway, around the backside of town. Unless you're really in a rush, follow the brown "Welcome to Historic Hale'iwa Town" sign into town because this is where it's all happening.

Many of the old buildings of town are of the single-story plantation-era variety from the early 1900s. Hale'iwa has managed to keep this old-style look fairly intact, and even the new North Shore Marketplace shopping mall has kept with the style and created mostly single-story false-front stores and covered wooden lanai.

Head through town going eastward and cross the graceful double-arch **Anahulu River Bridge.** Park for a moment and walk back over the bridge. Look upstream to see homes with tropical character perched on the bank of this lazy river. The scene is reminiscent of times gone by, and it is said that Queen Lili'uokalani once had a summer house on the riverbank here. The former Queen has left another mark on the town, this in the guise of the Lili'uokalani Protestant Church on the highway. Although the congregation is much older and the original church was from the late 1800s, the present church dates from 1961. Standing to the side in the cemetery are some headstones from the early days. If you're heading to between Waialua from Hale'iwa, take Hale'iwa Road, a back way through residential areas. Look for Pa'ala'a (Sacred Firmness) Road and take it past the Hale'iwa Shingon Mission temple, another old vestige from Hale'iwa's past. This Buddhist mission hosts an Obon festival yearly, traditionally observed in July, a colorful cultural event that honors the dead. This quiet town with a sugar past and lazy days of surfers and hippies is still strong on cultural activities. If you're in town during the Hale'iwa Arts Festi-val and the taro festival, don't miss them. These days, major activities revolve around surfing; some of the biggest surfing events in the country are held at the beaches up the coast.

## PARKS

Fronting town, **Hale'iwa Ali'i Beach Park** is on the western shore of Waialua Bay, set next to Hale'iwa Harbor. This beach park is improved with restrooms, a lifeguard tower, and a small boat launch. Lifeguards staff the tower throughout the summer, on weekends in winter. The shoreline is rocks and coral with pockets of sand, and although portions can be good for swimming, the park is primarily noted for surfing at a break simply called Hale'iwa. The park is popular with townspeople, and it became more widely known in the late 1990s because the then-popular TV program *Baywatch Hawaii* was based here, and some of the shows were filmed on the beach.

A little farther to the west, on Kaiaka Point, is **Kaiaka Beach County Park.** This is a good snorkeling beach, and you'll find restrooms and picnic areas here. Camping is allowed with a county permit.

**Hale'iwa Beach County Park,** clearly marked off the highway on the eastern side of Waialua Bay beyond the bridge, is right at the river mouth across from the marina. Here you'll find pavilions, picnic facilities, athletic grounds, restrooms, showers, lots of parking, and a food concession, but no camping. The area is good for fishing, surfing, and, most important, for swimming year-round! It's about the only safe place for the average person to swim along the entire North Shore during winter. You can often see the canoe club practicing in the bay during late afternoon.

**Kawailoa Beach** is the general name given to the waterfront stretching all the way from Hale'iwa Beach County Park to Waimea Bay. Cars park where the access is good. None of the shoreline is really suitable for the recreational swimmer. All are surfing areas, with the most popular being Chun's Reef.

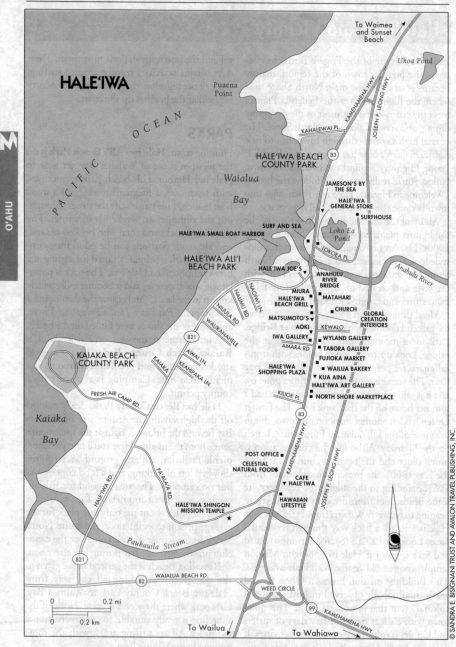

**HALEʻIWA**

PACIFIC OCEAN

Puaena Point

Waialua Bay

Kaiaka Bay

To Waimea and Sunset Beach

Ukoa Pond

KAHALEWAI PL.

HALEʻIWA BEACH COUNTY PARK

JAMESON'S BY THE SEA

HALEʻIWA GENERAL STORE

SURFHOUSE

Loko Ea Pond

LOKOEA PL.

SURF AND SEA

HALEʻIWA SMALL BOAT HARBOR

HALEʻIWA ALIʻI BEACH PARK

HALEʻIWA JOE'S

ANAHULU RIVER BRIDGE

Anahulu River

MIURA

MATAHARI

HALEʻIWA BEACH GRILL

CHURCH

MATSUMOTO'S

GLOBAL CREATION INTERIORS

AOKI

KEWALO

IWA GALLERY

WYLAND GALLERY

TABORA GALLERY

AMARA RD.

FUJIOKA MARKET

HALEʻIWA SHOPPING PLAZA

WAILUA BAKERY

KUA AINA

HALEʻIWA ART GALLERY

KILIOE PL.

NORTH SHORE MARKETPLACE

KAIAKA BEACH COUNTY PARK

NAOMI LN.

NAIMU RD.

NIUULA RD.

WAIKANAHELE

AWAI LN.

KEAHIPAKA LN.

KAIAKA

FRESH AIR CAMP RD.

POST OFFICE

CELESTIAL NATURAL FOODS

CAFE HALEʻIWA

HAWAIIAN LIFESTYLE

HALEʻIWA SHINGON MISSION TEMPLE

HALEʻIWA RD.

PAALAA RD.

Paukauila Stream

WAIALUA BEACH RD.

WEED CIRCLE

To Wailua

To Wahiawa

KAMEHAMEHA HWY.

JOSEPH P. LEONG HWY.

KAMEHAMEHA HWY.

0        0.2 mi
0     0.2 km

## ACCOMMODATIONS

On the back side of Lokoea Pond just at the edge of town is **Surfhouse**, 62-202 Lokoea Pl., Haleiwa, HI 96712, 808/637-7146, info@surf-house.com, www.surfhouse.com. A budget accommodation, the Surfhouse offers shared and private rooms in the main house, a detached bunkhouse, and a couple of cabins. The bunkhouse has six beds that run $15 per night or $95 per week; private rooms are $40–45 per night or $280 per week. Campers can find a space on the lawn for $9 per night ($15 per couple) or $56 per week. Washers and dryers are available, and the "Hale'iwa Yacht Club," with its stove, sink, refrigerator, couches, and chairs, serves as the communal eating, sitting, and entertainment area for guests. Bicycles and water equipment can be rented at inexpensive rates. There's adequate space to park cars. Mostly, young people come to hang out here for a few weeks or stay while looking for a job and more permanent housing or while surfing or watching surfing competitions, and often a real camaraderie develops among them. Make your arrangements with Sophie or Lee.

For vacation rentals, see the list of agents in the Accommodations section of the Waimea Bay and Vicinity section.

## FOOD

### Inexpensive

**Celestial Natural Foods**, 808/637-6729, open Mon.–Sat. 9 A.M.–6 P.M., Sun. 10 A.M.–6 P.M., is near the western end of town. Up front is a complete natural and health food store. In back, and called **Paradise Found**, is a lunch counter that's open until 5 P.M. that serves vegetarian meals. Some items are nachos for $4.95, tofu sauté wrap at $5.95, garden burger for $5.95, and tempeh calzone for $8.95. Smoothies, fresh juice drinks, teas, sodas, and sweets are also available. The food is healthful and nutritious, but portions are definitely not for the hungry.

**Cafe Hale'iwa**, 808/637-5516, a casual hole-in-the-wall eatery on your right just as you enter town, serves one of the best breakfasts on O'ahu.

Specials of the house are whole-wheat banana pancakes for $4.95, the Dawn Patrol, which is two buttermilk pancakes with two eggs for $3, off the wall omelettes $6.25–7.50, huevos rancheros at $6.50, Breakfast in a Barrel, which is an egg and potato burrito with home fries and rice or beans for $5.55, and steaming-hot Kona coffee. Lunch options include fish sandwiches, burritos with home fries and potato salad, and steak and eggs for $7.95. The café attracts many surfers, so it's a great place to find out about conditions. Hours are Mon.–Fri. 7 A.M.–12:30 P.M. and Sat. and Sun. until 2 P.M.

Another tiny place with great treats is **Kua Aina**, for a great assortment of sandwiches, salads, and—some claim—the best burgers on the island. Most items are under $6. There are a few tables out front on the lanai if you're lucky enough to find a spot among the hungry mob. Open 11 A.M.–8 P.M.

Almost next door is **Spaghettini**, 808/637-0104. With a take-out window and a few seats under the canopy, this restaurant dishes up full helpings of pasta, a few sandwich offerings, and New York–style pizza. It's quick and fun and draws those who want to fill up without spending too much. Pasta runs $8–9, pizza $5.45 and up, and combinations are also on the menu.

If the smells of fresh-baked bread and pastries don't bring you into the **Wailua Bakery,** nothing will. Aside from the breads, cookies, and muffins, the bakery makes filling and delicious sandwiches, smoothies, and juice, right for a "get-me-started" push in the morning or a "keep-me-going" nudge during the day. Although closed on Sunday, the bakery is open other days from 8 A.M.–4 P.M.

**Rosie's Cantina,** 808/637-3538, in the Hale'iwa Shopping Plaza, open daily for breakfast, lunch, and dinner, prepares hearty Mexican dishes for a decent price. The inside is "yuppie Mex" with brass rails, painted overhead steam pipes, and elevated booths. Breakfast is mostly eggs and grill items, but with a south-of-the-border edge, but the full lunch and dinner menus are more typically Mexican, from burritos to quesadillas and fajitas. Expect to pay $8–9 for most dishes. Full bar is available.

**Pizza Bob's,** 808/637-5095, also in the Hale'iwa Shopping Plaza, has an excellent local reputation, and its little pub serves not only delicious pizza, but also salads, pasta, burgers, and sandwiches. Dinner specials are offered nightly. People are friendly, there's plenty of food, and the price is right. Open most nights until 9 P.M., Fri.–Sat. until 10 P.M., and there's live music on Friday evenings.

You can tell by the tour buses parked outside that **Matsumoto's** is a famous store on the North Shore. What are all those people after? Shave ice. This is one of the best places on O'ahu to try this island treat. Not only do the tourists come here, but local families often take a Sunday drive just to get Matsumoto's shave ice. Try the Hawaiian Delight, a mound of ice smothered with banana, pineapple, and mango syrup, or any three of nearly two dozen flavors plus ice cream or sweet beans on the bottom. If lines are too long here or if you want to frequent the competition, try **Aoki's** shave ice or **Miura Store,** both only a few steps away. Shave ice cones run about $2.

Its bright colors and modernistic designs might make you think that you're in a modern art painting, but the food at the **Hale'iwa Beach Grill,** 808/637-3394, brings you back to reality. A casual place—plate lunches, sandwiches, burritos, and other simple fare all go for under $6. Order at the counter. The grill is open 11 A.M.–5 P.M.

If you're tired or just need a pick-me-up, head for the North Shore Marketplace, where you'll find the **Coffee Gallery,** 808/637-5571, open daily 6 A.M.–9 P.M., which has a large selection of fresh roasted gourmet coffee, including Kona coffees and international selections of organically grown coffee. You can enjoy a steaming cup from its full-service espresso bar, along with fresh carrot juice and vegan pastries made without dairy products or eggs. Every day there is a homemade soup, fresh salad, and a fine selection of deli sandwiches that range from a vegetarian garden burger on a whole wheat bun with lettuce and tomatoes, Maui onion, guacamole, and a side of tortilla chips to pita bread filled with eggplant, pesto, and veggies, all priced around $6. It's all vegetarian. Sit outside in the shaded and screened dining area and watch the characters of the North Shore come and go. Internet access is available.

For south-of-the-border food, try **Cholo's Homestyle Mexican Restaurant,** 808/637-3059, open 8 A.M.–9 P.M. Plate items, which include rice and beans, run $5.25–9.25; dinners include rice, beans, salad, chips, salsa, and a choice of meat and go for $7.50–11.75. Many combinations and a variety of nacho plates are also available. To help keep you interested while you wait for you food, the walls are festooned with masks, paintings, prints, crossed, figurines, and other works of art and crafts.

Up front at the Marketplace and along the highway, **Kono's Big Wave Cafe,** 808/637-9211, serves hearty burrito breakfasts, bagels, salads, sandwiches, and hot dogs for those with a healthy appetite. It's one of the few places in town that offers Internet access. Open weekdays 8 A.M.–6 P.M., Sat. until 7 P.M. and Sun. from 9 A.M.

If you're heading west and looking for a sweet treat, stop at **Paalaa Bakery** on the outskirts of Wahiawa for malasadas, pastries of all sorts, donuts, twists, turnovers, and the like. Open 5 A.M.–8 P.M. daily.

## Moderate

**Jameson's by the Sea,** 62-540 Kamehameha Hwy., 808/637-4336, open daily for lunch, dinner, and cocktails, is the best that Hale'iwa has to offer. At the north end of town overlooking the sea, its outdoor deck is perfect for a romantic sunset dinner, while inside the romantic mood is continued with shoji screens, cane chairs with stuffed pillows, candles with shades, and tables resplendent with fine linen. Appetizers include a salmon pâté, crab-stuffed mushrooms, fresh oysters, and a bowl of creamy clam chowder. Main dishes like mahimahi, baked stuffed shrimp, ocean scallops, and filet mignon range $18.50–25. For dessert have the lemon macadamia nut chiffon pie. The pub on the lower level serves lunch from a slightly different menu that includes sandwiches and a variety of imported beers. Breakfast is served Sat.–Sun. 9 A.M.–noon. Reservations are highly recommended. Request a window seat for the sunset.

**Haleʻiwa Joe's Seafood Grill,** 66-011 Kamehameha Hwy., 808/637-8005, open daily for lunch from 11:30 A.M. and dinner from 5:30 P.M., is in a green cinder-block building on the left before you cross the Anahulu River bridge. Although purely utilitarian on the outside, the inside is modern and tasteful with a touch of North Shore surfing decor. Located on the site of the area's first hotel and a precious *heiau*, this fine restaurant looks out over the Haleʻiwa boat harbor, and some of what's on the menu comes directly from the fishing boats. Dine inside or out. Appetizers like ahi spring roll, Thai fried calamari, and crunchy coconut shrimp run $7–10. Soups and salads are on the menu from a house salad at $3.95 to a grilled salmon spinach salad for $10.75. Main entrées here emphasize fish, but steak and ribs are also available. Fresh mahimahi is always a winner, grilled spicy shrimp starts the taste buds jumping, and the pork ribs marinated in soy-ginger and hoisin sauce tip the hat toward the Orient. Most entrées run $14–20, but the Alaskan king crab legs go for $24.95. Haleʻiwa Joe's is a good-time place with tasty food in a casual setting. Its full bar and live music (on some weekends) make this a lively hangout for the local crowd and visitors alike.

# SHOPPING
## In Town

In town you'll find **Miura** general store, in business since 1918, which has a few basic dry goods but mostly cloth and brightly colored clothing. **Matahari** carries women's fashions. **Global Creation Interiors** handles furniture, artwork, home accessories, and some hand-painted silk clothing.

Along the highway is **Haleʻiwa Shopping Plaza,** which provides all the necessities in one-stop shopping: boutiques, pharmacy, photo store, a Bank of Hawaii and First Hawaiian Bank, and general food and merchandise. For food and picnic supplies, try the **Haleʻiwa IGA,** open Mon.–Sat. 8 A.M.–8 P.M., Sun. 8:30 A.M.–5:30 P.M. Almost across the street is the smaller **Fujioka Super Market** with a smaller variety but nearly the same hours.

## North Shore Marketplace

The North Shore Marketplace, along the Kamehameha Highway between McDonald's and the Haleʻiwa Shopping Center, is a newer complex with some unique shops. Most shops are open 9 A.M.–6 P.M., with restaurants serving until late. One of the most interesting shops is **Jungle Gem's,** with a metaphysical assortment of crystals, crystal balls, African trading beads, and gems. The shop specializes in locally made jewelry that is reasonably priced and of excellent quality. The owners are knowledgeable gemologists and fine jewelers who do much of the work on display. **Silver Moon Emporium** has not only some jewelry but also a fine collection of boutique clothing. For something more gifty and more island-oriented, have a look at **Polynesian Handicrafts** and **Kamaʻainas Haleʻiwa.** Upstairs in the back is **Outrigger Trading Co.,** a shop specializing in gifts and souvenirs. Here you can find high-quality jewelry, prints, T-shirts, candles, books, and many more items. The shop is open daily 10 A.M.–10 P.M.

For water wear and ocean equipment, have a look at **Kitehigh Boardsports** and **Quicksilver. Patagonia** has high-quality outdoor wear and equipment.

To the left in the rear as you drive into the parking lot is **Barnfield's Raging Isle Surf and Cycle,** 808/637-7707, www.ragingisle.com, a full-service mountain bike and surf shop open daily 10 A.M.–6 P.M. The shop also manufactures surfboards here, the only major place on the North Shore doing so. Board repairs are also made. Casual clothing and surf wear are stocked.

**Twelve Tribes International Imports** is a multicultural emporium in the back with items from the global village. Although there are several craft and jewelry items, much is clothing. It's open Mon.–Fri. 10:30 A.M.–5:30 P.M., Sat. 10 A.M.–6 P.M., and Sun. noon–5 P.M.

Across the way is **North Shore Glass,** where hand-blown art glass is produced in the open-air studio. Most of what the artists make goes to the hotels, but they do have a good collection of retail items that they sell in the studio. Pyrex is used for these delicate figures, many of them dolphins and other sea creatures. Check them out to see how the work is done. Open 10 A.M.–6 P.M. daily.

Next door to North Shore Glass is the **North Shore Surf Museum.** A walk through this compact showplace will teach you a bit about the history of surfing on the North Shore, and you'll have a chance to examine surfboards, clothing, photographs, and other artifacts of surfing life and the culture of the North Shore. The sign says "open most afternoons."

## Art Galleries and Shops

'Iwa Gallery, open most days 10:30 A.M.–6:30 P.M., is across the street from the Protestant church, which was founded in 1892, and next door to Aoki's Shave Ice. This co-op shows the efforts of local artists who have been juried in order to place their artwork on consignment. Featured are the fine candle sculptures of Scott Bechtol. Other artists displayed at the gallery include Angela Kanas, a watercolor artist who does fanciful renditions of Hawaiian gods, goddesses, and traditional folk; Janet Stewart, who depicts island themes like Madame Pele lying with the blood of her hot lava flowing from her body or a *keiki* hula dancer with a look of concentration on her face; and Bill Cupid, who uses the bark of banana trees to create entire island scenes like ships departing a sheltered harbor. Serigraphs and cards by Janet Holiday are often depictions of flowers in bold primary colors; Peggy Pai, born and raised in China, creates silk batik with ephemeral, beautiful, cloudy landscapes; James Rack uses his palette and brush to catch scenes of idyllic Hawaii; and Norman Kelly catches children at play or surfers on towering waves in his fluid watercolors.

**Wyland Gallery,** across the street from the Hale'iwa Shopping Plaza, 808/637-7498, is open daily 9 A.M.–6 P.M. Wyland is a famous environmental artist known for his huge whale and marine life murals, in addition to watercolors and fine oil paintings. The gallery is large, spacious, and well lit, and is the first galley that he opened. Everything has a Hawaiian or sea theme. There are watercolors of Hawaiian maidens by Janet Stewart, the strong paintings of John Pitre and Scott Powers, and bronze sculptures of the sea by Scott

Hanson. If the original artwork is too expensive, there are posters, mini-prints, and postcards.

The **Tabora Gallery,** 808/637-2986, features the wonderfully evocative seascape paintings of Tabora. It's easy to see how the subtle color, movement, and expression in his scenes has propelled him to become one of the most sought-after contemporary Hawaiian artists. Also displayed in this gallery are paintings by Rudolf Gonzales, Tabora's cousin, who paints the same basic subjects with a slightly different feel. Landscape paintings of Gary Reed and fantasy-scapes of James Coleman, who once was a Disney artist, also grace the gallery walls.

At the North Shore Marketplace, **Hale'iwa Art Gallery,** 808/637-3368, shows mostly original works by island artists, many from O'ahu, mostly up-and-comers who have not yet made it big but who show obvious talent. Lots of paintings are features, with a smaller selection of other forms and mediums. Featuring more than 30 (mostly) island artists, **Britton Gallery,** 808/637-6505, has a good selection of high-quality work that's a combination of paintings, prints, photographs, sculpture, and woodwork, with the addition of some gift items.

A neighbor to Hale'iwa Cafe, **Hawaiian Lifestyle,** 808/637-3000, is a collection of koa woodwork and functional art pieces, like boxes and bowls, rocking chairs, lamps, and wall decorations that are done mostly by North Shore artists.

## Sporting Rentals and Activities

The following shops are all along the main drag through Hale'iwa.

**Barnfield's Raging Isle Surf and Cycle,** in the North Shore Marketplace, 808/637-7707, is primarily a surf shop and manufacturer of Barnfield's Raging Isle Boards. Aside from selling and repairing bikes, Barnfield's also rents mountain bikes at $40 for 24 hours.

**Island Bike Rentals** rents full-suspension mountain bikes for $40 per day, cruisers at $20 per day, one-person mopeds for $35 per day, and two-passenger scooters for $60 per day. They are a small shop that builds custom bikes to order and does bike repair. Find them behind the 'Iwa Gallery or call 808/637-9991.

For surfboards, sailboards, boogie boards, snorkeling equipment, scuba gear, and other water toys, try **Surf and Sea,** 62-595 Kamehameha Hwy., 808/637-9887, www.surfnsea.com. The most well-established place in town, Surf and Sea is a mustard yellow building near the bridge that offers great rentals and sales, boat trips, fishing charters, and daily scuba, surfing, and sailboarding lessons. Open daily 9 A.M.–6 P.M. Across the street next to the bridge, **Tropical Rush** has a great selection of surfboards and beachwear for sale and boards for rent.

Along the highway in the center of town is **Strong Currents,** a surf shop that also has clothing, but it's more than that. It's almost like a museum of surfing with all the collectibles on display. Also for boards, clothing, and accessories, try **HIC Hawaiian Island Creations** nearby. Another quality company doing scuba lessons is **Deep Ecology,** 66-456 Kamehameha Hwy., 808/637-7946, www.deepecologyhawaii.com.

There is not an overabundance of water activity companies on the North Shore, but **North Shore Catamaran Charters,** 808/638-8279, does offer cat rides throughout the year

from Hale'iwa harbor on its 40-foot *Ho'o Nanea.* Picnic snorkels run from May–Oct. and whale-watching rides from Jan.–May. An associated company, **The Watercraft Connection** 808/637-8006, rents personal watercraft and kayaks from a small booth at the entrance to the harbor. Also leaving from Hale'iwa harbor for part- or full-day charter fishing trips along the North Shore is **Chupu Charters,** 808/638-3474.

## INFORMATION AND SERVICES

The best sources of current specific information pertaining to the North Shore are the bulletin boards outside many of the shops and restaurants.

As you enter Hale'iwa from the west, you'll pass a gas station and a full-service post office; just east of the arched bridge is another gas station and the Hale'iwa General Store for basic supplies. Bank of Hawaii and First Hawaiian Banks are at the Hale'iwa Shopping Plaza. Hale'iwa Family Health Center, 808/637-5087, a walk-in clinic at the rear of the Haleiwa Shopping Plaza, is open Mon.–Sat. 8 A.M.–5 P.M.

# Waimea Bay and Vicinity

The two-lane highway along the North Shore is pounded by traffic; be especially careful around Waimea Bay. The highway sweeps around until you see the steeple of **St. Peter and Paul Mission** with the bay below. The steeple is actually the remnants of an old rock-crushing plant on the site. On the far side of the bay, the road enters **Waimea,** a small one-horse town with little more than a fire station, beach park, supermarket, and one shop that sells beachwear, gifts, and accessories, and rents bikes, snorkel and beach gear, and gives surf lessons.

## Waimea Bay Beach County Park

Waimea Bay has some of the largest rideable waves in the world. This is the heart of surfers' paradise. The park, improved with a lifeguard tower, restrooms, and a picnic area, covers the bay where the river enters the ocean. The

church steeple overlooks the beach's east end; kids dive off rocks at its western end. In summer, the bay is as calm as a lake. During big winter swells, the bay is lined with spectators watching the surfers ride the monumental waves. People inexperienced with the sea should not even walk along the shorebreak in winter. Unexpected waves come up farther than you'd think, and a murderous rip lurks only a few feet from shore. The area is rife with tales of heroic rescue attempts, many ending in fatalities. A plaque commemorates Eddie Aikau, a local lifeguard credited with making thousands of rescues. In 1978, the *Hokule'a,* the Polynesian Sailing Society's double-hulled canoe, capsized in rough seas about 20 miles offshore. Eddie was aboard and launched his surfboard to swim for help. He never made it, but his selfless courage lives on.

ROBERT NILSEN

winter at Waimea Bay Beach

## Waimea Falls Park

Look for the well-marked entrance to Waimea Falls Park, mountain side from the bay, and then drive into the lush valley before coming to the actual park entrance. The park is the most culturally significant travel destination on the North Shore, and while providing a wonderful day of excitement, education, and outdoor activity, it has not lost sight of its ancient *aloha* soul. Primarily a botanical garden, with a fascinating display of flowers and plants labeled for your edification, the **Waimea Arboretum** collects, grows, and preserves extremely rare specimens of Hawaii's endangered flora. If you choose not to walk, a free open-air tram will take you through, narrating all the way. Within this garden setting is Waimea Falls Park, which presents lessons, demonstrations, and other activities of cultural significance throughout the day at several locations. One thrilling event is the professional diving from the 55-foot rock walls into the pool below Waimea Falls. Culturally enlightening are displays of ancient hula *(kahiko)* performed by accomplished dancers, a display of Hawaiian games, carving demonstrations, and walks along forest paths that end at fascinating historical sites. All in

all, and amid the beauty of this valley, this is a wonderful learning experience while you have fun at the same time. On the property is **Hale o Lono Heiau,** one of the island's largest and most ancient *heiau*, dedicated to the god Lono, and numerous other sites of ancient Hawaiian life and ethnology. As a newer accompaniment to this cultural experience, the park offers outdoor tours for those who desire more physical activity. Horseback rides and mountain-bike tours are conducted over trails in the adjacent valley, and guided or self-guided kayak tours are operated down the lazy river toward the ocean. Some age and weight restrictions apply.

Waimea Falls Park is open 10 A.M.–5:30 P.M. daily, 808/638-8511. General admission, which allows you access to all shows and cultural tours, is $24 adults, $12 ages 4–12. Activities are sold as separate options and, except for one, do not require admission to the park. Horseback rides lasting one hour or 90 minutes go three times a day for $45 per hour. For the more physically fit, various 30-minute to two-hour mountain-bike rides run $20–45. Guided and self-guided kayaking trips along the stream are $15–45. Taking place inside the park, the Top of the Falls "hike, lean, and look" activity, which imparts a bird's-eye view of a cliff dive, is run several times a day for $20. In addition, the Discover Waimea Package puts general admission and lunch together for $32.95 adults and $18.95 children. At the visitors center, the Pikake Restaurant is open for buffet lunch only at $12.95 from 11 A.M.–2 P.M., but plate lunches and other foods can be had throughout the day from the Country Kitchen Snack Shop inside the park.

## Pupukea Beach Park

A perfect place to experience marine life is the large tidepool next to Pupukea Beach Park, the first one north of Waimea Bay, across the street from the Shell gas station. The beach park has restrooms, picnic facilities, and fair swimming in sandy pockets between coral and rock, but only in summer. A long retaining wall out to sea forms a large and protected pool at low tide. Wear footgear and check out the pools with a mask. Don't be surprised to find large sea bass. Be careful not to step on sea urchins, and stay away from the pool during rough winter swells, when it can be treacherous. The western end of this park is called Three Tables. The eastern section of the park is called Shark's Cove, although no more sharks are here than anywhere else. The area is terrific for snorkeling and a major destination for scuba tours in season. The Pupukea Marine Life Conservation District runs from Three Tables Cove past Shark's Cove to Kulalua Point and includes the tidal pools and shoreline. Most water activities are permitted, but spearfishing is not. If you had to pick a spot from which to view the North Shore sunset, Pupukea Beach Park is hard to beat. Convenient for those who are out for a bit of exercise, a jogging/bicycle path parallels the highway and links Pupukea Beach Park with Sunset Beach Park a couple of miles up the road.

Farther down the road, as you pass mile marker 9, you can't help noticing a mammoth redwood log that has been carved into a giant statue called *Maui Pohaku Loa*, representing an ancient Hawaiian. Peter Wolfe, the sculptor, has done a symbolic sculpture for every state in the union, this being his 50th. This statue is extremely controversial. Some feel that it looks much more like an American Indian than a Hawaiian, and that the log used should have been a native koa instead of an imported redwood from the Pacific Northwest. Others say that its *intention* was to honor the living and the ancient Hawaiians, and that is what's important.

## Pu'u O Mahuka Heiau

Do yourself a favor and drive up the mountain road leading to this *heiau*, even if you don't want to visit it. The vast and sweeping views of the coast below to the west are incredible. About one mile past Waimea Bay the highway passes a Foodland on the right. Turn here up Pupukea Road and follow the signs.

Pu'u O Mahuka Heiau, the largest on O'ahu, covers a little more than five acres. Designated as a national historical landmark, its three sections descend the hillside in huge steps, with one area dropping to another just below. The *heiau* was the site of human sacrifice. People still come to pray, as is evidenced by many stones wrapped in *ti* leaves placed on small stone piles lying about the grounds. In the upper section is a raised mound surrounded by stone in what appears to be a central altar area. The *heiau's* stonework shows a high degree of craftsmanship throughout, but especially in the pathways. The lower section of the *heiau* appears to be much older and is not as well maintained.

Drive past the *heiau* access road and in a minute or so make a left onto Alapio Road. This takes you through an expensive residential area called Sunset Hills and past a home locally called The Mansion—look for the English-style boxwood hedge surrounding it. The home was purported to be Elvis Presley's island hideaway. This area is a tremendous vantage point from which to view Fourth of July fireworks lighting up Waimea Bay far below. Next to it is a white sculpture called the World Unity Monument. The road straight up the hill leads to the Boy Scout Camp, beyond which a biking/hiking trail leads into the mountains.

## The Great Surfing Beaches

Beyond Waimea Bay lies a series of great surfing beaches, most powerful and dramatic in winter

**M**

**O'AHU**

when the big waves roll into shore. It is here, when the waves are at their best, that the big international surfing competitions are held and swarms of visitor drive up to watch. Unless you are familiar with the water and have experience in big waves, don't even think of going out. Just spend some time on shore admiring the power of the ocean and skill of those who know how to ride these monsters.

These beaches run end to end, and its hard to tell where one ends and the next begins. This is one of the longest white-sand beaches on O'ahu, and while the entire stretch is sometimes referred to as Sunset Beach, each world-famous surfing spot warrants its own name, although they're not clearly marked and are tough to find . . . exactly. Winter surf erodes the beach, with coral and lava fingers exposed at the shoreline, but in summer you can expect an uninterrupted beach usually 200–300 feet wide. In years past, the beaches were not always well maintained, and the restrooms, even at Waimea Bay, were sometimes atrocious. The reason was politics and money. Efforts all went into Waikiki, where the tourists are. Who cared about a bunch of crazy surfers on the North Shore? They're just a free curiosity for the tourists' enjoyment! Recently, however, some money has been put into this area to alleviate these problems, and a few new facilities have been constructed.

First up the line is **Banzai Beach,** probably the best-known surfing beach in the world. Its notoriety dates from *Surf Safari,* an early surfer film made in the 1950s, when it was dubbed "Banzai" by Bruce Brown, maker of the film. The famous tubelike effect of the breaking waves comes from a shallow reef just offshore, which forces the waves to rise dramatically and quickly. This forces the crest forward to create "the Pipeline," hence the term **Banzai Pipeline** for this break. Other breaks at this beach are **Back Doors, Off the Wall,** and **Log Cabins.** A lifeguard tower near the south end of the beach at the stream entrance is all you'll find in the way of improvements. Parking is along the roadway.

**'Ehukai Beach County Park** is the next area north. Look for Sunset Beach Elementary School on the inland side of the highway. There is a small parking lot here, but you can park in the school's lot on nonschool days. 'Ehukai has a lifeguard tower and restroom and provides one of the best vantage points from which to watch the surfing action on the Pipeline, as well as **Pupukea, Gas Chambers,** and **Kammie Land,** other breaks up the coast to the right. Surfing competitions will often have their headquarters set up here, and broadcasting companies will televise from this beach.

Don't expect much when you come to **Sunset Beach County Park,** except for a grand beach that curves around to the east to Sunset Point. Aside from a lifeguard tower, there's only a parking lot and bathrooms across the street. Almost as famous as the surfing break is the **Sunset Rip,** a notorious offshore current that grabs people every year. Summertime is generally safe, but never take *moana* for granted.

Farther to the east and just beyond the University Livestock Farm is **Waiale'e Beach County Park.** Its rocky shoreline makes it not so good for swimmers except for a small sandy spot at the southern end, but many fishermen come to try their luck. Off the shore here and to the south is **Vezlyland,** a well-known surfing spot. Across the street may be a stand selling fresh fruit and coconuts, and in the area you'll undoubtedly find others selling sweet corn.

# ACCOMMODATIONS
## Surfer Rentals
The North Shore of O'ahu has long been famous for its world-class surfing. The area attracts enthusiasts from around the world who are much more concerned with the daily surfing report than they are with deluxe accommodations. The Kamehameha Highway is dotted with surfer rentals from Hale'iwa to Turtle Bay. Just outside their doors are famous surfing breaks. Some of these accommodations are terrific, whereas others are barely livable, and you'll find that most of both types are taken throughout the winter surfing season.

**Shark's Cove Rentals,** 59-672 Kamehameha Hwy., 808/638-7980, info@sharkscoverentals.com, www.sharkscoverentals.com, offers shared and private rooms in its two houses directly across from Shark's Cove. Clean, safe, homey, and well-maintained, Shark's Cove contains a living room, full kitchen, and shared bathroom in each of its three areas, and an outdoor covered patio, pay phone, washer, and dryer for use by all guests. With a capacity of 20, it's small enough to get to know others easily yet large enough for some diversity. A bunk in the four-person room upstairs in the two-story house runs $30 per night ($25 May–Sept.). Other rooms with a single bunkbed or a double/single bunkbed run $60–75 per room ($50–60 in the summer). Weekly and monthly rates are available. No breakfast is served, and there is a small key and linen deposit. Contact John or Wilma Lane for information or reservations.

**Backpacker's Vacation Inn and Plantation Village,** 59-788 Kamehameha Hwy., 808/638-7838, fax 808/638-7515 (courtesy phone at airport), bpacker@maui.net, www.backpackers-hawaii.com, specializes in budget accommodations for surfers, backpackers, and families. It's in a perfect location, between Waimea Bay and the center of Waimea village, fronting Three Tables Beach. Find it at mile marker 6, the fourth driveway past the church tower coming from Waimea Bay. On the mountain side of the road are two three-story, pole-style houses that offer hostel and private room accommodation, while on the ocean side directly across is an additional building with studios. Basic rates in the main house are $15–18 for a bunk in the hostel-style rooms, which includes use of a kitchen, laundry facilities, and TV in the communal room. Each room has four bunks, a shower, and a bath. The feeling is definitely not deluxe, but it is adequate, and there can be a real communal vibe. The back house has several private rooms for two with shared kitchen and bath for $45–55. Studios in the building on the beach rent for $80–114 daily depending on the season, and each has a complete kitchen or kitchenette, two double beds, a roll-out couch, a ceiling fan, and a world-class view of the beach from the lanai. Weekly rates with discounts are offered, and all payments are to be made in advance—no refund policy. This inn and hostel is often full, so book ahead. It provides free boogie boards and snorkeling gear, Internet access, bike rental for $5–10 per day, and can arrange whale-watching or sunset sails, scuba lessons, kayak rental, and other activities and equipment often at reduced rates. Small valuables can be locked away in an office safe, and larger items can also be stored. Airport transportation for guests is free to and from, and The-Bus no. 52 stops directly in front. This friendly, laid-back place is a good choice.

About two hundred yards toward town is the **Plantation Village,** also operated by Backpacker's. The cluster of nine private cottages here, once the homes of real plantation workers, create a small community. These cottages are furnished with cable TV, linens, fans, and a full kitchen, and the lanai is a great place to catch the breezes. It's only a three-minute walk to the Foodland store for supplies. Everyone is free to use the washers and dryers and pay phone in the common area. One caveat, however: Some guests have complained that the cottages have, in some cases, been unkempt, in need of supplies, lacking in security, and generally not kept up to the best standards. Use your own judgment. Many of the fruit trees on the grounds provide the guests with complimentary bananas, papayas, and mangos. A bunk in the dorm here goes for $15–18. The larger, multibedroom cottages that sleep 4–10 people run $110–200. An inexpensive and nutritious evening meal is served two or three nights in the garden area of the village. During surfing season, the Plantation Village is booked up, so reserve well in advance. For information and reservations, contact Backpacker's (see previous paragraph).

## Vacation Rentals

**Ke Iki Beach Bungalows,** 59-579 Ke Iki Rd., Waimea, HI 96712, 808/638-8829, keikibeach-bungalows@hawaii.rr.com, www.keikibeach.com, is a small beachfront condo complex just past the Foodland supermarket heading east. The property has 200 feet of beach with a sandy bottom that goes out about 300 feet (half that in winter). The complex is quiet with a home-away-from-home atmosphere. Rates are $185–199 for a two-bedroom unit, $150–195 for a one-bedroom unit on the water, and $160 for a two-bedroom,

$95–110 for a one-bedroom, and $85 for a studio on the street side. A three-night minimum is required; weekly rates are available, with lower rates during low season and higher rates over the Christmas holiday. A one-time cleaning fee is charged, which ranges $45–85 depending on the size of unit.

Various agencies handle rental homes and condos along the North Shore, mostly between Hale'iwa and Turtle Bay. The range is broad and prices vary greatly, even season to season, but generally you might expect to pay about $100 per night for a studio or condo on the beach, up to $150 for a one-bedroom rental, up to $200 for a two-bedroom unit, and $200–500 for a three- or more bedroom home. These homes are fully furnished with all you'll need for a relaxing vacation. Cleaning deposits are usually applied, and rental agreements are often for a minimum of one week, although sometimes less. By and large, full payment is made in advance. To check on what is available, try the following agencies: **Sterman Realty,** 66-250 Kamehameha Hwy., Ste. D100, Haleiwa, HI 96712, 808/637-6200, fax 808/637-6100, www.sterman.com; **Team Real Estate,** 66-250 Kamehameha Hwy., Ste. D103, Haleiwa, HI 96712, 808/637-3507 or 800/982-8602, fax 808/637-8881, www.teamrealestate.com; **Sunset Homes, LLC,** 66-030 Kamehameha Hwy., Haleiwa, HI 96712, 808/638-7299, fax 808/637-4200, www.sunsethomes.net.

## FOOD

All food options in and near Waimea fall into the inexpensive to moderate range.

For a full selection of food supplies, shop **Foodland** along the highway in Waimea. In this town without a restaurant, the deli counter at Foodland could serve as a lunch stop, since you can get deli salads, cut meat, whole roasted chickens, chicken strips, and sandwiches there until 9 P.M. Foodland also has a bakery counter and a Starbucks. A *kaukau* wagon usually dispenses plate lunches across from Pupukea Beach Park.

The **Pikake Restaurant** at Waimea Falls Park is open daily for a lunch buffet 11 A.M.–2 P.M. for $12.95. It's fun to dine here even if you don't enter the park. From the dining room, you can look into some of the nicest gardens while feeding crumbs to the peacocks. A lunch window in the park serves cold sandwiches, burgers, and some hot entrées, mostly for under $6.

Behind the Maui Pohaku Loa statue in a covered garden setting is the **Taste of Paradise Surf Grill.** This outdoor eatery produces better than average grinds 11:30 A.M.–9:30 P.M. daily, with live music in the evenings on the weekends. Not inexpensive but not outrageous, some of what's on the menu includes shrimpetizers (6-, 12-, or 20-piece appetizer for $6–20), Haleiwa fish, pipeline eggplant, and Waimea veggie plates for $7–8.50, and grilled sandwiches for about $6.50. A down-to-earth operation that aims to please.

Less than half a mile west of Sunset Beach Park is **Sunset Pizza,** open throughout the day for burgers, sandwiches, some quick Italian meals, and pizza. Outdoor seating is available; place your order at the counter. It's next to Kammies market, which has some basic food supplies, drinks, and sundries, and a laundromat and gas station.

The Sunset Beach store has basic items but is the home of **Ted's Bakery,** where you can get a fine assortment of loaves, pies, and sinfully rich pastries and sweet treats. Ted's also does breakfast omelets and eggs for $3.50–4.50, and burgers, plate lunches, and sandwiches for lunch for $4.50–5.50. No seating, all take-out, open 7 A.M.–2 P.M.

# Turtle Bay

## TURTLE BAY RESORT

The Turtle Bay Resort, 57-091 Kamehameha Hwy., Kahuku, HI 96731, 808/293-8811 or 800/203-3650, fax 808/293-1286, www.turtle-bayresort.com, is a first-class resort on Turtle Bay, the northern extremity of the North Shore. This resort was built in the 1960s as a self-contained destination and is surrounded by sea and surf on Kuilima Point, which offers protected swimming year-round at Kuilima Cove. In all, it has about 880 acres and stretches for five miles along the coast. The entrance road to the hotel is lined by blooming hibiscus outlining a formal manicured lawn. Two 18-hole golf courses embrace the property, and there is also a professional tennis facility on the grounds with plexi-pave courts.

From 2001 to 2003, the hotel went through an extensive renovation that brought all exterior and interior public areas up to date. Along with a total room, restaurant, and meeting room renovation, the lobby was opened up to Kuilima Bay, letting in the light and making this enticing view part of the welcoming experience. The hotel offers a totally renovated and expanded swimming pool deck with hot tub and water slide; full water activities, including equipment rental and surfing and scuba lessons; horseback riding along the beach, through the oceanfront iron-wood forest, and across a wetland preserve; a small clutch of shops for jewelry, gifts, and sundries; and the fanciest dining on the North Shore. Because the hotel is an oasis unto itself, you should always call ahead to book any of the activities, even as a guest staying at the hotel, to avoid disappointment, and the concierge desk in the lobby can help with any on-site or off-site arrangements. By all means, however, take a hike along part or all of the 12 miles of trails that the resort has winding through its property. Ask for a copy of the resort's "Trail and Ocean Guide." Although each has its own character, the trail to the banyan tree and Kawela Bay is superb. The resort's seaside Wedding Pavilion is

splendid with open-beamed ceiling, stained glass, and eight-foot beveled windows that can be thrown open to allow the ocean breezes to waft through. As part of the remodel, the hotel now sports a spa that has its own fitness center, half a dozen treatment rooms, including a wet room and outdoor massage cabanas, and a beauty salon. Pamper yourself with one of the many massage, facial, or body treatment options. Several "spa rooms" on the floor above have direct access by dedicated elevator to the spa center. For a moderate additional fee, the summer Keiki Turtle Club kid's program will keep kids ages 5–12 busy throughout the day with arts, crafts, and age-appropriate activities.

All 400 guest rooms and two dozen suites in the three-wing main hotel building are ocean view, but not all are oceanfront. No matter where you are, however, you have a great view, especially Dec.–Apr., when humpback whales cavort in the waters off the point. Rooms are furnished with king or double beds, full baths, a mini-fridge, ample closets, a/c, remote-control cable TV, in-room safe, and high-speed Internet access. Suites come complete with a changing room, sitting area, and a large enclosed lanai. In addition, several dozen self-contained luxury cottages line Turtle Bay and offer more seclusion with direct access to lawn and shoreline. Rates are $139–289 for an oceanview or oceanfront room, $300–450 for a cottage, and suites cost $495–1,950; $39 for an extra person. The family plan allows children under 18 to stay free in a room with their parents. Numerous room and car, golf, tennis, and romance discount packages are always available. The Turtle Bay Resort is a first-class destination resort, but because of its fabulous yet out-of-the-mainstream location, you get much more than what you pay for. The Turtle Bay Resort is an excellent choice for a vacation with the feel of being on a Neighbor Island.

### Resort Dining

Because it is set in the country with little else around, the Turtle Bay Resort provides several

ROBERT NILSEN

**The refurbished Turtle Bay Resort has a spectacular location overlooking the North Shore.**

options for meals. The **Palm Terrace** is the main hotel restaurant for all-day dining. Best known for its sumptuous buffets, menu service is also an option. The Palm Terrace serves hearty American favorites, from simple to fancy, supplemented by dishes from around the world. Breakfast might be the full buffet for $16.95, eggs any style, omelettes, or Belgian waffles for around $9.50. Expect salads, sandwiches, and wraps for lunch, while dinner could be a theme buffet, pan-seared salmon at $17.50, sea salt–roasted prime rib for $21, or liliokoi barbecue chicken at $17. The views overlooking the pool and beyond to Turtle Bay combined with excellent value for the money make the Palm Terrace the best *ordinary* restaurant on the North Shore.

For that extra-special dinner, make reservations at **21° North**. Open Tues.–Sun. 6–10:30 P.M., this is the resort's redesigned fine-dining restaurant; resort wear is requested. Facing west and overlooking the charming Turtle Bay, it's a perfect place for sunset and a romantic retreat. Start with a soup or appetizer like Kahuku corn and lemongrass soup, seared foie gras, or ahi sashimi, mango, and heart of palm salad, all $7–13. Move to an entrée such as honey

soy–scented rack of lamb, potato-wrapped *moi* on baby bok choy, or grilled shrimp, lobster, and scallops, all priced at $23–26. A selection of wine would make a perfect match to the meal, while coffee, a cordial, or a luscious dessert would certainly finish it off in style.

The **Surf Room** is synonymous with Sunday brunch at the Turtle Bay Resort. It enjoys a wonderful reputation, and if friends or family come visiting, islanders take them here to impress. Brunch is buffet style 10 A.M.–2 P.M. and features mounds of fresh fruits and pastries, fresh-squeezed fruit juices, imported cheeses, eggs in several styles, fresh fish, seafood, sashimi, and more. Reservations are not taken; cost is $25 adults. Expect a wait, which goes quickly as you enjoy the magnificent scenery. The Surf Room is nearly as close as you can get at the resort without being in the water.

Located at the golf clubhouse, **Lei Lei's** bar and grill offers large portions of tasty food in a relaxed and casual setting. During the day, sandwiches, burgers, and other quick foods are prepared mainly for golfers, but in the evening this restaurant shines with such items as crab-stuffed salmon, crunchy coconut shrimp, double-cut pork loin chop, and prime rib, all served with fresh vegetables and either garlic smashed potatoes or white rice. Expect entrées in the $18–24 range.

Just off the lobby, the **Bay Club** is a casual lounge and bar offering drinks and *pu pu* nightly. It has a perfect spot overlooking Kuilima Bay. In the late evening, usually 10 P.M.–1 A.M., it offers either a DJ or live music.

When lounging by the pool, pick up a cool cocktail drink, lunch, or *pu pu* from the **Hang Ten** bar, which also has live evening entertainment. Down on the beach, the **Sand Bar** is open 11 A.M.–4 P.M. for light snacks and drinks.

## TURTLE BAY CONDOMINIUMS

Surrounded by golf links on the approach road to Turtle Bay Resort is a secure condominium complex of several hundred units that's split into two groups. Within this quiet and landscaped community at Kuilima are private tennis courts, swimming pools, and barbecue facilities, and you're only a short stroll away from the activity, shopping, and dining options at the resort. Vacation rentals in this tropical complex are studios to three-bedroom units, each with a full kitchen, one or more bathrooms, ceiling fans, washer and dryer, entertainment center with TV, telephone, and a lanai that opens onto the green lawn, palm trees, flowering bushes, and the fairway. Rates for these units run $90–105 studio, $110–145 one-bedroom, $165 two-bedroom, and $180 three-bedroom. Fees are slightly less during low season, which runs from mid-April through mid-December. There is a two-night minimum stay with a one-week minimum in place over the Christmas holiday. A downpayment is required, as is a "guest service fee." For information and reservations, contact one of the two following companies: **The Estates at Turtle Bay,** 56-565 Kamehameha Hwy., P.O. Box 366, Kahuku, HI 96731, 808/293-0600 or 888/200-4202, fax 808/293-0471, www.turtle-bay-rentals.com; or **Turtle Bay Condos,** 56-565 Kamehameha Hwy., P.O. Box 248, Kahuku, HI 96731, 808/293-2800, fax 808/293-2169, www.turtlebaycondos.com.

O'AHU

# Big Island of Hawai'i

*In what other land save this one is the commonest
form of greeting not "Good Day" . . . but "Love?" . . .
Aloha. . . It is the positive affirmation of
one's own heart giving.*

—Jack London, 1916

# Introduction

The island of Hawai'i is grand in so many ways. Its two nicknames, "The Orchid Island" and "The Volcano Island," are both excellent choices: the island produces more of the delicate blooms than anywhere else on earth, and Pele, the fire goddess who makes her mythological home here, regularly sends rivers of lava from the world's largest and most active volcanoes. However, to the people who live here, Hawai'i has only one real nickname, "The Big Island." Big isn't necessarily better, but when you combine it with beautiful, uncrowded, traditional, and inexpensive, it's hard to beat. More recently and with the growing connection with their cultural roots, some Hawaiians are again beginning to refer to the Big Island as Moku O Keawe ("Island of Keawe"), a traditional reference, after a well-loved former ruler of the island, Keawe'ikekahiali'iokamoku.

The Big Island was the first to be inhabited by the Polynesian settlers, yet it's geologically the youngest of the Hawaiian Islands at barely a million years old. Like all the islands in the Hawaiian chain, it's a mini-continent whose geographical demarcations are much more apparent because of its size. There are parched deserts, steaming fissures, jet-black sand beaches, raw semi-cooled lava flows, snow-covered mountains, upland pastures, littoral ponds, and lush valleys where countless waterfalls break through the rock faces of thousand-foot-high chasms. There are small working villages that time has passed by, the state's most tropical city, and an arid coast stretching

Waipi'o Valley

ROBERT NILSEN

more than 90 miles where the sun is guaranteed to shine. You'll find some of the islands' least expensive accommodations as well as some of the world's most exclusive resorts.

Historically, the Big Island is loaded with religious upheavals, the births and deaths of great people, vintage missionary homes and churches, reconstructed *heiau,* and even a royal summer palace. Here is the country's largest privately owned ranch, where cowboy life is the norm; America's most famous coffee-producing region; artist communities; and enclaves of the counterculture, where people with alternative lifestyles are still trying to keep the faith of the 1960s.

Sportspeople love it here, too. The Big Island is a mecca for triathletes and offers snow skiing in season, plenty of camping and hiking, the best marlin waters in all the oceans of the world, great horseback riding, and as much water sports activity as anyone would desire.

Direct flights are available to the Big Island, where the fascination of perhaps not "old" Hawaii, but definitely "simple" Hawaii, still lingers.

Kailua-Kona on the west coast and Hilo on the east side are the two ports of entry to the Big Island. At opposite ends of the island as well as of the cultural spectrum, the two have a friendly rivalry. It doesn't matter at which one you arrive, because a trip to the Big Island without visiting both is unthinkable. Better yet, split your stay and use each as a base while you tour. The Big Island is the only Hawaiian Island big enough that you can't drive around it comfortably in one day, nor should you try. Each of the six districts is interesting enough to spend at least one day exploring.

## Kona

Kona is dry, sunny, and brilliant, with large expanses of old barren lava flows. When watered, the rich soil blossoms, as in Holualoa and South Kona, renowned for its diminutive **coffee plantations.** Coffee is not the only thing that has blossomed here as **Holualoa** has grown from agricultural community to a small artist's enclave. The town of Captain Cook, named after the intrepid Pacific explorer, lies just above the very beach where he was slain because of a terrible miscommunication two centuries ago. Ironically,

nearby is the restored **Pu'uhonua o Honaunau Heiau,** where mercy and forgiveness were rendered to any *kapu*-breaker or vanquished warrior who made it into the confines of this safe refuge.

**Kailua-Kona** is the center of Kona. The airport is just north of town, and here lies a major concentration of condos and hotels; the town itself boasts an array of art and designer shops. World-class triathletes come here to train, and charter boats depart in search of billfish and other denizens of the deep. Within Kailua is **Moku'aikaua Church,** a legacy of the very first packet of missionaries to arrive in the islands, and **Hulihe'e Palace,** vacation home of the Kamehameha line of kings. Dominating this entire coastline, **Mt. Hualalai** rises to the east, and northward, the Kona District offers a string of fine beaches.

## Kohala

Up the coast in South Kohala is **Hapuna Beach,** one of the best on the island. In 1965, Laurence Rockefeller opened the Mauna Kea Resort near there. Since then, this resort, along with its sculptured, coast-hugging golf course, has been considered one of the finest in the world. Just south is the Kona Village Resort, whose guests can spend the night in a "simple" grass shack on the beach. Its serenity is broken only by the soothing music of the surf and by the not-so-melodious singing of "Kona nightingales," a pampered herd of wild donkeys that frequents this area. Over the years, other expansive resorts and golf courses have been added here, making this the island's luxury resort area, on a par with any in the state. Upcountry, at the base of the Kohala Mountains, is **Waimea** (Kamuela), center of the enormous **Parker Ranch.** Here in the cool mountains, cattle graze in chest-high grass, and *paniolo,* astride their sturdy mounts, ride herd in time-honored tradition. Hunters range the slopes of Mauna Kea in search of wild goats and boars, and the Fourth of July is boisterously acknowledged by the wild whoops of cowboys at the world-class Parker Ranch Rodeo.

North Kohala is primarily the hilly peninsular thumb on the northern extremity of the island. Along the coast are small beach parks, empty except for an occasional local family picnic. A series of *heiau* dot the coast, and on the northernmost tip a broad plain overlooking a sweeping panorama marks the birthplace of Kamehameha the Great. The main town up here is **Hawi,** holding on after the sugar companies pulled out a few years ago. Down the road is Kapa'au, where **Kamehameha's statue** resides in fulfillment of a *kahuna* prophecy. Along this little-traveled road, a handful of artists offer their crafts in small shops. At road's end is the overlook of **Pololu Valley,** where a steep descent takes you to a secluded beach in an area once frequented by some of the most powerful sorcerers in the land.

## The Saddle Road

This cross-island road begins just outside of Hilo. It slices across the island through a most astonishing high valley or "saddle" separating the mountains of **Mauna Loa** and **Mauna Kea.** Passable, but the bane of car rental companies, the Saddle Road slides down the western slope of Mauna Kea to meet the Belt Road, from where it's an easy drive to either Waimea or Kona. From the Saddle Road, a spur road heads up to the top of Mauna Kea at 13,796 feet, where **astronomical observatories** peer into the heavens through the clearest air on earth. Heading south, another road zigzags up the slope of Mauna Loa to a point where a hiking trail continues to the top.

## Hilo

Hilo is the oldest port of entry, the most tropical town in Hawai'i, and the only major city built on the island's windward coast. The city is one tremendous greenhouse where exotic flowers and tropical plants are a normal part of the landscape, and entire blocks canopied by adjoining banyans are taken for granted. The town, which hosts the yearly Merrie Monarch Festival, boasts Japanese gardens, several tropical gardens, the **Lyman Mission House and Museum,** and a profusion of natural phenomena, including **Rainbow Falls** and **Boiling Pots.** Plenty of rooms in Hilo are generally easily available, and its variety of restaurants will titillate anyone's taste buds. Both go easy on the pocketbook.

## Hamakua Coast

Hamakua refers to the entire northeast coast, where streams, wind, and pounding surf have chiseled the lava into towering cliffs and precipitous valleys known locally by the unromantic name of "gulches." Until recently, all the flatlands here were awash in a green sea of sugarcane; now, no commercial and few private fields remain. A spur road from the forgotten town of Honomu leads to **'Akaka Falls,** whose waters tumble over a 442-foot cliff—the highest sheer drop of water in Hawaii. North along the coastal road is **Honoka'a,** a one-street town of stores, restaurants, and crafts shops. The main road bears left here to the cowboy town of Waimea, but a smaller road inches farther north. It deadends at the top of **Waipi'o Valley,** cradled by cliffs on three sides with its mouth wide open to the sea. On its verdant floor a handful of families live simply by raising taro, a few head of cattle, and horses. Waipi'o was a burial ground of Hawaiian *ali'i,* where *kahuna* traditionally came to commune with spirits. The enchantment of this "power spot" remains.

## Puna

Puna lies south of Hilo and makes up the majority of the southeast coast. Here are the greatest lava fields that have spewed from Kilauea, the heart of **Hawaii Volcanoes National Park.** An ancient flow embraced a forest in its fiery grasp, entombing trees that stand like sentinels today in **Lava Tree State Monument. Cape Kumukahi,** a pointed lava flow that reached the ocean in 1868, is officially the easternmost point in Hawaii. Just below it a string of beaches feature ebony-black sand. The road skirts the coast before it dead-ends where it has been covered over by lava at the small village of Kaimu. Atop the volcano, miles of hiking trails crisscross the park and lead to the very summit of Mauna Loa. Kilauea Crater is circled by a rim drive that brings you up close to the sights near the park entrance and where you can lodge or dine at Volcano House, a venerable inn carved into the rim of the crater. From the rim drive, Chain of Craters Road spills off the mountain through a forbidding, yet vibrant, wasteland of old lava flows until it comes to the sea, where this living volcano fumes and throbs.

## Ka'u

Ka'u, the southern tip of the island, is an arid region with pockets of green. On one well-marked trail leading from the main road you'll discover an eerie set of footprints, the remnants of an ill-fated band of warriors who were smothered under the moist ash of a volcanic eruption and whose demise marked the ascendancy of Kamehameha the Great. Like Hamakua, Ka'u was a sugar-growing region. Sugar is no more and its loss created a tough economic environment, but macadamia nuts and other agricultural crops are being raised. Here are some lovely beaches and parks you'll have virtually to yourself. One at Punalu'u has jet-black sand and is known for turtles, while another farther south has a distinctly green color. From the highway, a narrow ribbon of road leads to **Ka Lae** (South Point), the most southerly piece of ground in the United States.

# The Land

The Big Island is the southernmost and easternmost of the Hawaiian islands—it is also the largest. This island dwarfs all the others in the Hawaiian chain at 4,028 square miles and growing. It accounts for about 63 percent of the state's total landmass; the other islands could fit within it two times over. With 266 miles of coastline, the island stretches about 95 miles from north to south and 80 miles from east to west. Cape Kumukahi is the easternmost point in the state, and Ka Lae is the southernmost point in the country.

Science and *The Kumulipo* oral history differ sharply on the age of the Big Island. Scientists say that Hawai'i is the youngest of the islands, being a little more than one million years old; the chanters claim that it was the first "island-child" of Wakea and Papa. It is, irrefutably, closest to the "hot spot" on the Pacific floor, evidenced by Kilauea's frequent eruptions and by the undersea Lo'ihi Seamount. The geology, geography, and location of the Hawaiian Islands, and their ongoing drifting and building in the middle of the Pacific, make them among the most fascinating pieces of real estate on earth. The Big Island is the *most* fascinating of them all—it is truly unique.

Separating Hawai'i from Maui to the northwest is the 'Alenuihaha Channel, which at about 30 miles wide and over 6,800 feet deep, is the state's second widest and second deepest channel.

## The Mountains

The tremendous volcanic peak of **Mauna Kea** (White Mountain), located in north-central Hawai'i, has been extinct for more than 3,500 years. Its seasonal snowcap earns Mauna Kea its name and reputation as a unique ski area in winter. More than 18,000 feet of mountain below the surface rises straight up from the ocean floor—making Mauna Kea actually 31,796 feet tall, a substantial 2,768 feet taller than Mt. Everest; some consider it the tallest

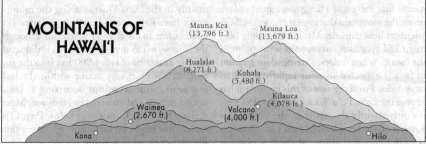

MOUNTAINS OF HAWAI'I

Mauna Kea (13,796 ft.)
Mauna Loa (13,679 ft.)
Hualalai (8,271 ft.)
Kohala (5,480 ft.)
Kilauea (4,078 ft.)
Waimea (2,670 ft.)
Volcano (4,000 ft.)
Kona
Hilo

© SANDRA E. BISIGNANI TRUST AND AVALON TRAVEL PUBLISHING, INC.

mountain in the world. At 13,796 feet above sea level, it is without doubt the tallest peak in the Pacific. Near its top, at 13,020 feet, is **Lake Waiau,** the highest lake in the state and third highest in the country. Mauna Kea was obviously a sacred mountain to the Hawaiians, and its white dome was a welcome beacon to seafarers. On its slope is the largest adze quarry in Polynesia, from which high-quality basalt was taken to be fashioned into prized tools. The atmosphere atop the mountain, which sits mid-Pacific far from pollutants, is the most rarefied and cleanest on earth. The clarity makes Mauna Kea a natural for astronomical observatories. The complex of telescopes on its summit is internationally staffed and provides data to scientists around the world.

The **Kohala Mountains** to the northwest are the oldest and rise only to 5,480 feet at Kaunu o Kaleiho'ohei peak. This section looks more like the other Hawaiian Islands, with deep gorges and valleys along the coast and a forested interior. As you head east toward Waimea from Kawaihae on Route 19, for every mile you travel you pick up about 10 inches of rainfall per year. This becomes obvious as you begin to pass little streams and rivulets running from the mountains.

**Mount Hualalai** at 8,271 feet is the backdrop to Kailua-Kona. It's home to many of the Big Island's endangered birds and supports many of the region's newest housing developments. Just a few years ago, Mt. Hualalai was thought to be extinct, since the last time it erupted was in 1801. It is now known that within the last thousand years, the mountain has erupted about every two or three centuries. In 1929 it suffered an earthquake swarm, which means that there was a large movement of lava inside the mountain that caused tremors. USGS scientists now consider Mt. Hualalai only dormant and very likely to erupt at some point in the future. When it does, a tremendous amount of lava is expected to pour rapidly down its steep sides. From the side of this mountain has grown the cone Pu'u Wa'awa'a. At 3,967 feet, it's only slightly shorter than the very active Kilauea on the far side of Mauna Loa. Obsidian is found here and is one of the few place in

Hawaii where this substance has been quarried in such quantities.

Even though **Mauna Loa** (Long Mountain) measures a respectable 13,679 feet, its height isn't its claim to fame. This active volcano, 60 miles long by 30 wide, comprises 10,000 cubic miles of iron-hard lava, making it the densest and most massive mountain on earth. In 1950, a tremendous lava flow belched from Mauna Loa's summit, reaching an astonishing rate of 6,750,000 cubic yards per hour. Seven lava rivers flowed for 23 days, emitting more than 600 million cubic yards of lava that covered 35 square miles. There were no injuries, but the villages of Ka'apuna and Honokua were partially destroyed along with the Magoo Ranch. Its last eruption in 1984 was small by comparison yet created fountaining inside the summit crater and a "curtain of fire" along its eastern rift.

The lowest of the island's major peaks, **Kilauea** rises only to 4,078 feet. Its pragmatic name means "The Spewing," and it is the world's most active volcano. In the last hundred years, it has erupted on the average once every 11 months. The Hawaiians believed that the goddess Pele inhabited every volcano in the Hawaiian chain, and that her home is now Halema'uma'u Crater in Kilauea Caldera. Kilauea is the most scientifically watched volcano in the world, with a permanent observatory built right on the crater rim. When it erupts, the flows are so predictable that observers run toward the mountain, not away from it! The flows, however, can burst from fissures far from the center of the crater in areas that don't seem "active." This occurs mainly in the Puna District along the mountain's East Rift Zone. In 1959, Kilauea Iki Crater came to life after 91 years, and although the flow wasn't as massive as others, it did send blazing fountains of lava 1,900 feet into the air. Kilauea has been very active within the last few years, with eruptions occurring at least once a month and expected to continue. Most activity has been from a vent below Pu'u O'o crater. You might be lucky enough to see this phenomenon while visiting.

# CLIMATE

The average temperature around the island varies between 72 and 78° F. Summers raise the temperature to the mid-80s, and winters cool off to the low 70s. Both Kona and Hilo seem to maintain a year-round average of about 74 degrees, and the South Kohala Coast is a few degrees warmer. As usual, it's cooler in the higher elevations, and Waimea sees most days in the mid-60s to low 70s, while Volcano maintains a relatively steady 60 degrees. Atop Mauna Kea, the temperature rarely climbs above 50° or dips below 30, while the summit of Mauna Loa is about 10 degrees warmer. The lowest recorded temperature on the Big Island (and for the state) was 1° F inside the Mauna Kea summit crater in January 1970, while the highest ever recorded was in April 1931 at Pahala in Ka'u—a scorching (for Hawaii) 100°.

## Precipitation

Weatherwise, the Big Island's climate varies not so much in temperature but precipitation. Hawai'i has some of the wettest and driest coastal areas in the islands. The line separating wet from dry can be dramatic. Waimea, for example, has an actual dry and wet side of town, as if a boundary line split the town in two! Houses on the dry side are at a premium. Kona and Hilo are opposites. The Kona Coast is almost guaranteed to be sunny and bright, receiving as little as 15 inches of rainfall per year but with an average of 28 inches. Both Kona and the Ka'u Desert to the south are in the rain shadow of Mauna Loa, and most rain clouds coming from east to west are pierced by its summit before they ever reach Kona. Hilo is wet, with predictable afternoon and evening showers—they make the entire town blossom. Though this reputation keeps many tourists away, the rain's predictability makes it easy to avoid a drenching while exploring the town. Hilo does get as much as 128 inches of rainfall per year, with a record of 153.93 inches set in 1971. It also holds the dubious honor of being the town with the most rainfall recorded by the National Weather Service in a 24-hour period—a drenching 22.3 inches in February 1979.

BIG ISLAND OF HAWAI'I

## BIG ISLAND TEMPERATURE AND RAINFALL

| Town | | Jan. | March | May | June | Sept. | Nov. |
|------|------|------|-------|-----|------|-------|------|
| **Hilo** | high | 79 | 79 | 80 | 82 | 82 | 80 |
| | low | 62 | 62 | 61 | 70 | 70 | 65 |
| | rain | 11 | 15 | 7 | 10 | 10 | 15 |
| **Kona** | high | 80 | 81 | 81 | 82 | 82 | 81 |
| | low | 62 | 64 | 65 | 68 | 68 | 63 |
| | rain | 4 | 3 | 2 | 0 | 2 | 1 |

Temperature is in degrees Fahrenheit; rainfall is in inches.

# Flora and Fauna

The indigenous plants and birds of the Big Island have suffered the same fate as those of the other Hawaiian Islands: they're among the most endangered species on earth and disappearing at an alarming rate. There are some sanctuaries on the Big Island where native species still live, but they must be vigorously protected. Do your bit to save them; enjoy but do not disturb.

## COMMON FLORA

The Hawaiians called the **prickly pear cactus** *panini,* which translates as "very unfriendly," undoubtedly because of the sharp spines covering the flat, thick leaves. The cactus is typical of those found in Mexico and the southwestern United States. It was introduced to Hawaii before 1810 and established itself coincidentally with the cattle brought in at the time; *panini* is very common in North Kohala, especially on the Parker Ranch lands. It is assumed that Don Marin, a Spanish advisor to Kamehameha I, was responsible for importing the plant. Perhaps the early *paniolo* (cowboys) felt lonely without it. The *panini* can grow to heights of 15

feet and is now considered a pest, but nonetheless it looks as if it belongs. It develops small, delicious, pear-shaped fruits. Hikers who decide to pick the fruit should be careful of small, yellowish bristles that can burrow under the skin and irritate. The beautiful yellow and orange flowers measure three inches across. An attempt is being made to control the cactus in *paniolo* country. *El cosano rojo,* the red worm found in the bottom of Mexican tequila, has been introduced to destroy the plant. It burrows into the cactus and eats the hardwood center, causing the plant to wither and die.

More species of **lobelia** grow in Hawaii than anywhere else in the world. A common garden flower elsewhere, it can grow to tree height in Hawaii. The lobelia flower is tiny and resembles a miniature orchid with curved and pointed ends, like the beak of the native *'i'iwi.* This bird feeds on the flower's nectar; it's obvious that both evolved in Hawaii together and exhibit the strange phenomenon of nature mimicking nature.

The Big Island has more species of **gesneriad,** the African violet family, than anywhere else on earth. Many don't have the showy flowers

---

## BIG ISLAND BOTANICAL GARDENS

The **Hilo Forestry Arboretum,** located along Kilauea Avenue between Lanikaula and Kawili Streets, is maintained by the Department of Natural Resources, Division of Forestry. Open Mon.–Fri. 8 A.M.–3 P.M.; free for self-guided tour. The site is used for the propagation of rare and endangered plant species, for research, and for experimental pursuits. This arboretum contains examples of most of the trees present in Hawaii, including indigenous and imported specimens.

**Nani Mau Gardens,** 421 Makalika St., Hilo, 808/959-3500, is open daily 8 A.M.–5 P.M. Admission is $10, $5 per person for an optional tram tour. The 20-acre gardens feature separate areas for hibiscus, anthurium, orchid, gardenia, bromeliad, and other tropical plants. This is the showiest garden on the island, a large, tame, and

beautiful display. Plants are labeled.

The **Hilo Tropical Gardens,** 808/969-9873, at 1447 Kalaniana'ole Ave. is the oldest botanical garden on the island, being established in 1948. Open daily except Thurs. and Sun., this garden is small and a bit overgrown in its profusion of plants. Lots of anthuriums and orchids. Entrance is $2 adult for a self-guided tour.

**Hawaii Tropical Botanical Gardens,** 808/964-5233, open daily 9 A.M.–5 P.M., is a few miles north of Hilo. Admission is $15, children 6–16 $5. Here you are in the middle of a tamed tropical rainforest jungle, walking along one mile of manicured paths among more than 2,000 different species of trees and plants. Admission is adults $15 and children 6–16 $5.

The **World Tropical Botanical Gardens,**

that you normally associate with African violets but have evolved into strange species with huge, fuzzy leaves.

The *pu'ahanui,* whose name means "many flowers," is Hawaii's native hydrangea; it is common in the upland forests of the Big Island.

## Ferns

If you travel to Volcanoes National Park you will find yourself deep in an amazing, high-altitude tropical rainforest. This unique forest exists because of the 120 inches of annual rainfall, which turns the raw lava into a lush forest. Besides stands of 'ohi'a and koa, you'll be treated to a primordial display of ferns. All new fronds on ferns are called "fiddleheads" because of the way they unfurl and resemble the scrolls of violin heads. Fiddleheads were eaten by Hawaiians during times of famine. The most common ferns are *hapu'u,* a rather large tree fern, and *'ama'uama'u,* a smaller type with a more simple frond. A soft, furry growth around the base of the stalks is called *pulu.* At one time *pulu* was collected for stuffing mattresses, and a factory was located near Kilauea. But *pulu* breaks down and forms a very fine dust after a few years, so it never really became generally accepted for mattresses.

At high altitudes, young ferns and other plants often produce new growth that turns bright red as protection against the sun's ultraviolet rays. You'll see it on new foliage before it hardens. Hawaiians called this new growth *liko.* Today, people still make lei from *liko* because it has so many subtle and beautiful colors. 'Ohi'a *liko* is a favorite for lei because it is so striking.

## BIRDS

You'll spot birds all over the Big Island, from the coastal areas to the high mountain slopes. Some are found on other islands as well, but the ones listed below are found only or mainly on the Big Island. Every bird listed is either threatened or endangered.

### Hawaii's Own

The *nene,* or Hawaiian goose, is making a comeback from the edge of extinction. Approximately 500 live on the Big Island. Good places to view *nene* are in Volcanoes National Park at Kipuka Nene, Summit Caldera, Devastation Trail, and at Volcanoes Golf Course, at dawn and dusk. They gather at the golf course because they love to feed on grasses. The places to view them on the Kona side are at Pu'ulani, a housing development north of Kailua-Kona, and at Kaloko

---

808/963-5427, near Laupahoehoe on the Hamakua Coast, is a garden in the making. While the plan is to cultivate some 30,000 species, arranged in evolutionary groupings, only small sections are open to the public. The impressive three-tier Umauma Waterfall is on the property. Open Mon.–Sat. 9 A.M.–5:30 P.M.; $7 adult and $3 teens.

**Amy B. H. Greenwell Ethnobotanical Garden,** 808/323-3318, along Rte. 11, between the communities of Kealakekua and Captain Cook. The garden is open Mon.–Fri. 8:30 A.M.–5 P.M. Guided tours are offered on the second Sat. of every month at 10 A.M., but visitors are welcome any time during daylight hours; $4 donation. This 12-acre interpretive ethnobotanical garden has indigenous Hawaiian plants, Polynesian introduced plants, and Hawaiian medicinal plants. The garden

has remnants of the Kona field system, which dates from pre-contact times.

The **Sadie Seymour Botanical Gardens** sits up above the coast in Kailua-Kona. Its plantings are grouped by areas of the world on nearly a dozen terraces. Small but well landscaped, this garden is a quiet retreat in the otherwise dry and hot upper Kona area. **Kealakowa'a Heiau,** an ancient sacred site dedicated to blessing canoes, is on the property. Open daily 9 A.M.–5 P.M. for self-guided tours; admission is free.

Specializing in plants that thrive in the arid zone, **Pua Mau Place,** 808/882-0888, has an appropriate spot in the dry hills just north of Kawaihae. Opened in 2000, it's still young but full of promise. Visit Wed.–Sun. only 10 A.M.–5 P.M.; $8 entrance fee.

Mauka, another housing development on the slopes of Mt. Hualalai. At the top of the road up Mt. Hualalai is a trail, a good place to see the *nene.* Unfortunately, as the housing developments proliferate and the residents invariably acquire dogs and cats, the *nene* will disappear.

The **Hawaiian crow,** or *alala,* is reduced to fewer than 12 birds living on the slopes of Hualalai and Mauna Loa above the 3,000-foot level. It looks like the common raven but has a more melodious voice and sometimes dull brown feathers. The *alala* breeds in early spring, and the greenish-blue, black-flecked eggs hatch from April to June. It is extremely nervous while nesting, and any disturbance causes it to abandon its young.

The **Hawaiian hawk** (*'io*) primarily lives on the slopes of Mauna Loa and Mauna Kea below 9,000 feet. This noble bird, the royalty of the skies, symbolized the *ali'i.* The hawk exists only on the Big Island, for reasons that are not entirely clear. The *'io* population was once dwindling, and many scientists feared that the bird was headed for extinction. The good news is that the *'io* is making a dramatic comeback.

The ***'akiapola'au,*** a honeycreeper, is a five-inch yellow bird hardly bigger than its name. It lives mainly on the eastern slopes in 'ohi'a and koa forests above 3,500 feet. It has a long, curved upper beak for probing and a smaller lower beak that it uses woodpecker-fashion. The *'akiapola'au* opens its mouth wide, strikes the wood with its lower beak, and then uses the upper beak to scrape out any larvae or insects. Listen for the distinctive rapping sound to spot this melodious singer. The *'akiapola'au* can be seen at the Hakalau Forest National Wildlife Refuge and along the Pu'u O'o Volcano Trail from Volcanoes National Park. It's estimated that only about 1,000 of these rare birds are left.

In addition, two other endangered birds of the Big Island are the *koloa maoli,* a duck that re-

**Hawaiian hawk**

sembles a mallard, and the slate gray or white *'alae ke'oke'o* coot.

## Marine Birds

Two coastal birds that breed on the high slopes of Hawaii's volcanoes and feed on the coast are the **Hawaiian dark-rumped petrel** (*'ua'u*) and the **Newell's shearwater** (*'a'o*). The *'ua'u* lives on the barren high slopes and craters, where it nests in burrows or under stones. Breeding season lasts from mid-March to mid-October. Only one chick is born per season and it is nurtured on regurgitated squid and fish. The *'ua'u* suffers heavily from predation. The *'a'o* prefers the forested slopes of the interior. It breeds April–November and spends its days at sea and nights inland. Feral cats and dogs reduce its numbers considerably. In addition, the *ae'o*, Hawaiian black-necked stilt, has become endangered.

## Forest Birds

Some native birds found in the upland forests of the Big Island are the common ***'elepaio, 'amakihi, 'i'iwi,*** and ***'apapane.*** Perhaps less commonly seen is the **Hawaiian thrush** (*'oma'o*), a bird found above 3,000 feet in the windward forests of Hawai'i. This eight-inch gray bird is a good singer, often seen perching with distinctive drooping wings and a shivering body. The best place to look for it is at the Thurston Lava Tube, where you can see it doing its baby-bird shivering-and-shaking act. A great mimic, it can sound like a cat or even like an old-fashioned radio with stations changing as you turn the dial.

The ***'akepa*** is a four- to five-inch bird. The male is a brilliant orange to red, the female a drab green and yellow. It is found mainly on Hualalai and in windward forests.

The six-inch, bright yellow ***palila*** is found only on Hawai'i in the forests of Mauna Kea above 6,000 feet. It depends exclusively upon *mamane* trees for survival, eating its pods, buds, and flowers.

BOB RACE

## MAMMALS

Hawaii had only two indigenous mammals: the monk seal or *'ilio holu I ka uaua* (found throughout the islands) and the hoary bat (found mainly on the Big Island), both of which are threatened or endangered. The remainder of the Big Island's mammals are transplants. But like anything else, including people, that has been in the islands long enough, they have taken on characteristics that make them "local."

The following animals are found primarily on the Big Island. The **Hawaiian hoary bat** *('ope'ape'a)* is a cousin of the Mainland bat. Its tail has a whitish coloration, hence its name. The hoary bat has a 13-inch wingspan. Unlike other bats, it is a solitary creature, roosting in trees. It gives birth to twins in early summer and can often be spotted over Hilo and Kealakekua Bays just around sundown.

The **feral dog** *('ilio)* is found on all the islands but especially on the slopes of Mauna Kea, where packs chase feral sheep. Poisoned and shot by local ranchers, their numbers are diminishing. Black dogs, thought to be more tender, are still eaten in some Hawaiian and Filipino communities.

The **feral sheep** are escaped descendants of animals brought to the islands by Captain Vancouver in the 1790s and of merinos brought to the island later and raised for their exceptional woolly fleece. These sheep exist only on the Big Island, on the upper slopes of Mauna Loa, Mauna Kea, and Hualalai. The fleece is a buff brown, and the sheep's two-foot-wide curved horns are often sought as hunting trophies. Feral sheep are responsible for the overgrazing of young *mamane* trees, which are essential to the endangered *palila* bird. In 1979, a law was passed to exterminate or remove the sheep from Mauna Kea so that the native *palila* could survive.

The **mouflon sheep** was introduced to Lana'i and Hawai'i to cut down on overgrazing and serve as a trophy animal. This Mediterranean sheep can interbreed with feral sheep to produce a hybrid. It lives on the upper slopes of Mauna Loa and Mauna Kea. Unfortunately, its introduction has not been a success. No evidence concludes that the smaller family groups of mouflon cause less damage than the herding feral sheep, and hunters reportedly don't like the meat as much as feral mutton.

The **feral donkey,** better known as the "Kona nightingale," came to Hawaii as a beast of burden. Domesticated donkeys are found on all islands, but a few wild herds still roam the Big Island along the Kona Coast, especially near the exclusive Kona Village Resort at Kaupulehu.

**Feral cattle** were introduced by Captain Vancouver, who gave a few domesticated head to Kamehameha; immediately a *kapu* against killing them went into effect for 10 years. The lush grasses of Hawaii were perfect and the cattle flourished; by the early 1800s they were out of control and were hunted and exterminated. Finally, Mexican cowboys were brought to Hawaii to teach the locals how to be range hands. From this legacy sprang the Hawaiian *paniolo.*

## MARINE LIFE

### Humpback Whales

Humpback whales, known in Hawaii as *kohola,* migrate to Hawaiian waters yearly, arriving in late December and departing by mid-March. The best places to view them are along the southern Kona Coast, especially at Kealakekua Bay and Ka Lae (South Point), with many sightings off the Puna coast around Isaac Hale Beach Park.

### Hawksbill Turtle

Hawaii Volcanoes National Park stretches from the top of Mauna Kea all the way down to the sea. It is here, around Apua Point, that three of the last-known nesting sites of the very endangered hawksbill turtle *(honu 'ea)* are found. This creature has been ravished in the Pacific, where it is ruthlessly hunted for its shell, which is made into women's jewelry, especially combs. It is illegal to bring items made from turtle shell into the United States, but the hunt goes on.

### Billfish

Although these magnificent game fish occur in various South Sea and Hawaiian waters, catching them is easiest in the clear, calm waters off the Kona Coast. The billfish—swordfish, sailfish, marlin, and *a'u*—share two distinctive common features: a long, spearlike or swordlike snout and a prominent dorsal fin. The three main species of billfish caught are the blue, striped, and black marlin. Of these three, the **blue marlin** is the leading game fish in Kona waters. The blue has tipped the scales at well over 1,000 pounds, but the average fish weighs in at 300–400 pounds. When alive, this fish is a striking cobalt blue, but when dead, its color changes to slate blue. It feeds on skipjack tuna; throughout the summer, fishing boats look for schools of tuna as a tip-off to blues in the area. The **black marlin** is the largest and most coveted catch for blue-water anglers. This solitary fish is infrequently found off the banks of Kona. Granddaddies can weigh 1,800 pounds, but the average is a mere 200. The **striped marlin** is the most common commercial billfish, a highly prized food served in finer restaurants and often sliced into sashimi. Its coloration is a remarkable royal blue. Its spectacular leaps when caught give it a great reputation as a fighter. The striped marlin is smaller than the other marlins, so a 100-pounder is a very good catch.

## THE HAKALAU FOREST NATIONAL WILDLIFE REFUGE

The Hakalau Forest National Wildlife Refuge, acquired with the help of the Nature Conservancy but administered solely by the U.S. Fish and Wildlife Service, is a 33,000-acre tract of land north of the Saddle Road that borders the Department of Hawaiian Home Lands land. It's up-

land forest and former ranchland that drifts down into solid rainforest that is the home of such birds as the endangered *'akiapola'au, 'akepa, 'io,* Hawaiian creeper, and *nene,* and the common *i'iwi, 'oma'o, 'apapane, 'amakihi, 'elepaio,* and *pueo.* The U.S. Fish and Wildlife Service is working hard to allow the upper abandoned pastures of this refuge to regenerate with native forests; efforts include fencing, snaring, and hunting to rid the area of feral pigs and cattle, and replanting with koa, 'ohi'a, opeka, pilo, and other native species while removing introduced and exotic foliage. It's a tremendous task that's mainly being shouldered by the U.S. Fish and Wildlife Service manager Dick Wass and his staff. The refuge is not adequately staffed to accept visits by the general public at all times, but the Maulau Tract, the northernmost section of the refuge, is open for hiking and birding—with prior permission—every month. This area is a two-hour drive from Hilo, half of which is over a rugged dirt road traversable only by a 4WD vehicle! Numerous volunteer opportunities are available for various ongoing projects, either in the field or at the greenhouse, for a weekend or week-long stint. If you *truly* have a dedication to help and aren't afraid to get your hands dirty, contact Dick for a very rewarding experience. To enter the refuge for any reason, contact the office at least three weeks in advance to make arrangements; call 808/933-6915, fax 800/933-6917, or write to the Refuge Manager, Hakalau Forest NWR, 32 Kinoole St., Suite 101, Hilo, HI 96720, or email at richard_wass@fws.gov. The refuge is a very beautiful diamond in the rough, encompassing an incredible rainforest.

# Government and Economy

The county of Hawai'i is almost entirely Democratic and currently has only two Republican elected state legislative members. The current mayor is Harry Kim, a Democrat. The mayor is assisted by an elected county council consisting of nine members, one from each council district around the island. Hilo is the county seat.

Of the 25 state senatorial districts, Hawai'i County comprises three, all represented by Democrats. The First District takes in the whole northern section of the island: the Hamakua Coast, Mauna Kea, North and South Kohala, and part of North Kona. The Second District is mainly Hilo and its outlying area. The Third comprises Puna, Ka'u, South Kona, and most of North Kona. Hawai'i County has six of 51 seats in the state House of Representatives. At this time, four representatives are Democrats, and the two Republicans represent the Kona and South Kohala strip. For internet information on Hawai'i County see www.hawaii-county.com.

For internet information on Hawai'i County see www.hawaii-county.com.

The Big Island's economy is the state's most agriculturally based. More than 5,000 farmhands, horticultural workers, and *paniolo* work the land to produce about one-third of the state's vegetables and melons, over 75 percent of the total fruit production, 95 percent of the papaya, 75 percent of the bananas, 95 percent of the avocados, and 50 percent of the guavas. Some of the state's taro is also produced on the Big Island, principally in the Waipi'o Valley and along the Hamakua Coast, and ginger production has become a major economic factor with more than six million pounds grown annually. The Big Island also produces 50 million pounds of macadamia nuts yearly, about 90 percent of that which is grown in the state. While that still is a respectable number, it's less than half the world's total. Hawai'i used to have the only commercial coffee plantations in the country, but now coffee is grown on all the major Hawaiian islands. Due to the increased interest in gourmet Kona coffee, the coffee industry's share in the economy of the island is increasing, and the Big Is-

land grows about three million pounds of coffee every year on about 2,500 acres. The Big Island is the only place in the country where cocoa beans for making chocolate are grown commercially. About 350 or more horticultural farms produce the largest number of orchids and anthuriums in the state, leaving the Big Island awash in color and fragrance. Other exotic flowers and foliage are also a growing concern. In the hills, entrepreneurs raise *pakalolo* (marijuana), which has become the state's most productive although illicit cash crop.

## Sugar

Hawai'i used to be the state's largest sugar grower, with more than 150,000 acres in cane. These commercial fields produced four million tons of refined sugar, 40 percent of the state's output. The majority of sugar land was along the Hamakua Coast, long known for its abundant water supply. At one time, the cane was even transported to the mills by water flumes. Another large pocket of cane fields was on the southern part of the island, mostly in Ka'u and Puna. With the closing of the last mill in 1996, sugar is no longer grown commercially on the island. Still, small entrepreneurial farms grow it on greatly reduced acreage. The big cane trucks have ceased to roll and the smokestacks stand in silent testimony to an era gone by.

## Coffee

Coffee has been grown on the Big Island since 1828. The Kona District is a splendid area for raising coffee; it gives the beans a beautiful tan. Lying in Mauna Loa's rain shadow, it gets dewy mornings followed by sunshine and an afternoon cloud shadow. Kona coffee has long been accepted as gourmet quality; it is sold in the better restaurants throughout Hawaii and in fine coffee shops around the world. It's a dark, full-bodied coffee with a rich aroma. Approximately 650 small farms produce nearly $15 million a year in coffee revenue. Few, however, make it a full-time business. The production of Kona coffee makes up only about one-tenth of 1 percent of the coffee grown around the world. As such a rare bean, it's often blended with other varieties. When sold unblended it is quite expensive.

## Cattle and Other Livestock

Hawai'i's cattle ranches produce more than five million pounds of beef per year, 50 percent of the state's total. More than 450 independent ranches dot the island, with total area over 650,000 acres, but they are dwarfed both in size and production by the massive Parker Ranch (now held as a public trust), which alone has 225,000 acres and is three-quarters the size of O'ahu. While beef is the largest player in the livestock market, pork, dairy products, eggs, poultry, sheep, goats, and bees also are components, constituting perhaps half of the island's livestock revenues.

## The Military

On average, about 60 military personnel are stationed on the Big Island at any one time, with about the same number of dependents. Most of these people are attached to the enormous Pohakuloa Military Reserve in the center of the island; a lesser number are at a few minor installations around Hilo and at Kilauea Volcano.

## Tourism

More than 3,000 island residents are directly employed by the hotel industry, and many more indirectly serve the tourists. There are slightly more than 9,500 hotel rooms, with the greatest concentration in Kona. Big Island hotels have the lowest occupancy rate in the state, rarely rising above 60 percent. The Big Island receives about 1.1 million tourists annually, about 21,000 on any given day, with 2.5 times as many people going to the Kona side as the Hilo side. Of the major islands, it ranks third in annual visitors, following O'ahu and Maui.

## Land Ownership

Hawai'i County comprises more than 2.5 million

**BIG ISLAND LAND OWNERSHIP**

Hawai'i
2,578,073 Acres

STATE

FEDERAL

HAWAIIAN HOMELANDS

SMALL PRIVATE

LARGE PRIVATE

acres. Of this total, the state owns about 800,000 million, mostly forest preserves and undeveloped land, and the federal government has nearly large acreage in the Hawaii Volcanoes National Park, Pohakuloa Military Training Area, and Hakalau

Forest National Wildlife Refuge. Large landowners control most of the rest except for about 116,000 acres of Hawaiian Homelands. The major large landowners are the Bishop Estate, Parker Ranch, and the Samuel Damon Estate.

# The People

With 149,000 people, the Big Island has the second-largest island population in Hawaii, just over 12 percent of the state's total. However, it has the smallest population density of the main islands, with about 37 people per square mile. Of these, 61 percent are urban dwellers while 39 percent live rurally. The Hilo area has the largest population with 47,000 residents, followed by North and South Kona with about 37,000, Puna

at 31,000, South Kohala at 13,000, and the Hamakua Coast, North Kohala, and Ka'u each between 6,000–8,000. Within the last dozen years, the areas of Puna and South Kohala have experienced the greatest increases in population. There is no ethnic majority on the Big island, however, population numbers include 32 percent Caucasian, 28 percent mixed, 27 percent Asian, 11 percent Hawaiian, and 2 percent other.

# Festivals and Events

The following events and celebrations are either particular to the Big Island, or they're celebrated here in a special way. Everyone is welcome to join in the fun, and most times the events are either free or nominally priced. There's no better way to enjoy yourself while vacationing than by joining in a local party or happening. Island-specific information is also available on the Web; check the calendar listing at www.bigisland.org for events on Hawai'i.

## January

During **The Volcano Wilderness Marathon and Rim Runs** the truly energetic run 26 miles through the desolate Ka'u Desert, while a 10-mile race around the Caldera Crater Rim and a five-mile run down into and out of the Kilauea caldera features more than 1,000 participants.

## February

The **Waimea Cherry Blossom Heritage Festival** showcases ethnic presentations, Japanese cultural events, a parade, and a tea ceremony.

## March

The month rumbles in with the **Kona Stam-**

## BIG ISLAND ARTS AND CULTURE INFORMATION

**East Hawai'i Cultural Council,** Box 1312, Hilo, HI 96721, 808/961-5711, publishes *Art Centering,* a monthly newsletter of what's happening artistically and culturally on the Big Island. The publication includes a good monthly calendar of events with listings from exhibit openings to movies. Associated groups are the East Hawai'i Cultural Center, Big Island Dance Council, Hawai'i Concert Society, Hilo Community Players, and Bunka No Izumi.

**Volcano Art Center,** 808/967-8222, promotes visual and performing arts at Volcano and offers community art classes and workshops. The Art Center publishes the *Volcano Gazette,* a monthly newsletter detailing events it sponsors.

**pede** at Honaunau Arena, Honaunau, Kona. *Paniolo* provide plenty of action during the full range of rodeo events.

## April

The **Merrie Monarch Festival** in Hilo sways

## BIG ISLAND MUSEUMS AND HISTORICAL SOCIETIES

**Pacific Tsunami Museum,** 130 Kamehameha Ave., 808/935-0926, open Mon.–Sat. 9 A.M.–4 P.M., is housed in the art-deco-style First Hawaiian Bank building near the bay front in Hilo. It's dedicated to those who lost their lives in the destructive tidal waves that hit and virtually destroyed the city in 1946 and 1960. Visual displays, video film, and computer links all add to the educational focus of this organization, but the most moving aspect are the photographs of the last two terribly destructive tsunami to hit the city. Admission for adults is $5.

**Lyman Mission House and Museum,** 276 Haili St. in Hilo, 808/935-5021, open Mon.–Sat. 9 A.M.–4:30 P.M., was first opened in 1932. The main building is a New England–style structure from 1839, the oldest wood frame house on the island. It contains furniture and household goods from Rev. and Mrs. Lyman and other missionary families on the island. In a modern annex are a collection of Hawaiian artifacts and items of daily use in the Island Heritage Gallery and a very fine collection of rocks and minerals in the Earth Heritage Gallery. Admission is $5 adults, $2.50 children 6–18.

**Hulihe'e Palace,** a Victorian-style building in downtown Kailua-Kona, 808/329-1877, open Mon.–Fri. 9 A.M.–4 P.M., Sat. and Sun. 10 A.M.–4 P.M., is one of three royal palaces in the state. Used by the Hawaiian monarchs until 1916, it now contains countless items owned and used by the royal families. It's a treasure house and well worth a look. Adult admission is $5, $4 senior, $1 student. Guided or self-guided tours.

**Parker Ranch Historic Homes** are located a few miles outside Waimea, 808/885-5433, open daily 10 A.M.–5 P.M.; $8.50 admission adults. Pu'opelu, the ranch home of the Parker family, is a structure to be appreciated in and of itself, but it also houses artwork of world-prominent European artists, Chinese glass art, and antique furniture collected by Richard Smart, the last of the Parker line. Reconstructed on the grounds is Mana House, the original Parker ranch home from 1847, also open for viewing.

**Kamuela Museum,** located west of downtown Waimea, 808/885-4724, open daily 8 A.M.–5 P.M.,

---

with the best hula dancers that the islands' *hula halau* have to offer. Gentle but stiff competition features hula in both its ancient *(kahiko)* and modern *(auana)* forms. The festival runs for a week on a variable schedule from year to year. It's immensely popular with islanders, so hotels, cars, and flights are booked solid. Tickets usually go on sale at the first of the year and sell out in a month. This is the state's most prestigious hula competition. For information call the HVB at 808/935-9168.

## May

**Honoka'a Annual Western Week End** at Honoka'a is a fun-filled weekend with a Western theme. It includes a cookout, parade, rodeo, and dance.

The annual **Spring Arts Festival** held at the Wailoa Center in Hilo is a juried art show featuring mixed media artwork by Big Island artists.

The **Annual Keauhou-Kona Triathlon** at Keauhou Bay is open to athletes unable to enter

the Ironman and to anyone in good health. Each of its three events is half as long as in the Ironman, and it allows relay-team racing for each grueling segment.

## June

Hilo flashes its brilliant colors with the **Annual Hilo Orchid Society Show,** at the Hilo Civic Auditorium, and the **Annual Big Island Bonsai Show,** Wailoa Center, Hilo. Both are sometimes scheduled for April or July.

**Bon Odori,** also called O Bon Festival, the Japanese festival of departed souls, features dances and candle lighting ceremonies held at numerous Buddhist temples throughout the island. These festivities change yearly and can be held anytime from late June to early August.

## July

Every year on the weekend closest to July 1, the week-long **Pu'uhonua O Honaunau National** is a wonderfully eclectic private collection of Hawaiiana, upcountry *paniolo* life, Asian artifacts, and photos of the Parker family. This museum has many items that you might expect to find in a much larger big-city museum. Admission is $5, $2 for children under 12.

**Parker Ranch Museum** in the visitor center at the Parker Ranch Shopping Center, 808/885-7655, is open daily 9 A.M.–5 P.M. (tickets sold until 4 P.M.); adult admission is $6. This is an exhibit of Parker family history and a brief history of ranching and *paniolo* life on the Big Island. Many display items plus a video are offered.

**Kona Historical Society Museum,** just south of the town of Kealakekua, 808/323-3222, is open Mon.–Fri. 9 A.M.–3 P.M.; $2 admission. Housed in a native stone and lime mortar general store from 1875, this museum has a small collection of glassware and photographs. An archive of Kona-area historical items is housed in the basement and is open by appointment only.

**Onizuka Space Center,** 808/329-3441, is located at the Kona International Airport. Its hours are 8:30 A.M.–4:30 P.M. daily except Thanksgiving, Christmas, and New Year's Day; $3 admission. This center is a memorial to Hawaii's first astronaut and a space education facility for adults and children. It includes interactive and static exhibits, models, audiovisual displays, and lots of reading material.

The **Laupahoehoe Train Museum,** 36-2377 Mamalahoa Hwy., near the Laupahoehoe Lookout, 808/962-6300, is a small but wonderful view into the life and times of trains and life along the train line of the Hamakua Coast. The museum is open Mon.–Fri. 9 A.M.–4:30 P.M., weekends 10 A.M.–2 P.M. Entrance is $3 adult, $2 for children and seniors.

The **Thomas A. Jaggar Museum** is a state-of-the-art venture with multimedia displays depicting the geology and volcanology of the Kilauea Caldera and entire volcano zone in Hawaii Volcanoes National Park. Open daily 8:30 A.M.–5 P.M., admission free.

**Historical Park Annual Cultural Festival** is held at the national park south of Kealakekua Bay. This free event features traditional Hawaiian arts and crafts, music, dance, and food, and everyone is welcome.

The week of the **Fourth of July** offers the all-American sport of rodeo along with parades. Don't miss the **Parker Ranch 4th of July Horse Race and Rodeo,** Paniolo Park, Waimea. The epitome of rodeo by Hawaii's top cowboys is set at the Parker Ranch.

The **Kilauea Volcano Wilderness Run** is held over rough lava, in and out of volcanic craters, and through ʻohiʻa and fern forests within the Hawaii Volcanoes National Park.

With well-known headliners and newcomers alike, the annual **Big Island Slack Key Guitar Festival** is held in Hilo, sponsored by the East Hawaiʻi Cultural Center.

Held in Kona, the **Na Pua ʻO Ke Kai** billfish tournament is a day-long fishing event for women.

## August

The **Pro-Am Billfish Tournament,** held in the waters off Kona, precedes and is a qualifying meet for the more famous annual **Hawaiian International Billfish Tournament,** held about one week later. A world-renowned tournament and the Big Daddy of them all, the HIBT has been held every year since 1959. Contact organizers at 808/329-6155 for information on either event, or see www.konabillfish.com.

On the weekend closest to Admission Day (August 17), a royal procession, traditional hula, lei workshops, games, and crafts are on the schedule at the **Hawaiian Cultural Festival** at Puʻukohola Heiau in Kawaihae.

The **International Festival of the Pacific** features a "Pageant of Nations" in Hilo. Folk dances, complete with authentic costumes from throughout Asia and the Pacific, add a rare excitement to the festivities. Other events include a parade, hula, and food from the Pacific.

**BIG ISLAND OF HAWAIʻI**

Kailua-Kona hosts the annual **Queen Lili'uokalani Long Distance Canoe Race** every Labor Day weekend. Single-hull, double-hull, and one-person events are held over a two-day period. Run between Kailua and Honaunau, this 18-mile race is the longest in the state, with more than 2,500 paddlers in competition.

## September

In early September don't miss the **Parker Ranch Round-Up Rodeo** at the ranch rodeo arena in Waimea.

The **Hawai'i County Fair** at Hilo is an old-time fair held on the grounds of Hilo Civic Auditorium.

## October

When they really "wanna have fun," super-athletes come to the **Ironman World Triathlon Championship** at Kailua-Kona. A 2.4-mile open-ocean swim, followed by a 112-mile bike ride, topped off with a 26.2-mile full marathon, is their idea of a good day. For information, contact the Ironman Office, 808/329-0063, or go to www.ironmanlive.com on the internet.

Lasting two weekends, the **Hamakua Music Festival** features island musicians and those of national fame. Always jazz, some classical

and Hawaiian music are also performed. For information, call 808/775-3378, or check www.hamakuamusicfestival.com.

## November

Taste the best coffee commercially grown in the United States at the annual **Kona Coffee Cultural Festival** in Kailua-Kona. This festival is the oldest and longest-running foods festival in the state—the 33th was held in 2003—and celebrates a product that's been growing in the region for about 175 years. It's the food festival in the state. Parades, arts and crafts, and ethnic foods and entertainment are part of the festivities. For information, call 808/326-7820; www.kona-coffeefest.com.

Celebrating another of the island's agricultural products, the **Taro Festival** is held yearly in Honoka'a.

## December

The people of Hilo celebrate a New England Christmas in memory of the missionaries with **A Christmas Tradition,** held at the Lyman House Memorial Museum, Hilo, 808/935-5021. To get a jump on it, the **Annual Waimea Christmas Parade** is held in Waimea toward the beginning of the month.

# Sports and Recreation

You'll have no problem having fun on the Big Island. Everybody goes outside to play. You can camp and hike, drive golf balls over lagoons, smack tennis balls at private and public courts, ski, snorkel, windsurf, gallop a horse, bag a wild turkey, spy a rare bird, or latch onto a marlin that'll tail-walk across a windowpane sea. Choose your sport and have a ball.

## BEACHES

The Big Island takes the rap for having poor beaches—this isn't true! Being the youngest island, Hawai'i has far fewer beaches than any of the other major Hawaiian islands, but they are spectacular. Except for a handful of these shore-

line retreats, they are small affairs often with volcanic rock intrusions, and the wave action hasn't had enough time to grind new lava and coral into sand.

A few county beaches have lifeguards. For lifeguard hours and locations, call the Department of Parks and Recreation, 808/961-8694.

## East Side

The east side has few accessible beaches. The best are in the Hilo area. Hilo Waterfront beach is a nice long crescent of gray-white sand, but few use this beach for swimming. Locals head east to **Onekahakaha Beach, Leleiwi Beach,** and **Richardson's Beach,** which are all small pockets of white sand bound by rugged lava

ROBERT NILSEN

The waves at Kamakahonu Beach, on Kailua Bay, are gentle enough for kids.

shoreline. The only other beaches of note along this coast are the long black-sand **Waipi'o Beach** in Waipi'o Valley and the smaller **Waimanu Beach** in a valley farther north. The use of either of these two valley beaches is discouraged unless the water is glassy smooth.

## South Side

Black sand typifies the beaches along the south coast. The best, near Kalapana and Kaimu, have been overrun by lava flows in the past 15 years, although new ones are being created. Beaches that still draw swimmers in Puna are **Isaac Hale Beach** (also called Pohoiki) and the half-hidden **Kehena Beach.** In Ka'u, the best in the region and easiest to get to is **Punalu'u Beach.** Near the windswept South Point is **Green Sand Beach,** an oddity for sure but more to look at than for swimming, unless it's totally calm.

## West Side

**Miloli'i** and **Ho'kena** are two local and fairly isolated beaches in South Kona. Although they're fine for a day out, you have to make an effort to get to either. North Kona has more beaches and is much more easily accessible: **Kahalu'u**

**Beach** is the first of these, and while the swimming is fine, the snorkeling is better. **Disappearing Sands Beach** (also called White Sand Beach) is also good when the sand is there; it's a popular spot for boogie boarders. Perhaps the most gentle for kids and an all-around good place to have your first dip into the Kona waters is **Kailua Bay Beach** in front of the King Kamehameha's Kona Beach Hotel. There are pockets of sandy beach at the Old Kona Airport State Recreation Area, but better beaches are found farther north at Kaloko-Honokohau National Historical Park and Kona Coast State Park.

The best beaches on the island dot the Kohala Coast. An almost perfectly crescent-shaped white-sand beach fronts the Kona Village Resort. The sandy bottom, clear water, and palm fringed shore will certainly let you know that you're floating in paradise. Longer and straighter is the ever-popular **'Anaeho'omalu Beach,** which fronts the Waikoloa Beach Marriott Resort. Not only is the swimming good here, but you can indulge in a wide variety of water sports. Diminutive beaches hug the coast at the Mauna Lani Resort, but the island's best beaches are just a few miles away. **Hapuna Beach** and **Kauna'oa**

**Beach** are the crown jewels of Big Island beaches: white sand, gentle slope, and long and narrow sand strips. Swimming is great and snorkeling is also noteworthy. If you had to choose one beach as the premier swimming beach on the island, it would definitely be one of these two. Both are fronted by first-class luxury hotels, and Hapuna Beach also has public facilities.

# SCUBA AND SNORKELING
## Scuba

Those in the know consider the deep diving along the steep drop-offs of Hawaii's geologically young coastline some of the best in the state. The ocean surrounding the Big Island has not had a chance to turn the relatively new lava to sand, which makes the visibility absolutely perfect, even to depths of 150 feet or more. There's also 60–70 miles of coral belt around the Big Island, which adds up to a magnificent diving experience. Only advanced divers should attempt deep-water dives, but beginners and snorkelers will have many visual thrills inside the protected bays and coves. While most people head to the west (Kona) side, there is very good diving on the east side as well.

## Scuba Shops and Tour Companies

There are about two dozen companies on the Big Island, mostly on the Kona side, that offer scuba instruction and escorted dives and rent scuba equipment.

One of the best outfits to dive with on the Big Island is **Dive Makai** in Kona, 808/329-2025, www.divemakai.com, operated by Tom Shockley and Lisa Choquette. These very experienced divers have run this service for years and have many dedicated customers. Both Tom and Lisa are conservationists who help preserve the fragile reef. They've worked very hard with the Diver's Council to protect dive sites from fish collectors and to protect the reef from destruction by anchors. Their motto, "We care," is not a trite saying, as they continue to preserve the reef for you and your children.

Another excellent diving outfit is **Jack's Diving Locker**, 75-5819 Ali'i Dr. in the Coconut Grove Marketplace, 808/329-7585 or 800/345-4807, www.jacksdivinglocker.com, a responsible outfit that does a good job of watching out for its customers and taking care of the reef. Owners Teri and Jeff Leicher, along with their crew, run diving and snorkeling excursions along the Kona Coast from Kealakekua Bay to Keahole Point, which takes in over 50 dive sites (most of which have permanent moorings to protect the reef from damage by anchoring). Jack's also specializes in snorkel sales and rentals, scuba equipment rentals, and certification classes. Dive run the gamut from a one tank beach dive at $50 to a multi-day, multi-dive arrangement for $265.

**Big Island Divers,** 75-5467 Kaiwi St., 808/329-6068 or 800/488-6068, www.bigislanddivers.com, departing from Honokohau Harbor on a custom-built 35-foot dive boat, offers a very inexpensive scuba certification course that's given on four consecutive Saturdays or Wednesdays, so you must intend to stay on the Big Island for that length of time. The normal four-day course costs about $499. Big Island Divers offers a two-tank two-location dive for $89, as well as introductory and night dives.

**Kohala Divers** along Route 270 in the Kawaihae Shopping Center, 808/882-7774, www.kohaladivers.com, open daily 8 A.M.–5 P.M., offers scuba certification, snorkel equipment rentals for $10, and scuba equipment rentals for $15. The company leads two-tank dives for $99, a night dive for $125, an introductory dive for $145, and will take snorkelers along for $45 if there's room on the boat. It's a bit far to go from Kailua-Kona but great if you're staying at one of the Kohala resorts or in Waimea. A full-service dive shop, this company is the farthest north along the Kohala coast.

Nearby in Kawaihae is **Mauna Kea Divers,** 808/882-1544, www.maunakeadivers.com, who have somewhat cheaper prices and will model a tour for you if you have special needs or desires.

**Kona Coast Divers,** 74-5614 Palani Rd., Kona, 808/329-8802 or 800/562-3483, www.konacoastdivers.com, is owned and operated by longtime Kona Coast diver Jim Robertson. This outfit is efficient and to the point. There are many dive options, but some rates are: two-tank boat dive, $80; night dive, $99; a manta ray dive, $65, and an introductory dive, $135. Full underwater gear is sold and rented.

**Sandwich Isle Divers,** 808/329-9188, www.sandwichisledivers.com, is owned and operated by Steve and Larry, longtime Kona coast divers who know all the spots. They have a custom, six-passenger dive boat, great for small, personalized trips for avid divers. They offer competitive rates for instruction and day and night dives: certified diver with all gear for $95, introductory dive at $120, and a night dive for $75. Their office is in the Kona Marketplace.

**Honu Sports,** 808/938-9795, near the Royal Kona Resort in Kailua, offers several shore and boat dives for $89–99 and an introductory boat dive for $139. The use of a propulsion torpedo scooter is an added $40.

**Eco-Adventures** at the King Kamehameha's Kona Beach Hotel in Kailua, 808/329-7116 or 800/949-3483, offers daily morning, afternoon, and night boat charters as well as beach dives and open water certification. Eco-Adventures is conveniently located and offers good value for your money.

If you only want a shore dive, try **Ocean Eco Tours,** 808/324-7873, www.oceanecotours.com. This company says it specializes in beginners, and certification courses are taught.

A twist on the usual snorkel adventure is offered by **Torpedo Tours Hawaii,** 808/938-0405, www.torpedotours.com, which does shore and boat dives as well as certification. Small groups are important here. To provide a little extra power, this company provides "torpedo" scooters, battery powered motors that pull you through the water at 2 mph, for some dives: $55–90 from shore or $129 for a torpedo dive from a boat.

For those still dancing to the primordial tune of residual DNA from our one-celled, ocean-dwelling ancestors, *Kona Aggressor II* is a "live-aboard" dive boat, 808/329-8182 or 800/344-5662, www.aggressor.com or www.pac-aggressor.com, departing Kona every Saturday for six days of diving along the Kona coast toward South Point. Passengers dive up to five times per day and night, as the Aggressor completely fulfills its motto of

"Eat, Sleep, and Dive." This is the Cadillac of dive cruises, and everything on board is taken care of. Rates run $1,995 per person.

The **Nautilus Dive Center,** 382 Kamehameha Ave., Hilo, 808/935-6939, www.downtown-hilo.com/nautilus, open Mon.–Sat. 9 A.M.–4 P.M., is one of the longest-established dive companies on the Hilo side. This full-service dive center offers instruction, rentals, and guided dives at prices less expensive than on the more frequented Kona side. But don't be fooled, the Hilo side has some very good diving. Two popular spots are Leleiwi Beach and Richardson Beach.

Two other shops in Hilo that offer a variety of boat and shore dives, as well as a multitude of other water activities, are **Aquatic Perceptions,** 808/933-1228; and **Planet Ocean Watersports,** 200 Kanoelehua Ave., 808/935-7277.

## Snorkeling

Kona's most popular snorkel sites include Kekaha Kai State Park, Pawai Bay, Disappearing Sands Beach, Kahalu'u Beach Park, Kealakekua Bay by the Captain Cook monument (often said to be the best on the island), and Pu'uhonua O Honaunau (outside the park boundaries), in Kona. In the Kohala area, seek out 'Anaeho'omalu Beach, Hapuna Beach Park, Mauna Kea Beach Park, Puako coastal area, Spencer Beach County Park, Mahukona Beach County Park, and Kapa'a Beach County Park. Leleiwi Beach County Park and Richardson's Beach in Hilo area are favorites, while Puna's best snorkeling spots are the Kapoho tidepools and Isaac Hale Beach Park.

## Snorkel Rental

Larger hotels and some condos often have snorkel equipment for guests, but if it isn't free, it always costs more than if you rent it from a dive shop. Many activities booths and virtually all dive shops rent snorkel gear at competitive rates. Depending upon the quality of gear, snorkel gear runs from about $3 an hour or $9 a day to $9 an hour or $30 a day. Many of the places that rent snorkel gear also rent boogie boards, usually at about $5–8 a day.

Good old **Snorkel Bob's,** in the parking lot in

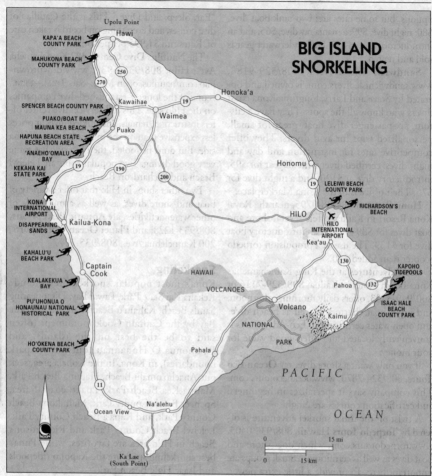

**BIG ISLAND SNORKELING**

© SANDRA E. BISIGNANI TRUST AND AVALON TRAVEL PUBLISHING, INC.

front of Huggo's Restaurant in Kailua-Kona, 808/329-0770, www.snorkelbob.com, offers some of the best deals for snorkel rental in Hawaii (free snorkeling maps and advice). This gear can be taken interisland and turned in at any Snorkel Bob's location. Depending on the type, snorkel gear will cost $2.50–9 a day or $9–35 a week.

At the beach in front of the King Kamehameha Kona Beach Hotel, the **Kona Beach Shack** not only rents snorkel gear at $7 a day, they also rent kayaks, peddle boats, boogie

boards, and other beach and water equipment. Open daily 9 A.M.–5 P.M.

The 1940 Pontiac woody wagon out front points you to **Kahalu'u Bay Surf and Sea,** 808/322-43338, located just down the road and across the street from Kahalu'u Bay and beach park. This shop can set you up with snorkel gear, surfboard, kayaks, and other water equipment at a fair price.

One of the cheapest for week-long rentals, **Miller's Snorkeling,** 808/326-1771, at the Kona Bali Kai condo, south of Kailua-Kona along

Aliʻi Drive, rents complete snorkel gear for $7 per day or $15 per week and other beach gear and accessories.

In Hilo, look for snorkel gear at **Nautilus Dive Center,** 382 Kamehameha Ave. at the edge of the downtown strip, 808/935-6939, where snorkel gear runs $5 a day.

## Snorkel Boats

Snorkel cruises can be booked through the various activities centers along the Kona and Kohala coasts and at your hotel travel desk. Snorkeling, scuba, and snuba excursions are also provided by the following.

**Fair Wind,** 808/322-2788 or 800/677-9461 off-island, www.fair-wind.com, a well-established company with the 60-foot catamaran *Fair Wind II,* has a great reputation and is sure to please. Its boat leaves daily from magnificent Keauhou Bay and stops at Kealakekua Bay in front of the Captain Cook monument. This boat has a diving platform and water slide, sunning deck, and easy access steps into the water. All equipment is on board, and scuba and snuba are options for an additional fee. The four-and-a-half-hour morning cruise runs $89 for adults, $50 for children 4–12; the three-and-a-half-hour afternoon tour is $55 and $35, respectively. A continental breakfast and lunch or snacks and beverages are served.

Departing from the Kailua pier and sailing north to Pawai Bay, **Body Glove Cruises,** 808/326-7122 or 800/551-8911, www.bodyglovehawaii.com, is a full-fledged snorkel and scuba company offering a bar and lunch. Costs for the morning and afternoon snorkel sails on the *Body Glove* run $84 adult/$46 child and $52 adult/$32 child, respectively. In season, whale watching trips may take the place of the afternoon snorkel sail.

**Kamanu Charters,** 808/329-2021 or 800/348-3091, www.kamanu.com, Kona's original snorkel sail, in business over 30 years, provides a full day of fun with beer and snacks included in the price. They pilot a true sailing catamaran and take fewer passengers—a maximum of 24. Sails leave from the Honokohau Marina for Pawai Bay at 9 A.M. and 1:30 P.M., $65 adults and $45 kids 12 and under. Kamanu

Charters is a good choice for a fun-filled sail and snorkel experience.

Leaving from Kailua pier on a morning snorkel tour is **Dream Cruises,** 808/326-6000, www.dream-cruises.com. On board are snorkel gear, a water slide, and a water trampoline. This ship provides a fun-filled adventure on its four-hour cruise for $75 adult and $40 children under 17.

At Waikoloa Beach Resort ʻAnaehoʻomalu Bay, there are two companies offering snorkel services, plus a wide range of other beach and water activities. **Ocean Sports and Activities,** 808/886-6666 or 888/742-5234, www.hawaiioceansports.com, and **Red Sail Sports,** 808/886-2878 or 877/733-7245, www.redsail.com, both run morning snorkel tours from the beach on sleek catamarans for about $65. Red Sail also has sailings from Hapuna Beach. At the Four Seasons Resort, **Hualalai Water Sports,** 808/325-8222, also offers various sail and/or snorkel options from $55–90. Other of the luxury resorts also operate their own boats.

Inflatable Zodiac rafts also offers daily snorkel tours down the Kona coast to Kealakekua Bay (see Zodiac below).

## Snuba

**Snuba Big Island, Inc.,** 808/326-7446, can set you up for this new adventure. Dives take place four times every day at the beach in front of King Kamehameha's Kona Beach Hotel or at one of the Kohala Coast beaches. The basic snuba experience costs about $59 per person, and you must be at least eight years old. Alternately, you can snuba (and snorkel) at Kealakekua Bay on the twice-daily sail with the Fair Wind sailing boat for the cost of their sail plus $49 per person.

# CATCHING WAVES
## Surfing

The surfing off the Big Island is rather uninspiring compared to that off the other islands. Overall, the reefs are treacherous and the surf is lazy. Some surfers bob around off Hilo Bay, and sometimes in Kealakekua and Kailua bays on the Kona side. Puna also attracts a few off Pohoiki Beach, and during the right conditions, others make the trip down to the beach in Waipi'o Valley. One spot that seems to have a good deal of interest for local surfers is Honoli'i Beach, a few miles north of Hilo. Generally, the north and west shores have better swells during the winter, the east and south shores in summer. If you're thinking about buying or renting a surfboard, try **Orchid Land Surfshop**, www.surfolhawaii.com, 262 Kamehameha Ave., in downtown Hilo, 808/935-1533, or **Honolua Surf Co.**, 808/329-1001, at the Kona Inn Shopping Village in Kailua-Kona for starters. Be sure to ask there about what's happening with the water when you're on island. For surf lessons, try **Ocean Eco Tours** in Kona, 808/324-7873; **Hawaii Lifeguard Surf Instructors** on the Kona side, 808/324-0442; or **Kahalu'u Bay Beach Rentals**, 808/322-4338, near Kahalu'u Beach Park in Keauhou.

## Sailboarding

The Big Island seems nearly bereft of good sailboarding locations. By all accounts, 'Anaeho'omalu Bay at Waikoloa Beach Resort on the Kohala Coast is the best place to sail. For instruction and rental equipment, check with **Ocean Sports and Activities**, 808/886-6666 or 888/742-5234 at the Waikoloa Beach Marriott Resort, which rent boards at $20 an hour and gives 60 minutes of instruction for $45.

## PARASAILING AND JETSKIING

**UFO Parasailing**, 808/325-5836 or 800/359-4836, offers boat platform take-off and landing that's safe and easy for young and old alike. A "400 feet for seven minutes" atmospheric ride runs $47 and the "800 feet for 10 minutes" stratospheric ride is $57. For those tempted to leave orbit, they'll let out 1,200 feet of rope for $67. Reduced rates are available for early birds, and boat ride-alongs are $18. You, too, can dangle from a parachute and put your life in the hands of these fun-filled Kona guys who will streak you through the air. The boat leaves from the Kailua pier; check in at the office across the street from the pier. Parasailing on the Big Island is done year-round.

If you want speed but know that staying on the water is more your style, try **Aloha Jet Ski Rentals**, 808-329-2745. To take a powerful Kawasaki jet ski for a spin around the bay any day except Monday, you must be 18 years old to drive and at least 12 to ride. Rate run $45 for one-half hour, $65 an hour, and $10 for a second person. No experience necessary.

## OCEAN TOURS

Whether it's skimming across the ocean surface on a trim sloop, diving by submarine to view coral fields, or watching whales breach and play, there are many and various ocean tours to excite visitors to the Big Island. Virtually all of these tours stay on the Kona side of the island. Some of the more popular options follow.

### Zodiac

**Captain Zodiac**, 808/329-3199 or 800/422-7824, www.captainzodiac.com, will take you on a fantastic ocean odyssey beginning at Honokohau Small Boat Harbor just north of Kailua-Kona, from where you'll skirt the coast south all the way to Kealakekua Bay. A Zodiac is a very tough, motorized rubber raft, sometimes with a rigid fiberglass bottom. It looks like a big, horseshoe-shaped inner-tube that bends itself and undulates with the waves like a floating waterbed. These seaworthy craft, powered by twin Mercury 280s, have five separate air chambers for unsinkable safety. Skippers take you and up to 15 others for a thrilling ride down the Kona coast, pausing along the way to whisk you into sea caves, grottoes, and caverns, and if the right time of year you have the added benefit of seeing whales. The Kona coast is also marked with ancient ruins and the remains of villages, which the captains point out, and about which they relate historical anecdotes as you pass by. You stop at Kealakekua Bay, where you can swim and snorkel in this underwater conservation park. Roundtrips departing at 8 A.M., and again at 1 P.M., take about four hours and cost $78 adults, $63 children 4–12. Captain Zodiac also provides a light tropical lunch of fresh exotic fruit, taro chips, fruit juice, iced tea, and sodas. All you need are a bathing suit, sun hat, towel, suntan lotion, camera, and sense of adventure.

**Fair Wind,** 808/332-2788 or 800/677-9461, www.fair-wind.com, does similar tours on its 28-foot, rigid-bottom Zodiac raft with inboard diesel, the *Orca,* but these tours leave from Kailua pier. Leaving at 8:30 A.M., morning tours run four hours with snorkel stops at Kealakekua Bay and one other location; $73 adult, $60 children 6–12. Three-hour afternoon tours start at 1 P.M. and make just one stop at Kealakekua Bay; $55 adult, $45 children.

**Sea Quest,** 808/325-7238, www.seaquesthawaii.com, runs a similar inflatable raft snorkel tour to Kealakekua Bay from Keauhou Bay with numerous stops along the way to explore sea caves and other coastline features. Morning and afternoon departures are available and cost $75 and $56, respectively. These smaller rafts take only up to six guests.

Using a smaller inflatable raft for more intimate groups, **Dolphin Discoveries,** 808/322-8000, www.dolphindiscoveries.com, also offers raft and snorkel trips to Kealakekua Bay from Keauhou Bay boat ramp. Morning and afternoon trips are given daily. The four-hour morning tour runs $74 adult and $59 kids 5–15; the three-hour afternoon tour is $55 per person. These folks are very focused on the study and research of dolphins, whales, and other sea animals, so your trip will be educational. Part of your fee goes to support marine conservation programs.

## Sailing

Sailing is a year-round adventure, and boats take advantage of the steady breezes and fine weather along the Kona Coast. In season (November–April), sailing companies offer fascinating whale-watching adventures as part of the bargain.

One of the only true mono-hull charter sailing ships on the island, the *Honu,* is put in the water by **Honu Sail Charters,** 808/896-4668, www.sailkona.com, which runs half-day, full-day, and sunset sailing tours on their sleek sailboat from Honokohau Marina. Half-day tours, including snorkeling and snacks, run $80, full-day

tours run $120, while the sunset tour with *pu pu* is $60; maximum of six guests.

The *Maile,* berthed at Kawaihae Harbor, P.O. Box 44335, Kamuela, HI 96743, 808/326-5174 or 800/726-SAIL, is a 50-foot Gulfstar sloop available for luxury sailing charters and shorter-term whalewatching, snorkeling, and fishing expeditions. Skippered by Ralph Blancato, a U.S. Coast Guard-certified Master, the sloop offers competitive prices on half- or full-day charters, sunset sails, and long-term rental. Offering more than just a sailing trip, Blancato teaches his guests about marine life, reef ecology, and island environment. Aside from her commercial use, the *Maile* also functions as the research boat for both the Ocean Mammal Institute and the Oceanic Society.

## Kayaking

Ocean kayaking has gained popularity in Hawai'i in the last several years. Although the entire coastline would offer adventure for the expert kayaker, most try sections of the coast near Kealakekua Bay and east out of Hilo that offer excellent shoreline variation and great snorkeling.

While you can rent kayaks and go where you want, a few companies offer guided trips to exceptional places. Open-cockpit rental kayaks generally run about $25 for a single or $45–50 for a tandem per day and come with all necessary gear and sometimes a car rack. Occasionally, companies will rent by the hour or week. Tours vary, but run about $65–80 for a half day.

In Captain Cook, **Adventures in Paradise,** 808/323-3005 or 866/824-2337, www.bigislandkayak.com, is the company to see. Contact Geoff Hand for kayak rentals or tours. Rentals run $25 per person and tours for $79 per person are usually run near Honaunau Bay or at Kealakekua Bay. Geoff knows the water and will make your tour an experience. As he allows time for snorkeling, he'll point out the many reef fish and other sea creatures that inhabit this coastline.

Also near Kealakekua Bay are **Aloha Kayak Co.,** 808/322-2868 in Honalo, www.alohakayak.com; **Kona Boy's Kayaks,** 808/328-1234, between Honalo and Kealakekua; and **Kealakekua Bay Kayak,** 808/323-3329, in the town of Kealakekua, www.konakayak.com.

In Kailua, try **Ocean Safaris,** 808/326-4699, www.oceansafariskayaks.com, for half-day guided tours in the Keauhou area for $59 or an early bird tour of Kailua Bay for $30. Otherwise, try **Honu Sports,** 808/938-9795, www.honusports.com.

For kayak rentals in the Hilo area, contact **Aquatic Perceptions,** 808/935-9997. Kayak rental starts at $15 for four hours single and goes up from there; tours start at $25 per person. **Planet Ocean Watersports,** 808/935-7277, at 100 Kamehameha Ave. also rents kayaks and offers kayak tours.

In Waimea, **C&S Outfitters,** 808/885-5005, rents kayaks at $25 for a half day, $30 per day, and $120 a week, and this includes a roof rack. From here, recommended paddle areas are Puako in the summer and Kealakekua in the winter.

A twist on the kayak business is offered by **Flum'in da Ditch,** 808/889-6922 or 877/449-6922, www.flumindaditch.com, located near the big banyan tree in Hawi. On an outing with this company, you'll float about three scenic miles of the Kohala irrigation flume, over small ravines, and through tunnels in the remote, private lands of North Kohala. Guided by experts and utilizing specially-designed five-person inflatable kayaks, you'll not only experience the beauty of the surrounding rainforest and rugged scenery but will also absorb a lesson in the history and culture of this area. No experience required. Bring an extra set of dry clothes. Tours go daily at 8:30 A.M. and 12:30 P.M. and run $85 for adults and $65 for children ages 5–18.

## Whale-Watching

Three-hour whale-watching tours on the 40-foot boat *Lady Ann* are offered by **Captain Dan McSweeney's Whale Watching Adventures,** 808/322-0028 or 888/942-5376, www.ilovewhales.com. While many are interested in looking only for the humpback whale, Dan, a marine biologist and whale researcher, takes visitors ye round so they can also learn about different kinds of whales and other ocean mammals that inhabit this coast. This is an educational trip, the best the island has to offer. If you want to see whales and learn about these beautiful mammals in the

process, go with Dan. The *Lady Ann* leaves from the Honokohau Marina every day from mid-December through mid-April, and Tuesday, Thursday, and Saturday the rest of the year. Tours run $54.50 adults and $34.50 children.

From December through May, most of the Zodiac, snorkel, scuba, catamaran, and sailing boats run whale-watching tours in addition to their other activities.

## Dinner Cruises

**Captain Beans' Polynesian Cruise,** 808/329-2955, is a Kona institution that will take you aboard its glass-bottom barge-like boat daily at 5:15 P.M. from Kailua Pier. During the very tame cruise you'll spot fish, listen to island music, and enjoy a sunset dinner. The cost is $52 (slightly more for those staying in the Kohala resorts), and this includes dinner, beverages, and transportation. This cruise is only open to those age 21 and older. Captain Bean's is the bus tour version of a water cruise.

The smaller trimaran *Kona Dream* runs more personal dinner cruises off the Kona coast nightly from 5:30–7:30 P.M. Dinner, beverages, and soft island music are all included for $50 adults and $33 children 4–12. A nice sunset is thrown in for free.

## Glass-Bottom Boats

*Marian* of the **Kailua Bay Charter Company,** 808/324-1749, does glass-bottom boat tours from the Kailua pier, daily on the hour from 10 A.M.–2 P.M. Taking only 44 passengers, this cruise runs $25 adults or $10 for kids ages 5–12. Sunset cruises are also available. **Aloha Adventure Cruise,** 808/331-2992, runs a two-hour dolphin watch/glass-bottom boat tour daily at 9:30 A.M. and noon from the Kailua pier. Monday, Wednesday, and Friday evenings, the crew turns its attention above water and runs a sunset cruise departing at 5:15 P.M. All cruises are aboard the *Coral Sea,* run $49, and feature island music, *pu pu,* two cocktails, and, of course, the fine sunset. **Ocean Sports and Activities** at 'Anaeho'omalu Bay at Waikoloa Resort offer half-hour glass-bottom boat trips for $15 and a similar tour is offered at Kona Village Resort.

## Submarines

**Atlantis Submarine,** 808/329-6626 or 800/548-6262, allows everyone to live out the fantasy of Captain Nemo on a silent cruise under the waves off Kailua-Kona. After checking in at the office at the King Square Shopping Center, you board a launch at Kailua Pier that takes you on a 10-minute cruise to the waiting submarine tethered offshore. You're given all of your safety tips on the way there. The underwater portion lasts about a half hour. As you descend to 120 feet, notice that everything white, including teeth, turns pink because the ultraviolet rays are filtered out. The only colors you can see clearly beneath the waves are blues and greens because water is 800 times denser than air and filters out the reds and oranges. Everyone gets an excellent seat with a viewing port; there's not a bad seat in this 48-passenger submarine, so you don't have to rush to get on. Don't worry about being claustrophobic, either—the sub is amazingly airy and bright, with aircraft-quality air blowers above the seats. Cruises run at 8:30 A.M., 10 A.M., 11:30 A.M., and 1:30 P.M., although the times may change according to the season, and cost $84 for adults and $42 for children. Atlantis joins with other island tour operators to offer discounted prices when you combine a submarine trip with a lu'au, a whale watch or snorkel cruise, or a helicopter ride.

## FISHING

### Fishing Boats and Charters

The fishing around the Big Island's Kona Coast ranges from excellent to outstanding! It's legendary for marlin fishing, but there are other fish in the sea. A large fleet of charter boats with skilled captains and tested crews is ready, willing, and competent to take you out. The vast majority are berthed at Honokohau Small Boat Harbor just north of Kailua-Kona. The best times of year for marlin are July–September and January–March (when the generally larger females arrive). August is the optimum month. Rough seas can keep boats in for a few days during December and early January, but by February all are generally out.

To charter a boat, contact the individual captains directly, check at your hotel activities desk, or book through one of the following agencies. **Charter Services Hawaii,** operated by Ed Barry, 808/334-1881 or 800/567-5662, www.konazone.com, fishing@aloha.net, offers more than 50 boats in all sizes and price ranges. Ed also offers complete packages including room, car, and boat along with a cash prize of $1 million if you book through his agency and top the world record. If you're after a company that's knowledgeable about getting you onto a boat that will bring you to waters where you'll have the opportunity to catch one of the twirling and gigantic "big blues," this is the place to come.

Located on the dock at Honokohau Harbor, the **The Charter Desk,** 808/329-5735 or 888/566-2487, www.charterdesk.com, charter@aloha.net, represents some 50 boats in the harbor. This is another well-respected and competent company that works hard at matching clients to boats.

The **Kona Charter Skippers Association,** 808/329-3600 or 800/762-7546, www.konabiggamefishing.com, konafish@hawaii.rr.com, is another agency that tries to match you and your desires with the right boat and captain.

Most of the island's 80 charter boats are berthed at Honokohau Harbor off Route 19, about midway between downtown Kailua and Kona Airport. Fish are weighed-in daily 11 A.M.–1 P.M. and again 3–5 P.M. Big fish are hardly ever weighed in at Kailua Pier in front of the King Kamehameha's Kona Beach Hotel as they used to be for the benefit of tourists. Honokohau Harbor has far eclipsed Kailua Pier, which is now tamed and primarily for swimmers, triathletes, and body-boarders. A few boats also leave from Keauhou Bay and Kawaihae Harbor on the west side, and some use the river mouth in Hilo.

An excellent publication listing some boats and general deep-sea fishing information is *Fins and Fairways,* P.O. Box 9014, Kailua-Kona, HI 96745, 808/325-6171, www.fishkona.com. This tabloid, published by Captain Tom Armstrong and available free at newsstands and in hotel and condo lobbies, is filled with descriptions of boats, phone numbers, captains' names, maps, and photos of recent catches. For general fishing information and a listing of tournaments throughout the islands, pick up a copy of *Hawaii Fishing News* at a newsstand or supermarket.

You can also contact **The Hawaiian International Billfish Association,** P.O. Box 4800, Kailua-Kona, HI 96740, 808/329-6155, www.konabillfish.com, for details on upcoming tournaments and on "what's biting and when."

Of course, the bar at the Harbor House Restaurant at the Honokohau Marina might be just as easy a place to get quick, reliable, and up-to-the-minute information on how the fish are biting as well as which boats seem to be having the best luck.

## Coastal and Freshwater Fishing

You don't have to hire a boat to catch fish! The coastline is productive too. *Ulua* are caught all along the coast south of Hilo, and at South Point and Kealakekua Point. Bays around the island produce *papio* and *halalu*, while *manini* and *'ama'ama* hit from Kawaihae to Puako. Hilo Bay is easily accessible to anyone, and the fishing is very exciting, especially at the mouth of the Wailuku River.

Licensed fishing is limited to the **Waiakea Public Fishing Area,** a state-operated facility in downtown Hilo. This 26-acre pond offers saltwater and brackish-water species. A license is required. You can pick one up at sporting goods stores or at the Division of Aquatic Resources, 75 Aupuni St., Hilo, HI 96720, 808/974-6201.

# CAMPING AND HIKING

The Big Island has the best camping in the state, with more facilities and less competition for campsites than on the other islands. Nearly three dozen parks fringe the coastline and sit deep in the interior; almost half offer camping. The others boast a combination of rugged hikes, easy strolls, self-guided nature walks, swimming, historical sites, and natural phenomena. The ones with campgrounds are state-, county-, and nationally operated, ranging from remote walk-in sites to housekeeping cabins. All require camping permits—inexpensive for the county and state parks, free for the national park. Camping permits can be obtained by walk-in application to the appropriate office or by writing. Although there is usually no problem obtaining sites, when writing, request reservations well in advance, allowing a minimum of one month for letters to go back and forth.

## General Information

Most campgrounds have pavilions, fireplaces, toilets (sometimes pit), and running water, but usually no individual electrical hookups. Pavilions often have electric lights, but sometimes campers appropriate the bulbs, so it's wise to carry your own. Drinking water is available, but at times brackish water is used for flushing toilets and for showers, so read all signs regarding water. Backcountry shelters have catchment water, but never hike without an adequate supply of your own. Cooking fires are allowed in established fire pits, but no wood is provided. Charcoal is a good idea, or bottled fuel for those hiking. When camping in the mountains, be prepared for cold and rainy weather. Women, especially, should never hike or camp alone, and everyone should take precautions against theft, though it's not as prevalent as on the other islands.

## County Parks

The county-maintained parks are open to the public for day-use, and permits are only required for overnight tent and RV camping. For information contact: Department of Parks and Recreation, County of Hawaii, 101 Pauahi St., Suite 6, Hilo, HI 96720, 808/961-8311. You can obtain a permit by mail or pick it up in person, Mon.–Fri. 7:45 A.M.–4:00 P.M. If you'll be arriving after hours or on a weekend, have the permits mailed to you. Branch offices (all with reduced hours) are located at Hale Halawai in Kailua-Kona, 808/327-3565; in Waimea Community Center in Waimea, 808/885-3014; in Yano Hall in Captain Cook, 808/323-3060; in Na'alehu, 808/939-2510, and in Pahala, 808/928-3102. Fees are $5 per day per adult; children 13–17, $2 per day; youngsters under 12, $1 per day. Pavilions for exclusive use are $25 per day with kitchen, $10 without. Camping is limited to one week for any one site June–August and for two weeks at any one site for the rest of the year. County parks that allow camping are as follows (counterclockwise around the island from Hilo): Kolekole, Laupahoehoe, Kapa'a, Mahukona, Spencer, Ho'okena, Miloli'i, Whittington, Punalu'u, and Isaac Hale.

## State Parks

Day-use of state parks is free, with no permit required, but you need one for tent camping and for cabins. Five consecutive nights is the limit for either camping or cabins at any one site. If you want a permit, at least one week's notice is required regardless of availability. You can pick up your permit at the state parks office Mon.–Fri. 8 A.M.–3:30 P.M., but again it saves time if you do it all by mail. Write: Department of Land and Natural Resources, Division of State Parks, P.O. Box 936 (75 Aupuni St., Room 204), Hilo, HI 96721, 808/974-6200.

Camping is permitted only at Kalopa and MacKenzie State Recreation Areas and Manuka State Wayside, where there is a $5 fee per campsite per night. Forest cabins are located at Kalopa

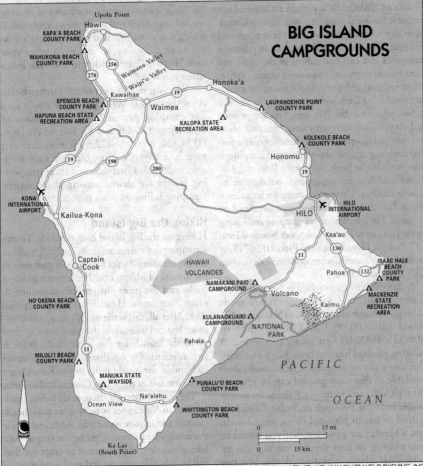

BIG ISLAND
CAMPGROUNDS

Upolu Point

Hawi

KAPA'A BEACH
COUNTY PARK

MAHUKONA BEACH
COUNTY PARK

270

250

Waimanu Valley

Waipi'o Valley

Honoka'a

19

Kawaihae

SPENCER BEACH
COUNTY PARK

Waimea

LAUPAHOEHOE POINT
COUNTY PARK

HAPUNA BEACH STATE
RECREATION AREA

KALOPA STATE
RECREATION AREA

19

190

200

KOLEKOLE BEACH
COUNTY PARK

Honomu

19

KONA
INTERNATIONAL
AIRPORT

Kailua-Kona

HILO
INTERNATIONAL
AIRPORT

HILO

Kea'au

130

Captain
Cook

HAWAII
VOLCANOES

11

ISAAC HALE
BEACH
COUNTY
PARK

132

Pahoa

NAMAKANI PAIO
CAMPGROUND

Volcano

Kaimu

MACKENZIE
STATE
RECREATION
AREA

HO'OKENA BEACH
COUNTY PARK

KULANAOKUAIKI
CAMPGROUND

NATIONAL
PARK

Pahala

11

MILOLI'I BEACH
COUNTY PARK

PACIFIC

MANUKA STATE
WAYSIDE

PUNALU'U BEACH
COUNTY PARK

OCEAN

Ocean View

Na'alehu

WHITTINGTON BEACH
COUNTY PARK

0        15 mi

0        15 km

Ka Lae
(South Point)

BIG ISLAND OF HAWAI'I

SRA, and A-frame cabins are at Hapuna Beach SRA. The four-person A-frames are a flat $20 per night. The group housekeeping cabins at Kalopa SRAs are $55 for up to eight people. When writing for permits, specify exactly which facility you require, for how long, and for how many people. Located along the Saddle Road near Pohakuloa Military Camp, Mauna Kea State Park is now closed to overnight use but day use is still permitted.

## Hawaii Volcanoes National Park

For overnight back-country camping in Hawaii Volcanoes National Park, permits are required but available for free through the park Visitors Center. Your stay is limited to seven days per campground per year. There are a half dozen walk-in primitive campsites and two trail cabins in the park; you can't reserve them and you should expect to share them with other hikers. Applications for camping and hiking are taken only one day in advance before your first day. No open fires are permitted. At primitive campsites along the coast, there are three-sided, open shelters that offer only a partial covering against the elements. Camping is also available at both Namakani Paio and Kulanaokuaiki drive-in campgrounds, but there are no shower facilities. There is no charge for tent camping at these two campsites and no reservations are required. For information on camping and hiking in the park, write Hawaii Volcanoes National Park, P.O. Box 52, Hawaii National Park, HI 96718, or stop by the Visitors Center, 808/985-6000, open daily 7:45 A.M.–5 P.M.

A-frame cabins are provided at Namakani Paio Campground, and arrangements are made through Volcano House, Hawaii Volcanoes National Park, HI 96718, 808/967-7321 or 800/325-3535. It's first-come, first-served. A cooking pavilion has fireplaces, but no wood or drinking water are provided. The 10 small cabins available at this campground can be reserved through Volcano House. Each sleeps up to four people and costs $40 single or double, $8 each for a third or fourth person. Linens, soap, towels, and a blanket are provided, but you would be wise to bring an extra sleeping bag as it can get cold. Each cabin contains one double bed, two

single bunk beds, and an electric light, but no electrical outlets. There is a picnic table and barbecue grill for each cabin, but bring your own charcoal and cooking utensils. Check in at Volcano House after 3 P.M. and check out by noon.

## Other Camping Areas

Camping is allowed by permit at three campsites on Kamehameha Schools Bishop Estate land in Waipi'o Valley. For specific information and to obtain a free permit, contact the Bishop Estate's Kona office, 808/332-5300, 78-6831 Ali'i Dr., Suite 232, Kailua-Kona, HI 96740, at least two weeks in advance of your intended trip. They will send you an application, which you must sign and return. There are no toilets in the valley, so you must bring your own "Port-A-Potty" with you and take it out when you leave!

Camping is also permitted farther north along the coast in Waimanu Valley. Apply for a free camping permit from the Division of Forestry and Wildlife, P.O. Box 4849, Hilo, HI 96720, 808/974-4221, no more than one month in advance. Nine campsites are available, each with a fireplace, and three composting toilets are shared among the campers. Camping is limited to six nights.

## Hiking the Big Island

Hiking on the Big Island is stupendous. There's something for everyone, from civilized walks to the breathtaking 'Akaka Falls to huff-puff treks to the summit of Mauna Loa. The largest number of trails, and the most outstanding according to many, lace across Hawaii Volcanoes National Park. After all, this is the world's most active volcano. You can hike across the crater floor, spurred on by the knowledge that it can shake to life at any moment. Or dip down off the mountain and amble the lonely trails in the Ka'u Desert or the remains of the King's Coastal Trail in Puna.

The most important thing to do before heading out in Volcanoes is to stop at park headquarters and inquire about trail conditions. Make absolutely sure to register, giving the rangers your hiking itinerary. In the event of an eruption, they will be able to locate you and send a helicopter if

ROBERT NILSEN

The trail to Kapaloa Falls cuts across the steep walls of Pololu Valley.

necessary. Follow this advice; your life may depend upon it! Everyone can enjoy vistas on Devastation Trail, Sulfur Bank, or at the Thurston Lava Tube without any danger whatsoever.

In the north sit Waipi'o, Waimanu, and Pololu Valleys. All offer secluded hiking and camping where you can play Robinson Crusoe on your own beach and gather island fruits from once-cultivated trees gone wild. The State Division of Forestry and Wildlife also maintains a number of trails in various locations around the island that cater to all levels of hikers. Check with them for details and maps.

## Bird-Watching and Hiking Tours

Hawaii has its fair share of birds. One type or other of the state's many species can be seen and heard wherever you are on the island, whether sunbathing along the shore, putting on a golf green, or hiking high on the mountainside. The most common will soon be obvious, but to see some of Hawaii's rare winged creatures you have to be adventurous, quiet, and willing to walk. Be sure to bring your binoculars. Anyone can appreciate birds where they are, but hard-core birders might want to go to spots where the chance

of getting a fleeting glimpse of that "rare one" will be greater.

If you're not familiar with good birdwatching spots on Hawai'i, contact Rob or Cindy Pacheco at **Hawaii Forest and Trail,** 74-5035B Queen Ka'ahumanu Hwy., Kailua-Kona, HI 96740, 808/331-8505 or 800/464-1993, fax 808/331-8704, www.hawaii-forest.com, info@hawaii-forest.com. This well-established naturalist company uses powerful 4WD vans to get you to where the less common birds are found. Its three exclusive birdwatching tours take you to the rainforests of the Pu'u O'o Ranch, the Hakalau National Wildlife Refuge on the eastern slope of Mauna Kea, and the forests on the leeward slope of Mauna Kea. Other tours include the Valley Waterfall Adventure to the spectacular Pololu Valley of North Kohala, a mule ride along the rim of the Pololu Valley, a tour to Hawaii Volcanoes National Park, and the Mauna Kea Summit and Stars adventure. All tours are kept to a Maximum of 10 people, are guided by knowledgeable naturalists, include food and beverage, provide all necessary equipment, and include pick-up and drop-off from specified locations on the Kona side. The trip to

Pololu Waterfall and the mule ride, both half-day affairs, are $95 adult or $85 for children ages 8–12. The rest are full-day tours that run $145 adult and $105 child. Children are welcome on all trips except for the Mauna Kea Summit adventure, which has an age limit of sixteen. Any of these tours will certainly be a highlight of your vacation.

A well-established and reputable hiking company that will help you stretch your legs in the great outdoors yet have minimal impact on the land is **Hawaiian Walkways,** 808/775-0372 or 800/457-7759, www.hawaiianwalkways.com, hiwalk@aloha.net. Run by Hugh Montgomery and his wife Kaulana, this company will teach you about the land you walk through and help you appreciate its diversity and sanctity. Hikes are easy to moderate and generally last three to five hours. Four basic hikes take you to the rim of Waipi'o Valley for a peek into the Valley of Kings, into Hawaii Volcanoes National Park to discover the secrets of Kilauea volcano, up on the mist-shrouded slopes of Mt. Hualalai, and to the many *kipuka* along the Saddle Road. Custom hikes can also be arranged. The Waipi'o rim hike is offered daily, while the others can be arrangement and customized to the guests needs. Both the Waipi'o Waterfall Adventure and the Kona Cloud Forest Botanical Walk run $85 per person. The Kilauea Volcano Discovery and Saddle Road Exploration are $175 for the first person, $100 for each additional adult, and $50 for children. A small day pack, walking stick, raingear, lunch, and drinks are provided, as is expert commentary by the knowledgeable owner/guides. A hike with Hawaiian Walkways is not only good physical exercise, it's an excellent introduction to the natural world of the Big Island. Two thumbs up.

For a more educational, "guided geologic adventure" on one of the earth's most changeable pieces of real estate, try **Hawaii Volcano GeoVentures,** P.O. Box 816, Volcano, HI 96785, tel./fax 808/985-9901, http://planet-hawaii.com/hea/volcano, geoventures@aloha.net. With a focus on the Kilauea volcano area and guided by a geologist/educator, these trips take you nose to nose with the wonders of the living earth.

**Island Outfitters** offers a more out-of-the-way adventure with helicopter flights from the Kohala resorts to remote Honokane Nui Valley on the Hamakua Coast and then a naturalist-lead hike within the valley. The 3.5-hour tour runs $380 per person and the 6.5-hour tour is $680. Contact Island Outfitters at P.O. Box 4441, Hilo, HI 96720, 808/966-7933 or 800/840-9974, fax 808/966-6931; www.islandoutfittershawaii.com, islehike@aloha.com.

With 8- and 10-day hiking and multi-sport tours to the Big Island and/or Maui and Kaua'i, **Hawaiian Adventure Tours** offers a different sort of opportunity for those who want more of a long-term catered excursion. These two tours run $1750–2000 per person with a minimum of three or four, include all arrangements and most costs within the islands, and are run roughly on a monthly basis. For information and reservations, contact the company at P.O. Box 1269, Kapa'au, HI 96755, 808/889-0227 or 800/659-3544; www.hawaiiadventuretours.com, advtours@aloha.net.

The **Kona Hiking Club,** 808/325-0012, is a fairly loosely-organized group of individuals that offers no-cost hikes on the first Saturday of the month. Meet at 8 A.M. at the parking lot behind the Sibu Restaurant in Kailua-Kona and bring your own lunch. Hikes run to various destinations, some to private land that cannot be accessed any other way.

## Maps

On the Big Island, **Basically Books,** in downtown Hilo at 160 Kamehameha Ave., 808/961-0144, has an unbeatable selection of maps, including topographical maps for hikers, NOAA nautical and aeronautical charts, and Defense Mapping Agency charts of the Pacific. On the Kona side, try **Big Island Marine, Inc.,** 73-4840 Kanalani St., #A-1, Kailua-Kona, HI 96740, 808/329-3719; or **Kona Marine,** 808/329-1012, in the Honokohau Small Boat Harbor, for nautical charts. The **Hawaii Forest and Trail** retail store, 808/331-8505, in Kailua across from the entrance to Honokohau Marina, carries USGS maps.

# HORSEBACK RIDING

**Waipi'o Na'alapa Stables,** 808/775-0419, offers one of the most unique rides on Hawai'i, with stables in the valley. The owner and her family have lived in Waipi'o Valley for over 25 years and know its history, geology, and legends intimately. There is pick-up service from Kukuihaele "up top" for the 9:30 A.M. and 1 P.M. rides; $75 per person for two and a half hours. If you have time, don't miss this wonderful adventure!

**Waipi'o On Horseback,** 808/775-7291, also offers horseback riding through fabulous Waipi'o Valley. These 2.5-hour, morning and afternoon sightseeing rides, $75 for adults and $55 for kids, are good for all riding levels.

For a ride up on Waipi'o's rim, looking down into Hawai'i's largest and most spectacular valley, try **Waipi'o Ridge Stables,** 808/775-1007, www.topofwaipio.com/horse.htm. This outfit offers a 2.5-hour rim ride to valley vistas, through former sugarcane land for $75. The 5.5-hour ride adds a side trip to a waterfall where you stop for lunch and a swim. It runs $145. Rides leave at 8:45 A.M. and 12:45 P.M. from Waipi'o Valley Artworks in Kukuihaele.

Enjoyable rides are also offered by the **Mauna Kea Resort Stables** (for nonguests also), 808/882-4288, located in Waimea—turn between K.M. Seeds and Ace Hardware and follow the signs. The Parker Ranch lends the resort a *paniolo* to guide you over the quarter-million acres of open range on the slopes of Mauna Kea, morning or afternoon. The stable is open Mon.–Sat. 9 A.M.–3 P.M. Rates are $40 per person for a one-hour ride and $70 for the two-hour ride; special trail rides available on request. Eight years old is the minimum age for riders; 210 pounds is the maximum weight.

**Paniolo Riding Adventures,** 808/889-5354, offers horseback riding on a working ranch in the Kohala Mountains north of Waimea. With your comfort in mind, they offer chaps, rain slickers, cowboy hats, and fleece saddle covers to keep you happy where the sun don't shine. Prices vary according to the ride, from novice to cowpoke, but a typical 2.5-hour open range ride will run about $89. After your guide matches

you with an appropriate steed, you head out onto the 11,000 acre range. Aside from the horseback rides, the ranch also offers mountain biking, hiking, and archery.

**Kohala Na'alapa Stables,** 808/889-0022, offers open range rides onto the historic Kahua Ranch, high in the Kohala Mountains. Rides are offered daily at 9 A.M. and 1:30 P.M.; two-and-a-half-hour rides are priced $75, hour-and-a-half rides $55.

Using horses from its own working ranch in Waimea, **Dahana Ranch,** 808/885-0057, gives riders free range rides on its own property. Rides leave five times a day; 1.5-hour rides are $55, 2.5-hour rides are $100 and include a barbecue lunch. Experienced or not, no problem; riders age three and up and up to 300 pounds are okay. For those with lots of experience, a two-hour advanced rider only ride also runs $100. Good upcountry range landscape.

**Kings' Trail Rides O'Kona,** 808/323-2388, has an office along Route 11, at mile marker 111, high above the Kona Coast between Kealakekua and Captain Cook. The wranglers will lead you (four to six people maximum) on a custom trail ride down to Captain Cook's Monument on the shores of Kealakekua Bay. This four-hour trip, departing at 9 A.M. (two hours of actual riding), includes snorkeling in the bay, along with a delicious picnic lunch. The price is $95. No riders over 230 pounds or under age seven, please.

**Rain Forest Trailrides,** 808/322-7126, takes you on horseback across the face of the Hualalai Mountains. Open daily 9 A.M.–5 P.M., it offers rides several rides each day from about $35 an hour.

**Kapapala Ranch,** 808/968-6585, offers excursions on its working ranch in Ka'u just outside the town of Pahala. Rides run $75 for the two-hour experience. The ranch will also arrange overnight camping trips on the property that can be done by horse, hiking, pack mules, or 4WD vehicle.

Not a horse ride per se, a Kohala Mule Trail Adventure is offered by **Hawaii Forest and Trail,** 808/331-8505. These three-hour rides leave daily at 8:30 A.M. and 12:30 P.M. from near the Pololu

Lookout and head uphill for a look into this old and historic valley. Rates are $95 adults and $85 for kids 8–12.

## Wagon Rides

**Waipio Valley Wagon Tours,** 808/775-9518, is a mule-drawn tour of the magnificent Waipi'o Valley. The one-and-a-half-hour tours leave four times daily at 9:30 and 11:30 A.M., and 1:30 and 3:30 P.M. The cost is $40 for adults or $20 for children under 12 and includes transportation down into the valley.

# BICYCLING

Pedaling around the Big Island can be both fascinating and frustrating. If you circle the island, it's nearly 300 miles around on its shortest route. Most pick an area and bike there. Generally, roads are well paved, but the shoulders are often torn up. With all the triathletes coming to Hawaii, and all the fabulous, little-trafficked roads, you'd think the island would be great for biking! It is, but you are better off bringing your own bike than renting. If you do rent, instead of a delicate road bike, you'll be better with a cruiser for pedaling around town or along the beach or a mountain bike that can handle the sometimes poor road conditions as well as open up the possibilities of off-road biking. Even experienced mountain bikers should be careful on the often extremely muddy and rutted trails.

For off-street trails, pick up a copy of the Big Island Mountain Bike Association's comprehensive off-road, public-access trail guide at either HVB office or at most bike shops on the island. This guide is also available online at www.interpac.net/~mtbike. In addition to an introduction to the organization and safety tips, each trail is briefly described and accompanied by a rudimentary map, directions to the start of the trail, and any additional information that's necessary to complete the ride. The type of ride, length in distance, ride time, elevation change, and level of expertise needed are also listed. Trails vary from flat shoreline jaunts to rugged mountain workouts, for beginners to the advanced rider. Check it out before you ride; this information comes

from experienced island riders. For additional information contact BIMBA at P.O. Box 6819 Hilo, HI 96720-8934, or call 808/961-4452.

## Bicycle Shops and Rentals

**Hawaiian Pedals,** 808/329-2294, in the Kona Inn Shopping Plaza, rents mountain bikes at $15 for five hours, $20 for 24 hours, with discounted rates for longer needs. Bike racks and baby seats are also for rent. Open daily.

The **Bike Works,** 74-5599 Lehua St., Suite F-3, next to Gold's Gym in the Old Kona Industrial Area, 808/326-2453, sells, services, and rents mountain and road bikes and bike gear. This Kailua-Kona full-service shop is perhaps the best on the island. Daily rates run $20–30 an hour; five-hour and multi-day rates can also be arranged. Closed on Sunday, so Saturday rentals are for two days.

**B&L Bike and Sports,** 808/329-3309, handles lots of rental road and mountain bikes, as well as sales and repair. Bikes generally run $30 a day to $150 a week. The official Ironman Triathlon bike shop, B&L is located across from the Hilo Hattie shop in Kailua-Kona.

**Dave's Bike and Triathlon Shop,** 808/329-4522, owned and pedaled by triathlete Dave Bending, is just a long stride or two from the beginning of the Ironman Triathlon in the Kona Square Shopping Center, 75-5669 Ali'i Dr. Dave's rents road, mountain, hybrid, and suspension bikes from $15 a day to $60 a week. All rentals include a helmet, water bottle, map, bicycle lock, and, and road advice. Dave is a font of information, one of the best bicycle men on the island.

When in Hilo, check out **Hilo Bike Hub,** 808/961-4452, at 318 E. Kawila, for sales and service of all kinds of high-quality bikes and accessories. This shop and its owner are heavy into the mountain biking scene, including the Big Island Mountain Biking Association, and have information about all the island races. Crossbreed mountain bikes rent for $25 a day, front suspension bikes are $20, and full suspension bikes run $45. Closed Sunday, so Saturday rentals are for two days.

Also in Hilo is **Mid Pacific Wheels,** 1133C

Manono St., 808/935-6211, where you can get a more standard bike for $15 a day; and **Aquatic Perceptions,** 808/933-1228, where you can rent a mountain bike or cross for about $30 a day or a recumbent tandem for a bit more.

In Waimea, try either **C&S Outfitters,** 808/885-5005, for wheels that will get you up to the high country. Rental rates are $25–35 for five hours, $30 for 24 hours, or $130 for a week; helmet, pump, and patch kit are included. Bike carriers and trailers can also be arranged.

## Bicycle Tours

**Mauna Kea Mountain Bikes** runs four different group tours, for beginners to advanced riders. The beginner tour runs for 21 miles down Hwy. 250 over the shoulder of the Kohala Mountains to Hawi. This is a morning tour for a minimum of four riders; transportation back from Hawi is included. An intermediate ride on backroads around Waimea lets you get a feel for upcountry range country and farmland. The technical rainforest ride is a challenge, not long but lots of ups and downs through muddy single-track trails. The real crowning ride, however, is the ride down Mauna Kea from the summit to the Saddle Road. On this one you have to be in very good shape and be focused. Rides vary from two to four hours and rates range from $50 to $120. For details, call 808/883-0130 or 888/682-8687.

**Aquatic Perceptions** of Hilo, 808/935-9997, www.multi-sport-hawaii.com, a multi-sport activity company, offers a bicycle "Jungle Coastal Tour" of Puna. Starting in Pahoa, the group mounts mountain bikes and heads down the leisurely country roads to the south coast. From there, it's along the sometimes-canopied, sometimes-steamy coastal road as far as the new black sand beach and lava fields of Kaimu. The return to Hilo is by van. Four other bike tours are also offered, ranging from a ride around Kilauea Caldera to one along the North Kohala Coast. These rides are designed for an average rider, run four to eight hours, and cost $70–135.

**Kona Coast Cycling Tours,** 808/327-1133 or 877/592-2453 in Kona offer a number of different tours to various parts of the island; www.cyclekona.com. The Kohala Mountain

Downhill, Coffee Country Ride, and Old Mamalahoa Highway Ride all run six–eight hours and cost $95 per person. The North Kohala Adventure is a bit longer and runs $145. Custom rides and support can also be arranged.

**Paniolo Adventures,** 808/889-5354, does off road mountain biking on their ranch outside Waimea for $85 per person for an average ride. While beginners and moderate rides are given, technical rides can be accommodated for advanced riders. All equipment, drinks, and snacks provided.

Three Mainland-based companies that also do multi-day bicycle touring are the following. **Backroads,** 801 Cedar St., Berkeley, CA 94710, 510/527-1555 or 800/462-2848, fax 510/527-1444, www.backroads.com, goactive@backroads.com, goes easy on the environment with its bicycle and multi-sport trips to the Big Island. The six-day circle-island bike tour concentrates on the Kona Coast, Volcano, and North Kohala. It's offered Oct.–April and costs $2,298. Backroads also does a six-day multi-sport trip that takes you into major scenic area of the island; it runs $2,398, available Oct.–April. All on-island arrangements are included.

**Bicycle Adventures,** P.O. Box 11219, Olympia, WA 98508, 800/443-6060, www.bicycleadventures.com, office@bicycleadventrues.com, also organizes road trips around the Big Island, mostly on less-used roads that take in many of the best sights that the island offers. The eight-day trip circles the island form Hilo, with departures monthly October to June. Rides average 45 miles a day with overnights planned mostly at inns and small hotels. These all-inclusive tours cover everything you'll need while on the island and the cost is $2,354 plus $144 bike rental.

**Getaway Adventures** also offers similar six- and eight-day round island rides from Nov.–April that includes swimming, kayaking, and snorkeling. These trips start in Hilo and head around the bottom of the island. Rates are $1,699 and $1,999, respectively, with a bike rental fee of $130. For additional information and reservations, contact the company at 1117 Lincoln Ave., Calistoga, CA 94515, 800/499-2453, www.getawayadventures.com.

# SKIING

Bored with sun and surf? Strap the "boards" to your feet and hit the slopes of Mauna Kea for one of the most unique ski adventures in the world. Numerous popular runs have been named by those who ski the mountain often. There are no lifts, and you'll need a 4WD to get to the top and someone willing to pick you up again down slope. You can rent 4WDs from a number of car-rental agencies, but if that seems like too much hassle, contact **Ski Guides Hawaii**, P.O. Box 1954, Kamuela, HI 96743, 808/885-4188, www.skihawaii.com. Here you can rent skis, and they'll provide the "lifts" to the top. Skis, boots, and poles (or snowboards and shoes) rent for $50 a day; the popular full-day ski/snowboard tour with equipment, ride and driver, ski guide, and lunch goes for $250 per person (minimum three). Other ski packages and cross-country ski tours are available and priced on request. For additional information, check out the Ski Association of Hawaii at www.hawaiisnowskiclub.com.

You can expect snow Dec.–May, but you can't count on it. It's most probable during February and March, and occasionally it stays as late as June or July. Generally speaking, your chances for skiable snow are better the few days after a moisture-laden front has moved across the island, blanketing the top with a white covering. More snow comes in La Niña years and less during El Niño. A few points of note: The top of Mauna Kea is over 13,500 feet, so nearly everyone suffers from some sort of altitude sickness. This is exacerbated by heavy physical exercise, so you should be in top physical condition if you plan to ski. There is nothing under the snow except unforgiving lava rock, so ski with caution. Also, there are no services above the 9,000-foot level on the mountain, so bring food and lots of water, and enough gas to get you there and back again.

# GOLF

The Big Island has some of the most beautiful golf links in Hawaii. The Kohala-area courses taken together are considered by some to be the crown jewel of the state's golf options. Robert Trent Jones Sr. and Jr. have both built exceptional courses here. Dad built the Mauna Kea Beach Hotel course, while the kid built his at the Waikoloa Beach Resort. The Mauna Kea course bedevils many as the ultimate challenge. If the Kohala courses are too rich for your blood, a few in the Kailua area are less expensive, or you play a round in Hilo for $20 and hit nine holes in Honoka'a for $15. How about golfing at Volcano Golf Course, where if you miss a short putt, you can blame it on an earthquake?

# TENNIS

Many tennis courts dot the Big Island, and plenty of them are free. County courts are under the control of the Department of Parks and Recreation, which maintains a combination of lighted and unlit courts around the island. Usually of cement, these county courts can be reserved by calling the number listed in the accompanying chart. No fees are charged for these public courts, but play is on a first-come, first-served basis. Court rules apply and only soft-sole shoes are allowed. Please care for equipment and stick to time limits, especially if there are other players waiting. Some private and hotel courts are open to the public for a fee, while others restrict play to guests only. Most private courts have a plexi-pave or similar surface. Although each facility differs, private clubs usually have pro shops, offer equipment rental, and arrange clinics and lessons. Court play is regulated according to accepted rules, and proper attire is required, including proper shoes.

# HUNTING

Huge unpopulated expanses of grassland, forest, and scrubby mountainside are very good for hunting. The Big Island's game includes feral pig, sheep, and goats, plus pheasant, quail, dove, and wild turkey. Public game lands are spread throughout the island; a license is required to take birds and game. For full information, contact the Department of Land and Natural Resources, Division of Forestry and Wildlife Office, 19 E. Kawili, Hilo, HI 96720, 808/974-4221.

## LAND TOURS

### Bus and Shuttle Tours

Most tour companies run vans, but some larger companies also use buses. Though cheaper, tours on full-sized coaches are generally less personalized. Wherever a bus can go, so can your rental car—but on a tour you can relax and enjoy the scenery without worrying about driving. Also, tour drivers are very experienced with the area and know many stories and legends with which they annotate and enrich your trip. Tours gener-

ally run $40–70 per person and either circle the island or have Kilauea Volcano as their main feature. Narrated and fairly tame bus tours are operated by **Roberts Hawaii,** 808/329-1688 (Kona), 808/966-5483 (Hilo), or 800/831-5541, www.robertshawaii.com; and by **Polynesian Adventure Tours,** 808/329-8008 or 800/622-3011, www.polyad.com. **Jack's Tours,** 808/961-6666 or 808/329-2555, also runs various group bus tours to major sites on the island. **Dieter's Creative Hawaiian Isle Tours,** 888/290-1000, www.dieters-hawaii.com, does guided minibus tours of

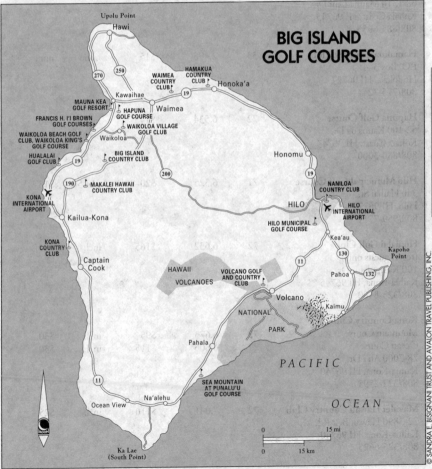

BIG ISLAND
GOLF COURSES

## BIG ISLAND GOLF COURSES

| Course | Par | Yards | Fees | Cart | Clubs |
|---|---|---|---|---|---|
| **Big Island Country Club**<br>71-1420 Mamalahoa Hwy.<br>Kailua-Kona, HI 96740<br>808/325-5044 | 72 | 6,510 | $85 | incl. | $30 |
| **Frances H. I'i Brown Golf Courses** | | | | | |
| South Course | 72 | 6,938 | $185 | incl. | $37.50 |
| North Course<br>68-1310 Mauna Lani Dr.<br>Kohala Coast, HI 96743<br>808/885-6655 | 72 | 6,913 | $185 | incl. | $37.50 |
| **Hamakua Country Club**<br>P.O. Box 344<br>Honoka'a, HI 96727<br>808/775-7244 | 33 | 2,496<br>(9 holes) | $15 | none | none |
| **Hapuna Golf Course**<br>62-100 Kauna'oa Dr.<br>Kohala Coast, HI 96743<br>808/880-3000 | 72 | 6,534 | $145 | incl. | $40 |
| **Hilo Municipal Golf Course**<br>340 Haihai St.<br>Hilo, HI 96720<br>808/959-7711 | 71 | 6,325 | $20–25 | $14.50 | $15 |
| **Hualalai Golf Club**<br>(resort guests only)<br>100 Ka'upulehu Dr.<br>Kailua-Kona, HI 96745<br>808/325-8480 | 72 | 6,632 | $165 | incl. | $60 |
| **Kona Country Club** | | | | | |
| Mountain Course | 72 | 6,673 | $95 | incl. | $30 |
| Ocean Course<br>78-7000 Ali'i Dr.<br>Kailua-Kona, HI 96740<br>808/322-2595 | 72 | 6,806 | $115 | incl. | $30 |
| **Makalei Hawaii Country Club**<br>72-3890 Hawaii Belt Rd.<br>Kailua-Kona, HI 96740<br>808/325-6625 | 72 | 7,041 | $110 | incl. | $25 |

| Course | Par | Yards | Fees | Cart | Clubs |
|---|---|---|---|---|---|
| **Mauna Kea Golf Course** <br> 62-100 Mauna Kea Beach Dr. <br> Kohala Coast, HI 96743 <br> 808/882-5400 | 72 | 6,737 | $195 | incl. | $40 |
| **Naniloa Country Club** <br> 120 Banyan Dr. <br> Hilo, HI 96720 <br> 808/935-3000 | 35 | 2,740 <br> (9 holes) | $25–30 <br> (18 holes) | $7.50 <br> (9 holes) | $10 |
| **Sea Mountain at** <br> **Punalu'u Golf Course** <br> P.O. Box 190 <br> Pahala, HI 96777 <br> 808/928-6222 | 72 | 6,416 | $32–35 | incl. | $25 |
| **Volcano Golf and Country Club** <br> Pi'i Mauna Dr. <br> Hawaii Volcanoes Nat'l Park, HI 96718 <br> 808/967-7331 | 72 | 6,547 | $62.50 | incl. | $16 |
| **Waikoloa Beach Golf Club** <br> 1020 Keana Pl. <br> Waikoloa, HI 96738 <br> 808/885-6060 | 70 | 6,566 | $150 | incl. | $35 |
| **Waikoloa King's Golf Course** <br> 600 Waikoloa Beach Dr. <br> Waikoloa, HI 96738 <br> 808/886-7888 | 72 | 6,594 | $150 | incl. | $35 |
| **Waikoloa Village Golf Club** <br> 68-1792 Melia St. <br> Waikoloa, HI 96738 <br> 808/883-9621 | 72 | 6,814 | $80 | $20 | $35 |
| **Waimea Country Club** <br> P.O. Box 2155 <br> Kamuela, HI 96743 <br> 808/885-8053 | 72 | 6,661 | $65 | incl. | $25 |

## BIG ISLAND TENNIS COURTS

### County Courts

Under jurisdiction of the County Department of Parks and Recreation, 25 Aupuni St., Hilo, HI 96720, 808/961-8740. No fee for use, and no reservations are necessary but might be appropriate on weekends.

| Town | Location | No. of Courts | Lighted |
|------|----------|---------------|---------|
| Hilo | Ainaole Park | 1 | No |
| Hilo | Hakalau Park | 2 | No |
| Hilo | Ho'olulu Park | 8 | Yes |
| Hilo | Lincoln Park | 4 | Yes |
| Hilo | Lokahi Park | 2 | Yes |
| Hilo | Malama Park | 2 | No |
| Hilo | Mohouli Park | 2 | No |
| Hilo | Pana'ewa Park | 2 | No |
| Honoka'a | Papa'aloa Park | 2 | Yes |
| Honoka'a | Honoka'a Park | 2 | No |
| Puna | Kurtistown Park | 1 | No |
| Puna | Shipman Park | 2 | No |
| Ka'u | Ka'u High School | 2 | No |
| Ka'u | Na'alehu Park | 2 | No |
| Captain Cook | Greenwell Park | 1 | Yes |
| Keauhou | Higashihara Park | 1 | No |
| Kona | Old Kona Airport | 4 | Yes |
| Kona | Kailua Playground | 1 | Yes |
| Waimea | Waimea Park | 2 | Yes |
| Kapa'au | Kamehameha Park | 2 | Yes |

Hilo and the volcano areas in German (other languages on request). Dieter's German-language tours area also offered on Maui and O'ahu.

### Adventure Van Tours

**Waipio Valley Shuttle,** 808/775-7121, offers a 90-minute tour down to Waipi'o Valley ($40 adult, $20 children under 11). The air-conditioned 4WD vans leaves from Waipi'o Valley Artworks in Kukuihaele Mon.–Sat. twice in the morning and twice in the afternoon. This is the easiest way into the valley and the guys know what they're doing as they've been at it since 1970.

For a trip to the rim for a look down into Waipi'o Valley, contact **Waipi'o Rim Backroad Adventures,** 808/775-1122 or 877/757-1414, www.topofwaipio.com/4x4.htm. This three-hour tour, for $85 adult or $40 for kids 12 and under, takes in former sugarcane land, backcountry roads, and unparalleled vistas overlooking the valley. A short hike is included that brings you to a small waterfall and pool. On this adventure, you ride in comfort and lunch is provided.

## Hotel and Private Courts Open to the Public

| Town | Location | Fee | No. of Courts | Lighted |
|------|----------|-----|---------------|---------|
| Pahala | Sea Mountain Resort 808/928-6200 | None | 4 | No |
| Keauhou | Keauhou Beach Resort 808/322-6112 | $5/hr | 6 | Yes |
| Kailua-Kona | Royal Kona Resort 808/334-1093 | $10/day | 6 | Yes |
| Kailua-Kona | King Kamehameha's Kona Beach Hotel 808/334-9889 | $5/hr | 4 | Yes |
| Waikoloa | Waikoloa Village 808/883-9704 | none | 2 | Yes |
| Waimea | Hawaii Prep Academy 808/881-4037 | $20 | 4 | Yes |
| Kohala | Outrigger Waikoloa Beach Resort 808/886-6666 | $10/hr | 6 | No |
| Kohala | Hilton Waikoloa Village Resort 808/881-2222 | $30/hr | 8 | No |
| Kohala | Mauna Lani Tennis Garden 808/885-1485 | $20/hr | 10 | No |
| Kohala | Mauna Kea Beach Resort 808/882-5420 | $25/day | 13 | No |
| Kohala | The Orchid at Mauna Lani Tennis Pavilion 808/887-7532 | $30/day | 10 | No |

**BIG ISLAND OF HAWAI'I**

**Mauna Kea Summit Adventures,** 808/322-2366 or 888/322-2366, www.maunakea.com, owned and operated by Pat Wright, has been taking visitors on high-adventure trips around the Big Island for the last 20 years. Your comfort and safety, as you roam the Big Island, are ensured as you ride in sturdy turbo diesel Ford vans with 4WD, air conditioning, sound system, first aid kit, and oxygen! The premier tour is an eight-hour journey to the top of Mauna Kea. Pat or one of his drivers not only fill your trip with stories, anecdotes, and fascinating facts during the ride, they top off the safari by setting up an eight-inch telescope not far from the Onizuka Center so you can get a personal view of the heavens through the rarefied atmosphere atop the great mountain. Mauna Kea Summit Adventures picks you up at your hotel in Kailua-Kona at about 4 P.M. If you're staying on the Hilo side, you'll be met at a predetermined spot along the Saddle Road. The price is $150, with hot savory drinks, soup, sandwiches, and good warm parkas included. Special trips for photography, hiking, astronomy, and shore fishing can also be tailored to your needs.

**Hawaii Forest and Trail,** 808/331-8505 or 800/464-1993, www.hawaii-forest.com, offers much the same summit and stargazing tour from the Kona side at $145 per person.

**Arnott's Lodge and Hiking Adventures,** 98 Apapane Rd., Hilo, HI 96720, 808/967-7097, www.arnottslodge.com/activity.html, offers a variety of hiking adventures to its guests and nonguests alike who are looking for more than an ordinary group tour. While the tours offered do change periodically, several have remained popular. They include a hike to the lava flow at Hawaii Volcanoes National Park, a waterfall and valleys hike, and the sunset and stargazing trek to the top of Mauna Kea. These are full eight-hour trips—some longer—and the cost is $48 for those staying at Arnott's Lodge in Hilo and $75 for others. Each trip takes only as many as the van will carry and goes only when the weather is cooperative. Some restrictions on age and physical condition apply, so be sure to check with the staff at Arnott's Lodge, or check out the website for the current list of adventures.

## ATV Tours

**ATV Outfitters Hawaii,** 808/889-6000, www.outfittershawaii.com, runs breezy four-wheel motorcycle tour across former Kohala sugar plantation land to rainforest and coastal sights at the northern tip of the island. The 1.5-hour ride is $90 and the five-hour ride costs $250. You'll ride over back roads and fields, through lush gullies to waterfalls, come to the edge of ocean cliffs, or dip down to a pebble beach. These fully equipped machines let you get to places that you wouldn't be able to access otherwise. Safe and reliable, the four-wheelers are easy to operate even for those who have had no experience on a motorcycle. Helmets, gloves, and goggles are supplied and instruction is given. To ride, you must be at least 16 years old and weigh 90–300 pounds. Wear long pants and closed-toe shoes.

# AIR TOURS
## Helicopter Tours

Air tours are a great way to see the Big Island, but they are expensive, especially when the volcano is putting on a mighty display. Expect to spend a minimum of $100 for a front-row seat to watch the amazing light show from the air. Some discounts may be offered seasonally or for booking over the Internet. Kilauea volcano erupting is like winning the lottery for these small companies, and many charge whatever the market will bear. To get the best view of the volcanic activity, schedule your flight for the morning, or no later than 2 P.M. Later, clouds and fog can set in to obstruct your view. While the volcano is the premier focus of these tour companies, some also offer tours up the Hamakua Coast for a view of the sea cliffs, deep valleys, waterfalls, and the North Kohala Mountains, and some do a modified round-island tour that takes in the volcano, east and west coastlines, and Hamakua valleys and waterfalls. Helicopter flights from the Hilo Commuter Terminal are very competitively priced, with savings on volcano tours over the companies operating out of the Kona Commuter Terminal. However, more flights leave out of Kona as there are more tourists on that side. Additionally, flights by Blue Hawaiian Helicopters also leave out of the Waikoloa Heliport, located across the highway from the entrance to Waikoloa Resort at the intersection of Queen Ka'ahumanu Highway and Waikoloa Road.

Everyone has an opinion as to which company offers the best ride, the best narration, or the best service. All the helicopter companies on Hawai'i are safe and reputable—nearly all pilots have been trained by the military—and most fly five- or six-seat A-Stars, with a few four-passenger Bell Jet Rangers and Hughes 500s still in use. Most have two-way headphones so you can communicate with the pilot. Each gives a pre-flight briefing to go over safety regulations and other details. Remember that the seating arrangement in a helicopter is critical to safety. The pre-flight crew is expertly trained to arrange the chopper so that it is balanced, and with different people of various sizes flying every day, their job is very much like a chess game. This means that the seating goes strictly according to weight. If you are not assigned the seat of your choice, for safety's sake, please do not complain. Think instead that you are part of a team whose goal is not only enjoyment but also to come back safe and sound. It's very difficult not to have a fascinating flight—no matter where you sit.

Nearly everyone wants to take photographs of their helicopter tour. Who wouldn't? Here are a few things to consider. Most of the newer helicopters are air-conditioned, which means that the windows don't open, so you might experience glare or some distortion. If you need absolutely clear shots, choose a chopper where the windows open or go with one that flies with its doors off. Also, if you are the only one taking pictures on a tour and you're seated in the middle of the rear seat, you won't be happy. Again, ask for a ride in a smaller rig where everyone gets a window seat.

Flying out of the Hilo Airport in a four-passenger Bell Jet-Ranger III helicopter is **Tropical Helicopters,** 808/961-6910, www.tropicalhelicopters.com. Tropical is a small company that gives personal attention to passengers. Its popular 40-minute volcano flight runs $99. An expanded 50-minute flight runs the same basic route but gives you additional overflight of waterfalls in the Hilo area for $138. The ultimate Feel the Heat flight, $158, takes you for an up-close look at the volcano activity—with the doors off!

**Safari Helicopters,** 808/969-1259 or 800/326-3356, www.safariair.com, info@safariair.com, also flies only from Hilo. Flights run 45 and 60 minutes, $149–199, and concentrate on the volcano and nearby waterfalls. Safari uses new air-conditioned A-Star craft. This is a reputable company with a good reputation, and pilots give you a memorable flight. Safari also flies on Kaua'i.

With its spotless safety record and large operation, **Blue Hawaiian Helicopters,** 808/961-5600 (Hilo), 808/886-1768 (Waikoloa), or 800/745-2583, www.bluehawaiian.com, operates several A-Star helicopters from the Waikoloa Heliport on the Kona side and additional A-Stars from the Hilo Airport. Volcano flights from Hilo go for $165 and last about 50 minutes. From Waikoloa, a two-hour circle island flight costs $340 and a shorter Kohala Mountain and valley tour goes for $175. Blue Hawaiian also offers flights on Maui.

Flying out of Kona, **Sunshine Helicopters,** 808/882-1233 or 800/622-3144, www.sunshinehelicopters.com, runs a 45-minute Kohala Mountain and Hamakua Valley tour at $160, a 45-minute volcano flight for $175, and a two-hour circle-island flight for $390. Sunshine offers a package with Atlantis Submarine and Body Glove snorkel trips for reduced rates on activities. Sunshine also operates helicopter flights on Maui.

Leaving from the Hilo airport, **Paradise Helicopters,** 808/969-7392, is close to the volcano and offers tours there for $145.

## Fixed-Wing Air Tours

For fixed-wing air tours, try one of the following. **Big Island Air,** 808/329-4868 or 800/303-8868, offers small-plane flights from Kona Airport, two-person minimum. A volcano tour in an eight-passenger Cessna costs $135 per person, and a round-island/volcano flight is $185. Every seat is a window seat, and the wings in the new plane are set above the windows. The plane can be chartered for $550 an hour from Kona or $660 an hour from Hilo.

For smaller planes, also with wings above the windows, try **Island Hopper,** 808/969-2000, which offers flights from both the Hilo and Kona Airports. Volcano and waterfall tours, $69–79, go from Hilo, but the longer flights from Kona are $149 for a volcano tour and $189 for a circle-island tour.

With similar flights and prices is **Mokulele Flight Service,** 808/326-7070 or 866/260-7070, www.mokulele.com. Circle-island tours, $203, go from Kona, while the volcano tours, $75, run from Hilo.

## Ballooning

Dawn hot air balloon rides over the Parker Ranch in Waimea are offered by **Paradise Balloons,** 808/877-6455 or 866/887-6455, www.paradiseballoons.com. Take off and landing (hopefully) are from near Pu'opelu just outside of town. The tour begins around 6:30 A.M. and offers you an unparalleled view of the ranch and western side of the Big Island. Flights cost $240 adults or $190 for children 5–12; reservations are necessary. Dress warmly as it can be quite cold that early and that high.

## Accommodations and Food

### ACCOMMODATIONS

Finding suitable accommodations on the Big Island is never a problem. The 9,500-plus rooms available at the island's 170 properties have the lowest annual occupancy rate of any in the islands at only 60 percent. Except for the height of the high seasons and during the Merrie Monarch Festival in Hilo, you can count on finding a room at a bargain. The highest concentration of rooms is strung along Ali'i Drive in Kailua-Kona—more than 5,000 in condos, apartment hotels, and standard hotels. Hilo has almost 2,000 rooms; many of its hotels have "gone condo," and you can get some great deals. The rest are scattered around the island in small villages from Na'alehu in the south to Hawi in the north, where you can almost count on being the only off-island guest. You can comfortably stay in the cowboy town of Waimea or perch above Kilauea Crater at one of the oldest hotel sites in the islands. There are bed and breakfasts, a handful of hostels, and camping is superb, with a campsite almost guaranteed at any time.

The Big Island has a tremendous range of accommodations. A concentration of the state's greatest luxury resorts are within minutes of each other on the Kohala Coast. All are superb, with hideaway "grass shacks," exquisite art collections as an integral part of the grounds, picture-perfect gardens, world-ranked golf courses, and perfect crescent beaches. Kona has fine reasonably priced hotels like the King Kamehameha's Kona Beach Hotel and Royal Kona Resort in downtown Kailua, and the Keauhou Beach Resort just south toward Keauhou. Interspersed among the big hotels are smaller hotels and condominiums with homey atmospheres and great rates. Hilo offers the best accommodations bargains. The first-class Hilo Hawaiian Hotel is priced like a mid-range hotel on the other islands, and then there are gems like the Dolphin Bay Hotel that give you so much for your money it's embarrassing. And

for a real treat, head to Hawaii Volcanoes National Park and stay at one of the bed-and-breakfasts tucked away there, or at Volcano House where raw nature has thrilled kings, queens, and luminaries like humorist Mark Twain for more than a century. If you want to get away from everybody else, it's no problem, and you don't have to be rich to do it. Pass-through towns like Captain Cook and Waimea have accommodations at very reasonable prices. Or try a self-growth or yoga retreat in Puna at Kalani Oceanside Resort or Yoga Oasis, or a meditation retreat at the Wood Valley Buddhist Temple above Pahala.

Operating strictly for establishments on the Big Island, the **Hawaii Island Bed and Breakfast Association** monitors its members for quality standards. For information about HIBBA, contact P.O. Box 1890, Honoka'a, HI 96727; www.stayhawaii.com, hibba@stayhawaii.com. The association's brochure lists member accommodations with addresses, telephone and fax numbers, email and website addresses, rates, and descriptions.

### FOOD

#### Lu'au

**Tihati's Drums of Polynesia Lu'au** at the Royal Kona Resort, 808/331-1526, occurs Monday, Friday, and Saturday. It's lots of fun but not too traditional.

**Island Breeze Lu'au** at the beach in front of King Kamehameha's Kona Beach Hotel, 808/326-4969, is held Sunday, Tuesday, Wednesday, Thursday, and Friday evening on the grounds of King Kamehameha's last residence.

The **Friday Night Lu'au** at Kona Village Resort, 808/325-5555, is the longest-running lu'au on the island and always offers a sumptuous meal. Highly recommended.

**Royal Lu'au** at the Waikoloa Beach Marriott, 808/886-6789, is offered on Sunday and Wednesday. 'Anaeho'omalu Bay makes a nice backdrop for this lu'au and the performance is rousing. Gets good mention from locals.

**Old Hawaii Aha'aina Lu'au** at the Mauna Kea Beach Hotel, 808/822-5810, is held on Tuesday. Perhaps the most traditional of the bunch, performance is by *Kumu Hula* Nani Lim and company. It gets high marks for the food and a fine seaside setting.

Every Friday, **Legends of the Pacific** is performed at Hilton Waikoloa Village, 808/885-1234.

# Getting There

Almost all travelers to the Big Island arrive by air. A few lucky ones come by private yacht, or by the cruise ships that dock at Hilo and Kona. For the rest, the island's two major airports are at Hilo and Kona. While a few airlines offer flights directly to the Big Island, most routings will still take you through Honolulu.

## Flights to the Big Island

Most island flights in the past landed at Hilo International Airport. With the Kona Coast gaining popularity, domestic flights from the Mainland have shifted to that side of the island, and the only direct international connection to the Big Island lands there as well. United Airlines operates nonstop flights to the Big Island from the Mainland—daily flights from San Francisco and Los Angeles to Kona International Airport. In past peak seasons, United has run a flight to Hilo International Airport, but it's an on-and-off affair depending on the number of travelers. Aloha Airlines flies from Oakland, California to Kona and Japan Airlines offers daily flights from Tokyo.

All other major domestic and foreign carriers fly you to Honolulu and have arrangements with either Hawaiian Airlines or Aloha Airlines for getting you to the Big Island. This sometimes involves a plane change, but your baggage can be booked straight through. If you fly from the Mainland with Hawaiian or Aloha, you have the added convenience of dealing with just one airline. Several charter airlines also fly to the Big Island nonstop from the Mainland.

## Big Island Airports

The largest airport on the Big Island is **Hilo International Airport,** which services Hilo and the eastern half of the island. Formerly known as Gen. Lyman Field, it was named after Gen.

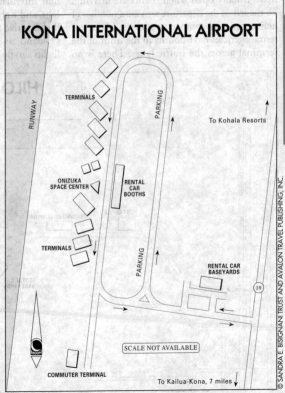

## KONA INTERNATIONAL AIRPORT

RUNWAY

TERMINALS

PARKING

To Kohala Resorts

ONIZUKA SPACE CENTER

RENTAL CAR BOOTHS

TERMINALS

PARKING

RENTAL CAR BASEYARDS

19

SCALE NOT AVAILABLE

COMMUTER TERMINAL

To Kailua-Kona, 7 miles

BIG ISLAND OF HAWAI'I

Albert Kuali'i Brickwood Lyman, the first ethnic Hawaiian to become a brigadier general (1942) in the U.S. Army. This airport is remarkably close to downtown Hilo. It's a modern facility with full amenities, and its runways can handle jumbo jets. Interisland flights from here connect directly to Kona, Kahului, and Honolulu, from where you can get to any other airport in the state. The two-story terminal has an information center, a restaurant, a number of vendors, restrooms, and telephones. There is no bank, money exchange, or post office. As you look at the terminal building, the departure lounge is in the center beyond the check-in counters and agricultural inspection station. Arrivals are on the right and the arrival area has baggage claim, restrooms, public telephones, and a small tourist information booth that's usually open when flights are arriving. To the left of the departure area are a number of helicopter tour company counters. Major car rental agencies have booths to the front of the terminal across the traffic lanes. There is no

public transportation to or from the airport; a taxi for the three-mile ride to town costs about $8–12. Public parking is in a large lot behind the car rental booths. Parking fees run $1 for the first half hour, $1 for each additional hour, and a maximum of $7 per day. Along the airport road, a short way in toward town, is the old commuter terminal building where one more helicopter companies has its office and where you check in for their tours.

**Kona International Airport** is nine miles north of Kailua-Kona and handles the air traffic for Kona, Kohala, and the west side of the island. The Kona Airport is surrounded by fields of black lava. This airport handles a growing amount of air traffic from other island cities and all the Mainland and international flights, eclipsing Hilo as the island's major air transportation hub. Interisland flights arrive from Hilo, Honolulu, and Kahului; Mainland and international flights arrive from San Francisco, Los Angeles, Oakland, and Tokyo. During winter, charter flights also fly in from Vancouver. The terminal is

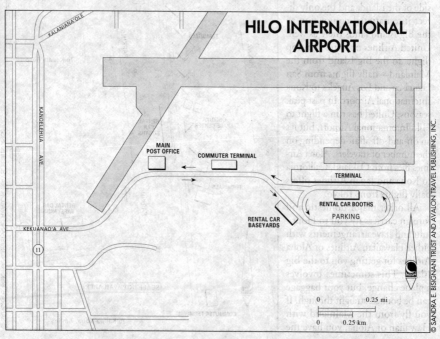

a series of open-sided, non-connected, Polynesian-style buildings. There are no jetways; everyone boards and deplanes by stairway onto the tarmac. Departures leave near the center of this cluster, where you also find the agricultural inspection station; arrivals come to either end. Most Hawaiian, American, and Japan airlines departures are from the left-hand side; Aloha and United airlines use mostly the right-hand side. Here too are lockers, telephones, restrooms, visitor information booths near both baggage claim areas, various food vendors, lei stands, and other shops. Car-rental agencies have booths across the circle road. Access to the public parking lot is 5:30 A.M.–9 P.M.; it costs $1 for the first half hour, $1 each hour after that, and $7 maximum for 24 hours. There is no public transportation to the airport. A private cab to your hotel in Kailua-Kona will be $12 or more. The commuter terminal just down the road is for helicopter and fixed-wing tourist flight check-in.

**Waimea-Kohala Airport** is just outside Waimea (Kamuela). There are few amenities and no public transportation to town. Only a few weekly commuter flights are scheduled between Waimea and Honolulu. **Upolu Airport** is a lonely strip on the extreme northern tip of the island, with no facilities whatsoever and no scheduled flights. Both airports are serviced on request by small charter airlines.

## Interisland Carriers

**Hawaiian Airlines** can be contacted at 800/367-5320 Mainland and Canada, 800/882-8811 statewide, or on the Big Island at 808/935-0858 in Hilo or 808/326-1214 in Kona, www.hawaiianair.com. The majority of flights to the Big Island with Hawaiian Airlines run between Honolulu

and Kona; 14 flights (about 40 minutes) are spread throughout the day from approximately 5:15 A.M. to 8 P.M. One of these flights stops at Kahului, Maui. A similar schedule applies to Hilo. All other Hawaiian Airlines flights originating in Hilo or Kona go through Kahului or Honolulu. Hawaiian Airlines partners with American Airlines, Continental Airlines, and Northwest Airlines.

**Aloha Airlines**, 800/367-5250 Mainland and Canada, 808/935-5771 on the Big Island, www.alohaair.com, also services the Big Island with flights from the neighboring islands. Its 15 daily Honolulu-Kona runs start at 5:10 A.M., with the last at 6:50 P.M.; one dozen Honolulu-to-Hilo flights depart throughout the day, 5:10 A.M.–6:30 P.M. Connecting through Honolulu, there are 10 daily flights to Lihu'e, Kaua'i from Kona and Hilo. Aloha also flies once a day from both Kona and Hilo to Kahului, Maui, and once a day between Hilo to Kona. Aloha Airlines partners with United Airlines.

**Pacific Wings** is a local and reputable commercial airline that seems to fill the gaps that the bigger airlines often miss. On the Big Island, it services only the Waimea Airport on regularly scheduled flights. Daily flights depart Honolulu and arrive in Waimea at 5:55 P.M. These flights deplane and depart at 6:10 P.M. for Kahului, Maui, where they arrive at 6:50 P.M. Every day except Sunday, a plane leaves Waimea at 8 A.M. direct for Honolulu, arrival at 9:10 A.M. On Sunday, the flight leaves at 3:10 P.M. and arrives in Honolulu at 4:20 P.M. Pacific Wings also does flightseeing tours from its base on Maui and is available for charters. For other information and flight schedules, contact the airline at Kahului Airport Commuter Terminal, Kahului, HI 96732, 808/873-0877; www.pacificwings.com.

# Getting Around

The first thing to remember when traveling on the Big Island is that it *is* big, more than four times larger than Rhode Island. A complete range of vehicles is available for getting around, everything from rental cars to mopeds. Hawai'i, like O'ahu and Kaua'i, has some public transportation. Hitchhiking, while illegal, is still used by some to get around. Choose the conveyance that fits your style, and you should have no trouble touring the Big Island.

## Highway Overview

Getting around the Big Island is fairly easy. There is one main highway called the Hawai'i Belt Road (also called Mamalahoa Highway) that circles the island, one cross-island highway called the Saddle Road, and a limited number of other highways and secondary roadways. The Hawai'i Belt Road has different numbers in various sections around the island, and this may lead to some confusion. Connecting Kailua-Kona and Hilo around the south end, the number is Highway 11. Major roads that lead off of it are Napo'opo'o Road, which runs down to Kealakekua Bay; Ke Ala O Keawe Road to Pu'uhonua O Honaunau National Historical Park; South Point Road, which drops down to the southernmost tip of the island; Chain of Craters Road, which leads through Hawaii Volcanoes National Park to the lava-covered littoral Puna Coast; and Kea'au-Pahoa Road (Highway 130) from Kea'au to the hinterland of Puna. In Puna, Kapoho-Pahoa Road (Highway 132) and Kapoho-Kalapana Beach Road (Highway 137) make a circle with Highway 130 from Pahoa, down along the shore, and back again.

Going north from Kailua-Kona, the Hawai'i Belt Road (Highway 190), which starts off for the first few miles as Palani Road, cuts across the upper slopes of the volcanoes to Waimea. Slicing through coffee country, as part of the Belt Road, is Highway 180. From Honalo, Route 11 heads down toward Kailua, first as Kuakini Highway, which itself makes a tangent into town, and then continues as Queen Ka'ahumanu Highway.

Heading north from Kailua, Queen Ka'ahumanu Highway becomes Route 19. In Kawaihae, it turns uphill to Waimea, becoming Kawaihae Road. In Waimea, Highways 19 and 190 merge, and Highway 19 becomes the designation as the Hawai'i Belt Road continues along and down the Hamakua Coast back to Hilo. Connecting Highway 19 and Highway 190 through the town of Waikoloa is Waikoloa Road. In Honoka'a, Highway 240 leaves the Belt Road and runs north to the edge of Waipi'o Valley. North Kohala is cut by two roads. Akoni Pule Highway (Highway 270) runs along the coast up and around the tip as far as the Pololu Valley. Connecting this road and the town of Waimea is the Kohala Mountain Road (Highway 250). Off-limits to most rental cars, the Saddle Road (Highway 200) rises to about 6,500 feet between the tall peaks of Mauna Loa and Mauna Kea, making a shortcut between Hilo and Waimea or the Kohala Coast. From along the Saddle Road, rugged 4WD roads lead up to the observatories atop Mauna Kea and nearly to the top of Mauna Loa.

# CAR RENTALS

The best way to tour the island is in a rented car, but keep these tips in mind. Most car companies charge you a fee if you rent the car in Hilo and drop it off in Kona, and vice versa. The agencies are prejudiced against the Saddle Road and the spur road leading to South Point, both of which offer some of *the* most spectacular scenery on the island. Their prejudice is unfounded because both roads are paved, generally well maintained, and no problem if you take your time. They'll claim the insurance will not cover you if you have a mishap on these roads. A good automobile policy at home will cover you in a rental car, but definitely check this before you take off. The road to the top of Mauna Kea is a 4WD only road. Heed the signs, not so much for going up, but for needed braking power coming down. Don't even hint of these intentions to the car-rental agencies, or they won't rent you a car. Avis and Harper allow you to drive the Saddle Road, and Harper rents 4WDs for the Mauna Kea road.

No way whatsoever should you attempt to drive down to Waipi'o Valley in a regular car! The grade is unbelievably steep, and only a 4WD can make it. Put simply, you have a good chance of being killed if you try it in a car.

Gas stations are farther apart than on the other islands, and sometimes they close very early. As a rule, fill up whenever the gauge reads half full.

Both Hilo International Airport and Kona International Airport have a gauntlet of car rental booths and courtesy phones outside the terminals.

## Auto Rental Companies

The following are major firms represented at both the Hilo and Kona airports. Kona numbers begin with "3" while Hilo numbers state with a "9."

**Dollar,** 808/961-6059 or 808/329-2744.
**Alamo,** 808/961-3343 or 808/329-8896.
**National,** 808/935-0891 or 808/329-1674.
**Avis,** 808/935-1290 or 808/327-3000.
**Budget,** 800/527-0700 nationwide.
**Hertz,** 808/935-2896 or 808/329-3566.
**Thrifty,** 808/961-6698 or 808/329-1339.

Some years ago, local companies abounded, but today only one has survived with any significance. At **Harper,** in Hilo at 808/969-1478, Kona at 808/329-6688, or 800/852-9993 off-island, you can rent a car, truck, seven- to 15-passenger van, RV, or 4WD for driving up to Mauna Kea. Good competitive rates.

## Motorcycles and Mopeds

**DJ's Rentals,** 808/329-1700 or 800/993-4647, http://harleys.com, open daily 7:30 A.M.–6 P.M., is located directly across from King Kamehameha's Hotel in Kailua-Kona in an outdoor booth. DJ's rents mopeds, scooters, and motorcycles. Costs are: one-person mopeds $15 half day, $25 daily, and $125 a week; two-person scooters (capable of attaining highway speeds), $25 half day, $45 daily, and $225 a week. Big Twin Harleys run $145 daily or $90 half day, and others rent for about 20 percent less. A half day is 7:30 A.M.–noon or noon–6 P.M.

## Motor Homes

If you don't want to stop at a hotel every night, why not take your hotel with you? **Island RV,** 73-4820 Kuakini Hwy., Kailua-Kona, HI 96740, 808/334-0464 or 800/406-4555, lets you do just that when you rent a motor home RV so can go at your own pace and stop where you want. The RVs sleep up to six and come with all the necessary cooking and sleeping gear. The rental rate runs about $250 a day or $1,500 a week, but the weekly rate includes airport pickup, itinerary planning, park registration fees, and the last night in a Kona hotel.

**Harper** car rental company also rents RVs, 808/969-1478 in Hilo, 808/329-6688 in Kona, or 800/852-9993 Neighbor Islands, Mainland, or Canada.

# ALTERNATIVE TRANSPORTATION

## Hele-On Bus

The county of Hawai'i maintains the Mass Transit Agency, known throughout the island as the Hele-On Bus. For information, schedules, and fares contact the Mass Transit Agency at 25 Aupuni St., Hilo, HI 96720, 808/961-8744. open Mon.–Fri. 7:45 A.M.–4:30 P.M. The main bus terminal is in downtown Hilo at Mo'oheau Park, just at the corner of Kamehameha Avenue and Mamo Street. Recently, it's been completely rebuilt and modernized. Like bus terminals everywhere, it has a local franchise of derelicts and down-and-outers, but they leave you alone. The Hele-On Bus system now has a mostly modern fleet of large buses that are clean and comfortable. The Hele-On operates Mon.–Fri. approximately 6 A.M.–6 P.M., depending on the run, except for the route to Kona and Kohala, which also operate Saturdays, and the route from North Kohala to the Kohala resorts, which operates daily. There are a number of intra-Hilo routes with additional intercity routes to points around the periphery of the island, but these all operate on a very limited schedule, sometimes only once a day. If you're in a hurry then definitely forget about taking it, but if you want to meet the people of Hawai'i, there's no better way. The base fare is 75 cents, which increases whenever you go into another zone. Transfers are given free if you must change buses, but these must be used within an hour. A number of discount fares (monthly, round-trip, multiple-ticket, disabled, senior citizen, student) are available. Have exact change for the fare when you board. You can also be charged an extra $1 for a large backpack or suitcase. Don't worry about that—the Hele-On is one of the best bargains in the country. Large items like surf boards, boogie boards, and bicycles are not allowed.

There are four basic intercity routes connecting to Hilo. One—the longest bus route—goes from Kealia, south of Captain Cook, all the way to Hilo on the east coast via Kailua-Kona, Waikoloa, Waimea, Honoka'a, and Laupahoehoe. Operating Mon.–Sat., this journey covers 110 miles in just over four hours and costs $6 for the entire distance, the most expensive fare in the system. Additional intra-Kona buses run just between Kealia and Kailua on weekdays. You can take the southern route from the Ocean View post office through Ka'u, Na'alehu, and Hawaii Volcanoes National Park to Hilo. This trip takes just 2.5 hours and costs $5.25. A third route to Hilo runs from Pahoa through Kea'au, while the fourth starts in Waimea then proceeds down the coast through Honoka'a and Honomu to Hilo. In the Kohala district, a daily bus runs every weekday morning from Kapa'au through Hawi to the various Kohala resorts and returns in the late afternoon.

## Shuttle Services

Kona and Kohala are serviced by a three-part shuttle system that together is called the **Kona Coast Express,** 808/329-1688 or 800/831-5541. The Kona Town Trolley runs from Keauhou pier at its southern end to King Kamehameha's Kona Beach Hotel, stopping at a number of condos along this stretch as well as at Keauhou Shopping Center, Hilo Hattie, and the Kona Inn Shopping Village. The Kohala Coast-Waikoloa Resort Express Bus makes stops at all the Kohala resorts and at the King's Shopping Center. The Kona Coast Express Bus connects passengers between these southern and northern sections of the system. Transfer stations are located at the

King's Shopping Center in Waikoloa and the King Kamehameha's Kona Beach Hotel in Kailua. An all-day pass on either the Kona Town Trolley or the Kohala Coast-Waikoloa Resort Express Bus is $5 per person. A $15 all-day pass lets you transfer from one section to the other and use the entire system. Tickets are available from the driver. The Kona Town Trolley runs 8:45 A.M.–10:15 P.M., the Kohala Coast-Waikoloa Resort Express Bus runs 6:15 A.M.–11 P.M., and the connecting Kona Coast Express Bus runs 8 A.M.–10:15 P.M.; each runs at approximately 90-minute intervals.

Kailua-Kona also has the **Ali'i Shuttle,** 808/775-7121, which cruises Ali'i Drive but makes different stops than the Kona Town Trolley. This white bus runs about every 90 minutes, 8:40 A.M.–7:40 P.M. At the north end it stops at the Lanihau Center, King Kamehameha's Hotel, Kona Inn Shopping Village, Hulihe'e Palace, and Royal Kona Resort. On the way south, pickups are at Magic Sands Beach and Kahalu'u Beach Park. On the south end it stops at Keauhou Shopping Center, and Kona Country Club. Rides are $2 each way, $5 for a day pass, $20 for a weekly pass, or $40 for a monthly pass.

## Taxis

Both the Hilo and Kona airports always have taxis waiting for fares. Fares are regulated. From Hilo's airport to downtown costs about $12, to the Banyan Drive hotels about $8. From the Kona Airport to hotels and condos along Ali'i Drive in Kailua fares run $19–32, north to Waikoloa Beach Resort they run about $40, and are approximately $60 as far north as the Mauna Kea Resort. Obviously, a taxi is no way to get around if you're trying to save money. Most taxi companies, both in Kona and Hilo, also run sightseeing services for fixed prices. In **Kona** try: Kona Airport Taxi, 808/329-7779; Paradise Taxi, 808/329-1234; Laura's Taxi, 808/326-5466; or C&C Taxi, 808/329-6388. In **Hilo** try: Hilo Harry's Taxi, 808/935-7091; A-1 Bob's Taxi, 808/959-4800; and Percy's Taxi, 808/969-7060.

An alternative in the Kona area is **Speedy Shuttle,** 808/329-5433. Operating 7 A.M.–10 P.M. daily, Speedy Shuttle runs multi-seat vans, so its prices are cheaper per person the more people you have riding. It also would be appropriate if you have lots of luggage. Sample rates from the Kona Airport are $17 to downtown Kailua-Kona, $24 to the south end of Kailua and the Keauhou area, and $30 for a ride up to Waikoloa Beach Resort. Speedy Shuttle has a courtesy phone at the airport for your convenience. Reservations a day ahead are not necessary but may be helpful to get a ride at the time you want.

## Hitchhiking

The old thumb works on the Big Island about as well as anywhere else. Although hitchhiking is technically illegal, the police seem to have much more important things to pay attention to than going after those just trying to get down the road. Stay off the roadway, be low-key, but make your intentions known. Some people hitchhike rather than take the Hele-On Bus not so much to save money but to save time! It's a good idea to check the bus schedule (and routes), and set out about 30 minutes before the scheduled departure. If you don't have good luck hitching a ride, just wait for the bus to come along and hail it. It'll stop.

# Information and Services

## Emergencies

For **police, fire, and ambulance** anywhere on the Big Island, dial **911.** For **nonemergency police** assistance and information call 808/935-3311.

**Civil Defense:** In case of natural disaster such as hurricanes or tsunamis on the Big Island, call 808/935-0031.

**Coast Guard Search and Rescue:** 800/552-6458.

**Sexual Assault Crisis Line:** 808/935-0677.

For recorded information on **local island weather,** call 808/961-5582; for the **marine report,** call 808/935-9883; and for **volcano activity,** call 808/985-6000. For time of day, dial 808/961-0212.

## Medical Services

On the east side, 24-hour medical help is available from Hilo Medical Center, 808/974-4700. While in Ka'u, seek help from the Ka'u Hospital in Pahala, 808/928-8331. On the west side, try Kona Community Hospital in Kealakekua, 808/322-9311. The new North Hawaii Community Hospital in Kamuela, 808/885-4444, services the northern part of the island.

For minor emergencies and urgent care in Kona, try **Kona-Kohala Medical Associates,** 808/327-4357 and **Kaiser Permanente,** 808/334-4400. In Hilo, try **Kaiser Permanente,** 808/934-4000, or **Hilo Medical Associates,** 808/934-2000. In Waimea, use the **Lucy Hen-**rigues Medical Center, 808/885-7351, and in Honoka'a, see the **Hamakua Health Center,** 808/775-7204.

GB>Longs Drugs, KTA Super Stores, and **Kmart** all have pharmacies. Others that should meet your needs are: **Village Pharmacy,** 808/885-4418, in Waimea; **Hilo Pharmacy,** 808/961-9267, along the bay front; **Kealakekua Pharmacy,** 808/322-1639, in Kealakekua; **Waikoloa Pharmacy,** 808/883-8484 in Waikoloa; and **Kamehameha Pharmacy,** 808/889-6161, in Kapa'au.

## Consumer Protection

If you encounter problems with accommodations, bad service, or downright rip-offs, try the following: the Chamber of Commerce in Hilo, 808/935-7178, or in the Kona/Kohala area, 808/329-1758; the Office of Consumer Protection, 808/933-0910; or the Better Business Bureau of Hawaii on O'ahu, 877/222-6551.

## Tourism Information

The best information on the Big Island is dispensed by the HVB Hilo Branch, 250 Keawe St., Hilo, HI 96720, 808/961-5797 or 800/648-2441, and HVB Kona Branch, 250 Waikoloa Beach Drive, Suite B15, Waikoloa, HI 96738, 808/886-1655; www.bigisland.org.

The **visitor information booths** at the two island airports, 808/934-5838 in Hilo and

808/329-3423 in Kona, are good sources of information available on arrival. The Wailoa Center in downtown Hilo, 808/933-4360, open 8 A.M.–4:30 P.M. Mon.–Fri., also maintains visitor information and brochures about the island.

## Post Office
The central post office on Hawai'i is in Hilo, and there are 25 branch post offices in towns around the island.

## Reading Material
**Libraries** are located in towns and schools all over the island. The main branch is at 300 Waianuenue Ave., Hilo, 808/933-8888. This location can provides information regarding all libraries. In Kailua-Kona, the library is at 75-140 Hualalai Rd., 808/327-4327. Branch libraries are located in all major towns.

Free **tourist literature** is available at the airport, many hotels, and most restaurants and shopping centers around the island. They come out monthly or quarterly and contain money-saving coupons, information on local events and activities, shopping and restaurants, and island maps. The small-format magazine-style *Coffee Times* focuses on cultural and historical topics, while the newspaper-format *Hawai'i Island Journal* concentrates on issues of the day and has very good island calendars of events section. With a focus on activities and fun things to do, *101 Things to do on Hawaii the Big Island* is a great resource and also has money-saving coupons. Publications with local orientation are *Kohala Mountain News, Kona Times, Hamakua Times* and *The Waimea Gazette. Big Island Drive Guide* is available

from the car rental agencies and contains tips, coupons, and good maps. The Hawaii AAA *Tourbook* is also very useful.

Daily island newspapers include *Hawaii Tribune-Herald,* a Hilo publication (www.hilo-hawaiitribune.com), and *West Hawaii Today,* published in Kona (www.westhawaiitoday.com), both owned by the same parent company and each costing 50 cents daily and $1 on Sunday. Providing an alternative and progressive view on island issues is the *Ka'u Landing,* a monthly out of Ocean View (www.kau-landing.com).

## Island Radio
More than a dozen radio stations broadcast on the Big Island. Most broadcast only on either the Hilo or Kona side, while a few send signals to both sides. Among the most popular are:
**KIPA 620 AM:** Rainbow Radio: easy listening contemporary
**KPUA 670 AM:** news and sports
**KHPR 90.7 FM** Hawaii Public Radio
**KAOE 92.7 FM** rock and roll
**KWXX 94.7 FM:** island music, light contemporary rock, Jawaiian
**K-BIG 97.9 and 106.1 FM:** contemporary adult
**KAPA 99.1 and 100.3 FM:** Hawaiian and island tunes

## Island Facts
Hawai'i has three fitting nicknames: the Big Island, the Volcano Island, and the Orchid Island. It's the youngest, most southerly, and largest (4,028 square miles) island in the Hawaiian chain. Its color is red, the island flower is the red 'ohi'a lehua, and the island lei is fashioned from the lehua blossom.

BIG ISLAND OF HAWAI'I

# Kona

Kona is long and lean and takes its suntanned body for granted. This district *is* the west coast of the Big Island and lies in the rain shadows of Mauna Loa and Mauna Kea. You can come here expecting brilliant sunny days and glorious sunsets, and you won't be disappointed; this reliable sunshine has earned Kona the nickname "The Gold Coast." Offshore, the fishing grounds are legendary, especially for marlin that lure game-fishing enthusiasts from around the world. There are actually two Konas, north and south, and both enjoy an upland interior of forests, ranches, and homesteads while most of the coastline is low, broad, and flat. If you've been fantasizing about swaying palms and tropical jungles dripping with wild orchids, you might be in for

"Kona shock," especially if you fly directly into the Kona Airport. Around the airport the land is raw black lava that can appear as forbidding as the tailings from an old mining operation. Don't despair. Once in town, trees form a cool canopy and flowers add color at every turn.

The entire Kona district is old and historic. This was the land of Lono, god of fertility and patron of the Makahiki Festival. It was also the spot where the first missionary packet landed and changed Hawaii forever, and it's been a resort since the 19th century. In and around **Kailua** are restored *heiau*, a landmark lava church, and a royal summer palace where the monarchs of Hawaii came to relax. The coastline is rife with historical sites: lesser *heiau*, petroglyph fields,

ROBERT NILSEN

cultural historic park Pu'uhonua O Honaunau

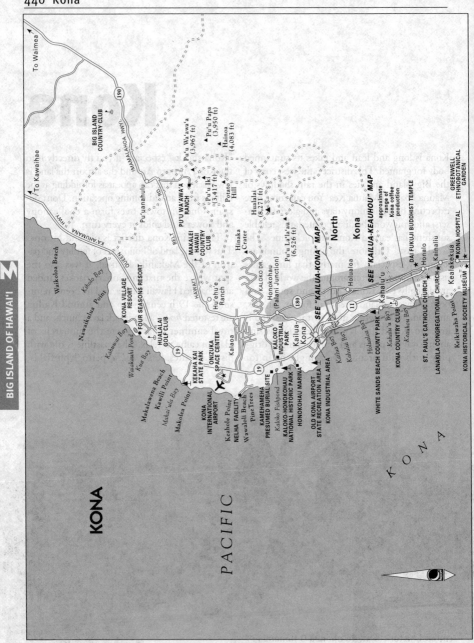

KONA

PACIFIC

To Waimea

To Kawaihae

BIG ISLAND
COUNTRY CLUB

(190)

MAMALAHOA HWY

Pu'u Wa'awa'a
(3,967 ft)

Pu'u Papa
(3,950 ft)

Hainoa
(4,083 ft)

PU'U WA'AWA'A
RANCH

Pu'uanahulu

Pu'u Iki
(3,417 ft)

Potato
Hill

MAKALEI
HAWAII
COUNTRY
CLUB

Hinaka
Crater

Hualalai
(8,271 ft)

Pu'u La'la'au
(6,526 ft)

KA'AHUMANU HWY

QUEEN

BELT
RD

Waikoloa Beach

Kiholo Bay

Nawaikulua Point

KONA VILLAGE
RESORT

FOUR SEASONS RESORT

HUALALAI
GOLF CLUB

Kahuwai Bay

Waiaka'ili Pond

Kua Bay

Makalawena Beach

Kawili Point

Mahai'ula Bay

Makolea Point

ONIZUKA
SPACE CENTER

KEKAHA KAI
STATE PARK

Kalaoa

19

Hu'ehu'e
Ranch

Honokohau
(Palani Junction)

KALOKO DR

Kailua
Kona

HAWAII

BELT

RD

North
Kona

Holualoa

SEE "KAILUA-KEAUHOU" MAP

SEE "KAILUA-KONA" MAP

approximate
range of
Kona coffee
production

DAI FUKUJI BUDDHIST TEMPLE

Honalo

Kahalu'u

Kainaliu

(11)

GREENWELL
ETHNOBOTANICAL
GARDEN

KONA HOSPITAL

Kealakekua

KONA HISTORICAL SOCIETY MUSEUM

LANAKILA CONGREGATIONAL CHURCH

ST. PAUL'S CATHOLIC CHURCH

Krikiwaha Point

Ke'ei

Kealakekua Bay

KONA COUNTRY CLUB

Kahalu'u Bay

Kahului Bay

Holualoa Bay

WHITE SANDS BEACH COUNTY PARK

KONA INDUSTRIAL AREA

OLD KONA AIRPORT
STATE RECREATION AREA

HONOKOHAU MARINA

KALOKO-HONOKOHAU
NATIONAL HISTORIC PARK

Kaloko Fishpond

KAMEHAMEHA
PRESUMED BURIAL SITE

Pine Trees

Wawaloli Beach

NELHA FACILITY

Keahole Point

KONA
INTERNATIONAL
AIRPORT

KALOKO
INDUSTRIAL
PARK

K  O  N  A

K  O  N  A

(180)

(19)

(11)

North

Kona

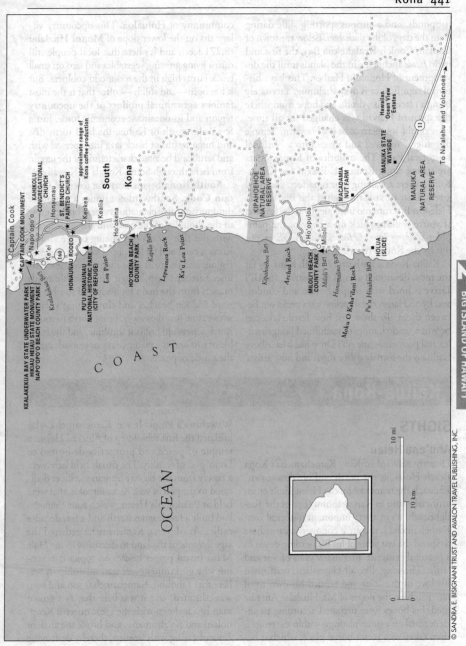

BIG ISLAND OF HAWAI'I

fishponds, and a curious sporting slide dating from the days of the *makahiki*. Below the town of Captain Cook is **Kealakekua Bay,** the first and main *haole* anchorage in the islands until the development of Honolulu Harbor. This bay's historical significance is overwhelming, alternately being a place of life, death, and hope from where the spirit of Hawaii was changed for all time. Here on the southern coast is a Hawaiian "temple of refuge," restored and made into a National Historical Park. The majority of Kona's sights are strung along Route 11. Except for Kailua-Kona, where a walking tour is perfect, you need a rental car to visit the sights; the Big Island's Hele-On Bus runs too infrequently to be feasible. If you're walking, pick up a copy of the pamphlet *Walking Tour of Historic Kailua Village,* put out by the Kona Historical Society.

Kailua-Kona is the heart of North Kona, by far the most developed area in the district. Its **Ali'i Drive** is lined with shops, hotels, and condos, and by and large, the shoreline vista peeks out between them. To show just how fertile lava can be when tended, miles of multihued bougainvillea and poinsettias line Ali'i Drive like a lei. Above Kailua is the former coffee town and now artists' community of **Holualoa.** This upcountry village sits on the lower slope of **Mount Hualalai** (8,271 feet), and it's here that local people still earn a living growing vegetables and taro on small truck farms high in the mountain coolness. But it has been—and still is—coffee that is the most famous agricultural product of the upcountry region and its dominant economic force. Just a few miles north of Kailua, the land turns dry, and huge swaths of black lava interspersed with arid scrubland become characteristic of the terrain from here through South Kohala to Kawaihae.

**South Kona** begins near the town of **Captain Cook.** Southward continues a region of diminutive coffee plantations where bushes grow to the shoulder of the road and the air is heady with the rich aroma of roasting coffee. South Kona is rural and far less populated. It's a rugged region, and the road stays high above the coastline. Farther south, rough but passable roads branch from the main highway and tumble toward hidden beaches and tiny fishing villages where time just slips away. From north to south, Kona is awash in brilliant sunshine, and the rumble of surf and the plaintive cry of seabirds create the music of peace.

## Kailua-Kona

### SIGHTS

#### Ahu'ena Heiau

Directly seaward of King Kamehameha's Kona Beach Hotel, at the north end of "downtown" Kailua, is the restored Ahu'ena Heiau. Built on an artificial island in Kamakahonu (Eye of the Turtle) Beach, it's in a very important historical area. Kamehameha I, the great conqueror, came here to spend the last years of his life, settling down to a peaceful existence after many years of war and strife. The king, like all Hawaiians, reaffirmed his love of the *'aina* and tended his own royal taro patch on the slopes of Mt. Hualalai. After he died, his bones were prepared according to ancient ritual on a stone platform within the temple, then taken to a secret burial place, which is believed to be just north of town somewhere near Wawahiwa'a Point. It was Kamehameha who initiated the first rebuilding of Ahu'ena Heiau, a temple of peace and prosperity dedicated to Lono, god of fertility. The rituals held here were a far cry from the bloody human sacrifices dedicated to the god of war, Kuka'ilimoku, that were held at Pu'ukohola Heiau, which Kamehameha had built a few leagues north and a few decades earlier. At Ahu'ena, Kamehameha gathered the sage *kahuna* of the land to discourse in the Hale Mana (main prayer house) on topics concerning wise government and statesmanship. It was here that Liholiho, Kamehameha's son and heir, was educated, and it was here that as a grown man he sat down with the great queens, Keopuolani and Ka'ahumanu, and broke the ancient *kapu* of eating with women, thereby destroying the old order.

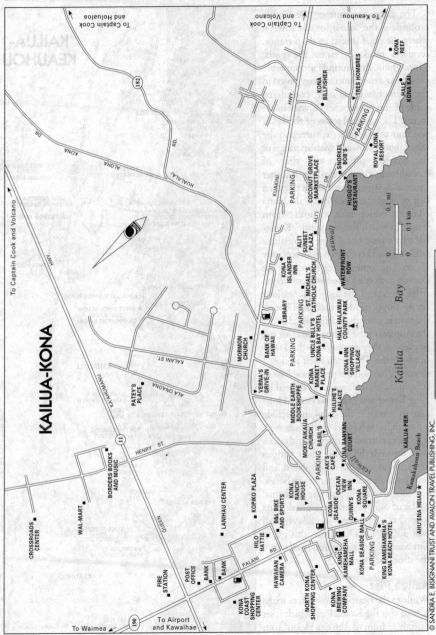

KAILUA-KONA

To Captain Cook and Volcano

To Waimea
To Airport and Kawaihae

BIG ISLAND OF HAWAI'I

Kailua Bay

0       0.1 mi
0       0.1 km

© SANDRA E. BISIGNANI TRUST AND AVALON TRAVEL PUBLISHING, INC.

The tallest structure on the temple grounds is the 'anu'u (oracle tower), where the chief priest, in deep trance, received messages from the gods. Throughout the grounds are superbly carved kia akua (temple image posts) in the distinctive Kona style, considered some of the finest of all Polynesian art forms. The spiritual focus of the heiau was humanity's higher nature, and the tallest figure, crowned with an image of the golden plover, was that of Koleamoku, a god of healing. Another interesting structure is a small thatched hut of sugarcane leaves, Hale Nana Mahina, which means "house from which to watch the farmland." Kamehameha would come here to meditate while a guard kept watch from a nearby shelter. The commanding view from the doorway affords a sweeping panorama from the sea to the king's plantations on the slopes of Mt. Hualalai. Though the temple grounds, reconstructed under the auspices of the Bishop Museum, are impressive, they are only one-third their original size. The heiau itself is closed to visitors but you can get a good look at it from the shore. Free tours offered by King Kamehameha's Kona Beach Hotel take you down to the heiau and include a tour of its own hotel grounds as well. The hotel portion of the tour includes a walk through the lobby, where various artifacts and artworks are displayed, and features an extremely informative botanical tour that highlights the medicinal herbs of old Hawaii. The hotel tours begin at 1:30 P.M. weekdays; call 808/329-2911. Don't miss this excellent educational opportunity, well worth the time and effort!

## Kailua Pier

While in the heart of downtown, make sure to visit the Kailua Pier, which is set directly in front of Ahu'ena Heiau. Tour boats and the occasional fishing boat

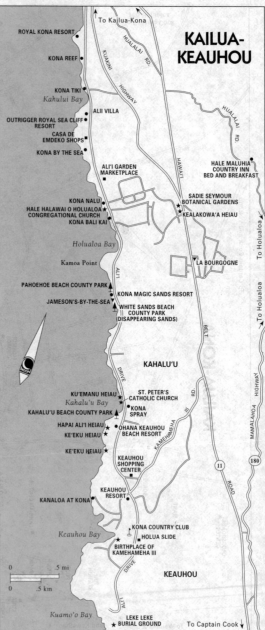

KAILUA-KEAUHOU

use this facility, so there is some activity on and off all day. Shuttle boats also use this pier to ferry passengers from cruise ships to town for land excursions. While it varies throughout the year, more of these large ships make Kailua a port of call during the late spring and autumn months than the rest of the year, but an interisland cruise ship makes a regular stop here once a week.

## Moku'aikaua Church

Kailua is one of those towns that would love to contemplate its own navel if it could only find it. It doesn't really have a center, but if you had to pick one, it would be the 112-foot steeple of Moku'aikaua Church. This highest structure in town has been a landmark for travelers and seafarers ever since the church was completed in January 1837. Established in 1820, the church claims to be the oldest house of Christian worship in Hawaii. The site was given by King Liholiho to the first Congregationalist missionaries, who arrived on the brig *Thaddeus* in the spring of that year. Taking the place of two previous grass structures, the construction of this building was undertaken in 1835 by the Hawaiian congregation under the direction of Rev. Asa Thurston. Much thought was given to the orientation of the structure, designed so the prevailing winds blow through the entire length of the church to keep it cool and comfortable. The walls of the church are fashioned from massive, rough-hewn lava stone, mortared with plaster made from crushed and burned coral that was bound with *kukui* nut oil. The huge cornerstones are believed to have been salvaged from a *heiau* built in the 15th century by King Umi that had occupied this spot. The masonry is crude but effective—still sound after more than 165 years.

Inside, the church is extremely soothing, expressing a feeling of strength and simplicity. The resolute beams are native 'ohi'a, pegged together and closely resembling the fine beamwork used in barns throughout 19th-century New England. The pews, railings, pulpit, and trim are all fashioned from koa, a rich brown, lustrous wood that begs to be stroked. Although the church is still used as a house of worship, it also has the air of a museum, housing paintings of historical

personages instrumental in Hawaii's Christian past. The crowning touch is an excellent model of the brig *Thaddeus*, painstakingly built by the men of the Pacific Fleet Command in 1934 and presented to the church in 1975. The church is open daily from sunrise to sunset, and volunteer hostesses may be around to answer your questions from late morning to mid-afternoon.

## Hulihe'e Palace

Go from the spiritual to the temporal by walking across the street from Moku'aikaua Church and entering Hulihe'e Palace. This two-story Victorian structure commissioned by Hawaii's second governor, John Kuakini, dates from 1838. A favorite summer getaway for all the Hawaiian monarchs who followed, especially King Kalakaua, it was used as such until 1914. At first glance, the outside is unimpressive, but the more you look the more you realize how simple and grand it is. The architectural lines are those of an English country manor, and indeed Great Britain was held in high esteem by the Hawaiian royalty. Inside, the palace is bright and airy. Most of the massive furniture is made from koa. Many pieces were constructed by foreigners, including the German Wilhelm Fisher. The most magnificent pieces include a huge formal dining table, 70 inches in diameter, fashioned from one solid koa log. Upstairs is a tremendous four-poster bed that belonged to Queen Kapi'olani, and two magnificent cabinets that were built by a Chinese convict serving a life sentence for smuggling opium. King Kalakaua heard of his talents and commissioned him to build the cabinets. They proved to be so wonderfully crafted that after they were completed the king pardoned the craftsman.

Prince Kuhio, who inherited the palace from his uncle, King Kalakaua, was the first Hawaiian delegate to Congress. He decided to auction off all the furniture and artifacts to raise money, supposedly for the benefit of the Hawaiian people. Providentially, the night before the auction each piece was painstakingly numbered by the royal ladies of the palace, and the name of the person bidding for the piece was dutifully recorded. In the years that followed, the **Daughters of**

BIG ISLAND OF HAWAI'I

**Hawai'i,** who now operate the palace as a museum, tracked down the owners and convinced many to return the items for display. Most of the pieces are privately owned, and because each is unique, the owners wish no duplicates to be made. It is for this reason, coupled with the fact that flashbulbs can fade the wood, that a strict *no photography* policy is enforced. The palace was opened as a museum in 1928!

Historical artifacts are displayed in a downstairs room. Delicate and priceless heirlooms on display include a tiger-claw necklace that belonged to Kapi'olani. You'll also see a portrait gallery of Hawaiian monarchs. Personal and mundane items are on exhibit as well—there's an old report card showing a 68 in philosophy for King Kalakaua—and lining the stairs is a collection of spears reputedly belonging to the great Kamehameha himself.

Hulihe'e Palace, 808/329-1877, is on the *makai* side of Ali'i Dr., open Mon.–Fri. 9 A.M.–4 P.M., Sat. and Sun. 10 A.M.–4 P.M. You can look around on your own or ask the staff for a tour, which usually lasts 45 minutes. Admission is $5 adults, $4 seniors, $1 students. A hostess knowledgeable in Hawaiiana is usually on duty to answer questions.

The **Palace Gift Shop,** small but with quality items, is on the grounds next door to the palace. Open daily except Sunday. It offers a fine selection of koa sculptures of fish, sharks, and even a turtle, along with Hawaiiana books and postcards. Just outside is a saltwater pond with tropical fish.

## Historical Walking Tour

The Kona Historical Society offers a leisurely one- to 1.5-hour guided walking tour of the Ahu'ena Heiau, Moku'aikaua Church, Hulihe'e Palace, and other nearby sights Mon.–Fri. at 9 and 11 A.M., for $15 per person. Advance reservations are necessary. You can tour each of these sites on your own, but you can learn so much more from a knowledgeable guide. Make reservations at 808/323-3222, and wear comfortable shoes and a hat.

## Up Above Town

At the intersection of Kuakini and Queen Ka'ahumanu Highways, on the grounds of the Kona Outdoor Circle Education Center, is a landscaped sliver of land called the **Sadie Seymour Botanical Gardens.** Grouped and planted on nearly a dozen terraces are typical plants that grow in Hawaii that are originally from other areas of the world. Small but well landscaped, this garden is a quiet retreat in the otherwise dry and hot upper Kona area. Open daily 9 A.M.–5 P.M. for self-guided tours, there is no admission but donations are accepted.

Adjacent to the botanical gardens is **Kealakowa'a Heiau,** an ancient sacred site dedicated to blessing canoes. This blessing was done after the rough shape had been cut in the upland forest but before the final work was completed at the beach. Consisting of four separate platforms, this *heiau* was reputedly built around 1600 by King Umi. There is currently no admittance to the *heiau* as the area is being preserved, but it is easily seen when looking over the surrounding stone wall.

## Along Ali'i Drive

Ali'i Drive heads south from Kailua, passing the majority of Kona's accommodations on its way to **Keauhou.** On the mountain side of the road, a continuous flow of flowers drapes the shoulder like a femme fatale's seductive boa, while seaside the coastline slips along, rugged and bright, making Ali'i Drive a soothing sight.

At your first stop, near White Sands Beach, look for the historic **Hale Halawai O Holualoa Congregational Church** built in 1855 by Rev. John D. Paris. Services are still held every Sunday at 9 A.M. The base of the church is mostly original lava rock topped with a new roof. The cemetery area is peaceful and quiet and offers a perfect meditative perch from which to scan the coast below. Back on the road, look for signs to Kahalu'u Beach Park; pull in and park here. On the rocky northern shore of this bay is **St. Peter's Catholic Church.** Its diminutive size, capped by a blue tin roof that winks at you from amidst the lava like a bright morning glory in an ebony vase, has earned it the nickname Little Blue Church. Built in 1889 on the site of an old, partially reclaimed *heiau*, the church is a favorite spot for snapshots. Inside,

J.D. BISIGNANI

**St. Peter's Church**

simplicity reigns with bare wood walls and a plain crucifix. The only splash of color is a bouquet of fresh flowers on the altar. To the right of the church as you face it are the remains of **Ku'emanu Heiau,** a temple where chiefs would pray for good surfing conditions. Their prayers must have worked, as surfers today still gracefully ride the waves offshore within sight of this rock platform. On the grounds of the Ohana Keauhou Beach Resort, a 10-minute walk south along the coast, are the remains of **Kapuanoni Heiau** and **Hapai Ali'i Heiau.** Just beyond that, at water's edge and fronting the abandoned Kona Lagoons hotel property, is the **Ke'eku Heiau.** All are unrestored historical sites that still show signs of being used, and all offer vantage points from which to view the coast.

Near the end of the road is **Keauhou Bay.** Here you'll find a cluster of historical sites, and the small boat harbor and boat ramp. Look for a monument marking the birthplace of Kamehameha III in 1814. Local people come to fish from the pier around 5 P.M. for *halalu,* a tough

little fish to catch. Along the shoreline are a number of partially developed *heiau* sites. A small home stuck on a point of land on the edge of the bay is where John Wayne married his wife Pilar in 1954, and it marks the site of the first modern house built on the bay. Opposite the harbor, at the end of King Kamehameha III Road is Keauhou Park and beach access, an area of lawn, pavilion, sand volleyball court, and restrooms.

At the very end of the Ali'i Drive, past the Kona Country Club golf course, is the **Leke Leke Burial Grounds.** Laid to rest here are troops that fought under the leadership of Kekuaokalani, keeper of the war god Ku after the death of King Kamehameha I, in an attempt to sustain the traditional religious and social order of the Hawaiian people. More than 300 died here at Kuano'o Bay, using firepower obtained from the foreigners. This battle was the violent end to the old ways and symbolized the shaky introduction of the Western overlay on Hawaiian society.

## North of Town

**Honokohau Harbor,** three miles north of Kailua-Kona, is a huge small-boat harbor and deep-sea fishing facility that has eclipsed the old Kailua Pier. This is the premier fishing harbor on the island, is used by other water-sport activity companies and sailboats, and is frantic with energy during the various "billfish tournaments" held throughout the year. The harbor area is full of fishing-oriented shops, including Kona Marine for nautical charts, and is also home to the Harbor House Restaurant, where you can hear a yarn from Kona's old salts. Primarily, this is where you come to see huge fish caught that day and talk to the skippers of the deep-sea fishing boats that go after them. When you pull into the marina, you'll see a road that goes off to the left. Head that way toward the tan building, to where the pier and the weigh-station are located. The huge fish will be hoisted, measured, and photographed while the skippers and their crews clean and prepare the boats for the next day's outing. **Weigh in** is every day 11 A.M.–1 P.M. and 3–6 P.M., basically when the boats return from their half-day and full-day trips; call 808/334-1881 for information. If you are fascinated by deep-sea fishing, this is your chance to pick a likely boat and to get acquainted with the crew.

The future is now at the amazing Ocean Technology facilities located just south of the airport between mile markers 95 and 94, where you'll find a turnoff heading toward the sea. This is the **Natural Energy Laboratory of Hawaii Authority (NELHA),** www.nelha.org. Incredible things are being done here. For example, cold water from 2,000 feet below the surface of the ocean is placed in a turbine with warm surface water, a process that generates electricity and also provides desalinated water. In addition, the cold water is used for raising very un-Hawaiian things such as alpine strawberries, lobsters, abalone, sea cucumbers, commercial black pearls, and Japanese flounder, as well as for raising *limu,* a local edible seaweed, oysters, clams, and shrimp. Others use its alternative energy source to make fish jerky, to grow shiitake mushrooms, and even to raise tropical fish that will become living bouquets of color in fish tanks around the world. Cyanotech, a leading manufacturer of marine products for worldwide nutrition and pharmaceutical markets, uses the

## ANCIENT SPORT OF HOLUA

In principle, *holua* was similar to snow sledding, and mostly a "chiefly" sport of the *ali'i.* Sleds were long two-runner affairs, perhaps six inches wide and eight feet long or longer, stabilized by cross bracing and grab bars on which the person would lie. These sleds were launched down a slope that was up to one mile in length and ended at or near the ocean. Only a few of these slopes remain, largely fallen into disrepair or taken apart to make way for modern constructions. Most prominent on the Big Island, the largest known sledding course was Kaneaka in Keauhou, the remains of which lie on the Kona Country Club *makai* golf course. Look for it across the road from the club house. These slopes were constructed of volcanic rock and filled in with small pebbles to make a flat top. It is believed that this flat top was then covered with layers of large leaves (maybe banana or *ti*) or thatching to provide a slippery surface for sledding. Once on the runway, there was no stopping until the sled got to the bottom—or went over the side. The danger associated with this sport must have been an important component of its thrill. With no steering mechanism, the chance of disaster seems large. *Holua* seems to have slowly died out through the 1800s, perhaps, as some have suggested, after the Makahiki Festival—which may have been its principle forum—ceased to be a central component of the Hawaiian cultural tradition. No one in living memory is purported to have actually seen the sport in action. Only recently has there been much attention turned to its understanding. Few examples of a *holua* sled have survived—the best is displayed at the Bishop Museum in Honolulu—and few accounts relate anything about the sport. Aside from a few brave, modern souls who have tried short sections of slope for the thrill, this sport has not yet been brought back by the resurgence of ancient Hawaiian culture. Perhaps its time is still to come.

facilities to make spirulina, available in health food stores, as well as numerous other products and ingredients. Tours are offered Wed. and Thurs. at 10 A.M.; call 808/329-7341 for reservations. Tours run about one hour in length; donations are accepted. If you choose to take a tour, don't be overwhelmed by the size of the complex; the products are brought to a central area for your viewing. A short self-guided tour will introduce you to the basics of what is done here. Behind this facility is the Ho'ona Historic Preserve, an area of home sites and graves from a late-19th-century Hawaiian community. Cutting across the NELHA area up near the highway is a section of the old King's Trail. The NELHA access road is open 6 A.M.–8 p.m.

Dedicated to Hawaii's own Col. Ellison S. Onizuka and to the men and women who tragically perished aboard the spacecraft *Challenger* on January 28, 1986, the **Onizuka Space Center** is located at Kona International Airport, P.O. Box 833, Kailua-Kona, HI 96745, 808/329-3441, www.planet-hawaii.com/astronautonizuka. Hours are daily 8:30 A.M.–4:30 P.M. except Thanksgiving, Christmas, and New Year's Day; admission is $3 adults, $1 children. From this tragedy, a living memorial and space education facility was erected. Inside the modern, well-appointed building children and adults alike can marvel at human exploration of space by viewing exhibits like a "moon rock," a scale model of a space shuttle and space station, an interactive staffed maneuvering unit, a real space suit, and a theater showing educational videos throughout the day. There is a gift shop with plenty of fascinating reading material concerning the international effort to explore the heavens. Stop in before flying out.

# BEACHES AND PARKS

If Kona is short on anything, it is beaches. The ones that it has are adequate and quite striking in their own way, but they tend to be small, few, and far between. People expecting a huge expanse of white sand will be disappointed. These beaches do exist on the Big Island's west coast, but they are north of Kailua-Kona in the Kohala district. Kona does, however, have beaches alive with marinelife,

providing excellent and safe snorkeling and top-notch tidepool exploration opportunities.

The following are the main beaches in and around Kailua-Kona. For descriptions of South Kona beaches see below.

## Kamakahonu Beach

You couldn't be more centrally located than at "Eye of the Turtle" Beach. Find it in downtown Kailua-Kona next to Kailua Pier, in front of King Kamehameha's Kona Beach Hotel. Local people refer to it as "Kids' Beach" because it is so gentle and safe, perfect for a refreshing dip. Big kids come here to play too, when every year world-class athletes churn the gentle waters into a fury at the start of the Ironman Triathlon. Rent snorkel gear, kayaks, and other water gear for reasonable prices from the Beach Shack, located in front of the hotel, or from other shops nearby. Restrooms and telephones are located at the inland end of the pier.

## Ali'i Drive Beaches

**White Sands Beach County Park** (a.k.a. **Magic Sands** or **Disappearing Sands**) is an excellent spot for a dip—if the sand is there. Every year, usually in winter, the sands are stripped away by heavy seas and currents, exposing rough coral and making the area too rugged for the average swimmer. People still come during those months because it's a good vantage point for observing migrating humpback whales. The sands always come back, and, when they do, the beach is terrific for all kinds of water sports, including body-surfing and snorkeling. White Sands is known locally as a great boogie-boarding and bodysurfing spot. The best board surfing is just north of the beach in a break the locals call "Banyans." White Sands' amenities include drinking water, showers, and restrooms, making the beach a favorite spot with local people and tourists.

Just before White Sands park is the small and narrow **Pahoehoe Beach County Park.** With its seawall, lawn, palm trees, and walkways, its a good place to suntan on the grass or picnic in the shade, but the rocky shoreline is not a place to swim.

**Kahalu'u Beach Park** on Kahalu'u Bay has always been a productive fishing area. Even today, fishermen come to "throw net." You'll occasionally see large family parties surrounding their favorite fish with a huge *hukilau* net, then sharing their bounty among all participants. Because of this age-old tradition, the area has not been designated a marine conservation district. Kahalu'u became a beach park in 1966. This ensured that the people of Kona would always have access to this favorite spot, which quickly became surrounded by commercial development. Ohana Keauhou Beach Resort occupies the land just to the south. Amenities at the park include picnic tables, showers, restrooms, a lifeguard, and even a basketball court. Often a *kaukau* wagon and snorkel rental truck are also there for those who didn't prepare well enough. The swimming is very good, but the real attraction is snorkeling. The waters are very gentle, and Kahalu'u is a perfect place for families or beginning snorkelers, as the water is generally only six to eight feet deep. However, stay *within* the bay because a powerful and dangerous rip current lurks outside. The shoreline waters are alive with tropical fish: angelfish, parrotfish, unicorn fish, the works. Unfortunately, Kahalu'u is often crowded, but it is still worth a visit. The reef offshore makes great waves and this bay has been a great surfing spot for centuries.

## Old Kona Airport State Recreation Area

In 1970 the old Kona Airport closed and the state of Hawaii turned it into a beach park. Take Kuakini Highway north from downtown until it ends. Often used on weekends by families for picnics and other gatherings, facilities include showers, restrooms, and a picnic area near the water, plus athletic fields, a gymnasium and aquatic center, and a children's playground near the entrance. Parking is unlimited along the old runway, where you can also walk, bike, in-line skate, or jog. The park gate closes at 8 P.M. The white-sand beach is sandwiched between the black lava at water's edge and the runway. You can enter the water at some shallow inlets, but the bottom is often rocky (be sure to wear water shoes) and the waters can be treacherous during high surf. The safest spot is a little sandy cove at the south-

ern end of the beach. Swimming is generally not good here, but sunbathing is great. Tidepooling is good when the water is low. Snorkeling is fine at the northern end of the beach, and offshore a break at "Shark Rocks" makes the old airport popular with Kona surfers. The waters in front of the park are a 217-acre marinelife conservation district protected from motorized boat usage but open to scuba divers and snorkelers.

## Kaloko-Honokohau National Historical Park

All types of people come to **Honokohau Beach,** including fishermen, surfers, and snorkelers, but it was primarily known as a clothing-optional beach. That status drastically changed when the area officially became part of Kaloko-Honokohau National Historical Park. At the Honokohau Small Boat Harbor, stay to the right and park at the end of the access road in a dirt parking lot near the Kona Sailing Club. Follow the well-worn path into the vegetation on the far side of the berm, and keep walking for a few minutes to the beach.

This area, more toward Kaloko just up the coast, was heavily populated during old Hawaiian days, and plenty of archaeological sites—mostly fishponds, ruins of houses, *heiau,* a small *holua* slide, and a few petroglyphs—are found along the shoreline. Most of these sites are protected; if you come to an archaeological area, obey all posted signs and approach with great care and respect. Remember, it is imperative that you do not touch, disturb, or remove any historical artifacts. The coarse, gray-sand beach offers safe swimming in somewhat shallow water. There are no facilities except bathrooms at each entrance.

Nudity is officially illegal within the park. Camping and open fires, also illegal, are citable offenses under federal regulations. Near the north end of the beach and over the dunes is "Queen's Bath" (called "Anchialine Bath" by the park service). Because it is under consideration as a historical site, swimming in the pond is prohibited. **Kaloko Beach,** about a 10-minute hike north of Queen's Bath, has great snorkeling in only 10–20 feet of water. Here, you can explore a series of sea arches. The entire area is a favorite with green sea turtles, which make their presence known mainly in the evenings. Two large fishponds in the park have been rehabilitated to a more natural environment and are home to several endangered waterbirds that include the *ae'o* (stilt) and the *alae ke'oke'o* (Hawaiian coot).

Dedicated in 1978, the 1,160-acre Kaloko-Honokohau National Historical Park can be entered either from Honokohau Small Boat Harbor or via Kaloko Gate, just off Hwy. 19 across from the Kaloko Industrial Park, and a mile-long hike. The gate is open daily 8 A.M.–3:30 P.M. For information, call the park office at 808/329-6881.

## North Kona Beaches

The next beach you come to heading north is the famous **Pine Trees** surfing beach, located near the NELHA facility just south of the airport. Where the long access road turns abruptly to the right, look for a well-worn dirt road leading to the left away from NELHA, and follow it to Pine Trees. Although famous with surfers and the site of many competitions, Pine Trees (none of which are in evidence) is not a good swimming beach. There are a few one-towel coves along the rocky shoreline where you can gain access to the water, but mostly it's a place from which to observe the action. You can also follow the road toward the NELHA facility a short way to **Wawaloli Beach,** a large, sandy, public beach, fronted by rock and coral. Here are a few volleyball nets, a restroom, and some picnic tables.

## Kekaha Kai State Park

Recently opened and well marked, the Kekaha Kai (Kona Coast) State Park stretches north, encompassing several sandy secluded beaches in its 1,642-acre domain. The first is about two miles north of the airport between mile markers 91 and 90; open 9 A.M.–7 P.M., except Wed. Follow the rugged but passable dirt road for about 1.5 miles to one of the closest beaches to Kailua-Kona. The semi-improved area has toilets and picnic tables built around palm trees. The land rises before getting to the coarse, salt-and-pepper sand beach. The swimming is usually safe here

except in winter and some come to snorkel, but always be careful.

Before you get to the official parking area, notice a walking path off to the right. It is a 10-minute walk to Mahai'ula Bay and its magnificent **Mahai'ula Beach.** This crescent of tan sand stretches for about 200 yards, with shade trees coming down almost to the water's edge. Completely unimproved and fairly secluded, it's a great beach to "get away from it all" for the day. Back from the water here are the remains of an abandoned red beach house that once belonged to the Magoon family, longtime island residents and major stockholders in Hawaiian Airlines. These buildings have appeared as a movie set over the years. Walk north from Mahai'ula Beach along an arrow-straight path across a hot stretch of rough lava for about 15 minutes to the smaller and more secluded white-sand **Makalawena Beach.** Local boys love to bodysurf here in winter. Alternatively, drive two miles farther north, between mile markers 89 and 88, look for the Pu'u Ku'ili cinder cone, whose vegetation has been given a crew cut by the trade winds. Turn here on a very rugged, 4WD-only dirt road that takes you down to Makalawena. En route to this totally secluded area, you'll pass over rough lava and coral and eventually come to a gate, where you park. Proceed on foot, and you'll have your choice of three wonderful beaches; all are frequented by green sea turtles. At the north end of these beaches is a small brackish but mostly freshwater pond, the domain of *nanini* fish and a harmless brine shrimp. If you do not have 4WD, you can still enjoy this area, but it means a hike of about 30 minutes. Be sure to bring water, especially if you intend to spend the day.

A few minutes farther north by car, just past the cinder cone, you'll find another rugged lava and coral road. If you have 4WD you can go to the end of the road and then walk to the beach, but you can also walk for about 15 minutes from the turnout near the highway. The well-worn path leads you to **Kua Bay,** a famous swimming and boogie-boarding beach. Kua Bay can also be reached in about 30 minutes by a path over coral and lava from Kukio Beach, which is next to the Four Seasons Resort.

# ACCOMMODATIONS

Almost all of Kona's accommodations lie along the six miles of Ali'i Drive from Kailua-Kona to Keauhou. Most hotels/condos fall in the moderate to expensive range. A few inexpensive hotels are scattered here and there along Ali'i Drive, and back up in the hills are a "sleeper" or two, cheap but decent. The following list should provide you with a good cross section.

It's sad but true: except for the limited beach parks at Ho'okena and Mili'li'i, south of Kailua-Kona, there is *no official camping* in all of the Kona district. Campers wishing to enjoy the coast must go north to the Kohala district to find a campground, or south to Ka'u. Some unofficial camping does exist in Kona, but as always, this generates certain insecurities. Bivouacking for a night or two in any of the unofficial camp spots should be hassle-free. Good luck!

## Hostel

**Patey's Place,** 75-195 Ala Ona Ona St., Kailua-Kona, HI 96740, 808/326-7018, fax 808/326-7640, www.hawaiian-hostels.com, is a reasonably priced and friendly hostel. Upon arrival, it will appear as though a section of the living sea was taken from the coast and moved whole into a residential area of Kona. You will be cohabiting with whales, mermaids, and dolphins, all rendered by airbrush *air*tist Paul Fullbrook, an Aussie artist who was undoubtedly a green sea turtle in his past life. Rates are bunk room $19.50, semiprivate $27.50, private room $35 single, and big room $46. No meals are provided. A $10 key and linen deposit is returned on departure. Patey's also provides transportation to and from the airport for $10. There are body boards, fishing gear, snorkel gear, and bike rentals at reasonable fees; lockers; safe deposit box; inexpensive email access; and free and invaluable information. All rooms are clean, lockable, and cooled by cross ventilation and ceiling fans. The hostel is also outfitted with four full bathrooms, three kitchens, a 2nd-floor sunset deck, laundry facilities, gas barbecues, and an activities desk. You shouldn't expect, nor will you find, the standards of a five-star resort, but Patey's is an excellent choice for the adventurer, budget traveler, or anyone who enjoys a dynamic international crowd.

## $50-150

For a reasonable and homey hotel, try the **Kona Tiki Hotel,** 75-5968 Ali'i Dr., Kailua-Kona, HI 96740, 808/329-1425, fax 808/327-9402, one of the first accommodations south of "downtown." At more than 50 years old, this is one of the oldest vacation hotels along the coast, and although of an old style without the luxury, the place is kept up. Sandwiched between the ocean and the road, it's a bit noisy during the day but quiets down at night except for the lullaby of the rolling surf. The Kona Tiki features refrigerators in all rooms, some kitchenettes, a complimentary continental breakfast daily, and a small guest pool. The 15 refurbished rooms are clean, with ceiling fans but no phones or televisions, and all units face the ocean so everyone gets a view. Prices are $59–65 for a standard room with queen or queen and twin bed, and $70 for a kitchenette; extra person $8, three-day minimum, no credit cards.

**Kona Seaside Hotel** is a basic but well-cared-for downtown hotel at 75-5646 Palani Rd., Kailua-Kona, HI 96740, 808/329-2455 or 800/560-5558, fax 808/329-6157, www.konaseasidehotel.com. Part of the island-owned Sand and Seaside Hotel chain, most rooms here have a/c, cross ventilation, and lanai, and there's self-service laundry on the premises. A sundeck and central courtyard surround one swimming pool; a second pool is located near the front entrance. Prices range from $98 standard to $120 deluxe, with AAA and AARP discounts and room and car packages available. The Kona Seaside operates two adjacent restaurants, one that serves a self-service continental breakfast, and the second that serves lunch and dinner. The Seaside Shopping Center is located next door.

**Uncle Billy's Kona Bay Hotel,** at 75-5744 Ali'i Dr., Kailua-Kona, HI 96740, 808/329-1393 or 800/367-5102, resv@unclebilly.com, www.unclebilly.com, is a locally owned hotel in the center of town, run by Uncle Billy and his Kona family. Its best feature is the friendly and warm staff. The hotel is a remaining wing of the old Kona Inn, the rest of which was torn down to accommodate the shopping center across the road. The semicircular hotel is built around a central courtyard and garden containing Kimo's Family Buffet, a bar, and a swimming pool. Uncle Billy's is a bit of a throwback to Kona's earlier days, still it's comfortable, clean, and convenient, but not plush. The rooms are a combination of moderate and superior with a/c, TV, and mini-fridge. Rates begin at $84–94, and $94 with kitchenette; many discounts and package rates are available.

## $150–250

**King Kamehameha's Kona Beach Hotel** in downtown Kailua-Kona at 75-5660 Palani Rd., Kailua-Kona, HI 96740, 808/329-2911 or 800/367-6060, reservations@hthcorp.com, www.konabeachhotel.com, is one of the only Kona hotels that has its own beach and is located on a spot favored by Hawaiian royalty; Kamehameha the Great spent the last days of his life here and it's adjacent to the restored Ahu'ena Heiau. The walls of the lobby are lined with historical artifacts; portraits of the Kamehameha royal family beginning with the great chief Kamehameha are displayed in the reception area; two *kahili* stand nearby as signs of royalty; and a feather cape and hat also adorn one wall. Other displays make up this mini-museum, and it's worth a look even if you are not staying here. Pick up a brochure about these artifacts at the front desk. In addition, weekly events are put on to introduce guests to aspects of Hawaiian art and culture. Rooms each feature a lanai with a sweeping panorama of the bay or Mt. Hualalai. Prices for the 460 rooms are $135–200 for standard to oceanfront rooms and up to $550 for a three-bedroom suite, additional person $30, and children under 18 stay free when sharing their parents' room. The hotel features the Kona Beach Restaurants, Billfish Bar, Island Breeze lu'au, tennis courts, a plethora of shops, a freshwater pool, and a beach, as well as an activities desk, guided historical tours, Internet access for guests, and self-service laundry. The King Kamehameha's Kona Beach Hotel is an older property, but its well run by a proud staff, well maintained to keep a high standard, and good value for your money.

The **Royal Kona Resort,** 75-5852 Ali'i Dr., Kailua-Kona, HI 96740, 808/329-3111 or 800/919-8333, www.royalkona.com, has figuratively and literally become a Kona landmark. The hotel, built like rising steps with the floor below larger than the one above, commands a magnificent view from its perch atop a beautiful promontory of black lava that anchors the south end of downtown Kailua. All 450 rooms are spacious, and each includes a lanai. Standard rates run from $160 for a garden view to $180 for an ocean view and $240 for an oceanfront room, with the oceanfront corner king rooms costing $260. Many packages are available. On the property, you can dine for breakfast or dinner in the Tropics Cafe Restaurant, which has a lovely sun-soaked veranda with a sweeping view of the surrounding coastline. The Windjammer, an open-air lounge next door, features entertainment several evenings each week. The hotel pool has an upper kiddies' pool and a lower, re-tiled main pool adjacent to the rolling surf, and an ocean-fed beach lagoon is sheltered from the force of the waves by huge black lava boulders. Between the main building and the beach tower is the small coconut grove. Here, the *imu* is fired up every Monday, Wednesday, and Friday evening, creating delectable morsels for the famous Kona sunset lu'au that comes complete with island entertainment that fills the grounds with music and laughter. The tennis courts, attended by a professional staff, are lit for nighttime play. Other full-service amenities include a self-serve laundry, free parking, exercise spa classes, baby-sitters, and no charge for children under 17 years of age sharing a room with their parents. The Royal Kona Resort keeps alive the tradition of quality service at a quality hotel.

The **Ohana Keauhou Beach Resort,** 78-6740 Ali'i Dr., Kailua-Kona, HI 96740, 808/322-3441 or 800/462-6262, is built on a historic site that includes the remains of two *heiau,* a reconstruction of King Kamehameha III's summer cottage, two freshwater springs, and several fishponds. Kahalu'u Beach Park is adjacent with its white-sand beach, and the entire area is known for fantastic tidepools. This famous Kona hotel underwent an extensive renovation in 1999 and the result is a wonderful feeling of old-fashioned Hawaii. To set the mood, paintings by Hawaii's Herb Kane hang on the walls and reflect the heritage of the two dugout canoes in the lobby. Throughout the hotel, soothing greens and sand-beige colors coordinate with the period-style furniture to make this a restful retreat. Rates range from $199 for a garden view up to $299 for deluxe oceanfront room, with suites at $600; rates are lower during value season and many special discounts are available all year. Each of the 311 rooms has a/c, TV, phone, private lanai, and small refrigerator. The hotel has the Kama'aina Terrace restaurant that's open for breakfast and dinner; the Kalanikai lunch café near the water, which serves wraps, sandwiches, and other light fare; and a lobby lounge where you'll hear free music most nights. The resort also has a swimming pool, activities desk, the Lamont's sundries store, Kailua Artists Gallery, Kolona salon and day spa, and a fitness center. In keeping with the new outlook, the hotel is offering daily activities and presentations in Hawaiian dance, music, arts and crafts, and a torch lighting ceremony. A free cultural tour is offered daily that takes you around to the historical sites on the hotel grounds. For the tennis player, Island Slice Tennis is on the property. Although not the largest, the Keauhou Beach Hotel is the finest hotel property in the Kailua area.

## Condominiums

**Economy:** A few reasonably priced and attractive condominium apartments include the following. **Kona Islander Inn** hotel-style condominium apartments, 75-5776 Kuakini Hwy., Kailua-Kona, HI 96740, 808/329-3181, are well appointed for a reasonable price. Conveniently located within walking distance of downtown Kailua-Kona, they're tucked into a tight but well-landscaped garden next door to St. Michael's and Kealoakamalamalama Churches. The style is "turn-of-the-20th-century plantation" shaded by tall palms. All rental units have phone, off-road parking, a/c, TV, and refrigerators. Rates are $70–80. Reservations for this and the following two condos can also be made through Hawaii Resorts Management,

800/622-5348, www.konahawaii.com, which manages units in more than a dozen other mostly economical to moderate condos along this coast.

**Kona Billfisher,** 808/329-9277, offers apartment-style condos with full kitchens, pool, barbecues, limited maid service, and gazebo. One-bedroom units cost $85 daily for up to four persons, two-bedroom units $110 for up to six guests. Weekly and monthly rates and discounts are available; minimum three days.

**Kona Magic Sands Resort,** 808/329-9393, couldn't get closer to the water. It sits on oceanside lava directly adjacent to White Sands Beach. Here, you can lounge poolside and eat at Jameson's Restaurant without leaving the property. The studios have full kitchens, color TV, and phones. Rates run $125 during high season or $95 during low season; three nights minimum.

Set next to the Royal Kona Resort is the small and quiet **Hale Kona Kai,** 75-5870 Kahakai Rd., Kailua-Kona, HI 96740, tel./fax 808/329-2155 or 800/421-3996. These one-bedroom, oceanfront apartments are fully equipped condo units with lanai, and a swimming pool and laundry facilities are on the premises. Room rates are $125–135 a night, three-night minimum, $10 for each additional person over two.

On a narrow property that slides down to the sea, the contemporary-style **Alii Villa,** 808/329-1288, look as if they came out of the 1960s with their straight lines and architectural concrete blocks. Set amidst plentiful vegetation, with a swimming pool and two barbecue grills in the middle of the property, these condos run in the $75–145 range during high season.

Small in comparison, **Kona Seaspray** rents condo units in its two-building complex at 78-6665 Ali'i Dr., with an exceptional setting across from Kahalu'u Bay and St. Peter's Church. Spacious, well-kept, with all amenities, and a small pool on property, these units start at $700 a week. Kona Seaspray is popular so call well in advance; 808/322-2403, fax 808/322-0105, seaspraykona@aol.com, www.konaseaspray.com.

Set kitty-corner to the Keauhou Shopping Center and just a short walk from the Kona Country Club Golf Course is the **Keauhou Resort,** 78-

7039 Kamehameha III Rd., Kailua-Kona, HI 96740, 808/322-9122 or 800/367-5286, fax 808/322-9410, keauhouresort@konanet.net, a town house complex of low-rise units in a garden of bougainvillea and other tropical plants. One- and two-bedroom units have electric kitchens, washers and dryers, telephones, and color TV, and there are two pools on the property. Reasonable rates run $85 a day for a one-bedroom garden unit to $117 for a two-bedroom ocean-view unit; five night minimum stay.

**Moderate:** Just outside the central Kailua area, at the start of "condo row," is **Kona Reef,** a Castle Resort property at 75-5999 Ali'i Dr., Kailua-Kona, HI 96740, 808/329-2959. Finely appointed units look out over the central garden and pool to the sea beyond. Each unit is set up with full kitchen, washer and dryer, and all you need for an easy stay. One-, two-, and three-bedroom suites run $190–230 high season, slightly less during low season, and can sleep four to eight people. For reservations, contact the condo direct or call Castle Resorts at 800/272-5275 in Hawaii, 800/367-5004 nationwide, www.castleresorts.com.

Only steps from the stone church Hale Halawai O Holualoa is **Kona Nalu.** A small property with a few more than a dozen units, it's not only quiet but relatively central on this Kona strip. Expect rates in the $215–235 range for two-bedroom oceanfront units. Contact Sunquest Vacations, 800/357-5168, for information and reservations.

A Marc Resort property, **Kona Bali Kai,** 76-6246 Ali'i Dr., Kailua-Kona, HI 96740, 808/329-9381 or 800/535-0085, fax 808/326-6056, is a very decent, comfortable place with a swimming pool, activities desk, concierge, and sundries shop on property. The studio, one-, and two-bedroom units have a fully equipped kitchen, TV and VCR, and phone for local calls. All apartments are individually owned so the decor differs, but most have muted colors and a tropical feel. Rates run $169–299. While some units are directly on the ocean, others are on the mountain side of Ali'i Drive, so they may or may not have an ocean view. This is a good choice for being close to town but not in the center of the hubbub.

**Expensive:** The **Outrigger Royal Sea Cliff Resort,** 75-6040 Ali'i Dr., Kailua-Kona, HI 96740, 808/329-8021 or 800/688-7444, winner of the AAA Three-Diamond Award, offers classy condo apartments. The alabaster contemporary building features rooms fronting a central garden courtyard, and the stark white color inside and out provide a Mediterranean feel. The unobstructed views of the black lava coast from most rooms are glorious, and a perfect day-ending activity is sunsets enjoyed on your private lanai. Amenities include free tennis, daily maid service, cable color TV, freshwater and seawater swimming pools, jet spa and sauna, and activities desk. Units here are spacious and regular season rates start with a studio at $233 and move to one bedrooms $263–310, two bedrooms $298–363, with a few oceanfront villas at $803. The "family plan" allows children under 18 to stay at no charge when using existing beds; otherwise there's a $20 daily extra person charge.

**Kona by the Sea,** 75-6106 Ali'i Dr., Kailua-Kona, HI 96740, 808/327-2300 or 800/321-2558 in Hawaii, 800/922-7866 Mainland and Canada, is a beautifully situated condominium with extraordinary coastal views. Like many of Kona's properties, it has no beach, but there is a pool on the premises and an activities desk. From the balcony of your suite overlooking a central courtyard, you can watch the aqua-blue surf crash onto the black lava rocks below. Each spacious one- or two-bedroom unit has two bathrooms, tiled lanai, modern full kitchen, living room with fold-out couch, dining room, color cable TV, and central air. Like its near neighbor, this property is also a AAA Three-Diamond Award winner. Regular season prices are $300–335 for one-bedroom units and $370–390 for two-bedroom units.

Outrigger's **Kanaloa at Kona,** 78-261 Manukai St., Kailua-Kona, HI 96740, 808/322-9625 or 800/688-7444, is situated in a quiet upscale residential area away from traffic at the southern end of Kailua-Kona in Keauhou. This is one of those special places where you feel you get more than you pay for. The one- and two-bedroom units are enormous. Bigger isn't always better, but in this case it is. Each individually owned and decorated unit comes equipped with a complete and modern kitchen, two baths, a lanai with comfortable outdoor furniture, a wet bar for entertaining, and a washer and dryer. Rates for the tastefully furnished units range from $250 for one-bedroom, fairway-view villas to $360 for two-bedroom units with loft on the ocean; the rooms can accommodate four and six people, respectively, at no extra charge. Two nights minimum. Many package rates and discounts are available. A security officer is on duty at all hours, and on the grounds you'll find three swimming pools and whirlpool spas, two lighted tennis courts for guest use only, gas barbecue grills, an activities desk with free morning coffee, and even a fine-dining restaurant and cocktail lounge overlooking the black rocky shore. The complex itself consists of some three dozen low-rise units that lie between the Kona Country Club and the water, and the grounds are finely landscaped. This is a place that feels like vacation. If you would like to escape the hustle and bustle but stay near the action, the Kanaloa at Kona is the place. It's a winner.

## Vacation Rental Agencies

With the multitude of condos and rental houses along this coast, there are plenty of agencies to do the looking for you. It's often better the first time around to let one of the agencies find one to fit your needs and then look for something else for next time while you're on the island. Try one of the following for condominium units or rental homes.

**Sunquest Vacations,** 77-6435 Kuakini Hwy., Kailua-Kona, HI 96740, 808/329-6488 or 800/367-5168 in the U.S., 800/800-5662 in Canada, fax 808/329-5480, www.sunquest-hawaii.com, manages over 200 units in some 30 condo properties in the Kona area, with nearly two dozen homes. By and large, these units are midrange. They also arrange car rentals, tours, and activities. This company is one of the "big boys" and has a well-deserved reputation.

**Century 21 All Islands,** 75-5689 Ali'i Dr., Kailua-Kona, HI 96740, 808/326-2121 or 800/546-5662, fax 808/329-6768, www.island-srentals.com/BigIsland/Aloha-C21.html, handles

mostly economy to midrange condo units in Kailua and Keauhou.

**Property Network,** 75-5799 Ali'i Dr., Kailua-Kona, HI 96740, 808/329-7977 or 800/358-7977, fax 808/329-1200, vacation@hawaii-kona.com, www.hawaii-kona.com, handles the full range of condos along the Kona Coast in about two dozen different properties plus a handful of homes; economy to midrange.

For mostly upper-end condo units in the Keauhou area, try **Keauhou Property Management Company,** 76-6225 Kuakini Hwy., Ste. C-105, Kailua-Kona, HI 96740, 808/326-9075 or 800/745-5662, fax 808/326-2055.

**Knutson and Associates,** 75-6082 Ali'i Dr., Ste. 8, Kailua-Kona, HI 96740, 808/329-6311 or 800/800-6202, fax 808/326-2178, www.kona-hawaiirentals.com, manages midrange condo units and a few vacation homes mostly in the central Kona area.

With roughly 150 properties, of which about two dozen are homes, **West Hawaii Property Services, Inc.,** 78-6831 Ali'i Dr., Ste. 234A, Kailua-Kona, HI 96740, 808/322-6696 or 800/799-5662, fax 808/324-0609, whps@il-hawaii.com, www.konarentals.com, has a good range of places from economy to deluxe.

A smaller company with about half condo units and half homes is **C. J. Kimberly Realtors,** 75-5875 Kahakai Rd., Kailua-Kona, HI 96740; 808/329-4321 or 888/780-7000, fax 808/329-5533, cjkimberly@aloha.net, www.cjkimberlyrealtors.com.

**Action Team Realty,** 75-5660 Kopiko St., Ste. B4, Kailua-Kona, HI 96740, 808/329-8626 or 800/335-3347, www.konacondo.com, handles many condo units in about a dozen and a half properties, as well as a number of individual homes, in Kona.

# FOOD

## Inexpensive

"So, for the budget traveler," you've been asking yourself, "which is the best restaurant in town, with the most food at the lowest prices, with that down-home atmosphere?" **The Ocean View Inn,** 808/329-9998, is it! The gigantic menu of

Chinese, American, Japanese, and Hawaiian food is like a mini-directory. Lunch and dinner range $8–12, and a huge breakfast goes for about $5. It's open daily except Mon., 6:30 A.M.–2:45 P.M. and 5:15–9 P.M., with the bar open daily 6:30 A.M.–9 P.M. Located across from the seawall near King Kamehameha's Kona Beach Hotel, it's always crowded with local people, a sure sign that the food is good.

The **Royal Jade Garden,** in the Lanihau Center, 808/326-7288, open daily 10:30 A.M.–9:30 P.M., is a Chinese restaurant where you get an amazing amount of well-prepared food for a moderate price. Run-of-the-mill chow mein, noodle soup, and meat dishes of chicken, duck, pork, or beef cost $6–9. More expensive items include lobster with black bean sauce and a variety of fresh fish and seafood. In the Royal Jade there's no decor, but if you are hungry and on a tight budget, this is one of the best values in town.

**Aki's Cafe,** 808/329-0090, located across from the seawall, is a moderately priced Japanese/American restaurant offering breakfast, lunch, and dinner. Breakfast can be three-egg omelettes, an eggs Benedict scramble, pancakes, or a Japanese breakfast with eggs, miso soup, rice, and your choice of meat. Lunch can be California-roll sushi, fried noodles to which you can add chicken or shrimp, or curry with rice. The dinner menu offers marinated New York steak, chicken teriyaki, garlic pasta, and its well-known fish and chips. Aki's is a centrally located, simple restaurant that adds a nice touch to ordinary food.

**King Yee Lau,** 808/329-7100, located in the Ali'i Sunset Plaza across from the seawall and open Mon.–Sat. 11 A.M.–2 P.M., nightly 5–9 P.M., offers an all-you-can-eat lunch buffet and the usual Chinese dishes like pressed crispy duck, beef with ginger sauce, and shrimp with seasoned vegetables, most priced under $9. Many vegetarian selections are offered.

**Kimo's Family Buffet,** located in the heart of Kailua in the courtyard of Uncle Billy's Kona Bay Hotel, 808/329-1393, serves very reasonably priced breakfast and dinner buffets. The breakfast buffet runs $5.95, dinner buffet $10.95, and a Sunday brunch $6.95. These prices can't be beat, but don't expect a lavish layout or a gourmet production.

Part of a small chain on the island, **Verna's Drive-In** on Kuakini Hwy. is where many local people go for inexpensive fast food like plate lunches, sandwiches, omelettes, burgers, and drinks. Open all day. Totally local.

In a freestanding booth in the Lanihau Center, **Chili by Max,** open Tues.–Sat. 10 A.M.–4 P.M., is famous for its award-winning oven-baked chili, made with beef or sautéed tofu. Also on the bill of fare are kosher hot dogs, chili dogs, chili nachos, baked potatoes, chicken breast sandwiches, tacos, and ice cream.

In the Kopiko Plaza, along Palani Rd. and just down from the Lanihau Center, you'll find several places to eat, including Hama Yu and Kona Mix Plate. **Kona Mix Plate,** 808/329-8104, open Mon.–Sat. 10 A.M.–8 P.M., is a no-frills counter restaurant serving standard Japanese, Korean, and American breakfasts, sandwiches, and plates like teriyaki beef, *kalbi* ribs, and shrimp platters for about $8, with a few items up to $15. While not special, the food is acceptable and inexpensive, and there always seems to be a line at lunch—a good sign. Stop by **Hama Yu Japanese Restaurant,** 808/331-8888, daily except Sun. for lunch and dinner. Lunch meals might be noodles, *donburi*, or tempura, while dinner is usually a bit fuller with items like teriyaki and *kobayashi* for $16–25 or sushi and sashimi for $25–35. Hama Yu has a sister restaurant up the coast at the King's Shops in Waikoloa.

Although the Kona industrial area doesn't sound inviting, it is a great place to find inexpensive food, along with stores where the *people* shop. To get to the industrial area, head for the airport, and about one minute north of the junction of Rte. 19 (the airport road) and Palani Rd., make a left on Kaiwi St. Or follow Kuakini Rd., a major intersection off Palani Rd. just a minute from the seawall, to Kaiwi St. The triangle formed by Kaiwi and Kuakini is primarily the old industrial area. Behind the Kailua Candy Company in this area is the **Orchid Thai Cuisine** restaurant, 808/327-9437. Located in a small strip-mall setting, the ambience is plain pedestrian but the food is better than average. Open

Mon.–Fri. 11 A.M.–9 P.M., you'll find all your usual favorite Thai dishes like chicken *satay;* papaya salad; *pad thai* noodles; red, green, and yellow curries; plus a host of other items. Most main dishes run $7.50–8.50; takeout is available on all orders.

If you're hungry for a quick bite while up at the Crossroads Shopping Center, stop in **Manna Korean Barbecue** for inexpensive Korean/American/Hawaiian foods where most items are under $7.

**Harbor House,** at the Honokohau Small Boat Harbor, 808/326-4166, open daily 10:30 A.M.–8:30 P.M., features one of Kona's longest bars. Harbor House is more or less an open-air pavilion, but it is actually quite picturesque as it overlooks the harbor. If you are interested in a charter fishing boat, this is the best place to come to spin a yarn with the local skippers who congregate here daily in the late afternoon. Over the bar hangs a gigantic 1,556-pound marlin, almost as big as the Budweiser sign. Strategically placed TVs make it a good sports bar, and the jukebox has a great selection of oldies and contemporary tunes. You can not only quaff a variety of draft beers here, you can order off the bill of fare for grilled bacon cheeseburgers with fries, shrimp and chips, crab-salad sandwiches, clam chowder, and the like. Harbor House is one of the truly *colorful* places in Kailua-Kona, and one of the best places to relax and have a hassle-free brew. It's also a place where the fish stories you tell might easily become exaggerated with the number of beers you drink.

## Bakeries, Delis, and Coffee

You can't get "hotter" than **Lava Java,** 808/327-2161, one of Kona's popular coffeehouse/restaurants, open daily 6 A.M.–10 P.M. in the Ali'i Sunset Plaza across from the seawall. Here, local people and tourists alike come to kick back, read the papers, and actually engage in the lost art of conversation. Sandwiches, soups, and salads are major menu items. Try the turkey and ham for $7.95, a garden burger for $6.95, Polish dog for $3.75, Greek wrap for $5.95, chicken salad for $6.95, or chips and salsa for $4.95. Lava Java

has a counter offering muffins, cookies, root-beer floats, Kona coolers made with tropical fruit sorbet, Italian sodas, ice cream, and bulk 100 percent Kona coffee by the pound. Reasonable Internet access is available.

Down the road next to Huggo's is **Java on the Rock,** an early morning coffee bar serving freshly brewed Kona coffee, espresso, and a variety of fresh-baked pastries. Takeout is an option, but perhaps it would be better to sit along the waterfront and savor your drink while you enjoy the harbor scene. A friendly place with lots of "Aloha." Open daily 6–11 A.M. except major holidays. For something a bit more substantial at the same great location, try lunch or the late lunch menu from 2:30–4:30 P.M.

**Buns in the Sun** bakery and deli, 808/326-2774, at the back of the Lanihau Center, is open daily from 5 A.M. but closes by mid-afternoon. Buns not only sells fresh-brewed gourmet coffee, pastries, and bread, it also makes American-standard and Hawaiian-style breakfasts, unique lunch sandwiches, tasty wraps, and more. If you're out and about, this is a good stop.

The **French Bakery,** 808/326-2688, open weekdays 5:30 A.M.–3 P.M., Sat. 5:30 A.M.–2 P.M. in the Old Kona Industrial Area, is a budget gourmet deli/restaurant where the food is great and the prices are low. Not only does it have the full range of pastries, breads, and other goodies you would expect, it has wonderful and inexpensive sandwiches and coffee.

Nearby is **Pot Belli Deli,** 808/329-9454, open weekdays 7 A.M.–4 P.M. The refrigerated deli case holds such things as chicken, ham, or tuna salad sandwiches, spinach pie, and bagels with cream cheese. The shelves hold all the condiments and extras you need for a terrific picnic lunch. You can get your order to go or eat at one of the few booths inside.

If you're looking for pastries and sandwiches while at the Keauhou Shopping Center, head for **Daylight Donuts and Deli,** 808/324-1833; open from 6 A.M.

## Moderate

**Cafe Sibu,** in the Kona Banyan Court, 808/329-1112, open daily 11:30 A.M.–2 P.M. for lunch and 5–9 P.M. for dinner, is an Indonesian restaurant serving savory marinated meats and vegetables spiced with zesty sauces and flame grilled. The restaurant, across from the seawall under the big banyan tree, has only a few outside tables and makes a light attempt at decor with a few antique Indonesian masks. If you're hungry, go for the *gado gado* for $11.50, an Indonesian salad layered with spices and peanut sauce that can be dinner for one or an appetizer salad for two or three. *Saté*, curry, and stir-fry dishes can be made with chicken, beef, pork, shrimp, or vegetables for $10.25–14.25, or try the truly authentic *ayam panggang pedis,* a grilled and marinated spicy chicken. Although slightly more expensive, the combination plates are good deals, as they let you try a number of items. Lunch prices are a couple bucks cheaper. Cafe Sibu definitely serves some of the tastiest and most interesting, moderately priced food in Kailua-Kona.

Look for a bright *akachochin,* a red paper lantern, marking the entrance to **Bistro Yokohama** in the Ali'i Sunset Plaza, 808/329-9661, open Mon.–Fri. 11:30 A.M.–1:30 P.M. and Mon.–Sat. 5:30–9 P.M. for dinner. Inside is simplicity: Japanese kites, light wood furniture, and a few glowing lanterns. The classic lunches include *soba* sukiyaki, *teishoku, donburi,* or a fixed-plate lunch, such as *donkatsu* pork cutlets, that includes an appetizer, salad, rice, and miso soup. Some traditional dinner entrées are cooked right at your table, like sukiyaki or *shabu shabu,* thin slices of beef and assorted vegetables boiled in stock, and most dinners are in the $20 range. Although in a shopping plaza, both the atmosphere and cuisine are genuine.

A few steps away is **Thai Rin Thai Restaurant,** 808/329-2929. Open Mon.–Sat. for lunch and dinner and Sun. for dinner only, this restaurant offers lunch for under $8 and dinners for around $10, with chef's specials like crab stir-fry and deep-fried fish for $13–21. Located in the heart of the strip, this is a convenient choice.

The **Kona Ranch House,** 808/329-7061, located at the corner of Kuakini Hwy. and Ololi Rd., is a delightful restaurant with something for everyone. It has two rooms: the family-oriented Paniolo Room, where hearty appetites are filled family-style; and the elegant Plantation Lanai, where both your palate and sense of beauty are satiated. This cheery restaurant is well regarded in town and epitomizes plantation dining. The Kona Ranch House is the type of establishment where you get more than you pay for. The menu is mostly standard American fare with a heavy dollop of fish and seafood. It's a popular place, you may need reservations for breakfast on the weekends. Open 6:30 A.M.–2 P.M. for breakfast and lunch, and Sun. for brunch. Reservations are taken for dinner, served 4:30–9 P.M. Meats are a large part of the extensive menu—some are from the Parker Ranch—and most dinner entrées run $14–20.

**Basil's Pizzeria and Restaurant** in downtown Kailua-Kona, 808/326-7836, open daily 11 A.M.–10 P.M., is a place that makes its own pizza dough. Individual gourmet pizzas are $5.95–10.95, depending upon your choice of toppings; New York–style pizza, 14-inch and 16-inch, is $10.95–17.95. Besides pizza, Basil's offers soup of the day for $3.50, Italian antipasto at $7.95, angel hair primavera for $10.95, shrimp marinara for $14.95, eggplant parmigiana at $10.95, and an assortment of other fine Italian foods. A nightly "fresh catch special" is priced around $15, or you can order any number of sandwiches for under $7. Pizza by the slice is available 11 A.M.–5 P.M. only, and you can do takeout. If you don't care to come down, Basil's offers free delivery of any menu item in the Kailua area. So go ahead, recline on your condo lanai and call Basil's, and they'll be over *molto rapido.*

**Cassandra's Greek Taverna,** 808/334-1066, open daily 7 A.M.–10 P.M., on the 2nd floor directly across from the Kona pier, is decorated in a predominant blue and white motif reminiscent of the Greek Isles. Breakfast runs 7–11 A.M., and lunch is served 11 A.M.–4 P.M., with most items under $9. Dinner expands the lunch menu and includes such offerings as traditional appetizers like dolmades (grape leaves stuffed with meat and rice) and *keftedes* (pan-fried Greek meatballs), and savory entrées like a gyro plate, Greek-style baby-back pork ribs, shrimp *posidonian,* or souvlaki made with chicken, beef, or lamb. Prices are usually $14–25, a platter for two runs $45; full bar. This is the place to come to for eastern Mediterranean food. Earthy, vibrant Greek music to stir the soul wafts through the air, and belly dancing is performed for guests on Friday and Saturday evenings.

**Quinn's,** across from King Kamehameha's Kona Beach Hotel, 808/329-3822, is Kona's socially eclectic bar and grill where everyone from local bikers to pink-roasted tourists and tournament anglers are welcomed. It's also a roost for night owls who come here to munch and have a beer or mixed drink when everything else in town is closed. The inside bar is cozy, friendly, and sports-oriented. Quinn's is open daily for lunch 11 A.M.–5 P.M. and for dinner 5–11 P.M. For lunch, a gigantic mound of shrimp and crab salad is wonderful. The fresh catch-of-the-day sandwiches with salad or charbroiled burgers are a deal. Fill up for under $10. Dinner entrées are juicy filet mignon, chicken stir-fry, and fresh catch sautéed or broiled. Main entrées are $19–23 and all include soup or dinner salad, vegetable, rice, and Quinn's home-fried potatoes. For the less hearty eater, reasonably priced specialties include tenderloin tips sautéed in brandy with onions, shrimp and chips, and fish and chips, all for less than $10.50.

Cool down with a frosty margarita and watch life go by as you perch on a stool at the upstairs location of **Pancho and Lefty's,** 808/326-2171, near the summer palace. Happy hour, running 3–6 P.M., offers 12-ounce drafts for $1 and big, potent 16-ounce margaritas for $2.75. Open daily 11 A.M.–10 P.M. for food, menu selections begin with appetizers such as buffalo wings, skinny dippers (potatoes covered with bacon and cheese, guacamole and sour cream, or refried beans and cheese), and nachos. Full dinners include taco salad, seafood salad with crisp greens, enchiladas, or fajitas—steak, chicken, or seafood (fresh catch). Specials are enchilada rancheros, *carne asada,* seafood Vera Cruz, or a tamale dinner. Most everything is in the $10–17 range, with a few items for two over $20. Pancho and Lefty's is a good-time place with satisfying food that's easy on the budget.

When you enter the Kaloko Industrial Park, just past mile marker 97 and about three miles north from Kailua-Kona, the setting makes you think you're after plumbing supplies. That's here too, but you'll also find terrific food prepared by one of Hawaii's greatest chefs at **Sam Choy's Kaloko Restaurant,** 808/326-1545, open daily 6 A.M.–2 P.M. and Sun. from 7 A.M. To get there, turn right onto Hinalani St., go up one block and take a right onto Kanalani St., and a left two blocks down onto Kauhola St. Look for Sam's in a nondescript gray building halfway up the hill on the right. The atmosphere is pleasant enough, but those who have dined on Sam's sumptuous creations come for the food! Breakfasts like the ultimate stew omelette (a three-egg omelette filled with Sam's beef stew) for $7.50, steak and eggs for $10.95, or any one of the various "loco moco" will keep you going most of the day. The lunch menu includes fresh island fish prepared *poke* style and then flash-fried for $7.50, saimin at $3, and Kaloko noodle mania for $7.50. While not the cheapest in town, the portions are large and the flavors perfect.

Up in the Crossroads Shopping Center on Henry St. is a wonderful gourmet restaurant that serves meals at moderate prices. This is Amy Ota's **Oodles of Noodles,** 808/329-9222. Don't be put off by the shopping center location—the food is great and the rich colorful decor, low light, and dark tile floor are conducive to a fine meal. Oodles serves a fusion of East and West, with such items as Japanese *udon,* Thai rice noodles, and Italian pasta, that leads to unique and surprising flavors. Almost everything has noodles of some sort in it, including the appetizers, soups, and salads, and with many items you can create your own combinations. Some menu selections include crisp Thai calamari in noodle nest, red miso *ramen* with shiitake mushrooms and tofu, Asian risotto, Peking duck with herbs and spices, and *aglio olio* linguini with shellfish, and there are always featured specials. Most lunch entrées cost under $12, dinners from $14–24, while the appetizers, soups, and salads run $7–15. Food here is a treat for the taste buds, and the variety of noodle dishes is outstanding. Amy's restaurant is an excellent choice.

With a menu that's at least twice as long as you might expect to find, **Bangkok House** Thai restaurant, 808/329-7764, serves plentiful food in a pleasing setting in the King Kamehameha Mall. Your choices include standard Thai fare, with soups, curries, rice, noodles, and vegetarian dishes, plus many surprises. Most entrées run $8–10, with specials up to $15. The lunch menu is a few bucks cheaper.

Overlooking the Royal Kona Resort tennis courts is **Tres Hombres,** 808/329-2173, a Mexican restaurant with a strong island influence. *Taquitos,* tostadas, burritos, *chili rellenos,* fajitas, and all the usual offerings are on the menu, as are steak, fish, and seafood items. Lunch and dinner have roughly the same menu, with few items more than $17. Before dinner, stop at the bar for a cool one and watch the sunset. Open Sun.–Thurs. 11:30 A.M.–9 P.M. and Fri. and Sat. until 10 P.M. This is a good choice for Mexican. For a more local Mexican restaurant, try **Reuben's,** 808/329-4686, down on Kuakini Hwy.

**Bubba Gump's,** adjacent to Waterfront Row, is one of the newest of the midrange restaurants along Ali'i Dr. It's a fun, family restaurant that, of course, does shrimp and seafood.

Moving back a generation brings you to the **Hard Rock Cafe,** 808/329-8866, upstairs in the Coconut Grove Marketplace, where the 1970s and 1980s is the theme. Music accompanies your meal and memorabilia covers the walls. The Hard Rock has standard American fare with many burger and sandwich choices, plus items like hickory barbecued chicken, smoked pork chops, and fresh catch of the day, mostly under $10. Of course, there is a bar to serve drinks and a counter that sells Hard Rock merchandise. Open daily 11 A.M.–11 P.M., 11:30 P.M. on Fri. and Sat.

Upstairs in another of the Coconut Grove Shopping Center buildings is **Lulu's,** 808/331-2633, a breezy, open-air place with food as pleasing as the setting. *Pu pu,* sandwiches, burger, and sides are mostly under $10, and the signature ribs and pork chops go for $13.95. After dinner, move to the long bar for a good-time brew.

Downstairs from Lulu's is **Durty Jake's,** 808/329-7366. Open all day, food here is easy, and dinner specials are barbecue chicken and Cajun fish and shrimp. A long list of *pu pu* are on the menu for those who don't care for a full meal. As it's on the sidewalk level, Durty Jake's has plenty of walk-by traffic, runs happy hour 4–6 P.M. daily, and offers live music Tues.–Sat. nights.

Up above the sand volleyball court at the rear of Coconut Grove Marketplace is the **Outback Steakhouse,** 808/326-2555. An eatery from down under, this is an easygoing place—appropriate for Hawaii—that's open for dinner daily 4:30–10 P.M., with happy hour until 7 P.M. Start your meal with bloomin' onions, kookaburra wings (buffalo chicken wings), or Brisbane caesar salad. Ranging $12–22, main entrées include Ayers Rock steak, ribs on the barbie, Alice Springs chicken, or Walhalla pasta. A theme restaurant with an adventurous clientele, Outback Steakhouse is worth a try.

South of town in the Keauhou Shopping Center is the breezy, easygoing **Drysdale's Too** restaurant, 808/322-0070, where you can get burgers, sandwiches, hot dogs, gyros, and any number of meat and meatless dishes, plus soups, salads, tropical drinks, and beer. A friendly, comfortable place, it's somehow familiar, and you'll be happy that it won't cost an arm and a leg. Burgers and sandwiches run $6–10, while most entrées are less than $15.

## Expensive

At **Huggo's Restaurant,** on Ali'i Dr. next door to the Royal Kona Resort, 808/329-1493, it's difficult to concentrate on the food because the setting is so spectacular. If you were any closer to the sea, you'd be in it, and of course the sunsets are great. Because it is built on a pier, you can actually feel the floor rock. Huggo's is open Mon.–Fri. 11:30 A.M.–2:30 P.M. for full lunch service, 2:30–4:30 P.M. for late-lunch sandwiches only served at the bar, and 5:30–10 P.M. for dinner, with entertainment most nights. Lunch is reasonable, with tasties like Huggo's club, a pizza with your choice of toppings for around $10, or a classic Huggo's burger. The dinner menu is superb and starts with fresh sashimi and seafood chowder made from clams and fresh fish and seasoned with sherry, cream sauce, and butter. The best entrées come from the sea just outside the door and are priced daily at around $26.

Also worth trying is shrimp scampi, Australian lobster tail, and chicken with ginger orange sauce. Huggo's has been in business for more than 30 years and is consistently outstanding. Enjoy free *pu pu* Mon.–Fri. 4–6 P.M. while sipping a cocktail as the red Kona sun dips into the azure sea.

**The Kona Inn Restaurant** at the Kona Inn Shopping Village, 808/329-4455, open daily for lunch and dinner, is a lovely but lonely carry-over from the venerable old Kona Inn. On entering, notice the marlin over the doorway and a huge piece of hung glass through which the sunset sometimes forms prismatic rainbows. The bar and dining area are richly appointed in native koa and made more elegant with a mixture of turn-of-the-20th-century wooden chairs, polished hardwood floors, and sturdy open-beamed ceilings. If you want to enjoy the view, try a cocktail and some of the *pu pu* served until closing. Lunch is reasonable at the café grill, serving mostly light foods, sandwiches, burgers, soups, and salads. Dinner is served 5:30–9:30 P.M., reservations recommended. The menu is heavy on fish and meat but offers a few Asian stir-fry dishes and pastas. Expect dinner entrées to run $15–25. The Kona Inn Restaurant epitomizes Kona beachside dining, and the view is simply superb.

**Michaelangelo's,** in Waterfront Row, 808/329-4436, is run by Mike Medeiros—a true *Mediterraneo* if there ever was one. It is open for lunch daily 11 A.M.–4 P.M. and for dinner until 10 P.M., with happy hour 11 A.M.–5 P.M. Every night of the year from 10 P.M. until 2 A.M., the restaurant converts into a disco, so there's music and dancing for late-night revelers. Savory selections include antipasto for $9.95–15.95, soup of the day for $5.95, and specialty salads that could make a meal. The lunch menu is a simplified and slightly less expensive version of the evening menu. The dinner menu, with most entrées in the $16–25 range, includes spaghetti marinara, chicken parmesan, lava-fire calamari, or cioppino. A children's menu helps keep costs down for families. The large oceanfront room is appointed with open-beamed ceilings joined by distinctive copper couplings, with Casablanca fans.

Also in Waterfront Row, **Beachcomber's,** 808/329-2451, open daily for lunch

11 A.M.–2 P.M. and dinner 5–9 P.M., has a good reputation for service, value, and well-prepared food. Primarily, it is a steak and seafood house with most dinner entrées costing $20–28, with lobster or combination plates with lobster much pricier. Several options are prime rib, rack of lamb, spiced yellowfin *'ahi,* and Australian cold-water lobster tail. The Sunday brunch menu is a variation of the daily lunch fare. The location is very pleasant, away from the street noise and with a good view of the sea.

The **Kona Beach Restaurant,** at King Kamehameha's Kona Beach Hotel, 808/329-2911, is open daily for breakfast and dinner and is especially known for its Sunday champagne brunch served 9 A.M.–1 P.M., $25.95 for adults. The long tables are laden with fruit, vegetables, pasta salad, peel-and-eat shrimp, omelettes, waffles, hot entrées from fresh catch to sashimi, and desserts so sinful you'll be glad that someone's on their knees praying at Sunday services. Friday and Saturday nights are very special because of the Prime Rib & Seafood Buffet at $24.95, which brings hungry people from around the island. Other nights also have their special buffets: Monday is Hawaiian for $13.95, Tuesday features crab and tempura at $19.95, Wednesday brings Chinese delicacies for $15.95, and Thursday is an Italian buffet priced at $15.95. Dinner is served 5:30–8 P.M., until 9 P.M. on Fri. and Sat. Served 6–10 A.M., the breakfast buffet for $11.95 is a deal, and there are children's prices for all meals. The Kona Beach Restaurant is sure to please. The restaurant itself is tasteful, but the best feature is an unobstructed view of the hotel's beach, especially fine at sunset.

If you're staying out near Keauhou, rather than driving into town, reserve a seat at the casually elegant **Kama'aina Terrace Restaurant,** 808/322-3441, at the Ohana Keauhou Beach Resort. Open to the ocean breezes, from your table you can look out across the grass lawn to the rocky shoreline. While the restaurant is open for breakfast, it is perhaps best in the evening. Appetizers, soups, and salads run $7–12. For an entrée, choose from such items as chili-crusted *'ahi,* oven-roasted chicken, marinated rib-eye steak, or a lamb chop, all in the $18–25 range.

Also out in Keauhou, located at the Outrigger

Kanaloa at Kona condominium, is **Edward's at Kanaloa,** 808/322-1434. Edward's provides outdoor seating under a covered arbor at the oceanside, nearly on the rocks. This is a perfect spot for a sunset dinner: small, intimate, and romantic. The staff is attentive, there is an extensive wine list, and a bar can set you up with any drink that you wish. While American-style breakfasts and light lunches are served, the restaurant is best known for dinner. Start your evening meal with a stuffed mussel appetizer and move on to a chilled gazpacho soup. All in the $20–24 range, the short menu has medallions of pork with prunes, rack of lamb, tenderloin of beef *gaufrettes,* grilled chicken breast, and local fresh fish. Choosing dessert is a difficult task, as your choices include praline chocolate mousse cake, crème brûlée, roasted Kea'au banana tiramisu, and the like. An excellent choice for a night out, reservations are required and a guest pass to the property is necessary.

## Fine Dining

*Oui oui, Monsieur,* but of course we have zee restaurant *français.* It is **La Bourgogne,** 808/329-6711, open Mon.–Sat. 6–10 P.M., located at the corner of Nalani St., about three miles south of downtown Kailua-Kona along Rte. 11. For those who just can't live without escargot or real French onion soup, you've been saved. How much will it set you back? Plenty, *mon petit!* Cold and hot appetizers include *pâté du chef* for $8.95, and escargots de Bourgogne for $7.95, while scrumptious French onion soup for $6.95 or homemade lobster bisque for $7.50 will follow. For salads, order greens with local goat cheese or greens with mango and lobster. Titillating seafood and poultry entrées, $25–32, feature fresh catch of the day; lobster braised with shallots, tomato, brandy, and cream; and roast duck breast with raspberries and pine nuts. Meat courses, $26–32, include delectable roast rack of lamb with creamy mustard sauce, tenderloin of venison with sherry and pomegranate sauce, and osso bucco veal shank in red wine. Top off your gourmet meal with fresh, made-in-house desserts like crème brûlée or a lemon tartlet. This restaurant, small and slightly out of the way, is definitely worth a visit for those who enjoy exceptional food—a memorable gastronomic experience. Definitely call for reservations, perhaps a couple of days in advance.

**Jameson's-by-the-Sea,** 77-6452 Ali'i Dr., 808/329-3195, is open for lunch weekdays 11 A.M.–2:30 P.M. and dinner every evening 5:30–9:30 P.M. Jameson's makes a good attempt at elegance with high-backed wicker chairs, crystal everywhere, white linen table settings, and a back-lit fish tank in the entry. The sea foams white and crashes on the shore just outside the restaurant's open windows. The quality of the food is very good, just shy of gourmet. People come here for fish, and they are never disappointed. The lunch menu lists appetizers like sashimi, salmon pâté, and fried calamari, and a variety of sandwiches. The dinner menu offers the same appetizers but adds a seafood platter with sashimi, shrimp, and fresh oysters. The dinner entrées range from fresh catches like *opakapaka, ono,* and mahimahi to fried shrimp and scallops with oyster sauce and Chinese pea pods. Other full meals include filet mignon with béarnaise sauce, baked stuffed shrimp, sesame chicken, and shrimp curry with mango chutney, mostly under $27. For dessert, save room for the assortment of homemade chiffon pies.

## Brewery

The **Kona Brewing Company** has been creating quality beer since the mid-1990s. It produces nearly a dozen varieties from a light lager to a dark porter, perhaps the best known of which are Pacific Golden Ale, Fire Rock Pale Ale, and Longboard Lager, with additional seasonal brews. Bar beer is brewed on the premises at a rate of about 150 barrels a week, but retail bottled beer is brewed in California according to Kona Brewing Company's recipe. Free brewery tours and tastings are given weekdays at 10:30 A.M. and 3 P.M., but if you miss the tour, stop by the brewery and café anyway to try a beer or two. The café serves mostly pizza, salads, and sandwiches, nothing elegant, but a good complement to the brew. A seat at the bar gets you up close to all the action there, or you may choose a booth inside or a table out on the lanai where you can watch the sun go down as easily as the beer in your tall, cool glass. The kitchen is open until 10 P.M., the

BIG ISLAND OF HAWAI'I

bar later. Periodic live music is performed, mostly on Sundays. Located behind Zac's Business Center in the North Kona Shopping Center, Kona Brewpub is open for lunch and dinner daily.

## ENTERTAINMENT

The most memorable evening experience for most is free: watching the sunset from Kailua Pier and taking a leisurely stroll along Ali'i Drive. Otherwise, Kona nights come alive mainly in the restaurants and dining rooms of the big hotels and fancier restaurants. The two lu'au have "Polynesian Revues" of one sort or another, which are generally good, clean, sexy fun, but of course these shows are limited only to the lu'au guests. For those who have "dancin' feet" or wish to spend the evening listening to live music, there's a small but varied selection from which to choose.

**Huggo's Restaurant,** with its romantic waterfront setting along Ali'i Dr., and the attached Huggo's on the Rocks, feature music 8:30 P.M.–12:30 A.M. The entertainment changes nightly: karaoke, smooth Jawaiian, other mellow contemporary sounds, or a touch of rock or jazz now and again.

For other music over the dinner hour and beyond, try **Durty Jake's** at the Coconut Grove Marketplace or the **Kona Brewpub,** which has live music, particularly on Sunday.

The **Aston Keauhou Beach Resort** soothes you with easy listening, Hawaiian style, at the veranda bar, nightly except Sunday and Monday.

At the Royal Kona Resort's open-air **Windjammer Lounge,** sip a flavorful tropical concoction while watching the sun melt into the Pacific. Entertainment is offered several evenings a week, featuring hula at sundown.

In downtown Kailua-Kona, the **Billfish Bar** at King Kamehameha's Kona Beach Hotel has live entertainment Friday and Saturday 6–9 P.M., featuring mellow Hawaiian music.

**Kimo's Family Buffet** at the Kona Bay Hotel offers a free hula show 6–8 P.M. Tues.–Sun. during dinner. As the entertainment is performed outdoors near the pool, passersby are also treated to lovely strains of Hawaiian music and swaying hips.

From 6–7 P.M. on Friday, stop by for a free Polynesian show at the Keauhou Shopping Center.

After all the other bars and restaurants have closed, head to **Michaelangelo's** for disco dancing every night 10 P.M.–2 A.M. at Waterfront Row.

For a quiet beer, sports talk, or just hanging out with the local people, try the bars at **Quinn's** or **Ocean View Inn,** both in downtown Kailua-Kona.

**Makalapua Stadium Cinemas,** 808/327-0444, located up by the Kmart, or the **Keauhou 7 Cinemas,** 808/324-7200, at the Keauhou Shopping Center, both show first-run movies. Tickets run $7.50 for adults. Call for times and current showings.

### Lu'au

**Tihati's Drums of Polynesia Lu'au,** at the Royal Kona Resort, 808/329-3111, held every Monday, Wednesday, and Friday, offers an evening of entertainment and feasting, Hawaiian style. The lu'au begins at 5:15 P.M. and is followed by an open bar, lavish buffet, and thrilling entertainment for three fun-filled hours. Many supposedly authentic lu'au play-act with the *imu*-baked pig, but here it is carved and served to the guests. Prices are $55 adults, $25 children ages 6–12, free for children under age five. For the show only, which starts at 7 P.M., the rates are $28 adult and $18 children 6–12. Reservations are strongly recommended.

King Kamehameha's Kona Beach Hotel, 808/326-4969, sways with Hawaiian chants during its famous **Island Breeze Lu'au** held every Sunday, Tuesday, Wednesday, Thursday, and Friday on the beach and grounds of King Kamehameha's last residence, Ahu'ena. The pig is placed into the *imu* every morning at 10:15 A.M. and the festivities begin in the evening with a lei greeting at 5:30 P.M., followed by a crafts demonstration, torch-lighting, and an *imu* ceremony at 6 P.M. Cocktails flow 6–8 P.M.; the 22-course lu'au dinner is served 6:30–8:30 P.M., with the Polynesian show starting at 7:30 P.M. Prices are $55 adults, $21 children 6–12, free for children five and under. Limited cocktail and show seating runs $30 adult and $14.50 children. Reservations are required. Call 808/326-4969 or stop by the lu'au desk in the lobby of the hotel; www.islandbreezeluau.com.

## RECREATION

### Snorkeling and More

For snorkeling equipment rental, try **Snorkel Bob's,** 808/329-0770, www.snorkelbob.com, located across from Huggo's; it has some of the best prices, equipment, and services on the island. Gear, which includes mask, snorkel tube, and fins, is rented for a 24-hour day or by the week. The snorkel set runs $2.50–9 a day or $9–35 a week, depending on the quality. Rental boogie boards are also available, and Bob and his crew can arrange tours as well.

The **Kona Beach Shack,** 808/329-7494, at the King Kamehameha's Kona Beach Hotel, not only rents snorkel gear at $7 a day, they also rent kayaks, paddleboats, boogie boards, and other beach and water equipment. The Beach Shack also can arrange guided kayak and snorkel tours, outrigger canoe rides, snuba, an underwater tour that involves wearing a diver's helmet, and most

activities that take place from the Kailua Pier. Open daily 9 A.M.–5 P.M.

**Miller's Snorkeling,** 808/326-1771, at the Kona Bali Kai condo, rents complete snorkeling gear for $7 per day or $15 per week. It also rents boogie boards and beach accessories and is open daily 8 A.M.–5 P.M.

Next to Snorkel Bob's in a small freestanding building is **Honu Sports,** 808/938-9795. Honu Sports does snorkel, scuba, and kayak rental and tours.

Others in town that rent scuba equipment and/or offer guided tours are **Jack's Diving Locker,** 808/329-7585, **Kona Coast Divers,** 808/329-8802, **Sandwich Isle Divers,** 808/329-9188, and **Big Island Divers,** 800/329-6068. Most dive shops also rent snorkel gear.

### Bicycling

**Dave's Bike and Triathlon Shop,** 808/329-4522, owned and pedaled by triathlete Dave Bending, is located just a long stride or two from the beginning of the Ironman Triathlon across from King Kamehameha's Kona Beach Hotel in the Kona Square Shopping Center. Dave rents mountain bikes, hybrids, full-sus-

ROBERT NILSEN

**boats anchored in Kailua Bay**

pension bikes, and a few road bikes from $15 a day to $60 a week. Prices include helmet, water bottles, map, bicycle lock, and, most importantly, road advice. Dave knows his stuff, so pay heed! If you want to do more than just pedal along the beach, come see Dave.

**Hawaiian Pedals,** at the Kona Inn Shopping Village, 808/329-2294, rents basic mountain bikes and hybrids. A sister store, the **Bike Works,** 808/326-2453, 74-5599 Lehua St., Ste. F-3, up in the industrial area, rents suspension mountain bikes and road bikes. Rates for 24 hours are $20 for mountain and hybrids, $25 for road and front-suspension bikes, and $30 for full-suspension mountain bikes. Five-hour and multi-day rates can also be arranged. Hawaiian Pedals is open daily; the Bike Works is closed on Sunday, so if you rent a bike there on Saturday you must rent it for two days.

**B&L Bike and Sports,** 808/329-3309, offers bike sales, repair, and as many rental bikes as any other shop in town. Located just across the street from Hilo Hattie's, B&L rents road and mountain bikes for $30 a day or $150 a week.

## Submarine Tour

One company in Kailua offers a once-in-a-lifetime, below-the-surface-of-the-water experience to view undersea life at the fish eye level. **Atlantis Submarine,** 808/329-6626 or 800/548-6262, allows everyone to live out the fantasy of Captain Nemo on a silent cruise under the waves. This underwater dive lasts about a half hour and descends to 120 feet, where everything seems to turn to blues and greens. You cruise in air-conditioned comfort and have great viewing out the two-foot-diameter windows. Cruises run four times a day 8:30 A.M.–1:30 P.M.; the price is $84 adults and $42 children. Find the office across the street from the pier.

## Sunset Dinner Cruise

**Captain Beans' Polynesian Cruise** departs Kailua Pier daily at 5:15 P.M. and returns at about 8 P.M. If you are after a pleasant but not adventurous sunset cruise, take this one, but keep in mind that this is the bus tour equivalent of a boat ride. On board, you are entertained while the bar dispenses liberal drinks and the deck groans with an all-you-can-eat buffet. The best part—after the sunset—is that you get a terrific panorama of the Kona Coast from the sea. You can't help having a good time on this cruise, and if the boat sinks with all that food and booze in your belly, you're a goner—but what a way to go! Minimum age is 21 years, $52 includes tax, tip, and transportation from area hotels. Reservations suggested; call 808/329-2955.

## Tennis

The Royal Kona Resort has four latexite courts, three of which are lighted for night play, that are open to resort guests and nonguests alike. Court fees are a reasonable $10 per day. Avid tennis players should check the weekly rates. Instruction can be arranged and racquets rented for $3–8. Call the pro shop at 808/334-1093 to reserve court time, particularly for night play.

Island Slice Tennis, 808/322-6112, at the Keauhou Beach Hotel, offers reserved tennis play on six lighted courts for $5 for the first hour and $10 after that. Round robins are held at various times throughout the week and instruction runs $40 an hour.

## Golf

The **Kona Country Club** is a lovely golf course near the end of Ali'i Drive that has 18-hole ocean and mountain courses, with grand views over this eminently rocky coast. Greens fees run $95 for the mountains course and $115 for the ocean course, $75 and $85, respectively, after noon. The pro shop is open daily and the adjacent Vista Restaurant at the clubhouse serves breakfast and lunch. Call 808/322-2595 for tee times.

If the local golf courses are just too expensive or if you're just not sure enough about your game, spend some time first at the **Swing Zone** miniature golf course and practice at the Menehune Country Club 18-hole grass putting course that's shaped like the Big Island itself. One round runs $6 and includes a putter and balls, no players under age 12; golf rules apply. This course has no lights so it's daytime play only. Also at the Swing Zone is a full-size driving range that's lit at night; a pail of 60 balls costs $6. If these two aren't enough to wear you out, try the batting cage, also lit, where $1 buys 10 pitches. Open daily until 9 P.M., the Swing Zone is located across the street from the Old Airport Beach Park; 808/329-6909.

# SHOPPING

The Kailua-Kona area has an abundance of two commodities near and dear to a tourist's heart: sunshine and shopping malls. Below is a selection of Kona-area shopping centers and malls, including a general idea of what they contain.

### Shopping Along Ali'i Drive
**King Kamehameha's Kona Beach Hotel Mall,** fully air-conditioned, features a cluster of specialty shops which include an ABC Store, selling wine, liquor, and beer along with suntan lotions, gift items, magazines, novels, and T-shirts; Jewel Palace, sparkling with watches and fine jewelry fashioned from gold and silver; Silver Reef, featuring Hawaiian-motif jewelry, glassware, Japanese dolls, and porcelainware; and a host of other gift, craft, and apparel shops. The most intriguing of the bunch is the Made on the Big Island store, with its large sampling of local crafts and gifts.

Kitty-corner to King Kamehameha's Hotel is the **Kona Seaside Mall,** where most shops open daily 9 A.M.–6 P.M. Here you'll find Neptune's Garden, creating rainbows with its display of stained glass art fashioned into lamps, creative hangings, and vases, plus a few paintings. For clothing, try Tropical Tees for casual wear, Sandal Stop, Eel Skin Liquidators, and Bubi's Sportswear Center of Kona. Other shops are the Kona Coast Sunglass Company, Goldfish Jewelry, and DJ's Rentals for motorcycles and scooters.

The **Kona Square Shopping Center,** next to the Seaside Mall, features Mermaid's By The Sea, a distinctive ladies' and children's clothing boutique bright with alohawear, pareu, sundresses and evening dresses, and a ceiling hung with cherubic angels if you're not sharing your Hawaii vacation with one of your own. Directly across from Mermaid's is Island Silversmiths, Kona's oldest modern-day shop, in business since 1973, so you know it's doing something right. This tiny mall also has Dave's Bike and Triathlon Shop, UFO Parasail, and Maui Divers Jewelry.

Just down the way, the **Kona Banyan Court** has a dozen shops with a medley of goods and services. Unison is a surfing shop with T-shirts, sandals, hats, and boogie boards. The most impressive shop in the complex is Big Island Jewelers, owned and operated by brothers Flint and Gale Carpenter, master goldsmiths. The shop motto, "Have your jewelry made by a Carpenter," applies to custom-made jewelry fashioned to their or your personal design. Big Island Jewelers, in business since 1983 and open daily, does repairs and also carries a full line of pearls and loose stones that you can have mounted into any setting you wish. Cafe Sibu is located in the rear.

Kitty-corner from Hulihe'e Palace is **Kona Marketplace,** which offers a variety of shops in several adjacent buildings selling everything from diamonds to bathing suits. The restaurant Poncho and Lefty's has a prominent spot on the 2nd floor of one of the buildings. Here too is Kona Jewelers, specializing in fine jewelry and ceramics; Serendipity for fashions; the jam-packed Aloha From Kona specializes in baubles, bangles, postcards, handbags, and purses; and the Kona Flea Market stuck to the rear of the mall sells inexpensive travel bags, shells, beach mats, suntan lotion, and all the junk that you could want. For art, look at Kim Taylor Reece Gallery, Rapozo Gallery, or Aloha Art. Sandwich Isle Divers can set you up for a dive along this exciting coast. In the alley behind Poncho and Lefty's is the Middle Earth Bookshoppe, one of the best on the island.

One of the largest malls in Kailua is the **Kona Inn Shopping Village.** It spreads south from Hulihe'e Palace in a long meandering series of buildings, taking the place of what was the old Kona Inn Hotel. This shopping village boasts more than 40 shops selling fabrics, fashions, art, gems and jewelry, food, bicycles, souvenirs, and gifts. One shop in this mall is Hula Heaven, which specializes in vintage Hawaiian shirts and modern reproductions, plus some Hawaiiana collectibles. Prices for these fashionable shirts range from $50 for the "look-alikes" to $1,000 for the rarest of the classics. Because many of the items on display date from the 1940s and

1950s, the shop is like a trip back in time. Other stores include Kona Jewelry Factory, featuring island-inspired jewelry; Pacific Fine Art has an array of paintings and graphics from around the country; Surf N' Sandals for an amazing collection of coverings for your feet and head; Fare Tahiti Fabrics for incidental travel bags, pareu, and fabrics; Island Salsa featuring one-of-a-kind designer T-shirts, alohawear for the entire family, ladies' evening wear, swimwear, and dinner clothes; Golden Orchid Originals, a women's resort wear and casual wear shop; Kona Inn Jewelry, for worldwide treasures—one of the oldest and best-known shops for a square deal in Kona; Flamingo's for contemporary island clothing and evening wear mainly for women, Honolua Surf Co. and Sgt. Leisure for tropical wear, and an ABC Store for sundries.

**Waterfront Row** is a shopping and food complex in the center of downtown Kailua-Kona. Built of rough-cut lumber, it's done in period architecture reminiscent of an outdoor promenade in a Boston shipyard at the turn of the 20th century. Here, Crazy Shirts sells unique island creations that are wearable memories of your trip to the island, Bad Ass Coffee Company dispenses black brew by the cup or by the pound, and Wyland Galleries of Hawaii displays island-inspired paintings and sculpture. Restaurants include Beachcomber's for steaks and seafood and Michaelangelo's for fine Italian cuisine.

The smaller **Ali'i Sunset Plaza** has Japanese and Thai restaurants, the Lava Java coffee shop, and other shops that include the Kipuka Smoke Shop for cigars and accessories, Mana Beads and Jewelry, and Kilauea Clothing Company for vintage prints and alohawear.

Newest to the Kailua strip, located just down from the Royal Kona Resort, is **Coconut Grove Marketplace.** This shopping plaza, with its sand volleyball court, has about a dozen shops that include Rift Zone Gallery for a great collection of artwork. You can find coverings for your eyes at Sunglass Hut, fine clothing and alohawear at Malia Kane and Tropics, jewelry from Pia Moana Pearls, and Jack's Diving Locker can set you up on a scuba tour. Hungry? You'll find Hard Rock Cafe, Lulu's Restaurant, Durty Jack's, and Outback Steakhouse here.

## Shopping Along Palani Road

There are several malls on both sides of Palani Road, which heads away from the water, starting at the King Kamehameha Hotel. They include the following.

Backing up against King Kamehameha's Kona Beach Hotel is the small **King Kamehameha Mall,** where you will find, among other shops, the Kona Wine Market, with the town's largest selection of wines, Bangkok House Restaurant, and a couple of small shops for flowers, lei, and gift baskets.

Up from the King Kamehameha Mall is the **North Kona Shopping Center,** where Video Showplace, Body Glove cruises, Zac's Business Center, Kona Brewing Company and Brewpub, and Hele Mai laundry are located.

In the **Kona Sports Center** is B&L Bike and Sports shop. The official Ironman store, it has one of the largest selections of sporting equipment in town. Across the road is the Kona location of **Hilo Hattie's,** 808/329-7200, open 9:30 A.M.–5:30 P.M., where you can find family fashions, gifts, souvenirs, music, and packaged island foods. Hilo Hattie's offers free transportation to and from hotels in the area. Just around the corner is the **Kopiko Plaza,** a small mall with a smattering of inexpensive restaurants.

The **Lanihau Center,** along Palani Road between Kuakini Hwy. and Queen Ka'ahumanu Hwy., offers Longs Drugs for sundries and photo supplies; an assortment of restaurants including Buns in the Sun, Chili by Max, and Royal Jade Garden. Here as well are a Sack 'n Save supermarket, three banks, and the Kailua-Kona post office.

Across Palani Road, **Kona Coast Shopping Center** features a KTA Super Store for groceries and sundries, Starbucks Coffee, a couple of inexpensive eateries, a handful of fashion shops, and a Blockbuster Video where you can rent a movie for the evening. Blockbuster is open 10 A.M.–midnight weekend, until 11 P.M. on weekdays.

## Along Queen Kaʻahumanu Highway

At the corner of Queen Kaʻahumanu Hwy. and Henry Street is the new **Crossroads Center.** The two big stores here are Wal-Mart and Safeway, but other places of note are the fine restaurant Oodles of Noodles, Kona Natural Foods, and a Bank of Hawaii branch office. Across Henry Street in its own building is a huge Borders Books and Music store for the town's largest selection of books, CDs, and maps.

The new **Makalapua Center** above the old Kona Industrial Area has a huge Kmart which is open 6 A.M.–midnight daily for all general shopping needs, including clothing, household goods, and camping and athletic supplies. Macy's also has a big store here for family fashions, and the multiplex **Makalapua 7 Cinemas** has a screen to explore your every fantasy.

For those with a membership, Costco is located at the back of the Kaloko Industrial Park, north of Kailua-Kona on the way to the airport.

## Keauhou Shopping Center

If, god forbid, you haven't found what you need in Kailua, or if you suddenly need a "shopping fix," the Keauhou Shopping Center is at the corner of Aliʻi Drive and Kamehameha III Road in Keauhou. Look for flags waving in the breeze high on the hill marking the entrance. This mall houses over 40 shops and is one of the newest in the area. You can find all your food and prescription needs at KTA Super Store, the largest in the area, and mail your postcards at a branch post office. Head to Longs Drugs for everything from foot care products to photo developing, and Ace Hardware for nuts and bolts. For food, Drysdale's Too is an indoor/outdoor bar and grill where you can relax over a cold beer or choose from an extensive sandwich menu; you could also have a pizza at Rocky's Pizza, a taste of Asia at Royal Thai Cafe, a morning pick-me-up at Daylight Donuts and Deli, or a jolt at Bad Ass Coffee. Other shops include the Showcase Gallery, for glassware, paintings, ceramics, and local crafts; Borderlines and Paradise Found Boutique for apparel; and Alapaki's Hawaiian Gifts for a fine sampling of island gifts and souvenirs from black coral jewelry to koa bowls, and a replica of a Hawaiian double-hulled canoe made of coconut and cloth with traditional crab-claw sails to *tutu* dolls bedecked in colorful muʻumuʻu. Alapaki's represents some one hundred artist and craftspeople from all the major islands.

## Art and Specialty Shops

The **Palace Gift Shop** is located on the grounds of Huliheʻe Palace. Open daily except Sunday, it has quality Hawaiian craft items nice enough for gifts or memorabilia and a good collection of postcards and books on Hawaiiana.

One of the few art galleries in Kailua is the **Rift Zone Gallery,** 808/331-1100, located in the Coconut Grove Marketplace. This gallery displays the whole spectrum of artwork, almost exclusively from Big Island artists, including ceramics by Robert Joiner, bronze sculpture, paintings, wood art, furniture, and art glass. If you're looking to purchase art made in Hawaii, this is an excellent place to start.

Two other shops to look at for island art are **Wyland Galleries** at Waterfront Row, 808/334-0037, and **Kailua Village Artists Galleries,** 808/329-6653, a co-op gallery of Big Island artists at the Ohana Keauhou Beach Resort.

**Hawaii Forest and Trail** is a tour company that leads wonderful bird-watching, hiking, and mule ride eco-adventures around the island. It now has a retail store just up from the entrance to Honokohau Harbor that carries a small selection of hiking and outdoor supplies, adventure clothing, first-aid supplies, books, and USGS maps. While you're here, look into the company's tours. They are excellent.

**Kailua Candy Company,** 808/329-2522, www.kailua-candy.com, is located in the old Kona Industrial area on the corner of Kuakini Hwy. and Kiawi Streets. It was recognized as one of the "top 10 chocolate shops in the United States" in the February 1993 issue of *Bon Appetit* magazine. All the chocolates are made of the finest ingredients available, and all would try the willpower of Gandhi, but the specialty is the macadamia nut *honu,* Hawaiian for turtle. Shipping of all boxed candy is available at the cost of postage plus a handling fee. Open Mon.–Sat. 8 A.M.–6 P.M., until 4 P.M. on Sunday, have a peek through the plate glass windows into the kitchen to watch the work being done on weekdays and nibble samples of the products any day.

The **Banyan Tree Bazaar** (not really the name, but no one has bothered to give it one yet) is along Ali'i Drive across from the seawall. Look for local merchants selling locally made necklaces, earrings, and bracelets. Others sell various artworks, along with an array of inexpensive but neat tourist junk.

## Food Markets

**KTA Super Stores,** open daily 6 A.M.–midnight, are generally the cheapest markets in town and are located at the Kona Coast Shopping Center along Palani Rd. and at the Keauhou Shopping Center, at the extreme south end of Ali'i Drive at its junction with Kamehameha III Road. They're well stocked with sundries; an excellent selection of Asian foods, fresh veggies, fish, and fruit; and a smattering of health food. The market also contains a full-service pharmacy.

You'll also find a **Sack 'n Save** supermarket in the Lanihau Center, open 5 A.M.–midnight; and a **Safeway** in the newer Crossroads Center up on Henry Street.

**Kona Wine Market,** in the small King Kamehameha Mall, 75-5626 Kuakini Hwy., 808/329-9400, open Mon.–Sat. 9 A.M.–8 P.M., Sunday 10 A.M.–6 P.M., is the best wine shop on the Kona Coast. It features an impressive international selection of wine and varietals and a large cooler holds a fine selection of beer, both domestic and imported. Store shelves also hold wonderful gourmet munchies like Indian chutney, Sicilian olives, mustards, dressings, marinades, smoked salmon, hearty cheeses, and even pasta imported from Italy. Cigar smokers will also appreciate the humidor filled with fine cigars from around the world.

**Kona Reef Liquor and Deli** is south of town center at the Casa De Emdeko condominium. It's well stocked with liquor, drink, and packaged groceries, but at convenience-store prices, and the deli does simple food items. Open until 10 P.M., 8 P.M. on Sundays.

## Outdoor Markets

You'll find the **Kona Farmers' Market,** held every Wednesday, Friday, Saturday, and Sunday 7 A.M.–3 P.M. at the parking lot across from Hale Halawai County Park and Uncle Billy's Kona Hotel. A great place for locally grown fruits and vegetables, flowers, coffee, and crafts, this market has many booths that sell non-food items.

About two miles south of the pier on the *mauka* side of Ali'i Drive is the outdoor **Ali'i Gardens Marketplace,** open 9 A.M.–5 P.M. Wed.–Sunday. Vendors sell local produce, flowers, crafts, and some clothing and jewelry.

## Health Food Stores

Kona keeps you healthy with **Kona Natural Foods** in the Crossroads Shopping Center on Henry Street, 808/329-2296, open Mon.–Sat. 9 A.M.–9 P.M., Sunday until 7 P.M. Besides a good assortment of health foods, there are cosmetics, books, and dietary and athletic supplements. Vegetarians will like the ready-to-eat and inexpensive sandwiches, salads, soups, smoothies, and juices. Shelves are lined with teas, organic vitamins and herbs, and packaged foods. A cooler is filled with organic juices, cheeses, and soy milk. A refrigerator holds organic produce, while bins are filled with bulk grains. Overall a good store, there seems to be a greater emphasis on nutrition than natural organic foods.

A **General Nutrition Center,** located in the Lanihau Center and open daily from 10 A.M., is stocked with vitamins, food supplements, and minerals.

## Bookstores

In Kailua-Kona be sure to venture into **Middle Earth Bookshoppe,** 808/329-2123, tucked back in behind Kona Marketplace next to St. Michael's Church along Ali'i Drive. Open Mon.–Sat. 9 A.M.–9 P.M., Sunday to 6 P.M., this jam-packed bookstore has shelves laden with fiction, nonfiction, paperbacks, hardbacks, travel books, Hawaiiana, and lots of good maps. A great place to browse, much more intimate than the big chain stores.

In the North Kona Shopping Center, around back behind Zac's, is **Bargain Books,** 808/326-7790. Open daily, this shop has shelves stacked full of used books at half the cost of new books. If you're looking for a cheap read or just like browsing, have a look here.

The largest bookstore in town, however, is **Borders Books and Music,** 808/331-1668, at the corner of Queen Ka'ahumanu Hwy. and Henry Street. As at all Borders, you have a huge selection of paperbacks and hardcover books in all genres, a great Hawaiiana section, and a wide selection of maps, postcards, magazines, newspapers, and CDs. Special readings and musical events are held throughout the month, and Cafe Espresso is there for you when you get thirsty.

## Photo Needs

**Zac's Business Center,** 808/329-0006, in the North Kona Shopping Center, is open Mon.–Fri. 8 A.M.–7 P.M., Saturday 9 A.M.–6 P.M., and Sunday 10 A.M.–4 P.M. Although Zac's offers excellent photo lab services and sells a variety of film, this is much more than a photo store. Other services available are copies, fax, wrapping and shipping, printing, computer rental, and Internet connection.

**Longs Drugs'** photo departments at both the Lanihau Center and Keauhou Shopping Center have excellent prices on film and camera supplies. Both **Kmart** and **Wal-Mart** have one-hour photo finishing departments.

Located above the Kona Divers shop on Palani Road, **Hawaiian Camera Supply,** 808/326-7355, offers sales, service, and repair of cameras and sells a limited selection of film.

# INFORMATION AND SERVICES

## Emergencies and Health

The **Kona Community Hospital,** 808/322-9311, is located in Kealakekua, about 10 miles south of central Kailua-Kona with 24-hour emergency care.

For minor emergencies and urgent care, try **Hualalai Urgent Care,** at the Crossroads Medical Center on Henry Street, 808/327-4357; or **Kaiser Permanente,** 75-184 Hualalai Rd., 808/334-4400.

**Longs Drugs** in Kailua and Keauhou, **KTA Super Stores** in Keauhou, and **Kmart** at the Makalapua Center all have pharmacies.

## Information

Numerous activity information gazebos are located at the various malls in town, usually open until early evening, that can handle your questions about everything from dining to diving.

The **Kailua-Kona Public Library,** 808/327-4327, is at 75-140 Hualalai Rd., up from Hale Halawai Park. Open Tues. 10 A.M.–8 P.M., Wed. and Thurs. 9 A.M.–6 P.M., Fri. 11 A.M.–5 P.M., and Sat. 9 A.M.–5 P.M.; closed Sunday and Monday.

## Services

The First Hawaiian Bank, Bank of Hawaii, and the American Savings Bank all have branches and ATM machines at or next to the Lanihau Center on Palani Road. Bank of Hawaii also maintains ATM machines at KTA Super Stores and the Safeway supermarket.

The Kailua-Kona **post office** is at 74-5577 Palani Rd., at the Lanihau Center.

**Zac's Business Center,** 808/329-0006, is a full-service business, computer, shipping, printing, and photo developing shop at the North Kona Shopping Center. Internet access runs $8 an hour or $2.75 for 15 minutes.

**Mailboxes, The Business Center,** 808/329-0038, in the Crossroads Shopping Center also does packing, shipping, copies, and offers Internet access.

There are other Internet cafés in town, such as Lava Java, which generally charge $2–3 for 15 minutes or $7–8 an hour.

For a self-serve Laundromat, try **Hele Mai Laundromat** at the rear of the North Kona Shopping Center, open 6 A.M.–8:45 P.M.; **Tyke's Laundromat** at 74-5483 Kiawe St. in the old Kona Industrial Area, open 6:30 A.M.–9:30 P.M. daily; or the **Kona Wash Tub** along Alapa Street, which is open daily 8 A.M.–8 P.M. All have drop-off service.

# TRANSPORTATION

If you want to concentrate on the scenery and not the driving, take the **Ali'i Shuttle,** 808/775-7121. Painted white, the bus runs daily every 90 minutes (more or less) along Ali'i Drive

8:40 A.M.–7:40 P.M. and charges $2 each direction ($5 for a day pass, $20 weekly). The terminal points are Lanihau Shopping Center on the north end and Keauhou Shopping Center on the south end, with pickups at major hotels and beaches along the way. You can hail the bus and it will stop if possible.

Taxis will also do the trick for getting around town but can be quite expensive when going long distances. An alternative that works particularly well with groups is **Speedy Shuttle,** 808/329-5433, operating 7 A.M.–10 P.M. daily. Speedy Shuttle mainly services Kailua, Keauhou, and Kohala resort areas but will go farther for a price. It has a courtesy phone at the airport for your convenience in getting into town. Rates for single travelers from the airport to downtown Kailua run about $17 or $24 as far south as the Keauhou Beach Hotel. Going north, rates are about $30 to the Waikoloa Beach Resort or $38 to the Mauna Lani Resort area. Rates for groups are higher but the price per person drops dramatically.

# Holualoa

Holualoa (The Sledding Course) is an undisturbed mountain community perched high above the Kailua-Kona Coast with many of the island's most famous artists creating art in galleries that line up paintbrush to easel along its vintage main street. Prior to its transformation to an art community, Holualoa had another history. In days past, general stores, hotels, restaurants, bars, and pool halls lined its streets. Before Hawaii found its potential for tourism and started to develop its coastal areas, rural Hawaii was primarily agricultural, and the farms, and consequently most of the people, were located on the mountainsides. Large agricultural areas sustained working communities, and Holualoa was one such population center. While agriculture is still a big part of the local economy, it has been bolstered by tourism and the arts. Get there by taking the spur Rte. 182, known as **Hualalai Road,** off Rte. 11 (Queen Ka'ahumanu Hwy.) from Kailua-Kona, or by taking Rte. 180 (Mamalahoa Hwy.) from Honalo in the south or from Palani Junction in the north (where Rte. 190 and Rte. 180 meet). Nine-mile-long Rte. 180, a narrow mountain road that parallels Rte. 11, gives you an expansive view of the coastline below. Climbing Hualalai Road also affords glorious views of the coast. Notice the immediate contrast of the lush foliage against the scant vegetation of the lowland area. On the mountainside, bathed in tropical mists, are tall forest trees interspersed with banana, papaya, and mango trees. Flowering trees pulsating in the green canopy explode in vibrant reds, yellows, oranges, and purples. This is coffee country, so you'll see acres of coffee trees at numerous plantations and several coffee stands along Rte. 180, with more along Rte. 11 farther to the south. If you want to get away from the Kona heat and dryness, head up to the well-watered coolness of Holualoa at 1,400 feet in elevation. When leaving Holualoa for points south, stay on Rte. 180, the Mamalahoa Hwy., a gorgeous road with great views from the heights. Going north, take Rte. 180 until it meets Rte. 190, which leads around the western flank of Mt. Hualalai and very gradually uphill to Waimea. For the coast, Kaiminani Drive cuts down through the residential area of Kalaoa just north of Kailua-Kona, or, farther north, take Waikoloa Road to the South Kohala coastal region.

For the past one hundred years or so, a string of small dry goods and general merchandise stores dotted what are now Routes 180 and, south of Honalo, 11. Many of these stores were built by new immigrants to cater to the then-growing number of coffee workers and small-time farmers. Along this 20-mile stretch were some 90 stores. Most are now gone, some have been converted to other uses, but a few still function as they always have. Some are still operated by the original family, but most have different names, different owners, or different uses. Some of the best known are Komo Store, Kimura Lauhala Shop, Ushijima Store, Oshima Store, Kamigaki Market, and Fujihara Store. As you drive this road, stop in to get a sense of what these stores were like and consider what impact they had on the economy of the area. To help you along, pick up a copy of the *Guide to Kona Heritage Stores* put out by the Kona Historical Society.

## Galleries and Shops

After you wind your way up Hualalai Road through this verdant jungle area, you suddenly enter the village and are greeted by the **Kimura Lauhala Shop,** 808/324-0053, open weekdays 9 A.M.–5 P.M., Saturday until 4 P.M., closed Sunday. The shop, still tended by the Kimura family, has been in existence since 1915. In the beginning, Kimura's was a general store, but it always sold *lau hala* and became famous for its hats, which local people would make to barter for groceries. Famous on, and later off, the island, only *Kona-side* hats have a distinctive pull-string that makes the hat larger or smaller. The older generation Kimuras, and most of the friends who helped manufacture the hats, are getting on in age and can no longer keep up with the demand. Many hatmakers have passed away, and few young people are interested in keeping the art alive. Kimura's still has handmade hats, but the stock is dwindling. All *lau hala* weavings are done in Kona, while some of the other gift items are brought in. Choose from authentic baskets, floor mats, handbags, slippers, and of course an assortment of the classic sun hats. Also for an authentic souvenir, look for a round basket with a strap, the original Kona coffee basket.

After Kimura's follow the road for a minute or so to enter the actual village, where the library, post office, and a cross atop a white steeple welcome you to town. The tiny village, complete with its own elementary school, is well kept, with an obvious double helping of pride put into this artists' community by its citizens. In the center of town is **Paul's Place,** a well-stocked country store, open weekdays 7 A.M.–8 P.M., weekends 8 A.M.–8 P.M.

Along the main road is a converted coffee mill, gaily painted and decorated, and currently the home of the nonprofit **Kona Arts Center,** open Tues.–Sat. 10 A.M.–4 P.M., which began as a labor of love by husband and wife artist team Robert and Carol Rogers. Uncle Bob, as he was affectionately known, passed away, but Aunt Carol is still creating art at the center. Both had an extensive background in art teaching. They moved from San Francisco to Holualoa in 1965 and began offering community workshop classes. Workshops and exhibitions continue, and there is always some class or other going on. Much of the work is displayed in the small gallery at the entrance, where you may find everything from hobby crafts to serious renderings, including paintings, basketry, pottery, sculptures, and even tie-dyed shirts. The center is very friendly and welcomes guests with a cup of Kona coffee. Stop by to view the art or observe a class in progress. For those who desire to put hand to piece, $35 gets you a month's membership, and you can attend workshops any or all days; a different project is done every day. The building is rickety and old, and the floor incredibly uneven, but it's obviously filled with good vibrations and love.

Next to Kona Arts Center is **Cinderella's,** 808/322-2474, an antiques and collectibles shop open Tues.–Sat. noon–5 P.M. Here you find furniture, art, knickknacks, jewelry, and much from estate sales.

At the upper end of town is the **Shelly Maudsley White Gallery,** 808/322-5220, open Monday, Tuesday, Thursday, and Friday, or other days by appointment. The gallery displays the works of accomplished watercolorist Shelly Maudsley White. Tropical flora and fauna is the theme, and the hibiscus, exotic birds, plumeria-scented forests, and hilarious yet pointed marine works confirm her philosophy that "there is more happening on this earth than what meets the eye." Also shown are meticulous and artistic fine woodwork by a local furniture maker.

A premier shop in town, **Studio 7,** 808/324-1335, open Tues.–Sat. 11 A.M.–5 P.M., is owned and operated by Hiroki and Setsuko Morinoue, who both studied at the Kona Art Center. The shop showcases Setsuko and Hiroki's work, along with that of about two dozen other Big Island artists. Hiroki works in many media but primarily does large watercolors or woodblock prints. Setsuko, Hiroki's wife, is a ceramicist and displays her work with about six other potters. Check out the "neoclassical" silk-screen prints, free-form bowls, and wooden bracelets. Strolling from room to room in Studio 7 is like following a magic walkway where the art is displayed simply but elegantly, a legacy of the owners' very Japanese sense of style.

"He's a potter, I'm a painter," is the understatement uttered by Mary Lovein, the female half of the artistic husband and wife team of Mary and Matthew Lovein. They produce and display their lovely and inspired artwork at **Holualoa Gallery,** 808/322-8484, www.lovein.com, open Tues.–Sat. 10 A.M.–5 P.M. Mary uses acrylics and airbrush to create large, bold, and bright seascapes and landscapes of Hawaii. Matthew specializes in *raku:* magnificent works of waist-high vases, classic Japanese-style ceramics glazed in deep rose, iridescent greens, crinkled gray, and deep periwinkle blue. Mary and Matthew collaborate on some of the larger pieces. Matt creates the vessel and, while it is still greenware, Mary paints its underglaze. Other artists featured in the shop are Cecilia Faith Black, who does delicate jewelry; Patricia Van Asperen-Hume, who creates fused glassworks; Frances Dennis, who hand-paints romantic Hawaiian imagery on porcelain, and multi-media artist Charles Corda who creates metal sculpture and acrylic images. Also displayed are works in ceramic, glass, wood, and carved Plexiglas; most of the inspiring works are done in a contemporary or modernist style.

The flora and fauna of Hawaii come alive in **Ululani,** 808/322-7733, www.ululani.com, open Tues.–Sat. 10 A.M.–4 P.M. The bright and airy studio, once the home of "grease monkeys," showcases original paintings, many of the flora, fauna, and scenery of the islands, by the shop's owners. Also displayed is artwork by Herb Kane, world renowned for his dream-reality paintings of Hawaii and its people. Aside from the paintings, you'll find prints, posters, and cards created from original works, T-shirts, pottery, and jewelry.

Nearly across the street is **Hawaii Color Fine Art** gallery, 808/324-1590, which features impressionist paintings mostly by owners Darrell and Pat Hill.

Using Hawaiian woods, David Reisland shows his skill at working and turning wood to create innovative designs. See the result at the **David Reisland Fine Woodworking** gallery, 808/325-6863, on the main street of town.

Holualoa's original post office, toward the south end of the community, houses both **Hale O Kula** goldsmith gallery, 808/324-1688, and **Capell Gallery,** 808/937-8893. Sam, the goldsmith, doesn't need much room, so he has the back. He works mostly in gold, silver, and precious stones; he also creates bronze sculptures and ceramics… very, very small sculptures. Doing mostly commission work, his shop is only open by appointment, but he does display a few other island jewelers' works outside his door. The Capell Gallery up front treats you to original works by the owner—*plein air* oil paintings of tropical scenes, some of contemporary style, and multiple-block, wood block prints.

A side road, easily spotted along Holualoa's main street, leads you up to **Koyasan Daishiji Shingon,** a Japanese Buddhist mission with distinctive red-orange buildings and a stone-lantern lined entrance that was 100 years old in 2002. The mission is basic, simple, and unpretentious, combining Japanese Buddhism with a Hawaiian air. The roof has the distinctive shape of a temple, but unlike those found in Japan, which are fashioned from wood, this is corrugated iron. Getting to the temple takes only a few minutes, and coming back down the road rewards you with an inspiring vista of Kona and the sea.

**Note:** Keep in mind that it is customary for most of the galleries to be *closed on Monday.*

## Coffee Plantation

Holualoa and the mountainside south of here is prime coffee growing area. Literally hundreds of small farms produce beans to be turned into America's most favorite drink. The farms in this region produce about one third of the state's total coffee production, and there are several mills along the strip that process the beans. Everyone knows Kona coffee and those who drink this black brew hold it in high esteem for its fine character. Every year in November, the Kona Coffee Cultural Festival is held to celebrate coffee, the importance this agricultural crop has had on the region for some 175 years, and the people of the area who make it possible.

One mile south of Kimura's is the **Holualoa Kona Coffee Company** plantation and mill, 77-6261 Mamalahoa Hwy., Holualoa, HI 96725, 808/322-9937 or 800/334-0348, www.konalea.com. This mill is open to visitors weekdays 7:30 A.M.–4 P.M. for a free tour of the milling and roasting process and coffee tasting. If you haven't ever been introduced to how coffee gets from tree to cup, this would be a good opportunity to discover how it's done. Although a small operation, this mill handles coffee beans from dozens of area farmers. A retail shop on site sells estate coffee; it can also be ordered by mail.

In this upland area, other coffee producers that have retail shops are UCC Hawaii, www.ucc-hawaii.com, Ferrari, and Blue Sky, www.konablueskycoffee.com. The Ferrari shop is located in Holualoa, UCC Hawaii has a stand a couple of miles north of the village, and Blue Sky is situated along Hualalai Rd. just below Mamalahoa Highway. Blue Sky also offers tours of its mill weekdays and Saturdays.

## Accommodations

The shocking pink **Kona Hotel,** along Holualoa's main street, 808/324-1155, primarily rents its 11 units to local people who spend the workweek in Kailua-Kona's seaside resorts and then go home on weekends. They are more than happy, however, to rent to any visitor passing through and are a particular favorite with Europeans. The Inaba family opened the hotel in 1926, and it is still owned and operated by Goro Inaba with his wife Yayoko, who will greet you at the front desk upon arrival. A clean room with bare wooden floors, a bed and dresser, no phone or television in the room, and shared baths down the hall goes for $20 single, $26 double, and $30 with twin beds. Call ahead for reservations. No meals are served, but Mrs. Inaba will make coffee in the morning if you wish. The hotel is simple, clean, and safe, and while not stupendous, the view from the back rooms is more than worth the price.

A wooden jewel box nestled in velvet greenery waits to be opened as it rests on the edge of Holualoa high above the wide, rippling, cerulean Pacific. **The Holualoa Inn Bed and Breakfast,** at 76-5932 Mamalahoa Hwy., P.O. Box 222, Holualoa, HI 96725, 808/324-1121 or 800/392-1812, fax 808/322-2472, inn@aloha.net, www.konaweb.com/HINN, was the retirement home of Thurston Twigg-Smith, CEO of the *Honolulu Advertiser* and member of an old *kama'aina* family. Mr. Twigg-Smith built the original home in 1978, but tragically, it burned to the ground. Undaunted, he rebuilt, exactly duplicating the original. After living here a few years Mr. Twigg-Smith decided it was too quiet and peaceful and went back to live in Honolulu. In 1987 it was converted into a B&B. The home is a marvel of taste and charm—light, airy, and open. Follow the serpentine drive from Holualoa's main road into the midst of vibrant foliage daubed with red hibiscus, manicured thickets of ripening coffee, sun-yellow papaya, and wind-swirled palms. The home at the end of the drive pleasantly shocks the senses. Top to bottom, it is the natural burnished red of cedar and eucalyptus. Here the Hawaiian tradition of removing your shoes upon entering a home is made a pleasure. The eucalyptus floors, softly polished, cool, and smooth, massage your feet; the roof rides above the walls so the air circulates easily. The front lanai is pure relaxation, and stained glass puncturing the walls here and there creates swirls of rainbow light. Throughout the home are original artworks done by the Twigg-Smith family. A pool table holds king's court in the commodious games room, as doors open to a casual yet elegant sitting room where breakfast is served. A back staircase leads to a gazebo, floored with tile and brazenly open to the elements, while the back lanai is encircled by a roof made of copper. From here, Kailua-Kona glows with the imaginative mistiness of an impressionist painting, and, closer by, 40 acres are dotted with coffee trees and cattle raised by the family. Just below is the inn's swimming pool, tiled in blue with a torch ginger motif, and off to the side the hot tub. The six island-theme rooms run $175–225 and all differ in size and decor, discounts for stays longer than seven days, and breakfast is served to all guests. Some years back, Mr. Twigg-Smith was offered $7 million for the home. Much to our benefit, he declined. This is a gem.

Above Kailua on the road to Holualoa, surrounded by lush tropical foliage that permeates the air with a sweet perfume, perches **Hale Maluhia Country Inn Bed and Breakfast,** 76-770 Hualalai Rd., Kailua-Kona, HI 96740, 808/329-1123 or 800/559-6627, fax 808/326-5487, kona@hawaii-inns.com, www.hawaii-inns.com/hi/kna/hmh, a hideaway lovingly tended by hosts Ken and Sue Smith. Built and furnished in rustic Hawaiian style with a Victorian twist, this Christian B&B offers accommodations in the main house or the separate Banyan Cottage. The interiors of the central house and cottage feature open-beamed ceilings, plenty of natural wood trim, koa cabinets, and full kitchens. On the property are an outdoor stone-and-tile Japanese *ofuro* (spa) with massage jets, and a massage table where your cares and aches will float away on the evening breeze. Two relaxing common areas are outfitted with board games, a pool table, a large library, and surround sound color TV/VCR (with a large video library), while five lanai present the natural drama of a Michelangelo sunset nightly; all are wheelchair friendly. Ken spoils you every morning with a sumptuous home-cooked breakfast buffet laden with tropical fruits and juices, fresh bread and pastries, savory breakfast meats, herbal teas, and robust Kona coffee. All rooms are decorated with Hawaiian and provincial antique furniture and feature private baths. Rates are $90–125 for a guest room in the main house, and $150 for the Banyan Cottage; discounts are offered for longer stays. Hale Maluhia (House of Peace) is all that its name implies.

## KONA COFFEE

A coffee belt runs like a band through Kona. Generally speaking, it's a swath of mountainside 800–1,400 feet in elevation, about two miles inland from the coast, from one to two miles wide, and perhaps 25 miles long. In this warm upland region, watered by cool morning mists and rains, warmed by the afternoon sun, and cooled by evening breezes, coffee trees have an ideal climate in which to grow. Within this band, about 2,500 acres are planted in coffee, producing about 2.5 million pounds of the beans, which amounts to about one-third of the state's production. Most coffee estates here are small, in the 3–20 acre range, and there are about 600 individual growers. Kona has been known for decades as a region that produces exceptional coffee. Until a few short years ago, it was the only area in the state (and country) that grew coffee. Now, farms on each of the main Hawaiian Islands also produce the bean.

Arabica coffee trees are grown in Kona. Trees will produce beans at a young age and keep producing until at least 80 years old if properly tended. Newly formed, coffee "cherries" are green. Most contain two beans, but a small portion have single, more or less round beans called peaberries. When the cherries ripen they turn red. Kona coffee beans are picked by hand, a tough and tedious job, but one that produces quality fruits. Harvest generally takes place for the five months from September through January, with the lower elevation fields starting earlier and the higher elevation fields ending later. After picking, the beans are brought to the mill to be processed. The first step is wet milling, where the outer covering is removed and the slimy inner liquid released. The beans are then rinsed and dried to a specific moisture content, and the silver skin-like covering is taken off. Beans are then separated according to their shape and size by a shaker, graded by quality and substance, bagged, and weighed before they are certified for bulk shipping. Roasting is another matter. Most roasting is done either the traditional way in a drum roaster or by a newer hot air method. Various roasts include light, medium, dark, and the result is determined primarily by the temperature while the length of roasting time is less of a factor. After waiting a few hours for carbon dioxide to off-gas, roasted coffee is packaged. Roughly seven pounds of hand picked coffee cherries are required to make one pound of roasted coffee.

About a dozen Kona coffee plantations are open for year-round visitation of their property and mills. A few are listed in the text; others have signs along the road you will see as you drive through this region. To help you on your way, pick up a copy of the *Kona Coffee Country Driving Tour* brochure, put out by the Kona Coffee Cultural Festival.

## Food

The enticing aroma of rich coffee has been wafting on the breeze in this mountain community ever since the **Holuakoa Cafe** opened its doors in 1992. Just up the hill from the Kona Hotel, the cafe, 808/322-2233, open Mon.–Fri. 6:30 A.M.–3 P.M., and weekends 8 A.M.–3 P.M., serves wonderful coffee, juices, and herbal teas, salads, sandwiches, and smoothies. The cafe also serves as a revolving art gallery for local artists and displays a few boutique, souvenir, and craft items. You can sit inside at a table or enjoy your coffee and pastry alfresco on the veranda, from where the two-block metropolis of Holualoa sprawls at your feet.

# South Kona

Kailua-Kona's Ali'i Drive eventually dead-ends in Keauhou. Before it does, King Kamehameha III Road turns up the mountainside and joins Rte. 11, which in its central section is called the Kuakini Highway. This road, heading south, quickly passes the towns of **Honalo, Kainaliu, Kealakekua,** and **Captain Cook,** and farther on whisks through the smaller communities of **Honaunau, Keokea,** and **Kealia.** These mountainside communities lie along a 10-mile strip of Rte. 11, and if it weren't for the road signs, it would be difficult for the itinerant traveler to know where one village ends and the next begins. You'll have ample opportunity to stop along the way for gas, food, or sightseeing. These towns have some terrific restaurants, fine bed-and-breakfast accommodations, specialty shops, and unique boutiques. If you are up for some off-the-beaten-track sightseeing, you won't be disappointed. At Captain Cook, you can dip down to the coast and visit Kealakekua Bay, or continue south to **Pu'uhonua O Honaunau,** a reconstructed temple of refuge, the best in the state. Farther south still, little-traveled side roads take you to the sleepy seaside villages of **Ho'okena** and **Miloli'i,** where an older, slower lifestyle is still the norm.

## HONALO AND KAINALIU

This dot on the map is at the junction of Routes 11 and 180. Not much changes here, and the town is primarily known for the red and white **Dai Fukuji Soto Buddhist Mission** temple at the beginning of town. This temple is open during the day for those who care for a look. Inside are two ornate altars; feel free to take photos but please remember to remove your shoes. A short distance down a side road is the older **St. Paul's Catholic Church** (1864). Also up the way, and again on the ocean side of the highway, is **Lanakila Congregational Church,** erected in 1867.

Kainaliu is larger and more of a town, with a choice of shopping, restaurants, and a theater. It's just a mile or less up the road from Honalo, and it seems as if these two communities mesh into one.

ROBERT NILSEN

**Dai Fukuji Soto Buddhist Mission**

## Food

**Teshima's Restaurant** in Honalo is open daily 6:30 A.M.–1:45 P.M. and 5–9 P.M. Here, in unpretentious surroundings, you can enjoy a full American, Hawaiian, or Japanese lunch for about $7 and dinner for $10–15. A lunch specialty is the bento box lunch for $6.75 that includes rice balls, luncheon meat, fried fish, teriyaki beef, kamaboku (fish cake), and Japanese roll. Evening meals include fresh catch, tempura, donburi, udon noodles, and a teishoku full meal. Since 1940, Teshima's has been a mom-and-pop (and kids) family restaurant. If you're interested in a good square meal, you can't go wrong here.

**Aloha Angel Café,** 808/322-3383, open daily 8 A.M.–3 P.M. for breakfast and lunch, is part of the lobby of the Aloha Theater in Kainaliu. The enormous yet economical breakfasts feature locally grown eggs, homemade muffins, and potatoes. Lunchtime sandwiches, around $8, are super-stuffed with varied morsels, from tofu and avocado to turkey breast. There are also a variety of soups, salads, and wraps. For a snack choose from an assortment of homemade baked goods that you can enjoy with an espresso or cappuccino. Order at the counter and then sit on the lanai that overlooks a bucolic scene. There is table service for dinner, served 5–9 P.M. daily inside the newer dining room to the side. The dinner menu changes periodically, but may include items like taro-crusted fresh *ahi,* Cajun spice chicken, filet mignon, and scampi with basil pesto, all of which run $14–22. This is an excellent place for food any time of the day.

At the south end of town, in the Mango Court, is **Evie's Natural Foods,** 808/322-0739, open weekdays 8 A.M.–7 P.M., weekends 9 A.M.–5 P.M. This full-range health food store serves freshly made, organic and wholesome sandwiches, soups, and other delicious foods at its deli. It also has "grab 'n go" items in a cooler. Evie's stocks plenty of coffee, herbs, vitamins and minerals, some fresh produce, packaged natural foods, and an assortment of bulk grains.

The **Standard Bakery** in town has breads, baked goods and wonderful hot *malasadas* to take for the road.

## Entertainment

The **Aloha Theater** in Kainaliu hosts productions of the semi-professional local repertory company, Kona Association of the Performing Arts, which puts on about six plays per year that run for about three weeks each. Check the local newspaper, HVB office, or look for posters here and there around town. The theater periodically hosts other types of stage performances, live music, dance, and art films and is a venue for the Hawaii International Film Festival in November. Show times and ticket prices differ for all performances in this completely refurbished and well-appointed theater (built 1929–32), so call the box office for details at 808/322-2323.

## Shopping

There is not much in the way of shopping in Honalu except for a gas station and kayak rental shop. You'll have much better luck in Kainaliu.

The **Blue Ginger Gallery,** 808/322-3898, open Mon.–Sat. 9 A.M.–5 P.M., showcases the art of owners Jill and David Bever, as well as over 100 artists' works from all over the island. David creates art pieces in stained glass, fused glass, and wood. Jill paints on silk, creating fantasy works in strong primary colors. Using her creations as base art, she then designs one-of-a-kind clothing items that can be worn as living art pieces. The small but well-appointed shop brims with paintings, ceramics, sculptures, woodwork, fiber art, and jewelry. As a compliment to the local artwork, about one half the gallery holds imported Asian art and craft items, including Polynesian masks, carved elephants, Buddha heads, and batiks from Indonesia. The Blue Ginger Gallery is a perfect place to find a memorable souvenir of Hawaii.

A wonderful assemblage of paintings, line drawings, and other forms of art are on display at **Lavender Moon Gallery,** 808/324-7708. Along with the works of owners Patricia and Dux Missler, you'll find the captivating pencil sketches of Kathy Long, the contemporary paintings of Megan Long, her daughter, and the renderings of Hawaiian children by Mary Koski, her mother.

In the Basque Building across from Kimura's are the Eternal Wave and Capstone galleries. The **Eternal Wave Gallery,** 808/322-3203, displays pottery, prints, candles, woodwork, and more by mostly local artists. An intriguing collection, it has perhaps more common quality pieces than the works in other galleries in town. Next door is **Capstone Gallery,** 808/322-3377, which displays local and mainland painters of a contemporary style, including those of owner Eric Tore.

**Paradise Found,** 808/332-2111, has "clothing for the adventurous." This shop is an eclectic mix of women's and men's clothing, alohawear, accessories, and some furniture and art objects. All are new but some are reproduction pieces of masterful older designs.

For those looking for antiques and collectibles, have a peek at **Creative Costumes,** 808/322-9600, in the Vintage Eye Plaza building. Not only does this shop have clothing and accessories, it handles a wide variety of other old treasures.

**Surfin' Ass Coffee Company,** 808/324-7733, open daily 7 A.M.–9 P.M., is a coffee and espresso bar where they roast their own beans on the premises in a Royal No. 4 Roaster manufactured in 1910, probably the last operational roaster of its type left in the state. After watching the roasting, take your cup of coffee and a homemade pastry to the rear of the shop, where you'll find an indoor stone grotto area away from the noise of the street. This was the original Bad Ass coffee shop. From here, the revolution spread.

**Big Island Crafts & Gifts,** 808/322-0642, open daily 10 A.M.–6 P.M., has a very surprising interior, filled as it is with authentic jewelry, shells, and beadwork. Many of the items are purchased from local people and include hula instruments, *lau hala* weavings, Ni'ihau shellwork, Hawaiian fishhook pendants, *kukui* nut lei, and even an assortment of Hawaiian food products like mustard and salad dressings. Hanging on the walls are carvings of tikis, dolphins, turtles, and owls, the *'aumakua* of ancient Hawaii. For the children, there are Hawaiian dolls, and children of all ages will love a replica of a sea-going canoe with the distinctive crab claw sail. For those who can't live without another T-shirt, you'll find them, as well as artificial flower lei. Look for this down-home craft shop across from Surfin' Ass Coffee Company.

**Oshima Dry Goods** is well stocked with drugs, fishing supplies, magazines, a huge collection of fabric, and some wines and spirits. Also in town is **Kimura Market,** a general grocery store with some sundries, and **H. Kimura Store** for bolts of fabric. Oshima's and H. Kimura's are two of the stores along this road that still function pretty much the same as they have for decades.

As you are leaving the built-up area of Kainaliu, look for the **Island Books** "Used Books Bought and Sold" sign. Open daily 9 A.M.–7 P.M. (usually), this shop stocks a general mix of titles, but history, geography, Hawaiiana, and a good selection of used travel books are the specialty. Here's a great place to purchase some casual reading material and save money at the same time; 808/322-2006.

At the south end of town in the Mango Court is a shop selling hemp products: clothing, oils, and other items. All material is imported due to the U.S. prohibition on the production of hemp fiber. Stop in to have a look at the items for sale and to learn about this, one of mother nature's most versatile and useful natural gifts.

## KEALAKEKUA

Kealakekua is one of the old established towns along the road, but it has a newer look with more modern buildings and small subdivisions. In town are a post office and library, a small shopping center, gas station, several eateries, a few gift shops, and an antiques store. Just south of town on the road up to the schools is **Christ Church Episcopal,** established in 1867 as the first Episcopal church in the islands. Newer is the Kona Hongwanji Mission.

As coffee farms do in other areas of Kona, the **Greenwell Farm Coffee Mill** grows and roasts its own estate coffee. Located downhill from the Kona Historical Society Museum, the mill runs tours of its orchard and processing facility Mon.–Sat. 8 A.M.–4 P.M., and its retail stand is only happy to sell half-pound, one-pound, and five-pound packages of its best roast.

### Kona Historical Society Museum

The main building of the Kona Historical Society Museum was originally a general store built

ROBERT NILSEN

coffee mill and drying shed at the D. Uchida Coffee Farm, a typical small operation from the 1900s

around 1875 by local landowner and businessman H. N. Greenwell using native stone and lime mortar made from burnt coral. Now on both the Hawaii and National Registers of Historic Places, the building served many uses, including the warehousing and packaging of sweet oranges raised by Greenwell, purported to be the largest, sweetest, and juiciest in the world. The museum, 808/323-3222, open weekdays 9 A.M.–3 P.M. with a $2 donation for admission, is located one-quarter mile south of Kealakekua. The main artifact is the building itself, but inside, you will find a few antiques like a surrey and glassware, and the usual photographic exhibits with themes like coffee growing and ranching—part of the legacy of Kona. The basement of the building houses archives filled with birth and death records of local people, photographs both personal and official, home movies, books, and maps, most of which were donated by the families of Kona. The archives are open to the public by appointment only. To the rear is the Kona Historical Society office.

The **Kona Historical Society,** P.O. Box 398, Captain Cook, HI 96704, www.konahistorical.org, is a non-profit organization whose main purpose is the preservation of Kona's history and the dissemination of historical information. Sometimes the society sponsors lectures and films, which are listed in the local newspapers. They also offer 4WD tours of the Kona area ($55) three times per year, usually in March, July, and November, and a historical boat tour in late January ($20) that takes you from Kailua-Kona south along the coast. There is no fixed schedule, but if you are in the area during those times of year, it would be well worth the trouble to contact the museum to find out if these excellent tours are being offered. A Captain Cook lecture tour at Kealakekua Bay and an archaeological tour of Keauhou can also be arranged by appointment only, with a minimum of three people. However, walking tours of the historical district of Kailua ($15) are regularly scheduled Mon.–Fri. at 9 A.M. and 11 A.M.: 24-hour advance reservation, please. The tours usually last about 1.5 hours at a leisurely pace. Wear a hat and comfortable walking shoes.

Another excellent tour is the walking tour conducted at the historic **D. Uchida Coffee**

**Farm,** now listed on the National Register of Historic Places, but begun by Japanese immigrants in the early years of the 1900s. The Living History Farm guided tour ($15), offered weekdays on the hour from 9 A.M.–1 P.M., takes you to a working farm with original authentic buildings, machinery, and live animals, and explains how the farm and its workers fit into the multiethnic Kona community. With groups of 12 or more, costumed interpreters will perform chores typical of such a farm from that era, so the tour is a representation of what daily life was like when the farm operated from 1925 to 1945. Look for it at mile marker 110. For any of these fine historical society tours, make reservations by calling 808/323-2005.

Although not up and running yet, future plans of the historical society call for the reconstruction of a ranching homestead and the establishment of a living history museum there.

## Amy B. H. Greenwell Ethnobotanical Garden

You can not only smell the flowers but feel the history of the region at the Amy B. H. Greenwell Ethnobotanical Garden, along Rte. 11 south of Kealakekua at mile marker 110, 808/323-3318, www.bishopmuseum.org/greenwell. The garden is open Mon.–Fri. 8:30 A.M.–5 P.M., with guided tours on the second Saturday of every month at 10 A.M.; suggested donation, $4. Greenwell died in 1974 and left her lands to the Bishop Museum, which then opened a 12-acre interpretive ethnobotanical garden, planting it with indigenous Hawaiian plants, Polynesian introduced plants, and Hawaiian medicinal plants. At the beginning of the walking path through the lower section of the garden, take a fact sheet that describes the garden, complete with self-guided tour map. Represented here are four zones: coastal, agricultural, lowland dry forest, and upland wet forest. Within these sections are plants typical of the zone. The garden contains remnants of the Kona field system, dating from precontact times when a broad network of stone ridges delineated intensive agriculture fields that were spread over some 30 square miles and sustained a large population.

## Food

The **Korner Pocket Bar and Grill,** 808/322-2994, serving lunch and dinner weekdays 11 A.M.–10 P.M., is a family-oriented restaurant and friendly pool bar where you can get excellent food and drink at very reasonable prices. The Korner Pocket sits below the highway in the small shopping center on Haleki'i Street. Grill selections are a poolroom burger, fresh catch, or scrumptious bistro burger of grilled beef on crusty sourdough topped with fresh mushrooms sautéed in wine garlic sauce. Dinners are tempting items like fresh catch for $14, top sirloin for $10, and baby back ribs for $12, its encore entrée. The complete bar is well stocked with wines and spirits, or you can wash down your sandwich with an assortment of draft beers. The Pocket rocks with live music on weekends and hosts a pool tournament on Tuesdays. The Korner Pocket looks as ordinary as a Ford station wagon, both inside and out, but the food is surprisingly good.

At the crest of the hill is the tiny **Kona Mountain Cafe,** 808/323-2700, open daily from 6:30 A.M. Kona Mountain Cafe is a coffee shop with some tasty and nutritious sandwiches, pastries, and other eats. A full range of drinks, smoothies, ice cream, are also on the menu. A good stop for a longer trip down the highway, there is a fine view off the back lanai, and Internet access for a minimal charge.

Near the south end of town is the **Peacock House** Chinese restaurant, 808/323-2366. Open Mon.–Sat. for lunch and dinner and Sunday for dinner only, this is a reasonably priced local eatery with a typically long list of menu selections. No MSG upon request.

On your way out of town going south, stop by **Chris's Bakery** and pick up a snack for the road. A variety of pastries are available here, but Chris's is best known for *malasadas,* made fresh daily. Don't come by too late, however. While open daily at 6 A.M., they close up shop at 1 P.M.

## Shopping

The **Grass Shack,** a.k.a. The Little Grass Shack, 808/323-2877, open Mon.–Sat. 9 A.M.–5 P.M., sometimes Sunday noon–5 P.M., is an institution in Kealakekua, owned and operated by *kama'aina* Lish Jens. It looks like a tourist trap, but don't let that stop you from going in and finding some authentic souvenirs, most of which come from the area or from Ms. Jens's many years of traveling and collecting. The items *not* from Hawaii are clearly marked with a big sign that says, Sorry These Items Were Not Made In Hawaii. But the price is right. There are plenty of trinkets and souvenir items, as well as a fine assortment of artistic pieces, especially wooden bowls, hula items, exquisite Ni'ihau shellwork, and Hawaiian masks. A shop specialty is items made from curly koa. Each piece is signed with the craftsperson's name and the type of wood used. Others are made from Norfolk pine and *milo*. A showcase holds jewelry and tapa cloth imported from Fiji, and a rack holds tapes of classic Hawaiian musicians from the 1940s and '50s. The shop is famous for its distinctive *lau hala* hats, the best hat for the tropics.

The full-service **Kamigaki Market** is open most days 7 A.M.–9 P.M. and from 8:30 A.M. on Sunday.

## Horseback Riding

**Kings' Trail Rides O'Kona**, 808/323-2388, www.konacowboy.com, is located along the highway at mile marker 111. Rides from here go down a jeep and hiking trail to Kealakekua Bay and the Captain Cook monument. With morning departures, the four-hour trip includes two hours of riding followed by snorkeling in the bay and a picnic lunch. The price is $95 per person, limited to six riders. The ride office doubles as a retail shop and is open daily 7:30 A.M.–5 P.M. There you can purchase koa boxes, plantation coffee, Tropical Temptation chocolates like chocolate-covered coffee beans, along with cowboy items like spurs, western belts, and a full assortment of tack.

## Kayaking

Just before Kealakekua is **Kona Boys** kayak rental and tour outfit, 808/328-1234. Rental kayaks run $25 single or $45.50 double and a guided tour of Kealakekua Bay for $125 per person. If you're just after rental snorkel gear, they have it for $5–7.50 a day.

# CAPTAIN COOK AND VICINITY

Captain Cook is the last of the big towns along this highway. You can get gas, food, and lodging here, shop for some arts and crafts, and wash your clothes. Captain Cook is the gateway to the sights on the coast. In town is the Greenwell County Park with its numerous athletic fields, and next door is the county administration sub-office. Beyond this, the smaller towns are each but a few houses that create wide spots in the road. If you're in the area in March, have a look at the yearly Kona Stampede Rodeo at the Honaunau Rodeo Grounds, located at the big bend in the road going down to Pu'uhonua O Honaunau, and watch the local cowboys rope steers.

## Coffee Mills and Candy Factory

South of Captain Cook, you can't help noticing the trim coffee bushes planted along the hillside. On the highway almost to Honaunau, you find the **Royal Kona Coffee Mill and Museum**, 808/328-2511, www.royalkonacoffee.com, open daily for self-guided tours 8 A.M.–5 P.M. The tantalizing smell of roasting coffee and the lure of a "free cup" are more than enough stimulus to make you stop. Mark Twain did! The museum is small, of the non-touch variety. Mostly they're old black-and-white prints of the way Kona coffee country used to be. Some heavy machinery is displayed. The most interesting item is a homemade husker built from an old automobile. More or less integrated into the museum, is a small gift shop. You can pick up the usual souvenirs, but the real treats are gourmet honeys, jellies, jams, candies, and of course coffee. You can't beat the freshness of getting it right from the source. Refill anyone? Be sure to have a look at the mill while you are here, particularly during coffee processing season. You can witness the entire process from harvest to roast.

Two other coffee farms in the area that also offer tours of their mills are: **Bayview Farm**, a half mile north of St. Benedict's Church along Painted Church Road, 808/328-9658, www.bayviewfarmcoffees.com; and **Kona Pacific Farmers Cooperative**, on the way down to Napo'opo'o, 808/328-2411, www.kpfc.com.

Bayview Farm also has an outlet for its coffee, gifts, and craft items up on the Hawaiian Belt Road highway. The Farmers Cooperative has a retail shop that sells local products and a Thursday farmers' market.

Is that sweet tooth of yours starting to crave a little attention? Stop for a visit to the **Kona Coast Macadamia Nut and Candy Factory,** 808/328-8141, near the intersection of the belt road and Middle Ke'ei Road, where you can slack the craving with roasted macadamia nuts, chocolate-covered nuts, and macadamia cookies and candy. For something not so sinful, go for the Kona coffee or other gift items.

## Painted Church

Whether going to or coming from Pu'uhonua O Honaunau, make sure to take a short side trip off Rte. 160 to **St. Benedict's Painted Church.** This small house of worship is fronted by latticework, and with its gothic-style belfry looks like a little castle. Inside, a Belgian priest, John Berchman Velghe, took house paint and, with a fair measure of talent and religious fervor, painted biblical scenes on the walls and tropical skies and palm fronds on the ceiling. His masterpiece is a painted illusion behind the altar that gives you the impression of being in the famous Spanish cathedral in Burgos. Father John was pastor here 1899–1904, during which time he did these paintings, similar to others that he did in small churches throughout Polynesia. Before leaving, visit the cemetery to see its petroglyphs and homemade pipe crosses.

## Napo'opo'o

In the town of Captain Cook, Napo'opo'o Road branches off Rte. 11 and begins a roller-coaster ride down to the sea, where it ends at Kealakekua Bay. Many counterculture types once took up residence in semi-abandoned "coffee shacks" throughout this hard-pressed economic area, but the cheap, idyllic, and convenience-free life isn't as easy to arrange as it once was. The area is being "rediscovered" and getting more popular. Near the bottom, you pass **Kahikolu Congregational Church** (1852), the burial site of Henry Opukaha'ia, a young native boy taken to New England, where he was educated and converted to Christianity. Through impassioned speeches begging for salvation for his pagan countrymen, he convinced the first Congregationalist missionaries to come to the islands in 1820.

Continue down Napo'opo'o Road to the once-thriving fishing village of Napo'opo'o (The Holes), now just a circle on the map with a few houses fronted by neat gardens. During much of the last century, Napo'opo'o was a thriving community and had an active port where commodities and animals were shipped. Now only remnants of the old pier remain. When Napo'opo'o Road nears the water, turn right for Kealakekua (Pathway of the God) Bay. At the end this short road is the rather ill-kept **Napo'opo'o Beach County Park,** with showers, picnic tables, and restrooms. The beach here is full of cobbles with a little sand strip along the water, but it draws locals and visitors alike who come to sunbathe. Fronting the beach is Hikiau Heiau. Taking a side road around the south side of the bay will bring you to the more secluded white-sand **Manini Beach.**

Just south of Napo'opo'o, down a narrow and very rugged road is the sleepy seaside village of **Ke'ei.** This side trip ends at a canoe launch area and a cozy white-sand beach good in spots for swimming. The wide reef here is a fine snorkeling spot and a favorite of surfers. A channel to an underwater grotto has been sliced through the coral. On the shore are the remains of Kamaiko Heiau, where humans were once sacrificed. In 1782, on the flats beyond this village, the **Battle of Moku'ohai** was fought, the first battle in King Kamehameha I's struggle to consolidate power not only over the island of Hawai'i but eventually all the islands.

## Kealakekua Bay

Kealakekua Bay has been known as a safe anchorage since long before the arrival of Captain Cook and still draws boats of all descriptions. The entire bay is a 315-acre **Marine Life Conservation District,** and it lives up to its title by being an excellent scuba and snorkeling site. Organized tours from Kailua-Kona often flood the area with boats and divers in the area just off the

Captain Cook monument, but the bay is vast and you can generally find your own secluded spot to enjoy the underwater show. The area between Napo'opo'o and Manini Beach, an area at the southern tip of the bay, is also excellent for coral formations, lava ledges, and fish. If you've just come for a quick dip or to enjoy the sunset, look for beautiful, yellow-tailed tropicbirds that frequent the bay.

Relax a minute and tune in all your sensors because you're in for a treat. The bay is not only a Marine Life Conservation District with topnotch snorkeling, but it drips with history. *Mauka*, at the county park parking lot, is the well-preserved **Hikiau Heiau**, dedicated to the god Lono, who had long been prophesied to return from the heavens to this very bay to usher in a "new order." Perhaps the soothsaying *kahuna* were a bit vague on the points of the new order, but it is undeniable that at this spot of initial contact between Europeans and Hawaiians, great changes occurred that radically altered the course of Hawaiian history.

The *heiau* lies at the base of a steep *pali* that form a well-engineered wall. From the temple priests had a panoramic view of the ocean to mark the approach of Lono's "floating island," heralded by tall white tapa banners. The *heiau* platform was meticulously backfilled with smooth, small stones; a series of stone footings, once the bases of grass and thatch houses used in the religious rites, is still very much intact. The *pali* above the bay is pocked with numerous burial caves that still hold the bones of the ancients.

Captain James Cook, leading his ships *Resolution* and *Discovery* under billowing white sails, entered the bay on the morning of January 17, 1778, during the height of the Makahiki Festival, and the awestruck natives were sure that Lono had returned. Immediately, traditional ways were challenged. Shortly after their arrival, an old crew member, William Watman, died, and Cook was invited to bury him and perform a Christian burial atop the *heiau*. This was, of course, the first Christian ceremony in the islands, and a plaque at the *heiau* entrance commemorates the event. On February 4, 1778, a few weeks after open-armed welcome, the goodwill camaraderie

that had developed between the English voyagers and their island hosts turned sour, due to terrible cultural misunderstandings. The sad result was the death of Captain Cook. During a final conflict, this magnificent man, who had resolutely sailed and explored the greatest sea on earth, stood helplessly in knee-deep water, unable to swim to rescue boats sent from his waiting ships. Hawaiians, provoked to a furious frenzy because of an unintentional insult, beat, stabbed, and clubbed the great captain and four of his marines to death. A 27-foot obelisk of white marble erected to Cook's memory in 1874 "by some of his fellow countrymen" is at the far northern end of the bay.

The land immediately surrounding the monument is actually under British rule, somewhat like the grounds of a foreign consulate. Once a year, an Australian ship comes to tend it, and sometimes local people are hired to clear the weeds. The monument fence is fashioned from old cannons topped with cannon balls. Here too is a bronze plaque, often awash by the waves, that marks the exact spot where Cook fell. You can see the marble obelisk from the *heiau*, but actually getting to it is tough. Most people kayak across or take a tour boat from up the coast. Expert swimmers have braved the mile swim to the point, but be advised it's through open water. A rugged jeep/foot trail leads down the hill to the monument, but it's poorly marked and starts way back near the town of Captain Cook, almost immediately after Napo'opo'o Road branches off from Rte. 11. Behind the monument are the ruins of the Ka'awaloa village site, some of which can be seen in the trees. Ruins of a lighthouse and a boat launch are nearby.

## Pu'uhonua O Honaunau National Historical Park

This historical park, the main attraction in the area, shouldn't be missed. Though it was once known as City of Refuge Park, the official name of Pu'uhonua O Honaunau is coming into more use in keeping with the emergence of Hawaiian heritage. One way to get there is to bounce along the narrow four miles of coastal road from Kealakekua Bay. The other more direct and much better road is Rte. 160, where it branches off Rte. 11 at Keokea around mile marker 104, a short distance south of Honaunau.

The setting of Pu'uhonua O Honaunau couldn't be more idyllic. It's a picture-perfect cove with many paths leading out onto the sea-washed lava flow. The tall royal palms surrounding this compound shimmer like neon against the black lava so prevalent in this part of Kona. Planted for this purpose, these beacons promised safety and salvation to the vanquished, weak, and war-tossed, as well as to the *kapu*-breakers of old Hawaii. If you made it to this "temple of refuge," scurrying frantically ahead of avenging warriors or leaping into the sea to swim the last desperate miles, the attendant *kahuna*, under pain of their own death, had to offer you sanctuary. *Kapu*-breakers were particularly pursued because their misdeeds could anger the always-moody gods, who might send a lava flow or tsunami to punish all. Only the *kahuna* could perform the rituals that would bathe you in the sacred mana and thus absolve you from all wrongdoing. This *pu'uhonua* (temple of refuge) was the largest in all Hawaii, and be it fact or fancy, you can feel its power to this day.

The temple complex sits on a 20-acre finger of lava bordered by the sea on all sides. A massive, 1,000-foot-long mortarless wall, measuring 10 feet high and 17 feet thick, borders the site on the landward side and marks it as a temple of refuge. Archaeological evidence dates use of the temple from the mid-16th century, and some scholars argue that it was a well-known sacred spot as much as 200 years earlier. Actually, three separate *heiau* are within the enclosure. In the mid-16th century, Keawe, a great chief of Kona and the great-grandfather of Kamehameha, ruled here. After his death, his bones were entombed in *Hale O Keawe Heiau* at the end of the great wall, and his mana re-infused the temple with cleansing powers. For 250 years the *ali'i* of Kona continued to be buried here, making the spot more and more powerful. Even the great Queen Ka'ahumanu came here seeking sanctuary. As a 17-year-old bride, she refused to submit to the will of her husband, Kamehameha, and defied him openly, often wantonly giving herself to lesser chiefs. To escape Kamehameha's rampage, she made for the temple. Ka'ahumanu chose a large rock to hide under, and she couldn't be found until her pet dog barked and gave her away.

## KONANE

**K**onane is a traditional board game played by Hawaiians that is similar to checkers. Old boards have been found at various locations around the islands, often close to the water. The "board" is a flat rock with small depressions ground into it. These depressions usually number around 100, but may be as many as 200. Each of the depressions is filed with an alternating white and black stone or shell. Although there are many variations to the game, one is as follows. Each of two players removes one of his stones, creating two blank spots. One of the two players starts by jumping an opponent's stone, capturing it and taking it off the board. Play then moves to the other person, who in turn jumps the opposite color stone, removing it. The game continues like this, each person alternately jumping the opponent's stones, until one player is no longer able to make a jump, which ends the game.

*Konane* board

Kaʻahumanu was coaxed out only after a lengthy intercession by Capt. George Vancouver, who had become a friend of the king. The last royal personage buried here was a son of Kamehameha who died in 1818. Soon afterwards, the "old religion" of Hawaii died and the temple grounds were abandoned but not entirely destroyed. The foundations of this largest city of refuge in the Hawaiian Islands were left intact.

On the landward side of the refuge wall was the "palace grounds" where the *aliʻi* of Kona lived. Set here and there around the sandy compound are numerous buildings that have been re-created to let you sense what it must have been like when *aliʻi* walked here under the palms. The canoe shed, set directly back from the royal canoe landing site on the beach, was exceedingly important to the seagoing Hawaiians, and the temple helped sustain the mores and principles of the highly stratified and regimented society. Several fishponds lie in this compound that raised food for the chiefs, and a *konane* stone set next to the water—*konane* is a game similar to chess—is a modern version of one of the games that the old Hawaiians played. It is easy to envision this spot as one of power and prestige. Feel free to look around, but be respectful and acknowledge that Hawaiians still consider this a sacred spot.

In 1961, the National Park Service opened Puʻuhonua O Honaunau after a complete and faithful restoration was carried out. Careful consultation of old records and vintage sketches from early ships' artists gave the restoration a true sense of authenticity. Local artists used traditional tools and techniques to carve giant ʻohiʻa logs into faithful renditions of the temple gods. They now stand again, protecting the *heiau* from evil. All the buildings are painstakingly lashed together in the Hawaiian fashion, but with nylon rope instead of traditional cordage, which would have added the perfect touch.

Stop at the visitor center to pick up a map and brochure for a self-guided tour. Exhibits line a wall, complete with murals done in heroic style. Push a button and the recorded messages give you a brief history of Hawaiian beliefs and the system governing daily life—educate yourself. For additional information, see www.nps.gov/puho. The visitor center, 808/328-2288, is open daily 8 A.M.–4:30 P.M. Entrance to the 180-acre park is $5 per person. The beach park section to the south of the compound is open 6 A.M. to midevening. Swimming, sunbathing, and picnicking are allowed there, while snorkeling and kayaking can be done in the bay right in front of the refuge. Kayaks and small boats can be launched from the boat ramp in the village just to the north and adjacent to the refuge.

Every year on the weekend closest to July 1 (the first was held in 1971), the free three-day Puʻuhonua O Honaunau Cultural Festival is held here, featuring traditional Hawaiian arts and crafts, music and dance, canoe rides, and food. Be sure to stop by for a peek into the past if you are in the area during this time.

## Hotel

**Manago Hotel,** P.O. Box 145, Captain Cook, Kona, HI 96704, 808/323-2642, fax 808/323-3451, www.managohotel.com, has been in the Manago family since 1917, and anyone who puts his name on a place and keeps it there that long is doing something right. The Manago Hotel is clean and unpretentious with an old-Hawaii charm. There is nothing fancy going on here, just a decent room for a decent price. The old section of the hotel along the road is clean but a little worse for wear. The rooms are small with wooden floors, double beds, and utilitarian dressers, no fans, and shared bathrooms. Walk through to find a bridgeway into a garden area that's open, bright, and secluded away from the road. The new section features rooms with wall-to-wall carpeting, new furniture, private baths, louvered windows, ceiling fans, and private lanai. The rates are $25 single or $28 double for a room with a shared bath, $42–47 single and $45–50 double in the new section, plus $3 for an extra person. There is also one Japanese room that goes for $61 single or $64 double. Weekly and monthly discounts are available on all rooms. The views of the Kona Coast from the hotel grounds are terrific. Downstairs in the old building, the restaurant serves breakfast, lunch, and dinner every day except Monday.

## Bed-and-Breakfasts

**Areca Palms Estate Bed and Breakfast**, P.O. Box 489, Captain Cook, HI 96704, 808/323-2276 or 800/545-4390, fax 808/323-3749, arecapalms@konabedandbreakfast.com, www.konabedandbreakfast.com, is considered, even by other B&B owners, to be one of the best on the island. Innkeepers Janice and Steve Glass are more than happy to share their home with you. The house itself is sprinkled with antiques and fine furniture. A smooth wood floor and area rugs cover the spacious living and dining rooms under a cathedral ceiling. The house is always perfumed by fresh cut flowers, and Hawaiian music plays in the background to set the mood. Bedspreads are thick, the quilts in floral designs, and carpets cover the bedroom floors. Set in a broad manicured lawn surrounded by tropical flowers and palms, the outdoor hot tub and deck is the premier spot on the property. Rates for the four rooms range $80–125, inclusive of the sumptuous breakfast feast, two nights minimum.

In the quiet of the hills above town along a narrow residential lane is **Cedar House** bed-and-breakfast and coffee farm. Guest rooms at this home of cedar and redwood overlook the farm's coffee trees with views of the ocean in the distance. Two rooms have queen beds and share a bath, two others downstairs are larger with king beds and separate baths. To the side is a detached, remodeled, and brightly painted cottage with two bedrooms and a full kitchen that serves the needs of a small family or for those who desire a bit more privacy. Rates are $70–95 for the rooms, breakfast included, and $110 for the cottage—no breakfast. Your hosts, Diana and Nik Von der Lühe, will gladly show you around the farm and tell you about raising coffee. For reservations, contact them at P.O. Box 823, Captain Cook, HI 96704, tel./fax 808/328-8829, cedrhse@aloha.net, www.cedarhouse-hawaii.com.

Just a few steps from the Royal Kona Coffee Mill is **Affordable Hawaii at Pomaika'i "Lucky" Farm B&B**, 83-5465 Mamalahoa Hwy., Captain Cook, HI 96704, 808/328-2112 or 800/325-6427, fax 808/328-2255, nitabnb@kona.net, www.luckyfarm.com. This B&B is part of a working coffee and macadamia nut farm that has views of the coast from the back lanai of the main house. The one rental room in the farmhouse runs $55 a night, has its own bathroom, and lies off the sitting room with its TV and library. This room is a little close to the road and so may be a bit noisy during the day, but it all quiets down at night. The greenhouse, a newer addition down below, runs $65 a couple for each of its two rooms. Both have queen beds, futons for an extra two people, private entrances, and private baths. Then there's the coffee barn. Converted to a bedroom, it's been left with its rough-sawn framing and bare walls, but a half-bath has been added inside and a shower set up just outside the door. Renting for $65, it's just right for a romantic honeymoon couple. All guests are served a farm-healthy, homemade breakfast each morning and you can pick fruit from the trees on the property. Pomaika'i Farm offers relaxation, affordability, and great food. For reservations, contact Nita Isherwood, innkeeper.

Also on a working coffee and macadamia nut farm is **Rainbow Plantation B&B**, P.O. Box 122, Captain Cook, HI 96704, 808/323-2393 or 800/494-2829, fax 808/323-9445, sunshine@aloha.net, www.aloha.net/~konabnb, a peaceful country place where chickens, potbellied pigs, and peacocks rule the yard. Each of the rooms in the main house and detached cottages has a private entrance and bathroom. Rooms in the main house run $75–85, while the cottages, one a converted fishing boat, are $85–95. The Kukui Cottage rents for $250 for five nights. Breakfast is served each morning on the lanai, and all may use the "gazebo" kitchen.

**Lion's Gate,** owned by Diane and Bill Shriner, P.O. Box 761, Honaunau, HI 96726, 808/328-2335 or 800/955-2332, fax 808/328-1123, inkeeper@coffeeofkona.com, www.coffeeofkona.com, offers bed-and-breakfast rooms on a working macadamia nut and Kona coffee farm. Follow the long row of tall palm trees down to the house. Minutes from the Pu'uhonua O Honaunau National Historical Park, Lion's Gate features a queen bed, refrigerator, TV, and microwave in each of the two rooms, great views of the coast from the wraparound deck, a gazebo for relaxing, a hot tub, and, of course, complimentary Kona coffee and macadamia nuts. Either of the rooms can be combined with a third room to create a suite. The rooms run $110, or $165 as a suite.

**The Dragonfly Ranch,** P.O. Box 675, Honaunau, HI 96762, 808/328-9570 or 800/487-2159, dfly@dragonflyranch.com, www.dragonflyranch.com, owned and operated by Barbara Moore, offers "tropical fantasy lodging" that's set amongst thick vegetation on the way down to Pu'unonua O Honaunau. Rooms are intriguing and range from the Honeymoon Suite featuring a king bed in a lattice room, the airy Lomi lomi and more private Writer's studios, to the smaller Pele and Dolphin rooms. All rooms include a small refrigerator and basic cooking apparatus, indoor bathroom, private outdoor shower, cable TV, stereo, and small library. Rates run $100–200 with substantial discounts for longer stays. This is an open, airy place, where the outside and inside boundaries begin to blur. To some, the touted tropical fantasy may be a "tropical nightmare." The hosts are very friendly and inviting, indeed, but definitely have an alternative, counter-culture, new-age leaning. Free-spirited adventurers will feel comfortable here; others may not. Dragonfly Ranch is one of those places people totally adore or else dash away from. Rainbow streamers and a Buddha in a butterfly banner greet you as you turn in the drive.

In Napo'opo'o there are several options. On the inland side of the road is a house with cottage. The house has three bedrooms and one bath and rents for $630 a week; with one bedroom, the smaller cottage goes for $525 a week. Call 808/328-2151 for information and reservations. Directly on the bay and much larger and newer are two other rental homes. The four-bedroom, three-bath home sleeps up to 10 and runs $2,650–2,950 a week depending upon the season. A three-bedroom, three-bath house that sleeps up to 12 goes for $2,450–2,750. Not cheap, but the location can't be beat. For information, try 808/247-3637, fax 808/235-2644, hibeach@lava.net, www.hotspots.hawaii.com/beachrent1.html.

The least expensive place to stay in the area is **Pineapple Park,** tel./fax 808/323-2224 or 877/865-2266, ppark@aloha.net, www.pineap-ple-park.com. This clean and commodious hostel/B&B accommodation is in a converted plantation-era house along the main highway. Upstairs are the B&B rooms. Located around a common area, they run $40–65. Running $20 a bed, the dorm rooms are located in the converted walk-out basement which also has a TV lounge and inexpensive Internet access. All guests share baths, have use of laundry facilities and a large kitchen, and can rent kayaks and snorkel gear for minimal fees.

## Food

Try the legendary pork chop dinner served at the **Manago Hotel Restaurant,** 808/323-2642, in downtown Captain Cook. This meal and other offerings on the menu are plain old American food with a strong Hawaiian overlay. Other items are New York steak, the most expensive at $11.50, beef teriyaki, teri chicken, and four or five fish selections. All come with three side dishes and rice. This food won't set your taste buds on fire, but you won't be complaining about being hungry or not having a wholesome meal. The restaurant is open for breakfast 7–9 A.M., lunch 11 A.M.–2 P.M., and dinner 5–7:30 P.M.; closed Monday.

On the highway just as you cruise into town is **Billy Bob's Park 'n Pork** barbecue restaurant, 808/323-3371, where you can order up barbecued ribs, chicken, hot biscuits, coleslaw, and salad. Also available, partner, are prime rib, veggie enchiladas, a mean Caesar salad, hog fries, and chili. Everything on the menu is less than $10, and you can order anything for takeout. Those in the know say it's the best barbecue on the Kona side. Lasso that little missus of yours and come on down any night except Wednesday.

A local stop for a quick meal like a plate lunch or bowl of saimin is **Cap's Drive-In.**

Perhaps the best view down onto the Napo'opo'o/Kealakakua Bay area is from the back lanai of **The Coffee Shack,** 808/328-9555, and aside from its superb view it has delicious treats at a fair price. Open 7 A.M.–5 P.M. daily, the Coffee Shack has a full list of coffee, simple breakfasts, soup, sandwiches, and pizza, but best of all, a wide variety of luscious cakes, pies, pastries, and a host of other sweet treats all made fresh daily here in the kitchen. Eat in or take out.

Looking for authentic Hawaiian food served by delightful people? Try **Super Js** takeout in Honaunau for *lomi lomi* salmon, *laulau*, macaroni salad, *poi*, and a variety of plate lunches that run about $6. Don't go too late, however, as it usually closes around sundown. Closed on Sundays.

People in the know give the **Ke'ei Cafe**, 808/328-8451, rave reviews. But, you'll ask yourself: What's a fine restaurant serving fusion foods doing way out here in the very ordinary and tiny community of Honaunau? Seemingly set on the edge of the world, this little eatery has a wonderful location as the mountainside drops off below it toward Kealakekua Bay and the National Historical Park. Small in size but big in stature, the Ke'ei Cafe has made a name for itself and is very popular. Open 5:15–8 P.M. for dinner only, you'll need to call for reservations. Start with a Greek salad or Brazilian seafood chowder, both $6.95. Entrées run $10–19 and include seafood pasta with heady herbs and spices, roast half chicken in white wine peppercorn gravy, pan-seared rib-eye steak, and fresh catch prepared with red Thai curry, pan seared in lemon caper butter, or sautéed, market price. Follow this with a coconut flan or tropical bread pudding dessert. Yum! While the menu is short, there is a sufficient but limited selection of domestic and imported beers and wines. This will be a memorable meal, and the drive will be worth it. No credit cards.

On the road down to Pu'umonua O Honaunau is **Wakefield Garden and Restaurant.** Open daily 11 A.M.–4 P.M., this is more or less a pie and coffee shop that also sells cold drinks, soups, and sandwiches. In the back is the garden. You can tour for free, however, it may be well-kept or not depending upon how much care has been put into it lately.

## Shopping
The **Kealakekua Ranch Center,** in Captain Cook, is a two-story utilitarian mall with a few small shops, an Ace Hardware store, and a Choice Mart supermarket. Choice Mart is the last of the large markets along this road going south, so pick up supplies here. Open 7 A.M.–9 P.M.

Mon.–Sat., until 8 P.M. on Sunday, this full-service grocery store also has a small deli section.

Along the highway as you enter town is **Antiques and Orchids** collectibles shop. With a wide selection of furniture and housewares (many small items too) and an amazing variety of potted orchids, this is a great shop for any discriminating shopper.

A few steps away is **The Rainbow Path,** 808/323-3828, an intriguing shop specializing in books on Hawaii, metaphysics, self-help, personal discovery, and books for children. You can also find tapes and CDs that include Hawaiian chants, Native American Indian music, Celtic music, and music especially composed to induce relaxation and relieve stress. Your body is taken care of with Ayurvedic medicine, incense, beeswax candles, bath and body products, and natural perfumes of island scents. The soul will stir with crystal pendants, pyramids, beaded necklaces, and dream catchers. Several evenings a week, metaphysical readings are given by appointment; see the monthly calendar of events. Check the bulletin board for information about alternative healing and new-age practitioners. All who are on the path will find this shop an oasis.

Virtually the only such shop in town, the **Art Farm** displays all sorts of arts and crafts in various mediums.

**Bong Brothers,** 84-5227 Mamalahoa Hwy., on the *makai* side of the road near mile marker 106, 808/328-9289, is open Mon.–Fri. 8:30 A.M.–6 P.M., Sunday 10 A.M.–6 P.M. It's housed in a coffee mill complex circa 1920, one of the oldest in Honaunau, and sells not only coffee but organic produce and health food deli items. The shelves hold dried mango, candied ginger, bulk coffee, chocolate-covered coffee beans, Puna honey, dried pineapple, apples, bananas, special sauces, and—no shop is complete without them—T-shirts. Also look for a stack of burlap coffee bags, some bearing the Bong Brothers logo, that make a nifty souvenir. Adjacent is **Gold Mountain Mill,** a functional roasting mill tended by Tom Bong and his dog Bear; if time permits they'll show you around the operation. Coffee from the surrounding area comes in to be roasted in the still functional, vintage 1930s roaster.

Also in Honaunau, **Scotty's** mini-mart has a Korean barbecue take-out window.

At the Rte. 160 turnoff, look for **Merv's** for basic supplies. A short way past is the **Higashi Store,** also for a limited supply of food and snack items. In Kealia, the **Fujihara Store** has a slightly wider selection and is the last chance for packaged food and drinks until you get to Ocean View.

## Kayaking

In Captain Cook, **Adventures in Paradise,** 808/323-3005 or 866/824-2337, www.bigislandkayak.com, is the company to see for kayak rentals or tours.

# FARTHER SOUTH

## Ho'okena

If you want to see how the people of Kona still live, visit Ho'okena. A mile or two south of the Pu'uhonua O Honaunau turnoff, or 20 miles south of Kailua-Kona, take a well-marked spur road *makai* off Rte. 11 and follow it to the sea. The village is somewhat in a state of disrepair, but a number of homey cottages and some semi-permanent tents are used mostly on weekends by local fishermen. Ho'okena also boasts the **Ho'okena Beach County Park** with pavilions, restrooms, and picnic tables, but no potable water. Camping is allowed with a county permit. For drinking water, a tap is attached to the telephone pole near the beginning of your descent down the spur road. The gray-sand beach is broad, long, and probably *the* best in South Kona for both swimming and body surfing. If the sun gets too hot, some palms and other trees lining the beach provide not only shade but a picture-perfect setting. Until the road connecting Kona to Hilo was finally finished in the 1930s, Ho'okena shipped the produce of the surrounding area from its bustling wharf. At one time, Ho'okena was the main port in South Kona and even hosted Robert Louis Stevenson when he passed through the islands in 1889. Part of the wharf still remains, and nearby a fleet of outrigger fishing canoes is pulled up on shore. The surrounding cliffs are honeycombed with burial caves. If you walk a half mile north, you'll find the crumpled walls and steeple of **Maria Lanakila Church,** built in 1860 but leveled in an earthquake in 1950. The church was another "painted church" done by Father John Velghe in the same style as St. Benedict's.

## Miloli'i

This active fishing village is approximately 15 miles south of Pu'uhonua O Honaunau. Again, look for signs to a spur road off Rte. 11 heading *makai.* The long and winding road, leading through bleak lava flows, is narrow but worth the detour. Miloli'i (Fine Twist) earned its name from times past when it was famous for producing *'aha,* a sennit made from coconut-husk fibers; and *olona,* a twine made from the *olona* plant and mostly used for fishnets. This is one of the last villages in Hawaii where traditional fishing is the major source of income and where old-timers are heard speaking Hawaiian. Fishermen still use small outrigger canoes, now powered by outboards, to catch *opelu,* a type of mackerel that schools in these waters. The method of catching the *opelu* has remained unchanged for centuries. Boats gather and drop packets of chum made primarily from poi, sweet potatoes, or rice. No meat is used so sharks won't be attracted.

The **Miloli'i Beach County Park** is a favorite with local people on the weekends; camping is allowed by permit. Tents are pitched in and around the parking lot, just under the ironwoods at road's end. There are flushing toilets, a basketball court, and a brackish pond in which to rinse off, but no drinking water, so bring some. Swimming is safe inside the reef and the tidepools in the area are some of the best on the south coast. A 15-minute trail leads south to the coconut tree–fringed Honomalino Bay, where there's a secluded gray-sand and black-pebble beach great for swimming. But always check with the local people first about conditions! In the village, the small, understocked Miloli'i Grocery Store has little more than drinks and snacks but the price is right for being so far out.

For those looking for peace and quiet, try **Kaimana Guest House and Hostel,** P.O. Box

946, Captain Cook, HI 96704, 808/328-2207, kaimanavacations@msn.com, www.kaimanavacations.com, a two-story oceanside house in Miloli'i that has a kitchen, shared bath, and covered lanai. There's plenty of water equipment to borrow and great free stargazing. Hostel beds run $20, a private single room is $30, and a private double room is $40. A small detached cottage goes for $55 a night. No breakfast is served so if you're not cooking, the closest place for a meal is Ocean View. As remote as it is, you'll definitely need a rental car.

## Macadamia Nut Farm

When back on the highway heading south, you'll notice a long stretch of macadamia nut trees on both sides of the road. Now a division of Blue Diamond Growers, Mac Nut Farms of Hawaii is the largest single-owner macadamia nut farm in the state. Unfortunately, the company offers no tours of its facility nor do they have an outlet to sell their products. You'll just have to satisfy yourself with the view of acre after acre of trees and wait until you get to town to make that nutty purchase.

**BIG ISLAND OF HAWAI'I**

# South Kohala

The Kohala district is the peninsular thumb in the northwestern portion of the Big Island. At its tip is Upolu Point, only 40 miles from Maui across the 'Alenuihaha Channel. Kohala was the first section of the Big Island to rise from beneath the sea. The long-extinct volcanoes of the Kohala Mountains running down its spine have been reduced by time and the elements from lofty, ragged peaks to rounded domes of 5,000 feet or so. Kohala is divided into North and South Kohala. South Kohala boasts *the* most beautiful swimming beaches on the Big Island, along with world-class hotels and resorts. Inland is Waimea (Kamuela), the *paniolo* town and center of the massive Parker Ranch. Between the coast and Waimea lies the newer planned community of Waikoloa, with its clusters of condominiums, family homes, and a golf course. North Kohala, an area of dry coastal slopes, former sugar lands, a string of sleepy towns, and deeply incised lush valleys, forms the northernmost tip of the island.

South Kohala is a region of contrast. It's dry, hot, tortured by wind, and scored by countless old lava flows. The predominant land color here is black, and this is counterpointed by scrubby bushes and scraggly trees, a seemingly semi-arid wasteland. This was an area that the ancient Hawaiians seemed to have traveled through to get somewhere else, yet Hawaiians did live here—along the coast—and numerous archaeological sites dot the coastal plain. Still, South Kohala is stunning with its palm-fringed white-sand pockets of beach, luxury resorts, green landscaped golf courses, a proliferation of colorful planted flowers, and its deep blue inviting water. You don't generally travel here to appreciate the stunning landscape, although it too has its attraction, you come here to settle into a sedate resort community, to be pampered and pleased by the finer things that await at luxury resorts that are destinations in and of themselves.

Kiholo Bay shows greenery and turquoise lagoons—an exception on this coastline often covered by lava flows.

ROBERT NILSEN

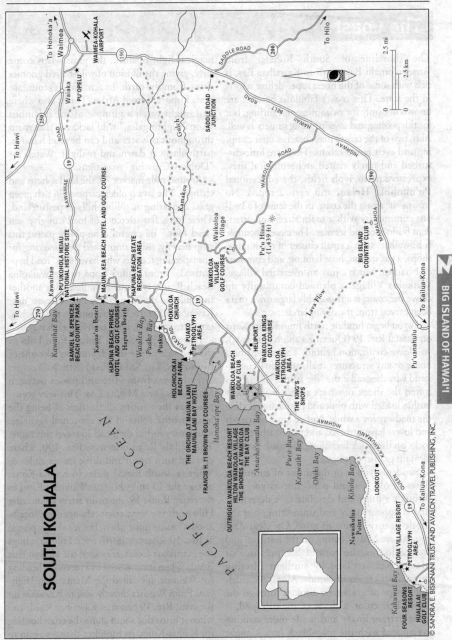

SOUTH KOHALA

PACIFIC OCEAN

To Hawi
To Honoka'a
To Hilo

SADDLE ROAD

WAIMEA-KOHALA AIRPORT
Waiaka
PU'OPELU

SADDLE ROAD JUNCTION

HAWAI'I BELT ROAD

Kamakoa Gulch

WAIKOLOA ROAD

PU'UKOHOLA HEIAU NATIONAL HISTORIC SITE

Kawaihae Bay
SAMUEL M. SPENCER BEACH COUNTY PARK

Kauna'oa Beach
MAUNA KEA BEACH HOTEL AND GOLF COURSE

HAPUNA BEACH PRINCE HOTEL AND GOLF COURSE
Hapuna Beach
HAPUNA BEACH STATE RECREATION AREA

Waialea Bay
Puako Bay
Puako
PUAKO RD.
PUAKO PETROGLYPH AREA

HOKULOA CHURCH

HOLOHOLOKAI BEACH PARK

THE ORCHID AT MAUNA LANI
MAUNA LANI BAY HOTEL

FRANCIS H. I'I BROWN GOLF COURSES
Honoka'ope Bay

WAIKOLOA BEACH GOLF CLUB

OUTRIGGER WAIKOLOA BEACH RESORT
HILTON WAIKOLOA VILLAGE
THE SHORES AT WAIKOLOA
THE BAY CLUB

WAIKOLOA PETROGLYPH AREA
THE KING'S SHOPS

HELIPORT
WAIKOLOA KINGS GOLF COURSE

WAIKOLOA VILLAGE
WAIKOLOA VILLAGE GOLF COURSE

Pu'u Hinai (1,439 ft)

Lava Flow

BIG ISLAND COUNTRY CLUB

MAMALAHOA

To Kailua-Kona

'Anaeho'omalu Bay

Puco Bay
Keawaiki Bay
Ohiki Bay
Kiholo Bay

QUEEN KA'AHUMANU HIGHWAY

Pu'uanahulu

To Kailua-Kona

LOOKOUT

Nawaikulua Point

KONA VILLAGE RESORT
PETROGLYPH AREA

Kahuwai Bay
FOUR SEASONS RESORT
HUALALAI GOLF CLUB

To Hawi
To Hawi
To Honoka'a
Waimea

190
250
270
19
200

KAWAIHAE ROAD

N

BIG ISLAND OF HAWAI'I

2.5 mi
2.5 km

© SANDRA E. BISIGNANI TRUST AND AVALON TRAVEL PUBLISHING, INC.

# The Coast

The shoreline of South Kohala, from 'Anaeho'omalu Bay north to Kawaihae Bay, is rich with some of the finest super-deluxe resorts in the state. This coast's fabulous beaches are known not only for swimming and surfing, but for tidepooling and awe-inspiring sunsets as well. Also, two of the coast's main beaches offer camping and even rental cabins. There are little-disturbed and rarely visited archaeological sites, expressive petroglyph fields, the educational **Pu'ukoholā Heiau,** and even a rodeo. No "towns" lie along the coast, in the sense of a laid-out community with a main street and attendant businesses and services. The closest facsimile is Kawaihae, with a small cluster of restaurants, shops, a gas station, boat landing, and commercial harbor, but it's just an oversized village. Waikoloa Village, a planned community up above the coast, is a reasonably large town that's been carved from the dry uplands.

As you begin heading north from Kailua-Kona on coastal Rte. 19 (Queen Ka'ahumanu Hwy.), you leave civilization behind. There won't be a house or any structures at all, and you'll understand why they call it the "Big Island." Perhaps to soften the shock of what's ahead, magnificent bushes loaded with pink and purple flowers line the roadway for a while. Notice too that friends and lovers have gathered and placed white coral rocks on the black lava along the road, forming pleasant graffiti messages.

Suddenly you're in the midst of enormous flows of old 'a'a and pahoehoe as you pass through a huge and desolate lava desert. At first it appears ugly and uninviting, but the subtle beauty begins to grow. On clear days you can see Maui floating on the horizon, and *mauka* looms the formidable presence of Mauna Kea streaked by sunlight filtering through its crown of clouds. Along the roadside, wisps of grass have broken through the lava. Their color, a shade of pinkish gold, is quite extraordinary and made more striking juxtaposed with the inky-black lava. Caught by your headlights at night, or especially in the magical light of dusk, the grass wisps come alive, giving the illusion of wild-haired gnomes rising from the earth. In actuality, it's fountain grass imported from Africa. This is also where you might catch a glimpse of the infamous "Kona nightingales," wild jackasses that roam throughout this area and can be road hazards, particularly at dawn and twilight. Watch for "Donkey Crossing" road signs.

Around mile marker 70, the land softens and changes. The lava is older, carpeted in rich green grass appearing as rolling hills of pastureland. These long, flat stretches of road can give you "lead foot." Be careful! The police patrol this strip heavily, using unmarked cars, looking for unsuspecting tourists who have been "road hypnotized." From Kailua-Kona to the Waikoloa Beach Resort is about 25 miles, with another five miles to the Mauna Kea Beach Resort near Kawaihae. If you're day-tripping to the beaches, expect to spend an hour traveling each way.

If you're approaching Kohala from Hilo or the east side of the island, you can take one of two routes. The Saddle Road (Rte. 200) comes directly west from Hilo and passes between Mauna Kea and Mauna Loa. This very scenic road has the alluring distinction of being the least favorite route of the car-rental agencies, which may forbid their cars to travel this route. The Saddle Road intersects Rte. 190, where you can turn north and drive for six miles to Waimea, south for 33 miles to Kailua-Kona, or take the 13-mile shortcut Waikoloa Road to the coast. Route 19, the main artery connecting Hilo with the west coast, changes its "locally known" name quite often, but it's always posted as Rte. 19. Directly north from Hilo as it hugs the Hamakua Coast, it's called the Hawaii Belt Road. When it turns west in Honoka'a, heading for Waimea, it's called the Mamalahoa Highway. From Waimea directly west to Kawaihae on the coast Rte. 19 becomes Kawaihae Road, and when it turns due south along the coast heading for Kailua-Kona, its moniker changes again to Queen Ka'ahumanu Highway.

# SIGHTS

The following sights and beaches are listed from south to north. All lie along coastal Rte. 19.

## Ka'upulehu Petroglyphs

Located just back from the ponds at the Kona Village Resort is a cluster of approximately 440 lava rock carvings, near where the ancient Kings Highway must have passed. This group of petroglyphs contains designs, many of them different from others along this coast. There are numerous human figures, some with paddles and fishing lines held in their hands, a turtle figure, and dozens that illustrate the lines of crab-claw sails of sailing canoes. While some of these carvings are speculated to be as much as 900 years old, others are obviously newer, as you can discern the date 1820 and some Western script—obviously done after contact with early white sailors. In 1998, the resort constructed a wooden boardwalk around the majority of these carved figures in order to protect the integrity of these fine works of art. Please stay on the wooden pathway during your self-guided tour. As this field lies on Kona Village property, you may need to contact the hotel in order to get permission to enter the property. Tours can be arranged through the concierge desk, 808/325-5555, where printed information and a map of the site are available.

## Waikoloa Petroglyphs

Set along a reconstructed section of the King's Trail and surrounded by the Beach Course golf course is the Waikoloa Petroglyph field. Unlike others nearby, this grouping is done in an undulating area and also includes remains of temporary structures. While many and varied designs are seen here, a circular pattern is much in evidence. Cinder rock paths have been constructed throughout this petroglyph field. Stay on the paths; do not walk on the carvings. Approach this area from the King's Shops for a self-guided tour or take one of the free guided tours conducted by the shopping center, Tues.–Fri. at 10:30 A.M. or Saturday at 8:30 A.M. Wear sturdy shoes, a hat, and bring drinking water.

## Puako Petroglyphs

These rock carvings, approximately 3,000 individual designs, are considered some of the finest and oldest in Hawaii, but carvings of horses and cattle signify ongoing art that happened long after Westerners appeared. Circles outlined by a series of small holes belonged to families who placed the umbilical cords of their infants into these indentations to tie them to the 'aina and give them strength for a long and good life. State archaeologists and anthropologists have reported a deterioration of the site due to vandalism, so please look but don't deface, and stay on established paths. Access is by a well-marked, self-guiding trail starting from Holoholokai Beach Park, located on the north side of the Orchid at Mauna Lani Hotel.

## Puako

Puako and its environs receive about 10 inches of rain a year, making it one of if not the driest areas of the state. This alluring area is located *makai* on a side road off Rte. 19 about four miles south of Kawaihae. Hawaiians lived here in times past, but a modern community has been building along the three-mile road past Puako Bay since the 1950s. This quiet, no-frills community is a mixture of working class homes, rental properties, and discreet vacation hideaways. Services amount to one reasonably well-stocked general store, a public telephone, and a vacation rental agency. A thin ribbon of white sand runs the length of the beach near the boat ramp that provides fair swimming. Sunsets here are magnificent, and you'll usually have the beach to yourself. The remainder of the shoreline through this community is mostly rock shelf with inlets and tidepools, for good fishing, snorkeling, and some surfing. Near-shore scuba diving is excellent, with huge caverns and caves to explore, and a colorful concentration of coral and marine life. There are half a dozen shoreline access routes along this strip road.

Along Puako Road is **Hokuloa Church,** built by Rev. Lorenzo Lyons in 1859. This musically talented reverend mastered the Hawaiian language and composed lovely ballads such as

**BIG ISLAND OF HAWAI'I**

"Hawaii Aloha," which has become the unofficial anthem of the islands. The church is a thick-walled structure with a plain simple interior. Sunday service is held at 9 A.M.

Between here and Hapuna Beach State Recreation Area just up the coast is **Waialea Bay Marine Life Conservation District,** a 35-acre preserve. Turn off Puako Road onto Old Puako Road and then turn down a rough road near pole number 69 to reach the shore. The white sand beach here is best in summer. The reef is wonderful for snorkeling, better at its southern end. Although a bit hard to get to, it's a favorite for the local community.

## Pu'ukohola Heiau

Don't miss this restored Hawaiian temple, a National Historical Site located one mile south of Kawaihae where coastal Rte. 19 turns into Rte. 270 heading into North Kohala. This site, covering 77 acres, includes **Mailekini Heiau** and the **John Young's Homestead** site. Below the *heiau,* in the trees near the sea, Kamehameha I kept a royal household, and a short way offshore in the bay is an older *heiau* dedicated to the shark god. The shark god *heiau* silted over in the 1950s due, at least in part, to

construction of the harbor facilities nearby, but to this day an inordinant number of black-tip reef sharks can be spotted near where this site was. Administered by the National Park Service, this sacred ground is open daily 7:30 A.M.–4 P.M.; free admission; website: www.nps.gov/puhe. As you enter, pick up a map highlighting the points of interest. It's worthwhile checking out the visitor center, 808/882-7218, where the rangers provide excellent information and pertinent informative books are available. The one trail through the park leads to its notable sites, and from it, a short section of a coastal trail runs to Spencer Beach County Park nearby. It's hot and dry at this site, so bring water and wear a hat. Pu'ukohola (Whale Hill) received its name either because the hill itself resembles a whale, or because migrating whales pass very close offshore every year. It was fated to become a hill of destiny. For the best views of the *heiau,* enter the Kawaihaw Small Boat Harbor and take an immediate left down a crushed coral drive to the flats alongside the bay opposite the park land.

Kamehameha I built Pu'ukohola Heiau in 1790–01 on the advice of Kapoukahi, a prophet

Pu'ukohola Heiau from across the bay

ROBERT NILSEN

from Kaua'i who said that Kamehameha would unify all the islands only after he built a temple to his war-god Kuka'ilimoku. Kamehameha complied, building this last of the great Hawaiian *heiau* from mortarless stone that when finished measured 100 by 224 feet. The dedication ceremony of the *heiau* is fascinating history. Kamehameha's last rival was his cousin, Keoua Kuahu'ula. This warlike chief realized that his *mana* had deserted him and that it was Kamehameha who would rise to be sovereign of all the islands. Kamehameha invited him to the dedication ceremony, but en route Keoua, in preparation for the inevitable outcome, performed a death purification ceremony by circumcising his own penis. When the canoes reached the beach, they were met by a hail of spears and musket balls. Keoua was killed and his body laid on Kuka'ilimoku's altar as a noteworthy sacrifice. Kamehameha became the unopposed sovereign of the Big Island and, within a few years, of all Hawaii.

Every August on the weekend closest to Establishment Day, a free two-day Hawaiian Cultural Festival is held on the *heiau* grounds, including arts and crafts exhibitions, games, hula demonstrations, music and dance, and re-creation of ancient ceremonies in traditional dress.

Near the *heiau*, but on the upland side of the highway, is the house site of John Young, an English seaman who became a close adviser to Kamehameha. Young, dubbed 'Olohana, "All Hands" by Kamehameha, taught the Hawaiians how to use cannons and muskets and fought alongside Kamehameha in many battles. He turned Mailekini Heiau into a fort, and over a century later the U.S. Army used it as an observation area during World War II. Young became a respected Hawaiian chief and grandfather of Queen Emma. Only he and one other white man have the honor of being buried at the Royal Mausoleum in Nu'uanu Valley on O'ahu. Little remains of the house itself, but it was certainly one of, if not the first, Western-style home and the first plastered structures in the islands. Apparently, John Young's wife didn't like the house too much; she had traditional-style structures built to the side for her use.

## BEACHES AND PARKS

There are a number of excellent beaches along this coast, most with good to excellent facilities. In addition, all resorts offer access to their beaches with (limited) public parking.

### Kahuwai Bay to Kua Bay

The picturesque Kahuwai Bay has a sandy bottom bounded by rocky shorelines on either side. It is a spot often chosen by green sea turtles to relax on the sand or to lay their eggs. Give them wide berth. Kona Village Resort fronts this bay and creates a fine Polynesian village background. Offshore is a fine reef for snorkeling and scuba. Next door, the Four Seasons Resort sits on a narrow strip of sandy beach and one swimming lagoon. Anchialine ponds here have been set aside as a fish management area. Beyond the Four Seasons is Kuki'o Beach, reachable by public access at the side of the Four Seasons Resort, and farther on is Kua Bay. Walking through hotel property, you can easily go between Kahuwai Beach and Kuki'o Beach.

**Kuki'o Beach** is bounded by rocky points, the aquamarine water pushes the steep and narrow brown sand beach up the dune, beyond which are more anchialine ponds. At the far end of this beach and tucked into the rocks is a much more protected and much smaller beach, just right for kids. Beyond this is a larger rocky cove. If you're adventurous, follow the very rough path across the a'a cobbles and around the point over broken coral. The path is not distinct and not easy, but once you get a ways around (it may take a half hour) you're rewarded with a fine view of the more isolated Kua Bay.

### Kiholo Bay

Near mile marker 81 on the highway is a pull-off and overlook that offers a good glimpse of this stark lava-covered coast. Down on the coast just north of the pull-off you'll see Kiholo Bay and Luahinewai Pond. The pond was a favorite stop for Hawaiian sailors going up the coast, who would have a swim in its cool turquoise waters before continuing on. Look for a stand of royal palms marking the spot, and follow the rough but passable 4WD road down to the beach, where you will find a large round wooden house that once belonged to Loretta Lynn. Close by, a path leads over the lava to a tiny cove made more dramatic by a black-sand beach.

## 'Anaeho'omalu Bay

After miles of the transfixing monochrome blackness of Kohala's lava flows, a green standout of palm trees beckons in the distance. Turn near mile marker 76 at the Waikoloa Beach Resort entrance, and follow the access road to historic 'Anaeho'omalu Bay, referred to locally as "A-Bay." Set back from the beach here is the Waikoloa Beach Marriott. The bay area, with its freshwater springs, coconut trees, blue lagoon, and white-sand beach, is a picture-perfect seaside oasis. Between the large coconut grove and the beach are two well-preserved fishponds where mullet was raised for consumption only by the royalty who lived nearby or were happening by in seagoing canoes. Throughout the area along well-marked trails are petroglyphs, a segment of the cobblestoned King's Highway, and numerous archaeological sites including house sites and some hard-to-find bur-

ial caves. The white-sand beach is open to the public, with access, parking, picnic tables, and beautiful lava stone showers/bathhouses. Although the sand is a bit grainy, the swimming, snorkeling, scuba diving, sailboarding, and just about any water sport are great. A walk north along the bay brings you to an area of excellent tidepools and waters heavily populated by marinelife.

## Holoholokai Beach Park

Located adjacent to the Orchid at Mauna Lani Hotel on a well-marked access road, this picturesque beach park is open to the public daily 6:30 A.M.–7 P.M. and is improved with a bathroom, running water, picnic tables, and resort-quality landscaping. Unfortunately, the beach itself is mostly coral boulders with only tiny pockets offering very limited water access. However, the park is used very little and is perfect for relaxing under a palm tree or for a leisurely stroll to explore the many tidepools. A shoreline path leads to the sand beach fronting the Orchid at Mauna Lani and past that to the wider sand beach at the Mauna Lani Bay Hotel, which fronts Makaiwa Bay. From the back side of the parking

Wide and long, Hapuna Beach is one of the finest strands of sand on the island.

lot at the public beach park, a trail heads into the *kiawe* and leads to Puako Petroglyphs.

## Hapuna Beach State Recreation Area

Approximately seven miles north of 'Anaeho-'omalu is the *second*-best (some rate this the best), but most accessible, white-sand beach on the island. Hapuna Beach is wide and spacious, almost 700 yards long by 70 wide in summer, with a reduction by heavy surf in winter. A lava finger divides the beach into almost equal halves. During good weather the swimming is excellent and lifeguards are on duty. During heavy weather, usually in winter, the rips are fierce, and Hapuna has claimed more lives than any other beach park on all of Hawaii! At the north end is a small cove almost forming a pool that is usually safe, a favorite for snorkeling with families and children. Many classes in beginning scuba and snorkeling are held in this area, and shore fishing is good throughout. At the south end, good breaks make for tremendous body surfing (no boards allowed), and those familiar with the area make spectacular leaps from the seacliffs. Picnic tables, pavilions, restrooms, and plenty of parking are available in this nicely landscaped park.

Camping is available in six A-frame screened shelters that rent for $20 per night and accommodate up to four. Provided are sleeping platforms (you bring your own bedding), electric outlets, cold-water showers, and toilets in separate comfort stations, plus a shared range and refrigerator in a central pavilion. Although the spot is a little run-down, the A-frames are very popular, so reservations and a deposit are required. You can receive full information from the Division of State Parks, P.O. Box 936, Hilo, HI 96721, 808/974-6200; or visit the office at 75 Aupini St., Room 204, in Hilo.

## Kauna'oa Beach

Better known as Mauna Kea Beach because of the nearby luxury hotel of the same name, Kauna'oa is less than a mile north of Hapuna Beach and is considered the best beach on the Big Island by not only the local population, but also by those who judge such things from a broader perspective. In times past, it was a nesting and mating ground for green sea turtles, and although these activities no longer occur because of human pressure on the habitat, turtles still visit the south end of the beach. Mauna Kea Beach is long and wide, and the sandy bottom makes for excellent swimming within the reef. It is more sheltered than Hapuna but can still be dangerous. Hotel beach boys, always in attendance, are unofficial lifeguards who have saved many unsuspecting tourists. During high surf, the shoreline is a favorite with surfers. Like all beaches in Hawaii, this one is public, but to keep the number of nonguests down, only 10 parking passes are handed out each day on a first-come, first-served basis. Pick up a pass at the guardhouse as you enter the hotel grounds. This entitles you to spend the day on the beach, but on weekends they're gone early. Alternately, park at Hapuna Beach and return via an easy mile-long trail connecting Hapuna and Mauna Kea Beaches.

## Spencer Beach County Park

The entrance for this park is the same as that for Pu'ukohola Heiau on Rte. 19 just south of Kawaihae. A coastal trail leads from the beach park up to the *heiau,* so you can combine a day at the beach with a cultural education. The park is named after Samuel Mahuka Spencer, a longtime island resident who was born in Waimea, served as county mayor for 20 years, and died in 1960 at Honoka'a. The park provides pavilions, restrooms, cold-water showers, electricity, picnic facilities, and even tennis courts. Day use is free, but tent and trailer camping are by county permit only. Spencer Beach is protected from wind and heavy wave action by an offshore reef and by breakwaters built around Kawaihae Bay. These make it the safest swimming beach along South Kohala's shore and a favorite with local families with small children. The wide, shallow reef is home to a wide spectrum of marinelife, making the snorkeling entertaining. The shoreline fishing is also excellent.

# LUXURY RESORTS

The South Kohala Coast has four resort areas, all providing luxury accommodations, fine dining, golf courses, full-service resort amenities, the best beaches on the island, and a smattering of historical and cultural sites. They are, in effect, self-sufficient mini-villages. The first north of Kailua-Kona is not referred to by one name, but encompasses the adjacent properties of **Kona Village Resort** at Ka'upulehu and the **Four Seasons Resort** at Hualalai. A new time-share property with golf course is rising from the lava to the south and this development fronts Kuki'o Beach. These resorts are actually situated in the North Kona district but are discussed here as they are more similar to the South Kohala luxury resorts than to any hotel complex in Kailua or Keauhou to the south. Kona Village Resort, the oldest resort along this coast, is designed like a Polynesian village: low-slung, thatch roofs, palm trees, white-sand beach, and shoreline ponds. It's a welcome oasis in a land of stark black lava; it has kept up with the times and still offers one of the best get-away destinations in the state. The Four Seasons Resort is the island's newest, a modern complex of tasteful buildings, a counterpoint to Kona Village, where you will find golf, tennis, and water sport opportunities. It's new and fresh, a delight for the senses.

Next up the way is **Waikoloa Resort,** the largest, busiest, and most commercial of the resort complexes. Here you have the Waikoloa Beach Marriott, a redesigned hotel that reflects the grandeur of Hawaii from the 1930s and '40s, the gargantuan Hilton Waikoloa Village, and three high-class condominiums. Here as well are the King's Shops, the only shopping center in the area, two superb golf courses, a multitude of tennis opportunities, a petroglyph field, remnants of the ancient King's Trail, anchialine ponds, and one of the best beaches on the coast. Just across the road is a commercial heliport. To ease getting around between shops, hotels, and condos, the Waikoloa Shuttle runs every 10 minutes between 10 A.M. and 9 P.M. at $1 per ride.

**Mauna Lani Resort** comes next, also big but not as commercial. Here too you find two magnificent hotels, five (and counting) condominiums, two golf courses, tennis, beaches, fishponds, two petroglyph fields, and a long history. There is no shopping complex here, but each hotel has a bevy of retail shops. This is a quality high-end resort, without glitz or hype.

Farthest to the north is the **Mauna Kea Resort.** Smaller and more intimate, it contains the grande dame of Kohala hotels, the Mauna Kea Beach Hotel, and its more recent addition, the Hapuna Beach Prince Hotel. Like bride and groom, these two hotels with their golf courses are sufficient unto themselves, and they sit on the two finest beaches on the island. While there are no major historical sites on the property, they lie a mile or two south of one of the most significant and well-kept *heiau* on this island.

## Kona Village Resort

So you want to go "native," and you're dreaming of a "little grass shack" along a secluded beach? No problem! The Kona Village Resort, P.O. Box 1299, Kailua-Kona, HI 96745, 808/325-5555 or 800/432-5450 in Hawaii, 800/367-5290 Mainland, kvr@aloha.net, www.konavillage.com, is a once-in-a-lifetime dream experience. Located on Kahuwai Bay, a picture-perfect cove of white sand dotted with coconut palms, the village lies seven miles north of the Kona Airport, surrounded by acres of seclusion. The accommodations are 125 distinctive "hales," individual renditions of thatch-roofed huts found throughout Polynesia and Hawaii. They are simple but luxurious, and in keeping with the idea of getting away from it all, have no TVs, radios, or telephones. All, however, do have ceiling fans and louvered windows to let the tropical breezes blow through. Beds are covered with distinctive quilts and pillows. Each hut features a wet bar, refrigerator, coffeemaker, and extra-large bathroom, and is either located along the water, around the lagoon, or back in a garden setting. At one time you had to fly into the hotel's private airstrip, but today you arrive by car. Almost exactly at mile marker 87, turn in, make a right within 100 yards, and follow the access road that leads through coal-black lava fields. Don't despair! Down by the sea you can see the shimmering green palm trees as they beckon you to the resort. Kona Village gives you your money's worth, with a lei greeting, free valet service, a private tennis center, water sports, numerous cultural activities, and a lu'au. Guided tours are also offered to the petroglyph field on property, complete with history and legends of the area.

Meals are served in the Hale Moana, the main dining room, and at the Hale Moana Terrace, where a famous luncheon buffet is served daily. Hale Samoa is the fine dining restaurant, open daily except Wednesday and Friday for dinner only. Upon entering Hale Samoa, your spirits rise immediately with the sweep of cathedral ceiling. On the walls is an original painting by Herb Kane, Hawaii's foremost artist, that depicts *The Fair American,* a tiny ship commandeered by King Kamehameha that was instrumental in changing the history of old Hawaii. The walls also hold portraits of the hotel's original owner, Johnno Jackson, an oil geologist from Texas, who in 1960 sailed in with his wife Helen, their Labrador dog, a monkey, and a parrot—all in a 42-foot schooner—landed on these shores and declared, "This is the spot!" Also on the grounds are Hale Ho'okipa "House of Hospitality," where a lu'au is held on Friday nights as it has for over 30 years, and an international buffet dinner every Wednesday. Drinks and tropical libations are offered throughout the afternoon at the Shipwreck Bar next to the beachfront pool, and at the Bora Bora Bar in the evening next to Hale Moana, where soft musical entertainment soothes guests every evening.

Rates per night start at $505 per couple with full American plan (includes three meals), and go up to $895 for oceanfront huts. Two-room units for three adults run $825–1,500. Deduct $113 for single occupancy and add $38 for children 3–5, $143 for children 6–12, and $193 for an extra adult. There is a strict reservations and refund policy, so check. These rates also include transportation to and from the airport if you need it, all scheduled activities, use of the tennis and fitness centers, water sport equipment, and all activities except scuba, snuba, massage, and the Friday night lu'au. The hotel's Na Keiki in Paradise is a children's program included in the room price that will entertain and educate children ages six and up throughout the day. The beach shack is open every day for your pleasure, as are the jewelry store and gift shop. Hotel manager Fred Duerr has

been at the facility since 1966, and most of his highly professional and seasoned staff tend to stay for years. They take pride in the hotel and do everything to help you have a rewarding, enjoyable, and relaxing stay at this premier resort. The Kona Village is a serene Hawaiian classic that deserves its well-earned reputation for excellence, and as a consequence gets 65 percent repeat visitors and 25 percent honeymooners.

## Four Seasons Resort

The Four Seasons Resort, Hualalai, 100 Ka'upulehu Drive, Kailua-Kona, HI 96740, 808/325-8000 or 888/340-5662, fax 808/325-8100, www.fourseasons.com/hualalai, at historic Ka'upulehu, opened in late 1996. This 243-room AAA Five-Diamond resort is split into 36 low-rise bungalows in four crescent groups that front a half-mile beach and several natural lagoons just down from Kona Village Resort. Located in among old lava flows from the Hualalai volcano, 32 of these units have ocean access and four are located along the 18th green of the accompanying golf course. Contemporary Polynesian in style, the units are a mixture of dark mahogany wood, light wall colors and carpeting, pleasing medium brown rattan furniture, and gray slate flooring. Authentic Hawaiian art pieces from the late 1700s to the present are displayed throughout the hotel. There is no skimping on space, furnishings, or amenities in any of the rooms or suites. Large as well are the bathrooms, each of which looks out onto a private garden, lanai, or patio. The slate floors of the main rooms are covered with seagrass mats and the beds with material reminiscent of tapa cloth. An exceptional place, this all-inclusive destination resort is not cheap. Rooms run $500–725 per night, suites $850–6,450, $110 for a third adult in a room. Numerous attractive packages are always offered, so inquire.

The resort's three restaurants will fill your every culinary need for all three meals of the day. Both the elegant AAA Four-Diamond **Pahu I'a Restaurant** and the casual **Beach Tree Bar and Grill** are set oceanside. With setting inside and out, Pahu I'a opens in the morning with local and international favorites, buffet or à la carte, and transforms in the evening into a more formal eatery with an emphasis on cuisines of the Pacific and the imaginative combinations of food and flavorings. Resort wear is required and reservations are necessary. Serving lunch and dinner, the Beach Tree offers grill items near the main pool. Several evenings a week, this restaurant offers theme nights with regional foods of the world. Nightly music is also a part of this venue, with a hula dancing performance several nights of the week. In addition, the **Hualalai Club Grille and Bar** at the golf clubhouse across the main entrance drive serves lunch and fine-dining dinners in a sophisticated but informal setting. For drinks and convivial late-night companionship there are several options. The Lava Lounge at the Pahu I'a is open evenings only and offers light music every night except Sunday. Set as close as you can get to the water without being in it, the Beach Tree bar dispenses libations throughout the day under its canopy roof and is an easy-going place to sit and watch the sun set.

On the ocean side of the meeting room building and the outdoor Hoku stage theater is Kids for all Seasons, the hotel's service of supervised care for five- to 12-year-olds that provides a wide variety of fun-filled and indoor and outdoor activities. For teens, Tsunami is the activity center for indoor games and it organizes outdoor excursions. Hualalai Tennis Club is open for hotel guests only. Located adjacent to the tennis courts is the Sports Club and Spa, a full-service facility that offers a variety of instructional classes, a 25-meter lap pool, exercise machines, massage and spa therapies, and sand volleyball and half-court basketball courts. For the duffer, the private Hualalai Golf Club offers 18 holes of challenging play along the ocean. A second course opened its front nine in 2002, with the back nine soon to come. Be sure to check out the Cultural Center with its 1,200-gallon reef aquarium just downstairs from the lobby, where you can learn about the surrounding waters, the Ka'upulehu area, and the life and lifestyle of ancient Hawaiians. In addition to the natural lagoons, the resort has both freshwater and saltwater swimming pools set just back from the beach. For those interested, a water sport kiosk on the beach can fix you up with needed gear or water activities.

## Waikoloa Beach Marriott Resort

Following a $25 million renovation and facelift, the former Royal Waikoloan re-emerged as the artful Waikoloa Beach Marriott, 69-275 Waikoloa Beach Dr., Waikoloa, HI 96738, 808/886-6789 or 800/688-7444, www.outriggerwaikoloabeach.com. On a perfect spot fronting the palm-fringed 'Anaeho'omalu Bay, the hotel looks out over ponds that once stocked fish for passing *ali'i*. The hotel lobby is a spacious open-air affair that lets the trade winds blow through across its cool sandstone floor. Six floors of rooms extend out in wings on both sides, flanking the landscaped courtyard with swimming pool and water slide. Greeting you as you enter the lobby is a marvelous old koa outrigger canoe set in front of a three-part mural by renowned Hawaiian artist Herb Kane of a royal canoe and Western frigate meeting off the Kona coast. Walk farther and gaze down upon the landscaped courtyard, heavy with greenery and the pungent smell of tropical plants. The renovation has bequeathed a look and feel reminiscent of the 1930s and '40s with its decorative artistic touches and imparts a sense of less hectic times. The Waikoloa Beach Marriott Resort is a class act.

All 545 hotel rooms and suites are tastefully decorated in light soothing colors, with king-size beds, rattan furnishings, custom quilts, and island prints of a mid-20th century art deco style. Each room has a/c, color TV, *yakuta* robes, in-room safe, small refrigerator, marble vanities, and a private lanai. Rooms are reasonably priced at $315–485, while suites run $965–3,100 per night. Hotel services and amenities include an activities desk for all on-site and off-property excursions and several retail shops and boutiques, and a Kahn Galleries shop for fine art. You can take part in daily Hawaiian cultural programs, use the business center, or have your kids properly cared for at the children's program. Enjoy the garden swimming pool, spa and fitness center, six tennis courts, and a grand beach with plenty of water activities. The hotel is just a few minutes' stroll past the royal fishponds to the beach or to the remains of a nearby ancient but now restored *heiau*.

The Waikoloa Beach Marriott also has new dining facilities. Harking back to the days when Hawaiian music and news of the islands was transmitted to the world by radio, and when Pan Am Clipper Ships flew travelers to the islands, is **Hawaii Calls Restaurant,** the hotel's main dining room. Open for breakfast and dinner, the decor says yesteryear but the menu is thoroughly modern with a mix of Continental and Asian cuisine. As part of this open-air restaurant, the **Clipper Lounge** serves tropical drinks as smooth as a Clipper's landing on a mirror lagoon. This lounge serves up a late bistro menu and nightly entertainment 5–11:30 P.M., while the more casual poolside **Nalu Bar and Grill** is open 10 A.M.–sunset for snacks, fill-'er-ups, and drinks. Fit for the royalty who once called this bay their home, the twice weekly Royal Lu'au draws appreciative guests for food and entertainment.

## The Shores at Waikoloa

The Shores at Waikoloa, 69-1035 Keana Place, Waikoloa, HI 96738, 808/885-5001—or contact Aston Hotel and Resorts, 800/321-2558 in Hawaii, 800/922-7866 Mainland and Canada—are secluded luxury condominiums nestled away in the planned community of Waikoloa. Enter through a security gate to see the peaceful and beautifully manicured grounds of these white-stucco and red-tile-roof condominiums. A few minutes away are the best beaches on Hawaii and all of the activities offered by the large luxury hotels, if you wish to participate. The condominium offers an activities desk where your outings can be arranged, a swimming pool and hot tub, two complimentary tennis courts, and outdoor barbecues. The condos are decorated by the individual owners so each room is unique, but there are guidelines and standards so every unit is tasteful and comfortable. All units are extremely spacious, with many boasting marble and terra cotta floors. All have huge bathrooms, full modern kitchens, laundry facilities, and light and airy sitting rooms complete with state-of-the-art entertainment centers. Rates range $275 for a one-bedroom to $700 for a three-bedroom golf villa. Low season brings a 10 percent reduction, and a number of packages are available. If you are

after a luxury vacation within a vacation where you can get away from it all after you've gotten away from it all, The Shores at Waikoloa is a superb choice. The Shores is a AAA Three-Diamond award winner.

## The Bay Club

Surrounded by golf links, The Bay Club, 69-450 Waikoloa Beach Drive, Kamuela, HI 96743, 808/886-7979 or 800/305-7979, has an ideal location. Like all other accommodations in this planned community of Waikoloa Beach Resort, The Bay Club is luxury living in a secure environment. On the property are tennis courts, a swimming pool with poolside cafe, a sauna and spa, fitness center, and activities center. You can partake in as much as you like or just lounge to your heart's content. The Bay Club is a time-share property, however, units are rented based on availability but no more than 30 days in advance. One-bedroom units run $300 while those with two-bedrooms go for $400.

## Hilton Waikoloa Village

At the Hilton Waikoloa Village, 425 Waikoloa Beach Dr., Waikoloa, HI 96738, 808/886-1234 or 800/445-8667, fax 808/886-2900, www.waikoloavillage.hilton.com, the idea was to create a reality so beautiful and naturally harmonious that anyone who came here, sinner or saint, would be guaranteed a glimpse of paradise. The architecture is "fantasy grand," and the grounds are grandly fantastic. The three main towers, each enclosing a miniature fern-filled botanical garden, are spread over the grounds almost a mile apart and are linked by pink flagstone walkways, canals navigated by hotel launches, and a quiet, space-age tram. Attention to the smallest detail is immediately apparent, and everywhere sculptures, art treasures, and brilliant flowers soothe the eyes. The museum promenade displays choice artworks from Hawaii, Oceania, and Asia—pick up a brochure from the sundries shops at the hotel explaining this $7 million collection—and here and there around the property are brilliant artistic flourishes. Nearly everywhere you look you delight in beauty. Songs of rare tropical birds and the wind whispering through a bamboo forest create the natural melody that surrounds you. The beach fronting the property offers excellent snorkeling, while two gigantic pools and a series of lagoons are perfect for water activities and sunbathing. You can swim in a private lagoon accompanied by dolphins, dine in first-rate restaurants, relax to a message at the spa, leave your kids for the day in the experienced hands of the Camp Menehune staff, pick up a memento at the retail shops, sweat over a game of tennis, or just let your cares slip away as you lounge in perfect tranquillity.

Like the hotel in general, its seven restaurants are culinary powerhouses, and every taste is provided for. **Donatoni's** features classic Northern Italian cuisine; **Palm Terrace** presents breakfast and dinner buffets, with a different theme nightly; **Imari** serves traditional Japanese fare; The Chinese **Kirin** restaurant offers dim sum lunches and seafood dinners; **Kamuela Provision Co.** specializes in steak and seafood; **Orchid Cafe** provides light breakfasts and lunches; and **Lagoon Grill** has casual lunches and tropical drinks. The hotel's bars, lounges, and casual poolside dining are other options, while twice weekly the **Legends of the Pacific** lu'au delights guests with fine food and an extravagant dinner show.

With all this splendor, the most talked-about feature at the hotel is still **Dolphin Quest.** A specially constructed saltwater pond is home to Atlantic bottlenose dolphins from Florida's Gulf Coast. Daily, on a lottery basis for adults, but with two months in advance reservations available to children up to 19 years of age, guests are allowed to interact with the dolphins. Dolphin Quest is an educational experience. Here you don't ride the dolphins and they don't do tricks for you. In the half-hour session, guests wade in chest-deep water with the dolphins gliding by while a staff member imparts information concerning not only dolphins, but all marinelife and human interdependence with it. The experience is voluntary on the dolphins' part—*they* choose to swim with *you* as a guest in their domain. Much of the proceeds from the program go toward marine research.

This resort is definitely a distinctive undertaking, a step apart from any other resort complex in the state. It has cut its own path and gone its own way. Yet with all the grandeur, it seems a bit like Disneyland on a lava flow; beautiful and expansive, yet incongruous and overblown. Forget intimacy. You don't come here to get away, you come here to participate. With 1,240 rooms on a 62-acre property, it's so big that entering the lobby can be like walking into Grand Central Station and navigating certain walkways like pushing through throngs at a fair. For all that, the Hilton still offers plenty for everyone and gives you unlimited options for a great vacation. You be the judge: is this paradise or something else?

This futuristic hotel complex has set a new standard; as you would expect, all this luxury comes at a price, but for the most part not unreasonable. Room rates are $189–450 for garden/mountain rooms, $229–540 for partial ocean views, $249–620 for deluxe ocean rooms, and $950–5,530 for suites!

## The Orchid at Mauna Lani

In a tortured field of coal-black lava made more dramatic by pockets of jade-green lawn rises ivory-white The Orchid at Mauna Lani, One N. Kaniku Dr., Kohala Coast, HI 96743, 808/885-2000 or 800/845-9905, www.orchid-maunalani.com. A rolling drive lined with *haku lei* of flowering shrubs entwined with stately palms leads to the open-air porte cochère. Enter to find koa and marble reflecting the diffused and soothing light of the interior. Straight ahead, off the thrust-proscenium Sunset Terrace, a living blue-on-blue still-life of sea and sky is perfectly framed. Nature, powerful yet soothing, surrounds the hotel. Stroll the grounds, where gentle breezes always blow and where the ever-present surf is the back beat of a melody created by trickling rivulets and falling waters as they meander past a magnificent free-form pool and trimmed tropical gardens of ferns and flowers. The hallways and lobbies open from the central area like the delicate ribs of a geisha's fan; walls are graced with Hawaiian quilts and excellent artwork on view everywhere; and every set of stairs boasts a velvety smooth koa banister carved with the pineapple motif, the Hawaiian symbol of hospitality. The Orchid is casually elegant, a place to relax in luxury and warm *aloha*.

Located in two six-story wings off the main reception hall, the 539 hotel rooms, each with private lanai and sensational view, are a mixture of kings, doubles, and suites. Done in neutral tones, the stylish and refined rooms feature hand-crafted quilts, twice-daily room attendance, an entertainment center, fully stocked honor bar, in-room safe, and spacious marble bathrooms. Room rates begin at $435 for a garden view to $705 for a deluxe oceanfront room. One-bedroom executive suites run $900 and the two magnificent Presidential Suites are … well, very expensive.

Dining at The Orchid can be everything from poolside casual to haute cuisine, prepared in various styles, using locally grown produce, herbs, meats, and seafood. The culinary results are not only mouth-watering but healthy and wonderfully nutritious. The Orchid's fine dining restaurant is **The Grill,** where crystal and dark koa wood set the scene and most dishes are either steak or fish. The Grill is open for dinner only; evening or alohawear requested. The **Orchid Court,** a casual restaurant featuring Pacific Rim and California cuisine, is the hotel's main dining room and is open for breakfast and dinner. Breakfasts are either à la carte or buffet, and a wide range of sandwiches, pizza, fish, meat, and pasta dishes are your choices for dinner. Poolside, **Brown's Beach House** is the most casual restaurant, where you dine alfresco in a garden setting for lunch and dinner, and where dinner entrées are inspirations of the islands and the Orient. Soft Hawaiian music accompanies a hula dancer in the evening. For a relaxing evening of drinks, a cigar, or billiards, and periodic live entertainment, lower yourself into an overstuffed leather chair at the Paniolo Lounge and Polo Bar.

The hotel offers first-rate guest services, amenities, and activities that include a small shopping mall with everything from sundries to designer boutiques, complimentary shuttle to and from Mauna Lani's famous championship golf courses, golf bag storage, 11 tennis courts (with seven lit for evening play), complimentary use of fitness center and snorkel equipment, a day spa with massage,

body treatments, and exercise, an enormous swimming pool and sun deck, bicycles for short tours, double-hull canoe sailing, safe-deposit boxes, on-property car rental, baby-sitting, Keiki Aloha, a special instructional day-camp program for children ages 5–12, and much, much more.

## Mauna Lani Bay Hotel and Bungalows

As soon as you turn off Rte. 19, the entrance road, trimmed in purple bougainvillea, sets the mood for Mauna Lani Bay Hotel and Bungalows, 68-1400 Mauna Lani Dr., Kohala Coast, HI 96743, 808/885-6622 or 800/367-2323, fax 808/885-1484, www.maunalani.com, a 350-room hotel that opened in 1983. Enter through a grand portico, whose blue tile floor, a mimic of the ever-present sea and sky, immediately creates a sense of sedate but beautiful grandeur. Below is a central courtyard, where full-size palms sway amidst a lava-rock water garden; cascading sheets of clear water splash through a series of koi ponds, making naturally soothing music. A short stroll leads you past the swimming pool and through a virtual botanical garden to a white-sand beach perfect for island relaxation. From here, any number of water sport activities can be arranged. Nearby are convoluted lagoons, and away from the shore you find the Sports Center with tennis courts, a lap pool, and weights, a full-service health spa, and exclusive shops. Surrounding the hotel is the marvelous Francis I'i Brown Golf Course, whose artistically laid-out fairways, greens, and sand traps make it a modern landscape sculpture.

The Mauna Lani offers superb dining options. The **Bay Terrace,** open daily for breakfast and dinner, offers the most casual dining, with a weekend seafood dinner buffet that shouldn't be missed and a Sunday brunch that draws visitors and locals alike. Set within the arms of a lagoon and overlooking the ocean is **CanoeHouse,** the hotel's signature restaurant. Open daily for dinner only, it delights you with Pacific Rim cuisine. Resort wear is required and reservations are highly recommended. Up at the golf clubhouse overlooking the fairways, **The Gallery Restaurant** serves lunch and dinner Tues.–Sat., while **Knickers Bar and Lounge** serves libations, sandwiches, and snacks. For lunch and cocktails, try the informal **Ocean Grill,** where you'll be comfortable in a bathing suit and cover-up. On the far side of Makaiwa Bay, the **Beach Club** also serves light lunches in an open-air environment until mid-afternoon. And for a perfect place to relax after a day of golf or tennis, seek out the **Honu Bar,** just off the atrium, where you will find a pool table and dance floor, an excellent selection of liqueurs, wine, and fine cigars, and be able to order light late-night meals and desserts.

Rooms at the AAA Five-Diamond award-winning Mauna Lani Bay Hotel run $375 mountain view to $725 for corner oceanfront, suites are $1,100. Rooms are oversized, the majority come with an ocean view, and each includes a private lanai, remote color TV and VCR, honor bar, in-room safe, and all the comforts of home. The very exclusive 4,000-square-foot, two-bedroom bungalows rent for $4,400–4,900 a night but each comes complete with a personal chef, butler, and swimming pool. In addition, one-, two-, and three-bedroom home-like villas go for $550–910, three-night minimum required. Weekly rates are available on the villas and bungalows. Guest privileges include complimentary use of snorkeling equipment, Hawaiian cultural classes, hula lessons, complimentary morning coffee, and resort and historic tours. For parents with young children who have come to the realization that "families who want to stay together don't always play together," the hotel offers a break from those little bundles of joy with Camp Mauna Lani for children ages 5–12. While you play, the kids are shepherded through games and activities. One of the favorite evening activities at the hotel takes place once a month at the Eva Parker Woods cottage. For this free event, Hawaiian musicians, dancers, and storytellers gather to share their cultural talents with community and resort guests. Ask the concierge for particulars and for information about the numerous daily activities.

## Mauna Lani Condominiums

Sitting in the lap of luxury are two secure, private, modern, and very high-end condo properties. They are **Mauna Lani Point,** which is surrounded by golf fairways at oceanside, and **The Islands**

**at Mauna Lani,** also surrounded by golf links but set away from the water. Each has superbly built, spacious units that leave nothing lacking. The Mauna Lani Point has one- and two-bedroom units that run $305–505 a night, while The Island rents two- and three-bedroom units for $495–695; three-night minimum. All guests can make use of the activities and amenities located within the Mauna Lani Resort complex. For reservations and information about either, contact Classic Resorts, 68-1050 Mauna Lani Point Dr., Kohala Coast, HI 96743, 808/885-5022 or 800/542-6284, fax 808/885-5015, info@classicresorts.com, www.classicresorts.com.

## The Mauna Kea Beach Hotel

This hotel has set the standard of excellence along Kohala's coast ever since former Hawaii Governor William Quinn interested Laurance Rockefeller in the lucrative possibilities of building a luxury hideaway for the rich and famous. Beautiful coastal land was leased from the Parker Ranch, and the Mauna Kea Beach Hotel, 62-100 Mauna Kea Beach Drive, Kohala Coast, HI 96743, 808/882-7222 or 800/882-6060, www.maunakeabeachhotel.com, opened in 1965. The Mauna Kea was the only one of its kind for a few years, until others saw the possibilities, and more luxury hotels were built along this coast. Over the years, the Mauna Kea grew a bit aged and suffered stiff competition from newer resorts nearby. After an extensive restoration, the Mauna Kea reopened with youthful enthusiasm in December 1995 and shines again as the princess it always was. Class is always class, and the Mauna Kea again receives very high accolades as a fine resort hotel.

The Mauna Kea fronts the beautiful Kauna'oa Beach, one of the best on the island. Million-dollar condos also grace the resort grounds, and hotel guests tend to come back year after year. The hotel itself is an eight-story terraced complex of simple, clean-cut design. The grounds and lobbies showcase more than 1,000 museum-quality art pieces from throughout the Pacific, and more than a half million plants add greenery and beauty to the surroundings. The landings and lobbies, open and large enough to hold full-grown palm trees, also display beautiful tapestries, bird cages with their singing captives, and huge copper pots on polished brick floors. The award-winning Mauna Kea Golf Course surrounds the grounds, and a multi-court tennis park overlooks the ocean. Swimmers can use the beach or the round courtyard swimming pool, set just off the small fitness center, and horseback riding is available at the Parker Ranch up in Waimea. A host of daily activities are scheduled, including a twice-weekly star gazing program, but perhaps the most unusual activity at the hotel is the evening manta ray viewing off Lookout Point.

Exceptional food is served in this exceptional environment. Serving classic Euro-Asian cuisine for dinner only is the **The Batik,** the hotel's finest restaurant. Dining here is truly a treat. For breakfast and dinner in an open-air setting with grand views of the coast, try the **Pavilion** restaurant. Near the beach, the **Hau Tree** does salads and sandwiches for lunch daily, and the **19th Hole** is a more casual spot at the golf course clubhouse that serves food from the East and West through midday. Three lounges also grace the grounds, each with its own entertainment. At the Saturday-evening clambake at the Hau Tree, you can feast

buffet-style on Maine lobster, garlic shrimp, sumptuous steamed clams, and much, much more; Tuesday evenings are extra special as a lu'au is performed at the Lu'au Gardens at North Pointe; and Sunday Brunch is legendary for its selection and quality. For dining reservations, call 808/882-5810.

The 310 beautifully appointed rooms, starting at $360, feature an extra-large lanai and specially made wicker furniture. From there, rates rise to $530 for beachfront units, and suites run $950–1,400. Numerous packages are available. The rooms are, like the rest of the hotel, the epitome of understated elegance. A television-free resort at its inception, the hotel now has TVs in most of the rooms as part of the recent restoration. A resort shuttle operates between here and the Hapuna Beach Resort Hotel, where Mauna Kea guests have signing privileges.

## Hapuna Beach Prince Hotel

Opened in 1994, the Hapuna Beach Prince Hotel, 62-100 Kauna'oa Dr., Kohala Coast, HI 96743, 808/880-1111 or 800/882-6060, www.hapunabeachprincehotel.com, fronts Hapuna Beach about one mile down the coast from

ROBERT NILSEN

**The Hapuna Beach Prince Hotel overlooks one of the finest beaches on the island.**

the Mauna Kea Hotel. These two hotels are separate entities but function as one resort, joined as if in marriage. The princess, Mauna Kea, has finally found her prince. Long and lean, this hotel steps down the hillside toward the beach in eight levels. A formal portico fronts the main entryway, through which you have a splendid view of palm trees and the ocean. This entryway is simple in design yet welcoming in spirit. Chinese flagstone, stained reddish by iron oxide, paves the main entry floor. Walls are the color of sand, and the wood throughout is light brown or dark teak. Lines are simple and decoration subtle. An attempt has been made to simplify and let surrounding nature become part of the whole. As at the Mauna Kea, visitors are not overwhelmed with sensory overload. A shuttle connects the Hapuna Beach to the Mauna Kea and all services available at one are open to guests of the other.

Carpeted bedrooms are spacious, allowing for king-size beds, and the bathrooms have marble floors. Each of the 350 large and well-appointed rooms has an entertainment center, comfy chairs, live plants, prints on the walls, and a lanai. Although rooms are air-conditioned, they all have louvered doors, allowing you to keep out the sun while letting breezes flow through. Rates for the 350 guest rooms start at $360 and go up to $595 a night; suites run $1,200–7,000.

Of the hotel's four restaurants, the oceanfront **Coast Grill** is its signature establishment. It specializes in fresh seafood, mixing flavors and preparations from the Pacific and Asia. The Oyster Bar here is renown and sushi is always top notch. Open only for dinner, reservations are recommended and resort attire is required. Serving buffet and à la carte breakfasts from its location overlooking the pool and ocean, the **Ocean Terrace** also does an evening Seafood feast buffet. Located in the clubhouse and catering mainly to the golfers, **Arnie's** serves standard American and health-conscious food with a few Oriental touches. Open for lunch only, with cocktails until late afternoon. In addition, you can get lunch items, afternoon snacks, and drinks at the **Beach Bar** down by the pool. Aside from the Beach Bar, the Reef Lounge serves up tropical drinks and nightly entertainment, and the Splash

at Hapuna cocktail lounge and nightclub rounds out the evening with late night drinks, appetizers, music, and dancing. Splash is open Wednesday through Saturday 8:30 P.M.–12:30 A.M., music is a different style every evening, and there is a $5 cover. Every Friday is Paniolo Night, and this Western buffet and dinner show, served at the Kohala Gardens, is always a hit.

The Prince Keiki Club at the Hapuna offers a reprieve to parents who desire some time away from their energetic kids. Children 5–12 years old can fill their time with fun activities and educational projects. For Mom and Dad are the links-style Hapuna Golf Course and the hotel's physical fitness center. While the spa and fitness center has weights, its main focus is on dance, yoga, stretching, and alignment techniques, with various massage therapies and body treatments also available. Set in the garden below the lobby, the swimming pool is great recreation during the day and reflects the stars at night. Speaking of the stars, four nights a week, the hotel hosts a star gazing program for hotel guests, and numerous other activities are scheduled through the week. Shops include the Amaury St. Gilles contemporary fine art.

## VACATION RENTAL AGENCIES

Along with a few high-end condos, luxury resorts are the mainstay of accommodations in coastal South Kohala. There are, however, a number of vacation rental homes and individual condo units available for those who want more privacy but still want the sun. Try the following agencies for options.

**Hawaii Vacation Rentals,** 7 Puako Beach Dr., Kamuela, HI 96743, 808/882-7000 or 800/332-7081, fax 808/882-7607, seaside@aloha.net, www.bigisland-vacation.com, handles properties almost exclusively in Puako, with a few others up and down the coast, that range from a studio cottage at $125 a night to a three-bedroom oceanfront mansion for $1,000 a night. A five- to seven-night minimum stay applies. This company also represents one or two units in Puako Beach Condominium, the only condo in this residential neighborhood and the only moderately priced, multiple-unit accommodation in this diamond-studded neck of the woods. The three-bedroom units run $135 a night, three nights minimum, with a kitchen, laundry, TV, and swimming pool.

For exclusive condo units and mansion-style homes at various resort complexes along the South Kohala Coast, try **South Kohala Management,** P.O. Box 384900 Waikoloa, HI 96738, 808/883-8500 or 800/822-4252, fax 808/883-9818, info@southkohala.com, www.southkohala.com. It handles premium properties only, with prices to match. Three nights minimum for condos and five nights minimum for homes.

**MacArthur & Company,** with an office in Waimea at the Historic Spencer House, 808/885-8885 or 877/885-8285, manages numerous rental homes mostly in the Kohala resort area, Puako, North Kohala, and Waimea with a few others south in Kona, that range mostly $500–1,000 a night, with several under $150 and a few over $3,500 a night. Write 65-1148 Mamalohoa Highway, Kamuela, HI 96743, info@letsgohawaii.com, www.letsgohawaii.com.

**Kohala by the Sea Realty,** 808/882-1991, fax 808/882-1994, P.O. Box 44550 Kawaihae, HI 96743, www.kohalacoast.com, has several condos from $100 a night to homes that mostly run $500–700. Many are booked months in advance so make your inquiry early.

## FOOD

Except for a few community-oriented restaurants in Waikoloa Village, a handful of reasonably priced roadside restaurants in Kawaihae, and a gaggle of eating establishments in the King's Shops, all of the food in South Kohala is served in the elegant but expensive restaurants of the luxury resorts. The resort hotels also provide the lion's share of the entertainment along the coast, mostly in the form of quiet musical combos and dinner shows.

### Restaurants at the King's Shops

**Hama Yu Japanese Restaurant,** 808/886-6333, is open daily 11:30 A.M.–3 P.M. and 5:30–9 P.M. With strikingly contemporary decor, Hama Yu serves authentic Japanese cuisine that's not cheap. Choose appetizers like soft-shell crab, yakitori,

and a variety of sashimi and sushi. Dinners, mostly $25–38, include tempura, Japanese steak, and tonkatsu. Sit at western-style tables or choose the sushi bar. Lunches are simpler with less expensive soups, noodles, donburi, sushi, and other similar dishes.

The **Grand Palace Chinese Restaurant,** 808/886-6668, open daily 11 A.M.–9:30 P.M., serves appetizers ranging from deep fried won ton for $5 to a cold platter for $16. Soups run $9 for pork with mustard cabbage all the way up to $56 for shark's fin soup with shredded crabmeat. Chicken and duck dishes range from $9 for sweet and sour chicken to $48 for a whole Peking duck. Seafood includes sautéed shrimp with asparagus for $15 and squid with bean sprouts for $10. There are also your standard beef, pork, and vegetable dishes, as well as the unusual hot pot dishes and sizzling platters. With over 150 items on the menu and prices that are above average, this is not your ordinary Chinese restaurant but a dining experience.

The **Big Island Steakhouse,** 808/886-8805, featuring the Merry Wahine Bar, is open daily from 5 P.M., serving items like a *pu pu* platter with baby-back ribs and a variety of salads from simple onion and tomato to aloha salads with fish, chicken, or beef. Entrées, mostly $16–19, include New York strip steak, filet mignon, prime rib, teriyaki pork chops, coconut prawns, and fresh fish.

**Roy's Waikoloa Bar and Grill,** 808/886-4321, is well known throughout the islands for blending ingredients from East and West. Roy's produces imaginative cuisine that will titillate your taste buds. The menu changes daily and always features nightly specials, but some of what you might expect to find are cassoulet of escargot appetizers and ginger chicken and sesame shrimp salad. For main entrées, look for braised garlic parmesan lamb shank, lemongrass chicken breast, and blackened 'ahi. Most dinner entrées are in the $21–28 range, with lunches somewhat less. Open 11:30 A.M.–2 P.M. and again from 5:30–9:30 P.M.; reservations are definitely recommended.

A separate area called **The Food Pavilion** will satisfy anyone on the run with everything from a Subway Sandwich to pizza and espresso coffee.

## Beach Grill

More than just a clubhouse eatery, the Beach Grill restaurant at the Waikoloa Beach Course golf clubhouse, 808/886-6131, is a diverse dining establishment with a better than average wine list. Lunch items are mostly light sandwiches, *pu pu*, and salads, with few surprises, but dinner is a different story. Here you can order fresh catch done any number of ways at market price, Hawaiian *huli huli* chicken, teriyaki top sirloin, scampi Alfredo, or sautéed calamari, mostly in the $17–24 range. Each dinner comes with potatoes, rice, vegetables, and warm bread. The Beach Grill is conveniently located for all guests at Waikoloa Resort and is open for lunch 11 A.M.–4 P.M., dinner 5:30–9 P.M., and for appetizers and cocktails until midnight.

## Lu'au

A sumptuous old-style feast is held at the **Kona Village Resort.** It's worth attending this lu'au just to visit and be pampered at this private hotel beach. Adults pay around $76, children 6–12 $46, children 3–5 $22. This lu'au is held every Friday by reservation only and as it's so popular you should call well in advance, perhaps even when you make your room reservation; 808/325-5555. The *imu* ceremony is at 6:30 P.M., followed by cocktails; the lu'au stars at 7 P.M. and the entertainment gets going at 8 P.M. The Kona Village Resort lu'au has been happening every Friday night for over 30 years, making it the longest-running lu'au on the island.

The **Royal Lu'au** at the Waikoloa Beach Marriott, 808/886-6789, is offered on Sunday and Wednesday from 5:30 P.M., with the *imu* ceremony beginning at 6 P.M. followed by an open bar, dinner, and Polynesian entertainment of song and dance that ends about 8:30 P.M. Prices are adults $65, children 6–12 $33, free for children five and under.

**Legends of the Pacific** at the Hilton Waikoloa Village is performed by Tihati Productions each Friday evening 6–9 P.M. A full buffet dinner, one cocktail, and a rousing show of Tahitian music and dance is performed at the Kamehameha Court on the resort grounds. Tickets are $65 adults, $32 kids 5–12. Call 808/886-1234 for reservations.

The Mauna Kea **Old Hawaii 'Aha'aina** Lu'au is presented every Tuesday at the North Pointe Lu'au Grounds. While dinner and entertainment start at 6 P.M., you may watch the *imu* preparation at 9 A.M. and the *imu* opening ceremony at 5:30 P.M. Dinner is a veritable feast, followed by entertainment by Nani Lim and her award-winning *hula halau*. Adults pay $72, children 5–11 are half price. For reservations, call 808/882-5810.

# SHOPPING

## The King's Shops

The Waikoloa Beach Resort community has its own small but very adequate shopping center. The King's Shops, open daily 9:30 A.M.–9:30 P.M., feature more than 40 different shops and restaurants, along with entertainment, special events, a Hawaiian Visitors Bureau office, and a gas station. A number of Hawaiian artifacts and exhibits are displayed here and there around the center. Many shops carry clothing: Crazy Shirts has distinctive tops and tees; Kunahs has casual tropical wear, shorts, T-shirts, hats, and classic aloha shirts for men; Noa Noa has an excellent selection of imported fashions from throughout Southeast Asia and some *tapa* from the South Pacific; Malia carries fine women's wear; and Kane By Malia is for men. It's obvious what Zac's Photo and Copy Center handles; Whaler's General Store carries light groceries and sundries; Pacific Rim Collections is where you will find Hawaiian quilts, masks from throughout the South Pacific, and carved whales and dolphins; and the Endangered Species shop stocks items from T-shirts to sculptures, many with an animal or floral motif, where a portion of the proceeds goes to the World Wildlife Foundation. For artwork, try either Dolphin Galleries or Genesis Galleries, where you'll see pieces by Tabora, Lau Chun, and glass work by Chuhuly; Under the Koa Tree showcases Hawaiian artists who have turned their hands to koa woodwork and fine jewelry; Indochine has jewelry, gifts and art from the Orient; and at The UkuleleHouse you can find an amazing collection of these musical instruments in all styles and sizes plus an assortment of quilts made in the Philippines. If all this shopping hasn't worn you out, head for Macy's or the Galleria, where its many departments carry goods from around the world. The center wouldn't be complete without a place to eat, and you can find everything from fast food to a fine meal. There's something for everyone.

Although the schedule changes periodically, **free entertainment** is offered at the King's Shops every Tuesday 5:30–6:30 P.M. and Thursday 6–8 P.M. when a local *hula halau* comes to perform, and Sunday 4–6 P.M. when local musicians play traditional and contemporary Hawaiian music. These events are popular with both tourists and locals and are an excellent chance to have fun Hawaiian style.

**Guided tours** of native Hawaiian plants and the nearby petroglyph field start at 10:30 A.M. Tues.–Fri. from in front of the food pavilion. Additionally, a petroglyph tour also runs on Saturday from 8:30 A.M. These petroglyphs offer a link to the mythology and lore of ancient Hawaii. Wear comfortable clothing and bring water for this two-hour walk.

## Puako

Basically the only other shopping option, aside from the stores in Kawaihae and Waikoloa, is at the **Puako General Store.** Open daily 8 A.M.–7 P.M., this small shop carries a limited but sufficient assortment of groceries and sundries for those staying in this coastal community.

# RECREATION
## Golf

The resorts in South Kohala offer half a dozen of the best golf courses in the state, and they are all within a few miles of each other.

Surrounding the Mauna Lani Bay Hotel are the marvelous **Francis H. I'i Brown Golf Courses** (North and South courses), whose artistically laid-out fairways, greens, and sand traps make it a modern landscape sculpture. The courses are carved from lava, with striking ocean views in every direction. Call the Pro Shop at 808/885-6655 for information and tee times.

The Mauna Kea's classic, trend-setting **Mauna Kea Golf Course** was designed by the master, Robert Trent Jones, has been voted among America's 100 greatest courses and Hawaii's finest. It lies near the ocean and has recently been joined by the **Hapuna Golf Course,** designed by Arnold Palmer and Ed Seay, which has been cut into the lava up above the hotels. Both 18-hole courses give even the master players a challenge. For tee times at Mauna Kea, call 808/882-5400 and for Hapuna, call 808/880-3000.

Like rivers of green, the Waikoloa Beach **King's Golf Course** and **Beach Golf Course** wind their way around the hotels and condos of Waikoloa Beach Resort. Both have plenty of water and lava rock hazards. For the King's Course, call 808/886-7888 and for the Beach Course, call 808/886-6060.

The last minus one to be constructed along the coast is the Four Seasons' **Hualalai Golf Club.** This Jack Nicklaus course seems to be set in the starkest surroundings. Starting inland, you wind over the tortured lava, finally returning to the water. The Pro Shop handles reservations at 808/325-8480. A second course at Hualalai opened its front nine in 2002 and this will be followed in due course by a back nine.

On the windy slope of Mauna Kea at Waikoloa Village is **Waikoloa Village Golf Club.** No slouch for difficulty, this Robert Trent Jones Jr. course is the most economical of the bunch. Call 808/883-9621 for a tee time.

If you are on vacation without your golf clubs and plan to play more than a round or two, consider renting clubs from **Island Discount Golf,** 75-5565 Luhia St., in Kailua-Kona, 808/334-1771, open daily. Rental rates start at $18 per day but go down for longer rental periods. These rental rates are cheaper than those at the golf courses.

## Tennis

Virtually every hotel and condominium has at least a couple of tennis courts on its property. Most are for use by guests only, but a few tennis centers are open to the public, and these can always arrange lessons, round robins, and match play. All the following are non-lighted, day-use only courts. The Waikoloa Beach Marriott tennis center has six courts with a $10 per hour court

BIG ISLAND OF HAWAI'I

fee. Call 808/886-6666 for a court time. More expensive, at $30 an hour, are the eight courts at the Hilton Waikoloa Village Resort, 808/881-2222. Court time at the Mauna Lani Tennis Garden, 808/885-1485, is $20 an hour. With 13 courts, the largest court complex is at the Mauna Kea Beach Resort. Play for $12.50 per person a day; call 808/882-5420 to make arrangements. The Tennis Pavilion at the Orchid at Mauna Lani has 10 courts at $15 per person a day; call 808/887-7532.

## Outrigger Canoe Ride

A 35-foot replica double-hull outrigger sailing canoe takes guests for rides along the Kohala Coast. Be part of the crew for a voyage. The *Halalua Lele* leaves from the beach in front of the Orchid at Mauna Lani; rides cost $95 per person. Call 808/885-2000 for reservations and departure times.

## Water Sports

For general water sports activities including scuba dives, snorkel gear rental and tours, catamaran or mono-hull sailing cruises, kayak rental, hydro bikes, boogie boards, sailboarding, and more, check with either **Ocean Sports Waikoloa**, 808/886-6666 or 888/724-5234, or **Red Sail Sports,** 808/886-2876 or 877/733-7245. These companies operate from 'Anaeho'omalu Beach, and Red Sail also has a few activities happening at Hapuna Beach.

At the Four Seasons Resort, **Hualalai Water Sports,** 808/325-8222, can put you onto a snorkel cruise, into the water for scuba diving, or aboard a catamaran for a sunset sail. Snorkel gear rental is available as is scuba instruction and certification.

## VISITORS INFORMATION

The **Big Island Visitors Bureau,** 808/886-1655, maintains their West Side office at the King's Shops. It's open regular hours for brochures and inquiries.

# Towns

## Kawaihae

This port town marks the northern end of the South Kohala Coast. Here, Rte. 19 turns eastward toward Waimea, or turns into Rte. 270 heading up the coast into North Kohala. Not really more than a village, Kawaihae town is basically utilitarian, with wharves, fuel tanks, and a boat ramp. A service cluster has numerous shops, restaurants, and a gas station. Unless you're stopping to eat, you'll probably pass right through.

The small **Kawaihae Shopping Center** can take care of your rudimentary shopping needs. There's a 7-Eleven convenience store, a couple clothing shops, Mountain Gold Jewelers, Black Pearl Gallery jewelers, and the Harbor Gallery art and gift shop. Restaurants are located on both levels. Across the highway, you can stop for fresh fish from local waters at Laau's Fish Market, open Mon.–Sat. 6 A.M.–6 P.M. Down the road a short way is Arts Pacifica, an art gallery and shop associated with the Amaury St. Gilles shop in the Hapuna Prince Hotel.

## Pua Mau Place

Pua Mau Place botanical and sculpture garden has an unlikely location here in arid Kohala, but that's one of its drawing cards. Two decades in the making and still a work in progress, about 12 acres of Pua Mau (Ever Blooming) Place opened to the public in 2000. The focus here is on flowering plants, ones that thrive and flourish in an arid environment. While many plants have established, some of the most showy are the hibiscus, plumeria, and date palm. With so much sunshine and so little rain, this is a harsh environment and only certain types of plants survive. A greater challenge for the plants is that no pesticides are sprayed and brackish water is used for irrigation. Only the hearty make it, and those that do seem to love it. Heavy mulch guides you along the well-signed paths and plant numbers correspond to a book you take on your self-guided tour. A bit of whimsy is added by a fair number of giant bronze sculptures of insects that dot the garden here and there. Payable at the gift shop, the entrance fee of $8 helps to support the nonprofit foundation that maintains the garden. Pua Mau is open Wed.–Sun. only 10 A.M.–5 P.M. For additional information, contact the gardens at 808/882-0888, P.O. Box 44555, Kawaihae, HI 96743, www.puamau.org.

## Accommodation

Set high above the ocean a few miles north of Kawaihae (turn onto Ala Kahua street at mile marker 6) is **Hale Ho'onanea** bed-and-breakfast. Modern in design, with new amenities, all three detached suites on this property have private entrances and baths, a small kitchenette, and perhaps best of all, plenty of privacy. A continental breakfast will be waiting for you each morning when you get up. Just over 1.5 miles from the coast, there are great ocean views out over the surrounding ranch land, whale-watching in season, and unbeatable stargazing any time of the year. The Hale Suite, with its king bed and queen sofa sleeper, runs $120. Tranquillity Suite has a king bed and queen futon and goes for $100. The smallest, with a queen bed and queen futon, is the Garden Suite and it rents for $90. For information and reservations, contact Jeanne or Larry Roppolo at P.O. Box 6568, Kamuela, HI 96743, tel./fax 808/882-1653 or 877/882-1653, jroppolo@houseofrelaxation.com, www.houseofrelaxation.com.

## Kawaihae Food

Who'd expect an upscale yuppie restaurant in the sleepy village of Kawaihae? **Café Pesto**, 808/882-1071, open Sun.–Thurs. 11 A.M.–9 P.M., Fri.–Sat. 11 A.M.–10 P.M., has a chic interior design with black-and-white checkerboard flooring and black tables trimmed with wood, similar to its sister café in Hilo. The bold gourmet menu tantalizes you with starters like crostini (French bread with a fresh, creamy herb garlic butter) and a host of freshly made salads from $3. Pasta dishes are scrumptious, including smoked-salmon pasta with mushrooms and sun-dried tomatoes, and fettucine in saffron cream sauce. Lunch, served 11 A.M.–4 P.M., brings an assortment of calzones and hot sandwiches that includes everything from smoked ham to a chicken pita. Café Pesto also

serves gourmet pizza with crust and sauces made fresh daily, all ranging in price up to about $18. Among its best pizzas are shiitake mushrooms and artichokes with rosemary Gorgonzola sauce. Dinner entrées are wild, with North Kohala fresh catch that can be grilled or sautéed for $19–22, and seafood risotto sumptuous with morsels of Keahole lobster, tiger prawns, and jumbo scallops for $19. Café Pesto is a perfect place to stop for a civilized meal as you explore the Kohala Coast.

Pancho Villa in aloha shirt and sombrero and riding a surfboard (!) would be instantly at home in **Tres Hombres Beach Grill**, 808/882-1031, located on the upper level of the Kawaihae Center and open Sun.–Thurs. 11:30 A.M.–9 P.M., until 10 P.M. on weekends. Besides being a south-of-the-border restaurant, Tres Hombres is an unofficial surfing museum filled with a fine collection of surfboards and surfing memorabilia donated by such legendary greats as Dewey Weber, Greg Knoll, and Jack Wise. The bamboo-appointed interior has a relaxed tropical effect. The extensive menu offers antojitos such as nachos, nachitos, calamari, and chimichangas for under $12. Substantial meals include all the Mexican favorites for $9–15, plus the grill also offers fish in tomato, pepper, and onion sauce, shrimp basted in lime butter, honey mustard chicken, and more unusual items like crab enchiladas, for up to $21. The full bar serves not only a range of beers and all the island favorites, but adds special concoctions like the Kawaihae Sunsets that will help you go down for the evening, and Mauna Kea Sunrises that, with a great deal of wishful thinking, will pop you back up. *Pu pu* are served 3–6 P.M. daily. Relax with an ice-cold margarita on the lanai of this casual restaurant, and experience an excellent change of pace from the luxury hotels just down the road.

A few steps away is the smaller **Akizuka's** which serves quick eats like *loco moco,* pot roast, fried saimin, plate lunches, sushi, coffee, and smoothies. While there are a few tables inside, most use this as a take-out place. Just down the way is the **Anuenue** pizza, ice cream, and shave ice window counter.

**Kawaihae Harbor Grill** serves lunch 11:30 A.M.–2:30 P.M. and dinner daily

5:30–9:30 P.M.; 808/882-1368. Climb the steps to the large veranda from where you have a bird's-eye view of Kawaihae and unfortunately an unobstructed view of the petrochemical tanks across the road. Dinners include fresh catch, steak and seafood combo, *huli*-style half chicken, and charbroiled rib eye steak, all $14–24. Lighter fare is also offered like a *pu pu* sampler, veggie platter, and crab cakes. Inside, the onetime village store is quite tasteful, with *lau hala* mats, lava lamps, and a glass partition that has been etched with an octopus and tropical fish. The Kawaihae Harbor Grill is tasteful and presented with pride.

Set at the edge of town along Rte. 270 is the **Blue Dolphin Restaurant,** 808/882-7771, open for dinner Wed.–Sat. 5–10 P.M., Friday until 11:30 P.M. Seating is all outdoors, but in the dry climate of Kawaihae that hardly matters. Dinner, mostly $13–22, begins with the soup of the day and appetizers like sautéed mushrooms and fresh ceviche. Entrées include crispy macadamia nut pork loin, *pulehu* (broiled) chicken breasts, nori-wrapped tempura ahi, and fresh catch. While the food is okay, the Blue Dolphin is perhaps best known for its music.

## Kawaihae Activities

**Kohala Divers,** 808/882-7774, www.kohaladivers.com, open daily 8 A.M.–5 P.M., is a full-service dive shop that offers open-ocean certification for $550, two-tank boat dives for $99, an introductory dive for $145, scuba rentals for $15, and snorkeling gear rentals for $10. If there's room on the boat, Kohala Divers will take snorkelers along for $40. Kohala Divers is also a retail shop where you can buy boogie boards, fins, masks, snorkels, and scuba equipment. If you are a scuba enthusiast, you can come here to get your tanks refilled or overhaul your diving gear. It's a bit far to go from Kailua-Kona—much closer from the Kohala resorts—but rates are competitive. Divers are taken up the coast from Kawaihae. On the lower level of the Kawaihae Shopping Center.

**Mauna Kea Divers,** 808/882-1544, www.maunakeadivers.com, also rents scuba and snorkel gear in Kawaihae and offers comparable scuba tours. Two-tank dive run $90, certification is $600, and scuba gear rental $24. Mauna Kea Divers will work with you to give you the experience that you want. Mauna Kea Divers is located along the highway.

Also on the lower level of the shopping center is **Paniolo Adventures,** 808/889-5354, an outfit that offers a variety of outings, including open-range horseback rides, mountain biking through cattle country, and hikes into the upper part of their ranch.

## Waikoloa Village

If you're interested in visiting Waimea as well as seeing the South Kohala coast, you might consider turning right off Rte. 19 near mile marker 75 onto Waikoloa Road. This route cuts inland for 13 miles, connecting coastal Rte. 19 with inland Rte. 190, which leads to Waimea. About halfway up, you pass the planned and quickly growing community of Waikoloa Village about six miles inland from Waikoloa Resort. Try to overlook the condo complexes along the road and head into the village itself, which is low-rise and quite tasteful. Waikoloa Village is a mixture of condominiums and single-family homes that is also home to Waikoloa Village Golf Club, whose course is open to the public, and Roussels restaurant at the clubhouse.

Waikoloa sits below the saddle that runs between Mauna Kea and the North Kohala Mountains. When the trade winds blow from the northeast, they funnel over this saddle and race down the slope, creating windy conditions that challenge golfers. For the dubious distinction of being a windy community, Waikoloa is sometimes jokingly called "Waiko-blow-a." The village is serviced by the **Waikoloa Highlands Shopping Center,** a small but adequate shopping mall with a gas station, full-service supermarket, First Hawaiian Bank, postal service store, small medical center, and a few restaurants and shops.

Fronting the ninth fairway of the golf course, you'll find **Waikoloa Villas,** 808/883-9144, or call Marc Resorts at 800/535-0085 for reservations. Rates for these condo units are one bedroom $169–189, two bedrooms $189–209, and three bedrooms $239–269, with a two-night minimum stay. Amenities include two swimming pools, spa, nearby golf, and weekly maid service. All units are fully furnished with complete kitchens, TV, and washers and dryers. The condo offers a money-saving condo/car package, as well as other discount packages. Check in at the Marc Resorts office in the Waikoloa Highlands Shopping Center, Suite 213.

**Paniolo Greens,** 808/883-0600 or 888/450-4646, a timeshare property nearby rents units when space is available. Starting at $230 a night, two-bedroom, two-bath condos come with a complete kitchen, washer and dryer, and entertainment center, and have tennis courts, exercise gym, and swimming pool on property.

Waikoloa has at least eight other condo/apartment properties that offer rental units, most in the economy and mid-range. For information about some of what is available, contact Triad Management at 808/329-6402 or Certified Management at 808/329-6063. **Aldridge Associates,** 808/883-8300, www.waikoloa.net, has vacation rentals in Waikoloa.

For those wanting to stay along the coast, **Roussels Waikoloa Village** is a bit out of the way, but for those willing to venture inland, the restaurant lies like a pot of gold at the end of the rainbow. In Waikoloa Village, turn onto Paniolo Avenue, then onto Lua Kula Street, and finally onto Malia Street and follow it to the golf course clubhouse where the Roussels sign will direct you to the restaurant. Roussels, 808/883-9644, is open seven days a week, for lunch 11 A.M.–2:30 P.M., appetizers 2–9:30 P.M., and dinner Tues.–Sat. 5–10 P.M. Reservations recommended. Roussels' niche is spicy Cajun food. It's the only restaurant on the island whose main emphasis is food from the Creole South. The shrimp, oyster, and okra gumbo at $6.95 a cup is outstanding and a specialty, as is the shrimp Creole for $17.95, or whet your appetite with crabmeat crepe, $8–9. A salad selection is the next course before you move to the Cajun entrées, which include chicken Pontalba, duck in hunter's sauce, trout meunière amandine, and blackened fresh catch, $17–25. All entrées are served with salad, vegetables, and fresh-baked bread. Complement the meal with a choice wine, choose from an assortment of cakes, pies, and mousses baked daily, and end with a wonderful liqueur. Lunches are a bit faster and geared toward the local golf clientele. Salads, burgers, and sandwiches are main menu items, but a few dinner selections also appear on the lunch menu in smaller, less expensive portions. This is upscale Cajun cooking in an upcountry island setting.

# Waimea

Waimea (also called Kamuela) is in the South Kohala district, but because of its inland topography of high mountain pasture on the broad slope of Mauna Kea, it can be considered a district in its own right. It also has a unique culture inspired by the range-riding *paniolo* of the expansive **Parker Ranch.** This spread, founded early in the 19th century by John Palmer Parker, dominates the heart and soul of the region. Waimea revolves around ranch life and livestock. Herds of rodeos and "Wild West shows" are scheduled throughout the year. But a visit here isn't one-dimensional. In town are homey accommodations and inspired country dining, and the town supports arts and crafts in fine galleries, and a scientific community to staff a number of the observatories high on the mountain above. For fun and relaxation there's a visitor and ranch center; Pu'opelu, the Parker mansion and art collection; a wonderful museum

operated by John Parker's great-great-granddaughter and her sons; a litany of historic shrines and churches; and an abundance of fresh air and wide-open spaces, the latter not so easily found in the islands.

The town, at elevation 2,670 feet, is split almost directly down the center—the east side is the wet side, and the west is the dry side. Houses on the east side are easy to find and reasonable to rent; houses on the dry side are expensive and usually unavailable. You can literally walk from verdant green fields and tall trees to semi-arid landscape in a matter of minutes. This imaginary line also demarcates the local social order: upper-class ranch managers (dry), and working-class *paniolo* (wet). However, the air of Waimea, refreshed and cooled by *kipu'upu'u* (fine mists) and wind, combines

J.D. BISIGNANI

Waimea rangeland

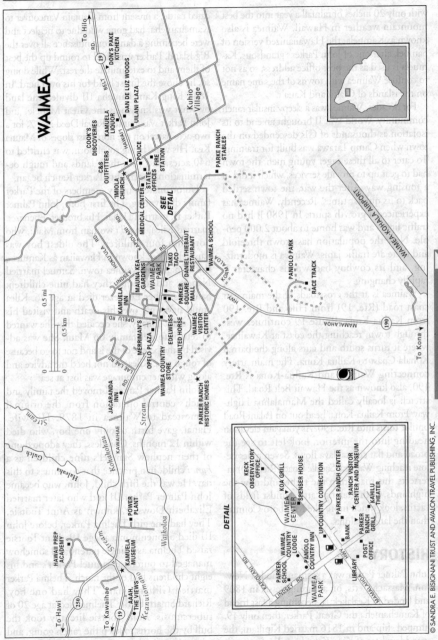

WAIMEA

To Hilo

DON'S PAKE
KITCHEN

BELT RD.

DAN DE LUZ WOODS

UILANI PLAZA

Kuhio
Village

HAWAII BELT (19)

KAMUELA
LIQUOR

COOK'S
DISCOVERIES

C&S
OUTFITTERS

POLICE

STATE
OFFICES

FIRE
STATION

PARKE RANCH
STABLES

'IMIOLA
CHURCH

MEDICAL CENTER

WAIMEA-KOHALA AIRPORT

SEE
DETAIL

TAKO
TACO

DANIEL THIEBAUT
RESTAURANT

WAIMEA SCHOOL

MAUNA KEA
GARDENS

WAIMEA
PARK

PARKER
SQUARE

PARKER RANCH
MALL

WAIMEA
VISITOR
CENTER

KAMUELA
INN

MERRIMAN'S

EDELWEISS

QUILTED HORSE

OPELO PLAZA

WAIMEA
COUNTRY STORE

JACARANDA
INN

KAMUELA
MUSEUM

HAWAII PREP
ACADEMY

POWER
PLANT

AAAH,
THE VIEWS

To Kawaihae

To Hawi

PANIOLO RANCH

RACE
TRACK

MAMALAHOA (190)

To Kona

PARKER RANCH
HISTORIC HOMES

LINDSEY RD.

KAPIOLANI RD.

OPELU RD.

MAMALAHOA HWY.

LAE LAE RD.

KAWAIHAE RD.

NOKUULA RD.

KAWAIHAE

Kohokohau Stream

Waihaloa Stream

Keanuiomano Stream

Haleaka Gulch

(250)

(19)

0.5 mi
0.5 km

N

BIG ISLAND OF HAWAI'I

DETAIL

KECK
OBSERVATORY
OFFICE

KOA GRILL

SPENSER HOUSE

UPCOUNTRY CONNECTION

WAIMEA
COUNTRY
CENTER

PARKER RANCH
VISITOR CENTER
AND MUSEUM

KAHILU
THEATER

PARKER
SCHOOL

WAIMEA
COUNTRY
LODGE

PANIOLO
COUNTRY INN

BANK

PARKER
RANCH
GRILL

POST
OFFICE

LIBRARY

WAIMEA
PARK

MAMALAHOA HWY.

LINDSEY RD.

KAPIOLANI BLVD.

with only 20 inches of rainfall a year into the best mountain weather in Hawaii. Waimea is also known as Kamuela, the Hawaiianized version of Samuel, after one of John Parker's grandsons. Kamuela is used as the post office address, so as not to confuse Waimea with towns of the same name on the islands of O'ahu and Kaua'i.

For decades, Waimea was a sleepy insular ranch community. World War II brought an end to its isolation as thousands of GIs descended on the town when Camp Tarawa was built for training. To cater to all these eager young men, the town had to gear up to provide services, which it did in a rousing way. After the war, the town settled back to its quieter times. Recently, Waimea has experienced a growth spurt. In 1980 it had no traffic lights and was home to about 2,000 people. Now the population has grown threefold and there are traffic jams. Waimea is modernizing, and its cowboy backwoods character is rapidly changing.

Waimea is at the crossroads of the main east coast road (Rte. 19) from Hilo and Rte. 190 from Kailua-Kona. Route 19 continues west through town, reaching the coast at Kawaihae, where it turns south and cuts along the barren Kohala Coast to Kailua-Kona. The main artery connecting Waimea and Kailua-Kona is Rte. 190, also known as the Hawaii Belt Road. This stretch is locally called the Mamalahoa Highway. From Kailua-Kona, head out on Palani Road until it turns into Rte. 190. As you gain elevation heading into the interior, look left to see the broad and flat coastal lava flows. Seven miles before reaching Waimea, Saddle Road (Rte. 200) intersects this road from the right, and now the highlands, with grazing cattle amidst fields of cactus, look much more like Marlboro Country than the land of aloha.

## HISTORY

John Palmer Parker was a seaman who left Newton, Massachusetts, on a trading vessel in 1809 and landed in Kealakekua, becoming a fast friend of Kamehameha the Great. Parker, then only 19, jumped ship and in 1816 married Kipikani, the granddaughter of King Kamehameha. Domesti-

cated cattle, a present from Captain Vancouver to Kamehameha, had gone wild due to neglect and were becoming a dangerous nuisance all over the Big Island. Parker was hired to round up the best of them and to exterminate the rest. While doing so, he chose the finest head for his own herd. In 1847 King Kamehameha III divided the land by what was known as the Great Mahele, and John Parker was granted Royal Deed No. 7, for a two-acre parcel on the northeast slopes of Mauna Kea. His wife, being royal born, was entitled to 640 acres, and with these lands and tough determination, the mighty Parker Ranch began.

Unfortunately, many members of the Parker family died young. The first-born, John Palmer Parker II, married Hanai. His brother, Ebenezer, married Kilea, an *ali'i* woman from Maui, who bore him four children. The oldest boy was Samuel Parker, known in Hawaiian as Kamuela, the co-name of Waimea town. Samuel married Napela, and together they had nine children. Samuel's father Ebenezer died at age 26. Kilea could never get over his death and visited his grave daily. Finally, she decided that she wanted to return to her family on Maui. She was advised by the people of the island not to go because of rough seas. Kilea did not heed the advice and along with her entourage was lost at sea.

John Palmer Parker II moved the family and ranch's central operation from the original homestead to Waimea in 1879. His wife, Hanai, gave birth to only one boy, who died within 12 months. Childless, they adopted one of their nephew Samuel's nine children as a *hanai* child, in a practice that continues to this day. He was the fifth child, John, who became John Palmer Parker III and who later married Elizabeth Dowsett, known as Aunt Tootsie. They had one girl, Thelma Parker, before John III died of pneumonia at age 19. Aunt Tootsie raised Thelma as a single parent and somehow managed to purchase Samuel Parker's and his eight children's half of the ranch. Thelma Parker married Gillian Smart. They had one boy, Richard Smart, before Thelma died at age 20 of tuberculosis. Aunt Tootsie literally took the bull by the horns to keep the ranch going, and when she passed away in 1943, she left everything to her grandson Richard. The ranch prospered under his ownership. After his death, the ranch became a charitable trust called the Parker Ranch Foundation Trust that benefits the people of Waimea and local communities long associated with its operation. Although the ranch at one time was a huge 500,000 acres, it is now down to 225,000 acres. When Richard Smart was alive, the Parker Ranch was the largest privately owned, single-owner ranch in the United States. Today, still at that size, it has 400 horses and 50,000 head of cattle that supply fully one-third of the beef in the Hawaiian Islands. The Parker Ranch Foundation Trust is the second largest landowner in the state, following the Bishop Estate. Find more information about the ranch and family at www.parkerranch.com.

# Sights

## Parker Ranch Historic Homes

Richard Smart, last heir to the gigantic Parker Ranch, opened **Pu'opelu,** a century-old family mansion, to the public just a few years before he passed away on November 12, 1992. On the grounds, the ranch's reconstructed original home is also open to visitors. Pu'opelu is located off Rte. 190 a few minutes southeast of town and is open daily 10 A.M.–5 P.M., admission $8.50 adults, $7.50 seniors, $6 children; 808/885-5433.

A formal drive lined with stately eucalyptus trees leads to the mansion. The home was begun in 1862 by an Englishman but bought by John Palmer Parker II in 1879. In 1910, Richard Smart's grandmother, Aunt Tootsie, added the living room, kitchen, and fireplace. In 1960, Richard Smart, who inherited the ranch lands and home from Aunt Tootsie, replaced the living room and raised its ceiling to 16 feet to accommodate his art collection, and he landscaped the grounds. He added elegant French doors and skylights, and the koa doorways were installed to match. Smart grew up in San Francisco and became enamored with the theater at a young age. He studied at the Pasadena Playhouse in the late 1920s and later appeared on Broadway with such famous names as Carol Channing and Nanette Fabray. Smart performed in plays all over the United States, and recordings of his singing provide the background music as you tour the house.

Enter an elegant sitting room illuminated by a crystal chandelier to begin your tour. Inside this living museum, the works of prominent European artists are displayed, but since Smart's death, some artworks have been sold off and the collection diminished. The tour is self-guided, with all art pieces named. Besides paintings by famous artists, there are magnificent pieces of wooden furniture, tall cabinets holding yellow Chinese Peiping glass from the 19th century, silver tea sets, glassware, figurines, and magnificent chandeliers. Make sure to see the little side bedroom, called the Venetian Room, aptly decorated with paintings of gondolas and appointed with treasures from Venice. Lighting the room are two chandeliers, one pink and the other turquoise. Here, the filigreed art-deco mirrors are also fabulous. The feeling is of genteel elegance, but notice that the walls are rather rough board-and-batten covered with beautiful artwork. Recently opened is Richard Smart's bedroom, which is loaded with memorabilia from his stage performances and mementos given by the people he knew on Broadway. You get the feeling of class, but it's obvious that you are on a ranch. In the emerald-green kingdom that is the Parker Ranch, Pu'opelu is the crown jewel.

Just outside Pu'opelu is the reconstructed New England "saltbox" **Mana Hale,** the original Parker Ranch homestead. The home was built in 1847 by family patriarch John Palmer Parker from the durable native koa found at high elevations on the ranch lands. The sons, who were by then married, built two homes, and as children came, added more rooms in the sprawling New England tradition. They also built one large community kitchen, at which the entire family cooked and dined. A replica shows how the home grew over the years, and it is a good indicator of how the Parker fortunes grew along with it. As the children's children got older, they needed a schoolhouse, so they built one at the corner of the original site. It still stands and is maintained by a *paniolo* and his family who live there. The exterior of the original home, covered by a heavy slate roof, was too brittle to move from its original site 12 miles away, but the interior was removed, numbered, and put back together again like a giant jigsaw puzzle in the reconstructed home. A model in the living room shows you what the original site looked like back in the 1800s. To preserve the rich wood interior of the home, all that's required is to wipe it down once a year with lemon oil. At first the home seems like a small cabin, just what you'd expect from the 1850s, but in actuality it's a two-story home with one bedroom downstairs and three upstairs.

## SIGHTS IN TOWN

### Parker Ranch Visitor Center and Museum

This is the first place to stop while in town if you want an overview of the evolution of this upcountry domain. The visitor center, 808/885-7655, at the Parker Ranch Center, is open daily 9 A.M.–5 P.M. (last tickets sold at 4 P.M.); admission is adults $6, $5 seniors, children $4.50. Tickets for joint admission to the visitor center, museum, and historic homes are $12, $12, and $9.50, respectively; for the visitor center, museum, homes, and wagon ride, prices run $42, $40, and $35, respectively.

After spending an hour at the center's museum and taking in the slide presentation, you'll have a good overview of the history of the Parker Ranch and, by extension, Waimea. Exhibits at the John Palmer Parker Museum depict the history and genealogy of the six generations of Parkers who have owned the ranch. In the museum, old family photos include one of Rev. Elias Bond, who presided over the Christian marriage of John Palmer Parker and his Hawaiian wife in 1820. Preserved also are old Bibles, clothing from the era, and an entire koa hut once occupied by woodcutters and range riders. There are fine examples of quilting, stuffed animals, an arsenal of old weapons, and even a vintage printing press.

The 15-minute video in the comfortable Thelma Parker Theater begins whenever enough people have assembled after going through the museum. The video presents a thorough and professional rendition of the Parker Ranch history, along with sensitive glimpses of ranch life of the still very active *paniolo.* To the rear of the shopping center is an old wood-and-stone corral.

### 'Imiola Church

Head east on Rte. 19 to "church row," a cluster of New England–style structures on the left, a few minutes past the Parker Ranch Visitor Center. Most famous among these old structures is 'Imiola (Seeking Life) Congregational Church. It was built from 1855 to 1857 by the Rev. Lorenzo Lyons, who mastered the Hawaiian language and translated some of the great old Christian hymns into Hawaiian, as well as melodic Hawaiian chants into English. Restored in 1976, the yellow clapboard church with white trim would be at home along any New England village green. When you enter, you'll notice an oddity: the pul-

'Imiola Church

pit is at the near side and you walk around it to face the rear of the church. Nearly all inside surfaces are of rich brown koa. The hymnals contain many of the songs translated by Father Lyons. Outside is a simple monument to Rev. Lyons, along with a number of his children's gravesites. Have a look inside or stop by for one of the two Sunday worship services.

Also along this row are the Ka Ola Mau Loa Hawaiian Church, the Kamuela Hongwanji Mission, the First Baptist Church, and the Waimea Chapel of the Church of Jesus Christ of Latter-day Saints.

## Kamuela Museum

The Kamuela Museum, 808/885-4724, open every day of the year 8 A.M.–5 P.M., the largest privately owned museum in Hawaii, is a fantastic labor of love. For the founders and curators, Albert and Harriet Solomon (Albert died in 2001 while in his nineties), it was a vocation that started in 1968 and fulfilled a prophecy of Albert's grandmother, who was pure Hawaiian and a renowned *kahuna* from Pololu Valley. When Albert was only eight years old, his grandmother foretold that he would build "a great longhouse near three mountains and that he would become famous, visited by people from all over the world." This prediction struck him so much that he wrote it down and kept it throughout his life. When grown, he married Harriet, the great-great granddaughter of John Palmer Parker, and the two lived in Honolulu for most of their adult lives, where Albert was a policeman. For 50 years the Solomons collected, collected, and collected! Harriet, being a Parker, was given heirlooms by family members, which are also on exhibit. The museum is west of town center on Rte. 19, 50 yards west of the junction with Rte. 250 heading toward Hawi. Admission to the museum, dedicated to Mary Ann Parker, John Parker's only daughter, is adults $5, children under 12, $2. Plan on spending at least an hour.

As you enter, the screen door bangs like a shot to signal that another visitor has arrived. Inside it's easy to become overwhelmed as you're confronted with everything from sombreros to a stuffed albatross, moose head, and South American lizard. An extensive weapons collection includes Khyber rifles, Japanese machine guns, swords, and knives. If you enjoy Hawaiiana, check out the *kahili* and *konane* boards, poi pounders, stone sinkers and hooks, wooden surfboards, and a very unique "canoe buster." The museum has a few extremely rare stone idols and a good collection of furniture from Hawaiian nobility, including Prince Kuhio's council table. Antiques of every description include Japanese and Hawaiian feathered fans, carved Chinese furniture, a brass diving helmet, some of the first Hawaiian Bibles, and even buffalo robes used by the pioneers. Everywhere are old photos commemorating the lives of the Parkers down through the years. Before you leave, go into the front room, where the view through a huge picture window perfectly frames a pond and three round-topped mountains in *paniolo* country.

# Practicalities

## ACCOMMODATIONS

### Inns

The **Kamuela Inn,** P.O. Box 1994, Kamuela, HI 96743, 808/885-4243 or 800/555-8968, fax 808/885-8857, kaminn@aloha.net, www.hawaii-bnb.com/kamuela.html, a onetime basic cinder-block motel, has been transformed into a bright and airy 31-unit boutique hotel. It is located down a short cul-de-sac off Rte. 19 just before Opelu Road. The owner takes personal pride in the hotel and offers each guest a complimentary continental breakfast each morning in the art gallery on premises. The pleasant grounds are appointed with flowers and manicured trees, and you'll find a swing to lull you into relaxation. The basic motel rooms are small, neat, and tidy with twin or double beds with wicker headboards, private bathrooms, and color TV, but no a/c (not needed) or phones. About one third of the units have kitchens. The deluxe Penthouse is upstairs and breaks into two joinable units that can accommodate up to five guests. The newer wing has tasteful larger rooms with hardwood floors, king-size or twin beds, and features deluxe Executive Suites with full kitchens. Prices range from $59 for a basic room and $72–85 for a deluxe, to $89–99 for suites with kitchenettes. The Penthouse suites, when sleeping five, and the Executive suites are $185. Smoking and non-smoking rooms are available. Reserve well in advance.

The Waimea Country Lodge, 65-1210 Lindsey Rd., Kamuela, HI 96743, 808/885-4100 or 800/367-5257, fax 808/885-6711, www.castleresorts.com, is located in "downtown" Waimea, but don't let "downtown" fool you because it's very quiet. Renovated in 1997, the rooms, many with kitchenettes and vaulted ceilings, have full baths and are well appointed with knotty pine furnishings, king- or queen-size beds with turned pine lamps, wicker easy chairs, fans and portable heaters, phones, and TVs. The barn-red board-and-batten inn sits off by itself and lives up to its place in *paniolo* country by giving the impression of a gentleman's bunkhouse. The view out the back toward the mountain is an added bonus. Rates are $95 standard, $100 superior, $110 with a kitchenette, $120 deluxe, and $10 for an additional person.

Built in 1897 as the Parker Ranch manager's house, this plantation estate has gone through several metamorphoses and most recently been renovated, expanded, and turned into The Jacaranda Inn, 65-1444 Kawaihae Rd., Kamuela, HI 96743, 808/885-8813, fax 808/885-6096, tji@ilhawaii.net, www.jacarandainn.com. This estate, with its raspberry-colored roof, dominates a broad lawn. A white ranch fence and bougainvillea hedge separate it from the road. Set amidst towering trees, the main house retains the original Hawaii Victorian flavor, with rich koa wood and numerous antiques. Enter the huge living room with its imposing fireplace, and from there you can move to the dining rooms, library, billiard room, bar, or terrace. Separate oversized suites have also been constructed to the rear as guest rooms. They are all decorated according to different themes and colors,

and while each shows individual character and style, they all have a similar romantic feel. These are not ordinary rooms; they are designed to pamper guests in luxury. The eight guest rooms, with pretty flower names like White Lily, Iris, Orchid, and Passion Flower, rent for $95–225 or $189–300 a night depending upon the option. One option is daily hot breakfast and maid service, along with a bottle of wine on arrival and no minimum stay; the second option is a daily continental breakfast, maid service every three days, and a two night minimum. In addition, a three-bedroom, three-bath cottage that can sleep up to six goes for $550 or $650 a night with a five night minimum.

## Bed-and-Breakfasts

No place could be more appropriately named than **aaah, The Views,** P.O. Box 6593, Kamuela, HI 96743, 808/885-3455 or 866/885-3455, fax 808/885-4031, tommare@aloha.net, www.beingsintouch.com. This bed-and-breakfast, located in a quiet residential neighborhood just downhill from central Waimea, has unimpeded views of Mauna Kea, Mauna Loa, and Mt. Hualalai to the south, and, of course, the ocean off the Kohala Coast to the west. Fine for the sunrise over the mountains, the sunsets on clear days are stupendous, and clear nights illuminate a star-studded sky. Aaah, The Views sits along a stream next to Parker Ranch land, so you may see cattle grazing nearby. Rooms in the two-bedroom suite of the detached house can be booked individually or together. Each has a sleeping room with a cozy loft and a small deck, and they share a good-sized bathroom with tub and shower. New and modern, these rooms are tastefully appointed and laid with berber carpet. Also in this detached building is a newer, tidy and compact garden studio, with its queen-bed room, loft, bath, and kitchen. While each room has a small refrigerator, microwave unit, and coffeemaker, a continental breakfast with plenty of fruits, pastries, cereals, and coffee is served each morning in the main house dining area or on a lanai that overlooks the stream. In the main house, the small Skylight Room is just big enough for one or a romantic couple. Room rates are $65–110, add $15 for an additional person.

Set along a pleasant stream a couple miles west of downtown Waimea is **Waimea Garden Cottage,** 808/885-8550. This lovely B&B is a quality professional place with plentiful modern amenities and a style that speaks of yesteryear with wainscoting, antique furniture, hardwood floors, and French doors. The two rooms run $145–155 double, $15 for one additional person in a room; three nights minimum.

Occupying the downstairs walkout apartment of a home in a quiet residential section east of the center of town is **Waimea Suite Bed and Breakfast,** 808/937-2833. This finely decorated apartment with its welcoming colors has two bedrooms, one with a king bed and the second with two twins, one pleasant bathroom, a full and modern kitchen stocked with necessities, and a koa-wood paneled living room with some antique furniture and a lava rock fireplace—wood provided. There is plenty of room inside and out on the lanai, where the lawn slopes away is a wooded expanse and beyond which is a good view of Mauna Loa. As the owner is a shopkeeper in town, there is no cooked breakfast, but all breakfast supplies and more are provided. No smoking is allowed indoors and no pets are accepted, but what this unit does offer in plenty is privacy, convenience, and comfort. Just right for one or two couples, or a small family, the rate is $125 a night for two, $25 for each additional adult or $15 for kids under age 12. Two nights minimum; weekly rates are available.

With great views over the long and broad Kohala Coast and up to Mauna Loa, Mauna Kea, and Hualalai, **Belle Vue** has a location that's just right. Spacious suites with living rooms, kitchenette, and fireplaces rent for $85–165 and this includes a fine breakfast. French and German spoken. Contact the owners at P.O. Box 1295, Kamuela, HI 96743, tel./fax 808/885-7732 or 808/772-5044, bellvue@aloha.net, www.hawaii-bellevue.com.

### Vacation Rental Agency

With an office at the Historic Spencer House, **MacArthur & Company,** 808/885-8885 or 877/885-8285, fax 808/885-5538, handles several rental homes in Waimea, with prices from $75 to $250 a night. Contact the company at 65-1148 Mamalohoa Highway, Kamuela, HI 96743, info@letsgohawaii.com, www.letsgohawaii.com.

## FOOD
### Inexpensive

The cafeteria-style **Kamuela Deli** offers sirloin steak, grilled ham steak, and boneless spicy chicken, all priced around $7. They also have breakfasts like corned beef hash or hamburger patties with eggs and hash browns. Deli sandwiches, priced under $5, include teriyaki beef, shrimp burgers, and ham sandwiches. Plate lunches are also available. The good price and good food make this a favorite spot for locals.

Also in the Waimea Center is **Young's Kalbi,** a Korean restaurant open daily except Sunday, that serves dishes like kalbi chicken, shrimp tempura, oyster-sauce chicken, and spicy pork, all priced under $8. Young's is very basic but clean, and the food is tasty.

**Don's Pake Kitchen,** about one mile east of town on Rte. 19 and open daily 10 A.M.–8:30 P.M., Sunday from 3 P.M., is a Chinese family restaurant that has a good reputation for food at reasonable prices even though most of its selections are of the steam-table variety. Some items are ginger beef, oyster chicken, and shrimp-sauce pork, but many people come for the saimin. Don's also specializes in large pans of food that can feed entire families.

**Waimea Coffee Company,** in the Parker Square, is open Mon.–Fri. 7 A.M.–5 P.M., Saturday 8 A.M.–4 P.M. Order coffee beans in bulk and coffee by the cup. Lunch is served 11 A.M.–3 P.M., including turkey, ham, or tuna sandwiches, Caesar salad, quiches, and homemade soups.

The **Hawaiian Style Café,** in a modest building across from Parker Square, is open Mon.–Fri. 6 A.M.–12:45 P.M., Sunday 7:30–11 A.M., but closed the last Sat., Sun., and Mon. of the month. It offers local and American standard food at very reasonable prices. Inside the blue-painted interior, chairs line a low counter where the menu offers breakfasts of two eggs with Spam or bacon, a three-egg omelette with a side of pancakes, Hawaiian-style loco moco, and Belgian waffles with whipped butter, strawberries, and maple syrup, mostly under $6. Plate lunches, around $9, served with rice and potato or macaroni salad include curry stew, *lau lau*, chicken, pickled veggie, or a steak plate. A little short on Martha Stewart panache but long on pride, the Hawaiian Style Café will fill you up while being easy on your wallet.

Back up the highway a ways and across from the park is **Tako Taco**, 808/887-1717, a Mexican taqueria that's open Mon.–Sat. 11 A.M.–8 P.M. Here you can get regular tacos, burritos, tostadas, and the like, along with vegetarian items and those made with tofu. Sit inside or out. Tako Taco has gained a reputation for quick, fresh, and wholesome food.

## Moderate

**Paniolo Country Inn,** on Lindsey Street, 808/885-4377, open daily for breakfast, lunch, and dinner, specializes in full country-style breakfasts, burgers, lunch platters, and flame-broiled steaks. Breakfast selections include omelettes, hotcakes, waffles, huevos rancheros, loco moco, and the *wiki wiki* breakfast of English muffin, banana bread or wheat toast, coffee, and small fruit juice. Breakfast selections generally run $3–7. Sandwiches and burgers cost around $7, with cowboy-size pizza for $7–27. More substantial Paniolo Platters like teriyaki short ribs, top sirloin, or porterhouse steak are mostly $10–18, and a selection of Mexican dishes is thrown in for good measure. Prime rib dinners are served Friday through Sunday evenings. The food is wholesome, the atmosphere American country, and the service prompt and friendly. Don't miss having a look at the cattle brands hanging on the walls.

**Maha's Cafe,** 808/885-0693, in the vintage Historic Spencer House at the Waimea Center, open Thurs.–Mon. 8 A.M.–4:30 P.M., offers coffee, tea, island-style food and desserts made fresh daily. The owner, "Maha," learned to cook for her large Hawaiian family but has worked professionally as a pastry chef and a sous chef at a number of resorts including the Mauna Lani Bay Resort. Maha's has window service but also sit-down service inside. From her diminutive kitchen comes breakfasts of poi pancakes with coconut syrup for

$3.75 and an assortment of too-tempting pastries including homestyle banana bread, papaya coffee cake, croissants, or pan biscuits $2.75, and always-fresh Kona coffee. Lunch can be any number of sandwiches, or Waipi'o Ways, a plate of broiled fresh fish with sliced and steamed Waipi'o taro and sweet potato on a bed of Kahua greens with ginger vinaigrette dressing for $9.25, smoked 'ahi with *lilikoi* salsa at $10.75, or Kohala Harvest, a mounded delight of vegetables with feta cheese for $7.75. Aloha Ahiahi, a version of afternoon tea served 3–4:30 P.M., brings a sampler of Maha's pastries, including croissants, open-faced finger sandwiches, shortbreads, and cobblers. The classic and restored Spencer House was the first frame house ever built in Waimea, in 1852. Once the home of a Judge Bickerton, it was also put to use as a court-house and as a hotel. The house was once surrounded by the lush green grasses of *paniolo* country but is now in the middle of the black asphalt of the Waimea Center's parking lot!

Perhaps slightly ignominiously located inside and at the back of the Waimea Country Store and gas station across from the Opelo Plaza is **Zappa's,** 808/885-1511. A glorified pizza joint, Zappa's also does hearty breakfasts, plate lunches, pasta, soups, salads, and sandwiches. Breakfast starts daily at 6:30 A.M. and runs through lunch until 1:30 P.M.; nightly except Tuesday, dinner hours are 4:30–8 P.M. Zappa's is a very local eatery that puts out tasty food in large portions at reasonable prices. Anything on the menu can be ordered for take-out.

**Morelli's Pizza** at the Waimea Center, 808/885-8557, is open daily from 11 A.M. Besides whole pizzas, the oven yields pizza by the slice ($2.25), garlic bread, and oven-baked sandwiches like turkey, pastrami, ham, or veggie, most for around $7. The pizzas range from a small cheese pizza for $6.75 to a three-topping monster tray at $18.50. Set items run $11.50–21.75. To round out your meal, you can also order garden and chef salads and homemade soup. A small dining room with picnic tables is provided if you choose to eat there.

## Expensive

Located adjacent to Waimea Center is **Koa**

**House Grill,** 808/885-2088, a well-liked casual place for Parker Ranch steak and ribs, lamb, chicken, and local greens. This is good standard American food at moderate prices, and has the only salad bar in town. While lunch meals are substantially cheaper, dinner entrées run mostly $14–25. The Koa House is open daily for lunch 11:30 A.M.–2 P.M. and 5:30–9 P.M. Lighter food is served all day at the bar, where happy hour is 5–6 P.M. Live music on Friday and karaoke on Saturday both run 9 P.M.–midnight.

**Aioli's Restaurant,** at Opelo Plaza, 808/885-6325, serves quick but tasty soups, salads, and sandwiches for lunch for under $10. The dinner menu changes every three weeks, and there is always a vegetarian entrée or two on the menu. The type of item that you might find on the menu includes herb crusted prime rib, seared scallops in a lime cream sauce, pan seared duck, and eggplant pasta. BYOB if you want—no corkage fee. Open at 11 A.M. except Sunday and Monday, the restaurant closes at 4 P.M. on Tuesday, 8 P.M. on Wednesday and Thursday, 9 P.M. on Friday and Saturday; on Sunday, hours are 8 A.M.–2 P.M. Definitely make dinner reservations as Aioli's is popular and there are only about a half dozen tables.

## Fine Dining

**The Edelweiss** on Rte. 19 across from the Kamuela Inn, 808/885-6800, is Waimea's established gourmet restaurant, where chef Hans-Peter Hager, formerly of the super-exclusive Mauna Kea Beach Hotel, serves gourmet food in rustic but elegant surroundings. The Edelweiss is open Tues.–Sat. for lunch 11:30 A.M.–1:30 P.M. and for dinner 5–9 P.M. Inside, heavy posts and beams and dark wood plank paneling exude that "country feeling," but fine crystal and pure white tablecloths let you know you're in for some superb dining. The wine cellar is extensive, with selections of domestic, French, Italian, and German wines. Affordable lunches include offerings like soup, turkey sandwiches, and chicken salad in papaya. Dinner starts with appetizers such as melon with prosciutto, escargot, onion soup, and Caesar salad. Some Edelweiss specialties are sautéed veal, lamb, beef, and bacon with pfefferling; roast duck braised with a light orange sauce; half spring chicken diablo; and of course Swiss and German favorites like Wiener schnitzel and roast pork and sauerkraut, mostly $20–25. In addition to the short standard evening menu, there are often over a dozen specials. The cooking is rich and delicious, the proof a loyal clientele who return again and again.

**Merriman's,** in the Opelo Plaza, 808/885-6822, has received a great deal of well-deserved praise from travelers and residents alike for its excellent food. The restaurant, resembling a small house from the outside, is stylish with its tablecloths, table settings, and cushioned chairs of bent bamboo. Here, chefs create fusion cuisine from local organic ingredients when available. The menu changes every few months, but perennial appetizer and salad favorites that run $8–12 are sweet corn and shrimp fritters, vine-ripened Lokelani tomatoes with Maui onions, and spinach salad with balsamic vinaigrette dressing. Lunch fare, mostly $7–11, includes coconut curry grilled chicken with peanut dipping sauce and rice; grilled eggplant sandwich with Puna goat cheese, basil, and hot sauce; and grilled shrimp on Asian linguine. Entrées from $16 to $35 are superb and might be Peking duck and stir-fry noodles with lop chong sausage, vegetables, and spicy Hoisin sauce; wok-charred *ahi;* shrimp linguine, and prime New York steak. Vegetarians can graze on pan-fried Asian cake noodles and grilled tofu asparagus and mushroom donburi. Some of the most delicious offerings, however, are the fresh catch at market price, prepared in various gourmet styles including herb-grilled sesame-crusted and sautéed with *lilikoi* sauce, or sautéed with pineapple vinaigrette. Owned and operated by Peter Merriman, one of Pacific Rim Cuisine's originators, Merriman's is a Big Island classic. Open for lunch weekdays 11:30 A.M.–1:30 P.M. and dinner daily 5:30–9 P.M.; call for reservations.

The newest of the fine dining restaurants in town is the **Daniel Thiebaut Restaurant,** 808/887-2200, located along Rte. 19 near the Parker Square Mall in the renovated and rambling plantation-era Chock In Store building. Open Mon.–Fri. for lunch 11:30 A.M.–1:30 P.M. and dinner nightly 5:30–9:30 P.M., reservations are usually necessary. Chef Daniel and his attentive staff serve a fusion of French and Asian cuisine with excellent flavors and textures. While the lunch menu is much simpler, dinner entrées include such items as Hunan-style rack of lamb, Provençal crusted tenderloin of beef in balsamic vinegar–red wine sauce with wild mushrooms ragout and herb polenta, sautéed macadamia nut chicken breast with gingered dijon mustard sauce, pickled pineapple and pavà potatoes, and wok-fried sea scallops with Asian style risotto and warm coconut crab dressing. There is a long wine list to accompany each different entrée, but save room for one of the scrumptious desserts or an after-dinner liqueur.

## RECREATION

Located behind the Parker Ranch Center is the Mauna Kea Ranch Stables, 808/885-4288, which has been offering horse rides over parts of the Parker Ranch for nearly three decades. Trail rides go several times a day Monday through Saturday and run $40 an hour or $70 for two hours. All rides are guided. Long pants and close-toe shoes are necessary.

You can pretend that you're a *paniolo* riding the range at the **Dahana Ranch,** 808/885-0057 or 888/399-0057. Spend a few hours tending cattle on this working ranch and learn about the history and culture of ranching the Big Island. Dahana Ranch will take just about anyone "three years to 300 pounds."

**Kohala Carriages** offers a tame 45-minute ranch wagon tour on Parker Ranch land, Tues.–Sat. every hour on the hour 10 A.M.–2 P.M., leaving from the Parker Ranch Visitor Center. Rides cost $15 adult, $12.50 seniors over 60, and $12 ages 4–11. Reserve a seat by calling 808/885-7655.

Every 4th of July, the Parker Ranch hosts a **rodeo** that is one of the best in the state.

Does a sunrise flight over the ranch sound like fun? It's a possibility with **Paradise Balloons, LLC,** 808/887-6455. Take off is from near Pu'opelu before the sun peaks over the mountains and the flight ends before lunch with a return celebration. Rides run $240 adult or $190 ages 5–12. All flights are weather permitting.

The best place in town to shop for good qual-

ity bikes and water gear is **C & S Outfitters,** 808/885-5005, located behind Cook's Discovery near the police station. This is a full-service shop that rents, sells, and repairs bicycles and rents kayaks. Stop here first if you're in need of such things.

Several miles east of town on the way to Honoka'a is the **Waimea Country Club** golf course, a pleasantly rolling Scottish links-style course carved from rangeland at over 2,000 feet in elevation. Enter between mile markers 51 and 52.

Periodically throughout the year, movies, plays, music, and a variety of other events are held at the Kahilu Theater at the rear of the Parker Ranch Center. Call 808/885-6868 for what's currently on schedule.

### Waipi'o Ridge Hike

It is possible once again to hike a portion of the Hamakua Ditch Trail, constructed a century ago when water was needed to irrigate the Hamakua sugar plantations. Drive along Hwy. 19 to the outskirts of Waimea and turn left onto White Road. Proceed to the end of the road and park as much off the roadway as possible. This is a narrow road and residents dislike cars parked on the roadway. If the way is not blocked, leave a donation at the trailhead and cross through the gate—you are crossing Hawaiian Homelands property. A gravel track leads around a water reservoir and on into the forest to the flume, which is in the forest reserve and open to the public. Follow the flume and hiking trail about an hour upstream, where it eventually skirts the edge of the upper reaches of the Waipi'o Valley and from where there are superb vistas (on a clear day) into the valley and a long thin waterfall. About a half hour farther along the trail, you can look back down the valley to the ocean and beach. This area often clouds in by late morning, so hit the trail early.

## SHOPPING

Waimea's accelerated growth can be measured by the shopping centers springing up around town. These mostly small malls house boutiques that add to the shopping possibilities in Waimea's established centers.

## Parker Ranch Center

This long-established mall was totally rebuilt in 2002, completely changing the face of the center of town. With more of a country look, the mall now has more store space than it originally held. A new Foodland grocery store occupies a spot along the highway on the Honoka'a end and nearby are KFC and Blockbuster Video. For an alternative food store, try Healthways II. The Parker Ranch Store has moved from its back location up to the front. Focused on its country cowboy heritage, the shop sells boots, cowboy hats, shirts, skirts, and buckles and bows, and many hand-crafted items are made on the premises. Also moved to the front is Reyn's for island fashions and alohawear. Reopening after a long hiatus and occupying a prominent location is the Parker Ranch Grill. For a mix of quicker foods, stop by the food court, or head to Starbucks or Dairy Queen for a cup of coffee or ice cream cone. As always, the Parker Ranch Visitor Center and Museum is open and available to give visitors a brief overview of this historic area.

## Waimea Center

Well marked along the Mamalahoa Hwy. behind McDonald's, most Waimea Center stores are open weekdays 9 A.M.–5 P.M. and Saturday 10 A.M.–5 P.M. Among its shops you will find a KTA Super Store with everything from groceries to pharmaceuticals; Leilani Bakery has pastries and breads; head to Pack, Ship and Copy Depot, for copies, shipping, Internet access, and other business needs; the Men's Shop, whose name says it all; It's All Good, for women's fashions; Kamuela Kids for children's clothing; Big Island Surf has boards, swimsuits, and beachwear; and the intriguing Without Boundaries has an eclectic mix of gifts, travel items, and all around fun things. To keep you going through all this shopping are Morrelli's Pizza and some inexpensive restaurants.

For the photographer, Waimea Photo sells film and does photo developing. Just around the corner and along the highway, Positive Image also carries and develops film. Both shops are open Monday through Saturday only.

## Parker Square

Located along Rte. 19, heading west from town center, this small mall has a collection of fine boutiques and shops. Here, like an old trunk filled with family heirlooms, the **Gallery of Great Things,** 808/885-7706, really is loaded with great things. Inside you'll find novelty items like a carousel horse, silk dresses, straw hats, koa paddles, Ni'ihau shellwork, vintage kimonos, an antique water jar from the Chiang Mai area of northern Thailand, Japanese woodblock prints, and less expensive items like shell earrings and koa hair sticks. The Gallery of Great Things represents about 200 local artists on a revolving basis, and the owner, Maria Brick, travels throughout the Pacific and Asia collecting art, some contemporary, some primitive. With its museum-quality items, the Gallery of Great Things is definitely worth a browse. But remember, most items are one of a kind—"now you see them, now you don't."

**Sweet Wind,** 808/885-0562, open daily, is packed with books, beads, and unique gifts. This "alternative thought and resource center" also sells incense, aromatherapy tinctures, and crystals. The beads come from the world over, and a display case holds Native American rattles, drums, and silver and amber jewelry. Visiting Sweet Wind is soothing for body and soul.

The **Silk Road Gallery,** 808/885-7474, open daily except Sunday, is resplendent with an exceptional collection of Asian antiques and craft items, specializing in creations from Japan and China. In this tasteful shop you will discover such treasures as carved ivory *netsuke,* a favorite of the well-dressed samurai; ornate silk kimonos; Sung Dynasty vases; and Satsumayaki painted pottery from Japan. As you look around you may spot lacquer tables and bowls, ornate *tansu* (chests), straw sandals, an actual water wheel, sacred scrolls that hang in a place of honor in Japanese homes, a Chinese jade bowl with elaborate dragon handles, and an 18th-century Chinese mogul lotus bowl. The owners make frequent trips to Asia, where they personally pick all the items in their shop, at which the artistic wonders of the ancient Silk Road are still on display.

Other stores in the center include **Bentley's Home and Garden Center,** with crockery, glassware, books, *lau hala* bags, and ceramics; **Imagination Toys,** hung with kites, Hawaiian dolls, stuffed gorillas, parrots, and puzzles; **Fine Jewelry by Jock,** where custom-made jewelry or stones can be procured; and **Waimea Coffee and Company,** for small estate Kona coffee and light food and drink. The **Waimea General Store** sells mostly high-end sundries with plenty of stationery, children's games, stuffed toys, books on Hawaiiana, and gadgets.

## Other Shops

The word *kama'aina* was invented with Patti Cook in mind. The proprietor of **Cook's Discoveries,** 808/885-3633, open daily 10 A.M.–6 P.M., Patti has filled her shop with personally chosen items displaying her impeccable taste and knowledge about all things relating to Hawaii. Everything inside Cook's Discoveries, fashioned by craftspeople from throughout the state, says "Hawaii." Shelves hold lustrous koa boxes, bracelets, cribbage boards, and pen sets, all easily transportable. Look for traditional pieces, including a carved ivory pendant (fossilized walrus tusk) representing a human tongue, the "voice of authority," traditionally worn only by the highest *ali'i,* hung from a necklace of woven black silk (substituting for human hair). Other traditional pieces are *lei o mano* (lei of sharks' teeth), a clublike war weapon yielded in battle or when absolute and immediate persuasion was necessary, *kukui* nut lei, distinctive warrior helmets with mushroomlike protuberances atop, poi bowls, and decorated gourds once used for food storage. Contemporary "made in Hawaii" articles include handmade coconut lotion and soap, plenty of jewelry, carved tiki walking sticks, and brush and mirror sets. You'll also find *mu'umu'u* and pareu in tropical designs and colors, T-shirts emblazoned with Nenewe the shark god, exquisite Hawaiian quilts, books on Hawaiian subjects, gourmet jars of jams, jellies, and sauces made from *lilikoi, ohelo* berries, and Waimea's famous strawberries, and the shop's own oatmeal, coconut, macadamia nut cookies. This is one-stop shopping for memorable Hawaiian gifts. Look for Cook's kitty-corner from the police station, just beyond 'Imiola Church.

Who would have thought that one of the best wine and liquor stores on the island would be in a country town like Waimea? Look for **Kamuela Liquor Store** east along the highway just past Cook's Discovery. It's been in business since 1946. Open 8 A.M.–7:30 P.M. Mon.–Sat. and 9 A.M.–5 P.M. on Sun., it has a great selection of bottled beers along with its wines and liqueurs.

Across from the liquor store is **Dan De Luz's Woods,** a fine shop and showroom selling large bowls and small boxes made from native woods. These pieces are roughed out in Mountain View, where De Luz has another shop, and the blanks are finished in Waimea after a year of drying.

Perhaps the best place in town, and one of the best of the island, to see authentic Hawaiian antiques and collectibles is **Mauna Kea Galleries,** 808/887-2244 or 877/969-4852. Line drawings from the early years, prints from the 1930s, Aloha shirts from the 1950s, jewelry, books, artifacts, furniture, and more are all here, but don't expect to pinch pennies. These fine-quality items may cost a bundle.

A few doors away is **Waimea Antiques and Collectibles,** 808/887-0024, a varied collection with average prices.

Up the road is **Antiques by...,** 808/887-6466. One room here is filled with Hawaiiana, the rest of the house has more ordinary collectibles. Good pricing.

Near the main intersection in town is the **Upcountry Connection** art gallery, 808/885-0623. Open daily except Sunday, this gallery focuses on two basic themes, cultural Hawaiiana and cowboy art and crafts, and has a very decent collection of both. Well worth a stop.

Located directly to the front of the Waimea Visitors Center, **The Quilted Horse,** 808/887-0020, is a fun shop full of household items, gift, prepared food items, Christmas ornaments, knickknacks, and one of the best selections of quilts on the island. Reasonably priced, the quilts are made in the Philippines but designed in Hawaii.

## Food Markets

For food shopping try the **KTA Super Store** at the Waimea Center, for everything from groceries to pharmaceuticals. Across the highway at the Parker Ranch Center, the newer **Foodland** also has a full range of options, plus **Kamuela Meat Market** features fine cuts of Parker Ranch beef.

The **Waimea Homestead Farmers' Market** is held every Saturday 7 A.M.–noon, when local farmers come to sell their produce, much of which is organic. Flowers, baked goods, and crafts are usually available. Look for the stalls in front of the Hawaiian Homelands office located along Rte. 19, about two miles east of town center heading toward Honoka'a.

Alternately, try the **Parker School Farmers' Market,** held Saturday 8 A.M.–noon at the Parker School.

## INFORMATION AND SERVICES

The post office is located in the Parker Ranch Center. The U.S. Postal Service designates Waimea as Kamuela, so as not to confuse it with the Waimeas on O'ahu and Kaua'i.

The **Waimea Visitor Center,** 808/885-6707, is west of town along Rte. 19, next to Parker Square. Operated by the nonprofit Waimea Main Street organization, this office provides free maps and brochures of the area and public restrooms. This is a good stop to learn about the rich cultural history of the area and what's happening in town today.

The Police and Fire departments and district court are located in the civic center complex across the highway from Church Row.

### Medical Services

The full-service **North Hawaii Community Hospital,** 808/885-4444, is located across from the Keck Observatory Office along Rte. 19. Physicians are available at the **Lucy Henriques Medical Center,** 808/885-7921, also along the highway, and at the **Kaiser Permanente Waimea Clinic,** 808/881-4500, on Lindsey Road.

### Airport

The **Waimea-Kohala Airport,** 808/887-8126, is along Rte. 190 just a mile or so before you enter town. This airport is used by private planes and a few daily flights by a small commuter airline. Facilities amount to a waiting lounge and basic restrooms. Unless a flight is scheduled, even these may be closed.

BIG ISLAND OF HAWAI'I

# North Kohala

In North Kohala, jungle trees with crocheted shawls of hanging vines stand in shadowed silence as tiny stores and humble homes abandoned by time melt slowly back into the muted earth. This secluded region changes very little, and very slowly. It also has an eastward list toward the wetter side of the island, so if you're suffering from "Kona shock" and want to see flowers, palms, banana trees, and Hawaiian jungle, head for the north coast. Here the island of Hawai'i lives up to its reputation of being not only big, but bold and beautiful as well.

North Kohala was the home of Kamehameha the Great. From this fiefdom he launched his conquest of all the islands. The shores and lands of North Kohala are rife with historical significance, and with beach parks

where only a few local people ever go. Here cattle were introduced to the islands in the 1790s by Captain Vancouver, an early explorer and friend of Kamehameha. Among North Kohala's cultural treasures is **Lapakahi State Historical Park,** a must-stop offering a walk-through village and "touchable" exhibits that allow you to become actively involved in Hawaii's traditional past. Northward is **Kamehameha's birthplace**—the very spot—and within walking distance is **Mo'okini Luakini,** one of the oldest *heiau* in Hawaii and still actively ministered by the current generation of a long line of *kahuna.*

**Hawi** was a sugar town whose economy turned sour when the last of the five sugar mills in

North Kohala coastline, beyond the mouth of Pololu Valley

ROBERT NILSEN

the area stopped operations in the mid-1990s. Hawi is making a slow comeback, along with this entire northern shore, which has seen an influx of small, boutique businesses and art shops. In **Kapaʻau,** a statue of Kamehameha I peering over the chief's ancestral dominions fulfills an old *kahuna* prophecy. On a nearby side road stands historic **Kalahikiola Church,** established in 1855 by Rev. Elias Bond. On the same side road is the old Bond Homestead, one of the most authentic missionary homes in all of Hawaii. The main coastal road ends at **Pololu Valley Lookout,** where you can overlook one of the premier taro-growing valleys of old Hawaii.

A walk down the steep *pali* into this valley is a walk into timelessness, with civilization disappearing like an ebbing tide.

In Kawaihae, at the base of the North Kohala peninsula, Rte. 19 turns east and coastal Rte. 270, known as the Akoni Pule Hwy., heads north along the coast. It passes through both of North Kohala's two major towns, Hawi and Kapaʻau, and ends at the *pali* overlooking Pololu Valley. All the historical sites, beach parks, and towns in the following sections are along this route.

Route 250, the back road to Hawi, is a delightful country lane that winds through gloriously green grazing lands for almost 20 miles

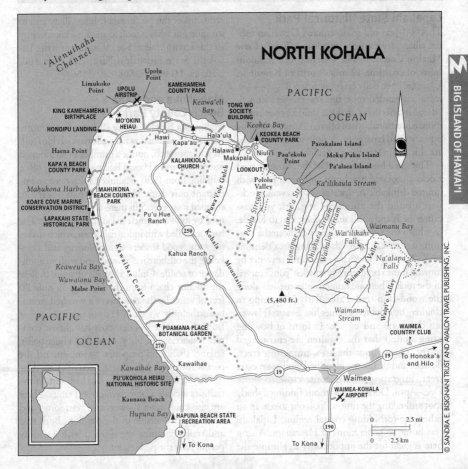

BIG ISLAND OF HAWAIʻI

along the leeward side of the Kohala Mountains. It begins in the western outskirts of Waimea and ends in Hawi. One of the most picturesque roads on the island, it's lined with ironwood trees, dotted with mood-setting cactus and small "line shacks," and herds of cattle graze in the pastures of the several ranches along the way. Vistas open to the west and far below are expansive panoramas of rolling hills tumbling to the sea. Just outside Hawi, Rte. 250 splits; going right takes you to Kapa'au, left to Hawi. If you're

coming along coastal Rte. 270 from Kapa'au toward Hawi, look for the H. Naito Store, and make a left there to go back over Rte. 250 to Waimea; you don't have to go all the way to Hawi to catch Rte. 250.

Upolu airstrip is a lonely runway at Upolu Point, the closest spot to Maui. A sign points the way at mile marker 20 along coastal Rte. 270. Here, you'll find only a bench and a public telephone. The strip is serviced only on request by small propeller planes.

## Kawaihae Coast

### Lapakahi State Historical Park

This 600-year-old reconstructed Hawaiian fishing village, combined with adjacent **Koai'e Cove Marine Conservation District,** is a standout hunk of coastline 12 miles north of Kawaihae. Gates are open daily except holidays 8 A.M.–4 P.M. for a self-guided tour, but the ranger's knowledgeable anecdotes make a guided tour much more educational, when offered. Arrive at least by 3 P.M. so you have enough time to fully appreciate this site before the gate is locked.

The small hut at the end of the entrance road stocks annotated brochures and water jugs with limited drinkable freshwater. As you walk clockwise around the numbered stations, you pass canoe sheds and a fish shrine dedicated to Ku'ula, to whom the fishermen always dedicated a portion of their catch. A salt-making area demonstrates how the Hawaiians evaporated seawater by moving it into progressively smaller "pans" carved in the rock. There are numerous homesites along the wood-chip trail. Particularly interesting to children are exhibits of games like *konane* (Hawaiian checkers) and *ulimika* (a form of bowling using stones) that the children are encouraged to try. Throughout the area, numerous trees, flowers, and shrubs are identified, and as an extra treat, migrating whales come close to shore Dec.–April. Don't leave without finding a shady spot and taking the time to look out to sea. In an otherwise forbidding coastal region, Lapakahi was home to generations of Hawaiians. A stop here is great for the opportunity to glimpse the

remnants of this precontact fishing village and to imagine just what it took to sustain a community in this environment. For information write Lapakahi State Historical Park, P.O. Box 100, Kapa'au, HI 96755, 808/889-5566.

### Mahukona and Kapa'a Beach County Parks

Mahukona Beach County Park is a few minutes north of Lapakahi down a well-marked side road. As you approach, notice a number of abandoned warehouses and a Hawaii Railroad Company office building from 1930. Mahukona was once an important port from which the Kohala Sugar Co. shipped its goods. Still there is a pier with a hoist used by local fishermen to launch their boats. The harbor is filled with industrial debris, which makes for some good underwater exploring, and snorkeling the offshore reef rewards you with an abundance of sealife. Only 150 yards offshore (follow the anchor chain from the landing) in only 20 feet of water lie the remains of a wrecked steamboat, the only wreck in Hawaii that's accessible from shore. The wooden boat has almost completely deteriorated, but you will find a huge boiler, engine, shaft, and propeller. Swimming off the pier is also good, but all water activities are dangerous during winter months and high surf. Picnic facilities include a large pavilion and tables. There are also cold-water showers and restrooms, and electricity is available in the pavilion. Both tent and trailer camping are allowed with a county permit near the parking lot.

Kapa'a Beach County Park is five minutes farther north. Turn *makai* on a side road and cross a cattle grate as you head toward the sea. This park is even less visited than Mahukona. The rocky beach makes water entry difficult. It's primarily for day use and fishing, but there is a pavilion, some barbecue grills, and a restroom. Camping is allowed with a county permit. Neither of these two beaches are spectacular, but they are secluded and accessible. If you're interested in a very quiet spot to contemplate a lovely panorama of Maui in the distance, this is it.

## Mo'okini Luakini Heiau

At mile marker 20, turn down a one-lane road to Upolu airstrip. Follow it until it reaches the dead end at the runway. Turn left here on a *very* rough dirt road to Mo'okini Luakini—this road may not be passable. This entire area is one of the most rugged and isolated on the Big Island, with wide windswept fields, steep seacliffs, and pounding surf. Pull off at any likely spot along the road and keep your eyes peeled for signs of cavorting humpback whales, which frequent this coast Nov.–May. After bumping down the road for about two miles, look for a tall transmission

tower pointing its bony metal finger skyward, which marks the road to the *heiau*. Sometimes the road is closed with a locked gate and you'll have to walk five minutes uphill to gain access, but if the gate is open, you can drive in.

Only *ali'i nui* were allowed to came to the *heiau* to purify themselves and pray, sometimes offering human sacrifices. In 1963, Mo'okini Luakini was the first Hawaiian site to be listed in the National Historical Sites Registry. Legend says that the very first temple at Mo'okini was built as early as A.D. 480. This incredible date implies that Mo'okini must have been built immediately upon the arrival of the first Polynesian explorers, who many scholars maintain arrived in large numbers a full two centuries later. According to oral tradition, this original *heiau* was enlarged by the Tahitian high priest Pa'ao, who came with conquering warriors from the south in the 12th century, bringing the powerful *mana* of the fierce war-god Kuka'ilimoku. The oral tale relates that the stones for the temple were fitted in a single night, passed hand to hand by a human chain of 18,000 warriors for a distance of 14 miles from Pololu Valley. They created an

ROBERT NILSEN

According to oral tradition, Mo'okini Luakini Heiau was one of the first built on the island—and still stands strong today.

irregular rectangle measuring 125 by 250 feet, with 30-foot-high and 15-foot-thick walls in some sections. Regardless of its age, the integrity of the remaining structure is remarkable and shows great skill in construction.

When you visit the *heiau*, pick up a brochure from a box at the entrance (often empty); if none are available, a signboard nearby gives general information. The entire *heiau* is surrounded by a stone wall erected for its protection in 1981. In one corner of the enclosure is a traditional Hawaiian structure used in some of the temple ceremonies. On occasion, this building is blown down by the strong winds that lash this coast. Be aware of the integration of its stone platform and how perfectly suited this thatched structure is to provide comfort against the elements in Hawaii. Look through the door at a timeless panorama of the sea and surf. Notice that the leeward stones of the *heiau* wall are covered in lichens, giving them a greenish cast and testifying to their age. A large, flat stone outside the wall was used to prepare victims for the sacrificial altar. Next to it and embedded in the ground is Kapakai, the guardian god in stone of the nearby King Kamehameha birthsite. This stone was removed here in the mid-1900s for protection, but will be returned to its original place when the time is right. The only entrance to the *heiau* itself is in the wall roughly facing southwest. Entering here, you pass the enclosure used by the *Mu,* the person responsible for finding and catching the human sacrifices that were offered at the temple. Once a closed temple, the *kapu* of restriction has been lifted so that all may now enter. However, please be respectful as you walk around, as this temple is still in use, and stay on the designated paths that are cordoned off by woven rope. Along the short wall closest to the sea is a "scalloped" altar, reputedly set up and used by Pa'ao, but where recent offerings are often seen. When you visit, bring a lei to place in respectful offering on the altar. Inside the *heiau* are remnants of enclosures used by the *ali'i* and space set aside for temple priests. The floor of the temple is carpeted with well-

placed stones and tiny green plants that give a natural mosaic effect. By oral tradition, members of the Mo'okini family have been the priests and priestesses of the temple for at least 15 centuries, with the family line and duties of maintaining temples for the Polynesian rulers as they moved throughout the Pacific region that go back to the mists of time. Today, the inherited title of *kahuna nui* rests with Leimomi Mo'okini Lum, who has gone to great lengths to offer visitors information about the temple and particularly to instruct school children about its historical and religious significance.

## Kamehameha's Birthplace

A few minutes' walk from the *heiau* along the dirt road, an HVB Warrior points to Kamehameha's birthplace, **Kamehameha 'Akahi 'Aina Hanau.** The entrance to the area is at the back side, away from the sea. Inside the low stone wall, which always seems to radiate heat, are some large boulders believed to be the actual "birthing stones" where the high chieftess Kekuiapoiwa, wife of the warrior *ali'i* Keoua Kupuapaikalananinui, gave birth to Kamehameha sometime around 1752. This male child, born as his father prepared a battle fleet to invade Maui, would grow to be the greatest of the Hawaiian chiefs—a brave, powerful, but lonely man, like the flat plateau upon which he drew his first breath. The temple's ritual drums and haunting chants dedicated to Ku were the infant's first lullabies. He would grow to accept Ku as his god, and together they would subjugate all of Hawaii. In this expansive North Kohala area, Kamehameha was confronted with unencumbered vistas and sweeping views of neighboring islands, unlike most Hawaiians, whose outlooks were held in check by the narrow, confining, but secure walls of steep-sided valleys. Only this man with this background could rise to become "The Lonely One," high chief of a unified kingdom.

Together, Mo'okini Heiau, King Kamehameha's birthplace, and several other nearby historical sites make up the seven-acre **Kohala Historical Sites State Monument.**

# North Coast Towns

## HAWI

As you come into Hawi along Rte. 270, you'll see a line of false-front buildings leaning shoulder-to-shoulder like patient old men knowing that something *will* happen, and it has! Introducing you to the town are Sacred Heart Church, Hawi Jodo Buddhist Mission, and the Kohala Seventh-Day Adventists Church, lovely temples of worship and symbols of Hawaii's diversified spirituality. In the middle of town at the gas station, Rte. 250, crossing the Kohala Mountains from Waimea, intersects the main road.

Hawi was once a bustling sugar town that boasted four movie theaters in its heyday. In the early 1970s, the Kohala Sugar Co. pulled up stakes, leaving the one-industry town high and dry. Still standing is the monumental stack of the sugarworks, a dormant reminder of what once was. The people of Hawi have always had grit, and instead of moving away they toughed it out and have revitalized their town. Spirit, elbow grease, and paint were their chief allies. Hawi has risen from its slumber and is now making a comeback with new restaurants and galleries opening their doors. Here, too, are a handful of local shops selling food and fashions, some remarkable craft shops, an area information center, and the only functioning hotel in North Kohala.

A glowing example of Hawi's modern restoration and revitalization is the N. Takata building, now occupied by the Bamboo Restaurant and Gallery. This venerable old building was built by the Harada Family sometime before 1915 and served as a hotel for contract workers on their way to plantation work camps in the area. As the sugar trade took root, merchants came to town, and the hotel began catering to this more upscale clientele. These traveling salesmen were the epitome of the stereotype, and they desired evening entertainment. "Ladies of the night" took up residence in a few back rooms, and, with the proximity to the cane fields, might aptly have been known as "sugar babies." The fortunes of the Harada family took a turn for the worse, and the

building was bought in 1926 by the Takata family, who converted it to a grocery and dry goods store that served the community until 1991, when they moved shop, building a new store about one mile down the road. The old building fell into disrepair but was reopened as a restaurant after 16 months of restoration. New touches were added, like the old wicker chairs that once rocked wealthy vacationers into a light slumber at Waikiki's Moana Hotel, but they left the best alone, preserving the original feel of the building. Upon entering, notice the floor, heavily trodden over the decades, every nick marking a memory. The original wavy window glass is intact and still bears the original painted signs reading, "Fruits, Groceries, Cigars, Candy, Meats, and Coca Cola." The restaurant section, to the left as you enter, is perfect for an evening of dining; to the right is a gallery selling artworks. Browse before or after dinner and appreciate that this little community is finding a way to restore itself.

The Kohala Visitor Center dispenses maps, information, and *aloha*. It's open daily and located just west of the junction between Routes 270 and 250 in Hawi. The area post office is a large new facility on Rte. 270 between Hawi and Kapa'au near the H. Naito Store.

## Accommodations

Long known as Luke's Hotel, the 18-room **Kohala Village Inn**, 55-514 Hawi Rd., Hawi, HI 96755, 808/889-0419, has always catered to local working people or island families visiting the area, as well as passing tourists. Located just up from the intersection in Hawi, this old plantation-style building, white with blue trim and a blue roof, has a quiet central courtyard encircled by a wide and airy lanai. Most rooms have a television but none have phones; all have private baths. Standard rooms run $58–68; connecting rooms that share a bath are $88–98. Clean, adequate, and somewhat spartan, the hotel has a friendly, quiet atmosphere and evokes the spirit of the past.

Overlooking horse pastures and out across the channel toward Maui is **Cabin in the Treeline,**

808/884-5105, P.O. Box 190591, Hawi, HI 96719, cwej@vacationhi.com, www.vacationhi.com. Cabin in the Treeline has two buildings literally set at treeline at the edge of a pasture. These modern buildings with all modern amenities and conveniences have been designed in an old-style rustic *paniolo,* combination mainland mountain cabin, architectural style. The main house has a large living room, kitchen, two bathrooms, a master bedroom downstairs, and an upstairs bedroom. The barn-like Loft has one large bedroom upstairs with a queen bed and futon, television, and refrigerator. The bathroom with shower is downstairs with laundry facilities. Rates run $155–225 per night depending upon the number of guests.

If a larger, private home with space enough for a family is more what you need or if you just want more privacy, contact MacArthur and Company, 65-1148 Mamalahoa Highway, Kamuela, HI 96743, 808/885-8885 or 877/885-8285, info@letsgohawaii.com, www.letsgohawaii.com. This company offers a number of luxury properties in the Hawi area including several in a gated private ranch development that run $500–895 a night. Many of these homes have their own swimming pools and at least one has a private tennis court. Another option is the restored six-bedroom, six-bath plantation manager's house in Hawi, which runs $700 a night.

## Food

Occupying the renovated N. Takata building is the **Bamboo Restaurant,** 808/889-5555, open Tues.–Sat. 11:30 A.M.–2:30 P.M. for lunch, 6–9 P.M. for dinner, and Sunday for brunch 11 A.M.–2 P.M., with live music on Friday and Saturday evenings. Lunch at the Bamboo can be a salad, sandwich, or one of the many entrées, like *kalua* pork and cabbage, herb-grilled fresh fish, or a Kohala quesadilla with your choice of main ingredient. Dinner begins with *pu pu* such as margaritaville prawns, calamari strips, or seared *poke,* but the restaurant is best known for its pot stickers, which are Thai seasoned chicken pieces with herbs and peanuts served with a sweet chili mint sauce. From the land comes flame-broiled rib-eye steak, pork tenderloin, or pineapple bar-

becued chicken. However, as you're so close to the sea, why not try the fish, which come in different preparations like herb-grilled in Thai flavors, crusted with macadamia nuts and pan fried, or sautéed and covered with margarita sauce and papaya relish. Sesame-nori crusted shrimp, shrimp alfredo, local-style stir-fry noodles, and teri chicken are also options. Sunday brunch is a crowd-pleaser, with the regular lunch menu plus platters like eggs Bamboo—poached egg on a toasted English muffin with a slice of smoked ham or vegetables and topped with *lilikoi* hollandaise sauce and served with fried potatoes or rice. While moderately expensive, the food at the Bamboo Restaurant is the finest and most sophisticated on the north coast. Reservations are often necessary, and while you wait try one of their famous passion fruit margaritas.

For a south-of-the-border taste treat, stop at **Hula La's Mexican Kitchen,** 808/889-5668, located at the back of the Kohala Trade Center building. Hula La's is known for its gut-filling burritos, tasty concoctions with beans, pork, chicken, or fish, fresh greens, other tasty morsels, and homemade salsa, $5.50–7.50. The Mexican-style plate lunches are also filling. If a burrito or plate lunch sounds like too much, choose a quesadilla or an order of nachitos, nachos, or tacos, or one of the menu specials. At this neat little eatery you can fill up for under $10 including a drink and be on your way in no time. Open weekdays 10 A.M.–9 P.M. and weekends from 8 A.M.

In tiny Hawi, you can find island-style food with an Asian touch and Mexican treats, so why not German food? On the *mauka* side is **Aunty's Place,** 808/889-0899, where you can enjoy wienerschnitzel, jagerschnitzel, schweinbraten, and bratwurst, along with a few selections from the rest of the continent, like chicken Cordon Bleu, lasagna, and pizza. For those with less of an appetite, Caesar, Greek, chef, and Chinese chicken salads are also on the menu. Most entrées run $9–13, so it goes easy on the wallet. Aunty's bar is at the front of this tiny restaurant. Happy hour is 4–6 P.M. and occasionally there will be live music in the evenings.

Sun, surf, and the trek to Hawi made you a bit droopy? Salvation is at hand at the **Kohala Cof-**

fee **Mill** in downtown Hawi; open daily. Inside the remodeled vintage building, order Kona coffee, espresso, cappuccino, pastries, and soft drinks, or a Tropical Dreams ice cream cone. Shelves hold T-shirts, herbal teas, fruit jelly and jam, honey, and other packaged food and gifts. Whether you sit inside in the cool of the shade or out on the sidewalk, this is a perfect place to watch the slow life of Hawi amble by.

## North Coast Recreation

There is little in the way of organized recreation along the north coast, but what there is can be exciting. Perhaps the most unusual activity is a kayak ride down a section of the Kohala Ditch. Completed in the early part of the 20th century and considered a feat of engineering, this 22-mile-long irrigation system supplied the Kohala Sugar mills with a steady supply of water until the plantation ceased business. Specially designed five-person inflatable kayaks put in above Makapala and drift down the flume, into and out of tunnels and over gullies for about three miles. Prepare to get wet. Tours go daily at 8:30 A.M. and 12:30 P.M. and run $85 for adults and $65 for children ages 5–18. Make reservations with **Flum'in da Ditch,** 808/889-6922 or 877/449-6922, www.flumindaditch.com, or stop into its office up from the banyan tree in the center of Hawi.

**HMV Tour** also takes you into the back mountain areas of the Kohala district but you ride in the relative luxury of a formidable 4WD Hummer. Morning and afternoon rides are offered weekdays, $95 for adults and $65 for children 5–15. Contact 808/889-6922 or 877/889-6944; http://hmvtours.com.

**ATV Outfitters Hawaii** will take you to out-of-the-way places along the coast and up into the rainforest on former Kohala sugar plantation land on its rugged four-wheel motorcycles. Several daily rides are offered, from a 1.5-hour ride for $90 to a five-hour ride for $250. Contact ATV Outfitters at 808/889-6000 or 888/288-7288, www.outfittershawaii.com.

**Hawaii Forest and Trail** offers a hiking experience along the Kohala Ditch trail to Kapoloa waterfall at the back of the Pololu Valley and a mule ride down the steep cliff face to the Pololu Valley floor and beach. Contact Hawaii Forest and Trail, 808/331-8505 or 800/464-1993, www.hawaii-forest.com.

## Shopping

The **Nakahara Store** has been serving people of Hawi for decades, near the main intersection in town. One part of the store has groceries, while the other is a basic dry goods shop. **K. Takata** store is the best-stocked grocery store in Hawi. It's located along the highway about one mile east of the town center. At the intersection of highways 270 and 250 is **H. Naito Store,** another general grocery, dry goods, and fishing supplies store. **Kohala Health Food** in downtown Hawi, to the side of the Kohala Coffee Mill, is open Mon.–Fri. 10 A.M.–6 P.M. and Sat. 11 A.M.–4 P.M., closed Sundays. A small but vibrant establishment, its shelves hold herbs, vitamins, minerals, some packaged natural foods, and local organic produce and fruit when available. If you're looking for something not as healthy, **Kohala Spirits** stocks all sorts of beers, wines, and liquors. Across from the health food store, **Kohala Flowers** is alive with flowers and plants. Inside are small gift items and a cooler holding lei, perfect for brightening the day of that "special person," and perhaps for brightening the evening prospects for you.

Proof that two establishments can occupy the same place at the same time, the **Bamboo Gallery,** open when the restaurant is open, shares the vintage N. Takata Building with the Bamboo Restaurant. The gallery is lustrous with all types of artwork: koa furniture, covered photo albums, jewelry boxes, and sculptures, representing the work of many island artists. The furniture includes rocking chairs that beg to be sat in and fine koa dining room tables. Works of other well-known artists on display include lovely boxes, creamy white hand-thrown crystalline-glazed ceramics with flower or fish motifs, tapa-covered notebooks, replicas of sailing canoes, a smattering of aloha shirts, hand-painted silkwear, jewelry with an ocean motif, and bright prints.

Across the street and down a bit in the renovated Toyama Building is **As Hawi Turns,** a small but intriguing shop for fashions and distinctive gifts. Women will find dresses, skirts, wraps,

BIG ISLAND OF HAWAI'I

sarongs, hats, slippers, jewelry, and accessories here and men have a selection of aloha shirts. Most everything is brightly colored with wild or distinctive designs. Other neat novelty items, gifts, crafts, and post cards are also carried.

The **L. Zeidman Gallery** shows an amazing collection of turned wooden bowls, some sculpted wooden pieces, and emotive paintings of Hawaiian subjects. If you haven't seen the work of Hawaiian woodturning craftsmen or a sampling of native and introduced Hawaiian woods, this is a good place to stop for a look.

Also worth a stop is **Hawi Gallery** for its fine furniture and boxes, and **Mother's Antiques and Fine Cigars** for collectibles and burnables. For more antiques and collectibles, head to **Kohala Fine Furniture and Collectibles** right at the main intersection.

Along the highway just east of the main intersection are several more galleries and gift shops. With hand-crafted works of art in clay, the small **Sugar Moon** gallery features the works of owners Tom and Julie Kostes. **Passion Flower** has art, antiques, and collectibles, while **Treaures of the Earth ... and Beyond** will entice you with crystals, stones and other more metaphysical objects.

## KAPA'AU

Kapa'au is a sleepy community, the last town for any amenities on Rte. 270 before you reach the end of the line at Pololu Overlook. In town are a library, bank, and police station, and the historic Nambu Building (1898) has recently been renovated. Some distance outside of town in either direction are the Union Market and the Arakawa Store. Most young people have moved away seeking economic opportunity, but the old folks remain, and macadamia nuts are bringing some vitality back into the area. Here too, but on a smaller scale than in Hawi, local artists and some new folks are starting shops and businesses catering to tourists.

The main attraction in town is **Kamehameha's statue**, in front of the Kapa'au Courthouse. The statue was commissioned by King Kalakaua in 1878, at which time an old *kahuna* said that the statue would feel at home only in the lands of

Kamehameha's birth. Thomas Gould, an American sculptor living in Italy, was hired to do the statue, and he used John Baker, part Hawaiian and a close friend of Kalakaua, as the model. Gould was paid $10,000 to produce the remarkable and heroic sculpture, which was sent to Paris to be cast in bronze. It was freighted to Hawaii, but the ship carrying the original statue sank just off Port Stanley in the Falkland Islands, and the nine-ton statue was thought lost forever. With the insurance money, Gould was again commissioned and he produced another statue that arrived in Honolulu in 1883, where it still stands in front of the Judiciary Building. Within a few weeks, however, a British ship arrived in Honolulu, carrying the original statue, which had somehow been salvaged and unceremoniously dumped in a Port Stanley junkyard. The English captain bought it there and sold it to King Kalakaua for $850. There was only one place where the statue could be sent: to the then-thriving town of Kapa'au in the heart of Kamehameha's ancestral homelands. Every year, on the night before Kamehameha Day, the statue is painted with a fresh coat of house paint; the bronze underneath remains as strong as the great king's will.

**Kamehameha County Park,** down a marked side road, has a full recreation area, including an Olympic-size pool open to the public, basketball courts, and weight rooms in the main building along with outside tennis courts with night lighting and a driving range. There are restrooms, picnic tables, and a kiddie area, all free to use.

### Kalahikiola Church

A few minutes east of town, a county lane leads to Kalahikiola Congregational Church. The road is delightfully lined with palm trees, pines, and macadamias like the formal driveway that it once was. Pass the weathering buildings of the Bond Estate and follow the road to the church on the hill. This church was built by Rev. Elias Bond and his wife Ellen, who arrived at Kohala in 1841 and dedicated the church in 1855. Rev. Bond and his parishioners were determined to overcome many formidable obstacles in building Kalahikiola (Life from the Sun) Church, so that they could "sit in a dry and decent house in Jehovah's presence." They hauled timber for miles, quarried and carried stone from distant gulches, raised lime from the sea floor, and brought sand by the jarful all the way from Kawaihae to mix their mortar. After two years of backbreaking work and $8,000, the church finally stood in God's praise, 85 feet long by 45 feet wide. The attached bell tower, oddly out of place, looks like a shoebox standing on end topped by four mean-looking spikes. Note that the doors don't swing, but slide—some visitors leave because they think it's locked. Inside, the church is dark and cool and, inexplicably, the same type of spikes as on the bell tower flank both sides of the altar. There is also a remarkable koa table.

## The Bond Estate

The *most* remarkable and undisturbed missionary estate still extant in Hawaii (and one of two undisturbed mission districts in the world—the other is in Nepal) is the old Bond Homestead and its attendant buildings, including the now defunct but partially renovated Kohala Girls' School up the road and the Kalahikiola Church. All three of these wonderful structures are on the National Historical Register. No tours are given, but you can have a look at the outside of the buildings on the homestead grounds and at the girls' school if the gate on the drive in is not locked.

## Tong Wo Society Building

Behind the Rankin Gallery in Halawa is the lovely and historically significant Tong Wo Society building (1886) and cemetery—well worth a visit. As the third Chinese Triad hall in Hawaii, Tong Wo Kung Ssu, as it was called and as the placard over the door still reads, was one of the early formal meeting places for the Chinese immigrant workers, a place to push for the overthrow of the Manchu government in China, an organizational force for community action and mutual support, and a social center. Since 1970, work has been done to restore the building to its former splendor, and it now stands as a shining example, not only of the renovation of a structure, but also of the reinvigoration of a social organization, and the will of the community to remake one of its own.

**Tong Wo Society Building**

## Keokea Beach County Park

Two miles past Kapa'au toward Pololu you pass a small fruit stand and an access road heading *makai* to secluded Keokea Beach County Park. The park, on the side of the hill going down to the sea, is a favorite spot of North Kohala residents, especially on weekends, but it receives little use during the week. The rocky shoreline faces the open ocean, so swimming is not advised except during summer calm, yet there is a protected cove for the little ones. Amenities include a pavilion, restrooms, showers, and picnic tables. No camping is permitted.

## Accommodations

Located a quarter-mile above Kapa'au is the **Kohala Country Adventures Guest House,** an island home with three units that could be your base for exploring North Kohala. The upstairs unit has a living area with king-size futon and double bed, a combination dining area and efficiency kitchen, a bath with shower, and sun deck. It rents for $135 a night, multiple-night rentals preferred. Basically a room with a double bed and a bathroom, the economy room rents for $70 and can be adjoined to the suite for a larger family. The downstairs garden room, with its queen-size bed and single bed, kitchenette, full bath with spa tub, also has a deck off the bedroom and rents for $99. Each unit has its own private entrance and views of the garden. All guests receive a light continental breakfast in the morning to have at their leisure, or can elect not to have breakfast for a slightly reduced room rate. Two nights minimum requested. For reservations, call Bobi Moreno at 808/889-5663 or 866/892-2484, write P.O. Box 703, Kapa'au, HI 96755, or go to www.kcadventures.com.

Located near Kapa'au, *mauka* of the highway in a residential neighborhood, is **Cook's Cottage,** a studio with a full kitchen and bath, TV, laundry facilities, and separate entrance, available for $65 a night or $350 a week. Sleeps up to four. Contact Sue Cook at 808/889-0912.

In the village of Niuli'i, on the road down to Keokea Beach Park is **Kohala's Guest House,** P.O. Box 172 Hawi, HI 96719, 808/889-5606, fax 808/889-5572, http://home1.gte.net/svendsen, where you have a choice of studio or either half of a duplex. The studio comes with a queen-size bed and bath, kitchenette, color TV, and private entrance. Both halves of the duplex are fully contained houses with a full kitchen, living and dining areas, three bedrooms, two bathrooms, TV, and laundry facilities. The studio rents for $49 a night. The houses run up to $125 a night or $600 a week, depending upon the number of bedrooms that you need.

## Food

**Nambu Courtyard Café,** 808/889-5546, is located in the historic Nambu Building. Open for breakfast and lunch Mon.–Fri. 6:30 A.M.–4 P.M., Sat. until 4 P.M., and Sun. until 1:30 P.M., this little café offers such items as bagels and English muffins with various toppings for breakfast. Grilled sandwiches like stuffed focaccia, spicy Italian, and Swiss beef, plus pastries and ice cream are best for lunch. Have these inside or with any number of coffees or other drinks in the back garden. The Nambu Courtyard Café is a great spot for a morning pick-me-up or a tasty bite during the day.

**Jen's Kohala Cafe,** 808/899-0099, open daily 10 A.M.–5 P.M. across the street from the Kamehameha Statue in Kapa'au, is the place to stop for wraps, sandwiches, burgers, soups, and smoothies. Some Saturdays and Sundays of the year, the cafe stays open 4:30–8:30 P.M. for Thai food nights.

**J&R's Place** offers local food, pizza, and coffee. You can't go wrong at this simple, clean, good, and inexpensive eatery.

## Shopping

For food shopping in Kapa'au try **Union Market,** along Rte. 270 coming into Kapa'au, which sells not only general merchandise and meats, but also a hefty assortment of grains, nuts, fruits, and locally made pastries and breads. To the east of town is the **Arakawa Store,** also with a combination of groceries, general merchandise, and dry goods. The **Kamehameha Pharmacy** in downtown Kapa'au is a full-service pharmacy, 808/889-6161.

In Kapa'au, across from the Kamehameha statue, is **Ackerman Gallery,** 808/889-5971, open daily 9 A.M.–5:30 P.M., owned and operated by artist Gary Ackerman. Besides showcasing some of his own sensitive, island-inspired paintings, he displays local pottery, carvings, woven baskets and other natural fiber works, and one-of-a-kind jewelry. He also carries a smattering of artwork from throughout the Pacific. The artwork selections are tasteful and expensive. You can also choose a reasonably priced gift item, especially from the handmade jewelry section. Make sure to check out the display of beautiful hand-blown glass. The distinctive, iridescent glaze is achieved by using volcanic cinders—you can bring home a true island memento that includes a bit of Madame Pele herself. Gary has expanded by opening a second Ackerman Gallery just down the street. This lovely gallery, housed in a turn-of-the-century building, showcases only his paintings, known for their dramatic colors and textures, giclé and lithographs of his work, and is a testament to the man and his enduring popularity.

Occupying another renovated old building along the highway is the **Sue Swerdlow Art Gallery,** 808/889-0002. Swerdlow, "a colorist," displays her own works of bold and bright colors, plus a selection of pieces by other artists.

In the renovated Nanbu Building is **Kohala Book Shop,** 808/889-6400, fax 808/889-6344, kohalabk@gte.net, reputedly the largest used bookstore in the state. It handles fiction and non-fiction, rare and unusual books, books on Hawaii and the Pacific, and even some cards and other gift items. Thousands of volumes line the shelves, and if you can't find what you're looking for, the owners will try to locate a copy by searching their sources for it. You can also search their listing of books by logging onto the www.abebooks.com website and finding the Kohala Book Shop link. If you want to visit the shop, stop by Tues.–Sat. 11 A.M.–5 P.M.

Also in the same building are the **Nambu Galleries,** the **Elements** jewelry and crafts shop, and **Victoria Fine Arts** gallery. Nambu Galleries shows landscapes by the owner and other paintings by artists from diverse places like California, China, and Colombia. Elements is more gift oriented with a diverse collection of pottery, wind chimes, jewelry, prints, painted scarves, Christmas ornaments, and much more.

The **Rankin Gallery,** 808/889-6849, occupies the historic Wo On (Harmony and Peace) general store in Halawa, which served the Chinese community during plantation days. This gallery displays a wide range of island-inspired paintings, turned wooden bowls, and some American Southwest art. Around the side and in the back is the Tong Wo Society building.

## POLOLU VALLEY

Finally you come to Pololu Valley Overlook. It's about 12 miles from Pololu Valley to Waipi'o Valley, with five deep-cut valleys in between, including the majestic Waimanu, the largest. From the lookout it takes about 20 minutes to walk down to the floor of Pololu. The trail is well maintained as you pass through a heavy growth of *lau hala,* but it can be slippery when wet. **Kohala Ditch,** a monument to labor-intensive engineering, runs along the walls of this valley to its rear. It carried precious water to the sugar plantations, and today carries adventurous kayakers for a very unusual thrill ride. Pololu and the other valleys were once inhabited and were among the richest wet taro plantations of old Hawaii. Today, abandoned and neglected, they have been taken over by introduced vegetation. The black-sand beach fronting Pololu is lined with a thick forest of trees. The rip current here can be very dangerous, so enter the water only in summer months. The rip fortunately weakens not too far from shore; if you're caught, go with it and ride the waves back in. Many people hike into Pololu for seclusion and back-to-nature camping. Make sure to boil the stream water before drinking. Plenty of wild fruits can augment your food supply, and the shoreline fishing is excellent.

# The Saddle Road

Slicing across the midriff of the island in a gentle arch from Mamalahoa Hwy. near Waimea to Hilo is Rte. 200, the Saddle Road. Everyone with a sense of adventure loves this bold cut across the Big Island through a broad high valley separating the two great mountains, Mauna Loa and Mauna Kea. Along this stretch of some 55 miles you pass rolling pastureland, broad swaths of lava flows, arid desert-like fields that look a bit like Nevada, a *nene* sanctuary, trailheads for several hiking trails, mist-shrouded rainforests, an explorable cave, and spur roads leading to the tops of Mauna Kea and Mauna Loa. Here as well is the largest military training reserve in the state, with its live firing range, and the Bradshaw Army Airfield. What you won't see

is much traffic or many people. It's a great adventure for anyone traveling between Kona and Hilo. Keep your eyes peeled for convoys of tanks and armored personnel carriers as they sometimes sally forth from Pohakuloa Military Camp, and also watch out for those who want to make this a high-speed shortcut from one side of the island to the other.

## Road Conditions

The Saddle Road was constructed in 1942 and left as gravel until about 25 years ago. While the road up both sides is at a good incline, the saddle itself is reasonably flat and at about 6,000–6,500 feet. Car-rental companies cringe when you mention the Saddle Road. Most still do not allow their cars on

**Mauna Kea Observatory**

ROBERT NILSEN

this road even though it is paved and well engineered. Check your rental agreement, as it'll be very specific on this point. They're terrified you'll rattle their cars to death. For the most part, these fears are groundless, as there are only short sections that may be rough, due mostly to military use. By and large, it's a good road, no worse than many others around the island—the Hilo side is wider and has better shoulders than the Kona side. However, it *is* isolated, and there are no facilities whatsoever along its length. If you do have trouble, you'll need to go a long way for assistance, but if you bypass it, you'll miss some of the best scenery on the Big Island. On the Kona side, the Saddle Road turnoff is about six miles south of Waimea along Rte. 190, about halfway between Waimea and Waikoloa Road. From Hilo, follow Waianuenue Avenue inland. Saddle Road, Rte. 200, also signed as Kaumana Drive, splits left

after about a mile and is clearly marked. Passing Kaumana Caves County Park, the road steadily gains elevation as you pass into and then out of a layer of clouds. Expect fog or rain.

## MAUNA KEA

There is old lava along both sides of the road as you approach the broad tableland of the saddle. Much of the lava here is from the mid-1800s, but some is from a more-recent 1935 flow. About 25 miles up from the Kona side, and 28 miles out of Hilo, a clearly marked access road to the north leads to the summit of 13,796-foot Mauna Kea (White Mountain). A sign warns you that this road is rough, unpaved, and narrow, with no water, food, fuel, restrooms, or shelters. Moreover, you can expect wind, rain, fog, hail, snow, and altitude sickness. Intrigued? Proceed—it's not as

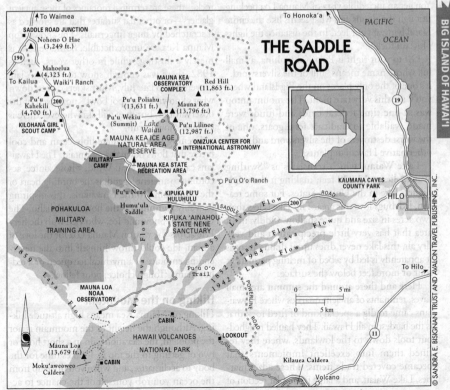

bad as it sounds. In fact, the road, while steep, is well paved for the first six miles to the **Onizuka Center for International Astronomy and Visitor Information Center** at 9,300 feet, where there are restrooms and drinking water. Beyond there, the road is gravel for several miles, but paved again at the very top. A 4WD vehicle is required beyond the visitor center, and if there's snow, the road may not be passable at all.

Just beyond the Onizuka Center is **Hale Pohaku** (House of Stone), which looks like a ski resort; many of the scientists from the observatory atop the mountain live here. From here, the road is graded, banked, and well maintained, with the upper four miles paved so that dust is kept to a minimum to protect the sensitive "eyes" of the telescopes. As you climb, you pass through the clouds to a barren world devoid of vegetation. The earth is a red, rolling series of volcanic cones. You get an incredible vista of Mauna Loa peeking through the clouds and what seems like the entire island lying at your feet. In the distance the lights of Maui flicker.

Off to your right is Pu'u Kahinahina, a small hill whose name means "hill of the silversword." It's one of the only places on the Big Island where you'll see this very rare plant. The mountaintop was at one time federal land, and funds were made available to eradicate feral goats, one of the worst destroyers of the silversword and many other native Hawaiian plants.

**Lake Waiau,** which translates as "Swirling Water," lies at 13,020 feet, making it the third-highest lake in the United States. For some reason, ladybugs love this area. This lake is less than two acres in size and quite shallow. Oddly, in an area that has very little precipitation and very dry air, this lake never dries up or drains away as it apparently is fed by a bed of melting permafrost four or more feet below the surface.

Here and there around the summit are small caves, remnants of ancient quarries where Hawaiians came to dig a special kind of fired rock that is the hardest in all Hawaii. They hauled roughed-out tools down to the lowlands, where they refined them into excellent implements that became coveted trade items. These adze quarries, Lake Waiau, and a large triangular section of

the glaciated southern slope of the mountain have been designated **Mauna Kea Ice Age Natural Area Reserve.**

A natural phenomenon is the strange thermal properties manifested by the cinder cones that dot the top of the mountain. Only 10 feet or so under their surface is permafrost that dates back 10,000 years to the Pleistocene Epoch. If you drill into the cones for 10–20 feet and put a pipe in, during daylight hours, air will be sucked into the pipe. At night, warm air comes out of the pipe with sufficient force to keep a hat levitating.

Mauna Kea is the only spot in the tropical Pacific that was thought to be glaciated until recent investigation provided evidence that suggests that Haleakala on Maui was also capped by a glacier when it was higher and much older. The entire summit of Mauna Kea was covered in 500 feet of ice. Toward the summit, you may notice piles of rock—these are terminal moraines of these ancient glaciers—or other flat surfaces that are grooved as if scratched by huge fingernails. The snows atop Mauna Kea are unpredictable. Some years it is merely a dusting, while in other years, such as 1982, there was enough snow to ski from late November to late July. Most skiers careen down what's known as the "poi bowl," northwest of the observatories, but they will ski wherever there is enough snow to run.

Evening brings an incredibly clean and cool breeze that flows down the mountain. The Hawaiians called it the Kehau Wind, whose source, according to ancient legend, is the burning heart of the mountain. To the Hawaiians, this inspiring heavenly summit was the home of Poliahu, The Goddess of Snow and Ice, who vied with the fiery Pele across the way on Mauna Loa for the love of a man. He could throw himself into the never-ending embrace of a mythical ice queen or a red-hot mama. Tough choice, poor fellow!

## Hiking on the Mountain

Hiking on Mauna Kea means high altitude hiking. Although the height of the mountain is not the problem, the elevation gain in a short hour or two of getting to the top is. It takes time for the body to acclimatize, and when you drive up from the ocean you rob yourself of the chance to acclimatize easily. What you may expect to experience normally are slight dizziness, a shortness of breath due to reduced oxygen levels, and reduced ability to think clearly and react quickly. Some people are more prone to elevation problems, so if you experience more severe symptoms, get to a lower elevation immediately. These symptoms include prolonged or severe headache, loss of appetite, cramped muscles, prolonged malaise or weakness, dizziness, reduced muscle control and balance, and heart palpitations. Use your head, know your limits, and don't push yourself. Carry plenty of water (more than you would at a lower elevation) and food. Wear a brimmed hat, sunglasses, sunscreen, and lip balm, a long-sleeved shirt and long pants, and sturdy hiking boots or shoes. Carry a windbreaker, sweater, and gloves, as it can be cold and windy at and near the top. Don't alter the natural environment. Take out all that you take in.

There are a few good day hike trails on the mountain. About six miles above the Visitor Center, a dirt track heads off the access road to the west and downhill to a parking lot. From the parking area, it's about one mile farther west, over the saddle between two small hills, to Lake Waiau and its placid waters. On the way, a trail from the top (about a 30-minute hike) crosses this path and heads down the mountain back to the Visitor Center. A couple of miles down this cross path is an adze quarry site. Perhaps the most convenient hike is that to the true summit of the mountain. Start from the roadway across from the University of Hawaii 2.2-meter Telescope, cross over the guardrail, and follow the rough path down into the saddle and steeply up the hill, a distance of less than half a mile.

## MAUNA KEA OBSERVATORY COMPLEX

Atop the mountain is a mushroom grove of astronomical observatories, as incongruously striking as a futuristic earth colony on a remote planet of a distant galaxy. The crystal-clear air and lack of dust and light pollution make the Mauna Kea Observatory site *the* best in the world. At close to 14,000 feet, it is above 40 percent of the earth's at-mosphere and 98 percent of its water vapor. Temperatures generally hover around 40–50 degrees during the day, and there's only 9–11 inches of precipitation annually, mostly in the form of snow. The astronomers have come to expect an average of 325 crystal-clear nights per year, perfect for observation. The state of Hawaii leases plots at the top of the mountain, upon which various institutions from all over the world have constructed telescopes. Those institutions in turn give the University of Hawaii up to 15 percent of their viewing time. The university sells the excess viewing time, which supports the entire astronomy program and makes a little money on the side. Those who work at the top must come down every four days because the thin air makes them forgetful and susceptible to making minor calculation errors. Scientists from around the world book months in advance for a squint through one of these phenomenal telescopes, and institutions from several countries maintain permanent outposts here.

The first telescope that you see on your left is the United Kingdom's **James Clerk Maxwell Telescope** (JCMT), a radio telescope with a primary reflecting surface more than 15 meters in diameter. This unit was operational in 1987. It was dedicated by Britain's Prince Philip, who rode all the way to the summit in a Rolls Royce. The 3.6-meter **Canada-France-Hawaii Telescope** (CFHT), finished in 1979 for $33 million, was the first to spot Halley's Comet in 1983.

A newer eye to the heavens atop Mauna Kea is the double **W. M. Keck Observatory.** Keck I was operational in 1992 and Keck II in 1996. The Keck Foundation, a philanthropic organization from Los Angeles, funded the telescopes to the tune of over $140 million, among the world's most high-tech, powerful, and expensive. Operated by the California Association for Research in Astronomy (CARA), a joint project of the University of California and Cal Tech, the telescopes have an aperture of 400 inches and employ entirely new and unique types of technology. The primary reflectors are fashioned from a mosaic of 36 hexagonal mirrors, each only three inches thick and six feet in diameter. These "small" mirrors have been very carefully joined together to form one incredibly huge, actively controlled light reflector surface. Each of the mirror segments is capable of being individually positioned to an accuracy of a millionth of an inch; each is computer-controlled to bring the heavenly objects into perfect focus. These titanic eyeballs have already spotted both the most distant known galaxy and the most distant known object in the universe, 12 and 13 billion light years from earth, respectively. The light received from these objects today was emitted not long after the "Big Bang" that created the universe theoretically occurred. In a very real sense, scientists are looking back toward the beginning of time! The Keck Observatory includes a gallery that's open to the public Mon.–Fri. 10 A.M.–4 P.M., a video presentation of the telescope, displays, a viewing area inside one of the domes, and restrooms. Alternately, one may visit the Keck Observatory office in Waimea for complete information about the telescope, without having to make the trek up to the top of the mountain.

In addition to these are the following: The **NASA Infrared Telescope Facility** (IRTF), online since 1979, does only infrared viewing with its three-meter mirror. Also with only infrared capabilities, the **United Kingdom Infrared Telescope** (UKIRT), in operation since 1979 as well, searches the sky with its 3.8-meter lens. Directly below it is the **University of Hawaii .6-meter Telescope.** Built in 1968, it was the first on the mountaintop and has the smallest reflective mirror. Completed in 1970, the **University of Hawaii 2.2-meter Telescope** was a huge improvement over its predecessor but is now the second smallest telescope at the top. The **Caltech Submillimeter Observatory** (CSO) has been looking into the sky since 1987 with its 10.4-meter radio telescope. **Subaru** (Japan National Large Telescope) is a monolithic 8.3-meter mirror capable of both optical and infrared viewing. It is the most recently completed telescope on the mountain, fully operational since 2000. The **Gemini Northern 8.1-meter Telescope,** also with both optical and infrared viewing, is run by a consortium from the United States, United Kingdom, Canada, Chile, Argentina, and Brazil. Its southern twin is located on a mountaintop in Chile, and together they

have been viewing the heavens since 1999. Situated to the side and below the rest is the **Submillimeter Array,** a series of eight six-meter-wide antennae. About two miles distant from the top is the **Very Long Baseline Array,** a 25-meter-wide, centimeter wavelength radio dish that is one in a series of similar antennae that dot the 5,000-mile stretch between Hawaii and the Virgin Islands.

While the state is considering expansion of the complex to include additional telescopes and support facilities, a number of groups, including The Hawaiian-Environmental Alliance, are calling upon the state to proceed in a culturally and environmentally friendly manner or to not proceed at all.

The entire mountaintop complex, plus almost all of the land area above 12,000 feet, is managed by the University of Hawaii. Visitors are welcome to tour the complex and stop by the Visitor Center at the **Onizuka Center for International Astronomy,** www.ifa.hawaii.edu/info/vis, at the 9,300-foot level. Named in honor of astronaut Ellison Onizuka, born and raised on

## MAUNA KEA OBSERVATORIES ONLINE

**University of Hawaii 2.2-meter Telescope:** www.ifa.hawaii.edu/88inch

**NASA Infrared Telescope Facility:** http://irtfweb.ifa.hawaii.edu

**Canada-France-Hawaii Telescope:** www.cfht.hawaii.edu

**United Kingdom Infrared Telescope:** www.jach.hawaii.edu/UKIRT/home.html

**James Clerk Maxwell Telescope:** www.jach.hawaii.edu/JACpublic/JCMT/home.html

**Caltech Submillimeter Observatory:** www.submm.caltech.edu/cso

**Very Long Baseline Array:** www.nrao.edu/vlba/html/VLBA.html

**W. M. Keck Observatory:** www2.keck.hawaii.edu

**Subaru:** www.naoj.org

**Gemini Northern 8.1-meter Telescope:** www.gemini.edu

**Submillimeter Array:** sma2.harvard.edu

the Big Island, who died in the *Challenger* space shuttle tragedy in 1986, this center is a must-stop for stargazers. Inside are displays of astronomical and cultural subjects, informational handouts, and computer links to the observatories on the hill above, as well as evening videos and slide shows. Often, small 11- to 16-inch telescopes are set up outside during the day to view the sun and sunspots and in the evening to view the stars and other celestial objects. The Visitor Center is about one hour from Hilo and Waimea and about two hours from Kailua-Kona. A stop here will allow visitors a chance to acclimatize to the thin, high-mountain air—another must. A stay of one hour here is recommended before you head up to the 13,796-foot summit. (Because of the high altitude and the remoteness of the mountaintop from emergency medical facilities, children under age 16 are prohibited from venturing to the summit. People with cardiopulmonary or respiratory problems or with physical infirmities or weakness, women who are pregnant, and those who are obese are also discouraged from attempting the trip. In addition, those who have been scuba diving should not attempt a trip to the top until at least 24 hours have elapsed.) The Visitor Center provides the last public restrooms before the summit and is a good place to stock up on water, also unavailable higher up. The Visitor Center is open Mon.–Fri. 9 A.M.–noon, 1–5 P.M., and 6–10 P.M., and Saturday and Sunday 9 A.M.–10 P.M. Free stargazing tours are offered daily 6–10 P.M. and a summit tour every Saturday and Sunday 1–5 P.M. (weather permitting). These programs are free of charge. For either activity, dress warmly. Evening temperatures will be 40–50 degrees in summer and might be below freezing in winter, and winds of 20 miles per hour are not atypical. For the summit tour, you must provide your own 4WD transportation from the Visitor Center to the summit. For more visitor and program information, call 808/961-2180; call 808/974-4203 for road conditions. For information on the Internet about the mountaintop observatories or the individual telescope installations, log onto the University of Hawaii Institute for Astronomy website (www.ifa.hawaii.edu/) and follow the links from there.

If you plan on continuing up to the summit, you must provide your own transportation and it must be a 4WD vehicle. As the observatories are used primarily at night, it is requested that visitors to the top come during daylight hours and leave by a half hour after sunset to minimize the use of headlights and reduce the dust from the road, both factors that might disrupt optimum viewing. For rental vehicles, contact **Harper Car and Truck Rentals** in Hilo, 808/969-1478, which offers 4WD rentals certified for driving to the mountaintop. Alternately, make arrangements for a guided tour to the top. From the Kona side, try **Mauna Kea Summit Adventures,** 808/322-2366 or 888/322-2366, www.maunakea.com; **Hawaii Forest and Trail,** 808/331-5805 or 800/464-1993, www.hawaii-forest.com; or **Hawaiian Eyes Land Tours,** 808/326-2434. In Hilo, contact **Arnott's Hiking Adventures,** 808/969-7097, www.arnottslodge.com. Take extra layers of warm clothing and your camera. Photographers using fast film get some of the most dazzling shots *after* sunset. During the gloaming, the light show begins. Look down upon the clouds to see them filled with fire. This heavenly light is reflected off the mountain to the clouds and then back up like a celestial mirror in which you get a fleeting glimpse of the soul of the universe.

# SIGHTS ALONG ROUTE 200
## Pohakuloa
The broad, relatively flat saddle between Mauna Kea and Mauna Loa is an area known as Pohakuloa (Long Stone). At an elevation of roughly 6,500 feet, this plain alternates between lava flow, grassland, and semi-arid desert pockmarked with cinder cones. About seven miles west of the Mauna Kea Road, at a sharp bend in the road, you'll find a cluster of cabins that belong to the now-closed Mauna Kea State Recreation Area. No overnight services are available here, but you can stop for a picnic and potty break. Nearby is a game management area, so expect hunting and shooting of wild pigs, sheep, and birds in season. A few minutes west is the **Pohakuloa Military**

**Camp,** whose maneuvers can sometimes disturb the peace in this high mountain area.

## Kipuka Pu'u Huluhulu

Bird-watchers or nature enthusiasts should turn into the Kipuka Pu'u Huluhulu parking lot across the road from the Mauna Kea Road turn-off. A *kipuka* is an area that has been surrounded by a lava flow, but never inundated, that preserves an older and established ecosystem. Here you will find a hunters' check-in station. From the parking lot, a hiking trail leads into this fenced, 38-acre nature preserve. Several loop trails run through the forest on the hill, and there are two exits on Mauna Loa Observatory Road, on its eastern edge. Pu'u Huluhulu means "Shaggy Hill," and this diminutive hill is covered in a wide variety of trees and bushes, which include *mamame, naio, 'iliahi* (sandalwood), koa, and 'ohi'a. Some of the birds most often seen are the greenish-yellow *'amakihi,* the red *'i'iwi* and *'apapane,* the dull brown and smoky-gray *'oma'o.* In addition, you may be lucky enough to spot a rare *'io,* Hawaiian hawk, or the more numerous *pueo,* short-eared owl. Even if you are not particularly drawn to the birds or the trees, this is a good place to get out of the car, stretch your legs, and get acclimatized to the elevation.

## Pu'u O'o Trail

Just after mile marker 24 on the way up from Hilo is the trailhead for Pu'u O'o Trail. From the small parking lot along the road, this trail heads to the south about four miles where it meets Powerline Road, a rough 4WD track, and returns to the Saddle Road. This area is good for bird-watching, and you might have a chance to see the very rare *'akiapola'au* or *'apapane,* and even wild turkeys. This area is frequently shrouded in clouds or fog, and it could very well rain on you. You may want to walk only part way in and return on the same trail, rather than making the circle.

## MAUNA LOA

The largest mass of mountain to make up the Big Island is Mauna Loa (Long Mountain). It lies to the south of Mauna Kea and dominates the southern half of the island. At 13,677 feet, it is about 100 feet shorter than Mauna Kea. The top of this mountain is the huge **Moku'aweoweo Caldera,** virtually as big as Kilauea Crater near Volcano. Connected to this caldera are the smaller but equally impressive North and South pits, each about as big as Halema'uma'u, which is within Kilauea Crater. Unlike Mauna Kea, Mauna Loa has had some recent volcanic activity, spilling lava in 1949, 1950, 1975, and 1980. The top of this mountain is within the Hawaii Volcanoes National Park boundary. One of the longest and perhaps the most difficult hiking trail in the park runs up from the Volcano area to Red Hill cabin and from there on up to the top of the mountain. A 2.6-mile trail skirts the western edge of the caldera to the actual summit. Just over two miles long, another trail reaches the Mauna Loa cabin, perched on the eastern edge of the rim and directly across from the summit.

Mauna Loa Observatory Road, a rough gravel road maintained by the state, turns south off Rte. 200 and leads about 19 miles to the **Mauna Loa NOAA Observatory,** at 11,150 feet. This atmospheric observatory is not open to the public, but you can park near it. From the observatory, a rigorous 3.5-mile-long trail rises some 2,000 feet to the caldera rim. If you intend to hike the observatory trail, be aware that this is a very remote area. There are no services, restrooms, or water along the way. It can be cold and moist, snow and winter conditions can happen at any time of year, and there is virtually no protection from the weather until you get to the cabin on the eastern rim. Park officials estimate that about half of all hikers taking this trail get some degree of altitude sickness.

# Hilo

Hilo is a blind date. Everyone tells you what a beautiful personality she has, but . . . But? It rains—130 inches a year. Mostly the rains come in winter and spring and are limited to predictable afternoon showers, but they do scare some tourists away, keeping Hilo reasonably priced and low-key. In spite of, and because of, the rain, Hilo is gorgeous. It's one of the oldest permanently settled towns in Hawaii, and the largest on the windward coast of the island. Hilo's weather makes it a natural greenhouse. Botanical gardens and flower farms surround Hilo like a giant lei, and shoulder-to-shoulder banyans canopy entire city blocks. To counterpoint this tropical explosion, Mauna Kea's winter snows backdrop the town. The crescent of

Hilo Bay blazes gold at sunrise, while a sculpted lagoon, Asian pagodas, rock gardens, and even a tiny island connected by a footbridge line its shores. Downtown's waterfront has perfect historical buildings that always need a paint job. They lean on each other like "old salts" who've had one too many. Don't make the mistake of underestimating Hilo, or of counting it out because of its rainy reputation. For most, the blind date with this exotic beauty turns into a fun-filled love affair.

Hilo is a unique town in a unique state in America. You can walk down streets with names like Pu'u'eo and Keawe, and they could be streets in Anywhere, U.S.A., with neatly painted houses surrounded by white picket fences. Families live

Pe'epe'e Falls

here. At just over 40,000, Hilo has the second-largest population in the state after Honolulu. It is the county seat, has a bustling commercial harbor, has a long tradition in agriculture and industry, boasts a branch of the University of Hawaii, and is home to the Hawai'i Community College. It was once the terminus of railway lines that stretched north along the Hamakua Coast, and south to Mt. View and Pahoa. There are roots and traditions, but the town is changing. Fishermen still come for the nightly ritual of soul-fishing and story-swapping from the bridge spanning the Wailuku River, while just down the street newly arrived chefs prepare Cajun blackened fish at a yuppie restaurant and midnight philosophers sip gourmet coffee and munch sweets elsewhere. Hilo is a classic tropical town. Some preserved buildings, proud again after new facelifts, are a few stories tall and date from the turn of the 20th century when Hilo was a major port of entry to Hawaii. Sidewalks in older sections are covered with awnings because of the rains, which adds a turn-of-the-20th-century gentility. Because Hilo is a town, most Americans

can relate to it: it's big enough to have one-way streets and malls, but not so big that it's a metropolis like Honolulu, or so small that it's a village like Hana. You can walk the central area comfortably in an afternoon, but the town does sprawl. Teenagers in "boom box" cars cruise the main strip, which is lined with restaurants, antiques and collectibles shops, professional businesses, and mom-and-pop shops. This once vibrant town looks half dead in sections, with stores and shops falling silent due to the modern phenomena of new and large shopping malls in the outlying areas. Yet, there is a movement toward revival, and some old buildings are being enlivened with new uses and bold new shops are taking the places of the old and gone. There's even a down-and-out section where guys hunker down in alleyways, smoking cigarettes and peering into the night. In the still night, there's the deep-throated sound of a ship's foghorn, a specter of times past when Hilo was a vibrant port. Hilo is the opposite of Kailua-Kona both spiritually and physically. There, everything runs fast; it's a clone of Honolulu. In Hilo the old beat, the old

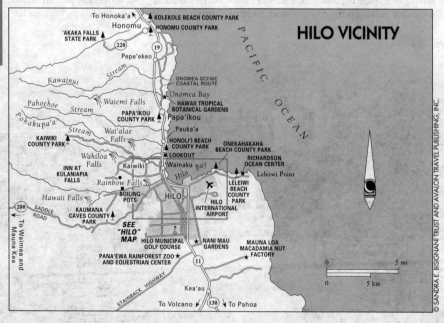

music, that feeling of a tropical place where rhythms are slow and sensual, still exist. Hilo nights are alive with sounds of the tropics and the heady smell of fruits and flowering trees wafting on the breeze. Slow down and relax; you'll start to feel at home. Hilo remains what it always was—a town, a place where people live.

Hilo is the eastern hub of the island. Choose a direction, and an hour's driving puts you in a time-lost valley deep in *paniolo* country, or on the blackness of a recent lava flow, or above the steaming fumaroles of Hawaii Volcanoes National Park. In and around town are museums, riverbank fishing, a cultural center, plenty of gardens, waterfalls, a potholed riverbed, and lava caves. Aside from the bay beach, which is generally not used for swimming, Hilo's beaches are small and rocky—perfect for keeping crowds

away. Hilo is bite-size, but you'll need a rental car to visit most of the sights around town.

The main thoroughfares through the downtown area are Kamehameha Avenue, Kilauea Street, which merges into Keawe Street, and Kino'ole Street, all of which run parallel to the bay. The Bayfront Highway, Rte. 19, skirts the water and runs north up the Hamakua Coast and east past the Banyan Drive area to the beaches out in Keaukaha. Heading inland from the water from the river mouth to Rainbow Falls and Boiling Pots is Waianuenue Avenue, and off it branches Kaumana Drive, Rte. 200, which continues over the mountain as the Saddle Road. Kaneolehua Avenue starts at Banyan Drive and runs inland to Volcano. On both sides of this main thoroughfare are the town's newer commercial districts and the airport.

## Sights

## DOWNTOWN

### Lyman Mission House and Museum

The preserved New England–style homestead of David and Sarah Lyman, Congregational missionaries who built it in 1839, is the oldest frame building still standing on the Big Island. In 1856, a second story was added, which provided more room and a perfect view of the harbor. In 1926, Haili Street was extended past the home, and at that time the Wilcox and Lyman families had the house turned parallel to the street so that it would front the entrance. The building is now on the National and State Registers of Historic Places.

The Lyman Mission House opened as a museum in 1932! The furniture is authentic "Sandwich Isles" circa 1850, the best pieces fashioned from koa. Much of it has come from other missionary homes, although many pieces belonged to the original occupants. The floors, mantels, and doors are deep, luxurious koa. The main door is a "Christian door," built by the Hilo Boys Boarding School. The top panels form a cross and the bottom depicts an open Bible. Many of the artifacts on the deep windowsills are tacked down because of earthquakes. One room was used as a school-

room/dayroom where Mrs. Lyman taught arithmetic, mapmaking, and proper manners. The dining room holds an original family table that was set with the "Blue Willow" china seen in a nearby hutch. Some of the most interesting exhibits are of small personal items like a music box that still plays and a collection of New England autumn leaves that Mrs. Lyman had sent over to show her children what that season was like. Upstairs are bedrooms that were occupied by the parents and the seven children. Their portraits hang in a row. Mrs. Lyman kept a diary and faithfully recorded eruptions, earthquakes, and tsunami. Scientists still refer to it for some of the earliest recorded data on these natural disturbances. The master bedroom has a large bed with pineapples carved into the bedposts, crafted by a ship's carpenter who lived with the family for about eight months. The bedroom mirror is an original, in which many Hawaiians received their first surprised look at themselves. A nursery holds a cradle used by all eight children. It's obvious that the Lymans did not live luxuriously, but they were comfortable in their island home.

The Lyman House is at 276 Haili St., 808/935-5021, www.lymanmuseum.org, and is

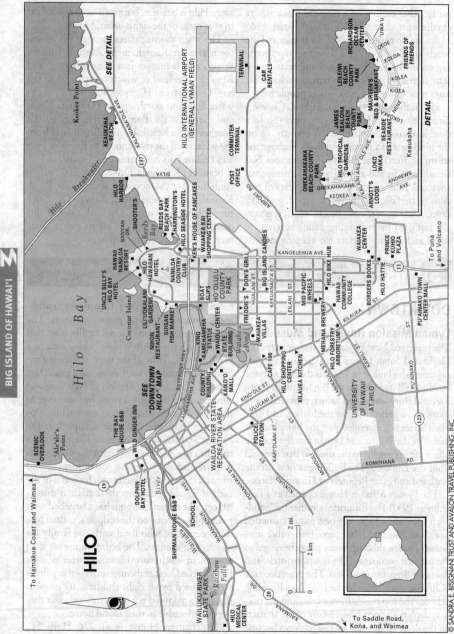

SEE DETAIL

Keokea Point

KEAUKAHA BEACH

Hilo Breakwater

Hilo Harbor

KALANIANA'OLE AVE.

137

HILO INTERNATIONAL AIRPORT
(GENERAL LYMAN FIELD)

TERMINAL

CAR RENTALS

COMMUTER TERMINAL

POST OFFICE

AIRPORT RD.

SILVA

KEN'S HOUSE OF PANCAKES

HILO HARBOR

REEDS BAY BEACH PARK

HARRINGTON'S

HILO SEASIDE HOTEL

WAIAKEA KAI SHOPPING CENTER

KANOELEHUA AVE.

WAIAKEA CENTER

PRINCE KUHIO PLAZA

11

To Puna and Volcano

SHOOTER'S

Reeds Bay

Banyan Dr.

HILO HAWAIIAN HOTEL

UNCLE BILLY'S HILO BAY HOTEL

HAWAII NANILOA RESORT

LILI'UOKALANI GARDENS

Coconut Island

NANLOA COUNTRY CLUB

BIG ISLAND CANDIES

HILO BIKE HUB

HAWAII COMMUNITY COLLEGE

HILO HATTIE

BORDERS BOOKS

DON'S GRILL

HUALANI ST.
KEKUANAO'A ST.
HUALANI ST.

MID PACIFIC WHEELS

PU'AINAKO TOWN CENTER MALL

Hilo Bay

NIHON RESTAURANT

SUISAN FISH MARKET

BOAT SLIPS

HO'OLULU COUNTY PARK

FREDDIE'S

WAIAKEA' VILLAS

Waiakea Pond

KING KAMEHAMEHA STATE BUILDING

WAIOLI CENTER

KAMEHAMEHA AVE.

BAYFRONT HWY.

LEILANI ST.

KILAUEA ST.

MEHANA BREWERY

HILO FORESTRY ARBORETUM

KILAUEA

KILAUEA KITCHEN

LANIKAULA ST.
LANIKAULA ST.

UNIVERSITY OF HAWAII AT HILO

123

'Ale'ale'a Point

SCENIC OVERLOOK

THE BAY HOUSE B&B

WILD GINGER INN

COUNTY BUILDING

KAIKO'O MALL

CAFE 100

HILO SHOPPING CENTER

KINO'OLE ST.
ULULANI ST.

KAPI'OLANI ST.

MOHOULI ST.

KUKUAU ST.

KOMOHANA RD.

DOLPHIN BAY HOTEL

WAILUKU RIVER STATE RECREATION AREA

POLICE STATION

PONAHAWAI ST.

River

19

To Hamakua Coast and Waimea

SHIPMAN HOUSE B&B

SCHOOL ST.

WAIANUENUE AVE.

KAWILI ST.

HILO MEDICAL CENTER

KAUMANA DR.

WAILUKU RIVER STATE PARK

Rainbow Falls

DR.

20

HILO

To Saddle Road, Kona, and Waimea

0    2 mi
0    2 km

BIG ISLAND OF HAWAI'I

DETAIL

'UWA'U

RICHARDSON OCEAN CENTER

FRIENDS OF FRIENDS

'O'OE
'O'OE

KOLOA

KALANIANA'OLE AVE.

LEILEIWI BEACH COUNTY PARK

KOLEA

KIOEA

MAUREEN'S BED & BREAKFAST

SEASIDE RESTAURANT

JAMES KEALOHA BEACH COUNTY PARK

KANE

'IENE

LOKO WAKA

ONEKAHAKAHA BEACH COUNTY PARK

HILO TROPICAL GARDENS

KAILANI ANA 'OLE AVE.

ONEKAHAKAHA

ARNOTT'S LODGE

ANDREWS AVE.

KEOKEA

Keaukaha

© SANDRA E. BISIGNANI TRUST AND AVALON TRAVEL PUBLISHING, INC.

SEE "DOWNTOWN HILO MAP"

open Mon.–Sat. 9 A.M.–4:30 P.M., admission $5 adults, $2.50 children 6–18. Guided tours are given six times a day by experienced and knowledgeable docents who relate many intriguing stories about the building and its occupants.

Next door to the Lyman House, in a modern two-story building, is the Lyman Museum. The 1st floor is designated the **Earth Heritage Gallery.** The mineral and rock collection here is rated one of the top 10 in the entire country, and by far the best in Polynesia. Marvel at thunder eggs, agates, jaspers, India blue mezolite, aquamarine lazurite from Afghanistan, and hunks of weirdly shaped lava. These displays are the lifelong collection of the great-grandson of the original Rev. Lyman. Anything coming from the earth can be exhibited here: shells named and categorized from around the world, petrified wood, glass paperweights, and crystals. Other exhibits explain the geology and volcanology of Kilauea and Mauna Kea, and a section is dedicated to the vanishing flora and fauna of Hawaii.

Upstairs is the **Island Heritage Gallery,** where a replica of a Hawaiian grass house, complete with thatched roof and floor mats, is proudly displayed. Nearby are Hawaiian tools: hammers of clinkstone, chisels of basalt, and state-of-the-art "stone age" polishing stones with varying textures used to rub bowls and canoes to a smooth finish. Hawaiian fiberwork, the best in Polynesia, is also displayed, as well as coconut, pandanus, and the pliable air root of the *'ie'ie.* The material, dyed brown or black, was woven into intricate designs. You'll also see fishhooks, stone lamps, mortars and pestles, *lomi lomi* sticks, even a display on *kahuna,* with a fine text on the *kapu* system. Precontact displays give way to kimonos from Japan, a Chinese herbal medicine display, and displays dedicated to Filipino, Portuguese, and Korean heritage. In adjoining rooms are galleries dedicated to Chinese art, with a fine grouping of ceramic and jade pottery and statuary from the last three centuries with a few pieces as old as 2,000 years, and a collection of artwork by Hawaiian artists. Periodic exhibitions are shown in a third gallery. Saying good-bye is a bust of Mark Twain, carved from a piece of the very monkeypod tree he planted in Wai'ohinu in

1866. The museum is educational and worth some time, and the gift shop a good place to look for authentic Hawaiian products and books.

## Pacific Tsunami Museum

Hilo suffered a devastating tsunami in 1946 and again in 1960. Both times, most of the waterfront area of the city was destroyed, but the 1930 Bishop National Bank building survived, owing to its structural integrity. Appropriately, the Pacific Tsunami Museum, 130 Kamehameha Ave., 808/935-0926, www.tsunami.org, is now housed in this fine art-deco structure and dedicated to those who lost their lives in the devastating waves that raked the city. The museum has numerous permanent displays, an audio-visual room, computer linkups to scientific sites, and periodic temporary exhibitions. While there is general scientific information, what's perhaps the most moving feature of this museum are the photographs of the last two terrible tsunamis that struck the city and the stories retold by the survivors of those events. Stop in Mon.–Sat. 9 A.M.–4 P.M. for a look, it's well worth the time. Admission is $5 adults, $4 seniors, and $2 students. Other permanent displays of photos relating to the tsunamis are hung in the Kress Building farther down Kamehameha Avenue and on the lower level of Wailoa Center.

## Downtown Walking Tour

Start your tour of Hilo by picking up a pamphlet/map entitled *Walking Tour of Historic Downtown,* free at the HVB office and many restaurants, hotels, and shops. This self-guiding pamphlet takes you down the main streets and back lanes where you discover the unique architecture of Hilo's glory days. The majority of the vintage buildings have been restored, and the architecture varies from the early 20th-century Kress and S. Hata Building to the continental style of the Hawaiian Telephone Building and the Zen Buddhist Taishoji Shoto Mission. Older is the Lyman House and nearby the New England–style Haili Congregational Church (1859; congregation founded in 1824) and St. Joseph's Catholic Church.

On the median strip between the Bayfront

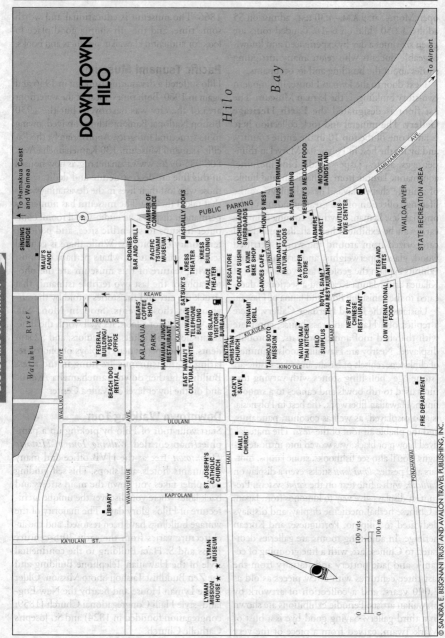

DOWNTOWN HILO

Hilo Bay

To Airport

KAMEHAMEHA AVE.

To Hamakua Coast and Waimea

19

SINGING BRIDGE

MAUI'S CANOE

Wailuku River

PUBLIC PARKING

BUS TERMINAL

MO'OHEAU BANDSTAND

WAILOA RIVER

STATE RECREATION AREA

CHAMBER OF COMMERCE

CRONIES BAR AND GRILL

PACIFIC TSUNAMI MUSEUM

BASICALLY BOOKS

KRESS THEATER

KRESS BUILDING

PESCATORE

OCEAN SUSHI

ORCHIDLAND SURFBOARDS

DA KINE BIKE SHOP

CANOES CAFE

REUBEN'S MEXICAN FOOD

S. HATA BUILDING

FARMERS MARKET

NAUTILUS DIVE CENTER

BYTES AND BITES

KEAWE

BEARS' COFFEE SHOP

SATSUKI'S

PALACE THEATER

HAWAIIAN TELEPHONE BUILDING

BIG ISLAND VISITORS BUREAU

ABUNDANT LIFE NATURAL FOODS

FURNEAUX

KTA SUPER STORE

KEKAULIKE

KALAKAUA

KALAKAUA PARK

HAWAIIAN JUNGLE RESTAURANT

TSUNAMI GRILL

KILAUEA

ROYAL SIAM THAI RESTAURANT

NEW STAR CHINESE RESTAURANT

FEDERAL BUILDING/ POST OFFICE

EAST HAWAI'I CULTURAL CENTER

CENTRAL CHRISTIAN CHURCH

TAISHOJI SOTO MISSION

NAUNG MAI THAI KITCHEN

HILO SURPLUS

MAMO

LOW INTERNATIONAL FOOD

DRIVE

WAILUKU

BEACH DOG RENTAL

KINO'OLE

SACK'N SAVE

FIRE DEPARTMENT

AVE.

ULULANI

PONAHAWAI

HAILI CHURCH

HAILI

ST. JOSEPH'S CATHOLIC CHURCH

KAPI'OLANI

LIBRARY

WAIANUENUE

KA'IULANI ST.

LYMAN MUSEUM

LYMAN MISSION HOUSE

100 yds

100 m

0

0

BIG ISLAND OF HAWAI'I

Highway and Kamehameha Ave. is a bandstand and main city bus stop. The **Mo'oheau Bandstand** is all that's left of the dozens of structures that lined the ocean side of Kamehameha Avenue before the 1946 tsunami. Miraculously, this structure survived. The bandstand is sometimes used by the Hawai'i County Band for concerts and for other community events. A **tourist information kiosk** near the bandstand and bus stop has brochures and maps to dispense about the city.

A remarkable building, the "Old Police Station" is located at 141 Kalakaua St., opposite Kalakaua Park. Built in 1932 and placed on the National and State Registers of Historic Places and Buildings in 1979, this old colonial structure is now the home of the **East Hawai'i Cultural Center,** 808/961-5711, a nonprofit organization that supports local arts and hosts varying festivals, performances, and workshops throughout the year, here and at other locations on the island. It also hosts Shakespeare in the Park performances by a local repertory group that stages, directs, designs, and enacts Shakespearean plays under the large banyan tree in Kalakaua Park, across the street, during the month of July. If you're in Hilo at this time, it shouldn't be missed. Monthly juried and non-juried art exhibits are shown on the main floor gallery; a venue for various performing artists is upstairs. The bulletin board is always filled with announcements of happenings in the local art scene. Stop in as there is always something of interest on the walls, and because this organization is worthy of support. The Big Island Dance Council, Hawai'i Concert Society, Hilo Community Players, and Bunka No Izumi are all member groups. The center is open 10 A.M.–4 P.M. Mon.–Sat., donations acceped. For more information, see www.lastplace.com/EXHIBITS/EHCC.index.htm.

Set aside for public use by King Kalakaua himself, **Kalakaua Park** is a grassy area overseen by a huge banyan tree, a midtown oasis. A seated statue of King David Kalakaua, the Merrie Monarch, takes center stage. Across Waianuenue Avenue is the solid and stately **Federal Building** with its offices and downtown post office. This stone structure dates from 1917.

A short walk up the street brings you to the **Hilo Public Library,** 300 Waianuenue Avenue. Sitting at the entrance are two large stones. The larger is called the **Naha Stone,** known for its ability to detect any offspring of the ruling Naha clan. The test was simple: Place a baby on the stone, and if the infant remained silent, he or she was Naha; if the baby cried, he or she wasn't. It is believed that this 7,000-pound monolith was brought from Kaua'i by canoe and placed near Pinao Temple in the immediate vicinity of what is now Wailuku Drive and Keawe Street. Kamehameha the Great supposedly fulfilled a prophecy of "moving a mountain" by budging this stone. The smaller stone is thought to be an entrance pillar of the Pinao Temple. Just behind the library is the Wailuku River. Pick any of its bridges for a panoramic view down to the sea. Often, local fishermen try their luck from the Wailuku's grassy banks. The massive boulder sitting near the river's mouth is known as **Maui's Canoe.** During the tsunami of 1946, the railroad bridge that crossed the river at bay's edge was torn from its base like a weak Tinker Toy construction. The metal bridge that crosses the river today is known as the "singing bridge" because the mesh that creates the roadway hums or "sings" as rubber tires spin across it.

## Around Banyan Drive

If your Hilo hotel isn't situated along Banyan Drive, go there. This bucolic road skirts the edge of the Waiakea Peninsula that sticks out into Hilo Bay. Lining the drive is an almost uninterrupted series of banyan trees forming a giant canopy, while the fairways and greens of the Naniloa Country Club golf course take up the center of the tiny peninsula. Skirting its edge are the Lili'uokalani Gardens, a concentration of hotels, and Reed's Bay. This peninsula was once a populated residential area, an offshoot of central Hilo. Like much of the city, it too was destroyed during the tsunami of 1960. Park your car at one end and take a stroll through this park-like atmosphere. The four dozen banyans that line this boulevard (the first planted in 1933, the last in 1972) were planted by notable Americans and foreigners, including Babe Ruth, President Franklin D. Roosevelt, King George V, Hawaiian

Lili'uokalani Gardens

ROBERT NILSEN

volcanologist Dr. Jaggar, Hawaiian Princess Kawananakoa, pilot Amelia Earhart, and then-senator Richard Nixon. A placard in front of each tree gives particulars. Time has taken its toll here, however, and as grand as this drive once was, it is now a bit overgrown and unkempt in spots, with much of the area needing a little sprucing up.

**Lili'uokalani Gardens** are formal Japanese-style gardens located along the west end of Banyan Drive. Meditatively quiet, they offer a beautiful view of the bay. Along the footpaths are pagodas, torii gates, stone lanterns, and half-moon bridges spanning a series of ponds and streams. Along one side sits a formal Japanese Tea House where women come to be instructed in the art of the tea ceremony. Few people visit this 30-acre garden, and if it weren't for the striking fingers of black lava and the coconut trees, you could easily be in Japan.

**Coconut Island** (Moku Ola) is reached by footbridge from a spit of land just outside Lili'uokalani Gardens. It was at one time a *pu'uhonua* (place of refuge) opposite a human sacrificial *heiau* on the peninsula side. Coconut Island has restrooms, a pavilion, and picnic tables shaded by tall coconut trees and ironwoods. A favorite picnic spot for decades, kids often come to jump into the water from stone abutments here and older folks come for a leisurely dip in the cool water. The only decent place to swim in Hilo Bay, it also offers the best panorama of the city, bay, and Mauna Kea beyond.

Until 2001 when it closed, Suisan Fish Auction was at the corner of Banyan Drive and Lihiwai Street, which crosses Kamehameha Avenue near the rivermouth. This fish auction drew island fishermen of every nationality and was great entertainment for visitors. Boats would tie up and fishermen would talk quietly about the prices; restaurateurs and housewives gathered before 6 A.M. to eyeball the catch of the day; and when the sale started, the auctioneer's staccato was pure pidgin. Later tourists would amble by, and it usually wound up a bit past 8 A.M. As colorful as it was, government regulations pressured its closure. While the auction no longer operates, the fish market next door is still open daily except Sunday to sell the fresh fish catch by the same local fisherman.

Cross Kamehameha Avenue heading south and you'll see **Ho'olulu County Park,** with the Civic Center Auditorium, numerous athletic stadiums, and a city nursery brimming with orchids. This is the town's center for organized athletic events, large cultural festivals, and the annual county fair. To the west is **Waiakea Pond,** a brackish lagoon where people often fish. The **Wailoa River State Recreation Area,** which encompasses the lagoon, is a 132-acre preserve set along both sides of this spring-fed pond in the center of Hilo. City residents use this big broad area for picnics, pleasure walks, informal get-togethers, fishing, and launching boats. On the eastern side are picnic pavilions and barbecue grills. Arching footbridges cross the river connecting the halves. Stop at the **Wailoa Center** on the western side for tourist information and cultural displays (open weekdays only). The walls in the upstairs gallery of this 10-sided building are used to display works of local artists and cultural/historic exhibits, changed on a regular basis. On the lower level hang astonishing pictures of the 1946 and 1960 tsunamis that washed through the city. The Wailoa Center sits in a broad swath of greenery, an open, idyllic park-like area that used to be a cramped bustling neighborhood known as Shinmachi. It, like much of the city, was almost totally destroyed during the tsunami of 1960. Nearby stands the **Tsunami Memorial** to the residents of this neighborhood who lost their lives in that natural disaster. Also close by is the county **Vietnam War Memorial,** dedicated to those who died fighting that war, and a new **statue of King Kamehameha I,** a replica of that which graces the town of Kapa'au at the northern tip of the island. Park at the Wailoa Center on Piopio Street, off Pauahi Street. Additional parking for this landscaped area is on the western side along Park Street at the end of Pi'ilani Street.

## Farther Afield

A few miles out of town, heading west on Waianuenue Avenue, are two natural spectacles definitely worth a look. Just past Hilo High School a sign directs you to Wailuku River State Park. Here is **Rainbow Falls,** a most spectacular yet easily visited natural wonder. You'll look down on a circular pool in the river below that's almost 100 feet in diameter; cascading into it is a lovely

waterfall. The 80-foot falls deserve their name because as they hit the water below, their mists throw flocks of rainbows into the air. Underneath the falls is a huge cavern, held by legend to be the abode of Hina, mother of the god Maui. Most people are content to look from the vantage point near the parking lot, but if you walk to the left, you can take a stone stairway leading to a private viewing area directly over the falls. Here the river, strewn with volcanic boulders, pours over the edge. Follow the path for a minute or so along the bank to a gigantic banyan tree and a different vantage point. The falls may be best seen in the morning when the sunlight streams in from the front.

Follow Waianuenue Avenue for two more miles past Hilo Medical Center to the heights above town. A sign to turn right onto Pe'epe'e Falls Street points to the **Boiling Pots,** another section of Wailuku River State Park. Few people visit here. Follow the path from the parking lot past the toilets to an overlook. Indented into the riverbed below is a series of irregularly shaped depressions that look as though a peg-legged giant left his peg prints in the hot lava. Seven or eight resemble naturally bubbling whirlpool tubs as river water cascades from one into the next. This phenomenon is best after a heavy rain. Turn your head upriver to see **Pe'epe'e Falls,** a gorgeous, five-spouted waterfall. Although signs warn you not to descend to the river—risky during heavy rains—locals hike down to the river rocks below to sunbathe and swim in pools that do not have rushing water.

In 1881, Mauna Loa's tremendous eruption discharged a huge flow of lava. The river of lava crusted over, forming a tube through which molten lava continued to flow. Once the eruption ceased, the lava inside siphoned out, leaving the tube now called **Kaumana Caves.** The caves are only five miles out of downtown Hilo along Rte. 200, clearly marked next to the road. Oddly enough, they are posted as a fallout shelter. Follow a steep staircase down into a gray hole draped with green ferns and brightened by wildflowers. Smell the scent of the tropical vegetation. You can walk only a few yards into the cave before you'll need a strong flashlight. It's a thrill to turn around and look at the entrance, where blazing sunlight shoots through the ferns and wildflowers.

Not many travelers can visit a zoo in such a unique setting, where the animals virtually live in paradise. The 150 animals at this 12-acre zoo, where it rains about 130 inches a year, are endemic and introduced species that would naturally live in such an environment. While small and local, the zoo is a delight. The road to the **Pana'ewa Rainforest Zoo,** 808/959-7224, www.hilozoo.com, is a trip in itself, getting you back into the country. Follow Rte. 11 south past mile marker 4 until you see the sign pointing right up Stainback Hwy. to the zoo. Near the zoo is the **Pana'ewa Equestrian Center,** with a full-size horse racing track. On a typical weekday, you'll have the place much to yourself. The zoo, operated by the county Department of Parks and Recreation, is open daily 9 A.M.–4 P.M., closed Christmas and New Year's Day. Feedings are usually done around 9 A.M. and 3:15 P.M. and the petting zoo activities happen around 1:30 P.M., so you may want to be around for them. Admission is free, although donations to the nonprofit Friends of the Pana'ewa Zoo are appreciated. Here you have the feeling that the animals are not "fenced in" so much as you are "fenced out." The collection of about 75 species includes ordinary and exotic animals from around the world. You'll see pygmy hippos from Africa, a rare white Bengal tiger named Namaste, a miniature horse and steer, Asian forest tortoises, water buffalo, monkeys, and a wide assortment of birds like pheasants and peacocks. The zoo hosts many endangered animals indigenous to Hawaii like the *nene,* Laysan duck, Hawaiian coot, *pueo,* Hawaiian gallinule, and even a feral pig in his own stone mini-condo. There are some great iguanas and mongooses, lemurs, and an aviary section with exotic birds like yellow-fronted parrots and blue and gold macaws. The back central area is a tigers' playground; a tall fence marks this rather large area where the tiger still rules his domain. It's got its own pond and tall grasses that make the tigers feel at home. The zoo makes a perfect side trip for families and will certainly delight the little ones.

**Mauna Loa Macadamia Nut Factory,**
808/966-8618, is located several miles south of Hilo off Rte. 11, nearly to Kea'au. Head down Macadamia Road for about three miles until you come to the Visitors Center. Inside is an informative free video explaining the development and processing of macadamia nuts in Hawaii. Walkways outside the windows of the processing center and chocolate shop let you view the process of turning these delicious nuts into tantalizing gift items, but this is best viewed from August through January when most of the processing is done. Then return to the snack shop for macadamia nut goodies like ice cream and cookies, and the gift shop for samples and an intriguing assortment of packaged macadamia nut items. While you're here, step out back and take a self-guided tour of the small garden where many introduced trees and plants are identified. The Visitors Center is open daily 8:30 A.M.–5 P.M.

## GARDENS

Along Kilauea Avenue, between Lanikaula and Kawili Streets, the Department of Natural Resources, Division of Forestry maintains the **Hilo Forestry Arboretum,** open Mon.–Fri. 8 A.M.–3 P.M., closed Saturday, Sunday, and holidays; no charge. This arboretum and tree nursery contains many of the trees present in Hawaii, including indigenous and imported specimens. Have a look at the diagram map of the grounds in the office before you head out back for a self-guided tour. The map attempts to name the trees by matching them with points on the map as you pass by, instead of referring to signs on each specimen. The trees are magnificent, and you will have this quiet area virtually to yourself. Originally the site was an animal quarantine station operated by the Territory of Hawaii; the 19.4 acres of the arboretum were established in 1920 by Brother Mathias Newell. Brother Newell was a nurseryman employed by the Catholic boys' school in Hilo. At that time the Division of Forestry was already actively introducing plant species from all over the world. For the 40 years between 1921 and 1961 the department was engaged in the development and maintenance of arboretums consisting primarily of plant species from Australia and Africa. Arboretum sites ranged from sea level to Mauna Kea. Plant materials were exchanged, and thousands of breadfruit cuttings were exported. Over 1,000 different tree species and 500 different fruit trees were field-tested. Here at the Hilo Arboretum over 1,000 trees were planted. A few trees such as the paper bark and some pines are more than 50 years old. Presently a small number of timber species are grown for reforestation purposes. Essentially the Hilo site is utilized for the propagation of rare and endangered plant species, for research, and for experimental pursuits.

**Nani Mau Gardens** is the largest in Hilo, and touring these spectacular displays is well worth an afternoon. Located at 421 Makalika St., Hilo, HI 96720, 808/959-3500, the gardens are open daily 8 A.M.–5 P.M. Admission is $10 adult, $5 children ages 4–10, and $5 per person for an optional tram tour. The gardens consist of 20 sculpted acres. More than a botanical garden, Nani Mau is a "floral theme park" designed as a tourist attraction. Walks throughout the garden are very tame but very beautiful; umbrellas are provided during rainy weather, which adds its own dripping, crystalline charm to the experience. Plants are labeled in English, Latin, and Japanese. The gardens are a huge but ordered display of flowers, flowering trees, and shrubbery. The wildly colored plumage of tropical birds here and there competes with the colors of the exotic blooms. The gardens are broken off into separate areas for hibiscus, anthurium, orchid, gardenia, and bromeliad, along with a Japanese garden, a fruit orchard, and stands of bamboo, palms, and other trees. It also features floral sculptures, a small reflective pond, and an assortment of flowers and shrubs laid out in geometric patterns, and even "aloha" and "Hilo Hawaii" spelled out. The Nani Mau Restaurant

## MACADAMIA NUTS

Hawaii produces about 40 percent of the world's supply of macadamia nuts, and the majority of the state's crop is raised on the Big Island. About one million macadamia nut trees produce these tasty nuts at the Mauna Loa Macadamia Nut property outside Hilo, with a larger property producing nuts in South Kona. Smaller growers raise this crop at different locations on the Big Island, as well as on Moloka'i, O'ahu, and Kaua'i.

A native of Australia, macadamia nut trees were first brought to Hawaii and planted in Honoka'a in 1881 by the British agriculturist W. H. Purvis. One of these trees is still bearing! A number of these trees were again introduced to Hawaii in 1921 for study but failed to produce an acceptably significant and even-quality product. However, W. Pierre Naquin, then manager of the Honoka'a Sugar Co., thought that the nut might have some potential and started the first commercial nut farm in 1924. After years of grafting and experimentation on the island of O'ahu, over half a dozen varieties of the tree proved to yield acceptable nuts, and this led to large-scale commercial ventures in the 1950s. Macadamia nut trees can grow to about 40 feet tall, branch out to about the same width, and have dark green leaves. Trees require at least five years before they begin to produce nuts, and perhaps five to 10 additional years before they are in full production. Once mature, they can produce for years. Trees flower at different times over many months and produce nuts most of the year. This requires harvesting on a periodic basis. While some nuts are shaken from the trees, most fall naturally and are picked up from the ground. The nuts have a leathery skin that breaks open to reveal a very hard brown shell. This shell is cracked open to give forth the fruit itself, a light-colored, crisp and creamy orb about the size of a marble. In larger commercial ventures, the nuts are collected, dried, cracked, and sorted mechanically, while small-time growers may do some of this work by hand. Many of the nuts are roasted and salted, but some are set aside to be put into a brittle, glazed with various concoctions, or dipped in chocolate. Additionally, the nuts are often added to sauces, desserts, pastries, and confections. Some now are pressing the nut for its oil. Macadamia nuts contain mostly monounsaturated fat and traces of several minerals. Its high burn and smoke temperature makes it great for cooking and its smooth texture is appropriate for lighter foods.

provides lunch only, 10:30 A.M.–1:30 P.M., and the tourist shop is exactly like a Japanese omiyagi (souvenir) shop. No wonder, since it's owned by ethnic Japanese, and the tour buses coming here are all filled with Japanese visitors. If you enjoy a clean outdoor experience surrounded by magnificent flowers, this is the place.

Established in 1948, apparently as the oldest botanical garden on the island, **Hilo Tropical Gardens**, 808/969-9873, has recently reopened at 1447 Kalaniana'ole Ave. and is slowly being brought back to life after a number of years of neglect; open daily except Thursday and Sunday. A thick profusion of tropical plants greet you as you enter this garden and a maze of walkways leads through its somewhat overgrown grounds. The garden is compact so not overwhelming and some of the plants are marked so you can know what you're looking at. Among the many are a host of anthuriums and orchids. Aside from the flowers, here and there along the walkways are pools in lava sinks and a hidden lava tube or two. Entrance is $2 adult for a self-guided tour and free for children; enter through the gift shop, where you can find flowers, lei, gifts, and crafts, all of which can be shipped for you. When you're finished, stop next door for a scoop of Hilo Homemade Ice Cream.

Just a few minutes north of town, on the Onomea scenic coastal route, is the **Hawaii Tropical Botanical Gardens**, 808/964-5233, www.htbg.com, open daily 9 A.M.–5 P.M. for self-guided tours. Admission is adults $15, children 6–16 $5, and kids five and under are free. Remember that the entrance fee not only allows you to walk through the best-tamed tropical rainforest on the Big Island but helps preserve this wonderful area in perpetuity. The gardens were established in 1978 when Dan and Pauline Lutkenhouse purchased the property in order to educate the public to the beauty of tropical plants in their natural setting. The gardens have been open for viewing since 1984. Mr. Lutkenhouse, a retired San Francisco businessman, purchased the 25-acre valley and personally performed the work that transformed it into one of the most exotic spots in all of Hawaii. The locality was amazingly beautiful but inaccessible because it was so rugged.

Through a personal investment of nearly $1 million and six painstaking years of toil aided by only two helpers, he hand-cleared the land, built trails and bridges, developed an irrigation system, acquired more than 2,000 different species of trees and plants, and established one mile of scenic trails and a water lily lake stocked with *koi* and tropical fish. Onomea was a favorite spot with the Hawaiians, who came to fish and camp for the night. The valley was a fishing village called Kahali'i in the early 1800s. Later on it became a rough-water seaport used for shipping sugarcane and other tropical products. A remake of *Lord of the Flies* was filmed here some years ago, and it's easy to see why the area made the perfect movie set.

Start at the visitors center along the road, where you'll find a gift shop, the tiny Onomea Museum, self-guided tour maps, drinking water, restrooms, umbrellas for your convenience, and jungle perfume—better known as mosquito repellent! Cross the road to the garden entrance and descend into this lush valley. The steep trail into the valley is about 500 feet long; once into the heart of the garden, the trails are more level. Plants from the four corners of the globe, including Iran, Central China, Japan, tropical Africa, India, Borneo, Brazil, East Indies, South Pacific Islands, tropical America, and the Philippines, are named with a full botanical description. Native plants from Hawaii are included. As you walk, listen for the songs of the native birds that love this ancient spot. Choose one of the aptly named trails like Fern Circle, Heliconia Trail, or Waterfall Trail and lose yourself in the beauty of the surroundings. You are in the middle of a tamed jungle, walking along manicured paths. Stroll the Ocean Trail down to the sea, where the rugged coastline is dramatically pummeled by frothy waves, a sea arch provides dramatic sculpture, and turtles swim the bay. You can hear the waves entering submerged lava caves, where they blow in and out like a giant bellows. Away from the sea you'll encounter screened gazebos filled with exotic birds like cockatoos from Indonesia and blue-fronted Amazon parrots. Walk the inland trails past waterfalls, streams, ponds, a bamboo grove, palms, and innumerable flowers. For at least a brief time you get to feel the power and beauty of a living Garden of Eden.

# BEACHES

If you define a beach as a long expanse of white sand covered by a thousand sunbathers and their beach umbrellas, then Hilo doesn't have any. If a beach, to you, can be a smaller, more intimate affair where a good number of tourists and families can spend the day on pockets of sand between fingers of black lava, then Hilo has plenty. Hilo's best beaches all lie to the east of the city along Kalaniana'ole Avenue, an area known as the Keaukaha Strip, which runs six miles from downtown Hilo to its dead end at Leleiwi Point. Not all beaches are clearly marked, but even those are easily spotted by cars parked along the road.

**Hilo Bayfront Park** is a thousand yards of gray-black sand that narrows considerably as it runs west from the Wailoa River toward downtown. At one time it went all the way to the Wailuku River and was renowned throughout the islands for its beauty, but commercialism of the waterfront ruined it. By 1960, so much sewage and industrial waste had been pumped into the bay that it was considered a public menace, and then the great tsunami came. Reclamation projects created the Wailoa River State Recreation Area at the east end, and shorefront land became a buffer zone against future inundation. Few swimmers come to the beach because the water is cloudy and chilly, but the sharks don't seem to mind! The bay is terrific for fishing and picnicking, and the sails of small craft and sailboards can always be seen. It's a perfect spot for canoe races, and many local teams come here to train. Notice the judging towers and canoe sheds. In the early 1800s, King Kamehameha I reputedly had 800 canoes made and launched from this beach for an assault on Kaua'i to bring that distant island under his control. The armada never made it, but eventually Kaua'i came under the great king's influence by diplomatic means. Toward the west end, near the mouth of the Wailuku River, surfers catch long rides during the winter months, entertaining spectators. There is public parking along the eastern half near the canoe clubs or at the Wailoa river mouth where the fishing boats dock.

**Reeds Bay Beach Park** is a largely undeveloped area on the east side of the Waiakea Peninsula. Technically part of Hilo Bay, the water is notoriously cold because of a constantly flowing freshwater spring, hence the name Ice Pond at its innermost end. Mostly frequented by fishermen, some sailors park their private boats here.

Keaukaha Beach at **Carlsmith Beach County Park,** located on Puhi Bay, is the first in a series of beaches as you head east on Kalaniana'ole Avenue. Look for Baker Avenue and pull off to the left into a rough parking area. This is a favorite spot with local people, who swim at "Cold Water Pond," a spring-fed inlet at the head of the bay. A sewage treatment plant fronts the western side of Puhi Bay. Much nicer areas await you just up Kalaniana'ole Avenue.

**Onekahakaha Beach County Park** has it all: safe swimming, white-sand beach, lifeguards, and all amenities. Turn left onto Onekahakaha Road and park in the lot of Hilo's favorite "family" beach. Swim in the large, sandy-bottomed pool protected by a man-made breakwater. Outside the breakwater the currents can be fierce, and drownings have been recorded. Walk east along the shore to find an undeveloped area of the park with many small tidal pools. Beware of sea urchins.

**James Kealoha Beach County Park,** also known locally as "Four Mile Beach," is next; people swim, snorkel, and fish here, and during winter months it's a favorite surfing spot. A large grassy area is shaded by trees and a picnic pavilion. Just offshore is an island known as Scout Island because local Boy Scouts often camp there. This entire area was known for its fishponds, and inland, just across Kalaniana'ole Avenue, is the 60-acre Loko Waka Pond. This site of ancient Hawaiian aquaculture is now a commercial operation that raises mullet, trout, catfish, perch, tilapia, and others. The Seaside Restaurant operates here.

**Leleiwi Beach County Park** lies along a lovely residential area carved into the rugged coastline. This park with its parking lot, life guard, three pavilions, trees, and rock wall is a favorite local spot for scuba divers. The shore here is open to the ocean, and currents may be strong. Plentiful sealife make this a good snorkeling spot. Almost adjacent is Richardson Ocean Park, known locally

BIG ISLAND OF HAWAI'I

as **Richardson's Beach Park.** Richardson Ocean Center is located here. Use a shower that's coming out of the retaining wall surrounding the house to wash off. A seawall skirts the shore and a tiny cove with a black-sand beach is the first in a series. This is a terrific area for snorkeling, with plenty of marinelife, including *honu* (green sea turtles). Walk east to a natural lava breakwater. Behind it are pools filled and flushed by the surging tide. The water breaks over the top of the lava and rushes into the pools, making natural whirlpool tubs. This is one of the most picturesque swimming areas on the island.

Just beyond is the end of the road and undeveloped parkland. When the pavement stops, follow the dirt track. This unofficial camping area has no amenities whatsoever, and seems like a homeless settlement. A series of pools like those at Richardson's are small, sandy-bottomed, and safe. Outside of the natural lava breakwater, currents are treacherous. Winter often sends tides surging inland here, making this area unusable.

Going north out of Hilo a few miles brings you to **Honoli'i Beach County Park.** Turn right onto Nahala Street, then left onto Kahoa, and follow it around until you see cars parked along the road. The water is down a steep series of steps, and while the black-sand beach is not much appreciated for swimming, it is known as one of the finest surfing spots on this side of the island.

## Practicalities

## ACCOMMODATIONS

Accommodations in Hilo are hardly ever booked up, and they're reasonably priced. Sounds great, but some hotels have "gone condo" to survive while others have simply shut their doors, so there aren't as many choices as there once were. During the Merrie Monarch Festival in April, the entire town is booked solid! The best hotels are clustered along Banyan Drive, with a few gems tucked away on the city streets.

### Hostel

**Arnott's Lodge,** 98 Apapane Rd., Hilo, HI 96720, 808/969-7097, fax 808/961-9638, info@arnottslodge.com, www.arnottslodge.com, is a reasonably priced budget accommodation, safe, clean, and friendly, that offers most everything that a traveler might expect while on the road. Follow Kamehameha Avenue east until it turns into Kalaniana'ole Avenue; in about five minutes you'll see a lighted yellow sign pointing to Arnott's. Those without private transportation can be picked up by a free shuttle service operating 8 A.M.–8 P.M., with outbound departures set at 8 A.M., 12:30 P.M., and 5:30 P.M. A ride downtown or to the airport costs only $2, or $3 round-trip. Arnott's also offers inexpensive expeditions that are some of the best guided tours on the island. Other services are coin laundry, telephones, reasonable Internet access, safe storage of valuables and backpacks at no cost, and free use of bicycles and snorkel gear. Dormitory bunks—male, female, and coed—at $17 are spotlessly clean and cooled by cross ventilation and ceiling fans. Single rooms with bath, kitchen, and living room shared with one other room are $37; a double room with the same setup is $47. With private baths, the singles and doubles run $57. A self-contained suite with two bedrooms, one with a double bed and the other with twins, includes a bathroom, kitchen, and living room for $120 for up to five people; each additional person is $15. Check-in is until 8 P.M.; late check-in is $5 extra, and no check-in after 10 P.M. Camping on the lawn with your own tent is now an option for $9 per person. Leisure time can be spent in a large entertainment area, where you can watch one of a huge selection of videos. A covered lanai with picnic tables has barbecue grills for your convenience, and to the side is a lanai platform built in a tree. Arnott's is an excellent hostel/lodge offering a quality, hassle-free stay with an international clientele.

### Bed-and-Breakfasts

B&Bs are located here and there around town. Several are strung out along the highway north of town, a number are out toward Richardson's Beach, and a handful are scattered above town in residential pockets.

A short way past the "singing bridge," take the first right turn to get to **The Bay House B&B,** 42 Pukihae St., Hilo, HI 96720, 808/961-6311 or 888/235-8195, bigbayhouse@excite.com, www.bayhousehawaii.com. This new house with its three guest rooms sits on the cliff over Hilo Bay, as close as you can get to downtown Hilo. Rooms run $120 a night and each has a king or queen bed, private bath, television, telephone, and oceanside lanai, and from each you can watch the cruise ships come and go from port or the full moon shining on the bay. Decorations and accoutrements bring out the individual color and character of each room. Guests share a common entrance room with books, magazines, and refrigerator, and receive a breakfast of fruit, juice, pastries, coffee, and other goodies which you can have at your leisure when you wake up. Set even closer to the edge of the cliff is a hot tub, perfect for a starry-night soak. The Bay House is comfortable, plush, very clean, and quiet. No credit cards are accepted.

Accepting paying guests for 20 years and others for longer that that, Amy Gamble Lannan's **Lihi Kai** bed-and-breakfast, 30 Kahoa Road, Hilo, HI 96720, 808/935-7865, is a treasure and the longest running B&B in town. This sedate, contemporary-style house sits on the edge of a cliff just north of town and has a million-dollar view of Hilo Bay; it's less than two miles north of the "singing bridge." Guests of the two rooms share a bathroom and partake with Amy of a filling breakfast of fruit, pastries, and coffee to start the day. A small swimming pool occupies part of the yard. While Lihi Kai is a treasure, Amy is the jewel. Full of life and love, with a witty sense of humor, she can offer you insight on where to eat, what to see, how to get around, and where to find adventure. Rooms are $55 a night plus $5 a night for less than three nights. Cash or personal check, please; no credit cards. Because the house is so close to the cliff edge, she's reluctant to take children under age eight. Make reservations well in advance, as her guests keep coming back again and again.

Set on a bluff overlooking the ocean just over two miles north of town is **Hale Kai,** 111 Honoli'i Pali, Hilo, HI 96720, 808/935-6330, fax 808/935-8439, bjornen@interpac.net, www.interpac.net/~halekai. This modern house has a small pool and hot tub. A sitting room for guests is shared, but each of the four rooms has its own bath and looks out over the ocean. Room rates run $90–100 a night with the suite at $110—no credit cards. The house is very comfortable, and the breakfast of fruits, pancakes, and sausages gives you a good start on the day.

**Holmes' Sweet Home B&B,** 107 Ko'ula St., Hilo, HI 96720, 808/961-9089, fax 808/934-0711, homswhom@gte.net, www.stayhawaii.com /holmes.html, is the residence of John and Charlotte Holmes. On a quiet residential cul-de-sac high above town (more than 700 feet in elevation) with a view of Hilo Bay and the city lights, this B&B provides two comfy rooms priced $60–70 that feature a private entrance to a common room, guest refrigerator and microwave, and private bathrooms. A tropical continental breakfast is included.

The first place out along the Keaukaha strip is **Maureen's Bed and Breakfast,** 1896 Kalaniana'ole Ave., 808/935-9018 or 800/953-9018, fax 808/961-5596, maureen@maureenbnb.com, www.maureenbnb.com. Surrounded by landscaped lawns and koi ponds, this B&B was built in 1932 from redwood and cedar brought from the Mainland. With its high-ceilinged living room, arched windows and doors, balconies, and a Japanese tea room, it has plenty of charm in an East meets West kind of way. Comfortable and pleasingly decorated, the rooms rent for $50 single, $75 double with a shared bath, and $100 double with a private bath. A filling breakfast is always included. This is a bargain and an all around good place.

**Friends of Friends,** P.O. Box 5731, Hilo, HI 96720, 808/961-6556, bbell@aloha.net, http://vrbo.com/vrbo/1335.htm, is a basement studio that's been converted into a homey living area. While it has a low ceiling, everything else is standard. Two entrances open into the sitting and sleeping areas with its queen bed and single bed, and the full kitchen and bathroom are to

## THE SHIPMAN HOUSE

A house can have presence, and, if it's brushed by magic like the Tin Man in *The Wizard of Oz*, it can even attain a heart. The home we're referring to was a purchase motivated by love and occupied by a large, dynamic family. The Shipman House, known locally as "the Castle," perched on five verdant acres high above Hilo, has such a heart.

After a quarter century on the Mainland, Barbara Ann Andersen, great-granddaughter of William H. "Willie" Shipman, the original owner, returned with her children and her husband Gary to restore to its former grandeur the residence where she spent her childhood summers, Easters, and Christmases. The house was figuratively stripped to its petticoats and outfitted in grand style.

To appreciate Shipman House B&B Inn fully, you must know its history, which goes back as far as the first tall ships that arrived from New England bearing the missionaries and their faith to the old kingdom. The first members of the family to reside in Hawaii were the Rev. William C. Shipman and his wife Jane, who arrived in the 1850s. The Rev. Shipman died young, leaving Jane alone and in need of a means to support herself and their three children; she accomplished this by opening a Hawaiian girls' boarding school in Hilo. Later she met and married Mr. Reed, a famous engineer responsible for most of Hilo's bridges and for whom, by strange coincidence, "Reed's Island," the section of Hilo where the mansion sits, was named.

One of the boys, William H. "Willie" Shipman, married Mary Melekahuia Johnson, one of the young Hawaiian ladies at his mother's school. Mary was descended from the ruling *ali'i*. Willie originally determined to study medicine, but one day his stepfather, Mr. Reed, made him an offer he couldn't refuse, saying, "Son, if you will give up medicine and take up the study of business, I'll give you a ranch to run." Willie knew a good opportunity when he saw it, and over the years he became one of the largest landholders on the Big Island, founding W. H. Shipman, Ltd.

Around the turn of the 20th century, Mary often implored Willie to take her for a drive, which would invariably pass by a lovely home being built on Ka'iulani Street. Holding his hand and looking into his eyes she would ask, "Willie, won't you buy me that house?" and he would reply, "I can't. The Wilsons own it." Finally, one day as they passed the house, Mary asked once again, but this time Willie smiled and said, "Yes, my dear. It's been ours for 30 days." They moved into the house in April 1901.

Mary was a dear friend of Hawaii's last queen, Lili'uokalani, who would visit at the Shipman house whenever she was in Hilo. While there the queen would preside over simple but elegant "poi luncheons," always seated at the place of honor at the huge round koa dining room table, where she could look out the bay windows at Hilo below. After lunch, Lili'uokalani would slip away to the "Library" to clandestinely savor a fine cigar.

To arrive at the Castle, ascend Waianuenue Avenue to Ka'iulani Street. There, turn right, cross the bridge, veer left, and you'll see the Shipman House on the rise. Climb the steps to the wraparound lanai, a necessity even for well-to-do families, who,

the side. The unit comes with its own phone and cable TV, and opens onto a covered lanai. The rate is $275 a week, one week minimum. Sleeps two to three.

Located on 22 acres of macadamia nut and tropical fruit orchards north of the Boiling Pots, with views over Hilo and the ocean, and with the 120-foot Kulaniapia Waterfall on the property, is **The Inn at Kulaniapia Falls,** P.O. Box 11338, Hilo, HI 96721, 808/966-6373 or 888/838-6373, waterfall@hilo.net, www.waterfall.net. This contemporary-style B&B features four large second-story suites with private, granite-tiled baths and covered balconies: two face the ocean, two face inland. The room rate is $99 double, with $15 for an additional guest, and an expanded continental breakfast of tropical fruits, pastries, and coffee comes with an egg dish. Guests share the 1st-floor common room, a blend of island-style and Japanese motifs, and can use the kitchen and a barbecue grill. A good distance up from the highway, partially over an unpaved road, only the sound of the waterfall and the birds disturb the quiet.

Just four miles north of town is **Our Place Papaikou's B&B,** P.O. Box 469, Papa'ikou, HI like all Hawaii residents, spend a great deal of time outdoors. The broad landing provides a wonderful view of Hilo and the sea in the distance, with wild flowers and tangled greenery cascading into a tropical bowl at your feet. Two stained glass windows, encircled by a laurel wreath, the classic sign of a congenial home, greet you on entering. The Double Parlor, the 1st floor of the rounded three-story Tower that caps the home, is magnificent. Everywhere is glass—old-fashioned, hand-made curved glass—its mottled and rippled texture giving a surrealistic twist to the panorama.

Pad along on the burnished fir flooring past koa-wainscoted walls to enter the Dining Room, where an enormous dining table and *pune'e* (movable couch) are still very functional. The back area of the home is called the Conservatory, really the center of the home for day-to-day life, where the family took their meals. Just off it is a Solarium and the Butler's Pantry, next to an "Otis in-home elevator," installed in the 1930s and probably Hilo's first. Here, too, is a bedroom, formerly reserved for guests like Jack London and his wife Charmian. The peaceful Library, waiting to engulf an afternoon reader within its impressive 12-foot ceilings, is warmed by a brick fireplace with a koa mantel and is fringed by built-in koa bookcases.

Ascend the central staircase to the 2nd floor, where once upon a time a ballroom adorned in white wallpaper with twinkling stars swayed with dancing and music; nowadays part has been converted into a bedroom. At the back near the elevator, a window opening to a catwalk led to a small

room built over the water tank. That room served as great-grandfather Willie's "Office," his haven from the clamor of 10 children! In the back corner is a second bedroom. A spiral staircase ascends to the attic where a "canvas room" was the children's dormitory. A large, free-standing credenza holds hats and antique clothing. Also in the attic is the entrance to the Tower, a wine barrel of a room with wraparound windows.

Shipman House is once again one of *the* finest homes in all Hawaii in which to spend a quiet and elegant visit.

96781, tel./fax 808/964-5250, rplace@aloha.net, www.ourplacebandb.com. Set among thick vegetation in a little gulch, the three rooms of this cedar home open onto a large lanai that overlooks Kupua Stream, but if you can imagine it, the house would be just as much at home on a high Colorado mountainside. The Early American (double bed) and Oriental Room (queen bed) run $60 a night and share a bathroom, while the Master Bedroom with its king bed and day bed is $80 a night, two-night minimum. The lofty Great Room, open to all guests, has a cozy fireplace, TV, stereo, and a grand piano that

loves to be tickled by someone who really knows how to play. When traveling up Hwy. 19, turn left at Pinky's convenience store, take the next two lefts, and turn down the driveway.

**Shipman House B&B Inn,** 131 Ka'iulani St., Hilo, HI 96720, tel./fax 808/934-8002 or 800/627-8447, bighouse@bigisland.com, www.hilo-hawaii.com, is the grandest B&B in all Hawaii. The main house offers three guest rooms with antique beds, private bath, and stately views through enormous windows. Other guests will lodge in the Cottage, a separate building on the grounds, originally built for the express purpose of accommodating visitors. The Cottage contains two spacious bedrooms, each with queen bed, window seats, and private bath. Both rooms have private entrances, ceiling fans, and a small refrigerator. This is strictly a no smoking establishment and a "no TV zone," and children are not encouraged as there are so many antiques in the house and a steep ravine outside. Room rates are $154–184 single or double; $25 per extra person, add $25 for a single-night stay.

The Library is open to guests, along with use of the 1912 Steinway piano whose keys were once tickled by Lili'uokalani, and you can look around the house on your own in those areas where the doors are open. On Tuesday and Wednesday evenings, hula classes are held on the lanai and guests can participate. Breakfast, served 7:45–9 A.M. (earlier upon request, and special diets are accommodated), is an expanded continental with homemade cereals, hot cereals on request, assorted local fruits (there are 20 varieties of fruit trees on the property), fruit juices, Kona coffee, yogurt, fruit bread, muffins, popovers, or cinnamon rolls. Check in is 3–6 P.M., and checkout is at 10 A.M.

## Banyan Drive Hotels

The following hotels lie along Banyan Drive. They range from moderate to a bit more than moderate. There are no luxury hotels in Hilo.

The **Hilo Seaside Hotel,** 126 Banyan Way, 808/935-0821 or 800/560-5557 in Hawaii, fax 808/969-9195, www.sand-seaside.com, is owned by the Kimi family. Like the others in this small island chain, it's clean and well kept and has Polynesian-inspired decor with a '60s or '70s feel. On the property is Luci's Grill, which serves basic Japanese and American breakfasts and dinners. Room prices are $88 standard, $100 superior pool view, $110 deluxe pool view, and $110 garden kitchenette; third person charge is $10 and breakfast is included for all but the standard rooms. Add approximately $25 for a room/car package. Ask about off-season, AAA, and AARP rates, and a better rate is sometimes offered depending on the amount of business at the time. Each room has a lanai, air conditioner and ceiling fan, television, and small refrigerator, and there is

a coin laundry facility on premises. The grounds are laid out around a well-tended central courtyard garden, and the pool is secluded and away from the street; to the front, a large koi pond lies in another garden. While flash and polish are not part of the routine, the place is very clean and well kept, and you will find two scoops of dignity and pride. At this family-style hotel with a motel atmosphere, the friendly staff goes out of its way to make you feel welcome. Located across from the Ice Pond, this is a good choice for a moderate price at a convenient location.

**Uncle Billy's Hilo Bay Hotel** is sandwiched between two larger hotels at 87 Banyan Dr., Hilo, HI 96720, 808/935-0861, 800/442-5841 in Hawaii, 800/367-5102 Mainland, resv@unclebilly.com, www.unclebilly.com,. The Hilo Bay's blue metal roof and white louvered shutters make it look a bit like "Long John Silver's Meets Polynesia." The lobby's rattan furniture and thatched longhouse theme are pure '50s-kitsch Hawaii. Definitely have a look. There is free parking and a guest pool. This is a no-frills establishment, but all rooms are clean and air-conditioned with a TV and phone. Rooms run $84–94 or studio kitchenettes $94–104, good value for the money, but don't expect anything too modern or too luxurious. Numerous discounts are available, so be sure to ask. The in-house Fish and Steakhouse restaurant serves reasonably priced food for breakfast and dinner only, and a free hula show is presented every evening at 6 P.M. in the lounge off the lobby. Uncle Billy's General Store, where you can buy everything from beer to sundries and ice cream to resort wear, is part of the complex.

The **Hilo Hawaiian Hotel,** 71 Banyan Dr., Hilo, HI 96720, 808/935-9361, 800/272-5275 in Hawaii, 800/367-5004 Mainland and Canada, occupies the most beautiful grounds of any hotel in Hilo. From the vantage of the hotel's colonnaded veranda, you overlook formal gardens, Coconut Island, and Hilo Bay. Designed as a huge arc, the hotel's architecture blends well with its surroundings and expresses the theme set by the bay, that of a long, sweeping crescent. While neat, clean, well maintained, and with all necessary amenities, the hotel still has somewhat of a '70s feel. If you want flash and glamour, try one of the new resorts on the Kona side. However, for down-home quality with a touch of class in Hilo, you can't do better than the Hilo Hawaiian. Prices at this property run $119 for a standard room, $139 for a superior, $149 for an ocean-view room, and $183–360 for suites; all rooms have a/c, phone, and cable color TV, plus there's a swimming pool on the property. Guest services include a gift shop, Laundromat, free parking, and a front-desk safety deposit box. The Queen's Court restaurant, Wai'oli Lounge, and the Tranquil Waters day spa are all on the property for guests' convenience. Along Banyan Drive out front, the Banyan General Store for sundries and Bayview Farm Coffee shop are other options. This is the best accommodation Hilo has to offer.

**Hawaii Naniloa Resort,** 93 Banyan Dr., Hilo, HI 96720, 808/969-3333, 800/442-5845 in Hawaii, 800/367-5360 Mainland and Canada, hinani@aloha.net, www.naniloa.com, is a large, 325-room hotel. Rates start at $100 for garden view, $120 for partial ocean view, and $140 for oceanfront rooms; suites are available for $160–190. Numerous discounts are offered. The Naniloa offers air conditioning and a TV in all rooms, but only the higher end rooms have balconies. Other amenities include hotel parking, the Sandalwood and Ting Hao restaurants, a lounge, periodic entertainment at the Crown Room, a gift shop, Laundromat, and two pools. The original hotel dates back more than 60 years and over the years built a fine reputation for value and service. Unfortunately, the Naniloa has not kept up its facility as one might expect and has gotten a bit raggedy around the edges. It's become "very tired" and is much in need of a thorough overhaul to bring back the high standard that it once maintained.

## Accommodations near Downtown

**Dolphin Bay Hotel** is a sparkling little gem—simply the best hotel bargain in Hilo, one of those places where you get more than you pay for. It sits on a side street in the Pu'u'eo section of town at the north end of Hilo Bay, at 333 'Iliahi St., Hilo, HI 96720, 808/935-1466, fax 808/935-1523, johnhilo@gte.net, www.dolphinbayhilo.com. John Alexander, the owner/manager, is at the front desk nearly every day. He's a font of information about the Big Island and will happily dispense advice on how to make your day trips fulfilling. The hotel was built by his father, who spent years in Japan, and you'll be happy to discover this influence when you sink deep into the *ofuro*-type tubs in every room. All 18 units have small but sufficient modern kitchens. Rates are $66 single and $72 double for a standard room, $76 and $79 for a superior room, $89 for a one-bedroom, and $99 for a two-bedroom fully furnished unit; additional guests $10. Weekly rates can be arranged. The more deluxe units upstairs have open-beamed ceilings and lanai and, with three spacious rooms, feel like apartments. No swimming pool or a/c here, but there are color TVs and fans with excellent cross ventilation. The grounds and housekeeping are immaculate. Hotel guests can partake of free bananas, papayas, and other exotic fruits found in hanging baskets in the lobby, as well as free coffee. Make reservations, because everyone who has found the Dolphin Bay comes back again and again.

**The Wild Ginger Inn,** 100 Pu'u'eo St., Hilo, HI 96720, 808/935-5556 or 877/212-8276, fax 808/593-8183, wildgingerinn@usa.com, www.wildgingerinn.com, is a bubble-gum pink and vibrant green plantation-style hotel from the 1940s, so don't expect the floors to be level or everything to be spotless. It's located a short two blocks from the north edge of downtown, a few steps from the Dolphin Bay Hotel. An open-air lobby leads to a corridor veranda overlooking the thick greenery of the side yard, with a small view of the bay in the distance. A double hammock and vintage rattan chairs in the lobby area are for your relaxation. Each of the more than 30 rooms, very basic but reasonably clean, has a ceiling fan, but no telephones; some also have TVs and microwaves, and most have small refrigerators and private baths. Room rates run $45–99 single or double, $64–94 triple, and $89–99 quad, depending upon the type of room: budget, standard, superior, lanai, deluxe, or suite. Discounts are available for longer stays. Every morning, fruit, juice, and pastries are put out for guests. The inn is completely non-smoking, with a special area provided for smokers in the garden. Internet access, laundry facilities, and front-desk security boxes are available to guests. New management promises to make long-needed repairs to the old building.

Near the Kaiko'o Mall is a funky, barebones place called **Off The Wall Mini Hotel,** 10 Wilson St., 808/934-8000. Rooms have been partitioned in this older house to make private and bunk rooms. One room has a bathroom, the others share, and the covered shower is in the garden out back. This is a no smoking place, and everyone shares a common TV lounge. Rooms run $25–35 a night; a bunk in the dorm goes for $15 with a three night minimum. There is no luxury here whatsoever and you get only the most basic of accommodations, but is a place to hang out for someone on a tight budget.

## FOOD

### Inexpensive

Named after the famous all-Japanese fighting battalion that predated even the famous "442," the **Cafe 100,** 969 Kilauea Ave., 808/935-8683, open Mon.–Thurs. 6:45 A.M.–8:30 P.M., Fri.–Sat. until 9:30 P.M., is a Hilo institution. The Miyashiro family has been serving food at its indoor-outdoor restaurant here since the late 1950s. Although the loco moco, a cholesterol atom bomb containing a hamburger and egg atop rice smothered in gravy, was invented at Hilo's Lincoln Grill, the Cafe 100, serving it since 1961, has actually patented this belly-buster and turned it into an art form. There are the regular loco moco, teriyaki loco, spam loco, hot dog loco, oyako loco, and for the health conscious, the mahi loco. So, if your waistline, the surgeon general, and your arteries permit, this is *the* place to have one. With few exceptions, they cost $6 or less. Breakfast choices include everything from bacon and eggs to coffee and donuts, while lunches feature beef stew, salmon mixed plate, and fried chicken, or an assortment of sandwiches from teriyaki beef to good old BLT. Make your selection and sit at one of the picnic tables under the veranda to watch the people of Hilo go by.

All trips to Hilo must include a brief stop at **Low International Food,** 808/969-6652, long occupying the corner of Kilauea and Ponahawai Streets and open daily except Wednesday 9 A.M.–8 P.M., where *everyone* comes for the unique bread. Some of the more fanciful loaves are made from taro, breadfruit, guava, mango, passion fruit, coconut, banana, pumpkin, and cinnamon. The so-you-want-to-taste-it-all rainbow bread is a combination of taro, guava, and sweet bread. Loaves cost around $6, and arrangements can be made to ship them anywhere in the country. Breakfast, lunch, and dinner plates, most under $6, range from the shrimp black bean to grilled mahi mahi, *lau lau,* and Korean chicken. Choose a table under the pavilion and enjoy your picnic in downtown Hilo.

Open every day 7 A.M.–9 P.M. and a place that gets praise from local people is **Freddie's,** 454 Manono St., 808/935-1108. The decor might be called upscale Formica, but Freddie's serves down-home food, all for under $7. Lunch and all entrées are served with two scoops of rice, fries, or mashed potatoes. Among the items on the menu are saimin, teriyaki steak sandwich, chili dogs, and burgers.

Another favorite of locals and, at 485 Hinano St., not far away is **Don's Grill,** 808/935-9099, open daily except Monday 10:30 A.M.–9 P.M., until 10 P.M. on Friday. This American/Hawaiian family-style basic restaurant is known for a good square meals at reasonable prices. Inside find wood-trimmed blue Formica tables in a very modern yet functionally tasteful setting with additional seating is in the solarium. Here you find everything from *saimin* to sandwiches and fish to rotisserie chicken. Most entrées run $6.50–10.

If you want to eat anything but uninspired "American standard" in Hilo after 9 P.M., go to **Nori's Saimin and Snacks,** 688 Kino'ole St., 808/935-9133, stuck away and hard to spot (but worth it) in a little strip business across from the bowling alley. Here you can have a totally "island experience" in a humble, honest restaurant that specializes in authentic "local grinds." Inside, where the service is slow but friendly, are Formica tables and chairs, counter stools, and the "that's what you really look like" glow of fluorescent lighting. Boiling pots hold saimin of all sorts, which is generously ladled into steaming bowls and topped with fresh vegetables. Or order a plate lunch with a scoop of macaroni salad. Two people can eat until they waddle at Nori's for about $15. There's no atmosphere, but the food is authentic and good.

**New Star Chinese Restaurant** 808/934-8874, is at 172 Kilauea Ave. and open daily 10 A.M.–9 P.M. except Tuesday. If you want to eat with "the people," this is the spot. The servings are generous and for $8 you can fill up. This large restaurant is clean, the service is friendly, and the dining experience, while certainly not fancy, is definitely authentic. Takeout available.

When at the Prince Kuhio Plaza, stop at **Dotty's Family Restaurant,** 808/959-6477. Open for breakfast daily 7–11 A.M., for lunch Mon.–Sat. 10:30 A.M.–2 P.M., and for dinner Mon.–Thurs. 5–8 P.M., Friday 5–9 P.M., Dotty's is an institution where local people come for the hearty portions and the homestyle cooking. Breakfast favorites are corned beef hash and eggs or French toast made with thick slices of Punalu'u sweet bread. Lunch includes the grilled chicken supreme with mushrooms and Swiss cheese or Dotty's ultimate steak sandwich. Those in the know come for Dotty's famous oven-roasted turkey, fresh catch of the day, or barbecued pork ribs with house-made smoke-flavored sauce for dinner. Fresh vegetables, real mashed potatoes, and homemade soups (great chowder on Friday) come with all full meals, and there's plenty of homemade pie for dessert.

**Bears' Coffee Shop,** 106 Keawe, 808/935-0708, is an upscale coffee shop renowned for its breakfasts, served 7 A.M.–2:30 P.M. Mon.–Sat., 8 A.M.–noon on Sunday, but coffee is available 5:30 A.M.–5 P.M. Bears' features Belgian waffles (made with malted flour), bagels, and an assortment of egg dishes. Lunch is hearty deli sandwiches of turkey, pastrami, chicken fillet, tuna, or ham, along with "designer" bagels and salads. You can get most anything for under $5. Beverages include Italian sodas, homemade lemonade, and a large selection of coffee, cappuccino, and café latte from the full espresso bar. All are perfect with desserts like carrot cake, Bear's

brownies, cheesecake, and pies. A great place to relax, read the morning paper, check out the Teddy Bears on the wall, or watch Hilo life go by from the sidewalk bistro tables.

**Satsuki's,** 808/935-7880, at 180 Keawe St. receives the highest recommendation because when local people want a good meal at an inexpensive price they head here. It's open for lunch 11 A.M.–2 P.M., dinner 5–8:30 P.M., closed Tuesday. Specialties are oxtail soup and the Okinawa soba plate lunch. There are plenty of traditional favorites, and all meals come with miso soup, Japanese pickles and condiments, rice, and tea. Spotlessly clean and friendly. This is excellent food at excellent value.

**Tsunami Grill and Tempura,** 250 Keawe St., 808/961-6789, is open Mon.–Sat. 10:30 A.M.–2 P.M. and 4:30–8 P.M. On Sunday, it's only open for dinner, and then only for the buffet. Like many of the restaurants in town, the Tsunami Grill has its own loyal local clientele. The food is excellent and the prices are unbeatable. You'll walk away stuffed on traditional Japanese food like udon, soba, katsu, tempura, donburi, and saimin, or bento for about $10, or if you order the buffet, it is $24.95 on Sunday and $14.95 the rest of the week.

For food of the raw variety, head across the street to **Ocean Sushi,** Tsunami Grill's sister shop, 808/961-6625, where most sushi on the menu is $2.50–4 and the many kinds of rolls run about $4.50. There is a laundry list of possibilities, both traditional and contemporary. Also on the menu are the more expensive sushi boxes and sashimi platters, salads, miso soup, and the like. Open 10 A.M.–2:30 P.M. and 4:30–9 P.M. Mon.–Saturday.

**Miyo's,** 808/935-2273, overlooks Waiakea Pond from its second story location at Waiakea Villas. Here you find "homestyle Japanese cooking" done the way you might find in Japan, in simple surroundings, at a very reasonable price. Fresh fish daily, and vegetarian options are available. You can't go wrong here. Open for lunch 11 A.M.–2 P.M. and for dinner 5:30–8:30 P.M., closed Sunday.

The **Happy Valley Seafood Restaurant,** 808/933-1083, at the Hilo Shopping Center, has a typically Chinese long list of menu items and reasonably priced live lobster. Serves Mandarin and Szechwan, mixed plate, dim sum, and has take-out; open daily.

**Ken's House of Pancakes** is a place to get a good standard American meal for a good price. Open 24 hours every day of the year, it's conveniently located on the way to the airport at 1730 Kamehameha Ave., 808/935-8711.

Kitty-corner across the intersection is the local **Verna's,** 808/935-2776, for plate lunches, burgers, sandwiches, and a multitude of inexpensive fast local food with nothing much more than $5. Take-out or sit at the picnic table to the side.

Located on Furneaux Ave., **Canoes Cafe,** 808/935-4070, has a large variety of inspired sandwiches, wraps, and salads available Mon.–Sat. 8 A.M.–3 P.M., 10 A.M.–2 P.M. on Sunday.

**Ono Hawaiian** serves plate lunches, burgers, and vegetarian entrées from its lunch wagon at the bayfront beach.

## Pastries and Treats

**Lanky's Pastries,** Hilo Shopping Center, 808/935-6381, open 6:30 A.M.–9 P.M., deli side from 6 A.M., is a perfect place to head if you have a sweet tooth that *must* be satisfied. The deli/bakery is especially known for its "long johns,"—long, thin sugar donuts filled with custard—but it also has all kinds of baked goods from bread to apple turnovers.

Places for a refreshing scoop of ice cream are **Tropical Dreams Ice Cream** at the refurbished Kress Building downtown (you can get baked goods here too), **Hilo Homemade Ice Cream** either at 41 Waianuenue Ave. or at Hilo Tropical Gardens along Kalaiana'ole Ave. on the way to the beaches, and the **Big Island Candies** shop on Hinano Street. Both Tropical Dreams and Hilo Homemade ice creams are local brands made in town.

**Hilo Seeds and Snacks** at 15 Waianuenue Ave. and **Kilauea Preserve Center** at 187 Kilauea Ave. sell authentic crackseed. If you've never tried this unique island snack, here's your opportunity.

## Moderate

**Restaurant Miwa,** at Hilo Shopping Center, 808/961-4454, is open 11 A.M.–2 P.M. and again 5–10 P.M., until 9 P.M. on Sunday. Very beautifully appointed, Miwa is a surprise, especially since it's stuck back in the corner of the shopping center. Enter to find traditional shoji screens and wooden tables adorned with fine linens, along with a classic sushi bar. The menu is excellent, with appetizers like sake-flavored steamed clams and crab sunomono (seaweed, cucumber slices, and crab meat). A specialty is nabemono, a hearty and zesty soup/stew prepared at your table for a minimum of two people. Traditional favorites popular with Westerners include beef sukiyaki and shabu shabu, and there's also a variety of combination dinners that give you a wider sampling of the menu at good value. Restaurant Miwa is an excellent choice for a traditional meal at a reasonable price in a congenial setting.

Near Hilo Shopping Center, at 1438 Kilauea Ave. is **Kilauea Kitchen,** 808/935-6664. Open for three meals a day, this simple eatery offers great food at very reasonable prices. Breakfast might be French toast, pancakes, *loco moco,* or a Japanese-style breakfast; the lunch menu includes sandwiches, burgers, and wraps. Dinners are a bit more sophisticated with entrées like pan seared mahi mahi, sweet chili chicken, and grilled New York steak, most under $8. In the same building is **Hilo-Shi-Bento-Ya and Bakery,** where noodles, udon, saimin, and sushi are available. Menu items here have been created with the help of the well-known Honolulu chef Russell Siu of 3660 On The Rise.

Very clean and down-home proud, the **Royal Siam Thai Restaurant,** 70 Mamo St., 808/961-6100, serves up tasty Thai treats daily 11 A.M.–2 P.M. and 5–8:30 P.M. Appetizers include a crispy Thai noodle dish for $6 and two of the several soups are coconut chicken soup for $6 and a seafood soup for $9. Entrées range from simple fried rice dishes through curries and meat dishes to seafood selections, mostly in the $7–10 range. There are specials nightly. Vegetarian selections are numerous and portions are large. This little restaurant gets good reviews and has a local following.

The tiny **Naung Mai Thai Kitchen,** 808/934-7540, at 86 Kilauea Ave. is open weekdays except Wednesdays for lunch and Monday–Saturday for dinner, and puts out some of the best Thai food in the state at very reasonable prices. Although nicely decorated, people come for the flavors and fresh ingredients. Once you try, you'll want to go back, but go early as the half dozen tables and booths tend to fill up fast.

**Fiasco's**, at the Waiakea Kai Shopping Plaza, 200 Kanoelehua St., 808/935-7666, serves good square meals Sun.–Thurs. 11 A.M.–10 P.M., weekends to 11 P.M. Featuring a country inn flavor, Fiasco's has a cobblestoned entrance that leads you to the cozy, post-and-beam dining room appointed with stout wooden tables, with semi-private booths lining the walls. The menu begins with appetizers, mostly $4–7, like fried mozzarella, escargot, or a big plate of onion rings. Lighter appetites might enjoy the huge and well-regarded soup and salad bar buffet at $9, or a grilled chicken Caesar salad for $8. Sandwiches and burgers also run about $8. Entrées include Mexican fare and American standards, with a few pasta dishes thrown in to round out the selection. Many are under $10, while the most expensive item on the menu is only $18; Friday night prime rib is $16. Families can save money with a special children's menu. The English-style pub has a full mahogany bar, a classic with polished lion's-head brass rails, offers comfortable stools with black leather booths, and serves up wine, mixed drinks, and perhaps the largest selection of beer on the island—island-made, domestic, and imports.

Along Kamehameha Avenue is a hole-in-the-wall eatery with a handful of tables called **Honu's Nest**, 808/935-9321, that's gained a good reputation and strong local clientele. Served are a variety of Japanese dishes like tempura, donburi, soba, curry, and full dinners with salad, miso, and rice. Nothing on the menu is over $10. Open Mon.–Sat. 11 A.M.–3 P.M., Honu's Nest is popular so you may have to wait for a table.

**Nihon Restaurant**, 808/969-1133 (reservations recommended), a second story establishment raised up on pilings at 123 Lihiwai St. and overlooking both Lili'uokalani Gardens and the bay, presents authentic Japanese meals, an excellent sushi bar, and combination dinners along with cultural and artistic displays. What you get

here is like what you'd expect in Japan, with most everything under $17. Open daily except Sunday for lunch 11 A.M.–1:30 P.M. and dinner 5–9 P.M., sushi bar until 10 P.M.

**Reuben's Mexican Food**, 336 Kamehameha Ave., 808/961-2552, open Mon.–Fri. 11 A.M.–9 P.M., Saturday noon–9 P.M., will enliven your palate with its zesty dishes. The interior has the feel of Old Mexico with its bright murals and collection of sombreros and piñatas. Mariachi music wafts through the room, and you better like it because Pancho Villa is keeping an eye on you from the wall! The lengthy menu is reasonable, mostly $8–10, with selections like carne asada, steak tacos, chicken flautas, crab enchiladas, and a vegetarian bean chili verde burrito. All are served with beans and rice, and the portions are huge. The bar has a large selection of Mexican, American, and European *cerveza* for $2–3, but Reuben's is most famous for its margaritas—more than one will get you acting like a human chimichanga. ¡Olé!

Near Kalakaua Park is **Hawaiian Jungle**, 808/934-0700, open daily 11 A.M.–9 P.M. for Mexican and Peruvian dishes. Many of the usual Mexican dishes are on the menu as are more substantial dinners. Unique here, however, are empanadas chillenas, a ham or spinach and cheese filled pastry, and lomo saltano, a Peruvian fajita, and there is a Peruvian special every night. Entrées run $9–17. Live music on the weekends.

## Expensive

**Queen's Court Restaurant** at the Hilo Hawaiian Hotel on Banyan Drive, 808/935-9361, offers a nightly buffet that is *the* best in Hilo. Connoisseurs usually don't consider buffets to be gourmet quality, but the Queen's Court proves them wrong, and there's even nightly dinner music to match. Throughout the week, buffets include a prime rib and crab buffet Mon.–Thurs., a legendary seafood buffet on Friday, and a Hawaiian seafood buffet on Sunday. All are extraordinary and would give the finest restaurants anywhere a run for their money. The buffets run $24–27, with a 25 percent discount for seniors. The dining room is grand, with large archways and windows overlooking Hilo Bay. Sunday champagne brunch is more of the same quality at $24. Breakfast is served Mon.–Sat. 6:30–9:30 A.M., $10 for the buffet or à la carte with such items as eggs any style, a short stack of griddle cakes, an "Omelette by the Bay," or a local scramble. Lunch is also reasonably priced and served 11:15 A.M.–1:15 P.M. except Sunday, when the brunch runs 10:30 A.M.–1:30 P.M. Make reservations, especially on seafood night, because the Hilo Hawaiian attracts many Hilo residents who love great food.

Modern and chic with a black and white checkerboard floor, linen on the tables, an open-air kitchen, a high ceiling with ceiling fans, and the calming effect of ferns and flowers, is **Café Pesto**, at 308 Kamehameha Ave. in the historic S. Hata Bldg., 808/969-6640, open Sun.–Thurs. 11 A.M.–9 P.M., Fri.–Sat. until 10 P.M. One of Hilo's established restaurants, it offers affordable gourmet food in an open, airy, and unpretentious setting that looks out across the avenue to the bay. Pizzas from the 'ohi'a wood-fired oven can be anything from a simple cheese pie for $8 to a large Greek or chili-grilled shrimp pizza for $18; you can also create your own. Lunch calzones run about $11 but at dinner go for $15 with soup and salad. Lunchtime also features sandwiches and pasta. For dinner, try an appetizer like Asian Pacific crab cakes or sesame-crusted Hamakua goat cheese. Heartier appetites will be satisfied with the main dinner choices, which might be mango-glazed chicken, island seafood risotto, or a combination beef tenderloin and tiger prawns with garlic mashed potatoes for $15–29. Follow this with a warm coconut tart, liliko'i cheesecake, or creme brûlée and you'll be set for the evening. Café Pesto also has a brass-railed bar where you can order caffé latté or a fine glass of wine to top off your meal in one of the best island-cuisine restaurants in Hilo.

Sicilian fishermen would feel right at home at **Pescatore**, 235 Keawe St., 808/969-9090, open daily for breakfast 7:30–11 A.M., lunch 11 A.M.–2 P.M., dinner 5:30–9 P.M. for some of the finest Italian pasta and sandwiches in Hilo. The building has had multiple uses over the years and, as part of its colorful past, served as a house of ill repute. It is now a bright and cheery room with high-backed, red velvet armchairs and for-mally set tables with green linen tablecloths. Italian-style chandeliers, lace curtains, and koa trim add to the elegance. When the Italian in you desires antipasti, minestrone soup, cioppino classico alla pescatore, gamberetti Alfredo, or any number of other seafood dishes, head for Pescatore. Many dinner entrées run $16–25.

**Harrington's**, 135 Kalaniana'ole Ave., 808/961-4966, is open nightly for dinner 5:30–9:30 P.M., Sunday until 9 P.M., and lunch Mon.–Fri. 11 A.M.–3:30 P.M.; the lounge opens at 4 P.M. The restaurant overlooks the Ice Pond at Reed's Bay in a convivial setting. A sunset cocktail or dinner is enhanced with the melodic strains of live jazz, contemporary, or Hawaiian music playing softly in the background on the weekends. The continental cuisine of mostly steak and seafood features appetizers like seafood chowder, mushroom tempura, and escargot in casserole that run $4–9. Although the eggplant parmigiana at $15 is vegetarian, other mostly meat entrées include prawns scampi, scallops chardonnay, calamari meunière, Slavic steak, prime rib au jus, and chicken marsala for $16–20. Much appreciated by locals, the menu hasn't changed much since the 1970s. While not inspired, Harrington's turns out eminently pleasing food in a pleasant atmosphere.

**The Seaside Restaurant**, 808/935-8825, appropriately named, is located out along the Keaukaha strip at 1790 Kalaniana'ole Ave. at a fish farm operation. If you want, have a look at the ponds before you head in for your meal. About a dozen varieties of freshwater and saltwater fish are available on the menu in a number of preparations, and for those who would rather, a few steak, chicken, and pasta selections are also available. For fish, come to the Seaside. Most fish dinners range from $17.95 to $25.95. All dinners come complete with salad, vegetables, rice, and apple pie. This is a popular place with locals, so make a reservation; open Tues.–Sun. 5–8:30 P.M.

## Brewery

Hilo has its own microbrewery, **Mehana Brewing Company,** 275 E. Kawili St., 808/934-8211, www.mehana.com. A small operation—about 1,200 barrels a year—in business since 1996, this microbrewery crafts five varieties of light beer with no preservatives, brewed especially for the tropical climate. Stop at the small tasting room for a sample any day except Sunday. If it's not too busy, someone may show you around. Open Mon.–Fri. 9 A.M.–5:30 P.M. and Sat. 10 A.M.–4 P.M.

## ENTERTAINMENT

Hilo doesn't have a lot of nightlife, but neither is it a morgue.

One of the best places for weekend music and dancing, and quick easy food every night of the week except Sunday is the large and lively **Cronies Bar and Grill,** 808/935-5158, at the corner of Waianuenue and Kamehameha Avenues. Hamburgers, sandwiches, and *pu pu* in the $6–8 range, with a handful of more expensive entrées, are on the menu, and Cronies offers a full complement of drinks. On Friday and sometimes other nights of the week there's live music. Belly up to the bar, toss some darts at the electronic dartboard, or use the billiard table in the back while the music plays up front. Open at 11 A.M.

If you're looking for a night out in the Banyan Drive area, try **Shooter's,** 808/969-7069, at 121 Banyan Drive. Open 11 A.M.–2 A.M., Shooters is a bar and restaurant where you can dance seven nights a week. DJ music ranges from reggae to rock to rap depending upon the crowd and the night, with live music (cover charge) a couple times a month. The cavernous interior is like a giant rumpus room with cement floors, neon beer signs, a graffiti wall, and TVs at every angle; the decor is industrial chic. Don't be put off by the atmosphere, which can seem a bit stark and hard at first glance. Shooter's is friendly, has security, and boasts that "there hasn't been one confrontation since the day we opened." That's nice!

**Wai'oli Lounge** at the Hilo Hawaiian Hotel offers live contemporary Hawaiian music Fri.–Sat. nights, karaoke Sun.–Thurs, and complimentary *pu pu* daily 5–7 P.M. In the cocktail lounge at the Naniloa hotel, live music and dancing are an option on Friday and Saturday evenings. **Uncle Billy's Fish and Steakhouse** at the Hilo Bay Hotel has a free hula show nightly

6–7:30 P.M. **Harrington's** offers live jazz, contemporary, or Hawaiian music Thurs.–Sat.; good for dinner or just for relaxing.

At Waiakea Villas, the **Karaoke Box,** 808/935-6269, is a place to sing to your heart's content. Open Mon.–Thurs. 5–10 P.M., Fri.–Sat. until 2 A.M., closed Sunday. Right next door is the **Hale Inu Sports Bar.** Stop in for a cold one and a game on the big screen.

### Movie Theaters

To catch a flick, try the **Prince Kuhio Theaters,** at the Prince Kuhio Plaza, 808/951-3456, with eight screens and tickets for $7 adult or $5 student. Downtown in the refurbished Kress Building is the newer four-screen **Kress Cinemas,** 808/961-3456, where tickets cost $5.50. The renovated **Palace Theater** 38 Haili St., 808/934-7777, shows art films, is the venue of the yearly Hawaii International Film Festival, and hosts periodic live performances. Here you have stadium seating, a proscenium stage, and wonderful old murals. If you're into art-deco buildings and old cinemas, make this a stop. It's mostly open weekends at 7:30 P.M.; movie tickets are $6 adult and $5 student.

## RECREATION

### Bicycling

The **Hilo Bike Hub,** 318 E. Kawila, 808/961-4452, is perhaps the best shop in town for quality mountain bikes and accessories; sales, repair, and rentals. Stop here for information about island races and ideas for where to bike on-road or off-road on the island. Crossbreed mountain bikes rent for $25 a day, front suspension bikes are $20, and full suspension bikes run $45; rent for seven days at the price of four. Closed on Sunday, so if you rent a bike on Saturday, you must rent it for two days.

**Mid Pacific Wheels,** at 1133-C Manono St., 808/935-6211, sells and rents mid-range mountain bikes. Bikes rent for $15 a day; helmets, tubs, and bike rack are extra. Open daily.

**Aquatic Perceptions,** 808/933-1228, arranges bicycle tours to various locations on the island, including one through the tropical district of Puna

BIG ISLAND OF HAWAI'I

and another around Kilauea Crater rim drive, for about $100 per person.

For recycled bicycles, sales, repair, or rentals, stop and talk with the owner of **Da Kine Bike Shop,** at 12 Furneaux Lane, 808/934-9861, just a few steps from Kamehameha Avenue in downtown Hilo. Nothing is new here, but you might find a bike to cruise the beach or one maybe to buy and sell back at the end of your trip. Open Tues.–Sat. only.

## Scuba

The **Nautilus Dive Center,** 382 Kamehameha Ave., Hilo, 96720, 808/935-6939, derooy @gte.net, www.downtownhilo.com/nautilus, open Mon.–Sat. 9 A.M.–4 P.M., Sunday by appointment, owned and operated by certified instructor William DeRooy, is one of the longest established dive companies on the Hilo side. This full-service dive center offers three- to five-day PADI certification at a very reasonable $125 per person for a group of at least four or $300 for private lessons, and shore dives at $55 for one tank or $75 for two tanks for certified divers, including transportation. Boat dives can be arranged. New and used dive gear, scuba rental equipment, and snorkel gear rental at $5 for 24 hours are also available. DeRooy is willing to provide information over the phone for anyone coming to the Hilo side to dive or snorkel. He updates you on ocean conditions, suggests spots compatible with your ability, and even offers a free dive and snorkel map whether you're a customer or not. Bill is a font of information about the Big Island's water sports and shares it in the true *aloha* spirit. Definitely stop in!

With a wider range of water equipment for sale or rent can be found at **Planet Ocean Watersports,** 808/935-7277, at 100 Kamehameha Ave. Snorkel gear, scuba gear, and kayaks can be rented, and dive and kayak tours can be arranged.

## Golf

The only county-maintained golf course on the island is located high above downtown Hilo. **Hilo Municipal Golf Course,** 340 Haihai St., 808/959-7711, is a 6,325-yard, par-71 undulating course where non-residents can golf for

$20 weekdays and $25 weekends. There are reduced rates for state and island residents. Cart rental is separate, and rental clubs are available. This is definitely a local course but does provide some challenge. Call ahead for tee times.

Occupying the center of the Waiakea Peninsula and surrounded by Banyan Drive is the **Naniloa Country Club** golf course, 808/935-3000. Maintained by the Naniloa hotel, this small nine-hole course is a par 35 over a flat 2,740 yards; $30 for two times around on weekends or $25 during the week. It's an easygoing place where lots of people come to learn and practice.

## Arnott's Expeditions

Arnott's Lodge, 808/969-7097, www.arnotts lodge.com/activity.html, offers a variety of hiking adventures to its guests and to those who do not stay at the lodge but want more of an adventure than organized tours usually offer. Although the schedule of offerings changes periodically, some of Arnott's mainstays are the hikes to the lava flow in Volcanoes National Park, a waterfall and valleys hike of Saturday, and the sunset and stargazing trek from the top of Mauna Kea. These van tours each run a full eight hours and take only as many as the van will hold. Rates run $48, higher for those not staying at the lodge. All trips are made weather permitting and only if there are enough takers to make a go of them. Some restrictions apply, so be sure to check with the staff at Arnott's Lodge, or check out its website for the current list of adventures.

# SHOPPING
## Shopping Malls

Hilo has the best general-purpose shopping on the island. **Prince Kuhio Plaza,** at 111 E. Pua'inako, open weekdays 10 A.M.–9 P.M., Saturday 9:30 A.M.–7 P.M., Sunday 10 A.M.–5 P.M., is the island's largest shopping mall with over 75 shops. It's basically an indoor covered mall with the addition of several large detached buildings. Jewelry shops, fashion and shoe stores, music and books, sporting goods, fast-food restaurants, and large department stores like Sears, JC Penney, and Macy's make this a one-stop shopping experience. Here too you'll find Longs Drugs, Safeway, and a Hilo Hattie's store in their own separate buildings. Across Maka'ala is the newer **Waiakea Center** with a Borders Books and Music, Island Naturals natural food store, Wal-Mart, and Office Max. These two malls together make the greatest concentration of Hilo shopping.

The strip mall **Pua'inako Town Center** is located a little farther up Kanoelehua Avenue (Rte. 11) and on the other side of the street, with lots of small shops, a Sack 'n Save Market, KTA Superstore, and one fast-food outlet after another.

The older shopping plazas are closer in toward the downtown area. **Kaiko'o Mall** is at 777 Kilauea Avenue near the state and county buildings. Once a thriving full-service mall, many of its shopping spaces are now vacant; however, one end has been remodeled and filled with several county offices, including the Department of Parks and Recreation. Still full of local shops and some excellent inexpensive restaurants, the **Hilo Shopping Center** sits along Kilauea Avenue at the corner of Kekuanao'a Street.

## Downtown Shops

If you're looking for a simple yet authentic gift or souvenir try the **Lyman Museum gift shop,** which also has an excellent collection of books on Hawaiian subjects.

**Ets'ko,** 35 Waianuenue Ave., 808/961-3778, is Ginza and Paris in Hilo. This classy, eclectic little shop sells all sorts of expensive but very nice arts and craft items, gifts, furniture, jewelry, and a small selection of silk and natural fiber clothing. Perhaps a hand-painted silk tie for him or a Japanese *tansu* chest for her is just the piece you're looking for. Open Mon.–Sat. 9 A.M.–6 P.M. and until 4 P.M. on Sunday in a small and very compact shop.

**Old Town Printers,** 160 Kamehameha Ave., open Mon.–Sat., has been in business since 1962 selling stationery, office supplies, postcards, and a terrific selection of calendars. It is in the same shop as Basically Books, the best book shop in town for Hawaiiana and maps.

**Sig Zane Design,** at 122 Kamehameha Ave., 808/935-7077, open Mon.–Sat. 9 A.M.–5 P.M., is one of the most unique and distinctive shops on the island. Here, owner and designer Sig Zane creates distinctive island wearables in 100 percent cotton. All designs are not only Hawaiian/tropical but also chronicle useful and medicinal Hawaiian plants and flowers. Sig's wife, Nalani, who helps in the shop, is a *kumu hula* who learned the intricate dance steps from her mother, Edith Kanakaole, a legendary dancer who has been memorialized with a local tennis stadium that bears her name. You can get shirts, dresses, and pareu, as well as affordable house slippers, sweatshirts, T-shirts, *hapi* coats, and even futon covers. The shelves also hold *lau hala* hats, hand-bound koa notebooks, and basketry made from natural fibers.

After having moved down to Kamehameha Avenue, business at **Fabric Impressions** has picked up. Stop here for bulk fabric, sewing accessories, quilt supplies, and quilts. Sewing classes and quilting workshops are also offered on a regular basis. Open except Sunday until 5 P.M.

If you're looking for surfboards ($20 a day), boogie boards, or surfwear, or just want to find out about surfing conditions in the area, stop by **Orchid Land Surfshop,** at 262 Kamehameha Ave., 808/935-1533, www.surfolhawaii.com. Established in 1972 and run by an avid surfer, this place will have what you need. Check its website for surf reports, conditions, and weather forecast.

**Dreams of Paradise,** 808/935-5670, is a gallery located in the restored S. Hata Building, erected in 1912. Some artists showcased in the gallery specialize in the flora and fauna of Hawaii, produce fine koa furniture, offer distinctive acrylic paintings, catch the sun in stained glass renditions of breadfruit, lotus blossoms, and various Hawaiian flowers, and produce lava sculptures and renditions of animal life. Shelves also hold gourmet food items, incidental bags, distinctive cooking aprons, and plenty of inexpensive but tasteful souvenirs. Also of interest in the S. Hata building are Kipuka Smoke Shop for cigars, Bugado's Fine Woods for turnings and furniture, and a Black Pearl jewelry shop.

**Caravan Town** at 194 Kamehameha Ave. is open daily except Sunday. It is one of the most interesting junk stores in Hilo. The shelves hold an internationally eclectic mix of merchandise that includes pendulum clocks, plaster Greek goddesses, luggage, and paper lanterns. Also, the shop specializes in over-the-counter Chinese herbs and medicines purportedly effective for everything from constipation to impotence. Other antique and collectible shops along this street worth a look are **Pink Elephant, The Most Irresistible Shop in Hilo,** and the venerable old **Oshima's.**

**Hilo Surplus Store,** featuring raincoats, hats, military supplies, knives, backpacks, rubber rafts, plenty of old and new military uniforms, and some camping equipment can be found at 148 Mamo Street.

North of town several miles and just before the Hawaiian Tropical Botanical Gardens along the scenic coastal road is **Hawaiian Artifacts and Antiques,** 808/964-1729, open daily 9 A.M.–5 P.M., a shop owned and operated by Paul Gephart. Paul creates small wood boxes and ornaments, mainly from koa and 'ohi'a, and sculptures of whales, dolphins, birds, and poi bowls. He also has a small collection of tasteful jewelry and seashells, all at very decent prices. Most intriguing perhaps are the reproductions of old Hawaiian weapons.

Hilo's twice-weekly farmers market is a great place for farm-fresh fruits and vegetables.

## Food Markets

For groceries and supplies try: **KTA Super Store,** downtown at 321 Keawe Ave. or in the Pu'ainako Town Center; **Safeway,** 111 E. Pu'ainako; or **Sack 'n Save** at Pu'ainako Town Center or 250 Kino'ole. **Suisan Fish Market,** at 85 Lihiwai St., is open 8 A.M.–5 P.M. daily except Sunday. Pick up a copy of the *Hawaii Fishing News* and *Fisherman's News* at the counter.

Since 1977, **Abundant Life Natural Foods** has been doing business in downtown Hilo at 292 Kamehameha Ave., 808/935-7411, open weekdays 8:30 A.M.–6:30 P.M., Wednesday and Saturday from 7 A.M., and Sunday 10 A.M.–4 P.M. The store's kitchen puts out daily specials of smoothies, soup, salads, sandwiches, and *bento,* most for under $6, while the shelves are stocked with an excellent selection of fresh fruits and veggies, bulk foods, cosmetics, vitamins, and herbs. The bookshelves cosmically vibrate with a selection of tomes on metaphysics and new-age literature.

In the Waiakea Center next to Borders Books is **Island Naturals** market and deli, 808/935-5533. This full-service shop is open Mon.–Sat. 8:30 A.M.–8 P.M. and Sunday 10 A.M.–7 P.M. Fresh fruit and produce line the shelves, as do packaged, refrigerated, and frozen natural foods, plus personal care items, supplements, vitamins, and minerals. The deli has ready to order foods and pre-made items. You'll get wholesome healthy foods here, with a good vibe from people who care about what they sell.

All you folks with that affinity for chocolate will certainly be pleased by the **Big Island Candies** factory and gift shop at 585 Hinano St., 808/935-8890 or 800/935-5510, www.bigislandcandies.com. Stop by to look through the glass at the delicacies being produced and choose your favorite off the many shelves of possibilities. Hawaiian macadamia nut cookies, chocolate-dipped shortbread, and macadamia nut biscotti only start the selections. This store also sells Hilo Homemade ice cream and is open every day 8:30 A.M.–5 P.M. You can even peruse the offerings and order off the Web.

On Wednesday and Saturday mornings, stop by the corner of Kamehameha Avenue and Mamo Street for the **Hilo Farmers' Market.** This is a lively affair, great for local color, where you can get healthy locally grown produce and bouquets of colorful flowers at bargain prices. Across the street at The Market Place and also a few steps up the road under the big tents are more vendors selling flowers, arts and crafts, and other gift items.

## Bookstores

Hilo has some excellent bookstores. **Basically Books,** downtown at 160 Kamehameha Ave., 808/961-0144, www.basicallybooks.com, open Mon.–Fri. 9 A.M.–5 P.M., Saturday until 3 P.M., has a good selection of Hawaiiana, out-of-print books, and an unbeatable selection of maps and charts. You can get anywhere you want to go with these nautical charts, road maps, and topographical maps, including sectionals for serious hikers. The store also features a very good selection of travel books, and flags from countries throughout the world. Owner and proprietress Christine Reed can help you with any of your literary needs.

The **Book Gallery,** at Prince Kuhio Plaza, 808/959-7744, is a full-selection bookstore featuring Hawaiiana, hardcovers, and paperbacks. Also at the Prince Kuhio Plaza is **Waldenbooks,** 808/959-6468, one of the city's largest and best-stocked bookstores.

The largest bookstore in Hilo is **Borders Books and Music,** 808/933-1410, open daily at the Waiakea Center, across Maka'ala Street from the Prince Kuhio Plaza. Borders has tens of thousands of hardcover and paperback books, full Hawaiiana and travel sections, plenty of road maps, and over a dozen newspapers from around the world. Readings, music performances, book and CD signings, and other special events are scheduled throughout the month. If browsing makes you thirsty, stop for a snack at the shop's Cafe Espresso.

# INFORMATION AND SERVICES

## Medical

**Hilo Medical Center,** 1190 Waianuenue Ave., 808/974-4700, has both outpatient services and a 24-hour emergency room. Just up the street at 1292 Waianuenue Avenue is a **Kaiser Permanente** clinic, 808/934-4000.

The **Hilo Pharmacy,** at 308 Kamehameha Ave. in the S. Hata Bldg., 808/961-9267, open Mon.–Fri. 8:30 A.M.–5:30 P.M., Saturday 8:30 A.M.–12:30 P.M., is a full-service pharmacy that also has a photo developing service. Others in town are **Shiigi Drug,** at the Kaiko'o Mall, 808/935-0001; **Windward Pharmacy,** 808/981-2055, at the Pua'inako Center, **Longs Drugs,** 555 Kilauea Ave., 808/935-3357; and the pharmacies at the **KTA Super Store** and **Wal-Mart.**

## Information

Good sources of maps and helpful brochures are **Big Island Visitors Bureau,** at the corner of Keawe and Haili Streets, 808/961-5797, open Mon.–Fri. 8 A.M.–noon and 1–4:30 P.M.; the **Chamber of Commerce,** 106 Kamehameha Ave., 808/935-7178, and the **tourist information kiosk** next to the bus station.

## Schools and Libraries

The **Hilo Public Library** is located at 300 Waianuenue St., 808/933-8888. The **University of Hawaii at Hilo,** 200 W. Kawili, 808/974-7311, is a branch of the state university system that has a strong Hawaiian language program. The **Hawaii Community College,** in a separate campus a short distance away, is a more skills-focused facility.

## Banking and Post Office

All the state's big banks have branches in Hilo. Try **City Bank** at Kaiko'o Mall, 808/935-6844; **Central Pacific Bank,** 525 Kilauea Ave., 808/935-5251; **Bank of Hawaii,** 120 Pauahi St., 808/935-9701; **First Hawaiian Bank,** 1205 Kilauea Ave., 808/969-2211; or **American Savings Bank,** 100 Pauahi St., 808/935-0084.

The **Hilo Main Post Office,** open weekdays

9 A.M.–4:30 P.M., Saturday 9 A.M.–12:30 P.M., is an efficiently run, modern post office, clearly marked on the access road to the airport. It is extremely convenient for mailings prior to departure. A downtown postal station is located in the federal building on Waianuenue Avenue.

## Internet Connection

**Bytes and Bites** is open daily 10 A.M.–10 P.M. for your Internet connection to the world at $2.50 for 15 minutes or $8 an hour, and for faxing, scanning, office programs, games, and computer instruction. Find it at 223-A Kilauea Ave., on the corner of Ponahawai across from Low International bakery and restaurant.

On the corner of Waianuenue and Kino'ole, across from the post office, **Beach Dog Rental** offers Internet access at $2 for 20 minutes or $6 an hour.

A number of accommodations around town also offer inexpensive Internet services. Try Arnott's Lodge or the Wild Ginger Inn.

# Hamakua Coast

Along the shore, cobalt waves foam into razor-sharp valleys where cold mountain streams meet the sea at lonely pebbled beaches. Inland, the Hamakua Coast, once awash in a rolling green sea of sugarcane, is starting to be put to other uses. Along a 50-mile stretch of the Hawai'i Belt Road (Rte. 19) from Hilo to Waipi'o, the Big Island grew its cane for 100 years or more. Water was needed for sugar, a ton to produce a pound, and this coast has plenty. Huge flumes once carried the cut cane to the mills. In the 19th century so many Scots worked the plantations hereabouts that Hamakua was called the "Scotch Coast." Now most residents are a mixture of Scottish, Japanese, Filipino, and Portuguese ancestry. Side roads dip off Rte. 19 into one-family valleys where the modest, weather-beaten homes of plantation workers sit surrounded by garden plots on tiny, hand-hewn terraces. These valleys, as they march up the coast, are unromantically referred to as "gulches." From the Belt Road's many bridges, you can trace silvery-ribboned streams that mark the valley floors as they open to the sea. Each valley is jungle, lush with wildflowers and fruit trees transforming the steep sides to emerald-green velvet. This is a spectacular drive, and the coast shouldn't be missed.

This stretch of the island has recently been named the "Hilo-Hamakua Heritage Coast" in an effort to draw attention to its historic and cultural significance. When in Hilo, pick up a copy of *A Driver's*

ROBERT NILSEN

Waipi'o Valley

*Guide to the Hilo-Hamakua Heritage Coast* pamphlet and look for brown and white road signs indicating points of interest as you proceed along Route 19.

## Onomea Scenic Drive

Route 19 heading north from Hilo toward Honokaʻa is a must, with magnificent inland and coastal views one after another. Only five minutes from Hilo, you'll come to Papaʻikou town. Look for Pinky's convenience store on the right. Within a half mile, a road posted as a scenic drive dips down toward the coast. Take it. Almost immediately signs warn you to slow your speed because of the narrow winding road and one-lane bridges, letting you know what kind of area you're coming into. Start down this meandering lane past some very modest homes and into the jungle that covers the road like a living green tunnel. Prepare for tiny bridges crossing tiny valleys. Stop, and you can almost hear the jungle growing. This four-mile-long Onomea Scenic Drive is like a mini-version of Maui's Hana Road. Along this route are sections of an ancient coastal trail and the ruins of a former fishing village. Drive defensively, but take a look as you pass one fine view after another. This road runs past the Hawaii Tropical Botanical Gardens and rejoins Rte. 19 at Pepeʻekeo, a workers' village where you can get gas or supplies. For those requiring a stop along this route, try What's Shakin' for fresh smoothies, juices, and a few simple and quick eats.

# Honomu to Honokaʻa

The ride alone, as you head north on the Belt Road, is gorgeous enough to be considered a sight. But there's more! You can pull off the road into sleepy one-horse towns where dogs are safe snoozing in the middle of the road. You can visit plantation stores in Honomu on your way up to ʻAkaka Falls, or take a cautious dip at one of the seaside beach parks. If you want solitude, you can go inland to a forest reserve and miles of trails. The largest town on the coast is Honokaʻa, with supplies, handmade mementos, restaurants, accommodations, and even a golf course. You

can veer west to Waimea from Honoka'a, but don't—yet. Take the spur road, Rte. 240, to Kukuihaele, and from there drop down into Waipi'o Valley, known as the "Valley of Kings," one of the most beautiful in all of Hawaii.

## HONOMU AND VICINITY

During its heyday, Honomu (Silent Bay) was a bustling center of the sugar industry boasting saloons, a hotel/bordello, and a church or two for repentance, and was even known as "Little Chicago." Now Honomu mainly serves as a stop as you head elsewhere, but definitely take the time to linger. Honomu is 10 miles north of Hilo and about a half mile or so inland on Rte. 220, which leads to 'Akaka Falls. On entering, you'll find a string of false-front buildings that are doing a great but unofficial rendition of a "living history museum." The town has recently awoken from a long nap and is now bustling—if that's possible in a two-block town—with wonderful art galleries, craft shops, and small cafés. At the south end of town, just at the turn to 'Akaka Falls, notice the **Odaishisan,** a beautifully preserved Buddhist Temple. Honomu is definitely worth a stop. It takes only minutes to walk the main street, but those minutes can give you a glimpse of history that will take you back 100 years.

### Accommodation

Nestled into three oceanfront acres of fruit and nut trees, with the driveway lined in palms, is the luxuriant, neo-Victorian **The Palms Cliff House,** 808/963-6076, fax 808/963-6316, P.O. Box 189, Honomu, HI 96728, palmscliffhouse@aol.com, www.palmscliffhouse.com. Overlooking a small bay where you can see whales in the winter and spinner dolphins all year round, this bed-and-breakfast caters to the discriminating crowd. The eight rooms, all done in individual themes (Orchid Suite, Bombay Nights, Bellisimo, Tropical Splendor…), are decorated with antique beds, custom-made Italian sheets, coordinated furniture, and artwork on the walls. Marble entryways and bathrooms, fireplaces in four rooms, whirlpool tubs in several, a wide lanai facing the ocean for each room that is blocked from the others for privacy, an entertainment center, and all plush amenities are what you might expect from such a high-end establishment. And to ensure a peaceful and uninterrupted getaway, there are no phones in the rooms and a separate hot tub sits in the garden. Gourmet breakfast specialties are cooked every morning in addition to fruits, juice, and other drinks. With all this luxury, room rates are not cheap. Set up for no more than two individuals in a room, they run $175–375 a night; six have king beds, one has a queen, and one has twins. With prior arrangement, special dinners, cooking classes or outings, weddings, massage, yoga, and other activities can be arranged.

### Food

Before entering town proper you'll spot **Jan's,** a convenience store selling cold beer, groceries, and sundries. At the upper end of town is a small grocery store and bakery in the old Ishigo Building.

On the left as you drive along the main street are several shops for sit-down or take-out food. First up is **Akaka Cafe,** a little eatery serving such things as saimin, sandwiches, and plate lunches, all for easy-on-the-pocketbook prices. The interior of the old building holds a few tables with chairs salvaged from Honomu's defunct theater and a counter with little red stools. Akaka Cafe is clean, friendly, and caught in a time warp harkening back to the days when a burger was the treat of the week!

The **Woodshop Gallery/Café** has a more modern and artsy atmosphere as its part of the gallery. After perusing the fine artwork, sit down for a sandwich, burger, smoothie, or coffee. Choose a table inside, or head for the lanai where you can watch the "action" in the two-block downtown of Honomu.

Set out back behind the 'Ohana Gallery and surrounded by greenery is the **Bamboo Lanai Café.** Stop here to soothe your sweet tooth with a smoothie, cookie, ice cream, float, or a cup of coffee.

Open daily 11:30 A.M.–7:30 P.M., Friday and Saturday until 8 P.M., at the upper end of town, is **Pizza Hawaii.** Pick up a slice for $1.90 or a whole pie for $14–22, or satisfy your hunger

BIG ISLAND OF HAWAI'I

with hot and cold sandwiches, hot dogs, or bagels with a variety of toppings.

## Shopping

The **Woodshop Gallery/Café,** 808/963-6363 or 877/479-7995, www.woodshopgallery.com, open daily 10:30 A.M.–6 P.M., along Honomu's main street, offers a wonderful opportunity for browsing among fine tropical wood furniture and artworks. This is one of the island's finest collections of arts and crafts. Shelves shine with the lustrous patina of bowls, mirrors, and furniture fashioned from koa, mango, *milo,* and macadamia wood, as well as from Norfolk pine, which can be turned to a translucent thinness. All pieces can be shipped, as can wood planks if you desire to create your own furniture or art piece. Jeanette and Peter McLaren, the shop owners, create stained glass works and furniture, respectively. Other artists produce additional furniture, art glass, ceramics, pottery, prints, paintings, and a great selection of turned bowls. Less expensive items include chopsticks, wooden spoons made of coconut and wood, combs, barrettes, and lovely vanity mirrors that come in a velvet bag.

More craftsy than the Woodshop Gallery next door, **Honomu Plantation Gallery** has a whole host of arts and crafts that make perfect gifts from your trip. Open 9:30 A.M.–5:30 P.M. daily.

The **'Ohana Gallery,** 808/963-5467, operates with the philosophy that Hawaii's culture, history, and beauty are alive in the art of its people. Open daily except Sun. and Mon. 10 A.M.–4 P.M., this is a combination fine arts cooperative gallery and gift shop that occupies part of the Ishigo Building, built in 1880 and the oldest building in Honomu. Gracing the shelves and walls of the two-story gallery are works of wood, clay, pottery, paint, paper, glass, stone, and other mediums, all by island artists.

The small **Hawaiian Creations** shop has a fine collection of boxes and other small wooden pieces that fall into the fine furniture category. Some jewelry is also displayed. Also showing jewelry and creations in wood is **Circle A Gifts,** where much of the work is done on premise.

Another establishment worth a visit is **Glass**

**From the Past,** with vintage bottles, dug locally, and a variety of other collectibles.

One of the most unusual collections in town is at **Tribal Arts and Crafts of the South Pacific,** where clothing, crafts, carvings, woven goods, and numerous other objects are sold.

The **Flying Mermaid Gallery** sells clothing, gifts, post cards, and some packaged food items. It's located next to the **Honomu Emporium,** where you'll find almost anything connected to the Teddy Bear and dolls.

## 'Akaka Falls State Park

Follow Rte. 220 from Honomu past former sugarcane fields for three miles to the parking lot of 'Akaka Falls, at a little more than 1,000 feet in elevation. From here, walk counterclockwise along a paved "circle route" that takes you through everybody's idea of a pristine Hawaiian valley. For the 40-minute hike, you're surrounded by heliconia, *ti,* ginger, orchids, azaleas, ferns, and bamboo groves as you cross bubbling streams on wooden footbridges. Many varieties of plants

'Akaka Falls

that would be in window pots anywhere else are giants here, almost trees. An overlook provides views of Kahuna Falls spilling into a lush green valley below. The trail becomes an enchanted tunnel through hanging orchids and bougainvillea. In a few moments you arrive at 'Akaka Falls. The mountain cooperates with the perfect setting, forming a semicircle from which the falls tumble 442 feet in one sheer drop, the tallest single-tier waterfall in the state. After heavy rains, expect a mad torrent of power; during dry periods marvel at liquid-silver threads forming mist and rainbows. The area, maintained by the Division of State Parks, is one of the most easily accessible forays into Hawaii's beautiful interior.

## Kolekole Beach Park

Look for the first tall bridge (100 feet high) a few minutes past Honomu, where a sign points to a small road that snakes its way down the valley to the beach park below. Slow down and keep a sharp eye out as the turnoff is right at the end of the bridge and easy to miss. Amenities include restrooms, grills, electricity, picnic tables, pavilions, and a camping area (county permit); no drinking water is available. Kolekole is very popular with local people, who use its pavilions for all manner of special occasions, usually on weekends. A black-sand beach fronts an extremely treacherous ocean. The entire valley was inundated with more than 30 feet of water during the great 1946 tsunami. The stream running through Kolekole comes from 'Akaka Falls, four miles inland. It forms a pool complete with waterfall that is safe for swimming but quite cold.

## Wailea

Just a few miles beyond Kolekole Beach Park, above the highway on the old road, is the tiny community of Wailea. A former sugar town, it's now a sleepy village. Yet, despite this sleepiness there is much energy and direction. Occupying one of the old storefronts, The WaiOla Community Wellness Center has set its sights on community involvement, health and wellness issues, and the preservation of cultural crafts. Also in town is the easygoing and casual **Akiko's Buddhist Bed and Breakfast,** P.O. Box 272,

Hakalau, HI 96710, tel./fax 808/963-6422, msakiko@aloha.net, www.alternative-hawaii.com/akiko. You need not be a Buddhist to stay, but you should come with an open mind and open heart. The bright yellow main house clues you in to the cheeriness and energy inside. Akiko's offers four Japanese-style rooms in the main building, a common kitchen, and bathroom with shower. This building is called the Monastery and is set aside for silence during the day. An adjacent two-story plantation house also has four rooms, plus a living room, kitchen, and a basic bathroom with shower. A retreat studio is also available in a third building, with basic cooking appliances for longer stays. Breakfast is a group affair in the main house with fruits from the garden, fresh-baked bread, and other goodies created by the talented Akiko. While it is not required, you may want to attend one of the informal meditations held every morning at 5 A.M. in the main house meditation room, or tag along on one of the morning walks. Yoga is done every Sunday morning. The rooms in the main house have futons on the floor; the plantation house has both beds and futons. Rates are $40 single or $55 double per night, and the plantation house can be rented for $155 a night. Weekly and monthly rates are $260 and $555 single or $355 and $750 double. The upstairs retreat studio has a two-week minimum and goes for $420 single or $585 double for that period. An easy place with good vibes and always plenty going on, you can rest and relax, participate or not, or head out to explore the countryside yourself. Check the website for an activity calendar.

## World Tropical Botanical Gardens

With such an impressive name, this garden promises to be good. But wait, the gardens are only in their infancy! Created on land that was sugarcane just a few short years ago, the gardens, which opened in 1995, are destined to be a wonderful sight. So far, however, and until the collection starts to mature and new plants are put in, there are only small sections worth seeing near the entrance of this 300-acre tract. By far, the most impressive sight on the property is the three-tier Umauma Waterfall—and it is sure to please. The plan is to cultivate some 30,000 species—arranged in evolutionary grouping—and every year the gardens grow a little more in stature toward that goal. These gardens are open Mon.–Sat. 9 A.M.–5:30 P.M., and the entrance fee—which helps to further the cause—is $7 adults or $3 for teens. For more information, call 808/963-5427 or check out the website at www.wbgi.com. Follow the signs up from the highway near mile marker 16 to the visitor center.

## LAUPAHOEHOE

This wave-lashed peninsula is a finger of smooth pahoehoe lava that juts into the bay. Located about halfway between Honomu and Honoka'a, the valley at one time supported farmers and fishermen who specialized in catching turtles. Laupahoehoe was the best boat landing along the coast, and for years canoes and, later, schooners would stop here. A plaque commemorates the tragic loss of 20 schoolchildren and their teacher who were taken by the great tsunami of 1946. Afterwards, the village was moved to the high ground overlooking the point. **Laupahoehoe Point County Park** now occupies the low peninsula; it has picnic tables, showers, electricity, and a county camping area. The sea is too rough to swim in but many fishermen come here, along with some daring surfers. Laupahoehoe makes a beautiful rest stop along the Belt Road. Turn near mile marker 27, after the highway comes back out of the valley. The road down to the park is narrow and winding and runs past several rebuilt homes and a restored Jodo Mission.

Near the Laupahoehoe scenic overlook, at 36-2377 Mamalahoa Hwy., is the **Laupahoehoe Train Museum,** 808/962-6300. Open weekdays 9 A.M.–4:30 P.M. and weekends 10 A.M.–2 P.M., with an entrance fee of $3 adult or $2 children and seniors, this museum treats you to a taste of the olden days when trains hauled sugarcane, commercial goods, and people up and down this rugged coast. The museum once was the home of the Superintendent of Maintenance for this division, and is now filled with train memorabilia, photographs, books, and furniture that were either from the house or typical of the era, and two

videos give insight into the train line and sugar era. The house itself has been lovingly restored as has the track "wye" on the grounds, and you can see remnants of a loading platform out front. Biding their time, several train cars wait to be rebuilt. This museum is a worthy enterprise that gives you a glimpse into late-19th-century and early-20th-century coastal culture and is a fine place to stop on your way up the road. This line was part of the railroad that ran down to Hilo and beyond to Pahoa and up to Mountain View, but this rail system came to an abrupt halt on the first day of April 1946 when a tsunami washed ashore and destroyed track, bridges, and other property. The railroad company never recovered.

Ten miles inland from Laupahoehoe Point along a very rugged jeep trail is **David Douglas Historical Monument.** This marks the spot where the naturalist, after whom the Douglas fir is named, lost his life under mysterious circumstances. Douglas, on a fact-gathering expedition on the rugged slopes of Mauna Kea, never returned. His body was found at the bottom of a deep pit that was used at the time to catch feral cattle. Douglas had spent the previous night at a cabin occupied by an Australian who had been a convict. Many suspected that the Australian had murdered Douglas in a robbery attempt and thrown his body into the pit to hide the deed. No hard evidence of murder could be found, and the death was officially termed accidental.

### Practicalities

As you drive up the highway, you dip into and out of the **Maulua Gulch,** the biggest and one of the most impressive so far up this coast. Just before Laupahoehoe, look for a sign to **Papa'aloa.** Although now silent, you can almost imagine the hubbub of activity when this town, and others like it on the coast such as Niu and 'O'okala, were alive with sugar production. Turn here, and head down the road to the **Papaaloa Store,** where local people go to buy the area's *best* smoked meats and fish, and *laulau* made right at the store; macaroni salad and meals to go are also available.

In Laupahoehoe along Rte. 19, look for **M. Sakado Store,** open 7 A.M.–9 P.M., an old-fashioned convenience store. It sells basic items like milk, bread, and soft drinks, enough for a picnic. There's not too much else here but a post office, police station, and schools.

**Maxi's Place,** 808/972-0011, open 6 A.M.–6 P.M., in a white and turquoise, vintage gas station in Laupahoehoe Village, is a plate lunch restaurant. Plate lunches are the standard, from mahimahi to teriyaki beef, but burgers, loco moco, and snacks are also on the menu. Desserts are homemade cheesecake and ice cream, and drinks include shakes. The atmosphere is as local as you can get!

## Pa'auilo

About 10 miles past Laupahoehoe is Pa'auilo, another ghost of a sugar town. Set close to the highway, the new town has a post office, several schools, and a former plantation manager's house. In business for about 100 years, **Paauilo Store** serves sundries, a few groceries, soda, sandwiches, and plate lunches. Down toward the sea were plantation workers' camps but are now just quiet forgotten neighborhoods, and on the coast are the old abandoned mill site and docks where raw sugar was loaded for transport.

## Kalopa State Recreation Area

This spacious natural area is 12 miles north of Laupahoehoe, five miles southeast of Honoka'a, three miles inland on a well-marked secondary road, and 2,000 feet in elevation. Little used by tourists, it's a great place to get away from the coast and up into the hills. Hiking is terrific throughout the park and adjoining forest reserve on a series of nature trails where some of the flora has been identified. Most of the forest here is endemic, with few alien species. Some of what you will see are 'ohi'a, koa, the *hapu'u* tree fern, and *kopiko* and *pilo*, both species of the coffee tree family. Near the entrance and camping area is a young arboretum of Hawaiian and Polynesian plants. Beyond the arboretum is an easy three-quarter-mile nature loop trail through an 'ohi'a forest, and three-mile loop trail takes you along the gulch trail and back to camp via an old road. All trails are well marked and vary widely in difficulty. Birdlife here may not be as varied as high up the mountainside, but still you can catch sight of 'elipaio, auku'u (a night heron), the white-eye, cardinal, and the Hawaiian hoary bat. The park provides an excellent opportunity to explore some of the lush gulches of the Hamakua Coast, as well as day-use picnicking, tent camping, and furnished cabins (state permit required) that can house up to eight people. Camping and cabin use is limited to five consecutive days per party. The bunk-style cabins, each with a bathroom and shower, rent for $55 for one to eight campers. Linens and blankets are provided, and you may cook in the recreation hall. For reservations, contact the State Park office, 75 Aupuni St. #204, Hilo, HI 96721, 808/974-6200.

BIG ISLAND OF HAWAI'I

# Honoka'a to Kukuihaele

## HONOKA'A AND VICINITY

With a population of around 2,000, Honoka'a (Rolling Bay) is the major town on the Hamakua Coast. In the past, it was a center for cattle, sugar, and macadamia nut industries and a place where GIs stationed at Camp Tarawa in Waimea would come for R&R. Now it's mainly a tourist town and a center for controversy about land use issues now that sugar is no longer the economic behemoth of the region. One issue which has caused some uproar is the 18,000 acres of former cane land, now owned by the Bishop Estate after the Hamakua Sugar Mill went bankrupt in the mid-1990s, that's been turned into a huge eucalyptus tree farm. From here, you can continue on Rte. 19 for 16 miles to Waimea or take Rte. 240 north for nine miles to the edge of Waipi'o Valley, which you should not miss. First, however, stroll the main street of Honoka'a, Mamane Street, where there are a number of shops specializing in locally produced handicrafts, a gallery or two, restaurants, and general merchandise stores next to antiques shops. Also in town are a small health center, a post office, two banks, a movie theater, public library, a nine-hole golf course, and a small visitor information center. It's also the best place to stock up on supplies or gasoline—there are stations on both Routes 19 and 240. If you are proceeding north along Rte. 240, the coastal route heading to Waipi'o Valley, just past mile marker 6 on the left, keep an eye peeled for a lava-tube cave right along the roadway. This is just a tease of the amazing natural sights that follow.

## Festivals

The **Hamakua Music Festival,** 808/775-3378, www.hamakuamusicfestival.com, held yearly in early October and lasting two weekends, attracts not only island musicians but musicians of national and international fame. While there is always jazz, classical, and Hawaiian music on the schedule, other genres of music are sometimes also performed. Major concerts are performed on the weekends at the Honoka'a People's Theater, with related events and local musical groups performing during the week. Tickets usually run about $20 per concert, very reasonable for big name performers, and excess profits from the festival are used to fund local music scholarships and the salary for a local music teacher.

The annual **Taro Festival** is held in November and it celebrates the most cherished of traditional Hawaiian foods. Events include Hawaiian music, hula, chanting, taro exhibits, food made from taro, and crafts and games. The whole town gets into the swing of things and this daylong event is a hit.

**Western Days Weekend** is scheduled for the end of May. Genuine cowboys as well as city slickers from the Mainland pretending to be *paniolo* will throw their Stetsons in the air and yell "yippie yi yo kai yea!" when this event rolls around. It's a time for all cowboys to gather for fun and games. Two rodeos are held during the weekend at the Honoka'a Arena for those who like that sort of rough and tumble affair—and for those who just like to watch. Aside from a lively parade that makes its way through town, there's horseshoe pitching, craft displays, a dinner and dance, and—everyone's favorite—the Saloon Girl contest. For information about either the Western Days Weekend or the Taro Festival, contact the Honoka'a Business Association, P.O. Box 474, Honoka'a, HI 96727, www.alternative-hawaii.com/hba.

## Accommodations

Centrally located along Rte. 240 in downtown Honoka'a is the **Hotel Honoka'a Club,** P.O. Box 247, Honoka'a, HI 96727, 808/775-0678 or 800/808-0678, honokaac@gte.net, http://home1.gte.net/honokaac. Built in 1908 as the plantation manager's club, it's still infused with the grace and charm of the old days. Yet, what it lacks in elegance it makes up for in cleanliness and friendliness. The hotel, mostly used by local people, is old and well used but clean and comfortable, and the only accommodation right in town. Follow a wainscoted hallway from the front office to your room. All rooms are upgraded with carpeting and fluffy quilts; each features a view and TV. From the back rooms, you get a view over the tin roofs of residential Honoka'a and the ocean. There are more spartan but very clean rooms downstairs. Rooms run $80 for a two-room suite, $55–65 for an ocean view room with TV, private bath and, queen bed, and $45–50 for an economy room with a private bath. Rates include a simple continental breakfast. Hostel rooms, located in the basement, all with shared bath and kitchen facilities, are separated into three private rooms at $35 and two communal rooms (one sleeping three people and the other six people) that rent for $15, add $5 if you do not supply your own linens. The basement hostel rooms, although a bit dungeonesque, are clean, with windows to catch the breeze.

About four miles up above town in the pasture and forest land of Ahualoa is **Mountain Meadow Ranch B&B,** P.O. Box 1697, Honoka'a, HI 96727, tel./fax 808/775-9367, bill@mountainmeadowranch.com, www.mountainmeadowranch.com. Perfect for peace and quiet, the lower level of the ranch home has a living room with TV and VCR, sitting room with microwave and small refrigerator, two bedrooms, a dry sauna, tub, and shower, and its own entrance. A light continental breakfast left on the sideboard is included in the room price. This unit with one room runs $80 or $130 for the two bedrooms. A separate guest cottage with full kitchen, two bedrooms with queen beds, bath, wood stove, full entertainment center, and laundry room is also available, but no breakfast is included. There is a three-night minimum, and the rate is $125 a night or $800 a week. No smoking inside either unit.

The **Log Cabin** guesthouse in Ahualoa, P.O. Box 1994, Kamuela, HI 96743, 808/885-4243 or 800/555-8968, kaminn@aloha.net, www.hawaii-bnb.com/kamuela.html, is associated with Kamuela Inn in Waimea. It sits on a five-acre forested property in a cool mountain setting at about 2,500 feet. The log-style walls and framing and barn roof give this large house a welcoming country feel. This house has a large living room with fireplace, upstairs library, full kitchen, five guest bedrooms, and a hot tub stuck in a garden gazebo. Room rates are $59 with shared bath, $99 with private bath, or $375 a night for the whole house, continental breakfast included.

Surrounded by pastureland just outside Kalopa State Recreation Area, **Mauka Bed and Breakfast,** P.O. Box 767, Honoka'a, HI 96727, tel./fax 808/775-9983, maukabb@gte.net, www.stayhawaii.com/mauka/mauka.html, is a quiet spot. At 1,700 feet in elevation, it is also cool and refreshing. There is one studio here with a private entrance, queen bed, bathroom, TV, and VCR. The room rate of $60 a night includes a simple continental breakfast. No credit cards. This is a basic, simple, inexpensive place with no frills, but it is near hiking and horse pastures.

## Food

Local people thought that Jolene was such a good cook, they talked her into opening **Jolene's Kau Kau Corner** in downtown Honoka'a, 808/775-9498, open Mon.–Sat. 10:30 A.M.–3 P.M., closed Sunday. Most tried-and-true recipes were handed down by her extended family, who lends a hand in running the restaurant. The restaurant, located in a vintage storefront, is trim and neat, and the menu includes a variety of plate lunches like beef tips teriyaki and breaded shrimp, a steaming bowl of beef stew, saimin, and burgers and fries, all under $8. Jolene's is as down-home and local as you can get, with friendly service, hearty dishes, and reasonable prices. This is one of the best places to eat along the northern Hamakua Coast!

Follow the comforting aroma of fresh-baked bread to **Mamane Street Bakery & Café,** 808/775-9478, open Mon.–Sat. 6 A.M.–5 P.M., closed Sunday, owned and operated by Eliahu "Ely" Pessah. Ely bakes goodies including coconut turnovers, Danish pastries, and ensemada, a special type of cinnamon roll, but what the local people come in for are the honey-nut bran muffins, crunchy with chunks of macadamia nuts. Ely's oven also turns out ham and cheese croissants, mozzarella or marinara focaccia, or three-cheese focaccia. Eat in or take out while enjoying your purchase with a cup of steaming coffee or tea.

Almost across the street is **Cafe Il Mondo,** 808/775-7711, an Italian pizzeria and coffee bar that's open Mon.–Sat. 11 A.M.–8 P.M. This is a cheery place with Italian music on the sound system and Hawaiian prints on the walls. Here you feel the spirit of Italy. While pizzas, mostly $10–18, are the main focus, you can also get tasty calzones for $8, lasagna, sandwiches, salads, soup, ice cream, and gourmet coffee, of course! If you're on the road, ask for your pizza to go.

"On a Wing and a Prayer" is part of the logo welcoming you to **Simply Natural Ice Cream Parlor and Deli,** 808/775-0119, open Mon.–Sat. 9 A.M.–4 P.M. Besides ice cream in tropical and standard flavors, a board offers a full sandwich menu with plenty of soups and vegetarian items, and breakfasts of omelettes and pancakes. Beverages include soft drinks, fresh-squeezed carrot juice, Kona coffee, espresso, and cappuccino.

**Tex Drive In,** 808/775-0598, open daily 5 A.M.–9 P.M. and a little later on weekends, is an institution in town. Everyone knows it and everyone's been there—many times. The long-established Hamakua restaurant is known for its fresh malasadas (sugared, holeless Portuguese donuts), production of which is showcased behind plate glass windows inside. Get some! They're a treat. But ask before 7 P.M. or they'll probably be sold out. Every month, 15,000 of these tasty treats are sold—sometimes many more. Tex has a fast-food look, a drive-up window, walk-up counter, and inside and outside tables, but the cavernous dining room in the back is still there and the food is still as filling and reasonable as ever. Serving "Ono Kine" food, it specializes in inexpensive local food like *kalua* pork, teriyaki chicken and beef, hamburgers, and fresh fish, and there are many ethnic items on the menu. Prices are very reasonable, with most dinners around $7 and sandwiches less. Local people and (an even better sign) the local police come here to chow down on good, easy-on-the-wallet food, and more than that, it's very clean. Tex Drive In is located along Route 19, at the corner of Pakalana Street.

**Herb's Place,** in downtown Honoka'a, is open for breakfast, lunch, and dinner daily from 5:30 A.M. You get basic meals and cocktails in this little roadside joint.

**C.C. Jon's,** a local ethnic eatery open for breakfast and lunch, is right on the road as you enter town. Most of the plate lunch dishes are under $5.

## Entertainment

The once run-down but classic "Last Picture Show" **Honoka'a People's Theater,** along the main drag, has been renovated to its old 1930s splendor. It's a big-screen theater, seating about 500, that has a new surround sound system. First-run movies generally show Fri.–Sun. evenings, with art movies shown on Tuesday and Wednesday. Showtime is 7 P.M. and tickets run $6 for adults, $4 for seniors, and $3 for children. This theater is also used as a venue for the yearly Hawaii International Film Festival, for the autumn Hamakua Music Festival, and for other community events throughout the year. Call 808/775-0000 to hear what's showing.

## Shopping

If you are at all interested in the history of Hawaii, make sure to stop by the **Hawaiian Artifacts and Antiques** shop along the main drag in downtown Honoka'a. This amazing curio and art shop is owned and operated by Lokikamakahiki "Loki" Rice, who ran it for many years with her husband James, who passed away in the spring of 1996. Loki, elderly and in failing health, keeps no set hours, opening when she feels like it, usually for a few hours in the afternoon, but never before 2 P.M. At first glance the shop may look inauthentic, but once you're inside, that impression quickly melts away. Loki, a full-blooded Hawaiian, was born and raised in Waipi'o Valley, and James traveled the Pacific for years. The stories from the old days are almost endless. Notice a tiki that serves as a main beam, and two giant shields against the back wall. They belonged to Loki's father, a giant of a man just under seven feet tall and more than 450 pounds—he had to have a special coffin made when he was buried on the island of Ni'ihau. Local people bring in their carvings and handicrafts to sell, many of which are hula implements and instruments like drums and rattles. Some of the bric-a-brac is from the Philippines or other South Sea islands, but Loki will identify them for you. Mingled in with what seems to be junk are some real artifacts like poi pounders, adzes, and really good drums. Many have come from Loki's family, while others have been collected by the Rices over the years. But the real treasure is Loki, who will share her *aloha* as long as time and the call from above permits.

Toward the east end of the downtown row, **Seconds To Go,** open daily except Sunday 9:30 A.M.–5 P.M., is owned and operated by Elaine Carlsmith. The collectibles and antiques shop specializes in Hawaiian artifacts; it brims with classic Hawaiian ties and shirts from the 1950s, dancing hula-doll lamps, antique hardware and building materials, clawfoot bathtubs, old books, Japanese bowls, a good collection of plates and saucers, and a ukulele. Elaine also sells used fishing gear in case you want to try your luck. If you like collectibles of any sort, you'll love it here.

**The Honoka'a Trading Company,** 808/775-0808, open daily 10 A.M.–5 P.M., is a discovery shop owned and operated by Denise Walker. Items come and go, but you can expect to find classic artwork from the Matson Steamship Lines, hula dolls, Japanese netsuke, poi bowls, costume jewelry, pots and pans, bottles, and old crockery. Denise has also filled this rambling building with a good selection of old books, Hawaiian instruments, Japanese fans, and vintage signs. Denise focuses not only on things *from* Hawaii, but on things brought *to* Hawaii. Much of the furniture and many of the antique items were brought to Hawaii by *kama'aina* and GI families.

If these shops haven't been enough for your antiques and collectibles needs, make your last stop at **Honoka'a Market Place,** 808/775-8255, where you can browse through furniture, clothing, and all sorts of old castoffs that now command a stiff price, and actually are, collectively, a window on the past. Here as well is a great selection of (imported) quilts and clothing.

Several shops that sell clothing, accessories, lotions, and gifts items are **Taro Patch Gifts, Maya's Clothing and Gifts** and **Mary Guava Designs.**

**Kama'aina Woods,** 808/775-7722, in Honoka'a a hundred yards down the hill from the post office, is usually open daily 9 A.M.–5 P.M. except Sunday but this depends on the weather, the owner's inclination, and how the spirits are moving on any particular day. The shop is owned and operated by Bill Keb, a talented woodworker who specializes in fabulous bowls turned from native woods like koa, *milo,* extremely rare *kou,* and a few introduced woods like mango and Norfolk Island pine. Boxes, platters, and other items are made by different island craftsmen. All of the wooden art pieces, priced from affordable to not-so-affordable, are one-of-a-kind and utilitarian. Less expensive items are koa or *milo* bracelets, letter openers, and rice paddles.

Farther down toward the ocean, in the old macadamia nuts factory, is **Hawaii's Only Live Arts Gallery.** Open 9 A.M.–5 P.M. daily, a large gallery shows works of local artists, some of whom do work here. On different days, you might see glass blowing, wood carving, oil painting, or pottery. A whole assortment of gifts are sold and coffee is roasted for the snack bar, where you have your choice of ice cream or other tasty treats.

The **Bamboo Gallery,** 808/775-0433, is a spacious showroom on the main drag where you will find an eclectic mix of wood, bamboo, fiber, canvas, multi-media, and glass art, all displayed in a sparse Oriental style. Nearby is **Hamakua Art Glass** with many more lovely examples of this art form. Toward the east end of town is **Starseed** for beads and gems.

**S. Hasegawa** has a few racks of local fashions and a few bolts of traditional Japanese cloth, as well as gifts and candies, cards, and cosmetics. This is an old-time general dry goods store. Next door is the very ethnic **Filipino Store;** stop in to soak up a cultural experience and to find an array of exotic spices and food ingredients.

For groceries and even a few health food items, stop at **T. Kaneshiro Store** and the much smaller **K.K. Super-Mart,** two well-stocked markets in town. A small selection of mostly local and organic produce, fruits, packaged and canned health foods, supplements and vitamins is available at the **Taro Junction** next to Hotel Honoka'a Club. Small but very healthy, it's open weekdays 10 A.M.–8:30 P.M. and 9 A.M.–5 P.M. on Saturdays.

## KUKUIHAELE

For all of you looking for the "light at the end of the tunnel," Kukuihaele (Traveling Light) is it. A small plantation town, Kukuihaele now subsists on tourism. The new highway bypasses town. Take the old road down and in; it pops out again on the other side. At the far edge of town, on the cusp of the valley wall, is the **Waipi'o Valley Overlook,** an exceptional location for peering into this marvelous, mysterious, and legend-filled valley. For most tourists, this is as close as you'll get to the "Valley of Kings." But, oh, what a sight! Stand a while and soak in the surroundings: the valley and ocean, the black sand beach, the coastal cliffs, and the ever-changing clouds. During winter months you might be treated to a special sight when mama humpbacks bring their newborn babies to the bay below to teach them how to be whales.

On the old road just before town, the **Last Chance Store,** open daily except Wednesday and Sunday 9 A.M.–5 P.M., stocks basic grocery supplies plus a small assortment of handicrafts and gift items. The Last Chance has an excellent selection of domestic and imported beers, along with light snacks for a picnic lunch. The Last Chance Store is just that; there is no other shop beyond.

**Waipi'o Valley Artworks,** 808/775-0958 or 800/492-4746, open daily 9 A.M.–5:30 P.M., is an excellent shop in which to pick up an art object. There are plenty of offerings in wood by some of the island's best woodworkers that include carvings and bowls, but the shop also showcases various Hawaii-based artists working in different media. Definitely check out inspired prints, paintings, line drawings, pottery, and jewelry. You'll also find crafts, a smattering of souvenir items, a fairly extensive collection of books mostly on Hawaiiana, designer T-shirts, and other wearables. This is one of those wonderful finds, an out-of-the-way place that carries a good selection of excellent artwork—and they'll ship. The shop also features a counter serving ice cream, sandwiches, and soft drinks. Waipi'o Valley Artworks is the meeting place for Waipio Valley Shuttle, which will take you down to the valley, and for the biking, horseback, and van tours that explore the valley rim. All in all, Waipi'o Valley Artworks is the hub of activity in this not so bustling town.

## Accommodations

A vintage home of a one-time plantation manager, **Waipio Wayside**, P.O. Box 840, Honoka'a, HI 96727, tel./fax 808/775-0275 or 800/833-8849, wayside@ilhawaii.net, www.waipiowayside.com, is owned and operated by Jackie Horne as a congenial B&B Inn. Look for the Waipio Wayside sign hung on a white picket fence exactly two miles toward Waipi'o from the Honoka'a post office. You enter through double French doors onto a rich wooden floor shining with a well-waxed patina. The walls are hand-laid vertical paneling, the prototype that modern paneling tries to emulate. Here is a formal dining area and an informal seating area with books, a television, videos, and music. The home contains five bedrooms, each with private bathroom, ranging in price $95–145, $25 extra for an additional person beyond two. The Birds Eye Room has a three-night minimum and the Library Room a two-night minimum, with a $10 surcharge for single-night stays. Spacious and airy, all rooms are individually decorated by theme and hung with beautiful Battenburg lace curtains. The back deck, where you will find hammocks in which to rock away your cares, overlooks manicured grounds that gently slope to a panoramic view of the coast. Jackie, whose meticulous and tastefully appointed home is straight from the pages of a designer magazine, is also a gourmet

cook. Breakfast is sometimes waffles with strawberries and whipped cream, sometimes omelettes and biscuits, with fresh fruit from the property. Beverages are pure Hamakua coffee, juices, and gourmet teas from around the world, and there is always an assortment of snacks. A stay at Waipio Wayside is guaranteed to be civilized, relaxing, and totally enjoyable. As a benefit, Jackie will gladly arrange island activities for her guests.

**Hale Kukui**, 808/775-7130 or 800/444-7130, P.O. Box 5044, Honoka'a, HI 96727, info@halekukui.com, www.halekukui.com, owned and operated by Bill and Sarah McCowatt. This is a secluded vacation rental on four acres that's perched high on the *pali,* from where you get a sweeping view down onto the Waipi'o Valley beach, up the rugged coast, and out to the wide Pacific. Follow the main road *through* Kukuihaele and look for a sign pointing you down a private drive that leads about 200 yards to the finely landscaped yard and two comfortable cottages and a studio. The rental units are separate from the main house and each has a hot tub on the lanai. Inside, the units are tastefully decorated with comfy furniture and ceiling fans, and there are large windows on the lanai side that provide the exceptional views. Full kitchens contains all that you'll need to cook a meal, and that's good as all meals are your responsibility. The studio has a queen-size bed and a queen-size pull-out sofa; the cottages have king beds with additional queen-size beds. Rates run $125 for the studio and $160 or $175 for the cottages; two nights minimum and the seventh night free. For the use of guests, a simple trail leads down to the semiprivate stream where you'll find a small but refreshing pool.

Enjoy the privacy of **Hamakua Hideaway**, P.O. Box 5104, Kukuihaele, HI 96727, 808/775-7425 or 808/775-0995 weekdays, jhunt@gte.net, http://home1.gte.net/jhunt. This rental is only a 15-minute walk from the Waipi'o Valley overlook, tucked into trees with a lush garden surrounding. With living room, kitchenette, bath, television, and phone, the "treehouse" runs $95 a night or $85 a night for two nights or more, with reduced weekly and monthly rates available.

Surrounded by green acres of pasture on the edge of the sea cliff next to the Waipi'o Valley

Overlook is the **Cliff House,** 808/775-0005 or 800/492-4746, P.O. Box 5045, Kukuihaele, HI 96727. This two-story, two-bedroom house has a living room, full kitchen, laundry room, one bathroom, and lanai that looks over the ocean. This house runs $175 a night for a couple, two nights minimum, with an extra person charge of $20 for up to four. No credit cards. Check-in is at the Waipi'o Valley Artworks shop.

With its ridgeside location, **Waipio Ridge Vacation Rental,** 808/775-0603, has an exceptional spot. From the front lawn, you can peer down onto the valley and out to the blue ocean with unobstructed views. This little studio has one bedroom, one bath, two queen beds and rents for $85 a night or $75 a night for two or more nights, with a $15 extra person charge.

## Waipi'o Valley

Waipi'o is the way the Lord would have liked to fashion the Garden of Eden, if he hadn't been on such a tight schedule. You can read about this incredible valley, but you really can't believe it until you see it for yourself. Route 240 ends a minute outside of Kukuihaele at an overlook, and 900 feet below is Waipi'o (Curving Water), the island's largest and most southerly valley of the many that slice the harsh Kohala Mountains. The valley is a mile across where it fronts the sea at a series of sand dunes, and six miles from the ocean to its back end. It's vibrantly green, always watered by Waipi'o Stream and lesser streams that spout as waterfalls from the *pali* at the rear and to the side of the valley. The green is offset by a wide band of black-sand beach. The far side of the valley ends abruptly at a steep *pali* that is higher than the one on which you're standing. A six-mile trail leads over it to Waimanu Valley, smaller, more remote, and more luxuriant.

Travelers have long extolled the amazing abundance of Waipi'o. From the overlook you can make out the overgrown outlines of garden terraces, taro patches, and fishponds in what was Hawai'i's largest cultivated valley. Every foodstuff known to the Hawaiians once flourished here; even Waipi'o pigs were said to be bigger than pigs anywhere else. In times of famine, the produce from Waipi'o could sustain the populace of the entire island (estimated at 100,000 people). On the valley floor and alongside the streams you'll still find avocados, bananas, coconuts, passion fruit, mountain apples, guavas, breadfruit, tapioca, lemons, limes, coffee, grapefruit, and pumpkins. The old fishponds and streams are alive with prawns, wild pigs roam the interior, as do wild horses, and there are abundant fish in the sea. Carrying on the traditions of farmers of old, some farmers in the valley still raise taro, and this has once again become one of the largest taro-producing regions on the island and one of the principal production centers in the state.

But the lovingly tended order, most homes, and the lifestyle were washed away in the tsunami

looking down into Waipi'o Valley

ROBERT NILSEN

BIG ISLAND OF HAWAI'I

of 1946. Now Waipi'o is largely unkempt, a wild jungle of mutated abundance. The valley is a neglected maiden with a dirty face and disheveled, windblown hair. Only love and nurturing can refresh her lingering beauty.

# HISTORY

## Legend and Oral History

Waipi'o is a mystical place. Inhabited for more than 1,000 years, it figures prominently in old Hawaiian lore. In the primordial past, Wakea, progenitor of all the islands, favored the valley, and oral tradition holds that the great gods Kane and Kanaloa dallied in Waipi'o, intoxicating themselves on 'awa. One oral chant relates that the demigod Maui, that wild prankster, met his untimely end here by trying to steal baked bananas from these two drunken heavyweights. One flung Maui against the rear valley wall, splattering blood everywhere, hence the distinctively red color of the earth at the far back reaches of the valley. Lono, god of the Makahiki, came to Waipi'o in search of a bride. He found Kaikilani, a beautiful maiden who lived in a breadfruit tree near **Hi'ilawe Waterfall,** which tumbles 1,000 feet in a cascade of three drops to the valley below and is the island's tallest waterfall.

Nenewe, a shark-man, lived near a pool at the bottom of another waterfall on the west side of Waipi'o. The pool was connected to the sea by an underwater tunnel. All went well for Nenewe until his grandfather disobeyed a warning never to feed his grandson meat. Once Nenewe tasted meat, he began eating Waipi'o residents after first warning them about sharks as they passed his sea-connected pool on their way to fish. His constant warnings aroused suspicions. Finally, the cape he always wore was ripped from his shoulders, and there on his back was a shark's mouth! He dove into his pool and left Waipi'o to hunt the waters of the other islands.

Pupualenalena, a *kupua* (nature spirit), takes the form of a yellow dog that can change its size from tiny to huge. He was sent by the chiefs of Waipi'o to steal a conch shell that mischievous water sprites were constantly blowing, just to irritate the people. The shell was inherited by

Kamehameha and is now in the Bishop Museum. Another dog-spirit lives in a rock embedded in the hillside halfway down the road to Waipi'o. In times of danger, he comes out of his rock to stand in the middle of the road as a warning that bad things are about to happen.

Finally, a secret section of Waipi'o Beach is called **Lua o milu,** the legendary doorway to the land of the dead. At certain times, it is believed, ghosts of great *ali'i* come back to earth as "Marchers of the Night," and their strong chants and torch-lit processions fill the darkness in Waipi'o. Many great kings were buried in Waipi'o, and it's felt that because of their *mana,* no harm will come to the people who live here. Oddly enough, the horrible tsunami of 1946 and a raging flood in 1979 filled the valley with wild torrents of water. In both cases, the devastation to homes and the land was tremendous, but not one life was lost. Everyone who still lives in Waipi'o will tell you they feel protected.

The remains of **Paka'alana Heiau** is in a grove of trees on the right-hand side of the beach as you face the sea. It dates from the 12th century and was a "temple of refuge" where *kapu* breakers, vanquished warriors, and the weak and infirm could find sanctuary. Paka'alana was a huge *heiau* with tremendous walls that were mostly intact until the tsunami of 1946. The tsunami sounded like an explosion when the waters hit the walls of Paka'alana, according to first-hand accounts. The rocks were scattered, and all was turned to ruins. Nearby, **Hanua'aloa** is another *heiau* in ruins. Archaeologists know even less about this *heiau,* but all agree that both were healing temples of body and spirit, and the local people feel that their positive *mana* is part of the protection in Waipi'o.

## Recorded History

Great chiefs have dwelt in Waipi'o. King Umi planted taro just like a commoner and fished with his own hands. He went on to unite the island into one kingdom in the 15th century. Waipi'o was the traditional land of Kamehameha the Great and in many ways was the basis of his earthly and spiritual power. It was here that he was entrusted with the war god, Kuka'ilimoku, as King Kalani'opu'u was dying. Kamehameha came here to rest after heavy battles, and offshore was the scene of the first modern naval battle in Hawaii. Here, Kamehameha's war canoes faced those of his nemesis, Keoua. Both had recently acquired cannons bartered from passing sea captains. Kamehameha's artillery was manned by two white sailors, Davis and Young, who became trusted advisors. Kamehameha's forces won the engagement in what became known as the "Battle of the Red-Mouthed Gun."

When Captain Cook came to Hawaii, 4,000 natives lived in Waipiʻo; a century later only 600 remained. At the turn of the 20th century many Chinese and Japanese moved to Waipiʻo and began raising rice and taro. People moved in and out of the valley by horse and mule, and there were schools, stores, a post office, churches, and a strong community spirit. Waipiʻo was painstakingly tended. The undergrowth was kept trimmed and you could see clearly from the back of the valley all the way to the sea. World War II arrived and many people were lured away from the remoteness of the valley by a changing lifestyle and a desire for modernity. The tsunami in 1946 swept away most of the homes, and the majority of the 200 people who lived there then pulled up stakes and moved away. For 25 years the valley lay virtually abandoned. The Peace Corps considered it a perfect place to build a compound in which to train volunteers headed for Southeast Asia. This too was later abandoned. Then in the late 1960s and early '70s a few "back to nature" hippies started trickling in. Most only played "Tarzan and Jane" for a while and moved on, especially after Waipiʻo served them a "reality sandwich" in the form of the flood of 1979.

Waipiʻo is still very unpredictable. In a three-week period from late March to early April of 1989, 47 inches of rain drenched the valley. Roads were turned to quagmires, houses washed away, and more people left. Part of the problem is the imported trees in Waipiʻo. Until the 1940s, the valley was a manicured garden, but now it's very heavily forested. All of the trees you will see are new; the oldest are mangroves and coconuts. The trees are both a boon and a blight. They give shade and fruit, but when there are floods, they fall into the river, creating logjams that in-

crease the flooding dramatically. Waipiʻo takes care of itself best when humans do not interfere. Taro farmers too have had problems because the irrigation system for their crops was washed away in the last flood. But, with hope and a prayer to Waipiʻo's spirits, they rebuild, knowing full well that there will be a next time. And so it goes.

## Waipiʻo Now

Waipiʻo is at a crossroads. Many of the old people are dying or moving topside (above the valley) with relatives. Those who live here learned to accept life in Waipiʻo and genuinely love the valley, while others come only to exploit its beauty. Fortunately, the latter underestimate the raw power of Waipiʻo. Developers have eyed the area for years as a magnificent spot in which to build a luxury resort. But even they are wise enough to realize that nature rules Waipiʻo, not humankind. For now the valley is secure. A few gutsy families with a real commitment have stayed on and continue to revitalize Waipiʻo. The valley now supports perhaps 40 residents. More people live topside but come down to Waipiʻo to tend their gardens. On entering the valley, you'll see a lotus-flower pond, and if you're lucky enough to be there in December, it will be in bloom. It's tended by an elderly Chinese gentleman, Nelson Chun, who wades into the chest-deep water to harvest the sausage-linked lotus roots by clipping them with his toes! Margaret Loo comes to harvest wild ferns. Seiko Kaneshiro is perhaps the most famous taro farmer because of his poi factory that produces Ono Ono Waipiʻo Brand Taro. Another old-timer is Charlie Kawashima, who still grows taro the old-fashioned way, an art form passed from father to son. He harvests the taro with an *oʻo* (digging stick) and after it's harvested cuts off the corm and sticks the *huli* (stalk) back into the ground, where it begins to sprout again in a week or so.

## Aloha Distress

In the summer of 1992, the Bishop Museum requested an environmental impact survey on Waipiʻo Valley because the frequency of visitors to the valley had increased tremendously. Old-time residents were complaining not only about the overuse of the valley, but about the loss of their quiet and secluded lifestyle. Some tour operators cooperated fully and did their best to help in the preservation and reasonable use of one of Hawaii's grandest valleys; others did not. Because of the impact study, commercial tours are not allowed to go to the beach area on the far side of the stream, which is now open to foot traffic only, and the valley is closed on Sunday to commercial tours.

There also seems to be some kind of socio-ethnic battle evolving in the valley. Long-term residents, mostly but not exclusively of Hawaiian descent, are staking out the valley as their own and have largely withdrawn the spirit of *aloha* from the melanin-challenged visitors to their wonderful valley. Their dissatisfaction is not wholly without basis, as some who have come to the valley have been quite disrespectful, trespassing on private property, threatening to sue landowners for injuries caused by themselves, or finding themselves stuck in a river that no one in their right mind would try to cross in a vehicle. Many wonderful, open, and loving people still live in the valley, but don't be too surprised to get the "stink face" treatment from others. Be respectful and stay on public property. If the sign says *Kapu* or Keep Out, believe it. It is everyone's right to walk along the beach, the switchback that goes to Waimanu, and generally waterways. These are traditional free lands in Hawaii open to all people, and they remain so. It's really up to you. With proper behavior from visitors, Waipi'o's mood can change, and *aloha* will return.

## Driving

The road leading down to Waipi'o is outrageously steep and narrow, averaging a 25 percent gradient! If you attempt it in a regular car, it'll eat you up and spit out your bones. More than 20 fatalities have occurred since people started driving it, and it has only been paved since the early 1970s. You'll definitely need 4WD, low range, to make it; vehicles headed downhill yield to those coming up. There is very little traffic on the road except when surfing conditions are good. Sometimes Waipi'o Beach has the first good waves of the season, and this brings out the surfers en masse.

**Waipio Valley Shuttle,** 808/775-7121, has its office at Waipi'o Valley Artworks in Kukuihaele. It's best to make a reservation. Comfortable air-conditioned 4WD vans make the 90-minute descent and tour, Monday through Saturday at 9 A.M., 11 A.M., 1 P.M., and 3 P.M. Along the way, you'll be regaled by legends and stories and shown the most prominent sights in the valley by drivers who live in the area. The tour costs $40 for adults, $20 for children under 11. Buy your ticket at the Artworks. This is the tamest, but safest, way to enjoy the valley. These guys know what they're doing—they've been in business since 1970. If you decide to hike down or stay overnight, you can make arrangements for the van to pick you up or drop you off for an added cost.

# RECREATION
## Hiking
If you have the energy, the hike down the paved section of the road is just over one mile, but it's a tough mile coming back up! Once you're down in the valley, make a hard right and follow the dirt road to the beach or head straight ahead and plunge into the heart of the valley. You should remember before you go too far that you will have to cross one or more of the valley streams. There are no bridges; you'll have to wade through. None are deep or wide and are not usually a problem, but when steady rains swell the streams, stay out for your own sake, as you could easily be swept downstream.

## Waipi'o Beach
Stretching over a mile, this is the longest black-sand beach on the island. A tall and somewhat tangled stand of trees and bushes fronts this beach. The surf here can be very dangerous, and there are many riptides. If there is strong wave action, swimming is not advised. It is, however, a good place for surfing and fishing. The road to the beach leads along the east wall of the valley and opens onto plenty of space to picnic under the trees. In order to get to the long expanse of beach across the mouth of the stream, you have to wade across it, stepping carefully over the boulders that lay on the bottom. To compound matters, waves

sometimes wash water up the mouth of the stream. Be advised and be careful. Alternately, walk into the valley and find a public path that leads to the beach on the far side of the stream.

## Horseback Riding in the Valley

For a fun-filled experience guaranteed to please, try horseback riding with **Waipiʻo Naʻalapa Stables,** 808/775-0419. Sherri Hannum, a mother of three who moved to Waipiʻo from Missouri almost 30 years ago, and her husband Mark, own and operate the trail rides. The adventure begins at Waipiʻo Valley Artworks in Kukuihaele, where you begin a 4WD ride down to the ranch, which gives you an excellent introduction to the valley. When you arrive, Sherri has the horses ready to go. She puts you in the saddle of a sure-footed Waipiʻo pony and spends two hours telling you legends and stories while leading you to waterfalls, swimming holes, gravesites, and finally a *heiau.* She knows the trails of Waipiʻo intimately. The lineage of the horses of Waipiʻo dates from the late 1700s. They were gifts to the *aliʻi* from Capt. George Vancouver. Waipiʻo was especially chosen because the horses were easy to corral and could not escape. Today, more than 150 semi-wild progeny of the original stock roam the valley floor. If the fruits of Waipiʻo are happening, Sherri will point them out and you can munch to your heart's delight. Tours lasting 2.5 hours cost $75 and start at 9:30 A.M. and 1 P.M. Full-day tours can be arranged, but a minimum of two and a maximum of four riders is required. Sorry, no children under eight years old or riders weighing more than 230 pounds. Go prepared with long pants, shoes, and swimsuit.

**Waipiʻo On Horseback,** 808/775-7291, also offers horseback riding through fabulous Waipiʻo Valley. These sightseeing rides for all skill levels start at 9:30 A.M. and 1:30 P.M. and last about 2.5 hours. The cost of $75 for adult and $55 for kids under age 12 includes transportation from the Last Chance Store in Kukuihaele to the valley floor. Make reservations 24 hours in advance.

## Wagon Tour

**Waipio Valley Wagon Tours,** P.O. Box 1340, Honokaʻa, HI 96727, 808/775-9518, owned and operated by Peter Tolin, is one of the most fun-filled ways of exploring Waipiʻo. This surrey-type wagon, which can hold about a dozen people, is drawn by two Tennessee mules. The fascinating 90-minute tours depart four times daily at 9:30 A.M., 11:30 A.M., 1:30 P.M., and 3:30 P.M. Cost is $40, children under 12 half price, children two and under free. To participate, make reservations 24 hours in advance, then check in 30 minutes before departure at the Last Chance Store, where a 4WD vehicle will come to fetch you. If you just drop by, you can ask at the store to see if there is space for you, but a last-minute opening is definitely not guaranteed. Lunch is not included, but if you bring your own, you can walk down to the beach and have a great picnic. The original wagon was built by Peter himself from parts ordered from the Mainland. Unfortunately, every part he ordered broke down over a nine-month trial period. Peter had all new parts made at a local machine shop, three times thicker than the originals! Now that the wagon has been "Waipiʻonized," the problems have ceased. The only high-tech aspect of the wagon ride is a set of small speakers through which Peter narrates the history, biology, and myths of Waipiʻo as you roll along.

## Upper Rim Adventures

The valley itself doesn't get all the attention. Recently, several other opportunities have opened for people to explore the east rim of the valley. You have your choice of hiking, horseback riding, mountain biking, and 4WD van exploration. Each adventure takes a different route, although some may overlap trails. All include a trip through former sugarcane land, and each brings you to wonderful vistas that overlook the broad expanse of the Waipiʻo Valley from a height of over 1,000 feet. As you go, you'll be told stories and legends of the valley and vignettes of the culture and history of the area; some tours may even include a dip in a secluded pool under a tumbling waterfall.

Tours with **Hawaiian Walkways,** 808/775-0372 or 800/457-7759, hiwalk@aloha.net, www.hawaiianwalkways.com, led by Hugh Montgomery or one of his able staff, guide you through the rim-edge forest and over a long-abandoned former flume construction trail to the very edge of the valley. Here you can sneak up on and look down upon Hiʻilawe Waterfall and get to spots overlooking the valley that cannot be reached any other way. This is not just good physical exercise but also an education in the flora and fauna of the region, as Hugh is a proverbial fount of knowledge about the area. The Waipiʻo Waterfall Adventure hike is moderate, takes about four hours, and goes daily for $90 per person. Lunch, drinks, and all necessary equipment are supplied. Meet at their office in Honokaʻa.

**Waipiʻo Ridge Stables,** 808/775-1007, offers a 2.5-hour rim ride for $75 and a six-hour valley rim and hidden waterfall ride for $145. Check-in is at 8:45 A.M. or 12:45 P.M. An **ATV Adventure** takes you over backroads and dirt trails to the edge of the valley. Tours leave at 9:30 A.M. and 1 P.M. The ride is about two hours long and includes a snack. No riders under 100 pounds or over 300 pounds please. Reserve your spot by calling 808/775-1701. Starting at 9:30 A.M., a three-hour 4WD tour is offered by **Waipiʻo Rim Backroad Adventures,** 808/775-1122, that takes you in comfort to many of the same spots for exceptional vistas into the Waipiʻo Valley. This catered ride runs $85 per adult or $40 for kids 12 and under and is less physical but just as rewarding as the other adventures. The ATV, horseback riding, and 4WD tours meet at Waipiʻo Valley Artworks in Kukuihaele. Additional information and reservations for all three are available at 877/757-1414 or get information on the Web at www.topofwaipio.com.

### Camping in Waipiʻo

For camping in Waipiʻo Valley you must get a permit from the Kamehameha Schools Bishop Estate, Kona Office, 78-6831 Aliʻi Drive, Suite 232, Kailua-Kona, HI 96740, 808/322-5300. To get the permit, you must call at least two weeks in advance, giving the dates requested (four-day maximum) and number of people in your party. You will be mailed or faxed an application, and all adult members in your party must sign a "liability waiver" (parents or legal guardians must sign for any children) before the no-cost permit will be granted. Also, you must provide your own "Port-A-Potty" (yes, it's true) or "chemical toilet" and remove it when you leave. A small "camper style" potty, available in Hawaii at sporting goods stores, is sufficient. Camping is allowed in three designated areas only on the east side of Waipiʻo Stream. A resident caretaker in the valley will check on campers. Many hikers and campers have stayed in Waipiʻo overnight without a permit and usually have had no problem, but it is illegal! Remember, however, that most of the land, except for the beach, *is* privately owned.

The Waipiʻo Overlook has a 24-hour parking limit. That's good for day use of the valley, but not sufficient for most campers or for those attempting the trek to Waimanu Valley beyond. Check with Waipiʻo Valley Artworks for longer-stay parking arrangements.

## WAIMANU VALLEY

The hike down to Waipiʻo and over the *pali* to Waimanu Valley is considered by many to be one of the top three treks in Hawaii. You must be fully prepared for camping and in excellent condition to attempt this hike. Also, water from the streams and falls is not good for drinking due to irrigation and cattle grazing topside; bring purification tablets or boil or filter it to be safe. To get to Waimanu Valley, a switchback trail, locally called the Z trail, but otherwise known as the **Muliwai Trail,** leads up the 1,200-foot *pali,* starting about 100 yards inland from the west end of Waipiʻo Beach. The beginning of the switchback trail has a post with a painting that reads "Caution Menehune." Waimanu was bought by the State of Hawaii some years ago, and it is responsible for trail maintenance. The trail ahead is rough, as you go in and out of more than a dozen gulches before reaching Waimanu. After the ninth gulch is a trail shelter. Finally, below is Waimanu Valley, half the size of Waipiʻo but more verdant, and even wilder because it has been uninhabited for a longer time. Cross Waimanu Stream in the shallows where it meets the sea. The trail then continues along the beach and back into the valley about 1.5 miles, along the base of the far side, to Waiʻilikahi Falls, some 300 feet high. For drinking water (remember to treat it), walk along the west side of the *pali* until you find a likely waterfall. The Muliwai Trail to the Waimanu Valley floor is about 15 miles round-trip from the trailhead at the bottom of the *pali* in Waipiʻo Valley, or 19 miles round-trip from Waipiʻo Lookout. To stay overnight in Waimanu Valley you must have a (free) camping permit available through the Division of Forestry and Wildlife, P.O. Box 4849, Hilo, HI 96720, 808/974-4221, open Mon.–Fri. 8 A.M.–4 P.M. Apply not more than one month in advance. Your length of stay is limited to seven days and six nights. Each of the nine designated campsites along the beach has a fireplace, and there are three composting outhouses in the valley for use by campers. Carry out what you carry in!

Early in the 19th century, because of economic necessity brought on by the valley's remoteness, Waimanu was known for its *ʻokolehau* (moonshine). Solomon, one of the elders of the community at the time, decided that Waimanu had to diversify for the good of its people. He decided to raise domesticated pigs introduced by the Chinese, who roasted them with spices in rock ovens as a great delicacy. Solomon began to raise and sell the pigs commercially, but when he died, out of respect, no one wanted to handle his pigs, so they let them run loose. The pigs began to interbreed with feral pigs, and after a while there were so many pigs in Waimanu that they ate all the taro, bananas, and breadfruit. The porkers' voracious appetites caused a famine that forced the last remaining families of Waimanu to leave in the late 1940s. Most of the trails you will encounter are made by wild-pig hunters who still regularly go after Solomon's legacy.

According to oral tradition the first *kahuna lapaʻau* (healing doctor) of Hawaii was from Waimanu Valley. His disciples crossed and recrossed Waipiʻo Valley, greatly influencing the development of the area. Some of the *heiau* in Waipiʻo are specifically dedicated to the healing of the human torso; their origins are traced to the healing *kahuna* of Waimanu.

# Puna

The Puna district, south of Hilo on the southeast coast, was formed from rivers of lava spilling from Mauna Loa and Kilauea again and again over the last million years or so, and continues to be the most volcanically active part of the island today. The molten rivers stopped only when they hit the sea, where they fizzled and cooled, forming a chunk of semi-raw land that bulges into the Pacific—marking the state's easternmost point at **Cape Kumukahi.** These titanic lava flows have left phenomenal reminders of their power. The earth here is raw, rugged, and jagged. It has not yet had sufficient time to age and smooth. Black lava flows streak the land and grudgingly give over to green vegetation. On the coast, cliffs stand guard against the relentless sea,

and here and there lava tubes punctuate the coastline, leaving telltale signs of the mountains' might. Yet, the greatest of these features is the rift zone, where rupture lines dart out like streamers from a volcano's central crater. It is here along this zone that the unstable ground has slumped away and fallen into the ocean in great cataclysmic landslides and later settled to create benches of lowlands and the present coastline. It is along this rift zone that the mountain still shows its volatility, for the current active lava flow is disgorging from a vent along this line.

**Pahoa** is the major town in this region. It was at one time the terminus of a rail line that took commodities and people to Hilo. This was timber country and later sugarcane land, but since

Puna's coastal road

ROBERT NILSEN

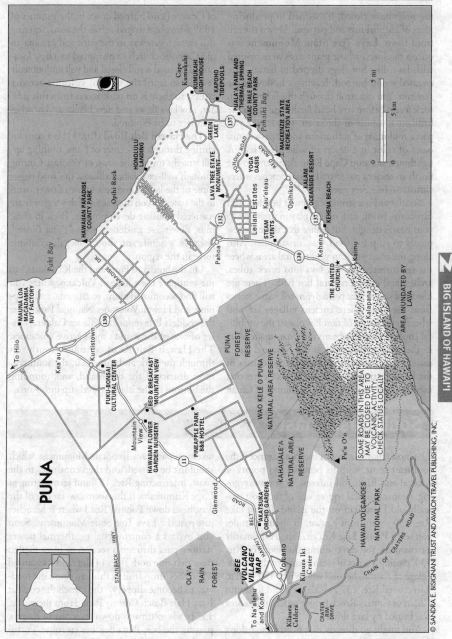

BIG ISLAND OF HAWAI'I

the mills have closed, it's turned to producing acres of anthuriums and papayas. Down the hill from town, **Lava Tree State Monument** was once a rainforest whose giant trees were covered with lava, like hot dogs dipped in batter. The encased wood burned, leaving a hollow stone skeleton. You can stroll through this lichen-green rock forest before you head farther east into the brilliant sunshine of the coast. Roads take you past a multitude of anthurium and papaya farms, oases of color in a desert of solid black lava. A lighthouse sits atop Cape Kumukahi, and to the north an ancient paved trail passes beaches where almost no one ever goes.

Southward is a string of popular beaches. You can camp, swim, surf, or just play in the water to your heart's delight, but realize that there are few places to stop for food, gas, or supplies. Also along the coast you can visit natural areas where the sea tortured the hot lava into caves, tubes, arches, and even a natural hot bath. There are historical sites where petroglyphs tell vague stories from the past, where ancient villages lay, and where generations of families placed the umbilical cords of their newborns into man-made holes in the rock. Hawaii Volcanoes National Park's eastern end covers the southwestern corner of the Puna district. The park's Visitors Center that used to stand just before the beginning of Chain of Craters Road burned down in the summer of 1989 when lava surged across the road, severing this eastern gateway to the park and causing an old Catholic church to be moved to a new location. This road is still closed and will undoubtedly remain so until the current volcanic activity ceases, so there is no park access from this side. Yet, raw lava flows and new black-sand beaches are there to be explored.

The **Hawaii Belt Road** (Rte. 11) is a corridor cutting through the center of Puna, running uphill straight toward the town of Volcano. Cutting through well-established villages, this road passes some of the largest and best-known flower farms in the state, and on both sides of this highway are scattered housing developments. Back in these hills, new-wave gardeners grow "Puna Butter" *pakalolo,* a significant, though illegal, economic force in the region.

On the border of Puna and the Ka'u district to the south are the village of **Volcano,** where you will find accommodations, restaurants, and shopping, and Hawaii Volcanoes National Park. Here the goddess Pele resides at Kilauea Caldera, center of one of the world's most active volcanoes. The Hawaii Belt Road continues southwest through the park and into Ka'u, the southernmost district of the Big Island, and, rounding the bottom of the island, travels up into Kona.

## Southeast Coast

The most enjoyable area in the Puna district is the southeast coast, with its beaches and points of natural and historical interest. It is an easygoing, steamy, tropical region, one of the most typically old Hawaiian on the island. If you take Rte. 130 south from Kea'au, in about 12 miles you reach Pahoa. Like Kea'au, Pahoa is primarily a crossroads. You can continue due south on Rte. 130, passing a series of steam vents, to the seaside village of Kaimu, beyond where Rte. 130 used to join coastal Rte. 137 at Kalapana and feed into Chain of Craters Road, before much of this area was buried by lava flows.

You might go directly east from Pahoa along Rte. 132. This lovely, tree-lined country road takes you past Lava Tree State Monument, which shouldn't be missed, and then continues to the coast, intersecting Rte. 137 and terminating at Cape Kumukahi. If this seems *too* far out of the way, head down Pohoiki Road where it branches just past the Lava Tree State Monument. Soon you bypass a controversial geothermal power station, pass through a section of huge mango trees that line both sides of the road (be careful when they drop fruit as this can cause the roadway to become slippery), then reach the coast at Isaac Hale Beach County Park. From there, Rte. 137 heads southwest down the coast to Kaimu, passing the best Puna beaches en route. Fortunately for you, this area of Puna is one of those places where no matter which way you decide to go, you really can't go wrong.

## PAHOA AND VICINITY

You can breeze through this "one-street" town, but you won't regret stopping if even for a few minutes. A raised wooden sidewalk passing false-front shops is fun to walk along to get a feeling of the early 20th century. Yet, a revitalized 1960s counterculture element thrives in town along with the workaday local population. The shops here are an eclectic mix of food vendors, restaurants, and antiques and crafts stores. The rest of town is a bit more utilitarian with a lumberyard, supermarkets, gas stations, more restaurants, clothing stores, a church, schools, police and fire departments, post office, Olympic-size swimming pool, and the island's oldest operating movie theater. At one time Pahoa boasted *the* largest sawmill in America. Its buzz saw ripped 'ohi'a railway ties for the Santa Fe and other railroads. It was into one of these ties that the golden spike uniting the East and West coasts of the Mainland was supposedly driven. Many local people earned their livelihood from 'ohi'a charcoal

that they made and sold all over the island until it was made obsolete by the widespread use of kerosene and gas introduced in the early 1950s. Pahoa's commercial heart went up in flames in 1955. Along the main street was a tofu factory that had a wood-fired furnace. The old fellow who owned the factory banked his fires as usual before he went home for the night. Somehow, they got out of control and burned all the way down to the main alley dividing the commercial district. The only reason the fire didn't jump the alley was because a papaya farmer happened to be around and had a load of water on the back of his truck, which he used to douse the buildings and save the town.

Pahoa is attempting to protect and revitalize its commercial center and bring new life to vintage buildings like the Akebono Theater, where classic movies are once again being shown. Pahoa has one of the highest concentrations of old buildings still standing in Hawaii that are easily accessible. Although the center of town has been bypassed by a new road, make sure to enter the town and stroll along the tiny backroads.

To replace timber and sugar, Pahoa is in the process of becoming the anthurium capital of

Pahoa's main street, with its raised walkways and old storefronts, is a reminder of days gone by.

the world. As you get close to Pahoa, coming from Kea'au, you'll see black shade cloth draping anthurium nurseries, sheltering magnificent specimens of the usually red flowers, plus plenty of white, green, and even black anthuriums. Papaya is also grown here in large quantities, and a number of farms are located below town toward the coast.

## Lava Tree State Monument

In 1790, slick, fast-flowing pahoehoe lava surged through this 'ohi'a forest, covering the tree trunks from the ground to about a 12-foot level. The moisture inside the trees cooled the lava, forming a hardened shell. At the same time, tremors and huge fissures cracked the earth in the area. When the eruption ended, the still-hot lava drained away through the fissures, leaving the encased tree trunks standing like sentinels, only to burn away later. The floor of the forest is so smooth in some areas that the lava seems like asphalt. Each lava tree has its own personality; some resemble totem poles, and it doesn't take much imagination to see old, craggy faces staring back at you. Many still stand, while others have tumbled to the ground where you can look inside their pipelike structure. The most spectacular part of the park is near the entrance. Immense trees loom over cavernous cracks (*puka*) in the earth and send their roots, like stilled waterfalls, tumbling down into them. A 20-minute walk around this park makes a pleasant stop on your journey. To get to Lava Tree, take Rte. 132 east from Pahoa and on about three miles through a tree tunnel of towering albizia trees to the well-marked entrance on the left. Drinking water is not available but toilets are.

## Accommodations

Right downtown, occupying the upper floor of a building erected in 1910, is the **Pahoa Orchid Inn,** 808/965-9664. The stairway leads to a 2nd floor lobby above Luquin's Mexican Restaurant; as you ascend imagine how many others have grasped that rail over the decades. This small hotel has a handful of rooms, most with cable TV, lace curtains, and white wicker furniture like grandma used to have on her porch. Other furniture is reminiscent of the 1930s and '40s, and ceiling fans help cool the rooms. While simple, everything is neat and clean, and it went through a renovation a few years ago. Rooms run $35–55 a night with a shared bath or $65 with a private bath.

There are a number of bed-and-breakfasts in the general Pahoa area. One in the Leilani Estates just south of town is **Pearl's Shell B&B,** 808/965-7015 or 877/202-4255, at 13-3432 Kupono St., pearlsh@aloha.net, www.pearl-shellbb.com. Pearl's Shell has three rooms, two larger rooms with queen beds, and private entrances and baths, and a smaller room off the common room with a double bed and private bath. A full breakfast on the lanai is included in the room prices, which run $55 for the small room and $70 for the two larger rooms. An ordinary place in an extraordinary location, this bed-and-breakfast has a finely landscaped yard where flowers will delight your eyes and birds will call out in melodies from the surrounding thick forest.

## Food

**Luquin's Mexican Restaurant,** 808/965-9990, open daily until 9 P.M., is a reasonably priced Mexican restaurant that offers the usual enchiladas, burritos, tacos, combination platters, and Mexican and American breakfasts, most in the $6–8 range but with some up to $15. Some say it's the best on the island. Margaritas are a house specialty at the cantina. A local favorite, you'll be hard pressed to find a seat on Friday or Saturday evenings.

**Paolo's Bistro** Tuscan Italian restaurant, 808/965-7033, open Tues.–Sun. 5:30–9 P.M., is the place for fine dining in town. Dine inside at tables topped with fine tablecloths or have a seat in the patio outside. Start with an appetizer, $7–8, like a bowl of minestrone soup or fresh mozzarella antipasto, and follow that with ravioli with spinach and ricotta or pasta with prawns. Other entrées might be chicken Marcella, cioppino, raviolli gorgonzola, or pasta al pesto, mostly in the $13–18 range, and there are always desserts like tiramisu or strawberries marinated in chardonnay. To round out the meal, have a cup of espresso or a caffé latté. A bit pricier than other places in town, Paolo's serves wonderfully tasty food that's worth the extra cost.

Almost next door is **Sawasdee Thai Cuisine,** 808/965-8186. Open daily except Sunday 5–8:30 P.M., this intimate eatery serves memorable Thai food with a fine blend of herbs and spices. Your mouth will not be disappointed. Using local organic ingredients, menu choices include appetizers like po pia spring rolls, soups such as po tak hot and sour seafood soup, and a variety of salads. Rice, noodle, and curry dishes make up the main entrée choices, most in the $7–12 range, and any can be made vegetarian if you wish.

Across the street is **Papa's,** a café with nearly everything under $6 and all choices are organic, healthy, and nutritious. Open every day except Sunday.

Other eateries in town include **Ludi's** for Filipino and local grinds and **Big Jake's Island BBQ. Jo Mama** is a bar that occasionally has music but features a local-style breakfast all day long. For the late night drinkers and revelers, try the very local **Punatix Lounge.**

## Shopping

When you pull into Pahoa you are greeted by the **Pahoa Village Center,** a small shopping center where you'll find a Laundromat, a video store, pharmacy, and the Black Rock Restaurant. Across the street is a 7-Eleven, and just down the road is the full-service **Pahoa Cash and Carry** grocery store, which has enough for any supplies or incidentals that you may need.

**Pahoa Natural Groceries,** 808/965-8322, now in a new building on a side street just off the main drag, is open weekdays 7:30 A.M.–8 P.M., Sunday until 6 P.M. The store specializes in organic food items and is one of the finest health food stores on the Big Island. It has an excellent selection of fresh veggies, organic bulk grains, herbs and minerals, deli items, a hot food table, and a very good bakery selection. There's a kitchen on the premises, so the food is not only healthful but very fresh.

At the corner is **Pahoa Natural Emporium,** 808/965-6634, open daily 10 A.M.–6 P.M., with a small but excellent selection of jewelry, Guatemalan clothing, Balinese batik, Yucatan hammocks, gifts, magazines, and cards. The Emporium also displays artwork, some by local artists, and a colorful selection of rugs. The shirts and dresses are all cotton and rayon. Some of the clothing is designed or handmade here in Puna. The back room displays a profusion of these vibrant rainbow-colored clothes.

You'll find two **farmers' markets** in town. On Saturday 7:30 A.M.–noon at the Sacred Heart Catholic Church is the more typical of these markets, with a variety of food and flowers. More a combination farmers' market and flea market, the other is held Sunday 9 A.M.–1 P.M., down the highway near mile marker 8. Very popular, look for the signs and the crowds.

# ALONG THE COAST

All of Puna's beaches, parks, and campgrounds lie along coastal Rte. 137 stretching for 20 miles from Kumukahi to Kaimu. Route 137 is also called Kapoho-Kalapana Beach Road or simply the "Red Road" because of its distinctive crushed red lava rock color. Surfers, families, transients, even nude-sunbathing "buffs" have their favorite spots along this southeast coast. For the most part, swimming is possible, but be cautious during high tide. There is plenty of sun, snorkeling sites, and good fishing, and the campgrounds are almost always available.

## Cape Kumukahi

It's fitting that Kumukahi means "First Beginning" since it is the easternmost point of Hawaii and was recognized as such by the original Polynesian settlers. Follow Rte. 132 past Lava Tree for about 10 miles to the coast, where a lighthouse sits like an exclamation point on clinker lava. Along the way, get an instant course in volcanology: You can easily chart the destructive and regenerative forces at work on Hawaii. At the five-mile marker you have a glimpse of the lava flow of 1955. Tiny plants give the lava a greenish cast, and shrubs are already eating into it, turning it to soil. Papaya orchards grow in the raw lava of an extensive flat basin. The contrast between the

**BIG ISLAND OF HAWAI'I**

black, lifeless earth and the vibrant green trees is startling. In the center of the flatland rises a cinder cone, a caldera of a much older mini-volcano unscathed by the modern flows; it is gorgeous with lush vegetation. Farther on is the lava flow of 1960, and you can see at a glance how different it was from the flow of five years earlier. When Rte. 132 intersects Rte. 137, continue straight ahead down the unpaved road for about two miles to the Cape Kumukahi Lighthouse. People in these parts swear that on the fateful night in 1960 when the nearby village of Kapoho was consumed by the lava flow, an old woman (a favorite guise of Madame Pele) came to town begging for food and was turned away by everyone. She next went to the lighthouse asking for help and was cordially treated by the lighthouse keeper. When the flow was at its strongest, it came within yards of the lighthouse and then miraculously split, completely encircling the structure but leaving it unharmed as the flow continued out to sea for a considerable distance.

Route 137 continues north and in short order plunges into a forest of trees; the road turns into a rugged and rutted dirt lane that is often full of potholes and pools of water. Proceed with caution, this stretch is not kind to low-slung rental cars. If you continue, you will pass secluded private property and as-yet-undeveloped county park land and pop out on the other side at the bottom of the Hawaiian Shores Estates subdivision, which cascades down the hill from Pahoa. You're better off to turn south and enjoy other sights of the coast.

## Kapoho Tidepools

Although the old village of Kapoho was covered by lava a few short decades ago, a new community has been rebuilt to take its place. This new village has a mixture of retirees, working-class families, and vacation rentals. The section closest to the lighthouse is a gated community; the next one south is open. You can snorkel in the tidepools along the coast fronting this village. They can be enjoyed by anyone who takes the time to seek them out. Remember that this is a quiet rural community with pride in its natural resources, so be respectful when you visit. Turn

onto Kapoho Kai Drive and head down into this small development. Park off the roadway along the road farthest down toward the water. It's a short way across the lava field toward the ocean before these pools become apparent. Wear shoes, as the lava is sharp. Best at high tide or when the tide is coming in, the pools provide good snorkeling in a safe environment.

Across the highway from the entrance road to the gated community is Kapoho Crater, sometimes called Green Mountain. This is a low volcanic cone that is thickly covered in trees and that has a small natural lake in its caldera known as Green Lake.

## Puala'a Park and Thermal Spring

Back on Rte. 137, continue south under the dense tree cover. Between mile markers 10 and 11, just after the road narrows, you come upon **Puala'a Park,** also known as Ahalanui. Quietly opened by the County of Hawai'i on July 4, 1993, this lovely, 1.3-acre park was an ancient fishing village where a few families still maintain homes. The park features a sand-bottom pond that's been formed into a pool, thermally heated to a perfect temperature. Step in and relax in its soothing warmness. Some people use the pond to do watsu, a type of in-water massage. The swimming is safe except during periods of very high surf, when ocean water washes in over the outer cement wall. The park is perfect for families with young children. The pond is now watched over by a lifeguard, and toilets have been set up for your convenience. The new parking area is open 7 A.M.–7 P.M.; otherwise park across the street in the old lot.

## Isaac Hale Beach County Park

You can't miss this beach park (often referred to as Pohoiki) located on Pohoiki Bay at the junction of Rte. 137 and Pohoiki Road. Just look for a jumble of boats and trailers parked under the palms. At one time Pohoiki Bay served the Hawaiians as a canoe landing, then later became the site of a commercial wharf for the Puna Sugar Company. It remains the only boat launching area for the entire Puna Coast, used by pleasure boaters and commercial fishermen. Due to this dual role, it's often very crowded. Amenities include a pavilion, restrooms, and a picnic area; potable water is not available. Camping is permitted with a county permit. Experienced surfers dodge the rip-current in the center of the bay. Pohoiki Bay is also one of the best scuba and snorkel sites on the island. Within walking distance of the salt-and-pepper beach is another thermal spring in a lava sink surrounded by lush vegetation. It's popular with tourists and residents alike and provides a unique and relaxing way to wash away sand and salt. To find it, face away from the sea and go to the left along a small but well-worn path that leads between the water and a beach house. Be sure to ask permission if someone is around. The pools are warm, small, and tranquil. Harmless, tiny brine shrimp nibble at your toes while you soak.

## MacKenzie State Recreation Area

This state park was named for forest ranger A. J. MacKenzie, highly regarded throughout the Puna district. He was killed in the area in 1938. The park's 13 acres sit among a cool grove of ironwoods originally planted by MacKenzie. A portion of the old King's Hwy., scratched out by prisoners in the 19th century as a form of community service, bisects the area. In the past, many people who first arrived on the Big Island hung out at MacKenzie until they could get their start. Consequently, the park received its share of hard-core types, which has earned it a reputation for rip-offs. Mostly it's safe, rather deserted, and not particularly well looked after now, but if you're camping, take precautions with your valuables. The entire coastline along MacKenzie is bordered by low but rugged black-lava seacliffs. Swimming is dangerous, but the fishing is excellent. Be extremely careful when walking along the water's edge, especially out on the fingers of lava; over the years, people have been swept away by freak waves. Within the park is a skylight of a collapsed lava tube, one end of which exits at the seacliff and the other a stone's throw inland and across the road. Take a flashlight and be careful if you venture inside. MacKenzie Park is located along Rte. 137, two miles south of Pohoiki. Picnic facilities are available, but there is no drinking water. A state permit is required for overnight camping.

## Kehena Beach

Pass the tiny village of 'Opihikao, where Kama'ili Road drops down from Rte. 130 to the Red Road. 'Opihikao was a major town along this coast in the 1800s but has faded away into quaint quietude. Just beyond this community the close canopy of trees opens, the road becomes wider, and the vistas broaden. Here are picture postcard coastal scenes as good as any on the island. Cross over two sections of the 1955 lava flow and soon you come upon Kehena Beach. Kehena is actually two pockets of black-sand beach below a low seacliff. Entrance to the beach is marked only by a scenic pulloff, about four miles south of 'Opihikao; usually a half dozen cars are parked there. At one time Kehena was very popular, and a stone staircase led down to the beach. In 1975 a strong earthquake jolted the area, breaking up the stairway and lowering the beach by three feet. Now access is via a well-worn path, but make sure to wear sneakers because the lava is rough. The ocean here is dangerous, and often pebbles and rocks whisked along by the surf can injure your legs. Once down on the beach, head north for the smaller patch of sand, because the larger patch is open to the sea and can often be awash in waves. The black sand is hot, but a row of coconut palms provides shade. The inaccessibility of Kehena makes it a favorite "no-hassle" nude beach with many "full" sunbathers congregating here.

## End of the Road

Just near the lava-inundated village of Kalapana, Routes 130 and 137 come to an abrupt halt where Madame Pele has repaved the road with lava. At the end of the line near the village of Kaimu you come to a barricaded area. Volcanic activity has continued virtually unabated beyond here since January 1983, when lava fountains soared 1,500 feet into the sky and produced a cone more than 800 feet tall. The initial lava flow was localized at Pu'u O'o vent, but after dozens of eruptive episodes it shifted eastward to Kupa'ianaha, which continuously produced about half a million cubic yards of lava per day. Today, it is mostly erupting once again from flank vents on Pu'u O'o. The lava flows eight

BIG ISLAND OF HAWAI'I

miles to the sea, mostly through lava tubes. It has inundated almost 40 square miles, caused $61 million worth of property damage, and added more than 500 acres of new land to the Puna Coast—and it's still growing. Unfortunately, these lava flows have also completely covered the very popular Kaimu Beach Park (also known as Black Sand Beach), Harry K. Brown Beach Park, the national park's visitors center, and 13th-century **Waha'ulu Heiau**. For a full description of **Chain of Craters Road** and recent volcanic activity, see the following chapter on Hawaii Volcanoes National Park. Parts of the road are still open, but only *within* the park and from the other end.

Volcanic activity has pretty much ceased in the Kaimu area and the lava solidified. You can walk out over the new lava directly toward the sea to a new black-sand beach but you are prohibited from going west where you can experience difficulty if you walk too far toward where the lava still flows. Some hazards you may encounter are brushfires, smoke, ash, and methane gas, which is extremely explosive. You can also fall through the thin-crusted lava into a tube, which will immediately reduce you to a burnt offering to Pele and unceremoniously deposit your ashes into the sea! New lava can cut like broken glass, and molten lava can be flung through the air by steam explosions, especially near the coastline. Seacliffs collapse frequently, and huge boulders can be tossed several hundred feet into the air. The steam clouds contain minerals that can cause burning eyes, throat and skin irritations, and difficulty breathing.

If you are still intrigued, realize that you are on the most unstable piece of real estate on the face of the earth. For those maniacs, fools, adventurers, and thrill-seekers who just can't stay away, give yourself up for dead, and proceed. Follow the old roadbed, up and down, over the lava. When you can no longer discern the road, pick your way across the undulating lava field, but don't get too close to the sea or the active flows. Observers say that every day, huge chunks fall off into the sea. As you look back at the mountain you can see heat waves rising from the land upon which you are standing. A camera with a zoom lens or a pair of binoculars accentuates this phe-

nomenon. The whole mountain waves in front of you. As you walk closer to the sea, the lava cools and you can see every type there is: rope lava, lava toes, lava fingers. The tortured flow, which may crinkle as you walk over it, has created many imaginative shapes: gargoyles, medieval faces, dolphins, and mythical creatures. At the coast, when lava pours into the sea, it may create a white spume of steam lifting 200–300 feet into the air. No other place in the world gives you the opportunity to be the first person to tread upon the earth's newest land.

In Kaimu, you can safely walk the short distance over the lava to the ocean. At the end of the road, head straight toward the water and in 15 minutes you are there. The new beach is seaward about a quarter mile from where Kaimu Beach Park used to be. Now, raw and rugged lava meets the sea and is slowly being turned into black sand once again.

In August 2001, the mayor allowed a road to be plowed from the end of Route 130 toward the lava flow for a better view of the activity. Many island people applauded this effort to open access to the inundated area of Kalapana, but the road was closed in March 2002 when part of the new access route was destroyed by additional lava flow. Time will tell if and when this area will again be opened to traffic.

## The Painted Church

Star of the Sea Catholic Church is a small but famous structure better known as "The Painted Church." Originally located near Kalapana, this church was in grave danger of being overrun by a lava flow. An effort to save the historic church from the lava was mounted, and it has been moved to a location along Rte. 130, just above Kaimu. A brief history of the area asserts that the now-inundated Kalapana was a spiritual magnet for Roman Catholic priests. Old Spanish documents support evidence that a Spanish priest, crossing the Pacific from Mexico, actually landed very near here in 1555. Father Damien, famous priest of the Molokai Leper Colony, established a grass church about two miles north and conducted a school when he first arrived in the islands in 1864. The present church dates from 1928, when Father Everest Gielen began its construction. Like an inspired but much less talented Michelangelo, this priest painted the ceiling of the church, working mostly at night by oil lamp. Father Everest was transferred to Lanai in 1941, and the work wasn't completed until 1964, when George Heidler, an artist from Atlanta, Georgia, came to Kalapana and decided to paint the unfinished altar section. The artwork itself can only be described as gaudy but sincere. The colors are wild blues, purples, and oranges. The ceiling is adorned with symbols, portraits of Christ, the angel Gabriel, and scenes from the Nativity. Behind the altar, a painted perspective gives the impression that you're looking down a long hallway at an altar that hangs suspended in air. The church is definitely worth a few minutes.

## Steam Vents

Along Rte. 130, about halfway between Pahoa and Kaimu, look for a small, unobtrusive sign that reads Scenic Overlook. Pull off and walk about 75 yards toward the sea until you find four non-toxic steam vents. Low mounds of lava with warm steam issuing from cracks in the earth, they are used by many local people as natural saunas. People come here to climb into the openings and relax in the warmth. On occasion, these vents will be overused, garbage is left around, or the surrounding area soiled as a toilet, but by and large they provide a wonderful natural experience.

## Accommodations

For vacation rental homes at Kapoho, contact **A Piece of Paradise**, P.O. Box 1314, Pahoa, HI 96778, 808/965-1224, www.apoParadise.com. Located in the oceanfront gated community, a one-bedroom cottage here rents for $99 a night while several two- and three-bedroom homes run $120–195 a night; three nights minimum. Each is completely furnished with full kitchen and living areas and located a few short steps from the ocean and tidepools.

The embracing arms of the Puna rainforest surround you as you make your way down the driveway to the quiet and secluded **Yoga Oasis** re-

treat center. Set on 26 acres of forest, with plenty of fruit and nut trees and numerous stands of bamboo, this yoga center and alternative accommodation offers yoga workshops and, on occasion, other health related retreats. While you can come for the accommodation only, the optional morning yoga classes are a treat and the seclusion is perfect for those who just want a little time to themselves, but the location offers easy access to coastal Puna sights, restaurants in Pahoa, and is close enough to both Hilo and Hawaii Volcanoes National Park for easy day trips. Private rooms with shared bath in the main building or a tentalow run $60 single or $80 double, a little higher with a yoga package (morning yoga class and a vegetarian breakfast). The secluded Coconut Grove tentalow with its outdoor shower runs $125 single or $145 double, and this includes breakfast and yoga class. Two nights minimum for these. Sleeping up to four, the redwood and cedar "treehouse" runs $225 a night for a couple, breakfast and morning yoga included; each additional person $25, three nights minimum. Healthy, home-made vegetarian meals are created three times a day and run $10–15, while massage and other activities are added features at additional cost. Workshops and classes are held in the large screened exercise rooms on the 2nd floor of the main building. For information about yoga classes and reservations for staying, call 800/965-8460 or 800/274-4446, info@yogaoasis.org, www.yogaoasis.org.

**Kalani Oceanside Resort**, RR 2 Box 4500, Pahoa Beach Rd., HI 96778, 808/965-7828 or 800/800-6886, kalani@kalani.com, www.kalani.com, is a nonprofit, international conference and holistic retreat center, a haven where people come when they truly want to step aside for a time. The entrance is located a few miles east of Kaimu on Rte. 137 between mile markers 17 and 18, on the mountain side of the road. Look for a large Visitors Welcome sign and proceed uphill until you see the office and sundries shop. Depending upon the yearly schedule, a variety of activities include massage, hula, meditation, yoga, lei-making, *lau hala*-weaving, and hikes, for men, women, couples, and families, gay and straight. The grounds have a botanical atmosphere, with a rain-fed swimming pool (clothing optional after 7:30 P.M.), a watsu pool, hot tub, whirlpool tub, assembly studios, classrooms, cottages, and cedar lodges with kitchen facilities. Kalani is not an oceanfront property and only some rooms have an ocean view over the trees. Rates are $60 single for a dorm room with shared bath, $105 single and $110 double for a private room with shared bath, $125 single and $135 double for a private room with private bath, $135 single and $150 double for a guest cottage, and $210 single and $240 double for the tree house. Rates are $10 higher from November through the end of April. You can also camp for $20 a night, or cheaper than that per person as a family. A blown conch shell calls you to breakfast at 8 A.M., lunch at noon, and dinner at 6 P.M. (nonguests welcome). The meals cost $8, $10, and $16 respectively, with a meal ticket pre-purchased at the office. Food is served from the buffet line in the open-air dining hall, and fruits and vegetables from the property are used when possible. Entertainment by resident or local musicians is performed in a very casual setting at the Olelo Cafe next to the office some evenings until 11 P.M. The generator (and hence the lights) goes off at 11 P.M., but candles are provided for night owls. Kalani is not for everyone, but if you are looking for unpretentious peace and quiet, healthful food, and inner development, this is one place you may find it.

During a recent eruption of the volcano, lava stopped about 20 feet from the front of **Hale Kipa O Kiana,** 808/965-8661 or 800/682-3592, RR 2 Box 4874 Kalapana Shores, Pahoa, HI 96778, haleokiana@aol.com, www.halekipao kiana.com. Open again, the one downstairs room

with a private entrance and bath goes for $335 a week with a modified continental breakfast each morning; one week minimum, monthly rates available. No credit cards. The room has a small refrigerator and microwave, television, phone, and laundry facilities. Located on a cul de sac, this house is quiet, fairly secluded, and perfect for naturists, although anyone is welcome.

For a larger house to rent, contact **Kaimu Bay Vacation Rentals,** 808/878-6682, fax 808/878-3204, kaufman@maui.net. Located at the end of the road, across from new lava and near the new black-sand beach, this basic contemporary style house has a kitchen, living area, with two bedrooms and a bath upstairs and an additional bedroom and bath down, television, phone, and laundry facilities. Rent runs $83 a night for the two bedroom or $105 for the entire house; weekly rates are available.

Set next to the steam vents is **Steam Vent Inn,** a large home with rental rooms that also has a couple of steam vents on its property. Each of the four rooms has two queen beds and runs $75–120, including a continental breakfast. Four hostel rooms with private or shared baths run $17–35. For information, contact 808/965-8800 or look at www.steamventinn.com.

## Food

Right where the roads ends you'll find **Verna's V Drive In** for quick and easy local eats. Have yourself a plate lunch, loco moco, or burger, fries, and a drink, before you head out for the short jaunt over the lava to the water. Usually open until 5 P.M., this is a favorite lunch spot for tour buses that bring guests to view the new lava and beach.

# Along the Hawai'i Belt Road

## KEA'AU

Kea'au is the first town south of Hilo on Rte. 11, and although pleasant enough, it's little more than a Y in the road. Before the sugar mill closed in the mid-1990s, this was a bustling town with great swaths of the surrounding land in cane. Kea'au and the numerous subdivisions that have mushroomed on both sides of the highway running to Pahoa and up to Volcano have become bedroom communities to Hilo. At the junction of Rte. 11 (Hawai'i Belt Road) and Rte. 130 is **Kea'au Shopping Center,** a small shopping mall with a handful of variety stores, a Laundromat, a post office, restaurants, a Bank of America, and gas station. Here, the Sure Save Supermarket has not only groceries but plenty of sundries and a decent camera department. Route 130 heads southeast from here to the steamy south coast, while Route 11 (Hawai'i Belt Road) heads southwest and passes through the mountain villages of Kurtistown, Mountain View, Glenwood, and Volcano at approximately 10-mile intervals, then enters Hawaii Volcanoes National Park. The Belt Road, although only two lanes, is straight, well surfaced, and scrupulously maintained. When heading to the Puna coast, it's easiest now to take the Kea'au Bypass Road around the east side of town, right past the old sugar mill, so you don't get bogged down in town traffic.

### Food

The local Dairy Queen, in the Kea'au Town Center, not only makes malts and sundaes but serves breakfast, lunch, and dinner. Also in the shopping center is **Kea'au Natural Foods,** 808/966-8877, with a large stock of organic food items, herbs, and grains but no juice or snack bar. However, pre-made sandwiches from the deli case are always available. Have a look at the bulletin board for information on alternative happenings in the community. Open Mon.-Fri. 8:30 A.M.–8 P.M., Saturday until 7 P.M., and Sunday 9:30 A.M.–5 P.M. Have a beer while you wait for your laundry to wash at the Suds 'n Duds Laundromat.

For a more congenial environment, try **Charley's Bar and Grill,** 808/966-7589, for a cool one or a light meal. Serving sandwiches, burgers, pasta, and a few other entrées, Charley's is open Wed.-Sat. until 2 A.M. and other nights until midnight. Several nights a week there are live bands and dancing (cover), and on other evenings you can still sing along to the karaoke music, shoot pool, or throw darts. This is perhaps the nicest place in town for a relaxing evening out.

**Lemongrass,** a simple unadorned Vietnamese and Thai restaurant, serves ethnic foods in filling portions with hardly anything more than $8. Just as basic, just as cheap, but even smaller, the **Kea'au Chop Suey House** next door has a good variety in its menu, including several vegetarian dishes.

On the far side of the shopping center, **Verna's Drive-In** serves plate lunches and drinks.

## MOUNTAIN TOWNS

### Kurtistown

Near the highway in what might be considered the center of town are the post office, B. J.'s 76 Service Station, and the **J. Hara Store,** the best-stocked store on the highway for sundries and groceries.

Just south of there, down 'Ola'a Road is the **Fuku-Bonsai Cultural Center.** This institution is a combination nursery, mail-order shop, bonsai display garden, and bonsai exhibition center. It is also the nonprofit Mid-Pacific Bonsai Foundation's Hawaii State Bonsai Repository. Have a walk through the garden and marvel at the miniature trees and plants demonstrating Japanese, Chinese, and Hawaiian styles, and note the similarities and differences. There are some 200 specimens in formal exhibition. Inside are educational displays of tools, techniques, and more plants. Diminutive plants can be purchased in the shop to carry away, or they can be shipped anywhere in the country. Fuku-Bonsai is open Mon.-Sat. 8 A.M.–4 P.M. For anyone interested in raising bonsai or simply looking at these wonderfully sculpted

**BIG ISLAND OF HAWAI'I**

## ANTHURIUM

Originally a native of Central America, the anthurium was introduced into Hawaii in 1889 by Samuel M. Damon, an English missionary. Damon discovered that Hawaii's climate and volcanic soil made an ideal environment for this exotic flower. Over the years since then, anthurium production has turned into a million-dollar export industry with all the major growers located on the Big Island. Anthurium grow on a tall stock as a glossy and heart-shaped flower bract, with a yellowish flower spike arising from the stock at the bract's base, and accompanied by large shiny green leaves. The most common anthurium has dark red bracts about the size of the palm of a hand, but they have been bred in a variety of colors, from lily white to green, purple, and black, and from silver dollar size to as big as a plate.

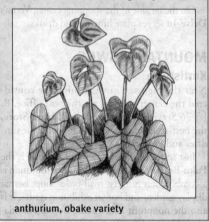

anthurium, obake variety

DIANA LASICH HARPER

plants, this is a worthy stop. For a mail-order catalog, contact P.O. Box 6000, Kurtistown, HI 96760, 808/982-9880, sales@fukubonsai.com, www.fukubonsai.com.

Just over two miles up the road is the **Dan De Luz's Woods** showroom, 808/968-6607, which displays all sorts of turned wooden bowls, small wood boxes, and other small objects made of tropical island woods. With such a variety, one look here gives you a good sense of the types of wood that are grown on the island.

Look for a vintage plantation house painted blue a short ways beyond and on the opposite side of the highway. This is **Tinny Fisher's Antique Shop,** owned and operated by Charles and Dorothy Wittig. What started as "yard sale treasures" turned into a unique curio, antiques, and collectibles shop. Open daily except Monday noon–6 P.M., the shop has all kinds of antiques and collectibles from Asia and Hawaii, including glass balls, Asian furniture, jewelry, and glassware galore. Tinny's also features a good Hawaiiana collection, with artifacts from the ancient days like *kukui* nut lamps, poi pounders, and stone knives.

## Mountain View

Mountain View is a village of nurseries specializing in anthuriums. Many of them sport signs and some invite you to look around. **Hawaiian Flower Gardens Nursery,** 808/968-8255 or 877/434-0555, open daily except Sunday, is one. There you can learn a little about the history of these fancy exotic flowers and see all sizes and colors. This is the home of the Toyama Red Anthurium, but they come in all shades from stark white to green and deep purple, and sizes from delicate tiny petals and those as big as a spade. Several other nurseries that not only grow but ship these lovely flowers are **Albert Isa Nursery,** P.O. Box 17, Mt. View, HI 96771, 808/968-6125; and **Hale Ohia Gardens,** P.O. Box 1042, Mt. View, HI 96771, 800/273-3848, fax 808/968-6892. For mail-order flowers, prices generally range $35–75 plus shipping costs, depending upon the mix.

Along the highway is a mini-mart, a post office, gas station, and **Verna's Too Drive In** serving plate lunches, sandwiches, burgers, and shakes. As you pass through, take a minute to explore the short side road into the village itself. It seems that every house has a garden of ferns, flowers, and native trees. On this old road through the village is **Mt. View Bakery,** open 8 A.M.–3:30 P.M. except Sunday, home of the famous stone cookies—have them with milk!

## Accommodations

**Bed & Breakfast Mountain View,** P.O. Box 963, Kurtistown, HI 96760, 808/968-6868 or

888/698-9896, fax 808/968-7017, info@bbmt view.com, www.bbmtview.com, is owned and operated by Jane and Linus Chao, both internationally known artists. The couple's inspired artwork graces the home. A residence and artist studio, this B&B lies just outside the village of Mountain View along S. Kulani Road, on a landscaped four-acre parcel with a marvelous view north to Mauna Kea. Enter through an iron gate under a canopy of trees. The spacious guest rooms are modern in all amenities and equipped with king, queen, or twin beds; two have private bathrooms, two others share. Everyone has use of the common room for reading, TV, or simply appreciating the fine view. A full breakfast is served each morning in the dining room, and each day the offering is different. Room rates run $55–95 daily. For peace and serenity and inspiration of the artistic soul, there is no better place than Bed & Breakfast Mountain View.

Farther into this labyrinth of roads south of Mt. View, down along Pikake Street, is **Pineapple Park B&B Hostel,** P.O. Box 639, Kurtistown, HI 96760, 808/968-8170 or 877/865-2266, park@aloha.net, www.pineapple-park.com. This is country living in modern style. A bed in the bunkroom runs $20 a night and a double room runs $55; these rooms share kitchen and bath facilities and have use of the common room where there's Internet access. No breakfast is provided. A private room for $85 is available with breakfast, and a detached bungalow large enough for six people can be rented for $175 a night. Tenting runs $12 and old buses

converted into sleeping rooms with shared detached toilets run $35. Check-out is before 10 A.M., check-in until 9 P.M., and quiet time after 11 P.M. This is a smoke-free environment.

## Glenwood

Located between mile markers 19 and 20, this town offers a gas station and **Hirano's General Store** for a few basic provisions. Tours of the Kazumura Lava Tube, reputedly the longest lava tube system in the world, are offered three times daily except Sunday. Call 808/969-9622 for reservations; pick up is across the street from Hirano's store. Alternately, call Harry Shick, 808/967-7208, for a guided tour of a portion of the cave. Volcano Cave Adventures, 808/968-0763 or 808/968-8606, also offers unpretentious personalized tours into a rainforest cave. These underground adventures travel several hundred feet through undeveloped lava tubes for a raw glimpse of the bowels of Mother Nature. Each trip runs about 1.5–2 hours.

A few minutes beyond town you pass **Akatsuka Orchid Gardens,** 808/967-8234, open daily 8:30 A.M.–5 P.M., except major holidays. If tour buses don't overflow the parking lot, stop in for a look at how orchids are grown. In the covered showroom, an incredible variety of orchids are on display and for sale, and neat little souvenirs are sold in the gift shop. Akatsuka ships cut flowers and potted orchids anywhere in the country. For a mail-order catalog, contact P.O. Box 220, Volcano, HI 96785, 888/967-6669, fax 808/967-7140.

# Volcano Village

You shouldn't miss taking a ride through the village of Volcano, a beautiful old settlement with truly charming houses and cottages outlined in ferns. Follow the signs off the main highway near mile marker 26 to the Old Volcano Highway, which is the main drag through the village. Tiny one-lane roads lace this community, which sits virtually atop one of the world's undeniable "power spots." This is a heavily forested area with no sidewalks or street lights. Lighting is gener-

ally subdued, so it can be very dark at night. At about 4,000 feet, it gets surprisingly cool and, of course, it often rains—over 150 inches a year. Summer daytime temperatures average 75°F, around 65°F in winter. At night it drops to 55°F in summer and into the 40s or less in winter. The fog rolls in most late afternoons, obscuring distant views but bestowing on the village an otherworldly charm. The area is so green and so vibrant that it appears surrealistic. With flowers, ferns, and trees

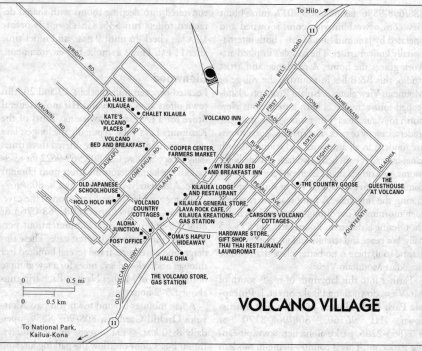

WRIGHT RD.

HAUNINI RD.

KA HALE IKI KILAUEA

KATE'S VOLCANO PLACES

CHALET KILAUEA

VOLCANO BED AND BREAKFAST

OLD JAPANESE SCHOOLHOUSE

HOLO HOLO IN

KEONELEHUA RD.

LAUKAPU RD.

KILAUEA RD.

VOLCANO INN

COOPER CENTER, FARMERS' MARKET

MY ISLAND BED AND BREAKFAST INN

KILAUEA LODGE AND RESTAURANT

VOLCANO COUNTRY COTTAGES

KILAUEA GENERAL STORE, LAVA ROCK CAFE, KILAUEA KREATIONS, GAS STATION

ALOHA JUNCTION

POST OFFICE

OMA'S HAPU'U HIDEAWAY

HALE OHIA

HARDWARE STORE, GIFT SHOP, THAI THAI RESTAURANT, LAUNDROMAT

CARSON'S VOLCANO COTTAGES

OLD VOLCANO HWY.

THE VOLCANO STORE, GAS STATION

HAWAII BELT ROAD

To Hilo

FIRST

JADE AVE.

RUBY AVE.

PEARL AVE.

LIONA

SIXTH

EIGHTH

NAHELENANI

FOURTEENTH

ALAOHIA

THE COUNTRY GOOSE

THE GUESTHOUSE AT VOLCANO

To National Park, Kailua-Kona

0    0.5 mi
0    0.5 km

**VOLCANO VILLAGE**

© SANDRA E. BISIGNANI TRUST AND AVALON TRAVEL PUBLISHING, INC.

everywhere, it is hard to imagine a more picturesque village in all of America. But even in this little parcel of paradise, things are changing, if slowly. The town of about 1,500 people boasts two general stores, a hardware store, two small gift shops/galleries, a post office, a farmers' market, a winery, several restaurants, an abundance of accommodations, several artists' studios, and newer and larger subdivisions south of the highway.

## Volcano Golf and Country Club

What's most amazing about this course is where it is. Imagine! You're teeing off atop an active volcano surrounded by one of the last pristine forests in the state. At the right time of year, the surrounding 'ohi'a turn scarlet when they are in bloom. The fairways are carved from lava, while in the distance Mauna Loa looms. Hit a poor shot and you can watch your ball disappear down a steam vent. Just kidding—you're not that close! The course began about 80 years ago when a group of local golfers hand-cleared three "greens,"

placing stakes that served as holes. Later this was improved to sand greens with tin cans for holes, and after an eruption in 1924 blanketed the area with volcanic ash that served as excellent fertilizer, the grass grew and the course became a lush green. After World War II the course was extended to 18 holes, and a clubhouse was added. Finally, Jack Snyder, a well-known course architect, redesigned the course to its present par-72 layout. Rates are $62.50 with shared cart; reduced rates for Big Island residents. The course is located just north of the Belt Road, about two miles west of the park entrance. Turn on Pi'i Mauna Drive, sometimes called Golf Course Road. Phone 808/967-7331 for more information and tee times. After a round of golf, stop for lunch at the clubhouse restaurant.

## Volcano Winery

About one mile beyond the golf course at the end of Pi'i Mauna Road and off to your left are the buildings of the Volcano Winery, 808/967-

7479, www.volcanowinery.com. This is the only winery on the Big Island and the southernmost in the United States. It's a hands-on operation where everything is done manually. Because the land is at an elevation of about 4,000 feet, the patented Symphony grape (a combination of grenache gris and muscat of Alexandria grapes) is grown to take best advantage of the climatic conditions, which are similar to those in Oregon and Washington. About 14 acres of this rough countryside are currently being cultivated with grapes, producing about three tons of grapes per acre, and another four acres have been planted in half a dozen other varieties to see if they too will produce acceptable wine. Bottled are dry and semi-dry wines, and three wine and fruit blends including guava/chablis, jaboticaba/chablis, and a macadamia honey wine. A local favorite, the jaboticaba blend is made with a Brazilian fruit of that name; the honey "wines" are made without any grapes. All bottles cost $13–16 apiece. Although no tours of the winery are available, a tasting room is open daily 10 A.M.–5:30 P.M. Have a sip at the glass-covered koa bar and maybe you'll want to purchase a bottle for later in the evening or a six-bottle case to share with friends when you get home. There also is a small boutique on the premises selling T-shirts, jewelry, *kukui* nut leis, postcards, and other gift items.

## ACCOMMODATIONS

There are a great number of accommodations in and around Volcano Village. While most are near the heart of the village, several are located in the fern forests south of the highway and a few are located around the golf course about two miles west of town. Most are bed-and-breakfasts, some are vacation homes where you take care of your own meals, and there is one hostel. These places run from budget and homey to luxurious and elegant, but most are moderate in price and amenities. Some of these establishments also act as agents for other rental homes in the area, so your choices are many. See also the Volcano House listing in the National Park chapter below.

### Hostel

Volcano has a hostel, and a fine one it is! Although a modern structure, this all-wood forest house is an old-style place with a comforting, traditional hostel feel. **Holo Holo In,** P.O. Box 784, Volcano Village, HI 96785, 808/967-7950, fax 808/967-8025, holoholo@inter-pac.net, www.enable.org/holoholo, snuggles under the towering trees in a residential area of the village, next to the old Japanese schoolhouse at 19-4036 Kalani Honua Road. Owned, operated, and built by Satoshi Yabuki, a world traveler himself when he was younger, this is a one-man operation; his office hours are 6:30–9 A.M. and 4:30–9 P.M. Having taken guests for over a dozen years, this hostel has been an AYH member for about half that time. On the downstairs level is a huge kitchen with all needed appliances and utensils and a library of books and information. You are more than welcome to cook, but please clean up after yourself. Here too are a laundry facility and a sauna ($4 per person per use). Upstairs are the men's and women's dorms and the TV room, and there are bathrooms up and down. Rates are $17 per person for the dorm ($15 for AYH members), or $40 per couple for the one private room (can sleep four, so good for a small family). Please bring your own sheets or there will be a nominal extra charge. This is a great little accommodation at a bargain price—a real find.

### $50–100

Down the lane behind the post office is **Aloha Junction,** a renovated bed-and-breakfast surrounded by green lawns and *hapu'u* ferns. A converted plantation manager's home, this house has three bedrooms upstairs, one down, and a suite in a separate building to the rear. Each bedroom has comfortable queen or twin beds with quilts and old-style lace curtains on the windows. All three main floor bedrooms share one bathroom. In the common room, the fireplace is warm and welcoming, and the huge television and entertainment center or quick Internet access computer will keep you occupied in the evening if you don't care to venture out. Out back, under a patio cover in case of rain, is the hot tub. All guests receive a filling home-cooked breakfast—different every morning—that's served family style with friendly conversation that makes a pleasant way to start the day. Room rates are $75 a night. For information and reservations, contact Robert or Susan Hughes at 808/967-7289 or 888/967-7286, relax@bbvolcano.com, http://bbvolcano.com.

A B&B with an excellent reputation is **My Island Bed and Breakfast Inn,** P.O. Box 100, Volcano, HI 96785, 808/967-7216, fax 808/967-7719, myisland@ilhawaii.net, www.myislandinnhawaii.com. The main house, the oldest in the village, is a New England–style three-level house from 1886 that was the Lyman summer home for many years. Rooms in this building rent for a reasonable $45–55 single to $60–70 double; some share a bathroom. A few steps away, the two garden units go for $70–95. A fully furnished vacation house on the property, plus four other vacation homes in the village and up near the golf course, go for $125 double with an extra charge for additional guests. No credit cards are accepted. All guests are served a "world-class" breakfast each morning in the main house. Spend some time in the exquisite seven-acre flower garden here as it is a wonderful extra benefit to this property.

Located at the end of Old Volcano Highway on the lower end of town, **Volcano Inn,** 808/967-7293 or 800/997-2292, fax 808/985-7349, volcano@volcanoinn.com, www.volcanoinn.com, has four rooms and several cottages at separate locations. The main three-story house is of modern design, with a common room and huge dining room where complimentary breakfasts are served to all guests. Rooms run $65–85 a night single, $85–105 a couple. Each has a private entrance and bath, TV and VCR, refrigerator, and coffeemaker. The cottages, at locations on the south side of the highway in a fern forest, go for $80–155, and two are big enough for a small family. A 10 percent discount is given for AAA members. The inn also operates horseback riding tours. Inquire about what's currently offered.

Located on the downhill side of the highway, the **Country Goose Bed and Breakfast,** P.O. Box 597, Volcano, HI 06785, 808/967-7759 or 800/238-7101 Mainland, fax 808/985-8673, cgoose@interpac.net, www.countrygoose.com, is a very pleasant place with lots of knickknacks on the walls. The knotty pine on the walls, open-beamed ceiling, and decor all say easy country living. Comfortable and homey, rooms include private baths and entrances, and the common room is open to all guests. Everyone is served a hearty country-style breakfast each morning in the dining room. Nestled under 'ohi'a trees and ferns, half a mile from the highway, this little place is quiet. The gracious owner, Joan Early, has built herself a fine retreat here and loves to share it with others who love the area. Rooms rent for $75 a night for two, with an extra $10 for a third person. Joan also represents several one-, two-, and three-bedroom homes in the village and out near the golf course that are available for nightly, weekly, or longer stays.

Owned and operated by Bonnie Goodell, **The Guest House at Volcano,** P.O. Box 6, Volcano, HI 96785, 808/967-7775 or 866/886-5226, fax 808/967-8295, innkeeper@volcanguesthouse.com, www.volcanoguesthouse.com, is a very friendly hideaway on the farthest back road of Mauna Loa Estates subdivision, south of the highway from Volcano Village. The fully furnished cottage is designed as a self-sufficient unit where guests are guaranteed peace and quiet on a lovely six-acre homesite. Bring your own food. Bonnie grew up in Hawaii and was for many years the education director for the Honolulu Botanical Gardens. She *knows* her plants and is willing to chat with her guests. The two-story guest home is bright and airy. Enter into a combo living room, kitchen, and dining area, with twin beds in a bedroom. Upstairs is a sleeping area with two twin beds and a queen bed. Futons can sleep even more. In the main house, a one-bedroom apartment called Claudia's Place has its own entrance and bathroom. It's completely handicapped-accessible and will sleep up to three. Two newer units have been built down the drive. They are mirror footprints of each other and face one another across a covered patio. The Twins are also fully accessible, each has a living room, kitchen, queen and twin beds, and sleeps up to four. The rate for Claudia's Place is $75, $85 for either of the Twins, and $95 for the cottage, $15 for each additional adult over two,

$10 for kids. Two nights minimum, with the seventh night at no charge. Sometimes Bonnie will allow an emergency one-night stay, but then there is a $15 surcharge.

## $100–150

**Kilauea Lodge,** P.O. Box 116, Volcano Village, HI 96785, 808/967-7366, fax 967-7367, stay@kilauealodge.com, www.kilauealodge.com, owned and operated by Lorna and Albert Jeyte, is the premier restaurant and lodge atop Volcano, as well as one of the very best on the island. The solid stone and timber structure was built in 1938 as a YMCA camp and functioned as such until 1962, when it became a "mom and pop operation," often failing and changing ownership. It faded into the ferns until Lorna and Albert revitalized it in 1987, opening in 1988. The lodge is a classic, with a vaulted, open-beamed ceiling. A warm and cozy "international fireplace" dating from the days of the YMCA camp is embedded with stones and plaques from all over the world. This building houses the restaurant and the office. An assortment of rooms, ranging $125–145 and including a complete breakfast for all guests in the restaurant, are lo-

cated in three adjacent buildings on the property, and there is a hot tub for guests in the rear garden. The brooding rooms of the original guesthouse section were transformed into bright, cozy, and romantic suites. The rooms, all differently appointed, range in decor from Hawaiian-European to Asian with a motif of Japanese fans. Each room has a bathroom with vaulted 18-foot ceilings and a skylight, a working fireplace, queen or twin beds, and swivel rocking chair. A separate one-bedroom cottage, set in the ferns to the side, features a wood-burning stove (central heat too), wet bar, a queen-size bed, private bath, and small living room with queen-size pull-out sofa. In 1991, Kilauea Lodge opened the Hale Aloha building with its seven new units centered around a commodious common room where you can read and snooze by a crackling fire. All rooms in the new section are very spacious, with vaulted ceilings (upstairs) and tastefully furnished with wicker furniture, white curtains, and fluffy quilts to keep off the evening chill. Many are hung with original artwork by Gwendolyn O'Connor. Check-in is 3–5 P.M. at the office; after that, check in at the restaurant. The Kilauea Lodge provides one of the most *civilized* atmospheres in

ROBERT NILSEN

**Kilauea Lodge**

Hawaii in one of its most powerful natural areas. The combination is hard to beat.

Just up the road from the Kilauea Lodge is the cute little two-bedroom cottage, **Tutu's Place.** Built in 1929 by the Uncle Billy of hotel chain fame for "tutu" (grandma), it was bought several decades later by the Warner family. Mr. Warner was a minister and was involved in Hawaiian politics. His wife, Ruth Warner, lived in the cottage for 30 years until it was bought in 1995 by Lorna Larson-Jeyte, the owner of the Kilauea Lodge, who used to visit as a child. Although it's been completely refurbished, people in the know say that the cottage is still imbued with the spirit of Ruth Warner. It's done in a theme of rattan and koa, with a fireplace in the living room, a full kitchen, and a wonderful little bathroom. For a small place, it has a surprisingly roomy feel. The rate is $155 for two people, including breakfast at the Kilauea Lodge, plus $15 for each additional person. To make reservations, call the Kilauea Lodge, and ask for Tutu's Place.

Next door to Tutu's Place, and conveniently located near stores and restaurants, is **Oma's Hapu'u Hideaway,** a modern semi-A-frame mountain house of cedar that's great for a family. Here you have all you need: a full kitchen, living room, bathroom, two bedrooms downstairs, one with bunks that's great for kids, and a master bedroom loft upstairs. The house comes with TV and VCR and phone. It's a cozy place that goes for $105 a night. The owners live across the street in a plantation house, and in the rear is **The Maid's Quarters,** a self-contained cottage with full kitchen, living room tiled with marble, fireplace, spacious bedroom, completely updated bathroom, and a hot tub. This is a lovely place, just right for a romantic couple. This cottage runs $95 a night. Next door is the refurbished **Haunani House.** Also good for a family, it has three bedrooms, two baths, a full kitchen, living room with gas fireplace, washer and dryer, and television, and rents for $115 a night. All three are good value for the money. Each has a two night minimum with a fifth night free; $15 for each additional person over two. No breakfast is served. For information, write P.O. Box 611, Volcano, HI

96785; 808/985-8959, todd@volcanovillage.net, www.volcanovillage.net.

**Kate's Volcano Places** is a winner! A pleasant, homey, and cozy place, the cottage is a modern reconstruction with full attention to detail that combines Western cabin and Scandinavian styles with a touch of the Orient. One large room, this cottage has a king bed, separate bathroom, and full kitchen equipped with all conveniences and stocked with supplies. The sitting area sports a built-in entertainment center and opens onto the back deck. Up front, the reconditioned island-style Kahi Malu house has two bedrooms, one bathroom, and a full kitchen; the living room, amazingly, is solid koa. Like the cottage, it too has been brought up to snuff with all modern conveniences. This house and cottage are set toward the back of the village and are very quiet and private. At a separate location, the three-bedroom Hiiaka house from 1939 is surrounded by a large yard. This house is perfect for a family of up to eight with its huge living room and fireplace, full kitchen, and three bedrooms. Rental rates are $95 for the cottage, $125 for Kahi Mahi, and $135 for Hiiaka, and this includes breakfast goodies stocked in the refrigerator for each morning that you'll be there. For information and reservations, contact Kathryn Grout, P.O. Box 159 Volcano, HI 96785, 808/967-7990 or 877/967-7990, kathryn@volcanoplaces.com, www.volcanoplaces.com.

**Volcano Country Cottages,** P.O. Box 545, Volcano, HI 96785, 808/967-7960 or 800/967-7960, aloha@volcanocottages.com, www.volcanocottages.com, are conveniently located in the heart of the village at one of its oldest homes. Available are the Ohelo Berry Cottage for $95 for one night and the two-bedroom Artist's House for $120; $15 for each additional person beyond two. The studio cottage is a cozy one-room affair with kitchenette, bathroom, and room heater that snuggles into the back vegetation. It's perfect for a couple but can also sleep two kids on futons. A covered lanai outside the front door is a wonderful spot to sit during a light rain. Each morning, a filling and tasty breakfast of fruits and baked goods is left for you to have at your leisure. Set closer to the front of the property under towering tsugi trees, the Artist's House contains a full kitchen, also stocked with morning treats, a woodstove, and washer and dryer. It sleeps four comfortably and up to four more on pull-out futons. For use by all guests, the hot tub sits behind the main house in the fern forest. This is a gracious place, one of peace and tranquillity, with the added gift of artwork hung on the walls. Check-in is 3–5 P.M. The Wellspring Center for yoga and stress reduction operates on property.

Follow a private mountain lane for a few minutes into an enchanted clearing where the artwork of a meticulous Japanese garden surrounds a New England gabled and turreted home and its attendant cottages of red-on-brown rough-cut shingles. Once the hideaway of the Dillinghams, an old and influential *kama'aina* family, **Hale Ohia**, P.O. Box 758, Volcano Village, HI 96785, 808/967-7986 or 800/455-3803, fax 808/967-8610, haleohia@bigisland.com, www.haleohia.com, is now owned and operated by Michael D. Tuttle, who purchased the property after falling hopelessly in love at first sight. The main house holds the Dillingham Suite, $110 per night, with its own sitting room, bath, and glass-covered lanai. Simple and clean, with hardwood floors and wainscoted walls, the home is the epitome of country elegance, Hawaiian style. Adjacent in the main house, occupying one bedroom, a big bath, and the main living room, is the Master Suite for $140. Hale Ohia Cottage, once the gardener's residence, has two stories, with the bottom floor front occupied by the Iiwi and Camellia suites, $95, which are wheelchair-accessible and can be combined for larger groups. Stained-glass windows with a calla lily-and-poppy motif add a special touch, while the low ceilings are reminiscent of the captain's quarters on a sailing ship. The 1st floor rear has a full kitchen and a covered lanai complete with barbecue grill that makes it perfect for evening relaxation. Narrow stairs lead to a full bath located on the first landing, and the upstairs opens into a bright and airy parlor and adjacent bedrooms that can sleep five comfortably, $130. Hale Lehua, once a private study, is secluded down its own lava footpath and rents for $110. The interior is cozy with its own fireplace, bamboo and wicker furniture,

self-contained bathroom, covered lanai, partial kitchen, and leaded glass windows through which the surrounding fern forest will emit its emerald radiance. Similar but more luxurious is the Ihilani Cottage, at $125. Newest of the units is Cottage #44—created from a water tank! The round redwood tank has been turned into the bedroom, and attached to it in a newly built structure are the living room, efficiency kitchen, bathroom with shower and whirlpool tub, and covered lanai. No expense was spared for this cute little unit and it rents for $150. To make your stay even more delightful, room rates include an "extended" continental breakfast, and guests are welcome to immerse themselves in the bubbling whirlpool tub that awaits under a canopy of Japanese cedars and glimmering stars. No TV and no smoking, but there is an on-site phone in the wisteria-covered gazebo.

Embraced within the arms of ferns and 'ohi'a are the three cottages of **Volcano Rainforest Retreat**, 808/985-8696 or 800/550-8696, volrain@bigisland.net, www.volcanoretreat.com, a luxury accommodation for discriminating guests wanting privacy for their stay in the rainforest. Constructed in an open style of cedar and redwood, these buildings are warm and welcoming and rich in color and detail. Hale Kipa has a living room with kitchen and sleeping loft. The octagonal Hale Nahele is one large room with a bed, seating area, and a kitchenette. The six-sided Hale Ho'ano, smallest and with the most obvious Japanese influence, has the benefit of an outdoor ofuro tub and shower. Rates are $170, $140, and $95, respectively; discounts for three nights or longer.

**Ka Hale Iki Kilauea** is a very romantic home away from home, canopied by the forest trees, screened from the road by tall ferns, and 50 feet through the jungle from the driveway. Much like a cabin with a porch all around, the inside opens to a high open-beamed ceiling, living room with a woodstove, and full kitchen. Sliding doors and picture windows all around frame the living green tapestry outside. In the bath is a huge tub fit for two; bathe by candlelight and open the full-length windows to let in the night air. Up the ladder-like narrow stairway is the bedroom and queen

BIG ISLAND OF HAWAI'I

bed, where you can drift away with the moon and starlight gently filtering through the skylight windows. The rental rate is $135 a night for a couple and $15 more for an extra person, or $700 a week, breakfast included. For reservations, contact Joan Early at the Country Goose, 808/967-7759 or 800/238-7101, www.vrbo.com/vrbo/1438.htm.

Deep in the fern forest, **Carson's Volcano Cottages,** P.O. Box 503, Volcano, HI 96785, 808/967-7683 or 800/845-LAVA, fax 808/967-8094, carsons@aloha.net, www.carsonscottage.com, owned and operated by Tom and Brenda Carson, offers two B&B rooms in the main house, but by far the nicer accommodations are in the detached cottages. The suites in the main house are located upstairs and run $125–155 a night. The cottage accommodations all have private baths, entrances, and decks, and in the garden is a hot tub for everyone to use. The one-acre property is naturally landscaped with 'ohi'a and fern, and moss-covered sculptures of Balinese gods peek through the foliage. Nick's Cabin #19, $125 double, a miniature plantation house with corrugated roof and woodstove, has a mini-kitchen and a bath with a skylight—rustic country charm. The three-room cottage, $105–110 per room, has vaulted ceilings and queen beds, and rooms decorated in Hawaiian Monarchy, Oriental, and tropical floral styles. Leaded glass windows open to a private porch. Tom and Brenda provide an extended continental breakfast for all guests in their dining room that might include banana bread, French toast, passion fruit juice, bagels and lox, or strawberry crepes. You'll be comfortable in front of the living room fireplace or enjoying the evening sky from the hot tub. The Carsons also rent out four other one- and two-bedroom, fully furnished cottages in the village that run $125–165 and a seaside retreat down in Kapoho if you are going that direction.

## $150 and up

Peeking from the *hapu'u* fern forest in a manicured glen is **Chalet Kilauea,** 998 Wright Road, Volcano Village, HI 96785, 808/967-7786 or 800/937-7786, fax 808/967-8660 or 800/577-1849, reservations@volcano-hawaii.com, www.volcano-hawaii.com, where you will be cordially

accommodated by owners Lisha and Brian Crawford and their staff. Downstairs there's an outdoor lounge area, and a black-and-white checkerboard dining room where wrought-iron tables sit before a huge picture window. A three-course candlelight breakfast is served here every morning. Enter the second level of the main house to find a guest living room where you can while away the hours playing chess, listening to a large collection of CDs, or gazing from the wraparound windows at a treetop view of the surrounding forest, ferns, and impeccable grounds. Beyond the koi pond in the garden, a free-standing gazebo houses an eight-person hot tub available 24 hours a day.

The main house, called The Inn at Volcano, is known for elegance and luxury. It holds four suites and two theme rooms, $139–399. The Oriental Jade Room is richly appointed with Chinese folding screens, samurai murals, Oriental carpet, and jade-green bedspread. The green marble bathroom adds to the green theme of the surrounding vegetation. The lanai outside is shared with the Out of Africa Room, which has a strong color theme of burgundy and brass, and appointed with bold wood carvings and some basketwork. The Continental Lace Suite is fluff and lace, the bridal suite. Here the colors are white, gold, and pink; a wedding dress hangs in the corner to accentuate the theme. Located on the 1st floor, the Owners' Suite is designed for up to three people. Pink carpet covers the floor and a green floral spread covers the bed. With two shower heads in the shower stall, a couple can be happy showering together. Connected by a deck to the main house is the Treehouse Suite, a two-story unit with bath, sitting room, wet bar, and kitchenette downstairs, and a large bedroom on the upper floor. The surrounding glass makes the living forest part of the decor. A private lanai overlooks the garden, and a hand-crafted wooden circular staircase connects the two floors. An adjacent "cabin" is the Hapu'u Suite. It has a fireplace in the cozy living room but perhaps its best feature is the master bathroom which looks out onto the back garden.

Chalet Kilauea also has many other accommodations in Volcano Village including Castle Suites at Mauna Loa, a modern Victorian home set on the golf course, where three suites range $189–249. Lokahi Lodge has four rooms that run $99–149, or $590 for a group of up to 14 people. For those on a tighter budget, the Volcano Bed and Breakfast rents rooms for $49–69 and still has plenty of common space. The entire house can be rented for $293 a night and can sleep 13. In addition, five vacation homes dotted here and there about town in the secluded privacy of the forest are available for $139–379. Whatever your price range and whatever your needs, Chalet Kilauea will have something for you, and breakfast is an option at most accommodations.

## FOOD

The **Kilauea Lodge Restaurant,** open for dinner 5:30–9 P.M. nightly (reservations a must), is an extraordinary restaurant serving gourmet continental cuisine—the premier restaurant in Volcano Village. A large fireplace dominates one side of the room with an inviting couch at its front. The hardwood floor reflects light from the two chandeliers that hang from the open-beamed wooden ceiling. Prints of Hawaiian scenes hang from the walls, and beer mugs line the stone mantle. A warm, welcoming, and homey place, the Kilauea Lodge Restaurant has fine dining in an unpretentious setting. A very friendly and professional staff serves the excellent food prepared by Albert, the owner, and his kitchen help. Although the menu changes a bit every night, you'll start off with fresh bread—studded like the fireplace, but with sunflower and sesame seeds. Appetizers such as mushroom caps stuffed with crab and cheese will titillate your palate, or try the baked brie cheese, a specialty. Entrées, ranging $17–28, include soup, salad, and vegetables. The menu is strong on the meats, with its heavy German influence, but vegetarians will be delighted with their options too. Dinner features seafood Mauna Kea (succulent pieces of seafood served atop a bed of fettuccine) and paupiettes of beef (prime rib slices rolled around herbs and mushrooms in a special sauce). Always a great choice, the catch of the day is blackened, broiled, or sautéed with a savory sauce. There is always a nightly special, and each dish is infused with herbs and pungent seasonings. To match any meal, you can select from the extensive wine list, which includes a special reserve section. Desserts are wonderful, and the meal can be topped off with a cup of Irish or Italian coffee.

Situated behind the Kilauea General Store is **Lava Rock Cafe,** 808/967-8526, the most local of the eateries in the village. The Lava Rock is open 7:30–10:30 A.M. for breakfast, until 5 P.M. for lunch (4 P.M. on Sunday), and dinner is served Tues.–Sat. until 9 P.M. Start your day with eggs, griddle items, or loco moco. For lunch you can get a plate lunch, burger, or sandwich, along with sides, fountain drinks, and coffee. Dinners are a bit heartier with the likes of teriyaki chicken and New York steak, and almost everything is under $12, except for a few of the meat dishes that run up to $17.50. While not gourmet, this is good food. You get plentiful portions at a good price in pleasant surroundings—and there's even Internet access.

A fine addition to the restaurant scene in Volcano is **Thai Thai Restaurant,** 808/967-7969, open for dinner 5–9 P.M. every day except Wednesday. This restaurant puts out food that will transport you to the Orient. It has established a good reputation in town for tasty food and large portions. Start with an appetizer (some as big as entrées), like deep-fried tofu or chicken satay. Traditional soups and salads come next, followed by curries or stir-fried selections, most of which can be made with your choice of shrimp, chicken, beef, or pork. Almost everything on the menu is in the $9–13 range, so it's not exorbitant. Take-out available.

Around the side and behind the Volcano Store is **JP's Volcano Cafe.** This quick-serve café has eggs and local favorites for breakfast and sandwiches, salads, and soup for lunch, plus lots of coffee all day long. Open 6 A.M.–4 P.M. Seating is outside under the awning.

You can get away from the crowds and have a satisfying breakfast or lunch at **Volcano Country Club Restaurant,** 808/967-8228, at the golf course clubhouse. No dinner meals are served. The green and white interior complements the fairways, which can be seen through the surrounding plate glass windows. A fireplace fills

BIG ISLAND OF HAWAI'I

the center of this country kitchen style room. Complete breakfast is served daily 8–10 A.M. (6:30 A.M. on weekends), a full lunch menu daily 10:30 A.M.–2 P.M. For breakfast choose omelettes, hotcakes, or other standard American fare. Lunch selections include hearty sandwiches, salads, and burgers, as well as local favorites like teriyaki beef, saimin, or loco moco. Many stop by just for the Portuguese bean soup. Most everything on the menu is under $9. The bar is well stocked, so enjoy an exotic drink, beer, or glass of wine after your round of golf. Good choice for lunch.

Wouldn't it be fun to have a full multi-course gourmet dinner prepared and delivered to your door by a trained chef and served on linen and fine china, with the dishes whisked away after you're finished so you can turn your attention to more romantic matters? Well, you can do just that here in the tiny village of Volcano for $30 per person plus gratuity and wine. Call the **Culinary Crusaders,** 808/985-7167, 24-hour advance notice requested. It is not inexpensive, but an experience to be remembered.

If you're looking for something faster and not so gourmet, try **Big O's Pizza,** 808/985-9995. The basic 12-inch pie runs $12.50 with each extra at 50 cents. Open 5–10 P.M. Tues.–Sat. and 4–6:30 P.M. Sunday and Monday. Call in your order and pick it up at the Kilauea General Store.

See also Volcano House Restaurant in the National Park chapter below.

## SHOPPING

A **farmers' market** open every Sunday 8:30–11 A.M. sells local produce, fruit, flowers, baked goods, soups and other prepared foods, used books, and other items. It's located along Wright Road at the Cooper Center. Come early

for the food. This is a wonderful community event. Don't miss it.

**Volcano Store,** 808/967-7210, also called the "upper store," is open daily 5 A.M.–7 P.M. and sells gasoline, film, a few camping supplies, tropical flowers, a good selection of basic foods, and general dry goods items. For events happening around the village, see the community bulletin board on the wall outside. There are public telephone booths out front, and a few steps away is the full-service post office.

Just down the road, **Kilauea General Store,** 808/967-7555, also called the "lower store," is open daily 7 A.M.–7:30 P.M. (until 7 P.M. on Sundays). This store also sells gas, and although it is not as well stocked as a grocery, it does have a deli case, a good selection of beer and liquor, postcards, videos, an ATM machine, and an excellent community bulletin board. It's here that you can order and pick up your Big O's pizza.

Set between these two is **True Value Hardware** for all your home and yard needs. Open daily 7 A.M.–5:30 P.M., 5 P.M. on weekends.

In a separate building behind the Kilauea General Store is **Kilauea Kreations,** a shop that carries gifts, crafts, and art by local artists. Perhaps best of what they have is quilts, quilting supplies, and materials. For other arts and crafts by local artists, souvenirs (much imported), as well as information about the area, have a look at the **Village Art Store** above the hardware store.

**Volcano Wash and Dry** sits behind the hardware store and is open 8 A.M.–7 P.M. Buy soap up front at the hardware store.

Many artists have found a home at Volcano, and a few studios dot the backroads. Ask at one of the stores for a map of those studios open to guests.

For Internet access, check at the Lava Rock Cafe.

# Hawaii Volcanoes National Park

Hawaii Volcanoes National Park (HVNP) is an unparalleled experience in geological grandeur. The upper end of the park is the summit of stupendous Mauna Loa, the most massive mountain on earth. Mauna Loa Road branches off Hwy. 11 and ends at a foot trail for the hale and hearty who trek to the 13,679-foot summit. The park's heart is **Kilauea Caldera,** almost three miles across, 400 feet deep, and encircled by 11 miles of **Crater Rim Drive.** At the park **Visitors Center** you can give yourself a crash course in geology while picking up park maps, information, and backcountry camping permits. Nearby is **Volcano House,** Hawaii's oldest hotel, which has hosted a steady stream of adventurers, luminaries, royalty, and heads of state ever since it opened its doors in the 1860s. Just a short drive away is a pocket of indigenous forest, providing the perfect setting for a bird sanctuary. In a separate detached section of the park is **'Ola'a**

Halema'uma'u Crater seems small in the immense expanse of Kilauea Caldera.

ROBERT NILSEN

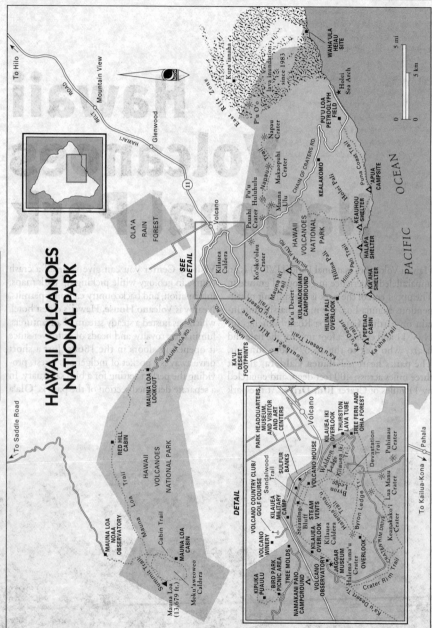

# HAWAII VOLCANOES NATIONAL PARK

To Hilo

BELT ROAD

Mountain View

Glenwood

HAWAII 11

Volcano

OLA'A RAIN FOREST

SEE DETAIL

East Rift Zone

Kupaʻianaha

Puʻu ʻŌʻō

Lava inundation since 1983

WAHAʻULA HEIAU SITE

Holei Sea Arch

5 mi

5 km

Napau Crater

PUʻU LOA PETROGLYPH FIELD

Makaopuhi Crater

Mauna Ulu

CHAIN OF CRATERS RD.

KEALAKOMO

Holei Pali

Puna Coast Trail

APUA CAMPSITE

PACIFIC OCEAN

Puʻu Huluhulu

Pauahi Crater

Napau Trail

KEAUHOU SHELTER

HILINA PALI RD.

Koʻokoʻolau Crater

Kilauea Caldera

HALAPA SHELTER

Hilina Pali Trail

KAʻAHA SHELTER

Mauna Iki Trail

Kaʻu Desert

KILAUANOKUAIKI CAMPGROUND

HAWAII VOLCANOES NATIONAL PARK

PEPEIAO CABIN

Kaʻu Desert Trail

HILINA PALI OVERLOOK

Hilina Pali Trail

Kaʻu Desert Trail

Kaʻu Desert Trail

Kaʻaha Trail

Southwest Rift Zone

HAWAII BELT RD.

KAʻU DESERT FOOTPRINTS

Mauna Loa Trail

MAUNA LOA LOOKOUT

Mauna Loa Trail

MAUNA LOA BD.

To Saddle Road

RED HILL CABIN

HAWAII VOLCANOES NATIONAL PARK

Mauna Loa Cabin Trail

MAUNA LOA NOAA OBSERVATORY

MAUNA LOA CABIN

Summit Trail

Mauna Loa (13,679 ft.)

Mokuʻaweoweo Caldera

BIG ISLAND OF HAWAIʻI

© SANDRA E. BISIGNANI TRUST AND AVALON TRAVEL PUBLISHING, INC.

## DETAIL

Volcano

PARK HEADQUARTERS, VISITOR AND ART CENTERS

VOLCANO COUNTRY CLUB/ GOLF COURSE

Sandalwood Trail

KILAUEA IKI OVERLOOK

THURSTON LAVA TUBE

TREE FERN AND OHIA FOREST

Puhimau Crater

VOLCANO WINERY

KILAUEA MILITARY CAMP

SULFUR BANKS

VOLCANO HOUSE

Waldron Ledge

Kilauea Iki

Kilauea Iki Trail

Lua Manu Crater

Devastation Trail

KILAUEA STEAM VENTS

Halemaʻumaʻu Trail

Byron Ledge

Keanakakoʻi Crater

To Kailua-Kona

Steaming Bluff

Byron Ledge Trail

KIPUKA PUAULU

BIRD PARK PICNIC AREA

TREE MOLDS

KILAUEA OVERLOOK

VOLCANO OBSERVATORY

JAGGAR MUSEUM

Halemaʻumaʻu Overlook

Kilauea Caldera

Crater Rim Drive

Crater Rim Trail

Kaʻu Desert Trail

NAMAKANI PAIO CAMPGROUND

To Pahala

**Forest,** a pristine wilderness area of unspoiled flora and fauna.

Crater Rim Drive circles Kilauea Caldera past steam vents, sulfur springs, and tortured fault lines that always seem on the verge of gaping wide and swallowing. On the way you can peer into the maw of **Halema'uma'u Crater,** home of the fire goddess, Pele, and you'll pass **Hawaiian Volcano Observatory** (not open to public), which has been monitoring geologic activity since the turn of the 20th century. Adjacent to the observatory is the **Thomas A. Jaggar Museum,** an excellent facility where you can educate yourself on the past and present volcanology of the park. A fantastic walk is **Devastation Trail,** a paved path across a desolate cinder field where gray, lifeless trunks of a suffocated forest lean like old gravestones. Within minutes is **Thurston Lava Tube,** a magnificent natural tunnel *"leid"* by amazingly vibrant fern grottoes at the entrance and exit.

The southwestern section of the park is dominated by the **Ka'u Desert,** not a plain of sand but a semi-arid slope of lava flow, cinder, scrub bush, and heat that's been defiled by the windblown debris and gasses of Kilauea Volcano and fractured by the sinking coastline. It is a desolate region, an area crossed by a few trails that are a challenge even to the sturdy and experienced hiker. Most visitors, however, head down the **Chain of Craters Road,** first through the 'ohi'a and fern forests, then past numerous secondary craters and down the *pali* to the coast where the road ends abruptly at a hardened flow of lava and from where visitors can glean information about current volcanic activities from the small ranger station and try to glimpse the current volcanic activity in the distance.

The indomitable power of Volcanoes National Park is apparent to all who come here. Mark Twain, enchanted by his sojourn through Volcanoes in the 1860s, quipped, "The smell of sulfur is strong, but not unpleasant to a sinner." Amen, brother! Wherever you stop to gaze, realize that you are standing on a thin skin of cooled lava in an unstable earthquake zone atop one of the world's most active volcanoes.

Established in 1916 as the 13th U.S. na-

tional park, HVNP now covers 377 square miles. Based on its scientific and scenic value, the park was named an International Biosphere Reserve by UNESCO in 1980 and given World Heritage Site status in 1982 by the same organization, giving it greater national and international prestige. With about 2.5 million visitors a year, this is one of the top visitor attractions in the state.

Admission to the park is $10 per vehicle (good for multiple entries over a seven-day period), $20 for an annual permit, $5 for bicycle and motorcycle traffic and hikers, and free to those 62 and over with a Golden Age, Golden Eagle, or Golden Access passport. These "passports" are available at the park headquarters and are good at any national park in the United States. For information about the park, write to Hawaii Volcanoes National Park, P.O. Box 52, Hawaii National Park, HI 96718-0052; call 808/985-6000 for a recorded message; or visit www.nps.gov/havo.

## Geologic History: Science Versus Madame Pele

The goddess Pele is an irascible old dame. Perhaps it's because she had such a bad childhood. All she wanted was a home of her own where she could house her family and entertain her lover, a handsome chief from Kaua'i. But her sea goddess sister, Namakaokaha'i, flooded her out wherever she went after Pele seduced her husband, and the pig god, Kamapua'a, ravished Pele for good measure. So Pele finally built her love nest at Halema'uma'u Crater at the south end of Kilauea Caldera. Being a goddess obviously isn't as heavenly as one would think, and whenever the pressures of life get too much for Pele, she blows her stack. These tempestuous outbursts made Pele one of the most revered gods in the Hawaiian pantheon because her presence and might were so easily felt.

For a thousand years Pele was appeased by offerings of pigs, dogs, sacred *'ohelo* berries (her favorite), and now and again an outcast man or two (never women) who would hopefully turn her energy from destruction to more comfortable pursuits. Also, if Pele was your family's personal goddess, your remains were sometimes allowed to be thrown into the fire pit as a sign of great respect. In the early 1820s, the chieftess Kapi'olani, an ardent convert to Christianity, officially challenged Pele in an attempt to topple her like the other gods of old. Kapi'olani climbed down into Pele's crater and ate the sacred *'ohelo* berries, flagrantly violating the ageless *kapu*. She then took large stones and defiantly hurled them into the fire pit below while bellowing, "Jehovah is my God. It is He, not Pele, that kindled these flames."

Yet today, most residents, regardless of background, have an inexplicable reverence for Pele. The Volcano Post Office receives an average of three packages a week containing lava rocks taken by tourists as souvenirs. Some hold that Pele looks upon these rocks as her children and taking them from her is kidnapping. The accompanying letters implore the officials to return the rocks because ever since the offender brought them home, luck has been bad. The officials take the requests very seriously, returning the rocks with the customary peace offering. Many follow-up "thank you" letters have been written to express relief that the bad luck has been lifted. There is no reference in Hawaiian folklore to this phenomenon, although Hawaiians did hold certain rocks sacred. Park rangers will tell you that the idea of "the bad-luck rocks" was initiated a few decades back by a tour bus driver who became sick and tired of tourists getting his bus dirty by piling aboard their souvenirs. *Voilà!* Another ancient Hawaiian myth! Know, however, that the rocks in Hawaii Volcanoes National Park are protected by federal law, much meaner and more vindictive than Pele.

Pele is believed to take human form. She customarily appears before an eruption as a ravishing beauty or a withered old hag, often accompanied by a little white dog. She expects to be treated cordially, and it's said that she will stand by the roadside at night hitching a ride. After a brief encounter, she departs and seems to mysteriously evaporate into the ether. Kindness on your part is the key; if you come across a strange woman at night, treat her well—it might not help, but it definitely won't hurt.

## Eruptions

The first white man atop Kilauea was Rev. William Ellis, who scaled it in 1823. Until the 1920s, the floor of the caldera was exactly what people thought a volcano would be: a molten lake of lava. Then the forces of nature changed, and the fiery lava subsided and hardened over. Today, Kilauea is called the only "drive-in" volcano in the world, and in recent years it has been one of the most active, erupting almost continuously since 1983 at vents along its eastern fault. When it begins gushing, the result is not a nightmare scene of people scrambling away for their lives, but just the opposite; people flock *to* the volcano. Most thrill-seekers are in much greater danger of being run over by a tour bus hustling to see the fireworks than of being entombed in lava. The volcanic action, while soul-shakingly powerful and not really predictable, is almost totally safe. The Hawaiian Volcano Observatory has been keeping watch since 1912, making Kilauea one of the best-understood volcanoes in the world. The vast volcanic field is creased by rift zones, or natural pressure valves. When the underground magma builds up, instead of *kaboom!* as in Mt. St. Helens, it bubbles to the surface like a spring and gushes out as a river of lava. Naturally, anyone or anything in its path would be burned to a cinder, but scientists routinely walk within a few feet of the still-flowing lava to take samples and readings. In much the way canaries detected mine gas, longtime lava observers pay attention to their ears. When the skin on top begins to blister, they know they are too close. The lava establishes a course that it follows much like an impromptu mountain stream caused by heavy rains.

This does not mean that the lava flows are entirely benign, or that anyone should visit the area during an eruption without prior approval by the park service. When anything is happening, the local radio stations give up-to-the-minute news, and the park service provides a recorded message at 808/985-6000. In 1790 a puff of noxious gases was emitted from Kilauea and descended on the Ka'u Desert, asphyxiating a rival army of Kamehameha's that just happened to be in the area. Eighty people died in their tracks.

In 1881 a flow of lava spilled toward undeveloped Hilo and engulfed an area within today's city limits. In 1942, a heavy flow came within 12 miles of the city. Still, this was child's play in comparison with the unbelievable flow of 1950. Luckily, this went down the western rift zone where only scattered homes were in its path. It took no lives as it disgorged well over 600 million cubic yards of magma that covered 35 square miles! The flow continued for 23 days and produced seven huge torrents of lava that sliced across the Belt Road in three different areas. At its height, the lava front traveled six miles per hour and put out enough material to pave an eight-lane freeway twice around the world. In 1960, a flow swallowed the town of Kapoho on the east coast. In 1975, an earthquake caused a tsunami to hit the southeast coast, killing two campers and sinking a section of the coast by three feet.

The most recent—and very dramatic—series of eruptions that spectacularly began on January 3, 1983, has continued virtually unabated ever since, producing more than one cubic kilometer of lava. Magma bubbled to the surface about two miles away from Pu'u O'o. The gigantic fissure fountained lava and formed Pu'u O'o Cinder Cone, now 800 feet high and almost 1,000 feet across. Over a 3.5-year period, there were 47 episodic eruptions from this vent. On July 20, 1986, a new fissure broke upon the surface at Kupa'ianaha just outside the park in a nature reserve and formed a lava lake about one acre in surface size

## VOLCANO ACTIVITY

For current information on volcano activity in the area, check the Hawaiian Volcano Observatory "Volcano Watch" website at http://hvo.wr.usgs.gov/volcanowatch. Related volcano and earthquake information for the Big Island is also available at http://hvo.wr.usgs.gov and from the Hawaii Center for Volcanology website at www.soest.hawaii.edu/GG/HCV/kilauea; or by calling 808/985-6000 for the Park Service's recorded message. Should there be any major increase in activity, local radio stations give up-to-the-minute news.

and 180 feet deep. At the end of April 1987 all activity suddenly stopped and the lava drained from the lake and tube system, allowing scientists to accurately gauge the depth. About three weeks later, it started up again when lava poured back into the lake, went through the tube system, and flowed back down to the ocean.

More episodic eruptions followed and from that point the flow turned destructive and started taking homes. It flowed about seven miles to the coast through tubes and on the surface, wiping out Kapa'ahu, parts of Kalapana, and most of the Royal Gardens Subdivision, with more than 180 homes incinerated. In May 1989 it moved into the national park proper, and on June 22, it swallowed the park Visitors Center at Waha'ula. Since 1992, lava has been flowing into the ocean within the park. Unexpectedly, in January 1997 the dramatic activity shifted two miles westward to the Napau Crater, where lava erupted in spouts of fire and flows, and Pu'u O'o ceased spewing. Since February 1997, the majority of activity moved back to Pu'u O'o Cinder Cone, where there has been a continual shift of vent locations on the west and southwestern flanks and constant renewed activity inside the crater. Until 1997, remote Waha'ula Heiau was spared, but in August of that year lava inundated and buried the sacred spot. The destruction has caused more than $61 million worth of damage. Many of the homesteaders in the worst areas of the flow were rugged individualists and back-to-nature alternative types who lived in homes that generally had no electricity, running water, or telephones. The homes were wiped out. Some disreputable insurance companies with legitimate policyholders tried to wiggle out of paying premiums for lost homes, although the policies specifically stipulated loss by lava flow. The insurance companies whined that the 2,200°F lava never really touched some of the homes, and therefore they were exonerated from covering the losses. Their claims were resoundingly repudiated in the courts, and people were paid for their losses.

At its height, the output of lava was estimated at 650,000 cubic yards per day, which is equal to 55,000 truckloads of cement, enough to cover a football field 38 miles high. Since this activity started in 1983, it has averaged 300,000–600,000 cubic yards a day (that's over two billion cubic yards!!), added 560 acres of new land to the park and greater acreage to the areas outside the park, and buried about 13 miles of the Chain of Craters Road. For a history of the park's volcanic activity plus up-to-the-minute reports on current activity, see http://hvo.wr.usgs.gov. Related information is also available at www.soest.hawaii.edu/GG/HCV.

## Mauna Loa

At 13,679 feet, this magnificent mountain is a mere 117 feet shorter than its neighbor Mauna Kea, which is the tallest peak in the Pacific, and by some accounts, tallest in the world. Measured from its base, 18,000 feet beneath the sea, it would top even Mt. Everest. Mauna Loa is the most massive mountain on earth, containing 19,000 cubic miles of solid, iron-hard lava, and it's estimated that this titan weighs more than California's entire Sierra Nevada mountain range! In fact, Mauna Loa (Long Mountain), at 60 miles long and 30 miles wide, occupies the entire southern half of the Big Island, with Hawaii Volcanoes National Park merely a section of its great expanse.

The summit of Mauna Loa with its mighty **Maku'aweoweo Caldera** and a broad swath of wilderness on the flank of the mountain rising up to it from Kilauea Caldera are all within park boundaries. This is the least visited part of the park, and in a sense the most separate. In order to visit here you have to hike.

The 17-mile hike to the summit of Mauna Loa is the most grueling in the park. The trailhead (6,662 feet) is at the lookout at the end of the pavement of Mauna Loa Road. Hikers in excellent condition can make the summit in three days round-trip, but four would be more comfortable. There is a considerable elevation gain, so expect freezing weather even in summer and snow in winter. Altitude sickness can also be a problem. En route you pass through *nene* country, with a good chance to spot these lava-adapted geese. Fences keep out feral goats, so remember to close gates after you. The first cabin is at Red Hill (10,035 feet) and the second is on the rim of Moku'aweoweo Caldera (13,250 feet) at the mountaintop. Water is from roof catchments

and should be boiled. Mauna Loa's oval-shape Moku'aweoweo Caldera is more than three miles long and 1.5 miles wide and has vertical walls towering 600 feet. At each end is a smaller round pit crater. From November to May, if there is snow, steam rises from the caldera. The two-mile-long **Cabin Trail** runs along the south rim of the summit caldera, while the 2.5-mile-long **Summit Trail** slips along the north rim to the highest point. The 3.5-mile **Observatory Trail** will also get you to the summit from the Mauna Loa NOAA Weather Observatory on the north slope, but you must ascend via the Saddle Road. The summit treats you to a sweeping panorama that includes the great majority of the Big Island and Haleakala on Maui.

## Special Notes

Everything in the park—flora and fauna, rocks, buildings, trails, etc.—is protected by federal law. Be respectful and do not carry anything away with you! Do not climb on any ancient rock structures and do not deface any petroglyph carvings. The *nene*, Hawaii's state bird, is endangered. By feeding these birds, visitors have taught them to stand in parking lots and by the roadside. What appears to be a humane and harmless practice actually helps kill these rare birds. Being run over by automobiles has become the leading cause of death of adult birds in the park. Please look, but do not try to approach, feed, or harass the *nene* in any way.

Bicycles are permitted in the park on paved roads only and paved sections of the Crater Rim Trail.

## Hiking

There are over 150 miles of hiking trails within the park. One long trail heads up the flank of Mauna Loa to its top; a spiderweb of trails loops around and across Kilauea Caldera and into the adjoining craters; and from a point along the Chain of Craters Road, another trail heads east toward the source of the most recent volcanic activity. But by far the greatest number of trails, and those with the greatest total distance, are those that cut through the Ka'u Desert and along the barren and isolated coast. Many have shelters, and trails that require overnight stays provide cabins or primitive campsites.

Because of the possibility of an eruption or earthquake, it is *imperative* to check in at park headquarters, where you can also pick up current trail information and excellent maps. In fact, a hiking permit is required for most trails outside the Crater Rim Drive area and the stretch along the coast beyond the end of Chain of Craters Drive. Pick up your free permit no more than one day in advance. When hiking, wear long pants and closed-toe shoes or boots. Much of the park is hot and dry, so carry plenty of drinking water. Wear a hat, sunscreen, and sunglasses, but don't forget raingear because it often rains in the green areas of the park. Stay on trails and stay away from steep edges, cracks, new lava flows and any area where lava is flowing into the sea.

If you will be hiking along the trails in the Kilauea Caldera, the free park maps are sufficient to navigate your way. To aid with hikes elsewhere, it's best to purchase and use larger and more detailed topographical maps. Two that are readily available and of high quality are the *Hawaii Volcanoes National Park* by Trails Illustrated and the Earthwalk Press's *Hawaii Volcanoes National Park Recreation Map.*

# Kilauea Caldera

Many sights of Hawaii Volcanoes National Park are arranged one after another along **Crater Rim Drive.** Most of these sights are the "drive-up" variety, but plenty of major and minor trails lead off here and there.

Expect to spend a long full day atop Kilauea to take in all the sights, and never forget that you're on a rumbling volcano where a misstep or loss of concentration at the wrong moment can lead to severe injury or even death. Try to arrive by 9 A.M. with a picnic lunch to save time and hassles. Kilauea Caldera, at 4,000 feet, is about 10°F cooler than the coast. It's often overcast, and there can be showers. Wear walking shoes and bring a sweater and/or windbreaker. Binoculars, sunglasses, and a hat will also come in handy.

Small children, pregnant women, and people with respiratory ailments should note that the fumes from the volcano can cause problems. Stay away from sulfur vents and don't overdo it, and you should be fine.

A very dramatic way to experience the awesome power of the volcano is to take a helicopter tour. The choppers are perfectly suited for the maneuverability necessary to get an intimate bird's-eye view. The pilots will fly you over the areas offering the most activity, often dipping low over lava pools, skimming still-glowing flows, and circling the towering steam clouds rising from where lava meets the sea. When activity is really happening, tours are jammed, and prices, like lava fountains, go sky-high. Remember, however, that these tours are increasingly resented by hikers and anyone else trying to have a quiet experience, and that new regulations might limit flights over the lava area.

## VISITORS CENTER AREA

The best place to start is at the Visitors Center and Park Headquarters. The turn-off is clearly marked along Hwy. 11 at mile marker 30. By midmorning it's jammed, so try to be an early bird. The center is well run by the National Park Service, which offers a free film about geology and volcanism, with tremendous highlights of past eruptions and plenty of detail on Hawaiian culture and natural history. It runs every hour on the hour starting at 9 A.M. Free ranger-led tours of the nearby area are also given on a regular basis, and their start times and meeting places are posted near the center's front doors. Also posted are After Dark in the Park educational interpretive program activities. A self-guided natural history museum gives more information about the geology of the area, with plenty of exhibits on flora and fauna. You will greatly enrich your visit if you take a half-hour tour of the museum, even though more volcano-specific information is available at the state-of-the-art Thomas A. Jaggar Museum a few minutes up the road.

For safety's sake, anyone trekking to the backcountry *must* register with the rangers at the Visitors Center, especially during times of eruption. Do not be foolhardy! There is no charge for camping, and rangers can give you up-to-the-minute information on trails, backcountry shelters, and cabins. Trails routinely close due to lava flows, tremors, and rock slides. The rangers cannot help you if they don't know where you are. Many day trails leading into the caldera from the rim road are easy walks that need no special preparation. The backcountry trails can be very challenging, and detailed maps (highly recommended) are sold at the center along with special-interest geology and natural history publications prepared by the Hawaii Natural History Association. The Visitors Center is open daily 7:45 A.M.–5 P.M.; call 808/985-6000 for trail, camping, or volcanic activity information.

For those who are not traveling by rental car, the public Hele-On Bus stops once a day in front of the Visitors Center Monday–Friday. There are no scheduled stops on weekends. Pick-up for the bus going to Hilo is at 8 A.M. and the cost is $2.25 for a ticket and $1 for a backpack. Coming from Hilo, the bus leaves at 2:40 P.M. from the Mo'oheau Bus Terminal downtown and arrives at Volcano about 3:45 P.M.

## Volcano House

Have you ever dreamed of sleeping with a goddess? Well, you can cuddle up with Pele by staying at Volcano House. If your plans don't include an overnight stop, go in for a look. Sometimes this is impossible, because not only do tour buses from the Big Island disgorge here, but tour groups are flown in from Honolulu as well. A stop at the bar provides refreshments and a tremendous view of the crater. Volcano House still has the feel of a country inn. This particular building dates from the 1940s, but the site has remained the same since a grass hut was perched on the rim of the crater by a sugar planter in 1846. He charged $1 a night for lodging. A steady stream of notable visitors has come ever since: almost all of Hawaii's kings and queens dating from the mid-

dle of the 19th century, as well as royalty from Europe. Mark Twain was a guest, followed by Franklin Roosevelt. Most recently, a contingent of astronauts lodged here and used the crater floor to prepare for walking on the moon. In 1866 a larger grass hut replaced the first, and in 1877 a wooden hotel was built. It is now the Volcano Art Center and has been moved just across the road. In 1885, an expansion added 14 rooms and the dining room, and 35 more rooms were constructed in the mid-1920s. An accident caused the hotel to burn down in 1940, but it was rebuilt the next year.

The person who owned/operated Volcano House the longest was George Lycurgus, who took over management of the hotel in the 1890s. His son, Nick, followed him and managed the hotel until 1969. Since 1986, the hotel has once again been under local management as a concessionaire to the park service.

## Volcano Art Center

Art and history buffs should walk across the street to the Volcano Art Center, 808/967-7565, which is the original 1877 Volcano House, Hawaii's oldest hotel. You not only get to see some fine arts and crafts, but you can take a self-guided tour of this mini-museum, open daily 9 A.M.–5 P.M. except Christmas. A new show featuring one of the many superlative island artists on display is presented monthly, and there are always ongoing demonstrations and special events. Artworks on display are in a variety of media, including canvas, paper, wood, glass, metal, ceramic, fiber, and photographs. There is also a profusion of less expensive but distinctive items like posters, cards, and earthy basketry made from natural fibers collected locally. One of the functions of the art center is to provide interpretation for the national park. All of the 350 or so artists who exhibit here do works that in some way relate to Hawaii's environment and culture. Volcano Art Center is one of the finest art galleries in the entire state, boasting works from the best the islands have to offer. Definitely make this a stop.

As a community-oriented organization, the Volcano Art Center sponsors classes and workshops in arts, crafts, and language; an Elderhostel program; and a season of performing arts, which includes musical concerts, dance performances, and stage plays. Some involve local performers, while others headline visiting artists. Performances, classes, and workshops take place at the Kilauea Theater at the military camp or in town at the Old Japanese Schoolhouse. Tickets for performances are sold individually at local outlets or you can buy a season ticket. For current information and pricing, call the center office at 808/967-8222 or check out the art center website at www.volcanoartcenter.org for what's happening.

## CRATER RIM DRIVE

There are so many intriguing nooks and crannies to stop at along Crater Rim Drive that you'll have to force yourself to be picky if you intend to cover the park in one day. Crater Rim Drive is a circular route; it matters little which way you proceed. Take your choice, but the following sights are listed counterclockwise beginning from Kilauea Visitors Center. Along this road you will travel from a tropical zone into desert, then through a volcanic zone before returning to lush rainforest. The change is often immediate and differences dramatic. Keep this in mind as you travel around the caldera. Your biggest problem on this route will be timing your arrival at the "drive-in" sights to avoid the steady stream of tour buses. Also remember that the Jaggar Museum closes at 5 P.M., so be sure to get around to that point with time enough to allow yourself to appreciate what it has to offer.

### Sulfur Banks

You can easily walk to Sulfur Banks from the Visitors Center along a 10-minute trail. If you're driving, signs along Crater Rim Drive direct you, and your nose will tell you when you're close. As you approach these fumaroles, the earth surrounding them turns a deep reddish-brown, covered over in yellowish-green sulfur. The rising steam is caused by surface water leaking into the cracks where it becomes heated and rises as vapor. Kilauea releases hundreds of tons of sulfur gases every day, with Sulfur Banks being an example.

This gaseous activity stunts the growth of vegetation. And when atmospheric conditions create a low ceiling, the gases sometimes cause the eyes and nose to water. The area is best avoided by those with heart and lung conditions.

### Steam Vents

Within a half mile you'll come to Steam Vents, which are also fumaroles, but without sulfur. The entire field behind the partitioned area steams. The feeling is like being in a sauna. There are no strong fumes to contend with here, just the tour buses. A short hike from here leads to the Crater Rim Trail, where you can view the Steaming Bluff, which is more pronounced when the temperature is cooler, such as early in the morning. **Kilauea Military Camp** is located beyond the vents and is not open to the public except for community events at the theater, the bowling alley, and the cafeteria. The camp serves as an R&R facility for active duty and retired military personnel, and certain other government employees.

### Observatory and Museum

Some distance farther is **Kilauea Overlook,** as good a spot as any to get a look into the caldera, and there are picnic tables near the parking lot. Here too is **Uwekahuna (Wailing Priest) Bluff,** where the *kahuna* made offerings of appeasement to Pele. A Hawaiian prayer commemorates their religious rites. Unless you're stopping for lunch or making your own (appropriate) offering, it's perhaps better to continue on to the observatory and museum, where you not only have the view outside but get a scientific explanation of what's happening around you.

The **Hawaiian Volcano Observatory,** http://hvo.wr.usgs.gov, has been keeping tabs on the volcanic activity in the area since the turn of the 20th century. The actual observatory is filled with delicate seismic equipment and is closed to the public, but a lookout nearby gives you a dentist's view into the mouth of Halema'uma'u Crater (House of Ferns), Pele's home. Steam rises and you can feel the power, but until 1924 the view was even more phenomenally spectacular: a lake of molten lava. The lava has since crusted over and the floor is again black. Scientists do not predict a recurrence in the near future, but no one knows Pele's mind. This is a major stop for the tour buses. Information plaques in the immediate area tell of the history and volcanology of the park. One points out a spot from which to observe the perfect shield volcano form of Mauna Loa—most times too cloudy to see. Another reminds you that you're in the middle of the Pacific, an incredible detail you tend to forget when atop these mountains.

The newest addition to the national park is located next door to the observatory, and offers a fantastic multi-media display of the amazing geology and volcanology of the area. The state-of-the-art **Thomas A. Jaggar Museum,** complete with a miniseries of spectacular photos on movable walls, topographical maps, inspired paintings, and video presentations, is open daily 8:30 A.M.–5 P.M., admission free. The expert staff constantly upgrades the displays to keep the public informed on the newest eruptions. The 30–45 minutes it takes to explore the teaching museum will enhance your understanding of the volcanic area immeasurably. Do yourself a favor and visit this museum before setting out on any explorations, and stop at the book/gift shop for something to take home.

## Halema'uma'u Crater

A string of interesting stops follows the observatory. One points out the Ka'u Desert, an inhospitable lava plain studded with a few scraggly plants. Next comes the **Southwest Rift,** a series of cracks running from Kilauea's summit to the sea. You can observe at a glance that you are standing directly over a major earthquake fault. Dated lava flows follow in rapid succession until you arrive at **Halema'uma'u Overlook** parking lot. A well-maintained cinder trail to the overlook is only one-quarter mile long and gives an upclose view of the crater. The area is rife with fumaroles leaking sulfur dioxide and should be avoided by those with respiratory problems. At the end you're treated to a full explanation of Halema'uma'u. Until this crater crusted over after an explosion in 1942, Halema'uma'u could be seen as a red glow and sometimes as a fabulous display of spouting lava from the Volcano House

Hotel. From here, two trails make tracks across the caldera floor to the far side and back to park headquarters. Farther along the road is a spot that was once an observation point that caved in. You won't take the ground under your feet for granted!

## Keanakako'i Crater

**Keanakako'i Overlook** is set on the rim of the diminutive crater of the same name. This was a prehistoric adze quarry from which superior stone was gathered to make tools. It was destroyed by a flow in 1877. If that seems in the remote past, realize that you just crossed a section of road that was naturally paved over with lava from a "quickie" eruption in 1982!

## Devastation Trail

Most visitors hike along the half-mile Devastation Trail, which could aptly be renamed "Regeneration Trail." The half mile it covers is fascinating, one of the most-photographed areas in the park. It leads across a field devastated by a tremendous eruption from **Kilauea Iki** (Little Kilauea) in 1959, when fountains of lava shot 1,900 feet into the air. The area was once an 'ohi'a forest that was denuded of limbs and leaves, then choked by black pumice and ash. The vegetation has regenerated since then, and the recuperative power of the flora is part of an ongoing study. Blackberries, not indigenous to Hawaii, are slowly taking over. The good news is that you'll be able to pick and eat blackberries as you hike along the paved trail, but the rangers are waging a mighty war against them. Notice that many of the trees have sprouted aerial roots trailing down from the branches: this is total adaptation to the situation, as these roots don't normally appear. As you move farther along the trail, tufts of grass and bushes peek out of the pumice. Then the surroundings become totally barren and look like the nightmare of a nuclear holocaust.

## Thurston Lava Tube

If the Devastation Trail produced a sense of melancholy, the Thurston Lava Tube, otherwise called Nahuku, makes you feel like Alice walking

ROBERT NILSEN

ROBERT NILSEN

**'ohi'a and fern forest**

through the looking glass. Inside is a fairy kingdom. As you approach, the expected signboard gives you the lowdown on the geology and flora and fauna of the area. Take the five minutes to educate yourself. The paved trail starts as a steep incline, which quickly enters a fern forest. All about you are fern trees, vibrantly green, with native birds flitting here and there. As you approach the lava tube, it seems almost man-made, like a perfectly formed tunnel leading into a mine. Ferns and moss hang from the entrance, and if you stand just inside the entrance looking out, it's as if the very air is tinged with green. If there were such things as elves and gnomes, they would surely live here. The walk through takes about 10 minutes, undulating through the narrow passage. At the other end, the fantasy world of ferns and moss reappears.

## Hikes

The **Crater Rim Loop Trail** begins at Volcano House and parallels Crater Rim Drive. Hiking the entire 11.5 miles takes a full day, but you can take it in sections as time and energy permit. It's a well-marked and well-maintained trail, mostly paved or cinder; all you need are proper clothing, water, and determination. For your efforts, you'll get an up-close view of all of the sights outlined along Crater Rim Drive plus other views and vistas.

**Halema'uma'u Trail** provides some of the best scenery for the effort. It begins at park headquarters and descends into Kilauea Caldera, running about 2.5 miles to the Halema'uma'u Crater pit and crossing lava fields that are only 20–25 years old. Circle back via the Byron Ledge Trail, about three miles long, or arrange to be picked up at the Halema'uma'u parking area on the south side of the Crater Rim Drive.

**Kilauea Iki Trail** begins at the Thurston Lava Tube parking lot or at the Kilauea Iki Overlook. One of the most popular, easiest, and picturesque hikes in the park, this four-mile trail generally takes two hours round-trip and passes over the floor of Kilauea Iki Crater, which was a sea of lava in 1959 when an exceedingly tall spume of lava spouted from the crater rim, creating the most spectacular show the volcano has performed in memory. Start by taking the section of the Crater Rim Trail that follows the rim of the Kilauea Iki Crater, then branch west and descend the western edge of the crater wall. From there it's back across the crater floor, where you pass the spouting site and adjacent ash hill, and a zigzag up the eastern side. Or do it in the reverse. If conditions are right, the cracked and buckled floor of the pit might steam as you walk across. It's easy to link up with the Byron Ledge Trail near the west end of this loop, from where you can walk into Halema'uma'u Caldera or back to park headquarters.

On the south side of Kilauea Iki Crater, the one-mile-long **Devastation Trail** links Pu'u Pua'i Overlook and the Devastation Trail parking area, from where there is a link trail to the Byron Ledge Trail on the Kilauea Caldera rim.

A shorter hike that takes you along the north edge of the rim and back via the Sulfur Banks is the **'Iliahi (Sandalwood) Trail,** a hike of just over one mile round-trip. Along this hike, you're not only treated to the sights and sounds of trees and birds, but also to the mysteries of steam vents, faults, and cracks.

Alternately, go left out of Volcano House and follow the **Earthquake Trail,** a section of the Crater Rim Loop Trail, along **Waldron Ledge.** The easy trail takes you along a paved section of the old Chain of Craters Road that was damaged by a 6.6 magnitude quake in 1983. Sections of the road are buckled, and parts have slid down the edge of the rim.

# Chain of Craters Road

The Chain of Craters Road that once linked the park with Kalapana village on the coast was severed by an enormous lava flow in 1995 and can now only be driven to where the flow crosses the road beyond the Holei Sea Arch. Remember that the volcanic activity in this area is unpredictable, and that the road can be closed at a moment's notice. As you head down the road, every bend— and they are uncountable—offers a panoramic vista. There are numerous pull-offs; plaques provide geological information about past eruptions and lava flows. The grandeur, power, and immensity of the forces that have been creating the earth from the beginning of time are right before your eyes. Although the road starts off in the 'ohi'a forest, it opens to broader views and soon cuts diagonally across the *pali* to reach the littoral plain. Much of this section of the road was buried under lava flows from 1969 to 1974. When the road almost reaches the coast, look for a roadside marker that indicates the Puna Coast Trail. Just across the road is the Pu'u Loa Petroglyph Field trailhead. The lower part of the road is spectacular. Here, blacker-than-black seacliffs, covered by a thin layer of green, abruptly stop at the sea. The surf rolls in, sending up spumes of sea water. In the distance, steam billows into the air where the lava flows into the sea. At road's end you will find a barricade and an information hut that's staffed by park rangers throughout the afternoon and into the evening. Read the information and heed the warnings. The 20-mile drive from atop the volcano to the barricade takes about 30 minutes and drops 3,700 feet in elevation.

While hiking to the lava flow is not encouraged, park staff do not stop you from venturing out. They warn you of the dangers and the reality ahead. Many visitors do make the hike (more than three miles one-way), but there is no trail. The way is over new and rough lava that tears at the bottom of your shoes. If you go in the evening when the spectacle is more apparent, a flashlight with several extra batteries is absolutely necessary. To hike there and back could take three to four hours. If you decide to hike, bring plenty of water. There is no shade or water along the way, and the wind often blows along this coast. Do not hike to or near the edge of the water, as sections of lava could break off without warning. Depending upon how the lava is flowing, it may or not be worth the effort. When the lava is flowing, it is often possible to see the reddish glow at night from the end of the road, but you probably won't see much that's distinguishable unless you use high-power binoculars.

## Craters
As you head down Chain of Craters Road you immediately pass a number of depressions for

which the road is named. First on the right side is **Lua Manu Crater,** a deep depression now lined with green vegetation. Farther is **Puhimau Crater.** Walk the few steps to the viewing stand at the crater edge for a look. Many people come here to hear the echo of their voices as they talk or sing into this pit. Next comes **Ko'oko'olau Crater,** then **Hi'iaka Crater** and **Pauahi Crater.** Just beyond is a turn-off to the east, which follows a short section of the old road. This road ends at the lava flow, and from here a trail runs as far as **Napau Crater.**

The first mile or more of the Napau Trail takes you over lava from 1974, through forest *kipuka,* past lava tree molds, and up the treed slopes of **Pu'u Huluhulu.** From this cone you have a view down on Mauna Ulu, from which the 1969–74 lava flow disgorged, and east toward **Pu'u O'o** and the currently active volcanic vents, some seven miles distant. Due to the current volcanic activity farther along the rift zone, you will need a permit to day hike beyond Pu'u Huluhulu; the trail itself may be closed depending upon where the volcanic activity is taking place. However, the trail does continue over the shoulder of Makaopuhi Crater to the primitive campsite at Napau Crater, passing more cones and pit craters, lava flows, and sections of rainforest. A four-hour ranger-led hike out this way runs on Wednesday afternoon only. It's popular and limited to a dozen people, so call to reserve a place at 808/985-6017.

## Roadside Sights

For several miles, Chain of Craters Road traverses lava that was laid down about 40 years ago; remnants of the old road can still be seen in spots. There are long stretches of smooth pahoehoe lava interspersed with flows of clinker 'a'a. Here and there, a bit of green pokes through a crack in the rock, bringing new life to this stark landscape. Everywhere you look, you can see the wild "action" of these lava flows, stopped in all their magnificent forms. At one vantage point on the way is **Kealakomo,** a picnic overlook where you have unobstructed views of the coast. Stop and enjoy the sight before proceeding. Several other lookouts and pull-offs have been cre-

ated along the road to call attention to one sight or another.

The last section of road runs very close the edge of the sea, where cliffs rise up from the pounding surf. Near the end of the road is the **Holei Sea Arch,** a spot where the wave action has undercut the rock to leave a bridge of stone. This is small but a dramatic sight. Enjoy the scene, but don't lean too far out trying to get that perfect picture!

## Pu'u Loa Petroglyphs

The walk out to Pu'u Loa Petroglyphs is delightful, highly educational, and takes less than one hour. The trail, although it traverses solid lava, is discernible. The tread of feet over the centuries has smoothed and discolored the rock. As you walk along, note the *ahu,* traditional trail markers that are piles of stone shaped like little Christmas trees. Most of the lava field leading to the petroglyphs is undulating pahoehoe and looks like a frozen sea. You can climb bumps of lava, from eight to 10 feet high, to scout the immediate territory. Mountainside, the *pali* is quite visible and you can pick out the most recent lava flows—the blackest and least vegetated. As you approach the site, the lava changes dramatically and looks like long strands of braided rope.

The petroglyphs are in an area about the size of a soccer field. A wooden walkway encircles most of them and helps to ensure their protection. A common motif of the petroglyphs is a circle with a hole in the middle, like a donut; you'll also see designs of men with triangular-shaped heads. Some rocks are entirely covered with designs, while others have only a symbolic scratch or two. These carvings are impressive more for their sheer numbers than the multiplicity of design. If you stand on the walkway and trek off at the two o'clock position, you'll see a small hill. Go over and down it, and you will discover even better petroglyphs that include a sailing canoe about two feet high. At the back end of the walkway a sign proclaims that Pu'u Loa meant "Long Hill," which the Hawaiians turned into the metaphor "Long Life." For countless generations, fathers would come here to place pieces of their infants' umbilical cords into small holes as offerings to the gods to grant long life to their children. Concentric circles surrounded the holes that held the umbilical cords. The entire area, an obvious power spot, screams in utter silence, and the still-strong *mana* is easily felt.

The Big Island has the largest concentration of petroglyphs in the state, and this site holds its greatest number. One estimate puts the number at 28,000!

## Waha'ula Heiau

Waha'ula Heiau (Temple of the Red Mouth) radically changed the rituals and practices of the relatively benign Hawaiian religion by introducing the idea of human sacrifice. The 13th century marked the end of the frequent comings and goings between Hawaii and the "Lands to the South" (Tahiti), and began the isolation that would last 500 years until Captain Cook arrived. Unfortunately, this last influx of Polynesians brought a rash of conquering warriors

carrying ferocious gods who lusted for human blood before they would be appeased. Pa'ao, a powerful Tahitian priest, supervised the building of Waha'ula and brought in a new chief, Pili, to strengthen the diminished *mana* of the Hawaiian chiefs due to their practice of intermarriage with commoners. Waha'ula became the foremost *luakini* (human sacrifice) temple in the island kingdom and held this position until the demise of the old ways in 1819. Not at all grandiose, the *heiau* was merely an elevated rock platform smoothed over with pebbles.

Waha'ula lay along the coast road near the eastern end of the park. This entire area is now completely inundated by recent lava flows. Until 1997, the *heiau* itself was a small island in a sea of black lava that miraculously escaped destruction, but in August of that year lava oozed over these 700-year-old walls and filled the compound. Madame Pele has taken back her own.

# Other Park Areas

## KA'U DESERT

### Hilina Pali Road

About two miles down the Chain of Craters Road, the Hilina Pali Road shoots off to the southwest over a narrow roughly paved road all the way to the end at **Hilina Pali Lookout**—about nine miles. Soon after you leave the Chain of Craters Road the vegetation turns drier and you enter the semi-arid Ka'u Desert. The road picks its way around and over old volcanic flows, and you can see the vegetation struggling to maintain a foothold. On the way you pass the Mauna Iki trailhead, Kulanaokuaiki Campground, and former Kipuka Nene Campground—closed to help the *nene* recover their threatened population. You should see geese here, but please leave them alone and definitely don't feed them. The road ends right on the edge of the rift, with expansive views over the benched coastline, from the area of current volcanic flow all the way to South Point. From here, one trail heads down the hill to the coast

while another pushes on along the top of the cliff and farther into the dry landscape. At the pali lookout is a pavilion and restrooms, but no drinking water. This is not a pleasure ride as the road is rough, but it is passable. For most it probably isn't worth the time, but for those looking for isolation and a special vantage point, this could be it.

### Ka'u Desert Trails

**Ka'u Desert Trail** starts along Crater Rim Drive past the Jaggar Museum and heads southwest into the desolation. It runs for about six miles before it meets the Mauna Iki Trail. A second entry to the desert trail starts about eight miles south of the park entrance along Rte. 11, between mile markers 37 and 38. It's a short 20-minute hike from this trailhead to the **Ka'u Desert Footprints**. The trek across the small section of desert is fascinating, and the history of the footprints makes the experience more evocative. The trail is only 1.6 miles round-trip, but allow at least an hour, mostly for observation. The predominant foliage is *'ohi'a* that contrasts with the bleak sur- roundings—the feeling throughout the area is one of foreboding. You pass a wasteland of 'a'a and pahoehoe lava flows to arrive at the foot- prints. A metal fence in a sturdy pavilion sur- rounds the prints, which look as though they're cast in cement. Actually they're formed from pisolites: particles of ash stuck together with moisture, which formed mud that hardened like plaster. Eroded and not very visible, the story of these footprints is far more exciting than the prints themselves.

In 1790 Kamehameha was waging war with Keoua over control of the Big Island. One of Keoua's warrior parties of approximately 80 peo- ple attempted to cross the desert while Kilauea was erupting. Toxic gases descended upon them, and the warriors and their families were en- veloped and suffocated. They literally died in their tracks, but the preserved footprints, al- though romanticism would have it otherwise, were probably made by a party of people who came well after the eruption. This unfortunate oc- currence was regarded by the Hawaiians as a di- rect message from the gods proclaiming their support for Kamehameha. Keoua, who could not deny the sacred signs, felt abandoned and shortly thereafter became a human sacrifice at Pu'ukohola Heiau, built by Kamehameha to honor his war god, Kuka'ilimoku.

From the footprints, **Mauna Iki Trail** heads east, crossing a 1974 flow to connect with the Hilina Pali Road at Kulanaokuaiki Camp- ground. You'll have to follow rock cairns some of the way. The Ka'u Desert Trail continues south and swings around to the east, passing Pepeiao Cabin on the way to the Hilina Pali Overlook. From the cabin, **Ka'aha Trail** heads down to and along the coast to Ka'aha Shel- ter, where it meets a trail coming down from the overlook. From here, the **Puna Coast Trail** mostly parallels the coast, passing Halape and Keauhou shelters and 'Apua Point campsite be- fore it meets the Chain of Craters Road near the petroglyph site. At the shelters, rain catch- ment tanks provide drinking water. In 1975, an earthquake rocked this area, generating a tsunami that killed two campers; more than

30 others had to be helicoptered to safety. All campers must register at the Kilauea Visitors Center. Registering will alert authorities to your whereabouts in case of a disaster. Hiking in the Ka'u Desert requires full hiking and camping gear. Bring plenty of water.

## SMALL DETOURS
### Mauna Loa Road

About 2.5 miles west of the park entrance on the Belt Road, Mauna Loa Road turns off to the north. This road will lead you to the Tree Molds and a bird sanctuary, as well as to the trailhead for the Mauna Loa summit trail. As an added in- centive, a minute down this road leaves 99 per- cent of the tourists behind.

**Tree Molds** is an ordinary name for an ex- traordinary place. Turn right off Mauna Loa Road soon after leaving the Belt Road and fol- low the signs for five minutes. This road runs in to the tree molds area and loops back onto it- self. At the loop, a signboard explains what oc- curred here. In a moment, you realize that you're standing atop a lava flow, and that the scattered potholes were entombed tree trunks, most likely the remains of a once-giant koa forest. Unlike at Lava Tree State Monument, where the magma encased the tree and flowed away, the opposite action happened here. The lava stayed put while the tree trunk burned away, leaving the 15- to 18-foot-deep holes. While the "sights" of this site may not excite some visitors, realizing what happened here and how it happened is an eye-opener.

**Kipuka Puaulu** is a sanctuary for birds and nature lovers who want to leave the crowds behind, just under three miles from Rte. 11 up Mauna Loa Road. The sanctuary is an is- land atop an island. A *kipuka* is a piece of land that is surrounded by lava but has not been inundated by it, leaving the original vegeta- tion and land contour intact. A few hundred yards away, small scrub vegetation struggles, but in the sanctuary the trees form a tower- ing canopy a hundred feet tall. The first sign takes you to an ideal picnic area called Bird Park with cooking grills; the second, 100 yards beyond, takes you to Kipuka Puaulu Loop Trail. As you enter the trail, a bulletin board describes the birds and plants, some of the last remaining indigenous fauna and flora in Hawaii. Please follow all rules. The dirt trail is self-guided, and pamphlets describing the stations along the way may be dispensed from a box near the start of the path. The loop is only one mile long, but to really assimilate the area, especially if you plan to do any bird-watching, expect to spend an hour minimum. It doesn't take long to realize that you are privileged to see some of the world's rarest plants, such as a small, nondescript bush called 'a'ali'i. In the branches of the towering 'ohi'a trees you might see an 'elepaio or an 'apapane, two birds native to Hawaii. Common finches and Japanese white eyes are imported birds that are here to stay. There's an example of a lava tube, a huge koa tree, and an explanation of how ash from eruptions provided soil and nutrients for the forest. Blue morning glories have taken over entire hillsides. Once considered a pest and aggressively eradicated, they have recently been given a reprieve and are now considered good ground cover—perhaps even indigenous. When you do come across a native Hawaiian plant, it seems somehow older, almost prehistoric. If a precontact Hawaiian could come back today, he or she would recognize only a few plants and trees seen here in this preserve. As you leave, listen for the melodies coming from the treetops, and hope the day never comes when no birds sing. To hear the birds at their best, come in early morning or late afternoon.

Mauna Loa Road continues westward and gains elevation for approximately 10 miles. It passes through thick forests of lichen-covered koa trees, cuts across **Kipuka Ki,** and traverses the narrow **Ke'amoku Flow.** At the end of the pavement, at 6,662 feet, you find a parking area and lookout. If the weather is cooperating, you'll be able to see much of the mountainside; if not, your field of vision will be much restricted. A trail leads from here to the summit of Mauna Loa. It takes two long and difficult days to hike. Under no circumstances should it be attempted by novice hikers or those unprepared for cold alpine conditions. At times, this road may be closed due to extreme fire conditions.

## 'Ola'a Forest

Off Rte. 11 close to Volcano village, turn on Wright Road (or County Rd. 148) heading toward Mauna Loa. On a clear morning you can see the mountain dead ahead. Continue for approximately three miles until you see a barbed-wire fence. The fence is distinctive because along it you'll see a profusion of *hapu'u* ferns that are in sharp contrast to the adjacent ranch property. Here is an 'ola'a rainforest, part of the national park and open to the public, although park biologists like to keep it quiet. Be aware that the area is laced with cracks and lava tubes. Most are small ankle twisters, but others can open up under you like a glacial crevasse. Here is a true example of a quickly disappearing native forest. What's beautiful about an endemic forest is that virtually all species coexist wonderfully. The ground cover is a rich mulch of decomposing ferns and leaves, fragrant and amazingly soft.

Although open to the public, entrance to this area is *not* encouraged. There are no maintained trails, no well-recognized and marked trailheads, and no services whatsoever. It's a thick, dense forest that provides no easy visible clues to direction or location, and the park has no maps of the forest that it gives out to visitors. While there are some hunting trails that lace the area, it is not user-friendly and it's very easy to get lost. If you get lost and if no one knows you're in there, it could be life threatening. If you do venture in, bring a compass, a cell phone, plenty of water, warm clothing, and rain gear. Leave your name and telephone number with someone on the outside and set aside a time to contact that person. Also, be aware that you may be trampling native species or inadvertently introducing alien species. The park service is trying to bring the area back to its native Hawaiian rainforest condition through eradication of alien plants and elimination of feral pigs.

# Practicalities

## ACCOMMODATIONS

If you intend to spend the night atop Kilauea, your choices of accommodations are few and simple. Volcano House provides the only hotel, but cabins are available at the campgrounds, and there are a handful of tent campsites along the hiking trails. For military personnel, lodging is offered at the Kilauea Military Camp.

### Cabins and Camping

The main campground in Volcanoes, **Namakani Paio,** clearly marked off Rte. 11, is situated in a stately eucalyptus grove. There is no charge for tent camping and no reservations are required. It's first-come, first-served. There are cooking grills by each campsite, but no wood or drinking water is provided. While there are toilets, there are no shower facilities for those camping and hiking within the park, so make sure you're with people who like you a whole bunch. Ten small **cabins** are available here through Volcano House. Each accommodates four people and costs $40 single

or double, and $8 each for a third or fourth person. A $12 refundable key deposit gives access to the shower and toilet, and a $20 refundable deposit gets you linens, soap, towels, and a blanket (extra sleeping bag recommended). Each cabin contains one double bed and two single bunk beds and an electric light, but no electrical outlets. Outside are a picnic table and barbecue grill, but you must provide your own charcoal and cooking utensils. Check in at Volcano House after 3 P.M. and check out by noon.

There are also camping spaces and restrooms at **Kulanaokuaiki,** located halfway down Hilina Pali Road. As at Namakani Paio, these are on a first-come, first-served basis. No reservations are required and no fee is charged. As it sits in the middle of this arid desert, it's hot, dry, and has little shade. No drinking water is provided.

For backcountry overnight camping, apply at the Kilauea Visitors Center (7:45 A.M.–4:45 P.M.) for a free permit no earlier than the day before you plan to hike. Camping is permitted only in established sites and at trail shelters. No open

cabins at Namakani Paio Campground

fires are permitted. Carry all the drinking water you will need, and carry out all that you take in.

## Volcano House

If you decide to lodge at Volcano House, P.O. Box 53, Hawaii Volcanoes National Park, HI 96718, 808/967-7321 or 800/325-3535, don't be frightened away by the daytime crowds. They disappear with the sun. Since the mid-1980s, Volcano House has gone through a slow renovation and once again shines as what it always has been: a quiet country inn. The 42 rooms are comfy but old-fashioned. Who needs a pool or TV when you can look out your window into a volcano caldera? To the left of the reception area indoors, a crackling fireplace warms you from the chill in the mountain air, and this fire has burned virtually nonstop since the early days of the hotel. In front of the fireplace are stuffed leather chairs and a wonderful wooden rocker. Paintings and vintage photographs of the Hawaiian kings and queens of the Kamehameha line and magnificent photos of eruptions of the mountain hang on the walls. The hotel, owned and operated by a *kama'aina* family, is an authorized concession of the park. Room rates are main building with crater view $165–185, non-crater view $135; Ohia Wing standard room $85, garden view $95; $15 extra for each additional person. No charge for children 12 and under occupying the same room as their parents. Rooms include koa wood furniture, Hawaiian quilted comforters, a telephone, and room heater, and each has a private bath or shower. Efficiently run, the hotel has a restaurant, lounge, two gift shops, 24-hour front desk service, maid service, and safe-deposit boxes. Besides that, you could hardly get closer to the crater if you tried.

## Kilauea Military Camp

One mile west of the park entrance, within the park boundary, is the Kilauea Military Camp. Offering rooms and meals, this facility is open to active duty and retired military personnel, civilian employees of the Department of Defense, and their families. Available are dormitory rooms, one-, two-, and three-bedroom cottages, and apartments. Services include a lounge bar, recreation facility, tennis courts, athletic fields, a general store, post office, Laundromat, and gas station—all for guests only. Open to the public are the cafeteria, which serves three meals a day; the theater, which hosts community events; a bowling alley with state-of-the-art equipment and its snack bar, open daily 3–10 P.M. Tours of the island can be arranged by the front office staff, and shuttle pick-up from the Hilo airport can also be arranged with advance notice. For additional information, availability, and fees, write KMC Lodging, A Joint Services Recreation Center, Attn.: Reservations, Hawaii Volcanoes National Park, HI 96718; 808/967-8333, fax 808/967-8343, reservations@kmc-volcano.com, www.kmc-volcano.com.

# FOOD AND SHOPPING

## Food

**Volcano House Restaurant** offers a breakfast buffet daily 7–10:30 A.M. for $9.50 or $5.50 for children ages 2–11, that includes cereals, milk, and juices, an assortment of pastries, pancakes topped with fruit and macadamia nuts, sweet bread French toast, scrambled eggs, and Portuguese sausage. A lighter continental breakfast is $5.50. The lunch buffet, $12.50 adult or $7.50 per child, is served daily 11 A.M.–2 P.M. Often terribly crowded because of tour buses, the lunch buffet offers tossed greens and assorted vegetables, fresh fruit platters, stuffed mahimahi, pot roast, honey-dipped chicken, and drinks. If there are too many tour buses parked outside during the lunch hour, give it a miss and try later. Dinner, nightly 5:30–9 P.M., starts with appetizers like sautéed mushrooms and a fruit platter. It moves on to entrées like seafood linguine, scampi, New York steak, catch of the day, and roast prime rib, the specialty. Most entrées run $15–22. A child's menu is also available with dishes under $8. The quality is good, portions large, and the prices reasonable; reservations are recommended. More than the food, however, the view out the big picture window over the caldera is worth the price.

For a nightcap, Uncle George's Lounge, just off the main entry, is a perfect spot to relax and watch the crater disappear into the dark. It closes when the restaurant stops serving.

The **KMC cafeteria** is open to the public for buffet-style dining three meals a day: 7–9:30 A.M., 11 A.M.–1 P.M., and 5:30–8 P.M. Fairly nondescript, this cafeteria is pleasant enough and scrupulously clean. Warmers on the buffet line keep the food trays steaming like the steam vents down the road. While not exceptional in any way, the food is hearty, filling, military fare that's very easy on the pocketbook.

## Shopping

If you are after an exquisite piece of art, a unique memento, or an inexpensive but distinctive souvenir, be sure to visit the **Volcano Art Center.** It's a treat.

When your little tummy starts grumbling, head for the snack shop at the hotel to appease it; it's open 9 A.M.–5 P.M. The hotel also has two gift shops that carry a wide assortment of tourist gifts, crafts, postcards, film, souvenirs, and a selection of logo wear. They are open 7 A.M.–7:15 P.M. Along the road, the Jaggar Museum has a small gift shop that carries a fine selection of books and gifts relating to Hawaii's natural environment.

BIG ISLAND OF HAWAI'I

# Ka'u

The Ka'u district is as simple and straightforward as the broad, open face of a country gentleman. It's not boring, and it does hold pleasant surprises for those willing to look. Formed entirely from the massive slopes of Mauna Loa, the district presents some of the most ecologically diverse land in the islands. The bulk of it stretches 50 miles from north to south and almost 30 miles from east to west, tumbling from the snowcapped mountains through the cool green canopy of highland forests. The domain of sugar until 1995, its middle elevations now support stands of macadamia nut trees, eucalyptus, koa, and coffee. At lower elevations it becomes pastureland of belly-deep grass ending in blistering-hot black sands along the coast that are encircled by a necklace of foamy white sea. Much has been scored by recent lava flows and shaken by powerful earthquakes—the worst in 1868. At the bottom of Ka'u is **Ka Lae** (South Point), the southernmost tip of Hawaii and the southernmost point in the United States. It lies at a latitude 500 miles farther south than Miami and twice that below Los Angeles. Ka Lae was probably the first landfall made by the Polynesian explorers on the islands, and the entire area, particularly the more watered coastal spots, seems to have been heav-

Punalu'u's black-sand beach

ily populated by early immigrants. A variety of archaeological remains support this belief.

Most people dash through Ka'u on the Hawaii Belt Road, heading to or from Volcanoes National Park. Its main towns, **Pahala** and **Na'alehu,** are little more than pit stops. The Belt Road follows the old Mamalahoa Trail where, for centuries, nothing moved faster than a contented man's stroll. Ka'u's beauties, mostly tucked away down secondary roads, are hardly given a look by most unknowing visitors. If you take the time and get off the beaten track, you'll discover black- and green-sand beaches, turtles basking on the shore, Wild West rodeos, a Tibetan Buddhist temple, and an electricity farm sprouting windmill generators. The upper slopes and broad pasturelands are the domain of hunters, hikers, and *paniolo,* who still ride the range on sure-footed horses. In Ka'u are sleepy plantation towns that don't even know how quaint they are, and beach parks where you can count on finding a secluded spot to pitch a tent. Time in Ka'u

moves slowly, and *aloha* still forms the basis of day-to-day life.

The majority of Ka'u's pleasures are accessible by standard rental car, but many secluded coastal spots can be reached only by 4WD. For example, **Ka'iliki'i,** just west of Ka Lae, was an important fishing village in times past. A few archaeological remains are found here, and the beach has a green cast due to the lava's high olivine content. Few tourists ever visit, although hardy souls come to angle the coastal waters. Spots of this type abound, especially in Ka'u's remote sections. But civilization has found Ka'u as well: When you pass mile marker 63, look down to the coast and notice a stand of royal palms and a large brackish pond. This is Luahinivai Beach, one of the finest on the island, where country and western star Loretta Lynn built a fabulous home. Those willing to abandon their cars and hike the sparsely populated coast or interior of Ka'u are rewarded with areas unchanged and untouched for generations.

## Towns and Sights

### PAHALA

Some 22 miles southwest of Volcano is Pahala, clearly marked off Rte. 11. The Hawaii Belt Road flashes past this town, but if you drive into it, you'll find one of the best-preserved examples of a classic sugar town in the islands. Not long ago, the hillsides around Pahala were blanketed by fields of cane and dotted with camps of plantation workers. It was once gospel that sugar would be "king" in these parts forever, but the huge mill is gone, and the background whir of a modern macadamia nut-processing plant now breaks the stillness.

With 1,500 people, Pahala has the largest population in the district, even though some people left with the closing of the mill. In town you'll find the basics—a gas station, district hospital, small shopping center, post office, several churches and temples, a Bank of Hawaii office, Mizuno's Superette, and a plate lunch restaurant. Recently, Tex Drive-In of Honoka'a has

opened a branch in Pahala, so now you're able to get excellent quality local food and hot *malasadas* at a reasonable price. On the outskirts of town, just beyond where the mill used to stand, is Pahala Plantation Store. This shop is open daily, selling gifts, souvenirs, some artwork, coffee, snacks, T-shirts, books, and more.

### Pahala Plantation Cottages

When the sugar mill closed, many people left Pahala and the surrounding area. The town slumped but never disappeared. It has hung on and has slowly managed to infuse life back into itself. Recently, travelers have started to discover what a peaceful area of the island this is and what a fine example Pahala is of a former plantation community. To cater to the traveling public, Pahala Plantation Cottages offers a number of vacation rental accommodations in town, including the renovated seven-bedroom, four-bath plantation manager's house, which rents for $500 a night or $85 a room. Other nearby renovated and spacious one- to four-bedroom plantation cottages run $85–185 a night and are sizable enough for a family. As each has a full kitchen, no meals are provided. For information, contact Julie Neal at P.O. Box 940, Pahala, HI 96777, 808/928-9811, mahalo@aloha.net, www.pahala-hawaii.com.

## Wood Valley Temple

Also known as Nechung Dorje Drayang Ling, or Immutable Island of Melodious Sound, the Wood Valley Temple, P.O. Box 250, Pahala, HI 96777, 808/928-8539, fax 808/928-6271, nechung@aloha.net, www.planet-hawaii.com /nechung, is true to its name. This simple vermilion and yellow Tibetan Buddhist temple sits like a sparkling jewel surrounded by the emerald-green velvet of its manicured grounds, which are scented by an aromatic stand of majestic eucalyptus trees. The grounds, like a botanical garden, vibrate with life and energy.

The Buddha gave the world essentially 84,000 different teachings to pacify, purify, and develop the mind. In Tibetan Buddhism there are four major lineages, and this temple, founded by Tibetan master Nechung Rinpoche, is a classic synthesis of all four. Monks, lama, and scholars from different schools of Buddhism are periodically invited to come and lecture as resident teachers. The Dalai Lama came in 1980 to dedicate the temple and graced the temple once again in 1994 when he addressed an audience here of more than 3,500 people. Programs vary, but people genuinely interested in Buddhism come here for meditation and soul-searching as well as for peace, quiet, relaxation, and direction. Morning and evening services at 7 A.M. and 6:30 P.M. are led by the Tibetan monk in residence. Formal classes depend upon which guest teacher is in residence.

Buddhists strive to become wise and compassionate people. The focus of the temple is to bring together all meditation and church groups in the community. Plenty of local Christian and Buddhist groups use the nonsectarian facilities. Any group that is spiritually, socially, and community oriented and that has a positive outlook

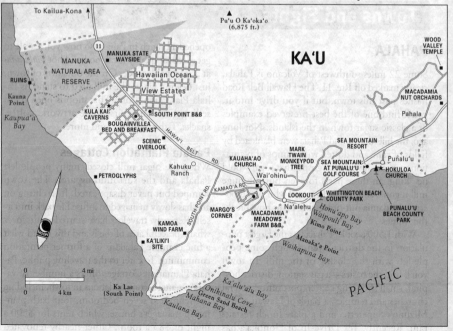

KA'U

To Kailua-Kona

Pu'u O Ka'oka'o (6,875 ft.)

WOOD VALLEY TEMPLE

11

MANUKA STATE WAYSIDE

MANUKA NATURAL AREA RESERVE

RUINS

Kauna Point

*Kaupua'a Bay*

Hawaiian Ocean View Estates

MACADAMIA NUT ORCHARDS

Pahala

KULA KAI CAVERNS

SOUTH POINT B&B

BOUGAINVILLEA BED AND BREAKFAST

SCENIC OVERLOOK

HAWAI'I BELT RD.

Kahuku Ranch

SEA MOUNTAIN RESORT

KAUAHA'O CHURCH

MARK TWAIN MONKEYPOD TREE

SEA MOUNTAIN AT PUNALU'U GOLF COURSE

Puñalu'u

HOKULOA CHURCH

Wai'ohinu

KAMAO'A RD.

PETROGLYPHS

SOUTH POINT RD.

LOOKOUT

WHITTINGTON BEACH COUNTY PARK

Na'alehu

KAMOA WIND FARM

MARGO'S CORNER

MACADAMIA MEADOWS FARM B&B

*Honu'apo Bay*

*Waipouli Bay*

Kimo Point

PUNALU'U BEACH COUNTY PARK

KA'ILIKI'I SITE

Manaka'a Point

Waikapuna Bay

0      4 mi

0      4 km

Ka Lae (South Point)

Ka'alu'alu Bay

Onikinalu Cove

Green Sand Beach

Mahana Bay

Kaulana Bay

PACIFIC

MOON

is welcome. Wood Valley Temple can't promise nirvana, but they can point you to the path.

The retreat facility is called the Tara Temple and at one time housed a Japanese Shingon Mission in Pahala. When the Shingon sect moved to a new facility in Kona, this building was abandoned and given to Wood Valley Temple. A local contractor moved it to its present location in 1978, cranked it up one story, and built dormitories underneath. The grounds, hallowed and consecrated for decades, already held a Nichiren temple, the main temple here today, that was dismantled in 1919 at its original location and rebuilt on its present site to protect it from lowland flooding.

If you wish to visit, please do so on weekends and be respectful, as this is a retreat center. For those staying, either as guests or as part of a program, rates at the retreat facility are private room single $50, double room $70; bunk in the dorm $35, with use of a large communal kitchen and shared bath. Meals are not provided. All require a two-night minimum stay or a $10 surcharge for only one night. Weekly discounts and group rates are available. Definitely call or write to make reservations and get directions.

## Kapapala Ranch

Even though sugar is gone, ranching is not. The 24,000-acre Kapapala Ranch still manages a working enterprise between the town of Pahala and the national park and offers excursions onto the property. A two-hour trail ride runs $75 per person, a 4WD day-long work adventure with the owner is $100 per person, limit two, while a 4WD tour runs $150 an hour with a two-hour minimum for up to five passengers. Also offered is an overnight camping experience on ranch land that can be done by horse, hiking with pack mules, or vehicle. Arrange cost with the ranch. Near the ranch home, several of the ranch hand cabins have been refurbished and turned into cozy and homey guest cottages. Able to sleep up to six, each has a full kitchen, bathroom, and bedrooms. For reservations, rates, and other inquiries, call 808/968-6585, fax 808/968-6059, pre@bigisland.net, www.kapapala.com.

## PUNALU'U

Along the coast just south of Pahala are the small communities of Punalu'u and Ninole. Punalu'u was an important port during the sugar boom of the 1880s and even had a railroad. Notice the tall coconut palms in the vicinity, unusual for Ka'u. Punalu'u means "Diving Spring," so named because freshwater springs can be found on the floor of the bay. Native divers once paddled out to sea, then dove with calabashes that they filled with fresh water from the underwater springs. This was the main source of drinking water for the region.

What was Ninole is now home to the **Sea Mountain Resort and Golf Course,** built in the early 1970s by a branch of the C. Brewer Company. The string of flat-topped hills in the background is the remains of volcano cones that became dormant about 100,000 years ago. In sharp contrast with them is **Lo'ihi Seamount,** 20 miles offshore and about 3,000 feet below the surface of the sea. This very active submarine volcano is steadily building and should reach

the surface in just a few tens of thousands of years. Near Ninole is **Hokuloa Church,** which houses a memorial to Henry Opukaha'ia, the Hawaiian most responsible for encouraging the first missionaries to go to Hawaii to save his people from damnation.

## Punalu'u Beach County Park

Punalu'u Beach Park (near mile marker 56) is a county park with full amenities and famous for its black-sand beach. Here you'll find a pavilion, bathrooms, showers, drinking water, telephone, and open camping area (permit required). During the day there are plenty of tourists around, but at night the beach park empties, and you virtually have it to yourself. Punalu'u boasts some of the only safe swimming on the south coast, but that doesn't mean that it can't have its treacherous moments. Head for the northeast section of the black-sand beach near the boat ramp. Stay close to shore because a prevailing rip current lurks just outside the bay. Hawaiian green sea turtles and hawksbill turtles use this beach for building their nests and they're often seen swimming in the bay. When they're around, please give them plenty of room and don't harass them—it's the law.

A *kaukau* wagon often parks at Punalu'u Beach, offering island sandwiches, shave ice, cold drinks, and snacks.

## Sea Mountain Resort

Sea Mountain Resort, P.O. Box 70, Pahala, HI 96777, 808/928-8301 or 800/488-8301, fax 808/928-8008, is a time-share condominium that also rents available units to the general public—but only up to 60 days in advance. Options include a studio at $80 garden view or $100 ocean view, one bedroom $100–125, and two bedrooms $125–155. Because of its rural location, Sea Mountain can offer secluded accommodations for reasonable prices. Your condo unit will be a low-rise, Polynesian-inspired bungalow with a shake roof. The standard units, all tastefully furnished, offer remote color TVs, full kitchens, full baths, ceiling fans, and a lanai. The resort itself has a swimming pool and spa pool, laundry facilities, four unlit tennis courts, and a golf course. Although the units vary, all are furnished in island theme, typically with rattan couches and easy chairs. The feeling throughout the resort is a friendly, home-away-from-home atmosphere. Outside your door are the resort's fairways and

Another view of Punalu'u's black-sand beach

greens, backdropped by the spectacular coast. If you're after peace and quiet, Sea Mountain is hard to beat.

Ninole Cove Park, part of the Sea Mountain Resort, is within walking distance and open to the public. For day use, you might consider parking near the pro shop. As you walk to the beach from here you pass a freshwater pond, quite cold but good for swimming.

The **Sea Mountain at Punalu'u Golf Course,** 808/928-6222, is a 6,416-yard, 18-hole, par-72 course. As it's set right on the coast, the winds can be strong and usually blow across the fairways, creating challenging play. Greens fees are $32 weekdays and $35 weekends for guests, $42 and 45, respectively, for visitors; clubs are available to rent. Range balls are $5 a bucket and golf lessons $25 an hour. The clubhouse offers morning coffee at 7 A.M., serves a limited menu of sandwiches and *pu pu* from 10 A.M.–2 P.M., and has a full bar that's open later.

# NA'ALEHU AND VICINITY

Between Punalu'u and Na'alehu, the coastal area is majestic; stretching into the aqua-blue sea is a tableland of black lava with waves crashing against it in a surrealistic seascape that seems to go on forever.

## Whittington Beach County Park

Three miles north of Na'alehu is a county park with full amenities and camping, but no drinking water. To its side are ponds and palm trees, a spot sometimes used by fishermen. This park is tough to spot from the road because it's not clearly marked. Before the hill going up to Na'alehu you'll see a bridge at the bottom. Turn right and proceed down the access road. The park is never crowded. Here you'll encounter some old ruins from the turn of the 20th century when Honu'apo Bay was an important sugar port. Before that, this was a sizable Hawaiian settlement. On the way up the hill, pause at the lookout, enjoy the seascape, and consider that only the tiny specks of the South Pacific islands are between here and Antarctica! If that starts a chill on your shoulders, also know that Ka'u is the

warmest region of the island, and Na'alehu hit 100 degrees in 1931, the highest temperature recorded in the state.

Open daily across from Whittington Beach is a souvenir and neat tourist junk shop. Inside, find hula skirts, wooden boxes, *kukui* nut lei, wooden platters, straw hats, and tiki carvings.

## Na'alehu

Na'alehu, the largest town in the area and the most southern town in the United States, is lush. Check out the overhanging monkeypod trees. They form a magnificent living tunnel as you go down Rte. 11 through the center of town. Every Fourth of July, a down-home rodeo is held in town for all the amateur riders of the district. Come and enjoy. Na'alehu is a former sugar town, but it still maintains a small downtown business area, has a post office, and supports a gas station.

### Na'alehu Practicalities

**Becky's Bed & Breakfast,** P.O. Box 673, Na'alehu, HI 96772, tel./fax 808/929-9690 or 866/422-3259, beckys@hi-inns.com, http://1bb .com/Beckys, is about 100 yards east of the theater, *mauka* of the road. Available in this modest but cheery plantation home, built originally for the company doctor in 1937, are two spacious rooms with queen beds and one room with two double beds. Each room has a private bath, and two have private entrances. They run $70 single or $75 double. To help you relax, the B&B features a backyard deck. To get you started, a full breakfast of juice, fruit, and a griddle entrée is served every morning except Sunday.

On the west side of town, at the intersection with the Na'alehu Theater, grocery and hardware stores, a large, easily spotted sign marks the **Punalu'u Bake Shop and Visitor Center,** 808/929-7343, open daily 9 A.M.–5 P.M. The bake shop, tempting with all kinds of pastries, is especially known for its *pao dolce,* sweet bread. Park and follow daily busloads of tourists down a cement pathway to the retail shop for baked goods, sandwiches, ice cream, coffee, cold drinks, and a smattering of souvenirs. Punalu'u sweet bread is well known throughout the island. Have a look at the operation through the viewing windows. The cool and pleasing gardens here make a fine rest stop for the long stretches through this part of the island.

For a quick sandwich or full meal try the **Na'alehu Coffee Shop,** 808/929-7238, open until 8 P.M. except Wednesdays and Sundays. Many of the local people call this restaurant "Roy's," after the owner's first name. The menu is typical island cuisine with a Japanese flavor; the best item is the fresh fish from local waters. The restaurant is basic and clean, with most meals on the menu around $9. In the attached Menehune Treasure Chest shop there's a wide assortment of souvenirs and tourist junk. Look for the big yellow building near the shopping center as you enter town.

With more diversity in its menu, **Shaka Restaurant,** 808/929-7404, is the second local eatery in town and located just up from the theater. Open daily except Monday 10 A.M.–9 P.M., this eatery is clean and well run, with tapa patterns on the tablecloths and chair cushions. Friday brings live evening entertainment and a prime rib special. Extensive breakfast and lunch menus feed hungry folks during the day and in the evening your choices include grilled chicken fillet, baby back ribs, fresh catch, New York steak, and veggie stir-fry. Meals come with soup and a dinner salad, and a kid's menu helps keep the prices down for families. Not gourmet by any means, you won't go away hungry or disappointed.

**Na'alehu Fruit Stand,** 808/929-9009, open Mon.–Thurs. 9 A.M.–6 P.M., Friday and Saturday until 7 P.M., Sunday until 5 P.M., is a favorite with local people, always a tip-off that the food is great. Along with fresh fruit, it sells submarines, hot dogs, pizza, quiche, salads, soda, tea, coffee, fresh baked goods, and a good selection of grains, minerals, vitamins, and health foods. If you're staying in the area, check out the rental video collection. Outside is a bulletin board for local events. This is the best place on the south coast for a light meal or picnic lunch.

About 100 yards from the Na'alehu Fruit Stand, notice the baseball park. Here **Kalaiki Plate Lunch,** open daily 6:30 A.M.–3 P.M., run by the Hanoa family, serves hearty sandwiches and island favorites ready to go. This place is especially known for its full breakfasts, only $5.

If you are in town on Saturday morning, stop by the **farmers market** at the theater.

**Na'alehu Shopping Center** is along the road at the west end of town. In the small complex you'll find the small but full-service, open daily **Island Market** grocery store and Ed's Laundromat. Across the street is an Ace Hardware store.

The **Na'alehu Theater,** 808/929-9133, is a large building along the highway in front of the shopping center. It's a classic old-time theater usually open on weekends, and a venue of the Hawaii International Film Festival. Call for what's showing.

## Wai'ohinu

A tall church steeple welcomes you to the small town of Wai'ohinu. There's nothing remarkable about this village, except that as you pass through you'll be seeing an example of the real Hawaiian country lifestyle as it exists today. Wai'ohinu was an important agricultural region in centuries past, and King Kamehameha even had personal land here. Just before the well-marked Shirakawa Motel on the *mauka* side of the road is the **Mark Twain Monkeypod Tree.** Unfortunately, Wai'ohinu's only claim to fame—except for its undisturbed peace and quiet—blew down in a heavy windstorm in 1957. Part of the original trunk, carved into a bust of Twain, is on display at the Lyman House Museum in Hilo. A shoot from the original trunk has grown to become a sizable descendant of the town's original attraction.

## Wai'ohinu Practicalities

The **Shirakawa Motel,** P.O. Box 467, Na'alehu, HI 96772, 808/929-7462, is a small, clean, comfortable, "hang loose bruddah" motel where your peace and quiet are guaranteed. The Shirakawa has been open since 1928. The original two-story hotel has now been converted to the home of the retired second-generation owners. Their son now runs the dozen-room, dark green, red roof motel, which consists of clean and utilitarian single-story detached buildings to the side. Prices are a reasonable $30 single, $35 double, $42 kitchenette, $8 for "rollaway children" and $10 for "rollaway adult" (if only it were that easy!). There's a 10 percent discount for a one-week stay, 15 percent for longer.

A short hop west of town is **Macadamia Meadows Farm B&B**, P.O. Box 756, Na'alehu, HI 96772, tel./fax 808/929-8097 or 888/929-8118, kaleena@aloha.net, www.macadamiameadows.com, set as you might expect, in the middle of an eight-acre working macadamia nut farm. But this is more than just a B&B. With the full-size tennis court, swimming pool, and basketball court, it seems like a mini-resort, and when you get restless, you can stroll through the orchard. The huge main house, with open kitchen, dining and living areas, and wraparound lanai, looks out on the back lawn and nut trees. In the main house are the spacious Mukupuni Room for $75, Volcano Room for $75, and smaller Hawaiian Room at $65. Downstairs is the Honeymoon Suite with its canopy queen bed and clawfoot tub for $125. In the newer detached building, the Pauli room with its queen and king beds runs $85, but when combined with an adjacent room and its full bed goes for $120 for up to four people. All rooms have private entrances and television, and only the Hawaiian and Volcano rooms share a bathroom. A hearty and taste-tempting breakfast is served to all guests, and the owners will gladly show you around the farm and introduce you to the world of nut farming.

Margo Hobbs and Philip Shaw of **Margo's Corner**, P.O. Box 447, Na'alehu, HI 96772, 808/929-9614, margos@bigisland.com, can accommodate you in their strikingly original pentagonal guesthouse for $60 single or $75 double. The guesthouse, with a private bath and shower, has a queen-size bed. Brightly painted outside, it's also a rainbow of cheery colors on the inside. Two nights minimum is preferred. Down below, the Adobe Suite, with its private bath and sauna, sleeps four to six people. A bit like a cave, with its curved walls and earthen feel, it's not dark and confining but bright and intriguing with all its detail. This suite has a queen-size futon in the living area and two raised beds in the bedroom. It rents for $100 a night single and $15 for each additional person; two nights minimum. The rate for indoor guests includes full gourmet vegetarian

dinners and breakfast every day. Touring bicyclists and backpackers can camp for $25 per person in the yard among Norfolk pines; a shower is available. An organic vegetable garden is out back—food for your meals. No smoking and no excessive drinking, please. For your extra food needs, Margo's maintains a small but well-stocked health food store that's open in the afternoon. Margo's is about halfway between Na'alehu and the South Point Road, just south of Kama'oa Road in the Discovery Harbor subdivision. Call for exact directions and reservations.

You can pick up supplies and buy gas at **Wong Yuen Store** and gas station, 808/929-7223, open Mon.–Sat. 8 A.M.–7 P.M., Sunday to 5 P.M.

## SOUTH POINT

The Hawaiians simply called this Ka Lae (The Point). Some scholars believe Polynesian sailors made landfall here as early as A.D. 150, and that their amazing exploits became navigating legend long before colonization began. A paved, narrow, but passable road branches off from Rte. 11 approximately six miles west of Na'alehu, and it drops directly south for 12 miles to land's end. Luckily the shoulders are firm, so you can pull over to let another car go by. Car-rental agencies may warn against using this road, but their fears are unfounded. You proceed through a flat, treeless area of rangeland for cattle and horses. Suddenly, incongruously, huge mechanical windmills appear, beating their arms against the sky. This is the **Kamoa Wind Farm.** Notice that this futuristic experiment at America's most southern point uses windmills made in Japan by Mitsubishi! The trees here are bent over by the prevailing wind, demonstrating the obviously excellent wind-power potential of the area. However strong the potential, the wind can also be a liability. You will notice that some of the windmills have been damaged by winds that were too strong. Farther along, you enter countryside controlled by the Hawaiian Homelands agency, some of which you are forbidden to enter. That means that you are not welcome on the land, but you do have the right to remain on the road.

Here the road splits left and right. Go right

until road's end, where you'll find a parking area usually filled with the pickup trucks of local fishermen. Walk to the cliff and notice attached ladders that plummet straight down to where fishing boats can anchor. Local skippers moor their boats here and bring supplies and their catch up and down the ladders, or transfer loads via rope. Nearby is a tall white structure with a big square sign turned sideways like a diamond and a navigational light on its top. It marks the true **South Point,** the southernmost tip of the United States. Directly below this marker is an ancient *heiau* and at water's edge are holes curiously carved into some rocks. These are reputed to be **anchor points** used by early Hawaiians to secure their canoes to shore by long ropes while the current carried them a short way offshore. In this manner, they could fish without being swept away. Usually, a few people are line-fishing from the point, and today fishermen use floats or tiny boats to carry only their lines out to sea. The *ulua,* tuna, and *ahi* fishing is renowned throughout this area. The fishing grounds here have always been extremely fertile, and thousands of shell and bone fishhooks have been found throughout the area. Scuba divers say that the rocks off South Point are covered with broken fishing line that the currents have woven into wild macramé. The rocks are covered with Hawaiian dental floss—monofilament fishing line that has been snapped. Survey the mighty Pacific and realize that the closest continental landfall is Antarctica, 7,500 miles to the south.

Back where the road Ys, follow the road left and pass a series of WWII barracks being reclaimed by nature. This road, too, leads to a parking area and small Hawaiian Homelands office and information center where you pay a few bucks to park. Out front stands a short statue of a native Hawaiian wrapped in chains, symbolic of their situation as a disenfranchised people in their own land. Beyond is Kaulana boat ramp (*kaulana* means "boat landing") where a few seaworthy craft are bobbing away at their moorings and still farther is the trail to Green Sand Beach.

When the Kona winds blow out of the South Pacific, South Point takes it on the chin. The weather should always be a consideration when

fishing at South Point

ROBERT NILSEN

you visit. In times past, any canoe caught in the wicked currents was considered lost. Even today, only experienced boaters brave South Point, and only during fine weather.

There is no official camping or facilities of any kind at South Point, but plenty of boat owners bivouac for a night to get an early start in the morning. The lava flow in this area is quite old and grass-covered, and the constant winds act like a natural lawn mower.

## Green Sand Beach

The trail to Green Sand Beach starts near the boat ramp at Kaulana Bay. Head east from there past the gate. All along are remnants of precontact habitation, including the remains of a *heiau* foundation. If you walk for three miles, you'll come to Papakolea, better known as Green Sand Beach, at Mahana Bay. The lava in this area contains olivine, a green semiprecious stone that weathered into sand-like particles distributed along the beach. You're walking into the wind going there, but it's not a rough go—there's no elevation gain to speak of. The lava in the area is 'a'a, weathered and overlaid by thick ground cover. An ancient eruption deposited 15–18 feet of ash right here, and the grasses grew.

About three miles on, you see what is obviously an eroded cinder cone at the edge of the sea. Peer over the edge to have a peek at the beach with its definite green tinge. This is the only beach along the way, so it's hard to mistake. Green Sand Beach definitely lives up to its name, but don't expect emerald green. It's more like a dull army olive green. Getting down to it can be treacherous. Around the side of the cove, you'll be scrambling over tough lava rock, and you'll have to make drops of four to five feet in certain spots—or you could slide down the sand at the back end. Once you get over the lip of heavy-duty rock, the trail down is not so bad. When you begin your descent, notice overhangs, almost like caves, where rocks have been piled up to extend them. These rocked-in areas make great shelters, and you can see remnants of recent campfires in spots perfect for a night's bivouac. Down at the beach, be very aware of the wave action. The currents can be wicked here, and you should only enter the water on very calm days. No one is around to save you, and you don't want to wind up as flotsam in Antarctica.

# OCEAN VIEW

Before you get to Ocean View, you have a sense of what the area is like when you stop at the highway scenic lookout spot near mile marker 75 and view the strong black lava flows that fill the horizon. Ocean View is often referred to as the largest subdivision in the state. In fact, it is a conglomeration of five subdivisions that is several miles wide and that pushes up the mountain about six miles and down toward the ocean another three. The highest lots are at about 5,000 feet. This unincorporated town of self-sufficient individuals who don't want to be bothered by anyone has been carved out of rough volcanic rubble with an overlay of trees and bush. While not the most scenic, it is attractive in its own untamed way. If you're curious, have a drive through.

Services are located in two small shopping centers that flank the highway. Above the highway, you'll find an Ace Hardware, Ocean View Pizzaria, and the Kahuku Market. Below the highway is a second gas station, the post office, the full-service Ocean View Market, Desert Rose Cafe, and a laundromat. Down the road a piece is Mister Bell's Restaurant and bar. Aside from house lots and a community center, there's not much else here. This area was hit hard by the downturn in the state economy during the 1990s, and often people had to drive long distances to get work—if they could find it at all. Now the area seems to be growing in a slow and steady manner, but people still have a long distance to commute.

There frankly is little to do in Ocean View itself if you are a visitor, but as there are few lights and little air pollution, this is one of the greatest locations for stargazing in the islands without going up to the top of the mountain.

## Kula Kai Caverns

The newest and perhaps most curious offering of this region is the Kula Kai Caverns, P.O. Box 6313, Ocean View, HI 96737, 808/929-7539, www.kulakaicaverns.com. In contrast to the Ka'eleku Caverns on Maui, which are about 30,000 years old, the Kula Kai Cavern system—13 miles of tunnel have been surveyed—is a mere baby at about 1,000 years old. A tour underground here gives you a look at the bowels of the largest mountain in the world, once used for shelter and as a place to collect water in this region of low rainfall. Like other lava tubes in the world, the Kula Kai Caverns shows fine examples of lava shelves, pillars, lava balls, and other customary lava formations. As these interconnected tubes are so close to the surface in some spots, roots of 'ohi'a trees have penetrated the ceiling of the cave and hang like hairy tendrils. The inside cave temperature averages 68°F year round. An easy 30-minute interpretive walking tour ($12 for adults and $8 for kids) leads through the lighted section of the caverns. The more rigorous two-hour spelunking tour ($45, age eight and above) takes you deeper into the maze. On either, the intent is to be an educational and cultural experience. More than to just have a look, it's preferable to learn of the island's volcanic history, how lava tubes form, and how they have been used by man. Other cave tours can be arranged, depending upon your interest and skill level, and all tours are given be prior arrangement only. Long pants and closed-toe shoes are required; gloves, knee pads, hard hats, and lights are provided.

## Accommodations

**Bougainvillea Bed and Breakfast,** P.O. Box 6045, Ocean View, HI 96737, tel./fax 808/929-7089 or 800/688-1763, peaceful@interpac.net, www.hi-inns.com/bouga, has views of the ocean and South Point. The inn is quiet and romantic, with fine landscaping all around, and each room has a private entrance and bath. Guests share the swimming pool, hot tub, barbecue area, TV, and the game and video library. There is nothing out here to block your view, so at night there is unbeatable stargazing! As your sightseeing options are limited in Ocean View, owners Martie and Don Nitsche gladly offer suggestions for activities and can make arrangements for you. A full nutritious homemade breakfast—different each day—is served every morning. Rooms are $65 single or $69 double; $15 for an extra person; two night minimum.

Set just above the highway, **South Point Bed and Breakfast,** 808/939-9049, fax 808/939-7557, P.O. Box 6589, Ocean View, HI 96737, southpointbandb@aol.com, also has views of South Point. As it's reasonably close to the road, there is some traffic noise, but this is somewhat muffled by the tall trees and thick vegetation on property. The bed-and-breakfast rooms run $55–65 double, while one room with a mini-kitchen and no served breakfast has the same rate. A discount of 10 percent is offered for two nights

and 15 percent for five nights or longer; no credit cards. For the starry nights you find here, there's no better place to be in the evening than soaking in the hot tub contemplating the universe.

## Food

**Ocean View Pizzaria,** 808/929-9677, is open Sun.–Thurs. 11 A.M.–7 P.M. and weekends until 8 P.M. While the focus is pizza, smalls run $8 and large pies go for $10, with extra cost for the toppings of your choice, you can also get a salad, hot and cold sandwiches, and even a few baked goods.

The **Desert Rose Cafe,** 808/939-7673, is down below the highway. Advertised as "the southernmost cafe in the USA," the Desert Rose is open for three meals a day. Expect eggs and scrambles for breakfast, sandwiches and burgers for lunch, and a variety of fish and red meat entrées in the $12–15 range for dinner. Basic and clean, this eatery puts out fine nutritious food.

## Manuka State Wayside

The Manuka State Wayside is 12 miles west of South Point Road and just inside the Ka'u district. This civilized scene has restrooms, a pavilion, and a two-mile trail through a native and introduced forest, all of which lies within the Manuka Natural Area Reserve. The forested slopes above Manuka provide ample habitat for introduced, and now totally successful, colonies of wild pigs, pheasants, and turkeys. Shelter camping (no tents) is allowed on the grounds. This is an excellent rest or picnic stop, but bring your own drinking water. Within a couple of miles, you're in South Kona, heading up the coast past the world's largest single-owner macadamia nut farm, toward Captain Cook and Kailua.

# Introduction

# Maui

*How shall we account for this nation spreading it-
self so far over this vast ocean? We find them from
New Zealand to the south, to these islands to the
north and from Easter Island to the
Hebrides. . . how much
farther is not known. . . .*

—Captain James Cook

# Introduction

The *Kumulipo,* the ancient genealogical chant of the Hawaiians, sings of the demigod Maui, a half-human mythological sorcerer known and revered throughout Polynesia. Maui was a prankster on a grand scale who used guile and humor to create some of the most amazing feats of derring-do ever recorded. A Polynesian combination of Paul Bunyan and Hercules, Maui had adventures known as "strifes." He served humankind by fishing up the islands of Hawaii from the ocean floor, securing fire from a tricky mud hen, lifting the sky so humans could walk upright, and slowing down the sun god by lassoing his genitals with a braided rope of his sister's pubic hair. Maui accomplished this last feat on the summit of the great mountain Haleakala (House of the Sun), thus securing more time in the day to fish and to dry tapa. Maui met his just but untimely end between the legs of the great goddess, Hina. This final prank, in which he attempted to crawl into the sleeping goddess's vagina, left his feet and legs dangling out, causing uproarious laughter among his comrades, a band of warrior birds. The noise awakened Hina, who saw no humor in the situation. She unceremoniously squeezed Maui to death. The island of Maui is the only island in Hawaii and throughout Polynesia named after a god. With such a legacy the island couldn't help but become known by the slogan *"Maui no ka 'oi"* ("Maui is the best").

sunset over Ka'anapali

In a land of superlatives, it's quite a claim to call your island *the* best, but Maui has a lot to back it up. Maui has more miles of swimmable beach than any of the other islands. Haleakala, the massive mountain that *is* East Maui, is the largest dormant volcano in the world, and its hardened lava rising more than 30,000 feet from the sea floor makes it one of the heaviest concentrated masses on the face of the earth. There are legitimate claims that Maui grows the best onions and potatoes, but the boast of the best *pakalolo* may only be a pipe dream, since all the islands have great soil and weather and many enterprising gardeners.

## West Maui

If you look at the silhouette of Maui on a map, it looks like the head and torso of the mythical demigod bent at the waist and contemplating the uninhabited island of Kaho'olawe. The head is West Maui, and its profile is that of a wizened old man whose wrinkled brow and cheeks are the West Maui Mountains. The highest peak here is **Pu'u Kukui**, at 5,788 feet, located just about where the ear would be. If you go to the top of the head you'll be at **Kapalua**, a resort community that's been carved from pineapple fields. Fleming Beach begins a string of beaches that continues down over the face, stopping at the chin, and picking up again at the throat, covers the chest, which is South Maui. **Ka'anapali** is at the forehead; its massive beach continues almost uninterrupted for four miles, an area that in comparison would take in all of Waikiki, from Diamond Head to Ala Moana. The resort properties here are cheek to jowl, but the best are tastefully done with uninterrupted panoramic views and easy and plentiful access to the beach. Between Ka'anapali and Kapalua, pineapple fields fringe the mountain side of the road, while condos are strung along the shore throughout the communities of **Honokowai, Kahana,** and **Napili.**

**Lahaina** is located at the Hindu "third eye." This town is where it's "happening" on Maui, with concentrations of craftspeople, artists, museums, historical sites, restaurants, and nightspots. Used in times past by royal Hawaiian *ali'i* and then by Yankee whalers, Lahaina has always been somewhat of a playground, and the good-times mystique still lingers. It's from Lahaina, across the waters of the 'Au'au Channel, better known as the "Lahaina Roads," that people can catch a glimpse of the island of Lana'i. At the tip of the nose is **Olowalu**, where a lunatic Yankee trader, Simon Metcalfe, decided to slaughter hundreds of curious Hawaiians paddling toward his ship just to show them he was boss. From Olowalu you can see four islands: Moloka'i, Lana'i, Kaho'olawe, and a faint hint of Hawai'i far to the south. The back of Maui's head is little known, but for the mildly adventurous it presents tremendous coastal views and Kahakuloa, a tiny fishing village reported to be a favorite stomping ground of great Maui himself.

## Central Maui: The Isthmus

A low, flat isthmus planted primarily in sugarcane is the neck that connects the head of West Maui to the torso of East Maui, which is Haleakala. The Adam's apple is the little port of **Ma'alaea,** which has a good assortment of pleasure and fishing boats as well as the new **Maui Ocean Center.** Ma'alaea provides an up-close look at a working port not nearly as frenetic as Lahaina. The nape of the neck is made up of the twin cities of **Wailuku,** the county seat, and **Kahului,** where most visitors arrive at Maui's principal airport. These towns are where the "people" live. Some say the isthmus, dramatically separating east and west, is the reason Maui is called "The Valley Isle." Head into **'Iao Valley** from Wailuku, where the West Maui Mountains have been worn into incredible peaked monolithic spires. This stunning valley area played a key role in Kamehameha's unification of the Hawaiian Islands, and geologically it seems to be a more fitting reason for Maui's nickname.

## East Maui/Haleakala

Once you cross the isthmus you're on the immensity of **Haleakala,** the one mountain that makes up the entire bulging, muscled torso of the island. A continent in microcosm, its geology encompasses alpine terrain, arid scrub desert, moonscape, blazing jungle, pastureland, and lava-encrusted wasteland. The temperature, determined by altitude, ranges from subfreezing to subtropical. If you head east along the spine, you'll find world-class sailboarding beaches, the artist and surfer village of **Pa'ia,** last-picture-show towns, and a few remaining family farms planted in taro. Route 360, the only coastal road, rocks and rolls you over more than 600 curves and shows you more waterfalls and pristine pools than you can count. After crossing more than 50 bridges, you come to **Hana.** Here, the dream Hawaii that people seek still lives. Farther along is **Kipahulu,** then **'Ohe'o Gulch,** known for its fantastic pools and waterfalls. Close by is where Charles Lindbergh is buried, and many celebrities have chosen the surrounding hillsides for their special retreats and hideaways.

On Haleakala's broad chest is the macho cowboy town of **Makawao,** complete with a Wild West rodeo contrasting with the gentle but riotous colors of carnation and protea farms down the road in **Kula. Polipoli Spring State Recreation Area** is

here, a thick forest canopy with more varieties of imported trees than anywhere else in Oceania. A weird cosmic joke places **Kihei** just about where the armpit would be. Kihei is a mega-growth condo area ridiculed as an example of what developers shouldn't be allowed to do. Oddly enough, **Wailea,** just down the road, exemplifies a reasonable and aesthetic planned, although much more exclusive, community and is highly touted as a "model" development area. Just at the belly button, close to the kundalini, is **Makena,** long renowned as Maui's alternative beach, but rapidly losing its status as the island's last "free" beach.

Finally, when you pilgrimage to the summit of Haleakala, it'll be as if you've left the planet. It's another world: beautiful, mystical, raw, inspired, and freezing cold. When you're alone on the crater rim with the world below garlanded by the brilliance of sunrise or sunset, you'll know that you have come at last to great Maui's heart.

# The Land

After the Big Island of Hawai'i, Maui is the second largest and second youngest of the main Hawaiian Islands. The land was formed from two volcanoes: the West Maui Mountains and Haleakala. The **West Maui Mountains** are geologically much older than Haleakala, but the two were joined by subsequent lava flows that formed a connecting low, flat isthmus. **Pu'u Kukui,** at 5,788 feet, is the tallest peak of the West Maui Mountains. It's the lord of a mountain domain whose old weathered face has been scarred by a series of deep crags, verdant valleys, and inhospitable gorges. Rising more than 30,000 feet from the ocean floor, **Haleakala** is by comparison an adolescent with smooth, rounded features looming 10,023 feet above sea level, with a landmass four times larger than West Maui. The two parts of Maui combine to form 727 square miles of land with 120 miles of coastline. At its farthest points, Maui is 26 miles from north to south and 48 miles east to west. The coastline has the largest number of swimmable beaches

in Hawaii, and the interior is a miniature continent with almost every conceivable geological feature evident.

## Rivers and Lakes

Maui has no navigable rivers, but there are hundreds of streams. Two of the largest are **Palikea Stream,** which runs through Kipahulu Valley forming 'Ohe'o Gulch, and **'Iao Stream,** which has sculpted the amazing monoliths in 'Iao Valley. The longest, at 18 miles, is Kalialinui-Wai'ale Stream, which starts just below the summit of Haleakala, runs through Pukalani, and empties into the ocean near Kahului airport. A few reservoirs dot the island, but the two largest natural bodies of water are the 41-acre **Kanaha Pond,** on the outskirts of Kahului, and 500-acre **Kealia Pond,** on the southern shore of the isthmus; both are major bird and wildlife sanctuaries. Hikers should be aware of the countless streams and rivulets that can quickly turn from trickles to torrents, causing flash floods in valleys that were the height of hospitality only minutes before.

## CLIMATE

Maui has similar weather to the rest of the Hawaiian Islands, though some aficionados claim that it gets the most sunshine of all. The weather on Maui depends more on where you are than on what season it is. The average daily temperature along the coast is about 78° F (25.5° C) in summer and during winter is about 72° F (22° C). On Haleakala summit, that average is 43–50° F (6–10° C). Nights are usually no more than 10 degrees Fahrenheit cooler than days. Since Haleakala is a main feature on Maui, you should remember that altitude drastically affects the weather. Expect an average temperature drop of three degrees for every 1,000 feet of elevation, so at the top, Haleakala is about 30 degrees cooler than at sea level. The lowest temperature ever recorded on Maui was atop Haleakala in 1961, when the mercury dropped well below freezing to a low, low 11° F. In contrast, sunny Kihei has recorded a blistering 98° F.

Maui has wonderful weather, and because of near-constant breezes the air is usually clear and clean. Traffic and weather conditions never create smog, but because of burning cane fields Maui air will at times become smoky, a condition that usually rectifies itself in a day when the winds are blowing. On rarer occasions, a volcanic haze, known as "vog," filters over the island, being blown in from the Big Island. If it's hazy, doesn't smell of smoke, and nothing has been burning, it's probably vog.

### Precipitation

Rain on Maui is as much a factor as it is elsewhere in Hawaii. On any day, somewhere on Maui it's raining, while other areas experience drought. A dramatic example of this phenomenon is a comparison of Lahaina with Pu'u Kukui, both on West Maui and separated by only seven miles. Lahaina, which translates as "Merciless Sun," is hot, arid, and gets only 15 inches of rainfall annually, while Pu'u Kukui can receive close to 400 inches (33 *feet!*) of precipitation. This rivals Mt. Wai'ale'ale on Kaua'i as the wettest spot on earth. Other leeward towns get a comparable amount of rain to Lahaina, but as you move Upcountry and around the north coast, the rains become greater. Finally, in Hana, rainfall is about five times as great as on the leeward side, averaging more than 80 inches a year. The windward (wet) side of Maui, outlined by the Hana Road, is the perfect natural hothouse. Here, valleys sweetened with blossoms house idyllic waterfalls and pools that visitors treasure when they happen upon them. On the leeward (dry)

## MAUI TEMPERATURE AND RAINFALL

| Town | | Jan. | March | May | June | Sept. | Nov. |
|------|------|------|-------|-----|------|-------|------|
| Lahaina | high | 80 | 81 | 82 | 83 | 84 | 82 |
| | low | 62 | 63 | 68 | 68 | 70 | 65 |
| | rain | 3 | 1 | 0 | 0 | 0 | 1 |
| Hana | high | 79 | 79 | 80 | 80 | 81 | 80 |
| | low | 60 | 60 | 62 | 63 | 65 | 61 |
| | rain | 9 | 7 | 2 | 3 | 5 | 7 |
| Kahului | high | 80 | 80 | 84 | 86 | 87 | 83 |
| | low | 64 | 64 | 67 | 69 | 70 | 68 |
| | rain | 4 | 3 | 1 | 0 | 0 | 2 |

Note: Temperature is in degrees Fahrenheit; rainfall in inches.

MAUI

side are Maui's best beaches: Kapalua, Ka'anapali, Kihei, Wailea, and Makena. They all sit in
Haleakala's rain shadow. If it happens to be
raining at one beach, just move a few miles

down the road to the next. Anyway, the rains
are mostly gentle, and the brooding sky, especially at sundown, is even more spectacular
than usual.

## Flora and Fauna

Maui's indigenous and endemic plants, trees, and
flowers are both fascinating and beautiful, but unfortunately, like everything else that was native,
they are quickly disappearing. The majority of
flora considered exotic by visitors was introduced
either by the original Polynesians or by later white
settlers. Maui is blessed with state parks, gardens,
undisturbed rainforests, private reserves, and commercial nurseries, all of which offer brilliant and
dazzling colors to the landscape.

### 'Ahinahina (Silversword)

Maui's official flower is a tiny pink rose called a
*lokelani*. The island's unofficial symbol, however,
is the silversword. The Hawaiian name for silversword is *'ahinahina*, which translates as "gray
gray," and the English name derives from a sil-
verfish, whose color the plant is said to resemble.
The *'ahinahina* belongs to a remarkable plant
family that claims 28 members, with five in the
specific silversword species. It's kin to the common sunflower, and botanists say the entire family evolved from a single ancestral species.
Hypothetically, the members of the *'ahinahina*
family can interbreed and produce remarkable
hybrids. Some plants are shrubs, while others
are climbing vines, and some even become trees.
They grow anywhere from desert conditions to
steamy jungles. On Maui, the *'ahinahina* is only
found on Haleakala, above the 6,000-foot level,
and is especially prolific in the crater. Each plant
lives from five to 20 years and ends its life by
sprouting a gorgeous stalk of hundreds of pur-
plish-red flowers. It then withers from a majestic
six-foot plant to a flat gray skeleton. An endangered species, *'ahinahina* are totally protected.
They protect themselves, too, from radiation
and lack of moisture by growing fuzzy hairs all
over their swordlike stalks. You can see them
along the Haleakala Park Road at Kalahaku Over-

look or by hiking along Silversword Loop on the
floor of the crater.

### Protea

These exotic flowers are from Australia and South
Africa. Because they come in almost limitless
shapes, sizes, and colors, they captivate everyone who sees them. They are primitive, almost
otherworldly in appearance, and they exude a
life force more like an animal than a flower. The
slopes of leeward Haleakala between 2,000 and
4,000 feet are heaven to protea—the growing
conditions could not be more perfect. Here live
the hardiest, highest-quality protea in the world.
The days are warm, the nights are cool, and the
well-drained volcanic soil has the exact combination of minerals on which protea thrive.
Haleakala's crater even helps by creating a natural
air flow that produces cloud cover, filters the
sun, and protects the flowers. Protea make excellent gifts that can be shipped anywhere. As
fresh-cut flowers they are gorgeous, but they have
the extra benefit of drying superbly. Just hang
them in a dark, dry, well-ventilated area and they
do the rest. You can see protea, along with other
botanical specialties, at the gardens, flower farms,
and gift shops in Kula.

### Carnations

If protea aren't enough to dazzle you, how about
fields of carnations? Most Mainlanders think of
carnations stuck in a groom's lapel, or perhaps
have seen a table dedicated to them in a hothouse, but not fields full of carnations! The Kula
area produces carnations that grow outside nonchalantly, in rows, like cabbages. They fill the
air with their unmistakable perfume, and they
are without doubt a joy to behold. You can see
family and commercial plots throughout the
upper Kula area.

# MAUI'S BOTANICAL GARDENS

**Kula Botanical Gardens,** 808/878-1715, has some 2,000 varieties of tropical and semitropical plants, including orchids, bromeliads, fuchsia, protea, *kukui* and sandalwood trees, and numerous ferns, on more than five acres. Located at 3,300 feet near the junction of Routes 377 and 37 at the south end, this privately owned garden is open daily 9 A.M.–4 P.M. for self-guided tours; $5 admission.

**Enchanting Floral Gardens,** 808/878-2531, is located along Route 37 just south of Pukalani at mile marker 10. This private garden features about 2,000 species of native Hawaiian plants as well as exotic plants from around the world on eight acres. Open daily 9 A.M.–5 P.M. for self-guided tours; $5 admission.

**University of Hawaii Experimental Station** offers 20 acres of constantly changing, quite beautiful plants, although the grounds are uninspired, scientific, rectangular plots. Located on Mauna Place just off Copp Road above Route 37 in Kula, this garden is open Mon.–Thur. 7:30 A.M.–3:30 P.M., closed for lunch. Although admission is free, visitors should check in with the station manager.

**Garden of Eden,** along the Hana Highway, is a 26-acre private garden of tropical plants and flowers, many labeled. Open daily 9 A.M.–3 P.M.; $7.50 admission.

**Ke'anae Arboretum,** above Ke'anae Peninsula on the Hana Highway, is always open with no fee. In a natural setting with walkways, many identifying markers, and mosquitoes, this six-acre arboretum is split into two sections: ornamental tropical plants and Hawaiian domestic plants. The native forest swaths the surrounding hillsides.

**Kahanu Gardens,** a branch of the Pacific Tropical Botanical Gardens, is located on the rugged lava coast west of Hana at the site of Pi'ilanihale Heiau. In this 123-acre garden, you'll find stands of breadfruit and coconut trees, a pandanus grove, and numerous other tropical plants from throughout Polynesia. Open Mon.–Fri. 10 A.M.–2 P.M. for self-guided tours; $10 admission. Call 808/284-8912 for information.

**Maui Nui Botanical Gardens** in Keopuolani Park in Kahului is a new garden that focuses on coastal and dryland forest plants from the four islands of Maui County. Open Mon.–Fri. 8 A.M.–4 P.M. and Saturday 9:30 A.M.–2:30 P.M. Free admission. Call 808/249-2798 for information.

**Maunalei Arboretum** is accessible to guided hikes only. Located above Kapalua, this private botanical garden was started in the 1930s.

While not a botanical garden, **Polipoli Spring State Recreation Area** has some magnificent stands of redwoods, eucalyptus, conifers, ash, cypress, cedar, *sugi* and other pines. Various trails lead through the forest. Always open, but way off the beaten track. Similarly, **Hosmer Grove,** within Haleakala National Park at 6,800 feet in elevation, is an experimental forest project from the early 20th century that has fine examples of introduced trees like cedar, pine, fir, juniper, and *sugi* pine that were originally planted in hopes of finding a commercial, economically marketable wood for Hawaii. A short trail now winds through the no-longer-orderly stands of trees. Hike on your own or take a periodic ranger-guided tour. For recorded park information, call 808/572-4400.

## Maui's Endangered Birds

Maui's native birds are disappearing. The island is the last home of the crested honeycreeper (*'akohekohe*), which lives only on the windward slope of Haleakala from 4,500 to 6,500 feet. It once lived on Moloka'i, but no longer. The Maui parrotbill is another endangered bird, found only on the slopes of Haleakala above 5,000 feet. The *po'ouli* is a very rare dark brown bird that was saved from extinction through efforts of the Sierra Club and Audubon Society, who successfully had it listed to the Federal List of Endangered Species. The bird has one remaining stronghold deep in the forests of Maui.

Two endangered waterbirds found on Maui

are the Hawaiian stilt *('ae'o)* and the Hawaiian coot *('alae ke'oke'o)*.

## Whale-Watching

From shore you're likely to see whales anywhere along Maui's south coast. If you're staying at any of the hotels or condos along Ka'anapali or Kihei and have an ocean view, you can spot them from your lanai or window. Two good vantage spots are Papawai Point and McGregor Point along Route 30 just west of Ma'alaea.

During whale-watching season, a Pacific Whale Foundation naturalist may be at McGregor Point daily from 8:30 A.M.–3:30 P.M. with a display van to help people locate whales and answer questions. Ma'alaea Bay is another favorite nursing ground for female whales and their calves. Another excellent viewpoint is Makena Beach, on the spit of land separating Little and Big Beaches. If you time your arrival near sunset, even if you don't see a whale you'll enjoy a mind-boggling light show.

# Government and Economy

Maui County encompasses Maui island, as well as Lana'i, Moloka'i, and the uninhabited island of Kaho'olawe. Of the 25 State Senatorial Districts, Maui County is represented by three, all Democrats. The county also has six House districts of the 51 total, represented by three Democrats and three Republicans. Not surprisingly, the districts with the Republican representatives are the heavily touristed areas of West Maui and South Maui., and Upcountry. West Maui, with Ka'anapali and Lahaina, is one of the most developed and financially sound areas in all of Hawaii. It's a favorite area with tourists and is one of the darlings of developers. South Maui, with the tourist areas of Kihei, Wailea, and Makena has a similar orientation. With both the Senate and House districts, the islands of Lana'i, Moloka'i, and Kaho'olawe are pared with the sparsely populated but heavily "local" area of East Maui. Lana'i has a tiny population, a growing tourist industry, and, in comparison, a minuscule economy. Moloka'i has the largest per capita concentration of native Hawaiians, a "busted economy" with a tremendous share of its population on welfare, and a grassroots movement determined to preserve the historical integrity of the island and the dignity of the people.

Following four years of Democratic control of the mayor's office, Republicans once again control the mayor seat. In 2002, Alan Arakawa won over then incumbent James "Kimo" Apana, who, at age 36, became the youngest mayor in Maui's history in 1998. Although Maui, like the rest of the state, is overwhelmingly Democratic, the Republicans had had their candidate in the mayor's office for most of the 30 years prior to 1998. The mayor is assisted by an elected county council consisting of one member from each council district around the county. For online information pertaining to Maui County, see www.co.maui.hi.us.

Maui's economy is a mirror image of the state's economy: it's based on tourism, agriculture, and government expenditures. The primary growth is in tourism, with Maui being the second most frequently chosen Hawaiian destination after O'ahu. On average, Maui attracts about two million tourists per year, and on any given day there are about 40,000 visitors enjoying the island. More than 17,000 rooms are available on Maui in all categories, and they're filled 75 percent of the time. The majority of the rooms are in Kihei to Wailea and the Ka'anapali to Kapalua strip. With tourists finding Maui more and more desirable every year, and with agriculture firmly entrenched, Maui's economic future is bright.

## Agriculture and Ranching

Maui generates revenue through cattle, sugar, pineapples, and flowers, along with a substantial subculture economy in *pakalolo*. **Cattle grazing** occurs on the western and southern slopes of Haleakala, where 35,000 acres are owned by the Haleakala Ranch, and more than 23,000 acres belong to the Ulupalakua Ranch. The upper slopes of Haleakala around Kula are a gardener's dream. Delicious onions, potatoes, and all sorts of garden vegetables are grown, but they are secondary to large plots of gorgeous flowers, mainly carnations and the amazing protea.

**Sugar,** actually a member of the grass family, is still very important to Maui's economy, but without federal subsidies it wouldn't be a viable cash crop. The largest acreage is in the central isthmus area, which is virtually all owned by the Alexander and Baldwin Company. Maui's one remaining operating mill is located at Pu'unene; the mill in Pa'ia is not being used but has not been dismantled. The Lahaina mill closed in 1996, and the cane fields on the Ka'anapali side have all been abandoned, the land given to pineapple production, developed into residential subdivisions, or simply left fallow. Those lodging in Ma'alaea and north Kihei will become vividly aware of the cane fields when they're burned off just prior to harvesting, putting tons of black smoke and ash into the air, which is otherwise known as black snow. Making these unsightly burnings even worse is the fact that the plastic pipe used in the drip irrigation of the fields is left in place. Not cost-efficient

to recover, it is burned along with the cane, adding its noxious fumes to the air. Luckily, the wind blows strong and constantly across the isthmus of Maui, so the smoke doesn't hang around long, but the ash and smell stay longer.

Maui Land and Pineapple Company grows **pineapples** in central east Maui between Pa'ia and Makawao and on substantial acreage in Kapalua in the far northwest. Some of the pineapples shipped throughout the state and to the Mainland are whole fruits, while much is canned. Maui's first cannery (1914–1920) was in Honokohau, north of Kapalua. From 1920 to 1962, canning was done at the cannery in Lahaina. Today, Maui's only cannery is in Kahului, behind the Ka'ahumanu Shopping Center. With slightly fewer acres in production than sugarcane, pineapple now garners a larger value in total sales of the two.

## Military
The small military presence on Maui amounts to

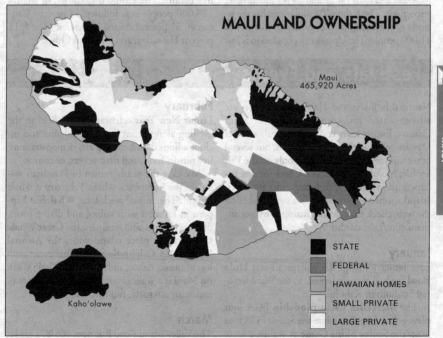

MAUI LAND OWNERSHIP

Maui
465,920 Acres

Kaho'olawe

■ STATE
■ FEDERAL
□ HAWAIIAN HOMES
□ SMALL PRIVATE
▨ LARGE PRIVATE

a tiny Army installation near Kahului and the Coast Guard facility at Ma'alaea.

## Land Ownership

Maui County is about 750,000 acres in size, and of that 465,000 belongs to Maui, 165,000 to Moloka'i, 90,000 to Lana'i, and 28,800 to the uninhabited island of Kaho'olawe. Almost 30,000 acres is owned by the federal government—Haleakala National Park. The state controls about four times that acreage in its various forest and protected land holdings. In three separate sizable sections, the large chunks of Hawai-

ian Home Lands are on the south slope of Haleakala near Kaupo, above Kihei on the western slope of the mountain, and on Moloka'i between Kaunakakai and Mo'omomi Beach. Land held by large landowners is greater than that held by small landowners. On Maui these players are Alexander and Baldwin, C. Brewer, Amfac, Maui Land and Pineapple Company, Haleakala Ranch, and Ulupalakua Ranch. The two largest landowners on Moloka'i are the Moloka'i Ranch, which owns about one-third of the island, and Pu'u O Hoku Ranch. Lana'i is owned 98 percent by Castle and Cooke.

## The People

With 128,000, Maui has the third-largest island population in Hawaii, about 10.5 percent of the state's total; about 7,200 people live on Moloka'i, and just over 3,200 live on Lana'i. Maui's population density is 176 people per square mile, with Moloka'i and Lana'i at 27 and 23 per square mile, respectively. The Kahului/Wailuku area has the island's greatest density of population, with about 41,000 people. The Upcountry population is just

over 22,500, some 18,000 live along the west coast, 20,000 make South Maui their home, while some 10,000 live along the Hana Highway, less than 2,000 of which live in Hana itself. For Maui County, 78 percent are urban while 22 percent live rurally. The ethnic breakdown of Maui's 128,000 people is as follows: 34 percent Caucasian, 31 percent Asian, 22 percent Mixed, 11 percent Hawaiian, and 1 percent Other.

## Festivals and Events

National holidays and Hawaii state events are all celebrated and commemorated in Maui County. Events such as Aloha Festivals and Lei Day are celebrated on all the islands, but several other unique happenings occur only on the Valley Isle, Moloka'i, and Lana'i. Check local newspapers and the free island magazines for dates. Island specific information is also available on the web; check the calendar listing at www.visit-maui.com/calendar.html.

### January

Late January brings the college all-star **Hula Bowl** football game (televised) to the War Memorial Stadium in Kahului.

The **Mercedes Championship** PGA tour plays golf at Kapalua, while the Senior PGA tour hosts the **Senior Skins Game** at Wailea.

### February

**Lunar New Year** celebrations are held in the evening along Front Street in Lahaina and include a lion's dance, martial arts demonstrations, live music, food, and firecrackers, of course.

Marking the yearly return to Hawaiian waters of the humpback whale, February is whale month. The annual week-long **Whalefest** happens in Lahaina with sailing and diving tours, demonstrations, and seminars; the **Great Whale Count** takes place island-wide; the **Annual Whale Day Celebration** is a Kihei event with lots of music, dance, and food; and **Whale Week on Maui** is a Wailea event with all sorts of events, including a regatta, fun run, and parade.

### March

The Valley Island Road Runners, 808/871-6441,

sponsor the **Maui Marathon** in mid-March from Queen Ka'ahumanu Center in Kahului to Whalers Village in Ka'anapali.

The **East-Maui Taro Festival,** 808/248-8972, www.tarofestival.org, is celebrated in Hana with traditional ceremonies, music, food markets, symposiums, demonstrations, and exhibitions to honor one of the island's most basic food sources and the resurgence of Hawaiian cultural traditions.

## April

The **Da Kine Classic Windsurfing Event** professional windsailing competition for men and women is held at Kanaha Beach. Call 808/877-2111 for information. This is part of the Maui Race series.

The "Ulupalakua Thing," also called the **Maui Agricultural Trade Show and Sampling,** is the largest event for displaying and promoting Hawaii-grown and -manufactured products. Held at the Tedeschi Winery at the Ulupalakua Ranch, admission is charged. Call 808/878-1266 for information; www.mauiag.org.

## May

Lahaina's signature cultural event is **In Celebration of Canoes.** This cultural gathering honors the voyaging canoe, which brought the ancestors of modern Hawaiians from the South Pacific. Cultural arts demonstrations, lu'au, musical performances, and the carving of canoes from logs are some of the activities. Representatives from Pacific island nations participate.

## June

The **Annual Upcountry Fair** at the Eddie Tam Center, Makawao, is an old-fashioned farm fair right in the heart of Maui's *paniolo* country. Crafts, food, and competitions are all part of the fair, as are the county 4-H championship and auctions.

The annual **Slack Key Guitar Festival** at the Maui Arts and Cultural Center in Kahului features some of Hawaii's best musicians.

The **Maui Film Festival** shows a handful of art films in December and January at the Maui Arts and Culture Center in Kahului and then weekly throughout the rest of the year. Outdoor film

events take place in Wailea in June. Call 808/572-3456 or 808/579-9244 for information on current year showings, or visit the festival's website at www.mauifilmfestival.com.

## July

Head for the coolness of Upcountry Makawao for the annual **Makawao Rodeo.** *Paniolo* are an old and very important tradition in Hawaiian life. Held at the Oskie Rice Arena, this old-time Upcountry rodeo can't be beat for fun and entertainment anywhere in the country. It's always accompanied by the Paniolo Parade through town.

The **4th of July** brings the best fireworks display on Maui to the Lahaina Roads. Thousands congregate for the show.

July brings the annual **Kapalua Wine and Food Symposium** where foods prepared by local master chefs get paired with international wines. Call 808/669-0244 for information.

Late July or early August brings the **Quicksilver Cup Windsurfing Championship** competitions to Kanaha Beach in Kahului.

## August

The Japanese **Bon Odori** takes place in late July–August at Buddhist temples throughout the island, featuring dance, drumming, and lantern boats. Everyone is invited to participate.

**Maui Onion Festival,** at Whalers Village in Ka'anapali, celebrates the island's most famous commercial herb. All sorts of music, chef's demonstrations, and cooking-related events take place.

## September

Labor Day weekend brings the well-respected **Maui Writers Conference,** usually held at one of the fancy hotels on the island.

The annual **Maui Marathon** takes runners from Kahului down to Ma'alaea and then along the ocean to Ka'anapali. For information, call 808/871-6441.

A culinary event featuring some of the best chefs in the islands, **A Taste of Lahaina** is not only a tasty treat of food, wine, and beer, but also offers cooking demonstrations and local music.

Head back up to Makawao for another excellent

## MAUI'S MUSEUMS AND HISTORICAL SOCIETIES

**Alexander and Baldwin Sugar Museum,** at the corner of Pu'unene Ave. and Hansen Rd. in Pu'unene, 808/871-8058, is a small but highly informative museum on the history and culture of sugar and sugar production on Maui and the corresponding plantation life. See a functioning sugar mill across the street. Open Mon.–Sat. 9:30 A.M.–4:30 P.M.; $5 admission.

**Baldwin Home,** on Front St. across from the harbor in Lahaina, is the two-story home of medical missionary Rev. Dwight Baldwin. This showcase museum is the oldest stone structure on the island, and it portrays the early days of the missions on Maui. Open daily 10 A.M.–4 P.M.; $3 admission.

**Hale Pa'i** is a printing house located on the grounds of Lahainaluna School on the hillside above Lahaina. It has an operational replica printing press, original Lahainaluna Press publications, and exhibits about the early days of Western contact in Lahaina. Open Mon.–Fri. 10 A.M.–4 P.M.

**Bailey House Museum,** at 2375-A Main St., Wailuku, is a repository of Hawaiian historical precontact objects, artifacts from the early days of the missionaries on Maui, and the paintings of Edward Bailey. From the 1830s, this stone house itself is of interest. Once Bailey's home, it also served at one time as a dormitory for the Wailuku Female Seminary boarding school. Open Mon.–Sat. 10 A.M.–4 P.M.; $5 admission.

**Maui Historical Society,** 808/244-3326, is housed in the lower level of the Bailey House Museum. This organization promotes interest in and knowledge of the history of Maui County and maintains an invaluable historical archive. Sponsors free lectures, classes, and events during the year.

**Hana Cultural Center,** 808/248-8622, is located across from the entrance to Hana Bay. It preserves and restores historical artifacts, photos, and documents from the Hana area. On the grounds are a restored courthouse and jail. This cultural center also has four traditional-style buildings and maintains an ethnobotanical garden. Open daily 10 A.M.–4 P.M.; $2 admission.

The private and nonprofit **Paper Airplane Museum** in Kahului, 808/887-8916, is a collection of model paper airplanes, photographs and artifacts from Maui's aviation history, and a collection of planes and other objects made from tin cans. An eclectic display, this museum will not fail to please and educate. Open daily at a storefront in the Maui Mall; donation suggested.

The **Whale Museum,** 808/661-4567, at the Whalers Village shopping mall in Ka'anapali, displays whaling artifacts and portrays the history and culture of whaling in Hawaii, and the whaler's life. This excellent display includes a reconstructed fo'castle (ship's quarters) and many photographs. In the courtyard is a 40-foot sperm whale skeleton. Self-guided learning experience while you shop. Open daily 9:30 A.M.–10 P.M.; free.

---

**Maui County Rodeo** as well as plenty of good happenings during the statewide **Aloha Week.**

## October
**Maui County Fair,** at the Wailuku War Memorial Complex, brings out the kid in everyone. An old-fashioned fair with Western and homespun flavor, this event offers rides, booths, and games.

Wild costumes and outlandish behavior set the mood for **Halloween** in Lahaina, the largest celebration of Halloween in Hawaii, often called the "Mardi Gras of the Pacific." For information, call 808/667-9194.

The **Kaanapali Classic Senior PGA Golf Tournament** lures some of the game's living legends to the Ka'anapali links.

The **XTERRA World Championships** are held yearly in Wailea. This off-road triathlon combines a 1.5-mile ocean swim, 30K mountain bike ride, and an 11K run.

## November
The **Maui Invitational Basketball Tournament**

# MAUI'S ARTS AND CULTURE ORGANIZATIONS

**Lahaina Arts Society,** 808/661-0111, is a non-profit organization that has two galleries in the Old Lahaina Courthouse, open daily 9 A.M.–5 P.M. All artwork displayed there is juried artwork by the groups 175 members. Every other weekend, members also display their artwork under the banyan tree behind the courthouse. The Lahaina Arts Society also organized a year-round outreach program at a dozen sites throughout the island where classes are taught by society members.

The **Lahaina Town Action Committee,** 808/667-9175, www.visitlahaina.com, organizes cultural events and other activities in Lahaina, including the ever-popular Friday evening Art Night. This group also sponsors the **Lahaina Visitor Center,** which has its office on the first floor of the Old Lahaina Courthouse.

The **Maui Historical Society,** 808/244-3326, www.mauimuseum.org, collects and preserves artifacts and disseminates information about the history and culture of Maui. It is located in the basement of the Bailey House Museum in Wailuku.

**The Lahaina Restoration Foundation,** 808/661-3262, is a community organization in Lahaina created to preserve the flavor and authenticity of old Lahaina without the context of continued growth and development. They own and maintain numerous historical buildings as museums and try to educate the visiting public about the history of the area.

**Friends of Moku'ula,** 808/661-3659, www.mokuula.com, is a nonprofit organization with the goal of bringing to the attention of the public the importance of the old royal compound of Moku'ula in Lahaina and to its eventual re-creation.

holds a pre-season college team playoff at the Civic Center in Lahaina.

Each year the Ka'anapali Beach Hotel hosts **Hula O Na Keiki,** the state's only children's solo and partner hula contest. Two days of competition make this an entertaining event for everyone.

## December

This month remembers Maui of old with the **Na Mele O Maui** festival in Lahaina and Ka'anapali. Hawaiian music, dance, arts, and crafts are featured.

The **Festival of Art and Flowers** in Lahaina incorporates displays of flowers grown on the island (including the beautiful protea), demonstrations, workshops, and music, plus the **Holiday Lighting of the Banyan Tree** and decorating the Old Courthouse for Christmas.

# Sports and Recreation

Maui won't let you down when you want to go outside and play. More than just a giant sandbox for big kids, its beaches and surf are warm and inviting, and there are all sorts of water sports from scuba diving to parasailing. You can fish, hunt, camp, or indulge yourself in golf or tennis to your heart's content. The hiking is marvelous and the horseback riding on Haleakala is some of the most exciting in the world. The information offered in this chapter is merely an overview. Have fun!

## BEACHES

Since the island is blessed with 150 miles of coastline, more than 32 of which are wonderful beaches, your biggest problem is to choose which one you'll grace with your presence. But before you romp, pick up and read the brochures *Maui Beach Safety Tips,* by the American Red Cross, and *Beach and Ocean Safety Information,* found at some free information stands around the island.

M

MAUI

## West Maui

The most plentiful and best beaches for swimming and sunbathing are on West Maui, strung along 18 glorious miles from Kapalua to Olowalu. For an all-purpose beach you can't beat **D.T. Fleming Beach, Kapalua Bay Beach,** or **Napili Beach** on Maui's western tip. They have everything: safe surf (except in winter), great swimming, snorkeling, and bodysurfing in a first-class, family-oriented area. Then comes **Ka'anapali Beach,** bordered by the hotels and condos, the most well-known beach on the island. Black Rock, at the Sheraton, is the best for snorkeling. In Lahaina, **Lahaina Beach** is convenient but not private and just so-so. **Puamana Beach** and **Launiupoko Beaches** have only fair swimming, but great views and picnic areas. The beach at **Olowalu** has very good swimming and is one of the best and most accessible snorkeling spots on the island, while farther down, **Papalaua Wayside** offers camping and a narrow beach fringed by *kiawe* trees that surround tiny patches of white sand.

## Kihei and Wailea

The 10 miles stretching from Ma'alaea to Wailea are dotted with beaches that range from poor to excellent. **Ma'alaea Beach** and **Kealia Beach** extend four miles from Ma'alaea to Kihei. These are excellent for walking, sailboarding, and enjoying the view, but little else. **Kama'ole Beach I, II,** and **III** are at the south end of Kihei. Top-notch beaches, they have it all—swimming, snorkeling, and safety. **Keawakapu Beach** is more of the same. Then come the great little crescent beaches of Wailea, which get more secluded as you head south: **Mokapu, Ulua, Wailea,** and **Polo.** All are surrounded by the picture-perfect hotels of Wailea, and all have public access. **Makena Beach,** down the road from Wailea, is very special. It's one of the island's best. At one time, alternative-lifestyle people made Makena a haven, and it still attracts free-spirited souls. There's nude bathing in secluded coves, unofficial camping, and freedom.

## Wailuku and Kahului

Poor ugly ducklings! The beaches in town are shallow, unattractive ones, and no one spends any time there. However, **Kanaha Beach** near the airport isn't bad at all, and it's a favorite of beginning sailboarders and kitesurfers. **H.P. Baldwin Beach** in Pa'ia has a reputation for hostile locals protecting their turf, but the beach is good, and you won't be hassled if you "live and let live." **Ho'okipa Beach** just east of Pa'ia isn't good for the average swimmer, but it is the "Sailboarding Capital" of Hawaii, and you should visit here just to see the exciting, colorful spectacle of people skipping over the ocean with bright sails.

## Hana

Everything about Hana is heavenly, including its beaches. There's **Kaihalulu Beach,** small but almost too pretty to be real with red cinder sand. Black-sand **Wai'anapanapa Beach,** surrounded by the state park and good for swimming and snorkeling, even provides a legendary cave whose waters turn blood red. **Hana Bay** is well protected and safe for swimming and kayaking. Just south of town is the white-sand **Hamoa Beach,** described by James Michener as looking like the South Pacific.

# SCUBA AND SNORKELING

Maui is as beautiful from under the waves as it is above. There is world-class snorkeling and diving at many coral reefs and beds surrounding the island. You'll find some of the best, coincidentally, just where the best beaches are: mainly from Kihei to Makena, up around Napili and Kapalua bays, and especially around Olowalu. For a total thrill, try diving Molokini, the submerged volcano off Makena, just peeking above the waves and designated a Marine Life Conservation District. There are underwater caves at Nahuna (Five Graves) Point, just up from Makena landing; magnificent caves, arches, and lava tubes out at Lana'i. *Only* advanced divers should attempt the back side of West Maui, the coast at Kipahulu, and beyond Pu'uiki Island in Hana Bay. For these and other locations, with a brief description, check out the Maui Dive Shop's pamphlet, *Maui Dive Guide.*

Chuck Thorne is a diver who lives on Maui; he receives the highest accolades for *The Diver's Guide to Maui,* the definitive book on all the

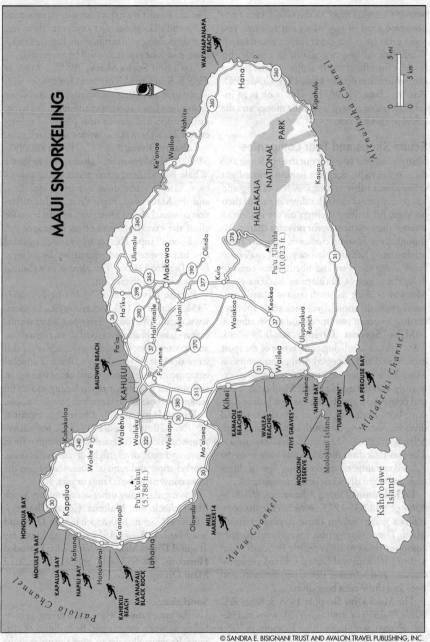

# MAUI SNORKELING

HALEAKALA
NATIONAL
PARK

Pu'u 'Ula'ula
(10,023 ft.)

Hana

Kipahulu

Kapo

Alenuihaha Channel

Wai'anapanapa Beach

Nahiku

Wailua

Ke'anae

Ulumalu

Makawao

Olinda

Kula

Keokea

Kekea

Waiakoa

Ulupalakua
Ranch

Wailea

Kihei

Kamaole
Beaches

Wailea
Beaches

"Five Graves"

Makena

Molokini
Reserve

Ahihi Bay

"Turtle Town"

La Perouse Bay

Molokini Island

Kaho'olawe
Island

'Alalakeiki Channel

'Au'au Channel

Mile
Marker 14

Ma'alaea

Olowalu

Lahaina

Ka'anapali

Honokowai

Kahana

Kapalua

Kahakuloa

Waihe'e

Wailuku

Waiehu

Waikapu

Pu'unene

Kahului

Pa'ia

Ha'iku

Hali'imaile

Pukalani

Pu'u Kukui
(5,788 ft.)

Honolua Bay

Mokule'ia Bay

Kapalua Bay

Napili Bay

Kahekili
Beach

Ka'anapali
Black Rock

Baldwin Beach

Pailolo Channel

© SANDRA E. BISIGNANI TRUST AND AVALON TRAVEL PUBLISHING, INC.

MAUI

5 mi

5 km

Hana

36

340

30

30

30

30

31

31

31

37

37

377

378

390

390

398

365

360

360

360

360

320

380

311

370

best dive/snorkel spots on the island. He's a no-nonsense kind of guy who's out to show you some great spots but never forgets about safety. While he's no longer available as a guide, his book is for sale at many scuba outlets, or you can write for it direct: Maui Dive Guide, P.O. Box 40, Hana, HI 96713. This book is an invaluable resource, well worth the money and the effort to check it out.

## Scuba Shops and Tour Companies

Many boats will take you out diving. Some also do snorkel trips, deep-sea fishing, moonlight cruises, and other charters. A few rafting and kayak companies also offer dives as part of their package. All activities centers on the island can arrange these excursions for no extra charge. Although there is some crossover, typically boats leaving from Lahaina Harbor go to Lana'i or to spots along the west and north Maui coast to dive; those out of Ma'alaea or Makena go to Molokini or along the south coast of Maui. Companies that do shore dives pick their spot according to ocean conditions and the weather.

**Mike Severns Diving,** 808/879-6596, www.mikesevransdiving.com, is one of the most experienced and respected diving companies on Maui. Mike is a marine scientist/explorer who's extremely knowledgeable about Maui both above and below the waves. He has his own boat and accepts both beginning and advanced divers, and dives mostly along the south coast. Diving with Mike is an extraordinary educational experience. The two-tank dives run $120 and leave from the Kihei boat ramp; no snorkel tours. Special three-tank and night dives can be accommodated.

**Ed Robinson's Diving Adventures,** 808/879-3584 or 800/635-1273, www.mauiscuba.com, offers a great deal for those staying in South Maui. The company runs tours from two fully equipped boats to spots mostly in South Maui and to Molokini and Lana'i. Offered are introductory and refresher dives, certification, and two- and three-tank boat dives.

The **Maui Dive Shop,** at 1455 S. Kihei Rd., 808/879-3388 or 800/542-3483, www.mauidiveshop.com, with its six other locations in Kihei and Lahaina, is Maui's largest scuba operation.

The retail outlet is a full-service water sports store, and it and all locations offer a variety of shore and boat dives along with certification. Rates are moderate, and your experience will be memorable.

You'll find **Scuba Shack,** 808/879-3483, at 2349 S. Kihei Road. This outfit has a shops with all the gear and offers numerous boat and shore dives plus classes at competitive rates. No hype, just personalized service with plenty of experience. Check them out at www.scubashack.com.

**Lahaina Divers,** 808/667-7496 or 800/998-3483, 143 Dickenson St., Lahaina, next to Pacific Whale Foundation, offers a snorkeling experience, various scuba dives to Lana'i, Molokini, and the Maui coast, night dives, and certification courses. Lahaina Divers uses its own boats for all of the excursions and offers beverages and snacks on all trips. This company is well regarded and has an established reputation. Boats leave from Lahaina Harbor. The company's website is at www.lahainadivers.com.

**Pacific Dive,** 808/667-5331 or 877/667-7331, located at 150 Dickenson St., Lahaina, www.pacificdive.com, offers open-water certification classes, beach dives, boat dives, night dives, and scooter dives. This full-service scuba/snorkel store does daily rentals on scuba and snorkel equipment, boogie boards, and other water gear, and also has a complete repair facility and air fill station for those already certified. Nitrox available.

**Dive Maui,** at 900 Front St., Lahaina, 808/667-2080 or 866/281-7450, www.divemauiscuba.com, covers the whole range from shore and boat dives, night dives, certification, snorkel trips, and rentals. Boats leave from the most convenient boat ramp or pier.

Among the many other companies in South Maui check out **Makena Coast Charters,** 808/874-1273 or 800/833-6483, or **Dive and Sea Maui,** 808/874-1952. In West Maui, try **Tropical Divers Maui,** 808/669-6284; **Extended Horizons,** 808/667-0611 or 888/348-3628; or **Maui Diving,** 808/667-0633 or 800/959-7319.

## Snorkeling

Use the same caution when scuba diving or snorkeling as when swimming. Be mindful of currents. It's generally safer to enter the water in the center of a bay than at the sides where rip currents are more likely to occur. The following sites are suitable for beginners to intermediates: on Maui's western tip, Honolua Bay and nearby Mokule'ia Bay, both part of a Marine Life Conservation District; Kapalua and Napili Bays for usually good and safe conditions; in Ka'anapali, Black Rock at the Sheraton Hotel; and at Olowalu, where the ocean is very gentle with plenty to see. Also try the rocky headlands between the Kama'ole beaches in Kihei and farther down between the beaches in Wailea. 'Ahihi Bay and La Pérouse Bay in South Maui are great spots, and fairly isolated. On the windward side Baldwin Beach in Pa'ia and Wai'anapanapa State Park beach near Hana are both generally good. Under no circumstances should you miss taking a boat out to Molokini. It's worth every penny, even though it's getting rather crowded! Some boats also stop at **Turtle Town** off of Maui's last lava flow. Manele and Hulopo'e bays on Lana'i are like aquariums, both also marine life conservation districts. And there are plenty more.

## Snorkel Equipment

Sometimes condos and hotels have snorkeling equipment free for their guests, but if you have to rent it, don't do it from a hotel or condo; go to a snorkel or dive shop where it's much cheaper. Expect to spend $5–10 a day for mask, fins, and snorkel, or $25–30 a week.

One of the best snorkel deals is through **Snorkel Bob's**, www.snorkelbob.com, 808/879-7449 in Kihei, 808/667-2553 in Lahaina, and 808/669-9603 in Napili. Old Snorkel Bob will dispense information and full snorkel gear for only $9–29 a week. Add $7 a week if you add a dry snorkel tube. You can return it to any store on Maui or on a Neighbor Island if you'll be heading off Maui before the week is up. Daily rates are similarly reasonable. Slick-bottom boogie boards run $26 a week, and other water gear are also available for rent.

**A & B Rentals and Sportswear,** 808/669-0027, in Honokowai at the Da Rose Mall, open daily 9 A.M.–5 P.M., rents snorkel gear for $2.50 per day and $9 per week, as well as boogie boards.

Located in the Kahana Plaza, **Boss Frogs**

808/669-6700, has snorkel gear for $2.50–9 per day or $9–30 per week. This shop also rents surfboards, boogie boards, and bikes. Boss Frogs also has shops in Napili, Lahaina, and Kihei.

**West Maui Sports,** 808/661-6252, behind Lahaina Cannery mall, rents ordinary snorkel gear for $2.50 a day or $10 a week. Also rent body boards, kayaks, beach gear, and golf clubs.

In Lahaina, try **Duke's Rental Shop,** along Front Street at the south end of downtown, for snorkel gear at $3 a day, as well as surfboards, bikes, golf clubs, and an assortment of other items.

Numerous other shops on the island also rent snorkel gear at comparable but variable rates depending upon the quality of the equipment. Some also sell snorkel gear, as do the Sports Authority, Wal-Mart, and other large shops in Kahului, where you can find a set from about $20 and up depending upon the quality.

## Snorkel Excursions

For a pure snorkeling adventure, unlike those offered by the tour boats, try **Snorkel Maui,** 808/572-8437, with Ann Fielding, the naturalist author of *Hawaiian Reefs and Tide Pools* and *An Underwater Guide to Hawai'i,* which detail many of the invertebrates and reef fish you will encounter on one of her fantastic dives. Ms. Fielding instructs you in snorkeling and in the natural history and biology of what you'll be seeing below the waves. She tailors the dive to fit the participants. A basic half-day snorkel dive costs $85 adults or $75 kids. The company's website is at www.maui.net/~annf.

Dozens of snorkel boat excursions take place in Maui's waters every week. Most boats leave either from Lahaina or Ma'alaea Harbor, while others leave from the beaches fronting the large hotels of Ka'anapali, Wailea, and Makena. Catamarans, mono-hulls, sailing ships, power boats, or rafts: snorkeling vessels come in all shapes and sizes. Prices range $50–80 for half-day adventures; full-day tours with lunch and sail could be $150.

For a magnificent day of sailing, exploring, and snorkeling, you can't beat **Trilogy Excursions,** 808/661-4743 or 888/628-4800, whose sleek catamarans leave Lahaina Harbor for a day trip to Lana'i, Ma'alaea Harbor for Molokini, or Ka'anapali Beach for trips up the coast.

Others to check out are: **Pride of Maui,** 808/242-0955; **Classic Charters'** *Four Winds II,* 808/879-8188; **Island Marine Activities'** *Lahaina Princess,* 808/661-8397; **Prince Kuhio,** 808/242-8777; **Blue Dolphin,** 808/661-3333; or **Boss Frogs'** *Frogman,* 808/874-6325.

**Snuba** excursions are also a possibility on some snorkel boats. Try **Four Winds,** 808/879-8188, which goes to Molokini Crater, **Island Scuba,** 808/667-4608, or the kayak company **Maui Eco-tours,** 808/891-2223. A snuba experience will run $45–70, depending whether it's part of a boat tour or an activity by itself.

## CATCHING WAVES

### Bodysurfing

All you need are the right wave conditions and a sandy beach to have a ball bodysurfing and boogie boarding. Always check conditions first—bodysurfing has led to some very serious neck and back injuries for the ill-prepared. The following are some decent beaches: Ulua, Wailea, Polo, or Makena, the north end of Kama'ole Beach Park I in Kihei, Napili Bay, D.T. Fleming, and Baldwin Park. Typical boogie board rental prices are $5 a day to $25 a week—similar to the rate for snorkel gear.

### Surfing

While the north coast of O'ahu is known as the best surfing area in Hawaii—and arguably the best in the world—Maui has a few decent spots for the enthusiast. Try Honolua Bay, Napili Bay, Lahaina Harbor, Launiupoko Park, Ma'alaea Harbor, and Ho'okipa Beach. Many beginners stay at the more gentle beaches between Lahaina and Olowalu, Laniupoko Park, and the beaches in Kihei.

Maui does have one spot, however, that has gained worldwide notoriety over the last several years. This is "Jaws." On a good day, waves at Jaws rise 30–50 feet high! The conventional method of catching a wave—paddling belly down on your board until you gain enough speed and momentum to slip down the front of the wave—

## OUTRIGGER CANOES

Historically, outrigger canoes have been made from the trunks of koa trees. Koa trees large enough to build a canoe out of are scarce these days, however, and most are legally protected. To have one made today from available logs would run $40,000–100,000. By far the majority of outrigger canoes in the islands these days are made from fiberglass. Much cheaper, they still must meet rigorous specifications. On Maui there are eight or nine canoe clubs, and most have 100-plus members. In all of Hawaii, outrigger canoeing is the team sport that has the greatest participation, with more than 10,000 active canoe club members in about 60 canoe clubs throughout the state.

doesn't work here because of the height and speed of these waves. Ingenious (and maybe a bit crazy) surfers have come up with a solution—use a jet ski to gain speed and tow the surfer to the right spot before dashing out of harm's way. Some surfers use the tow rope as a big slingshot to propel themselves even faster from behind the jet ski. Some surfboards used at Jaws have straps for the feet similar to a sailboard. So far, no one has died in this highly risky endeavor, but it seems likely that over time someone will bite it big. Jaws is about 10 minutes past Ho'okipa Beach on the road to Hana and then down a road toward the ocean. People are reluctant to give the exact location, although locals know the spot well. Some fear, and rightly so, that inexperienced surfers will give this monster a try, but homeowners in the area just don't like the traffic and congestion. On a high surf day, there may be as many as 350 cars parked on the approach road.

### Surfing Instruction

More than two dozen shops on Maui rent surfboards, and perhaps a dozen or more companies and individuals teach the basics of surfing. Some are listed below. You can get surfing lessons in groups or individually. Lessons generally run in the vicinity of $60–80 for a group lesson that lasts about two hours or about $100–160 for a private lesson. Many lessons are taught directly south of Lahaina Harbor, while some instruction is done at the beach parks between Lahaina and Olowalu or in Kihei. The surfing schools offer a number of multi-day packages.

A "learn in one day" guarantee is offered by the well-respected **Nancy Emerson School of Surfing,** 808/244-7873 or 808/662-4445, www.surfclinics.com. Nancy and her instructors offer lessons just to the side of Lahaina harbor. The **Surf School on Kaanapali Beach,** 808/244-6858, www.mauisurfschool.com, offers lessons in Ka'anapali Beach. Also in Lahaina are **Goofy Foot,** 808/244-9283; **Surf Dog Maui,** 808/250-7873, www.surfdogmaui.com; and **Outragious Adventures,** 808/669-1400, www.youcansurf.com. In Kihei, give a call to **Maui Waveriders,** 808/875-4761, www.mauiwaveriders.com; or **Big Kahuna,** 808/875-6395, www.bigkahunaadventures.com.

## Sailboarding

Ho'okipa Beach, just east of Pa'ia, is the "Sailboarding Capital of the World," and the big-money championship used to be held here every year in March and April. Today, the **Aloha Classic,** held in late October or early November is as big as it gets. Smaller local and national competitions are held in spring and winter, usually at Kooks Beach, Kanaha Beach Park, in Kahului, but for details ask at any of the big sailboarding shops on the island.

Kanaha Beach Park has perfect gentle winds and waves for learning the sport, and the beach at Spreckelsville has virtually the same characteristics. Summer is best for sailboarding because of the winds, which blow steadily from the east. Mornings are good for the novice because winds are lighter. As winds and chop pick up in the afternoon the more advanced board riders hit the water. Any sailboard shop will point you in the right direction for location and gear according to your skill level. When the winds come from the south, most sailboarders head to the north end of Kihei and set in at Mai Poina 'Oe La'u Beach Park to sail on Ma'alaea Bay. Sometimes in the winter, you'll see boarders out on the water with the whales. Wherever you decide to try the water,

ROBERT NILSEN

**Strong, consistent trade winds make the beaches of central Maui some of the best in the world for sailboarding.**

pick up a copy of *Guidelines For Windsurfing on Maui,* if you can find one, before you put together your gear.

Rental equipment with a board and one mast runs roughly $30 a day or $50 with two sails, to $350 and $550 for two weeks, depending upon the quality of gear. Group lessons for three or more usually run 2–3 hours, and private lessons that run 1–2 hours cost about $70–80. Remember—start with a big board and a small sail! Take lessons to save time and energy. To rent equipment or take lessons, try **Maui Windsurf Company,** 808/877-4816 or 800/872-0999. Several others to try, with comparable rates for lessons and rentals, are **Hi-Tech Surf Sports,** 808/877-2111, www.htmaui.com; **Second Wind,** 808/877-7467 or 800/936-7787, www.maui.net/~secwind; **Neilpryde Maui,** 808/877-7443 or 800/321-7443, www.neilprydemaui.com; **Extreme Sports Maui,** 808/871-7954 or 877/376-6284, www.extremesportsmaui.com; **Hawaiian Island Surf and Sports,**

808/871-4981 or 800/231-6958, www.hawai-iianisland.com; **Sailboards Maui,** 808/579-8432; and **Simmer Hawaii,** 808/879-8484.

For lessons only, inquire at one of the shops or directly with **Alan Cadiz's HST,** 808/871-5423 or 800/968-5423, www.hstwindsurfing.com; or **Action Sports Maui,** 808/871-1590, www.actionsportsmaui.com. **Al West's,** 808/877-0090 or 800/870-4084, www.mauivans.com, also does lessons and rents vans to transport your gear.

## Kitesurfing

A cross between wakeboarding and flying a kite, kiteboarding (also known as kitesurfing) is one of the newest water sports to hit the island. If you want to see it, head for "kite beach," just west of Kanaha Beach park in Kahului.

Lessons by several shops in Kahului run from a two-hour kite control class to three-hour introductory lessons to a five-day advanced course. For most, the three-hour course works best and runs about $240. Rental gear is also available at local shops. If you decide to really get into the sport, you can get set up for about $1,000. Perhaps the premier organization offering lessons and equipment is **Kiteboarding School of Maui,** at 22 Hana Hwy., www.ksmaui.com. Others are: **Second Wind,** 808/877-7467 or 800/936-7787, www.secondwindmaui.com; and **Hawaiian Islands Surf and Sport,** 808/871-4981 or 800/231-6958, www.kitesails.com. If you are new on the island, be sure to familiarize yourself with kitesurfing regulations. Pick up a copy of the *Safe Kiteboarding Guidelines* printed by the Maui Kiteboarding Association and available at shops that rent or sell kite-boarding equipment, or check the association's website at www.maui.net/~hotwind/mka.html.

## THRILL CRAFT

Usually the term "thrill craft" refers to jet skis, water-ski boats, speedboats, parasailing, and other such motorized watercraft. In years past, a controversy raged about their use. The feeling among conservationists was that these craft disturb humans, and during whale season they disturb the whales that come to winter over in the rather small Lahaina Roads and Ma'alaea Bay. This is definitely a case of "one person's pleasure is another person's poison." On March 31, 1991, a law was passed that bans these types of craft from operating in west and south Maui waters during whale season: December 15 through May 15. Although you might assume that this is due to the sound of the motors roaring through the waters—research has been done to determine if this too is a problem—the restriction was set in place because of the speed and unpredictable nature of these water craft.

## Jet Skis

To try this exciting sport in season, contact **Pacific Jet Sports,** 808/667-2001, for use of jet skis and wave runners. From 9 A.M.–4 P.M. daily, you can meet their shuttle boat on the beach in front of the Hyatt Hotel in Ka'anapali and it will take you out to their pontoon and riding area where you'll get instruction on how to operate these machines. Rates are $50 for a half hour or $78 an hour, and $13 extra for each additional person up to three for the wave runners. You must be 15 years old to operate.

## Parasailing

If you've ever wanted to soar like an eagle, here's your chance with no prior experience necessary. Basically, a parasail is a parachute tethered to a speedboat. And away we go! The most dangerous part seems to be getting in and out of the boat when you leave the harbor or shore. On the powerboat a special harness attaches to a parachute. You're put in a life vest and strapped to the harness, which forms a cradle upon which you sit while aloft. Make sure, once you're up, to pull the cradle as far under your thighs as you can. It's much more comfortable. Don't be afraid to loosen your steel grip on the guide ropes, because that's not what's holding you anyway. In the air, you are as free as a bird and the unique view is phenomenal. You don't have time to fret about going up. The boat revs and you're airborne almost immediately. Once up, the feeling is very secure. The technology is simple, straightforward, and safe. Relax and have a ball. Cost is about $60–70 for a 10-minute joyride that lets out about 800 feet of line or $40–50 for a seven-minute ride where you are at the end of a 400-foot line. Some pull singles only, others take doubles. **UFO Parasail,** 808/661-7UFO or 800/359-4UFO operates on Kaʻanapali Beach, **Parasail Kaanapali,** 808/669-6555, leaves from Mala Wharf, while **Parasail in Paradise,** 808/661-4060, uses a slip in the Lahaina Harbor.

## OCEAN TOURS

You haven't really seen Maui unless you've seen it from the sea. Tour boats take you fishing, sailing, whale-watching, dining, diving, and snorkeling. You can find powerboats, sailboats, catamarans, and Zodiac rafts that offer a combination of some or all of these options or just sail you around for pure pleasure—Maui presents one of the premier sailing venues in the Pacific. Many take day trips to Lanaʻi. Others visit Molokini, a submerged volcano with only half the crater rim above water; it has been designated a marine life conservation district. The majority of Maui's pleasure boats are berthed in Lahaina Harbor, and most have a booth right there on the wharf where you can sign up. A substantial number of other boats come out of Maʻalaea Harbor, and a few companies are based in Kihei. The following are basically limited to sailing/dining/touring activities, with snorkeling often part of the experience. To add to the mix, there are even a few submarine tour possibilities, where you can see underwater sights without getting wet.

### Excursions and Dinner Sails

**Trilogy,** 808/661-4743 or 888/628-4800, www.sailtrilogy.com, founded and operated by the Coon Family, is a success in every way and its cruises are the best on Maui. Although the handpicked crews have made the journey countless times, they never forget that it's your first time. They run catamarans that carry up to 50 passengers, and once aboard, you're served refreshments and Mama Coon's famous cinnamon rolls. The Discover Lanaʻi tour leaves Lahaina Harbor weekdays. Once at Lanaʻi, you can frolic at Hulopoʻe Bay, which is great for swimming and renowned as an excellent snorkeling area. Scuba

and kayaking are also options too. All gear is provided. While you play, the crew is busy at work preparing a delicious barbecue at the picnic facilities at Manele Harbor. You couldn't have a more memorable or enjoyable experience than sailing with Trilogy. But don't spoil your day; be sure to bring along (and use!) a wide-brim hat, sunglasses, sunscreen, a long-sleeve shirt, and a towel. For this full day's experience, adults pay $169, children (3–15) half price. Leaving later in the day is the Discover Lanaʻi Sunset Sail for the same price. Trilogy Excursions also runs a popular half-day trip to Molokini Crater, sailing daily from Maʻalaea Harbor, adults $95, children half price, which includes breakfast, lunch, and all snorkeling gear; a five-hour midday picnic sail from Kaʻanapali Beach for $95; two-hour whale-watching sails during whale season, also from Kaʻanapali Beach for $39; and a Saturday all-day zodiac tour to Lanaʻi with jeep tour of the island for $199. Trilogy periodically adds new adventures to its lineup so explore the options.

If you've had enough of Front Street Lahaina, **Club Lanai,** 808/667-9595 or 800/531-5262, is a Maui-based company with two boats that runs day excursions, and does whale-watching, sunset cocktail, and sunset dinner cruises, too. You board your catamaran at Lahaina Harbor, leaving at 7 A.M. and returning at around 3:30 P.M. after a full day. En route you're served a breakfast. The club provides you with snorkel gear, and scuba diving can also be arranged at an extra charge. Family oriented with plenty of activities for children of all ages, Club Lanai lets you set your own pace . . . do it all, or do nothing at all. Departing in the late afternoon, the sunset cocktail and dinner cruises bring an easy end to a busy day.

Pacific Whale Foundation, 808/249-8811, runs four powered catamarans out of the Lahaina and Maʻalaea harbors. All trips to Lanaʻi and Molokini involve snorkeling and dolphin encounters, with whalewatching in season. Trips to Lanaʻi run $37–75, a snorkel trip to Molokini is $64, and a dozen and a half whale-watch trips in season from Lahaina and Maʻalaea harbors go for $20. In addition, the *Manuteʻa,* a 50-foot catamaran runs from Lahaina Harbor for a sunset dinner sail for $49.95. Kids 4–12 go free with a paying adult

MAUI

and it's half price for additional children the same age. This is eco-friendly company with great credibility. Three of their boats are powered by biofuel—reprocessed vegetable oil. For more information, check www.pacificwhale.org.

The *Prince Kuhio*, 800/242-8777 or 800/468-1287, offers a different kind of trip altogether. Comfort, luxury, and stability come with this 92-foot monohull ship. Departing from Ma'alaea Harbor daily, the *Prince Kuhio* does a four-hour snorkel cruise to Molokini and turtle town ($84 adults, $48 children 5–15) including a continental breakfast, buffet lunch, open bar, and champagne on the return voyage. In season, the *Prince Kuhio* also does whalewatch cruises for $21. A similar large ship that also does the Molokini trip is *Lahaina Princess*, 808/667-6165.

The 44-foot catamaran *Frogman*, 808/662-0075 and its partner *Blue Dolphin* depart from Ma'alaea Harbor for trips to Molokini. The glass-bottom *Four Winds* does similar morning and afternoon cruises for $40–78, as do *The Pride of Maui*, 808/242-0955, and Friendly Charter's *Lani Kai*, 808/244-1979. The quickest way to Molokini, which means more time in the water, is aboard the catamaran *Kai Kanani*, 808/879-7218, which departs from in front of the Maui Prince Hotel in Makena. Equipment and food are provided. Other resort catamarans leave from west side beaches, all doing a combination of snorkel sails, sunset cruises, and private charters. These sunset tours generally run about $60 and half-day snorkel tours around $80. *Teralani* and *Teralani II* leave from Ka'anapali Beach in front of Whalers Village, *Gemini* from the Westin Maui, and *Kiele V* from the Hyatt Regency. Up the coast, the *Kapalua Kai* sails from the Kapalua Bay Hotel.

**Scotch Mist Sailing Charters,** 808/661-0386, has one racing yacht, *The Scotch Mist II*. It is the oldest sailing charter on Maui (since 1970) and claims to have the fastest mono-hull sailboat in Lahaina Harbor, boasting the lightest boat, the biggest sail, and the best crew. A sail/snorkel in the morning costs $60 per person; the afternoon sailing trip is best to catch the trade winds; or take the sunset sail (up to 25 passengers) for $35 per person. A champagne and chocolate sunset cruise

also runs for $40. When the season is right, whale-watching sail are also offered for $25–40.

Other sailing ships that do a variety of snorkel, sunset, or sailing tours include the following. The sloops *Flexible Flyer,* 808/244-6655, and *Cinderella,* 808/244-0009, also leave from Ma'alaea Harbor. The *Flexible Flyer* charges $142 per person with a six guest capacity to $660 for the boat on a five-hour run. Also with six passengers maximum, the *Cinderella* charges $135 per person for short tours. The entire ship can be chartered at the rate of $400 for four hours, $800 for a full day, or $360 for a two-hour sunset run. America's Cup contender *America II,* 808/667-2195, sailing out of Lahaina Harbor, can carry up to 28 passengers, leaves twice daily at $33 a person, and runs $32.95 for a sunset sail. **Paragon Sailing Charters,** 808/244-2087, runs their two catamarans on a twice daily snorkel and sail schedule with evening sunset sails for $51–149 per person. Running private charters only, the rate for *Island Star,* 808/669-7827, runs $500–3,000.

Sunset cruises are very romantic and very popular. They last for about two hours and cost $40–70 for the basic cruise, but for a dinner sail expect to spend $70–90. Remember, too, that the larger established companies are usually on Maui to stay, but that smaller companies come and go with the tide! The big 149-passenger *Maui Princess,* 808/667-6165, offers dinner cruises aboard its sleek 118-foot motor yacht for $79 ($59 children), which includes open bar, dinner, entertainment, and dancing. **Windjammer,** 808/661-8600, also does a salmon and prime rib dinner cruise for $75 on its 93-passenger three-masted schooner, with sailings daily at 5:30 P.M. and 7:30 P.M. Others to check out are the sunset cocktail cruise on the *Pride of Maui,* Island Marine's barefoot buffet sunset cruise, and sunset cruise, dinner sail, and dance party hosted by Club Lanai.

Some companies offer a variety of cocktail sails and whale-watches for much cheaper prices, but many tend to pack people in so tightly that they're known derisively as "cattle boats." Don't expect the personal attention you'd receive on smaller boats, and always check the number of passengers when booking.

## Whale-Watching

Anyone on Maui from November to April gets the added treat of watching humpback whales as they frolic just off Lahaina, one of the world's major wintering areas for the humpback. Almost every boat in the harbor runs a special whalewatch during this time of year. If you're susceptible to seasickness, take a ride in the morning as the water usually get a little choppier in the afternoon.

Highly educational whale-watch trips are sponsored by the **Pacific Whale Foundation,** located at Ma'alaea Harbor Village, 300 Maalaea Road, Suite 211, 96793, 808/249-8811, open daily 6 A.M.–10 P.M. A nonprofit organization founded in 1980, it is dedicated to research, education, and conservation, and is one of the only research organizations that has been able to survive by generating its own funds through membership, donations, and excellent whale-watch cruises. The foundation has one of the best whale-watches on the island aboard its own ships, berthed for your convenience at Ma'alaea and Lahaina Harbors. The scientists and researchers who make up the crew rotate shifts and come out on the whale-watch when they're not out in the Lahaina Roads getting up close to identify,

and make scientific observations of, the whales. Most of the information that the other whale-watches dispense to the tourists is generated by the Pacific Whale Foundation, www.pacificwhale.org. Departures from Ma'alaea and Lahaina Harbors are several times daily. The foundation also offers an "Adopt-a-Whale Program" and various reef and snorkel cruises that run throughout the year.

## Rafting

For a totally different experience, try a rafting trip. Numerous rafting companies have sprung up in the last decade or more so there's plenty of competition. These rafts are small rigid-bottom crafts with a sun shade that mostly seat 6–24 people. The vessels are highly maneuverable, totally seaworthy, high-tech motorized rafts whose main features are their speed and ability to get intimate with the sea as the supple form bends with the undulations of the water. You're right on the water, so you'll get wet, and you often ride right on the inflatable rubber tubes. Like boat tours, these rafts do one or a combination of tours that involve whale-watching, snorkeling, scuba, sea caves, coastal cruises, or the circumnavigation of Lana'i. For

The humpback whale visits Hawaiian waters every year to mate, give birth, and raise its young before beginning its long summer and autumn migration to feed in Alaskan waters.

half-day rides, you can expect a charge of about $70–80; $110–135 for a full day adventures. Some shorter whale watch runs last about two hours and run around $40–50. The first company in Maui waters was **Blue Water Rafting,** 808/879-7238, www.bluewaterrafting.com, departs from the Kihei Boat Ramp for trips down along the rugged Makena coast or out to Molokini. Other options: **Ocean Rafting,** 808/661-7238 or 888/677-7238, www.hawaiioceanrafting.com, heads to Lana'i; **Hawaiian Rafting Adventures,** 808/661-7333, www.hawaiianrafting.com, leaves from Mala Wharf for Lana'i; **Ultimate Rafting,** 808/667-5678, www.ultimatewhalewatch.com, leaves from the Lahaina Harbor and goes to Lana'i; and **Ocean Riders,** 808/661-3586, leaves Mala Wharf for Lana'i or Moloka'i depending upon the weather.

## Kayaking

Kayaking has also become quite popular over the last decade and more. Much of the kayaking is done in the Makena area, but some companies take trips to the north coast and other locations. Located in the Rainbow Mall at 2439 S. Kihei Rd., **South Pacific Kayaks,** 808/875-4848 or 800/776-2326, www.southpacifickayaks.com, offers a half-day introductory trip (with drinks and snacks) for $59, an advanced explorer trip along the remote coastline of South Maui (including drinks and full lunch) for $89, a shorter sunset trip for $55, and several location options. Tours include plenty of snorkeling opportunities as you glide in and out of tiny bays fashioned from jutting lava rock fingers. South Pacific Kayaks offers rentals and sales of single and double kayaks, snorkel sets, and also offers hiking adventures. **Kelii's Kayak Tours,** 808/874-7652, www.keliiskayak.com, has several tours to various sites around the island ranging $49–99. See also **Makena Kayak,** 808/879-8426, which has two-to four-hour trips at Makena or the west side cliffs for $55–85; **Big Kahuna Kayak,** 808/875-6395, www.maui.net/~paddle, has two kayak tours in South Maui for $60–85, but also does surfing lessons, hiking tours, and outrigger canoe rides; **Maui Eco-tours,** 808/891-2223, www.mauiecotours.com, departs from La Per-ouse Bay; and **Pacific Coast Kayak,** 808/879-2391, which also tours various Makena sites. Out in Hana, you can explore Hana Bay and the nearby coastline with **Hana-Maui Sea Sports,** 808/248-7711. If renting a kayak to go on your own, expect single kayaks to go for about $25 a day while tandem kayaks will be about $40 a day.

## Submarines

Undersea adventures have also come to Maui. With *Atlantis Submarine,* 808/667-2224 or 800/548-6262, www.atlantisadventures.com, you can dive to more than 130 feet to view the undersea world through glass windows. The basic tour in this 48-passenger true submarine starts at $85 adult and $43 for kids; you must be at least three feet tall to board. These trips leave from the Lahaina Harbor pier every hour from 9 A.M. and travel to the sub loading area about two miles east of town. The trip under lasts about 50 minutes. Atlantis offers several combo packages with other island activity vendors.

The 34-passenger *Reefdancer,* 808/667-2133, www.galaxymall.com/stores/reefdancer, is a submersible that lets you view the underwater from the depth of no more than 10 feet—but it's a great view nonetheless and you might see more fish. The *Reef dancer* leaves from Lahaina Harbor and fares run $33–45 for 60- and 90-minute tours.

# FISHING

## Fishing Charters

The fishing around Maui ranges from very good to excellent. A sizable fleet of charter boats with skilled captains and tested crews is ready, willing, and competent to take you out. Most are berthed at Lahaina Harbor while others are at Ma'alaea Harbor.

Some of the best boats at Ma'alaea Harbor include: *Carol Ann,* 808/877-2181; *No Ka Oi III* and *Maka Kai,* 808/879-4485, run by Ocean Activities Center; and *Makoa Kai,* 808/875-2251, captained by Dave Ventura, who does only private fishing charters. In Lahaina you can't go wrong with the *Judy Ann,* 808/667-6672; *Aerial III* or *No Problem,* 808/667-9089; *The*

*Finest Kind* and *Reel Hooker,* 808/661-0338; or *Lucky Strike II,* 808/661-4606.

# CAMPING AND HIKING

Maui offers limited camping, and most of it is easily accessible. Camping facilities sit along the coast and amid the scenic forest areas of Haleakala. They range in amenities from housekeeping cabins to primitive hike-in sites. All require camping permits—inexpensive for the county and state parks, free for the national park. Camping permits can be obtained by walk-in application to the appropriate office or by writing. Although there is usually no problem obtaining sites, when writing, request reservations well in advance, allowing a minimum of one month for letters to go back and forth.

## Haleakala National Park

Camping at Haleakala National Park is free, but there is an automobile entrance fee of $10, $5 for bikers and hikers. Permits are not needed to camp at Hosmer Grove, just a short drive from park headquarters, or at Kipahulu Campground along the coastal road 10 miles south of Hana. Camping is on a first-come, first-served basis, and there's an official three-day stay limit, but it's a loose count, especially at Kipahulu, which is almost always empty. The case is much different at the campsites inside Haleakala Crater proper. On the floor of the basin are two primitive tenting campsites, one at Paliku on the east side and the other at Holua on the northwest corner. For these you'll need a wilderness permit from park headquarters, picked up on the first morning of your trip. Because of ecological considerations, only 25 campers per night can stay at each site, and a three-night, four-day per month maximum stay is strictly enforced, with tenting allowed at any one site for only two consecutive nights. However, because of the strenuous hike involved, campsites are open most of the time. You must be totally self-sufficient and equipped for cold-weather camping to be comfortable at these two sites.

Also, Paliku, Holua, and another site at Ka-palaoa on the south edge of the basin offer cabins.

Fully self-contained with stoves, water, and nearby pit toilets, they can handle a maximum of 12 campers each. Bunks are provided, but you must have your own warm bedding. The same maximum-stay limits apply as in the campgrounds. Stays at these cabins are at a premium—they're popular with visitors and residents alike. Reservations must be made at least two months in advance by mail using only a special cabin reservation request form. A lottery of the applicants chosen for sites keeps it fair for all. These cabins are geared toward groups, with rates of $40 for one to six people or $80 for up to the limit of 12. To have a chance at getting a cabin, write well in advance for complete information to: Haleakala National Park, P.O. Box 369, Makawao, HI 96768, or call 808/572-4400.

## State Parks

Of the eight state parks on Maui, two have overnight camping. **Polipoli Spring State Recreation Area** and **Wai'napanapa** offer free tenting, and housekeeping cabins are available; reservations highly necessary. Permits are required at each, and RVs technically are not allowed. Day use is free and open to everyone.

The dozen housekeeping cabins at Wai'anapanapa have a maximum capacity of six and have all necessary amenities, while the one at Polipoli Spring (gas stove, no electricity) can handle up to 10 persons. As with camping, permits are required with the same five-day maximum stay (the cabin at Polipoli Spring is closed on Tuesday night). Reservations are absolutely necessary, especially at Wai'anapanapa, and a 50 percent deposit at time of confirmation is required. There's a three-day cancellation requirement for refunds, and payment is to be made in cash, by money order, certified check, or personal check, the latter only if it's received 30 days before arrival so that cashing procedures are possible. The balance is due on arrival. Cabins are $45 per night for up to four people, and $5 for each additional person up to the limit. These are completely furnished down to the utensils, with heaters for cold weather and private baths.

Usually, tent camping permits are no problem to secure on the day you arrive, but reserving

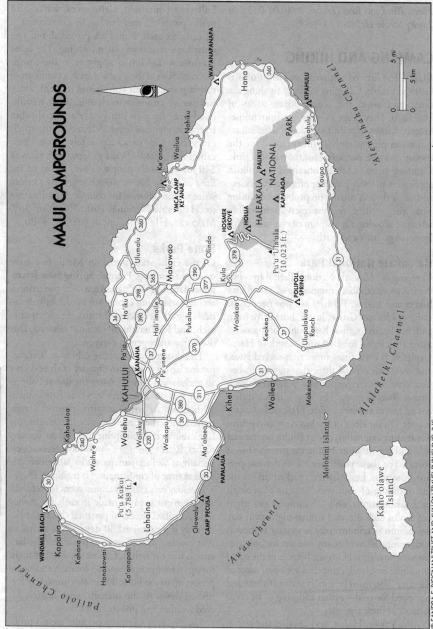

# MAUI CAMPGROUNDS

WINDMILL BEACH
Kapalua
Kahana
Honokowai
Ka'anapali

Kahakuloa
340
Waihe'e
30

320
Waiehu
Waikapu
30

Waiheu
WAILUKU
KAHULUI
Pa'ia

PAPALAUA
Ma'alaea
380
30

Pu'u Kukui
(5,788 ft.)
Olowalu
CAMP PECUSA
Lahaina

'Au'au Channel

Pailolo Channel

Molokini Island

Kaho'olawe Island

'Alalakeiki Channel

311
370
Pu'unene
KANAHA
37
Hali'imaile
390
36
Ha'iku
398
365
390
377
Makawao
Olinda
Kula
Waiakoa
Keokea
37
Ulupalakua Ranch
31
Kihei
Wailea
Makena

POLIPOLI SPRING
Pu'u 'Ula'ula
(10,023 ft.)
378
HOSMER GROVE
HOLUA
KAPALAOA
HALEAKALA NATIONAL PARK
PALIKU

360
Ulumalu
Ke'anae
Wailua
Nahiku
YMCA CAMP KE'ANAE

WAI'ANAPANAPA
Hana
360

Kipahulu
KIPAHULU
Kaupo
31

'Alenuihaha Channel

0    5 mi
0    5 km

MAUI

ensures you a space and alleviates anxiety. Permits are available from the Maui Division of State Parks, 54 S. High St., Room 101, Wailuku, HI 96793, 808/984-8109. Office hours are Mon.–Fri. 8 A.M.–4 P.M. This office also issues permits for camping at Pala'au State Park on Moloka'i.

## County Parks

Maui has 16 county parks. Only **Kanaha Beach Park** in Kahului and **Papalaua Beach Park** near the Lahaina Tunnel have overnight camping, but be aware that Kanaha Beach park is closed every Tuesday and Wednesday for maintenance. Camping fees are quite reasonable at $3 per night per adult, 50 cents for children, with no more than three consecutive nights at each park. To get a permit and pay your fees, either write in advance and an application will be mailed to you or visit the Department of Parks and Recreation permit issuing office Mon.–Fri. 8 A.M.–4 P.M. at 1580-C Ka'ahumanu Ave. (at the front of the War Memorial Gym) Wailuku, HI 96793. Call 808/270-7389 for more information.

## Private Campgrounds

**YMCA Camp Keanae** is perhaps the best known private campground on the island, and it's a beauty. It lies on the rugged north shore, halfway along the Hana Highway. This camp offers bunkhouses (you must provide your own bedding), tenting space, bathrooms with showers, and a gymnasium. Tents can be pitched on the broad grassy lawn. Bring your own cooking gear. The dining room and kitchen are open for large group use only. Check-in is 3–7 P.M. A fee of $15 per person or $30 per family is charged, with a three-day maximum stay. Y members get reduced rates. All accommodations are by reservation only. For information and reservations, call the camp at 808/248-8355; YMCACampKeanae@aol.com, YMCACampKeanae@aol.com.

**Camp Pecusa** is located about one-quarter mile east of Olowalu, along the coast east of Lahaina. Owned and operated by The Episcopal Church in Hawaii, this camp often fills with groups staying in the cabins during the summer. Tent space is open any time of the year for public use. A fee of $5 is charged per person per night. No reservations are taken, but it's best to call to see if space is available. For information, call 808/661-4303 or write Camp Pucusa, 800 Olowalu, HI 96761.

Camping is also permitted at **Windmill Beach,** just north of Honolua Bay on the northwest coast, on land owned by Maui Land and Pineapple Company. This is primitive camping—there are *no* facilities. No reservations are necessary, but a permit is. Camping permits are issued by the company office at 4900 Honoapi'ilani Hwy. (across the highway from Napili Plaza), Mon.–Fri. 7 A.M.–3:30 P.M. Fees are $5 per party with three nights maximum. For information, call 808/669-6201.

## Hiking

The hiking on Maui is excellent. Most times you have the trails to yourself, and the hikes range from a family saunter to a strenuous trek. There is no access problem on the more-established routes, but for others you'll need special permission from the landowners. However, many public access trails skirt the coast and penetrate deep into the interior.

Perhaps the most adventurous hiking on Maui is along the 27 miles of trails within Haleakala National Park. This is all high-elevation hiking with virtually no shade cover or water available, so you must be well prepared. Two trails start at different locations along Haleakala Highway and drop into the crater basin, traversing it to its far end. Several secondary trails connect these two main trails, while a third heads out and over the Kaupo Gap to descend the mountain to the south.

Not all hiking on the island requires such preparation or endurance. The Polipoli Spring area offers many miles of trails much lower in elevation and through sheltered forests, yet they give you great views over the countryside. There are also short hikes at 'Iao Needle near Wailuku and longer hikes up the Waihe'e Stream and Waihe'e Ridge, both north of Wailuku. Longer, drier, and more exhausting is the Lahaina Pali Trail, which cuts across the mountain ridge from Ma'alaea to the coast road heading toward Lahaina.

Coastal trails are also an option, and the easiest to approach are sections of the old King's Highway at Wai'anapanapa State Park. Another section of this ancient paved trail can be accessed from the end of the road at La Pérouse Bay.

Refer to the appropriate travel chapter for specific information about each of these hikes.

## Tour Companies

**Hike Maui,** P.O. Box 330969, Kahului, Maui, HI 96733, 808/879-5270, fax 808/893-2515, www.hikemaui.com, hikemaui@hikemaui.com, as its name implies, offers walking tours to Maui's best scenic areas accompanied by Ken Schmitt, a professional nature guide, or one of his fine staff. Ken has dedicated years to hiking Maui and has accumulated an unbelievable amount of knowledge about this awesome island. He's proficient in Maui archaeology, botany, geology, anthropology, zoology, history, oceanography, and ancient Hawaiian cosmology, and the hikes are actually workshops in Maui's natural history. Ken has expanded his operation to include a small hand-picked staff of assistants, each trained in the sciences, with the soul of an adventurer and the heart of an environmentalist. The hikes require a minimum of four people and a maximum of eight. All special equipment is provided, but you are requested to wear comfortable walking/hiking shoes. Gourmet lunches and fruits are provided. These hikes take in sights from Hana to West Maui, the coast, forest, and crater summit of Haleakala, and range from the moderate to the hardy ability level. Good physical conditioning is essential. Half-day hikes last about five hours and all-day hikes go for eight hours or more. The rates vary from $61 to $140. A day with Ken Schmitt or one of his dedicated guides is a classic outdoor experience. You'll be in the hands of experts. Don't miss it!

**Mango Mitch Ecotours** is another well-established company that offers small groups customized half-day, full-day, and overnight hikes, kayak trips, 4WD excursions, as well as multiple-day expeditions to other islands. Half-day hikes and snorkel trips run $60–70; the full-day Hana-area hike and swim is $90. An overnight in Haleakala Crater runs $120. Call for information on other options and multi-day trips. For Maui tours, refreshments and some gear are provided; all meals and equipment are provided on the overnight tours. Aside from the hiking experience itself, Mango Mitch imparts knowledge about Hawaii's natural history and culture to all his guests. For more information, contact P.O. Box 2511, Wailuku, HI 96793, 808/873-1848.

**Maui Hiking Safaris,** P.O. Box 11198, Lahaina, HI 96761, 808/573-0168 or 888/445-3963, fax 808/572-3037, www.mauihiking safaris.com, mhs@maui.net, also offers organized group hikes for $59–69 a half day or $89–99 a full day, all gear, snacks, and beverages provided. Various hikes are offered through valleys and forests, to waterfalls and up along ridges, and each hike is narrated with special attention to history and botany. Hikes generally are 4–8 miles in length and groups go with no more than six people. Tours led by Randy Weaver.

**Paths in Paradise** offers a full range of hikes, easy to strenuous, from half day to full day, most on Haleakala and its slope, with an emphasis on natural history and birds. Fees run $95–150. All food and necessary gear are provided. Hikes are led by Renate Gassmann-Duvall, Ph.D.; tours in German available. For information and reservations, contact P.O. Box 667, Makawao, HI 96768, 808/573-2022, fax 808/573-2021, www.maui.net/~corvusco, renate@lava.net.

**Latitudes & Attitudes** offers hikes on West Maui and Haleakala. Usually 4–6 hours in length, covering 2–6 miles, these hikes take you to a private arboretum tucked up the mountainside, into a valley used by ancient Hawaiians, through the thick jungle to a waterfall, and the crater of Haleakala. Hikes are easy to moderate in endurance. Rates are $80–120 for adults, with a minimum of four needed for a hike to go. All hiking equipment, breakfast and/or lunch is provided, and there is hotel pickup in the Kapalua and Ka'anapali area. For information and reservations, contact the company at 808/661-7720 or 877/661-7720 or 877/661-7720, www.ecomaui.com.

# HORSEBACK RIDING

Those who love sightseeing from the back of a horse are in for a big treat on Maui. Stables dot the island, so all you have to do is choose the terrain for your trail ride: a breathtaking ride through Haleakala Crater, across rangeland, or a backwoods ride into the rainforest. No riding is allowed on the beach. Choose the stable by area or type of ride offered. Unfortunately, none of this comes cheap, but you won't be disappointed by either the quality of trail guide or scenery. It's advisable to wear jeans (jogging suit bottoms will do) and a pair of closed-toe shoes. Sunscreen and a hat are also recommended on most rides. All stables have age and weight restrictions, so be sure to check with them directly for all details.

You'll have your choice of rides at **Ironwood Ranch:** sunset, mountain, pineapple field, or extended rides for experienced riders. The West Maui Journey, for all skill levels, costs 80 for 90 minutes and runs through the foothills of the mountains. Also for all riders are the two-hour sunset ride for $110 and a two-hour Hawaiian Excursion also runs $110. No one over 220 pounds please. Horses are matched to the rider's experience level and all rides are escorted. Ironwood Ranch, 808/669-4991 or 887/699-4529, is located at mile marker 29 along Route 30 above Napili. As all rides are conducted on private ranch land, meet at the pickup point across the highway from Napili Plaza. Check out their website at www.ironwoodranch.com.

**Makena Stables,** 808/879-0244, www.makenastables.com, is located at the end of the road at the edge of La Perouse Bay. Owners Helaine and Pat Borge will take you on a two-hour introductory ride through low-elevation rangeland, lava flows, and along the mountain trails of Ulupalakua Ranch; on three-hour morning or sunset rides; or on a five- to six-hour bay and lunch ride. Rides range from $120–165, and only one ride goes a day. Must be at least 13 years old and no more than 205 pounds.

**Pony Express Tours** offers trail rides into Haleakala Crater—full day $190, partial day $155, lunch provided. One- and two-hour rides ($60–105) are also offered across Haleakala

Ranch land at the 4,000-foot elevation. Riders must be at least 10 years old and not more than 235 pounds. Contact Pony Express Tours, 808/667-2200, www.maui.net/~ponex.

**Thompson Ranch Riding Stables,** a family-operated stable that will even mount up children under 10, guides you over the lower slopes of Haleakala on one of Maui's oldest cattle ranches. Located at 3,700 feet, just outside of Keokea, rides go downhill from here. A 1.5-hour ride runs $60, while the two-hour ride is $70 and the sunset ride is $80. Contact Thompson Stables at 808/878-1910.

**Adventures On Horseback** offers waterfall rides along the north coast over lands of a private estate in Haʻiku for $185. Rides go with a maximum of six riders, who must be at least 12 years old and five feet tall, and not over 225 pounds. Bring your own swimming suit and towel. A full-day "horse whisperer" program is also offered for $300. For reservations and information, call 808/242-7445. The company's website is at www.mauihorses.com.

Hotel guests are given priority for use of the horses at the **Hana Ranch Stables,** but you can call ahead to arrange a trail ride on this truly magnificent end of the island. The one-hour easy guided rides and two-hour rides go either along the coast or into the upper pastureland. Cost is $50 or $90 per person; riders must be seven years old. Private rides can be arranged. For information, call 808/248-8811.

In Kipahulu you'll find **Oheo Stables,** 808/667-2222, www.maui.net/~ray. Two rides (10:30 A.M. and 11 A.M.) are given every day, both three hours on the trail, and the destination is the highland above Makahiku and Waimoku Falls in Haleakala National Park. Only six riders maximum per ride; must be 12 years old and not more than 225 pounds. Both rides include snacks, and drinks, and both run $129.

**Mendes Ranch** offers two different rides daily over their 3000-acre working cattle ranch on the rugged north coast of Maui; $85 and $130 per person. Riders must be at least 11 years old and no more than 250 pounds. On both these rides, you'll have a look at the shoreline, pastureland, lush valleys, and waterfalls, and a real *paniolo* barbecue picnic is provided on the longer ride. This is a local experience led by real cowboys. Mendes Ranch is located just past mile marker 6 on Route 330 north of Wailuku. Check-in is at 8:15 A.M. and 12:15 P.M. For reservations, call 808/871-5222; www.mendesranch.com.

Fun for the whole family, rides at the **Piiholo Ranch,** 808/357-5544, in Makawao take you over a small working cattle ranch. Groups are limited to six riders. A morning picnic ride runs $140, while the afternoon ride with refreshments is $120; private rides can be arranged as well. Daily except Sunday. See www.piiholo.com.

## BICYCLING

Bicycle enthusiasts should be thrilled with Maui, but the few flaws might flatten your spirits as well as your tires. The countryside is great, the weather is perfect, but the roads are heavily trafficked and the most interesting ones are narrow and have bad shoulders. Pedaling to Hana will give you an up-close personal experience, but for bicycle safety this road is one of the worst. Haleakala is stupendous, but with a rise of more than 10,000 feet in less than 40 miles it is considered one of the most grueling rides in the world—going up. It's superb coming down. Cycling on Maui as your primary means of transportation is not for the neophyte; because of safety considerations and the tough rides, only experienced riders should consider it.

### Bicycle Rentals

Some bicycle rental shops will tell you that the Park Service does not allow you to take your bike up to Haleakala National Park—horse pucky! You *cannot* ride the bike on the hiking paths, but going up the road (40 miles uphill) is okay if you have the steam. You are given this misinformation because the bike rental shops don't want the wear and tear on their bikes, but for the prices they charge, they shouldn't squawk. For off-road riding, try the trails in Kula Forest Reserve near Polipoli Spring State Recreation Area.

**South Maui Bicycles,** 808/874-0068, 1993 S. Kihei Rd. across from Kalama Park and open Mon.–Sat. 10 A.M.–6 P.M., Sunday until 2 P.M., is

a rental and bike repair shop that boasts the largest fleet on Maui from which to choose. Rates are: street bikes $22 per day, $99 per week; road bike $29 per day or $129 per week, and simple mountain bikes $19 a day or $89 a week. Frank Hackett, the shop owner, will take time to give you tips including routes and the best times to travel.

**West Maui Cycles,** 808/661-9005, at 840 Waine'e St. in Lahaina, is a full-service bike sale and rental store that also carries other sporting equipment. The store has mostly Cannondale, GT, and Schwinn bikes. Standard road bike rates run from $30 a day to $120 a week, tandems run $55–65 a day or $220–260 a week, and cruisers are $15 a day or $60 a week. Mountain bikes vary from $30 a day to $160 a week, depending on suspension.

Cruisers can also be rented in Lahaina from **Duke's Rental Shop,** across from Kamehameha School along Front Street, for $10 a day.

In Kahului, **The Island Biker,** 808/877-7744, at 415 Dairy Rd., rents mostly mountain bikes along with its sales and repair services. They go for $29 a day, $95 a week, or $250 a month. Open Mon.–Sat. 9 A.M.–6 P.M. Also try **Extreme Sports Maui,** 808/871-7954, which has mountain bikes for $29–39 a day or $162–218 a week.

For other bike rentals, try **A & B Rental and Sales,** in Honokowai at 3481 Lower Honoapi'ilani Rd., 808/669-0027, open daily 9 A.M.–5 P.M., which rents basic mountain bikes at $15 for 24 hours or $60 per week. Aside from running bike tours, **Haleakala Bike Company,** 808/572-2200, in Ha'iku also rents Gary Fisher mountain bikes, all equipment, and a rack if you need one for $45 a day or $120 a week.

### Haleakala Bicycle Tours

An adventure on Maui that's become famous is riding a specially equipped bike from the summit of Mt. Haleakala for 40 miles to the bottom at Pa'ia. These bikes are mountain bikes or modified cruisers with padded seats, wide tires, and heavy-duty drum brakes, front and back. Typically, these tours take about eight hours with about three hours on the bike. Most offer a shuttle pickup and drop-off at your hotel. For tours that go to the top of the mountain for sunrise, expect to get picked up about 3 A.M.—get to bed early! Every bike rider on tours that ride through the national park must wear a full motorcycle helmet. Other tours that start outside the park will provide you with a regular bicycle helmet. Warm, layered clothing is a must, long pants and closed toe shoes recommended. All bike companies have some guidelines—no pregnant women, minimum age of 12, must be at least five feet tall—but each company's requirements may be slightly different, so check. These safety requirements are not without reason. No one wants to take a chance of your safety. Although comparatively safe, a few deaths have occurred on these bike trips over the years.

A pioneer in this field is **Maui Downhill,** 199 Dairy Rd., Kahului, 808/871-2155 or 800/535-BIKE, www.mauidownhill.net. Included in the bike ride for $150 you get two meals (continental breakfast, brunch or a gourmet picnic lunch), and a windbreaker, gloves, and helmet to use. To drench yourself in the beauty of a Haleakala sunrise, you have to pay your dues. You arrive at the base yard in Kahului at about 3:30 A.M. after being picked up at your condo by the courtesy van. Here, you'll muster with other bleary-eyed but hopeful adventurers and munch donuts and coffee, which at this time of the morning is more like a transfusion. Up the mountain, in the van, through the chilly night air takes about 90 minutes, with singing and storytelling along the way. Once atop, find your spot for the *best* natural light show in the world: the sun goes wild with colors as it paints the sky and drips into Haleakala Crater. This is your first reward. Next comes your bicycle environmental cruise down the mountain with vistas and thrills every inch of the way, with stops for sightseeing, food, and to let cars pass. For the not-so-early risers, other mountain descent tours are available for $150 and $104.

**Maui Mountain Cruisers** of Kahului, 808/871-6014 or 800/232-6284, www.mauimountaincruisers.com; **Mountain Riders,** 808/242-9739 or 800/706-7700, www.mountainriders.com; **Cruiser Phil's,** 808/893-2332 or 877/764-2453, www.cruiserphil.com; **Emerald**

**Island Bicycle Rides,** 808/573-1278 or 800/565-6615, www.mauibiking.com; and **Hawaii Downhill,** 808/893-2332, are other major bike touring companies that offer pretty much the same guided bike services at competitive rates.

A twist to this convoy guided bike tour is offered by **Haleakala Bike Company,** 808/575-9575, www.bikemaui.com, in Ha'iku. With this outfit, you meet at the bike store and get fitted with your bike and are given all necessary equipment. For the sunrise tours, the van leaves at about 4:15 A.M. and brings you to the top of the mountain in the park for your sunrise experience. When the riders start down the mountain, the company van stays with them until they are comfortable with the bikes and route and then lets them go the rest of the way by themselves, taking their time or zipping down the hill as they like, stopping when they want and eating where they desire. All that is required is that they return by about 4 P.M. It's bike freedom. Later in the morning, another drop-off goes to the crater rim. These rides are $84 and $74. Later drop-offs at the park entrance go for $65, but you can do the "take away option" for $45.

Another company that encourages a go-at-your-own-pace unguided tour is **Upcountry Cycles,** 808/573-2888 or 800/373-1678, www.bikemauihawaii.com.

**Aloha Bicycle Tours,** 808/249-0911, www.maui.net/~bikemaui, does trips through upcountry.

For going off road with a guided tour, see **Maui Eco-adventures,** 808/661-7720, www.eco-maui.com, who have access to private ranch land on the side of Haleakala.

## Bicycle Touring

For long-distance bicycle touring, contact **Go Cycling Maui,** 808/572-0259. This company provides all the gear and the know-how for small group tours of one to five days in length for $135–575 per person. You just need to show up and enjoy; routes can be negotiated. Fit and experienced bicyclists only. Call for rates.

For those who like to strike out on their own, two routes are recommended. One takes you for a 50-mile loop from Wailuku (or Lahaina) up the

Ka'anapali coast and around the head of Maui back to Wailuku. The road starts out in good repair, but the traffic will be heavy until you pass Kapalua. Here the road begins to wind along the north coast. Since this road has been paved, traffic around the north end has picked up, so the road will not be just yours anymore. Around the north end there is no place to get service. Go prepared, and be on the lookout for cars. The second route is from Kahului up to Kula or Pukalani via Pulehu Road and back down the mountainside via Pa'ia, Ha'iku, or Ulumalu, taking you through irrigated cane fields, the cool Upcountry region, the lush, and sculpted north slope of Haleakala.

## GOLF AND TENNIS

Maui has 10 golf courses with 16 links; all but one have 18 holes. These range from modest municipal courses to world-class private clubs.

Some are along the coast, while others back against the mountain with sweeping views of the lowlands. The high-class resort areas of Ka'anapali, Kapalua, and Wailea are built around golf courses. Refer to the accompanying chart for specific information.

Deciding at the last minute to golf? Want a discount rate? Willing to golf where it may not necessarily be your first choice? Try **Stand-by Golf,** 888/645-2665, where you can arrange tee times for great savings. Call one day in advance or the morning you want to play. **Maui Golf Shop,** 808/875-4653, also offers some reduced-rate greens fees on short notice. If you want to rent clubs other than at the golf course, try **Maui Golf Shop** 808/875-4653, at the Kihei Gateway Center in Kihei, **Maui Golf Repair,** 808/661-0889, or **West Maui Sports,** 808/661-6252, in Lahaina.

There are many tennis courts on Maui, and

## MAUI GOLF COURSES

| Course | Par | Yards | Fees | Cart | Clubs |
|---|---|---|---|---|---|
| **The Dunes at Maui Lani** | 72 | 6,413 | $95 | Incl. | $30 |
| Kuihelani Highway | | | | | |
| Kahului, 808/873-0422 | | | | | |
| **Elleair Maui Golf Club** | 70 | 5,979 | $85 | Incl. | $30 |
| 1345 Pi'ilani Highway | | | | | |
| Kihei, 808/874-0777 | | | | | |
| **Kaanapali Golf Courses** | | | | | |
| 2290 Kaanapali Pkwy. | | | | | |
| Kaanapali, 808/661-3691 | | | | | |
| North Course | 71 | 6,136 | $150 | Incl. | $35 |
| South Course | 71 | 6,067 | $142 | Incl. | $35 |
| **Kapalua Golf Club** | | | | | |
| 300 Kapalua Drive (Bay) | | | | | |
| Kapalua, 808/669-8044 | | | | | |
| Bay Course | 72 | 6,051 | $180 | Incl. | $40 |
| Village Course | 71 | 5,753 | $180 | Incl. | $40 |
| Plantation Course | 73 | 6,547 | $220 | Incl. | $40 |
| **Makena Golf Courses** | | | | | |
| 5415 Makena Alanui | | | | | |
| Makena, 808/879-3344 | | | | | |

plenty of them are free. The accompanying chart is a partial listing of what's available.

# HUNTING

Maui's game includes wild pigs and feral goats; hunted birds are pheasant, partridge, francolin, quail, dove, and wild turkey. There are several public hunting sections around the island, and a license is required. For full information, write the Department of Land and Natural Resources, Division of Forestry and Wildlife Office, 54 S. High St., Rm. 101, Wailuku, HI 96793, 808/984-8100. Office hours are 8 A.M.–3:30 P.M.

## Sporting Clays

Maui County has two sporting clay grounds, one on Maui and one on Lana'i. Each is designed differently but both provide the same basic service. Open daily 8:30 A.M.–dusk, **Pa-**paka Sporting Clays,** 808/879-5649, is located in Makena. Call for reservations and directions. For Lana'i Pine Sporting Clays, see the Lana'i chapter below.

# LAND TOURS
## Bus and Van Tours

It's easy to book tours to Maui's famous areas, such as Lahaina, Hana, 'Iao Valley, and Haleakala. Normally they're run on either half- or full-day schedules (Hana is always a full day) and range anywhere from $40 to $85 with hotel pickup included, kids at reduced rates. Some even do special cultural tours to such places as Kahakuloa Valley on the north shore. Big bus tours are run by **Roberts Hawaii,** 808/871-6226, 800/831-5541, www.roberts-hawaii.com, and they're quite antiseptic—you sit behind tinted glass in an air-conditioned bus. Other companies with smaller tour

| Course | Par | Yards | Fees | Cart | Clubs |
|--------|-----|-------|------|------|-------|
| North Course | 72 | 6,914 | $155 | Incl. | $35 |
| South Course | 72 | 7,014 | $175 | Incl. | $35 |
| **Maui Country Club** Sprecklesville, 808/877-7270 | 72 | 6,339 | $75 $38 (9 holes) | Incl. | $20 |
| **Pukalani Country Club** 360 Pukalani Street Pukalani, 808/572-1314 | 72 | 6,882 | $50 | Incl. | $20 |
| **Sandalwood Golf Course** 2500 Honoapi'ilani Highway Wailuku, 808/242-4653 | 72 | 6,469 | $80 | Incl. | $35 |
| **Waiehu Municipal Golf Course** Wailuku, 808/270-7400 | 72 | 6,330 | $26 (weekdays) $30 (weekends) | $8 | $15 (18) $10 (9) |
| **Wailea Golf Club** 120 Kuakahi Street (Blue) Wailea, HI 96753 | | | | | |
| Blue Course 808/875-5155 | 72 | 6,797 | $140 | Incl. | $35 |
| Gold Course 808/875-7450 | 72 | 6,653 | $160 | Incl. | $35 |
| Emerald Course | 72 | 6,407 | $150 | Incl. | $35 |

MAUI

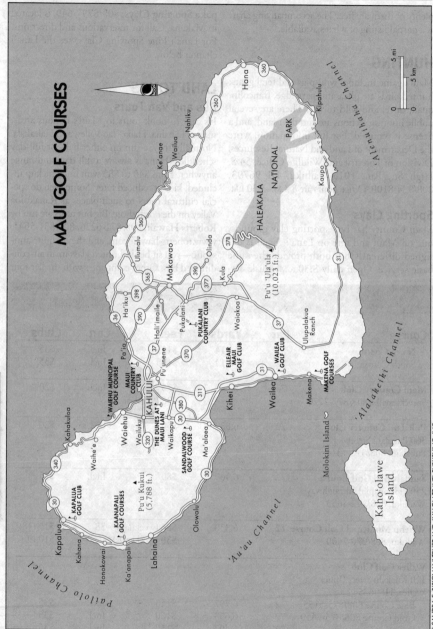

# MAUI GOLF COURSES

HALEAKALA NATIONAL PARK

Pu'u 'Ulaula (10,023 ft.)

Pu'u Kukui (5,788 ft.)

Kaho'olawe Island

Molokini Island

Kapalua

KAPALUA GOLF CLUB

Kahakuloa

Kahana

Honokowai

Ka'anapali

KAANAPALI GOLF COURSES

Lahaina

Olowalu

Waihe'e

WAIEHU MUNICIPAL GOLF COURSE

MAUI COUNTRY CLUB

Waiehu

Waikapu

THE DUNES AT MAUI LANI

KAHULUI

Wailuku

Pa'ia

SANDALWOOD GOLF COURSE

Ma'alaea

Pu'unene

Ha'iku

Hali'imaile

Makawao

Olinda

Kula

PUKALANI COUNTRY CLUB

Pukalani

Waiakoa

ELLEAIR MAUI GOLF CLUB

Kihei

Wailea

WAILEA GOLF CLUB

Makena

MAKENA GOLF COURSES

'Ulupalakua Ranch

Ke'anae

Wailua

Nahiku

Hana

Kipahulu

Kaupo

Ulumalu

Pa'uwela Channel

'Au'au Channel

'Alalakeiki Channel

'Alenuihaha Channel

0 5 mi
0 5 km

MAUI

# MAUI TENNIS COURTS

## County Courts

Under jurisdiction of the Department of Parks and Recreation, 808/270-7230. Courts listed are in or near visitor areas and open to the public.

| Town | Location | No. Of Courts | Lighted |
|---|---|---|---|
| Hali'imaile | Hali'imaile Park | 1 | Yes |
| Hana | Hana Ball Park | 2 | Yes |
| Kahului | Kahului Community Center | 2 | Yes |
| Kihei | Kalami Park | 4 | Yes |
| | Waipu'ilani Park | 6 | Yes |
| Lahaina | Lahaina Civic Center | 5 | Yes |
| | Malu'ulu O Lele Park | 4 | Yes |
| Makawao | Eddie Tam Center | 2 | Yes |
| Pukalani | Pukalani Park | 2 | Yes |
| Wailuku | Wailuku War Memorial Complex | 4 | Yes |
| | Wells Park | 7 | Yes |

## Hotel and Private Courts Open to the Public

| Town | Location | No. of Courts | Lighted |
|---|---|---|---|
| Ka'anapali | Hyatt Tennis Center 808/661-1234 | 6 | Yes |
| | Maui Marriott Tennis Club 808/661-6200 | 5 | No |
| | Royal Lahaina Tennis Ranch 808/667-5200 | 10 | 6 |
| | Sheraton Maui Tennis Club 808/667-9200 | 3 | Yes |
| Kapalua | Kapalua Tennis Center 808/665-0112 | 10 | 5 |
| | Kapalua Tennis Garden 808/669-5677 | 10 | 4 |
| Makena | Makena Tennis Club 808/879-8777 | 6 | 2 |
| Napili Bay | Napili Kai Beach Resort 808/669-6271 | 2 | No |
| Wailea | Wailea Tennis Club 808/879-1958 | 11 | 3 |

MAUI

buses and vans also hit the high points but have specialty tours. Try **Ekahi Tours,** 808/877-9775 or 888/292-2422, www.ekahi.com; **Polynesian Adventure Tours,** 808/877-4242 or 800/622-3011, www.polyad.com; **Akina Aloha Tours,** 808/879-2828 or 800/800-3989, www.akina-tours.com, and **Valley Isle Excursions,** 808/661-8687 or 877/871-5224, www.tourmaui.com.

**Temptation Tours,** 808/887-8888 or 800/817-1234, www.temptationtours.com, operates the ultimate in luxury van tours for the discriminating traveler. The deluxe vans, more like limousines, seat each of the eight passengers in a comfortable captain's chair for trips to Hana and Haleakala. This outfit runs more than a half dozen tours, all out to Hana or up to Haleakala, many combined with other activities. One Hana tour combines with a great cave tour, while a second lets you fly by helicopter one way. The Haleakala trips take you up for sunrise or let you experience a day on the mountain. Rates run $134–239.

## Offroad Tours

**Maui ATV Tours** has opened tours across the uplands of the Ulupalakua Ranch. These *mauka* tour take you up on the hillsides of this working cattle ranch, through pastures and past lava caves to panoramic scenes of the island, with a good chance of seeing wildlife. Tours are conducted on single-passenger, four-wheel automatic ATVs. Instruction is given on the operation of these machines, so no experience is necessary. Each trip runs in a circular route so there are new sights through the entire trip. A morning four-hour ride starts at 7:30 A.M. and runs $125 while the two-hour afternoon ride is $90 and begins at 1:30 P.M. Refreshments are provided. Must be 16 years old to ride on your own, but youngsters can be taken on a three-passenger ATV. All protective gear is provided but you should wear long pants and close-toe shoes. No one over 300 pounds, pregnant women, or those with back problems are allowed to ride. Private tours can be accommodated. For those who do not care to drive an ATV machine, a 4WD Pinzgauer truck tour is offered that also takes you to places that you can not ordinarily go. These three-hour tours go morning and afternoon and run $125 per person. For all activities,

meet at the office across from the Ulupalakua Store near the winery. For reservations, call 808/878-2889; www.mauiatvtours.com.

Haleakala Ranch also offers ATV tours across the vast acreage of its ranch. Meet at the office on the highway up to the summit and from there head into the ranch property. These tours start at about 4000 feet and go up from there so the views can be wonderful. Morning and afternoon tours are offered. Two-hour tours run $90 while the 3.5-hour tours go for $130. Call 808/661-0288 for information and reservations or see the website www.atvmaui.com.

## Personal Guided Tours

For a personalized tour where a guide drives your rental car and takes you to "local" places, try the following. **Guides of Maui,** 808/877-4060 or 800/231-8022, www.guidesofmaui.com, offers a Hana tour, circle-island tour, or Hana and Haleakala combination tour, a honeymooner's tour, and others. Trips start at 8 A.M. and return late afternoon and the rate is $235 per car with your rental car.

A similar service is provided by **Hapa Papa's Tours,** 808/242-8500, where a trip to Hana, 'Iao Valley, or Haleakala runs $75–95 per person depending on the tours, and they supply the van.

## Tape Tours

For those who desire a go-at-your-own-pace alternative to van tours, yet want the convenience of an escort, **Best of Maui Cassette Tours** may be for you. Buy a quality tape $13 or CD for $17 describing the Hana Highway and what to see and do along the way. This rental comes with a small pamphlet of sights, history, and legends, a route map, a video, and coupons. Pick up your cassettes 5 A.M.–1 P.M.; reservations are appreciated. Call Best of Maui at 808/871-1555 or stop by at 333 Dairy Rd., Kahului. You can also get one of these tapes at **Woo-wee Maui's Cafe** next door, where they will also provide you with a boxed lunch for the road for $8.95.

Offering roughly the same service at a similar price is **Hana Cassette, CD Guide,** 808/572-0550. Pick up your tape and all the extras from 5 A.M. at their booth at the Shell gas station along

Dairy Road in Kahului, or inside the station after the booth closes.

You will also find that a number of condos and other accommodations, as well as some other activities, have these tapes for use by their guests for free.

# AIR TOURS

Maui is a spectacular sight from the air. A few small charter airlines, a handful of helicopter companies, and a hang gliding outfit swoop you around the island. These joyrides are literally the highlight of many people's experiences on Maui, but they are expensive.

## Helicopter Tours

Chopper companies are competitively priced, with tours of West or East Maui at around $125, with a Hana/Haleakala flight at about $180. Circle-island tours are approximately $225, but the best might be to include a trip to Moloka'i at approximately $225 in order to experience the world's tallest sea cliffs along the isolated windward coast. While the most spectacular ones take you over Haleakala Crater, or perhaps to the remote West Maui Mountains, where inaccessible gorges lie at your feet, the 45-minute east Maui tour is the most popular. Know, however, that many hikers have a beef with the air tours: after they've spent hours hiking into remote valleys in search of peace and quiet, out of the sky comes the mechanical whir of a chopper to spoil the solitude.

All flights leave from the heliport at the back side of Kahului Airport—access off Haleakala Highway extension road. Each company has an office at the Kahului Airport where you check in and receive your pre-flight instructions. There is a parking lot here: free the first 15 minutes, $1 for 15-30 minutes, $1 each additional hour, maximum of $7 a day.

**Air Maui,** 808/877-7005 or 877/238-4942, www.airmaui.com, is one of the "little guys" but it works hard to please by offering many options at competitive prices with a great safety record. Family owned and operated. Air Maui offers all the standards and can customize a tour for you. A great choice.

**Alex Air,** 808/871-0792 or 888/418-8455, www.helitour.com, is a small personable company that runs a tight ship. It offers a wide variety of flights on two types of helicopters, the A-Star and a smaller Hughes 500. Two of its flights make landings at a black sand beach.

**Sunshine Helicopter,** 808/871-0722 or 800/469-3000, www.sunshinehelicopters.com, is another local, family-run outfit that flies the "Black Beauties." The seating is two-by-two, and each pilot goes out of his way to give you a great ride. Aside from the usual tours, this company does charters and combinations with Atlantis Submarine tours. Sunshine Helicopters also operates on the Big Island.

**Blue Hawaiian Helicopters,** 808/871-8844 or 800/745-2583, www.bluehawaiian.com, operates on Maui and the Big Island. It's a company that does lots of advertising, gets a lot of passengers, and has done work for film companies. Standard flights plus one that touches down and a combination fly/drive to/from Hana tour with Temptation van tours.

If you want a private flight, try **Mauiscape Helicopters,** 877-7272 or 888/440-7272, www.mauiscape.net. This company uses a four-seat Robinson Raven and usually takes two passengers although three passengers can fit, so everyone has a window seat. Other options are a four-set EC110, or a six-seat A-Star. With East Maui, West Maui, Haleakala, and Circle Island flights, tours run $180–250. The Mauiscape office is near the corner of Dairy Road and Hana Highway in Kahului.

## Fixed-Wing Tours

For a Maui joyride out of Kahului Airport, contact **Paragon Air,** 808/244-3356 or 800/248-1231, www.paragon-air.com. Paragon offers several different options, like a flight to Moloka'i with a tour of Kalaupapa for $210 or a flight to Moloka'i coupled with the mule ride down to Kalaupapa for $279. Others include a four-hour Big Island volcano tour for $495, and a five-island tour for $165. Paragon Air can also be hired for point-to-point charter travel for those who don't want to wait in lines at the airport.

An alternate for a Big Island volcano tour, a

sunset tour, or private charter is **Maui Air,** 808/877-5500, www.volcanoairtours.com. Maui Air runs the two-hour volcano tour from either Kahului or Kapalua airports at $279 per person. Taking a slightly different route to the Big Island, the sunset tour leaves from Kahului Airport only and is $255 per passenger. Flights are conducted in nine-passenger air-conditioned, twin-engine planes and everyone gets a comfortable window seat with stereo headset for the tour narration.

## Motorized Hang Gliding and Paragliding

For motorized hang gliding, contact **Hang Gliding Maui,** 808/572-6557, www.hanggliding-maui.com. These powered flights run $115 for 30 minutes and $190 for an hour. Long tours and instruction can be arranged. Flights leave from the Hana Airport only. Call for reservations.

Want to try paragliding off the side of Haleakala? Contact **Proflyght Hawaii Paragliding,** 808/874-5433 or 877/463-5944, www.paraglidehawaii.com, which will set you up on a tandem flight with a certified instructor. Depending upon launch site, flights can be 5–10 minutes or up to 40 minutes; rates are $75–275. All necessary equipment is provided, but you should wear warm comfortable clothing and sturdy shoes.

# BOOKING AGENCIES

**Ocean Activities Center,** 808/879-4484, is one of the biggest agencies for booking any and all kinds of activities on Maui. For much of the fun events like snorkeling, scuba diving, whale-watching, sunset cruises, and deep-sea fishing, the center has its own facilities and equipment, which means it not only provides you with an excellent outing, but offers very competitive prices. Ocean Activities can also book you on helicopters and land tours, and rent boogie boards, snorkel equipment, sailboards, surfboards, and kayaks. It has booking agencies in the Kihei area at the Mana Kai Maui Resort, Maui Hill Resort, and the Kamaole Shopping Center, at the Ma'alaea Harbor Village Shops, and at the Maui Marriott in Ka'anapali. Prices on all of their activities are very reasonable, and the service is excellent. If you had to choose one agency for all your fun needs, this would be a good bet.

Another very reputable outfit with one booking office in Lahaina is **Barefoot's Cashback Tours,** 808/661-8889 or 888/222-3601, www.tombarefoot.com. Barefoot's gives you up to a 10 percent discount on all your activities if you pay by cash or travelers checks or 7 percent discount with credit cards. It too can set you up with virtually any activity around the island or throughout the state. Stop in at 834 Front St. to see what adventure awaits at a reduced rate. Shop here; you'll be glad you did.

**Activity Warehouse** can provide the same service, often with last-minute reservations, and it also rents some ocean equipment. You can find Activity Warehouse in Lahaina, 808/667-4000, at 900 and 602 Front St., at the Embassy Vacation Resorts in Honokowai, 808/667-6062, and in Kihei, 808/875-4000, at 247 Pi'ikea Ave., Suite 103. **Activity World,** 808/667-7777, has a dozen and a half booths throughout the island, many at condos and resorts. They're convenient and offer good reductions in prices for all sorts of activities on the island. These are legitimate venders with solid reputations. You will, however, find a horde of other activities desks up and down Front Street and in other locations; you don't have to search for them—they'll find you, especially to make an exhausting high-pressured pitch for time shares! Avoid them—unless you want to listen to the rap in exchange for your reduced ticket price.

One of the easiest ways to book a fishing activity and sightsee at the same time is to walk along the Lahaina Wharf—there's an information booth here operated by many of the companies who rent slips at the harbor. Check it out first, and then plan to be there when the tour boats return. Asking the passengers, right on the spot, if they've had a good time is about the best you can do. You can also check out the boats and do some comparative pricing of your own.

For boats out of quiet Ma'alaea Harbor and a full range of activities around the island, contact the **Ma'alaea Activity Center,** 808/242-6982, www.activityshack.com. The center does it all, from helicopters to horseback, but specializes in the boats berthed at Ma'alaea.

# Accommodations and Food

## ACCOMMODATIONS

With about 18,000 rooms available, in some 225 properties, Maui is second only to O'ahu in the number of visitors it can accommodate. There's a tremendous concentration of condos, approximately 9,000 units, predominating in Kihei, Ma'alaea, Honokowai, Kahana, and Napili; and plenty of hotels, the majority in Ka'anapali and Wailea. To round things out, numerous B&Bs sit here and there around the island, and three hostels in Wailuku and one in Lahaina cater to the alternative traveler. Camping is limited to a handful of parks, but what it lacks in number it easily makes up for in quality.

More than 90 hotels and condos have sprouted on West Maui, from Lahaina to Kapalua. The most expensive are along some of Maui's best beaches in Ka'anapali and Kapalua and include the Hyatt Regency, Westin Maui, Sheraton, Kapalua Bay, and Ritz-Carlton. The older condos in Honokowai are cheaper, with a mixture of expensive and moderate as you head north. Lahaina itself offers only a handful of places to stay: condos at both ends of town, three renovated old-style inns, and a handful of bed-and-breakfasts. Most people find the pace a little too hectic, but you couldn't get more in the middle of *it* if you tried. Ma'alaea Bay, between Lahaina and Kihei, has 11 quiet condos. Prices are reasonable, the beach is fair, and you're within striking distance of the action in either direction.

Kihei is "condo row," with close to 100 along the six miles of Kihei Road, plus a few hotels. This is where you'll find top-notch beaches and the best deals on Maui. Wailea, just down the road, is expensive, but the hotels here are world-class and the secluded beaches are gorgeous. Kahului often takes the rap for being an unattractive place to stay on Maui. It isn't all that bad. You're smack in the middle of striking out to the best of Maui's sights, and the airport is minutes away for people staying only a short time. Prices are cheaper and Kanaha Beach is a sleeper, with great sand, surf, and few visitors. Hana is an experience in itself. You can camp, rent a cabin, or stay at an exclusive hotel. Always reserve in advance and consider splitting your stay on Maui, spending your last few nights in Hana. You can really soak up this wonderful area, and you won't have to worry about rushing back along the Hana Highway.

## FOOD

### Lu'au

**Old Lahaina Lu'au,** 808/667-1998, www.old-lahainaluau.com, on the beach at its location near the Lahaina Cannery Mall, has an excellent reputation because it is as close to authentic as you can get. Doors open at 6 P.M. daily, 5:30 P.M. during winter months, but reserve at least three to six days in advance to avoid disappointment, perhaps two weeks in advance during peak season. The lu'au, featuring a "locals' favorite," all-you-can-eat buffet and all-you-can-drink bar, costs $79 adults, $49 children 2–12. The traditional hula dancers use *ti*-leaf skirts, and the music is *fo' real*. The Old Lahaina Lu'au is one of the oldest and it gets the nod from nearly everyone as being the best lu'au on the island.

**Renaissance Wailea Beach Resort,** 808/891-7811, recounts tales of old Hawaii with its professional hula show and lu'au every Tuesday, Thursday, and Saturday at 5:30 P.M. Hawaiian music, hula, drumming, and a fire dancer entertain as you dine through the evening on a wonderful assortment of foods expertly prepared by the chefs. Price includes open bar at $70 adults, $33 children 3–12. Reservations are required.

The Royal Lahaina Resort has been offering the nightly **Royal Lahaina Lu'au** for years in their Lu'au Gardens starting at 5 P.M. While definitely designed for the tourist, the show is entertaining and the food offered is authentic and tasty. Prices are $67 adults, free for children 12 and under with a paying adult; reservations at 808/661-3611.

**Wailea's Finest Lu'au,** 808/879-1922, at the Wailea Marriott Resort, has garnered awards for its

MAUI

lu'au fare and Polynesian show, and its fire/knife dancer is an international award winner for his skill. Held Monday, Tuesday, Thursday, and Friday 5–8 P.M., $68 adults, $30 children 6–12.

Hyatt Regency Maui's **Drums of the Pacific,** 808/667-4420, is held every evening 5–8 P.M., for $78 adults and $37 kids 6–12. This meal and show always gets high marks from those who know on the island.

The **Maui Marriott** also presents its version of the lu'au and Polynesian show, starting the night with Polynesian games and activities. The Marriott's niche is its funny and entertaining twists. The evening starts at 5 P.M. and runs until 8 P.M. Cost is $78 adults, $38 children 3–8. Call 808/661-5828 for reservations.

While not the typical lu'au, per se, **The Feast at Lele** does a wonderful job of combining food with entertainment. Each of the five courses of this sit-down, served meal is accompanied by a Hawaiian, Tongan, Tahitian, or Samoan music and dance performance. Prepared under the direction of chef James McDonald, who also owns and operates the i'o and pacific'O restaurants, the food is top-notch, and the show, designed by those who bring you the Old Lahaina Lu'au, is well coordinated with the meal. This evening runs $95 adult and $65 for children, daily from 6–9 P.M. (5:30–8:30 P.M. during winter) at the beachfront 505 Front Street Mall venue in Lahaina. Reservations a must; call 808/667-5353 or see www.feastatlele.com.

# Getting There

## BY AIR

Almost all travelers to Maui arrive by air. A few lucky ones come by private yacht, the interisland ferries from Lana'i or Moloka'i, or one of the cruise ships that docks at Kahului. A limited number of direct air flights from the Mainland United States, Canada, and Japan are offered, but most airlines servicing Hawaii, both domestic and foreign, land in Honolulu and then carry on to Maui or offer connecting flights on "interisland carriers." More than 100 flights per day pass through Kahului Airport, while less than a dozen a day fly to Kapalua-West Maui airport.

### Maui's Airports

There are three commercial airports on Maui, but the vast majority of travelers will be concerned only with **Kahului Airport,** which accommodates 95 percent of the flights in and out of Maui. Kahului Airport is only minutes from Kahului city center, on the north-central coast of Maui. A full-service facility with all amenities, it has a few gift and snack shops, a restaurant, two tourist information booths, a newsstand, display cases of Hawaiian arts and crafts, a lost and found office, bathrooms, public telephones, car rental agencies, and limited

private transportation. Of the tourist information booths, one of which is in the arrival lounge and the other in the upstairs courtyard, at least one will be open from 6:30 A.M.–10 P.M. daily. As you face the terminal building, the departure lounge is on your right, the arrival lounge is on your left, and splitting the two is an upper-level courtyard with shops, a restaurant, and lounge. For your entertainment, a hula and music show is performed here for two hours at midday. Between the baggage claim and car rental booths is a 10 by 20 foot, 1,200-gallon state-of-the-art aquarium with accompanying signboards, constructed and maintained by the Maui Ocean Center, that presents to visitors a sample of the lively and colorful world that surrounds the island. A few steps beyond the rental car booths at the front of the arrival building is the commuter terminal, and on the far side of the runway is the heliport. Public parking at the airport costs $1 for the first half hour, $1 for each additional hour, or $7 maximum per day. There is metered parking at the commuter terminal. In 1990, the Kahului Airport underwent a major expansion that allows it to land large commercial planes and handle a great increase in traffic, including direct international flights. An additional runway expansion was then considered, but this plan has been permanently shelved due to sustained and overwhelming popular disapproval. Major roads lead from Kahului Airport to all primary destinations on Maui.

Hawaiian Airlines opened the one-strip **Kapulua-West Maui Airport** in early 1987. You fly in over pineapple fields. This facility is conveniently located between the Ka'anapali and Kapalua resort areas, on the *mauka* side of the Honoapi'ilani Highway at Akahele Street, just a few minutes from the major Ka'anapali hotels and condos of Honokowai and Kahana. As convenient as it is to this area of West Maui, it is not heavily used. Hawaiian Airlines no longer operates connecting flights to West Maui with the rest of Hawaii. There is on again-off again scheduled service with both Island Air and Pacific Wings, but you can't always count on it, and some charter companies use this strip for

their flights. The small terminal is user–friendly with a snack bar, sundries shop, tourist brochures, and courtesy phones for car rental pickup in the baggage claim are. Parking is in the metered lot: $1 for the first one-half hour, $1 for each additional hour, or $7 maximum for the day.

The third airstrip is **Hana Airport,** an isolated runway with a tiny terminal on the northeast coast just west of Hana, serviced only by Pacific Wings. It has no amenities aside from a bathroom and telephone, and transportation is available only to the Hotel Hana-Maui via the hotel shuttle. People flying into Hana Airport generally plan to vacation in Hana for an extended period and have made prior arrangements for being picked up. The only car rental available in Hana is by Dollar Rent A Car at 808/248-8237—call before you arrive!

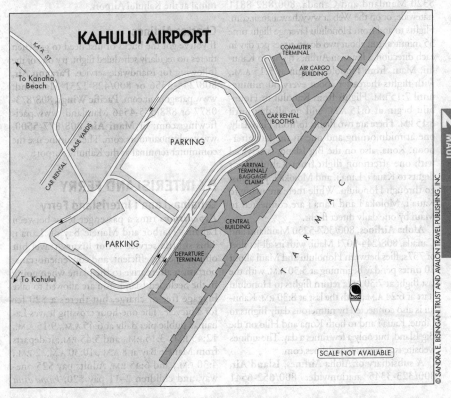

KAHULUI AIRPORT

KAA ST.

To Kanaha Beach

CAR RENTAL BASE YARDS

COMMUTER TERMINAL

AIR CARGO BUILDING

CAR RENTAL BOOTHS

PARKING

ARRIVAL TERMINAL/ BAGGAGE CLAIMS

PARKING

CENTRAL BUILDING

DEPARTURE TERMINAL

To Kahului

HANA HWY

MOON

SCALE NOT AVAILABLE

MAUI

© SANDRA E. BISINGANI TRUST AND AVALON TRAVEL PUBLISHING, INC.

### Flights to Maui

Until not too long ago, United Airlines was the only carrier that offered nonstop flights from the Mainland to Maui. Now, Delta Air Lines, American Airlines, Hawaiian Airlines, and Aloha Airlines offers daily flights from various Mainland cities to Maui. All other major domestic and foreign carriers fly you to Honolulu and have arrangements with either Hawaiian Airlines or Aloha Airlines for getting you to Maui. This involves a plane change, but your baggage can be booked straight through. If you fly from the Mainland with Hawaiian or Aloha, you have the added convenience of dealing with just one airline. Several charter airlines also fly to Maui nonstop from the Mainland.

### Interisland Carriers

**Hawaiian Airlines** can be reached at 800/367-5320 Mainland and Canada, 800/882-8811 statewide, or on the Web at www.hawaiianair.com. Flights to and from Honolulu (average flight time 35 minutes) run about two dozen times per day in each direction. Hawaiian Airlines flights to Kahului, Maui, from Honolulu begin at 5:15 A.M., with flights thereafter about every 30 minutes until 7:15 P.M. Flights from Kahului to Honolulu begin at 6:15 A.M. and go all day until 8:15 P.M. There are two flights to/from Hilo daily, one at midmorning and one in the late afternoon. Kona, also on the Big Island, is serviced with one afternoon flight from Kahului. For flights to Kaua'i, Lana'i, and Moloka'i, you must go through Honolulu. While there are many to Kaua'i, Moloka'i and Lana'i are connected to Maui by one daily direct flight.

**Aloha Airlines,** 800/367-5250 Mainland and Canada, 808/244-9071 Maui, with its all-jet fleet of 737s, flies between Honolulu and Maui about 20 times per day beginning at 5:30 A.M. with the last flight at 7:30 P.M.; return flights to Honolulu start at 6:24 A.M., with the last at 8:30 P.M. Kahului is also connected by numerous daily flights to Lihue, Kaua'i and to both Kona and Hilo on the Big Island, but only a few times a day. The airline's website is at www.alohaairlines.com.

A subsidiary of Aloha Airlines, **Island Air,** 800/323-3345 nationwide, 800/652-6541 statewide, connects Honolulu, Kahului, and Kona with the state's smaller airports, including Kapalua–West Maui, Lana'i, Ho'olehua on Moloka'i. About half the flights are on jet aircraft and half on Dash-8 turboprop airplanes. Four flights a day connect Honolulu to Kahului, making a stop on Moloka'i or Lana'i. Direct flights to and from Honolulu and Kapalua–West Maui Airport run five times daily from 7:25 A.M. to 4:40 P.M.

A local company operating eight-seat, twin-engine Cessna 402C planes, **Pacific Wings,** 888/575-4546 or 808/873-0877, www.pacificwings.com, does the pickup routes. They connect Kahului nonstop with Hana, Lana'i, Moloka'i, and Kamuela on the Big Island. To Honolulu, flights are either nonstop or through one of these other airports. Pacific Wings also flies from Hana, Moloka'i, and Kalaupapa to Honolulu. Pacific Wings uses the commuter terminal at the Kahului Airport.

### Charter Airlines

If you've got the bucks or just need to go when there's no regularly scheduled flight, try one of the following for islandwide service. **Paragon Air,** 808/244-3356 or 800/428-1231 Mainland, www.paragon-air.com. **Pacific Wings,** 808/873-0877 or 888/575-4546 Mainland, www.pacificwings.com; or **Maui Air,** 808/877-5500, www.volcanoairtours.com. These airline use the commuter terminal at the Kahului Airport.

## BY INTERISLAND FERRY

### Lahaina–Lana'i Interisland Ferry

*Expeditions* runs a passenger ferry between Lahaina Harbor and Manele Bay on Lana'i. This shuttle service is not luxury travel but offers a speedy, efficient, and convenient transportation alternative to the plane when going to the Secluded Island. You are allowed to take luggage free of charge, but there's a $20 fee for a bicycle. The one-hour crossing leaves Lahaina's public pier daily at 6:45 A.M., 9:15 A.M., 12:45 P.M., 3:15 P.M., and 5:45 P.M.; it departs from Manele Bay at 8 A.M., 10:30 A.M., 2 P.M., 4:30 P.M., and 6:45 P.M. Adults pay $25 one-way, and children 2–11 pay $20; *kama'aina* rates are available. It's best to reserve your place. As only two bikes are permitted on each ferry, be sure to let the company know well ahead of time if you're planning to take one. Ground transportation on Lana'i from the pier at Manele Bay is provided by Lana'i City Service, which will take you up to Lana'i City for $20 round-trip or $10 round-trip to the Manele Bay Hotel. An added perk of this trip is that you will see dolphins from the boat most of the year and there's good whale-watching during the winter months. For information and reservations, call 808/661-3756 on Maui or 800/695-2624 on Lana'i and elsewhere, or write 658 Front St., Suite 127, Lahaina, HI 96761. Visit the company website at www.go-lanai.com.

## Maui–Moloka'i Interisland Ferry

The *Maui Princess* used to sail daily between Kaunakakai and Lahaina, but for economic reasons the service was stopped in 1997, affecting many businesses on Moloka'i. Island Marine, the company which operates this ship, started ferry operation again in 2001 with the refurbished and faster *Molokai Princess,* which makes the crossing in about 75 minutes. Although the schedule is open to change, the yacht currently runs daily, leaving Kaunakakai at 5:45 A.M. and 3:30 P.M., and returning from Lahaina at 7:45 A.M. and 5:15 P.M. The fares are $40 one-way for adults and $20 for kids. Bikes are an extra $15 each way, but don't need to be packed. For information and reservations, contact Island Marine at 808/667-6165 or 800/275-6969; www.molokaiferry.com.

---

# Getting Around

If it's your intention to *see* Maui when you visit, and not just to lie on the beach in front of your hotel, the only efficient way is to rent a car. A few shuttles, taxis, and the good old thumb are available, but all these are flawed in one way or another. Other unique and fun-filled ways to tour the island include renting a bike or moped, but these conveyances are highly specialized and are more in the realm of sports than touring.

## RENTAL CARS

Maui has about two dozen car rental agencies that can put you behind the wheel of anything from an exotic convertible to a used station wagon with chipped paint and torn upholstery. There are national companies, interisland firms, good local companies, and a few fly-by-nights that'll rent you a clunker. The national firms have booths at Kahului Airport. No rental agency has a booth at the Kapalua-West Maui Airport (there are courtesy phones), but one company has a booth at the Hana Airport. The rest are scattered around the island, with a heavy concentration in Kahului, on Halawai Dr. in Ka'anapali, and along S. Kihei Road. Those without an airport booth have either a courtesy phone

or a number to call; some will pick you up and shuttle you to their lots.

## Auto Rental Agencies

The following major firms have booths at Kahului Airport—exit the arrival terminal and go to your right. Many pre-booked cars are waiting at these booths, but if you want to rent a car upon arrival, you must take a company shuttle to the base yard behind the airport parking lot or in town to arrange for your car.

**Dollar Rent A Car,** 808/877-2731 in Kahului, 808/667-2651 in Ka'anapali, 808/248-8237 in Hana

**Alamo,** 808/871-6235 in Kahului and 808/661-7181 in Ka'anapali.

**National Car Rental,** 808/871-8851 in Kahului, 808/667-9737 in Ka'anapali.

**Avis,** 808/871-7575 in Kahului, 808/661-4588 Ka'anapali.

**Budget,** 800/527-7000 on Maui.

**Hertz,** 808/877-5167 Kahului, 808/661-7735 in Ka'anapali.

**Enterprise,** 808/871-1511 Kahului, 808/661-8804 in Ka'anapali.

**Thrifty,** 808/871-2860.

The following local companies are based in

MAUI

Maui. None have a booth at the airport but a few have pickup service through courtesy phones. **Word of Mouth Rent-A-Used Car,** at 150 Hana Hwy., 808/877-2436 or 800/533-5929, www.mauirentacar.com, pickup van provided, offers some fantastic deals on their used, but not abused, cars. They're a reputable agency, having been around for more than 25 years. Office hours are 8 A.M.–5 P.M., but they will leave a car at the airport at earlier or later hours with prior arrangement. Others include: **Kihei Rent A Car,** 808/879-7257 or 800/251-5288, www.kiheirentacar.com, at 96 Kio Loop behind the Maui Dive shop in Kihei; and **Maui Cruisers,** 808/249-2319 or 877/749-7889 Mainland, 800/488-9083 Canada, www.mauicruisers.net, who will put you in a car that will make you "look local."

## Four-Wheel Drive

Though much more expensive than cars, some people might feel safer in 4WDs for completely circling Maui or driving some roads in Upcountry. Also, unlike for cars, the rental companies offering 4WDs put no restrictions on driving past 'Ohe'o Gulch. Four-wheel drives can be obtained from **Dollar** and a few other of the "big boys," as well as the following. **Maui Rent A Jeep,** 808/877-6626 or 800/701-JEEP, www.mauijeep.com; **Kihei Rent A Car;** 808/879-7257 or 800/251-5288, www.kiheirentacar.com; or one of the fantasy vehicle dealers listed below. Rates vary from company to company but are mostly around $75–100 per day, dependent on availability, model, and length of rental.

## Vanity Vehicles

If you feel like stepping out in *style,* consider renting a flashy sports cars. **Island Riders,** 808/661-9966 in Lahaina or 808/874-0311 in Kihei, www.islandriders.com, rents a Dodge Viper, Ferrari 348TS, Prowler, Porsche, Cabriolet, and Corvette convertible, as well as a few jeeps, vans, and Mazda Miatas. These cars are classy but they're not cheap, and you may have to be 25 years old to rent. However, for that one night of luxury, it may be worth it to you. Rates run from $200 a day to $850 a day depending upon the type of car. Rental by the hour is also

possible. The **Aloha Toy Store,** 640 Front St., 808/661-1212, www.alohatoystore.com, also has a variety of these fancy cars at comparable rates, as does **Hawaiian Riders,** 808/662-4386 at 196 Lahainaluna Street in Lahaina and 808/891-0889 in Kihei, www.hawaiianriders.com.

## Motorcycles

A few companies also rent motorcycles for the intrepid traveler. Virtually all rental bikes are Harley-Davidson big hogs or sportsters. Rates vary but run around $100 for half a day and $140–190 for 24 hours; longer rentals can be arranged. All drivers must be at least 21 years old, have a valid motorcycle endorsement on your license, and be in possession of a major credit card. Insurance is available. Companies want you to stay on good paved roads and don't usually allow trips to Hana. Although it is not required by state law to wear them, helmets are available, but you must wear eye protection. For riding one of these big steeds, contact **Mavriks',** 808/661-3099, at Halawai Drive in Ka'anapali. Also try **Island Riders,** 808/661-9966 in Lahaina or 808/874-0311 in Kihei; the **Aloha Toy Store,** 808/662-0888 or 808/661-1212 in Lahaina, The shops at Wailea, 808/891-0888, or The Fairway Shops in Ka'anaplai, 808/661-9000; **Hawaiian Riders,** 808/662-4386 in Lahaina or 808/891-0889 in Kihei; or **Hula Hogs,** 808/875-7433 in Kihei.

## Mopeds

Just for running around town or to the beach mopeds are great. Expect to pay about $25 for two hours, $35 for four hours, and $45 for eight hours; some offer weekly rates. Most will ask for a cash deposit; some will not let you have them overnight. You must be at least 18 years old. Check with **Hawaiian Island Cruzers,** 808/879-0956, at 2395 S. Kihei Rd.; **Mavriks',** 808/661-3099, at Halawai Drive in Ka'anapali; **Aloha Toy Store,** 808/662-0888, at 640 Front Street, Lahaina, the Shops at Wailea in Wailea, 808/891-0888, or The Fairway Shops in Ka'anapali, 808/661-9000; or **Hawaiian Riders,** 808/662-4386, at 196 Lahainaluna Rd. in Lahaina or in Kihei, 808/891-0889.

# ALTERNATIVE TRANSPORTATION

## Maui Bus System

There is limited public bus service on Maui that operates between Wailuku and Kahului, within the South Maui and West Maui areas, between these two regions, with a connection up to Wailuku and Kahului through Ma'alaea. Unfortunately, there is still no public bus service to Upcountry or along the Hana Highway. This public transportation system is operated by MEO (Maui Economic Opportunity, Inc.) and Akina Aloha Tours: the MEO Public Shuttle and the Akina Holo Ka'a Transit.

The MEO Public Shuttle runs two circular routes between Kahului and Wailuku six to eight times a day Monday through Saturday allowing for easy access between these two towns. Overlapping seven of these stops is the Akina Holo Ka'a Transit Route 5 which runs down to Ma'alaea and on to Lahaina Harbor, Whaler's Village in Ka'anapali, and the Ritz-Carlton in Kapalua or from Ma'alaea down to the Shops at Wailea in Wailea. Four of these overlapping stops are the State office building in Wailuku and the Queen Ka'ahumanu Center, the Maui Mall, and Kmart in Kahului. There is no fare for the MEO Public Shuttle, although donations are accepted.

The Holo Ka'a Transit buses operate within the South Maui and West Maui areas and between these two areas. The point to point one-way fare for rides within the Lahaina-Ka'anapali section is $1, $2 for the routes between Kapalua and Ka'anapali as well as the Kihei to Makena route, $5 one-way to or from Ma'alaea, and an all day systemwide pass is $10, which includes the connection from Wailuku or Kahului.

West Maui Route 1 runs approximately one dozen times a day between Kapalua and Ka'anapali from 9 A.M. Route 2 starts at 8:45 A.M. and goes more than a dozen times a day between Ka'anapali and Lahaina. The Route 3 Express runs six times a day from Ka'anapali Whaler's Village to Lahaina, then on to Ma'alaea and finally through Kihei to The Shops at Wailea. An Early Bird Route also runs twice a morning between Kihei at Kapalua, via Ma'alaea, Lahaina, and Ka'anapali. Route 4 runs seven times a day within South Maui, stopping at nearly a dozen and a half stops on the way. The Suda's Store is at the north end and the Maui Prince in Makena is at the south end.

For information on routes, schedules, and fares for this public transit system, contact MEO at 808/877-7651, www.meoinc.com or Akina Aloha Tours, 808/879-2828, www.akinatours.com. Systemwide schedules and timetables are also printed in some of the free tourist literature available across the island.

## Shuttle Service

**Speedi Shuttle,** 808/875-8070, connects the Kahului Airport to virtually anywhere on the island. It operates daily during the hours that the planes fly. Pickup can be from either the airport or any hotel or condo if going to the airport. Use the telephone next to the information booth in the baggage claim area when at the airport. Rates vary according to distance and how many are in your party, but as an example, a party of two from the airport to Wailea would run about $32, to Ka'anapali $46, to Kapalua $60, and between Wailea and Lahaina $45.

**Executive Airport Shuttle,** 808/669-2300, offers virtually the same service to and from the airport and to points around the island for nearly the same rates, like $30 from the airport in Kahului to the harbor in Lahaina. While these companies will service their calls as soon as they can, they prefer several hours or even 24 hours advance notice if possible in order to best facilitate use of their vehicles.

The free **Kaanapali Trolley** runs along the Ka'anapali strip about every half hour 10 A.M.–10 P.M., stopping at all major resorts, the golf course, and the Whaler's Village shopping complex. Look for the green jitneys. Pick up free printed tourist literature or ask at any hotel desk for the schedule.

The **Wailea Shuttle** is a complimentary van that stops at several of the major hotels and condos in Wailea, The Shops at Wailea, and golf course clubhouses in Wailea every 30 minutes. It operates 6:30 A.M.–8 P.M. Be sure to check with

**MAUI**

the driver about the last pickup times if you are out in the evening.

## Taxis

About two dozen taxi companies on Maui operate pretty much as island-wide service. Some operate by area. Most, besides providing normal taxi service, also run tours all over the island. While sedans predominate, some minivans are being used as well. Taxis are expensive and metered by the distance traveled. For example, a ride from Kahului Airport to Lahaina is $49, Ka'anapali is $55, to Kapalua $75, and about $40 to Wailea. Expect $5–10 in and around Kahului, and about $12 to the hostels in Wailuku. Any taxi may drop off at the airport, but only those with permits may pick up there. In the Kihei/Wailea area, try: **Wailea Taxi,** 808/874-5000; or **Kihei Taxi,** 808/879-3000. **Kahului Taxi Service,** 808/877-5681, operates in central Maui. In West Maui, options include **Alii Cab,** 808/661-3688; **AB Taxi,** 808/667-7575; and **Island Taxi,** 808/667-5656. Operating on the west side, **Classy Taxi,** 808/665-0003, uses renovated old cars from the 1920s and '30s. A ride from Lahaina to Ka'anapali runs about $11, and from there to Kapalua it's about $18.

Several companies on the island offer limo service. These are expensive rides, however, and will run, for example, more than $120 one-way from the Kahului Airport to Ka'anapali. Private tours might run $60 for two persons for two hours or $90 for a full load for the same time frame. Ask your hotel concierge for assistance in arranging for this service, or contact one of the following: **Wailea Limousine,** 808/875-4114; **Executive Service,** 808/669-2300; or **Bob and Sons Limousine Service,** 808/877-7800.

## Hitchhiking

Hitchhiking is once again legal in Maui County. Use the old tried-and-true method of thumb out, facing traffic, with a smile on your interesting face. You can get around quite well by thumb, if you're not on a schedule. Hitching short hops along the resort beaches is easy. Catching longer rides to Hana or up to Haleakala can be done, but it'll be tougher because the driver will know that you'll be with him or her for the duration of the ride. Under no circumstances should women hitch alone.

# Information and Services

## Emergencies

For **police, fire, and ambulance** anywhere on Maui, dial **911.**

For **non-emergency police** assistance and information: 808/244-6400.

**Civil Defense:** In case of natural disaster such as hurricanes or tsunamis on Maui, call 808/270-7285.

**Coast Guard:** 800/552-6458.

**Sexual Assault Crisis Line:** 808/873-8624.

For recorded information on **local island weather,** call 808/877-5111; for the **marine report,** call 808/877-3477; and for conditions on Haleakala, call 808/571-5054. For **time of day,** dial 808/242-0212.

## Medical Services

**Maui Memorial Medical Center** is located at 221 Mahalani St., Wailuku, 808/244-9056. It is the only full-service hospital on the island.

There are several clinics around the island, including the following. **Urgent Care Maui/Kihei Physicians,** 808/879-7781, at 1325 S. Kihei Rd., Suite 103, where doctors, a clinical lab, and X-rays are available from 6 A.M.–midnight daily. **Kihei-Wailea Medical Center,** 808/874-8100, in the Pi'ilani Village Shopping Center, has physicians, a pharmacy, physical therapy, and a clinical laboratory and is open Mon.–Fri. 8 A.M.–8 P.M., Saturday and Sunday until 5 P.M. **Kaiser Permanente** has a clinic in Lahaina at 910 Waine'e, 808/662-6900, in Wailuku at 80 Mahalani St., 808/243-6000, and in Kihei at 1279 S. Kihei Rd., 808/891-6800; open Mon.–Fri. 8 A.M.–5 P.M., closed noon–1 P.M., weekends, and holidays. At Dickenson Square in Lahaina, **Aloha Family Prac-**

tice Clinic, 808/662-5642, has hours weekdays 8:30 A.M.–4:30 P.M. for preventative and urgent care needs. In the center of Wailuku at 2180 Main St., try Maui Medical Group, 808/249-8080; they also have clinics in Lahaina and Pukalani. The West Maui Healthcare Center maintains an office at the Whalers Village shopping mall, 808/667-9721; open 8 A.M.–8 P.M. daily.

Of the numerous drugstores throughout the island, the following should meet your needs: Longs Drug in Kihei, Lahaina, and Kahului; Kihei Pharmacy, 808/879-8499, at 41 E Lipoa; and Lahaina Pharmacy, 808/661-3119, in the Lahaina Shopping Center.

## Consumer Protection and Tourism Complaints

If you encounter problems with accommodations, bad service, or downright rip-offs, try the following: Maui Chamber of Commerce, 250 Ala Maha, Kahului, 808/871-7711; the Office of Consumer Protection, 808/984-8244; or the Better Business Bureau (O'ahu), 877/222-6551.

## Tourism Information

The best information on Maui is dispensed by the Maui Visitors Bureau, 1727 Wili Pa Loop, Wailuku, HI 96793, 808/244-3530 ro 800/525-6284, www.visitmaui.com. For general information about Maui and specific accommodation and activities listings, ask for the official vacation planner, or check it on the Web at www.hshawaii.com/mvp.

The state operates two visitors information booths at Kahului Airport, one in the center building upper level and the other in the baggage claim area of the arrival terminal. One or the other should be open daily 6:30 A.M.–10 P.M., offering plenty of practical brochures and helpful information. Call 808/872-3892. Also, scattered around the arrival terminal lower level are numerous racks of free brochures, magazines, and other tourist literature.

## Post Offices

The main post office on Maui is at 250 Imi Kala St. in Wailuku. In addition, there are 11 branch post offices on Maui, five on Moloka'i, and one on Lana'i.

## Reading Material

The main branch of the library is at 251 High St., Wailuku, 808/243-5766; other branches are in Kahului, Lahaina, Makawao, Kihei, and Hana. The libraries hold a hodgepodge of hours through the week.

Free tourist literature is well done and loaded with tips, discounts, maps, happenings, etc. Found in hotels, restaurants, and street stands, they include: This Week Maui, Maui Gold, Maui Magazine, Maui Beach and Activity Guide, Maui Activities and Attractions, and The Best Guidebook. Published three times a year, the Drive Guide, with excellent maps and tips, is given out free by all car rental agencies; similar is the Driving Magazine of Maui. Maui Menus and Menu are all about food; 101 Things to do Maui is a great resource and also has money-saving coupons; and Maui Visitor is worth a look.

The major local paper available on Maui is the Maui News. Published Mon.–Fri., it has good "Datebook" listings of local events; www.mauinews.com. Lahaina News, www.west-maui.com, is a daily community paper of news, feature stories, and entertainment listings. Free local papers include the Maui Times, Haleakala Times, Gold Coast, and Maui Weekly.

## Island Radio

More than a dozen radio stations broadcast on Maui. Popular ones: KHPR 88.1 FM (also 90.7 FM) broadcasts from Honolulu and is the island's public radio station; KPOA 93.5 FM out of Lahaina does a mix of contemporary Hawaiian and standard rock; the format on KAOI 95.1 FM in Wailuku is mostly adult rock with a request line; KAPA 99.1 FM offers island sounds; KNUI 900 AM does traditional Hawaiian; and KAOI 1110 AM does news, talk, and sports.

## Maui Facts

Maui is the second youngest and second largest Hawaiian Island after Hawai'i. Its nickname is the Valley Island. Its color is pink and its flower is the lokelani, a small rose.

MAUI

# Central Maui: The Isthmus

## Kahului

It is generally believed that Kahului means "The Winning," but perhaps it should be "The Survivor." Kahului suffered attack by Kamehameha I in 1790, when he landed his war canoes here in preparation for battle at 'Iao Valley. In 1900 it was purposely burned to thwart the plague, and then rebuilt. Combined with Wailuku, the county seat just up the road, this area is home to 38,800 Mauians, more than one-quarter of the island population. Here's where the people live. It's a practical, homey, commercial town, the only deep-water port from which

Maui's sugar and pineapples are shipped out and other commodities shipped in, and it now has the island's only pineapple cannery. Although Kahului was an established sugar town by 1880, it's really only grown up in the last 40 years. In the 1960s, Hawaiian Commercial and Sugar Co. began building low-cost housing for its workers, which became a model development for the whole of the United States. Most people land at the airport, blast through for Lahaina or Kihei, and never

ROBERT NILSEN

'Iao Needle

# CENTRAL MAUI

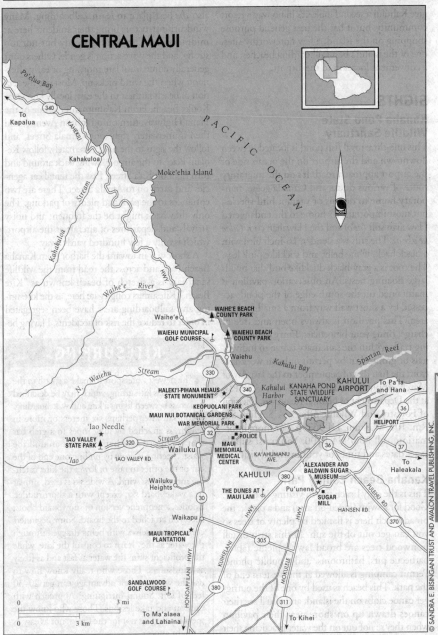

PACIFIC OCEAN

Po'elua Bay

To Kapalua

Kahakuloa

Moke'ehia Island

Kahakuloa Stream

KAHEKILI HWY

Waihe'e River

Waihe'e

WAIHE'E BEACH COUNTY PARK

WAIEHU MUNICIPAL GOLF COURSE

WAIEHU BEACH COUNTY PARK

Waiehu

N. Waiehu Stream

Kahului Bay

Spartan Reef

Kahului Harbor

KANAHA POND STATE WILDLIFE SANCTUARY

KAHULUI AIRPORT

To Pa'ia and Hana

HALEKI'I-PIHANA HEIAUS STATE MONUMENT

KEOPUOLANI PARK

MAUI NUI BOTANICAL GARDENS

WAR MEMORIAL PARK

POLICE

Kahului

HELIPORT

'Iao Needle

'IAO VALLEY STATE PARK

'Iao Stream

'IAO VALLEY RD.

Wailuku

MAUI MEMORIAL MEDICAL CENTER

Ka'AHUMANU AVE.

KAHULUI

To Haleakala

Wailuku Heights

ALEXANDER AND BALDWIN SUGAR MUSEUM

THE DUNES AT MAUI LANI

Pu'unene

SUGAR MILL

HANSEN RD.

Waikapu

MAUI TROPICAL PLANTATION

PUEHU RD.

SANDALWOOD GOLF COURSE

To Ma'alaea and Lahaina

To Kihei

0        3 mi

0        3 km

Highways: 340, 330, 32, 320, 30, 36, 37, 370, 380, 305, 311

MAUI

give Kahului a second look. It's in no way a resort community, but it has the best general-purpose shopping on the island, a few noteworthy sites, one of the island's best sailboarding beaches, and a convenient location to the airport.

## SIGHTS

### Kanaha Pond State Wildlife Sanctuary

This one-time royal fish pond is located between downtown and the airport on the ocean side of the airport approach road. It's on the migratory route of various ducks and Canada geese, temporary home to dozens of vagrant bird species, but most important it's home to the endangered Hawaiian stilt (*ae'o*) and the Hawaiian coot (*'alae ke'oke'o*). The stilt is a slender, 16-inch bird with a black back, white belly, and sticklike pink legs. The coot is a gray-black ducklike bird that builds large floating nests. An observation pavilion is maintained on the south edge of the pond, accessed by a short walkway from a small parking area. This pavilion is always open and free of charge. Bring your binoculars. Entry to the walking trails within the sanctuary is free to individuals or groups but by permit only on weekdays from the first day of September to the last day of March. Apply Monday–Friday 8 A.M.–3:30 P.M. at the Department of Natural Resources, Division of Forestry and Wildlife office, 54 S. High St., Rm. 101, Wailuku, HI 96793. For more information, call 808/984-8100. You must supply exact dates and times of your intended visit.

### Kanaha Beach County Park

This is the only beach worth visiting in the area. Good for a swim (roped-off area) and a picnic, the broad beach here is flanked by plenty of trees so you can get out of the sun. In this strip of tall ironwood trees are broad lawns, picnic tables, barbecue pits, bathrooms, and a public phone. Permit camping is allowed at the western end of the park. This beach is used by one of the outrigger canoe clubs on the island, and you'll see their canoes drawn up on shore near their pavilion when they're not out on the water practicing their strokes. Kanaha is a favorite of sailboarders, and it's

also *the* best place to learn sailboarding. Many windsurf instructors bring their students here at midmorning. The wind is steady but not too strong, and the wave action is gentle. Others don't generally come until late morning or early afternoon when the wind picks up. Most use the section of beach farthest to the east, locally known as Kooks Beach. From Ka'ahumanu Avenue or the Hana Highway, turn onto Hobron Avenue, and then immediately right onto Amala Street, and follow the signs to the park. Alternately, follow Keolani Place to the airport, swing back around and turn right on Ka'a Street. Pass the rental car agencies and carry on to Amala Street. There are two entrances to the park and plenty of parking. The only drawback might be the frequent and noisy arrivals and departures of aircraft at the airport, which is only a few hundred yards away.

A short way in toward the harbor from Kanaha Beach Park and across the road from the wildlife sanctuary is a stretch of beach known as "Kite Beach." Kitesurfers congregate here, as the kitesurfing and sailboarding areas have been segregated in order to reduce the risk of accidents. Having be-

## KITESURFING

The newest watersport to make a splash in the islands is kitesurfing, which may be described as a cross between flying a kite and wakeboarding. A foil-sail kite, perhaps six meters or more in length, is attached by long ropes to a grab bar that is clipped to a harness worn around the waist. Steering is done by pulling one end of the bar or the other to raise or lower the kite, catching more or less wind. A wide ski is used, similar to a wakeboard ski, except with a short rudder. Booties, a neoprene version of snowboard boots, keep you attached to the board. Some beginners content themselves with being dragged through the water as they learn to control the kite, while the proficient skim the water as fast and as freely as windsufers. Those who really know how to use the wind to their advantage can get 20–30 feet of loft. Sound intriguing? Approach with caution and take lessons. Those who know the sport say that it's not for the timid, nor as easy as it might appear.

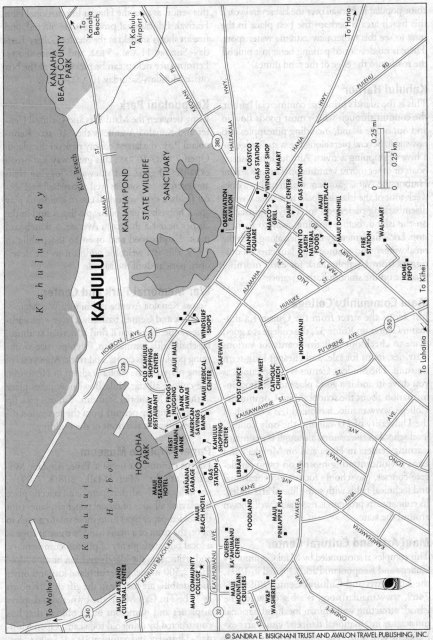

KAHULUI

*Kahului Bay*

*Kahului Harbor*

KANAHA BEACH COUNTY PARK

KANAHA POND STATE WILDLIFE SANCTUARY

To Kanaha Beach

To Kahului Airport

OBSERVATION PAVILION

COSTCO
GAS STATION
WINDSURF SHOP
KMART
MARCO'S GRILL
DAIRY CENTER
GAS STATION
MAUI MARKETPLACE
MAUI DOWNHILL
WAL-MART
DOWN TO EARTH NATURAL FOODS
FIRE STATION
TRIANGLE SQUARE
HOME DEPOT

To Kihei

WINDSURF SHOPS

OLD KAHULUI SHOPPING CENTER
MAUI MALL
HIDEAWAY RESTAURANT
TWO FROGS HUGGING
BANK OF HAWAII
MAUI MEDICAL CENTER
AMERICAN SAVINGS BANK
FIRST HAWAIIAN BANK
SAFEWAY
POST OFFICE
SWAP MEET
CATHOLIC CHURCH

To Lahaina

KAHULUI SHOPPING CENTER
LIBRARY
MANANA GARAGE
GAS STATION

HOALOHA PARK

MAUI SEASIDE HOTEL
MAUI BEACH HOTEL

FOODLAND
MAUI PINEAPPLE PLANT

MAUI ARTS AND CULTURAL CENTER
MAUI COMMUNITY COLLEGE
QUEEN KA'AHUMANU CENTER
MAUI MOUNTAIN CRUISERS
W&F WASHERETTE

To Waihe'e
To Waihe'e

Kite Beach

AMALA ST.
KEOLANI PL.
HALEAKALA HWY
HANA HWY
PULEHU RD.
KEOLANI PL.
HOBRON AVE.
HANA HWY
ALAMAHA
HUIILIKE
PU'UNENE AVE.
HONGWANJI
KAULAWAHINE ST.
LAIO PL.
DAIRY RD.
PAPA PL.
LALO PL.
KANE
KA'AHUMANU AVE.
KA'AHUMANU
QUEEN
LONO AVE.
HINA AVE.
WAKEA AVE.
LANAI AVE.
MAHA
KEA ST.
ONEHE'E
KAMEHAMEHA

0      0.25 mi
0      0.25 km

N

MAUI

come popular in Hawaii over the last several years, this beach area is perhaps the best place in the state to see this rather new extreme water sport. There is no developed parking here; just pull off the road onto the edge of the sand dune.

## Kahului Harbor

This is the island's principal commercial harbor, the conduit through which most goods flow in and out of the island, including pineapples and raw sugar. Several piers along the water's edge are a hive of shipping activity. Although no fishing boats or other tourist ventures operate at Kahului Harbor, the *Norwegian Star,* which makes a one-week tour of the islands, docks here once a week, disembarking passengers for a day's sightseeing on the island, before floating away to its next stop. Local fishermen try their luck along both the breakwaters, and a canoe club launches its outriggers from Hoaloha Park for early morning practice on the smooth harbor waters.

## Maui Community College

Just across the street from the Queen Ka'ahumanu Center on Route 32, the college is a good place to check out bulletin boards for various activities, items for sale, and cheaper long-term housing. The Student Center is conspicuous as you drive in and is a good place to get most information about the school. Maui Community College, www.mauicc.hawaii.edu, is a branch of the University of Hawaii and the only college-level school in the county, although it maintains learning centers in Hana and on Moloka'i and Lana'i. Concentrating mostly on two-year-degree courses, the school's focus is on vocational and technical fields with some liberal arts added. Its culinary arts program is reasonably well known around the state.

## Maui Arts and Cultural Center

This complex is surrounded by Maui Community College and Keopuolani Park. Opened in 1994, the Maui Arts and Cultural Center, 808/242-7469, www.mauiarts.org, is a big draw for the island, attracting well-known local and national musicians, international dancers, visual arts exhibitions, and films. The Maui Film Festival uses this venue, as does the Hawaii International Film Festival. Educational programs are offered, and free art shows are held at the Shaffer Gallery Tuesday–Sunday 11 A.M.–5 P.M. and before shows. Performance tickets can be picked up at the box office Monday–Saturday 10 A.M.–6 P.M.

## Keopuolani Park

Lying between the Maui Arts and Cultural Center and Kanaloa Avenue is the 110-acre Keopuolani Park, the largest county park on the island. Open 7 A.M.–10 P.M., this greenway has broad expanses of grass and sidewalks, jogging trails and exercise stations, as well as baseball and soccer fields, a sand volleyball court, children's play areas, horseshoe pits, picnic pavilions, and in the corner near Ka'ahumanu Avenue, a skateboard park. Landscaped and open to the public in 1999, this is a welcome addition to the developed parklands of the island.

## War Memorial Park and Center

Across Kanaloa Avenue is Wailuku War Memorial Park and Center, basically a large-arena athletic venue. Here you'll find a football stadium, baseball field, gymnasium, Olympic-size swimming pool, tennis courts, and track. After years of being played at the Aloha Stadium in Honolulu, the college all-star Hula Bowl now takes place at the War Memorial Stadium. You can pick up county camping permits from the recreation director's office at the front of the building.

## Paper Airplane Museum

For the curious, the unusual Paper Airplane Museum at the Maui Mall, 808/877-8916, www.flex.com/~edynray/pam, is an eclectic place displaying all sizes of model paper airplanes (not the folded-paper type) from those small enough to fit on the palm of a man's hand to those as large as a local boy, with plenty of photos, commentary, and artifacts on the island's aviation history. More than 2,500 model paper airplane kits and other memorabilia are for sale in the gift shop. Known as "The Tin Can Man," the owner also displays airplanes and numerous other objects that he's constructed by using old soda cans. Open Monday–Thursday and Saturday 10 A.M.–6 P.M., Friday until 8 P.M., and Sunday until 4 P.M. Admission is free to this nonprofit museum, yet donations are gladly accepted and will be used to support their children's outreach programs.

## Alexander and Baldwin Sugar Museum

The museum, 808/871-8058, www.sugarmuseum.com, is located at the intersection of Pu'unene Avenue (Route 311) and Hansen Road, about one-half mile from Dairy Road. Hours are Monday–Saturday 9:30 A.M.– 4:30 P.M.; admission $5 adults, $2 children 6–17, ages five and under free. (Avoid the area around 3 P.M. when the still-working mill across the street changes shifts.) This small but highly informative museum could easily be your first stop after arriving at Kahului Airport only 15 minutes away, especially if you're heading to Kihei. Once you get off the plane, you'll realize that you're in the midst of sugarcane fields. If you want to know the history of this crop and the people who worked and developed it, visit the museum. The vintage museum building (circa 1890) was the home of the sugar plantation superintendent, who literally lived surrounded by his work. Outside on the lawn are several old pieces of machinery from decades past, once used at the plantation. Inside is a small but well-stocked bookstore and gift shop featuring Hawaiiana and handmade clothing and artifacts, with goodies like guava and coconut syrups and raw sugar.

As you begin your tour, notice the ancient refrigerator in the hallway that the staff still uses. In the first room, you are given a brief description of the natural history of Maui, along with a rendition of the legends of the demigod Maui. Display cases explain Maui's rainfall and use of irrigation for a productive sugarcane yield. There is an old-fashioned copper rain gauge along with pragmatic artifacts from the building of the Haiku Ditch. A collection of vintage photos features the Baldwin and Alexander families, while a historical plaque recalls when workers lived in ethnic camps, each with its own euphemistic name (Chinese at Ah Fong, Japanese at Nashiwa, Portuguese at Cod Fish). This setup was designed to discourage competition (or cooperation) among the ethnic

groups during labor disputes and to ease the transition to the new land. These people are represented by everything from stuffed fighting cocks to baseball mitts from the '30s. Included is an educational video on sugarcane production. The museum is in the shadow of the state's largest and the island's only active sugar mill, and you can hear the wheels turning and the mill grinding. It's not an antiseptic remembrance, but a vital one where the history still continues. No tours are given at the mill across the street, but you can view a scale model of the crushers to get an idea of what goes on inside its hulking exterior.

# ACCOMMODATIONS

Kahului features two economical hotels, just right for the traveler looking for a good deal away from the island's tourist hubs, yet in a convenient location to many island sites, the airport, and business and government offices. These accommodations are west of Hoaloha Park on the harbor side of Ka'ahumanu Avenue (Rte. 32).

The **Maui Beach Hotel,** 808/877-0051 or 888/649-3222, fax 808/871-5797, is a low-rise affair with a Polynesian-style peaked roof over its lobby. On the lobby level are the front desk, small gift shop, and a banquet hall. Upstairs, daily buffets at the Rainbow Dining Room are a good value, and cocktails and *pu pu* are served at the Lokelani Lounge near the dining room from 5:30 P.M., with entertainment on the weekends. Open 9 A.M.–5:30 P.M., the small swimming pool is located on the second floor next to the pool. Lying between two arms of rooms, the central lawn leads down to the narrow beach fronting Kahului Harbor. Rates are $98–185 for standard to oceanfront rooms and $450 for an oceanfront suite. Each room has a small refrigerator, color television, safe for valuables, a lanai, and air-conditioning. For the convenience of its guests, a complimentary shuttle runs to the airport every hour 6:30 A.M.–9 P.M.; reservations necessary. The Maui Beach Hotel has offered the same friendly hospitality to *kama'aina* and visitors alike since the 1960s.

About 100 yards to the east is the **Maui Seaside Hotel,** 808/877-3311 or 800/560-5552, fax

808/877-4618, www.mauiseasidehotel.com, part of the Sand and Seaside Hotels, a small island-owned chain. Friendly and economical, this too is a two-story facility with a swimming pool in the central courtyard, access to the beach, and Vi's Restaurant for breakfast and dinner. All rooms hold two double beds or a king-size bed, have a color TV, small refrigerator, ceiling fan, and air-conditioning. Some kitchenettes are available, and there is a self-service laundry on premises. More motel-like than the Maui Beach, the Maui Seaside is clean, neat, and well cared for, and the owners show obvious pride in the way they keep up the property. AAA approved, rates are $98–135, or $105–125 with rental car; numerous discounts, including through the Internet, are offered.

## FOOD

The Kahului area has an assortment of inexpensive to moderate eating establishments and one that is a notch above the rest. Many are found in the shopping malls.

### Inexpensive

Several basic restaurants and other food purveyors are located along Dairy Road. If you're looking for a wholesome, natural deli item, fresh salad, hot entrée, or freshly baked pastry, there's not a better place to look than the deli counter at **Down to Earth Natural Foods,** 305 Dairy Rd. Prices for items from the hot bar and salad bar run just over $6 per pound; prices for other items are marked and moderate. Open daily, it's also a full-service grocery store.

At the Dairy Center just up the road, you'll find the inexpensive eateries **Koko Ichiban Ya** for Japanese food and **Piñata's** Mexican restaurant. In the second half of this complex, around the corner and fronting Hana Highway, is **Maui Coffee Roasters,** 808/877-2877, for those who want a hot brew or take-home beans, available from all the islands. Tea, cold drinks, smoothies, sandwiches, wraps, soups, salads, veggie burgers, and baked goods are also available in this good-time, upscale, yuppie-ish coffeehouse-type place. Open weekdays at 7 A.M. and weekends at 8 P.M.

With an unlikely location in an industrial area

among car repair shops is **Ajiyoshi Okazuya,** 385 Hoohana St., Unit 5C, 808/877-9080. Once here, try grilled fish, oxtail soup, or any of the other inexpensive Japanese dishes.

Follow your nose in the Queen Ka'ahumanu Center to **The Coffee Store,** 808/871-6860, open Mon.–Fri. 7:30 A.M.–9 P.M., Saturday 8 A.M.–7 P.M., and Sunday 8 A.M.–5 P.M. Light lunches include savories like a hot croissant or a spinach roll pastry puff, mostly in the $6–7 range. Coffee by the cup is $1.25 and up. The coffees, roasted on the premises, are from more than 20 gourmet varieties hand-picked in Hawaii and from around the world. Gifts and giftwear are sold too. In addition, the Queen Ka'ahumanu Center also has a food court with half a dozen international fast-food outlets. You'll be sure to find something you can eat here.

The Maui Mall has a selection of inexpensive fast-food-type shopping center restaurants that include **Siu's Chinese Kitchen,** where most of their typical Chinese dishes are under $5, **Maui Mixed Plate** for local hot entrées, **Island Breeze Cafe,** and **IHOP.** All are good choices for a quick lunch during the day. Other fast-food eateries can be found in the food courts at Maui Marketplace.

Finally, for those who need their weekly fix of something fried and wrapped in Styrofoam, Kamehameha Avenue and adjacent streets behind the Maui Mall are dotted with a slew of fast-food chain restaurants.

### Moderate

The Maui Beach Hotel serves food in its second-floor, open-air **Rainbow Dining Room** restaurant. You can fill up here at the breakfast buffet from 7–9:30 A.M. Monday–Saturday for $5.99, or try the Sunday buffet for $7.99. A lunch buffet is served 11 A.M.–2 P.M. daily for $10.95. Nearly every evening there's a different theme buffet from 5:30–8 P.M. for $21.99, except for the special Thursday king crab, prime rib, seafood, and lobster buffet for $28.99. At the Rainbow Dining Room, you'll have no complaint about value for price.

**Vi's Restaurant,** at the Maui Seaside Hotel, 808/871-6494, serves a standard American fare breakfast 7–9 A.M. for $6 or less and dinner

6–8 P.M. for under $13.50. Vi's offers more than 20 dinners such as fresh fish and steak, and breakfasts include their well-known omelets and hotcakes, and other island favorites.

In the Kahului Shopping Center you'll find **Ichiban Restaurant,** 808/871-6977, an authentic and inexpensive Japanese eatery, open daily except Sunday 7 A.M.–2 P.M. (Saturday from 10:30 A.M.), dinner 5–9 P.M., featuring full and continental breakfast, along with Japanese, American, and local specialties. Much of the breakfast menu is typically American, like eggs and bacon, omelets, and pancakes, most around $5. The lunch menu includes teriyaki chicken or shrimp tempura, chicken cutlet, don buri dishes, a variety of udon, and basic noodles, most $5–8. Dinner features combination plates, with your choice of any two items like shrimp and vegetable tempura, sashimi, or teriyaki chicken for around $14, along with more expensive special combinations like steak and lobster, the most expensive item on the menu, for $20–27. In addition, the sushi bar is open for lunch and dinner, with individual pieces ranging $3.75–6.75.

**Koho Grill and Bar,** 808/877-5588, at the Queen Ka'ahumanu Center, is an easygoing, good-time family dining place. The breakfast menu items are fairly standard, but Koho combines appetizers and salads with burgers, plate lunches, a few Mexican and Italian dishes, plus fish and standard American meat entrées for lunch and dinner. The food is not special, but you won't be disappointed either.

At the corner of Dairy Road and the Hana Highway is **Marco's Grill and Deli,** 808/877-4446, a casual place with black and white leather booths and cane chairs set around tiled tables. It's very Italian, and you might hear Tony Bennett being played as background music. For breakfast try chocolate cinnamon French toast for $6.95, pancakes, omelets, or pastries. A quick lunch might be one of the many deli sandwiches or a hot sandwich from the grill, most for under $13. Among the usual Italian fare items are Italian sausage and linguini for $16.95, pasta and basil for $14.95, and veal parmigiano for $22.95. Other specialties are vodka rigatoni for $16.95 and grilled salmon for $20.95. Take-out is available for

anything on the menu, or choose something from the deli case. Open daily 7:30 A.M.–10 P.M.

The only on-the-water dining in Kahului is the **Hideaway** restaurant, 808/873-6555, next to Hoaloha Park. Hideaway does breakfast, lunch, and dinner buffets along with their à la carte menu, which has a combination of American standard and local dishes. The dinner menu is heavy on the meats and seafood, with pork ribs a signature item. Entrées run $13–23, and the *keiki* menu makes this a more affordable place for families. The Sunday breakfast buffet and the Monday–Saturday lunch buffets runs $10.99, while the nightly dinner buffet is $18.99. With dark wood overtones and low lighting, the Hideaway might also be a romantic spot for those who don't want to spend a bundle.

Perhaps the best of the bunch, and with the most outstanding menu, is **Mañana Garage,** 808/873-0220, located at the corner of Lono and Ka'ahumanu avenues. This trendy "nuevo latino" eatery serves lunch and dinner inside and out on the patio, and mixed drinks and Mexican beer at the bar. Fitting with its name, the Mañana Garage has a semi-industrial look mixed with bright Latin colors. While the lunch and dinner menus differ somewhat, a few items you will find are fried calamari and quesadilla con queso appetizers and entrées like fresh fish chimichanga, roasted habanero chicken, Cuban fried steak, chili adobo pulled pork, and pumpkin seed crusted shrimp. Lunch items run $8–13, while dinner entrées are $14–25. Weekdays, lunch is served 11 A.M.–2:30 P.M. with an abbreviated midday menu available 2:30–5 P.M. Dinner is served nightly from 5–9 P.M., but evening revelers can get food off the late-night menu until 10:30 P.M. Wednesday–Saturday, when the place is filled with the sounds of sultry live jazz or Latin instrumental music. While not the most romantic spot—the restaurant sits across from a gas station on a busy street—it does, however, have tasty food with a south-of-the-border zing in a vibrant and visually pleasing atmosphere. Call for reservations.

## Groceries

For basic grocery items, try any of the following full-service stores in Kahului: **Star Market** at the

Maui Mall, **Ah Fooks** at the Kahului Shopping Center, **Foodland** at the Queen Ka'ahumanu Center, and **Safeway** at 170 E. Kamehameha Avenue behind the Maui Mall. **Down to Earth Natural Foods,** 305 Dairy Rd., across from Maui Marketplace, is open Monday–Saturday 7 A.M.–9 P.M. and Sunday 7 A.M.–8 P.M. A full-service natural foods grocery with bulk items, canned and boxed goods, fresh vegetables and fruit, vitamins, minerals, and supplements, and health and beauty items, the store also has a deli counter, salad bar, hot entrée bar, and a bakery.

For a quick stop at a basic bottle shop, try Ah Fooks at the Kahului Shopping Center, Star Market at the Maui Mall, or the **Hawaii Liquor Superstore** at the Maui Marketplace.

## ENTERTAINMENT

The six-plex **Kaahumanu Theater,** on the second floor of the Queen Ka'ahumanu Center, 808/875-4910, screens shows for $7.75 adults, $4.50 teens, and $2 children. At the Maui Mall, the **Maui Mall Megaplex Cinemas,** 808/249-2222, has eight screens and tickets run $7.50 adults, $4.50 ages 3–11.

You can hear free musical entertainment at both the Maui Mall and Queen Ka'ahumanu Center, usually over the lunch hour or early evening. These schedules vary throughout the month, but definitely stop and listen if the music is going when you are there shopping.

The **Maui Arts and Cultural Center,** 808/242-7469, has a varied program of music, dance, film, and visual arts showings at their complex near the harbor. This is one of the finest arts venues in the state. The box office is open 10 A.M.–6 P.M. Monday–Saturday.

## RECREATION

Kahului is by no means a recreational center on the island, but it does offer a variety of options for sports and recreation. Nearby beaches are known throughout the world for excellent sailboarding and kitesurfing. Although the mountain is a distance away, you can start your journey for a bike ride down the mountain here.

Located southwest of downtown Kahului in the rolling sand hills of the isthmus is the "Irish Linksland Design" **The Dunes at Maui Lani,** the island's newest golf course. Undulating over the sand dunes, with plenty of elevation change, this course is a welcome addition to the range of courses offered on the island. Designed by Nelson and Haworth, the facility opened in 1999 with rudimentary facilities, but a full-service pro shop, restaurant, and driving range were added in 2000. Located north and south of Wailuku, respectively, are the shoreline **Waiehu Municipal Golf Course,** a family-friendly course used mostly by locals. This course is beautiful to play yet open to the bay, so it can get strong winds. The more challenging **Sandalwood Golf Course** lies on the lower slope of the West Maui Mountains.

## SHOPPING

Because of its malls, Kahului has the best all-around shopping on the island. Combine this with the smaller shopping plazas, Kmart, Wal-Mart, Costco, and individual shops around town, and you can find absolutely everything you might need. For something different, don't miss the **Maui Swap Meet,** 808/877-3100, on Pu'unene Avenue next to the post office, every Saturday 7 A.M.–noon.

You can also shop almost the minute you arrive or just before you leave at two touristy but good shops along Keolani Place. Less than one-half mile from the airport are the **T-shirt Factory,** with original Maui designs and custom inexpensive T-shirts, as well as aloha shirts, sarongs, and pareu; and **Coral Factory,** for pink and black coral and jewelry sets with semiprecious stones. The Coral Factory seems to be set up largely to cater to Japanese tour groups.

On Dairy Road between Haleakala and Hana highways are the two huge stores housing **Kmart** and **Costco.** Farther down Dairy Road are the equally as large **Wal-Mart** and **Home Depot** stores. Mainland American mercantilism has invaded!

The two-story **Queen Ka'ahumanu Center** along Ka'ahumanu Avenue is Kahului's largest mall, with the widest selection of stores on the island with goods priced for the local market and plenty of free parking. The mall's central courtyard is covered with a big skylight and a huge sail-like expanse of canvas—a good way to let the light and breezes through. You'll find the big stores like **Macy's** and **Sears** anchoring this mall, with the smaller **Shirokiya** here as well. Numerous apparel, shoe, jewelry, and specialty stores and three restaurants fill this center, and a half dozen inexpensive international fast-food eateries are located in the food court. In addition, the center hosts a farmers market on Fridays 8 A.M.–3 P.M. Several of the specialty shops are a large **Waldenbooks** for one of the best selections of books on Maui; **Serendipity** for oriental furniture, home accessories, and inspired clothing; **Ho'opomaika'i**, which carries Hawaiian gifts and crafts; **Maui Hands** for arts and crafts; a **Whaler's General Store** for sundries; and **GNC** for nutritional supplements. On the upper level, you can relax in the cool, dark comfort of the **Kaahumanu Theater** and catch a movie. For something free, entertainment is often offered at the center stage over the lunch hour and at about 7 P.M. on Fridays.

The low-rise, open-air, and renovated **Maui Mall** is more pedestrian, yet it has a pleasant ambiance as its buildings are set around courtyards. At the intersection of Hana Highway and Ka'ahumanu Avenue, Maui Mall has **Longs Drugs** for everything from aspirin to film, a **Star Market**, the unusual **Paper Airplane Museum** (see the Sights section), a megaplex theater, a handful of clothing and specialty shops, and a couple places for quick foods. On Fridays, there is free live entertainment at the mall's center stage.

While **Kahului Shopping Center**, 47 Ka'ahumanu Ave., has lost much of its vitality, you'll still find **Ah Fooks** supermarket, open daily from 6:30 A.M. and specializing in Asian foods, the smaller **Ji-Mi Asian Food Mart,** the moderate and pleasant **Ichiban Restaurant**, a **Salvation Army Thrift Store**, and **Central Pacific Bank.** Maui Organic Farmers Market holds court here on Wednesdays 8 A.M.–noon. This mall is less distinctive than the other two along Ka'ahumanu Avenue and seems to have suffered most because of the newer and larger malls in town.

**The Old Kahului Shopping Center**, 55 Ka'ahumanu Ave., just across from the Maui Mall, is just that, an old building from 1916 that held a bank and a series of shops that was modernized and brought back to life in the late '80s. Once full of boutiques and specialty shops, it now has only two ordinary shops and a chiropractic office. **Lightning Bolt** specializes in surfboards and surf attire, modern fashions, women's apparel, hats, and sunglasses, while **Fabric Mart** has miles of cloth and craft and sewing supplies.

The newest mall in Kahului, with a style from Anywhere U.S.A., occupies a huge area along Dairy Road. This is **Maui Marketplace,** and here you'll find such stores as **Borders Books and Music** for the best selection of books on the island; **The Sports Authority** for a large selection of athletic clothing and equipment, bicycles, and camping and fishing supplies; the clothing stores **Hawaiian Island Creations** and **Old Navy;** a **Sunglass Hut** outlet; the huge **Lowe's** home improvement warehouse for anything you might need for your house or yard; **OfficeMax** for your business needs; **Pier 1 Imports** for home furnishings; several jewelry stores; other smaller shops; and a food court.

Kahului has the greatest concentration of sailboarding and watersport shops on the island, many of them at or near the corner of Hana Highway and Dairy Road. Shop here and comparison shop before going anywhere else. **Hawaiian Island Surf and Sport** carries a multitude of water sports equipment, new and used, for sale and rental. Next door is **Island Biker,** which sells and services road bikes and mountain bikes and rents mountain bikes. A boardsail away at the **Triangle Square** mall across from Kahana Pond, you'll find **High Tech Surf Sport** for all water sports equipment and information, and across Hana Highway is **Neilpryde Maui.** Several other water sport shops are located within a stone's throw of the Kanaha Pond near Kamehameha Avenue.

At the **Dairy Center,** at the intersection of Dairy Road and Hana Highway, you'll find **Extreme Sports Maui** and **Kinko's** along with several eateries, **Marco's Grill** and **Maui Coffee Roasters.** Extreme Sports rents the usual water equipment, plus skateboards and bikes, and has a small climbing wall.

Of the freestanding shops in town, **Two Frogs Hugging,** 808/873-7860, at the corner of Ka'ahumanu and Pu'unene Avenues, is one of the most unusual with its collection of wooden furniture and wood and stone carvings imported mostly from Indonesia. Look for the two hugging frogs stone sculpture out front.

## SERVICES

### Medical Services

For medical emergencies, try **Maui Memorial Medical Center,** 808/244-9056, at 221 Mahalani. Clinics include **Kaiser Permanente,** 808/243-6000, at 20 Mahalani. Both of these facilities are located between downtown Kahului and downtown Wailuku, the medical center up behind the county police station, the clinic across the road from the police station.

### Banking

Kahului has numerous **banks,** most with ATMs, and the majority are near the intersection of Ka'ahumanu and Pu'unene Avenues. There is a Bank of Hawaii, 808/871-8250, at 27 S. Pu'unene Avenue and at the Maui Marketplace; First Hawaiian Bank, 808/877-2311, at 20 W. Ka'ahumanu Avenue; American Savings Bank branches at 73 Pu'unene Avenue, 808/871-8411, and at the Queen Ka'ahumanu Center; and Central Pacific Bank, 808/877-3387, at 85 W. Ka'ahumanu Avenue.

### Post Office

The Kahului **post office,** 138 S. Pu'unene Ave. (Rte. 350), is open Monday–Friday 8:30 A.M.–5 P.M. and Saturday 9 A.M.–noon. For information, call 800/275-8777.

If you need to check your email while on Maui, stop at **Kinko's,** 395 Dairy Rd. 808/871-2000, and use a computer for $.20 per minute, or avail yourself of any of the facility's other numerous copy and office services. Open daily 7 A.M.–11 P.M. For other copy, postal, and business services, try **Mail Boxes Etc.,** 415 Dairy Rd., 808/877-0333, across from Kmart.

### Library

The **library,** 808/873-3097, tucked quietly under the trees at 90 School Street, is open Mondays, Thursdays, Fridays, and Saturdays 10 A.M.–5 P.M., and Tuesdays and Wednesdays 10 A.M.–10 P.M.; closed Sundays.

### Laundry

The **W & F Washerette,** 125 S. Wakea, 808/877-0353, features video games to while away the time as well as a little snack bar. Soap and change machines, drop-off service, and dry cleaning are available. Open daily 6 A.M.–9 P.M.

# Wailuku

Historical towns often maintain a certain aura long after their time of importance has passed. Wailuku is one of these. Maui's county seat since 1905, the town has the feel of one that has been important for a long time. Wailuku earned its name, "Water of Destruction," from a ferocious battle fought by Kamehameha I against Maui warriors just up the road in 'Iao Valley. The slaughter was so intense that more than four miles of the local stream literally ran red with blood. In the 1800s, the missionaries settled in Wailuku, and their architectural influences, such as a white-steeple church and the courthouse at the top of the main street, give an impression of a New England town. Later in the 19th century, sugar came to town, and this vast industry grew with muscle and pumped great vitality into the community. After the turn of the 20th century, Wailuku strengthened its stance as the island's center of government, business, and industry, and the wealthy and influential built homes here. Wailuku maintained this strong position until the 1960s when the sugar industry declined and the growth of tourism began to create other centers of population and industry on the island. Although still a vibrant government and population center, much of Wailuku's importance to the island's economy has been eclipsed.

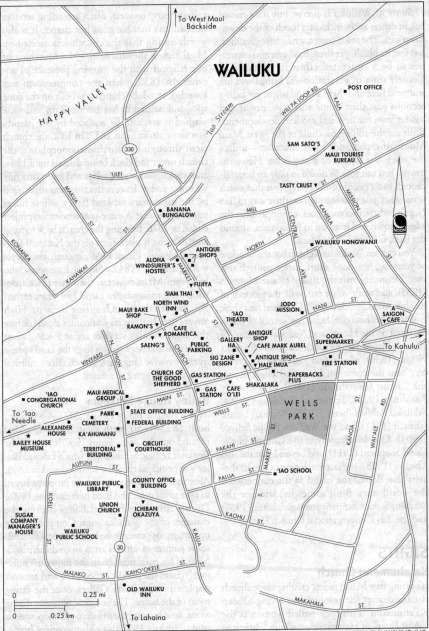

# WAILUKU

To West Maui
Backside

To Lahaina

To Kahului

To 'Iao
Needle

HAPPY VALLEY

'Iao Stream

330

'ULEI PL.

WILI PA LOOP RD.

POST OFFICE

KALA ST.

SAM SATO'S

MAUI TOURIST BUREAU

MISSION ST.

TASTY CRUST ▼

MILL ST.

CENTRAL AVE.

KANIELA ST.

MOON

MAKUA ST.

KAHAWAI ST.

KONAHEA ST.

BANANA BUNGALOW

N. MARKET ST.

NORTH ST.

ANTIQUE SHOPS

ALOHA WINDSURFER'S HOSTEL

▼ FUJIYA

SIAM THAI ▼

NORTH WIND INN

MAUI BAKE SHOP

RAMON'S ▼

CAFE ROMANTICA

SAENG'S ▼

VINYARD ST.

HIGH ST.

N. CHURCH ST.

'IAO THEATER

GALLERY HA

ANTIQUE SHOP

CAFE MARK AUREL

ANTIQUE SHOP

SIG ZANE DESIGN

▼ HALE IMUA

PUBLIC PARKING

CHURCH OF THE GOOD SHEPHERD

GAS STATION

GAS STATION

CAFE O'LEI

SHAKALAKA

PAPERBACKS PLUS

WAILUKU HONGWANJI

JODO MISSION

NANI ST.

A SAIGON CAFE

OOKA SUPERMARKET

FIRE STATION

E. MAIN ST.

WELLS ST.

WELLS PARK

'IAO CONGREGATIONAL CHURCH

ALEXANDER HOUSE

BAILEY HOUSE MUSEUM

MAUI MEDICAL GROUP

PARK

CEMETERY

KA'AHUMANU

STATE OFFICE BUILDING

FEDERAL BUILDING

CIRCUIT COURTHOUSE

TERRITORIAL BUILDING

AUPUNI ST.

COUNTY OFFICE BUILDING

WAILUKU PUBLIC LIBRARY

UNION CHURCH

ICHIBAN OKAZUYA

WAILUKU PUBLIC SCHOOL

SUGAR COMPANY MANAGER'S HOUSE

KOELI ST.

30

MALAKO ST.

KAHO'OKELE ST.

OLD WAILUKU INN

S. MARKET ST.

PAKAHI ST.

PALUA ST.

KAOHU ST.

KAIUA ST.

'IAO SCHOOL

KANOA ST.

WAI'ALE RD.

MAKAHALA ST.

0        0.25 mi

0        0.25 km

MAUI

Some of Wailuku is pretty, but it's a mixed bag in others areas, including much of the downtown area. The town center, while once dignified, has lost its blush, yet there has been and continues to be a concerted effort to revitalize it. Comely rows of plantation-era bungalows are scattered here and there around town, yet fading sections past their prime also exist, not always too far from the new and modern developments. Built on the rolling foothills of the West Maui Mountains, this adds some character—unlike the often-flat layout of many other Hawaiian towns. You can tour Wailuku in only an hour, although most people don't even give it that much time. They just pass through on their way to 'Iao Needle, where everyone goes, or simply skirt the edge of town and head on to Kahakuloa, around the back side, and West Maui.

You can see Wailuku's sights from the window of your car, but don't shortchange yourself this way. Definitely visit the Bailey House Museum (1833), and while you're out, walk the grounds of Ka'ahumanu Church (1876). Clustered near these two are other historical buildings, several of which are listed on the Hawaii and National Registers of Historic Places. These include the small Alexander House (1836), which is set just above the cemetery near the corner of Main and High streets, the Circuit Courthouse (1907), Old County Building (1925), Territorial Building (1930), Wailuku Public Library (1928), Wailuku Union Church (1911), and the Wailuku Public School (1904). One block away is the Church of the Good Shepherd (1911), and beyond that the 'Iao Theater (1928), the last remaining of the 19 theaters that dotted the island in the era between the world wars. Built somewhat later are the Wailuku Sugar Company manager's house (1936) and the 'Iao Congregational Church (1936).

## SIGHTS
### Ka'ahumanu Church
It's fitting that Maui's oldest existing stone church is named after the resolute but loving Queen Ka'ahumanu. This rock-willed woman is the "Saint Peter" of Hawaii, upon whom Christianity in the islands was built. She was *the* most im-

portant early convert, often attending services in Kahului's humble grass-hut chapel. It is also worth noting that the church was erected on Maui king Kahekili's *heiau*—the squashing of one religion with the growing presence of another. In 1832, when the congregation was founded, an adobe church was built on the same spot and named in her honor. Rain and time washed it away, to be replaced by the island's first stone structure in 1837. In 1876 the church went through its fourth metamorphosis, the church tower and clock being delayed until 1884, and what remains is the white and green structure we know today. Its construction was supervised by the missionary Edward Bailey, whose home stands to the rear. A three-year renovation project ended in 1976, bringing the church back to form and allowing it placement on the National Register of Historic Places. Oddly enough, the steeple was repaired in 1984 by Skyline Engineers, who hail from Massachusetts, the same place from which the missionaries came 150 years earlier! You can see the church sitting there on High Street (Rte. 30), but it's sometimes closed during the week. Sunday services are at 9 A.M., when the Hawaiian congregation sings the Lord's praise in their native language. An excellent cultural and religious event to attend!

### Bailey House Museum
This is the old Bailey House, 2375-A Main St., built 1833–1850, with various rooms added throughout the years. From 1837 it housed the Wailuku Female Seminary, of which Edward Bailey was principal until the school closed in 1849. After that, the Baileys bought the property, began to raise sugar cane, and lived here until the 1890s. During this time, Edward Bailey became the manager of the Wailuku Sugar Company. More important for posterity, he became a prolific landscape painter of various areas around the island. Most of his paintings, 26 in the museum's holdings, record the period 1866–1896 and are now displayed in the Bailey Gallery, once the sitting room of the house. The one-time seminary dining room, now housing the museum gift shop, was his studio. In July 1957 this old missionary homestead formally became the Maui Historical So-

ROBERT NILSEN

the Bailey House, a museum of Hawaii's missionary era

ciety Museum, at which time it acquired the additional name of Hale Hoikeike, "House of Display." It closed in 1973 when it was placed on the National Register of Historic Places, then was refurbished and reopened in July 1975.

You'll be amazed at the two-foot-thick walls the missionaries taught the Hawaiians to build, using goat hair as the binding agent. Years of whitewashing make them resemble new-fallen snow. The rooms inside are given over to various themes. The Hawaiian Room houses excellent examples of the often practical artifacts of pre-contact Hawaii like stone tools, bone fishhooks, and wooden weapons; especially notice the fine displays of tapa cloth and calabashes. Hawaiian tapa, now nearly a lost art, was considered Polynesia's finest and most advanced. Upstairs is the bedroom. It's quite large and dominated by a four-poster bed. In this and an adjoining room, there's a dresser with a jewelry box, other pieces of furniture, toys for children, and clothes including hats and fine lace gloves. Downstairs you'll discover the sitting room and kitchen, the heart of the house: the "feelings" are strongest here, and perhaps more so because original paintings by Edward Bailey adorn the walls. The solid 'ohi'a

lintel over the doorway is as stout as the spirits of the people who once lived here. The stonework on the floor is well laid but now covered for preservation, and the fireplace is totally homey.

Now look outside: The lanai runs across the entire front and down the side. Around back is the canoe shed, housing a refurbished sennit-sewn outrigger canoe from the late 1800s, as well as Duke Kahanamoku's redwood surfboard from about 1910. On the grounds you'll also see exhibits of sugarcane, sugar pots, *konane* boards, and various Hawaiian artifacts around the lush and landscaped lawn. Open Monday–Saturday 10 A.M.–4 P.M. Admission is well worth the $5 adults, $4 seniors, and $1 children 7–12. Upon arrival, a docent will introduce you to the house and then let you make a self-guided tour at your leisure. Adjacent in the gift shop is a terrific selection of high-quality souvenirs, books, music, and Hawaiiana at better-than-average prices. All are done by Hawaiian artists and craftspeople, and many are created specifically for this shop.

The office of the **Maui Historical Society**, 808/244-3326, office@mauimuseum.org, www.mauimuseum.org, is in the basement of the Bailey House. It seems appropriate that

MAUI

this society, which collects and preserves artifacts and disseminates information about the history and culture of Maui, should be located on the grounds where Kahekili, Maui's last king, had his compound.

## Kepaniwai Park

As you head up Route 320 to 'Iao Valley, you're in for a real treat. Two miles after leaving Wailuku, you come across Kepaniwai Park and Heritage Gardens. Here the architect, Richard C. Tongg, envisioned and created a park dedicated to all of Hawaii's people. See the Portuguese villa and garden complete with an outdoor oven, a thatch-roofed Hawaiian grass shack, a New England "salt box," a Chinese pagoda, a Japanese teahouse with authentic garden, a Korean pavilion, and a bamboo house—the little "sugar shack" that songs and dreams are made of. Admission is free and there are pavilions with picnic tables often used by families for a Sunday picnic. This now-tranquil spot is where the Maui warriors fell to the invincible Kamehameha and his merciless patron war god, Ku. Kepaniwai means "Damming of the Waters"—literally with corpses. Kepaniwai is now a monument to man's higher nature: harmony and beauty.

## Hawaii Nature Center, 'Iao Valley

Located at the upper end of Kepaniwai Park is the Hawaii Nature Center, 'Iao Valley, 808/244-6500, www.hawaiinaturecenter.org, a private, nonprofit educational and interactive science center—good for kids and grown-ups alike and highly recommended. Open daily 10 A.M.–4 P.M., $6 adults, $4 children, this center boasts 30 exhibits that will beg you to participate, challenge your mind, and teach you about all aspects of Hawaiian nature at the same time. This seems an appropriate spot for a nature center because the West Maui Mountains harbor 12 distinct plant communities, about 300 species of plants, of which 10 are endemic to this locale, and literally thousands of varieties of animals and insects. One-mile, 1.5-hour nature walks are guided through the valley daily to bring you face to face with some of the wonders this valley has to offer. These hikes generally start at 1:30 P.M. and cost $25 adults, $23 children, which includes entrance to the exhibits. Reservations are required.

## The Changing Profile

Up the road toward 'Iao Valley you come to a scenic area long known as Pali 'Ele'ele, or Black Gorge. This stream-eroded narrow slit canyon has attracted attention for centuries. It was one of the places in 'Iao Valley where ali'i were buried, so that no one would discover their final resting place. Amazingly, after President Kennedy was assassinated, people noticed his likeness portrayed there by a series of large boulders on one side of the valley wall; mention of a profile had never been noted or recorded there before. Bring your binoculars, as the pipe that once served as a rudi-

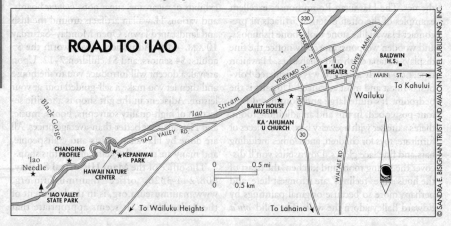

mentary sighting instrument is gone. The likeness—with eyes closed in deep repose—is uncanny and easily seen, unlike most of these formations, where you have to stretch your imagination to the breaking point. Recently, however, the powers that be (a committee of the State Department of Land and Natural Resources) have pronounced that this image is really that of the late-15th-century *kahuna* Kauaka'iwai. Legend has it that he was turned to stone to protect the *ali'i* buried in this valley. Go figure. You obviously see what you want to in these stones anyway.

## 'Iao Valley State Park

This valley has been a sacred spot and a place of pilgrimage since ancient times. Before Westerners arrived, the people of Maui, who came here to pay homage to the "Eternal Creator," named this valley 'Iao, "Cloud Supreme" or "Supreme Light." Facing almost directly east, the valley catches the warming morning sunlight. According to legend, the gods Maui and Hina raised their daughter 'Iao in this valley. As 'Iao grew, she became entranced with a half-man, half-fish god, and they became lovers. This arrangement did not please her father, who, in revenge, turned 'Iao's lover into a stone pinnacle, the peak we know as 'Iao Needle.

Historically, 'Iao Valley was a place set aside and did not belong to the traditional *ahupua'a* land-division system. No commoners were allowed into the valley except on special occasions, and royalty were buried here in secret graves. During the Battle of Kepaniwai in 1790, when King Kamehameha defeated Maui's King Kahekili, this valley was valiantly defended but overrun. Countless commoners perished while the *ali'i* escaped over the mountains to Olowalu.

In the center of this velvety green amphitheater-like valley is a pillar of stone rising more than 1,200 feet (actual height above sea level is 2,250 feet), its grassy top at one time a natural altar and lookout for defense. Kuka'emoku, now commonly called "The Needle," is a tough basaltic ridge that remained after water swirled away the weaker stone surrounding it, leaving only a saddle that connects it to the valley wall,

ROBERT NILSEN

One of the most unusual natural features on the island, 'Iao Needle draws great numbers of visitors every year.

unseen from below. 'Iao Valley is actually the remnant of the volcanic caldera of the West Maui Mountains, whose grooved walls have been smoothed and enlarged by the restlessness of mountain streams. Robert Louis Stevenson had to stretch poetic license to create a word for 'Iao when he called it "viridescent."

The road ends in a parking lot. Signs point you to paved paths, tame and well maintained, with plenty of vantage points for photographers. If you take the lower path to the river below, you'll find a good-size, popular swimming hole; but remember, these are the West Maui Mountains, and it can rain at any time, causing water to rise rapidly. Pu'u Kukui, West Maui Mountains' tallest peak, lies on the western edge of this crater rim and gets about 400 inches of rain per year! On the east side of the stream below the bridge, a loop path leads though a garden of native plants. Beyond the bridge, steps lead up to an observation pavilion. You can escape the crowds, however, even in this heavily touristed area. As you head back, take the paved path that bears

MAUI

## MAUI SAND DUNES

The isthmus of Maui connects the island's two great mountains. This low, broad plain was formed by lava that spewed over thousands of years, connecting the two mountains (and at one time also connecting Maui to Lana'i and Kaho'olawe) before the fire ceased and Maui drifted to the northwest. Over the eons, coral and sand formed along the periphery of the island, and strong winds from the northeast lifted this mixture off the beaches along the isthmus's north shore and deposited it inland forming sand dunes. The isthmus is windswept and fairly flat, but dunes have formed as mostly low, rounded hills, principally on the western side of the isthmus, that rise to about 200 feet in height where they push against the mountainside at Wailuku.

to the right skirting the river and the tourists magically disappear. Here are several pint-size pools where you can take a refreshing dip. A rudimentary path continues up this valley. About one mile up is a fork in the stream, beyond which it is not recommended to go.

'Iao is for day use only; hours are 7 A.M.–7 P.M. On your way back to Wailuku you might take a five-minute side excursion up to Wailuku Heights. Look for the road on your right. There's little here besides a mid- to upper-end residential area, but the view below over the isthmus is tops!

### Maui Tropical Plantation and Country Store

This attraction is somewhat out of the ordinary. The 60-acre Maui Tropical Plantation, 808/244-7643, presents a model of a working plantation that you can tour by small tram. Most interesting is the up-close look at Maui's agricultural abundance. Displays of each of these products are situated around the taro patches at the plantation village. A 40-minute tram ride takes you through fields of cane, banana, guava, mango, papaya, pineapple, coffee, and macadamia nuts; flowers here and there add exotic color. Leaving every 45 minutes 10 A.M.–3:15 P.M., the tram ride is $9.90 adults, $3.65 children 3–12. The planta-

tion, with its restaurant, gift shop, and tropical flower nursery, is near Waikapu, a small village along Route 30 between Wailuku and Ma'alaea. If you visit over the noon hour, stop by the Plantation Cafe for lunch, open 11 A.M.–2 P.M. daily. The Country Store here sells Maui-produced goods and can mail gift packages of fruits, nuts, and coffee, while the nursery will ship flowers to anywhere in the country. Look for the windmill! Open daily 9 A.M.–5 P.M.

## ACCOMMODATIONS

Visitors to Wailuku mostly stay elsewhere on Maui because there are only a few specialized and humble hostels and one historic bed-and-breakfast inn.

### Bed-and-Breakfast

The only fine place to stay in Wailuku is at the attentively renovated **Old Wailuku Inn at Ulupono,** 2199 Kaho'okele St., 800/305-4899 or 808/244-5897, fax 808/242-9600, Maui bandb@aol.com, www.mauiinn.com, now on the Hawaii Register of Historic Places. Built in 1924 for the son and daughter-in-law of Maui's first bank president, this was the queen of homes in one of Maui's most posh neighborhoods. Refurbished in 1997, this house was brought back to its early charm, lovingly detailed, filled with period furniture that evokes the feeling of grandma's house, and decorated with Hawaiian and Asian antiques and artwork. It's a gem. Yet no modern amenity or comfort is left out. Each room has a TV, VCR, telephone, private bath, ceiling fan, and gorgeous Hawaiian quilt on its spacious bed. A fax machine, photocopier, and computer are also available for use. The house has central air-conditioning, but the cooling trade winds are generally enough to moderate the temperature. Catching the morning sun, the screened breakfast room looks out over the rear garden. The open-air front porch is a perfect spot for afternoon tea or reading a book from the extensive house library, and the living room is a fine place to relax in the evening. Each of the seven guest rooms is named for a Hawaiian flower, and their color and design motifs follow. The four upstairs rooms are spacious and grand, with native hardwood floors and 10-foot ceilings. The downstairs rooms are cozier, and two have their own courtyards. In the back garden, the Vagabond House was built on the site of an old garage and opened for guests in 2002. It contains three rooms that, like the rest of the house, are in keeping with the period of the 1920s and '30s. A gourmet breakfast accompanies each night's stay and, no matter what the offering, is tasty, filling, nutritious, and well presented. You'll be pampered. Born and raised on the island, the gracious and personable hosts, Janice and Tom Fairbanks, have intimate knowledge of what to do, what to se, and where to eat throughout the island and will gladly share their knowledge and recommendations with you. Rooms in the main house run $120–180 double occupancy, $140–160 for the Vagabond House; two nights minimum. Parking is on property.

## Hostels

The **Banana Bungalow**, 310 N. Market St., 808/244-5090 or 800/846-7835, fax 808/244-3678, info@mauihostel.com, www.mauihostel.com, is located on the edge of Happy Valley. It's a clean and spartan hostel, with a coat of (yellow) paint, some artistic decorations, refurbished bathrooms up and down, and a renovated common room. Typically, you're liable to hear languages from a half dozen countries, and if you're into sailboarding or just after a cross-cultural experience, this is the spot. The Banana Bungalow offers basic accommodations, and if you care more about your experience than your sleeping arrangements, it's the place for you. Rates are $32 single, $40 double, $50 triple, or $17.50 for a bunk in a four- to six-person dorm (co-ed and female-only), which includes the bed linens but not towels. All rooms and dorms share bathrooms. Monthly rates can be arranged for dorm use. A departure air ticket and/or a foreign passport are required to stay. Extra services include a free and convenient morning airport/beach shuttle; laundry and storage facilities; a common room for conversation, TV, or music; free Internet access; a hot tub, barbecue grill, hammocks in the garden under tropical fruit trees; discount rates on water equipment and lessons; and dis-

count car rental deals. Because the Banana Bungalow is in a residential neighborhood, the 10 P.M.–8 A.M. quiet hours are enforced. Also, no smoking and no drugs are allowed. The hostel's no-cost adventure van tours, different every day, are sign-up tours open to anyone, guests or not, on a first-come, first-served basis. Tours change periodically due to interest, but typical outings include a hike over swinging bridges into a lush nearby valley, a road trip to Hana, a snorkel and sunset tour to a marine sanctuary, an 'Iao Valley walk, and a drive to Haleakala for sunset. There is no cost for these tours, but you should tip the driver. Reception hours are 8 A.M.–11 P.M.; there is no curfew. The Banana Bungaow is the premier hostel accommodation on Maui.

The **North Wind Hostel,** 2080 Vineyard St., tel/fax 808/242-1448 or 866/946-7835, maui@northwind-hostel.com, www.northwind-hostel.com, is easily spotted with its row of international flags fluttering from the second-floor balcony. Enter via the alley sidewalk; 24-hour access. With a capacity of about 45, this single-floor hostel caters mostly to young, independent travelers and surfers. Bunk rooms go for $18 a bed, single rooms $32, and double rooms $38, exclusive of tax but including bed linens; all rooms share four bathrooms with showers. You'll need an air ticket off Maui or a foreign passport to check in. Good for socializing, the lounge has a television and a computer for Internet access. There are laundry facilities; a safe for valuables; storage facilities for sailboards, backpacks, and large items, and much more. No smoking is permitted inside the hostel. In a previous incarnation, this hostel won the respect of the community for transforming the former fleabag Wailuku Grand Hotel into a viable business and dealing equitably with the locals; however, the hostel has gone through several changes of ownership in the last few years, so only time will tell if it manages to maintain its integrity.

The newest inexpensive accommodation in town is the **Aloha Windsurfers' Hostel,** 167 N. Market St., 808/249-0206 or 800/249-1421, fax 808/249-0705, alohawindsurf@yahoo.com, www.accommodations-maui.com. With only 16 places, this remodeled old structure is small and

MAUI

quiet, with a common room, kitchen, and several bathrooms. The rate for a dorm bed is $17.50, $42–49 for a single private room, and $46–56 for a private double room. Weekly, monthly, and room and car rates are also available. Amenities include a free simple breakfast, Internet access, and local calls, as well as airport and beach pickup and drop-off.

## FOOD

### Downtown

Wailuku has some of the best and most inexpensive restaurants on Maui. The establishments listed as follows are all in the bargain or reasonable range. The decor in most is basic and homey, with the emphasis placed on the food. Even here in this nontouristy town, however, some of the restaurants are sprucing up and becoming a bit gentrified.

**Saeng's,** 2119 Vineyard, 808/244-1567, serves excellent Thai food at great prices. Dishes include appetizers like Thai crisp noodles for $4.95 and green papaya salad for $6.50. The savory soups, enough for two, include spicy coconut shrimp soup for $9.50 and po teak, a zesty seafood combination soup for $10.95. Thai specialties such as pad thai vegetables, chicken Thai curry, and eggplant shrimp are all under $10, while vegetarian selections like stir-fry vegetables and Evil Prince tofu are under $7.50. Only some seafood plates are more expensive at $12.95. Although the interior is quite tasteful with linen tablecloths and paisley booths, the best seating is outside in the covered garden patio, where a small waterfall gurgles pleasantly. Open Monday–Friday for lunch 11 A.M.–2:30 P.M. and dinner nightly 5–9:30 P.M., except for Sunday when it closes at 8:30 P.M.

**Siam Thai,** 123 N. Market, 808/244-3817, is a small restaurant (open Mon.–Sat. 11:30 A.M.–2:30 P.M., daily 5–9:30 P.M.). It serves excellent Thai food with an emphasis on vegetarian cuisine, at prices that are comparable with Saeng's. Extensive menu; a perennial favorite.

**Ramon's Restaurant,** 2102 Vineyard, 808/244-7243, is open from 8 A.M. and serves food throughout the day. It also has the only bar in town and provides live music on some weekends. Ramon's has a good mix of Mexican and Hawaiian dishes, with plenty of plate dishes, specials, combinations, and burritos. Some items off the menu are teriyaki chicken plate for $6.95, fiesta combination plates for $9.95, a bean burrito for $7.95, and enchilada del mar for $14.95.

**Maui Bake Shop and Deli,** 2092 Vineyard St., 808/242-0064 (open weekdays 7 A.M.–3 P.M., Saturday 7 A.M.–1 P.M., closed Sunday) has a full selection of home-baked goods, and sandwiches for about $3.95, with soup du jour $6.75. Daily specials can be pizza, quiche, filled croissants, or even lox and bagels for under $5. Tantalizing baked goods include apple strudel, coconut macaroons, apricot twists, fruit tarts, and homemade pies. Enjoy your selection with an espresso, cappuccino, or hot tea. Maui Bake Shop is a common stop for morning nourishment.

Kitty-corner across the intersection and open Tuesday–Friday 11 A.M.–3 P.M. for vegetarian cuisine is **Cafe Romantica,** 808/249-0697. Short on hours, but heavy on quality, they offer a variety of soups and salads, pastries, samosa, crepes, lasagna, and quiche.

The tiny **Ichiban Okazuya** take-out restaurant is located just around the corner from the county office building on Kaohu Street. They're open 10 A.M.–2 P.M. and 4–7 P.M. for katsu, teriyaki, and other quick eats. They have a good reputation that's growing.

An unassuming little storefront shop that serves wonderful food and that's been a hit with local patrons is **Cafe O'lei On Main Street,** 808/244-6816. Stop by Monday–Friday 10:30 A.M.–3:30 P.M. for coffee, sandwiches, and other entrées. Most everything is under $7.

Just down the street on the corner of Main and Market streets, **Shakalaka Fish and Chips,** 808/986-0855, serves up quick and inexpensive eats Monday–Friday 10:30 A.M.–8 P.M.

For a spot of coffee, tea, pastries, bagels, or light lunches, head to the sophisticated **Cafe Mark Aurel,** 28 N. Market St., 808/244-0852 (open Mon.–Fri. 7 A.M.–6 P.M., Saturday and holidays 7 A.M.–1 P.M.).

One block down on the corner of Maluhia Street is **Hale Imua Internet Cafe,** 808/242-

1896, which not only offers Internet access but also serves all manner of coffee and other drinks, sandwiches, and salads. Open Monday–Friday 9 A.M.–5:30 P.M., Saturday until 4 P.M.

A little out of the way but well worth the effort to find is **A Saigon Cafe,** 1792 Main St., 808/243-9560. A great family place, clean but not fancy, this may be the best Vietnamese cuisine on the island. It gets a thumbs up from everyone. Although there's no large sign yet advertising its location, it's a favorite local stop, and you'll know why once you try. Start with spring rolls at $5.75 or shrimp pops for $7.25 and move on to one of the tasty soups like hot and sour fish soup for $9.20 or a green papaya salad for $5.50. Entrées, all under $10 except the Saigon fondue, which is cooked at your table, include a wide range of noodle, meat, fish, and vegetarian dishes, all with good portions. The menu is extensive. Open daily 10 A.M.–10 P.M., Sunday until 8:30 P.M., this restaurant is behind Ooka Super Market, below the bridge.

On the edge of town toward Kahului near the underpass is **Stillwell's Bakery and Cafe,** 1740 Ka'ahumanu Ave., 808/243-2243. Having established a fine reputation with locals, it's now becoming known to visitors. The surroundings are nothing special, but the food is worthy of the reputation, and the breads, baked goods, and cakes are delicious—and served at some fine restaurants on the island. Stop in for a pastry and coffee, cookies, a lunch sandwich and soup, or other hot entrée. Open Monday–Saturday 6 A.M.–4 P.M.

## Off the Main Drag

If you get out of downtown, you'll be rewarded with some of the *most* local and *least* expensive restaurants on West Maui, many of them along Mill Street and Lower Main. They are totally unpretentious and serve hefty portions of tasty, homemade local foods. If your aim is to *eat* like a local, search out one of these.

The **Tasty Crust Restaurant,** 1770 Mill St., 808/244-0845, opens daily 5:30 A.M.–11 P.M., Friday and Saturday until midnight. Similar to a diner, with bar stools at the counter, booths, and a few tables, the welcome sign says "This is where

old friends meet." If you have to carbo-load for a full day of sailing, snorkeling, or sailboarding, order the famous giant homemade hotcakes.

**Sam Sato's,** 1750 Wili Pa Loop Rd. in the Mill Yard, 808/244-7124, is famous for *manju,* a pufflike pastry from Japan usually filled with lima or adzuki beans. This is one of those places that, if you are a local resident, you *must* bring Sato's manju when visiting friends or relatives off-island. Aside from the manju there are noodles, saimin, sandwiches, and plate lunches for lunch, and omelets and banana hotcakes for breakfast. Many think that Sam serves the best dry mein noodles on the island. Most everything is under $5.50. Open Monday–Saturday 7 A.M.–4 P.M., pickup until 2 P.M. A highly specialized place, but worth the effort.

Another well-established local place is **Nazo's Restaurant,** 1063 Lower Main St., 808/244-0529, on the second floor of the Puuone Plaza, an older yellowish two-story building. Park underneath and walk upstairs. Daily specials cost under $9, but Nazo's is renowned for its oxtail soup, a clear-consommé broth with peanuts and water chestnuts floating around, a delicious combination of East and West. Open Monday–Saturday 10 A.M.–2 P.M. and again 5–9 P.M.

**Tokyo Tei,** 808/242-9630, in the same complex but downstairs, is another institution that has been around since 1937 serving Japanese dishes to a devoted clientele. Eating here is as consistent as eating at grandma's kitchen, with traditional Japanese dishes like tempura, various don buri, and seafood platters. If you want to sample real Japanese food at affordable prices, come here! Open daily 11 A.M.–1:30 P.M. for lunch, 5–8:30 P.M. dinner, open Sunday for dinner only.

**Romeo's Café,** 740 Lower Main St., 808/242-5957, is in a no-nonsense part of town, in a place of local atmosphere, where the inside is pink, white, and yellow, with booths and a few tables. Breakfast starts at 6 A.M. and includes items like pancakes, omelets, and loco moco. Lunch is also served (but not dinner), and nothing on the menu is more than $7.

For a different taste treat, try the traditional-style manju and mochi made fresh daily at Wailuku's **Shishido Manju Shop,** 758 Lower

Main St., 808/244-5222. If you're in the mood for a more contemporary manju with new flavors or hot malasadas, traditional or fancy, try **Home Maid Bakery,** 1005 Lower Main St.,808/244-7015.

## Groceries

For general grocery shopping, go to **Ooka Super Market,** 1870 Main St., where you'll find not only the usual groceries but also a deli section and many ethnic foods. For decades, this has been Wailuku's major food supplier. A new addition, **Sack 'N Save,** is located in the Wailuku Town Center on the north edge of town along Waiehu Beach Road. In Happy Valley, you can get a few basic necessities, including sashimi and plate lunches to go, at the tiny **Takamiya Market** along Market Street from 6 A.M.–5 P.M.

You can pick up fresh produce at the tiny **Wailuku Town Open Market,** held along Market Street near Sig Zane Design and open Monday–Friday 7 A.M.–7 P.M.

# ENTERTAINMENT

Wailuku is not a hotbed for entertainment by any stretch of the imagination, yet there are a few items worthy of note. Live theater is offered by **Maui Onstage,** 68 N. Market St., 808/242-6969, in the remodeled 'Iao Theater building. Major productions occur several times a year, while traveling stage performances and other events take the stage periodically. Plays are generally performed in the evening, with some matinee shows on the weekends. Tickets run $15 adult, $13 seniors and students.

The only bar in town and about the only place for live entertainment is **Ramon's** restaurant on Vineyard Street.

# SHOPPING

Most shopping in this area is done in Kahului at the big malls, but for an interesting diversion, some people shop closer to home. Wailuku's attic closets used to overflow with numerous discovery shops all in a row hung like prom-night tuxedos, limp with old memories, and

each with its own style. Today, most of these specialty shops are gone, but the few that hang on are all along Market Street. Here you'll find **Brown-Kobayashi,** 808/242-0804, for Asian art and furniture; **Bird of Paradise,** 808/242-7699, which handles blue willow china, vintage bottles, Depression and carnival glass, license plates from around the world, and even a smattering of antique furniture; and **Gottling, Ltd.,** 808/244-7779, specializing in Oriental art and furnishings. If you're still on a roll, other shops are **Ali'i Antiques,** 808/243-9497; **Old Daze Antiques and Collectibles,** 808/249-0014; and **Sheila's Junktique,** 808/244-9610.

Lucky for those who live or visit here, **Sig Zane Designs,** 808/249-8997, a well-known women's apparel and fabric design store from Hilo, has opened a shop here, and a few steps up Market Street, **Gallery Ha,** 808/244-3993, has opened it doors. **Paperbacks Plus,** 1977 Main St., 808/242-7135, is the only book purveyor in town, dealing mostly in used titles and some new Hawaiiana.

The best place in Wailuku to pick up a high-quality gift to take home is at the **Bailey House Museum gift shop.** Here you'll find books, CDs, and a wide assortment of crafts made by island artists with native materials at a decent price.

# SERVICES

For **banking,** there's a Bank of Hawaii branch office at 2105 Main, 808/871-8200, and an American Savings Bank, 808/244-9148, at 69 N. Market Street. The state office building, county office building, federal building, old courthouse, and library are all situated along High Street in the center of town, and the **post office** is out in the Mill Yard near the **Maui Visitors Bureau** office, 808/244-3530, both on Wili Pa Loop Road.

**Camping permits** for county parks are available at the War Memorial Gym, 808/270-7389, Monday–Friday 8 A.M.–4 P.M. They cost $3 adults, $.50 children, per person per night. State park permits can be obtained from the State Building, 54 S. High St., Rm. 101, Wailuku, HI 96793, 808/984-8109, weekdays 8 A.M.–4:15 P.M. only.

# Kahakuloa: West Maui's Back Side

To get around to the back side of West Maui you can head north from Ka'anapali or north from Wailuku. A few short years ago, this road was in rugged shape, closed to all but local traffic, and forbidden to rental cars by their companies. It's still narrow and very windy in part—there are still a few short one-lane sections near the Wailuku end—but now it's paved all the way. What once took three hours might all now take only an hour. Because many people drive it these days, there is more traffic, so it still has hazards. Additionally, loose rock tumbles onto the roadway from embankments (particularly after rainfalls), so be mindful and aware of debris. Drive slowly, carefully, and defensively. In large part, the road is the journey.

## Sights

Route 340, or Kahekili Highway, runs north from Kahului to Kahakuloa Bay and beyond, where it changes number to Route 30 not too much before reaching Kapalua. Before you start this 18-mile stretch, make sure you have adequate gas and water. From Wailuku, head north on Market Street through the area called Happy Valley. This road continues out of town as Route 330. Before it meets Route 340, you'll see an overgrown macadamia nut farm on the upland side of the road, a failed attempt at diversifying the agricultural base of this region.

Just north of the bridge over 'Iao Stream along Route 340 will be Kuhio Place on your left. Turn here and then again onto Hea Place to **Haleki'i and Pihana Heiau State Monument,** which sits on a bluff overlooking lower 'Iao Stream. This was a place of great prominence during the centuries that Maui kings called Wailuku home and when a large population filled the surrounding land cultivating it in taro. Although uninspiring, this 10-acre site is historical and totally unvisited. Originally constructed around 1240 for other reasons, Haleki'i became a house of images. Pihana was made a temple of war and rededicated to the war god Ku by Kahekili, Maui's last king. Legend says that the last human

sacrifice on Maui was performed here for Kamehameha I as a demonstration of his control over the island. These *heiau* are on the National Register of Historic Places.

A short way north and down Lower Waiehu Road toward the water—a Shoreline Access sign will point the way—you'll reach **Waiehu Beach County Park.** This strip of sand meets the southern end of the Waiehu Golf Course and is a decent place for sunbathing, as well as swimming when the water is calm. Surfers sometimes come for the waves, but people mostly come to use the athletic fields.

Back on Route 340 you come shortly to the small town of **Waihe'e** (Slippery Water), where you'll find the reconstructed **Waihe'e Protestant Church,** established in 1828 as one of the first churches on the island, standing next to the Waihe'e School. Turn at the town Park (softball on Saturday) and follow the sign pointing you to **Waiehu Municipal Golf Course;** call 808/243-7400 for tee times. Mostly local people golf here; it's full of kids and families on the weekend. The fairways, strung along the sea, are beautiful to play. Waiehu Inn Restaurant is an adequate little eatery at the golf course.

Like its sister on the south edge of the golf course, **Waihe'e Beach County Park** is tucked into its northern corner. It too is secluded and frequented mostly by local people. Some come here to picnic or snorkel and spear fish inside the reef. The reef is quite a ways out and the bottom is rocky, but the shore is sandy. Although both parks are for day use only, they'd probably be okay for an unofficial overnight stay. To reach this park, go left and follow the fence just before the golf course parking lot.

At mile marker 5, the pavement narrows and begins to climb the hillside. The road hugs the coastline and gains elevation quickly; the undisturbed valleys are resplendent. Here are several one-lane sections. Slow down and use the pull-offs if you want to take pictures of the wild coastline below or Haleakala in the distance. Soon you pass Maluhia Road, the access road to a Boy Scout camp and the

MAUI

Waiheʻe Ridge trail, which leads up into the West Maui Mountains. Across from the entrance to Maluhia Road is Mendes Ranch, and beyond that—oddly enough—is the new upper-end residential subdivision of Maluhia Country Ranches. With the paving of this coastal road, several commercial establishments have been opened along this back route. One of these is **Aina Anuhea Tropical Gardens,** a private garden between mile markers 8 and 9. While not spectacular, this garden is fine for a short stop. Walkways take you through the diminutive gardens, from where you're able to see not only the bay below but also Haleakala off in the distance. Smitty will greet you as you come up the driveway, collect your $5 entrance fee, and set you on the right path.

In a few miles you skirt a tall headland—easily seen from Paʻia and points along the north shore—and pass the **Kaukini Gallery,** 808/244-3371, probably the most remote gallery on the island. A place of arts, crafts, and gifts, the gallery displays the work of more than four dozen island artists. From here the road rounds the shoulder and drops down to the fishing village of **Kahakuloa** (Tall Lord), with its dozen weather-worn houses and two tiny churches. St. Francis Xavier Mission, above the village on the east side of the stream, was founded in 1846. Being on the north coast, the turbulent waters constantly wash the beach of round black stones. Although a tiny community (you are greeted with Aloha, Welcome, and Farewell all on one sign), each house is well kept with pride, and a new house or two have popped up in the last decade or so. To cater to the increased through traffic, several roadside stands have popped up selling fruit, shave ice, banana bread, and other delicacies. Over-

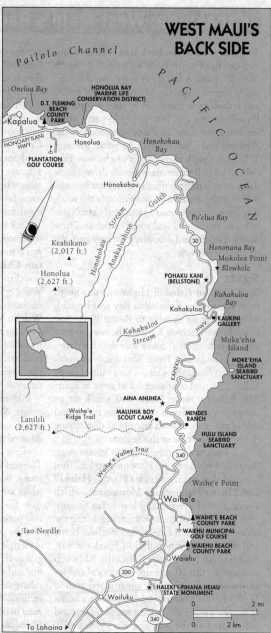

WEST MAUI'S BACK SIDE

Pailolo Channel

PACIFIC OCEAN

Oneloa Bay

HONOLUA BAY (MARINE LIFE CONSERVATION DISTRICT)

D.T. FLEMING BEACH COUNTY PARK

Kapalua

HONOAPIʻILANI HWY

Honolua

Honokohau Bay

PLANTATION GOLF COURSE

Honokohau

Honokohau Stream

Anakaluahine Gulch

Poʻelua Bay

Keahikano (2,017 ft.)

30

Hononana Bay
Mokolea Point
★ Blowhole

Honolua (2,627 ft.)

POHAKU KANI (BELLSTONE)

Kahakuloa Bay

Kahakuloa

KAUKINI GALLERY

Kahakuloa Stream

KAHEKILI HWY

Mokeʻehia Island

MOKEʻEHIA ISLAND SEABIRD SANCTUARY

Lanilili (2,627 ft.)

Waiheʻe Ridge Trail

AINA ANUHEA
MALUHIA BOY SCOUT CAMP

MENDES RANCH

HULU ISLAND SEABIRD SANCTUARY

Waiheʻe Valley Trail

340

Waiheʻe Point

Waiheʻe

WAIHEʻE BEACH COUNTY PARK

WAIEHU MUNICIPAL GOLF COURSE

★ ʻIao Needle

WAIEHU BEACH COUNTY PARK

Waiehu

330

HALEKIʻI-PIHANA HEIAU STATE MONUMENT

Wailuku

340

To Lahaina

0        2 mi

0     2 km

looking Kahakuloa on the western side is a pullout and promontory where you have good views over the rugged coast and back at the village. Here the road is at its absolute narrowest. The valley is very steep-sided and beautiful. Supposedly, great Maui himself loved this area.

A mile or so past Kahakuloa and near mile marker 15, you come to **Pohaku Kani,** the bell stone. It's about six feet tall and the same in diameter, and it sits directly on the inland edge of the road. The seascapes along this stretch are tremendous. The surf pounds along the coast below and sends spumes skyward, roaring through a natural blowhole. **Nakalele blowhole** sits near the Nakalele Lighthouse coast guard beacon site. Park at the entrance road to the lighthouse at mile marker 38 or about one-half mile to the east of there. From the road, it's a short walk down to the water-a good spot for the family. Enjoy the spume close-up, but be aware that it's a rough coastline with occasional heavy surf, churning seas, and lots of wind and spray. After the bell stone, the road becomes wider again but still curvy, the mileage markers start over and reduce in number, and you're soon at D. T. Fleming Beach Park. Civilization comes again too quickly.

## Hiking Trails

The **Waihe'e Valley Trail** runs into this picturesque narrow valley. North of the town of Waihe'e, turn left onto Waihe'e Valley Road, just before mile marker 5 and the Waihe'e Stream bridge. Proceed to the village and park in the pulloff near the middle of this community. Leave a couple of bucks in the collection box! Walk right at the T-intersection and go to a gate. Inside the gate, the trail first follows the maintenance road that skirts the stream, with the flume on the opposite bank. This level track then takes you over two suspension footbridges, through a bamboo forest, and under huge banyan trees until you reach the head dam, where you can leap off a rope swing into the pool. Count on at least two hours, more if you intend to swim in the pool.

**Waihe'e Ridge Trail** is a 2.5-mile trek leading up Kanoa Ridge on the windward slope of the West Maui Mountains. Follow Route 340

on the swinging bridge trail

around the back side to Maluhia Road at the Mendes Ranch. Turn inland here and follow the road up about one mile—almost to the Boy Scout camp—where there's a parking area, trail sign, and vehicular gate. Walk through the adjacent trail gate, go *steeply* up the hill on the cement track, cross the pasture, and head for the trees and another gate where the trail actually begins. This trail starts innocently enough but does become a switchback farther up and crosses some areas that are boggy during the rains. The trail rises swiftly to over 2,560 feet. Along the way, views into Waihe'e and Makamaka'ole valleys are spectacular, and you even get distance views of Wailuku, the isthmus, and Haleakala. Maintained and marked by mileage markers, the trail continues on to Lanilili summit, where on clear days you can see the northern slope of the mountain. This trail takes energy; count on three hours for the more than five miles there and back. If you think you'll be on the trail after 5:30 P.M. or so, park your car down near the highway at the entrance to Maluhia Road because the gate across this road closes at 6 P.M.; for those wanting an early start, it opens at 7 A.M.

**MAUI**

# West Maui

## Lahaina

Lahaina (Merciless Sun) is and always has been the premier town on Maui. It's the most energized town on the island as well, and you can feel it from the first moment you walk down Front Street. Maui's famed warrior-king Kahekili lived here and ruled until Kamehameha, with the help of newfound cannon power, subdued Kahekili's son in 'Iao Valley at the turn of the 19th century. When Kamehameha I consolidated the island kingdom, he chose Lahaina as his seat of power. It served as such until Kamehameha III moved to Honolulu in the mid-1840s. Lahaina is where the modern world of the West and the old world of Hawaii collided, for better or worse. The *ali'i* of

Hawaii loved to be entertained here; the royal surf spot, mentioned numerous times as an area of revelry in old missionary diaries, is just south of the Small Boat Harbor. Kamehameha I built in Lahaina the islands' first Western structure in 1801, known as the Brick Palace; the site, near the harbor entrance, still remains. Queens Ke'opuolani and Ka'ahumanu, the two most powerful wives of the great Kamehameha's harem of more than 20, were local Maui women who remained after their husband's death and helped to usher in the new order.

The whalers came preying for "sperms and humpbacks" in 1819 and set old Lahaina Town a-reelin'. Island girls, naked and willing, swam out to meet the ships, trading their favors for baubles from the modern world. Grog shops flourished, and drunken sailors owned the debauched town.

Lahaina Harbor

ROBERT NILSEN

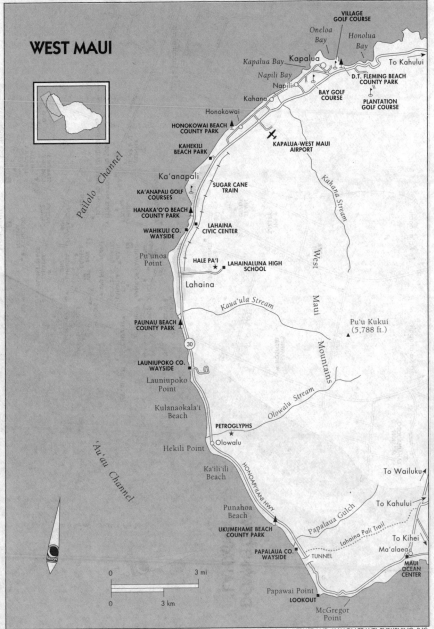

# WEST MAUI

VILLAGE GOLF COURSE

*Oneloa Bay*

*Honolua Bay*

*Kapalua Bay* Kapalua

To Kahului

*Napili Bay*

D.T. FLEMING BEACH COUNTY PARK

Napili

BAY GOLF COURSE

PLANTATION GOLF COURSE

Kahana

Honokowai

HONOKOWAI BEACH COUNTY PARK

KAPALUA-WEST MAUI AIRPORT

*Pailolo Channel*

*Kahana Stream*

KAHEKILI BEACH PARK

Ka'anapali

KA'ANAPALI GOLF COURSES

SUGAR CANE TRAIN

HANAKA'O'O BEACH COUNTY PARK

*West*

LAHAINA CIVIC CENTER

WAHIKULI CO. WAYSIDE

Pu'unoa Point

HALE PA'I

LAHAINALUNA HIGH SCHOOL

*Maui*

Lahaina

*Kaua'ula Stream*

Pu'u Kukui
(5,788 ft.)

PAUNAU BEACH COUNTY PARK

*Mountains*

30

LAUNIUPOKO CO. WAYSIDE

Launiupoko Point

*Olowalu Stream*

Kulanaokala'i Beach

PETROGLYPHS

'Au'au Channel

Olowalu

Hekili Point

To Wailuku

Ka'ili'ili Beach

To Kahului

*HONOAPI'ILANI HWY*

Punahoa Beach

*Papalaua Gulch*

To Kihei

UKUMEHAME BEACH COUNTY PARK

Lahaina Pali Trail

Ma'alaea

PAPALAUA CO. WAYSIDE

TUNNEL

MAUI OCEAN CENTER

MOON

0        3 mi

0        3 km

Papawai Point
LOOKOUT

McGregor Point

MAUI

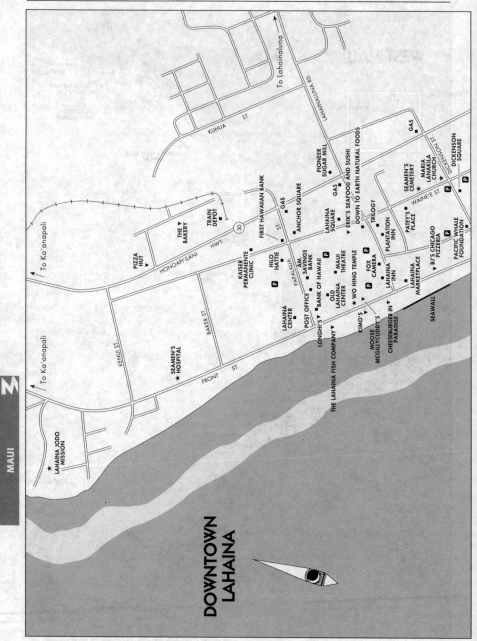

DOWNTOWN LAHAINA

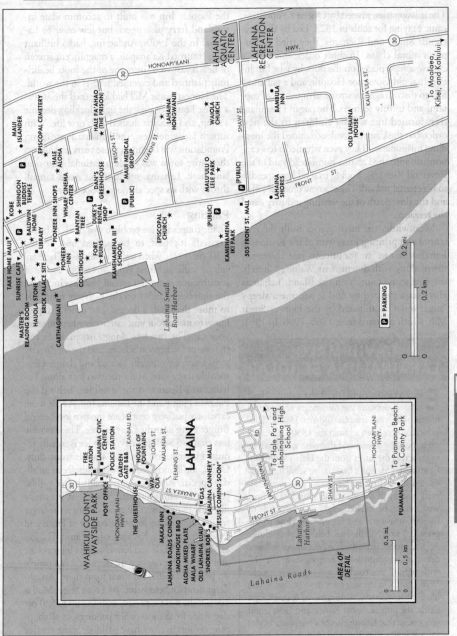

MAUI

© SANDRA E. BISIGNANI TRUST AND AVALON TRAVEL PUBLISHING, INC.

The missionaries, invited by Queen Keʻopuolani, came praying for souls in 1823. Led by the Reverends Stuart and Richards, they tried to harpoon moral chaos. In short order, there was a curfew, a *kapu* placed on the ships by wise but ineffectual old Governor Hoapili, and a jail and a fort to discourage the strong-arm tactics of captains and unruly seamen. The pagan Hawaiians transformed like willing children to the new order, but the Christian sailors damned the meddling missionaries. They even whistled a few cannonballs into the Lahaina homestead yard of the Reverend Richards, hoping to send him speedily to his eternal reward. Time, a new breed of sailor, and the slow death of the whaling industry eased the tension.

Meanwhile, the missionaries built the first school and printing press west of the Rockies at Lahainaluna in the mountains just above the town, along with downtown's Waineʻe Church, the first stone church on the island. Lahaina's glory days slipped by and it became a sleepy "sugar town" dominated by the Pioneer Sugar Mill, which operated from 1860–1996. In 1901,

the Pioneer Inn was built to accommodate interisland ferry passengers, but few *came* to Lahaina. In the 1960s, Amfac Inc. had a brilliant idea. It turned Kaʻanapali, a magnificent stretch of beach just west, into one of the most beautifully planned and executed resorts in the world. The Pioneer Sugar Mill had long used the area as a refuse heap, but now the ugly duckling became a swan, and Lahaina flushed with new life. With superb farsightedness, the Lahaina Restoration Foundation was begun in those years and almost the entire town was made a national historical landmark. Lahaina, subdued but never tamed, throbs with its special energy once again.

## Parking

Traffic congestion is a problem that needs to be addressed. It's best to be parked and settled 4:30–5:30 P.M., when traffic is heaviest. There are still no traffic lights on Front Street, but a spree of construction in the last several years has increased the number of lights on the highway from two to more than half a dozen. The other thing to know to make your visit carefree is where to stash your car. The two lots along Dickenson Street, the one at Dickenson Square, and the lot directly to its south are centrally located and charge a reasonable daily rate, as do the two lots along Lahainaluna Road and the small lots behind the Baldwin Home and the Lahaina Inn. A little more expensive but very central are the two lots behind Burger King near the Banyan Tree. These private lots charge $5–10 per day; exact fee is usually required because few lots have attendants on duty. Often, you'll find a reduced overnight fee or an all-day special. Also close is a smallish free public parking lot along Luakini Street, but it usually fills early in the day. A bit more distant is the larger free public parking lot at the corner of Front and Prison streets, but it has a three-hour limit. The lots at Maluʻulu O Lele and Kamehameha Iki parks are also free and for use by park users only, but people do park and walk into town from there. An underground lot below the 505 Front Street Mall is safe but the most expensive with fees up to $20 per day. Aside from these public parking lots, all shopping centers in town have parking: Some are free with time limits, some charge beyond a certain

## DAVID MALO: LAHAINALUNA SCHOLAR

Every year, in April, the Lahainaluna High School celebrates the anniversary of the death of one of its most famous students, David Malo. Educated here as an adult in the 1830s, he stayed on to become a teacher. His house was down in town across the street from the Hale Paʻi Prison. Considered Hawaii's first native scholar, he authored the definitive *Hawaiian Antiquities,* an early history of the Hawaiian islands. His final wish was to be buried "high above the tide of foreign invasion," and his grave is close to the giant "L" atop Mount Ball, behind Lahainaluna. At graduation, students from the school follow a decades-old tradition of surrounding the "L" with lighted tiki torches, making quite a sight from town. On the way back down to town, you have an impressive panorama of former cane fields, the port, Lahaina Roads, and Lanaʻi, and you realize that Lahaina is not a big place, as you can see it all easily from end to end.

## THE LAHAINA RESTORATION FOUNDATION

Begun in 1961 by Jim Luckey, a historian who knows a great deal about Lahaina and the whaling era, the **Lahaina Restoration Foundation,** 808/661-3262, is now headed by Keoki Freeland, an old Maui resident and grandson of the builder of the Pioneer Inn. Its office is the upstairs of the Baldwin Home. The main purpose of the foundation is to preserve the flavor and authenticity of Lahaina without stifling progress—especially tourism. The foundation is privately funded and has managed to purchase or lease many of the important historical sites in Lahaina for their continued maintenance. It owns the Baldwin Home, Masters' Reading Room, and the Seaman's Hospital, leases the Wo Hing Temple and the old Courthouse, and maintains Hale Pa'i, Hale Aloha, and the old prison. The people on the board of directors come from all socioeconomic backgrounds. You don't get on the board by how much money you give but by how much effort and time you are willing to invest in the foundation; the members are extremely dedicated. Merchants approach the foundation with new ideas for business and ask how they can best comply with the building codes. The townspeople know that their future is best served if they preserve the feeling of old Lahaina rather than rush headlong into frenzied growth. The historic village of Williamsburg, Virginia, is sometimes cited as Lahaina's model, except that Lahaina wishes to remain a "real" living, working town.

---

time, and some offer validated parking. All are reasonably priced. Street parking has a three-hour limit. Watch your time as the "meter patrol" is very efficient, and your car may wind up in the pound if you're not careful! Parking fines are $35, and it will cost more than $100 if your car is towed. Those staying in Ka'anapali should leave cars behind and take the Holo Ka'a shuttle for the day or hop on the Sugar Cane Train.

## SIGHTS

In short, strolling around Lahaina offers the best of both worlds. It's busy, but it's bite-size. It's engrossing enough, but you can see it in half a day. The main attractions are mainly downtown within a few blocks of each other. Lahaina technically stretches, long and narrow, along the coast for about four miles, but you may only be interested in the central core, a mere mile or so. All along Front Street, the main drag, and the side streets running off it are innumerable shops, restaurants, and hideaways where you can browse, recoup your energy, or just wistfully watch the sun set. Go slowly and savor, and you'll feel the dynamism of Lahaina past and present all around you. Enjoy!

### The Banyan Tree

The best place to start your tour of Lahaina is at this magnificent tree at the corner of Hotel and Front streets. You can't miss it because it spreads its shading boughs over almost an entire acre. It is the largest banyan in the state. Use the benches to sit and reconnoiter while the sun, for which Lahaina is infamous, is kept at bay. Children love it, and it seems to bring out the Tarzan in everyone. Old-timers sit here chatting, and on Saturdays and Sundays, various artists gather here to display and sell their artwork under the tree's broad branches. Every Christmas, the tree is covered in lights, and numerous other festivities are held in its shade. This banyan was planted in April 1873 by Sheriff Bill Smith in commemoration of the Congregationalist Missions' golden anniversary. One hundred years later, a ceremony was held here and more than 500 people were accommodated under this natural canopy. Symbolic as it is, this banyan is truly the heart of Lahaina.

### Courthouse

Behind the banyan tree on Wharf Street is the old county Courthouse. Built in 1859 from coral blocks recycled from Kamehameha III's ill-fated palace, Hale Piula, it also served as governor's office, post office, customs office, and the police station, complete with a jail in the basement. The jail is now home to the Lahaina Arts Society's **Old Jail Gallery,** where paintings and artifacts are kept behind bars, waiting for patrons to liberate them. The society has its main **Banyan Tree**

**Gallery** on the first floor. Since its renovation in 1998, another project of the Lahaina Restoration Foundation, the **Lahaina Visitor Center,** 808/667-9193, has also occupied a room on the main floor, and here anyone can come for all sorts of tourist information and brochures about the town. Located in the old courtroom on the second floor, a small museum displays historical and cultural objects pertaining to the area; open daily from 9 A.M.–5 P.M. with free entrance. Public bathrooms are located upstairs; use either the stairway or the elevator.

Adjacent is the **Fort,** built in the 1830s to show the sailors that they couldn't run amok in Lahaina. Even with its 20-foot-high walls, it was not much of a deterrent. When it was torn down, the blocks were hauled over to Prison Street to build the real jail, Hale Pa'ahao. A corner battlement of the fort was restored, but that's it, because restoring the entire structure would mean mutilating the banyan. The cannons, from a military vessel sunk in Honolulu harbor a few years prior and now set along the wharf in front of the courthouse, are in approximately the location that they had been when they were fixtures on the fort wall.

Just south of the fort was one of the several canals that ran through Lahaina. At one point, this canal was widened to land small boats coming in from the ships anchored offshore. Just beyond it, in what is now part of the school yard, was the Government Market. A notorious place, all kinds of commodities, manufactured and human, were sold here during the whaling days, and it was given the apt name of "Rotten Row."

## Small Boat Harbor

Walking along the harbor stimulates the imagination and the senses. The boats waiting at anchor sway in confused syncopation. Hawser ropes groan and there's a feeling of anticipation and adventure in the air. Here you can board for all kinds of seagoing excursions. In the days of whaling there was no harbor; the boats tied up one to the other offshore in the "roads," at times forming an impromptu floating bridge. The whalers came ashore in their chase boats; with the winds always up, departure could be made at a moment's notice. The activity here is still dominated by the sea.

## THE CARTHAGINIAN II

**T**he masts and square rigging of this ship were a replica of the enterprising freighters that braved the Pacific some two hundred years ago. Everyone was drawn to it. Until its demise in 2003, it was the only truly square-rigged ship left afloat on the seas. It replaced the *Carthaginian I* after that ship went aground in 1972 while being hauled to Honolulu for repairs. The Lahaina Restoration Foundation found the steel-hulled ship that became the *Carthaginian II* in Denmark; built in Germany in 1920 as a two-masted schooner, it tramped around the Baltic under converted diesel power. The foundation had it sailed 12,000 miles to Lahaina, where it underwent extensive conversion until it became the beautiful replica of those older vessels. The *Carthaginian II* was a floating museum dedicated to whaling and to whales. On deck, it was easy to check out the rigging, masts, and steering platform, and try to imagine sailing on a ship of this size for months around Cape Horn and then up and across the broad Pacific to Hawaii. Below decks was a museum containing artifacts and implements from the whaling days. After years of good use, this trusty old ship began to give way and in its later years began to sink at its moorings. In 2003, the ship was towed out to sea and sunk as a diving site, so its usefulness lives on in another capacity.

Although whaling has long since ceased to be, and commercial fishing is not really a player either, the Lahaina Roads still plays host to some big ships. More than four dozen modern cruise ships make a stop annually at Lahaina so their fun-seeking voyagers can taste a bit of what West Maui has to offer. Without a large pier, all ships park out in the deep water and, as in the days of old, passengers are tendered from ship to shore in smaller boats. These cruise ships tend to come in the winter, when the weather is warm and the waters of Alaska are just too cold.

Just as today, the old commercial and whaling boats used a light to guide their way to port. At the harbor's mouth is the site of Lahaina's first lighthouse. In 1840, before any were built along what would later be the West Coast of the United States, King Kamehameha III ordered a lighthouse to be constructed here. The original wooden nine-foot structure was rebuilt to 26 feet in 1869, and the present concrete structure was installed in 1916. As might be expected, a whale oil lamp was first used for light, later to be supplanted by electricity.

## The Brick Palace Site

A rude structure was commissioned by Kamehameha I in 1801 and slapped together by two forgotten Australian ex-convicts. It was the first Western structure in Hawaii, but unfortunately the substandard materials have all disintegrated or been moved and only the site remains, marked by a slab in front of the library. Kamehameha never lived in it, but it was occupied and used as a storehouse until the 1850s. Inland from this site was a taro patch (now occupied by the library), said to have been tended by King Kamehameha I and/or Kamehameha III as an inspiration of labor to his subjects. Just to the right of the Brick Palace site, as you face the harbor, is **Hauola Stone.** Formed like a chair, it was believed by the Hawaiians to have curative powers if you sat on it and let the ocean bathe you. One legend says it was a woman who was turned to stone and saved by the gods as she tried to escape those who were pursuing her. Best view is at low tide.

## Pioneer Inn

This vintage inn, situated at the corner of Hotel and Wharf streets, is just exactly where it belongs. Stand on its veranda and gaze out at the banyan tree and harbor. Presto . . . it's magic time! You'll see. It was even a favorite spot for actors like Errol Flynn and later Spencer Tracy when he was in Lahaina filming *Devil at Four O'clock.* The green and white inn was built in 1901 to accommodate interisland ferry passengers, but its style seems much older. If ironwork had been used on the veranda, you'd think you were in New Orleans. A new and larger wing of rooms and shops was built behind it in 1965 and the two form a courtyard. Make sure to read the hilarious rules governing behavior that

are posted in the main lobby, and give your regards to the old salt who's greeted guests at the front door for years. Although the second-floor rooms of the old section are no longer used, the inn still retains character and atmosphere despite its recent major renovation.

## Baldwin Home

One of the best attractions in Lahaina is the Baldwin Home, on the corner of Front and Dickenson streets. It was occupied by Doctor/Reverend Dwight Baldwin, his wife Charlotte, and their eight children, two of whom died in infancy. He was a trained teacher, as well as the first doctor/dentist in Hawaii. The building also served from the 1830s to 1868 as a dispensary, meeting room, and boarding home for anyone in need. The two-foot-thick walls are of cut lava, and the mortar was made of crushed coral over which plaster was applied. Originally, the downstairs had four rooms; only later were the side rooms and upstairs added. The men slept downstairs in the boys room; upstairs were rooms for the girls. When needed, the upstairs was used by guests, boarders, or the sick and could be occupied by several dozen at one time. As you enter, notice how low the doorway is and that the doors inside are "Christian doors"—with a cross forming the upper panels and an open Bible at the bottom. The Steinway piano that dominates the entrance was built in 1859. In the bedroom to the right, along with all of the period furniture, is a wooden commode. Also notice the lack of closets; all items were kept in chests. Most of the period furniture and other items were not owned or used by the Baldwins but are representative of the era.

The doctor's fees are posted and are hilarious. Payment was by "size" of sickness: very big $50, diagnosis $3, refusal to pay $10! The Reverend Baldwin was 32 when he arrived in Hawaii from New England, and his wife was 25. She was supposedly sickly, and he had heart trouble, so they moved to Honolulu in 1868 to receive better health care. The home became a community center, housing the library and meeting rooms. Today, the Baldwin Home is a showcase museum of the Lahaina Restoration Foundation.

It's open daily 10 A.M.–4 P.M., admission $3 adults, $2 seniors, $5 couples or families.

The oldest coral-block house in Hawaii was built in 1827 for Rev. William Richards and his family who had come to serve in Lahaina three years earlier. Now gone, the house occupied the site of Campbell Park next door to the Baldwin Home.

## Masters' Reading Room

Originally a missionaries' storeroom, the uniquely constructed coral-stone Masters' Reading Room was converted to an officers' club in 1834. It was restored to original condition in 1970, becoming the office of the Lahaina Restoration Foundation. For a short while in the 1990s, it was used as a native Hawaiian craft shop, but it is not used presently. Located next door to the Baldwin Home, these two venerable buildings constitute the oldest standing Western structures on Maui.

## Wo Hing Temple

This structure on Front Street is a Lahaina Restoration Foundation reconstruction. Built in 1912 as a social and religious hall for Chinese workers and residents in the area, it's perhaps the best example of such a structure in the state and has been placed on the National Register of Historic Places. Leased from the Chee Kung Tong Chinese fraternal society, it was opened to the public in 1984 and shows the Chinese influence in Lahaina. Downstairs are displays, upstairs is the altar. In the cookhouse next door, you can see film clips of Hawaii taken by the Edison Company in 1899 and 1906. It's open daily 10 A.M.–4 P.M.; admission is by donation ($1).

## Hale Pa'ahao

This is Lahaina's old prison, located midblock on Prison Street, and its name literally means "Stuck-in-Irons House." It was constructed by prisoners in 1852 from blocks of stone salvaged from the old defunct Fort. It had a catwalk for an armed guard and cells complete with shackles for hardened criminals, but most were drunks who yahooed around town on the Sabbath, wildly spurring their horses. The cells were rebuilt in 1959, the gatehouse in 1988, and the structure is maintained by the Lahaina Restoration Foun-

Wo Hing Temple

dation. The cells, curiously, are made of wood, which shows that the inmates weren't that interested in busting out. Have a look at the prison rules posted on the gatehouse wall on your way in. It's open daily; admission is free but donations are accepted.

## Kamehameha Iki Park

Across the street from Malu'ulu O Lele Park was the site of Hale Piula (Iron-roof House), a two-story royal stone palace built in the late 1830s for King Kamehameha III. Never finished, its stones were later used to construct the old courthouse that now stands between the banyan tree and harbor. This mostly barren spot is now known as Kamehameha Iki Park. On this site the 62-foot double-hulled sailing canoe, Mo'o Kiha (Sacred Lizard), has been built by the cultural group Hui O Wa'a Kaulua and is considered by them to be "Maui's flagship of Hawaiian culture and goodwill." Future plans for the park include additional canoes, canoe sheds, traditional-style buildings, landscaping, and educational and cultural training programs. Access to one of the two in-town beaches is here.

## Waiola Church and Cemetery

The church is not impressive, but its history is. This is the spot where the first Christian services were held in Hawaii, in 1823. A Waine'e stone church was built here in 1832 that could hold 3,000 people, but it was razed by a freak hurricane in 1858. Rebuilt, it survived until 1894, when it was deliberately burned by an angry mob, upset with the abolition of the monarchy in Hawaii and the islands' annexation by the United States. Another church was built, but it too was hit not only by a hurricane but by fire as well. The present structure was built in 1951 and renamed Waiola. In the cemetery is a large part of Maui's history: Buried here are Hawaiian royalty. Lying near each other are Queen Ke'opuolani, her star-crossed daughter, Princess Nahi'ena'ena, and old Governor Hoapili, their royal tomb marked by two large headstones surrounded by a wrought-iron fence. Other graves hold missionaries such as William Richards and many infants and children.

## Churches and Temples

You may wish to stop for a moment at Lahaina's other churches and temples dotted around town. They are reminders of the mixture of faiths and peoples that populated this village and added their particular cultural styles. **Holy Innocents Episcopal Church,** built in 1927, is on Front Street, near Kamehameha III school. Known for its "Hawaiian Madonna," its altar and pulpit are resplendent with paintings of fruits, plants, and birds of the islands. Stop by on Sundays when the church is full and hear the sermon preached and hymns sung in Hawaiian. **The Episcopal Cemetery** (from 1863) on Waine'e Street shows the English influence in the islands. Many of the royal family, including King Kalakaua, became Anglicans. This cemetery holds the remains of many early Maui families, and of Walter Murray

## MALU'ULU O LELE

This park, a nondescript area at the corner of Shaw and Front, holding tennis and basketball courts, a baseball field, and a parking lot, was at one time the most important spot in Lahaina—"The Breadfruit Shelter of Lele." ("Lele" was the former name of Lahaina.) Here was a small pond with a diminutive island in the center. The 17-acre pond, Mokuhinia, was inhabited by a *mo'o*, a lizard spirit, said to be the deceased daughter of a proud Maui king, and protector of the tiny one-acre island, Moku'ula, home of Maui royalty and the Kamehamehas when they were in residence. King Kamehameha III and his sister Princess Nahi'ena'ena were raised together in Lahaina. They fell in love, but the new ways caused turmoil and tragedy. Instead of marrying and producing royal children, a favored practice only 20 years earlier, they were wrenched apart by the new religion. He, for a time, numbed himself with alcohol, while she died woefully from a broken heart. She was buried here, and for many years Kamehameha III could frequently be found at her grave, quietly sitting and meditating. Shortly afterward, the government of Hawaii moved to Honolulu, and although part of this island remained a royal mausoleum, it slowly fell into disrepair. By the early years of the 20th century, water that fed this pond had been largely diverted for use in irrigating the surrounding sugarcane fields. By 1918, all of the remains of the island were taken away, the pond was filled, and the ground was leveled for use as a park.

Friends of Moku'ula, www.mokuula.com, is a nonprofit organization based in Lahaina, which is trying to bring the historical and cultural significance of Malu'ulu O Lele to the public eye, and eventually to re-create the pond and island to its former physical shape. In association with this organization, the group Maui Nei offers an historical walking tour of Lahaina daily except Sunday for $37 per person. These tours are led by a *kupuna* and stop at more than a dozen sites around town, but there is a focus on Moku'ula and its significance. Tours last about 2 hours and start at 9:30 A.M. from the steps of the old Courthouse. Reservations are required, preferably 24 hours in advance.

**M**

MAUI

Gibson, the notorious settler, politician, and firebrand of the 1880s. Just behind is **Hale Aloha,** "House of Love," a small structure built by Maui residents in thanksgiving for being saved from a terrible smallpox epidemic that ravaged Oʻahu but largely bypassed Maui in 1853–54. The structure was restored in 1974. Also on Waineʻe is **Maria Lanakila Church,** the site of the first Roman Catholic Mass in Lahaina, celebrated in 1841. The present structure dates from 1928. Next to the church's cemetery is the **Seamen's Cemetery,** where many infirm from the ships that came to Lahaina were buried after failing to recover. Most stones have been obliterated by time, and only a few remain. Herman Melville came here to pay his last respects to a cousin buried in this yard. **Hongwanjii Temple** is also on Waineʻe, between Prison and Shaw. It's a Buddhist temple with the largest congregation in Lahaina and dates from 1910, although the present structure was raised in 1927. Down Luakini Street is the tall clapboard plantation-era structure **Hokuji Mission Shingon Buddhist Temple.**

The **Lahaina Jodo Mission** is near Mala Wharf on Ala Moana Street. When heading west, you'll leave the main section of town and keep going until you see a sign over a building that reads "Jesus Coming Soon." Turn left toward the beach and you'll immediately spot the three-tiered wooden pagoda. The temple bell welcomes you at the entrance gate, and a giant bronze Buddha sits exposed to the elements on a raised stone platform nearby. The largest outside of Asia, this seated Amita Buddha image was dedicated in 1968 in commemoration of the centennial of the arrival of Japanese workers in Hawaii. The grounds are impeccable and serenely quiet. You may stroll around, and while the buildings are closed to the public, you can climb the steps of the main building to peek into the temple. The entire area is a perfect spot for solitary meditation if you've had enough of frenetic Lahaina. Buddha's birthday is celebrated here every April. The Puʻupiha Cemetery is across the street along the beach. It seems incongruous to see tombstones set in sand.

## Mala Wharf

Built in 1922 and once an integral part of La-

haina commerce, the old Mala Wharf now stands decaying at the northern end of town. Next to it is a new boat launch ramp, which is used by local fishermen and some ocean activities companies. There are restrooms here but no other amenities or services.

## U.S. Seamen's Hospital

This notorious hospital from 1833 was reconstructed by the Lahaina Restoration Foundation in 1982. Here is where sick seamen were cared for under the auspices of the U.S. State Department. Allegations during the late 1850s claimed that the care here extended past the grave! Unscrupulous medicos supposedly charged the U.S. government for care of seamen who had long since died. The hospital is located at Front and Baker, heading toward Kaʻanapali, near the Jodo Mission. The stony exterior of this building has been maintained, but the building now houses a company that produces the visitor channel for television. In the front yard is a 10,000-pound, swivel-end Porter anchor, found off Black Rock in Kaʻanapali. This building was supposedly constructed for King Kamehameha III as a place where he could gamble, carouse, and meet his sister Nahiʻenaʻena for love trysts away from the puritanical eyes of the missionaries.

## Lahainaluna

Head up the mountain behind Lahaina on Lahainaluna Road for approximately two miles. On your left you'll pass the **Pioneer Sugar Mill,** in operation until 1996. Once at Lahainaluna (Above Lahaina) you'll find the oldest school west of the Rockies, opened by the Congregationalist missionaries in 1831. Children from all over the islands, and many from California, came here if their parents could afford to send them away to boarding school. Today, the school is West Maui's public high school, but many children still come here to board. The first students were given not only a top-notch academic education but a practical one as well. They built the school buildings, and many were also apprentices in the famous Hale Paʻi (Printing House), which turned out Hawaii's first newspaper (1834) and made Lahaina famous as a printing center.

One look at **Hale Pa'i** and you think of New England. It's a white stucco building with blue trim and a wood-shake roof. It houses a replica printing press and copies of documents once printed there. Placed on the National Register of Historic Places in 1976 and restored in 1982, it's open Monday–Friday 10 A.M.–4 P.M. Owned by the state, Hale Pa'i is maintained by the Lahaina Restoration Foundation. If you visit the campus when school is in session, you may go to Hale Pa'i, but if you want to walk around, please sign in at the vice principal's office. Lahainaluna High School is still dedicated to the preservation of Hawaiian culture.

## Heading East

Five miles east of Lahaina along the coastal road (Route 30) is the little village of **Olowalu.** Today, little more than the Olowalu General Store and Chez Paul French Restaurant are here. This was the place of the Olowalu Massacre perpetrated by Captain Metcalfe, whose far-reaching results greatly influenced Hawaiian history. Two American seamen, Young and Davis, were connected with this incident, and with their help Kamehameha I subdued all of Hawaii. Only the remains of a pier and a few storage buildings mark the site of a once busy cane harbor and port facilities.

Behind the general store a dirt track leads about one-half mile to **petroglyphs;** make sure you pass a water tower at the start because there are three similar roads here. After about 20 minutes, you'll come to the dilapidated remains of a wooden stairway going up to a rock face on an outcrop. Etched into the flat face of this deep red rock are a small group of human figures and one crab claw sailing canoe, which are believed to be about 300 years old. Some modern graffiti defaces this rock, so it's a little difficult to determine just what's what, but these petroglyphs are still perhaps the most easily accessible of all such rock art on the island.

Near mile marker 14 is good snorkeling, some of the best on the island. Other good snorkeling is done near the highway tunnel, where boats come to anchor just off shore. You will see them from the road as you pass by. Just east of mile marker 11, the old **Lahaina Pali Trail** heads up the rugged dry hillside to cross the ridge and drop down to the isthmus north of Ma'alaea.

If you continue east on Route 30, you'll pass **Papawai** and **McGregor Point,** both noted for their vistas (here you can see South Maui, Molokini, Kaho'olawe, and Lana'i) and as excellent locations to spot whales in season. The road sign merely indicates a scenic lookout.

# BEACHES

The best beaches around Lahaina are just west of town in Ka'anapali, or just east toward Olowalu. A couple of adequate places to spread your towel are right in Lahaina, but they're not quite on a par with the beaches just a few miles away.

## In-Town Beaches

One beach stretches east of the harbor starting at Kamehameha Iki Park. It's crowded at times, on occasion used for beach volleyball, and there may be "wash up" at certain times of the year. It's cleaner and quieter at the east end down by Lahaina Shores Hotel. Close to the old royal compound, it was a favorite with the *ali'i.* There are restrooms, the swimming is fair, it's gentle for kids, and the snorkeling is acceptable past the reef. **Lahaina Beach** is at the west end of town near Mala Wharf. Follow Front to Pu'unoa Place and turn down to the beach. This is a good place for families with tots because the water is clear, safe, and shallow. There is beach access also at the turnaround on Kai Pali Place, the next two streets in toward town.

## Puamana Beach County Park

About two miles before you enter Lahaina from the southeast along Route 30, you'll see signs for this beach park, a narrow strip between the road and the sea. The swimming and snorkeling are only fair. The setting, however, is quite nice with picnic tables shaded by ironwood trees. The views are terrific, and this is a great spot to eat your plate lunch only minutes from town.

## Launiupoko Wayside Park

One mile farther southeast, this park has restrooms and showers, but only a small enclosed kiddie beach that's best at high tide when it fills with water. This is more of a picnic area than anything else, although many come to sunbathe on the grass below the coconut trees. Beginning surfers like this spot, and some beginning surf lessons are taught here because the waves are gentle.

South of here you'll see lots of shore fishermen and others out for a quiet afternoon. Although not a designated park, the water is adequate for swimming. Find parking where you can under the trees.

## East of Olowalu

Between Olowalu and the highway tunnel are **Ukumehame Beach County Park** and **Papalaua Wayside**. The first is a small park with picnic tables, barbecue pits, toilets, and a tiny lawn for sunbathing; swimming is okay. At mile marker 11, Papalaua Wayside is a mostly unimproved area with lots of ironwood trees for shade, but there are toilets. This long, narrow beach is a favorite of shore fishermen, and camping is allowed with a county permit.

## Wahikuli Wayside Park

Along Route 30 between Lahaina and Ka'anapali, this county park is a favorite with local people and excellent for a picnic. It has a rocky shore and a short, narrow sand beach, but is known as a good swimming spot. The drawback is that it's right on the busy highway. With three parking areas, it's as if the park was split into three units. Tennis courts are located up across the street behind the main Lahaina post office.

Just up the highway, as if connected to this wayside park, is **Hanaka'o'o Beach County Park**. This beach, which is actually the south end of Ka'anapali Beach, runs north past some of the most exclusive hotels on the island. Local canoe clubs put their canoes in the water here, and at certain times of the year paddling events will be held at this beach.

## ACCOMMODATIONS

Lodging in Lahaina is not of the usual tourist resort variety that people head to Ka'anapali for. Lahaina tends to be hot and hot to trot, espe-

cially at night. You can find good bargains here, and if you want to be in the thick of the action, you're in the right spot.

The hotels in Lahaina are small, more along the lines of inns, as there names suggest. The only true hotel in town is the Pioneer Inn. Both the Lahaina Inn and Plantation Inn are much smaller, more intimate, and each serves a complimentary breakfast to all guests.

### $100–150

The **Pioneer Inn,** 658 Wharf St., Lahaina, HI 96761, 808/661-3636 or 800/457-5457, fax 808/667-5708, info@pioneerinnmaui.com, www.pioneerinnmaui.com, is the oldest hotel on Maui still accommodating guests, and it was the only hotel on West Maui until 1963. The inn has undergone more than a facelift since its early days. The semiseedy, old-timey essence has now been spiffed and polished. Now a Best Western hotel, the Pioneer Inn had $500,000 poured into it in 1997–98, but all renovation was done in early-1900s taste. For decades, the Pioneer Inn had absolutely no luxury whatsoever, only a double scoop of atmosphere. It was the place to come if you wanted to save money and be the star of your own movie with the Inn as the stage set. Creaky stairways, threadbare carpets, low-light hallways, shared baths, and questionable merrymakers and occupants—the place had it all. Now the stairway doesn't creak anymore, new carpet has been laid, TVs installed, baths have shiny new tiles and some period fixtures, bedrooms have new furniture, trim and wall coverings renewed, and all rooms have air-conditioning. What does remain the same are the lanai, which, depending on the room, look out over the banyan tree or the hotel courtyard and pool, the posted house rules, and the old salt who still stands at the front door. Rooms run $115–180; AAA and Best Western Gold Club discounts are available. Downstairs, food and drink are served daily at the grill and bar, and local live music in always on the menu. Shops occupy the perimeter of the ground floor fronting the banyan tree and Front Street.

Another reborn classic is the **Lahaina Inn,** 127 Lahainaluna Rd., Lahaina, HI 96761, 808/661-0577 or 800/669-3444, fax 808/667-

9480, inntown@lahainainn.com, www.lahainainn.com. Completely renovated and re-modeled, this one-time dowdy orphan, the old, down-at-the-heels traveler's classic, Lahainaluna Hotel, emerged in 1989 as a lovely lady. Gone from this cockroach paradise are the weather-beaten linoleum floors, bare-bulb musty rooms, and rusted dripping faucets. In their place are antique-stuffed, neo-Victorian, tastefully appointed rooms that transport you back to the late 1800s. Each room is individually decorated, and period pieces include everything from wardrobes to nightstands, rugs, ceramic bowls, mirrors, pictures, lamps, and books. The only deference to modernity are the bathrooms with their new-but-old-style fixtures, the air-conditioning, telephones, and safes—no TV. You can still peer from the balcony of this vintage hotel—each room has a lanai with two hardwood rocking chairs and a table—or observe the masses below from behind heavy drapes and lace curtains. The 12 units include three spacious suites. Rates are $119–129 for the rooms and $169 for parlor suites ($10 less during regular season) and include a complimentary continental breakfast, served every morning from about 7:30 A.M. at the sideboard at the end of the hall. There is a two-night minimum stay only on Fridays and Saturdays; children older than age 15 are welcome. For dinner, you might try downstairs at the renowned David Paul's Lahaina Grill, which offers Inn guests a discount. Free to guests, parking is in the public parking lot directly behind the inn.

## $150–200

If Agatha Christie were seeking inspiration for *the* perfect setting for one of her mysteries, **The Plantation Inn**, 174 Lahainaluna Rd., Lahaina, HI 96761, 808/667-9225 or 800/433-6815, fax 808/667-9293, info@theplantationinn.com, www.theplantationinn.com, is where she would come. The neo-Victorian building is appointed with posted verandas, hardwood floors, natural wood wainscoting and trim counterpointed by floral wall coverings, bedspreads, and deep-cushioned furniture. Rays of sunlight stray through stained-glass windows and wide double doors. Each uniquely decorated room is comfortable,

with four-poster beds and private tiled baths with bold porcelain and brass fixtures; most have sofas. The complete illusion is turn of the 20th century, but the modern amenities of air-conditioning, remote TV and VCR, a fridge, daily maid service, and a soothing spa and pool are included. The back addition brings the total room count to 19. Most of the back 12 units have lanai overlooking the garden courtyard with its pool, spa, and guest pavilion. Prices are a reasonable $157 standard, $177 superior, $197 deluxe, $220–240 suites (some with kitchenette and hot tub), and all include a filling continental breakfast at poolside. Rates are slightly higher during the peak Christmas season, when there is a seven-night minimum, and special packages are available. The Plantation Inn also offers a money-saving option for dinner at Gerard's, the fine French restaurant on the first floor. While now associated with the Ka'anapali Beach Hotel in Ka'anapali, it still maintains great autonomy. Set off the main drag and away from the bustle, it's simply one of the best accommodations that Maui has to offer, and although a relatively new building, it fits well into the 19th-century whaling port ambiance that Lahaina fosters.

## Condominiums

Lahaina's few condos are listed from least expensive to most expensive. One is modern, new, and pricey. One is a more affordable renovated older place. The rest fall in between.

Out beyond the Lahaina Roads is **The Makai Inn**, 1415 Front St., 808/662-3200, fax 808/661-9027, info@makaiinn.net, www.makai-inn.net, a former concrete block two-story apartment building turned into rental units. Compact and landscaped in a pleasing manner, this neat and tidy complex is set right on the water where there's nothing blocking you from the sunset. Each of the more than one dozen units is small, yet all have full kitchens and bathrooms, queen or double beds, and a sitting room. While furnished in tropical style, there are no TVs or phones in the units nor daily maid service, but there is a laundry room on premises, a pay phone, and off-street parking. Units run $70–105 per night, $10 extra for each person more than two, and a discount is offered after seven nights. The Makai Inn offers an affordable option for staying in this exciting town.

The **Lahaina Roads,** 1403 Front St., is a condo/apartment at the far north end of town where all units have fully equipped kitchens, TV, and maid service on request. One-bedroom units (for two) run $125; two-bedroom units (for four) are $200. There is a three-night minimum stay and a deposit required to hold your reservation. There is no beach here because it sits right along the seawall, but there is a freshwater pool, and you couldn't have a better view, with every unit facing the ocean. Parking is on ground level below the rooms. Rentals are handled through Klahani Resorts, P.O. Box 11108, Lahaina, HI 96761, 808/667-2712 or 800/669-6284, fax 808/661-5875.

Located a few blocks away from the hubbub, the **Ohana Maui Islander,** 660 Waine'e St., Lahaina, HI 96761, 808/667-9766 or 800/462-6262, fax 808/661-3733, is an adequate hotel offering rooms with kitchenettes, studios, and one- and two-bedroom suites. Originally intended as a residential condo complex, these units are more spacious than most visitor accommodations. All have daily maid service, air-conditioning and TV, plus there's a swimming pool, lighted tennis court (hotel guests only), coin laundry facility, and a barbecue and picnic area on premises. The low-rise design in a garden setting lends a homey atmosphere; an activity desk at the front can help arrange your outings. Basic hotel rooms start at $149, family studios $179, and suites $199-279. Studios and suites all have kitchens. Suites will take three guests, one-bedroom, one-bath suites will hold four guests, and the two-bedroom, two-bath suites up to six individuals. Take a botanical walk through the garden, where there are many varieties of exotic plants and flowers. This fine little hideaway is an Ohana Hotels property.

A six-story condo, the **Lahaina Shores,** at the south end of town, 475 Front St., Lahaina, HI 96761, 808/661-4835 or 800/642-6284, was constructed before the Lahaina building code limited the height of new structures. The condo has become a landmark for incoming craft. The Shores offers a swimming pool and spa and is the only accommodation in Lahaina located on a beach. From a distance, the Southern-mansion facade is striking; up close, though, it becomes painted cement blocks and false colonnades. The fully air-conditioned rooms, however, are good value for the money. The basic room contains a full bathroom, large color TV, and modern kitchen. They're all light and airy, and the views of the harbor and mountains are the best in town. Studios run $180 mountain-view and $215 oceanfront; one-bedroom suites are $250 mountain-view and $280 oceanfront. The penthouse suites run $290 and $315 for mountain and ocean views, respectively. Other amenities include a front desk, daily maid service, laundry facilities, and an activities desk. This facility is associated with the Classic Resorts group, info@classicresorts.com, www.classicresorts.com.

A 28-acre private community of condos located on the south edge of town along the ocean, **Puamana** is a quiet hideaway away from the hustle and bustle of town, definitely a high-end property. The clubhouse here was the Pioneer Sugar Company's former plantation manager's residence (built 1923), and it's a beauty. Surrounding it are broad lawns and the townhouses. One-bedroom condo units run $140-200, two-bedroom units $175-275, and three-bedroom townhouses $350-500; three- to five-night minimum stay. Discounts are given for long stays, and all rates are somewhat lower during the low season. All units have fully equipped kitchens, all linens, TVs and VCRs, air-conditioning, and outdoor barbecue grills. Puamana also features an oceanside swimming pool plus two others on property; a sauna, reading parlor, and lending library in the clubhouse; a guests-only tennis court; badminton and volleyball courts; and children's play areas. The only drawback is that it's wedged against the highway, but a thick hedge blocks out much of the noise. For rentals, contact Klahani Resorts, P.O. Box 11108, Lahaina, HI 96761, 808/667-2712 or 800/669-6284, fax 808/661-5875; or Whaler's Realty Management, 808/661-3484 or 800/676-4112, fax 808/661-8338.

## B&Bs and Guesthouses

By and large, the B&Bs in Lahaina are clumped together in two areas of town: south of downtown near the water, and halfway to Ka'anapali and up above the highway in the area known as Kapunakea.

Barbier's **Old Lahaina House,** P.O. Box 10355, Lahaina, HI 96761, 808/667-4663 or 800/847-0761, fax 808/669-9199, info@oldlahaina.com, www.oldlahaina.com, is a big salmon-colored house, surrounded by a wall of the same color, has four rooms, all with private baths, that range $69–115 but $10–20 higher in the busy season. No breakfast is served. All rooms include air-conditioning, telephone, TV, small refrigerator and microwave, and everyone has access to the garden and the refreshing swimming pool and deck, which occupy the front yard. Reduced rental car rates can be arranged. Old Lahaina House is a relaxing, homey place, lived in by the family (so there may be kids around).

In a street behind, you'll find the **Bambula Inn** bed and breakfast, 518 'Ilikahi St., Lahaina, HI 96761, 808/667-6753 or 800/544-5524, fax 808/667-0979, bambula@maui.net, www.bambula.com. Here, a cottage and studio are separated at the back of the house so you're independent from the family, while a smaller studio is set to the side. Each unit has a full kitchen, queen-size beds, private bath, TV, phone, and lanai. The detached cottage for $110 has air-conditioning, while both studios have fans. The rear studio runs $100 and the side studio is $79; $20 for each additional person more than two, three nights minimum. Breakfast is brought to your room, and a complimentary sunset sail aboard the family sailboat *Bambula* is offered every evening, weather permitting. Contact Pierre for information and reservations. If these rooms are full, ask about his other accommodation options.

The peach color of the **Garden Gate Bed And Breakfast,** 67 Kaniau Rd., Lahaina, HI 96761, 808/661-8800 or 800/939-3217, fax 808/661-0209, jaime@gardengatebb.com, www.gardengatebb.com, beyond its private courtyard garden lets you know that this is an easygoing, restful, and welcoming place. There are three bedrooms in the main house, one larger unit off an upstairs lanai to the side, an efficiency unit under that, and a newer room at the front. All have private baths, and although each is different from the other, all are comfy and decorated in island style. Only the efficiency has a kitchen. The others have microwaves and refrigerators, but a breakfast of pastries, fruit, and drinks is served daily except Sunday on the patio unless the weather doesn't permit. All guests may use the barbecue and laundry facilities, and you can borrow bikes and beach gear. Rates run $79–139; three-night minimum stay. Knowledgeable and ready to share information about their island and what to see, the owners make you feel like part of the family.

**The GuestHouse,** 1620 Ainakea Rd., Lahaina, HI 96761, 808/661-8085 or 800/621-8942, fax 808/661-1896, relax@mauiguesthouse.com, www.mauiguesthouse.com, is a well-appointed contemporary B&B where the host will provide free snorkel gear and even scuba lessons for a fee. The GuestHouse caters largely to honeymooners and scuba enthusiasts. All rooms have queen beds, air-conditioning, ceiling fans, TVs, refrigerators, phones, and private lanai, and all have private baths with a hot tub or whirlpool tub. Full breakfast is provided. Everyone shares the living room, kitchen, barbecue, and laundry facility. Each of the four rooms runs $129 per couple or $115 single.

**Wai Ola Vacation Paradise,** 1565 Ku'uipo, 808/662-0812 or 800/572-5642, fax 808/661-8045, waiola@maui-vacations.com, www.waiola.com, is a private home with three units, all with private entrances; however, the entire house may also be rented. Located just off the pool, the large one-bedroom Makai Apartment is more than 1,000 square feet, with full kitchen and amenities. It runs $150 per couple and $15 each extra person up to four. The Malanai Suite is about half as big but also has a full kitchen and all amenities. Located in the garden, it runs $135 per couple. With its own private lanai and large king bed, the Honeymoon Ohana room goes for $175 per night. If the two-bedroom, two-bath upper portion of the house is rented, the rate is $400 per night. Depending on the number of bedrooms, the entire house goes for $550–850 per night.

M

MAUI

The minimum stay is five nights. All units are well-appointed and have air-conditioning, TV, VCR, and phones, and everyone has use of the free laundry facilities and the swimming pool. As a vacation rental, no food is served, but all kitchens are stocked with basics. Very private; booked mostly by honeymooners.

The **House of Fountains,** 1579 Lokia St., Lahaina, HI 96761, 808/667-2121 or 800/789-6865, fax 808/667-2120, private@aloha-house.com, www.alohahouse.com, is farther up in this neighborhood. A large modern house, with tile floor throughout, native wood furniture, and overall Hawaiian-style decor, this B&B is a restful and relaxing spot that also has a pool and hot tub on the back patio. Room rates for the six suites are $95–145 per night, with $20 for extra individuals, which includes a filling breakfast of fruits and other goodies.

## Hostel

If you're looking for the least expensive place in town, try **Patey's Place Maui Hostel,** 761 Waine'e St., 808/667-0999, maui@hawaiian-hostels.com, www.hawaiian-hostels.com, the only hostel-type accommodation in town. This single-story house, with additional rooms added to the side for space, is spartan and reasonably clean. There's no luxury at this easygoing hostel, but it's serviceable. Guests can hang out on the cushions in the common TV room, a kitchen is available for simple food preparation and storage, there's coin laundry available, and there are shared bathrooms with showers. Drugs and smoking are forbidden in the rooms, and quiet time is after 10 P.M. A bunk in the dorm room runs $20 per night, the small single room $45, a private room with shared bath $50–55, and the private room with private bath $60. Used by those visiting the island on the cheap and by those who've come to find work, this could be a good place to garner information about what to see and do on Maui.

# FOOD

Lahaina's menu of restaurants is gigantic. All palates and pocketbooks can easily be satisfied: There's fast food, sandwiches, sushi, happy hours,

vegetarian, and elegant cosmopolitan restaurants. Because Lahaina is a dynamic tourist spot, restaurants and eateries come and go with regularity. The following is not an exhaustive list of Lahaina's food spots—it couldn't be—but there is plenty listed here to feed everyone at breakfast, lunch, and dinner. *Bon appétit!*

## Quick Food and Snacks

Hawaii's own **Lappert's Ice Cream,** next to the library, not only has rich ice cream, shave ice, and cookies, but also serves fat- and sugar-free ice cream—about the only thing on Maui that is fat-free! **Häagen-Dazs** can also serve up your favorite flavor at both the Pioneer Inn shops and near Lahaina Market Place.

A good spot for a quick snack is **Mr. Sub Sandwiches,** 129 Lahainaluna Rd., which features double-fisted sandwiches and packed picnic lunches. Your sweet tooth will begin to sing the moment you walk into **The Bakery,** 911 Limahana, 808/667-9062, near the Sugar Cane Train. You can't beat the stuffed croissants for under $3 or the sandwiches for under $5. The pastries, breads, and bagels are goooood! Open daily at 5:30 A.M. and closes at 2 P.M. weekdays, 1 P.M. on Saturday, and noon Sunday.

**Take Home Maui,** 121 Dickenson St., 808/661-8067 or 800/545-MAUI from the Mainland for mail order, is a food store and delicatessen that specializes in packaging agriculturally inspected Maui produce such as pineapples, papayas, Maui onions, protea, potato chips, macadamia nut products, and even Kona coffee, which they will deliver to you at the airport before your departing flight. For an on-the-spot treat, they prepare deli sandwiches for under $6, a variety of quiches, and sides of macaroni and potato salad. Take Home Maui is famous for its fresh-fruit smoothies, homemade soups, and picnic lunches. Choose a shaded spot on the veranda and enjoy your lunch while taking a break from the jostle of Front Street. Open 7:30 A.M.–6:30 P.M.

## Inexpensive

Across from the Banyan Tree is **Swiss Cafe,** 808/661-6776, a simple European-style eatery with seating outside under the trellis, where you can order hot and cold sandwiches, pizzas, coffee, and juice for reasonable prices—nothing is over $8. Perhaps a bagel with cheese and tomato or fresh croissant will satisfy you for breakfast. All sorts of sandwiches and personal-size pizzas can be made for lunch, but the "melts" are the focus. Some stop by just for an espresso or iced mocha, while others come to cool off with a smoothie or ice cream. Open 9 A.M.–6 P.M., and while you're here, check your email—from $.10 per minute depending on the length of use.

Tacos, burritos, and other south-of-the-border foods are served up with a Hawaiian attitude at **Maui Taco,** 808/661-8883, at Lahaina Square Shopping Center. This is excellent Mexi-waiian food with a punch, and everything on the menu is less than $7.

**Smokehouse BBQ,** 1307 Front St., 808/667-7005, serves baby back ribs, chicken, and fish smoked over a kiawe grill and smothered in special barbecue sauce. Also available for lunch are a variety of burgers and sandwiches, and always sides like rice, barbecued beans, and cole slaw. This is where local people and those in the know come for a very good but no-frills meal. If eating hearty without caring about the ambiance (actually the sunset view couldn't be better) is your aim, come here. Open daily 11 A.M.– 9 P.M. Takeout available.

The **Thai Chef,** 808/667-2814, will please any Thai food lover who wants a savory meal at a good price. Search for this restaurant stuck in a corner at the Old Lahaina Center (open Mon.–Fri. 11 A.M.–3 P.M. for lunch, dinner nightly 5–10 P.M.). As in most Thai restaurants vegetarians are well taken care of with plenty of spicy tofu and vegetable dishes. The extensive menu offers everything from scrumptious Thai soups with ginger and coconut for $8.95 (enough for two) to curries and seafood. Most entrées are under $14 with a good selection under $10. It's not fancy, but food-wise you won't be disappointed. Takeout is available. When in Kihei, visit the second Thai Chef restaurant in the Rainbow Mall.

**Zushi's** is a reasonably priced Japanese restaurant selling sushi and various other Japanese dishes in Lahaina Square Shopping Center on Waine'e Street. Zushi's serves lunch (take-out too) 11 A.M.–2 P.M., dinner 5–9:30 P.M. Authentic with most items under $6. Also in this shopping center is **Denny's,** which serves up inexpensive standard American fare.

**Sunrise Cafe,** 808/661-8558, open 6 A.M.–6 P.M. at 693 Front Street to the side of the library, is the kind of place locals keep secret. It's a tiny restaurant where you can have excellent coffee and a sandwich or more substantial gourmet food at down-home prices. The nutritious and wholesome food includes breakfast specials like freshly baked quiche for $6.95, and lunch salads from Chinese chicken to fresh island fruit all priced under $9. Those with heartier appetites can choose various hot or cold sandwiches for under $8, soups for $3.95, *kalua* pork, tofu dish, roasted beef, or other main entrée for under $12. The kitchen closes at 4 P.M. A deli case holds scrumptious award-winning pastries that are complemented by fine coffee selections always freshly brewed and a good selection of herbal teas. Eat inside or out on the back patio.

At the 505 Front Street Mall is **Bamboo Bar and Grill,** 808/667-4051, which serves inexpensive Thai and Vietnamese dishes for lunch and dinner until 11 P.M., with only a few items on the menu over $13. Many of the well-known seafood, meat, and vegetarian dishes are available plus a few that might not be familiar, like fish or shrimp simmered in a clay pot.

Next door to the new Old Lahaina Lu'au venue near Mala Wharf is **Aloha Mixed Plate,** 808/661-3322, a great spot for a simple, authentic, and award-winning meal and a cold drink. While noodle dishes, burgers, and sandwiches are on the menu, the specialties are the plate lunches. Available in three sizes, most run $2.95–8.95. Open 10:30 A.M.–10 P.M.; happy hour 3–6 P.M. You can't beat it.

Among the several eateries at the Wharf Cinema Center is the unpretentious **Yakiniku Lahaina,** which serves a fine rendition of Korean food.

Aside from the full range of produce, vitamins, health foods, and bulk foods, the **Down To Earth Natural Foods,** on Lahainaluna Rd., 808/667-2855, has some reasonably priced and healthily prepared hot and cold foods, fruit

MAUI

drinks, and smoothies. Items at the salad bar and hot-food counter are priced $6.50 per pound. Open Monday–Saturday 7 A.M.–9 P.M., Sunday 8:30 A.M.–8 P.M.

**Penne Pasta Cafe,** 808/661-6633, at the Dickenson Square, is an inexpensive Italian restaurant that serves quality food quickly at reasonable prices. Order at the counter and your meal will be brought to your table. Pastas include linguine pesto, baked penne, and chicken piccata. Pizza and flatbreads are also available, as are salads, and a few sandwiches, like prosciutto, pepper, onion, and provolone, and open-face roasted eggplant parmesan. Nothing on the menu is over $10. Run by Mark Ellman, a perennial favorite island chef who has started and run numerous restaurants over the years, Penne Pasta is a winner.

The trendiest of the inexpensive eateries in town, the open-air **Cheeseburger in Paradise,** 811 Front St., 808/661-4855, open 10:30 A.M.–11 P.M., with live music nightly, is a joint down by the sea overlooking the harbor out back. Served are a whole slew of burgers priced $6.75–8.50, Portuguese turkey burger for $8.50, the jumbo cheese dog covered with cheese and sautéed onions for $6.50, or the Maui classic BLT for $6.75. Other selections include the aloha fish and seasoned fries at $10.25, a huge Upcountry salad for $7.50, and calamari scallop gumbo for $6.95. Cheeseburger also has a full bar that sells a range of both imported and domestic beer, along with tropical concoctions. If you were going to pick one spot to have a beer, soak in the sights, and capture the flavor of old Lahaina, "the Burg" has all the trimmings.

Also a trendy place and up at the top end of the inexpensive spots is the **Hard Rock Cafe,** 808/667-7400, at the Lahaina Center on the corner of Front and Papalaua streets. Open daily from 11:30 A.M., this is a large breezy, screened restaurant keeping the rock-and-roll faith. Over the bar is a '59 Cadillac convertible woody, and on the walls are prints of rock stars and electric guitars, including a Gibson autographed by the Grateful Dead. The floors have a shiny patina, and the raised stools and round-top tables give you a view of the street and the sea beyond.

Menu prices are moderate, with homemade onion rings at $4.29, Caesar salad for $7.79, Cajun chicken sandwich at $9.19, barbecued ribs for $15.99, and grilled burger for $7.59. Sit inside at the bar or dining section or outside under the umbrellas. Food is served until 10 P.M. Sunday–Thursday, until 10:30 Friday and Saturday; the bar is open two hours longer every night, and there's live music on Saturday.

Also reasonably cheap and an institution is **Moose McGillycuddy's,** 808/667-7758. A wild and zany place, there is music nightly (live on Fridays and Saturdays), the sports channel on the many TVs hanging here and there, daily specials, early-bird specials (both breakfast and dinner), and a happy hour 3–6 P.M. The large portions are filling, and the menu reads like a book, with burgers, sandwiches, fajitas, *pu pu,* and much else, most under $10. Take a moment (or an hour) and have a look at all the stuff hanging on the walls.

## Moderate

**Kobe Japanese Steak House,** 136 Dickenson at the corner of Luakini, 808/667-5555, is open daily for dinner from 5:30 P.M. Service is teppanyaki-style, which means that the chef comes to you. His sharp blade flashes through the air and thumps the table, keeping the culinary beat as it slices, dices, and minces faster than any Veg-o-matic you've ever seen. The delectables of marinated meat, chicken, and vegetables are then expertly flash-fried at your own grill, often with aplomb in a ball of sake-induced flame. The experience is fun, the food very good, and the interior authentic Japanese. Teppan meals come complete with rice, soup, and tea. Expect to spend at least $18 for an entrée (less for the early-bird specials), $11 for an appetizer, and from $15 for four pieces of sushi. Other style fish and meat entrées are also available for up to $37. Complement your meal with a glass of sake or Japanese beer. Aside from the food, karaoke entertainment on the weekend draws a lively crowd.

Set right at the harbor, the **Pioneer Inn Bar and Grill,** 808/661-3636, at the historic Pioneer Inn, has a marine theme. It serves breakfast

6:30–11:30 A.M., offering two buttermilk pancakes for $6.25, eggs Benedict for $7.25, and a three-egg omelet for $8.25. Lunch and dinner, served noon–11 P.M., start with such items as a hearty bowl of Portuguese soup for $5.50 or Caesar salad for $8, and moves on to a full selection of sandwiches for under $9, pepper-grilled steak for $20.25, oven-roasted chicken for $13.95, sesame-seared ahi for $22.50, or primavera Alfredo for $12.50. In addition, the saloon is open for drinks from noon–midnight, with happy hour 3–7 P.M., and there's live music most evenings. Because the Pioneer Inn is the oldest hotel in town, and a true landmark with a great lanai from which you can view the harbor, the experience is really one of history and atmosphere.

The **Whale's Tail Bar and Grill,** 808/667-4044, is a casual, easygoing, open-air restaurant that overlooks the banyan tree from above the ABC Discount Store at the Wharf Cinema Center. Open 11 A.M.–11 P.M. daily for lunch and dinner, there is a full bar with happy hour from 2:30–5 P.M. and live entertainment nightly 4–7 P.M. At the Whale's Tale you'll find mostly salads, burgers, and sandwiches in the $6–9 range, with seafood dishes up to $11.

At the back of the Wharf Cinema Center is the fun-loving **Poncho and Lefty's Cantina and Restaurante,** 808/661-4666. Amble back and sit awhile for a margarita or cerveza, or stop by at lunch or dinner for tasty Mexican *comidas*. Food runs the gamut from nacho appetizers to two-fisted burritos to sizzling fajita plates. Most dishes run $8–15, but the more complex fajitas are priced around $25.

**Kimo's,** 845 Front St., 808/661-4811, is friendly and has great harbor and sunset views on the lower level. If you're in Lahaina around 6 P.M. and need a break, head here to relax with some "Kimo therapy." Popular, but no reservations taken. Kimo's offers seafood from $16.95, with most entrées $15–19 and is known for the catch of the day, usually the best offering on the menu; limited menu for children. Lunch prices are half the dinner prices, and you can get an assortment of *pu pu*, burgers, and sandwiches. Dine upstairs or down. The downstairs bar has top-notch well drinks featuring brand-name liquors. Kimo's is

one of the well-established restaurants in town with a great reputation.

**The Lahaina Fish Company,** 831 Front St., 808/661-3472, open daily from 11 A.M. for lunch and 5–10 P.M. for dinner, buys from local fishermen so the fish is guaranteed fresh. Belly up to the Hammerhead Bar, fashioned from glass and brass, or choose a table that looks directly out onto Lahaina Harbor. Notice the vintage Coca-Cola vending machine and a display of knots that were tied by the old salts who visited Lahaina. The limited lunch/grill menu has sandwiches and other light foods, mostly for under $10. The evening dinner menu starts with dinner salads at $3.99, a fried calamari appetizer at $9.99, or a bowl of fresh seafood chowder for $3.95. Entrées can be island fish and chips at $9.99, fisherman's pasta with fish and vegetables for $12.99, or sautéed sea scallops for $16.99. Meat and poultry dishes include Hawaiian teriyaki chicken for $12.99, luau-style pork ribs for $15.99, or top sirloin steak for $12.99. The fresh fish, of which there might be half a dozen varieties to select from depending on what's caught that day, is grilled and basted, oven broiled, or blackened Cajun style and offered at market price. Every day brings a chef's special.

At 505 Front Street is **Hecock's,** 808/661-8810, open daily 8 A.M.–10 P.M. for food service, bar open until 2 A.M., owned and operated by Tom and Nancy, a husband and wife team who bring good food at reasonable prices. Hecock's breakfast could be ranch eggs with a broiled mahimahi for $8.75 or a three-egg omelet for $6.95, along with the classics like French toast or buttermilk pancakes with the trimmings for under $7. The lunch menu offers a chef salad for $8.95, assorted burgers and sandwiches priced under $9.95. The dinner bill of fare includes fettuccine Alfredo for $16.95, scampi for $24.95, and rack of lamb for $24.95. A children's menu, happy hour, daily specials, and an early-bird special offered 5–6 P.M. help keep prices down.

**Lahaina Coolers,** 808/661-7082, at Dickenson Square, presents quick, easy meals throughout the day in an open-air setting. Try pancakes, omelets, or eggs Benedict for breakfast; salads, sandwiches, and burgers for lunch; and pasta,

MAUI

pizzas, fresh fish, steaks, and burgers for dinner. Few items on the evening menu are over $15.95. Coolers is a casual place, great for late-night revelers who can get food until midnight and drinks until 2 A.M.

**BJ's Chicago Pizzeria**, 808/661-0700, on the second floor overlooking the seawall at 730 Front St., is known throughout the island for its deep-dish pizzas. Various choices, ranging from the ordinary cheese and tomato to shrimp thermador and "the works," run about $10–24. All made to order, they take some time, but everyone agrees they're worth the wait. Along with the pizza are various calzone and pasta dishes, and fine salads. Eat in or take out. BJ's has one of the largest beer selections on the island and live contemporary music every evening.

**Compadres Mexican Bar and Grill**, 808/661-7189, at the Lahaina Cannery Mall, has a full menu ranging from nacho appetizers through soups, salads, and sandwiches to a complete list of entrées, most in the $10–18 range. Sit down, relax, and enjoy your meal and the surroundings, or have a beer or margarita at the spacious long bar.

**Café Sauvage**, 808/661-7600, has an intimate spot in the courtyard at 844 Front Street below Moose McGillycuddy's. Food prepared here has a definite Pacific Rim twist, with such offerings as shrimp cocktail in lemon juice, yellow ginger, toasted coconut, and fresh chilis, Thai chicken roulade, and braised veal shank with saffron risotto. Main entrées run $17–26. Call for reservations.

## Fine Dining

When you feel like putting a major dent in your budget and satisfying your desire for gourmet food, you should be pleased with one of the following.

You won't be a pawn when you walk onto the black-and-white-checkered floor at **Longhi's**, 888 Front St., 808/667-2288, open daily 7:30 A.M.–10 P.M. Longhi owns the joint and he's a character. He feels that his place has healing vibes and that man's basic food is air. Longhi's has been around since 1976, and it's many people's favorite. Prices at Longhi's may seem expensive, but the portions are enormous and can easily fill

two. If you don't want to stuff yourself, ask for a half-order. Mornings you can order frittatas, like spinach, ham, and bacon, eggs Benedict, or lox and bagels. A good lunch choice is pasta Siciliana with calamari, spicy with marinara sauce, a corned beef sandwich, or Greek salad; for dinner, the prawns amaretto and shrimp Longhi are signature dishes, but numerous pasta, meat, and other seafood dishes are on the menu. Dinner entrées generally run $19–30 with pastas somewhat less. Save room for the fabulous desserts or a cooling cocktail. Longhi's is a winner. It's hard not to have a fine meal here, and the wine list is outstanding. There's always a line, reservations accepted, never a dress code, and always complimentary valet parking! Live music is provided only on Friday and Saturday evenings.

After two decades of operating in Kahana, **Erik's Seafood and Sushi** moved into Lahaina and opened anew at the back end of the Old Lahaina Center. The entire staff came with the move, and the superb menu has stayed the same, but there is now the addition of a sushi bar. The new restaurant has kept the decoration in an appropriately nautical theme, with fish tanks, divers' helmets, and mounted trophy fish. Erik's is open weekdays for lunch 11 A.M.–2 P.M. and dinner nightly 5–10 P.M., and a light bar menu is available throughout the afternoon; call 808/662-8780 for reservations. Lunch is a variety of reasonably priced dishes. The early-bird specials, which run at the bargain price of $12.95 and $13.95, are offered 5–6 P.M. Bouillabaisse, cioppino, and seafood curry are among the chef's specialties, but you shouldn't forget to try one of the many appetizers first. Shellfish, lobster, steak, and poultry are on the menu, but the real focus is on the wide variety of fish that can be prepared in numerous ways. Most dinners run $21–30, with all fish quoted at the daily market price. Erik's is known to have the *best* selection of fresh fish on Maui—always more than half a dozen selections nightly. Sushi is created in its own section, but it can also be ordered from the main dining room. This is a quality restaurant with delicious food and excellent service.

**Ruth's Chris Steak House**, 808/661-8815, has captured the attention of those Midwestern corn-fed-beef lovers. If you're wanting a meal of meat and potatoes, this is your place. Entrées run $24–37 and include filet, rib eye, T-bone, and strip steaks, and pork, veal, and lamb chops. A few seafood items also appear on the menu at market price. A semi-formal affair with crystal on the linen-clad tables and a full bar, Ruth's is open for dinner only 5–10 P.M. in the Lahaina Center; reservations are a necessity.

The pacific'O Cafe, 808/667-4341, at 505 Front Street, has garnered a solid reputation. Foods and flavors from the West, the East, and the Pacific are blended together, using only the freshest ingredients from the islands, to create a delectable contemporary Pacific cuisine. Start with a fine Thai coconut seafood chowder for $6.50 or roasted Maui onion and Puna goat cheese salad for $9.50. Lunch entrées, like the seared fish or sautéed prawn pasta, are all reasonable at less than $15. Dinner entrées run $22–29 and might be fish tempura wrapped in wakame, pan-roasted scallops and pork, coconut macadamia nut–crusted fish, or sesame-crusted lamb. Comfortable seating, attentive servers, and the views out over the ocean might tempt you to linger over your meal and savor an excellent bottle of wine. Open daily for lunch 11 A.M.–4 P.M. and dinner 5:30–10 P.M. Dinner runs until 10:30 on Friday and Saturday, when there's live jazz 9 P.M.–midnight.

The i'o restaurant next door, 808/661-8422, is open 5:30–10 P.M. for dinner only; reservations are a must. Like pacific'O, i'o is owned by Chef James McDonald, but unlike its neighbor, i'o is more experimental with its food and the ambiance is more modern. Start your evening with tomato bread, served each night with a different dipping sauce. Appetizers include the "silken purse" steamed wonton, scallops on the half shell, and the signature i'o crab cakes, $8–12. The main entrée might be a luscious crispy ahi, another signature dish, the foie gras–crusted and pan-fried fresh fish, or the wok stir-fried lobster Thai-hitian with mango curry sauce, $23–34. No matter your choice, each dish is artfully inspired and the symphony of flavors, particularly the sauces, compliment one another. If you think you've tried all manner of desserts, order the goat cheese ice cream for a new expe-

rience, or have your meal with one of the many tropical-flavored martinis that the restaurant is known for. Sleek, open, and airy inside, there is also seating outside on the patio where, if you time it right, you can watch the sunset paint the sky in bands of pink and red or the crescent moon rise into the inky night sky.

David Paul's Lahaina Grill, 127 Lahainaluna Rd. under the Lahaina Inn, 808/667-5117, open for dinner nightly 6–10 P.M., is one of Lahaina's finest gourmet restaurants. Here owner David Paul Johnson, famous for his sauces, presents "artwork on a plate." The dining room is quite lovely, with coved and pressed-metal ceilings from which hang punchbowl chandeliers illuminating the starched-white table settings that surround the central bar. With low lighting and soft music, this well-appointed room is meant for a long romantic evening of salubrious relaxation. The professional and friendly servers definitely give you attentive service. The menu is diverse and can be served at the bar as well. Start with a bowl of Maui onion soup for $9, a Kona lobster-crab cake appetizer for $15, or baby romaine Caesar salad for $11. Entrées include David Paul's signature dishes, tequila shrimp and firecracker rice, made from tiger prawns marinated in chili oil, lemons, cilantro, cumin, and brown sugar in a blend of vanilla bean and chili rice for $29, and Kona coffee–roasted rack of lamb for $39, plus others like Maui onion-crusted seared ahi for $38 and kalua duck with a plum sauce reduction for $29. Vegetarians will find at least one meatless entrée on each menu, and other dietary restrictions can be accommodated by the masterful chefs. No matter what is on the changing menu, you can be assured that the ingredients are the freshest available. The very wicked dessert tray, with everything priced $10–12, combined with a cup of rich roasted coffee, ends a wonderful meal.

Gerard's elegant restaurant is in the Plantation Inn, 174 Lahainaluna Rd., 808/661-8939, open daily for dinner only 6–9 P.M., with validated free parking nearby. The epitome of neo-Victorian charm, the room is comfortable with puff-pillow wicker chairs and always set with fine crystal atop starched linen. Fronting the

MAUI

building is a small dining garden, and inside the interior is rich with hardwood floors and oak bar. Chef Gerard Reversade, trained in the finest French culinary tradition since age 14, creates masterpieces. He feels that eating is *the* experience of life, around which everything else that is enjoyable revolves. Gerard insists that the restaurant's servers share his philosophy, so along with the excellent food comes excellent service. The menu changes, but it's always gourmet. Gerard's is not cheap, but it's worth every penny because nothing on the menu is less than excellent. Appetizers range $10.50–24.50, entrées $32.50–42.50, and desserts are $8.50. Some superb salad choices are the island greens with heart of palm, or spinach salad with grilled scallops, shaved reggiano cheese, and balsamic vinaigrette. Appetizers feature mouth-watering choices like shiitake and oyster mushrooms in a puff pastry and duck foie gras. Full entrées like Confit of duck with fingerling potato cakes, venison cutlets with Jamaica pepper and an akala berry port sauce, or roast Hawaiian snapper with star anise and savory titillate the palate. The grilled rack of lamb with mint crust is one of Gerard's superb signature dishes. Even if you possess great self-control, you have less than an even chance of restraining yourself from choosing a luscious dessert like crème brûlée, chocolate mousse in cream puffs with raspberry sabayon, or even fresh strawberries glazed with suzette butter and macadamia nut cream. *C'est bon!*

**Chez Paul,** 808/661-3843, five miles east of Lahaina in Olowalu, is secluded, romantic, very popular, and French—what else! Owner Patrick Callarec emphasizes Provençale regional cuisine with flavors of traditional French cooking. Chez Paul is open nightly 6–9 P.M.; reservations are a must. Local folks who are into elegant dining give it two thumbs up. The wine list is tops, the desserts fantastic, and the food *magnifique!* Start with luscious hors d'oeuvres like chilled leek and potato soup with chives or oven-roasted eggplant and tomatoes, or a warm appetizer such as Borgogne escargot in their shells or wild mushroom and brie cheese baked in a puff pasty, all priced $10–26. Salads lead to delightful entrées, which might be fresh island fish poached in

champagne, bouillabaisse, filet mignon in caviar sauce, boneless crispy duck with tropical fruits and pineapple sauce bigarade, or herbed veal loin, all priced $30–45. If you have room after such a feast, try one of the fine desserts. Hot and runny chocolate cake is a favorite, but pineapple and vanilla crème brûlée in a pineapple shell or ice cream soufflé with mandarin liquor flavor will do as well. This is fine dining at its best. Chez Paul is definitely worth the trip from Lahaina, with a short stroll along the beach recommended as a perfect aperitif.

# ENTERTAINMENT

Lahaina is one of those places where the real entertainment is the town itself. The best thing to do here is to stroll along Front Street and people-watch. As you walk along, it feels like a block party with the action going on all around you—as it does on Halloween. Some people duck into one of the many establishments along Front Street for a breather, a drink, or just to watch the sunset. It's all free, enjoyable, and safe.

## Art Night

Friday night is Art Night in Lahaina. In keeping with its status as the cultural center of Maui, Lahaina opens the doors of its galleries 7–10 P.M., throws out the welcome mat, sets out food and drink, provides entertainment, and usually hosts a well-known artist or two for this weekly party. It's a fine social get-together where the emphasis is on gathering people together to appreciate the arts and not necessarily on making sales. Take your time and stroll Front Street from one gallery to the next. Stop and chat with shopkeepers, munch the goodies, sip the wine, look at the pieces on display, corner the featured artist for comment on his or her work, soak in the music of the strolling musicians, and strike up a conversation with the person next to you who is eyeing that same piece of art with the same respect and admiration. It's a party. People dress up, but don't be afraid to come casually. Take your time and immerse yourself in the immense variety and high quality of art on display in Lahaina.

## Halloween

This is one of the big events of the year. As many as 30,000 people head to town for the night. It seems that everyone dresses in costume, strolls Front Street, parties around town, and gets into the spirit of the evening. It's a party in the street with throngs of people, dancing, live music, swirling color, a costume contest at the banyan tree, an arts festival, and other activities that include a haunted house, a clown show, and *keiki* parade for the little ones. For the adults, the parade goes on all evening. Halloween in Lahaina has become so popular with some revelers that they fly in from Honolulu just for the night. To accommodate the fun, Front Street is closed to traffic from the Banyan Tree all the way past the Lahaina Center from midafternoon until past midnight.

## Fourth of July

There is some musical entertainment and other special activities to celebrate this occasion, but the biggest excitement is created by the fireworks celebration out over the Lahaina Roads, with its multicolor puffballs, showers of streaming light, and blazing rocket trails. This is the best show on the island and can be seen for miles. Plenty of people crowd into town, sit along the seawall, or stop along the roadways to have an up-close look at the color show. On this day, it may be difficult to get to Lahaina if you're not staying there or haven't arrived by midafternoon, and parking can be a struggle or simply unattainable.

## Nightspots and Dancing

All of the evening musical entertainment in Lahaina is in restaurants and lounges, except for the acclaimed Old Lahaina Lu'au and The Feast at Lele.

You, too, can be a disco king or queen on **Longhi's** black-and-white chessboard dance floor every weekend. Longhi's has live music on Friday and Saturday nights featuring island groups.

**Moose McGillycuddy's** (just listen for the loud music on Front Street) is still a happening place with occasional music, although it's becoming more of a cruise joint for post-adolescents. Those who have been around Lahaina for a while usually give it a miss, but if you want to get your groove on with a younger crowd, this place is for you.

The open-air **Cheeseburger in Paradise** rocks with live music nightly until 11 P.M. There's no cover charge, and you can sit upstairs or down listening to the tunes.

Similarly, you can hear live soft rock during dinner at the **Whale's Tail Bar and Grill** at the Wharf Cinema Center across from the banyan tree, at **BJ's Chicago Pizzeria** overlooking the water, and at the **Pioneer Inn Grill and Bar** at the Pioneer Inn. Live jazz happens every Thursday–Saturday evening at **pacific'O** restaurant at 505 Front Street Mall.

**Maui Brews** not only has a long bar—up to 16 beers on tap, half from Hawaii—a restaurant serving breakfast, lunch, and dinner, and a game room, but the back room becomes a nightclub with loud music, colored lights, and plenty of people. There's music and dancing nightly until 2 A.M., and this seems to be the most happening place in town. Music ranges from rock to techno to reggae, and while a DJ sets the stage most evenings, there are live acts on Fridays and occasionally on other nights.

## Theater Shows

Lahaina is lucky to have two theater shows: one large, the other more intimate. Performed at the 700-seat Maui Theatre with its thrust stage and amphitheater seating is 'Ulalena, a 1.5-hour historical review, cultural journey, and tale of legend and myth that is in essence the story of the Hawaiian people. While the content is thoroughly Hawaiian, it's told in a manner that's modern and Western—and that's part of its magic. Colorful, captivating, and imaginative, it is full of fun visuals, dramatic dance, and superbly moving music. This is a show not to be missed. Tickets run $48 standard, $58 for preferred seating in the middle, and $68 for premium seats, a cocktail, and backstage pass; $28, $38, and $48, respectively for kids. Showtimes are 6 P.M. and 8:30 P.M. Tuesdays and 6 P.M. Wednesday–Saturday. The Maui Theatre is located at 878 Front Street, in the Old Lahaina Center; call 808/661-9913 for information and reservations or see the website: www.mauitheatre.com.

**Warren and Annabelle's** is a slight-of-hand, up-close magic show that's performed in a 78-seat theater at 900 Front Street, upstairs at the Lahaina Center. Before the show, guests gather in the theater's cocktail lounge for gourmet appetizers and drinks to be serenaded on piano by Annabelle, a 19th-century resident "ghost." Anyone who loves magic will be thrilled by this show, and it's particularly captivating because it all happens just a few feet from where you're sitting. You'll leave wondering, "How did he do that?" This show is open to those 21 years of age and older. Tickets for the show run $40 per person, and shows are performed every evening Monday–Saturday. Packages with various drinks and appetizers included are also available. Call 808/667-6244 for information and reservations.

## Lu'au

Lahaina has two of the best dinner shows anywhere on the island. The **Old Lahaina Lu'au** is the most authentic lu'au on the island, and the all-you-can-eat buffet and all-you-can-drink bar has a well-deserved reputation. Located on the beach near the Lahaina Cannery Mall, it is the only lu'au on the island not associated with a hotel. Seating is daily at 6 P.M. (from 5:30 P.M. in winter), but because it's so popular, be sure to reserve tickets several days in advance, perhaps two weeks in advance during peak season; 808/667-1998. Tickets are $79 adults, $49 children 2–12.

The **Feast at Lele** combines food and entertainment. While not a lu'au per se, the five-course meal is masterfully coordinated with music and dance from the islands of Hawaii, Tonga, Tahiti, and Samoa. Reservations are a must; 808/667-5353. The dinner and show runs $95 adults, $65 children, daily 6–9 P.M. (from 5:30 in winter) on the beach at the 505 Front Street Mall.

## Cinemas

**Lahaina Cinemas,** once the only multiplex theater on West Maui, is located on the third floor of the Wharf Cinema Center. Showing only first-run features, movies start at about noon and run throughout the day. Adults $7.25, kids 2–11 $4.25, seniors $4.75; all seats $4 until 5 P.M. Lahaina's second cinema is **Front Street Theaters.** Located at the Lahaina Center, this four-screen theater charges $7.25 adults, $4.25 kids, and $4.75 matinee. Call 808/249-2222 for what's showing at either theater.

**The Hawaii Experience Domed Theater,** 824 Front St., 808/661-8314, has continuous showings on the hour daily 10 A.M.–9 P.M. (40-minute duration); $6.95 adults, $3.95 children 4–12. The idea is to give you a total sensory experience by means of the giant, specially designed concave screen. You sit surrounded by it. You will tour the islands as if you were sitting in a helicopter or diving below the waves. And you'll be amazed at how well the illusion works. If you can't afford to fly through Kaua'i's Waimea Canyon, dive with the humpback whales, watch the sunrise over Haleakala, or view the power of an oozing volcano, this is about as close as you can get. A second film on a different subject is sometimes offered during the day. For both shows, tickets run $11.90 and $5.90, respectively. The lobby of the theater doubles as a gift shop where you can pick up souvenirs such as carved whales, T-shirts, and a variety of inexpensive mementos.

## Hula and Polynesian Shows

For a different type of entertainment, stop to see the free *keiki* hula shows, Wednesdays at 2:30 P.M. and Fridays at 6 P.M., at Hale Kahiko in the parking lot of the Lahaina Center. Various singers also perform on Tuesdays and Thursdays around sunset. Hale Kahiko is a reproduction Hawaiian village displaying implements and items of everyday use; open daily 9 A.M.–6 P.M.

Various weekly shows are also offered at center stage at the Lahaina Cannery Mall. Tuesdays and Thursdays at 7 P.M. there's a free Polynesian show, and a *keiki* hula show is presented Saturdays and Sundays 1–2 P.M.

# RECREATION

Lahaina is a center particularly for ocean-based activities on Maui. For further details on activity providers, see the Sports and Recreation section in the On the Road chapter.

**Snorkel Bob's,** at 1217 Front St. near the Mala Wharf, 808/661-4421, rents snorkel gear for $15 per week (daily rental also), which you can take to a neighboring island and return there for a small extra fee. Boogie boards are available at $13 per day or $26 per week, and Snorkel Bob's advice, whether you need it or not, is plentiful and free. Open 8 A.M.–5 P.M. daily, Snorkel Bob's can also fix you up with virtually any activity on the island through their activity desk.

Across from the banyan tree is **Duke's Rental Shop,** where snorkel gear runs $3 per day. Ordinary surfboards and longboards go for anywhere from $7 for two hours to $20. Water equipment are not the only items you can rent here; look also for cruiser bikes from $10 per day, golf clubs from $15, and a whole assortment of other items.

**West Maui Cycles,** at the Lahaina Square Shopping Center below Denny's Restaurant, 808/661-9005, rents snorkel gear, surfboards, and boogie boards, but its big thing is the sale, service, and rental of road and mountain bicycles. Mountain bikes run $30–40 per day, depending on the quality. Also available are cruisers at $15, road bikes at $30, and tandems at $55–65, car racks extra. Weekly rates are available. All bike rentals come with a helmet, pump, tool kit, and lock. Stop here for all of your cycling needs on West Maui.

**West Maui Sports,** 808/661-6252, rents snorkel gear for $2.50–10 per day or $10–35 per week. Boogieboards are $20 per day or $75 per week, single kayaks $35 per day and $120 per week, tandem kayaks $50 per day or $150 per week. If you haven't brought them from home, beach chairs, coolers, umbrellas, other beach gear, fishing poles, and golf clubs can also be rented. Look for them behind Lahaina Cannery Mall next to Aloha Mixed Plate.

## Activity Companies

Companies that can set you up with almost any activity offered on the island include the following: **Tom Barefoot's Cashback Tours,** 834 Front St., 808/661-8889 or 888/222-3601, www.tombare-foot.com, is a one-shop business that has a great handle on all types of tourist activities on Maui and throughout the state. They reduce the fee for activities by 10 percent for those who pay in cash or traveler's checks and a 7 percent discount is given for payment by credit card. You can also explore information and book activities before you come to town. This company has been around for more than 25 years and is a leader in the business.

The purveyor with the largest number of activity booths around the island (over a dozen—mostly at condo resorts and shopping centers) is **Activity World,** 808/667-7777 or 800/624-7771, www.hawaiiactivityworld.com. In Lahaina, look for them at 910 Honoapiʻilani Highway, the Wharf Cinema Center, Lahaina Shores, and Maui Islander. **Activity Mart,** 808/667-6278 or 800/450-7736, www.activitymart.com, has an office at 624 Front Street and another at the Lahaina Cannery Mall. **Activity Warehouse,** 808/667-4000 or 800/343-2087, www.travel-hawaii.com, across from Kamehameha III School along Front St., can also set up your activity schedule. The **Lahaina Ticket Company,** 764 Front St. at the Pioneer Inn shops, 808/662-3430, can also arrange activities for you. For purely ocean activities, try the **Pier 1** booth at Lahaina Harbor, 808/667-0680.

A few of these companies and others not mentioned greatly discount their activities, but there is a trade-off. Usually, in order to get this vastly reduced fare for an activity, you must attend a time-share presentation and sit through the hard sell that follows. If you are interested in buying into a time-share property anyway, getting cheap tickets in the process may not be a bad idea. However, most people just give it a miss because they have better things to do on their vacations than be bombarded by high-pressure salespeople.

## The Sugar Cane Train

The old steam engine puffs along from Lahaina to Puʻukoliʻi Depot in Kaʻanapali pulling old-style open-air passenger cars through cane fields and the Kaʻanapali golf course. The six miles of narrow-gauge track are covered in 25 minutes (each way), and the cost round-trip is $15.95

ROBERT NILSEN

The cane is now gone, but a ride on the Sugar Cane Train still evokes images of the muscled farming economy that once dominated this coast.

adults, $9.95 children 3–12. The train runs throughout the day 10:15 A.M.–4 P.M. It's very popular, so book in advance—more than 400,000 people ride the train every year. All rides are narrated and the conductor even sings. It's not just great fun for children; everybody has a good time. On Tuesdays and Thursdays, the dinner train leaves Pu'ukoli'i Depot at 5 P.M. for a sunset ride, followed by a paniolo barbecue dinner at the Ka'anapali Depot; $65 adults, $39 kids. All kinds of combination tours with other activity vendors are offered as well; they're tame, touristy, and fun. Contact the Lahaina Kaanapali and Pacific Railroad at 808/667-6851 or 800/499-2307; www.sugarcanetrain.com.

## Hiking Trail

The **Lahaina Pali Trail** is a Na Ala Hele (Hawaii Trail and Access System) trail. Five miles in length, it starts near mile marker 11, about one-half mile west of the Lahaina Tunnel. Following an old established trail, it crosses the Kealaloloa Ridge at 1,600 feet and then descends to an access road that meets the highway near the junction of Highways 30 and 380. Starting at nearly sea level, you have a steady but not steep climb, yet overall you might consider this a rigorous climb. The trail passes in and out of several small and one deeper gulch, the largest of which is Malalowai'ole Gulch. This trail is hot and dry, with no shade, so bring plenty of water and wear a hat and sturdy hiking shoes because it's fairly rocky. If you're lucky, there will be some breeze blowing up the hill. On the way you might see cattle in the upland pastures or *nene* hiding in the grass near the trail. Near the halfway point, the trail flattens out as it rounds the bend of the hill, and for a short way it follows a Department of Land and Natural Resources (DLNR) road before it zigzags down the east slope to the Ma'alaea side trailhead. If starting from the east side, park about 100 yards south of the turnoff to Kahului and walk about one-half mile in from the highway to the trailhead. Expect a hike of at least three hours one way. Several markers along the way indicate cultural and historical sites. If you're interested in more than just a hike, pick up a copy of the *Tales From the Trail: Maui History and Lore From the Lahaina Pali Trail: A Trail Guide* brochure put out by the DLNR, Division of Forestry and Wildlife, and available at their office in the state office building in Wailuku.

# SHOPPING

Once learned, everybody loves to do the "Lahaina Stroll." It's easy. Just act cool, nonchalant, and give it your best strut as you walk the gauntlet of Front Street's exclusive shops and boutiques. The fun is just in being there. If you begin in the evening, go to the south end of town and park down by Prison Street; it's much easier to find a spot and you walk uptown, catching the sunset.

## The Lahaina Stroll

On Prison Street, check out **Dan's Green House,** 808/661-8412, open daily 9 A.M.–5 P.M., specializing in *fuku-bonsai,* miniature plants originated by David Fukumoto. They're mailable (except to Australia and Japan), and when you get them home, just plop them in water and presto . . . a great little plant; from $26. Dan's also specializes in exotic birds like African gray parrots, macaws from Australia, common cockatoos, and various cheeky parrots, and has a few other miniature animals. Dan's is a great place to browse, especially for families.

Near the corner is **Mermaid's Dowry,** 113 Prison St., 808/662-3697, a small antique shop that has an amazingly diverse collection for the space—all collected by the owner (open Wed.–Sun. 9 A.M.–5 P.M.).

As you head up Front Street, the first group of shops includes **Activity Warehouse** and **Duke's Rental Shop,** where you can rent everything from snorkel gear and surfboards to cruiser bikes and golf clubs. Visit the "pin and ink" artist upstairs at **Skin Deep Tattooing,** 626 Front St., 808/661-8531, open daily 10 A.M.–10 P.M., until 6 P.M. Sunday, where you can get a permanent memento of your trip to Maui. Skin Deep features "new-age primal, tribal tattoos," Japanese-style intricate beauties, with women artists available for shy female clientele. The walls are hung with sample tattoos you can choose from. A sobriety test is necessary to get tattooed. No wimps allowed! This is a legitimate place where

the artists know what they're doing; they've been in business now for more than 20 years.

Up a ways are **Camellia** with a treasure chest laden with gifts and jewelry made from gold, silver, and ivory, and **Original Maui Divers,** which has some fancy jewelry including its specialty, black tree coral. Around the side are the **Aloha Toy Store,** with its motorcycle rentals, and **Swiss Cafe,** which offers early morning coffee and breakfast and other goodies during the day.

## Moving Down the Line

The following shops are all located along Front Street. By no means exhaustive, this list just gives you an idea of some of the unique shops here.

Between the Pioneer Inn and the seawall, walk onto the sandy floor of the Polynesian-style **Gecko Store,** where all of the items, including shorts, T-shirts, bathing suits, and sweatshirts, bear the bug-eyed sucker-footed logo of Hawaii's famous clicking geckos. Next door is the **Lahaina Hat Co.,** where you can find the perfect chapeau to shield your head from the "merciless" Lahaina sun; and at **Maui Mercantile** you can find all sorts of clothing fit for the sun.

**Golden Reef,** 695 Front St., is open daily 10 A.M.–10 P.M. Inside is all manner of jewelry from heirloom quality to costume baubles made from black, gold, red, and pink coral, malachite, lapis, and mother of pearl. All designs are created on the premises. Everyone will be happy shopping here because prices range from $1–1,000 and more. Contrast these gems with **Bijoux Pour Vous** heirloom Hawaiian jewelry only a few steps away.

Noah himself would have been impressed with the **Endangered Species Store,** open daily 9 A.M.–10:30 P.M., where a lifesize mountain gorilla, coiled python, flitting butterflies, and fluttering birds bid you welcome to this lovely jam-packed menagerie. The shelves hold world globes, maps, cuddly panda bears, posters of trumpeting elephants, sculptures of soaring eagles, parlor games, postcards, and memento flora- and fauna-inspired T-shirts of 100 percent cotton designed by local artists. A percentage of the profits from every purchase is set aside to advance environmental issues. Moreover, the store tries to deal with vendors who also contribute to the well-being of endangered species and the environment.

Back on the mountain side of the street, **Tropical Blues,** 754 Front, presents fine aloha shirts and women's alohawear. Next door at 752 Front, one of the four **Serendipity** shops on the island offers a unique collection of casual islandwear, furniture, wood carvings, and accouterments of an Asian and Hawaiian nature. In this stretch you will also find **Island Woodcarving** gallery, a prefect spot to choose a hand-carved art piece done in an island wood in a Hawaiian style, and both an **ABC Discount Store** and **E-Z Discount** for sundries, gifts, snacks, and liquor.

The **Whaler's Locker,** 780 Front St., 808/661-3775, open 9 A.M.–10 P.M., is a sea chest filled with hand-engraved scrimshaw on fossilized walrus and mammoth ivory. Lahaina, historically a premier whaling port, has long been known for this sailor's art etched on everything from pocket knives to whale-tooth pendants. Display cases also hold gold and amber jewelry, Ni'ihau shellwork, Japanese *netsuke,* shark's teeth, and even some coral necklaces. If you are looking for a distinctive folk-art gift that truly says Maui, the Whaler's Locker is an excellent store from which to make your choice. The 780 Front Street building is the second oldest shop in modern Lahaina, dating back to 1871.

Sharing the same address is **The South Seas Trading Post,** open daily 8:30 A.M.–10 P.M. It has artifacts from the South Pacific, like tapa cloth from Tonga, but also colorful rugs from India, primitive carvings from Papua New Guinea, and Burmese *kalaga* wall hangings with their beautiful and intricate stitching, jade from China, and bronze from Tibet. You can pick up a one-of-a-kind bead necklace for only a few dollars or a real treasure that would adorn any home, for a decent price. Both antiques and reproductions are sold; the bona fide antiques have authenticating dates on the back or bottom sides.

In the courtyard just off Front Street and Lahainaluna Road is **The Lahaina Market Place,** a collection of semi-open-air stalls and a handful of storefronts, open daily 9 A.M.–9 P.M. Some vendors have roll-up stands and sell trinkets and

baubles. Some is junk, but it's neat junk, and they all compete for your business. A mainstay of this alleyway market, **Maui Crystal** has fine examples of handmade glass sculpture and some crystals that are not made on premises. Pyrex and softer colored glass is used to form these creations, an activity you can watch through the glass windows of the small workshop. Two art galleries, facing Lahainaluna Road, back up against this courtyard.

## The Far End

On both sides of Front Street beyond Lahainaluna Road, the shops continue. In the Old Poi Factory, 819 Front St., is **David's of Hawaii.** The "sexually incorrect" will love David's, where you can find all kinds of lewd postcards, T-shirts, and souvenirs. If T-shirts bearing sexually implicit puns offend you, keep strolling—it's nasty in there. Funky and audacious. Open daily 9 A.M.–10:30 P.M. This little nook also has jewelry and gift shops.

The **Old Lahaina Book Emporium,** 808/661-1399, the best used bookstore on this side of the island, is crammed full of hardcover and paperback books, just right for a poolside read or serious study. Down the valley at 834 Front Street, this shop also has some new books and new and used CDs, with trades welcome; open Mon.–Sat. 10 A.M.–9 P.M. and Sunday until 6 P.M.

Scrimshaw is the art of carving and/or coloring ivory. Whaling and nautical scenes are perhaps the most common, but other designs are also found. **Lahaina Scrimshaw,** 845 Front St. (across from Wo Hing temple), 808/661-8820, open daily 9 A.M.–10 P.M., boasts its own master scrimshander who works in the window every day from about 7:30 A.M.–noon, and who is willing to answer questions about this seaman's art. Most of the scrimshaw is done on antique whale's teeth from the whaling era or on fossilized walrus and mastodon tusks. The scrimshaw offered is authentic and made by about 40 artists, most of whom are from Hawaii.

**Elephant Walk** is a gift and clothing store that's fairly representative of others you'll find along Front Street, and the prices are good. **Crazy Shirts** also has a great assortment of distinctive T-shirts and other clothes. Also in this store at 865 Front Street is the tiny but intriguing display of antiques, nautical instruments, scrimshaw, and whaling-related pictures.

Across the street is **The Whaler** for mostly new marine and nautical objects and some art glass. At the **Sunglass Hut** shop, you can pick up shades for the strong tropical sun. Depending on the type, these sunglasses run $40–350. Also available are a wide range of watches—waterproof and not—some economical and others that will bust your budget.

## Off the Main Drag

**Fox Camera,** 139 Lahainaluna Rd., 808/667-6255, open daily, is a full-service, one-hour-developing camera store. It's good in West Maui for any specialized photo needs. A second one-hour lab is down the street and around the corner at 820 Front Street. Technicians here can do some camera repair or arrange to have it done.

Even if you haven't been out on a whale-watching tour, stop in at the Pacific Whale Foundation's **Ocean Store,** 143 Dickenson St., 808/667-7447, for a look at all the clothing, posters, jewelry, and gift items relating to the whale and other sea creatures. It's almost an education having a look here, and the proceeds help support this worthy organization.

The **Salvation Army Thrift Shop,** on Shaw St. just up from Front St., has the usual collection of inexpensive used goods but occasionally some great buys on older aloha shirts. Open Monday–Saturday, regular business hours.

## 505 Front Street

With most shops open daily 9 A.M.–9 P.M., this mall offers a barrel full of shops and restaurants at the south end of Front Street, away from the heavy foot traffic. The complex looks like a New England harbor village, and the shopping is good and unhurried with validated underground parking for customers. Some shops include a **Whalers General Store** for sundries; **Foreign Intrigue Imports; Maui to Go** for arts and crafts; **Colors of Maui Clothing;** and the wonderful **Elizabeth Doyle Gallery,** which has a superb collection of art glass, ceramics, and paintings—some island artists.

Check your email at **Ali'i Espresso Cafe** as you linger over a snack and coffee. Rates are $.20 cents per minute, $6 per half-hour, or $12 per hour; printouts are extra. Several other shops inhabit this mall, as do half a dozen restaurants.

## The Wharf Cinema Center

The Wharf Cinema Center at 658 Front offers three floors of fast-food eateries, clothing and jewelry stores, souvenir shops, and a movie theater. Most shops are open 9 A.M.–9 P.M. Playing first-run movies, the triplex **Lahaina Cinemas** occupies much of the third floor. Browse **Crazy Shirts** with its excellent selection of quality T-shirts or the **Red Dirt Shirt** shop for distinct T's from Kaua'i. **Hawaiian Styles and Creations** offers tropical sportswear, and **Island Swimwear** carries bathing suits for men and women. For a ready-made bed covering or cloth to sew your own tropical dress, head for **Quilts 'N Fabric Land,** and if a take-home souvenir is what you're after, look at **A Piece of Maui Gallery and Gifts.**

**Island Coins and Stamps** on the third floor is a shop as frayed as an old photo album. It specializes in philatelic supplies. Also on the third floor is the **Atlantis submarine** office, where you can arrange a memorable underwater Maui adventure. If all of this shopping gets you down, sit and relax at **Maui Island Coffee** or have a bite to eat at **The Blue Lagoon** in the central courtyard. For postal needs and gifts, stop by the **Lahaina Mail Depot** on the lower level at the rear; open weekdays 10 A.M.–4:30 P.M., Saturday until 1 P.M. Across the walk is **Island Sandals,** 808/661-5110, a small shop run in the honest old-style way that produces fully adjustable leather tie sandals, styled from the days of Solomon. As the gregarious sandal maker says, he creates the right sandal for $155 ($135 women's) and gives you the left as a gift. Stop in and have him trace your feet for an order. As he works, he'll readily talk about political, social, or local island issues, and definitely tell you why it's much better to have leather on the bottom of your feet than any man-made material. See his work at www.islandsandals.com. Out front is an **ABC Discount Store.** For those coming from Ka'anapali, the West Maui Shopping Express stops at the rear of this complex.

MAUI

## Pioneer Inn Shops

Below Pioneer Inn is a clutch of shops that includes **Products of Hawaii Too** for gift and craft items; a **Lifestyle** alohawear clothing shop; and a **Whalers General Store.** Several other clothing stores are here, as are **Trouvaille Gallery** for jewelry, gifts, and artwork, **Maui Divers** for unique jewelry made from the harvest of the sea, and **Häagen-Dazs** for ice cream treats. Most shops are open 9 A.M.–9 P.M.

On the sidewalk in front of these shops is a stand where you can get your picture taken with a multicolored macaw on your shoulder (or with one on each shoulder and one sitting on your head!). Taken one day, the photos are ready the next day. The fee ranges upward from $20, depending on the number and size of your photographs.

## Old Lahaina Center

The Old Lahaina Center, in front of the midtown post office and between Front and Waine'e streets, has an **Ace Hardware,** a new **Foodland,** the **Lahaina Ticket Company,** and a **Starbuck's Coffee** shop. In the midst of this complex is the **Maui Theatre,** where the 'Ulalena theater show is performed, while along Papalaua Avenue are **Bank of Hawaii** and **American Savings Bank** branches. In the portion closest to Waine'e Street, you'll find **Nagasako General Store, Lahaina Pharmacy, Lahaina Fishing Supplies** for fishing gear and marine hardware, and **Ji Mi's Asian Food Mart.**

Across Waine'e Street is the **Lahaina Square Shopping Center,** with its several inexpensive eateries, **West Maui Cycles,** and **Gold's Gym.** You'll find an Activity Warehouse center and additional eateries next door at the small **Anchor Square** center.

## The Lahaina Center

Lahaina's newest shopping center is at the corner of Front and Papalaua streets at the north edge of downtown. The signature establishments of this mall are the **Hard Rock Cafe,** filled with memorabilia of rock-and-roll greats and serving American standards and cold beer; a **Banana Republic** for livable fashions; and **Hilo Hattie** for Hawai-

ian clothing and gifts. In the center you will also find **Local Motion,** a hip clothing store selling tank tops, swimwear, and locally designed T-shirts; **Wet Seal** for young women's clothing; several other fashion shops; an **ABC Discount Store** for sundries and inexpensive beach gear; a **Dive Maui** outlet for water activities and equipment; **Diamond Head Gallery** and **Pictures Plus** for art; and several activity companies. You can also cool down at the long bar at **Maui Brews,** have a meal at the restaurant, spend some extra change in the game room, or come in the evening for music and dancing at their nightclub. For finer food, try **Ruth's Chris Steak House** and follow that with an evening of magic at **Warren and Annabelle's.** Lahaina's second cinema complex, the **Front Street Theaters,** occupies one of the center buildings. There is a pay parking lot here that's free with validation. The Holo Ka'a shuttle stops at the Hilo Hattie store more than 10 times per day on its route between Lahaina and Ka'anapali; $1 per person each way.

After shopping, stop by **Hale Kahiko** and have a look at the traditional-style Hawaiian buildings and items of everyday use displayed as a cultural showcase in a landscaped enclosure to the side of the parking lot. Open daily 9 A.M.–6 P.M. While here enjoy the *keiki* hula shows at 2:30 P.M. on Wednesdays and 6 P.M. on Fridays.

## Lahaina Cannery Mall

As practical looking as its name on the outside—it is a converted pineapple cannery, after all—the center's bright, well-appointed, and air-conditioned interior features some of the best and most convenient shopping on West Maui; open daily 9:30 A.M.–9 P.M. The mall is located at 1221 Honoapi'ilani Highway, near Mala Wharf. If you'll be staying at a condo and doing your own cooking, the largest and generally least expensive supermarket on West Maui is **Safeway,** open daily 24 hours. To book any activities, from a whale-watch to a dinner cruise, you'll find **Activity Mart** offering the right price. Sundries can be picked up at the **ABC Discount Store,** and you can beat the sun's glare by stopping into **Shades of Hawaii.** Some of the clothing shops you'll find here are **Crazy Shirts, Maui WaterWear, Escape to Maui,**

**Panama Jacks,** and **Blue Ginger Designs.** Food is available at **Compadres Mexican Bar and Grill,** as well as half a dozen smaller stalls for international food in the food court.

**Waldenbooks** has one of its excellent, well-stocked stores in the mall. One of the most unusual shops is **The Kite Fantasy,** featuring kites, windsocks, and toys for kids of all ages. You can buy kites like a six-foot flexifoil for more than $100 or a simple triangular plastic kite for only a few bucks. Cloth kites are made from nylon with nice designs for a reasonable $15.95. Another unique shop, well worth the effort to explore, is **Na Mea Hawai'i Store.** This unique shop carries only native Hawaiian arts and crafts, block prints, clothing, printed fabric, tapa fabric, feather and shell lei, and food items, as well as a good selection of local music and books on Hawaiian subjects. This is the real thing. You won't find tourist junk or imported goods here. Open daily 10 A.M.–7 P.M., stop in for an authentic gift from the island. Along the same lines, **Totally Hawaiian Gift Gallery** carries quilts, carved bowls, shellwork, woodwork, and other fine gift items.

If you're into designer coffees and cigars, come to **Sir Wilfred's.** It's one of the few places on this side of the island for such delicacies. If you're hungry, try the deli case for pastries and the like, or order a cup of soup, quiche, lasagna, or a sandwich. A good assortment of gift items round out what's sold here. **Longs Drugs** is one of the cheapest places to buy and develop film. You can also find a selection of everything from aspirin to boogie boards. There's plenty of free parking at this mall, but the Holo Ka'a shopping shuttle stops here a dozen times a day shuttling between Lahaina and Ka'anapali; $1 per person each way or $2 for a trip all the way from Kapalua.

Booths are set up in the mall Monday–Friday 10 A.M.–4 P.M., displaying and selling Hawaiian art and crafts. Also, a free **Polynesian Show** is presented every Tuesday and Thursday evening 7–8 P.M., and there's a **Keiki Hula Show** every Saturday and Sunday 1–2 P.M.

## Arts

Dubbed the "Art Capital of the Pacific," it's said that Lahaina is the world's third-largest art mar-

ket. Who determined that to be so is a question unanswered, yet it is certain that you can view countless works of art here and spend a fortune acquiring it. Many artists on display at the galleries in Lahaina are local island artists and others from the state, although other Americans and numerous foreigners are also represented. Although not all, many of the galleries in town are open until 10 P.M.

The Lahaina Arts Society has its **Old Jail Gallery** in the basement of the Old Lahaina Courthouse and its **Banyan Tree Gallery** on the first floor. Both are open daily 9 A.M.–5 P.M. The Lahaina Arts Society is a nonprofit venture, and all artworks hung in its galleries are juried pieces of its 175 members, all island residents. You can get some good bargains here. Contact the Lahaina Arts Society at 808/661-0111 for information. Every other Saturday and Sunday 8 A.M.–5 P.M., society members display and sell their art at **Banyan Tree Craft Fair,** under the big banyan behind the courthouse. On alternate weekends, other artists and craftspeople display their wares at the same location at the **Na Kupuna O Maui He U'i Cultural Arts Festival.** Sometimes you'll get demonstrations and music to boot. Many of the artists here are up and coming, and the prices for sometimes remarkable works are reasonable. They're trying to make a living by their skills, and most are not displayed at the well-known galleries in town.

**The Village Galleries,** with two locations open daily 9 A.M.–9 P.M. at 120 Dickenson St., 808/661-4402, and at 180 Dickenson St., 808/661-5559, were founded by Lynn Shue in 1970 and are among the oldest continuous galleries featuring original works of Maui artists. At the original gallery at 120 Dickenson, enter to find everything from raku pottery to hand-blown glass and sculptures done in both wood and metal. Some of the accomplished painters on display are George Allan, who works in oils; Joyce Clark, another oil painter noted for her seascapes; Betty Hay-Freeland, a landscape artist; Fred KenKnight, who uses watercolors to depict island scenes; and Lowell Mapes, who also uses oil to render familiar landmarks and island scenes. The galleries also have inexpensive items like

**M**

**MAUI**

postcards, posters, and limited-edition prints, all perfect as mementos and souvenirs. The gallery at 180 Dickenson features more contemporary and abstract works.

With several shops around the islands, **Dolphin Galleries,** 697 Front St., 808/661-5000, has a wide collection of internationally known artists, many from Hawaii. One of the most unusual is the teenage sensation Alexandra Nechita, who produces abstract impressionist pieces not unlike Picasso.

**The Wyland Gallery,** 711 Front St., 808/667-2285, showcases the works of Wyland, renowned worldwide for his "whaling wall" murals of cavorting whales. Wyland's visionary oil and watercolor paintings of marvelous aquatic scenes adorn the walls, while his compassionate bronze renderings of whales and dolphins sing their soul songs from white pedestals. Other featured paintings are done by Al Hogue, William DeShazo, Neolito, Steven Power, and John Pitre. Also displayed are the organic sculptures of Dale Joseph Evers, a pioneer in functional furnishings, who has turned bronze and acrylic into dolphin-shaped tables. A second Wyland Gallery, 136 Dickenson St., 808/661-0590, vibrates with fantastic colors and images. Galleries are open 9 A.M.–9 P.M. daily.

The two **Galerie Lassen,** 700 and 844 Front St., 808/661-1101 and 808/667-7707, showcase original and limited-edition prints by Christian Riese Lassen, who boldly applies striking colors to bring to life his landscapes and two-worlds perspective of sea and earth. Complementing the exaggerated hues of Lassen's mystical works is the subtle patina of Richard Steirs' cast-iron sculptures of supple whales and dolphins. Mr. Steirs, an Upcountry resident, is among the most admired sculptors on Maui with his limited-edition castings.

After many successful years in Kula, Curtis Cost has opened a second gallery, the **Curtis Wilson Cost Gallery,** 808/661-4140, at 710 Front Street. All works on display are by Cost, and his style is one of realism, portraying bucolic country scenes in rich colors with strong greens.

Displaying only contemporary oil paintings is the **Elizabeth Edwards Fine Art** gallery, 808/667-6711, at 716 Front Street. **The La-** **haina Galleries,** 728 Front St., 808/667-2152, is one of the oldest galleries on the island. The gallery, with a central room and two in the rear, is hung with the works of Dario Campanile, Lau Chun, Guy Buffet, Aldo Luongo, and other widely acclaimed painters, and the mesmerizing acrylic sculptures of Frederick Hart. Branch galleries are located at the Kapalua Shops in Kapalua and at The Shops at Wailea.

At **Celebrities** gallery, 764 Front St., 808/667-0727, you can find paintings, drawings, photographs, and other artworks by well-known personalities who are generally not known for their artwork. Some of those whose works are shown include Bob Dylan, John Lennon, Tony Bennett, Anthony Quinn, and David Bowie. Surprisingly, much of it is reasonably good. Stop in for a look.

**Robert Lynn Nelson Studio,** 802 Front St. near the corner of Lahainaluna Road, 808/667-2100, shows originals and prints only of Robert Lynn Nelson, the father of the modern marine art movement, which splits the canvas between land and undersea scenes. Although most well-known for his marine scenes, Nelson pursues other styles and themes that he is not known for, like landscapes and abstracts, that you may only find displayed in this gallery. A second gallery is found at the West Maui Center on the mountain side of Honoapi'ilani Highway.

Showing modern art with bright colors is **Sargents Fine Art** gallery right on the corner of Front Street and Lahainaluna Road. Some of what hangs on these walls are abstract sailing ships by Rick Lawrence, impressionist landscapes by Anne Good, surreal scenes by Vladimir Kush, portraits by Bill Mack, fairies by St. Clair, impressionist pieces by Andrea Smith, and immense brightly painted fruit by Carmelo Sortino.

Nearly across Lahainaluna Road is the **Martin Lawrence Gallery,** 808/661-1788, which shows an eclectic and pleasing collection of pop and contemporary art by such artists as Warhol, Chagall, Picasso, Miro, Etré, and Kordakova. Around the corner at 126 Lahainaluna Road, in a one-man shop, is **Island Art Collection,** 808/667-6782, showing island scenes by owner Jim Kingwell.

The **One World Gallery,** 816 Front St.,

808/661-3984, is a zany collection of modern art, jewelry, glass, ceramics, and multimedia art pieces, full of fun and with a sense of humor. Clown faces by Red Skelton, African wildlife scenes by Craig Bone, and portraits of Hawaiians by Lori Higgins are some of what you will find at **Addi Galleries,** 844 Front St., 808/661-4900.

Displaying idyllic home scenes, waterfalls, snowscapes, and the like by Thomas Kinkade are the **Thomas Kinkade Galleries,** 808/667-7175, at 780 Front Street. Closed on Sunday.

### Food/Liquor Stores
The following markets/supermarkets are in and around Lahaina. The larger ones also stock beer, wine, and liquor. **Safeway,** at the Lahaina Cannery Mall, open 24 hours, is a large supermarket complete with deli, fish market, floral shop, and bakery. **Foodland,** at the Old Lahaina Center, is a new and well-stocked supermarket. **Nagasako General Store,** also at the Old Lahaina Center, open daily 7 A.M.–10 P.M., Sunday until 7 P.M., has a smaller selection of ethnic Hawaiian, Japanese, Chinese, and Korean foods, along with liquor selections, fresh fish, and produce.

For bulk foods, health food items, vitamins, minerals, and supplements, and hot and cold prepared foods, try the full-service **Down To Earth Natural Foods,** 808/667-2855, at the corner of Lahainaluna Road and Waine'e Street. Open Monday–Saturday 7 A.M.–9 P.M. and Sunday 8:30 A.M.–8 P.M.

**The Olowalu General Store,** 808/661-3774, located five miles east of Lahaina along Rte. 30, open Mon.–Fri. 6 A.M.–6:30 P.M., Sat. 7 A.M.–6:30 P.M., Sun. 7 A.M.–5 P.M., is fairly well stocked and the only place to pick up supplies in this area. It also has light snacks, including sandwiches and hot dogs, making it a perfect stop if you are snorkeling or swimming on the nearby beaches.

**Mr. Wine,** on the corner of Lahainaluna Road and Waine'e Street, 808/661-5551, not only has a huge selection of wines, and some beer, liquors, and liqueurs, but also keeps the better wines and champagnes under cellar conditions in a climatically controlled room at 55°F and 70 percent humidity. While classic wines are stocked, the shop also has many economical wines just right

for any wallet. Beat the hot Lahaina sun and stop in for a perfect bottle for the evening. Open Monday–Saturday 11 A.M.–7 P.M.

## INFORMATION AND SERVICES
### Information
The following groups and organizations should prove helpful: Lahaina Restoration Foundation, P.O. Box 338, Lahaina, HI 96761, 808/661-3262. The foundation is a storehouse of information about historical Lahaina; be sure to pick up its handy brochure, *Lahaina, A Walking Tour of Historic and Cultural Sites,* for an introduction to historically significant sites around town.

The Lahaina Town Action Committee, 648 Wharf St., Lahaina, HI 96761, 808/667-9175, sponsors cultural events and other activities throughout the year, including Art Night and Halloween, and can provide information about what's happening in the area. It operates the **Lahaina Visitor Center** on the first floor of the Old Lahaina Courthouse. For popular events and activities happening in Lahaina, contact the events hotline at 808/667-9194 or 888/310-1117, or visit the center's website at www.visitlahaina.com. Pick up its *Maui Historical Walking Guide* brochure. It has information mostly on Lahaina and Ka'anapali.

The nonprofit Lahaina Arts Society, 808/661-0111, las@mauigateway.com, has information about the art scene and art events in town. They maintain two galleries at the old Courthouse and run an art program for children.

The Lahaina **public library,** 680 Wharf St., 808/662-3950, is open Tuesday noon–8 P.M., Wednesday and Thursday 9 A.M.–5 P.M., and Friday and Saturday 10:30–4:30 P.M.

### Medical Services
A concentration of all types of specialists is found at the Maui Medical Group, 130 Prison St., 808/661-0051 (open Mon.–Fri. 8 A.M.–5 P.M. and Saturday 8 A.M.–noon); call for emergency hours. Professional medical care can also be found at the Kaiser Permanente clinic, 910 Waine'e St., 808/662-6900, during the same hours. Alternatively, the Aloha Family Practice Clinic, 180

Dickenson St. at Dickenson Square, Ste. 205, 808/662-5642, offers scheduled and urgent care services.

Pharmacies in Lahaina include the Lahaina Pharmacy at the Old Lahaina Center, 808/661-3119; Longs Drugs at the Lahaina Cannery Mall, 808/667-4390; and Valley Isle Pharmacy, 130 Prison St., 808/661-4747.

## Banking

In Lahaina during normal banking hours, try the Bank of Hawaii, 808/661-8781, or the American Savings Bank, 808/667-9561, in the Old Lahaina Center; or First Hawaiian Bank, just a few steps away at 215 Papalaua St., 808/661-3655.

## Post Office

The main post office is on the very northwest edge of town where Ka'anapali begins; the midtown postal branch is located at the Old Lahaina Center. Both are open Monday–Friday 8:30 A.M.–5 P.M. and Saturday 9 A.M.–1 P.M.

Lahaina Mail Depot is a post office contract station located at The Wharf Cinema Center, 808/667-2000. It's open weekdays 10 A.M.–4:30 P.M. and Saturday until 1 P.M., and along with the normal stamps and such, it specializes in sending packages home. Mailing boxes, tape, and packaging materials are all available, as are souvenir packs of coffee, nuts, candies, and teas, which might serve as a last-minute purchase, but are expensive.

# Ka'anapali

Five lush valleys, nourished by streams from the West Maui Mountains, stretch luxuriously for 10 miles from Ka'anapali north to Kapalua. All along the connecting **Honoapi'ilani Highway** (Rte. 30), the dazzle and glimmer of beaches is offset by black volcanic rock. This is West Maui's resort coast. Two sensitively planned and beautifully executed resorts are at each end of this drive. Ka'anapali Resort is 500 acres of fun and relaxation at the south end. It houses six luxury hotels, a handful of beautifully appointed condos, a shopping mall and museum, 36 holes of world-class golf, tennis courts galore, and epicurean dining in a chef's salad of cuisines. Two of the hotels, the Hyatt Regency and Sheraton, are inspired architectural showcases that blend harmoniously with Maui's most beautiful seashore surroundings. At the northern end is another gem, the Kapalua Resort, 1,650 of Maui's most beautifully sculpted acres with its own showcases, prime golf, fine beaches, exclusive shopping, and endless activity.

Ka'anapali, with its four miles of glorious beach, is Maui's westernmost point. It begins where Lahaina ends and continues north along Route 30 until it runs into the village of Honokowai. Along this shore, Maui flashes its most captivating pearly white smile. The sights here are either natural or man-made, but not historical. This is where you come to gaze from mountain to sea and bathe yourself in natural beauty. Then, after a day of surf and sunshine, you repair to one of the gorgeous hotels or restaurants for a drink or dining, or just to promenade around the grounds.

## History

Western Maui was a mixture of scrub and precious *lo'i*, irrigated terrace land reserved for taro, the highest life-sustaining plant given by the gods. The farms stretched to Kapalua, skirting the numerous bays all along the way. The area was important enough for a "royal highway" to be built by Chief Pi'ilani, and it still bears his name.

Westerners used the lands surrounding Ka'anapali to grow sugarcane, and **The Lahaina, Kaanapali, and Pacific Railroad,** known today as the "Sugar Cane Train," chugged to Ka'anapali Beach to unburden itself onto barges that carried the cane to waiting ships. Ka'anapali, until the 1960s, was a blemished beauty where the Pioneer Sugar Mill dumped its rubbish. Then Amfac, who owned the mill and this land, decided to put the land to better use. In creating Hawaii's first planned resort community, it outdid itself. Robert Trent Jones, Sr. was hired to mold the golf course along this spectacular coast, while

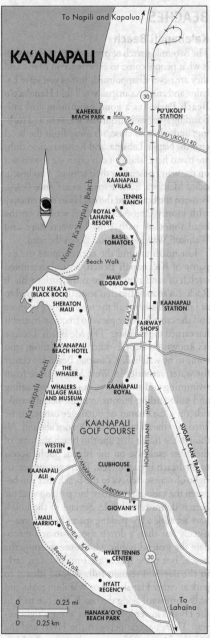

# KA'ANAPALI

To Napili and Kapalua

KAHEKILI BEACH PARK

PU'UKOLI'I STATION

KAI
ALA DR.
PU'UKOLI'I RD.

MAUI KAANAPALI VILLAS

TENNIS RANCH

ROYAL LAHAINA RESORT

BASIL TOMATOES

Beach Walk

MAUI ELDORADO

KAANAPALI STATION

PU'U KEKA'A (BLACK ROCK)

SHERATON MAUI

KEKA'A DR.

FAIRWAY SHOPS

KA'ANAPALI BEACH HOTEL

THE WHALER

WHALERS VILLAGE MALL AND MUSEUM

KAANAPALI ROYAL

North Ka'anapali Beach

Ka'anapali Beach

KAANAPALI GOLF COURSE

HONOAPI'ILANI HWY.

SUGAR CANE TRAIN

WESTIN MAUI

KAANAPALI PARKWAY

CLUBHOUSE

KAANAPALI ALII

GIOVANI'S

MAUI MARRIOT

NOHEA KAI DR.

Beach Walk

HYATT TENNIS CENTER

HYATT REGENCY

To Lahaina

HANAKA'O'O BEACH PARK

0    0.25 mi
0    0.25 km

© SANDRA E. BISIGNANI TRUST AND AVALON TRAVEL PUBLISHING, INC.

the Hyatt Regency and its grounds became an architectural counterpoint. The Sheraton Maui was built atop, and integrated with, Pu'u Keka'a, "Black Rock," a wave-eroded cinder cone, and the architects used its sea cliffs as part of the walls of the resort. Here, on a deep underwater shelf, daring divers used to descend to harvest Maui's famous black coral trees. The Hawaiians believed that Pu'u Keka'a was a very holy place where the spirits of the dead left this earth and migrated into the spirit world. Kahekili, Maui's most famous 18th-century chief, often came here to leap into the sea below. This old-time daredevil was fond of the heart-stopping activity and made famous "Kahekili's Leap," an even more treacherous sea cliff on nearby Lana'i. Today, the Sheraton puts on a daily sunset show where this "leap" is reenacted.

## Pu'u Keka'a

One of the most easily accessible and visually engaging snorkeling spots on Maui is located at the Sheraton's Black Rock. Approach this either from the beach in front of the hotel, where you can snorkel west around the rock, or from around back. The entire area offshore is like an underwater marine park. There are schools of reef fish, rays, and even lonely turtles. Follow the main road past the Sheraton until it begins to climb the hill. Walk along the pathway that leads to the North Ka'anapali Beach and head for the remnants of an old pier. This pier was built as the end of a spur line of the sugarcane railroad and used to ship bags of sugar. After the Mala Wharf was constructed closer to Lahaina in the 1920s, the rail lines were taken up and cattle were shipped off island from here. There is limited free public parking in Ka'anapali, so you may have to park in one of the few pay lots. Alternately, park at Kahekili Beach Park at the far north end of Ka'anapali near the Maui Kaanapali Villas, from where it's only a 15-minute walk.

## Whale Museum

The free Whale Museum, at Whaler's Village shopping mall, 808/661-5992, has a few outside displays, but most items are inside on the

MAUI

upper level of the mall. The most dramatic outside display is the skeleton of a 40-foot sperm whale. This big boy greets you at the entrance to the mall as you come up the steps. There is also a whaling boat in a side courtyard. The compact display area upstairs on the mezzanine level is full of whaling history, photographs, drawings, artifacts from whaling ships, a reconstructed forecastle, a video on whaling, and many informative descriptions and stories about the whaling industry, whaling life, and the whalers themselves. After a walk through the museum, pick up a memento at the museum gift shop. Open 9 A.M.–10 P.M. daily. This is a must-see stop for anyone who wishes to have a better understanding of whales, sailors, life on board, and this integral aspect of Hawaiian history.

## Transportation

Ka'anapali is serviced by the free **Kaanapali Trolley** within the resort area. It runs throughout the day from 10 A.M.–10 P.M. on a prescribed schedule and stops at each resort and at the Whalers Village.

**Holo Ka'a** public transit shuttle runs south between Ka'anapali and Lahaina Harbor in Lahaina and north to Kapalua. Shuttles operate about a dozen times a day between 9 A.M.–10 P.M., stopping at hotels, condos, and shopping centers on the way. Rides between Ka'anapali and Lahaina are $1 each way and between Ka'anapali and Kapalua are $2 each way. Several times a day, shuttles connect the West Maui and South Maui regions through Ma'alaea. Fares are $5 either way to/from Ma'alaea and $10 per day for the entire system.

Fun for the entire family, the **Sugar Cane Train** takes the scenic route between Ka'anapali and Lahaina.

The Kapalua–West Maui Airport is the most convenient for air travel to this end of the island, but there are only a limited number of daily flights in and out of this airstrip. Most air traffic to Maui still goes via Kahului. For access to the airport in Kahului from Ka'anapali and Lahaina, try **Speedy Shuttle** or **Executive Shuttle.** From Lahaina, the fare will be about $35 one way, a bit more from Ka'anapali.

# BEACHES

## Ka'anapali Beach

The two-mile stretch of pristine sand at Ka'anapali is what people come to experience in Maui, and they are never disappointed. Just as you leave Lahaina and enter Ka'anapali you'll find **Hanaka'o'o Beach Park.** It's a good swimming and sailboarding spot, with lifeguards, showers, and parking; and while so close, it's away from the hotel crowds. Napili, Lahaina, and Kahana canoe clubs are based here, and you can often see rowers out on the water practicing their strokes. This beach, called Makaiwa, is also referred to as Canoe Beach. Between the beach and the road is an old cemetery with mostly Chinese characters written on the headstones. A path runs between here and Wahikuli Wayside Park just down the road.

Just north around the corner opens the expanse of **Ka'anapali Beach,** an uninterrupted stretch of sand running from the park to Black Rock. Ka'anapali Beach is sometimes referred to as Little Waikiki for all the resorts along its shore and the crowds of people who frequent it, and it has earned the moniker "Dig Me Beach" because it's known for people-watching and those who come to be watched. Ka'anapali Beach is a center for water activities in West Maui. Aside from swimming and snorkeling, you can take surfing and sailboarding lessons, rent an ocean kayak, ride on a catamaran or outrigger canoe, or be lifted into the air by parasail. Options abound. Although the hotels that line this beach are some of the most exclusive on the island, public access to the beach is guaranteed. There are numerous right-of-way walkways to the beach that run between the various properties, but parking your car here is definitely a hassle. Several of the hotels have set aside a few parking spaces in their area— usually less than a dozen spots—to accommodate the general public who come to enjoy the beach, but these spaces are usually taken early in the day and remain full. A good idea is to park at either Hanaka'o'o or Wahikuli parks and walk northward along the beach. You can park in the Hyatt's lower lot and enter along a right-of-way. There's access between the Hyatt and the Marriott's pay parking ramp, between the Mar-

ROBERT NILSEN

Broad sand, gentle water, a plethora of activities, and nearby accommodations and restaurants make Ka'anapali Beach Maui's best known vacation spot.

riott and the Kaanapali Alii, which also has limited parking, and between the Kaanapali Alii and the Westin Maui. There is also some parking near the Sheraton and at the Whalers Village parking ramp, but you must pass through the gauntlet of shops.

## North Ka'anapali Beach

Continue past Black Rock and the beach continues north. Quieter than the main Ka'anapali Beach, it's much less frequented, has no lifeguards, and only the Royal Lahaina Resort has frontage here. In the early 20th century, pigs and cattle were raised where the Royal Hawaiian Hotel now stands, and before that some of the area back from the beach was a village site. This North Ka'anapali Beach is also known as Keka'a Beach, and the section fronting and just north of Kahekili Beach Park is locally called Airport Beach because the small Ka'anapali airstrip and terminal were located here during the 1960s and '70s.

Located just north of the Royal Lahaina Resort, **Kahekili Beach Park** is dedicated to Maui's last major king, Kahekili. Open 6 A.M. to 30

minutes past sunset, this small park is a commodious place with a broad lawn, palm trees, a pavilion for cooking, and tables for a picnic. The large shaded parking area can accommodate many cars, and you can count on always finding someone here. The beach, sometimes used for scuba lessons and not bad for snorkelers, runs uninterrupted to Black Rock.

## Beach Walk

As in Wailea, a beach walkway has been created in Ka'anapali that parallels the edge of the sand from the Hyatt Regency in the south to the Sheraton in the north. This walkway is a convenient way to pass from one property to another: Peruse your neighbor hotel, try one of the restaurants down the line, or walk to shop. During the cool hours of the day and at sunset, this walkway is also used by joggers out for exercise and those who want the perfect location to watch the sun go down. If you cut through the Sheraton property and duck out the other side, you can connect with a similar pathway that skirts the golf course and runs along the North Ka'anapali Beach into the Royal Lahaina Resort.

MAUI

# LUXURY HOTELS

The Ka'anapali Resort offers hotels that are all in the luxury category—no budget or midrange accommodations here. The following should give you an idea of what's available.

## Ka'anapali Beach Hotel

Not as large or as luxurious as its chain-hotel neighbors, but an excellent hotel nonetheless, the Ka'anapali Beach Hotel, 2525 Ka'anapali Pkwy., 808/661-0011 or 800/262-8450, fax 808/667-5978, www.kbhmaui.com, is a bargain and the least expensive hotel property on the beach. This is undoubtedly the most Hawaiian of the hotels in Ka'anapali and perhaps in the state. As you arrive, you'll be greeted with *ho'okipa* (hospitality), and throughout your stay experience the *po'okela* (excellence) of the staff. There is no glitz here, just warm and friendly service, reasonably priced restaurants, a wonderful beachfront location, and nearly as many amenities as the big boys down the line. Guest service provides many free activities and demonstrations, including lei-making, hula lessons, *lau hala* weaving, and a free torchlighting ceremony and sunset hula show nightly. The tour desk can always hook you up with any activity on the island, and the gift and sundries shop has items that you forgot to bring with you or you want to take back as souvenirs.

A delight is the 11 A.M. music and dance performance put on by the hotel staff on Mondays, Wednesdays, and Fridays—they even have their own CD! On these days, and also on Sundays, a craft fair is held in the lobby 9–11 A.M. If you're staying here, don't miss it; if you're not, drop on by anyway—everyone is welcome. Have a swim in the hotel's distinctive whale-shaped pool or check with the Trilogy Ocean Sports activity booth for water equipment to rent and water tours. Over the past few years, most of the rooms have been totally renovated with new wicker furniture, island-inspired wall coverings, a unique sliding-glass door arrangement for the lanai, and larger and updated bathrooms, and the rest of the property repainted and spiffed up. The two restaurants and one snack shop provide a wide variety of food for everyone's taste, and the courtyard bar offers libations into the evening. The Aloha Passport for Kids program will keep the little ones busy as they go from spot to spot around the property collecting mementos from each "destination." Standard rooms range $195–265 for an ocean view, oceanfront rooms are $290, and suites are priced $255–600. Numerous special packages are available.

## Sheraton Maui

The 510 rooms and suites of the Sheraton Maui, 2605 Ka'anapali Pkwy., Lahaina, HI 96761, 808/661-0031 or 800/782-9488, fax 808/661-0458, www.sheraton-maui.com, are built around Ka'anapali's most conspicuous natural phenomenon, Pu'u Keka'a, "Black Rock." Originally opened in 1963, the Sheraton reopened in 1997 after a two-year complete and extensive renovation. Open, bright, and breezy, the lobby looks out over the finely landscaped gardens and an enticing meandering pool with a water slide and spa. Two classy restaurants grace the hotel, as does one indoor lounge, where you can shoot billiards in the evening, and one bar situated at poolside, which features evening entertainment. The guest activities desk can arrange almost any activity that the island offers, and you can rent water equipment and have lessons from the beach activity booth. The snorkeling around Black Rock is the best in the area, and every evening there is a torchlighting ceremony and cliff dive from the rock.

As a guest, you can avail yourself of several daily catamaran rides aboard the *Teralani* or head for some sporting competition at the resort's tennis club. The fitness center, day spa, business center, and clothing and sundries shops are all for guest use. Kids ages 5–12 can be taken care of as well through the daily Keiki Aloha program, which operates half-day, full-day, and evening services that combine arts and crafts with history and culture. The north end of the Ka'anapali beach walk ends at the Sheraton, so you can stroll all the way to the Hyatt at the south end without leaving the oceanside. Most rooms at the Sheraton face the ocean; all are air-conditioned and have full amenities. Rates are $350–420 for garden and mountain-view rooms, $510–610 for oceanview and oceanfront rooms, $750 for an Ohana family suite, and other suites from $825. The extra adult charge is $50, but children 17 years old and under stay free in the same room as an adult if existing bedding is used. The Sheraton Maui has a superb location and is a superb property. You'll be entranced by the beauty, welcomed by the friendly and helpful staff, and thoroughly enjoy your well-deserved vacation.

## Hyatt Regency Maui

The moment you enter the main lobby of this luxury hotel, the magic begins. A multithread architectural extravaganza opens to the sky, birds fly freely, and magnificent potted plants and full-size courtyard palm trees create the atmosphere of a modern Polynesian palace located at Ka'anapali's southern extremity, at 200 Nohea Kai Dr., Lahaina, HI 96761, 808/661-1234 or 800/554-9288, fax 808/667-4498, www.maui.hyatt.com. Nooks and crannies abound and wildlife inhabits the impeccable landscaped gardens and ponds. The swimming pools are inspired by the islands: grottoes, caves, waterfalls, and a 150-foot slide are all built in. A swinging wooden bridge connects sections of the pool deck. There are four fine restaurants on property, half a dozen lounges (one is a swim-up bar at the pool), and the Drums of the Pacific lu'au. The covey of specialty shops and boutiques will please parents, and the little kids will love it here too. Camp Hyatt for children ages 5–12 runs daily 9 A.M.–3 P.M. and includes activities and excursions that change daily. An evening camp 6–10 P.M. is also available, so put those little kiddies in the care of professionals and have a romantic night out.

All beach activities, equipment rentals, and lessons, including a sail/snorkel ride on the *Kiele V* catamaran, can be arranged through the beach activities center at oceanside. Expend some energy at the health club and tennis center, or try the oceanfront Spa Moana for the relaxing royal treatment. For those with less physical activity in mind, check out the daily Hawaiian demonstrations in the lobby, the hotel wildlife tour, the art and garden tour ($2 million worth of art—most from Asia and the Pacific), or the nightly as-

tronomy show ($25 per person) on the hotel roof. The lobby activity desk or Aloha Services will help you make reservations for activities throughout the island, and if you're here on business, the business center can help take care of your office needs. Rates for the 806 rooms and suites are $345 for terrace rooms, $385 for golf/mountain rooms, $445 for oceanview rooms, and $565 for oceanfront rooms. Rates are higher for the special Regency floors, and suites run $900–4,500. If you visit, valet parking is in front of the hotel. Or you can self-park out front or around in the back. From here, both the north end of Lahaina, pretty at night with its colored lights reflecting on the water, and Lana'i, floating across the Lahaina Roads, are easily visible.

## Westin Maui

The Westin Maui, 2365 Ka'anapali Pkwy., Lahaina, HI 96761, 808/667-2525 or 866/500-8313, fax 808/661-5764, www.westinmaui.com, is actually a phoenix, risen from the old Maui Surf Hotel. True to the second life of that mythical bird, it is a beauty. Westin is known for its fabulous entranceways, lobbies, and quiet nooks, and you won't be disappointed here. A series of strolling paths takes you through resplendent manicured grounds that surround an extensive multipool area, one of the largest on Maui. Waterfalls, water slides, and natural rock formations all blend to create civilized paradise. To the left of the main lobby is a collection of exclusive boutique shops and a business center. You'll find just what you want to eat or drink at any time of the day at one of the hotel's three restaurants and three lounges. The ocean activity center can set you up with all sorts of rentals on the beach or a ride on *Gemini,* the hotel's sailing catamaran. The kids are taken care of at the supervised daily Keiki Kamp. The daily kids' program runs 9 A.M.–3 P.M., with an evening program from 6:30–9:30.

For the experience of all, each Friday 8 A.M.–4 P.M. brings Ho'olauna, a Hawaiian culture and arts program, and throughout the week are other activities set up especially for the guests. Perhaps a soothing massage or healing facial is what you're looking for. The Health Spa and Beauty Salon is open daily 6 A.M.–8 P.M. for your

MAUI

needs. If you just want to soak in some beauty, have a tour of the hotel's art collection. The Westin Maui has more than 750 guest rooms. Standard terrace rooms run $350, a garden-view room $380, golf/mountain-view $420, ocean-view $445–510, oceanfront $580, and suites go upward from $850.

## Royal Lahaina Resort

Twenty-seven idyllic acres surround 542 rooms at the Royal Lahaina Resort, 2780 Keka'a Dr., Lahaina, HI 96761, 808/661-3611 or 800/222-5642, fax 808/661-6150, www.2maui.com, the largest complex in Ka'anapali. Here the tropical landscaping leads directly to the sun-soaked beach. One of the first properties to be developed, the Royal Lahaina is divided into cottages and a tower. Rates range from a standard room at $320 to an oceanfront room at $460. Cottages rent for $390 and $500, suites $550–750; condo/car and other deals and packages are available. The renovated rooms are decorated in a comfortable Hawaiian style with all amenities and private lanai; some of the cottages have kitchens. The adjacent and newly remodeled Royal Hale building also has rooms for $240–270. There are two restaurants at the resort, a poolside grill, a nightly lu'au, music in the lounge, and two swimming pools on the well-maintained grounds. A handful of sundries shops are located at the hotel entrance for your convenience. The beach activities booth rents snorkel equipment, sailboards, and kayaks, and arranges scuba lessons. The resort is also home to the **Royal Lahaina Tennis Ranch,** boasting 11 courts and a 3,500-seat stadium along with special tennis packages for those inclined.

## Maui Marriott

The Maui Marriott, 100 Nohea Kai Dr., Lahaina, 96761, 808/667-1200 or 800/763-1333, fax 808/667-8300, www.marriott.com, recently finished a year-long reconstruction process, which included, among other things, renovating the lobby, building a new courtyard and pool area, and turning some rooms into time-share units. With nearly 400 rooms, a Trilogy Ocean Sports beach activity booth for water recreation activities

and tours, on-site tennis courts, two dozen shops, three restaurants, one bar, an evening lu'au, and indoor and outdoor parking, the Marriott is one of the largest properties on West Maui. Open to the beach and facing the setting sun, the hotel is graced with cooling breezes that waft across its manicured gardens and through the open atriums of its buildings. Indoors, the many flowers and potted plants bring the outdoors inside; outdoors, the grounds are more finely landscaped and tended than ever. The centerpiece of the reconstruction is the courtyard and swimming pool area, which incorporates a huge pool with lagoons, waterfalls, a water slide, and a children's beach area. It is now one of the premier courtyard garden areas in Ka'anapali. The hospitable staff orchestrates the numerous daily handicraft and recreational activities, and there's plenty to keep every family busy. Snorkel sets, boogie boards, and kayaks can be rented at the beach activities center, and scuba lessons are given. Room rates are $329 for a standard room, $369 oceanfront, and $414 deluxe oceanfront; suites run $579–1,499. Special honeymoon, tennis, golf, and family plans are available.

# CONDOMINIUMS

Generally less expensive than the hotels, but still in the luxury category, most of these condos offer full kitchens, TVs, some maid service, swimming pools, tennis courts, and often a convenience store and laundry facilities. Combinations of the above are too numerous to mention, so it's best to ask all pertinent questions when booking. Off-season rates and discounts for longer stays are usually offered.

Located right on the water amid the hotels are the fancy high-rise Kaanapali Alii and The Whaler condos. Set along the golf links and following the lay of the land are the low-rise Kaanapali Royal and Outrigger Maui Eldorado Resort. A short way north up the beach and off on a road by itself is Maui Kaanapali Villas.

## Kaanapali Alii

The Kaanapali Alii, 50 Nohea Kai Dr., Lahaina, HI 96761, 808/667-1400 or 800/642-6284, fax

808/661-5686, www.kaanapalialii.com, managed by Classic Resorts, lies in a finely landscaped yard right on the ocean. The four high-rise towers are aesthetically pleasing and are set off by flowers and greenery hanging from many of the balconies. If you need space, try staying here because each of the 200 or so large one- and two-bedroom units runs 1,500–1,900 square feet. All have full kitchens, dining and living rooms, two bathrooms, air-conditioning, and washers and dryers. Services include free parking on premises, a beach activity center, complimentary tennis, daily maid service, room service, and many area activities, and restaurant bills can be put on your room charge as a service. On the property are an exercise room, a swimming pool that overlooks the beach, a whirlpool spa, and barbecue grills. Room rates are $350–740 per night, three-night minimum.

## The Whaler on Kaanapali Beach

The Whaler, 2481 Ka'anapali Pkwy., Lahaina, HI 96761, 808/661-4861 or 800/922-7866, fax 808/661-8315; www.the-whaler.com, comprises two high-rise buildings set right on the beach next to Whalers Village shopping mall. Outwardly, it has less character than the Kaanapali Alii but offers numerous amenities. On property are a pool and spa, exercise room, tennis courts for guests, sundries shop, and concierge desk. These units run from a 640-square-foot studio to a 1,950-square-foot two-bedroom, two-bath suite. Rates are $235–700, with substantially lower rates during the low season. There is a two-night minimum stay, and several car/condo, honeymoon, and senior packages are available. Covered parking is offered and signing privileges are granted at some nearby restaurants. The Whaler is managed by Aston, but some units are available through **Whalers Realty Management,** 808/661-3484 or 800/676-4112.

## Maui Eldorado Resort

An Outrigger Hotels and Resorts property, the Maui Eldorado Resort, 2661 Keka'a Dr., 808/661-0021, fax 808/667-7039, www.outrigger.com, drapes the hillside along the fourth and fifth fairways of the golf course and has a beach-front cabana on the water. Guests can avail themselves of three small swimming pools and a sundries store on property, and an activity desk will help you plan your day. These privately owned studios and one- and two-bedroom suites run $195–395 year-round. All have full kitchens, air-conditioning, TV, in-unit safes, washers and dryers, and daily maid service. For toll-free reservations and information, call Outrigger direct at 800/688-7444. Some units here are also offered for rent directly by their owners or through independent agents, such as Whalers Realty Management, 808/661-3484 or 800/367-4112.

## Kaanapali Royal

A golfer's dream right on the course, the Kaanapali Royal, 2560 Keka'a Dr., 808/667-7200, has only two-bedroom, two-bath, privately owned units that run about $280 per night during peak season but less during the regular season. Each suite has a full kitchen and a lanai that faces the fairway, a sunken living room, an entertainment center, and washer and dryer. Take advantage of the guest-only swimming pool, lighted tennis courts, and barbecue pit. Units are rented through agents only. Contact Whalers Realty Management, 808/661-3484 or 800/676-4112; Maui Beachfront Rentals, 808/661-2684 or 888/661-7201; Chase'n Rainbows, 808/667-7088 or 800/367-6093; or Maui Resort Rentals, 808/879-5973 or 800/441-3188.

## Aston Maui Kaanapali Villas

Enjoy the surroundings of 11 sculpted acres at this affordable condo at 45 Kai Ala Dr., 808/667-7791 or 800/922-7866, fax 808/667-0366. The extensive grounds of cool, swaying palms harbor three pools, a beach service booth, the Castaway Restaurant, an activity desk, and a sundries shop. Rates begin at $220 for a hotel room with refrigerator. Studios with kitchens run $285–375, and it's $385–600 for one- and two-bedroom suites with air-conditioning, cable TV, full kitchens, plus maid service daily. This property, located at the far north end of the Ka'anapali development, has an added bonus of peace and quiet, although you remain just minutes from the action and a short stroll from Black Rock.

M

MAUI

These units are very large with spacious bedrooms; even the studios are capable of handling four people. A good choice.

## FOOD

Every hotel in Ka'anapali has at least one restaurant, with several others scattered throughout the area. Some of the most expensive and exquisite restaurants on Maui are found in these hotels, but surprisingly, at others you can dine very reasonably. The only cheap eats in the area are the few fast-food restaurants at Whalers Village shopping mall.

### Nonresort Restaurants

**Reilley's Steak and Seafood,** an Irish restaurant and bar, is located in the clubhouse at Ka'anapali Golf Courses, 808/667-7477. Open for lunch and dinner, Reilley's is known for its twice-weekly prime rib dinner. Other meat and seafood entrées are generally in the $19–28 range. Nightly dinner specials are offered, as is lobster on Sundays. During the day, a simple pub menu is offered at the bar. Reilley's has a full bar—their single-malt Scotch selection is remarkable—so come and have a drink after a round of golf or just to watch the sun set over the fairway. Live jazz is on tap every Monday and Tuesday.

**Giovani's Tomato Pie,** 808/661-3160, a moderately priced "Italian American Ristarante," is located at the entrance to Ka'anapali Resort. Here you'll find everything you'd expect at such a restaurant and much more. Start your meal with a fine antipasto, salada, or zupa, most in the $4–9 range. Pizza and pasta selections of all kinds are numerous, but full-course meals like veal parmigiana, seafood pescatore, calamari and peas with bacon, and shrimp scampi are also great choices. Basic pizzas run $9–15, pasta dishes are in the same range, and full meals run up to $20. This is a pleasant, family-oriented restaurant, and the kid's menu makes the bill easier on mom and dad. Open for dinner 5:30–9:30 P.M.

Downstairs is **Jonny's Burger Joint,** open 11:30 A.M.–2 A.M. for cold drinks from the bar, fist-size burgers until midnight, and games. Jonny's serves meat, veggie, fish, and chicken burgers with all the trimmings and a variety of deep-fried side items. This is a good-time place to relax after a day in the sun.

### At Whalers Village

This shopping mall has three restaurants and a clutch of fast-food joints. You can find everything from pizza and frozen yogurt to lobster tails. Prices range from bargain to pricey.

The well-established **Leilani's On The Beach,** 808/661-4495, has a downstairs Beachside Grill open 11 A.M.–11 P.M., while the upstairs fine-dining section is open for dinner only 5–10 P.M. A daily dinner special is featured 5–6:30 P.M. The Beachside Grill offers plate lunches of barbecued ribs, *paniolo* steak, or stir-fry chicken all priced around $10, along with appetizers like sashimi at a daily quote, and creamy seafood chowder for $4. The burgers range $7–9.50. A more formal dinner from the upstairs broiler can be fresh fish of the day, filet mignon for $23 from the lava rock broiler, baby back pork ribs at $17 from the kiawe-wood smoker, or fried coconut prawns for $16. A children's menu helps keep prices down. Cocktails are served until midnight at the bar, and there's entertainment daily 2:30–5:30 P.M.

Another favorite here is the partially indoors but mostly outdoors **Hula Grill and Barefoot Bar,** 808/667-6636. Open 11 A.M.–11 P.M., with dinner served 5–9:30 P.M. You can eat either in the casual Barefoot Bar under a thatch cabana or in the more formal dining area. Reservations are taken for inside but not for the barefoot bar outside. No matter where you sit, however, the sunsets are always great. At the Barefoot Bar, try burgers, sandwiches, salads, and pizza. The dining room features seafood and steak. Expect entrées in the $20–25 range, with such choices as firecracker mahimahi, shrimp scampi, and black angus New York steak. Music runs 3–5 P.M. at the Barefoot Bar and 6:30–9 P.M. in the dining room.

The **Rusty Harpoon,** 808/661-3123, offers a pleasing atmosphere, a dozen satellite TVs showing sports events, and plenty of seafood items. It also has a bar that claims to serve the best daiquiris on Maui, along with a happy hour 2–6 P.M. and again from 10 P.M.–2 A.M. Breakfast served 8–11 A.M. gets you started for the day with create-your-own three-egg omelets for $8.95, a homestyle breakfast with potatoes, eggs, and sausage links for $7.95, continental breakfast for $7.95, and a Belgian waffle bar with your choice of various fruit toppings and garnishes for $7.95. Lunch, served 11 A.M.–5 P.M., is an extensive menu starting with appetizers like a house salad for $4.95 or crab-stuffed mushrooms for $9.95. Sandwiches are priced $8.95–9.95, burgers around the same. Dinner, served 5–10 P.M., offers entrées mostly in the $22–28 range, including linguine Mediterranean, pineapple teriyaki chicken, and rack of lamb, and lighter bistro fare is served from the bar until midnight. Don't forget about the sushi and seafood bar or the luscious desserts. To save money, the Rusty Harpoon has a $14.95 early-bird special from 5–6 P.M. and a children's menu.

## Ka'anapali Beach Hotel

The restaurants here are down-to-earth, reasonably priced, and provide some food from the native Hawaiian diet that's unlike anything else in the area. The **Tiki Terrace** is the main food venue of the Ka'anapali Beach Hotel and offers casual dining in an open-air setting. Breakfast can be à la carte or buffet style ($9–12) and consists mostly of American standards, but a local-style breakfast is on the menu. It runs 7–11 A.M. daily, except for Sunday when it gives way to a champagne Sunday brunch that runs 9 A.M.–1 P.M. More Hawaiian-inspired dishes are on the table for this brunch, $28.95, and the whole affair is accompanied by Hawaiian music. Dinner in the Tiki Terrace runs 5:30–9 P.M. and reservations are recommended, 808/667-0124. Most entrées run $17–33. Aside from more usual items on the menu, there is a Hawaiian combo selection that consists of poi, taro, steamed fish or chicken, sweet potatoes, and Pahole fern salad, that is totally Hawaiian in essence. On Fridays the Tiki Terrace does a *huli huli* barbecue of whole pig. Aside from the eats, a free hula show is given nightly at 6:30 P.M.

Open daily 6 A.M.–2 P.M., and again 4–9 P.M., the **Ka'anapali Mixed Plate** restaurant serves all-you-can-eat breakfast and lunch buffets for $9.75 and a dinner buffet for $12.95. An early-

bird prime rib plate runs $10.95. In the courtyard next to the whale-shaped pool, have a salad, sandwich, or burger from the **Tiki Grill,** 11 A.M.–6 P.M., or just stop for a drink at the **Tiki Bar** when the *pu pu* are put out 3–6 P.M. The bar stays open until 10 P.M.

## Royal Lahaina Resort

The **Royal Ocean Terrace,** the resort's only dining room, is open daily for breakfast and dinner. The breakfast buffet runs $11.50 and is a very good deal—à la carte also. Most evening entrées are in the $13–20 range and include fresh catch, top sirloin, and island-style chicken that can be prepared in half a dozen ways. Sunday brunch 9 A.M.–2 P.M. is a winner. The attached lounge serves *pu pu* in the afternoon and provides entertainment every evening. It overlooks the ocean. When the resort is very busy, a second restaurant and pool grill may also be open for business. You can get ice cream, sandwiches, and pastries from the **Royal Scoop Ice Cream Parlor.**

Located at the entrance to the Royal Lahaina Resort, but an independent establishment, is **Basil Tomatoes,** 808/662-3210, an Italian grill that's open for dinner only 5:30–9 P.M.; reservations suggested. Basil's has garnered a fine reputation for its wonderful Northern Italian food. Start with an antipasto of fried green tomatoes at $8 or cheese-stuffed artichokes at $12 and move on to the house salad for $9 or another fine bowl of greens. The entrées cover the whole range of meats, poultry, and fish, and are generally in the $22–30 range, with pastas $17–22. To complement any dinner selection, choose from a variety of beers, wine, or aperitifs, and round out your meal with a cup of coffee and a sweet dessert.

## Westin Maui

Located on the pool level, the **'Ono Surf Bar and Grille** is open all day for bistro dining. While the à la carte menu is an option, the 'Ono is known especially for its breakfast buffet at $19.95. For lunch, sandwiches rule, but dinner entrées are more substantial with fish, meats, and poultry in the $18–25 range. Just as well attended as the breakfast buffet is the Saturday evening prime rib and seafood buffet that runs

MAUI

$29.95. The 'Ono bar runs a happy hour daily 5–7 P.M., during which time there is musical entertainment with the addition of a hula show on Fridays and afternoon music on Fridays and Saturdays. Perhaps the most well-known dining at the Westin is the champagne Sunday brunch, $29.95, served 9:30 A.M.–1 P.M. at the oceanfront **tropica** restaurant. The Sunday brunch at this open-air venue is a tradition at the Westin, and it too is always accompanied by live music. For those with smaller eyes (and stomachs), the **Colonnade Cafe** along the lobby-level open-air hallway to the pool serves pastries, fruits, and coffee from 6–11:30 A.M. More formal evening dinners are also served at the tropica, and entrées might be filet mignon, roasted lobster, guava-crusted rack of lamb, or any of several fish selections done in one of five different preparations. The early-bird special runs $24.95. Reservations are a must; 808/667-2525.

## Maui Marriott

Serving casual food all day at poolside is the **Beachwalk Market and Pantry.** With mostly light fare on the menu, it's perfect for a midday snack. Open, airy, and very pleasant, **Va Bene** serves a bit more elegant breakfast, but in the evening turns into the hotel's fine-dining Italian restaurant. The à la carte menu has items in the $19–28 range as well as two prix fixe menus for $22 and $28. Special to this restaurant is the Friday night prime rib buffet dinner for $28 and the Saturday night Alaskan king crab buffet dinner at $35. Expanding the bar and its scope of appetizers, **Nalu Sunset Bar** (formerly the Makai Bar) is still a great place for excellent *pu pu,* sushi, and entertainment some evening as you watch the sun set into the distant horizon. *Pu pu* run $6–12, sushi mostly $4–8 with specials up to $10, and there are specials some evenings. The Nalu Sunset Bar is open daily 5–10:30 P.M.

## Hyatt Regency Maui

The **Swan Court** is the Hyatt's signature restaurant. Save this one for a very special evening. You don't come here to eat, you come here to dine! Anyone who has been enraptured by those old movies where couples regally glide down a central staircase to make their grand entrance will have his or her fantasies come true. Although expensive, with entrées up to $38, you get your money's worth not only with the many wonderful tastes but also with the attention to detail. Dinner, served 6–10 P.M., is grand and the style is continental; reservations are recommended, and resort attire is required. The Swan Court offers a sumptuous breakfast buffet daily and much-talked-about Sunday brunch. For reservations, call 808/667-4727.

**Spats Trattoria,** open for dinner only, is downstairs near the entrance and decorated in heavy dark wood and carpets, premodern artwork, and intimate low light. Spats specializes in "country homestyle" Northern Italian food, with the average entrée around $20 for pasta dishes and $25 for fish and meat. Casual attire, reservations recommended. Set in the more casual setting of the garden, yet overlooking the grotto pool, is the open-air **Cascades Grille and Sushi Bar,** with a full complement of selections for lunch and dinner from about $22–34, yet some come especially for the sushi. Stop by **Pavilions** at the garden level during the day for light food and quick dining. After a full and pleasing meal, you might want to try **Cascade Lounge** or **Swan Court Lounge** for an aperitif, or the **Weeping Banyan Lounge** off the main lobby for a nightcap and soft music before heading off for a stroll along the beach.

## Sheraton Maui

A blend of Asia and America, in theme, decor, and cuisine, **Teppan Yaki Dan** is the hotel's signature restaurant. Appetizers like blackened ahi or Oriental duck salad get you ready for the main meal of meat or fish, all cooked at your table teppanyaki style. It's a delight for the eyes and taste buds, but not cheap, as most entrées run $22–32. Teppan Yaki Dan serves Tuesday–Saturday 6–9 P.M., reservations recommended. Less formal is the **Keka'a Terrace** restaurant, where you can order all day long while surveying the gardens, pool, and Black Rock. Aside from the à la carte menu, regular and continental breakfast buffets can be selected. Lunch is mostly salads, sandwiches, and wraps in the under $13 range. More extensive and heartier, evening entrées run $20–32, and include fresh catch of the day on one of four preparations, coconut shrimp, barbecued baby back ribs, and roast boneless pork loin. To reserve at either restaurant, call 808/661-0031. In addition, the poolside Lagoon Bar offers light barbecued eats throughout the day, music until 7 P.M., and the perfect seating for the evening torchlight and cliff dive performance at Black Rock.

## Maui Kaanapali Villas

This is the only Ka'anapali condo that has a restaurant. The casual and moderately priced **Castaway Cafe,** 808/661-9091, is located only steps from the beach and is open for breakfast, lunch, and dinner. Breakfast items include omelets, items from the griddle, and fruit, most for under $8.50. Burgers, sandwiches, and salads are served for lunch, and for dinner, a variety of seafood, pasta, chicken, and steaks go for $15–24. Every day there are specials, and the full bar can set you up with a drink any time until 9:30 P.M.

# ENTERTAINMENT

## Lu'au

The dinner show accompanying the lu'au at the Hyatt Regency features pure island entertainment. **Drums of the Pacific** is a musical extravaganza that you would expect from the Hyatt. There are torch-lit processions and excitingly choreographed production numbers, with all the hula-skirted *wahines* and *malo*-clad *kanes* you could imagine. Flames add drama to the setting and the grand finale is a fire dance. The Hyatt lu'au, 808/667-4720, is held every evening 5–8 P.M.; $78 adults, $37 kids 6–12.

Similarly, the lu'au at the Royal Lahaina Resort and Maui Marriott entertain you with music and dance while you stuff yourself on fine island cuisine. These two are fairly tourist-oriented but great fun nonetheless. Follow your nose nightly at 5 P.M. to the Luau Gardens for the **Royal Lahaina Lu'au** banquet and show, where the biggest problem after the Polynesian Revue is standing up after eating mountains of

traditional food. Reservations needed, 808/661-3611; adults $67, children 12 and under free with a paying adult. The **Maui Marriott Lu'au** presents its version nightly except Monday, starting with an *imu* ceremony and Polynesian games. The Marriott's niche is its funny and entertaining twists. The evening starts at 5 P.M. and runs until 8 P.M.; $78 adults, $38 children 3–8; 808/661-5828.

## Musical Entertainment

The Ka'anapali Beach Hotel presents a free hula and music show in its courtyard at 6 P.M. for everyone's pleasure. In addition, Monday, Wednesday, and Friday around 11 A.M., the staff of this hotel put on a music and hula show for guests. It's good fun in a family atmosphere.

Hawaiian music is also presented outdoors at 7 P.M. Monday, Wednesday, and Saturday on the center stage at Whalers Village. If you are into lively music, try the **Hula Grill** at the shopping center. Across the way, **Leilani's on the Beach** has softer music in the afternoon. The **'Ono Grille** at the Westin has music nightly 5–7 P.M. and during the afternoons on Friday and Saturday. Several of the bars and lounges, like the Weeping Banyan Lounge and Swan Court Lounge at the Hyatt and the Lagoon Bar at the Sheraton, also have live late afternoon and/or evening music.

Away from the hotels, live jazz on Monday and Tuesday evenings at **Reilley's** at the Kaanapali Golf Clubhouse is about the only option.

## Illusion Show

Sunday through Thursday, the Ka'anapali Beach Hotel hosts the **Black Rock Illusions** dinner show at its Kanahele Room. This show is not only one of slight of hand, but also presents larger magic tricks and special effects. Hula and Hawaiian legends are woven into the fabric of the show making, this a nonillusory Hawaiian experience. Seating starts at 5:30 P.M. for the full buffet dinner, and the main show is preceded by tricks done at your table by a wandering magician. Dinner and show are by reservation only; call 808/661-3424; adults $69–79, children $29–49. Entrance at 6 P.M. for cocktails and the show runs $35 adults, $25 kids.

# RECREATION

## Golf

Ka'anapali Resort, www.kaanapali-golf.com, is dominated by two gold courses. Designed by Robert Trent Jones, Sr., the North Course is a challenge and requires masterful putting. While a bit shorter, the South Course by Arthur Snyder calls for more overall accuracy. The clubhouse for both sits right at the resort entrance, and the pro shop rents clubs, arranges lessons, and can set you up on a putting green or the driving range. The Kaanapali Classic Senior PGA Tournament is played here. For nonresidents, greens fees run $150 for the North Course and $142 for the South Course, with twilight rates at half the regular fee. Call 808/661-3691 for tee times.

## Tennis

The Royal Lahaina Tennis Ranch, Sheraton Maui Tennis Club, and the Maui Marriott Tennis Club are all operated by the same company. Rates are the same for all, and it rents racquets, balls, machines, and can arrange round robins, lessons, and clinics. The court fee runs $10 per person daily, racquets go for $2.50, and ball machines are $20 per hour. The Tennis Ranch at the Royal Lahaina has a 3,500-seat stadium that's rated for non-pro tournaments (it's occasionally used for concerts) and 10 other courts. Open 8 A.M.–noon and again 2–7 P.M. Call 808/667-5200 for court time. The Sheraton has three lighted courts open 8 A.M.–noon and 2–8 P.M.; 808/667-9200. Five courts are open at the Marriott 7 A.M.–8 P.M.; 808/661-6200 to arrange time on a court.

The Hyatt runs its own tennis center of five courts that's open from 7 A.M. until dusk. All equipment is available, and lessons and clinics can be arranged. Court time runs $12 per hour for guests or $20 for nonguests. To set a time for play, call 808/661-1234.

## Water Activities

A whole variety of water activities and gear are available at Ka'anapali, some from established activity booths, some from the hotels, and some from private vendors that operate right on the beach. Not all provide all services. The following is a sampling of what you might expect to find somewhere along the beach: Hobie Cats $45 per hour or $69 for a one-hour lesson; single kayak $15 per hour, tandem kayak $25 per hour; sea cycle (pedal boat) $25 per hour; windsurf board $20 per hour or a 90-minute lesson for $69; boogie board $5 per hour; and snorkel gear $10 per day. Jet Ski rental and parasailing are other options. Scuba lessons and a variety of rentals can be arranged at the beach activity booths at each hotel. The *Gemini* at the Westin Maui, the *Kiele V* from the Hyatt, the *Teralani* at the Sheraton, and others leaving from the beach in front of Whalers Village make sailings every day that weather permits. For a full listing, contact any of the activity desks at the hotels on this strip, or the Maui Ocean Activities booth on the beach at Whalers Village, 808/667-2001. You can arrange water activities and all other activities islandwide at reduced rates at Activity World, located on Halawai Drive just off the highway north of the main Ka'anapali strip.

# SHOPPING

Ka'anapali provides a varied shopping scene: the **Whalers Village** shopping complex, which has a mix of the affordable and exorbitant; the **Royal Lahaina Resort** for some distinctive purchases; and the **Hyatt Regency, Westin Maui,** and **Maui Marriott,** where most people get financial jitters even window-shopping.

## Whalers Village

Open daily 9:30 A.M.–10 P.M., you can easily find anything at this shopping complex that you might need. Some of the shops are **Reyn's,** for upscale tropical clothing; **Giorgiou** and others for expensive women's fashions; the exclusive **Louis Vuitton** for designer luggage; **Blue Ginger Designs,** for women's and children's resortwear and alohawear; **Dolphin Gallery,** with beautiful creations in glass, sculptures, paintings, and jewelry; **Lahaina Scrimshaw,** for fine scrimshaw pieces and other art objects ranging from affordable to expensive; **Endangered Species Store,** where you are greeted by a stuffed python and proceeds go to help endangered species; **Eyecatcher Sunglasses,** where you can take care of your eyes with shades from $150 Revos to $5 cheapies; **Jessica's Gems,** featuring the work of designer David Welty, along with coral jewelry and black Tahitian pearl rings; **Ritz Camera** for film developing; **Waldenbooks,** a full-service book shop; and an **ABC Discount Store** for sundries. There are many other shops tucked away here and there.

A fascinating shop is **Lahaina Printsellers,** www.printsellers.com, featuring original and reproduction engravings, drawings, maps, charts, and naturalist sketches. The collection comes from all over the world, but the Hawaiiana collection is amazing in its depth, with many works featuring a nautical theme reminiscent of the amazing explorers who opened the Pacific or naturalist theme showing the flora and fauna of the islands.

The Whalers Village also has plenty of fast-food shops, three fine restaurants, the West Maui Healthcare Center, the Whale Museum, and ATMs. The Kaanapali Trolley and the westside public shuttle make stops at the mall.

Be sure to catch the free entertainment performed at 7 P.M. at the center stage some evenings of the week, and the weekly creation of sand sculpture in front of the stage on the lower level during the day. Every year in late July or early August, the Maui Onion Festival is held here at the mall, celebrating the most well known of Maui's agricultural crops with chef's demonstrations, food products, and music. Everyone is welcome.

There is free parking for three hours at the parking structure with validation from one of the mall shops. For others, the Whaler's Village parking lot charges $2.50 per hour or $20 maximum for the day, making parking an expensive proposition in Ka'anapali unless you have free parking as a guest of one of the hotels or condos here.

## Fairway Shops

A new group of shops located along the highway across from the Ka'anapali train depot is called the Fairway Shops. Access is from both Honoapi'ilani Highway and Keka'a Drive. Two of the shops that might be of interest to visitors are the **Toy Store** for car and motorcycle rentals and **Maui Dive Shop,** which rents gear and offers tours.

# INFORMATION AND SERVICES

## Information

All hotels have concierge desks and/or activity desks that offer guests free information about their hotels and the Ka'anapali area.

For a source of general information on all aspects of the Ka'anapali area as well as several brochures, contact Kaanapali Beach Resort Association, 2530 Keka'a Dr., Ste. 1-B, Lahaina, HI 96761, 808/661-3271 or 800/245-9229, kbra@kaanapaliresort.com, www.kaanapaliresort.com.

## Car Rentals

Between Ka'anapali and Honokowai, along the edge of the highway on Halawai Drive, are several rental companies that service all of West Maui. Dollar, Budget, Avis, Alamo, Hertz, and National car rental companies have offices and small lots here, as does Mavrik Motorcycles. While the availability is somewhat limited, the car rental companies do carry sedans and jeeps. Renting here eliminates one fee that is charged at the airport lots in Kahului. Mavrik only rents motorcycles and scooters.

## Medical Services

The West Maui Healthcare Center maintains an office on the upper level at the Whalers Village shopping mall, 808/667-9721; open 8 A.M.–8 P.M. daily. Doctors On Call, 808/667-7676, operates daily 8 A.M.–9 P.M. out of the Hyatt Regency, Westin Maui, and at the Kapalua Resort but makes house calls.

## Banking

There are no banks in Ka'anapali; the closest are in Lahaina. Most larger hotels can help with some banking needs, especially with cashing traveler's checks. An ATM is located on the lower level of the Whalers Village mall.

# Honokowai, Kahana, and Napili

Between Ka'anapali and Kapalua are the villages of Honokowai, Kahana, and Napili, which service the string of condos tucked away here and there along the coast. After Ka'anapali started to be built, developers picked up on Amfac's great idea and built condos here. Unfortunately, they seemed to be interested more in profit than beauty, earning this strip the dubious title of "condo ghetto." While somewhat softened over time by a great deal of thoughtful landscaping, some redevelopment, and the addition of private homes, beaches, and markets, this stretch remains overwhelmingly a string of condominium accommodations and vacation rentals. Each of these villages is a practical stop where you can buy food, gas, and all necessary supplies to keep your vacation rolling. You head for this area if you want to enjoy Maui's west coast and not spend a bundle of money. These towns are not quite as pretty as Ka'anapali or Kapalua, but proportionate to the money you'll save, you come out ahead. These areas are not clearly distinct from one another, so you may have some trouble determining where one ends and the next begins, but generally they are separated by some stretch of residential neighborhood. With the development of the new Ka'anapali Ocean Resort at the far northern end of Ka'anapali, the boundary between Ka'anapali and Honokowai will become less distinct. Napili, at the far north end of this strip, adjoins and in some ways is connected to Kapalua. To get to this area, travel north along Honoapi'ilani Highway past Ka'anapali and then take Lower Honoapi'ilani Road through Honokowai, and continue on it to Kahana and Napili. Three short connector roads link the new highway with the old road. For those who need to use it, the Kapalua–West Maui Airport sits above the highway in Kahana surrounded by acres of pineapple fields.

## Beaches

The whole strip here is rather rocky and full of coral, so not particularly good for swimming except in a few isolated spots.

**Honokowai Beach Park** is right in Honokowai just across from a small shopping plaza and the well-cared-for and still used Lahuiokalani Ka'anapali Congregational Church (1850). The park has a large lawn with palm trees and picnic tables, but a small beach with a reef in close. The water is shallow and tame—good for tots. While the swimming is not as nice as at Ka'anapali, snorkeling is fair and you can get through a break in the reef at the north end.

**Kahana Beach** is near the Kahana Beach Resort; park across the street. Nothing spectacular, but the protected small beach is good for catching some rays and it's decent swimming between the bands of rock when the waves are not too strong. There's a great view of Moloka'i, and the beach is never crowded. Just south of there is **Pohaku Park.** It's a narrow strip with only a few parking stalls but is often used for picnics or by surfers—no restroom.

Napili Bay is one of the best on the island for swimming and snorkeling.

ROBERT NILSEN

By far the best beach in this area, and one of the best on the island, is that at **Napili Bay.** This gentle crescent slopes easily into the water, and its sandy bottom gives way to coral, so snorkeling is good here as well. There are rights-of-way to this perfect, but condo-lined, beach. Look for beach access signs along Napili Place and on Hui Drive. They're difficult to spot, but once on the beach there's better-than-average swimming, snorkeling, and a good place for beginning surfers and boogie boarders.

## ACCOMMODATIONS

At last count there were more than three dozen condos and apartment complexes in the four miles encompassing Honokowai, Kahana, and Napili. There are plenty of private homes out there as well, which gives you a good cross-section of Hawaiian society. A multimillion-dollar spread may occupy a beach, while out in the bay is a local fisherman with his beat-up old boat trying to make a few bucks for the day—and his house may be up the street. Many of the condos built out here were controversial. Locals refused to work on some because they were on holy ground, and a few actually experienced bad-luck jinxes as they were being built. The smarter owners called in *kahuna* to bless the ground and the disturbances ceased.

As usual, condos are more of a bargain the longer you stay, especially if you can share costs with a few people by renting a larger unit. As always, you'll save money on food costs. Most of these are in the $200 per night and up category. Only a handful fall into the $100 per night or less group, with a remainder falling somewhere in between. Because of the mixture of studio, one-, two-, and three-bedroom units, some properties have a wide price range. The following should give you an idea of what's available in this area, starting from the south end moving north.

### Mahana at Kaanapali

Aston's Mahana at Kaanapali, 110 Ka'anapali Shores Place, 808/661-8751 or 800/922-7866, is billed as an "all oceanfront resort," and in fact all units have an ocean view at no extra cost because

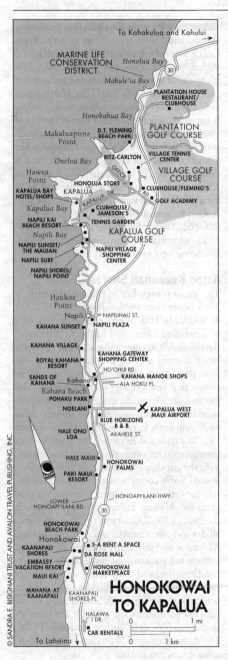

To Kahakuloa and Kahului

MARINE LIFE
CONSERVATION
DISTRICT

Honolua Bay

Mokule'ia Bay

PLANTATION HOUSE
RESTAURANT/
CLUBHOUSE

Honokahua Bay

Makaluapuna
Point

D.T. FLEMING
BEACH PARK

PLANTATION
GOLF COURSE

Oneloa Bay          RITZ-CARLTON

VILLAGE TENNIS
CENTER

VILLAGE GOLF
COURSE

Hawea
Point

HONOLUA STORE        CLUBHOUSE/FLEMING'S

KAPALUA BAY
HOTEL/SHOPS

KAPALUA

GOLF ACADEMY

Kapalua Bay

CLUBHOUSE/
JAMESON'S

NAPILI KAI
BEACH RESORT

TENNIS GARDEN

Napili Bay

KAPALUA GOLF
COURSE

NAPILI SUNSET/
THE MAUIAN

NAPILI VILLAGE
SHOPPING
CENTER

NAPILI SURF

NAPILI SHORES/
NAPILI POINT

Haukoe
Point

Napili        NAPILIHAU ST.

KAHANA SUNSET        NAPILI PLAZA

KAHANA VILLAGE

KAHANA GATEWAY
SHOPPING CENTER

ROYAL KAHANA
RESORT

HO'OHUI RD.

SANDS OF
KAHANA

KAHANA MANOR SHOPS

ALA HOKU PL.

Kahana

Kahana Beach

POHAKU PARK

NOELANI

KAPALUA WEST
MAUI AIRPORT

BLUE HORIZONS
B & B

HALE ONO
LOA

AKAHELE ST.

HALE MAUI        HONOKOWAI
PALMS

PAKI MAUI
RESORT

HONOAPI'ILANI HWY.

LOWER
HONOAPI'ILANI RD.

HONOKOWAI
BEACH PARK

HONOKOWAI

5-A RENT A SPACE

KAANAPALI
SHORES

DA ROSE MALL

EMBASSY
VACATION RESORT

HONOKOWAI
MARKETPLACE

MAUI KAI

MAHANA AT
KAANAPALI

KAANAPALI
SHORES PL.

**HONOKOWAI
TO KAPALUA**

HALAWA
I DR.

0          1 mi

CAR RENTALS

0        1 km

To Lahaina

© SANDRA E. BISIGNANI TRUST AND AVALON TRAVEL PUBLISHING, INC.

MAUI

the two long and tall buildings parallel the shoreline. The second you walk into the entry of this condo and look through a large floor-to-ceiling window framing a swimming pool and the wide blue sea, your cares immediately begin to slip away. A AAA three-diamond property, this condo sits on a point of beach and is one in the first group of condos north of Ka'anapali. Enjoy a complete kitchen plus heated pool, sauna, two tennis courts, maid service, activities desk, and a money-saving family plan. Restaurant signing privileges and the kids Camp Kaanapali are available at and in coordination with the Aston Kaanapali Shores just up the way. Rates begin with studios at $295, one-bedroom suites at $385, and huge two-bedroom suites (up to six people) for $625, but greatly reduced rates are offered during the spring and autumn "value seasons."

## Maui Kai

Smaller and older, yet offering great value, is the Maui Kai condominium resort, 106 Ka'anapali Shores Place, 808/667-3500 or 800/367-5635, fax 808/667-3660, reservation@mauikai.com, www.mauikai.com. These well-kept and privately owned units each have a full kitchen, an entertainment center, air-conditioning, a lanai that overlooks the water, daily maid service, and tile throughout. Relax at the swimming pool or inquire at the activity desk to arrange off-property tours. Studios run $155, one-bedrooms $188–198, and two-bedrooms $294, with rates reduced by about 10 percent during the value season. Two nights' minimum stay except for the last two weeks of December, when there is a seven-night minimum. The Maui Kai is an intimate place that gives you a good location and great value for the money.

## Embassy Vacation Resort

Open, airy, and with an atrium courtyard, this huge pink pyramid occupies a sliver of beach. Each of the more than 400 air-conditioned suites has a kitchen, separate living area, large-screen TV, and lanai. Daily maid service is offered, as are a children's program, two restaurants, an activity desk, a Maui Ocean Activities ocean sports booth, and laundry facilities. Kids will love the water slide at the pool, while the adults may gravitate to the spa and fitness center. The resort's Ohana Grill is a casual restaurant that serves quick food such as burgers, salads, and pizza for under $10. It's open for lunch and dinner and features live entertainment from 6–9 P.M. The North Beach Grille, a dinner-only restaurant, is the resort's better eatery, where you'll find a greater variety of entrées in the under $25 range and a nightly all-you-can-eat buffet. In a way, the Embassy is like a smaller version of the more exclusive resorts down the beach in Ka'anapali. Rates run $349–489 for a one-bedroom suite and $629 for a two-bedroom suite that sleeps six. The Embassy is located at 104 Ka'anapali Shores Place, 808/661-2000 or 800/669-3155, fax 808/667-1353, www.mauiembassy.com. There is shoreline access next to this resort.

## Aston Kaanapali Shores

The green tranquility of this created oasis at 3445 Lower Honoapi'ilani Road, 808/667-2211 or 800/922-7866, offers an unsurpassed view of sun-baked Lana'i and Moloka'i just across the channel. You enter a spacious and airy open lobby, framing a living sculpture of palms and ferns that's protected by the two arms of guest rooms that reach nearly to water's edge. The grounds are a trimmed garden in large proportions dappled with sunlight and flowers. Soak away your cares in two whirlpools, one tucked away in a quiet corner of the central garden area for midnight romance, the other near the pool. Visit the gift shop, sundries store, fitness center, lighted tennis courts, and activities desk, or enroll the little ones in Camp Kaanapali, a program for children. Enjoy a romantic dinner at the Beach Club Restaurant, which serves meals all day and offers entertainment in the evening. All studios and suites have been refurbished and include full kitchens, sweeping lanai, TVs, air-conditioning, and daily maid service. Prices range from a studio at $300 to a two-bedroom oceanfront suite for $730. Several hotel rooms with refrigerators are also available at a more affordable $200, as are suites for $900–1,000. The Aston Kaanapali Shores is a AAA three-diamond accommodation.

## Paki Maui Resort

At 3615 Lower Honoapi'ilani Road, 808/669-8235 or 800/922-7866, this Aston-managed, excellent-value condo presents airy and bright rooms with sweeping panoramas of the Lahaina Roads. Well-appointed studios for two begin at $210, up to $345 for a two-bedroom oceanfront apartment for up to six people; additional guests are $20. Amenities include maid service, air-conditioning, cable TV, complete kitchens, pool with spa, and coin laundry facilities. Every unit in this gracefully curved building has a private lanai overlooking a gem of a courtyard or the ocean. You can save money by getting a garden-view unit without sacrificing that delightful feeling that you are in the tropics. A complimentary mai tai party is held weekly for all guests. Although the Paki Maui is in town, it feels secluded the moment you walk onto this property, which forms a little oasis of tranquility. There is no sand beach fronting the condo, but the snorkeling along the reef is excellent.

## Honokowai Palms

At 3666 Lower Honoapi'ilani Road, this condo is an old standby for budget travelers. A basic two-story cinder block affair, originally used as housing for workers constructing the Sheraton down the road, it's basically a long-term place now with a few rental units. The Palms is older, but not run-down; no tinsel and glitter, but neat, clean, and adequate. There is no view. Fully furnished with kitchens, TVs, full baths, and queen- or king-size beds. A swimming pool and coin laundry are on the premises. The least expensive condos along the coast, a one-bedroom unit runs $80; three nights minimum. Contact the Klahani Resorts Corp. for details and reservations, 808/667-2712 or 800/669-6284, fax 808/661-5875.

## Hale Maui

This very reasonably priced mustard-yellow apartment hotel, owned and operated by Hans Zimmerman, offers one-bedroom apartments that can accommodate up to five people. All have a full kitchen, private lanai, color TV, and limited maid service, with coin washers and dryers, barbecue grills, and beach access available to guests. All units are bright, tasteful, clean, and neat as a pin. One of the most reasonable condos along the coast, rates are $85–105, extra person $15, weekly and monthly discount rates available; three nights minimum. The Hale Maui is an excellent choice for budget travelers who would rather spend money on having fun than on a luxurious hotel room. Contact Hale Maui at P.O. Box 516 Lahaina, HI, 96767, 808/669-6312, fax 808/669-1302, halemaui@maui.net, www.maui.net/~halemaui.

## Hale Ono Loa

Four floors high with a pool in the garden, this place will give you a basic condo experience. Amenities include complete kitchens, separate living and dining areas, TVs, lanai, partial maid service, and laundry facility. Hale Ono Loa, 3823 Lower Honoapi'ilani Rd., has peak- and low-season rates with about a $20 difference. High-season one-bedroom, ocean-view is $116, a two-bedroom oceanview runs $173; three nights minimum, discounts for stays more than 28 days. For information and reservations, contact Maui Lodging, 808/669-0089 or 800/487-6002, fax 808/669-3937.

## Noelani

This AAA-approved condo located at 4095 Lower Honoapi'ilani Road, 808/669-8374 or 800/367-6030, fax 808/669-7904, www.noelani-condo-resort.com, is last in the line before Kahana. All units are oceanfront, with fully equipped kitchens, ceiling fans, color TVs, VCRs (video rental available), washer/dryers in the non-studio units, and midweek maid service. On the grounds are two heated pools, a hot tub, and a barbecue area. You're welcomed on the first morning with a complimentary continental breakfast served poolside, where you are given an island orientation by the concierge. You'll find peace and quiet here; you can't go wrong. Studios rent from $122–135, one bedrooms are $165, two and three bedrooms for $217 and $267; 10 percent discount offered after 28 days. Car/condo, senior, AAA, and honeymoon discounts are given.

## Sands of Kahana

You know you're in Kahana when you pass Pohaku Park and spot the distinctive blue roofs of this gracious complex, which forms a central courtyard area at 4299 Lower Honoapi'ilani Road. The condo boasts the poolside Kahana Terrace Restaurant, which serves breakfast, lunch, and dinner daily. The narrow sandy-bottomed beach fronting the property is very safe and perfect for swimming and sunbathing. The Sands of Kahana gives you extraordinarily large units for the money, with lots of glass for great views, and to sweeten the pot, they're beautiful and well appointed, mostly in earth tones and colors of the islands. Some studios in this complex are timeshare units. Of the rental units, one bedrooms at $150–225, two-bedroom units at $205–285, and three-bedroom units at $305–350 are massive with two lanai, two baths with a tub built for two, walk-in closets, and great ocean views. Each unit offers a gourmet kitchen, cable TV, daily maid service, and washer/dryer units. The property, with pool, three tennis courts, putting green, barbecue area, fitness center, and spa, exudes a sense of peace and quiet, and although there are plenty of guests, you never feel crowded. This is where you come when you want to get away from it all but still be within reach of the action. All arrangements are made through Sullivan Properties, P.O. Box 55, Lahaina, HI 96767; 808/669-0423 or 800/332-1137, fax 808/669-8409; www.sands-of-kahana.com.

## Royal Kahana Resort

A tall, imposing structure in a flying V-wing shape gives all rooms a perfect view of the ocean and the islands across the channel. Light in color and accented by floral patterns, all units have full kitchens, living areas, and washers and dryers, plus there are two tennis courts on the property for guest use only, a swimming pool by the beach, an activities desk, and a fitness center. Regular-season rates are $210–230 for a studio, $265–400 for a one bedroom, and $320–460 for a two-bedroom unit; value season has rates reduced 10–15 percent with more drastic discounts at certain times of the year. The Royal Kahana is located at 4365 Honoapi'ilani Road. Call 808/669-5911, fax 808/669-5950, or Outrigger Hotels and Resorts direct at 800/668-7444.

## Kahana Village

Up the road at 4531 Lower Honoapi'ilani Road, 808/669-5111 or 800/824-3065, fax 808/669-0974, www.kahanavillage.com, this graceful vacation condominium is a group of low beach houses surrounded by well-manicured lawns on three acres. Each of the pleasantly comfortable units is individually owned, so all have a slightly different character. All are light and breezy, appointed in earth tones, and each has a complete kitchen, color TV, VCR, and large lanai. Ground-level apartments are large at 1,700 square feet and feature three bedrooms and two baths. The upper-level units are a bit smaller but still spacious at 1,200 square feet and have two bedrooms (one as a loft), two baths, and high open-beam ceilings. There is a narrow pebble beach out front, and the property has a swimming pool, hot tub, and barbecue grills. Rates are $240–280 for second-floor units, $330–395 for ground-level units, and $20 per night for each extra person; five nights minimum. Low-season rates are about 20 percent less; 10 percent discount for stays longer than 14 days.

## Kahana Sunset

This property has a superb spot on a wonderful little beach. Set alone on the small and protected Keoninue Bay, the finely sculpted gardens and trellised lanai set off the attractive and privately owned condo units that step down to the water. All units have full kitchens, private lanai, color TVs, washers and dryers, and daily maid service. Ceiling fans are used in each unit, and louvered windows catch the cooling sea breezes. Rates are $130–240 for one-bedroom, garden- and oceanview units, two bedroom oceanview units run $195–275, while two-bedroom oceanfront units run $280–370. Substantial off-season and monthly discounts are offered and some packages are available. There is a two-night minimum, except during the year-end holidays. Some credit cards accepted. Kahana Sunset, 4909 Lower Honoapi'ilani Rd., 808/669-8700 or 800/669-1488, fax 808/669-4466, www.kahanasunset.com, is managed by Premier Resort.

## Napili Point Resort

Napili Point, 5295 Honoapi'ilani Rd., 808/669-9222 or 800/669-6252, fax 808/669-7984, www.napili.com, is one of the most beautifully situated complexes on Maui. This low-rise property sits on its own promontory of black lava separating Kahana and Napili. The reef fronting the condo is home to a colorful display of reef fish and coral, providing some of the best snorkeling on the west end. Not graced with a sand beach (it's only 100 yards north along a path), nature, however, was generous in another way. Each room commands an unimpeded panorama with a breathtaking sunset view of Lana'i and Moloka'i. You get a deluxe room for a standard price. Because of the unique setting, the condo is secluded although convenient to shops and stores. The two-story buildings offer fully furnished one- and two-bedroom units from an affordable $229–399, less during regular season, with full kitchens, washers and dryers, walk-in closets, and large dressing and bath areas. Amenities include maid service, two pools, and barbecue grills. Two-bedroom units on the second floor include a loft with its own sitting area. Floor-to-ceiling windows frame the living still life of sea and surf so you can enjoy the view from every part of the apartment.

## Napili Shores

Next door to Napili Point and overlooking Napili Bay from the lava-rock shoreline is the two-story Napili Shores condominium, 5315 Lower Honoapi'ilani Rd., 808/669-8061 or 800/688-7444, fax 808/669-5407, an Outrigger property. All units surround a tropical garden, fish pond, manicured lawn, hot tub, and two swimming pools. Although not large or ostentatious, each unit is comfortable and contains a full kitchen, color TV, and large lanai. Rates run $182–238 for studios, $216–244 for one-bedroom units, with many packages available. There are two restaurants on the premises: the Orient Express Thai Restaurant and the Gazebo; an activity desk; and a guest laundry.

## Napili Surf Beach Resort

Located at 50 Napili Place, these are reasonably priced full condo units at the south end of Napili Beach that attract mostly an older crowd with some younger families, particularly during the summer. Both the buildings and grounds have been upgraded recently. The grounds are not luxurious but nicely manicured and have two pools and three shuffleboard lanes. Very clean rooms with full kitchens have ceiling fans, TVs, and their own lanai. Daily maid service is provided, and there's a laundry facility on premises. Garden-view studio units run $130, oceanview and oceanfront studios are $175–190, while the one-bedroom units range $205–280. Minimum stay is five nights, 10 during the Christmas holiday season; 10 percent discount for 30 days or longer. Car/condo packages and other special deals are offered. Contact Napili Surf at 808/669-8002 or 800/541-0638, fax 808/669-8004, relax@napilisurf.com, www.napilisurf.com.

## Napili Sunset

At 46 Hui Drive, this AAA-approved condo has two buildings on the beach and one away from the water. All units have fully equipped kitchens, ceiling fans, color TVs, and daily maid service and share the pool, the beachfront barbecue grill, and a laundry area. Studio apartments in the building away from the beach go for $120, one bedrooms $225, and two bedrooms $315; all have reduced rates during the low season. For additional information and reservations, contact Napili Sunset at 808/669-8083 or 800/447-9229, fax 808/669-2730, www.napilisunset.com.

## The Mauian

Opened in 1959, this property is the oldest on the bay, and it couldn't have a better location. Don't let the age fool you, however, because all 44 units have been attentively renovated with new kitchens and bathrooms, pleasing period-style reproduction bamboo and hardwood furniture, and Hawaiian artwork that helps conjure up the feeling of a slower, more hospitable Hawaii. And you'll find hospitality here—lots of it. This is a gem. The '50s-era buildings blend well with the garden, in which you'll find not only tropical flowers and bushes, but also taro and medicinal plants. The open central lawn holds a pool and shuffleboard courts (join a tournament), and every unit has a lanai with a view of the beach and ocean. It's the kind of place where you might expect to hear slack-key guitar wafting across the garden, and you'll certainly hear the water lapping at the shore, lulling you to sleep at night. Ceiling fans and louvered windows create air flow; there is no air-conditioning. There also are no TVs or phones in the studios, but there is a TV and a phone as well as video and book libraries in the community Ohana Room, where a complimentary continental breakfast is served daily 7:30–9 A.M. and the sunset Thursday Aloha Party is a tradition. Because of the hospitality and sense of *ohana* (family), many guests return year after year. Based on double occupancy, rates for low and high seasons are $180/$195 for a beachfront unit, $165/$185 for beach-view units, and $145/$165 for garden units; $10 each extra person. The Mauian is located at 5441 Lower Honoapi'ilani Road, 808/669-6205 or 800/367-5034, fax 808/669-0129, info@mauian.com, www.mauian.com.

## Napili Kai Beach Resort

At 5900 Honoapi'ilani Road, 808/669-6271 or 800/367-5030, fax 808/669-0086, www.napilikai.com, this accommodation is the last in Napili before you enter the landscaped expanse of Kapalua. The Napili Kai Beach Resort, the dream-come-true of now-deceased Jack Millar, was built before regulations forced properties back from the water. Jack Millar's ashes are buried near the restaurant under a flagpole bearing the United States, Canadian, and Hawaiian flags. The setting is idyllic, with the beach a crescent moon with gentle wave action. The bay is a swim-only area with no pleasure craft allowed. Rates run $190 for a garden-view hotel room up to $700 for an oceanfront luxury two-bedroom suite, but amenities include a kitchenette (refrigerators in the hotel rooms), private lanai, air-conditioning in most units, complimentary snorkel gear, daily tea party, activities desk, and all the comforts of home. Several special packages are available. There are four pools, "Hawaii's largest whirlpool," an exercise room, a croquet lawn, putting greens, and tennis courts on property, and the Kapalua Bay Golf Course is just a nine-

iron away. All rooms have Japanese touches complete with shoji screens. There's fine dining, dancing, and entertainment at the on-site Sea House Restaurant overlooking the beach.

## Bed-and-Breakfasts

True to its name, the **Blue Horizons B&B,** 3894 Mahinahina St., P.O. Box 10578, Lahaina, HI 96761, 808/669-1965 or 800/669-1948, fax 808/665-1615, innkeeper@bluehorizonsmaui.com, www.bluehorizensmaui.com, has good views of the blue Pacific looking to the west over Honokowai and Kahana. Set in a residential neighborhood below the Kapalua–West Maui Airport, this modern-style bed-and-breakfast offers three rooms. All have private bathrooms, one has a kitchenette, and all have refrigerators. The living room, kitchen, screened lanai, lap pool, barbecue grill, and washer/dryer are for everyone's use. Breakfast is included Monday–Saturday. Room rates run $99–129 for two, $15 per additional person; two nights minimum. The Blue Horizon is perhaps the only B&B north of Lahaina on the west coast.

## Agencies

Aside from booking a room direct, you can work through a condo booking agenc,y which will do all the arranging for you. For condos and homes throughout West Maui, try the following:

**Whalers Realty Management,** 808/661-3484 or 800/676-4112, fax 808/661-8338, www.vacation-maui.com, has more units in Ka'anapali properties than Honokowai, but does have a presence here.

With condos stretching from Lahaina to Napili is **Maui Beachfront Rentals,** 808/661-3500 or 888/661-7200, www.mauibeachfront.com.

With units in seven properties, **Klahani Resorts,** 808/667-2712 or 800/669-6284, fax 808/661-5875, www.klahani.com, deals mostly in the low to midrange places.

**Sullivan Properties,** P.O. Box 55, Lahaina, HI 96767, 808/669-0423 or 800/332-1137, fax 808/669-8409, www.kapalua.com, has rental units in a handful of condo properties along this stretch and in Kapalua up the coast.

**Maui Lodging,** 808/669-0089 or 800/487-

6002, fax 808/669-3937, www.mauilodging.com, concentrates on a dozen oceanfront condo properties in the Honokowai area of West Maui.

# FOOD AND ENTERTAINMENT
## Inexpensive

At Da Rose Mall, just as you enter Honokowai proper, **Lourdes Kitchenette,** 808/669-5725, offers take-out or delivery service along with a few picnic tables out front where you can eat. Open daily 10 A.M.–4 P.M., they prepare plate lunches and simple Filipino food such as adobo, with everything under $7. Lourdes is small, simple, clean, and adequate. Across the parking lot is **Cha Cha's Place,** a basic eatery for local-style grinds and priced, like Lourdes, with nothing over $7.

For a quick bite, **Honokowai Okazuya and Deli,** 808/665-0512, is available for an amazing selection of Chinese, Japanese, Italian, Mexican, and vegetarian foods at very affordable prices. Located in 5-A Rent a Space mall, 3600 Lower Honoapi'ilani Rd., Honokowai Okazuya has well-deserved popularity. Eat in or take out. Open Monday–Saturday only 10 A.M.–2:30 P.M. and again 4:30–9 P.M.

The following three restaurants are all located at Napili Plaza. **Maui Tacos** has reasonably priced, health-conscious fast food and a variety of drinks. Try a chimichanga for $5.99, a tostada for $5.25, tacos for about $3.50, or a two-fisted burrito that will keep you full all day for $6.95 or less. The salsa and guacamole are made fresh daily. No MSG or lard is used. Food is served form 9 A.M. For those who need a little pick-me-up during the day, stop at **The Coffee Shop,** open 6:30 A.M.–6 P.M. Down at the end of the line is **Mama's Ribs 'N Rotisserie,** a small takeout place that does all their cooking on the spot from fresh ingredients. Try a plate meal of ribs or chicken, done teriyaki- or traditional-style, with rice and barbecue beans, or choose a full rack of ribs or whole chicken. Side dishes are barbecue beans, macaroni salad, or rice. Aside from the full rack of ribs at $18.99, virtually everything else is under $11.75. This is a local eatery of good repute. Open Monday–Saturday 11 A.M.–6 P.M. Mama knows best.

The **Gazebo,** 808/669-5621, open daily 7:30 A.M.–2 P.M., one of the best-kept secrets in the area, is a little brown gazebo with louvered windows next to the pool at the Napili Shores Resort. Be prepared for a line. Locals in the know come here for a breakfast of the Gazebo's famous banana, pineapple, and especially the macadamia nut pancakes for $6.50. There are also eggs and omelets of all sorts under $8.95. The lunch menu features a range of sandwiches from $6.25–8.25, along with burgers and lunch plates under $8.25. You can enjoy a world-class view sitting inside or outside the Gazebo for down-home prices.

## Moderate

Whether you're a guest or not, a quiet and lovely restaurant in which to dine is **The Beach Club** at the Aston Kaanapali Shores. One of Honokowai's best-kept secrets, the restaurant is centered in the condo's garden area and opens directly onto the sea. The restaurant changes throughout the day from a casual café in the morning to a more formal candlelit room in the evening, but the service is always friendly. Breakfast, served 7–11:30 A.M., with early-bird specials until 9 A.M., is mostly standard American fare. Lunch, served 11:30 A.M.–3 P.M., offers sandwiches and lighter fare. The evening dinner menu, served 5:30–9:30 P.M., whets your appetite with scrumptious appetizers. Soup of the day and salad lead to main entrées such as chicken Marsala, grilled scallops, or clams pesto with linguine, with most in the $15–20 range. A children's menu is also offered, and entertainment is provided several nights a week.

Under the blue roof by the pool at the Sands of Kahana Resort, the open-air and moderately priced **Kahana Terrace Restaurant,** 808/669-5399, is just right for sunsets. Breakfast offerings feature omelets and items from the griddle; lunch is mostly sandwiches and burgers that go for less than $10. Appetizers like coconut shrimp and hot buffalo wings and various salads precede dinner entrées that can be fresh catch of the day for $19.95, New York strip steak for $19.95, or chicken-fried steak for $13.95. Every night brings early-bird specials where you get even more for your money, and on Sunday an all-you-can-eat poolside barbecue packs them in.

While not haute cuisine, food here is nutritious and satisfying. Live music nightly 5–7 P.M.

Located at the Kahana Manor Shops, **Dollie's Pub and Café,** 808/669-0266, is open daily 11 A.M.–midnight, with happy hour 3–6 P.M. Dollie's features several TVs with satellite hookup for sporting events, cappuccino, and weekend entertainment. The good food and fair prices on Dollie's menu feature more than a dozen sandwiches from which to choose, all priced $5.25–8.95; *pu pu* like nachos and potato skins; plates of various fettuccine from $9.95–11.95; and pizza by the tray for $15–21 or by the slice for $1.50 from 3–6 P.M. and 10 P.M. to closing. The sandwiches and other entrées are good, but the pizza is the best. The bar has a wide selection of domestic and imported beers, wines, and a daily exotic drink special. One of the few eateries in the area, Dollie's is usually a laid-back pub/pizzeria but can get hopping on the weekends and is perhaps the most happening place for late-night get-togethers in Kahana.

The **China Boat** restaurant, 4474 Lower Honoapi'ilani Hwy. in Kahana, 808/669-5089, is open Monday–Saturday for lunch 11:30 A.M.–2 P.M. and daily for dinner 5–9 P.M. It's almost elegant with its highly polished, black-lacquer furniture, pink tablecloths, scroll paintings, and island-inspired prints, but the food quality is variable. A typically large MSG-free Chinese menu offers seafood, beef, chicken, vegetables, pork, and noodle dishes at a reasonable price. Most entées run $10–15, with some vegetarian and rice dishes less.

At the Kahana Gateway Shopping Center, the **Outback Steakhouse,** 808/665-1822, is an Australian meat house serving down under grilled and flame-broiled favorites. The Outback is open 4–10 P.M. for dinner, until midnight for drinks. Get your meal going with a Kookaburra wings appetizer or bonzer Brisbane Caesar salad. Sirloin, porterhouse, and tenderloins are favorites, as are smoked and grilled baby back ribs and seasoned and grilled chicken and shrimp. Most entrées run $16–22.

The **Orient Express,** at the Napili Shores Resort, 808/669-8077, is open daily for dinner only 5:30–10 P.M. The restaurant serves Thai and Chinese food with a flair for spices; duck salad and stuffed chicken wings are a specialty. The early-bird special, served before 6:30 P.M., is a five-course dinner for $11.95. The full menu of finely spiced foods includes Orient Express's well-known curry dishes; take-out is available. Most entrées are in the $12–15 range. Overlooking the koi pond at the resort, this restaurant is a good choice. Sharing the same space is Harry's sushi and *pu pu* bar, where everything is prepared before you at the counter. Nigiri sushi orders run $4.50–7, sashimi $9.50–15, with a few other items on the menu.

## Expensive

Finally McDonald's has a culinary purpose: to landmark **Roy's Kahana Bar and Grill,** 808/669-6999, located at the Kahana Gateway Shopping Center and open daily for dinner 5:30–10 P.M. At Roy's, the executive chef works kitchen magic preparing the best in Pacific Rim cuisine. Roy Yamaguchi, the inspirational founder, has a penchant for locating his Hawaii restaurants in pragmatic shopping malls. At Roy's Kahana, the surroundings are strictly casual, like a very upscale cafeteria. The enormous room, reverberating with the clatter of plates and the low hum of dinner conversations, has 40-foot vaulted ceilings, a huge copper-clad preparation area, heavy koa tables and booths, track lighting, and windows all around. Roy's philosophy is to serve truly superb dishes post haste, but impeccably, focusing on the *food* as the dining experience, not the surroundings. Although part of the menu changes every night, you could start your culinary extravaganza with island-style pot stickers with a spicy almond satay peanut sauce, grilled Sichuan-spiced baby back ribs, crispy Upcountry green salad with a creamy spinach and tarragon dressing, or an individual *imu* pizza, all for less than $12. Move on to main dishes like lemongrass chicken, grilled filet mignon, or blackened yellowfin ahi. Expect entrées to be $22–30. Desserts feature the chocolate macadamia tart or the signature fluffy dark-chocolate soufflé (allow 20 minutes to prepare). The full bar serves beer, mixed drinks, and personally selected wine by the bottle or glass. Eating at Roy's is no place to linger over a romantic cocktail. It's more like sipping the world's finest champagne from a beer mug, but the best by any other name is still the best!

Nicole Yamaguchi has a restaurant named in her honor, just next door to her dad's place at the Kahana Gateway Shopping Center, open daily from 5:30 P.M., 808/669-5000. **Roy's Nicolina Restaurant** features Euro-Asian cuisine heavily spiced with California and Southwestern dishes. For example, try a gourmet pizzalike flatbread covered in red onions, tomatoes, and pesto, or Cajun shrimp and handmade sausage. Appetizers can be pan-fried calamari with anchovy mayonnaise, or seared goat cheese and eggplant with cilantro pesto and red pepper vinaigrette. Entrées are delicious and fascinating, with offerings like roasted orange-ginger plum duck, or Yankee pot roast with mashed potatoes and garlic spinach. While much of the menu at Nicolina's is the same as across the hall at Roy's, about half is created only for this restaurant, and it too changes nightly. If dad's place is filled up, you'll love the quieter Nicolina's, a "Sichuan-spiced taco chip off the old block."

Since 1998 you've been able to get handcrafted beer on Maui's west side at the **Fish and Game Brewing Company and Rotisserie,** 808/669-3474, at the Kahana Gateway Shopping Center. Of the half-dozen, brewed-on-property varieties that are always on tap, you could try the Plantation Pale Ale, Wild Hog Stout, or the lighter Honolua Lager. Beers run $3.75 a glass, or $5 for a sampler of five. The sports bar is in the back, and to its front is the deli counter and a sit-down space for lunch. Order your sandwiches and drink at the counter and have a look at the gourmet cheeses, seafood, and specialty meats that line the deli case. In the evening, the dark paneled dinner room is opened for full meals, and set behind glass in that room is the brewing apparatus. Start your dinner with spiced tomato steamed mussels, grilled brewers sausage, or oyster chowder. For the heart of the meal, try fresh fish in one of four preparations, which includes steamed Oriental and habanero cornmeal–crusted dungeness crab, or cioppino pasta. From the rotisserie and grill come such items as hoisin-glazed duckling, marinated pork loin, and rack of lamb,

and most entrées are in the under $27 range. The rich surroundings, fine food flavors, and quality beer will make for a satisfying evening.

At the Napili Kai Beach Resort, the **Sea House Restaurant,** 808/669-1500, is open daily for breakfast 8–10:30 A.M., lunch 11:30–2 P.M., and dinner 6–9 P.M. (5:30 P.M. in winter); reservations suggested. Inside the semi-open-air restaurant, breakfast is standard American fare and lunch is sandwiches, salads, soups, and a few entrées. The restaurant shines more at night and has a list of appetizers that's nearly as long as the list of entrées. Dinner choices, served with vegetables and rice pilaf or potato, include fresh catch for $27, Sea House scampi for $26, seasoned and broiled rack of lamb for $27, and ancho chili chicken breast for $24. Besides the normal menu, every night brings a special dinner menu, but the best is the lobster tail dinner on Thursdays. A full wine list includes selections from California and France. There are the sweet sounds of Hawaiian music nightly and a wonderful Friday night Napili Kai Foundation children's Polynesian show put on by local children who have studied their heritage under the guidance of the foundation. Dinner seating is at 6 P.M., the show at 7:30 P.M.; $50 adults, $25 children. If you just want to soak up the rays and gorgeous view of Napili Bay, you can wear your swimwear and have a cool drink or light fare at the Whale Watcher's Bar, where you can also get lunch and *pu pu.*

# SHOPPING
## Honokowai Marketplace

This shopping plaza, located at the intersection where Lower Honoapi'ilani Road splits off from Honoapi'ilani Highway, is a new mall in the spirit of the Kahana Gateway Shopping Center and the Napili Village Shopping Center farther up the highway. Modern in design and convenient in location, it provides services for tourists and residents alike. Here you'll find a large **Star Market** for all basic food needs and deli items, a **Maui Dive shop, Java Jazz** coffee shop, a video rental shop, and a dry cleaners. **Maui Arts and Gifts** provides souvenirs and take-home art,

M

MAUI

**Aloha Shirt Shack** can set you up with something to wear, you can buy and develop film at **Imagine Photo,** and **Pizza Paradiso, Soup Nutz,** and **Hula Scoops** will give you something quick to eat and drink.

## Da Rose Mall

Look for this tiny mall located oceanside at the south end of town at 3481 Lower Honoapi'ilani Road, where you'll find **A & B Rental and Sales,** 808/669-0027, open daily 9 A.M.–5 P.M., specializing in bicycles, snorkel gear, boogie boards, and surfboards. Prices are mountain bikes $15 for 24 hours, $60 per week; snorkeling gear $2.50 per day and $9 per week. Boogie boards, surfboards, and even fishing poles are rented by the day or week. The sportswear includes board shorts, sundresses, sarongs, aloha shorts, T-shirts, and sunglasses. In front is **Lourdes Kitchenette,** around the side are **Treasures From the Sea** gift shop and **Blooming Rose Boutique** studio for women's fashions, and across the parking lot is **Cha Cha's Place** restaurant. Maui No Ka Oi farmers sell their produce at a **farmers market** in the parking lot of Da Rose Mall Sunday–Friday 7:30 A.M.–3:30 P.M. This is a good chance to pick up locally grown foods. Next door is an **ABC Store,** open daily 6:30–11 P.M., a minimarket selling everything from resort wear to wine.

## 5-A Rent a Space Mall

At 3600 Lower Honoapi'ilani Highway, this mall is usually located by reference to the Pizza Hut here. **Honokowai Okazuya and Deli** is the other eatery in this strip of shops, while **The Fish Market Maui** sells fresh fish, seafood, and prepared, ready-to-eat, or ready-to-cook items. Here you'll also find **Snorkels N' More,** 808/665-0804, open daily 8 A.M.–5 P.M., which has reasonable rates for sales and rental of snorkel gear, boogie boards, surfboards, other water equipment, and some golf clubs. There are usually a few bikes for rent as well, and same-day film processing is available.

Monday, Wednesday, and Friday 7–11 A.M. you'll find the West Maui **farmers market** in the parking lot across from Honokowai Beach Park. Pick up fresh fruit, produce, flowers, and other food products for a day on the beach or dinner ingredients for those staying at the condos nearby. Also in this small complex are **Gina's Food Mart** and **Boss Frog's,** where you can rent snorkel gear or sign up for a boat ride.

## Kahana Manor Shops

Aside from **Dollie's,** in the Kahana Manor Shops, there is the **Kahana Manor Groceries,** a one-stop sundries and liquor store open Monday–Saturday 8 A.M.–10 P.M.; the **Women Who Run With Wolves** boutique for beach and athletic wear and accessories for active women; the **Wiki Wiki One-Hour Photo** for all your camera needs; and **Boss Frogs** water activity shop that rents snorkel gear and kayaks, and does activity reservations.

## Kahana Gateway Shopping Center

At this newest shopping addition to the Kahana area, easily spotted along Route 30 by McDonald's golden arches, you'll find a **gas station,** a **Whalers General Store, Bank of Hawaii,** and the **Koin-Op Laundromat.** However, the premier stop is **Roy's Kahana Bar and Grill,** one of the finest gourmet restaurants on Maui, and **Roy's Nicolina Restaurant** next door. But these aren't the only eateries here. Also try the **Fish and Game Brewing Company and Rotisserie,** one of only two on the island, and its accompanying restaurant where you can get gourmet foods and specialty meats, and the more casual **Outback Steakhouse.** Also at the center is the **Maui Dive Shop,** 808/669-3800, a full-service water activities store where you can rent snorkel equipment, scuba gear, and beach accessories; **Gallerie Hawaii** for contemporary international artwork; **Hutton's Jewelry; Leslie's Family Funwear** for contemporary fashions; and **Ashley's Internet Cafe** for ice cream, yogurt, hot and cold drinks, and sandwiches while you check your email ($.25 per minute, minimum $3).

## Napili Plaza

Napili's shopping center offers the full-service **First Hawaiian Bank; Napili Supermarket,** open daily 6:30 A.M.–11 P.M., featuring fresh fish; and **Mail Services Plus,** open Monday–Saturday 8 A.M.–6 P.M., Saturday until 1 P.M., closed Sunday, for all your postal and shipping needs. You may want to pick up a video for the night at **Cinemagic Video** or snorkel gear at **Boss Frog's.** For food, the center has **Maui Tacos,** the **Coffee Store,** and **Mama's Ribs 'N Rotisserie.** If you stop by on Wednesday or Saturday from 9 A.M.–4 P.M., have a look at the craft fair for arts, crafts, gifts, and collectibles.

## Napili Village Shopping Center

At 5425 Lower Honoapi'ilani Road, this tiny cluster of shops is hardly big enough to warrant the moniker "shopping center." The **Napili Village General Store,** 808/669-6773, is a well-stocked little store and known landmark, good for last-minute items, with fairly good prices for where it is. You can pick up picnic items and sandwiches, groceries, sundries, and liquor. Open daily 7 A.M.–9 P.M. Next door is **Snorkel Bob's,** 808/669-9603, open daily 8 A.M.–5 P.M., where you can rent snorkel equipment (prescription masks available) for as little as $9 per week and boogie boards for only $26 per week. Bob lets you return your gear at any of his shops for free. Snorkel Bob also arranges island tours.

# Kapalua

Kapalua sits like a crown atop Maui's head. One of the newest areas on Maui to be developed, the 1,650-acre Kapalua Resort, www.kapalua-maui.com, was begun in 1975 as a vision of Colin Cameron, one of the heirs to the Maui Land and Pineapple Company. It's been nicely done. Within the resort are the Kapalua Bay and Ritz-Carlton luxury hotels, a half-dozen upscale condominium communities, exclusive shops, three championship golf courses, a golf academy, two tennis centers with multiple courts, sweeping vistas, and terrific beaches. Nearby are horseback-riding stables and plenty of water activity options. All of this has been carved out of the former Honolua Ranch, an outgrowth of land granted to Rev. Baldwin (of Lahaina) in 1836, that eventually grew to be 24,500 acres by 1902. From the beginning, the Honolua Ranch grazed cattle and farmed fruits and coffee. This is pineapple country now, and these golden fruits have been raised here since 1912. Following the introduction of this crop, a cannery was built; camps, a store, and a church were set up for plantation workers; and a railroad was established for transporting the goods. Currently, Maui Land and Pineapple Company has about 9,000 acre of pineapple under cultivation, here and near Makawao, and is the largest producer of these sweet fruits in the United States.

Of the annual special events that take place at Kapalua, a few have broad interest. Held in late June, the Kapalua Wine and Food Festival showcases culinary works of island chefs and couples these with select wines from around the world. The yearly Earth Maui Nature Summit conference is presented by the Kapalua Nature Society, which also sponsors an Earth Maui 5K Fun Run and Kapalua Fun Swim Challenge. These bring out plenty of enthusiastic local athletes, and part of the proceeds go to environmental organizations around the island. Both the Kapalua Open Tennis Tournament in September and the Senior Tennis Championship earlier in the year draw admiring crowds, but perhaps the most well-known event that takes place in Kapalua is the nationally broadcast Mercedes Championship golf tournament.

In 1993, the Bay Course was the first golf course in the nation to be certified by the Audubon Society as a cooperative sanctuary; by the next year, the Village and Plantation courses also had that designation. This certification means that, among other things, measures are taken to protect and promote wildlife habitat, plant native species of vegetation, reduce water consumption, and restrict the use of chemicals for fertilizers and pest control. For another example of the lengths that the landowners are willing to go in their stewardship of the natural environment, one need only look to a secluded and rather unusual sanctuary high above the West Maui Airport. There, land has been set aside and infrastructure begun on a gorilla preserve that will be the future home to Koko, the well-known great ape who talks in sign language.

## Transportation

The complimentary **Kapalua Shuttle** runs throughout the resort for use by resort guests on an on-demand basis from 6 A.M.–11 P.M. While there is no regular schedule, it will make stops at the hotels and villas, tennis courts, golf courses, and the Kapalua–West Maui Airport. For information or pickup, call 808/669-3177. A dozen times a day, the Holo Ka'a public transit shuttle runs between the two hotels in Kapalua and the Ka'anapali Resort, stopping at nine points along the way in Napili, Kahana, and Honokowai. The fare is $2 one way.

## BEACHES AND BAYS

### Kapalua Beach

Just past Napili Bay is the equally as nice Kapalua Bay with its fine crescent beach that's popular although usually not overcrowded. Look for access just past the Napili Kai Beach Resort. Park in the public lot and follow the path through the tunnel below the Bay Club restaurant to the beach. The well-formed reef has plenty of fish for snorkeling, but swimming is good here too. Also here are restrooms, showers, and a hotel beach concession.

### Oneloa Beach

Located around the point from Kapalua Beach, Oneloa is a small sandy beach down a steep path between condos, where swimming is good and locals come to surf. Seldom visited and private; parking available at the entrance to The Ironwoods.

### D. T. Fleming Beach Park

One of Maui's best—a long, wide beach backed by wonderful shade trees. This beach park is on Honoapi'ilani Highway just past the Ritz-Carlton, where the road dips back down to the coast. Here you'll find parking, showers, barbecue grills, and excellent swimming except in winter, when there's a pounding surf. There's fair snorkeling here and good surfing, but many younger kids come for body boarding. This is the beach for the Ritz-Carlton, so the south end closest to the hotel has become a bit exclusive, while the rest maintains its very local flavor.

### Mokule'ia Bay

Mokule'ia Bay is about 200–300 yards after mile marker 32. There is limited parking along the road, where cement stairs lead down to the water through a stand of trees. This beach has great bodysurfing but terribly dangerous currents in the winter when the surf is rough. Be careful. The surf here is known as "Slaughterhouse." This en-

## PU'U KUKUI PRESERVE

High in the hills above Kapalua is the **Pu'u Kukui Preserve.** Donated by the Maui Land and Pineapple company and managed by the Nature Conservancy, this 8,661-acre tract of rainforest real estate was dedicated in 1992 and is said to be the largest privately owned preserve in the state. It borders the remainder of the 13,000 acres that make up the whole of the West Maui Mountains rainforest, one of the most environmentally diverse areas in the state. Within its boundaries are several endangered species of birds, five endangered and brightly colored tree snails, and 15 distinct plant communities. Thickly wooded hillsides and deep ravines, a mist-shrouded mountaintop, boggy upland plateaus, and a swampy crater characterize this area. It is pristine wilderness that gets nearly as much rain (more than 400 inches per year) as Mt. Wai'ale'ale on Kaua'i (said to have the highest rainfall in the world), and has, in miniature, characteristics similar to the Alaka'i Swamp on Kaua'i. There is no public access to this preserve, except for a once-a-year guided group hike arranged by lottery and sponsored by the Kapalua Nature Society. In response to this rich environment and the deep cultural and historical past of the region, the Kapalua Nature Society was formed to promote an awareness and appreciation for the diversity of the land and a respect for holding it in trust for future generations.

ROBERT NILSEN

Situated within a marine life conservation district, Mokule'ia Bay is a great spot to snorkel.

tire area, plus all of adjacent Honolua Bay, is a **Marine Life Conservation District** and the underwater life is fabulous—some of the best snorkeling in the area. Fish, crabs, eels, rays, octopus, and numerous other sea creatures use the bottom sand, multihued coral, and volcanic rock to play out their rhythm of life.

## Honolua Bay

Just past Mokule'ia Bay heading north, look for a dirt road, then park, or park just after crossing the bridge. It's about a 10-minute walk to the beach from either spot. The bay is good for swimming, snorkeling, and especially surfing. Some people stay the night without much problem. For good views of the surfers, drive a little farther along the road and park along the cliff just as the road reaches the top, or drive down the dirt road at the edge of the pineapple field for a spot—there will be lots of cars on a good wave day.

## Honokohau Bay

This rather sizable bay faces north and is the last

bay before the "wilds" of the backside become predominant. Into the bay drains the water of the narrow but deep Honokohau Valley, from which water is taken by flume to irrigate the extensive fields of West Maui. A few houses constitute the community of Honokohau near mile marker 36. A rocky beach and thin strip of gray sand are located where the stream enters the bay, which generally has a sandy bottom close to shore. In the uplands above this valley are extensive pineapple fields, and from 1914–20 the island's first pineapple cannery canned fruit here to be distributed to the world. Canning operations moved to Lahaina and continued there until 1962, when the business moved again to a new cannery in Kahului, which is still in operation.

# LUXURY HOTELS

As in Ka'anapali, all accommodations in Kapalua fall into the luxury classification.

## Kapalua Bay Hotel and Ocean Villas

This, like other grand hotels, is more than a place to stay; it's an experience. The hotel steps down the hillside from its sixth-level entrance. The main lobby is partially open, letting through the gentle breezes and opening up the ocean vista. Plants accent the lobby, and the walls are hung with paintings by Peggy Hopper. All colors are soothing and subdued. To one side is the Lehua Lounge, which is open for cocktails and light snacks. A tiny brook splits the Gardenia Court restaurant on the lower level, and the view over the garden lawns and out to sea is spectacular. The clean lines of the hotel, its sparse decoration, and contemporary elegance let the view speak for itself without distraction. The ocean view vies for your attention here, while the pool pulls you down to the garden, and the beach lures you to the water. Not overly ornamented, guest rooms are done in muted colors—off-whites, tans, and tropical greens. Each spacious room is neatly laid out with an entertainment center, three telephones, electronic safe, a soft couch and easy chairs, and louvered doors to the lanai. The well-lit bathrooms have his and hers sinks at each end of the room, separate dressing

M

MAUI

closets, and individual areas for the tub, shower, and commode. Marble, tile, and chrome are used throughout. Concierge service and twice-daily maid service are additional amenities.

There are three restaurants and a lobby lounge in the complex, a business center, fitness room, swimming pool and spa, beach activity center, arcade of shops, and a multitude of daily activities and cultural programs including Kamp Kapalua for kids. Every day from 9 A.M.–3 P.M. in the lobby, craftspeople and artisans share their work with hotel guests. The least expensive rooms in the hotel are ones with a garden view at $360–390. Oceanview rooms run $450–620, and suites from $1,200; $75 each additional person 18 and older. In addition, a dozen one- and two-bedroom oceanfront villa suites go for $530–800 per night. For reasonable sums, numerous packages are available. The Kapalua Bay Hotel is part of the Luxury Collection of Starwood Hotels and Resorts. Contact the Kapalua Bay Hotel at One Bay Drive, Kapalua, HI 96761, 808/669-5656 or 800/367-8000, www.kapaluabayhotel.com.

## Ritz-Carlton Kapalua

The green sweep of tended lawns fading into the distant sea foaming azure heralds your entrance into an enchanted realm as you wind your way down the roadway leading to the Ritz-Carlton Kapalua, a AAA five-diamond property at One Ritz-Carlton Drive, Kapalua, HI 96761, 808/669-6200 or 800/262-8440, fax 808/665-0026, www.ritzcarlton.com. At the porte cochere, a waiting bellman will park your car. Enter the main hall and relax in the formal parlor of overstuffed chairs, marble-topped tables, and enormous flower arrangements. Evenings in the hall bring mellow entertainment under soft illumination. Through a huge set of double doors is a terrace of Chinese slate. Below, in the floral heart of the hotel grounds, are the trilevel seashell-shaped swimming pools and fluttering palms. Reminiscent of the Orient, the roof line of this great hotel covers the two wings that descend the hill toward the sea, creating an enormous central area between them. All this, coupled with the dark and rich woodwork, thick patterned carpets, floral drapery, pineapple-pattern wallpaper, and halls hung with fine works by prominent island artists and 19th-century reproductions, define the Ritz as the epitome of elegance and luxury.

On the beach, a sweeping crescent of white sand is embraced by two sinewy arms of jet-black lava. It becomes immediately obvious why the diminutive promontory was called Kapalua, "Arms Embracing the Sea," by the ancient Hawaiians who lived here. Notice on the rise above the sea a rounded shoulder of banked earth separated from the main hotel grounds by a low hedge of beach naupaka: The spirits of ancient *ali'i* linger here. This 13.5-acre burial ground harbors perhaps 2,000 graves from around 850 to the 1800s, and it also contains a section of the old paved King's trail that at one time circled the island. With the discovery of this site, the original construction plans were altered, and the hotel was moved away from the area in an attempt to protect it. A *kahuna* was asked to perform the ancient *mele* to appease the spirits, and to reconsecrate the land, passing the *kahu* (caretaking) of it to the Ritz-Carlton. Although the small parcel was deeded to the state as the **Honokahua Preservation Site,** the hotel management and staff alike take their responsibility very seriously. Public access is restricted.

For those with physical fitness and pampering on their minds, the hotel has a fitness center complete with exercise machines, yoga classes, massage therapy, a beauty salon, sauna, and steam rooms. Other hotel offerings include the Ritz Kids children's program, the Aloha Fridays program of cultural activities, a croquet lawn, a putting green, a business center, and a clutch of exclusive shops. At the corner of the property, the Kumulani Chapel or adjacent gazebo can be arranged for weddings.

Located in two wings off the main reception hall, the nearly 550 luxury rooms and suites, all with their own private lanai and sensational view, are a mixture of kings and doubles. Done in muted neutral tones of coral or celadon, the rooms feature hand-crafted quilts, twice-daily room attendance, turndown service, color TVs,

24-hour room service, a fully stocked honor bar, and an in-room safe. The spacious marble bathrooms offer wide, deep tubs, separate shower stalls and commodes, and double sinks. Rates begin at $340 for a garden view to $535 for a deluxe ocean view. The Ritz-Carlton Club, an exclusive floor with its own concierge, and featuring continental breakfast, light lunch, cocktails, cordials, and a full spread of evening hors d'oeuvres, is $635. Suites from a one-bedroom garden view to the magnificent two-bedroom Ritz-Carlton Suite run $610–2,700. Many special packages are offered.

## CONDOMINIUMS

Several groups of upscale condominiums dot this spacious resort, either fronting the water or overlooking the golf fairways. Condos in the Bay Villas, Ridge Villas, and Golf Villas range from one-bedroom fairway units to two-bedroom oceanfront hideaways—and a handful of luxury homes are thrown into the mix. Each is individually owned, so all are decorated differently, but all are equipped with full kitchens, air-conditioning and fans, washers and dryers, telephones, and TVs, and all amenities that you'll need for your vacation. Daily maid service can be arranged. All groups of villas also have swimming pools, barbecue grills, and maintained gardens. One-bedroom villas with a fairway view start at $199 and climb rapidly to the three-bedroom oceanfront villas for $499. Daily rates for the luxury homes run $1,650 for three bedrooms to $4,000–7,000 for five-bedroom ones. Some golf and tennis packages and car/condo deals are also offered. Check-in is at the Kapalua Villas Reception Center in a structure built in 1912 and used for decades as the plantation office. For information and reservations, contact Kapalua Villas, 550 Office Rd., Kapalua, HI 96761, 808/669-8088 or 800/545-0018, fax 808/669-5234, www.kapaluavillas.com. For rental options throughout the remainder of this luxury resort, contact Kapalua Vacation Rentals, 808/669-4144, and Sullivan Properties, 808/669-0423.

## FOOD
### Kapalua Bay Resort Restaurants

The resort has four dining spots. The elegant **Bay Club,** 808/669-8008, offers fine dining for dinner 6–9:30 P.M. on a promontory overlooking the beach and Moloka'i in the distance. Traditionally elegant, there is a dress code, and the soft evening entertainment creates a superb atmosphere. With selections like the signature crab and rock shrimp cake appetizer, Kona lobster, porcini mushroom–dusted opakapaka, seafood paella, and Basque-style rack of lamb, expect to spend at least $35 for a superbly prepared entrée with overtones of flavors from the Pacific and Asia. The menu changes seasonally.

The open-air and contemporary **Gardenia Court** on the lower lobby level of the main building is the principal dining room of the hotel. It serves breakfast daily 6–11 A.M., with a Sunday brunch overlapping from 9:30 A.M.–1:30 P.M. Sunday brunch runs $32 per person. Dinners run Tuesday–Saturday 6–9 P.M., while the Friday seafood buffet starts at 5:30 P.M. Most entrées are $24–32, and the seafood buffet is $38. Resortwear required.

For lunch, light favorites are served at **The Plumeria Terrace,** a relaxing poolside café open 11 A.M.–5 P.M. for food and until 5:30 P.M. for cocktails. In the entrance lobby, the **Lehua Lounge** serves *pu pu* and a light à la carte menu 4:30–9 P.M. and drinks until 10 P.M., with relaxing music in the evening to help let the cares of the day slip away.

### Ritz-Carlton Restaurants

Dining at the Ritz-Carlton is a wonderful gastronomic experience, with two main restaurants from which to choose, plus a lobby lounge, sushi bar, and both beachside and poolside cafés. **The Terrace Restaurant,** set below the main lobby and open daily for breakfast 7–11 A.M., informal and relaxed, overlooks the central courtyard with the dramatic sea vista beyond and features fish and seafood with undertones of Asian flavors. Although there is an extensive à la carte breakfast menu, the house specialty is a breakfast buffet for $24.

**The Banyan Tree,** a semiformal outdoor restaurant oceanside of the swimming pool, is open for lunch 11:30 A.M.–3:30 P.M. and dinner 5:30–9 P.M., with live entertainment at dinnertime Friday–Tuesday. Food is a mix of Asian and Hawaiian. Fashioned like a Mediterranean court, the restaurant offers seating in high-backed chairs at teakwood tables, with mood lighting reminiscent of old oil lamps. Dine al fresco on the redwood deck and watch cavorting whales just offshore. Start with a spicy pesto grilled shrimp, chilled island gazpacho, or warm asparagus and crab salad. Entrée selections include a Hawaii sea bass, Colorado rack of lamb, pineapple-glazed chicken, bouillabaisse, and many more, most from $24–34.

Down by the beach, on a patio surrounded by a manicured coconut grove, is **The Beach House,** serving tropical libations, healthy fruit smoothies, burgers, and sandwiches for under $16 from 11:30 A.M.–4 P.M. Similarly, the **pool bar and café** offers light food and beverages 11:30–4 P.M.

From noon to midnight at the **lobby lounge** you'll find light appetizers, desserts, drinks, and complimentary coffee while you sit and gaze out over the courtyard from the patio. Nearby in the lobby and open 5–10 P.M. is the **Kai** sushi bar with the freshest of sushi.

## Sansei

Located in the Kapalua Bay Shops is the exceptional **Sansei** seafood restaurant and sushi bar, 808/669-6286, which serves not only Japanese sushi, but also a whole variety of Pacific Rim food and drinks from the bar. Open daily 5:30–10 P.M. for dinner, and Thursday and Friday for a late-night dinner and laser karaoke from 10 P.M. until closing, which is usually around 2 A.M. For those who like to dine early, an early-bird special is offered 5:30–6 P.M. Sansei offers an extensive menu of sushi rolls and appetizers. Although traditional sushi (and sashimi) can be ordered, the Sansei has made its reputation by taking these Japanese morsels to a higher level with eclectic combinations of ingredients and sauces, as in the mango crab salad handroll with its spicy Thai vinaigrette sauce, and the Kapalua

Butterfly, which is snapper, smoked salmon, crab, and veggies in a crisp panko batter roll with tangy ponzu sauce. An award-winning appetizer is the Asian rock shrimp cake, which is shrimp crusted with crispy noodles with ginger-lime-chili butter and cilantro pesto. The sushi and appetizers could certainly fill you up, but save room for an entrée. These delicacies include a special seafood pasta with tiger prawns, onion scallops, and Japanese noodles, a Szechwan-crusted ahi tuna, Peking duck breast with mushroom and potato risotto and foie gras demi-glaze, and Colorado lamb T-bone chop. Sushi rolls run $4–16, appetizers up to $13, and main entrées $16–24. The menu items are imaginative and the blends of flavors exceptional.

## Jameson's Grill and Bar

Don't underestimate this excellent restaurant just because it's located between the golf clubhouse and tennis center. The Kapalua Bay Golf Course provides the backdrop, and the restaurant provides the filling, delicious food. The main room with its flagstone floor and open-beam ceiling is richly appointed with koa wood, and large windows frame a sweeping view of the supergreen fairways of the golf course. Sit inside or out on the patio. Breakfast and lunch are mostly light and easy meals; the real treat comes in the evening from 5–10 P.M., when a more substantial dinner meal is served. Start with an appetizer such as stuffed mushrooms for $8.95 or seared sashimi for $12.95, and move on to a soup or one of the many fine salads. Entrées include fish of the day at market price, lemon pepper chicken for $18.95, rack of lamb for $27.95, and New York strip steak for $25.95. Follow your meal with dessert or sip wine selected from an extensive list. All items can be ordered take-out. An excellent restaurant with a lovely setting at 200 Kapalua Drive. Call 808/669-5653 for reservations.

## The Plantation House

Above Kapalua at the Plantation Golf Course Clubhouse, you'll find the lovely Plantation House Restaurant, 808/669-6299, open daily 8–11 A.M. for breakfast, 11 A.M.–3 P.M. for lunch, and 5:30–10 P.M. for dinner. Inside, the split-level floor, gabled roof, natural wood, fireplace, and carpeted and marbled floor add elegance, but the real beauty is the natural still life that pours through the floor-to-ceiling French doors. Kapalua lies at your feet and the West Maui Mountains rise behind. For breakfast, the extensive menu offers fare like a hearty rancher's breakfast of two eggs, toast, two scoops of rice or breakfast potatoes, grilled ham, bacon, or Portuguese sausage all for $8; or smoked salmon Benedict for $10. For lunch, start with pan-fried crab cakes served with basil pepper aioli for $8.50 or a Greek chicken salad for $11.50. A half-pound double-fisted Plantation House burger is available for $8 and a chicken breast sandwich for $9. The dinner menu tempts your palate with scallop skewers and prawn and pork pot stickers. The chef prepares pasta al giorno for $16, or tops it with scallops or shrimp for $21, and sautéed jumbo prawns with garlic mashed potatoes run $22. However, fish is the focus here, and one of the most popular of the many signature entrées is sautéed fish with braised asparagus and Alaskan snow crab meat. The food, with flavors and ingredients influenced by the Mediterranean, is a winner, and the views make it even more special.

### Fleming's Restaurant

Fleming's "On the Greens at Kapalua" is the restaurant at the Village Golf Course clubhouse, 808/665-1000. As with the other clubhouse eateries at this resort, it has surprisingly good food, providing what can casually be referred to as golf gourmet. Breakfast, served 8–11 A.M., is mostly eggs and griddle items. A lanai menu that's mostly *pu pu*, soup, salad, and sandwiches is served 11 A.M.–3 P.M. Dinner from 5 P.M. is definitely fine dining with a fancier twist. Start with crispy crab cakes, portobella mushroom ravioli, or Upcountry pear salad in the $7–12 range, and move on to such entrées as fish of the day, grilled pork chop, filet mignon Wellington, or pan-roasted rack of lamb that run mostly $20–29. Spiced with the flavors of the people who have migrated to the islands, your meal will be satisfying no matter your choice.

### Honolua Store

Set next to the entrance of the Ritz-Carlton, this small general store also serves reasonably priced light meals and sandwiches. The breakfast menu, served 6–10 A.M., offers "The Hobo"—eggs, sausage, and rice for $3.95—or two pancakes for $2.95. Plate lunches, sandwiches, grilled items, and salads all run under $7 and are served 10 A.M.–3 P.M., or pick something out of the deli case or take away a box lunch. Sit at a table on the front porch and overlook the broad lawns and tall pine trees of the exclusive planned community of Kapalua. This is by far the cheapest place in the area to eat.

## SHOPPING

### Kapalua Shops

A cluster of exclusive shops service the resort, including **McInerny** with fine women's apparel, **@Reyn's** for islandwear, **Kapalua Kids** for the younger set, and **Kapalua Logo Shop** if you want to show off that you've at least been to the Kapalua Resort, since all items of clothing sport the butterfly logo. Visit **La Perle** for pearls, diamonds, and other fashionable jewels, and **South Seas Trading Post** for antiques, art, and more ethnic jewelry. For fine examples of Hawaiian quilts and other stitchery, try **Hawaiian Quilt Collection. Lahaina Galleries** has a wonderful collection of island and off-island artists on display, while the **Elizabeth Doyle Gallery** features art glass, and **W.H. Smith** has all your sundry supplies. For a bit more of an intellectual stop, try **Kapalua Discovery Center** for a short historical, cultural, and natural-history lesson about the area; open 10 A.M.–5 P.M. daily, free. When you get hungry from all the shopping, stop into the **Sansei** restaurant and sushi bar for a taste of Japan and the Pacific with an eclectic twist. Adjacent to the Kapalua Bay hotel, these shops are open from 9 A.M. daily.

If you're here on Tuesday at 10:30 A.M., come and listen to slack-key guitar or ukulele and stories. On Thursdays 10–11 A.M., be sure to see the free ancient hula show, and on Fridays 10:30–11:30 A.M., you can participate in a hula lesson. Some Mondays and Wednesdays, crafts

M

MAUI

are taught, and Fridays at 9:45 A.M. a cultural history lesson is presented by the resort's Hawaiian Cultural Advisor. These shops are connected to those in Ka'anapali and Lahaina by the Holo Ka'a public transit shuttle.

## Honolua Store

This well-stocked, reasonably priced general store, open daily 6 A.M.–8 P.M., is a rare find in this expensive neck of the woods. The shelves hold beer, wine, and liquors, basic food items from bananas to sweets, books and gifts, and even a smattering of sunglasses, shorts, hats, aloha shirts, and logo wear. Breakfast and lunch are dispensed from the deli in the back, and boxes of preinspected pineapples can be purchased here to be taken back to the Mainland. Built in 1929 and metamorphosed over the years, this shop has served the needs of this community for nearly as long as there has been a community here, and it functioned in more than one way as the center of village life until the village was eclipsed by the Kapalua Resort in the mid-1970s.

# RECREATION
## Golf

Kapalua's three golf courses combine to make one of the finest golfing opportunities in the state. The Bay Course is an ocean course that extends up the hill into the trees. The signature hole 5 is a challenge, with the fairway laid out around the curve of a bay. Pushing up against the surrounding pineapple fields, the Village Course is a mountain course that offers vistas over the distant ocean. At more than 7,000 yards, the Plantation Course is the longest and is used by the PGA for professional championships. For information and tee times, call 808/669-8044. In addition, the new Kapalua Golf Academy, 808/669-6500, is the largest such instructional facility in the state, offering clinics and lessons. Outdoors are target greens, putting greens, wedge areas, bunkers, a short game area, and an 18-hole putting course.

## Tennis

The Kapalua Resort boasts 20 plexipave courts in two tennis centers, representing the largest private tennis facility in the state. Both offer pro shops, equipment rental, clinics, lessons, and tournaments. Some courts are lighted so evening play is possible. Courts times run $10 per person for resort guests or $12 for others; call for reservations. The Tennis Garden, 808/669-5677, is located near the Bay Course clubhouse, while the Village Tennis Center, 808/665-0112, is ensconced near the water below the Ritz-Carlton.

## Other Activities

**Kapalua Dive Company,** 808/669-3448 or 877/669-3448, www.kapaluadive.com, services guests at both the Kapalua Bay Hotel and the Ritz-Carlton. Aside from the gear it rents, this company offers lessons and various dives, which include shore dives, scooter dives, and a kayak dive. Also of interest is its kayak/snorkel trip that cruises the coast from Kapalua Bay to Honolua Bay.

**Ironwood Ranch** has the only riding opportunities on this side of the island, from an easy jaunt through the lower foothills to a more advanced ride up the mountain. Rides range $80–110 for up to two hours. To reserve a spot and get information on where to meet, call the ranch at 808/669-4991.

## Tours

Above the Kapalua Resort, **The Maunalei Arboretum** is open to tours. Within this private garden is a two-mile loop trail that takes you up to about 2,600 feet. This garden is the work of D. T. Fleming, a former Honolua Ranch manager, who collected a multitude of tropical plants from around the world. Hikes leave daily at 8 A.M. for the four-hour trip. Contact Maui Eco-adventures, 808/661-7720, to reserve your spot.

Kapalua is pineapple country, and what would be better than to take a walk through pineapple fields and learn about this sweet golden fruit, its production, and the pineapple industry as a whole? Sponsored by the Kapalua Nature Society, plantation tours are held weekdays except holidays from 9:30 A.M.–noon and again from 12:30–3 P.M. if there is enough interest and demand; $29 per person. Wear a hat, closed-toe shoes, and clothes that you don't mind getting a little dusty. Tours leave from the Kapalua Villas reception center; call 808/669-8088 for additional information and reservations.

## Kapalua Art School

Located in the former plantation blacksmith shop at 800 Office Road, the Kapalua Art School is a community center open to residents and resort guests alike that offers a variety of classes on a rotating basis, including watercolor, drawing, weaving, ceramics, dance, and yoga. In operation since 1995, this school functions on a drop-in basis, and fees run about $30 for three-hour sessions. Call 808/665-0007 for information about what's currently being offered.

# South Maui

## Ma'alaea

Ma'alaea is a small community located in the southwestern corner of the Maui isthmus that is home to a small harbor, a handful of houses, a row of condominiums, several fine restaurants, the Maui Ocean Center aquarium, and a new and expanding shopping plaza. It sits on the edge of the huge and beautiful Ma'alaea Bay, often referred to as a whale's nursery because so many mother whales head here to birth and raise their young during their winter and spring stay in the islands. Until the advent of plane travel to and between the islands, Ma'alaea was a busy port for interisland steamer traffic, principally serving the Ma'alaea and Kihei areas. Constructed in its current configuration in 1952, **Ma'alaea Harbor** is a bite-size working port, one of two on the island where tour boats dock (the other being Lahaina Harbor). With the comings and goings of all types of craft, the harbor is colorful, picturesque, and always busy; and it has the dubious distinction of being the second windiest harbor in the world, with sustained winds averaging 25 knots. Upon entering the harbor, you are greeted by a small U.S. Coast Guard installation at the east end and Buzz's Wharf, a well-known restaurant, at the other. Between these two, you'll find restrooms and the Ma'alaea Activities booth at harborside, which can book all sea, land, and air tours and activities for you. Across the street from the Coast Guard Station is Ma'alaea Store (est. 1946), and tucked in beside it is the Shinto

the beaches of Kihei

**SOUTH MAUI**

To Wailuku

To Kahului

MOKUELE HWY

KEALIA POND WILDLIFE REFUGE

311

Kealia Pond

Lahaina Pali Trail

HAYCRAFT PARK

MAUI OCEAN CENTER

31

Ma'alaea

Ma'alaea Beach

KEALIA BEACH PLAZA

To Lahaina

30

Ma'alaea Harbor

KIHEI WHARF

McGregor Point

MAI POINA 'OE IA'U BEACH COUNTY PARK

Ma'alaea Bay

CAPTAIN VANCOUVER MONUMENT

KALEPOLEPO BEACH PARK

PI'ILANI HWY

MAUI RESEARCH AND TECHNOLOGY PARK

AZEKA PLACE SHOPPING CENTER

31

ELLEAIR MAUI GOLF CLUB

To Kula

Kihei

KALAMA PARK

KIHEI HWY

KAMA'OLE BEACHES COUNTY PARKS

Maui Meadows

Keokea

KIHEI BOAT RAMP

MOKAPU BEACH PARK

37

ULUA BEACH PARK

WAILEA SHOPPING VILLAGE

WAILEA BEACH PARK

WAILEA ALANUI RD

POLO BEACH PARK

Wailea

WAILEA GOLF COURSE

PALAUEA BEACH PARK

MAKENA LANDING

Makena Bay

KEAWALA'I CHURCH (1832)

Onouli Beach

Makena

Pu'u Ola'i

MAKENA GOLF COURSE

Oneloa Beach

Ulupalakua Ranch

TEDESCHI WINERY

MARINE LIFE CONSERVATION DISTRICT

SEABIRD SANCTUARY

Molokini Island

MAKENA ALANUI RD

MAUI'S LAST VOLCANIC ERUPTION SITE (1790)

Kanahena

31

'Ahihi Bay

'AHIHI-KINA'U NATURAL AREA RESERVE

To Hana

'Alalakeiki Channel

Cape Kina'u

La Perouse Bay

Ancient Paved Road

0    3 mi

0    3 km

MAUI

© SANDRA E. BISIGNANI TRUST AND AVALON TRAVEL PUBLISHING, INC.

fishermen's shrine Ebesu Kotohira Jinsha, which was constructed in 1914 and rebuilt in 1999. Up above the shrine and store are the aquarium and new gaggle of shops. The condominiums line Hauoli Street, which culminates in Haycraft Park, the western end of Ma'alaea Beach. Outside the breakwater is Ma'alaea's only well-known surf spot, called Freight Trains by locals and Ma'alaea Pipeline by others for its fast break.

For decades, Ma'alaea was little more than a sleepy village and harbor. It's still small, but the influx of money and development is changing the face and character of the community. With greater traffic, Ma'alaea is busier and its visitors require more services. More than just a place to get on a snorkel boat or pass by on your way from Ka'anapali to Kihei, it's beginning to form an integrated identity all its own—a destination, not a byway. Luckily for those who live here, most changes are taking place up by the highway.

Maui's electric power generation plant sits outside of Ma'alaea. While not particularly conspicuous, you will recognize the towers that rise above the surrounding sugarcane fields along Route 31 as it descends down to the ocean east of the village as you approach the Kealia Pond Natural Wildlife Refuge. Two power-generation units have been built, with only one currently in operation. Another unit is being planned, perhaps in anticipation of future island growth.

## SIGHTS
### Maui Ocean Center
The most radical change for the community in years was the opening of the Maui Ocean Center. The Ocean Center is a large aquarium and marine park with several dozen indoor and outdoor displays and hands-on exhibits. Explore the realm of the reef in the Living Reef building, handle tide pool creatures at the Touch Pool, and learn about the fascinating turtles, stingrays, and whales in their separate exhibits. As an added benefit during winter, whales can be seen cavorting and breaching in the bay beyond the harbor. Perhaps the most unique feature at the center is the Underwater Journey, where you walk through a four-inch-thick, 54-foot-long transparent acrylic tunnel in the 750,000-gallon "open ocean" tank, Hawaii's largest aquarium, which offers a 240-degree view

ROBERT NILSEN

Walk through the tunnel at the Maui Ocean Center—with fish all around you, you'll feel as though you're submersed in a coral reef.

of the waterlife. There are no trained animal shows here, only periodic feedings and presentations by ocean naturalists at various locations throughout the center. No matter what your focus, this will be an enjoyable and educational experience as you'll learn about Hawaii's unique marine culture; all animals are indigenous or endemic. A stop here could easily be a half-day affair, so when you get hungry, have a quick bite at the Reef Cafe snack bar, or try the Seascape Ma'alaea Restaurant for a more substantial lunch meal. Before leaving, pick up a memento of your day's visit at the gift shop. The Maui Ocean Center, 808/270-7000, www.mauioceancenter.com, is open daily 9 A.M.–5 P.M. (until 6 P.M. in summer); $19 adults, $13 children 3–12, $17 seniors. Audio guides are available in English and Japanese for an additional $2. If you're without transportation, ride the Holo Ka'a public transit shuttle from either the South Maui or West Maui areas, $5 one way to either section or $10 for a one-day systemwide pass.

## Ma'alaea Beach

Consisting of three miles of windswept sand partially backed by Kealia Pond National Wildlife Refuge, Ma'alaea Beach has many points of access between Ma'alaea and Kihei along Route 31. The strong winds make this thin beach less desirable for sunbathing than others on the island, but it's a sailboarder's dream. The hard-packed sand is a natural track for joggers, which are profuse in the morning and afternoon. Few come here except locals to picnic, fish, or play games in the sand with kids. The beachcombing and strolling are quiet and productive. From the Ma'alaea end, you can access the beach from Haycraft Park. If you're up by 6 A.M. you can see the Kihei canoe club practice at the Kihei end; they put their canoes in the water near the old Kihei wharf just across the road from Suda's Store.

## Kealia Pond National Wildlife Refuge

Established in 1992, this refuge stretches between Ma'alaea and Kihei, mostly on the inland side of Route 31. Now set aside for stilts, coots, and other wildlife, this pond was once two productive fish ponds used by Hawaiians living around the bay. Aside from the stilt and coot, other birds and fowl that inhabit the pond are Hawaiian duck, black-crowned night heron, golden plover, and ruddy turnstone. Migratory waterfowl such as the pintail and shoveller visit the refuge, and hawksbill turtles come to shore to lay eggs. The refuge entranceway is off Mokulele Highway near mile marker 6, between Kihei and Kahului. A short walkway to the pond starts from the refuge headquarters, which is open weekdays 8 A.M.–4:30 P.M. Because of the birds' breeding and nesting season, it's perhaps best to visit from Aug.–April. As with most such refuges, this environment lies in a delicate balance and changes according to the season. With the winter rains and runoff the pond may increase in size to more than 400 acres; during periods of drought, parts of it may dry up all together, shrinking the size by over half and leaving a salty residue on exposed ground. One of Maui's first airstrips, the old Ma'alaea Airport used to occupy the flats near here.

# PRACTICALITIES
## Accommodations

There are no hotels in Ma'alaea. Condominiums stand one after another along the water east of the harbor. For rooms, check with the **Maalaea Bay Rentals** agency, 808/244-7012 or 800/367-6084, fax 808/242-7476, www.maalaeabay.com. This agency has an office at the Hono Kai Resort, 280 Hauoli St., Ma'alaea, HI 96793, and handles more than 100 units in a majority of the condos along this road. All units are fully furnished with complete kitchens, TVs, telephones, and lanai; and each property has a pool and laundry facility. Rates run $125–225 from mid-December to the end of April, with substantial discounts for summer and fall; five-night minimum, 10 nights during the Christmas holidays. Rates are reduced by 10 percent for monthly stays.

## Food

The award-winning **Waterfront Restaurant** at the Milowai Condo, 808/244-9028, has a well-deserved reputation and a great view of the harbor and bay. It's owned and operated by the Smith brothers, who work both the front and the kitchen.

The Waterfront is open for lunch 10 A.M.–1:30 P.M. daily except Saturday and daily from 5 P.M. for dinner. Choose a horseshoe-shaped booth tucked around the room's perimeter or a table out on the deck with sea breezes and the setting sun, and order a bottle of wine from the extensive international list. For starters, consider the Caesar salad for $8.95, Pacific oysters on the half shell at $10.95, or imported French escargot for $8.95. Definitely order the Maine lobster chowder, a famous specialty, for $8.50. The entrée scampi is $24.95, medallions of tenderloin is $25.95, while rack of lamb in a Sichuan peppercorn sauce is $28.95. However, the best choice is the fresh island fish, priced daily, of which there might be 5–8 varieties available each night and which can be prepared in a variety of ways: Sicilian; à la meuniere in a white wine sauce with lemon; Bastille, which is imprisoned in angel hair potato and sautéed and topped with fresh scallions; Southwestern; Cajun; baked with crab stuffing; baked in parchment paper; or sautéed, broiled, baked, or poached. Save room for one of the prize-winning desserts. The Waterfront provides an excellent dining experience, from the fine service to the wonderful food, and is well worth the price. Free parking in designated spots in the Milowai lot.

**Buzz's Wharf** restaurant, 808/244-5426, open daily 11 A.M.–11 P.M., specializes in seafood. The waterfront atmosphere and second-story views are first rate. It's a favorite spot and often busy. *Pu pu* selections include steamed clams for $11.95, escargot on the shell for $8.95, and coconut panko shrimp for $11.95. The lunch menu offers an assortment of sandwiches for under $12, fish and chips for $13.95, and fish and meat plates. For dinner, try prawns Tahitian, the seafood medley, or a mouthwatering rib eye for $18–27. Enjoy a liter of house wine for $12 or cocktail for $6. End your meal with dessert followed by a stroll around the moonlit harbor.

Bamboo predominates in the tables, chairs, and room dividers of the **Ma'alaea Grill** at the Ma'alaea Harbor Village next to the Maui Ocean Center. Hardwood floors, old-style lighting and ceiling fans, and large French doors that let in the ocean breezes and let you look out over the harbor add to the ambiance. A full bar greets you as

you enter this restaurant, and you can see into the kitchen through a plate-glass window on the way to your seat. Ma'alaea Grill is open for lunch 10:30 A.M.–3 P.M., dinner daily except Monday 5:30–9 P.M., and it has a simpler café menu from 3–5 P.M. Lunch is casual with salads, sandwiches, and several light entrées for under $10. Dinner is more formal and pricier, but expect larger portions and a touch more class. Try fried ahi stuffed calamari or tempura potato cake appetizer before moving on to a full entrée, like sautéed mahimahi, macadamia nut–crusted duckling, grilled jumbo shrimp, or *kiawe* grilled New York steak, all $14–23. Like its sister restaurants in Wailuku, Lahaina, and Makawao, the Ma'alaea Grill offers quality food at a decent price.

More casual is the **Blue Marlin** grill and bar, an open-air eatery located on the lower level of Ma'alaea Harbor Village and looking out over Ma'alaea Harbor. Hanging on the wall at the entrance is a stuffed blue marlin, a grander size approaching 1,200 pounds caught by one of the boats at the harbor. Not surprisingly, fish and seafood are the mainstay of the menu, but steaks, burgers, and sandwiches also make an appearance. Open from 11 A.M. for lunch and dinner, most entrées run $15–25.

The **Tradewinds Deli and Mart,** located at the Maalaea Mermaid condo, carries groceries, drinks, and alcohol, creates deli sandwiches (from $3.99), and also rents snorkel equipment and boogie boards. Hours are Monday–Thursday 9 A.M.–8 P.M. and Friday 9 A.M.–9 P.M.

Located directly across from the Coast Guard station and open daily except Monday 8 A.M.–5 P.M., the **Ma'alaea Store** is where you have a much better chance of buying fishing tackle than you do a loaf of bread, but it does have some very limited groceries, snacks, and sundries.

## Shopping

Following the opening of the Maui Ocean Center, the two-level **Ma'alaea Harbor Village** opened next to the aquarium, with a **Whalers General Store** for sundries and food items, **Moonbow Tropics** for tropical clothing, and an **Island Soap and Candle Works** store for scents and perfumes of the tropics. You can book your water tours with the ocean activities center, eat at two restaurants, or snack on ice cream and cookies at **Hula Cookies.** On the lower level is a **Maui Dive Shop.**

The **Pacific Whale Foundation** also has a store here where you can pick up logowear, books on whales and other marine subjects, look at the exhibit area, or garner information about water tours and educational programs run by the foundation. It's definitely worth a stop to see what this organization is offering. Next door is the Pacific Whale Foundation's new Ocean Science and Discovery Center, which conducts numerous classes, programs, video presentations, and activities for kids and adults alike throughout the week.

In a booth at the edge of the harbor is **Ma'alaea Activities Center,** 808/242-6982. Not only can the staff here book you on a fishing boat or other water excursion from this harbor, but they can also take care of all your activity needs for the entire island. Having been around since 1981, they know their business. Stop by 8 A.M.–4 P.M. daily.

At the far end of this triangular commercial area are a gas station, fast-food eatery, and the Maui Golf and Sports Park, open 10 A.M.–10 P.M. daily, where you can putt around a miniature golf course.

# Kihei

Kihei (Shoulder Cloak) takes it on the chin whenever antidevelopment groups need an example at which to wag their fingers. From the 1960s to the 1980s, construction along both sides of Kihei Road, which runs the length of town, was unabated. Because there was no central planning for the development, mostly high-rise condos and a few hotels were built wherever they could be squeezed in: some lovely, some crass.

ROBERT NILSEN

**outrigger canoes ready for launch near the old Kihei Wharf**

Building continued in the 1990s, although at a slower pace and with more restrictions, and in the 2000s much of the new construction has been inland. There's hardly a spot left where you can get an unobstructed view of the beach as you drive along. That's the "slam" in a nutshell. The good news is that Kihei has so much to recommend it that if you refrain from fixating on this one regrettable feature, you'll thoroughly enjoy yourself, and save money, too.

The developers went hyper here because it's perfect as a tourist area. The weather can be counted on to be the best on all of Maui. Haleakala, looming just behind the town, catches rainclouds before they drench Kihei. Days of blue skies and sunshine are taken for granted. On the other side of the condos and hotels are gorgeous beaches, every one open to the public. Once on the beachside, the condos don't matter anymore. The views out to sea are unobstructed vistas of Lana'i, Kaho'olawe, Molokini, and West Maui, which gives the illusion of being a separate island. The buildings are even a buffer to the traffic noise! Many islanders make Kihei their home, so there is a feeling of real community here. It's quieter than Lahaina with not as much action; but for sun and surf activities, this place has it all.

The six-mile stretch bordered by beach and mountain that makes up Kihei has always been an important landing spot on Maui. Hawaiian war ca-

MAUI

noes moored here many times during countless skirmishes over the years; later, Western navigators such as Captain George Vancouver found this stretch of beach a congenial anchorage. A totem pole across from the Maui Lu Resort marks the spot where Vancouver landed. During World War II, when a Japanese invasion was feared, Kihei was considered a likely spot for an amphibious attack. Overgrown pillboxes and rusting tank traps are still found along the beaches. Kihei is a natural site with mountain and ocean vistas. It's also great for beachcombing up toward Ma'alaea, but try to get there by morning because the afternoon wind is notorious for creating minor sandstorms.

Kihei's commercial sections are separated by residential areas. There is no one town center as such, although the highest concentration and greatest number of businesses are near the post office and the Azeka Place shopping centers. The new Maui Research and Technology Park has been built above the Elleair Maui Golf Club in Kihei, sprucing up the image of the area a little and bringing in some high-tech white-collar jobs at the same time, particularly with the creation of the Maui High Performance Computing Center. While only three shiny glass and steel office buildings have been built at this office park so far, land has been set aside for many more.

# BEACHES
## Mai Poina 'Oe Ia'u Beach County Park
On Kihei's northern fringe, this beach offers only limited paved parking, otherwise just along the road. Showers, tables, and restrooms front the long and narrow white-sand beach, which has good, safe swimming but is still plagued by strong winds by early afternoon. These trade winds are a delight for sailboarders and kiteboarders alike, and here you can see more than 100 sporting enthusiasts out trying the wind when conditions are optimal.

## Kalepolepo Beach Park
Next to the Humpback Whale National Marine Sanctuary office, this park has a small beach that's good for kiddies. Centuries ago, the thriving com-

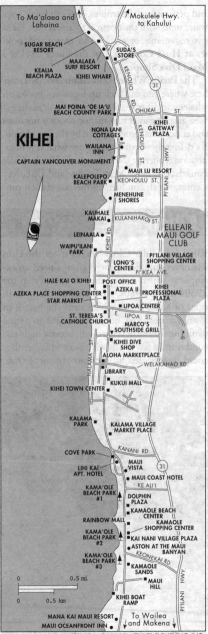

© SANDRA E. BISIGNANI TRUST AND AVALON TRAVEL PUBLISHING, INC.

munity of Kalepolepo occupied this area of Kihei and farmed the three-acre royal fish pond **Ko'ie'ie Loko I'a,** small but best preserved of the royal fish ponds on Maui. Remnants of its rock wall can still be seen arcing through the water. Now much reduced in size, the walls once stood higher than high tide and wider than two men abreast. It's estimated that more than 2,000 pounds of fish per year were harvested from these waters when it was a functioning fish pond in the late 1500s.

## Waipu'ilani Park

Just south of Kalepolepo is this park with its narrow beach, broad lawn, tennis courts, smattering of coconut trees, great sunsets, and sailboarders in season. Rather infrequented, it's like a big greenway to the sea for the condos that front it. The shoreline for over one-half mile south has been set aside as a State Beach Preserve. Access to it is at the end of West Lipoa Street. Off the coast here were three large fish ponds that have now all but disappeared.

## Kalama Park

This park is more suited to family outings, athletic games, and enjoying the vista than it is for beach activities. Kalama has a large lawn ending in a breakwater, a small beach in summer, and none in winter. However, there are 36 acres of pavilions, tables, barbecue pits, volleyball, basketball, and tennis courts, a baseball diamond, a soccer field, and plenty of expanse to throw a frisbee. With its great views of Molokini and Haleakala, it is considered the best family park in the area. At its extreme southern end, just across the highway bridge, is the diminutive Cove Park, where locals put small boats in the water and others come to surf.

## Kama'ole I, II, and III

These beach parks, often referred to as Kam I, II, and III, are at the south end of town. All three have beautiful white sand, picnic tables, lifeguards, and all the amenities. The swimming and body-surfing are good. At the north end of Kam I is an area called Charley Young Beach. Snorkeling is good here and for beginners on the reef between II and III, where much coral and many colorful reef fish abound. Kama'ole III has a kids' playground. Shopping and dining are nearby.

## Kihei Boat Ramp

Just south of Kama'ole III Beach is the Kihei Boat Ramp, used by many ocean activity companies in the area to launch boats and rafts.

# ACCOMMODATIONS

The emphasis in Kihei is on condos. With keen competition among them, you can save some money while having a more homey vacation. Close to 100 condos, plus a smattering of vacation apartments, cottages, and even a few small hotel resorts, are all strung along Kihei Road. As always, you pay more for ocean views. Don't shy away from accommodations on the *mauka* side of Kihei Road. You have total access to the beach, some superior views of Haleakala, and you usually pay less money. The accommodations that follow are listed north to south. By and large, these places are located north of the Azeka Place shopping centers and south of Kalama beach park, leaving the central section of town for businesses and homes.

## Hotels

**Maui Lu Resort,** 575 S. Kihei Rd., Kihei, HI 96753, 808/879-5881 or 800/922-7866, fax 808/879-4627, a 28-acre Aston-managed property at the north end of Kihei, attempts to preserve the feeling of old Hawaii with its emphasis on *ohana*. The Maui Lu is not designed as an ordinary hotel—it looks more like condo units—but none of the rooms have kitchens. Amenities here include an activities desk, tennis and volleyball courts, a Maui-shaped swimming pool, and two tiny pocket beaches. While three buildings are located next to the water, most rooms are located in the newer wings up the hill near the entrance lobby. Rooms are priced $108–180 during value season and $131–215 during regular season. All hotel-style rooms include TV, air-conditioning, refrigerator, and daily maid service.

The **Maui Coast Hotel,** 2259 S. Kihei Rd., Kihei, HI 96753, 808/874-6284 or 800/895-6284, fax 808/875-4731, www.mauicoasthotel.com, is Kihei's only true "high-rise" hotel. Completed in 1993 and renovated in 1999, the 265 rooms and suites here are bright and cheerful, blending Southwestern pastels and Hawaiian-style furniture. Adding to your comfort are standard amenities like remote-control color TV, air-conditioning and ceiling fans, complimentary in-wall safes, coffeemakers, refrigerators, slippers to pad around in, full bathrooms that include a jacuzzi bathtub, and a "who asked for one?" bathroom scale. A wet bar is in all the larger suites. Guests are also treated to morning coffee, and washers and dryers are on every other floor. This seven-story hotel offers two spas with whirlpools, a swimming pool, lighted guests-only tennis courts, Spices Restaurant, the Tradewinds poolside bar with nightly entertainment, sundries shop, and free parking. Rates are reasonably priced at $165–175 for a standard room, $195–350 for a suite, $20 each additional person, with discounted off-season and weekly rates. Rental car packages are also available, and a fifth night free is offered on some rooms. The Maui Coast Hotel, set back from busy Kihei Road, offers a small oasis of peace and tranquility with excellent rates for the amenities offered.

**Best Western Maui Oceanfront Inn,** 2980 S. Kihei Rd., 808/879-7744 or 800/263-3387, fax 808/874-0145, www.mauioceanfrontinn.com, is located at the entrance to Wailea. In 2000, this intimate complex was given a complete makeover including buildings, furnishings, and grounds, and reborn as a boutique hotel where low-rise, multiunit buildings run from the road down to the water. Each air-conditioned room and suite has a TV and entertainment center, air-conditioning and ceiling fans, in-room safe, and a small refrigerator. None has cooking facilities. Rates are $151 for a mountain-view room, $159 for garden-view, $215–231 for garden-view and oceanview suites, and $240 for oceanfront suites.

## Condos and Cottages

One of the several condos at the far north end of Kihei, at the eastern end of Ma'alaea Beach, is **Sugar Beach Resort,** 145 N. Kihei Rd., 808/879-7765. All one- and two-bedroom units have full kitchens, ceiling fans and air-conditioning, TVs, and lanai, with guest-only tennis courts, swimming pool, spa, sauna, barbecue grills, sundries shop, sandwich shop, and activities desk on property. The activity desk can book you

on virtually any land and sea excursion, while the sundry shop offers rental bikes, kayaks, snorkel gear, and beach equipment. All units are individually owned and decorated. Rates run about $125–195 for one-bedroom and $220–325 for two-bedroom suites, but these rates vary a bit according to the rental agency. Contact the following agents for rooms here and at other nearby condos: Condominium Rentals Hawaii, 808/879-2778 or 800/367-5242 Mainland, 800/663-2101 in Canada; Rainbow Rentals, 808/244-1688 or 800/451-5366; or Maui Condominium and Home Realty, 808/879-5445 or 800/451-5008.

The Polynesian-style roofs and dark wooden siding might draw you to the two-story, luxury **Maalaea Surf Resort,** 12 S. Kihei Rd., 808/879-1267 or 800/423-7953, fax 808/874-2884, but the fully furnished bright interiors, well-tended lawns, tennis courts, swimming pools, and white-sand beach will captivate you. Each unit has air-conditioning and daily maid service. One-bedroom suites run $205–230, and two-bedroom units are $277–350. A fifth night is offered free during their value season. This condo is near the intersection of Highways 31 and 311.

The first place south of Suda's Store is **Nona Lani Cottages,** 455 S. Kihei Rd., 808/879-2497 or 800/733-2688, www.nonalanicottages.com, owned and operated by Dave and Nona Kong. These eight clean and neat units on the *mauka* side of the road have full kitchens and baths, queen beds, and daybeds. Laundry facilities, public phones, hammocks, chaise lounges, and barbecues are on the premises, and each unit has a raised lanai with tables. Rates are $90 per night during low season, $15 per additional person and four-night minimum, and $99 per night during high season when there's a seven-night minimum stay. Weekly and monthly rates are available. These individual plantation-style units are about as down-home Hawaiian as you can get, a good place to come if you're looking for relaxation. The Nona Lani also has three rooms (no kitchens) in the main house, which run $65 and $75, respectively, for low- and high-season, three- and four-night minimum rental.

A few steps away is **Wailana Inn,** 14 Wailana Place near the Vancouver Monument, 808/874-

3131 or 800/399-3885, fax 808/874-0454, www.wailanabeach.com, an apartment turned condo rental. This two-story building has less than a dozen units so it's quiet, and it's just a minute's walk to the beach. Each unit has a king or queen bed, kitchen or kitchenette, TV with DVD player, air-conditioning, and telephone. A sun deck with a hot tub is located on the roof, and there is a washer and dryer on premises for your use. Spacious enough, these units have been totally remodeled and run $140 per night for a room with kitchen and $100 for the kitchenettes.

**Menehune Shores,** 760 S. Kihei Rd., mailing address P.O. Box 1327, Kihei, HI 96753, 808/879-3428 or 800/558-9117, fax 808/879-5828, is a huge, family-oriented and moderately priced high-rise condo on the beach overlooking an ancient fish pond. The building is highlighted with replicas of Hawaiian petroglyphs. On the oceanside is a new swimming pool. The Menehune is used mostly by seniors, except during Christmas when families come. All units have an ocean view, and rates are $130–220 for one- to three-bedroom condos in high season, three-day minimum. Low-season rates are about 10 percent less, discounts are given for week-long and month-long stays, and special car/room packages can be arranged. Full kitchens with dishwashers, and washers and dryers are in each unit, which are individually owned, so furnishings vary. All units have recently been remodeled.

**Kauhale Makai,** 938 S. Kihei Rd., has fully furnished, individually decorated studios and suites that are a mixture of garden, mountain, and ocean view. All are clustered around a central courtyard garden and lawn. A swimming pool, kiddie pool, barbecues, putting green, and sauna are available, making it good for the family. Rates from $85–110 studio, $95–120 one bedroom, and $130–190 two bedroom, four-night minimum; weekly and monthly discounts given. All reservations are handled through Maui Condominium and Home Realty, P.O. Box 1840 Kihei, HI 96753, or call 808/879-5445 or 800/451-5008, fax 808/874-6144.

The boxy four-story **Leinaala** condos, 998 S. Kihei Rd., 808/879-2235 or 800/334-3305, may not attract everyone, but don't let the ap-

pearance fool you. Each of the 24 fully appointed units faces the beach across the lawns of the Waipu'ilani Park, and all are narrow units that run from the front of the building to the back so cooling breezes can waft right through. Set back from the road, this is a quiet spot where you can splash in the pool in peace. Winter rates are $135 and $180 for one- and two-bedroom units during high season. The best time for space is during the summer, when rates are $30–50 less; four nights minimum. Weekly and monthly rates can be adjusted and car rental packages arranged. Other reduced rates are available.

Off the main thoroughfare, **Hale Kai O Kihei,** 1310 Uluniu Rd., Kihei, HI 96753, www.hkok-maui.com, is a three-floor apartmentlike cinder block affair, simple and utilitarian, clean, well-kept, and cute for what it is—and it's recently been spruced up. Each furnished unit has a direct ocean view with a lanai that looks over the pool, garden, and beach. There is also shuffleboard, barbecue grills, and coin laundry, with maid service on request. Reasonable rates are $132 for a one-bedroom unit ($112 for low season) and $168 for two bedrooms ($135 low season); three nights minimum—15 percent discount for stays of one month or greater. For information, contact AA Oceanfront Condo Rental, 808/879-7288 or 800/457-7014, fax 808/879-7500.

The following condos are all south of Kalama Park. First is **Lihi Kai Cottages,** 2121 Ili'ili Rd., Kihei, HI 96753, 808/879-2335 or 800/544-4524, set across the road from the tiny Cove Park. These nine cottages are such a bargain that they're often booked by returning guests, particularly during winter. They're not plush, there's no pool, and they've been around a while, but they're homey and clean, with little touches like banana trees growing on the property. Rates are $90 daily for 3–6 nights, $80 for seven or more nights; three nights minimum. Monthly rates are available on request, no credit cards accepted. For reservations, call or write well in advance c/o Manager, at the above address.

**Maui Vista,** 2191 S. Kihei Rd., 808/879-7966 or 800/535-0085, fax 808/874-5612, is a pleasing 10-acre condo complex on the *mauka* side of the main road that has units managed by

**M**

**MAUI**

Marc Resorts. Three swimming pools, six tennis courts, barbecue grills, and an activities desk are available to all guests. All studios and one- and two-bedroom suites have kitchens, are modern in their appointments, spacious in layout, have air conditioning, contain in-room washers and dryers, and have maid service. Studios run $169, one-bedroom suites $169–189, and two-bedroom suites $229–239, $20 less during "value" periods, $15 each extra person.

Stretching up from the road long and lean is **Aston at the Maui Banyan,** 2575 S. Kihei Rd., 808/875-0004 or 808/922-7866, fax 808/874-4035. Several multiple-unit buildings climb the hill, and set to the side are two patio areas with swimming pools, hot tubs, barbecue grills, and plenty of space to catch the sun. While there are some hotel rooms in this complex, most are one-, two-, and three-bedroom condo units with kitchens for $250–365 per night. All are pleasantly modern in decor, spacious, and have all needed amenities for a restful and relaxing vacation.

At **Kamaole Sands,** 2695 S. Kihei Rd., 808/874-8700 or 800/367-5004, fax 808/879-3273, all apartments come completely furnished with a full bath and kitchen, roomy living area, and lanai. Prices are $167–220 one bedroom, $252–335 two bedrooms, $366–410 three bedrooms, fifth night free; winter season rates slightly higher and rental car packages available. Stepping down the hillside, the Kamaole Sands is a full-service, family-oriented condo geared toward making the entire family comfortable. The Sandpiper Grill, situated poolside and for guests only, serves inexpensive breakfasts, lunches, and dinners on Friday featuring fresh island fish and pasta. One of the main features of the Kamaole Sands is its wonderful tennis courts, free to guests, with a tennis instructor to help you work on the fine points of your game. Here as well are a swimming pool, kid's pool, a jet spa, volleyball courts, and barbecue areas. The Kamaole Sands is bright, cheerful, and gives you a lot for your money.

If you want to rise above it all in Kihei, come to **Maui Hill,** 2881 S. Kihei Rd., 808/879-6321 or 800/922-7866, an upbeat Aston-managed condo with a Spanish motif. This condo resort sits high on a hill and commands a sweeping view of the entire area. The one-, two-, or three-bedroom suites are spacious, bright, and airy; all have ceiling fans and air-conditioning, cable TV, daily maid service, and full kitchens. A concierge service helps with your every need, and all sun and surf activities can be arranged at the activity desk. The grounds are secluded, beautifully maintained, and offer a pool with whale mosaic on the bottom, tennis courts, and spa. Regular-season rates are one bedroom from $280 (up to four people), two bedrooms from $365 (up to six people), and three bedrooms from $495 (up to eight people); *substantial* savings during low-season. A weekly complimentary mai tai party complete with games, singing, and door prizes is held for guests, along with a continental breakfast at 8 A.M. that offers an orientation on island activities. Guests can also enjoy a weekly afternoon lei-making class and a poolside scuba orientation several days per week.

At the very south end of Kihei is **Mana Kai Maui** oceanfront resort, 2960 S. Kihei Rd. On-site features include an activities desk, daily maid service, a sundries store, swimming pool, and the Five Palms oceanside restaurant and bar. Condo units have full kitchens, TV, private lanai, and ceiling fans. All hotel rooms, with outdoor access, air-conditioning, and refrigerators, are on the garden level. Winter rates run $116–140 for the hotel rooms, $210–247 for a one-bedroom, and $247–303 for a two-bedroom suite. Summer rates (until Dec. 15) are substantially cheaper, Christmas rates are 10 percent higher, and there is a 10 percent discount for stays of one month or more at any time of year. For rentals and information, contact Condominium Rentals Hawaii, 808/879-2778 or 800/367-5242 Mainland, 800/663-2101 Canada, fax 808/879-7825.

## Rental Agencies

Numerous rental agencies handle condo units and rental homes in Kihei and South Maui. Several of these agencies are as follows:

**Condominium Rentals Hawaii,** 362 Huku Li'i Place, #204, Kihei, HI 96753, 808/879-2778 or 800/367-5242 Mainland, 800/663-2101 Canada, fax 808/879-7825, www.crhmaui.com, can arrange your stay in 10 condos in Kihei.

**Kihei Maui Vacations,** P.O. Box 1055, Kihei,

HI 96753, 808/879-7581 or 888/568-6284, fax 808/879-2000, www.kmvmaui.com, has units in more than two dozen condos, mostly in Kihei, but a few in Ma'alaea and Wailea.

**Maui Condominium and Home Realty,** P.O. Box 1840, Kihei, HI 96753, 808/879-5445 or 800/451-5008, fax 808/874-6144, www.mauicondo.com, manages mostly economical to midrange units in Kihei.

**Maui Resort Vacation Rentals,** P.O. Box 1755, Kihei, HI 96753, 808/879-5973 or 800/441-3187, fax 808/879-1357, www.mauiresort4u.com, handles units in more than two dozen condos along the Kihei coast and also has a few rental homes.

**AA Oceanfront Condo Rentals,** 1279 S. Kihei Rd., Ste. 107, Kihei, HI 96753, 808/879-7288 or 800/488-6004, fax 808/879-7500, www.aaoceanfront.com, manages properties from north Kihei to Makena, economy to deluxe.

**Kumulani Vacations and Realty,** P.O. Box 1190, Kihei, HI 96753, 808/879-9272 or 800/367-2954, fax 808/874-0094, www.kumulani.com, handles rentals in 10 condos in Kihei and Wailea.

### Bed-and-Breakfasts

At 815 Kumulani Drive in the quiet neighborhood of Maui Meadows is **Eva Villa,** tel/fax 808/874-6407 or 800/884-1845 Mainland and Canada, pounder@maui.net, www.maui.net/~pounder. Built with the clean lines of contemporary design, Eva Villa is set in a finely landscaped yard sporting an attractive koi pond. Here you'll find a studio and two-room apartment that overlook the swimming pool. In a separate structure is a small cottage with its own kitchen. All units have phones and TV, a small refrigerator and eating area, and a private entrance. Rates run $115–140. The roof-top deck, pool, and hot tub are open to all guests, and everyone is provided with a simple continental breakfast left in your room to have at your leisure.

A few blocks lower is **Anuhea Bed and Breakfast,** 3164 Mapu Place, 808/874-1490 or 800/206-4441, fax 808/874-8587, lodging @anuheamaui.com, www.anuheamaui.com. Owned and operated by Russell and Cherie Kolbo,

Anuhea has three comfortable rooms in the upper floor with private bathrooms and air-conditioning and two garden-level rooms with fans that share a bath. Each room has a king-size bed, small refrigerator, and television. Everyone can share the living room, use the washer and dryer, as well as relax in the garden with its hot tub and hammock. A health-oriented breakfast of grains and eggs is served each morning on the lanai. The upper rooms run $115 per night, the garden rooms $105. No children under 12 years old please.

One block closer to the highway but still away from the noise of traffic is **Dreams Come True on Maui,** 3259 Akala Dr., 808/879-7099 or 877/782-9628, staymaui@aol.com, www.maui.net/~tcroly. Two rooms in the main house, situated off the garden and each with a private entrance and kitchenette, run $75–85 during low season and $10 more per night during high season, mid-December into spring; three- or four-night minimum stay. Out front, with a view down onto the coast, is a detached vacation cottage, which has a six-night minimum and rents for $650 per week.

## FOOD

With few exceptions, restaurants listed as follows are all located at shopping centers in Kihei.

### Inexpensive

At the north end, the first inexpensive eatery is **Suda's Snack Shop,** open Mon.–Sat. 6 A.M.–12:30 P.M., for burgers, plate lunches, and drinks. Adjacent to the Suda's Store, the snack shop is nothing special but is a good spot for a quick bite to eat.

Heat-flushed tourists hoping to chill out should head for **Stella Blue's Cafe,** located at Longs Shopping Center, 808/874-3779, open daily 7:30 A.M.–9 P.M. This is an economical place, good for the family, where the kids will love the selections and adults can still order a beer or wine. Breakfast, served 8–11 A.M., features a continental breakfast for $7.95, French toast for $6.95, and a "create your own" omelet starting at $5.95. Sandwiches, everything from a BLT to hot pastrami and turkey breast, average about $8.50. From the grill you can have a tuna melt, blues burger, grilled chicken, or Reuben for under $9.75. Dinners are more complete, with such offerings as spinach lasagna, scampi Provençale, baby back ribs, and charbroiled taro burger all for $8–20.

**Kal Bi House,** 808/874-8454, in a corner of Longs Shopping Center and open Wed.–Sun. 10:30 A.M.–9 P.M., offers a full range of Americanized Korean standards like barbecued short ribs, fried squid, noodles, stews, and small intestine soup, as well as plate lunches and combination plates, and a few Japanese dishes like chicken teriyaki. Most everything is under $12 except for the full-meal bulgogi for $24.99; takeout is available. This restaurant is basic but clean.

**Azeka's Ribs and Snack Shop,** at Azeka Makai next to Ace Hardware, is an institution and is very famous for its specially prepared (uncooked) ribs, perfect for a barbecue. Also available are plate lunches, burgers, sushi, and saimin. Open 7–3:30 (until 5 P.M. for ribs).

For Asian food that's still a bit out of the ordinary for most, try **Vietnamese Cuisine** restaurant in the Azeka Makai shopping center, 808/875-2088. A full range of dishes include pho ga or pho tai, chicken and beef soups; lau cai do bien, seafood combo soup; bun bo xao, sautéed lemongrass and beef over vermicelli noodles; com chien tom, shrimp fried rice; and plenty of dishes prepared in the wok.

Let the rich aroma of roasting coffee lure you to **The Coffee Store,** 808/875-4244, open daily 6 A.M.–10 P.M. at Azeka Mauka. Breakfast fare features quiche for $3.75 or a breakfast quesadilla for $6.95. Lunch selections, always served with crusty homemade bread, include a Caesar salad for $4.95—or $6.95 for the large size that can easily feed two—and sandwiches like tuna, turkey, or vegetarian for $5.50–6.50. Daily homemade soup for $3.95 including bread and coffee, stuffed quesadillas of all sorts for $4–6, and wraps complete the menu. Enjoy coffee drinks that range in price $1–2.50, along with hot and iced herbal teas, hot chocolate, and Italian cream sodas. A deli case is filled with luscious desserts sure to satisfy any sweet tooth, and, of course, you can purchase bulk coffee. You can dine inside or sit outside, especially in the evening to hobnob with local residents who come here to chat and enjoy a rich cup of coffee and snack or to check the Internet.

The fountain bar, jukebox, Formica tabletops, leatherette booths, distinctive color scheme, period decorations, and music peg **Peggy Sue,** at Azeka Mauka, 808/875-8944, as a classic, theme hamburger joint—with a modern twist. You can order your Big Bopper burger for $9.25 or the Earth Angel garden burger for $8.25, or sample one of the salads, sandwiches, hot dogs, or other menu items, mostly for under $11. No '50s joint worth its name would be without that cool summer favorite, so Peggy Sue serves ice cream, shakes, sundaes, and fountain drinks. Stop in for the nostalgia rush.

If you've been having too much fun and need a reviving cup of espresso, stop in at the **Kihei Caffe,** at Kalama Village Marketplace, 808/878-2230, open daily at 5 A.M., Sunday at 6 A.M., and enjoy your coffee along with an excellent assortment of sandwiches and baked goods. Order a complete breakfast of eggs, bacon, home fries, and biscuits with gravy for $6, or a giant raisin muffin for $2.75. Sandwiches, all under $6.50, are served on your choice of homemade bread—only cold sandwiches after 2 P.M. The café provides a few tables and stools inside and more outside, where you can watch the action on Kihei Road or across the road through Kama'ole Beach Park to the ocean.

**Sushi Go,** 808/875-8744, has a different concept than most Japanese restaurants. Chairs here are located around a bar that has a conveyor carrying ready-made sushi selections. Select what you want and pay for what you've eaten. All plates are color coded by price, so you should have a rough idea of where you stand when the bill comes. Wednesday 4–8 P.M. is an all-you-can-eat special for $22.99. Take-out platters are also available. Sushi Go is located in the Kukui Mall and open daily for lunch and dinner.

A few steps away is **Alexander's,** 808/874-0788, open 11 A.M.–9 P.M. This local long-term establishment is definitely a cut above most fast-food restaurants and has taken a few steps along the upscale, yuppie, health-conscious road. The menu offers fresh fish, shrimp, and chicken sandwiches for $6.50–7.75. Plate lunches for $10 or under, sides, salads, and drinks, as well as larger baskets for $16.25–19.95, are also on the menu. Full meals are served with coleslaw and french fries or rice. All deep frying is done in canola oil, but you can request broiling instead. You can't go wrong here. There's not much decor or atmosphere, but the food is delicious and makes a perfect take-out meal that can be enjoyed at the beach.

**Sports Page Bar and Grill,** at the Kamaole Beach Center, 808/879-0602, open 11 A.M.–midnight for cocktails and until 10 P.M. for food service, scores big with a full bar, a large-screen TV, and foosball and a pool table in the back. Order a mug of beer and a light snack like oyster shooters for $1.25 or teriyaki chicken breast strips for $7.95. The burger and sandwich menu goes all the way with a San Francisco '49er burger topped with bacon and cheese, a Chicago Cubs hot dog, or a Boston Celtics turkey sandwich, all for under $8.50. There's music some evenings, and a cover may be charged. Mostly a working man's bar, although visitors are certainly welcome, its walls are covered with sports pictures, pennants, and posters. Families and even the athletically challenged will be comfortable here.

Also at Kamaole Beach Center is **Hawaiian Moon's Deli and Natural Foods,** open Mon.–Sat. 8 A.M.–9 P.M., Sunday until 7 P.M. Stop for a healthy bite to eat (the hot bar and salad bar run $5.99 per pound), juice or espresso, or shop for groceries, vitamins, and bulk foods.

Also at the Kamaole Beach Center is **Maui Tacos,** 808/879-5005, open daily 9 A.M.–9 P.M. and serving Mexican food with definite Hawaiian bump. Here you can get soft tacos, big burritos, chimichangas, enchiladas, and other typical Mexican treats for under $7.

Open 7:30–11 A.M., **Annie's Cafe and Deli** at Kai Nani Village Plaza serves smoothies, juices, coffees, and a variety of quick snack deli items, mostly for less than $8.

## Moderate

**Margarita's Beach Cantina,** 101 N. Kihei Rd. in the Kealia Beach Plaza, 808/879-5275, open daily 11:30 A.M.–11:30 P.M., has a well-deserved reputation for good food at fair prices. Formerly vegetarian, it now serves a variety of meat and chicken dishes but still uses the finest ingredients, cold-pressed oils, and no lard or bacon in the bean dishes. The decor is classical Mexican with white stucco walls and tiled floors. There's an outdoor deck affording a great sunset view and sea breezes, or stop by for live music and dancing Friday 5–7 P.M. The *carta* offers taco salads for $11.95, combination plates for $11.95–16.95, money-saving daily fish specials, and live Maine lobster on Monday evenings. Most entrées are in the $12–15 range, with nothing more than $20. Look for reduced-price well drinks, beers, and margaritas during the 2:30–5 P.M. happy hour.

**Restaurant Isana,** 515 S. Kihei Rd., 808/874-5700, is open daily for the best Korean food in the area and also has Japanese sushi from 4–8 P.M. You can either sit at the sushi bar or have dinner cooked at your table. Upstairs is the bar, which has a karaoke sing-along after 10 P.M. Most dinners are in the $14–19 range.

While you can order hoagies, hot sandwiches, and calzone at **Shaka Sandwich and Pizza,** 808/874-0331, it's perhaps best known for pizza. New York–style thin crust, a Sicilian crust, and gourmet pizzas with various kinds of crusts are all available from $14 on up. Located behind Jack In The Box across from Star Market. Delivery is available.

With a grander scale and pleasing decor of vaulted ceilings, piano music in the evening, and inside and outside seating, **Marco's Southside Grill,** 1445 S. Kihei Rd., just across from Maui Dive Shop, 808/874-4041, is much different than its sister restaurant in Kahului, but it has a similar menu. Marco's serves fine Italian food all day long. Breakfast specialties are omelets, lunch brings deli and grill sandwiches, but dinner is finer dining. Pizza and all sorts of pasta are on the menu, but other entrées, like chicken parmigiano and ribeye steak, are good choices. Dinner entrées run mostly $13–19.

Although you can get appetizers, salads, sandwiches, burgers, shrimp, and chicken at **Tony Roma's,** at the Kukui Mall, 808/875-1104, Tony's is especially known for ribs, ribs, and more ribs. Prepared in several different ways, rib entrées run about $16, with most other entrées less. For those who want just a little extra, try the combo meals for $17–29. Open for lunch and dinner daily.

In the Rainbow Plaza, **The Thai Chef Restaurant,** 808/874-5605, offers you a full menu of tasty Thai food at reasonable prices. Like its sister restaurant in Lahaina, you can get appetizers like spring rolls for $7.50 or green papaya salad at $6.50, and various soups for around $10. Entrées include red, green, or yellow curries from $9–11, with noodle, rice, and seafood dishes up to $14. There's a hefty selection for vegetarians, and desserts run $2–3. Well maintained, Thai Chef has a casual decor.

In the Kihei Kalama Village you'll find **Pita Paradise,** 808/875-7679. Stuck in the back of the center, Pita Paradise offers a variety of pita items, served with roasted potatoes or rice pilaf, but also serves kebabs, pasta, and salad. Pita run mostly in the under $11 range, and most other items run $13–19. Open for lunch and dinner until 9:30 A.M.

Upstairs at the Rainbow Plaza is **Dean O's Maui Pizza Cafe,** 808/891-2200. Dean O's serves lunch of pizza and sandwiches before 5 P.M. and again after 9 P.M. Available 5 P.M.–9 P.M., dinner is pizza and pasta in small and large portions. Sandwiches include barbecue pork and chicken parmesan for around $9.50. Pizzas run $12.50–16.25, and pasta might be fettuccine or a Big Kahuna Bolognese. The full-service bar can take care of you for after-dinner drinks.

In the Kamaole Center, **Canton Chef,** 808/879-1988, offers the usual long list of choices from appetizers to meat and seafood dishes. Several spicy Sichuan items are on the menu to fire up your day. Most entrées are in the $7–13 range.

**KKO Kai Ku Ono,** 808/875-1007, a semi-sports bar casual dining place below Harlow's at Kai Nani Village Plaza, is open 8 A.M.–midnight with entertainment nightly. Grab a pizza and beer and cool off after a day at the beach with a game of pool or darts. A variety of *pu pu,* sandwiches, and pasta is available, as are heartier selections in the evening and a seafood bar until closing. Most items are under $15. The full bar will set you up with drinks, while you kick back and catch your favorite sporting event on one of the televisions.

Tucked into the rear of Kai Nani Village Plaza

is **Ziziki's Restaurant and Bar,** 808/879-9330, where the flavors and textures of the Greek and Mediterranean dishes will excite your palate. Dinner only is served 5–10 P.M. and includes chicken souvlakia, spanakopita, moussaka Alaniki, and leg of lamb, all ranging $18–25. Other items are stuffed grape leaves for $8, Grecian village salad for $9, and several pasta dishes. If you're in doubt as to what would be tasty, try the A Taste of Greece platter, a sampling of several homemade entrées on the menu. Sit inside or out.

## Expensive

Upstairs at the Kai Nani Village Plaza toward the south end of Kihei is **Harlow's,** 808/879-1954. Specializing in prime rib and seafood, Harlow's is open for dinner only from 5 P.M., offering most entrées for $22–36, including black angus prime rib, opakapaka macadamia nut, and braised brisket of beef. Located on the second floor, Harlow's also offers great sunset views.

**Sansei** seafood restaurant and sushi bar, at the Kihei Town Center, 808/879-0004, has the same excellent menu as the original restaurant in Kapalua. Entrées include shichimi-seared fresh Atlantic salmon, Sansei seafood pasta, and spicy crab-stuffed whole lobster tail, all ranging $16–24. More numerous are the appetizers, like tee duck egg roll, miso garlic prawns, and Japanese calamari salad. Sansei is best known for its innovative and exceedingly pleasing sushi, which run $4–16. Sansei is open daily 5:30–10 for dinner and 10 P.M.–2 A.M. on Thursday, Friday, and Saturday for late-night dining and free karaoke.

**Roy's Kihei Bar and Grill,** at the new Pi'ilani Village Shopping Center, 808/891-1120, is a great addition to food options in town. Reservations are recommended and casual resortwear is preferred. Open 5:30–10 P.M. for dinner, Roy's Kihei has many of the same features as those at his other restaurants, like an open kitchen, a regular menu with specials that change nightly, and food that blends the flavors of Hawaii and Asia. Some regulars on the menu include hibachi teriyaki salmon and seared shrimp on a stick with wasabi cocktail sauce appetizer, poached D'anjou pear salad, and entrées like roasted macadamia nut mahimahi, "jade pesto" steamed seabass, herb-grilled chicken breast, and *kiawe* grilled rack of lamb. Specials of the night are just as inventive and usually greater in number. Save room for dessert.

Overlooking the beach, the casual **Five Palms** restaurant, located at the Mana Kai Maui Resort at the extreme south end of Kihei, 808/879-2607, is open for brunch daily 8 A.M.–2:30 P.M., with a *pu pu* menu and happy hour from 3–6 P.M. Dinner runs 5–9:30 P.M. Brunch includes the usual breakfast items such as eggs, omelets, and griddle fare, but also gives you the wider options of soups, salads, sandwiches, and some fish and meat dishes. Dinner is more romantic, and the kitchen turns it up a few notches. Start with a roasted artichoke, crispy Kahuku prawn, or hichimi-spiced and seared ahi appetizer. Move on to slow-roasted prime rib, Hawaiian seafood bouillabaisse, seared duck breast, oven-roasted lobster tail, or fresh fish, the specialty of the house. Appetizers are $8–13 while main entrées run $22–40, but you can come before the rush for the $20 early-bird special. Set so close to the water, the location and scenery are an integral part of the dining experience here.

Only steps from Wailea is the fine-dining restaurant called **Sarento's On The Beach**, 808/875-7555. Open for dinner only 5:30–10 P.M., with a full bar from 5 P.M., all parking is complimentary valet only because of limited space. The excellent reputation and proximity draw many guests from the resorts and condos of Wailea. The seating couldn't be better, with the restaurant set right on the beach, and it's the water and sparkling light off the waves rather than the interior decoration that draws your attention most. However, the interior's contemporary design and modern touches certainly render a warm and friendly atmosphere. The anticipation starts when guests walk past a glassed-in wine cooler on the way to their tables. Appetizers like grilled prawns and pancetta with fire-roasted sweet pepper sauce or mussels in garlic white wine parmesan sauce tempt the palate, which one of the fine salads will clear before the main entré. Main dishes might include baked potato ravioli, seafood "Fra Diavolo," osso bucco, swordfish "saltimbocco," grilled beef filet, or rack of lamb, and run $26–40. Whatever the choice, the flavors and tastes are sure to be impeccable. Sar-

ento's sister restaurants are Nick's Fishmarket down the road at the Fairmont Kea Lani Maui in Wailea, and Aaron's Atop the Ala Moana and Sarento's Top of the "I," both in Honolulu.

# ENTERTAINMENT

Kihei isn't exactly a hot spot when it comes to evening entertainment, although several venues do provide options. **Margarita's Beach Cantina** has live-band dancing on Friday evenings 5–7 P.M. Try **Tradewinds** poolside bar at the Maui Coast Hotel for nightly music in a relaxed setting. **Kahale Beach Club** at the Kihei Kalama Village Market Place, a local bar for people who work in the area, is a place that offers music and dancing on an occasional basis. To its front is the fun little bar **Life's a Beach,** which serves up evening entertainment along with burgers, sandwiches, salads, and *pu pu.* Next door is the intimate **La Creperie** café, the premier jazz venue in the area, with live music nightly 8 P.M.–1 A.M. A bit more upscale is **Bocalino** bistro in the Azeka Makai shopping center, where live music and dancing happens 10 P.M.–1 A.M. Up for Karaoke? Try the **Isana** restaurant after 10 P.M. Many of the restaurants in the area offer entertainment on a hit-and-miss basis, usually one artist with a guitar, a small dinner combo, or some Hawaiian music. These acts are usually listed in the free tourist brochures.

**Hapa's Brew Haus,** 41 E. Lipoa St. in the Lipoa Center, is a big place that once brewed its own beer. Now it serves a variety of others' beers and offers a good-time atmosphere with games, entertainment, and dancing until the wee hours of the morning on its big dance floor. While the schedule changes monthly, local live bands often perform from about 9 P.M., and occasionally a big-name musician will stop by. Willie K has played here for years. On other nights, DJs spin the music. Different covers for different events.

The **Kukui Mall Theater** at the Kihei Town Center is the only movie theater on this side of the island. It's a four-screen theater with shows starting at about noon. Admission is $8 adults, $5 seniors and kids, and $5.50 matinee.

Into billiards? Visit **Dick's Place** at the Kamaole Shopping Center, on the second floor.

MAUI

Open 11 A.M.–midnight, Dick's also serves food and has a full bar.

## SHOPPING

While driving the length of Kihei, you will find shopping centers, both large and small, strung along the entire coastal area like shells on a dime-store lei. At many you can buy food, clothing, sporting goods, picnic supplies, sundries, photo equipment, cosmetics, resortwear, ice cream, pizza, dinner, and liquor. You can also book activities, order a custom bikini, or just relax with an ice-cold beer while your partner satisfies his or her shopping addiction. In Kihei, you have more than ample opportunity to spend your hard-earned vacation money that would be a sin to take back home. Aloha!

### North End Shopping

At the very north end of Kihei, as you approach from Wailuku or Lahaina, is the **Sugar Beach General Store,** with a small clutch of shops selling resortwear, snacks, and gifts. The activities company here can set you up for a fun afternoon or rent you a bicycle or water gear.

**Suda's Store,** 61 S. Kihei Rd., is a basic little market with limited food items, but with cold beer, fresh fish, and deli items. Open Monday–Friday 7:30 A.M.–5 P.M., Saturday until 4 P.M., and Sunday 8 A.M.–3 P.M., it sits along the *mauka* side, across from the Kihei Canoe Club. Locally grown produce is sold in the parking lot here from 1:30–5:30 P.M. on Monday, Wednesday, and Friday. A few minutes down the road from Suda's heading for Kihei, look for the **Nona Lana Cottages,** where you can pick up a fresh-flower lei for a reasonable price.

Set along Pi'ilani Highway (Route 31), the main thoroughfare above Kihei that parallels Kihei Road, is **Kihei Gateway Plaza.** Even with the **Aloha Gifts and Gallery** shop and **Maui Clothing Outlet** store, its perhaps most useful for its gas station, minimart, and video rental outlet.

### Pi'ilani Village Shopping Center

The newest shopping center in town, and one of the largest, is set along Pi'ilani Highway at the corner of Pi'ikea. This is a big place with a little of everything for local residents and visitors. You can buy gas, clothing, food, and sundries. Several of the largest stores are **Roy's Kihei** restaurant for fine dining, **Hilo Hattie** for Hawaiian fashions and gifts, and a **Safeway** supermarket for groceries and a pharmacy. Aside from these, **Waldenbooks** has a good selection of books, **Blockbuster Video** has evening entertainment for rent, **ABC Stores** for sundries, **Flash Back Photo** for film, **Tropical Disk** for music, and the **Kihei-Wailea Medical Center** has an office here.

### Longs Shopping Center

Located at 1215 S. Kihei Road, almost opposite the post office, this shopping center is dominated by a huge **Longs Drugs,** stocked with electronics, photo equipment and film developing, sundries, cosmetics, stationery, a pharmacy, and even sporting goods. Around the center you will find the **T-Shirt Factory** featuring all kinds of discounted wearable take-home gifts, and you can do everything from faxing to packing and shipping at **Mail Boxes Etc. American Savings Bank** is conveniently located here for all the shopping that you may be doing in this center and along the Kihei strip. A **farmers market** is held here in the parking lot every Saturday from 8 A.M.–noon.

### Azeka Place

Adjacent to the post office is the Azeka Place Shopping Center, now also referred to as Azeka Makai, in what might be considered the center of town. Once filled with small boutique shops, you now mostly find small restaurants and fast-food eating establishments, as well as the **Kihei Ace Hardware** and **B&B Scuba.** Just down the street is a **Star Market** for all your grocery needs.

The Kihei **post office,** 1254 S. Kihei Rd., is open Monday–Friday 8:30 A.M.–4:30 P.M. and Saturday until 1 P.M.

### Azeka Place II

This newer and larger shopping center is located just across the street from the original Azeka Place and is now also called Azeka Mauka. Featured here are **The Coffee Store,** a great place for a cup of coffee, a light lunch or late-night snack, or to check your email; **Cyber Surf Lounge** also for Internet access; and **Bank of Hawaii,** a full-service bank with ATMs. For vitamins, minerals, and supplements, try **General Nutrition Center,** and **Hula Hogs** rents motorcycles, which can be filled at the **gas station** at the corner. Started in 1950 as a one-store, mom-and-pop operation, the two Azeka Place shopping centers comprise more than 50 shops and make the largest shopping complex in South Maui.

## Lipoa Center

Until Pi'ilani Village Shopping Center was built, the Lipoa Center was the only major shopping center not on the main drag. Lipoa Center is located a hop, skip, and a jump up Lipoa Street, just around the corner from Azeka Place II. Here you'll find a **First Hawaiian Bank, Kihei Professional Pharmacy, Shell gas station,** and **Gold's Gym.** Perhaps more of interest for the traveler are **Hapa's Brew Haus** for music and drinks and the **Lipoa Laundry Center,** a clean and modern full-service laundry that's open daily from 8 A.M. and Monday–Saturday until 9 P.M., Sunday 5 P.M.

## Kukui Mall

At the Kukui Mall, across from Kalama Park, is the apparel store **Local Motion.** Tired of the beach, or just need to beat the heat? Stop at the multiscreen **Kukui Mall Theater.**

Across the street at the corner is the **Aloha Marketplace.** Once just a bunch of stalls under awnings and trees, it's now an open-air courtyard building ringed with stalls where you can shop daily 9 A.M.–9 P.M. for jewelry, clothing, carvings, and other touristy gifts.

## Kihei Town Center

This small shopping center just south of the Kukui Mall offers a 24-hour **Foodland, Cyberbean** for drinks and Internet access, the **Rainbow Attic** consignment shop, and several eateries.

## Kihei Kalama Village Market Place

Look for this bargain-filled, semi-open-air warren of stalls under a tall roof superstructure at 1945 S. Kihei Road, offering everything from tourist trinkets to fine art; clothes, crafts, and jewelry pre-

dominate. This is the best open-air market in South Maui and perhaps on the island. Around the periphery are other shops. Among them you will find **Serendipity,** a small, well-appointed boutique that displays imported items mainly from Malaysia and Brazil, and **Clementines** for one-of-a-kind women's clothing. Out front at the corner, **Maui Discount Activity World** will set you up with your day's activity. If you're hungry, you'll find all sorts of food options here as well.

## Dolphin Shopping Plaza

This small, two-story plaza at 2395 S. Kihei Road includes **Boss Frogs,** where you can rent snorkel gear at a reasonable price, and **Hawaiian Island Cruisers** can provide you with a rental bike or moped. In the back are several small restaurants. Upstairs, you'll find **Kihei Chiropractic.**

## Kamaole Beach Center

A small group of shops between Dolphin and Rainbow plazas, this center has **Honolulu Surf Company** clothing store for local fashions and **Snorkel Bob's** to pick up snorkel gear for the week. You can get groceries and deli food at **Hawaiian Moon's Natural Foods** or come by after a warm day on the beach for a cool beer at **The Sports Page Grill and Bar.**

## Rainbow Mall

Yet another small mall just up the road at 2439 S. Kihei Road features **South Pacific Kayaks and Outfitters** and **Aloha Destination's Auntie Snorkel** for the sales and rental of snorkel gear, boogie boards, kayaks, and camping and hiking gear for very reasonable prices. Other shops in the mall are **Maui Custom Beachwear,** where you can buy off the rack or have a bikini made especially for you; **Haleakala Trading Company** for Hawaii-made gifts and souvenirs; **Premiere Video** for evening entertainment if you're staying in a condo; and **Topaz,** a fine jewelry and watch store. **Aloha Discount Liquor** is located at the back of the mall.

## Kamaole Shopping Center

Last in this quick succession of small malls is the slightly larger Kamaole Shopping Center at 2463

S. Kihei Road. This mall has several inexpensive eateries and various clothing, souvenir, and sundries stores. From its two floors of shops you can buy baubles, beads, and some nicer pieces at **Unique Jewels;** tropical fashions at **Panama Jack's;** sunglasses at **Shades of Hawaii;** and liquor, gifts, and souvenirs at **Whalers General Store.** Lappert's Aloha Ice Cream sells island-made delights and fat-free yogurt. Also in the center is a **Maui Dive Shop,** a complete diving and water sports store offering rentals, swimwear, snorkels, cruises, and sailboarding lessons, and an **Ocean Activities Center** booth for booking water sports. **Postal Plus,** open Mon.–Sat. 9 A.M.–6 P.M., can take care of your stamp, box, and shipping needs, and offers computer connections, as does **Hale Imua Internet** next door.

## Kai Nani Village Plaza
This small cluster of restaurants sits at the south end of Kihei. Aside from the eateries, you'll find the **Sunshine Mart** for sundries and food items.

## Farmers Markets
A small farmers market is held in the parking lot in front of Suda's Store at 61 S. Kihei Road, every Monday, Wednesday, and Friday 1:30–5:30 P.M. Besides fresh produce, stalls sell shells, T-shirts, and knickknacks of all kinds. There is also a farmers market in the Longs Shopping Center every Saturday 8 A.M.–noon.

## Food/Liquor Stores
**Foodland,** at Kihei Town Center (open 24 hours), **Star Market** (5 A.M.–2 A.M.) at 1310 S. Kihei Road, and **Safeway** (open 24 hours) at Pi'ilani Village Shopping Center, are full-service supermarkets with a complete liquor, wine, and beer selection.

**Hawaiian Moon's Natural Foods** at the Kamaole Beach Center is a small but full-service natural health-food store. Stop in for bulk foods, groceries, herbs, organic fruits and vegetables, vitamins, minerals and supplements, juices, bottled water, soy drinks, and beer. There's even a freezer case for ice cream and a deli case for takeout sandwiches.

At the very south end of Kihei are two small

markets. Smaller and more basic, the **Sunshine Mart** is located at the Kai Nani Village Plaza. At Mana Kai Maui Resort, try **Keawakapu General Store** for groceries, sundries, snacks, and spirits. Open daily 7 A.M.–9 P.M.

At the Rainbow Mall, **Aloha Discount Liquor** has a good selection of liquor, imported beers, and wine.

# RECREATION
## Golf
Associated with the Maui Beach Hotel in Kahului, the only golf course in Kihei is **Elleair Maui Golf Club,** 808/874-0777. Set along Pi'ilani Highway, this course has been totally reworked over the past few years, so it now presents a new face. Young and open, there are good views over town to the coast. Greens fees are an economical $85. After a round of golf, stay for dinner or a drink at The Palm Restaurant at the clubhouse, open Tues.–Sun. 5–10 P.M.

## Water Gear and Rentals
The **Maui Dive Shop,** 808/879-3388, has a main store and office at 1455 S. Kihei Road near the Star Market in Kihei and offers a full range of equipment, lessons, and rentals. Open daily 7:30 A.M.–9 P.M., it is one of the oldest and most respected companies in the business. Another location along this coast is at the Kamaole Shopping Center, 808/879-1533.

**Dive and Sea Maui,** 1975 S. Kihei Rd., 808/874-1952, is also a full-service dive shop offering dives, certification, air refills, equipment rentals, and dive/snorkel boat trips to Molokini Crater.

**Snorkel Bob's,** 808/879-7449, is easy to spot at the Kamaole Beach Center. Open daily 8 A.M.–5 P.M., Bob has some of the best deals around for some very good gear. The weekly prices can't be beat at $9–36 for snorkel gear and about the same for boogie boards. Daily rentals are available too, as are prescription lenses. You also get snorkel tips and Bob's semi-soggy underwater humor. Looking for an above-water activity? Bob can arrange that too.

**Auntie Snorkel,** 808/879-6263, located at

the Rainbow Mall, rents snorkel gear, along with boogie boards, beach chairs, and even ice chests at prices that are among the lowest in the area.

Also at the Rainbow Mall, **South Pacific Kayaks and Outfitters,** 808/875-4848 or 800/776-2326, open daily 8 A.M.–4 P.M., offers half a dozen kayak options from a half-day introductory trip for $59 to an advanced explorer tour along the remote South Maui coastline for $89. The longer tours include lunch, and all have plenty of snorkeling opportunities as you glide in and out of tiny bays fashioned from jutting lava rock fingers. South Pacific Kayaks offers rentals of single kayaks at $30 and double kayaks at $40 per day. For those who love the land more, several hiking trips can also be arranged.

# INFORMATION AND SERVICES
## Information
The member organization South Maui Destination Association has some information about South Maui: hotels, B&Bs, restaurants, activities, shopping, services, real estate, and more. Contact the association at 101 N. Kihei Rd., Ste. 4, Kihei, HI 96753, 808/874-9400, fax 808/879-1283, info@southmauivacations.com, www.kihei.org. Their *Maui Guide* can be seen online at www.mauiguide.com.

## Medical Services
For minor medical emergencies, try **Urgent Care Maui/Kihei Physicians,** 1325 S. Kihei Rd., Ste. 103, 808/879-7781, where doctors, a clinical lab, and X-rays are available from 6 A.M.–midnight daily. **Kihei-Wailea Medical Center,** 808/874-8100, in the Pi'ilani Village Shopping Center, has physicians, a pharmacy, physical therapy, and a clinical laboratory and is open Monday–Friday 8 A.M.–8 P.M., Saturday and Sunday until 5 P.M.

Chiropractic services are available at the **Chiropractic Clinic of Kihei,** 1847 S. Kihei Rd., 808/879-7246, which specializes in nonforce techniques, and **Kihei Chiropractic Center,**

at the Dolphin Plaza, 808/879-0638. There's also **Kihei Acupuncture Clinic,** 1051 S. Kihei Rd., 808/874-0544, specializing in gentle needling techniques and offering a full selection of Chinese herbs.

## Transportation
The **Holo Ka'a public transit shuttle** connects Kihei with Wailea and Makena to the south and west to the Maui Ocean Center in Ma'alaea, from where you can carry on to Lahaina, Ka'anapali, and Kapalua in West Maui. The shuttle runs daily approximately 9 A.M.–10 P.M. Fares are $1 point to point, $5 for Makena–Ma'alaea, and $10 for a one-day pass for the whole system.

## Banking
There are several branch banks in Kihei. **Bank of Hawaii,** 808/879-5844, is at Azeka Place II; **First Hawaiian Bank,** 808/875-0055, is at the Lipoa Center; **American Savings Bank,** 808/879-1977, is at the Longs Center; **Hawaii National Bank,** 808/879-8877, is at 1325 S. Kihei Road; and **City Bank,** 808/891-8586, is at the Kukui Mall.

## Post Offices
The main **post office** in Kihei is located at Azeka Place, 1254 S. Kihei Road. **Mail Boxes Etc.,** at Longs Shopping Center, open weekdays 8 A.M.–6 P.M., Saturday 9 A.M.–5 P.M., Sunday 10 A.M.–3 P.M., offers fax services, copies, notary, and packing and shipping.

## Laundry
**Lipoa Laundry Center** at the Lipoa Center, 808/875-9266, is also a full-service laundry and dry cleaning establishment. Open 8 A.M.–8 P.M. with shorter hours on Sunday.

## Library
The **Kihei Public library,** 808/875-6833, is across the street and down from the Kukui Mall. It has variable daily hours.

# Wailea

Wailea (Waters of Lea) isn't for the hoi polloi. It's a deluxe resort area custom-tailored to fit the egos of the upper class like a pair of silk pajamas. This section of South Maui was barren and bleak until Alexander and Baldwin Co. decided to landscape it into an emerald 1,450-acre oasis of world-class golf courses and destination resorts. Every street light, palm tree, and potted plant is a deliberate accessory to the decor so that the overall feeling is soothing, pleasant, and in good taste. To dispel any notions of snootiness, the five sparkling beaches that front the resorts were left open to the public and even improved with better access, parking areas, showers, and picnic tables—a gracious gesture even if state law does require open access! You'll know when you leave Kihei and enter Wailea. The green, quiet, and wide tree-lined avenues give the impression of an upper-class residential suburb. Wailea is where you come when quality is the most important aspect of your vacation. The brilliant five-star resorts are first-rate architecturally, and the grounds are exquisite botanical jewel boxes.

Aside from the beaches, the two main attractions in Wailea are the fantastic golf and tennis opportunities. Three magnificent golf courses have been laid out on Haleakala's lower slopes, all open to the public. Tennis is great at the Wailea Tennis Club, and many of the hotels and condos have their own championship courts.

To keep up the quality, a few years ago Wailea Shopping Village was completely razed and rebuilt as The Shops at Wailea and in a fashion that would outdo even the fine upscale shops of Ka'anapali and Kapalua on the west end of the island.

Running along the water from one end of Wailea to the other is a 1.5-mile-long beach walk. This cement path cuts across all properties from the Renaissance Wailea Beach Resort to the Kea Lani, and like the beaches, it's open to the public. Used often in the early morning or late afternoon for exercise by walkers and joggers, it's a convenient way to get to the next beach or to the next resort for lunch or dinner. Even if you're not staying in the area, take a stroll down the path and have a look at the wonderfully landscaped gardens and resort properties here.

You can get to Wailea by coming straight down South Kihei Road through the strip of condos and shopping centers. To miss this area and make better time, take Pi'ilani Highway, Route 31. This route takes you up on the hillside, where you

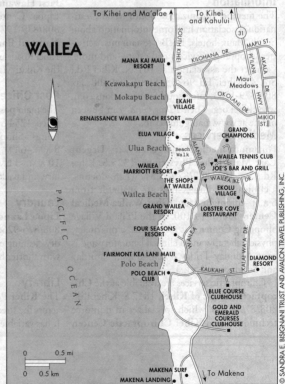

have some nice views out over the water and can watch Kihei slip by in a blur below. Where this highway stops, Wailea Ike Drive snakes down the hill to Wailea Alanui Drive and deposits you in the heart of Wailea at the new shopping center.

For greater information on Wailea, have a look at the website: www.wailea-resort.com.

## Onward and Backward

If you turn your back to the sea and look toward Haleakala, you'll see its cool, green forests and peak wreathed in mysterious clouds. You'll want to run right over, but you can't get there from here! Outrageous as it may sound, you have to double back 18 miles to Kahului and then head up Route 37 for another 20 miles just to get to the exact same spot on Route 37 that you can easily see. Some maps show a neat little road that connects the Wailea/Makena area with Upcountry in a mere three-mile stretch, but it's a private 4WD road that's never open to the public because it traverses ranchland. If this appalling situation is ever rectified, you'll be able to travel easily to the Tedeschi Winery and continue on the "wrong way" to Hana, or go left to Kula and Upcountry. For now, however, happy motoring!

## BEACHES

If you're not fortunate enough to be staying in Wailea, the best reason for coming here is its beaches. These little beauties are crescent moons of golden sand that usually end in lava outcroppings on both ends. This makes for sheltered, swimmable waters and good snorkeling and scuba. Many of the hotel guests in Wailea seem to hang around the hotel pools, maybe peacocking or just trying to get their money's worth, so the beaches are surprisingly uncrowded. The following beaches are listed from north to south.

### Keawakapu

The first Wailea beach, almost a buffer between Kihei and Wailea, is just past the Mana Kai Resort. Turn left onto Kamala Place, or proceed straight on South Kihei Road until it dead-ends. Plenty of parking is available at both accesses, but no amenities are provided. Keawakapu is a lovely beach with a sandy bottom. Good swimming and fair snorkeling. There's also a beginner's dive spot offshore.

## Mokapu and Ulua

These two beaches are shoulder to shoulder, separated only by a rock outcropping. Turn right off Wailea Alanui at the first turn past the Renaissance Wailea Beach Resort. The beach is clearly marked, and there's a parking area, showers, and restrooms. Being resort beaches, they're both particularly well-kept. Beautiful sand and protected waters are perfect for swimming. There's good snorkeling at the outcropping separating the beaches, or swim out to the first reef just in front of the rocks for excellent snorkeling.

## Wailea Beach

The Outrigger, Grand Wailea, and Four Seasons resorts front this beach. One-half mile past The Shops at Wailea, turn right onto a clearly marked access road between the Grand Wailea and the Four Seasons; at the end of the drive there's good parking, as well as showers and toilets. A short but wide beach, Wailea offers good swimming and bodysurfing, but the snorkeling is only fair.

## Polo Beach

Follow Wailea Alanui toward Makena. Turn right on Kaukahi Street just past the Fairmont Kea Lani Maui and right again at the clearly marked sign near the Polo Beach condo. Here also are paved parking, showers, and toilets. Polo Beach is good for swimming and sunbathing, with few tourists. There's excellent snorkeling in front of the rocks separating Polo from Wailea Beach—tremendous amounts of fish, and one of the easiest spots to get to.

## LUXURY ACCOMMODATIONS

### Renaissance Wailea Beach Resort

Always a beauty, the Renaissance Wailea, 3550 Wailea Alanui, Wailea, HI 96753, 808/879-4900 or 800/992-4532, fax 808/874-5370, www.renaissancehotels.com, is like a rich red cabernet that has aged superbly. The Renaissance is a superbly appointed resort with attention given to

MAUI

the most minute details of comfort and luxury. When you enter the main lobby, you're actually on the fifth floor; the ones below terrace down the mountainside to the golden sands of Mokapu Beach. The lobby has original artworks on the walls and a sweeping marble staircase leading down to the Palm Court Restaurant. A bubbling spa fashioned from lava rock is surrounded by vines and flowering trees; another spa contains three little pools and a gurgling fountain, so that while the therapeutic water soothes your muscles, the music of the fountain soothes your nerves. The impeccable grounds have grown into an actual botanical garden. And everywhere there is water, cascading over tiny waterfalls, tumbling in brooks, and reflecting the amazing green canopy in tranquil lagoons.

The 345 white-on-tan rooms are appointed with koa and rattan furniture. Beds are brightened with quilted pillows, and each room is accented with standing lamps, paintings of Hawaiian flora, an entertainment center with VCR and remote-control TV, wall safe, a glass-topped writing desk, even matching *happi* coats for an evening of lounging. Sliding doors lead to a lanai, where you can relax or enjoy a quiet in-room meal. The bathrooms are small but adequate, with double marble-topped sinks and a queen-size tub. The hotel features the very private Mokapu Beach Club, a detached low-rise wing complete with its own pool and daily continental breakfast, where the hotel's impeccable service rises yet higher with valet service and 24-hour concierge. Room rates are $345 terrace view, $400 garden view, $450 ocean view, and $600 Mokapu Beach Club; $40 each additional person over age 18. Suites run $1,050–4,000 for one and two bedrooms. Varying rates include a family plan, where children under 18 stay free if they're in their parents' room, and also a variety of golf and tennis packages.

You will enjoy the Palm Court, Hana Goin Japanese, and poolside Maui Onion restaurants, the lobby cocktail lounge, where there's live music nightly, and the Wailea Sunset Luau held three times weekly. The Renaissance offers valet parking, 24-hour room service, a business center, a fitness center, therapeutic massage and body care,

the part-day Camp Wailea children's program, free daily newspaper, a small shopping arcade, a twice-weekly arts and crafts mini-fair, and a concierge desk to book you into every kind of outdoor Maui activity. The most amazing feature about the resort is its feeling of peace and tranquility. The Renaissance is part of the Marriott family of hotels.

## Wailea Marriott Resort

The Wailea Marriott, an Outrigger Resort property branded with the Marriott name, is a class act, and since its remodel in 2000, its an even finer place. The entryway has been opened to let more light into the main building and reception area, and other public areas of the hotel have been reconfigured into new lounges and restaurants. The main lobby, supported by gigantic wooden beams, is still inviting with its informal setting and frames a wide panorama of the sea and Lana'i floating on the horizon. Walk out onto a stone-tiled portico and below, in a central courtyard ringed by palms, is a series of quiet lily ponds highlighted with red torch ginger and alive with serenading bullfrogs in the evening. Stroll the 22 meticulously landscaped acres and dip into one of the pools, take the kids to the new family pool with its waterslide and play areas, or have a look at the Hawaiian fishermen's shrine near the shore. All rooms have been totally remodeled with simple and suitable furnishings and decorations, and throughout the property designs in the carpet, light fixtures, and other decorative features have been taken from Hawaiian mythology and symbolism.

The Wailea Marriott was the first large hotel property in Wailea. It has roots here. Not only that, but it makes the claim of being the "most Hawaiian hotel in Wailea." From the little touches to the large efforts, most would say that it is so. The hotel has established a position of Director of Hawaiian Culture and runs a Hawaiian cultural program called Ho'olokahi that not only educates the staff about its own Hawaiian heritage but also shares the Hawaiian culture with guests and brings the community to the hotel for cultural exchanges. The Hawaiian cultural program has a varied schedule of activities and workshops presented by knowledgeable Hawaiian elders and teachers. All you need to do to attend is sign up. Some activities are hula demonstrations and contests, lei making, and ukulele instruction. On Aloha Friday, arts and crafts are displayed and sold, and hula is performed in the hotel lobby. The resort also hosts a Hawaiian sailing canoe regatta, which is accompanied by numerous cultural activities and events. In addition, the restaurant Hula Moons is dedicated to Don Blanding, an early enthusiast of Hawaii and Hawaiian culture from the early 20th century, and it proudly displays some of Blanding's personal belongings and mementos of the times.

At least 80 percent of the resort's 521 rooms have ocean views, which in most cases are actually oceanfront. Rooms are coordinated with light pastel tones of green-on-tan and beige. All have a large entertainment center with remote-control TV and small refrigerator. Granite bathrooms are well-proportioned with a full bath and shower, sinks, and separate dressing area. Doors open to a terra cotta–floored lanai, flushed with sunshine and sea breezes, from where you have a private view of the Lahaina Roads. More amenities include room service, the Mandara Spa, a business center, a row of shops, self-service laundry, and complimentary valet parking in a covered parking lot. For children, the Cowabunga Kids Club fills the day with supervised activities for a nominal fee.

For food and entertainment, head to the newly redesigned lobby-level Hula Moons Restaurant or poolside Kumu Bar and Grill, pop into the new Mele Mele Lounge next to Hula Moons for a drink or *pu pu* while you chat or watch the sunset, or attend the award-winning lu'au and Polynesian show, "Wailea's Finest Luau," down by the water. Outings and activities can be arranged at the concierge desk in the lobby. Room rates run $325 for a standard garden room to $525 for a deluxe oceanfront room; suites are available at $650–1,500; $40 per extra person. Special family plans, room and car, honeymoon, golf, and other packages are available. The Wailea Marriott Resort is located at 3700 Wailea Alanui, Wailea, Maui, HI 96753, 808/879-1922 or 800/688-7444, fax 808/874-8331, www.outriggerwailea.com.

## Grand Wailea Resort Hotel & Spa

A sublime interplay of cascading water, light diffused and brilliant, and the music of natural sound have been entwined with fine art, sculpted landscaping, and brilliant architecture to create the intangible quality of grandeur so apparent at the astounding Grand Wailea Resort Hotel & Spa, 3850 Wailea Alanui, Wailea, HI 96753, 808/875-1234 or 800/888-6100, fax 808/879-4077, www.grandwailearesort.com. On arrival the spume of a thunderous waterfall, misting a heroic sculpture of the warrior king, Kamehameha, is the tangible spirit of the grand hotel. Inside the towering reception atrium, the water and sculpture interplay continues. Hula dancers both male and female, some with arms outstretched to the sun, others in repose or in a stance of power, are the visual *mele* singing of the ancient times. A mermaid, bronzed, bare-breasted, offers a triton shell of sweet water, and behind, sleek canoes float on a pond of blue. Ahead the glimmering sea, foaming surf, and wind-tossed palms dance to their immortal tune. Left and right, Fernando Botero's sculpted women—enormous, buxom, and seductive—lie in alluring repose.

In the garden, a formal fountain, surrounded by royal palms, is reflected in a rectangular pool inlaid with white and gold tile forming a giant hibiscus. The pool area surrounds a "volcano" and fronts Wailea beach. Here, a canyon river, complete with gentle current, glides you through a series of pools and past small grottoes where you can stop to enjoy a hot tub, swing like Tom Sawyer on a suspended rope, swim up to a bar for your favorite drink, or just slip along until you are deposited in the main pool. Waiting is the world's only water elevator, to lift you to the top again and again. Other meandering waterways and pools dot the property.

If Nero had the health and relaxation resources found at the hotel's Spa Grande, his fiddle playing would have vastly improved and Rome never would have burned. The magic begins as soon as you enter this marble-clad facility, the largest in the state and arguably the best equipped. Dip first into a Japanese *ofuro* that unjangles nerves and soothes muscles. From there, a cold dip to revitalize and then into the termé baths, followed by a cascading waterfall shower or jet rinse. Awaiting you are private massage rooms where you can choose a multitude of different massage, facial, and body treatments. Each room opens to the sea, whose eternal rhythm helps create complete relaxation.

The Grand Wailea is a huge complex of five separate wings and a tower, with 780 guest rooms. These rooms feature private lanai that look out over the water and flower gardens below, while inside they are sanctuaries of pure luxury. All are appointed in soothing earth tones with complete entertainment centers, a bar (some have mini refrigerators), in-room safes, and twice-daily maid service. Rates are $450–760 for standard rooms, and $1,575–2,000 for suites. Guests of the Napua Tower have concierge service and many special amenities. Rooms here run $800, suites $2,000–10,000. Numerous packages are offered.

For the dining and entertainment pleasure of its guests, the Grand Wailea has six restaurants, four bars and lounges, and one nightclub. To make a family visit perfect, **Camp Grande** holds court for children ages 5–12. Run by professionals, both day and evening camps feature movies, a preschool playroom, arts and crafts, a computer learning center, a videogame room, and a kids' restaurant. The Grand Wailea has Wailea's largest collection of resort shops, and if that's not enough, you are only a 10-minute walk from the Shops at Wailea next door. For those unfortunate enough to be in Hawaii on business, the hotel's business center is set up to take care of all equipment and service needs.

Scuba diving lessons, a catamaran sail, and other water activities and rentals are arranged by an outside concession on hotel property near the beach. Periodic tours of the grounds and hotel art are offered—worth some $30 million when collected; some now say it's worth $75 million. The garden tour is free and given Thursday at 10 A.M. and starts at the concierge desk; sign-up is required. Beginning from the Napua Gallery, the art tour is offered Tuesdays and Fridays at 10 A.M.; free to hotel guests, but $6.25 for nonguests. Finally, there is a nondenominational **chapel** that's used for weddings (the hotel does about 500 per year), a miniature cathedral with floor-to-ceiling stained-glass windows.

## Four Seasons Resort Maui at Wailea

AAA five-diamond award winner the Four Seasons, 3900 Wailea Alanui, Wailea, Maui, HI 96753, 808/874-8000 or 800/334-6284, fax 808/874-6449, www.fourseasons.com/maui, situated on 15 acres at the south end of Wailea Beach, is oriented to the setting sun and opens itself up to the sweet sea breezes. Casually elegant, the open-air lobby is full of cushy chairs and couches, fountains, flowers, fans, and a grand staircase that glides down to the huge pool at beach level. On the way down, say "hello" to Ricky and Lucy, the hotel parakeets who make their home below the staircase. The pool and the colonnade of lobby pillars above it hint at a Romanesque architectural influence, yet the ambiance and colors of the hotel say island natural. Original artwork and reproductions hang throughout the lobby and hallways, while huge fossilized sea anemones are displayed on lobby tables, and birds and plants bring the outdoors inside. Countless little details make this resort pleasant and special.

The Four Seasons is a study of cream-on-cream, and this color scheme runs throughout the resort, offset by coral, almond, muted greens, and other pastels. Each large room has a bedroom and sitting area, an exceptionally large bath with separate shower and deep tub, a well-stocked wet bar, TV, room safe, and private lanai; 85 percent of the rooms have an ocean view and all have twice-daily room service. While air-conditioning is standard, rooms also have sliding screen doors or louvered French doors and overhead fans. Double rooms and suites are even more spacious, with the addition of a second bathroom and/or a dining area. Rates for the standard rooms run $335 for a mountain view up to $665 for a prime ocean view, $100 per extra person. Depending on the number of bedrooms and location, suites run $755–6,700. Rates on the Club Floor, which includes on-floor check-in, complimentary continental breakfast, afternoon tea, sunset cocktails and hors d'oeuvres, and a personal concierge, run $750–2,450, $160 per extra person. The club lounge on this floor also provides books, newspapers, magazines, and board games. Golf, family, room and car, romance, and two-island packages are also available.

Other resort amenities include three top-notch restaurants, a lobby lounge that has entertainment nightly except Sunday, five shops, a game room with a fine collection of surfing memorabilia, meeting rooms for conventions, complimentary valet parking, 24-hour room service, and an early-arrival/late-departure lounge where you can relax and enjoy the hotel services, store a small bag, or shower off the grit of travel. In addition, the supervised "Kids for all Seasons" program can keep your little ones ages 5–12 busy for all or part of the day, 9 A.M.–5 P.M., with games and activities. On site are two tennis courts and lawn croquet (for guests only); an expanded health club with exercise machines and a steam room that offers massage and personal training; and organized beach activities. Down by the beach, all beach chairs, cabanas, snorkel equipment (free rental for one hour), boogie boards, and the like are complimentary—added value for guests. These and most hotel amenities are included in the room charge. Although not cheap, you get a lot for your money and great service.

## Fairmont Kea Lani Maui

While Aladdin napped and dreamed of high adventure, his genie was at work building a pleasure dome more splendid than the great Khan's Xanadu. The Fairmont Kea Lani Maui, 4100 Wailea Alanui, Wailea, HI 96753, 808/875-4100 or 800/441-1414, fax 808/875-1200, www.fairmont.com, is an alabaster fantasy bazaar where turrets and cupolas cover vaulted and coved ceilings suspended above towering pillars. Enter the central lobby, an open-air court with a bubbling fountain, completely sculpted and gilded; sultan's slippers would be appropriate here to pad around on the mosaic floors. One level down is the lounge, formal but comfortable, with giant shoji-like mirrors and sculpted harps and lyres embedded in the walls. A staircase leads down from there to a tranquil pool area fronting a wide sweep of grass and perpetual blue sea. Three restaurants, a deli, and a lounge bar service the food needs of the guests.

Lodging at the Kea Lani is in one-bedroom luxury suites with separate living area priced $339–629, or in opulent two- and three-bedroom villas set closer to the water and priced $1,400–2,400, with several room/car, room/meal, and romance packages as options. Enter the suites, very roomy at just under 900 square feet, to find a richly embossed carpet contrasting with white-on-white walls. These units sleep four. Double doors open to the master bedroom. The sitting room, formal but comfy, is appointed with puff-pillow chairs, a queen-size sleeper sofa, entertainment center, marble-topped tables, and a full bar with microwave and coffeemaker. All rooms are air-conditioned, but there are also ceiling fans. The bathroom, marble from floor to ceiling, features an oversize tub, two pedestal sinks, a huge stall shower, and cotton *yukata* for a day of lounging. The bi-level villas, sleeping 6–8, include more of the same but have greater floor space and more bedrooms. They are completely furnished with full and modern kitchens and laundry rooms. Outside each villa in its private courtyard is a plunge pool, slightly heated and perfect for two, and a gas barbecue.

The hotel's pool area is grand, just right for frolicking or for savoring an afternoon siesta. A free-form upper pool, boasting a swim-to bar, and serviced by the Polo Beach Grill, is connected to the lower pool by a 140-foot water slide. The lower area is family oriented with a football-shaped children's pool, but escape is at hand at the casbah pool, inlaid with multihued tiles forming an entwined moon and sun around it; adults can shelter in Camelot-like tents providing shade and privacy or relax in one of two jet spas. Other amenities include a beach activities booth, an activities desk, in-house doctor's office, business center, complimentary fitness center, health and body spa, and a clutch of swank boutiques. The children have their own Keiki Lani children's program, open daily 9 A.M.–3 P.M., where children ages 5–12 are entertained with a mixture of fun and educational activities and even given lunch.

## Destination Resorts Hawaii

This complex is made up of six separate villages that are scattered along the coast or up around the golf course. Check-in is handled at the Destination Resorts office on the lower level of The Shops at Wailea near the front. For those properties that have a peak season, it runs from mid-December to the end of April. Year-round and high-season rates are quoted; low-season rates will be approximately 10 percent cheaper. **Ekolu Village,** located near the Blue Course, has one- and two-bedroom condo units for $195–275. Also on the golf links, next to Wailea Tennis Club, is **Grand Champions,** with one-, two-, and three-bedroom units for $200–385. At the entrance to Wailea and with oceanfront and hillside units, **Ekahi Village** has studio, one-, and two-bedroom condos for $180–410. Tucked between the Renaissance and Outrigger hotels, **Elua Village** fronts Ulua Beach and has one-, two-, and three-bedroom condos ranging $295–825. Right on Polo Beach is **Polo Beach Club,** the only high-rise condo building in the bunch. Rates here are $350–515 for one- or two-bedroom units. The newest and perhaps the most exclusive is **Makena Surf,** on a private section of coast a short way down the road toward Makena. Here one-, two-, and three-bedroom units run $417–775.

All rates are based on double occupancy, with children 12 years and younger free; an additional $20 is assessed for each extra adult. Special golf, tennis, car, and romance packages are available. There is a three- to five-night minimum stay, 10–14 nights during the Christmas–New Year's season. The fifth or seventh night is free depending on the village. An additional resort fee may be charged on check-in with each reservation. All units are plush and fully furnished, with kitchens, daily housekeeping service, a swimming pool or pools, barbecue grills, and some with tennis courts on the premises. All have gated entrances. The beach, two golf courses, and additional tennis courts are nearby. Amenities include concierge services; reservations for dinners and all air, land, and sea activities; and arrangements for rental vehicles and water equipment. For information and reservations, contact Destination Resorts Hawaii at 808/879-1595 or 800/367-5246, fax 808/874-3554, www.drhmaui.com.

## Diamond Resort

Formerly a member-only resort, this condo property is now open to all but gets plenty of Japanese visitors. The Diamond Resort, 555 Kaukahi St.,

Wailea, HI 96753, 808/874-0500 or 800/800-0720, fax 808/874-8778, www.diamondresort.com, sits high above the Wailea Blue Golf Course and has a wonderful view over the ocean. The slate roof and stone exterior on the round portion of the main building make a wonderful first impression, and the pools and stream that cascade down between the buildings create a restful feeling. Let the resort's three restaurants fill your belly, the training center help you work out, and the spa soothe your muscles. The spa features Japanese *ofuro,* Scandinavian saunas, and various baths. The 72 large, air-conditioned, one-bedroom guest suites have ocean, partial-ocean, or garden views and come with kitchenettes, TV and VCRs, and lanai. Rates run $240–340 per night, with numerous packages available, and this includes daily maid service and complimentary spa use.

# FOOD
## At the Renaissance

The **Palm Court** is the main dining room at the Renaissance, a first-rate restaurant. Walk though the lobby and look over the rail to the partially open-air restaurant below. The Palm Court is open for breakfast 6–11 A.M. and for dinner nightly from 5:30 P.M. Breakfast is Mediterranean à la carte or American buffet. The evening menu offers a blend of East and West, featuring theme buffets and à la carte entrées ranging from pizza to porterhouse steak to prawns linguine, all $16–30.

The **Sunset Terrace** in the lobby is a delightful perch on which to have a drink and survey the grounds and beach below. Every evening brings a dramatic torch-lighting ceremony. The drums reverberate and the liquid melancholy of the conch trumpet sends a call for meditation at day's end. Drinks include the full complement of island specialties, and you can order wonderful gourmet-quality *pu pu* while listening to the sweet sounds of island music.

**Maui Onion** is a convenient snack-type restaurant at poolside that's open 11 A.M.–6 P.M. for light lunches. Burgers, sandwiches, salads, smoothies, and Maui onion rings, the specialty, are on the limited menu. Prices are reasonable, especially if you don't want to budge from your lounge chair.

Last but not least, **Hana Gion** offers Kyoto-style Japanese food daily except Tuesday and Thursday from 5:30–9 P.M. in a small and intimate restaurant off the lobby. The focus here is on teppanyaki and sushi, but the à la carte menu is an option. Not cheap, but memorable.

## Wailea Marriott Resort

Serving contemporary Hawaiian cuisine is **Hula Moons Restaurant,** the Outrigger's main dining establishment. Open daily for breakfast buffet and à la carte or buffet dinner, this casual restaurant is on the lobby level next to the Mele Mele Lounge. While fish is the main focus here, many other entrées are also on the menu. Wednesday is a prime rib buffet, Friday a seafood buffet, and every night a well-stocked salad bar. The name Hula Moons derives from the writings of Don Blanding, Hawaii's poet laureate, who arrived by steamship in 1924, dead broke, and remained for more than 40 years, all the while singing the island's praises. A few of the poet's personal belongings are still displayed—all whispering of the time when Hawaii was a distant land where only the rich and famous came to escape. Nice nostalgic touch.

Newly created next to Hula Moons, the **Mele Mele Lounge** serves tropical drinks and *pu pu* 11 A.M.–11 P.M. Low-lit, comfortable, full of bamboo and tropical designs, it serves as a place to relax, ponder your next outing, or just watch the sun set into the water beyond the garden. Open daily 11 A.M.–9 P.M., the **Kumu Bar and Grill** is a casual poolside eatery that serves light lunches and more substantial evening fare, accompanied by nightly music and hula. While appetizers and salads hold court during the day, in the evening seafood, steak, and ribs are the main offerings.

For the little ones, the **Wailele Snack Bar** is located next to the kids activity pool and serves a children's menu from 10 A.M.–4 P.M., with lots of goodies that are easy and fun to eat.

## Grand Wailea Resort Hotel & Spa

The resort has an eclectic mix of restaurants, all landscaped around the central theme of water, art, and flowers, offering a variety of cuisines catering to all tastes and appetites. **The Grand Dining Room Maui** has perhaps the best seat in the house, overlooking the gardens and the sea. Open for breakfast only, both a daily buffet and à la carte menus are offered. A fun and informal restaurant is the open-air **Bistro Molokini**. Island fusion, with a dash of the health conscious, items include wood-fired pizza, light sandwiches, and grilled seafood dinners. Open 11:30 A.M.–9:30 P.M. **Cafe Kula,** open daily 6 A.M.–6 P.M., specializes in casual terrace dining. Here the freshest fruits, organic vegetables, and whole grains provide the foundation for most dishes. Enjoy salads and sandwiches, fruits, pastries, and desserts.

**Humuhumunukunukuapua'a,** the resort's signature restaurant, is a thatched-roof Polynesian restaurant afloat on its own lagoon complete with tropical fish in a huge aquarium. The specialties prepared at the Humu come from throughout the Pacific. *Pu pu* like coconut prawn or crispy crab and lobster shrimp cakes are great to nibble on while enjoying a special exotic drink. Entrées are delightful, with offerings like pan-seared ahi, roasted duck breast, and vegetable coconut curry. Delectable but not cheap; entrées in the $22–30 range. Open Tuesday–Saturday 5:30–9 P.M. for dinner only, with nightly entertainment.

Perhaps the most elegant restaurant at the hotel is **Kincha,** serving superb Japanese cuisine. Enter over stepping stones past a replica of a golden tea kettle used by Toyotomi Hideyoshi, who was revered as both a great warrior and a master of the *chanoyu,* the tea ceremony. Follow the stones past stone lanterns that light your way over a humpbacked bridge. Inside a raised tatami area awaits, with sushi chefs ready to perform their magic, and private rooms are perfect for a refined full meal. Sushi and tempura are prominent on the menu. Entrées are Japanese favorites like hotategai, a broiled sea scallop and sake-broiled salmon, or seared Hawaiian snapper with Japanese spices and a lemon-miso butter sauce, with prices from $26 on up. Open Saturday–Monday, 6–9 P.M. only.

## Four Seasons Resort

Located at the Four Seasons Resort, **Spago** restaurant is an experience in fine dining. Elegant but

MAUI

not stuffy, its windows open to let in sea breezes and moonlight. Start the experience with an appetizer such as spicy ahi tuna "poke" in sesame-miso cones, sautéed oysters with hot-sweet Chinese mustard, or local goat cheese with organic greens. Main delicacies include Chinois lamb chops grilled with Hunan eggplant and chili-mint vinaigrette, steamed Big Island moi fish with chili, ginger, and baby bok choy, roasted duck with wild huckleberries, star anise, and black pepper, and pan-seared scallops. This dinner-only restaurant has entrées in the $29–42 range. Reservations are recommended, and proper resort dress is required.

The casual **Pacific Grill** restaurant combines a large selection of foods from Asia and the West. The breakfast buffet is a long-established special, but an à la carte menu is also available. For dinner, some entrées are cooked in view of the guests. Pacific Rim entrée specialties include sautéed mahimahi, Hawaii salt-crusted rotisserie prime rib of beef, and a seafood stir-fry, most $26–36. At the Pacific Grill, alohawear and activewear are the norm.

The remodeled and expanded **Ferraro's at Seaside** serves food throughout the day. For breakfast, you can choose from an à la carte menu or have coffee and something lighter from the coffee and pastry bar. For lunch, served 11 A.M.–4 P.M., light fare of salads, sandwiches, and pizza are good options. Light lunch is served from 4–6 P.M. when dinner starts. Dinner is more formal and features the new *kiawe* wood-burning oven. As Italian as Italian can be, Ferraro's throws in Italian music for free, Monday–Saturday. Start with an antipasti such as oven-baked clams and mussels, and move on to fresh black truffle alla parmagiana risotto, potato gnocchi with creamy Genovese pesto, sautéed veal scaloppini, or Maine lobster and Tuscan-style seafood stew, with most entrées in the $25–30 range. Set almost on the water, Ferraro's is a great place to watch the sunset.

## Fairmont Kea Lani Maui

An elegant breakfast at the Kea Lani happens at the **Kea Lani Restaurant,** 808/879-7224, where you can order à la carte or dive into the full-scale buffet from 6:30–11 A.M. For a casual lunch or early dinner, with outdoor poolside seating from 11 A.M.–5 P.M., try the **Polo Beach Grill and Bar** for a light salad, sandwich, or kiawe-grilled burger. If you're in the pool, you can swim up to the bar until 7 P.M. for a cool-down drink.

For casual dining any time of day, visit the **Ciao Deli** rich with the smell of espresso, where the shelves hold homemade jellies, jams, chutney, peppercorn ketchup, and Italian olives. Choose fresh-baked bread, pastries, or a spicy focaccia from the bakery, pesto salad or a sandwich from the deli. For a sit-down lunch or dinner meal, try the outdoor trattoria **Caffe Ciao** across the walk, where you'll find hot and cold appetizers, sandwiches, and fresh island fish for lunch, and pizza from the wood-fired oven, pasta and risotto dishes, and other entrées like pesca alla Isolana, pollo alla Florentina, and ossobusso di Vitello in the evening, ranging $22–32.

The fine-dining restaurant at the Kea Lani is **Nick's Fishmarket,** which produces Hawaiian regional cuisine with an emphasis on fish and seafood. A selection of entrées includes roasted salmon, seafood paella, grilled ahi with cracked pepper, and seared swordfish with candied peanut crust. Expect entrées from $27–37 and quality to match. Open nightly 5:30–10 P.M., there is a dress code and reservations are highly recommended.

## Diamond Resort

The two resort restaurants are the Taiko and the Le Gunji. With a Frank Lloyd Wright feel in the architecture and appointments, **Taiko** serves breakfast, lunch, and dinner nightly except Tuesday and is open 7–10 A.M., 11 A.M.–1:45 P.M., and 6–9 P.M. The day starts with a Japanese- or Western-style breakfast for $13; lunch includes sandwiches and burgers, or Japanese soba, udon, or other traditional dishes for less than $13. Dinner entrées, like teriyaki chicken, onaga shioyaki, and lobster daiyaki, run $21–35; a whole range of sushi is also available. The more intimate **Le Gunji** has limited seating of up to 16 people at 6 P.M. and 8 P.M. only; reservations are a necessity and a dress code is enforced. Choose from five set menus, ranging $50–70. Food is a unique blend of French cuisine prepared in a Japanese teppanyaki style. Call 808/874-0500 for reservations.

An independent establishment, **Capische?**, 808-879-8255, offers sophisticated Italian food evenings only 5:30–8:30 P.M., except Sunday. Seating is limited, so definitely call for reservations. The relatively small menu has sautéed calamari, quail saltimbocca, and seafood antipasti for appetizers and soups and salads for $8–16. Pasta and risotto like cioppino and shrimp carbonara run $28–30. Meat and fish entrées include seared scallops, crispy Pacific snapper, lamb osso bucco, and filet mignon for $29–35. This sophisticated restaurant has dishes that will certainly please. Capische?

## Nonresort Restaurants

The following restaurants are located along the golf links in the area, except for Joe's, which is located at the Wailea Tennis Club.

On the 15th fairway of the Wailea Blue Course, just up from The Shops at Wailea, is the **Lobster Cove Restaurant,** 808/879-6677, a seafood restaurant that shares space with **Harry's Sushi Bar.** Appetizers include garlic clams for $10.95, sweet and sour crispy shrimp for $11.95, and lobster cakes for $11.95. These tasty treats would go well with the Caesar salad for $6.95. Entrées, limited but wonderful, might be seafood penne pasta for $20.95, blackened ribeye steak with king crab for $32, fresh island fish at market price, or a filet mignon for $25. Choose from an adequate wine list for a bottle to accompany your meal. You can order *pu pu* or make a meal from the offerings at Harry's. The choices of sushi are numerous and run mostly $4.25–7 per order and are double that for a plate of sashimi. Also consider such items as California rolls or bowls of noodles. These restaurants are open daily 5:30–10 P.M.

A little up the hill and across the road at the Wailea Tennis Club is **Joe's Bar and Grill,** 808/875-7767. Open for dinner every evening from 5:30–10 P.M., Joe's serves large and tasty portions of honest American, homestyle comfort food in a relaxing atmosphere. Joe's is set directly above the tennis courts in a wood-floored, open-beamed room, and cool breezes waft through the sliding-glass partitions. Chief schmoozer Joe Gannon is the other half to Haliimaile General Store restaurant's chef Beverly

Gannon. While the ambiance and lighting set a welcome mood, the real treat is the food. Ahi carpaccio, Asian fried calamari, and Joe's gazpacho come first, with other appetizers and salads. Entrées include grilled thick-cut pork chop, pan-seared New York steak, and Joe's famous meatloaf, one of the best sellers; all range from $24–32. You know this is a family affair because Joe's daughter makes the mouth-watering desserts. The bar has a full range of beers and can make any mixed drink you desire. Martinis are specialties. Eat at Joe's, and have food the way you wish your mother used to make it.

At the Blue Golf Course clubhouse is **Mulligan's on the Blue** bar and pub restaurant, 808/874-1131. Mulligan's serves pancakes, corn beef and hash, an Irish breakfast, and other such dishes as breakfast for $7–11. Later in the day, a full pub menu of burgers, fish and chips, shepherd's pie, and many other items are available, as are tap beer and mixed drinks at the long bar. Long after the golfers are gone, the drinks continue to flow, and nearly every evening you can hear Hawaiian, contemporary, or Irish tunes until 1:30 A.M. Stop by for a pint, Paddy.

The **SeaWatch,** 808/875-8080, at the Emerald Golf Course clubhouse, looks out over the fairway, but the most outstanding feature of its location is the view over Molokini and Kaho'olawe. The SeaWatch serves Hawaiian regional cuisine, and many selections are prepared over a kiawe-wood grill. Breakfast and lunch are served 8 A.M.–3 P.M. and are mostly egg and other grill items, or salads and sandwiches. Dinner, served 6–10 P.M., is more refined, focusing on well-balanced flavors and ingredients. Start with chilled tiger prawns and brandied blue crab salad or a macadamia nut–crusted brie with pineapple relish on crostini. A sweet Kula organic green salad might complement your main entrée, which could be parmesan-crusted chicken breast on cappelini pasta, roasted rack of lamb, or miso-glazed tiger prawns. Fresh fish, prepared with a mango chutney macadamia crust, kiawe grilled, or peppered and sautéed, are all always fine choices. Entrées run $23–30. The servers are attentive, the service is professional, and dinner is enhanced by classical piano accompaniment.

**M**

**MAUI**

## At The Shops at Wailea

At the ocean end of this center are three fine-dining restaurants and one that's more casual; two upstairs and two down.

**Tommy Bahama's,** 808/875-9983, is casual yet sophisticated, open to the ocean breezes, a perfect spot for lunch or dinner or an evening drink at the bar. Its tropical colors and rattan furniture lend it an island feel, and these combined with evening entertainment create a relaxing and welcoming place.

At the other side on the upper level is **Ruth's Chris Steak House,** 808/874-8880. Just like its restaurant in Lahaina, the dark wood, table linens, crispness of dress and service, and huge wine rooms lend this restaurant a semiformal feeling. The emphasis here is meat, and you'll find it in many permutations from petit filets to ribeye, New York strip, and lamb chops, mostly $24–36. Potatoes, rice, and vegetables are ordered separately, but don't skimp on the mouth-watering desserts. Ruth's Chris has a huge selection of wines, one to go with any entrée. Reservations are definitely recommended, and resortwear is appropriate.

After having run a very successful operation in Lahaina for many years, **Longhi's,** 808/891-8883, opened a second restaurant here to great anticipation—and no one is disappointed. This spacious eatery with its classic black-and-white-checkered marble floor is open, airy, and has a full bar. Food is served from 8 A.M. (7:30 A.M. on weekends) until 10 P.M., and the emphasis is on pasta, seafood, and steak. Some of what you might find on the menu are mussels in marinara sauce, corned beef sandwich, Bolognaise rigatoni pasta, grilled New York steak, fresh island fish Veronique, prawns amaretto, or a simpler eggplant parmesan. Expect lunch sandwiches and pasta in the $8–16 range and dinner entrées mostly $27–30.

The most casual of the restaurants is **Cheeseburger, Mai Tais, & Rock N Roll,** 808/874-8990. With a tropical bar, lots of rattan, and hoards of knickknacks and other decorations hanging from the walls and ceiling, you know that Cheeseburger is a place to hang loose, enjoy your meal, or slowly sip one of those special mai tais. While the day starts with eggs, pancakes, and other griddle items, burgers, burgers, and more burgers are what it's really all about here. Of course, the cheeseburger and double cheeseburger are on the menu, but chicken, turkey, garden, and veggie burgers are all options, as are a calamari steak sandwich, various salads, and a few fish selections. Don't forget the sides. Most burgers and sandwiches run $8.25–10.

# ENTERTAINMENT

## Lu'au

Wailea has two lu'au that have been favorites of guests for years. At the Renaissance, the **Wailea Sunset Lu'au** shows Tuesday, Thursday, and Saturday from 5:30 P.M.; $70 adults, $33 kids 5–12, An open bar accompanies the island-style foods that include *poi, lomi lomi* salmon, and *kalua* pig. Entertainment by the Tihati company is a Polynesian revue of hula and drumming that ends in a fiery knife dance. If you don't go away full and with a smile on your face, it's your own fault. Call 808/891-7811 for reservations.

**Wailea's Finest Lu'au** is performed at oceanside by the Outrigger resort every Monday, Tuesday, Thursday, and Friday from 5–8 P.M.; $68 adults, $30 children 6–12. An *imu* ceremony and torch-lighting ceremony kick off the affairs. A sumptuous buffet dinner of Hawaiian favorites and hula show follow, and the night is finished by an enthralling fire knife dancer. To reserve, call 808/874-7831.

## Music

If you haven't had enough fun on the Wailea beaches during the day, you can show off your best dance steps at the **Tsunami** nightclub at the Grand Wailea. This venue hops to Top 40 DJ music every Friday and Saturday 9:30 P.M.–1:30 A.M. Complimentary for resort guests, the cover for others is $10. For men, long pants are required with covered shoes; for the ladies, dressy resortwear is fine.

Easy-listening music is performed every evening at the **Sunset Terrace** lounge on the lobby level of the Renaissance Resort overlooking the gardens, and all hotels provide some venue for soft Hawaiian music, often with a little hula show included, like the **Kumu Bar** at the Outrigger Wailea, **Botero Lounge** at the Grand Wailea, or the lobby lounge at the Four Seasons.

# RECREATION

## Golf and Tennis

The 54 links to the Wailea golf course should not disappoint anyone. Studied and demanding, each offers its own challenges plus the beauty of the surrounding area. At more than 7,000 yards (from the gold tee), the Gold Course demands attention to natural and man-made obstacles and design. It's consistently rated one of the top courses in the state. Sharing a clubhouse, the Emerald Course is the most compact but perhaps provides the most stunning scenery. Much tamer, the oldest of the three, and ranging the farthest, the Blue Course meanders like a lazy brook through the surrounding condominiums. Greens fees run between $115–135, club rentals $35, and the driving range $6; lessons are also available. For tee times, call 808/875-7450.

Aside from its award-winning golf courses, Wailea Resort sports an 11-court tennis facility, with one championship court that can seat nearly 1,000 fans. Court fees run $27 per hour for resort guests and $30 for nonguests. Private lessons, clinics, and round robins can be arranged, and equipment is rented. For information or court times, call 808/879-1958.

# SHOPPING

## The Shops at Wailea

Each major hotel in the resort has an arcade of shops for quick and easy purchases, but the real shopping opportunity in Wailea is at The Shops at Wailea, a new upscale, open-air shopping center with sophisticated shops that rivals any on the island. International retailers like **Louis Vuitton, Gucci, Tiffany & Co., Fendi,** and **Cartier** are here, as are local and national firms like **Banana Republic, Crazy Shirts, Reyn's** and **Martin & MacArthur.** Clothing stores make up a bulk of the shops, but jewelry shops, art galleries, camera shops, and sundry stores have also found a place here. Head to **Island Camera** or **Ritz**

**Camera Center** for all your photographic needs, **Lapperts** for sweet ice cream treats, and set up island excursions at **Activity Warehouse.** Even the ubiquitous **ABC Stores** and **Whaler's General Store,** for such items as suntan lotion that you inadvertently left at home, gifts, and sweet treats, are a bit more upscale here than at other locations around the island.

As you might expect, there are a handful of art galleries in this center, including **Lahaina Galleries, Lassen Gallerie, Dolphin Gallery,** and **Wyland Galleries,** which each display many painted works by Hawaiian artists and others. **Ki'i Galleries** shows art glass; **Kela** hangs nature photographs, turned wooden bowls, and some impressionist paintings; and **Elan Vital Galleries** has totally unique jewels of vibrant, swirling, and flowing canvases of shimmering color. **Destination Resorts,** the management company for most of the condo units in Wailea, has its reservations office on the lower level.

Wednesday evenings at The Shops at Wailea are special. A "Festival of the Arts," called **Wailea on Wednesdays,** is held here 6:30–9:30 P.M. Taking after the Friday evening festivities in Lahaina, galleries at The Shops at Wailea have special showings, put out goodies and wine, and sometimes host artists for discussions and demonstrations, all while music is played in the central courtyard for the enjoyment of all who wander through. At times, other festivities and activities of the art world will also be hosted to create broader appeal for this event.

# SERVICES

There are no banks or post offices in Wailea, but there are two ATMs at The Shops at Wailea. For money exchange or postal needs, ask for assistance from your hotel front desk, or use facilities up the road in Kihei.

## Transportation

The **Wailea Resort Shuttle** is a complimentary jitney that stops at most major hotels, The Shops at Wailea, and golf clubhouses in Wailea about every 30 minutes. It operates 6:30 A.M.–8 P.M.

MAUI

Be sure to check with the driver about the last pickup times if you are out in the evening. With a little walking, this is a great way to hop from one beach to the next.

The **Holo Ka'a** public transit shuttle runs throughout the Makena, Wailea, and Kihei area seven times a day from 7 A.M.–7 P.M., with additional service several times a day up to Ma'alaea, and on to Lahaina, Ka'anaplai, and Kapalua. The one-way fare within South Maui is $1. It's $5 as far a Ma'alaea, and $10 for a daily pass throughout the system.

# Makena

Just a skip south down the road is Makena Beach, but it's a world away from Wailea. This was a hippie enclave during the '60s and early '70s, and the freewheeling spirit of the times is still partially evident in the area, even though Makena is becoming more refined, sophisticated, and available to visitors. For one thing, "Little Makena" is a famous (unofficial) clothing-optional beach, but so what? You can skinny-dip in Connecticut. The police come in and sweep the area now and again, but mostly it's mellow, and they've been known to arrest nude sunbathers on Little Makena to make the point that Makena "ain't free no more." Rip-offs can be a problem, so lock your car, hide your camera, and don't leave anything of value. Be careful of the *kiawe* thorns when you park; they'll puncture a tire like a nail. What's really important is that Makena is *the last* pristine coastal stretch in this part of Maui that hasn't succumbed to undue development . . . yet. The Maui Prince Hotel and its adjacent golf course and tennis courts comprise the 1,600-acre Makena Resort. Carved from land that was used for generations to graze cattle, this resort is as yet much less developed than Wailea up the road but has great potential for expansion.

Aside from the sundries shop at the Maui Prince Hotel, there's nothing in the way of amenities past Wailea, so make sure to stock up on all supplies. In fact, there's nowhere to get *anything* past the hotel except for the lunch wagon that's usually parked across from the state park entrance. The road south of the Maui Prince Hotel to La Pérouse Bay is by and large fairly good with a decent surface. It does, however, narrow down to almost a single lane in spots, particularly where it slides past small coves. Drive carefully and defensively.

Makena Beach is magnificent for bodysurfing if you have experience, and for swimming, but only when the sea is calm. Whales frequent the area and come quite close to shore during the season. Turtles waddled on to Makena to lay their eggs in the warm sand until early in the 19th century, but too many people gathered the eggs and the turtles scrambled away forever. The sunsets from **Pu'u Ola'i** (Red Hill), the cinder cone separating the big Makena beach from Oneuli Beach, are among the best on Maui; you can watch the sun sink down between Lana'i and West Maui. The silhouettes of pastel and gleaming colors are awe-inspiring. Oranges, russets, and every shade of purple reflect off the clouds that are caught here. Makena attracts all kinds: gawkers, burn-outs, adventurers, tourists, free spirits, and a lot of locals. It won't last long, so go and have a look now!

## Keawala'i Church

This Congregational Church was established in 1832. The present stone structure was erected in 1855 and restored in 1952. Services are held every Sunday at 9:30 A.M. and 5 P.M., and many of the hymns and part of the sermon are still delivered in Hawaiian. Notice the three-foot-thick walls and the gravestones, many with a ceramic picture of the deceased. A parking lot, restrooms, and showers are across the road for the beach access, which is just down the road. Take Honoiki Road from the main highway, or come down the old coast road from Polo Beach past Makena Boat Landing. The church is almost at the road's dead end, beyond which is the Maui Prince Hotel property.

## Small Beaches

You'll pass by the local **Palauea** and **Po'olenalena** beaches, via the coastal Old Makena Road, as

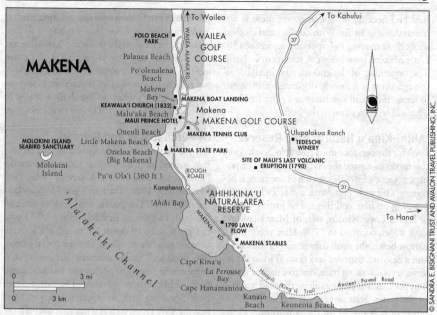

MAKENA

To Wailea
POLO BEACH PARK
Palauea Beach
Po'olenalena Beach
Makena Bay
MAKENA BOAT LANDING
KEAWALA'I CHURCH (1832)
Malu'aka Beach
MAUI PRINCE HOTEL
Oneuli Beach
Little Makena Beach
Oneloa Beach (Big Makena)
Pu'u Ola'i (360 ft.)
Kanahena

MOLOKINI ISLAND SEABIRD SANCTUARY
Molokini Island

'Alalakeiki Channel

WAILEA ALANUI RD.
WAILEA GOLF COURSE

Makena
MAKENA GOLF COURSE
MAKENA TENNIS CLUB
MAKENA STATE PARK
(ROUGH ROAD)
'Ahihi Bay
'AHIHI-KINA'U NATURAL AREA RESERVE
1790 LAVA FLOW
MAKENA STABLES
Cape Kina'u
La Perouse Bay
Cape Hanamanioa
Kanaio Beach
Keoneoio Beach

To Kahului
37
Moon
Ulupalakua Ranch
TEDESCHI WINERY
SITE OF MAUI'S LAST VOLCANIC ERUPTION (1790)
31
To Hana
MAKENA RD.
Ho'opili (King's) Trail
Ancient Paved Road

0    3 mi
0    3 km

© SANDRA E. BISIGNANI TRUST AND AVALON TRAVEL PUBLISHING, INC.

MAUI

you head toward Makena. There is no development here yet, no amenities, and usually few people, but good swimming and white, sloping sands. **Nahuna (Five Graves) Point** is just more than a mile past Polo. An old graveyard marks the entrance. Not the best for swimming, it's great for scuba and snorkeling because of the underwater ridges of lava and caves, and the fish and turtles that hang out there. A short distance farther on is the **Makena Boat Landing** (water, restrooms, showers), a launch site for kayakers and scuba divers. Makena Landing was a bustling port in the mid-1800s and a principal point for shipping goods and cattle from this end of the island to other major island seaports.

**Oneuli,** on the north side of Pu'u Ola'i, actually has a salt-and-pepper beach, with a tinge of red from the dirt of the hill. Turn down a rough dirt road for one-third mile. Not good for swimming, but good diving, unofficial camping, and shore fishing. Open 5 A.M.–9 P.M.; no amenities and not many people. Signs warn you not to climb the hill—also from the Big Beach side—but obvious trails lead to the top and over its sides. The Maui Prince fronts **Malu'aka Beach.**

There is public access from the end of the road near Keawala'i Church and from the end of a dead-end road just past the resort, that swings back toward the hotel.

## Makena State Park

A few minutes past the Maui Prince Hotel, look for a *kaukau* wagon or fruit stand on the left, where you might pick up a snack before turning right onto the park access road. Negotiate the excessive speed bumps for a few hundred yards to the parking lot and a few portable toilets; a second beach access is a few hundred yards farther on. This is **Oneloa Beach,** generally called Big Beach or Makena Beach, a nice long, golden strand of fine sand that's open 5 A.M.–9 P.M. daily. Right leads you to **Pu'u Ola'i** (Earthquake Hill), a 360-foot cinder cone. When you cross over the point from Big Makena Beach you'll be on **Little Makena,** a favorite clothing-optional beach for locals and tourists alike. You'll know that you're on the right beach by the bare bums. Both beaches are excellent for swimming (beware of currents in winter), bodysurfing, and superb snorkeling in front of the hill (sometimes called

Red Hill because of its color), yet there is not much shade at either. With families and clothed sunbathers moving in (especially on weekends), Little Makena is no longer so remote or isolated. The beginning of the end may be in sight, although there is a loosely organized movement to retain this small sanctuary as a place for those who still wish to swim in the buff.

## 'Ahihi-Kina'u Natural Area Reserve

Look for the sign four miles past Polo Beach. Even this far down toward the end of the road—or perhaps because of it—this stretch of the coast is becoming a bit more populated, and fancy homes are popping up here and there. The jutting thumb of lava is **Cape Kina'u,** part of Maui's last lava flow, which occurred in 1790. Here you'll find a narrow beach, the small community of Kanahena, and a desolate, tortured lava flow. Within the reserve, several walking trails, one to a natural aquarium pool, start at pullouts along the road and lead to the water. Start at pole no. 18 for the "fishbowl" or pole no. 24 for the "aquarium." Please stay on established paths and wear sturdy hiking shoes or boots. Dolphins often play off this point,

and whales can be seen near shore during winter. Aside from the lava fields, 'Ahihi-Kina'u is also an underwater reserve, so the scuba and snorkeling are first-rate. The best way to proceed is along the reef toward the left, or along the reef to the right if you enter at La Pérouse Bay. Beware not to step on the many spiny urchins in the shallow water. If you do, vinegar or urine will help with the stinging.

## La Pérouse Bay and Beyond

On the far side of Cape Kina'u is La Pérouse Bay, named after the French navigator Jean de François La Pérouse, first Westerner to land on Maui in May 1786. The bay is good for snorkelers and divers. The public road ends at the entrance to La Pérouse Bay, but with a 4WD you can get a distance down the rough track from here for good shore fishing and unofficial camping. If you walk farther around to the south you'll come across a string of pocket-size beaches, some with pebbles, others with sand. The currents can be tricky along here, so be careful. Beyond the bay, the 4WD road ends at a navigational light on the point, below which are a coral beach and several small coves.

ROBERT NILSEN

**The archaeological remains of an old Hawaiian village can be found near Kanaio Beach.**

Past the bay is a remnant of the **Hoapili Trail**, now part of the state Na Ala Hele trail system and still hikable for perhaps two miles. Two trailheads, both indicated by gates—the first through a metal fence, the second through a rock wall—are marked by signs and an area map. This trail, sometimes referred to as the "King's Trail," leads over a rough stone bed that was at one time trudged by royal tax collectors. While parts have recently been refurbished, notice the neat rock curb; this trail is still in very good condition after nearly 200 years. Along the way, a spur trail leads down to Kanaio Beach and the sea, where you get a view of Cape Hanamanioa and its Coast Guard navigational light. At the end of the refurbished section of this trail you reach Keoneoia Beach. Set just inland are many ancient house sites, *heiau,* and canoe sheds in very good condition, and other tangible remains are strewn throughout this archaeological district and beyond to the east. Stay on the trail and leave everything as you find it! Beyond Keoneoia Beach is private land, over which a torturous 4WD road leads across and eventually up to Highway 31 between Ulupalakua and Kaupo. It could easily be a good day's hike exploring out this way, but remember that no help is available. Wear good shoes, bring a hat, and carry plenty of water, water, and more water.

## ACCOMMODATIONS

### Maui Prince Hotel

A gleaming wing-shaped building, understated and almost stark on the outside, the Maui Prince Hotel, 5400 Makena Alanui, Makena, HI 96753, 808/874-1111 or 800/321-6248, fax 808/879-8763, is a fabulous destination resort that opens into an enormous central courtyard, one of the most beautiful in Hawaii. Japanese in its architecture and its sense of beauty, the courtyard is a protected haven of cascading waters, black lava rock, stone lanterns, breeze-tossed palms, and raked Zen-like gardens. Lean over the hardwood rails of the balconies on each floor and soak in the visual pleasure of the landscape below, where from these balconies cascade flowers and ferns in sympathetic mimicry of Maui's waterfalls.

All 310 rooms have an alcove door, so you can open your front door yet still have privacy and allow the breeze to pass through. Oceanview and oceanfront rooms ranging $310–480 are beautifully accentuated in earth tones and light pastels. One-bedroom suites, priced $600 and $1,500, feature a giant living room, three lanai, a large-screen TV and VCR, and white terrycloth robes for lounging. The master bedroom has its own TV, listening center, and king-size bed. A nonsmoking wing is also available. The bathrooms have a separate commode and a separate shower and tub. The Prince also offers the very reasonable Prince Special that includes an oceanview room and midsize rental car priced only $350 per night per couple; other honeymoon, golf, tennis, and car packages are also available. For your food and entertainment needs, the Prince has three restaurants and one lounge at the hotel and one restaurant at the golf clubhouse.

The Maui Prince faces fantastic, secluded Malu'aka Beach, almost like a little bay, with two points of lava marking it as a safe spot for swimming and snorkeling. Sea turtles live on the south point and come up on the beach to nest and lay their eggs. To the left you can see Pu'u Ola'i, a red cinder cone that marks Makena. The pool area is made up of two circular pools—one for adults, the other a wading pool for kids—two whirlpools, cabanas, and a poolside snack bar. There's volleyball, croquet, and six plexipave tennis courts with a pro on staff, but the 36 holes of the Makena Golf Course are the main athletic attraction of the Prince. The concierge desk offers a variety of complimentary activities including a snorkel and scuba introduction, plus several fee activities. For the little ones, the Prince Keiki Club children's program can be arranged for healthy and supervised morning and/or afternoon activities. For the big people, see what the complimentary fitness center and spa can do for you. The boat *Kai Kanani* arrives each morning and will take you snorkeling to Molokini or arrange other activities throughout the island.

The Makena Resort **shuttle** runs on an on-demand basis for resort guests only and can take you to and fetch you from the Makena golf course and tennis courts and all facilities in the

Wailea resort. Arrange your ride through the hotel concierge.

# FOOD

## At the Prince

The Prince has three restaurants. The fanciest restaurant is the **Prince Court**, featuring fine dining nightly for dinner only 6–9:30 P.M., except for the truly exceptional Sunday champagne brunch, which is served 9 A.M.–1:30 P.M. The evening fare is Hawaiian regional cuisine and then some. Start with appetizers like ginger duck pot stickers and Kona lobster summer rolls, or soups and salads that include Ma'alaea asparagus bisque and tomato and portabello mushroom salad. From the grill, entrées include Hawaiian fresh catch, butterflied lamb chops, and grilled Thai pork tenderloin, most for $22–30. In addition, Friday night brings a prime rib and seafood buffet for $40, and the Sunday brunch runs $39. The room is subdued, elegant, and highlighted with snow-white tablecloths and sparkling crystal. The view is serene facing the courtyard or dramatic looking out to sea.

**Hakone** is a superb and traditional Japanese restaurant and sushi bar. Open Tuesday–Saturday 6–9 P.M., it serves complete dinners like sukiyaki, isaribi, shabu shabu, and haruyama for $36 and under, and it also serves sushi and sashimi, plus traditional *kaiseki* dinners for $45–58. A special Monday night dinner buffet is offered at $42, where you have your choice from a panoply of delightful dishes. In keeping with the tradition of Japan, the room is subdued and simple, with white shoji screens counterpointed by dark, open beams. The floor is black slate atop packed sand, a style from old Japan.

The main dining room, serving breakfast and lunch, is the more casual and affordable **Cafe Kiowai**. Located on the ground level, it opens to the courtyard and fish ponds. Breakfast brings a breakfast buffet or an à la carte menu of griddle items and eggs, while you can get salads, sandwiches, wraps, and pizza until 3 P.M.

For now, food and accommodations in Makena mean the Maui Prince. The only exceptions are the **Makena Clubhouse** restaurant at the golf course, which serves sandwiches and grilled items for lunch, mostly for under $12, and late afternoon *pu pu* until sunset.

For evening entertainment in Makena, the only option is the **Molokini Lounge** at the hotel. Live entertainment is performed nightly 6–10:30 P.M. with the addition of a hula show on Mondays, Wednesdays, and Fridays.

# RECREATION

Because the Maui Prince Hotel is a destination resort, on-site recreation possibilities include the beach, beach activity booth, a sailing catamaran, and the swimming pool. Golf at **Makena Golf Course** and tennis at **Makena Tennis Club** are just across the road and offer world-class courts and links. The golf course offers 36 holes; greens fees for hotel guests run $125–150, with twilight rounds cheaper. The six-court tennis club has two lighted courts for night play. Lessons, matches, and rentals are handled at the pro shop. Court fees run $20 per hour for resort guests and $24 for nonguests.

Loading from the beach in front of the hotel, the *Kai Kanani* sailing catamaran takes passengers to Molokini (the shortest route) for a half day of fun, food, and snorkeling. The ship runs Tuesday–Saturday 7–11:30 A.M. for $79 per person.

**Makena Stables** offers trail rides through this dry, remote region at its location near the end of the road at La Pérouse Bay. Rides range from $120–195, and you must be at least 13 years old and weigh no more than 205 pounds. Call 808-879-0244 for the different rides available.

# Upcountry

Upcountry is much more than a geographical area to the people who live there: It's a way of life, a frame of mind. You can see Upcountry from anywhere on Maui by lifting your gaze to the slopes of Haleakala. There are no actual boundaries, but this area is usually considered as running from Makawao in the north all the way around to Kahikinui Ranch in the south, and from below the cloud cover down to about the 1,500-foot level. It swathes the western slope of Haleakala like a large, green floral bib patterned by pasturelands and festooned with wild and cultivated flowers. In this rich soil and cool-to-moderate temperatures, cattle ranching and truck farming thrive. Up here, *paniolo* ride herd on the range of the enormous 35,000-acre Haleakala Ranch, spread mostly around Makawao, and the smaller but still sizable 23,000 acres of the Ulupalakua Ranch, which *is* the hills above Wailea and Makena.

While Makawao retains some of its real cowboy town image, it has become more sophisticated, with some exclusive shops, fine-dining restaurants, art galleries, and alternative healing practitioners. Pukalani, the largest town and expanding residential area, is a waystation for gas and supplies, and is pineapple country. Kula is Maui's flower basket. This area is one enormous garden, producing brilliant blooms and hearty vegetables. Polipoli Spring State Recreation Area is a forgotten wonderland of tall forests, a homogenized stand of trees from around the world. Tedeschi Winery in the south adds a classy touch to Upcountry—a place where you can taste wine and view the winemaking process. There are plenty of commercial greenhouses and flower farms to visit all over Upcountry, but the best activity is a free Sunday drive along the mountain roads and farm lanes, just soaking in the scenery. The purple mists of mountain jacaranda and the heady fragrance of eucalyptus encircling a mountain pasture manicured by herds of cattle portray the soul of Upcountry.

ROBERT NILSEN

Upcountry rangeland

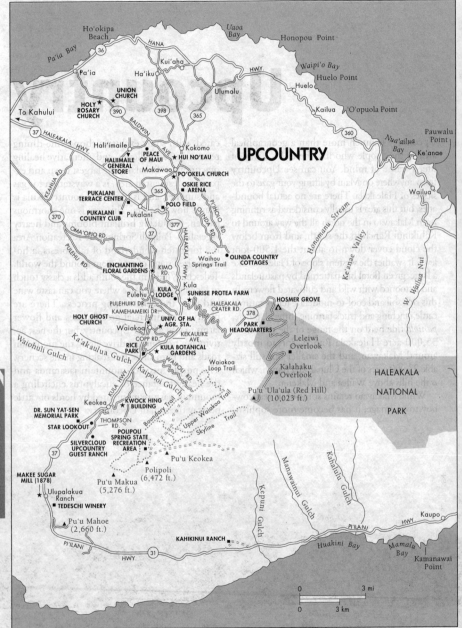

UPCOUNTRY

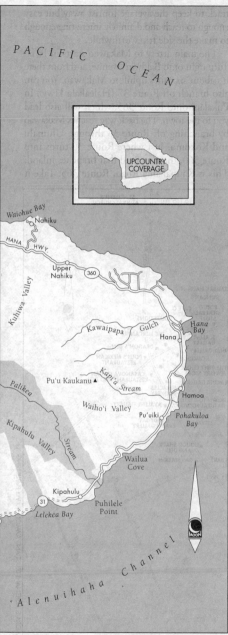

© SANDRA E. BISIGNANI TRUST AND AVALON TRAVEL PUBLISHING, INC.

# Makawao

Makawao is proud of itself; it's not *like* a cowboy town, it *is* a cowboy town. Depending on the translation that you consult, Makawao means "Eye of the Dawn" or "Forest Beginning." Both are appropriate. Surrounding lowland fields of cane and pineapples give way to upland pastures rimmed with tall forests, as Haleakala's morning sun shoots lasers of light through the town. Makawao was settled in the late 19th century by Portuguese immigrants who started raising cattle on the upland slopes. It loped along as a *paniolo* town until World War II, when it received an infusion of life from a nearby military base below Kokomo. After the war, it settled back down and became a sleepy village again, where as many horses were tethered on the main street as cars were parked. Most of its false-front, one-story buildings are a half-century old, but their prototype is strictly "Dodge City, 1850." During the 1950s and '60s, Makawao started to decline into a bunch of worn-out old buildings. It earned a reputation for drinking, fighting, and cavorting cowboys, and for a period was derisively called "Macho-wao."

In the 1970s it began to revive. It had plenty to be proud of and a good history to fall back on. Makawao is *the* last real *paniolo* town on Maui and, with Kamuela on the Big Island, is one of the last two in the entire state. At the Oskie Rice Arena, it hosts the largest and most successful rodeo in Hawaii. Happening at the same time, the Paniolo Parade is a marvel of homespun humor, *aloha,* and an old-fashioned good time, when many people ride their horses to town, leaving them to graze in a public corral. They do business at stores operated by the same families for 50 years or more. Although many of the dry goods are country-oriented, a new breed of merchant has come to town. You can buy a wood stove, art glass, Asian medicine, homemade baked goods, designer jeans, contemporary painting, and espresso coffee all on one street. At its eateries you can have fresh fish, a steamy bowl of saimin, Italian pasta, a plate lunch, or a Mexican quesadilla. Artists of all mediums have found

MAUI

Makawao and the surrounding area fertile ground for their work, and the town has become a hotbed of alternative healing practitioners. Look on any bulletin board in town and you'll see a dozen fliers advertising formulas for better life, better health, reawakening of the spirit, Asian health therapies, and new-age, new-health concepts.

Everyone, old-timers and newcomers alike, agrees that Makawao must be preserved, and they work together to do so. They know that tourism is a financial lifeline, but they shudder at the thought of Makawao becoming an Upcountry Lahaina. It shouldn't. It's far enough off the track to keep the average tourist away but easy enough to reach and definitely interesting enough to make the side trip worthwhile.

The main artery to Makawao starts in Pa'ia. Turn right onto Baldwin Avenue, and from there it's about six miles uphill to Makawao. You can also branch off Route 37 (Haleakala Hwy.) in Pukalani onto Route 365, which will also lead you to the town. The back way reaches Makawao by branching off Route 36 through Ulumalu and Kokomo. Just where Route 36 turns into Route 360, there's a road that branches inland: This is Kaupakalua Road, Route 365. Take it

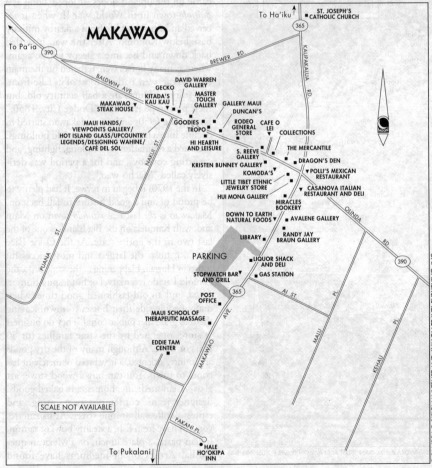

MAKAWAO

To Ha'iku

St. Joseph's Catholic Church

To Pa'ia

BREWER RD.

BALDWIN AVE.

KAUPAKALUA RD.

DAVID WARREN GALLERY

GECKO

KITADA'S KAU KAU

MASTER TOUCH GALLERY

MAKAWAO STEAK HOUSE

GALLERY MAUI

DUNCAN'S

MAUI HANDS/ VIEWPOINTS GALLERY/ HOT ISLAND GLASS/UPCOUNTRY LEGENDS/DESIGNING WAHINE/ CAFÉ DEL SOL

GOODIES

TROPO

RODEO GENERAL STORE

CAFÉ O LEI

COLLECTIONS

HI HEARTH AND LEISURE

S. REEVE GALLERY

THE MERCANTILE

KRISTEN BUNNEY GALLERY

KOMODA'S

DRAGON'S DEN

POLLI'S MEXICAN RESTAURANT

LITTLE TIBET ETHNIC JEWELRY STORE

CASANOVA ITALIAN RESTAURANT AND DELI

HUI MONA GALLERY

MIRACLES BOOKERY

DOWN TO EARTH NATURAL FOODS

AVALENE GALLERY

OLINDA RD.

LIBRARY

RANDY JAY BRAUN GALLERY

PARKING

LIQUOR SHACK AND DELI

390

NAKUI ST.

PIANA ST.

STOPWATCH BAR AND GRILL

GAS STATION

POST OFFICE

MAUI SCHOOL OF THERAPEUTIC MASSAGE

AI ST.

MAUU PL.

KEHAU PL.

EDDIE TAM CENTER

MAKAWAO AVE.

SCALE NOT AVAILABLE

PAKANI PL.

To Pukalani

HALE HO'OKIPA INN

MAUI

through backcountry Maui, where horses graze around neat little houses and Haleakala looms above. At one Y intersection there's Hanzawa's Variety Store; continue on through Kokomo to Makawao. Notice the mixture of old and new houses—Maui's past and future in microcosm. Here, the neat little banana plantation on the outskirts of the diminutive town says it all. Pass St. Joseph's Catholic Church and you've arrived through Makawao's back door. This is an excellent off-track route to take on your way to or from Hana. Alternately, you can also come up Kokomo Road, Route 398, through Haiku from the Hana Highway.

### Events

Makawao has a tremendous rodeo season every year—2003 was the 48th annual. Most meets are sponsored by the Maui Roping Club. They start in the spring and culminate in the massive **Makawao Rodeo,** held over three days on the weekend nearest July 4. These events attract the best cowboys from around the state, with substantial prize money as reward. Both males and females try their luck in separate groupings. The numerous competitions include barrel racing, breakaway, team, and calf roping, and bull and bronco riding. Organization of the event is headed by long-time resident Brendan Balthazar, who welcomes everyone to participate with only one rule: "Have fun, but maintain safety." General admission is $10, $5 for seniors and children; call 808/572-2076 for information. Every year the rodeo is accompanied by the fun-loving Paniolo Parade, which is in its 38th year.

The day-long **Upcountry Fair** happens at the Eddie Tam Center in mid-June. A real county event, you'll find all sorts of craft displays, games, ethnic dances, competitions, and food booths, as well as the 4-H judging and animal auction.

Upcountry plays **polo.** The Maui Polo Club, 808/877-7744, www.mauipolo.com, sponsors matches in the spring and fall. From Apr.–June, matches are held at the Haleakala Ranch polo arena, about one mile above Pukalani and just off Highway 377. The Sept.–Nov. matches take place above Makawao at the Olinda outdoor polo field next to Oskie Rice rodeo arena. All matches are held on Sundays at about 1 P.M. and admission runs $3 per person.

## SIGHTS

### Up From Pa'ia

En route on Baldwin Avenue (Route 390) you pass the Pa'ia **sugar mill,** a real-life Carl Sandburg poem. A smaller sister mill to the one at Pu'unene, it was until a few short years ago a green monster trimmed in bare lightbulbs at night, dripping with sounds of turning gears, cranes, and linkbelts, all surrounded by packed, rutted, oil-stained soil. Now it stands silent and unused, a testimony to better economic times. Farther along Baldwin Avenue sits **Holy Rosary Church** and its sculpture of Father Damien. The rendering of Damien is idealized, but the leper, who resembles a Calcutta beggar, has a face that conveys helplessness while at the same time faith and hope. It's worth a few minutes' stop. Coming next is **Makawao Union Church** (1916), and it's a beauty. Like a Tudor mansion made completely of stone with lovely stained-glass windows and a

**Makawao Union Church**

MAUI

heavy slate roof, the entrance is framed by two tall and stately royal palms. Farther up is tiny **Rainbow County Park,** one of the few noncoastal parks on Maui. Set in the bend of the road, the grassy lawn here would be okay for a picnic.

At mile marker 5 along Baldwin Avenue, Hali'imaile Road turns to the south and leads to the small pineapple town of **Hali'imaile.** This tiny community, a combination of old plantation town and new development, offers a wonderful restaurant, the Haliimaile General Store—well worth the drive—a farm-fresh pineapple and produce market, and a well-shaded county park that features picnic tables, ball fields, and lighted tennis courts.

Farther up the street is the **Hui No'eau Visual Arts Center,** 2841 Baldwin Ave., 808/572-6560, www.huinoeau.com, a local organization that features traditional and modern arts housed at Kaluanui, a mansion built in 1917 by the Baldwin family on their 10-acre estate. The member artisans and craftspeople produce everything from ceramics to *lau hala* weaving, and drawings to sculpture. The old house is home to the center office, gift gallery, and periodic shows, while the former stable and carriage house have become studios. Throughout the year classes, lectures, and exhibits are offered, along with an annual Christmas Fair featuring their creations. One of the best features of visiting Hui No'eau (Club of Skills) is the resplendent mansion. Built in a neo-Spanish motif with red-tiled roof and light pink stucco exterior, Kaluanui sits among the manicured grounds that feature a reflection pond just in front of the portico. The gift shop and gallery are open daily 10 A.M.–4 P.M. (a $2 donation is suggested), and you'll often find someone around working in the studios.

## Nearby Attractions

Take Olinda Road out of town. All along it custom-designed houses have been built. Look for **Po'okela Church,** a coral-block structure built in 1843. **Seabury Hall,** a private boarding school for grades 6–12, sits among trees above Makawao. In May, it hosts a day-long arts and crafts fair, with entertainment, food, games, and auctions. An annual event for nearly 30 years, it has be-

come the best-known and best-subscribed crafts fair on the island. In four miles you pass **Rainbow Acres,** 808/573-8313. Open Tuesday and Thursday 9 A.M.–4 P.M., this nursery specializes in cacti and succulents. Then shortly you come to the Maui Bird Conservation Center and Maui Forest Bird Recovery Project office—neither open to the public. Near the top of Olinda, turn left onto Pi'iholo Road, which loops back down. Along it is **Aloha O Ka Aina,** 808/572-9440, a nursery specializing in ferns. Open Wednesday–Saturday 9 A.M.–4 P.M.

## Hiking Trail

The **Waihou Spring Trail** is the easiest hiking access in the area, but in reality it is little more than a good walk. The trailhead is just below the intersection of Olinda Road and Pi'iholo Road. Running entirely through a forest canopy of pine and eucalyptus, this trail, flat and wide for most of its length, only narrows when it drops steeply down into a ravine as it gets close to the spring, which is now virtually always dry. The trail starts out by running through an experimental tree-growing area. Shortly you come to a T-intersection. Going right, you keep to the main trail; left brings you in a half-mile loop back to the main trail. From an overlook on the main path, the trail zigzags down to the boulder-strewn bottom of a narrow ravine, a cool and quiet sanctuary. Usually dry, a dripping curtain of water must cover the back wall during the rains. Neither strenuous nor lengthy, this one-mile hike is nonetheless good exercise.

# PRACTICALITIES

## Accommodations

Built in 1924 and used by a Portuguese family to raise 13 children, the plantation house **Hale Ho'okipa Inn,** 32 Pakani Place, 808/572-6698 or 877/572-6698, fax 808/573-2580, mauibnb@maui.net, www.maui-bed-and-breakfast-inn.com, has been turned into a lovely B&B. Not a modern rendition, this well-loved place has real-world, lived-in charm and is filled with comfortable period-style and antique furniture and furnishings and artwork by Hawaiian artists. Three rooms on one side of the house have their own private baths, while the two-bedroom suite on the other side shares a bath and has use of the big country kitchen. A continental breakfast with fruit from the garden is served each morning in the parlor. Rates run $95–125 per night for the rooms and $150–165 for the suite. The inn is within walking distance of town, not far beyond and above the highway from the Eddie Tam Center. For those who like to hike, the owner offers guided tours up into Haleakala or over to the West Maui Mountains for a reasonable fee.

**Olinda Country Cottages and Inn,** 2660 Olinda Rd., 808/572-1453 or 800/932-3435, fax 808/573-5326, olinda@mauibnbcottages.com, www.mauibnbcottages.com, is up above Makawao past mile marker 11. Located on an old protea farm at about 4,000 feet in elevation, and backed up against Haleakala Ranch, this B&B is secluded, spacious, and homey. The main house has two rooms upstairs and a suite below, with two separate cottages for plenty of privacy. The two bedrooms in the house have a private entrance and share a sitting room, and each has a private bath. Breakfast is provided each morning for these rooms. The downstairs suite and individual cottages are more like small homes with all the amenities. Because each has a kitchen, breakfast is served only the first morning. All have plenty of country-style furnishings and antiques, and the color and design work well. The bedrooms run $140 per night, the suite $140, and the cottages $195–245. The rooms and suite have a two-night minimum, the cottages three. No smoking is permitted inside, and no children under eight years old are allowed to stay here. Highly recommended for quiet and seclusion, yet close enough to get to a fine restaurant in town. With gregarious hosts and good value, the only drawback for some folks might be the windy road leading up to the B&B.

Down near Hali'imaile is **Peace of Maui** vacation rentals, 1290 Hali'imaile Rd., Makawao, HI 96768; 808/572-5045 or 888/475-5045, pom@maui.net, www.maui.net/~pom. Peace of Maui overlooks the broad pineapple fields of this agricultural region, and from the property you have views of the north coast, the West Maui Mountains, and the great mountainside sweep of Haleakala. Rooms in the main house are not extravagant but clean and serviceable at $40 single or $45 double. Guests share a bathroom, comfy living room and kitchen, and the outdoor patio with barbecue grill. A separate cottage across the yard sleeps 1–4, has a bright and efficient kitchen, small living room with TV, a lanai, and washer and dryer. At $85 per night for two and $5 extra for an additional person, it's a bargain. Breakfast is not included because you have full use of the kitchen.

## Food

**Inexpensive: Kitada's Kau Kau Korner,** 808/572-7241, makes the best saimin on Maui—according to all the locals. It's a town institution and located across from the Makawao Steak House in a small plantation-style wood-frame building. Very local, nothing fancy, it's open Monday–Saturday 6 A.M.–1:30 P.M. The sharp slap of the screen door announces your entry. Order at the counter, then pour yourself a glass of water and take a seat. The saimin is inexpensive, and there are also plate lunches, burgers, and sandwiches that mostly run less than $6.

**Komoda's** is a general store that has been in business for more than 80 years. It sells a little of everything, but the bakery is renowned far and wide. It's open 7 A.M.–5 P.M. except Tuesday and Sunday, and until 2 P.M. on Saturday. People line up outside to buy their cream puffs and homemade cookies, which are all gone by late morning.

Sheltered down a short alley behind the Reeve Gallery is **Café O'Lei,** 808/573-9065, which offers simple but filling soups, salads, and sandwiches daily for lunch 11 A.M.–4 P.M. Menu items run $6.25–8 and include a snow crab and avocado sandwich, vegetarian chili, and curry chicken salad. Courtyard seating is available.

Just down the street is **Duncan's Coffee Company,** 573-9075, open most days 6:30 A.M.–9 P.M. for coffee (by the cup or pound), sodas, juices, salads, bagels, and wraps, and ice cream. Duncan's makes a great pit stop in the morning for a pick-me-up or a rest stop later in the day.

If you need a break from looking at all the art and glass, head to the **Café del Sol,** 808/572-4877, in the courtyard behind Viewpoints Gallery.

MAUI

This little eatery is open Monday–Saturday until 11 A.M. for breakfast and 11 A.M.–5 P.M. for lunch. People come just for the coffee, but you can also get granola, lox and bagels, fresh pastries, and egg breakfasts, or hot or cold sandwiches that run mostly $5.50–8.25.

**Moderate:** At 1127 Makawao Avenue you'll find the **Stopwatch Sports Bar & Grill,** 808-572-1380. Open for lunch and dinner, a variety of inexpensive burgers and sandwiches are served along with more substantial steak, fried chicken, fish entrées, and evening specials. Most items on the menu are under $10. There's live entertainment and dancing on Friday and Saturday evenings, and the bar holds happy hour daily 4–7 P.M.

An excellent place to eat is **Polli's Mexican Restaurant,** 808/572-7808, open daily 11 A.M.–10 P.M. The sign, Come In and Eat or We'll Both Starve, greets you at the front. The meals are authentic Mexican, using the finest ingredients. Formerly vegetarian—they'll still prepare any menu item in a vegetarian manner—they use no lard or animal fat in their bean dishes. You can have full lunch dishes for under $10 or dinner entrées for $10–17. Margaritas are large and tasty, the cervezas cool and refreshing. Monday night is barbecue night; Tuesday is kid's night. Still down home, still wholesome meals, still a happening place, this is one of Makawao's favorites.

**Makawao Steak House,** 808/572-8711, near the bottom end of town, is open daily for dinner from 5:30 P.M., with early-bird specials until 6:30. Casual, with wooden tables, salad bar, and good fish selections, dinners run to around $26. The steak dishes, and especially the Monday night special prime rib, are the best, and it has one of the only standard salad bars in the area. The Makawao Steak House has been around a long time and maintains a good, solid reputation. Even if you're not up for a meal, you might consider stepping into the lounge for a drink.

**Expensive:** A surprising and delicious dining experience, the best restaurant in town is found at **Casanova Italian Restaurant and Deli,** 808/572-0220, located across from Polli's at the main intersection of town. The deli is open daily for breakfast and lunch 7:30 A.M.–6 P.M. The interior is utilitarian—a refrigerated case loaded with salads, chocolates, cheese, and juice, and a few tables for eating. A real gathering spot in the morning, breakfast brings waffles, omelets, and pastries; lunch is sandwiches and hot entrées. Order your meal at the counter. The best place to sit is on the front porch, where you can perch above the street and watch Makawao life go by. Upcountry-yuppie-elegant, Casanova's restaurant occupies the adjoining section of the building, open daily except Sunday, for lunch 11:30 A.M.–2 P.M. and nightly for dinner 5:30–9 P.M., featuring pizza, pasta, and other fine Italian cuisine. Of course, pasta is the staple, but meat, fish, and poultry entrées are also popular. While you wait, you can watch the pizza maker toss the dough before putting it in the wood-burning oven. Expect pasta and pizza entrées in the $12–16 range, others $20–24. While the food is as good as the deli fare next door, many come for the music and dancing, which starts around 9:45 P.M. and runs until 1 A.M. Wednesday–Saturday. Having a nightclub atmosphere, a large dance floor, and a first-class sound system, it draws people not only from Upcountry but also from Central and South Maui. Casual attire is fine, but remember, Upcountry gets cool at night, so you might need something to cover your arms and shoulders.

The **Haliimaile General Store,** 808/572-2666, open Mon.–Fri. 11 A.M.–2:30 P.M., and again 5:30–9:30 P.M., with a Sunday brunch 10 A.M.–2:30 P.M. and a mini-menu 2:30–5 P.M., serves elegant gourmet food to anyone lucky enough to find this Upcountry roadhouse. Located in Hali'imaile village along Hali'imaile Road between Baldwin Avenue and the Haleakala Highway, the restaurant is housed in what was this pineapple town's general store. Climb the steps to a wide veranda and enter to find the vintage utilitarian wood-floored interior transformed into an airy room with tropical fish hung from the ceiling, primitive ceramics and sculptures placed here and there, and original paintings of brilliant colors. It's as if the restaurant is part contemporary boutique and art gallery, and the old grocery shelves are filled with distinctive gift and gourmet food items. Choose a table in the casual front room, perch on a canvas chair at the copper-top bar in front of the open kitchen, or ask for a table in the back room, more formal with dark wood paneling, ceiling fans, track lighting, and floral displays. Master chef Beverly Gannon presents creative "Hawaiian regional cuisine with an American and international twist," while her Irish husband, master schmoozer Joe Gannon, presents an equally magnificent Blarney Stone atmosphere! While the menu changes seasonally, a sampling of what you might expect includes appetizers like the sashimi Napoleon, Asian pear and duck taco, or Bev's crab dip served on boboli bread, all under $17. These are an experience in themselves but serve to prepare you for the main course to come. Entrées include *paniolo* barbecue ribs, coconut seafood curry, aged Midwest beef rib eye, rack of lamb Hunan style, or chili verde enchiladas, all of which range in price from $22–32. Save room for a masterful dessert created by pastry chef and daughter Teresa Gannon. Piña colada cheesecake anyone? The food is always healthy and fresh and the portions are plentiful. Whatever your choice, you'll leave with a full belly and a smile on your face. The setting is casual and alohawear is okay, but because of the elevation, long sleeves and pants might be in order. The Haliimaile General Store has been reborn, and its spirit lives on in this wonderful restaurant.

## Food Markets

**Down To Earth Natural Foods,** 1169 Makawao Ave., 808/572-1488, open daily 8 A.M.–8 P.M., is a first-rate health food store that originated in Wailuku and later opened a branch here in Makawao. Inside you'll find shelves packed with minerals, vitamins, herbs, spices, and mostly organic fruits and vegetables. Bins hold bulk grains, pastas, honey, and nut butters, while a deli case holds sandwiches and drinks. You can even mix up a salad from the salad bar to take out, or choose a hot entrée from the food bar. At $6.49 per pound, the hot entrées are one of the best bargains in town for a meal. Down to Earth has a philosophy by which it operates: "To promote the living of a healthy lifestyle by eating a natural vegetarian diet; respect for all forms of life; and concern for the environment."

**Rodeo General Store,** 3661 Baldwin Ave., is a one-stop shop with a wide selection of natural foods, deli items, pastries, produce, fresh fish, wines, spirits, and cigars. Open 7 A.M.–10 P.M. daily. The **Liquor Shack and Deli,** 1143 Makawao Ave., provides plate lunches for about $6.75 and a full range of liquid refreshments daily 9 A.M.–10:30 P.M.

In Hali'imaile, **Maui Fresh** is an outlet for Maui Pineapple Company. Available are fresh and canned pineapples and a variety of seasonal fruits and vegetables. A small plantation museum offers visitors a snapshot of the pineapple industry and the company operation. Open Monday–Friday, 10 A.M.–6 P.M., Saturday 9 A.M.–5 P.M., this store is located next to the plantation office along Hali'imaile Road and only a few steps from the Haliimaile General Store restaurant. This shop sponsors a flea market every first and third Saturday and an annual pineapple picnic in May for food, games, crafts, music, and plantation tours.

## Art Galleries

**The Courtyard of Makawao** is a consortium of shops at 3620 Baldwin Avenue near the bottom end of town where you can dine, peruse fine art, collect country craft, or watch as glassblowers pursue alchemical art. In the reconstructed Makawao Theater building, **Maui Hands,** 808/572-5194, is open daily except Sunday 10 A.M.–6 P.M. This artists' "consignment shop" specializes in Maui-made art and crafts like semiprecious stone necklaces, sterling and gold jewelry, prints, bamboo work, raku pottery, primitive basketry, and even some T-shirts. **Viewpoints Gallery,** 808/572-5979, open daily 10 A.M.–6 P.M. (Sunday until 4 P.M.), is an artists' cooperative specializing in locally created paintings, sculptures, handicrafts, and jewelry. Most of the artists live in the area, and with enough notice they will come to meet you if time permits. This shop is a perfect place to spend an hour eyeing the contemporary art scene that is so vibrant in Upcountry. Every month brings a new exhibit. Outside is a pleasant courtyard, around which are several more shops.

In the back you will find artisans making magic

at **Hot Island Glass,** 808/572-4527, open daily 9 A.M.–5 P.M., with glass being blown most days 10 A.M.–4 P.M. These very talented glassblowers turn molten glass into vases, platters, sea creatures, and some small items like paperweights. Just line up at their window and watch the artists work. Incidental pieces run as cheap as $10, but the masterpieces go for several thousand. Don't worry about shipping or packing glass; they're also masters at packing so things don't break on the way home. In the back corner, **Upcountry Legends,** 808/572-3523, open daily 10 A.M.–6 P.M., Sunday 11 A.M.–5 P.M., sells hand-painted silk shirts, ladies apparel, sterling silver jewelry, huggable teddy bears and other stuffed animals, greeting cards, candles, and baskets.

For more fine art, painting, pottery, wood sculpture, and more, check out **David Warren Gallery** across from the Courtyard and the **Master Touch Gallery** for fine jewelry. Up the street a bit and behind Tropo is the small **Gallery Maui,** with a wide selection of art and wood furniture by island artists. Farther up Baldwin Avenue is the **Sherri Reeve Gallery,** where you'll find the inspiring watercolor florals of the artist. Nearly across the street, **Kristen Bunney Gallery** hangs paintings by the owner, displays woodwork, gifts, and jewelry by others, and sells Tibetan rugs. At the corner, you're sure to find something that catches your eye at the **Hui Mona Gallery** "art collective."

Although Baldwin Avenue has been the scene of most studios and shops, a few newer businesses have slowly begun to occupy buildings along Makawao Avenue. The **Randy Jay Braun Gallery,** 1156 Makawao Ave., displays Braun's photo art, plus plenty of art in other media, gifts, rugs, and wood crafts. Next door is **Avalene Gallery,** open Mon.–Sat. 10–6 P.M., where they have whimsical pottery sculpture on Smeltzer, paintings by Kasprzycki, and wood, metal, glass, and ceramic pieces by other fine island artists.

## Shopping

Makawao is changing quickly, and nowhere is this more noticeable than in its local shops. The population is now made up of old-guard *paniolo,* yuppies, and alternative people. What a combo! Some unique and fascinating shops here can provide you with distinctive purchases.

When Mimi Merrill opened **Miracles Bookery,** 3682 Baldwin Ave., 808/572-2317, she put her heart, soul, and all of her resources into the place. Miracles Bookery specializes in books on new-age spiritualism, astrology, Tarot, self-discovery, children's classics, Hawaiiana, poetry, and "preloved" books. Miracles also has unique gift items: angels, petroglyph reproductions, candles, puzzles, Native American jewelry, bumper stickers with an attitude, posters, and music of all kinds from spiritual to rock. Open Monday, Thursday, and Sunday 8 A.M.–8 P.M., Wed.–Sat. until 9 P.M.

At the corner is the tiny **Little Tibet Ethnic Jewelry Store,** open Mon.–Sat. 10 A.M.–5 P.M., for brass and bronze jewelry and religious art and accouterments.

**Collections Boutique,** open daily until 6 P.M., Saturday until 4, imports items from throughout Asia: batiks from Bali, clothes from India, silk Hawaiian shirts, and jewelry, lotions, cosmetics, accessories, sunglasses, and handicrafts from various countries. Next door, **The Mercantile** also deals in women's fashions, as do several other shops along Baldwin Avenue.

**HI Hearth and Leisure,** 808/572-4569, has the largest line of wood-burning and gas stoves in Hawaii. That's right, stoves! Nights in the high country can get chilly, and on top of Haleakala it's downright cold. Here as well are barbecue grills, fireplaces, chimneys and accessories, a good selection of cutlery, and a large variety of hot sauces and rubs.

Listen for tinkling wind chimes to locate **Goodies,** open 9:30 A.M.–5:30 P.M., Sunday 10 A.M.–5 P.M., a boutique that looks like a spilled treasure chest. Crystals, silk and cotton casual and elegant clothing, dolls, children's wear, stuffed animals, locally crafted trays, and magic wands fill this shop. Just down the way, **Gecko** carries an eclectic collection of mostly imported gifts, some jewelry, and wearable accessories.

About the only shop in town for men's clothing is **Tropo,** where you can find shorts, polo shirts, aloha shirts, and even hats and ties. Open Monday–Saturday 10 A.M.–6 P.M., Sunday 11 A.M.–4 P.M.

At the front of The Courtyard of Makawao building is the **Designing Wahine** shop, where you can find kid's clothing, gifts, home decoration, and plenty of other nifty island-style gifts.

Down a narrow alley a few steps from the intersection of Baldwin and Makawao avenues is **The Dragon's Den Herb Store,** 808/572-2424, a shop stuffed full of Chinese herbs and medicines, minerals, crystals, teas, gifts, and books on Eastern healing arts. The **Dragon's Den Heal-** ing Center, 808/572-5267, occupies the same building. Also in the alley is **Grace Health Clinic,** 808/572-6091, which specializes in chiropractic care, massage, and traditional Asian medicine, and half a dozen other health professionals. Check the bulletin board here for medical practices and community events. For an alternative practice, contact **Maui School of Therapeutic Massage,** 1043 Makawao Ave., 808/572-2277.

# Pukalani

This waystation town, at the intersection of the Old Haleakala Highway and Route 365, is a good place to get gas and supplies for a driving trek through Kula or a trip up Haleakala. It's a rapidly growing community with many new housing developments around its periphery. There are no outstanding cultural or historical sights in Pukalani, but a fine golf course graces its southern edge. Across the street from the major shopping center is a large community park with ball fields, basketball courts, and a great swimming center with an Olympic-size swimming pool.

At the **Pukalani Terrace Center,** the largest shopping mall in Upcountry, are an **Ace Hardware, Foodland** grocery store (open 24 hours), **Paradise Video,** a **Bank of Hawaii** and **American Savings Bank,** both of which have ATMs, a **Maui Medical Group** clinic office, and a **post office.** In the corner of the mall, the full-service **Upcountry Laundry and Dry Cleaning** is open daily 8 A.M.–9 P.M. except Sunday, when it closes at 5 P.M. There are a variety of economical eateries here, including **Royal King's Garden** Chinese restaurant (no MSG) and **Ono Loco Food** mixed-plate shop, along with several fast-food places.

One of the best restaurants in the area is the **Pukalani Country Club Restaurant,** 808/572-1325, open daily 7:30 A.M.–2 P.M. and 5–9 P.M. It has a salad bar and sandwiches but specializes in local and Hawaiian foods such as *kalua* pig and *lau lau* plates at reasonable prices. Most patrons are local people, so you know that they're doing something right. The only Upcountry golf course on Maui, **Pukalani Country Club,** offers 18 holes of inexpensive golf. In the bargain come spectacular views over the isthmus and up toward Haleakala. Turn south at the Pukalani Terrace Center and follow the road for four or five blocks to reach the golf course.

Farther up the road at the corner of Aewa Place is the **Cow Country Cafe,** 808/572-2395, in a faded pink and gray building. Open daily 7 A.M.–2 P.M. and again for dinner Wednesday–Sunday 5:30–9 P.M., the café has brought wholesome and unpretentious dining to Upcountry. Inside, wooden tables, bent-back chairs, a tiled counter, and a black-on-white Holstein motif set the ambiance in this American/island standard restaurant. The Cow Country Cafe is a perfect economical breakfast or lunch stop while touring Kula.

At the intersection of Makawao Avenue is the **Pukalani Superette,** a well-stocked grocery store, especially for this neck of the woods, that's open Monday–Friday 6:30 A.M.–9 P.M. with shorter hours on the weekends. Down from the superette, going toward Makawao, is a second smaller shopping center, the **Pukalani Square,** where you'll find an **'Ohana Physicians** clinic, **Paradise Pharmacy,** the Maui **Nature Conservancy** office, and a **First Hawaiian Bank.**

Located at 112 Ho'opalua Drive, not far out of Pukalani on the way toward the lower Kula area, is the **Kula Hula Inn,** 808/572-9351 or 888/485-2466, fax 808/572-1132. This Christian B&B has three rooms in the main house and two separate units. The rooms have their own bathrooms, and one has a separate entrance and lanai. They rent for $90–130. For $125 you can get the three-room Suite Plumeria. The larger and more private two-bedroom Hula Moon Cottage with full bath and kitchen goes for $145. An extra $15 per person is added to the bill when there are more than two people in a unit. Breakfast is included daily except Sunday for all except the cottage, where it's optional for an additional charge. This is a secure gated property surrounded by a large lawn, so it's good for kids.

# Kula

Kula (Open Country) could easily provide all of the ingredients for a full-course meal fit for a king. Its bounty is staggering: vegetables to make a splendid chef's salad, beef for the entrée, flowers to brighten the spirits, and wine to set the mood. Up here, soil, sun, and moisture create a garden symphony. Sweet Maui onions, cabbages, potatoes, tomatoes, apples, pineapples, lettuce, herbs, asparagus, and artichokes grow with abandon. Herefords and Black Angus graze in knee-deep fields of sweet green grass. Flowers are everywhere: Beds of proteas, camellias, carnations, roses, hydrangeas, and blooming peach and tangerine trees dot the countryside like daubs from van Gogh's brush. As you gain the heights along Kula's lanes, you look back on West Maui and a perfect view of the isthmus. You'll also enjoy wide-open spaces and rolling green hills fringed with trees like a lion's mane. Above, the sky changes from brooding gray to blazing blue, then back again. During light rainy afternoons, when the sun streams in from the west, you could easily spot a rainbow on the hillside, as if sprouting from the rich green pastureland. Kula is a different Maui—quiet and serene.

## Getting There

The fastest way is the route to Haleakala. Take Route 37 through Pukalani, turn onto Route 377, and when you see Kimo Road on your left and right, you're in Kula country. Following Route 37 a few miles past Pukalani gets you to the same area, only lower on the mountain slope. If you have the time, take the following scenic route. Back in Kahului start on Route 36 (Hana Highway), but shortly after you cross Dairy Road look for a sign pointing to Pulehu-Oma'opio Road on your right. Take it! You'll wade through acres of sugarcane, and in six miles this road

splits. You can take either because at the top they deposit you in the middle of things to see. Once the road forks, you'll pass some excellent examples of flower and truck farms. The cooperative vacuum cooling plant is in this neighborhood, a place where many farmers store their produce. Cross Route 37 (Kula Highway) and turn onto Lower Kula Road. Explore this road for a while before heading straight uphill via (Lower) Kimo Drive, Pulehuiki Drive, Kamehameiki Road, or Copp Road, which bring you through some absolutely beautiful countryside to Route 377.

## SIGHTS

### Botanical Gardens

Follow Route 377 south—it turns into Kekaulike Avenue after Haleakala Crater Road, Route 378, turns up the mountain. Look for the **Kula Botanical Gardens,** 808/878-1715, on your left just before the road meets again with Route 37. These privately owned gardens are open daily 9 A.M.–4 P.M.; be sure to start by 3 P.M. to give yourself enough time for a thorough walk-around. Admission is $5 adults, $1 children 6–12. Here are nearly six acres of identified tropical and semitropical plants on a self-guided tour. There is also a stream that runs through the property, a koi pond, and a small aviary. Some of the 2,000 different varieties of plants include protea, orchid, bromeliad, fuchsia, and ferns, and the native koa, *kukui,* and sandalwood. First opened to the public in 1971, the gardens are educational and will give names to many flowers and plants that you've observed around the island. It makes for a relaxing afternoon—a wonderful spot. Enter through the gift shop.

Located across from mile marker 10 on the Kula Highway, the privately owned **Enchanting**

**Floral Gardens,** 808/878-2531, is newer and more commercial than Kula Botanical Garden, yet worthy of a look. Its eight acres are neatly laid out, with many of the 2,000 varieties of flowers and plants identified. Stroll down the path and be captivated by the abundance. Plan on taking about an hour to see the entire lot. Open daily 9 A.M.–5 P.M.; entrance $5 adults, $1 children.

The University of Hawaii maintains an **agriculture experimental station** of 20 acres of flowers and other agricultural plants that change with the seasons. Located on Mauna Place above Route 37; open Monday–Thursday 7 A.M.–3:30 P.M. Check in with the station manager at the office—closed during the lunch hour. A self-guided tour map is available at the office. While there are experimental plots for other ornamental flowers, vegetables, and fruits, the main focus of this facility is hybridized protea for commercial production. Perhaps best from Oct.–May, it's more a stop for scholarly interest because you can find more showy plants at the botanical gardens and flower shops nearby.

### Flower Shops

**Upcountry Harvest,** 808/878-2824 or 800/575-6470, www.upcountryharvest.com, sits next door to the Kula Lodge and is open daily 8 A.M.–5:30 P.M. Don't miss seeing the amazing fresh and dried flowers and arrangements. Here you can purchase a wide range of protea and other tropical flowers that can be shipped back home, or you can order off the Internet. Live or dried, these flowers are fantastic. Gift boxes starting at $45 are well worth the price. The salespeople are friendly and informative, and it's educational just to visit.

The **Sunrise Protea Farm,** 808/876-0200 or 800/222-2797, www.sunriseprotea.com, and gift shop is less than one-half mile up Haleakala Crater Road. The shop sells gift items, local Maui produce, homemade sweets, sandwiches, and fruit juices. In the flower shop you'll find fresh and dried flowers and arrangements that can be sent anywhere in the country; fresh bouquets from $50, dried arrangements from $42. An easy stop on the way back from Haleakala. Open daily 7:30 A.M.–4 P.M.

The nursery and flower shop **Proteas of Hawaii,** 808/878-2533 or 800/367-7768, www.hawaii-exotics.com, is located across the road from the University of Hawaii agricultural experimental station; hours are 8 A.M.–4:30 P.M. Fresh protea baskets, tropical bouquets, and individual flowers can be purchased and shipped anywhere. Prices start at about $40, or $20 for lei.

## Polipoli Spring State Recreation Area

If you want quietude and mountain walks, come here, because few others do. Just past the Kula Botanical Gardens look for the park sign on your left leading up Waipoli Road. This 10-mile stretch is only partially paved; the first half zigzags steeply up the hill, and the second half, although fairly flat, is dirt and can be very rutted, rocky, or muddy. Hang gliders use this area, jumping off farther up and landing on the open grassy fields along the lower portion of this road. Hunting is also done in the forests here, and several trails lead off this road to prescribed hunting areas. As usual, the trip is worth it. Polipoli has an established forest of imported trees from around the world: eucalyptus, redwoods, cypress, ash, cedar, and sugi pines. Much of the area was planted in the 1920s by the state and in the 1930s by the Civilian Conservation Corps. These trees do well here because the park lies right in that band where moisture-laden clouds seem to hang around the mountain. There is a great network of trails in the immediate area and even one that leads up to the top of the mountain. One of the most popular is the Redwood Trail, which you can take to a shelter at the end. These trails are for hiking and mountain biking only—no motorcycles or horses.

At 6,200 feet, the camping area can be brisk at night. Camping is free, but permits are required and are available from the Division of State Parks, 54 S. High St., Rm. 101, Wailuku, HI 96793, 808/984-8109. Water, picnic tables, and outhouses are provided at the camping spot, which is a small, grassy area surrounded by tall eucalyptus trees. The cabin here is a spacious three-bedroom affair with bunks for up to 10 people. It starts at $45 per night for 1–4 people and goes up $5 per additional person. It's rustic, but all camping and cooking essentials are provided, including a wood-burning stove. If you want to get away from it all, this is your spot.

## Hiking Trails

Most of these trails form a network through and around Polipoli Spring State Recreation Area and are all accessible from the camping area at 6,200 feet. **Redwood Trail,** 1.7 miles, passes through a magnificent stand of redwoods, past the ranger station and down to an old Civilian Conservation Corps camp at 5,300 feet where there's a rough old shelter. **Tie Trail,** one-half mile, joins Redwood Trail with **Plum Trail,** so named because of its numerous plum trees, which bear fruit during the summer. **Skyline Trail,** 6.5 miles, starts atop Haleakala at 9,750 feet, passing through the southwest rift and eventually joining the **Haleakala Ridge Trail,** 1.6 miles, at the 6,500-foot level, then descends through a series of switchbacks. You can join with the Plum Trail or continue to the shelter at the end. Both the Skyline and Ridge trails offer superb vistas of Maui.

Other trails throughout the area include **Polipoli,** 0.6 miles, passing through the famous forests of the area; **Boundary Trail,** four miles, leading from the Kula Forest Reserve to the ranger's cabin, passing numerous gulches still supporting native trees and shrubs; and **Waiohuli Trail,** descending the mountain to join Boundary Trail and overlooking Keokea and Kihei with a shelter at the end. **Waiakoa Trail,** seven miles, begins at the Kula Forest Reserve Access Road. It ascends Haleakala to the 7,800-foot level and then descends through a series of switchbacks, covering rugged territory and passing a natural cave shelter. It eventually meets up with the three-mile **Waiakoa Loop Trail.** All of these trails offer intimate forest views of native and introduced trees, and breathtaking views of the Maui coastline far below.

## Other Sights

In the basement of the Kula Lodge, tucked away as if in a wine cellar, is the **Curtis Wilson Cost Gallery,** 808/878-6544 or 800/508-2278, www.costgallery.com. One of Maui's premier artists, Cost captures scenes reflecting the essence of Upcountry Maui; handles color, light, and

Built by Portuguese immigrants in 1897, Holy Ghost Catholic Church continues to serve this multiethnic community after more than a century of use.

shadow to perfection; and portrays the true pastoral nature of the area. This is traditional realism with a touch of imagination. Stop in and browse daily 8:30 A.M.–5 P.M., or visit his other shop on Front Street in Lahaina.

**Holy Ghost Catholic Church,** on Lower Kula Road in Waiakoa, is an octagonal house of worship (Hawaii's only) raised in 1897 by the many Portuguese who worked the farms and ranches of Upcountry. It was rededicated in 1992 after extensive renovation and has many fine hand-carved and hand-painted statues and an elaborate altar that was sent by the king and queen of Portugal when the church was built. This church is worth a look, not only for the museum-quality woodwork inside, but also for the great view over the isthmus. In 1983, it was placed on the National Register of Historic Places.

Near the intersection of Highways 37 and 377 is **Rice Park,** a grassy wayside rest area that has a few picnic tables, bathrooms, and a public phone. From here, you get a good view over the lower mountain slope, the coast at Kihei and Wailea, and the isthmus.

In Waiakoa, there's a gas station; down on the main highway is the **post office.** Across the highway from there is a Montessori School, which hosts a Christmas Faire every year just before the holiday season.

## Accommodations and Food

The **Kula Lodge,** RR 1, Box 475, Kula, HI 96790, 808/878-1535 or 800/233-1535, fax 808/878-2518, info@kulalodge.com, www.kulalodge.com, is on Route 377 just past Kimo Road and just before Haleakala Crater Road. Lodging here is in five detached chalets ranging $100–165; check-in is at the lodge restaurant. Two of the chalets have fireplaces with wood provided, four have lofts for extra guests, and all have lanai and excellent views of lower Maui. With their dark wood, carpets, and cathedral ceilings, they are almost contemporary in appearance. The Kula Lodge is a fine establishment with a wonderful location at 3,200 feet in elevation. Perhaps the only drawback is the clamor created when riders on the Haleakala downhill bike trips arrive in a large group for breakfast. Be up early so as not to be disturbed.

The lobby and dining area of the **Kula Lodge Restaurant,** 808/878-1535, are impressively rustic, with open beamwork and framing, dark wood, and stone. This building started as a private residence when it was built more than 50 years ago. The walls are covered with high-quality photos of Maui: sailboards, silverswords, sunsets, cowboys, and horses. The large main dining room has giant plate-glass windows with a superlative view. Breakfast is served daily 6:30–11:15 A.M., lunch 11:45 A.M.–4:15 P.M., and dinner 4:45–9 P.M.; Sunday brunch runs 6:30 A.M.–noon. The menus are surprisingly large. Try Hawaiian buttermilk griddle cakes or vegetarian Benedict for breakfast, or a fresh fish sandwich or grilled chicken breast for lunch. Start dinner with miso oyster Rockefeller or a Kula farm green salad, and move on to a fresh fish, New York steak, or macadamia nut pesto pasta. The assortment of gourmet desserts includes a tasty mango pie, and one of these should

round out your meal. There may be entertainment in the evenings. Before or after dinner, sit at the bar for a drink or warm yourself on the couches that front the stone fireplace.

Just up the road is **Kula Sandalwoods** restaurant, 808/878-3523, serving breakfast from about 7:30 and lunch until 2:30 P.M. or 3 P.M. Set on the hillside above the road, Kula Sandalwoods has a great view out over the isthmus. Breakfast might be eggs Benedict for $9.75, omelets for $8.95, or griddle items. Lunch is mostly burgers and sandwiches that run $8.50–9.75.

**Kula View Bed & Breakfast,** 808/878-6736, at 600 Holopuni Road below Highway 37, offers a room on the upper level of the home with private entrance, private lanai, and sweeping views of Upcountry and across the isthmus to the West Maui Mountains. Surrounded by two lush acres, peace is assured in your bright and cheery room appointed with queen-size bed, wicker furniture in a breakfast nook, and a shower; telephone and TV are available upon request. The rate is $85 per night, single or double occupancy, which includes a simple continental breakfast. Weekly discounts are available; cash and traveler's checks only. For reservations, contact host Susan Kauai at P.O. Box 322, Kula, HI 96790, sfkauai@mauigateway.com, www.kulaview.com.

In the tiny community of Waiakoa on Lower Kula Road you'll find **Morihara Store,** open daily 7 A.M.–8 P.M. for basic necessities. Across the street is the spacious but spartan **Cafe 808,** open daily 6 A.M.–8 P.M., serving down-home local food, with nothing on the menu more than $8.95.

## CONTINUING SOUTH
### Keokea

Continue south on Route 37 through the town of Keokea, where you'll find gas, a small selection of items at Henry Fong's and Ching's general stores, two rural churches, including St. John's Episcopal Church, and an excellent park for a picnic. At the far end of the village are **Keokea Gallery,** open Tues.–Sat. 9 A.M.–5 P.M., which displays modern art by Maui artists, and next door is **Grandma's Maui Coffee.** Grandma's is open every day, 7 A.M.–5 P.M. You can enjoy fresh pastries for breakfast until 10 A.M. and sandwiches, taro burgers, and pies for lunch. The real treat, however, is the coffee, grown on the slope below and roasted in an old-fashioned, hand-crank, 115-year-old coffee machine in the shop. Stop in for a sip or take a package to go. Partway down Thompson Road south of town are the Thompson Ranch Riding Stables corral, Silvercloud Upcountry Guest Ranch bed-and-breakfast, and Star Lookout cottage.

For the diehard history buff, there is an old structure up above town that represents a link to the past, when Chinese workers inhabited the area in greater numbers than they do today. This is the **Kwock Hing Society Building** on Middle Road, a two-story green structure with cream trim that has signboards on either side of the front door that are carved with Chinese characters. A smaller plantation-style building sits to the side. Both have been well maintained. Here, local Chinese would congregate for all sorts of social purposes.

Almost as evidence of that Chinese connection is **Dr. Sun Yat-sen Memorial Park,** farther along the highway. A small triangular county park, here you'll find a statue to this famous Chinese physician/politician, two carved stone lions, and picnic tables. Dr. Sun Yat-Sen spent some of his younger years studying in Honolulu and also had a brother who lived on Maui. It seems that Dr. Sun's movement to overthrow the Manchu Dynasty, which ruled China until 1911, germinated here in Hawaii.

## Tedeschi Winery

Past Keokea you'll know you're in ranch country. The road narrows and herds of cattle graze in pastures that seem like manicured gardens highlighting *panini* (prickly pear) cactus. You'll pass Ulupalakua Ranch office and store and then almost immediately come to the Tedeschi Winery tasting room on the left, 808/878-6058, www.mauiwine.com. Open for tastings daily 9 A.M.–5 P.M., the winery sells bottles of all its wines and cushioned boxes for transporting them. Here, Emil Tedeschi and his partner Pardee Erdman, who also owns the 23,000-acre Ulupalakua Ranch, offer samples of their wines. This is one of

two wineries in Hawaii, the only one on Maui. When Erdman bought the ranch and moved here in 1963, he noticed climatic similarities to the Napa Valley and knew that this country could grow decent wine grapes. Tedeschi comes from California, where his family has a small vineyard near Calistoga. The partners have worked on making their dream of Maui wine a reality since 1974.

It takes time and patience to grow grapes and turn out a vintage wine. While they waited for their carnelian grapes (a cabernet hybrid) to mature and be made into a sparkling wine, they fermented pineapple juice, which they call Maui Blanc. If you're expecting this to be a sickeningly sweet syrup, forget it. Maui Blanc is surprisingly dry and palatable. In 1984 the first scheduled release of the winery's carnelian sparkling wine, Maui Brut, celebrated the patience and craftsmanship of the vintners. Maui Blush, a zinfandel-like light-pink dinner wine, and Maui Nouveau, a young red wine that's no longer available, were then added to the list. Most recently, Plantation Red, a very dry, oaky, red wine; Maui Splash, a sweet dessert wine that is a combination of pineapple and passion fruit; the mellow Ulupalakua Red table wine; and the dry salmon-colored Rose Ranch Cuvée have made their debut. On occasion, special varietals are bottled. You can taste these wines at the white ranch house set among the tall, proud trees just off the highway, once visited by King Kalakaua in 1874.

From here, free tours run at 10:30 A.M. and 1:30 P.M. to the working winery buildings just a few steps away. Hugging the ground closer to the road is a 100-year-old plaster and coral building that used to be the winery's tasting room. Formerly, it served as the jailhouse of the old Rose Ranch owned by James Makee, a Maui pioneer sugarcane planter. Look for the 25-acre vineyard one mile before the tasting room on the ocean side of the highway. Tedeschi wines are available in restaurants and stores around the island and on the Internet.

Across the street are remains of the old **Makee Sugar Mill.** A few steps away is the Ulupalakua Ranch store and office and the ranch store and deli, which is open regular business hours. Hanging around the store like old plantation workers after a hard day's work are several carved and painted lifelike figures, representing various groups of people who have contributed to Maui's past. Sit down and say hello.

The ranch runs two-hour and four-hour **ATV Tours** over its property, either down close to the water or up on the mountain side. These rides give guests an unprecedented view of a sizable section of Maui that is normally off limits. For information, contact **Maui ATV Tours** at 808/878-2889.

At the end of April, an agricultural trade show called **The Ulupalakua Thing** gives growers and producers an opportunity to show their goods and hand out samples. Products grown and manufactured throughout the state are on display, making this the largest such agricultural event in Hawaii. The Ulupalakua Thing is held at the Ulupalakua Ranch on the grounds of the Tedeschi Winery.

## Accommodations

A good place for groups and couples, the **Silvercloud Upcountry Guest Ranch,** 1373 Thompson Rd., Kula, HI 96790, 808/878-6101 or 800/532-1111, fax 808/878-2132, slvrcld@maui.net, www.silvercloudranch.com, is located just out of Keokea and lies just up the slope from the Thompson Ranch horse corral. This fine country accommodation has six rooms in the main house and five studios in an adjoining building. The cottage on the hillside up behind is very private and an excellent retreat for newlyweds. Appropriately ranch-style, all rooms are surrounded by pastureland, and at nearly 3,000 feet in elevation, have unobstructed views down on the green lower slopes of the mountain, Ma'alaea Bay, and West Maui. Rooms in the large well-appointed main house run $110–162, and everyone has access to the kitchen, living room, and dining room. Each bedroom has a private bath but no telephone, and the upstairs rooms have a balcony that overlooks the front lawn. The studios run $132 and $188, and come with a bath, kitchen, and private lanai. Renting for $195 per night, the cottage is a fully furnished unit with its own woodstove for heat. A full breakfast is included for all guests and is served on the back lanai of the main house, surrounded by a flower garden. There is a $15 surcharge for one-night stays. Rates increase about 10 percent from December 15 to the end of February.

Just down the road is the **Star Lookout,** tel/fax 907/346-8028, www.starlookout.com, a single cottage, semi-ranch-style "retreat" that's just right for a quiet and restful stay. This cottage has a kitchen, great views, and plenty of privacy, and rents for $150 per night, two nights minimum.

# Haleakala National Park

**Haleakala** (House of the Sun) is spellbinding. Like seeing Niagara Falls or the Grand Canyon for the first time, it makes no difference how many people have come before you; it's still an undiminished, powerful, personal experience. What is perhaps the most profound aspect of this astounding spot is it grandeur and diversity. The arid volcanic mountaintop "crater" basin is grand in its immensity and that which draws the greatest number of visitors, but the park holds within its boundary numerous other climactic zones and geologic regions, which include frigid alpine peaks, sparsely vegetated upper mountain slopes, a thick and nearly undisturbed tropical forest valley, and a warm coastal littoral strip. Within these differing areas is a great biodiversity that in many respects is quite fragile and in great need of care and protection.

At just over 10,000 feet in elevation, Haleakala is one of the world's largest dormant volcanoes, composed of amazingly dense volcanic rock, almost like poured cement. Counting the 20,000 feet or so of it lying under the sea makes it one of the tallest mountains on earth. The park's boundaries encompass 30,183 variable acres, which stretch from Hosmer Grove on the west end to Kipahulu on the east. Of these, nearly 28,000 acres have wilderness status. The most impressive feature is the "crater" basin itself. It's 3,000 feet deep, 7.5 miles east to west, and 2.5 miles north

# HALEAKALA NATIONAL PARK

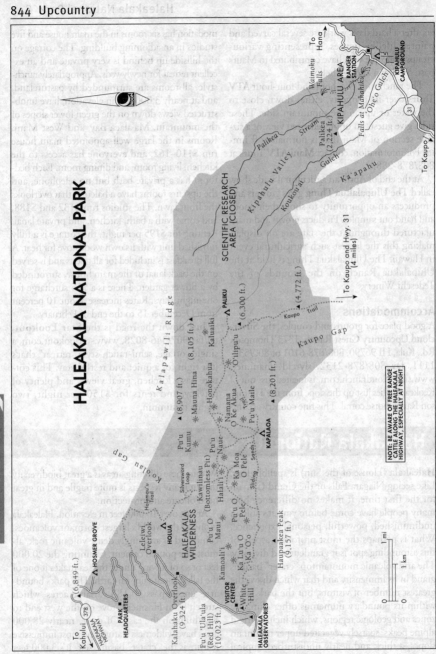

**NOTE: BE AWARE OF FREE RANGE CATTLE ALONG THE HALEAKALA HIGHWAY, ESPECIALLY AT NIGHT**

To Kahului

HALEAKALA HIGHWAY

378

**PARK HEADQUARTERS**

6,849 ft.

HOSMER GROVE

Leleiwi Overlook

Kalahaku Overlook
9,324 ft.

HALEAKALA WILDERNESS

HOLUA

Halemau'u Trail

Silversword Loop

Kawilinau

Pu'u
Kumu

Mauna Hina
8,907 ft.

Pu'u
Naue

Honokahua

Pu'u O
(Bottomless Pit)

Pu'u O
Maui

Halali'i

Ka Moa
O Pele

Ka Lu u O
Ka 'O'o

Kamoali'i

Pu'u O
Pele

Sliding Sands

White Hill

**VISITOR CENTER**

Pu'u 'Ula'ula
(Red Hill)
10,023 ft.

HALEAKALA
OBSERVATORIES

Haupaakea Peak
9,157 ft.

Namana
O Ke Akua

Pu'u Maile

KAPALAOA
8,201 ft.

'O'ilipu'u

Koolau Gap

PALIKU
6,300 ft.

Kalua iki

Kaupo Trail

Kaupo Gap

4,772 ft.

To Kaupo and Hwy. 31
(4 miles)

Kalapawili Ridge

Koukou at a

Ka apahu

Kipahulu Valley

Palikea Stream

Palikea
Gulch

SCIENTIFIC RESEARCH
AREA (CLOSED)

Palikea
(2,224 ft.)

Waimoku Falls

Falls at Makahiku

Ohe'o Gulch

KIPAHULU AREA

KIPAHULU AREA
RANGER STATION

KIPAHULU
CAMPGROUND

To Hana

31

To Kaupo

1 mi

1 km

© SANDRA E. BISIGNANI TRUST AND AVALON TRAVEL PUBLISHING, INC.

to south, accounting for 19 square miles, with a circumference of 21 miles. A mini mountain range of nine prominent and additional smaller cinder cones marches across the basin floor. They look deceptively tiny from the observation area, but the tallest at about 600 feet is Pu'u O Maui.

In 1916, much of the mountaintop area of the present Haleakala National Park, along with a large portion of what is now Hawaii Volcanoes National Park, some 100 miles distant on the Big Island of Hawai'i, was created as Hawaii National Park. Kipahulu Valley was brought within the park boundary in 1951. The Maui and Hawai'i sections were split into separate entities in 1961 and Haleakala National Park was born. In 1969, the coastal Kipahulu section was added to the park, and in the late 1990s, 52 additional acres were added along the coast. An additional 2,000 acres were acquired in 2001 between 'Ohe'o and Kaupo, and this Ka'apahu section runs in a swath from the basin ridge down to the ocean.

The entire park is a nature preserve dedicated to Hawaii's quickly vanishing indigenous and endemic plants and animals, and it was recognized as an International Biosphere Reserve by the United Nations in 1980. Two of the endangered species at home here are the *nene*, the Hawaiian wild goose, and the *'ahinahina*, the a fantastically adapted yet fragile silversword plant. Within the park boundaries are six endangered bird species and perhaps 35 endangered plant species. To help mitigate the negative effects of large introduced animals, miles of fence has been raised and, over the years, thousands of goats, cattle, pigs, and other animals removed from the park.

Aside from the *nene*, other endangered birds within the park are the *pueo* (owl), often seen soaring above open scrubland hunting for rodents, and the *'ua'u* (petrel), which nests on cliffs at about 8,000 feet but spends much of its time at sea fishing for food. Common forest birds that might be seen in native stands of trees, such as at Hosmer Grove, are the red *'apapane* and *'i'iwi*, and the yellowish green *'amakihi* and *'alauahio*. Also common, but introduced species, and more often seen along the road or on land with some cover are the ring-necked pheasant and chukar. Perhaps 400 or so species of insects live within the

park, and it's estimated that some 20 percent of these are found nowhere else than on Haleakala.

**Note:** A discussion of the Kipahulu section of the national park and its hiking and camping options is found in the Beyond Hana section of the East Maui Chapter.

## Weather

As high as it is, Haleakala helps create its own weather. Sunshine warms air that rises up the mountainside. When this moisture-laden air pushes into a cooler strata, it creates a band of clouds that moisten the forest and create what is known as the cloud forest. These clouds often push up into the basin itself, gushing up through the Ko'olau and Kaupo gaps, sometimes obscuring the basin from view. When there are clouds, they retreat back down the mountainside in the cool of the evening, leaving the basin clear once again. As air temperature drops about three degrees for every 1,000 feet, the top may be more than 30 degrees cooler than the sunny beaches along the Kihei coast below. Haleakala also traps moisture from the trade winds, so the high mountain slopes above Hana get about 400 inches of rain per year, creating thick forest cover, while the slopes above Makena and farther around to Kaupo, mostly dry and scrubby, get only a dozen inches yearly. Average temperatures at the park headquarters run 52°F in winter and 59°F in summer, with minimum and maximum of 30°F and 80°F, respectively. Monthly rainfall averages 1–2.5 inches May–Oct. and 4.5–10 Nov.–Apr. at park headquarters. The average annual rainfall is slightly less at the summit, but substantially more at the east end of the basin and nearly 200 inches per year in the Kipahulu area and valley above. In 2001, Haleakala received snow that stayed for three days. It was the first snow in a decade.

## The Experience

If you're after *the* Haleakala experience, you must see the sunrise or sunset. Both are magnificent and both perform their stupendous light show with astonishing speed. The sun, as it rises or sets, infuses the clouds with streaks, puffs, and bursts of dazzling pastels, at the same time backlighting and edging the basin in glorious golds and reds. If conditions are right, a rainbow may hang over the basin at sunset. Prepare for an emotional crescendo that will brim your eyes with tears at the majesty of it all. Engulfed by this magnificence, no one can remain unmoved. For this show of shows, the weather must be cooperative, and you may not be able to tell how it will be from down below. Misty, damp clouds can surround the basin, blocking out the sun, or pour into the basin, obscuring even it from view. Don't forget the wind. It's usually breezy at the top, which tends to drop the temperature even more, so wear appropriate clothing: jacket, hat, and gloves. The *Maui News* prints the hours of sunrise and sunset (on a daily basis) because they vary with the season, so make sure to check. The National Weather Service provides a daily weather recording at 808/877-5111. For more specific information, you can call the park headquarters at 808/572-4400 for a recorded message. Plan on taking a minimum of 90 minutes to arrive from Kahului, and to be safe, arrive at least 30 minutes before dawn or dusk, because even one minute is critical. For sunrise, the view from the edge of the basin is best. For sunset, hike up to the enclosure on top of Red Hill or sit just over the edge of the hill so you're out of the wind, on the west side of the parking lot.

**Note:** If you want to avoid downhill bikers and tourists, you can also get a great view from the Kalahaku Overlook. When you drive back down the mountain, shift into a low gear to control your speed to prevent riding the brakes.

### "Crater" Facts

Haleakala was formed by flow upon flow of lava. Lava is the hottest natural substance on earth, and it can run like a swift, fiery river. Because of the high viscosity of its lava and the generally nonexplosive nature of the volcanoes in Hawaii, they form classic shield volcanoes. Primarily smooth pahoehoe in form, plenty of 'a'a is also found in the mountain's composition. You'll be hiking over both, but be especially careful on 'a'a because its jagged edges will cut you as quickly as coral. While most activity ceased long long ago, some volcanic activity has been suspected within the basin as recently as 800 years ago. The basin is primarily formed from erosion, not from caving in on itself—hence not a crater, per se. The erosion on Hawaii is quite accelerated due to carbonic acid buildup, a by-product of the quick decomposition of abundant plant life. The rocks break down into smaller particles of soil, which are then washed off the mountain by rain or blown off by wind. Natural drainage

## HALEAKALA SPIRITUALITY

Although some doubt their authenticity, stories have led others to believe that certain *kahuna* brought their novitiates to Haleakala to perform final rites of initiation. Legends have said that intense power struggles took place atop the mountain between the healing practitioners, the *kahuna lapa'au*, and their rivals the *kahuna ana'ana*, the "black magic" sorcerers of old Hawaii. **Kawilinau,** a sulfur vent on the basin floor that's sometimes referred to as the "Bottomless Pit," was the site of an ancient battle between Pele and one of her siblings, and thus held tremendous significance for both schools of *kahuna*. Average Hawaiians did not live on Haleakala, but came now and again to quarry tool-stones. Only *kahuna* and their apprentices may have lived here for any length of time, as a sort of spiritual preparation and testing ground.

For some in the modern age, Haleakala is a power spot, a natural conductor of cosmic energy that attracts students of higher consciousness from around the world. They claim that it accelerates personal growth, and they compare it to remote mountain and desert areas in the Holy Lands. It is held that not only is there an energy configuration coming from the earth itself, but there is also a high focus of radiation coming from outside the atmosphere. Perhaps the mountain's mass accounts for the strange power ascribed to Haleakala as it sits like a mighty magnetic pyramid in the center of the North Pacific. No one is guaranteed a spiritual experience on Haleakala, but if you're at all sensitive, this is fertile ground.

Haleakala's crater basin is one of the most awe-inspiring sights on the island.

patterns form, and canyons begin to develop and slowly eat their way to the center. The two largest are **Koʻolau Gap** at the upper end of the Keʻanae Valley in the north and **Kaupo Gap** in the south. These canyons, over time, moved their heads past each other to the center of the mountain, where they took several thousand feet off the summit. Following this great erosion, the mountain erupted time and again, forming a huge amphitheater-like basin, most often referred to as Haleakala Crater. Extra spilled into and filled up both major canyons, hence the solidified flow that appears today coming from both ends of the crater. For more information on Haleakala's volcanic history, see http://hvo.wr.usgs.gov/volcanoes/haleakala.

Some stones that you encounter while hiking will be very lightweight. They once held water and gases that evaporated. If you knock two together, they'll sound like crystal. Also, look out for Maui diamonds, a crystalline mineral called pyroxene.

The cinder cones in the basin are fascinating. They're volcanic vents with a high iron content. Climbing them violates park rules made to protect endangered plants and threatened insects that pollinate them. Notice the color of the compacted earth on the trails. It's obvious why you should remain on them. Plants like the *ʻahinahina* (silversword) are shallow-rooted and live by condensing moisture on their leaves. Don't walk too close to them because you'll compact the earth around them and damage the roots. The ecosystem on Haleakala is very delicate, so please keep this in mind to better preserve its beauty for future generations.

## SIGHTS

You'll start enjoying Haleakala long before you reach the top. Don't make the mistake of simply bolting up the mountain without taking time to enjoy what you're passing. Route 37 from Kahului takes you through Pukalani, the last big place to buy supplies. There it branches to clearly marked Route 377. In six miles the zigzag Route 378 or **Haleakala Highway** heads more steeply up the mountain. Along the way are forests of indigenous and introduced trees, including eucalyptus, beautifully flowering jacaranda, and stands of cactus. The vistas change rapidly from one vantage point to the next. Sometimes it's the

MAUI

green rolling hills of Ireland, and then instantly it's the tall, yellow grass of the plains. This is also cattle country, so don't be surprised to see herds grazing as you roll past or on the road itself. Before ranchers and farmers cleared this land, the entire mountainside from Pukalani all the way up to Hosmer Grove was native forest.

## Headquarters

Admission to the park is $10 per car, $5 for bikers, hikers, and motorcycles, and is good for seven days; national park discount passes are honored. After paying your entrance fee, the first stopping point in the park is **Hosmer Grove Campground** (see Camping section), a short way down a secondary park road on your left. Proceed past this turnoff a few minutes and you'll arrive at **park headquarters,** elevation 7,000 feet, open daily 8 A.M.–4 P.M. Campers can get their permits here, and others will be happy to stop for all manner of brochures and information concerning the park, for water, or to use the toilet or pay phone. There are some 'ahinahina outside, and a few nene can occasionally be seen wandering the area. After you pass the park headquarters, zig and zag a couple more times, there's parking for Halemau'u Trail (see Hikes section). Following are two overlooks, **Leleiwi** and **Kalahaku.** Both offer tremendous views and different perspectives on the basin. They shouldn't be missed, especially Kalahaku, where there are 'ahinahina and the remnants of a travelers' lodge from the days when an expedition to Haleakala took two days.

## Visitors Center

Near road's end is the visitors center, elevation 9,740 feet, approximately 10 miles up the mountain from headquarters and a half-hour drive. You get one of the best views into the basin from here. It's open from sunrise to 3 P.M. and contains a clear and concise display featuring the basic geology of Haleakala. Maps and books are available, and ranger talks are particularly informative, delving into geology, natural and cultural history, and legends pertaining to this great mountain. A 15–20-minute ranger talk takes place daily at 9:30 A.M., 10:30 A.M., and 11:30 A.M. at the summit above the visitors center. Various ranger-

led hikes are also given, including the hike down Sliding Sands Trail and the Hosmer Grove forest walk. Additional interpretive talks and ranger-led hikes are conducted at the Kipahulu ranger station. Check with the park headquarters or the visitors center for times and days of programs. All horse rides into the basin and bike trips down the mountainside through the park start from the parking lot to the front of the visitors center. By 10 A.M., there will be lots of people at the top, so enjoy the time between when the bikers leave and the buses arrive. Before going farther, have a stop at the potty.

Bikes going down the mountain travel about 20–25 miles per hour, sometimes faster. If you're caught behind a string of bikes on your way down, just slow down and wait for them to pull over and let you pass.

# HIKING AND CAMPING
## Walks

One of the topside paths leads to **Pa Ka'oao** (White Hill). An easy quarter-mile hike will take you to the summit, and along the way you'll pass stone shelters and sleeping platforms from the days when Hawaiians came here to quarry the special tool-stone. It's a type of whitish slate that easily flakes but is so hard that when you strike two pieces together it rings almost like iron. Next comes **Pu'u 'Ula'ula** (Red Hill), the highest point on Maui at 10,023 feet. Atop is a glass-encased observation area (open 24 hours). This is where many people come to view the sunset. From here, if the day is crystal clear, you can see all of the main Hawaiian Islands except Kaua'i. To add some perspective to size and distance, it's 100 miles from the top of Haleakala to the volcanic peak Mauna Loa on the Big Island to the southeast. O'ahu is seldom seen and then only as a small bump on the horizon because it's some 140 miles away. Behind you on the slope below is **Maui Space Surveillance Complex,** a research facility with eight telescopes that's used by the University of Hawaii, and a satellite tracking station that's staffed by the U.S. Air Force. Closed to the public, tours of these facilities are no longer given. For more information, check www.ifa.hawaii

.edu/haleakala in reference to the research site and www.maui.afmc.af.mil for the military site.

The easy **Hosmer Grove Nature Trail** leads you through a stand of introduced temperate zone trees planted in 1910 to see if any would be good for commercial lumber use. There are perhaps a dozen different species of trees here, and the walk should take a half hour or so over mostly level ground. Originally planted in separate areas, these trees and others have intermingled now. Here you will see Jeffrey pine, ponderosa pine, lodgepole pine, incense cedar, eucalyptus, Norway spruce, eastern red cedar, Douglas fir, and Japanese sugi. Several signs are posted along the trail to explain what the trees are and how the forest developed. This is a good spot to look for native birds.

Halfway up the hill and a completely different environment, a one-quarter-mile **nature walk** leads you from a parking lot to the Leleiwi Overlook. Along the way you find low shrubs and alpine plants rather than trees and thick vegetation. Views from the overlook into the crater basin are well worth the walk.

Various **ranger-led walks** are given during the week, leaving either from the visitors center or from Hosmer Grove campground. On Mondays and Thursdays at 9 A.M., a naturalist leads a hike down into the Waikamoi cloud forest from Hosmer Grove, and on this hike you'll learn about trees, birds, and natural features of the area. This hike is three hours, three miles, and moderately strenuous. A ranger-led hike also goes down the Sliding Sands trail on a Cinder Desert Hike on Tuesdays and Fridays at 9 A.M. from the trailhead at the visitors center parking lot. The two-mile walk takes about two hours and is moderately strenuous.

## Hikes

There are three major trails in Haleakala Wilderness Area (Halemau'u, Sliding Sands, and Kaupo) and several connecting trails—about 27 miles of trails in all. **Halemau'u Trail** starts at the 8,000-foot level along the road about three miles past the park headquarters. It descends quickly by way of switchbacks to the 6,600-foot level on the basin floor, offering expansive views of Ko'olau Gap along the way. En route you'll pass

Holua Cabin, Silversword Loop and Kawilinau sulfur vent (the "Bottomless Pit"—a mere 65 feet deep), and junctions with both the Sliding Sands and Kaupo trails before you reach Paliku Cabin. If you go out via the Sliding Sands Trial and visitors center, you shouldn't have any trouble hitching back to your car left at the Halemau'u trailhead.

**Sliding Sands** begins at the summit of Haleakala near the visitors center. This could be considered the main trail into the basin and gives you the best overall hike, with up-close views of cinder cones, lava flows, and unique vegetation. It joins the Halemau'u Trail more than one mile west of the Paliku Cabin. Near Kapalaoa Cabin, you can turn left to Kawilinau and exit via Halemau'u Trail, or circle around by way of other connecting trails and exit the way you came. Exiting the Halemau'u Trail is a good choice, but you'll have to hitch back to your car at the visitors center.

The **Kaupo Trail** is long and tough. It descends rapidly through the Kaupo Gap to the park boundary at 3,880 feet. Below 4,000 feet the lava is rough and the vegetation thick. It then crosses private land, which is no problem, and after a steep and rocky downhill grade along well-marked trails deposits you in the semi-ghost town of Kaupo, on the dry rugged southern slope of the mountain. You'll have to hitch west just to get to the scant traffic of Route 31, or head nine miles east to Kipahulu and its campground, and from there back along the Hana Road.

For those inclined, Pony Express offers horse tours into the basin. Hikers should also consider a day with the professional guide service Hike Maui. The guide's in-depth knowledge and commentary will make your trip not only more fulfilling, but enjoyably informative as well.

## Hikers

Serious hikers or campers must have sturdy shoes, good warm clothes, raingear, plenty of water, down sleeping bags, and a serviceable tent (unless you've reserved one of the cabins). Hats and sunglasses are needed. Compasses are useless because of the high magnetism in the rock, but binoculars are particularly rewarding. No cook-fires are allowed in the basin, so you'll need a stove. Don't burn any dead wood because the soil needs all of the decomposing nutrients it can get. Water is usually available at all of the cabins within the basin, but the supply is limited and must be treated before use, so bring what you will need. This environment is particularly delicate. Stay on the established trails so you don't cause undue erosion. Leave rocks and especially plants alone. Don't walk too close to 'ahinahina or any other plants because you'll compact the soil. Leave your pets at home; ground-nesting birds here are easily disturbed. If nature calls, dig a very shallow hole, off the trail, and pack out your used toilet paper because the very dry conditions are not conducive to it biodegrading. Best is to use the pit toilets at the campsites if at all possible.

## Camping

Camping is free with a necessary camping permit from park headquarters. The **Hosmer Grove campground,** named after Ralph Hosmer, is at the 6,800-foot level, just before park headquarters; the free camping here is limited to three nights and to 50 people, but there's generally room for all. There's water, pit toilets, picnic tables, grills, and a pavilion. While here take a stroll along the half-mile forest loop that threads its way through the grove of trees that Hosmer planted.

**Kipahulu Campground** is a primitive camping area on the coast near 'Ohe'o Stream. It's part of the park, but unless you're an intrepid hiker and descend all the way down the Kaupo Trail, you'll come to it via Hana.

There are cabins in the basin at **Holua, Kapalaoa,** and **Paliku,** each with twelve padded bunk beds and a pit toilet. Tent camping is allowed at Holua and Paliku. Cabins at any of these sites are extremely popular, and reservations must be sent in advance by mail at least three months ahead. Each cabin is reserved for one group of up to 12 people only. A lottery of the applicants chosen for sites keeps it fair for all. Environmental impact studies limit the number of campers to

25 per area per day. Camping is limited to a total of three days per month, with no more than two consecutive days at each spot. Rates for cabin use are $40 for up to six persons and $80 to a maximum of 12 people. For complete details and reservation form, contact Haleakala National Park, P.O. Box 369, Makawao, HI 96768, 808/572-4400. If writing by mail, include the note "attn. cabins" on the outside of the envelope. Visit the park's website at www.nps.gov/hale.

## Making Do

If you've come to Hawaii for sun and surf and you aren't prepared for alpine temperatures, you can still enjoy Haleakala. For a day trip, wear a windbreaker or jacket and your jogging suit or a sweater, if you've brought one. Make sure to wear socks, and even bring an extra pair as makeshift mittens. Use your dry beach towel to wrap around inside your sweater as extra insulation, and even consider taking your hotel blanket, which you can use Indian fashion. Make raingear from a large plastic garbage bag with holes cut for head and arms; this is also a good windbreaker. Take your beach hat, too. Don't worry about looking ridiculous in this get-up—you will! But you'll also keep warm! Remember that for every thousand feet you climb, the temperature drops three degrees Fahrenheit, so the summit is about 30 degrees cooler than at sea level. As the sun reaches its zenith, if there are no rain clouds, the basin floor will go from about 50°F to 80°F. It can flip-flop from hot to dismal and rainy several times in the same day. The nights may drop below freezing, with the coldest recorded temperature inside the basin a bone-chilling 14°F. Dawn and dusk are notorious for being bitter. Because of the altitude, be aware that the oxygen level will drop, and those with any impairing conditions should take precautions. The sun is ultra-strong atop the mountain, and even those with deep tans are subject to burning. Noses are particularly susceptible.

# East Maui

## The Road to Hana

On the long and winding road to Hana's door, most people's daydreams of paradise come true. A trip to Maui without a visit to Hana is like ordering a sundae without a cherry on top. The 50 miles from Kahului to Hana are some of the most remarkable in the world. The Hana Highway (Route 36) starts out innocently enough, passing Pa'ia. The inspiration for Pa'ia's gaily painted storefronts looks like it came from a jar of jelly beans. Next come some north-shore surfing beaches where sailboarders fly, doing amazing aquabatics. Soon there is a string of "rooster towns," so named because that's about all that seems to be stirring. Then Route 36 be-

comes Route 360, and at mile marker 3 the *real* Road to Hana begins.

The semiofficial count tallies more than 600 rollicking turns and 57 one-lane bridges, inducing everyone to slow down and soak up the sights of this glorious road. It's like passing through a tunnel cut from trees. The ocean winks with azure blue through sudden openings on your left. To the right, streams, waterfalls, and pools sit wreathed with jungle and wildflowers. Coconuts, guavas, mangos, and bananas grow everywhere on the mountainside. Fruit stands pop up now and again as you creep along. Then comes Ke'anae with its arboretum and taro farms, indicating that many ethnic Hawaiians still live along the road. There are places to camp, picnic, and swim, both in the ocean and in freshwater streams.

ROBERT NILSEN

**sailboarding at Ho'okipa Beach**

Along with you, every other car traveling the Hana Highway is on the road to take in the beauty that this coast has to offer. Nearly all visitors pass through, some stay a day or a week, while others take up residence. Islanders, mainlanders, and foreigners alike are enticed by the land, and under its spell they put down roots. George Harrison had a house a few miles down the coast in Nahiku, and Jim Nabors, Kris Kristofferson, and Carol Burnett maintain homes here.

Then you reach Hana itself, a remarkable town, the birthplace of the great Queen Ka'ahumanu. Past Hana, the road becomes even more rugged and besieged by jungle. It opens up again around 'Ohe'o Gulch. Here waterfalls cascade over stupendous cataracts, forming a series of pools until they reach the sea. Beyond is a rental car's no-man's land, where the passable road toughens and Haleakala shows its barren, volcanic face scarred by lava flows and covered by dryland forest.

# PA'IA

Pa'ia (Noisy) was a bustling sugar town that took a nap. When it awoke, it had a set of whiskers and its vitality had flown away. At the beginning of the 19th century, many groups of ethnic field workers lived here, segregated in housing clusters called camps that stretched up Baldwin Avenue. Pa'ia was the main gateway for sugar on East Maui, and even a plantation railroad functioned here until about 30 years ago. During the 1930s, its population, at more than 10,000, was the largest on the island. Then fortunes shifted toward Kahului, and Pa'ia lost its dynamism—until recently. Pa'ia was resuscitated in the 1970s by an influx of paradise-seeking hippies, and then again in the '80s came another shot in the arm from sailboarders. These two groups have metamorphosed into townsfolk and have pumped new life into Pa'ia's old muscles. The practical shops catering to the pragmatic needs of a plantation town were replaced. The storefronts were painted and spruced up. A new breed of merchants with their eyes on passing tourists has taken over. Now Pa'ia focuses on boutiques, crafts, artwork, and food. It also has a golf course in Spreckelsville, a high-end residential neighborhood to the west. Opened in

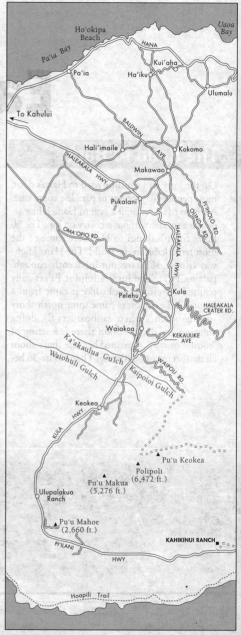

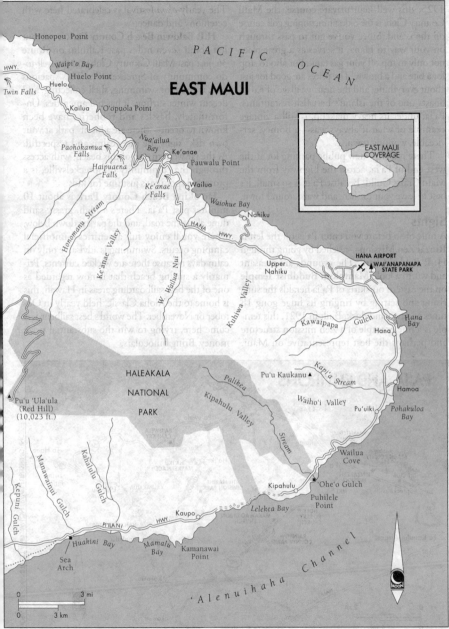

PACIFIC          OCEAN

Honopou Point

Waipi'o Bay
HWY.          Huelo Point
Twin Falls    Huelo
              Kailua    'O'opuola Point

Paohokamua
Falls              Nua'ailua
                   Bay        Ke'anae
Haipuaena                Pauwalu Point
Falls
       Ke'anae    Wailua
       Falls                Waiohue Bay
                                Nahiku

**EAST MAUI**

EAST MAUI
COVERAGE

HANA
HWY.

HANA AIRPORT
WAI'ANAPANAPA
STATE PARK

Upper
Nahiku

Hana
Bay

Kawaipapa   Gulch   Hana

Kuhiwa Valley                        Kapi'a Stream

Honomanu Stream

Ke'anae Valley

W. Wailua Nui

HALEAKALA

NATIONAL

PARK

Pu'u 'Ula'ula
(Red Hill)
(10,023 ft.)

Palikea        Pu'u Kaukanu

Kipahulu Valley

Waiho'i Valley

Hamoa

Pu'uiki
Pohakuloa
Bay

Stream

Wailua
Cove

Maiiawainui Gulch

Kahalulu Gulch

Kepuni Gulch

Kipahulu        'Ohe'o Gulch
                Puhilele
Lelekea Bay     Point

P'ILANI   HWY.   Kaupo

Huakini Bay      Mamalu
                 Bay   Kamanawai
Sea              Point
Arch

'Alenuihaha    Channel

0        3 mi
0        3 km

MOON

M

MAUI

© SANDRA E. BISIGNANI TRUST AND AVALON TRAVEL PUBLISHING, INC.

1925, this well-kept private course, the Maui Country Club, is the oldest functioning golf course on the island. Since you've got to pass through on your way to Hana, it serves as a great place not only to top off your gas tank, but also to stop for a bite and a browse. The prices are good for just about everything, and the nearby village of Ku'au boasts one of the island's best fish restaurants. Pa'ia, under its heavy makeup, is still a vintage example of what it always was—a homey, serviceable, working town.

There is a large new public parking lot at the west end of Pa'ia, across the highway from the Maui Crafts Guild. Because Pa'ia is so small, it's best to leave your car here and walk around town.

## Sights

A mile or so before you enter Pa'ia on the left is **Rinzai Zen Mission**—reached by going through H. P. Baldwin Park. The grounds are pleasant and worth a look. **Mantokuji Buddhist Temple** on the eastern outskirts of Pa'ia heralds the sun's rising and setting by ringing its huge gong 18 times at dawn and dusk. Built in 1921, this temple is a fine example of a Zen mission structure and perhaps the best representative on Maui.

The yearly *obon* festival is celebrated here with ceremony and dance.

**H.P. Baldwin Beach County Park** is on your left about seven miles past Kahului on Route 36, just past Maui Country Club and the well-to-do community of Spreckelsville. This spacious park is good for swimming, shell-collecting, and decent winter surfing. It has full amenities. Unfortunately, hassles and robberies have been known to occur—there are a lot of "park at your own risk" signs. Be nice, calm, and respectful. At the far western end of this beach, with access through the community of Spreckelsville, is a protected spot that's just fine for kids.

**Ho'okipa Beach County Park** is about 10 minutes past Pa'ia. There's a high, grassy sand dune along the road, and the park is down below, where you'll enjoy full amenities—unofficial camping occurs. Swimming is advisable only on calm days because there are wicked currents. Primarily a surfing beach that is now regarded as one of the best sailboarding areas in Hawaii, this is home to the Aloha Classic, held yearly in October or November. The world's best sailboarders come here, trying to win the substantial prize money. Bring binoculars.

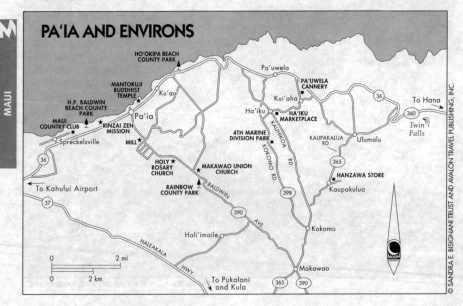

PA'IA AND ENVIRONS

© SANDRA E. BISIGNANI TRUST AND AVALON TRAVEL PUBLISHING, INC.

## Accommodations

One of the few place to lodge in Pa'ia is at the **Nalu Kai Lodge,** 808/579-8009, located down the alley just off the T intersection where Baldwin Avenue meets the Hana Highway; ask for Myrna. This plain and simple two-story cement-block building offers clean, quiet, adequate rooms. Don't expect anything fancy, just the necessities; no TV and no telephones, linoleum floors, and fans in some rooms. Rates vary—Myrna bargains—but expect to spend about $40 for one night or $350 for a month. There are seven units, one double and six singles. Many people stay long-term.

Surfers and others looking for very inexpensive accommodations can find space in a house at 151 Hana Highway, only a few steps from the center of Pa'ia. Basically a house turned into a rental pad, where dorm beds go for $20 per day and a private room $40 per day. Call 808/579-8015 for more information.

Just east of Pa'ia, before you get to Ku'au, is **The Spyglass House,** 367 Hana Hwy., Paia, HI 96779, 808/579-8608 or 800/475-6695, relax @spyglassmaui.com, www.spyglassmaui.com. With rooms and suites, or combinations thereof, in three houses, it has plenty of options to choose from. Set nearly on the water with a hot tub in the yard, this is a restful, breezy, modern place with bright colors and a marine motif. Rooms in the main house run $120–150 per night, in the Dolphin House $90–120. Next door, the Blue Tile House has rooms and two suites for $90–250. Rentals for fewer than three nights are charged a $30 cleaning fee.

About a mile away in the tiny community of Ku'au is the **Kuau Plaza Condo,** 808/579-8080, fax 808/579-8533. Rooms have private baths and color televisions. Laundry facilities are located on premises. These rooms are nothing special, but they get you close to Maui's best surfing spots, and it's just a skip down the road from Pa'ia. Rooms and suites generally run $40–70 per night.

Fronting the beach next to Mama's Fish House is **The Inn at Mama's Fish House,** 799 Poho Place, Paia, HI 96779, 808/579-9764 or 800/860-4852, fax 808/579-8594, www.mamasfishhouse.com. Close to the action but not bothered by the hubbub of town, this is very much a tropical hideaway. Hidden by foliage from the restaurant and the neighbor houses, one-bedroom and two-bedroom units, each nicely furnished, come complete with a modern kitchen and entertainment center, air-conditioning, telephone, and lanai with gas grill. The one-bedroom unit runs $175 per night, while the larger units go for $350; three nights minimum.

For all sorts of vacation rentals in Pa'ia, the Northshore, and other areas of the island, contact **Ho'okipa Haven Vacation Services,** 808/579-8282 or 800/398-6284, fax 808/579-9953, info@hookipa.com, www.hookipa.com. This company has rental units from studios along a stream for $70 per night to luxury homes for more than $1,000 per night.

## Food

There are more than a handful of restaurants in and around Pa'ia that cater to all type of palates. The following is a sampling, listed roughly from inexpensive to expensive.

Offering an alternative for the java jock is the easygoing **Anthony's Coffee,** on Baldwin Avenue, 808/579-8340, where you can get coffee by the cup or a pound to go. Come for breakfast and pastries or try a lunch sandwich or ice cream as you hang out and read the paper.

**Picnic's,** 30 Baldwin Ave., 808/579-8021, is open daily 7 A.M.–3 P.M. Breakfast and lunch offer everything from eggs and pancakes to plate lunches and vegetarian sandwiches, like the famous spinach nut burger, all under $8. The best options are boxed picnic lunches that add a special touch if you're heading to Hana. They start from the basic Upcountry Picnic, which includes sandwiches and sides at $8.50 per person, to the Holo Holo Pikiniki for four, with all the fixings for sandwiches, herb-roasted chicken, sides, condiments, dessert, and even a tablecloth all in a Styrofoam ice chest for $52. Picnic's is one of the best stops along the Hana Road even for a quick espresso, cappuccino, or frozen yogurt. Or treat yourself with the fresh-baked pastries like macadamia nut sticky buns and the apple and papaya turnovers: worth the guilt!

The **Hokus Pokus,** 115 Baldwin Ave.,

808/579-9144, open daily 3–9 P.M., is an extraordinary health-conscious restaurant that those into healthy food frequent. You won't come here for the decor, you'll come for the large portions of incredibly delicious food. Hokus Pokus serves only vegetarian food made with organic products and uses no meat; the food is mostly cholesterol-free. Standard menu items include hummus salad at $6.50, the tempeh burger for $5.95, tofu soft tacos for $9.50, curry veggies at $10.95, and polenta au gratin for $9.95; specials nightly. Luscious smoothies are priced at $3.25. Sit at one of the few tables inside, or call ahead for orders to go.

At the corner is the **Paia Fish Market,** 808/579-8030, a casual sit-down restaurant with picnic tables inside. Specializing in charbroiled fish, the menu also includes more than a dozen types of fish and seafood, all at market price, that can be prepared in one of four different manners. You can also have charbroiled chicken, blackened sashimi, seafood salad, or fresh fish to take home and prepare yourself. Open for lunch and dinner 11 A.M.–9:30 P.M., the menu also includes burgers, pasta, and fajitas. Most lunch and dinner plates run $7–15, but the fish entrées may be more expensive. This is a perennial favorite.

**Cafe des Amis,** 42 Baldwin Ave., 808/579-6323, is a small eatery featuring a mixture of French and Indian foods. On the menu are crepes, like spinach with feta, ham and gruyere, or roast vegetables, feta, and pesto for $6–8. Dinner entrées might include beef and mushroom, shrimp, or vegetable curries in the $9–12 range. Coffee, tea, smoothies, and lassi are available to drink, but you can bring your own bottle of wine if you like. Open 8:30 A.M.–8:30 P.M., you'll find Cafe des Amis an intimate place with energetic music and food that will delight your taste buds.

For a quick bite, you have **Charley's,** 808/579-9453, a restaurant specializing in pizza, pasta, and sandwiches that's open 7 A.M. for breakfast, from 11:30 for lunch, and from 5 P.M. for dinner. Charley's is a gathering place for breakfast and has items like huevos rancheros for $7.95. For lunch, select a fish sandwich for $8.25 or burgers for around $9. Some dinner specials, like fettuccini Alfredo at about $15, are more pricey but still

very reasonable. Soups, salads, and appetizers are priced equally well. In the back is a saloon with a long bar, booths, pool tables, and occasional live music. This is a big, rambling, amiable place, a town institution, where tourists and locals alike come for a pleasant time, and the bar is a good afternoon hangout for locals.

Across the street and also on the corner, a great place to people-watch or be watched is **Milagros Bar and Restaurant,** 808/579-8755. Milagros does burgers, sandwiches, and fish; eat inside or outside on the patio along the sidewalk. This is semi-Mexican fare with sandwiches and burgers in the $6–8 range and dinners like seafood enchiladas and grilled ahi burritos mostly $12–16. Milagros has a full bar so you can ease into the evening with a tropical margarita, south-of-the-border beer, glass of fine wine, or well drink.

Having moved up the street, reworked the menu, and created a whole new environment, **Jacques Northshore,** 808/579-8844, is now a festive, colorful, happening restaurant and bar with outdoor lanai seating under umbrellas and an indoor sushi bar. Whether it's meat or fish, Jacques serves the freshest. Lunch brings a long list of appetizers, many sandwiches, and a few main entrées all under $12, but perhaps the dinner menu is more memorable. Start with a pumpkin coconut soup with diced scallops or shiitake salmon shrimp coconut ravioli appetizer, or a fried tofu salad or salad Niçoise. Several pasta dishes are favorites, but entrées like fresh fish, oven-roasted pork, spicy peanut chicken, sautéed beef, or seafood curry are special. Dinner entrées run mostly $16–20. A lively place with food at a reasonable price make Jacques a winner.

**Moana Bakery and Cafe,** 71 Baldwin Ave., 808/579-9999, is another good choice. Food is served 8 A.M.–9 P.M., and baked goods are always available from the deli case. Breakfast is mostly egg dishes, griddle items, and saimin, while lunch choices include salads, sandwiches, and wraps. Dinner is more substantial, with dishes like island pesto pasta, chili-seared ahi, and medallions of filet mignon, $11–27. To top it off, there's live jazz or Hawaiian music on some evenings—no cover.

**Mama's Fish House,** 808/579-8488, where

reservations are highly recommended, is just past Pa'ia in Ku'au and on the left heading toward Hana. Look for the turnoffs near the blinking yellow light; you'll see a vintage car with a sign for Mama's, a ship's flagpole, and a fishing boat marking the entranceway. There's plenty of off-road complimentary valet parking. Mama's, serving lunch 11 A.M.–2:30 P.M., cocktails and *pu pu* until dinner at 5 P.M., has earned the best reputation possible—it gets thumbs up from local people even though it is expensive. It's perhaps the best upscale beach shack on the island, set right on the water surrounded by coconut trees and tiki torches with outrigger canoes drawn up on the lawn out front. The fish is caught fresh daily, with some broiled over *kiawe,* while the vegetables come from local gardens and the herbs are Mama's own. Fish entrées run $30–39 for dinner, other items are $29–49. For a meal with the same special flavors but a bit easier on the pocketbook, stop by for lunch. Special Hawaiian touches, wonderful food, friendly professional service, and a great view of Maui's north shore add to the enjoyment of every meal. A terrific idea is to make reservations here for the evening's return trip from Hana.

For groceries and foodstuffs, try the following: **Mana Natural Foods,** 49 Baldwin Ave., 808/579-8078, open daily 8:30 A.M.–8:30 P.M., is a well-stocked health food store, one of the best on Maui, that's kind of funky and still not "modernized." Inside the old building you'll find shelves full of local organic produce, vitamins, grains, juices, bulk foods, and more. For takeout, try the salad bar for about $5 per pound or the hot entrée bar with items at various prices, or look for picnic items in the cooler. Outside, check out the great community bulletin board for what's selling and happening around Pa'ia and to find rental housing.

Just before Baldwin Avenue along the Hana Highway is **Nagata Store,** a general grocery store with a seafood department that's open Monday–Friday 6 A.M.–7 P.M., Saturday 6 A.M.–6 P.M., Sunday 6 A.M.–1 P.M.

The **Wine Cooler,** at the corner of Baldwin Ave. and the Hana Hwy., is a well-stocked bottle shop with a superb selection of wines, liquor, and ice-cold beer. Microbreweries are well represented. Open 11 A.M.–9:30 P.M. most days and until 10 P.M. on some days.

## Shopping

**Maui Crafts Guild,** 43 Hana Hwy., P.O. Box 609, Pa'ia, HI 96779, 808/579-9697, www.mauicraftsguild.com, is on the left just as you enter Pa'ia. Open daily 9 A.M.–6 P.M., the Crafts Guild is one of the best art outlets in Hawaii. It's owned and operated by the artists themselves, now numbering more than two dozen, all of whom must pass a thorough jurying by present members. All artists must be islanders, and they must use natural materials found in Hawaii to create their work except for some specialized clay, fabrics, and printmaking paper. Items are tastefully displayed, and you'll find a wide variety of artwork and crafts, including pottery, prints, woodwork, stone art, bamboo work, fiber art, silk painting, and jewelry. Different artists staff the shop on different days, but business cards and phone numbers are available if you want to see more of something you like. Prices are reasonable, and this is an excellent place to make that one big purchase.

Along the Hana Highway before you get to Baldwin Avenue is **Paia Trading Co.,** a discovery shop open Monday–Friday 9 A.M.–5 P.M. with collectibles like glass, telephones, aloha shirts, lanterns, jewelry, license plates, oil lamps, flotation balls, old bottles, and a smattering of pottery and antique furniture. Next door is **Boutique II,** open daily 10 A.M.–6 P.M., Sunday to 4 P.M., filled with ladies' apparel and alohawear. **Nuage Bleu,** a boutique open daily 10 A.M.–5 P.M., features distinctive fashions and gift items, mostly for women. **Jaggers,** open daily 9 A.M.–5 P.M., carries alohawear, fancy dresses, replicas of vintage aloha shirts for men, and some umbrellas. **Maui Hands** is nearby and has prints, turned wood, and some paper art pieces. Across the street is a shaved ice shop and **Sand and Sea,** primarily a sculpture gallery featuring dolphins.

Around the corner and open daily until 6 P.M. is **Paia Mercantile,** displaying a collection of quilts, wooden boxes, hand-blown glass, jewelry, and many more intriguing craft items. Nearby is the **Hemp House,** a shop that carries hemp clothing, bags, accessories, soap, smoking

MAUI

paraphernalia, and information on hemp fiber and its uses. Here too is **Moon Beam Tropics,** carrying women's sundresses, men's aloha shirts, shorts, T-shirts, and other islandwear. Walk along the opposite side of Baldwin Avenue for a half block and you'll find a drawerful of boutiques and fashion shops, including **Old Plantation Store** for Hawaiian gifts, crafts, and clothing; **Lotus Moon** for jewelry, **Neccesaries Boutique** antique and curio shop of "Hawaiian Bohemian Funk;" and **Mandala Ethnic Arts,** which carries furniture, clothing, gifts, statues, and alternative art from South and Southeast Asia. All are interesting shops and worth a peek.

A bit farther along Baldwin Avenue is a branch **Bank of Hawaii** building and quite a bit farther up the new **post office** and laundromat. For the sailboarder, look for boards and gear at **HT High Tech Surf Sports.** At this and other surf shops in town, you can dress yourself for the beach and get a board to ride over those waves.

Pa'ia has three **gas stations: 76,** which has made-to-order sandwiches at its minimart, a **Chevron,** and a newer **Shell** station on the west end of town with a mini-mart. These gas stations are the last places to fill your tank before reaching Hana. Next door to the 76 station is **Paia General Store** (open until 9 P.M.) for groceries, supplies, and sundries, with a take-out snack window called the **Paia Drive Inn** (6 A.M.–2 P.M.), where most "local food" is under $7. Next to that, in what was at one time the Lower Pa'ia Theater, is **Simmer** sailboard shop. Simmer sells clothing, boards, components, and accessories, does sail repair, and rents boards. Lessons can also be arranged. Across the street is the **Pa'ia Mercantile Shopping Complex,** a collection of little shops ranging from surfing equipment to beads and gifts.

Heading down the road to Hana you'll see a community center on your right, the Mantokuji Buddhist temple on your left, and a little farther on the **Kuau Market,** a convenience store to get snacks for the road that's open daily 6 A.M.–7 P.M. Just around the bend is **Mama's Fish House,** and shortly after Ho'okipa Beach,

near mile marker 14 on the mountain side of the highway, you'll come across **Maui Grown Market and Deli.** Housed in a vintage corrugated roof plantation-style building with a porch out front, it carries mostly sandwiches, plate lunches, salads, smoothies, drinks, and packaged food items, with a limited supply of fresh produce. Lunch boxes are a specialty. Open daily 6:30 A.M.–6 P.M., this is the last place you'll see before you really start to wind your way down the Hana Highway. A public phone is out front. Aside from side trips to Ha'iku, Kui'aha, and Ulumalu, you'll have clear sailing down the road to Hana.

## HA'IKU

Around mile marker 11, Ha'iku Road heads up the hill to the little community of Ha'iku. From Upcountry, follow Kokomo Road down the hill after turning off Route 365 below Makawao. Kokomo Road runs past the 4th Marine Division Park, a community park of athletic fields and a few picnic tables that was the site of the World War II 4th Marine Division camp. Ha'iku is an old cannery town, canning, boxing, and sending millions of pineapples and guavas to the world over the decades. After the cannery companies stopped production, their industrial buildings were renovated and turned into shops and studios, and have become, along with the Pa'uwela Cannery down the road, a center for artists and craftspeople. In the largest of the old cannery buildings, the pineapple cannery, now called **Ha'iku Marketplace,** you'll find among the many shops here a **True Value Hardware** store, the **Haleakala Bike Company** shop for sales and rental, **Haiku Video, Ha'iku Pharmacy, Ha'iku Laundromat, Postal Plus, Colleen's Bakeshop and Haiku Cannery Pizza,** and the **Ha'iku Grocery Store,** open daily and a good place to pick up supplies. For what's happening in and around town, check out the community bulletin board around the side. To the side of the huge parking lot in a separate building is **Hana Hou Cafe,** 808/575-2661, a wonderful local-style eatery that has indoor and patio seating with a take-out window with the same menu. And what's more, there's live music by the owner on Thursday, Friday, and Saturday evenings. The menu contains mostly plate lunches, but pasta, burgers, and full meal dinners are also available, and most items run $7–17.

Also at the main intersection is **Fukushima Store,** a mini-mart that's open daily 6:30 A.M.–8 P.M., Sunday until 5 P.M. Here too you'll find a community bulletin board. For a quick bite to eat, stop around the corner at **Haiku Gourmet Takeout and Deli,** a small place with only a few tables inside. Open 6 A.M.–8 P.M., you have your choice of breakfast items, deli salads, pastries, and sandwiches, and in the evening, more substantial entrées like prime rib, spicy chicken, and Thai veggie stir-fry for around $12. Across Ha'iku Road is the **post office,** and tucked behind it is **Ha'iku Town Center,** the second of the big remodeled cannery buildings that's been turned into space for other use. This was the guava cannery. Among other shops you'll find **The Hemp Stock,** a small shop dealing almost entirely with the numerous and various products made from the hemp plant. Stop by daily 10 A.M.–5 P.M. to see what great products they carry, most of it made in the studio in back. Check out what they have or order online at www.sativahempwear.com. Just up the line is **Veg Out,** 808/575-5320, a vegetarian restaurant open Monday–Friday 10:30 A.M.–7:30 P.M. and Saturday 11:30–6. Every Saturday from 8 A.M.–noon, you can find a **farmers market** in front of this center for local produce and crafts.

Ha'iku Road runs east, wending its way in and out of gulches, over bridges, and through thickly vegetated forests to the community of Kui'aha. This is a great way to see the back roads of lower mountain Maui. There are lots of roads in this area, and many people have settled here, carving out their little bit of paradise. An alternate road to Kuiaha from the Hana Highway starts just past mile marker 12. Look for West Kui'aha Road and make a right heading for the old **Pa'uwela Cannery,** which is less than five minutes up the road. This huge tin can of a building has been divided into a hon-

eycomb of studios and workshops housing fine artists, woodworkers, potters, T-shirt makers, and surfboard and sailboard makers. These artists and craftspeople come and go, so you're never sure just who will be occupying the studios. **Hawaiian Fish Prints Gallery** is one of these places. It's unique focus is making color prints from actual sea creatures. While here, be sure to stop at the **Pauwela Cafe** for a cold drink, hot coffee, salad, sandwich, or pastry. Sit inside or out. Open Monday–Saturday 7 A.M.–3 P.M., Sunday 8 A.M.–2 P.M. For other needs, try the small **Ohashi General Store** across and a bit up the street; open 8 A.M. to about 6 P.M.

Not situated along the coast but in the forest above Ulumalu is **Lanikai Farm,** P.O. Box 797, Ha'iku, HI 96708, 808/572-1111 or 800/484-2523, fax 808/572-3498, lanibb@maui.net, www.maui.net/~lanibb. This "Victorian-European style" newer home lies next to the Ko'olau Forest Reserve and is surrounded by tropical fruit trees. The guest rooms have private entrances, TVs, small refrigerators, and lanai, and there is use of the washer/dryer and barbecue grill. A scrumptious breakfast of European-style breads and fresh fruit is served every morning. Rates are $65 single, $70 double, or $100 for two rooms; two nights minimum. A studio rental without breakfast runs $80 or two rooms for $105. The athletically inclined might want to have a turn on the squash court on property.

Just down the road at 81 Lanikai Place is **Lanikai Vacation Rentals.** Set next to a stream and small waterfall, this property has two rental units. The Garden Suite is a quiet two-bedroom, two-bath unit with full kitchen that goes for $95 per night or $600 per week. Around back and more secluded is Hale Nahele, a one-room unit with a small kitchen and deck that overhangs the streambank. Perfect for a romantic couple, this unit runs $75 per night or $450 per week. Three nights minimum for either unit; cash or traveler's checks please. For information and reservations, contact Dharmo Feldmann, tel/fax 808/573-0750, lanikaivacations@maui.net, www.maui.net/~dharmo/lanikai.

MAUI

## THE ROAD BEGINS

The Road to Hana holds many spectacles and surprises, but one of the best is the road itself . . . it's a marvel! The road was hacked out from the coastline and completed in 1927, every inch by hand using pick and shovel. Crushed volcanic rock was the first surface material. Rebuilt and partially paved in 1962, only in 1982 was the road fully paved. Mother nature and man's machines have taken their toll on the road, and in the early '90s, the Hana Highway was widened and again resurfaced. Today it's smooth sailing, although stretches are periodically closed for repair. An ancient Hawaiian trail followed the same route for part of the way, but mostly people moved up and down this coastline by boat. What makes the scenery so special is that the road snakes along Maui's windward side. There's abundant vegetation and countless streams flowing from Haleakala, carving gorgeous valleys. There are a few scattered villages with a house or two that you hardly notice, and the beaches, although few, are empty. Mostly, however, it's the feeling that you get along this road. Nature is close and accessible, and it's so incredibly "South Sea island" that it almost seems artificial—but it isn't.

## SIGHTS

### Twin Falls

A favorite of locals, the trail to Twin Falls should take about 20–30 minutes. It's one of the first places to stop and enjoy along the road. Park near mile marker 2 just before the Ho'olawa Bridge. A metal gate marks the jeep trail. This is private property and people live back here, but everyone seems to use it as if it were open to all. There's even a fruit stand at the entrance and a sign along the jeep trail pointing to the falls. On the way, a couple of side trails go off to the left and down to the stream. Guavas grow in this area, and you might find ripe fruit at the right time of the year—there used to be a guava cannery in Ha'iku not far away. Before you get to an irrigation ditch, a small trail heads off to the left and leads to the stream and falls. The first pool is fed by two falls that give the area its name. A trail to the right

Twin Falls makes a refreshing stop along the road to Hana.

ROBERT NILSEN

goes up to the top of the falls and on to a second falls a short distance above. There you'll have more privacy. If you continue on to the irrigation ditch, cross it, and enter a secondary ravine, the trail will lead you to another small falls.

### Huelo

A few miles past the new bridge and pulloff for Twin Falls is Huelo. Huelo means "Famous Owl," a name given for the birds that used to inhabit trees in the area. In the 1840s, Huelo was a bustling sugar town surrounded by cane fields and even sustained a mill. Later, the area grew pineapples and then reverted to a quiet "rooster town." Now it's not a town at all anymore, just a collection of homes and hobie ranches, but it's still known for the **Kaulanapueo Church,** built in 1853. This structure is made from coral that was hauled up block by block from Waipi'o Bay below and is reminiscent of New England architecture. It's still used on the second and fourth Sundays of each month at 10 A.M., and a peek through the

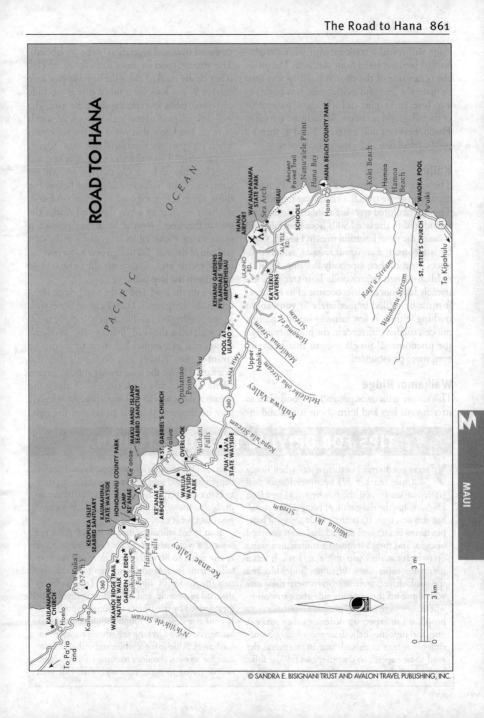

## ROAD TO HANA

PACIFIC

OCEAN

To Pa'ia and

KAULANAPUEO CHURCH

Huelo

Kailua

Pu'u Kuka'i (574 ft)

360

WAIKAMOI RIDGE TRAIL NATURE WALK

GARDEN OF EDEN

Puohokamoa Falls

Haipua'ena Falls

Ni'ili'ili'ehu Stream

KEOPUKA ISLET SEABIRD SANCTUARY

KAUMAHINA STATE WAYSIDE

HONOMANU COUNTY PARK

MAKU MANU ISLAND SEABIRD SANCTUARY

Ke'anae

CAMP KE'ANAE

ST. GABRIEL'S CHURCH

KE'ANAE ARBORETUM

Ke'anae Valley

WAILUA WAYSIDE PARK

Wailua

OVERLOOK

Waikani Falls

PUA'A KA'A STATE WAYSIDE

Opuhanao Point

Nahiku

Upper Nahiku

Wailua Iki Stream

Kapa'ula Stream

Helelike'oha Stream

Mokulehua Stream

Honomaele Stream

HANA HWY

360

Kuhiwa Valley

POOL AT ULAINO

KEHANU GARDENS PI'ILANIHALE 'HEIAU

Airport/Heiau

ULAINO RD.

HANA AIRPORT

WAI'ANAPANAPA STATE PARK

Sea Arch

HEIAU

Ancient Paved Trail

Nanu'ale Point

Hana Bay

HANA BEACH COUNTY PARK

Hana

SCHOOLS

'ALA'ELE RD.

KA'ELEKU CAVERNS

Kapi'a Stream

Waiohonu Stream

Koki Beach

Hamoa

Hamoa Beach

WAIOKA POOL

Pu'uiki

ST. PETER'S CHURCH

To Kipahulu

31

3 mi

0   3 km

0

© SANDRA E. BISIGNANI TRUST AND AVALON TRAVEL PUBLISHING, INC.

door will reveal a stark interior with straight-backed benches and a front platform. The pit on the ocean side of the church building was used to make the lime and mortar mix. Few bother to stop here, so it's quiet and offers good panoramas of the village and sea below. At the broad turnoff to Huelo, between mile markers 3 and 4, there's a public telephone and a row of mailboxes.

## Kailua

The next tiny community is Kailua. Plenty of mountain apple trees flourish along this stretch. The multicolored trees are rainbow eucalyptus, introduced in the late 1800s from Australia and some of the most beautiful trees in Hawaii. Close by is a cousin, *Eucalyptus robusta,* which produces great timber, especially flooring, from its reddish-brown heartwood. This tree gets extremely hard once it dries because of its resins, so it must be milled immediately or you can do nothing with it. A few minutes beyond Kailua, notice a sudden difference in the humidity and in the phenomenal jungle growth that becomes even more pronounced.

## Waikamoi Ridge

This nature walk (mosquitoes!) is a good place to stretch your legs and learn about native and introduced trees and vegetation (some are labeled). The turnout, good for about half a dozen vehicles, is not clearly marked along the highway past mile marker 9, but look for a metal gate at roadside and picnic tables in a clearing above the road. The well-defined, gradual trail leads through tall stands of trees. You know that you're on the right path when you pass the signboard that says "Quiet, trees at work." This trail is about one mile long and takes less than an hour. On the way, you will get glimpses of the highway and stream below. For those never before exposed to a bamboo forest, it's most interesting when the wind rustles the trees so they knock together like natural percussion instruments. Picnic tables are available at the start and end of the trail. Tall mango trees tower over the upper picnic area. Return via the same trail or walk down the jeep path.

Back on the road, and at the next bridge, is excellent drinking water. There's a stone barrel with a pipe coming out, and local people come to fill jugs with what they call "living water." It doesn't always run in summer but most times can be counted on. About one-half mile beyond Waikamoi Ridge the road crosses another stream where there's limited parking. Walk along the stream a short way to this waterfalls. Although it may be slippery, you can go around the right

## TIPS FOR DRIVING THE ROAD TO HANA

You've got 30 miles of turns ahead when Route 36 (mile marker 22) becomes Route 360 (mile marker 0) and the fun begins. The Hana Highway has the reputation of being a "bad road," but this isn't true. It's narrow, with plenty of hairpin turns, but it's well banked, has clearly marked bridges, and there's frequent maintenance going on (which can slow you up). Years back, it was a harrowing experience. When mudslides blocked the road, drivers were known to swap their cars with those on the opposite side and carry on to where they were going. The road's reputation sets people up to expect an ordeal, so they make it one, and unfortunately, drive accordingly. Sometimes it seems as though tourists demand the road to be rugged, so that they can tell the folks back home that they, too, "survived the road to

Hana." This popular slogan appears on T-shirts, copyrighted and sold by Hasegawa's famous store in Hana, and perpetuates this belief. You'll have no problem, though, and you'll see much more if you just take it easy.

Your speed will often drop below 10 miles per hour and will rarely exceed 25. Cloudbursts occur at any time, so be ready for slick roads. A heavy fall of fruit from roadside mango trees can also coat the road with slippery slime. Look as far up the road as possible, and don't allow yourself to be mesmerized by the 10 feet in front of your hood. If your tire dips off a rough shoulder, don't risk losing control by jerking the wheels back on immediately. Ride it for a while and either stop or wait for an even shoulder to come back on. Local people trying to make time will often ride your side and up to another falls and cascade. Back on the road, you can see still other falls that are much farther up this valley.

## Garden of Eden

This finely landscaped property is a private arboretum and botanical garden. Entrance $7.50; open daily 8 A.M.–3 P.M. Have a stroll here among the 26 acres of tropical trees and flowering bushes, more than 500 of which are labeled for easy identification, or walk out to the Puohokamoa Falls overlook, where you have a fine view down onto this graceful waterfall. There are restrooms here and a place to picnic, so make a stop on your way down the road.

## Puohokamoa Falls

At mile marker 11, you'll find this nice pool and picnic table. A short trail will take you to the pool and its 30-foot cliff, from which local kids jump off. You'll also find a trail near the falls, and if you go upstream about 100 yards you'll discover another invigorating pool with yet another waterfall. Swimming is great here, and the small crowd may be gone. If you hike downstream about one-half mile *through* the stream (no trail), you come to the top of a 200-foot falls from where you can peer over the edge. Be very conscious of water conditions and the dangers of being near the cliff edge.

## Wayside Rest and Park

Less than two miles past Waikamoi Ridge are **Kaumahina State Wayside,** along the road, and the largely undeveloped **Honomanu County Park** down at Honomanu Bay. Some people camp here unofficially with splendid views out to sea overlooking the rugged coastline and the black-sand and rock beach of Honomanu Bay. Honomanu is not good for swimming because of strong currents but is good for surfing. Two dirt roads, one on either side of the stream, lead to it. There are no amenities at Honomanu, but Kaumahina has picnic tables and restrooms. From Kaumahina, you're rewarded with splendid views down the coast to the Ke'anae Peninsula. Slicing deep into the heart of the mountain, Honomanu Valley has 3,000-foot cliffs and 1,000-foot waterfalls.

## Ke'anae

Running back about five miles toward the center of the mountain, Ke'anae Valley is the largest on the north side of Haleakala. It and the Kaupo Valley on the mountain's southern slope were filled in by lava flows or landslides, greatly reducing their original size.

rear bumper, but generally they won't honk. Pull over and let them by when possible. Pulloffs on this road are not overabundant, so be sure to choose your spot carefully. As a safety measure and courtesy to others, yield to all oncoming traffic at each bridge.

Driving from Kahului to Hana will take three hours, not counting some recommended stops. The greatest traffic flow is 10 A.M.–noon; returning "car trains" start by 3 P.M. and are heaviest around 5 P.M. Many white-knuckled drivers head for Hana as if it were a prized goal, without stopping along the way. This is ridiculous. The best sights are before and after Hana; the town itself is hardly worth the effort. Expect to spend a long day exploring the Hana Road. To go all the way to 'Ohe'o Stream and take in some sights, you'll have

to leave your hotel at sunup and won't get back until sundown. If your budget can afford it, plan on staying the night in Hana (reservations definitely) and return the next day. This is a particularly good plan if you have an afternoon departing flight from Kahului Airport. Also, most tourists seem terrified of driving the road at night. Actually, it can be easier. There is far less traffic, road reflectors mark the center and sides like a runway, and you're warned of oncoming cars by their headlights. Those in the know make much better time after dark! In case of **emergency,** roadside telephones are located *makai* between mile markers 5 and 6, at the Halfway to Hana roadside stand, and at Pua'a Ka'a State Wayside. Less than 3,000 people live along the entire north coast of East Maui leading to and including Hana.

Usually clearly marked on the right side of the highway—the sign at times has gone missing—will be the six-acre **Keʻanae Arboretum,** established in 1971. A hike through this facility will exemplify Hawaiian plant life in microcosm. There are two sections, one of ornamental tropical plants (identified) and the other of Hawaiian domestic plants. Toward the upper end of the arboretum are taro fields, and the hillsides above are covered with the natural rainforest vegetation. You can picnic along Piʻinaʻau Stream. Although the trail is hard to pick out, hardier hikers can continue for another mile or so through the rainforest; at the end of the trail is a pool and waterfall. Because there is a gate across the entrance to the arboretum (located at a sharp curve in the road), pull well off the road to park your car and walk in.

**YMCA Camp Keanae,** 808/248-8355, fax 808/248-8492, YMCACampKeanae@aol.com, is just before the arboretum. It looks exactly as its name implies, set on a gorgeous, grassy slope. There are three bunkhouses (you must provide your own bedding), two bathrooms with showers, a gymnasium, and for large groups only, a dining room and kitchen. Tent camping is allowed on the lawn; bring your own cooking gear. Arrival time is between 3 and 9 P.M., three-day maximum stay, $15 per person or $30 per family. Y members have reduced rates. Overlooking the entire area with views over the ocean are two cottages that sleep up to four and rent for $115 per unit. All accommodations and camping space are by reservation only.

**Keʻanae Peninsula** is a thumblike appendage of land formed by a lava flow that came down the hollowed-out valley from Haleakala Crater. Its rocky shoreline is a favorite of local fishermen, perhaps appropriate because *keʻanae* means "mullet." A fantastic lookout is here—look for a telephone pole with a tsunami loudspeaker atop it at mile marker 17, and pull off just there. Below you'll see neat little farms, mostly raising taro. Shortly before this lookout, and about 200 yards past the arboretum, a public road heads down into the peninsula, arcing around to a turnaround and parking area past the church. If you walk, park well off the roadway just as you get down the

Keʻanae Peninsula is one of the most productive taro producing areas of the island.

hill. About one mile, this stroll should take less than half an hour, but you may want to stop to chat. Most people living here are native Hawaiians. They still make poi the old-fashioned way: Listen for the distinctive thud of poi-pounding in the background. Although *kapu* signs abound, most people are friendly, and someone has even set up a fruit stand. If you visit, be aware that this is one of the last patches of ground owned by Hawaiians and tended in the old way. Be respectful, please. Notice the lava-rock missionary church. Built in 1860, **Lanikili ʻIhi ʻIhi O Lehowa O na Kaua Church** was rebuilt in 1969. Neat and clean, it has straight-back, hardwood pews and a pleasant altar inside. Services are held twice a month. The cemetery to the side is groomed with tropical flowers, while the grounds are rimmed by tall coconut trees. A ballpark and public telephone stand next to the church.

## Fruit Stands

Past Keʻanae between mile markers 17 and 18

is the **Halfway to Hana** roadside refreshment stand, where you can buy banana bread, shave ice, ice cream, sandwiches, fruit, and something to drink. Notice the picture-perfect, idyllic watercress farm on your left.

Do yourself a favor and look for **Uncle Harry's Fruit Stand,** clearly marked on the left past the Ke'anae Peninsula just beyond the Ke'anae school. Unfortunately, this *kahuna*, who knew a great deal of the natural pharmacology of old Hawaii and was a living encyclopedia on herbs and all their healing properties, has passed away, but his spirit lives on.

Other fruit stands pop up now and again on this road. It's just a down-home cottage industry. No definite times necessarily, just open when they are. Look for them as you pass, stop to refresh yourself, and leave a little for the local economy.

## Wailua

At mile marker 18, you come to Wailua, a picturesque spot. Similar to Ke'anae, it too is covered in taro but not to as great an extent. Turn left here on Wailua Road and proceed to **St. Gabriel's Church.** Set at the back of the lawn to the side near the cemetery you'll find the **Miracle of Fatima Shrine,** so named because a freak storm in the 1860s washed up enough coral onto Wailua Beach that the church could be constructed by the Hawaiian congregation. There is a lovely and relatively easy-access waterfall nearby. Pass the church, turn right when you get to the bottom of the hill, and park by the large field. Look for a worn path (may be private, but no signs or hassle) that leads down to the falls. Look inland up the valley and you'll see a long sliver of a falls just below the roadway that clings to the *pali*. You can look down on this village and valley from several pulloffs and the Wailua Wayside Park, all past the Wailua Road turnoff along the Hana Highway.

## Wailua Wayside Park

Cut into the ridge directly along the roadway is the small parking lot of this tiny wayside park. Drive slowly and keep your eyes peeled because the sign comes up quickly and you have little time to signal your turn to get off the road. A short series of steps leads up under a canopy of overhanging *hao*

tree branches to a flat, grassy area about 20 feet above the road. From here you have an expansive view down onto Wailua and up along the face of the *pali*. From the rear of the parking area, you can peer into the adjoining *mauka* valley, and when it rains you can see several waterfalls cascading down the valley walls inland. No facilities are available. From here, you can see the Ke'anae Valley and Ko'olau Gap. Look closely. From this vantage point it is obvious how lava and rubble from the Haleakala basin poured down the mountain, filling this once deep-cut valley. A pulloff on the ocean side of the roadway about one-half mile farther provides you with perhaps a better view down into Wailua Valley.

## Pua'a Ka'a State Wayside

This spot is about 14 miles before Hana. There's no camping, but there are a few picnic tables and restrooms. Across the road from the parking lot is a short path that leads to Kopili'ula and Waikani Falls. A very public place, it's not the best scenery along the road, and these are not the best pools for swimming.

## Nahiku

The village, named after the Hawaiian version of the Pleiades, is reached by a steep but now paved three-mile road and has the dubious distinction of being one of the wettest spots along the coast. Turn near mile marker 25. The well-preserved and tiny little church near the bottom of the road was constructed in 1867 (renovated in 1993) and is just big enough for a handful of pews. You may see school kids playing ball in the yard next to the church, the only place in the community that's open and large enough. The turnaround at oceanside is where many locals come to shore-fish. Often during the summer, an extended family pod of dolphins enters Nahiku Bay in the afternoon to put on an impromptu performance of water acrobatics just for the joy of it. At one time Nahiku was a thriving Hawaiian village with thousands of inhabitants. Today it's home to only about 70 people. A few inhabitants are Hawaiian families, but mostly the people are wealthy Mainlanders seeking isolation. After a few large and attractive homes went up, the real estate agents changed the description from "desolate" to "secluded." What's the difference? About $1 million per house! In the early 1900s, this was the site of the Nahiku Rubber Co., the only commercial rubber plantation in the United States. Many rubber trees still line the road, although the venture collapsed in 1912 because the rubber was poor as a result of the overabundance of rainfall. Some people have augmented their incomes by growing *pakalolo* in the rainforest of this area; however, the alternative-lifestyle people who first came here and have settled in have discovered that there is just as much money to be made raising ornamental tropical flowers and have become real "flower children." Many have roadside stands along the Hana Highway, where payment for the flowers displayed is on the honor system. Leave what is requested—prices will be marked.

Near mile marker 29 in Upper Nahiku, you'll come upon **Nahiku Ti Gallery** for gifts and crafts, a pastry and refreshment shop, and a little stand selling baked breadfruit bread and smoked fish kebabs.

## ACCOMMODATIONS

Several bed-and-breakfast establishments and similar accommodations lie along the road to Hana, many at or near Huelo. Only a few are listed as follows.

Surrounded by trees, bamboo, and wildflowers, **Halfway to Hana House,** P.O. Box 675, Haiku, HI 96708, 808/572-1176, fax 808/572-3609, gailp@maui.net, www.maui.net /~gailp, is a small and peaceful getaway with views over the lush north coast. As a one-studio apartment on the lower level of the house, there are no distracting noises. Its private entrance leads into a comfortable room with double bed and mini kitchen. In a separate room is the bath, and a breakfast patio is out the back. Breakfast of pastries and fruit from the property is waiting every morning if you desire. The room rate is $100 double with breakfast, $85 without; three nights minimum, 10 percent discount for a week or more. A kayak and scuba

enthusiast, the owner can tell you about good ocean spots to visit.

**Hono Hu'aka Tropical Plantation,** P.O. Box 600, Haiku, HI 96708, 808/573-1391, fax 808/573-0141, info@retreatmaui.com, www.retreatmaui.com, down behind Kaulanapueo Church on a 300-foot cliff above Waipi'o Bay, is a peaceful 38-acre retreat and alternative working plantation farm. This place retains a connection to the past in the guise of a *heiau* while it looks toward the peace and tranquility of the future. The property is dotted with tropical permaculture orchards and gardens, and the stream was blocked to form a naturally heart-shaped pond. Set amid bamboo, a globelike kiva meditation hall sits about the main house and office, below which is a heated swimming pool and spa. The two suites on the garden level of the house rent for $60 per night, or together for $110. The gazebo suite at poolside below the nine-sided office is often used by newlyweds; it runs $100. Overlooking much of the farm and surrounding forested hillsides, the bamboo octagons go for $75–85. Much more of an adventure is the two-story treehouse for $135. The cliff house, set on the precipice of the 300-foot *pali* next to a waterfall, with a commanding view of the bay, is yours for $150. High-season rates run about 20 percent more. Any stay less than three nights requires an additional housekeeping fee. Breakfast of organic fruits from the property, home-baked muffins and croissants, juice, and tea will be placed in your refrigerator for your first morning. After the first day, there is a nominal charge for breakfast if you desire to order it, but you can fix whatever you want because each unit is equipped with a kitchenette. Come, relax, refresh, and reinvigorate, or participate in one of the activities offered.

Also in the community of Huelo, with a spectacular view up the coast toward Hana, is **Huelo Point Lookout,** P.O. Box 790117, Paia, HI 96779, 808/573-0914 or 800/871-8645, fax 808/573-0227, dreamers@maui.net, www.maui.net/~dreamers. Here, the main house and three cottages are scattered around the acreage, which is finely landscaped with tropical trees and bushes. The rock-wall swimming pool is inviting, and a soak in the hot tub under a cloudless night sky befits a day on the island. Wake up to the sound of birds singing in the trees, have your breakfast on the lanai, and spend your day leisurely hanging out here or venture out to see the island sights. Once a fisherman's cottage, surrounded by banana trees and heliconia, the remodeled Star Cottage has an indoor/outdoor bathroom, a solarium, and a queen-size bed and double futon, $185–225. A bit smaller and with views of the mountain, Haleakala Cottage studio has a full kitchen and king-size bed in one room, $185–195. Outside is an enclosed shower and a covered lanai. The Rainbow Cottage is a newer building, renting for $275–345. Downstairs are the living room and kitchen; a 22-foot-tall wall of glass offers the best views of the coast from either floor. Make your way up the handmade wooden spiral staircase to the upstairs bedroom, where a king-size bed lies under a large skylight. Outside is your own private hot tub. The Sunrise Suite in the main house has a wall of sliding-glass doors that faces east for perfect sunrise views, its own kitchen, and a large bath. This suite rents for $345–360 per night, but the entire main house can also be rented for families or groups of up to eight people for $2,650–2,850 per week, one-week minimum. Cash or traveler's checks only; no credit cards accepted.

About one mile down a dirt road near Twin Falls is **Maluhia Hale B&B**, 808/572-2959, P.O. Box 687 Haiku, HI 96708, djg@maui.net, www.maui.net/~djg/cottage.htm. Off the main route, this 2.5-acre quiet and relaxing spot is enveloped by greenery, yet has the wide ocean vista spreading at your feet. A detached open-beam plantation-style cottage, dressed in white, with screened porch and a sitting room has a king-size bed, a nearly full kitchen, and a detached bathing room that has a clawfoot tub and shower; very commodious. The cottage can accommodate three. Light, open, and airy, it rents for $115 per night with breakfast, $20 for an extra person; two nights minimum.

Down at the end of the road is the **Tea House Cottage**, P.O. Box 335, Ha'iku, HI 96708, 808/572-5610, teahouse@maui.net, www.mauiteahouse.com. This B&B is "off the grid," generating its own power by photovoltaic cells and collecting its own water. Quiet, with no distractions, from here you have broad views of the ocean. The one cottage has a Japanese feel, with a living room, kitchen, bedroom, and screened lanai; a few steps away is the redwood bathhouse. Art on the walls is by the owner/artist, and it complements the rattan furniture and oriental rugs. The room rate is $120 double or $105 single per night; two nights minimum, seventh night no charge. A daily breakfast is provided. A tunnel through the trees leads you to the house, and walkways run throughout the property, one to a small stupa built some 30 years ago by a Tibetan monk.

The lush and verdant grounds of the **Kailua Maui Gardens,** Box 790189, Paia, HI 96779, 808/572-9726, fax 808/572-3409, info@kailua-mauigardens.com, www.kailuamauigardens.com, is located in the tiny community of Kailua. Set amid a landscape of tropical trees and flowering plants are three cottages and one garden apartment, yet surprisingly each unit maintains a great deal of privacy. The swimming pool, two spas, and two barbecue grills are for everyone's use. With a full kitchen, queen-size bed, full-size futon, and twin bed on the porch, the Aloha Cottage is the largest, sleeps up to five, and goes for $120 for two nights or $110 for three or more. The Jungle Bungalow has a full kitchen and king-size bed; rates are $110 for two nights or $90 for three or more. Smallest is The Love Shack. More intimate yet very comfortable, it has a queen-size bed, and like the Jungle Bungalow, it has a private outdoor shower. It rents for $95 for two nights or $75 for three or more. With one bedroom, a full kitchen and sitting area, and its own entrance, the Garden Apartment is located below the main house but is completely separate and rents for $110 for two nights or $90 for three nights or more. Two nights minimum; weekly rates can be arranged. A continental breakfast is served each morning by the pool.

MAUI

# Hana

Hana is about as pretty a town as you'll find anywhere in Hawaii, but if you're expecting anything stupendous you'll be sadly disappointed. For most it will only be a quick stopover at a store or beach en route to 'Ohe'o Stream: The townsfolk refer to these people as "rent-a-car tourists." The lucky who stay in Hana, or those not worried about time, will find plenty to explore throughout the area. The town is built on rolling hills that descend to Hana Bay; much of the surrounding lands are given over to pasture, while trim cottages wearing flower corsages line the town's little lanes. Before the white man arrived, Hana was a stronghold that was conquered and reconquered by the kings of Maui and those of the north coast of the Big Island. The most strategic and historically laden spot is Ka'uiki Hill, the remnant of a cinder cone that dominates Hana Bay. This area is steeped in Hawaiian legend, and old stories relate that it was the demigod Maui's favorite spot. It's said that he transformed his daughter's lover into Ka'uiki Hill and turned her into the gentle rains that bathe it to this day.

Hana was already a plantation town in the mid-1800s when a hard-boiled sea captain named George Wilfong started producing sugar on his 60 acres there. Later, Danish brothers August and Oscar Unna came to run the plantation, and over the years the laborers came from the standard mixture of Hawaiian, Japanese, Chinese, Portuguese, Filipino, and even Puerto Rican stock. The *luna* were Scottish, German, or American. All have combined to become the people of Hana. After having grown to half a dozen plantations and producing for decades, sugar production faded out by the 1940s and Hana began to die, its population dipping below 500. Just then, San Francisco industrialist Paul Fagan purchased 14,000 acres of what was to become the **Hana Ranch.** Realizing that sugar was *pau*, he replanted his lands in *pangola* range grass and imported 300 Hereford cattle from another holding on Moloka'i. Their white faces

staring back at you as you drive past are now a standard part of Hana's scenery. Today, Hana Ranch has about 3,000 acres and raises more than 2,000 head of cattle. Hana's population, at 1,850, is about 48 percent Hawaiian.

Fagan loved Hana and felt an obligation to and affection for its people. He also decided to retire here, and with enough money to materialize just about anything, he decided that Hana could best survive through limited tourism. He built the Ka'uiki Inn, later to become the Hotel Hana-Maui, which catered to millionaires, mostly his friends, and began operation in 1946. Fagan owned a baseball team, the San Francisco Seals, and brought them to Hana in 1946 for spring training. The community baseball field behind the hotel was made for them. This was a brilliant publicity move because sportswriters came along; becoming enchanted with Hana, they gave it a great deal of copy and were probably the first to publicize the phrase "Heavenly Hana." It wasn't long before tourists began arriving.

Unfortunately, the greatest heartbreak in modern Hana history occurred at just about the same time, on April 1, 1946. An earthquake in Alaska's Aleutian Islands sent huge tsunamis that raked the Hana coast. These destroyed hundreds of homes, wiping out entire villages and tragically sweeping away many people. Hana recovered but never forgot. Life went on, and the menfolk began working as *paniolo* on Fagan's spread and during roundup would drive the cattle through town and down to Hana Bay, where they were forced to swim to waiting barges. Other entire families went to work at the hotel, and so Hana lived again. It's this legacy of quietude and old-fashioned *aloha* that attracted people to Hana over the years. Everyone knows that Hana's future lies in its uniqueness and remoteness, and no one wants it to change. The people as well as the tourists know what they have here. What really makes Hana heavenly is similar to what's preached in Sunday school: Everyone wants to go there, but not everyone makes it.

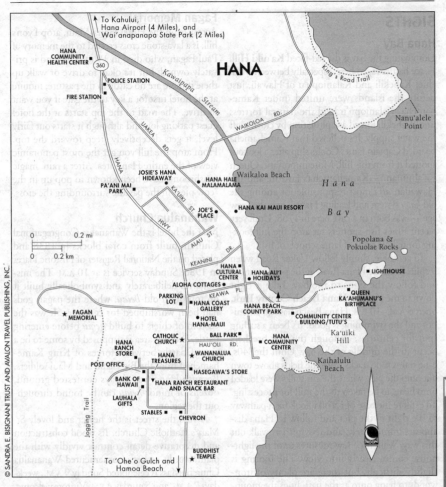

To Kahului,
Hana Airport (4 Miles), and
Wai'anapanapa State Park (2 Miles)

HANA COMMUNITY HEALTH CENTER
360
POLICE STATION
FIRE STATION

Kawaipapa Stream

HANA

King's Road Trail

WAIKOLOA RD.

Nanu'alele Point

UAKEA RD.

HANA HWY

KA'UIKI ST.

JOSIE'S HANA HIDEAWAY
PA'ANI MAI PARK

HANA HALE MALAMALAMA
JOE'S PLACE

Waikaloa Beach

Hana Bay

HANA KAI MAUI RESORT

Popolana & Pokuolae Rocks

ALAU ST.

KEANINI DR.

HANA CULTURAL CENTER
ALOHA COTTAGES
PARKING LOT
HANA COAST GALLERY
HOTEL HANA-MAUI
BALL PARK
CATHOLIC CHURCH
HANA RANCH STORE
POST OFFICE
BANK OF HAWAII
HANA TREASURES
LAUHALA GIFTS
HANA RANCH RESTAURANT AND SNACK BAR
STABLES
CHEVRON

KEAWA PL.

HANA ALI'I HOLIDAYS

HANA BEACH COUNTY PARK

HAU'OLI RD.
WANANALUA CHURCH
HASEGAWA'S STORE

COMMUNITY CENTER BUILDING/TUTU'S
HANA COMMUNITY CENTER

LIGHTHOUSE
QUEEN KA'AHUMANU'S BIRTHPLACE

Ka'uiki Hill

Kaihalulu Beach

FAGAN MEMORIAL

Jogging Trail

0   0.2 mi
0   0.2 km

To 'Ohe'o Gulch and Hamoa Beach

BUDDHIST TEMPLE

Moon

© SANDRA E. BISIGNANI TRUST AND AVALON TRAVEL PUBLISHING, INC.

MAUI

## Hana Festivals

As is the case in most Hawaiian towns, Hana has many local festivals and events. First in the year is the fireworks on New Year's Eve over Fagan's cross. In late March, the weekend **Taro Festival,** with its traditional ceremonies, games, music, authentic foods and a food market, arts and crafts exhibitions, and hula demonstrations, thrills everyone. People come from all over the state to watch and participate; make plans well in advance. Later in June or early July, the chil-

dren of town get treated to the **Makeke,** a children's festival, when all sorts of games and celebrations are held. For decades, Hana has had a tie with the great American sport of baseball. To honor this connection, a softball tournament is held over the Labor Day weekend, pitting families and friends against one another in friendly but serious competition. As with all of the state, the **Aloha Festival** is celebrated with gusto. Parades, lu'au, a fishing tournament, and many other activities are organized.

# SIGHTS

## Hana Bay

Dominating the bay is the red-faced **Ka'uiki Hill.** Fierce battles raged here, especially between Maui chief Kahekili and Kalaniopu'u of Hawaii, just before the islands were united under Kamehameha. Kalaniopu'u held the natural fortress until Kahekili forced a capitulation by cutting off the water supply. It's believed that Kamehameha boarded Captain James Cook's ship after a lookout spotted it from this hill. More important, Queen Ka'ahumanu—Kamehameha's favorite and the Hawaiian *ali'i* most responsible for ending the old *kapu* system and leading Hawaii into the "new age"—was born in a cave here in 1768. Until very recent times fish-spotters sat atop the hill looking for telltale signs of large schools of fish.

To get there, simply follow Uakea Road when it splits from the Hana Road at the police station, and follow the signs to the bay. Take it right down to the pier and **Hana Beach County Park,** open 6 A.M.–10 P.M. Hana Beach has full amenities and the swimming is good. It's been a surfing spot for centuries, although the best breakers occur in the middle of the bay. Until the '40s, cane trains rode tracks from the fields above town out onto the pier, where the cut stalks were loaded onto boats to be taken to the mill for processing. To explore the base of Ka'uiki, look for a pathway to the right of the pier and follow it. Hana disappears immediately, and few tourists walk out this way. Walk for a few minutes until the lighthouse comes clearly into view. The footing is slightly difficult, but there are plenty of ironwoods to hang onto as the path hugs the mountainside. A few pockets of red-sand beach eroded from the cinder cone are below. A copper plaque erected in 1928 commemorates the spot of Ka'ahumanu's birth. Proceed straight ahead to the lighthouse sitting on a small island. To cross, you'll have to leap from one jagged rock to another. If this doesn't suit you, take your bathing suit and wade across a narrow sandy-bottomed channel. Stop for a few moments and check the wave action to avoid being hurled against the rocks. When you've got it timed, go for it! The view from up top is great.

## Fagan Memorial

Across from the Hotel Hana-Maui, atop Lyon's hill, is a lava-stone cross erected to the memory of Paul Fagan, who died in 1960. The land is privately owned, but it's okay to drive or walk up there if there are no cattle in the pasture; inquire at the hotel first for a key to the gate if you want to drive. The road to the top starts at the hotel guest parking lot, and although it starts out fairly level, it gets deceptively steep toward the top. From atop the hill you get the most panoramic view of the entire Hana area. After a rain, magic mushrooms have been known to pop up in the "cow pies" in the pasture surrounding the cross.

## Wananalua Church

Near the hotel is the Wananalua Congregational Church, built from coral blocks in 1838 and placed on the National Register of Historic Places in 1988. Sunday service is at 10 A.M. The missionaries deliberately and symbolically built it on top of an old *heiau,* where the pagan gods had been worshipped for centuries. It was the custom of chiefs to build *heiau* before entering battle, and this area is supposed by some to be a site of battle between forces of King Kamehameha I from the Big Island and Maui soldiers. Because Hana was always contested ground, dozens of minor *heiau* can be found throughout the region.

Across the street is the newer and lovely St. Mary's Catholic Church. Its wood construction and decorative detail contrast vividly with the plain, sturdy, rather unornamented Wananalua Church. Mass is celebrated Sunday 9 A.M., weekdays 7 A.M., and Saturday 4 P.M. Visitors welcome.

## Hana Cultural Center

Located along Uakea Road on the right, kitty-corner from the Hana Bay entrance road, this center is open daily 10 A.M.–4 P.M. (but may open at noon on Sunday); $2 donation gladly accepted. Founded in 1971, the Hana Cultural Center, 808/248-8622, www.planet-hawaii.com/hana, occupies an unpretentious building (notice the beautifully carved koa doors, however) on the grounds of the old courthouse and jail. The center houses fine examples of quiltwork: one, entitled "Aloha Kuuhae," was done by Rosaline Keli-noi, a Hana resident and the first woman voted into the state legislature. There are precontact stone implements, tapa cloth, and an extensive shell collection. Your donation entitles you to visit the courthouse and jail next door. Simple but functional, with bench and witness stand, it makes Andy of Mayberry look like big time. This tiny courthouse was used regularly 1871–1978 and is still used monthly for the same purpose. It's been placed on the Hawaii Register of Historic Places. The jail, "Hana Lockup," was also built in 1871 and finally renovated in 1997. The towns-folk knew whenever it held an inmate because he became the groundskeeper and the grass would suddenly be mowed.

In the ancient Hawaiian style and using tradi-tional materials, a sleeping house, cook house, meeting house, and canoe shed have been con-structed to the side and below the center to give you an idea of what types of buildings were used in Hawaii in the past. On the terrace below these structures is a small **ethnobotanical garden** of medicinal and agricultural native plants. Pick up a brochure about the plants inside the museum. Be sure to stop at the cultural center while in Hana to learn a bit about local history and culture.

## Ka'eleku Caverns

One of Hana's unique adventures is spelunking. There are 50 known caves on Maui and 150 on the Big Island. Only a short section of the Thurston Lava Tube in Hawaii Volcanoes Na-tional Park and two to three others can be en-tered. Some 30,000 years old, Ka'eleku (Standing in the Dark) Cave near Kahanu Gardens in Hana is the only cave on Maui that's open to the public, and it's a beauty. This cave, like all others in Hawaii, is actually a lava tube 30–40 feet below the surface, so the cave follows the lay of the land up and down the mountainside. No matter what the temperature is outside, it's always a moderate 64–72°F inside. You enter through a skylight and make your way down the steps to the floor of the cave, which once flowed with molten lava. Here you must let your eyes adjust to the darkness be-fore proceeding downhill. As liquid lava surged through this tube it scored the walls, leaving stri-

ations. Here and there, you will also see benches and ledges along the sides, where lava cooled faster on the periphery than the middle. Some rubble has fallen from the ceiling or off the walls, creating small mounds, but the trail skirts or tra-verses these obstructions. You can walk upright all the way, no kneeling or crawling involved.

Other natural features that occur in this cave are lava stalactites and stalagmites, drip columns, a bowling alley–like channeling with gutters down both sides, ropy pahoehoe lava levees, clinkers of rough 'a'a, side loops, convergent channels, and over tubes. A very unusual feature found in certain portions of the cave, and perhaps peculiar to this cave alone, are delicate, filigreed grapelike botryoid clusters. And the colors, who would have thought? There is gray, blue, brown, gold, and copper—quite astounding. One of the mysteries of this cave is that the air flows in two different directions. Through the lower portion, the flow is downward and out a series of sky-lights; in the upper section, the air flows uphill, exiting at a yet undiscovered spot. Because this cave has only recently been open to visitors, it's still in pristine condition. Care must be taken not to touch delicate formations or accidentally crush or break anything fragile. "Cave softly and carry a big light" is the owner's motto.

Maui Cave Adventures, P.O. Box 40, Hana, HI 96713, 808/248-7308, info@mauicave.com, www.mauicave.com, is run by Chuck Thorne, and he can set you up with a tour. All tours are guided, very informative, and safe. Chuck is happy to share with you what he knows about this cave as well as other caves in the state. Check-in is at the kiosk at the cave entrance, located about one-half mile along Ulaino Road after turn-ing off the Hana Highway. An informative schematic drawing of the cave, with explanation, is displayed at the parking lot. A hard hat, light, and drinks are provided. Wear long pants, closed-toe shoes, and a T-shirt—something that you don't mind getting a little dirty. If you have any in-terest in caving or have never even been under-ground before, you'll be glad you had a look at this one. A one-hour walking tour costs $29 per per-son, and adventurers must be at least seven years old. The two-hour "wild" tour is $69 per person, with an age requirement of 15 years old. Two-person minimum for tours to run. Contact the company (open 8 A.M.–8 P.M.) for information, advanced reservations, and departure times.

## Kahanu Gardens

Turn off Hana Highway onto Ulaino Road and proceed toward the ocean. Here, the pavement soon gives way to a dirt track and leads about 1.5 miles to Kahanu Gardens, 808/248-8912, www.ntbg.org, located just past a shallow stream. The gardens are open Monday–Friday 10 A.M.–2 P.M., but may be closed at any time if, because of heavy rains, the stream (no bridge) is too high or moving too swiftly to cross. This 123-acre tropical garden runs down to the tortured lava coastline. Part of the National Tropical Botanical Garden system, the Kahanu Gardens contain a variety of domestic and imported tropical plants, including a huge native pandanus forest and large and varied collections of breadfruit and coconut trees. While one of the purposes of the garden is to propagate and protect Hawaiian and Polynesian ethnobotanical plants, within its property is Pi'ilanihale Heiau, Hawaii's largest, with massive walls that rise more than 50 feet and a broad top that's twice as long as a football field and half that wide. A National Historical Landmark, this *heiau* is probably from the 14th century and possibly a royal compound associated with Pi'ilani, a Maui king from around 1500 who seems to have unified the island as one political unit. You may walk through on your own for $10. The walk is level, but leave yourself 1–1.5 hours for the tour.

Just before the Kahuna Gardens is the private **Hana Maui Tropical Botanical Garden,** a 10-acre site open daily 9 A.M.–5 P.M. for self-guided tours; $3 entrance fee.

## Pool at Ulaino

Past Kahanu Gardens, Ulaino Road continues to roughen, crosses two more streams, passes several homesites carved out of the bush, and ends after more than a mile at a parking area near the ocean. This may not be drivable during heavy rains with a 2WD rental car but may be passable with a 4WD vehicle. Walk across the boulders that form the beach at the mouth of the stream and stay along the *pali* for 100 yards or so until you come upon what some people call Blue Pond or Blue Pool tucked behind some larger rocks. This hideaway is an old local favorite, a clothing-optional swimming spot where a waterfall drops fresh water into an oceanside pool. Not always blue, it's sometimes murky when water brings large amounts of sediment down from the hillside above. As always at pools, be aware of stones and branches that might come over the top and give you a knot on your noggin as a souvenir of your time in paradise.

## Hana Airport

Less than a mile in toward town from Ulaino Road, on Ala'ele Road, a sign points left to Hana Airport, where **Pacific Wings,** 808/873-0877, schedules some flights. Most flights to Hana go through Kahului, although there are a few from Honolulu. Hotel Hana-Maui operates a shuttle between the airport and the hotel for its guests and will take others when not full. There is no public transportation in Hana, and only **Dollar Rent A Car,** 808/248-8237, can provide wheels for you, so make reservations *before* arriving in Hana. Their booth is open 8 A.M.–5 P.M. daily at the airport. Aside from the airline counters, there is only a public telephone and restrooms here at this tiny terminal.

**Blue Hawaiian** helicopters makes one run up the Hana coast that stops at the Hana Airport. Here, it connects with ground transportation by **Temptation Tours,** so you can go one way by air and the other by land, a fly-drive offering. Neither company has an office at the Hana Airport.

The real adventurer may want to take note that power hang-gliding flights are offered at the Hana Airport, but by appointment only. Contact Hang Gliding Maui, 808/572-6557, to arrange a 30- or 60-minute flight over the Hana Coast.

## Wai'anapanapa State Park

Only three miles outside Hana, and down a road that's clearly marked along the highway at mile marker 32, this state park offers not only tent and RV camping but also housekeeping cabins sleeping up to six. Set some distance from the beach and tenting area, the cabins offer hot water, electricity, a full kitchen, bathroom, bedrooms, and bedding, and rent for $45 per night for up to four people and $5 for each additional person. A deposit is required. They're very popular, so book far in advance by writing to the Division of State Parks or visiting its office at 54 S. High St., Rm. 101, Wailuku, HI 96793, 808/984-8109. The grassy camping area has picnic tables, water, showers, and restrooms. Even for those not camping, Wai'anapanapa is a "must stop." Pass the office to get to the beach park and its black-sand beach. The swimming is dangerous during heavy surf because the bottom drops off quickly, but on calm days it's mellow. The snorkeling is excellent, and it should be, because Wai'anapanapa means "Glistening Waters." Just offshore is a clearly visible natural stone bridge. Some very brave local kids come and jump off the rocks here—for the thrill, no doubt.

A short, well-marked trail leads to **Wai'anapanapa Caves.** The tunnel-like trail passes through a thicket of vines and *hau,* a bush used by the Hawaiians to mark an area as *kapu.* The two small caves are formed from lava. The water trapped inside is clear. These caves mark the site of a Hawaiian legend, in which a lovely princess named Popu'alaea fled from her cruel husband Ka'akae. He found her hiding here and killed her. Bringing a sense of truth to this legend, hordes of tiny red shrimp occupy these caves at certain times of the year, turning the waters red, which the Hawaiians take as a reminder of the poor slain princess.

Along the coastline here are remnants of an ancient paved Hawaiian trail known as the **King's Highway.** You can follow it for a short distance. To get to the section running north toward the airport, cross the black-sand beach and head up the far side. This trail is reasonably well maintained but fairly rugged because of lava and cinders and stays on or near the cliffs most of the way. This walk takes about two hours. A section of the trail also runs south past the cabins along the coast toward Hana. Along the way you'll pass small bays, lava cliffs, blowholes, and an old *heiau.* The vegetation is lush, and long fingers of black lava stretch out into cobalt-blue waters. Expect about a three-hour hike. Along this road to the state park and at various spots along the Hana Highway, you'll find small roadside stands with flowers or fruits for sale on the honor system.

# BEACHES
## Kaihalulu Beach
Named Kaihalulu (Roaring Sea) but also known as Red Sand Beach, this is a fascinating and secluded beach area. Follow Uakea Road past the turnoff to Hana Bay. Proceed ahead until you pass the public ballpark and tennis courts on your right and the community center on your left. The road deadends shortly. Head through the open lot between the community center and hotel property, where you pick up a worn path. Ahead is a Japanese cemetery with its distinctive headstones, some now being lost to wave erosion and a degrading shoreline. Below are pockets of red sand amid fingers of black lava washed by sky-blue water. There are many tide pools here. Stay close to the water and walk the shoreline path around Ka'uiki Head until you are obviously in the hollowed-out amphitheater of the red cinder cone. Pat the walls to feel how crumbly they are—the red "sand" is eroded cinder. The water in the cove is fantastically blue against the redness. There is another trail that leads over the edge of the cliff and *steeply* down to the beach, but unfortunately the walk down can be treacherous. This path clings to the side of a cliff, and the footing is made tough because of unstable and crumbly cinders. Grave accidents have occurred, and even locals often won't make the trip. Use the shoreline path.

Across the mouth of the bay are jagged fingers of stone, jutting up like castle parapets from a fairy kingdom, that keep the water safe for swimming. This is a favorite fishing spot for local people, and the snorkeling is good, too. The beach is best in the morning before 11 A.M.; afterward it can get hot if there's no wind and rough if the wind is from the north—remember the beach's name. The coarse red sand massages your feet, and there's a natural jacuzzi area in foamy pools of water along the shore. This secluded beach is unofficially clothing optional, so if you're going to be upset by nude sunbathers, it may be better to head somewhere else.

## Koki Beach

The beach is a mile or so out of town heading toward 'Ohe'o. Look for Haneo'o Road on your left with a sign directing you to Koki and Hamoa Beaches. Koki is only a few hundred yards on the left, at the first set of pullouts by the water. This beach is a mixture of white sand and red sand from the hill next to it. The riptides are fierce in here, so don't swim unless it's absolutely calm, but locals surf here when conditions are right—usually in summer. The winds can whip along here, too, even though at Hamoa Beach, less than a mile away, it can be dead calm. Koki is excellent for beachcombing and for a one-night unofficial bivouac.

A very special person named Smitty lived in a cave on the north side of the beach. A distinguished older man, he "dropped out" years back and came here to live a simple monk's existence. He kept the beach clean and saved several people from the riptide. He was a long-distance runner who would tack up a "thought for the day" on Hana's public bulletin board. People loved him and he loved them in return. In 1984 the roof of his cave collapsed and he was killed. When his body was recovered, he was in a kneeling position. At his funeral, all felt a loss, but there was no sadness because all were sure that Smitty had gone home.

## Hamoa Beach

Follow this loop road a few minutes past Koki Beach to the other side of this small thumb of a peninsula to Hamoa Beach. Between Koki and Hamoa are the remnants of the extensive Haneo'o fish pond, part of which is still discernible. This entire area is an eroding cinder cone known as **Kaiwi O Pele** (the Bones of Pele). This is the spot where the swinish pig god, Kamapua'a, ravished her. Pele also fought a bitter battle with her sister here, who dashed Pele on the rocks, giving them their anatomical name. Out to sea is the diminutive 'Alau Island, a remnant left over by Maui after he finished fishing up the Hawaiian Islands.

You can tell that the gray-sand Hamoa Beach is no ordinary beach the minute you start walking down the paved walkway. This is the semipri-

vate beach of the Hotel Hana-Maui, but don't be intimidated, because no one can own the beach in Hawaii. Hamoa is terrific for swimming and snorkeling on calm days or bodysurfing or surfing on days when the wind is up a little. The hotel guests are shuttled here by buses throughout the day, so if you want this lovely beach to yourself arrive before midmorning and stay after late afternoon. There is a pavilion that the hotel uses as well as restrooms and showers for its guests, but there are public toilets as well.

# ACCOMMODATIONS

## Hotel Hana-Maui

The legacy of Paul Fagan who built it in the late '40s, **Hotel Hana-Maui,** 808/248-8211 or 800/321-4262, fax 808/248-7202, www.hotel-hanamaui.com, is as close to a family-run hotel as you can get. Most personnel have either been there from the beginning or their jobs have passed to their family members, and the hotel has had fewer than 10 managers in the last 60 years. Guests love it that way, proven by an astonishing 80 percent in repeat visitors, most of whom feel as if they're staying with old friends. Unfortunately, the hotel suffered a downturn in the late '90s, but after a change of ownership in 2001, renovation of rooms and restaurants, and a new executive chef, it's on the upswing once again. The public areas in the hotel are done in muted beige and browns with touches of blues, greens, and other light colors. It's open and airy with flagstone floors and easy furniture of hardwood and colorful leather. The low-slung Bay Cottages cluster around the lawn, eight spa suites have been renovated below the main building, while the newer plantation-style Sea Ranch Cottages overlook the ocean on land that slopes down to the water. Rooms, all with their own lanai, surround the beautifully appointed grounds, where flowers add a splash of color to the green-on-green blanket of tropical plants and gently sloping lawn. All suites have a wet bar and large, comfortable sitting area with hardwood, bamboo, and coconut furniture and furnishings. The floors, a rich natural wood, are covered here and there with natural pandanus

Hotel Hana-Maui's Sea Ranch Cottages look out over the water and allow guests to relax in luxurious ranch-style accommodations.

mats. The beds, all king-size or two twins, are covered with quilts, while overhead fans provide all the cooling necessary. These quilts, plus some of the wallpaper in the units and design details in other parts of the hotel, were inspired by traditional 18th- and 19th-century Hawaiian *kapa,* patterns. The guest-cottage rooms have king-size beds and freestanding armoires. The bathrooms, as large as most sitting rooms, are tiled with earth-tone ceramic. You use the walk-in shower or climb a step to immerse yourself in the huge tub, then open eye-level windows that frame a private mini-garden like an expressionist's still life.

The hotel staff adds an intangible quality of friendliness and *aloha.* In the main building, there is a library for use by guests, a few shops for clothes, necessities, and gifts, and a superb art gallery. The refurbished hotel restaurant is open for breakfast, lunch, and dinner, and the Paniolo Bar serves drinks from the late morning until 10 P.M. Thursday. Sunday bring a free hula show to the dining room at 7 P.M., and Thursday–Sunday 6:30–9:30 P.M., the soft lilt of Hawaiian music and song wafts through the house from the bar. Other facilities and activities include a wellness center, dedicated spa facilities, two heated swimming pools, a hot tub, tennis courts, superb horseback riding, a three-hole practice golf course, a croquet lawn, free bicycle use by guests, hikes to nearby sites, and daily transportation to the hotel's facilities on Hamoa Beach, where there is an attendant on duty and water gear to use. All activities are easily arranged by visiting the activities desk, which can be counted on to keep family and children happy with lei-making, swaying hula lessons, and other such interests. Free shuttle service is provided by the hotel throughout the area as well as to the airport for those arriving and leaving.

The Bay Cottages have rates starting at $295 for a garden-view suite and progress up to $365 for an oceanview suite. The Sea Ranch Cottages run $395–725 and include all activities and in-room snacks. For large families or groups, the plantation house, the former plantation manager's home, goes for $1,500 per night. From December 20 through January 5, holiday rates on all rooms are approximately 20 percent higher. There is a $50 extra charge for each additional adult in a room; kids 18 and younger stay free with existing bedding. The entire scene isn't stiff or fancy, but it is a memorable first-class experience!

## Vacation Rentals

**Joe's Place,** 808/248-7033, is on Uakea Road not far from the entrance to the bay. A very modest but clean self-serve guesthouse, this is a home that's been split into eight guest rooms. Rooms for singles or doubles cost $45, $55 with a private bath. Also available is a room for $65 that can sleep three. Cash or traveler's checks only. Check-out time is at 10 A.M. and check-in is at 3 P.M. or as soon as your room is available. Reservations are held until 6 P.M. There's kitchen access, a communal TV room, daily towel change, and maid service on request at an extra charge. If no one is in the office, ring for assistance.

Located across from the Heavenly Hana Inn on the north end of town, **Hana Maui Vacation Rental,** P.O. Box 455, Hana HI, 96713, tel/fax 808/248-8087 or 800/991-2422, www.maui-hana.com, is a small place with three units. Neat, tidy, and inexpensive, one has a kitchen while the other two have only microwaves and mini-refrigerators. All have bedrooms separate from the cooking area, bathrooms with showers, and separate entrances. While not large, it's certainly adequate, and the price is right. The room with a kitchen runs $65 per night, with the microwave $55; maximum three guests per room.

**Kulani's Hideaway,** 808/248-8234, has two units that rent for $65 double occupancy that are conveniently located on the road down to the state park. While nothing special, they are comfortable and each has a bedroom, bathroom, and a small kitchen.

Adjacent to the Hana Cultural Center, the **Aloha Cottages,** P.O. Box 205, Hana, HI 96713, 808/248-8420, are owned and operated by Zenzo and Fusae Nakamura and are the best bargain in town. The studio and cottages are meticulously clean, well built, and sparsely appointed. For $65–95, $10–25 per additional guest, you get two bedrooms and bath, a full kitchen, living room, linoleum floors throughout, a deck, and outdoor grills, but no television or phones. Mrs. Nakamura is very friendly and provides daily maid service. In season, fruit trees on the property provide free fruit to guests.

**Josie's Hana Hideaway,** P.O. Box 265, Hana HI, 96713, 808/248-8418 or 808/248-7727, offers two spartan rooms in the rear of her house and one up at the front. Each large and comfy unit (the front unit is smaller than the ones behind) has a bedroom/sitting room with a kitchenette in the corner, color TV by the queen bed, a full bathroom, and a separate entrance. If you want, you can prepare your meal in the kitchenette on the upper lanai. No breakfast is served. The daily room rate is $75 single or $85 double, $10 for an extra person, and five- and seven-day rates are available. Owner Josie Diego also rents the one-bedroom house next door for $125 per night and a cabin behind it for $95 per night. Aside from these, Josie also rents five other houses and cottages in town from 1–3 bedrooms that range from $100–150 per night. No credit cards or personal checks are accepted. To find Josie's, turn off the Hana Highway onto Ka'uiki Street, near Pa'ani Mai Park, and go down to the bend in the road.

Located on the road that leads to the airport, **Tradewinds Cottages,** P.O. Box 385, Hana, HI 96713, 808/248-8980 or 800/327-8097, twt@maui.net, www.hanamaui.net, rents two detached houses set in a tropical flower garden that have full kitchens and bathrooms, queen-size beds and sleeper sofas, color TVs, ceiling fans, and a hot tub on each desk. The Tradewinds Cottage runs $145 per night, maximum of six, while the smaller Hana Cabana is $120 per night, maximum of four; $10 each additional person after the first couple. No meals are provided, but you can pick fruit from the trees on property when it's ripe. In addition, the owner has a new rental house in town with an unobstructed view over the bay, where rooms go for $135–$210, depending on the number needed.

A magnificent place on the lower road into town, **Hana Hale Malamalama,** P.O. Box 374, Hana, HI 96713, 808/248-7718, hanahale@maui.net, www.hanahale.com, overlooks an ancient, rebuilt fish pond. This is a culturally significant site, and numerous artifacts have been found here. Great care has been taken to aesthetically landscape the property so that the buildings seem to fit in as if they've been here for years. Four buildings make up the compound. Set next to the pond, the Royal Lodge is a two-floor, 1,800-square-foot house made in the Philippines of hardwood, transported here, and reconstructed. Upstairs is the Royal Suite; downstairs, the Garden Suite. Up on the bluff are the two-story Tree House Cottage, Poolside Bungalow, and Banana Cabana. The Royal Suite runs $225 and the Garden Suite $125, but these two can be rented together as a complete unit. The Poolside Bungalow is $160, the Tree House Cottage $175, and the Banana Cottage runs $150. There is a two-night minimum for all units, and a continental breakfast comes with each. This is a perfect place for a honeymoon or for a couple who just wants a little luxury and class without spending an arm and a leg. Two units next door are also rented, the Bamboo Inn Suite at $150 and the two-story, two-bedroom Bamboo Inn Villa for $200. Call John Romain for reservations.

**Hana Accommodations,** 808/248-7868 or 800/228-4262, fax 808/248-8240, info@hana-maui.com, www.hana-maui.com, rents two private houses and two studios on the lush, tropical Hana coast just beyond town near Waioka Pool. Your choices include a three-bedroom, one-bathroom house with a full kitchen that can sleep up to eight for $150 and sits on its own property. Next door is a two-bedroom cottage with a full kitchen and an outdoor shower in the garden for $120. Located in the garden, the smaller units are both cozy studios for up to two people, one with an efficiency kitchen and the other with only a few cooking appliances, that run $76–95. Rates drop slightly after four days. Contact Tom Nunn for reservations.

**Hana Ali'i Holidays,** P.O. Box 536, Hana, HI 96713, 808/248-7742 or 800/548-0478, fax 808/248-8595, info@hanaalii.com, www.hanaalii.com, a second and larger agency in Hana, rents everything from a seaside cottage to large plantation homes scattered throughout the Hana area, offering more than a dozen homes, cottages, and studios to choose from.

One of the smallest is the Hauoli Lio Cottage, which is situated on a horse ranch and perfect for two at $80 per night. At the other end are Hale Kilohana, which is a two-story, three-bedroom island house with all amenities, and only a short walk to Hamoa beach, for $250 per night, and the Hamoa Beach house, also a two-story affair with three bedrooms, that rents for $300 per night or $100 more with a detached studio. All others, oceanfront, secluded, budget, fall in between, and several can be rented together for larger groups. Weekly and monthly rentals are also available. Some units are nonsmoking, some have a minimum of two nights' stay. Contact Duke; he'll set you up with something that's just right for your needs. He runs a quality business with quality homes.

**Hamoa Bay House and Bungalow,** P.O. Box 773, Hana, HI 96713, 808/248-7884 or fax 808/248-7047, hamoabay@maui.net, www.hamoabay.com, sits in a copse of trees and bamboo just off the Hana Highway above Hamoa Beach. Inspired by the architecture of Bali, two stone lions holding umbrellas greet you at the driveway. The main house and a second-story studio in the back are both for rent. The main house has two bedrooms, while the upstairs unit has a living room/bedroom. Both have full kitchens and baths, plus ceiling fans, TVs, phones, and barbecues. The studio has a hot tub/shower on the screened porch, while the house has an outdoor shower. Laundry facilities are available. Either makes a fine romantic getaway. Rates for the house are $250 for two or $350 for four, with a three-night minimum. For the upstairs studio, it's $195 per night, with a three-night minimum. Cash, personal and traveler's checks only; no credit cards. No smoking, and no children under 14.

**Hana Oceanfront Cottages,** P.O. Box 843 Hana, HI 96713, 808/248-7558 or 877/871-2055, dansandi@maui.net, www.hanaocean-frontcottages.com, sits above and overlooks Hamoa Beach. The downstairs one-bedroom suite in the main house is a large 1,100-square-foot unit with Hawaiian decoration fronted by a covered lanai. It rents for $195 per night. The Hamoa Beach Cottage is a separate unit, also large and also in Hawaiian decor, that goes for $235 per night. Each has a complete kitchen and all necessities, a gas grill, an entertainment center, and a outdoor showers; two nights minimum.

Beyond Hamoa Beach is Waioka Pool. High above the highway near this pool, with a million-dollar view out over the ocean, is the new **Hana's Heaven** vacation rental, P.O. Box 1006, Hana, HI 96713, 808/248-8854 or 888/205-3030, www.hanasheaven.com, great for a sunrise because it faces east. Hana's Heaven is one studio unit, bright, clean, and cheery, with a full kitchen, tiled bathroom, washer and dryer, and screened porch. Huge picture windows front the unit for the best views. This studio runs $150 per night for a couple and $20 extra for each additional person. For information and reservations, contact the owners who live on property.

Set high above the west end of town, the luxurious vacation rental **Ekena**, P.O. Box 728, Hana HI 96713, tel/fax 808/248-7047, ekena@maui.net, www.maui.net/~ekena, is owned and operated by Robin and Gaylord Gaffney. The upper and lower floors are separate, but only one level is rented at a time—unless the entire building is desired—so you won't be disturbed by anyone. So spacious are these units that each floor could be rented by two couples, one on each end, who want to share the cost and enjoy each others' company. Both floors have large living rooms, fully equipped kitchens, two master bedrooms, and spacious bathrooms. Ekena is a wonderful pole building with a huge deck and spectacular views both down to the coast and up the mountainside. Because it sits high up the hill, it is almost always graced with trade winds, so even if it's dead calm in town it may be breezy up there. At the upper end of the vacation rental bracket, it's not cheap, but it's good value for the money. The Jasmine level with one bedroom goes for $185 per night, two bedrooms $250. The Sea Breeze level is $350. Both together for up to eight guests run $600 per night. Three nights minimum, no kids younger than 14. For information and reservations, contact T. Isetorp.

The second most famous Hana accommodation, the **Heavenly Hana Inn**, P.O. Box 790, Hana, HI 96713, tel/fax 808/248-8442, hanainn@maui.net, www.heavenlyhanainn.com, resembles a Japanese *ryokan*. It's located within the bamboo fence, just past the schools on the way into town. Walk through the formal garden and remove your shoes on entering the open-beamed main dining hall. Skylights brighten this central dining area. The inn is homey and delightful, and tea and meditation rooms flank the front entrance, adding a sense of tranquility. Having undergone renovations, the inn is more beautiful than ever in its simplicity. A variety of woods give warmth to the living areas, shoji screens hide what need not always be present, and the decoration is perfectly authentic. The three suites seem like little apartments broken up into sections by shoji screens. Each has a sleeping room, bathroom with soaking tub, a sitting room with television but no telephone, and its own private entrance. One suite has a second bedroom. No children under age 15 and no smoking is allowed inside. Special gourmet breakfasts are served at $15 per person with at least one week prior notice, and lunch or tea service can also be accommodated upon request with advance notice. These suites run $185–250 per night, with a two-night minimum.

## Hana Kai Maui Resort

These resort condos, the only condo rentals in town at 1533 Uakea Road, and AAA approved, are all well maintained and offer a lot for the money. Because there are only 16 rental units on property, you know this is an intimate place. Rates are studios $125–145, deluxe one-bedrooms $145–195; fifth night free, and weekly and monthly rates available. All have private lanai with exemplary views of the bay, maid service, laundry facilities, and barbecues, but no phone or television. The views couldn't be better because the grounds, laid out in a lovely garden highlighting the interplay of black lava rock and multihued blooms, step down the mountainside to Popolana Beach on Hana Bay. For additional information, contact: P.O. Box 38, Hana, HI 96713, 808/248-8426 or 800/346-2772, fax 808/248-7482, hanakai@maui.net, www.hanakaimaui.com.

# FOOD

## Hotel Hana-Maui

As far as dining out goes, there's little to choose from in Hana. The Hotel Hana-Maui main dining room offers breakfast, lunch, and dinner. Prices vary according to your choice of options, but expect to spend $10–15 for breakfast and lunch and $24–37 for a dinner entrée. Reservations are highly recommended; call 808/248-8211. Light food and appetizers are also served at the Paniolo Bar 2:30–9 P.M. The bar menu includes such items as paniolo baby back ribs, Hana cobb salad, teriyaki burger, and furikake shoestring fries. Served 7:30–10:30 A.M., breakfast is all manner of fresh fruits and juices, hot pastries, eggs Benedict, pancakes, and omelets. Lunch, served 11:30 A.M.–2:30 P.M., includes hoisin-orange glazed duck salad, steamed pork and vegetable gyoza, plus a variety of burgers and sandwiches. Special dinner menus are prepared daily, but you can begin with ahi sashimi, Hana breadfruit cakes, or shiitake mushroom soup, and then move on to an assortment of grilled, seared, or roasted chicken and seafood, or locally grown beef and lamb, all basted in a variety of sauces. Desserts are too tempting to resist. Dinner is served 6–9 P.M.

If you're going the Hamoa Beach for the day, the hotel can prepare a picnic lunch for you at $18.50 per person. Make reservations at the activities desk in the hotel lobby.

Entertainment at the hotel—and that, quite frankly, is it for the whole town—is an informal hula and Hawaiian music shows put on by local families during dinner on Thursday and Sunday at 7 P.M. Aside from that, music is performed Thursday–Sunday at the Paniolo Bar, usually by one or two local musicians on ukulele and/or guitar, who fill the entire building with good cheer and melodious song before and after dinner. The Paniolo Bar is open daily 11:30 A.M.–10:30 P.M. For alternate entertainment, try the frequent evening baseball games at the ballpark behind the hotel.

## Hana Ranch Restaurant

The Hana Ranch Restaurant, 808/248-8255, serves very tasty meals, but it can be stampeded by ravenous tourists heading up or down the Hana Road. Reservations are recommended. Seating is inside or on the lanai under a timber framework. A buffet lunch is served daily 11 A.M.–3 P.M. Dinner is served Friday and Saturday evenings 5:30–8:30 P.M., and Wednesday is pizza night. The dinner menu includes appetizers like crispy crab cakes and homemade onion rings. Follow this with your choice of salad and an entrée, which might include fish chowder, grilled salmon, and baby back pork ribs, mostly in the $17–23 range. A short wine list is available, or you can choose some other drink or beer from the bar. A notch or two below the hotel restaurant, the food here is tasty, filling, and decently priced. Besides the Hotel Hana-Maui, the Hana Ranch Restaurant is the only place in Hana to have an evening meal. The outside take-out window is open 6:30 A.M.–7 P.M. for plate lunches, burgers, sandwiches, and saimin, but is only open until 4 P.M. on nights that the restaurant serves dinner inside. Shaded picnic tables are to the side.

## Tu Tu's

Tu Tu's Snack Shop, open Mon.–Sat. 8 A.M.–4 P.M. at the community center building fronting the beach, offers window service and a few tables on the porch. Eggs, *loco moco*, French toast, and other breakfast items are all under $4.50, sandwiches to $4, and plate lunches under $6.50. Other items include salads, saimin, hamburgers, drinks, and ice cream. This building, which has bathrooms, was donated to the community by Mrs. Fagan, the wife of Paul Fagan, the original owner of the Hotel Hana-Maui.

# SHOPPING

## Hasegawa's General Store

In the ranks of general stores, Hasegawa's would be commander-in-chief. This institution, run by Harry Hasegawa, had been in the family for 80 years before it burned to the ground in the fall of 1990. While your gas tank was being filled, you could buy anything from a cane knife to a computer disk. There

MAUI

were rows of food items, dry goods, and a hardware and parts store out back. Cold beer, film, blue jeans, and picnic supplies—somehow it was all crammed in there. Everybody went to Hasegawa's, and it was a treat just to browse and people-watch. Now revived and housed in the old movie theater building, this store still serves the community and visitors that sustained it for so long. It's just as packed as ever, has the only one-day film processing in town, and its only ATM. Open Monday–Saturday 7 A.M.–7 P.M., Sunday 8 A.M.–6 P.M.; 808/248-8231.

### Hana Ranch Store

From the Hana Road, make the first right past St. Mary's Catholic Church and go up to the top of the hill to find the Hana Ranch Store, 808/248-8261, open daily 7 A.M.–7 P.M., a general store with an emphasis on foodstuffs. It carries a supply of imported beers, a wide selection of food items, film, videos, and some gifts. The bulletin board here gives you a good idea of what's currently happening in town.

In the small complex next to the Hana Ranch Restaurant, look for **Hana Treasures,** open Mon.–Fri. 9 A.M.–4 P.M., Saturday and Sunday until 3 P.M. The small shop features airbrushed T-shirts by Hana artists, an assortment of Hawaiian gifts and souvenirs, particularly those made in the Hana area, and a display case of silver necklaces, bracelets, and rings. Also in this complex look for **Lauhala Gifts,** the small flower shop, gift, and craft store across the way.

### Hana Coast Gallery

Located at Hotel Hana-Maui, this gallery displays an excellent collection of fine art by Hawaiian residents. Not only is the work of very high quality, but the whole gallery is set up in a way that's conducive to show off each piece to its fullest. The list is long, but some of what you'll find here is watercolors, turned wood bowls, Asian brush paintings, bronze sculpture, woodblock prints, jewelry, basketry, and wood furniture. The gallery, 808/248-8636, is open daily 9 A.M.–5 P.M.

## ACTIVITIES

### Hana-Maui Sea Sports

Arranged through the Hotel Hana-Maui activities desk or by calling 808/248-7711, this kayak adventure heads to Hana Bay for a two-hour session and can take as many as eight people. Kayak and snorkel tours are given at 9:30 A.M. and 2 P.M.; $79 per person, half price under age 12. They'll even snap pictures underwater for you as you snorkel and print them before you leave.

### Horseback Riding

Horseback rides are given at the Hana Ranch Stables. A one-hour trail ride, either along the coast or in the upper pastures, leaves at various times throughout the day, and a two-hour ride goes at 9 A.M. on Tuesdays and Thursdays. The short rides cost $50 per person, the longer ride $90, and riders must be at least seven years old. Private rides can also be arranged.

### Jogging Trail

A walking, jogging, bicycling trail is maintained on Hana Ranch property, on what was the narrow-gauge sugarcane railroad bed. The trail runs for a bit more than two miles and starts partway up the path to the Fagan Memorial. Walk south. The trail meets the highway near where Haneo'o Road turns down to Koki Beach.

### Power Hang Gliding

The only commercial ultralight motorized paragliding on the island runs out of the Hana Airport, and only then by appointment. **Hang Gliding Maui,** 808/572-6557, offers tandem flights that run 30–60 minutes for $115–190. This open-cockpit, slow-speed tour gets you as close to a bird's-eye view of the area as is possible.

## SERVICES

### Medical Services

Along the Hana Road at the Y intersection, clearly marked on the right just as you enter town, is **Hana Community Health Center,** 808/248-8294. Open weekdays 8:30 A.M.–4:30 P.M. Walk-in, nonemergency treatment is available. For emergencies, use the phone at the hospital entrance or dial 911.

## Police Station

The police station is at the Y intersection between Hana Highway and Uakea Road, just as you enter town. For emergencies call 911; otherwise, 808/248-8311.

## Bank, Post Office, and Library

The Bank of Hawaii, 808/248-8015, is open Monday–Thursday 3–4:30 P.M., Friday 3–6 P.M.; cash advances on Visa and MasterCard can be made there. For an ATM, go to Hasegawa's store.

The **post office** is open weekdays 8 A.M.–4:30 P.M.; a community bulletin board is posted outside. Both are next door to the Hana Ranch Restaurant. The excellent Hana school/public **library**, 808/248-7714, is located at the new Hana School on the western edge of town; open Monday, Tuesday, and Friday 8 A.M.–4 P.M. (from

9 A.M. on Tuesday), Wednesday and Thursday 11 A.M.–7 P.M.

## Gas

There is one gas station in town. The Chevron station next to the horse stables is open daily 7:30 A.M.–6:30 P.M. It has a public bathroom and telephone. Gas in Hana is expensive, about $.40 per gallon higher than elsewhere on the island. Be sure to fill up before leaving town because the nearest gas station west is in Pa'ia; going south around the bottom, the closest is in Keokea in Upcountry.

## Car Rental

Located at the airport, **Dollar Rent A Car,** 808/248-8237, is the only show in town. It's best to call in advance to ensure a reservation. Cars may be available on short notice during low season, but don't count on it. If you're staying at the Hotel Hana-Maui, the activity desk there can also help arrange this service.

# Beyond Hana

About one-half mile south of Hana is mile marker 51. From there, the mile markers decrease in number as you continue around the south coast back to Kahului. Now you're getting into adventure. The first sign is that the road becomes narrower, then the twists and turns begin again. After 'Ohe'o Gulch, a few miles are still unpaved, which is followed by a long stretch that's nothing more than a patchwork quilt of filled potholes. You know you're in a rural area with not much traffic when you come across the sign "Caution: Baby Pigs Crossing." There is one phone, no gas, only a fruit or flower stand or two, and one store until you reach Ulupalakua Ranch. Although the road is good for most of the year, during heavy rains sections do still wash out and become impassable. The fainthearted should turn back, but those with gumption are in for a treat. There are roadside waterfalls, thick luscious forests, cascading streams filling a series of pools, pocket-size ranches, a hero's grave, tiny plantation communities, some forgotten towns,

isolated homesteads, million-dollar retirement retreats, and desolate scrubby ranchland. If you persevere all the way, you pop out at the Tedeschi Winery, where you can reward yourself with a glass of bubbly before returning to civilization.

## Waioka Pool

A myth-legend says Waioka Pool, also referred to by some as Venus Pool, was once used exclusively by Hawaiian royalty. At the Waiohonu bridge just past mile marker 48, cross over the fence and hike (public-access trail) through the fields above the river to its mouth. There you'll find a series of waterfalls below the bridge and a freshwater pool scoured out of the solid rock walls of this water course. Used by Hawaiian royalty during centuries past, it's now a refreshing, usually solitary, place for a swim or to sunbathe on the smooth rocks. Be safe and stay out of the ocean because the surf, which can be just over the narrow sandbar, is strong. At certain times of the year you may see giant turtles just off the rocks a short way farther down the coast. In the fields above and to the north of Waiohino Stream are the remains of an old sugar mill and part of the King's Highway, a paved pathway that once ran along the coast. In 2002, Hana Ranch set aside 41 acres of the oceanfront property running north from the stream as a "perpetual conservation easement" that cannot be developed in the future but may still be grazed by ranch cattle. Just down the road in Pu'uiki is the refurbished **St. Peter's Church** (1859).

## Wailua Falls

About six miles after leaving Hana, Wailua and Kanahuali'i Falls tumble over steep lava *pali,* filling the air with a watery mist and filling their pools below. They're just outside your car door, and a minute's effort will take you to the mossy grotto at the base. There's room to park. If not for 'Ohe'o up ahead, this would be a great picnic spot, but wait! Sometimes roadside artists park here, and basket makers or fruit sellers ply their trade. Check out the taro fields that have been created on the ocean side of the road. If you are going back toward Hana on this road, you will see another falls high above Wailua Falls on the mountain above. In a few minutes, about one-half mile before you enter the park, you pass a little shrine cut into the

mountain. This is the **Virgin by the Roadside.** It's usually draped with a fresh lei.

## KIPAHULU

This is where the enormous **Kipahulu Valley** meets the sea. It's also the coastal boundary of Haleakala National Park. Most of this valley, about one-third of the national park area, is off limits to the public, set aside as a biological preserve. Palikea Stream starts way up on Haleakala and steps its way through the valley, leaving footprints of waterfalls and pools until it spends itself in the sea. The area was named the Seven Sacred Pools by some unknown publicity person in the late '40s. The area should have been held sacred, but it wasn't. Everything was right here. You can feel the tremendous power of nature: bubbling waters, Haleakala red and regal in the background, and the sea pounding away. Hawaiians lived here—there are remains of housing sites—but the numerous *heiau* that you might expect seem to be missing. Besides that, there aren't seven pools—there are a few dozen! The name "Seven Sacred Pools" is falling into disfavor because it is inaccurate. Local people and the National Park Service prefer the proper name Kipahulu, Pools of 'Ohe'o, and 'Ohe'o Gulch, instead. In the late '90s, 52 acres were added to

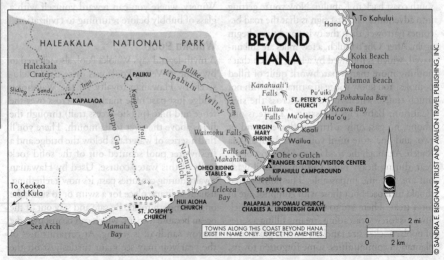

the park near the pools, including additional shoreline and the Kanekauila Heiau.

## Visitors Center

About 10 miles out of Hana you'll come to a large cement arched bridge (excellent view) and then a parking area to your left with a ranger's station/visitors center, restrooms, and public telephone. Pay your $10 entrance fee at the visitors center. From the visitors center lanai you can see the Big island looming on the horizon on a clear day. Information on the Kipahulu district of the national park, area trails and their conditions, the native Hawaiian people who lived in the area and their lifestyle, and the natural resources of the district are all well explained by displays inside. The center also stocks a selection of books about the area. A small bulletin board outside displays other information. The center is open daily 9 A.M.–5 P.M. The rangers are friendly and informative, so before doing any exploring stop in and ask about trail conditions. They know a tremendous amount of natural history concerning the area and can inform you about the few dangers in the area, such as the flash flooding that occurs in the pools. Interpretive talks are given at the ranger station daily at 12:30, 1:30, 2:30, and 3:30 every afternoon, and occasional cultural programs are offered every Thursday. Call the ranger station, 808/248-7375, for information. You can hike the trail by yourself, but ranger-led hikes are also given. A short one-mile hike goes to the Bamboo Forest daily except Saturday at 9:30 A.M. Those intending to hike or camp should bring their own water. Most people go to the easily accessible lower pools, but a stiff hike up the mountain takes you to the upper pools, a bamboo forest, and a fantastic waterfall; 99 percent of park visitors are gone by sundown. From the parking lot, a short dirt track leads down to the large, grassy camping area.

## The Lower Pools

Head along the clearly marked **Kuloa Point Loop Trail** from the parking area to the flat, grass-covered peninsula. The winds are heavy here as they enter the mouth of the valley from the sea. A series of pools to choose from is off

relaxing at the lower pools, 'Oheo Gulch

to your left. It's delightful to lie in the last one and look out to the sea crunching the shore just a few yards away. Move upstream for the best swimming in the largest of the lower pools. Be careful, though, because you'll have to do some fairly difficult rock climbing. The best route is along the right-hand side as you face up the valley. Once you're satiated, head back up to the road along the path on the left-hand side and above the riverbank. This trail will take you back to the ranger station, or you can walk up to the arch bridge that you crossed when arriving, one of the best vantage points from which to look up and down this amazing valley. This trail is a half-mile loop from the ranger station. From near the point, the **Kahakai Trail** runs along the coast to the campground.

## Waterfalls

Few people head for the waterfalls, buat those who will be delighted. The trail is called **Waimoku Falls Trail,** and it begins at the ranger station. The falls at Makahiku are one-half mile uphill, and Waimoku Falls is two miles distant. The toughest part is at the beginning as you huff-puff your way uphill. Soon, the trail brings you to an overlook, from where you can see the lace-like **Falls at Makahiku** as it plummets 181 feet to the rugged valley floor below. A short way beyond this is a shorter second falls, where the pool has undercut the opposite bank and the water then cascades down through a narrow gorge and series of stepped pools. During summer, guava and other fruit drops to the ground, creating a pungent or downright smelly fragrance along the trail. The path continues over two new metal bridges that cross more cascades and pools, and then zigzag up the opposite bank. After passing some enormous mango trees, you head through a high jungle area. Suddenly you're in an extremely dense bamboo forest—an incredible experience in itself. The trail is well cut as you pass through the green darkness of this stand. If the wind is blowing, the bamboo will sing a mournful song for you. Here you get the first glimpse of the waterfall—a tease of what's ahead. This trail gets somewhat sloppy and slippery in sections, and about one-quarter mile of boardwalk had been built over small streams and the worst of the soggy ground. Emerge into more mangos and thimbleberries and there's the creek again. Turn left and follow the creek, without crossing yet, and the trail will become distinct again. There's a wooden walkway, and then, eureka!—Waimoku Falls. It cascades over the *pali* and is so high that you have to strain your neck back as far as it will go. It's more than a waterfall; it's silver filigree. You can stand in the shallow pool below surrounded by a sheer rock amphitheater. The sunlight dances in this area and tiny rainbows appear and disappear. If you are there during the rains, you may see more than one extra waterfall coming off the cliff above.

One word of warning: As at all such waterfalls on the islands, where the pool beckons to slack the heat and the surrounding scenery is so captivating, rocks and boulders periodically dislodge from the *pali* above and tumble into the pool below. How else have the boulders in the pool gotten to where they are? Usually, although not always, these falling rocks are accompanied by sounds of rock striking rock. Always keep an ear out for danger and an eye upward. At popular

and oft-visited waterfalls, warning signs are posted to warn you of such dangers and to keep you out of harm's way. Know the dangers and heed the warnings.

## Camping

Kipahulu is part of Haleakala National Park, and camping is free (obtain permit at the visitors center) in designated sites only for a three-day limit. No backcountry camping or camping along the streams is allowed. Groups of more than 12 should obtain permits from the park superintendent at Park Headquarters, P.O. Box 369, Makawao, HI 96768, 808/572-9306. The campground (maximum 100) is primitive and mostly empty, except for holiday weekends, when they can be packed. From the parking lot follow the camping sign and continue down the hill on the rutted dirt track. Bear right to a large, grassy area overlooking the sea, where signs warn you not to disturb an archaeological area. Notice how spongy the grass is here. Move to the trees to escape the wind. Here are clean outhouses, a few picnic tables and barbecue grills, but no potable water, so make sure to bring plenty of your own to drink.

## BEYOND 'OHE'O GULCH

Some of Route 31 beyond 'Ohe'o is genuinely rugged and makes the car companies cry. But it can be driven, and even the tourist vans make it part of their regular route. Be aware, however, that rough weather can bring landslides; the road may be closed by a locked gate with access available only for official business and local residents. Check the bulletin board at the ranger station for road conditions! If the road is closed, a sign in Hana will warn you of this condition. In 1.5 miles you come to the well-kept clapboard **St. Paul's Church,** which sits right next to the highway. Services are conducted here twice a month. To its side are the smokestack and ruins of the long-silenced sugar mill that once processed cane from this area. A little farther along and down a side road is **Palapala Ho'omau Church** (founded 1864) and its tiny cemetery, where Charles Lindbergh and Sam Pryor are buried. People, especially those who are old enough to remember

ROBERT NILSEN

Looking at the Kaupo Gap, it's easy to imagine hot molten lava flowing out of the Haleakala crater basin, as it did in ages past.

the "Lone Eagle's" historic flight, are drawn here like pilgrims. The public is not really encouraged to visit, but the human tide cannot be stopped. If you go, please follow all of the directions posted. Right next to the church cemetery is the tiny **Kipahulu Lighthouse Point County Park,** which sits on the edge of the cliff overlooking the frothy ocean below. Several trees and picnic tables provide a quiet and shaded place for a bite to eat and a rest. Up the road is Samuel F. Pryor's Kipahulu Ranch. Mr. Pryor was a vice president of Pan Am and a close chum of Lindbergh's. It was he who encouraged Lindbergh to spend his last years in Hana.

Kipahulu Ranch has seen other amazing men. Last century a Japanese samurai named Sentaro Ishii lived here. He was enormous, especially for a Japanese of that day, more than six feet tall. He came in search of work, and at the age of 61 married Kehele, a local girl. He lived in Kipahulu until he died at the age of 102.

Past Sam Pryor's place is **Oheo Riding Stables,** up a long driveway from the road. From here two rides a day are taken through the lush vegetation to spots overlooking Makahiku and

Waimoku Falls, both in the national park. About three hours are spent in the saddle; six guests maximum per ride.

A few dozen yards past the Kukuiula Bridge is a great spot for a view of the coastline and the roadway carved into the side of the hill. Park near the bridge and walk up the road to take pictures. Past here the road really begins to get rugged and narrow, but only about eight miles remain partially unpaved. If the road is dry, continue cautiously; if it's been raining hard, consider turning back. At the Kalena Bridge, a couple of miles ahead, the road designation changes to Pi'ilani Highway, Route 31.

## Kaupo

The vistas open up at the beginning of the Kaupo Gap just when you pass **Hui Aloha Church.** Built in 1859, this church sits on a level, grassy spot below the road near the sea. Depending on the weather and how long since it was last graded, the road down may be very rough and impassable except with a 4WD vehicle. Eight miles from 'Ohe'o, the village of **Kaupo** and the Kaupo Store follow Hui Aloha Church. Kaupo means

MAUI

Landing at Night and may refer to travelers from other islands who landed by canoe at night on this south shore of Maui. Both the coastline and inland areas of Kaupo sustained substantial Hawaiian communities for hundreds of years.

After so many years of erratic hours and unpredictable closures, Kaupo Store once again has regular hours, Monday–Saturday 10 A.M.–5 P.M. A real anachronism, the store serves double duty as unofficial dusty museum and convenience store. Along with the antiques hanging on the walls and filling the shelves (not for sale), the store stocks cold juices and beer, ice cream, candy, and chips—mostly snacks and traveling food—but it also has a few gifts.

Only a few families live in Kaupo, old ones who ranch and new ones trying to live independently. During decades past, Kaupo Store, which was established in the mid-1920s, was the center of this community. If only the walls could talk, what stories they would tell. Kaupo Store is the last of a chain of stores that once stretched all the way from Ke'anae and were owned by the Soon Family. Nick Soon was kind of a modern-day wizard. He lived in Kaupo, and among his exploits he assembled a car and truck brought piecemeal on a barge, built the first electric generator in the area, and even made from scratch a model airplane that flew. He was the son of an indentured Chinese laborer.

A short distance past Kaupo is **St. Joseph's Church.** Built in 1862, it was renovated in 1991. Services are held on the fifth Sunday of the month, so only a few times per year. In 2002, this church hosted a wedding, the first in 47 years! The abandoned rectory stands to the side.

Once you get to the Kaupo Gap, the tropical vegetation suddenly stops and the landscape is barren and dry for most of the year. Here Haleakala's rain shadow creates an environment of yellow grassland dotted with volcanic rock. Everywhere are *ahu,* usually three stacked stones, that people have left as personal prayers and wishes to the gods. Just after Kaupo, the dirt road becomes a beat-up patchwork that wheels along past range land and ranches with the ocean far below. When the road dips to the ocean, you are in Kaupo Ranch. Near the mouth of the deepest valley to slit this side of the island, you'll find a pebble beach that seems to stretch a mile. At mile marker 32, look down to the coast and see two rough volcanic peninsulas. On the westernmost sits a *heiau.* A short way beyond, before the road dips down the hillside, is a pulloff where you can walk out on a bluff and overlook these peninsulas. A good but distant view of these peninsulas is also possible from another pulloff near mile marker 29. Near here, looking west, is a good spot to view a sea arch, and by mile marker 28 you get a good look at the bottom end of one of the mountainside's deepest gulches. Beyond that, the road gains elevation and the landscape becomes more arid except for the green carpet of trees high up on the mountainside. From there, you can look down on Maui's last lava flow and La Pérouse Bay. Near mile marker 23, the new road surface starts, and before the road tucks back into the trees you get great views of the coast. Be aware of free-range cattle, which can be in the middle of the road around any turn, all the way along this road through Kaupo. Enjoy the road, because in a few minutes you'll be back in the civilized world.

# Lana'i

Lana'i (Day of Conquest), in the long, dark past of Hawaiian legend-history, was a sad, desolate, and secluded place inhabited by man-eating spirits and fiendish blood-curdling ghouls. It was redeemed by spoiled but tough Prince Kaulula'au, exiled there by his kingly father, Kaka'alaneo of Maui. Kaulula'au proved to be not only brave, but wily too; he cleared Lana'i of its spirits through trickery and opened the way for human habitation. Lana'i was for many generations a burial ground for the *ali'i* and therefore filled with sacred *mana* and *kapu* to commoners. Later, reports of its inhospitable shores filled the logs of old sailing vessels. In foul weather, captains navigated desperately to avoid its infamously treacherous waters, whose melancholy whitecaps still outline Shipwreck Beach and give credence to its name.

Most people visiting the Hawaiian Islands view Lana'i from Lahaina on West Maui but never actually set foot on this lovely, quiet island. For two centuries, first hunters and then lovers of the humpback whale have come to peer across the waters of the 'Au'au Channel, better known as the Lahaina Roads, in search of these magnificent giants. Lana'i is a victim of its own reputation. Most visitors were informed by even longtime residents that Lana'i, nicknamed The Pineapple Island, was a dull place covered in one large pineapple plantation: endless rows of the porcupine plants, sliced and organized by a labyrinth of roads, contoured and planted by improbable-looking machines, and tended by mostly Filipino workers in wide-brimmed hats and goggles. It's true that Lana'i had the largest pineapple plantation in the world, 15,000 cultivated acres, which accounted for about 90 percent of U.S.

ROBERT NILSEN

**Picture-perfect Hulopo'e Bay**

production, but production stopped in the mid-1990s and the carpet of pineapples is gone. The remnants of these fields are still obvious in the swirls of grass as you approach the island by air. Now only about 100 acres remain in cultivation out by the airport—as a testimony to a bygone era—and these fruits are raised for local consumption only. All other pineapples on the island are raised by local gardeners. But the island has 74,000 acres that remain untouched and perfect for exceptional outdoor experiences, ranging from golf to mountain biking to snorkeling.

Because of its past reputation as a place where almost no one went and recent shift from pineapple production to tourism that caters to the well-to-do who want their peace and quiet, Lana'i is once again becoming known as the "Secluded Island."

The people of Lana'i live in one of the most fortuitously chosen spots for a working village in the world: Lana'i City. All but about two dozen of the island's 3,200 permanent residents make their homes here. Nestled near the ridge of mountains in the northeast corner of the Palawai Basin, **Lana'i City** (elev. 1,600 feet) is sheltered, cooled, and characterized by a mature and extensive grove of Cook pines planted in the early 1900s by the practical New Zealand naturalist George Munro. This evergreen canopy creates a parklike atmosphere about town while reaching tall green fingers to the clouds. A mountainous spine tickles drizzle from the water-bloated bellies of passing clouds for the thirsty, red, sunburned plains of Lana'i below. The trees, like the bristled hair of an annoyed cat, line the **Munro Trail** as it climbs Lana'ihale, the highest spot on the island (3,370 feet). The Munro Trail's magnificent panoramas encompass sweeping views of no less than five of the eight major islands as it snakes along the mountain ridge, narrowing at times to the width of the road itself.

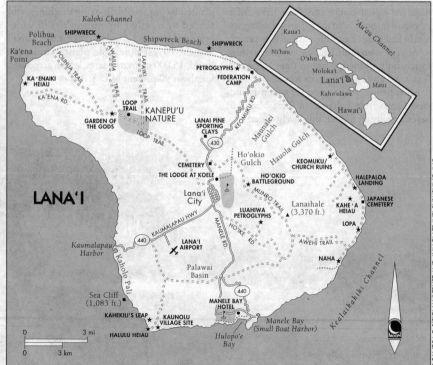

**Maunalei Gulch,** a vast precipitous valley, visible from "The Trail," was the site of a last-ditch effort of Lana'i warriors to repel an invasion by the warrior king of the Big Island at the turn of the 18th century. Now its craggy arms provide refuge to mouflon sheep as they execute death-defying leaps from one rocky ripple to the next. On the valley floors roam axis deer, and, until recently, on the northwest grasslands were the remnants of an experimental herd of pronghorn antelope brought from Montana in 1959. After saturating yourself with the glories of Lana'i from the heights, descend and follow a well-paved road from Lana'i City to the southern tip of the island. Here, **Manele** and **Hulopo'e** bays sit side by side. Manele is a favorite spot of small sailing craft that have braved the channel from Lahaina. Hulopo'e Bay, just next door, is as salubrious a spot as you can hope to find. It offers camping and all that's expected of a warm, sandy, palm-lined beach. With its virtually untouched underwater marine park, Hulopo'e is regarded as one of the premier snorkeling spots in the entire island chain.

You can hike or drive a 4WD vehicle to **Kaunolu,** one of the best-preserved ancient Hawaiian village sites. Kamehameha the Great came to this ruggedly masculine shore to fish and frolic his summers away with his favorite cronies. Here, Kahekili leaped from a sea cliff to the ice-blue waters below and challenged all other warriors to prove their loyalty to Kamehameha by following his example and hurtling themselves off what today is known as **Kahekili's Leap.**

You can quickly span a century by heading for the southeast corner of Lana'i and its three abandoned villages of **Lopa, Naha,** and **Keo-muku.** Here legends abound. *Kahuna* curses still guard a grove of coconut trees, which are purported to refuse to let you down if you climb for their nuts without offering the proper prayers. Here also are the remnants of a sugar train believed to have caused its cane enterprise to fail because the rocks of a nearby *heiau* were disturbed and used in its track bed. Nearby, a decaying abandoned Hawaiian church, the only remnant of the town of Keomuku, insists on being photographed.

You can head north along the east shore to **Shipwreck Beach,** where the rusting hulk of a ship, along with timbers and planks from the great wooden square-riggers of days gone by, lie along the beach, attesting to the authenticity of its name. Shipwreck Beach is a shore-stroller's paradise, a real beachcomber's boutique. Also along here are some thought-provoking **petroglyphs.** Other petroglyphs are found on a hillside overlooking the former "pine" fields of the Palawai Basin.

If you hunger for a totally private beach, head to the northwest corner of the island. En route, you'll pass through a scarce remnant of Hawaiian dryland forest at **Kanepu'u Preserve** and a fantastic area of ancient cataclysm aptly called **The Garden of the Gods.** This raw, baked area of monolithic rocks and tortured earth turns incredible shades of purple, red, magenta, and yellow as the sun plays on it from different angles. If you're hot and dusty and aching for a dip, continue north to trail's end, where the desolation of the garden suddenly gives way to the gleaming brightness of virtually unvisited **Polihua Beach.**

After these daily excursions, return to the green serenity of Lana'i City. Even if you're only spending a few days here, you'll be made to feel like you're staying with old friends. You won't have to worry about bringing your dancing shoes, but if you've had enough hustle and bustle and yearn to stroll in quietude, sit by a crackling fire, and look up at a crystal-clear sky, head for Lana'i. Your jangled nerves and ruffled spirit will be glad you did.

# THE LAND

The sunburned face of Lana'i seems parched but relaxed as it rises in a gentle, steady arc from sea level. When viewed from the air it looks like an irregularly shaped kidney bean. The sixth largest of the eight main islands, Lana'i is roughly 140 square miles, measuring 18 miles north to south and 13 miles east to west at its longest points, with 47 miles of coastline. A classic single-shield volcano, at one time Lana'i was probably connected to Maui, Moloka'i, and Kaho'olawe as a single huge island when the sea level was much lower. Its rounded features appear more benign

MAUI

than the violent creases of its closest island neighbors; this characteristic earned it the unflattering appellation of "Hump." More lyrical scholars, however, claim the real meaning has been lost to the ages or may in fact mean "Day of Conquest," but Lana'i does look like a hump when viewed from a distance at sea.

Its topography is simple. A rugged mountain ridge runs northwest to southeast through the eastern half of the island, and much of its length is traversed by the Munro Trail. The highest peak is Lana'ihale (3,370 feet). This area is creased by precipitous gulches on its windward side: The two deepest are Maunalei and Hauola at more than 2,000 feet. The topography tapers off steadily as it reaches the sea to the east. Beaches stretch from the white sands of Polihua, past Shipwreck Beach in the north, terminating at the salt-and-pepper sands of Naha on the east. Beyond a short section of sea cliff lie the beautiful rainbow arches of Manele and Hulopo'e in the south. Marine fossils found at the 1,000-foot mark and even higher in the mountains indicate its slow rise from the sea.

Until 1993, Palawai, Lana'i's central basin, was completely cultivated in manicured, whorled fields of pineapple. Before pineapple production, Palawai was covered in cactus, cattle were grazed, and some wheat was grown. Now it's nearly all gone fallow in tall grass. The southwest and west coasts have phenomenal sea cliffs accessible only by boat. Some of the most majestic are the **Kaholo Pali,** which run south from Kaumalapau Harbor, reaching their most amazing ruggedness before Kaunolu Bay. At many spots along this stretch the sea lies more than 1,500 feet below. Starting at Lana'i City in the center, a half hour of driving in any direction presents a choice of this varied and fascinating geography.

The southern and western shores of Lana'i are characterized by sheer cliffs that drop into deep blue water.

## Climate

The daily temperatures are quite balmy, especially at sea level, but it can get blisteringly hot in the basin and on the leeward side, so be sure to carry plenty of water when hiking or four-wheel-driving. At 1,600 feet, Lana'i City gets refreshingly cool in the evenings and early mornings, but a light jacket or sweater is adequate, although thin-blooded residents bundle up. While it's sunny most days, fog rolls into town occasionally, evoking an ethereal, mysterious feel and sense of magic. The average summer temperature along the coast of Lana'i is about 80°F while the average winter tempera-

## LANA'I CITY TEMPERATURE AND RAINFALL

|          | Jan. | March | May | June | Sept. | Nov. |
|----------|------|-------|-----|------|-------|------|
| High     | 70   | 71    | 75  | 80   | 80    | 72   |
| Low      | 60   | 60    | 62  | 65   | 65    | 62   |
| Rainfall | 3    | 3     | 2   | 0    | 2     | 4    |

Note: Temperature is in degrees Fahrenheit; rainfall in inches.

ture is about 70°F. It can be as much as 10 degrees cooler in Lana'i City.

## Water

Lying in the rain shadow of the West Maui Mountains, even Lana'i's windward side receives only 40 inches of rainfall per year. The central basins and leeward shores taper off to a scant 12 inches, not bad for pineapples and sun worshippers. Lana'i has always been short of water, but wells now help satisfy the needs of the residents. Its scruffy vegetation and red-baked earth are responsible for its inhospitable reputation. There are no rivers, and the few streams, found mostly in the gulches of the windward mountains, carry water only when the rains come and are otherwise dry. Most ventures at colonizing Lana'i, both in ancient and modern times, were kept to a minimum because of this water shortage. The famous Cook pines of Lana'i City, along with other introduced greenery, greatly helped the barrenness of the landscape and provided a watershed. They tickle the underside of and drink water from the clouds that graze the highland ridge. But the rust-red earth remains unchanged, and if you get it onto your clothes, it'll remain there as a permanent souvenir.

# FLORA AND FAUNA

Most of Lana'i's flora and fauna have been introduced. In fact, the Cook pine and the regal mouflon sheep were a man-made attempt to improve the natural, often barren habitat. These species have adapted so well that they now symbolize Lana'i, as the ubiquitous pineapple once did. Besides the mouflon, Lana'i boasts axis deer and a few feral goats. A wide variety of introduced game birds include the Rio Grande turkey, ring-necked pheasant, and an assortment of quail, francolins, and doves. Like the other Hawaiian islands, Lana'i, unfortunately, is home to native birds that are headed for extinction. Along the Munro Trail and on the windward coast you pass through forests of Cook pines, tall eucalyptus stands, shaggy ironwoods, native koa, and silver oaks. Everywhere, dazzling colors and fragrances are provided by Lana'i's flowers.

## Flowers

Although Lana'i's official flower is the *kauna'oa,* it's not really a flower, but an airplant that grows wild. It's easily found along the beach at Keomuku. It grows in conjunction with *pohuehue,* a pinkish red, perennial seashore morning glory. Native to Hawaii, the *pohuehue* grows in large numbers along Lana'i's seashore. It's easy to spot, and when you see a yellow-orange vinelike airplant growing with it, you've found Lana'i's *kauna'oa,* which is traditionally fashioned into lei. The medicinal *'ilima,* used to help asthma sufferers, is found in large numbers in Lana'i's open fields. Its flat, open yellow flower is about one inch in diameter and grows on a waist-high shrub. Two other flowers considered by some to be pests are the purple *koali* morning glory and the miniature red and yellow flowering lantana, known for its unpleasant odor. Both are abundant on the trail to the Garden of the Gods.

## Cook Pines

These pines were discovered by Captain Cook in the South Pacific, and some say that the first were brought here by Captain Vancouver as a future supply of ship masts. Imported in great numbers by George Munro, they adapted well to Lana'i and helped considerably to attract moisture and provide a firm watershed. Exquisitely ornamental, they can also be grown in containers. Their perfect cone shape makes them a natural Christmas tree, used as such in Hawaii; some are even shipped to the Mainland for this purpose.

## Endemic Birds

The list of native birds still found on Lana'i gets smaller every year, and those still on the list are rarely seen. The *'amakihi* is about five inches long with yellowish green plumage. The males deliver a high-sounding tweet and a trilling call. Vegetarians, these birds live mostly on grasses and lichen, building their nests in the uppermost branches of tall trees. Some people believe that the *'amakihi* is already extinct on Lana'i.

The *'ua'u* or Hawaiian petrel is a large bird with a 36-inch wingspan. Its head and back are shades of black with a white underbelly. This "fisherbird" lives on squid and crustaceans, which it regurgitates to its chicks. Unfortunately, the Hawaiian petrel nests on the ground, sometimes laying its eggs under rocks or in burrows, which makes it easy prey for predators. Its call is reported to sound like a small yapping dog.

The 'apapane is abundant on the other main islands but dwindling rapidly on Lana'i. It's a chubby red-bodied bird about five inches long with a black bill, legs, wingtips, and tail feathers. It's quick, flitty, and has a wide variety of calls and songs from beautiful warbles to mechanical buzzes. Its feathers were sought by Hawaiians to produce distinctive ornate featherwork.

## Axis Deer

This shy and beautiful creature came to Lana'i via Moloka'i, where the first specimens arrived in 1868 as a gift from the Hawaiian consul in Hong Kong. Its native home is the parkland forests of India and Sri Lanka. The coats of most axis deer are golden tan with rows of round lifetime spots, along with a black stripe down the back and a white belly. They stand 3–4 feet at the shoulder, with bucks weighing an average of 160 pounds and does about 110. The bucks have an exquisite set of symmetrical antlers that always form a perfect three points. The antlers can stand 30 inches high and more than 20 inches across, making them coveted trophies. Does are antlerless and give birth to one fawn, usually between November and February, but Hawaii's congenial weather makes for good fawn survival anytime of the year. Axis deer on Lana'i can be spotted anywhere from the lowland *kiawe* forests to the higher rainforests along the Munro Trail. Careful and proper hunting management should keep the population stable for many generations. The meat from axis deer is reported to have a unique flavor, different from Mainland venison—one of the finest tasting of all wild game.

## Mouflon Sheep

Another name for these wild mountain sheep is Mediterranean or European bighorn. One of only six species of wild sheep in the world, mouflon are native to the islands of Sardinia and Corsica, whose climates are quite similar to Hawaii's. They have been introduced throughout Europe, Africa, and North America. Although genetically similar to domestic sheep, they are much more shy, lack a woolly coat, and only infrequently give birth to twins. Both rams and ewes are a similar tannish brown, with a snow-white rump, which is all that most people get to see of these always-alert creatures as they quickly and expertly head for cover. Rams weigh about 125 pounds (ewes a bit less) and produce a spectacular set of recurved horns. They need little water to survive, going for long periods on only the moisture in green plants. On Lana'i they are found along the northwest coast in the grasslands and in the dry *kiawe* forests.

# HISTORY

Kaka'alaneo peered across the mist-shrouded channel between West Maui and Lana'i and couldn't believe his eyes. Night after night, the campfire of his son Kaulula'au burned, sending its faint but miraculous signal. Could it be that the boy was still alive? Kaulula'au had been given every advantage of his noble birth, but still the prince had proved to be unmanageable. King Kaka'alaneo had even ordered all children born on the same day as his son to be sent to Lahaina, where they would grow up as his son's friends and playmates. Spoiled rotten, young Kaulula'au had terrorized Lahaina with his pranks and one day went too far: He destroyed a new planting of breadfruit. Even the chief's son could not trample the social order and endanger the livelihood of the people. So finally the old *kahuna* had to step in. Justice was hard and swift: Kaulula'au must be banished to the terrible island of Lana'i, where the man-eating spirits dwelled. There he would meet his fate, and no one expected him to live. But weeks had passed and Kaulula'au's nightly fires still burned. Could it be some ghoulish trick? Kaka'alaneo sent a canoe of men to investigate. They returned with incredible news. The boy was fine! All the spirits were banished! Kaulula'au had cleansed the island of its evil fiends and opened it up for the people to come and settle.

## Oral History

In fact, it's recorded in the Hawaiian oral genealogical tradition that a young Kaulula'au did open Lana'i to significant numbers of inhabitants in approximately 1400. Lana'i passed through the next few hundred years as a satellite of Maui, accepting the larger island's social, religious, and political dictates. During this period, Lana'i supported about 3,000 people, who lived by growing taro and fishing. Most inhabited the eastern shore facing Maui, but old home sites show that the population became established well enough to homestead the entire island. Lana'i was caught up in the Hawaiian wars that raged in the last two decades of the 1700s and was ravaged and pillaged in 1778 by the warriors of Kalaniopu'u, aging king of the Big Island. These hard times marked a decline in Lana'i's population; accounts by Western sea captains who passed by even a few years later noted that the island looked desolate, with no large villages evident.

Lana'i began to recover and saw a small boost in population when Kamehameha the Great established his summer residence at Kaunolu on the southern shore. This kept Lana'i vibrant for a few years at the beginning of the 19th century, but it began to fade soon thereafter. The decline continued until only a handful of Hawaiians remained by the 20th century. The old order ended completely when one of the last traditional *kanaka*, a man named Ohua, hid the traditional fish god, Hunihi, and died shortly thereafter in his grass hut in the year 1900.

## Early Foreign Influences

No one knows his name for sure, but all historians agree that a Chinese man tried his luck at raising sugarcane on Lana'i in 1802. He brought boiling pots and rollers to Naha on the east coast, but after a year of hard luck gave up and moved on. About 100 years later a large commercial sugar enterprise was attempted in the same area. This time the sugar company even built a narrow-gauge railroad to carry the cane. A story goes that after disrupting a local *heiau* to make ballast for the rail line, the water in the area, never in great abundance to begin with, went brackish. Again sugar was foiled.

In 1854 a small band of Mormon elders tried to colonize Lana'i by starting a "City of Joseph" at Palawai Basin. This began the career of one of Hawaii's strangest, most unfathomable yet charismatic early leaders. Walter Murray Gibson came to Palawai to start an idyllic settlement for the Latter-day Saints. He energetically set to work improving the land with funds from Utah and the hard work of the other Mormon settlers. The only fly in Gibson's grand ointment occurred when the Mormon Church discovered that the acres of Palawai were not registered to the church at all but to Walter Murray Gibson himself! He was excommunicated and the bilked settlers relocated. Gibson went on to have one of the strangest political careers in Hawaiian history, including championing native rights and enjoying unbelievable influence at the royal Hawaiian court as Prime Minister to King Kalakaua. His land at Palawai passed on to his daughter, who became possessed by the one evil spirit Kaulula'au failed to eradicate: She tried to raise sugarcane, but was fated, like the rest, to fail.

A few other attempts proved uneconomical, and Lana'i languished. The last big attempt at cattle raising produced The Ranch, part of whose lands make up the Cavendish Golf Course in Lana'i City. This enterprise did have one bright note. A New Zealander named George Munro was hired as the manager. He imported all manner of seeds and cuttings in his attempt to foliate the island and create a watershed. The Ranch failed, but Munro's legacy of Cook pines stands as a proud testament to this amateur horticulturist.

## The Coming of Pineapples

The purchase of Lana'i in 1922 was one of the niftiest real estate deals in modern history. James D. Dole, the most enterprising of the pineapple pioneers, bought the island—lock, stock, and barrel—from the Baldwins, an old missionary family, for $1.1 million. That comes to only $12 per acre, although many of those acres were fairly scruffy, not to mention Lana'i's bad economical track record. Dole had come from Boston at the turn of the 20th century to figure out how to can pineapple profitably. Dole did such a remarkable job of marketing the "golden fruit" on the Mainland that in a few short years, Midwestern Americans who'd never even heard of pineapples before were buying cans of it regularly from the shelves of country grocery stores. In 1922, Jim Dole needed more land for his expanding pineapple fields, and the arid basin of Palawai seemed perfect.

Lana'i Plantation was an oligarchy during the early years, with the plantation manager as king. One of the most famous of these characters was H. Broomfield Brown, who ran Lana'i Plantation in the '30s. He kept watch over the fields from his house through a telescope. If anyone loafed, he'd ride out into the fields to confront the offender. Mr. Brown personally "eyeballed" every new visitor to Lana'i: All prostitutes, gamblers, and deadbeats were turned back at the pier. An anti-litter fanatic, he'd even reprimand anyone who trashed the streets of Lana'i City.

During the labor strikes of the 1960s, workers' grievances were voiced, and Lana'i began to function as a more fair enterprise. With pineapple well established on the world market, Lana'i finally had a firm economic base. From a few thousand fruits in the early days, the flow at its peak reached a million fruits per day during the height of the season. They were shipped from the manmade port at Kaumalapau, which was specially built in 1926 to accommodate Lana'i's "pines."

## Crushed Pineapples

At its height, Lana'i had 18,000 acres of pineapples under production (15,000 acres for most of its heyday). These acres made up the largest single pineapple plantation in the world. Virtually the entire island was operated by the Dole Co., whose name had become synonymous with pineapples. In one way or another, everyone on Lana'i owed their livelihood to pineapples, from the worker who twisted his ankle in a pine field to the technician at the community hospital who X-rayed it. Now, all has changed and only a few plots remain, mostly for use by the hotels.

Foreign production, especially in the Philippines, has greatly increased, and the Lana'i pineapple industry has folded. As acreage was taken out of pineapple production, and as the population of the island and number of visitors have increased, the company has experimented, without much success, with raising various organic vegetables, grains, and cattle to diversify the island's economy. This seems to be a pet project of the owner, and the hope is to make the economy of Lana'i more locally sustainable and less dependent on imports from the other islands and the Mainland.

## Changing Lana'i

Most are amazed that George Munro's pines still shelter a tight-knit community that has remained untouched for so long. But all that's changing, and changing quickly. Two new hideaway luxury hotels have risen, and they're beauties. The coming of these resorts has brought the most profound changes to Lana'i since James Dole arrived at the turn of the 20th century. Castle and Cooke, practically speaking, owns the island— 98 percent of it anyway. David Murdoch is the CEO and owner of Castle and Cooke, and the hotels are his babies. He developed them and the two golf courses and continues to develop residential lots (up to 700 in the next 10 years) through a permutation of companies that is now called the Lana'i Company. This company employs a staff of about 1,200 or so, more than all the workers needed to tend the pineapple fields, which was just over 500 people. The hotels have brought an alternative job market, new life to the downtown area, and a housing spurt. One fact was undeniable concerning Lana'i: If you wanted to make a living you either had to work the pineapple fields or leave. Now that has changed. To stop the disenfranchisement of the local people, which was generally the case with rapid development, the Lana'i Company has built several new housing projects, which have come with a promise. Local people, according to seniority with the company and length of residence on Lana'i, had first choice. One group of houses is multiple-family, geared to the entry-level buyer, and the second is single-family homes. Million-dollar homes are also starting to pop up above town and now begin to line the fairways of the new golf courses. This isn't all heart on the part of the Lana'i Company. It wants to ensure that the hotels will have a steady and contented workforce to keep them running without a hitch and to make the whole venture economically viable.

Downtown Lana'i is inadequate. It couldn't possibly handle the hotel guests and all of the new workers and their families who have moved to the island. Old buildings have been refurbished, some torn down and replaced, with more upscale businesses taking their place. The tired little shops in town are on Lana'i Company property, most with month-to-month leases. The Lana'i Company again promises to be fair, but like the rest of Lana'i, they'll have a choice: progress or perish. Most islanders are optimistic, keeping an open mind and adopting a wait-and-see attitude concerning the inevitable changes and the promises that have been made for a better life, but so far it looks promising.

## THE PEOPLE

Lana'i is characterized by the incredible mix of racial strains so common in Hawaii—Filipino, Japanese, Hawaiian, Chinese, and Caucasian. It is unique, however, in that 60 percent of its people are Filipino. The Filipinos, some recent immigrants, were solicited by Castle and Cooke to work as laborers on the pineapple plantation. Mostly single young men, the majority Ilocano, some may have come to join relatives already on Lana'i. Here they learned English and from Lana'i they spread out. As workers they were perfect: industrious and quiet. At night you wonder where they all are. Because of the tremendous shortage of eligible women, most workers stay home or fish or have a beer in the backyard with buddies. And on Sundays, there is the illegal (officially nonexistent) cockfight. For high living, everyone heads for Maui or O'ahu.

The next largest racial groups are Japanese (14 percent), Hawaiian (12 percent), and whites (11 percent). The Japanese started as the field workers before the Filipinos, but now, along with the whites, are Lana'i's professionals and middle management. The races coexist, but there are still unseen social strata. There's even a small Chinese population (1 percent), who continue their traditional role as shopkeepers. Finally, about 2 percent fall into the "mixed" category, with many of these Filipino-Hawaiian.

## Community

Lana'i has a strong sense of community and uniqueness that keeps the people close. For example, during a bitter three-month strike in 1964, the entire community rallied and all suffered equally: laborers, shopkeepers, and management. All who remember say that it brought out the best in the island tradition of *aloha*. If you really want to meet Lana'ians, just sit in the park in the center of Lana'i City for an hour or two. You'll notice a lot of old-timers, who seem to be very healthy. You could easily strike up a conversation with some of them.

## Other Faces

It once might have struck you that most of the people you saw around Lana'i were men. That in itself was a social comment about Lana'i, where men worked the fields and women stayed at home in their traditional roles, nurturing and trying to add to the pleasantries of life. Now you will see more and more women about, many who work at the hotels. You might notice that there are no famous crafts of Lana'i and few artists working commercially. This is not to say there is no art on Lana'i, but the visitor rarely sees it until they stop at the Lana'i Art Center in town. One reason that Lana'i produces so little commercial art is that it's a workers' island with virtually no unemployment, so everyone is busy making a living. Old-timers are known to make superb fishing poles, nets, and even their own horseshoes. The island ladies are excellent seamstresses, and with the rising interest in hula, make lovely lei from the beautiful *kauna'oa*, Lana'i's flower. If you turn your attention to the young people of Lana'i, you'll see the statewide problem of babies having babies. Although the situation is getting better, teenage parents are still not uncommon. Young guys customize their cars, although there's no place to go. If as a young person you wish to remain on Lana'i, then in almost every case your future will be tied to the Lana'i Company. If you have other aspirations, it's "good-bai to Lana'i." These islanders are some of the most easygoing and relaxed people you'll encounter in Hawaii, but with the electronic age extending its long arms of communication, even here they're not nearly as "backwater" as you might think.

## Events

All official holidays are honored and celebrated. As anywhere in the state, Lana'i celebrates special events in its own unique way, and each ethnic group has festivities that the whole island participates in. Some community events include **Community Kite Flying** day, held at Lana'i City in March. **May Day** is important throughout the state, and events here take place at Lana'i High School. The **Fourth of July** (or another day in early July) brings the **Pineapple Festival** to Hulopo'e Beach on Lana'i, when all the town gathers to enjoy music, crafts, demonstrations, and, of course, lots of pineapple. A farmers market is held for produce and home-baked goods, and a cooking contest is conducted for amateurs and professionals alike. To cap off the event, fireworks light the night sky. As everywhere in the state, **Aloha Festivals** happens on the island with a parade and other activities.

# SPORTS AND RECREATION

No question that Lana'i's forte is its natural unspoiled setting and great outdoors. Traffic jams, neon lights, blaring discos, shopping boutiques, and all that jazz just don't exist here. The action is swimming, hiking, snorkeling, fishing, horseback riding, and some hunting. Tennis and golf round off the activities. Lana'i is the place to revitalize your spirits. You want to get up with the birds, greet the sun, stretch, and soak up the good life.

## Camping

The only official camping permitted to nonresidents is located at Hulopo'e Bay, administered by the Lana'i Company. Reservations for one of the six official campsites on the grass up from the beach are a must, although unbelievably there's usually a good chance of getting a space. Lana'i Company officials state that they try to accommodate any overflow unreserved visitors, but don't count on it. Because Lana'i is largely privately owned by Castle and Cooke, the parent company of the Lana'i Company, you really have no recourse but to play by their rules. It seems they want to hold visitors to a minimum and keep strict tabs on the ones that do arrive.

Nonetheless, the campsites at Hulopo'e Bay are great. Lining the idyllic beach, they're far enough apart to afford some privacy. The showers are designed so that the pipes, just below the surface, are solar heated. This means a good hot shower during daylight and early evening. Campsite use is limited to six nights, and you must be 18 years of age or older to make an application. The fee includes a one-time $5 registration, plus $5 per person per night. For reservations write to the Lana'i Company, P.O. Box 310, Lanai City, Lanai, HI 96763, attn. Camping, or call 808/565-3982. Permits, if not mailed in advance, are picked up at the Lana'i Company office, and payment of fees are made to the ranger at the camp site. If visiting on the spur of the moment from a neighboring island, it's advisable to call ahead.

**Note:** While hiking or four-wheel-driving the back roads of Lana'i, especially along Naha, Shipwreck, and Polihua beaches, a multitude of picture-perfect camping spots will present themselves, but they can be used only by Lana'i residents, although there's little supervision. A one-night bivouac would probably go undetected. No other island allows unofficial camping, and unless it can be statistically shown that potential visitors are being turned away, it seems unlikely that the Lana'i Company will change its policies. If you're one of the unlucky ones who have been turned down, contact parent company Castle and Cooke with your protest: 650 Iwilei Rd., Honolulu, HI 96817, 808/548-4811.

## Hiking and Jogging

All of the paved roads and many of the gravel roads in Lana'i City are decent for walking and jogging. Although the traffic is not heavy, be careful if you're on the roadway.

One trail on the island has been marked, the **Koloiki Ridge Trail.** Pick up a map at either of the resort front desks. Start at the rear of the Lodge at Koele and head up through the golf course into a tall stand of pine trees. Cross under the power lines and into Hulopo'e Valley, where an abandoned road heads up to the Munro Trail. Once there, turn right and head south, walking into and out of Kukui Gulch, until you round an eroded "moonscape" on your right. A short way farther, turn left down an old jeep trail for per-haps 5–10 minutes. Head through a tunnel in the trees to the flat, open Koloiki lookout. From here, you can look down into Naio and Mau-nalei gulches and out toward Maui and Moloka'i. This trail is about five mile round-trip and should take at least three hours. An organized group hike also does this route for $15 per person, and on the way you get treated to historical and cul-tural anecdotes about the island. Contact the concierge for details.

Shorter and easier is **Fisherman's Trail,** a 1.5-mile one-way shoreline trail that runs from Hu-lopo'e Bay, below the Manele Bay Hotel, west to the end of the golf course. A project of the State Na Ala Hele trail system, this was once part of an ancient trail that circled the island.

## Snorkel and Scuba

Lana'i, especially around Manele/Hulopo'e Bay, has some of the best snorkeling and scuba in Hawaii. If you don't have your own equipment, and you're not a guest at one of the hotels, you could buy gear from Pine Isle or Richards stores or rent from the Adventure Lana'i Ecocentre. If you're the adventurous sort, you can dive for spiny lobsters off Shipwreck, but make absolutely sure to check the surf conditions because it can be super-treacherous. It would be best to go with a local person.

**Trilogy Ocean Sports,** 808/565-2387 or 888/628-4800, www.sailtrilogy.com, operates a catamaran and a rigid-bottom inflatable raft from Manele Boat Harbor for several sailing and snorkel options. The four-hour snorkel/sail ($110) leaves Mondays, Wednesdays, and Fridays at 8:45 A.M., and Saturdays at 10 A.M. A scuba adventure runs at the same time and on the same days for $159–169, or there is the option of an early morning scuba dive at Cathedrals, one of the island's best dive sites, for $95. Rafting tours for scuba divers run three days a week for $130, while the four-hour Sunday raft adventure runs $125. For those who don't care to start from a boat, beach dives are also offered daily at Hulopo'e Beach for $65–75. Book directly or through the concierge desk at the Manele Bay Hotel or at the Lodge at Koele.

Trilogy, in the business for years, has worked out all the kinks, and their boat, crew, and ser-vices are truly state-of-the-art. No matter how many times they make the trip, they never seem to forget that it's a new and exciting adventure for you, and they go out of their way to be helpful, upbeat, and caring without being intrusive. The catamaran's aft is set up for easy entry and exit, with steps going down to the water level. Just make like a seal and slither in and out! If the winds are up, the captain will be happy to set sail as they head toward Kahekili's Leap and other famous Lana'i landmarks. The experience is not just underwater, but also in the magnificent views of this pristine island that hasn't changed much since the days of the Polynesian explorers. On morning sails, you return in the early afternoon with plenty of time left for more sightseeing or just relaxing. For those on Trilogy boats coming from Lahaina, the company has a pavilion at Manele Harbor that's used to feed their guests and from where they are taken to Hulopo'e Bay to snorkel and swim or tour the island by van.

**Spinning Dolphin Charters,** 808/565-6613, owned and operated by Capt. Jeff Menze, a long-time Lana'i resident, will take you fishing (chil-dren welcome), snorkeling, and whale-watching in season; six person maximum. Captain Jeff is a commercial fisherman and master diver who knows all of the best spots in Lana'i's waters. Of-fered are whole-day and half-day adventures, special off-the-beaten-path dives, and private boat charters. Rates run $400 for a half-day trip to $800 for a full-day trip.

The **Kila Kila** also offers sunset cruises, whale-watch trips in season, and full- and half-day fishing expeditions for $825–1,200 (for up to six people). Contact either hotel concierge for reservations.

## Swimming

Lana'i City has a fine swimming pool. Located in town near the high school, it's open to the public during summer, usually 10:30 A.M.–5 P.M. daily except Wednesday and on a limited schedule during other seasons. Each of the two resorts has its own swimming pool and spa—for use by reg-istered guests only. By far the best swimming beach on Lana'i is at Hulopo'e Bay, but a few other spots for a dip can be found along the coast from Shipwreck Beach to Naha.

## Other Outdoor Adventures

An independent company that caters largely to hotel guests, **Adventure Lana'i Ecocentre**, P.O. Box 1394, Lanai City, HI 96763, 808/565-7373, www.adventurelanai.com, can take you along the north coast of Lana'i on a kayak/snorkel trip, on a 4WD expedition of the highlights around the island, biking down to Shipwreck Beach, a shore dive for scuba enthusiasts, or on several other outings on the island. Half-day outings cost $79 per person, the scuba trip is $129. Guided tours and introduction are provided, and private tours can be arranged. Rentals can be accommodated. Adventure Lana'i has camping gear, kayaks, mountain bikes, and snorkel gear at competitive prices. See your hotel concierge or arrange reservations directly.

Hotel Lanai rents mountain bicycles for $24 on a day-by-day basis, 7 A.M.–7 P.M. If you are staying at the Lodge at Koele, check with the concierge about their rental bicycles and accompanying picnic backpack.

## Tennis and Golf

You can play **tennis** at two lighted courts at the Lana'i School from 7 A.M.–8:30 P.M. They have rubberized surfaces called royal duck and are fairly well maintained—definitely okay for a fun game. The Lodge at Koele and the Manele Bay Hotel have plexipave courts, and their use is complimentary for hotel guests but $25 per hour for nonguests. The six courts at Manele Bay are newer than the three at the Lodge and in better condition. Equipment rental (rackets and ball machines), court times, and fees can be arranged at the pro shops or through the concierge desks. Private lessons and clinics are available.

Golfers will be delighted to follow their balls around **Cavendish Golf Course** on the outskirts of Lana'i City. This nine-hole, 3,058-yard, par-36 course (use the blue tees the first time around, the white tees if you want to go a second nine holes) is set among Cook pines and has been challenging local residents since the 1930s. It's free to all, but visitors to the island are requested to leave a donation for maintenance at the first tee, which, unless you're familiar with the course, could be a bit hard to find. Ask—it's straight up from the clubhouse. Even this unassuming community course has a signature hole with some difficulty. It's the ninth hole, and its green is about 50 feet higher than the tee, plus you must golf through a narrow opening in the trees to reach the green. You'll find this course at the end of Nani Street.

The **Experience at Koele,** 808/565-4653, a Greg Norman–designed course, won the *Fortune Magazine* Best New Golf Course of 1991 award. This magnificent course, set in the mountains above the Lodge, offers not only challenging links

## LANA'I GOLF AND TENNIS

| Golf Course | Par | Yards | Fees | Cart | Clubs |
|---|---|---|---|---|---|
| Cavendish Golf Course | 36 | 3,058 | Donation | None | None |
| The Challenge at Manele 808/565-2222 | 72 | 7,039 | $205 nonguest $165 hotel guest | Incl. | $50 |
| The Experience at Ko'ele 808/565-4653 | 72 | 7,014 | $205 nonguest $165 hotel guest | Incl. | $50 |

| Tennis Court | No. of courts | Lighted |
|---|---|---|
| The Lodge at Ko'ele Tennis Courts | 3 | Yes |
| Manele Bay Hotel Tennis Center | 6 | No |
| Lana'i School (Lana'i City) | 2 | Yes |

ROBERT NILSEN

The unique eighth hole at the Experience at Koele drops from ridge to valley.

but also a fantastic series of views of Moloka'i and Maui on a shimmering canvas of sea. With four sets of tees ranging from forward to tournament, the course yardage varies accordingly from 5,425–7,014 yards. The course also boasts the only bent-grass greens in the state. Two of the finest holes are the number 8, par four, which cascades 250 feet from ridgetop to glen below, and the short but maximum water-challenged number 9.

**The Challenge at Manele,** 808/565-2222, designed by the legendary Jack Nicklaus, officially opened on Christmas Day 1993. Employing the five-tee concept, the par-72 course ranges in length 5,024–7,039 yards. This course is set above the cliff edge, along the sparkling ocean at the Manele Bay Hotel. Three of the main holes, including the signature number 12, par-three hole, demand a tee shot over the greatest water hazard in the world, the wide Pacific.

## Horseback Riding

**The Stables at Koele,** 808/565-4424, open daily and just a few minutes from the Lodge at Koele, offers a variety of mounted excursions. Trail rides run 1–3 hours for $50–110. Three- and four-hour trail rides with lunch are $110–140. Private rides can be arranged for $75–260, as can a full-day ride to the top of the mountain for $400 or a sunset ride for $150. Other rides are available, including a 10-minute children's pony ride and a carriage ride through town for $75. Lana'i enjoys a ranching heritage that goes back to the 1870s. Many of the trails you'll be following date from those early days. Riders must be in good health, weigh less than 250 pounds, and be at least nine years old and stand four foot, six inches tall—except for the pony rides. Everyone must wear long pants and close-toed shoes. Safety helmets will be provided for all riders.

## Hunting

The first cliché you hear about Lana'i is that it's one big pineapple plantation. The second is that it's a hunter's paradise. The first was true, and the second still is. Both private and public hunting are allowed. Because virtually all of Lana'i is privately owned, about two-thirds of the island is set aside as a private reserve, and one-third is leased to the state for public hunting and is cooperatively managed.

The big-game action for public hunting is provided by mouflon sheep and axis deer. Various days are open for hunting game birds, which include ring-necked and green pheasant; Gambel's, Japanese, and California quail; wild turkey; and a variety of doves, francolins, and partridges. The public hunting area is restricted to the northwest corner of the island. Brochures detailing all necessary information can be obtained free of charge by writing to the Department of Land and Natural Resources, 1151 Punchbowl St., Honolulu, HI 96813. Contact Derwin Kwon at the Lana'i regional office, P.O. Box 732, 911 Fraser Ave., Lanai City, HI 96763, 808/565-7916. Licenses are required ($20 residents, $105 nonresidents) and can be purchased by mail from the Department of Land and Natural Resources or picked up in person at the office on Lana'i.

Public archery hunting of mouflon sheep is restricted to the last Saturday in July and first Saturday in August. The muzzleloader rifle season occurs on the second and third Saturday in August,

MAUI

and for rifles, shotguns, and bows and arrows for the nine following Saturdays. Tags are required and hunters are restricted by public drawing. Regular season for axis deer (rifle, shotgun, and bows) opens on the nine consecutive Saturdays starting from the third Saturday in March; it's also restricted by public drawing. Muzzleloader season is the two Saturdays before that, and archery season for axis deer is the two Saturdays and days in between preceding the muzzleloader season. Bag limits are one mouflon ram and one buck.

On the private land, only axis deer are hunted. Hunting is done year-round, although the best trophy season is May–November. Hunting dates must be mutually agreed upon by the hunter and the rangers because there are a limited number of rangers and this is a three-day process, although the hunt is only one long day affair. Write 3–6 months in advance for best results. The rate is $275 per day for a regular hunting permit or $50 for an archery hunting permit that is good until the Hawaiian hunting license expires. Guide service is not officially mandatory, but you must prove that you have hunted Lana'i before and are intimately knowledgeable about its terrain, hunting areas, and procedures. If not, you *must* acquire the services of a guide. Guide service is $750 per day, which includes a permit and all necessities, except lodging and meals, from airport pickup to shipping the trophy. For all hunters, a Hawaii state hunting license and a hunter safety card are required. For full details, write to Gary Onuma, Chief Ranger, The Lana'i Company, Game Management, P.O. Box 310, Lanai City, HI 96763, 808/565-3981, fax 808/565-3984.

## Sporting Clays

An outgrowth of hunting, sporting clays is a sport that helps develop and maintain your hand-eye coordination. Shooting is done from different stations around a course, and the object is to hit a small, round clay disk. Different from trap or skeet shooting, sporting clays relies on moving targets that mimic different animal and bird movements, hopping along the ground like a rabbit, springing off the ground like a quail, or flying high like a pheasant. Here you can have all the enjoyment of hitting a target without the guilt of killing a living animal. **Lana'i Pine Sporting Clays,** 808/563-4600, is a high-tech operation that services both beginners and advanced shooters. To satisfy everyone's needs, there are skeet and trap ranges here as well and an airgun station for kids. Several shooting competitions are held here every year, including the Hawaii Pacific Open Ducks Unlimited Shoot in October.

Register at the pro shop and pick up your needed supplies and accessories there. A paved path connects each of the 14 stations; take a golf cart or walk the course. The basic package, including 100 targets, gun rental, cartridges, eye and ear protection, and safety vest, runs $145 per person; $85 for 50 targets. For experienced shooters, guns, cartridges, targets, and carts can be rented separately, and you may use your own gun. Instruction is also given for beginners at $75; private lessons are available. Pull!

## Archery

Set up next to Lana'i Pine Sporting Clays is the newer **Lana'i Pine Archery** course, 808/565-3800. With 12 targets set 15 and 35 yards from the firing line, this is enough to give everyone a challenge. Open 9:15 A.M.–2:30 P.M.daily, the pro shop will set you up with all the needed equipment for your ability. Instruction runs $45, and course use for those who already know how to shoot is $35 or $25 with your own gear.

## Fishing

**Spinning Dolphin Charters,** 808/565-6613, operates a fishing boat out of Lana'i for full- or half-day charters from 1–6 people. Similarly, the *Kila Kila* also offers fishing expeditions.

One of the island's greatest pastimes is the relaxing sport of fishing. Any day in Lana'i City Park, you'll find plenty of old-timers to ask where the fish are biting. If you have the right approach and use the right smile, they just might tell you. Generally, the best fishing and easiest access on the island is at Shipwreck Beach running west toward Polihua. Near the lighthouse ruins is good for *papio* and *ulua,* the latter running to 50 pounds. Many of the local fishermen use throw-nets to catch the smaller fish such as *manini,* preferred especially by Lana'i's elders. Throw-netting takes skill usually learned from childhood, but don't be afraid to try even if you throw what the locals call a "banana" or one that looks like Maui (a little head and a big body). They might snicker, but if you laugh too, you'll make a friend.

Mostly you'll fish with rod and reel using frozen squid or crab, available at Lana'i's general stores. Bring a net bag or suitable container. This is the best beachcombing on the island, and it's also excellent diving for spiny lobster. There is good shore fishing (especially for *awa*) and easy accessibility at Kaumalapau Harbor, from where the pineapples used to be shipped and where the supplies for the island now come. There is also superb offshore fishing at Kaunolu, Kamehameha's favorite angling spot on the south shore. You can catch *aku* and *kawakawa*, but to be really successful you'll need a boat. Finally, Manele Hulopo'e Marine Life Conservation Park has limited fishing, but as the name implies, it's a conservation district, so be sure to follow the rules prominently posted at Manele Bay.

## GETTING THERE

### By Air

**Hawaiian Airlines,** 800/882-8811 on Lana'i, 800/367-5320 Mainland and Canada, flies to Lana'i. It currently has a direct daily early morning flight from Honolulu that returns via Moloka'i. The daily afternoon flight from Honolulu comes through Moloka'i, returning directly to Honolulu. Morning and afternoon flights to Kahului go via Moloka'i and/or Honolulu.

Daily flights are available to and from Lana'i by **Island Air,** 800/652-6541 on Lana'i or 800/323-3345 elsewhere. Using some jets and some turboprops, Island Air flies to and from Honolulu seven times daily, with twice-daily flights between Lana'i and Kahului, Maui.

Based in Kahului, the small commuter and tour operator **Pacific Wings,** 888/575-4546, also flies regularly scheduled flights to and from Lana'i twice daily on weekdays with an abbreviated schedule on weekends. Flights also connect Lana'i twice a day direct to Honolulu.

**Lana'i Airport** is a practical little strip about four miles southwest of Lana'i City, out near the remaining pineapple fields. The pleasing new terminal offers a departure lounge, gift shop, bathrooms, and public phones. If you are staying at any of the three hotels, a shuttle will transport you into town and drop you at the appropriate place for a $10 use fee. Complimentary airport pickup can also be arranged with Dollar Rent A Car if you rent from them. Otherwise, Rabaca's Limousine Service, 808/565-6670, rabaca@aloha.net, can shuttle you into town for $5 per seat or $10 minimum for ride.

### By Boat

The passenger ferry *Expeditions,* 808/661-3756 on Maui or 800/695-2624 on Lana'i and elsewhere, www.go-lanai.com, plies daily between Lahaina and Manele Bay. This shuttle offers speedy and convenient alternative transportation to the island. The crossing takes less than one hour, and the ferry leaves Manele Bay at 8 A.M., 10:30 A.M., 2 P.M., 4:30 P.M., and 6:45 P.M. From Lahaina's public loading pier, ferries leave at 6:45 A.M., 9:15 A.M., 12:45 P.M., 3:15 P.M., and 5:45 P.M. The adult fare is $25 one-way while children 2–11 are $20; *kama'aina* rates are available. It's best to reserve a place. Luggage is taken free of charge, except for a $20 fee for bicycles. Because only two bikes are permitted on each ferry, be sure to let the company know well ahead of time so your bike can go with you. Ground transportation on Lana'i from the pier at Manele Bay is provided by Lana'i City Service, which will take you up to Lana'i City for $20 round-trip or $10 round-trip to the Manele Bay Hotel. An added perk of this trip is that you will see dolphins from the boat most of the year, and there's good whale-watching during the winter.

## GETTING AROUND

### Shuttle and Limousine Service

No public bus service operates on Lana'i, but **Lana'i City Service,** 808/565-7227, operates a free airport shuttle service during their business hours (7 A.M.–7 P.M.) if you're renting a vehicle from them. Lana'i City Service also meets all ferries at the pier at Manele Bay and shuttles passengers to Manele Bay Hotel for $10 round-trip or up to Lana'i City for $20 round-trip.

Otherwise, shuttle service is handled by **Rabaca's Limousine Service,** 808/565-6670, rabaca@aloha.net. To/from the airport or anywhere in and around Lana'i City, the charge is $5 per seat, and from Lana'i City to Manele Bay Hotel or the pier at Manele Harbor it's $10 per seat; two-seat minimum on all rides. Rabaca has three stretch limos that are available 24 hours a day. Itineraries are set by the guest.

## Lana'i Resort Shuttle

A shuttle service is offered for guests of the two big resorts and Hotel Lanai. This shuttle runs daily 7 A.M.–11 P.M. every hour during the day and every 30 minutes on the hour and half hour in the evening, and picks up passengers at the front of each hotel. A connecting shuttle runs to and from the airport, $10 per person round-trip, meeting all arriving and departing planes.

## Car Rental

For a car—or better yet, a jeep—try **Lana'i City Service, Dollar Rent A Car,** 1036 Lana'i Ave. in Lana'i City, 808/565-7227. You'll be outfitted with wheels and given a drive guide with information about road conditions and where you're allowed and not allowed to drive with their vehicles. Pay heed! Make sure to tell them your plans, especially if you're heading for a remote area. Lana'i City Service is a subsidiary of Trilogy Excursions and has a franchise with Dollar Rent A Car. It rents compacts for $59.99 per day, full-size cars for $79.99, eight-passenger minivans for $129.99, and 4WD Jeep Wranglers for $129.99 per day; all prices are exclusive of tax. Ask about weekly, monthly, and *kama'aina* rates. No insurance is available for vehicles rented on Lana'i, except for no-fault insurance, which is required by law. Lana'i City Service offers free shuttle service to and from the airport if you rent with them. This service operates only during their regular business hours, 7 A.M.–7 P.M. If you need to be at the airport before they start in the morning or after they close in the evening, there will be a $10 pickup charge if you drop off the vehicle at

the airport. A fee of $20 is charged for picking up a vehicle left at the ferry pier.

Lana'i City Service has the only gas station on the island, and it's open daily 7 A.M.–7 P.M. With the few roads on the island, you won't be using much gas, but you'll have to fill the tank up on a rental vehicle when you return it. The price of gas varies but is usually $.50 per gallon more expensive on Lana'i than the average price on Maui.

## Using a 4WD Rental

With only 30 miles of paved road on Lana'i and rental cars firmly restricted to these, there is no real reason to rent one unless you are here just to golf. The *real* adventure spots of Lana'i require a 4WD vehicle, which on Lana'i is actually useful and not just a yuppie showpiece because mind-boggling spots on Lana'i are reachable only on foot or by 4WD. Unfortunately, even the inveterate hiker will have a tough time because the best trailheads are quite a distance from town, and you'll spend as much time getting to them as hiking the actual trails.

Many people who have little or no experience driving 4WDs are under the slap-happy belief that they are unstoppable. Oh, would that it were true! They do indeed get stuck, and it's usually miserable getting them unstuck. The rental agency will give you up-to-the-minute information on the road conditions and a fairly accurate map for navigation. It tends to be a bit conservative on where they advise you to take their vehicles, but the staff also live on the island and are accustomed to driving off-road, which balances out their conservative estimates. Also, remember that road conditions change rapidly: A hard rain on the Munro Trail can change it from a flower-lined path to a nasty quagmire, or wind might lay a tree across a beach road. Keep your eye on the weather, and if in doubt, don't push your luck. If you get stuck, you'll not only ruin your outing and have to hike back to town, but you'll also be charged for a service call, which can be astronomical, especially if it's deemed to be a result of your negligence. Most of your dirt road driving will be in 2WD, but certain sections of some roads and other roads during inclement weather will require 4WD. Only on the rarest occasion will you need low-range gearing.

## Jeep Tours

Personalized, escorted jeep tours on the island can be arranged through **Rabaca's Limousine Service,** 808/565-6670, rabaca@aloha.net. Let them know your preferences and they'll tailor a tour for you. The rate is $50 per hour with a maximum of four passengers. There is a two-hour minimum, but it usually takes at least three hours to get to some place on the island, have a look around, and get back. If you are unsure about driving dirt roads or may not want to rent a jeep for the out-of-the-way places, leave the driving to the professionals. It can be a good deal. You can also inquire here about kayaking, mountain biking, hiking, photography, fishing, and hunting options. Rabaca can either arrange this for you or send you in the right direction to match your needs.

## Hitchhiking

Hitching is legal in Maui County, and that includes Lana'i. Islanders are friendly and quite good about giving you a lift. Lana'i, however, is a workers' island, and the traffic is really skimpy during the day. You can only reasonably expect to get a ride from Lana'i City to the airport or to Manele Bay because both are on paved roads and frequented by normal island traffic, or to Shipwreck Beach on the weekends. There is only a very slim chance of picking up a ride farther afield, toward the Garden of the Gods or Keomuku, for example, so definitely don't count on it.

# INFORMATION AND SERVICES

The following phone numbers may be useful as you visit Lana'i: Emergency: 911; police, 808/565-6428; weather and surf conditions, 808/565-6033; Lana'i City Service gas station, 808/565-7227; Department of Land and Natural Resources, 808/565-7916; Lana'i Airport, 808/565-6757; Lana'i Community Hospital 24-hour emergency service, 808/565-6411; Lana'i Family Health Center, 808/565-6423

## Information

For general information about Lana'i, and activities and services on the island, contact Destination Lana'i, P.O. Box 700, Lanai City, HI 96763,

808/565-7600 or 800/947-4774, fax 808/565-9316, dlanai@aloha.net, www.visitlanai.net.

Additionally, maps, brochures, and pamphlets on all aspects of staying on Lana'i are available free from the Lana'i Company, P.O. Box 310, Lanai City, HI 96763, 808/565-3000.

For an up-close look at local news and what's happening in the community, have a look at the monthly *Lana'i Times* newspaper.

## Banking

Try full-service **First Hawaiian Bank,** in Lana'i City, 808/565-6969, for your banking needs. **Bank of Hawaii,** 808/565-6426, also has a branch here. Banks are open Monday–Thursday 8:30 A.M.–3 P.M. (4:30 P.M. for Bank of Hawaii) and Friday until 6 P.M., but they may be closed for lunch. Both have ATMs outside their offices for after-hours banking. All major businesses on the island accept traveler's checks, and many now also accept credit cards.

## Post Office

The Lana'i post office, 808/565-6517, at its new location on Jacaranda Street, just a few steps off the city park, is open weekdays 9 A.M.–4 P.M. and Saturday 10 A.M.–noon. You can find boxes and padded mailers for your beachcombing treasures at the two general stores in town.

## Library

Located at 6th Street and Fraser Avenue next to the school, the public library is open Tuesday, Thursday, and Friday 8 A.M.–4 P.M., Wednesday 1–8 P.M., and Saturday 11 A.M.–4 P.M.

## Cinema

On the corner of Lana'i Avenue and 7th Street, Lana'i Playhouse, 808/565-7500, is the only theater on the island; it runs current-release movies. Open Friday–Tuesday; tickets run $7 adults, $4.50 kids and seniors.

## Laundry

Located on the north side of Dole Park in the middle of Lana'i City, the only laundromat on the island is open every day from "morning until nighttime": 5 A.M.–8:30 P.M. Bring coins.

M

MAUI

# Lana'i City

Lana'i City would be more aptly described and sound more appealing if it were called Lana'i Village. A utilitarian town, it was built in the 1920s by Dole Pineapple Company. The architecture, field-worker plain, has definitely gained character in the last 70 years. It's an excellent spot for a town, sitting at 1,600 feet in the shadow of Lana'ihale, the island's tallest peak. George Munro's Cook pines have matured and now give the entire town a green, shaded, parklike atmosphere. It's cool and breezy—a great place to launch from in the morning and a welcome spot to return to at night. Most visitors head out of town to the more spectacular sights and never take the chance to explore the back streets.

As you might expect, most houses are square boxes with corrugated roofs, but each has its own personality. Painted every color of the rainbow, they'd be garish in any other place, but here they break the monotony and seem to work. The people of Lana'i used to make their living from the land and can still work wonders with it. Around many homes are colorful flowerbeds, green gardens bursting with vegetables, fruit trees, and flowering shrubs. When you look down the half-dirt, broken-pavement roads at a line of these houses, you can't help feeling that a certain nobility exists here. The houses are mud-spattered where the rain splashes red earth against them, but inside you know they're sparkling clean. Many of these narrow lanes are one-way streets—watch for signs!

The modern suburban homes that line the few blocks at the extreme south end of town are mostly from the late 1980s and early '90s. Most of these belong to Lana'i's miniature middle class and would fit unnoticed in any up-and-coming neighborhood on another island. On the north edge of town are a few new apartments and multifamily buildings that were put up in the mid-1990s. On the slope above town, set along the golf course fairways, are the more recent townhouses and luxury homes that will, over the years, become more predominant if development goes as planned. Similarly, a luxury home development is growing along the golf fairways to the side of Manele Bay Hotel.

## Around Town

Lana'i City streets running east-west are numerical starting with 3rd Street and running to 13th Street; the streets running north-south have alphabetical first letters and include Fraser, Gay, Houston, Ilima, Jacaranda, Ko'ele, and Lana'i avenues, with a few more streets beyond this central grid. If you manage to get lost in Lana'i City you should seriously consider never leaving home.

If you sit on the steps of Hotel Lanai and peer across its huge front yard, you can scrutinize the heart of downtown Lana'i City. Off to your right are offices, the community hospital and health center sitting squat and solid. In front of them, forming a type of town square, is Dole Park, where old-timers come to sit and young mothers bring their kids for some fresh air. No one in Lana'i City rushes to do anything. Look around and you'll discover a real fountain of youth: The many octogenarians walk with a spring in their step. Years of hard work without being hyper or anxious is why they say they're still around. The park is surrounded by commercial Lana'i. There's nowhere to *go* except over to the schoolyard to play some tennis or to Cavendish Golf Course for a round of nine holes. Lana'i City has a movie theater, and its now showing pictures once again. You can plop yourself at the Blue Ginger Cafe or Tanigawa's for coffee or stay in the park if you're in the mood to strike up a conversation—it shouldn't take long.

Meander down Lana'i Avenue past a complex of former agricultural buildings and shops. Once full of heavy equipment, this is where Lana'i showed its raw plantation muscle. Part of it has now been tamed and is the site of a new senior citizen's housing complex. Beyond the commercial buildings on both sides of the downtown park are the rows of plantation houses, now with newer subdivisions farther to each end. Do yourself a favor: Get out of your rental car and walk around town for at least 30 minutes. You'll experience one of the most unique villages in America.

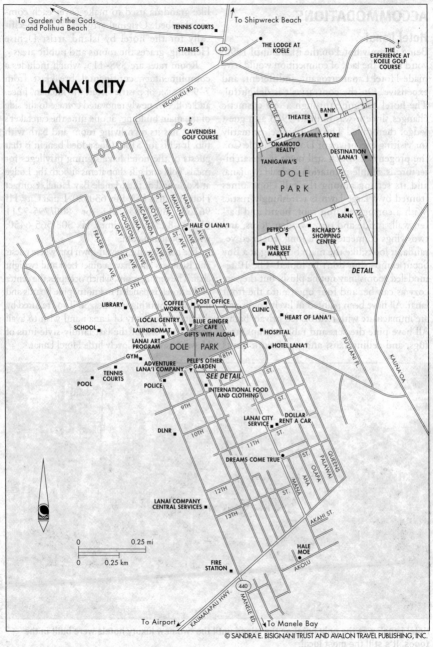

# LANA'I CITY

To Garden of the Gods and Polihua Beach

To Shipwreck Beach

TENNIS COURTS

STABLES

THE LODGE AT KOELE

THE EXPERIENCE AT KOELE GOLF COURSE

KEOMUKU RD.

CAVENDISH GOLF COURSE

**DETAIL**

KOELE AVE.

7TH ST.

THEATER

BANK

LANA'I FAMILY STORE

OKAMOTO REALTY

DESTINATION LANA'I

TANIGAWA'S

LANA'I AVE.

DOLE PARK

8TH ST.

BANK

PETRO'S

RICHARD'S SHOPPING CENTER

PINE ISLE MARKET

3RD ST.

FRASER AVE.

HOUSTON AVE.

GAY AVE.

ILIMA AVE.

JACARANDA AVE.

KOELE AVE.

LANA'I AVE.

MAHANA AVE.

NANI AVE.

HALE O LANA'I

4TH AVE.

5TH AVE.

6TH ST.

LIBRARY

SCHOOL

COFFEE WORKS

POST OFFICE

CLINIC

HEART OF LANA'I

LOCAL GENTRY

BLUE GINGER CAFE

GIFTS WITH ALOHA

LAUNDROMAT

HOSPITAL

DOLE PARK

8TH ST.

HOTEL LANA'I

GYM

PELE'S OTHER GARDEN

ADVENTURE LANA'I COMPANY

LANAI ART PROGRAM

TENNIS COURTS

POOL

POLICE

**SEE DETAIL**

INTERNATIONAL FOOD AND CLOTHING

9TH ST.

LANAI CITY SERVICE

DOLLAR RENT A CAR

DLNR

10TH ST.

11TH ST.

DREAMS COME TRUE

MANA ST.

AHA ST.

OLAPA ST.

PALAWAI ST.

QUEENS ST.

12TH ST.

LANAI COMPANY CENTRAL SERVICES

13TH ST.

AKAHI ST.

HALE MOE

AKOLU

FIRE STATION

KAUNAKOA

PUUIANI PL.

0       0.25 mi

0       0.25 km

To Airport

KAUMALAPAU HWY.

MANELE RD.

To Manele Bay

MAUI

## ACCOMMODATIONS

### Hotel Lanai

Being the only hotel on the island until 1990, you'd think the lack of competition would have made Hotel Lanai arrogant, indifferent, and expensive. On the contrary: It is delightful. The hotel has gone through a few cosmetic changes since it was built in 1923 as a guest lodge, then called The Clubhouse, primarily for visiting executives of Dole Pineapple Co., the progeny of which still owns it. Its architecture is simple plantation-style Hawaiiana, and its setting among the tall Cook pines fronted by a large lawn is refreshingly rustic. With a corrugated iron roof, board and batten walls inside and out, wooden floors, and two wings connected by a long, enclosed veranda, it looks like the main building at a Boy Scout camp—but don't be fooled. The 10 remodeled rooms may not be plush, but they are cozy as can be, and four open onto the front lanai. All have been painted in lively colors and are immaculate with refurbished private baths. All have pine dressers and tables, lamps, area rugs, and ceiling fans, and patchwork quilts like grandma used to make cover each comfortable bed. Original artwork, done specifically for the hotel by island artist Denise Henning, graces the rooms and public areas.

Room rates are $98–115, which includes a complimentary continental breakfast from 7–9:30 A.M. of pastries from the kitchen, juice, and coffee. A newly renovated cottage to the side of the main building, at one time the caretaker's house, has its own living room and bath with tub. It rents for $150. One added benefit is that guests of the hotel have signing privileges for meals, golf, and gift shop items at both the Lodge at Koele and at the Manele Bay Hotel. Contact Hotel Lanai at P.O. Box 630520, Lanai City, HI 96763, 808/565-7211 or 800/795-7211 (7 A.M.–8 P.M. local time), fax 808/565-6450, www.hotellanai.com.

The hotel has the only in-town bar, where guests and islanders alike have a quiet beer and twilight chat. The dining room, which occupies the center of the hotel, is paneled in knotty pine boards and lined with hunting trophies. So if you're lured by the quiet simplicity of Lana'i and wish to avail yourself of one of the last family-style inns of Hawaii, stay at the lovely little Hotel Lanai.

Hotel Lana'i was the only hotel on the island until the two new luxury hotels were built in the 1990s. It's still the most local.

## The Lodge at Koele

A stately row of Cook pines bids welcome as they line the red-brick driveway leading to this grand manor house perched in genteel quietude just a 15-minute walk from downtown Lana'i City. An upland country hotel befitting this area of trees and cool summers, it's gracefully done in neo-Victorian style. Here, a huge pineapple mural painted above the front entrance greets everyone upon arrival. The name for this section of the island, Ko'ele, means dark sugarcane. The Lodge at Koele, P.O. Box 310, Lanai City, HI 96763, 808/565-7300 or 800/321-4666, www.lodgeatkoele.com, with its encircling veranda and sweep of broad lawn, exudes gracious relaxation. You enter into the Great Hall, where the back ceiling is a translucent skylight through which the sun casts diffused beams onto the formal Victorian parlor below. Encircled by a rich koa balcony, the Great Hall holds two immense fireplaces, the largest in Hawaii. Parlor settings of velvet chairs, cushy couches, wicker lounges, credenzas covered in flowers and ferns, and lustrous end tables are perfect for a lazy afternoon of perusing the newspapers and magazines of the world or listening to soft island music every evening. At each corner of the spacious Great Hall is a hexagonal room of beveled windows: one for dining; one for music; one a library; and the last a game room with backgammon, chess, and dominoes. Afternoon tea by reservation is served in the tea room or on the terrace.

Out front is a croquet pitch, to the side a lawn bowling green. Out back through glass French doors are two more croquet lawns, the swimming pool and fitness/healing center, gazebo and reservoir, Japanese strolling garden, orchid house, palm and fruit gardens, and an executive putting green—a professionally designed "miniature" but real golf course. Here, with putter and a glass of chilled champagne and chocolate-dipped strawberries, you can test your skill against tiny sand traps, puddle-size water traps, and challenging Chihuahua-inspired doglegs both left and right.

Walk along the wide, covered veranda past a row of rocking chairs to the two wings off the Great Hall, where you will find the 102 guest rooms, which range in price from $375 for a garden view to $3,000 for the best suite. A renewal project of the entire property was completed in 2000. Once inside, you can take the brass-doored elevator, but you should climb instead the sweeping wooden staircases bearing carved pineapples, the symbol of hospitality, and walk the broad hardwood hall hung with the works of island artists (ask the concierge for an art list for the hotel), letting period wall lamps light your way. Rooms are furnished in a combination of wicker and heavy knotty pine, with a four-poster bed—each topped with a carved pineapple—covered by a downy quilt, while billowy printed curtains flutter past a window seat. Along with this early-1900s charm comes a full entertainment center, in-room safe, and wet bar. Each room has its own lanai with tile floor and wooden furniture. The bathroom, perhaps blue- or black-on-white marble, features a sink and deep soaking tub with old-fashioned brass knobs, and separate commode. Each room also has multiple phones, ceiling fans, and even umbrellas to borrow and walking sticks for an afternoon foray into the surrounding hills.

An unexpected favorite for many guests is the hotel's Visiting Artist Program. Started in 1992, this ongoing cultural event brings writers, musicians, chefs, poets, filmmakers, and a whole host of other creative people to the hotel for free informal gatherings and presentations about one weekend a month. Two in-house restaurants are here to serve the guests. You can find sundries (and film developing) at the hotel shop, open 8 A.M.–9 P.M. All hotel and island activities, including croquet, tennis, golf, hunting, horseback riding, jeep tours, sporting clays, and beach and boating activities, as well as Internet connection, can be arranged by the concierge. There is regular and frequent shuttle service to meet all arriving and departing planes, to and from Lana'i City, Hotel Lanai, and to Manele Bay Hotel.

## The Manele Bay Hotel

Although it's located overlooking Manele Bay, this hotel property is dealt with here because it's the only other hotel accommodation on the island.

Glass doors curved in a traditional Roman arch sympathize with the surging Pacific as you enter the seaside 250-room Manele Bay Hotel,

P.O. Box 310, Lanai City, HI 96763, 808/565-7700 or 800/321-4666, www.manelebayhotel.com, fashioned in a fusion of Mediterranean, Asian, and Hawaiian design and motif. The open reception area, all marble and glass, with cushy chairs and couches, a huge colorful rug, and carved elephant tusks, holds two massive murals of Lana'i and the wide Pacific dotted with islands. Heroic paintings depict pioneering Polynesians in a double-hulled canoe sighting the Hawaiian Islands and the rascal Prince Kaulula'au, redeemer of Lana'i, standing triumphantly on a windswept beach after banishing the vexatious specters of Lana'i. The lower lobby in contrast has a decidedly Asian feel, with hints of Hawaii. High on the upper walls are painted huge murals depicting Chinese scenes. Below, salubrious chairs and cushions invite you to relax, Asian-style adornments please the eye, and a huge Hawaiian-theme chandelier provides light. For an elegant evening, order a drink or come to hear the evening entertainment at the Hale Aheahe Lounge. The hotel library is a genial room filled with leather-bound tomes, globes, and models of sailing ships. Overhead, the recessed wooden ceiling has been painted with various emblems of Hawaii; the floor is the intricate paisley of tasseled Persian carpets. Sit in a high-backed chair just near the balcony and enjoy the vantage point overlooking Hulopo'e Court below.

From the main reception area, descend a grand staircase and pass a formidable lava rock wall draped with the purples and pinks of living bougainvillea. Here is the grand cloverleaf pool encircled by a marble apron, open for use 24 hours a day. On the lawn below the pool lies an archeological site. Nearby, the newly renovated hotel spa is complete with steam rooms, saunas, and professional staff. The fitness machines and free weights have been moved to one of the open but covered patios. The formal gardens, two on the east and three on the west, and each with its own theme, are tranquil oases where rivulets drop into koi ponds surrounded by patches of broad-leafed taro and swaying stands of bamboo. It's a marvelous setting, but perhaps the best outdoor feature of all is the unobstructed natural beauty of Hulopo'e Bay.

The hotel rooms and suites are mainly in wings east and west. East rooms bear marine names derived from the sea; the west rooms are named after flowers. These oversize guest rooms ranging in price $375–525, designed with Mediterranean and Asian themes, offer four-poster mahogany beds covered with thick quilts, wicker lounge chairs, wet bars, and user-friendly entertainment centers. Marble-tiled bathroom features extra-deep soaking tubs, double sinks and vanity, separate commodes, and glass-enclosed shower stalls big enough for two. Each room has its own private lanai that either overlooks one of the gorgeous gardens or offers an ocean panorama. The hotel also offers several suites that range in price $725–2,200. A typical midrange suite offers a formal parlor and separate master bedroom with a dressing room attached. On the Butler Floor, someone will pack and unpack clothing, draw a hot bath, pour cold champagne, make dinner reservations, and act as your personal liaison at the hotel.

The hotel also offers valet parking, tennis courts, a beach kiosk, a children's program, a gift shop, three restaurants, and a cocktail lounge, where music is performed nightly 5:30–9:30 P.M. Saturdays and Sundays are special with *keiki* hula dancers who come to perform their special magic in the Hulopo'e Court. Another treat is to walk a few minutes to the hotel's **Lana'i Conference Center,** where the antechamber holds museum-quality artifacts. In glass cases, you will find stone implements ranging from *'ulu maika,* Hawaiian bowling stones similar to Italian boccie, to *poho kukui* (*kukui* nut oil lamps). Most of these implements, including a petroglyph stone, have been gathered from Lana'i. There is also an impressive replica of a Hawaiian double-hulled canoe.

## B&Bs and Vacation Rentals

For a more homey stay on the Pineapple Island, try one of the few bed-and-breakfast inns or vacation rentals on Lana'i, all of which are in Lana'i City. These places offer a substantially cheaper alternative to staying on Lana'i than the resorts, and they get you into the community.

**Dreams Come True,** 808/565-6961 or 800/566-6961, fax 808/565-7056, hunter

@aloha.net, www.dreamscometruelanai.com, is a guesthouse in the oldest part of town at 12th Street and Lana'i Avenue. Four rooms in this comfortable plantation house are rented to guests, each with its own bathroom (Italian marble and whirlpool tub) and use of the common room and full kitchen. Decent size for the island, one room has two queen beds, two have one queen bed, and the fourth has two singles. An expanded continental breakfast, with fresh-squeezed lilikoi juice, is served each morning. The rate is $98.50 single or double per night; $35 extra for a child in the same room as parents, or $380 for the entire house. In-house massage can be arranged by appointment only; the owners sell their handmade jewelry; and 4WD vehicles can be rented (inquire as to rates). Find out more about these properties by contacting the owners, Michael and Susan Hunter.

**Hale Moe,** on the south side of town at 502 Akolu St., P.O. Box 196, Lanai City, HI 96763, 808/565-9520, www.staylanai.com, rents three rooms, each with a bathroom, or the entire house. Usually no breakfast is served, but guests can use the kitchen. Two rooms go for $80 and the third is $90. The whole house can be rented for $300.

Several fully equipped houses can be rented from Phylis McOmber, 808/565-6071. One is a two-story affair that can sleep up to eight; the others sleep 5–6 persons. Call for rates.

**Hale O Lana'i,** 808/247-3637, fax 808/235-2644, hibeach@lava.net, www.hibeach.com, is a newer two-bedroom, two-bath house on 4th Street and Lana'i Avenue that has all the amenities for a fine vacation stay. It rents for $115–135 per night, two nights minimum; or $685 on a weekly basis.

Aside from these, try Dolores Fabrao, 808/565-6134, who rents rooms in the family house, 538 Akahi St., for $50 single, $60 double. She also has a larger room that's often used by hunting groups; $25 per person with four or more.

## Rental Agents

**Okamoto Realty,** 730 Lana'i Ave., #112, P.O. Box 630552, Lana'i City, HI 96763, 808/565-7519, fax 808/565-6106, was Lana'i's first house rental agency, and it handles upscale property.

Although the number of houses in its listing varies, you're likely to find three-bedroom affairs at $150–175 per night for up to seven people or a four-bedroom, three-bath cedar house for $495 per night that will sleep 10. All houses are completely furnished, including linens and kitchen utensils, and most have washer/dryer and TV. Houses are rented by the day (with a two-night minimum), week, or month.

Handling some vacation rental properties on the island is **Lana'i Realty,** P.O. Box 676, Lanai City, HI 96763, 808/565-6597 or 800/943-0989. They have homes for $100–145 per night with a two-night minimum.

# RESTAURANTS

Aside from the resort hotels, Lana'i City is the only place on the island where you can dine, shop, and take care of business. The food situation on Lana'i used to be discouraging. Most everything had to be brought in by barge, and the fresh produce, fish, and meat was at a premium. People surely ate differently at home, but in the two tiny restaurants open to travelers, the fare was restricted to the "two-scoop rice and teri beef" variety, with fried noodles and Spam as the pièce de résistance. But, the times they are a-changin'! Now there are more options from which to choose and more culinary variety.

By far the best restaurant in town is **Henry Clay's Rotisserie** at the Hotel Lanai, 808/565-7211; open for dinner daily 5:30–9 P.M. Set just off the entry porch is the barrel-vaulted dining room; guests are also seated in the adjacent back room and bar and on the back patio. Evening appetizers run the gamut from oyster shooters at $1.75 apiece to Cajun shrimp for $10.95. A soup or salad prepares the way for an entrée, be it eggplant creole and angel hair pasta for $18.95, "Louisiana style" barbecue ribs for $19.95, rotisserie roasted whole chicken for $25.95, or either fresh catch and roasted free-range venison loin at a daily quote. Gourmet pizzas are also served, and don't forget the homemade desserts. This is down-home country cooking with a Cajun twist and island influence. Have a look through the glass window into the kitchen to see the large commercial rotisserie full of chicken and other meat. Order a variety of beers or a glass of wine with your meal or simply stop by the bar for a drink from 5:30 P.M. until closing.

The banging screen doors announce your presence as you enter the plantation-era wainscoted **Blue Ginger Cafe,** 808/565-6363, open daily 6 A.M.–2 P.M. and 3–9 P.M., which could actually be called chic for Lana'i. Upon entering, baked goods let you know that not long ago it was Dahang's Bakery, a Lana'i institution whose motto, "Mo betta grind ova hea," has also survived. It offers a full breakfast menu with choices like two eggs with sausage for $4.75, along with plenty of side orders, and fresh pastries. Plate lunches are $6.50 or so, while a bowl of saimin goes for $2.95. Burgers, sandwiches, pizza, and ice cream are also on the menu at comparable prices. Varying nightly, dinner specials, served with rice "toss" salad or macaroni salad, run $8–16. Eat inside or on the front veranda, where you can see everything there is to see in Lana'i City. If you *really* like it here, take home one of their T-shirts. Look for the blue roof.

An authentic workers' restaurant, **Tanigawa's,** open daily except Wednesday for breakfast and lunch 6:30 A.M.–1 P.M., is one of those places that you must visit at least for morning coffee. Totally down-home, but a pure cultural experience, you can also get hot cakes, omelets, burgers, and plate lunches, most for under $7. Arrive before 7 A.M., when many of the older people come to "talk story." Just one look around at the crinkled faces will reveal the tough but sweet spirit of Lana'i.

For a healthy, quick, light meal, try **Pele's Other Garden,** 8th St. and Houston Ave., 808/565-9628. This deli and pizzeria is open Monday–Saturday 9 A.M.–3 P.M. for lunch and 5–9 P.M. for dinner. Eat in or take out. Try a turkey, veggie wrap, or other sandwich for $8 or less, or a hot entrée, like a cheese quesadilla or grilled chicken breast, for $4.50–7.99. More substantial dinner entées run $13–19. Individual or family-size pizzas run $7–22, or choose a salad or something else from the deli case, which also holds gourmet meats, olives, and cheeses. Be sure to check the special board because you never

know what scrumptious delicacy will be offered each day.

Occupying the old Akamai Trading Company shop is **Petro's,** 808/565-6622, serving pizza and sub sandwiches. Open 10 A.M.–8 P.M., Petro's serves pizza by the slice or you can "build your own."

The **Coffee Works,** 604 Ilima St., 808/565-6962, offers espresso, latte, or cappuccino, herb tea, or refreshing ice cream. Open Monday–Friday 6 A.M.–6 P.M., Saturday until 5 P.M., and Sunday until 1 P.M.

## Hotel Restaurants

In harmony with the rest of the Lodge at Koele, the dining rooms are impeccably furnished. Serving all day, **The Terrace,** set in a section off the Great Hall and the more casual of the two restaurants, looks out over the exotic gardens, while the separate dinner-only Formal Dining Room lends itself to evening attire—jackets required. Breakfast selections at The Terrace include continental breakfast, eggs Benedict, and sweet rice waffles with *lilikoi*-coconut chutney. At midday satisfy your hunger with light fare. Dinner, like the other daily fare, is made from the freshest island ingredients. Choose standards like roasted veal chop, braised short ribs, grilled fresh prawns on pasta, or a superbly prepared catch of the day.

In the **Formal Dining Room** you'll have a grand dining experience. It always gets rave reviews form diners who are into serious eating. Once again, the freshest island ingredients are used to prepare each meal that leaves the kitchen. Not only are they sumptuous, but they are also presented in a pleasing manner. All of this elegance doesn't come cheap, however. Expect prices in the $40–50 range for an entrée, which includes butter-braised Maine lobster, seared Hawaiian snapper, and herb-crusted rack of Colorado lamb.

The **Clubhouse** at the Experience at Koele golf course is open daily 10:30 A.M.–3:30 P.M., serving excellent soups, sandwiches, and salads at reasonable prices. Everyone is welcome, and the standing room only lets you know that the food is very good. Try a Korean barbecued beef sandwich, Caesar salad, or one of the many pasta dishes for $7–13. Indoor or outdoor seating is available, with a great view of the 18th green.

The master chef at the Manele Bay Hotel's formal **Ihilani Restaurant** offers a prix fixe menu nightly, along with a complete menu of à la carte suggestions. Expect most entrées in the $32–44 range, with the six-course prix fixe menu at $100 per person. The Ihilani serves dinner only Tuesday–Saturday 6–9:30 P.M.—jackets recommended. Begin with ravioli of Hawaiian goat cheese in a sauce of cilantro and sun-dried tomatoes or gratinée of South Pacific blue prawns. Second courses can be Mediterranean antipasto or Provençale saffron lobster fish soup. Entrées include lavender honey–glazed Muscovy duck breast, grilled catch of the day, and baked onaga and citrus in a sea salt crust. All of this, with a superb view of the bay and beach, is magnifique!

The less formal but still extremely elegant **Hulopo'e Court** offers breakfast and dinner of contemporary Hawaiian regional cuisine, with prices similar to the Ihilani. This is perhaps the best breakfast spot on the island. Begin the day with a continental breakfast, choose all manner of traditional favorites from the breakfast buffet, or make an à la carte selection. Dinner begin with appetizers like crispy fried calamari and cilantro hummus. Soups and salads introduce the entrées, like smoked chicken penne pasta, Hawaiian seafood stew, tarragon-crusted center-cut pork chop, and pan-seared mahimahi. An excellent selection of domestic and imported beer and wine completes the meal.

The least formal dining setting is poolside at **The Pool Grille,** an al fresco restaurant serving lunch and afternoon snacks 11 A.M.–5 P.M. daily. Start with an appetizer such as a chicken quesadilla or cocktail of Pacific shrimp. Lighter appetites will enjoy main-course salads, including marinated grilled vegetables, Cobb salad, or seafood salad. The sandwich board features a good old-fashioned club, a grilled beef burger, or a hot dog. Special offerings are Hawaiian favorites like grilled fresh catch or a steamy bowl of savory saimin.

Overlooking the pool, the **Hale Aheahe Lounge** is open every evening 5–11, serves appetizers until 10 P.M., and has sweet sounds of soft piano music playing until 9:30 P.M.

One must not forget the **Clubhouse Restaurant** at the Challenge at Manele golf course, which has superb underwater scene murals painted on its walls by John Wulbrandt. The view from here is perhaps the best on the property, overlooking both the hotel and bay, with Haleakala on Maui in the background, particularly on a night when the full moon is rising early. Food is served daily 11 A.M.–3 P.M., dinner Thursday–Sunday 6–9 P.M. Small plates are the theme here. Some selections on this hot and cold *pu pu* menu are shrimp satay, spiced lamb, and grilled *ahi* with white bean cassoulet, all for under $15 a plate.

# SHOPPING

Except for the clutch of shops at the Lodge at Koele and Manele Bay Hotel, and the gift shop at the airport, shopping on Lana'i means shopping in Lana'i City. Be aware that all but a few shops are closed on Sunday, and remember that some shops in town may close their doors for an hour or longer at midday for a siesta.

The two grocery stores in town are fairly well stocked with basics. The markets are almost next door to each other. **Pine Isle Market,** 808/565-6488, run by Kerry Honda and open 7 A.M.–10 P.M. every day except Sunday, is Lana'i's closest equivalent to a supermarket, although it also carries hardware and general merchandise. It has a good community bulletin board outside. **Richards Shopping Center,** 808/565-6047, is open Monday–Saturday 8:30 A.M.–5:30 P.M. A small grocery and sundries store, it supplies all your basic camping, fishing, and general merchandise needs, including clothing and medicines, some groceries, liquor, and odds and ends.

Around the corner is **International Food and Clothing Center,** 808/565-6433, where you can pick up not only things to eat, but also hardware and hunting supplies. They have their own butcher, but not much in the way of clothing anymore. This is an old-fashioned general store, definitely a local place; open weekdays 8 A.M.–6 P.M., until 1:30 on Sunday, closed Saturday. On the next street over are a couple of small new shops that

**M**

**MAUI**

sell CDs and tapes and a few snacks. On the far side of the city park is the **Lana'i Family Store,** 808/565-6485, for video rentals and furniture.

**Gifts With Aloha,** 808/565-6589, a shop that carries art and craft items from local and other Hawaii residents, is just down the road. Some items include cloth and clothing, jewelry, quilts, and candles. You should be able to find something for that special occasion here, Mon.–Sat. 9:30 A.M.–6 P.M. Behind Gifts With Aloha is **The Local Gentry,** 808/565-9130, a clothing boutique for women that's open Monday–Friday 10 A.M.–6 P.M. and Saturday until 5 P.M.

Nearby is the **Lana'i Art Program** gallery, 808/565-7503, open daily at irregular hours because it's staffed by volunteers, which has taken the spirit of the Zimbabwe saying "If you can walk, you can dance," and changed it into "If you've got life, you've got art." This co-op of local Lana'i citizens has created a nonprofit organization dedicated to developing the artistic talents of its members and has a strong kids program. Classes, chaired by guest artists, are periodically offered in photography, woodworking, Japanese doll-making, fabric-making, drama and cultural arts, painting, glass, ceramics, and pen and ink drawing. The showroom offers purchases such as hand-dyed silk scarves, stenciled T-shirts, naturally dyed incidental bags, notecards, and lovely pareu for women. Pottery and silk painting seem to predominate. The work is always changing, but you are sure to find a distinctive island memento that couldn't be more genuine. All are welcome, resident or not, so you can drop in on a workshop, pay for your supplies, and create your own art.

Now in a bright yellow plantation-era house at 758 Queen Street, behind Hotel Lanai, **Heart of Lana'i Art Gallery,** 808/565-6678, features watercolors of island scenes by Denise Henning, wooden bowls and ukuleles by Cyrus Keanini, and oil paintings by Macauio Pascual and Pam Andelin. The works are casually displayed but of top quality. With no fixed hours, it's best to call ahead to be sure that the gallery is open. Tuesday–Saturday 2:30–4:30 P.M., Denise hosts an afternoon tea, not only to open her gallery but also to invite special island *kapuna* to talk story. Reservations are requested.

Are you looking for fresh food to cook yourself? Try the **farmers market** at Dole Park, Saturday morning 7–9 A.M. For snacks and sundries, you can also try the Lana'i Plantation Store at the Lana'i City Service gas station. For last-minute souvenirs, have a look at the **airport gift shop** in the terminal building.

# Exploring Lana'i

## MUNRO TRAIL

The highlight of visiting Lana'i is climbing the Munro Trail to its highest point, Lana'ihale (3,370 feet), locally called **The Hale.** As soon as you set foot on Lana'i, the silhouette of this razorback ridge with its bristling coat of Cook pines demands your attention. Set off for The Hale and you're soon engulfed in its cool stands of pines, eucalyptus, and ironwoods, all colored with ferns and wildflowers. George Munro, a New Zealander hired as the manager of the Lana'i Ranch a short time before Jim Dole's arrival, is responsible for this lovely flora. With a pouch full of seeds and clippings from his native New Zealand, he trudged all over Lana'i planting, in an attempt to foliate the island and create a permanent watershed. Driven by that basic and primordial human desire to see things grow, he climbed The Hale time and again to renew and nurture his leafy progeny. Now, all benefit from his labors.

### The Trail

There are two basic ways to go to The Hale, by foot or 4WD. Some local people go on horseback. Head out of town on Keomuku Road toward Shipwreck Beach. It's preferable to start in the morning; cloud cover is common by early afternoon. At mile marker 1, still on the Lana'i City side of the mountains, take the first major road to the right. The sign here should read Cemetery Road. In about one-quarter mile the

ROBERT NILSEN

**on the Munro Trail**

road comes to a Y intersection—go left. You immediately start climbing and pass through a forested area. Continue and the road forks; again bear left. Always stay on the more obviously traveled road, and don't be fooled by the shortcuts that have been constructed for water drainage. The side roads may look muddy or be overgrown, and it's obvious which is the main one. Robert Frost would be disappointed.

As you climb, you pass a profusion of gulches, great red wounds cut into Lana'i's windward side. First comes deep and brooding **Maunalei (Mountain Lei) Gulch,** from where Lana'i draws its water through a series of tunnels bored through the mountains. It's flanked by **Ko'oLana'i Trail,** a rugged and dangerous footpath leading all the way to the coast. Past the communication towers is **Ho'okio Gulch,** a battleground where Lana'i's warriors were vanquished in 1778 by Kalaniopu'u and his ferocious fighters from the Big Island. All that remains are a few room-size notches cut into the walls where the warriors slept and piled stones to be hurled at the invaders. After

Ho'okio Gulch, a trail bears left, bringing you to the gaping mouth of **Hauola Gulch,** more than 2,000 feet deep. Keep your eyes peeled for axis deer, which seem to defy gravity and manage to cling and forage along the most unlikely and precipitous cliffs. Be very careful of your footing—even skilled Lana'i hunters have fallen to their deaths in this area.

The jeep trail narrows on the ridge to little more than 10 feet across. On one side are the wild gulches, on the other the whorling fingerprints of the former pineapple fields. At one point along the way, there's even a picnic table with a view down the west side at one of the short pulloffs. Along the trail, in season, you can munch strawberries, common guavas, and as many thimbleberries as you can handle. At the crest of The Hale, let your eyes pan the horizon to see all of the main islands of Hawaii, except for Kaua'i and Ni'ihau. Rising from the height-caused mirage of a still sea is the hazy specter of O'ahu to the north, with Moloka'i and Maui clearly visible just 10 miles distant. Haleakala, Maui's magical mountain, has a dominant presence viewed from The Hale. Sweep right to see Kaho'olawe, bleak and barren, its body shattered by years of bombs, a victim of controversial war games now ended, that with great volunteer help is slowly on the mend. Eighty miles southeast of Kaho'olawe is the Big Island, its mammoth peaks, Mauna Loa and Mauna Kea, looming like ethereal islands floating in the clouds.

Just past the final lookout is a sign for **Awehi Trail,** which leads left to Naha on the beach. It's extremely rough, and a drive down would definitely require 4WD in compound low gear. Access to this road is not permitted by the rental car company, so you'll have to walk if you want to explore this route. Follow the main road down this dusty decline and take either Ho'ike Road, which flattens out and joins with Route 440 just south of Lana'i City, or head straight ahead and join the highway near where it heads down the hill to Manele Bay. If you have time for only one outing on Lana'i or funds budgeted for only one day of 4WD rental, make sure to treat yourself to the unforgettable Munro Trail.

MAUI

# HEADING SOUTH

Joseph Kali'ihananui was the last of the free Hawaiian farmers to work the land of Lana'i. His great-grandson, Lloyd Cockett, lived in Lana'i City until a few years ago. Joseph made his home in the arid but fertile Palawai Basin, which was later bought by Jim Dole and turned into the heart of the pineapple plantation. Just south of Lana'i City on Route 440 (Manele Road), the Palawai Basin is the crater of the extinct single volcano of which Lana'i is formed. Joseph farmed sweet potatoes, which he traded for fish. He gathered his water in barrels from the dew that formed on his roof and from a trickling spring. His lands supported a few cattle among its now-extinct heavy stands of cactus. Here, too, Walter Murray Gibson attempted to begin a Mormon colony, which he later aborted, supposedly because of his outrage over the idea of polygamy. Nothing noteworthy remains of this colony, but on a hillside overlooking Palawai are the Luahiwa Petroglyphs.

## Luahiwa Petroglyphs

Heading south on Manele Road, look to your left for six tall pine trees and the back side of a stop sign at Ho'ike Road. Ho'ike Road was once paved but has now disintegrated into gravel. Parenthetically, during the pineapple days, major roads that ran through the pineapple fields were paved in order to keep the big trucks running from field to warehouse even when rains made the fields slick with mud. These roads were lines with stone, quarried and set in place by Korean stone masons in the early 1900s. While the rows of pineapples are gone, whorls of grass still grow in the fields. A telltale sign that these fields were recently cultivated are the ever-present bits and pieces of black plastic irrigation pipe and weed cloth that can be seen here and throughout the Palawai basin, an ugly remnant of the plantation days that will be around for years.

After turning left onto Ho'ike, head straight down the road about one mile. When the road comes up a low rise, turn left and follow this secondary road, keeping the ditch on your right. Proceed about one-half mile until you come to a silver water pipe about 12 inches in diameter.

Follow this pipe, heading back toward Lana'i City, jogging right up onto the dike, crossing the pipe, and continue on the upper road about three-tenths mile to rocks on your right at the base of the hill.

Scamper up the hill to the boulders on which appear the petroglyphs. Once brownish black and covered in lichen, their appearance has changed somewhat following an accidental grass fire, which, oddly enough, exposed additional petroglyphs in a ravine to the south that had not been remembered by island residents. Their natural arrangement resembles an oversize Japanese rock garden. Dotted on the hillside are sisal plants that look like bouquets of giant green swords. As you climb to the rocks be very careful of your footing because the ground is crumbly and the vegetation slippery. The boulders cover a three-acre area; most of the petroglyphs are found on the south faces of the rocks. Some are hieroglyphics of symbolic circles, others are picture stories complete with canoes gliding under unfurled sails. Dogs snarl with their jaws agape, while enigmatic triangular stickmen try to tell their stories from the past. Equestrians gallop, showing that these stone picture-books were done even after the coming of the white man. The Luahiwa Petroglyphs are a very special spot where the ancient Hawaiians still sing their tales across the gulf of time. Unfortunately, some modern graffiti now mars the stones.

## Hulopo'e and Manele Bays

Proceed south on Route 440 to Lana'i's most salubrious spots, the twin bays of Manele and Hulopo'e. At the crest of the hill, just past the milepost, you can look down on the white, inviting sands of Hulopo'e to the right and the rockier small-boat harbor of Manele on the left. The island straight ahead is Kaho'olawe, and on very clear days you might be able to glimpse the peaks of Hawai'i's Mauna Loa and Mauna Kea. Years and years ago, Manele was the site of an ancient Hawaiian village, and it was the principal port for the island until the current commercial harbor was built at Kaumalapa'u. **Manele Bay** is a picture-perfect anchorage where a dozen or so small boats and yachts are tied up on any given day. Ferries from

Maui drop off passengers here, and tour boats also tie up here. In the trees overlooking the harbor are a few picnic tables and a public bathroom. Manele and Hulopo'e are a Marine Life Conservation District, with the rules for fishing and diving prominently displayed on a large bulletin board at the entrance to Manele. Because of this, the area is superb for snorkeling, and you can often see a pod of spinner dolphins playing in the water. The tidepools here are also past of this marine reserve and can provide great fun and exploration. No boats are allowed within Hulopo'e Bay except for Hawaiian outrigger canoes, and you may see the canoe club using the bay for practice.

**Hulopo'e Bay** offers gentle waves and soothing, crystal-clear water. The beach is a beautiful expanse of white sand fringed by palms with a mingling of large boulders that really set it off. Aside from the day-use picnic areas with lawns and grills, this is Lana'i's official camping area, and six sites are available. All are well spaced, each with a picnic table and fire pit. A series of shower stalls made of brown plywood provides solar-heated water and just enough privacy, allowing your head and legs to protrude. After refreshing yourself you can fish from the rock promontories on both sides of the bay, or explore the tide pools on the left side of the bay out near the point. It's difficult to find a more wholesome and gentle spot anywhere in Hawaii. For the more adventurous, walk the path that skirts the headland around to Flat Rock, where you have a direct view out to Pu'upehe Rock. Easily seen on top of this pinnacle are the remains of a fishing **heiau.** Some snorkel tours bring their guests to dive just below this headland. Alternately, take the Na Ala Hele Fisherman's Trail from the beach and along the shore below the hotel and golf course to the farthest fairway.

### Kaumalapa'u Harbor

A side trip to Kaumalapa'u Harbor might be in order. This man-made facility, which used to ship more than a million pineapples a day during peak harvest, was the only one of its kind in the world. Activity is now way down, with only one ferry a week on Thursday to deliver supplies, yet it is still Lana'i's lifeline for off-island goods. As you've probably already rented a vehicle, you might as well cover these few paved miles from Lana'i City on Route 440 just to have a quick look. En route you pass Lana'i's odoriferous garbage dump, which is a real eyesore. Hold your nose and try not to notice. The harbor facility is no-nonsense commercial, but the coastline is reasonably spectacular, with a glimpse of the island's dramatic sea cliffs. Also, this area has super-easy access to some decent fishing, right off the pier. An added bonus for making the trek to this lonely area is that it is one of the best places on Lana'i from which to view the sunset, and you usually have it all to yourself.

# KAUNOLU: KAMEHAMEHA'S GETAWAY

At the southwestern tip of Lana'i is Kaunolu Bay, a point where currents from both sides of the island converge. At one time, this vibrant fishing village surrounded Halulu Heiau, Lana'i's most important religious spot, and a sacred refuge where the downtrodden were protected by the temple priests who could intercede with the benevolent gods. Halulu Heiau is perhaps named after the man-eating bird Halulu from Tahiti, one of the legendary birds that guided Polynesians from the south to the Hawaiian islands. Kamehameha the Great would escape Lahaina's blistering summers and come to these fertile fishing waters with his loyal warriors. Some proved their valor to their great chief by diving from Kahekili's Leap, a man-made opening in the rocks 60 feet above the sea.

The remains of more than 80 house sites and a smattering of petroglyphs dot the area. The last inhabitant was Ohua, elder brother of Joseph Kali'ihananui, who lived in a grass hut just east of Kaunolu in Mamaki Bay. Ohua was entrusted by Kamehameha V to hide the *heiau* fish-god, Kuniki; old accounts by the area's natives say that he died because of mishandling this stone god. The natural power still emanating from Kaunolu is obvious, and you can't help feeling the energy that drew the Hawaiians to this sacred spot.

### Getting There

Proceed south on Manele Road from Lana'i City

through Palawai Basin until it makes a hard bend to the left. Here, a sign points you to Manele Bay. Do not go left to Manele, but proceed straight and stay on the once-paved pineapple road. The rental car company doesn't allow their vehicles on this and most other former plantation roads, but you can hike. Head straight through the old pineapple fields until you come upon two orange pipes (like fire hydrants) on the left and right. Turn left here onto a rather small road. Follow the road left to a sign that actually says Kaunolu. This dirt track starts off innocently enough as it begins its plunge toward the sea, and you pass two abandoned dryland farms along the way that once experimented with herbs and vegetables that didn't require much water. Only two miles long, the local folks consider it the roughest road on the island. It *is* a bone-cruncher, so take it super slow if you are in a vehicle. Plot your progress against the lighthouse on the coast. This road is not maintained. Because of natural erosion; it may be too rugged for any vehicle to pass. This area is excellent for spotting axis deer and wild turkeys. The deer are nourished by *haole koa*, a green bush with a brown seed pod that you see growing along the road. This natural feed also supports cattle but is not good for horses, causing the hair on their tails to fall out.

## Kaunolu

The village site lies at the end of a long, dry gulch that terminates at a rocky beach, suitable in times past as a canoe anchorage. This entire area is a mecca for archaeologists and anthropologists. The most famous was the eminent Dr. Kenneth Emory of the Bishop Museum; he filed an extensive research report on the area in the 1920s. A more recent research team covered the area in the mid-1990s. In response to its importance, Kaunolu has been designated an Archaeological Interpretive Park and been given the status of a National Historical Landmark. At its terminus, the road splits left and right. Go right to reach a large *kiawe* tree with a picnic table under it. Just in front of you is a large pile of nondescript rocks purported to be the ruined foundation of Kamehameha's house. Numerous other stone remnants dot the slope on both sides of the gulch. Unbe-

lievably, this sacred area is sometimes trashed by disrespectful and ignorant picnickers. Hurricane 'Iwa also had a hand in changing the face of Kaunolu, as its tremendous force hit this area head on and even drove large boulders from the sea onto the land. As you look around, the ones that have a whitish appearance were washed up on shore by the fury of 'Iwa.

The villagers of Kaunolu lived mostly on the east bank and had to keep an ever-watchful eye on nature because the bone-dry gulch could suddenly be engulfed by flash floods. In the center of the gulch, about 100 yards inland, was Pa'ao, the area's freshwater well. Pa'ao was *kapu* to menstruating women, and it was believed that if the *kapu* was broken, the well would dry up. It served the village for centuries, but it's totally obliterated now. In 1895 a Mr. Hayselden tried to erect a windmill over it, destroying the native caulking and causing the well to turn brackish—an example of Lana'i's precious water being tampered with by outsiders, causing disastrous results.

## The Sites

Climb down the east bank and cross the rocky beach. The first well-laid wall close to the beach on the west bank is the remains of a canoe shed. Proceed inland and climb the rocky bank to the remains of Halulu Heiau. Just below in the undergrowth is where the well was located. The *heiau* site has a commanding view of the area, best described by the words of Dr. Emory himself:

> *The point on which it is located is surrounded on three sides by cliffs and on the north rises the magnificent cliff of Palikaholo, terminating in Kahilikalani crag, a thousand feet above the sea. The ocean swell entering Kolokolo Cave causes a rumbling like thunder, as if under the* heiau. *From every point in the village the* heiau *dominates the landscape.*

As you climb the west bank, notice that the mortarless walls are laid up for more than 30 feet. If you have a keen eye you'll notice a perfectly square fire pit right in the center of the *heiau*.

This area still has treasures that have never been catalogued. For example, you might chance upon a Hawaiian lamp, as big and perfectly round as a basketball, with an orange-size hole in the middle where *kukui* nut oil was burned. Old records indicate that Kuniki, the temple idol, is still lying here face down no more than a few hundred yards away. If you happen to discover an artifact, do not remove it under any circumstance. Follow the advice of the late Lloyd Cockett, a *kapuna* of Lana'i, who said, "I wouldn't take the rock because we Hawaiians don't steal from the land. Special rocks you don't touch."

### Kahekili's Leap

Once you've explored the *heiau,* you'll be drawn toward the sea cliff. **Kane'apua Rock,** a giant towerlike chunk, sits just offshore at the end of the cliff. Below in the tide pool are basin-like depressions in the rock-salt evaporation pools, the bottoms still showing some white residue. Follow the cliff face along the natural wall obstructing your view to the west. You'll see a break in the wall about 15 feet wide with a flat rock platform. From here, **Shark Island,** which closely resembles a shark fin, is perfectly framed. This opening is Kahekili's Leap, perhaps named after a Lana'i chief, not the famous chief of Maui. Here, Kamehameha's warriors proved their courage by executing death-defying leaps into only 12 feet of water and clearing a 15-foot protruding rock shelf. Scholars also believe that Kamehameha punished his warriors for petty offenses by sentencing them to make the jump. Today, daredevils plunge from the cliff for fun in a yearly cliff-diving competition. Kahekili's Leap is a perfect background for a photo. Below, the sea surges in unreal aquamarine colors. Off to the right is Kolokolo Cave, above which is another, even more daring leap at 90 feet. Evidence suggests that Kolokolo is linked to Kaunolu Gulch by a lava tube that has been sealed and lost.

### Petroglyphs

To find the petroglyphs, walk directly inland from Kane'apua Rock, using it as your point of reference. On a large pile of rocks are stick figures, mostly with a bird-head motif. Some heads even look like a mason's hammer. This entire area has a masculine feeling to it. There aren't the usual swaying palms and gentle, sandy beaches. With the stones and rugged sea cliffs, you get the feeling that a warrior king would enjoy this spot. For their enjoyment, the vacationing chiefs often played *konane,* and a few stone boards can still be found from this game of Hawaiian checkers. Throughout the area is *pili* grass, used by the Hawaiians to thatch their homes. Children would pick one blade and hold it in their fingers while reciting *"E pili e, e pili e, 'au hea ku'u hale."* The *pili* grass would then spin around in their fingers and point in the direction of home. Pick some *pili* and try it yourself before leaving this wondrous, powerful area.

## THE EAST COAST: KEOMUKU AND NAHA

Until the 20th century, most of Lana'i's inhabitants lived in the villages of the now-deserted east coast. Before the coming of Westerners, 2,000 or so Hawaiians lived along these shores, fishing and raising taro. It was as if they wanted to keep Maui in sight so they didn't feel so isolated. Numerous *heiau* from this period still mark the ancient sites. The first white men also tried to make a go of Lana'i along this stretch. The Maunalei Sugar Co. tried to raise sugarcane on the flat plains of Naha but failed and pulled up stakes in 1901—the last time this entire coastline was populated to any extent even though some cattle ranching was done here following the demise of the sugar plantation. Today, the ancient *heiau* and a decaying church in Keomuku are the last vestiges of habitation, holding out against the ever-encroaching jungle. You can follow a jeep trail along this coast and get a fleeting glimpse of times past.

The shallow coastline that wraps around the north and east coast of Lana'i opposes the shallow south coast of Moloka'i. Although many fewer than on that coast of Moloka'i, most ancient fish ponds of Lana'i were located here, and their remnants can still be seen. Because of the shallow nature of the water and its rocky bottom, swimming is not particularly good along most of this coast except for a few isolated sandy spots. In

MAUI

fact, the water cannot be seen well from the road most of the way to Naha because of the growth of trees and bushes along the beach. Numerous pullouts and shore access roads have been created, however, so you can get to the water. Unfortunately, inconsiderate visitors have left these pullouts a bit trashy with junk tossed to the ground rather than taken out.

## Getting There

Approach Keomuku and Naha from one of two directions. The most straightforward is from north to south. Follow Keomuku Road from Lana'i City until it turns to dirt and branches right (south) at the coast, about one-half hour. This road meanders for about 12 miles all the way to Naha, another 30–60 minutes. Although the road is partially gravel and packed sand and not that rugged, you will need a 4WD in spots. Watch for washouts and fallen trees. Because of storm wash or flooding from the hills, this road is sometimes closed to traffic and not safe to traverse. The road is paralleled by a much smoother beach route partway along the coast, but it can only be used at low tide. Many small roads connect the two, so you can hop back and forth between them every 200–300 yards. Consider three tips: (1) If you take the beach road, you can make good time and have a smooth ride, but could sail past most of the sights because you won't know when to hop back on the inland road; (2) dry sand can easily bog down even a 4WD vehicle, making an expensive rescue mission for a tow truck, so be wise and only drive where sand is hard-packed; and (3) be careful of the *kiawe* trees because the tough, inch-long thorns can puncture tires as easily as nails.

The other alternative is to take Awehi Trail, a rugged jeep track, about halfway between Lopa and Naha. This route is not open to rental jeeps, but you can hike it. This trail leads up the mountain to the Munro Trail, but because of its ruggedness it's best to take it down from The Hale instead of up. A good long day would take you along the Munro Trail, down Awehi Trail, then north along the coast back to Keomuku Road. If you came south along the coast, it would be better to retrace your steps instead of heading up

Awehi. When you think you've suffered enough, remember that this trail and others were carved out by Juan Torqueza. He trailblazed alone on his bulldozer, unsupervised, and without benefit of survey.

## Keomuku Village

There isn't much to see in Keomuku Village other than an abandoned Hawaiian church. This village was the site of the Maunalei Sugar Co. The town was pretty much abandoned after 1901 when the sugar company ceased operations, but a ranching operation did utilize this area until midcentury. Most all of the decaying buildings were razed in the early 1970s. A few hundred yards north and south of the town site are examples of some original fish ponds. They're tough to see because they're overgrown with mangrove, but a close observation gives you an idea of how extensive they once were. The **Hawaiian church** is worth a stop, and it almost pleads to be photographed. From outside, you can see how frail it is, so if you go in, tread lightly. The altar area, a podium with a little bench, remains. A banner on the fading blue-green walls reads *"Ualanaano Jehova Kalanakila Malamalama,* October 4, 1903." Only the soft wind sounds where once strong voices sang vibrant hymns of praise.

A few hundred yards south of the church is a walking trail. Follow it inland to **Kahe'a Heiau** and a smattering of petroglyphs. This is the *heiau* disturbed by the sugarcane train; its desecration was believed to have caused the sweet water of Keomuku to turn brackish. The people of Keomuku learned to survive on the brackish water and kept a special jug of fresh water for visitors.

## Heading South

Farther south a Japanese cemetery and monument were erected for the deceased workers who built **Halepaloa Landing,** from where the cane was shipped. Today, only rotting timbers and stonework remain, but the pier offers an excellent vantage point for viewing Maui, and it's a good spot to fish.

The road continues past **Lopa,** ending at **Naha.** Both were sites of ancient fish ponds; the one at Naha can still be discerned at low tide.

On the way, you'll pass several roads heading inland that lead to hunting areas. You also pass a few coconut groves. Legend says that one of these was cursed by a *kahuna*—if you climb a tree to get a coconut you will not be able to come down. Luckily, most tourists have already been cursed by "midriff bulge" and can't climb the tree in the first place. When you get to Naha, check out the remnants of the paved Hawaiian walking trail before slowly heading back from this decaying historical area.

## SHIPWRECK BEACH

Heading over the mountains from Lana'i City to Kaiolohia Beach (Shipwreck Beach) offers you a rewarding scenario: an intriguing destination point with fantastic scenery and splendid panoramas on the way. Head north from Lana'i City on Keomuku Road. In less than 10 minutes you crest the mountains, and if you're lucky the sky will be clear and you'll be able to see the phenomenon that guided ancient navigators to land: the halo of dark brooding clouds over Maui and Moloka'i, a sure sign of landfall. Shorten your gaze and look at the terrain in the immediate vicinity. Here, in the gulches and gullies, wounded earth bleeds red while offering patches of swaying grass and wildflowers. It looks like the canyons of Arizona have been dragged to the rim of the sea. As you wiggle your way down Keomuku Road, look left to see the decaying hull of a World War II oiler sitting on the shallow reef almost completely out of the water. Made of concrete, this ship has not rusted apart like others that have foundered here, but it too is slowly disintegrating. Curiously, this ship was deliberately beached here when it apparently outlived its usefulness. For most, this derelict is the destination point on Shipwreck Beach.

As you continue down the road, little piles of stones, usually three, sit atop a boulder. Although most are from modern times, these are called *ahu,* a traditional Hawaiian offering to ensure good fortune while traveling. Under no circumstances should you disturb them. Farther down, the lush grasses of the mountain slope disappear, and the scrub bush takes over. The pavement ends and the dirt road forks left (west) to Shipwreck Beach or straight ahead (south) toward the abandoned town of Naha. If you turn left you'll be on an adequate sandy road, flanked on

Abandoned on Lana'i's north reef, this ship is the destination of many island kayaking adventures.

MAUI

both sides by thorny, tire-puncturing *kiawe* trees. In less than a mile is a large, open area to your right. If you're into unofficial camping, this isn't a bad spot for a one-night bivouac—the trees here provide privacy and an excellent windbreak against the constant strong ocean breezes. About two miles down the road is Federation Camp, actually the remains of a tiny village of unpretentious beach shacks built by Lana'i's workers as getaways and fishing cabins. Charming in their humbleness and simplicity, they're made mostly from recycled timbers and boards that have washed ashore. Some have been worked on quite diligently and skillfully and are actual little homes, but somehow the rougher ones are more attractive. You can drive past the cabins for a few hundred yards to park and begin your walk.

## Petroglyphs

Near the very end of the road is a cabin that a local comedian has named the "Lana'i Hilton." Park your car to the end of the sand road and walk a short way up the coast to a cement base for a long-since-gone lighthouse. Look closely and you can see that two workers of days gone by, John Kapau and Kam Chee, put their names and initials in the wet cement of this foundation on November 28, 1929. Behind the cement block, arrows point you to "The Bird Man of Lana'i Petroglyphs." Of all the petroglyphs on Lana'i, these are the easiest to find; trail-marking rocks have been painted white by Lana'i's Boy Scouts. Running almost directly inland, follow them for a couple hundred yards to a large rock bearing the admonition Do Not Deface. Climb down the path into a small gully and look with a keen eye— the rock carvings are small, most only about one foot tall. Little childlike stick figures, some have intriguing bird heads whose symbolic meaning has been lost. Dog or other animal figures are also found here as well as a larger two-foot-high figure on a rock on the opposite side of the wash.

## Hiking the Beach

The trail along the beach goes for eight long, hot miles to Polihua Beach. That trip should be done separately, but at least walk as far as the ship, about a mile from the end of the road. The area has some of the best beachcombing in Hawaii; no telling what you might find. The most sought-after treasures are glass floats that have bobbed for thousands of miles across the Pacific, strays from Japanese fishnets. You might even see a modern ship washed onto the reef, like the Canadian yacht that went aground in spring 1984. Navigational equipment has improved, but Shipwreck Beach can *still* be a nightmare to any captain caught in its turbulent whitecaps and long, ragged coral fingers. This area is particularly good for lobsters and shore-fishing, and you can swim in shallow sandy-bottom pools to refresh yourself as you hike.

Just inland of the beach and west of the end of the road is an overgrown section of an old trail that once connected villages along this coast, now nearly lost among the *kiawe* trees and buried under sand. Named the Kaiolohia-Kahue Trail and part of the state's Na Ala Hele trail system, it awaits funding to be restored for its cultural significance and as an alternate means of access to this area.

Try to time your return car trip over the mountain for sundown. The tortuous terrain, stark in black and white shadows, is awe-inspiring. The larger rocks are giant sentinels: It's easy to feel the power and attraction they held for the ancient Hawaiians. As you climb the road on the windward side with its barren and beaten terrain, the feelings of mystery and mystique attributed to spiritual Lana'i are obvious. You come over the top and suddenly see the plateau—manicured, rolling, soft, and verdant—and the few lights of Lana'i City beckoning.

## THE GARDEN OF THE GODS AND POLIHUA

The most ruggedly beautiful, barren, and inhospitable section of Lana'i is out at the north end. After passing through a broad stretch of former pineapple fields, you come to Kanepu'u Preserve, the island's only nature reserve and best example of dryland forest. Just as you pop out the far side of the preserve, you reach Keahi Kawelo, the appropriately named Garden of the Gods. Waiting is a fantasia of otherworldly landscapes—barren red earth, convulsed ancient lava flows, tortured pinnacles of stone, and psychedelic striations of vibrating colors, especially moving at sunrise and sunset. Little-traveled trails lead to Ka'ena (The Heat) Point, a wasteland dominated by sea cliffs where adulterous Hawaiian wives were sent into exile for a short time in 1837. Close by is Lana'i's largest *heiau*, dubbed Ka'enaiki, so isolated and forgotten that its real name and function were lost even to Hawaiian natives by the middle of the 19th century. After a blistering, sun-baked, 4WD drubbing, you emerge at the coast on Polihua, a totally secluded, white-sand beach where sea turtles once came to bury their eggs in the natural incubator of its soft, warm sands (Polihua means "eggs in bosom").

## Getting There

Lana'i doesn't hand over its treasures easily, but they're worth pursuing. To get to the Garden of the Gods, head past the Lodge at Koele, and turn left onto the road that runs between the tennis courts and the riding stable. After about one minute, there's an intersection where you should turn right. Follow this road through former pineapple fields, keeping the prominent ridge on your right. Proceed for about 20 minutes until you pass through the Kanepu'u dryland forest preserve. Disregard the roads to the right and the left. Once out the back side of the preserve, you soon begin to see large boulders sitting atop packed red earth, the signal that you're entering the Garden of the Gods. It's about another hot half hour drive down to Polihua Beach, and on the way you'll find a marker on the left for Ka'ena Road, which leads to magnificent sea cliffs and Ka'enaiki Heiau. Basically, you're heading toward the western tip of Moloka'i, which you can keep in your sights in the distance across the channel. Have no illusions about this road. It's long and bumpy, but if you want a beach to yourself, persevere. Definitely do not attempt the lower reaches of this road without 4WD.

## Kanepu'u Preserve

Straddling the road leading to the Garden of the Gods, this 590-acre preserve is the best remaining example of dryland forest on Lana'i and a sampling of what covered much of the lower leeward slopes of the Hawaiian Islands before the coming of humans. In this forest you'll find *olopua,* a native olive tree; *lama,* a native ebony; *na'u,* Hawaiian gardenia; the *'iliahi* sandalwood tree; and numerous other plant varieties, 49 species of which are found only in Hawaii, as well as many species of birds. Over the centuries, these dryland forests were reduced in size by fire, introduced animals, and the spread of non-native weeds and trees. Erosion control measures, such as the planting of native shrubs and seeds, have been implemented to cover bare spots and fill contour scars. Under the care of The Nature Conservancy and local conservation groups, this forest and others like it are being protected.

As you pass through this preserve, stop at the self-guided loop trail to get a close-up look at some of the trees in the forest. It's about a 15-minute walk over level ground, if you stop and read the posted signs. Overlooking this trail and set on a nearby rise is Kanepu'u (Kane's Hill) Heiau.

Guided hikes through the preserve are occasionally offered. For more information about these hikes or for general information about the preserve, try 808/565-7430.

## The Garden of the Gods

There, a shocking assault on your senses, is the bleak, red, burnt earth, devoid of vegetation, heralding the beginning of the garden—a Hawaiian Badlands. The flowers here are made of rock, the shrubs are the twisted crusts of lava, and trees are baked minarets of stone, all subtle shades of orange, purple, and sulfurous yellow. Although most is obviously created by natural erosion, some piles of stone are just as obviously erected by man. The jeep trail has been sucked down by erosion and the garden surrounds you. The beginning seems most dramatic, but much more spreads out before you as you proceed down the hill. Stop often to climb a likely outcropping and get a sweeping view. While you can't see Lana'i's coastline from here, you do have a nice view of Moloka'i across the channel. The wind rakes these badlands and the silence penetrates to your soul. Although eons have passed, you can feel the cataclysmic violence that created this

MAUI

haunting and delicate beauty. The Garden of the Gods is perhaps best in the late afternoon when slanting sunlight enriches colors and casts shadows that create depth and mood.

## Polihua Beach

After leaving the Garden of the Gods, you can bear left to lonely **Ka'ena Point,** where you'll find Lana'i's largest *heiau,* a brooding setting full of weird power vibrations. Straight ahead, the trail takes you down to the coast. Abruptly the road becomes smooth and flat. Like a mirage too bright for your eyes, an arch is cut into the green jungle, framing white sand and moving blue ocean. As you face the beach, to the right it's flat, expansive, and the sands are white, but the winds are heavy; if you hiked eight miles, you'd reach Shipwreck Beach. A few shade trees edge the sand so you can get out of the heat. More interesting is the view to the left, which has a series of lonely little coves. The sand is brown and coarse, and large black lava boulders are marbled with purplish gray rock embedded in long, faulted seams. Polihua is not just a destination point where you come for a quick look. It takes so much effort coming and going that you should plan on having a picnic and a relaxing afternoon before heading back through the Garden of the Gods and its perfectly scheduled sunset light show.

# Moloka'i

Moloka'i is a sanctuary, a human time capsule where the pendulum swings inexorably forward, but more slowly than in the rest of Hawaii. It has always been so. In ancient times, Moloka'i was known as Pule O'o, "Powerful Prayer," where its supreme chiefs protected their small underpopulated refuge, not through legions of warriors but through the chants of their *kahuna*. This powerful, ancient mysticism, handed down directly from the goddess Pahulu, was known and respected throughout the archipelago. Its *mana* was the oldest and strongest in Hawaii, and its practitioners were venerated by nobility and commoners alike—they had the ability to "pray you to death." The entire island was a haven, a refuge for the vanquished and *kapu*-breakers of all the islands. It's still so today, beckoning to determined escapees from the rat race!

The blazing lights of supermodern Honolulu can easily be seen from the west end of Moloka'i, while Moloka'i as viewed from O'ahu is fleeting and ephemeral, appearing and disappearing on the horizon. The island is home to the largest number of Hawaiians. In effect it is a tribal homeland: More than 3,000 of the island's 7,400 inhabitants have more than 50 percent Hawaiian blood and, except for Ni'ihau, it's the only island where they are the majority. The 1920s Hawaiian Homes Act allowed *kuleana* of 40 acres to anyone with more than 50 percent Hawaiian ancestry. *Kuleana* owners form the grassroots organizations that fight for Hawaiian rights and battle the colossal forces of rabid developers who have threatened Moloka'i for decades.

ROBERT NILSEN

This steep cliff separates Kalaupapa Peninsula from the rest of the island.

Moloka'i has had several sobriquets through the years. Many decades ago, it was know as the Lonely Isle, undoubtedly because so many leprosy patients were dumped on its shore. These individuals were truly lonely people, sent away from family, friends, and loved ones, abandoned by society to the netherworld of the kingdom. Perhaps in an effort to shift its image to a positive one, Moloka'i became know as the Friendly Isle because of the nature of its inhabitants, a characteristic that they certainly still exhibit today. Within the last couple of decades, and coinciding with the resurgence of a popular interest in the Hawaiian culture, people began to call Moloka'i the Most Hawaiian Island because it has the largest percentage of Hawaiian residents for its population, aside from the private island of Ni'ihau. Most recently, and in a bid to play up its natural potential as a place to come and play outdoors, officials in the tourism business have given to Moloka'i the phrase Hawaiian by Nature. Most Hawaiians know the monikers Friendly Isle and Most Hawaiian Isle. Time will tell if its new name will stick.

## Kaunakakai and West

Kaunakakai, the island's main town, once looked like a Hollywood sound stage where Jesse James or Wyatt Earp would feel right at home. The town is flat, with few trees, and three blocks long. Ala Malama, its main shopping street, is lined with false-front stores; pickup trucks are parked in front where horses and buggies ought to be. To the west are the prairie-like plains of Moloka'i, some sections irrigated and now planted in profitable crops. The northern section of the island contains **Pala'au State Park,** where a campsite is always easily found, and **Phallic Rock,** a natural shrine where island women came to pray for fertility. Most of the west end is owned by the mammoth 54,000-acre **Molokai Ranch.** Part of its lands supports several thousand head of cattle and herds of axis deer imported from India in 1867.

The 40-acre *kuleana* are here on the uplands beyond the airport, as well as abandoned Dole and Del Monte pineapple fields. The once-thriving pineapple company town of **Kualapu'u** is now a semi-ghost town since Del Monte pulled up stakes in 1985, and coffee is now grown on some of the fields. This area attracts its scattered Filipino workers mostly on weekends, when they come to unofficially test

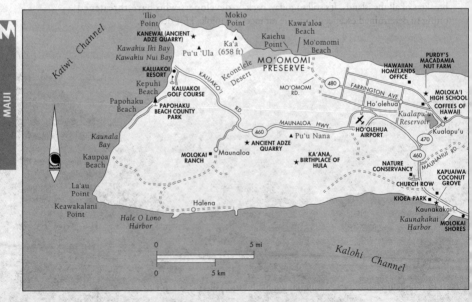

their best cocks in the pit. Look for the small A-frame shelters in yards here that house these creatures. Dole shut down the pineapple fields around **Maunaloa** in 1975, after which the town took a swift nose dive into neglect. Having recently undergone a massive facelift, Maunaloa is holding on as the Molokai Ranch is expanding its operations to include more tourism-related activities.

On the western shore is the **Kaluakoi Resort,** perched above the island's best beach. Here, 6,700 acres sold by the Molokai Ranch to the Louisiana Land and Exploration Company, later sold to another concern, and most recently bought back by the ranch, are *slowly* being developed as homesites, but so far houses are only scattered here and there. This area, rich with the finest archaeological sites on the island, is a hotbed of contention between developers and preservationists. The Kaluakoi Resort with its golf course and the low Polynesian-style architecture of its hotel and condominiums that blend well with the surroundings was pointed to as a well-planned development, but unfortunately it has gone through economic trouble and fallen on hard times.

## The East Coastal Road

Highway 450 is a magnificent coastal road running east from Kaunakakai to Halawa Valley. A slow drive along this bucolic country thoroughfare rewards you with easily accessible beach parks, glimpses of fish ponds, *heiau,* wildlife sanctuaries, and small one-room churches strung along the road like rosary beads. Almost every mile has a historical site, like the **Smith and Bronte Landing Site** where two pioneers of trans-Pacific flight ignominiously alighted in a mangrove swamp, and **Paikalani Taro Patch,** the only one from which Kamehameha V would eat poi.

On Moloka'i's eastern tip is **Halawa Valley,** a real gem accessible by car. This pristine gorge has two lovely waterfalls and their pools, and a beach park where the valley meets the sea. Most of the population of Halawa moved out in 1946 after a 30-foot tsunami washed their homes away and mangled their taro fields, leaving a thick, salty residue. Today only a handful of those from the old families and a few alternative lifestylers live in the valley among the overgrown stone walls that once marked the boundaries of manicured and prosperous family gardens. On Pu'u O Hoku Ranch property is **Kalanikaula,** the sacred *kukui*

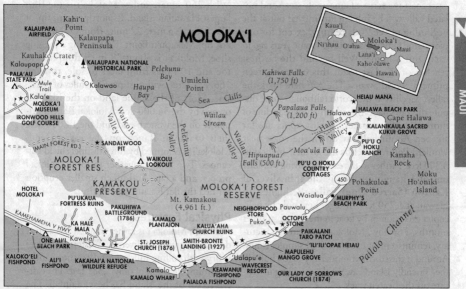

© SANDRA E. BISIGNANI TRUST AND AVALON TRAVEL PUBLISHING, INC.

grove of Lanikaula, Moloka'i's most powerful *kahuna* of the classic period. This grove was planted at his death and became the most sacred spot on Moloka'i.

## The Windward Coast

**Kalaupapa** (Flat Leaf) is a lonely peninsula formed by lava flow from the 400-foot-high Kauhako Crater, the highest spot on this relatively flat nub of land. Kalaupapa colony for leprosy patients, completely separated from the world by a hostile, pounding surf and a precipitous 1,600-foot *pali*, is a modern story of human dignity. Kalaupapa, and Kalawao before it, was a dispossessed settlement of dispossessed people where the unfortunate victims of leprosy were banished to die. Here humanity reached its lowest ebb of hopelessness, violence, and depravity, until one tiny flicker of light arrived in 1873— Joseph de Veuster, a Belgian priest known throughout Hawaii as Father Damien. In the greatest example of pure *aloha* yet established on Hawaii, he became his brothers' keeper. Tours of Kalaupapa operated by well-informed residents are enlightening and educational.

East of Kalaupapa along the windward (northeast) coast is a series of amazingly steep and isolated valleys. The inhabitants moved out at the beginning of the 20th century, except for one pioneering family that returned some years ago to carve out a home. Well beyond the farthest reaches of the last road, this emerald-green primeval world awaits. The *pali* here mark the tallest sea cliffs in the world (although some dispute this designation), with an "average incline of more than 55 degrees." Many spots are far steeper. About halfway down the coast near Umilehi Point, the cliffs are at their highest at 3,300 feet. Farther to the east and diving headfirst out of a hanging valley is the thin sliver of **Kahiwa (Sacred One) Falls,** the highest in Hawaii at 1,750 feet. You get here only by helicopter excursion or by boat in the calmer summer months. For now, Moloka'i remains a sanctuary, reminiscent of the Hawaii of simpler times. Around it the storm of modernity rages, but still the "Friendly Island" awaits those willing to venture off the beaten track.

Moloka'i's north shore has some of the highest sea cliffs in the world.

## THE LAND

With 260 square miles, Moloka'i is the fifth largest Hawaiian island. Its northwestern tip, at 'Ilio Point, is a mere 22 miles from O'ahu's eastern tip, Makapu'u Point. Resembling a jogging shoe, Moloka'i is about 38 miles from heel to toe and 10 miles from laces to sole, totaling 166,425 acres, with just over 88 miles of coastline. Most of the arable land on the island is owned by the 54,000-acre Molokai Ranch, primarily on the western end, and the 14,000-acre Pu'u O Hoku Ranch on the eastern end. Moloka'i was formed by three distinct shield volcanoes. Two linked together to form Moloka'i proper, and a later and much smaller eruption formed the flat Kalaupapa Peninsula.

### Physical Features

Although Moloka'i is rather small, it has a great deal of geographical diversity. Western Moloka'i is dry with rolling hills, natural pastures, and a maximum elevation of only 1,381 feet. The eastern sector of the island has heavy rainfall. The tallest sea cliffs in the world, and craggy, narrow valleys perpetually covered in a velvet cloak of green plants edge its northern front. Viewed from the sea it looks like a 2,000-foot vertical wall from surf to clouds, with tortuously deep chasms along the coastline. Mount Kamakou is the highest peak on Moloka'i, at 4,961 feet, and lying below it on the south shore is a narrow littoral of farms and fields. Moloka'i's south shore is also worthy of note as it has about 28 miles of reef, the state's only continuous barrier reef. The south-central area is relatively swampy, while the west and especially northwest coasts around Mo'omomi have rolling sand dunes. Papohaku Beach, on the west end of Moloka'i, is one of the most massive white-sand beaches in Hawaii. A controversy was raised when it was discovered that huge amounts of sand were dredged from this area and hauled to O'ahu; the Molokai Ranch was pressured and the dredging ceased. A hefty section of land in the north-central area is a state forest where new species of trees are planted on an experimental basis. The 240-acre Pala'au State Park is in this cool upland forested area.

## Man-Made Marvels

Two man-made features on Moloka'i are engineering marvels. One is the series of 62 ancient fish ponds strung along the south shore like pearls on a string—best seen from the air as you approach the island by plane. The outlines of dozens can still be seen, but the most amazing is the enormous **Keawanui Pond,** covering 54 acres and surrounded by a three-foot-tall, 2,000-foot-long wall. It's on the National Register of Historic Places. The other is the modern **Kualapu'u Reservoir** completed in 1969. The

world's largest rubber-lined reservoir, it can hold 1.4 billion gallons of water. Part of its engineering dramatics is the Moloka'i Tunnel, which feeds it with water from the eastern valleys. The tunnel is eight feet tall, eight feet wide, and almost 27,000 feet (five miles) long.

## Climate

The average island daytime maximum temperature runs 75–85°F (24–29°C), winter to summer. The yearly average rainfall is 27 inches; the east receives a much greater percentage than the west.

# FLORA AND FAUNA

Land animals on Moloka'i were brought by humans: pigs, goats, axis deer, and cattle. The earliest arrival still extant in the wild is the *pua'a* (pig). Moloka'i's pigs live in the upper wetland forests of the northeast, but they can actually thrive anywhere. Hunters say the meat from pigs that have lived in the lower dry forest is superior to those that acquire the muddy taste of ferns from the wetter upland areas. Pigs on Moloka'i are hunted mostly with the use of dogs, who pin them by the ears and snout while the hunter approaches on foot and skewers them with a long knife.

Offspring from a pair of **goats** left by Captain Cook on the island of Ni'ihau spread to all the islands; they were very well adapted to life on Moloka'i. Originally from the arid Mediterranean, goats could live well without any surface water, a condition quite prevalent over most of Moloka'i. They're found primarily in the mountainous area of the northeast.

The last free-roaming arrivals to Moloka'i were **axis deer.** Moloka'i's deer came from the upper reaches of the Ganges River, sent to Kamehameha

| MOLOKA'I TEMPERATURE AND RAINFALL | | | | | | |
|---|---|---|---|---|---|---|
| | Jan. | March | May | June | Sept. | Nov. |
| High | 79 | 79 | 81 | 82 | 82 | 80 |
| Low | 61 | 63 | 68 | 70 | 68 | 63 |
| Rain | 4 | 3 | 0 | 0 | 0 | 2 |
| Note: Temperature is in degrees Fahrenheit; rainfall is in inches. | | | | | | |

V by Dr. William Hillebrand while on a botanical trip to India in 1867. Kamehameha V sent some of the first specimens to Moloka'i, where they prospered. Today they are found mostly on western Moloka'i, although some travel the south coast to the east.

## Birdlife

A few of Hawaii's endemic birds can be spotted by a determined observer at various locales around Moloka'i. They include the Hawaiian petrel (*'ua'u*); Hawaiian coot (*'alae ke'oke'o*), prominent in Hawaiian mythology; Hawaiian stilt (*ae'o*), a wading bird with ridiculous stick legs that protects its young by feigning wing injury and luring predators away from the nest; and the Hawaiian owl (*pueo*), a bird that helps in its own demise by being easily approached. Moloka'i has a substantial number of introduced game birds that attract hunters throughout the year.

The nonprofit organization **Nene O Moloka'i** operates a facility that breeds, releases, and monitors the state bird, the *nene*. Located about four miles east of Kaunakakai, it offers free tours daily at 9 A.M., but you must make an appointment to visit. To learn more about these friendly geese, call 808/553-5992 or visit the organization's website at www.aloha.net/~nene.

## Flora

The *kukui* or candlenut tree is common to all of the Hawaiian Islands; along with being the official state tree, its tiny white blossom is Moloka'i's flower. The *kukui*, introduced centuries ago by the early Polynesians, grows on lower mountain slopes and can easily be distinguished by its pale green leaves. Low and dry, the western end of Moloka'i is typified by shrubby bushes and gnarled trees. Only in the windy desertlike Mo'omomi sand dune area does hearty native shore vegetation still survive. In the upper reaches of the north shore valleys, the vegetation is as rich, diverse, and luxuriant as the wet areas of the other islands.

## Conservation Controversy

It has long been established and regretted that introduced animals and plants have destroyed Hawaii's delicate natural balance, leading to the extinction of many of its rare native species. Several well-meaning groups and organizations are doing their best to preserve Hawaii habitat, but they don't always agree on the methods employed. Feral pigs, indiscriminate in their relentless hunt for food, are ecological nightmares that virtually bulldoze the rainforest floor into fetid pools and gouged earth, where mosquitoes and other introduced species thrive while driving out the natives. Moloka'i's magnificent Kamakou Preserve, Upper Pelekunu Valley, and the central Moloka'i ridges are some of the last remaining pockets of natural habitat on the island. The Kamakou Preserve, 2,774 pristine acres, is covered, like the others, in 'ohi'a forest, prime habitat for the almost-extinct *oloma'o* (Moloka'i thrush), *kakawahie* (creeper), and the hearty but beleaguered *'apapane* and *'amakihi*. No one disagrees that the wild boar must be managed to protect these areas, but they do not agree on *how* they should be managed. The Nature Conservancy in its dedication to preserving the rainforest backed a policy to snare the wild boar, maintaining that this was the best possible way of eliminating these pests while placing the forest under the least amount of stress. In opposition to the practice of snaring is Pono, a local organization of native Moloka'i hunters that maintains snaring pigs is inhumane, causing the animals to starve to death or to die slowly from strangulation. Pono also abhors the wasting of the meat and the indiscriminate killing of sows.

Aside from the **Kamakou Preserve**, the Nature Conservancy also maintains 5,759 acres of the upper Pelekunu Valley on the remote north coast of the island, where there is no public access. There is access, however, to the **Mo'omomi Preserve**, a 921-acre area of sand dunes west of Mo'omomi Beach that is safe harbor for several species of endangered coastal plants, seabirds, and green sea turtles. You can walk in on your own, but the Nature Conservancy conducts guided hikes once a month into the Kamakou and Mo'omomi preserves. These hikes run $10 for members and $25 for nonmembers (who then become members for one year). If you wish to attend, call well in advance for dates and to reserve your spot; 808/553-5236. For more information, log onto the organization's website at www.tnc.org.

# HISTORY

The oral chant *"Moloka'i nui a Hina . . ."* ("Great Moloka'i, child of Hina") refers to Moloka'i as the island-child of the goddess Hina and the god Wakea, male progenitor of all the islands; Papa, Wakea's first wife, left him in anger as a result of this unfaithfulness. Hina's cave, just above Kalua'aha on the southeast coast, can still be visited and has been revered as a sacred spot for countless centuries. Another ancient spot, Halawa Valley, on the eastern tip of Moloka'i, is considered one of the oldest settlements in Hawaii. As research continues, settlement dates are pushed farther back, but for now scholars agree that early wayfarers from the Marquesas Islands settled Halawa in the mid-7th century.

Moloka'i, from earliest times, was revered and feared as a center for mysticism and sorcery. In fact, an ancient name for the island is Moloka'i Pule O'o (Moloka'i of the Potent Prayers). **'Ili'ili'opae Heiau** was renowned for its powerful priests, whose incantations were mingled with the screams of human sacrifice. Commoners avoided 'Ili'ili'opae, and even powerful *kahuna* could not escape its terrible power. One, Kamalo, lost his sons as sacrifices at the *heiau* for their desecration of the temple drum. Kamalo sought revenge by invoking the help of his personal god, the terrible shark deity Kauhuhu. After the proper prayers and offerings, Kauhuhu sent a flash flood to wipe out Mapulehu Valley where 'Ili'ili'opae was located. All perished except for Kamalo and his family, who were protected by a sacred fence around their home.

This tradition of mysticism reached its apex with the famous Lanikaula, "Prophet of Moloka'i." During the 16th century, Lanikaula lived near Halawa Valley and practiced his arts, handed down by the goddess Pahulu, who predated even Pele. Pahulu was the goddess responsible for the "old ocean highway," which passed between Moloka'i and Lana'i and led to Kahiki, lost homeland of all the islanders. Lanikaula practiced his sorcery in the utmost secrecy and even buried his excrement on an offshore island so that a rival *kahuna* could not find and burn it, which would surely cause his death. Hawaiian oral history does not say why Palo, a sorcerer from Lana'i and a friend of Lanikaula, came to spy on Lanikaula and observed him hiding his excrement. Palo burned it in the sacred fires, and Lanikaula knew that his end was near. Lanikaula ordered his sons to bury him in a hidden grave so that his enemies could not find his bones and use their *mana* to control his spirit. To further hide his remains, he had a *kukui* grove planted over his body. **Kalanikaula** (Sacred Grove of Lanikaula) is still visible today.

## Incursions from Outside

Captain James Cook first spotted Moloka'i on November 26, 1778, but because it looked bleak and uninhabited, he decided to bypass it. It wasn't until eight years later that Capt. George Dixon sighted the island and decided to land. Very little was recorded in his ship's log about this first encounter, and Moloka'i slipped from the attention of the Western world until Protestant missionaries arrived at Kalua'aha in 1832 and reported the native population at approximately 6,000.

In 1790, Kamehameha the Great came from the Big Island as a suitor seeking the hand of Keopuolani, a chieftess of Moloka'i. Within five years he returned again, but this time there was no merrymaking: He came as a conquering chief on his thrust westward to capture O'ahu. His war canoes landed at Pakuhiwa Battleground, a bay just a few miles east of Kaunakakai between Kawela and Kamalo; it's said that warriors lined the shores for more than four miles. The grossly outnumbered warriors of Moloka'i fought desperately, but even the incantations of their *kahuna* were no match for Kamehameha and his warriors. Inflamed with recent victory and infused with the power of their horrible war-god Ku ("of the Maggot-dripping Mouth"), they slaughtered the Moloka'i warriors and threw their broken bodies into a sea so filled with sharks that their feeding frenzy made the waters appear to boil. Thus subdued, Moloka'i slipped into obscu-

MAUI

rity once again as its people turned to a quiet life of farming and fishing.

## Molokai Ranch

Moloka'i remained almost unchanged until the 1850s. The Great Mahele of 1848 provided for private ownership of land, and giant tracts were formed into the Molokai Ranch. About 1850, German immigrant Rudolph Meyer came to Moloka'i and married a high chieftess named Dorcas Kalama Waha. Together they had 11 children, with whose aid he turned the vast lands of the Molokai Ranch into productive pastureland. A man of indomitable spirit, Meyer held public office on Moloka'i and became the island's unofficial patriarch. He managed Molokai Ranch for the original owner, Kamehameha V, and remained manager until his death in 1897, by which time the ranch was owned by the Bishop Estate. In 1875, Charles Bishop had bought half of the 70,000 acres of Molokai Ranch, and his wife, Bernice, a Kamehameha descendant, inherited the remainder. In 1898, the Molokai Ranch was sold to businessmen in Honolulu for $251,000. This consortium formed the American Sugar Co., but after a few plantings the available water on Moloka'i turned brackish, and once again Molokai Ranch was sold. Charles Cooke bought controlling interest from the other businessmen in 1908 and remained in control of the ranch until 1988, when it was sold to Brierly Investments, a business concern from New Zealand.

## Changing Times

Very little happened for a decade after Charles Cooke bought the Molokai Ranch from his partners. Moloka'i did become famous for its honey production, supplying a huge amount to the world up until World War I. During the 1920s, political and economic forces greatly changed Moloka'i. In 1921, Congress passed the **Hawaiian Homes Act,** which set aside 43,000 acres on the island for people who had at least 50 percent Hawaiian blood. By this time, however, all agriculturally productive land in Hawaii had already been claimed. The land given to the Hawaiians was very poor and lacked adequate water. Many Hawaiians had long since left the land

and were raised in towns and cities. Now out of touch with the simple life of the taro patch, they found it very difficult to readjust. To prevent the Hawaiians from selling their claims and losing the land forever, the Hawaiian Homes Act provided that the land be leased to them for 99 years. Making a go of these 40-acre *(kuleana)* parcels was so difficult that successful homesteaders were called "Moloka'i Miracles."

In 1923 Libby Corporation leased land from Molokai Ranch at Kaluako'i and went into pineapple production; Del Monte followed suit in 1927 at Kualapu'u. Both built company towns and imported Japanese and Filipino field laborers, swelling Moloka'i's population and stabilizing the economy. Many of the native Hawaiians subleased their *kuleana* tracts to the pineapple growers, and the Hawaiian Homes Act seemed to backfire. Instead of the homesteaders working their own farms, they were given monthly checks and lured into a life of complacency. Those who grew little more than family plots became, in effect, permanent tenants on their own property. Much more importantly, they lost the psychological advantage of controlling their own future and regaining their pride, as envisioned in the Hawaiian Homes Act.

## Modern Times

For the next 50 years life was quiet. The pineapples grew, providing security. Another large ranch, **Pu'u O Hoku** (Hill of Stars) was formed on the eastern tip of the island. It was originally owned by Paul Fagan, the amazing San Francisco entrepreneur who later developed the Hana Ranch on Maui. In 1955, Fagan sold Pu'u O Hoku to George Murphy, a Canadian industrialist, for a meager $300,000. The ranch, under Murphy, became famous for beautiful white Charolais cattle, a breed originating in France.

In the late 1960s, things started quietly happening on Moloka'i. The Molokai Ranch sold 6,700 acres to the Kaluakoi Corp., which they controlled along with the Louisiana Land and Exploration Company. In 1969 the long-awaited Moloka'i reservoir was completed at Kualapu'u; finally west Moloka'i had plenty of water. Shortly after Moloka'i's water problem appeared to be finally under control, Dole Corp. bought out Libby in 1972, lost millions in the next few years, and shut down its pineapple production at Maunaloa in 1975. By 1977 the acreage sold to the Kaluakoi Corp. started to be developed, and the Molokai Sheraton (later called the Kaluakoi Hotel, but now closed) opened along with low-rise condominiums and 270 fee-simple home sites ranging 5–43 acres. Plans then for this area included two more resorts, additional condominiums, shopping facilities, bridle paths, and an airstrip (it's only 20 minutes to Honolulu). Lo and behold, it seemed that sleepy old Moloka'i with the tiny Hawaiian Homes farms was now prime real estate and worth a fortune.

To complicate the picture even further, Del Monte shut down its operations in 1982, throwing more people out of work. In 1986 it did resume planting 250-acre tracts, but now all of the pineapple is gone. Recently, coffee has been put into production near the old pineapple town of Kualapu'u, some experimental plots of fruits and vegetables have been planted, and the Molokai Ranch has brought in sheep and cattle. After Brierly Investments bought the Molokai Ranch, other changes started to take place, including a total facelift for the town of Maunaloa and greater emphasis on tourism for a slice of the ranch's income. These new avenues of diversification are still in their infant stages but might possibly lead to greater economic strength and stability. In 2002, Molokai Ranch bought back the acreage it sold in the 1960s, and it remains to be seen if other changes will happen on the west end. Moloka'i is in a period of flux in other ways. There is great tension between developers, who are viewed as carpetbaggers interested only in a fast buck, and those who consider themselves the last remnants of a lost race holding on desperately to what little they have left.

# ECONOMY

If it weren't for a pitifully bad economy, Moloka'i would have no economy at all. At one time the workers on the pineapple plantations had good, steady incomes and the high hopes of the working class. With all of the pineapple jobs gone, Moloka'i was transformed from an island with virtually no unemployment to a hard-luck community with a high rate of people on welfare. With the start of the coffee plantation, this bleak economic situation lessened somewhat, but the more recent downturn in tourism has dealt the island a blow. Inexplicably, Moloka'i also has the highest utility rates in Hawaii. Some say this is because the utility company built a modern biomass plant and didn't have enough biomass to keep it operating, so the people were stuck with the fuel tab. The present situation is even more ludicrous when you consider that politically Moloka'i is part of Maui County. It is lumped together with Ka'anapali on Maui's western coast, one of Hawaii's poshest and wealthiest areas, where most people are recent arrivals from the Mainland. This amounts to almost no political/economic voice for grassroots Moloka'i.

## Agriculture

The word that is now bandied about is "diversified" agriculture. What this means is not pinning all hope on one crop like the ill-fated pineapple, but planting a potpourri of crops. Attempts at diversification are evident as you travel around Moloka'i, and many fields are set off by long rows of tall trees as windbreaks. Fields of corn, wheat, fruits, nuts, and coffee are just west of Kaunakakai; many small farmers are trying truck farming by raising a variety of garden vegetables that they hope to sell to the massive hotel food industry in Honolulu. Watermelon, bell pepper, onions, and herbs are perhaps the most well known, and one farm—some say the largest in the state—grows sweet potatoes. Maui Community College, part of the University of Hawai'i system, also has some acreage here for experimentation in raising native trees. The problem is not in production, but transportation. Moloka'i raises excellent crops, but not enough established transport exists for the perishable vegetables. A barge service, running on a loose twice-weekly schedule, is the only link to the market. The lack of proper storage facilities on Moloka'i makes it tough to compete in the hotel food business, which requires the freshest produce. Unfortunately, vegetables don't wait well in the heat for late barges.

MAUI

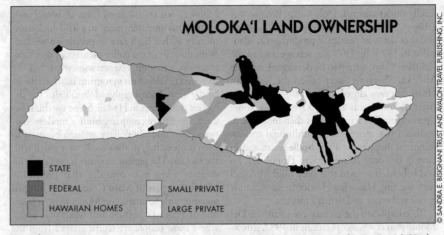

**MOLOKA'I LAND OWNERSHIP**

STATE

FEDERAL

HAWAIIAN HOMES

SMALL PRIVATE

LARGE PRIVATE

## Development

When development was new, a debate raged between those in favor of tourist development, which they said would save Moloka'i, and grassroots organizations, which insisted that unchecked tourism development would despoil Moloka'i and give no real benefit to the people. A main character in the debate was the Kaluakoi Corp., which wanted to build condos and sell more home lots. It claimed that this, coupled with a few more resorts, would bring in jobs. The people know that they will be relegated to service jobs (maids and waiters), while all the management jobs go to outsiders. Most islanders felt that only rich people from the Mainland could afford million-dollar homes and condos and that eventually they will become disenfranchised on their own island. Claims were that outsiders have no feeling for the 'aina (land) and would destroy important cultural sites whenever growth dictates. While quieted much over the years, this issue is only barely under the surface and erupts quickly when any talk of development is in the winds.

Some years back the Kaluakoi Corp. hired an "independent" research team to investigate the area around Kawakiu Iki Bay, known to be an ancient adze quarry. After weeks of study, this Maui-based research team reported that Kawakiu was of "minor importance." Hawaii's academic sector went wild. The Society of Hawaiian Archaeology

dispatched its own team under Dr. Patrick Kirch, who stated that Kawakiu was one of the richest archaeological areas in Hawaii. In one day they discovered six sites missed by the "independent" research team and stated that a rank amateur could find artifacts by merely scraping away some of the surface. Reasonable voices call for moderation. Both sides agree Moloka'i must grow, but the growth must be controlled, and the people of Moloka'i must be represented and included as beneficiaries.

## THE PEOPLE

Aside from the tiny island of Ni'ihau, Moloka'i has the largest percentage of Hawaiian population, perhaps partly because of relatively small commercial development on the island throughout its history, which did not bring in large numbers of ethnic workers. Although sugar was tried early on with some success, it never grew to vast size, and the pineapple production on the island was also limited. Only ranching has really persevered, and this doesn't require any large number of laborers. More recently, with the slow development of tourism, white-collar workers have filtered into the workforce, and there has been a small increase in tourism-related jobs. Local Hawaiians make up 48 percent of Moloka'i's population; 21 percent are Filipino, 18 percent Caucasian, 9 percent Japanese, 1 percent Chinese, and 3 percent various other groups.

Moloka'i is obviously experiencing a class struggle. The social problems hinge on the economy—the collapse of pineapple cultivation and the move toward tourism. The average income on Moloka'i is quite low, and the people are not consumer-oriented. Tourism, especially getaway condos, brings in the affluent. This creates friction; the have-nots don't know their situation until the haves come in and remind them. Today, most people hunt a little, fish, and have small gardens. Some are small-time *pakalolo* growers who get over the hard spots by making a few dollars from some backyard plants. There is no organized crime on Moloka'i. The worst you might run into is a group of local kids drinking on a weekend in one of their favorite spots. It's a territorial thing. If you come into their vicinity, they might feel that their turf is being invaded, and you could be in for some hassles. All this could add up to a bitter situation except that the true nature of most of the people is to be helpful and friendly. Just be sensitive to smiles and frowns and give people their space.

### Ethnic Identity

An underground link exists between Moloka'i and other Hawaiian communities such as Waianae on O'ahu. Moloka'i is unusual in that it is still Hawaiian in population and influence, with continuing culturally based outlooks that remain unacceptable to Western views. Ethnic Hawaiians are again becoming proud of their culture and heritage, as well as politically aware and sophisticated, and are just now entering the political arena.

Social problems on Moloka'i relate directly to teenage boredom and hostility in the schools, fueled by a heavy drinking and drug scene. A disproportionate rate of teen pregnancy is a direct by-product. The traditional educational approach is failing.

*Ho'oponopono* is a fascinating family problem-solving technique still very much employed on Moloka'i. The process is like "peeling the onion," where a mediator, usually a respected

*kapuna,* tries to get to the heart of a problem. Similar to group therapy, it's a closed family ordeal, never open to outsiders, and lasts until all emotions are out in the open and all concerned feel "clean."

## FESTIVALS AND EVENTS

Like all of the other islands, Moloka'i celebrates all federal and state holidays and major events. In addition to these, specific events have particular importance on this island. A few of these follow.

### January

The day-long **Makahiki Festival,** held at Kaunakakai Park, includes food, arts, crafts, and games in a revived version of the ancient Hawaiian Olympics.

### May

Music, song, and hula contests are the focus of the day at the **Moloka'i Ka Hula Piko,** held at Papohaku Beach Park on the west end of Moloka'i. This event, which includes craft and art demonstrations and Hawaiian foods, is held to honor the birth of hula, traditionally held to have been on top of Ka'ana Hill above Maunaloa.

### July

The annual **Moloka'i to O'ahu Paddleboard Race,** a 32-mile paddle race on longboards, runs across Kaiwi Channel from Papohaku Beach to Maunaloa Beach Park in Hawaii Kai on O'ahu.

### September

The **Wahine O Ke Kai Outrigger Canoe Race** for women takes off at the end of September in Hawaiian-style canoes from the remote Hale O Lono Beach on Moloka'i's west end to Kahanamoku Beach in Waikiki. In crossing, the teams must navigate the always-rough Kaiwi Channel.

### October

The **Moloka'i Hoe Outrigger Canoe Race** is the men's version of this canoe contest, which also starts from Hale O Lono Beach and races to Kahanamoku Beach on O'ahu.

MAUI

## SPORTS AND RECREATION

Because Moloka'i is a great place to get away from it all, you would expect an outdoor extravaganza. In fact, Moloka'i is a "good news, bad news" island when it comes to recreation, especially in the water. Moloka'i has few excellent beaches, with the two best, Halawa and Papohaku, on opposite ends of the island; Papohaku Beach on the west end is treacherous during the winter but generally good the rest of the year. Surfers and sailboarders will be disappointed with Moloka'i except at a few locales at the right time of year, while bathers, sun worshippers, and families will love the few small, secluded beaches with gentle waves located mostly on the south shore.

Moloka'i has a small population and plenty of undeveloped "outback" land. This *should* add up to great hiking and camping, but the land is mostly privately owned, camping spots are few, and you need permission or must enter with an organized activity company for most of the trails. However, those bold enough to venture into the outback on open trails will virtually have it to themselves. Moloka'i has tame, family-oriented beach parks along its southern shores, superb hunting and fishing, two golf courses, and a handful of tennis courts. Couple this with clean air, no industrial pollution, no city noise, and a deliciously casual atmosphere, and you wind up with the epitome of relaxation.

### Camping

The best camping on Moloka'i is at **Pala'au State Park** at the end of Route 470, in the cool mountains overlooking Kalaupapa Peninsula. It's also the site of Moloka'i's famous Phallic Rock. Here you'll find pavilions, grills, picnic tables, and fresh water. What you won't find are crowds; in fact, most likely you'll have the entire area to yourself. The camping here is free, but you need a permit, good for seven days, from the park headquarters office in Kalae, 808/567-6923, or from the Division of State Parks in Wailuku on Maui, 808/984-8109.

Camping is permitted for two days at **Waikolu Lookout** in the Moloka'i Forest Reserve, but you'll have to follow a tough dirt road (Main Forest Road) for 10 miles to get to it. Bring your own water because none is available there. A free permit must be obtained from the Division of Forestry and Wildlife, 54 S. High St., Wailuku, HI 96793, 808/984-8100, or if you write, allow at least a week.

County park, seaside camping is allowed at **One Ali'i Park,** just east of Kaunakakai, and at **Papohaku Beach Park,** on the west end. These parks have full facilities. Papohaku is isolated and quiet, but because of its location and easy access just off the highway, One Ali'i is often noisy. Also, you are a target here for any rip-off artists. A county permit is required and available from County Parks and Recreation at the Mitchell Pauole Center in Kaunakakai, 808/553-3204, open Mon.–Fri. 8 A.M.–4 P.M.; fees are $3 per day for adults, $.50 for children under age 17. Camping is limited to three consecutive days and a total of 15 days per year.

Until renovation is completed, camping is not permitted at the Hawaiian Home Lands' **Kioea Park,** one mile west of Kaunakakai, the site of one of the most amazing royal coconut groves in Hawaii.

### Hiking

Moloka'i should be a hiker's paradise, and there are a few well-maintained and easily accessible trails, but others cross private land, skirt guarded *pakalolo* patches, are poorly maintained, and/or are tough to follow. This section provides a general overview of some hiking possibilities available on Moloka'i.

One of the most exciting hassle-free trails descends the *pali* to the **Kalaupapa Peninsula.** You follow the well-maintained mule trail down, and except for some "road apples" left by the mules, it's a totally enjoyable experience suitable for in-shape hikers. Because this trail is within the boundary of the National Historical Park, you *must* have a reservation with the guide company to descend this trail and tour the peninsula.

Another excellent trail is at **Halawa Valley,** following Halawa Stream to cascading Moaula Falls, where you can take a refreshing dip if the famous *mo'o,* a mythical lizard said to live in the pool, is in the right mood. This trail is strenuous enough to be worthwhile and thrilling enough to be memorable. Halawa Valley is one of the most ancient populated sites in the islands, and many remnants of the past still dot the floor of the valley. In years past, anyone could walk up into Halawa Valley; however, because of abuse, disrespect, degradation of the land, and a few lawsuits, it was closed to the public for two years. It has been opened again, and you can go in with a group booked by the Molokai Ranch Outfitters Center, 808/552-2791. These trips run daily at 9:30 A.M. for $75 per person, and each guide not only shows you the way but also gives you a private historical and cultural lesson on the way. Call for reservations and all particulars. Some valley residents are willing to guide the curious for about $20, and, while you are not supposed to go in without permission because it is private land, some people do make the trip in by themselves. If you know the way and go in by yourself, leave a donation ($5 should be sufficient) at the flower stand by the wooden bridge over the stream in appreciation for those in the valley who maintain the trail.

Moloka'i Forest Reserve, which you can reach by driving about 10 miles over the rugged Main Forest Road (passable by 4WD only in the dry season), has fine hiking. On the way you'll find the Sandalwood Measuring Pit and just at the reserve boundary the Waikolu Lookout. The hale and hearty who push on for several more miles will find themselves in the Nature Conservancy's **Kamakou Preserve** overlooking Pelekunu and Wailau, two fabulous and enchanted valleys of the north coast.

The Molokai Ranch offers the greatest number of diverse and unique cultural hiking tours across its land at the west end of the island. For schedules, times, and fees, call the Ranch Outfitters Center at 808/552-2791 or 888/729-0059.

For guided hiking tours to other parts of the island, try the services of Eddie Tanaka, 808/558-8396, a Moloka'i native who knows all of the good trails, or either of the outdoor adventure companies, Molokai Outdoors, 808/553-4477, or Molokai Rentals and Tours, 808/553-5663.

## Beaches

**East End:** The beaches of Moloka'i have their own temperament, ranging from moody and rebellious to sweet and docile. Heading east from Kaunakakai along Route 450 takes you past a string of beaches that vary from poor to excellent. Much of this underbelly of Moloka'i is fringed by a protective coral reef that keeps the water flat, shallow, and at some spots murky. This area was ideal for fish ponds but leaves a lot to be desired as far as beaches are concerned. The farther east you go, the better the beaches become. The first one you come to is at **One Ali'i Park,** about four miles east of Kaunakakai. Here you'll find a picnic area, campsites, good fishing, and family-class swimming where the kids can frolic with no danger from the sea. Next you pass **Kakahai'a Beach Park,** but perhaps the best beach along the road is **Murphy's Beach** at mile marker 20. **Halawa Bay,** on Moloka'i's far east end, is the best all-around beach on the island. It's swimmable year-round, but be extra careful during the winter. The bay protects the beach for a good distance; beyond its reach the breakers are excellent for surfing. The snorkeling and fishing are good to very good.

**West End:** The people of Moloka'i favor the isolated beaches on the northwest section of the island. **Mo'omomi Beach** is one of the best and features good swimming in summer, fair surfing, and pleasurable snorkeling along its sandy, rocky bottom. You have to drive over a very rutted dirt road to get there. Although car rental agencies are against it, you can make it, but only in dry weather. From Mo'omomi you can walk west along the shore and find your own secluded spot in a series of small and large beaches. Very few visitors go south from Maunaloa town, but it is possible and rewarding for those seeking a secluded area. As you enter Maunaloa town a crushed coral track goes off to your right. Follow it through Molokai Ranch land and down the hill to **Hale O Lono Harbor,** start of an Outrigger Canoe Race. The swimming is only fair, but the fantasy feeling of a deserted island is pervasive. **Kepuhi Beach** just below the Kaluakoi Hotel is excellent, and **Papohaku Beach** beyond the headland farther to the south is renowned for its vast expanse of sand. Unfortunately, both are treacherous in the winter, with giant swells and heavy rips, which make them a favorite for surfers. Anyone not accustomed to strong sea conditions should limit themselves to sunning and wading only to the ankles. During the rest of the year, this area is fairly good for swimming, sometimes becoming like a lake in the summer, but still exhibits areas of undertow and shore break. Stay on the safe side and limit yourself to walks along the sand. About one-half mile north of Kepuhi Beach is an ideal spot named **Kawakiu Beach,** good for swimming, depending on tide conditions, secluded sunbathing, and unofficial camping. This area is well established as an archaeological site, and access to the beach was a hard-fought controversy between the people of Moloka'i and the Molokai Ranch.

## Snorkel and Scuba

Some charter fishing boats arrange scuba and snorkeling excursions, but scuba and snorkeling on Moloka'i are just offshore, and you don't need a boat to get to it. Beginners will feel safe at **One Ali'i Park,** where the sea conditions are mild, although the snorkeling is mediocre. The best underwater area is the string of beaches heading east past mile marker 18 on Route 450, and especially at mile marker 20. Mo'omomi Beach on the northwest shore is very good, and Kawakiu Beach out on the west end is good around the rocks, but stay away during winter. For those staying at Molokai Ranch, Halena and Kolo beaches along the south coast also offer decent snorkeling.

**Moloka'i Fish and Dive** in Kaunakakai, 808/553-5926, is a full-service snorkel shop. It has very good rental rates at $9 a set per day and can give you directions to the best spots.

**Bill Kapuni's Snorkel and Dive Adventure,** P.O. Box 1962, Kaunakakai, HI 96748, 808/553-9867, cpgroup@aloha.net, www.molokai.com/kapuni, is an excellent way to enjoy Moloka'i's underwater spectacle. Owner Bill Kapuni, a native Hawaiian, is intimately familiar with both the marine life you will encounter and the Hawaiian myths and legends of his heritage. Bill's trips, including complimentary snacks, are $65 for snor-keling and $95 for a two-tank dive. Bill offers professional PADI instruction and has a compressor to fill tanks for certified divers. Other water activities can be accommodated. All trips operate on a Boston Whaler, six-person maximum.

## Ma'a Hawaii, Moloka'i Action Adventures

Walter Naki knows Moloka'i—its mountains, seas, shores, trails, flowers, trees, and birds. His one-man action-adventure company, Ma'a Hawaii, P.O. Box 1269, Kaunakakai, HI 96748, 808/558-8184, loosely translates as "used to, accustomed to, or familiar with." A native Hawaiian raised on the island and versed in its myths and mysteries, Walter has won the Hawaiian decathlon five times and has won renown in statewide spearfishing and free-diving contests. If it has to do with the outdoors, Walter does it. Walter's north shore boat trip is his number-one activity. He's one of the few who takes guests to the "backside" of the island. The boat goes summer or winter—summer is best—but only when the water is safe, and the trip costs $100 per person. In summer, the water on the north shore is a bit choppy, but there is no surf so you can get close to shore and land, swim, and hike in Wailua Valley. In winter, the water is smoother, but there are larger—sometimes immense—swells, and it's not possible to land or even get very close to the shore because of the strong surf.

Walter is a certified boat captain as well as a certified scuba diver. For a scuba trip, you must bring your own gear. Deep-sea fishing excursions, kayaking, whale-watching, snorkeling, spear fishing, and reef fishing tours are also available on request. Walter can arrange other activities, such as hunting for axis deer, wild boar, or goats on private land, which costs $200 per day for bow hunters (you supply the equipment) and $300 per day for rifle hunters (two hunters per day only, Walter suppies the guns and ammunition). Hiking and "camera safaris" over many of the same hunting trails cost $50 for a half day (up to six people only) and are often guided by Walter's friend Eddie Tanaka; call 808/558-8396. Walter is a great guide, but he is definitely "fo real," absolutely genuine with no glitz or glamour.

He will do everything he can to make your day safe and enjoyable, even stopping at his friend's taro patch to give you a glimpse of preserved island life. If you seek a unique experience where you can touch the spirit of Moloka'i, travel for a day with Walter Naki.

## Kayaking

The Molokai Ranch **Outfitters Center,** 808/552-2791 or 888/729-0059, runs a rather tame but thoroughly fun kayak tour along the south shore inside the reef for $65, or $45 if you are a guest at the ranch.

If you want to take off on your own or be guided through the placid reef, try **Moloka'i Outdoors,** 808/553-4477. Guided trips run $78 for the coastline tour and $45 for the sunset tour. Single and double rental kayaks are available at $10 per hour or $25 per day, or $15 per hour or $40 per day, respectively. See them at Hotel Moloka'i.

**Molokai Rentals and Tours,** 808/553-5663, offers a morning kayak tour along the south shore for $45, as well as rents kayaks for those who care to go on their own. Daily rentals run $25 for a single and $40 for a tandem.

## Sailing

Moloka'i is nearly devoid of charter sailboats; however, for those who like to feel the salty sea breeze in their hair, hear the snap of a full-furled sail, or enjoy the sunset from the deck of a sailing ship, try an excursion with **Moloka'i Charters,** P.O. Box 1207, Kaunakakai, HI 96748, 808/553-5852. The only charter sailing ship on the island is its 42-foot sloop *Satan's Doll,* berthed at the Kaunakakai wharf. Tours offered are a two-hour sunset sail for $40 and a full-day sail to Lana'i for swimming and snorkeling for $90. In season, whale-watching tours are also run for $50. Four-person minimum; priced per person.

## Surfing

The best surfing that's easily accessible is out on the east end past mile marker 20. Pohakuloa Point has excellent breaks, which continue eastward to Halawa Bay. Mo'omomi Beach has decent breaks, as does Kepuhi Beach in front of Kaluakoi Resort

(also good for sailboarding) and Papohaku farther down; Kawakiu's huge waves during the winter are suitable only for experts. For gear and accessories, stop at **Molokai Surf** along the highway in Kaunakakai. If you need to rent a surfboard, try **Moloka'i Outdoors,** 808/553-4477, or **Molokai Rentals and Tours,** 808/553-5663.

## Horseback and Mule Rides

The **Molokai Ranch,** 808/552-2791, offers a variety of rides over its lands for ranch guests and nonguests. Included are a *paniolo* roundup for $80 and three different trail rides for $80–125. An inexpensive, tame wagon ride around part of the property is also an option.

On the far eastern tip of the island, **Pu'u O Hoku Ranch,** 800/558-8109, offers several trail rides through its working ranch, which range from a one-hour ride for $50 to a full-day waterfall excursion for $145. Other specialized rides are also offered, like a beach ride for $120 and an early morning sunrise ride for $80. These rides let you see scenery that is generally not open to others than those who work on the ranch.

Coupled with a tour of the Kalaupapa settlement, the **Molokai Mule Ride,** P.O. Box 200, Kualapuu, HI 96757, 808/567-6088 or 800/567-7550, muleman@aloha.net, www.muleride.com, runs tours from topside down to the peninsula. The well-trained mules will transport you round-trip down and up the 1,600-foot *pali* face, negotiating the switchbacks with ease. The ride each way is about 90 minutes. Conducted 8 A.M.–3:30 P.M. daily except Sunday, this tour is $150 per person and includes the ground tour of the settlement and lunch; add $9 per person (minimum two) if you need transportation from the Moloka'i Airport if you're flying in for the day for the tour. No riders who weigh more than 240 pounds, please; all must be at least 16 years old and in good physical shape. Molokai Mule Ride can also arrange the ground tour for you ($40) if you desire to hike down the hill, or a fly-in from Ho'olehua Airport to the peninsula and ground tour for $119. Other options are the ground tour and a fly-in from either Maui for $224 or Honolulu for $215.

## Biking

For the only sales and repair of bikes on Moloka'i, and for guided bike tours of Pu'u O Hoku ranchland way out on the eastern tip of the island, see **Moloka'i Bicycle,** 808/553-3931 or 800/709-2453, www.bikehawaii.com/molokaibicycle. Open Monday, Tuesday, and Thursday 3–6 P.M. and Saturday 9 A.M.–2 P.M., this bike shop is located in a warehouse-type building at 80 Mohala Street, just up from the highway. It hardly looks like a bike shop, so keep your eyes peeled. Moloka'i Bicycle has the largest rental pool on the island, aside from those at the Mokola'i Ranch. Rental rates are regular mountain bikes, $15 per day or $70 per week; mountain bikes with front suspension, $20 per day or $85 per week; road bikes, $24 per day or $100 per week. Bicycle drop-off is possible around the island for a small fee. Guided-ride rates run $65 per person (minimum two) for three- to five-hour rides and $45 per person for one- to three-hour rides. Call 808/553-5740 for reservations.

Molokai Ranch offers several levels of bike riding over numerous courses across their ranch land. Half- and full-day guided tours are run for $35 and $80, respectively, and traverse a great deal of the rugged ranch land. These courses offer trails for the beginner to the advanced rider. A night ride is also an option. Renting bikes from the Outfitters Center is $20 per day or $30 for full suspension. For information, call 808/552-2791.

**Moloka'i Outdoors,** 808/553-4477, located at Hotel Moloka'i, rents bikes for $27 per day and mopeds for $25 per day. **Molokai Rentals and Tours,** 808/553-5663, has mountains bikes for $20 per day.

## Golf

Moloka'i's two golf courses are as different as custom-made and rental clubs. When the **Kaluakoi Golf Course** opened in 1977, it was a picture-perfect beauty that would challenge any top pro. Laid out by master links designer Ted Robinson and located out at the Kaluakoi Resort at the extreme west end of the island, this par-72 wound through a dry but beautiful setting, including five holes strung right along the beach. Unfortunately, years of decline finally caused the course to close, but after being purchased by the Molokai Ranch, the first nine holes reopened in 2002 with plans for eventually opening the rest of the course. Although still in need of much work, the front nine are playable, and greens fees run $20 for nine or $35 if you want to go around twice. For tee times, call the pro shop at 808/552-0255.

Moloka'i's other golf course is the homey **Ironwood Hills Golf Course,** 808/567-6000, originally built for pineapple company executives. Open 7 A.M.–5 P.M. daily, this rarely used but well-maintained mountain course is nine holes, par 34, and 3,088 yards long. Pay the affordable greens fee to the office manager or to a groundskeeper who will come around as you

## MOLOKA'I GOLF AND TENNIS

| Golf Course | Par | Yards | Fees | Cart | Clubs |
|---|---|---|---|---|---|
| **Ironwood Hills Golf Course** | 34 | 3,088 | $18/9 holes | $7 (9 holes) | $8 |
| 808/567-6000 | | | (18 holes) | $3 (pullcart) | $25 |
| **Kaluakoi Golf Course** | 36 | 3,138 | $20/9 holes | $10 | $10 |
| 808/552-0255 | | | $35/18 holes | $5 (pullcart) | |

| Tennis Court | Location | No. of Courts | Lighted |
|---|---|---|---|
| **Kaunakakai** | Community Center | 2 | Yes |
| **Ho'olehua** | Moloka'i High School | 2 | Yes |

play; $18 for nine holes or $25 if you want to loop the course twice. Twilight rates, club rental, riding and hand carts are also available. The course is located up in the hills in Kala'e at 1,200 feet in elevation, just before the Meyer Sugar Mill—look for the sign. Ironwood Hills is turning from a frog to a prince. Recent work has concentrated on improving the grounds. Even today there is no pro shop or snack shop available—all these will come in time—and only a small trailer as an office.

## Tennis

Public courts are available at Moloka'i High School in Ho'olehua and at the Community Center in Kaunakakai, but you may have to reserve a spot with the office in the Mitchell Pauole Center next door for the courts in town. Condo tennis courts are reserved for guests only. Two courts are available at the **Ke Nani Kai Condos,** at the Kaluakoi Resort, and two courts are at the **Wavecrest Condo** east of Kaunakakai on Route 450.

## Fishing

The Penguin Banks of Moloka'i are some of the most fertile waters in Hawaii. Private boats as well as the commercial fishing fleets out of O'ahu come here to try their luck. Trolling produces excellent game fish such as marlin, mahimahi, *ahi* (a favorite with sashimi lovers), and *ono,* with its reputation of being the best-tasting fish in Hawaii. Bottom fishing, usually with live bait, yields *onaga* and *uku,* a gray snapper favored by local people. Moloka'i's shoreline, especially along the south and west, offers great bait-casting for *ulua* and *'ama 'ama. Ulua* is an excellent eating fish, and with a variance in weight from 15–110 pounds, it can be a real whopper to catch from shore. Squidding, *limu* gathering, and torch-fishing are all quite popular and productive along the south shore, especially around the old fish pond sites. These remnants of Hawaii's one-time vibrant aquaculture still produce mullet, the *ali'i's* favorite; an occasional Samoan crab; the less desirable, introduced tilapia; and the better-left-alone barracuda.

The *Alyce C.,* 808/558-8377, www.world-widefishing.com/hawaii/b225/index.html, is a 31-foot, fully equipped diesel-powered fishing boat, owned and operated by Captain Joe Reich, who can take you for full- ($400), three-quarter ($350), or half-day ($300) charters and offers whale-watching tours in season.

**Fun Hogs Hawaii,** 808/567-6789, www.molokai-rentals.com/funhogs also offers half- or full-day fishing excursions, as well as two-hour sunset cruises, and whale-watching trips in season. This company will also take a group bodyboarding, give instruction, and provide gear. Charters for other purposes are welcome.

The **Moloka'i Fish and Dive Co.,** 808/553-5926, www.molokaifishanddive.com, also arranges deep-sea charters as well as excursions and shoreline sailing.

## Hunting

Public hunting lands on Moloka'i are open to anyone with a valid state hunting license. Wild goats and pigs can be hunted in various hunting units year-round on weekends and state holidays, except when bird hunting is in effect. Bag limits are two animals per day. Hunting game birds (ring-necked pheasants, various quails and doves, wild turkeys, partridges, and francolins) is open on public lands from the first Saturday in November to the third Sunday in January. A special dove season runs late January through March. For full information, license, and fees, contact the Division of Forestry and Wildlife, P.O. Box 347, Kaunakakai, HI 96748, 808/533-1745.

Some of the best hunting on Moloka'i is on the private lands of the 54,000-acre **Molokai Ranch.** The ranch now has Hawaiian Kine Hunting coordinate its hunting operation. Call 808/336-0095 and speak with Joey Joao about all the particulars. From Jan.–Sept., hunting is open for axis deer only, and the rate is $650 per day without guide and $400 per day extra for guide service. Following state rules and regulations, game bird hunting is also offered on the ranch during regular state hunting season. The fee then is $100 per day without a guide and $300 per day extra with guide service. All hunters must be in possession of a Hawaii state hunting license. Ecological conditions may affect hunting at certain times of the year.

## Land Tours

Only a few limited tours are offered on Moloka'i. Mostly, it's you and your rental car. **Moloka'i Off-road Tours and Taxi,** 808/553-3369, offers a six-hour narrated tour ($59) by air-conditioned van, which hits many of the highlights of the island. They can also tailor a tour to your needs; reservations are required.

## Air Tours

An amazing way to see Moloka'i—particularly its north coast—is by helicopter. This method is admittedly expensive, but dollar for dollar it is *the* most exciting way of touring and can get you places that no other means can. A handful of companies operate mostly from Maui and include overflights of Moloka'i. Although a helicopter trip will put a big hole in your budget, most agree they are among the most memorable experiences of their trip. Try **Air Maui,** 808/877-7005; **Sunshine Helicopters,** 808/871-0722; and **Blue Hawaiian Helicopters,** 808/871-8844.

If you are lucky, your regularly scheduled flight from Kahului to Ho'olehua will also fly along the north coast and give you a glimpse, although not real close, of this spectacular line of *pali* and valley.

## Activity Desk/Rentals

The **Moloka'i Outdoors** activity desk, 808/553-4477 or 877/553-4477, outdoors@aloha.net, www.molokai-outdoors.com, basically handles everything. The staff members here are well versed on what recreational possibilities are available on the island, and they go out of their way to make it happen for you. From them you can rent bikes and kayaks, snorkel gear, surfboards and sailboarding equipment, camping gear, and a host of accessories. They can guide you on a bike tour of the coffee plantation, kayak tour inside the fringe reef, or teach you how to surf or windsurf. This company can set you up with any of the other activity providers on the island, connect you with activities on other islands, shuttle you to and from the airport, and as a travel agency, can arrange transportation, lodging, and car rental. Contact them for all of your island activity needs. Open Monday–Saturday 8 A.M.–6 P.M., Saturday until 5 P.M.

**Molokai Rentals and Tours,** 808/553-5663 or 800/553-9071, also offers numerous options for rental equipment, rental cars, arranges kayak, hiking, and bike tours, other island activities, accommodation, and travel to and from the island.

## SHOPPING

Coming to Moloka'i to shop is like going to Waikiki and hoping to find a grass shack on a deserted beach. Moloka'i has only a handful of shops where you can buy locally produced crafts and Hawaiiana. Far and away, most of Moloka'i's shopping is centered **along Ala Malama Street** in downtown Kaunakakai—all three blocks of it! Here you'll find the island's only health food store, two very good food markets, and a clutch of souvenir shops. Away from Kaunakakai the pickin's get mighty slim. Heading west you'll find the **Kualapu'u General Store** off Route 470 on the way to Kalaupapa, and a sundries store and gift shop in Kaluakoi Hotel on the far west end. The Maunaloa Road (Route 460) basically ends in Maunaloa town. Go there!

The best and most interesting shop, **The Big Wind Kite Factory,** is in town and is worth a visit in its own right. It's accompanied by the **Plantation Gallery,** an intriguing souvenir shop of Hawaiian and imported items. Heading east from Kaunakakai is another shoppers' wasteland with only the sundries store at the Molokai Shores condo, the gift shop at Hotel Molokai, and the Puko'o Neighborhood Store for anything to buy.

## ACCOMMODATIONS AND FOOD

One quick overview can paint, in broad strokes, the picture of where accommodations are located and where food can be found on Moloka'i. While seemingly enough for visitors, places to stay are not numerous. The main town of Kaunakakai has one fine renovated and refurbished island-style hotel and one condominium. To the east is another condominium, and in this eastern section of the island are the bulk of its vacation rentals, cottages, and B&Bs, not surprising since the greatest number of people live in Kaunakakai and along the southeast coastline. The west end has the upper-end accommodations. Opened some 30 years ago as a top-notch hideaway resort, the Kaluakoi Hotel (now closed) and Golf Club (reopened) had many good years and then gradually began a slide into disrepair. Within the resort are three mid- to upscale condominiums. Up the hill in Maunaloa are the newest and most unusual accommodation options on the island. The Molokai Ranch started a high-end camping/activity experience several years ago that, through its ups and downs, has been a great experience for those lucky enough to have made the trek. In 1999, the ranch opened the lodge, and it is now the most luxurious accommodation on the island. Built in retro island ranch style, this operation is a gem.

Food is another item all together. Kaunakakai has a handful of small eateries, mostly geared toward the local population, but the best of the bunch is the restaurant at Hotel Moloka'i. To the east of town, there is only one place to eat: the Neighborhood Store in Puko'o. After years of successful operation, the Kualapu'u Cookhouse, headquarters of "The Slow Food Chain," closed. Now Kamuela's Cookhouse has taken its place. Places to eat at the west end are few and far between. The Kaluakoi Hotel restaurants closed when the hotel ceased operation, so those staying at the resort condos and vacation homes must go into Kaunakakai or up the hill to Maunaloa if they want to eat out. There are three options: In the lodge are the upscale Maunaloa Room and the Paniolo Lounge; the local-style Paniolo Cafe is in the theater building in town. Those who stay at the ranch camps are provided food on site.

## GETTING THERE

Only Hawaiian Airline, Island Air, and Pacific Wings have regularly scheduled flights to Ho'olehua Airport on Moloka'i. Molokai Air Shuttle, Commercial Flyer, and Paragon Air also fly to the island, but on an on-call or charter basis. Pacific Wings, Molokai Air Shuttle, and Commercial Flyer also fly to Kalaupapa, to connect with tours of the peninsula.

**Hawaiian Airlines,** 808/567-6510 on Moloka'i, 800/882-8811 in Hawaii, or 800/367-5320 Mainland, has daily flights each way connecting Moloka'i and Honolulu. Weekend morning flights from Honolulu and afternoon flights to Honolulu go through Lana'i. Flights to all other cities in Hawaii go through Honolulu.

**Island Air,** 808/567-6115 or 800/652-6541 Hawaii, 800/323-3345 Mainland, offers flights connecting Moloka'i with O'ahu and Maui. There are nine daily flights to/from Honolulu 6:25 A.M.–8 P.M. Morning and afternoon flights connect Moloka'i to Kahului, Maui.

**Pacific Wings,** 800/867-6814, connects Moloka'i with Kahului and Honolulu once a day, using eight-seat, twin-engine Cessna 402C aircraft. It also has morning and afternoon flights between Honolulu and Kalaupapa Peninsula.

**Molokai Air Shuttle,** 808/567-6847 Moloka'i or 808/545-4988 O'ahu, flies a Piper Aztec to/from Honolulu and Moloka'i for $69.95 round-trip or $39.95 one way. This is not a scheduled route: You call and let them know when you want to fly and they will tell you what's available that day. Molokai Air Shuttle offers a great fare; however, arrival/departure in Honolulu is along Lagoon Drive, which is on the opposite side of the runways from the main terminal building, so it's not convenient for connecting flights but is fine if you're just being picked up in the city. Molokai Air Shuttle also flies unscheduled flights from Honolulu to Kalaupapa for $49 one way and to Lana'i for $175 one way.

**Commercial Flyer,** 888/266-3597 or 808/833-8014 in Honolulu, also does nonscheduled flights from Honolulu to topside Moloka'i and to Kalaupapa. Rates are $70 round-trip and $40 one way to Ho'oluhua and $110 round-trip to Kalaupapa. Call to see what is flying when.

**Paragon Air,** 808/244-3356 on Maui or 866/946-4744 Mainland, also does on-demand flights between Moloka'i and Honolulu, plus islandwide air charters in small aircraft to any island destination.

## Moloka'i Airport

The **Ho'olehua Airport** has a small terminal with an open-air baggage claim area to the far right, check-in counters next to that, and the waiting lounge on the left side. In the baggage claim area, Dollar and Budget have rental car booths, and each has a base yard a few steps away across the public parking lot out front. There is no public transportation on Moloka'i, but two companies offer taxi service. Also at the terminal you'll find a snack bar run by the Moloka'i Coffee Company, toilets, and public telephones in the baggage claim area and in the lobby. Pick up a loaf of excellent Moloka'i bread, the best souvenir available, or a lei from the small gift shop. Tourist brochures are available from a rack in the arrival area. On your way out of the airport, you are greeted first thing with the sign "Aloha. Slow Down. This is Moloka'i."

## By Sea

The Maui Princess used to sail daily between Kaunakakai and Lahaina, but for economic reasons the service was stopped in 1997, affecting many businesses on Moloka'i. Island Marine, 808/667-6165 or 800/275-6969, www.molokai-ferry.com, the company that operates this ship, started ferry operation again in 2001 with the refurbished and faster *Moloka'i Princess,* which is able to make the crossing in about one hour and 15 minutes. Although the schedule is subject to change, the yacht runs daily, leaving Kaunakakai at 5:45 A.M. and 3:30 P.M., returning from Lahaina at 7:30 A.M. and 5:15 P.M. The fares are $40 one way for adults and $20 for kids. Also offered are several day tour packages to Moloka'i from Maui. The cruise/car and cruise/van tour packages run $139 per person.

## GETTING AROUND

### Car Rental

Moloka'i offers a limited choice of car rental agencies, so make reservations to avoid being disappointed. Rental car booths at the air terminal close after the last flight of the day has arrived. Rental car companies on Moloka'i dislike their cars being used on dirt roads (there are plenty) and strongly warn against it. Sedans, economy through full-size, are the most numerous, but SUVs, small trucks, minivans, and full-size vans are also available in limited numbers.

**Dollar Rent A Car,** 808/567-6156 or 800/800-4000, provides professional and friendly service; **Budget Rent A Car,** 808/567-6877 or 800/527-7000, is another option. These two companies have booths and base yards only at the airport. Pick up a copy of the *Molokai Drive Guide* magazine for maps and useful information on sights and activities.

The local company called **Island Kine Auto Rental,** P.O. Box 1018, Kaunakakai, HI 96748, 808/553-5242 or 866/527-7368, fax 808/553-3880, info@molokai-car-rental.com, www.molokai-car-rental.com, is located in Kaunakakai. Its slant is to rent the kind of vehicle that the big companies don't and to be competitive in pricing with the kind they do. It has a sizable fleet of two- and four-door sedans, 4WDs, 10- and 15-passenger vans, and pickups, all used but well maintained. Although these cars can be taken off paved roads, a cleaning fee may be tacked onto your bill depending on how much time is involved in putting the vehicle back in service. Let them know what kind of car you need and for how long, and they'll let you know what the rate will be. They even do a courtesy pickup at the airport or pier and give you a brief introduction of what's to see and do on the island. Island Kine gives personalized service, treats you well, and offers competitive rates.

Also offering a few rental vehicles at competitive rates is **Molokai Rentals and Tours,** 808/553-5663 or 800/553-9071, www.molokai-rentals.com.

There are only three **gas stations** on the island: two in Kaunakakai and one in Maunaloa. Fill your tank before turning in your rental car because there is not a station at or near the airport. Gas prices are generally $.40–50 higher on Moloka'i than on Maui.

### Public Transportation

No public bus transportation services Moloka'i. **Moloka'i Off-road Tours and Taxi,** 808/553-3369, does transfers to and from the airport 8 A.M.–6 P.M. for $7 per person ($8 after hours), minimum of three passengers. Alternately, **Molokai Outdoors,** 808/553-4477, also offers shuttle service between the airport and Kaunakakai for $22.50. Shuttle service to other parts of the island, as well as off-road touring, are options for both of these companies.

## Hitchhiking

The old thumb gives fair to good results on Moloka'i. Most islanders say they prefer to pick up hitchhikers who are making an effort by walking along, instead of lounging by the side of the road. It shows that you don't have a car but do have some pride. Getting a ride to or from Kaunakakai and the airport is usually fairly easy. To other destinations, it's more problematic.

# INFORMATION AND SERVICES

Telephone numbers for service agencies that you might find useful: emergency, 911; police, 808/553-5355; County Parks and Recreation, 808/553-3204; Division of Forestry, 808/553-1745; Hawaiian Homelands, 808/560-6104; Kaunakakai post office, 808/553-5845.

## Information

The **Moloka'i Visitors Association** (MVA), 808/553-3876 or 800/800-6367 Mainland and Canada, mva@aloha.net, www.molokai-hawaii .com, can help with every aspect of your trip to Moloka'i. From their office at the Kamo'i Professional Center, they dispense up-to-the-minute information on accommodations, transportation, dining, activities, and services, and some brochures and island maps. The MVA should be your first contact if you are contemplating a visit to Moloka'i. Open Monday–Friday 8:30 A.M.–4:30 P.M.

For additional general information about the island, try the websites www.molokai-aloha.com, www.molokai.com, and www.visitmolokai.com.

## Medical Services

Moloka'i is a small place with a small popula-

tion, so there is not as much available here in the way of medical treatment as on Maui or the other larger islands. Yet Moloka'i has Moloka'i General Hospital, 808/553-5331, which is located at the end of Home 'Olu Street just above Ala Malama Avenue in Kaunakakai. There are half a dozen doctors on the island and half as many dentists. Try Molikai Drugs, 808/553-5790, in the Kamo'i Professional Center, one block off the main drag, for prescription drugs, first-aid items, potions, lotions, and sundries. Open Monday–Saturday 8:45 A.M.–5:45 P.M.

## Banking

There are two banks on the island, both in downtown Kaunakakai and each open Monday–Thursday 8:30 A.M.–4 P.M., Friday until 6 P.M. Each has an ATM. They are Bank of Hawaii, 808/553-3273, and American Savings Bank, 808/553-3263.

## Library

The Moloka'i Public Library (1937), 808/553-1765, is located next to the government buildings at the west end of Kaunakakai. Hours are Tuesday, Thursday, and Friday 10 A.M.–5 P.M. and Monday and Wednesday 12:30–8 P.M.

## Newspapers

For a local look at what's happening on the island of Moloka'i, check out either of the island's two newspapers. The larger and more mainstream is *The Dispatch* (www.aloha.net/~mkkdisp), published in Maunaloa, while the more humble *Mokokai Advertiser-News* (www.molokaiadvertisernews.com) is published in Kaunakakai by solar power.

## Laundry

Across from the Moloka'i Drive Inn, the Ohana Laundromat is open daily 6 A.M.–9 P.M. There is also a small laundromat behind Outpost Natural Foods, open daily 7 A.M.–9 P.M.

# Kaunakakai

No matter where you're headed on the island, you have to pass through Kaunakakai (Beach Landing), the tiny port town and economic and government center that is Moloka'i's hub. An hour spent walking the three blocks of Ala Malama Street, the main drag, and its side streets gives you a good feeling for what's happening. If you need to do any banking, mailing, or shopping for staples, Kaunakakai's the place. Hikers, campers, and even day-trippers should get all they need here because shops, both east and west, are few and far between and mostly understocked. Evenings are quiet here, with no neon or glamour and no traffic lights, and that's just the way that people want to keep it.

## SIGHTS

Head toward the water and you'll see **Kaunakakai wharf** stretching out into the shallow harbor for one-half mile. Not a natural harbor, the approach to the wharf had to be cleared through coral. Townsfolk like to drive their cars onto the causeway, but it's much better to walk out. On the landing are the harbor office, public toilets, boat moorings, and a boat launch. The ferry from Lahaina pulls into port here, the twice-weekly barge to the island stops here, and the few private and commercial sailing and fishing boats are tied up at its moorings. Fishing from the wharf isn't great, but it's handy and you never can tell. If you decide to stroll out, look for the raised platform surrounded by stone west of the approach road that was the site of Lot Kamehameha's summer house, "Malama" (circa 1864). Lot Kamehameha was King Kamehameha V, the last of the direct line of Kamehameha rulers. This site and the adjacent land is now part of the as-yet-undeveloped Malama Cultural Park, which only has restrooms, parking, and access to the water. To its side is the Moloka'i Voyaging Canoe Society building.

## Kapuaiwa Coconut Grove

A five-minute drive or a 20-minute walk west brings you to this 11-acre royal coconut grove planted in the 1860s for Kamehameha V, or Kapuaiwa to his friends. Kapuaiwa Coconut Grove was originally built because there were seven pools here in which the *ali'i* would bathe, and the grove was planted to provide shade and seclusion. The grove also symbolically provided the king with food for the duration of his life. The grove has diminished from the 1,000 trees originally planted, but more than enough remain to give a sense of grandeur to the spot. Royal coconut palms are some of the tallest of the species, and besides providing nuts, they served as natural beacons pinpointing the spot inhabited by royalty. These that remain are more than 80 feet tall. After years of becoming overgrown, this parklike grove is slowly being renovated and brought back into more beautiful shape. Mostly you'll have it to yourself. Pay heed to the signs warning of falling coconuts. An aerial bombardment of hefty five-pounders will rudely customize the hood of your rental car. Definitely do not walk around under the palms if the wind is up.

## Church Row

Sin has no chance against the formidable defensive line of churches standing altar to altar along the road across from Kapuaiwa Coconut Grove. A grant from Hawaiian Homelands provides that a church can be built on this stretch of land to any congregation that includes a minimum number of Hawaiian-blooded parishioners. The churches are basically one-room affairs that wait quietly until Sunday morning, when worshippers come from all over the island. Let there be no doubt: Old Satan would find no customers around here, as all spiritual loopholes are covered by one denomination or another. Visitors are always welcome, so come join in. Be wary of this stretch of road, though, because all services seem to let out at the same time on Sunday morning, causing a minuscule traffic jam.

## In-Town Parks

Right in the center of town is the Mitchell Pauole Center, which has the police, fire, county, and

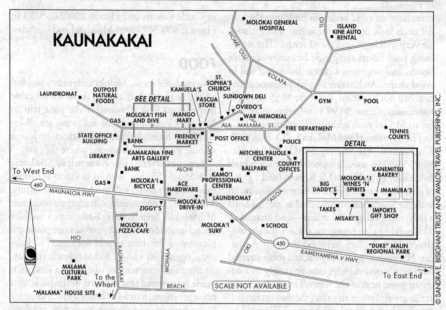

KAUNAKAKAI

MOLOKAI GENERAL HOSPITAL

ISLAND KINE AUTO RENTAL

LAUNDROMAT

OUTPOST NATURAL FOODS

SEE DETAIL

KAMUELA'S

ST. SOPHIA'S CHURCH

SUNDOWN DELI

OVIEDO'S

PASCUA STORE

GYM

POOL

GAS

MOLOKA'I FISH AND DIVE

MANGO MART

WAR MEMORIAL

ALA MALAMA ST.

FIRE DEPARTMENT

TENNIS COURTS

STATE OFFICE BUILDING

BANK

FRIENDLY MARKET

POST OFFICE

POLICE

DETAIL

LIBRARY

KAMAKANA FINE ARTS GALLERY

To West End

460

BANK

MOLOKA'I BICYCLE

ALOHI

KAMO'I

MITCHELL PAUOLE CENTER

BALLPARK

COUNTY OFFICES

BIG DADDY'S

MOLOKA'I WINES 'N SPIRITS

KANEMITSU BAKERY

IMAMURA'S

GAS

MAUNALOA HWY.

ACE HARDWARE

KAMO'I PROFESSIONAL CENTER

LAUNDROMAT

TAKES

MISAKI'S

IMPORTS GIFT SHOP

ZIGGY'S

MOLOKA'I DRIVE-IN

HIO

MOLOKA'I PIZZA CAFE

MOLOKA'I SURF

SCHOOL

450

OKI

KAMEHAMEHA V HWY.

"DUKE" MALIN REGIONAL PARK

MALAMA CULTURAL PARK

To the Wharf

KAUNAKAKAI

MOHALA

BEACH

To East End

"MALAMA" HOUSE SITE ★

SCALE NOT AVAILABLE

parks and recreation offices. Directly across the street is the Kaunakakai Ball Park; behind it are the community tennis courts and swimming pool and more open spaces for athletic games. Adjoining this county land, but with access from the highway, is the new "Duke" Malin Regional Park, which has additional ball fields, restrooms, and a pavilion with picnic tables.

### Classic Fish Ponds

Moloka'i is known for its fish ponds, which were a unique and highly advanced form of aquaculture prevalent from at least the early 13th century. Because of an abundance of shallow, flat waters along its southern shore, Moloka'i was able to support a network of these ponds numbering more than five dozen during their heyday. Built and tended by the commoners for the royal *ali'i,* they provided succulent fish that could easily be rounded up at any time for a meal or impromptu feast. The ponds were formed in a likely spot by erecting a wall of stone or coral. It was necessary to choose an area that had just the right tides to keep the water circulating, but not so strong as to destroy the encircling walls. Openings

were left in the wall for this purpose. **Kaloko'eli Pond** is about two miles east of Kaunakakai along Route 450. Easily seen from the road, it's an excellent example of the classic fish pond. You can proceed a few more minutes east until you come to a coconut grove just one-half mile before One Ali'i Beach Park. Stop here for a sweeping view of **Ali'i Fishpond,** another fine example.

## ACCOMMODATIONS

Besides camping, Kaunakakai has only two places to stay. Head here for adequate accommodations if you want to save money.

**Molokai Shores,** a Marc Resorts Hawaii management property, 808/553-5954 or 800/535-0085, fax 808/533-3241, www.marcresorts.com, only 1.5 miles east of downtown Kaunakakai, has full kitchens, large living rooms, and separate bedrooms. The white walls contrasting with the dark brown floors are hung with tasteful prints. Plenty of lounge furniture is provided, along with a table for outside dining and barbecues. The upper floor of the three-story building offers an open-beam ceiling including a full loft. Some units have an extra bedroom built into the loft. All units look out over the ocean. The grounds are very well kept, quiet, and restful. The swimming pool fronts the gentle but unswimmable beach, and nearby is a classic fish pond still in good shape. Architecturally, it's pragmatic and neat but not beautiful. Rates are $155 one-bedroom oceanfront, $199 two-bedroom oceanfront; $15 for each additional person.

The 45-room **Hotel Moloka'i**, P.O. Box 1020, Kaunakakai, HI 96748, 808/553-5347, fax 808/553-5047, www.hotelmolokai.com, was built in 1966 by an architect (Mr. Roberts) and a group of guys who wanted a place to vacation. Enamored with the South Seas, they wanted to give his hotel a Polynesian village atmosphere—and succeeded. The buildings are two-story, semi-A-frames constructed largely with redwood from the American Northwest, with sway-backed roofs covered with split-wood shingles that fit snugly in a coconut grove next to the water. The upstairs units are larger and more airy than the downstairs studios, but both feature lanai, phone, TV, a small refrigerator, and daily housekeeping service. This hotel had its heyday before the big resort and the big money came to the island. After a change of ownership in 1998, Hotel Moloka'i was closed for extensive room renovation and landscaping. By the beginning of 1999, the hotel was once again entertaining guests and has again become a happening place on the island. In a way, it's a throwback to the casual and slower '60s.

Not only tourists come looking for this slice of Hawaii, but also Hawaiian residents come to visit. Hotel Moloka'i was always known for good dining, weekend live entertainment, a well-appointed gift shop, a swimming pool, and a poolside bar, and it now continues that tradition. The restaurant and bar are open daily, and rooms run $85–140. For the convenience of guests, there is an on-site laundry facility and the island's most comprehensive activities desk. Hotel Moloka'i is located just before mile marker 2, east of town. The only drawback is that the hotel is located next to the highway, but overall traffic noise is not much of a concern. Hotel Molokai is a great choice. For current information on dining and room availability, contact Hotel Moloka'i directly

or Castle Resorts and Hotels, 800/272-5275 in Hawaii, 800/367-5004 Mainland and Canada.

## FOOD

Like the hotel scene, Moloka'i has only a handful of places to eat, but among these are veritable institutions that if missed make your trip to Moloka'i incomplete. The following are all located on Kaunakakai's main street or just a minute away. Just ask anyone where they are.

**Inexpensive:** The **Kanemitsu Bakery**, 808/553-5855, has been in business for more than 70 years and is still run by the same family. The bakery is renowned for its numerous varieties of Moloka'i breads. Mrs. Kanemitsu's cookies are scrumptious, and anyone contemplating a picnic or a day hike should load up. The bakery is open 5:30 A.M.–6:30 P.M.; closed Tuesday. At the front counter you can order a sandwich made from bread that is baked in the back, and none are more than $4. There's a lunch counter too, where you can get eggs, pancakes, omelets, and local Hawaiian foods, open 5:30–11:30 A.M. daily except Tuesday. Kanemitsu Bakery is known far and wide for its "hot bread." In fact, this is one thing that you had to bring back for family and friends if you made a trip to Moloka'i. Fresh-baked hot bread is available from the bakery only from 10 P.M.–3 A.M. Go down the alley next to Imamura's to reach the bakery's back door. If the door isn't open, you may have to bang on it. Tell the person how many loaves you want and they'll be brought to the door. It's perhaps best to check out the price of bread during the day.

**Big Daddy's**, 808/553-5841, serves a variety of inexpensive Filipino food, in addition to the eggs and omelets for breakfast, local-style plate lunches for lunch, and ice cream. Next door is Big Daddy's Market for a limited selection of groceries, some prepared foods, and a few true Filipino delicacies like balut. The restaurant is open Monday–Friday until 4 P.M., the market daily 7:30 A.M.–10 P.M.

Sister restaurant to Kamuela's Cookhouse in Kualapu'u, **Kamuela's in Kaunakakai**, 808/553-4286, serves wholesome inexpensive down-home cooking to happy customers in a clean, friendly, family-oriented environment. Breakfast is mostly standard American, like eggs, omelets, and corn beef hash, while lunch and dinner bring sandwiches and burgers, mostly in the $4–7 range. Open daily from 7 A.M.–3 P.M. and Monday–Saturday 5–9 P.M. The art on the wall is by a local artist.

**Oviedo's Lunch Counter,** 808/553-5014, in the last building on the left across from the war memorial, is a strictly Filipino restaurant where every item on the menu is only about $7.75. Choose from ethnic selections like pork adobo, chicken papaya, tripe stew, sweet and sour ribs, pig's feet, mongo beans, and eggplant pimakbet. Oviedo's is small and run-down but clean. The decor is worn linoleum floors and Formica tables. Basically a take-out place, there are a few tables inside if you care to eat there.

Next door to Oviedo's is the **Sundown Deli,** 808/553-3713. Making reasonably priced sandwiches for about $5, salads, and soups in a shop that's hardly big enough to turn around in, this place is establishing a fine reputation. Open Monday–Saturday 7 A.M.–4 P.M.; order at the counter or call your order in to pick up.

**Outpost Natural Foods,** 808/553-3377, serves wholesome, healthy, nutritious quick foods from its inside window Monday–Friday 10 A.M.–3 P.M. Here you can find various sandwiches for less than $6, burritos for up to $4.25, salads, veggie and tempeh burgers for around $5, and the daily lunch specials for under $6. This is the best vegetarian food on the island. In addition, there is an assortment of fresh juices and smoothies. While there, pick up any groceries you'll need for your time on the island.

**Kamo'i Snack 'N Go** is in the Kamo'i Professional Center. Stop here for Dave's ice cream, candies, cold drinks, and other snacks. Open daily until 9 P.M.

The **Moloka'i Drive-In,** 808/553-5655, open daily 6 A.M.–10 P.M., is along Kamehameha V Highway in a green, flat-roofed building that has the look of the '60s. You order from the window and then take your meal to eat under an awning, or step into the air-conditioned inside to find a few tables. Breakfast offers omelets, eggs, Spam, bacon, or ham along with sides of rice,

hashbrowns, or toast for under $5. Lunch is chili dogs, nachos, subs, fish, shrimp, plate lunches, and chicken burgers, with a special featured every day. The drive-in is actually tasteful, bright, and clean. It's a local place with decent food and very affordable prices, but you won't find food for the health-conscious here. It would make a great stop for a picnic lunch to go, especially if you're heading to Halawa and points east.

**Ziggy's,** 10 Mohala St., 808/553-8166, is split into two halves: one, the restaurant, the other, a sports bar and pool room. The restaurant half is open Monday–Thursday 6 A.M.–9 P.M., Friday and Saturday until 10 P.M., while the bar is open 11 A.M.–11 P.M., and Friday and Saturday until 2 A.M. While not memorable, the food here is standard American with a heavy dash of local "grind." Breakfasts can be griddle items, omelets, and corn beef and hash. For lunch and dinner, you can choose meals like kalbi ribs, mahimahi, hamburger steak, burgers, and nightly specials for $7–15.

**Moderate:** Don't let the name **Moloka'i Pizza Cafe,** 808/553-3288, fool you! Although this bright and cheery air-conditioned restaurant makes designer pizza, the emphasis is on *café*. Located wharfside of the town's main intersection, this eatery is open daily 10 A.M.–10 P.M. (until 11 P.M. on Friday and Saturday, from 11 A.M. on Sunday). The café does food with a flare. Pizzas come in three sizes and range in price from a Moloka'i small for $9.50 up to their giant Big Island with everything including green peppers, onions, sausage, beef, and bacon for $23.50. Sandwiches can be an Italian sub laden with turkey, ham, and roast beef, or a plump fresh-baked pocket sandwich. Hearty appetites will enjoy meals like pasta in marinara sauce, barbecued spare ribs (great!), or the fresh catch. Order it! Caught in these waters, the fish comes in the back door, is filleted, cooked, and served to you as fresh as it can be. Wednesday, Thursday, and Sunday specials are Mexican, Hawaiian *laulau,* and prime rib. Desserts too! The Moloka'i Pizza Cafe delivers—perfect for anyone staying in a condo. Take-out is also available.

The **Hotel Moloka'i Restaurant,** 808/553-5347, is the fanciest place in town and the best restaurant on the island east of Maunaloa.

Located right on the water, it has a superb location. Breakfast, lunch, and dinner are served every day of the week, and there are always specials. Breakfasts are a mixture of standard American and island treats, while lunch is mostly salads and sandwiches with a few plate entrées. The kitchen shines best at dinner, when you can order such items as fresh catch of the day, coconut shrimp, *paniolo*-style pork ribs, or misoyaki charbroiled chicken breast, all for less than $20 an entrée. Friday and Saturday nights only there is a prime rib special. This is tasty food at good value. Entertainment happens on the weekends, when local and off-island bands play live dance music into the night, but a special tradition and authentic treat are the songs sung by local ladies from 4–6 P.M. on Aloha Friday. Aloha Friday is also a special at the bar, which is one of three on the island.

## SHOPPING

**Moloka'i Fish and Dive,** in downtown Kaunakakai, 808/553-5926, sounds very practical, and it is, but it has a good selection of souvenirs, T-shirts and fashions, books (including a couple written by shop owner James Brocker), maps of Moloka'i, island music, jewelry, a good assortment of film, along with its fishing, hunting, and camping equipment. Basically, they stock a little bit of everything. They can give you detailed information about fishing and water sports on Moloka'i, arrange island tours, and rent some water gear like snorkel sets, boogie boards, or a rod and reel. Open Monday–Saturday 8 A.M.–6 P.M., Sunday until 2 P.M.

**Moloka'i Island Creations,** connected to Moloka'i Fish and Dive and open the same hours, features authentic Moloka'i designs on ladies' blouses, tank tops, and T-shirts. It also has original Moloka'i glassware, china, and porcelain, along with Hawaiian cards and notebooks. Fashions also include pareu, children's alohawear, shorts, hats, aloha shirts, **mu'umu'u,** swimwear, a good selection of jewelry, and a rack of cosmetics and perfumes in island scents.

**Imamura's,** open daily except Sunday 8:30 A.M.–5:30 P.M. and Sunday until noon, is a very friendly down-home shop that sells everything from flip-flops to fishnets. It also specializes in lei-making needles and has a great selection of inexpensive luggage. The shelves hold beach mats and hats, T-shirts, pots and pans, and kitchen utensils. The sales staff are all friendly and slow-paced; when you return, they'll smile a welcome.

Across the street is the newer **Imports Gift Shop,** which has an assortment of clothing, gifts, souvenirs, postcards, and a few snacks. Open Monday–Saturday until 9 P.M. and Sunday until 4 P.M.

**Moloka'i Mango,** open Mon.–Sat. 9 A.M.–7:30 P.M., is a place to find entertainment for the evening as well as packaged foods and some household supplies. There is no movie theater in Kaunakakai, but since 1998 there has been one in Maunaloa. People who want to watch a big-screen show must now travel to the west end for it—and they do. If not, rent your movie here.

For those who are into wholesome health food, **Outpost Natural Foods,** 70 Makaena Place across from the government buildings, 808/553-3377, is the only store of its kind on Moloka'i, but it's excellent. It's open Monday–Friday 9 A.M.–6 P.M., Sunday 10 A.M.–5 P.M.; closed Saturday. The fruits and vegetables are locally and organically grown as much as possible. Along with the usual assortment of health foods, you'll find bulk grains, granola, nuts, and dried fruits. The jam-packed shelves also hold rennetless cheese, fresh yogurt, nondairy ice cream, vitamins, minerals, supplements, and a good selection of herbs, oils, spices, and natural health care products. If you can't find what you need, ask Dennis, the owner, or the general manager on duty. The juice bar, open weekdays only 10 A.M.–3 P.M., is a great place for a healthy lunch and cold drink.

For general shopping along Ala Malama Street, the **Friendly Market,** open Mon.–Fri, 8:30 A.M.–8:30 P.M., Saturday to 6:30 P.M., is by far the best-stocked grocery store on Moloka'i. There's a community bulletin board outside. It might list cars for sale, Hawaiian genealogies, or fund-raising sushi sales. Have a look!

Just down the street, **Takes Variety Store,** which also carries hardware and general merchandise, is open daily except Saturday. **Misaki's Groceries and Dry Goods** a few steps farther along sells just about everything in food and general merchandise that you'll require. Open daily from 8:30 A.M. but closes at noon on Sunday.

For that special evening, try **Moloka'i Wines 'N Spirits,** 808/553-5009, open daily until late evening, which has a very good selection of vintage wines, beer, and liquor, as well as gourmet treats. Although not the only place on Moloka'i that sells wine and beer, it is the only shop on the island with such selection. For a limited supply of drinks, candy, and other snacks, try **Pascua Store.**

On the second floor of the Moloka'i Center across from the library is **Kamakana Fine Arts Gallery,** 808/553-8520, www.kamakana-gallery.com. This gallery is the only such art gallery on the island and one of the best such gallery/gift shops in the state. The gallery is an important forum for the approximately 140 Moloka'i island artists to display their work, which includes hand-painted, "quilt design" paper, turned wooden bowls, exquisite pencil drawings, cloth quilts, photographs, alohawear, jewelry, and ukulele. The gallery is open Monday–Friday 9:30 A.M.–5:30 P.M., Saturday until 2 P.M. Stop in and support Moloka'i artists or at least just peruse what's being shown. You'll certainly find something that pleases.

**Moloka'i Drugs,** 808/553-5790, open daily 8:45 A.M.–5:45 P.M., closed Sunday, is the only full-service pharmacy and drugstore on the island. Don't let the name fool you, because it sells much more than potions and drugs. You can buy anything from sunglasses to film, watches, toys, baby food, small appliances, and garden supplies. It has the best selection of film on Moloka'i, with a very good selection of books, especially Hawaiiana. Film processing, including slides, takes 48 hours. It's located in the small Kamo'i Professional Center, one street back from the main drag.

**Moloka'i Surf,** open daily except Sunday 9 A.M.–6 P.M. in its shop along the highway, has bathing suits, sandals, T-shirts, shorts, alohawear, and surfing gear.

If you're in town on Saturday morning, be sure to have a look at the **farmers market,** held 7 A.M.–noon on the sidewalk in front of the bank buildings, for local produce and craft items.

The two full-service gas station and mechanic shops on the island are **Rawlin's Chevron Service,** 808/553-3214, at the corner of the highway and the wharf road; and **Kalama Service,** 808/553-5586, one block up. Larger and newer, Rawlins is generally open later and is the only one open on Sundays.

## East to Halawa Valley

The east end of Moloka'i, from Kaunakakai to Halawa Valley, was historically the most densely populated area of the island. At almost every milepost is an historical site or point of interest, many dating from precontact times. A string of tiny churches attests to the coming of the missionaries in the mid-1800s, and a crash-landing site was an inauspicious harbinger of the deluge of Mainlanders bound for Hawaii in the 20th century. This entire stretch of Route 450 is almost entirely undeveloped, and the classical sites such as *heiau,* listening stones, and old battlegrounds are difficult to find, although just a stone's throw from the road. The local people like it this way because most would rather see the south shore of Moloka'i

remain unchanged. A determined traveler might locate the sites, but unless you have local help, it will mean hours tramping around in marshes or on hillsides with no guarantee of satisfaction. Some sites such as **'Ili'ili'opae Heiau** are on private land and require permission to visit. It's as if the spirits of the ancient *kahuna* protect this area.

### SIGHTS

It's a toss-up whether the best part about heading out to the east end of Moloka'i is the road itself or the reward of Halawa Valley at the end. Only 30 miles long, it takes 90 minutes to drive. The road slips and slides around corners, bends

ROBERT NILSEN

the mouth of Halawa Valley and its bay

around huge boulders, and dips down here and there into coves and inlets. Out on the far end, the cliff face and protruding stones have been painted white so that you can avoid an accident, especially at night. Sometimes the ocean and road are so close that spray splatters your windshield. Suddenly you'll round a bend to see an idyllic house surrounded by palm trees with a gaily painted boat gently rocking in a protected miniature cove. Behind is a valley of verdant hills with colors so vibrant they shimmer. You negotiate a hairpin curve, and there are Lana'i and Maui, black on the horizon, contrasted against the waves as they come crashing in foamy white and blue. Down the road chugs a pickup truck full of local people. They wave you a "hang loose" as their sincere smiles light up your already glorious day. Out in one of the innumerable bays are snorkelers, while beyond the reef, surfers glide in exhilarating solitude.

The local people think of the road as "their road." Why not? They use it as a sidewalk, playground, and extension of their backyards. Dogs snooze on it, while the rumps of grazing stock are only inches away from your fender. The speed limit is 35, but go slower and enjoy it more. The mile markers stop at mile 17, then four miles farther you come to the best part. Here, the well-tended two-lane highway with the yellow stripe plays out. The road gets old and bumpy, but the scenery gets much more spectacular. It's about nine miles from where the bumpy part begins until you reach the overlook at Halawa Valley. Come with a full tank of gas, plenty of drinking water, a picnic lunch, and your sense of wonder.

## One Ali'i Beach Park

A few minutes east of Kaunakakai, the road brings you to a stand of perhaps 80 coconut palms, a place where you can get a view of one of the string of fish ponds that are famous in this area. One Ali'i Beach Park, only a few minutes farther along near mile marker 3, is actually split into two units. Although this park is open for camping, it's too close to the road, not well shaded, and a bit too overused to be comfortable. The swimming here is only fair for those who like a challenging surf, but excellent for families with little children who want calm waters. Restrooms and showers are available, and the grounds are generally in good shape. Those not camping here would find it pleasant enough for a short stop, but it's nothing compared with what's farther east along the road.

## View from the Heights

About two minutes past One Ali'i, Makanui Road (the sign says Kawela Plantation I) leads up the hillside on the *mauka* side of the road. A two-minute ride up this road exposes the beginnings of a high-end residential development. As you gain height (one of the only roads that allows you to do so), you'll have an excellent view of the coastline with a panorama of the fish ponds below and Lana'i and Maui floating on the sea. Beyond this road are two others just like it, leading into a largely undeveloped subdivision with much the same overview.

## Kawela

The Kawela area was a scene of tragedy and triumph in Moloka'i's history. Here was **Pakuhiwa,** the battleground where Kamehameha I totally vanquished the warriors of Moloka'i on his way to conquering O'ahu. In nearby Kawela Gulch are the remains of **Pu'ukaua,** the fortress that Kamehameha overran. The fortress oddly doubled as a *pu'uhonua,* a temple of refuge, where the defeated could find sanctuary. Once the battle had been joined, and the outcome was inevitable, the vanquished could find peace and solace in the very area that they had so recently defended.

Today the area offers refuge as **Kakahai'a Beach County Park** and across the highway, the **Kakahai'a National Wildlife Refuge.** The beach park is not used heavily: It, too, is close to the road. This is also an excellent area for coconut trees, with many nuts lying on the ground for the taking. The refuge is an area where birdwatchers can still be captivated by the sight of rare endemic birds.

## Kamalo to Puko'o

This six-mile stretch is loaded with historical sites. Kamalo is one of Moloka'i's natural harbors and was used for centuries before most of the island commerce moved to Kaunakakai. In the late 1800s, **Kamalo Wharf** was the island's principal landing site—turn off the highway at mile marker 10, just at the bend on the road. There

may be some fishing shacks here and outrigger canoes from a local club. Tracks once ran out on the wood and stone "mall" to help unload ships. Only remnants of this pier remain. From here, turn around and have a look at the mountains. You'll be facing the highest point on the island.

**Saint Joseph Church,** next in line, was built in 1876 by Father Damien and restored in 1995. It's small, no more than 16 by 30 feet, and very basic. Inside is a small wooden altar adorned with flowers. A picture of Father Damien and one of St. Joseph adorn the walls. Outside is a black metal sculpture of Damien and a small graveyard. It is said that Father Damien purposefully located the church here, to offer the Hawaiians an alternative to giving offerings at Pu'ili Heiau, which lies just inland.

One mile or so past St. Joseph's is the **Smith and Bronte Landing Site.** These two aviators safely crash-landed their plane here on July 14, 1927, completing the first trans-Pacific civilian flight in just over 25 hours. All you can see is a mangrove swamp, but it's not hard to imagine the relief of the men as they set foot even on soggy land after crossing the Pacific. They started a trend that would bring more than six million people a year to the islands. A mile or beyond that is **Keawanui Fishpond.** At 54 acres and with a 2,000-foot-long wall, it is the largest on the island. The Wavecrest Resort Condominium is nearby at mile marker 13, and just before you reach it you pass a shrimp farm on the ocean side of the highway.

Before Puko'o are three noteworthy sites. **Kalua'aha Church** looks like a fortress with its tiny slit windows and three-foot-thick plastered walls and buttresses. Built in 1844 by the Protestant missionaries Reverend and Mrs. Hitchcock, it was the first Christian church on Moloka'i and is considered by some to be the most significant building on the island. Used for worship until the 1940s, it has since fallen into disuse. In 1967, the bell and steeple came down, the roof is caving in, and the rest is mostly in ruins. While parishioners had repair plans, it is doubtful that the structure can be saved without major rehabilitation.

**Our Lady of Sorrows Church,** another built by Father Damien in 1874 and rebuilt in 1966, is next. Inside are beautiful pen-and-ink drawings of the Stations of the Cross imported from Holland. Mass is held on Sunday at 7:15 A.M. Across the street is a fine example of a fish pond.

Following on the ocean side is the deep shade of the **Mapulehu Mango Grove,** one of the largest in the world with more than 2,000 trees and 32 varieties. Planted by the Hawaiian Sugar Co. in the 1930s in an attempt to diversify, but now owned by the Bishop Estate, the trees came from all over the world, including Brazil, India, and Formosa. Unfortunately, most of the United States was not educated about eating exotic fruits, so the mangos rotted on the tree unpicked, and the grove became overgrown. While mangos are now well known and these trees still produce prodigiously, it seems that the cost would be too high to trim this grove back into shape to make it economical. So the grove still stands unused and uncared for. To compound matters, the Mediterranean fruit fly has become a problem.

Then comes **'Ili'ili'opae Heiau,** one of Hawaii's most famous human-sacrifice temples, and a university of sorcery, as it were, where *kahuna* from other islands were tutored. All of the wooden structures on the 286-by-87-foot stone platform have long since disappeared. Legend holds that all of the stone was carried across the island from Wailau Valley and perfectly fitted in one night of amazing work. Legend also holds that the sorcerers of 'Ili'ili'opae once sacrificed two sons of a local *kahuna* for some childish misbehavior at the temple. Outraged, he appealed to a powerful shark-god for justice. The god sent a flash flood to wipe out the evil sorcerers, washing them into the sea, where the shark-god and other sharks he had called for the feast waited to devour them. Because the temple is now on private land, it is necessary to receive permission to visit it. This *heiau* is now on the National Register of Historic Places.

At Puko'o, near mile marker 16, is the private **Mana'e Canoe Club** with its well-tended lawns and tiny inlets. There have been controversies about public access to the beach on the bay across from the canoe club, which has been the norm for generations. The situation culminated in public protests and walks to the beach. There is, however, public access to the old wharf area directly west of the canoe club, but this spot is only fair for swimming. There is also beach access on the east side of this lagoon, where there is better swimming.

Just past Puko'o is the **octopus stone,** a large stone painted white next to the road. It is believed that this stone signifies a cave inhabited by a mythical octopus and that it still retains magical powers. Across the road are the remains of **Paikalani Taro Patch,** reputed to have been three acres in size. Said to have been constructed by Pi'ilani, king of Maui, both Kamehameha I and Kamehameha V got taro to make poi from it.

## More East End Beaches

**Waialua Beach,** also called Peabody Beach, almost at mile marker 19, is one of the best beaches on the island for swimming, snorkeling, and beginner surfing. A freshwater stream entering the ocean is convenient for rinsing off. Two minutes past mile marker 19 is a sand and coral beach where you can walk knee-deep out to the reef. At high tide, it's chest high.

Just before mile marker 20, a stone fish pond perimeter wall has been restored to near its original form, with a six-foot-wide flat top, outlet gate, and shrine to the fish deity. A grassroots restoration project, this is perhaps the best example of what a functioning fish pond looked like in centuries past. Slowly, others along the coast are also being restored with community involvement.

**Mile Marker 20 Beach,** known locally as Murphy's Beach, with its strand of white sand and protected lagoon, is the main beach on the east end. Pull off at a handy spot and enjoy the great snorkeling, although the swimming is only mediocre. It's very safe and perfect for a family outing. Just past the beach there is a pulloff parking area on a rock point. At times, local youngsters come here to jump off the rocks into the water. In and out of another bay, you come to Pohakuloa, also called Rock Point, a well-known surf spot.

**Note:** All of these beaches are sand, but once you reach the water much of the bottom is sharp coral. Wear a pair of reef walkers or old sneakers. You do not want to go out there barefoot!

## On to Halawa Valley

Past Puko'o, the road gets spectacular. Many blow-your-horn turns pop up as you wend around the cliff face following the natural roll of the coastline. Coming in rapid succession are incredibly beautiful bays and tiny one-blanket beaches, where solitude and sunbathing are perfect. Be careful of surf conditions! Some of the fruitful valleys behind them are still cultivated in taro. Offshore is the crescent of **Moku Ho'oniki Island,** now a seabird sanctuary but used at times during World War II for bombing practice. The road swerves inland, climbing the hills through pastureland to the 14,000 acres of **Pu'u O Hoku Ranch.** The ranch office at mile marker 25 doubles as the tiny Last Chance Store, which sells drinks, candy, and other snacks for the day until midafternoon. As you pass through the pasture on your way to the valley, you can see the famous and sacred *kukui* grove where Lanikaula, one of the most powerful sorcerers of Moloka'i, is buried on the highest hill ahead of you and on the oceanside. The different-looking cattle grazing these hilly pastures are Brangus, a cross between Angus and Brahman, imported by Pu'u O Hoku (Hill of Stars) Ranch and now flourishing on these choice pasturelands. In addition to cattle and horses, the ranch has about five organic acres planted in several varieties of *awa,* papaya, bananas, and vegetables. The road comes to a hairpin turn where it feels like you'll be airborne. Before you is the magnificent chasm of Halawa Valley with its famous waterfalls sparkling against the green of the valley's jungle walls. Hundreds of feet below, frothy aquamarine breakers roll into the bay.

## Halawa Valley and Bay

This choice valley, rich in soil and watered by Halawa Stream, is believed to be the first permanent settlement on Moloka'i, dating from around A.D. 650. Your first glimpse is from an overlook along the road, from which you get a spectacular panorama across the half-mile valley to Lamaloa Head forming its north wall, and westward, deep into its two-mile cleft, where lies Moaula Falls. Many people are so overwhelmed when they gaze from the overlook into Halawa

that they don't really look around. Turn to your right and walk only 15 yards directly away from Halawa. This view gives a totally different perspective of a deep-V valley and the pounding surf of its rugged beach—so different from the gently arcing haven of Halawa Bay. For centuries, Halawa's farmers carved geometric terraces for taro fields until a tsunami of gigantic proportions inundated the valley in 1946 and left a plant-killing deposit of salt. Most people pulled out and left their homes and gardens to be reclaimed by the jungle.

Follow the winding paved road into the valley until you see Ierusalema Hou Church (1948). Go a little farther to the beach park pavilion, park your car, and walk out to the beach. Here you have a choice of bathing in the cool freshwater stream or in the surf of the protected bay. Alternately, take the road past the church. It curves to the right, crosses Halawa Stream, and continues to the opposite side of the bay. Don't venture out past the mouth of the bay because the currents can be treacherous. This area is great for snorkeling and fishing and is one of the good surfing beaches on Moloka'i.

Halawa Bay is a beach park, but it's not well maintained. Near the pavilion are toilet facilities and a few dilapidated picnic tables, but no official overnight camping is allowed and the water is not potable. People do bivouac for a night on Pu'u O Hoku Ranch land at the north end of Halawa Bay under a canopy of ironwood trees, but it's frowned upon. Be aware that this area attracts rip-offs, and it's not safe to leave your gear unattended.

Near the bridge over the stream is a flower farm, which runs the **Tea in the Valley** botanical tour. Offered at 10 A.M. and 2 P.M., the cost for the farm tour is $15 adults, $10 kids. This tour can be combined with a guided hike to Moa'ula Falls. For information, call 808/658-0117.

## Moa'ula Falls

One of *the* best walks on Moloka'i, mosquitoes notwithstanding, is to the famous 250-foot Moa'ula (Red Chicken) Falls. Halawa Stream can be a trickle or torrent, depending on recent rains. If Moa'ula Falls is gushing, the stream too will

Moa'ula Falls, Halawa Valley

be roaring. The entire area up toward the falls harbors the remains of countless terraces, rock walls, taro patches, and home sites. Leave everything as you find it. Groves of *kamani* trees mark the sites where *ali'i* were buried; their tall trunks at one time were used by Hawaiian fishermen and later by sailors as a landmark. Legend recalls that a female lizard, a *mo'o*, lives in the gorgeous pool at the bottom of the falls. Sometimes she craves a body and will drag a swimmer down to her watery lair. The only way to determine her mood is to place a *ti* leaf (abundant in the area) in the pool. If it floats, you're safe, but if it sinks, the lady lizard wants company—permanently! Minor gods who live in the rocks above Moa'ula Falls pool want to get into the act too. They'll drop tiny rocks on your head unless you make an offering (a penny under a *ti* leaf will do). Above Moa'ula Falls you can see **Upper Moa'ula Falls,** and in the next valley to the side the cascading brilliance of 500-foot **Hipuapua Falls.** For some years the trail to these waterfalls was closed because it goes across private property. You can once again gain access

through a guided tour, by going with a resident of the valley, or if you are a guest of the Pu'u O Hoku Ranch cottages or lodge.

## ACCOMMODATIONS AND FOOD

First down the line is **Ka Hale Mala,** just less than five miles east of Kaunakakai on Kamakana Place. This vacation rental is the ground floor of a family house, set amid a tropical garden. Here you have a large living room, full kitchen and bath, and a laundry room, plus use of snorkel gear. Rates are $70 without breakfast or $80 with. For more information, contact Cheryl or Chuck Corbiell, P.O. Box 1582, Kaunakakai, HI 96748, 808/553-9009, cpgroup@aloha.net, www.molokai-bnb.com.

Depending on your point of view, the **Wavecrest Resort** is either a secluded hideaway or stuck out in the sticks away from all the action. It's east of Kaunakakai on Route 450 just at mile marker 13. You'll find *no* hustle, bustle, anxiety, nightlife, or restaurants, and only basic supplies at the Wavecrest general store at the entrance. This condominium sits on five well-tended acres fronting a lovely-to-look-at lagoon that isn't good for swimming. It catches the morning sun and looks directly across the Pailolo Channel to Ka'anapali on Maui. Enjoy a putting green, shuffleboard court, newly refurbished swimming pool, and two lighted tennis courts free to guests. Be aware that there are no phones in any of the units. For those who need to call, there are two pay phones at the front office. In each unit is a fully furnished kitchen, spacious living room, ceiling fan, television, and lanai. A laundry room is located on each floor for guest use. Even if you feel that you're too far from town, remember that nothing is going on there anyway. Another attraction is that local fishermen may put in just next to the Wavecrest and sell their fish for unbeatable prices. Guests can barbecue on gas grills. Rates are one-bedroom ocean or garden view $70, one-bedroom oceanfront $80, two-bedroom oceanfront $135; $15 per extra person. Car/condo packages are also available. Attractive monthly and low-season discounts are available. Call Friendly Isle

Realty, 808/553-3666 or 800/600-4158, fax 808/553-3867, www.molokairesorts.com, which manages numerous other units in each of the condominiums on the island and also several homes on the west end and along the beaches on the east end.

**Kamalo Plantation,** HC 01, Box 300, Kaunakakai, HI 96748, tel/fax 808/558-8236, kamaloplantation@aloha.net, www.molokai.com/kamalo, is a five-acre tropical garden, where Glenn and Akiko Foster welcome guests. About 10 miles east of Kaunakakai, and across from Father Damien's St. Joseph Church, Kamalo Plantation is surrounded by well-vegetated grounds and even has a *heiau* on the property. The Fosters can accommodate you in a fully contained private studio cottage with king-size bed, full kitchen, indoor and outdoor showers, and deck for $85, two-night minimum. The cottage is secluded on the property and has a sitting area, necessary cooking appliances, an outside deck, and a barbecue grill in its own little gazebo. The tropical decor makes this comfy cottage a home away from home. A breakfast of fruit and baked breads and a tour of the grounds are part of the price. A fine place, perfect for a quiet getaway. The Fosters also have the **Moanui Beach House** for rent across from the beach at mile marker 20. This renovated A-frame sits up on the hillside overlooking a horse pasture and the water. With two bedrooms, 1.5 baths, and a full kitchen, this house is just right for a small family and goes for $140 double occupancy, with $20 for each additional person, three-night minimum.

Just past the Puko'o Neighborhood Store, going east, is a casual oceanfront house with two bedrooms and two baths, a full kitchen, and only steps from the water. This cute little place runs $180 per night, three-night minimum. This and a half dozen other homes and cottages nearby on the east end that generally run $125–330 per night with a three-night minimum, plus one big house on Papohaku Beach, and condo units at different properties across the island, are handled by Swenson Real Estate, P.O. Box 1979, Kaunakakai, HI 96748, 808/553-3648 or 800/558-3648, fax 808/553-3783, rent@island-realestate.com, http://molokai-vacation-rental.com.

Some distance farther is the **Waialua Beach House,** 808/599-3838 or 888/579-9400, fax 808/537-2322, hawaiibeachhouse@hotmail.com, www.hawaiibeachhouse.org, a three-bedroom, two-bath, oceanfront home with all the conveniences. This island-style house sleeps up to six and runs $165 per night, three nights minimum, $1,055 per week, with an $85 cleaning fee.

At the far eastern end of the island, overlooking the lands of Pu'u O Hoku Ranch, P.O. Box 1889, Kaunakakai, HI 96748, 808/558-8109, fax 808/558-8100, hoku@aloha.net, www.puuohoku.com, is **Pu'u O Hoku Country Cottages.** Check in at the ranch office along the highway at mile marker 25. If you're looking for a place to really be away, this is it. The spacious Sunrise Cottage, once a guest cottage at the ranch manager's residence, is a large two-bedroom house that has been renovated but is still charming in its simplicity. It has a living room with a wall of glass, dining room, and full kitchen. Each of the two bedrooms has a private bath. With a couch and a bed in the living room, it can sleep six. You are on your own for food, but there is a television and a telephone. Feel free to use the swimming pool at the main lodge up the hill. Facing east and unencumbered by ambient light, it's just right for sunrise and star gazing. The rental rate is $125 per night for two, $20 for each extra person, or $750 per week.

Up the hill, the lodge is also available for group rental and would make a great place for a conference or retreat. The lodge has 11 bedrooms, seven bathrooms, a huge main room, and an industrial kitchen. Originally built for Paul Fagan, who later built Hotel Hana-Maui, this lodge will house up to 23 individuals and is surrounded by acres of lawn and trees. The rate for the lodge is $1,000 per night. Set in a small grove of trees at the edge of the pasture on the oceanside of the office is the Grove Cottage. Nearly twice as large as the Sunrise Cottage, this house has four bedrooms, three bathrooms, a full kitchen, and a large living room with a fireplace, as well as a television and telephone. For the Grove Cottage, the

MAUI

rental rate is $125 per night for two people, $165 for four, or $990 per week. Two nights minimum for any unit.

The only place to find food on this end of the island is the **Neighborhood Store N Counter,** 808/558-8498, in Puko'o. This con- venience store carries basic necessities. Con- nected is a lunch window that serves breakfasts and lunches, such as sandwiches for $4 and plate lunches for $6–7. The store is open 8 A.M.–6 P.M. daily, and the lunch window has the same hours except that it's closed on Wednesday.

## Middle Moloka'i and Kalaupapa

As you head west from Kaunakakai on Route 460 toward Ho'olehua Airport you pass fields planted in various crops. These are Moloka'i's attempt at diversified agriculture since the demise of pineapple. The cultivated fields give way to hundreds of acres filled with what seems like skeletons of dead trees. It's as if some eerie specter stalked the land and devoured their spirits. Far- ther along and just before a bridge, the **Main Forest Road** intersects, posted for 4WD vehicles but navigable in a standard car only during dry weather and if the road has been graded. As much as the traction of a 4WD, in spots you need the clearance of a high-profile truck or jeep to get through the ruts and puddles. This road is no joke. It's a long way for help and costly for a tow. This track leads to the Sandalwood Measuring Pit, a depression in the ground that is a perma- nent reminder of the furious and foolhardy trad- ing of two centuries ago. Farther on is the Kamakou Preserve, a largely intact region of na- tive trees and wildlife. Here too along little-used trails are spectacular views of the lost valleys of Moloka'i's inaccessible northeast shore.

West on Route 460, another branch road, Route 470, heads north through Kualapu'u, Del Monte's diminished pineapple town, to road's end at Pala'au State Park, Moloka'i's best camping area and home to the famous Phallic Rock. Near the state park en- trance is the lookout for **Kalaupapa Peninsula** and the beginning of the mule trail, which switch- backs down more than 1,600 feet to the hum- bling and uplifting experience of Kalaupapa.

### MAIN FOREST ROAD

Head west on Route 460 from Kaunakakai, and just before mile marker 4 turn right before the bridge. After a few hundred yards you pass the Homelani Cemetery. Here, a red dirt road called Main Forest or Maunahui Road heads into the mountains. Your car rental agency will tell you that this road is impassable except in a 4WD, and they're right—if it's raining or has rained re- cently! But, even if it's dry, this road is rough. Follow the rutted road up into the hills and you'll soon be in a deep forest of 'ohi'a, pine, eucalyptus, and giant ferns thriving since their planting in the early 1900s. The cool, pleasant air mixes with rich earthy smells of the forest. At 5.5 miles you enter the Moloka'i Forest Preserve. At just under six miles there's a bend to the right. Proceed a few hundred yards, and on your left is a wood shop with turned wood bowls for sale! Ignore many small roads branching off.

After nine miles is the **Sandalwood Measuring Pit** (Lua Moku 'Iliahi), or Pit of the Sandalwood Ship, a depression in the ground in the shape of a ship's hull. Now bordered by a green pipe fence, it's not very spectacular, and this is a long way to go over a rough road to see a shallow hole in the ground, but the Sandalwood Pit is a permanent reminder of the days of mindless exploitation in Hawaii when money and possessions were more important than the land or the people. Hawaiian chiefs had the pit dug to measure the amount of sandalwood necessary to fill the hold of a ship. They traded the aromatic wood to Yankee cap- tains for baubles, whiskey, guns, manufactured goods, and tools. The traders carried the wood to China, where they made huge profits. The trading was so lucrative that the men of entire villages were forced into the hills to collect it, even to the point where the taro fields were ne- glected and famine gnawed at the door. It only took a few years to denude the mountains of their copious stands of sandalwood, which is even more incredible when you consider that all of the work was done by hand and all of the wood was carried to the waiting ships on the coast using the *maka'ainana* as beasts of burden.

Travel past the Sandalwood Pit (beware of the mud) for about one mile, and you'll come to **Waikolu (Three Waters) Overlook.** From here you can peer down into the pristine valley 3,700 feet below. If rains have been recent, hundreds of waterfalls spread their lace as they fall to the green jungle. The water here seeps into the ground, which soaks it up like a huge, dripping sponge. Father Damien tapped a spring at the bottom end of this valley to supply fresh water to his flock at Kalawao. A water tunnel, bored into the valley, collects the water and conducts it for more than five miles until it reaches the 1.4 billion-gallon Kualapu'u Reservoir. Drive to this area only on a clear day because the rain will not only get you stuck in mud but also obscure your view with heavy cloud cover. Camping is allowed at the overlook park. Get your free permit from the Division of Forestry and Wildlife office in Wailuku, on Maui, before you come.

Past the Waikolu Overlook is the Kamakou Reserve. **Hanalilolilo Trail** begins not far from Waikolu Lookout and winds through high mountain forests of 'ohi'a. Hiking trails through this area are poorly marked, poorly maintained, and strenuous—great qualifications for those who crave solitude and adventure. Alternately, continue walking the 4WD road into the preserve. After about 4.5 miles, at a spot where the road makes a sharp right turn, the **Pepe'opae Trail** heads into the Pepe'opae Bog over a boardwalk, ending after 1.5 miles at the Pelekunu Lookout, where you are rewarded with a breathtaking view into Pelekunu Valley. Pelekunu means "smelly" (due to no sunshine). Don't let the name fool you, though. Hawaiians lived happily and well in this remote, north shore valley for centuries. Time, aided by wind and rain, has turned the 3,300-foot sea cliffs of Pelekunu into some of the tallest in the world. Today, Pelekunu is more remote and isolated than ever. There are no permanent residents, although islanders come sporadically to camp in

the summer, when the waters are calm enough to land on the coast.

The 2,774-acre **Kamakou Preserve,** established by the Nature Conservancy of Hawaii in 1982, seeks to preserve this unique forest area, home to five species of endangered Hawaiian birds, two of which are endemic only to Moloka'i. There are 250 species of Hawaiian plants and ferns, 219 of which grow nowhere else in the world. Even a few clusters of sandalwood trees are tenaciously trying to make a comeback. The land was donated by the Molokai Ranch, which controls the water rights. Most trails have been mapped, and hunting is encouraged throughout most of the area. Up-to-the-minute information and maps are available from the preserve manager by writing to P.O. Box 220, Kualapuu, HI 96757, 808/553-5236.

# KUALAPU'U AND KALA'E

Kualapu'u was a vibrant town when pineapple was king and Del Monte was headquartered here. Now, coffee is king and some of the town's former vibrancy has resurfaced. The coffee plantation produces about one-half million pounds of unroasted coffee beans per year, second only in the state to the much larger Kaua'i Coffee company on Kaua'i. It is the only town where you can find basic supplies and a post office on the way to Kalaupapa.

Right at the turnoff onto Farrington Avenue is the restored Plantation Store and an adjacent espresso bar. Displayed in the store are many attractive gifts, arts, and crafts done by Moloka'i and other island residents. The lunch counter has pastries, sandwiches, and various coffee (free samples) and juice drinks. This is now coffee country, so pick up a bag of Mululani Estate or Muleskinner coffee at the store or try a cup at the lunch counter. Both are open Monday–Friday 7 A.M.–4 P.M., Saturday from 8 A.M., and Sunday from 10 A.M.

Walking tours are given at the 500-acre **Coffees of Hawaii** coffee plantation that take you through the fields for an up-close look at the coffee plants, then head to the mill and roasting room to see what happens to the beans once they're picked. These 45- to 60-minute tours are generally offered Monday–Friday 9:30 A.M. and 11:30 A.M. and cost $7 per person; 24-hour advance reservations requested. For more information, contact the plantation at 808/567-9241 or 800/709-2326, www.molokaicoffee.com.

A minute down Farrington Avenue you'll come to the **Kualapu'u Market,** open daily 8:30 A.M.–6 P.M. except Sunday. Here you'll find a selection of foodstuffs, fresh produce and beef, and general merchandise.

Across the road from the market is the **Kamuela's Cookhouse,** the only restaurant in town. Open 7 A.M.–3 P.M., Kamuela's offers simple food in an unpretentious environment. Most choices are eggs, griddle items, lunch plates, and burgers. Order at the counter and sit either inside at one of the few tables or outside at the picnic table under the canopy.

Notice also the world's largest rubber-lined reservoir across the highway from town. Holding 1.4 billion gallons, its water comes via a five-mile-long, eight-foot-round tunnel from the water-filled valleys to the east.

## Purdy's Macadamia Nut Farm

A few miles west of Kualapu'u, on Lihi Pali Avenue, is **Purdy's Na Hua 'O Ka Aina Farm,** www.molokai.com/eatnuts. A former airline employee, Mr. Purdy grew up just down the road. When the airline pulled out of Moloka'i, he decided to stay home, become a farmer, and teach people about the exquisite macadamia nut. His farm has 50 trees that are about 80 years old. These trees still produce nuts prodigiously and continuously for 10 months of the year— Sept.–June—with nuts at all different stages of maturity on the tree at one time. When mature, nuts fall to the ground. Harvested from the ground, they are taken to be cracked and either kept raw or roasted and lightly salted. This one-acre grove of trees is farmed naturally, but Mr. Purdy has put in about 250 trees at another location on the island that are fertilized and treated with pesticides. Purdy's is the only mac nut farm on Moloka'i, and his yield is about 250–300 pounds of unshelled nuts per tree, as opposed to the 150–200 pounds on the thousand-acre

farms of the Big Island. Visit the shop at the farm, where Mr. Purdy tells everyone about the trees. Have a go at cracking one of the nuts, and have a taste of its rich fruit. Bags of nuts are sold at his gift shop—a little treat to yourself for the road—and can be mailed anywhere in the country. Free admission; open Tuesday–Friday 9:30 A.M.–3:30 P.M. and Saturday 10 A.M.–2 P.M.

## Moloka'i Museum and Cultural Center

Along Route 470, two miles past Kualapu'u in the village of Kala'e, you'll discover the old R. W. Meyer Sugar Mill, now part of the Moloka'i Museum and Cultural Center, 808/567-6436. Open Monday–Saturday 10 A.M.–2 P.M., the self-guided mill tour is $2.50 adults, $1 students 5–18, which includes the cultural center building with its displays, gift and book shop, and historical video. Proceeds go into a fund to construct a new museum building. Built in 1878, the restored mill (1988) is on the National Register of Historic Places. It is in functioning order and clearly shows the stages of creating sugar from cane. As the smallest commercial mill in the state, it was used only until 1889, and it ground cane from 30 nearby upland acres. The museum and cultural center focus on preserving and demonstrating Hawaiian arts and handicrafts like quilting, *lau hala* weaving, wood carving, plus demonstrations of lei-making and hula. The idea is to share and revive the arts of Hawaii, especially those of Moloka'i, in this interpretive center. As an outgrowth, the center is used as the Elderhostel campus for Moloka'i. In August, the annual Moloka'i music and dance festival takes place at the center. Hula is performed, local musicians play, and the whole community turns out.

Just beyond the center is the Meyer cemetery. You can enter, but be respectful. Rudolph Meyer, his wife, and children are buried here. Up in among the trees above the mill is the Meyer home, which is not open to the public. Partially restored in 1973, it's now in disrepair. Perhaps one day it will be restored again and preserved as another tangible link to the family that helped shape the history and economy of the island. The three acres that the cultural center sits on were graciously donated by the Meyer family. Aside from sugarcane, coffee, vegetables, fruits, and dairy cattle were raised on Meyer land, and the present Meyer Ranch still occupies a large tract of the surrounding upland area.

A minute or two past the sugar mill in a bucolic scene of highland fields of knee-deep grass is the tiny community of Kala'e.

## Pala'au State Park

A few minutes past Kala'e are the stables for Molokai Mule Rides, which take you down to Kalaupapa. Even if you're not planning on taking a mule ride, make sure to stop and check out the beauty of the countryside surrounding the mule stables. Follow the road until it ends at the parking lot for Pala'au State Park.

In the lot, two signs direct you to the Phallic Rock and to the Kalaupapa Overlook (which is not the beginning of the trail down to the peninsula). Pala'au State Park offers the best camping on Moloka'i, although it's quite a distance from the beach. Follow the signs from the parking lot for about 200 yards to **Phallic Rock** (Kauleo Nanahoa), one of the best examples of such a stone in the state. Nanahoa, the male fertility god inhabiting the anatomical rock, has been performing like a champ and hasn't had a "headache" in centuries! Legend says that Nanahoa lived nearby and one day sat to admire a beautiful young girl who was looking at her reflection in a pool. Kawahua, Nanahoa's wife, became so jealous when she saw her husband leering that she attacked the young girl by yanking on her hair. Nanahoa became outraged in turn and struck his wife, who rolled over a nearby cliff and turned to stone. Nanahoa also turned to stone in the shape of an erect penis, and there he sits pointing skyward to this day. Barren women have come here to spend the night and pray for fertility. At the base of the rock is a tiny pool the size of a small bowl that collects rainwater. The women would sit here hoping to absorb the child-giving *mana* of the rock. You can still see offerings and of course graffiti.

Return to the parking lot and follow the signs to **Kalaupapa Overlook.** Jutting 1,600 feet below, almost like an afterthought, is the penin-sula of Kalaupapa, which was the home of the lost lepers of Hawaii, picked for its remoteness and inaccessibility. The almost-vertical *pali* served as a natural barrier to the outside world. If you look to your right you'll see the mule trail switchbacking down the cliff. Look to the southeast sector of the peninsula to see the almost perfectly round **Kauhako Crater,** remnant of the separate volcano that formed Kalaupapa.

## THE KALAUPAPA EXPERIENCE

No one knew how the dreaded disease came to the Hawaiian Islands, but they did know that if you were contaminated by it your life would be misery. Leprosy has caused fear in the hearts of humans since biblical times, and King Kamehameha V and his advisors were no exception. All they knew was that those with the disease had to be isolated. Kalawao Cove, on the southeast shore of Kalaupapa Peninsula, was regarded as the most isolated spot in the entire kingdom. So, starting in 1866, the lepers of Hawaii were sent to Kalawao to die. Through crude diagnostic testing, anyone who had a suspicious skin discoloration, ulcer, or even bad sunburn was rounded up and sent to Kalawao. The islanders soon learned that once someone was sent, there was no return. So the afflicted hid. Bounty hunters roamed the countryside. Babies, toddlers, teenagers, wives, grandfathers—none were immune to the bounty hunters. They hounded, captured, and sometimes killed anyone who had any sort of skin ailment. The captives were torn from their families and villages and loaded on a ship. No one would come near them on board, and they sometimes sat open to the elements in a cage. They were allowed only one small tin box of possessions. As the ship anchored in the always choppy bay at Kalawao, the cage was opened and the victims were tossed overboard, followed by a few sealed barrels of food and clothing that had been collected by merciful Christians. Those too weak or sick or young drowned; the unlucky made it to shore. While it wasn't always this way, at times the crew waited nervously with loaded muskets in case any of those on shore attempted to board the ship.

## Hell on Earth

Waiting for the newcomers were the forsaken. Abandoned by king, country, family, friends, and apparently the Lord himself, some became like animals—beasts of prey. Young girls with hardly a blemish were raped by reeking, deformed men in rags. Old men were bludgeoned, their tin boxes ripped from their hands. Children and babies cried and begged for food. The arrivals made rude dwellings of sticks and stones, while others lived in caves or on the beach open to the elements. Finally, the conscience of the kingdom was stirred, and while the old dumping ground of Kalawao was not abandoned, new patients were mostly exiled to the more hospitable Kalaupapa side of the peninsula, just a mile or so to the west.

## The Move to Kalaupapa

Those sent to Kalaupapa were treated more mercifully. Missionary groups provided food and rudimentary clothing, and *kokua* (helpers) provided aid. An attempt was made to end the lawlessness and depravity and to provide some semblance of civilized society. Still, the leprosy patients were kept separate, and for the most part lived outdoors or in very rude huts. They could never come in direct contact with the *kokua* or anyone else who came to the peninsula. Many *kokua*, horrified by Kalaupapa, left on the next available boat. With little medical attention, death was still the only release from Kalaupapa.

## Light in Hell

It was by accident or miracle that Joseph de Veuster, **Father Damien**, a Catholic priest, came from Belgium to Hawaii. His brother, also a priest, was supposed to come, but he became ill and Father Damien came in his place. Damien spent several years on the Big Island of Hawai'i, building churches and learning the language and ways of the people, before he came to Kalaupapa in 1873. What he saw touched his heart. He was different from the rest, having come with a sense of mission to help those with the disease and bring them hope and dignity. The other missionaries saw Kalaupapa not as a place to live, but to die. Damien saw these people as children of God who had the right to live and be comforted.

Father Damien just weeks before his death from Hansen's disease

When they hid under a bush at his approach, he picked them up and stood them on their feet. He carried water all day long to the sick and dying. He bathed their wounds and built them shelters with his own two hands. When clothes or food or materials ran short, he walked topside and begged for more. Other church groups were against him, and the government gave him little aid, but he persevered. Damien scraped together some lumber and fashioned a flume pipe to carry water to his people, who were still dying mainly from pneumonia and tuberculosis brought on by neglect. Damien worked long days alone, until he dropped exhausted at night.

Father Damien modified **St. Philomena Church,** a structure that was originally built in Honolulu by Brother Bertrant in 1872 and shipped to Moloka'i in segments. Father Damien invited his flock inside, but those grossly afflicted could not control their mouths, so spittle would drip to the floor. They were ashamed to soil the church, so Damien cut squares in the floor through which they could spit onto the ground. Slowly a light began to shine in the hearts of the shunned residents, and the authorities began to take notice. Conditions began to improve, but there were those who resented Damien. Robert Louis Stevenson visited the settlement, and after meeting Damien wrote an open letter that ended "he is my father." Damien of course eventually contracted leprosy, but by the time he died in 1889 at age 49, he knew his people would be cared for. In 1936, Damien's native Belgium asked that his remains be returned. He was exhumed and his remains sent home, but a memorial still stands where he was interred at Kalaupapa. After lengthy squabbles with the Belgian government, Father Damien's right hand was returned to Kalaupapa in 1995 and has been reinterred as a religious relic. In 1995, he was beatified by Pope John Paul II. Several books have been written about Damien's life; perhaps the best of the bunch is *Holy Man, Father Damien of Molokai,* by Gavan Daws, while numerous others have been written about life at Kalaupapa as a leprosy patient.

## The Light Grows Brighter

Brother Dutton, who arrived in 1886, and Mother Marianne Cope, a Franciscan nun from Syracuse, New York, who came in 1888 with two other Sisters of Saint Francis, carried on Damien's work. In addition, many missionary groups sent volunteers to help at the colony. Thereafter the people of Kalaupapa were treated with dignity and given a sense of hope. In 1873, the same year that Damien arrived at Kalaupapa, Norwegian physician Gerhard Hansen isolated the bacteria that causes leprosy, and shortly thereafter the official name of the malady became Hansen's disease. By the turn of the 20th century, adequate medical care and good living conditions were provided to the patients at Kalaupapa. Still, many died, mostly from complications. Families could not visit members confined to Kalaupapa unless they were near death, and any children born to the patients—who were now starting to marry—were whisked away at birth and adopted, or given to family members on the outside. Even until the 1940s, people were still sent to Kalaupapa be-

cause of skin ailments that were never really diagnosed as leprosy. Many of these indeed did show signs of the disease, but there is always the haunting thought that they may have contracted it after arrival at the colony.

In the mid-1940s sulfa drugs were found to arrest most cases of Hansen's disease, and the prognosis for a normal life improved. By the 1960s further breakthroughs made Hansen's disease noncontagious, and in 1969 the quarantine on patients was eliminated. Patients at Kalaupapa were then free to leave and return to their homes. No new patients were admitted, but most, already living in the only home they'd ever known, opted to stay. In total over the years, about 8,000 unfortunate individuals were exiled to this forgotten spit of land. Almost as if it were an accident of fate designed to expunge evidence of the damning past, the community hospital along with all its records burned to the ground in the early '90s. No help was afforded by the local fire truck, which was unable to be started.

Nonetheless, medical treatment continues and all needed care is still provided. The community of resident patients numbers less than 45 today (down from a high of about 1,800 in 1917)—the average age is about 70—and state caretakers and federal employees in the community now outnumber patients. In all of Hawaii today, there are about 450 people registered with Hansen's disease; all but those at Kalaupapa live at home with their families. Each year on average, about 18 new cases are diagnosed in the state. Still the number of patients continues to drop as the old-timers die. In 1980, Kalaupapa and adjoining lands were designated Kalaupapa National Historical Park, jointly administered by the state Department of Health, but the residents are assured lifetime occupancy and free care.

The Kalaupapa Peninsula and its three adjoining valleys are technically a separate county within the state structure called Kalawao. There is a sheriff but no elected officials, but residents can and do vote in state and national elections. Of this area, 12 acres have been designated parkland, about 500 are Hawaiian Homelands, and the rest is state property. In the past, much of the peninsula was fenced off as rangeland for cattle, but more recently the cattle and goats have pretty much destroyed the native vegetation, which is now overgrown by alien species.

## Getting There

It shouldn't be a matter of *if* you go to Kalaupapa, but *how* you go. You have choices. You can fly, walk, or ride a mule. No matter how you go, you *cannot* walk around Kalaupapa unescorted. You *must* take an official tour, and children under 16 are not allowed. If you're going by mule, arrangements are made for you by the company, but if you're walking down or flying in, you have to call ahead to Richard Marks at **Damien Tours,** 808/567-6171, and he will give you an exact place and time to meet once down on the peninsula. Typically, this is a 9:45 A.M. pickup at the Kalaupapa Airport for those who fly in, followed by a 10 A.M. pickup at the bottom end corral for those who hike or ride the mules down. Damien Tours charges $32 for a fascinating, four-hour tour conducted by one of the residents. Definitely worth the money; the insight you get from the resident tour guide is priceless and unique. No food or beverages, except water, are available to visitors, so make sure to bring your own.

"I'd rather be riding a mule on Moloka'i" is an eye-catching T-shirt sported by some who have been lucky enough to have made the descent to Kalaupapa aboard the sure-footed mules of the **Molokai Mule Ride.** The well-trained mules will transport you down the 1,600-foot *pali*, expertly negotiating 26 hairpin switchbacks on the trail to the bottom. After your tour of the settlement, these gutsy animals carry you right back up so you too can buy your T-shirt and claim your ride-completion certificate. You are on the mule about 90 minutes each way. Operating daily except Sunday from 8 A.M., this tour runs $150 and includes the ground tour of the settlement and lunch. No riders weighing more than 240 pounds, please; you must be at least 16 years old and in good physical shape. For reservations, call 808/567-6088 or 800/567-7550.

If you're **hiking** to Kalaupapa, follow the mule trail cut by Manuel Farinha in 1886 and renovated in the late 1990s. Go about 200 yards past the stables and look for a road to the right. Follow this track down past pasture land to the trailhead, where there is a small metal building with an odd, faded sign that reads Advance Technology Center Hawaii USA, near an old overgrown observation point for the peninsula. The 3.8-mile, 90-minute trail going down the steep north face of the *pali* is well maintained and only mildly strenuous. You should be in good physical condition to hike it, however, because it can take a toll on your knees going down and requires strength and endurance on the way up. It may be preferable to leave before the mules do in the morning (around 8:15 A.M.), but in any case give yourself enough time to make it to the bottom before the tour pickup at 10 A.M. The trail will be rutted and muddy in spots, and you'll have to step around the road apples, so wear hiking boots if possible, sneakers at a minimum. A zigzag of 26 turns (they're numbered) gets you down to the bottom, and one long zag will bring you to the beach and the mule corral beyond. There is no swimming at this beach, which is pending status as a turtle sanctuary and is an area where monk seals have been known to give birth.

You can **fly** directly from Ho'olehua, top side Moloka'i, walk down and fly up, or fly both ways from Honolulu or Kahului, Maui. From topside to Kalaupapa with Molokai Air Shuttle, 808/567-6847, will run $49.90 one way. A round-trip flight from Honolulu to Kalaupapa (with one leg that goes through Ho'oluhua) via Pacific Wings runs about $140. For information and reservations, contact Pacific Wings, 800/867-6814 or 888/575-4546. Commercial Flyer, 888/266-3597 or 808/833-8014 in Honolulu, makes a Honolulu–Kalaupapa round-trip for $110. Paragon Air, 808/244-3356 on Maui or 866/946-4744 elsewhere, offers round-trip charter flights from both Kahului and Kapalua, Maui, for $210, which includes your airfare, tour fee, and a simple lunch. All flights get you to Kalaupapa in time for the start of your tour and pick you up when your tours ends at about 3 P.M. for your return flight. If you want to fly in, you must still arrange for the ground tour through Damien Tours (or be sponsored by someone who lives in Kalaupapa) before you will be sold a ticket. If you decide to fly, notice the breakers at the end of the runway sending spray high into the air. The pilots time their takeoffs to miss the spray!

## The Tour

Damien Tours will pick you up by bus either at the airport or at the mule corral. From there, you start your tour by a drive into the main Kalaupapa settlement, where all residents live, and where the hospital, park service office, post office, several churches, and pier are located. Driving past the old visitors center, you arrive at the pier. Although many supplies come by plane, a ferry comes once a year to bring bulkier goods. Across from the pier is the remodeled St. Francis Church and next to it, the unassuming Father Damien Memorial Hall, a mini-museum dedicated to Father Damien, Brother Dutton, and Sister Marianne Cope. Both can be visited if time permits. The tour then takes you past the remains of the old burnt hospital and the Bishop Home, a residence for female patients, to a stop at the new visitors center. This new center has displays of the settlement and a few books and other items for sale.

From there, you head over the flank of Pu'u 'Uao (405 feet), the highest point on the peninsula, to the old Kalawao settlement site for a stop at St. Philomena Church. This is perhaps the most moving part of the tour because the church and its cemetery are about the only physical remains of the works of Father Damien. During Father Damien's time, there were nearly 300 mostly small and humble buildings in Kalawao, many of which were constructed with the help of this holy man. Lunch is at Judd Park nearby, located next to where the first leprosy hospital stood, and from this bluff you have a great view overlooking the precipitous north Moloka'i coast. Pu'u 'Uao was the volcanic caldera out of which lava flowed to create the Kalaupapa Peninsula. Its crater top contains a small lake about the size of a baseball infield that is said to be more than 800 feet deep. On your return, you'll pass several graveyards that line the road to the airport, the last resting place to the thousands of victims who were cruelly treated by their disease and the society in which they lived.

# Moloka'i's West End

Long before contact with the Europeans, the west end of Moloka'i was famous throughout the Hawaiian Islands. The culture centered on Maunaloa, the ancient volcanic mountain that formed the land. On its slopes the goddess Laka learned the hula from her sister and spread its joyous undulations to all of the other islands. Not far from the birthplace of the hula is Kaluako'i, one of the two most important adze quarries in old Hawaii. Without these stone tools, no canoes, bowls, or everyday items could have been fashioned. Voyagers came from every major island to trade for this dense, hard stone. With all of this coming and going, the always-small population of Moloka'i needed godly protection. Not far away at Kalaipahoa, the "poison wood" sorcery gods of Moloka'i lived in a grove that supposedly sprouted to maturity in one night. With talismans made from this magical grove, Moloka'i kept invading warriors at bay for centuries.

Most of the island's flat, usable land is out that way. The thrust west began with the founding of the Molokai Ranch, whose 54,000 acres make up about 50 percent of the good farm and range land on the island and about one-third of the island. The ranch was owned in the 19th century by Kamehameha V, and after his death it was sold to private interests, who began the successful raising of Santa Gertrudis cattle imported from the famous Texas King Ranch. The ranch still employs a few *paniolo*. Today, anywhere between 6,000–10,000 head of Brahman and Brangus cattle roam ranch land, with about 80 horses to do the work.

## THE NORTHWEST

The northwest section of Moloka'i, centered at **Ho'olehua,** is where the Hawaiian Home Land parcels are located. The entire area has a feeling of heartland America, and if you ignore the coastline in the background you could easily imagine yourself in the rolling hills of Missouri. Don't expect a town at Ho'olehua. All that's there is a little post office and a government office.

## Mo'omomi Beach

The real destination is Mo'omomi Beach. Follow Route 460 until it branches north at Route 480 one mile east of the airport. Follow Route 480 until it turns left onto Farrington Avenue in Ho'olehua, and continue for about four miles until it turns into a red dirt road. This road can be extremely rutted, even tipping your car at a precarious angle. Be advised! Continue for 10–15 minutes, veer right, and shortly you come to a Hawaii Home Lands recreational pavilion. When the bottom section of this road washes out, traffic is directed onto a secondary road called Anahaki Road, which also takes you to the pavilion at the beach. Below you is Mo'omomi Beach. This area is a favorite with local people, who come here to swim, fish, and surf. The swells are good only in winter, but the beach becomes rocky at that time of year. The tides bring the sand in by April and the swimming until is good November. Unofficial camping is probably okay on this grassy area, and a toilet and water are available at the pavilion.

Mo'omomi Beach goes back to Hawaiian legend. Besides the mythical lizards that inhabited this area, a great shark-god was born here. The mother was a woman who became impregnated by the gods. Her husband was angry that her child would be from the spirit world, so he directed her to come and sit on a large rock down by the beach. She went into labor and began to cry. A tear, holding a tiny fish, rolled down her cheek and fell into the sea and became the powerful shark-god. The rock on which his mother sat is the large black one just to the right of the beach.

If you feel adventurous, you can head west along the shore, where you come to tiny beaches that you have entirely to yourself. Farther on is the isolated and much larger **Kawa'aloa Beach** and bay. Because this area is so isolated, be extremely careful of surf conditions. Inland from Kawa'alo and to the west is **Keonelele**, a miniature desert strip of sand dunes. The wind whips through this region and pushes the sand into rows. Geologists haunt this area trying to piece together Moloka'i's geological history. The Hawaiians used Keonelele as a burial site, and strange footprints found in the soft sandstone supposedly foretold the coming of white men. Today, Keonelele is totally deserted; although small, it gives the impression of a vast wasteland. A 921-acre plot west of Kaiehu Point, including much of the Keonelele area, is now overseen by the Nature Conservancy as the **Mo'omomi Preserve.** This coastal ecosystem, mostly unaltered over the centuries, safeguards 22 native plant species—four of which are endangered—that do well in this harsh, wind-blown environment. The Hawaiian green sea turtle also frequents these sands, making this preserve a sanctuary for this creature. Although the Hawaiian owl, plover, and numerous sea birds visit this distant stretch of shore, numerous birds that used to live here are now extinct, leaving only their bones in the sand to tell of their presence here. Within the preserve, use only the beach or the marked trails and 4WD roads.

## Papohaku Beach

The best attraction in the area doesn't have a price tag. Papohaku Beach is the giant expanse of white sand running south from the Kaluakoi Resort. The sands here are so expansive that some was dredged and taken to O'ahu in the 1950s. During the winter a great deal of sand is stripped away and large lava boulders and outcroppings are exposed. Every spring and summer the tides carry the sand back and deposit it on the enormous beach. Camping is permitted at the **Papohaku County Beach Park** just past the resort. Pick up your permit at the Mitchell Pauole Center in Kaunakakai, 808/553-3204, before you come all the way out here. Here you'll find a large, grassy play area, toilets, showers, picnic tables, grills for cooking, and a virtually empty beach. A sign on the road past the park tells you to watch out for deer. This road runs through a huge Papohaku Ranch lands home development area, with several beach access roads and parking areas that lead to other spots along this huge expanse of beach.

The last beach access at the end of the paved

road leads to a secluded and protected small bay and fine sand beach that is even safe during winter when other beach areas are not. Locals refer to this beach as Dixie Maru Beach because a fishing boat of that name once sunk in the bay. The Kaupoa Trail starts from the south end of this beach and runs into Molokai Ranch lands—about a 30- to 40-minute walk.

One of the attractions of Moloka'i is its remoteness. Here the sky is clear, and at night the stars are brilliant. Yet, even here you know that you're not too far from the crush of humanity because directly across the Kaiwi Channel you can clearly see the glow of Honolulu, Wailua, and Kaneohe shimmering in the distance, and, closer at hand, the more muted lights of Maunaloa on the hill above.

## Kawakiu Beach

This secluded and pristine beach on the far northwestern corner of Moloka'i was an item of controversy between the developers of the Kaluakoi Corp. and the grassroots activists of Moloka'i. For years access to the beach was restricted, and the Kaluakoi Corp., which then owned the land, planned to develop the area. It was known that the area was very important during precontact times and rich in unexplored archaeological sites. The company hired a supposed team of "experts," who studied the site for months and finally claimed that the area had no significant archaeological importance. Their findings were hooted at by local people and by scholars from various institutions who knew better. This controversy resulted in Kawakiu Beach being opened to the public with plans of turning it into a beach park; the archaeological sites will be preserved.

The swimming at Kawakiu is excellent, with the sandy bottom tapering off slowly. To get there go to the Paniolo Hale Condo at Kaluakoi Resort and park at the end of the dirt road that heads toward the sea, past the last paved parking lot of the condo. Walk across the golf course fairway to the beach. Follow it north for three-quarters mile, dodging the tide until you come to the very private Kawakiu Beach—definitely not recommended during periods of high surf, when

swimming would be too dangerous anyway. No rules or prying eyes here, so if you would like to swim au naturel, this is the place. If you have lots of time and energy, walk on farther to the smaller and rocky but more private Kawakiu Iki Beach, or farther on to the ancient adze quarry and abandoned Coast Guard station on 'Ilio Point. The hike is mildly strenuous, but Kawakiu is definitely worth it.

## Practicalities

Much of the west end of Moloka'i is the Kaluakoi Resort. This complex includes three resort condominiums, the Kaluakoi Golf Course, private home sites, and Papohaku Beach. After years of decline, the Kaluakoi Hotel closed its doors in 2001. Although the hotel no longer accepts guests, several of its shops are still doing business. You'll find the small **A Touch of Molokai** clothing shop, along with the **West End Sundries** store, which sells snacks, magazines, and liquor. The **Laughing Gecko** shop stocks antiques, art, jewelry, Hawaiiana, and locally designed T-shirts made on Moloka'i.

Some of the units at the resort complex, collectively called the **Kaluakoi Villas,** 1131 Kaluako'i Rd., Maunaloa, HI 96770, 808/552-2721 or 800/367-5004 mainland, are managed by the Castle Group. Each studio, suite, and cottage has been tastefully decorated and includes a color TV, lanai, kitchen or kitchenette, and guests can use the hotel swimming pool. Rates range $135–155 for a studio, $160–190 for a one-bedroom suite, and $240 for the ocean cottages on the golf course; fourth night is free.

Built in 1981, the **Ke Nani Kai** condos, a Marc Resorts Hawaii management property, P.O. Box 289, Maunaloa, HI 96770, 808/552-2761, or 800/535-0085, fax 808/553-3241, www.marcresorts.com, are *mauka* of the road leading to the Kaluakoi Hotel. They cost $155–169 for one of the fully furnished one-bedroom apartments; two bedrooms rent at $189–209. All apartments are large and in excellent condition. On property are a swimming pool and two tennis courts, and you're only a few steps away from the Kaluakoi golf course.

M

MAUI

Newer yet, **Paniolo Hale,** P.O. Box 190, Maunaloa, HI 96770, 808/552-2731 or 800/367-2984, fax 808/552-2288, stay@paniolohaleresort.com, www.paniolohaleresort.com, is another condo complex set in the trees surrounded by fairways. These buildings have more style than others on the area, and the whole complex is a little classier. The swimming pool, paddle tennis, and barbecue grill are for the use of all guests. Maid service is provided for stays of one week or longer, and each unit has a washer and dryer. Garden and ocean studios run $95–155, $115–230 for one bedroom, and $145–265 for two bedrooms; three-night minimum except over the Christmas holiday season, when it's one week. Two-bedroom units have a hot tub and enclosed lanai.

## MAUNALOA AND THE SOUTHWEST COAST

According to legend, the hilltop area Ka'ana above Maunaloa was the first place in the islands that the Hawaiians received hula instruction. Today, there are many *hula halau* on Moloka'i, and the yearly Moloka'i Hula Ka Piko festival is held down the hill at Papohaku State Park to honor this ancient music and dance form.

Most people heading east-west between Kaunakakai and the Kaluakoi Resort never used to make it into Maunaloa town because Route 460 splits just east of Maunaloa, and Kaluako'i Road heads north toward the Kaluakoi Resort and away from the town. Until recently, with the pineapples gone and few visitors, the town barely hung on. Built in 1923, Maunaloa was a wonderful example of a plantation town. It was a little patch of humble workers' houses carved into a field. In front you were likely to see a tethered horse, a boat, or glass fishing floats hanging from the lanai. Overhead you could see a kite flying—a sign that you had arrived in Maunaloa. The townsfolk were friendly, and if you were looking for conversation or a taste of Hawaiian history, the old-timers hanging around under the shaded lean-to near the post office were just the ticket.

But the winds of change have started to blow in Maunaloa and the force increases. The Molokai Ranch, which owns the town, has instituted a new grand development scheme to completely "rejuvenate" the town. Most of the old homes, many falling apart and maybe uninsurable, have been torn down and have been replaced by new, similar-style homes. Bunched together away from the downtown area, these homes are set closer together than the old houses were. They are affordable for many and well below the state average. Local people have been given first choice, and many have taken the deal. Additionally, streets have been paved and new ones laid out. A new sewer system and water reservoir have been installed, along with other segments of a modern infrastructure. While several of the old standby commercial establishments have remained, like the post office, general store, church, and *The Dispatch* newspaper office, the town has gotten a new face. A movie theater, local-style eatery, gas station, ranch activities center, and the ranch lodge with its rooms, restaurant, and bar have been built. An open-air "museum" features several renovated old buildings moved from other locations in town, and the Maunaloa Cultural Park is a spot where community events are staged. Future plans include more business establishments and new residential areas for custom homes, but only time will tell when those wil actually appear. With all these changes, there is certain to be some disagreement about their effect. Many people take a wait-and-see attitude, but others who live and/or work in town seem to think that the changes are for the better.

The only public shore access on this corner of the island is **Hale O Lono** harbor and beach. Turn just after the ranch outfitter and follow Mokia Street past the ranch lodge south out of town and keep to the major track of crushed coral. This road runs for a couple of miles down to the harbor. Hale O Lono is an old harbor that services the ranch, a few commercial boats related to the ranch, and the occasional passing ship. From here, the sand of Papohaku Beach was shipped to O'ahu in the 1950s. With its small but fine white-sand beach, Hale O Lono is the launch point for the annual Bankoh Moloka'i outrigger canoe championship races to Waikiki.

If you are staying at the Molokai Ranch, other

spots along the coast might be of interest. About one mile east of Hale O Lono is **Halena Beach,** where there is an old Boy Scout camp and pavilion. East of there down the coastal dirt track is **Kolo Beach,** a fine, long strand that sports the dilapidated **Kolo Wharf** at its far end. Kolo Wharf was where Moloka'i once shipped its pineapples. Now only naked pilings stand to mark the spot. On the far western end of the island is **Kaupoa Beach,** a once distant and secluded old-time favorite of island residents that is now the site of a modern-day camp.

## Molokai Ranch Accommodations

The only place to stay in Maunaloa is at the Molokai Ranch, but you don't just sleep there; you also find food and activities. Accommodations are either in the lodge or at Kaupoa Camp, located at Kaupoa Beach, a perfect white-sand double crescent at the extreme west end, a place that's good for swimming and tidepooling, with an occasional monk seal on the beach or dolphin in the bay. Kaupoa Camp has 40 two-bedroom "tentalows." Wood-frame structures covered with heavy canvas, all are set up on wooden platforms that hold umbrella-covered patio tables, chairs, and benches. Inside are comfortable queen beds, a chest of drawers, and a chair. Set off to the side of the lanai is a composting toilet and half-roof shower that uses solar energy to heat the water. Electricity in each camp is powered by solar batteries; no televisions or phones. All this is done to impact the environment as little as possible. This is rustic simplicity—but luxurious camping. Rates are $275–295 per day, with reduced rates for children and *kama'aina*. These prices include a hearty morning breakfast served at an open-air pavilion on site, daily maid service, and transportation within the ranch; lunches run $12 and dinners $25.

In 2000, The Lodge at Molokai Ranch, now the **Sheraton Molokai Lodge,** 100 Maunaloa Hwy., Maunaloa, HI 96770, 808/552-2741 or 877/726-4656, fax 808/552-2773, www.sheraton-molokai.com, opened for the greater pleasure and comfort of those visiting the ranch who desired more than the rustic Kaupoa Camp had to offer. This two-story, 22-room lodge reflects the days of the 1920s and '30s, with its early ranch decor and Hawaiiana tourist memorabilia. It's a Hawaiian ranch lodge in the true sense of the word, with a central hall flanked by wings of bedroom suites. In the main hall, you can easily make yourself comfortable as you sit back on a fine leather coach or wicker chair in front of the warming stone fireplace beneath the high ceiling that rises above you on the shoulders of rough-hewn timber posts and beams. Deep-patterned tropical foliage fabric covers the furniture and pillows, and artwork reflecting earlier years of tropical Hawaii, the golden glow of table lamps, rustic accessories, and a chandelier made from deer horn fill the room. Relax to the live entertainment every evening or grab a book from the upstairs library and sit yourself down in one of the second-floor nooks that overlook this hall. The bedrooms are as salubrious, also done in the decor of days past, but with all modern amenities. Room rates are $360–425. For anyone staying at the ranch needing transportation to and from the airport, there is an additional $20 fee. The lodge also has a restaurant, bar with billiard table, fitness center, massage service at the spa, an outdoor swimming pool, and the island's only elevator. A wide variety of activities on ranch property and along the coast are offered through the Outfitters Center.

## Food

**Maunaloa Room** is the lodge's restaurant, serving the island's most upscale cuisine, with a superb vista over ranchland and a view of O'ahu and the lights of Honolulu at night (so near, yet so far!). This is Moloka'i cuisine, gourmet ranch food. When the temperature is warm and balmy, sit outside on the verandah; when it cools down in the evening, move to one of the tables inside. Open for breakfast, Sunday brunch, and dinner, the lounge takes care of guests for lunch. Try an appetizer like salt-fried Molokai shrimp or "kahlua" duck lumpia, and entrées such as saffron-scented Pacific snapper, center-cut New York steak, and lemongrass-mango breast of chicken for $20–28. The **Paniolo Lounge** offers an easygoing atmosphere, whether sitting on a rawhide bar stool or at a table along the lanai. This full-service bar also offers lunch

**M**

10 A.M.–4 P.M. and *pu pu* from then until 9 P.M. for light evening fare. for those staying at Kaupoa Camp, all three meals of the day are served at the camp pavilion, with plenty of salads and greens and main dishes like New York steak, fresh fish, and chicken breast.

A few steps away in the theater building, the **Paniolo Cafe** serves inexpensive local food and is open daily 11 A.M.–7:30 P.M. This is the only other option in town and the only nonranch restaurant on the west end of the island.

## Activities and Recreation

There was a theater is Maunaloa until the mid-1970s, after which the only one on the island was in Kaunakakai. When that one closed, the island was without until the new **Maunaloa Town Cinemas,** 808/552-2707, was built in 1997. This triplex theater shows first-run movies and draws people not only from Maunaloa but also from Kaluako'i and Kaunakakai. Tickets run $6.50 adults, $4 children and seniors.

For outdoor adventure, you must go to the Molokai Ranch **Outfitters Center,** 808/552-2791 or 888/729-0059, where all sorts of outdoor activities can be arranged. If you're staying at one of the camps, activities are arranged through the camp staff. These activities include horseback riding (corral roundup and trail rides), ocean kayaking, full or half-day mountain-biking tours, cultural walks, a wagon ride, archery and sporting clay shooting, whale-watching in season, arts and crafts, and a children's program; all equipment is provided. A separate charge is made for each activity; mostly $30–90 apiece. Those staying at the ranch get priority for activities, but anyone may participate. For those not staying at the ranch, the rates are somewhat higher. While at the Outfitters Center, choose a souvenir at the logo shop or have a peek at the mini-museum for a survey of the island's history and culture and a small display of photos and artifacts. The Outfitter Center is open daily 7 A.M.–7 P.M.

## Shopping

A good reason to make the trek to Maunaloa is to visit the **Big Wind Kite Factory,** 808/552-2364, www.molokai.com/kites, open Mon.–Sat. 8:30 A.M.–5 P.M., Sunday 10 A.M.–2 P.M., owned and operated by Jonathan Socher and his wife Daphne. The hand-crafted kites and windsocks from this down-home cottage industry are the same ones that sell at outlets around the state. All are made on the premises by Jonathan, Daphane, son Zach, and a few workers, who come up with designs like butterflies, rainbow stars, and hula girls in *ti*-leaf skirts—ask for a free factory tour. Jonathan will give you a lesson in the park next door on any of the kites, including the stunt ones. They make beautiful, easily transportable gifts that'll last for years. The shop is ablaze with beautiful colors, as if you've walked into the heart of a flower. This is a happy store. The Big Wind Kite Factory is *the* most interesting shop on Moloka'i.

In the second half of this building, **The Plantation Gallery** sells a variety of crafts by local artists—Hawaiian quilt pillowcases, Pacific isle shell jewelry, scrimshaw (on deerhorn), earrings, bracelets, boxes, bamboo xylophones, and other wood objects. Part of the boutique has batiks, Balinese masks, wood carvings, quilts, and sarongs; especially nice are carved mirror frames of storks, birds, and flowers. And if you just can't live without a blowgun from Irian Jaya, this is the place. Here too you'll find perhaps the island's best selections of books on Hawaii, postcards, and a selection of T-shirts, Hawaiian shirts, and sarongs. After you've run through a million tourist shops and are sick of the shell lei, come here to find something truly unique.

**Maunaloa General Store,** 808/552-2346, is open Monday–Saturday 8 A.M.–6 P.M. It's a well-stocked store where you can pick up anything you'll need if you'll be staying in one of the condos at Kaluako'i. You can buy liquor, wine, beer, canned goods, meats, and vegetables.

Across from the theater and tucked into the side of the general store is the west end's only **gas station.** The price of gas here is virtually no different than anywhere else on the island. Open Monday–Friday 7 A.M.–1 P.M. and Saturday 10 A.M.–2 P.M., this station also carries drinks, sundries, and has an ATM. There is no bank in Maunaloa.

# Kahoʻolawe

The island of Kahoʻolawe (the Carrying Away—as if by currents), known as Kanaloa in ancient days, is clearly visible from many points along Maui's south shore. From Lahaina and Maʻalaea, the outline of Kahoʻolawe on the horizon resembles the back and dorsal fin of a whale half out of the water, ready to dive. In fact, many whales and dolphins do congregate around the island in summer to calve their young and mate for the coming year. Until recently Kahoʻolawe was a target island, uninhabited except for a band of wild goats that refused to be killed off.

Kahoʻolawe was a sacred island born to Wakea and Papa, the two great mythical progenitors of Hawaii. The birth went badly and almost killed Papa, and it hasn't been any easier for her ill-omened child ever since. Kahoʻolawe became synonymous with Kanaloa, the man-god. Kanaloa was especially revered by the *kahuna ʻanaʻana,* the "black sorcerers" of old Hawaii. Kanaloa, much like Lucifer, was driven from heaven by Kane, the god of light. Kanaloa held

dominion over all poisonous things and ruled in the land of the dead from his power spot here on Kahoʻolawe. Kanaloa was also revered as the god of voyaging by early Polynesians and as such held an important place in their cast of deities.

For years, a long, bitter feud raged between the U.S. Navy, which wanted to keep the island as a bombing range, and Protect Kahoʻolawe Ohana, a Hawaiian native-rights organization, which wanted the sacred island returned to the people. The Navy finally agreed to stop bombing and returned the island to the state of Hawaii, bringing the Ohana one step closer to its goal. However, Kahoʻolawe remains closed to outside visitors, who must be content to view it from across the water.

## The Land

Kahoʻolawe is 11 miles long and six miles wide, with 29 miles of coastline. Its 45 square miles make it the seventh largest of the main Hawaiian islands, larger only than Niʻihau, and its mean elevation of about 600 feet is lower than all of the

ROBERT NILSEN

Kahoʻolawe

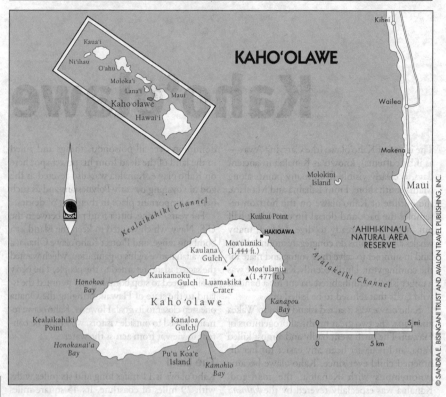

KAHO'OLAWE

other islands except for that small, private enclave. The tallest hill, Moa'ulanui, is in the eastern section at 1,477 feet. Across the shallow Luamakika Crater is the nearly-as-tall hill Moa'ulaniki, at 1,444 feet. There are no natural lakes or ponds on the island, and all streams except for one or two are seasonal. Because Kaho'olawe lies in Maui's rain shadow (it's six miles across to South Maui), it receives only about 25 inches of rain per year.

The land is covered by sparse vegetation and is cut by ravines and gulches. Much of the island, particularly the south and east coasts, is ringed by steep *pali*, but the land slides off more gradually to the north and west. There are few beaches on the island, but the best are at the west end between Honokoa Bay and Honokanai'a Bay (some references say Hanakanaea Bay). Also known as Smuggler Cove, Honokanai'a Bay is said to be the

site of a treasure buried on the beach in 1880 and as yet unclaimed. Kealaikahiki (the Way to Foreign Lands) Point is the island's western tip, and this rock was said to be used as a beacon during centuries past for canoe travelers to and from the island to the south.

Kaho'olawe's official color is gray and its plant is the *hinahina,* a low, spreading beach heliotrope with narrow silvery-gray leaves and small, white flowers.

## HISTORY

It's perfectly clear that small families of Hawaiians lived on Kaho'olawe for countless generations and that religious rites were carried out by many visiting *kahuna* over the centuries, but mostly Kaho'olawe was left alone. There are scores of archaeological sites and remnants of *heiau* all over the bomb-cratered face of Kahoʻolawe, perhaps from as early as A.D. 1150. Most of these sites are close to water near the area known as Hakioawa in the northeast corner of the island, but a few others have been discovered inland. One site of archaeological interest is an adze quarry, located up top and said to be the second largest in the state.

In the early 1800s, Kahoʻolawe was used as a place of banishment for criminals. It was a harsh sentence because the island had little food and less water. Yet, many survived and some managed to raid the nearby islands of Maui and Lanaʻi for food and women! The first attempt at sheep ranching was started in 1858 but was not successful. This was followed by a second venture, which also proved largely unproductive because of the great numbers of wild goats that had by that time established themselves on the island. By the turn of the 20th century, Kahoʻolawe was already overgrazed, and a great deal of its bare topsoil was blown away into the sea.

In 1917, Angus MacPhee, a cattleman, leased Kahoʻolawe from the territorial government for $200 per year. The lease would run until 1954 with a renewal option, if by 1921 MacPhee could show reasonable progress in taming the island. Harry Baldwin bought into the **Kahoʻolawe Ranch** in 1922, and with his money and MacPhee's know-how, Kahoʻolawe turned a neat profit. Within a few years Kahoʻolawe Ranch cattle were being shipped regularly to markets on Maui. MacPhee did more than anyone to reclaim the land. He got rid of many of the goats and introduced horses and game birds. While the island supported indigenous vegetation such as ʻohiʻa, mountain apples, and even Hawaiian cotton and tobacco, MacPhee planted eucalyptus and range grass from Australia, which caught on well and stopped much of the erosion. Gardens were planted around the homestead and the soil proved to be clean and fertile.

## The Navy Arrives

In 1939, with the threat of war on the horizon, MacPhee and Baldwin, stimulated by patriotism, offered a small tip of Kahoʻolawe's southern shore to the U.S. Army as an artillery range. One day after the attack on Pearl Harbor, the U.S. Navy seized all of Kahoʻolawe "to further the war effort" and evicted MacPhee, immediately disenfranchising the Kahoʻolawe Ranch. During World War II, the Navy praised Kahoʻolawe as being *the* most important factor in winning the Pacific War. The island was supposed to be returned after the war, but when the lease ran out in 1954 the island was appropriated by presidential decree for use solely by the military. No compensation was ever given to MacPhee or his family. Throughout its military stewardship, Kahoʻolawe became the most bombarded piece of real estate on the face of the earth. The U.S. government held the island until the fall of 1990.

## The Protect Kahoʻolawe Ohana

Founded in 1976, the Protect Kahoʻolawe Ohana (PKO) is an extended group favoring traditional values based on *aloha ʻaina* (love of the land), which is the primary binding force for all Hawaiians. They would like the island to return to Hawaiian Lands inventory, with the *kahu* (stewardship) in the hands of native Hawaiians. The point driven home by the PKO is that the military has totally ignored and belittled native Hawaiian values, which are now beginning to be asserted. They maintain that Kahoʻolawe is not a barren wasteland, but a vibrant part of their history and religion. Kahoʻolawe was placed on the National Register of Historic Sites in 1981.

In a formal agreement with the PKO and the state of Hawaii in 1980, the U.S. Navy granted legal access to the island for four days per month. The PKO built a *halau* (longhouse), and members used the time on Kahoʻolawe to dedicate themselves to religious, cultural, and social pursuits. The Ohana look to Kahoʻolawe as their *puʻuhonua* (refuge), where they gain strength and knowledge from each other and the *ʻaina*. Hopefully, Kahoʻolawe's future as a sacred island is now secure.

## Changing Hands

In 1990, then-president George Bush, Sr. issued an order to immediately halt the bombing of Kahoʻolawe, and at the same time established a congressional commission to create the terms and conditions for returning the island to the state. At that time, Ka Lahui Hawaii, the Native Nation of

Hawaii, founded in Hilo in 1987, demanded that the island, as "totally ceded lands," be given to them as part of their sovereign nation. The PKO, in a more moderate stance, suggested "land banking" the island under the control of the state or federal government until the United States recognizes the sovereignty of the Ka Lahui Hawaii. In the meantime, the PKO continues to lobby for exclusive rights to the stewardship of Kaho'olawe. On May 7, 1994, Kaho'olawe was returned to the state of Hawaii.

## Transition
With the transfer of the island back to state protection, Kaho'olawe has become an "island reserve." The U.S. Congress dedicated $400 million over a 10-year period toward cleaning the island of scrap and unexploded ordnance and for the rejuvenation of the environment. What appeared to be a huge amount of money soon turned out to be woefully inadequate for the task and only enough to start the process of making the island safe and healthy. The Kaho'olawe Island Reserve Commission (KIRC) was established by state law to oversee and manage this effort. The reserve includes the island of Kaho'olawe plus the waters surrounding it to a distance of two miles. This total area is one of restricted access.

Now that the goats are gone and some of the ordnance cleaned up, the greatest problem seems to be erosion. While vegetation has a hold in some valleys and clings to spots where goats could not feed, much of the soil covering the island's plateau and gentle slopes has been blown off, exposing red, hardpan earth. Much work has been done; various approaches have been tried to establish grasses and other plants, and dams of grasses have been placed to prevent dirt from washing down gullies to the sea. Still, much more needs to be done. Introduced species are overtaking the dwindling native plants, and field mice are swiftly eating native seeds. Two other serious problems that must be overcome are the remaining unexploded ordnance, which is both expensive and risky to remove and dispose of, and the perpetual lack of water. While the ordnance cleanup effort continues by the military,

Mother Nature must be coaxed to help out with water. With similar natural conditions as those of South Maui, the island gets only minimal rain each year. Freshwater comes from rain catching, and few streams ever run.

The only habitation sites on Kaho'olawe are the traditional structures put up by the PKO near Hakioawa and the military installation on the west end of the island. There is currently virtually no infrastructure on the island except for a few rutted dirt roads. Over the years, several thousand people have visited the island, mostly to help with the cleanup efforts or to participate in religious and cultural activities. Kaho'olawe might become a great cultural resource, a place where Hawaiians could go to practice age-old traditions in a sympathetic environment, but it probably will never be a place for any large-scale habitation.

Although exact plans for the future are still undecided, it seems most likely that the island will be kept out of the hands of developers and open to visitors for cultural purposes if the risk factor finally drops low enough. How the island will be managed and what status it will eventually attain is still to be determined.

## The Book on Kaho'olawe
Inez MacPhee Ashdown lived on the island with her father and was a driving force in establishing the homestead. She has written a book, *Recollections of Kaho'olawe*, that chronicles the events from 1917 until the military takeover and is rife with myths, legends, and historical facts about Kaho'olawe.

## Information
Only a lucky few set foot on Kaho'olawe. For information about current happenings relating to this tortured island, log on to the PKO's website: www.kahoolawe.org. Alternately, try that of the KIRC at www.state.hi.us/kirc (or www.hawaii.gov/kirc), or the Navy information site at www.efdpac.navfac.navy.mil/news/kaho/hp1.htm. To contact the PKO, write: P.O. Box 152, Honolulu, HI 96810. For the KIRC: 811 Kolu St., Ste. 201, Wailuku, HI 96793, 808/243-5020 or 800/468-4644, administrator@kirc.state.hi.us.

# Kaua'i

*O, how my spirit languishes to step
ashore in the Sanguishes. . . .*

—Robert Louis Stevenson, circa 1888

# Introduction

This is the oldest of the main Hawaiian Islands, perhaps six million years old, and nature has had ample time to work, sculpting Kaua'i into a beauty among beauties. Flowers and fruits burst from its fertile soil, but the "Garden Island" is much more than greenery and flora—it's the poetry of land itself. Its mountains have become rounded and smooth, and its streams tumbling to the sea have cut deep and wide, giving Kaua'i the only navigable river in Hawaii. The interior is a dramatic series of mountains, valleys, and primordial swamp. The great gouge of Waimea Canyon, called the "Grand Canyon of the Pacific," is an enchanting layer of pastels where uncountable rainbows form prismatic necklaces from which waterfalls hang like silvery pendants. The northwest is the sea cliffs of Na Pali, mightiest in all of Oceania, looming nearly 4,000 feet above the pounding surf.

Only 100 miles by air from Honolulu, everything seems quieter here, rural but upbeat, with the main town being just that, a town. The pursuit of carefree relaxation is unavoidable at five-star hotels, where you're treated like a visiting *ali'i*, or at campsites deep in interior valleys or along secluded beaches where reality *is* the fantasy of paradise.

Kaua'i is where Hollywood comes when the script calls for "paradise." The island has several dozen major films to its credit, everything from idyllic scenes in *South Pacific* to the lurking horror of Asian villages in *Uncommon Valor*. *King Kong* tore up this countryside in search of love, and Tattoo

ROBERT NILSEN

Kilauea Lighthouse

spotted "de plane, boss" in *Fantasy Island*. In *Blue Hawaii*, Elvis's hips mimicked the swaying palms in a famous island grove, while torrid love scenes from *The Thorn Birds* were steamier than the jungle in the background. More recently, parts of *Outbreak* and *Jurassic Park* were filmed here. Perhaps the greatest compliment is that Kaua'i is where other islanders come to look at the scenery.

Kaua'i is the most regularly shaped of all the major islands—more or less round, like a partially deflated beach ball. The puckered skin around the coast forms bays, beaches, and inlets, while the center is a no-man's-land of mountains, canyon, valleys, and swamp.

## Lihu'e

Almost everyone arrives at the airport in Lihu'e, although some fortunate individuals step ashore at Lihu'e's port, **Nawiliwili Harbor.** Lihu'e is the county seat and major town with government agencies, full amenities, and an array of restaurants, shopping, and accommodations; however, most visitors head north to the resort areas of Wailua/Kapa'a or Princeville/Hanalei, or west to the fabulous Po'ipu Beach area. Lihu'e's **Kaua'i Museum** is a must-stop, where you'll learn the geological and social history of the island, immensely enriching your visit.

On the outskirts of town is the remarkably preserved **Grove Farm Homestead,** a classic Hawaiian plantation so intact that all that seems to be missing is the workers. At Nawiliwili Bay you can see firsthand the Menehune's handiwork at the **Alakoko (Menehune) Fishpond,** still in use. A short distance uphill from there on the west edge of town is the bedroom community of **Puhi,** home of **Kaua'i Community College,** the island's only higher educational institution. Just north past the tiny valley community of **Kapaia** is the suburb of **Hanama'ulu.** In Kapaia is the junction of Route 583 which leads inland through several miles of former sugarcane fields, terminating at the engaging panorama of **Wailua Falls.**

## East Coast

Heading northeast from Lihu'e along Route 56 takes you to **Wailua** and **Kapa'a,** a region known as the Coconut Coast. Wailua is built along the Wailua River, the only navigable stream in Hawaii. At the mouth of the river are two beach parks, a temple of refuge, and petroglyphs, while upstream are more *heiau,* royal birth stones, the heavily touristed yet beautiful **Fern Grotto,** and the **Kamokila Hawaiian Village,** all within the **Wailua River State Park.** Here too are remarkable views of the river below and the cascading **'Opaeka'a Waterfalls.** Beyond the falls, the squat compact mountain ridge called the **Sleeping Giant** still presides over town in humble repose. Beyond the giant are upland residential communities and, farther, the **Keahua Arboretum,** the start of several good hiking trails. Heavily damaged by Hurricane 'Iniki, Wailua's Coco Palms Resort was an island institution set in the heart of the most outstanding coconut grove on Kaua'i. While it still lies in devastated disarray, its myth and legend live on.

Along Route 56 toward Kapa'a you pass **The Coconut Marketplace** and half a dozen smaller shopping malls. In the vicinity, a clutch of affordable condos line the beach. Kapa'a, built on pineapple and sugarcane, is a workers' town with more down-home shopping and good, inexpensive restaurants. Heading north, you pass **Kealia Beach,** an excellent surfing spot; **Anahola Beach,** where the water is fine; and **Moloa'a Bay,** a secluded spot that you can have mostly to yourself. The only town along the way is tiny **Anahola,** where a community of Hawaiian residents advertise lei strung from flowers grown in their yards.

## North Coast

**Kilauea,** the first town in the Hanalei District and a former sugarcane plantation, begins the north shore. A narrow coastal road leads you through town to **Kilauea Lighthouse,** a beacon of safety for passing ships and for a remarkable array of birds that populate the surrounding **wildlife sanctuary.** In the vicinity, numerous side roads lead to "secret beaches," excellent snorkeling spots, and wild surf. **Princeville** is next, one of the largest planned resorts in Hawaii, featuring its own airstrip. Here an entire modern village is built around superb golf courses and an exclusive deluxe resort.

Down the narrowing lane and over a single-lane steel-strut bridge is **Hanalei.** Inland is a terraced valley planted in taro just like in the old days. Oceanside is **Hanalei Bay,** a safe anchorage and haven to seagoing yachts that have made it a port of call ever since Westerners began coming to Hawaii. On the outskirts is **Wai'oli Mission House,** a preserved missionary home dating from 1837. Then comes a string of beaches, uncrowded and well-known for snorkeling. You pass through the tiny village of **Wainiha** and then **Ha'ena,** with the island's "last resort." Just before the end of the road at **Ke'e Beach** are the **wet and dry caves.** Commanding a superb view above the beach are **Kaulu Paoa** and **Kaulu O Laka** *heiau,* dedicated to hula and the veneration of Laka, its bestower. This location is where the beach scenes from *The Thorn Birds* were filmed. From here only your feet and love of adventure take you down the **Kalalau Trail** to back-to-nature camping. You pass along a narrow foot trail down the **Na Pali Coast,** skirting emerald valleys cut off from the world by impassable 4,000-foot sea cliffs. All along here are *heiau,* ancient village sites, caves, lava tubes, and the romantic yet true **Valley of the Lost Tribe** just beyond trail's end.

## South Shore

From Lihu'e west is a different story. Route 50 takes you past the coastal **Ha'upu (Hoary Head) Ridge,** where **Queen Victoria's Profile** squints down at you. **Maluhia Road,** famous for its tunnel-like line of eucalyptus, branches off toward **Koloa,** a sugar town now rejuvenated with shops, boutiques, and restaurants. At the coast is **Po'ipu Beach,** the best on Kaua'i with its bevy of beautiful hotels and resorts. This sunny south coast is where many first-time visitors to Kaua'i head, and it's easy to understand why. At the west end of this strip resort is the **Spouting Horn,** a blowhole in the ceiling of a lava tube that spouts water with each inrushing wave, as regularly as Old Faithful in Yellowstone. In the lower Lawa'i Valley is the **National Tropical Botanical Garden,** managed for the propagation of the earth's tropical plants. Inland, 'Oma'o, Lawa'i, and Kalaheo are strung along the highway running west, each a former sugar town.

Packed with tight valleys, the rugged Na Pali Coast has little room for beaches.

ROBERT NILSEN

The largest is **Kalaheo,** where an island philanthropist, Walter McBride, gave the munificent land gift that has become **Kukui O Lono Park.** Here excellent views and a little-played golf course surround a small Japanese garden.

## West End

West on Route 50 brings you to **Hanapepe,** a good supply stop famous for its art galleries and inexpensive restaurants. Outside town are **Port Allen Harbor** and **Burns Field** airstrip, both used by numerous activity companies. The best beach between Po'ipu Beach and the far west end is **Salt Pond Beach,** where from ancient times, Hawaiians have harvested salt from evaporated sea water. From there, the road skirts the shore, passing **Kaumakani,** a dusty sugar plantation workers' village; **Olokele,** a perfect caricature of a sugar town with its neatly trimmed managers' homes; and **Pakala,** an excellent surfing beach. Quickly comes **Waimea,** where Captain Cook first came ashore, and on the outskirts is the **Russian Fort,** dating from 1817, when major world powers of the day were present in Hawaii, jockeying to influence this Pacific gem.

In Waimea and farther westward in **Kekaha,** the road branches inland, leading along the rim of **Waimea Canyon.** This is what everyone comes to see, and none are disappointed. The wonderfully winding road serves up lookout after lookout and trail after trail. You end up at **Koke'e State Park** and the **Kalalau Valley Lookout,** where you're king of the mountain,

and 4,000 feet below is your vast domain of the Na Pali Coast. West of the sugar town of Kekaha is a flat stretch of littoral farmland vast enough for cane and corn fields, and the military's **Pacific Missile Range Facility** at Barking Sands. The pavement ends and a good tourist-intimidating "cane road" takes over, leading you to the seclusion of **Polihale Beach,** where you can swim, camp, and luxuriate in privacy. If Madame Pele had had her choice, she never would have moved.

# The Land

Kaua'i, 100 miles northwest of O'ahu, is the northernmost and westernmost of Hawaii's six major islands and the fourth largest. It is approximately 33 miles long and 25 miles wide at its farthest points, with an area of 552 square miles and 90 miles of coastline. The island was built by one huge volcano that became extinct about five million years ago. Speculation holds that Ni'ihau, a separate and smaller shield volcano 20 miles off the west coast, may have been connected to Kaua'i at one time.

A simplified but chronologically accurate account of Kaua'i's emergence is found in a version of the Pele myth retold in *The Kumulipo.* It depicts the fire goddess as a young, beautiful woman who visits Kaua'i during a hula festival and becomes enraptured with Lohiau, a handsome and mighty chief. She wants him as a husband and determines to dig a fire pit home where they can reside in contented bliss. Unfortunately, her unrelenting and unforgiving sea-goddess sister pursues her, forcing Pele to abandon Kaua'i and Lohiau. Thus, she wandered and sparked volcanic eruptions on O'ahu, Maui, and finally atop Kilauea Crater on Hawai'i, where she now resides.

## Phenomenal Features of Kaua'i
Almost smack-dab in the middle of the island are **Mount Kawaikini** (5,243 feet) and adjacent **Mount Wai'ale'ale** (5,148 feet), the highest points on Kaua'i. These two high points are thought to be the western rim of the island's collapsed main volcanic crater. Mount Wai'ale'ale

is an unsurpassed "rain magnet," drawing an estimated 450 inches (37.5 feet) of precipitation during the approximately 350 days it rains per year, and earning itself the dubious distinction of being "the wettest spot on earth." Don't be intimidated—this rain is amazingly localized, with only 20 inches per year falling just 20 miles away. Visitors can now enter this mist-shrouded world aboard helicopters that fly through countless rainbows and hover above a thousand waterfalls. The top of the island is buffeted by strong winds, which, along with the cool temperatures, keep the plants that grow here close to the ground.

Draining Wai'ale'ale is **Alaka'i Swamp,** a dripping sponge of earth covering about 30 square miles of trackless bog. This patch of mire contains flora and fauna found nowhere else on earth. For example, 'ohi'a trees, mighty giants of upland forests, grow here as natural bonsai that could pass as potted plants. Bordering the Alaka'i Swamp on the west is **Waimea Canyon,** where eons of whipping winds, pelting rain, and incessantly grinding streams and rivulets have chiseled the red bedrock to depths of 3,000 feet and expanses two miles wide. Up and over the canyon wall from there is the **Na Pali Coast,** an incredibly scalloped, undulating vastness of valleys and *pali* forming a bulwark 4,000 feet high.

Other mountains and outcroppings around the island have formed curious natural formations. The **Ha'upu Ridge,** a diminutive range barely 2,000 feet tall south of Lihu'e, forms a profile of Queen Victoria. Above Wailua, the

**Nounou Ridge** gives the impression of a man in repose and has been dubbed The Sleeping Giant. Another small range in the northeast, the **Anahola Mountains,** had until recently an odd series of boulders that formed "Hole in the Mountain," mythologically created when a giant hurled his spear through sheer rock. Erosion has collapsed the formation, but another hole is forming, as if to continue the legend.

## Channels, Lakes, and Rivers

Kaua'i is separated from O'ahu by the **Kaua'i Channel.** Reaching an incredible depth of 10,900 feet and a width of 72 miles, it is by far the state's deepest and widest channel. On the far side, Kauai and Ni'ihau lie some 17 miles apart across the 3,570-foot-deep **Kaulakahi Channel.** Inland, man-made **Waita Reservoir** north of Koloa is the largest body of fresh water in Hawaii, covering 424 acres with a three-mile shoreline. The **Waimea River,** running through the floor of the canyon, is the island's longest at just under 20 miles, while the **Hanalei River** moves the greatest amount of water, emptying 140 million gallons per day into Hanalei Bay. But the **Wailua River** has the distinction of being the state's only navigable river, although passage by boat is restricted to a scant three miles upstream. The flatlands around Kekaha were at one time Hawaii's largest body of inland water. These ponds were brackish and were drained in the 19th century to create cane fields.

## CLIMATE

Kaua'i's climate will make you happy. Along the coastline the average temperature is 80° F in spring and summer, and about 75 during the remainder of the year. The warmest areas are along the south coast from Lihu'e westward, where the mercury can hit the 90s in midsummer. Nighttime temperatures usually drop 10–15°, and may drop into the upper 50s in winter, even along the coast. To escape the heat any time of year, head for Koke'e in the mountains, where the weather is always moderate, and may be down-right chilly.

## Precipitation

Although Mt. Wai'ale'ale is "the wettest spot on earth," in the areas most frequented by visitors, rain is generally not a problem. The driest section of Kaua'i is the arid Maha Plain near Polihale Beach in the west. From there across the south shore to the Po'ipu Beach resort area, rainfalls run from five inches per year up to a mere 20 inches. Lihu'e receives about 30 inches. As you head northeast to Kapa'a and then swing around the coast past Kilauea toward Hanalei, rainfall becomes more frequent but is still a tolerable 45 inches per year. Farther down the coast it may reach 75 inches a year. Cloudbursts in winter are frequent but short-lived.

## Hurricanes 'Iwa and 'Iniki

The Garden Island is much more than just another pretty face—the island and its people have integrity. Thanksgiving was not a very nice time on Kaua'i back in November 1982. Along with the stuffing and cranberries came an unwelcome guest who showed no *aloha,* Hurricane 'Iwa. What made this rude 80-mph party-crasher so unforgettable was that she was only the fourth such storm to come ashore on Hawaii since records have been kept and the first since the late 1950s. All told, 'Iwa caused $200 million worth of damage. A few beaches were washed away, perhaps forever, and great destruction was suffered by beach homes and resorts, especially around Po'ipu. Thankfully, no lives were lost. The people of Kaua'i rolled up their sleeves and set about rebuilding. In short order, the island recovered, and most residents thought "that was that."

Unfortunately, on Friday, September 11, 1992, Hurricane 'Iniki, with unimaginable ferocity, ripped ashore with top wind speeds of 175 mph and slapped Kaua'i around like the moll in a Bogart movie. "'Iniki" has two meanings in Hawaiian: "piercing winds" and "pangs of love," both devastatingly painful in their own way. The hurricane virtually flattened or tore to shreds everything in its path. No one was immune from the savage typhoon. Renowned director Steven Spielberg and his cast, including Laura Dern, Jeff Goldblum,

## TEMPERATURE AND RAINFALL

| Town | | Jan. | March | May | June | Sept. | Nov. |
|------|------|------|-------|-----|------|-------|------|
| **Hanapepe** | high | 79 | 80 | 81 | 84 | 82 | 80 |
| | low | 60 | 60 | 61 | 65 | 62 | 61 |
| | rain | 5 | 2 | 0 | 0 | 2 | 3 |
| **Lihu'e** | high | 79 | 79 | 79 | 82 | 82 | 80 |
| | low | 60 | 60 | 65 | 70 | 68 | 65 |
| | rain | 5 | 3 | 2 | 2 | 5 | 5 |
| **Kilauea** | high | 79 | 79 | 80 | 82 | 82 | 80 |
| | low | 62 | 64 | 66 | 68 | 69 | 65 |
| | rain | 5 | 5 | 3 | 3 | 1 | 5 |

Note: Temperature is in degrees Fahrenheit; rainfall is in inches.

Richard Attenborough, and Sam Neill, were on the island filming scenes for the blockbuster *Jurassic Park*. They, along with other guests, bellmen, maids, groundskeepers, and cooks, rode out the storm huddled in the ballroom of the Westin Kauai Lagoons, now the Kaua'i Marriott. Afterward, then-mayor JoAnn Yukimura and her staff worked day and night from her roofless office in Lihu'e. Hanalei taro farmers opened their humble doors to homeless neighbors and strangers alike, while a general manager of a luxury resort on the eve of his wedding pleaded with invited guests to give donations to various charitable organizations in lieu of gifts. There was hardly a structure on the entire island that wasn't damaged in one way or another. Proud yachts were thrown like toy boats into a jangled heap; cars were buried whole in the red earth; a full third of Kaua'i's 20,000 homes were broken into splinters; and 4,200 hotel rooms became a tangled heap of steel and jagged glass. By the grace of god, and because of a very competent warning system, only eight lives were lost, and fewer than 100 people had to be admitted to the hospital due to injury. Psychologically, however, many people who lost everything were scared; special counseling services were set up to offer techniques to deal with the stress and sense of loss. Insurance companies were stressed to the breaking point; some were very slow to pay, and a few literally went broke trying to pay all of the claims brought against them. Undaunted and with pride and will that far surpassed the fury of the storm, Kaua'i's inhabitants rebuilt, while nature took care of the rest. Some philosophical souls believe that *Kaua'i* wasn't hurt at all—only a bunch of buildings were destroyed. They contend that in its millions of years of existence, Kaua'i has been through many storms, and Hurricane 'Iniki was merely a "$1.5 billion pruning . . . for free." Though trees were twisted from the ground and bushes were flattened, Kaua'i is strong and fertile and the damage was temporary. Now, 'Iniki is mostly a memory and Kaua'i has emerged a touch more self-assured and as beautiful as ever.

KAUA'I

# Flora and Fauna

Kaua'i exceeds its reputation as the Garden Island. It has had a much longer time for soil building and for rooting of a wide variety of plant life, so it's lusher than the other islands. Lying on a main bird migratory route, lands such as the Hanalei National Wildlife Sanctuary have long since been set aside for their benefit. Impenetrable inland regions surrounding Mt. Wai'ale'ale and dominated by the Alaka'i Swamp have provided a natural sanctuary for Kaua'i's own bird and plant life. Because of this, Kaua'i is home to the largest number of indigenous birds extant in Hawaii, though even here they are tragically endangered. As on the other Hawaiian Islands, a large number of birds, plants, and mammals have been introduced in the past 200 years. Most have either aggressively competed for, or simply destroyed, the habitat of indigenous species. As the newcomers gain dominance, Kaua'i's own flora and fauna slide inevitably toward oblivion.

## Birds of the Alaka'i Swamp

The following scarce birds are some of the last indigenous Hawaiian birds, saved only by the inhospitableness of the Alaka'i Swamp. All are endangered species and under no circumstances should they be disturbed. The last survivors include: the **'o'u,** a chubby seven-inch bird with a green body, yellow head, and lovely whistle ranging half an octave; the relatively common **Hawaiian creeper,** a hand-size bird with a light green back and white belly, which travels in pairs and searches bark for insects; the *puaiohi,* a dark brown, white-bellied seven-inch bird so rare its nesting habits are unknown.

**'O'o'a'a,** although its name may resemble the sounds you make getting into a steaming hot tub, is an eight-inch black bird that played a special role in Hawaiian history. Its blazing yellow leg feathers were used to fashion the spectacular capes and helmets of the *ali'i.* Even before white people came, this bird was ruthlessly pursued by specially trained hunters who captured it and plucked its feathers. Finally there is the **'akialoa,** a seven-inch greenish-yellow bird with a long, slender, curved bill.

The **nukupu'u,** extinct on the other islands except for a few on Maui, is found in Kaua'i's upper forests and on the borders of the Alaka'i Swamp. It's a five-inch bird with a drab green back and a bright yellow chest.

## Marine and Water Birds

Among the millions of birds that visit Kaua'i yearly, some of the most outstanding are its marine and water birds. Many beautiful individuals are

## ROOSTER ALERT

An ever-present entity on Kaua'i, and to a lesser extent on the other islands, is the feral rooster. Early Polynesians brought chickens with them on their journeys from the South Pacific. Later, Europeans and others brought different varieties of fowl, and the Filipinos brought their fighting cocks. Over the years these animals mingled, mixing breeds. Many were kept in people's backyards for their meat, eggs, or ability to slit the throats of other cocks. As in any rural place, these animals would herald the dawn by crowing.

Hurricane 'Iniki changed this bucolic setting in a dramatic way. In its fury, it set many of these previously caged animals free to wander where they might—and they did with abandon. In essence, they've become the island animal kingdom's homeless. Today they seem to be everywhere, and more than that, make a racket at all times of the day. It was impossible to round up all these fugitive birds, so now they roam. To make matters worse, many of the cane fields they used to hunt in search of food are gone, given over to other crops or let grow fallow. They look for food where they still can find it, often near residential areas. Many island residents now consider these birds a nuisance, and some hope the state will open a hunting season on them to help control their increasingly obnoxious population. In the meantime, if you hit one on the road, probably few will care.

# KAUA'I'S BOTANICAL GARDENS

For those interested in the flora of Kaua'i, beyond what can be seen out of the car window, a visit to the following will be both educational and inspiring.

**National Tropical Botanical Garden,** in Po'ipu, 808/332-7361, is the only research facility for tropical plants in the country and the premier botanical garden on Kaua'i. Guided tours of the Allerton Garden lasting about 2.5 hours are given daily except Sunday for $30 a person. Self-guided tours of the McBryde Garden run $15. The visitor center/museum/gift shop is open Mon.–Sun. 8 A.M.–5 P.M. for walk-in visitors. You can take a short self-guided walk around the visitor center garden, but to go into the main gardens you need advance reservations. Pricey but exceptional. See www.ntbg.org.

**Moir Gardens** is at the Kiahuna Plantation Resort in Po'ipu. Over a 27-year period during the mid-1900s, five acres of this former plantation site were cultivated with about 2,500 plants from Africa, the Americas, the Pacific, and India, and include cactus and orchid sections. Open daily for free during daylight hours for self-guided walks.

**Smith's Tropical Paradise,** 808/821-6892, a finely manicured and well-kept private botanical and cultural garden with a bountiful, beautiful collection of ordinary and exotic plants, is on 30 riverfront acres adjacent to the Wailua Marina. Have a look here before heading upcountry. Open daily 8:30 A.M.–4 P.M.; admission is $5.25 adults, $2.50 children.

**Limahuli Botanical Garden,** on Kaua'i's extreme north shore, 808/828-1053, open Tues.–Fri. and again on Sunday 9:30 A.M.–4 P.M., showcases tropical plants both ancient and modern. It's part of the National Tropical Botanical Gardens, and there are both self-guided and guided walking tours, $10 and $15, respectively. As you walk this three-quarter-mile loop trail, you'll pass patches of taro plants introduced to Hawaii by early Polynesians, living specimens of endangered native species, and post-contact tropicals, all while enjoying listening to the legends of the valley.

The private 240-acre **Na 'Aina Kai Botanical Gardens** near Kilauea has numerous individual gardens of various themes, a large tropical hardwood plantation, and bronze sculptures set throughout. Guided tours are given Tuesday, Wednesday, and Thursday only, and range from a 90-minute stroll for $25 to a five-hour walk and ride for $70. For information, call 808/828-0525; www.naainakai.com.

**Limahuli Botanical Garden**

seen at Kilauea Point National Wildlife Refuge, where they often nest in the trees on the cliff or on Moku'ae'ae Islet. Among them are the **Laysan albatross** *(moli)*, which also nests along Barking Sands; the **wedge-tailed shearwater** *(ua'u kani)*; and the **red-footed booby.** Kiting from the same cliffs is the **white-tailed tropic bird,** and one of the most amazing is the **great frigate bird,** which nests at Kilauea Point and is also seen along the Kalalau Trail and even at Po'ipu Beach.

## Government and Economy

Kaua'i County is composed of the inhabited islands of Kaua'i and Ni'ihau and the uninhabited islands of Ka'ula and Lehua. Lihu'e is the county seat. It's represented by one state senators elected from the 7th District and three state representatives, from the 14th, 15th, and 16th districts, currently all Democrats. The current mayor of Kaua'i is Bryan J. Baptiste, a Republican who won his first term of office in 2002. For internet information on the government of Kauai County see http://kauaigov.org.

### Tourism

Kaua'i is the fourth most visited island after O'ahu, Maui, and the Big Island. Regaining momentum after Hurricane 'Iniki, it is once again attracting just over one million visitors annually. That means that on any given day, on average, there will be about 19,000 visitors on the island. Approximately 6,800 accommodation units are available, averaging a 74 percent occupancy rate. At one time, Kaua'i was the most difficult island on which to build a resort because of a strong grassroots anti-development faction. This trend has been changing due to the recession that hit everyone after Hurricane 'Iwa and then 'Iniki scared off many tourists. Island residents realized how much their livelihood was tied to tourism, so tourists are now viewed more as visitors rather than unwelcome invaders. Also, the resorts on Kaua'i are first rate, and the developers are savvy enough to create "destination areas" instead of more high-rise boxes of rooms. That doesn't mean that development on Kaua'i is easy. It's not, as there are many strict regulations to meet, and there is still a vocal opposition to unplanned development.

### Agriculture

Agriculture still accounts for a hefty portion of Kaua'i's income. While **sugar,** for decades the backbone of the island's economy, has taken a downward dip, it's still grown commercially on the island although fewer acres are in production and only one mill still processes cane. Kaua'i produces about 12 percent of the state's diversified agricultural crop, with a strong yield in **papayas.** In 1982, California banned the importation of Kaua'i's papayas because they were sprayed with EDB, a fumigant used to control fruit flies. The chemical is no longer used, and the papaya market has rebounded. Hanalei Valley and many other smaller areas produce four million pounds of taro, which is quickly turned into poi, and the county produces two million pounds of guavas, as well as pineapples, beef, and pork for its own use. A growing aquaculture industry produces prawns, and a tropical flower sector is now emerging. In the mid-1980s, nearly 4,000 acres stretching from 'Ele'ele to Kalaheo were put into coffee, tea, and macadamia nut production. This was, reputedly, the largest economic rediversification project in the state. Since then, coffee on Kaua'i has turned into a thriving industry, and the island now produces more coffee beans— about 50 percent of the state total—than anywhere in the state, including the famed Kona Coast. On the south shore, some corn is raised and two huge seed production facilities west of Kekaha grow seed corn to be shipped all over the world.

### Military

The military influence on Kaua'i is small but vital. With about 125 military personnel and nearly one thousand civilian contract workers, the only sizable military facility on the island is **Pacific Missile Range Facility** at Barking Sands

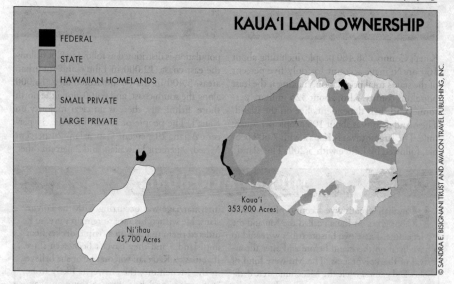

## KAUA'I LAND OWNERSHIP

- ■ FEDERAL
- ■ STATE
- ☐ HAWAIIAN HOMELANDS
- ☐ SMALL PRIVATE
- ☐ LARGE PRIVATE

Kaua'i
353,900 Acres

Ni'ihau
45,700 Acres

on the far west end of the island, which supports the testing of missiles, underwater warfare, and communications. In addition, an associated tracking facility sits on Makaha Ridge overlooking the south end of the Na Pali Coast. Operated by the Navy, this facility is available to all branches of the U.S. military, the Department of Defense, NASA, the Department of Energy, and select foreign military units.

## Land Ownership
Of Kaua'i County's total usable land area of approximately 399,000 acres, about 45,700 acres are on the privately owned island of Ni'ihau. The federal government owns just over 3,000 acres; the state has approximately 150,000 acres, of which 20,000 are Hawaiian Home Lands; and the county controls 600 acres, largely in parks. About 196,000 acres are privately owned, or 49 percent of the island. Of this, almost three-quarters is controlled by only half a dozen or so large landholders, mainly the Robinson Family, Amfac, Alexander & Baldwin, Grove Farm, Kamehameha Schools, Knudsen Estate, and Princeville Development Corporation.

## The People

Kaua'i County's 58,460 people, including about 160 on Ni'ihau, account for only five percent of the state's total population, making it the least populous county. Also, about 325 military personnel and their dependents live on the island. The island density is about 105 people per square mile. The largest town is Kapa'a with 7,600 people, followed by Lihu'e with 5,200. The island's population is distributed as follows: 18,500 along the east coast, 12,000 in Lihu'e and suburban areas, 5,400 in the Po'ipu/Koloa area, 16,000 along the south coast, and 6,400 along the north shore. Ethnically, there is no clear majority on Kaua'i. The people of Kaua'i include: 35 percent Asian, 29 percent Caucasian, 24 percent Mixed, 9 percent Hawaiian, and 2 percent other.

## MU AND MENEHUNE

Hawaiian legends give accounts of dwarf-like aborigines on Kaua'i called the Mu and the Menehune. These two hirsute tribes were said to have lived on the island before and after the arrival of the Polynesians. The Mu were fond of jokes and games, while the Menehune were dedicated workers, stonemasons par excellence, who could build monumental structures in just one night. Many stoneworks that can still be seen around the island are attributed to these hard-working nocturnal people.

Anthropological theory supports the legends that say that some non-Polynesian peoples actually did exist on Kaua'i. According to oral history, their chief felt that too much interplay and intermarriage was occurring with the Polynesians. He wished his race to remain pure, so he ordered them to leave on a "triple-decker floating island," and they haven't been seen since. If you ask a Kaua'ian whether he or she believes in the Menehune, the answer is likely to be, "Of course not! But, they're there anyway." Speculation holds that they may have been an entirely different race of people, or perhaps the remaining tribes of the first Polynesians. It's possible that they were cut off from the original culture for so long they developed their own separate culture, and the food supply became so diminished their very stature became reduced in comparison to other Polynesians.

## Festivals and Events

Island-specific information is also available on the web; check the calendar listings at www.kauaivisitorsbureau.org for events on Kaua'i.

### January
The annual Koke'e Natural History Museum **bird count** is held just at the new year. For avid birders. Call for information, 808/335-9975.

### February
The two-day **Waimea Town Celebration** is held at Waimea, the spot where Captain Cook first made contact. Food, entertainment, canoe races, and a partial marathon add to the fun. This annual event has been held for more than two decades.

### March
Midmonth features feminine beauty and grace at the **Miss Kaua'i Pageant,** at the Kaua'i Community College in Lihu'e.

The **Prince Kuhio Festival,** at Prince Kuhio Park in Po'ipu and in Lihu'e, features festivities from the era of Prince Kuhio along with a canoe regatta, music and dance, a 10K run, and a royal ball in period dress. A member of the royal family, Prince Kuhio was Hawaii's first delegate to the

## KAUA'I ARTS AND CULTURE INFORMATION

**State Foundation on Culture and the Arts,** 250 South Hotel Street., Honolulu, HI 96813, 808/586-0300, www.state.hi.us/sfca, was begun by the State Legislature in 1965 to preserve and promote Hawaii's diverse cultural, artistic, and historical heritage. It manages grants, maintains programs in folk arts and art in public places, and supports an events calendar.

**Garden Island Art Council,** 3116 Elua St., Lihu'e, HI 96766, 808/246-4561, www.kauai.net, giac@hawaiian.net, promotes arts and cultural events around the island.

For more than two decades, the **Kauai Community Players** troupe, P.O. Box 343, Lihu'e, HI 96766, 808/245-7700, www.hawaiian.net/~kcp, has been entertaining audiences year-round with adult and children's theater.

The **Kaua'i Society of Artists,** P.O. Box 3344, Lihu'e, HI 96766, 808/822-7179, ksa@hawaiian.net, holds public exhibitions at least three times a year. The Kaua'i Society of Artists periodically prints *Guide to Kaua'i Artists,* a magazine-size brochure on Kaua'i resident artists including brief descriptions of their work, studio addresses, contact information, and where their work can be found.

**Hawaii Children's Theater,** 808/246-8985, presents various live performances during the year.

College, community, and state events, and concerts, film, theater, and pageants are performed year-round at the **Kaua'i Community College Performing Arts Center** on the college campus in Puhi, 808/245-8270, www.kauaiarts.org.

U.S. Congress. Held for more than 30 years on March 26, his birthday.

## April

Enjoy the best that the island has to offer at the **Annual School Art Festival,** at the Kaua'i Museum.

## May

**Armed Forces Week** brings military open houses, concerts, and displays in and around the islands.

The four-day **Prince Albert Music Festival** takes place at the Princeville Hotel on the north shore and features a combination of classical music, slack-key guitar, and hula demonstrations, plus fashions, food, and crafts.

## June

**Banana Poka Festival** at the Koke'e Natural History Museum is an outdoor educational fair that also features foot and bike races.

## July

**Fourth of July** offers parades and other events, including the island's best fireworks show at Vidinha Stadium in Lihu'e. Fireworks are also shot off at the Pacific Missile Range Facility west of Kekaha.

The **Garden Island Championship Canoe Races** takes place at different locations on the island in late July. This and other canoe events are sponsored by Garden Island Canoe Racing Association.

**Koloa Plantation Days** celebrates Hawaii's plantation life with a parade, crafts fair, music and dance entertainment, ethnic foods, rodeo, and sports competitions. Events take place in and around Koloa.

## August

The annual **Kaua'i-Tahiti Fete** includes musical performances, hula competitions, and arts and crafts.

At the **Kaua'i County Fair** in late-August, gardeners, stockmen, and craftspeople of the Garden Island display their wares at Vidinha Stadium in Lihu'e. There are pageantry, great local foods, and terrific bargains to be had. Admission is $3 adults and $2 for kids.

## September

The **Mokihana Festival,** a week-long event

## KAUA'I'S MUSEUMS AND HISTORICAL SOCIETY

**Grove Farm Homestead**, P.O. Box 1631, Lihu'e, HI 96766, 808/245-3202, is open by reservation for guided tours Monday, Wednesday, and Thursday at 10 a.m. and 1 p.m. Donations requested are adults $5 and children 2–12 $2. This is the homestead of early sugar planter George N. Wilcox. Plantation owner's house, workers' cottages, outbuildings, and garden. Definitely worth a visit.

**Kaua'i Historical Society**, P.O. Box 1778, Lihu'e, HI 96766, 808/245-3373, www.kauaihistorical-society.org, was established in 1914. The society remains Kaua'i's only general historical archive, preserving printed and audio material, photographs, maps, and a variety of other objects. Members work toward the preservation of historical and cultural sites, offer educational programs, and organize periodic tours. Located in the historic county building in Lihu'e, the archives are free and open to the public for research weekdays by appointment.

**Kaua'i Museum**, 4428 Rice St., Lihu'e, HI 96766, 808/245-6931, www.kauaimuseum.org, is open Mon.–Fri. 9 A.M.–4 P.M. and Saturday 10 A.M.–4 P.M. Admission is adults $5, seniors $4, students 13–17 $3, children 6–12 $1. Monday, Tuesday, and Thursday a free tour at 10 A.M. is included with admission. The story of Kaua'i and Ni'ihau is told through art and ethnic exhibits. Hawaiiana books, maps, and prints are available at the museum shop.

**Koke'e Natural History Museum**, P.O. Box 100, Kekaha, HI 96752, 808/335-9975, www.aloha.net/~kokee, is open daily 10 A.M.–4 P.M.; $1 donation. Exhibits interpret the geology and unique plants and animals of Kaua'i's mountain wilderness.

Great to visit while at Waimea Canyon and Koke'e State Park.

**Wai'oli Mission House**, 808/245-3202, run by the same group that shows Grove Farm Homestead, is open Tuesday, Thursday, and Saturday 9 A.M.–3 P.M. No reservations are needed. Entrance by donation.

The **Hawaiian Art Museum**, 808/827-8383, at the Princeville Center, is a small collection of cultural artifacts from Hawaii and the Pacific that belong to Aloha International, an organization dedicated to the Hawaiian practice of *huna*. Open by appointment only.

The **Kaua'i Children's Discovery Museum**, 808/823-8222, under the whale tower at the Kauai Village Shopping Center in Kapa'a, is a hands-on museum dedicated to science, culture, and the arts as it relates to Hawaii, its past, and its environment. Open Tues.–Sat. 9 A.M.–5 P.M., and Monday 9 A.M.–5 P.M. during special events; admission $3.50 for children, $4.50 for adults.

The **Faye Museum** at the Waimea Plantation Cottages, 808/338-1625, is a small museum presenting photographs and artifacts of the sugar plantation years of west Kaua'i. Open daily 9 A.M.–9 P.M.; entrance free.

For a short historical perspective on coffee, a few artifacts, and the story on coffee production and processing on Kaua'i, stop in at the **Kauai Coffee Company Museum** in Numila, 808/335-0813.

with festivities at various locations along the south coast, is a grassroots festival featuring lei-making, hula, music competition and performance, along with folk-arts workshops and local entertainment.

## October

The annual one-day **Coconut Festival** held in on the Coconut Coast at Kapaʻa Beach park includes food, games, crafts, and performances.

**Eo E Emalani I Alakaʻi** commemorates Queen Emma's journey to Kokeʻe and the Alakaʻi Swamp. Activities include hula performances, chants, Hawaiian music, and craft demonstra-tions. Held at the Kokeʻe Natural History Museum at Kokeʻe State Park.

## November

November 11 is **Veterans Day.** All islands have parades. Get information through the local newspaper or contact the Kauaʻi Chamber of Commerce.

## December

The **Christmas Craft Fair** is an annual event known for attracting the island's best in hand-crafted items and home-baked goodies. At the Kauaʻi Museum, Lihuʻe, 808/245-6931.

# Sports and Recreation

Kauaʻi is an exciting island for all types of sports enthusiasts, with hiking, golf, tennis, hunting, and all manner of water sports, and it's a magnificent island to explore by land, sea, or air. You can ride a horse, camp at hidden reaches of the Na Pali Coast, or simply relax on a cruise. The following should start the fun rolling.

## BEACHES

Kauaʻi has more beach per shoreline mile than any of the other major Hawaiian Islands—about 50 miles of it. With so many beaches to choose from, the problem on Kauaʻi is picking which one to visit. If you venture farther than the immediate area of your hotel, the following will help in deciding just where you'd like to romp about. This is a simple listing only. For more details see the specific listings in the appropriate travel chapters.

### Lihuʻe Area

**Kalapaki Beach** in Lihuʻe is one of the best on the island, convenient to Kauaʻi's principal town center. This beach's gentle wave action is just right for learning how to bodysurf or ride the boogie board; snorkeling is fair. Two small crescent beaches lie near Ninini Lighthouse just below the Kauai Lagoons golf course. Water is rougher there, with much exposed rock; snor-keling should be done on calm days only. Also accessible but less frequented is **Hanamaʻulu Beach,** just up the coast, with a lagoon, picnic spots, and camping.

### East Side

**Lydgate Beach** has two pools bounded by large lava rocks, and the beaches below Wailua Municipal Golf Course offer seclusion in sheltered coves where there's fine snorkeling. **Wailua Beach,** fronting the Coco Palms, is also fine but best during calm weather. **Waipouli Beach** and **Kapaʻa Beach** flank the well-developed town of Kapaʻa, and both are better for beach combing than swimming. North of there are **Kealia Beach** and the little-frequented **Donkey Beach,** both known for good surfing. The undertow is quite strong at Donkey Beach, so don't venture out too far if you don't swim well. **Anahola Beach,** at the south end of Anahola Bay, has safe swimming in a protected cove, freshwater swimming in the stream that empties into the bay, picnicking, and camping. Snorkel a short distance up the shore to where the reef comes in close—an area where locals come for shore fishing. Still farther north is **Moloaʻa Beach,** a little-visited, picture-perfect, half-moon swath of sand.

### North Kauaʻi

Just beyond Kilauea is **Secret Beach,** all that its

name implies. At the end of a tiny dirt road, the start of which eludes many people, and down a steep back, is this huge stretch of white sand. You're sure to find it nearly empty. Exposed to the open ocean, waves at this beach can be furious. A bit farther on is **Kalihiwai Beach,** great for swimming and bodysurfing during the right conditions. The park at **'Anini Beach** is a great place to snorkel because it has the longest exposed reef in Kaua'i, and it's a wonderful place to learn sailboarding because of the shallow water inside the reef.

**Hanalei Bay** is a prime spot on the north coast. Swim at the mouth of the Hanalei River or at various spots along this long crescent. Experienced surfers ride the waves below the Princeville Hotel; snorkeling is good closer to the cliffs. West of Hanalei is **Lumaha'i Beach,** a beautiful curve of white sand backed by cliffs and thick jungle that was the silent star of the movie *South Pacific.* The inviting water here has a fierce riptide, so enter only when the water is calm. **Ha'ena Beach** and nearby **Tunnels** are terrific swimming and snorkeling spots. At the end of the road is **Ke'e Beach,** a popular place with some amenities, fine swimming in summer, and good snorkeling.

Many secluded beaches at the foot of the Na Pali cliffs dot the coast to the west along the Kalalau Trail. **Hanakapi'ai Beach** is reached after one hour on the trail and is fine for sunbathing; the water, especially in winter, can be torturous, so stay out. **Kalalau Beach** is a full day's hike down this spectacular coast. Beyond that, Nu'alolo Kai and Miloli'i beaches can only be reached by boat.

## South Kaua'i

The **Po'ipu Beach** area is the most developed on the island—accommodating, tame, and relaxing. You can swim, snorkel, and bodysurf here to your heart's content. The eastern end of this beach is referred to as **Brennecke Beach.** Fronting the Hyatt Regency is **Shipwreck Beach,** a place where many find the boogie boarding the best. Beyond that is the lonely expanse of **Maha'ulepu Beach** with its windswept dunes and silence.

Down the coast are **Salt Pond Beach,** one of the island's best and good for swimming and sailboarding, and **Pakala Beach,** popular with surfers but also good for swimming and snorkeling. The golden strand of **Kekaha Beach** runs

Polihale Beach spreads out from the south end of the Na Pali cliffs.

for miles with excellent swimming, snorkeling, and surfing, and stretches into the Pacific Missile Range Facility at Barking Sands, where you can go, with permission, for swimming, surfing, and sunning, and good views of Ni'ihau when no military exercises are in progress.

**Polihale Beach** is the end of the road. Swimming is not the best as the surf is high and the undertow strong, but walk along the shore for a view of the south end of the great Na Pali cliffs. It's a treat.

# SCUBA AND SNORKELING
## Scuba

Kaua'i is an excellent place to scuba dive. Several dozen frequented dive spots surround the island. Most on the south and north shores are good for all levels of divers, and the few off the east and west coasts are generally for experienced divers. The south shore dive sites are mostly between Po'ipu Beach and Spouting Horn, while the north shore dive sites lie between Hanalei and Ke'e Beach. By and large, boat dives go to the south shore in winter and the north shore in summer. There is only one good shore dive spot on Kaua'i and that's at Koloa Landing on the south shore. In addition, some dive tours go to Lehua Island off the north point of Ni'ihau. Not only is Lehua undisturbed, but there is very little runoff from the islands to cloud the water. Lehua reputedly has some of the best diving in the state with exceptionally clear water and deep drop-offs, but it's definitely for experienced and advanced divers only. Companies that offer dive tours vary their sites depending upon weather and water conditions and the skill level of the group.

## Scuba Shops and Tour Companies

**Fathom Five Divers,** 808/742-6991 or 800/972-3078, www.fathomfive.com, open daily 9 A.M.–6 P.M. in Koloa, is a retail store and complete diving center offering lessons, certification, rentals, and tours. Maximum of six passengers per boat.

Down the road at Po'ipu Plaza is **Seasport Divers,** 808/742-9303 or 800/685-5889, www.kauaiscubadiving.com, a scuba/snorkel shop that does sales, rental, certification, and both diving and snorkeling tours.

Other south shore diving companies are **Ocean Odyssey,** 808/245-8661, and **Mana Divers,** 808/742-9849.

A fine shop with a good reputation in Kapa'a is **Dive Kauai,** 808/822-0452 or 800/828-3483, www.divekauai.com, with retail, rental, certification classes, and tours.

Also in Kapa'a are **Bubbles Below,** 808/822-3483, www.aloha.net/~kaimanu; **Sunrise Diving Adventures,** 808/822-7333; and **Wet and Wonderful,** 808/822-0211.

On the north shore, try **North Shore Divers,** 808/826-1921.

In addition, many hotels have these or other companies run scuba classes at their hotel pools or organize tours from their beach activities booths.

## Snorkeling

The following are some of the best and safest snorkeling sites on Kaua'i. **Ke'e Beach,** at the end of the road at Ha'ena, is tops (definitely stay inside the reef). **Tunnels** has a wonderful view of the mountains (*experienced snorkelers only* at the reef edge; beginners should stay on top of the reef). **'Anini Beach,** almost always gentle and friendly for day outings, is terrific for sailboarding as well. **Lydgate State Park** is the safest for families and children. **Po'ipu Beach,** which is also safe for children, has the best entry to the right of the sand spit. **Koloa Landing,** an entry point for scuba shore dives, is a frequent haunt of sea turtles and eels. **Prince Kuhio Park** is best known for the turtles; and **Lawa'i Beach,** along Lawa'i Rd. leading to the Spouting Horn, has good coral and fish, and sometimes seals.

Before you put your mask on, however, ask at a snorkel shop which locations are best for the season and water conditions. Inquire about types of fish and other sea creatures you might expect to see, water clarity, entry points, surf condition, water currents, and parking.

## Snorkel Rentals and Tours

Good old **Snorkel Bob's,** at 4-734 Kuhio Hwy. in Waipouli, 808/823-9433, and also in Koloa at 3236 Po'ipu Rd., 808/742-2206, www.snorkel-

KAUA'I

bob.com, offers some of the best deals for snorkel gear rental in Hawaii (free snorkeling maps and advice). Gear runs $2.50 a day or $9 a week for a low-end set, $4.50 a day or $19 a week for mid-range gear, to $6.50 a day or $29 a week for the best Bob has to offer. Dry snorkel and prescription lenses are available. This gear can be taken to other islands and turned in at any Snorkel Bob's location. Shops are open daily 8 A.M.–5 P.M., but there is a night drop box at both locations.

**Kauai Water Ski and Surf Co.,** in the Kinipopo Shopping Village, 4-356 Kuhio Hwy. in Kapa'a, 808/822-3574, open daily 9 A.M.–7 P.M., is a complete water-sports shop that offers quality snorkel gear by the day or week at competitive prices. Clothing and other water sport gear is available.

At a perfect location across from Po'ipu Beach County Park is **Nukumoi Surf Co.,** 808/742-8019. Open daily 8:30 A.M.–7 P.M., the store rents complete sets of snorkel gear or fins and masks separately. Also available are boogie boards,

surfboards, and an assortment of umbrellas, chairs, coolers, and life preservers. A full line of water equipment and clothing is for sale.

The **Captain's Cargo Company,** in downtown Waimea (also the office of Liko Kaua'i Cruises), 808/338-0333, rents snorkel gear, arranges boat tours, and sells water clothing.

Other shops to check for snorkel gear are **Seasport Divers,** 808/742-9303 in Po'ipu; **Pedal and Paddle,** 808/826-9069, the **Hanalei Surf Co.,** 808/826-9000, and **Kayak Kaua'i,** 808/826-9844, all in Hanalei.

**Sea Fun Kauai,** 808/245-6400, offers half-day, shore-based, guided snorkeling tours, with equipment and snacks included, for $75 adult and $62.50 for children 5–12. Locations change depending upon the weather.

Many sailing boats and catamarans incorporate snorkeling into the sailing trip (see below), and some diving and fishing companies also offer snorkeling as an option.

For those interested in snuba, try **Snuba**

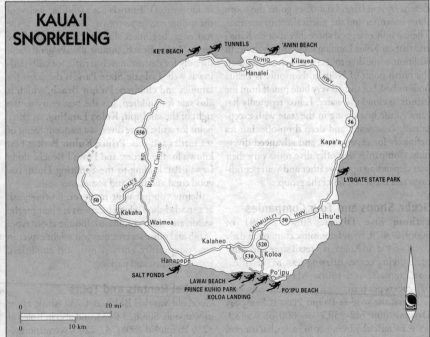

KAUA'I SNORKELING

Tours of Kaua'i, 808/823-8912, www.hshawaii.com/kvp/snuba, which offers guided tours off Po'ipu's Lawa'i Beach. The cost is $55 for 90 minutes.

## CATCHING WAVES

### Surfing

Surfing has long been the premier water sport in Hawaii. Locals and, now, "surfies" from all over the world know where the best waves are and when they come. While Anahola Beach was a traditional surfing spot on Kaua'i for Hawaiians of yesterday, the north shore has the beaches of choice today. The east side of Hanalei Bay provides a good roll in winter for experts, as does Tunnels. Quarry Beach, near Kilauea, and Kealia Beach and Donkey Beach, both north of Kapa'a, are used mostly by locals. On the south coast, the surfers' favorite is the west end of Po'ipu Beach, or west of there, near Pakala. Both Lawa'i Beach and Salt Ponds Beach are used if conditions are right, and waves for all levels can be found along the lengthy Kekaha Beach on the west end.

Boogie boarding is also a fun sport on smaller waves close to shore. Some well-known boogie board beaches are Brennecke Beach and Shipwreck Beach in Po'ipu, Kalihiwai Beach near Kilauea, and Black Pot Beach on Hanalei Bay.

### Surfing Lessons and Surf Shops

Surfing lessons are available; they include the free use of a surf board that fits your level, a 60- to 90-minute lesson with free surf time after that, and dry land instruction before entering the water. Most beginning lessons are in small groups of fewer than half a dozen and usually run about $35–50 an hour, although some companies offer private instruction. Try world champion Margo Oberg and her staff at **Margo Oberg's Surfing School** on Po'ipu Beach. Make reservations through Nukumoi Surf Co., 808/742-8019. **Kauai Surf School,** 808/332-7411, also uses Po'ipu Beach. In Lihu'e, **Pete's Surf School,** 808/639-4109, or **Aikane Surf School,** 808/652-7873, are two to try. **Hanalei Surf School,** 808/826-9283, and **Learn To Surf,** 808/826-7612, are two that operate in Hanalei.

**Kauai Water Ski and Surf Co.,** in the Kinipopo Shopping Village, Wailua, 808/822-3574, is a complete water-sports shop that offers surfboard and boogie board rentals by the day or week. Boogie boards run $5/day, surfboards $10–20/day, and a car rack with board rental is $5 a day.

**Seasport Divers,** located at the Po'ipu Plaza, 2827 Po'ipu Rd., 808/742-9303 or 800/685-5889, offers rental boards and surfing lessons.

Across from Po'ipu Beach, **Nukumoi Surf Co.,** 808/742-8019, rents hard board surfboards for experiences riders only at $25 a day or $75 a week.

**Hanalei Surf Co.,** 808/826-9000, just a few minutes from a great beginners' surfing area at Hanalei, offers surfing lessons or board rentals without lessons (boogie boards, too). Hanalei Bay goes completely flat in summer, so call ahead for surfing conditions.

Just down the road in Hanalei, **Kai Kane,** 808/826-5594, also sells and rents surfboards and boogie boards.

### Sailboarding

Sailboarding has become very popular on Kaua'i in the last few years. The best spots for beginners are 'Anini Beach on the north coast, Po'ipu Beach on the south, and Kalapaki Beach in Lihu'e. More challenging is Salt Ponds Beach on the west end, and for the advanced only, Ha'ena Beach on the north coast is preferred, or Tunnels just down the way. On the south shore, try Maha'ulepu Beach east of Po'ipu. Ask at water sport shops for other local favorites that would match your ability.

**Anini Beach Windsurfing,** 808/826-9463, is a one-man operation. Owner Keith Kabe will load his truck with sailboarding gear and come to you. Well known on the north shore, Keith will tailor your sailboarding lesson to fit your ability. Rentals for all levels available.

**Windsurf Kauai,** owned by Celeste Harvel, 808/828-6838, specializes in beginner lessons. Three-hour group lessons (six people maximum) are $70 with equipment. Those who already know how can rent sailboards here as well.

**Kalapaki Beach Boys,** at the Marriott in Lihu'e, 808/246-9661, rents sailboards and offers lessons.

KAUA'I

## WATER-SKIING

When you think of recreation on Kaua'i, water-skiing doesn't necessarily come to mind. **Kauai Water Ski and Surf Co.,** at Kinipopo Shopping Village in Wailua, is the island's only water-skiing company, and there is only one place where skiing it's permitted. Skimming placid Wailua River, freshwater skiers pass tour boats and kayaks going to and from the Fern Grotto. Water-skiing fees run $30 for one tow, $55 a half hour, and $100 an hour, including boat, driver, gas, skis, and other equipment. Instruction at all levels can be arranged; weekdays only.

## OCEAN TOURS

You've only seen half of Kaua'i until you've seen it from the sea. Ocean tours include fishing, sailing, whale-watching, diving, and snorkeling on sailboats, catamarans, and Zodiacs. Most ocean tours run along the Na Pali Coast, but when weather conditions are not good they may travel along the south-central coast. Some run out to

An ocean tour is one of the best ways to get close to the impressive Na Pali Coast.

Lehua Island, and fishing boats go even farther afield. The majority of tour boats run out of Port Allen Harbor on the south shore near Hanapepe, while others use Nawiliwili Harbor in Lihu'e, Kukui'ula Harbor near Po'ipu, and Kikiaola Harbor west of Waimea.

### Zodiacs

The exact opposite experience from the tame Wailua River trip is an adventurous ride down the Na Pali Coast in a very tough, motorized rubber raft. A Zodiac looks like a big horseshoe-shaped inner tube that bends and undulates with the waves like a floating waterbed. Most now come with a rigid bottom. These seaworthy craft, powered by twin engines, have separate air chambers for unsinkable safety. Seating a dozen or so, they take you for a thrilling ride down the coast, pausing along the way to whisk you into caves and caverns. The wind generally picks up in the afternoon, so for a more comfortable ride, book the morning cruise. Other tours run along the south. All are popular so make reservations. Bring a bathing suit, snorkel gear, camera (in a plastic bag for protection), and a windbreaker for the return ride; snacks are provided. Summer weather permits excursions almost every day, but winter's swells are turbulent, and these experienced seamen won't go if it's too rough. Take their word for it! Pregnant women and individuals with bad backs are advised not to ride.

Oldest and best known of the Zodiac companies is **Captain Zodiac,** 808/826-9371 or 800/422-7824, www.captainzodiackauai.com, owned and operated by "Captain Zodiac," Clancy Greff—which also operates on the Big Island of Hawai'i. From Port Allen Harbor, Captain Zodiac runs a 36-foot craft, one of the largest in the islands, making morning and afternoon trips up the Na Pali coast for $115–129. Whale-watching tours are also offered in season.

**Napali Explorer,** 808/338-9999 or 877/335-9909, www.napali-explorer.com, runs its expeditions from Waimea on ridged-bottom rafts. One of their boats is a souped-up version of the typical zodiac, with cushion seats, a shade canopy, swim step and a restroom. Five-hour morning and afternoon rides up the Na Pali Coast with a possible snorkeling stop at Nu'alolo Kai run $118. If the seas are just too rough to snorkel, they may give you a ride the full length of the coast. A winter scenic ride and the two-hour whalewatching tours are both offered for $79. All water equipment is provided, and snacks are offered on the longer trips.

Leaving from Kikiaola Harbor in Kekaha, **Na Pali Riders,** 808/742-6331, www.na-paliriders.com, run morning and afternoon trips for $120

Another reputable company is **Kauai Sea Tours,** 808/826-7254 or 800/733-7997, www.kauaiseatours.com, which runs comparable tours from Port Allen Harbor.

**Poipu Zodiaz Tourz,** 808/742-7422, www.ztourz.com, runs year-round from Kukui'ula Harbor near Po'ipu and offers trips along the south coast. Morning and afternoon trips, plus whalewatching tours in winter run $79.

## Catamarans and Sailboats

For an adventure with a smooth ride, try a catamaran or a sailboat. Many of the companies that do water adventures on Kaua'i run power catamarans—only one true sailing ship plies these waters. Catamarans (cats) ride on two widely spaced hulls with a superstructure between; some, called trimarans, have a third hull down the middle. Each comes with some shaded seating area to protect from the sun and on-board toilets and freshwater showers. All provide smooth sailing down the coast and get you back in great comfort. Some of the cats are set up with sails and take advantage of it when the winds are right. These ships primarily run swim/snorkel tours up the Na Pali Coast, but some also have sunset tours along the south coast and, during winter, whale-watching tours. A few offer scuba dives for an extra charge. They offer plenty of fun, give you great views of the coast, and provide complimentary snacks along the way. Those with sails throw in the added experience of slicing through the water without the distraction of motors. Most tour companies run their boats out of Port Allen Harbor, although one goes out of Kikiaola Harbor, and a few use Hanalei as a base. Options vary, so when calling, be sure to ask about the particulars of each trip.

**Liko Kaua'i Cruises,** 808/338-0333 or 888/732-5456, www.loko-kauai.com, is a cruise company owned and operated by native Hawaiian Captain Liko Ho'okano. Unlike all the other cruises, Liko Kaua'i takes you on a 49-foot power catamaran down the Na Pali Coast from the west end, departing from Kikiaola Harbor just two miles from Waimea. The four- to five-hour tour meets at 7 A.M. at the offices of Captain's Cargo Company in Waimea. The rates are $125 for adults and $80 for children 4–14. During the summer months, afternoon snorkel tours are given and sunset tours are also available at $95 adult and $60 children.

**A Na Pali Eco Adventures,** 808/826-6804 Or 800/659-6804, www.napali.com, provides environmentally responsible interpretive tours in its specially outfitted catamarans (they burn recycled vegetable oil) and sails from Port Allen harbor. In addition to snorkeling activities, the crew will teach you about marine ecology and the culture of the island. Rates are $129 for a six-hour tour and $115 for a five-hour tour, both snorkel tours, and $85 for a four-hour cruise. In season, whalewatching tours run $49–105 depending upon length.

**Blue Dolphin Charters,** 808/335-5553, welcomes you aboard its 63-foot power catamaran on which you can sail, snorkel, scuba dive, use the water slide, photograph spinning dolphins, and watch the sun go down. All trips depart from Port Allen Harbor except for Po'ipu Sunset cruise which leaves from Kukui'ula Harbor. Tours include a five- to six-hour Na Pali Coast snorkel and scuba run for $109 and a seven-hour Ni'ihau snorkel and scuba trip for $149 that also takes in part of the Na Pali coast. The additional fee for diving is $25. Blue Dolphin is one of only two companies that head to the north end of Ni'ihau and Lehua Rock. Also offered are a three-hour Na Pali sunset cruise for $75 and the two-hour Po'ipu sunset tour for $50. All tours run daily except for the Ni'ihau trip which goes on Tues., and Friday.

Running under sail is possible with Captain Andy of **Capt. Andy's Sailing Adventures,** 808/335-6833 or 800/535-0830, www.sailing-hawaii.com. He lets the wind power his 65-foot catamaran as much as possible. Capt. Andy will take you for a morning of sailing up the Na Pali coast, snorkeling, and beachcombing, or an afternoon snorkel and sunset cruise also along the Na Pali coast, either for $109. Both these tours leave from Port Allen. The two-hour sunset cruise for $59 leaves from Kukui'ula Harbor near Po'ipu. Whalewatching tours along the south coast are available in season. Kids always get discounts.

**Holoholo Charters,** 808/335-0815 or 800/848-6130, www.holoholo-charters.com, also runs out of Port Allen Harbor. Its two cats, one motorized and one for sailing, offer various options including a three-hour sunset cruise for $79, a full-day cruise to Ni'ihau for snorkeling and sightseeing for $156, and morning and afternoon sailing snorkel trips up the Na Pali coast for $109.

Also try **Catamaran Kahanu,** 808/335-3577 or 888/213-7711, www.catamarankahanu.com, at Port Allen. Operated by a family whose ancestors may have lived along the Na Pali coast, you'll get an intimate experience on the morning Na Pali Coast tour for $105 or the afternoon sightseeing tour for $85.

**Kauai Sea Tours,** 808/826-7254 or 800/733-7997, www.kauaiseatours.com, also offers similar catamaran tours at similar prices out of Port Allen.

One of the few companies to use Hanalei Bay is **Na Pali Catamarans,** 808/826-6853. Here you must canoe from shore to a waiting power catamaran, which is smaller at 32 feet and only holds 15 passengers. From there you cruise the Na Pali Coast from the east. A four-hour snorkeling tour runs $125 and a three-hour whale-watching tour is $90.

For a larger catamaran, the only sailing cat out of Hanalei, try **Captain Sundown,** 808/826-5585, www.captainsundown.com. Captain Sundown has a morning snorkel tour for $130 and an afternoon sunset tour for $75.

While in Lihu'e, ride with **Rainbow Runner,** 808/632-0202, which offers a 1.5-hour sail out of Nawiliwili Harbor for $59.

**Bluewater Sailing,** 808/828-1142, runs the 42-foot ketch-rigged yacht *Lady Leanne II* out of Port Allen. This is Kaua'i's only monohull charter sailing vessel. Half-day rates are $105 for adults or $85 for kids, and sunset sails run $60 for adults or $55 for kids. All-day private charters can also be arranged.

## Whale-Watching Cruises

Boats generally run from January through April, but it all depends on how many whales are about and how long they stay. Many of the above Zodiac and catamaran charter companies run whale-watching tours in season.

## Kayaking

Kayaking has become very popular in Hawaii, and kayaking in Kaua'i is good. Sea kayaking is predominant, but on Kaua'i, at least three rivers can be kayaked as well. Wailua River runs up to Fern Grotto from the town of Wailua, Hule'ia River slides by the Alakoko Fishpond outside Lihu'e, and the Hanalei River skirts the Hanalei Wildlife Reserve on the north shore. The two stretches of ocean most popular with kayakers on Kaua'i are the Kipu Kai area just south of Lihu'e on the south shore and the magnificent Na Pali Coast on the north shore. Kipu Kai is a secluded bowl-shaped valley that opens onto a fine beach and is backed by a jagged mountain ridge—only one private road runs to the cattle ranch that occupies this property. It's less than an hour over the water from Lihu'e. Because of water conditions, this stretch is best in the winter. North shore water conditions are better in the summer; water is generally flattest then so you'll be fighting the wind and waves less. Because the north coast sea current runs from east to west, kayak along the Na Pali Coast from Ha'ena to Polihale, not the other way around. Make sure you save enough strength for the return trip.

Check with one of the kayak shops to get the latest information about sea conditions and consider taking an organized tour, offered by many of the kayak shops around the island. At times, permits for tours along both the north and south shores are rescinded, so check to see what's happening when you are there. Whether you paddle on the river or ocean, wear a swimsuit or shorts and T-shirt you don't mind getting wet, and tabi or some type of water shoe or sandal. Be sure to take a brimmed hat and sunglasses, put on sunscreen, take a towel and a dry change of clothes (a dry bag is usually provided on tours), and don't forget drinking water and snacks. A windbreaker is recommended for the open ocean. Most shops want day-rental kayaks back by 5 P.M.

Kayaks (the sit-upon kind) generally rent for about $25 single or $50 tandem. Some shops rent carriers to haul the kayak yourself. A few are near a launch site, but many have shops away from the water, so you have to strap the kayak to a rack and drive to the put-in point.

**Outfitters Kauai** in Po'ipu, 808/742-9667 or 888/742-9887, www.outfitterskauai.com, offers a seven-hour South Shore Trip for $119 for those in good physical condition, and a full-day summertime-only Na Pali Day Trip Tour for $165 that runs the whole length of the coast from Ha'ena to Polihale. Also offered are tours on both the Hule'ia and Wailea rivers for $80 and $94, respectively.

Also offering a full-day tour along the Na Pali Coast from May–Sept. is **Na Pali Kayak Tours,** 808/826-8968; www.kauai-kayaking.net. Launching from the Ha'ena State Park beach, the group heads down the coast for a day of exploration and returns to the set-in point by late afternoon. Groups are limited to half a dozen or so and the fee is $165 per person. This is a strenuous 12-hour day, so you must be physically fit. Meet in Hanalei at 6 A.M. Transportation to/from the launch site is provided as are snacks and drinks.

**Kayak Kauai** in Hanalei, 808/826-9844 or 800/437-3507, www.kayakkauai.com, open daily 8 A.M.–5 P.M., has extensive experience-its owners are world-class kayak experts and the staff are sensitive people who provide good service while having a good time. Two-person river kayaks rent for $50 per day and one-person kayaks for $26; sea kayaks are $60 and $35, respectively. Lessons, shuttle service, and storage are also available. From May to September, the company leads ocean kayak tours up the Na Pali coast for $165. An all-day affair, this tour is for those who are in good shape and do well on the water. During the winter, tours are done on the south coast for $115. A half-day Hanalei River tour is offered year-round for $60, and a paddle up the Wailua River to the Secret Falls runs $85. Multi-day trips are also available. All of the above provide good

family-style fun. Kayak Kauai also rents and sells surfboards, boogie boards, snorkel gear, other beach and water equipment, and camping gear. Staff will rig your car to carry the kayak and will provide drop-off and pick-up service at Ke'e Beach for $15 or at Polihale State Park for $225 for five persons or less, otherwise $45 per person—when it's safe to be on the ocean.

**Kauai Water Ski and Surf,** 808/822-3574, in the Kinipopo Shopping Village, Wailua, is a complete water-sports shop that offers daily kayak rentals: $50 a day tandem, $25 a day single seat. Others in the Wailua/Kapa'a area for tours and rentals are: **Paradise Outdoor Adventures,** 808/822-1112, http://kayakers.com; **Wailua River Kayak Adventures,** 808/822-5795; **Kayak Wailua,** 808/822-3388, http://kayakwailua.com; and **Duke's Kayak Adventures,** 808/822-4000.

For the Hule'ia River tours, try **Aloha Canoes and Kayak,** 808/246-6804, www.hawai-ikayaks.com, at the Kalapaki Marketplace in Nawiliwili, or **Island Adventures,** 808/245-9662, www.kauaifun, at Nawiliwili Harbor. In Hanalei, **Kayak Adventures,** 808/826-9340, www.extreme-hawaii.com/kayak, will take care of you.

## RIVER CRUISE

Kaua'i has the only navigable river in Hawaii. Covered barges cruise the Wailua River, where *ali'i* once ruled, leaving the Wailua Marina and proceeding a couple of miles upriver to the Fern Grotto. This is a tourist activity, pure and simple, but the setting is lovely if you can get beyond the hype and hordes of people. Two companies service this route and run several trips a day for a reasonable fee. See the **Wailua** chapter for details.

## FISHING
### Deep-Sea Fishing Charters

There are excellent fishing grounds off Kaua'i, especially around Ni'ihau, and a few charter boats for hire. Most are berthed at Nawiliwili Harbor, with some on the north coast and at least one in Kekaha.

The following charter boats have good reputations, and all leave from Nawiliwili Small

**KAUA'I**

Boat Harbor. **Wild Bill's Fishing Charters,** 808/822-5963, offers a modern 28-foot Radon Sportfisher. **Hana Pa'a Charters,** 808/823-6031, www.fishkauai.com, has a 38-foot Betram for trolling, bottom fishing, or night fishing. **True Blue Charters,** 808/246-9662, has the biggest and most luxurious fishing boat on the island, the 55-foot *Konane Star.* Also luxurious are the 38- and 42-foot Bertrams run by **Kai Bear Sportfishing Charters,** 808/652-4556, www.kaibear.com.

**Sport Fishing Kauai,** 808/742-7013, www.fishing-kauai-hawaii.com, with 28- and 38-foot Bertrams, *Kauai Kai* and *Vida Del Mar II* leave out of Port Allen Harbor and Kukui'ula Harbor. Farther to the west, **Kekaha Fishing Company,** 808/337-2700, takes the *Susan Lee* out of the Kikiaola Harbor at Kekaha.

*Sea Breeze V* from **Anini Fishing Charters,** 808/828-1285, with skipper Bob Kutkowski, specializes in sport and bottom fishing. He and Robert McReynolds of **North Shore Charters,** 808/828-1379, both leave from 'Anini Beach and fish the waters of the north coast. Going with either of these guys is perhaps the best introduction to sportfishing in Kaua'i.

## Freshwater Fishing

Kaua'i has trout and bass. Rainbow trout were introduced in 1920 and thrive in 13 miles of fishable streams, ditches, and reservoirs in the Koke'e Public Fishing Area. Large and small bass and the basslike *tucunare* are also popular game fish on Kaua'i. Introduced in 1908, they're hooked in reservoirs and in the Wailua River and its feeder streams.

Commercial freshwater fishing operations go for large- and small-mouth bass and peacock bass. For full- and half-day bass fishing excursions, mostly in the reservoirs around Kalaheo and Koloa, but sometimes on the east side, contact **Cast & Catch,** 808/332-9707. Its 17-foot bass boat fishes one of Kaua'i's lovely freshwater reservoirs. All tackle, bait, and soft drinks are provided along with airport/hotel pickup and delivery. Fares vary, but half-day trips run $150–300 for one to three persons and full day trips go for $250–350, three people maximum.

Also try **J.J.'s Big Bass Tours,** 808/332-9219, with 1993 Big Bass Hawaii State Champion, John Jardin. Tackle, license, refreshments, and hotel pickup are included.

# CAMPING AND HIKING

Kaua'i is very hospitable to campers and hikers. More than a dozen state and county parks and forest reserves offer camping, and a network of trails leads into the interior. There are different types of camping to suit everyone: you can drive right up to your spot at a convenient beach park, hike for a day through incredible country to camp in total seclusion, or boat to secluded spots along the Na Pali Coast. A profusion of "secret beaches" have unofficial camping; this cannot be recommended, but it's definitely done. Koke'e State Park provides affordable self-contained cabins, and RV camping is permitted at Koke'e and Polihale State Parks and at Ha'ena and Hanama'ulu County Parks.

Hikers can take the Kalalau Trail—perhaps the premier hiking experience in Hawaii—or go topside to Koke'e and follow numerous paths to breathtaking views over the bared-teeth cliffs of Na Pali. Hunting trails follow many of the streams into the interior; or, if you don't mind mud and rain, you can pick your way across the Alaka'i Swamp. Other fine trails are found in the Wailua area. Wherever you go, enjoy but don't destroy, and leave the land as beautiful as you find it.

## General Information

All campgrounds, except for those along the Na Pali Coast and the forest reserve campsites in Waimea Canyon, provide grills, pavilions (some with electricity), picnic tables, cold-water showers, and drinking water. Unfortunately, at some parks, toilets and showers have been vandalized and no longer function, but this may vary according to park maintenance schedules. Camping fuel is not provided, so bring your own wood or charcoal for the grill. No one can camp "under the stars" at official campgrounds; all must have a tent. Campsites are unattended, so be careful with your gear—especially radios, stereos, and cameras—but your tent and sleeping bag are generally okay. Always be prepared for wind and rain, especially along the north shore.

At times, police aggressively issue tickets and hefty fines for illegal camping, especially along north shore beaches. *Sometimes* they merely issue a warning, but definitely do not count on it! Multiple offenders can even be sentenced to jail time.

## County Parks

A permit is required for camping at all county-maintained parks with camping facilities, and these are Ha'ena, Hanalei Black Pot, 'Anini, Anahola, Hanama'ulu, Salt Pond at Hanapepe, and Lucy Wright in Waimea; RV camping is permitted at only the Ha'ena and Hanama'ulu parks. Permits are good for up to seven nights per campground. Camping is limited to 60 days total in any one-year period. The permit-issuing office is the Division of Parks and Recreation, 4444 Rice St., Moikeha Bldg., Suite 150, Lihu'e, HI 96766, 808/241-6660, open Mon.–Fri. 8 A.M.–4:15 P.M.

At all other times, including weekends and holidays, you can pick up your permit at the Kaua'i Police Dept., Lihu'e Branch, 3060 'Umi St., 808/241-6711. An application must include the name, address, and telephone number of the principal adult, names and a copy of official identification for all adults in the party, and number of tents that will be used. The cost is $3 per person per day (except Hawaii residents); children under 18 are free if accompanied by parent or guardian. Park rangers can issue permits on the spot, but these cost $5 per person per day. If you write in advance for information and reservations, you'll be sent an application. Return it with the appropriate information, and your request will be logged in the reservations book. You'll also receive brochures and maps of the campgrounds. When you arrive, you must pick up and pay for your permit at the Parks and Recreation office or the police station. Be aware that each beach park is closed one day a week for maintenance, except for Hanalei Black Pot Park, which is only open Friday,

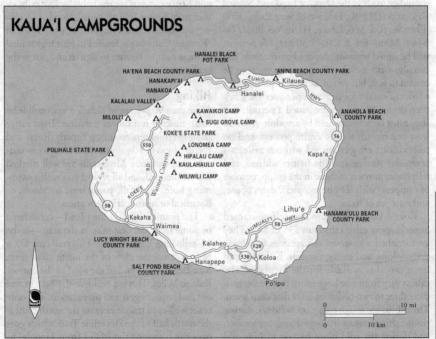

**KAUA'I CAMPGROUNDS**

HANALEI BLACK POT PARK
HA'ENA BEACH COUNTY PARK
HANAKAPI'AI
HANAKOA
'ANINI BEACH COUNTY PARK
KUHIO
Kilauea
KALALAU VALLEY
MILOLI'I
KAWAIKOI CAMP
SUGI GROVE CAMP
Hanalei
HWY
ANAHOLA BEACH COUNTY PARK
KOKE'E STATE PARK
56
POLIHALE STATE PARK
550
LONOMEA CAMP
HIPALAU CAMP
KAULAHAULU CAMP
WILIWILI CAMP
Kapa'a
KOKE'E RD.
Waimea Canyon
Lihu'e
HANAMA'ULU BEACH COUNTY PARK
Kekaha
Waimea
50
KAUMUALI'I HWY
50
LUCY WRIGHT BEACH COUNTY PARK
Kalaheo
520
SALT POND BEACH COUNTY PARK
Hanapepe
530
Koloa
Po'ipu
N
0          10 mi
0          10 km

**KAUA'I**

Saturday, and holidays. When you make your application to camp, ask the parks office for its current closure schedule.

## State Parks

Camping is allowed at three state parks on Kaua'i—Koke'e, Na Pali Coast, and Polihale—and a no-cost camping permit is required; RV camping is allowed at Koke'e and Polihale only. Permits run $5 per campsite per night at Polihale and Koke'e and $10 per night for the Na Pali Coast sites. Camping is restricted to five consecutive nights within a 30-day period per campground, with one night allowed at Hanakapi'ai when going in along the Kalalau Trail and one night when coming out from the valley, and three-night maximum at Miloli'i farther along the coast. At Polihale, campsites perch on top of the dunes that back the beach, and at Koke'e, the campsite is in the open meadow at the far end from the museum. Permits are issued no more than one year in advance. An application for a permit should be made at the Dept. of Land and Natural Resources (DLNR), Division of State Parks, 3060 'Eiwa St., Rm. 306, Lihu'e, HI 96766, 808/274-3444, Mon.–Fri. 8 A.M.–3:30 P.M. *No* permits will be issued without proper identification. You can also write well in advance for permits to be mailed to you, but you must include photocopies of identification for each camper over 18. Children under 18 will not be issued a permit, and they must be accompanied by an adult. Allow at least one month for the entire process, and no reservations are guaranteed without at least a seven-day notice. Include name, address, and telephone numbers of those in the group, number of campers (with ID photocopies), dates of use, and number of tents.

Koke'e Lodge also provides self-contained housekeeping cabins that run $35 or $45. They are furnished with stoves, refrigerators, hot showers, cooking and eating utensils, bedding, and linen; wood is available for the fireplaces. The cabins vary from one large room that accommodates three to two-bedroom units that sleep seven. The cabins are tough to get on holidays, during trout-fishing season in August and September, and during the wild plum harvest in June and July. For reservations, write Koke'e Lodge, P.O. Box 819, Waimea, HI 96796, or call 808/335-6061 daily 9 A.M.–3:45 P.M.

## Forest Reserves

Camping is allowed in specified sites only within the Na Pali Kona and Pu'u Ka Pele forest reserves. These reserves encompass Waimea and adjacent canyons and the upper Koke'e region. Permits are required and issued free of charge. Applications may be made at the State Division of Forestry and Wildlife, 3060 'Eiwa St., Rm. 306, Lihu'e, 96766, 808/274-3433, Mon.–Fri. 8 A.M.–4 P.M., and must include the names of all campers and the exact dates for which the campsite is requested. Be sure to pick up the very useful *Recreational Map of Western Kauai* when making your application. Accessible by 4WD vehicles along Camp 10 Road are the Kawaikoi and Sugi Grove campsites. Camping at these camps is limited to three nights total within a 30-day period. The four campsites in Waimea and Koai'e canyons are reachable by foot only, either from Kukui Trail off Koke'e Road or by hiking up the Waimea Canyon from the town of Waimea. Camping is limited to four nights total at these camps. Be sure to sign in and out at the trailheads.

## Hiking

More than 90 percent of Kaua'i is inaccessible by road, making it a hikers' paradise. Treks range from overnighters requiring superb fitness and preparedness to 10-minute nature loops just outside your car door. Most trails are well marked and maintained, and all reward you with a swimming hole, waterfall, panoramic overlook, or botanical or historical information.

The premier hike on the island—considered by some to be the best hike in the state—is the 11-mile long Kalalau Trail. This trail cuts like a ribbon across the cliffs of the north coast from Ke'e Beach at the end of the road to the remote Kalalau Valley. This is a multiple-day hike in and out and requires gear and preparation. The only other well-used trail of note on the north coast is the north half of the Powerline Trail, which goes over the hump of the island from Hanalei to

Keahua Arboretum above Wailua. Around the east side are several good day hikes offering plenty of exercise and good vistas. Perhaps the most popular are the three trails on the Sleeping Giant. Farther up onto the mountainside are the Kuilau Trail, Moalepe Trail, and the southern end of the Powerline Trail. By far the greatest concentration of hiking trails on Kaua'i, the trails of Waimea and Koke'e State Parks provide some of the prettiest and most awesome scenery. Here, you have a choice of forest, canyon, or coastal view hikes. It seems that one could walk for a month and not cover all the trails in this area. Further description of each of these trails is found in the appropriate travel chapter below.

Through its various divisions, the Department of Land and Natural Resources, 3060 'Eiwa St., Lihu'e, HI 96766, provides free detailed maps and descriptions of most trails. For state park trails, direct letters to the Department's Division of State Parks; for forest reserve trails, the Division of Forestry.

## Tips and Warnings

You *cannot* go from Koke'e down to the valleys of Na Pali. Every now and again someone attempts it and is killed. The cliffs are impossibly steep and brittle, and your handholds and footholds will break from under you. Don't be foolish.

If you're going into the Alaka'i Swamp, remember that all the birds and flora you encounter are unique, and most of them are fighting extinction. Also, your clothes will become permanently stained with swamp mud—a wonderful memento of your trip. Before attempting any of the trails, please sign in at park headquarters.

## Rental Equipment and Sales

**Kayak Kaua'i Outbound,** P.O. Box 508, Hanalei, HI 96714, 808/826-9844 or 800/437-3507, open daily 8 A.M.–5 P.M., sells and rents camping equipment. There you can find all sorts of camping gear including metal cups and dishes, packaged foods, insect repellent, backpacks ($8/day, $32/week), day packs, ground cloths, stove ($6/day, $24/week), camping gas, candles, sleeping bags and pads ($10/day, $40/week), and two-person tents ($8/day, $32/week).

**Pedal and Paddle,** 808/826-9069, open daily in Hanalei's Ching Young Center, also rents and sells backpacking equipment at roughly the same prices as Kayak Kaua'i. A rental day begins at the time you rent and ends at 5 P.M. the following day. Bikes, snorkel gear, surfboards, boogie boards, and kayaks are also available.

Other camping supply outlets are **Kmart,** in the Kukui Grove Center, and **Wal-Mart,** near the hospital on the north end of Lihu'e. These shops have basic camping supplies, mostly for the car-camping crowd and not so much for the backpack/hiker variety, but they do carry reasonably inexpensive goods including dome tents, lanterns, outdoor stoves and fuel, and flannel sleeping bags.

## Guided Hikes

**Koke'e Natural History Museum** offers guided hikes through a variety of trails in the state park on weekends during summer. Trails will differ each week according to the weather. These hikes leave from the museum at 12:30 P.M.; bring water and all needed equipment. Call 808/335-9975 to reserve your spot; the fee is $3 a head.

**Sierra Club** announces group hikes in the Garden Island newspaper. You can also find the Kaua'i group outing schedule on the net at www.hi.sierraclub.org/kauai/kauai.html. Some hikes are along well used trails, while others are to destinations seldom seen. Hikes are lead by local volunteers and a waiver must be signed to join. A minimal donation is requested.

The most education-oriented hikes on the island are done by **Kaua'i Nature Tours.** Full-day hikes, all in the easy to moderate level, focus on the natural environment; hikers learn about Kaua'i's geology, natural history, and flora and fauna. Various hikes throughout the week go to Waimea Canyon, the Na Pali Coast, Maha'ulepu Beach and dune area, and other beaches around the island. If you want your day to be more than a physical adventure, these hikes may be for you. All hikes run most of the day and cost $82–97 including lunch. For information, call 808/742-8305 or 888/233-8365, or go to www.kauainaturetours.com.

Guided hikes to a waterfall and scenic overlooks of Hanalei are offered on the **Princeville Ranch,** daily except Sunday. Hikes run about three hours and the cost is $59–74. Drinking water and all equipment is provided. For information or to reserve, call 808/826-7669.

**Aloha Kauai Tours,** 808/245-6400 or 800/452-1113, www.alohakauaitours.com, offers one combination 4WD van and hiking tour. Their half-day, weekday only Blue Hole tour heads to the interior of the island to the base of Mt. Wai'ale'ale. The rate is $65 adult or $50 for kids age 5–12.

Combining hikes to various locations with some time spent in a kayak, **Hawaiian Adventure Tours,** 808/889-0227 or 800/659-3544, offers multiple-day, multiple-island guided tours. Locations include Kaua'i, the Big Island, and/or Maui, and while not cheap (the 8–10 trips run about $2000), nearly all expenses are covered once in the islands. For additional information, check out the website, www.hawaiianadventuretours.com.

## HORSEBACK RIDING

All horseback tours on Kaua'i are guided. Most of the guides are extremely knowledgeable about the area's unique flora and fauna and are able to talk story about the ancient tales and legends pertaining to the ride site. For your safety and comfort, wear long pants (jeans are best) and closed-toe shoes. Bring a hat and sunblock as well. Most riding stables take riders 10 years old or older, and some have a weight limit—usually around 220 pounds. Snacks and drinks are provided on most rides that go more than a couple of hours. Horseback riding is not allowed on beaches in Hawaii.

**Silver Falls Ranch,** on the north shore off Rte. 56 just west of Kilauea, 808/828-6718, www.hawaiian.net/~sfr, offers rides daily through private property below Mt. Mamahana, in the shadow of Kalihiwai Ridge. You can choose a one-and-a-half-hour Greenhorn's Trail Ride for $69; the Hawaiian Discovery Ride, two hours long with refreshments provided for $78; or the Silver Falls Ride, a three-hour ride including a picnic and swim at a private falls for $105. All riders are matched with their horses, and the guides are experienced instructors. More than

just a tour operator, the Silver Falls Ranch offers full equestrian services, including lessons, and maintains a stable of only quarter horses. Silver Falls Ranch is a reputable company, offering enjoyable rides in a beautiful setting.

**Princeville Ranch Stables,** located between Princeville and the Princeville Airport, 808/826-6777, www.princevilleranch.com, closed Sunday, offers a variety of rides through the ranch property and along the bluff that overlooks 'Anini Beach. The deluxe, four-hour ride costs $120 and meanders across verdant interior land, ending at an inland waterfall for a swim and picnic. A shorter ride takes you to lookouts over Hanalei Valley and into the foothills of the surrounding mountains for $65, while the 1.5-hour "cattle drive" at $120 calls for participation in getting the herd into its pen. All riders must be over age eight.

**Esprit De Corps Riding Academy,** 808/822-4688, www.kauaihorses.com, located in the upper Kapa'a area near the end of Olohena Road, will take you on a three-hour ride for $148, a five-hour ride with snacks for $215, and a deluxe eight-hour ride with lunch and a swim in a mountain stream for $345. These rides are geared to riders with some experience, and to those who can handle being on a horse for hours. A slower, shorter ride, great for those with less skill and for photographers, runs $112. Reservations are necessary. Riders must be age 10 or older. You'll head deep into the mountains above Kapa'a, to relatively unfrequented spots with good vantage points across the foothills to the coast as well as up toward the island's highest peaks.

You can hire mounts from **CJM Country Stables,** located about 1.5 miles past the Hyatt in Po'ipu, 808/742-6096, www.cjmstables.com. CJM offers three rides: a secret beach breakfast ride Tues., Thurs., and Sat. starting at 8:30 A.M. and lasting three hours for $80; a two-hour hidden beach ride twice daily, mid-morning and early afternoon, for $70; and a beach, swim, and picnic ride on Mon., Wed., and Fri. for three hours starting at noon, for $90. No rides are given on Sunday. All rides are taken in the Maha'ulepu Beach and nearby coastal area.

**Keapana Horsemanship,** 808/823-9303, www.keapana.com, is located along Ma'alo Road, on the way to Wailua Falls. This is the most convenient stable to Lihu'e. Rides include an introductory ride for $59, a waterfall view ride for $89, a three-hour picnic swim ride for $150, and a six-hour ride up to the Keahua Arboretum for $250.

## BICYCLING

Riding a bike around Kaua'i is fairly easy, thanks to the lack of big hills—except for the road up to Koke'e State Park. Traffic is moderate, especially in the cool of early morning, when it's best for making some distance. Roads are generally good, but shoulders aren't wide and are sometimes nonexistent, particularly on the back roads. Peak season brings a dramatic increase in traffic and road congestion. Take care! Some bike lanes have been constructed, but these are mostly near tourist resorts. Wherever you ride, watch for rocks, sticks, wet surfaces, crumbled asphalt, and, on gravel back roads, bumps, ruts, and mud puddles.

Mountain biking on most cane roads is not encouraged because you are riding through private property and there is the chance of encountering heavy equipment. Stay off of other private property and do not go beyond locked gates. Some roads leading off the main highways are Route 583 to Wailua Falls (easy); the upland residential roads above Wailua and Kapa'a (easy to moderate); roads uphill between Lawa'i and Kalaheo (slow, steep, and tough); the coastal trail from Kapa'a Beach Park to Anahola (relatively easy), about six miles one-way; and Po'ipu Road past the Hyatt Regency Resort to Maha'ulepu Beach (easy). Others to try are Kealia Road from Kealia up the mountain to the Spaulding Monument and from there down to Anahola (moderate uphill and easy down), the back road past the end of Hauaala Road to the Spaulding Monument (moderate—you must walk the bike a short ways due to the deteriorating condition of the road), and Ko'olau Road near Moloa'a Beach (easy). The 4WD dirt tracks in Koke'e State Park and the adjacent forest reserves are easy to moderate and give you a good workout. Some hiking trails on state forest reserve land are also open to mountain biking, including the 13-mile Powerline

Trail over the mountain from Keahua Arboretum to Hanalei (strenuous), the Kuilau and Moalepe Trails, the Kuamo'o Trail on the Sleeping Giant, and the Waimea Canyon Trail on the west end. Remember that there is no biking allowed on any state park trail or forest reserve trail other than those listed above.

### Bike Shops

**Outfitters Kauai,** an ecology-minded sports shop specializing in kayaking and mountain biking, is owned and operated by Rick and Julie Havilend in the Po'ipu Plaza, at 2827-A Po'ipu Rd., P.O. Box 1149, Po'ipu Beach, HI 96756, 808/742-9667 or 888/742-9887, www.outfitterskauai.com, open daily 9 A.M.–5 P.M. Mountain-bike rentals include helmet, a water bottle, lock, and a map and cost $25–40 a day, while cruisers run $20 and road bikes $33, with multi-day discounts available. Biking and kayaking incidentals are also available for purchase, along with Patagonia clothing. These guys have lots of information and will do their best to match you and your interests with a great place to ride.

An excellent choice is **Bicycle John's,** a full-service bicycle shop offering sales and repair. Located along Rte. 56 in the Kuhio Business Center building as you enter Lihu'e, 808/245-7579, the shop is open 10 A.M.–6 P.M. on Mon., Wed., and Fri. and until 4 P.M. on Saturday.

The only bike shop in Kapa'a is the full-service **Kauai Cycle and Tour,** at 1379 Kuhio Hwy. in Kapa'a, 808/821-2115, www.bike-hawaii.com/kauaicycle, open Mon.–Fri. 9 A.M.–6 P.M., Sat. 9 A.M.–4 P.M. These guys do sales, repairs, and rentals, and can tell you where best to ride on the island. Beach cruisers rent for $15 for 24 hours, front-suspension mountain bikes run $20 a day or $95 per seven-day week, and full-suspension mountain bikes are $35 a day and $150 a week. Each rental includes a helmet, lock, and water bottle. A car rack is available for $5. Even though their name says it, they don't run tours anymore.

You're not required to salute John Sargent, the **Bike Doctor,** in Hanalei, 808/826-7799, open Tues.–Fri. 9 A.M.–5 P.M. and Sat. 10 A.M.–4 P.M., who has a shop stocked with everything for both

KAUA'I

casual and serious cyclists. John sells road bikes, sells and rents Marin mountain bikes, and offers special *wiki wiki* repair service to visiting cyclists whose equipment has broken down. Rental prices for high-quality mountain bikes only are $25 a day or $100 per seven-day week, including helmet, tool box, and water bottle. The Bike Doctor is intimately familiar with roads and trails all over the island and is happy to give advice on touring. Happy pedaling!

**Kayak Kaua'i,** in Hanalei at 808/826-9844, www.kayakkauai.com, rents mountain bikes and cruisers for $15–20 a day, with multiple-day rates available.

**Pedal and Paddle,** in the Ching Young Center in Hanalei, 808/826-9069, rents cruisers at $10 per day or $40 per week, and $20 and $100 for a mountain bike; prices include lock, helmet, and car rack if desired.

Various activity centers around the island also rent bikes for around $15 per day for a mountain bike and $10 per day for a beach cruiser.

## Bicycle Tours

A miniature version of the great Haleakala downhill bike ride is offered on Kaua'i by two tour companies. The 11-mile ride on Kaua'i starts in the cool mountain air on the rim of Waimea Canyon at about 3,400 feet elevation. From there the group skirts the rim and then heads down the foothills to the coast at Kekaha. All tours are done in groups, and each member is given a helmet and jacket to wear. A sag wagon follows for those who need a rest and to alert traffic that comes from behind. Snacks are provided. Closed-toe shoes are a necessity, and long pants may be recommended. Don't forget to bring sunglasses and sunscreen. The cruiser bikes are cushy, with big easy-chair seats, raised handlebars, and extra strong brakes. Sunrise and

## KAUA'I GOLF COURSES

| Course | Par | Yards | Fees | Cart | Clubs |
|---|---|---|---|---|---|
| **Kaua'i Lagoons Golf Club** 3351 Ho'olaule'a Way Lihu'e, HI 96766 808/241-6000 800/634-6400 | 72 | 6,960 (Mokihana) 7,070 (Kiele) | $120 $170 | incl. | $35 |
| **Kiahuna Golf Club** 2545 Kiahuna Plantation Drive Po'ipu, HI 96756 808/742-9595 | 70 | 6,366 | $45–75 | incl. | $30 |
| **Kukuiolono Golf Course** 854 Pu'u Road Kalaheo, HI 96741 808/332-9151 | 36 | 2,981 | $7 | $6 $2 handcart | $6 |
| **Poipu Bay Golf Course** 2250 Ainako St. Koloa, HI 96756 808/742-8711 800/858-6300 | 72 | 7,034 | $65–185 | incl. | $40–60 |

sunset rides are available and run about $80 per person with reduced rates for kids; count on four and a half to five hours for the entire trip although actual bike time is about one hour. If this sounds like a trip for you, contact **Bicycle Downhill,** 808/742-7421, www.outfitters-kauai.com; or **Kauai Coasters,** 808/639-2412, www.aloha.net/~coast.

## GOLF

Kaua'i offers varied and exciting golfing around the island at eight golf courses. Kukuiolono Golf Course, a mountaintop course in Kalaheo, is never crowded and is worth visiting just for the scenery. Wailua Municipal Golf Course is a public course with reasonable greens fees; it's considered excellent by visitors and residents—one of the best municipal courses in the country and the longest running on the island. Princeville

boasts 45 magnificent holes sculpted above Hanalei Bay. A favorite for years, Kauai Lagoons Golf Club in Lihu'e has added its Kiele Course. Also in Lihu'e is the up-and-coming, currently 10-hole Puakea Golf Course. In Po'ipu, Kiahuna Plantation Golf Course and the new Po'ipu Bay Resort Golf Course are fabulous courses on the sunny south coast.

## TENNIS

The accompanying chart lists private and public tennis courts. Public courts, usually cement, are run by the county and reservations can be made by calling the number listed. No fees are charged for these public courts, but play is on a first-come, first-served basis. Court rules apply and only soft-sole shoes are allowed. Please care for equipment and stick to time limits, especially if there are others waiting to play. Many hotel tennis courts

| Course | Par | Yards | Fees | Cart | Clubs |
|---|---|---|---|---|---|
| **Princeville Makai Golf Course** <br> P.O. Box 3040 <br> Princeville, HI 96722 <br> 808/826-5070 <br> 800/826-1105 | 36 <br> 36 <br> 36 | 3,430 (Ocean) <br> 3,445 (Woods) <br> 3,456 (Lake) | $125 | incl. | $35–85 |
| **Princeville Prince Course** <br> P.O. Box 3040 <br> Princeville, HI 96722 <br> 808/826-5070 <br> 800/826-1105 | 72 | 7,309 | $120–175 | incl. | $35 |
| **Puakea Golf Course** <br> 4315 Kalepo Street <br> Lihu'e, HI 96766 <br> 808/245-8756 | 40 | 3,803 | $15–65 | incl. | $15 |
| **Wailua Municipal Golf Course** <br> 3-5350 Kuhio Hwy. <br> Lihu'e, HI 96766 <br> 808/241-6666 | 72 | 6,981 | $32–44 | $14 | $15 |

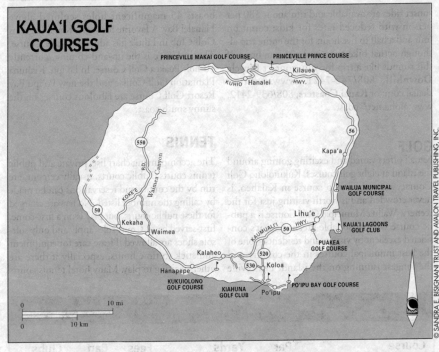

## KAUA'I GOLF COURSES

PRINCEVILLE MAKAI GOLF COURSE
PRINCEVILLE PRINCE COURSE
Kilauea
KŪHIO  Hanalei  HWY.
550
KŌKE'E RD.
Waimea Canyon
56
Kapa'a
WAILUA MUNICIPAL GOLF COURSE
50
Kekaha
Lihu'e
KAUMUALI'I
KAUA'I LAGOONS GOLF CLUB
Waimea
50
HWY.
PUAKEA GOLF COURSE
Kalaheo
520
Hanapepe
530
Koloa
PO'IPU BAY GOLF COURSE
KUKUIOLONO GOLF COURSE
KIAHUNA GOLF CLUB
Po'ipu
0        10 mi
0        10 km

© SANDRA E. BISIGNANI TRUST AND AVALON TRAVEL PUBLISHING, INC.

are open to nonguests, usually for a fee; by and large condo tennis courts are reserved for guests only. All private courts are a hard court plexi-pave surface. Although each facility differs, private clubs usually have pro shops, offer equipment rental, and arrange clinics and lessons. Court play is regulated according to accepted rules, and proper attire is required, including proper shoes.

## HUNTING

All game animals on Kaua'i have been intro-duced. Hunters go for feral pigs and goats, and black-tailed deer, which are found only on Kaua'i. Black-tailed deer come from Oregon. Forty were released on Kaua'i in 1961; the herd is now sta-bilized at around 700 and they're hunted in Oc-tober by public lottery. Because they thrive on island fruits, their meat is sweeter and less gamy than that of Mainland deer.

A number of game birds are found on Kaua'i. Bag limits and hunting seasons vary, so check with the Department of Land and Natural Resources, Division of Forestry and Wildlife for details at 3060 'Eiwa St., Lihu'e, HI 96766, 808/274-3433. Ring-necked pheasants are one of the best game birds. Also on the list are francolins—gray, black, and Erkel's—chukar, quail, including the Japanese and California varieties, and doves.

### Hunting Excursions

Ni'ihau Safaris, Ltd., 808/338-9869, owned and operated by the Robinson family, offers hunt-ing trips to the forbidden island of Ni'ihau. The rate is a very stiff $1,650 and includes round-trip helicopter flight, a personal hunting guide, and a bag limit of one ram and one wild boar. If caught, they are skinned, packed, and readied for mounting. Although the game is plentiful, expect an arduous hunt with the straight-shoot-ing skills left up to you. Also, do not expect to come into contact with any of the island's 160 Hawaiian residents. What you pay for, you get, and that's it!

# KAUA'I TENNIS COURTS

## County Courts

Under jurisdiction of the County Division of Parks and Recreation, 4444 Rice St., Suite 150, Lihu'e, HI 96766, 808/241-6277. No fee for use. Reservations are recommended but most often not necessary. All courts are lighted.

| Town | Location | No. of Courts |
|------|----------|---------------|
| Hanapepe | next to stadium | 2 |
| Kalaheo | Kalawai Park | 2 |
| Kapa'a | New Park | 2 |
| Kekaha | Faye Park | 2 |
| Koloa | Knudsen Park | 2 |
| Wailua | Wailua Homelots Park | 4 |
| Wailua | Wailua Homesteads Park | 4 |

## Hotel and Private Courts Open to the Public

| Town | Location | Fee | No. of Courts | Lighted |
|------|----------|-----|---------------|---------|
| Lihu'e | Tennis Club at Kaua'i Lagoons 808/245-3323 | $20 | 8 | No |
| Po'ipu | Poipu Kai Resort 808/742-8706 | $10 | 8 | No |
| Po'ipu | Hyatt Regency 808/742-1234 | $20 | 4 | Yes |
| Po'ipu | Kiahuna Tennis Club 808/742-9533 | $10 | 10 | Yes |
| Princeville | Hanalei Bay Resort 808/826-6522 | $6 | 8 | Yes |
| Princeville | Princeville Tennis Club 808/826-3620 | $15 | 6 | No |
| Wailua | Kauai Coconut Beach Hotel 808/822-3455 | $7 | 3 | No |

KAUA'I

# LAND TOURS

## Bus Tours

Most tour companies run vans, but some larger companies also use buses. Though cheaper, tours on full-sized coaches are generally less personalized. Coach tours vary, but typical trips go to the north shore, to Waimea Canyon and south coast sights, or combine one of these tours with a trip to the Wailua River and the Fern Grotto. Each agency has its own routes and schedules, but all hit the major tourist sites. Rates sometimes include entrance fees and lunch. A trips to the Waimea Canyon will run about $40, and it will be about the same for the Fern Grotto. Combining these two or going to the North Shore runs about $60. Children's fares are about 25 percent less. Fares may vary according to the area of pickup. Often a tour to the Fern Grotto is considered the highlight. Companies offering these tours include **Polynesian Adventure Tours,** 808/246-0122; **Kaua'i Island Tours,** 808/245-4777; **Roberts Hawaii Tours,** 808/831-5541; and **Kaua'i Paradise Tours,** 808/246-3999, which specializes in German-speaking narration.

Kaua'i has been used to set the scene for nearly 60 feature films, and now there's a van tour that will escort you to the location of many of these, providing you with details of the movies' making and the actors who made them, in a 15-passenger van that's at least as comfortable as the cush seats in any silver screen multiplex. **Hawaii Movie Tours,** 808/822-1192 or 800/628-8432, www.hawaii-imovietour.com, runs a five-hour van tour around the periphery of the island from its Kapa'a office and a six-hour tour that heads inland for part of the run. The costs are $95 for adults and $76 for kids 11 and under, and $113 and 103, respectively; lunch included.

## Adventure Van Tours

One unique tour company is **Aloha Kauai Tours,** 808/245-6400 or 800/452-1113, www.alohakauaitours.com. It alone is licensed to operate tours in the Na Pali Kona Forest Reserve. Knowledgeable guides take you into the back country over dirt roads by air-conditioned, 12-passenger 4WD vans, with an informed narrative on the way. They let you see a part of Kaua'i not reached by anyone who doesn't walk or bike in. Traveling is rough, but the sights are unsurpassed; truly, this is one of the few ways in Kaua'i to get off the beaten path. The company's guides, all local people, are excellent and have a tremendous amount of knowledge about the island's flora, fauna, and history. The eight-hour adventure costs $125 plus tax ($90 for children age 12 and under) and includes a deli/picnic lunch (vegetarian too!). Tours start at 9 A.M. in Puhi. This same company also does an excellent Kauai Backroads tour in 4WD vans through cane fields up to Kilohana Crater, with commentary about the area on the way. From the crater, the tour then heads to the east Po'ipu seashore near Maha'ulepu through the tunnel in the Ha'upu Ridge, constructed in 1946–47 by Grove Farm to transport cane to the Koloa mill from fields in the Kipu area. Virtually the whole route is on private cane land, behind locked gates, and inaccessible to those without the needed permission. Morning and afternoon tours start at Kilohana, last four hours, and cost $60 for adults or $50 for chil-

## MOVIES MADE ON KAUA'I

For decades, filmmakers have been drawn to Kaua'i. About five dozen feature films or parts of films have been made on the island. While Kaua'i is varied in its topography and climate, most filmmakers use the lush vegetation, waterfalls, beaches, sheer cliffs, and tropical scenery as backdrops. Everyone seems to know that Kaua'i was used in *South Pacific* with Mitzi Gaynor in 1958 and in *Blue Hawaii* with Elvis in 1961, but others include scenes from *Raiders of the Lost Ark, King Kong, Outbreak, Jurassic Park, Islands in the Stream, Hook, Uncommon Valor,* and *The Man with the Golden Gun.*

To fill in the details and the trivia, pick up a copy of *The Kaua'i Movie Book* by Chris Cook, published in 1996 by Mutual Publishing of Honolulu. Alternately, have a look at www.filmkauai.com for a complete list of movies made on the Garden Island and additional information and trivia about moviemaking on Kaua'i.

KAUA'I

dren, snacks included. Their Blue Hole tour into the interior of the island beyond the Keahua Arboretum is a half-day 4WD and hiking trek that only runs on weekdays. The rate is $65 or $50 for kids age 5–12.

## ATV Tour

**Kauai ATV,** P.O. Box 800, Kalaheo, HI 96741, 808/742-2734 or 877/707-7088, www.kauaiatv.com, runs four-wheel ATV (all terrain vehicle) tours through former cane land around Koloa, from the ocean at Maha'ulepu to the Ha'upu Ridge. Three times a day, the three-hour tours take a route that runs along former cane haul roads, past the Waita Reservoir, and into the half-mile-long tunnel cut through the mountain above the reservoir. Rides are $90 a person; riders 16 years old and older are welcome. Helmets, face shields, gloves, beverages, and instructions are provided; long pants, a long-sleeved shirt, and closed-toe shoes are a must. When weather conditions are right, a waterfall tour is also offered for a bit more. The office is on the corner of Weliwlei and Waikomo roads in Koloa.

Running a similar operation on the far side of the Ha'upu Range is **Kipu Ranch Adventures,** 808/246-9288. The three-hour ATV rides here run through the still-active Kipu Ranch, over ground that has been used on numerous occasions by movie makers.

## Kaua'i Backcountry Adventures

As one of the newest tour operators on the island, Kaua'i Backcountry Adventures has found a niche for itself by providing group tubing tours down a section of the Hanama'ulu Ditch, built around 1870 and part of the water collection system for the now-silent Lihu'e sugar plantation. Guests are transported to the put-in point and from there ride brightly-colored inner tubes some two miles down the flume, in and out of tunnels (head lamps provided), and along a lush stretch of backcountry Kaua'i that is impossible to see on your own as it's on private property. Tubers are rewarded with a picnic lunch at the conclusion of the ride. Wear a swimming suit or clothes that you don't mind getting wet and put water shoes on your feet. Tours run once in the morning at

9 A.M. and again in the early afternoon at 1 P.M. The rate for this mountain tubing adventure is $85 per person, with a minimum age of five and no one over 300 pounds. Kids 14 and younger must be accompanied by an adult and those with claustrophobia (there are tunnels) should think twice about participating. Plans for future activities on other parts of the plantation property include kayaking, hiking, mountain biking, and ATV tours, so call to see what's happening when. For information and reservations, contact Kaua'i Backcountry Adventures at P.O. Box 183, Hanama'ulu, HI 96715, 808/245-2506 or 888/270-0555; www.kauaibackcountry.com, adventure@kauaibackcountry.com.

# AIR TOURS

## Helicopter Tours

Flying in a chopper is a thrilling experience, like flying in a light plane—with a twist. It can take you into all kinds of otherwise inaccessible little nooks and crannies. Routes cover the entire island, but the highlights are flying through colorful gorge of the Waimea Canyon, along the giant sea cliffs of the Na Pali Coast, and into the Mt. Wai'ale'ale crater—where it almost never stops raining and where you see dozens of waterfalls and even 360-degree rainbows floating in midair. Earphones cut the noise of the aircraft and play soul-stirring music as a background to the pilot's narration. Each pilot's stories are as different as the pilots themselves, so it's pot luck in that regard, but all are skilled in bringing you up-close to the island. All flights run in a clockwise circle around the island along the same basic route. Longer flights linger at certain scenic spots and dart into more valleys. The basic one-hour around-the-island flight runs about $175 per person; a shorter 45-minute flight is around $125, and longer 75- to 90-minute flights run about $210; most offer internet discounts. Some give complimentary videos of your flight or a professionally-made "standard" flight, while others charge for a video if you want one. Ni'ihau Helicopters also flies periodically to points on Ni'ihau. Its flights are more expensive, but it's the only way to get to see that island up close.

**Safari Helicopters offer excellent, unobstructed views.**

Discounts of up to 15 percent from some of the companies are always featured in the ubiquitous free tourist brochures and occasionally available through activities and information centers.

Of the dozen helicopter companies on Kaua'i, the majority operate from Lihu'e Airport, with a handful flying from Burns Field in Hanapepe and one flying from the Princeville Airport. For those companies without offices adjacent to the heliports, vans shuttle guests to the tarmac.

The granddaddy of them all is **Jack Harter Helicopters,** located along Ahukini Rd. halfway between the airport and downtown Lihu'e, 808/245-3774 or 888/245-2001, www.heli-copters-kauai.com. Jack, along with his wife, Beverly, literally started the helicopter business on Kaua'i and has been flying the island for around 40 years. He and his pilots know countless stories about Kaua'i and just about everywhere to go on the island. Jack Harter runs both six-passenger a/c and four-passenger open-window helicopters, and 60- and 90-minute flights. His old slogan—"Imitated by all, equaled by none"-says it all.

**Safari Helicopter,** 808/246-0136 or 800/326-3356, www.safariair.com, is owned and operated by pilot Preston Myers, who learned to fly in

the '60s and has been flying over Kaua'i since 1987. Safari prides itself on offering a luxury tour in its state-of-the-art ASTAR helicopters, complete with two-way sound system, unobstructed view, air-conditioned compartments, and an all-seeing video camera system that records your trip for future enjoyment. A video of your personal tour costs $25. Preflight instruction takes place in Myers' Lihu'e office.

**'Ohana Helicopter Tours,** at the Anchor Cove Shopping Center, 808/245-3996 or 800/222-6989, www.ohana-helicopters.com, is an owner-operated company that gives personalized service. 'Ohana offers complimentary shuttle service from its office to the heliport. The staff want you to have the time of your life-not hard to achieve with this experience. The owner, Bogart Kealoha, has years of commercial and military experience and *knows* this island of his birth. His company has a flawless flight record and has grown into one of the largest and best-regarded helicopter companies on the island. From smooth liftoff to gentle landing, you are in good hands with 'Ohana.

Following are descriptions of a few other companies with good reputations and competitive prices that fly out of Lihu'e Airport. **Island Heli-**

**copters,** 808/245-8588 or 800/829-5999, www.islandhelicopters.com, flies about 16 flights a day and has an office near the old air terminal. **South Sea Helicopters,** 808/245-2222 or 800/367-2914, www.southseahelicopters.com, is owned and operated by Dennis Esaki, a local pilot with plenty of knowledge and experience. **Will Squyres Helicopters,** 808/245-8881 or 888/245-4354, www.helicopters-hawaii.com, is a small operation with personalized service from an owner who loves his work. At **Air Kauai,** 808/246-4666 or 800/972-4666, www.airkauai.com, owner and pilot Charles DiPiazza takes personal care of you in his air-conditioned AS350B with oversize and extra windows; he offers seven flights per day.

Two reputable companies fly from Burns Field in Hanapepe. **Bali Hai Helicopters,** 808/335-3166 or 800/325-8687, www.balihai-helitour.com, has an office along the highway in town. Bali Hai offers 45- and 60-minute flights for $110 and $139 on their four-passenger Bell Ranger machines. **Inter-Island Helicopters,** 808/335-5009, www.hawaiian.net/~interisland, flies a Hughes 500, four-seater with the doors off to give you a real open-air experience. Along with the basic one-hour tour at $170, it also offers a waterfall picnic stop on private land for $225. You can find the Inter-Island office at the airfield.

The only company flying out of Princeville is **Heli USA,** 808/826-6591, www.heliusa.com. It flies similar round-island routes, but skips some of the residential and farming area on the south shore.

**Ni'ihau Helicopters,** P.O. Box 450, Kaumakani, HI 96747, 808/335-3500 or 877/441-3500, has an office in the old sugar town of Kaumakani but flies out of Burns Field. The primary purpose of Ni'ihau Helicopters is to provide medical and emergency treatment for the residents of Ni'ihau. However, to defray costs, daily tourist charters are offered on its twin-engine Agusta 109A, when there are enough passengers. The flight runs three to four hours, one hour of flight time with the remainder on a beach. The rate is $280 per person. While it cannot compete for scenery with helicopter companies that regularly fly only over Kaua'i, it does offer you the only way to land on Ni'ihau except for the hunting safaris run by the same company.

## Ultralight Power Hang Gliding

**Birds in Paradise,** 808/822-5309, www.birdsinparadise.com, instructs you how to soar above the emerald green and azure blue of Kaua'i in a 70 horsepower ultralight power glider. Instructor Gerry Charlebois has thrilled over 10,000 brave and slightly wacky souls in the skies above Kaua'i. He describes his apparently skyworthy craft as a "motorcycle with wings," and advertises that it's "the most fun you can have with your clothes on." Safety features include a backup rocket parachute that will bring the entire craft safely to the ground, and a surprising structural strength certified twice as strong as a Cessna and capable of withstanding 6 Gs positive load and 3 Gs negative. This state-of-the-art tandem glider needs only about 100 feet for takeoff and landing, and Gerry has mounted both a video and a still camera so you can write back home, "Look, Mom-no hands"-and, as she's always said, not much sense either. For those who enjoy pushing the envelope in a contraption soaring at 55 mph, prices are $100 for a 30-minute lesson, $175 for one hour. Advanced instructional flights run $255 for 90 minutes and $330 for two hours, which is enough time to get you around the island. All flights leave from Burns Field in Hanapepe.

## Accommodations and Food

### ACCOMMODATIONS

Kaua'i is very lucky when it comes to places to stay. It's been blessed by a combination of happenstance and planning. The island was not a major Hawaiian destination until the early 1970s. By that time, all concerned had wised up to the fact that what you *don't do* is build endless miles of high-rise hotels and condos that blot out the sun and ruin the view of the coast. Besides that, a very strong grassroots movement here insisted on tastefully done low-rise structures that blend into and complement the surrounding natural setting. This concept mandates "destination resorts," the kind of hotels and condos that lure visitors because of their superb architecture, artistic appointments, and luxurious grounds. There is room for growth on Kaua'i, but the message is clear: Kaua'i is the most beautiful island of them all, and the preservation of this delicate beauty benefits everyone.

Kaua'i has about 7,000 accommodation units in roughly 175 properties, some 3,000 of which are condominium and timeshare units. There are three major resort areas on Kaua'i: the Coconut Coast, Po'ipu south shore, and Princeville. The Coconut Coast is the oldest of these areas and has a concentration of condominiums; its occupancy rate and price per room are the lowest of the three main resort areas. Po'ipu, which has the best general-purpose beach and is the most popular destination on Kaua'i, was the first big resort development on the island, and it has a good mix of hotel, condo, B&B, and vacation rental properties. The average price per room here and at Princeville is roughly the same. The north shore Princeville development has mostly high-end condos and hotel rooms. In addition to these three areas, Lihu'e, which had the island's first major high-rise hotel, has one excellent destination resort and many modest family-run hotel and motels. On the outskirts of town are two affordable hotel and condo properties. Vacation rentals and B&Bs along the north shore are located primarily in Kilauea, Hanalei, and Ha'ena,

**Whether right on the water or inland with a view, condominiums offer visitors plenty of amenities and good value.**

ROBERT NILSEN

KAUA'I

# TIME-SHARES

While time-share accommodations are a factor on all the major islands except Lana'i, Kaua'i has taken to the concept in a big way. Nearly 50 percent of the state's total time-share units are on the Garden Island. Whether condo apartments or hotel suites, these units are handled in various ways. Generally speaking, specific units are bought for a specified length of time during the year, usually in one-week increments, guaranteeing you vacation accommodations year after year—whether you use them or not. With some organizations, these units can be traded for rooms in other associated time-share complexes around the country (or world). If you do not use your time-share during your time slot, most overseeing companies can rent it for you for that time. With some time-share groups, no specific units are negotiated, but points are bought and these can be used to reserve space wherever the company has properties.

The price of purchasing a time-share unit varies based on its luxury and location, and there will be some additional annual fees involved for maintenance and administration. Units are sold directly through time-share companies, some real estate agents, and time-share resale offices. Time-share companies have requirements for sales that may include, among other things, ownership of a house, specific minimum income level, and U.S. citizenship.

One of the favorite means employed by time-share companies to get you to look at their properties is to offer greatly reduced activity prices—you'll see these activity booths all over the island—in exchange for your attendance at a seminar and sales session. If you don't mind the sales pitch and accompanying pressure to purchase, try one out. Others wouldn't waste their time with such dealings while on vacation, even if it meant reduced activity rates.

and there is one condominium in Ha'ena, literally the last resort. Along the south shore, some rooms are available in Kalaheo, but there is not much from there to the west end, except one relaxing cottage-type property in Waimea. Scattered throughout the rest of the island are mostly vacation rental and B&B accommodations, and the island's one hostel is located in Kapa'a. Long stretches along the coast between the major centers have very little lodging.

# FOOD

## Lu'au

When asked about recommendations for a lu'au on Kaua'i, nearly everyone suggests **Smith's Tropical Paradise Garden Lu'au**, held within the Tropical Paradise Gardens along the banks of the Wailua River. As with most such lu'au, this one starts with an *imu* ceremony, followed by drinks and a full buffet meal. While the food is not necessarily better than anywhere else, the entertainment is different and separate from the meal. Not the typical Polynesian review, here the spectacle includes Hawaiian music, a fiery volcanic eruption, and dances from all the major

ethnic groups that have made Hawaii their home. Held Monday, Wednesday, and Friday, the gates open at 5 P.M.; the price is $56 for adults, $28.50 for children 7–13, and $18.75 for ages 3–6. Check-in for the music pageant only is at 7:30 P.M.; $15 for adults, $7.50 for kids under age 12. Call 808/821-6895 or 808/821-6896 for reservations-a must-or pick up tickets at the garden entrance or at the Smith's booth across from the entrance to the Coco Palms on the north side of the river mouth.

The **Kauai Coconut Beach Resort** presents a daily lu'au, 6–8:30 P.M., at its *lu'au halau* under a canopy of stars and palm trees. The *imu* ceremony takes place at 6:15 P.M. so you can see the pig taken from the pit and readied for the meal. Hawaiian- and local-style food is served from 6:30 P.M., with cocktails ongoing until the show begins. Afterward, lean back and watch Hawaiian-only music and dance-no extravaganza, just fine sights and sounds. The enthusiastic entertainment is a combination of *kahiko* (ancient hula) and *awana* (modern hula), performed by an accomplished troupe of both men and women. Most numbers are *kahiko*—dignified, refined, and low-key portrayals of the tales and myths of ancient

KAUA'I

Hawaii. Intermixed are *awana* numbers, startling, colorful, and reminiscent of the days when Elvis was still the gyrating king of *Blue Hawaii*. Admission for adults is $55, $50 for seniors, $33 for children age 12–17, and $23 for the little ones 3–11; call 808/822-3455 for reservations.

Every Monday only at 5:30 P.M., the Radisson Kauai Beach Resort presents the Old Hawaiian Style Lu'au. Unless the weather precludes, this event is held in the central garden by the pool. A full buffet dinner is followed by song and dance of the ancestors. Rates run $55 for adults and $27.50 for kids age 6–12; call 808/355-5828 for reservations.

**Reflections of Paradise** takes place at the Kilohana Carriage House, Tuesday and Thursday at 6:15 P.M. The evening starts here with a roast pig and other goodies being taken from the *imu*. The full buffet is followed by a show of music and dance from all of Polynesia, both ancient and modern, that you may be invited to participate in. Adults are $58, seniors and teens $54, and children 4–12 $30; 808/245-9593 for reservations.

**Pa'ina 'O Hanalei** beachside lu'au is per-formed at the Princeville Hotel on Monday and Thursday evenings at 6 P.M. near the swiming pool at the hotel. Food is prepared by the hotel kitchen and the performance is a rousing Polynesian review. Adults $68, children 6–12 $33; seniors $55. Call 808/826-2788 for reservations.

Down-home and thoroughly local, **Tahiti Nui** presents a full buffet and Polynesian show every Wednesday 5–8 P.M. in Hanalei. Since 1963, this family-run operation serves real Hawaiian food and offers a show that's not glitzy extravaganza or slick production. This lu'au is very casual Kaua'ian, and everybody has a good time. Adults $52, $30 teens, and $20 for children 3–11; call 808/826-6277 for reservations.

The only lu'au on the south coast is **Drums of Paradise,** 808/742-1234, held at the Hyatt Regency in Po'ipu every Thursday and Sunday evening 6–8 P.M. Presented on the lawn of the lower garden, the full buffet dinner is followed by an elaborate and high-energy Polynesian show. Adults $65, Juniors $50, and children 6–12 years $32.

# Getting There

Until very recently, there were no nonstop flights to Kaua'i. All passengers had to go through Honolulu to get to Kaua'i. Since 1999, United Airlines has run daily fights from Los Angeles to Kaua'i and has added a flight from San Francisco. All other major domestic and foreign carriers fly to Honolulu and have arrangements with either Hawaiian Airlines or Aloha Airlines for getting you to Kaua'i. If you fly from the Mainland with Hawaiian or Aloha, you have the added convenience of dealing with just one airline to get you to Kaua'i. Several charter airlines also fly to Kaua'i nonstop from the Mainland.

## Kaua'i's Airport
**Lihu'e Airport,** less than two miles from downtown Lihu'e, receives the vast majority of Kaua'i's commercial flights. On arrival, you're immediately struck by the warm balmy temperature and gentle island breezes. No public transportation to or from the airport is available, so you must either rent a car or hire a taxi. The terminal, long and low, has arrival lounges at both ends and the departure lounge in the middle. In the departure lounge are a restaurant and cocktail lounge, snack shop, flower shop, gift shop, restrooms, public telephones, and ATM machines. The gift shop sells pre-inspected island fruit that's boxed and ready to transport. For your entertainment, Hawaiian music is performed several mornings each week in the main lobby 9–11:30 A.M., and historical and cultural displays are located here and there around the terminal. Baggage pickup is at either end, Aloha and United to the left as you enter the terminal from the plane, Hawaiian Airlines and others to the right—follow the signs. In each baggage claim area are restrooms, public telephones, and free tourist brochures. Outside the baggage claim areas are tourist information booths (usually staffed) with additional brochures and a courtesy

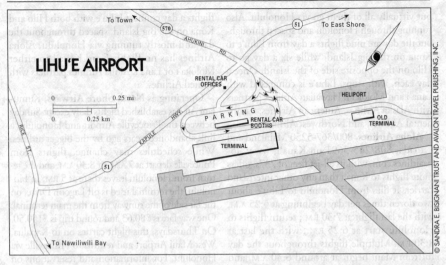

LIHU'E AIRPORT

phone for information. Check-in counters are along the outside corridor of the central section—Hawaiian Airlines on the left and Aloha and United on the right as you look at the terminal building. Additional space is used by charter airlines. All non-carry-on baggage must go through an agricultural inspection at the terminal entrance; carry-on luggage is run through X-ray machines. All major car rental agencies maintain booths just outside the main entranceway, and each has a base lot beyond the airport ring road that is serviced by van pick up. Public parking is 5:30 A.M.–9:45 P.M. Parking fees run $1 for the first half hour, $1 for each additional hour, with a $7 maximum up to 24 hours. Taxi stands are at both ends of the terminal, and a courtesy taxi phone can be found at each outside tourist information counter.

The old terminal at the Lihu'e Airport, a few hundred yards down Ahukini Road, is now used by flight-see airplane and interisland charter companies. Across the street is the heliport, used actively by more than half a dozen helicopter companies offering sightseeing tours of the island.

**Burns Field** (Port Allan Airport) in Hanapepe was the first commercial airstrip on the island, but it hasn't been used as such for years. There are no facilities here whatsoever, and the strip is used only by three helicopter and one ultralight aircraft tour companies.

**Princeville Airport,** along Route 56 just east of Princeville, served commercial commuter air flights until the mid-1990s, when those routes were discontinued. After a few years hiatus, North Shore Airways began passenger airline service between Princeville and Honolulu, with connection to Kapalua, Maui. The Princeville Airport is used by an occasional private plane that only needs a short runway, but much more frequently by the HeliUSA helicopter company, and is often referred to by residents of the area as the heliport. The terminal is a cute little building made inconspicuous by the immense beauty surrounding it. Here you'll find a toilet, telephone, an Avis car rental office, and Amelia's Cafe and lounge (upstairs).

## Interisland Carriers

The majority of flights from **Hawaiian Airlines,** 800/367-5320 Mainland and Canada, 800/882-8811 statewide, or 808/245-4516 on Kaua'i, www.hawaiianair.com, are to and from Honolulu, with about a dozen and a half per day in each direction. Hawaiian Airlines flights to Lihu'e from Honolulu begin at 5:35 A.M., with flights thereafter about every hour until 7:30 P.M. Flights from Lihu'e to Honolulu begin at 6:35 A.M. and go all day until 8:30 P.M. About a dozen flights run to/from Kahului, Maui, starting around 6:30 A.M. and running until almost 6:30 P.M., but virtually all of them go via Honolulu. Also running through Honolulu and spaced throughout the day are nine flights a day from Lihu'e to Kona on the Big Island, while six a day go to Hilo on the opposite side of the island. Once a day each, with stops, Lihu'e is connected with Lana'i and Moloka'i. Hawaiian Airlines partners with Alaska Airlines, American Airlines, Continental Airlines, and Northwest Airlines.

**Aloha Airlines,** 800/367-5250 Mainland and Canada, 808/245-3691 on Kaua'i, www.alohaairlines.com, with its all-jet fleet of 737s, offers more flights to Kaua'i than any other interisland carrier. It flies from Honolulu to Lihu'e about two dozen times per day beginning at 5:25 A.M. with the last flight at 7:30 P.M.; return flights to Honolulu start at 6:25 P.M., with the last at 8:30 P.M. Multiple flights throughout the day to/from Maui begin at around 6:30 A.M. and run until after 6:30 P.M., and all but a handful stop in Honolulu on the way. About a dozen

flights a day connect Lihu'e with both Hilo and Kona on the Big Island, spaced throughout the day and mostly running via Honolulu. Aloha Airlines has no flights from Kaua'i to either Moloka'i or Lana'i. Aloha Airlines partners with United Airlines.

Operating as **North Shore Airways,** Kumulani Air has established flights daily except Sunday between the Princeville Airport and Honolulu, a link abandoned years ago by the bigger airlines. While schedules may change, flights from Princeville depart at 7 A.M. or 8:30 A.M. and the return from Honolulu leaves there at 5 P.M. In Honolulu, the terminal used is off Lagoon Drive, on the far side of the runway from the main terminal. One way fare is $80.63 and round trip is $150.50. On Thursdays, this flight carries on to Kapalua, West Maui Airport and returns to Princeville via Honolulu. For information and reservations on Kaua'i, call 808/826-7499 or 866/867-4673, or check online at www.northshoreairways.com.

## Getting Around

The most common way to get around Kaua'i is by rental car. The abundance of agencies keeps prices competitive. As always, reserve during peak season, but in the off-season you may take your chances by shopping around to score a good deal. Kaua'i also has limited shuttle-bus service; expensive taxis; reasonable bicycle, moped, and scooter rentals; and the good old (legal) thumb.

### Highway Overview

Kaua'i is nearly round, and one major highway nearly circles the island. Starting in Lihu'e and running north, Highway 56 (Kuhio Highway) goes as far as Ke'e Beach past Hanalei; running west, Highway 50 (Kaumuali'i Highway) runs past Kekaha nearly to Polihale. From the far northern end to the west end, it's about 70 miles and will take about two hours of driving time at a comfortable speed. Only a few major roadways lead off of this coast highway. In and near Lihu'e, they are: Route 570, which runs from the center of town to the airport; Route 51, Kapule Highway, leading from Hanama'ulu to Nawili-

wili Harbor; Route 58, Nawiliwili Road, from Kukui Grove Shopping Center also to Nawiliwili Harbor; and Route 583, Ma'alo Road, which goes to Wailua Waterfall from Kapaia. North of Lihu'e, Route 580, Kuamo'o Road, runs inland from Wailua, and Route 581, Kamalo Road, circles inland from Kapa'a around the backside of the "Sleeping Giant" to meet Route 580. Along the south shore, Route 520, Maluhia Road, leaves Route 50 at the Tunnel of Trees and runs down to Koloa and Po'ipu; Route 530, Koloa Road, connects Lawa'i and Koloa; and Route 540, Halewili Road, sweeps down through the coffee plantation, running from Kalaheo to 'Ele'ele. The longest and most significant highway running off of the coast road is Route 550, Waimea Canyon Drive, connecting Kekaha to Koke'e State Park.

### Auto Rental Agencies

The following major firms maintain booths at the Lihu'e Airport. Some companies have cars waiting at the airport, but most shuttle guests to the baseyard just beyond the airport circle road or close by in town to pick up their vehicle.

**Dollar,** 808/245-3651.

**Alamo,** 808/246-0646.

**National Car Rental,** 808/245-5636.

**Avis,** 808/245-3512. Avis is the only company that maintains a small booth at the Princeville Airport, 808/826-9773.

**Budget,** 800/527-0700 worldwide.

**Hertz,** 808/245-3356.

**Thrifty,** 808/246-6252.

A local company with a reputation for being reliable is **Westside-U-Drive,** 808/332-8644.

## Vanity Cars

**Hawaiian Riders,** 808/822-5409 or 888/527-9484, www.hawaiianriders.com, has a rental office on Kaua'i across from the Waipouli Town Center, open 8 A.M.–5 P.M. daily. If you want to splurge or have a need to impress, this company has something that will do the job. How about a bright yellow Corvette convertible? Maybe a new Plymouth Prowler or the Dodge Viper is more your style. These cars are not cheap; if you want the look, you have to pay. They run from $300 a day for the 'vette to $550 a day for the Viper; part-day rentals can also be arranged. To rent one of these babies, you must be 21 years old and have a credit card in your name. Hawaiian Riders also rents motorcycles, mopeds, and bikes.

## Motorcycles

In business since 1986, **Ray's Motorcycle Rentals,** 808/822-4644, has only Harley-Davidsons. They're very well maintained and come with a spit shine. You need four things to rent and ride one of these bikes: a valid driver's license with motorcycle endorsement, to be 21 years old or older, to wear long pants, and to wear closed-toe shoes. Aside from that, you must know how to ride—you may get a short test in the parking lot! Bikes run $100 per day (tax included, no hidden costs), and all equipment is supplied: helmets, goggles, glasses, and jackets. While helmets are not required by law in the state of Hawaii, they are recommended. The shop opens at 8 A.M. and all bikes must be back by 5 P.M.

Now and again, other motorcycle rental companies open up shop on the island. Try **Hawaiian Riders,** 808/822-5409 or 888/527-9484, in Waipouli, which has half a dozen Harley models that run from $39 for three hours to $199 for 24 hours.

## Mopeds

These tiny two-wheelers are available from **Hawaiian Riders,** 808/822-5409 or 888/527-9484, at their office in Waipouli across from the Waipouli Town Center. Rental rates range from $20 for two hours to $39 for eight hours. The store also rents full-size motorcycles, exotic cars, and bicycles. To rent a moped or motorcycle, you must be 21 years old; a credit card is required for some rentals, while a cash deposit is all right for others.

# ALTERNATIVE TRANSPORTATION

## The Kaua'i Bus

One of the benefits to come out of the destruction caused by Hurricane 'Iniki was the establishment of limited public bus transportation. The 'Iniki Express, set up after the hurricane and free at one time, has morphed into **The Kaua'i Bus,** run by the Transportation Agency of the county Offices of Community Assistance, 3220 Hoolako St., Lihu'e, HI 96766, 808/241-6410. Write or call Mon.–Sat. 7 A.M.–5 P.M. for a current route schedule. Operating times are Mon.–Sat. 5:15 A.M.–8 P.M. (no operation Sunday and holidays). The regular fare is $1.50 ($15 for a monthly pass) or 75 cents for seniors, students, and people with disabilities if carrying I.D. The bus will pick up and drop off only at designated bus stops, and it does not allow large bags or items such as backpacks and boogie boards, but baby strollers are okay.

Each bus displays a route sign at the front and on its curb side. The Kaua'i Bus runs two main routes along the coast highway, north to Hanalei and west to Kekaha, with the addition of one circle route in Lihu'e and one route up to Kapahi above Kapa'a. Although buses have scheduled times, they do not run on regular intervals; there may be as little as one-half hour or as much as 2.5 hours between runs. Please check a current printed bus schedule. Route 100 runs from Kekaha to Lihu'e, and Route 200 makes the reverse run. One bus a day in each direction—early morning and late afternoon—dips down for a circle of Koloa and Po'ipu via Lawa'i before proceeding. Route 400 connects Hanalei to Lihu'e, and Route 500 does the reverse, while Route 600 runs from Lihu'e to Kapahi via Kapa'a and returns. The Lihu'e Extension, Route 700, 8 A.M.–3 P.M. only, starts at the Kukui Grove Shopping Center, runs down to Nawiliwili Harbor, and travels up Rice Street to the County Building. From there it goes along the highway to the Wilcox Hospital before returning to the center of town, Nawiliwili Harbor, and Kukui Grove Shopping Center. Saturday service is reduced by about half, with no service at all on routes 600 and 700. One wonders just how long this bus system will maintain funding—most of the buses seem to run nearly empty. If you do not have a rental car, it is possible to get around by bus, but it will not be convenient nor will it necessarily take you where you want to go.

## Taxi

Taxis are all metered and charge a hefty price for their services; all have the same rates. While many are still sedans, minivans are increasing in num-ber. Airport taxis have a monopoly on pick-ups at the airport, although others can drop off there. Sample fares: $5–6 from Lihu'e to the airport; $30–35 from Po'ipu to Lihu'e; $12–15 from Lihu'e to Wailua; $18–20 from Lihu'e to Kapa'a; $55 from Lihu'e to Waimea; $62 from Lihu'e to Princeville; and $22 from Princeville to Ke'e Beach and the Kalalau trailhead. Reputable taxi companies include **Akiko's,** 808/822-7588, in Kapa'a; **City Cab,** 808/245-3227, in Lihu'e; **Kauai Taxi,** 808/246-9554, also in Lihu'e; **Southshore Cab,** 808/742-1525 in Poi'pu; and **North Shore Cab,** 808/639-7829, and **Taxi Hanalei,** 808/639-1188, in Hanalei.

For limousine service, try **Kauai Limo Corporation,** 808/ 808/245-4855 or 800/764-7213. On the North Shore, call **Kauai North Shore limousine,** 808/826-6189.

## Hitchhiking

Using your thumb to get around is legal on Kaua'i, but you must stay off the paved portion of the road. For short hops in and around the towns—like from Koloa to Po'ipu or from the airport to Lihu'e—thumbing may not be difficult. But getting out to the Kalalau Trail or to Polihale on the west end when you're toting a backpack and appear to be going a longer distance is tough. As on all the islands, you're most likely to be picked up by a visiting or local *haole*. Sometimes locals in pickup trucks will stop to give you a ride for short distances. Women *should not* hitch alone!

# Information and Services

## Emergencies

For **police, fire,** and **ambulance** anywhere on Kaua'i, dial 911.

**Non-emergency police** assistance and information: 808/241-6711.

**Coast Guard Search and Rescue:** 800/552-6458.

**Civil defense:** In case of natural disaster such as hurricanes or tsunami on Kaua'i call 808/241-6336.

**Sexual Assault Crisis Line:** 808/245-4144.

For recorded messages 24 hours a day: **weather,** 808/245-2919, or the National Weather Service, 808/245-6001; **marine and surf report,** 808/245-3564; and **time of day,** 808/245-0212.

## Medical Services

The island's principal medical facility is the full-service **Wilcox Memorial Hospital,** 3420 Kuhio Hwy., Lihu'e, 808/245-1100; dial 808/245-1010 for 24-hour emergencies. Smaller facilities are **West Kaua'i Medical Center,** in Waimea at 808/338-9431, which is also open for 24-hour medical emergencies; and **Samuel Mahelona Memorial Hospital,** in Kapa'a, 808/822-4961.

Medical services are also available from **Kaua'i Medical Group,** 3420 B Kuhio Hwy., Lihu'e, 808/245-1500; after hours call 808/245-1831. The urgent-care walk-in clinic runs Mon.–Sat. 9 A.M.–4 P.M. and Sunday 10 A.M.–3 P.M.; the regular clinic runs weekdays 8 A.M.–5 P.M. and weekends 8 A.M.–noon. There are additional offices in 'Ele'ele, Kapa'a, Koloa, Kukui Grove Shopping Center, and Kilauea.

Additional options include the **Hale Le'a Family Medicine** clinic, 808/828-2885, in Kilauea and open daily except Sunday; the **Princeville Medical Clinic,** 808/826-7228, at the Princeville Center; and the **Kalaheo Clinic,** 808/332-8523 in Kalaheo. In Kapa'a, the Samuel Mahelona Hospital sponsors a **walk-in clinic,** 808/823-4175, weekdays 9 A.M.–5 P.M.

For the **Natural Health and Pain Relief Clinic** in Kapa'a, call 808/245-2277.

Many pharmacies give senior discounts. Options include **Southshore Pharmacy,** 808/742-7511, in Koloa; **Westside Pharmacy,** 808/335-5342, in Hanapepe; **Shoreview Pharmacy,** 808/822-1447, in Kapa'a; and **Longs Drugs,** in the Kukui Grove Shopping Center, 808/245-7771, and in Kapa'a, 808/822-4915. All the hospitals and medical groups also have their own pharmacies.

## Consumer Protection

If you encounter accommodations problems, bad service, or downright rip-offs while on Kaua'i, try the following: Chamber of Commerce, 808/245-7363; Office of Consumer Protection, O'ahu, 808/586-2630; and the Better Business Bureau of Hawaii on O'ahu, 808/536-6956.

## Tourist Information

The best information on Kaua'i is dispensed by Kaua'i Visitors Bureau, 4334 Rice St., Suite 101, Lihu'e, HI 96766, 808/245-3971 or 800/262-1400, www.kauaivisitorsbureau.org.

## Post Offices

The central post office on Kaua'i is at 4441 Rice St., Lihu'e. Main branches are at Kapa'a, Koloa, and Waimea, with more than a dozen others scattered around the island.

## Reading Material

The Kaua'i central **library** is at 4344 Hardy St., Lihu'e, 808/241-3222. Branch libraries are in Hanapepe, Kapa'a, Koloa, Princeville, and Waimea. Check with the main library for times and services.

Free **tourist literature** and the narrow-format, magazine-style *This Week Kauai, Spotlight's Kauai Gold,* and *Kauai Activity and Attractions* are available at the airport, many hotels, and most restaurants and shopping centers around the island. They come out monthly or quarterly and contain money-saving coupons, island maps, and information on local

KAUA'I

events, activities, shopping, and restaurants. *Kauai Beach Press* has similar content with the addition of stories but is in a newspaper format. Other such magazines and guides appear now and again at the same locations. With a focus on activities and fun things to do, *101 Things to do on Kauai* is a great resource and also has money-saving coupons. *Menu* is an informative magazine that lists restaurants and details of their menus. *Kauai Drive Guide* is available from the car rental agencies and contains tips, coupons, and good maps. The Hawaii AAA *Tourbook* is also very useful. Other publications of interest are the *Kauai Magazine* and the in-flight magazines of Aloha and Hawaiian Airlines.

There is one main island newspaper, *The Garden Island*, www.kauaiworld.com, published daily, 50 cents daily and $1 on Sunday. It can be picked up at numerous stands around the island.

## Kaua'i Radio Stations

The following stations are broadcast on Kaua'i.

Some high-powered stations from O'ahu can be picked up on Kaua'i as well.

**KONG 570 AM:** news, talk, and sports

**KUAI 720 AM:** contemporary, sports, surf reports, requests, some Hawaiian oldies

**KKCR 91.9 and 90.9 FM:** nonprofit community radio station with various formats

**KONG 93.5 FM:** the "big gorilla" on the island—contemporary and requests.

**KSRF 95.9 FM:** "Surf." island sounds

**KFMN 96.9 FM:** adult contemporary

**KITH 98.9 FM:** Travelhost. Island sounds and commercial travel information

**KTOH 99.9 FM:** oldies from the 50s to the 90s

**KSHK 103.3 FM:** "Shaka." classic rock and roll

## Island Facts

Kaua'i's nickname is "The Garden Island," and it is the oldest of the main Hawaiian Islands. The official island color is purple, and its lei is made from the *mokihana,* a small native citrus fruit with a slight anise-fragrance that changes color from green to brown as it matures.

# Lihu'e

The stacks of the Lihu'e sugar mill let you know where you are: in a former plantation town on one of the world's most gorgeous islands. Lihu'e (Cold Chill) began growing cane in the 1840s, and its fields were among Hawaii's most productive. Until 1996, when the Lihu'e mill shut down, cane from the surrounding fields was crushed here. Fields around town still grow cane that's trucked elsewhere for processing. Lihu'e, the county seat, has 5,200 residents, with an additional 6,800 in the nearby bedroom communities of Puhi and Hanama'ulu. With this strong agricultural base and its standing as the county seat, the town has flourished and boasts all the modern conveniences, including shopping centers, a library, museum, a hospital, and the island's principal airport and commercial harbor. But the feel is still somewhat of a company town that's only slowly expanding its opportunities. Only a few short years ago Lihu'e had but two

traffic lights; it now has nearly a dozen, with a growing rush-hour traffic problem. It isn't the geographical center of the island, but it is halfway along the coastal road that encircles the island, making it a perfect jumping-off point for exploring the rest of Kaua'i. It has a great concentration of local restaurants, a major resort, right-priced accommodations, some entertainment, and the most varied shopping. One of the island's best beaches is within a five-minute drive of downtown, and you can be out of town and exploring long before your shave ice begins to melt.

Lihu'e's two bedroom communities, Puhi to the west and Hanama'ulu to the north, add to the strength and importance of this area. Puhi has the island's only higher educational institution, Kaua'i Community College, and a growing industrial park. Hanama'ulu, an old sugar community, has a stronger past than present but hangs on because of its close proximity to Lihu'e. Its small center has

The Lihue Lutheran Church is the oldest in the islands.

a handful of well-established stores and a restaurant with a great reputation, and down at the coast is a fine beach park. Between Lihu'e and Hanama'ulu is the tiny settlement of Kapaia, a wide spot in the road in the Hanama'ulu Stream valley that has two additional fine shops and two churches, the 1884 Immaculate Conception Catholic Church, and Lihu'e Hongwanji Buddhist Tem-ple. Both religious buildings, fine examples from days gone by, are well kept for present use. Stop for a look. Kapaia Stitchery is perhaps the best shop on the island for sewing and quilting supplies, and, oddly enough, the other store, Wailua Falls Gallery, sells handmade woodwork and fine cigars. From Kapaia, Ma'alo Road (Rte. 583) runs up through former cane fields to Wailua Falls.

# Sights

## KAUA'I MUSEUM

If you really want to enrich your Kaua'i experience, this is the first place to visit. Spending an hour or two here infuses you with a wealth of information regarding Kaua'i's social and cultural history. The two-building complex is at 4428 Rice St. in downtown Lihu'e, 808/245-6931, open Mon.–Fri. 9 A.M.–3 P.M. and Saturday 10 A.M.–2 P.M.; admission is $5, $4 seniors 65 and older, $3 students 13–17, $1 children 6–12, and free under six. For greater enrichment, museum staff conduct one-hour tours, free with admission, Monday, Tuesday, and Thursday at 10 A.M.

Dedicated in 1924 to Albert Spencer Wilcox, son of pioneer missionaries in Hanalei, the main building has a Greco-Roman facade and was the public library until 1970. Its two floors house the main gallery, devoted to ethnic heritage and island art exhibits that are changed on a regular basis. Included here is a small but fascinating exhibit of calabashes, koa furniture, quilts, and feather lei. One large calabash belonged to Princess Ruth, who gave it to a local child. Its finish, hand-rubbed with the original *kukui* nut oil, still shows a fine luster. The rear of the main floor is dedicated to the Senda Gallery, with its collection of vintage photos shot by W. J. Senda, a Japanese immigrant from Matsue who arrived in 1906. These black and whites are classics, opening a window onto old Kaua'i. Upstairs in the small Oriental Art Gallery is a fine selection of art objects, mostly from China and Japan. Revolving shows, sometimes of contemporary art and crafts or children's art, are held in a second gallery on this floor.

On the far end of the first floor, the Museum Shop sells books, cards, Hawaiiana prints, a wonderful selection of Hawaiian craft items, and a fine selection of detailed U.S. Geological Survey maps of the entire island. Some inexpensive but tasteful purchases include baskets, wooden bowls, and pieces of tapa.

Kaua'i's fascinating natural and cultural history begins to unfold when you walk through the courtyard into the second half of the museum, the William Hyde Rice Building. Notice the large black iron pot used to cook sugarcane. The exhibits are self-explanatory, chronicling Kaua'i's development over the centuries. The windows of the Natural History Tunnel show the zones of cultivation on Kaua'i, along with its beaches and native forests. Farther on is an extensive collection of Kaua'i shells, old photos, and the history and genealogy of Kaua'ian royalty and the ruling class. The central first-floor area has a model of a Hawaiian village, a collection of weapons, some fine examples of adzes used to hollow canoes, and a model of the HMS *Resolution* at anchor off Waimea. An excerpt from the ship's log records Captain Cook's thoughts on the day that he discovered Hawaii for the rest of the world.

As you ascend the stairs to the second floor, history continues to unfold. Missionaries stare from old photos, their countenances the epitome of piety and zeal. Most old photos record the plantation era. Be sure to see the Spalding Shell Collection, gathered by Colonel Spalding, an Ohio veteran of the Civil War who came to Kaua'i and married the daughter of Captain James Makee, owner of the Makee Sugar Company. Shells from around the world join examples

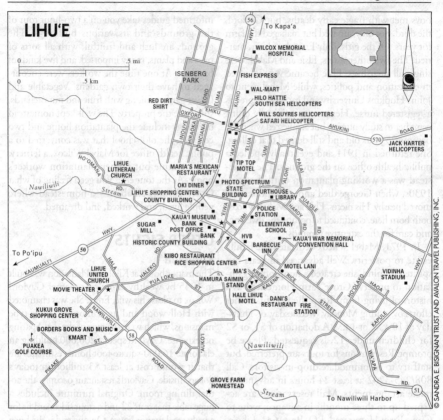

of magnificent koa furniture, table settings, children's toys, dolls, and photos of Ni'ihau—about all that the outside world ever sees. Follow the stairs back to the ground floor and notice the resplendent examples of feather capes on the wall. On the main floor, in an alcove by the front door, push the button to immerse yourself in a short video of Kaua'i. This pictorial is a treat for the eyes; soothing Hawaiian chanting in the background sets the mood.

## GROVE FARM HOMESTEAD

Grove Farm is a plantation started in 1864 by George Wilcox, the son of Congregational missionary teachers, who worked for the original owner of the surrounding acreage. The first owner

saw no future in the parched land and sold around 500 acres to Wilcox for $12,000, which he had 10 years to repay in a lease-to-purchase arrangement. Through a system of aqueducts, Wilcox brought water down from the mountains and began one of the most profitable sugar plantations in Hawaii. During the years following, he bought additional surrounding land, and at its height the property encompassed 27,000 acres. Currently it stands at slightly less than 22,000 acres—still sizable, and one of the five largest landholdings on the island.

George Wilcox never married. In 1870, his brother Sam came to live on the homestead, and in 1874, Sam married Emma, the daughter of missionaries from the Big Island. The couple had six children—three boys and three girls. Two of the boys met with tragic early deaths, but Gaylord, the third, not only survived but managed the farm for years. Of the girls, only Etta, the oldest, married. The two other sisters, Elsie and Mabel, were single all their lives. Elsie became very involved in education and politics, while Mabel went to Johns Hopkins University and earned a degree as a registered nurse. Her parents originally didn't want her to study nursing but acquiesced when she became 25 years old and still desired that calling. She returned in 1911 and eventually opened a public health office on the grounds. The homestead was a working plantation until the mid-1930s, when George died and operations were moved nearby. His nieces, Elsie and Mabel Wilcox, both born here, continued to occupy the dwellings and care for the extensive grounds.

In 1971, Mabel Wilcox dedicated the family estate to posterity. Well advanced in years but spirited in mind, she created a nonprofit organization to preserve Grove Farm Homestead as a historical living farm. Reap the benefits of her efforts by visiting Monday, Wednesday, or Thursday at 10 A.M. or 1 P.M. A donation of $5, or $2 for children under 12, is requested. Please be prompt! Reservations for tours are preferred, but staff try to accommodate drop-in visitors. Call 808/245-3202 at least 24 hours in advance to make arrangements. Mail reservations are accepted up to three months in advance; write to Grove Farm Homestead, P.O. Box 1631, Lihu'e, HI 96766. The homestead is off Nawiliwili Road; precise directions are given when you call. Group size is limited to give full attention to detail and minimize wear and tear on the buildings.

The first thing you might notice when entering Grove Farm is the remains of a narrow-gauge railroad track. The tracks meant sugar, and sugar meant prosperity and change for old Hawaii. A low stone wall partially surrounds the homestead, and beyond the walls are orchards, pasture, and gardens. This is no "glass-case" museum. It's a real place with living history, where people experienced the drama of changing Hawaii. It is part of what was the oldest intact sugar plantation in Hawaii. You meet at the plantation office, where you should notice the old maps on the walls showing the extent of the Wilcox landholdings. Well-informed guides take you on a two-hour tour of the grounds and its various buildings. The grounds are lush and fruitful, with all sorts of trees and plants, many imported, and five kinds of bamboo. At one time the workers were encouraged to have their own gardens. Vegetable and flower gardens, along with fruit and nut orchards, still grace the property. The well-kept homestead buildings include the plantation home and two cottages, the old school that was converted to a public health office for Mabel Wilcox, a fernery, and a simple but homey plantation worker's home. As the tour ends you get a feeling of what Grove Farm is all about—a homestead where people lived, and worked, and dreamed.

## OTHER SIGHTS

### Kilohana

The manor house at Kilohana Plantation was built in 1935 by wealthy *kama'aina* planter Gaylord Wilcox to please his wife, Ethel. She was enamored with Hollywood and its glamorous Tudor-type mansions, which were the rage of the day. Sparing no expense, Gaylord spent $200,000 building an elaborate 16,000-square-foot home; estimates are that it would cost at least $3 million in today's dollars. Inside, Gaylord's restaurant occupies the actual dining room. Original furniture includes a huge table that seats 22 and a stout sideboard fit for a truly regal manor house. On one end is the huge living room, a grand room, almost museum-like, filled with period furniture, rugs, and art pieces on the walls. As you pass from room to room—some of which are occupied by fine gift boutiques and art galleries—notice the coved ceiling, wood molding, and grand staircase. A mirror from the 1930s (mirrors in Hawaii have a tough time holding up because of the moisture) still hangs just inside the tiled main entranceway. From the flagstone rear veranda (also occupied by Gaylord's for alfresco dining), view a living tapestry of mountain and cloud, even more ethereal when mist shrouds magical Mt. Wai'ale'ale in the distance.

For a small fee, a horse and carriage takes guests through part of the 35 lush acres that surround the home, which was the center of a working farm—a feeling that lingers because of the back gardens

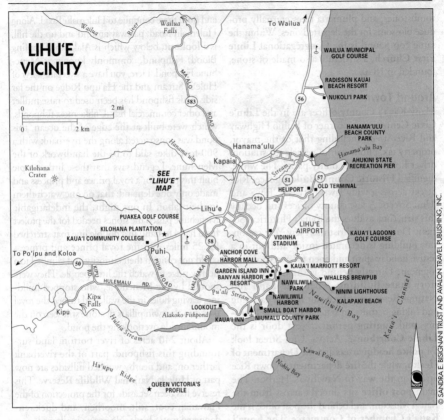

# LIHU'E VICINITY

To Wailua

Wailua River

Wailua Falls

MA'ALO ROAD

583

WAILUA MUNICIPAL GOLF COURSE

56

RADISSON KAUAI BEACH RESORT

NUKOLI'I PARK

HANAMA'ULU BEACH COUNTY PARK

Hanama'ulu Stream

51

Hanama'ulu

Kapaia

SEE "LIHU'E" MAP

Hanama'ulu Bay

AHUKINI STATE RECREATION PIER

57

HELIPORT

OLD TERMINAL

570

Lihu'e

Kilohana Crater

PUAKEA GOLF COURSE

KILOHANA PLANTATION

KAUA'I COMMUNITY COLLEGE

Puhi

To Po'ipu and Koloa

50

KIPU RD.

HULEMALU RD.

HALEHAKA RD.

PUHI ROAD

58

LIHU'E AIRPORT

VIDINHA STADIUM

KAUA'I LAGOONS GOLF COURSE

ANCHOR COVE HARBOR MALL

GARDEN ISLAND INN

BANYAN HARBOR RESORT

KAUA'I MARRIOTT RESORT

WHALERS BREWPUB

NAWILIWILI PARK

NINIINI LIGHTHOUSE

NAWILIWILI HARBOR

KALAPAKI BEACH

Nawiliwili Bay

Pu'ali Stream

Kipu Falls

Kipu

Huleia Stream

LOOKOUT

Alakoko Fishpond

KAUA'I INN

SMALL BOAT HARBOR

NIUMALU COUNTY PARK

Kawai Point

Kauai Channel

Ha'upu Ridge

QUEEN VICTORIA'S PROFILE

Nohu Bay

0    2 mi
0    2 km

© SANDRA E. BISIGNANI TRUST and AVALON TRAVEL PUBLISHING, INC.

and the remaining workers' cottages. To reach Kilohana, take Rte. 50 (Kaumuali'i Hwy.) west from Lihu'e for about two miles toward the tiny village of Puhi, and look on the mountain side for the clearly marked entrance.

## Lihu'e's Old Churches

When Rte. 56 becomes Rte. 50, just as you pass the Lihu'e Sugar Mill, look for the HVB Warrior pointing you to the **Lihue Lutheran Church.** Just before the bridge, follow Ho'omana Road up the hill through a well-kept residential area. Rebuilt following Hurricane 'Iwa in 1982, the current building is a faithful copy of the original structure built in 1885. It has everything a church should have, including a bell tower and spire, but it's all miniature. The church reflects a strong

German influence that dominated Lihu'e and its plantation until World War I. The early 20th century pastor was Hans Isenberg, brother of the plantation founder and husband to Dora Rice from the old *kama'aina* family. The outside of the church is basic New England, but inside nautical influences are visible, and the more ornate altar is reminiscent of baroque Germany. Headstones in the yard to the side indicate just how old this congregation is. In fact, with an active congregation since 1881, it is the oldest Lutheran church in the islands.

Across from the Kukui Grove Shopping Center behind the car dealership along Nawiliwili Avenue is the lava stone **Lihue United Church,** which was mostly attended by cane workers and their families. Its cemetery is filled with simple

KAUA'I

tombstones, and plumeria trees eternally produce blossoms for the departed ones. Within the same compound is the Congregational **Lihue First Church,** a structure also made of stone, founded in 1840.

## Around Town

Many Kaua'i County offices are in the **Lihu'e Civic Center** on the corner of Kuhio Highway and Rice Street, including that of the mayor, property tax, public works, vehicle registration, driver licensing, and county parks. The white, dignified **Historic County Building** faces Rice Street across a wide lawn between 'Eiwa and 'Umi Streets. A few county offices still occupy this structure, as does the Kaua'i Historical Society. During the Christmas/New Year season, this building is decorated inside and out in a festive holiday spirit and open for everyone's enjoyment. Directly behind is the newer three-story **State Building,** where the Land and Natural Resources office can handle camping and hiking permits on state land, fishing licensing, and hunting permits. Next door is the **Lihu'e Courthouse.** Across 'Umi Street look for **police headquarters** and the **Department of Health,** while the **fire department** is down Rice Street on the way to Nawiliwili Harbor. The main **post office** sits directly across from the Kaua'i Museum, and behind the post office is the **Kaua'i Chamber of Commerce.** The **Kaua'i Visitors Bureau** has its office in the Watamull Plaza building, 4334 Rice Street. Following Hardy Street back around past the Kaua'i War Memorial Convention Hall, you'll locate the main **library** across the street from Wilcox Elementary School. Look for the sweep of its roof—like the sail of an outrigger canoe. The library is open Monday and Wednesday 10 A.M.–8 P.M., Tuesday and Thursday 9 A.M.–5 P.M., Friday 10 A.M.–5 P.M., and Saturday 9 A.M.–1 P.M. East along the main drag (Kuhio Hwy.) are three gas stations, and farther out beyond Hilo Hattie and Wal-Mart is Wilcox Memorial Hospital.

## Alakoko Fishpond

From Nawiliwili Harbor, follow Wa'apa Road south through the little community of Niumalu, and from there continue to Hulemalu Road. Along Hulemalu Road, partway around and up the hill, is a **lookout,** below which is Alakoko (Rippling Blood) Fishpond, commonly known as Menehune Fishpond. Here, you have a sweeping view of Hule'ia Stream and the Ha'upu Ridge on the far side. This fishpond has been used to raise mullet and other commercial fish. Unlike most fishponds, which were built at the edge of the ocean, this pond was constructed along the riverbank with a 900-foot dike, said to be the handiwork of the Menehune. Legend says that these little people built this pond for a royal prince and princess and made only one demand: that no one watch them in their labor. In one night, the indefatigable Menehune passed the stones needed for the project from hand to hand in a double line that stretched for 25 miles. But the royal prince and princess could not contain their curiosity and climbed to a nearby ridge to watch the little people. They were spotted by the Menehune, who stopped building, leaving holes in the wall, and turned the royal pair into the twin pillars of stone still seen on the mountainside overlooking the pond.

About 240 acres of river bottom land surrounding this fishpond, part of the riverbank farther on, and nearby wooded hillsides are now part of **Hule'ia National Wildlife Reserve.** This reserve has been set aside for the protection of the Hawaiian coot, stilt, moorhen, and duck, endangered water birds. No access is allowed.

## Wailua Falls

In Kapaia, Rte. 583 (Ma'alo Road) branches from the highway and heads north into the interior. This paved road lifts up to rolling terrain with a backdrop of lofty mountain peaks. Route 583 runs through abandoned cane fields, passes a valley overlook, and ends in a parking area about four miles up, where there are always people selling crafts. Below, Wailua Falls tumbles as two spouts, flowing 80 feet over a ledge into a large round pool, while white-tailed tropicbirds circle above. It's said that the *ali'i* would come here to dive from the cliff into the pool as a show of physical prowess; commoners were not considered to be infused with enough mana to perform this feat.

ROBERT NILSEN

**Wailua Falls**

Many of the trees here are involuntary trellises for rampant morning glory. Pest or not, the blossoms are still beautiful as the weed climbs the limbs. A trail down to the falls is particularly steep and often slippery because the sun doesn't penetrate to dry the ground. Look for it about 100 feet back from the end of the guardrail, but be very careful. If you make it down, you may have the falls to yourself, but you'll be like a goldfish in a bowl with the tourists—perhaps jealously—peering down at you. This falls and the river gorge down from here are part of the Wailua River State Park.

# BEACHES AND PARKS

Lihu'e has very convenient beaches. You can sun yourself within 10 minutes of anywhere in town, with a choice of beaches on either Nawiliwili or Hanama'ulu Bay. Few tourists head to Hanama'ulu Bay, while Nawiliwili Bay is a classic example of "beauty and the beast." There is

hardly a more beautiful harbor than Nawiliwili's, with a stream flowing into it and verdant mountains all around. However, it is a working harbor complete with dock storage and petrochemical tanks. Private yachts and catamarans bob at anchor with their bright colors reflecting off dappled waters, and as your eye sweeps the lovely panorama it runs into the dull tan wall of a warehouse on the hill where raw sugar was stored before being shipped to the Mainland to be processed. It's one of those places that separates perspectives: some see the "beauty," while others focus on the "beast."

## Kalapaki Beach

This most beautiful beach at Nawiliwili fronts the lavish Kaua'i Marriott. Just follow Rice Street down until it becomes Rte. 51; you'll soon see the entrance to the hotel on your left. Park in the visitors' area at the hotel entrance, at the rear of the hotel, or at the north end of Nawiliwili Park, where a footbridge leads across Nawiliwili Stream to the hotel property and the beach. Access to the beach is open to anyone. The wave action at Kalapaki is gentle at most times, with long swells combing the sandy-bottomed beach. Kalapaki is one of the best swimming beaches on the island, only fair at best for snorkeling, but a great place to try bodysurfing, sailboarding, or begin with a surfboard. From here there are great views of the Ha'upu Range and the bay. If you're there on the right day, you can watch cruise ships sail into or out of port on their rounds of the islands.

## Nawiliwili Park

This park fronts Nawiliwili Bay, beyond the seawall to the side of Kalapaki Beach. Its lawn provides room for picnic tables, toilets, play equipment for kids, a sand volleyball court, and plenty of space for an impromptu game of football, and although it has palm trees and ironwoods for shade, it is not nearly as visually pleasing as the landscaped hotel property directly fronting the beach. Local swimmers and surfers come here for beach access, a few come to spearfish, and others come to drink beer and while away the hours under the trees. On occasion, turtles play off the rocks. Follow the road

KAUA'I

past the enclosed port area to the end of the breakwater for a good view of the inner harbor and Haʻupu Ridge.

## Niumalu County Park

Just west of the Nawiliwili Small Boat Harbor, this county-maintained park lies along the Huleʻia Stream. It's a very local park, home of the Kaiola Canoe Club, with pavilions, showers, and toilets, but no camping.

## Ninini Beach

Located to the harbor side of Ninini Point and the lighthouse, this small, unfrequented spot, with a narrow sandy beach backed up against the low cliff below Whalers Brewpub, is gentle most of the year, except when the kona winds blow in from the south. A second smaller beach is closer to the Marriott below the golf course. These secluded beaches are generally frequented by locals. Head past the hotel and turn right, going past the few private homes that overlook the bay. Walk along the edge of the golf course until you see the two beaches below, both good for sunbathing. There is also access from the brewpub parking lot.

To get to **Ninini Point Lighthouse,** take the paved road across from Vidinha Stadium and follow it around between the airport runways

and Kauaʻi Lagoons Golf Course. This road soon turns to red dirt and is used by joggers. Near the end, one fork leads to the back of the brewpub while the other runs out to the rocky point on which the lighthouse sits. It's about 2.5 miles. The lighthouse, now automated, has operated since 1897; the present yellow structure was built in 1932. There is shoreline access here and a few battered picnic tables.

## Ahukini State Recreation Pier

As the name implies, Ahukini is simply a pier from which local people fish. And it's some of the best pole fishing around. With the airport to your right, proceed down Ahukini Road until the road ends at a large circular parking lot and breakwater. The airport flight path is directly overhead. The scenery is only fair, and the spot itself is rather unkempt and littered. A skeletal cement framework remains of the old pier, so if you're not into fishing give it a miss. On the way down, sections of train tracks cross the road, a vestige of the sugar era and the means by which cane was transported to waiting ships. Ahukini Pier was used for about 100 years as a major port to ship sugarcane from the island to be processed elsewhere, and as such played an important role in the economy of the island.

# Practicalities

## ACCOMMODATIONS

If you like simple choices, you'll appreciate Lihuʻe; it holds only two fancy resorts and two condo complexes. The rest of the accommodations are small family-run hotel/motels or apartment hotels. In the smaller places, prices are good because Lihuʻe isn't considered a prime resort town. Yet it makes an ideal base, because from Lihuʻe you can get *anywhere* on the island in less than an hour. Although it's the county seat, the town is quiet, especially in the evenings, so you won't have to deal with noise or hustle and bustle.

## Under $50

The pink **Motel Lani,** owned and operated by

Janet Naumu, offers clean, inexpensive rooms at 4240 Rice St.; for reservations write Motel Lani, P.O. Box 1836, Lihuʻe, HI 96766, or call 808/245-2965. There are nine units, and, although close to the road, they're surprisingly quiet. Each room has a small desk, dresser, bath, fan, and refrigerator and is cross-ventilated. Some have air-conditioning. Janet usually doesn't allow children under three years old, but she's reasonable and will make exceptions. A small courtyard with a barbecue is available to guests. Rates for two nights or more are $32–50 double, $50 and up triple, $14 for an additional person, slightly more for one night. Deposit required.

The **Tip Top Motel,** 3173 ʻAkahi St., Lihuʻe, HI 96766, 808/245-2333, is a combination motel, restaurant, and bakery popular with local folks. It's a functional, two-story, cinder-block building painted light gray. The check-in lobby/café/bakery is open Tues.–Sun. 6:30 A.M.–3 P.M. and 5:30–9 P.M.; on Monday the hours are 7:30 A.M.–3 P.M. At other hours, check in at Chrissy and Charley's Bar around the side of the building. The rooms are antiseptic in every way—a plus, as your feet stay cool on the bare linoleum floor—and there's virtually no decoration, but there is a TV in every room and all are air-conditioned. Just to add that mixed-society touch, instead of a Gideon's Bible in the dresser drawer, you get *The Teachings of Buddha,* placed by the Sudaka Society of Honolulu. Rates are $45 per room, plus a $10 refundable key deposit.

The **Hale Lihue Motel,** 2931 Kalena St., Lihu'e, HI 96766, 808/245-2751, has made an excellent comeback. Don't expect anything fancy from this mocha-colored, 20-room, two-story, cinder-block building, but the manager runs a clean hotel with a screened-in lobby. There are no TVs or phones in the rooms; the television is in the lobby, a pay phone on the front lanai. Perfect for no-frills, budget accommodations. Used mostly by construction workers, backpackers, bicyclists, and budget travelers. Rates are approximately $28 single, $32 double, or $38 for three people; weekly rates available.

## $50–100

Steve and Susan Layne, owners of the attractive **Garden Island Inn** at 3445 Wilcox Rd., Lihu'e, HI 96766, 808/245-7227, fax 808/245-7603 or 800/648-0154, www.gardenislandinn.com, info@gardenislandinn.com, did a wonderful job of turning the once character-laden but worse-for-wear Ocean View Motel into a bright and cheery inn, with a green-on-white color scheme. Head down Rice Street toward the harbor; the inn is on a cul-de-sac across from Nawiliwili Beach Park, just a stroll from Kalapaki Beach. Each room has color cable TV, a microwave, small refrigerator, and coffeemaker with complimentary Kona-blend coffee. There is tile throughout. The inn also provides boogie boards, snorkeling gear, beach mats, and ice chests for a day's outing. The garden-view, ground-floor rooms, $65–80

double, are appointed with island prints and flowers from the garden and are cooled by louvered windows and ceiling fans. Second floor rooms, $85–95 double, are about the same, but each has a/c and its own lanai. The best rooms, $95–125, are on the third floor. More like mini-suites, these one- and two-room units have kitchenettes, a/c, and balconies and give you two full rooms that can easily accommodate four people comfortably. All 21 rooms are nonsmoking. In addition, a two-bedroom condo unit behind the inn with a fully furnished kitchen, cable TV, washer/dryer, and suburb views of the harbor rents for $145–200/day depending on the number of people (maximum of 6) plus a $75 cleaning fee; four-night minimum. From the front of the inn, you can watch the goings-on in Nawiliwili Harbor and dock area. For the money, the Garden Island Inn is one of the best deals on Kaua'i.

Down the road at 2430 Hulemalu Road in Niumalu is **The Kaua'i Inn,** 808/245-9000 or 800/808-2330, www.kauai-inn.com, info@kauai-inn.com. Originally built in Lihu'e, then relocated to Kalapaki Beach, this hotel was moved to its present location when the old Kauai Surf Hotel was constructed at the beach. Badly damaged during Hurricane 'Iniki, this old standby has reopened and been fully modernized after six years of reconstruction, transforming it once again into a lovely lady. The 48 guest rooms surround a newly landscaped courtyard with a small swimming pool, and each room has a private bath, refrigerator, microwave, and cable TV. Rooms run $79 for a king bed, $99 for two double beds, and $99 for a suite, and that rate includes a basic continental breakfast at the pool house. Quiet and a bit out of the way, the Kaua'i Inn offers clean and comfortable accommodation at reasonable prices.

## $100–150

Down the street from the Garden Island Inn are the **Banyan Harbor Resort** condominiums, 3411 Wilcox Rd., 808/245-7333 or 800/422-6926, fax 808/246-3687, www.vacation-kauai.com; email: banyan@aloha.net. Stepping up the hillside in two- and three-story buildings, many of the 148 one- and two-bedroom units in this complex have views of Nawiliwili Harbor. Each is outfitted with a fully equipped kitchen and dining room, separate living room, TV and VCR, and a washer and dryer; most units have air conditioning. Queen beds and sofa beds (double beds in some units) allow for up to four persons in the smaller units and a maximum of six in the larger. Maid service is offered every third day, and the swimming pool, tennis courts, and barbecue grills are for guest use only. Although standard rates run $110 for the smaller units and $140 for two-bedrooms, be sure to inquire about the numerous discounts, package rates, and extended stay deals. This is good value at a convenient location.

## $150–250

Midway between the airport and Kapa'a, down the tree-lined entrance road to and along a series of ponds that separate it from the adjacent Pahio time-share property, the **Radisson Kaua'i Beach Resort,** 4331 Kauai Beach Dr., Lihu'e, HI 96766, www.radisson.com/kauaihi, 808/245-1955 or 800/333-3333, fax 808/246-9085, is a low-lying complex on 25 landscaped acres that's isolated from the three major resort areas on the island. Its 340 rooms lie in two- and three-story units that spread from the entrance and lobby like arms around the central garden, where tall coconut trees tower over four swimming pools, one with a sand bottom, and a "mini-mountain" with grotto and artificial waterfall. Free and open to the public, a torch-lighting ceremony with hula presentation is performed in the garden nightly. Rooms are spacious and tastefully appointed, with a full bathroom, entertainment centers, cable TV, a sitting area, and an ocean- or garden-view lanai. Dining amenities include the casual Naupaka Terrace restaurant, which serves up satisfying if not memorable breakfasts and dinner, and the Driftwood Sandbar and Grill by the pools for lunch options. In the evening, Shutters lobby lounge serves libations and presents periodic soft Hawaiian music. A wide range of activities can be scheduled at the concierge desk, and the Pahio spa and fitness center is there for those who want to pamper themselves. Visit the lobby gift shop for sundries, reading material, and food items, view artwork while sipping Kaua'i-grown and -brewed coffee at A Piece of Paradise Gallery, or stop in to the

Remember Kauai shop for a wearable jewelry memento of your trip. Large-group meetings and banquets can be accommodated in the function rooms, which otherwise regularly present the hotel lu'au Polynesian revue every Monday and dinner theater shows on Thursday. Rates range from $209 for a mountain/garden-view room to $299 for an oceanfront room; suites run $299–800. Special packages and discounts are available.

## $250 and Up

The **Kaua'i Marriott Resort and Beach Club,** Kalapaki Beach, Lihu'e, HI 96766, 808/245-5050 or 800/220-2925, fax 808/245-5049, is a testament to humans' perseverance coupled with the forgiving personality of Mother Nature. Kaua'i's first high-rise hotel was built on Kalapaki Beach in the 1960s as the Kauai Surf. This structure still stands as the Kilohana wing of the Marriott. In 1987, the hotel was completely refurbished and rebuilt, emerging as the Westin—at the time the most luxurious property on Kaua'i. Hurricane 'Iniki then furiously blew ashore in 1992, raking the island and mangling the hotel. Afterward, the Marriott chain purchased the property and set about restoring it to its former grandeur. The result is, once again, a fabulous hotel, where about half the rooms are time-share properties. Although 10 floors tall, the Marriott doesn't seem to dominate the surroundings, as it's tucked into the bottom of the hill below town. Upon arrival, you enter through a grand foyer. Descending the escalator you emerge on a flagstone path, along the perimeter of Ka Mala O Kalapaki, a formal garden that says "Hawaii" unmistakably. This garden is surrounded by ballrooms and convention rooms. You'll soon descend a flight of marble stairs on your left into the reception area. Displayed here is a lustrous original koa canoe that belonged to Prince Kuhio. In the care of a local Hawaiian family over the generations, the canoe was leased to Marriott with the understanding that funds be used in a scholarship that directly benefits a child of Hawaiian ancestry.

The beachside area of the hotel includes an extensive doughnut-shaped swimming pool (ostensibly the largest in Hawaii) surrounded by five neoclassical thrust proscenium porticos bubbling with soothing whirlpools and cascades of water; greenery and small private gardens fill other spaces. Overall the hotel is decorated in muted salmon, light green, periwinkle, and island pastel colors, and the halls, walkways, and other public spaces are dotted with an extensive collection of Asian and Hawaiian artworks. Although you're surrounded by luxury at the Marriott, you experience the feeling of a quieter, more casual place. The hotel is very much like the stunning sister who decided to stay close to home instead of heading for the bright lights where her beauty would easily have dazzled everyone.

The resort's 345 rooms are classified as garden view, $299; pool/ocean view, $354; ocean view, $414; and suites, $649–2,600; $35 for an additional adult. Romance, golf, and breakfast packages are also available. Rooms are pure luxury: each has a private lanai, and most overlook the pool or ocean. A comfy bed faces an entertainment center complete with remote-control color TV, while a writing desk, table, chairs, and floor lamps fill out the room. Each room boasts air-conditioning, a mini-fridge, tiled full bath, a steam iron and ironing board, in-room safe, and coffeemaker with complimentary Kona coffee.

The Marriott has four restaurants, one to fit your every need. Amenities include room service, an activities desk, concierge service, a fitness center, golf course and tennis center, children's program, and complimentary airport shuttle. Shops include Lamonts Gifts and Sundries, Collectors Fine Art, Grande's Gems, and Tropical Tantrum and Taro Fields for fashions. Everything from hair styling to facials, body treatments, and massages is available at the full-service Alexander Day Spa. The Ala Lani Spa, a few steps up the road at the tennis club, also offers basically the same services. At one end of the quarter-mile-long beach promenade, the Kalapaki Beach Boys activity center has gear for all water activities and can arrange activities like scuba, sailing, kayaking, and fishing.

### Vacation Rental Agencies
**Kauai Vacation Rentals,** 3-3311 Kuhio Hwy., Lihu'e, HI 96766, 808/245-8841 or 800/367-5025, www.KauaiVacationRentals.com, aloha

@kvrre.com, handles condos and vacation rental homes throughout the island, with only a handful of condo units overlooking Kalapaki Beach next to the Marriott.

## FOOD
Dining in Lihu'e is a treat—good to your palate and your budget. The town has many local eateries and a few fast-food chains. Stepping up in class, there are continental, Italian, and Japanese restaurants, while moderately priced establishments serve up hearty dishes of Mexican, Chinese, and good old American fare. Fancier dining is found at the big hotels and a few select restaurants around town.

### Inexpensive
If you ask anyone in Lihu'e where you can chow down for cheap, they'll send you to **Ma's Family Inc.,** 4277 Halenani St., 808/245-3142, an institution owned and operated by matriarch Akiyo Honjo, a third-generation Kaua'ian, who is assisted at times by her great-grandchildren. Turn off Rice Street onto Kress and follow it to the corner, where you'll find Ma's. Ma's is open weekdays 5 A.M.–1:30 P.M. and Saturday, Sunday, and holidays 5–11:30 A.M. (or until customers stop coming). The building is old and has seen some wear but is clean. A few tourists find it, but mostly it's local working people who come here for a hearty and filling meal. Lunches are good, but the super deals are breakfast and the Hawaiian specialties. The coffee, free with breakfast and served with condensed milk, arrives in a large pot about as soon as your seat hits the chair. The menu is posted above the kitchen window. You can start the day with The Works, which includes either potatoes or fried noodles, bacon or sausage, and toast for $6. If that's too much, ask for an omelette, French toast, or pancakes. From the Hawaiian menu, try *kalua* pork with two eggs and rice, poi, and *lomi* salmon, or Kaua'i sausage—all for under $6. Ma's also serves hamburgers, an assortment of sandwiches including teriyaki beef, loco moco, and noodles.

**Hamura Saimin Stand,** 2956 Kress St., 808/245-3271, is just around the corner from

KAUA'I

Ma's. It's open from 10 A.M., and people flock to the orange countertops and pale yellow interior of this restaurant all day long, where they perch on short stools to eat steaming bowls of saimin. To get an idea just how frequented this little shop is, have a look at the well-worn thresholds of its doors. Sunday the shop closes at 9:30 P.M., Mon.–Thurs. at 11 P.M., and Fri.–Sat. it stays open until 1 A.M., when all the bars let loose their revelers. There is no decor here (beyond the sign admonishing "Please do not stick gum under counter"), just good food. Your first time, try the Saimin Special, which gives you noodles, slivers of meat and fish, vegetables, won ton, and eggs, all floating in a golden broth. Other items on the small menu are variations on the same theme, with nothing more than $6. The bowl size determines your portion: small, medium, large, extra large, special, extra large special. On the counter sit hot sauce, mustard, and shoyu—condiments that you mix yourself in the small bowls that accompany your soup. Enjoy not only the saimin, but also the truly authentic Kaua'i experience. Also available as sides are crispy wonton, skewers of beef or chicken, *manapua,* and *liliko'i* (passion fruit) pie for $1.50 a slice.

**Halo Halo Shave Ice** occupies a second counter in the same building 10 A.M.–4 P.M.—use the side entrance. Here you can get some of the best throat coolers on the island.

**Oki Diner,** 3125 Kuhio Hwy., 808/245-5899, just up from the county government office building, has become another favorite for locals in town, and it's open 21 hours a day—closed only 3–6 A.M. This is a spartan place, simple but pleasant. Everything on the menu is available at any time—good quality food at reasonable prices, mostly under $8. A counter at the entrance sells baked goods, so you can leave with sweets for the road or come in to pick up a cake.

Down the street and almost across from the Garden Island Newspaper office is **Maria's Mexican Restaurant,** 808/246-9122, open for lunch and dinner with the best Mexican food in Lihu'e (some claim the best on the island). Maria prepares all ingredients in the kitchen from personal recipes, and the food is as traditional as you can get. A bit farther down is **Local Boy Restaurant,** 808/246-8898, for friendly service and generous portions of local food.

**Tip Top Cafe/Bakery,** 3173 'Akahi St., 808/245-2333, open daily except Monday 6:30 A.M.–2 P.M., doubles as the downstairs lobby of the Tip Top Motel. A local favorite with unpretentious but clean surroundings, the food is wholesome but uninspired—just like the service. Breakfast is the best deal, at around $5, and the macadamia nut pancakes are delish! They are known throughout the island. Plate lunches are under $6, but they say the oxtail soup is the best seller. You can choose anything from pork chops to teriyaki chicken, and you get soup, salad, rice, and coffee. Visit the bakery section and let your eyes tell your stomach what to do. The *malasadas* are fresh daily. Both the bakery and café have been in business since 1916. Sharing this space is the **Sushi Katsu** Japanese restaurant, 808/246-0176, also an inexpensive local eatery. Open daily except Monday 11 A.M.–2 P.M. for sushi only and 5:30–9:30 P.M. for sushi and other Japanese food.

**Dani's,** 4201 Rice St., toward Nawiliwili near the fire department, 808/245-4991, is open Mon.–Fri. 5 A.M.–1:30 P.M., Saturday 5 A.M.–1 P.M., closed Sunday. Another favorite with local people, it's been around a while and has a good reputation for giving you a hearty meal for a reasonable price. The food is American-Hawaiian-Japanese. Most full meals range $6–10, and you have selections like *lomi* salmon, tripe stew, teriyaki beef and chicken, and fried fish. Unpretentious, the cafeteria-style interior displays Formica-topped tables and linoleum floors.

Look for an anchor chain marking the two-tone blue **Kalapaki Beach Hut,** open daily 7 A.M.–7 P.M. at the bottom of Rice Street, just before Nawiliwili Harbor. This window-restaurant offers limited seating on the porch or in the upstairs "crow's nest," from where you get a view of the harbor. With a good reputation among local clientele, it serves breakfast, like omelettes, eggs, and loco moco, 7–10:30 A.M. Lunches of fish and chips and a variety of sandwiches run $4–8. The specialty is large, juicy buffalo burgers with all the fixings, but turkey burgers and traditional beef burgers are also offered. The Beach

Hut is an excellent, laid-back choice for a simple lunch in the Nawiliwili area.

For a cool ice cream, shave ice, or smoothie, head around behind the Kalapaki Beach Hut to the **Cool Spot.**

**The Fish Express,** 3343 Kuhio Hwy., across from Wal-Mart, 808/245-9918, is a retail sales store with a full selection of fresh and frozen fish and seafood that's open daily 10 A.M.–7 P.M., until 5 P.M. on Sunday. If you're looking for something for the road, try the lunch counter and grill Mon.–Fri. 10 A.M.–3 P.M. for plate lunches, sandwiches, and seafood platters, mostly in the $5–8 range. Takeout only.

The Kukui Grove Shopping Center has a number of sit-down and sidewalk restaurants. They include the **Deli and Bread Connection,** a kitchenware store with a deli counter offering sandwiches and an assortment of soups and salads; **Joni-Hana,** a walk-up counter with *bento* and plate lunches priced reasonably; **Myron's Filipino & Local Food;** and **Ho's Chinese Kitchen** for Cantonese food at very reasonable prices.

## Moderate

**Kiibo Restaurant,** 2991 'Umi St., 808/245-2650, serves authentic Japanese meals without a big price tag. Many Japanese around town come here to eat. The low stools at the counter are reminiscent of a Japanese *akachochin* or *sushiya*. The menu listing savory offerings of *udon, donburi,* teriyaki, and a variety of *bento* (simple boxed lunch) and *teishoku* (full meal with soup and rice) includes pictures showing you just what you'll get. Sushi is also served. The service is quick and friendly; most offerings are under $12. Restaurant Kiibo is *ichiban!* What it lacks in ambiance, it makes up for in good food. Just off Rice Street, it's open for lunch 11 A.M.–1:30 P.M. and for dinner 5:30–9 P.M., closed Sunday and holidays.

The **Barbecue Inn,** 2982 Kress St., 808/245-2921, open Mon.–Sat. 7 A.M.–1:30 P.M., then 5–8:30 P.M. Mon.–Thurs. and 4:30–8:45 P.M. Fri.–Sat., has been in business and run by the Sasaki family since 1940, and if you want a testimonial, just observe the steady stream of local people, from car mechanics to doctors, heading for this restaurant. The atmosphere is "leatherette

and Formica," but the service is homey, friendly, and prompt. More than 30 entrées—Japanese, American, and local—include tempura, seafood, prime rib, and a dinner plate special. The scampi is perhaps the best for the price on the island. Most meals come complete with soup, salad, a beverage, and dessert, mostly in the $9–17 range. There's always a list of specials, longer than some restaurant's menus. Breakfast and lunch are at bargain prices, the homemade pies are luscious, and cocktails are available.

**Tokyo Lobby,** 3501 Rice St., in Nawiliwili at the Harbor Mall, 808/245-8989, is open Mon.–Fri. for lunch 11 A.M.–2 P.M., dinner daily 4:30–9 P.M. It prides itself on the freshness of the food, especially the seafood. Appointed with shoji screens, a pagoda-style roof over the sushi bar, paper fans, and paper lanterns, the Tokyo Lobby creates an authentic Japanese atmosphere. Most meals are presented in small wooden boats, the signature of the restaurant. Lunch might be *nigiri* sushi or sashimi, various *don buri,* a bowl of rice with savory bits of meat, egg, and vegetables on top, or *nabeyaki,* assorted seafood with vegetables, and noodles in a broth. The dinner menu includes sashimi and sushi platters, calamari steak, curried chicken, and beef teriyaki, most around $15, or combination dinners like sesame chicken with sashimi for a bit more.

Only a few steps away at the Harbor Mall is **Kauai Chop Suey,** 808/245-8790, open daily except Monday for lunch 11 A.M.–2 P.M. and for dinner 4:30–9 P.M. This is a reasonably priced Cantonese restaurant. The restaurant's two dining rooms, separated by a keyhole archway, are alive with plants and brightened by Chinese lanterns hanging from the open-beamed ceiling. Entrées include sizzling shrimp with lobster sauce (Mama Lau, the owner, says this is the best!), boneless chicken with mushrooms, or beef or pork with tomato. House specials are Kauai Chop Suey and a variety of noodle dishes. Kauai Chop Suey also offers plate lunches and dinners to go and has a steady local clientele, a sure sign of good food at reasonable prices.

If you're in the mood for cuisine from south of the border while out playing on Kalapaki Beach, head to the **Nuevo España Restaurant,** 808/632-

0513, at Anchor Cove Shopping Center, where you can sit on the deck and look out over the water. Basic Mexican dishes here run $8.50–13. Open 8 A.M.–9 P.M.

The **Whalers Brewpub,** 808/245-2000, at the Kaua'i Lagoons Golf Course serves up a full menu, but most come for the location and the beer. Turn at the Marriott entrance and follow the signs for about one mile. One of two brewpubs on the island, Whalers brews 550–800 barrels of beer every year—it's served only on the premises. As you enter, you can see the brewing apparatus through the glass windows to your left. Depending on the season, between three and eight varieties are available. Lunches include mostly salads, sandwiches, and burgers in the $8–13 range, while ribs, chicken, fish, and vegetable dishes are available for dinner for $15–25. The restaurant is situated about 90 feet above outer Nawiliwili Bay, so great sunsets are on the menu nearly every day, as is whale-watching from November to May. Live music usually happens every other weekend, but DJ tunes are more frequent.

## Expensive

**JJ's Broiler,** 808/246-4422, at the Anchor Cove Shopping Center, is open daily 11 A.M.–5 P.M. for lunch, until 10 P.M. for dinner, and from 5 P.M. for cocktails and light meals. The menu offers grain-fed aged beef from the Midwest and daily choices of fish caught by local captains and delivered fresh. The living landscape of Nawiliwili Bay glistening through the huge windows creates the backdrop for the bi-level interior. The first level is more casual, with a full bar, wooden tables, and bentwood chairs, or you can dine alfresco on the veranda under large umbrellas. The upstairs offers horseshoe booths and intimate tables, along with another full bar and wraparound windows that open to cooling sea breezes. Hanging from the ceiling are replicas of 12-meter racing yachts, exactly like those entered in the America's Cup. Lunch at JJ's starts with appetizers, mostly $8–9, like potato skins, teriyaki chicken sticks, and breaded and deep-fried calamari. Soups include the specialties French onion and Hawaiian Ocean Chowder, each for $6.25. Classic sandwiches and burgers run $8.95–12.95.

Aside from its famous Slavonic Steak (a thin broiled tenderloin dipped in butter, wine, and garlic sauce) at $21.95 or fresh fish at market price, dinner can be roasted macadamia lamb rack for $23.95, New York steak at $24.95, black bean shrimp with Asian polenta for $21.95, or broiled chicken fettuccine for $17.95. Daily specials for both lunch and dinner are offered to help save money, but no matter what you order, large portions will arrive.

**Duke's Canoe Club,** 808/246-9599, on Kalapaki Beach at the Kaua'i Marriott Resort, open daily 5–10 P.M. upstairs for dinner and 11:30 A.M.–11:30 P.M. for drinks, *pu pu,* and light meals at the downstairs **Barefoot Bar,** is as much a Hawaiian class act as its namesake, the legendary Duke Kahanamoku. Duke's is one of those places, with an exemplary setting just off the beach path and a lustrous wood and thatched interior illuminated by torches and moonlight, that pleasantly overwhelm you with the feeling that you're *really in Hawaii.* At the Barefoot Bar, you feel compelled to quaff a frothy brew and, well... kick off your shoes as you listen to the natural melody of wind and waves just a palm tree away. You can order sandwiches, plate lunches, pizza, burgers, and salads, most for well under $10, and you can enjoy a variety of island drinks prepared at the full-service bar (open until midnight). Upstairs, still casual but elegant enough for a romantic evening, the menu offers fresh catch, prepared in your choice of five different ways. You can also order shrimp and other seafood, various pasta, or *huli huli* chicken at a reasonable $14.95. The most expensive entrée is the herb-roasted prime rib for $24.95. Soft music upstairs accompanies dinner nightly, while livelier Hawaiian music fills the downstairs bar on Thursday, Friday, and Saturday. Duke's is Hawaii at its best: relaxed, charming, idyllic, and offering fine cuisine.

The Marriott has three in-house restaurants with better than average fare. **Kukui's Restaurant,** the hotel's open-air main dining room, is open for breakfast, lunch, and dinner and serves Pacific Rim cuisine near the pool. Specials include the Friday night prime rib and seafood buffet, Saturday night Pacific Rim sampler buffet, and a Sunday champagne brunch—all $34.95. Live

Hawaiian music is performed here every evening, with the addition of a torch-lighting ceremony on Monday and Thursday, and a short hula show on Saturday. At the far side of the pool is the **Kalapaki Grill,** which serves up broiled burgers, sandwiches, salads, sides, and drinks during the day. Overlooking the central pool from the promenade is **Aupaka Terrace.** Cocktails are served on the terrace, as is a continental breakfast, and sushi and Hawaiian *pu pu* in the evening.

Dining inside beyond the open shuttered windows or outside on the patio is a pleasure at the Naupaka Terrace Steak House at the Radisson. While open for breakfast, the Naupaka shines in the evening with a wide range of offerings that include Midwestern-raised beef. Start with appetizers like Hanama'ulu chicken fritters for $9.75 or Naupaka quesadillas at $8.75 before moving on to your entrée. Heavy on the meats, the menu includes filet mignon, strip steak, top sirloin, or ribeye done in various taste-tempting preparations. Prime rib, lamb chops, fish, and plenty of seafood are also on the menu, and there is always something for the vegetarian. Most meat and fish entrées run $22.95–32.75. For lunch, try the Driftwood Sandbar and Grill, alongside the sand-bottom pool, for sandwiches and other lighter foods.

## Fine Dining
The heady aroma of sautéed garlic mixed with the sweet scents of oregano and rosemary floats from the kitchens of **Café Portofino,** 808/245-2121, on the second level of the Harbor Mall. This authentic Italian restaurant, owned and operated by Giuseppe Avocadi, is open daily for dinner only 5–9:30 P.M. Sliding wooden doors open to the distinctive wooden bar—a bold statement of high chic—under the open-beamed wooden ceiling and fancy fans. The main dining room, encased in beveled glass windows, is studded with tables, formally set, and counterpointed by a black-and-white tiled floor. Candlelight and wall sconces set the mood, flowers and ferns add island color, and an outdoor veranda is perfect for a romantic evening. The dinner menu begins with antipasto Portofino for $8, while other appetizer choices run $8–10. Salads include the mixed green house

salad for $5; soups, like minestrone or gazpacho, are priced at $4. Tempting Italian entrées include spaghetti alla marinara at $13.50, eggplant parmigiana or pollo porcini (sautéed chicken breast in brandy with a light wild mushroom sauce) for $15, and specialties of the house like osso buco (veal shank) over fettuccine for $26. Fresh fish (daily quote), broiled, baked, or sautéed, is served with fresh homemade condiments. There is a full wine list, and desserts complement a cup of coffee or cappuccino from the full espresso bar. Every night, you are serenaded with live contemporary music on saxophone, piano, or harp. Café Portofino is an excellent choice for an evening of romance and fine dining. *Buon appetito!*

The rear flagstone veranda and original dining room at Kilohana, the restored 1935 plantation estate of Gaylord Wilcox, have been turned into the breezy **Gaylord's,** 808/245-9593, open Mon.–Sat. for lunch 11 A.M.–3 P.M., dinner daily from 5 P.M., and Sunday for brunch 9:30 A.M.–3 P.M. Reservations are recommended. Lunch might include items like a Kilohana fruit platter, sesame chicken or Greek roasted vegetable salad, or more substantial dishes like baby-back ribs, fresh fish, or a Reuben sandwich. Dinners begin with a wide selection of appetizers, salads, and soups from $3.95. Mostly in the 21.95–31.95 range, entrées include herb-crusted whole rack of lamb; chicken breast with papaya, pineapple, and macadamia nut sauce; and Greek-style linguine with grilled chicken, sun-dried tomatoes, olives, and feta cheese. Fish and game lovers will greatly enjoy the seafood rhapsody, fish, prawns, and lobster in a light creamy butter sauce; one of several choices of fresh fish (market price) that can be char-broiled, sautéed, or crusted; or Gaylord's famous farm-raised venison, which may be offered in a number of daily preparations. Save room for one of Gaylord's memorable desserts and finish your meal with a cappuccino or caffe mocha prepared on a century-old espresso machine, resplendent in its battered yet burnished glory. Gaylord's also prides itself on having one of the largest wine cellars on Kaua'i, featuring more than 100 vintages from around the world representing more than two dozen varietals. The à la carte Sunday brunch features a hearty Plantation Breakfast, strawberry French toast, Gaylord's eggs Benedict, and a vegetarian quiche. Prices for a complete brunch are $8.95–14.95 and include a fresh-baked sweet roll and fruit plate. Gaylord's is a wonderful restaurant to visit just to spend a quiet afternoon or as a special treat for a honeymoon or anniversary. For that romantic occasion, ask for a table at the end of the portico; at one step down, it sets you off a bit by yourself. Whether outdoors on the more casual veranda or indoors in the formal dining room, with its starched linens and stemware, the feeling is one of gentility.

## Farmers' Market

If you're making your own meals while visiting Kaua'i, remember that locally grown fresh fruit and vegetables are available from vendors at the farmers' market every Friday at 3 P.M. at Vidinha Stadium parking lot in Lihu'e.

A private farmers' market is held every Monday at 3 P.M. at the Kukui Grove Shopping Center.

# ENTERTAINMENT

Lihu'e is not the entertainment capital of the world, but if you have the itch to step out at night, there are a few places where you can scratch it.

At the Marriott, stop by Kukui's Restaurant or Duke's Canoe Club and Barefoot Bar for Hawaiian and contemporary music every evenings. Kukui's also has a sunset hula show on Saturday and a torch-lighting ceremony every Monday and Thursday.

The Radisson also hosts a free nightly torch-lighting and hula show at the grotto in its central courtyard. This is accompanied by a Polynesian revue of music and dance, the lu'au is held outdoors by the pool, weather permitting, otherwise inside the ballroom. For a less Hawaiian evening, try the "A Night of Broadway" dinner show at the Radisson, where three musical acts are performed between courses of your buffet meal. The evening's entertainment runs $68 for adults, with kids age 6–12 about half price. For information and reservations, call 808/245-1955.

**Reflections of Paradise,** the second lu'au performed in the area, takes place at the Kilohana Carriage House on Tuesday and Thursday. The evening starts around 6:15 P.M. with a full buffet that's followed by a musical Polynesian revue. Adults are $58, seniors and teens $54, and children 4–12 $30; call 808/245-9593 for reservations.

Enjoy a night of shared karaoke fun (free on Monday nights) at **Rob's Good Times Grill,** open nightly until 2 A.M. in the Rice Street Shopping Center. A funky, dark little place with booths and Formica tables, it's become a local hangout. A would-be crooner is given the microphone and sings along with the music—the video and words to which are projected on a screen in the corner. Even if your mom used to ask you to stop singing in the shower, here you can join in the fun. Everyone gets applause, and beer and drinks are reasonably priced. Rob's Good Times Grill is one of Lihu'e's only "neighborhood bars," where you can watch sports on the big screen TVs, shoot a round of pool, hobnob with the locals, and have a reasonable meal.

**The Nawiliwili Tavern,** housed in the old Hotel Kuboyama, at the bottom of Rice St. along Paena Loop Rd., 808/245-7267, open 2:30 P.M.–1 A.M., is a friendly neighborhood bar and restaurant where you can mix with local people and tourists alike who are having fun playing pool or darts; music alternates with satellite sports broadcasts. Enjoy a cold beer at the long bar, or satisfy your appetite by ordering any number of plate lunches or pu pu. The grill is open until late evening, and happy hour runs weekdays 4–6 P.M.

If you're lucky, you can "strike out" at the **Lihue Bowling Center,** in the Rice Shopping Center, 808/245-5263. It's the only bowling alley on the island. The lanes stay open until 11:30 P.M. on Friday and Saturday but usually close about 10:30 P.M. on weekdays depending on how busy things are. Scoring is done with an automatic system.

For movies, try the **Kukui Grove 4 Cinemas,** behind the gas station across Nawiliwili Road from the big Kukui Grove Shopping Center. Call 808/245-5055 for what's playing.

For more than two decades, the **Kauai Com-**

**munity Players** have presented the island with theatrical performances. Four times a year, this nonprofessional community theater group puts on well-known and experimental plays, usually in the Lihu'e Parish Hall across Nawiliwili Road from the Kukui Grove Shopping Center. For information on what's currently showing, call 808/245-7700.

If you happen to be on Kaua'i on the Fourth of July, don't fail to see the fireworks at Vidinha Stadium in Lihu'e. A "do not miss" event, it's reputedly one of the best light shows in the state.

## RECREATION

Lihu'e is not the recreational center on the island, but it does offer a variety of options. When games are happening, spectator sports can by watched at Vidinha Stadium, which has baseball diamonds and football/soccer fields.

Ho'olaule'a Road runs past the Marriott and leads over two arching bridges to Whalers Brewpub. This road serves as a **jogging path** and, beyond the brewpub, connects with a dirt road that runs in one direction to the Ninini Point Lighthouse and in the other direction circles around to Rte. 51.

### Golf and Tennis

**Kaua'i Lagoons Golf Club**, 808/241-6000 or 800/634-6400, is one of the premier golf courses on the island. Located between the Kaua'i Marriott and the airport, the fairways of its two courses are strung along 40 acres of freshwater meandering ponds. The older Mokihana course is a links course for recreational play, while the Kiele course has been designed as a more challenging championship course. While launches don't cruise these lagoons as they did during the Westin days, the water is still a pleasing backdrop for play. Greens fees run $170 for the Kiele and $120 for the Mokihana—substantially less for resort guests. Golf instruction is available, and clinics are held daily at $25 per person, limit 10. Open 6:30 A.M.–6 P.M., the clubhouse (with restaurant) overlooks one of these lagoons; call ahead for tee times.

The **Puakea Golf Course**, 808/245-8756,

has been carved from former cane fields just west of the Kukui Grove Shopping Center. The current 10 holes lie on rolling ground and contain a deep ravine, volcanic outcrops, and other natural hazards. Greens fees for nonresidents are $45 or $65 for two times around, $50 twilight. Call the clubhouse/grill for tee times.

Next to the Kaua'i Lagoons golf clubhouse, the eight plexipave courts of the **Tennis Club at Kaua'i Lagoons Resort**, 808/245-3323, are open to any single or group for a $20 per hour court fee. Ball machines are available for an additional fee, as are private and semi-private instruction, daily clinics, and round robin mixers. Call for information, times, and pricing. Except for the 600-seat stadium, these courts are not lighted, so the hours of operation are 7 A.M.–dusk. Operating out of the same office and using the same telephone number, open daily 7 A.M.–7 P.M., is the **Ala Lani Spa,** where you can treat your skin, nails, hands, or whole body to sensual delights and comforts.

### Kayaks and Sailboats

Located at Nawiliwili Small Boat Harbor, **Island Adventures,** 808/245-9662, www.kauaifun.com, rents single- and double-seat kayaks, $10–15/hour or $30–45/day, for a trip up Hulei'a Stream. This is the same group—different name—as the Kalapaki Beach Boys, who run the Marriott beach activities center. For a guided tour on the river, try **Aloha Canoes and Kayak,** at the Kalapaki Marketplace in Nawiliwili, 808/246-6804. **Outfitters Kauai,** 808/742-9667 or 888/742-9887, offers a seven-hour Kipu Kai Daytrip Tour from September to May for $119 for those in good physical condition, and a Kipu Falls tour for $80, which requires a two-mile kayak paddle plus a 1.5-mile hike to and from the falls.

Few tour boats cruise this part of the island, but **Rainbow Runner,** 808/632-0202, runs its trimaran from Kalapaki Beach for 90-minute sails for $59 adult.

### Fishing

Charter fishing boats operate out of Nawiliwili Small Boat Harbor. One of these is the 55-foot *Konane Star* run by **True Blue Charters,**

808/246-6333, which is associated with Island Adventures. When not fishing, they will do snorkeling and whale-watching trips. Other fishing tour companies are **Kai Bear Sportsfishing Charters,** 808/826-4556; **Sea Lure Fishing Charters,** 808/822-5963; and **Sport Fishing Kauai,** 808/742-7013.

# SHOPPING

Many good selections and bargains are found in the city. Kaua'ians shop in Lihu'e, and the reasonable prices that local purchasing generates are passed on to you.

## Shopping Centers

Not much is left of the **Lihu'e Shopping Center** in downtown Lihu'e except the Big Save Supermarket. Along Rte. 56 just up from there, you'll see a classic building dating from 1923. Once the home of Garden Island Motors Limited, this and adjacent buildings make up a small strip mall housing Photo Spectrum, offering one-hour film processing, and a few eateries and offices. The **Rice Shopping Center,** 4303 Rice St., features a laundromat, a bowling alley, inexpensive eateries, a health-food store, and a neighborhood bar. The real shopping now is done at the newer centers and at the huge Wal-Mart and Kmart stores.

The **Kukui Grove Shopping Center,** at the intersection of Kaumuali'i Hwy. and Nawiliwili Rd., just a few minutes west of downtown Lihu'e, is Kaua'i's largest all-purpose shopping mall. The center's main stores include Macy's and Sears, for general merchandise and apparel; Longs Drugs for sundries, sporting goods, medicines, and photo needs; and Star Market for groceries. Deja Vu is a surf shop with T-shirts, sun hats, glasses, wraparound dresses, bikinis, boogie boards, surfboards, sandals, and a smattering of dress shirts and shoes. Zales and Prestige Jewelers offer fine jewelry. For anything that beeps or buzzes, head for Radio Shack. Other shops include Dan's Sports Shop, for golf clubs, tennis racquets, baseball caps, mitts, dartboards, and water gear; General Nutrition Center for the health-conscious; the Deli and Bread Connection for kitchen gadgets and wholesome

eats; the Kauai Products Store, which offers quality, mostly island-made goods of all sorts; and half a dozen small eateries. For something more artistic, stroll through the Garden Island Arts Council exhibition hall to peruse the paintings and sculptures. General hours are 9:30 A.M.–7 P.M. Mon.–Sat., until 9 P.M. on Friday, and 10 A.M.–6 P.M. on Sunday. In a separate section to the side are Borders Books and Music and Kmart.

The **Anchor Cove Shopping Center,** at Kalapaki Beach, is a compact shopping and dining mall with a great location. Among the semi-detached kiosks, you will find an ABC Store, open daily 7 A.M.–10:30 P.M., selling sundries, beachwear, groceries, film, drugs, cosmetics, and also liquor; Crazy Shirts, open daily 9 A.M.–9 P.M., with well-made and distinctive T-shirts; and Honolua Surf Co. for casual clothing and resortwear; and at Tropic Isle Music Company you will find CDs of classic, traditional, contemporary, and modern island music and any number of island-inspired gifts. For a look at what Tropic Isle Music offers, call 800/685-0413 for a catalog ($3) or visit www.tropicislemusic.com. Maui Divers Jewelry stocks all sorts of ornaments for a take-home gift; Sophisticated You, owned and operated by former beauty queen Therese Jasper, features ladies' fine apparel for sale or rent, including wedding gowns and tuxedos, just in case the tropical sun goes to your head and you decide to tie the knot. Other establishments in the center include Ohana Helicopters' office and reservations desk, JJ's Broiler, Nuevo España Restaurant, and Shipwreck Sub and Pizza for a quick meal. Park out front. From another parking lot to the side, a footbridge over the stream connects to Duke's Canoe Club restaurant and the Marriott property.

Next to Anchor Cove is the small **Kalapaki Marketplace,** with a handful of shops that include the Aloha Canoe and Kayak office, Endless Summer for fruit and smoothies, Lappert's Ice Cream, a souvenir shop, and a billiards parlor.

Just up the road and across the street from the Anchor Cove is the **Harbor Mall.** While landscaped and remodeled to let the breeze in, many of its shops are still empty, but Red Dirt Shirt has a store in the back near a footwear shop, and the restaurants Tokyo Lobby, Kauai Chop Suey, and Café Portofino all have space up front.

## Kilohana

On the outskirts of Lihu'e, just west of Kukui Grove Shopping Center, Kilohana is a unique collection of shops in a unique setting. Around the time that Gaylord Wilcox moved the business office of Grove Farm from the homestead site, he had the 16,000-square-foot Kilohana plantation house built. After decades of family use, the building was renovated in 1986 and turned into shops that sell arts and crafts. Shops are open 9:30 A.M.–9:30 P.M., until 5 P.M. on Sunday.

The longest-lasting part of a journey is the memory. One of the best catalysts for recapturing your trip is an inspirational work of art or handicraft. The Country Store specializes in Hawaiian-inspired souvenirs, wind chimes, wicker picnic baskets, cutlery, pillows, vintage fabric handbags, aloha shirts, hand-blown and hand-etched glass, lovely silver jewelry, and plenty of other eye pleasers. Master crafts from local artists include koa boxes, turned bowls, quilted throws, and cobalt blue hand-blown and -etched glass. Upstairs and down you will also find Sea Reflections, glimmering with glass, jewelry, coral, shells, and marine sculpture; Grande's Gems, for that impulse purchase of a gold bracelet or pearl necklace; and the Kilohana Galleries Artisan's Room, offering more artwork. In separate buildings out back are Clayworks at Kilohana, which not only sells artists' work but is a place where you can create your own masterpiece, and Kilohana Clothing Company, which carries island-inspired alohawear.

Artwork isn't the only thing offered here, for Gaylord's restaurant serves some of the most exquisite meals on this side of the island. It also presents the Reflections of Paradise lu'au every Tuesday and Thursday. Appreciate the house as you wander from shop to shop, but also treat yourself to a short ride around the plantation grounds in a horse-drawn carriage that operates from 11 A.M.–6 P.M. Just show up and stand in line near the front entrance. The cost of this 20-minute ride is $10 for adults and $5 for kids. For a more extensive look at the grounds and an introduction to the history of the plantation and

culture of sugar, try the one-hour sugarcane carriage tour for $24 adults and $12 kids; call 808/246-9529 for reservations.

## Specialty Shops

Don't pass up **Hilo Hattie**, 3252 Kuhio Hwy., at the intersection of Ahukini Rd., 808/245-3404, open every day 8:30 A.M.–6:30 P.M., an institution of alohawear, to at least educate yourself on products and prices. Though the designs may not be one-of-a-kind, nor all made in the state, Hilo Hattie clothing is very serviceable and well made. Specials are always offered in the free tourist literature and on clearance racks at the store itself. There is a great selection of gifts and souvenirs, food items, books, and many other Hawaii-inspired products. Among the abundance of incentives to get you in is the free hotel pick-up from Po'ipu to Kapa'a, free juice at the door, and free hemming.

Also at the intersection of Kuhio Hwy. and Ahukini Road is a **Red Dirt Shirt** outlet. Like its sister stores in Waimea and Kapa'a, this shop carries the famous dirt red T-shirts. Dozens of island designs are available in S–XXXXL. These make good gifts and wearable mementos of your trip to the island.

In a move from Kapa'a, **Two Frogs Hugging**, 808/246-8777, open Mon.–Sat. 10 A.M.–6 P.M., has taken up residence along Kuhio Hwy. near the intersection with Ahukini Road. Two Frogs carries a wonderfully eclectic collection of imported arts, crafts, and furniture from Indonesia, including teak outdoor furniture, mahogany chairs, rattan accessories, pottery pots, bamboo window shades, woven bags, knickknacks, and stone carvings. Look for the two hugging frogs statue out front.

You knew that it had to happen here as well. Both the big box stores **Kmart** and **Wal-Mart** have outlets in Lihu'e. These stores carry everything that the Mainland stores carry with the addition of island-specialty sections. Their introduction has put local stores out of business, but residents can get clothing and household items cheaper here than they were able to previously. In addition, each has a large sporting goods section and offers one-hour film developing.

You can find everything you need to try your luck in Kaua'i's waters at **Lihue Fishing Supply,** 2985 Kalena St., 808/245-4930, open Mon.–Saturday.

## Arts, Crafts, and Souvenirs

**Kaua'i Museum Shop** at the Kaua'i Museum has authentic souvenirs and Hawaiian items with competitive prices, which include tapa, wooden bowls, books, cards, prints, and maps.

The **Kauai Products Store,** at the Kukui Grove Shopping Center, 808/246-6753, is a gem. This shop carries art and crafts items, mostly made in Kaua'i, that include paintings, wooden boxes, quilts, metal sculpture, T-shirts, a smattering of jewelry, and food products. It's fine quality at reasonable prices. A good place to stop for a preview of what the island has to offer.

**Kapaia Stitchery,** 808/245-2281, open 9 A.M.–5 P.M. Mon.–Sat., is where you find handmade quilts and distinctive fashions. This shop is along Rte. 56 in Kapaia. The owner is Julie Yukimura, who, along with her grandmother and a number of very experienced island seamstresses, creates fashions, quilts, and embroideries that are beautiful, painstakingly made, and priced right.

Hung from the ceiling for better display, the quilts are awe-inspiring. If you are considering purchasing a quilt while on the island, this is definitely one of the best places to start your search. Ready-made aloha shirts and dresses are mostly 100 percent cotton, and, given a couple of days, these can be made to order from most any material in the store. For those who sew, the range and quality of material is outstanding, and sewing accessories, patterns, and books are all available. You can't help but be pleased with this fine shop!

The aroma of wood and premium cigars wafts from the small **Wailua Falls Gallery** and cigar shop, 808/245-2711, at the big dip along Rte. 56, just at the turnoff to Wailua Falls, next to Kapaia Stitchery, open 9 A.M.–5:30 P.M. Mon.–Sat. or until they want to close. The swirl of burly koa lends natural luster to the handmade humidors and the limited number of furniture pieces and smaller wood artwork, while paintings hang on the wall and earrings on racks.

## Bookshops

Your best bet for all kinds of books in Lihu'e is **Borders Books and Music,** 808/246-0862. Open every day at 8:30 A.M., it closes

**Kaua'i Museum**

Mon.–Thurs. at 10 P.M., Fri.–Sat. at 11 P.M., and Sunday at 8 P.M. Borders carries one of the best Hawaiiana sections on the island. After finding your favorite book, browse the CD racks for music or peruse the map section for guidance. Borders also carries select Mainland and international newspapers. Cafe Espresso, within the store, serves up drinks and snacks.

A great place for books relating to Kaua'i and Hawaii is the **Kaua'i Museum Shop,** open museum hours only. Wal-Mart and Kmart both have book sections, but your selection is limited to generic titles.

### Photo Needs

For film developing, try **Longs Drugs, Kmart** or **Wal-Mart. Photo Spectrum,** 808/245-7667, offers one-hour film processing and also does studio portraits. No shops on the island do camera repair or servicing.

### Supermarkets and Health Food Stores

The **Big Save Supermarket,** near the county government building, is open daily 7 A.M.–11 P.M., and a well-stocked **Star Super Market,** open daily 6 A.M.–11 P.M., is at the rear

of Kukui Grove Shopping Center. Also at Kukui Grove is **General Nutrition Center** for vitamins, minerals and supplements.

**Vim 'N Vigor,** in the Rice Shopping Center, 808/245-9053, open Mon.–Fri. until 5 P.M. and Sat. until 2 P.M., specializes in vitamins, minerals, and other supplements. The shelves are stocked with a good but limited selection of whole-wheat flour, spices, organic pastas, and teas. The back deli case holds a small selection of fresh organic vegetables and prepared deli sandwiches.

### Other Needs

As the principal population center of the island, and its county seat, Lihu'e has five major banks, four of which are within a few steps of each other along Rice Street; the other one is across the highway from Kukui Grove Shopping Center. The main post office is across the street from the museum.

For business services, including packing, shipping, printing, copying, and Internet access, see **Hale 'Oihana,** 808/245-3442, behind the post office.

The **Lihue Laundromat** is an open-air, 24-hour, self-service laundromat at the Rice Shopping Center.

## The Environs

## PUHI

Sustaining substantial residential growth over the past decade, Puhi has become a bedroom community of Lihu'e. Two road signs tip you off that you're in Puhi—one for **Kaua'i Community College** and the other for the **Queen Victoria's Profile** scenic overlook turnout. It's beneficial to keep abreast of what's happening at the college by reading the local newspaper and free tourist brochures. Often, workshops and seminars concerning Hawaiian culture, folk medicine, and various crafts are offered; most are open to the general public and free of charge. The Hawaii International Film Festival and local theater groups use the college's Performing Arts Center for their performances. About 5,000 stu-

dents are enrolled at this two-year community college, part of the University of Hawaii system, most in the fields of business education, health, liberal arts, and vocational technology. Call 808/245-8225 for information about registration and course offerings or visit the college's website: www.kauaicc.hawaii.edu.

Queen Victoria's Profile isn't tremendously remarkable, but a definite resemblance to the double-chinned monarch has been fashioned by nature on the ridge of the Hoary Head Mountains to the south. East and below the tallest peak is a short single rock outcrop. Along the edge of this profile you can imagine the face—the short protuberance about halfway down is the nose and the bump on top the crown. Use your imagination.

Also in Puhi is the head office for Grove Farms

Co., a Shell station, one restaurant, a deli, and a warehouse/business park.

## Food

**Paradise Seafood and Grill** is an easygoing eatery on the highway in Puhi with dining inside or out on the covered veranda at booths or tables. Quick eats include burgers and fish and chips for under $8, with a more extensive evening menu of fish, meats, chicken, and pasta for $15–20.

Across from the gas station at the intersection is **Puhi Fish and Catering Company**, a small deli. Open Mon.–Sat. 6 A.M.–7 P.M., Friday until 8 P.M.; the deli is open until 3 P.M. Stop by for an inexpensive plate lunch, box lunch, drinks, or a selection of fresh fish. This place does lots of takeout, but you're welcome to eat inside at one of the tables.

To its side are the small **Hanalima Baking** shop for pastries, breads, and sandwiches, and the even smaller **People's Market,** which carries some fruit, flowers, and lei.

## Hiking Trail

The hike to Kipu Falls is short and easy. From the Kipu bridge, head back uphill about 100 yards and park off this narrow road. Walk for about 15 minutes down the dirt trail on the east side of the stream that skirts an old cane field. Look for a side trail that heads down the bank to the top of the falls. The main trail continues on a ways for a head-on look at the falls and its pool. About five yards high and perhaps 30 yards wide, Kipu Falls is broad and muscular and creates a pleasing picture as water pours over its craggy face.

# HANAMA'ULU

Hanama'ulu is like a "suburb" of Lihu'e and has always been tied to sugar. It holds a post office, an elementary school, a great local restaurant, gas station, and several other shops. From the center of town, follow Hanama'ulu Road and then Hehi Road down under the highway to Hanama'ulu Beach County Park.

## Hanama'ulu Dining and Services

Heading north, in Hanama'ulu and clearly marked along Rte. 56, is the **Hanamaulu Restaurant Tea House and Sushi Bar,** 808/245-2511, where they must be doing something right—they've lasted in the same location for more than 70 years! Open 10 A.M.–1 P.M. for lunch Tues.–Fri. and 4:30–8:30 P.M. for dinner Tues.–Sun. (sushi Tues.–Sat. only). The menu, which includes sushi, *yakiniku,* and a variety of full-meal Japanese and Chinese dishes, is priced right. An Oriental Buffet is served Sunday evening. Ho Tai, the pudgy happy Buddha, greets you as you enter the main dining room, which has shiny parquet flooring and is partitioned by shoji screens and hanging plants. Through the back and part of the same restaurant is the sushi bar, and beyond that are the elevated tatami-floored rooms (with space for your feet to dangle down) made private by sliding screens that look over a fishpond and a lovely Japanese garden. The gardens behind and to the side of the restaurant are small and wonderful and well worth a stroll. This is a local favorite—authentic food at appropriate prices.

In the large green Hanama'ulu Trading Co. building next door (built 1908) is the post office, as well as the **Big Wheel Donut Shop,** open early for a quick sugar fix. Across the street sit a 7-Eleven and a Shell gas station.

Clearly marked along Rte. 56, the Hanama'ulu Plaza is right at the intersection of Kuhio Highway and Hanama'ulu Road. It's a small but practical shopping center featuring a laundromat and deli. **Ara's Sakanaya,** 808/245-1707, open Mon.–Sat. 9 A.M.–7 P.M. and Sunday 9 A.M.–5 P.M., is a takeout deli-restaurant that offers plate lunches until 1:30 P.M., Japanese *bento,* and fresh fish daily. Neat and tidy, **Plaza Laundry** is a full-service laundry with wash, dry, and fold service for those who don't care to do their own. One of the best on the island, it's open Mon.–Sat. 7:30 A.M.–8:30 P.M. and Sunday until 4:30 P.M.

## Hanama'ulu Beach County Park

With a gradual decline, the beach here is fine, and although it's very accessible and good for swimming, few tourists come. To the right of the beach is a small lagoon formed by Hanama'ulu Stream. Local families frequent this broad grassy park, and it's particularly loved by children because they can play Tom Sawyer on the banks of the heavily forested stream. If you're lucky, you may see dolphins jumping and spinning at the opening of the bay. There are picnic tables, showers, toilets, a pavilion, and camping (with a county permit) under the ironwood trees that front the beach. At times, homeless people stake out semi-permanent camps here, so it may not be the best for camping or the safest place to leave gear unattended. In Hanama'ulu, turn *makai* (toward the sea) off Rte. 56 onto Hanama'ulu Road at the 7-Eleven store, take the right fork onto Hehi Road, and follow it under the highway to the park. There is no access directly off the highway.

## Nukoli'i Beach Park

Between Hanama'ulu and Lydgate beach parks is a long and low windswept coastal area that is partially developed into one resort area and the Wailua Municipal Golf Course. Running along this coast is Nukoli'i Beach, a sand beach fronted almost immediately by a shore reef. Swimming is not encouraged as the shore and near shore areas are rocky, but snorkeling is fair on days when the trade winds are not too strong. Locals sometimes come here to shore fish. On the Hanama'ulu side of the Radisson Kaua'i Beach Resort is a mostly undeveloped beach park that has some parking, a toilet, and showers.

KAUA'I

# East Shore

## Wailua

The east coast of Kaua'i has been called the Coconut Coast, and it's obvious why when you pass through. Even with the extensive development in the area, numerous stands of coconut trees can be seen from the Wailua Municipal Golf Course all the way through Kapa'a. The greatest concentration of these stately nut trees, and a fine representation of the area, is at the Coco Palms near the mouth of the Wailua River. It is here that the coconut grove takes on a magical feel and captivates all who see it.

Wailua (Two Waters) is heralded by the swaying fronds of extra-tall royal palms; whenever you see these, like the *kahili* of old, you know you're entering a special place, a place of royalty. The Hawaiian *ali'i* knew a choice piece of real es-

tate when they saw one, and they cultivated this prime area at the mouth of the Wailua River as their own and referred to it as Wailua Nui Ho'ano (Great Sacred Wailua). This was an important gathering place, a spiritual center for the islands, and through the centuries many *heiau* were built in the area, some where unfortunates were slaughtered to appease the gods, others where the weak and vanquished could find succor and sanctuary. The road leading inland along the Wailua River was called the King's Highway. Commoners were allowed to travel along this road and to approach the royal settlement by invitation only. The most exalted of the island's *ali'i* traced their proud lineage to Puna, a Tahitian priest who, according to the oral tradition, arrived in the earliest migrations and settled here.

Even before the Polynesians came, the area was purportedly settled by the semi-mythical

**Sleeping Giant**

ROBERT NILSEN

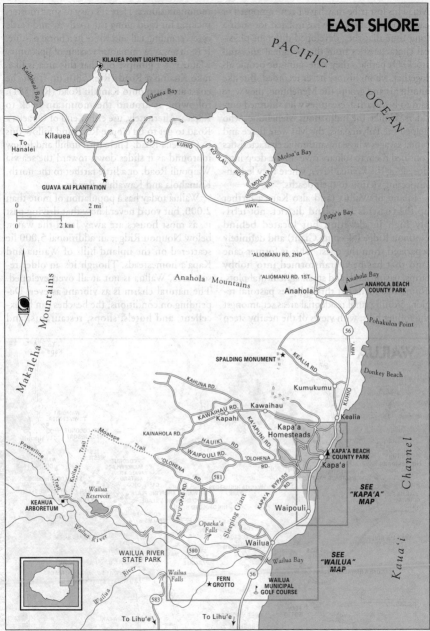

# EAST SHORE

PACIFIC

OCEAN

KILAUEA POINT LIGHTHOUSE

Kalihiwai Bay

Kilauea Bay

To
Hanalei

Kilauea

KUHIO 56

KO'OLAU RD.

Moloa'a Bay

MOLOA'A RD.

HWY.

Papa'a Bay

GUAVA KAI PLANTATION

0        2 mi

0      2 km

MOON

'ALIOMANU RD. 2ND

'ALIOMANU RD. 1ST

Anahola Bay

Anahola Mountains

Anahola

ANAHOLA BEACH
COUNTY PARK

Makaleha Mountains

Pohakuloa Point

56

KEALIA RD.

Donkey Beach

SPALDING MONUMENT

Kumukumu

KAHUNA RD.

KUHIO HWY.

Kawaihau

Kealia

KAWAIHAU RD.

Kapahi

Kapa'a
Homesteads

KAPUNI RD.

KAINAHOLA RD.

HAUIKI RD.

WAIPOULI RD.

'OLOHENA RD.

'OLOHENA RD.

KAPA'A BEACH
COUNTY PARK

Kapa'a

Moalepe Trail

Powerline Trail

Kuilau Trail

Wailua
Reservoir

581

SEE
"KAPA'A"
MAP

Waipouli

KAPA'A BYPASS RD.

KEAHUA
ARBORETUM

PU'UOPAE RD.

Opaeka'a
Falls

Sleeping Giant

Wailua River

WAILUA RIVER
STATE PARK

580

Wailua
Falls

FERN
GROTTO

Wailua

56

Wailua Bay

SEE
"WAILUA"
MAP

Kaua'i Channel

WAILUA
MUNICIPAL
GOLF COURSE

583

To Lihu'e

To Lihu'e

KAUA'I

Mu. This lost tribe may have been composed of early Polynesians who were isolated for such a long time that they developed different physical characteristics from their original ancestral stock. Or perhaps they were a unique people altogether, whom history never recorded. But like another island group, the Menehune, they were said to be dwarfish creatures who shunned outsiders. Unlike the industrious Menehune, who helped the Polynesians, the Mu were fierce and brutal savages whose misanthropic characteristics confined them to solitary caves in the deep interior along the Wailua River, where they led unsuspecting victims to their deaths.

Inland of Wailua (and also Kapa'a farther up the coast) is an upland district, not terribly high in elevation but located behind Nounou Ridge (Sleeping Giant) and definitely separated from the coast. This is former cane land that has been transformed into hobby farms, pastureland, and small agricultural plots. Numerous roads cut through this pastoral region, creating rural residential areas set amongst the rolling hills, with views of the nearby steep

mountain slopes. Here it's easy to spot roosters picking for food along the roadway and cattle egrets standing tall and white in a horse pasture. It is, in a way, a miniature version of upcountry Maui. For a glimpse of what this area is like, take Kuamo'o Road (Rte. 580) up from the coast and turn onto Kamalu Road (Rte. 581), following it around the mountain back to Kapa'a. Alternately, use either end of Opaeka'a Road to get to Pu'u'opae Road and follow this to Olohena Road. There turn uphill and follow it around as it slides down toward the sea via Waipouli Road, or a little farther to the north, Kainahola and Kawaihau Roads.

Wailua today has a population of more than 2,000, but you'd never know that driving past it, as most houses are away from the water, below Nounou Ridge; an additional 5,000 lie scattered on the upland hills of Wailua and Kapa'a homesteads. Though it's an older resort area, Wailua is not at all overdeveloped. The natural charm is as vibrant as ever. Depending on conditions, the beaches can be excellent, and hotels, shops, restaurants, and

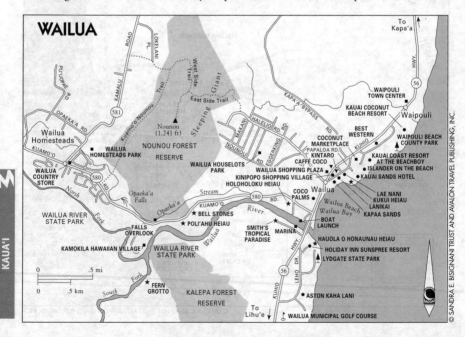

ROBERT NILSEN

inside Fern Grotto, looking out

nightlife are close at hand. With development increasing both to the north and south, perhaps now, as in days of old, the beauty of Wailua will beckon once again.

## SIGHTS

To the traveling public, Wailua is famous primarily for two attractions: one natural, Fern Grotto, the other man-made, Smith's Tropical Paradise. People flock to these, as they are indeed beautiful spots, but there also exist many other spots of historical and cultural significance. Most of these lie within the boundary of **Wailua River State Park,** which runs from the mouth of the Wailua River up the narrow valley, along its south fork to Wailua Falls and its north fork almost to Wailua Reservoir and Keahua Arboretum. Within the arms of this 1,093-acre park are several other waterfalls (including Opaeka'a Falls), half a dozen *heiau,* sacred birthing stones, and vantages for meditative views of the river below. For access to the river park, there is the Wailua Marina on its south bank and the boat/kayak launch on the north bank; the Lydgate Park and Wailua Beach sections front the bay.

## Fern Grotto

Nature's attraction is the Wailua River itself, Hawaii's only navigable stream, which meanders inland toward its headwaters at the foot of forbidding Mt. Wai'ale'ale. Along this route is the Fern Grotto, a tourist institution of legend, hype, and beauty rolled into one. Two local companies run sightseeing trips to the grotto on large motorized barges. As you head the two miles upriver, the crew tells legends of the area and serenades visitors with Hawaiian songs. A hula demonstration is given, and visitors are encouraged to get up and swing along. The grotto itself is a huge rock amphitheater, whose ever-misty walls create the perfect conditions for ferns to grow. And grow they do, wildly and with abandon, filling the cavern with their deep musty smell and penetrating green beauty. Partially denuded of its lush green coat and overhead tree canopy by Hurricane 'Iniki, the grotto is slowly filling in and becoming again the beauty it once was. Although the grotto is smaller than one might imagine, the resonating acoustics are wonderful from inside. Here in the natural cathedral, musicians break into the "Hawaiian Wedding Song"; over the years a steady stream of brides and grooms have come to exchange vows.

KAUA'I

The Fern Grotto trip is an amusement ride, and, aside from paddling yourself upriver in a kayak, it's the only way to get there. It's enjoyable and memorable, but you have to stay in the right frame of mind; otherwise, it's too easy to put down. (See Wailua River Cruises below for particulars.)

## Smith's Tropical Paradise

Along the Wailua River is this 30-acre botanical and cultural garden. A large entranceway welcomes you and proclaims it a "tropical paradise." Inside, most plants are labeled; many are ordinary island foliage, but others are rare and exotic even for the Garden Island. The entire area is sheltered and well watered, and it's easy to imagine how idyllic life was for the original Hawaiians. The two main buildings are a lu'au house and a lagoon theater used in the evenings for an international musical show and lu'au. The "villages"—Philippine- and Polynesian-inspired settlements—are merely plywood facsimiles. However, the grounds themselves are beautifully kept and very impressive. Peacocks and chickens pecking beneath the trees are natural groundskeepers, preventing insects and weeds from overpowering the gardens. This garden provides an excellent opportunity to familiarize yourself with Kaua'i's plants, flowers, fruits, and trees. You are welcome to walk where you will, but signs guide you along a recommended one-mile route. Scheduled mini-trams carry tourists around the grounds for an additional fee. Entrance fees are $5.25 adults, $2.50 children 2–11. Smith's Tropical Paradise, 808/821-6895, is open 8:30 A.M.–4:30 P.M., after which the gardens are readied for the evening lu'au and musical entertainment. To get to the gardens, follow the road past the Wailua Marina on the south side of the river.

## Kamokila Hawaiian Village

At a bend in the Wailua River on the way to the Fern Grotto sits Kaua'i's only re-created folk village. Kamokila (Stronghold) has been cut from the jungle on the site of an *ali'i* village, the first of seven ancient villages in this valley; the villages farther up were for commoners. The prominent ridge across the river indicates the boundary past which an ordinary man could not tread for fear of his losing his life.

The old village sat on terraces on the hillside above the river, and fields were cultivated where the village now lies. Kamokila has been resurrected to give visitors a glimpse of what island life was like for the ancient Hawaiians. Opened in 1981, it was destroyed almost immediately by Hurricane 'Iwa in 1982 and badly knocked around again by Hurricane 'Iniki in 1992. Here you find examples of buildings, agricultural plots, fruit trees and medicinal plants, and demonstrations of ancient crafts and activities of everyday life. Taro is grown and poi made, mats and skirts are woven, and traditional medicines prepared. A *hale noa* (chief's sleeping quarters), *hale koa* (warrior's house), *pahoku hanau* (birthing house), *hale ali'i 'akoakoa* (assembly hall), *hale lapa'au* (herbal medicine office), and *lana nu'u mamao* (oracle tower) have been erected. The *imu* pit for cooking is functional, and an athletic ground hosts games at festival times. There are also tikis (spirit containers) and *'aumakua* (ancestral spirit icons) set up at propitious spots around the village.

Use the informational sheet for a self-guided tour around the property and an explanation of the importance of each site. Ask the staff about the methods of creating handicrafts and tools, the uses of both the ordinary and medicinal plants, and how the village operated on a daily basis. You may drive down to the village by following a steep one-lane track that skirts the ridge—the turnoff is just above the Opaeka'a Falls overlook on Rte. 580. The entrance fee is $5 for adults, $2.50 for children under 12; open Mon.–Sat. 9 A.M.–5 P.M. A trip to this inspiring village is well worth the time and effort and will certainly add to your knowledge of the roots of Hawaiian life. For more information, call 808/823-0559. Combining this tour with a kayak trip up the river costs $25. As the closest entry point onto the river for Fern Grotto, the secret falls, and swimming spots along the riverbank, entry here knocks off several miles of paddling.

## Historical Sites and Heiau

The King's Highway (Rte. 580), running inland

from Wailua, and Rte. 56, the main drag, have a number of roadside attractions and historical sites dating from the precontact period. Most are just a short stroll from your car and well worth the effort. The mountains behind Wailua form a natural sculpture of a giant in repose, aptly called the **Sleeping Giant.** You have to stretch your imagination just a little to see him (his outline is clearer from farther up in Waipouli), and although not entirely a bore, like most giants, he's better left asleep. This giant and his green cover are part of the Nounou Forest Reserve.

Along Rte. 56, a tall stand of palms on the south side of the Wailua River is part of Lydgate State Park and marks the spot of **Hauola O Honaunau** (Pu'uhonua O Hauola), a temple of refuge that welcomed offending *kapu*-breakers of all social classes. Here miscreants could atone for their transgressions and have their spiritual slates wiped clean by temple priests, enabling them to return to society without paying with their lives. Both the refuge and **Hikina A Ka La Heiau,** a site of rituals and prayers to the rising sun, are marked by a low encircling wall. The area, where the Wailua River meets the sea, is extremely picturesque. Perhaps it's knowledge about the temple of refuge that creates the atmosphere, but here, as at all of these merciful temple sites, the atmosphere is calm and uplifting, as if some spiritual residue has permeated the centuries. It's a good spot to relax in the cool of the grove, and picnic tables are available. At the river mouth and shallowly incised into the river rock are a handful of Kaua'i's few petroglyphs— human and geometric figures. These can usually be seen at low tide and when not covered by sand. Over the road near the entrance to the marina is **Malae Heiau.**

On the low point that forms the northern extent of Wailua Bay, on Lae Nani condominium property, is **Kukui Heiau.** As this whole region was once populated by royalty and was a point of arrival and departure between the islands, and perhaps also for travelers from islands of the South Pacific, Kukui Heiau was used as a fire beacon site to direct canoes to a proper landing. Perhaps 500 years old and once about 230 feet long by 70 feet wide, only a fragment of its former stone

structure is evident today, affirming the skill of its builders and the importance of the site.

As Rte. 580 starts to meander inland, you pass the state park boat launch area. Almost immediately on your left look for **Holoholoku Heiau,** where the unfortunate ones who didn't make it to the temple of refuge were sacrificed to the never-satisfied gods. This temple is one of Kaua'i's most ancient; the altar itself is the large slab of rock near the front. As if to represent the universality of the life-death cycle, **Pohaku Ho'o Hanau,** the royal birthing stones, are within an infant's cry away. Royal mothers came here to deliver the future kings and queens of the island. The stones somehow look comfortable to lean against, and perhaps their solidity reinforced the courage of the mother. Behind the *heiau,* a silver guardrail leads up the hill to a small, neatly tended Japanese cemetery. The traditional tombstones chronicling the lives and deaths of those buried here have turned green with lichens against the pale blue sky.

Back on Rte. 580, you start to wend your way uphill. You can see how eroded and lush Kaua'i is from this upland perch. Notice, too, the dark green fresh water as it becomes engulfed by the royal blue of the ocean in the distance. As you climb, look for an HVB Warrior pointing to **Opaeka'a Falls.** The far side of the road has an overlook; below is the Wailua River and the Kamokila Hawaiian Village. Take a look around to see how undeveloped Kaua'i is.

Across the road and down a bit from the Opaeka'a turnoff is **Poli'ahu Heiau,** a one-acre site supposedly built by the Menehune and used by King Kaumuali'i, Kaua'i's last king. This is one of seven *heiau* known to have been constructed along the Wailua River from the river mouth to the moutaintop. While its use is not definitely known and all the structures inside are long since gone, it is assumed by the size to have been a *luakini heiau,* one that required a powerful leader and great manpower to build and one that may have been used for human sacrifice. Nothing is left but a rectangular wall enclosure with an enlargement at one corner that has once again been filled with rock to create a fairly level platform. Do not walk on the stones, as it's believed that the spirits of the ancestors are contained in the rocks.

Down the ridge at the end of a gravel track are **bell stones** (some contest this and say that these stones are *not* the bell stones). Whether these two stones were *the* bell stones or not, bell stones were historically pounded when a royal *wahine* gave birth, and their peals could be heard for miles. From here, there is a great view over the river and down to the coast. It's easy to see why this was a very productive region and one prized by the *ali'i*.

## Beaches and Parks

**Lydgate Beach** is a gem. It's on the south side of the Wailua River, behind the Holiday Inn SunSpree Resort complex. A large lava rock barrier makes for great swimming and snorkeling even in high surf. The pool is completely protected and perfect for tots, but stay off the slippery rock barrier. Overseeing the whole beach is a lifeguard. This beach is never overcrowded, and you can find more seclusion by walking along the coast away from the built-up area toward the golf course. If you head to the river, the brackish water is refreshing, but stay away from the point where it meets the ocean; the collision creates tricky, wicked currents. One of the best on the island, **Lydgate State Park** also provides sheltered picnic tables under a cool canopy provided by a thick stand of ironwoods, plus grills, restrooms, and showers, but no camping. Here at the park is **Kamalani Playground**, a wonderful kids' play structure created for the community with community input. This is a child's dream come true: slides, swings, steps, tubes, passageways, and different-level platforms.

Back down the coast and fronting the golf course is a secluded beach, a continuation of Nukoli'i Beach that's farther down. You can drive to it by following the paved road at the northern end of the course until it becomes dirt and branches toward the sea as a beach access road. Few people ever come here, and plenty of nooks and crannies are good for one night's bivouac.

**Wailua Beach,** fronting the Coco Palms, is part of the Kaumuali'i section of Wailua River

State Park. It can be treacherous and should only be entered on calm days when lifeguards are in attendance. It's a favorite for people who want to sunbathe, play in the water near shore, or stroll along the sand. Surfers come for the breaks on the northern edge of the bay, and bodyboarders can sometimes be seen near the river mouth. Park under the trees at either end.

**Waipouli Beach County Park** fronts the cluster of hotels near the Coconut Marketplace. Largely an undeveloped grassy area, the narrow beach is really not recommended for swimming because of the near shore reef but is fine for sunbathing and collecting driftwood.

A half-mile-long **beach walk,** partly over hotel sidewalks with the rest across the grassy sand of the county park, starts at the Kauai Sands Hotel on the south end and runs past the Kauai Coconut Beach Resort on the north end.

## ACCOMMODATIONS

### $100–150

Part of the Hawaiian-owned Sand and Seaside Hotels chain, **Kauai Sands Hotel,** to the side of Coconut Marketplace at 420 Papaloa Rd., Wailua, HI 96746, 808/822-4951 or 800/560-5553, fax 808/822-0978, www.kauaisandshotel.com, info@kauaisandshotel.com, is a better-than-average moderate hotel with a convenient location, spacious grounds, accommodating staff, a large relaxing lobby, the budget Aldon's Restaurant, two pools, beach access, and self-service laundry facilities. As with all four Sand and Seaside Hotels, this one is reminiscent of earlier days of Hawaiian tourism, a place that would seem familiar to someone who had visited Hawaii in the 1960s or '70s. All rooms have one king-size or two double beds, a small refrigerator, air-conditioning, ceiling fans, TVs, telephones, and lanai. What the hotel lacks in luster it makes up for in price. Daily rates are $98 for a standard room, $110 for a superior pool room, $130 for the deluxe room, and $130 for a room with kitchenette. Room and car packages are offered for about $30 more. Numerous discounts are offered, including AARP, AAA, military, and Internet booking.

## $150–200

Best Western has taken a former condo complex of 10 two-story buildings and turned the units into the comfortable **Best Western Plantation Hale Suites,** 484 Kuhio Hwy., Kapa'a, HI 96746, 808/822-4941 or 800/775-4253, fax 808/822-5599, www.plantation-hale.com, ph@aloha.net. Plantation Hale is across the street from Waipouli Beach Park just north of the Coconut Marketplace. While not an oceanfront property, it's only a stroll away. Accommodations are all one-bedroom, spacious, and eminently comfortable apartment suites with full kitchens, bath, and living area, each with color cable TV and daily maid service. An open-air hallway runs the length of each unit. There are three swimming pools on the property, two spas, a putting green, barbecue areas, and laundry facilities, and the front has an activities desk. While the road side has a border of trees and bushes, it's a bit close to the highway and some back units may get traffic noise. Rates are $165–175 for a basic suite, $175–185 for garden view, and $185–195 for scenic view rooms; $20 for each extra adult. Numerous discounts are offered. The Plantation Hale is a decent value all around.

Between the water and the Coconut Marketplace sits the **Aston Islander on the Beach,** 4-

## THE COCO PALMS

The Coco Palms was a classic Hawaiian hotel, one of the first tourist destinations built on the island, but it took a terrible beating during Hurricane 'Iniki. The Polynesian-inspired buildings are interspersed through a monumental coconut grove planted by a German immigrant in the early 1800s. His aspiration was to start a copra plantation, and although it failed, his plantings matured into one of the largest stands of coconut trees in the islands.

When Hollywood needed "paradise" it came here. The Coco Palms served as movie backdrop for Elvis in *Blue Hawaii* and for Rita Hayworth in the movie *Sadie Thompson,* bringing the hotel (and the island) notoriety. The chapel built for *Sadie Thompson* was left standing, and more than 2,000 marriages were performed there over the years. Some scenes from the movie *South Pacific* were filmed at the Coco Palms, and after Tattoo informed Mr. Roarke of the arrival of "da plane, Boss" in the popular TV series *Fantasy Island,* it was into the hotel coconut grove that he drove his jeep.

Nightly, the hostelry's famous torch-lighting ceremony took place under the palm canopy, which encircles a royal lagoon once used to fatten succulent fish for the exclusive use of the *ali'i*. Everyone, hotel guest or not, was welcome at the ceremony. Some dismissed the ceremony as "fake traditional," but it was the *best* "fake traditional" on the island—both dramatic and fun. This ceremony was started by the now-deceased Grace Guslander—a legend in her own right—a congenial hostess and old-time hotelier famous for her cocktail parties.

The Coco Palms was a peaceful garden brought to its knees by the hurricane. It was and still is a landmark. The greenery has rebounded, of course, but one wonders how much of the grounds and the buildings will be saved when the property is finally turned to other uses.

the coconut grove at the Coco Palms

484 Kuhio Hwy., Kapaʻa, HI 96746, 808/822-7417 or 800/922-7866, fax 808/822-1947, www.astonhotels.com, an easy eight-structure complex with a front veranda and decorative balustrades on all levels, giving it something of a Southern plantation look. All rooms come with air-conditioning, wet bars, refrigerators, coffeemakers, color TVs, room safes, and lanai, and each oceanfront unit has the addition of a microwave. Comfortable and up-to-date, each room is decorated with island flavor. Set right on the beach, this 198-room property has a pool with jet spa, pool bar, barbecue/picnic area, and sand volleyball net, in addition to an activity desk, gift shop, and guest laundry. The Jolly Roger Restaurant sits adjacent to the parking lot, and only a few steps farther are the myriad shops and eateries of the Coconut Marketplace. Slightly lower during the "value season," room rates run $145 for garden view to $198 for oceanfront, with suites at $240.

## $200–250

The 216-room oceanfront **Holiday Inn Sun-Spree Resort Kauaʻi**, 3-5920 Kuhio Hwy., Kapaʻa, HI 96746, 808/823-6000 or 888/823-5111, fax 808/823-6666, www.holidayinn-kauai.com, info@holidayinn-kauai.com, has a lovely setting at the mouth of the Wailua River just above Lydgate Park. Incorporated into the architecture is a series of cascading pools and a koi pond that boils with frenzied color at feeding time. The main lobby is a huge affair with swooping beams in longhouse style, and the wings of rooms run toward the ocean from there. The feeling you get here is spaciousness and welcome. The hotel facilities include two swimming pools and a whirlpool spa, a small fitness room, one tennis court for guests only, volleyball and shuffleboard courts, coin-operated laundry, and a picnic area. For food, there's The Palms Restaurant and lounge, and Kahanu poolside snack bar. The hotel rooms are large, and many have ocean views; sliding glass doors let in the breeze, but the rooms don't have balconies. The overall color scheme includes muted greens and peach. While the bathrooms are not large, they are tastefully done; one wing has showers and the other has bathtubs. Each room contains a small refrigerator, TV, room safe, and iron and ironing board—all the amenities needed. Room rates run $198–231 and $258 for suites; no charge for children 19 and under using existing bedding. Thirteen spacious two-room cabanas with kitchenettes are separate from the main facility and have unobstructed views of the beach park; they run $363 a night. Room and car and romance packages are available. This is a fine, quiet place, where you receive a lot for your money.

Amidst a huge grove of swaying coconut palms, a natural buffer offering peace and tranquillity, with wings encircling a central courtyard, sits the sand-colored **Kauai Coconut Beach Resort,** P.O. Box 830, Kapaʻa, HI 96746, 808/822-3455 or 800/222-5642, www.kcb.com. The palm grove once belonged to the family of the famous swimmer and actor Buster Crabbe, of *Buck Rogers* fame. He and his twin brother, Bud, were born and raised right here, and Buster learned to swim along this very coast. The lobby is alive with trees, flowers, and vines trellised from the balconies; stained glass depicting a sailing canoe departing at sunset and a 40-foot water cascade add comfort and grandeur. A bas-relief encircles the reception area, and as your eyes sweep from panel to panel it tells the story of how the Hawaiians became a "people," migrating originally from Indonesia until they found their fabled "homeland in the north." All rooms have color TVs, air-conditioning, mini-fridges, safes, coffeemakers with complimentary Kona coffee, and private lanai. Built in 1978 and well used, recent remodeling and upgrades in furniture and amenities keep it fresh and new. Pastels and earth tones predominate, and artwork with Hawaiian themes hangs throughout. Rooms are sizable, and the suites that front the ocean are larger yet. Rates are $140 for a standard room, $210 for an ocean view, and $280 for an oceanfront room; numerous package deals, specials, and discounts are also available. For your convenience, the hotel offers a full-service activity desk, concierge service, a summer children's program, and laundry services. The central courtyard swimming pool and spa are places to relax, and the hotel's three tennis courts, free to guests, offer rentals and lessons and are open to the public for a small fee. An indoor/outdoor restaurant serves breakfast, lunch, and dinner. As the sun sets, find a seat around the courtyard for the free torch-lighting ceremony, then move to the Royal Coconut Grove Lounge for a drink and nightly entertainment.

## Condos

The luxury **Aston Kaha Lani,** 4460 Nehe Rd., 808/882-9331, fax 808/822-2828, www.aston-hotels.com, between the Wailua golf course and Lydgate State Park, is a quiet place with a broad oceanfront lawn, large swimming pool, and tennis courts. These spacious units have living rooms that face the ocean across the lanai, fully equipped kitchens, and separate bedrooms. Each unit is equipped with ceiling fan, color cable TV, and room safe, and a laundry facility is on property. One-bedroom units run $225–265, two-bedroom units $325–355, and three-bedroom units $425–495; $35–75 less during value season.

A moderately priced condominium on Wailua Bay is the **Kapaa Sands,** 380 Papaloa Rd., Kapa'a, HI 96746, 808/822-4901 or 800/222-4901, fax 808/822-1556, www.kapaasands.com, ksresort@gte.net, with pool, laundry facilities, and maid service. The oldest condo on the island—open since 1968—the 24-unit Kapaa Sands is kept clean and up to date and has been completely refurbished since Hurricane 'Iniki. It is on old Japanese grounds that once housed a Shinto shrine. The Japanese motif is still reflected in the roofline of the units and the *torii* design above each door number. The well-landscaped grounds are rather compact but manage to include a swimming pool and a grass lawn that fronts a thin sand beach. Each unit has a full kitchen, ceiling fans in all rooms, telephone, TV, VCR, and a lanai. Two-bedroom units occupy two levels, with the bedrooms upstairs. Room rates are $100 and $117 for ocean view and oceanfront studios, and $134 and $152 for two-bedroom ocean view and two-bedroom oceanfront units. Monthly rates are available; the minimum stay is three days except during winter, when it is seven days.

The two classiest places along the north edge of Wailua Bay are Lae Nani and Lanikai. Managed by Outrigger Resorts, **Lae Nani** is a peach of a place. Located at 410 Papaloa Rd., Kapa'a, HI 96746, 808/822-4938, fax 808/822-1022, Outrigger central reservations 800/688-7777, it offers one- and two-bedroom units on the beach. The rich decor varies by unit, but all have full kitchens, lanai, ceiling fans, TVs, and one and a half baths; most have ocean views. All are immaculately clean. There is a laundry room, daily maid service, one tennis court for guests only, a swimming pool, and poolside barbecue grill. The small Kukui Heiau is on the property beachside, adjacent to a rock-enclosed swimming area that's perfect for kids and others unsure of the waves and tides. One-bedroom units for up to four people are $220–270, and the two-bedroom units are $240–330, maximum six; a two-night minimum stay is enforced. There is public shoreline access at the edge of this property.

Also three stories tall with many of the same amenities, the **Lanikai** is next door to the Lae Nani at 390 Papaloa Rd., 808/822-7700 or 800/755-2824, fax 808/822-7456. Here there are one- and two-bedroom units with kitchens that rent for $280–330 a day, $10–30 cheaper during low season. Ask about discounts. For additional information or reservations, contact Castle Resorts, 800/367-5004.

Newly renovated, the **Kauai Coast Resort at the Beachboy,** 808/822-3441 or 877/977-4355, fax 808/822-0843, www.kauaicoastresort.com, is an attractive oceanfront condominium complex with one- and two-bedroom units with full kitchen and laundry facilities, air-conditioning, daily maid service, and other amenities that make for a comfortable vacation. The property has a heated pool, children's pool, poolside bar, tennis courts, activity desk, fitness room, and on-site day spa. The Hukilau Lanai (operated by Gaylord's) serves food just off the lobby in the restaurant that overlooks the garden. Although primarily a timeshare property, rooms are rented to others when available. Studio/garden view rooms run $120, one-bedrooms $185–220, and two-bedroom units $245–295 a night.

## Vacation Rental Agencies

**Kauai Vacation Rentals,** 3-3311 Kuhio Hwy., Lihu'e, HI 96766, 808/245-8841 or 800/367-5025, www.KauaiVacationRentals.com, aloha @kvrre.com, handles condos and vacation rental

KAUA'I

homes throughout the island, but in Wailua it is nearly all condo units.

## Bed-and-Breakfasts

In the uplands behind the Sleeping Giant is **Rosewood Bed and Breakfast,** 872 Kamalu Rd., 808/822-5216, fax 808/822-5478, www.rosewoodkauai.com, rosewood@aloha.net. Creamy yellow with white trim and set behind a neat picket fence, Rosewood is a finely kept plantation-style house with a smaller Victorian house, thatched house, and bunkhouse on the property. Least expensive, at $40–50, are the three cozy bunkhouse rooms, which share a bathroom, but each has a refrigerator, microwave, and sink. The thatched cottage, one large room with kitchenette and an outdoor shower, runs $105, and the main house room with private bath goes for $85. With two floors, two bedrooms, a full kitchen, and porch, the Victorian house runs $125. It looks like a miniature of the main house. Breakfast is included for guests of the main house room; $10 extra for those in the bunkhouse and cottages. No credit cards. Three-night minimum stay.

Managed by Rosewood is **Hale Makani,** a full house with three bedrooms. Located in the residential area below Sleeping Giant, it has views of the ocean. Bedrooms are upstairs; downstairs is one large room split into living, dining, and kitchen areas. This place is great for a family. The rental rate is $150 a night for up to four people. Among the more than one dozen other properties that Rosewood manages is **Rainbows End,** a small one-bedroom plantation-style cottage with kitchenette and outside shower that's up on the rolling hills above Sleeping Giant. This property runs $115 a night. Contact Rosewood above for information and reservations.

A short distance from Rosewood B&B is **Hempey's Garden Island Bed and Breakfast,** 6078 Kolopua St., 808/822-0309, fax 808/822-4399. Recently remodeled, each room has its own bathroom, and all lie off the common room with its cushy chairs and couches, TV, audio equipment, and kitchenette. Separate from the other rooms and with its own entrance, the brightly painted studio is often requested by honeymooners. A full homemade breakfast is served on the lanai at 8:30 A.M. for all guests. Rooms run $55, the studio $65; $10 less for no breakfast. Two nights minimum. No credit cards or personal checks are accepted. For additional information, see www.hempeys.com, hempey@hawaiian.net.

**Aloha Country Inn** suites and cottages, 808/822-0168 or 866/822-0166, fax 808/822-0108, www.alohacountryinn.com, alohacountryinn@hawaiian.net, is at 505 Kamalu Road, at the road's big bend. The two large upstairs suites in the house run $75 and $85, and both have kitchenettes. In the spacious yard out back are separate units, a two-bedroom cottage for $95, two studio units at $80 and $85, and a larger suite for $140. All rooms have a two night minimum. No credit cards.

**Makana Crest** cottage, P.O. Box 3671, Lihu'e, HI 96766, 808/245-6500, has a small single unit with two bedrooms, a bath with shower, and a kitchen that runs $100 a day, three-day minimum, or $500 a week.

Across the road from Opaeka'a Falls is **House of Aleva,** 808/822-4606, offering two rooms that share a bath on the second level. Rates are $40 single or $55 double; no credit cards are accepted. Work out breakfast particulars with host.

# FOOD

## Inexpensive

Stark white with a few ethnic decorations, the **Korean Bar-B-Q Restaurant,** 808/823-6744, is in the Kinipopo Shopping Village; open daily 10 A.M.–9 P.M., Tues. from 4:30 P.M. While some items are authentic Korean, there is a mix of Hawaiian and American in the menu. Single plates like kalbi (short ribs) and chapchae (stir-fry clear noodles) mostly run $7–8, and the combo plates cost just a bit more. Plate dishes come with two-scoop rice and four vegetables, otherwise order à la carte for a few dollars less. Takeout is available.

Directly across the street is **Wailua Family Restaurant,** 808/882-3325. Open from early morning, this place becomes a fairyland of lights in the evening. A full menu is served all day, but many come for the very reasonably priced buffets (lunch, $8.99; dinner, $11.99) and salad bar. In addition to the regular menu, Masa's Sushi Bar, inside, offers a taste of the Orient.

Serving breakfast and dinner, **Aldon's Restaurant** at the Kauai Sands Hotel serves American standard food at very reasonable prices.

Surrounded by hotels and condos, the **Coconut Marketplace** has more than a dozen eateries. Among the many, check out **Eggbert's,** a family-style restaurant that's popular for breakfast and frequented by shoppers. Serving mostly light fare, Eggbert's is open 7 A.M.–3 P.M. and again 5 P.M.–9 P.M. Across from center stage, the **Palm Tree Terrace,** 808/821-1040, serves lunch and dinner daily, concentrating on sandwiches, pasta, seafood, and poultry. **Aloha Kauai Pizza** serves some of the best pizza on the island and is a hit with locals. A short menu of other Italian food is available, many items made from family recipes. Open daily 11 A.M.–9 P.M. **Harley's Ribs and Chicken** says it all with its name. For your sweet tooth, step up to **Zack's Frozen Yogurt** counter or **Lappert's Ice Cream** stand.

## Moderate

As the main dining room at the Holiday Inn SunSpree, **The Palm Restaurant** is open for breakfast and dinner. Sit inside or out on the lanai under tiki torches, where you can look out over the garden to the moon reflected off the water and hear soft evening sounds filter out through the huge open doors. While it serves an à la carte menu in the evening, it's perhaps best known for its very reasonably priced morning buffets, $10.95. Evening entrées include an *'ahi poki* appetizer, seafood linguine with wine sauce and citrus shoyu chicken for $17, and prime beef rib for $18. Adjacent to the dining room is the **Kuhio Lounge,** quiet most evenings except Friday when it's transformed into a disco for dancing. For salads, sides, sandwiches, burgers, and cocktails during the day, try the afternoon-only **Kahanu snack bar** at the ocean-view pool.

The **Wailua Marina Restaurant,** 808/822-4311, overlooking the Wailua River, offers moderately priced "local-style" food that's filling but not designed for the most refined palate. At the busy marina, the restaurant caters mostly to large tour groups during the day and couples and smaller groups in the evening. If you're going on a Fern Grotto boat trip, consider eating here for lunch 10:30 A.M.–2 P.M. Open 5–8:30 P.M. for dinner, except Monday. Entrées run the gamut from chuck ground steak to fillet of mahimahi and filet mignon. Most fall into the $12–20 range; only the lobster and lobster combination plates are more than $30. All entrées include rice or potatoes, a trip to the salad bar, and coffee or tea. Not gourmet, but convenient, and there's never a wait after the last boat upriver.

**Mema** 808/823-0899, across the highway from Kintaro's, is open Mon.–Fri. 11 A.M.–2 P.M. for lunch and nightly 5–9:30 P.M. for dinner. Serving Thai and Chinese cuisine, it's a casual family-operated restaurant with a touch of class. The ornate chairs and tables set the theme, while walls and cabinets are well appointed with decorations. Waiters, dressed in silky Thai clothing, carry their trays past a profusion of potted plants and flowers. The menu starts with crispy noodles and continues through nearly 50 appetizers, vegetable, chicken, and seafood items; curries; soups; and noodle and rice dishes. Appetizers run $6.95–10.95, and most main entrées and soups range $8.95–17.95. Entrées include broccoli with oyster sauce, seafood red curry cooked in coconut milk with basil and bamboo shoots, pad thai, and black bean sauce stir-fry. Most entrées can be prepared vegetarian, and spiciness can be adjusted. Mema's offers complete wine, beer, cocktail, and dessert menus. If you are looking for a restaurant with excellent exotic food where you can enjoy a pleasant evening for a reasonable price, Mema's should be at the top of your list. It's a winner.

Behind the Wailua Shopping Plaza in a converted plantation house, almost hidden under tall trees and behind a prolific bougainvillea, is **Caffé Coco,** 808/822-7990, open daily except Monday 4–9 P.M. Using local produce, fresh fish, and pork, the tiny kitchen puts nutritious food on your plate, a mix of European, Asian, Mexican, and American cuisine. Try penne d'alba pasta, cilantro pesto *'ahi,* or *ono* charmoula with curried vegetable samosa, rice, salad, raiita, and chutney. Full-platter dinners run $14–21. Lighter fare includes soup, focaccia, and green salad; a tofu, veggie, peanut wrap; barbecue pork sandwich; and seafood gumbo. Aside from the daily menu, numerous specials are posted. After dinner, pick one of the many tempting, homemade desserts from the deli case or order coffee from the espresso bar. This is island-casual cuisine at its best—tasty, wholesome, and healthy. Order at the counter and take a seat out back in the garden under the vine-covered canopy, amongst orchids, bananas, and lime trees. To add to the ambiance, live music is performed every evening of the week. As seating is outside, if the mosquitoes get too bothersome, feel free to use the organic "jungle juice" kept at the counter.

At the Coconut Marketplace is **Buzz's Steak and Lobster** restaurant, 808/822-0041, open for lunch noon–2:30 P.M. and dinner 4:30–10 P.M. *Pu pu* and happy hour are 3–4:30 P.M., and an early-bird special runs 4:30–6:30 P.M. Buzz's started serving steaks and seafood in Waikiki in 1957 and, with its signature restaurant still open on O'ahu, continues to do the same. You enter through large koa doors, where an open kitchen presides over a comfortable dining area, while palm fronds and a hanging canoe add a Polynesian flair. Take time to notice the collection of artifacts, paintings, basketry, lei, and antiques gathered from Tahiti and the islands of the South Pacific. Word on the street says the salad bar here is the best, and it's complimentary with dinner. For lunch, Buzz's offers such items as soup of the day at $2.95, mahimahi and teriyaki chicken sandwiches for $6.25. Desserts include New York–style cheesecake and homemade ice-cream pie, both priced at $3.95. Appetizers, served at both lunch and dinner, include sautéed mushrooms at $5.50 and teriyaki beef sticks at $4.95. Dinner entrées are mahimahi almondine for $11.95, Pacific shrimp for $17.95, various steaks for around $17.95, and lobster and fresh catch at market price.

Near the front entrance to Coconut Market Place is the open and breezy **Kauai Hula Girl** bar and grill, 808/822-4422, open daily for lunch and dinner. *Pu pu* run about $10, and entrées are mostly in the $15–25 range. Music accompanies dinner every night.

The **Jolly Roger Restaurant,** 808/822-3451, open 6:30 A.M.–10 P.M., claims to have the longest happy hour on the island—from opening to 8 P.M., when karaoke starts in the lounge. It's not known for exceptional food, but you always get hearty substantial portions no matter what time of day you come to dine, and there are always advertised special deals. Breakfast is served until noon, lunch 11 A.M.–4 P.M., and dinner 3–10 P.M. You can find Jolly Roger between the Coconut Marketplace and the Islander on the Beach.

## Expensive

The Japanese legend of Kintaro, a pint-size boy born to an old couple from inside a peach pit, is slightly less miraculous than the excellent and authentic Japanese restaurant named for him, owned and operated by a Korean gentleman, Don Kim. From the outside, **Restaurant Kintaro,** next to the Kinipopo Shopping Village Center, 808/822-3341, open daily except Sunday 5:30–9:30 P.M. for dinner only, is nothing special, but inside it transforms into the simple and subtle beauty of Japan. The true spirit of Japanese cooking is presented, with the food as pleasing to the eye as to the palate. For its variety, innovation, and quality, the sushi bar alone is worth stopping in for. The dinners are expertly and authentically prepared, equaling those served in fine restaurants in Japan. If you have never sampled Japanese food before, Restaurant Kintaro is Kaua'i's best place to start. Those who *are* accustomed to the cuisine can choose from favorites like tempura, sukiyaki, a variety of soba, and the old standby teriyaki. Most dinners run $14–19. Reservations are often necessary.

The **Voyage Room,** at the Kauai Coconut Beach Resort, 808/822-3455, offers a sumptuous breakfast buffet for $10.75, or an à la carte menu for both breakfast and lunch. Every evening 5:30–9:30 P.M., the Voyage Room transforms into **The Flying Lobster.** The surf-and-turf-oriented menu begins with appetizers for $4–9.95 and soup of the day. Seafood lovers will enjoy entrées like the Ali'i spiny lobster dinner for $24, coconut shrimp at $17, or fresh catch of the day at $15.95. From the broiler, you can dine on New York strip steak at $21.95 or teriyaki top sirloin for $14.95. Lighter fare, scrumptious desserts, and drinks are also on the menu, and don't forget the early-bird special 5:30–6:30 P.M. Follow the example of the locals who come to the Flying Lobster on Saturday evenings 5:30–9:30 P.M. for the seafood and prime-rib buffet—lobster, crab, shrimp, oysters, prime rib, and fresh fish cooked to order before your very eyes. Prices are reasonable at $24.95 adults, $15.95 children ages 12–17, and $1 per year for kids 6–11. Reservations are recommended because the buffet is popular with local people, who know quality, quantity, and a good price when they see them.

## ENTERTAINMENT

The **Kauai Coconut Beach Resort** offers a little of everything. You can enjoy free *pu pu* at Royal Coconut Grove Lounge, just off the gardens and pool deck—happy hour is 4–6 P.M. Follow that with the free torch-lighting ceremony in the central courtyard. Every evening 6:30–8:30 P.M., listen to island sounds by local musicians.

The dining room and lounge at the Holiday Inn SunSpree Resort come alive on Friday nights 9 P.M.–1 A.M. with the sounds of disco for dancing, so polish your shoes and practice your steps.

The Coconut Marketplace hosts a free **Polynesian Hula Show** daily at 5 P.M. The young local dancers and musicians put as much effort into their routines as if this were the big time.

The Coconut Marketplace also has something to offer moviegoers: the **Plantation Cinema 1 and 2.** Call 808/821-2324 for showings and movie times. Adult entrance is $6.50, seniors and children $3.50.

The lounge at the Jolly Roger Restaurant behind the Coconut Marketplace offers karaoke nightly. You can listen, sing, and even dance nightly 8 P.M.–2 A.M. "Happy hour" runs all day until karaoke begins, and the drinks are cheaper than at a hotel. The atmosphere is casual and the talk friendly.

A good watering hole, where you can find cool drinks, good conversation, and lively music nightly, is **Tradewinds—A South Seas Bar,** at the Coconut Marketplace, 808/822-1621, open 10 P.M.–2 A.M. On some nights with live bands there's a cover charge.

Two **lu'au** are performed along this coast. The Kauai Coconut Beach Resort holds its lu'au every evening in the *lu'au halau* amongst the coconut trees starting at 6 P.M. The buffet table is loaded with luscious island food and there is an open bar throughout the evening. Legends of the island are performed in music and dance. Adult tickets are $55, seniors $50, $33 for children 12–17, and $23 for those 3–11; call 808/822-3455 for reservations. Smith's Tropical Paradise Garden Lu'au hosts a buffet and presents the Golden People of Hawaii international pageant musical revue on Monday, Wednesday, and Friday starting at 5 P.M. on the banks of the Wailua River. Tickets are $56 for adults, $28.50 for children 7–13, and $18.75 for ages 3–6; for the show only with no buffet, entrance at 7:30 P.M., tickets run $15 adult and $7.50 children. Call 808/821-6895 or 808/821-6896 for reservations.

## RECREATION

### Golf

**Wailua Municipal Golf Course,** 808/241-6666, skirts the coast, fronting a secluded beach. Opened in 1920 but rebuilt several times, it is the oldest golf course on Kaua'i and supposedly the first built on an outer island. Because of its idyllic setting, it's perhaps the most beautiful public links in Hawaii, and it frequently gets cited as one of the finest municipal courses in the country. On occasion, tournaments are held here. Even if you're not an avid golfer, you can take a lovely stroll beside the fairways as they stretch out along the coastline. The greens fees for nonresidents are a reasonable $32 weekdays, $44 weekends, carts are $14, and club rental is $15. The driving range is open until 10 P.M. For the convenience of golfers, the clubhouse has a dining room and snack bar open daily.

### Wailua River Cruises

You too can be one of the many cruising up the Wailua River on a large, canopied, motorized barge. Anyone can fully enjoy this trip, most popular with middle-age and older tourists, if they let the beauty of the spot surround them. The Fern Grotto, where the boat docks, is a natural amphitheater festooned with hanging

ROBERT NILSEN

on the Wailua River, cruising to the Fern Grotto

ferns—one of the most tourist-visited spots in Hawaii. The oldest company is **Smith's Motor Boat Service,** 808/821-6892 or 808/821-6893, in operation since 1947. The extended Smith family still operates the business, and members serve in every capacity. During the 20-minute ride upriver on their green boats you're entertained with music and a recounting of legends, and at the Fern Grotto a small but well-done medley of island songs is performed. Daily cruises (90 minutes round-trip) depart every half hour from Wailua Marina 9–11:30 A.M. and 12:30–3 P.M. Monday, Wednesday, and Friday there's an additional 3:30 P.M. cruise. Adults cost $15, children (2–12) $7.50; discounts for seniors and *kama'aina* are available.

**Waialeale Boat Tours,** 808/822-4908, with the red barges, is Smith's only competition. Also at the marina, it's a smaller operation with fewer sailings but offers the same type of musical accompaniment and storytelling during the ride. While the daily tour schedule changes periodically depending on the volume of customers, generally boats leave every hour on the half hour between 9:30 A.M. and 1:30 P.M., with periodic additional tours. Tickets are available at the company's marina office and cost $15 adults, $7.50 children; senior and *kama'aina* rates available.

## Kayaking

Kayaking in Wailua means kayaking up the gentle and slow-moving Wailua River. The favorite route is to head to Fern Grotto or perhaps a bit beyond to a river's edge swimming hole. Do not use the boat dock at Fern Grotto, as they are maintained only for the river barges. Although it has caused some bank degradation, the only way to disembark there is to tie your kayak to a bush on the bank next to the dock and walk along the water to the paved walkway. A second route, now preferred by some, is to head to what is known as "Secret Falls" (or Misty Falls). Going upriver, turn right into the north fork of the river just past Kamokila Hawaiian Village. A short way up—stay to your left—look for the trailhead and tie your kayak up along the bank. From here it's about an hour's walk to the falls. Roughly, follow the south bank until you get to a water gauging station. Just beyond it, cross the stream that comes in from your left. Walk up this stream, cross the right branch, and recross the main stream for a short distance to the falls.

When going either upstream or down on the Wailua River, stay hard to the north bank, as there is frequent barge traffic and a periodic motorboat pulling water-skiers.

To rent kayaks for one of these adventures—be sure to ask for a river map—check with one of the following companies. **Wailua Kayak and Canoe,** 808/821-1188, is next to the Smith Motorboat Company booth on Wailua Road, which is the first left turn off Kuamo'o Road (Rte. 580) after turning inland off of Kuhio Highway (Rte. 56). As this is the closest place to the river, it's easy to carry the kayak to the launch site. Make your arrangements at the Smith booth or at the Coconut Coast Activity Center just up the road next to Mema's restaurant. Other shops that have rental kayaks, some of which run kayak tours, are **Kauai Water Ski and Surf Co.,** 808/822-3575, in the Kinipopo Shopping Village; **Kayak Wailua,** 808/822-3388, near the Shell gas station in the same center; **Duke's Kayak Adventures,** 808/822-4000, in Waipouli, and both **Rainbow Outdoor Adventures,** 808/822-1112, and **Wailua River Kayak Adventures,** 808/822-5795, farther up in Kapa'a. Rates for kayak rentals generally run $25–30 for a single and $50 for a tandem. If needed, car carriers can also be rented. All places require that you return kayaks by 5 P.M. Kayak launching and retrieval should be done at the state park unit launch site, the third driveway on the left off Rte. 580 up from Kuhio Highway. Kamokila Hawaiian Village also rents kayaks for $25, which includes entrance to the village. If you rent there, you don't have to paddle so far up the river.

## Water-Skiing

Ever thought of water skiing in paradise? Skimming the smooth waters of Wailua River is the only possibility on Kaua'i, and **Kauai Water Ski and Surf Co.,** in the Kinipopo Shopping Village in Wailua, 808/822-3574, has business to themselves. Open daily 9 A.M.–7 P.M., the shop offers one pull for $30, a half hour of skiing for $55, and one hour for $100. Prices include boat, gas, driver, and all equipment. This shop also sells beach clothes and water sports equipment. Rentals include kayaks, surfboards, boogie boards, and snorkeling equipment.

## East Kaua'i Hiking Trails

All these trails are in the mountains above Wailua. One trail system crisscrosses Nounou Ridge, otherwise known as the Sleeping Giant, while others are farther up into the hills.

**Nounou Mountain Trail, East Side,** begins off Haleilio Road just north of Wailua Beach, at the Kinipopo Shopping Village. Follow Haleilio Road for 1.2 miles until it begins to curve to the left. Near pole no. 38, park at the small trailhead parking lot. The trailhead leads to a series of switchbacks that scale the mountain for 1.75 miles. The trail climbs steadily through native and introduced forest and past one large volcanic outcrop. Near the top, it meets the west side trail coming in from the right, and shortly beyond that is a flat, grassy area with a picnic table, shelter, and bench. This is the "chest" of the giant. Stop here a while and take in the views down to Wailua and the coast or up toward the middle of the island. From the picnic area you can proceed along the spine of the mountain, the "throat," to the giant's "face." Although the going gets a little tougher and the mountain drops off quickly on both sides, the trail is passable and you may have it to yourself. From the face, you're rewarded with a superb 360-degree view but may not be able to see down the slope due to the thick brush cover.

A parking area and right of way for **Nounou Mountain Trail, West Side** is found at the end of Lokelani Street, off Rte. 581, north of Rte. 580. Alternately, a trail right of way leads directly up to this point from Rte. 581, but there is not much parking along the road. Follow the right of way until it joins the trail at the top end of the pasture. This trail leads you through a forest of introduced trees planted in the 1930s and includes Norfolk Pine, strawberry guava, and a forest of *hala* trees near the top. About a quarter mile from the start, a fork in the trail locates the junction of the **Kaumo'o Nounou Trail,** which traverses the west side of the mountain, through a bamboo forest and over Opaeka'a Stream, from its trailhead on Rte. 580 across from Melia Street. The West Trail joins the East Trail at the 1.5-mile marker and proceeds to the picnic table and shelter. This trail is slightly shorter and more forested than that on the ocean side. Bring water for both, as there is none on the way.

Follow Rte. 580 until you come to the University of Hawaii Agriculture Experimental Station. Keep going past the Wailua Reservoir until the pavement ends and then follow the dirt road for almost a mile to **Keahua Arboretum.** A developed picnic and fresh water swimming area is at the ford at Keahua Stream, about seven miles in from the highway. Two short trails run downstream on either side of the stream here, and another leads into the marshy area beyond the hill. It would be helpful to have trees in the arboretum named, but it isn't so. The southern end of the **Powerline Trail** starts at the arboretum. Cross the stream and walk up the steep road on the far side. At the crest of the road, a 4WD track heads uphill to the right. This is the start, and from here it's a long half-day's hike over the mountain to the trailhead on the Hanalei side, about 13 miles away. While there is some shade near the beginning, the majority of the trail is exposed to the sun virtually all day. For those without a car at the north trailhead or someone to pick you up on that side, hike up to the top and return back down this side. Of the two halves of the trail, this south side is the shortest and steepest, but the prettiest, and from the top you have relatively close views up to the top of Mt. Wai'ale'ale, the sheer mountainsides that swoop down from it, and numerous distant waterfalls. This trail, often used by mountain bikers and also by hunters during hunting season, takes you through the heart of the mountains that make up the eastern half of the island. On occasion a 4WD vehicle will attempt this trail, but several sections are virtually impassable due to erosion. Dirt bikers also like to use this trail, particularly on the weekend, so for the most peace and quiet it's perhaps best to walk this trail during the week.

The **Kuilau Trail** begins about 200 yards before the entrance to the arboretum, on the right. This gradual trail follows a muddy old roadway for a mile or so to a flat spot with a picnic area and shelter. Here are some magnificent views of the mountains, some of the best anywhere. You can look directly out at Mt. Wai'ale'ale and what's known as the Wai'ale'ale crater or farther afield to Kilohana and the Ha'upu Ridge, or follow the powerline as it marches up and over the pass. Like the arboretum below, this is a good area to listen to the birds. Continue on this trail, circling around the hill, and you'll eventually come to a small footbridge. At the bridge, about two miles from the trailhead, the Kuilau Trail meets the Moalepe Trail. After crossing the bridge, the trail climbs through a dense tunnel of trees to a small open flat spot and then turns to the east. The **Moalepe Trail** starts at the end of Olohena Road. From here a dirt track runs for some distance inland to a turnaround, but it may not be passable as it's extremely rutted and often slick in rainy weather. This route, a popular horseback-riding trail, gains the heights and offers some excellent panoramas before joining the Kuilau Trail at the footbridge, almost three miles from Olohena Road. Both these trails bring you to mid-elevation mountain slopes.

# SHOPPING
## Kinipopo Shopping Village

This diminutive mall, on the seaside of Kuhio Hwy. just beyond the end of Wailua Beach, offers most of Wailua's one-stop shopping. Aside from Korean, Chinese, and Japanese restaurants, you can find a handful of unique small shops. **Kauai Water Ski and Surf Co.,** 808/822-3574, open daily 9 A.M.–7 P.M., is a complete sales and rental water-sports shop. Bathing suits, bikinis, sun visors, men's shorts, surfboards, boogie boards, wet suits, fins, masks, snorkels, underwater watches, and even a few backpacks and day packs line the shelves of this small but jam-packed shop. Water-skiing can be arranged and kayaks rented.

If you are an aficionado of old Hawaii, drop in to the **Tin Can Mailman,** 808/822-3009, open daily except Sunday 10 A.M.–5 P.M. (some days until 4 P.M.). The Tin Can Mailman definitely has a heart for out-of-print books on Hawaii and Polynesia, battered travel guides filled with memories, antique maps, vintage menus, early botanical prints, rare missionary items, and even new books. The shop is small and bursting with ancient voices still quietly singing their songs.

**Reinventions Consignment Boutique,** open

daily, carries an assortment of previously used clothing, including aloha shirts and casual dresses. For something new, try **Kinipopo Fine Art** or **Goldsmith's Kauai** jewelry store; for a permanent memento, see what **Garden Isle Tattoo** has to offer. The **Shell Station Mini-Mart**, at the corner, sells sundries, snacks, beer, and packaged foods.

## Wailua Shopping Plaza

Across the highway from Kinipopo Shopping Village, in the Wailua Shopping Plaza, are several more eateries, including Mema's restaurant, the Wailua Family Restaurant, Aussie Tim's Texas Barbecue, and a TCBY yogurt shop. Set back in the trees in a separate building to the rear of this center, Caffé Coco serves scrumptious wholesome dinners. Next to Caffé Coco is **Bambulei,** 808/823-8641, an intriguing little shop that, along with a variety of antiques and collectibles, carries some women's clothing. Although there is an eclectic mix, much is Asian or Asian-inspired, and there's a heavy predominance of Hawaiiana from the middle decades of the 1900s. This is worth the stop if a step back in time is of interest to you. Open 10 A.M.–5 P.M.

## The Coconut Marketplace

Prices at this cluster of more than 70 shops, restaurants, and galleries are kept down because of the natural competition of so many businesses, each of which tries to specialize, which usually means good choices for what strikes your fancy. Any of the jewelry shops have enough stock on hand to drop even Mr. T to his knees. With so many apparel and footwear shops, the job of finding just the right aloha shirt, casual dress, sports clothing, or sandal shouldn't be a problem. Most shops are open 9 A.M.–9 P.M., Sunday 10 A.M.–6 P.M.

**Ship Store Gallery,** 808/822-7758, sets sail for adventure with nautical artwork of tall-masted ships and contemporary Japanese art in a gallery that's filled with cannons, pistols, and swords. This is an amazingly full place that will get the mariner in everyone away from the dock. In addition to the plentiful artwork are fine antiques and collectibles. Showing works by artists that have become synonymous with Hawaii, **Kahn Galleries,** 808/822-3636, has captivating paintings that might just be what you're looking for as a memento of your trip to the island.

At least stop in to browse at **Kauai Fine Arts,** open daily 9 A.M.9 P.M., until 6 P.M. on Sunday. Owned by Caribbean islander Mona Nicolaus, who operates the original Kauai Fine Arts in Hanapepe, the boutique specializes in original engravings, antique prints mainly of the Pacific Islands, antique maps, and vintage natural science photos from as far afield as Australia and Egypt. Also on display are hand-embroidered pillows and quilts, designed in Hawaii but made on Bali, and tapa imported from Tonga or Fiji. Kauai Fine Arts offers framing and worldwide shipping.

Some other shops include **Island Surf Shop,** where you can purchase a boogie board, travel bag, *pareu,* beach hat, and T-shirts; **Sole Mates,** for those slippers and hats that you forgot to bring with you; **Products of Hawaii, Too,** selling just that; **Happy Kauain** for gifts; and **Jungle Rain** for casual clothing and gifts. At **Hawaii's Keepsakes,** you can purchase any number of attractive craft items and peruse the collection of large and small Hawaiian quilts. For the ordinary purchase, head for **Whaler's General Store,** and the **Kaua'i Visitors Center** can give you information about things to see, places to go, and adventures to experience.

## Wailua Country Store

At the intersection of Rte. 580 and Rte. 581 to the back of the Sleeping Giant, this small country shop has basic grocery supplies and snacks, good for those in a vacation rental home in this area or as a last stop for those heading up to Keahua Arboretum or the Powerline Trail.

## Kapa'a

Kapa'a means "to hold," as in "to hold a canoe on course." In the old days, when the canoes set sail to O'ahu, they'd always stop first at Kapa'a to get their bearings, then make a beeline directly across the channel to O'ahu. Yachts still do the same today. It was probably a series of fishing villages in days past, but from 1913 to 1960 there was a huge pineapple cannery in Kapa'a, and much of the east shore bristled with these sweet golden fruits. More recently, sugarcane was raised, but that too is all but gone.

Old Town Kapa'a is where Rte. 56 and Rte. 581 meet. The heart of Kapa'a itself is a workers' settlement, a blue-collar community with modest homes, utilitarian shops, several churches, some down-home eateries, and modest accommodations. Only in the past few years has there been a move to yuppify shops and restaurants. Yet, the Kapa'a area is one of some contrasts. At the south end along the main drag is **Waipouli** (Dark Water), actually a separate community just north of Coconut Marketplace, though you'd never know it. Clustered here are newish condos, several full-service shopping malls, a multitude of restaurants, and some nightlife—sort of a live-in resort atmosphere. Inland from the center of town are newer, rural bedroom communities that string along the roads that track in toward the mountains. The population is nearly 8,000, and at least half again that number live in the upland communities, so about the same number of people live here as in the greater Lihu'e area, but the vibe in Kapa'a is definitely more local. What distinguishes Kapa'a is its unpretentiousness. This is "everyday paradise," where the visitor is made to feel welcome and stands in line with everyone else at the supermarket. Generally, the weather is cooperative, beaches are fair, and the pace is unhurried. Kapa'a isn't the choicest vacation spot on the island, but you can have a great time here and save money.

A **guided walking tour** of town, complete with snippets of history, culture, and legends, is offered by the Kaua'i Historical Society. These tours start at the Pono Kai Resort, run about 90 minutes, and go up as far as the Kapa'a Library before returning via the beach path. Tours are run Tuesday, Thursday, and Saturday at 10 A.M., and again at 4 P.M. if there is interest; $15 adults and $5 for children under age 12. Reservations are necessary; call 808/821-1778.

To ease traffic through the heart of this community, the **Kapa'a Bypass Road** skirts around from Wailua to the north edge of Kapa'a. It runs through the agricultural fields behind town and is open 5:30 A.M.–9 P.M. daily. From where this bypass meets Olohena Road near the New Kapa'a Park, jog toward the ocean and turn onto Lehua Street to miss the downtown intersection.

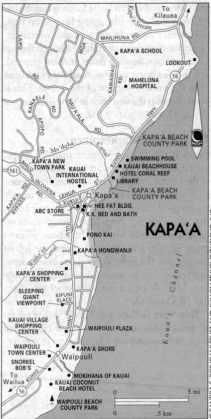

There are few sights per se, although near the middle of this strip, at Kipuni Place, is the **Sleeping Giant Viewpoint** pulloff. From this angle you get a reasonably good look at the mountain, and, using your imagination, you can distinctly see a recumbent figure with head, neck, and chest. Trails up both the front and back of this hill bring you to a picnic spot on the chest, from where a narrow trail leads over the throat to the chin and forehead. While in Kapa'a, spend your time checking out the shops, scanning the color-mottled mountains of the interior, and combing the beaches, especially those to the north. A few minutes up the coast, you're in wide-open spaces. Small oceanside communities pop up, their residents split between beach-house vacationers and settled *kama'aina*. The only town of size is Anahola.

## Beach Park

Central Kapa'a's beach begins near Waika'ea Canal, and **Kapa'a Beach County Park** runs north from there for almost a mile until it ends near a community swimming pool and the Kapa'a Library. A number of small roads lead to the beach through town from the highway. Kapa'a Beach County Park has just over 15 acres, with a pavilion, picnic tables, showers, toilets, and grills. At its south end, a footbridge connects both sides of the canal, where locals often come to fish. A boat ramp backs into the canal here, and there is a deep enough channel through the reef for boats to get in and out. This beach is pretty enough to look at, but it is not a typical resort beach. The feeling here is that this area belongs to the locals, although no undue hassles have been reported.

## ACCOMMODATIONS
### Under $50
**Kauai International Hostel,** 4532 Lehua St., Kapa'a, HI 96746, 808/823-6142, welcomes international guests with a friendly multilingual staff. Rates are $20 for a dorm bunk (no reservations, private female dorm available) and $50 for one of the five private rooms with double bed (reservations accepted); $10 key deposit. Reduced rates for those with hostel cards. Although the hostel is open 24 hours, quiet time is at 11 P.M.; checkout is by 10 A.M. Occasionally, staff members or guests organize an impromptu barbecue (everyone contributes to cover the cost), and the hostel runs van tours (tip the driver), mostly hikes to waterfalls, canyons, and pristine beaches, when there is enough interest and the van is running. Airport pick-up and delivery run $10 each way. Facilities include a large communal kitchen, an indoor lounge with comfortable couches and cable TV, a covered outdoor lanai with a pocket billiard table, and coin washers and dryers. Store your valuables in the office safe. Dorm rooms, each with a sink and private bath, contain either four or six bunks. The private rooms are small but sufficient, and they share a bath. With room for 42, the hostel is clean and well managed. While it has a nominal seven-night maximum stay, there have been some long-term residents. This is a good place to meet young people from all over the world.

Just past the park in Kapa'a, across the street from Kojima's Grocery is **Kauai BeachHouse on the Blue Lagoon,** 4-1552 Kuhio Hwy., Kapa'a, HI 96746, 808/822-3424, www.kauai-blue-lagoon.com, nvb@hawaiian.net. A real beach house converted into a hostel-like accommodation, it offers women's and coed dorms and a couple of private rooms. Most rooms look out across a grassy lawn to the still water "lagoon" inside the reef. The table on the second-floor lanai is a gathering place, and a mini-kitchen to the side is for guest use. Also for guests are cable TV, a washing machine (line dry), free weights, and a few exercise machines. The roof can also be used for relaxation. Rooms contain double bed bunks, each with a privacy curtain; rates are $23 single, $35 double, or $50 for a private room. The baths are shared. No smoking. The place sits amongst a tangle of trees behind a garage that barely escaped the last hurricane; look for a "Chiropractor" sign and turn in there. Walk up to the second floor to check in. The public bus stops out front. A funky place with easygoing island character, it's not for everyone, but might be right for backpackers, bicycle riders, budget travelers, or anyone who cares more about what they eat than where they sleep.

M

## $50–100

On a back street in downtown Kapaʻa, only one block from the water, is **K.K. Bed and Bath,** 4486 Kauwila St., Kapaʻa, HI 96746, 808/822-7348 or 800/615-6211 code 32, www.kkbedbath.com, kkbedbath@aloha.net. Owner/manager Richard Sugiyama has turned an old 1930s family warehouse into two clean and bright rental rooms, each with queen bed, refrigerator, color TV, ceiling fan, and bath with shower. Don't expect anything plush, but the place is neat as a pin and Richard is a very accommodating fellow. Daily room rates are $40 single, $50 double, $60 for three adults; no charge for children under 12 when using existing beds. Breakfast is not included. Three-night minimum, no credit cards. Reservations appreciated.

Women looking for an environment that is supportive of women travelers and seekers of self-enlightenment should try **Mahina's Women's Guest House,** 808/823-9364, www.mahinas.com, mahinas@hawaiian.net, a three-bedroom beach house near the center of Kapaʻa. The small private bedroom sleeps one for $47 or two for $60, while the master bedroom with a king bed runs $60–80. Between these two is a room that has either a king bed or two twins and runs $35–55 for one or $70–75 for two. In addition, the bed on the enclosed lanai goes for $45 single or $55 for two. Weekly and monthly rates are available. Everyone shares the rest of the house. There is no smoking inside. For availability, contact Sharon.

**Hotel Coral Reef,** at 1516 Kuhio Hwy., Kapaʻa, HI 96746, 808/822-4481 or 800/843-4659, fax 808/822-7705, is relatively inexpensive and definitely has character. Toward the north end of Kapaʻa between the main road and the beach, this 25-unit family-style hotel, one of the first built in the area, has a deluxe view of the ocean and a small grove of coconut trees on the lawn. The rates for the recently refurbished rooms are: ocean view $59, oceanfront $89, and two-room suite $79, with a $10 charge for additional guests. The hotel offers room and car packages and *kamaʻaina* and senior citizen discounts. Rooms feature single and double beds, refrigerators, cable TV, and lanai. Rooms downstairs have tile; upstairs, carpet. There is daily maid service, a pay telephone in the lobby, activity bookings, and equipment rental. The Hotel Coral Reef is neat as a pin and very affordable for a family vacation.

## Condos

The **Kapaʻa Shore** resort condominium is along the main road, across and just up from Kauai Village shopping center, at 4-0900 Kuhio Hwy. It's mostly a time-share property, but one- and two-bedroom ocean-view and oceanfront rental units are available per day or by the week. All units are bright and cheerful, with full kitchens. One-bedroom units run $115–125 per day or $700–750 a week. Two-bedroom units go for $145–155 per day and $850–930 per week. The property contains a swimming pool, hot tub, and tennis courts, and maid service is available on request. For reservations, call Garden Island Properties, 808/822-4871 or 800/801-0378.

The largest property on the Coconut Coast, the **Pono Kai,** at 4-1250 Kuhio Hwy., Kapaʻa, HI 96746, www.ponokai-resort.com, is a 241-unit property on 11 acres, just to the north of the Waikaʻea Canal. While principally a time-share, it has a good number of vacation rental units. Built in 1975 but kept up to date, all units are individually owned and decorated; one-bedrooms are $189–239, two bedrooms $209–279. All have full kitchens, cable TV, and lanai; many have a/c, and each building has laundry facilities. A few studios with partial kitchens are also available for $79–99. On the property you'll find a swimming pool, jet spa, sauna, shuffleboard lanes, lighted tennis courts for guests only, a small Japanese garden, and numerous barbecue areas. Various craft and cultural activities are offered throughout the week, and the activities desk can arrange excursions for you. For reservations, call RCI Management, 808/822-9831 or 800/456-0009. Marc Resorts manages many units in this complex and maintains front desk staffing 8 A.M.–5 P.M. daily. For information and reservations through Marc Resorts, call 808/823-8427 or 800/535-0085.

Two moderate condos in Waipouli are **Mokihana of Kauai,** 796 Kuhio Hwy., and **Kauai Kailani,** 856 Kuhio Hwy. Both are primarily time-share properties but do vacation rentals when space permits. The Mokihana has all studios with kitchenettes for $65 a day. Kauai Kailani has two-bedroom units with full kitchens for $75. Not luxury by any means, these properties are good value for the money and you're right on the water near restaurants and shopping. For information and reservations, call 808/822-3971 or 360/676-1434 if more than 30 days in advance.

## Bed-and-Breakfasts

Inland high above Kapaʻa on a working three-acre tropical flower farm in an area called Kawaihau is **Kakalina's Bed and Breakfast,** 6781 Kawaihau Rd., Kapaʻa, HI 96746, 808/822-2328 or 800/662-4330, fax 808/823-6833, www.kakalina.com, info@kakalina.com. Decorated with tropical motifs, Kakalina's has a two-bedroom, two-bath suite with a full kitchen, living room, and dining room on the ground floor of the main house, and a separate house with upstairs and downstairs units. The downstairs studio has a full kitchen that can open to a second bedroom if needed, while the upstairs one-bedroom unit with kitchenette has the best views. The Hale 'Ehu suite in the main house runs $155–175 a night for one or two couples, respectively, or $90 for a half-suite. In the second house, the upstairs Hale 'Kolu is $90, while the downstairs Hale 'Elua in $85. Rental includes a simple fruit, juice, pastry, and coffee breakfast for all guests. In addition, the Ginger Hale, a one-bedroom vacation rental house one mile down the road, has a complete kitchen and rents for $75 a day, no breakfast included. Two nights minimum.

Not far away is **Alohilani Bed and Breakfast,** 1470 Wanaʻao Rd., Kapaʻa, HI 96746, 808/823-0128 or 800/533-9316, www.hawaiian.net/~alohila, alohila@hawaiian.net. Alohilani has two suites, one for $99 and the other for $109 a night, with queen beds, private baths, ceiling fans, refrigerator and microwave, and a guest cottage for $109 that has an efficiency kitchen. The hot tub pool is shared, and a continental breakfast is served.

## Vacation Rental Agencies

**Garden Island Properties,** 4-928 Kuhio Hwy., 808/822-4871 or 800/801-0378, www.kauaiprop-erties.com, stricko@kauaiproperties.com, focuses its efforts on the east side of the island. It manages more than two dozen vacation rentals and numerous condo units mostly from Kapaʻa to Miloliʻi but also has several along the north shore as far as Haʻena and a few in Lihuʻe, everything from a $100/night casual oceanside "hut" to a sumptuous four-bedroom house that sleeps 12 for nearly $2,000 a week.

# FOOD

From the Waipouli Town Center to the north edge of Kapaʻa, there are dozens of places to eat. The vast majority are either inexpensive diners or midpriced restaurants, but there is also one fine dining restaurant, plus the ubiquitous fast-food chains, several bakeries, fruit stands, markets, and grocery stores.

## Inexpensive Food in Shopping Malls

The Waipouli Plaza has one of the best moderately priced restaurants on the island, **The King and I,** 808/822-1642, open daily for dinner. This Thai restaurant serves wonderful food that will make your taste buds stand up and be counted. Most dinners are $8–12. Serving the same basic type of food, with the addition of Chinese and Vietnamese dishes, at roughly the same prices is **Sukhothai** Thai restaurant, 808/821-1224, in the Kapaʻa Shopping Center up the road. Sukhothai is open 10:30 A.M.–9:30 P.M. daily.

In the Waipouli Complex, another tiny mall along Kuhio Hwy., is the **Aloha Diner,** 808/822-3851. Open daily except Sunday 11:30 A.M.–3 P.M. and 5:30–9 P.M., this diner serves Hawaiian food. It offers à la carte selections like *kalua* pig, chicken luʻau, *lomi* salmon, rice and poi, *haupia,* and *kulolo.* Dinner specials run $6–8, with full dinners around $10. Takeout is available. There is no atmosphere, the service is slow but friendly, and most people eating here are residents who know where to come for filling food.

**Papaya's,** a natural-food café and market below the Whale Tower at Kauai Village, 808/823-0190, open daily except Sunday 9 A.M.–8 P.M., is not only the largest, but also the best natural-food store and café on Kauaʻi. From the café section (the deli counter closes at 7 P.M.) come daily specials like marinated baked tofu over brown rice with green salad, soup du jour, and two-fisted sandwiches like grilled vegetable and a good old-fashioned tempeh burger. Papaya's is famous for its hot entrées, including spinach lasagna, fish tacos, and spicy kung pao stir-fry, priced under $8. Daily specials are always posted. Several American standard breakfasts with a veggie twist and an assortment of homemade pastries are available until 1 P.M. Gourmet coffees, herbal teas, sodas, fresh juices, and smoothies are also specialties. Outdoor tables are available, or sit on the grass in the courtyard. If you are into healthy organic food, there is no place better than Papaya's!

## Other Inexpensive Eateries

Marilyn Monroe, skirt tossed by the Kaua'i breeze, and the big bow tie and bigger smile of owner and chief soda jerk Kriss Erickson welcome you to **Beezers,** 808/822-4411, a vintage 1950s soda fountain, at the main intersection in downtown Kapa'a, open daily 11 A.M.–10 P.M. Kriss, a bartender for two decades, researched the soda-fountain idea for years before opening Beezers—and actually got his best idea after visiting Disneyland. He scoured Hawaii and then finally the Mainland before finding a real soda fountain. The floor of red, black, and white tiles leads to low stools facing a counter made from glass brick and featuring a light show inside that matches the tunes coming from a real jukebox in the corner. Let your eyes play over the splendid 16-foot mahogany back bar, cabinet, and mirror as you sip your soda, slurp your shake, or savor your sandwich. Besides standard cones, Beezers serves such scrumptious dishes as an old-fashioned banana split and a Mustang Sally—a rich chocolate brownie with two scoops of creamy vanilla, hot fudge, whipped cream, and nuts—both for $6.75. Handmade malts, shakes, and flavored Cokes can be created, or choose a soda, brownie wedge, homemade pie, sandwich, or sloppy joe. Kriss says that more substantial food service is on the way: breakfast all day, blue-plate specials, and old-fashioned diner food. Look for it. Beezers is the kind of place where, if you're not smiling going in, you're definitely smiling coming out.

Look for yellow and white umbrellas shading a few picnic tables across from the field at the town park that mark **Bubba's,** 808/823-0069, open daily 10:30 A.M.–8 P.M. Here you can have a Bubba burger for $2.95 or a Big Bubba for $4.95. Other menu items include a "Slopper," an open-faced burger smothered in Bubba's famous Budweiser beer chili, for $5.50; and fish and chips, chicken burger, or corn dog, all for under $4.25. Sides include french fries, onion rings, and chili fries. Burgers come on a toasted bun with mustard, ketchup-based relish, and diced onions. Anything else you want on it—cheese, teriyaki, lettuce, or tomatoes—you pay for. Hey, they've been doing things this way since 1936—it's worked for them. Bubba's is a throwback to the days when a diner owner was also the short-order cook and all the burgers were handmade. Yet, they've also kept up. Try the free WebTV Internet access or buy a Bubba shirt or hat to take with you. Rock and roll, grease, and Elvis lives, man! Enjoy!

When you don't want to fool around deciding where to get a good meal, head for the north end of Kapa'a and the local favorite, **Kountry Kitchen,** 1485 Kuhio Hwy., 808/822-3511, open daily 6 A.M.–9 P.M. (Tuesday until 2 P.M.). The tables are usually packed with regulars during peak dining hours. Breakfasts are full meals like hefty omelettes, mostly for under $6; lunches of salads, sandwiches, and specialty plates cost a few bucks more. Full homestyle dinners of country ribs, sesame shrimp, or baked ham served with soup, bread, potatoes or rice, and veggies are $8–10. The food is tasty, the service prompt and friendly, and the portions large. True to its advertising, you'll find "no fancy napkins, just good home cooking."

A few steps away is the smaller and more basic **Higashi Store.** A no-atmosphere place with formica tables, it serves inexpensive breakfast and lunch dishes like eggs, omeletes, and saimin from 6:30 A.M.

At the north end of Kapa'a, near the neighborhood center and community swimming pool, is the **Killer Juice Bar,** "the mother of all juice bars." A homespun place, operating out of a roadside stand and parked antique truck, it sells smoothies and fruit drinks, locally grown fresh fruits and vegetables, and homemade breads and pastries. A great stop. Look for the large green umbrella shading the produce.

## Moderate

The **Ono Family Restaurant,** next to the Pono Kai Resort, 808/822-1710, open daily 7 A.M.–1:30 P.M., is cozy and functional, with nice touches like carpeted floors, ceiling fans, and front lanai seating. An established business, the restaurant gives friendly service, pays attention to detail, and always serves large portions. Creative breakfasts include eggs Canterbury, with turkey, tomatoes, jack cheese, mushrooms, and hollandaise sauce over poached eggs on an English muffin; a tropical stack of pancakes with bananas, macadamia nuts, and coconut; and a variety of omelettes. For lunch, you can't go wrong with a sandwich or burger, meat loaf and mashed potatoes, or teriyaki chicken from the broiler. The daily fish special is always terrific, and everything is reasonably priced. The Ono Family Restaurant is a local favorite.

**Norberto's El Cafe,** 808/822-3362, near the intersection of Kukui St. and Rte. 56 in downtown Kapaʻa, is open Tues.–Sat. 5–9 P.M. This family-run Mexican restaurant has been doing business for over two decades. What's it doing in a small town on a Pacific Island, you ask? Gringo, don't look a gift burro in the mouth! Norberto's serves nutritious, delicious, wholesome food and caters to vegetarians—all dishes are prepared without lard or animal fats. The smell of food wafting out of the front door around dinnertime is its best advertisement. This is some of the best Mexican food on the island. Most full-course meals of burritos, enchiladas, and tostadas are under $16; children's plates and à la carte dishes are also available. The best deals are the chef's specials of burrito el café, rellenos tampico, fajitas, and enchiladas grande. Dinners are served with soup, beans, and rice; chips and salsa are complimentary. There's beer on tap or, if you really want to head south of the border (by way of sliding under the table), try a pitcher of margaritas. If you have room after

stuffing yourself like a chimichanga, try a delicious chocolate-cream pie or homemade rum cake. The café is extremely popular with local folks and tables don't stay empty.

The Anglicized version of Norberto's can be found at **Poncho and Lefty's,** 808/823-9244, on the second floor of the Hee Fat building across from the ABC store in downtown Kapaʻa. Nachos, buffalo wings, and a taco salad will warm you up for the big plates of taquitos, chimichangas, enchiladas rancheros, carne asada, or other south of the border favorites. Have a drink with dinner or just come up to sit at the open breezy window for a look down onto the street. Happy hour is 3–6 P.M. and there's live music on Friday and Saturday nights.

The **Olympic Cafe,** a fixture in downtown Kapaʻa for more than half a century but torn up by Hurricane ʻIniki, metamorphosed and came back to business at 1387 Kuhio Hwy., 808/822-2825, and is open daily 6 A.M.–3 P.M. for breakfast and lunch. This casual place has French doors that open onto the sidewalk, and contemporary music plays in the background. Breakfasts of pancakes, omelettes, or scrambles are mostly under $8, and lunches include sandwiches, burgers, salads, and wraps for $6–11. To accompany any meal are juices, smoothies, Italian sodas, specialty teas, and, of course, fine coffees and blends, the real reason that some people come by. Order at the counter.

Across the street are three small restaurants that serve large portions of wholesome food at decent prices. The **Mermaid Cafe** is a walk-up window restaurant with outside seating that does tacos and two-fisted wraps with flavorful sauces for the healthy, organic, veggie, bean sprout, brown rice, tofu-eating crowd. Most dishes are under $7.95. Open 11 A.M.–9 P.M. daily. **Wasabi's** sushi restaurant goes the Japanese route for lunch Tues.–Sat. and dinner nightly. Its main focus is affordable sushi rolls, but tempura and other dinners are also available. Between these two, the **Postal Internet Cafe** offers Internet connection along with its menu of wraps and other healthful food.

**La Playita Azul,** 808/821-2323, at the Kauai Village shopping center, open Mon.–Sat. 4:30–9 P.M., is an eat-in or takeout place that serves fresh Mexican fare. Look for the red chili peppers on the curtains in the windows. On the menu are the usual salads, tacos, burritos, tostadas, and enchiladas, with most items under $15, and every evening there are specials. This place offers healthy, wholesome food at decent prices. Give it a try.

Across the shopping center is **Camp House Grill and Bar,** open 6:30 A.M.–9 P.M. An offshoot of the original Camp House Grill in Kalaheo, this family-style place is known for its breakfasts, burgers, Hawaiian *huli* chicken, and barbecue pork ribs. With a more upscale menu, and prices to match, it seems to get better food reviews than the original restaurant in Kalaheo. Full bar.

## Expensive

Since 1973, the **Bull Shed,** 808/822-3791, has been serving happy customers on the Coconut Coast from its dining room overlooking the water at the Mokihana of Kauai condo in Waipouli. Heavy on the meats, the rack of lamb at $24 and prime rib at $20 are favorites. The Bull Shed also serves plenty of fish and seafood, priced mostly under $20. When available, Alaskan king crab and rock lobster tail go for whatever the market will bear.

One of the newest entries into the Waipouli/Kapa'a food scene is **Emerson's Seafood Restaurant,** 808/822-3662, at Kauai Village. Open on weekdays 11 A.M.–2 P.M. for lunch and nightly 5:30–9 P.M. for dinner, Emerson's focus is, not surprisingly, fish and other creatures of the sea. Appetizer and salad items include Caesar salad with seared pepper 'ahi, baked oysters crusted with artichokes, and crab cakes with roasted corn relish and mango remoulade. Main dishes, like baked mahimahi crusted in crab meat and covered in mango sauce, bamboo-steamed Hawaiian snapper, and a hearty bouillabaisse, run $16–25. Making a name for itself, Emerson's relies on fish from the nearby waters and local talent to prepare it. As the restaurant's not large, call for a reservation.

An easy-going place, with a sophisticated atmosphere, reasonable prices, and tasty food is **Coconuts,** 808/823-8777. You will pass through the front bar on the way to the dining room, which is softly lit to set the mood. Furniture is made from coconut, panels of reed grass cover the ceiling, while murals and paintings of tropical scenes adorn the walls. Seafood is the specialty at Coconuts, but meats are also served. Start with fried calamari, grilled herb polenta, or a salad before moving on to the main dish. Entrées can be from the sea, like grilled and teriyaki dipped salmon, seafood paella, or tempura 'ahi, $10–20, or meats like filet mignon, blackened New York steak, or cured pork chops for up to $22. Although the food is flavorful, the chef does not overindulge the spices. Table bread comes with a yummy hummus dip. Open 4–10 P.M. daily except Sunday.

While the **Lemongrass Grille,** 808/821-2999, has the appearance of a thoroughly Thai restaurant, it mixes Thai dishes with borrowings from other cultures and adds to this mix the wonderful seafood from Hawaiian waters. Some menu items are lemongrass seafood stew, fresh catch and Thai spiced eggplant, braised short ribs with Korean accompaniments, and *huli huli* chicken breast. A variety of sushi is always available. Entrées run $13–21, and sushi is generally in the $3.50–7.50 range. Full bar. The Lemongrass Grille has become popular, so call for reservations.

## Fine Dining

Master chef Jean-Marie Josselin knows a good thing when he sees it and, moreover, knows how to prepare it exquisitely. You can enjoy his excellent food at **A Pacific Cafe,** at Kauai Village, 808/822-0013, open 5:30–9:15 P.M. As it's very popular, call to reserve a table or come 5:30–6:30 when it's generally quieter. Although it's in a shopping center, A Pacific Cafe creates a casually elegant atmosphere appointed with a cove and molded ceiling, ferns and flowers placed here and there, bamboo chairs, and an open kitchen so that you can witness the food preparation. Although the menu changes nightly, items below are a sampling of what type of food the kitchen creates. Appetizers range $7–12.75 and include such delicacies as deep-fried tiger-eye 'ahi sushi with wasabi and mustard sauces and firecracker salmon with cucumber kimchee and sweet and sour sauce. Choose a savory soup and refreshing salad like roasted kabocha pumpkin soup, organic tomato salad, or baby organic hearts of romaine, $6.25–8.75. Order from the wood-burning grill—you can't go wrong! Try grilled coffee-smoked double pork chops for $21.95, lemon rosemary marinated chicken at $20.95, and linguine stir-fried rock shrimp for $18.95. One specialty of A Pacific Cafe includes wok-charred mahimahi with garlic sesame crust and lime ginger sauce for $23.75. If you can't decide, try the prix-fixe menu for $39 and get the works. Save room for one of the luscious desserts. A Pacific Cafe is an excellent restaurant with the perfect mixture of exceptional food, fine service, superb presentation, and a wonderful wine cellar; by far the best the area has to offer.

## ENTERTAINMENT

The night scene in Kapaʻa is less than extensive. For a cool island drink, canned music, and a local crowd try **Pau Hana Bar and Grill** at the Kauai Village shopping center or **Lizard Lounge** at the Waipouli Center.

The **Kauai Village Theater** has taken up residency in the small theater in Kauai Village shopping center. Open most evenings, this theater shows mostly art, foreign, and specialty films and the occasional live theater production. Call 808/823-6789 for the current schedule.

The grass courtyard in front of Papaya's at Kauai Village comes alive with the sound of music by Larry Rivera and his musical family every Friday afternoon at 3 P.M.

## RECREATION

### Water Sports

**Snorkel Bob's,** just beyond the Coconut Marketplace in Waipouli, 808/823-9433, open 8 A.M.–5 P.M. daily, offers some of the best deals for snorkel rental in Hawaii (and free snorkeling maps and advice). Gear, which includes mask, snorkel tube, and fins, is rented for a 24-hour day or by the week. The basic set is $2.50/day or $9/week. Upgrades in quality run $4.50/$19 and $6.50/$29, and for the ultimate optical correction mask the rate is $9 a day or $35 a week. For a "dry" tube add $2 a day. Bob's also rents boogie boards. If you'll be island-hopping, Snorkel Bob's allows you to take the gear with you

and drop it off at a Snorkel Bob's location on the next island. Bob is now booking various island activities, so you may get free rental on some equipment if you book through him.

**Dive Kauai,** 1038 Kuhio Hwy., 808/822-0452 or 800/828-3483, www.divekauai.com, is a full-service scuba and snorkel shop. Dive Kauai offers sales and rental of all equipment and carries some water-sport clothing and accessories. Scuba gear packages run $40–50, introductory dives are $98 for a one-tank boat or shore dive or $125 for two tanks. For certified divers, most other dives run $80–100. A variety of certification courses are offered, but a basic four- to five-day course runs about $395.

### Bicycling

One of the best bike shops on the island for sales, repair, and rental is **Kauai Cycle and Tour,** 1379 Kuhio Hwy., 808/821-2115, open Mon.–Fri. 9 A.M.–6 P.M., Saturday 9 A.M.–4 P.M. Beach cruisers rent for $15 for 24 hours, front-suspension mountain bikes run $20 a day or $95 per seven-day week, and full-suspension mountain bikes are $35 a day and $150 a week. Each rental includes a helmet, lock, and water bottle. A car rack is available for $5. Unfortunately, Kauai Cycle doesn't run tours anymore, but stop in and talk to the guys as they can give you great advice on where to ride for your type of bike and level of experience.

### Horseback Riding

**Esprit de Corps Riding Academy,** 808/822-4688, offers four basic rides, plus specialty rides on request, and riding lessons. These rides, which go into the mountains from upper Kapaʻa, tend to be long, so they are better suited to experienced riders. The three-hour Fast ride with trotting and cantering runs $148; the Wow!!! ride runs $215 for five hours, snack included; and the All Day ride is a full-day adventure, with time for a deli lunch and dip in a mountain pool, for $345. If you desire a shorter ride and love to take pictures on the trail, try the two- to three-hour A Taste of Kauai ride for $112. Riders must be age 10 or older for the trail rides, and no more than five riders are allowed per group.

KAUAʻI

## Activity Centers

**Chris "The Fun Lady,"** 4-746 Kuhio Hwy. across from the Waipouli Shopping Center, 808/822-7759, open daily 8 A.M.–6 P.M., offers boogie-board rentals at $5–15 a day; kayaks for $25 single, $50 double with coolers, dry bags, life vests, car racks, and waterproof maps included; and top-of-the-line snorkel gear (prescription masks, too), golf clubs, fishing equipment, and surfboards at competitive prices. Chris is an expert at arranging all ocean, air, and land activities and tours, and making lu'au reservations, claiming that her years of experience on Kaua'i don't always get you the cheapest but do always get you the best.

**Snorkel Bob's,** next door, has also started doing activities. If you rent snorkel equipment from him, he can also hook you up with other island activities for a reasonable price.

## Movie Tours

For movie buffs, **Hawaii Movie Tours,** 808/822-1192 or 800/628-8432 for reservations, www.hawaiimovietour.com, has luxury van trips for you. These escorted tours of the island stop at many of the sites used by Hollywood to make its feature films. On the way, you'll get regaled with stories of these movies and their actors, see scenes from the movies on the comfy van's TV monitor, sing along with songs from the movies, and be provided with lunch. The five-hour coastal tour starts in Kapa'a at the tour office behind Lemongrass Grille and costs $95 adult, $76 for kids 11 and under. A six- to seven-hour inland 4WD tour (except weekends) takes you to other movie locations back in lush valleys and on private land that are hard to get to otherwise; $113 for adults or $103 for children.

# SHOPPING

Kapa'a teems with shopping opportunities. Lining Kuhio Highway are several large and small shopping plazas along with the central downtown shops. All your needs are met by a variety of shops tucked away here and there. Like dealing with the sun in Hawaii, enjoy yourself but don't overdo it.

## Kauai Village

Built around a plantation-era main street theme, this modern, large, and very diverse shopping center, one of the newest and best that Kaua'i has to offer, is at 4-831 Kuhio Highway. It contains a **Safeway** supermarket, open 8 A.M.–8 P.M. Mon.–Fri. and 9 A.M.–6 P.M. Saturday and Sunday; **Longs Drugs,** open Mon.–Sat. 8 A.M.–9 P.M. and Sunday until 6 P.M., a complete variety store with photo equipment and a pharmacy; an **ABC** store, for everything from suntan lotion to beach mats; and **Waldenbooks,** 808/822-7749, open Mon.–Sat. 9 A.M.–8 P.M. and Sunday 9 A.M.–5 P.M., well stocked with everything from Hawaiiana to travel books.

Dining options here include the **A Pacific Cafe,** a fantastic restaurant featuring Pacific Island cuisine prepared by master chef Jean-Marie Josselin; **Papaya's,** the island's best natural health-food store and café; **Camp House Grill,** for food you might have seen on a plantation family's dining table; and **La Playita Azul,** for healthy Mexican with a touch of the islands.

Other stores are the always good **Crazy Shirts; Pai Moana Pearls,** for the increasingly popular Tahitian black pearls; and **V.J. Silver and Gold,** which claims to have the island's best selection of silver jewelry. Both **Kahn Galleries** and **Wyland Galleries** are resplendent with some of the finest artworks in Hawaii and offer art lovers a chance to just look or select a favorite to take home as a tangible memory of their island vacation. For paintings, crystals, jewelry, candles, and other eclectic gifts, stop at **Life's Treasures.**

Perhaps the best place in the area to look for authentic Hawaiian art and craft items is the **Kaua'i Heritage Center of Hawaiian Culture and the Arts,** 808/821-2070, open Mon.–Fri. 10 A.M.–6 P.M., Saturday until 4 P.M. Aside from the retail business, this organization also runs exhibits, workshops, lectures, demonstrations on aspects of Hawaiian culture, and displays of high-quality Hawaiian artifacts. Offered here are programs in hula, lei-making, painting, language, and legends for adults and children.

Under the Whale Tower toward the back of the center is **Kaua'i Children's Discovery Museum,** 808/823-8222, a hands-on adventure gallery where young kids can learn about science, nature, technology, and culture, particularly as it pertains to Hawaii and Polynesia. Kids can explore an underwater coral reef, learn to navigate an outrigger canoe by the stars, ride a flight simulator into space, try virtual reality games, or create arts and crafts. This community-based, volunteer-staffed organization is set up to involve children in their surroundings. On your way out, stop by the gift shop and look over the selection of science toys, educational games, and gifts. The museum is open Tues.–Sat. 9 A.M.–5 P.M., Monday for special events. Admission is $3.50 for children, $4.50 for adults.

## Kapaʻa Shopping Center

Marked by a Shell station and a Burger King at 4-1105 Kuhio Hwy. is this bite-size, functional shopping center. Here, you'll find a **Big Save,** a well-stocked food store open daily 7 A.M.–10 P.M.; the full-service Kapaʻa post office; an **Ace Hardware** store; an inexpensive restaurant or two; and the Kapaʻa clinic of the Kauaʻi Medical Group. Here as well is **Kapaʻa Laundry Center,** with self-service machines and drop-off service. The laundromat is open 7:30 A.M.–9:30 P.M. and has coin and boxed soap machines. It's the best in the area.

## Small Shopping Malls

Across the highway from another Shell station, the **Waipouli Complex** houses Aloha Diner for local Hawaiian food and Popo's Cookies. The nearby **Waipouli Plaza** contains Waipouli Variety, with clothing, gifts, and a great fishing/hunting section; The King and I Thai restaurant; and a seashell merchant selling retail and wholesale. Farther down the road, in the **Waipouli Town Center,** you'll find **Foodland,** open 5 A.M.–11 P.M., as well as a Fun Factory arcade for games, Blockbuster Video for home/condo entertainment, and the Lounge Lizard bar.

## Boutiques and Galleries

Ambrose of **Ambrose's Kapuna Surf Gallery,** 808/822-7112, in the bright yellow building across from Foodland in the Waipouli Town Center, is a surfers' advocate, philosopher, and gener-

ally good guy. He has one of the largest collections of big boards and old surfboards on the island, and some new ones, too, which he creates out back. After years of selling natural foods, fruits, and produce, Ambrose has turned his shop into an art galley that displays his creations of surf art. Stop in for a look at some of the funkiest and most unusual artwork on the island.

Next door to Ambrose's is **Marta's Boat,** 808/822-3926, open Mon.–Sat. 10:30 A.M.–6 P.M. This is primarily a children's boutique, but the overflowing shelves also hold handmade quilts by local ladies, T-shirts, shorts, casual wear, elegant evening wear, and beautiful lingerie. A rack of games and educational items offers help in keeping the little ones happy on a return plane voyage or during an evening in the condo.

Next to the Lemongrass Grille is **Jungle Girl,** a boutique of "funk and flash" that carries the odd and exotic island-inspired clothing and imports of a dizzying variety. This is an all-around fun shop for ladies looking for something out of the ordinary. Guys may find it fun too.

In the old Kawamura Store building, built 1949 and rebuilt 1993, is **Hula Girl,** 808/822-1950, for fine fashions, vintage alohawear, Hawaiian craft items, tropical Christmas ornaments, and much more. If you're looking for quality with island flavor, try here. Only a few steps away is **Jim Saylor Jewelry,** 808/822-3591, for hand-crafted jewelry and gemstones.

As shiny and glittering as the sunbeams pouring through the windows, **Kela's Glass Gallery,** in the Hee Fat Marketplace building, 4-1354 Kuhio Hwy., Kapaʻa, HI 96746, 808/822-4527, owned and operated by Larry Barton, is a showcase for more than 60 contemporary artists working in glass. The gallery features everything from classic vases to free-form sculptures ranging in price from affordable to not affordable. Kela's also sells and ships (disassembled, but with pieces numbered for easy reassembly) wooden flowers that are hand-carved and hand-painted in Indonesia. There are 30 different flowers including hibiscus, irises, calla lilies, various ginger, and heliconia.

Next door is **Kebanu Gallery,** 808/823-6820, a delightful stop to peruse one of the most unusual collections of contemporary art on the island, including engaging works of wood, metal, glass, fiber art, and other media.

In the same building is **South China Sea Trading Company,** 808/823-8655, with arts and crafts items and tropical furniture from Hawaii and Southeast Asia.

At the intersection across from the ABC Store, **Aloha Images** gallery, 808/821-1382, displays an incredibly wide variety and large number of paintings at affordable prices. There's bound to be something that you'd love to take home.

**Earth Beads,** 808/822-0766, owned by Angelika Riskin, open daily except Sunday 10 A.M.–6 P.M., specializes in beads and imported items from India, Africa, and South America. Shimmering in the tiny shop are earrings, belts, incidental bags, and sterling silver jewelry from Thailand, as well as locally made designs. Primitive basketry, incense, perfumed oils, T-shirts, "jungle" umbrellas and very unusual greeting cards complete the stock of this great little shop.

For a perfectly natural gift, slip down **Orchid Alley** for a beautiful potted plant. Send one home as a reminder of your tropical vacation—they ship. Back down the main drag next to Pono Market is **Flowers and Joys** for some of the best (although not the cheapest) lei on the island.

Next to Orchid Alley is **William & Zimmer Woodworkers,** 808/822-2850, which displays artfully crafted and finely finished furniture and smaller wooden objects, mostly made of koa. As you can't pack these babies into your suitcase, they'll gladly crate and ship anywhere in the states for you.

Walk into the **Island Hemp and Cotton Company,** 808/821-0225, open daily 10 A.M.–6 P.M., and suddenly you're in Asia. Stride across the reed mat floor while the soulful eyes of a Buddha sitting serenely atop a glass counter follow you in. Across from the ABC store in downtown Kapa'a, the shop is owned and operated by Nancee McTernan, a long-distance traveler and "old Asia hand" who has personally chosen every item in the store. Some special items include Buddhas from Borneo, baskets from Bali, carved bone necklaces from New Zealand, local puka shell jewelry, and antique wood carvings from all parts of Indonesia. Men's and women's clothing, all made from or-

ganic cotton, hemp, linen, and other natural fibers, includes everything from casual shirts to elegant dresses, hats to backpacks. If you are after a truly distinctive gift, one-of-a-kind clothing, or an original artifact, visit this shop.

Up near the north end of town, the **Original Red Dirt Shirt** outlet sells many fetching designs made right here on the island using Kaua'i's red earth as a dye. The store carries mostly T-shirts, up to size XXXXL, but also some kids' and toddlers' outfits. Take home the essence of Kaua'i. Several other small arts and crafts shops make up this little complex, and these and others put their wares out under tents Thurs.–Sun. 9 A.M.–5 P.M. at the **Kauai Products Fair.**

Look for **M. Miura Store** at the north end of Kapa'a, mountain side, open Mon.–Sat. 9 A.M.–5 P.M. Local people shop at this clothing and accessory store for alohawear, T-shirts, sunglasses, sandals, caps, men's and women's shorts, and a good selection of bikinis.

## Photo Needs

Try **Cameralab,** 808/822-7338, behind L&L Drive-In restaurant in Waipouli, or **Longs Drug** at Kauai Village for all your photo finishing needs.

## Food Shopping

For a full-service supermarket, try **Safeway** at Kauai Village, **Big Save** at the Kapa'a Shopping Center, or **Foodland** at the Waipouli Town Center. Older (since 1946) and more local is **Kojima's** grocery. This well-stocked store on the mountain side of the road beyond the Aloha Lumber yard at the north end of town carries produce, meat, liquor, beer, and picnic supplies.

**Papaya's,** at the Kauai Village, 808/823-0190, open daily except Sunday 9 A.M.–8 P.M., is a natural-food market and café. Coolers and shelves hold items like wild tropical guava juice, organic sprouted hot-dog buns, and mainstays like organic fruits and vegetables, yogurt, wholegrain bread, and bulk foods. There is also a good selection of organic teas, flavored coffees, and premium microbrewery beers, along with racks of fine wines. Spices, oils, vinegars, organic salad dressings, homeopathic medicines, cruelty-free cosmetics, vitamins, minerals, and an assortment of biodegradable cleaning products are also well represented. A large deli display case holds all kinds of goodies and desserts, and wholesome lunches can be ordered to be eaten outside. If you buy fruit from the produce section, the staff will cut it up for you so you can eat it out front.

Newer and smaller is **Poppy's** natural food market, 808/823-9313, open Tues.–Sun. 8 A.M.–8 P.M. at the north end of town across from the library. Poppy's carries fresh fruits and vegetables, a limited line of grocery items, vitamins, minerals, and other health aids, plus its small kitchen puts out smoothies, salads, bagels, sandwiches, and wraps 11 A.M.–5 P.M. While here, check on the yoga classes held upstairs.

Along the main highway, the local family-run **Pono Market,** open Mon.–Sat. 7 A.M.–7 P.M. (9 P.M. on Friday) and Sunday 8 A.M.–4 P.M., is stuffed to the gills with mini-mart items, along with takeout sushi, *bento,* and deli sandwiches.

As you approach the main intersection in Kapa'a, look for the **Sunnyside Farmers' Market,** open daily 8 A.M.–8 P.M., where you can get fresh fruits, vegetables, and flowers from around the island, pre-packaged and pre-inspected food items to take home, and gift, jewelry, clothing, and beach items. One of the specialties is locally grown non-acidic pineapples. The deli in the back, called A Marketplace Cafe, serves soups, salads, sandwiches, and other lunch items and drinks.

There's a county-sponsored **farmers' market** every Wednesday at 3 P.M. at the Kapa'a New Town Park, near the armory behind town. This is a lively, local event with great options for vegetables, fruit, and flowers. Stop and pick up food for your evening meal or try coconut milk right out of the shell.

## SERVICES

**Business Support Services,** across from the Kapa'a Hongwanji, 808/822-5504, open Mon.–Sat. 8 A.M.–6 P.M., can answer all of your shipping and packing needs. Also available are fax, photocopy, and Internet services, and you can rent time on a typewriter or computer. Internet use runs $2.50 for 15 minutes, so you can check your email here.

The two laundromats in the area are **Basuel's** just behind Snorkel Bob's (no soap or change machines) and the larger **Kapa'a Laundry Center** in the Kapa'a Shopping Center, which offers both self-serve and drop-off service. For dry cleaning, head to the **Pono Cleaners** on the main street next to Pono Market.

The **Kapa'a post office** is at the Kapa'a Shopping Center, pretty much in the middle of town.

Just north of the Kapa'a Beach County Park is the town **library.**

## Heading North

## ANAHOLA AND VICINITY

Route 56 north from Kapa'a is a visual treat. At first, the coastline glides along in an ever-changing panorama. Shortly, the road moves inland through former cane fields, then passes a large dairy farm before moving into orchard and pasture land. While there are a few new residential developments in the works, overall development is sparse until you get to Kilauea in the Hanalei District. To your left are the dominant **Anahola Mountains,** jagged, pointed, and intriguing. Until recently, you could crane your neck and see Hole-in-the-Mountain, a natural arrangement of boulders that formed a round *puka* (legend says it was formed by an angry giant who hurled his spear with such force that he made the hole), but time and storms have taken their toll, and the old hole has collapsed. More recently, a second hole has begun to open up just below the ridge; this is best seen from the highway beyond Anahola.

### Kealia

Just north of Kapa'a the road rises slightly around a point. On this point is a somewhat trashy **scenic lookout** from where you have decent views up and down the coast. As soon as you cross Kapa'a Stream you're in the village of Kealia; its school,

Donkey Beach is a quiet, secluded beach for those looking for an escape from the crowds.

store, and post office are now closed, but the rodeo corral still gets use. The wide, white strand of **Kealia Beach** curves along the coast for a half mile. It's not an official beach park, so there are no facilities, but during calm weather the swimming, bodysurfing, and boogie boarding are good—particularly near the jetty at the north end. Few people are ever here except some local anglers and surfers, who find the waves most challenging during winter swells but who come anytime of the year when the surf is right.

Inland, Kealia Road takes you up over patched asphalt, past the community of Kumukumu, and through former sugarcane fields to the deteriorating Spalding Monument. From this upcountry vantage point, now cowboy country, you can glimpse both the ocean and Anahola Mountains and perhaps see horseback riders and dirt bikers on the open grassland on the weekends.

### Donkey Beach

Continue along Rte. 56 heading north past mile marker 12 to a shoreline access parking lot. Follow the trail through the lots of the new Kealia Kai subdivision for 10 minutes until you come to a surfing beach that the locals call Donkey Beach. A tall stand of ironwoods shadows its south end.

Unfortunately, the undertow is severe, especially during rough weather, and only experienced surfers challenge the waves here. You can sunbathe and take dips, but remain in the shallows close to shore. This area is very secluded, and some come here to spend time au naturel, but the new housing development above the beach will certainly make this area more frequented in coming years. Bicycle riders who bike the shoreline cane road from Kapa'a to Anahola skirt this beach on their way north.

### Anahola

The first village that you come to is Anahola. While the old village is down along the bay, the commercial part of town and newer homes in the Hawaiian Homelands tract have been built up along the highway. As you approach 'Anahola, you'll likely see signs on the highway advertising **lei for sale.** Families here make a few extra dollars by selling these beautiful and fragrant symbols of *aloha*. Although prices vary, expect to pay up to $5 for a *ti*-leaf lei or $5–10 for a flower lei. Stop and pick one up for your sweetie; many last for several days if refrigerated.

Just before mile marker 14 is **Whaler's General Store,** open daily 6:30 A.M.–9:30 P.M., sell-

ROBERT NILSEN

ing groceries, souvenirs, vegetables, and liquor, as well as the Anahola post office and a well-known eatery. Anahola Road off Rte. 56 just before the Whaler's General Store leads to Anahola Beach, a long strand of white sand that forms a series of decent beaches. Just a minute up the road, look to your right for 'Aliomanu Road (first) and follow it for a few minutes to the mouth of the Anahola River as it spills into the bay. Along the curve of the bay north of the river mouth is the narrower and less-frequented section of the beach. Beyond the point is the more secluded 'Aliomanu Beach.

'Aliomanu Road used to run from the highway down to and along the coast before turning inland again to the highway. During one of the last hurricanes, the bridge over a small stream at the north end of 'Aliomanu Beach was washed out and hasn't been replaced. The result is that each section of 'Aliomanu Road is a cul-de-sac. 'Aliomanu Road (second) is the north section of this road, and there is access to 'Aliomanu Beach from that end as well.

## Anahola Beach County Park

Stretching from the river mouth along the south curve of the bay, this park has a developed picnic area, grills, showers, restrooms, and numerous camping spots—county permit required. Tall ironwood trees provide a natural canopy along the narrow strip of sand that slides gently into the water. The swimming is safe in the protected cove and in the fresh water river, good for a refreshing dip. As you walk north the waves and rips get tougher. It's not advisable to enter the deep water, although some experienced board riders do challenge the waves here, as the Hawaiians did long ago, in an area called Kanahawale, which means "Easily Broken." However, the reef comes close to shore at this end, and wherever you can find a sheltered pocket it's good for snorkeling. Local anglers love this spot for near-shore fishing, and families come to have a weekend sunset dinner and evening bonfire on the beach. The entire area is popular with local people and at times begins to look like a tent city of semi-permanent campers and squatters. Although the county works to maintain the park, these long-term residents tend to make the area messy at

times. This is a place to camp for a few days, or just to stop in for a refreshing plunge on the way to or from the north shore. If you camp, don't leave your stuff unattended for too long.

## Moloa'a Beach

The turnoff to Moloa'a (Matted Roots) Bay is between mile markers 16 and 17 near the dairy farm. Turn down the rough Ko'olau Road, follow it to Moloa'a Road, and take this narrow but paved road to the end. Look for the brilliant poinsettias blooming in early winter along Ko'olau Road—they are the island's clue that Christmas and the New Year are near. Moloa'a Bay has a magnificent but rarely visited beach. The road leading down is a luscious little thoroughfare, cutting over domed hillocks in a series of curves. The jungle canopy is thick and then opens into a series of glens and pastures. Off to the sides homes perch on stilts made from telephone poles. A short drive takes you to road's end and a small cluster of dwellings, where there is limited space to put your vehicle. Park here and follow the right-of-way signs to the beach. Here, a stream comes into the bay providing a great place to wash off the ocean water after a dip. The beach is lovely, bright, and wide, forming a crescent moon. To the north the beach ends in a grassy hillock; south, it's confined by a rocky headland where the swimming is best. As at all east and north shore beaches, swimming is advised only during calm weather. Snorkeling is good, but you'll have to swim the channel out to the base of the *pali,* which is inadvisable if the waves are rough. Although a few homes are around, Moloa'a is a place of peaceful solitude. Sunsets are light shows of changing color, and you'll probably be a solitary spectator.

## Larsen's Beach

From Moloa'a Bay, return to Ko'olau Road (the old coast road) and follow it north as it twists into and then out of the valley. As it comes up on the heights near an old cemetery, turn seaward and follow a narrow gravel road for half a mile to a small parking lot at the crest of the cliff. From here, a path leads down to Larsen's Beach, named after L. David Larsen, who was a manager of the Kilauea sugar plantation. He built a home for his family nearby. Not particularly good for swimming because of the rocky bottom and close-in reef, this beach is a place where locals come to harvest a type of seaweed or do throw-net fishing. The narrow sand shore may be good for sunbathing, however, and, except on weekends, you'll probably have the place to yourself.

## Accommodations

Several rental properties line 'Aliomanu Road. **Mahina Kai,** P.O. Box 699, Anahola, HI 96703, 808/822-9451 or 800/337-1134, www.mahinakai.com, reservations@mahinakai.com, is a Japanese-style house with a cobalt blue tile roof that's backed into a hillside and has views of the ocean. An indoor koi pond, open spaces, Oriental furnishings and artwork, and paper *shoji* screens help create the atmosphere. The finely landscaped yard is tended with care, and there is even a small *heiau* on the property. Down below the house, set in a walled garden amidst thick vegetation, is the very private free-form swimming pool. Above the main house, the "tea house" has enough room for workshop activities and small group meetings. Each of the three rooms in the house has its own bathroom and lanai; two have adjoining sitting rooms. These rooms share a kitchenette. The detached Bamboo Cottage has its own small kitchen and sitting room. Rooms run $125–225 a night with a three-night minimum. Mahina Kai is gay friendly.

**Paradise Vacation Rentals,** 4760 'Aliomanu Rd., 808/822-5754 or 800/569-3063, is on the beach side of the road in a quiet, relaxed compound. Here you have a choice of a studio at $75 or the house at $100 per night. The studio has a queen bed and small kitchenette, while the house has two king and three single beds and a full kitchen. For information, write P.O. Box 108, Anahola, HI 96703.

**Moloa'a Kai** on Moloa'a Bay gives you all the amenities of a two-bedroom, two-bath house right on the beach. This house can sleep up to seven and rents for a week at $885–985. Daily rental—four-night minimum—is also an option for $150 a night. Contact Hawaii Beachfront Vacation Homes, 46-535 Haiku Plantation Place, Kane'ohe,

HI 96744, 808/247-3637, fax 808/235-2644, www.hotspots.hawaii.com/beachrent1.html, hi-beach@lava.net.

**Jade Lily Pad** is tucked away a short distance up Moloa'a Stream and reachable via a dirt driveway by 4WD vehicles. Wood floors and a cathedral ceiling make this cottage seem larger than it is. Its two bedrooms are good for a family, and the full kitchen makes it easy and convenient to prepare meals and save a few bucks. The Jade Lily Pad rents for $250 a night. Contact Rosewood, 808/822-5216, fax 808/822-5478, www.rosewoodkauai.com, for additional information and reservations.

Other vacation rentals can be arranged through **Garden Island Properties,** 808/822-4871 or 800/801-0378 in Kapa'a.

## Food

**Duane's Ono Char Burger,** open Mon.–Sat. 10 A.M.–6 P.M. and Sunday 11 A.M.–6 P.M., is known far and wide. It's a clean, friendly roadside stand where you can get burgers, fish and chips, sides, and drinks. Some of the double-fisted burgers include the Ono; an Old Fashioned, with cheddar, onions, and sprouts on a Kaiser roll; the Local Boy, made with teriyaki, cheddar cheese, and pineapple; a Local Girl, made with teriyaki and Swiss cheese; and even a meatless Boca Burger. The burgers are oversize and heavy with cheese and trimmings, and most everything is under $6. For an extra treat, try a delicious marionberry shake. Umbrella tables are to the side, but hold your appetite for a few minutes and make it a picnic at the nearby beach.

Across the road from Duane's and up a bit, look for the Anahola Baptist Church and a small lane leading to the **Polynesian Hide-a-way,** a local Hawaiian restaurant, open daily 10 A.M.–5 P.M. The Hide-a-way is a hut in a grove of trees for eat-in or takeout that offers plate lunches such as *huli huli* chicken, *laulau,* *kalua* pig, and fish and chips. Polynesian Hide-a-way is down-home, clean, friendly, inexpensive, delicious, and filled with the *aloha* spirit. You can't go wrong.

# North Shore

The north shore is a soulful song of wonder, a contented chant of dream-reality, where all the notes of the Garden Island harmonize gloriously. The refrain is a tinkling melody, rising, falling, and finally reaching a booming climax deep in the emerald green of Na Pali. In so many ways this region is a haven: tiny towns and villages that refused to crumble when sugar pulled out; a patchwork quilt of diminutive *kuleana* of native Hawaiians running deep into luxuriant valleys, where ageless stone walls encircle fields of taro; a winter sanctuary for migrating birds and gritty native species desperately holding on to life; a refuge for myriad visitors—the adventuring, vacationing, life-tossed, or work-weary who come to its shores seeking a setting to find peace of body and soul.

The north shore is only 30 miles long, but, oh, what miles! Along its undulating mountains, one-lane roads, and luminescent bays are landlocked caves still umbilically tied to the sea; historical sites, the remnants of peace or domination once so important and now reduced by time; and living movie sets, some occupied by villas of stars or dignitaries. Enduring, too, is the history of old Hawaii in this fabled homeland of the Menehune, overrun by the Polynesians who set up their elaborate kingdoms built on strict social order. The usurpers' *heiau* remain, and from one came the

ROBERT NILSEN

Hanalei Bay is one of the most perfect in the islands.

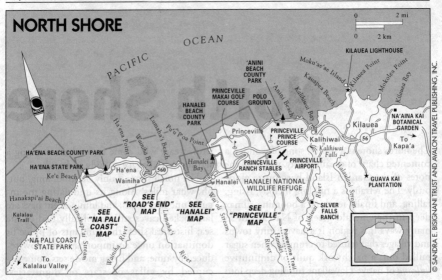

NORTH SHORE

PACIFIC OCEAN

KILAUEA LIGHTHOUSE

Moku'ae'ae Island · Kilauea Point
Kauapea Beach · Mokolea Point
'ANINI BEACH COUNTY PARK
PRINCEVILLE MAKAI GOLF COURSE
POLO GROUND
'Anini Beach · Kalihiwai Bay · Kilauea Bay
HANALEI BEACH COUNTY PARK
Princeville · Kilauea
PRINCEVILLE PRINCE COURSE · Kalihiwai
NA'AINA KAI BOTANICAL GARDEN
To Kapa'a
Ha'ena Point · Lumaha'i Beach · Pu'u Poa Point
Kalihiwai Falls
HA'ENA BEACH COUNTY PARK
HA'ENA STATE PARK
Ke'e Beach
Ha'ena · Wainiha · 560 · Hanalei
Hanalei Bay
PRINCEVILLE RANCH STABLES
PRINCEVILLE AIRPORT
HANALEI NATIONAL WILDLIFE REFUGE
GUAVA KAI PLANTATION
Hanakapi'ai Beach
Kalalau Trail
SEE "NA PALI COAST" MAP
SEE "ROAD'S END" MAP
SEE "HANALEI" MAP
SEE "PRINCEVILLE" MAP
SILVER FALLS RANCH
NA PALI COAST STATE PARK
To Kalalau Valley
Wainiha River · Lumaha'i River · Wai'oli Stream · Hanalei River · Kalihiwai River · Hanalei Stream
Powerline Trail

© SANDRA E. BISIGNANI TRUST AND AVALON TRAVEL PUBLISHING, INC.

hula, swaying, stirring, and spreading throughout the island kingdoms.

Starting in **Kilauea,** an old plantation town, you can marvel at the coastline from bold promontories pummeled by the sea and observe seabirds at the wildlife sanctuary. Then there are the north shore beaches—fans of white sand, some easily visited as official parks, others hidden, the domains of simplicity and free spirits. **Princeville** follows, a convenient but incongruous planned community, vibrant with its own shopping mall and flexing condo muscles. Over the rise is **Hanalei,** even more poetic than its lovely name, is

a tiny town, a yachties' anchorage with good food, spirited, slow, a bay of beauty and enchantment. Movie cameras once rolled at neighboring **Lumaha'i Beach,** and an entire generation shared the dream of paradise when they saw this spot in *South Pacific.* Next in rapid succession are **Wainiha** and **Ha'ena,** with their few amenities, a little of the world's most relaxed lifestyle. The road ends at **Ke'e Beach,** where adventure begins with the start of the **Na Pali Coast Trail.** The north shore remains for most visitors the perfect setting for seeking and maybe actually finding peace, solitude, the dream, yourself.

## Kilauea

There's no saying *exactly* where it begins, but Kilauea is generally considered the gateway to the north shore. The village proper was built on sugar, but that foundation melted away in the early 1970s. Now the town holds on as a way station to some of the most intriguing scenery along this fabulous coast. Notice the bright, cheery, well-kept homes as you pass through this community. The homeowners may be short on cash but are nonetheless long on pride and surround their

dwellings with lovingly tended flower gardens. The bungalows—pictures of homey contentment—are ablaze with color.

To get into town, look for mile marker 23 and a Shell gas station on your right, along with the Menehune Food Mart, a small store selling sundries and general groceries. This is where you turn onto Kolo Road, following the signs to Kilauea Lighthouse and the national wildlife refuge. The promontory that the lighthouse occupies,

KAUA'I

Kilauea Point, is the northernmost point of the main Hawaiian Islands. A second way into Kilauea is by turning off the highway just before mile marker 23 at Hookui Road. Go one block and turn left onto Kolo Street. Pass St. Sylvester's Church and proceed over a bridge, past the Kilauea School, and on into town. Kilauea's first commercial area is at the corner of Kolo Street and Kilauea Road near the gas station. Down Kilauea Road at Keneke Street are the Kong Lung Co. and other concerns, the real business hub of town. Behind this group of businesses is a small community park. One block away on Oka Street are two medical clinics and a bakery/café.

## SIGHTS

Just before you arrive at the turnoff to Kilauea, turn inland on Kuawa Road and follow the signs to the 480-acre **Guava Kai Plantation,** the largest guava-producing and -processing venture in the nation. Proceed along the access road lined with ferns, banana trees, ironwoods, and flowering bushes, and stop in at the visitor center/snack shop, 808/828-6121, open daily 9 A.M.–5 P.M., where you can learn about guava processing; taste guava juice, jams, and jellies; and purchase a guava product, T-shirt, or sundry item. The free self-guided tour is actually just a view of the beginning stages of fruit processing, as you are not allowed into the factory itself. Come early—much of the work in this outdoor receiving area starts before 6 A.M. You're invited to pick a handful of guava fruit from the orchard at no charge as a take-away treat—staff members will point you to an area where the fruit is ripe. Don't hurry away, however; treat yourself to a stroll through the small botanical garden. Follow a well-trodden path through a covered archway where tropical plants grow, and cross a tiny stream to find many of Hawaii's flowers and plants labeled by name. The path winds along for just five minutes and leads to a pond surrounded by taro, bird of paradise, hibiscus, torch ginger, ferns, and various palms. Before leaving, stop at the snack shop for guava juice, a juice float or slush, ice cream cone, or bowl of saimin.

Just east of Kilauea at the end of Wailapa Road,

**Na 'Aina Kai Botanical Gardens,** website: www.naainakai.com, is a botanical garden of grand proportions. Its 240 acres include well over 100 acres of a tropical hardwood plantation that includes nearly two dozen trees such as teak, mahogany, zebra wood, rosewood, and cocobolo, and another large tract of tropical fruit trees. In the heart of the property several theme gardens specialize in various types of plants, and throughout the gardens some 60 bronze sculptures add a playful touch. After years of loving preparation, this property has opened to the public for guided tours by reservation only; call 808/828-0525. Tours are given on Tuesday, Wednesday, and Thursday and involve some walking and/or a covered tram ride. They range from a 90-minute stroll for $25 to a five-hour walk and ride through all the sections of the property for $70. Adults and children 13 and above, please.

Where Kolo Road intersects Kilauea Road sits **Christ Memorial Episcopal Church** on the right. Hawaii seems to sprout as many churches as bamboo shoots, but this one is special. The shrubbery and flowers immediately catch your eye, their vibrant colors matched by the stained-glass windows, imported from England. The present church was built in 1941 from cut lava stone. Inside is a hand-hewn altar, and surrounding the church a cemetery holds several tombstones of long-departed parishioners. Go in, have a look, and perhaps meditate for a moment. Before turning on Kilauea Road have a look at **St. Sylvester's Catholic Church.** This house of worship is octagonal, with a roof resembling a Chinese hat. Inside are murals painted by Jean Charlot, a famous island artist. The church, built by Friar John Macdonald, was an attempt to reintroduce art as one of the bulwarks of Catholicism.

### Kilauea Point National Wildlife Refuge

Head down Kilauea Road (sometimes referred to as Lighthouse Road) past Kong Lung Co., following it as it makes a hard swing to the left, then winds around, ending at Kilauea Point National Wildlife Refuge and **Kilauea Lighthouse,** a designated national historical landmark. This facility, built in 1913, was at one time manned by

KAUA'I

ROBERT NILSEN

lighthouse at Kilauea Point National Wildlife Refuge

the Coast Guard but is now under the jurisdiction of the Department of the Interior's Fish and Wildlife Service. Stately and solid, it stands about 50 feet tall, the base more than 200 feet above the sea. Boasting the largest "clamshell lens" in the world, it was capable of sending a beam 20 miles out to sea. The clamshell lens was discontinued in 1976, when a small, high-intensity beacon was activated as the reference point for mariners.

The refuge, which encompasses the high cliffs from Kilauea Point past Crater Hill to Mokolea Point (one-half of an ancient and eroded crater rim), is alive with permanent and migrating seabirds. Keep your eyes peeled for the great frigatebird, kiting on its nearly eight-foot wingspan, and the red-footed booby, a white bird with black wingtips darting here and there, always wearing red dancing shoes. The *nene*, wedgetail shearwaters, and red- and white-tailed tropicbirds are also common here. The wildlife refuge is attempting to relocate albatross from the Midway Islands, where they have virtually taken over the island. More than 40 have been

successfully relocated, and you can watch them floundering around on nearby Albatross Hill. At certain times of the year, Hawaiian monk seals and green sea turtles can be seen along the shore and around Moku'ae'ae Island just off Kilauea Point. Dolphins are also spotted offshore during spring and summer, and whales play in these waters, part of the Hawaiian Islands Humpback Whale National Marine Sanctuary, during winter and spring.

A leisurely walk takes you out onto this amazingly narrow peninsula to the lighthouse and visitor center. Don't keep your eyes only in the air, however. Look for the coastal *naupaka* plants, which surround the parking lot and line the walk to the lighthouse. Common along the seashore and able to grow even in arid regions, these plants have bunches of bright green, moisture-retaining, leathery leaves; at their centers are white half-flowers the size of a fingernail and small white seeds. Information at the visitors center gives you a fast lesson in birdlife, plantlife, and a pictorial history of the lighthouse—worth reading. Also available is a good selection of books on Hawaiian flora, fauna, history, and hiking, as well as maps of the islands. There are usually informative docents in the yard, and the center often sets up binoculars on tripods trained on particular birds or nesting sites on the nearby cliffs.

The refuge has established a one-mile-long walking trail from Kilauea Point east to Crater Hill; it is used strictly for tours led by refuge personnel. The hiking tour leaves at 10 A.M. from the visitor center, Mon.–Fri. only; make your reservation by calling 808/828-0168. From Crater Hill, 568 feet straight up from the water, the wide Pacific stretches virtually unobstructed until it hits the Aleutian Islands of Alaska. A result of one of the last spates of volcanic activity on the island (perhaps some 12,000 years ago), this sea cliff is like a giant stack of pancakes, layered and jagged, with the edges eaten by age and covered with a green syrup of lichen and mosses. The cliff is undercut, giving the sensation of floating in midair. Profuse purple and yellow flowers spread all along the edge. Like Kilauea Point to the west and Mokolea Point to the east, these cliffs serve as a giant rookery for seabirds. The military found it a perfect spot, too, and erected a radar station here during World War II; the abandoned structures still remain.

This lighthouse and sanctuary are open daily 10 A.M.–4 P.M., except federal holidays. The entrance fee is $3 adults, free for children under 16; the cost of an annual refuge permit is $10. Golden Eagle, Golden Access, and Golden Age Passes, and a Federal Duck Stamp are honored for free entrance.

## Beaches

The Kilauea area has some fantastic beaches.

Kilauea Bay offers great fishing, unofficial camping, and beautiful scenery. Between mile markers 21 and 22, turn seaward on Wailapa Road and proceed for the better part of a mile. Follow the dirt road that veers off to the left and downhill to **Kahili Beach**, also known as Quarry Beach, on Kilauea Bay. This very pretty bay has headlands on each end, and the beach is split in the middle by a tongue of rock. Characteristic of Kaua'i, Kilauea Stream runs into the bay, and in this case meets the water on the west end of the beach, having first backed up against the sand bar to form a rather large pond. Swimming is good in the placid water of the stream, and some bring kayaks for a paddle around the pond. During calm periods, swimming is possible in the bay, but when the waves are up, local residents come to surf or use boogie boards. Plenty of places along the streambank or on the beach are good for picnicking and camping. It's especially popular on weekends when families come to play. At other times, the beach may be empty. Many local anglers come here to catch a transparent fish called 'o'io, which they often use for bait. It's too bony to fry, but they have figured out an ingenious way to get the meat. They cut off the tail and roll a soda pop bottle over it, squeezing the meat out through the cut. They then mix it with water, hot pepper, and bread crumbs to make delicious fish balls. This beach can also be reached from Kilauea town. Proceed past Kong Lung Co. and take the second dirt road to the right (if it's open to traffic), or walk; it angles through what used to be cane fields. Follow this rutted road a mile and a half down to the now-abandoned Kahili Quarry

at the end of the road, from where you must wade across the stream to the beach.

Kauapea Beach, more commonly called **Secret Beach,** deserves its name. After passing through Kilauea, look for Banana Joe's tropical fruit stand on the left; just past it is Kalihiwai Road. Make a right there and then take the very first dirt road on the right—through the cut in the roadbank—and down to a parking area. Follow the trail along the horse pasture barbed-wire fence and then steeply down the slippery ravine before emerging at the beach in less than 15 minutes. Even some local residents ruefully admit that the secret is out. However, if you venture to this beach, be conscious that there are private homes nearby and that it's a place locals come to enjoy themselves away from the crowds of tourists. If you expect Secret Beach to be small, you're in for a shock. This white-sand strand is huge and backed by steep cliff walls. Reasonably calm during summer months, waves thunder in and crash on the beach during winter. Dolphins seem to like this area as well—please give these intelligent animals plenty of space—and whales can be seen offshore during the winter months. Secret Beach is a de facto nude beach and is accepted as such by most local residents. Beyond the far end of the beach you can see Kilauea Lighthouse, proud and dominant and dazzling white in the sun. Along the beach a fine stand of trees provides shade perfect for pitching a tent, but be aware that police sometimes patrol here and issue tickets for camping without a permit. Nonetheless, some people make this beach home for a few weeks or months at a time—unofficially, of course. For drinking water, head along the beach and keep your eyes peeled for a freshwater spring coming out of the mountain. What more can you ask for?

**Kalihiwai Beach** is at the end of Kalihiwai Road. If you go over the Kalihiwai River, you've gone too far—even though another section of the Kalihiwai Road also leads from there down to the coast. This road was once part of the coastal road, but the devastating tsunami of 1946 took out the lower bridge, and the road is now divided by the river. As on many such rivers in Kaua'i, a ferry was used here to ease early transportation difficulties. Less than half a mile down the first Kalihiwai Road you come to an off-the-track, white-sand beach lined with ironwoods. The swimming, bodysurfing, and boogie boarding are outstanding here, given the right conditions. The river behind the ironwoods forms a freshwater pool for rinsing off, but there are no amenities whatsoever. People sometimes camp among the ironwoods. The second Kalihiwai Road—take the right fork in the road—leads you to the west side of the river, where locals come to fish. Some people put kayaks in the river here for a short paddle upriver, followed by a 10-minute hike to get to the waterfall that can be seen from the highway overlook.

On the way to the second Kalihiwai Road you cross Kalihiwai Stream. Just before the bridge is a scenic overlook where you can take in this lush valley and its waterfall. Before you get back into your car to head on, go back up the road a hundred yards or so where a tall thin waterfall slices through a tight ravine right at the road's edge, almost out of view of traffic. This spot is directly on the busy highway, so pull your car all the way off the roadway and be extra cautious as you walk along.

Go over the bridge and turn right on the second Kalihiwai Road. Follow this to a Y, take the left fork—'Anini Road—and follow it to its end at the remarkable **'Anini Beach County Park.** This area was known as one of the best fishing grounds and was reserved for the exclusive use of the *ali'i.* 'Anini was traditionally called *Wanini,* but time and sea air weathered a latter-day sign until the W rusted off completely. Newcomers to the area mistakenly called it 'Anini, and the name stuck. The reef here, at two miles, is the longest exposed reef off Kaua'i; consequently, the snorkeling is first-rate. It's amazing to snorkel out to the reef in no more than four feet of water and then to peer over the edge into waters that seem bottomless. Stay away from the boat landing and the route that boats take to cross the reef. Windsurfers also love this area, and their bright sails can be seen year-round. Those in the know say this is the best spot on Kaua'i for beginning sailboarders, as the trade winds generally blow gently and steadily toward the shore, the water is shallow, and the beach protected. Beginning lessons are often given here.

Longer than the reef, the beach is fine sand, and swimming is excellent. Follow the road to the end, where a shallow, brackish lagoon and a large sandbar make the area good for wading. This park has full amenities—toilets, picnic tables, grills, and a pavilion. Camping by county permit is allowed in designated areas; the day-use picnic spot is at the other end of the park. There are private homes and vacation rentals at both ends of this beach, so be considerate when coming and going.

A polo ground is across the road from the open camping area. On Sundays from April to August, matches are held here beginning at 3 P.M. and lasting until about 5 P.M. Admission is $3 per person or $6 per car. The exciting matches are both fun and stylish. The local horsemen are excellent players who team with their trusty mounts to perform amazing athletic maneuvers. Call the Kauai Polo Club, 808/828-0273, for information.

# PRACTICALITIES
## Accommodations
**Hale Ho'o Maha,** P.O. Box 422, Kilauea, HI 96754, 808/828-1341 or 800/851-0291, fax 808/828-2046, www.aloha.net/~hoomaha, hoomaha@aloha.net, is in Kalihiwai on five acres, a few minutes' walk from the bay and Secret Beach. This modern split-level home has four rooms at $65–90 a night, with breakfast included. The Pineapple room, with its round bed and private bath, and the Guava room, with its king bed, private bath and private entrance, have three-night minimums. The smaller two rooms share a bath. All guests have use of the full kitchen and common room with its TV and entertainment equipment, and the hosts will do their best to help you out arranging activities if you desire. Comfortable, contemporary island style.

Along 'Anini Beach Road are numerous vacation rentals. **'Anini Beach Hale,** P.O. Box 419, Kilauea, HI 96754, 808/828-6808 or 877/262-6688, www.yourbeach.com, aloha@yourbeach.com, is a modern two-bedroom, two-bath house, with full kitchen, laundry facilities, and entertainment center. It sleeps four adults and two children. Rates are $225 a night or $1,400 a week, plus a $75 cleaning fee.

For the large family, the 2,000-square-foot **Anini Hale,** P.O. Box 989, Hanalei, HI 96714, 808/826-6167, fax 808/826-6067, www.anini-hale.com, paradise@aninihale.com, will fit the bill for up to eight people with its three bedrooms, two baths, complete kitchen, laundry room, large living and dining rooms, and wraparound lanai. The house goes for $1,400 a week for two people, plus $100 for each additional person. A smaller cottage in the back, also with full amenities, rents for $115 a night or $700 a week.

## Vacation Rental Agencies

Also handling many vacation rentals from Anahola to Ha'ena is **Hanalei North Shore Properties,** 808/826-9622 or 800/488-3336, www.rental-sonkauai.com, hnsp@aloha.net.

Covering pretty much the same ground and offering upscale vacation rentals is **Kauai Vacation Rentals,** 3-3311 Kuhio Hwy., Lihu'e, HI 96766, 808/245-8841 or 800/367-5025, www.KauaiVacationRentals.com, aloha@kvrre.com, which handles many midrange homes in the Anahola to 'Anini Beach area.

**Bali Hai Realty,** 808/826-7244 or 800/404-5200, 5-5088 Kuhio Hwy., Hanalei, HI 96714, www.balihai.com, info@balihai.com., can set you up with an upper-end vacation home in Kilauea, Kalihiwai, or 'Anini.

## Food

Just behind Kong Lung Co. is **Kilauea Bakery and Pau Hana Pizza,** 808/828-2020, open daily 6:30 A.M.–9 P.M. (pizza from 11 A.M. except Sunday). Using all natural ingredients, Kilauea Bakery supplies some of the best restaurants along the north shore. The extensive selection of baked goods is tempting, the breadsticks famous, and occasionally something a bit offbeat, like pumpkin coconut muffins, is for sale. As with the other shops in this little complex, Kilauea Bakery succeeds in offering something special. The pizzas are made with garlic-infused olive oil, whole-milk mozzarella, and homemade sauce on a whole-wheat or sourdough crust. All are gourmet, topped with sautéed mushrooms, feta cheese, grated Parmesan, homemade pesto, sun-dried tomatoes, locally grown peppers, or the like, priced from $7.25 for a small cheese pizza to $27.85 for a 16-inch large with six toppings, or $2.75 by the slice. Specialty pizzas are also available. Enjoy your treat inside, or sit outside under a shade umbrella. Coffee, made by the cup, is served at the espresso bar. Before leaving, have a look at the bulletin board on the wall for alternative healing practitioners, naturopathic doctors, massage therapists, and local jacks and jills of all trades.

Next door to Kong Lung Co. is **Lighthouse Bistro,** 808/828-0480, the town's fine dining restaurant, open for lunch 11 A.M.–2 P.M. daily except Sundays. Choices include tacos, burgers, sandwiches, and the like, mostly in the $6–12 range. Dinners, nightly 5:30–9 P.M., are pricier. Appetizers and antipasti run $8–15. Entrées, $19–27, include stuffed shrimp in phyllo, chicken pesto, seafood linguine, and Cajun barbecue shrimp.

A few steps away is the Kilauea Theater, and beyond that **Kilauea Farmers' Market,** 808/828-1512, a deli/grocery store/lunch counter, open daily 8:30 A.M.–8:30 P.M., until 8 P.M. on Sunday. The deli carries food items and beverages and makes filling homemade soups, garden salads, and sandwiches. Much of the limited selection of produce is organic, and the market has packaged natural foods and a gourmet section with imported cheeses, fine food items, wines, and microbrews.

Look for the kiosk marking **Mango Mama's Cafe** at the Hookui Road turnoff along Rte. 56. Mango Mama's is ripe with papayas, bananas, macadamia nuts, fresh juices, smoothies, sugarcane, honey, and healthful sandwiches; open Mon.–Sat. 7:30 A.M.–6 P.M. Mango Mama has information on north shore activities as well.

After visiting all the sights, you need a rest. The perfect stop is just west of town at **Banana Joe's** fruit stand, *mauka* of the highway (toward the mountains), 808/828-1092, open 9 A.M.–6 P.M. daily. Run by Joe Halasey, his wife, and friends, this little yellow stand offers fresh fruit, smoothies and other drinks, packaged fruit baskets, baked goods with fruit, and locally produced honey. They have more kinds of fruit than you've ever heard of—try something new. After Banana Joe's and Mango Mama's, what's next in the related-to-a-tropical-fruit department? Sister Soursop and Brother Breadfruit?

Two **farmers' markets** are held each week in Kilauea. The county-sponsored market is Thursday at 4:30 P.M. at the Kilauea Neighborhood Center in the middle of town, and the private Saturday market is held along Lighthouse Road 9 A.M.–noon. Each has the usual collection of organic food and flower stands, but some say the Saturday market is bigger and better.

## Shopping and Services

In Kilauea across from the Shell station look for **Shared Blessing Thrift Shop,** open Tuesday and Thursday 2–5 P.M. and Wednesday and Saturday 9:30 A.M.–2:30 P.M. in a vintage plantation building, a good place to pick up secondhand treasures or curios from Kaua'i.

An institution in this area is **Kong Lung Co.,** along Kilauea Rd. at the intersection of Keneke St., 808/828-1822, open daily 10 A.M.–6 P.M., which has been serving the needs of the north shore plantation towns for more than a century. But don't expect bulk rice and pipe fittings. Rather, this is a collection of fine fashions and jewelry, bath products, antiques, art and crafts, and home accessories, much of which has a distinctive Asian flavor. It bills itself as an "exotic gift emporium," and you'll agree. The upstairs section of the store is called **Yin Yin Clothing Exchange** and sells consignment clothing for both men and women, as well as Hawaiian quilts and other quilted pieces.

Kilauea is also home to the **Island Soap and Candle Works,** behind the Kong Lung Co. store, 808/828-1955, www.handmade-soap.com, open Mon.–Sat. 9 A.M.–8 P.M., Sunday 11 A.M.–6 P.M. The owners, a husband and wife team, handpour the soap, perfuming the raw bars with coconut, plumeria, and ginger. They also produce

scented coconut oils, lotions, and bath gels capturing the scents of the islands, and a wide variety of scented candles. Business has been good, and the company has a second shop in Koloa on the south shore, with others on O'ahu and Maui. Island Soap products are available at boutiques throughout Hawaii and can also be purchased by mail: call 800/300-6067 or write 970 Kipuni Way, Kapa'a, HI 96746.

Next to the soap works is a fine art and jewelry shop called the **Lotus Gallery.** This store, along with its sister shop at the Beach House restaurant in Po'ipu, sells expensive and finely crafted items, many from Asia or designed with Asian themes.

The **Kilauea Theater** shows first-run films, including the annual International Film Festival films, and hosts many community events. Call 808/828-0438 for what's showing.

For medical emergencies while on the north shore, stop in at **Hale Le'a Family Medicine Clinic,** on Oka St., 808/828-2885. Next door is the **North Shore Pharmacy,** and a few steps away the **North Shore Clinic,** 808/828-1418.

## Recreation

On a 400-acre property, two miles into the mountains above the highway, is **Silver Falls Ranch,** 808/828-6718, a professional equine organization that treats its horses well, like it does its guests. Two horseback rides are offered: a two-hour Hawaiian Discovery Ride at $78 that takes you into the hills below Mt. Namahana and a three-hour Silver Falls Ride for $105 that includes a stop for lunch and a swim at the pool below a cascade falls. Private rides can be arranged. This is fun for every level of rider, and the rides surround you with wonderful scenery between Kalihiwai and Kamo'okoa Ridges.

# Princeville

Princeville is 9,000 acres of planned luxury overlooking Hanalei Bay. This bluff-top plateau was considered by the ancient Hawaiians as a place of mana and appropriately was the site of various *heiau*. This highland was also a great source of *hala* leaves because a forest of pandanus grew here, and these leaves were important for so many uses to the ancient Hawaiians. When Europeans first surveyed the island, they knew that this point could have strategic importance. In the early 1800s, the Russian Fur Trading Company built Fort Alexander on this headland, one of three forts it constructed on Kaua'i to establish and maintain influence over the independent Kaua'ian King Kaumuali'i. This fort served the company only for a few short months before the newcomers were forced to leave the island. It, and a fort erected in Hanalei below, fell into disrepair, and the stones were carted away for other purposes. All that remains are outlines of walls on the grassy lawn to the front of the Princeville

Hotel, a great place to watch the sunset. Only the stone walls at Fort Elizabeth in Waimea on the south coast of the island remain to hint at the scope of these Russian fortifications.

In the 1800s, the surrounding countryside was a huge sugar and coffee plantation—one of Kaua'i's oldest, established in 1853 by Scotsman R. C. Wyllie. After an official royal vacation to the ranch by Kamehameha IV and Queen Emma in 1860, the name was changed to Princeville in honor of the royal son, Prince Albert. The young heir unfortunately died within two years, and his heartbroken father soon followed. In 1865, Wyllie also died, and the plantation was sold. While coffee never really did well here, sugar continued to be raised and milled in Hanalei. The operation turned to cattle ranching around 1900, and this lasted until 1969 when the land changed hands again.

That year, Consolidated Gas and Oil of Honolulu took these acres and began developing

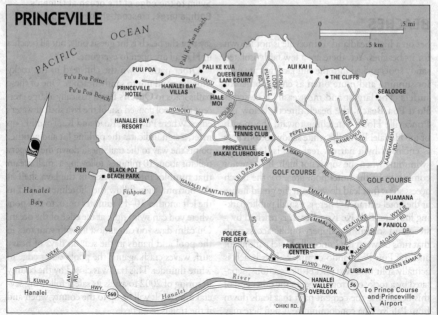

© SANDRA E. BISIGNANI TRUST AND AVALON TRAVEL PUBLISHING, INC.

them into a prime vacation community designed to keep the humdrum world far away. Bought by the Princeville Development Corporation, a subsidiary of Quitex Australia, the hotel went through a major renovation and other development was started. Then in 1990, the Princeville resort was taken over by the Japanese consortium of Suntory, Mitsui, and Nippon Shinpan. Unfortunately, Hurricane 'Iniki struck in 1992, necessitating major repairs to the hotel, condos, homes, and other facilities. The Princeville community now provides everything: accommodations, shopping, dining, a community park, the island's newest public library, golf and tennis facilities, a gas station, banks, and even a fire and police force. First-rate condos are scattered around the property, private luxury homes cluster around the golf links, and the refurbished multitiered Princeville Hotel perches on the hill over the bay. The guests expect to stay put, except for an occasional day-trip. Management and clientele are in league to provide and receive satisfaction. And without even trying, it's just about guaranteed. The community maintains a website at www.princeville.com.

ROBERT NILSEN

Swim to the edge of the ocean at Queen's Bath, a large, crescent-shaped tide pool.

## BEACHES

Set on a high headland, Princeville is not known for its beaches. Yet, there are a few fairly isolated sandy spots tucked into the cliff face that are used for sunning and more often as entry points for surfers. The largest and most easily accessed is **Pu'u Poa Beach,** the beach directly below the Princeville Hotel. Stretching toward the mouth of the Hanalei River, the white sandy bottom here is enclosed by a narrow reef and is decent for swimming when the surf is not high. If you're not coming from the hotel pool area, try the beach access steps that lead down from the guard house at the hotel entrance. There is a small public parking lot here. **Pali Ke Kua Beach** is reached by a steep and sometimes slippery public access path that runs between the Princeville Hotel parking lot and the Puu Poa condo complex. This beach is actually split into two pocket-like sections, separated by a rocky outcrop. To get to the other end of this beach, use the cement path that leads down from Pali Ke Kua condominium. A sign here may

say that the beach is for guests only, but all beaches in Hawaii are open to everyone.

Other paths down the cliff lead to the rocky shoreline and not to sandy beaches. One of these paths leads to **Queen's Bath,** basically a large crescent tide pool gouged out of the lava shelf at water's edge. Where Punahele Road and Kapi'olani Loop meet, a sign indicates the parking lot and another points the way to the trail. Head down the slippery trail for about 10 minutes, following a small stream that tumbles into a crevasse in the lava shelf at the bottom, then follow the shoreline around to the left another 10–15 minutes or so, to this pool where you can swim right at the edge of the ocean. On calm days you can almost lie with your toes in the pool and hands in the sea; on days of heavy surf, waves crash against the pool's outer edge in white thunder. This trail was closed by the county in spring of 2002 to assess its safety following several injuries. It will be up to the county when and if the trail is reopened.

# ACCOMMODATIONS

Virtually all the condos and hotel rooms in Princeville fall into the luxury range. The best deals naturally occur off season (fall), especially if you plan on staying a week or more. Oddly enough, a project like Princeville should make booking one of its many condos an easy matter, but it's sadly lacking on this point. Lack of a centralized organization handling reservations causes the confusion. Each condo building can have half a dozen booking agents, all with different phone numbers and widely differing rates. The units are privately owned, and the owners simply choose one agency or another. If you're going through a travel agent at home, be aware of these discrepancies and insist on the least-expensive rates. A situation that reduces the number of units available is that many of the condos are moving to exclusively time-share programs, while others still offer rental units along with the time-share units, so check out the possibilities.

## Princeville Hotel

The Princeville Hotel, 5520 Ka Haku Rd., Princeville, HI 96722, 808/826-9644 or 800/325-3589, fax 808/826-1166, www.princeville.com, is a dramatic architectural opus, built in four cascading tiers on the extreme point of this rugged peninsula. From its perch, all but 16 of the 252 rooms offer breathtaking views of the frothing azure of Hanalei Bay as it stretches toward the emerald green of Mt. Makana (Bali Hai) down the coast. The other rooms offer panoramic views of Pu'u Poa Marsh, a wildlife wetlands that offers sanctuary to exotic birdlife. This is one of Kaua'i's most opulent hotels, and the only hotel on the north shore. The main lobby offers elegance on a grand scale, with gold-capped Egyptianesque columns, teardrop chandeliers, and a central reflecting pool set in a floor of swirled black and white marble that's studded with Louis XIV chairs and plush couches. Here you'll find the concierge and activities desks. Opposite the front desk is the Living Room, a dignified area serving as library, cocktail lounge, and music room. Choose a plush chair just before sunset and sip a cocktail

as the sun streaks the sky with lasers of light dancing across the endless blue of the wide Pacific. There is entertainment every night: Hawaiian and contemporary music, and weekly sonorous Hawaiian chanting with hula. In addition, an artisans' program with demonstrations of Hawaiian arts and crafts is held daily. This lobby level has a small mini-mall with a cluster of shops, and the grand staircase at the far end leads to the hotel's two fine dining restaurants.

The hotel entrance is on level nine. Taking elevators and walkways to level one deposits you at the swimming pool and poolside Beach Restaurant and Bar, next to which the twice-weekly lu'au is performed. A few steps away is the beach and its activity center. The white-sand beach fronting the hotel is perfect for swimming, and the reef below, alive with tropical fish, is excellent for snorkeling. At dusk, descend to the pool area and immerse yourself in one of the hot tubs to watch the sun melt into the Pacific as you melt into the foaming bubbles.

The Keiki Aloha children's program will look after kids with entertaining excursions and arts and crafts. A free drop-off and pick-up shuttle service is offered anywhere in the Princeville resort area, including the Prince Golf Course clubhouse and the airport. Request a shuttle ride from the bell desk—be sure to ask for the telephone number to call for a return ride. No matter how formal the surroundings may seem, the staff infuse this property with the casual and genuine spirit of Hawaiian *aloha*.

All rooms feature bathrooms with double vanities, terry robes, slippers, and deep immersion tubs, some of which are mini-spas. Bathroom windows are of liquid crystal that can be controlled to change from opaque for privacy to clear so that you can enjoy the view while you soak. These finely decorated rooms in beige or green also feature king beds, refrigerators, remote-control color TVs, safes, ironing boards, and 24-hour room service; suites have an extra large and plush sitting area with dining table. A mountain/garden view room runs $405, partial ocean view and ocean view rooms $490–610, and junior suites are $705; other suites run $1,800–4,500. There is a $75 extra person charge, with a maximum of four to a room. Children under 18 room for free in existing beds. Numerous packages are available.

## Hanalei Bay Resort

Managed by Aston Hotels and Resorts, the Hanalei Bay Resort, 5380 Honoiki Rd., Princeville, HI 96722, 808/826-6522 or 800/827-4427, fax 808/826-6680, www.hanaleibaykauai .com, is a condo resort with some private units. You enter through a spacious open foyer paved with flagstone and face the front desk. To the side is the Happy Talk lounge, done in longhouse style with a palm-frond roof, koa long bar, and magnificent matching koa canoe. From the bar, you have a spectacular panorama of distant Bali Hai dappled by passing clouds and Hanalei Bay, a sheet of foam-fringed azure. Evening brings live music, with everything from jazz to a local slack-key combo. Just as good for views of the bay and the waterfalls on the mountains is the Bali Hai Restaurant. Stepping down the hillside from the front is the resort's free-form pool, complete with one sand edge, a 15-foot waterfall, and whirlpool grotto—all surrounded by landscaping inspired by the area's natural beauty. The cobalt blue tile of the second pool matches the color of the bay beyond. For a swim in the bay, take the beach path down the hill to the water. The resort's 16 buildings are situated along walking paths, and all units have a stupendous view. There is no driving on the property, so you must leave your car in the parking lot at the front and you and your luggage will be shuttled to your unit. The resort has amenities including TV, phone, and air-conditioning, full kitchens in the suites (only refrigerators in the hotel rooms), and laundry facilities. Daily cultural activities are scheduled. Sign up for these at the concierge desk, where other island activities can also be booked. The eight tennis courts here are open to guests and nonguests, and the pro shop arranges clinics and round robins. Single hotel rooms, studios with kitchenettes, and one-bedroom suites in mountain and ocean view categories are available; rates start at $185 for a room, run $215–240 for the studios, and $350–390 per night for the suites. A made-to-order breakfast and two afternoon cocktails daily are complimentary with each suite.

## Condos

There are more than a dozen and a half condominium properties in Princeville. Most of the high-end condos are far into the development near the Princeville Hotel or strung along the cliff edge overlooking the pounding surf. They are out to please and don't skimp on the luxuries. About a third are managed strictly as time-share properties, and several others have blocks of units that are also managed that way. Even in this luxury development there are a few small median-range complexes. Although low-end properties and subsidized housing were supposed to be incorporated into this development, it seems all of those have been shifted down the road to Kilauea. What follows is a sampling of what's available.

Marc Resorts Hawaii manages units in the five properties closest to the Princeville Hotel. Sleek and modernistic, with its curved exterior and step-terrace construction, **Puu Poa** is perhaps the most luxurious. It has spacious two-bedroom, two-bath units with complete kitchens that run $295–345 for up to six people, and guest-use tennis courts and a swimming pool. Next along the cliff is **Pali Ke Kua,** which boasts one of the best restaurants on the north coast. This property is a mix of one- and two-bedroom, garden, ocean-view, and oceanfront units, priced $219–345. Comfortable and well furnished, each unit has cable TV, washer and dryer, and a full kitchen—just right for families. Swim in the pool topside or walk the path down to the gazebo and secluded beach to sunbathe. Snug against this complex is the smaller and newer **Queen Emma Lani Court,** where deluxe one-bedroom units with full kitchens run $289. Across the road, overlooking the golf course, are Hale Moi cottages and Hanalei Bay Villas. Most economical are the **Hale Moi** cottages—four-plexes with pleasing mountain views. Hotel room–like master bedroom units, suites, and one-bedroom units cost $155–219. All except the master bedroom units have kitchens. The more luxurious **Hanalei Bay Villas** perch on stilts like bird cages overlooking the glen and fairway. Running $259–305, all units have two bedrooms, full kitchens, and mountain or bay views. All Marc Resort guests check in at the Pali Ke Kua office.

There is a two-night minimum for each of these properties. For information and reservations, call 800/535-0085.

Set high on the bluff overlooking the Pacific Ocean is **The Cliffs at Princeville,** 808/826-6219 or 800/3678024, www.cliffs-princeville.com. These one-bedroom condo units have two full-size baths, a fully equipped kitchen, and a large living room. Two large lanai, one at each end of the unit, offer both ocean and mountain views. Although all units are individually owned, furnishings are basically of a contemporary style. The bedrooms have king-size beds, and the cushy living-room couches pull out to sleep two more. Units have color TVs, video and stereo systems, compact washers and dryers, irons and ironing boards, small safes for valuables, and daily maid service. Some third-floor units have a loft, and the living-room ceiling slants up to the second floor. While this is largely a time-share property, units are rented when available. One-bedroom units are $200–225, with lofts $250–275; there's a two-night minimum. The property also has a pool with spa, putting green, volleyball court, four tennis courts free to guests, a breezy rec room with TV and reading material, and a laundry room. The activity desk will gladly arrange tours for you, offer suggestions for day-trips, or rent you a bicycle.

The weathered gray Cape Cod-ish **Sealodge** condos have one of the best locations for views along this coast. All individually owned, these units all have full amenities, and most have washers and dryers. Although rates vary a little, expect to pay $110 for a one-bedroom or $135 for a two-bedroom unit with a $50–60 cleaning charge; there may be a three-night minimum stay, and discounted weekly rates are available. Most of the units here are managed by Jack Waring, 800/446-4384; Herb Hubbard, 800/585-6101; and Carol Goodwin, 650/573-0636.

Like the above, the **Alii Kai II** is also on the cliff edge. Contact Oceanfront Realty, 800/222-5541, about rooms.

The **Paniolo,** 808/826-5525, and **Puamana,** 808/826-9768, are lower-end complexes for this development, where you would expect a better deal.

## Vacation Rentals

Handling vacation rentals in Princeville only is **Re/Max,** at the Princeville Center, 808/826-9675 or 877/838-8149, www.real-estate-kauai.com, rek@aloha.net. Most of these properties are high-end condos and homes that rent for $800–2,400 a week.

Also dealing almost exclusively with high-end condo and home properties in Princeville is **Pacific Paradise Properties,** 808/826-6530 or 800/800-3637, www.princeville-vacations.com, kaikona@hawaiian.net.

**Hanalei North Shore Properties,** 808/826-9622 or 800/488-3336, www.rentalsonkauai.com, hnsp@aloha.net, handles about 150 economy to high-end vacation rental homes and condos in Princeville and along the north shore from its office at the Princeville Center. This company can find the right place for you.

Also try **Hanalei Vacations,** 808/826-7288 or 800/487-9833, www.hanalei-vacations.com, rentals@aloha.net, which manages a full range of condos in Princeville and homes and cottages in Ha'ena.

# FOOD
## Fine Dining

Fine dining in Princeville means eating at the hotel restaurants. The **Bali Hai Restaurant,** at the Hanalei Bay Resort, 808/826-6522, enjoys an excellent reputation not only for its food but also for its superb atmosphere and prize-winning view of the sunset through the wraparound windows of this bi-level and informal yet elegant restaurant. Reminiscent of a Polynesian longhouse, with a vaulted thatched roof, it's open daily for breakfast 7–11 a.m., lunch 11:30 A.M.–2 P.M., and dinner 5:30–9 P.M. It's appropriately named; you look out between tall coconut trees, across the spectacular view of Hanalei Bay, and down the coast toward Bali Hai (Mt. Makana), the sentinel of the north coast. The Bali Hai chefs grow their own herbs on the premises and insist on fresh local vegetables, meat, and fish prepared in a mixture of continental and Pacific Rim cuisine. Start your day with chilled fresh fruit or a continental breakfast that includes fresh fruit juices, bakery items, and Kona coffee, or go local with a taro patch breakfast of two fried eggs, Portuguese sausage, poi pancakes, and taro hash browns. Lunchtime brings soups and salads, sandwiches, and an assortment of burgers. For dinner, you can start with appetizers like blackened 'ahi or Bali Hai crab cakes for $7–14.50. Entrée specialties include fresh island fish prepared with a variety of tempting sauces such as shiitake mushroom, chili and peanut satay, and pineapple fruit salsa. Standard but wonderful offerings are linguine with sautéed breast of chicken at $19.50, pan-seared shrimp and scallops for $25.75, and steak Olowalu for $32. For a lighter lunch, $9–12, try the breezy Happy Talk lounge, which also serves *pu pu* 5:30–9 P.M.

The Princeville Hotel is home to three restaurants. The **Cafe Hanalei,** open for breakfast 6:30–11 A.M., lunch 11 A.M.–2:30 P.M., dinner 5:30–9:30 P.M., offers indoor or outdoor seating in a casual setting. It's continental with a heavy dose of Oriental. Breakfast at Cafe Hanalei is either continental for $16.50 or full buffet for $22.95; à la carte and Japanese breakfasts are also available. The continental breakfast is much more than you might expect, and the full breakfast buffet is complete with an omelette station and an array of savory breakfast meats. On Sunday, breakfast stops early and gives way to Sunday brunch 10 A.M.–2 P.M. for $35 or $39 with champagne. Lunch may be a reasonably priced Japanese noodle salad with fish cake, Thai coconut curry with chicken and vegetables, a Caesar salad, or any of a number of gourmet sandwiches, wraps, or seafood dishes. Dinner entrées are barbecued lamb chop, Hawaiian bouillabaisse, grilled *ahi,* or breast of chicken, mostly in the $27–34 range. Finish with desserts like *liliko'i* (passion fruit) cheesecake, crème brûlée, or chocolate torte with minted truffle cream, all delicious and prepared daily. On Friday evening, a full seafood buffet is offered for $45. Just off the main lobby, the **Living Room** is a perfect place for a formal afternoon tea, a sunset cocktail, or evening *pu pu* and sushi bar. Beverage service runs until midnight, and there is soft musical entertainment through the mid-evening hours.

Also down a flight of steps from the main lobby, **La Cascata** offers tremendous views of the island's inland waterfalls and the setting sun. Open nightly for dinner 6–10 P.M., this is the hotel's most formal and upscale restaurant, the finest on the north shore and one of the premier dining experiences on the island. Designed after a famous restaurant in Positano, Italy, it features elegant decor, including hand-painted terra cotta floors, columns and arches, inspiring trompe l'oeil scenery murals, and formally set tables. After antipasti and insalata, the Italian menu features such items as sautéed lobster, shrimp, scallops, and clams over linguine pasta, pork tenderloin with candied red cabbage, fontina-stuffed breast of chicken, pesto-roasted pink snapper, and veal piccata with lemon and capers. Special attention is paid to the sauces, and a fine glass or bottle of wine from the well-stocked cellar can be chosen to accompany any entrée. Meals are perfectly finished with desserts like classic tiramisu, mango cheesecake, macadamia nut pie, or with a cup of espresso or cappuccino, or a glass of fine port. A dinner for two with wine can easily run $150.

For light meals 11 A.M.–5:30 P.M., try the hotel's casual, pavilion-type **The Beach Restaurant and Bar,** where you can order snacks, salads, or sandwiches, or swim up to the pool's water bar until sunset for a mid-lap mai tai. Try the crispy taco salad with black beans and vegetables, spicy buffalo wings, Black Angus burger, or fresh island fish sandwich, all priced $7.95–14.95. A children's menu helps keep prices down for the little ones. On Monday and Thursday from 6 P.M., the courtyard and accompanying stage area are transformed into the Pa'ina 'O Hanalei lu'au and Polynesian show.

The **Beamreach Restaurant,** 808/826-6143, in a freestanding building on the grounds of the Pali Ke Kua condo complex, is a casual fine dining restaurant where the chef offers a mix of island-style and classic American dishes. Open nightly for dinner 5:30–9 P.M.—reservations are suggested. Reduced-price Sunset Specials run 5:30–6:30 P.M. nightly. The bilevel dining room, subdued in shades of tan and brown, is lightly appointed with hanging baskets, throw nets, frescoes depicting Hawaiian mythology, and a display case holding ancient artifacts. A very good sign is

KAUA'I

that all soups, salad dressings, and rolls are made on the premises, and fresh organic greens and vegetables are used as much as possible. Stimulate your palate with appetizers like *poki,* sautéed mushrooms, or a pot of fresh steamed clams. Move on to entrées, priced $17–26, like South Sea pineapple shrimp, filet mignon, smoked pork tenderloin, macadamia nut chicken with tropical sauce, or fresh fish steamed, sautéed, broiled, or blackened. Your sweet tooth will be happy with desserts such as Tahitian Lime Pie, tropical fruit sherbet, or a rum, caramel, or chocolate sundae. The Beamreach also has a full-service bar stocked with fine wine, a good selection of beer, and house specialty tropical drinks.

## Princeville Center and Beyond

At the Princeville Center you'll find **Chuck's Steak House,** 808/826-6211, open for lunch Mon.–Fri. 11:30 A.M.–2:30 P.M., nightly for dinner 6–9:30 P.M. Chuck's has a very loyal clientele that comes not only for the juicy steaks but for the fresh fish as well. With an open-beamed ceiling, a choice of booth or table inside or on the lanai, and a few saddles and barrels placed here and there for effect, you might call Chuck's "casual country." The lunch menu has salads and *pu pu* such as "loaded fries," which are covered with bacon, cheese, and sour cream, and Caesar salad. Burgers and sandwiches go from a simple burger to a barbecue prime rib sandwich. Dinner is delicious, with the fresh catch charbroiled or sautéed for $22.95, shrimp Hanalei for $26.95, juicy prime rib for $19.95–27.95 depending on the cut, barbecued baby-back pork ribs for $23.50, teriyaki chicken breast at $18.95, and an assortment of combination dinners priced $23.95–29.95. A senior and children's menu relieves the bottom-line total. Chuck's has a full-service bar separate from the dining area, 11:30 A.M.–10:30 P.M., with music Thursday through Saturday. Chuck's is a good choice for a family-style restaurant offering hearty portions, but it's not inexpensive.

Also at the Princeville Center, you can get a reasonably inexpensive brew and burger, or something more sophisticated like garlic shrimp, beef tips, fish salad, and crab legs, at the **Paradise Bar and Grill.** Having the same menu for lunch and dinner means that an evening meal here is quite affordable. This is a friendly and easy-going place that locals frequent and send guests to. For that midday treat, **Lappert's Ice Cream** will gladly fill a cone for you.

The **Princeville Restaurant and Bar,** at the Prince Golf Course clubhouse, 808/826-5050, serves breakfast 8–11 A.M., lunch 11 A.M.–3 P.M., and cocktails 11 A.M.–6 P.M. The breakfast menu includes the usuals, like eggs, waffles, omelettes, and fruit plates. Salads, sandwiches (with names like Birdie, Double Eagle, and Bogey), and sides are served for lunch. In addition, the Sunday brunch and Monday night Japanese cuisine are still as popular as ever. This is a perfect spot in well-appointed surroundings for a day on the links.

# ENTERTAINMENT

There is little in the way of evening entertainment in Princeville; however, the following are definitely worth checking out.

The **Happy Talk Lounge,** with an outrigger canoe suspended from its ceiling, mixes its fantastic views of Hanalei Bay with exotic drinks, wine by the glass, and frothy beers for a night of relaxation and entertainment. A limited menu is served in the evening after the 4–6:30 P.M. happy hour with free *pu pu.* The bar swings with live entertainment Mon.–Sat. 6:30–9:30 P.M.—everything from contemporary music to Hawaiian ballads performed by slack-key artists. A very special performance that shouldn't be missed is the free jazz jam every Sunday 3–7 P.M. Local musical talent is fantastic, but to make things even better, top-name musicians who happen to be on the island are frequently invited to join in. If you love jazz, you can't find a more stunning venue than the Happy Talk.

The **Living Room,** in the main lobby of the Princeville Hotel, is a dignified venue of couches and stuffed chairs for a variety of island-theme entertainment, including Hawaiian music that's open to everyone 7–11 P.M. nightly. In addition, from 6:30 P.M. on Tues., Thurs., and Sun., there is a special Hawaiian ceremony of chanting and

KAUA'I

hula. In keeping with the grand setting, a formal afternoon tea is served 3–5 P.M., *pu pu* and desserts are available 5–10 P.M., and cocktails can be ordered until midnight.

Don't forget **Amelia's,** upstairs at the old Princeville Airport, open weekdays noon–8 P.M. and Fri.–Sun. 8:30 P.M.–1:30 A.M., with live music on the weekends. This friendly neighborhood-style pub serves sandwiches, hot dogs, chili, and nachos and has four TVs for live satellite sports.

**Pa'ina 'O Hanalei** beachside lu'au, performed Monday and Thursday at 6 P.M. near the swimming pool at the Princeville Hotel, is the only lu'au in this resort community. While not given the highest marks, the food is great and the island music and dance performance are rousing. Many show members also perform on Wednesday for the more casual Tahiti Nui lu'au down in Hanalei. Adult tickets are $68, seniors $55, and children 6–12 $33. Call 808/826-2788 for reservations.

The **Hawaiian Art Museum** at the Princeville Center on the second floor next to Foodland is open by appointment only; call 808/827-8383. It is home to Aloha International, www.huna.org, founded by Serge King and dedicated to the practice and philosophy of *huna.* The shelves and counters of this small collection hold artifacts like poi pounders and bowls, a remarkable carved statue of a god doing a handstand, a model village alive with dancers and warriors, descriptions of different canoes, *makini* masks with distinctive owl-like eyes, ferocious-looking *palau* war clubs, and Hawaiian musical instruments. On Sunday morning 10 A.M.–noon there is a session on Hawaiian philosophy and culture by Serge King, an internationally known author and lecturer proficient in his knowledge of *huna* and ancient Hawaiian arts and crafts. Throughout the week groups on hula, meditation, and healing meet. All activities are open to the public.

## SHOPPING

Aside from the shops at the hotels, the shopping in Princeville is clustered in the **Princeville Center,** with most shops open daily 8 A.M.–6 P.M.

Since Princeville is a self-contained community, many of these are practical shops: bank, hardware store, gas station, real-estate offices, post office, restaurants, and a medical clinic. **Foodland,** open daily 6 A.M.–11 P.M., is important because it offers the cheapest food on the north shore. Before it was built, the local people would drive to Kapa'a to shop; now they come here.

Some of the shops here include **Lappert's Ice Cream,** for a quick pick-me-up; **J Ms Jewels** for a quick pick-*her*-up; the **Kauai Kite and Hobby Company,** a bursting crayon box filled with stuffed animals, toys, and, of course, kites; **Hanalei Photo Company,** a full-service photography store offering developing, cameras, photo supplies, and gadgets; and **SanDudes Kauai,** a clothing boutique for men and women with sandals, sun hats, waterproof watches, perfume, ladies' dresses, jewelry, T-shirts, and beach bags.

## RECREATION

Those addicted to striking hard, dimpled white balls or fuzzy soft ones have come to the right spot. In Princeville, golf and tennis are the royal couple. However, they are not the only sporting options available. Horseback riding and hiking are becoming popular, and for those less inclined to the physical, a helicopter ride is better suited. To help keep yourself in condition or to ease your tired muscles after a hard day of exercise, pay a visit to the health spa.

### Golf

The **Princeville Makai Golf Course,** 808/826-5070, offers 27 holes of magnificent golf designed by Robert Trent Jones Jr. in 1971. This course, rated the #6 golf course in Hawaii by *Golf Digest* in 1998, has hosted the 26th annual World Cup in 1978, the LPGA Women's Kemper Open 1986–89, and the 1990 first Itoman LPGA World Match Play Championship. Radiating from the central clubhouse are three nine-hole, par-36 courses you can use in any combination. They include the Woods, Lake, and Ocean courses—the names highlighting the special focus of each. The cliff-top Ocean 7 is a challenging hole (you must shoot over a deep ravine), and the Lake 9 sets two lakes in your way, but the most difficult hole is Woods 6, which features a long dogleg into the trade winds. The pro shop will set you up with a tee time, and the snack shop offers reasonably priced sandwiches, burgers, and drinks. Greens fees are $125, with many discounts and packages available.

Opened in 1987, the 18-hole **Prince Course,** 808/826-5070, on the bluff above 'Anini Beach, also welcomes the public. It's off Hwy. 56 about one mile east of the Princeville Resort entrance and has its own clubhouse. For this course, accuracy and control are much more important than power and distance. Many expert golfers judge the Prince extremely difficult. With a course rating of 75.3 and slope of 145, it's one of the most challenging in Hawaii and is continually rated one of the top courses in the state and one of the top 50 in the country. Greens fees are $175. Fitting into its natural environment, thick tropical woods, deep ravines, and streams are among the obstacles. The driving range is open during daylight hours. The clubhouse has an extensive pro shop and houses the Princeville Health Club and Spa, and, on the lower level, the Princeville Restaurant and Bar.

The **Princeville Health Club and Spa,** at the Prince Course clubhouse, 808/826-5030, keeps you healthy with aerobics classes, free weights, a complete set of conditioning machines, a lap pool, hot tub, steam room, sauna, massage by appointment, and skin and body treatments. Nutrition programs can be set up with the staff, who also have information about running courses. One such **jogging path** runs between this clubhouse and the Princeville main entrance gate—about one mile. To enhance these offerings spectacular views out the plate glass windows look toward waterfall-draped mountains and over the rolling fairways to the Pacific Ocean. There's nothing like fabulous surroundings to add incentive to your aerobic exercise. The daily admission fee is $20; weekly and monthly rates are also available. Hours: Mon.–Fri. 6:30 A.M.–8 P.M., Saturday 8 A.M.–8 P.M., and Sunday 8 A.M.–6 P.M.

## Tennis

You can charge the net on six professional plexi-pave tennis courts at the **Princeville Tennis Club,** 808/826-3620. Open daily 8 A.M.–6 P.M. just down the rise from the Makai Golf Course clubhouse, the club offers a pro shop, private lessons by appointment, and racquet and ball machine rental. Court fees for a 90-minute reserved time are $15 ($12 for Princeville guests); weekly, monthly, quarterly, and annual memberships also available.

The **Hanalei Bay Resort Tennis Club,** 808/826-6522, has eight courts open to the public; court fee is $6 per person. Men's and women's clinics and round robins are scheduled, and equipment is rented. Call to reserve a court. Several condos in Princeville also have tennis courts for guests only.

## Princeville Ranch

**Princeville Ranch Stables,** 808/826-6777, a half mile east of Princeville Center, is open Mon.–Saturday. You can rent a mount here for group rides that take you throughout the ranch's fascinating countryside. Prices are $65, $110, and $120 for the scenic countryside ride, waterfall picnic ride, and participatory "cattle ride." Private rides can also be arranged. The Hanalei Stampede, Kaua'i's largest rodeo, is held at the stables in early August.

The ranch also offers **day hikes** on its property. The hiking office is across the highway from the stable office. Hikes include a waterfall excursion for $74, a combination hike and kayak trip for $89, and the Hidden Hanalei hike with views of Hanalei and the bay for $59. All hikes run about three hours; drinking water and all equipment are provided. No hikes on Sunday. Call 808/826-7669 to reserve a spot.

## Helicopter Tours

The only helicopter company currently operating at the Princeville Airport is **Heli USA,** 808/826-6591. Flying twin-engine machines, the company offers 35-, 45- and 60-minute circle-island flights for $99–179.

## SERVICES

**Princeville Service Center,** 808/826-7331, off the courtyard and the back of the Princeville Center, has postal, shipping, and packaging supplies and services, email access, and copy machines.

Akamai Computer's **Internet café,** 808/826-1042, on the second floor at the front of the center, is open Mon.–Fri. 10 A.M.–5 P.M.

The new **Princeville Library** is at the Princeville entrance. Open Tuesday, Thursday, Friday, and Saturday 9 A.M.–5 P.M., Wednesday noon–8 P.M.; closed Sunday and Monday. Its elegant design with arched ceiling and chandelier fits well in this resort community.

Both **Bank of Hawaii** and **First Hawaiian Bank** have branch offices with ATM machines at the Princeville shopping center.

The last **gas station** on the north shore is Princeville Chevron, open Mon.–Sat. 6 A.M.–10 P.M., Sunday until 9 P.M. If your gauge is low, make sure to tank up if you're driving back down the coast.

**Avis,** 808/826-9773, maintains a small rental car booth at the Princeville Airport.

After years of no service, the Princeville Airport has once again been opened to passenger air flights, with connections to Honolulu and Kapalua West Maui airports on North Shore Airways. For information on current flight schedules, call 808/826-7499 or 866/867-4673, or check online at www.northshoreairways.com.

# Hanalei

If Puff the Magic Dragon had resided in the sunshine of Hanalei instead of the mists of Hanalee, Little Jackie Paper would still be hangin' around. You know you're entering a magic land the minute you drop down from the heights and cross the Hanalei River. The narrow, one-lane bridge is like a gateway to the enchanted coast, forcing you to slow down and take stock of where you are.

Hanalei (Crescent Bay) compacts a lot into a little space. You're in and out of the town in two blinks, but you'll find plenty of shops, some terrific restaurants, the beach, ocean activities, and historical sites. You also get two superlatives for the price of one: the epitome of a laid-back north shore village, and a truly magnificent bay. In fact, if one were forced to choose the most beautiful bay in all of Hawaii, Hanalei would definitely be among the finalists.

Mile markers on Hwy. 56 going west are renumbered from one at Princeville. It is 10 miles from there to the end of the road at Ke'e Beach. On occasion, during periods of heavy rain when water threatens to swallow the bridge, it will be closed to traffic and the road blocked by gates. That means no cars in or out until the water recedes!

## SIGHTS

The sights around Hanalei are exactly that—beautiful sweeping vistas of Hanalei Valley and the sea, especially at sunset. People come just for the light show and are never disappointed. When you proceed past the Princeville turnoff, keep your eyes peeled for the Hanalei Valley **scenic overlook.** Don't miss it! Drifting into the distance is the pastel living impressionism of Hanalei Valley, most dramatic in late afternoon, when soft shadows from deeply slanting sun rays create depth in this quilt of fields. Down the center, the liquid silver Hanalei River flows until it meets the sea, where the valley broadens into a wide flat fan. Along its banks, impossible shades of green vibrate as the valley steps back for almost nine miles, all cradled in the protective arms of 3,500-foot *pali*. Controlled by rains, waterfalls either tumble over the *pali* like lace curtains billowing in a gentle wind or with the blasting power of a fire hose. Local wisdom says, "When you can count 17 waterfalls, it's time to get out of Hanalei." The valley has always been one of the most accommodating places to live in all of Hawaii, and its abundance was ever-blessed by the old gods. Madame Pele even sent a thunderbolt to split a boulder so that the Hawaiians

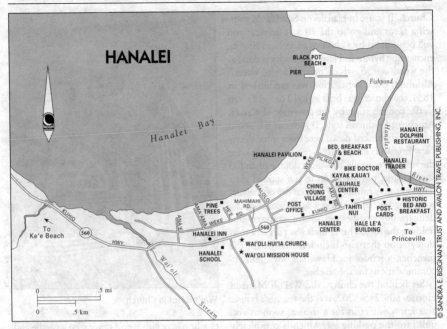

# HANALEI

BLACK POT BEACH
PIER
Fishpond
Hanalei Bay
HANALEI DOLPHIN RESTAURANT
HANALEI PAVILION
BED, BREAKFAST & BEACH
HANALEI TRADER
BIKE DOCTOR
KAYAK KAUA'I
KAUHALE CENTER
CHING YOUNG VILLAGE
PINE TREES
MAHIMAHI RD.
POST OFFICE
HISTORIC BED AND BREAKFAST
TAHITI NUI
POST-CARDS
To Ke'e Beach
KUHIO
560
HWY.
HANALEI INN
HANALEI CENTER
HALE LE'A BUILDING
To Princeville
HANALEI SCHOOL
WAI'OLI HUI'IA CHURCH
WAI'OLI MISSION HOUSE
Wai'oli Stream

could run an irrigation ditch through its center to their fields.

Unlike the Princeville bluff, Hanalei was an area for the common man. In the old days, Hanalei produced taro, and deep in the valley the outlines of the ancient fields can still be discerned. The bay produced great quantities of fish, and others were raised in ponds, one of which still remains between the town and a twist in the river. Then the white people came and planted coffee that failed and sugarcane that petered out, and finally raised cattle that over-grazed the land. During these times, Hanalei had to *import* poi from the Kalalau Valley to the west. Later, when Chinese plantation laborers moved in, the valley was terraced again, but this time the wet fields were given to rice. This crop proved profitable for many years and was still grown as late as the 1930s. Then, amazingly, the valley began to slowly revert back to taro patches.

In 1972, 917 acres of the Hanalei Valley were designated **Hanalei National Wildlife Refuge;** the endangered native water birds Hawaiian coot, black-necked stilt, *koloa* duck, and gallinule, as well as several migrant species, loved it and reclaimed their ancient nesting grounds. Today, the large, green, heart-shaped leaves of taro carpet the valley, and the abundant crop supplies about half of Hawaii's poi. You can go into Hanalei Valley; however, you're not permitted in the designated wildlife areas except to fish or hike along the river. Never disturb any nesting birds. Look below to where the one-lane bridge crosses the river. Just there, 'Ohiki Road branches inland. Drive along it slowly to view the simple and quiet homesteads, the historic Haraguchi Rice Mill, nesting birds, wildflowers, and terraced fields of this enchanted land.

In addition, and more recently, the **Hanalei River** itself has been designated an American heritage river, one of only 14 in the nation to be so noted and the only one whose total length is so designated. Federal money will help protect its unique character and enhance its preservation.

## Wai'oli Mission House Museum

As you leave town, look to your left to see the deep green clapboard and shingle **Wai'oli Hui'ia**

**Church.** If you're in Hanalei on Sunday, do yourself a favor and go to the 10 A.M. service; you will be uplifted by a choir of rich voices singing enchanting hymns in Hawaiian. Justice is done to the word *wai'oli,* which means "joyful water." Although the congregation was established in 1834, the church was built in 1912 on land given to the congregation by the governor of Kaua'i. American Gothic in style, it looks as if it could have been plunked down here from some sleepy New England community—except, perhaps, for the steeple's typically Hawaiian double pitch hip roof. Inside, pay attention to the stained glass windows that mimic the rich colors of the surrounding sea, land, and sky, and appreciate the delicate but sturdy open-beam supports upholding the roof. This church was part of a mission station that also included a home for the preacher, a school for Hawaiian boys, and accommodations for the teacher.

Set behind the church, the **Wai'oli Mission House,** 808/245-3202, was the teacher's house. You know you're in for a treat as soon as you pull into the parking lot, which is completely surrounded by trees, creeping vines, ferns, and even papaya. Walk over stepping-stones through a garden with the jagged mountains framing a classical American homestead; the acreage was also a self-sufficient farm where the resident teacher and family raised chickens and cattle. Most mission homes are New England–style, and this one is, too, inside. But outside, it seems somehow different. It was built by Rev. William P. Alexander, who arrived with his wife, Mary Ann, in 1834 by double-hulled canoe from Waimea. The home's second occupants moved in in 1837, and in 1846, Abner and Lucy Wilcox arrived and took up residence. They lived here until 1865, the year they both passed away on a trip to New England. This home became synonymous with the Wilcox family. Indeed, it was owned and occupied by the family until very recently. It was George, the son of Abner and Lucy, who founded Grove Farm on the south side in Lihu'e. His niece, Mabel, created the nonprofit organization that operates both the Wai'oli Mission House and the Grove Farm Homestead.

You enter the parlor, where Lucy Wilcox

Wai'oli Hui'ia Church

taught native girls who'd never seen a needle and thread to sew. In the background, an old clock ticks. Paintings of the Wilcoxes line the walls, and Abner's books line the shelves. Abner, in addition to being a missionary, was a doctor, teacher, public official, and veterinarian. His preserved letters show that he was a very serious man, not given to humor. He and Lucy didn't want to come to Wai'oli at first, but they learned to love the place. He worried about his sons and about being poor. He even wrote letters to the king urging that Hawaiian be retained as the first language, with English as the second.

During the time that this was a mission household, eight boys were raised here—four born in the main bedroom. Behind it is a nursery, the only room that has had a major change; a closet was built and an indoor bathroom installed there in 1921. Upstairs is a guest bedroom that the Wilcoxes dubbed the "room of the traveling prophet" because it was invariably occupied by visiting missionaries. It was also used by Abner Wilcox as a study, and the books in the room are the original primers printed on O'ahu.

The house has been added to several times and

is surprisingly spacious. Around the home are artifacts, dishes, knickknacks, and a butter churn from the last century. Lucy Wilcox churned butter, which she shipped to Honolulu in buckets and which brought in some good money. Most of the furniture is donated period pieces; only a few were actually used by the Wilcoxes. From an upstairs window, the view has remained unchanged from the last century: Hanalei Bay, beautifully serene and timeless. The Wai'oli Mission House is open Tuesday, Thursday, and Saturday 9 A.M.–3 P.M., and admission is free! At the end of the tour, there is a container for donations; please be generous.

## BEACHES

Since the days of the migrating Polynesians, Hanalei Bay has been known as one of the Pacific's most perfect anchorages. Used as one of Kaua'i's three main ports until very recently, it's still an occasional port of call for world-class yachts. They start arriving in mid-May, making the most of the easy entrance and sandy bottom, and stay throughout the summer. They leave by October, when even this inviting bay becomes rough, with occasional 30-foot waves. The Hanalei Pier was constructed in 1912 to transport rice from this fertile valley but was discontinued as a commercial port of call with the decline of that commodity. It has, however, continued to serve boaters and is still a favorite of fishermen. When you drive to the bay, the section under the trees between the pier and the river is called **Black Pot.** It received this name during an earlier time, when the people of Hanalei would greet the yachties with island *aloha,* which, of course, included food. A fire was always going with a large black pot hanging over it, into which everyone contributed and then shared in the meal. Across the road and upriver a few hundred yards is **Hanalei Canoe Club.** This small local club has produced a number of winning canoe teams in statewide competitions, oftentimes appearing against much larger clubs.

The sweeping crescent bay is gorgeous—nearly two miles of narrow beach that sweeps out gently to a sandy bottom. The Hanalei River and three smaller streams empty into it, and all around it's protected by embracing mountains. A long pier slices into it, and two reefs front the bay: Queen to the left and King to the right. The bay provides excellent sailing, surfing, and swimming—mostly in the summer when the water can be as smooth as a lake. The swimming is good near the river and at the west end, but rip currents can appear anywhere, even around the pier area, so be careful. The best surf rolls in at the outside reef below Pu'u Poa Point on the east side of the bay, but it's definitely recommended only for expert surfers who often come to catch the bigger waves of winter. Beginners should try the middle of the bay during summer, when the surf is smaller and gentler. The county maintains three parks on the bay: **Black Pot,** at the Hanalei River mouth, **Hanalei Pavilion,** in the middle of the bay, and **Pine Trees,** farther on. All three have picnic areas, grills, restrooms, and showers, although these amenities are sometimes vandalized and unusable, and Hanalei Pavilion and Pine Trees have lifeguards. You'll find beach access and parking for Pine Trees at the end of He'e, Ama'ama, and Ana'e roads, and more parking for beach access down the way at Waipa. Camping is permitted at Black Pot only on Friday, Saturday, and holidays. A small *kaukau* wagon selling plate lunches is often near the river here; local fishermen launch their boats in the bay and are often amenable to selling their catch.

## ACCOMMODATIONS

There are no hotels in Hanalei, only a handful of bed and breakfasts, one small motel-like inn, and plenty of vacation rental homes. Many of the rental homes, which range from economy to sumptuous, are right on the beach, while more are farther along the coast toward the end of the road. Wherever you stay, however, you're never far from the beach and always surrounded by exquisite scenery.

You can almost still smell the sweet incense that permeates the **Historic Bed and Breakfast,** 5-5067 Kuhio Hwy., P.O. Box 1684, Hanalei, HI 96714, 808/826-4622, www.historicbnb.com, historicbnb@hotmail.com. Housed in Kaua'i's oldest Buddhist Temple, the simple but elegant structure built in 1901 served the Japanese community until 1985, when it began to fall into disrepair. Neglected and deteriorating, the temple was saved by a consortium of local business people, who moved it from its original location in Lihu'e. It now has the distinction of being listed on both the national and state historic registers. This painstaking and extensive effort refurbished much of the original structure, including the lustrous hardwood floor, polished over the decades by the stockinged tread of devout parishioners. This B&B is owned and operated by Kelly Sato, who welcomes you to three bright and airy rooms cooled by ceiling fans. Decorated with Oriental-style hardwood furniture and exuding the character of the East, the three downstairs rooms are separated by shoji screens. You are free to relax in the comfortable common area—part of which serves as a dining room for breakfast—or to stroll outdoors to a small garden, perfect for an evening cup of tea. The shared indoor bathroom has a deep Japanese-style *ofuro* tub where you can soak away to your heart's content, or use the outdoor shower for a more natural experience. Rooms are priced $80 single or double, $15 for an additional person, with a discount for a stay of longer than seven days. Two nights minimum, no children under age nine, and no credit card payments. Breakfast is included; upon request and with 24-hour notice, a traditional Japanese breakfast can be prepared. Historic Bed and Breakfast is only a five-minute walk from the downtown area or the beach.

**Bed, Breakfast, and Beach,** P.O. Box 748, Hanalei, HI 96714, 808/826-6111, www.bestofhawaii.com/hanalei, hanaleibay@aol.com, owned by Carolyn Barnes, is a neo-classic trilevel plantation-style home in a quiet residential area only a minute's walk from the beach. It gives you a strong feeling that you are part of the community. Upstairs offers a wide, covered lanai, perfect for catching the breeze or listening to the soft patter of a morning shower while eating breakfast. On the upper levels you'll find plenty of windows from which to enjoy a postcard view of the surrounding mountains. The common area, a casual lounging parlor, is cool and inviting with smooth parquet floors, an open-beamed ceiling,

and knotty-pine paneling. The decor throughout is a mixture of classic Hawaiian and tasteful New England antique. Nooks and crannies are filled with objets d'art and plenty of reading material. From the common area, a staircase ascends to the Bali Hai Suite, a 700-square-foot unit that occupies the entire top floor. Off the central area are the Pualani Suite and Country Cedar Room—smaller, but alive, like a living floral arrangement with pastel blooms from ceiling to bedspread. Bed, Breakfast, and Beach is an excellent choice of accommodation for relaxation, a feeling of homeyness, and extremely good value. Rates are $80–135; children are welcome except in the Bali Hai Suite. If you're looking for a bit more privacy, ask about **Tutu's Cottage,** a small two-bedroom, one bath plantation-style house just a bit closer to downtown Hanalei. This cottage is rented by the week, $950 for a couple, plus $100 each for a third or fourth person. The cottage has all amenities, such as ceiling fans, TV, and telephone, and it has a full kitchen, so you have the freedom to fix your own meals.

The moderately priced **Hanalei Inn,** P.O. Box 1373, tel./fax 808/826-9333, Hanalei, HI 96714, www.hanaleiinn.com, is on the west side of town across from the school. It's tucked in among flowering bushes and trees, so it's not real obvious from the road. With only five studio apartments, it's a quiet place. Each unit has a living/bedroom area with queen-size bed, an efficiency kitchen sufficient to make light meals (one unit has no kitchen), a full bath, and a coin-operated washer and dryer to the rear of the overgrown pavilion. Room rates are $75 for the rooms with kitchens and $65 for the unit with no kitchen. For the budget conscious, a no-frills room with bed and bath runs $40. In addition, for larger groups, a house by Pine Trees runs $95 for one bedroom or about $300 for the whole house, which can sleep up to 10 in its three bedrooms and loft. No credit cards. Not exceptional in any way, nor with any particular character, it still offers some of the least expensive beds in town.

## Vacation Rental Agencies

With its office along the highway toward the west end of Hanalei, **Harrington's Paradise**

**Properties,** 808/826-9655 or 888/826-9655, chisholm@gte.net, offers many upscale vacation rentals in town and along the north shore.

**Na Pali Properties, Inc.,** at the Ching Young Village, 808/826-7272 or 800/715-7273, www.napaliprop.com, nal@aloha.net, has everything from $500-a-week cottages to $5,600-a-week homes on the beach.

**Hanalei North Shore Properties,** in the Princeville Shopping Center, 808/826-9622 or 800/488-3336, www.rentalsonkauai.com, hnsp@aloha.net, handles many vacation rentals in Hanalei as well as along the entire north shore from Anahola to Ha'ena.

**Century 21 All Islands—Kilauea,** 808/828-1234 or 800/828-1442, www.kauai-vacations-realty.com, can match you with a rental home anywhere along the north coast. This agency generally does bookings into individual homes, but it handles a few condo units as well.

**Kauai Vacation Rentals,** 3-3311 Kuhio Hwy., Lihu'e, HI 96766, 808/245-8841 or 800/367-5025, www.KauaiVacationRentals.com, aloha @kvrre.com, also has numerous rentals mostly in the medium to expensive range all the way to the end of the road.

Handling upper-end vacation homes along the entire north shore area, **Bali Hai Realty** can be contacted for information at 808/826-7244 or 800/404-5200, 5-5088 Kuhio Hwy., Hanalei, HI 96714, www.balihai.com, info@balihai.com.

## FOOD

Hanalei has a number of eating institutions, ranging from excellent restaurants to *kaukau* wagons. The food is great at any time of day, but those in the know time their meals to coincide with sunset. They watch the free show and then go for a great dinner.

### Inexpensive

Cubbyhole small, one of the few early morning places in town is **Hanalei Wake-Up Cafe,** 808/826-5551, open daily 6–11:30 A.M. The cheery help, the smell of freshly brewed coffee, and the good home cookin' should help start your day off on the right foot. With plastic chairs

and pictures on the walls, there is nothing high-class here, just good food.

In a freestanding building in the Hanalei Center follow the aroma of fresh brewed coffee to **Java Kai,** 808/826-6717, open daily 6:30 A.M.–6 P.M., where you can revitalize with a cup of espresso, cappuccino, latte, café au lait, or an old-fashioned hot chocolate. If you're in the mood for something else, try a flavored Italian soda or smoothie. Java Kai serves a limited breakfast and lunch menu that includes waffles, sandwiches, and quiche; you can eat inside or out on the lanai. Smaller items—all made on the premises—include muffins and cheesecake, or you might like to bring home a pound of bulk coffee. Occupying a window in the same building is **Shave Ice Paradise,** open 11:30 A.M.–5:30 P.M. Choose from a multitude of flavors of traditional shave ice, including coconut and papaya, with fruit cocktail and adzuki beans thrown in for good measure. There's ice cream and a signature drink called a Summer Breeze, somewhat like an Orange Julius with a special twist. Servers scoop the ice cream and make the shave ice as if they were doing it for family and friends. Your only problem is trying to lick faster than these hefty babies can melt.

Another quick stop for shave ice, smoothie, and juice is the truck stand in front of Kayak Kauai near the entrance of town.

**Hanalei Mixed Plate,** 808/826-7888, in a freestanding building in the Ching Young Village, serves up plate lunches of rice with one, two, or three entrées ($5.95–7.95) that might include shoyu ginger chicken, *kalua* pork and cabbage, and vegetable stir-fry. Hearty sandwiches ($6.95–10.95) of sautéed mahimahi, marinated and grilled teriyaki chicken, and the like are also on the menu, as are salads, flame-broiled (beef, buffalo, garden, or tempeh) burgers and fries, and hot dogs. Hanalei Mixed Plate is basically a walk-up counter with outdoor bar stool seating where prices are reasonable, servings generous, and the music free.

In the Hale Le'a building, next to Kai Kane, **Tropical Taco,** 808/527-8226, serves up tacos, burritos, and other quick Mexican fare for under $7.50.

**Bubba Burger,** 808/826-7839, open daily

10:30 A.M.–8 P.M., is still doing what it's always done: serving up double-fisted burgers, individually made, at great prices. It's mostly a window restaurant, but there is seating on the lanai, with a few tables inside. Bubba's burgers range in price $2.75–5.75, with other offerings on the menu like Italian sausage or a fish burger, and a Hubba Bubba—rice, a burger patty, and hot dog, all smothered with chili. Bubba's burgers come with mustard, relish, and onions; anything else you want on it is extra. Try side orders like chili fries or Caesar salad, all light on the wallet but not so light on the waistline.

In the Ching Young Village, **Pizza Hanalei,** 808/826-9494, is open daily 11 A.M.–9 P.M. Made with thin, white, or whole-wheat crust, these pizzas run $10.50 for plain cheese to $37.90 for the Lizzy Special. There is pizza by the slice ($2.75–3.15) 11 A.M.–4 P.M. Green salads, garlic bread, spinach lasagna, and pizzaritos (pizza filling rolled up in a pizza shell like a burrito) are also on the menu. Pizza Hanalei has garnered a good reputation.

## Moderate

The **Hanalei Gourmet,** in the old schoolhouse at the Hanalei Center, 808/826-2524, open daily 8 A.M.–10:30 P.M. for deli items, lunch, and dinner, is a born-again, one-stop, nouveau cuisine deli, semi-gourmet food vendor, and good-time bar. To top it off, it's friendly, the food is exceptionally good, the prices are right, and there's even live nightly entertainment. The restaurant is split into two sections; to the right is the deli, with cases filled with lunch meats, cheeses, salads, and smoked fish, while to the left is the dining area/bar. From the deli, you can also order a picnic lunch to go, side salads, plenty of baked goods, and even a fine bottle of wine. In the restaurant, ceiling fans keep you cool, while blackboards, once used to announce hideous homework assignments, now herald the daily specials. Behind the bar, windows through which kids once stared amid daydreams of summer now open to frame green-silhouetted mountains. Original wood floors, white walls bearing local artworks and hanging plants, two big-screen TVs for sports enthusiasts, and a wide veranda with a few tables

for dining alfresco complete the restaurant. Lunch sandwiches from $6–9 are huge wedges. Dinners are served 5:30–9:30 P.M. and feature specialty pastas, fresh fish, and ginger chicken. Most salad and grill items are under $9, and dinner entrées are under $20. The Hanalei Gourmet is the perfect spot for a meal or a social drink.

Brazilian food in Hanalei? Well, yes! Head for the rear of the Hanalei Center to **Neide's,** 808/826-1851, for Brazilian and Mexican food. It's open for lunch 11:30 A.M.–2 P.M. and dinner from 5 P.M. You can order such favorites as *muqueca,* a dish of fresh fish with coconut sauce, shrimp, and cilantro; *ensopado,* which is baked chicken and vegetables; or *bife acebolado,* an onion-smothered beef steak. A handful of Mexican standbys round out the reasonably priced menu.

At the first building on the right, flanking the bank of the Hanalei River as you enter town, look for a hanging dolphin sign marking the **Hanalei Dolphin Restaurant,** 808/826-6113, open daily 11 A.M.–10 P.M. The interior is casual, with an open-beamed ceiling, corrugated roof, shutters that hinge open to the garden, trophy fish, hanging glass floats, and ships' lanterns. Lunch is mostly salads, sandwiches, and sides. Dinner appetizers include ceviche at $6 and stuffed mushrooms for $8. Seafood, mainly from the owners' fish market around back, includes fresh catch at market price, teriyaki shrimp for $26, and calamari for $20. Fish, the specialty, is your best option, charbroiled or blackened, but Hawaiian chicken for $18, New York steak at $26, and other items are also on the menu. All entrées are served with family-style salads, pasta, steak fries or rice, and hot homemade bread. There's a full bar for tropical cocktails. Open for years, the Dolphin serves consistently good but not memorable food.

**Zelo's,** 808/826-9700, established in Princeville for seven years, moved to Hanalei in late 1995 after the hurricane. It's open daily 11 A.M.–9:30 P.M. with happy hour 3:30–5:30 P.M. and sometimes music on weekends. The interior of this indoor/outdoor restaurant is distinctive, with a long bamboo bar covered with a corrugated roof supported by old beams and tree trunks, *lau hala* matting on the walls, and ceiling fans rotating above. The lunch menu offers salads ranging from a petite to the Chinese chicken salad. Sandwiches, including a Philadelphia steak sandwich and turkey and cheese, plus a full range of burgers with all the fixings—including teriyaki, pesto, and a Cajun fish burger—are priced $7–10. Dinner brings a menu of items like beer-battered fish and chips at $14 or macadamia nut-crusted *ono* for $23. Other pasta, meat, and fish dishes run mostly in the $18–25 range. The atmosphere is pleasant, the staff friendly, and the food flavorful.

Upstairs in Ching Young Village, serving sushi, sashimi, rice rolls, and other Asian-inspired dishes, is **Sushi Blues,** 808/826-9701, open daily 6–10 P.M. Special rolls and sushi run $3.95–11.95, while entrées, mostly under $22, include such fine offerings as linguine and scallops, hibachi shrimp scampi, and grilled kiwi teriyaki chicken. Beverages include a full selection of beers, sake, wine, and tropical drinks, and there's live music on the weekends. Sit at the sushi bar and watch the magic being done or at one of the window tables overlooking main street Hanalei. Sushi Blues has a lively atmosphere and is perhaps the most happening place in town.

A great place to write home from is the covered veranda of the 100-year-old plantation home that was once the Hanalei Museum. The owners of **Postcards,** 808/826-1191, a gourmet natural food restaurant, have refurbished the building to a condition as close to the original as possible, and today it is listed on the national register. Enjoy breakfast here 8–11 A.M. (until noon on Sunday) with a steaming cup of cappuccino and a homemade muffin, bowl of granola, eggs, or bagels, and watch north shore life go by. Dinners are served daily 6–9 P.M., inside or out on the front and side porches. Tables are covered with old postcards under glass, and the restaurant is always full. Postcards is an upbeat, health-conscious vegetarian restaurant that prides itself on using organic ingredients and making every dish and sauce from scratch. While the menu changes periodically, vegetables, pasta, and seafood are the mainstays—no red meat or poultry is served. Dishes are simple but hearty, and while not inexpensive (mostly $16–21), the quality is excellent. Save room for dessert; they're all made here in the kitchen. Postcards is wheelchair-friendly,

and smokers are completely prohibited from lighting up—even outside. Reservations recommended. Postcards is an excellent choice.

**Bamboo Bamboo,** in the Hanalei Center, 808/826-1177, is a casually refined restaurant with seating inside and out on the lanai. Offering lunch and dinner daily, this open-air restaurant has a full bar and periodic weekend music. Crispy Thai spring rolls and fried calamari with papaya cocktail sauce appear as appetizers, and light dinners include fish and chips and Hanalei taro burgers. More substantial entrées, $18–25, include seafood pasta and potato-crusted mahimahi. For something quicker and easier, try fresh-baked pizza on Friday, Saturday, and Sunday evenings.

## Other Food Options

The **Hanalei Dolphin Fish Market,** around back behind the Hanalei Dolphin restaurant, is open daily 11 A.M.–8 P.M., selling fresh, locally caught fish, some ready-to-cook prepared items, sauces, and dressings. It can—with a day's notice—create a luscious sashimi and sushi platter.

**Hanalei Health and Natural Foods,** 808/826-6990, is open daily 8 A.M.–8 P.M. at the Ching Young Village. This small and tightly packed store sells bulk foods, fresh fruits and vegetables, baked breads, freshly squeezed juices, deli foods, and sandwiches, as well as books and vitamins. There is also a good selection of cosmetics, incense, candles, and massage oils. If you're into natural foods and healthful living, stop in, look around, and chat.

Every Tuesday 2–4 P.M., pick up some farmfresh fruit and vegetables from the Hawaiian Farmers of Hanalei **farmers' market,** a half mile west of town, in Waipa, on the road to Ha'ena. Look for the sign along the road *mauka.*

## ENTERTAINMENT

Hanalei is a quiet town, but there are a few options for at least some entertainment.

The **Hanalei Gourmet** offers light-hearted live music every night; Wednesday and weekend evenings bring music to **Sushi Blues and Grill,** upstairs in the Ching Young Village; and **Tahiti Nui** often has someone playing on Friday and

Saturday evenings from about 8 P.M. You've got to stop at the Tahiti Nui, if just to look around and have a cool drink. The owner, Louise Marston, a real Tahitian although her name doesn't sound like it, is dedicated to creating a friendly family atmosphere, and she succeeds admirably. The bar, open from noon to midnight, is the center of action; happy hour is 4–6 P.M. daily. Old-timers drop in to "talk story," and someone is always willing to sing and play a Hawaiian tune. The mai tai are fabulous. Just sit out on the porch, kick back, and sip away.

Perhaps the most down-home and local lu'au in the state is put on right here in Hanalei. **Tahiti Nui** presents a full buffet and Polynesian show every Wednesday 5–8 P.M. (unless there are not enough customers to make it a go). This is a family-run operation that's been going since 1963. The food is real Hawaiian and the show is no glitzy extravaganza or slick production. There's singing, dancing, and good cheer all around—a perfect time to mingle with the local people. This lu'au is very casual Kaua'ian, and everybody has a good time; adults $52, $30 teens, and $20 for children 3–11. Call 808/826-6277 for reservations.

## SHOPPING

The Hanalei Trader is the first building as you enter town. **Ola's,** 808/826-6937, open daily late morning to late evening, is an "American" craft store with eclectic assortment of items from many of the 50 states, like glass work from Oregon, ceramics from California, wood products from Hawaii, and jewelry from New York. Other items are wildflower honey, bath salts, greeting cards, hairbrushes, wooden boxes, leather purses, and pottery.

**Overboard Clothing** for casual islandwear for men and women, and **Black Pearl,** which sells jewelry made from those dark orbs from Tahiti, are also in the Hanalei Trader.

In the next streetfront building down **Kai Kane,** 808/826-5594, a.k.a. The Water Man, not only catches your eye but also helps keep the sun out of it with a display of hats for both men and women. It also sells a large selection of alohawear and casual beachwear. Glass cases hold watches and sunglasses, while two outrigger canoes hang overhead and paddles line the walls. Although Kai Kane is primarily a clothing shop, it does double duty as a surf shop filled with surfboards and a wide selection of wet suits, leashes, and shorts.

A small shop just near Tahiti Nui is **Kiki's Bikini's,** where ladies might find that just-right swimsuit. Around the side in the Kauhale Center is the **Royal Hawaiian Hammocks** store, selling that perfect item of comfortable relaxation in its many manifestations.

The **Ching Young Village Shopping Center** in the center of town includes a small shopping center plus nearby freestanding buildings. Among its attractions is a **Big Save Supermarket,** open daily 7 A.M.–9 P.M., the only food retailer from here to the end of the road. At **Hanalei Video and Music,** you can pick up some entertainment for the evening, and the **Artists Gallery of Kaua'i** sells art and crafts items done mostly on the island. Check **Pedal and Paddle** for sports equipment rental and clothing. Ching Young also offers a few other casual clothing stores and public restrooms. For a unique collection of gifts, crafts, clothing, and imports, stop at the eclectic, upscale shop **On the Road to Hanalei,** across the road from the old Hanalei school. Next door is **Evolve Love,** something like a co-op of area artists, where you'll find musings in paint, fine woodwork, artistic jewelry, and exquisite hand-painted silk cloth.

The **Hanalei Center,** located *mauka* of the highway across the street from Ching Young Village, has an excellent assortment of shops and boutiques. The original portion of this center is in the converted school building, but another section is in a newer structure to the west. Between them sit several freestanding buildings. Some of the many shops are **Rainbow Ducks,** specializing in children's wear; **Hula Beach** for fashions; and **Sand People,** which offers casual island clothing for men and women, gifts, and jewelry. **Yellowfish Trading Company,** a fascinating store neatly stuffed from floor to ceiling with Hawaiiana, antiques, collectibles, hula-doll lamps, classic Hawaiian aloha shirts, kuchi-kuchi dolls, costume and silver jewelry, floral day bags, candles, swords, antique hats, Matson Steamship Line posters, and koa carvings and incidentals is a veritable feast for the eyes for those interested in Hawaiiana. Here, too, is **Whalers General Store,** open daily 8 A.M.–8 P.M., selling groceries, liquor, sundries, and souvenirs. The old Hanalei School section of the center houses several additional shops, such as the **Hanalei Surf Company,** with boards, water gear, and clothing; and **Tropical Tantrum,** a small Hawaii chain that designs its own fabrics, which are then turned into original clothing in Indonesia. At Tropical Tantrum, women can rage in the most vibrant colors of purple, blue, red, green, and yellow, transforming themselves into walking rainforests. The most distinctive shop, **Kahn Galleries,** 808/826-6677, specializes in original artworks and limited edition prints created by some of the finest artists Hawaii has to offer.

# RECREATION

Hanalei is alive with outdoor activities. The following is merely a quick list of what's available.

Until August 1998 motorized boats could use Hanalei Bay for commercial purposes, many starting right from the river mouth. After that date, by governor's decree, only nonmotorized uses of the bay were allowed, to the consternation of many in the business sector. However, the reduced activity in the bay has made it a much quieter place, less busy, and more enjoyable for the nonmotorized recreational users.

The company to see for a kayaking adventure up the Hanalei River or, during summer, along the Na Pali Coast, is **Kayak Kaua'i,** 808/826-9844 or 800/437-3507. Rental rates per day are $26 for a single river kayak and $50 for a double; multiday and weekly rates are also available. Lessons, guide service, shuttle support, and storage can be arranged. Other water equipment—snorkel gear, surfboards, boogie boards—is also rented, as is camping gear and bikes. Mountain bikes run $20 a day while beach cruisers are $15; backpacks go for $8 a day, two-person tents $8, sleeping bags $6, and pads $4. If you want to

buy, Kayak Kaua'i is one of the few places on the island that sells good quality camping and backpacking equipment.

Also doing guided trips into the bay and up the river is **Kayak Hanalei,** 808/826-1881. Trips run 3–5 hours, including lunch, and cost $56–70 per person.

For catamaran adventures along the Na Pali Coast from Hanalei, try **Na Pali Catamarans,** 808/826-6853. This company offers three-hour tours with lunch that run $90–125.

The **Hanalei Surf Co.,** in the Hanalei Center, 808/826-9000, is a water-sports shop that rents and sells snorkeling equipment, boogie boards, surfboards, and other water equipment. Rental rates for surfboards run $15 per day or $65 a week, boogie boards are $5 or $7 with fins, and snorkel equipment is $4–5 or $17–20 a week; three- and five-day rates are also available on all rentals. Hanalei Surf Co. has a "rent to buy" option on its snorkel equipment—ask. The store is also stocked with a good selection of shirts, shorts, thongs, bathing suits, incidental bags, sunglasses, sunblock, and dresses.

**Pedal and Paddle,** in the Ching Young Village, 808/826-9069, open daily 9 A.M.–6 P.M., rents snorkel gear, boogie boards, kayaks, mountain bikes, and some camping gear. Prices are: snorkel gear $5 a day, $20 per week; boogie boards $5/$20; cruiser bikes $10/$40; ordinary mountain bikes $20/$100, two-person dome tents $12/$35; backpacks $5/$20; light sleeping bags $3/$10; and sleeping pads $3/$10. A rental day begins the hour you rent and ends at 5 P.M. the following day. Pedal and Paddle does not sell bikes or kayaks but has snorkel and camping gear, camp food, hats, and sandals for sale.

John Sargent's **Bike Doctor,** in Hanalei, 808/826-7799, open Tues.–Fri. 9 A.M.–5 P.M., Saturday 10 A.M.–4 P.M., does bike repair and is stocked with everything for the casual and serious cyclist. John is intimately familiar with roads and trails all over the island, has information on group rides and races, and is happy to give advice on touring. The Bike Doctor is the only shop in town that rents high-quality mountain bikes for the serious off-road rider, and these babies run $25 a day or $100 a week.

## North Coast Trail

The only hiking trail of length in the Hanalei area is the **Powerline Trail,** which runs across the island to the Keahua Arboretum above Wailua. Longer, more gradual, and overall less spectacular than the south side, this route gives you plenty of mountain views with only a peek here and there into the valley. Hot and dry, there is virtually no shade, yet the trail passes two small bogs on the way. Near the pass masterful views take in the Hanalei region and the core of the island's central mass, plus you have a view of both the north and south shores. Unless you have a car waiting at the arboretum, just hike up as far as you like—or the weather permits—and return to the north trailhead. About two hours from the trailhead, the pass is a good place to turn around. To reach the trailhead, turn at the Princeville Stables. Continue uphill about two miles until the pavement gives out. Proceed a bit farther until you reach an area to park near a green water tank. This trail is often used by mountain bikers. As there are sections that are virtually impassable, 4WD vehicles are not recommended.

## INFORMATION AND SERVICES

The **post office** in Hanalei is next to Ching Young Village.

**Kauai Adventure Activities,** 808/826-9998 or 877/266-8400, along the highway in Hanalei next to the post office, is the best place to stop for activity information and bookings for anywhere on the island. This is a full-service company that can put you not only on the water in a boat or kayak, but also on the back of a horse, up in a helicopter, at a lu'au, or into north shore accommodations. Kauai Adventure Activities offers the highest quality service, so your experience is a rewarding one.

Across from Zelo's is **Hanalei Town Activities and Information Center,** 808/826-7792, where you can collect information about the area, book an activity, or rent snorkel equipment or a boogie board.

For **Internet service** in Hanalei, see Bali Hai Photo shop, 808/826-9181.

**North Shore Cab,** 808/639-7829, and **Taxi Hanalei,** 808/639-1188, both do pick-up and delivery service on the north shore. The ordinary fare from Hanalei to Princeville runs about $12, to the end of the road at Ke'e Beach is $15, and to the Lihu'e Airport about $62. **Kauai North Shore Limousine,** 808/826-6189, offers luxury limo service with its stretch limos or Lincoln Towncars. You must pre-arrange this luxury service, and the driver will be waiting, resplendent in his casual chauffeur's uniform. Fares must be negotiated; two-hour minimum.

## Road's End

Past Hanalei you have six miles of pure magic until the road ends at Ke'e Beach. To thrill you further and make your ride even more enjoyable, you'll find historical sites; natural wonders; an oceanside resort; the *heiau* where hula was born, overlooking a lovely beach; and the trailhead to Kaua'i's premier hike, the Kalalau Trail. The Hanalei Valley is the largest along this coast; nearly as large but more serpentine is the Wainiha Valley. Between these lie the deep and green Wai'oli, Waipa, and Lumaha'i Valleys. At mile marker 7 is the tiny village of Wainiha, and beyond that the small community of Ha'ena, not a town per se, more a state of mind. The Wainiha Valley is said to have been inhabited long ago by the race of dwarfish Mu people. While many legends revolve around these mythical pre-Hawaiians, an official census from the late 1700s mentions 65 Mu living in Wainiha Valley. As you drive along, you cross one-lane bridges, travel through tunnels of trees, and pass little beaches and bays, one after another, invariably with small streams flowing into them. Try not to get jaded peering at "just another gorgeous north shore beach."

## SIGHTS

**Lumaha'i Beach** is a femme fatale, lovely to look at but treacherous. This hauntingly beautiful beach (whose name translates as "Twist of Fingers") is what dreams are made of: white sand curving perfectly at the bottom of a dark lava cliff with tropical jungle in the background. The riptides here are fierce even with the reef, and the water should never be entered except in very calm conditions during the summer. Look for a vista point after mile marker 5, just beyond the west end of Hanalei Bay. Cars invariably park here. It's a sharp curve, so make sure to pull completely off the road or the police may ticket you. An extensive grove of hala trees appears just as you set off down a steep and often muddy footpath leading down to the east end of the beach. The best, easiest, and safest place to park is among the ironwood trees at the west end of the beach near the bridge that crosses the Lumaha'i River; an emergency phone is across the road from this parking area. From here you can walk to the east end if you want seclusion.

About six-tenths of a mile past the YMCA, a short dead-end road turns off the highway and a trail through the trees leads to Makua Beach, commonly known as **Tunnels.** It's superb for snorkeling and scuba diving, perhaps the best on the island, with a host of underwater caves off to the left as you face the sea. Look for the small fish inside the reef; for the bigger fish (experienced snorkelers and divers only) you must go

into the sea caves or over the edge of the awesome drop-off. Both surfing and sailboarding are great, and so is the swimming if the sea is calm. Watch out for boats that come inside the reef. Off to the right and down a bit is a nude beach. There are no facilities here and parking is very limited along the roadway, but it's less than half a mile east down the beach from Ha'ena Beach Park.

**Ha'ena Beach County Park,** just a mile before road's end, is a large, flat, field-like area, where you stake out your own camping site. For your convenience, the county provides tables, a pavilion, grills, showers, and camping (permit required). The sand on this long crescent beach is rather coarse, and the swimming is good only when the sea is gentle, but in summertime a reef offshore is great for snorkeling. The cold stream running through the park is always good for a dip.

Across the road is the broad and low **Maniniholo dry cave.** Notice the gorgeous grotto of trees, and the jungle wild with vines. You walk in and it feels airy, like it would be nice living quarters, but it has never been suggested that the cave was used for permanent habitation. Luckily, even with all the visitors going in and out, it hasn't been trashed.

**Limahuli Botanical Garden,** 808/826-1053, in the last valley before the beginning of the Kalalau Trail, is a half mile past mile marker 9. Open Tues.–Fri. and again on Sunday 9:30 A.M.–4 P.M., the garden showcases tropical plants both ancient and modern. Presided over by the towering Mt. Makana, this garden is part of

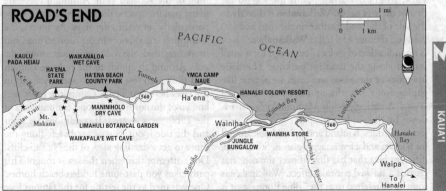

ROAD'S END

PACIFIC OCEAN

KAULU PAOA HEIAU
WAIKANALOA WET CAVE
HA'ENA STATE PARK
HA'ENA BEACH COUNTY PARK
Tunnels
YMCA CAMP NAUE
HANALEI COLONY RESORT
Ke'e Beach
Kalalau Trail
Mt. Makana
MANINIHOLO DRY CAVE
LIMAHULI BOTANICAL GARDEN
WAIKAPALA'E WET CAVE
Ha'ena
560
Wainiha
Wainiha Bay
Wainiha River
Lumaha'i Beach
Lumaha'i River
JUNGLE BUNGALOW
WAINIHA STORE
560
Hanalei Bay
Waipa
Waipa
To Hanalei

0   1 mi
0   1 km

MOON

KAUA'I

the National Tropical Botanical Gardens; the 14 original acres were donated by Juliet Rice Wichman in 1976, later expanded to 17 acres, and an additional 985-acre preserve in the valley above was donated by her grandson, Chipper Wichman, the garden's director, in 1994. There are both self-guided ($10) and guided ($15) walking tours of the gardens; guided tours are 10 A.M. and 2 P.M. only—by reservation. Wear good shoes; umbrellas are provided. Tours start at the visitors center, which has a fine collection of books on Hawaiian flora and other subjects. As you walk through this enchanted area you' pass taro patches growing behind stone terraces believed to be at least 900 years old, plants introduced to Hawaii by the early Polynesians, living specimens of endangered native Hawaiian species, and post-contact tropicals; your guide treats you to legends of the valley (or you can read them in your brochure) as you follow the three-quarter-mile loop trail. Only this garden with its trail is open to the public; the vast interior of the preserve is accessible only to biologists and botanists doing research. For those who love the living beauty of plants and flowers, a trip to Limahuli Botanical Garden is well worth the effort.

Just beyond the botanical garden driveway, the road dips and crosses a small stream. On the mountain side of the road is a shallow pool known as the "cool pond," where some come for a refreshing freshwater dip after their saltwater bath in the ocean.

Up the road, just after entering **Ha'ena State Park,** an HVB Warrior points the way to the first of the **wet caves. Waikanaloa** is directly to the side of the road. Farther up the road and 150 yards up the side of a hill is **Waikapala'e.** There is no indication of its location except for a small pulloff along the road for parking. The wide openings of these two wet caves are almost like gaping frogs' mouths, and the water is liquid crystal. Amazingly, while Maniniholo dry cave is down by the road, Waikapala'e wet cave, subject to the tides, is inland and uphill! Look around for *ti* leaves and a few scraggly guavas. Straight up, different lava that has flowed over the eons has created a stacked pancake effect. Waikapala'e is sometimes referred to as the "Blue Room" as it is

## ROAD ETIQUETTE

The narrow north shore highway beyond Hanalei, with its many one-lane bridges, requires that you drive with a certain degree of caution and road etiquette. First of all, slow down and enjoy the scenery. This road is full of curves, so drive defensively. If you need to stop, pull all the way off the roadway so other cars can get by safely.

White lines on the road and yield signs will alert you to where you must stop at one-lane bridges to let traffic from the other direction pass. There is not always a good line of sight at these bridges, so be cautious. If two cars approach a bridge at the same time, let the other car go first. If you are in a line of cars that is crossing the bridge when others are waiting to cross from the other direction, and if you are in the first half dozen of this line of cars, cross. Otherwise, stop and let the oncoming traffic cross before you proceed across the bridge. Above all, always be polite, smile, and give the other cars that wait the *shaka* sign.

said to take on an otherworldly blue hue from the back wall looking out toward the opening. If azure could bleed, it might be this color. The 66-acre Ha'ena State Park encompasses not only these caves but also Ke'e Beach and the trailhead for the Kalalau Trail.

The road ends at **Ke'e Beach,** a popular spot with restrooms and showers. Here is the beginning of the Kalalau Trail. Although there are many parking spaces, the lot begins to fill early, particularly on warm, dry days. As always, the swimming is good only in the summertime, but snorkeling inside the wide reef is great most of the year. Around the point to the right you might find the beach less crowded, and it was up in the trees here that Taylor Camp, the most well known of the north coast hippie communities of the 1960s, was located. If conditions are right and the tide is out, you can walk left along the shore to get a dazzling view of the Na Pali cliffs. Don't attempt this when the sea is rough! This path takes you past some hidden beach homes. One was used as the setting for the famous love rendezvous in the miniseries *The Thorn Birds*. Past the homes, another path takes you up the hill to the ancient sites of **Kaulu Paoa Heiau** and **Kaulu O Laka Heiau,** birthplace of the hula, where the goddess Laka bestowed to the Hawaiians this wonderful expression of dance and story. The views from up here are remarkable and worth the short climb, especially during winter, when the sun drops close to the cliffs and backlights Lehua Island, then sinks into its molten reflection. In the past, after novitiates had graduated from the hula *heiau,* they had to jump into the sea below, swimming around to Ke'e Beach as a sign of dedication. Tourists aren't required to perform this act.

## ACCOMMODATIONS AND FOOD

Over a small white bridge in the village of **Wainiha** (Angry Water) is the tiny **Wainiha Store,** 808/826-6251, open daily 9:30 A.M.–7 P.M., where you can pick up a few supplies and sundries. People from around the area come to the store to post flyers if they have rooms to rent. This way, you can still get a shack on the beach or in among the banana trees. Attached to the store is a sandwich window and a gift shop.

Aside from those few places listed below, rental homes—and there are dozens along this coast—can be arranged through any of the vacation rental agencies listed above in the Hanalei and Princeville sections.

If you're looking for a real quiet, secluded place to stay, you'll find it at the **Jungle Bungalow,** on the island in the Wainiha River, P.O. Box 1379, Hanalei, HI 96714, 808/826-9999 or 888/886-4969, www.junglebungalow.com, info@junglebungalow.com. Surrounded by thick tropical greenery and the sound of the rushing river, this two-story cottage offers a real tropical hideaway. Downstairs is a complete kitchen and living room, upstairs is the master bedroom and toilet. Outside, the lanai fronts a large private lawn, and around the side, surrounded by greenery for your privacy, is a clawfoot tub and shower. The bungalow goes for $135 for a couple, $10 each additional person up to five, and a one-

time $90 cleaning fee. A few yards up the driveway is the **Jungle Cabana,** www.junglecabana.com, a smaller single-level unit that sleeps two in a queen bed with a similar bathing setup outside. It holds a living/sleeping area, kitchen, and toilet; the cabana goes for $110 a night. The main house of the property is also a vacation rental unit; www.kauai-jungle-paradise.com, info@kauai-jungle-paradise.com. Raised off the ground for a view of the trees, this two-level house has three bedrooms, two baths, a full kitchen, dining room, and living room, as well as an outdoor shower and hot tub. This house runs $195 a night for up to four and $15 per each additional person up to eight, or $1300 a week with $75 per week for each of the additional person. A $120 out-cleaning fee is added and there is a $300 refundable damage deposit. All units require a four-night minimum stay.

Nearby, the **River Estate,** 808/826-5118 or 800/484-6030, fax 808/826-4616, P.O. Box 169, Hanalei, HI 96714, offers three self-contained homes that can be rented separately or together for a group of up to 20. With a five-night minimum and a cleaning fee, these homes run $175–200 a night.

---

## FIRE SHOWER

After Hanalei Bay, the most notable feature along the north coast is the towering spire of Mount Makana. Rising directly above Ke'e Beach at the end of the road, Mount Makana is popularly known as Bali Hai—made famous in the movie *South Pacific.* This peak was one of the two spots on the island—the other being the ridge end above Nu'alolo Beach just down the coast to the west—where, for special occasions, fire throwers would toss burning branches of *papala* or *hau* trees off the cliff at night in a Fourth of July–style spectacular similar to the old firefalls at Yosemite National Park. Updrafts of wind would carry these burning pieces of wood out to sea in a shower of red sparks. Crowds would gather along the shore and in canoes on the water to watch, and those whose firebrands went the farthest would be accorded great acclaim.

Next up, look for signs to the five-acre, 48-unit **Hanalei Colony Resort,** P.O. Box 206, Hanalei, HI 96714, 808/826-6235 or 800/628-3004, fax 808/826-9893, www.hcr.com, hcr@aloha.net—literally the last resort and the only resort on the beach along the north coast. You can rent very comfortable, spacious, two-bedroom condos here, each with a full kitchen, shower/tub, and lanai. The brown board-and-batten buildings blend into the surroundings. Now past 30 years old, this property is still well looked after but not luxurious, and the ocean-front units have some of the most spectacular views anywhere along this coast. The resort has a swimming pool and hot tub, barbecue grills, coin-operated washers and dryers, Hawaiiana classes, and twice-weekly maid service, but no TVs or phones in the rooms. The beach in front of the resort is great for a stroll at sunset, but be very careful swimming during winter months or periods of high surf. Based on single or double occupancy, units cost from $185 for a garden view to $300 for a premium oceanfront, $25–30 less during low season and $20 more during Christmas season, with the seventh night free for a weeklong stay.

There is a five-night minimum from the beginning of May through the beginning of September and again over the Christmas and New Year holiday season. Car-rental packages are available if arranged before arriving on Kaua'i.

Just past Hanalei Colony Resort, between mile markers 7 and 8 on the highway, look for the entrance to **YMCA Camp Naue.** Here, several buildings are filled with bunks with a separate toilet area and cooking facilities. The camp caters to large groups but is open to single travelers on a first-come, first-served basis for the staggering sum of $12 per night. The cost for tent camping is $10 per person. The bunkhouses lie under beach-side trees, and campers stay in the yard. All guests must provide their own sleeping bags or bedding. Hot showers are available to all, but the cooking facilities are only for groups. On the property is a pavilion with grills, but you must provide your own wood or bring a camp stove. As with most YMCAs, there are many rules to be followed. You can get full information from YMCA headquarters in Lihu'e or by writing YMCA of Kauai, P.O. Box 1786, Lihu'e, HI 96766, 808/246-9090, or 808/826-6419 in Ha'ena.

## Na Pali Coast

The Na Pali Coast, from Ke'e Beach on the north shore to Polihale Beach on the west end, is less than 15 miles long—but, oh, what miles! You must speak in superlatives to describe it. Here the seacliffs rise sharply out of the water to nearly 4,000 feet in height. Of the numerous valleys, the largest and most majestic is Kalalau Valley, the site of ancient habitation, archaeological remains, and many myths and legends. Deep cuts in this rock face have created numerous narrower chasms, including several hanging valleys, and these hold evidence of other inhabited sites. Rain is abundant along this coast, and streams course through each lush valley, creating many refreshing waterfalls; a few that fall directly into the sea were used by Hawaiians like faucets, to fill freshwater containers. While all sorts of huge trees (native and introduced), bushes, flowers, and vines fill the large Kalalau Valley and other valley floors, many of the steep valley walls are covered in ferns. A handful of sea caves, one with a collapsed ceiling, puncture this rampart at water level, and several beaches dot the coast. Fishing is good, particularly inside the fringe reefs at Ke'e, Nu'alolo Kai, and Miloli'i. The Na Pali Coast is home to a large community of spinner dolphins that often play in the wake of passing boats, and gracefully slow green sea turtles are spotted periodically. During winter months, whales migrate from the cold waters of the north Pacific to bask in the warmer Hawaiian waters to birth, nurse, and raise their young.

### Accessibility

No roads enter the Na Pali Coast area, so there is no option that way. However, it is not inaccessible. It can be approached by land, air, and water. Sea kayaks can be rented for a trip down the coast—during calm summer weather only. Nonmotorized

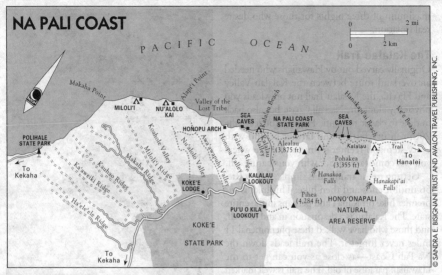

NA PALI COAST

PACIFIC OCEAN

0 — 2 mi
0 — 2 km

Makaha Point

POLIHALE STATE PARK

To Kekaha

MILOLI'I

NU'ALOLO KAI

'Alapi'i Point

Valley of the Lost Tribe

HONOPU ARCH

SEA CAVES

Kalalau Beach

NA PALI COAST STATE PARK

Hanakapi'ai Beach

SEA CAVES

Ke'e Beach

Koaie Valley

Koaie Ridge

Nu'alolo Valley

Honopu Valley

Kalepa Ridge

Awaawapuhi Valley

Alealau (3,875 ft)

Kalalau

Pohakea (3,355 ft)

Trail

To Hanalei

Kauhao Valley

Miloli'i Valley

Makaha Ridge

Ka'aweiki Ridge

Ha'ele'ele Ridge

Miloli'i Ridge

KOKE'E LODGE

KALALAU LOOKOUT

Hanakoa Falls

Hanakapi'ai Falls

To Kekaha

PU'U O KILA LOOKOUT

Pihea (4,284 ft)

HONO'ONAPALI NATURAL AREA RESERVE

KOKE'E STATE PARK

To Kekaha

and quiet, this is undoubtedly as close an experience to early Hawaiian outrigger canoe travel along the coast as most can get these days. Boat tours from the west end and south shore regularly make trips to this section of the island for a close-up look at the cliffs and valleys from the water—a truly awe-inspiring sight. Helicopters fly overhead, offering riders an unparalleled view of the entire coastline and dipping into valleys along the way, bringing you nose to nose with these green chasms. Even though there are flight restrictions, helicopter tours along this coast, as in other areas of the island, are not without critics, as they intrude on the serenity of an otherwise solitary and tranquil place. The Na Pali can also be seen by looking down from the Kalalau Valley overlooks and from several trails that traverse the razor ridges above the coast's deep valleys. Perhaps the best way to get up-close and personal with the Na Pali Coast is to hike in on the Kalalau Trail, which starts at road's end at Ke'e Beach.

## Na Pali Coast State Park

The Kalalau Valley and the trail leading to it, plus strips at Nu'alolo Kai and Miloli'i, are all part of the sprawling 6,175-acre Na Pali Coast State Park. The remainder of the coastline, cliffs, and valleys are either state forests or natural area

reserves. A ranger at Kalalau Valley oversees the park. For those hiking in, the trailhead has a box where you sign in. Day-use permits are required beyond Hanakapi'ai (two miles in); camping permits are required to stay overnight at Hanakapi'ai, Hanakoa, or Kalalau. You can camp for up to five nights, but no two consecutive nights are allowed at either Hanakapi'ai or Hanakoa. You need a good waterproof tent, sleeping bag, mosquito repellent, first-aid kit, biodegradable soap, food, and toiletries. There are many streams along the trail, but the water can be biologically contaminated and cause horrible stomach distress. Boil it or use purification tablets, or treat it with a filter. Little firewood is available, and you can't cut trees, so take a stove. Don't litter; carry out what you carried in.

Because of heavy use and environmental concerns, the Kalalau Trail and/or Hanakoa campsite have been closed from time to time during the past decade for repair and rejuvenation. Check with the DLNR State Parks office at 808/274-3444 for the current status on use and accessibility.

The Nu'alolo Kai and Miloli'i sections can only be reached by boat or kayak. While Nu'alolo Kai is reserved for day use only (commercial boat tours stop here during the summer months), primitive campsites are available at Miloli'i for a maximum of three nights for those who desire real isolation.

## The Kalalau Trail

Originally carved out by Hawaiians who needed an overland route between the Kalalau Valley and Ha'ena, the Kalalau Trail not only leads you physically along the Na Pali Coast, but also back in time to classic romantic Hawaii. You leave the 20th century farther and farther behind with every step and reenter a time and place where you can come face to face with your nature self.

Getting to the trailhead is simple: follow Rte. 56 until it ends and then hike. This hike is *the* premier hike on Kaua'i and perhaps in the entire state. The Kalalau is a destination in and of itself, and those who have walked these phenomenal 11 miles never forget it. The trail leads down the Na Pali Coast—as close as you can get to the Hawaiian paradise of old. The trail is well marked by countless centuries of use, so you won't get lost, but it's rutted, root strewn, and muddy. Remnants of mileage posts are all along the way. Streams become torrents during rains but recede quickly—just wait it out. Mountain climbing is dangerous because of the crumbly soil, and the swimming along the coast is unpredictable, with many riptides. Summers, when the wave action returns sand to the beach, are usually fine, but stay out of the water Sept.–April. At Hanakapi'ai, a grim reminder lists the names and ages of those who have lost their lives at this beach. Pay heed! Also, in keeping with the tradition of "Garden of Eden," many people go au naturel at Kalalau Beach. Private parts unaccustomed to sunshine can make you wish you hadn't, so cover up with either sunblock or clothing.

Many people hike in as far as **Hanakapi'ai**. This is a fairly strenuous two-mile hike, the first mile uphill to about 800 feet, the last down, ending at the beach. Camp at spots on the far side of the stream up from the beach. You can also camp in the caves at the beach, but only during the summer and at low tide. If you hike in and out, leave yourself three hours. From the west side of the stream, the unmaintained **Hanakapi'ai Trail** leads two miles up the valley to the splendid **Hanakapi'ai Falls**, taking you past some mag-

the Na Pali Coast, in all its raw beauty

ROBERT NILSEN

nificent mango trees and crumbling stone-walled enclosures of ancient taro patches. This trail crosses and recrosses the stream several times and is often overgrown. If the stream looks high and is running swiftly, turn back; the trail up ahead is narrow and dangerous during periods of high water. If it's low, keep going—the 300-foot falls and surrounding amphitheater are magnificent. You can swim in the pools away from the falls, but not directly under—rocks and trees can come over at any time. As a side trip from Hanakapi'ai camp, this trail should take about 2–3 hours round-trip, perhaps 5–6 hours from Ke'e Beach.

Hanakapi'ai to **Hanakoa** is 4.5 miles of serious hiking as the trail climbs steadily, not returning to sea level until reaching Kalalau Beach nine miles away. Switchbacks take you 600 feet out of Hanakapi'ai Valley. Although heavily traversed, the trail can be very bad in spots. Before arriving at Hanakoa, you must go through **Ho'olulu** and **Waiahuakua** hanging valleys. Both are lush with native flora and are parts of Hono'onapali Nature

Area Preserve. Shortly, Hanakoa comes into view. Its many wide terraces are still intact from when it was a major food-growing area. Coffee plants gone wild can still be seen. Hanakoa is rainy, but the rain is intermittent, and the sun always follows. The swimming is fine in the many stream pools. A one-third-mile hike up the east fork of the stream, just after the six-mile marker, takes you past more terraces good for camping before coming to **Hanakoa Falls.** The terraces are wonderful, but the trail is subject to erosion and is treacherous with many steep sections.

Hanakoa to **Kalalau Beach** is under five miles but takes about three tough hours. Start early in the morning; it's hot, and although you're only traveling five miles, it gets noticeably drier and more open as you approach Kalalau. The views along the way are ample reward. The power and spirit of the incomparable *'aina* predominate. Around the seven-mile marker you enter land that until the late 1970s was part of the Makaweli cattle ranch. The vegetation turns from lush foliage to lantana and sisal, a sign of the aridness of the land. After crossing Pohakuao Valley, you climb the *pali;* on the other side is Kalalau. The lovely valley, two miles wide and three deep, beckons with its glimmering freshwater pools. It's a beauty among beauties and was cultivated until the 1920s. Many terraces and house sites remain. Plenty of guava, mango, and Java plum trees can be found. You can camp only in the trees fronting the beach or in the caves west of the waterfall. You are not allowed to camp along the stream, at its mouth, or in the valley. The waterfall has a freshwater pool, where feral goats come in the morning and evening to water.

A *heiau* is atop the little hillock on the west side of the stream. Follow the trail here up-valley for two miles to **Big Pool,** making one stream crossing on the way. Big Pool is really two pools connected by a natural water slide. Riding it is great for the spirit but tough on your butt. Enjoy! Along the way you pass Smoke Rock, where *pakalolo* growers at one time came to smoke and talk story.

## Honopu, Nu'alolo Kai, Miloli'i

Less than a half mile to the west of Kalalau Valley is **Honopu Valley.** This valley is known as the "Valley of the Lost Tribe," as legend tells of a race of small people inhabiting it in great isolation. These Mu were also said to have lived in the Wainiha Valley to the east. The two-part beach at Honopu is unique in that it's split by a huge rock arch; it has been the setting of at least two movie sequences.

Beyond Awa'awapuhi Valley is **Nu'alolo Kai,** an area of beach and dunes backed up tight against the cliff. Nu'alolo Kai was inhabited by a small community of Hawaiians until 1919, and remains of their habitation still exist in stone enclosures, walls, and *heiau* platforms. Fishing was good within the protected reef, and taro was raised in the adjoining Nu'alolo 'Aina Valley. Between these two areas, however, is a sheer cliff, so a rope ladder was hung from a ledge above, from where a trail led around the point to the fields. Because of the reef, there was good anchorage here at Nu'alolo Kai, and it was often used as a rest stop by canoes going between Hanalei and Waimea.

About a mile to the west is **Miloli'i,** also an ancient inhabited site. Here the valley is more easily accessible, and small amounts of taro were cultivated to sustain a small population. There is anchorage on the beach for boats, a primitive camping area with restrooms and a shelter, and down the beach a *heiau* site. Notice that Miloli'i is much drier than the rest of the Na Pali Coast—the heavy rains that pelt Kalalau Valley peter out before they make it this far, and Miloli'i gets only about 20 inches a year.

# South Shore

The Kaumualiʻi (Royal Oven) Highway (Rte. 50) steps west from Lihuʻe, with the Haʻupu Ridge (Hoary Head Mountains) adding a dash of beauty to the south and Queen Victoria's Profile winking down from the heights. Inland is Kilohana Crater, and between it and the Haʻupu Ridge are still productive but ever diminishing cane fields. The road rises gently over the Knudsen Gap and you enter the Koloa District, which stretches to the east bank of the Hanapepe River. Soon, Maluhia (Peaceful) Road (Rte. 520) branches to the south through an open lei of fragrant eucalyptus trees lining the route to the old sugar town of Koloa and on to the much newer resort community of Poʻipu. Continuing west on the highway, coming in quick succession, are the small inland towns of ʻOmaʻo, Lawaʻi, and Kalaheo, way stations on the road. Hereabouts are the remains of the area's once vibrant sugar industry, wide acres of the area's new crop, coffee, an exquisite tropical botanical garden, beautiful white-sand beaches, and a few of the island's newest and most luxurious resorts.

Poʻipu sunset

ROBERT NILSEN

# Koloa

As you head down Maluhia Road, you pass through the **Tunnel of Trees,** a stand of rough-bark *Eucalyptus robustus,* sometimes referred to as "swamp mahogany." Brought from Australia and planted by the Knudsen family, the largest landowner in this area, to help stabilize the then soggy road over the Knudsen Pass, they're now well established, adding beauty, a heady fragrance, and shade to more than a mile of this country lane.

The town of Koloa attracts a large number of tourists and packs them into a small area. On the site of what was the island's oldest sugar mill, Koloa has been transformed from a tumble-down sugar town to a thriving tourist community where shops, restaurants, and boutiques line its wooden sidewalks. Nearly all the old shops are remodeled plantation buildings. Dressed in red paint and trimmed with white, they are festooned with strings of lights as if decorated for a perpetual Christmas festivity. Most businesses line the town's main street, but others are found along Po'ipu Road as it heads down toward the coast.

Traffic can be hectic with morning and evening mini-rush hours, and parking is always a problem. There are a few small parking lots, but you usually have to find a spot along the main drag or on one of the side streets—respect all signage.

In accord with its strong economic position, Koloa was the major population center on Kaua'i from 1835 to 1880. During this time, Koloa Landing in Po'ipu was reputedly one of the three most active whaling ports in Hawaii. Sugar and other agricultural products were shipped from the Koloa Landing, which was then one of the main ports of entry for the island. Sugar remained strong here throughout most of the last century, but the newest mill shut down in 1996, a victim of the statewide declining sugar industry, and its lifeless edifice can still be seen east of town at the end of Maha'ulepu Road. Active cane fields in this area are now gone, replaced by limited cattle ranching, coffee, papaya, and corn production.

One meaning for *koloa* is "duck"; the area was probably so named because of the preponderance of ponds throughout the district

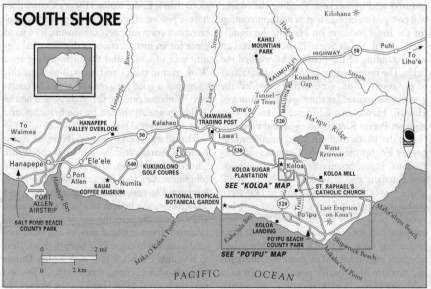

SOUTH SHORE

© SANDRA E. BISIGNANI TRUST AND AVALON TRAVEL PUBLISHING, INC.

that attract these water-loving fowl. In fact, before the development of the sugar industry, the Koloa District was known for its taro production, which employs flooded fields and necessitates much water. Today, numerous reservoirs dot the hillsides, including **Waita Reservoir** at the eastern edge of town, the largest man-made water catchment on the island and in the state.

A second meaning for *koloa* is "long sugarcane," and this seems appropriate because varieties of wild sugarcane grew throughout this area during the precontact times.

## SIGHTS

Just as you enter town, look to your right to see a weathered stone chimney standing alone in a little grassy field. Although of major historical significance, this unmarked edifice is what's left of the **Koloa Sugar Plantation,** established in 1835, site of the first successful attempt at refining sugar in the Hawaiian Islands. On this corner lot a simple circle plot contains more than a dozen varieties of sugarcane, along with a plaque and sculpture dedicated to the sugar industry and its workers. Reading the plaque will give you an explanation of and appreciation for the sugar industry on Hawaii, the significance of the Koloa Sugar Plantation, and an understanding of the people who worked the fields. The bronze sculpture portrays individuals of the seven ethnic groups that provided the greatest manpower for the sugar plantations of Hawaii: Hawaiians, Chinese, Japanese, Portuguese, Puerto Ricans, Koreans, and Filipinos. (From the 1830s to about 1910, smaller numbers of Englishmen, Scots, Germans, Scandinavians, Poles, Spaniards, American blacks, and Russians also arrived to work. All in all, about 300,000 immigrants came to Hawaii to make the sugar industry the success it has been.) Koloa is the birthplace of the Hawaiian sugar industry, the strongest economic force in the state for more than a century. More than anything else, it helped to shape the multiethnic mixture of Hawaii's population. To help celebrate Hawaii's plantation life, the annual

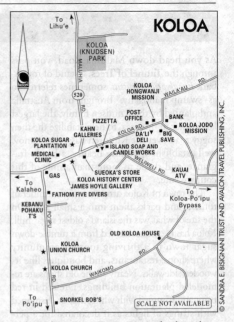

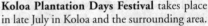

**Koloa Plantation Days Festival** takes place in late July in Koloa and the surrounding area.

While its name makes it sound more prestigious than it is, the **Koloa History Center** does have a few small displays and pictorials. Located in a courtyard near the stream, it's a good place for an introduction to the historical significance of Koloa and the surrounding area. With picnic tables and a small garden, this courtyard is good for a midday rest. The courtyard, Waikomo Stream, the roadway, and nearby buildings are all shaded by the branches of a huge monkeypod tree.

The tall steeple on the way to Po'ipu belongs to **Koloa Church,** locally known as the White Church. Its clapboard siding and colonial columns make it look like a transplant from New England. The congregation began in 1835, and this structure was built in 1859 and remodeled in 1929. For many years the steeple was an official landmark for many land surveys and was often used by sailors to direct their boats to shore. Next to it stands the black lava rock **Koloa Union Church,** with a heritage equally old. Up in town near the post office and bank are the Koloa Jodo

Mission and temple and the Koloa Hongwanji Mission, both founded in 1910 by Japanese immigrants to the plantation. If you take Weliweli Road out of town, then follow Hapa Road to its end, you come to **St. Raphael's Catholic Church,** marking the spot where a Roman Catholic mission was first permitted in the islands, in 1841. The stone church itself dates from 1856, when it was built by Friar Robert Walsh. This is a quiet spot, and the church has obviously done well. The roof of the church can be seen sticking above the trees from Kiahuna Golf Club in Po'ipu, a short distance away.

The one-mile-long Hapa Road is open again to foot traffic, and it runs through former cane fields to Po'ipu. Along it are a few remnants of ancient Hawaiian habitation sites.

Past Hapa Road, a continuation of Weliweli Road has been cut through the fields to become the **Koloa-Po'ipu Bypass,** a shortcut from just north of Koloa town to the eastern end of the Po'ipu strip, emerging near the Hyatt Regency Resort.

# ACCOMMODATIONS

**Old Koloa House,** 3327 Waikomo Rd., Koloa, HI 96756, 808/742-2099, www.oldkoloa-house.com, information@oldkoloahouse.com, was a plantation manager's house from the early 20th century. Originally located at Kukui'ula Harbor, it now sits on a quiet street in Koloa along a small stream. It offers one large suite that opens through a double French door to the back lawn and garden, and a smaller double-bed unit with a separate entrance and a deck off the side. The owners collect antiques, so a few older pieces of furniture and decorative items around the rooms elicit a sense of an older, slower time. It's a charming place. Mosquito netting, ceiling fan, TV, CD player, and books add to the homey, comfortable feel. Other amenities include a telephone, mini-fridge, microwave, coffeemaker, hair dryer, iron, and ironing board. Each room has a private bath, and a barbecue grill in the backyard gazebo is for guest use. For the first morning, a simple continental breakfast is left in the refrigerator; after that you're on your own.

The owners are helpful and engaging and can offer suggestions for activities and food. Old Koloa House seems a perfect place for newlyweds or other couples who desire a romantic escape. The room rate is $78 a night for either room; two nights' minimum.

Lying below the imposing Kahili peak, **Kahili Mountain Park,** P.O. Box 298, Koloa, HI 96756, 808/742-9921, www.kahilipark.com, is a gem, *if* you enjoy what it has to offer: it's like a camp for big people. To get there, follow Rte. 50 west about a half mile past the turnoff to Koloa, and look for the sign pointing mountainside up a well-graded dirt road. Follow it for about one mile to the entranceway. The surroundings are absolutely beautiful, and the only noises, except for singing birds, are from an occasional helicopter flying into Waimea Canyon and the children attending the school on the premises. The broad meadow is surrounded by mountains, with the coast visible and Po'ipu Beach about 15 minutes away. In the middle of the meadow is a cluster of rocks, a mini-replica of the mountains in the background. One strenuous trail from the property runs up to Kahili peak above; a shorter and much easier stroll brings you to a grove of Norfolk pines. A spring-fed pond is chilly for swimming but great for catching bass that make a tasty dinner. There are three types of accommodations: cabinettes, cabins, and new cabins. A cabinette is a one-room unit with five twin beds and kitchenette. A few of the original rustic cabinettes still remain, with bare wood walls, open ceilings, and cement floors, but the majority didn't survive Hurricane 'Iniki. The cabinettes are in a cluster facing a meadow, and each is surrounded by flower beds and trees. Bathrooms and showers are in a central building, with separate laundry facilities available. A relaxing Japanese *ofuro* (hot tub) is also open to guests. The cabins are raised, wooden-floored houses with full kitchens, inside toilets, outdoor showers, and bedrooms with chairs, tables, and dressers. Each has two twin beds and one double bed. New cabins, built after the hurricane, are a bit larger and upgraded with one queen-size and two twin beds, an indoor bathroom with shower, complete kitchen with large refrigerator, and a screened porch. Rates are based on double occupancy, with $10 extra for persons over eight years old: cabinette, $45–55; cabin, $65; new cabin, $75. Two cottages, a bit more luxurious, run $90 and $100, while the two-bedroom "canvasback" house runs $110 and sleeps up to eight. All linens, towels, toilet paper, and kitchen utensils are provided, but you must do all your own housekeeping. Kahili Mountain Park is owned and operated by the Seventh-Day Adventist Church, which also runs the school on the property. In 2002, Kahili Mountain Park experienced some land use issues with its landlord and was temporarily closed down. If this accommodation attracts you, call for the current status.

## FOOD

While there are not many restaurants in town, **Pizzetta,** 808/742-8881, is perhaps the best of the bunch and has established a fine reputation among locals. Right in the center of town, its front tiled section with a counter window gives way to a wood-floor raised back portion and lanai. Pictures of Italian scenes line the walls, soft jazz fills the air, and a full-service bar mixes drinks. Appetizers such as mozzarella sticks and stuffed mushrooms are $5.95–9.95; soups and salads are mostly under $10. Pasta, calzone, and baked casserole dishes are tempting and reasonably priced at $7.95–14.95. But Pizzetta is best known for its pizza—handmade crust, homemade sauce—which can be ordered as a whole pie or by the slice, eaten in or taken out; free delivery is available in the area. Standard or make-your-own pizzas run $12.95–22.95 or more depending on the number of toppings.

An easygoing casual place that's a hit with the tourist crowd is **Tomkat's Grill,** 808/724-8887. Enter via a hallway and proceed to the back, where seating is in two sections next to a small courtyard koi pond. The menu is heavy on sandwiches and burgers, most under $7.25, and deep-fried *pu pu.* Other lunch items are a chef salad, one-half rotisserie chicken, and a teriyaki steak plate. The limited dinner specials, served after 5 P.M., include barbecued pork ribs, garlic

seafood pasta, and fresh fish, all for under $17.95. A short children's menu helps keep prices down. Order drinks from the bar or pick out a fresh pastry from the case. Takeout is available on all items.

**Da'li Deli,** 808/742-8824, across from the post office, is open Mon.–Sat. 8 A.M.–3 P.M. for breakfast and lunch; eat in or takeout. Breakfast specials are mostly under $8, while lunch sandwiches are no more than $10. Others stop by for the bagels, pastries, bread, and deli items. This is a popular place offering healthy, gourmet food in an easy atmosphere. Tuesday through Saturday from 5:30 P.M., the deli transforms itself into the Italian restaurant **Cafe Cara,** creating traditional Italian dishes like mama used to make. Try dishes like bruschette antipasti, rucola salad, risotto porcini, or cannelloni di giorni. Entrées run $11–17. Bring your own wine.

A few steps down from Da'li Deli is **Koloa Fish Market,** open every day except Sunday, for the freshest whole fish and seafood in town, plate lunches, *pu pu,* and beer.

Next door to the fish market is **Mi Casita,** 808/742-2323, the only place in town that serves a full assortment of Mexican dishes.

For local atmosphere and inexpensive local food to match, try **Kauai Kitchens** next to the supermarket. Open for breakfast and lunch.

Adjacent to Sueoka's Store in downtown Koloa is a **plate-lunch window** that dishes out hearty, wholesome food Tues.–Sun. 9 A.M.–3 P.M. It's difficult to spend more than $6.

**Lappert's Aloha Ice Cream,** downtown Koloa, 808/742-1272, dishes up creamy scoops of delicious Kaua'i-made ice cream. Connoisseurs of the dripping delight consider it among the best in the world. The ice-cream parlor doubles as an espresso bar, with pastries thrown in for good measure.

In Koloa, a **Big Save Supermarket** is at the junction of Koloa and Waikomo Roads. A full-service grocery store, it's open 7 A.M.–11 P.M. daily. **Sueoka's Store,** in downtown Koloa, is a family-owned, local grocery and produce market, open 8 A.M.–9 P.M. Both carry everything you'll need for condo cooking.

Pick up fresh fruits and vegetables at the **farmers' market** held every Monday at noon at Koloa (Knudsen) Park. Depending on what's happening on the farms, you can get everything from coconuts to fresh-cut flowers while enjoying a truly local island experience.

## SHOPPING

In Koloa, shops and boutiques are strung along the road like flowers on a lei. You can buy everything from original art to beach towels. There are shops selling jewelry, swimwear, casual clothing, gifts, and even a specialty shop for candles; Old Koloa Town packs a lot of shopping into a little area. Besides, it's fun just walking the raised sidewalks of what looks very much like an old Western town.

Look for **Jungle Girl,** next to Lappert's Aloha Ice Cream, offering alohawear and casual clothing, and **Progressive Expressions** for surfboards, surf gear, and islandwear. Casual resortwear is available from **Paradise Clothing,** with a good assortment of bathing suits, beach dresses, men's and women's hats and shorts, and a sampling of clothing for children. Much more unique is **The Blue Orchid** at the upper end of town, a ladies' boutique selling dresses, alohawear, earrings, jewelry, and fresh-cut flowers. The owner handpaints the dresses and T-shirts, all of which are made from cotton, rayon, or silk.

Also along the strip, **Atlantis Gallery and Frames** features prints, posters, and framing, and **Kahn Galleries** offers an exceptional collection of paintings by some of the most prominent island artists.

Just before the elevated walkway begins, you'll find **Hula Moon Gifts.** The shelves at Hula Moon bear mostly arts and crafts made in Hawaii, with some of the gift items fashioned in Indonesia. Featured items include vests imprinted with a tapa design and antique print; lifelike Hawaiian dolls made from resin; tiles, platters, and red-dirt pottery; handmade (and numbered) ukulele; koa bowls; and less-expensive items like shark-teeth necklaces, barrettes, bracelets, mirror and comb sets, and koa bookmarks.

At the upper end of the raised walkway is

**Island Soap and Candle Works,** 808/742-1945, www.handmade-soap.com, open daily 9 A.M.–9 P.M. You can't miss this shop as the lovely aromas waft out of the store onto the sidewalk. It's a heady smell, and this is definitely not the place for those sensitive to fragrance. For others, head on in to an eye-popping variety of soaps, beeswax candles, lotions, gels, and oils. All handmade, these products are available at boutiques throughout Hawaii and can also be ordered by phone at 800/300-6067. A second store is at Kong Lung Co. in Kilauea on the north shore.

Beyond the stream and the monkeypod tree on the west end of the strip is **Crazy Shirts,** a Hawaiian firm selling some of the best T-shirts and islandwear available. Try **Emperors Emporium** for the usual postcards, cheap jewelry, outlet alohawear, and souvenirs, and **Koloa Country Store** for gifts and Internet access.

In the courtyard behind Crazy Shirts is the **James Hoyle Gallery,** 808/742-1010. After years of maintaining a studio and gallery in Hanapepe, James Hoyle packed up and moved everything to Koloa in 2002, but he maintains his tradition of painting locally inspired subjects. Hoyle has been able to capture the spirit of Hawaii through fantastic color and movement. The sense that permeates all of Hoyle's work is that in Hawaii, humanity cannot conquer nature but must learn to live in harmony with the 'aina. Hoyle uses bright colors, strong brush strokes, and heavy gobs of pastels in a manner similar to the impressionists like Van Gogh and Paul Gauguin. These fine works range in price from around $1,000 to $40,000. If you can't afford an original, serigraphs finished and embellished in vivid color by the artist go for around $700.

**Koloa One Hour Photo,** 808/742-8918, along Po'ipu Road in Koloa, offers camera needs, film, and processing. Farther down this road beyond Fathom Five Divers is **Kebanu,** a gallery of modern art pieces in wood, glass, stone, and pottery. **Pohaku T's** is more than a shop that sells T-shirts; it also designs its prints to bring awareness to the area, enhance its cultural legacy, and help slow the development of the remainder of this coastline.

# RECREATION

**Fathom Five Divers,** 808/742-6991, about 100 yards down from the Chevron station in Koloa, open daily 9 A.M.–6 P.M., is a complete diving center offering lessons, certification, and rentals. Two-tank boat dives for certified divers, including gear, are $129, shore dives $95. Introductory boat dives for the first-timer, including lesson and gear, are $145; a one-tank shore dive is $95. Certification courses take three to four days and run $395 with a small group or $495 for private instruction. Tank refills are also available. Boat dives go out of Kukui'ula Harbor near the Spouting Horn and shore dive at Koloa Landing. Fathom Five also does half-day snorkeling cruises and rents snorkel gear.

**Snorkel Bob's,** farther along Po'ipu Road, 808/742-2206, rents inexpensive snorkel gear that can be taken interisland. Snorkel Bob's has some of the best prices, equipment, and services on the island. Gear, which includes mask, snorkel tube, and fins, is rented for a 24-hour day or by the week. The snorkel set runs from $2.50/day or $9/week to $6.50 a day or $29 a week, depending on the quality. Prescription lenses, dry snorkels, and rental boogie boards are also available. This company is now booking various island activities, so you may get free or discounted equipment rental if you book through it. Open 8 A.M.–5 P.M.

**Kauai ATV,** on the corner of Weliweli and Waikomo Roads, 808/742-2734 or 877/707-7088, www.kauaiatv.com, info@kauaiatv.com, runs four-wheel ATV (all terrain vehicle) tours through former cane land surrounding Koloa. These tours run several times a day on two different three- and four-hour routes; $90 and $130 per person. Riders must be 16 years old or older and no more than 350 pounds. For safety reasons, no pregnant women or those with back injuries will be allowed to ride. Helmets, face shields, gloves, beverages, and instructions are provided; long pants, a long-sleeve shirt, and closed-toe shoes are a must.

Aside from its ball fields, Koloa Park has tennis courts that are open to the public, free, and lighted at night; they operate on a first-come, first-served basis.

# SERVICES

The Koloa **post office** is along Koloa Road across from the Big Save Supermarket. At the end of Koloa Road just beyond the post office is a branch of First Hawaiian Bank, the only bank in the Koloa-Po'ipu area. A self-serve coin **laundromat** is around the side of the supermarket. At the intersection of Koloa and Po'ipu Roads is the only **gas station** in town.

The Kaua'i Medical Group's **Koloa Clinic,** 808/742-1621 (808/245-1831 after hours), offers medical services Mon.–Fri. 8:30 A.M.–noon and 1:30–5 P.M. This clinic is by the stream next to the Koloa Sugar Mill chimney. The **Southshore Pharmacy** in downtown Koloa, 808/742-7511, open Mon.–Fri. 9 A.M.–5 P.M., not only has a prescription service but also first-aid supplies and skin- and health-care products. The **Koloa Chiropractic Clinic,** 3176 Po'ipu Rd., 808/742-9555, can also help with medical problems. (If they can't help, the Kauai Mortuary is right down the street.)

# Po'ipu

Po'ipu Road continues south from Koloa for two miles until it reaches the coast. En route it passes a private cane road, and a bit farther it branches at a Y. Here, Lawa'i (Beach) Road turns right and hugs the coast past condos, private homes, and a string of vacation rentals, terminating at the Spouting Horn and the entrance to the National Tropical Botanical Gardens. Po'ipu Road itself bends left past a string of condos and hotels, into what might be considered the town, except that nothing in particular makes it so. From Po'ipu Road, Kapili, Ho'owili, and Pe'e Roads lead to the beach. Ho'onani Road also runs along the water here, splitting from Lawa'i Road and crossing the Waikomo Stream just above Whaler's Cove. At the mouth of the stream you pass **Koloa Landing,** once the island's most important port. When whaling was king, dozens of ships anchored here to trade with the natives for provisions. Today nothing remains of the old wharf and storage buildings, but it is a favorite entry point for shore dives and a good place to watch for turtles in the morning and evening. Snorkeling and scuba diving are best to the sides of the bay, away from the sandy middle.

Po'ipu is the most well-established and developed tourist area on Kaua'i, but it fields competition from developments in Kapa'a and Princeville. On the oceanfront in Po'ipu, luxury accommodations and fine restaurants front the beaches, the water beckons, and the surf is gentle. Behind this resort community on the east end are the low volcanic cones of Pu'u Hi, Pu'u Hunihuni, and Pu'u Wanawana (a fourth such cone is now occupied by Po'ipu Crater Resort), where the last volcanic eruptions occurred perhaps 15,000–20,000 years ago. To the west, beyond Prince Kuhio's birthplace, is the Spouting Horn, a plume of water that jets up through an opening in the volcanic rock shore with every incoming wave, and beyond that, the National Tropical Botanical Gardens. Whether you're exploring the sights, cultivating a tan on the beach, combing the shops for your gift list, or sampling island treats, Po'ipu will not fail to provide.

Hurricane 'Iniki pummeled Po'ipu like a boxer hitting a punching bag. In the aftermath, it took years for the devastated Po'ipu area to recover and rebuild. By the end of 1999, all hotel and condo properties were again up and running, except for the former Waiohai Hotel. Only slowly have other properties been developed.

Although it continues to face some strident opposition by local activists and must meet strict county requirements, the largest new development planned in Po'ipu is for the Kukui'ula Bay area near Spouting Horn. Alexander and Baldwin plan a 200-room hotel fronting the lagoon basin, expansion of Kukui'ula Harbor facilities, greenways and bike paths, an 18-hole golf course, a shopping center, and over 3,000 condo units and residential lots that would stretch back to Po'ipu Road. To service this huge integrated development, a new road would have to be cut through former cane land to ease traffic on Lawa'i Road. While not directly fronting the water, this development will undoubtedly and dramatically change the face of Po'ipu, if and when it is completed.

# SIGHTS
## The Great Po'ipu Beaches

Although given a lacing by Hurricane 'Iniki, **Po'ipu Beach County Park** is on the mend and is Po'ipu's best-developed beach park. At the eastern end of Po'ipu, it provides a pavilion, tables, showers, toilets, a playground, walkways, and lifeguards on duty daily. There's plenty of parking along Ho'one Road or across the street. The swimming, snorkeling, and bodysurfing are great. Po'ipu Beach has something for just about everyone. A sheltered pool rimmed by lava boulders is gentle enough for any swimmer, and going just beyond it provides the more exciting wave action often used by local surfers. Follow the rocks out to Nukumoi Point, where there are a number of tide pools; snorkeling is best on the right side. Waves come in all sizes, and instructors use Po'ipu Beach for beginning surf lessons. The far eastern end of Po'ipu Beach is called **Brennecke Beach.** Popular with locals, it's one of the best spots on the island for boogie boarding and bodysurfing. Following the shoreline around to the west is an additional crescent beach, one that fronts the Kiahuna Plantation Resort and Sheraton Kauai Resort. It slopes gently into the water and is often the haunt of seals and turtles.

At the eastern end of the Hyatt an access road leads to **Shipwreck Beach,** now improved with a pavilion containing restrooms and showers. Shipwreck Beach is a half-mile strand of white sand on Keoneloa Bay. One of the only beneficiaries of Hurricanes 'Iwa and 'Iniki, the beach was broadened and widened with huge deposits of sand, making it bigger and better than ever. The swimming is good, but, as always, use caution. The beach is perhaps best known for boogie boarding and bodysurfing, and these usually take place at the far eastern end near the sandstone bluff. It is below this bluff that a boat wreck lay for many years. Now only the heavy motor still

lies here, exposed at times of heavy surf, the rest having been torn away by the last hurricane. Also near here, etched into the hardened sandstone and buried under beach sand most of the year, is one of the few petroglyph spots on the island. To see it, you have to be lucky enough to be there when the water pulls the sand away to expose these rock carvings. A pathway runs east along the golf course, affording fantastic seascapes as you amble along the bluff.

Continue along Po'ipu Road—no longer paved—past the golf course and turnoff to CJM Country Stables. Take the right turn onto another dirt road that runs down toward the water. Access to **Maha'ulepu Beach** is across private land. Be sure to note the time because this gate may be closed and locked 7 P.M.–7:30 A.M. The dirt access road leads down to a parking lot just behind the sand dunes; a track to the left behind the dunes leads to two smaller parking spots. Maha'ulepu Beach is long. Its western extent is rather straight and exposed; at the eastern

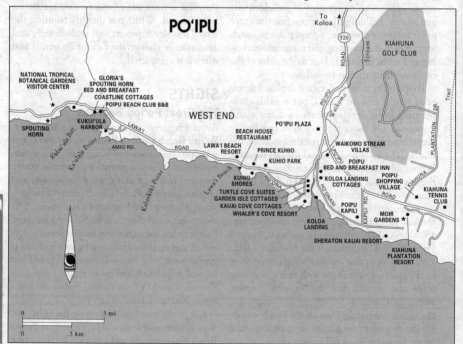

**PO'IPU**

To Koloa

KIAHUNA GOLF CLUB

NATIONAL TROPICAL BOTANICAL GARDENS VISITOR CENTER

GLORIA'S SPOUTING HORN BED AND BREAKFAST

COASTLINE COTTAGES

POIPU BEACH CLUB B&B

**WEST END**

SPOUTING HORN

KUKUI'ULA HARBOR

AMIO RD.

LAWA'I ROAD

Kukui'ula Bay

Ka'ula'ula Point

Kahekili Point

Lawa'i Beach

PO'IPU PLAZA

BEACH HOUSE RESTAURANT

LAWA'I BEACH RESORT

PRINCE KUHIO

KUHIO PARK

KUHIO SHORES

TURTLE COVE SUITES

GARDEN ISLE COTTAGES

KAUAI COVE COTTAGES

WHALER'S COVE RESORT

KOLOA LANDING

WAIKOMO STREAM VILLAS

POIPU BED AND BREAKFAST INN

KOLOA LANDING COTTAGES

POIPU KAPILI

MOIR GARDENS

SHERATON KAUAI RESORT

POIPU SHOPPING VILLAGE

KIAHUNA TENNIS CLUB

KIAHUNA PLANTATION RESORT

Waikomo Stream

POIPU RD

HO'ONA

HO'ONANI

KAPILI RD.

KIAHUNA PLANTATION DR.

Trail

MOON

0　　　.5 mi

0　　　.5 km

end it slips around into a nice protected cove, but the beach is not as nice here. Sand dunes back the beach through most of its length, and more are found beyond the beach before the mountains begin. Not many people frequent this beach—although George C. Scott came here to play Ernest Hemingway for the movie *Islands in the Stream*—but fishermen come, and, when the waves are right, surfers. When the waves are not too strong, swimming is good within the reef, which is also used by sailboarders. There is no official camping here and there are no facilities, but local people sometimes bivouac in the ironwoods at the east end. A trail along the lithified sandstone bluff runs by the golf course from Shipwreck Beach to near the CJM Country Stables, a distance of a mile or so, from where it's a short walk beyond to Maha'ulepu Beach. The owner of the Maha'ulepu area, AOL founder Steve Case (who also owns Grove Farm in Lihu'e, where his father was the manager several decades ago), has plans to develop this isolated beach

area, but there is strong local sentiment to leave the land undeveloped.

Just west of Kuhio Park, fronting Lawa'i Beach Resort, is the narrow, roadside **Lawa'i Beach,** also called Beach House Beach. Although the beach is not particularly good for swimming because of its rocky bottom and shoreline, these characteristics make it one of the best, and most family-safe, snorkeling spots in the area. Enter at the sandy end near the Beach House Restaurant. Surfers and body boarders also come here for the breaks created by the reef. Back down the coast a few hundred yards, on the east side of Kuhio Park, is **Keiki Beach** (Baby Beach). Somewhat protected by the reef, with a narrow sand strip, this beach is secluded and used mostly for sunbathing.

## East End

Along Po'ipu Road, look for the driveway into the Kiahuna Plantation Resort on the right across from the Po'ipu Shopping Village. This is the site of the **Moir Gardens.** These grounds,

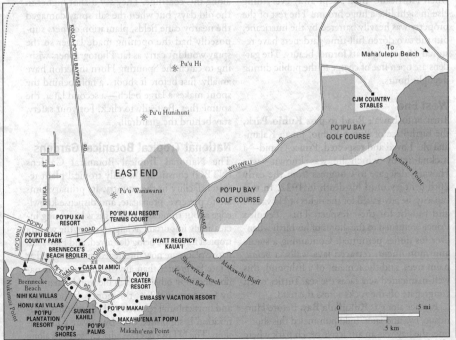

© SANDRA E. BISIGNANI TRUST AND AVALON TRAVEL PUBLISHING, INC.

originally part of the old Koloa Sugar Company manager's estate, were a "cactus patch" started by Sandie Moir, wife of the manager, Hector Moir, back in 1938. Over the years, the gardens grew more and more lavish, with the inclusion of succulents, orchids, bromeliads, dry land trees, and several ponds, until they became a standard Po'ipu sight. Mrs. Moir was a horticulturist enamored of cacti. Whenever she went to the Mainland she collected these amazing plants, mainly from Texas and the Southwest, and transported them back to Hawaii to be planted in her cactus garden. However, before planting them she would invite a *kahuna* to bless the land and to pray for their acceptance. The Kiahuna Plantation Resort has greatly expanded the original gardens; the property's 35 lovely acres are adorned with more than 3,000 varieties of tropical flowers, trees, and plants, and a lovely lagoon. The cactus garden has flourished and by magic or mystery was the only thing in the entire area left relatively untouched when Hurricane 'Iniki swept away everything else in sight like a huge broom. The rest of the property was heavily battered by the hurricane, but the two dozen full-time gardeners have restored everything to its former beauty. The gardens are open free of charge to the public during daylight hours.

## West End

Turn onto Lawa'i Road to pass **Kuhio Park,** the birthplace of Prince Kuhio, Jonah Kalaniana'ole. Loved and respected, Prince Cupid—a nickname by which he was known—was Hawaii's delegate to Congress from the early 20th century until his death in 1922. In this capacity, he advocated for the rights of Hawaiians and fought for their respect. This "People's Prince" returned to the shores of his birth whenever his duties permitted. Containing a statue and monument, terraced lava walls, a *heiau,* palm trees, and the remains of a fishpond, this well-manicured acre faces the sea. Turtles often congregate off the rocks across the road.

Farther along is **Kukui'ula Bay.** Before Hurricane 'Iwa and later 'Iniki pummeled this shoreline, the bay was an attractive beach park where many small boats anchored. The pier area has been put aright and is again functioning as before. A handful of sailing, diving, and fishing companies leave from the Kukui'ula Harbor, shore fishermen come to try their luck, and scuba divers explore the coral reef offshore. At the end of Amio Road, the park offers new and clean picnic tables, grills, and restrooms.

In a moment, you arrive at the **Spouting Horn.** A large parking area has many stalls marked for tour buses; at the flea market here, you can pick up trinkets, jewelry, and souvenirs. Don't make the mistake of looking just at the Spouting Horn. Have "big eyes" and look around at the full sweep of this remarkable coastline. The Spouting Horn is a lava tube that extends into the sea, with its open mouth on the rocky shore. The inrushing wave action causes the spouting phenomenon through a hole in the cave roof, which can blow spumes up to 60 feet high, depending on surf conditions, and resembles the spouting of whales that winter along this coastline. They say it shot higher in the old days, but when the salt spray damaged the nearby cane fields, plantation owners supposedly had the opening made larger so the spray wouldn't carry as far. Photographers wishing to catch the Spouting Horn in action have an ally. Just before it shoots, a hole behind the spout makes a large belch—a second later, the spume flies. Be ready to click. For your safety, stay behind the guardrail.

## National Tropical Botanical Gardens

The National Tropical Botanical Gardens (NTBG) constitute the only tropical plant research facility in the country. Its primary aims are to preserve, propagate, and dispense knowledge about tropical plants. This is becoming increasingly important as large areas of the world's tropical forests are being destroyed, and Hawaiian native plants are now threatened or endangered at a rate far greater than anywhere else in the nation and most other places in the world. Chartered by Congress in 1964, this nonprofit botanical and horticultural research and educational organization is supported only by private contributions. The NTBG has two adjacent sections along the south shore of Kaua'i: the McBryde Gardens and the Allerton Gardens. Aside from this location, the National Tropical Botanical Gardens also maintains the Limahuli Gardens on the north coast of Kaua'i; the Kahanu Gardens at Hana, Maui, which contains Pi'ilanihale Heiau, the largest *heiau* in the islands; and The Kampong in Coconut Grove, Florida.

Currently, the 259-acre **McBryde Gardens'** living collection has more than 6,000 species of tropical plants, and many additional plants are added to the collection each year. The staggering variety flourishing here ranges from common bamboo to romantic orchids. The gardens are separated into individual sections that include plants of nutritional and medicinal value, herbs and spices, and rare and endangered species in need of conservation; other groups include plants of special ethnobotanical interest, plants of unexploited potential, tropical fruits, and ornamentals.

Adjoining these gardens is 80-acre **Allerton Gardens,** started by John Allerton, a member of the Mainland cattle-raising family that founded the First National Bank of Chicago. This garden dates from the 1870s, when Queen Emma made the first plantings here at one of her summer vacation homes. In 1938, Robert Allerton bought this property, and for 20 years, he and adopted son John, helped by a host of gardeners, cleared the jungle and planted. John scoured the islands of the South Pacific to bring back their living treasures, and oftentimes, old *kama'aina* families would send cuttings of their rarest plants to be included in the collection. The Lawa'i River runs through the property, and pools, statuary, and garden "rooms" help set the mood.

These gardens are so enchanting that many visitors regard them as one of the real treats of their trip. The visitors center, 808/742-2623, open daily 8:30 A.M.–5 P.M., with its interpretive displays and small gift shop, is a restored plantation manager's house across from the Spouting Horn. Particularly nice are its selection of Ni'ihau shell lei, fine quilts, and books on Hawaii. This center opened in 1997, following the total destruction of the former visitors center by Hurricane 'Iniki. Feel free to take a self-guided walking tour of the demonstration gardens surrounding the center, which hold a variety of plants that might have been common around a plantation house during the sugar era. Trams run into the McBryde Gardens Mon.–Sat. 9:30 A.M.–2:30 P.M. every half hour for self-guided tours; $15. Guided tours of the Allerton Gardens are given Mon.–Sat. at 9 A.M., 10 A.M., 1 P.M., and 2 P.M., and each is led by knowledgeable horticultural staff or a Na Lima Kokua (Helping Hands) volunteer. The guided tours last about two and a half hours and cost $30—*kama'aina* rates are available. Wear good walking shoes, carry an umbrella if it looks like showers, and bring mosquito repellent! All tours leave from the visitors center. Reservations are a must and should be made four to five days in advance— longer during the Christmas and Thanksgiving seasons. Call the visitors center or write well in advance to the reservations secretary at P.O. Box 340, Lawa'i, HI 96765, tours@ntbg.org. Annual membership, $50 and up, entitles you to many benefits not given casual visitors— write to the development office at the address above or call 808/332-7324. Additional information is available at the website: www.ntbg.org.

## Koloa Heritage Trail

As in other places in the islands, Koloa and Po'ipu have begun to pay more attention to the cultural and historical significance of their past and have made efforts to educate residents and visitors alike to the importance of the area. One of the results has been the establishment of the Koloa History Center in Koloa, which gives a brief historical sketch of the area. The Po'ipu resorts have also put effort into establishing cultural programs and hosting learning events. More recently, the *Koloa Heritage Trail* brochure has been created to direct you to sites of significance in the Koloa/Po'ipu area, offering a map and description of each place of note. Pick up a brochure and follow along by car, bicycle, or on foot to learn more about this area, which is such a premier vacation area today.

# ACCOMMODATIONS

Most of Po'ipu's available rooms are in medium- to high-priced condos; however, options include a handful of cottages, several bed and breakfasts, and two first-class hotels.

## Luxury Hotels

Royal palms line the grand boulevard that ends at the elegant porte cochere where towering panes of glass open to a roiling sea frothing against periwinkle sky at the **Hyatt Regency Kauai Resort and Spa,** 1571 Po'ipu Rd., Koloa, HI 96756, 808/742-1234 or 800/554-9288, www.kauai-hyatt.com. The Hyatt is a grand hotel in grand dimension that bespeaks the luxury of 1920s and 1930s Hawaii. This magnificent, 600-room hotel, deceptive in size, is architecturally designed so that its five floors rise no taller than the surrounding palms. Through the entry are the main reception and concierge desks, and to the sides in both directions are the numerous resort shops. To one side of the inner courtyard is Stevenson Library, one of the Hyatt's bars and some claim the best hotel lounge in the state. The main courtyard opens onto a terrace that overlooks the oceanside grounds of the hotel. Walking paths scented by tropical blooms lead through acres of pools, both fresh and saltwater, featuring slides, a rivulet flowing through a "gorge," and the watery massaging fingers of cascading waterfalls and bubbling whirlpools. Through the heart of the hotel, greenery and flowers, both wild and tamed, compose a living lei of floral beauty. Lustrous koa tables bear flowers ablaze with color. Artworks, tapa wall hangings, and birdcages filled with flitting plumage and trilling songs line the hallways, while the interplay of marble floors and rich carpets is counterpointed by weathered bronze.

Heavy mahogany doors open into large guest rooms, all done in soothing pastels with white on tan textured wallpaper. Each room features a full entertainment center, private lanai with outdoor furniture, a mini-bar, double closets, and spacious bathrooms. Mahogany furniture, overstuffed chairs and footstools, and Chinese-style lamps ensure tasteful relaxation, and Hawaiian quilts cover the beds. Rates range from $395 for a garden view to $600 for a deluxe oceanfront room, $670 for a Regency Club room, and $1,000 to $3,600 for suites.

The five restaurants at the Hyatt range from casual to elegant, and five lounges offer libations in poolside to formal settings; additionally, there is the Poipu Bay Grill and Bar next door at the golf course clubhouse. Myriad cultural activities are scheduled throughout the week, and of great interest is the nightly Hawaiian music program accompanied by a torch-lighting ceremony and/or a *keiki* hula show. Drums of Paradise lu'au is held every Thursday and Sunday in the lower courtyard, and the on-property Anara Spa is perfect for those seeking a rejuvenative health retreat. Camp Hyatt keeps the kids busy while parents are off doing other things, and the hotel's tennis courts and adjacent golf links are for those who desire physical activity.

The **Sheraton Kauai Resort,** 2440 Ho'onani Rd., Po'ipu Beach, Koloa, HI 96756, 808/742-1661 or 800/782-9488, www.sheraton-kauai.com, reopened in 1997, the last of the major hotels on Kaua'i to do so after the devastating effects of Hurricane 'Iniki. Sheraton's two former properties were combined into a 414-room resort with ocean, beach, and garden wings, on 20 lovely acres. Casually elegant and elegantly modern, the Sheraton Kauai Resort is a tasteful, eminently comfortable accommodation, no taller than the coconut trees on property, where the tropics surround you and pretense is left at the door.

The porte cochere opens onto the open-air reception area. Check in and inquire about events or book activities at the concierge and activity desks. Notice the lovely mural of a Hawaiian family gracing the lobby. Around the courtyard beyond, look for the news library; retail shops for resortwear, sundries, fine art, and jewelry; a fitness center; beauty salon and massage center; and the hotel's main restaurant and lounge. The Shells restaurant is known for its breakfasts and seafood buffet dinners, and for the perfect sunset spot, find a seat at The Point lounge. In a quiet corner at the back of the Shells, the Naniwa restaurant offers tastes of Japan. Lighter fare is served throughout the day at the Oasis Bar and Grill by the oceanside pool. The property holds two swimming pools, one in the garden, surrounded by waterfalls, and the other, just off the beach, boasting a hot tub and water slide. The beach activities center offers rental of water equipment, and the tennis courts are open to guests only 7 A.M.–10 P.M. Kids 5–12 years old can have great fun in supervised play through the Keiki Aloha Club. A complimentary on-demand shuttle operates 10 A.M.–10 P.M. within a three-mile radius.

Each spacious room is appointed with amenities for your comfort, including a/c, entertainment center, refrigerator, personal safe, and private lanai. Room rates range from $320 for a garden view to $500 for an ocean luxury room; suites run $550–1,100. In addition, there is a daily $15 per room resort activities fee. Numerous packages are available. Guests at this resort can also use the facilities at the Princeville Hotel on the north shore and charge all expenses to their rooms.

## Condos

Although the prices in Po'ipu can be a bit higher than elsewhere on Kaua'i, you get a lot for your money. More than a dozen well-appointed modern condos are lined up along the beach and just off it, with thousands of units available. Most are a variation on the same theme: comfortably furnished, fully equipped, with a tennis court here and there, always a swimming pool, and maid service available. Most require a minimum stay of at least two nights, with discounts for longer visits. The following condos have been chosen to give you a general idea of what to expect.

**Embassy Vacation Resort Poipu Point,** managed by Marc Resorts Hawaii, 1613 Pe'e Rd., Po'ipu, HI 96756, 808/742-1888 or 800/535-0085, is a marriage of luxury condo and timeshare units that sits on 23 manicured, oceanfront cliff acres. The Embassy is grand in scope but not pretentious. Upon arrival, you enter through a white porte cochere to the main lobby with its guest reception and concierge desk, which opens to the cascading pools and falls of the gardens below. The 10 neoclassic plantation-style buildings surround a central courtyard where you will discover, fronting a sandy beach, a large pool with one side tiled and the other sand-bottomed. At

poolside is a hydrospa and, nearby, a complete fitness center. Mornings bring a complimentary healthy breakfast in an outdoor dining area near the pool. Here and there throughout the property you'll find little picnic nooks complete with tables and barbecue grills for your enjoyment. Notice a thick grove of ironwoods completely surrounded by a hedge; these protect the site of an ancient *heiau* that the resort is dedicated to preserving. Just below the pool area lies a stretch of dramatic coastline pounded by heavy wave action, frothing misty azure against the coal-black lava. These waters are too treacherous for recreational swimming, but a two-minute walk takes you to Shipwreck Beach. The one- and two-bedroom units, air-conditioned with ceiling fans throughout, feature full kitchens with marble-topped counters and all amenities and a dining/living room that opens to a wraparound lanai. Each unit has its own washer and dryer, along with steam iron and ironing board. Room charges (no extra charge for additional guests) range $349–489 for one-bedroom units and $389–583 for two-bedroom suites; package rates available.

The oceanfront condo complex of **Poipu Shores,** 1775 Pe'e Rd., Koloa, HI 96756; 808/742-7700 or 800/367-5004, is set along the rocky shoreline nearby, surrounded by other small condos. All units face the ocean, and the property offers a swimming pool and barbecue grills. The area's best beaches are only a short stroll away. Each unit has a complete kitchen, and all are clean, spacious, and airy. The one-bedroom units run $225–265, a standard two-bedroom is $265–300, a deluxe two-bedroom is $295–330, and a three-bedroom unit runs $325–360. There is a three-night minimum stay. Maid service is provided free every day. Poipu Shores is a Castle Resorts and Hotels property.

With 110 acres, **Po'ipu Kai Resort** has the largest grounds in the area—one corner of which runs down to the ocean. Through this finely landscaped property, a walking path connects Brennecke Beach with Shipwreck Beach. Set among broad gardens, most units look out onto a swimming pool or the tennis courts. There are one-, two-, three-, and four-bedroom units, in numerous floor plans. Some are Hawaiian in theme;

others are Spanish, with stucco and arched entryways; modern units show more glass and chrome; and a few may resemble your own Mainland abode. A handful of multi-bedroom homes are also available in the adjacent housing estate. Facilities on the grounds include nine tennis courts, a pro shop with a resident tennis pro, six swimming pools, two outdoor hot tubs, numerous barbecue grills, and an activity center. Next to the resort office is the House of Seafood, the area's premier seafood restaurant, open only for dinner. A complex structure of room rates exists, depending upon the season and length of stay, but generally the one-bedrooms run $115–274 during regular season, two-bedroom units $167–318, three-bedroom units $226–270, and four-bedrooms units $344. For larger groups, a number of five-bedroom units are also available; inquire. While a number of agencies handle rooms at the Po'ipu Kai, Suite Paradise handles the lion's share, and also manages units in half a dozen other condo properties in the Po'ipu area. For reservations, write to Po'ipu Kai Resort, 1941 Po'ipu Rd., Po'ipu-Koloa, HI 96756, or call 808/742-6464 or 800/367-8020, visit www.suite-paradise.com, or email mail@suite-paradise.com. Aston Hotels and Resorts also manages numerous units at Po'ipu Kai that range $280–445. For information on its units and rates, contact Aston at 1775 Po'ipu Road, Koloa, HI 96756, 808/742-7400 or 800/922-7866.

The **Kiahuna Plantation Resort,** 2253 Po'ipu Road, Koloa, HI 96756, 808/742-6411 or 800/688-7444, is operated by Hawaii's own Outrigger Resorts; some units are managed by Castle Resorts and Hotels, 800/367-5004. Prior to opening to the public in 1972, these grounds were the estate and gardens of Mr. and Mrs. Hector Moir, a manager of the Koloa Sugar Company. Their private home, now serving as the reception center, is a breezy but stout lava-rock structure in the classic plantation style. Their living room and adjoining rooms, appointed in lustrous koa, now serve as the dining room of the Plantation Garden Restaurant. Fronting the house is Moir Gardens, a unique mix of cacti and tropical flowers and trees. The property, comprising 35 lush acres fronting Po'ipu Beach, houses just over 300 units, divided into separate buildings. Contemporary in design, they are white inside and out with dark trim. Interior styling differs from one unit to another since each is individually owned, yet all are well appointed, as they must meet high standards. You enter the large one-bedroom units through louvered doors. Sliding doors at the far end allow breezes to filter through, assisted by ceiling fans in every room. The bedroom features a king- or queen-size bed, and across the hall, the bathroom has a shower and tub, dressing area, and handy hallway closets with complimentary safes. The comfy living room, separate dining area, and full modern kitchen are on the ocean side. Here you'll find all the amenities and comforts of home and, what's more, you have daily housekeeping service. Each unit has a covered lanai with table, chairs, and lounges overlooking the grounds. With the sea in the distance you'll feel like a transplanted flower in this magnificent garden, set amongst red ginger, yellow plumeria, and a painter's palette of greens. The two-bedroom units are bilevel and the size of most homes. All units are only a minute's walk from the beach, home to the Hawaiian monk seal March–July. Full beach service is provided, and the concierge desk can make arrangements for any activity on the island. Laundry facilities are on the premises. One-bedroom suites (maximum four guests) run $215–450, two-bedroom suites (for up to six) are $345–485. With several units located closer to the beach, Castle Resorts has some rooms that run up to $850 a night. Prices depend on the view; numerous packages are available. The Kiahuna Plantation Resort is a first-rate condominium, expertly managed, with a superb location.

**Poipu Kapili,** 2221 Kapili Rd., Koloa, HI 96756, 808/742-6449 or 800/443-7714, fax 808/742-9162, www.poipukapili.com, aloha @poipukapili.com, is a two- and three-story upscale condo complex with only 60 units on five acres. It has a touch of the Hawaiian plantation style, across the road from a rocky shoreline, beyond which waves continually break over the reef. All units have ocean views. The pool is in the center of the property, surrounded by flowering gardens and lawn. Free, lighted tennis courts are available, and racquets and balls are provided to guests. Each unit is huge, ranging from 1,200-

foot one-bedroom suites to 2,600-foot two-bedroom penthouses. Bedrooms have ceiling fans and wicker furniture, kitchens are spacious and furnished with modern appliances, and the large living area opens onto a private lanai, many of which overlook the pool and garden, some of which look directly onto the ocean. Regular season rates range $210–230 for a one-bedroom unit to $280–500 for a two-bedroom; high season and holiday rates are higher, but monthly and weekly discounts are available, as are several packages. The condo also offers a convenient activities desk that will book you into any activity that strikes your fancy.

On the far side of Koloa Landing is **Whaler's Cove**, 2640 Puuholo Rd., Koloa, HI 96756, 808/742-7571 or 800/225-2683, fax 808/742-1185, www.whalers-cove.com, whalers@hawaiian.net, a deluxe accommodation with only 38 units offering you an excellent sense of privacy and manageability. Set right on the point, Whaler's Cove opens to and embraces the sea. All individually owned, most units are tastefully decorated in a contemporary island style. Here you'll find full kitchens and baths with all the amenities, daily housekeeping, laundry facilities, and a private swimming pool set above the rocky water's edge. One-bedroom units here run $349–469, and two-bedroom units are $479–619.

Other condos also stretch along this wonderful shore. The smaller ones generally cluster at the east end of the beach; others are near Koloa Landing and Kuhio Park. **Makahu'ena at Poipu** sits on Makahu'ena Point, with the crashing waves below. Managed by Castle Resorts, this complex offers one-, two-, and three-bedroom units with full kitchens, and a swimming pool and tennis courts are on the property for guests to use. Rates run $190–390 during regular season, $10–20 less during low season. Call 808/742-2482 or 800/367-5004 for information.

**Poipu Crater Resort** snuggles inside a small seaside caldera. The Polynesian-inspired buildings are surrounded by greenery and the property includes a swimming pool and tennis courts. Units here are available through Suite Paradise, 808/742-7400 or 800/367-8020; Grantham, 808/742-2000 or 800/325-5701; Poipu Connection, 808/742-2233 or 800/742-2260; and R&R Realty, 808/742-7555 or 808/367-8022.

An older property with reasonable rates, **Sunset Kahili**, 808/742-7434 or 800/827-6478, www.sunsetkahili.com, sits high on the hill overlooking the east end of Po'ipu Beach. Just a few steps from Brennecke Beach is the newer and posher **Nihi Kai Villas**, 808/743-1412 or 800/742-1412, and on the west end, **Waikomo Stream Villas**, 808/742-7220 or 800/325-5701, is just inland and backs up against the stream above Koloa Landing. Both Nihi Kai and Waikomo Stream villas are managed by Grantham Resorts. Lawa'i Beach offers **Lawa'i Beach Resort**, 808/240-5100, a time-share property that rents out condo units for $125 a day when they are available, and the more spartan **Kuhio Shores**, 808/742-1391, and **Prince Kuhio**, 808/742-1409.

## East End B&Bs and Vacation Rentals

**Pua Hale** (Flower House), 2381 Kipuka St., Poi'pu Beach, Koloa, HI 96756, 808/742-1700 or 800/745-7414, www.portraitsofhawaii.com, poh@aloha.net, is a lovely, deluxe 750-square-foot house where your privacy and serenity are assured. With a touch of Japan, Pua Hale features shoji screens, cool wooden floors, a relaxing *ofuro*, custom furniture and decorating, and a complete kitchen and laundry. This self-contained unit, only minutes from Po'ipu, is surrounded by a privacy fence and a manicured garden, so you can choose whether you want to socialize or simply enjoy the glorious quietude on your own. Rates are a reasonable $120 per night, or $750 per week; four nights minimum. You can't find better.

Built in 1998 at the eastern end of Po'ipu is **Maluhia ma ka Honua.** With three bedrooms, four bathrooms, full kitchen, huge living/dining room, and wraparound lanai, this house is suited for families. It has all electric appliances in the kitchen and the amenities are modern throughout. Maluhia ma ka Honua makes you feel at home, and you can't help but relax and have a restful time. The rent rate is $1,890 per week, seven nights minimum, with a $200 cleaning fee. Contact Garden Island Rentals for reservations, 808/742-9537 or 800/247-5599.

KAUA'I

Right on the water just east of Brennecke Beach is the upscale **Honu Kai Villas**, 1871 Pe'e Road, Koloa, HI 96756, 808/742-9155 or 800/854-8363, fax 808/742-7940, www.honukai.com, rjr@honukai.com. The location couldn't be better. This tight compound contains five spacious units and a swimming pool. Modern in design with great attention to detail, each unit shows fine craftsmanship and material and has full kitchen and laundry facilities. Rates for one-bedroom units run $156–250 a day, two-bedroom units go for $250–282, and the three-bedroom oceanfront homes run $392–502; five nights minimum and a reduction per night after seven days. A $100–190 out cleaning fee is levied on all units. No breakfast is served.

Directly up from Brennecke Beach is **Plantation Cottage** vacation rental, 2254 Pane Rd., 808/245-8841. Built in 1924 and restored in 1996, this building evokes the sugar era with its spaciousness and front veranda. A two-bedroom, one-bath home that sleeps five, it rents for $165 a night or $825 a week; the rate changes depending on the season.

**Poipu Plantation Resort**, 1792 Pe'e Road, Koloa, HI 96756, 808/742-6757 or 800/634-0263, fax 808/742-8681, www.poipubeach.com, plantation@poipubeach.com, is a three-bedroom plantation-era home that's just up the street from Brennecke Beach. This home has three bed-and-breakfast rooms, all with different configurations, but each has a private bath, TV, and air-conditioning. The front lanai serves as a common room and is where breakfast is served. Rooms run $95–150 a night, three nights minimum. In three separate buildings tucked behind the front house are nine reasonably priced one- and two-bedroom condo units that have full kitchens, living rooms, and multiple amenities. The condo units range $105–135 a night, three nights minimum, and for the location are very reasonably priced.

Adjacent to the Hyatt Hotel and within easy walking distance of both Shipwreck and Brennecke Beaches is **Hale Hyette B&B**, which offers one room with private entrance and bath, a queen bed, partial kitchen, a lanai with views, and a simple fruit basket breakfast each morning. The

room rate is $85 a night; no credit cards. For reservations and information call 808/742-2877 or 866/764-7822, or check www.aalohakauai.com, halehyette@aol.com.

## West End B&Bs and Vacation Rentals

**Koloa Landing Cottages**, 2704-B Ho'onani Rd., Koloa, HI 96756, 808/742-1470 or 800/779-8773, www.koloa-landing.com, info@koloa-landing.com, is directly across the street from the Koloa Landing cove. These colorfully painted basic units are some of Po'ipu's least-expensive accommodations. The main house and five cottages, all two-bedroom, two-bath units, each sleep up to six people and have a full kitchen, lanai, and color television. Rates are $140 for the house and $125 for the cottages for up to four, with $10 for each additional person. For one bedroom it's $95, and the studio, also equipped with kitchen and color TVs, runs $85. A one-time cleaning fee of $20–60 is added to the price of the room. Four nights minimum. Coin laundry facilities are on the premises. The Treehouse and Beach House are two separate houses near the end of Nalo Road, above Brennecke Beach. Bright, open, airy, with a cathedral ceiling and a lanai facing the sea, the one-bedroom Treehouse is above a storage area below. It's great for couples and runs $150 a night. Directly behind is the Beach House. Perfect for a family, this very livable three-bedroom house has plenty of character and goes for $150 a night. Reservations are suggested well ahead of time. Contact Ellie or Bret for information or to reserve.

Next door to Koloa Landing Cottages is **Poipu Bed and Breakfast Inn**, 2720 Ho'onani Rd., Koloa, HI 96756, 808/742-1146 or 800/808-2330, www.poipu-inn.com, info@poipu-inn.net, a large and spacious renovated plantation house from the 1930s. Stained in tropical colors, this wooden house has all the comforts of home, plus antiques, art, and crafts from the island. If you have a childlike affection for carousel rides, you'll love this place because there are several carousel horses in the house. The bedrooms are on either side of the large, central sitting room. Each has a color TV, ceiling fan, and private bath. The sitting room has a TV, videotapes, books, and games.

Smoking is not allowed inside the house; sit out on the large, comfortable lanai or walk in the garden. Children are welcome. Daily room rates, including a continental breakfast, are $125–165. Rooms can be combined into two-bedroom, two-bath suites, and the entire house can be rented.

**Garden Isle Cottages,** 2660 Puuholo Rd., Koloa, HI 96756, 808/742-6717 or 800/742-6711, www.oceancottages.com, vacation@oceancottages.com, perches on the craggy rocks above Koloa Landing surrounded by lush foliage, offering privacy. The cottages are operated by artists Robert and Sharon Flynn, whose original works highlight each of the units. The cottages are two duplexes, each with upper and lower units. All the units have one bedroom and one bath and are self-contained and fully equipped; downstairs units have kitchens, upstairs units have kitchenettes. The price is $170 high season (mid-December to mid-April) and $140 low season, plus $10 for each person beyond two. Four nights' deposit is required; weekly and monthly rates can be arranged.

Contemporary **Turtle Cove Suites,** P.O. Box 1899, Koloa, HI 96756, 808/742-8978, fax 808/742-7071, planet-hawaii.com/poipubeach, turtles@aloha.net, has four units with full amenities overlooking Whalers Cove. Two have full kitchens and two have kitchenettes, and there's a small private swimming pool. Rates run $100–175, three nights minimum; $300 holds the reservation, and no credit cards are accepted.

Nearby along the same quiet residential road is **Kauai Cove Cottages,** 2672 Puuholo Rd. #A, Po'ipu, HI 96756, 808/742-2562 or 800/642-9945, www.kauaicove.com, info@kauaicove.com. Set close to the road and lined up like row houses, they are not much to look at from the outside, but they are a surprise on the inside. Not overly large, but modern in style and well designed in light-colored hardwood and bamboo, each of the three studios is adorned in island tropical decor with island-inspired artwork on the walls. Tall cathedral ceilings make the rooms appear more spacious, and a kitchen is set up for full meal preparations. Each room comes with color TV and a CD player with a selection of contemporary Hawaiian music, and old-style hanging mosquito netting surrounds the queen bed. These are comfortable units that remind you in every way that you are on vacation in the tropics. Rates are $75 a night with a $25 cleaning fee for stays of three days or less.

Nearly across the street, **Hale Pilialoha** is another pleasant house in this quiet neighborhood. Airy and spacious, the home's nine French doors open onto gardens and lanai. The main room and full kitchen complement the two bedrooms to accommodate a family. Rent is $200 a night for two people, $25 a person additional, plus $75 cleaning fee. Contact Rosewood, 872 Kamalu Rd., Kapa'a, HI 96746, 808/822-5216, fax 808/822-5478, website: rosewoodkauai.com, rosewood@aloha.net.

Along Lawa'i Road near Kukui'ula Harbor, three plantation-era buildings, aquamarine with white and yellow highlights, sun themselves contentedly on the well-landscaped lawn below tall palms and just back from the water, a perfect picture of old-style Hawaii from decades past. These renovated buildings are **Coastline Cottages,** and all have been brought up to date with modern comforts. The four units, a studio, a one-bedroom/two-bath, a two-bedroom/two-bath, and a three-bedroom/four-bath, run $185–650 a night with a three-night minimum. A barbecue grill and laundry facilities are on the premises. Contact P.O. Box 1214, Koloa, HI 96756, 808/742-9688, fax 808/742-7620, www.coastlinecottages.com, jds@aloha.net.

Directly across from Kukui'ula Harbor is the **Poipu Beach Club Bed and Breakfast,** 808/742-1639, 4560 Lawai Beach Rd., Koloa, HI 96756, www.poipubeachclub.com, info@poipubeachclub.com. Consisting of two buildings raised above the ground, the bed and breakfast offers views good not only out onto the water but also inland to the mountains. Of the three rooms, two run $125 and one is $160 a night, three nights minimum; no credit cards. Everyone shares the living room space. Full breakfast served.

You will find no bedroom closer to the gentle surf than at **Gloria's Spouting Horn Bed and Breakfast,** 4464 Lawa'i Beach Rd., Koloa, HI 96756, tel./fax 808/742-6995, www.gloriasbedandbreakfast.com. Leveled by Hurricane 'Iniki, the one-time humble plantation house has come back as a perfectly designed and highly attractive B&B, with your comfort and privacy assured. Created by Bob and Gloria with the help of a California architect, the stout, hurricane-resistant, natural-wood post-and-beam structure supports a Polynesian longhouse-style roof. None of the three guest rooms share a common wall, and the entire home is designed for maximum exposure to the outdoors. Wide bay windows with louvers underneath bring you as close as possible to the outdoors when opened simultaneously. A nubbed burgundy carpet (no shoes inside, please) massages your feet as you pad the hall to your cross-ventilated suite, which is further cooled by ceiling fans in the main bedroom and in your private bath. Skylights let in the sun or stars, and floral wallpaper and antique tables suggest a Victorian theme. Every suite opens to a private lanai where the rolling surf and dependable whoosh of the Spouting Horn serenade you throughout the evening. All baths are private, spacious, and offer a shower, commode, and Japanese *ofuro*. Descend a central stairway to a small bar that holds port, brandy, and different liqueurs for your evening enjoyment. Breakfast is a combination of fresh fruits, fresh juices, piping hot coffee and tea, and perhaps a pizza pancake crunchy with macadamia nuts and smothered with homemade banana topping. Room rates are $250 per night, $275 for less than seven nights, $300 over Christmas, three nights minimum; no credit cards. Only a few steps from the Spouting Horn, at this absolutely excellent accommodation traffic disappears at night and the quiet settles in.

## Vacation Rental Agencies

**R&R Realty and Rentals,** 808/742-7555 or 800/367-8022, fax 808/742-1559, www.r7r .com, randr@r7r.com, arranges only condo rentals in Po'ipu. R&R has more than four dozen units in half a dozen properties, mostly in the low to midrange complexes. Studios start about $75 a night, one-, two-, and three-bedroom units run $90–225, but rates are cheaper at four nights or longer.

**Poipu Connection Realty,** 808/742-2233 or 800/742-2260, fax 808/742-7382, www.poipu-connection.com, poipu@hawaiian.net, handles private vacation condo rentals and two homes exclusively along the Po'ipu coast. From the large complexes to a small six-plex, these units range from $75 a night for a studio to $275 a night for a deluxe oceanfront unit.

**Garden Island Rentals,** 808/742-9537 or 800/247-5599, fax 808/742-9540, www.kauai rentals.com, gir@kauairentals.com, rents mostly high-end vacation homes and a few condo units, exclusively in the Po'ipu area. Nearly all are on or very close to the water. The condo units run $125–250 a night with a four-night minimum stay, and the homes range up to $7,000 a week with a seven-night minimum.

**Grantham Resorts,** 808/742-2000 or 800/325-5791, fax 808/742-9093, www.grantham-resorts.com, info@grantham-resorts.com, is located in Koloa and manages both condo units and private homes, exclusively in Po'ipu. Most of its condo units are in the Waikomo Stream Villas and Nihi Kai Resort, but there are units in eight other complexes. Private home rentals run from a two-bedroom, two-bath bungalow near Keiki Beach for $175 a day to a four-bedroom, four-bath house that sleeps 10 for $925 a day. Well established and reputable, Grantham has been matching people with places since 1984.

**Kauai Vacation Rentals,** 3-3311 Kuhio Hwy., Lihu'e, HI 96766, 808/245-8841 or 800/367-5025, www.KauaiVacationRentals.com, aloha@kvrre.com, handles condo and vacation rental homes in Po'ipu, mostly low to midrange.

# FOOD

## Inexpensive

**Brennecke's Beach Deli** is just off Po'ipu Beach, below Brennecke's restaurant. The best deals are the takeout sandwiches, but it also has pastries, ice cream, and beer.

Joe Batteiger is a football fanatic from Cleveland, Ohio, who spent many a fall afternoon in that city's "Dog Pound." After the game, Joe and his buddies wanted to wrap their meaty fists around huge sandwiches and wash them down with cold ones. No froufrou food for these bruisers. So Joe moved to Kaua'i and opened a restaurant, which did so well when it was operating that he opened a second joint, **Joe's on the Green,** at the Kiahuna Golf Club clubhouse, 808/742-9696. Breakfast is served 7–11:30 A.M. with discounted specials until 9 A.M. Breakfast here is eggs Benedict, biscuits and gravy, corned beef hash, and omelettes, as well as pancakes, bagels, and loco moco. Lunch (until 2:30 P.M.) brings a personalized house salad that you build yourself for $6.50, beer battered fish and chips, and sandwiches priced $6.75–8.25. The grill serves up such treats as a Joe Mama burger for $7.50, a grilled chicken breast sandwich for $7.95, and A Dog Named Joe for $5.25; served with a wedge of kosher pickle and authentic stadium mustard imported from Cleveland. Happy hour for drinks runs 3–6 P.M., and dinners are now served Thursday 5:30–8:30 P.M. Joe's place is a sleeper, known mostly to local people who come time and again to get a fine breakfast or lunch at a reasonable price. Some swear it's the best breakfast in town.

## Moderate

An indoor/outdoor café, **Pattaya Asian Cafe,** at the Po'ipu Shopping Village, 808/742-8818, is open Mon.–Sat. 11:30 A.M.–2:30 P.M. for lunch and daily 5:30–9:30 P.M. for dinner. This is a very tasteful, moderately priced restaurant appointed with a flagstone floor and Thai mahogany tables and chairs. The ornate mahogany bar, covered by a pagoda roof, flashes with mirrors embedded in two gold and blue swans. The exotic menu starts with *mee grop,* a dish of crispy noodles, chicken, bean sprouts, and green onions; Bangkok wings, a concoction of long rice, onion, black mushrooms, carrots, and ground pork served with the house peanut sauce; and other appetizers that range $7.25–8.95. Soups and salads include spicy lemongrass soup, a Thai ginger coconut soup with chicken or seafood, and fresh island papaya salad. More substantial meals include pad thai, a traditional stir-fried noodle dish for $8.25–16.95; spicy fried rice ranging $8.95–11.25 depending upon ingredients; red, green, and yellow curry made with chicken, pork, beef, or shrimp for $8.95–16.95; and plenty of vegetarian selections. All dishes can be ordered to the spice

level you desire, and most come with your selection of tofu, beef, chicken, shrimp, or seafood. Pattaya Asian Cafe is a terrific and authentic restaurant with friendly service and good prices, and you know the food will be good because the owner uses herbs from his own garden.

At the rear of Po'ipu Shopping Village is the casual open-air **Tropical Burger** restaurant, 808/742-1808, with lots more on the menu than two-fisters. It opens for breakfast at 6:30 A.M. for eggs, omelettes, and griddle food; lunch starts at 11 A.M. with burgers, sandwiches, and salads. The dinner menu is more complete and great for the family. Entrées start at about $12.

You can find other midpriced restaurants at the hotels and clubhouses in Po'ipu. Try the **Poipu Bay Bar and Grill** at the Poipu Bay Golf Course clubhouse, 808/742-1515. Open 6:30 A.M.–2:30 P.M. for breakfast and lunch, with the bar serving until 4:30 P.M., this moderately priced restaurant serves mostly American standards, with the addition of a Japanese breakfast and various plate lunches. Seated inside or out, you'll have fantastic views over the fairways of the Ha'upu Ridge and coastline.

## Expensive

**Brennecke's Beach Broiler,** 808/742-7588, an open-air, second-story deck restaurant directly across from Po'ipu Beach County Park, offers a superb view. Seafood is the dinner specialty, but pasta and *kiawe*-broiled meat and chicken are also served; dinner prices range $17–26. Salads and sandwiches are served for lunch, and *pu pu* until closing. There is a children's menu for both lunch and dinner. Lunch is 11 A.M.–4 P.M., happy hour 2–5 P.M., dinner 4–10 P.M., with early dinner specials 4–6 P.M. Brennecke's is a fun, casual place with tasty food, a good choice for a family on vacation. As it's popular and not a big place, call for a reservation.

Up Nalo Road behind the Nihi Kai condominium is **Casa di Amici,** 808/742-1555, a fine Italian restaurant that relocated a few years back from its original location in Kilauea. Open nightly from 6 P.M. for dinner only, Casa di Amici offers a wide-ranging menu that includes a gnocchi quattro formaggio appetizer, sliced tomato salad, risotto Milanese, and various pasta dishes, or choose other entrées like fresh catch, black tiger prawns, medallions of beef filet, or porcini-crusted chicken. Most entrées fall into the $23–26 range with appetizers and salads for $5–8. The "light" selection offers smaller portions and saves a bit on the bill. Save room for bananas Foster, a chocolate torte, or tiramisu for dessert. Soft piano music is offered as an accompaniment on Friday and Saturday evenings. All in all, Casi di Amici is a reputable place, with a relaxing atmosphere and tasty food at prices that are not too outrageous.

**Keoki's Paradise,** at the Po'ipu Shopping Village, 808/742-7534, is an excellent choice for dinner or a night's entertainment. Enter past a small fountain into the longhouse-style interior with stone floor and thatched roof. Choose a seat at the long bar for a casual evening or at one of the tables overlooking the garden surrounding the restaurant. The varied menu lists savory items, including Thai shrimp sticks for $8.95; fresh catch for $19.95–23.95 prepared a variety of ways including baked, herb-sautéed, teriyaki-grilled, or in an orange ginger sauce; pesto macadamia shrimp for $16.95; or beef dishes like top sirloin at $18.95 and prime rib for $24.95. Keoki's renowned dessert is its Hula Pie, a mound of ice cream filling an Oreo cookie crust, that's big enough for at least two. Simpler and cheaper, the Cafe Menu (available 11 A.M.–11:30 P.M. at the bar) includes *pu pu,* burgers, salads, sandwiches, and plate lunches. "Aloha Fridays" bring food and drink specials 4:30–7 P.M. A great selection of beer and mixed drinks adds to an enjoyable evening. Have an island drink before going in to dinner, served 5:30–10 P.M. Live entertainment is offered Fri.–Sat. by local bands specializing in contemporary Hawaiian music. Keoki's is a feel-good place that fills you up with large portions of tasty food.

At the Po'ipu Shopping Village, culinary magic is created at **Roy's Poipu Bar and Grill,** 808/742-5000, open nightly for dinner 5:30–9:30 P.M. Here, in an open kitchen—one of Roy's trademarks—the chef de cuisine and a superbly trained staff create an array of marvelous dishes from the island's freshest meats, fish, poultry, fruits, and vegetables. The chef's "specials sheet" changes nightly, but a sampling of the delectable dishes that you may enjoy includes dim sum appetizers like crispy smoked duck gyoza, crispy Asian spring rolls, sweet basil-crusted beef sauté, and ravioli with shiitake and spinach. Healthy green salads and *imu*-baked pizzas are also available. A few entrées usually on the menu are lemongrass-crusted chicken, grilled shrimp, and pot roast trimmed with mashed potatoes and old-fashioned apple ginger pineapple sauce. The specials sheet always has fresh fish and seafood, like basil-seared *ono* with Thai red curry and lobster sauce, macadamia nut-crusted *hevi* with a mango and coconut sauce, and sesame-seared *uku* with a shiitake cream sauce, all at market price. Most entrées are in the $15–25 range. Roy's offers a memorable dining experience.

At the Kiahuna Plantation Resort in what once was the plantation manager's home, under towering trees and surrounded by lush greenery, **Plantation Gardens** restaurant and bar, 808/742-2216, serves up tempting fish and meat dishes, plus pasta and unique wood-fired pizzas. Try the apple-smoked bacon and three cheese or Puna goat cheese and pesto pizzas for $10.95–14.95. Perhaps more substantial are the full entrées, like pan-seared opakapaka with saffron lemon cream sauce, Hawaiian bouillabaisse, Parker Ranch New York steak, crispy rotisserie duck, or beef short rib stew, $20–27. The menu changes daily, but the full bar is always open for a complement to any meal.

## Fine Dining

Exquisite dining can be enjoyed at various restaurants, some overlooking Po'ipu's beaches—perfect for catching the setting sun—and others in elegant gardens bathed by tropical breezes. Prices are high, but you definitely get a full measure of what you pay for. Reservations are recommended at all these fine-dining establishments.

The **Beach House Restaurant,** 808/742-1424, with its superb location at Lawa'i Beach, is open daily for dinner only 6–10 P.M. (from 5:30 P.M. in winter). While the menu varies somewhat each night, expect a blending of East and West. Some entrées, mostly in the $22–27 range, might be a spinach-mushroom-stuffed chicken breast with boursin sauce, seared crab-stuffed pork medallions with Okinawan sweet potato mash and port demi sauce, Chinese-style roasted duck with lemon-orange Grand Marnier demi and seared miso shiitake risotto cake, and fire-roasted *ahi* with furikake mashed potatoes, cilantro black bean sauce, and beurre blanc. Sunset at the Beach House couldn't be better, so call well ahead of time and reserve a window seat, or stop at the lounge, which opens at 5 P.M., and order an appetizer for the show. The Beach House is now operated by the owners of the first-rate SeaWatch and Plantation House restaurants on Maui.

The **House of Seafood** at Po'ipu Kai Resort, 808/742-6433, has windows framing living still-lifes of palm fronds and flower gardens against a background of the distant ocean. It consistently has the largest selection of fresh fish in the area, often with at least 10 varieties, and its dishes are very creative—baked in puff pastry, sautéed with macadamia nut sauce, or steamed in a ginger sauce, to name a few. Ask the waiter for the best choice of the day. Although fish and seafood are its specialty, steak and chicken are also on the menu. Start your meal off with an appetizer, soup, or salad, and finish with a creamy island-fruit dessert or drink. Entrées run $25–43, with a children's menu $7–13. The House of Seafood is a restaurant for a special occasion; locals speak highly of the quality of its food. Open nightly for dinner only, with happy hour and *pu pu* 3–5 P.M.

The main dining room at the Hyatt is the **Ilima Terrace**, 808/742-1234, open daily for breakfast and lunch, with both buffet and à la carte menus. Descend a formal staircase and step onto a slate floor covered with an emerald green carpet. Floor-to-ceiling beveled glass doors look out onto the lovely grounds, and seating is pleasant inside or out. Start your day with a choice of fresh chilled juices, hearty omelettes, or griddle items, where most selections are under $10. If it's hard to choose, try the Ilima Breakfast Buffet at $19.75, or sleep in Sunday for the hearty champagne brunch for $30.95. Lunch is à la carte and brings starters like smoked chicken quesadillas, deli board items of soup, salad, and sand-wiches, or more substantial dishes like seared *'ahi*, prawn noodles, or your choice of pizza.

**Dondero's,** featuring classic Italian cuisine, is the Hyatt's signature restaurant, 808/742-1234, open for dinner only 6–10 P.M. The continental room is formal, and the view through floor-to-ceiling windows is of the manicured gardens. Dinner begins with antipasti, such as calamari fritti, for $8.50–12, and moves on to soups and salads, mostly under $10. Rigatoni alla Bolognese and other traditional pastas, osso buco, cioppino, and many other fish and meat selections fill the menu and cost $16.50–36. Round out your meal with tiramisu or another dessert, and coffee or cordials. In addition to dessert wines, Dondero's has table wine to complement any entrée. Resort attire is a must.

Slightly more casual is the Hyatt's **Tidepool Restaurant,** 808/742-1234, open for dinner only 6–10 P.M., a mushroom cluster of thatched South Sea "huts" supported by huge beams forming an indoor/outdoor restaurant overlooking the tide pools. Low-lit and romantic, the Tidepool boasts fresh fish, sautéed, seared, grilled, or steamed, with a medley of sauces and toppings to choose from. The signature dish is macadamia nut-crusted mahimahi with a kahlua, lime, and ginger butter sauce. This contemporary Hawaiian cuisine also includes grilled steak and ribs. Entrées run $23–36. While the food is memorable, the setting only adds to the experience.

The Sheraton also offers sumptuous food in fine settings. **Shells,** 808/742-1661, the Sheraton's signature restaurant, is set on a rocky point almost at water's edge. Facing east and commanding a superb view of the white sand and rich blue water of the bay, it's a perfect place to start the day. Served 6:30–11 A.M., Shells' breakfast has a well-deserved reputation. It includes traditional American and some international selections, off the menu or as a buffet. For an evening meal, items include any number of fresh fish, broiled, baked, steamed, or sautéed and covered in saffron cream, citrus glaze, teriyaki, beurre blanc, or tartar sauces. Other choices are roast prime rib, pork loin, macadamia- and panko-crusted chicken breast, and pasta dishes. The salad bar always includes locally grown greens. Entrées run mostly $25–35. In addition to the usual menu, the Friday Night Seafood Buffet has made a reputation for itself; it runs $37.50. Dinner is served 5:30–9:30 P.M. nightly.

The traditional-style Japanese restaurant **Naniwa,** 808/742-1661, is at the back corner of the Shells restaurant. Sushi is a favorite here, as are the fish preparations. Open 5:30–9:30 P.M. seven nights a week. Naniwa will not fail to please.

## ENTERTAINMENT

If, after a sunset dinner and a lovely stroll along the beach, you find yourself with dancing feet or a desire to hear the strains of your favorite tunes, Po'ipu won't let you down. Several hotel restaurants and lounges in the area feature piano music or small combos, often with a Hawaiian flair.

**The Point** lounge at the Sheraton gives you a ringside seat for sunset and perhaps the best coastal view in Po'ipu. This lounge is open for drinks and cocktails 11 A.M.–1 A.M. and offers nightly hula at 5 P.M. Light meals of soups, salads, and sandwiches are served 11 A.M.–3 P.M., and *pu pu* are offered 5–10 P.M. The Point follows sunset with the soft sounds of light contemporary music Mon.–Sat. until about 9 P.M.

For live jazz nightly from 9 P.M. try **Stevenson's Library** at the Hyatt. This is the poshest lounge on the island—resortwear requested—and it has a full range of excellent exotic drinks. With dark wood decor, a fancy bar, a saltwater aquarium, over-stuffed chairs, pool and billiard tables, a grand piano, and ornate chess sets waiting for the first move, this is a wonderful spot for evening relaxation.

Free Hawaiian music is presented nightly starting around sundown at the Hyatt's **Seaview Terrace,** and this show is accompanied by a torch-lighting ceremony every evening except Tuesday and Sunday, which bring a *keiki* hula show. Come for *pu pu* and cocktails and enjoy the captivating entertainment.

**Keoki's,** in the Po'ipu Shopping Village, gently sways with contemporary Hawaiian music Friday and Saturday evenings. Come for dinner or a quiet beer and *pu pu,* and let your cares drift away. The small dance floor is popular with those from the area.

The Po'ipu Shopping Village offers **free dance shows** performed every Tuesday and Thursday at 5 P.M. in the center's outdoor courtyard.

Every Thursday and Sunday evening 6–8:30 P.M., the **Drums of Paradise** lu'au is presented at the Ilima Garden at the Hyatt Regency. A full buffet dinner includes the usual complement of Hawaiian and Pacific foods, and the meal is followed by an enthusiastic and high-energy Polynesian show. Adult tickets are $65, $50 for those age 13–20, while children 6–12 years old get in for half the adult price. This is the only lu'au performed along the entire south coast.

## SHOPPING

Shopping in Po'ipu is varied and reasonably extensive for such a small area. The Po'ipu Shopping Village has the largest concentration of shops, but don't forget Po'ipu Plaza, the hotel arcades, and the Spouting Horn flea market.

### Po'ipu Shopping Village

The Po'ipu Shopping Village offers unique one-stop shopping, and most shops are open daily 9 A.M.–9 P.M. **Wyland Galleries** features some of

You can get a tee time at the Kukuiolono Golf Course—but you may have to share the green with wild roosters.

ROBERT NILSEN

the island's best painters and sculptors. **Hale Mana** handles Asian antiques, while a second Hale Mana carries fine arts. **The Black Pearl Collection** sells pearls and jewelry. **Xan** does designer jewelry. **Sand Kids** features distinctive children's wear, while half a dozen shops cater to adults. **Overboard** features casual to elegant alohawear, while two other shops carrying island clothing are **Crazy Shirts** and **Holuloa Surf Company. Bamboo Lace** offers dresses, blouses, hats, jewelry, and a smattering of alohawear. It's owned and operated by Nadine, who hand-picks fashionable clothing from the continent. Shelves also hold bath and skin-care products, gift items, lingerie, fancy shoes, and straw hats. For general merchandise items, stop at the **Whalers General Store.**

### Food Stores

Po'ipu is home to the generally well-stocked **Kukui'ula Store,** at Po'ipu Plaza, open Mon.–Fri. 8 A.M.–8:30 P.M. and Sat.–Sun. until 6:30 P.M., where you'll find groceries, produce, bakery goods, sundries, and liquor. **Whaler's General Store,** at Po'ipu Shopping Village, open daily 7:30 A.M.–10 P.M., is a well-stocked convenience store with a good selection of wines and liquors,

souvenirs, and gifts. **Brennecke's Beach Deli,** across from Po'ipu Beach County Park, has a small selection of packaged snack foods to go.

If you're staying in a Po'ipu condo and are buying large quantities of food, you may save money by making the trip to one of the larger markets in Koloa.

For fresh fruit and vegetables and ready-made gift baskets, try the open-air **Po'ipu Southside Market,** at the corner of Po'ipu Road and the Koloa-Po'ipu Bypass. Local farmers also have a stand set up along Po'ipu Beach Road near the cane haul road between Koloa and the coast.

### Photo Needs

**Poipu One Hour Photo,** inside the Seasport shop at the Po'ipu Plaza, 808/742-9303, does film developing.

## RECREATION
### Golf

Designed by Robert Trent Jones Jr., the **Kiahuna Golf Club,** 808/742-9595, is an 18-hole, par-70 course just up the road from Po'ipu Shopping Village. Undulating over land up from the coast,

KAUA'I

this course preserves several archaeological sites. The course is open for play 7 A.M. until sunset; the pro shop hours are 6:30 A.M.–6:30 P.M., and a restaurant is available throughout the day. Greens fees run $38 for 9 holes and $75 for a full 18 holes; midday, twilight, hotel guest, resident, junior, and package rates are also available. Lessons can be arranged.

The **Poipu Bay Golf Course,** 808/742-8711 or 800/858-6300, the site of the PGA Grand Slam of Golf since 1994, is a par-72 Scottish links-style course also designed by Robert Trent Jones Jr. and opened in 1991. With 7,034 magnificent yards (gold tees) rolling along the oceanside cliffs with the mountains as backdrop, it's noted for stunning views and is described as the Pebble Beach of the Pacific. Seven of the 18 holes have water hazards, making for challenging play. For practice, try the driving range, putting greens, and practice bunker. The excellent pro shop is open 6:30 A.M.–6 P.M.; call for tee times or for use of the driving range. At the clubhouse, the Poipu Bay Grill and Bar serves breakfasts and light lunches until 2:30 P.M. and drinks until the course closes. Fees run $185, $120 after noon, and $65 for twilight; reduced fees for Hyatt Regency guests. Lessons, club rental, and the practice range are extra.

## Tennis

Several hotels and condominiums in the Po'ipu area have tennis courts for their guests, but three are open to anyone. The largest is the **Kiahuna Tennis Club,** 808/742-9533, just east of the Po'ipu Shopping Village and across the street from the Kiahuna Plantation Resort. Kiahuna has 10 plexipave courts, a pro shop, rental equipment, and even a swimming pool. Court fees are $10, ball machines are $20 an hour, a basket of balls costs $10, and racquets are $5 apiece. Clinics are available for $10–12, and it's $45 for a one-hour lesson. Call for court times and inquiries about clinics and lessons. The tennis club is open 7:30 A.M.–6 P.M. daily.

The second well-equipped tennis facility is the **Po'ipu Kai Resort Tennis Center,** open 7 A.M.–6 P.M. with eight plexipave courts. While $5 for resort guests, there is a $10 an hour charge

for others. Although it's more relaxed here than at the Kiahuna Tennis Club, proper attire is required and you should leave the court ready for those who follow you. Round robins and clinics are held throughout the week for $10. Racquets and ball machines can be rented.

The Hyatt Regency **Tennis Garden,** 808/742-1234, has four hard courts and is open 8 A.M.–noon and 2–6 P.M. Court fees are $20 an hour, racquets can be borrowed, and a ball machine costs $10 an hour. Morning clinics are scheduled for $20 (minimum of three), and private lessons can be arranged for $65 an hour.

## Bicycling and Kayaking

**Outfitters Kauai,** in the Po'ipu Plaza, 808/742-9667 or 888/742-9887, www.outfitterskauai.com, open daily 9 A.M.–5 P.M., is a kayak and biking shop. Daily rental rates for bicycles are $20 for a cruiser, $33 for a road bike, and $25–40 for a mountain bike. All come with a helmet, lock, and water bottle. Outfitters Kauai also organizes a Bicycle Downhill bike ride that brings you up the Waimea Canyon so you can glide down to the coast. Rental kayaks and various guided kayak tours are also available. Outfitters Kauai retails biking and kayaking incidentals in its shop along with Patagonia clothing—shorts, sweatshirts, shirts, and even hats.

## Water Sports

**Seasport Divers,** at Po'ipu Plaza, 2827 Po'ipu Rd., 808/742-9303 or 800/685-5889, www.kauaiscubadiving.com, is a full-service snorkel/scuba/surf shop. Rentals include snorkel masks, fins, and snorkels at $5 per hour, $15 per day, and surfboard rentals differ depending on quality. Two-tank introductory boat or shore dives run $130 and $115, and a one-tank shore dive is $90. Morning and afternoon boat dives for certified divers run $100 each, and dive sites will be determined by the weather and water conditions. On calm days only, a full-day three-tank dive goes to Lehua Rock and the channel between there and Ni'ihau for $255. A three-day certification course for small groups goes for $375 or $595 for private lessons. Seasport Divers is a reputable company that gets the thumbs-up from locals. It's also a sports boutique with boogie boards, surfboards, and all sorts of water equipment, and the shop also has a clothing section and a one-hour photo finisher.

World surfing champion Margo Oberg or one of her staff members will teach you how to mount a board and ride gracefully over the shimmering sea. Beginning classes of one hour of instruction and a half hour of practice at Po'ipu Beach run $48 per person. Make reservations through Nukumoi Surf Co., 808/742-8019.

Across from Brennecke Beach is **Nukumoi Surf Co.,** 808/742-8019, open 8:30 A.M.–7 P.M. daily. Not only does this shop arrange surf lessons with Margo Oberg, it rents surfboards and other water equipment. Boogie boards or snorkel gear go for $5 a day or $15 a week. Nukumoi is very convenient to the beach. This is also a retail shop, so a full line of water equipment, sun glasses, and clothing is for sale.

**Kauai "Z" TourZ,** 808/742-7422, www.ztourz.com, does Zodiac snorkel tours from Kukui'ula Harbor to Kipu Kai and Lawa'i Kai. The cost is $69 adult and $59 for children for a three-hour tour, or $55 for the whale-watching tours in season.

### Horseback Riding

If you're into horseback riding, try **CJM Country Stables,** 808/742-6096, for any of its three scheduled rides. The two-hour, easy beach ride leaves at 9:30 A.M. and 2 P.M. daily and costs $75. Departing at 8:30 A.M. on Tuesday, Thursday, and Saturday, the beach breakfast ride takes you to a secluded beach girdled by high mountains where you relax while breakfast is prepared for you; it costs $80 and runs three hours. The longer beach, swim, and picnic ride leaves at noon on Monday, Wednesday, and Friday and costs $90. CJM is about 1.5 miles past the Hyatt Regency on Po'ipu Road.

### Guided Hikes

Every other Monday at 9 A.M., the Hyatt Regency offers a free two-hour informational guided hike along the coastal bluffs and dunes toward Maha'ulepu Beach. The Anara Spa, also

at the Hyatt, sponsors a "sunrise walk" every morning at 7 A.M.

### Spa

In its own facility at the Hyatt Regency is the distinctive green tile roof of the horseshoe-shaped **Anara Spa,** 808/742-1234. This spa offers total immersion into health and fitness, and general pampering of aching muscles and jangled nerves 6 A.M.–8 P.M. daily. The treatment rooms offer ancient Hawaiian and modern remedies for energy and rejuvenation. All rooms are indoor/outdoor, with mini-gardens and the serenade of falling waters to help relax and soothe. Various massages, facials, body treatments, and aromatherapies can be booked individually or as packages, and the salon offers hair, makeup, nail, and waxing services. The Anara Spa also offers a lap pool, aerobics room, complete training equipment, fitness assessment, personal training, and a morning walk along the beach or sand bluffs near the golf course. After a serious workout, relax at the spa's poolside Kupono Cafe for a health-conscious, low-calorie meal.

## INFORMATION

### General Information

The **Po'ipu Beach Resort Association,** P.O. Box 730, Koloa, HI 96756, 808/742-7444 or 888/744-0888, http://poipu-beach.org, info @poipu-beach.org, is an excellent nonprofit organization that can help you plan your trip in the Po'ipu area, arrange for accommodations, and point you in the right direction for activities and recreation. It can provide brochures and tips on everything from dining to accommodations and transportation; ask for its 36-page planning brochure, also available on the Web.

**Brennecke's Beach Center,** 808/742-7505, offers information and can set you up with any kind of activity on the island.

There are no banks in Po'ipu, but the two hotels will cash traveler's checks for their guests. The closest bank is in Koloa, as is the nearest post office and medical clinic.

KAUA'I

## Inland Towns

## LAWA'I

In times past, *ali'i* from throughout the kingdom came to Lawa'i to visit an ancient fishpond in the caldera of an extinct volcano. Legend says that this was the first attempt by Madame Pele to dig herself a fiery home. From more recent times, look into the valley below town to see an abandoned pineapple factory.

### Accommodations

Perched on a steep hillside above a broad green horse pasture and facing the high mountains toward the center of the island, **Marjorie's Kauai Inn**, P.O. Box 866, Lawa'i, HI 96765, 808/332-8838 or 800/717-8838, www.marjorieskauai-inn.com, marjorie@marjorieskauaiinn.com, has an unbeatable location. You have your choice of three private rooms, two with showers and one with a tub, each with private mini-kitchen, cable TV, phone, and its own entrance. Also included is access to a hot tub, a 50-foot lap pool and deck on the hillside below, beach equipment and accessories, and a barbecue grill. Fresh fruit, juice, and scrumptious homemade banana bread await in your room when you arrive. Light, bright, and cheery, all rooms open onto a lanai that overlooks the valley. Very accommodating, Marjorie takes the time to find out what you want to do and will gladly arrange activities for you. She encourages everyone to have wonderful adventures during their stay, and to "do more than one fun thing a day." Marjorie's Kauai Inn is a real find; quiet, rural, and relaxing. Room rates are $88 for the Tradewind room, and $96 for either the Valley View or Sunset View room; $15 for a third person.

Set amongst thick vegetation on a quiet cul-de-sac, with a fine view of the distant ocean, is **Victoria Place B&B**, P.O. Box 930, Lawa'i, HI 96765, 808/332-9300, fax 808/332-9465, www.hshawaii.com/kvp/victoria, edeev@aloha.net. Presided over by the gracious and warmhearted Edee Seymour, a transplant from the Mainland, Victoria Place is more like a home than a guest house. Edee fills you with a hearty breakfast and pastries, can clue you in on what to see and where to go, and always respects your privacy. The three rooms, one handicapped-accessible and another set up for a single traveler only, all have private bathrooms and run $60–80. These open onto the swimming pool at the front of the house. Down below, Victoria's Other Secret is a studio apartment with its own entrance, bath, and kitchen that goes for $100 a night. For any of the rooms, add $10 per room for one-night stays. No credit cards accepted. Everyone shares the back lanai and can borrow books from Edee's huge collection.

### Food

In town next to the post office, at mile marker 10, is the **Lawa'i Restaurant,** 808/332-9550, open until 2 P.M. for lunch and again from 4:30 P.M. until 8 P.M. (or 9 P.M.) for dinner, closed Sunday. This very local restaurant serves American standards and Asian food at very reasonable prices. You know this has to be a decent place because the police regularly make it their lunch stop. Next door is **Menehune Food Mart,** a reasonably well-stocked way station open daily.

A short way down Koloa Road past the Hawaiian Trading Post is **Lawa'i General Store,** for sundries and a few groceries.

### Shopping

At the intersection of Koloa Road and Kaumuali'i Highway (Rts. 50 and 530) is the **Hawaiian Trading Post** gift shop. Referred to by locals as "the tourist trap," the Hawaiian Trading Post sells a mind-boggling variety of hand-crafted items as well as a large selection of souvenirs, treasures, and tourist junk. Other selections include T-shirts, right-price aloha shirts, jewelry, black pearls, postcards, and carvings, and an excellent display of Ni'ihau shell lei that should be featured but are stuck away in the back. These Ni'ihau shell lei, some for display only and some for sale, are perhaps the best collection of shell lei on the island—worth the stop by themselves. Priced from several hundred to several thousand dollars, many of these beauties take a couple of years to string.

Occupying a portion of the same building is **Lee Sands,** featuring goods made from eel skin and other exotic leathers. Around the side you can still stand on a surfboard and have your picture taken at the fake wave fashioned from plaster, while across the parking lot is a pleasant grove of coconut, breadfruit, orange African tulip, and purple Hong Kong orchid trees.

# KALAHEO

The area around Kalaheo is springing up with many new housing subdivisions, and large tracts of coffee, tea, and macadamia nut trees are tinting the hillsides in new shades of green. Throughout the state there are pockets of population groups with heavier concentrations than elsewhere; for Kalaheo, it's the Portuguese. The town has three gas stations, a liquor store, post office, medical clinic and pharmacy, restaurants, a mini-mart, and a new office/shopping plaza, all along Rte. 50, making Kalaheo the first sizable town between Lihu'e and Hanapepe where you can pick up anything you may need before continuing west.

For a great view over the lowlands from the heights, take a drive up Puulima Road, Kikala Road, or Wawae Road above town. Drive slowly and cautiously—the roads are very steep and it is a residential area.

## Kukui O Lono Park

Kukui O Lono Park is a personal gift from Walter D. McBryde, the well-known plantation owner who donated the land to the people of Kaua'i in 1919. Accept it! It's off the beaten track but worth the trip. Turn left in Kalaheo at the Menehune Food Mart and go along Papalina Road for one mile until you come to the second Pu'u Road—the first turnoff to Pu'u Road skirts the hill below the park and circles back to the second Pu'u Rd. turnoff. A sharp right turn brings you through the large stone-and-metal gate (open 6:30 A.M.–6:30 P.M.). The park encompasses a public golf course and Japanese-style garden. The entrance road leads through a tunnel of eucalyptus trees to a commemorative plaque to McBryde. A flock of green parrots that nest in the tall eucalyptus

trees on the grounds can be heard in a symphony of sound in the early evening.

For the gardens and McBryde's memorial, go straight ahead to the parking lot; to get to the clubhouse, follow the road to your right for about a half mile. As the park is set on top of a hill, the sweeping views in all directions are striking. For the best view of the south coast, walk out to the pavilion but be watchful for golf carts. During the winter months, you may be able to spot whales spouting along the coast far below. Unfortunately, perfectly placed in the center of one of the nicest views is a microwave antenna and dish. Set amidst a grove of towering trees, the Japanese garden offers peace and tranquillity. Occasionally, weddings are held here. The whole scene is conducive to Zen-like meditation. Enjoy it. Just beyond the Japanese garden is a small collection of stones that were used by the Hawaiians for various purposes: for games, as a fish god, and for evaporating salt.

The **Kukuiolono Golf Course** clubhouse, 808/332-9151, houses a pro shop and snack bar. A round of golf on the par-36 course is $7; carts and clubs are rented at a similarly reasonable rate. Having opened in 1929 for the workers of the McBryde sugar plantation, this is the second oldest golf course on the island.

## Accommodations

**Classic Vacation Cottages,** P.O. Box 901, Kalaheo, HI 96741, 808/332-9201, fax 808/7645, www.classiccottages.com, clascot@hawaiian.net, comprises five homey units where you can expect low daily rates while enjoying excellent access to nearby attractions. Rates are $50 and $65 for the two studios, $75–80 for the two cottages, and $10 for each person more than two. The executive house sleeps up to six and rents for $175. Higher rates apply over the Christmas and New Year season. No credit cards accepted. Each unit has at least one stained-glass window, and all have kitchen facilities, cable TV, and ceiling fans. No breakfasts are served, but guests have free use of snorkel gear, tennis racquets, and golf clubs. Good value and seclusion.

The restored plantation home of District Judge Jardine, constructed in 1926, is now the **Aloha**

**Estates at Kalaheo Plantation,** tel./fax 808/332-7812, 4579 Pu'uwai Rd., P.O. Box 872, Kalaheo, HI 96741, www.kalaheo-plantation.com, kalaheo1@gte.net. Although some attempt has been made to keep with the old style, much of the renovation is modern in tone. The six suites, all named after beautiful tropical flowers, include private baths, kitchens or kitchenettes, seating areas, and lanai. All but one have king-size beds; the one has two full beds. Each has a private entrance, and all guests can use the screened front lanai. No breakfast is served. The owner creates stained glass pieces, some of which are displayed in the house. Rates run a reasonable $55–75 a night per room; weekly and monthly rates are available. The four downstairs rooms can be rented together for $199 a night, while the entire house can be yours for $350. No credit cards.

Behind the Kalaheo Steak House is the **Kalaheo Inn,** P.O. Box 584, Kalaheo, HI 96741, 808/332-6023, or 888/332-6023, fax 808/742-6432, www.kalaheoinn.com, chet@aloha.net. Once a ratbag dive for overnight and long-term stays, this inn has been totally remodeled into a bright and cheery place with lots of local character. These are basic apartment-like units, reasonably priced, and great for those who care more about what they eat and see than where they sleep. Each unit has separate living room, bedroom, and kitchen or kitchenette areas, queen or twin beds, ceiling fans, TV, and a bath with shower. New tile and vinyl flooring take the place of carpet. There are no phones in the rooms, but there is one in the laundry room for guest use. Rooms run $55–65 for one bedroom, $85 for two bedrooms, and $125 for the three-bedroom quiet house in the back.

## Food

Local people out for an evening meal at reasonable prices give the nod to **Kalaheo Steak House,** 4444 Papalina Rd., 808/332-9780, open daily 6–10 P.M., where you can get a well-prepared and hearty portion of steak, seafood, pork, or poultry, and, reputedly, one of the best dinner salads on the island. While you wait for your main dish, try the steamer clams, brought to your table in a bucket, or the wonderful Portuguese bean soup. Most menu items range $14–20. Make a left at the signal along Rte. 50 in Kalaheo and look for a green building on the left with an awning. The interior, very much in steakhouse motif, is completely knotty pine—simple, but tasteful, offering seating at a combination of black leatherette booths and tables with captain's chairs. A mural of tropical fish completes the decor. Local lore has it that when you leave the always busy Kalaheo Steak House, the *doggie bag* contains more food than you're usually served at most restaurants.

If you're interested in a pizza, stop in at **Brick Oven Pizza,** 808/332-8561, open Tues.–Sun. 11 A.M.–10 P.M., on the mountain side just as you enter Kalaheo. Pizzas range from $9.95 for a 10-inch cheese pizza to $29.75 for a large 15-inch deluxe with all the toppings, on whole wheat or white crust with garlic butter glazing. Brick Oven also prepares oven-baked sandwiches for around $7.50, pizza bread, and salads. Wine, beer, and soft drinks are available. If you're heading to Waimea or Polihale, call ahead to have a pizza ready for you. While a bit on the pricey side, Brick Oven has a well-deserved excellent local reputation. Many say it's the best on the island.

Chefs Tony and Rosario serve a mix of traditional northern and southern Italian cuisine at **Pomodoro Ristorante Italiano,** in the Rainbow Plaza on the left as you enter Kalaheo, 808/332-5945, open nightly 5:30–10 P.M. The menu opens with classics like mozzarella, prosciutto, or calamari antipasti, ranging in price $7.50–10.50, a mixed green salad at $5.95, and a Caesar for $6.95. Pasta is spaghetti with meatballs or Italian sausage for $12.95, linguine shrimp marinara at $16.95, fettuccine Alfredo for $12.95, and an assortment of ravioli, cannelloni, manicotti, and lasagna in different sauces priced at $13.95–14.95. Specialties are veal parmigiana or piccata at $19.95, eggplant parmigiana at $16.95, and chicken saltimbocca for $17.95. The wine list, by the bottle or glass, includes wines from California and Italy. Top off your meal with an espresso and an Italian dessert made fresh daily. The dining room is small, intimate, and island-flavored, and the waitstaff are professional. You'll be happy you came, and you'll leave well-fed.

Another option is the blue-and-white **Camp House Grill,** across from the Menehune Food Mart at the stoplight, 808/332-9755. Specializing in burgers and Hawaiian-style barbecued chicken, the Camp House Grill is open 6:30 A.M.–9 P.M. Menu items are basic American standards with a Hawaiian twist and include the famous Camp House breakfasts, like a flour tortilla stuffed with scrambled eggs, sausage, and cheeses, topped with salsa and served with rice or Camp House hash browns at $4.95; omelettes for around $6.95; and early-bird specials for as little as $2. Lunches and dinners start with salad, soup, and chili, but the restaurant is most famous for its burgers and fries, ranging $3.95–5.50, some with unusual toppings like grilled pineapple and teriyaki sauce. Evening specialties are barbecued pork ribs at $16.95 and *huli* chicken at $8.95. All the luscious homemade pies, like macadamia nut pie, pineapple cream cheese pie, and sour cream apple pie, are baked here in the kitchen. Although not gourmet, nor as clean as it could be, the Camp House Grill offers honest, filling, and moderately priced food.

For coffee in all its permutations, try the **Kalaheo Coffee Co. and Cafe,** 808/332-5858, near the main intersection in town. Aside from getting coffee by the cup, you can buy pound and half-pound packages of (mostly) Hawaiian coffee, whole bean or ground, blended or unblended, and even have it shipped. Breakfast items like omelettes, eggs, and pancakes are served until noon, and lunch runs 10:30 A.M.–3 P.M., 2 P.M. on Sunday for salads, sandwiches, and grill items you order at the counter. Wholesome, healthy, and filling, nearly everything on the menu is under $7.

At the signal along Rte. 50 in Kalaheo, **Menehune Food Mart** is across the street from **Steve's Mini Mart.** Both can supply sundries and light groceries.

Every Tuesday at 3:30 P.M. a **farmers' market** is held at the Kalaheo Neighborhood Center along the highway for locally grown produce, fruits, and flowers. Check it out for good fresh food and a local experience.

A couple of hundred yards up the road toward the gold course from the highway intersection is the **Madieros Farm** store, where you can pick up fresh eggs, meat, fish, and prepared Hawaiian foods. A great little place with lots to offer for those with a kitchen, Madieros is open 8 A.M.–5 P.M. weekdays, until 1 P.M. on Saturday, and closed Sunday.

## Services

Next to the post office near the traffic light, the **Kalaheo Clinic,** 808/332-8523, is open for checkups and minor emergencies Mon.–Fri. 8 A.M.–8 P.M. and Saturday 8 A.M.–noon.

# West End

After Kalaheo, the highway dips south again and passes 'Ele'ele, the still-active Port Allen Harbor, and Hanapepe at the mouth of the Hanapepe River, whose basin has long been known as one of the best taro lands in the islands. You pass tiny "sugar towns" and hidden beaches until you enter Waimea, whose east flank was once dominated by a Russian fort, the last vestige of a dream of island dominance gone sour. Captain Cook landed at Waimea in the midafternoon of January 20, 1778; a small monument in the town center commemorates the great event. Secondary roads leading in-

land from Waimea and Kekaha farther west converge, then meander along Waimea Canyon, the Pacific's most superlative gorge. Kekaha, with its now-silenced sugar stacks, marks the end of civilization, and the hard road gives out just past the Pacific Missile Range Facility. A cane road picks up and carries you to the wide, sun-drenched beach of Polihale, the end of the line, and the southernmost extremity of the Na Pali Coast.

This is the **Waimea District,** the broad and diverse west end of the island. Waimea means "red water," and the area was so named for the

sculpted Waimea Canyon

ROBERT NILSEN

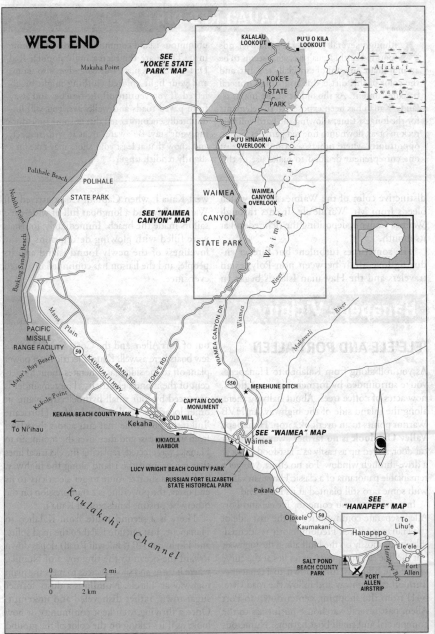

# WEST END

SEE "KOKE'E STATE PARK" MAP

Makaha Point

*Alaka'i Swamp*

KALALAU LOOKOUT

PU'U O KILA LOOKOUT

KOKE'E STATE PARK

PU'U HINAHINA OVERLOOK

Polihale Beach

POLIHALE STATE PARK

WAIMEA CANYON OVERLOOK

SEE "WAIMEA CANYON" MAP

WAIMEA CANYON STATE PARK

*Waimea Canyon*

Nohili Point

Barking Sands Beach

Mana Plain

Mana Plain

*Waimea River*

*Makaweli River*

PACIFIC MISSILE RANGE FACILITY

50

KAUMUALI'I HWY

MANA RD

KOKE'E RD

WAIMEA CANYON DR.

550

MENEHUNE DITCH

Major's Bay Beach

CAPTAIN COOK MONUMENT

Kokole Point

To Ni'ihau

KEKAHA BEACH COUNTY PARK

Kekaha

OLD MILL

SEE "WAIMEA" MAP

Waimea

KIKIAOLA HARBOR

LUCY WRIGHT BEACH COUNTY PARK

RUSSIAN FORT ELIZABETH STATE HISTORICAL PARK

Pakala

*Kaulakahi Channel*

Olokele

Kaumakani

Hanapepe

SEE "HANAPEPE" MAP

To Lihu'e

Ele'ele

Port Allen

*Hanapepe Bay*

SALT POND BEACH COUNTY PARK

PORT ALLEN AIRSTRIP

0        2 mi

0        2 km

KAUA'I

## KAUA'I RED DIRT

Although several of the Hawaiian Islands sport red earth, Kaua'i has what seems to be an inordinate amount of especially red dirt, and the color of this dirt is due to its high mineral bauxite content. As the oldest of the major islands, Kaua'i has been exposed to the elements for the longest time, allowing the hard volcanic rock to break down into fine red particles. Seeing opportunity where others see trouble, at least one entrepreneur decided to make use of this ubiquitous island commodity and dye clothing in it. These are the increasingly popular Red Dirt Shirts of Kaua'i. But what dyes also stains, and your light-colored clothing might be affected. If you venture off the beaches and away from paved roads and walkways, you will undoubtedly encounter red dirt at some time during your stay. Be aware, treat it with respect, and know that at least your shoes may take on a slightly reddish tinge.

distinctive color of the Waimea River, which bleeds from Mt. Wai'ale'ale. It cuts through Waimea Canyon, depositing the rich red soil at its mouth.

The sometimes turbulent but forever enduring love affair between non-Polynesian travelers and the Hawaiian Islands began in west Kaua'i, when Captain Cook arrived off Waimea Bay and a longboat full of wide-eyed sailors made the beach. Immediately, journals were filled with glowing descriptions of the loveliness of the newly found island and its people, and the liaison has continued unabated ever since.

## Hanapepe Vicinity

### 'ELE'ELE AND PORT ALLEN

As you roll along from Kalaheo to Hanapepe, you're surrounded by former sugarcane fields, now acres of coffee trees. About halfway there, along the inland side of the highway, an HVB Warrior points to an overlook. Stop. **Hanapepe Valley Overlook** is no farther away than your car door, served up as easily as a fast-food snack at a drive-through window. For no effort, you get a remarkable panorama of a classic Hawaiian valley, with some taro still planted at its lower end.

In a moment, you come to 'Ele'ele and Port Allen, separate communities on the east side of the Hanapepe River. Predominantly residential, 'Ele'ele sits mostly on the bluff along the highway, but the 'Ele'ele Shopping Center lies at the curve where the highway turns down to Hanapepe. Turn off the highway and follow the road (Rte. 541) from the shopping center down to Port Allen, past several warehouse businesses to the commercial and small boat harbors. Numerous tour boat companies and fishing charters run out of Port Allen, and the Coast Guard keeps a few boats here as well. Kauai Electric has a power plant off to the side that generates about 85 percent of the island's electricity. The remainder is produced by four small hydroelectric plants at other locations on the island. After Hurricane 'Iniki, the powerline that cuts across the island from west to east and then over the mountain to Hanalei was erected, replacing the electrical lines that ran around the island along the highway. Although a shorter route to get electricity to its end users, the powerline is a transgression on the otherwise pristine landscape of Kaua'i.

There is a second route from Kalaheo to Hanapepe. Just outside Kalaheo the road splits, and Highway 540 (Halewili Road) slopes down toward the ocean to the tiny town of Numila, where it turns and shoots across to meet the main highway at 'Ele'ele. **Numila** is a dusty former sugar town, rather disheveled and unkempt. Once a thriving, well-kept community, it now looks as if it's taking on the color of the ground on which it lies. Yet, it's still possible to see fine

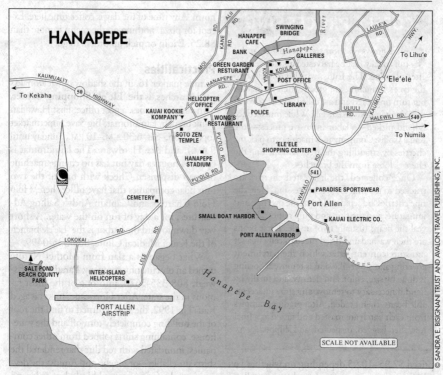

HANAPEPE

KAUMUALI'I
To Kekaha
50 HIGHWAY

ALII RD.
KANE RD.
MOI RD.
SWINGING BRIDGE
HANAPEPE CAFE
BANK
HANAPEPE RD.
GREEN GARDEN RESTURANT
KONA RD.
KOULA
HANAPEPE GALLERIES
POST OFFICE
LIBRARY
LAULE'A RD.
HWY.
To Lihu'e
'Ele'ele

HELICOPTER OFFICE
WONG'S RESTAURANT
POLICE
KAUAI KOOKIE KOMPANY
SOTO ZEN TEMPLE
HANAPEPE STADIUM
PU'OLO RD.
'ELE'ELE SHOPPING CENTER
ULIULI RD.
HALEWILI RD. 540
To Numila

CEMETERY
LOKOKAI RD.
LELE RD.
PU'OLO RD.
SMALL BOAT HARBOR
PORT ALLEN HARBOR
WAIALO RD.
541
PARADISE SPORTSWEAR
Port Allen
KAUAI ELECTRIC CO.

MOON
SALT POND BEACH COUNTY PARK
INTER-ISLAND HELICOPTERS
PORT ALLEN AIRSTRIP
Hanapepe Bay

SCALE NOT AVAILABLE

© SANDRA E. BISIGNANI TRUST AND AVALON TRAVEL PUBLISHING, INC.

examples of plantation-era vernacular housing here and imagine what it was like during the good years. The McBryde sugar mill once kept this town vibrant, but now its mill and offices house the Kauai Coffee Company.

If you use Rte. 540, and particularly if you're a coffee connoisseur, stop at the **Kauai Coffee Company Visitor Center and Museum,** just beyond Numila, 808/335-0813 or 800/545-8605, www.kauaicoffee.com. Over 150 years ago, coffee was planted in this region of Kaua'i as the first coffee plantation in the Hawaiian islands. After some years and little success, coffee production was discontinued here but took hold on the Big Island, at Kona. Today, coffee is grown not only on the Big Island, but also on Maui, Moloka'i, O'ahu, and once again on Kaua'i, where it's relatively big business. The Kauai Coffee Company has a 3,400-acre plantation of drip-irrigated Hawaiian *arabica* coffee bean plants and produces roughly five million

pounds of coffee as year. This is the largest single coffee estate in Hawaii and captures about 65 percent of the Hawaiian coffee market. Refurbished plantation buildings now hold the gift shop and museum, open daily 9 A.M.–5 P.M. Stop in to peruse the historical artifacts and learn how coffee is handled at each stage from tree to cup; sample tastes are always available. Aside from the usual gift items, you can purchase a bag or case of estate-grown ground or whole bean coffee in any of the numerous roasts.

## Food

**Toi's Thai Kitchen,** 808/335-3111, family operated and one of the best Thai restaurants on Kaua'i, is in the back corner of the 'Ele'ele Shopping Center. It's open Mon.–Sat. 10:30 A.M.–2:30 P.M. and 5:30–9:30 P.M. for dinner. Prepared by Mom and served by her lovely daughters, the menu starts with items like spicy sour soup with lemongrass and ginger,

## COFFEE PROCESSING

Coffee grows on short trees or bushes, and it can usually first be harvested about five years after planting. The fruits, which grow close to the tree's branches, are green when immature but turn bright red and are called "cherries" when they ripen in mid- to late fall. While much coffee is hand-picked—a labor-intensive process—the Kauai Coffee Company uses machines to pick the cherries by straddling the trees and shaking the cherries loose from the branches.

Once collected, the harvested cherries are trucked to the mill for wet processing. Here the ripe cherries are separated from the overripe and immature, and the skin and pulp removed to reveal the beans (usually two) inside. These beans are then washed and dried mechanically to a set moisture content, after which the parchment covering and silver-like skin is removed. Sorting is done by size, color, and density, and finally by hand if necessary to remove any stray unacceptable beans, then graded. After grading, samples from each batch are roasted and tasted as a final test, then bagged, inspected, and shipped.

priced $7.95–10.95 depending on whether you add pork, beef, or seafood, and spring rolls or deep fried tofu for $6.95. Entrées include stir-fried eggplant and tofu in a spicy sauce with your choice of meat, $7.95–10.95; savory satay priced $7.95–10.95; and yellow curry with your choice of meat for $7.95–9.95. For most items, you have your choice of meat, poultry, fish, seafood, eggplant, or vegetarian, and all can be adjusted to your preference in spiciness. One of the sweet Thai desserts comes with some meals, but if not, order one—it's a treat. Beer and wine are served. Although some Thai decorations adorn the walls, it's not for the decor that you come, but for the tasty and reasonably priced food.

In a separate building at the shopping center is **Grinds Espresso**, 808/335-6027, open daily 5:30 A.M.–9 P.M., a local place serving mostly local foods at reasonable prices. Egg and grill items are served up for breakfast; for the rest of the day, sandwiches and plate lunches are the

norm. Any time of the day is coffee time here. Except for pizza, nothing on the menu is more than $8.25. Eat in or pick up orders to go.

### Practicalities

At mile marker 16, in the shadow of McDonald's golden arches, is the **'Ele'ele Shopping Center**, with various eateries, a post office, First Hawaiian Bank branch, laundromat, Big Save Supermarket (open Mon.–Sat. 6:30 A.M.–10 P.M., Sunday until 9 P.M.), and Ace Hardware. The laundromat is open 24 hours a day but has no change machine or soap dispenser. Check with one of the two tour boat companies that have offices here, Holo Holo Charters and Captain Andy's Sailing Adventures, for a day of fun on the water. A short way down toward the harbor is the 'Ele'ele branch of the Kauai Medical Clinic, 808/335-0499.

What began as a slap from Mother Nature turned an obscure tiny company, **Paradise Sportswear,** 808/335-5670, into one of the most famous in the state. After Hurricane 'Iniki ravaged Kaua'i in 1992, the staff returned to find the roof of the building completely torn off and the warehouse, containing shirts jobbed from other companies, inundated with red dirt that rendered the shirts unsellable—or maybe not! Amidst the devastation, the future seemed bleak, but as legend would have it, one person said, in effect, "Ah, these shirts actually look pretty cool." Perhaps spurred by desperation, the forlorn faces, after rolling their eyes heavenward, slowly reconsidered and began to smile. Voilà, the **Red Dirt Shirt** was born. Dedicated to the community, Paradise Sportswear is a true cottage industry, employing local families who pick up ordinary white shirts, take them home, and repeatedly dip them in vats of Kaua'i's famous red dirt. After they bring them back, other local people working on the premises apply original silk-screen designs. Since absolutely no chemicals or dyes are used, no two shirts—which range in color from deep copper to burnt orange—are the same.

Tour the factory, in a large industrial building just before Port Allen Small Boat Harbor, daily 9 A.M.–noon and 1–4 P.M. to watch the silk-screening process, and make sure to stop in at the retail shop, which stays open until 5 P.M., where you can choose from countless designs and styles, ranging from tiny tank tops for tots to XXXXXLs for walking Sherman tanks, and take advantage of discounts on factory seconds and discontinued designs. The largest Red Dirt T-shirt made, a special order 8XL, was for a Hawaiian sumo wrestler! Retail outlets featuring Red Dirt T's are found on every island, with innumerable boutiques and shops carrying these very distinctive souvenirs. On Kaua'i, visit the outlet shops in Waimea, Lihu'e, and Kapa'a. Mainlanders can even find them at outlets in St. George and Moab, Utah—where, incidentally, you also find red dirt. For mail orders, call 800/717-3478 or go to www.dirtshirt.com. Recently, with new owners, the company has introduced a stonewashed Lava Blues line of dyed blue T-shirts with similar island-inspired designs.

In another section of the same warehouse is **Nite Owl T-shirts** company, which, aside from the racks of shirts with its own intriguing designs, does printing for other retailers on the island. Stop here for a wide selection and good deals on pricing. Although Nite Owl doesn't have the name that the Red Dirt Shirt company has, the quality and range of designs are equally as good.

## Recreation

For boating, scuba, and snorkel adventures, all of the following use Port Allen Harbor: **Blue Dolphin Charters,** 808/335-5553; **Capt. Andy's Sailing Adventures,** 808/335-6833; **Holoholo Charters,** 808/335-0815; **Captain Zodiac,** 808/826-9371; **Kauai Sea Tours,** 808/826-7254; **Na Pali Eco Adventures,** 808/826-6804; **Catamaran Kahanu,** 808/335-3577; and **Mana Divers,** 808/335-0881. The only true commercial sailing ship in Kaua'i, *Lady Leanne II,* run by **Bluewater Sailing,** 808/828-1142, uses Port Allen October through April.

## HANAPEPE

Hanapepe (Crushed Bay), billing itself as "Kaua'i's Biggest Little Town," has had a more glorious past than its present, although it has emerged as a center of the arts and has the greatest concentration of artists' studios on the island.

Hawaiians cultivated taro in Hanapepe Valley, making this a significant settlement. Later, the Chinese and others came to grow rice. From the early 1900s until just after World War II, Hanapepe was a bustling town. With a growing population, Hanapepe became an economic center, one of the largest towns on the island, with its main street chockablock with shops and businesses, two movie theaters, and three skating rinks. During the 1940s, thousands of GIs were trained and billeted here before being shipped to the Pacific for overseas duty. Burns Field became the first commercial airstrip on the island, now used only by air tour companies, and its harbor (Port Allen) remains the island's second largest commercial port and one of the principal harbors for boat tours.

Hanapepe is divided into two sections. As you approach town from the east, look up to your right; if it's early winter, you'll see an entire hillside of bougainvilleas ablaze with a multicolored patchwork of blossoms. The newer section to town lies along Rte. 50; the other is Old Hanapepe, a "must-see" along Hanapepe Road; the Y-intersections at both ends of town direct you by sign to the historic main street that parallels the highway. Along Rte. 50 the police and fire departments, a library, the Westside Pharmacy, the Hanapepe Hongwanji, a restaurant, and a gas station appear in rapid succession before the bridge. Beyond the bridge are more shops and restaurants, an ice cream shop, the Bali Hai Helicopter office, and the Hanapepe Park and stadium, often lit at night for ball games. A second helicopter company, **Inter-Island Helicopter,** has an office at the airstrip. Keep a lookout for the **Soto Zen Temple Zenshuji** on your left. It's quite large and interesting to people who haven't visited a temple before. At the western end of town is the famous **Kauai Kookie Kompany,** whose macadamia shortbread, Kona coffee, guava macadamia, and coconut krispies cookies, among others, are now available statewide. The Kookie Kompany retail shop is open Mon.–Fri. 8 A.M.–5 P.M., Saturday and Sunday 9 A.M.–5 P.M. Just beyond that, near the Y-intersection, is the large Mariko's gift shop, which often caters to tour buses; the Salt Ponds Country Store for sun-

ROBERT NILSEN

**Hanapepe's swinging foot bridge, built in 1911**

dries; and a small gift shop called Giorgio's where you'll find unique coconut postcards and painted surfboard art.

Old Hanapepe is a time-frozen still life of vintage false-front buildings housing art studios, local dry-goods stores, two banks, an excellent restaurant, a swinging foot bridge, and a gift shop or two like **Aloha Oe Island Gifts.** Like the newer section of town, it lies on both sides of "the bridge," but most businesses on the west side of this one-lane bridge (built 1911) have closed their doors or moved away.

## Friday Art Night

Following in the footsteps of Lahaina, Maui, Hanapepe has established Friday Art Night, to celebrate its strong and growing connection with the Hawaiian art community. Of the galleries in town, most are one-artist shops. Every Friday evening 6–9 P.M., those along the old main drag keep their doors open, catering to art lovers and others looking to peruse or buy. Most artists are available at their galleries and proudly display their latest works. Some may even pull their easels out on the sidewalk and demonstrate there. Refreshments are often available, and musical performances are usually given near the entrance to the swinging bridge. As casual a place as this is, the scene sometimes carries a main street block party atmosphere.

## Galleries

As you enter town on the right, **Kauai Fine Arts,** 808/335-3778, www.brunias.com, open 9 A.M.–5 P.M. daily, stocks prints, antique maps, and some tribal art from around the world. A great place to get lost in the age of exploration or early 20th-century Hawaii.

The **Kauai Village Gallery,** on the left as you enter town, 808/335-0343, www.hawaiiart.com, offers a collection of pottery and photographs by local artists, featuring gallery owner Lew Shortbridge and his surrealistic paintings. Prices are reasonable. Open Mon.–Sat. 10 A.M.–5 P.M.

The **Kim Starr Gallery,** 808/335-0381, shows the paintings and serigraphs of Kim Starr. Her cat series is becoming well known, as are her human figures. Open daily.

A few steps away is the **Kama'aina Cabinets/Koa Wood Gallery,** 808/335-5483, closed Sunday, showing fine examples of woodcarvings, furniture, and other wood pieces crafted with skill, experience, and a feeling of movement. Sharing the same storefront is **Uncle Eddie's Aloha Angels,** which features these celestial beings in all their manifestations.

Stop in at the fine art studio of **Dawn Traina Gallery,** 808/335-3993. Dawn, knowing she wanted to be an artist since childhood, pursued an education in art on both coasts. Working in multimedia with acrylics, pastels, and pencils, Dawn specializes in portraiture. She not only captures the feeling of what's current today, but somehow, since moving to Hawaii in 1979, has been able to tap into the lore of Hawaii and to visibly render the spirit of ancient chants, dances, legends, and the gentility of the plantation days.

Next door is the **Arius Hopman Studio Gallery,** 808/335-0227, featuring mostly landscape watercolors. Painted on location, each piece demonstrates a connectedness to the spot. Colors are vibrant and there is feeling in every stroke. Commissions accepted.

Almost across the street is **Hanapepe Art Center and Gallery,** 808/335-3442, which displays a wide eclectic collection of multimedia artwork and gifts, many by owners Rick and Anna Ramondi, but other artists are featured as well.

Although not on the main drag, **8-Bells Gallery,** 808/335-0550, features paintings and prints and some sculpture by local artists. This gallery can frame artwork.

## Beach

On the western outskirts of town, a sign points *makai* (toward the sea) down Rte. 543. Follow the sign past a small veterans' cemetery, where an HVB Warrior points down Lele Road to **Salt Pond Beach County Park,** the best beach and sailboarding spot on this end of the island. This beach is at the west end of the Port Allen Airport (Burns Field) runway, once the major airport for the island but now only an airstrip with no facilities that three helicopter companies and one ultralight aircraft company use.

Local people from around Hanapepe enjoy this popular beach park. The swimming is excellent— a natural breakwater in front of the lifeguard stand makes a pool safe for tots—and snorkeling is fair out on the periphery of the bay. Surfers enjoy the breaks here, and a constant gentle breeze makes the area popular with sailboarders. Bring a picnic lunch and make a day of it; on the weekends you might find a *kaukau* wagon parked here for light snacks. Amenities include several pavilions and picnic tables, toilets, and showers, and camping is allowed with a county permit.

Along the road to Salt Pond Beach, you pass the actual salt ponds, evaporative basins scraped out of the red earth that have been used for hundreds of years. The sea salt here is still harvested but isn't considered pure enough for commercial use. The local people know better; they harvest the salt in the spring and summer, and because of its so-called impurities (which actually add a special flavor), it is a sought-after commodity and an appreciated gift for family and friends. If you see salt in the basins, it belongs to someone, but there shouldn't be a hassle if you take only a *small* pinch

to taste. Don't scrape it up with your fingers because the sharp crystals can cut you—and you'll rub salt into your wounds in the process.

## Food

The **Green Garden Restaurant,** 808/335-5422, an old standby along the highway, is marked by a tangle of vegetation that almost hides the building. It's open except Tuesday for lunch 10:30 A.M.–2 P.M. and 5–9 P.M. for dinner, with breakfast from 7:30 A.M. on Sunday only. Since 1948, this family-owned restaurant has offered tourist-quality food in large portions, with *aloha* service. The new section of the restaurant is set up to hold busloads of tourists who arrive for lunch; go a little before or a little after noon. The old room has a few plants, but the name is really held up by the green decor and overgrown exterior. If you see anything on the menu that you might want to mix and match, just ask. Substitutions are made cheerfully. Breakfast is standard American fare with eggs, hotcakes, waffles, and the like; lunches run the gamut of American, Japanese, and Chinese dishes, mostly under $8; full-meal dinner selections include beverage for $9–16. The homemade pies are famous and always delicious.

Over the bridge and on your left is another island institution, **Wong's Restaurant,** 808/335-5066, open daily except Monday for breakfast, lunch, and dinner. Wong's is one giant dining room reminiscent of a small-town banquet hall that caters to local bowling leagues and wedding receptions. It's a favorite of the tour buses and can be crowded. The service is friendly, the portions large, and the food, while not memorable, is very reasonably priced; you won't complain, but you won't be impressed, either. Wong's specialties are Chinese and Japanese dishes, most $8–10. If that isn't enough, **Omoide's Deli and Bakery** occupies a second section of the same building where you can pick up a sandwich or pizza, birthday cake, or slice of its island-famous homemade *liliko'i* (passion fruit) chiffon pie.

Across the street from Wong's try the Atomic Clock Cafe, which along with the short menu has Internet access, or the small Olivia's Thai Noodle Soup shop. Next door is the larger and older **Lappert's Ice Cream,** the original establishment for this island-wide business, which now has outlets on O'ahu, Maui, and in Princeville, Koloa, and Kapa'a on Kaua'i. Rich and creamy, Lappert's ice cream has about 16 percent butterfat in its regular flavors and some 8 percent in its fruit flavors. Once you taste, you'll know why it's an island favorite.

As you come into the old town from the east, the first store on your left—in an old house—is **Taro Ko,** a tiny mom-and-pop, house-front shop selling taro chips. It's nothing to look at on the outside, but the flavors of the chips draw people here. While mama is inside looking after the deep-fryers, papa might be out lounging under the tree.

**Hanapepe Cafe and Espresso Bar,** 808/335-5011, open Tues.–Sat. 9–11 A.M. for breakfast, 11 A.M.–2 P.M. for lunch, and Fri. 6–9 P.M. for dinner with live music, is a fantastic eclectic restaurant for mind and body. Housed in the old town drugstore (circa 1939), the espresso bar/restaurant section is fashioned from the original soda fountain counter, tastefully modernized with a black-and-white checkerboard motif. All the food served is health-conscious vegetarian with an attempt at organic and locally grown whenever possible, but always fresh and definitely savory and satisfying. Breakfast is terrific, with eggs, scrambles, waffles, and multi-grain pancakes washed down with steaming cups of espresso, hot chocolate, cappuccino, caffe latte, and an assortment of herbal teas all reasonably priced. Lunch brings a garden burger, Caesar salad, and homemade soup, all served with fresh bread. Dinner is always vegetarian Italian à la Hawaii and could be baked lasagna al forno, linguine with pesto, or artichokes with cannelloni, all served with soup, salad, and bread for around $18. Dinner music is usually provided by a solo local performer playing anything from slack-key to classical flute music. If you are craving a snack, quiet cup of coffee, or a full meal, you can't beat the Hanapepe Cafe and Espresso Bar. Reservations recommended for dinner. Bring your own bubbly.

For local food at moderate prices, try **Linda's Restaurant,** offering breakfast specials and inexpensive dinners, or the **Da Imu Hut Cafe,** offering a full assortment of simple local grinds and refreshing drinks.

**Andy's Kine Catering,** 808/335-2810, is the newest venture into the food market in Hanapepe. Open 5 A.M.–1:30 P.M. to catch those starting early for boat tours and other activities, Andy's sells box lunches and deli sandwiches to go for $5.25–5.50. Look for Andy's near the bridge on the old town road.

On Thursday 3:30–5:30 P.M. a **farmers' market** is held at Hanapepe Town Park behind the fire station. Stop by for the freshest in local organic produce.

## Recreation

Bali Hai helicopter company has an office along the highway in Hanapepe, on the west side of the bridge next to Lappert's Ice Cream shop. **Bali Hai Helicopters,** 808/335-3166 or 800/325-8687, flies 45- and 60-minute circle island flights daily in its four-passenger Bell Ranger, which is painted in bright rainbow colors. Using Hughes 500 four-seater machines with their doors off for an open-air experience, **Inter-Island Helicopters,** 808/335-5009, also flies the circle-island route but adds one tour with a waterfall picnic stop. Its office is at the Burns Field airstrip.

Although based in Kaumakani, a few miles farther to the west, **Ni'ihau Helicopter,** 808/335-3500, office open Mon.–Sat. 8 A.M.–2 P.M., also uses Burns Field. Set up to provide medical services for the residents of Ni'ihau, the twin-engine Agusta 109A helicopter is also employed for sightseeing tours and hunting trips when there is enough interest. Ni'ihau Helicopter runs completely different tours from all other helicopter companies on Kaua'i. Its flight runs three to four hours, flies you to Ni'ihau and back, and gives you plenty of time on a Ni'ihau beach. Rates are $280 per person. This is virtually the only way to get to Ni'ihau unless you are an invited guest.

Also flying out of Burns Field in a 70-horsepower ultralight power glider is **Birds in Paradise,** 808/822-5309. With the instructor, you can have a truly unique experience soaring above terra firma in this "motorcycle with wings." Prices are $100 for a 30-minute lesson, $175 for one hour. Advanced instructional flights run $255 for 90 minutes and $330 for two hours.

# SUGAR TOWNS

The road hugs the coast after Hanapepe, bypassing a series of still-working sugar towns until you arrive in Waimea. **Kaumakani,** a small cluster of vernacular homes with a few dirt lanes where sugar plantation workers live, has a post office, mini-mart and bakery (closed Sunday), and the Ni'ihau Helicopter office. Here, everything seems to be tinged with red. *Mauka* of the highway, surrounded by cane fields, is the refurbished, plantation-style United Methodist Church, established 1901, the oldest Methodist church on the island.

Less than a half mile west is **Olokele.** As counterpoint to the disheveled and dusty look of Kaumakani, Olokele is a one-street community of larger and better-kept houses, wide green lawns, and towering canopy-like monkeypod trees. Manifesting an air of an easier life from earlier decades, quaint lampposts line this road as it dips down to the still-active sugar mill. At night the town displays a genteel quality. This is where the plantation managers and mill higher-ups live. Take a drive down toward the mill and draw your own conclusions about those who live here. Gay and Robinson, owners of the mill, offer two-hour bus and walking tours of the mill and surrounding fields as an overview of the sugar production process and everyday mill operation. Pants (or shorts) and closed-toe shoes must be worn, and it's a good idea to wear clothing that you wouldn't mind getting stained by the rich red dirt in the fields. Hard hats and goggles are provided for the part of the tour that goes through the mill. Perhaps the

best time to visit is April–October, when the mill is active. These **sugar plantation tours** start at the visitors center (open 8 A.M.–4 P.M. Mon.–Fri., 11 A.M.–3 P.M. Sat.), near the mill office, where there are displays of artifacts relating to the sugar industry. Tours are offered at 8:45 A.M. and 12:45 P.M. Mon.–Fri., except holidays, and run $30 per person, with a 30 percent discount for children 8–15. Gay and Robinson also offer **Olokele Canyon tours** by 4WD van, which include a seldom-seen view of Waimea Canyon from its east rim. Tours run Mon.–Fri. at 8:15 A.M. and include lunch. Rates are $60 for adults, $45 for kids; with minimum of two and a maximum of eight adults. Call 808/335-2824 for reservations; see www.gandrtours-kauai.com for additional information.

Next is **Pakala,** noted more for its surfing beach than for the town itself. At mile marker 21, a bunch of cars pulled off the road probably means the surf's up. Follow the pathway to try the waves yourself or just to watch the show. This beach is not a county park. Walk down past the bridge to a well-worn pathway leading through a field. In a few minutes is the beach, a 500-yard-long horseshoe of white sand. Off to the left is a rocky promontory popular with local anglers. The swimming is fair, and the reef provides good snorkeling, but the real go is the surf. The beach is nicknamed "Infinity" because the waves last so long; they come rolling in in graceful arcs to spill upon the beach, then recede in a regular, hypnotic pattern, causing the next wave to break and roll perfectly. Sunset is a wonderful time to come here for a romantic evening picnic.

KAUA'I

# Waimea

Like the Hanapepe Valley back down the coast, the area near the mouth of the Waimea River was historically a large settlement area, and the river valley was used for taro production, some of which carries on today. Kaumuali'i, the last great king of Kaua'i, maintained a household here, so Waimea for a time was a seat of power.

The town of Waimea has several sights of interest—pick up a copy of the *Historic Waimea Town* brochure to help you navigate. You can walk to see its old buildings, churches, the Captain Cook landing site, the sugar mill ruins, mill camp housing, and a royal coconut grove; a Russian fort lies across the river on the far bank. Waimea also has several fine accommodation, a brewpub, some reasonably good restaurants, and limited shopping. In addition, you'll find two supermarkets, two gas stations (last chance for gas), two boat tour companies, a laundromat, library, two banks, a sporting goods store, and a pharmacy. Near the western edge of the downtown area is a Red Dirt T-Shirt outlet, so if you haven't picked up one before now, you can get it here before heading out to the beach. As Waimea is the gateway to the Waimea Canyon and Koke'e State Parks, one of the two roads up the mountain starts here in town. This is Waimea Canyon Road (Rte. 550). A couple of blocks up Waimea Canyon Road is West Kaua'i Medical Center.

## SIGHTS

The remains of a Russian fort still guard the eastern entrance to Waimea town. Turn left at the sign for **Russian Fort Elizabeth State Historical Park;** the remains are right there. The fort, roughly shaped like an eight-pointed star, dates from 1817, when a German doctor, Georg Anton Schaeffer, built it in the name of Czar Nicholas of Russia, naming it after the potentate's daughter. Schaeffer, a self-styled adventurer and agent for the Russian-American Company, saw great potential in the domination of Hawaii and built two other forts on Kaua'i, one on the bluff at Princeville, which overlooks Hanalei Bay, and

the other down along the beachfront on the bay. Owing to political maneuverings with other European nations, Czar Nicholas never warmed to Schaeffer's enterprises and withdrew official support. For a time, Kaua'i's King Kaumuali'i flew the Russian flag, perhaps in a subtle attempt to play one foreign power against another. Soon, Schaeffer was unceremoniously kicked off Kaua'i, sent to Honolulu, and then forced to leave the islands altogether. The fort fell into disrepair and was virtually dismantled in 1864, when 38 guns of various sizes were removed. The stout walls, once 30 feet thick, are now mere rubble, humbled by encircling, nondescript underbrush. However, from points near its periphery you'll still get a reasonable view of Waimea Bay. Pick up a brochure at the entrance and walk the path inside and around the fortification.

Just after you cross the Waimea River, signs point to **Lucy Wright Beach County Park,** a five-acre park popular with the local folk. There's a picnic area, restrooms, showers, a playground, and tent camping with a county permit. The park is situated along the mouth of the river, which makes the water a bit murky. The swimming is fair if the water is clear, and the surfing is decent around the river mouth. The Kilohana Canoe Club launches here to practice on the bay. A few hundred feet to the west of this park is the **Waimea State Recreation Pier,** open for picnicking and good for open-ocean pole fishing and crabbing. Reach it by walking along the beach or down a backstreet behind the Waimea Library. The beach at both of these parks is not really recommended for swimming and is often full of driftwood.

Captain Cook's achievements were surely deserving of more than the uninspiring commemorative markers around Waimea. Whether you revere him as a great explorer or denigrate him as an opportunistic despoiler, his accomplishments in mapping the great Pacific were unparalleled and changed the course of history. In his memory, **Captain Cook's Landing** displays a modest marker attached to a boulder on the beach at

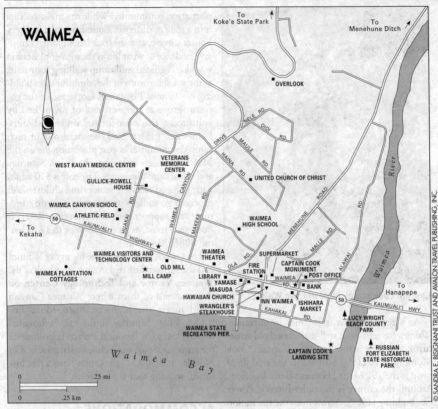

# WAIMEA

To Koke'e State Park

To Menehune Ditch

OVERLOOK

River

NELE RD.

DRIVE

MAULE RD.

OIOI RD.

HAINA RD.

WEST KAUA'I MEDICAL CENTER

VETERANS MEMORIAL CENTER

CANYON

UNITED CHURCH OF CHRIST

GULLICK-ROWELL HOUSE

WAIMEA CANYON SCHOOL

ATHLETIC FIELD

HUAKAI RD.

WAIMEA RD.

MAKEKE RD.

MENEHUNE ROAD

MALLE RD.

ALAWAI

Waimea

To Kekaha

50

KAUMUALI'I HIGHWAY

WAIMEA HIGH SCHOOL

To Hanapepe

WAIMEA VISITORS AND TECHNOLOGY CENTER

WAIMEA THEATER

OLA RD.

SUPERMARKET

CAPTAIN COOK MONUMENT

WAIMEA PLANTATION COTTAGES

OLD MILL MILL CAMP

LIBRARY

FIRE STATION

POST OFFICE

WAIMEA RD.

BANK

50

KAUMUALI'I HWY.

YAMASE MASUDA

HAWAIIAN CHURCH

INN WAIMEA

ISHIHARA MARKET

WRANGLER'S STEAKHOUSE

KAHAKAI RD.

LUCY WRIGHT BEACH COUNTY PARK

WAIMEA STATE RECREATION PIER

CAPTAIN COOK'S LANDING SITE

RUSSIAN FORT ELIZABETH STATE HISTORICAL PARK

Waimea Bay

0          .25 mi
0          .25 km

© SANDRA E. BISIGNANI TRUST AND AVALON TRAVEL PUBLISHING, INC.

Lucy Wright Beach Park, commemorating his "discovery" of the Sandwich Islands at 3:30 P.M. on September 20, 1778. A second landing marker and **Captain Cook's Monument** stand on the median strip Hofgaard Park in downtown Waimea.

If you're fascinated by Kaua'i's half-legendary little people, you might want to take a look at the **Menehune Ditch** (Kiki a Ola), a stone wall encasing an aqueduct curiously built in a fashion unused by and apparently unknown to the Polynesian settlers of Hawaii, in which mating stones are cut to match. The road now covers much of the ditch, which was cut into the riverside cliff face. The oral tradition states that the ditch was built by order of Ola, high chief of Waimea, and that he paid his little workers in 'opae, a tiny shrimp that was their staple. On payday, they

supposedly sent up such a great cheer that they were heard on O'ahu. Said to have once stretched 25 miles up the valley, today the site is greatly reduced as many of the distinctively hand-hewn boulders have been removed for use in buildings around the island, especially in the United Church of Christ building above the school grounds. Some steadfastly maintain that the Menehune never existed, but legends abound and works attributed to them are seen here and there around the island. To reach the ditch, follow the road in from the fire station. Similar to that in Hanapepe, a pedestrian footbridge crosses the river near the remnants of the ditch, used mostly in times of high water when it's impossible to drive a vehicle through the ford. It perhaps is a remnant of a time when Waimea was a much more thriving community.

Captain Cook statue in downtown Waimea

As a testament to its former importance, Waimea has numerous well-maintained **old structures.** Standing across from the Captain Cook Monument in Hofgaard Park in the middle of town is the 1929 First Hawaiian Bank Building. Around the corner is the older Electric Power Co. building (1907). Across from the fire station is the Hawaiian Church, built in 1865 and renovated in 1995—there's been a congregation since 1820. Across the street in two directions are the Fah Inn (1890), now a store for antiques and collectibles, and the old Ako Store (1909), now Wrangler's Steakhouse. The Yamase and Masuda buildings, one block up on either side of the intersection, date from 1919. The 1938 Waimea Theater, renovated in 1999, is a few steps up the road and once again open for movies Tues.–Sun. at 7:30 P.M. Established in 1859, the United Church of Christ building is the oldest church extant in town. Perhaps the oldest building is the Gullick-Rowell House (1829), on an overgrown lot at the entrance to the hospital. It's still occupied by descendants of the missionary family.

From 1884 to 1946, Waimea was the home of a thriving yet small sugar mill and center for a plantation community. While the mill structure is in a state of disrepair, a number of the workers' houses survive, and the back lanes of this "camp" give evidence of what life in the former plantation was like. A guided **mill camp walking tour** starts at the small museum in the administration building of Waimea Plantation Cottages, in the coconut grove at the west end of town. Led by volunteers, this tour focuses on the laborers' homes and gardens and the social role of such camp communities in past plantation life on the island. Tours are offered at 9 A.M. on Saturday and last about 90 minutes. The cost is $10 adult, with reduced rates for seniors and children. All proceeds go to help preserve the historic structures and support community events. Reservations are a must, as groups are kept to 12 or less; call 808/338-0006.

For a quick brief look at the history of Waimea and the surrounding region, stop for a look at the **Waimea Visitor and Technology Center,** on the west end of town where Waimea Canyon Road meets the highway, open Mon.–Fri. 9 A.M.–4 P.M., Saturday until 1 P.M. Audiovisual displays and a few historical artifacts help illustrate the area's sugar past and technological present. On Monday at 9:30 A.M., the center hosts a free historical walking tour around town.

## ACCOMMODATIONS

Aside from a few private rental homes and one inn, **Waimea Plantation Cottages,** 9400 Kaumuali'i Hwy. #367, Waimea, HI 96796, 808/338-1625 or 800/992-4632, fax 808/338-2338, www.waimea-plantation.com, info@kikiaola.com, is one of the few places to stay along the south shore west of Kalaheo—and what a place it is. Owned by the Kikiaola Land Company, Ltd., and managed by Aston Hotels and Resorts, this oceanfront property is set in a grove of more than 750 coconut palms and a few huge banyan trees at the west end of Waimea. Not victimized by big bucks or modern resort development, workers' and supervisors' cottages and the manager's house from the former Waimea sugar plantation have been renovated and preserved, and the grounds maintained in an old-style way. You are treated to

KAUA'I

a touch from the past. While some modern amenities such as color cable TVs and telephones have been added for comfort and convenience, an effort has been made to keep each unit as much in its original state (1920–30s era) as possible; period furniture and other furnishings add to the feel of that bygone era. Most buildings have bare wood floors and painted wood walls. Nearly all have ceiling fans and lanai. Housekeeping and linen service are included every three days. Complimentary washers and dryers are available on the premises. A swimming pool in the 1930s style has been constructed on the lawn, and there's croquet, horseshoes, and volleyball, along with a restaurant and brewpub. In accordance with this philosophy of preservation, some longtime employees of the plantation (no longer a functioning entity) are still offered low- or no-rent cottages in the mill camp rather than being turned out to make way for development of the land. On check-in at the administration building, have a look at the small **Faye Museum,** which presents artifacts and photographs of the early days of sugar in West Kaua'i.

Presently, there are 53 units, including 11 cottages moved from the Kekaha Plantation and others from the former town of Mana to the west. Rates for the cottages run $145 for a studio, $205 for a one-bedroom, $285 for a two-bedroom, $310 for a three-bedroom, and $385 for a four-bedroom; weekly discounts, specials, *kama'aina,* and value season rates are available. The two-story, five-bedroom, four-bath Manager's House is available for $575 a night. The average length of stay is 7–10 days, with a 35 percent return rate; make your reservations several months in advance. (A three-bedroom harbor house in Kekaha is also operated by Waimea Plantation Cottages.) Low-key and unpretentious, this institution aims to please and offers an opportunity for seclusion and serenity. What could be better than to relax and read a favorite book on your breezy lanai, watch the sunset through the coconut grove, or take a moonlight stroll along the gently lapping shore? Make reservations with Waimea Plantation directly or through Aston Hotels.

Right in town and up from the Hawaiian

Church is **Inn Waimea,** 808/338-0031, fax 808/338-1814, a remodeled two-story plantation-era home from the 1930s. A few steps from the business section of town and the beach, Inn Waimea is both convenient and quiet. Lovingly restored, modernized, and spacious, this comfy and attractive house offers one room and three two-room suites that have private bathrooms, cable TV, phones, ceiling fans, and a small refrigerator. The downstairs room and suite have king beds, upstairs are queen-size beds. Rates run $70 a night for the Taro room and $95 for the Bamboo, Hibiscus, and Banana suites; $10 extra for each additional guest. Included is a breakfast basket for each room.

# FOOD

It's easy to imagine a grizzled *paniolo* contentedly dangling his spurs over the banister of the distinctive veranda at **Wrangler's Restaurant,** in downtown Waimea at 9852 Kaumuali'i Hwy., 808/338-1218, open Mon.–Fri. for lunch 11 A.M.–4 P.M. and for dinner Mon.–Sat. 4–9 P.M. The interior is a large open-beamed room with hardwood floors, cooled by ceiling fans. You can dine inside at a private booth or table, or alfresco on the big veranda out front or in the red blaze—a ginger garden out back. To enhance the atmosphere, soft dinner music is played nightly. A full-service bar is stocked with a complete assortment of liquors, wines, and beers to complement all meals. The lunch menu has burgers, sandwiches, and Mexican plates, mostly under $10. As you might expect, the Wrangler dinner menu is heavy on the steaks and red meats, with some poultry, seafood, combinations, and a few Mexican selections. The house specialty is a sizzling 16-ounce New York steak served with sautéed mushrooms and baked potato. Entrées, $15–25, come with homemade chips and salsa and soup. Wrangler's is excellent and friendly. While you're there, take a few minutes and have a look at the gift shop and small *paniolo* museum.

For a simpler, quicker meal, try **Pacific Pizza and Deli,** 808/338-1020, for pizza, calzones, deli sandwiches, drinks, and ice cream. Along with the ordinary pizzas, you have your choice of

Thai, Japanese, Mexican, and other unusual pizza offerings. Refreshing drinks include Tropical Smoothies with pineapple, mango, or papaya, home-brewed ice tea, and coffee drinks from espresso to latte. Pacific Pizza shares the Wrangler's Restaurant building and is connected by double screen doors to the restaurant. Open daily 11 A.M.–9 P.M.

A fine place for coffee, pastries, and a light meal is **Waimea Bakery and Deli** across from the Captain Cook Monument. Open daily except Wednesday 6:30 A.M.–4 P.M. Many come for the espresso, but you can also get fountain drinks, juices, and smoothies. Good eats and good prices.

**Paulani's Farmers' Market** at the west end of town not only has local fruits and vegetables but also sandwiches, frosties, and smoothies. Directly across the street is **Big Bruddah's,** open daily for inexpensive and plentiful local grinds, sandwiches, and Italian dishes. Darri's Delites, for local grinds, and **Jo-Jo's Shave Ice,** which advertises 60 flavors, also do business along the highway.

The **Waimea Brewing Company,** 808/338-9733, is open daily for lunch and dinner on the property of Waimea Plantation Cottages, next to the registration office. The breezy plantation-style building has large open windows, high ceilings, and ceiling fans. The hand-crafted beers, ranging from Waialeale golden ale to Indian pale ale and Pakala porter, are brewed in a room seen through the glass window behind the bar. These beers can only be sold here. Stop for a repast and cool yourself down with one of these sudsy drinks. If you have trouble deciding which beer will fit your palate best, try the sampler first. Appetizers include smokin' wings, ale-steamed shrimp, and taro leaf goat cheese dip. Salads and sandwiches are favorites and run less than $10. Dinner entrées, such as fresh catch, honey mango-glazed ribs, furikake panko-crusted *ahi*, and Jawaiian chicken, range $14–20, and every evening there are specials. Save room for dessert. Sit inside so you can see the bar or outside on the veranda under the stars—either way it's a very pleasant, relaxing experience. Hours are 11 A.M.–11 P.M. daily, with food served until 9 P.M. Reservations are not always necessary but may be a good idea on the weekend, when there

is usually live music. Anything on the menu can be ordered to go.

Along the main road, facing Captain Cook's statue, is **Ishihara Market,** open 6 A.M.–8:30 P.M. on weekdays and from 7 A.M. on weekends, where you'll find all the necessities; it now sells some prepared hot meals. Across the street is a well-stocked **Big Save Supermarket** open 6 A.M.–10 P.M. daily. Its deli lunch counter, believe it or not, features terrific local dishes at very reasonable prices. For liquor of all sorts and a few eats, try **Da Booze Shop.**

# RECREATION

Captain Cargo's Company and the office of **Liko Kaua'i Cruises,** 808/338-0333 or 888/732-5456, www.liko-kauai.com, liko@aloha.net, are operated by Debra Hookano, wife of Captain Liko. Across from the Captain Cook monument in the center of town, the small but tasteful **Captain's Cargo Company** boutique, open daily 8 A.M.–5 P.M., offers jewelry, fashionable dresses, shorts, T-shirts, and even brocaded vests. The boutique also rents and sells surfboards, boogie boards, and snorkel equipment. Captain Liko runs his 49-foot power catamaran out of the tiny Kikiaola Harbor just up the road. This is the closest departure point for trips to the Na Pali Coast, so it gives you the shortest "commute." Born and raised on Kaua'i, Captain Liko worked for 10 years as a supervising lifeguard on the west end, and no one knows these waters better than he. After you board, Captain Liko begins telling Hawaiian tales, especially about Ni'ihau, the island of his ancestors. Captain Liko not only offers spectacular sights but also a chance to snorkel and swim if the weather is cooperating; he brings along snacks and drinks for the ride. If you are lucky, dolphins will play alongside the boat as you cruise, or you may see whales frolicking during the winter months. If sea conditions are right, the boat may go all the way to Ke'e Beach on the north shore. On the way back, since the boat is completely outfitted for fishing charters, some lucky person gets to reel in whatever bites. Morning cruises with check-in at 8 A.M. run about four hours long, $95 for adults and $60 for children 4–14 years. During the summer months, an afternoon cruise may be added, and, weather permitting, sunset cruises may also be run.

**Napali Explorer,** 808/338-9999 or 877/355-9909, www.napali-explorer.com, has an office in Waimea near the gas station. This company runs a 49-passenger, rigid-bottom inflatable raft up the Na Pali Coast year-round. The five-hour snorkel adventure, which stops at Nu'alolo Kai on the Na Pali Coast, runs $118 per person. The 3.5-hour scenic afternoon tour and the whale-watching expeditions (in season) go for $79.

## To the End of the Road

### KEKAHA

Back on Highway 50 going west, you enter Kekaha, passing the former plantation workers' homes trimmed in neat green lawns and shaded from the baking sun by palm and mango trees. Japanese gardens peek from behind fences. Kekaha was a planned plantation town, a model community by some regards, that was built and maintained by sugar and thrived for a century. The highway skirts town, running right along the water, while the main street, Kekaha Road, veers off near Kikiaola Harbor and runs into town past the old sugar mill to the shopping plaza at Alae Road. Along the main street look for **Thrifty Mini Mart** and the post office. Until 1996, cane trucks, like worker bees returning to the hive, carried their burdens into the ever-hungry jaws of the **Kekaha Sugar Company,** whose smokestack owns the skyline but belches black soot no more. The sweet molasses smell no longer lingers in the air. Even with the closing of the mill, the town remains well-trimmed and ostensibly prosperous, perhaps because of the work available at both Pioneer and Northrop King seed corn companies up the road and at Barking Sands, the Pacific Missile Range Facility farther on.

Koke'e Road, the western road leading to Waimea Canyon and Koke'e State Parks, branches off in the center of town. At this intersection you'll find the Waimea Canyon Plaza, a small mall with shops like the **Menehune Food Mart,** your last chance for snacks and sundries; **Obsessions Cafe** for burgers, *bento,* sandwiches, and plate lunches; **Lappert's Ice Cream;** and **Forever Kauai** and **Waimea Canyon General Store,** side-by-side shops for postcards, cheap jewelry, outlet alohawear, and souvenirs. Forever Kauai carries some of the best Ni'ihau shells on the island at prices that are better than at larger and more conveniently located outlets. At the first major cane road intersection on the road out of town toward the mountain, a traffic light was hung in 1957—the island's first. The dearth of traffic now makes you wonder why it's still functioning.

Route 50, Kaumuali'i Highway, proceeds west along the coast. When still in town, you pass **Kekaha Faye Park.** Across the road is **Kekaha Beach County Park** and **Kekaha Neighborhood Center,** site of the Saturday 9 A.M. **farmers' market,** with its pavilion, tables, toilets, and grills. At the western end of town is the lifeguard tower. Then the golden sands of the beach park stretch for miles, widening as you head west, with pulloffs and shade-tree clusters now and again. The sun always shines, so pick your spot anywhere along the beach. The area is good for swimming and snorkeling during calm weather, and fair for surfing, although the reef can be quite shallow in spots. The beach across the road from St. Theresa's Catholic church is perhaps the best for little kids. Since there's no tourist development in the area, it's generally quite empty.

At the east end of Kekaha, **Kikiaola Harbor** serves the needs of area residents with a boat launch and is where a few water tour companies launch their boats. There are a few picnic tables and restrooms here, but no camping is allowed.

There are no hotels or condominiums in Kekaha, only a handful of vacation rentals. **Kekaha Vacation Rentals,** 800/677-5959, www.kauai-vacationrentals.com/kekaha, offers six rental units ranging from a one-bedroom suite to a three-bedroom house; all are directly across the highway from the ocean. All units are comfortably furnished, supply all linens and towels, and have complete kitchens, TV, and washing machines. Bicycles and boogie boards are available for guests to use. These units range $85–150 a night, with an additional $75 cleaning fee; four nights minimum. They're often booked by return guests; inquire well in advance.

Try also **Kekaha Sunset Beach Vacation Rental,** 808/337-1054, kekahasunset@hotmail.com, which offers a three-bedroom house across the highway from the beach. With full kitchen, laundry facilities, TV, and phone, the house sleeps up to six and goes for $150 a night or $1,000 a week; four nights minimum. A one-

bedroom unit in the back, with kitchenette, is just right for a couple. It rents for $85 a night or $500 a week.

## PACIFIC MISSILE RANGE FACILITY

The sea sparkles, and the land flattens wide and long, with green cane billowing all around. Dry gulches and red buttes form an impromptu inland wall. Six miles down the road you come to the gates of the Pacific Missile Range Facility (PMRF), also known as **Barking Sands.** Here howl the dogs of war, leashed but on guard. Run by the Navy but used by all sectors of the U.S. military, allied foreign military units, and select civilian and educational agencies, PMRF is a training ground for air, surface, underwater, and coastal maneuvers, target practice, electronic warfare and communication, and tracking. In essence, it's a training facility for sea warfare. As one of its brochures states, "PMRF is the world's largest instrumented, multidimensional testing and training range." Its range covers 42,000 square miles to the west and south with the addition of 1,000 square miles underwater. Along with the main 2,000-acre facility along the coast, which boasts a 6,000-foot runway, an associated base, where training exercises are held, lies a short way up the Na Pali Coast on the end of Makaha Ridge. Built originally by NASA in 1960 to track the Mercury space craft, it's a state-of-the-art facility that is integral to maintaining the U.S. military's combat readiness.

In late 1996, NASA announced that one of the most advanced studies of the earth's atmosphere was to be conducted at the Pacific Missile Range Facility. That research featured "Pathfinder," an experimental remote-controlled light aircraft that was fueled entirely by solar power. This slow-speed "flying wing" was powered by six electric motors and reached a height of over 80,000 feet. It was followed by other high-altitude versions, including the Centurion, and in August 2001 the 14-propeller Hellios reached a height of 96,000 feet. NASA officials chose Kaua'i because its weather provides 360 clear days per year, offering perfect flying in virtually unobstructed air space. The program brought a sub-

## MANA PLAIN

Unlike the rest of the island, which is volcanic in nature, the Mana Plain is sedimentary, perhaps a combination of dirt swept down from the hills and sand pushed up from the sea. It stretches from the Waimea River to the Na Pali cliffs at Polihale, about 16 miles along its coastal periphery. Prior to the 1900s, the Mana Plain was marshy with numerous ponds and inland waterways—a great wildlife area for birds—and it was possible to boat from the former town of Mana on its west end to Waimea. The old town of Mana, which no longer exists, was a thriving sugar community in the middle of the 19th century but shrank to nothing with the decline of the sugar industry. The early Hawaiians lived along the coast and near the cliff, and when immigrants moved into the area, rice was cultivated. In the early 20th century, the wetlands were drained to create productive sugarcane land, and much is still used as such today.

Recently, some of this land has been turned over to other uses. One huge strip along the coast, the Pacific Missile Range Facility at Barking Sands, has been in military hands since World War II, and large acreage is planted in seed corn by two mainland companies. The Barking Sands airfield was originally built in 1928 by the Kekaha sugar plantation and later used by both Hawaiian Airlines interisland flights and Pan Am transpacific flights between the U.S. West Coast and Asia.

stantial amount of money into the local economy and provided hands-on experience for some lucky students at Kaua'i's community college.

PMRF is home to over 100 military personnel and their families, and nearly ten times that number of civilian workers are employed on the base. Most of its facilities are open only to these personnel, but some of the base is open to the public for swimming, camping, and fishing (see note below). The base maintains two recreational areas and the **Major's Bay Beach** for public use. Rec. I ("Barking Sands," Nohili dune area) and Rec. II (Kini Kini area) are open from 4 P.M. (6 P.M. for Rec. II) to 6 A.M. during the week and all day on weekends and holidays but may by closed at any time due to exercises and training maneuvers. Call 808/335-4229 for current information on closures. Major's Bay Beach, one of the broadest beaches on the island, is open 24 hours a day for swimming, surfing, and sunbathing—it's hot and shadeless. There is a new pavilion and toilet/shower facility up in the trees. You can camp here as well, but all camping must be done on the sand below the vegetation level. No camping permit is required, but you must get a recreation pass from the security guard at the front gate. Major's Bay Beach affords the best view of Ni'ihau, a purple Rorschach blot on the horizon—this is the closest you're likely to get to the "Forbidden Island." The Barking Sands has the largest sand dunes on Kaua'i, due to the ocean's shallowness between the two islands. Supposedly, if you slide down the dunes, made from a mixture of sand and ground coral, the friction will cause a sound like a barking dog, an effect that's most evident during the heat of the day when the sand is totally dry. Some locals come to the beaches at PMRF (and to Polihale Beach) to drive on the sand. If you choose to do so, be very cautious because vehicles can and do get stuck very easily. There is no tow service on the base—you would have to get assistance from town—and no gas service is available to guests, but if you've let air out of your tires to drive on the sand, you can refill your tires with air at the base service station. For any use of the base, you must register for a pass at the front gate security office, 808/335-4221. For nonresidents, your driver's license and rental car

agreement will be sufficient. The main gate is open 6 A.M.–6 P.M. Mon.–Fri.; at all other times go to the secondary gate about one mile back down the highway toward Kekaha.

On occasion, missile launches can be seen at the base. During these training operations, access to the base is restricted and the Navy blocks boat traffic past the facility. However, these launches can be seen from Polihale State Park and from the highway.

Aside from its beaches, most use of the base is for movies and stargazing, and for the annual Fourth of July fireworks show. The base movie theater, an outdoor affair with medium-size screen and stadium seats (you can bring your own lawn chair and sit on the grass), shows free first-run movies Wednesday to Sunday. All you need is a base pass. Showtime varies by season but is usually 7:30 P.M. in winter and 8 P.M. during the summer. Call 808/335-4210 for the current movie schedule.

The Kauai Educational Association for Science and Astronomy, a.k.a. **KEASA,** welcomes islanders and visitors of all ages to peer through its 14-inch computerized telescope every month on the Saturday nearest the new moon at its observatory on PMRF, beginning at sunset. When access to the base is restricted, a nearby location may be used instead. For further information and current meeting dates and times, call 808/245-8250. To get to either the movie theater or the observatory, use the base gate closest to Kekaha and inform the guard of your destination.

**Note:** Civilian access to the base was closed until further notice after September 11, 2001. Please call the above listed numbers for information on current access status.

## POLIHALE STATE PARK

Route 50 curves to the right after you pass the missile range. After the asphalt peters out, an HVB Warrior points left to Polihale State Park at a stop sign at a crossroads. You go in by four miles of dirt cane road that doesn't seem to get much attention. The earth is a definite buff color here, unlike the deep red that predominates throughout the rest of the island. You can day-trip to soak up the sights, and you'll find pavilions, showers, toilets, and grills. This area is hot and dry, so bring plenty to drink. Both RV and tent camping are allowed with a state park permit. The camping area is on the top of the dune on the left before you get to the day-use pavilions at the far end. There are generally no hassles, but the rangers do come around, and you should have a permit with you—it's a long way back to Lihu'e to get one.

From the parking area, walk over the tall dunes and down to the beach. The broad powdery white sand beach stretches for nearly three miles, pushing up against the Na Pali cliffs to the north and skirting a hill on the military base to the south. However, this beach actually continues around the bend, running uninterrupted (although it narrows substantially in spots) all the way to Kekaha, a distance of about 15 miles, basically edging the Mana Plain. It is the longest beach by far in the state. The swimming can be dangerous, as currents are strong, but the hiking is grand. With a small reef offshore, the most protected spot is known as Queen's Pond; it's at the southern end of Polihale Beach. You'll have your best chance to swim in summer. When the sea is not too rough, experienced surfers come to ride the waves.

Literally at the end of the road, this beach takes you away from the crowds, but you'll hardly ever be all by yourself. Here the cliffs come down to the sea, brawny and rugged with the Na Pali Coast beginning around the far bend. Where the cliffs meet the sea is the ruin of **Polihale Heiau.** This is a powerful spot, where the souls of the dead made their leap from land into infinity. Their goal was the land of the dead, a mythical submerged mountain a few miles off the coast. The priests of this temple chanted special prayers to speed them on their way, as the waters of life flowed from a sacred spring in the mountainside. Even if you are not pulled here because of the mystical, this is a marvelous place for a picnic and beach walk. As it rains so little here and distant clouds do not often hamper the view, sunsets are super, and seeing the green flash is a definite possibility. With no lights or air pollution to speak of, stargazing at Polihale can be exceptional.

## Mountain Parks

### WAIMEA CANYON STATE PARK

The "Grand Canyon of the Pacific" is an unforgettable part of any trip to Kaua'i, and you shouldn't miss it for any reason. Waimea Canyon Drive begins in Waimea, heading inland past sugarcane fields for seven miles, where it joins Koke'e Road coming up from Kekaha. This serpentine route runs along a good but narrow road into Kaua'i's cool interior, with plenty of fascinating vistas and turnouts along the way. Going up, the passenger gets the better view. Behind you, the coastal towns fade into the pale blue sea, while the cultivated fields are a study of green on green. Waimea Canyon Drive is narrower, windier, and steeper in parts than the more gradually graded and better paved Koke'e Road, a gentle roller coaster of a road. Either route is worthwhile, and you can catch both by going in on one leg and coming out on the other. Less than a mile before these two roads meet, you enter Waimea Canyon State Park, a ridgetop park of more than 1,800 acres that flanks the road to Koke'e and overlooks the canyon and ridges beyond, most of which lie within the boundaries of Pu'u Ka Pele and Na Pali Kona Forest Reserves.

Ever climbing, you feel as though you're entering a mountain fortress. The canyon yawns, devouring clouds washed down by drafts of sunlight. The colors are diffuse, a blended strata of gray, royal purple, vibrant red, russet, jet black, and bubble-gum pink. You reach the thrilling spine, where the trees on the red bare earth are gnarled and twisted. The road becomes a roller coaster whipping you past raw beauty, immense and powerful. Drink deeply, contemplate, and move on into the clouds at the 2,000-foot level, where the trees get larger again. This mountain fastness took the full brunt of Hurricane 'Iniki.

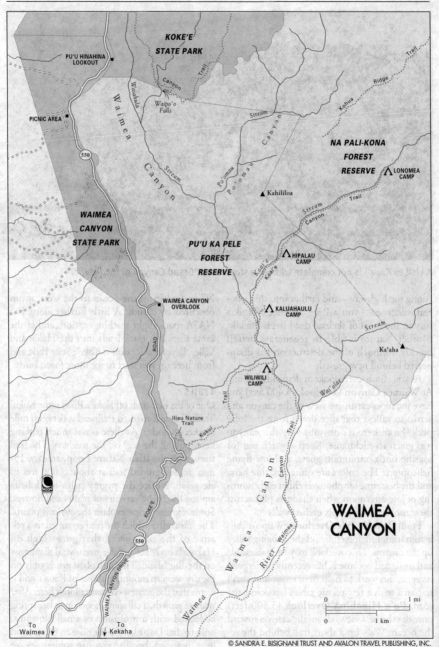

KOKE'E
STATE PARK

PU'U HINAHINA
LOOKOUT

Canyon

Trail

Waialula

Waipo'o
Falls

Stream

PICNIC AREA

Waimea

550

Canyon

Stream

NA PALI-KONA
FOREST
RESERVE

Po'omau

Kohua

Ridge

Trail

LONOMEA
CAMP

Po'omau

Kahililoa

Stream

Canyon

Trail

WAIMEA
CANYON
STATE PARK

PU'U KA PELE
FOREST
RESERVE

Koai'e

Koai'e

HIPALAU
CAMP

WAIMEA CANYON
OVERLOOK

Stream

KALUAHAULU
CAMP

ROAD

Ka'aha

WILIWILI
CAMP

Trail

Wai'alae

Iliau Nature
Trail

Kukui

Trail

Canyon

Trail

Waimea

KOKE'E

Canyon

WAIMEA
CANYON

550

Waimea

River

N

KAUA'I

WAIMEA CANYON DRIVE

0                    1 mi

0          1 km

To          To
Waimea    Kekaha

© SANDRA E. BISIGNANI TRUST AND AVALON TRAVEL PUBLISHING, INC.

ROBERT NILSEN

A visit to Kaua'i is not complete without a stop at the "Grand Canyon of the Pacific."

Along the highway—and farther into this arboreal wilderness—you will see evidence of 'Iniki's fury in the form of skeletal dead trees. Luckily, Mother Nature is able to regenerate herself quickly, so much of the destruction has disappeared behind new growth.

As you climb, every lookout demands a photo. At **Waimea Canyon Overlook** (3,400 feet) you have the most expansive view of the canyon and across to valleys that slice down from the lofty peak. From here it's obvious why this canyon was given its nickname. Keep a watch out for soaring birds, mountain goats, and low-flying helicopters. The colors are quite amazing here, and the best time for photos is either early morning or late afternoon when shadows play across these mottled and deeply etched walls.

From **Pu'u Ka Pele Overlook,** Waipo'o Falls is seen tumbling forcefully off the hanging valley up the canyon. This overlook may be inaccessible and unsigned because it has recently undergone revegetation work to help stem erosion. A small rest area with a few picnic tables lies across the road. **Pu'u Hinahina Overlook** (3,500 feet) provides the best views down the canyon toward the ocean. Walk up a short trail behind the restrooms and you may have a good view of

Ni'ihau adrift in the ocean to the west, if not obscured by clouds. A little farther along is a NASA space flight tracking station, and at the same turnoff a track leads into the Halemanu Valley. Beyond this point is Koke'e State Park, and from here on you start to see more forest birds.

## Trails

One of the best trails off Koke'e Road is the Kukui Trail. The well-marked trailhead is between mile markers 8 and 9. As there is not much parking here, pull all the way off the roadway. The trail starts with the **Iliau Nature Loop,** an easy, 15-minute, self-guided trail at about 3,000 feet in elevation. Notice the pygmy palm-like lobelia among the many varieties of plants and flowers. Some signage helps explain the various plants. The *iliau,* after which the trail is named, is a relative of the silversword that grows high on Haleakala on Maui and the greensword that grows on the Big Island. This rare plant grows only on the dry western mountain slopes of Kaua'i, and it seems that the greatest concentration is here. After years of growth, a tall spire shoots up in late spring bedecked with a profusion of small blossoms, only to die. Don't keep your nose to the ground here, however, because you can sometimes see white-tailed tropicbirds flying gracefully over the canyon or the brown-and-white *pueo* (Hawaiian owl) searching for its next meal.

The sign-in hut for the **Kukui Trail** is at the end of the Nature Loop; a pavilion stands nearby. Read some of the comments before heading down. The trail descends 2,000 feet through a series of switchbacks in two and a half miles. At the one-half-mile and one-mile points along the trail benches offer grand views of the canyon vistas. Turn around here if you think that the hike so far has been enough for you. Continuing down, the trail ends on the floor of the canyon at Wiliwili Campsite. From here the hale and hardy can head up the Waimea River for a half mile, either to the dam or on the opposite side of the river to Kaluahaulu Camp and the beginning of the **Koaiʻe Canyon Trail.** This three-mile trail takes you up the south side of Koaiʻe Canyon, where there are plenty of pools and two additional campsites. This trail *should not* be attempted during rainy weather because of flash flooding. You can also branch south from the Kukui Trail and link up with the **Waimea Canyon Trail,** which takes you eight miles, mostly via a 4WD track, to the town of Waimea. Because it crosses a game management area, you must have a special permit (available at the trailhead). There is no camping south of Waiʻalae Stream, the southern boundary of the forest reserve. The Waimea Canyon Trail is sometimes used by mountain bikers.

## KOKEʻE STATE PARK

After passing Puʻu Hinahina Overlook, you enter Kokeʻe State Park and soon reach park headquarters, the lodge, and museum. At the museum, helpful staff can provide a map of walking trails in the park and some information about the region's flora and fauna. Kokeʻe ranges 3,200–4,200 feet in elevation and is a huge 4,345 acres in area. Although its forest is mixed, koa and ʻohiʻa predominate. Temperatures here are several degrees cooler than along the coast and can be positively chilly at night, so bring a sweater or jacket. In January, the average daytime temperature is 45° and in July it's 68°. The average rainfall is 70 inches a year, with most of that coming

from October to May. Wild boar hunting and trout fishing are permitted within the park in prescribed areas at certain times of the year, but check with the Department of Land and Natural Resources on the third floor of the state office building in Lihuʻe about licenses, limits, season, etc., *before* coming up the mountain. Trout fishing permits are also issued at the park headquarters during fishing season only. To see wildlife anywhere in the park, it's best to look early in the morning or late in the afternoon when animals come out to feed. Aside from the views, the native forest birds attract many visitors to the park, and you don't always have to hike off the main roads to see them. You might see the reddish ʻapapane and ʻiʻiwi, the green-yellow ʻamakihi and ʻanianiau, and the brownish ʻelepaio. Of the nonnative birds, you probably will catch sight of the red-crested cardinal, the shama—a black bird with chestnut-colored breast and white on the tail—and, of course, the feral roosters.

Two spectacular lookouts await you farther up the road. At **Kalalau Lookout** (4,120 feet), mile marker 18, walk a minute and pray that the clouds are cooperative, allowing lasers of sunlight to illuminate the humpbacked, greencloaked mountains, silent and tortured, plummeting straight down to the roiling sea far, far below. There is a picnic area here with toilets. **Puʻu O Kila Lookout** (4,176 feet), another mile farther, is the end of the road. From here you not only get a wonderful view into the Kalalau Valley—the widest and largest valley along the Na Pali Coast—but also up across the Alakaʻi Swamp to Mt. Waiʻaleʻale if the clouds permit. One trail starts here and runs along an abandoned road construction project to Pihea, where it turns south into the Alakaʻi Swamp.

There is another fine viewpoint in this high mountain region that is not along Rte. 550, but a wonderful spot nonetheless. A short distance up from Puʻu Hinahina Lookout, take the only paved road leading off to the left as you go up the mountain. There is no sign at the intersection, but this is Makaha Ridge Road. This narrow road—drive defensively and watch for oncoming traffic—leads steeply down the ridge, passing **Kakio Keokeo Picnic Area** and continuing

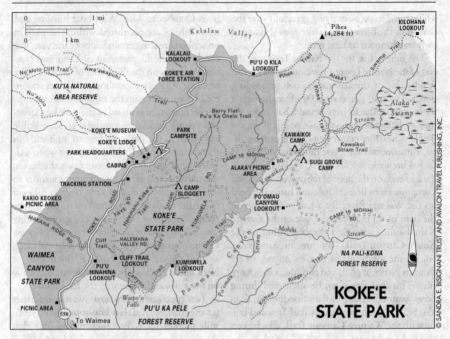

KOKE'E
STATE PARK

© SANDRA E. BISIGNANI TRUST AND AVALON TRAVEL PUBLISHING, INC.

about four miles to a PMRF tracking station—no entry. Cut through dense forest, the road affords no sweeping views. Almost to the end of the road, a secondary dirt road—for 4WD only—turns off to the left and runs for a little over one mile to the **Pine Forest Drive Picnic Area,** a great spot for a picnic and romantic sunsets.

## Koke'e Natural History Museum

Open 10 A.M.–4 P.M. daily, the Koke'e Natural History Museum, 808/335-9975, www.aloha.net /-kokee, is located to the side of a meadow just beyond the 15 mile marker. Be sure to stop; $1 suggested donation. It's a good place to get detailed hiking maps of the park and the surrounding national forest lands and additional information about the mountain environment of Kaua'i. Inside are informative displays of native birds, descriptions of plants and animals found in the park, Hawaiian culture, an exhibit on weather with a focus on Hurricane 'Iniki and its aftermath, books on Kaua'i and Hawaii, local Kaua'i crafts, and a relief map of the island. The non-

profit museum sponsors periodic work crews to help remove alien plants and maintain native species, conducts an annual environmental fair, and holds the annual Emmalani Festival. By reservation, the museum offers easy to moderate free guided walks appropriate for kids and adults on Sundays during summer months.

## Accommodations and Food

**Koke'e Lodge,** P.O. Box 819, Waimea, HI 96796, 808/335-6061, provides a dozen self-contained cabins, furnished with stoves, refrigerators, hot showers, cooking and eating utensils, and bedding; wood is available for woodstoves. The cabins cost $35 or $45 per night (five-night maximum; two-night minimum if one of the nights is Friday or Saturday) and vary from one large room for up to three people to two-bedroom units that sleep seven. The cabins are tough to get on weekends and holidays, in the Aug.–Sept. trout-fishing season, and during the wild plum harvest in June and July. For reservations, write well in advance (six months perhaps) and include an SASE, the number of people, and dates requested. Full payment is required within two weeks of making reservations, with a refund possible (less a $15 service fee) if reservations are canceled at least one week before arrival. Check-in is 2 P.M., check-out is 11 A.M. The lodge office is in the gift shop at the restaurant.

The Koke'e Lodge **restaurant and gift shop** are open 9 A.M.–4 P.M. daily. The restaurant serves a full breakfast 9–11 A.M. and lunch 11 A.M.–3:30 P.M. The cool weather calls especially for a slice of homemade pie, a steaming pot of coffee, or a cup of hot chocolate with a mountain of whipped cream. Prices for food and drink are on the high side, but, after all, everything has to be trucked up the mountain. The next nearest restaurant is 15 miles down the road at either Waimea or Kekeha. Also in the lodge is a shop that sells postcards, books, maps, T-shirts, snacks, sundries, and souvenirs; outside are a few picnic tables and a public telephone.

**Tent camping** is allowed with a permit at Koke'e State Park at a developed campground a few hundred yards across the meadow from the museum. Camping permits are issued for $5 per campsite at the state parks office in Lihu'e. Picnic tables and toilets are provided. In addition, two forest reserve campgrounds along Camp 10 Road and four primitive campgrounds in Waimea and Koai'e Canyons are open to campers with a free permit from the State Division of Forestry and Wildlife, which occupies the same office in Lihu'e as the state parks office.

The YWCA maintains **Camp Sloggett** within Koke'e State Park for group and individual hosteling and tent camping. Tent campers use raised platforms. Hostel guests use the bunkhouse on a first-come, first-served basis, unless a group of 20 or more has arranged to use the entire camp. The bunkhouse has single or bunk-style beds, and everyone has access to hot showers and a kitchen. Hostel guests must provide their own bedding and towels. Space can be arranged through the resident caretaker, who also has information about hiking. Rates are $10 for tent camping, $20 for hostel campers. Call 808/335-6060 for space availability or 808/245-5959 for group reservations. To reach the camp, take the first right turn after passing the Koke'e Lodge,

and follow the dirt road to a clearing and camp entrance. While this road may be somewhat rugged, it is open year-round and can be traversed by two-wheel-drive rental cars.

## Koke'e State Park Trails

Maps of Koke'e's trails are available at the Koke'e Natural History Museum. Two of the best are Hawaii Nature Guide's *Kokee's Trails* map and the more detailed and broader scope *Northwestern Kaua'i Recreational Map* by Earthwalk Press. The list of trails below is not meant to be comprehensive; these are only several of the many trails in the area. The trail entries are not detailed accounts but general descriptions to characterize the trails. Please check at the Koke'e museum for up-to-the-minute trail information and use one of the popular trail books listed in the Hiking section in the On the Road chapter of this book for more in-depth details of each trail.

Koke'e has about 45 miles of trails. Many start along Koke'e Drive or the dirt roads that lead off from it; most are marked and well maintained. Generally speaking, these trails are of four kinds: Na Pali Coast overlook trails; Alaka'i Swamp trails; forest trails; and canyon overlook trails. These trails are for hiking only. Bikes, horses, and motorcycles should be used on the park and forest reserve dirt roads only.

The first trails you encounter heading up from the coast are off Halemanu Road. **Cliff Trail** is only a few hundred yards long and leads to a spectacular overview of the canyon. Look for feral goats on the canyon ledges. **Canyon Trail** continues off Cliff Trail for 1.5 miles. It's a strenuous trail that dips down to Waipo'o Falls before climbing out of the canyon to the end of Kumuwela Road at Kumuwela Lookout, and it should take no more than three hours round-trip. Waipo'o Falls, in two sections and cascades, is the highest on the island at about 800 vertical feet. To make an easy circle, take Halemanu Road to its end. There, cross the wooded valley by the short **Unnamed Trail** to reach an undrivable section of Faye Road, which leads back up to the highway not too far from the Halemanu Road turnoff. **Halemanu-Koke'e Trail** leaves Halemanu Road and runs through the forest to a

ROBERT NILSEN

boardwalk along the Pihea Trail

secondary road off Camp 10 Road. It travels just more than a mile and is a self-guided nature trail. With plenty of native plants and trees, it's a favorite area for indigenous birds. Perhaps the easiest trail to access is the **Nature Trail** that starts near the Koke'e museum and requires less than half an hour to the end and back. This is a favorite and good for small children.

At pole no. 320 near park headquarters, you find the beginning of **Camp 10-Mohihi Road.** For this road, 4WDs are recommended, but it might be crossed with a two-wheel-drive car *only* in dry weather. It leads to a number of trails, mostly heading into the forest; others run out along ridges for canyon views, while still others head into the Alaka'i Swamp. **Berry Flat-Pu'u Ka Ohelo Trail,** an easy one-mile loop, gives you an up-close look at a vibrant upland forest. Under the green canopy watch for specimens such as *sugi* pine, California redwoods, Australian eucalyptus, and native koa. Locals come here to harvest

the methley plums, for which the area is famous. There is a midsummer season and limits for picking these plums, so check with the park headquarters first. Less than half a mile up ahead is the trailhead to the **Ditch Trail,** which gives views into Po'omau Canyon. Set aside at least a half day for this trail. A short way farther is **Sugi Grove,** where camping is limited to three days. This is the trailhead to the **Kawaikoi Stream Trail,** a 3.5-mile round-trip, moderate forest trail known for its scenic beauty. It follows the south side of the stream, crosses over, and loops back on the north side. Avoid it if the stream is high. About halfway up this trail, you can cross the stream to connect with the Pihea Trail.

The **Alaka'i Swamp Trail** is otherworldly and magical, crossing one of the most unusual pieces of real estate in the world. It begins off Camp 10 Road near the state park-forest reserve boundary. The nearby **Alaka'i Picnic Area** offers views into the Waimea Canyon. The trail heads into the swamp for 3.5 miles. Once you had to slog through the bogs, but now much of the way is over a raised walkway—easier for you and more protection for the fragile environment. Still, it's a rainy area, so be prepared to get wet and muddy. If you smell anise along the way, that's the *mokihana* berry, used with *maile* for fashioning wedding lei. This trail, great for the unique vegetation, is also very good for birding. The trail ends at the Kilohana Lookout, where there's an expansive vista of Wainiha and Hanalei Valleys on a very rare clear day; otherwise you'll be enveloped by thick clouds. This trail is a real gamble for views. An alternate route to the Alaka'i Swamp, providing easier access, starts by taking **Pihea Trail** from the end of the paved road near the Pu'u O Kila Overlook. This is a good general-interest trail because it gives you wonderful views into Kalalau Valley virtually all along its length. Don't forget to turn around, however, for the views over the inner valleys and up to Mt. Wai'ale'ale are superb. About one mile along, the trail turns south and descends into the forest where the Alaka'i Swamp Trail, which comes in from the right, bisects it. This trail is also good for birding, and aside from the native birds, you might run into *moa,* wild jungle fowl. Continuing straight through this trail intersection, the Pihea Trail eventually dips down to Kawaikoi Stream and ends at Kawaikoi Campsite, from where you can return via Camp 10 Road for an amazing loop of the area. Count on a long day to do the loop, or be dropped off at Pu'u O Kila Overlook and picked up at Kawaikoi campsite, a distance of about four miles.

One of the most rewarding trails for the time and effort is **Awa'awapuhi Trail.** The trailhead is after park headquarters, just past mile marker 17, beyond the crest of the hill. It's three miles long and takes you out onto a thin finger of *pali*, with the sea and an emerald valley 2,500 feet below. The sun dapples the upland forest, which still bears the scars of Hurricane 'Iniki. Everywhere flowers and fiddlehead ferns delight the eyes, while wild thimbleberries and passion fruit delight the taste buds. The trail is well marked, slightly strenuous, and steady down. Connecting with the Awa'awapuhi at the three-mile marker is the **Nu'alolo Cliff Trail,** which connects with the Nu'alolo Trail and has an open shelter about halfway along. The **Nu'alolo**

**Trail** starts near park headquarters and is the easiest trail to the *pali* with an overview of Nu'alolo Valley. It's 3.4 miles to the Nu'alolo Cliff Trail junction and 3.8 miles to the vista point at the Nu'alolo Trail terminus. In comparison, this trail is more open to the sun, hence hotter, than the more shaded and tree-covered Awa'awapuhi Trail. Either the Awa'awapuhi or Nu'alolo ridge trail can be done separately, without using the Nu'alolo Cliff Trail, but all three together make a nice loop. Remember that the trail going in is downhill and coming out is uphill—a more than 1,500-foot elevation gain. Pace yourself. It's over 10 miles, so give it a full day for sightseeing and a picnic, although it can be done in a strong half day. It's recommended that this loop be done clockwise, going in on the Nu'alolo Trail and coming out on the Awa'awapuhi Trail. It's perhaps safer to leave your car at the museum parking lot rather than at the trailhead, and anyway, the walk down the road from the Awa'awapuhi trailhead back to the museum is easier at the end of a long day than hiking up the road back to your car.

# Ni'ihau

The only thing forbidding about Ni'ihau is its nickname, "The Forbidden Island." Ironically, it's one of the last real havens of peace, tranquility, and tradition left on the face of the earth. This privately owned island, operating as one large cattle and sheep ranch, is home to many of the last remaining pure Hawaiians in the state. To go there, you must have a personal invitation by the owners or one of the residents. Some people find this situation strange, but it would be no stranger than walking up to an Iowa farmhouse unannounced and expecting to be invited in to dinner. The islanders are free to come and go as they wish and are given the security of knowing that the last real Hawaiian place is not going to be engulfed by the modern world. Ni'ihau is a reservation, but a *free-will* reservation—something you'll admire if you've ever felt that the world was too much with you.

## The Land and Climate

The 17-mile **Kaulakahi Channel** separates Ni'ihau from the western tip of Kaua'i. The island's maximum dimensions are 18 miles long by six miles wide, with a total area of 70 square miles. The highest point on the island, Pani'au (1,281 feet), lies on the east-central coast. The whole of Ni'ihau is the western crescent remains of an ancient and much larger island, most of which broke away along the eastern cliff line and

sank beneath the water. There are no port facilities on the island, but the occasional boats put in at Ki'i and Lehua Landings, both on the northern tip. Since Ni'ihau is so low and lies in the rainshadow of Kaua'i, it receives only 30 inches of precipitation per year, making it rather arid. Oddly enough, low-lying basins, eroded from the single shield volcano that made the island, act as a catchment system. In them are the state's largest naturally occurring lakes, 182-acre Lake Halulu and the larger, 841 acre, intermittent Lake Halali'i. Two uninhabited islets join Ni'ihau as part of Kaua'i County: Lehua, just off the northern tip and exceptional for scuba diving, and Ka'ula, a few miles off the southern tip; each barely covers one-half square mile.

## HISTORY

After the goddess Papa returned from Tahiti and discovered that her husband, Wakea, was playing around, she left him. The great Wakea did some squirming, and after these island-parents reconciled, Papa became pregnant and gave birth to Kaua'i. According to the creation chants found in the *Kumulipo,* Ni'ihau popped out as the afterbirth, along with Lehua and Ka'ula, the last of the low reef islands.

Ni'ihau was never a very populous island because of the relatively poor soil, so the islanders had to rely on trade with nearby Kaua'i for many necessities, including poi. Luckily, the fishing grounds off the island's coastal waters are the richest in the area, and Ni'ihauans could always trade fish. The islanders became famous for Ni'ihau mats, a good trade item, made from *makaloa,* a sedge plant that's plentiful on the island. Craftsmen also fashioned *ipu pawehe,* a geometrically designed gourd highly prized in the old days. When Captain Cook arrived and wished to provision his ships, he remarked that the Ni'ihau natives were much more eager to trade than those on Kaua'i, and he secured potatoes and yams that seemed to be in abundant supply. Today, aside from raising livestock, Ni'ihau residents make charcoal, gather honey, and produce excellent-quality (and very expensive) shell lei as their forebears have done for generations.

## Kamehameha IV Sells

Along with Kaua'i, Ni'ihau became part of the unified Hawaiian kingdom under Kamehameha I. It passed down to his successors, and in 1864, Kamehameha IV sold it to the Sinclair family for $10,000. Originally the king didn't want to sell this island and offered them another property, a swampy beach area, but much closer to the center of island power. That property was Waikiki. The Sinclairs turned the king down. Apparently, Ni'ihau was in great form after a fine spring and looked like a much better deal. This Scottish family, which came to Hawaii via New Zealand, has been the sole proprietor of the 46,000-acre island ever since, although they now live on Kaua'i. Through marriage, the Robinson family now owns Ni'ihau, as well as vast tracts of land on west Kaua'i. They began a sheep and cattle ranch, hiring the island's natives as workers. No one can say exactly why, but it's evident that this family felt a great sense of responsibility and purpose. Tradition passed down over the years dictated that islanders could live on Ni'ihau as long as they pleased, but that visitors were not welcome without a personal invitation. With the native Hawaiian population so

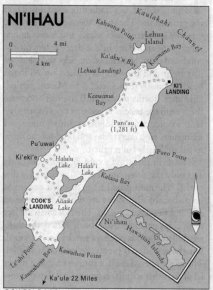

KAUA'I

devastated, the Robinsons (descendants of the Sinclairs) felt that these proud people should have at least one place to call theirs and theirs alone. To keep the race pure, male visitors to the island were generally asked to leave by sundown.

## Ni'ihau Invaded

During World War II, Ni'ihau was the only island of Hawaii to be occupied by the Japanese. A Zero pilot developed engine trouble after striking Pearl Harbor and had to ditch on Ni'ihau. At first the islanders took him prisoner, but he somehow managed to escape and commandeer the machine guns from his plane. He terrorized the island, and the residents headed for the hills. One old woman who refused to leave was like a Hawaiian Barbara Fritchie. She told the Japanese prisoner to shoot her if he wished, but to please stop making a nuisance of himself—it wasn't nice! He would have saved himself a lot of trouble if he had only listened. Fed up with hiding, one huge *kanaka*, Benehakaka Kanahele, decided to approach the pilot with *aloha*. He was convinced the intruder would see the error of his ways. This latter-day samurai shot Mr. Kanahele for his trouble. Ben persisted and was shot again. An expression of pain, disgust, and disbelief at the stranger's poor manners spread across Ben's face, but still he tried pleading with the prisoner, who shot him for the third time. Ben had had enough, and grabbed the astonished pilot and flung him headlong against a wall, cracking his skull and killing him instantly. This incident gave rise to a wartime maxim—"Don't shoot a Hawaiian three times or you'll make him mad"—and a song titled, "You Can't Conquer Niihau, Nohow." Mr. Kanahele lived out his life on Ni'ihau and died in the 1960s.

## LIFE TODAY

The only reliable connection that the islanders have with the outside world is a World War II-vintage landing craft, which they use to bring in

---

## NI'IHAU SHELLWORK

The finest shellwork made in Hawaii comes from Ni'ihau, in a tradition passed down over the generations. The shells themselves—tiny and very rare *kahelelani, laiki, momi,* and *kamoa* among them—are abundant in the deep waters off the windward coast. Sometimes, the tides and winds are just right and they are deposited on Ni'ihau's beaches, mostly from October to March, particularly after storms that disturb the reef and wash them onto the beach. When that does happen, island women and children, and now more and more men, stop everything and head for the shore to painstakingly collect them.

The shells are sorted according to size and color, and only the finest are kept: 80 percent are discarded. The most prized are so tiny that a dozen fit on a thumbnail. Colors are white, yellow, blue, red, and the very rare gold. The best shells are free from chips or cracks. After being sorted, the shells are drilled. Various pieces of jewelry are fashioned, but the traditional pieces are necklaces and lei. The lei are often done in a pattern imitating flower lei of the other islands, as few natural flowers grow on Ni'ihau. These works can be short, single-strand chokers or heavy multi-strand pieces. The rice motif is always popular; these are usually multi-stranded with the main shells clipped on the ends with various colored shells strung in as highlights.

A necklace takes long hours to create, with every shell connected by intricate and minute knots. Usually the women of Ni'ihau do this work. Clasps are made from a type of cowry shell found only on Ni'ihau. No two necklaces are exactly alike. They sell by the inch, and the pure white and golden ones are very expensive—most are handed down as priceless heirlooms. Although Ni'ihau shellwork is available in fine stores all over the state, Kaua'i, perhaps because it's closest or because family members live there, seems to get the largest selection. For an introduction, have a look at the collection at the Hawaiian Trading Company in Lawa'i. If you're after a once-in-a-lifetime purchase, consider Ni'ihau shellwork.

The most comprehensive book covering this artistic subject is *Ni'ihau Shell Leis,* by Linda Paik Moriarty, published by the University of Hawai'i Press.

supplies from Kaua'i, and an Agusta helicopter used for medical emergencies, supplies, and aerial tours. For years, homing pigeons were used to send messages, but they have been replaced by two-way radios. There's no communal electricity on the island, but people do have generators to power refrigerators and TVs. Radios are very popular, and most people get around either on horseback or in pickup trucks. The population numbers around 160 people, 95 percent of whom are Hawaiian, the other 5 percent Japanese, and the main community is Pu'uwai, about midway down the west coast. There is one elementary school, in which English is used, but most people speak Hawaiian at home. The children go off to Kaua'i for high school, but after they get a taste of what the world at large has to offer, a surprisingly large number return to Ni'ihau.

After Hurricane 'Iwa battered the island and Hurricane 'Iniki followed suit in 1992, the state was very eager to offer aid. The people of Ni'ihau thanked them for their concern but told them not to bother—that they would take care of things themselves. Ni'ihau was the only island to reject statehood in the plebiscite of 1959. In November 1988, when a group of environmentally conscious Kaua'ians took a boat to Ni'ihau to try to clear some of the beaches of the floating sea junk that had washed up on shore, the Ni'ihauans felt that the island was being trespassed—they didn't want such help in any case—and a few shots were fired, a warning to back off. Still unsettled, the controversy focuses on the question of who owns the beach—all beaches in Hawaii are open to free access, yet the whole island of Ni'ihau is privately owned. Occasionally, boaters still try to land on the island and some have their craft confiscated.

Today, some people accuse the Robinson family of being greedy barons of a medieval fiefdom, holding the Ni'ihauans as virtual slaves. This idea is utter nonsense. Besides the fact that the islanders have an open door, the Robinsons would make immeasurably more money selling the island off to resort developers than running it as a livestock ranch and hunting ground. As if the spirit of old Hawaii was trying to send a sign, it's interesting that Ni'ihau's official lei is fashioned from the *pupu*, a rare shell found only on the island's beaches, and the island's official color is white, the universal symbol of purity.

## Tours

**Ni'ihau Safaris** offers two different types of tours to the island, one a helicopter tour and the other a hunting tour. Aside from being invited to the island, these are the only ways to get a close-up look at Ni'ihau. Although it has no fixed schedule, **Ni'ihau Helicopters** flies charter tours on its twin-engine Agusta 109A when there are enough people to make a go of it. This three- to four-hour flight is not a sightseeing flight per se, but takes you to the island and lets you enjoy the beach for a couple of hours to play in the water and walk on the sand. Total flight time is about one hour. Don't expect to meet any island residents, however, as they usually set you down away from where the people live. Rates are $280 per person with lunch included. Alternately, a **hunting expedition** can be arranged for wild pig and feral sheep. The hunting rules for the island are strict but fair for a free chase hunt. Rates are $1,650 a day per hunter, with a maximum of four hunters, and this fee includes the helicopter flight to and ground transportation on Ni'ihau, guide, lunch, up to one animal each, and care and packing of all shot animals. For more information on either of these tours, call 808/335-3500 or 877/441-3500, or write P.O. Box 690270, Makaweli, HI 96769.

# The Northwestern Islands

Like tiny gems of a broken necklace, the Northwestern Hawaiian Islands spill across the vast Pacific. Popularly called the **Leewards,** most were discovered in the 19th century, oftentimes by hapless ships that ground to a sickening halt on their treacherous, half-submerged reefs. Even today, craft equipped with the most modern navigational devices must be wary in these waters. They remain among the loneliest outposts on the face of the earth.

## Land and Climate

The Leewards are the oldest islands of the Hawaiian chain, believed to have emerged from the sea 25–30 million years ago! Slowly they floated west-northwest past the suboceanic hot spot as the other islands were built. Measured from **Nihoa Island,** about 100 miles off the northwestern tip of Kaua'i, they stretch for just under 1,100 miles to **Kure Atoll.** There are a dozens of islets, shoals, and half-submerged reefs in this chain. Most have been eroded flat by the sea and wind, but a few tough volcanic cores endure. Together they make up a landmass of approximately 3,500 acres, the largest being the three Midway islands—taken together—at 1,580 acres, and the smallest the **Gardner Pinnacles** at six

acres. The climate is similar to that of the main islands with a slightly larger variance. Temperatures, usually 70–85 degrees, sometimes dip as low as 50 degrees and climb as high as 90 degrees. Rainfall can come any month of the year, but is more frequent in the winter. The average annual total is about 40 inches.

## Administration and History

Politically, the Leewards are administered by the City and County of Honolulu, except for the Midway Islands, which are under federal jurisdiction. None, except Midway, are permanently inhabited, but there are some lonely wildlife field stations on Kure and the French Frigate Shoals. All, except for Midway Atoll, are part of the **Hawaiian Islands National Wildlife Refuge,** established at the turn of the 20th century by Theodore Roosevelt. In 1996, following the closure of the Naval Air Base on Midway Island, Midway Atoll was turned over to the Department of the Interior and is now administered as the **Midway Atoll National Wildlife Refuge.**

In precontact times, some of the islands supported a culture markedly different from the one that emerged on the main Hawaiian Islands. Necker Island, for example, was the only island in

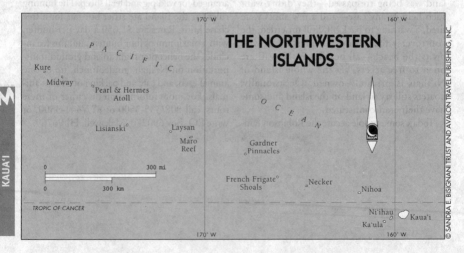

THE NORTHWESTERN ISLANDS

Kure
Midway
Pearl & Hermes Atoll
Lisianski
Laysan
Maro Reef
Gardner Pinnacles
French Frigate Shoals
Necker
Nihoa

PACIFIC OCEAN

0       300 mi
0    300 km

TROPIC OF CANCER

Ni'ihau   Kaua'i
Ka'ula

170° W     160° W

the entire Hawaiian archipelago on which the inhabitants carved stone figures with a complete head and torso. On others, remains of *heiau* and agricultural terracing allude to their colonization by precontact Hawaiians. Over the years, natives as well as Westerners have exploited the islands for feathers, fertilizer, seals, and fish.

The islands are now closely monitored by the U.S. Fish and Wildlife Agency. Permission to land on them is granted only under special circumstances. Studies are underway to determine if the waters around the islands can support commercial fishing, while leaving a plentiful supply of food for the unique wildlife of these lonely islands.

## Wildlife

Millions of seabirds of various species have found permanent sanctuary on the Leewards, using them as giant floating nests and rookeries. Today the populations are stable and growing, but it hasn't always been so. On Laysan, in the early 1900s, egg hunters came to gather countless albatross eggs, selling the albumen to companies making photographic paper. They brought their families along, and their children's pets, which included rabbits. The rabbits escaped and multiplied wildly. In no time they invaded the territories of the **Laysan honeycreeper, rail,** and **millerbird,** rendering them extinct. Laysan has recovered and is refuge to more than six million birds, including the rare and indigenous **Laysan teal** and **finch.**

An amazing bird using the rookeries is the **frigate bird.** During mating rituals, the male can inflate its chest like a giant red heart-shaped balloon. Also known as man-o'-war birds, they oftentimes pirate the catches of other birds, devour chicks, and even cannibalize their own offspring.

Some of the most prolific birds of the Leewards are terns, both the delicate all-white **fairy tern** and its darker relative the **sooty tern.** Other distinctive species include a variety of boobies, and the **Laysan albatross,** which has a wingspan of up to seven feet, one of the world's largest seabirds.

Besides birds, the islands are home to the **Hawaiian monk seal,** one of only two species of indigenous Hawaiian mammals. These beautiful and sleek animals were hunted to near extinc-

tion for their skins. Humans encroached on their territory, but now they are protected as an endangered species. About 1,000 individuals still cling to existence on various islands.

The **green sea turtle** is another species that has found a haven here. They were hunted to near extinction for their meat and leather, and of the few colonies around the world, the largest in the United States is on the French Frigate Shoals.

## MIDWAY ISLANDS

Midway Atoll is about 1,200 miles northwest of and an hour behind Honolulu. It is only 150 miles or so east of the international date line. The atoll is comprised of three separate islands, Sand, Eastern, and Spit, within a 25 square mile lagoon. Together, at about three square miles, the islands comprise about one half of the total land area of all the Northwestern Islands. These three islands and surrounding reef, only a dozen feet above the ocean level at their highest points, are coral growths that rise some 500 feet above the underlying volcanic peak.

First discovered in 1859 and named Brooks Islands, they were renamed Midway when annexed by the United States in 1867. In 1903, Pres. Theodore Roosevelt put the islands under the control of the U.S. Navy to help stem the loss of bird life by Japanese sailors, who gathered bird eggs and feathers there. In the first decade on the 1900s, employees of a cable company were the first permanent resident on the islands. This communications station was a strategic link between the United States and Asia. From 1935 until the early 1960s, Midway was a refueling station for most transpacific air routes to the Orient, first used by clipper seaplanes and later by prop and jet planes. With the growing concern about Japanese aggression in Asia, a naval base was begun on Midway in 1940. This installation was bombed on December 7, 1941, after the attack on Pearl Harbor earlier in the day. In June of the following year, the Battle of Midway took place in the ocean off the atoll, and was a turning point in the war of the Pacific. Until 1993, Midway continued to be used as a military base, housing up to 4,000 personnel during the 1960s. With the closure of the naval facility, Midway Atoll has become the Midway Atoll National Wildlife Refuge, administered from 1996 by the U.S. Fish and Wildlife Service for the Department of the Interior. Today, Midway has only several dozen permanent residents that run its facilities, maintain the refuge, and conduct scientific study. Limited tourism was allowed until 2002 when the concessionaire withdrew from its operations at Midway. One only hopes that at some time in the future the atoll will again be open to some tourist activities.

**Hawaiian monk seals, green sea turtles,** **spinner dolphins,** and close to 200 varieties of colorful **reef fish** inhabit the lagoon, while more than a dozen species of seabirds live and nest around the atoll. The world's large colony of **Laysan albatross,** about 2 million birds, inhabit the island, as do **great frigate birds, red-tailed tropic birds, terns, boobies, petrels,** and **wedge-tailed shearwaters.**

For more information on Midway Atoll, contact the Midway Atoll National Wildlife Refuge, 808/674-8237, P.O. Box 29460, Honolulu, HI 96820, or the U.S. Fish and Wildlife Service's office in Honolulu, 808/541-2749; http://midway.fws.gov.

# Resources

# Hawaiian Glossary

The list on the following pages gives you a "taste" of Hawaiian and provides a basic vocabulary of words in common usage that you are likely to hear. Becoming familiar with them is not a strict necessity, but they will definitely enhance your experience and make talking with local people more congenial. Many islanders spice their speech with certain words, especially when they're speaking "pidgin," and you too can use them just as soon as you feel comfortable. You might even discover some Hawaiian words that are so perfectly expressive they'll become regular parts of your vocabulary. Many Hawaiian words have been absorbed into the English dictionary. The definitions given are not exhaustive, but are generally considered the most common.

Words marked with an asterisk (*) are used commonly throughout the islands.

**'a'a\***—rough clinker lava. 'A'a has become the correct geological term to describe this type of lava found anywhere in the world.

**'ae**—yes

**ahupua'a**—pie-shaped land divisions running from mountain to sea that were governed by *konohiki*, local *ali'i* who owed their allegiance to a reigning chief

**aikane**—friend; pal; buddy

**'aina**—land; the binding spirit to all Hawaiians. Love of the land is paramount in traditional Hawaiian beliefs.

**akamai**—smart; clever; wise

**akua**—a god, or simply "divine"

**ali'i\***—a Hawaiian chief or noble

**aloha\***—the most common greeting in the islands; can mean both hello and good-bye, welcome and farewell. It can also mean romantic love, affection, or best wishes.

**'a'ole**—no

**'aumakua**—a personal or family god, often an ancestral spirit

**auwe**—alas; ouch! When a great chief or loved one died, it was a traditional wail of mourning.

**'awa,**—also known as *kava*, a mildly intoxicating traditional drink made from the juice of chewed *'awa* root, spat into a bowl, and used in religious ceremonies

**halakahiki**—pineapple

**hale\***—house or building; often combined with other words to name a specific place, such as Haleakala (House of the Sun), or Hale Pa'i at Lahainaluna, meaning Printing House

**hana\***—work; combined with *pau* means end of work or quitting time

**hanai**—literally "to feed." Part of the true *aloha* spirit. A *hanai* is a permanent guest, or an adopted family member, usually an old person or a child. This is an enduring cultural phenomenon in Hawaii, in which a child from one family (perhaps that of a brother or sister, and quite often one's grandchild) is raised as one's own without formal adoption.

**haole\***—a word that at one time meant foreigner, but which now means a white person or Caucasian

**hapa\***—half, as in a mixed-blooded person being referred to as *hapa haole*

**hapai\***—pregnant; used by all ethnic groups when a *keiki* is on the way

**haupia\***—a coconut custard dessert often served at a lu'au

**heiau\***—A platform made of skillfully fitted rocks, upon which temporary structures were built as temples and offerings made to the gods.

**holomu\***—an ankle-length dress that is much more fitted than a mu'umu'u, and which is often worn on formal occasions

**hono**—bay, as in Honolulu (Sheltered Bay)

**honu**—green sea turtle; endangered

**ho'oilo**—traditional Hawaiian winter that began in November

**ho'olaulea**—any happy event, but especially a family outing or picnic

**ho'omalimali\***—sweet talk; flattery

**huhu\***—angry; irritated

**hui\***—a group; meeting; society. Often used to refer to Chinese businesspeople or family members who pool their money to get businesses started.

**hukilau**—traditional shoreline fish-gathering in which everyone lends a hand to *huki* (pull) the huge net. Anyone taking part shares in the *lau* (food). It is much more like a party than hard work, and if you're lucky you'll be able to take part in one.

**hula\***—a native Hawaiian dance in which the rhythm of the islands is captured by swaying hips and stories told by lyrically moving hands. A *halau* is a group or school of hula.

**huli huli**—barbecue, as in *huli huli* chicken

**i'a**—fish in general. *I'a maka* is raw fish.

**imu\***—underground oven filled with hot rocks and used for baking. The main cooking method featured at a lu'au, used to steam-bake pork and other succulent dishes. The tending of the *imu* was traditionally for men only.

**ipo**—sweetheart; lover; girl- or boyfriend

**kahili**—a tall pole topped with feathers, resembling a huge feather duster. It was used by an *ali'i* to announce his or her presence.

**kahuna\***—priest; sorcerer; doctor; skillful person. In old Hawaii *kahuna* had tremendous power, which they used for both good and evil. The *kahuna ana'ana* was a feared individual who practiced "black magic" and could pray a person to death, while the *kahuna lapa'au* was a medical practitioner bringing aid and comfort to the people.

**kai**—the sea. Many businesses and hotels employ *kai* as part of their name.

**kalua**—means roasted underground in an *imu*. A favorite island food is *kalua* pork.

**kama'aina\***—a child of the land; an old-timer; a longtime island resident of any ethnic background; a resident of Hawaii or native son or daughter. Hotels and airlines often offer discounts called *"kama'aina* rates" to anyone who can prove island residency.

**kanaka**—man or commoner; later used to distinguish a Hawaiian from other races. Tone of voice can make it a derisive expression.

**kane\***—means man, but actually used to signify a relationship such as husband or boyfriend. Written on a lavatory door it means "men's room."

**kapu\***—forbidden; taboo; keep out; do not touch

**kaukau\***—slang word meaning food or chow; grub. Some of the best food in Hawaii comes from the *kaukau* wagons, trucks that sell plate lunches and other morsels.

**kauwa**—a landless, untouchable caste once confined to living on reservations. Members of this caste were often used as human sacrifices at *heiau*. Calling someone *kauwa* is still a grave insult.

**kava**—(see *'awa*)

**keiki\***—child or children; used by all ethnic groups. "Have you hugged your *keiki* today?"

**kiawe**—an algaroba tree from South America commonly found in Hawaii along the shore. It grows a nasty long thorn that can easily puncture a tire. Legend has it that the trees were introduced to the islands by a misguided missionary who hoped the thorns would coerce natives into wearing shoes. Actually, they are good for fuel, as fodder for hogs and cattle, and for reforestation, none of which you'll appreciate if you step on one of the thorns or flatten a tire on your rental car!

**ko'ala\***—any food that has been broiled or barbecued

**kokua**—help. As in "Your *kokua* is needed to keep Hawaii free from litter."

**kona wind\***—a muggy subtropical wind that blows from the south and hits the leeward side of the islands. It usually brings sticky hot weather and one of the few times when air-conditioning will be appreciated.

**konane**—a traditional Hawaiian game, similar to checkers, played with pebbles on a large flat stone used as a board

**ko'olau**—windward side of the island

**kukui**—a candlenut tree whose pods are polished and then strung together to make a beautiful lei. Traditionally the oil-rich nuts were strung on the rib of a coconut leaf and used as a candle.

**kuleana**—homesite; the old homestead; small farms. Especially used to describe the small spreads on Hawaiian Homelands on Moloka'i.

**Kumulipo\***—ancient Hawaiian genealogical chant that records the pantheon of gods, creation, and the beginning of humankind

**kupuna**—a grandparent or old-timer; usually means someone who has gained wisdom. The statewide school system now invites *kupuna* to talk to the children about the old ways and methods.

*la*—the sun. Often combined with other words to be more descriptive, such as *La*haina (Merciless Sun) or Haleaka*la* (House of the Sun).

**lanai***—veranda or porch. You'll pay more for a hotel room if it has a lanai with an ocean view.

*lani*—sky or the heavens

*lau hala**—traditional Hawaiian weaving of mats, hats, etc., from the prepared fronds of the pandanus (screw pine)

**lei***—a traditional garland of flowers or vines. One of Hawaii's most beautiful customs. Given at any auspicious occasion, but especially when arriving or leaving Hawaii.

*lele*—the stone altar at a *heiau*

*limu*—edible seaweed of various types. Gathered from the shoreline, it makes an excellent salad. It's used to garnish many island dishes and is a favorite at lu'au.

*lomi lomi*—traditional Hawaiian massage; also, raw salmon made into a vinegared salad with chopped onion and spices

*lua**—the toilet; the head; the bathroom

*luakini*—a human-sacrifice temple. Introduced to Hawaii in the 13th century at Waha'ula Heiau on the Big Island.

*lu'au**—a Hawaiian feast featuring poi, *imu*-baked pork, and other traditional foods. Good ones provide some of the best gastronomic delights in the world.

*luna*—foreman or overseer in the plantation fields. They were often mounted on horseback and were renowned for either their fairness or their cruelty. Representing the middle class, they served as a buffer between plantation workers and white plantation owners.

*mahalo**—thank you. *Mahalo nui* means "big thanks" or "thank you very much."

*mahele*—division. The "Great Mahele" of 1848 changed Hawaii forever when the traditional common lands were broken up into privately owned plots.

**mahimahi***—a favorite eating fish. Often called a dolphin, but a mahimahi is a true fish, not a cetacean.

*mahu*—a homosexual; often used derisively like "fag" or "queer"

*maile*—a fragrant vine used in traditional lei. It looks ordinary but smells delightful.

*maka'ainana*—a commoner; a person "belonging" to the *'aina* (land), who supported the *ali'i* by fishing and farming and as a warrior

*makai**—toward the sea; used by most islanders when giving directions

*make*—dead; deceased

*malihini**—what you are if you have just arrived: a newcomer; a tenderfoot; a recent arrival

*malo*—the native Hawaiian loincloth. Never worn anymore except at festivals or pageants.

*mana**—power from the spirit world; innate energy of all things animate or inanimate; the grace of god. Mana could be passed on from one person to another, or even stolen. Great care was taken to protect the *ali'i* from having their *mana* defiled. Commoners were required to lie flat on the ground and cover their faces whenever a great *ali'i* approached. *Kahuna* were often employed in the regaining or transference of *mana*.

*manini*—stingy; tight; a Hawaiianized word taken from the name of Don Francisco *Marin*, who was instrumental in bringing many fruits and plants to Hawaii. He was known for never sharing any of the bounty from his substantial gardens on Vineyard Street in Honolulu; therefore, his name came to mean "stingy."

*manuahi*—free; gratis; extra

*mauka**—toward the mountains; used by most islanders when giving directions

*mauna*—mountain. Often combined with other words to be more descriptive, such as Mauna Kea (White Mountain)

*mele*—a song or chant in the Hawaiian oral tradition that records the history and genealogies of the *ali'i*

**Menehune**—the legendary "little people" of Hawaii. Like leprechauns, they are said to shun humans and possess magical powers.

*moa*—chicken; fowl

*moana*\*—the ocean; the sea. Many businesses and hotels as well as places have *moana* as part of their name.

*moe*—sleep

*mo'olelo*—ancient tales kept alive by the oral tradition and recited only by day

*mu'umu'u*\*—a "Mother Hubbard," an ankle-length dress with a high neckline introduced by the missionaries to cover the nakedness of the Hawaiians. It has become fashionable attire for almost any occasion in Hawaii.

*nani*—beautiful

*nui*—big; great; large; as in *mahalo nui* (thank you very much)

*'ohana*—a family; the fundamental social division; extended family. Now often used to denote a social organization with grassroots overtones.

*'okolehau*—literally "iron bottom"; a traditional booze made from *ti* root. *'Okole* means "rear end" and *hau* means "iron," which was descriptive of the huge blubber pots in which *'okolehau* was made. Also, if you drink too much it'll surely knock you on your *'okole*.

*oli*—chant not done to a musical accompaniment

*ono*\*—delicious; delightful; the best. *Ono ono* means "extra or absolutely delicious."

*'opihi*—a shellfish or limpet that clings to rocks and is gathered as one of the islands' favorite *pu pu*. Custom dictates that you never remove all of the *'opihi* from a rock; some are always left to grow for future generations.

*'opu*—belly; stomach

*pahoehoe*\*—smooth, ropy lava that looks like burnt pancake batter. It is now the correct geological term used to describe this type of lava found anywhere in the world.

*pakalolo*—"crazy smoke"; grass; smoke; dope; marijuana

*pake*—a Chinese person. Can be derisive, depending on the tone in which it is used. It is a bastardization of the Chinese word meaning "uncle."

*pali*\*—a cliff; precipice. Hawaii's geology makes them quite common. The most famous are the *pali* of Oahu where a major battle was fought.

*paniolo*\*—a Hawaiian cowboy. Derived from the Spanish *espa-ol*. The first cowboys brought to Hawaii during the early 19th century were Mexicans from California.

*papale*—hat. Except for the feathered helmets of the *ali'i* warriors of old Hawaii, hats were generally not worn. However, once the islanders saw their practical uses and how fashionable they were, they began weaving them from various materials and quickly became experts at manufacture and design.

*pa'u*—long split skirt often worn by women when horseback riding. In the 1800s, an island treat was watching *pa'u* riders in their beautiful dresses at Kapi'olani Park in Honolulu. The tradition is carried on today at many of Hawaii's rodeos.

*pau*\*—finished; done; completed. Often combined into *pau hana*, which means end of work or quitting time.

*pilau*—stink; bad smell; stench

*pilikia*—trouble of any kind, big or small; bad times

*poi*\*—a glutinous paste made from the pounded corm of taro, which ferments slightly and has a light sour taste. Purplish in color, it's a staple at lu'au, where it is called "one-, two-, or three-finger" poi, depending upon its thickness.

*pono*—righteous or excellent

*pua*—flower

*puka*\*—a hole of any size. *Puka* is used by all island residents, whether talking about a pinhole in a rubber boat or a tunnel through a mountain.

*punalua*—a traditional practice, before the missionaries arrived, of sharing mates. Western seamen took advantage of it, leading to the spread of contagious diseases and eventual rapid decline of the Hawaiian people.

*pune'e*\*—bed; narrow couch. Used by all ethnic groups. To recline on a *pune'e* on a breezy lanai is a true island treat.

*pu pu*\*—an appetizer; a snack; hors d'oeuvres; can be anything from cheese and crackers to sushi. Oftentimes, bars or nightclubs offer them free.

*pupule*—crazy; nuts; out of your mind

***pu'u***—hill, as in Pu'u 'Ula'ula (Red Hill)

***tapa****—a traditional paper cloth made from beaten bark. Intricate designs were stamped in using beaters, and natural dyes added color. The tradition was lost for many years but is now making a comeback, and provides some of the most beautiful folk art in the islands. Also called Kapa.

***taro****—the staple of old Hawaii. A plant with a distinctive broad leaf that produces a starchy root. It was brought by the first Polynesians and was grown on magnificently irrigated plantations. According to the oral tradition, the life-giving properties of taro hold mystical significance for Hawaiians, since it was created by the gods at about the same time as humans.

***ti***—a broad-leafed plant that was used for many purposes, from plates to hula skirts. Especially used to wrap religious offerings presented at the *heiau.*

***tutu***—grandmother; granny; older woman. Used by all as a term of respect and endearment.

***ukulele****—*uku* means "flea" and *lele* means "jumping," so literally "jumping flea"—the way the Hawaiians perceived the quick fin-ger movements used on the banjo-like Portuguese folk instrument called a *cavaquinho.* The ukulele quickly became synonymous with the islands.

***wahine****—young woman; female; girl; wife. Used by all ethnic groups. When written on a lavatory door it means "women's room."

***wai***—fresh water; drinking water

***wela***—hot. *Wela kahao* is a "hot time" or "making whoopee."

***wiki****—quickly; fast; in a hurry. Often seen as *wiki wiki* (very fast), as in "Wiki Wiki Messenger Service."

**Useful Phrases**

***Aloha ahiahi***—Good evening

***Aloha au ia 'oe***—I love you

***Aloha kakahiaka***—Good morning

***Aloha nui loa***—much love; fondest regards

***Hau'oli la hanau***—Happy birthday

***Hau'oli makahiki hou***—Happy New Year

***Komo mai***—please come in; enter; welcome

***Mele kalikimaka***—Merry Christmas

***'Okole maluna***—bottoms up; salute; cheers; kampai

# Suggested Reading

Many publishers print books on Hawaii. Following are a few that focus on Hawaiian topics: **University of Hawai'i Press**, www.uhpress .hawaii.edu, has the best overall general list of titles on Hawaii. The **Bishop Museum Press**, www.bishopmuseum.org/bishop/press, puts out many scholarly works on Hawaiiana, as does **Kamehameha Schools Press**, www.ksbe.edu /newsroom/kspress. Also good, with a more general-interest list, are **Bess Press**, www.bess-press.com; **Mutual Publishing**, www.mutual publishing.com; and **Petrogylph Press**, www.ba-sicallybooks.com. A website specifically oriented toward books on Hawaii, Hawaiian music, and other things Hawaiian is **Hawaii Books** at www.hawaiibooks.com.

## Astronomy

Bryan, E.H. *Stars over Hawaii.* Hilo, HI: Petroglyph Press, 1977. An introduction to astronomy, with information about the constellations and charts featuring the stars filling the night sky in Hawaii, by month. A excellent primer.

Rhoads, Samuel. *The Sky Tonight—A Guided Tour of the Stars over Hawaii.* Honolulu: Bishop Museum, 1993. Four pages per month of star charts—one each for the horizon in every cardinal direction. Exceptional!

## Cooking

Alexander, Agnes. *How to Use Hawaiian Fruit.* Hilo, HI: Petroglyph Press, 1984. A slim volume of recipes using delicious and different Hawaiian fruits.

Beeman, Judy, and Martin Beeman. *Joys of Hawaiian Cooking.* Hilo, HI: Petroglyph Press, 1977. A collection of favorite recipes from Big Island chefs.

Choy, Sam. *Cooking from the Heart with Sam Choy.* Honolulu: Mutual Publishing, 1995. This beautiful, hand-bound cookbook contains many color photos by Douglas Peebles.

Fukuda, Sachi. *Pupus, An Island Tradition.* Honolulu: Bess Press, 1995.

Margah, Irish, and Elvira Monroe. *Hawaii, Cooking with Aloha.* San Carlos, CA: Wide World, 1984. Island recipes, as well as hints on decor.

Rizzuto, Shirley. *Fish Dishes of the Pacific—from the Fishwife.* Honolulu: Hawaii Fishing News, 1986. Features recipes using all the fish commonly caught in Hawaiian waters (husband Jim Rizzuto is the author of *Fishing, Hawaiian Style*).

## Culture

Dudley, Michael Kioni. *Man, Gods, and Nature.* Honolulu: Na Kane O Ka Malo Press, 1990. An examination of the philosophical underpinnings of Hawaiian beliefs and their interconnected reality.

Hartwell, Jay. *Na Mamo: Hawaiian People Today.* Honolulu: Ai Pohaku Press, 1996. Profiles 12 people practicing Hawaiian traditions in the modern world.

Heyerdahl, Thor. *American Indians in the Pacific.* London: Allen and Unwin Ltd., 1952. Theoretical and anthropological accounts of the influence on Polynesia of the Indians along the Pacific coast of North and South America. Although no longer in print, this book is fascinating reading, presenting unsubstantiated yet intriguing theories.

Kamehameha Schools Press. *Life in Early Hawai'i: The Ahupua'a.* 3rd ed. Honolulu:

Kamehameha Schools Press, 1994. Written for schoolchildren to better understand the basic organization of old Hawaiian land use and its function, this slim volume is a good primer for people of any age who wish to understand this fundamental societal fixture.

Kirch, Patrick V. *Feathered Gods and Fishhooks: An Introduction to Hawaiian Archaeology and Prehistory.* Honolulu: University of Hawai'i Press, 1997. This scholarly, lavishly illustrated, yet very readable book gives new insight into the development of precontact Hawaiian civilization. It focuses on the sites and major settlements of old Hawai'i and chronicles the main cultural developments while weaving in the social climate that contributed to change. A very worthwhile read.

## Fauna

Boom, Robert. *Hawaiian Seashells.* Honolulu: Waikiki Aquarium, 1972. Photos by Jerry Kringle. A collection of 137 seashells found in Hawaiian waters, featuring many found nowhere else on earth. Broken into categories with accompanying text including common and scientific names, physical descriptions, and likely habitats. A must-read for shell collectors.

Carpenter, Blyth, and Russell Carpenter. *Fish Watching in Hawaii.* San Mateo, CA: Natural World Press, 1981. A color guide to many of the reef fish found in Hawaii and often spotted by snorkelers. If you're interested in the fish that you'll be looking at, this guide will be very helpful.

Fielding, Ann, and Ed Robinson. *An Underwater Guide to Hawai'i.* Honolulu: University of Hawai'i Press, 1987. If you've ever had a desire to snorkel/scuba the living reef waters of Hawaii and to be familiar with what you're seeing, get this small but fact-packed book. The amazing array of marine life found throughout the archipelago is captured in

glossy photos with accompanying informative text. Both the scientific and common names of specimens are given. This book will enrich your underwater experience and serve as an easily understood reference guide for many years.

Goodson, Gar. *The Many-Splendored Fishes of Hawaii.* Stanford, CA: Stanford University Press, 1985. This small but thorough "fishwatchers" book includes entries on some deepsea fish.

Hawaiian Audubon Society. *Hawaii's Birds.* 5th ed. Honolulu: Hawaii Audubon Society, 1997. Excellent bird book, giving description, range, voice, and habits of the more than 100 species. Slim volume; good for carrying while hiking.

Hobson, Edmund, and E. H. Chave. *Hawaiian Reef Animals.* Honolulu: University of Hawai'i Press, 1987. Colorful photos and descriptions of the fish, invertebrates, turtles, and seals that call Hawaiian reefs their home.

Kay, Alison, and Olive Schoenberg-Dole. *Shells of Hawai'i.* Honolulu: University of Hawai'i Press, 1991. Color photos and tips on where to look.

Mahaney, Casey. *Hawaiian Reef Fish, The Identification Book.* Thailand: Planet Ocean Publishing, 1993. A spiral-bound reference work featuring many color photos and descriptions of common reef fish found in Hawaiian waters.

Nickerson, Roy. *Brother Whale, A Pacific Whalewatcher's Log.* San Francisco: Chronicle Books, 1977. Introduces the average person to the life of earth's greatest mammals. Provides historical accounts, photos, and tips on whalewatching. Well-written, descriptive, and the best "first time" book on whales.

Pratt, Douglas. *A Field Guide to the Birds of Hawaii and the Tropical Pacific.* Princeton, NJ: Princeton University Press, 1987. Useful field guide for novice and expert bird-watchers, covering Hawaii as well as other Pacific Island groups.

Tomich, P. Quentin. *Mammals in Hawai'i.* Honolulu: Bishop Museum Press, 1986. Quintessential scholarly text on all mammal species in Hawaii, with description of distribution and historical references. Lengthy bibliography.

van Riper, Charles, and Sandra van Riper. *A Field Guide to the Mammals of Hawaii.* Honolulu: Oriental Publishing. A guide to the surprising number of mammals introduced into Hawaii. Full-color pages document description, uses, tendencies, and habitat. Small and thin, this book makes a worthwhile addition to any serious hiker's backpack.

## Flora

Kepler, Angela. *Hawaiian Heritage Plants.* Honolulu: University of Hawai'i Press, 1998. A treatise on 32 utilitarian plants used by the early Hawaiians.

Kepler, Angela. *Hawai'i's Floral Splendor.* Honolulu: Mutual Publishing, 1997. A general reference to flowers of Hawaii.

Kepler, Angela. *Tropicals of Hawaii.* Honolulu: Mutual Publishing, 1989. This small-format book features many color photos of nonnative flowers.

Kuck, Lorraine, and Richard Togg. *Hawaiian Flowers and Flowering Trees.* Rutland, VT: Tuttle, 1960. A classic, although out-of-print, field guide to tropical and subtropical flora illustrated in watercolor. Succinct descriptions of Hawaiian plants and flowers with a brief history of their places of origin and their introduction to Hawaii.

Merrill, Elmer. *Plant Life of the Pacific World.* Rutland, VT: Tuttle, 1983. This is the defin-

itive book for anyone planning a botanical tour to the entire Pacific Basin. Originally published in the 1930s, it remains a tremendous work, worth tracking down through out-of-print book services.

Miyano, Leland. *Hawai'i, A Floral Paradise.* Honolulu: Mutual Publishing, 1995. Photographed by Douglas Peebles, this large-format book is filled with informative text and beautiful color shots of tropical flowers commonly seen in Hawaii.

Miyano, Leland. *A Pocket Guide to Hawai'i's Flowers.* Honolulu: Mutual Publishing, 2001. A small guide to readily seen flowers in the state. Good for the backpack or back pocket.

Sohmer, S. H., and R. Gustafson. *Plants and Flowers of Hawai'i.* Honolulu: University of Hawai'i Press, 1987. The authors cover the vegetation zones of Hawaii, from mountains to coast, introducing you to the wide and varied floral biology of the islands. They give a good introduction to the history and unique evolution of Hawaiian plantlife. Beautiful color plates are accompanied by clear and concise plant descriptions, with the scientific and common Hawaiian names listed.

Teho, Fortunato. *Plants of Hawaii—How to Grow Them.* Hilo, HI: Petroglyph Press, 1992. A small but useful book for those who want their backyards to bloom into tropical paradises.

Wagner, Warren L., Derral R. Herbst, and H. S. Sohner. *Manual of the Flowering Plants of Hawai'i,* revised edition, vol. 2. Honolulu: University of Hawai'i Press in association with Bishop Museum Press, 1999. Considered the scholarly Bible for Hawaii's botanical world.

Valier, Kathy. *Ferns of Hawaii.* Honolulu: University of Hawai'i Press, 1995. One of the few books that treat the state's ferns as a single subject.

# Health

Gutmanis, June. *Kahuna La'au Lapa'au,* revised edition. Honolulu: Island Heritage, 2001. Text on Hawaiian herbal medicines: diseases, treatments, and medicinal plants, with illustrations.

McBride, L. R. *Practical Folk Medicine of Hawaii.* Hilo, HI: Petroglyph Press, 1975. An illustrated guide to Hawaii's medicinal plants as used by the *kahuna lapa'au* (medical healers). Includes a thorough section on ailments, diagnosis, and the proper folk remedy. Illustrated by the author, a renowned botanical researcher and former ranger at Hawaii Volcanoes National Park.

Wilkerson, James A., M.D., ed. *Medicine for Mountaineering and Other Wilderness.* 4th ed. Seattle: The Mountaineers, 1992. Don't let the title fool you. Although the book focuses on specific health problems that may be encountered while mountaineering, it is the best first-aid and general health guide available today. Written by doctors for the layperson to use until help arrives, it is jam-packed with easily understandable techniques and procedures. For those planning extended hikes, it is a must.

# History

Apple, Russell A. *Trails: From Steppingstones to Kerbstones.* Honolulu: Bishop Museum Press, 1965. This "Special Publication #53" is a special-interest archaeological survey focusing on trails, roadways, footpaths, and highways and how they were designed and maintained throughout the years. Many "royal highways" from precontact Hawaii are cited.

Ashdown, Inez MacPhee. *Kaho'olawe.* Honolulu: Topgallant Publishing, 1979. The tortured story of the lonely island of Kaho'olawe by a member of the family who owned the island until it was turned into a military bombing target during World War II. It's also a first-person account of life on the island.

Barnes, Phil. *A Concise History of the Hawaiian Islands.* Hilo, HI: Petroglyph Press, 1999. An easy-to-read examination of the main currents of Hawaiian history and its major players, focusing on the important factors in shaping the social, economic, and political trends of the islands.

Cameron, Roderick. *The Golden Haze.* New York: World Publishing, 1964. An account of Captain James Cook's voyages of discovery throughout the South Seas. Uses original diaries and journals for an "on-the-spot" reconstruction of this great seafaring adventure.

Cox, J. Halley, and Edward Stasack. *Hawaiian Petroglyphs.* Honolulu: Bishop Museum Press, 1970. The most thorough examination of petroglyph sites throughout the islands.

Daws, Gavan. *Shoal of Time, A History of the Hawaiian Islands.* Honolulu: University of Hawai'i Press, 1974. A highly readable history of Hawaii dating from its "discovery" by the Western world to its acceptance as the 50th state. Good insight into the psychological makeup of influential characters who helped form Hawaii's past.

Dorrance, William H., and Francis S. Morgan. *Sugar Islands: The 165-Year Story of Sugar in Hawai'i.* Honolulu: Mutual Publishing, 2000. An overall sketch of the sugar industry in Hawaii from inception to decline, with data on many individual plantations and mills around the islands. Definitely a story from the industry's point of view.

Finney, Ben, and James D. Houston. *Surfing, A History of the Ancient Hawaiian Sport.* Los Angeles: Pomegranate, 1996. Features many early etchings and old photos of Hawaiian surfers practicing their native sport.

Fornander, Abraham. *An Account of the Polynesian Race; Its Origins and Migrations, and the Ancient History of the Hawaiian People to the*

*Times of Kamehameha I.* Rutland, VT: C.E. Tuttle Co., 1969. This is a reprint of a three-volume opus originally published 1878–1885. It is still one of the best sources of information on Hawaiian myth and legend.

Free, David. *Vignettes of Old Hawaii.* Honolulu: Crossroads Press, 1994. A collection of short essays on a variety of subjects.

Fuchs, Lawrence. *Hawaii Pono.* Honolulu: Bess Press, 1961. A detailed, scholarly work presenting an overview of Hawaii's history, based on ethnic and sociological interpretations. Encompasses most socioethnological groups from native Hawaiians to modern entrepreneurs. This book is a must for obtaining some social historical background.

Handy, E. S., and Elizabeth Handy. *Native Planters in Old Hawaii.* Honolulu: Bishop Museum Press, 1972. A superbly written, easily understood scholarly work on the intimate relationship of precontact Hawaiians and the *aina* (land). Much more than its title implies, this book should be read by anyone seriously interested in Polynesian Hawaii.

Ii, John Papa. *Fragments of Hawaiian History.* Honolulu: Bishop Museum, 1959. Hawaii's history under Kamehameha I as told by a Hawaiian who actually experienced it.

Joesting, Edward. *Hawaii: An Uncommon History.* New York: W.W. Norton Co., 1978. A truly uncommon history told in a series of vignettes relating to the lives and personalities of the first Caucasians in Hawaii, Hawaiian nobility, sea captains, writers, and adventurers. Brings history to life. Absolutely excellent!

Kamakau, S. M. *Ruling Chiefs of Hawaii,* revised edition. Honolulu: Kamehameha Schools Press, 1992.

Lili'uokalani. *Hawaii's Story by Hawaii's Queen,* reprint. Honolulu: Mutual Publishing, 1990.

Originally written in 1898, this moving personal account recounts Hawai'i's inevitable move from monarchy to U.S. Territory by its last queen, Lili'uokalani. The facts can be found in other histories, but none provides the emotion or point of view expressed by Hawaii's deposed monarch. This is a must-read to get the whole picture.

McBride, Likeke. *Petroglyphs of Hawaii.* Hilo, HI: Petroglyph Press, 1997. A revised and updated guide to petroglyphs found in the Hawaiian Islands. A basic introduction to these old Hawaiian picture stories.

Nickerson, Roy. *Lahaina, Royal Capital of Hawaii.* Honolulu: Hawaiian Service, 1978. The story of Lahaina from whaling days to present, spiced with ample photographs.

Takaki, Ronald. *Pau Hana: Plantation Life and Labor in Hawaii.* Honolulu: University of Hawai'i Press, 1983. The story of immigrant labor and the sugar industry in Hawaii until the 1920s from the worker's perspective.

## Introductory

Carroll, Rick, and Marcie Carroll, eds. *Hawai'i: True Stories of the Island Spirit.* San Francisco: Travelers' Tales, Inc., 1999. A collection of stories by a variety of authors that were chosen to elicit the essence of Hawaii and Hawaiian experiences. A great read.

Cohen, David, and Rick Smolan. *A Day in the Life of Hawaii.* New York: Workman, 1984. On December 2, 1983, 50 of the world's top photojournalists were invited to Hawaii to photograph the variety of daily life on the islands. The photos are excellently reproduced and accompanied by a minimum of text.

Day, A. G., and C. Stroven. *A Hawaiian Reader,* reprint. Honolulu: Mutual Publishing, 1984. A poignant compilation of essays, diary entries, and fictitious writings originally published in

1959 that takes you from the death of Captain Cook through the "statehood services."

Department of Geography, University of Hawai'i, Hilo. *Atlas of Hawai'i.* 3rd ed. Honolulu: University of Hawai'i Press, 1998. Much more than an atlas filled with reference maps, this book also contains commentary on the natural environment, culture, and sociology; a gazetteer; and statistical tables. Actually a mini-encyclopedia on Hawai'i.

Michener, James A. *Hawaii.* New York: Random House, 1959. Michener's fictionalized historical novel has done more to inform *and* misinform readers about Hawaii than any other book ever written. A great tale with plenty of local color and information, but read it for pleasure, not facts.

Piercy, LaRue. *Hawaii This and That.* Honolulu: Mutual Publishing, 1994. Illustrated by Scot Ebanez. A 60-page book filled with one-sentence facts and oddities about all manner of things Hawaiian. Informative, amazing, and fun to read.

Steele, R. Thomas: *The Hawaiian Shirt: Its Art and History.* New York: Abbeville Press, 1984.

## Language

Elbert, Samuel. *Spoken Hawaiian.* Honolulu: University of Hawai'i Press, 1970. Progressive conversational lessons.

Elbert, Samuel, and Mary Pukui. *Hawaiian Dictionary.* Honolulu: University of Hawai'i Press, 1986. The best dictionary available on the Hawaiian language. The *Pocket Hawaiian Dictionary* is a less expensive, condensed version of this dictionary and adequate for most travelers with a general interest in the language.

Pukui, Mary Kawena, Samuel Elbert, and Esther T. Mookini. *Place Names of Hawaii.* Honolulu: University of Hawai'i Press, 1974. The most current and comprehensive listing of Hawaiian and foreign place names in the state, giving pronunciation, spelling, meaning, and location.

Schutz, Albert J. *All About Hawaiian.* Honolulu: University of Hawai'i Press, 1995. A brief primer on Hawaiian pronunciation, grammar, and vocabulary. A solid introduction.

## Mythology and Legends

Beckwith, Martha. *Hawaiian Mythology,* reprint. Honolulu: University of Hawai'i Press, 1976. More than 60 years after its original printing in 1940, this work remains the definitive text on Hawaiian mythology. Beckwith compiled this book from many sources, giving exhaustive cross-references to genealogies and legends expressed in the oral tradition. If you are only going to read one book on Hawaii's folklore, this should be it.

Beckwith, Martha. *The Kumulipo,* reprint. Honolulu: University of Hawai'i Press, 1972. Translation of the Hawaiian creation chant, originally published in 1951.

Colum, Padraic. *Legends of Hawaii.* New Haven, CT: Yale University Press, 1937. Selected legends of old Hawaii, reinterpreted but closely based on the originals.

Elbert, S. H., ed. *Hawaiian Antiquities and Folklore.* Honolulu: University of Hawai'i Press, 1959. Illustrated by Jean Charlot. A selection of the main legends from Abraham Fornander's great work, *An Account of the Polynesian Race.*

Kalakaua, His Hawaiian Majesty, King David. *The Legends and Myths of Hawaii.* Edited by R. M. Daggett, with a foreword by Glen Grant. Honolulu: Mutual Publishing, 1990. Originally published in 1888, Hawaii's own King Kalakaua draws on his scholarly and formidable knowledge of the classic oral tradition to bring alive ancient tales from precontact Hawaii. A powerful yet somewhat Victorian voice from Hawaii's past speaks clearly and boldly, especially about the intimate role of pre-Christian religion in the lives of the Hawaiian people.

Melville, Leinanai. *Children of the Rainbow*. Wheaton, IL: Theosophical Publishing, 1969. A book on higher spiritual consciousness attuned to nature, which was the basic belief of pre-Christian Hawaii. The appendix contains illustrations of mystical symbols used by the *kahuna*. An enlightening book in many ways.

Pukui, Mary Kawena, and Caroline Curtis. *Hawaii Island Legends*. Honolulu: The Kamehameha Schools Press, 1996. Hawaiian tales and legends for youngsters.

Pukui, Mary Kawena, and Caroline Curtis. *Tales of the Menehune*. Honolulu: The Kamehameha Schools Press, 1960. Compilation of legends relating to Hawaii's "little people."

Pukui, Mary Kawena, and Caroline Curtis. *The Waters of Kane and other Hawaiian Legends*. Honolulu: The Kamehameha Schools Press, 1994. Tales and legends for adolescents.

Thrum, Thomas. *Hawaiian Folk Tales*, reprint. Chicago: McClurg and Co., 1950. A collection of Hawaiian tales originally printed in 1907 from the oral tradition as told to the author from various sources.

Westervelt, W. D. *Hawaiian Legends of Volcanoes*, reprint. Boston: Ellis Press, 1991. A small book originally printed in 1916 concerning the volcanic legends of Hawaii and how they related to the fledgling field of volcanism in the early 1900s. The vintage photos alone are worth a look.

## Natural Sciences and Geography

Carlquist, Sherwin. *Hawaii: A Natural History*.

National Tropical Botanical Garden, 1984. Definitive account of Hawaii's natural history.

Hazlett, Richard, and Donald Hyndman. *Roadside Geology of Hawai'i*. Missoula, MT: Mountain Press Publishing, 1996. Begins with a general discussion of the geology of the Hawaiian Islands, followed by a road guide to the individual islands offering descriptions of easily seen features. A great book to have in the car as you tour the islands.

Hubbard, Douglass, and Gordon Macdonald. *Volcanoes of the National Parks of Hawaii*, reprint. Volcanoes, HI: Hawaii Natural History Association, 1989. The volcanology of Hawaii, documenting the major lava flows and their geological effect on the state; originally printed in 1982.

Kay, E. Alison, comp. *A Natural History of the Hawaiian Islands*. Honolulu: University of Hawai'i Press, 1994. A selection of concise articles by experts in the fields of volcanism, oceanography, meteorology, and biology. An excellent reference source.

Macdonald, Gorden, Agatin Abbott, and Frank Peterson. *Volcanoes in the Sea*. Honolulu: University of Hawai'i Press, 1983. The best reference to Hawaiian geology. Well-explained for easy understanding. Illustrated.

## Periodicals

*Hawaii Magazine*. 3 Burroughs, Irvine, CA 92618. This magazine covers the Hawaiian islands like a tropical breeze. Feature articles on all aspects of life in the islands, with special departments on travel, events, exhibits, and restaurant reviews. Up-to-the-minute information, and a fine read.

*Naturist Society Magazine*. P.O. Box 132, Oshkosh, WI 54920. This excellent magazine not only *uncovers* bathing-suit-optional beaches throughout the islands, giving tips for naturalists visiting Hawaii, but also provides reports on local politics, environment, and conservation measures from the health-conscious nudist point of view. A fine publication.

## Pictorials

La Brucherie, Roger. *Hawaiian World, Hawaiian Heart.* Pine Valley, CA: Imagenes Press, 1989.

## Political Science

Bell, Roger. *Last Among Equals: Hawaiian Statehood and American Politics.* Honolulu: University of Hawai'i Press, 1984. Documents Hawaii's long and rocky road to statehood, tracing political partisanship, racism, and social change.

## Sports and Recreation

Alford, John, D. *Mountain Biking the Hawaiian Islands.* Ohana Publishing, 1997. Good off-road biking guide to the main Hawaiian islands.

Ambrose, Greg. *Surfer's Guide to Hawai'i.* Honolulu: Bess Press, 1991. Island-by-island guide to surfing spots.

Ball, Stuart. *The Hiker's Guide to the Hawaiian Islands.* Honolulu: University of Hawai'i Press, 2000. This excellent guide includes 44 hikes on each of the four main islands. Ball has also written *The Hikers Guide to O'ahu.*

Cagala, George. *Hawaii: A Camping Guide.* Boston: Hunter Publishing, 1994. Useful.

Chisholm, Craig. *Hawaiian Hiking Trails.* Lake Oswego, OR: Ferglen Press, 1999. Also *Oahu Hiking Trails.*

Cisco, Dan. *Hawai'i Sports.* Honolulu: University of Hawai'i Press, 1999. A compendium of popular and little-known sporting events and

figures, with facts, tidbits, and statistical information. Go here first for a general overview.

Lueras, Leonard. *Surfing, the Ultimate Pleasure.* Honolulu: Emphasis International, 1984. One of the most brilliant books ever written on surfing.

McMahon, Richard. *Camping Hawai'i: A Complete Guide.* Honolulu: University of Hawai'i Press, 1997. This book has all you need to know about camping in Hawaii, with descriptions of different campsites.

Morey, Kathy. *Oahu Trails.* Berkeley, CA: Wilderness Press, 1997. Morey's books are specialized, detailed hiker's guides to Hawaii's outdoors. Complete with useful maps, historical references, official procedures, and plants and animals encountered along the way. If you're focused on hiking, these are the best guides to take along. *Maui Trails, Kauai Trails,* and *Hawaii Trails* are also available.

Rosenberg, Steve. *Diving Hawaii.* Locust Valley, NY: Aqua Quest, 1990. Describes diving locations on the major islands as well as the marine life divers are likely to see. Includes many color photos.

Smith, Robert. *Hawaii's Best Hiking Trails.* Kula, Maui, HI: Hawaiian Outdoor Adventures, 1991. Other guides by this author include *Hiking Oahu, Hiking Maui, Hiking Hawaii,* and *Hiking Kauai.*

Sutherland, Audrey. *Paddling Hawai'i,* revised edition. Honolulu: University of Hawai'i Press, 1998. All you need to know about sea kayaking in Hawaiian waters.

Wallin, Doug. *Diving & Snorkeling Guide to the Hawaiian Islands.* 2nd ed. Houston: Pisces Books, 1991. A guide offering brief descriptions of diving locations on the four major islands.

# Travel

Clark, John. *Beaches of O'ahu.* Honolulu: University of Hawai'i Press, 1997. Definitive guide to beaches, including many off the beaten path. Features maps and black-and-white photos. Also *Beaches of the Big Island, Beaches of Kaua'i and Ni'ihau,* and *Beaches of Maui County.*

Stanley, David. *Moon Handbooks South Pacific.* 8th ed. Emeryville, CA: Avalon Travel Publishing, 2004. The model on which all travel guides should be based. Simply the best book in the world for travel throughout the South Pacific.

# Internet Resources

The following list of websites have information about the state of Hawaii that may be useful in preparation for a trip to the islands and for general interest.

**www.hawaii-county.com**
The official website of Hawai'i County. Includes, among other items, a county data book, information about parks and camping, and island bus schedules.

**www.co.maui.hi.us**
The official website of Maui County. Includes information on city government, the county-sponsored bus system, and a calendar of events.

**www.co.honolulu.hi.us**
The official website of the City and County of Honolulu. Includes information on city government, county data access, visitor information, and information on business and economic development.

**www.kauaigov.org**
The official website of Kaua'i County. Provides information about county government and agencies, business, parks and recreation, and the county bus system.

**www.gohawaii.com**
This official site of the Hawaii Visitors and Convention Bureau, the state-run tourism organization, has information about all the major Hawaiian islands: transportation, accommodations, eating, activities, shopping, Hawaiian products, an events calendar, a travel planner and resource guide for a host of topics, as well as information about meetings, conventions, and the organization itself.

**www.bigisland.org**
The official site of the Big Island Visitors Bureau, a branch of the Hawaii Visitors and Convention Bureau, has much the same information as the above website but specific to the island of Hawai'i. A very useful resource.

**www.visitmaui.com**
The official site of the Maui Visitors Bureau, a branch of the Hawaii Visitors and Convention Bureau, has information specific to the island of Maui. Tourist information specific to Moloka'i and Lana'i, can be found at the following sites: **www.molokai-hawaii.com** and **www.visitlanai.net.**

**www.visit-oahu.com**
The official site of the O'ahu Visitors Bureau, a branch of the Hawaii Visitors and Convention Bureau, has information specific to the island of O'ahu.

**www.kauai-hawaii.com**
The official site for Kauai tourist information. Has specific information for activities, sites, parks, and culture, and a calendar of events.

**www.bestplaceshawaii.com**
Produced and maintained by H&S Publishing, this first-rate commercial site has general and specific information about all major Hawaiian islands, a vacation planner, suggestions for things to do and places to see. For a non-government site, this is a great place to start a search for tourist information about the state or any of its major islands. One of dozens of sites on the internet with a focus on Hawaii tourism-related information.

**www.alternative-hawaii.com**
Alternative source for eco-friendly general information and links to specific businesses, with some cultural, historical, and events information.

**www.hawaiiecotourism.org**
Official Hawaii Ecotourism Association website. Lists goals, members, activities, and provides links to member organizations and related ecotourism groups.

**http://calendar.gohawaii.com**
For events of all sorts happening throughout the state, visit the calendar of events listing on the Hawaii Visitors Bureau website. Information can be accessed by island, date, or type.

**www.state.hi.us/sfca/culturecalendar.html**
This site of the State Foundation of Culture and the Arts features a calendar of arts and cultural events, activities, and programs held throughout the state. Information is available by island and type.

**www.hawaiianair.com,**
**www.alohaairlines.com,**
**www.pacificwings.com**
These websites for Hawaiian Airlines, Aloha Airlines, and Pacific Wings list virtually all regularly-scheduled commercial air links throughout the state.

**www.go-lanai.com, www.molokaiferry.com**
These websites for Expeditions and the Molokai Ferry list schedules and fares for and provide other information about the only two commercial ferries in the state. These ferries connect Lahaina, Maui to Lana'i and Moloka'i.

**www.mele.com**
Check out the Hawaiian music scene at Hawaiian Music Island, one of the largest music websites that focuses on Hawaiian music, books and videos related to Hawaiian music and culture, concert schedules, Hawaiian music awards, and links to music companies and musicians. Others with broad listings and general interest information are: Nahenahenet, **www.nahenahe.net;** and Hawaiian Music Guide, **www.hawaii-music.com.**

**www.uhpress.hawaii.edu**
This University of Hawai'i Press website has the best overall list of titles for books publishes on Hawaiian themes and topics. Other publishers to check for substantial lists of books on Hawaiiana are the Bishop Museum Press, **www.bishopmuseum.org/bishop/press;** Kamehameha Schools Press, **www.ksbe.edu/newsroom/kspress;** Bess Press, **www.besspress.com;** Mutual Publishing, **www.mutualpublishing.com;** and Petroglyph Press, **www.basicallybooks.com.**

**www.hawaiimuseums.org**
This site is dedicated to the promotion of museums and cultural attractions in the state of Hawaii with links to member sites on each of the islands. A member organization.

**www.bishopmuseum.org**
Site of the premier ethnological and cultural museum dedicated to Hawaiian people, their culture, and cultural artifacts.

**www.starbulletin.com,**
**www.honoluluadvertiser.com**
Websites for Hawaii's two main English-language dailies, the Honolulu Star Bulletin and the Honolulu Advertiser, both published in Honolulu. Both have a concentration of news coverage about O'ahu yet cover major news from the Neighbor Islands.

**www.honoluluweekly.com**
Site of Honolulu's principal alternative weekly newspaper. For years, this paper has been given local residents news with a different slant and often carries stories that the major newspapers do not print. Strong on local coverage with a conscience.

**www.mauinews.com**
Website of Maui's largest newspaper, Maui News. It has a concentration of news coverage about Maui yet covers major news from the Neighbor Islands.

**www.westhawaiitoday.com,
www.hilohawaiitribune.com**

Web presence for the newspapers, West Hawaii Today, published in Kona, and Hawaii Tribune-Herald, published in Hilo. Good for local and statewide news. Both have the same parent company.

**www.kauaiworld.com**

Website for the Garden Island, Kaua'i's major newspaper, published in Lihu'e. Focuses mainly of local news and events.

**www.nps.gov/havo**

This official site of Hawaii Volcanoes National Park is a wealth of general information about the park. Related sites are **www.nps.gov/puho**, for Pu'uhonua O Honaunau, a restored Hawaiian temple of refuge and **www.nps.gov/puhe**, for Pu'ukohola Heiau, a restored Hawaiian temple, both national historical sites on the Big Island administered by the National Park Service.

**www.nps.gov/hale**

This official website for Haleakala National Park has general information about the park:

transportation, camping, events, activities, and fees.

**www.state.hi.us/dlnr/dsp/dsp.html**

Pertinent information about the Hawaii state park system.

**www.oha.org**

Official site for the state-mandated organization that deals with native Hawaii-related affairs.

**www.hawaii-nation.org**

Site for Nation of Hawai'i, the oldest and largest organization of native Hawaiians who are advocating for sovereignty. While there are several dozen independent native Hawaiian rights organizations that are pushing for various degrees of sovereignty or independence for native Hawaiian people, some of the major groups are listed below: Reinstated Hawaiian Government, **www.reinstated.org;** Kingdom of Hawaii. **www.freehawaii.org;** (another) Kingdom of Hawaii, **www.pixi.com/~kingdom;** the Hawaiian Kingdom, **www.hawaiiankingdom.org.**

# Index

## Beaches

430–431; geography 5, 338, 391–392; government 399; Hamakua Coast 579–597; Hawaii Volcanoes National Park 621–639; Hilo 549–578; Ka'u 640–650; Kona 439–491; lei 85; National Wildlife Refuges 18; North Kohala 530–541; Puna 598–620; recreation 404–429; services, general 437–438; South Kohala 492–515; town populations 157; transportation to and on 431–437; Waimea 516–529

Big Pool: 1109
billfish: 397–398
billfishing: 98
Bingham, Reverend: 212
birds: 13–16; Big Island 395–396; endangered 14, 657–658; Kamakou Preserve 957; seabird

sanctuaries 953
bird-watching: Big Island 417–418; Hakalau Forest National Wildlife Refuge 398; Hanalei National Wildlife Refuge 1093; Kakahai'a National Wildlife Refuge 951; Kealia Pond National Wildlife Refuge 793; Kilauea Point National Wildlife Refuge 1077–1079; Kipuka Pu'u Huluhulu 548; Kipuka Puaulu 635–636; Koke'e State Park 1161; Pu'u O'o Trail 548
birthing stones: of Kamehameha the Great 534; Kukaniloko 315–316; Pohaku Ho'o Hanau 1047
Bishop Museum: 227–229, 266–267
Black Gorge: 712–713
Black Pot: 1095

**Index**

# Gardens

# Hiking

# Snorkeling

# Surfing

# Acknowledgments

Since the passing of J. D. Bisignani, the original author of *Moon Handbooks Hawaii,* I have taken on the great task of revising this book and others in his series of guides to Hawaii. Joe, you have been an inspiration to me and have laid a solid foundation for the present revision. Even though you are gone, you've been with me with each word. To you, my good friend, a big thank you.

As always, the staff at Avalon Travel Publishing has been professional in every way. A sincere thank you to everyone.

The following individuals require special thanks for their assistance in the revision of this book: Ellie, Tom Bartlett, Steve and Susan Layne, Tani Bova, Candy Aluli, Marjorie Ketcher, David Sayre, Katrina Souza, Patti Kimi Woodd, Rosemary Smith, Joe Moore, Stephanie Kaluahine Reid, Carolyn Barnes, Byron and Dot Fears, Jeremy, Nancy Daniels, Nita Isherwood, Don and Martie Nitsche, Charlene Cowan, Susan and Robert Hughes, Brian Crawford, Kathryn Grout, Star Townsend, Diana Allegra, Christine Jimenez, Barbara Anderson, John and Michele Gamble, Jackie Horne, Carolyn Cascavilla, Chris O'Connor, Joan Palmtag, Susan Bredo, Danny Breatchel, Laurence Montcastle, Doug Arnott, Geoff Hand, Thelma Akau, Ed Sullivan, Dick Neill, Bernie Worley, Sophie and Lee, John and Wilma Lane, Michele Lee, Gail Morris, Angela O'Malley Reed, Jubal Jones, Joyce Matsumoto, Bunny Look, Ethel Nada, Glen Manaba, Joseph Yamaoka, Merle Tokunaga, Karen Winpenny, George Hayward, Henry Nakahodo, Tom and Janice Fairbanks, Jim Heine, Kaui Dickson, Luana Pa'ahana, Nancy Brown, Jamie Mosley, Suzie Duro, Sherry Barbier, Elizabeth Marquez, Ellen Unterman, Shelley Drake, Bea Wolfe, Cherrie Attix, Henry Clay Richardson, Kirk Hansen, Maria Arceneaux, Keala, Eric Dixson, Randy Coon, Jim Coon, Virginia DiPiazza, Steve and Barbara Schonely, Stu Globerman, Lorene Suzuki-Nowicki, Haunani Vieira, Kathy Lane, and my wife, Linda Nilsen. A sincere *mahalo* to you all.

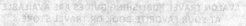

# U.S.~Metric Conversion

| | | |
|---|---|---|
| 1 inch | = | 2.54 centimeters (cm) |
| 1 foot | = | .304 meters (m) |
| 1 yard | = | 0.914 meters |
| 1 mile | = | 1.6093 kilometers (km) |
| 1 km | = | .6214 miles |
| 1 fathom | = | 1.8288 m |
| 1 chain | = | 20.1168 m |
| 1 furlong | = | 201.168 m |
| 1 acre | = | .4047 hectares |
| 1 sq km | = | 100 hectares |
| 1 sq mile | = | 2.59 square km |
| 1 ounce | = | 28.35 grams |
| 1 pound | = | .4536 kilograms |
| 1 short ton | = | .90718 metric ton |
| 1 short ton | = | 2000 pounds |
| 1 long ton | = | 1.016 metric tons |
| 1 long ton | = | 2240 pounds |
| 1 metric ton | = | 1000 kilograms |
| 1 quart | = | .94635 liters |
| 1 US gallon | = | 3.7854 liters |
| 1 Imperial gallon | = | 4.5459 liters |
| 1 nautical mile | = | 1.852 km |

To compute Celsius temperatures, subtract 32 from Fahrenheit and divide by 1.8. To go the other way, multiply Celsius by 1.8 and add 32.

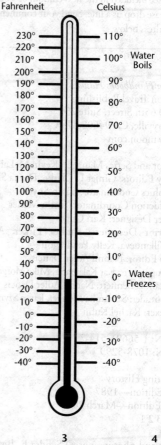

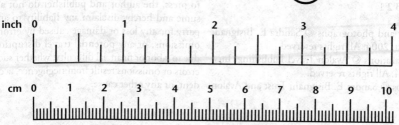

# Keeping Current

Although we strive to produce the most up-to-date guidebook humanly possible, change is unavoidable. Between the time this book goes to print and the moment you read it, a handful of the businesses noted in these pages will undoubtedly change prices, move, or even close their doors forever. Other worthy attractions will open for the first time. If you have a favorite gem you'd like to see included in the next edition, or see anything that needs updating, clarification, or correction, please drop us a line. Send your comments via email at atpfeedback@avalonpub.com, or use the address below.

*Moon Handbooks Hawaii*
Avalon Travel Publishing
1400 65th Street, Suite 250
Emeryville, CA 94608, USA
www.moon.com

Editor and Series Manager: Kevin McLain
Copy Editors: Ginjer L. Clarke, Deana Shields
Graphics Coordinator: Susan Snyder
Production Coordinator: Justin Marler
Cover Designer: Kari Gim
Interior Designers: Amber Pirker, Alvaro Villanueva, Kelly Pendragon
Map Editor: Naomi Adler Dancis
Cartographers: Kat Kalamaras, Mike Morgenfeld, Landis Bennett, Naomi Adler Dancis
Proofreader: Samantha Metzger, Jenica Szymanski
Indexer: Rachel Kuhn

ISBN: 1-56691-514-7
ISSN: 1078-5299

Printing History
1st Edition—1987
7th Edition—March 2004
5 4 3 2 1

Front cover photo: © Tomas del Amo/ Pacific Stock

Table of contents photos: Robert Nilsen

Printed in China through Colorcraft Ltd., Hong Kong.